Joyous ← not hand writting

WEBSTER'S Dictionary & Thesaurus for Students

WITH FULL-COLOR WORLD ATLAS

Joyous Terrell

Joyous

WEBSTER'S Dictionary & Thesaurus for Students

WITH FULL-COLOR WORLD ATLAS

Created in Cooperation with the Editors of
MERRIAM-WEBSTER

FEDERAL STREET PRESS

A Division of Merriam-Webster, Incorporated
Springfield, Massachusetts

This edition published by Federal Street Press
A Division of Merriam-Webster, Incorporated
P.O. Box 281
Springfield, MA 01102

Federal Street Press books are available for bulk purchase for sales promotion and premium use. For details write the manager of special sales, Federal Street Press, P.O. Box 281, Springfield, MA 01102

ISBN 13 978-1-59695-017- 7
ISBN 10 1-59695-017-X

Printed in the United States of America

07 08 09 10 5 4 3 2

Contents

A 48-page full-color world atlas follows page 502

Preface

The editors of this volume have created it with the student in mind. The dictionary and thesaurus are written in clear, precise language that is accessible to everyone. They serve as tools to enrich speech and writing and to make reading more rewarding.

The full-color atlas of the world has been carefully updated to show in detail the countries of the world as they exist today. It provides invaluable information to those studying world history and current events.

In addition, there are many special sections which provide useful information about our language, our country, and our world.

DICTIONARY

Preface to the Dictionary

This dictionary has been specially written for students. In this dictionary are the meanings and uses of more than 32,000 words and phrases. While this dictionary is written in simple language, it has the features of much larger dictionaries, and it is important to understand these features to allow you to make best use of your dictionary.

The **bold** word that begins an entry is known as the **main entry word**. All of the material in the entry is related to the main entry word or to derived words or phrases that also appear in the entry.

> **as·pen** *n* **:** a poplar tree whose leaves move easily in the breeze

Centered dots in the bold forms show where the words may be hyphenated at the end of a line on a page and they serve as an aid in sounding out the words.

Other bold forms may appear in this entry, such as **variant spellings** and **inflected forms** of the main entry word. Inflected forms are the plurals of nouns, the principal parts of verbs, or the comparative and superlative forms of adjectives.

Other bold items in the entry may be **defined run-on phrases** that have the main entry word in the phrase and **run-in entries**, that are being explained in the definition itself.

> **[1]stand** *vb* . . . — **stand by :** to be or remain loyal or true to — **stand for 1** : to be a symbol for . . . **2 :** to put up with . . .
>
> **chest·nut** *n* **1 :** a sweet edible nut that grows in burs on a tree (**chestnut tree**) related to the beech . . .

One of the more common bold forms appearing at an entry is the **undefined run-on entry**. This is a word at the end of an entry that is derived from the main entry by the addition of a common word ending (suffix).

> **har·mo·ni·ous** . . . — **har·mo·ni·ous·ly** *adv* — **har·mo·ni·ous·ness** *n*

Since you know the meaning of the main entry word and the meaning of the suffix, the meaning of the run-on entry is self-explanatory.

The way a word is used in a sentence, its *function*, sometimes called its *part of speech*, is indicated by any of several *italic* abbreviations: *n* for *noun*, *vb* for *verb*, *adj* for *adjective*, *adv* for *adverb*, *pron* for *pronoun*, *conj* for *conjunction*, *prep* for *preposition*, and *interj* for *interjection*. Others include *helping verb*, *prefix*, and *suffix*.

When there are two or more words that have the same spelling but are different in their meanings or how they function in a sentence, these are distinguished by a small superscript numeral in front of the spelling. The numeral is not part of the spelling; it is there in this dictionary to distinguish these identically spelled words (called **homographs**).

> **[1]seal** *n* **1 :** a sea mammal . . .
>
> **[2]seal** *n* **1 :** something (as a pledge) that makes safe or secure
>
> **[3]seal** *vb* **1 :** to mark with a seal . . .

One very important way a dictionary saves space when two or more words have the same meaning is by putting the definition at the more common word and linking to that entry by means of a **cross-reference** in SMALL CAPITALS. Look at the following.

> **ductless gland** *n* **:** ENDOCRINE GLAND

The treatment here tells you to look at the entry **endocrine gland** for a definition of both *ductless gland* and *endocrine gland*. And this treatment tells you also that *ductless gland* and *endocrine gland* are **synonyms**.

A

[1]**a** *n, pl* **a's** *or* **as** *often cap* **1 :** the first letter of the English alphabet **2 :** a grade that shows a student's work is excellent

[2]**a** *indefinite article* **1 :** some one not identified or known **2 :** the same **3 :** [1]ANY 1 **4 :** for or from each

a- *prefix* **1 :** on **:** in **:** at **2 :** in (such) a state, condition, or manner **3 :** in the act or process of

aard•vark *n* **:** an African animal with a long snout and a long sticky tongue that feeds mostly on ants and termites and is active at night

ab- *prefix* **:** from **:** differing from

aback *adv* **:** by surprise

aba•cus *n, pl* **aba•ci** *or* **aba•cus•es :** an instrument for doing arithmetic by sliding counters along rods or in grooves

abaft *adv* **:** toward or at the back part of a ship

ab•a•lo•ne *n* **:** a large sea snail that has a flattened shell with a pearly lining

[1]**aban•don** *vb* **1 :** to give up completely **:** FORSAKE **2 :** to give (oneself) up to a feeling or emotion — **aban•don•ment** *n*

[2]**abandon** *n* **:** a complete yielding to feelings or wishes

aban•doned *adj* **:** given up **:** left empty or unused

abash *vb* **:** to destroy the self-confidence of

abate *vb* **abat•ed; abat•ing :** to make or become less

ab•bess *n* **:** the head of an abbey for women

ab•bey *n, pl* **abbeys 1 :** MONASTERY, CONVENT **2 :** a church that once belonged to an abbey

ab•bot *n* **:** the head of an abbey for men

ab•bre•vi•ate *vb* **ab•bre•vi•at•ed; ab•bre•vi•at•ing :** to make briefer **:** SHORTEN

ab•bre•vi•a•tion *n* **1 :** a making shorter **2 :** a shortened form of a word or phrase

ab•di•cate *vb* **ab•di•cat•ed; ab•di•cat•ing :** to give up a position of power or authority

ab•di•ca•tion *n* **:** the giving up of a position of power or authority

ab•do•men *n* **1 :** the part of the body between the chest and the hips including the cavity in which the chief digestive organs lie **2 :** the hind part of the body of an arthropod (as an insect)

ab•dom•i•nal *adj* **:** of, relating to, or located in the abdomen

ab•duct *vb* **:** to take a person away by force **:** KIDNAP

ab•duc•tion *n* **:** the act of abducting

abeam *adv or adj* **:** on a line at right angles to a ship's keel

abed *adv or adj* **:** in bed

ab•er•ra•tion *n* **:** a differing from what is normal or usual

ab•hor *vb* **ab•horred; ab•hor•ring :** to shrink from in disgust **:** LOATHE

ab•hor•rent *adj* **:** causing or deserving strong dislike

abide *vb* **abode** *or* **abid•ed; abid•ing 1 :** to bear patiently **:** TOLERATE **2 :** ENDURE 1 **3 :** to live in a place **:** DWELL — **abide by :** to accept the terms of **:** OBEY

abil•i•ty *n, pl* **abil•i•ties 1 :** power to do something **2 :** natural talent or acquired skill

-abil•i•ty *also* **-ibil•i•ty** *n suffix, pl* **-abil•i•ties** *also* **-ibil•i•ties :** ability, fitness, or likeliness to act or be acted upon in (such) a way

ab•ject *adj* **:** low in spirit or hope — **ab•ject•ly** *adv* — **ab•ject•ness** *n*

ablaze *adj* **1 :** being on fire **2 :** bright with light or color

able *adj* **abler; ablest 1 :** having enough power or skill to do something **2 :** having or showing much skill

-able *also* **-ible** *adj suffix* **1 :** capable of, fit for, or worthy of being **2 :** tending or likely to — **-ably** *also* **-ibly** *adv suffix*

ably *adv* **:** in an able way

ab•nor•mal *adj* **:** differing from the normal usually in a noticeable way — **ab•nor•mal•ly** *adv*

[1]**aboard** *adv* **:** on, onto, or within a ship, train, bus, or airplane

[2]**aboard** *prep* **:** on or into especially for passage

[1]**abode** *past of* ABIDE

[2]**abode** *n* **:** the place where one stays or lives

abol•ish *vb* **:** to do away with **:** put an end to

ab•o•li•tion *n* **:** a complete doing away with

A–bomb *n* **:** ATOMIC BOMB

abom•i•na•ble *adj* **1 :** deserving or causing disgust **2 :** very disagreeable or unpleasant — **abom•i•na•bly** *adv*

abominable snow•man *n, often cap A&S* **:** a mysterious creature with human or apelike characteristics reported to exist in the Himalayas

abom•i•na•tion *n* **:** something abominable

ab•orig•i•ne *n, pl* **ab•orig•i•nes :** a member of the original race to live in a region **:** NATIVE

abound *vb* **1 :** to be plentiful **:** TEEM **2 :** to be fully supplied

[1]**about** *adv* **1 :** ALMOST, NEARLY **2 :** on all sides **:** AROUND **3 :** one after another **4 :** in the opposite direction

[2]**about** *prep* **1 :** on every side of **:** AROUND **2 :** on the point of **3 :** having to do with

[1]**above** *adv* **:** in or to a higher place

[2]**above** *prep* **1 :** higher than **:** OVER **2 :** too good for **3 :** more than

[3]**above** *adj* **:** said or written earlier

[1]**above•board** *adv* **:** in an honest open way

[2]**aboveboard** *adj* **:** free from tricks and secrecy

ab•ra•ca•dab•ra *n* **:** a magical charm or word

abrade *vb* **abrad•ed; abrad•ing :** to wear away by rubbing

[1]**abra•sive** *n* **:** a substance for grinding, smoothing, or polishing

[2]**abrasive** *adj* **:** having the effect of or like that of abrading

abreast *adv or adj* **1 :** side by side **2 :** up to a certain level of knowledge

abridge *vb* **abridged; abridg•ing :** to shorten by leaving out some parts

abridg•ment *or* **abridge•ment** *n* **:** a shortened form of a written work

abroad *adv or adj* **1 :** over a wide area **2 :** in the open **:** OUTDOORS **3 :** in or to a foreign country **4 :** known to many people

abrupt *adj* **1 :** happening without warning **:** SUDDEN **2 :** [1]STEEP 1 — **abrupt•ly** *adv* — **abrupt•ness** *n*

ab•scess *n* **:** a collection of pus with swollen and red tissue around it — **ab•scessed** *adj*

ab•sence *n* **1 :** a being away **2 :** [2]LACK 1, WANT

[1]**ab•sent** *adj* **1 :** not present **2 :** not existing **3 :** showing that one is not paying attention

[2]**ab•sent** *vb* **:** to keep (oneself) away

ab•sen•tee *n* **:** a person who is absent

ab•sent•mind•ed *adj* **:** not paying attention to what is going on or to what one is doing — **ab•sent•mind•ed•ly** *adv* — **ab•sent•mind•ed•ness** *n*

ab•so•lute *adj* **1 :** free from imperfection **:** PERFECT, COMPLETE **2 :** free from control or conditions **3 :** free from doubt **:** CERTAIN — **ab•so•lute•ly** *adv* — **ab•so•lute•ness** *n*

ab•so•lu•tion *n* **:** a forgiving of sins

ab•solve *vb* **ab•solved; ab•solv•ing :** to set free from a duty or from blame

ab•sorb *vb* **1 :** to take in or swallow up **2 :** to hold all of one's interest **3 :** to receive without giving back

ab•sor•ben•cy *n* **:** the quality or state of being absorbent

ab•sor•bent *adj* **:** able to absorb

ab•sorp•tion *n* **1 :** the process of absorbing or being absorbed **2 :** complete attention

ab•stain *vb* **:** to keep oneself from doing something — **ab•stain•er** *n*

ab•sti•nence *n* **:** an avoiding by choice especially of certain foods or of liquor

[1]**ab•stract** *adj* **1 :** expressing a quality apart from an actual person or thing that posseses it **2 :** hard to understand — **ab•stract•ly** *adv* — **ab•stract•ness** *n*

[2]**ab•stract** *n* **:** [2]SUMMARY

[3]**ab•stract** *vb* **1 :** to take away **:** SEPARATE **2 :** SUMMARIZE

ab•strac•tion *n* **1 :** the act of abstracting **:** the state of being abstracted **2 :** an abstract idea

ab•struse *adj* **:** hard to understand — **ab•struse•ly** *adv* — **ab•struse•ness** *n*

ab•surd *adj* **:** completely unreasonable or untrue **:** RIDICULOUS — **ab•surd•ly** *adv*

ab•sur•di•ty *n, pl* **ab•sur•di•ties 1 :** the fact of being absurd **2 :** something that is absurd

abun•dance *n* **:** a large quantity **:** PLENTY

abun•dant *adj* **:** more than enough **:** PLENTIFUL — **abun•dant•ly** *adv*

[1]**abuse** *n* **1 :** a dishonest practice **2 :** wrong or unfair treatment or use **3 :** harsh insulting language

[2]**abuse** *vb* **abused; abus•ing 1 :** to blame or scold rudely **2 :** to use wrongly **:** MISUSE **3 :** to treat cruelly **:** MISTREAT

abu•sive *adj* **:** using or characterized by abuse — **abu•sive•ly** *adv* — **abu•sive•ness** *n*

abut *vb* **abut•ted; abut•ting :** to touch along a border or with a part that sticks out

abut•ment *n* **:** something against which another thing rests its weight or pushes with force

abyss *n* **:** a gulf so deep or space so great that it cannot be measured

ac•a•dem•ic *adj* **1 :** of or relating to schools or colleges **2 :** having no practical importance — **ac•a•dem•i•cal•ly** *adv*

acad•e•my *n, pl* **acad•e•mies 1 :** a private high school **2 :** a high school or college where special subjects are taught **3 :** a society of learned persons

ac•cede *vb* **ac•ced•ed; ac•ced•ing :** to agree to

ac•cel•er•ate *vb* **ac•cel•er•at•ed; ac•cel•er•at•ing 1 :** to bring about earlier **:** HASTEN **2 :** to move or cause to move faster

ac•cel•er•a•tion *n* **:** a speeding up

ac•cel•er•a•tor *n* **:** a pedal in an automobile for controlling the speed of the motor

[1]**ac•cent** *vb* **1 :** to give a greater force or stress **2 :** to mark with a written or printed accent

[2]**ac•cent** *n* **1 :** a way of talking shared by a group (as the residents of a country) **2 :** greater stress or force given to a syllable of a word in speaking or to a beat in music **3**

: a mark (as ˈ or ˌ) used in writing or printing to show the place of greater stress on a syllable
ac·cen·tu·ate *vb* **ac·cen·tu·at·ed; ac·cen·tu·at·ing** **1 :** [1]ACCENT **2 :** EMPHASIZE
ac·cept *vb* **1 :** to receive or take willingly **2 :** to agree to
ac·cept·able *adj* **1 :** worthy of being accepted **2 :** ADEQUATE — **ac·cept·able·ness** *n* — **ac·cept·ably** *adv*
ac·cep·tance *n* **1 :** the act of accepting **2 :** the quality or state of being accepted or acceptable
ac·cess *n* **1 :** the right or ability to approach, enter, or use **2 :** a way or means of approach
ac·ces·si·ble *adj* **1 :** capable of being reached **2 :** OBTAINABLE — **ac·ces·si·bly** *adv*
ac·ces·sion *n* **:** a coming to a position of power
[1]**ac·ces·so·ry** *n, pl* **ac·ces·so·ries** **1 :** a person who helps another in doing wrong **2 :** an object or device not necessary in itself but adding to the beauty or usefulness of something else
[2]**accessory** *adj* **:** adding to or helping in a secondary way **:** SUPPLEMENTARY
ac·ci·dent *n* **1 :** something that happens by chance or from unknown causes **:** MISHAP **2 :** lack of intention or necessity **:** CHANCE
ac·ci·den·tal *adj* **1 :** happening by chance or unexpectedly **2 :** not happening or done on purpose — **ac·ci·den·tal·ly** *adv*
[1]**ac·claim** *vb* **:** [1]PRAISE 1
[2]**acclaim** *n* **:** [2]PRAISE 1, APPLAUSE
ac·cli·mate *vb* **ac·cli·mat·ed; ac·cli·mat·ing :** to change to fit a new climate or new surroundings
ac·cli·ma·tize *vb* **ac·cli·ma·tized; ac·cli·ma·tiz·ing :** ACCLIMATE
ac·com·mo·date *vb* **ac·com·mo·dat·ed; ac·com·mo·dat·ing** **1 :** to provide with a place to stay or sleep **2 :** to provide with something needed **:** help out **3 :** to have room for
ac·com·mo·dat·ing *adj* **:** ready to help — **ac·com·mo·dat·ing·ly** *adv*
ac·com·mo·da·tion *n* **1 :** something supplied that is useful or handy **2 accommodations** *pl* **:** lodging and meals or traveling space and related services
ac·com·pa·ni·ment *n* **:** music played along with a solo part to enrich it
ac·com·pa·nist *n* **:** a musician who plays an accompaniment
ac·com·pa·ny *vb* **ac·com·pa·nied; ac·com·pa·ny·ing** **1 :** to go with as a companion **2 :** to play a musical accompaniment for **3 :** to happen at the same time as
ac·com·plice *n* **:** a partner in wrongdoing
ac·com·plish *vb* **:** to succeed in doing **:** manage to do
ac·com·plished *adj* **:** skilled through practice or training **:** EXPERT
ac·com·plish·ment *n* **1 :** the act of accomplishing **:** COMPLETION **2 :** something accomplished **3 :** an acquired excellence or skill
[1]**ac·cord** *vb* **1 :** [1]GIVE 6 **2 :** to be in harmony **:** AGREE
[2]**accord** *n* **1 :** AGREEMENT 1, HARMONY **2 :** willingness to act or to do something
ac·cor·dance *n* **:** AGREEMENT 1
ac·cord·ing·ly *adv* **1 :** in the necessary way **:** in the way called for **2 :** as a result **:** CONSEQUENTLY, SO
ac·cord·ing to *prep* **1 :** in agreement with **2 :** as stated by
[1]**ac·cor·di·on** *n* **:** a portable keyboard musical instrument played by forcing air from a bellows past metal reeds
[2]**accordion** *adj* **:** folding or creased or hinged to fold like an accordion
ac·cost *vb* **:** to approach and speak to often in a demanding or aggressive way
[1]**ac·count** *n* **1 :** a record of money received and money paid out **2 :** a statement of explanation or of reasons or causes **3 :** a statement of facts or events **:** REPORT **4 :** [2]WORTH 1, IMPORTANCE — **on account of :** for the sake of **:** BECAUSE OF — **on no account :** not ever or for any reason
[2]**account** *vb* **1 :** to think of as **:** CONSIDER **2 :** to give an explanation **3 :** to be the only or chief reason
ac·coun·tant *n* **:** a person whose job is accounting
ac·count·ing *n* **:** the work of keeping track of how much money is made and spent in a business
ac·cu·mu·late *vb* **ac·cu·mu·lat·ed; ac·cu·mu·lat·ing** **1 :** COLLECT 1, GATHER **2 :** to increase in quantity or number
ac·cu·mu·la·tion *n* **1 :** a collecting together **2 :** something accumulated **:** COLLECTION
ac·cu·ra·cy *n* **:** freedom from mistakes
ac·cu·rate *adj* **:** free from mistakes **:** RIGHT — **ac·cu·rate·ly** *adv* — **ac·cu·rate·ness** *n*
ac·cu·sa·tion *n* **:** a claim that someone has done something bad or illegal
ac·cuse *vb* **ac·cused; ac·cus·ing :** to blame a fault, wrong, or crime on (a person) — **ac·cus·er** *n*
ac·cus·tom *vb* **:** to cause (someone) to get used to something
ac·cus·tomed *adj* **1 :** CUSTOMARY 2, USUAL **2 :** familiar with **:** USED

DICTIONARY

¹ace *n* **1 :** a playing card with one figure in its center **2 :** a person who is expert at something
²ace *adj* **:** of the very best kind
¹ache *vb* **ached; ach·ing 1 :** to suffer a dull continuous pain **2 :** YEARN
²ache *n* **:** a dull continuous pain
achieve *vb* **achieved; achiev·ing 1 :** to bring about **:** ACCOMPLISH **2 :** to get by means of one's own efforts **:** WIN
achieve·ment *n* **1 :** the act of achieving **2 :** something achieved especially by great effort
¹ac·id *adj* **1 :** having a taste that is sour, bitter, or stinging **2 :** sour in temper **:** CROSS **3 :** of, relating to, or like an acid — **ac·id·ly** *adv*
²acid *n* **:** a chemical compound that tastes sour and forms a water solution which turns blue litmus paper red
acid·i·ty *n, pl* **acid·i·ties :** the quality, state, or degree of being acid
ac·knowl·edge *vb* **ac·knowl·edged; ac·knowl·edg·ing 1 :** to admit the truth or existence of **2 :** to recognize the rights or authority of **3 :** to make known that something has been received or noticed
ac·knowl·edged *adj* **:** generally accepted
ac·knowl·edg·ment *or* **ac·knowl·edge·ment** *n* **1 :** an act of acknowledging some deed or achievement **2 :** something done or given in return for something done or received
ac·ne *n* **:** a skin condition in which pimples and blackheads are present
acorn *n* **:** the nut of the oak tree
acous·tic *or* **acous·ti·cal** *adj* **1 :** of or relating to hearing or sound **2 :** deadening sound
acous·tics *n sing or pl* **1 :** a science dealing with sound **2 :** the qualities in a room or hall that make it easy or hard for a person in it to hear clearly
ac·quaint *vb* **1 :** to cause to know personally **2 :** to make familiar **:** INFORM
ac·quain·tance *n* **1 :** personal knowledge **2 :** a person one knows slightly
ac·qui·esce *vb* **ac·qui·esced; ac·qui·esc·ing :** to accept, agree, or give consent by keeping silent or by not making objections
ac·qui·es·cence *n* **:** the act of acquiescing
ac·quire *vb* **ac·quired; ac·quir·ing :** to get especially by one's own efforts **:** GAIN
ac·qui·si·tion *n* **1 :** the act of acquiring **2 :** something acquired
ac·quis·i·tive *adj* **:** GREEDY 2 — **ac·quis·i·tive·ly** *adv* — **ac·quis·i·tive·ness** *n*
ac·quit *vb* **ac·quit·ted; ac·quit·ting 1 :** to declare innocent of a crime or of wrongdoing **2 :** to conduct (oneself) in a certain way
ac·quit·tal *n* **:** the act of acquitting someone
acre *n* **:** a measure of land area equal to 43,560 square feet (about 4047 square meters)
acre·age *n* **:** area in acres
ac·rid *adj* **1 :** sharp or bitter in taste or odor **2 :** very harsh or unpleasant
ac·ro·bat *n* **:** a person (as a circus performer) who is very good at stunts like jumping, balancing, tumbling, and swinging from things
ac·ro·bat·ic *adj* **:** of or relating to acrobats or acrobatics
ac·ro·bat·ics *n sing or pl* **1 :** the art or performance of an acrobat **2 :** stunts of or like those of an acrobat
acrop·o·lis *n* **:** the upper fortified part of an ancient Greek city
¹across *adv* **:** from one side to the other
²across *prep* **1 :** to or on the opposite side of **2 :** so as to pass, go over, or intersect at an angle
¹act *n* **1 :** something that is done **:** DEED **2 :** a law made by a governing body **3 :** the doing of something **4 :** a main division of a play
²act *vb* **1 :** to perform (a part) on the stage **2 :** to behave oneself in a certain way **3 :** to do something **:** MOVE **4 :** to have a result **:** make something happen **:** WORK
act·ing *adj* **:** serving for a short time only or in place of another
ac·tion *n* **1 :** the working of one thing on another so as to produce a change **2 :** the doing of something **3 :** something done **4 :** the way something runs or works **5 :** combat in war
action figure *n* **:** a small figure usually of a superhero used especially as a toy
ac·ti·vate *vb* **ac·ti·vat·ed; ac·ti·vat·ing :** to make active or more active
ac·tive *adj* **1 :** producing or involving action or movement **2 :** showing that the subject of a sentence is the doer of the action represented by the verb **3 :** quick in physical movement **:** LIVELY **4 :** taking part in an action or activity — **ac·tive·ly** *adv*
ac·tiv·i·ty *n, pl* **ac·tiv·i·ties 1 :** energetic action **2 :** something done especially for relaxation or fun
ac·tor *n* **:** a person who acts especially in a play or movie
ac·tress *n* **:** a woman or girl who acts especially in a play or movie
ac·tu·al *adj* **:** really existing or happening **:** not false
ac·tu·al·ly *adv* **:** in fact **:** REALLY

acute *adj* **acut·er; acut·est** **1 :** measuring less than a right angle **2 :** mentally sharp **3 :** SEVERE **4 :** developing quickly and lasting only a short time **5 :** CRITICAL 4, URGENT — **acute·ly** *adv* — **acute·ness** *n*

ad *n* **:** ADVERTISEMENT

ad·age *n* **:** an old familiar saying **:** PROVERB

ad·a·mant *adj* **:** not giving in

Ad·am's apple *n* **:** the lump formed in the front of a person's neck by cartilage in the throat

adapt *vb* **:** to make or become suitable or able to function — **adapt·er** *n*

adapt·abil·i·ty *n* **:** the quality or state of being adaptable

adapt·able *adj* **:** capable of adapting or being adapted

ad·ap·ta·tion *n* **1 :** the act or process of adapting **2 :** something adapted or helping to adapt

add *vb* **1 :** to join or unite to something **2 :** to say something more **3 :** to combine numbers into a single sum

ad·dend *n* **:** a number that is to be added to another number

ad·den·dum *n, pl* **ad·den·da :** something added (as to a book)

ad·der *n* **1 :** any of several poisonous snakes of Europe or Africa **2 :** any of several harmless North American snakes (as the **puff adder**)

[1]**ad·dict** *vb* **:** to cause to have a need for something

[2]**ad·dict** *n* **:** a person who is addicted (as to a drug)

ad·dic·tion *n* **:** the state of being addicted (as to the use of harmful drugs)

ad·di·tion *n* **1 :** the adding of numbers to obtain their sum **2 :** something added — **in addition :** [2]BESIDES, ALSO — **in addition to :** over and above **:** [1]BESIDES

ad·di·tion·al *adj* **:** [1]EXTRA — **ad·di·tion·al·ly** *adv*

[1]**ad·di·tive** *adj* **:** relating to or produced by addition

[2]**additive** *n* **:** a substance added to another in small amounts

ad·dle *vb* **ad·dled; ad·dling :** to make confused

[1]**ad·dress** *vb* **1 :** to apply (oneself) to something **2 :** to speak or write to **3 :** to put directions for delivery on

[2]**ad·dress** *n* **1 :** a rehearsed speech **:** LECTURE **2 :** the place where a person can usually be reached **3 :** the directions for delivery placed on mail **4 :** the symbols (as numerals or letters) that identify the location where particular information (as a home page) is stored on a computer especially on the Internet

ad·dress·ee *n* **:** the person to whom something is addressed

ad·e·noids *n pl* **:** fleshy growths near the opening of the nose into the throat

ad·ept *adj* **:** very good at something — **adept·ly** *adv* — **adept·ness** *n*

ad·e·quate *adj* **1 :** [1]ENOUGH **2 :** good enough — **ad·e·quate·ly** *adv* — **ad·e·quate·ness** *n*

ad·here *vb* **ad·hered; ad·her·ing** **1 :** to stay loyal (as to a promise) **2 :** to stick tight **:** CLING

ad·her·ence *n* **:** steady or faithful attachment

ad·her·ent *n* **:** a person who adheres to a belief, an organization, or a leader

ad·he·sion *n* **:** the act or state of adhering

[1]**ad·he·sive** *adj* **:** tending to stick **:** STICKY — **ad·he·sive·ly** *adv* — **ad·he·sive·ness** *n*

[2]**adhesive** *n* **:** an adhesive substance

adi·os *interj* — used instead of goodbye

ad·ja·cent *adj* **:** next to or near something — **ad·ja·cent·ly** *adv*

ad·jec·ti·val *adj* **:** of, relating to, or functioning as an adjective — **ad·jec·ti·val·ly** *adv*

ad·jec·tive *n* **:** a word that says something about a noun or pronoun

ad·join *vb* **:** to be next to or in contact with

ad·journ *vb* **:** to bring or come to a close for a period of time — **ad·journ·ment** *n*

ad·junct *n* **:** something joined or added to something else but not a necessary part of it

ad·just *vb* **1 :** to settle or fix by agreement **2 :** to move the parts of an instrument or a machine to make them work better **3 :** to become used to — **ad·just·er** *n*

ad·just·able *adj* **:** possible to adjust

ad·just·ment *n* **1 :** the act or process of adjusting **:** the state of being adjusted **2 :** a deciding about and paying of a claim or debt **3 :** something that is used to adjust one part to another

ad·ju·tant *n* **:** an officer who assists a commanding officer

ad–lib *vb* **ad–libbed; ad–lib·bing :** to improvise something and especially music or spoken lines

ad·min·is·ter *vb* **1 :** to be in charge of **:** MANAGE **2 :** to give out as deserved **3 :** to give or supply as treatment

ad·min·is·tra·tion *n* **1 :** the act or process of administering **2 :** the work involved in managing something **3 :** the persons who direct the business of something (as a city or school)

ad·min·is·tra·tive *adj* **:** of or relating to administration

ad·mi·ra·ble *adj* **:** deserving to be admired — **ad·mi·ra·bly** *adv*

ad·mi·ral *n* **:** a commissioned officer in the Navy or Coast Guard ranking above a vice admiral

ad·mi·ral·ty *adj* **:** of or relating to conduct on the sea

ad·mi·ra·tion *n* **:** great and delighted approval

ad·mire *vb* **ad·mired; ad·mir·ing :** to feel admiration for **:** think very highly of — **ad·mir·er** *n*

ad·mis·si·ble *adj* **:** deserving to be admitted or allowed **:** ALLOWABLE

ad·mis·sion *n* **1 :** an admitting of something that has not been proved **2 :** the act of admitting **3 :** the right or permission to enter **4 :** the price of entrance

ad·mit *vb* **ad·mit·ted; ad·mit·ting 1 :** [1]PERMIT 2, ALLOW **2 :** to allow to enter **:** let in **3 :** to make known usually with some unwillingness

ad·mit·tance *n* **:** permission to enter

ad·mon·ish *vb* **1 :** to criticize or warn gently but seriously **2 :** to give friendly advice or encouragement

ad·mo·ni·tion *n* **:** a gentle or friendly criticism or warning

ado *n* **:** fussy excitement or hurrying about

ado·be *n* **1 :** brick made of earth or clay dried in the sun **2 :** a building made of adobe

ad·o·les·cence *n* **:** the period of life between childhood and adulthood

ad·o·les·cent *n* **:** a person who is no longer a child but not yet adult

adopt *vb* **1 :** to take (a child of other parents) as one's own **2 :** to take up and practice as one's own **3 :** to accept and put into action — **adopt·er** *n*

adop·tion *n* **:** the act of adopting **:** the state of being adopted

ador·able *adj* **:** CHARMING, LOVELY — **ador·able·ness** *n* — **ador·ably** *adv*

ad·o·ra·tion *n* **:** deep love

adore *vb* **adored; ador·ing 1 :** [2]WORSHIP 1 **2 :** to be very fond of — **ador·er** *n*

adorn *vb* **:** to try to make prettier by adding decorations

adorn·ment *n* **1 :** DECORATION 1 **2 :** [1]ORNAMENT 1

adrift *adv or adj* **:** in a drifting state

adroit *adj* **:** having or showing great skill or cleverness — **adroit·ly** *adv* — **adroit·ness** *n*

ad·u·la·tion *n* **:** very great admiration

[1]**adult** *adj* **:** fully developed and mature

[2]**adult** *n* **:** an adult person or thing

adul·ter·ate *vb* **adul·ter·at·ed; adul·ter·at·ing :** to make impure or weaker by adding something different or of poorer quality

adult·hood *n* **:** the period of being an adult

[1]**ad·vance** *vb* **ad·vanced; ad·vanc·ing 1 :** to help the progress of **2 :** to move forward **3 :** to raise to a higher rank **4 :** to give ahead of time **5 :** PROPOSE 1

[2]**advance** *n* **1 :** a forward movement **2 :** IMPROVEMENT 1 **3 :** a rise in price, value, or amount **4 :** a first step or approach **5 :** a giving (as of money) ahead of time — **in advance :** [1]BEFORE 1 — **in advance of :** ahead of

ad·vanced *adj* **1 :** being far along in years or progress **2 :** being beyond the elementary or introductory level

ad·vance·ment *n* **1 :** the action of advancing **:** the state of being advanced **2 :** a raising or being raised to a higher rank or position

ad·van·tage *n* **1 :** the fact of being in a better position or condition **2 :** personal benefit or gain **3 :** something that benefits the one it belongs to

ad·van·ta·geous *adj* **:** giving an advantage **:** HELPFUL — **ad·van·ta·geous·ly** *adv*

ad·vent *n* **:** the arrival or coming of something

[1]**ad·ven·ture** *n* **1 :** an action that involves unknown dangers and risks **2 :** an unusual experience

[2]**adventure** *vb* **ad·ven·tured; ad·ven·tur·ing :** to expose to or go on in spite of danger or risk — **ad·ven·tur·er** *n*

ad·ven·ture·some *adj* **:** likely to take risks **:** DARING

ad·ven·tur·ous *adj* **1 :** ready to take risks or to deal with new or unexpected problems **2 :** DANGEROUS 1, RISKY — **ad·ven·tur·ous·ly** *adv* — **ad·ven·tur·ous·ness** *n*

ad·verb *n* **:** a word used to modify a verb, an adjective, or another adverb and often used to show degree, manner, place, or time

ad·ver·bi·al *adj* **:** of, relating to, or used an an adverb — **ad·ver·bi·al·ly** *adv*

ad·ver·sary *n, pl* **ad·ver·sar·ies :** OPPONENT, ENEMY

ad·verse *adj* **1 :** acting against or in an opposite direction **2 :** not helping or favoring — **ad·verse·ly** *adv* — **ad·verse·ness** *n*

ad·ver·si·ty *n, pl* **ad·ver·si·ties :** hard times **:** MISFORTUNE

ad·ver·tise *vb* **ad·ver·tised; ad·ver·tis·ing 1 :** to announce publicly **2 :** to call to public attention to persuade to buy **3 :** to put out a public notice or request — **ad·ver·tis·er** *n*

ad·ver·tise·ment *n* **:** a notice or short film advertising something

ad·ver·tis·ing *n* **1 :** speech, writing, pictures, or films meant to persuade people to buy something **2 :** the business of preparing advertisements

ad·vice *n* **:** suggestions about a decision or action
ad·vis·able *adj* **:** reasonable or proper to do **:** DISCREET — **ad·vis·ably** *adv*
ad·vise *vb* **ad·vised; ad·vis·ing** **1 :** to give advice to **:** COUNSEL **2 :** to give information about something — **ad·vis·er** *or* **ad·vi·sor** *n*
ad·vi·so·ry *adj* **1 :** having the power or right to advise **2 :** containing advice
1ad·vo·cate *n* **1 :** a person who argues for another in court **2 :** a person who argues for or supports an idea or plan
2ad·vo·cate *vb* **ad·vo·cat·ed; ad·vo·cat·ing** **:** to argue for
adz *or* **adze** *n* **:** a cutting tool that has a thin curved blade at right angles to the handle and is used for shaping wood
-aemia — see -EMIA
ae·on *or* **eon** *n* **:** a very long period of time **:** AGE
aer- *or* **aero-** *prefix* **:** air **:** atmosphere **:** gas
aer·ate *vb* **aer·at·ed; aer·at·ing** **1 :** to supply (blood) with oxygen by breathing **2 :** to supply or cause to be filled with air **3 :** to combine or fill with gas — **aer·a·tor** *n*
aer·a·tion *n* **:** the process of aerating
1ae·ri·al *adj* **1 :** of, relating to, or occurring in the air **2 :** running on cables or rails that are raised above the ground **3 :** of or relating to aircraft **4 :** taken from or used in or against aircraft — **ae·ri·al·ly** *adv*
2aer·i·al *n* **:** ANTENNA 2
ae·rie *n* **:** the nest of a bird (as an eagle) high on a cliff or a mountaintop
aero·nau·ti·cal *or* **aero·nau·tic** *adj* **:** of or relating to aeronautics
aero·nau·tics *n* **:** a science dealing with the building and flying of aircraft
aero·sol *n* **1 :** a substance (as an insecticide) that is dispensed from a container as a spray of tiny solid or liquid particles in gas **2 :** a container that dispenses an aerosol
aero·space *n* **1 :** the earth's atmosphere and the space beyond **2 :** a science dealing with aerospace
aes·thet·ic *or* **es·thet·ic** *adj* **:** of or relating to beauty and what is beautiful — **aes·thet·i·cal·ly** *adv*
1afar *adv* **:** from, at, or to a great distance
2afar *n* **:** a long way off
af·fa·ble *adj* **:** polite and friendly in talking to others — **af·fa·bly** *adv*
af·fair *n* **1 affairs** *pl* **:** BUSINESS 1 **2 :** something that relates to or involves one **3 :** an action or occasion only partly specified
1af·fect *vb* **1 :** to be fond of using or wearing **2 :** ASSUME 3
2affect *vb* **1 :** to attack or act on as a disease does **2 :** to have an effect on
af·fect·ed *adj* **:** not natural or genuine — **af·fect·ed·ly** *adv*
af·fect·ing *adj* **:** causing pity or sadness
af·fec·tion *n* **:** a feeling of attachment **:** liking for someone
af·fec·tion·ate *adj* **:** feeling or showing a great liking for a person or thing **:** LOVING — **af·fec·tion·ate·ly** *adv*
af·fi·da·vit *n* **:** a sworn statement in writing
af·fil·i·ate *vb* **af·fil·i·at·ed; af·fil·i·at·ing** **:** to associate as a member or branch
af·fin·i·ty *n, pl* **af·fin·i·ties** **:** a strong liking for or attraction to someone or something
af·firm *vb* **1 :** to declare to be true **2 :** to say with confidence **:** ASSERT
af·fir·ma·tion *n* **:** an act of affirming
1af·fir·ma·tive *adj* **1 :** declaring that the fact is so **2 :** being positive or helpful
2affirmative *n* **1 :** an expression (as the word *yes*) of agreement **2 :** the affirmative side in a debate or vote
1af·fix *vb* **:** FASTEN 1, 2, ATTACH
2af·fix *n* **:** a letter or group of letters that comes at the beginning or end of a word and has a meaning of its own
af·flict *vb* **:** to cause pain or unhappiness to
af·flic·tion *n* **1 :** the state of being afflicted **2 :** something that causes pain or unhappiness
af·flu·ence *n* **:** the state of having much money or property
af·flu·ent *adj* **:** having plenty of money and things that money can buy
af·ford *vb* **1 :** to be able to do or bear without serious harm **2 :** to be able to pay for **3 :** to supply one with
1af·front *vb* **:** to insult openly
2affront *n* **:** 2INSULT
afield *adv* **1 :** to, in, or into the countryside **2 :** away from home **3 :** outside of one's usual circle or way of doing **4 :** ASTRAY 2
afire *adj* **:** being on fire
aflame *adj* **:** burning with flames
afloat *adv or adj* **:** carried on or as if on water
aflut·ter *adj* **1 :** flapping quickly **2 :** very excited and nervous
afoot *adv or adj* **1 :** on foot **2 :** happening now **:** going on
afore·men·tioned *adj* **:** mentioned before
afore·said *adj* **:** named before
afraid *adj* **:** filled with fear
afresh *adv* **:** again from the beginning **:** from a new beginning
1Af·ri·can *n* **:** a person born or living in Africa
2African *adj* **:** of or relating to Africa or the Africans

African–American *n* : AFRO-AMERICAN — **African–American** *adj*
African violet *n* : a tropical African plant grown often for its showy white, pink, or purple flowers and its velvety leaves
Af•ro–Amer•i•can *n* : an American having African and especially black African ancestors — **Afro–American** *adj*
aft *adv* : toward or at the back part of a ship or the tail of an aircraft
[1]**af•ter** *adv* : following in time or place
[2]**after** *prep* **1** : behind in time or place **2** : for the reason of catching, seizing, or getting **3** : with the name of
[3]**after** *conj* : following the time when
[4]**after** *adj* **1** : later in time **2** : located toward the back part of a ship or aircraft
af•ter•ef•fect *n* : an effect that follows its cause after some time has passed
af•ter•glow *n* : a glow remaining (as in the sky after sunset) where a light has disappeared
af•ter•life *n* : an existence after death
af•ter•math *n* : a usually bad result
af•ter•noon *n* : the part of the day between noon and evening
af•ter•thought *n* : a later thought about something one has done or said
af•ter•ward *or* **af•ter•wards** *adv* : at a later time
again *adv* **1** : once more : ANEW **2** : on the other hand **3** : in addition
against *prep* **1** : opposed to **2** : as protection from **3** : in or into contact with
agape *adj* : wide open
ag•ate *n* **1** : a mineral that is a quartz with colors arranged in stripes, cloudy masses, or mossy forms **2** : a child's marble of agate or of glass that looks like agate
aga•ve *n* : a plant that has sword-shaped leaves with spiny edges and is sometimes grown for its large stalks of flowers
[1]**age** *n* **1** : the time from birth to a specified date **2** : the time of life when a person receives full legal rights **3** : normal lifetime **4** : the later part of life **5** : a period of time associated with a special person or feature **6** : a long period of time
[2]**age** *vb* **aged; ag•ing** *or* **age•ing** **1** : to grow old or cause to grow old **2** : to remain or cause to remain undisturbed until fit for use : MATURE
-age *n suffix* **1** : collection **2** : action : process **3** : result of **4** : rate of **5** : house or place of **6** : state : rank **7** : fee : charge
aged *adj* **1** : very old **2** : of age
age•less *adj* : not growing old or showing the effects of age — **age•less•ly** *adv*
agen•cy *n, pl* **agen•cies** **1** : a person or thing through which power is used or something is achieved **2** : the office or function of an agent **3** : an establishment doing business for another **4** : a part of a government that runs projects in a certain area
agen•da *n* : a list of things to be done or talked about
agent *n* **1** : something that produces an effect **2** : a person who acts or does business for another
ag•gra•vate *vb* **ag•gra•vat•ed; ag•gra•vat•ing** **1** : to make worse or more serious **2** : to make angry by bothering again and again
ag•gra•va•tion *n* **1** : an act or the result of aggravating **2** : something that aggravates
[1]**ag•gre•gate** *adj* : formed by the collection of units or particles into one mass or sum
[2]**ag•gre•gate** *vb* **ag•gre•gat•ed; ag•gre•gat•ing** : to collect or gather into a mass or whole
[3]**ag•gre•gate** *n* **1** : a mass or body of units or parts **2** : the whole sum or amount
ag•gre•ga•tion *n* **1** : the collecting of units or parts into a mass or whole **2** : a group, body, or mass composed of many distinct parts
ag•gres•sion *n* : an attack made without reasonable cause
ag•gres•sive *adj* **1** : showing a readiness to attack others **2** : practicing aggression **3** : being forceful and sometimes pushy — **ag•gres•sive•ly** *adv* — **ag•gres•sive•ness** *n*
ag•gres•sor *n* : a person or a country that attacks without reasonable cause
ag•grieved *adj* **1** : having a troubled or unhappy mind **2** : having cause for complaint
aghast *adj* : struck with terror or amazement
ag•ile *adj* **1** : able to move quickly and easily **2** : having a quick mind — **ag•ile•ly** *adv*
agil•i•ty *n* : the ability to move quickly and easily
aging *present participle of* AGE
ag•i•tate *vb* **ag•i•tat•ed; ag•i•tat•ing** **1** : to move with an irregular rapid motion **2** : to stir up : EXCITE **3** : to try to stir up public feeling — **ag•i•ta•tor** *n*
ag•i•ta•tion *n* : the act of agitating : the state of being agitated
agleam *adj* : giving off gleams of light
aglow *adj* : glowing with light or color
ago *adv* : before this time
agog *adj* : full of excitement
ag•o•nize *vb* **ag•o•nized; ag•o•niz•ing** : to suffer greatly in body or mind
ag•o•ny *n, pl* **ag•o•nies** : great pain of body or mind
agree *vb* **agreed; agree•ing** **1** : to give

one's approval or permission **2 :** to have the same opinion **3 :** ADMIT 3 **4 :** to be alike **5 :** to come to an understanding **6 :** to be fitting or healthful

agree•able *adj* **1 :** pleasing to the mind or senses **2 :** willing to agree — **agree•able•ness** *n* — **agree•ably** *adv*

agree•ment *n* **1 :** the act or fact of agreeing **2 :** an arrangement made about action to be taken

ag•ri•cul•tur•al *adj* **:** of, relating to, or used in agriculture

ag•ri•cul•ture *n* **:** the cultivating of the soil, producing of crops, and raising of livestock

aground *adv or adj* **:** on or onto the shore or the bottom of a body of water

ah *interj* — used to express delight, relief, disappointment, or scorn

aha *interj* — used to express surprise, triumph, or scorn

ahead *adv or adj* **1 :** in or toward the front **2 :** into or for the future

ahead of *prep* **1 :** in front of **2 :** earlier than

ahoy *interj* — used in calling out to a passing ship or boat

1aid *vb* **:** 1HELP 1, ASSIST

2aid *n* **1 :** the act of helping **2 :** help given **3 :** someone or something that is of help or assistance

aide *n* **:** a person who acts as an assistant

AIDS *n* **:** a serious disease of the human immune system in which large numbers of the cells that help the body fight infection are destroyed by a virus carried in the blood and other fluids of the body

ail *vb* **1 :** to be wrong with **2 :** to suffer especially with ill health

ai•le•ron *n* **:** a movable part of an airplane wing that is used to steer it to one side or the other

ail•ment *n* **:** SICKNESS 2

1aim *vb* **1 :** to point a weapon toward an object **2 :** INTEND **3 :** to direct to or toward a specified object or goal

2aim *n* **1 :** the directing of a weapon or a missile at a mark **2 :** 1PURPOSE

aim•less *adj* **:** lacking purpose — **aim•less•ly** *adv* — **aim•less•ness** *n*

1air *n* **1 :** the invisible mixture of odorless tasteless gases that surrounds the earth **2 :** air that is compressed **3 :** outward appearance **4 :** AIRCRAFT **5 :** AVIATION **6 :** a radio or television system **7 airs** *pl* **:** an artificial way of acting

2air *vb* **1 :** to place in the air for cooling, freshening, or cleaning **2 :** to make known in public

air bag *n* **:** an automobile safety device consisting of a bag that will inflate automatically in front of a rider to act as a cushion in an accident

air base *n* **:** a base of operations for military aircraft

air–con•di•tion *vb* **:** to equip with a device for cleaning air and controlling its humidity and temperature — **air con•di•tion•er** *n* — **air–con•di•tion•ing** *n*

air•craft *n, pl* **aircraft :** a vehicle (as a balloon, airplane, or helicopter) that can travel through the air and that is supported either by its own lightness or by the action of the air against its surfaces

air•drome *n* **:** AIRPORT

air•field *n* **1 :** the landing field of an airport **2 :** AIRPORT

air force *n* **:** the military organization of a nation for air warfare

air lane *n* **:** AIRWAY 2

air•lift *n* **:** a system of moving people or cargo by aircraft usually to or from an area that cannot be reached otherwise

air•line *n* **:** a system of transportation by aircraft including its routes, equipment, and workers

air•lin•er *n* **:** a large passenger airplane flown by an airline

1air•mail *n* **1 :** the system of carrying mail by airplanes **2 :** mail carried by airplanes

2airmail *vb* **:** to send by airmail

air•man *n, pl* **air•men 1 :** an enlisted person in the Air Force in one of the ranks below sergeant **2 :** AVIATOR

airman basic *n* **:** an enlisted person of the lowest rank in the Air Force

airman first class *n* **:** an enlisted person in the Air Force ranking above an airman second class

airman second class *n* **:** an enlisted person in the Air Force ranking above an airman basic

air•plane *n* **:** an aircraft with a fixed wing that is heavier than air, driven by a propeller or jet engine, and supported by the action of the air against its wings

air•port *n* **:** a place either on land or water that is kept for the landing and takeoff of aircraft and for receiving and sending off passengers and cargo

air•ship *n* **:** an aircraft lighter than air that is kept in the air by a container filled with gas and has an engine, propeller, and rudder

air•sick *adj* **:** sick to one's stomach while riding in an airplane because of its motion — **air•sick•ness** *n*

air•strip *n* **:** a runway without places (as hangars) for the repair of aircraft or shelter of passengers or cargo

air•tight *adj* **:** so tight that no air can get in or out — **air•tight•ness** *n*

air·wave *n* **:** the radio waves used in radio and television transmission — usually used in pl.

air·way *n* **1 :** a place for a current of air to pass through **2 :** a regular route for aircraft **3 :** AIRLINE

airy *adj* **air·i·er; air·i·est 1 :** of, relating to, or living in the air **2 :** open to the air **:** BREEZY **3 :** like air in lightness and delicacy

aisle *n* **:** a passage between sections of seats (as in a church or theater)

ajar *adv or adj* **:** slightly open

akim·bo *adv or adj* **:** with hands on hips

akin *adj* **1 :** related by blood **2 :** SIMILAR

[1]**-al** *adj suffix* **:** of, relating to, or showing

[2]**-al** *n suffix* **:** action **:** process

al·a·bas·ter *n* **:** a smooth usually white stone used for carving

à la carte *adv or adj* **:** with a separate price for each item on the menu

alac·ri·ty *n* **:** a cheerful readiness to do something

[1]**alarm** *n* **1 :** a warning of danger **2 :** a device (as a bell) that warns or signals people **3 :** the fear caused by sudden danger

[2]**alarm** *vb* **:** to cause a sense of danger in **:** FRIGHTEN

alas *interj* — used to express unhappiness, pity, or worry

al·ba·tross *n* **:** a very large seabird with webbed feet

al·bi·no *n, pl* **al·bi·nos 1 :** a person or an animal that has little or no coloring matter in skin, hair, and eyes **2 :** a plant with little or no coloring matter

al·bum *n* **1 :** a book with blank pages in which to put a collection (as of photographs, stamps, or autographs) **2 :** one or more phonograph records or tape recordings carrying a major musical work or a group of related pieces

al·bu·men *n* **1 :** the white of an egg **2 :** ALBUMIN

al·bu·min *n* **:** any of various proteins that are soluble in water and occur in plant and animal tissues

al·co·hol *n* **1 :** a colorless flammable liquid that in one form is the substance in fermented and distilled liquors (as beer, wine, or whiskey) that can make one drunk **2 :** a drink (as beer, wine, or whiskey) containing alcohol

[1]**al·co·hol·ic** *adj* **1 :** of, relating to, or containing alcohol **2 :** affected with alcoholism

[2]**alcoholic** *n* **:** a person affected with alcoholism

al·co·hol·ism *n* **:** a sickness of body and mind caused by too much use of alcoholic drinks

al·cove *n* **:** a small part of a room set back from the rest of it

al·der *n* **:** a tree or shrub related to the birches that has toothed leaves and grows in moist soil

al·der·man *n* **:** a member of a lawmaking body in a city

ale *n* **:** an alcoholic drink made from malt and flavored with hops that is usually more bitter than beer

[1]**alert** *adj* **1 :** watchful and ready to meet danger **2 :** quick to understand and act **3 :** ACTIVE 3, BRISK — **alert·ly** *adv* — **alert·ness** *n*

[2]**alert** *n* **1 :** a signal (as an alarm) of danger **2 :** the period during which an alert is in effect — **on the alert :** watchful against danger

[3]**alert** *vb* **:** to call to a state of readiness **:** WARN

al·fal·fa *n* **:** a plant with purple flowers that is related to the clovers and is grown as a food for horses and cattle

al·ga *n, pl* **al·gae :** any of a large group of simple plants and plant-like organisms that include the seaweeds and that include the seaweeds and that produce chlorophyll like plants but do not produce seeds and cannot be divided into roots, stems, and leaves

al·ge·bra *n* **:** a branch of mathematics in which symbols (as letters and numbers) are combined according to the rules of arithmetic

[1]**alias** *adv* **:** otherwise known as

[2]**alias** *n* **:** a false name

[1]**al·i·bi** *n, pl* **al·i·bis 1 :** the explanation given by a person accused of a crime that he or she was somewhere else when the crime was committed **2 :** [2]EXCUSE 2

[2]**alibi** *vb* **al·i·bied; al·i·bi·ing 1 :** to offer an excuse **2 :** to make an excuse for

[1]**alien** *adj* **:** FOREIGN 2

[2]**alien** *n* **:** a resident who was born elsewhere and is not a citizen of the country in which he or she now lives

alien·ate *vb* **alien·at·ed; alien·at·ing :** to cause (one who used to be friendly or loyal) to become unfriendly or disloyal

[1]**alight** *vb* **alight·ed** *also* **alit; alight·ing 1 :** to get down **:** DISMOUNT **2 :** to come down from the air and settle

[2]**alight** *adj* **:** full of light **:** lighted up

align *vb* **:** to bring into line — **align·er** *n* — **align·ment** *n*

[1]**alike** *adv* **:** in the same way

[2]**alike** *adj* **:** being like each other — **alike·ness** *n*

al·i·men·ta·ry *adj* **:** of or relating to food and nourishment

alimentary canal *n* **:** a long tube made up of the esophagus, stomach, and intestine into which food is taken and digested and from which wastes are passed out

al·i·mo·ny *n* **:** money for living expenses paid regularly by one spouse to another after their legal separation or divorce

alit *past of* ALIGHT

alive *adj* **1 :** having life **:** not dead **2 :** being in force, existence, or operation **3 :** aware of the existence of — **alive·ness** *n*

al·ka·li *n, pl* **al·ka·lies** *or* **al·ka·lis** **1 :** any of numerous substances that have a bitter taste and react with an acid to form a salt **2 :** a salt or a mixture of salts sometimes found in large amounts in the soil of dry regions

al·ka·line *adj* **:** of or relating to an alkali

¹all *adj* **1 :** the whole of **2 :** the greatest possible **3 :** every one of

²all *adv* **1 :** COMPLETELY **2 :** so much **3 :** for each side

³all *pron* **1 :** the whole number or amount **2 :** EVERYTHING

Al·lah *n* **:** the Supreme Being of the Muslims

all–around *adj* **1 :** having ability in many areas **2 :** useful in many ways

al·lay *vb* **1 :** to make less severe **2 :** to put to rest

al·lege *vb* **al·leged; al·leg·ing :** to state as fact but without proof

al·le·giance *n* **:** loyalty and service to a group, country, or idea

al·le·lu·ia *interj* **:** HALLELUJAH

al·ler·gen *n* **:** a substance that causes an allergic reaction

al·ler·gic *adj* **:** of, relating to, causing, or affected by allergy

al·ler·gist *n* **:** a medical doctor who specializes in treating allergies

al·ler·gy *n, pl* **al·ler·gies :** a condition in which a person is made sick by something that is harmless to most people

al·le·vi·ate *vb* **al·le·vi·at·ed; al·le·vi·at·ing :** to make easier to put up with

al·ley *n, pl* **al·leys** **1 :** a narrow passageway between buildings **2 :** a special narrow wooden floor on which balls are rolled in bowling

al·li·ance *n* **1 :** connection between families, groups, or individuals **2 :** an association formed by two or more nations for assistance and protection **3 :** a treaty of alliance

al·lied *adj* **1 :** being connected or related in some way **2 :** joined in alliance

al·li·ga·tor *n* **:** a large four-footed water animal related to the snakes and lizards

al·lot *vb* **al·lot·ted; al·lot·ting :** to give out as a share or portion

al·lot·ment *n* **1 :** the act of allotting **2 :** something that is allotted

al·low *vb* **1 :** to assign as a share or suitable amount (as of time or money) **2 :** to take into account **3 :** to accept as true **:** CONCEDE **4 :** to give permission to **5 :** to fail to prevent **6 :** to make allowance

al·low·able *adj* **:** not forbidden — **al·low·ably** *adv*

al·low·ance *n* **1 :** a share given out **2 :** a sum given as repayment or for expenses **3 :** the taking into account of things that could affect a result

al·loy *n* **:** a substance made of two or more metals melted together

all right *adj or adv* **1 :** satisfactory in quality or condition **2 :** very well

all–round *adj* **:** ALL-AROUND

all–star *adj* **:** made up mainly or entirely of outstanding participants

al·lude *vb* **al·lud·ed; al·lud·ing :** to talk about or hint at without mentioning directly

al·lure *vb* **al·lured; al·lur·ing :** to try to influence by offering what seems to be a benefit or pleasure

al·lu·sion *n* **:** an act of alluding or of hinting at something

¹al·ly *vb* **al·lied; al·ly·ing :** to form a connection between **:** join in an alliance

²al·ly *n, pl* **allies :** one (as a person or a nation) associated or united with another in a common purpose

al·ma·nac *n* **:** a book containing a calendar of days, weeks, and months and usually facts about the rising and setting of the sun and moon, changes in the tides, and information of general interest

al·mighty *adj, often cap* **:** having absolute power over all

al·mond *n* **:** a nut that is the edible kernel of a small tree related to the peach

al·most *adv* **:** only a little less than **:** very nearly

alms *n, pl* **alms :** something and especially money given to help the poor **:** CHARITY

aloft *adv or adj* **1 :** at or to a great height **2 :** in the air and especially in flight **3 :** at, on, or to the top of the mast or the higher rigging of a ship

¹alone *adj* **1 :** separated from others **2 :** not including anyone or anything else

²alone *adv* **1 :** and nothing or no one else **2 :** without company or help

¹along *prep* **1 :** on or near in a lengthwise direction **2 :** at a point on

²along *adv* **1 :** farther forward or on **2 :** as a companion or associate **3 :** throughout the time

DICTIONARY

along·shore *adv or adj* **:** along the shore or coast
[1]**along·side** *adv* **:** along or by the side
[2]**alongside** *prep* **:** parallel to
[1]**aloof** *adv* **:** at a distance
[2]**aloof** *adj* **:** RESERVED 1 — **aloof·ly** *adv* — **aloof·ness** *n*
aloud *adv* **:** using the voice so as to be clearly heard
al·paca *n* **:** a South American animal related to the camel and llama that is raised for its long woolly hair which is woven into warm strong cloth
al·pha·bet *n* **:** the letters used in writing a language arranged in their regular order
al·pha·bet·i·cal *or* **al·pha·bet·ic** *adj* **:** arranged in the order of the letters of the alphabet — **al·pha·bet·i·cal·ly** *adv*
al·pha·bet·ize *vb* **al·pha·bet·ized; al·pha·bet·iz·ing :** to arrange in alphabetical order
al·ready *adv* **:** before a certain time **:** by this time
al·so *adv* **:** in addition **:** TOO
al·tar *n* **1 :** a usually raised place on which sacrifices are offered **2 :** a platform or table used as a center of worship
al·ter *vb* **:** to change partly but not completely
al·ter·ation *n* **1 :** a making or becoming different in some respects **2 :** the result of altering **:** MODIFICATION
[1]**al·ter·nate** *adj* **1 :** occurring or following by turns **2 :** arranged one above, beside, or next to another **3 :** every other **:** every second — **al·ter·nate·ly** *adv*
[2]**al·ter·nate** *vb* **al·ter·nat·ed; al·ter·nat·ing :** to take place or cause to take place by turns
[3]**al·ter·nate** *n* **:** a person named to take the place of another whenever necessary
alternating current *n* **:** an electric current that reverses its direction of flow regularly many times per second
al·ter·na·tion *n* **:** the act, process, or result of alternating
[1]**al·ter·na·tive** *adj* **:** offering or expressing a choice — **al·ter·na·tive·ly** *adv*
[2]**alternative** *n* **1 :** a chance to choose between two things **2 :** one of the things between which a choice is to be made
al·though *conj* **:** in spite of the fact that
al·ti·tude *n* **1 :** height above a certain level and especially above sea level **2 :** the perpendicular distance from the base of a geometric figure to the vertex or to the side parallel to the base
al·to *n, pl* **altos 1 :** the lowest female singing voice **2 :** the second highest part in four-part harmony **3 :** a singer or an instrument having an alto range or part
al·to·geth·er *adv* **1 :** COMPLETELY **2 :** on the whole
al·tru·ism *n* **:** unselfish interest in others
al·um *n* **:** either of two aluminum compounds that have a sweetish-sourish taste and puckering effect on the mouth and are used in medicine (as to stop bleeding)
alu·mi·num *n* **:** a silver-white light metallic chemical element that is easily worked, conducts electricity well, resists weathering, and is the most plentiful metal in the earth's crust
alum·na *n, pl* **alum·nae :** a girl or woman who has attended or has graduated from a school, college, or university
alum·nus *n, pl* **alum·ni :** one who has attended or has graduated from a school, college, or university
al·ways *adv* **1 :** at all times **2 :** throughout all time **:** FOREVER
am *present 1st sing of* BE
amal·gam·ation *n* **:** the combining of different elements into a single body
amass *vb* **:** to collect or gather together
[1]**am·a·teur** *n* **1 :** a person who takes part in sports or occupations for pleasure and not for pay **2 :** a person who takes part in something without having experience or skill in it — **am·a·teur·ish** *adj*
[2]**amateur** *adj* **:** of, relating to, or done by amateurs **:** not professional
amaze *vb* **amazed; amaz·ing :** to surprise or puzzle very much
amaze·ment *n* **:** great surprise
am·bas·sa·dor *n* **:** a person sent as the chief representative of his or her government in another country — **am·bas·sa·dor·ship** *n*
am·ber *n* **1 :** a hard yellowish to brownish clear substance that is a fossil resin from trees long dead, takes a polish, and is used for ornamental objects (as beads) **2 :** a dark orange yellow
ambi- *prefix* **:** both
am·bi·dex·trous *adj* **:** using both hands with equal ease — **am·bi·dex·trous·ly** *adv*
am·bi·gu·i·ty *n, pl* **am·bi·gu·i·ties :** the fact or state of being ambiguous
am·big·u·ous *adj* **:** able to be understood in more than one way — **am·big·u·ous·ly** *adv*
am·bi·tion *n* **1 :** a desire for success, honor, or power **2 :** the aim or object one tries for
am·bi·tious *adj* **1 :** possessing ambition **2 :** showing ambition — **am·bi·tious·ly** *adv*
[1]**am·ble** *vb* **am·bled; am·bling :** to go at an amble
[2]**amble** *n* **:** a slow easy way of walking
am·bu·lance *n* **:** a vehicle meant to carry sick or injured persons
[1]**am·bush** *vb* **:** to attack from an ambush

²ambush *n* **:** a hidden place from which a surprise attack can be made

amen *interj* — used to express agreement (as after a prayer or a statement of opinion)

ame•na•ble *adj* **:** readily giving in or agreeing

amend *vb* **1 :** to change for the better **:** IMPROVE **2 :** to change the wording or meaning of **:** ALTER

amend•ment *n* **:** a change in wording or meaning especially in a law, bill, or motion

amends *n sing or pl* **:** something done or given by a person to make up for a loss or injury he or she has caused

ame•ni•ty *n, pl* **ame•ni•ties 1 :** the quality of being pleasant or agreeable **2** *amenities pl* **:** something (as good manners or household appliances) that makes life easier or more pleasant

¹Amer•i•can *n* **1 :** a person born or living in North or South America **2 :** a citizen of the United States

²American *adj* **1 :** of or relating to North or South America or their residents **2 :** of or relating to the United States or its citizens

American Indian *n* **:** a member of any of the first peoples to live in North and South America except usually the Eskimos

am•e•thyst *n* **:** a clear purple or bluish violet quartz used as a gem

ami•a•ble *adj* **:** having a friendly and pleasant manner — **ami•a•bly** *adv*

am•i•ca•ble *adj* **:** showing kindness or goodwill — **am•i•ca•bly** *adv*

amid *or* **amidst** *prep* **:** in or into the middle of

amid•ships *adv* **:** in or near the middle of a ship

ami•no acid *n* **:** any of numerous acids that contain carbon and nitrogen, include some which are the building blocks of protein, and are made by living plant or animal cells or obtained from the diet

¹amiss *adv* **:** in the wrong way

²amiss *adj* **:** not right **:** WRONG

am•i•ty *n, pl* **am•i•ties :** FRIENDSHIP

am•me•ter *n* **:** an instrument for measuring electric current in amperes

am•mo•nia *n* **1 :** a colorless gas that is a compound of nitrogen and hydrogen, has a sharp smell and taste, can be easily made liquid by cold and pressure, and is used in making ice, fertilizers, and explosives **2 :** a solution of ammonia and water

am•mu•ni•tion *n* **1 :** objects (as bullets) fired from guns **2 :** explosive objects (as bombs) used in war

am•ne•sia *n* **:** an abnormal and usually complete loss of one's memory

amoe•ba *n, pl* **amoe•bas** *or* **amoe•bae :** a tiny water animal that is a single cell which flows about and takes in food

among *also* **amongst** *prep* **1 :** in or through the middle of **2 :** in the presence of **:** WITH **3 :** through all or most of **4 :** in shares to each of

¹amount *vb* **1 :** to add up **2 :** to be the same in meaning or effect

²amount *n* **:** the total number or quantity

am•pere *n* **:** a unit for measuring the strength of an electric current

am•per•sand *n* **:** a character & standing for the word *and*

am•phet•amine *n* **:** a drug that causes the nervous system to become more active

am•phib•i•an *n* **1 :** any of a group of cold-blooded animals (as frogs and toads) that have gills and live in water as larvae but breathe air as adults **2 :** an airplane designed to take off from and land on either land or water

am•phib•i•ous *adj* **1 :** able to live both on land and in water **2 :** meant to be used on both land and water **3 :** made by land, sea, and air forces acting together — **am•phib•i•ous•ly** *adv* — **am•phib•i•ous•ness** *n*

am•phi•the•ater *n* **:** an arena with seats rising in curved rows around an open space

am•ple *adj* **:** more than enough in amount or size — **am•ply** *adv*

am•pli•fy *vb* **am•pli•fied; am•pli•fy•ing 1 :** to add to **2 :** to make louder or greater — **am•pli•fi•er** *n*

am•pu•tate *vb* **am•pu•tat•ed; am•pu•tat•ing :** to cut off

am•u•let *n* **:** a small object worn as a charm against evil

amuse *vb* **amused; amus•ing 1 :** to entertain with something pleasant **2 :** to please the sense of humor of

amuse•ment *n* **1 :** something that amuses or entertains **2 :** the condition of being amused

an *indefinite article* **:** ²A — used before words beginning with a vowel sound

¹-an *or* **-ian** *also* **-ean** *n suffix* **1 :** one that belongs to **2 :** one skilled in or specializing in

²-an *or* **-ian** *also* **-ean** *adj suffix* **1 :** of or relating to **2 :** like **:** resembling

an•a•con•da *n* **:** a large South American snake of the boa family

anal•y•sis *n, pl* **anal•y•ses :** an examination of something to find out how it is made or works or what it is

an•a•lyst *n* **:** a person who analyzes or is skilled in analysis

an•a•lyt•ic *or* **an•a•lyt•i•cal** *adj* **:** of, relating to, or skilled in analysis — **an•a•lyt•i•cal•ly** *adv*

DICTIONARY

an·a·lyze *vb* **an·a·lyzed; an·a·lyz·ing :** to examine something to find out what it is or what makes it work

an·ar·chist *n* **:** a person who believes in or practices anarchy

an·ar·chy *n* **1 :** the condition of a country where there is no government or law and order **2 :** a state of confused disorder or lawlessness

an·a·tom·i·cal *or* **an·a·tom·ic** *adj* **:** of or relating to anatomy

anat·o·my *n, pl* **anat·o·mies 1 :** a science that has to do with the structure of the body **2 :** the structural makeup especially of a person or animal

-ance *n suffix* **1 :** action or process **2 :** quality or state **3 :** amount or degree

an·ces·tor *n* **:** one from whom an individual is descended

an·ces·tral *adj* **:** of, relating to, or coming from an ancestor

an·ces·try *n, pl* **an·ces·tries :** one's ancestors

[1]**an·chor** *n* **1 :** a heavy iron or steel device attached to a ship by a cable or chain and so made that when thrown overboard it digs into the bottom and holds the ship in place **2 :** something that keeps something else fastened or steady

[2]**anchor** *vb* **1 :** to hold or become held in place with an anchor **2 :** to fasten tightly

an·chor·age *n* **:** a place where boats can be anchored

[1]**an·cient** *adj* **1 :** very old **2 :** of or relating to a time long past or to those living in such a time

[2]**ancient** *n* **1 :** a very old person **2 ancients** *pl* **:** the civilized peoples of ancient times and especially of Greece and Rome

-an·cy *n suffix, pl* **-an·cies :** quality or state

and *conj* **1 :** added to **2 :** AS WELL AS, ALSO — **and so forth :** and others or more of the same kind — **and so on :** AND SO FORTH

and·iron *n* **:** one of a pair of metal supports for firewood in a fireplace

an·ec·dote *n* **:** a short story about something interesting or funny in a person's life

ane·mia *n* **:** a sickness in which there is too little blood or too few red blood cells or too little hemoglobin in the blood

an·e·mom·e·ter *n* **:** an instrument for measuring the speed of the wind

anem·o·ne *n* **:** a plant related to the buttercup that blooms in spring and is often grown for its large white or colored flowers

an·es·the·sia *n* **:** loss of feeling or consciousness

[1]**an·es·thet·ic** *adj* **:** of, relating to, or capable of producing anesthesia

[2]**anesthetic** *n* **:** something that produces anesthesia

anew *adv* **1 :** over again **2 :** in a new or different form

an·gel *n* **1 :** a spiritual being serving God especially as a messenger **2 :** a person thought to be like an angel (as in goodness or beauty)

[1]**an·ger** *vb* **:** to make strongly displeased

[2]**anger** *n* **:** a strong feeling of displeasure and often of active opposition to an insult, injury, or injustice

[1]**an·gle** *n* **1 :** a sharp corner **2 :** the figure [redacted] by two lines meeting at a point **3 :** POINT OF VIEW

[2]**angle** *vb* **an·gled; an·gling :** to turn, move, or direct at an angle

[3]**angle** *vb* **an·gled; an·gling 1 :** to fish with hook and line **2 :** to try to get what one wants in a sly way

an·gler *n* **:** a person who fishes with hook and line especially for pleasure

an·gle·worm *n* **:** EARTHWORM

an·gling *n* **:** fishing with hook and line for pleasure

An·glo- *prefix* **1 :** English **2 :** English and

[1]**An·glo–Sax·on** *n* **1 :** a member of the German people who conquered England in the fifth century A.D. **2 :** a person whose ancestors were English

[2]**Anglo–Saxon** *adj* **:** of or relating to the Anglo-Saxons

an·go·ra *n* **:** cloth or yarn made from the soft silky hair of a special usually white domestic rabbit (**Angora rabbit**) or from the long shiny wool of a goat (**Angora goat**)

an·gry *adj* **an·gri·er; an·gri·est :** feeling or showing anger — **an·gri·ly** *adv*

an·guish *n* **:** great pain or trouble of body or mind

an·guished *adj* **:** full of anguish

an·gu·lar *adj* **1 :** having angles or sharp corners **2 :** being lean and bony

an·i·mal *n* **1 :** any of the great group of living beings (as jellyfishes, crabs, birds, and people) that differ from plants typically in being able to move about, in not having cell walls made of cellulose, and in depending on plants and other animals as sources of food **2 :** any of the animals lower than humans in the natural order **3 :** MAMMAL

animal kingdom *n* **:** a basic group of natural objects that includes all living and extinct animals

[1]**an·i·mate** *adj* **:** having life

[2]**an·i·mate** *vb* **an·i·mat·ed; an·i·mat·ing 1 :** to give life or energy to **:** make alive or lively **2 :** to make appear to move

an·i·mat·ed *adj* **1 :** full of life and energy

: LIVELY **2 :** appearing to be alive or moving

an·i·mos·i·ty *n, pl* **an·i·mos·i·ties :** [1]DISLIKE, HATRED

an·kle *n* **1 :** the joint between the foot and the leg **2 :** the area containing the ankle joint

an·klet *n* **:** a sock reaching slightly above the ankle

an·ky·lo·saur *n* **:** any of several plant-eating dinosaurs with bony plates covering the back

an·nals *n pl* **1 :** a record of events arranged in yearly sequence **2 :** historical records : HISTORY

an·neal *vb* **:** to heat (as glass or steel) and then cool so as to toughen and make less brittle

[1]**an·nex** *vb* **:** to add (something) to something else usually so as to become a part of it

[2]**an·nex** *n* **:** something (as a wing of a building) added on

an·nex·ation *n* **:** an annexing especially of new territory

an·ni·hi·late *vb* **an·ni·hi·lat·ed; an·ni·hi·lat·ing :** to destroy entirely **:** put completely out of existence

an·ni·ver·sa·ry *n, pl* **an·ni·ver·sa·ries :** the return every year of the date when something special (as a wedding) happened

an·nounce *vb* **an·nounced; an·nounc·ing 1 :** to make known publicly **2 :** to give notice of the arrival, presence, or readiness of

an·nounce·ment *n* **1 :** the act of announcing **2 :** a public notice announcing something

an·nounc·er *n* **:** a person who introduces radio or television programs, makes announcements, and gives the news and station identification

an·noy *vb* **:** to disturb or irritate especially by repeated disagreeable acts

an·noy·ance *n* **1 :** the act of annoying **2 :** the feeling of being annoyed **3 :** a source or cause of being annoyed

an·noy·ing *adj* **:** causing annoyance — **an·noy·ing·ly** *adv*

[1]**an·nu·al** *adj* **1 :** coming, happening, done, made, or given once a year **2 :** completing the life cycle in one growing season — **an·nu·al·ly** *adv*

[2]**annual** *n* **:** an annual plant

an·nu·ity *n, pl* **an·nu·ities :** a sum of money paid at regular intervals

an·nul *vb* **an·nulled; an·nul·ling :** to cancel by law **:** take away the legal force of — **an·nul·ment** *n*

an·ode *n* **1 :** the positive electrode of an electrolytic cell **2 :** the negative end of a battery that is delivering electric current **3 :** the electron-collecting electrode of an electron tube

anoint *vb* **1 :** to rub or cover with oil or grease **2 :** to put oil on as part of a religious ceremony

anon·y·mous *adj* **1 :** not named or identified **2 :** made or done by someone unknown — **anon·y·mous·ly** *adv*

[1]**an·oth·er** *adj* **1 :** some other **2 :** one more

[2]**another** *pron* **1 :** one more **2 :** someone or something different

[1]**an·swer** *n* **1 :** something said or written in reply (as to a question) **2 :** a solution of a problem

[2]**answer** *vb* **1 :** to speak or write in reply to **2 :** to take responsibility **3 :** [1]SERVE 5, DO

an·swer·able *adj* **1 :** RESPONSIBLE 1 **2 :** possible to answer

answering machine *n* **:** a machine that receives telephone calls by playing a recorded message and usually also recording messages from callers

ant *n* **:** a small insect related to the bees and wasps that lives in colonies and forms nests in the ground or in wood in which it stores food and raises its young

ant- *see* ANTI-

[1]**-ant** *n suffix* **1 :** one that does or causes a certain thing **2 :** thing that is acted upon in a certain way

[2]**-ant** *adj suffix* **1 :** doing a certain thing or being a certain way **2 :** causing a certain action

an·tag·o·nism *n* **:** a state of not liking and being against something

an·tag·o·nist *n* **:** a person who is against something or someone else **:** OPPONENT

an·tag·o·nis·tic *adj* **:** being against something or someone **:** HOSTILE, UNFRIENDLY — **an·tag·o·nis·ti·cal·ly** *adv*

an·tag·o·nize *vb* **an·tag·o·nized; an·tag·o·niz·ing :** to stir up dislike or anger in

ant·arc·tic *adj, often cap* **:** of or relating to the south pole or to the region around it

ante- *prefix* **1 :** before in time **:** earlier **2 :** in front of

ant·eat·er *n* **:** any of several animals that have long noses and long sticky tongues and feed chiefly on ants

an·te·cham·ber *n* **:** ANTEROOM

an·te·lope *n* **:** any of a group of cud-chewing animals that have horns that extend upward and backward

an·ten·na *n* **1** *pl* **an·ten·nae :** one of two or four threadlike movable feelers on the head of insects or crustaceans (as lobsters) **2** *pl* **an·ten·nas :** a metallic device (as a rod or wire) for sending or receiving radio waves

an·te·room *n* **:** a room used as an entrance to another

an·them *n* **1 :** a sacred song usually sung by a church choir **2 :** a patriotic song of praise and love for one's country

an·ther *n* **:** the enlargement at the tip of a flower's stamen that contains pollen

ant·hill *n* **:** a mound of dirt thrown up by ants in digging their nest

an·thol·o·gy *n, pl* **an·thol·o·gies :** a collection of writings (as stories and poems)

an·thra·cite *n* **:** a hard glossy coal that burns without much smoke

an·thrax *n* **:** a dangerous bacterial disease of warm-blooded animals that can affect humans

an·thro·poid *adj* **:** looking somewhat like humans

an·thro·pol·o·gy *n* **:** a science that studies people and especially their history, development, distribution and culture

anti- *or* **ant-** *prefix* **1 :** opposite in kind, position, or action **2 :** hostile toward

an·ti·bi·ot·ic *n* **:** a substance produced by living things and especially by bacteria and fungi that is used to kill or prevent the growth of harmful germs

an·ti·body *n, pl* **an·ti·bod·ies :** a substance produced by the body that counteracts the effects of a disease germ or its poisons

an·tic *n* **:** a wildly playful or funny act or action

an·tic·i·pate *vb* **an·tic·i·pat·ed; an·tic·i·pat·ing 1 :** to foresee and deal with or provide for beforehand **2 :** to look forward to

an·tic·i·pa·tion *n* **1 :** an action that takes into account and deals with or prevents a later action **2 :** pleasurable expectation **3 :** a picturing beforehand of a future event or state

an·ti·cy·clone *n* **:** a system of winds that is like a cyclone but that rotates about a center of high atmospheric pressure in a clockwise direction north of the equator and a counterclockwise direction south of the equator

an·ti·dote *n* **:** something used to reverse or prevent the action of a poison

an·ti·freeze *n* **:** a substance added to the liquid in an automobile radiator to prevent its freezing

an·ti·mo·ny *n* **:** a silvery white metallic chemical element

an·tip·a·thy *n, pl* **an·tip·a·thies :** a strong feeling of dislike

an·ti·quat·ed *adj* **:** OLD-FASHIONED 1, OBSOLETE

¹an·tique *n* **:** an object (as a piece of furniture) made at an earlier time

²antique *adj* **:** belonging to or like a former style or fashion

an·tiq·ui·ty *n* **1 :** ancient times **2 :** very great age

¹an·ti·sep·tic *adj* **:** killing or making harmless the germs that cause decay or sickness

²antiseptic *n* **:** an antiseptic substance

an·ti·so·cial *adj* **1 :** being against or bad for society **2 :** UNFRIENDLY

an·tith·e·sis *n, pl* **an·tith·e·ses :** the exact opposite

an·ti·tox·in *n* **:** a substance that is formed in the blood of one exposed to a disease and that prevents or acts against that disease

ant·ler *n* **:** the entire horn or a branch of the horn of an animal of the deer family — **ant·lered** *adj*

ant lion *n* **:** an insect having a larva form with long jaws that digs a cone-shaped hole in which it waits for prey (as ants)

an·to·nym *n* **:** a word of opposite meaning

an·vil *n* **:** an iron block on which pieces of metal are hammered into shape

anx·i·ety *n, pl* **anx·i·eties :** fear or nervousness about what might happen

anx·ious *adj* **1 :** afraid or nervous about what may happen **2 :** wanting very much **:** EAGER — **anx·ious·ly** *adv*

¹any *adj* **1 :** whatever kind of **2 :** of whatever number or amount

²any *pron* **1 :** any individuals **2 :** any amount

³any *adv* **:** to the least amount or degree

any·body *pron* **:** ANYONE

any·how *adv* **1 :** in any way, manner, or order **2 :** at any rate **:** in any case

any·more *adv* **:** NOWADAYS

any·one *pron* **:** any person

any·place *adv* **:** in any place

any·thing *pron* **:** a thing of any kind

any·way *adv* **:** ANYHOW

any·where *adv* **:** in, at, or to any place

any·wise *adv* **:** in any way whatever

A1 *adj* **:** of the very best kind

aor·ta *n* **:** the main artery that carries blood from the heart for distribution to all parts of the body

apace *adv* **:** at a quick pace **:** FAST

apart *adv* **1 :** away from each other **2 :** as something separated **:** SEPARATELY **3 :** into parts **:** to pieces **4 :** one from another

apart·ment *n* **1 :** a room or set of rooms used as a home **2 :** a building divided into individual apartments

ap·a·thet·ic *adj* **:** having or showing little or no feeling or interest — **ap·a·thet·i·cal·ly** *adv*

ap·a·thy *n* **:** lack of feeling or of interest **:** INDIFFERENCE

apato·sau·rus *n* **:** BRONTOSAURUS

[1]**ape** *n* **:** any of a group of tailless animals (as gorillas or chimpanzees) that are most closely related to humans — **ape•like** *adj*
[2]**ape** *vb* **aped; ap•ing :** to imitate (someone) awkwardly
ap•er•ture *n* **:** an opening or open space **:** HOLE
apex *n, pl* **apex•es** *or* **api•ces :** the highest point **:** PEAK
aphid *n* **:** any of various small insects that suck the juices of plants
apiece *adv* **:** for each one
aplomb *n* **:** complete freedom from nervousness or uncertainty
apol•o•get•ic *adj* **:** sorry for having done something wrong — **apol•o•get•i•cal•ly** *adv*
apol•o•gize *vb* **apol•o•gized; apol•o•giz•ing :** to make an apology
apol•o•gy *n, pl* **apol•o•gies :** an expression of regret (as for a mistake or a rude remark)
apos•tle *n* **1 :** one of the twelve close followers of Jesus sent out to teach the gospel **2 :** the first Christian missionary to a region **3 :** the person who first puts forward an important belief or starts a great reform — **apos•tle•ship** *n*
apos•tro•phe *n* **:** a mark ' used to show that letters or figures are missing (as in "can't" for "cannot" or " '76" for "1776") or to show the possessive case (as in "James's") or the plural of letters or figures (as in "cross your t's")
apoth•e•cary *n, pl* **apoth•e•car•ies :** DRUGGIST
ap•pall *vb* **:** to shock or overcome with horror
ap•pall•ing *adj* **:** being shocking and terrible
ap•pa•ra•tus *n, pl* **apparatus** *or* **ap•pa•ra•tus•es :** the equipment or material for a particular use or job
ap•par•el *n* **:** things that are worn **:** WEAR 2
ap•par•ent *adj* **1 :** open to view **:** VISIBLE **2 :** clear to the understanding **:** EVIDENT **3 :** appearing to be real or true — **ap•par•ent•ly** *adv* — **ap•par•ent•ness** *n*
ap•pa•ri•tion *n* **1 :** an unusual or unexpected sight **2 :** GHOST
[1]**ap•peal** *n* **1 :** a legal action by which a case is brought to a higher court for review **2 :** an asking for something badly needed or wanted **:** PLEA **3 :** the power to cause enjoyment **:** ATTRACTION
[2]**appeal** *vb* **1 :** to take action to have a case or decision reviewed by a higher court **2 :** to ask for something badly needed or wanted **3 :** to be pleasing or attractive
ap•pear *vb* **1 :** to come into sight **2 :** to present oneself **3 :** SEEM 1 **4 :** to come before the public **5 :** to come into existence
ap•pear•ance *n* **1 :** the act or an instance of appearing **2 :** way of looking
ap•pease *vb* **ap•peased; ap•peas•ing 1 :** to make calm or quiet **2 :** to give in to — **ap•pease•ment** *n* — **ap•peas•er** *n*
ap•pend *vb* **:** to add as something extra
ap•pend•age *n* **:** something (as a leg) attached to a larger or more important thing
ap•pen•di•ci•tis *n* **:** inflammation of the intestinal appendix
ap•pen•dix *n, pl* **ap•pen•dix•es** *or* **ap•pen•di•ces 1 :** a part of a book giving added and helpful information (as notes or tables) **2 :** a small tubelike part growing out from the intestine
ap•pe•tite *n* **1 :** a natural desire especially for food **2 :** [2]TASTE 4
ap•pe•tiz•er *n* **:** a food or drink usually served before a meal to make one hungrier
ap•pe•tiz•ing *adj* **:** pleasing to the appetite
ap•plaud *vb* **1 :** [1]PRAISE 1 **2 :** to show approval especially by clapping the hands
ap•plause *n* **:** approval shown especially by clapping the hands
ap•ple *n* **:** the round or oval fruit with red, yellow, or green skin of a spreading tree (**apple tree**) that is related to the rose
ap•pli•ance *n* **1 :** a device designed for a certain use **2 :** a piece of household or office equipment that runs on gas or electricity
ap•pli•ca•ble *adj* **:** capable of being put to use or put into practice
ap•pli•cant *n* **:** a person who applies for something (as a job)
ap•pli•ca•tion *n* **1 :** the act or an instance of applying **2 :** something put or spread on a surface **3 :** [1]REQUEST 1 **4 :** ability to be put to practical use
ap•pli•ca•tor *n* **:** a device for applying a substance (as medicine or polish)
ap•ply *vb* **ap•plied; ap•ply•ing 1 :** to put to use **2 :** to lay or spread on **3 :** to place in contact **4 :** to give one's full attention **5 :** to have relation or a connection **6 :** to request especially in writing
ap•point *vb* **1 :** to decide on usually from a position of authority **2 :** to choose for some duty, job, or office
ap•poin•tee *n* **:** a person appointed to an office or position
ap•point•ment *n* **1 :** the act or an instance of appointing **2 :** a position or office to which a person is named **3 :** an agreement to meet at a fixed time **4 appointments** *pl* **:** FURNISHINGS
ap•po•si•tion *n* **:** a grammatical construction in which a noun is followed by another that explains it
ap•pos•i•tive *n* **:** the second of a pair of nouns in apposition

DICTIONARY

ap·prais·al *n* **:** an act or instance of appraising

ap·praise *vb* **ap·praised; ap·prais·ing :** to set a value on

ap·pre·cia·ble *adj* **:** large enough to be noticed or measured — **ap·pre·cia·bly** *adv*

ap·pre·ci·ate *vb* **ap·pre·ci·at·ed; ap·pre·ci·at·ing 1 :** to admire greatly and with understanding **2 :** to be fully aware of **3 :** to be grateful for **4 :** to increase in number or value

ap·pre·ci·a·tion *n* **1 :** the act of appreciating **2 :** awareness or understanding of worth or value **3 :** a rise in value

ap·pre·cia·tive *adj* **:** having or showing appreciation — **ap·pre·cia·tive·ly** *adv*

ap·pre·hend *vb* **1 :** [1]ARREST 2 **2 :** to look forward to with fear and uncertainty **3 :** UNDERSTAND 1

ap·pre·hen·sion *n* **1 :** [2]ARREST **2 :** an understanding of something **3 :** fear of or uncertainty about what may be coming

ap·pre·hen·sive *adj* **:** fearful of what may be coming — **ap·pre·hen·sive·ly** *adv* — **ap·pre·hen·sive·ness** *n*

[1]**ap·pren·tice** *n* **:** a person who is learning a trade or art by experience under a skilled worker

[2]**apprentice** *vb* **ap·pren·ticed; ap·pren·tic·ing :** to set at work as an apprentice

ap·pren·tice·ship *n* **1 :** service as an apprentice **2 :** the period during which a person serves as an apprentice

[1]**ap·proach** *vb* **1 :** to come near or nearer **:** draw close **2 :** to begin to deal with

[2]**approach** *n* **1 :** an act or instance of approaching **2 :** a beginning step **3 :** a way (as a path or road) to get to some place

ap·proach·able *adj* **:** easy to meet or deal with

[1]**ap·pro·pri·ate** *vb* **ap·pro·pri·at·ed; ap·pro·pri·at·ing 1 :** to take possession of **2 :** to set apart for a certain purpose or use

[2]**ap·pro·pri·ate** *adj* **:** especially suitable — **ap·pro·pri·ate·ly** *adv* — **ap·pro·pri·ate·ness** *n*

ap·pro·pri·a·tion *n* **1 :** an act or instance of appropriating **2 :** a sum of money appropriated for a specific use

ap·prov·al *n* **:** an act or instance of approving

ap·prove *vb* **ap·proved; ap·prov·ing 1 :** to think well of **2 :** to accept as satisfactory

[1]**ap·prox·i·mate** *adj* **:** nearly correct or exact — **ap·prox·i·mate·ly** *adv*

[2]**ap·prox·i·mate** *vb* **ap·prox·i·mat·ed; ap·prox·i·mat·ing 1 :** to bring near or close **2 :** to come near **:** APPROACH

ap·prox·i·ma·tion *n* **1 :** a coming near or close (as in value) **2 :** an estimate or figure that is almost exact

apri·cot *n* **:** a small oval orange-colored fruit that looks like the related peach and plum

April *n* **:** the fourth month of the year

apron *n* **1 :** a piece of cloth worn on the front of the body to keep the clothing from getting dirty **2 :** a paved area for parking or handling airplanes

apt *adj* **1 :** just right **:** SUITABLE **2 :** having a tendency **:** LIKELY **3 :** quick to learn — **apt·ly** *adv* — **apt·ness** *n*

ap·ti·tude *n* **1 :** ability to learn **2 :** natural ability **:** TALENT

aqua *n* **:** a light greenish blue

aqua·ma·rine *n* **:** a transparent gem that is blue, blue-green, or green

aqua·naut *n* **:** a person who lives for a long while in an underwater shelter used as a base for research

aquar·i·um *n* **1 :** a container (as a tank or bowl) in which living water animals or water plants are kept **2 :** a building in which water animals or water plants are exhibited

Aquar·i·us *n* **1 :** a constellation between Capricorn and Pisces imagined as a man pouring water **2 :** the eleventh sign of the zodiac or a person born under this sign

aquat·ic *adj* **:** growing, living, or done in water

aq·ue·duct *n* **:** an artificial channel (as a structure that takes the water of a canal across a river or hollow) for carrying flowing water from one place to another

aque·ous *adj* **1 :** of, relating to, or like water **2 :** made of, by, or with water

-ar *adj suffix* **:** of or relating to

[1]**Ar·ab** *n* **1 :** a person born or living in the Arabian Peninsula **2 :** a member of a people that speaks Arabic

[2]**Arab** *adj* **:** of or relating to the Arabs **:** ARABIAN

[1]**Ara·bi·an** *n* **:** [1]ARAB 1

[2]**Arabian** *adj* **:** of or relating to the Arabian Peninsula or Arabs

[1]**Ar·a·bic** *n* **:** a language spoken in the Arabian Peninsula, Iraq, Jordan, Lebanon, Syria, Egypt, and parts of northern Africa

[2]**Arabic** *adj* **1 :** of or relating to Arabia, the Arabs, or Arabic **2 :** expressed in or making use of Arabic numerals

Arabic numeral *n* **:** one of the number symbols 1, 2, 3, 4, 5, 6, 7, 8, 9, and 0

ar·a·ble *adj* **:** fit for or cultivated by plowing **:** suitable for producing crops

Arap·a·ho *or* **Arap·a·hoe** *n, pl* **Arapaho** *or* **Arapahos** *or* **Arapahoe** *or* **Arapahoes :** a member of an Indian people of the plains region of the United States and Canada

ar·bi·ter *n* **1 :** ARBITRATOR **2 :** a person having the power to decide what is right or proper

ar·bi·trary *adj* **1 :** coming from or given to free exercise of the will without thought of fairness or right **2 :** seeming to have been chosen by chance — **ar·bi·trari·ly** *adv* — **ar·bi·trar·i·ness** *n*

ar·bi·trate *vb* **ar·bi·trat·ed; ar·bi·trat·ing 1 :** to settle a disagreement after hearing the arguments of both sides **2 :** to refer a dispute to others for settlement

ar·bi·tra·tion *n* **:** the settling of a disagreement in which both sides present their arguments to a third person or group for decision

ar·bi·tra·tor *n* **:** a person chosen to settle differences in a disagreement

ar·bor *n* **:** a shelter of vines or branches or of a frame covered with growing vines

ar·bo·re·al *adj* **1 :** of or relating to a tree **2 :** living in or often found in trees

ar·bo·re·tum *n, pl* **ar·bo·re·tums** *or* **ar·bo·re·ta :** a place where trees and plants are grown to be studied

ar·bor·vi·tae *n* **:** any of several evergreen trees with tiny scalelike leaves on flat branches shaped like fans

ar·bu·tus *n* **:** a plant that spreads along the ground and in the spring has bunches of small fragrant flowers with five white or pink petals

1arc *n* **1 :** a glowing light across a gap in an electric circuit or between electrodes **2 :** a part of a curved line between any two points on it

2arc *vb* **arced; arc·ing 1 :** to form an electric arc **2 :** to follow an arc-shaped course

ar·cade *n* **1 :** a row of arches with the columns that support them **2 :** an arched or covered passageway often between two rows of shops

1arch *n* **1 :** a usually curved part of a structure that is over an opening and serves as a support (as for the wall above the opening) **2 :** something suggesting an arch — **arched** *adj*

2arch *vb* **1 :** to cover with an arch **2 :** to form or shape into an arch

3arch *adj* **1 :** 2CHIEF 1, PRINCIPAL **2 :** being clever and mischievous — **arch·ly** *adv* — **arch·ness** *n*

ar·chae·ol·o·gy *or* **ar·che·ol·o·gy** *n* **:** a science that deals with past human life and activities as shown by fossils and the monuments and tools left by ancient peoples

ar·cha·ic *adj* **1 :** of or relating to an earlier time **2 :** surviving from an earlier period

arch·an·gel *n* **:** a chief angel

arch·bish·op *n* **:** the bishop of highest rank in a group of dioceses

ar·cher *n* **:** a person who shoots with a bow and arrow

ar·chery *n* **:** the sport or practice of shooting with bow and arrows

ar·chi·pel·a·go *n, pl* **ar·chi·pel·a·goes** *or* **ar·chi·pel·a·gos 1 :** a body of water (as a sea) with many islands **2 :** a group of islands in an archipelago

ar·chi·tect *n* **:** a person who designs buildings

ar·chi·tec·tur·al *adj* **:** of or relating to architecture — **ar·chi·tec·tur·al·ly** *adv*

ar·chi·tec·ture *n* **1 :** the art of making plans for buildings **2 :** a style of building

ar·chive *n* **:** a place in which public records or historical papers are saved

arch·way *n* **1 :** a passage under an arch **2 :** an arch over a passage

-archy *n suffix, pl* **-archies :** rule **:** government

arc·tic *adj* **1** *often cap* **:** of or relating to the north pole or to the region around it **2 :** very cold

ar·dent *adj* **:** showing or having warmth of feeling **:** PASSIONATE — **ar·dent·ly** *adv*

ar·dor *n* **1 :** warmth of feeling **2 :** great eagerness **:** ZEAL

ar·du·ous *adj* **:** DIFFICULT 1 — **ar·du·ous·ly** *adv* — **ar·du·ous·ness** *n*

are *present 2d sing or present pl of* BE

ar·ea *n* **1 :** a flat surface or space **2 :** the amount of surface included within limits **3 :** REGION 1 **4 :** a field of activity or study

are·na *n* **1 :** an enclosed area used for public entertainment **2 :** a building containing an arena **3 :** a field of activity

aren't : are not

ar·gue *vb* **ar·gued; ar·gu·ing 1 :** to give reasons for or against something **2 :** to discuss some matter usually with different points of view **3 :** to persuade by giving reasons — **ar·gu·er** *n*

ar·gu·ment *n* **1 :** a reason for or against something **2 :** a discussion in which reasons for and against something are given **3 :** an angry disagreement **:** QUARREL

ar·id *adj* **1 :** not having enough rainfall to support agriculture **2 :** UNINTERESTING, DULL

Ar·ies *n* **1 :** a constellation between Pisces and Taurus imagined as a ram **2 :** the first sign of the zodiac or a person born under this sign

aright *adv* **:** in a correct way

arise *vb* **arose; aris·en; aris·ing 1 :** to move upward **2 :** to get up from sleep or after lying down **3 :** to come into existence

ar·is·toc·ra·cy *n, pl* **ar·is·toc·ra·cies** **1 :** a government that is run by a small class of people **2 :** an upper class that is usually based on birth and is richer and more powerful than the rest of a society **3 :** persons thought of as being better than the rest of the community

aris·to·crat *n* **:** a member of an aristocracy

aris·to·crat·ic *adj* **:** of or relating to the aristocracy or aristocrats — **aris·to·crat·i·cal·ly** *adv*

[1]**arith·me·tic** *n* **1 :** a science that deals with the addition, subtraction, multiplication, and division of numbers **2 :** an act or method of adding, subtracting, multiplying, or dividing

[2]**ar·ith·met·ic** *or* **ar·ith·met·i·cal** *adj* **:** of or relating to arithmetic

ar·ith·met·ic mean *n* **:** a quantity formed by adding quantities together and dividing by their number

ark *n* **1 :** the ship in which an ancient Hebrew of the Bible named Noah and his family were saved from a great flood that God sent down on the world because of its wickedness **2 :** a sacred chest in which the ancient Hebrews kept the two tablets of the Law **3 :** a closet in a synagogue for the scrolls of the Law

[1]**arm** *n* **1 :** a human upper limb especially between the shoulder and wrist **2 :** something like an arm in shape or position **3 :** [1]POWER 1 **4 :** a foreleg of a four-footed animal — **armed** *adj*

[2]**arm** *vb* **1 :** to provide with weapons **2 :** to provide with a way of defense

[3]**arm** *n* **1 :** WEAPON, FIREARM **2 :** a branch of an army or of the military forces **3 arms** *pl* **:** the designs on a shield or flag of a family or government **4 arms** *pl* **:** actual fighting **:** WARFARE

ar·ma·da *n* **1 :** a large fleet of warships **2 :** a large number of moving things (as planes)

ar·ma·dil·lo *n, pl* **ar·ma·dil·los :** a small burrowing animal of Latin America and Texas whose head and body are protected by a hard bony armor

ar·ma·ment *n* **1 :** the military strength and equipment of a nation **2 :** the supply of materials for war **3 :** the process of preparing for war

ar·ma·ture *n* **:** the part of an electric motor or generator that turns in a magnetic field

arm·chair *n* **:** a chair with arms

arm·ful *n, pl* **arm·fuls** *or* **arms·ful :** as much as a person's arm can hold

ar·mi·stice *n* **:** a pause in fighting brought about by agreement between the two sides

ar·mor *n* **1 :** a covering (as of metal) to protect the body in battle **2 :** something that protects like metal armor **3 :** armored forces and vehicles (as tanks)

ar·mored *adj* **:** protected by or equipped with armor

ar·mory *n, pl* **ar·mor·ies** **1 :** a supply of arms **2 :** a place where arms are kept and where soldiers are often trained **3 :** a place where arms are made

arm·pit *n* **:** the hollow under a person's arm where the arm joins the shoulder

arm·rest *n* **:** a support for the arm

ar·my *n, pl* **armies** **1 :** a large body of men and women trained for land warfare **2** *often cap* **:** the complete military organization of a nation for land warfare **3 :** a great number of people or things **4 :** a body of persons organized to advance an idea

aro·ma *n* **:** a noticeable and pleasant smell

ar·o·mat·ic *adj* **:** of, relating to, or having an aroma

arose *past of* ARISE

[1]**around** *adv* **1 :** in circumference **2 :** in or along a curving course **3 :** on all sides **4 :** NEARBY **5 :** here and there in various places **6 :** to each in turn **7 :** in an opposite direction **8 :** in the neighborhood of **:** APPROXIMATELY

[2]**around** *prep* **1 :** in a curving path along the outside boundary of **2 :** on every side of **3 :** here and there in **4 :** near in number or amount

arouse *vb* **aroused; arous·ing** **1 :** to awaken from sleep **2 :** to excite to action

ar·range *vb* **ar·ranged; ar·rang·ing** **1 :** to put in order and especially a particular order **2 :** to make plans for **3 :** to come to an agreement about **:** SETTLE **4 :** to make a musical arrangement of — **ar·rang·er** *n*

ar·range·ment *n* **1 :** a putting in order **:** the order in which things are put **2 :** preparation or planning done in advance **3 :** something made by arranging **4 :** a changing of a piece of music to suit voices or instruments for which it was not first written

[1]**ar·ray** *vb* **1 :** to set in order **:** DRAW UP **2 :** to dress especially in fine or beautiful clothing

[2]**array** *n* **1 :** regular order or arrangement **2 :** a group of persons (as soldiers) drawn up in regular order **3 :** fine or beautiful clothing **4 :** an impressive group **5 :** a group of mathematical elements (as numbers or letters) arranged in rows and columns

ar·rears *n pl* **1 :** the state of being behind in paying debts **2 :** unpaid and overdue debts

[1]**ar·rest** *vb* **1 :** to stop the progress or movement of **:** CHECK **2 :** to take or keep in

one's control by authority of law **3 :** to attract and hold the attention of

²arrest *n* **:** the act of taking or holding in one's control by authority of law

ar·riv·al *n* **1 :** the act of arriving **2 :** a person or thing that has arrived

ar·rive *vb* **ar·rived; ar·riv·ing 1 :** to reach the place one started out for **2 :** to gain a goal or object **3 :** COME 2 **4 :** to gain success

ar·ro·gance *n* **:** a sense of one's own importance that shows itself in a proud and insulting way

ar·ro·gant *adj* **:** overly proud of oneself or of one's own opinions — **ar·ro·gant·ly** *adv*

ar·row *n* **1 :** a weapon that is made to be shot from a bow and is usually a stick with a point at one end and feathers at the other **2 :** a mark to show direction

ar·row·head *n* **:** the pointed end of an arrow

ar·row·root *n* **:** a starch obtained from the roots of a tropical plant

ar·se·nal *n* **:** a place where military equipment is made and stored

ar·se·nic *n* **:** a solid poisonous chemical element that is usually steel gray and snaps easily

ar·son *n* **:** the illegal burning of a building or other property

art *n* **1 :** skill that comes through experience or study **2 :** an activity that requires skill **3 :** an activity (as painting, music, or writing) whose purpose is making things that are beautiful to look at, listen to, or read **4 :** works (as pictures, poems, or songs) made by artists

ar·tery *n, pl* **ar·ter·ies 1 :** one of the branching tubes that carry blood from the heart to all parts of the body **2 :** a main road or waterway

ar·te·sian well *n* **1 :** a bored well from which water flows up like a fountain **2 :** a deep bored well

art·ful *adj* **1 :** done with or showing art or skill **2 :** clever at taking advantage — **art·ful·ly** *adv* — **art·ful·ness** *n*

ar·thri·tis *n* **:** a condition in which the joints are painful and swollen

ar·thro·pod *n* **:** any of a large group of animals (as crabs, insects, and spiders) with jointed limbs and a body made up of segments

ar·ti·choke *n* **:** a tall plant of the aster family with a flower head cooked and eaten as a vegetable

ar·ti·cle *n* **1 :** a separate part of a document **2 :** a piece of writing other than fiction or poetry that forms a separate part of a publication (as a magazine) **3 :** a word (as *a, an,* or *the*) used with a noun to limit it or make it clearer **4 :** one of a class of things

¹ar·tic·u·late *adj* **1 :** clearly understandable **2 :** able to express oneself clearly and well — **ar·tic·u·late·ly** *adv* — **ar·tic·u·late·ness** *n*

²ar·tic·u·late *vb* **ar·tic·u·lat·ed; ar·tic·u·lat·ing :** to speak clearly

ar·tic·u·la·tion *n* **:** the making of articulate sounds (as in speaking)

ar·ti·fice *n* **1 :** a clever trick or device **2 :** clever skill

ar·ti·fi·cial *adj* **1 :** made by humans **2 :** not natural in quality **3 :** made to look like something natural — **ar·ti·fi·cial·ly** *adv*

artificial respiration *n* **:** the forcing of air into and out of the lungs of a person whose breathing has stopped

ar·til·lery *n* **1 :** large firearms (as cannon or rockets) **2 :** a branch of an army armed with artillery

ar·ti·san *n* **:** a person (as a carpenter) who works at a trade requiring skill with the hands

art·ist *n* **1 :** a person skilled in one of the arts (as painting, sculpture, music, or writing) **2 :** a person who has much ability in a job requiring skill

ar·tis·tic *adj* **1 :** relating to art or artists **2 :** showing skill and imagination — **ar·tis·ti·cal·ly** *adv*

¹-ary *n suffix, pl* **-ar·ies :** thing or person belonging to or connected with

²-ary *adj suffix* **:** of, relating to, or connected with

¹as *adv* **1 :** to the same degree or amount **2 :** for example

²as *conj* **1 :** in equal amount or degree with **2 :** in the same way that **3 :** at the time that **4 :** BECAUSE, SINCE

³as *pron* **1 :** THAT, WHO, WHICH **2 :** a fact that

⁴as *prep* **1 :** ⁴LIKE 1 **2 :** in the position or role of

as·bes·tos *n* **:** a grayish mineral that separates easily into long flexible fibers and is used in making fireproof materials

as·cend *vb* **:** to go up **:** RISE

as·cen·sion *n* **:** the act or process of ascending

as·cent *n* **1 :** the act of rising or climbing upward **2 :** an upward slope **:** RISE

as·cer·tain *vb* **:** to find out with certainty

as·cribe *vb* **as·cribed; as·crib·ing :** to think of as coming from a specified cause, source, or author

asex·u·al *adj* **:** of, relating to, or being a process of reproduction (as the dividing of one cell into two cells) that does not involve

DICTIONARY

the combining of male and female germ cells — **asex·u·al·ly** *adv*

[1]ash *n* **:** a common shade tree or timber tree that has winged seeds and bark with grooves

[2]ash *n* **1 :** the solid matter left when something is completely burned **2 ashes** *pl* **:** the last remains of the dead human body

ashamed *adj* **1 :** feeling shame, guilt, or disgrace **2 :** kept back by fear of shame

ash·en *adj* **1 :** of the color of ashes **2 :** very pale

ashore *adv* **:** on or to the shore

ash·tray *n* **:** a container for tobacco ashes and cigarette and cigar butts

ashy *adj* **ash·i·er; ash·i·est 1 :** of or relating to ashes **2 :** very pale

[1]Asian *adj* **:** of or relating to Asia or the Asians

[2]Asian *n* **:** a person born or living in Asia

aside *adv* **1 :** to or toward the side **2 :** out of the way **:** AWAY **3 :** away from one's thought

aside from *prep* **:** with the exception of

as if *conj* **1 :** the way it would be if **2 :** the way one would if **3 :** [2]THAT 1

ask *vb* **1 :** to seek information **2 :** to make a request **3 :** to set as a price **4 :** INVITE 2 **5 :** to behave as if looking

askance *adv* **1 :** with a side glance **2 :** with distrust or disapproval

askew *adv or adj* **:** out of line

aslant *adv or adj* **:** in a slanting direction

[1]asleep *adj* **1 :** being in a state of sleep **2 :** having no feeling

[2]asleep *adv* **:** into a state of sleep

as of *prep* **:** [1]ON 5, AT

as·par·a·gus *n* **:** a vegetable that is the thick young shoots of a garden plant that is related to the lilies and lives for many years

as·pect *n* **1 :** a position facing a certain direction **2 :** a certain way in which something appears or may be thought of **3 :** the appearance of an individual **:** LOOK

as·pen *n* **:** a poplar tree whose leaves move easily in the breeze

as·phalt *n* **1 :** a dark-colored substance obtained from natural beds or from petroleum **2 :** any of various materials made of asphalt that are used for pavements and as a waterproof cement

as·phyx·i·ate *vb* **as·phyx·i·at·ed; as·phyx·i·at·ing :** to cause (as a person) to become unconscious or die by cutting off the normal taking in of oxygen whether by blocking breathing or by replacing the oxygen of the air with another gas

as·pi·rant *n* **:** a person who aspires

as·pi·ra·tion *n* **:** a strong desire to achieve something high or great

as·pire *vb* **as·pired; as·pir·ing :** to very much want something and especially something high or fine

as·pi·rin *n* **:** a white drug used to relieve pain and fever

ass *n* **1 :** an animal that looks like but is smaller than the related horse and has shorter hair in mane and tail and longer ears **:** DONKEY **2 :** a dull stupid person

as·sail *vb* **:** to attack violently with blows or words

as·sail·ant *n* **:** a person who attacks

as·sas·sin *n* **:** one who kills another person either for pay or from loyalty to a cause

as·sas·si·nate *vb* **as·sas·si·nat·ed; as·sas·si·nat·ing :** to murder a usually important person by a surprise or secret attack

as·sas·si·na·tion *n* **:** the act of assassinating

[1]as·sault *n* **1 :** a violent or sudden attack **2 :** an unlawful attempt or threat to harm someone

[2]assault *vb* **:** to make an assault on

[1]as·say *n* **:** an analyzing (as of an ore or drug) to determine the presence, absence, or amount of one or more substances

[2]as·say *vb* **:** to analyze (as an ore) for one or more valuable substances

as·sem·blage *n* **:** a collection of persons or things

as·sem·ble *vb* **as·sem·bled; as·sem·bling 1 :** to collect in one place or group **2 :** to fit (parts) together **3 :** to meet together — **as·sem·bler** *n*

as·sem·bly *n, pl* **as·sem·blies 1 :** a gathering of persons **:** MEETING **2** *cap* **:** a lawmaking body **3 :** the act of assembling **:** the state of being assembled **4 :** a collection of parts that make up a complete unit

assembly line *n* **:** an arrangement for assembling a product mechanically in which work passes from one operation to the next in a direct line until the product is finished

[1]as·sent *vb* **:** to agree to something

[2]assent *n* **:** an act of assenting **:** AGREEMENT

as·sert *vb* **1 :** to state clearly and strongly **2 :** to show the existence of — **assert oneself :** to insist strongly that others respect one's rights

as·ser·tion *n* **1 :** the act of asserting **2 :** a positive statement

as·sess *vb* **1 :** to decide on the rate or amount of **2 :** to assign a value to for purposes of taxation **3 :** to put a charge or tax on — **as·ses·sor** *n*

as·set *n* **1 assets** *pl* **:** all the property belonging to a person or an organization **2 :** ADVANTAGE 3

as·sid·u·ous *adj* **:** DILIGENT — **as·sid·u·ous·ly** *adv* — **as·sid·u·ous·ness** *n*

as·sign *vb* **1 :** to appoint to a post or duty

2 : to give out with authority 3 : to decide on definitely
as•sign•ment *n* 1 : the act of assigning 2 : something assigned
as•sim•i•late *vb* **as•sim•i•lat•ed; as•sim•i•lat•ing** : to take something in and make it part of the thing it has joined
as•sim•i•la•tion *n* : the act or process of assimilating
1as•sist *vb* : to give aid : HELP
2assist *n* : an act of assisting
as•sis•tance *n* 1 : the act of helping 2 : the help given
1as•sis•tant *adj* : acting as a helper to another
2assistant *n* : a person who assists another
1as•so•ci•ate *vb* **as•so•ci•at•ed; as•so•ci•at•ing** 1 : to join or come together as partners, friends, or companions 2 : to connect in thought
2as•so•ciate *adj* 1 : closely joined with another (as in duties or responsibility) 2 : having some but not all rights and privileges
3as•so•ciate *n* 1 : a fellow worker : PARTNER 2 : a person who is one's friend or companion
as•so•ci•a•tion *n* 1 : the act of associating : the state of being associated 2 : an organization of persons having a common interest 3 : a feeling, memory, or thought connected with a person, place, or thing
as•so•cia•tive *adj* 1 : serving to associate 2 : being a property of a mathematical operation (as addition or multiplication) in which the result is independent of the original grouping of the elements
as•sort *vb* : to sort into groups
as•sort•ed *adj* 1 : made up of various kinds 2 : suited to one another
as•sort•ment *n* 1 : the act of assorting : the state of being assorted 2 : a collection of assorted things or persons
as•sume *vb* **as•sumed; as•sum•ing** 1 : to take upon oneself : UNDERTAKE 2 : to take over usually by force 3 : to pretend to have or be 4 : to accept as true
as•sump•tion *n* 1 : the act of assuming 2 : something accepted as true
as•sur•ance *n* 1 : the act of assuring 2 : the state of being certain 3 : a being sure and safe : SECURITY 4 : confidence in one's own self
as•sure *vb* **as•sured; as•sur•ing** 1 : to make safe : INSURE 2 : to give confidence to 3 : to make sure or certain 4 : to inform positively
as•sured *adj* 1 : made sure or certain 2 : very confident — **as•sured•ly** *adv* — **as•sured•ness** *n*
as•ter *n* : any of various herbs related to the daisies that have leafy stems and white, pink, purple, or yellow flower heads which bloom in the fall
as•ter•isk *n* : a character * used in printing or in writing as a reference mark or to show that letters or words have been left out
astern *adv* 1 : behind a ship or airplane 2 : at or toward the stern 3 : 1BACKWARD 1
as•ter•oid *n* : one of thousands of small planets that move in orbits mostly between those of Mars and Jupiter and have diameters from a fraction of a kilometer to nearly 800 kilometers
asth•ma *n* : an ailment of which difficult breathing, wheezing, and coughing are symptoms
astir *adj* 1 : showing activity 2 : being out of bed : UP
as to *prep* 1 : with respect to : ABOUT 2 : ACCORDING TO 1
as•ton•ish *vb* : to strike with sudden wonder or surprise
as•ton•ish•ment *n* : great surprise : AMAZEMENT
as•tound *vb* : to fill with puzzled wonder
astray *adv or adj* 1 : off the right path or route 2 : in or into error
1astride *adv* : with one leg on each side
2astride *prep* : with one leg on each side of
as•trin•gent *adj* : able or tending to shrink body tissues — **as•trin•gent•ly** *adv*
astro- *prefix* : star : heavens : astronomical
as•trol•o•gy *n* : the study of the supposed influences of the stars and planets on human affairs by their positions in the sky in relation to each other
as•tro•naut *n* : a traveler in a spacecraft
as•tro•nau•tics *n* : the science of the construction and operation of spacecraft
as•tron•o•mer *n* : a person who is skilled in astronomy
as•tro•nom•i•cal *or* **as•tro•nom•ic** *adj* 1 : of or relating to astronomy 2 : extremely or unbelievably large — **as•tro•nom•i•cal•ly** *adv*
as•tron•o•my *n* : the science of celestial bodies and of their motions and makeup
as•tute *adj* : very alert and aware : CLEVER — **as•tute•ly** *adv* — **as•tute•ness** *n*
asun•der *adv or adj* 1 : into parts 2 : apart from each other in position
as well as *prep or conj* : in addition to : and also
asy•lum *n* 1 : a place of protection and shelter 2 : protection given especially to political refugees 3 : a place for the care of the poor or sick and especially of the insane
at *prep* 1 — used to indicate a particular place or time 2 — used to indicate a goal

DICTIONARY

3 — used to indicate position or condition **4** — used to tell how or why something is done

ate *past of* EAT

1-ate *n suffix* **:** one acted upon in such a way

2-ate *n suffix* **:** office **:** rank **:** group of persons holding such an office or rank

3-ate *adj suffix* **:** marked by having

4-ate *vb suffix* **:** cause to be changed or influenced by **:** cause to become **:** furnish with

athe•ist *n* **:** a person who believes there is no God

ath•lete *n* **:** a person who is trained in or good at games and exercises that require physical skill, endurance, and strength

athlete's foot *n* **:** a fungus infection of the foot marked by blisters, itching, and cracks between and under the toes

ath•let•ic *adj* **1 :** of, relating to, or characteristic of athletes or athletics **2 :** vigorously active **3 :** STURDY 2

ath•let•ics *n sing or pl* **:** games, sports, and exercises requiring strength, endurance, and skill

-ation *n suffix* **:** action or process **:** something connected with an action or process

-ative *adj suffix* **1 :** of, relating to, or connected with **2 :** tending to

at•las *n* **:** a book of maps

at•mo•sphere *n* **1 :** the gas surrounding a celestial body **:** AIR **2 :** the air in a particular place **3 :** a surrounding influence or set of conditions

at•mo•spher•ic *adj* **:** of or relating to the atmosphere

atoll *n* **:** a ring-shaped coral island or string of islands consisting of a coral reef surrounding a lagoon

at•om *n* **1 :** a tiny particle **:** BIT **2 :** the smallest particle of an element that can exist alone or in combination

atom•ic *adj* **1 :** of or relating to atoms **2 :** NUCLEAR 3

atomic bomb *n* **:** a bomb whose great power is due to the sudden release of the energy in the nuclei of atoms

at•om•iz•er *n* **:** a device for spraying a liquid (as a perfume or disinfectant)

atone *vb* **atoned; aton•ing :** to do something to make up for a wrong that has been done

atone•ment *n* **:** a making up for an offense or injury

atop *prep* **:** on top of

atro•cious *adj* **1 :** savagely brutal, cruel, or wicked **2 :** very bad — **atro•cious•ly** *adv* — **atro•cious•ness** *n*

atroc•i•ty *n, pl* **atroc•i•ties :** an atrocious act, object, or situation

at•tach *vb* **1 :** to take (money or property) legally in order to obtain payment of a debt **2 :** to fasten one thing to another **3 :** to bind by feelings of affection **4 :** to assign by authority **5 :** to think of as belonging to something

at•tach•ment *n* **1 :** connection by feelings of affection or regard **2 :** a device that can be attached to a machine or tool **3 :** a connection by which one thing is joined to another

1at•tack *vb* **1 :** to take strong action against **:** ASSAULT **2 :** to use unfriendly or bitter words against **3 :** to begin to affect or to act upon harmfully **4 :** to start to work on — **at•tack•er** *n*

2attack *n* **1 :** the act of attacking **2 :** beginning to work **3 :** a spell of sickness

at•tain *vb* **1 :** to reach as a desired goal **2 :** to come into possession of **3 :** to arrive at — **at•tain•able** *adj*

at•tain•ment *n* **1 :** the act of attaining **:** the state of being attained **2 :** ACCOMPLISHMENT 3

at•tar *n* **:** a sweet-smelling oil from flowers

1at•tempt *vb* **1 :** to try to do or perform **2 :** to try to do something

2attempt *n* **:** the act or an instance of attempting

at•tend *vb* **1 :** to pay attention to **2 :** to go with especially as a servant or companion **3 :** to care for **4 :** to go to or be present at **5 :** to take charge

at•ten•dance *n* **1 :** the act of attending **2 :** the number of persons present

1at•ten•dant *n* **:** a person who attends something or someone

2attendant *adj* **:** coming with or following closely as a result

at•ten•tion *n* **1 :** the act or the power of fixing one's mind on something **:** careful listening or watching **2 :** a state of being aware **3 :** careful thinking about something so as to be able to take action on it **4 :** an act of kindness or politeness **5 :** a military posture with body stiff and straight, heels together, and arms at the sides

at•ten•tive *adj* **1 :** paying attention **2 :** being thoughtful and polite — **at•ten•tive•ly** *adv* — **at•ten•tive•ness** *n*

at•test *vb* **:** to give proof of

at•tic *n* **:** a room or a space just under the roof of a building

1at•tire *vb* **at•tired; at•tir•ing :** to put clothes and especially fine clothes on

2attire *n* **:** clothing meant for a particular occasion

at•ti•tude *n* **1 :** the position of the body, or of the parts of the body, or of an object **2 :** a feeling or opinion about a certain fact or situation

at·tor·ney *n, pl* **at·tor·neys :** a person who acts as agent for another in dealing with business or legal matters
at·tract *vb* **1 :** to draw to or toward oneself **2 :** to draw by appealing to interest or feeling
at·trac·tion *n* **1 :** the act or power of attracting **2 :** something that attracts or pleases
at·trac·tive *adj* **:** having the power or quality of attracting **:** PLEASING — **at·trac·tive·ly** *adv* — **at·trac·tive·ness** *n*
[1]**at·tri·bute** *n* **1 :** a quality belonging to a particular person or thing **2 :** a word (as an adjective) indicating a quality
[2]**at·trib·ute** *vb* **at·trib·ut·ed; at·trib·ut·ing 1 :** to explain as the cause of **2 :** to think of as likely to be a quality of a person or thing
at·tri·bu·tion *n* **:** the act of attributing
at·tune *vb* **at·tuned; at·tun·ing :** to bring into harmony **:** TUNE
atyp·i·cal *adj* **:** not typical — **atyp·i·cal·ly** *adv*
au·burn *adj* **:** of a reddish brown color
[1]**auc·tion** *n* **:** a public sale at which things are sold to those who offer to pay the most
[2]**auction** *vb* **:** to sell at auction
auc·tion·eer *n* **:** a person in charge of auctions
au·da·cious *adj* **1 :** very bold and daring **:** FEARLESS **2 :** very rude **:** INSOLENT — **au·da·cious·ly** *adv* — **au·da·cious·ness** *n*
au·dac·i·ty *n, pl* **au·dac·i·ties :** the fact or an instance of being audacious
au·di·ble *adj* **:** loud enough to be heard — **au·di·bly** *adv*
au·di·ence *n* **1 :** a group that listens or watches (as at a play or concert) **2 :** a chance to talk with a person of very high rank **3 :** those of the general public who give attention to something said, done, or written
[1]**au·dio** *adj* **1 :** of or relating to sound or its reproduction **2 :** relating to or used in the transmitting or receiving of sound (as in radio or television)
[2]**audio** *n* **1 :** the transmitting, receiving, or reproducing of sound **2 :** the section of television equipment that deals with sound
au·dio·tape *n* **:** a tape recording of sound
au·dio·vi·su·al *adj* **:** of, relating to, or using both sound and sight
[1]**au·dit** *n* **:** a thorough check of business accounts
[2]**audit** *vb* **:** to make an audit of
[1]**au·di·tion** *n* **:** a short performance to test the talents of a singer, dancer, or actor
[2]**audition** *vb* **:** to test or try out in an audition
au·di·tor *n* **1 :** a person who listens especially as a member of a radio or TV audience **2 :** a person who audits business accounts
au·di·to·ri·um *n* **1 :** the part of a public building where an audience sits **2 :** a hall used for public gatherings
au·di·to·ry *adj* **:** of or relating to hearing
au·ger *n* **:** a tool used for boring holes
aught *n* **:** ZERO 1
aug·ment *vb* **:** to increase in size, amount, or degree
au·gust *adj* **:** being grand and noble **:** MAJESTIC — **au·gust·ly** *adv* — **au·gust·ness** *n*
Au·gust *n* **:** the eighth month of the year
auk *n* **:** a diving seabird of cold parts of the northern hemisphere with a heavy body and small wings
aunt *n* **1 :** a sister of one's parent **2 :** the wife of one's uncle
au·ra *n* **:** a feeling that seems to be given off by a person or thing
au·ral *adj* **:** of or relating to the ear or sense of hearing — **au·ral·ly** *adv*
au·ri·cle *n* **:** the part of the heart that receives blood from the veins
au·ro·ra bo·re·al·is *n* **:** broad bands of light that have a magnetic and electrical source and that appear in the sky at night especially in the arctic regions
aus·pic·es *n pl* **:** support and guidance of a sponsor
aus·pi·cious *adj* **1 :** promising success **2 :** PROSPEROUS 1 — **aus·pi·cious·ly** *adv*
aus·tere *adj* **1 :** seeming or acting harsh and stern **2 :** [1]PLAIN 1 — **aus·tere·ly** *adv*
aus·ter·i·ty *n, pl* **aus·ter·i·ties 1 :** an austere act or manner **2 :** lack of all luxury
[1]**Aus·tra·lian** *adj* **:** of or relating to Australia or the Australians
[2]**Australian** *n* **:** a person born or living in Australia
aut- *or* **au·to-** *prefix* **1 :** self **:** same one **2 :** automatic
au·then·tic *adj* **:** being really what it seems to be **:** GENUINE — **au·then·ti·cal·ly** *adv*
au·thor *n* **1 :** a person who writes something (as a novel) **2 :** one that starts or creates
au·thor·i·ta·tive *adj* **:** having or coming from authority — **au·thor·i·ta·tive·ly** *adv* — **au·thor·i·ta·tive·ness** *n*
au·thor·i·ty *n, pl* **au·thor·i·ties 1 :** a fact or statement used to support a position **2 :** a person looked to as an expert **3 :** power to influence the behavior of others **4 :** persons having powers of government
au·tho·rize *vb* **au·tho·rized; au·tho·riz·ing 1 :** to give authority to **:** EMPOWER **2 :** to give legal or official approval to
au·thor·ship *n* **:** the profession of writing

au·to *n, pl* **au·tos :** AUTOMOBILE
auto- — see AUT-
au·to·bi·og·ra·phy *n, pl* **au·to·bi·og·ra·phies :** the biography of a person written by that person
[1]**au·to·graph** *n* **:** a person's signature written by hand
[2]**autograph** *vb* **:** to write one's signature in or on (as a book)
au·to·mate *vb* **au·to·mat·ed; au·to·mat·ing :** to make automatic
[1]**au·to·mat·ic** *adj* **1 :** INVOLUNTARY **2 :** being a machine or device that acts by or regulates itself — **au·to·mat·i·cal·ly** *adv*
[2]**automatic** *n* **1 :** an automatic machine or device **2 :** an automatic firearm
au·to·ma·tion *n* **1 :** the method of making a machine, a process, or a system work automatically **2 :** automatic working of a machine, process, or system by mechanical or electronic devices that take the place of humans
[1]**au·to·mo·bile** *adj* **:** AUTOMOTIVE
[2]**automobile** *n* **:** a usually four-wheeled vehicle that runs on its own power and is designed to carry passengers
au·to·mo·tive *adj* **:** SELF-PROPELLED
au·tumn *n* **:** the season between summer and winter that in the northern hemisphere is usually the months of September, October, and November
au·tum·nal *adj* **:** of or relating to autumn
[1]**aux·il·ia·ry** *adj* **:** available to provide something extra
[2]**auxiliary** *n, pl* **aux·il·ia·ries 1 :** an auxiliary person, group, or device **2 :** HELPING VERB
[1]**avail** *vb* **:** to be of use or help
[2]**avail** *n* **:** help toward reaching a goal **:** USE
avail·able *adj* **1 :** SUITABLE, USABLE **2 :** possible to get **:** OBTAINABLE
av·a·lanche *n* **:** a large mass of snow and ice or of earth or rock sliding down a mountainside or over a cliff
av·a·rice *n* **:** strong desire for riches **:** GREED
av·a·ri·cious *adj* **:** greedy for riches — **av·a·ri·cious·ly** *adv* — **av·a·ri·cious·ness** *n*
avenge *vb* **avenged; aveng·ing :** to take revenge for — **aveng·er** *n*
av·e·nue *n* **1 :** a way of reaching a goal **2 :** a usually wide street
[1]**av·er·age** *n* **1 :** ARITHMETIC MEAN **2 :** something usual in a group, class, or series
[2]**average** *adj* **1 :** equaling or coming close to an average **2 :** being ordinary or usual
[3]**average** *vb* **av·er·aged; av·er·ag·ing 1 :** to amount to usually **2 :** to find the average of
averse *adj* **:** having a feeling of dislike
aver·sion *n* **1 :** a strong dislike **2 :** something strongly disliked
avert *vb* **1 :** to turn away **2 :** to keep from happening
avi·ary *n, pl* **avi·ar·ies :** a place (as a large cage) where birds are kept
avi·a·tion *n* **1 :** the flying of aircraft **2 :** the designing and making of aircraft
avi·a·tor *n* **:** the pilot of an aircraft
av·id *adj* **:** very eager — **av·id·ly** *adv*
av·o·ca·do *n, pl* **av·o·ca·dos :** a usually green fruit that is shaped like a pear or an egg, grows on a tropical American tree, and has a rich oily flesh
av·o·ca·tion *n* **:** an interest or activity that is not one's regular job **:** HOBBY
avoid *vb* **:** to keep away from
avoid·ance *n* **:** a keeping away from something
avow *vb* **:** to declare openly and frankly
avow·al *n* **:** an open declaration
await *vb* **1 :** to wait for **2 :** to be ready or waiting for
[1]**awake** *vb* **awoke; awo·ken** *or* **awaked; awak·ing 1 :** to arouse from sleep **:** wake up **2 :** to become conscious or aware of something
[2]**awake** *adj* **:** not asleep
awak·en *vb* **:** [1]AWAKE
[1]**award** *vb* **1 :** to give by judicial decision **2 :** to give or grant as deserved or needed
[2]**award** *n* **:** something (as a prize) that is awarded
aware *adj* **:** having or showing understanding or knowledge **:** CONSCIOUS — **aware·ness** *n*
awash *adv or adj* **1 :** washed by waves or tide **2 :** floating about **3 :** flooded or covered with water
[1]**away** *adv* **1 :** from this or that place **2 :** in another place or direction **3 :** out of existence **4 :** from one's possession **5 :** without stopping or slowing down **6 :** at or to a great distance in space or time **:** FAR
[2]**away** *adj* **1 :** [1]ABSENT 1 **2 :** DISTANT 1
[1]**awe** *n* **:** a feeling of mixed fear, respect, and wonder
[2]**awe** *vb* **awed; aw·ing :** to fill with awe
awe·some *adj* **:** causing a feeling of awe
aw·ful *adj* **1 :** causing fear or terror **2 :** very disagreeable or unpleasant **3 :** very great
aw·ful·ly *adv* **1 :** in a disagreeable or unpleasant manner **2 :** to a very great degree
awhile *adv* **:** for a while **:** for a short time
awk·ward *adj* **1 :** not graceful **:** CLUMSY **2 :** likely to embarrass **3 :** difficult to use or handle — **awk·ward·ly** *adv* — **awk·ward·ness** *n*

awl *n* **:** a pointed tool for making small holes (as in leather or wood)

aw•ning *n* **:** a cover (as of canvas) that shades or shelters like a roof

awoke *past of* AWAKE

awoken *past participle of* AWAKE

awry *adv or adj* **1 :** turned or twisted to one side **:** ASKEW **2 :** out of the right course **:** AMISS

ax *or* **axe** *n* **:** a tool that has a heavy head with a sharp edge fixed to a handle and is used for chopping and splitting wood

ax•i•om *n* **1 :** MAXIM **2 :** a statement thought to be clearly true

ax•is *n, pl* **ax•es :** a straight line about which a body or a geometric figure rotates or may be supposed to rotate

ax•le *n* **:** a pin or shaft on or with which a wheel or pair of wheels turns

ax•on *n* **:** a long fiber that carries impulses away from a nerve cell

1aye *adv* **:** 1YES 1

2aye *n* **:** an affirmative vote or voter

aza•lea *n* **:** a usually small rhododendron that sheds its leaves in the fall and has flowers of many colors which are shaped like funnels

azure *n* **:** the blue color of the clear daytime sky

B

b *n, pl* **b's** *or* **bs** *often cap* **1 :** the second letter of the English alphabet **2 :** a grade that shows a student's work is good

1baa *n* **:** the cry of a sheep

2baa *vb* **:** to make the cry of a sheep

1bab•ble *vb* **bab•bled; bab•bling 1 :** to make meaningless sounds **2 :** to talk foolishly **3 :** to make the sound of a brook — **bab•bler** *n*

2babble *n* **1 :** talk that is not clear **2 :** the sound of a brook

babe *n* **:** 1BABY 1

ba•boon *n* **:** a large monkey of Africa and Asia with a doglike face

1ba•by *n, pl* **babies 1 :** a very young child **2 :** the youngest of a group **3 :** an older person who acts like a baby

2baby *adj* **:** 1YOUNG 1

3baby *vb* **ba•bied; ba•by•ing :** to treat as a baby

ba•by•hood *n* **1 :** the time in a person's life when he or she is a baby **2 :** the state of being a baby

ba•by•ish *adj* **:** like a baby

ba•by–sit *vb* **ba•by–sat; ba•by–sit•ting :** to care for children usually during a short absence of the parents

ba•by–sit•ter *n* **:** a person who baby-sits

bach•e•lor : a man who has not married

ba•cil•lus *n, pl* **ba•cil•li 1 :** a rod-shaped bacterium that forms internal spores **2 :** a bacterium that causes disease **:** GERM, MICROBE

1back *n* **1 :** the rear part of the human body from the neck to the end of the spine **:** the upper part of the body of an animal **2 :** the part of something that is opposite or away from the front part **3 :** a player in a team game who plays behind the forward line of players — **backed** *adj*

2back *adv* **1 :** to, toward, or at the rear **2 :** in or to a former time, state, or place **3 :** under control **4 :** in return or reply — **back and forth :** backward and forward **:** from one place to another

3back *adj* **1 :** located at the back **2 :** not yet paid **:** OVERDUE **3 :** no longer current

4back *vb* **1 :** to give support or help to **:** UPHOLD **2 :** to move back — **back•er** *n*

back•bone *n* **1 :** the column of bones in the back **:** SPINAL COLUMN **2 :** the strongest part of something **3 :** firmness of character

1back•fire *n* **1 :** a fire that is set to check the spread of a forest fire or a grass fire by burning off a strip of land ahead of it **2 :** a loud engine noise that happens when fuel ignites with a valve open

2backfire *vb* **back•fired; back•fir•ing 1 :** to make a backfire **2 :** to have a result opposite to what was planned

back•ground *n* **1 :** the scenery or ground that is behind a main figure or object **2 :** a position that attracts little attention **3 :** the total of a person's experience, knowledge, and education

1back•hand *n* **1 :** a stroke made with the back of the hand turned in the direction in which the hand is moving **2 :** handwriting in which the letters slant to the left

2backhand *adv or adj* **:** with a backhand

back•hand•ed *adj* **1 :** 2BACKHAND **2 :** not sincere

back of *prep* **:** 2BEHIND 1

back•stage *adv or adj* **:** in or to the area behind the stage

back•track *vb* **:** to go back over a course or a path

1back•ward *or* **back•wards** *adv* **1 :** toward the back **2 :** with the back first **3 :** opposite to the usual way

2backward *adj* **1 :** turned toward the back

2 : BASHFUL 3 : slow in learning or development

back·wa·ter *n* **1 :** water held or turned back from its course **2 :** a backward place or condition

back·woods *n pl* **1 :** wooded or partly cleared areas away from cities **2 :** a place that is backward in culture

ba·con *n* **:** salted and smoked meat from the sides and the back of a pig

bac·te·ri·um *n, pl* **bac·te·ria :** any of numerous microscopic organisms that are single cells and are important to humans because of their chemical activities and as causes of disease

bad *adj* **worse; worst 1 :** not good **:** POOR **2 :** not favorable **3 :** not fresh or sound **4 :** not good or right **:** morally evil **5 :** not enough **6 :** UNPLEASANT **7 :** HARMFUL **8 :** SEVERE 4 **9 :** not correct **10 :** [1]ILL 4, SICK **11 :** SORRY 1 — **bad·ness** *n*

bade *past of* BID

badge *n* **:** something worn to show that a person belongs to a certain group or rank

[1]**bad·ger** *n* **:** a furry burrowing animal with short thick legs and long claws on the front feet

[2]**badger** *vb* **:** to annoy again and again

bad·ly *adv* **worse; worst 1 :** in a bad manner **2 :** very much

bad·min·ton *n* **:** a game in which a shuttlecock is hit back and forth over a net by players using light rackets

baf·fle *vb* **baf·fled; baf·fling :** to defeat or check by confusing

[1]**bag** *n* **1 :** a container made of flexible material (as paper or plastic) **2 :** [1]PURSE 1, HANDBAG **3 :** SUITCASE

[2]**bag** *vb* **bagged; bag·ging 1 :** to swell out **2 :** to put into a bag **3 :** to kill or capture in hunting

ba·gel *n* **:** a hard roll shaped like a doughnut

bag·gage *n* **:** the trunks, suitcases, and personal belongings of travelers

bag·gy *adj* **bag·gi·er; bag·gi·est :** hanging loosely or puffed out like a bag

bag·pipe *n* **:** a musical instrument played especially in Scotland that consists of a tube, a bag for air, and pipes from which the sound comes

[1]**bail** *vb* **:** to dip and throw out water from a boat — usually used with *out*

[2]**bail** *n* **:** a promise or a deposit of money needed to free a prisoner until his or her trial

[3]**bail** *vb* **:** to get the release of (a prisoner) by giving bail

bail out *vb* **:** to jump out of an airplane with a parachute

[1]**bait** *vb* **1 :** to torment by mean or unjust attacks **2 :** to put bait on or in

[2]**bait** *n* **:** something used in luring especially to a hook or a trap

bake *vb* **baked; bak·ing 1 :** to cook or become cooked in a dry heat especially in an oven **2 :** to dry or harden by heat

bak·er *n* **:** a person who bakes and sells bread, cakes, or pastry

baker's dozen *n* **:** THIRTEEN

bak·ery *n, pl* **bak·er·ies :** a place where bread, cakes, and pastry are made or sold

baking powder *n* **:** a powder used to make the dough rise in making baked goods (as cakes or muffins)

baking soda *n* **:** SODIUM BICARBONATE

[1]**bal·ance** *n* **1 :** an instrument for weighing **2 :** a steady position or condition **3 :** equal total sums on the two sides of a bookkeeping account **4 :** something left over **:** REMAINDER **5 :** the amount by which one side of an account is greater than the other

[2]**balance** *vb* **bal·anced; bal·anc·ing 1 :** to make the two sides of (an account) add up to the same total **2 :** to make equal in weight or number **3 :** to weigh against one another **:** COMPARE **4 :** to put in or as if in balance

bal·co·ny *n, pl* **bal·co·nies 1 :** a platform enclosed by a low wall or a railing built out from the side of a building **2 :** a platform inside a building extending out over part of a main floor (as of a theater)

bald *adj* **1 :** lacking a natural covering (as of hair) **2 :** [1]PLAIN 3 — **bald·ness** *n*

bald eagle *n* **:** the common North American eagle that when full-grown has white head and neck feathers

[1]**bale** *n* **:** a large bundle of goods tightly tied for storing or shipping

[2]**bale** *vb* **baled; bal·ing :** to make up into a bale — **bal·er** *n*

[1]**balk** *n* **:** HINDRANCE

[2]**balk** *vb* **1 :** to keep from happening or succeeding **2 :** to stop short and refuse to go

balky *adj* **balk·i·er; balk·i·est :** likely to balk

[1]**ball** *n* **1 :** something round or roundish **2 :** a usually round object used in a game or sport **3 :** a game or sport (as baseball) played with a ball **4 :** a solid usually round shot for a gun **5 :** the rounded bulge at the base of the thumb or big toe **6 :** a pitched baseball that is not hit and is not a strike

[2]**ball** *vb* **:** to make or come together into a ball

[3]**ball** *n* **:** a large formal party for dancing

bal·lad *n* **1 :** a simple song **2 :** a short poem suitable for singing that tells a story in simple language

ball–and–socket joint *n* **:** a joint (as in the

shoulder) in which a rounded part can move in many directions in a socket

bal·last *n* **1 :** heavy material used to make a ship steady or to control the rising of a balloon **2 :** gravel, cinders, or crushed stone used in making a roadbed

ball bearing *n* **1 :** a bearing in which the revolving part turns on metal balls that roll easily in a groove **2 :** one of the balls in a ball bearing

bal·le·ri·na *n* **:** a female ballet dancer

bal·let *n* **1 :** a stage dance that tells a story in movement and pantomime **2 :** a group that performs ballets

1bal·loon *n* **1 :** a bag that rises and floats above the ground when filled with heated air or with a gas that is lighter than air **2 :** a toy consisting of a rubber bag that can be blown up with air or gas **3 :** an outline containing words spoken or thought by a character (as in a cartoon)

2balloon *vb* **:** to swell or puff out like a balloon

1bal·lot *n* **1 :** an object and especially a printed sheet of paper used in voting **2 :** the action or a system of voting **3 :** the right to vote **4 :** the number of votes cast

2ballot *vb* **:** to vote or decide by ballot

ball·point *n* **:** a pen whose writing point is a small metal ball that inks itself from an inner supply

ball·room *n* **:** a large room for dances

balmy *adj* **balm·i·er; balm·i·est :** gently soothing

bal·sa *n* **:** the very light but strong wood of a tropical American tree

bal·sam *n* **1 :** a material with a strong pleasant smell that oozes from some plants **2 :** a plant (as the evergreen **balsam fir** often used as a Christmas tree) that yields balsam

bal·us·ter *n* **:** a short post that supports the upper part of a railing

bal·us·trade *n* **:** a row of balusters topped by a rail to serve as an open fence (as along the edge of a terrace or a balcony)

bam·boo *n* **:** a tall treelike tropical grass with a hard jointed stem that is used in making furniture and in building

1ban *vb* **banned; ban·ning :** to forbid especially by law or social pressure

2ban *n* **:** an official order forbidding something

ba·nana *n* **:** a yellow or red fruit that is shaped somewhat like a finger and grows in bunches on a large treelike tropical plant (**banana plant** or **banana tree**) with very large leaves

1band *n* **1 :** something that holds together or goes around something else **2 :** a strip of material around or across something **3 :** a range of frequencies (as of radio waves)

2band *vb* **1 :** to put a band on **:** tie together with a band **2 :** to unite in a group

3band *n* **1 :** a group of persons or animals **2 :** a group of musicians performing together

1ban·dage *n* **:** a strip of material used especially to dress and bind up wounds

2bandage *vb* **ban·daged; ban·dag·ing :** to bind or cover with a bandage

ban·dan·na *or* **ban·dana** *n* **:** a large handkerchief usually with a colorful design printed on it

ban·dit *n* **:** a lawless person **:** one who lives outside the law

band·stand *n* **:** an outdoor platform used for band concerts

band·wag·on *n* **1 :** a wagon carrying musicians in a parade **2 :** a candidate, side, or movement that attracts growing support

1bang *vb* **:** to beat, strike, or shut with a loud noise

2bang *n* **1 :** a violent blow **2 :** a sudden loud noise **3 :** 2THRILL 1

3bang *n* **:** hair cut short across the forehead — usually used in pl.

4bang *vb* **:** to cut (hair) short and squarely across

ban·ish *vb* **1 :** to force to leave a country **2 :** to drive away **:** DISMISS

ban·ish·ment *n* **:** a banishing from a country

ban·is·ter *n* **1 :** one of the slender posts used to support the handrail of a staircase **2 :** a handrail and its supporting posts **3 :** the handrail of a staircase

ban·jo *n, pl* **banjos :** a musical instrument with four or five strings and a fretted neck

1bank *n* **1 :** a mound or ridge especially of earth **2 :** something shaped like a mound **3 :** an undersea elevation **:** SHOAL **4 :** the rising ground at the edge of a river, lake, or sea

2bank *vb* **1 :** to raise a bank around **2 :** to heap up in a bank **3 :** to build (a curve) with the road or track sloping upward from the inside edge **4 :** to cover with fuel or ashes so as to reduce the speed of burning **5 :** to tilt an airplane to one side when turning

3bank *n* **1 :** a place of business that lends, exchanges, takes care of, or issues money **2 :** a small closed container in which money may be saved **3 :** a storage place for a reserve supply

4bank *vb* **1 :** to have an account in a bank **2 :** to deposit in a bank

5bank *n* **:** a group or series of objects arranged together in a row

bank·er *n* **:** a person who is engaged in the business of a bank

bank·ing *n* **:** the business of a bank or banker

1bank·rupt *n* **:** a person who becomes unable to pay his or her debts and whose property is by court order divided among the creditors

2bankrupt *adj* **:** unable to pay one's debts

3bankrupt *vb* **:** to make bankrupt

bank·rupt·cy *n, pl* **bank·rupt·cies :** the state of being bankrupt

1ban·ner *n* **1 :** 1FLAG **2 :** a piece of cloth with a design, a picture, or some writing on it

2banner *adj* **:** unusually good or satisfactory

ban·quet *n* **:** a formal dinner for many people often in honor of someone

ban·tam *n* **:** a miniature breed of domestic chicken often raised for exhibiting in shows

1ban·ter *vb* **:** to speak to in a friendly but teasing way

2banter *n* **:** good-natured teasing and joking

bap·tism *n* **:** the act or ceremony of baptizing

bap·tize *vb* **bap·tized; bap·tiz·ing 1 :** to dip in water or sprinkle water on as a part of the ceremony of receiving into the Christian church **2 :** to give a name to as in the ceremony of baptism **:** CHRISTEN

1bar *n* **1 :** a usually slender rigid piece (as of wood or metal) that has many uses (as for a lever or barrier) **2 :** a usually rectangular solid piece or block of something **3 :** something that blocks the way **4 :** a submerged or partly submerged bank along a shore or in a river **5 :** a court of law **6 :** the profession of law **7 :** a straight stripe, band, or line longer than it is wide **8 :** a counter on which liquor is served **9 :** a place of business for the sale of alcoholic drinks **10 :** a vertical line across a musical staff marking equal measures of time **11 :** 1MEASURE 6

2bar *vb* **barred; bar·ring 1 :** to fasten with a bar **2 :** to block off **3 :** to shut out

3bar *prep* **:** with the exception of

barb *n* **:** a sharp point that sticks out and backward (as from the tip of an arrow or fishhook) — **barbed** *adj*

bar·bar·i·an *n* **:** an uncivilized person

bar·bar·ic *adj* **:** of, relating to, or characteristic of barbarians

bar·ba·rous *adj* **1 :** not civilized **2 :** CRUEL 2, HARSH — **bar·ba·rous·ly** *adv*

1bar·be·cue *vb* **bar·be·cued; bar·be·cu·ing 1 :** to cook over or before an open source of heat **2 :** to cook in a highly seasoned sauce

2barbecue *n* **1 :** a large animal roasted whole **2 :** an outdoor social gathering at which food is barbecued and eaten

bar·ber *n* **:** a person whose business is cutting and dressing hair and shaving beards

bard *n* **1 :** a person in ancient societies skilled at composing and singing songs about heroes **2 :** POET

1bare *adj* **bar·er; bar·est 1 :** having no covering **:** NAKED **2 :** 1EMPTY 1 **3 :** having nothing left over or added **:** MERE **4 :** 1PLAIN 3

2bare *vb* **bared; bar·ing :** UNCOVER 1, 2

bare·back *adv or adj* **:** on the bare back of a horse **:** without a saddle

bare·foot *adv or adj* **:** with the feet bare

bare·head·ed *adv or adj* **:** with the head bare **:** without a hat

bare·ly *adv* **:** with nothing to spare

1bar·gain *n* **1 :** an agreement between persons settling what each is to give and receive in a business deal **2 :** something bought or offered for sale at a desirable price

2bargain *vb* **:** to talk over the terms of a purchase or agreement

barge *n* **:** a broad boat with a flat bottom used chiefly in harbors and on rivers and canals

bar graph *n* **:** a chart that uses parallel bars whose lengths are in proportion to the numbers represented

bari·tone *n* **1 :** a male singing voice between bass and tenor in range **2 :** a singer having a baritone voice **3 :** a horn used in bands that is lower than the trumpet but higher than the tuba

1bark *vb* **1 :** to make the short loud cry of a dog **2 :** to shout or speak sharply

2bark *n* **:** the sound made by a barking dog

3bark *n* **:** the outside covering of the trunk, branches, and roots of a tree

4bark *vb* **:** to rub or scrape the skin off

5bark *or* **barque** *n* **1 :** a small sailing boat **2 :** a three-masted ship with foremast and mainmast square-rigged

bark·er *n* **:** a person who stands at the entrance to a show or a store and tries to attract people to it

bar·ley *n* **:** a cereal grass with flowers in dense heads that is grown for its grain which is used mostly to feed farm animals or make malt

barn *n* **:** a building used for storing grain and hay and for housing farm animals

bar·na·cle *n* **:** a small saltwater shellfish that fastens itself on rocks or on wharves and the bottoms of ships

barn·yard *n* **:** a usually fenced area next to a barn

ba·rom·e·ter *n* **:** an instrument that measures air pressure and is used to forecast changes in the weather

bar•on *n* **:** a member of the lowest rank of the British nobility
bar•on•ess *n* **1 :** the wife or widow of a baron **2 :** a woman who holds the rank of a baron in her own right
bar•on•et *n* **:** the holder of a rank of honor below a baron but above a knight
ba•ro•ni•al *adj* **:** of, relating to, or suitable for a baron
barque *variant of* BARK
bar•racks *n sing or pl* **:** a building or group of buildings in which soldiers live
bar•rage *n* **:** a barrier formed by continuous artillery or machine-gun fire directed upon a narrow strip of ground
1bar•rel *n* **1 :** a round bulging container that is longer than it is wide and has flat ends **2 :** the amount contained in a full barrel **3 :** something shaped like a cylinder
2barrel *vb* **bar•reled** *or* **bar•relled; bar•rel•ing** *or* **bar•rel•ling :** to move at a high speed
1bar•ren *adj* **1 :** unable to produce seed, fruit, or young **2 :** growing only poor or few plants
2barren *n* **:** an area of barren land
bar•rette *n* **:** a clasp or bar used to hold a girl's or woman's hair in place
1bar•ri•cade *vb* **bar•ri•cad•ed; bar•ri•cad•ing :** to block off with a barricade
2barricade *n* **:** a barrier made in a hurry for protection against attack or for blocking the way
bar•ri•er *n* **1 :** something (as a fence) that blocks the way **2 :** something that keeps apart or makes progress difficult
bar•ring *prep* **:** aside from the possibility of
1bar•row *n* **:** a castrated male hog
2barrow *n* **1 :** WHEELBARROW **2 :** PUSHCART
1bar•ter *vb* **:** to trade by exchanging one thing for another without the use of money
2barter *n* **:** the exchange of goods without the use of money
1base *n* **1 :** a thing or a part on which something rests **:** BOTTOM, FOUNDATION **2 :** a line or surface of a geometric figure upon which an altitude is or is thought to be constructed **3 :** the main substance in a mixture **4 :** a supporting or carrying substance (as in a medicine or paint) **5 :** a place where a military force keeps its supplies or from which it starts its operations **6 :** a number with reference to which a system of numbers is constructed **7 :** a starting place or goal in various games **8 :** any of the four stations a runner in baseball must touch in order to score **9 :** a chemical substance (as lime or ammonia) that reacts with an acid to form a salt and turns red litmus paper blue
2base *vb* **based; bas•ing :** to provide with a base or basis
3base *adj* **bas•er; bas•est 1 :** of low value and not very good in some ways **2 :** not honorable **:** MEAN — **base•ness** *n*
base•ball *n* **1 :** a game played with a bat and ball by two teams of nine players on a field with four bases that mark the course a runner must take to score **2 :** the ball used in baseball
base•board *n* **:** a line of boards or molding extending around the walls of a room and touching the floor
base•ment *n* **:** the part of a building that is partly or entirely below ground level
bash *vb* **:** to hit very hard
bash•ful *adj* **:** uneasy in the presence of others
ba•sic *adj* **1 :** of, relating to, or forming the base of something **2 :** relating to or characteristic of a chemical base — **ba•si•cal•ly** *adv*
ba•sil *n* **:** a fragrant mint used in cooking
ba•sin *n* **1 :** a wide shallow usually round dish or bowl for holding liquids **2 :** the amount that a basin holds **3 :** a natural or artificial hollow or enclosure containing water **4 :** the land drained by a river and its branches
ba•sis *n, pl* **ba•ses :** FOUNDATION 2, BASE
bask *vb* **:** to lie or relax in pleasantly warm surroundings
bas•ket *n* **1 :** a container made by weaving together materials (as reeds, straw, or strips of wood) **2 :** the contents of a basket **3 :** something that is like a basket in shape or use **4 :** a goal in basketball — **bas•ket•like** *adj*
bas•ket•ball *n* **1 :** a game in which each of two teams tries to throw a round inflated ball through a raised basketlike goal **2 :** the ball used in basketball
bas•ket•ry *n* **1 :** the making of objects (as baskets) by weaving or braiding long slender pieces (as of reed or wood) **2 :** objects made of interwoven twigs or reeds
bas-re•lief *n* **:** a sculpture in which the design is raised very slightly from the background
1bass *n, pl* **bass** *or* **bass•es :** any of numerous freshwater and sea fishes that are caught for sport and food
2bass *n* **1 :** a tone of low pitch **2 :** the lowest part in harmony that has four parts **3 :** the lower half of the musical pitch range **4 :** the lowest male singing voice **5 :** a singer or an instrument having a bass range or part
bass drum *n* **:** a large drum with two heads

that produces a low booming sound when played

bas·soon *n* **:** a double-reed woodwind instrument with a usual range two octaves lower than an oboe

bass viol *n* **:** DOUBLE BASS

bass·wood *n* **:** a pale wood with straight grain from the linden or a related tree

[1]**baste** *vb* **bast·ed; bast·ing :** to sew with long loose stitches so as to hold the work temporarily in place

[2]**baste** *vb* **bast·ed; bast·ing :** to moisten (as with melted fat or juices) while roasting

[1]**bat** *n* **1 :** a sharp blow or slap **2 :** an implement used for hitting the ball in various games **3 :** a turn at batting

[2]**bat** *vb* **bat·ted; bat·ting 1 :** to strike with or as if with a bat **2 :** to take one's turn at bat

[3]**bat** *n* **:** any of a group of mammals that fly by means of long front limbs modified into wings

batch *n* **1 :** a quantity of something baked at one time **2 :** a quantity of material for use at one time or produced at one operation **3 :** a group of persons or things

bath *n, pl* **baths 1 :** a washing of the body **2 :** water for bathing **3 :** a place, room, or building where persons may bathe **4 :** BATHTUB **5 :** a liquid in which objects are placed so that it can act upon them

bathe *vb* **bathed; bath·ing 1 :** to take a bath **2 :** to go swimming **3 :** to give a bath to **4 :** to apply a liquid to **5 :** to cover with or as if with a liquid — **bath·er** *n*

bathing suit *n* **:** SWIMSUIT

bath·room *n* **:** a room containing a bathtub or shower and usually a washbowl and toilet

bath·tub *n* **:** a tub in which to take a bath

ba·ton *n* **1 :** a stick with which a leader directs an orchestra or band **2 :** a rod with a ball on one end carried by a drum major or drum majorette

bat·tal·ion *n* **1 :** a part of an army consisting of two or more companies **2 :** a large body of persons organized to act together

[1]**bat·ter** *vb* **1 :** to beat with repeated violent blows **2 :** to damage by blows or hard use

[2]**batter** *n* **:** a thin mixture made chiefly of flour and a liquid beaten together and used in making cakes and biscuits

[3]**batter** *n* **:** the player whose turn it is to bat

bat·tered *adj* **:** worn down or injured by hard use

bat·ter·ing ram *n* **1 :** an ancient military machine that consisted of a heavy beam with an iron tip mounted in a frame and swung back and forth in order to batter down walls **2 :** a beam or bar with handles used to batter down doors or walls

bat·tery *n, pl* **bat·ter·ies 1 :** two or more big military guns that are controlled as a unit **2 :** an electric cell for providing electric current or a group of such cells **3 :** a number of machines or devices grouped together

bat·ting *n* **:** cotton or wool in sheets used mostly for stuffing quilts or packaging goods

[1]**bat·tle** *n* **1 :** a fight between armies, warships, or airplanes **2 :** a fight between two persons or animals **3 :** a long or hard struggle or contest **4 :** WARFARE

[2]**battle** *vb* **bat·tled; bat·tling :** to engage in battle

bat·tle–ax *or* **bat·tle–axe** *n* **:** an ax with a broad blade formerly used as a weapon

bat·tle·field *n* **:** a place where a battle is fought or was once fought

bat·tle·ground *n* **:** BATTLEFIELD

bat·tle·ment *n* **:** a low wall (as at the top of a castle or tower) with openings to shoot through

bat·tle·ship *n* **:** a large warship with heavy armor and large guns

[1]**bawl** *vb* **1 :** to shout or cry loudly **2 :** to weep noisily

[2]**bawl** *n* **:** a loud cry

bawl out *vb* **:** to scold severely

[1]**bay** *n* **1 :** a reddish-brown horse **2 :** a reddish brown

[2]**bay** *vb* **:** to bark with long deep tones

[3]**bay** *n* **1 :** the baying of dogs **2 :** the position of an animal or a person forced to face pursuers when it is impossible to escape **3 :** the position of pursuers who are held off

[4]**bay** *n* **:** a part of a large body of water extending into the land

[5]**bay** *n* **:** the laurel or a related tree or shrub

bay·ber·ry *n, pl* **bay·ber·ries :** a shrub with leathery leaves and small bluish white waxy berries used in making candles

[1]**bay·o·net** *n* **:** a weapon like a dagger made to fit on the end of a rifle

[2]**bayonet** *vb* **bay·o·net·ted; bay·o·net·ting :** to stab with a bayonet

bay·ou *n* **:** a creek that flows slowly through marshy land

bay window *n* **:** a window or a set of windows that sticks out from the wall of a building

ba·zaar *n* **1 :** an Oriental marketplace containing rows of small shops **2 :** a large building where many kinds of goods are sold **3 :** a fair for the sale of goods especially for charity

ba·zoo·ka *n* **:** a portable shoulder gun consisting of a tube open at both ends that shoots an explosive rocket able to pierce armor

be *vb, past 1st & 3d sing* **was;** *2d sing* **were;** *pl* **were;** *past subjunctive* **were;** *past participle* **been;** *present participle* **be·ing;** *present 1st sing* **am;** *2d sing* **are;** *3d sing* **is;** *pl* **are;** *present subjunctive* **be** **1 :** to equal in meaning or identity **2 :** to have a specified character or quality **3 :** to belong to the class of **4 :** EXIST 1, LIVE **5** — used as a helping verb with other verbs

be- *prefix* **1 :** on **:** around **:** over **2 :** provide with or cover with **:** dress up with **3 :** about **:** to **:** upon **4 :** make **:** cause to be

[1]beach *n* **:** a sandy or gravelly part of the shore of the sea or of a lake

[2]beach *vb* **:** to run or drive ashore

beach·head *n* **:** an area on an enemy shore held by an advance force of an invading army to protect the later landing of troops or supplies

bea·con *n* **1 :** a guiding or warning light or fire on a high place **2 :** a radio station that sends out signals to guide aircraft

[1]bead *n* **1 :** a small piece of solid material with a hole through it by which it can be strung on a thread **2 :** a small round mass **3 :** a small knob on a gun used in taking aim

[2]bead *vb* **1 :** to cover with beads **2 :** to string together like beads

beady *adj* **bead·i·er; bead·i·est :** like a bead especially in being small, round, and shiny

bea·gle *n* **:** a small hound with short legs and a smooth coat

beak *n* **1 :** the bill of a bird **2 :** a part shaped like a beak — **beaked** *adj*

bea·ker *n* **:** a deep cup or glass with a wide mouth and usually a lip for pouring

[1]beam *n* **1 :** a long heavy piece of timber or metal used as a main horizontal support of a building or a ship **2 :** a ray of light **3 :** a constant radio wave sent out from an airport to guide pilots along a course

[2]beam *vb* **1 :** to send out beams of light **2 :** to smile with joy **3 :** to aim a radio broadcast by use of a special antenna

bean *n* **1 :** the edible seed or pod of a bushy or climbing garden plant related to the peas and clovers **2 :** a seed or fruit like a bean

[1]bear *n, pl* **bears** **1** *or pl* **bear :** a large heavy mammal with long shaggy hair and a very short tail **2 :** a grumpy or glum person

[2]bear *vb* **bore; borne; bear·ing** **1 :** [1]SUPPORT 4 **2 :** to have as a feature or characteristic **3 :** to bring forth **:** give birth to **4 :** to put up with **5 :** [2]PRESS 1 **6 :** to have a relation to the matter at hand

bear·able *adj* **:** possible to bear

beard *n* **1 :** the hair on the face of a man **2 :** a hairy growth or tuft

bear·er *n* **1 :** someone or something that bears, supports, or carries **2 :** a person holding a check or an order for payment

bear·ing *n* **1 :** the manner in which one carries or conducts oneself **2 :** a part of a machine in which another part turns **3 :** the position or direction of one point with respect to another or to the compass **4 bearings** *pl* **:** understanding of one's position or situation **5 :** CONNECTION 2

beast *n* **1 :** a mammal with four feet (as a bear, deer, or rabbit) **2 :** a farm animal especially when kept for work **3 :** a mean or horrid person

[1]beat *vb* **beat; beat·en** *or* **beat; beat·ing** **1 :** to strike again and again **2 :** [1]THROB 2, PULSATE **3 :** to flap against **4 :** to mix by stirring rapidly **5 :** to win against **6 :** to measure or mark off by strokes — **beat·er** *n*

[2]beat *n* **1 :** a blow or a stroke made again and again **2 :** a single pulse (as of the heart) **3 :** a measurement of time or accent in music **4 :** an area or place regularly visited or traveled through

[3]beat *adj* **1 :** being very tired **2 :** having lost one's morale

beat·en *adj* **:** worn smooth by passing feet

be·at·i·tude *n* **:** one of the statements made in the Sermon on the Mount (Matthew 5: 3-12) beginning "Blessed are"

beau *n, pl* **beaux** *or* **beaus :** BOYFRIEND

beau·te·ous *adj* **:** BEAUTIFUL

beau·ti·cian *n* **:** a person who gives beauty treatments (as to skin and hair)

beau·ti·ful *adj* **:** having qualities of beauty **:** giving pleasure to the mind or senses — **beau·ti·ful·ly** *adv*

beau·ti·fy *vb* **beau·ti·fied; beau·ti·fy·ing** **:** to make beautiful

beau·ty *n, pl* **beauties** **1 :** the qualities of a person or a thing that give pleasure to the senses or to the mind **2 :** a beautiful person or thing

beauty shop *n* **:** a place of business for the care of customers' hair, skin, and nails

bea·ver *n* **:** an animal related to the rats and mice that has webbed hind feet and a broad flat tail, builds dams and houses of sticks and mud in water, and is prized for its soft but strong fur

be·calm *vb* **:** to bring to a stop because of lack of wind

became *past of* BECOME

be·cause *conj* **:** for the reason that

because of *prep* **:** as a result of

beck *n* **:** a beckoning motion

beck·on *vb* **:** to call or signal by a motion (as a wave or nod)

be·come *vb* **be·came; become; be·com·ing** **1 :** to come or grow to be **2 :** to be suitable to : SUIT — **become of** : to happen to

be·com·ing *adj* : having a pleasing effect — **be·com·ing·ly** *adv*

[1]**bed** *n* **1** : a piece of furniture on which one may sleep or rest **2** : a place for sleeping or resting **3** : a level piece of ground prepared for growing plants **4** : the bottom of something **5** : LAYER 2

[2]**bed** *vb* **bed·ded; bed·ding** **1** : to put or go to bed **2** : to plant in beds

bed·bug *n* : a small wingless insect that sucks blood and is sometimes found in houses and especially in beds

bed·clothes *n pl* : coverings (as sheets and pillowcases) for a bed

bed·ding *n* **1** : BEDCLOTHES **2** : material for a bed

be·dev·il *vb* : to trouble or annoy again and again : PESTER, HARASS

bed·lam *n* : a place or scene of uproar and confusion

be·drag·gled *adj* **1** : limp and often wet as by exposure to rain **2** : soiled from or as if from being dragged in mud

bed·rid·den *adj* : forced to stay in bed by sickness or weakness

bed·rock *n* : the solid rock found under surface materials (as soil)

bed·room *n* : a room to sleep in

bed·side *n* : the place beside a bed

bed·spread *n* : a decorative top covering for a bed

bed·stead *n* : the framework of a bed

bed·time *n* : time to go to bed

bee *n* **1** : an insect with four wings that is related to the wasps, gathers pollen and nectar from flowers from which it makes beebread and honey for food, and usually lives in large colonies **2** : a gathering of people to do something together

bee·bread *n* : a bitter yellowish brown food material prepared by bees from pollen and stored in their honeycomb

beech *n* : a tree with smooth gray bark, deep green leaves, and small triangular nuts

beef *n, pl* **beefs** *or* **beeves** **1** : the flesh of a steer, cow, or bull **2** : a steer, cow, or bull especially when fattened for food — **beef-like** *adj*

beef·steak *n* : a slice of beef suitable for broiling or frying

bee·hive *n* : HIVE 1

bee·line *n* : a straight direct course

been *past participle of* BE

beer *n* : an alcoholic drink made from malt and flavored with hops

bees·wax *n* : wax made by bees and used by them in building honeycomb

beet *n* : a leafy plant with a thick juicy root that is used as a vegetable or as a source of sugar

bee·tle *n* **1** : any of a group of insects with four wings the outer pair of which are stiff cases that cover the others when folded **2** : an insect (as a bug) that looks like a beetle

beeves *pl of* BEEF

be·fall *vb* **be·fell; be·fall·en; be·fall·ing** **1** : to take place : HAPPEN **2** : to happen to

be·fit *vb* **be·fit·ted; be·fit·ting** : to be suitable to or proper for

[1]**be·fore** *adv* **1** : in front : AHEAD **2** : in the past **3** : at an earlier time

[2]**before** *prep* **1** : in front of **2** : in the presence of **3** : earlier than

[3]**before** *conj* **1** : ahead of the time when **2** : more willingly than

be·fore·hand *adv* : [1]BEFORE 1 : ahead of time

be·friend *vb* : to act as a friend to : help in a friendly way

beg *vb* **begged; beg·ging** **1** : to ask for money, food, or help as a charity **2** : to ask as a favor in an earnest or polite way

beg·gar *n* **1** : one who lives by begging **2** : PAUPER

be·gin *vb* **be·gan; be·gun; be·gin·ning** **1** : to do the first part of an action **2** : to come into existence

be·gin·ner *n* : a young or inexperienced person

be·gin·ning *n* **1** : the point at which something begins **2** : first part

be·gone *vb* : to go away : DEPART — used especially in the imperative mood

be·go·nia *n* : a plant with a juicy stem, ornamental leaves, and bright waxy flowers

be·grudge *vb* **be·grudged; be·grudg·ing** : to give or do reluctantly

begun *past of* BEGIN

be·half *n* : one's interest or support

be·have *vb* **be·haved; be·hav·ing** **1** : to conduct oneself **2** : to conduct oneself properly **3** : to act or function in a particular way

be·hav·ior *n* **1** : the way in which one conducts oneself **2** : the whole activity of something and especially a living being

be·head *vb* : to cut off the head of

[1]**be·hind** *adv* **1** : in a place that is being or has been departed from **2** : at, to, or toward the back **3** : not up to the general level

[2]**behind** *prep* **1** : at or to the back of **2** : not up to the level of

be·hold *vb* **be·held; be·hold·ing** : to look upon : SEE — **be·hold·er** *n*

beige *n* : a yellowish brown

be·ing *n* **1** : the state of having life or existence **2** : one that exists in fact or thought **3** : a living thing

be·la·bor *vb* **:** to keep working on to excess

be·lat·ed *adj* **:** delayed beyond the usual or expected time

1belch *vb* **1 :** to force out gas suddenly from the stomach through the mouth **2 :** to throw out or be thrown out violently

2belch *n* **:** a belching of gas

bel·fry *n, pl* **belfries :** a tower or room in a tower for a bell or set of bells

1Bel·gian *adj* **:** of or relating to Belgium or the Belgians

2Belgian *n* **:** a person born or living in Belgium

be·lief *n* **1 :** a feeling sure that a person or thing exists or is true or trustworthy **2 :** religious faith **:** CREED **3 :** something that one thinks is true

be·liev·able *adj* **:** possible to believe

be·lieve *vb* **be·lieved; be·liev·ing 1 :** to have faith or confidence in the existence or worth of **2 :** to accept as true **3 :** to accept the word of **4 :** THINK 2

be·liev·er *n* **:** one who has faith (as in a religion)

be·lit·tle *vb* **be·lit·tled; be·lit·tling :** to make (a person or a thing) seem small or unimportant

bell *n* **1 :** a hollow metallic device that is shaped somewhat like a cup and makes a ringing sound when struck **2 :** the stroke or sound of a bell that tells the hour **3 :** the time indicated by the stroke of a bell **4 :** a half-hour period of watch on shipboard **5 :** something shaped like a bell

bell·boy *n* **:** BELLHOP

bell·hop *n* **:** a hotel or club employee who answers calls for service by bell or telephone and assists guests with luggage

1bel·lig·er·ent *adj* **1 :** carrying on war **2 :** eager to fight

2belligerent *n* **1 :** a nation at war **2 :** a person taking part in a fight

bell jar *n* **:** a usually glass vessel shaped like a bell and used to cover objects or to contain gases or a vacuum

1bel·low *vb* **:** to give a loud deep roar like that of a bull

2bellow *n* **:** a loud deep roar

bel·lows *n sing or pl* **1 :** a device that produces a strong current of air when its sides are pressed together **2 :** the folding part of some cameras

1bel·ly *n, pl* **bellies 1 :** ABDOMEN 1 **2 :** the under part of an animal's body **3 :** STOMACH 1 **4 :** an internal cavity (as of the human body) **5 :** the thick part of a muscle

2belly *vb* **bel·lied; bel·ly·ing :** to swell out

belly button *n* **:** NAVEL

be·long *vb* **1 :** to be in a proper place **2 :** to be the property of a person or group of persons **3 :** to be a part of **:** be connected with **:** go with

be·long·ings *n pl* **:** the things that belong to a person

be·lov·ed *adj* **:** greatly loved **:** very dear

1be·low *adv* **:** in or to a lower place

2below *prep* **:** lower than **:** BENEATH

1belt *n* **1 :** a strip of flexible material (as leather or cloth) worn around a person's body for holding in or supporting clothing or weapons or for ornament **2 :** something like a belt **:** BAND, CIRCLE **3 :** a flexible endless band running around wheels or pulleys and used for moving or carrying something **4 :** a region suited to or producing something or having some special feature — **belt·ed** *adj*

2belt *vb* **1 :** to put a belt on or around **2 :** to strike hard

be·moan *vb* **:** to express grief over

bench *n* **1 :** a long seat for two or more persons **2 :** a long table for holding work and tools **3 :** the position or rank of a judge

1bend *vb* **bent; bend·ing 1 :** to make, be, or become curved or angular rather than straight or flat **2 :** to move out of a straight line or position **:** STOOP **3 :** to turn in a certain direction **:** DIRECT

2bend *n* **:** something that is bent **:** CURVE

1be·neath *adv* **:** in a lower place

2beneath *prep* **1 :** lower than **:** UNDER **2 :** not worthy of

bene·dic·tion *n* **1 :** an expression of approval **2 :** a short blessing by a minister or priest at the end of a religious service

ben·e·fac·tor *n* **:** one who helps another especially by giving money

ben·e·fi·cial *adj* **:** producing good results **:** HELPFUL — **ben·e·fi·cial·ly** *adv*

ben·e·fi·cia·ry *n, pl* **ben·e·fi·cia·ries :** a person who benefits or is expected to benefit from something

1ben·e·fit *n* **1 :** something that does good to a person or thing **2 :** money paid in time of death, sickness, or unemployment or in old age (as by an insurance company)

2benefit *vb* **ben·e·fit·ed** *or* **ben·e·fit·ted; ben·e·fit·ing** *or* **ben·e·fit·ting 1 :** to be useful or profitable to **2 :** to receive benefit

be·nev·o·lence *n* **:** KINDNESS, GENEROSITY

be·nev·o·lent *adj* **:** having a desire to do good **:** KINDLY, CHARITABLE

be·nign *adj* **1 :** of a gentle disposition **2 :** likely to bring about a good outcome — **be·nign·ly** *adv*

1bent *adj* **1 :** changed by bending **:** CROOKED **2 :** strongly favorable to **:** quite determined

2bent *n* **:** a strong or natural liking

be·queath *vb* **1 :** to give or leave by means of a will **2 :** to hand down

be·quest *n* **1 :** the act of bequeathing **2 :** something given or left by a will

[1]**be·reaved** *adj* **:** suffering the death of a loved one

[2]**bereaved** *n, pl* **bereaved :** a bereaved person

be·reft *adj* **1 :** not having something needed, wanted, or expected **2 :** [1]BEREAVED

be·ret *n* **:** a soft round flat cap without a visor

berg *n* **:** ICEBERG

beri·beri *n* **:** a disease caused by lack of a vitamin in which there is weakness, wasting, and damage to nerves

[1]**ber·ry** *n, pl* **berries 1 :** a small pulpy fruit (as a strawberry) **2 :** a simple fruit (as a grape or tomato) in which the ripened ovary wall is fleshy **3 :** a dry seed (as of the coffee tree)

[2]**berry** *vb* **ber·ried; ber·ry·ing :** to gather berries

berth *n* **1 :** a place where a ship lies at anchor or at a wharf **2 :** a bed on a ship, train, or airplane

be·seech *vb* **be·sought** *or* **be·seeched; be·seech·ing :** to ask earnestly

be·set *vb* **be·set; be·set·ting 1 :** to attack from all sides **2 :** SURROUND

be·side *prep* **1 :** by the side of **:** NEXT TO **2 :** compared with **3 :** [1]BESIDES **4 :** away from **:** wide of — **beside oneself :** very upset

[1]**be·sides** *prep* **1 :** in addition to **2 :** other than

[2]**besides** *adv* **:** in addition **:** ALSO

be·siege *vb* **be·sieged; be·sieg·ing 1 :** to surround with armed forces for the purpose of capturing **2 :** to crowd around — **be·sieg·er** *n*

besought *past of* BESEECH

[1]**best** *adj superlative of* GOOD **:** good or useful in the highest degree **:** most excellent — **best part :** [3]MOST

[2]**best** *adv superlative of* WELL **1 :** in the best way **2 :** [2]MOST 1

[3]**best** *n* **1 :** a person or thing or part of a thing that is best **2 :** one's greatest effort

[4]**best** *vb* **:** to get the better of

be·stir *vb* **be·stirred; be·stir·ring :** to stir up **:** rouse to action

be·stow *vb* **:** to present as a gift

[1]**bet** *n* **1 :** an agreement requiring the person who guesses wrong about the result of a contest or the outcome of an event to give something to the person who guesses right **2 :** the money or thing risked in a bet

[2]**bet** *vb* **bet** *or* **bet·ted; bet·ting 1 :** to risk in a bet **2 :** to be sure enough to make a bet

be·tray *vb* **1 :** to give over to an enemy by treason or fraud **2 :** to be unfaithful to **3 :** REVEAL 2, SHOW

be·troth *vb* **:** to promise to marry or give in marriage

be·troth·al *n* **:** an engagement to be married

[1]**bet·ter** *adj comparative of* GOOD **1 :** more satisfactory than another thing **2 :** improved in health — **better part :** more than half

[2]**better** *vb* **:** to make or become better — **bet·ter·ment** *n*

[3]**better** *adv comparative of* WELL **:** in a superior or more excellent way

[4]**better** *n* **1 :** a better person or thing **2 :** ADVANTAGE 1, VICTORY

bet·tor *or* **bet·ter** *n* **:** one that bets

[1]**be·tween** *prep* **1 :** by the efforts of each of **2 :** in or into the interval separating **3 :** functioning to separate or tell apart **4 :** by comparing **5 :** shared by **6 :** in shares to each of

[2]**between** *adv* **:** in a position between others

[1]**bev·el** *n* **:** a slant or slope of one surface or line against another

[2]**bevel** *vb* **bev·eled** *or* **bev·elled; bev·el·ing** *or* **bev·el·ling :** to cut or shape (an edge or surface) so as to form a bevel

bev·er·age *n* **:** a liquid that is drunk for food or pleasure

be·ware *vb* **:** to be cautious or careful

be·whis·kered *adj* **:** having whiskers

be·wil·der *vb* **:** to fill with uncertainty **:** CONFUSE — **be·wil·der·ment** *n*

be·witch *vb* **1 :** to gain an influence over by means of magic or witchcraft **2 :** to attract or delight as if by magic — **be·witch·ment** *n*

[1]**be·yond** *adv* **:** on or to the farther side

[2]**beyond** *prep* **1 :** on the other side of **2 :** out of the reach or sphere of

bi- *prefix* **1 :** two **2 :** coming or occurring every two **3 :** into two parts **4 :** twice **:** doubly **:** on both sides

[1]**bi·as** *n* **1 :** a seam, cut, or stitching running in a slant across cloth **2 :** a favoring of one way of feeling or acting over another **:** PREJUDICE

[2]**bias** *vb* **bi·ased** *or* **bi·assed; bi·as·ing** *or* **bi·as·sing :** to give a bias to

bib *n* **1 :** a cloth or plastic shield tied under a child's chin to protect the clothes **2 :** the upper part of an apron or of overalls

Bi·ble *n* **1 :** the book made up of the writings accepted by Christians as coming from God **2 :** a book containing the sacred writings of a religion

bib·li·cal *adj* **:** relating to, taken from, or found in the Bible

bib·li·og·ra·phy *n, pl* **bib·li·og·ra·phies** **:** a list of writings about an author or a subject
bi·car·bon·ate of soda **:** SODIUM BICARBONATE
bi·ceps *n, pl* **biceps** *also* **bi·ceps·es** **:** a large muscle of the upper arm
bick·er *vb* **:** to quarrel in a cross or silly way
bi·cus·pid *n* **:** either of the two teeth with double points on each side of each jaw of a person
[1]**bi·cy·cle** *n* **:** a light vehicle having two wheels one behind the other, a saddle seat, and pedals by which it is made to move
[2]**bicycle** *vb* **bi·cy·cled; bi·cy·cling** **:** to ride a bicycle
bi·cy·clist *n* **:** a person who rides a bicycle
[1]**bid** *vb* **bade** *or* **bid; bid·den** *or* **bid; bid·ding** **1 :** [1]ORDER 2, COMMAND **2 :** to express to **3 :** to make an offer for something (as at an auction) — **bid·der** *n*
[2]**bid** *n* **1 :** an offer to pay a certain sum for something or to do certain work at a stated fee **2 :** INVITATION 2
bide *vb* **bode** *or* **bid·ed; bid·ed; bid·ing** **:** to wait or wait for
[1]**bi·en·ni·al** *adj* **1 :** occurring every two years **2 :** growing stalks and leaves one year and flowers and fruit the next before dying — **bi·en·ni·al·ly** *adv*
[2]**biennial** *n* **:** a biennial plant
bier *n* **:** a stand on which a corpse or coffin is placed
big *adj* **big·ger; big·gest** **1 :** large in size **2 :** IMPORTANT 1 — **big·ness** *n*
Big Dipper *n* **:** a group of seven stars in the northern sky arranged in a form like a dipper with the two stars that form the side opposite the handle pointing to the North Star
big·horn *n* **:** a grayish brown wild sheep of mountainous western North America
big tree *n* **:** a very large California sequoia with light soft brittle wood
bike *n* **1 :** BICYCLE **2 :** MOTORCYCLE
bile *n* **:** a thick bitter yellow or greenish fluid supplied by the liver to aid in digestion
bi·lin·gual *adj* **:** of, expressed in, or using two languages
[1]**bill** *n* **1 :** the jaws of a bird together with their horny covering **2 :** a part of an animal (as a turtle) that suggests the bill of a bird — **billed** *adj*
[2]**bill** *n* **1 :** a draft of a law presented to a legislature for consideration **2 :** a record of goods sold, services performed, or work done with the cost involved **3 :** a sign or poster advertising something **4 :** a piece of paper money
[3]**bill** *vb* **:** to send a bill to
bill·board *n* **:** a flat surface on which outdoor advertisements are displayed
bill·fold *n* **:** a folding pocketbook especially for paper money **:** WALLET
bil·liards *n* **:** a game played by driving solid balls with a cue into each other or into pockets on a large rectangular table
bil·lion *n* **1 :** a thousand millions **2 :** a very large number
[1]**bil·lionth** *adj* **:** being last in a series of a billion
[2]**billionth** *n* **:** number 1,000,000,000 in a series
[1]**bil·low** *n* **:** a great wave
[2]**billow** *vb* **1 :** to roll in great waves **2 :** to swell out
bil·ly club *n* **:** a heavy club (as of wood) carried by a police officer
billy goat *n* **:** a male goat
bin *n* **:** a box or enclosed place used for storage
bi·na·ry *adj* **:** of, relating to, or being a number system with a base of 2
bind *vb* **bound; bind·ing** **1 :** to fasten by tying **2 :** to hold or restrict by force or obligation **3 :** [2]BANDAGE **4 :** to finish or decorate with a binding **5 :** to fasten together and enclose in a cover
bind·er *n* **1 :** a person who binds books **2 :** a cover for holding together loose sheets of paper **3 :** a machine that cuts grain and ties it into bundles
bind·ing *n* **1 :** the cover and the fastenings of a book **2 :** a narrow strip of fabric used along the edge of an article of clothing
bin·go *n* **:** a game of chance played by covering a numbered space on a card when the number is matched by one drawn at random and won by the first player to cover five spaces in a row
bin·oc·u·lar *adj* **:** of, using, or suited for the use of both eyes
bin·oc·u·lars *n pl* **:** a hand-held instrument for seeing at a distance that is made up of two telescopes usually having prisms
bio- *prefix* **:** living matter
bio·de·grad·able *adj* **:** possible to break down and make harmless by the action of living things (as bacteria)
bio·di·ver·si·ty *n* **:** biological variety in an environment as shown by numbers of different kinds of plants and animals
bio·graph·i·cal *adj* **:** of or relating to the history of people's lives
bi·og·ra·phy *n, pl* **bi·og·ra·phies** **:** a written history of a person's life
bi·o·log·i·cal *adj* **:** of or relating to biology
bi·ol·o·gist *n* **:** a specialist in biology
bi·ol·o·gy *n* **:** a science that deals with living things and their relationships, distribution, and behavior
bio·re·gion *n* **:** a region whose limits are

naturally defined by geographic and biological features (as mountains and ecosystems) — **bio·re·gion·al** *adj*

bio·tech·nol·o·gy *n* **:** the use of techniques from genetics to combine inherited characteristics selected from different kinds of organisms into one organism in order to produce useful products (as drugs)

bi·ped *n* **:** an animal (as a person) that has only two feet

bi·plane *n* **:** an airplane with two wings on each side of the body usually placed one above the other

birch *n* **:** a tree with hard wood and a smooth bark that can be peeled off in thin layers

bird *n* **:** an animal that lays eggs and has wings and a body covered with feathers

bird·bath *n* **:** a basin for birds to bathe in

bird dog *n* **:** a dog trained to hunt or bring in game birds

bird·house *n* **1 :** an artificial nesting place for birds **2 :** AVIARY

bird of prey : a bird (as an eagle or owl) that feeds almost entirely on meat taken by hunting

bird·seed *n* **:** a mixture of small seeds used chiefly for feeding wild or caged birds

bird's–eye *adj* **:** seen from above as if by a flying bird

birth *n* **1 :** the coming of a new individual from the body of its parent **2 :** the act of bringing into life **3 :** LINEAGE 1 **4 :** ORIGIN 2

birth·day *n* **1 :** the day on which a person is born **2 :** a day of beginning **3 :** the return each year of the date on which a person was born or something began

birth·mark *n* **:** an unusual mark or blemish on the skin at birth

birth·place *n* **:** the place where a person was born or where something began

birth·right *n* **:** a right belonging to a person because of his or her birth

bis·cuit *n* **1 :** CRACKER **2 :** a small cake of raised dough baked in an oven

bi·sect *vb* **1 :** to divide into two usually equal parts **2 :** INTERSECT

bish·op *n* **1 :** a member of the clergy of high rank **2 :** a piece in the game of chess

bis·muth *n* **:** a heavy grayish white metallic chemical element that is used in alloys and in medicine

bi·son *n, pl* **bison :** a large animal with short horns and a shaggy mane that is related to the cows and oxen

1bit *n* **1 :** a part of a bridle that is put in the horse's mouth **2 :** the cutting or boring edge or part of a tool

2bit *n* **1 :** a small piece or quantity **2 :** a short time **3 :** 1SOMEWHAT

3bit *n* **:** a unit of computer information that represents the selection of one of two possible choices (as *on* or *off*)

bitch *n* **:** a female dog

1bite *vb* **bit; bit·ten; bit·ing 1 :** to seize, grip, or cut into with or as if with teeth **2 :** to wound or sting usually with a stinger or fang **3 :** to cause to sting **4 :** to take a bait

2bite *n* **1 :** a seizing of something with the teeth or the mouth **2 :** a wound made by biting **:** STING **3 :** the amount of food taken at a bite **4 :** a sharp or biting sensation

bit·ing *adj* **:** producing bodily or mental distress **:** SHARP

bit·ter *adj* **1 :** sharp, biting, and unpleasant to the taste **2 :** hard to put up with **3 :** very harsh or sharp **:** BITING **4 :** caused by anger, distress, or sorrow — **bit·ter·ly** *adv* — **bit·ter·ness** *n*

bit·tern *n* **:** a brownish marsh bird which has a loud booming cry

1bit·ter·sweet *n* **1 :** a poisonous vine with purple flowers and red berries **2 :** a North American woody climbing plant with orange seedcases that open when ripe and show the red-coated seeds

2bittersweet *adj* **:** being partly bitter or sad and partly sweet or happy

bi·tu·mi·nous coal *n* **:** a soft coal that gives much smoke when burned

bi·zarre *adj* **:** very strange or odd

blab *vb* **blabbed; blab·bing :** to talk too much

1black *adj* **1 :** of the color black **2 :** very dark **3 :** of or relating to any peoples having dark skin and especially any of the original peoples of Africa south of the Sahara **4** *often cap* **:** of or relating to Americans having ancestors from Africa south of the Sahara **5 :** WICKED **6 :** very sad or gloomy **7 :** UNFRIENDLY — **black·ness** *n*

2black *n* **1 :** a black pigment or dye **2 :** the color of coal **:** the opposite of white **3 :** black clothing **4 :** a person belonging to a people having dark skin and especially a black African **5** *often cap* **:** an American having black African ancestors

3black *vb* **:** BLACKEN 1

black–and–blue *adj* **:** darkly discolored (as from a bruise)

black·ber·ry *n, pl* **black·ber·ries :** the black or dark purple sweet juicy berry of a prickly plant related to the raspberry

black·bird *n* **:** any of several birds of which the males are mostly black

black·board *n* **:** a hard smooth usually dark surface used especially in a classroom for writing or drawing on with chalk

black·en *vb* **1 :** to make or become black **2 :** 2SPOIL 2

black–eyed Su•san *n* **:** a daisy with yellow or orange petals and a dark center

black•head *n* **:** a dark plug of hardened oily material blocking the opening of a skin gland

black•ish *adj* **:** somewhat black

[1]**black•mail** *n* **1 :** the forcing of someone to pay money by threatening to reveal a secret that might bring disgrace on him or her **2 :** money paid under threat of blackmail

[2]**blackmail** *vb* **:** to threaten with the revealing of a secret unless money is paid — **black•mail•er** *n*

black•out *n* **1 :** a period of darkness enforced as a protection against air raids **2 :** a period of darkness caused by power failure **3 :** a temporary loss of vision or consciousness

black out *vb* **:** to lose consciousness or the ability to see for a short time

black•smith *n* **:** a person who makes things out of iron by heating and hammering it

black•snake *n* **:** either of two harmless snakes of the United States with blackish skins

black•top *n* **:** a black material used especially to pave roads

black widow *n* **:** a poisonous spider the female of which is black with a red mark shaped like an hourglass on the underside of the abdomen

blad•der *n* **1 :** a pouch into which urine passes from the kidneys **2 :** a container that can be filled with air or gas

blade *n* **1 :** a leaf of a plant and especially of a grass **2 :** the broad flat part of a leaf **3 :** something that widens out like the blade of a leaf **4 :** the cutting part of a tool or machine **5 :** SWORD **6 :** the runner of an ice skate — **blad•ed** *adj*

[1]**blame** *vb* **blamed; blam•ing 1 :** to find fault with **2 :** to hold responsible **3 :** to place responsibility for

[2]**blame** *n* **1 :** expression of disapproval **2 :** responsibility for something that fails — **blame•less** *adj*

blame•wor•thy *adj* **:** deserving blame

blanch *vb* **1 :** [1]BLEACH, WHITEN **2 :** to scald so as to remove the skin from **3 :** to turn pale

[1]**blank** *adj* **1 :** seeming to be confused **2 :** not having any writing or marks **3 :** having empty spaces to be filled in

[2]**blank** *n* **1 :** an empty space in a line of writing or printing **2 :** a paper with empty spaces to be filled in **3 :** a cartridge loaded with powder but no bullet

[1]**blan•ket** *n* **1 :** a heavy woven covering used for beds **2 :** a covering layer

[2]**blanket** *vb* **:** to cover with a blanket

[1]**blare** *vb* **blared; blar•ing 1 :** to sound loud and harsh **2 :** to present in a harsh noisy manner

[2]**blare** *n* **:** a harsh loud noise

[1]**blast** *n* **1 :** a strong gust of wind **2 :** a stream of air or gas forced through an opening **3 :** the sound made by a wind instrument **4 :** EXPLOSION 1

[2]**blast** *vb* **1 :** [2]BLIGHT **2 :** to break to pieces by an explosion **:** SHATTER

blast–off *n* **:** an instance of blasting off (as of a rocket)

blast off *vb* **:** to take off — used of vehicles using rockets for power

[1]**blaze** *n* **1 :** a bright hot flame **2 :** great brightness and heat **3 :** OUTBURST 1 **4 :** a bright display

[2]**blaze** *vb* **blazed; blaz•ing 1 :** to burn brightly **2 :** to shine as if on fire

[3]**blaze** *n* **:** a mark made on a tree by chipping off a piece of the bark

[4]**blaze** *vb* **blazed; blaz•ing 1 :** to make a blaze on **2 :** to mark by blazing trees

[1]**bleach** *vb* **:** to make white by removing the color or stains from

[2]**bleach** *n* **:** a preparation used for bleaching

bleach•er *n* **:** open seats for people to watch from (as at a game) usually arranged like steps — usually used in pl.

bleak *adj* **1 :** open to wind or weather **2 :** being cold and cutting **3 :** not hopeful or encouraging — **bleak•ly** *adv* — **bleak•ness** *n*

[1]**bleat** *vb* **:** to make the cry of a sheep, goat, or calf

[2]**bleat** *n* **:** the sound of bleating

bleed *vb* **bled; bleed•ing 1 :** to lose or shed blood **2 :** to feel pain or pity **3 :** to draw fluid from

[1]**blem•ish** *vb* **:** to spoil by or as if by an ugly mark

[2]**blemish** *n* **:** a mark that makes something imperfect **:** FLAW

[1]**blend** *vb* **1 :** to mix so completely that the separate things mixed cannot be told apart **2 :** to shade into each other **:** HARMONIZE

[2]**blend** *n* **1 :** a complete mixture **:** a product made by blending **2 :** a word formed by combining parts of two or more other words so that they overlap **3 :** a group of two or more consonants (as *gr-* in green) beginning a syllable without a vowel between

bless *vb* **blessed** *or* **blest; bless•ing 1 :** to make holy by a religious ceremony or words **2 :** to ask the favor or protection of God for **3 :** to praise or honor as holy **4 :** to give happiness or good fortune to

bless•ed *adj* **1 :** HOLY 1 **2 :** enjoying happiness — **bless•ed•ness** *n*

DICTIONARY

bless·ing *n* **1 :** the act of one who blesses **2 :** APPROVAL **3 :** something that makes one happy or content
blew *past of* BLOW
1**blight** *n* **1 :** a plant disease marked by drying up without rotting **2 :** an organism (as a germ or insect) that causes a plant blight
2**blight** *vb* **:** to injure or destroy by or as if by a blight
blimp *n* **:** an airship filled with gas like a balloon
1**blind** *adj* **1 :** unable or nearly unable to see **2 :** lacking in judgment or understanding **3 :** closed at one end **4 :** using only the instruments within an airplane and not landmarks as a guide — **blind·ly** *adv* — **blind·ness** *n*
2**blind** *vb* **1 :** to make blind **2 :** to make it impossible to see well **:** DAZZLE
3**blind** *n* **1 :** a device to reduce sight or keep out light **2 :** a place of hiding
4**blind** *adv* **:** with only instruments as guidance
1**blind·fold** *vb* **:** to shut light out of the eyes of with or as if with a bandage
2**blindfold** *n* **:** a covering over the eyes
blind·man's buff *n* **:** a game in which a blindfolded player tries to catch and identify one of the other players
blink *vb* **1 :** to look with partly shut eyes **2 :** to shut and open the eyes quickly **3 :** to shine with a light that goes or seems to go on and off
blink·er *n* **:** a light that blinks
bliss *n* **:** great happiness **:** JOY — **bliss·ful** *adj* — **bliss·ful·ly** *adv*
1**blis·ter** *n* **1 :** a small raised area of the skin filled with a watery liquid **2 :** a swelling (as in paint) that looks like a blister
2**blister** *vb* **1 :** to develop a blister or blisters **2 :** to cause blisters on
blithe *adj* **blith·er; blith·est :** free from worry **:** MERRY, CHEERFUL — **blithe·ly** *adv*
bliz·zard *n* **:** a long heavy snowstorm
bloat *vb* **:** to make swollen with or as if with fluid
blob *n* **:** a small lump or drop of something thick
1**block** *n* **1 :** a solid piece of some material (as stone or wood) usually with one or more flat sides **2 :** something that stops or makes passage or progress difficult **:** OBSTRUCTION **3 :** a case enclosing one or more pulleys **4 :** a number of things thought of as forming a group or unit **5 :** a large building divided into separate houses or shops **6 :** a space enclosed by streets **7 :** the length of one side of a block
2**block** *vb* **1 :** to stop or make passage through difficult **:** OBSTRUCT **2 :** to stop or make the passage of difficult **3 :** to make an opponent's movement (as in football) difficult **4 :** to mark the chief lines of
1**block·ade** *vb* **block·ad·ed; block·ad·ing :** to close off a place to prevent the coming in or going out of people or supplies
2**blockade** *n* **:** the closing off of a place (as by warships) to prevent the coming in or going out of persons or supplies
block and tackle *n* **:** an arrangement of pulleys in blocks with rope or cable for lifting or hauling
block·house *n* **:** a building (as of heavy timbers or of concrete) built with holes in its sides through which persons inside may fire out at an enemy
1**blond** *adj* **1 :** of a light color **2 :** having light hair and skin
2**blond** *or* **blonde** *n* **:** someone who is blond
blood *n* **1 :** the red fluid that circulates in the heart, arteries, capillaries, and veins of persons and animals **2 :** relationship through a common ancestor **:** KINSHIP — **blood·ed** *adj*
blood bank *n* **:** blood stored for emergency use in transfusion
blood·hound *n* **:** a large hound with long drooping ears, a wrinkled face, and a very good sense of smell
blood pressure *n* **:** pressure of the blood on the walls of blood vessels and especially arteries
blood·shed *n* **:** 1MURDER, SLAUGHTER
blood·shot *adj* **:** being red and sore
blood·stream *n* **:** the circulating blood in the living body
blood·suck·er *n* **:** an animal that sucks blood — **blood·suck·ing** *adj*
blood·thirsty *adj* **:** eager to kill or hurt — **blood·thirst·i·ly** *adv* — **blood·thirst·i·ness** *n*
blood vessel *n* **:** an artery, vein, or capillary of the body
bloody *adj* **blood·i·er; blood·i·est 1 :** smeared or stained with blood **2 :** causing or accompanied by bloodshed
1**bloom** *n* **1 :** 1FLOWER 1 **2 :** the period or state of blooming **3 :** a condition or time of beauty, freshness, and strength **4 :** the rosy color of the cheek **5 :** the delicate powdery coating on some fruits and leaves
2**bloom** *vb* **1 :** to produce blooms **:** FLOWER **2 :** to be in a state of youthful beauty and freshness
1**blos·som** *n* **1 :** 1FLOWER 1 **2 :** 1BLOOM 2
2**blossom** *vb* **1 :** 2BLOOM **2 :** to unfold like a blossom
1**blot** *n* **1 :** a spot or stain of dirt or ink **2 :** STIGMA 1, REPROACH
2**blot** *vb* **blot·ted; blot·ting 1 :** 2SPOT 1 **2**

: to hide completely **3 :** to dry with a blotter
blotch *n* **1 :** a blemish on the skin **2 :** a large irregular spot of color or ink — **blotched** *adj*
blot·ter *n* **:** a piece of blotting paper
blot·ting paper *n* **:** a soft spongy paper used to absorb wet ink
blouse *n* **1 :** a loose outer garment like a smock **2 :** the jacket of a uniform **3 :** a loose garment for women and children covering the body from the neck to the waist
1blow *vb* **blew; blown; blow·ing 1 :** to move or be moved usually with speed and force **2 :** to move in or with the wind **3 :** to send forth a strong stream of air from the mouth or from a bellows **4 :** to make a sound or cause to sound by blowing **5 :** to clear by forcing air through **6 :** to shape by forcing air into — **blow·er** *n*
2blow *n* **:** a blowing of wind **:** GALE
3blow *n* **1 :** an act of hitting (as with the fist or a weapon) **2 :** a sudden act **3 :** a sudden happening that causes suffering or loss
blow·gun *n* **:** a tube from which a dart may be shot by the force of the breath
blow·out *n* **:** a bursting of a container (as an automobile tire) by pressure of the contents on a weak spot
blow·pipe *n* **1 :** a small round tube for blowing air or gas into a flame so as to make it hotter **2 :** BLOWGUN
blow·torch *n* **:** a small portable burner in which the flame is made hotter by a blast of air or oxygen
blow up *vb* **1 :** EXPLODE 1 **2 :** to fill with a gas (as air)
1blub·ber *vb* **:** to weep noisily
2blubber *n* **:** the fat of various sea mammals (as whales) from which oil can be obtained
1blue *adj* **blu·er; blu·est 1 :** of the color blue **2 :** low in spirits **:** MELANCHOLY
2blue *n* **1 :** the color in the rainbow between green and violet **:** the color of the clear daytime sky **2 :** something blue in color — **out of the blue :** suddenly and unexpectedly
blue·bell *n* **:** a plant with blue flowers shaped like bells
blue·ber·ry *n, pl* **blue·ber·ries :** a sweet blue berry that has small seeds and grows on a bush related to the huckleberry
blue·bird *n* **:** any of several small North American songbirds more or less blue above
blue·bot·tle *n* **:** a large blue hairy fly
blue cheese *n* **:** cheese ripened by and full of greenish blue mold
blue·fish *n* **:** a bluish saltwater food fish of the eastern coast of the United States
blue·grass *n* **:** a grass with bluish green stems
blueing *variant of* BLUING
blue jay *n* **:** any of several crested and mostly blue American birds related to the crows
blue jeans *n pl* **:** pants usually made of blue denim
1blue·print *n* **1 :** a photographic print made with white lines on a blue background and used for copying maps and building plans **2 :** a detailed plan of something to be done
2blueprint *vb* **:** to make a blueprint of
blues *n pl* **1 :** low spirits **2 :** a sad song in a style that was first used by American blacks
blue whale *n* **:** a very large whale that is probably the largest living animal
1bluff *adj* **1 :** rising steeply with a broad front **2 :** frank and outspoken in a rough but good-natured way — **bluff·ly** *adv* — **bluff·ness** *n*
2bluff *n* **:** a high steep bank **:** CLIFF
3bluff *vb* **:** to deceive or frighten by pretending to have more strength or confidence than one really has — **bluff·er** *n*
4bluff *n* **1 :** an act or instance of bluffing **2 :** a person who bluffs
blu·ing *or* **blue·ing** *n* **:** something made with blue or violet dyes that is added to the water when washing clothes to prevent yellowing of white fabrics
blu·ish *adj* **:** somewhat blue
1blun·der *vb* **1 :** to move in a clumsy way **2 :** to make a mistake — **blun·der·er** *n*
2blunder *n* **:** a bad or stupid mistake
blun·der·buss *n* **:** a short gun that has a barrel which is larger at the end and that was used long ago for shooting at close range without taking exact aim
1blunt *adj* **1 :** having a thick edge or point **:** DULL **2 :** speaking or spoken in plain language without thought for other people's feelings — **blunt·ly** *adv*
2blunt *vb* **:** to make or become blunt
1blur *n* **:** something that cannot be seen clearly
2blur *vb* **blurred; blur·ring 1 :** to make hard to see or read by smearing **2 :** to make or become smeared or confused
blurt *vb* **:** to say or tell suddenly and without thinking
1blush *n* **1 :** a reddening of the face from shame, confusion, or embarrassment **2 :** a rosy color
2blush *vb* **1 :** to become red in the face from shame, confusion, or embarrassment **2 :** to feel ashamed or embarrassed
1blus·ter *vb* **1 :** to blow hard and noisily **2 :** to talk or act in a noisy boastful way
2bluster *n* **:** noisy violent action or speech

boa *n* **:** a large snake (as a python) that coils around and crushes its prey
boar *n* **1 :** a male pig **2 :** a wild pig
1board *n* **1 :** a sawed piece of lumber that is much broader and longer than it is thick **2 :** a dining table **3 :** meals given at set times for a price **4 :** a number of persons having authority to manage or direct something **5 :** a usually rectangular piece of rigid material used for some special purpose **6 :** BLACKBOARD **7 boards** *pl* **:** the low wooden wall enclosing a hockey rink **8 :** a sheet of insulating material carrying electronic parts (as for a computer) — **on board :** ABOARD
2board *vb* **1 :** to go aboard **2 :** to cover with boards **3 :** to give or get meals at set times for a price
board•er *n* **:** a person who pays for meals or for meals and lodging at another's house
board•ing•house *n* **:** a house at which people are given meals and often lodging
boarding school *n* **:** a school at which most of the students live during the school year
board•walk *n* **:** a walk made of planks especially along a beach
1boast *n* **1 :** an act of boasting **2 :** a cause for boasting or pride
2boast *vb* **1 :** to praise what one has or has done **2 :** to have and be proud of having
boast•ful *adj* **1 :** having the habit of boasting **2 :** full of boasts — **boast•ful•ly** *adv* — **boast•ful•ness** *n*
1boat *n* **1 :** a small vessel driven on the water by oars, paddles, sails, or a motor **2 :** 1SHIP 1
2boat *vb* **:** to use a boat — **boat•er** *n*
boat•house *n* **:** a house or shelter for boats
boat•man *n, pl* **boat•men :** a person who works on or deals in boats
boat•swain *n* **:** a warrant officer on a warship or a petty officer on a commercial ship who has charge of the hull, anchors, boats, and rigging
1bob *vb* **bobbed; bob•bing 1 :** to move or cause to move with a short jerky motion **2 :** to appear suddenly **3 :** to try to seize something with the teeth
2bob *n* **:** a short jerky up-and-down motion
3bob *n* **1 :** a float used to buoy up the baited end of a fishing line **2 :** a woman's or child's short haircut
4bob *vb* **bobbed; bob•bing :** to cut in the style of a bob
bob•by pin *n* **:** a flat metal hairpin with the two ends pressed close together
bob•cat *n* **:** an American wildcat that is a small rusty brown variety of the lynx
bob•o•link *n* **:** an American songbird related to the blackbirds
bob•sled *n* **:** a racing sled made with two sets of runners, a hand brake, and often a steering wheel
bob•tail *n* **1 :** a short tail **:** a tail cut short **2 :** an animal with a short tail
bob•white *n* **:** an American quail with gray, white, and reddish coloring
bode *past of* BIDE
bod•ice *n* **:** the upper part of a dress
bodi•ly *adj* **:** of or relating to the body
body *n, pl* **bod•ies 1 :** the material whole of a live or dead person or animal **2 :** the main part of a person, animal, or plant **3 :** the main or central part **4 :** a group of persons or things united for some purpose **5 :** a mass or portion of something distinct from other masses — **bod•ied** *adj*
body•guard *n* **:** a person or a group of persons whose duty it is to protect someone
1bog *n* **:** wet spongy ground that is usually acid and found next to a body of water (as a pond)
2bog *vb* **bogged; bog•ging :** to sink or stick fast in or as if in a bog
bo•gey *or* **bo•gy** *or* **bo•gie** *n, pl* **bogeys** *or* **bogies 1 :** GHOST, GOBLIN **2 :** something one is afraid of without reason
1boil *n* **:** a hot red painful lump in the skin that contains pus and is caused by infection
2boil *vb* **1 :** to heat or become heated to the temperature (**boiling point**) at which bubbles rise and break at the surface **2 :** to cook or become cooked in boiling water **3 :** to become angry or upset
3boil *n* **:** the state of something that is boiling
boil•er *n* **1 :** a container in which something is boiled **2 :** a tank heating and holding water **3 :** a strong metal container used in making steam (as to heat buildings)
bois•ter•ous *adj* **:** being rough and noisy — **bois•ter•ous•ly** *adv* — **bois•ter•ous•ness** *n*
bold *adj* **1 :** willing to meet danger or take risks **:** DARING **2 :** not polite and modest **:** FRESH **3 :** showing or calling for courage or daring — **bold•ly** *adv* — **bold•ness** *n*
bold•face *n* **:** a heavy black type — **bold–faced** *adj*
bo•le•ro *n, pl* **bo•le•ros 1 :** a Spanish dance or the music for it **2 :** a loose short jacket open at the front
boll *n* **:** the seedpod of a plant (as cotton)
boll weevil *n* **:** a grayish insect that lays its eggs in cotton bolls
bo•lo•gna *n* **:** a large smoked sausage usually made of beef, veal, and pork
1bol•ster *n* **:** a long pillow or cushion sometimes used to support bed pillows
2bolster *vb* **:** to support with or as if with a bolster

[1]**bolt** *n* **1 :** a stroke of lightning **:** THUNDERBOLT **2 :** a sliding bar used to fasten a door **3 :** the part of a lock worked by a key **4 :** a metal pin or rod usually with a head at one end and a screw thread at the other that is used to hold something in place **5 :** a roll of cloth or wallpaper

[2]**bolt** *vb* **1 :** to move suddenly and rapidly **2 :** to run away **3 :** to fasten with a bolt **4 :** to swallow hastily or without chewing

[1]**bomb** *n* **1 :** a hollow case or shell filled with explosive material and made to be dropped from an airplane, thrown by hand, or set off by a fuse **2 :** a container in which something (as an insecticide) is stored under pressure and from which it is released in a fine spray

[2]**bomb** *vb* **:** to attack with bombs

bom•bard *vb* **1 :** to attack with heavy fire from big guns **:** SHELL **2 :** to attack again and again

bomb•er *n* **:** an airplane specially made for dropping bombs

bon•bon *n* **:** a candy with a soft coating and a creamy center

[1]**bond** *n* **1 :** something that binds **2 :** a force or influence that brings or holds together **3 :** a legal agreement in which a person agrees to pay a sum of money if he or she fails to do a certain thing **4 :** a government or business certificate promising to pay a certain sum by a certain day

[2]**bond** *vb* **:** to stick or cause to stick together

bond•age *n* **:** SLAVERY

[1]**bone** *n* **1 :** the hard material of which the skeleton of most animals is formed **2 :** any of the pieces into which the bone of the skeleton is naturally divided — **bone•less** *adj*

[2]**bone** *vb* **boned; bon•ing :** to remove the bones from

bon•fire *n* **:** a large fire built outdoors

bong *n* **:** a deep sound like that of a large bell

bon•go *n, pl* **bongos** *also* **bongoes :** either of a pair of small drums of different sizes fitted together and played with the fingers

bon•net *n* **:** a child's or woman's hat usually tied under the chin by ribbons or strings

bon•ny *or* **bon•nie** *adj* **bon•ni•er; bon•ni•est** *chiefly British* **:** HANDSOME 3, BEAUTIFUL

bo•nus *n* **:** something given to somebody (as a worker) in addition to what is usual or owed

bony *adj* **bon•i•er; bon•i•est 1 :** of or relating to bone **2 :** like bone especially in hardness **3 :** having bones and especially large or noticeable bones

[1]**boo** *interj* — used to express disapproval or to startle or frighten

[2]**boo** *n, pl* **boos :** a cry expressing disapproval

[3]**boo** *vb* **:** to express disapproval of with boos

boo•by *n, pl* **boobies :** an awkward foolish person

[1]**book** *n* **1 :** a set of sheets of paper bound together **2 :** a long written work **3 :** a large division of a written work **4 :** a pack of small items bound together

[2]**book** *vb* **:** to reserve for future use

book•case *n* **:** a set of shelves to hold books

book•end *n* **:** a support at the end of a row of books to keep them standing up

book•keep•er *n* **:** a person who keeps accounts for a business

book•keep•ing *n* **:** the work of keeping business accounts

book•let *n* **:** a little book usually having paper covers and few pages

book•mark *n* **:** something placed in a book to show the page one wants to return to later

book•mo•bile *n* **:** a truck with shelves of books that is a traveling library

[1]**boom** *vb* **1 :** to make a deep hollow rumbling sound **2 :** to increase or develop rapidly

[2]**boom** *n* **1 :** a booming sound **2 :** a rapid increase in activity or popularity

[3]**boom** *n* **1 :** a long pole used especially to stretch the bottom of a sail **2 :** a long beam sticking out from the mast of a derrick to support or guide something that is being lifted

boom box *n* **:** a large portable radio and often tape player with two attached speakers

boo•mer•ang *n* **:** a curved club that can be thrown so as to return to the thrower

boon *n* **1 :** something asked or granted as a favor **2 :** something pleasant or helpful that comes at just the right time

[1]**boost** *vb* **1 :** to raise or push up from below **2 :** to make bigger or greater — **boost•er** *n*

[2]**boost** *n* **:** an act of boosting **:** a push up

[1]**boot** *n* **:** a covering usually of leather or rubber for the foot and part of the leg

[2]**boot** *vb* **:** [1]KICK 1

boo•tee *or* **boo•tie** *n* **:** an infant's knitted sock

booth *n, pl* **booths 1 :** a covered stall for selling or displaying goods (as at a fair or exhibition) **2 :** a small enclosure giving privacy for one person **3 :** a section of a restaurant consisting of a table between two backed benches

boo•ty *n* **:** goods seized from an enemy in war **:** PLUNDER

bo•rax *n* **:** a compound of boron used as a cleansing agent and water softener

¹bor·der *n* **1 :** the outer edge of something **2 :** a boundary especially of a country or state **3 :** an ornamental strip on or near the edge of a flat object

²border *vb* **1 :** to put a border on **2 :** to be close or next to

bor·der·line *adj* **:** not quite average, standard, or normal

¹bore *vb* **bored; bor·ing 1 :** to make a hole in especially with a drill **2 :** to make by piercing or drilling — **bor·er** *n*

²bore *n* **1 :** a hole made by boring **2 :** a cavity (as in a gun barrel) shaped like a cylinder **3 :** the diameter of a hole or cylinder

³bore *past of* BEAR

⁴bore *n* **:** an uninteresting person or thing

⁵bore *vb* **bored; bor·ing :** to make weary and restless by being uninteresting

bore·dom *n* **:** the state of being bored

bo·ric acid *n* **:** a weak acid containing boron used to kill germs

born *adj* **1 :** brought into life by birth **:** brought forth **2 :** having a certain characteristic from or as if from birth

borne *past participle of* BEAR

bo·ron *n* **:** a powdery or hard solid chemical element that melts at a very high temperature and is found in nature only in combination

bor·ough *n* **1 :** a self-governing town or village in some states **2 :** one of the five political divisions of New York City

bor·row *vb* **1 :** to take or receive something with the promise of returning it **2 :** to take for one's own use something begun or thought up by another **:** ADOPT — **bor·row·er** *n*

¹bos·om *n* **1 :** the front of the human chest **2 :** the breasts of a woman

²bosom *adj* **:** ³CLOSE 8, INTIMATE

¹boss *n* **1 :** the person (as an employer or foreman) who tells workers what to do **2 :** the head of a group (as a political organization)

²boss *vb* **1 :** to be in charge of **2 :** to give orders to

bossy *adj* **boss·i·er; boss·i·est :** liking to order people around

bo·tan·i·cal *adj* **:** of or relating to botany

bot·a·nist *n* **:** a specialist in botany

bot·a·ny *n* **:** a branch of biology dealing with plants

botch *vb* **:** to do clumsily and unskillfully **:** SPOIL, BUNGLE

¹both *pron* **:** the one and the other **:** the two

²both *conj* — used before two words or phrases connected with *and* to stress that each is included

³both *adj* **:** the two

¹both·er *vb* **1 :** to trouble (someone) in body or mind **:** DISTRACT, ANNOY **2 :** to cause to worry **3 :** to take the time or trouble

²bother *n* **1 :** someone or something that bothers in a small way **2 :** COMMOTION **3 :** the condition of being bothered

¹bot·tle *n* **1 :** a container (as of glass or plastic) usually having a narrow neck and mouth and no handle **2 :** the quantity held by a bottle

²bottle *vb* **bot·tled; bot·tling 1 :** to put into a bottle **2 :** to shut up as if in a bottle

bot·tle·neck *n* **:** a place or condition where improvement or movement is held up

bot·tom *n* **1 :** the under surface of something **2 :** a supporting surface or part **:** BASE **3 :** the bed of a body of water **4 :** the lowest part of something **5 :** low land along a river

bot·tom·less *adj* **1 :** having no bottom **2 :** very deep

bough *n* **:** a usually large or main branch of a tree

bought *past of* BUY

bouil·lon *n* **:** a clear soup made from meat (as beef or chicken)

boul·der *n* **:** a large detached and rounded or very worn mass of rock

bou·le·vard *n* **:** a wide avenue often having grass strips with trees along its center or sides

¹bounce *vb* **bounced; bounc·ing 1 :** to spring back or up after hitting a surface **2 :** to leap suddenly **3 :** to cause to bounce

²bounce *n* **1 :** a sudden leap **2 :** ²REBOUND 1

¹bound *adj* **:** going or intending to go

²bound *past of* BIND

³bound *vb* **:** to form the boundary of

⁴bound *adj* **1 :** tied or fastened with or as if with bands **2 :** required by law or duty **3 :** covered with binding **4 :** firmly determined **5 :** very likely to do something **:** CERTAIN, SURE

⁵bound *n* **:** a fast easy leap

⁶bound *vb* **:** to make a bound or move in bounds

bound·ary *n, pl* **bound·aries :** something that points out or shows a limit or end **:** a dividing line

bound·less *adj* **:** having no limits

bounds *n pl* **:** a point or a line beyond which a person or thing cannot go

boun·te·ous *adj* **1 :** LIBERAL 1 **2 :** ABUNDANT

boun·ti·ful *adj* **1 :** giving freely or generously **2 :** PLENTIFUL 2 — **boun·ti·ful·ly** *adv*

boun·ty *n, pl* **boun·ties 1 :** GENEROSITY 1

2 : generous gifts 3 : money given as a reward for killing certain harmful animals
bou•quet *n* : a bunch of flowers
bout *n* 1 : a contest of skill or strength between two persons 2 : [2]ATTACK 3
[1]**bow** *vb* 1 : [1]YIELD 8 2 : to bend the head or body as an act of politeness or respect
[2]**bow** *n* : the act of bending the head or body to express politeness or respect
[3]**bow** *n* 1 : a weapon used for shooting arrows and usually made of a strip of wood bent by a cord connecting the two ends 2 : something shaped in a curve like a bow 3 : a rod with horsehairs stretched from end to end used for playing a stringed instrument (as a violin) 4 : a knot made with one or more loops
[4]**bow** *vb* 1 : to bend into a bow 2 : to play with a bow
[5]**bow** *n* : the forward part of a ship
bow•el *n* 1 : INTESTINE — usually used in pl. 2 : a part of the intestine
bow•er *n* : a shelter in a garden made of boughs of trees or vines
[1]**bowl** *n* 1 : a round hollow dish without handles 2 : the contents of a bowl 3 : something in the shape of a bowl (as part of a spoon or pipe)
[2]**bowl** *n* : a rolling of a ball in bowling
[3]**bowl** *vb* 1 : to roll a ball in bowling 2 : to move rapidly and smoothly as if rolling 3 : to hit with or as if with something rolled
bow•legged *adj* : having the legs bowed outward
bow•line *n* : a knot used for making a loop that will not slip
bowl•ing *n* : a game in which balls are rolled so as to knock down pins
bow•man *n, pl* **bow•men** : ARCHER
bow•sprit *n* : a large spar sticking out forward from the bow of a ship
bow•string *n* : the cord connecting the two ends of a bow
[1]**box** *n* : an evergreen shrub or small tree used for hedges
[2]**box** *n* 1 : a container usually having four sides, a bottom, and a cover 2 : the contents of a box 3 : an enclosed place for one or more persons
[3]**box** *vb* : to enclose in or as if in a box
[4]**box** *vb* : to engage in boxing
box•car *n* : a roofed freight car usually having sliding doors in the sides
box elder *n* : an American maple with leaves divided into several leaflets
[1]**box•er** *n* : a person who boxes
[2]**boxer** *n* : a compact dog of German origin that is of medium size with a square build and has a short and often tan coat with a black mask
box•ing *n* : the sport of fighting with the fists
box office *n* : a place where tickets to public entertainments (as sports or theatrical events) are sold
boy *n* 1 : a male child from birth to young manhood 2 : a male servant
[1]**boy•cott** *vb* : to join with others in refusing to deal with someone (as a person, organization, or country) usually to show disapproval or to force acceptance of terms
[2]**boycott** *n* : the process or an instance of boycotting
boy•friend *n* : a regular male companion of a girl or woman
boy•hood *n* : the time or condition of being a boy
boy•ish *adj* : of, relating to, or having qualities often felt to be typical of boys — **boy•ish•ly** *adv* — **boy•ish•ness** *n*
Boy Scout *n* : a member of a scouting program (as the Boy Scouts of America)
bra *n* : a woman's undergarment for breast support
[1]**brace** *vb* **braced; brac•ing** : to make strong, firm, or steady
[2]**brace** *n* 1 : two of a kind 2 : a tool with a U-shaped bend that is used to turn wood-boring bits 3 : something that braces 4 : a usually wire device worn on the teeth for changing faulty position 5 : a mark { or } used to connect words or items to be considered together
brace•let *n* : a decorative band or chain usually worn on the wrist or arm
brack•en *n* : a large coarse branching fern
[1]**brack•et** *n* 1 : a support for a weight (as a shelf) that is usually attached to a wall 2 : one of a pair of marks [ ] (**square brackets**) used to enclose letters or numbers or in mathematics to enclose items to be treated together 3 : one of a pair of marks ⟨ ⟩ (**angle brackets**) used to enclose letters or numbers
[2]**bracket** *vb* 1 : to place within brackets 2 : to put into the same class : GROUP
brack•ish *adj* : somewhat salty
brad *n* : a slender wire nail with a small longish but rounded head
brag *vb* **bragged; brag•ging** : [2]BOAST 1
brag•gart *n* : a person who brags a lot
[1]**braid** *vb* : to weave together into a braid
[2]**braid** *n* : a length of cord, ribbon, or hair formed of three or more strands woven together
braille *n, often cap* : a system of printing for the blind in which the letters are represented by raised dots
[1]**brain** *n* 1 : the part of the nervous system that is inside the skull, consists of grayish nerve cells and whitish nerve fibers, and is

the organ of thought and the central control point for the nervous system **2 brains** *pl* **:** a good mind **:** INTELLIGENCE **3 :** someone who is very smart

[2]**brain** *vb* **:** to hurt or kill by a blow on the head

brain•storm *n* **:** a sudden inspiration or idea

brainy *adj* **brain•i•er; brain•i•est :** very smart

[1]**brake** *n* **:** a thick growth of shrubs, small trees, or canes

[2]**brake** *n* **:** a device for slowing or stopping motion (as of a wheel) usually by friction

[3]**brake** *vb* **braked; brak•ing :** to slow or stop by using a brake

brake•man *n, pl* **brake•men :** a crew member on a train whose duties include inspecting the train and helping the conductor

bram•ble *n* **:** any of a group of woody plants with prickly stems that include the raspberries and blackberries and are related to the roses

bran *n* **:** the broken coat of the seed of cereal grain separated (as by sifting) from the flour or meal

[1]**branch** *n* **1 :** a part of a tree that grows out from the trunk or from a large bough **2 :** something extending from a main line or body like a branch **3 :** a division or subordinate part of something — **branched** *adj*

[2]**branch** *vb* **:** to send out a branch **:** spread or divide into branches

[1]**brand** *n* **1 :** a mark of disgrace (as one formerly put on criminals with a hot iron) **2 :** a mark made by burning (as on cattle) or by stamping or printing (as on manufactured goods) to show ownership, maker, or quality **3 :** TRADEMARK **4 :** a class of goods identified by a name as the product of a certain maker

[2]**brand** *vb* **1 :** to mark with a brand **2 :** to show or claim (something) to be bad or wrong

bran•dish *vb* **:** to wave or shake in a threatening manner

brand–new *adj* **:** completely new and unused

bran•dy *n, pl* **brandies :** an alcoholic liquor made from wine or fruit juice

brass *n* **1 :** an alloy made by combining copper and zinc **2 :** the musical instruments of an orchestra or band that are usually made of brass and include the cornets, trumpets, trombones, French horns, and tubas

brat *n* **:** a naughty annoying child

[1]**brave** *adj* **brav•er; brav•est :** feeling or showing no fear — **brave•ly** *adv*

[2]**brave** *vb* **braved; brav•ing :** to face or take bravely

[3]**brave** *n* **:** an American Indian warrior

brav•ery *n* **:** COURAGE

[1]**brawl** *vb* **:** to quarrel or fight noisily

[2]**brawl** *n* **:** a noisy quarrel or fight

brawn *n* **:** muscular strength

brawny *adj* **brawn•i•er; brawn•i•est :** having large strong muscles

[1]**bray** *vb* **:** to make the loud harsh cry of a donkey

[2]**bray** *n* **:** a sound of braying

bra•zen *adj* **1 :** made of brass **2 :** sounding harsh and loud **3 :** not ashamed of or embarrassed by one's bad behavior **:** IMPUDENT

Bra•zil nut *n* **:** a dark three-sided nut with a white kernel

[1]**breach** *n* **1 :** a breaking of a law **:** a failure to do what one should **2 :** an opening made by breaking

[2]**breach** *vb* **:** to make a break in

[1]**bread** *n* **1 :** a baked food made from flour or meal **2 :** FOOD 1

[2]**bread** *vb* **:** to cover with bread crumbs

breadth *n* **1 :** distance measured from side to side **2 :** SCOPE 2

[1]**break** *vb* **broke; bro•ken; break•ing 1 :** to separate into parts suddenly or forcibly **2 :** to fail to keep **3 :** to force a way **4 :** [2]TAME 1 **5 :** to reduce the force of **6 :** to do better than **7 :** to interrupt or put an end to **:** STOP **8 :** to develop or burst out suddenly **9 :** to make known **10 :** SOLVE **11 :** [1]CHANGE 4

[2]**break** *n* **1 :** an act of breaking **2 :** something produced by breaking **3 :** an accidental event

break•down *n* **:** bodily or mental collapse **:** FAILURE 6

brea•ker *n* **1 :** a person or thing that breaks something **2 :** a wave that breaks on shore

[1]**break•fast** *n* **:** the first meal of the day

[2]**breakfast** *vb* **:** to eat breakfast

break•neck *adj* **:** very fast or dangerous

break out *vb* **1 :** to develop a skin rash **2 :** to start up suddenly

break•through *n* **:** a sudden advance or successful development

break up *vb* **1 :** to separate into parts **2 :** to bring or come to an end **3 :** to end a romance **4 :** to go into a fit of laughter

break•wa•ter *n* **:** an offshore wall to protect a beach or a harbor from the sea

[1]**breast** *n* **1 :** a gland that produces milk **2 :** the front part of the body between the neck and the abdomen — **breast•ed** *adj*

[2]**breast** *vb* **:** to face or oppose bravely

breast•bone *n* **:** the bony plate at the front and center of the breast

breast–feed *vb* **breast–fed; breast–feed•ing :** to feed (a baby) from a mother's breast

breast•plate *n* **:** a piece of armor for covering the breast

breast•work *n* **:** a wall thrown together to serve as a defense in battle

breath *n* **1 :** a slight breeze **2 :** ability to breathe **:** ease of breathing **3 :** air taken in or sent out by the lungs — **out of breath :** breathing very rapidly as a result of hard exercise

breathe *vb* **breathed; breath•ing 1 :** to draw air into and expel it from the lungs **2 :** ¹LIVE 1 **3 :** ¹SAY 1, UTTER

breath•er *n* **:** a pause for rest

breath•less *adj* **1 :** panting from exertion **2 :** holding one's breath from excitement or fear — **breath•less•ly** *adv*

breath•tak•ing *adj* **:** very exciting

breech•es *n pl* **1 :** short pants fastening below the knee **2 :** PANTS

¹**breed** *vb* **bred; breed•ing 1 :** to produce or increase (plants or animals) by sexual reproduction **2 :** to produce offspring by sexual reproduction **3 :** to bring up **:** TRAIN **4 :** to bring about **:** CAUSE — **breed•er** *n*

²**breed** *n* **1 :** a kind of plant or animal that is found only under human care and is different from related kinds **2 :** ¹CLASS 6, KIND

breed•ing *n* **:** training especially in manners **:** UPBRINGING

breeze *n* **:** a gentle wind

breezy *adj* **breez•i•er; breez•i•est 1 :** somewhat windy **2 :** lively and somewhat carefree — **breez•i•ly** *adv* — **breez•i•ness** *n*

breth•ren *pl of* BROTHER — used chiefly in some formal or solemn situations

breve *n* **:** a mark ˘ placed over a vowel to show that the vowel is short

brev•i•ty *n* **:** the condition of being short or brief

¹**brew** *vb* **1 :** to make (beer) from water, malt, and hops **2 :** to prepare by soaking in hot water **3 :** ²PLAN 2 **4 :** to start to form — **brew•er** *n*

²**brew** *n* **:** a brewed beverage

brew•ery *n, pl* **brew•er•ies :** a place where malt liquors are brewed

bri•ar *variant of* BRIER

¹**bribe** *n* **:** something given or promised to a person in order to influence a decision or action dishonestly

²**bribe** *vb* **bribed; brib•ing :** to influence or try to influence by a bribe

brib•ery *n, pl* **brib•er•ies :** the act of giving or taking a bribe

¹**brick** *n* **1 :** a building or paving material made from clay molded into blocks and baked **2 :** a block made of brick

²**brick** *vb* **:** to close, face, or pave with bricks

brick•lay•er *n* **:** a person who builds or paves with bricks

brid•al *adj* **:** of or relating to a bride or a wedding

bride *n* **:** a woman just married or about to be married

bride•groom *n* **:** a man just married or about to be married

brides•maid *n* **:** a woman who attends a bride at her wedding

¹**bridge** *n* **1 :** a structure built over something (as water, a low place, or a railroad) so people can cross **2 :** a platform above and across the deck of a ship for the captain or officer in charge **3 :** something like a bridge

²**bridge** *vb* **bridged; bridg•ing :** to make a bridge over or across

³**bridge** *n* **:** a card game for four players in two teams

¹**bri•dle** *n* **:** a device for controlling a horse made up of a set of straps enclosing the head, a bit, and a pair of reins

²**bridle** *vb* **bri•dled; bri•dling 1 :** to put a bridle on **2 :** RESTRAIN 2 **3 :** to hold the head high and draw in the chin as an expression of resentment

¹**brief** *adj* **:** not very long **:** SHORT — **brief•ly** *adv*

²**brief** *vb* **:** to give information or instructions to

brief•case *n* **:** a flat case for carrying papers or books

briefs *n pl* **:** short snug underpants

bri•er *or* **bri•ar** *n* **:** a plant (as the rose or blackberry) with a thorny or prickly woody stem

brig *n* **:** a square-rigged sailing ship with two masts

bri•gade *n* **1 :** a body of soldiers consisting of two or more regiments **2 :** a group of persons organized for acting together

brig•a•dier general *n* **:** a commissioned officer in the Army, Air Force, or Marine Corps ranking above a colonel

bright *adj* **1 :** giving off or filled with much light **2 :** very clear or vivid in color **3 :** INTELLIGENT, CLEVER **4 :** CHEERFUL — **bright•ly** *adv* — **bright•ness** *n*

bright•en *vb* **:** to make or become bright or brighter

bril•liance *n* **:** great brightness

bril•liant *adj* **1 :** flashing with light **:** very bright **2 :** very impressive **3 :** very smart or clever, — **bril•liant•ly** *adv*

¹**brim** *n* **1 :** the edge or rim of something hollow **2 :** the part of a hat that sticks out around the lower edge

²**brim** *vb* **brimmed; brim•ming :** to be or become full to overflowing

brin•dled *adj* **:** having dark streaks or spots on a gray or brownish background

brine *n* **1 :** water containing a great deal of salt **2 :** OCEAN

bring *vb* **brought; bring•ing 1 :** to cause to come with oneself by carrying or leading : take along **2 :** to cause to reach a certain state or take a certain action **3 :** to cause to arrive or exist **4 :** to sell for — **bring•er** *n*

bring about *vb* **:** to cause to happen : EFFECT

bring forth *vb* **:** to give birth to : PRODUCE

bring out *vb* **:** to produce and offer for sale

bring to *vb* **:** to bring back from unconsciousness : REVIVE

bring up *vb* **:** to bring to maturity through care and education

brink *n* **1 :** the edge at the top of a steep place **2 :** a point of beginning

briny *adj* **brin•i•er; brin•i•est :** of or like salt water : SALTY

brisk *adj* **1 :** very active : LIVELY **2 :** very refreshing — **brisk•ly** *adv* — **brisk•ness** *n*

[1]**bris•tle** *n* **1 :** a short stiff hair **2 :** a stiff hair or something like a hair fastened in a brush

[2]**bristle** *vb* **bris•tled; bris•tling 1 :** to rise up and stiffen like bristles **2 :** to show signs of anger

bris•tly *adj* **bris•tli•er; bris•tli•est :** of, like, or having many bristles

britch•es *n pl* **:** BREECHES

[1]**Brit•ish** *adj* **:** of or relating to Great Britain or the British

[2]**British** *n pl* **:** the people of Great Britain

brit•tle *adj* **brit•tler; brit•tlest :** hard but easily broken — **brit•tle•ness** *n*

broach *vb* **:** to bring up as a subject for discussion

broad *adj* **1 :** not narrow : WIDE **2 :** extending far and wide : SPACIOUS **3 :** [1]COMPLETE 1, FULL **4 :** not limited **5 :** not covering fine points : GENERAL — **broad•ly** *adv*

[1]**broad•cast** *adj* **1 :** scattered in all directions **2 :** made public by means of radio or television **3 :** of or relating to radio or television broadcasting

[2]**broadcast** *vb* **broadcast; broad•cast•ing 1 :** to scatter far and wide **2 :** to make widely known **3 :** to send out by radio or television from a transmitting station — **broad•cast•er** *n*

[3]**broadcast** *n* **1 :** an act of broadcasting **2 :** the material broadcast by radio or television : a radio or television program

broad•cloth *n* **:** a fine cloth with a firm smooth surface

broad•en *vb* **:** to make or become broad or broader : WIDEN

broad–mind•ed *adj* **:** willing to consider opinions, beliefs, and practices that are unusual or different from one's own — **broad–mind•ed•ly** *adv* — **broad–mind•ed•ness** *n*

[1]**broad•side** *n* **1 :** the part of a ship's side above the waterline **2 :** a firing of all of the guns that are on the same side of a ship

[2]**broadside** *adv* **1 :** with one side forward **2 :** from the side

broad•sword *n* **:** a sword having a broad blade

bro•cade *n* **:** a cloth with a raised design woven into it

broc•co•li *n* **:** an open branching form of cauliflower whose green stalks and clustered flower buds are used as a vegetable

broil *vb* **1 :** to cook or be cooked directly over or under a heat source (as a fire or flame) **2 :** to make or be extremely hot

broil•er *n* **:** a young chicken suitable for broiling

[1]**broke** *past of* BREAK

[2]**broke** *adj* **:** having no money

bro•ken *adj* **1 :** shattered into pieces **2 :** having gaps or breaks **3 :** not kept **4 :** imperfectly spoken

bro•ken•heart•ed *adj* **:** overwhelmed by grief : very sad

bro•ker *n* **:** a person who acts as an agent for others in the buying or selling of property

bro•mine *n* **:** a chemical element that is a deep red liquid giving off an irritating vapor of disagreeable odor

bron•chi•al *adj* **:** relating to the branches (**bronchial tubes**) of the windpipe

bron•chi•tis *n* **:** a sore raw state of the bronchial tubes

bron•co *n, pl* **bron•cos :** MUSTANG

bron•to•sau•rus *n* **:** a huge plant-eating dinosaur with a long thin neck and tail and four thick legs

[1]**bronze** *vb* **bronzed; bronz•ing :** to give the appearance or color of bronze to

[2]**bronze** *n* **1 :** an alloy of copper and tin and sometimes other elements **2 :** a yellowish brown color

brooch *n* **:** an ornamental pin or clasp for the clothing

[1]**brood** *n* **1 :** the young of birds hatched at the same time **2 :** a group of young children or animals having the same mother

[2]**brood** *vb* **1 :** to sit on eggs to hatch them **2 :** to think long and anxiously about something

brood•er *n* **1 :** one that broods **2 :** a building or a compartment that can be heated and is used for raising young fowl

brook *n* **:** a small stream — **brook•let** *n*

broom *n* **1 :** a woody plant of the pea family with long slender branches along which grow many drooping yellow flowers **2 :** a

brush with a long handle used for sweeping
broom•stick *n* **:** the handle of a broom
broth *n* **:** the liquid in which a meat, fish, or vegetable has been boiled
broth•er *n, pl* **brothers** *also* **breth•ren 1 :** a boy or man related to another person by having the same parents **2 :** a fellow member of an organization
broth•er•hood *n* **1 :** the state of being a brother **2 :** an association of people for a particular purpose **3 :** those who are engaged in the same business or profession
broth•er–in–law *n, pl* **broth•ers–in–law 1 :** the brother of one's husband or wife **2 :** the husband of one's sister
broth•er•ly *adj* **1 :** of or relating to brothers **2 :** 1KINDLY 2, AFFECTIONATE
brought *past of* BRING
brow *n* **1 :** EYEBROW **2 :** FOREHEAD **3 :** the upper edge of a steep slope
1brown *adj* **1 :** of the color brown **2 :** having a dark or tanned complexion
2brown *n* **:** a color like that of coffee or chocolate
3brown *vb* **:** to make or become brown
brown•ie *n* **1 :** a cheerful elf believed to perform helpful services at night **2** *cap* **:** a member of a program of the Girl Scouts for girls in the first through third grades in school **3 :** a small rectangle of chewy chocolate cake
brown•ish *adj* **:** somewhat brown
browse *vb* **browsed; brows•ing 1 :** to nibble young shoots and foliage **2 :** to read or look over something (as in a book or a store) in a light or careless way
brows•er *n* **1 :** one that browses **2 :** a computer program providing access to sites on the World Wide Web
bru•in *n* **:** 1BEAR 1
1bruise *vb* **bruised; bruis•ing :** to injure the flesh (as by a blow) without breaking the skin
2bruise *n* **:** a black-and-blue spot on the body or a dark spot on fruit caused by bruising (as from a blow)
1bru•net *or* **bru•nette** *n* **:** someone who is brunet
2brunet *or* **brunette** *adj* **:** having dark brown or black hair and dark eyes
brunt *n* **:** the main force or stress (as of an attack)
1brush *n* **:** BRUSHWOOD
2brush *n* **1 :** a tool made of bristles set in a handle and used for cleaning, smoothing, or painting **2 :** a bushy tail **3 :** an act of brushing **4 :** a light stroke
3brush *vb* **1 :** to scrub or smooth with a brush **2 :** to remove with or as if with a brush **3 :** to pass lightly across
4brush *n* **:** a brief fight or quarrel
brush•wood *n* **1 :** branches and twigs cut from trees **2 :** a heavy growth of small trees and bushes
brus•sels sprouts *n pl, often cap B* **:** green heads like tiny cabbages growing thickly on the stem of a plant of the cabbage family and used as a vegetable
bru•tal *adj* **:** being cruel and inhuman — **bru•tal•ly** *adv*
bru•tal•i•ty *n, pl* **bru•tal•i•ties 1 :** the quality of being brutal **2 :** a brutal act or course of action
1brute *adj* **1 :** of or relating to beasts **2 :** typical of beasts **:** like that of a beast
2brute *n* **1 :** a four-footed animal especially when wild **2 :** a brutal person
brut•ish *adj* **:** being unfeeling and stupid
1bub•ble *n* **1 :** a tiny round body of air or gas in a liquid **2 :** a round body of air within a solid **3 :** a thin film of liquid filled with air or gas
2bubble *vb* **bub•bled; bub•bling 1 :** to form or produce bubbles **2 :** to flow with a gurgle
bu•bon•ic plague *n* **:** a dangerous disease which is spread by rats and in which fever, weakness, and swollen lymph glands are present
buc•ca•neer *n* **:** PIRATE
1buck *n* **:** a male deer or antelope or a male goat, hare, rabbit, or rat
2buck *vb* **1 :** to spring or jump upward with head down and back arched **2 :** to charge or push against **3 :** to act in opposition to **:** OPPOSE
buck•board *n* **:** a lightweight carriage with four wheels that has a seat supported by a springy platform
buck•et *n* **1 :** a usually round container with a handle for holding or carrying liquids or solids **2 :** an object for collecting, scooping, or carrying something (as the scoop of an excavating machine) **3 :** BUCKETFUL
buck•et•ful *n, pl* **buck•et•fuls** *or* **buck•ets•ful 1 :** as much as a bucket will hold **2 :** a large quantity
buck•eye *n* **:** a horse chestnut or a closely related tree or shrub
1buck•le *n* **:** a fastening device which is attached to one end of a belt or strap and through which the other end is passed and held
2buckle *vb* **buck•led; buck•ling 1 :** to fasten with a buckle **2 :** to apply oneself earnestly **3 :** to bend, crumple, or give way
buck•shot *n* **:** coarse lead shot

buck•skin *n* **:** a soft flexible leather usually having a suede finish

buck•wheat *n* **:** a plant with pinkish white flowers that is grown for its dark triangular seeds which are used as a cereal grain

[1]**bud** *n* **1 :** a small growth at the tip or on the side of a stem that later develops into a flower or branch **2 :** a flower that has not fully opened **3 :** a part that grows out from the body of an organism and develops into a new organism **4 :** an early stage of development

[2]**bud** *vb* **bud•ded; bud•ding 1 :** to form or put forth buds **2 :** to grow or reproduce by buds

bud•dy *n, pl* **buddies :** [1]CHUM

budge *vb* **budged; budg•ing :** to move or cause to move from one position to another

[1]**bud•get** *n* **1 :** a statement of estimated income and expenses for a period of time **2 :** a plan for using money

[2]**budget** *vb* **1 :** to include in a budget **2 :** to plan as in a budget

[1]**buff** *n* **1 :** an orange yellow **2 :** a stick or wheel with a soft surface for applying polishing material

[2]**buff** *vb* **:** to polish with or as if with a buff

buf•fa•lo *n, pl* **buffalo** *or* **buf•fa•loes :** any of several wild oxen and especially the American bison

buffalo wing *n* **:** a deep-fried chicken wing coated with a spicy sauce and usually served with blue cheese dressing

[1]**buf•fet** *vb* **:** to pound repeatedly **:** BATTER

[2]**buf•fet** *n* **1 :** a cabinet or set of shelves for the display of dishes and silver **:** SIDEBOARD **2 :** a meal set out on a buffet or table from which people may serve themselves

bug *n* **1 :** an insect or other small creeping or crawling animal **2 :** any of a large group of insects that have four wings, suck liquid food (as plant juices or blood), and have young which resemble the adults but lack wings **3 :** FLAW **4 :** a person who is enthusiastic about something

bug•a•boo *n, pl* **bug•a•boos :** BUGBEAR

bug•bear *n* **1 :** an imaginary creature used to frighten children **2 :** something one is afraid of

bug•gy *n, pl* **buggies :** a light carriage with a single seat that is usually drawn by one horse

bu•gle *n* **:** an instrument like a simple trumpet used chiefly for giving military signals

bu•gler *n* **:** a person who plays a bugle

[1]**build** *vb* **built; build•ing 1 :** to make by putting together parts or materials **2 :** to produce or create gradually by effort **3 :** to move toward a peak

[2]**build** *n* **:** form or kind of structure **:** PHYSIQUE

build•er *n* **:** a person whose business is the construction of buildings

build•ing *n* **1 :** a permanent structure built as a dwelling, shelter, or place for human activities or for storage **2 :** the art, work, or business of assembling materials into a structure

built–in *adj* **:** forming a permanent part of a structure

bulb *n* **1 :** an underground resting form of a plant which consists of a short stem with one or more buds surrounded by thick leaves and from which a new plant can grow **2 :** a plant structure (as a tuber) that is somewhat like a bulb **3 :** a rounded object or part shaped more or less like a bulb

bul•bous *adj* **1 :** having a bulb **2 :** like a bulb in being round and swollen

[1]**bulge** *vb* **bulged; bulg•ing :** to swell or curve outward

[2]**bulge** *n* **:** a swelling part **:** a part that sticks out

bulk *n* **1 :** greatness of size or volume **2 :** the largest or chief part

bulk•head *n* **:** a wall separating sections in a ship

bulky *adj* **bulk•i•er; bulk•i•est 1 :** having bulk **2 :** being large and awkward to handle

bull *n* **:** the male of an animal of the ox and cow family and of certain other large animals (as the elephant and the whale)

[1]**bull•dog** *n* **:** a dog of English origin with short hair and a stocky powerful build

[2]**bulldog** *vb* **bull•dogged; bull•dog•ging :** to throw by seizing the horns and twisting the neck

bull•doz•er *n* **:** a motor vehicle with beltlike tracks that has a broad blade for pushing (as in clearing land of trees)

bul•let *n* **:** a shaped piece of metal made to be shot from a firearm — **bul•let•proof** *adj*

bul•le•tin *n* **:** a short public notice usually coming from an informed or official source

bulletin board *n* **:** a board for posting bulletins and announcements

bull•fight *n* **:** a public entertainment in which people excite bulls, display daring in escaping their charges, and finally kill them — **bull•fight•er** *n*

bull•finch *n* **:** a European songbird that has a thick bill and a red breast and is often kept in a cage

bull•frog *n* **:** a large heavy frog that makes a booming or bellowing sound

bull•head *n* **:** any of various fishes with large heads

bul·lion *n* **:** gold or silver metal in bars or blocks
bull·ock *n* **1 :** a young bull **2 :** [1]STEER, OX
bull's–eye *n* **1 :** the center of a target **2 :** a shot that hits the center of a target
[1]**bul·ly** *n, pl* **bul·lies :** a person who teases, hurts, or threatens smaller or weaker persons
[2]**bully** *vb* **bul·lied; bul·ly·ing :** to act like a bully toward
bul·rush *n* **:** any of several large rushes or sedges that grow in wet places
bul·wark *n* **1 :** a solid structure like a wall built for defense against an enemy **2 :** something that defends or protects
bum *n* **1 :** a person who avoids work and tries to live off others **2 :** [2]TRAMP 1, HOBO
bum·ble·bee *n* **:** a large hairy bee that makes a loud humming sound
[1]**bump** *n* **1 :** a sudden heavy blow or shock **2 :** a rounded swelling of flesh as from a blow **3 :** an unevenness in a road surface
[2]**bump** *vb* **1 :** to strike or knock against something **2 :** to move along unevenly **:** JOLT
[1]**bum·per** *adj* **:** larger or finer than usual
[2]**bump·er** *n* **:** a bar across the front or back of a motor vehicle intended to lessen the shock or damage from collision
bun *n* **:** a sweet or plain round roll
[1]**bunch** *n* **1 :** a number of things of the same kind growing together **2 :** [1]GROUP
[2]**bunch** *vb* **:** to gather in a bunch
[1]**bun·dle** *n* **:** a number of things fastened or wrapped together **:** PACKAGE
[2]**bundle** *vb* **bun·dled; bun·dling :** to make into a bundle **:** WRAP
bung *n* **1 :** the stopper in the bunghole of a barrel **2 :** BUNGHOLE
bun·ga·low *n* **:** a house with a single story
bung·hole *n* **:** a hole for emptying or filling a barrel
bun·gle *vb* **bun·gled; bun·gling :** to act, do, make, or work badly — **bun·gler** *n*
bun·ion *n* **:** a sore reddened swelling of the first joint of a big toe
[1]**bunk** *n* **1 :** a built-in bed **2 :** a sleeping place
[2]**bunk** *vb* **:** to share or sleep in a bunk
bunk bed *n* **:** one of two single beds usually placed one above the other
bun·ny *n, pl* **bunnies :** RABBIT
[1]**bunt** *vb* **:** to strike or push with the horns or head **:** BUTT
[2]**bunt** *n* **:** [2]BUTT, PUSH
[1]**bun·ting** *n* **:** any of various birds that are similar to sparrows in size and habits but have stout bills
[2]**bunting** *n* **1 :** a thin cloth used chiefly for making flags and patriotic decorations **2 :** flags or decorations made of bunting
[1]**buoy** *n* **1 :** a floating object anchored in a body of water so as to mark a channel or to warn of danger **2 :** LIFE BUOY
[2]**buoy** *vb* **1 :** to keep from sinking **:** keep afloat **2 :** to brighten the mood of
buoy·an·cy *n* **1 :** the power of rising and floating (as on water or in air) **2 :** the power of a liquid to hold up a floating body
buoy·ant *adj* **1 :** able to rise and float in the air or on the top of a liquid **2 :** able to keep a body afloat **3 :** LIGHT-HEARTED, CHEERFUL
bur *or* **burr** *n* **1 :** a rough or prickly covering or shell of a seed or fruit **2 :** something that is like a bur (as in sticking)
[1]**bur·den** *n* **1 :** something carried **:** LOAD **2 :** something that is hard to take **3 :** the carrying of loads **4 :** the capacity of a ship for carrying cargo
[2]**burden** *vb* **:** to put a burden on
bur·den·some *adj* **:** so heavy or hard to take as to be a burden
bur·dock *n* **:** a tall coarse weed related to the thistles that has prickly purplish heads of flowers
bu·reau *n* **1 :** a low chest of drawers for use in a bedroom **2 :** a division of a government department **3 :** a business office that provides services
bur·glar *n* **:** a person who is guilty of burglary
bur·glary *n, pl* **bur·glar·ies :** the act of breaking into a building to steal
buri·al *n* **:** the placing of a dead body in a grave or tomb
bur·lap *n* **:** a rough cloth made usually from jute or hemp and used mostly for bags and wrappings
bur·ly *adj* **bur·li·er; bur·li·est :** strongly and heavily built — **bur·li·ness** *n*
[1]**burn** *vb* **burned** *or* **burnt; burn·ing 1 :** to be on fire or to set on fire **2 :** to destroy or be destroyed by fire or heat **3 :** to make or produce by fire or heat **4 :** to give light **5 :** to injure or affect by or as if by fire or heat **6 :** to feel or cause to feel as if on fire
[2]**burn** *n* **:** an injury produced by burning
burn·er *n* **:** the part of a stove or furnace where the flame or heat is produced
bur·nish *vb* **:** to make shiny
burr *variant of* BUR
bur·ro *n, pl* **burros :** a small donkey often used as a pack animal
[1]**bur·row** *n* **:** a hole in the ground made by an animal (as a rabbit or fox) for shelter or protection
[2]**burrow** *vb* **1 :** to hide in or as if in a burrow

2 : to make a burrow **3 :** to make one's way by or as if by digging

[1]**burst** *vb* **burst; burst·ing 1 :** to break open or in pieces (as by an explosion from within) **2 :** to suddenly show one's feelings **3 :** to come or go suddenly **4 :** to be filled to the breaking point

[2]**burst** *n* **:** a sudden release or effort

bury *vb* **bur·ied; bury·ing 1 :** to put (a dead body) in a grave or tomb **2 :** to place in the ground and cover over for concealment **3 :** to cover up **:** HIDE

bus *n, pl* **bus·es** *or* **bus·ses :** a large motor vehicle for carrying passengers

bush *n* **1 :** a usually low shrub with many branches **2 :** a stretch of uncleared or lightly settled country

bush·el *n* **1 :** a unit of dry capacity equal to four pecks or thirty-two quarts (about thirty-five liters) **2 :** a container holding a bushel

bushy *adj* **bush·i·er; bush·i·est 1 :** overgrown with bushes **2 :** being thick and spreading

busi·ness *n* **1 :** the normal activity of a person or group **2 :** a commercial enterprise **3 :** the making, buying, and selling of goods or services **4 :** personal concerns

busi·ness·man *n, pl* **busi·ness·men :** a man in business especially as an owner or a manager

busi·ness·wom·an *n, pl* **busi·ness·wom·en :** a woman in business especially as an owner or a manager

[1]**bust** *n* **1 :** a piece of sculpture representing the upper part of the human figure including the head and neck **2 :** a woman's bosom

[2]**bust** *vb* **1 :** to hit with the fist **2 :** [1]BREAK 1

[1]**bus·tle** *vb* **bus·tled; bus·tling :** to move about in a fussy or noisy way

[2]**bustle** *n* **:** fussy or noisy activity

[1]**busy** *adj* **busi·er; busi·est 1 :** actively at work **2 :** being used **3 :** full of activity — **busi·ly** *adv*

[2]**busy** *vb* **bus·ied; busy·ing :** to make busy

busy·body *n, pl* **busy·bod·ies :** a person who meddles in the affairs of others

[1]**but** *conj* **1 :** except that **:** UNLESS **2 :** while just the opposite **3 :** yet nevertheless

[2]**but** *prep* **:** other than **:** EXCEPT

[3]**but** *adv* **:** [2]ONLY 1

[1]**butch·er** *n* **1 :** one whose business is killing animals for sale as food **2 :** a dealer in meat **3 :** a person who kills in large numbers or in a brutal manner

[2]**butcher** *vb* **1 :** to kill and dress (an animal) for food **2 :** [2]MASSACRE **3 :** to make a mess of **:** BOTCH

but·ler *n* **:** the chief male servant of a household

[1]**butt** *vb* **:** to strike or thrust with the head or horns

[2]**butt** *n* **:** a blow or thrust with the head or horns

[3]**butt** *n* **:** a target of ridicule or hurtful jokes

[4]**butt** *n* **1 :** the thicker or bottom end of something **2 :** an unused remainder

butte *n* **:** an isolated hill with steep sides

[1]**but·ter** *n* **1 :** a solid yellowish fatty food obtained from cream or milk by churning **2 :** a substance that is like butter in texture and use

[2]**butter** *vb* **:** to spread with or as if with butter

but·ter·cup *n* **:** a common wildflower with bright yellow blossoms

but·ter·fat *n* **:** the natural fat of milk that is the chief ingredient of butter

but·ter·fly *n, pl* **but·ter·flies :** an insect that has a slender body and large colored wings covered with tiny overlapping scales and that flies mostly in the daytime

but·ter·milk *n* **:** the liquid left after churning butter from milk or cream

but·ter·nut *n* **:** an eastern North American tree that has sweet egg-shaped nuts and is related to the walnuts

but·ter·scotch *n* **:** a candy made from sugar, corn syrup, and water

but·tock *n* **1 :** the back of the hip which forms one of the rounded parts on which a person sits **2 buttocks** *pl* **:** RUMP 1

[1]**but·ton** *n* **1 :** a small ball or disk used for holding parts of a garment together or as an ornament **2 :** something that suggests a button

[2]**button** *vb* **:** to close or fasten with buttons

but·ton·hole *n* **:** a slit or loop for fastening a button

but·ton·wood *n* **:** SYCAMORE 2

[1]**but·tress** *n* **1 :** a structure built against a wall or building to give support and strength **2 :** something that supports, props, or strengthens

[2]**buttress** *vb* **:** to support with or as if with a buttress

bux·om *adj* **:** having a healthy plump form

[1]**buy** *vb* **bought; buy·ing :** to get by paying for **:** PURCHASE — **buy·er** *n*

[2]**buy** *n* **:** [1]BARGAIN 2

[1]**buzz** *vb* **1 :** to make a low humming sound like that of bees **2 :** to be filled with a low hum or murmur **3 :** to fly an airplane low over

[2]**buzz** *n* **:** a sound of buzzing

buz·zard *n* **:** a usually large bird of prey that flies slowly

buzz·er *n* **:** an electric signaling device that makes a buzzing sound

¹by *prep* **1 :** close to **:** NEAR **2 :** so as to go on **3 :** so as to go through **4 :** so as to pass **5 :** AT 1, DURING **6 :** no later than **7 :** with the use or help of **8 :** through the action of **9 :** ACCORDING TO **10 :** with respect to **11 :** to the amount of **12** — used to join two or more measurements or to join the numbers in a statement of multiplication or division

²by *adv* **1 :** near at hand **2 :** ⁴PAST

by–and–by *n* **:** a future time

by and by *adv* **:** after a while

by·gone *adj* **:** gone by **:** PAST

by·gones *n pl* **:** events that are over and done with

¹by·pass *n* **1 :** a way for passing to one side **2 :** a road serving as a substitute route around a crowded area

²bypass *vb* **:** to make a detour around

by–prod·uct *n* **:** something produced (as in manufacturing) in addition to the main product

by·stand·er *n* **:** a person present or standing near but taking no part in what is going on

byte *n* **:** a group of eight bits that a computer handles as a unit

by·way *n* **:** a less traveled road off a main highway

C

c *n, pl* **c's** *or* **cs** *often cap* **1 :** the third letter of the English alphabet **2 :** 100 in Roman numerals **3 :** a grade that shows a student's work is fair

cab *n* **1 :** a light closed carriage pulled by a horse **2 :** TAXICAB **3 :** the covered compartment for the engineer and the controls of a locomotive or for the operator of a truck, tractor, or crane

ca·bana *n* **:** a shelter usually with an open side facing the sea or a swimming pool

cab·bage *n* **:** a garden plant related to the turnips that has a firm head of leaves used as a vegetable

cab·in *n* **1 :** a private room on a ship **2 :** a place below deck on a small boat for passengers or crew **3 :** a part of an airplane for cargo, crew, or passengers **4 :** a small simple dwelling usually having only one story

cab·i·net *n* **1 :** a case or cupboard with shelves or drawers for keeping or displaying articles **2 :** a group of persons who act as advisers (as to the head of a country)

¹ca·ble *n* **1 :** a very strong rope, wire, or chain **2 :** a bundle of wires to carry electric current **3 :** CABLEGRAM

²cable *vb* **ca·bled; ca·bling :** to telegraph by underwater cable

ca·ble·gram *n* **:** a message sent by underwater cable

ca·boose *n* **:** a car usually at the rear of a freight train for the use of the train crew and railroad workers

ca·cao *n, pl* **cacaos :** a South American tree with fleshy yellow pods that contain fatty seeds from which chocolate is made

¹cache *n* **1 :** a place for hiding, storing, or preserving treasure or supplies **2 :** something hidden or stored in a cache

²cache *vb* **cached; cach·ing :** to place, hide, or store in a cache

¹cack·le *vb* **cack·led; cack·ling 1 :** to make the sharp broken noise or cry a hen makes especially after laying an egg **2 :** to laugh or chatter noisily

²cackle *n* **:** a cackling sound

cac·tus *n, pl* **cac·tus·es** *or* **cac·ti :** any of a large group of flowering plants of dry regions that have thick juicy stems and branches with scales or prickles

¹cad·die *or* **cad·dy** *n, pl* **cad·dies :** a person who carries a golfer's clubs

²caddie *or* **caddy** *vb* **cad·died; cad·dy·ing :** to work as a caddie

cad·dis fly *n* **:** an insect that has four wings and a larva which lives in water in a silk case covered with bits of wood or gravel and is often used for fish bait

ca·dence *n* **:** the beat of rhythmic motion or sound (as of marching) **:** RHYTHM

ca·det *n* **:** a student in a military school or college

ca·fé *also* **ca·fe** *n* **1 :** ¹BAR 9 **2 :** RESTAURANT **3 :** NIGHTCLUB

caf·e·te·ria *n* **:** a restaurant where the customers serve themselves or are served at a counter but carry their own food to their tables

caf·feine *n* **:** a stimulating substance in coffee and tea

¹cage *n* **1 :** a box or enclosure that has large openings covered usually with wire net or bars and is used to confine or carry birds or animals **2 :** an enclosure like a cage in shape or purpose

²cage *vb* **caged; cag·ing :** to put or keep in or as if in a cage

ca·gey *adj* **ca·gi·er; ca·gi·est :** hard to trap or trick

cais·son *n* **1 :** a chest for ammunition usually set on two wheels **2 :** a watertight box or chamber used for doing construction work under water or used as a foundation

ca·jole *vb* **ca·joled; ca·jol·ing :** to coax or persuade especially by flattery or false promises : WHEEDLE

[1]**cake** *n* **1 :** a small piece of food (as dough or batter, meat, or fish) that is baked or fried **2 :** a baked food made from a sweet batter or dough **3 :** a substance hardened or molded into a solid piece

[2]**cake** *vb* **caked; cak·ing 1 :** ENCRUST **2 :** to form or harden into a cake

ca·lam·i·ty *n, pl* **ca·lam·i·ties 1 :** great distress or misfortune **2 :** an event that causes great harm

cal·ci·um *n* **:** a silvery soft metallic chemical element that is an essential for most plants and animals

calcium carbonate *n* **:** a solid substance that is found as limestone and marble and in plant ashes, bones, and shells

cal·cu·late *vb* **cal·cu·lat·ed; cal·cu·lat·ing 1 :** to find by adding, subtracting, multiplying, or dividing : COMPUTE **2 :** [1]ESTIMATE 1 **3 :** to plan by careful thought

cal·cu·la·tion *n* **1 :** the process or an act of calculating **2 :** the result obtained by calculating

cal·cu·la·tor *n* **1 :** a person who calculates **2 :** a usually small electronic device for solving mathematical problems

cal·cu·lus *n* **:** TARTAR 2

caldron *variant of* CAULDRON

cal·en·dar *n* **1 :** a chart showing the days, weeks, and months of the year **2 :** a schedule of coming events

[1]**calf** *n, pl* **calves 1 :** the young of the cow **2 :** the young of various large animals (as the elephant, moose, or whale) **3** *pl* **calfs :** CALFSKIN

[2]**calf** *n, pl* **calves :** the muscular back part of the leg below the knee

calf·skin *n* **:** the skin of a calf or the leather made from it

cal·i·ber *or* **cal·i·bre** *n* **1 :** the diameter of a bullet **2 :** the diameter of the hole in the barrel of a gun

[1]**cal·i·co** *n, pl* **cal·i·coes** *or* **cal·i·cos :** cotton cloth especially with a colored pattern printed on one side

[2]**calico** *adj* **:** marked with blotches of color

cal·i·per *or* **cal·li·per** *n* **:** an instrument with two adjustable legs used to measure the thickness of objects or the distance between surfaces — usually used in pl.

ca·liph *or* **ca·lif** *n* **:** an important official in some Arab countries

cal·is·then·ics *n sing or pl* **:** exercise to develop strength and grace that is done without special equipment

[1]**call** *vb* **1 :** to speak in a loud clear voice so as to be heard at a distance : SHOUT **2 :** to say in a loud clear voice **3 :** to announce with authority : PROCLAIM **4 :** SUMMON 12 **5 :** to bring into action or discussion **6 :** to make a request or demand **7 :** to get in touch with by telephone **8 :** to make a short visit **9 :** [2]NAME 1 **10 :** to estimate as — **call for :** to require as necessary or suitable

[2]**call** *n* **1 :** a loud shout or cry **2 :** a cry of an animal **3 :** a request or command to come or assemble **4 :** [1]DEMAND 1, CLAIM **5 :** [1]REQUEST 1 **6 :** a short visit **7 :** a name or thing called **8 :** the act of calling on the telephone

call down *vb* **:** [2]REPRIMAND

call·er *n* **:** one who calls

call·ing *n* **:** OCCUPATION 1, PROFESSION

cal·li·ope *n* **:** a keyboard musical instrument consisting of a set of steam whistles

calliper *variant of* CALIPER

cal·lous *adj* **1 :** having a callus **2 :** feeling no sympathy for others

cal·lus *n* **:** a hard thickened spot (as of skin)

[1]**calm** *n* **1 :** a period or condition of freedom from storm, wind, or rough water **2 :** a peaceful state : QUIET

[2]**calm** *vb* **:** to make or become calm

[3]**calm** *adj* **1 :** not stormy or windy : STILL **2 :** not excited or angry — **calm·ly** *adv* — **calm·ness** *n*

cal·o·rie *n* **1 :** a unit for measuring heat equal to the heat required to raise the temperature of one gram of water one degree Celsius **2 :** a unit equal to 1000 calories — used especially to indicate the value of foods for producing heat and energy in the human body

calve *vb* **calved; calv·ing :** to give birth to a calf

calves *pl of* CALF

ca·lyp·so *n, pl* **calypsos :** a folk song or style of singing of the West Indies

ca·lyx *n, pl* **ca·lyx·es** *or* **ca·ly·ces :** the outer usually green or leafy part of a flower

cam *n* **:** a device (as a tooth on a wheel) by which circular motion is changed to back-and-forth motion

cam·bi·um *n, pl* **cam·bi·ums** *or* **cam·bia :** soft tissue in woody plants from which new wood and bark grow

came *past of* COME

cam·el *n* **:** a large hoofed animal that chews the cud and is used in the deserts of Asia and Africa for carrying burdens and for riding

cam·era *n* **1 :** a box that has a lens on one side to let the light in and is used for taking pictures **2 :** the part of a television sending device in which the image to be sent out is formed

¹cam·ou·flage *n* **1 :** the hiding or disguising of something by covering it up or changing the way it looks **2 :** the material (as paint or branches) used for camouflage
²camouflage *vb* **cam·ou·flaged; cam·ou·flag·ing :** to hide or disguise by camouflage
¹camp *n* **1 :** a place where temporary shelters are erected **2 :** a place usually in the country for recreation or instruction during the summer **3 :** a group of people in a camp
²camp *vb* **1 :** to make or occupy a camp **2 :** to live in a camp or outdoors — **camp·er** *n*
¹cam·paign *n* **1 :** a series of military operations in a certain area or for a certain purpose **2 :** a series of activities meant to get a certain thing done
²campaign *vb* **:** to take part in a campaign — **campaign·er** *n*
Camp Fire Girl *n* **:** a member of a national organization for girls from seven to eighteen
cam·phor *n* **:** a white fragrant solid that comes from the wood and bark of a tall Asian tree (**camphor tree**) and is used mostly in medicine and in making plastics
cam·pus *n* **:** the grounds and buildings of a university, college, or school
¹can *helping verb, past* **could;** *present sing & pl* **can** **1 :** know how to **2 :** be able to **3 :** be permitted by conscience to **4 :** have permission to **:** MAY
²can *n* **1 :** a usually cylindrical metal container **2 :** the contents of a can
³can *vb* **canned; can·ning :** to keep fit for later use by sealing (as in an airtight jar)
¹Ca·na·di·an *adj* **:** of or relating to Canada or the Canadians
²Canadian *n* **:** a person born or living in Canada
ca·nal *n* **1 :** an artificial waterway for boats or for irrigation of land **2 :** a tubelike passage in the body
ca·nary *n, pl* **ca·nar·ies :** a small usually yellow songbird often kept in a cage
can·cel *vb* **can·celed** *or* **can·celled; can·cel·ing** *or* **can·cel·ling** **1 :** to cross out or strike out with a line **:** DELETE **2 :** to take back **:** WITHDRAW **3 :** to equal in force or effect **:** OFFSET **4 :** to remove (a common divisor) from numerator and denominator **:** remove (equivalents) on opposite sides of an equation or account **5 :** to mark (as a postage stamp) so as to make impossible to use again
can·cel·la·tion *n* **1 :** an act of canceling **2 :** a mark made to cancel something
can·cer *n* **1 :** a harmful growth on or in the body that may keep spreading and be fatal if not treated **2 :** a condition of the body characterized by a cancer or cancers
can·de·la·bra *n* **:** a candlestick or lamp that has several branches for lights
can·de·la·brum *n, pl* **can·de·la·bra** *also* **can·de·la·brums :** CANDELABRA
can·did *adj* **1 :** FRANK, STRAIGHTFORWARD **2 :** relating to photography of people acting naturally without being posed — **can·did·ly** *adv* — **can·did·ness** *n*
can·di·da·cy *n, pl* **can·di·da·cies :** the state of being a candidate
can·di·date *n* **:** a person who runs for or is nominated by others for an office or honor
can·died *adj* **:** preserved in or coated with sugar
¹can·dle *n* **:** a stick of tallow or wax containing a wick and burned to give light
²candle *vb* **can·dled; can·dling :** to examine (as eggs) by holding between the eye and a light — **can·dler** *n*
can·dle·light *n* **1 :** the light of a candle **2 :** a soft artificial light
can·dle·stick *n* **:** a holder for a candle
can·dor *n* **:** sincere and honest expression
¹can·dy *n, pl* **can·dies :** a sweet made of sugar often with flavoring and filling
²candy *vb* **can·died; can·dy·ing** **1 :** to coat or become coated with sugar often by cooking **2 :** to crystallize into sugar
¹cane *n* **1 :** an often hollow, slender, and somewhat flexible plant stem **2 :** a tall woody grass or reed (as sugarcane) **3 :** WALKING STICK 1 **4 :** a rod for beating
²cane *vb* **caned; can·ing** **1 :** to beat with a cane **2 :** to make or repair with cane
¹ca·nine *n* **1 :** a pointed tooth next to the incisors **2 :** a canine animal
²canine *adj* **1 :** of or relating to the dogs or to the group of animals (as wolves) to which the dog belongs **2 :** like or typical of a dog
can·is·ter *n* **:** a small box or can for holding a dry product
can·nery *n, pl* **can·ner·ies :** a factory where foods are canned
can·ni·bal *n* **1 :** a human being who eats human flesh **2 :** an animal that eats other animals of its own kind
can·non *n, pl* **cannon** *also* **cannons** **1 :** a heavy gun mounted on a carriage **2 :** an automatic gun of heavy caliber on an airplane
can·non·ball *n* **:** a usually round solid missile for firing from a cannon
can·not : can not
can·ny *adj* **can·ni·er; can·ni·est :** watchful of one's own interest — **can·ni·ly** *adv*
¹ca·noe *n* **:** a long light narrow boat with sharp ends and curved sides usually driven by paddles
²canoe *vb* **ca·noed; ca·noe·ing :** to travel or carry in a canoe — **ca·noe·ist** *n*

can·on *n* **1 :** a rule or law of a church **2 :** an accepted rule
can·o·py *n, pl* **can·o·pies 1 :** a covering fixed over a bed or throne or carried on poles (as over a person of high rank) **2 :** something that hangs over and shades or shelters something else
can't : can not
can·ta·loupe *n* **:** a muskmelon usually with a hard ridged or rough skin and reddish orange flesh
can·tan·ker·ous *adj* **:** QUARRELSOME
can·ta·ta *n* **:** a poem or story set to music to be sung by a chorus and soloists
can·teen *n* **1 :** a store (as in a camp or factory) in which food, drinks, and small supplies are sold **2 :** a place of recreation for people in military service **3 :** a small container for carrying liquid (as drinking water)
can·ter *n* **:** a horse's gait like but slower than the gallop
can·ti·le·ver *n* **1 :** a beam or similar structure fastened (as by being built into a wall) only at one end **2 :** either of two structures that extend from piers toward each other and when joined form a span in a bridge (**cantilever bridge**)
can·to *n, pl* **can·tos :** one of the major divisions of a long poem
can·ton *n* **:** a division of a country (as Switzerland)
can·tor *n* **:** a synagogue official who sings religious music and leads the congregation in prayer
can·vas *n* **1 :** a strong cloth of hemp, flax, or cotton that is used sometimes for making tents and sails and as the material on which oil paintings are made **2 :** something made of canvas or on canvas
can·vas·back *n* **:** a North American wild duck with reddish head and grayish back
1can·vass *vb* **:** to go through (a district) or go to (people) to ask for votes, contributions, or orders for goods or to determine public opinion — **can·vass·er** *n*
2canvass *n* **:** an act of canvassing
can·yon *n* **:** a deep valley with high steep slopes
1cap *n* **1 :** a head covering that has a visor and no brim **2 :** something that serves as a cover or protection for something **3 :** a paper or metal container holding an explosive charge
2cap *vb* **capped; cap·ping 1 :** to cover or provide with a cap **2 :** to match with something equal or better
ca·pa·bil·i·ty *n, pl* **ca·pa·bil·i·ties :** the quality or state of being capable
ca·pa·ble *adj* **1 :** having the qualities (as ability, power, or strength) needed to do or accomplish something **2 :** able to do one's job well **:** EFFICIENT — **ca·pa·bly** *adv*
ca·pa·cious *adj* **:** able to hold a great deal
ca·pac·i·ty *n, pl* **ca·pac·i·ties 1 :** ability to contain or deal with something **2 :** mental or physical power **3 :** VOLUME 3 **4 :** ROLE 1, STATUS
1cape *n* **:** a point of land that juts out into the sea or into a lake
2cape *n* **:** a sleeveless garment worn so as to hang over the shoulders, arms, and back
1ca·per *vb* **:** to leap about in a lively way
2caper *n* **1 :** a gay bounding leap or spring **2 :** a playful or mischievous trick **3 :** an illegal or questionable act
1cap·il·lary *adj* **1 :** having a long slender form and a small inner diameter **2 :** of or relating to capillary action or a capillary
2capillary *n, pl* **cap·il·lar·ies :** one of the slender hairlike tubes that are the smallest blood vessels and connect arteries with veins
capillary action *n* **:** the action by which the surface of a liquid where it is in contact with a solid (as in a capillary tube) is raised or lowered
1cap·i·tal *n* **:** the top part of an architectural column
2capital *adj* **1 :** punishable by or resulting in death **2 :** being like the letters A, B, C, etc. rather than a, b, c, etc. **3 :** being the location of a government **4 :** of or relating to capital **5 :** EXCELLENT
3capital *n* **1 :** accumulated wealth especially as used to produce more wealth **2 :** persons holding capital **3 :** profitable use **4 :** a capital letter **5 :** a capital city
cap·i·tal·ism *n* **:** a system under which the ownership of land and wealth is for the most part in the hands of private individuals
1cap·i·tal·ist *n* **1 :** a person who has capital and especially business capital **2 :** a person who favors capitalism
2capitalist *adj* **1 :** owning capital **2 :** CAPITALISTIC
cap·i·tal·is·tic *adj* **1 :** practicing or favoring capitalism **2 :** of or relating to capitalism or capitalists — **cap·i·tal·is·ti·cal·ly** *adv*
cap·i·tal·iza·tion *n* **1 :** the act or process of capitalizing **2 :** the amount of money used as capital in business
cap·i·tal·ize *vb* **cap·i·tal·ized; cap·i·tal·iz·ing 1 :** to write with a beginning capital letter or in capital letters **2 :** to use as capital (as in a business) **:** furnish capital for (a business) **3 :** to gain by turning something to advantage
cap·i·tol *n* **1 :** the building in which a state legislature meets **2** *cap* **:** the building in

Washington in which the United States Congress meets

ca•po *n, pl* **capos :** a bar that can be fitted on the fingerboard especially of a guitar to raise the pitch of all the strings

ca•pon *n* **:** a castrated male chicken

ca•price *n* **:** a sudden change in feeling, opinion, or action **:** WHIM

ca•pri•cious *adj* **:** moved or controlled by caprice **:** likely to change suddenly — **ca•pri•cious•ly** *adv* — **ca•pri•cious•ness** *n*

cap•size *vb* **cap•sized; cap•siz•ing :** to turn over **:** UPSET

cap•stan *n* **:** a device that consists of a drum to which a rope is fastened and that is used especially on ships for moving or raising weights

cap•sule *n* **1 :** a case enclosing the seeds or spores of a plant **2 :** a small case of material that contains medicine to be swallowed **3 :** a closed compartment for travel in space

[1]**cap•tain** *n* **1 :** a leader of a group **:** one in command **2 :** a commissioned officer in the Navy or Coast Guard ranking above a commander **3 :** a commissioned officer in the Army, Air Force, or Marine Corps ranking above a first lieutenant **4 :** the commanding officer of a ship

[2]**captain** *vb* **:** to be captain of

cap•tion *n* **1 :** the heading especially of an article or document **2 :** a comment or title that goes with a picture (as in a book)

cap•ti•vate *vb* **cap•ti•vat•ed; cap•ti•vat•ing :** to fascinate by some special charm

[1]**cap•tive** *adj* **1 :** taken and held prisoner especially in war **2 :** kept within bounds or under control **3 :** of or relating to captivity

[2]**captive** *n* **:** one that is captive **:** PRISONER

cap•tiv•i•ty *n* **:** the state of being a captive

cap•tor *n* **:** one that has captured a person or thing

[1]**cap•ture** *n* **:** the act of capturing

[2]**capture** *vb* **cap•tured; cap•tur•ing 1 :** to take and hold especially by force **2 :** to put into a lasting form

car *n* **1 :** a vehicle (as an automobile) that moves on wheels **2 :** the compartment of an elevator

ca•rafe *n* **:** a bottle that has a lip and is used to hold water or beverages

car•a•mel *n* **1 :** burnt sugar used for coloring and flavoring **2 :** a firm chewy candy

car•at *n* **:** a unit of weight for precious stones equal to 200 milligrams

car•a•van *n* **1 :** a group (as of merchants or pilgrims) traveling together on a long journey through desert or in dangerous places **2 :** a group of vehicles traveling together one behind the other

car•a•vel *n* **:** a small sailing ship of the fifteenth and sixteenth centuries with a broad bow and high stern and three or four masts

car•a•way *n* **:** an herb related to the carrots that is grown for its seeds used especially as a seasoning

car•bine *n* **:** a short light rifle

car•bo•hy•drate *n* **:** a nutrient that is rich in energy and is made up of carbon, hydrogen, and oxygen

car•bol•ic acid *n* **:** a poison present in coal tar and wood tar that is diluted and used as an antiseptic

car•bon *n* **:** a chemical element occurring as diamond and graphite, in coal and petroleum, and in plant and animal bodies

carbon di•ox•ide *n* **:** a heavy colorless gas that is formed by burning fuels and by decay and that is the simple raw material from which plants build up compounds for their nourishment

carbon mon•ox•ide *n* **:** a colorless odorless very poisonous gas formed by incomplete burning of carbon

carbon tet•ra•chlo•ride *n* **:** a colorless poisonous liquid that does not burn and is used for dissolving grease

car•bu•re•tor *n* **:** the part of an engine in which liquid fuel (as gasoline) is mixed with air to make it burn easily

car•cass *n* **:** the body of an animal prepared for use as meat

[1]**card** *vb* **:** to clean and untangle fibers and especially wool by combing with a card — **card•er** *n*

[2]**card** *n* **:** an instrument usually with bent wire teeth that is used to clean and untangle fibers (as wool)

[3]**card** *n* **1 :** PLAYING CARD **2 cards** *pl* **:** a game played with playing cards **3 :** a flat stiff piece of paper or thin pasteboard that can be written on or that contains printed information

card•board *n* **:** a stiff material made of wood pulp that has been pressed and dried

car•di•ac *adj* **:** of, relating to, or affecting the heart

[1]**car•di•nal** *n* **1 :** a high official of the Roman Catholic Church ranking next below the pope **2 :** a bright red songbird with a crest and a whistling call

[2]**cardinal** *adj* **:** of first importance **:** MAIN, PRINCIPAL

cardinal flower *n* **:** the bright red flower of a North American plant that blooms in late summer

car•di•nal•i•ty *n, pl* **car•di•nal•i•ties :** the number of elements in a given mathematical set

cardinal number *n* **:** a number (as 1, 5, 22)

that is used in simple counting and answers the question "how many?"

cardinal point *n* **:** one of the four chief points of the compass which are north, south, east, west

[1]**care** *n* **1 :** a heavy sense of responsibility **2 :** serious attention **3 :** PROTECTION 1, SUPERVISION **4 :** an object of one's care

[2]**care** *vb* **cared; car·ing 1 :** to feel interest or concern **2 :** to give care **3 :** to have a liking or desire

ca·reer *n* **1 :** the course followed or progress made in one's job or life's work **2 :** a job followed as a life's work

care·free *adj* **:** free from care or worry

care·ful *adj* **1 :** using care **2 :** made, done, or said with care — **care·ful·ly** *adv* — **care·ful·ness** *n*

care·less *adj* **1 :** CAREFREE **2 :** not taking proper care **3 :** done, made, or said without being careful — **care·less·ly** *adv* — **care·less·ness** *n*

[1]**ca·ress** *n* **:** a tender or loving touch or hug

[2]**caress** *vb* **:** to touch in a tender or loving way

care·tak·er *n* **:** a person who takes care of property for another person

car·fare *n* **:** the fare charged for carrying a passenger (as on a bus)

car·go *n, pl* **cargoes** *or* **cargos :** the goods carried by a ship, airplane, or vehicle

car·i·bou *n* **:** a large deer of northern and arctic North America that is closely related to the Old World reindeer

car·ies *n, pl* **caries :** a decayed condition of a tooth or teeth

car·il·lon *n* **:** a set of bells sounded by hammers controlled by a keyboard

car·nage *n* **:** [1]SLAUGHTER 3

car·na·tion *n* **:** a fragrant usually white, pink, or red garden or greenhouse flower that is related to the pinks

car·ne·lian *n* **:** a hard reddish quartz used as a gem

car·ni·val *n* **1 :** a traveling group that puts on a variety of amusements **2 :** an organized program of entertainment or exhibition **:** FESTIVAL

car·ni·vore *n* **:** an animal that feeds on meat

car·niv·o·rous *adj* **1 :** feeding on animal flesh **2 :** of or relating to carnivores

[1]**car·ol** *n* **:** a usually religious song of joy

[2]**carol** *vb* **car·oled** *or* **car·olled; car·ol·ing** *or* **car·ol·ling 1 :** to sing in a joyful manner **2 :** to sing carols and especially Christmas carols — **car·ol·er** *or* **car·ol·ler** *n*

[1]**car·om** *n* **:** a bouncing back especially at an angle

[2]**carom** *vb* **:** to hit and bounce back at an angle

[1]**carp** *vb* **:** to find fault

[2]**carp** *n* **:** a freshwater fish that lives a long time and may weigh as much as eighteen kilograms

car·pel *n* **:** one of the ring of parts that form the ovary of a flower

car·pen·ter *n* **:** a worker who builds or repairs things made of wood

car·pen·try *n* **:** the work or trade of a carpenter

[1]**car·pet** *n* **1 :** a heavy woven fabric used especially as a floor covering **2 :** a covering like a carpet

[2]**carpet** *vb* **:** to cover with or as if with a carpet

car·riage *n* **1 :** the manner of holding the body **:** POSTURE **2 :** a vehicle with wheels used for carrying persons **3 :** a support with wheels used for carrying a load **4 :** a movable part of a machine that carries or supports some other moving part

car·ri·er *n* **1 :** a person or thing that carries **2 :** a person or business that transports passengers or goods **3 :** one that carries disease germs and passes them on to others

car·ri·on *n* **:** dead and decaying flesh

car·rot *n* **:** the long orange edible root of a garden plant (**carrot plant**)

car·ry *vb* **car·ried; car·ry·ing 1 :** to take or transfer from one place to another **2 :** [1]SUPPORT 4, BEAR **3 :** WIN 4 **4 :** to contain and direct the course of **5 :** to wear or have on one's person or have within one **6 :** to have as an element, quality, or part **7 :** to hold or bear the body or some part of it **8 :** to sing in correct pitch **9 :** to have for sale **10 :** PUBLISH 2 **11 :** to go over or travel a distance

car·ry·all *n* **:** a large bag or carrying case

carry away *vb* **:** to cause strong feeling in

carry on *vb* **1 :** MANAGE 1 **2 :** to behave badly **3 :** to continue in spite of difficulties

carry out *vb* **:** to put into action or effect

car seat *n* **:** a portable seat for a small child that attaches to an automobile seat and holds the child safely

[1]**cart** *n* **1 :** a heavy vehicle with two wheels usually drawn by horses and used for hauling **2 :** a light vehicle pushed or pulled by hand

[2]**cart** *vb* **:** to carry in a cart — **cart·er** *n*

car·ti·lage *n* **:** an elastic tissue that makes up most of the skeleton of very young animals and is later mostly changed into bone

car·ti·lag·i·nous *adj* **:** of, relating to, or made of cartilage

car·ton *n* **:** a cardboard container

car·toon *n* **1 :** a drawing (as in a newspaper) making people or objects look funny or foolish **2 :** COMIC STRIP **3 :** a movie composed of cartoons

car·toon·ist *n* **:** a person who draws cartoons

car·tridge *n* **1 :** a case or shell containing gunpowder and shot or a bullet for use in a firearm **2 :** a case containing an explosive for blasting **3 :** a container like a cartridge

cart·wheel *n* **:** a handspring made to the side with arms and legs sticking out

carve *vb* **carved; carv·ing 1 :** to cut with care **2 :** to make or get by cutting **3 :** to slice and serve (meat) — **carv·er** *n*

cas·cade *n* **:** a steep usually small waterfall

cas·cara *n* **:** the dried bark of a western North American shrub used as a laxative

[1]case *n* **1 :** a particular instance, situation, or example **2 :** a situation or an object that calls for investigation or action (as by the police) **3 :** a question to be settled in a court of law **4 :** a form of a noun, pronoun, or adjective showing its grammatical relation to other words **5 :** the actual situation **6 :** a convincing argument **7 :** an instance of disease or injury **8 :** [2]PATIENT

[2]case *n* **1 :** a container (as a box) for holding something **2 :** a box and its contents **3 :** an outer covering **4 :** the frame of a door or window

ca·sein *n* **:** a whitish to yellowish material made from milk especially by the action of acid and used in making paints and plastics

case·ment *n* **1 :** a window sash opening on hinges **2 :** a window with a casement

[1]cash *n* **1 :** money in the form of coins or bills **2 :** money or its equivalent (as a check) paid for goods at the time of purchase or delivery

[2]cash *vb* **:** to pay or obtain cash for

cash·ew *n* **:** an edible nut that is shaped like a kidney and comes from a tropical American tree

[1]ca·shier *vb* **:** to dismiss from service especially in disgrace

[2]cash·ier *n* **:** a person who is responsible for money (as in a bank or business)

cash·mere *n* **:** a soft yarn or fabric once made from the fine wool of an Indian goat but now often from sheep's wool

cas·ing *n* **:** something that covers or encloses

cask *n* **1 :** a container that is shaped like a barrel and is usually used for liquids **2 :** the amount contained in a cask

cas·ket *n* **1 :** a small box for storage or safekeeping (as for jewels) **2 :** COFFIN

cas·se·role *n* **1 :** a deep dish in which food can be baked and served **2 :** the food cooked and served in a casserole

cas·sette *n* **1 :** a container holding photographic film or plates that can be easily loaded into a camera **2 :** a container holding magnetic tape with the tape on one reel passing to the other

[1]cast *vb* **cast; cast·ing 1 :** [1]THROW 1 **2 :** to throw out, off, or away **:** SHED **3 :** to direct to or toward something or someone **4 :** to put on record **5 :** to assign a part or role to **6 :** to give shape to liquid material by pouring it into a mold and letting it harden **7 :** to make by looping or catching up — **cast lots :** to take or receive an object at random in order to decide something by chance

[2]cast *n* **1 :** an act of casting **:** THROW, FLING **2 :** the form in which a thing is made **3 :** the characters or the people acting in a play or story **4 :** the distance to which a thing can be thrown **5 :** something formed by casting in a mold or form **6 :** a stiff surgical dressing of plaster hardened around a part of the body **7 :** a hint of color **8 :** [2]SHAPE 1 **9 :** something (as the skin of an insect) thrown out or off

cas·ta·net *n* **:** a rhythm instrument that consists of two small ivory, wooden, or plastic shells fastened to the thumb and clicked by the fingers in time to dancing and music — usually used in pl.

[1]cast·away *adj* **1 :** thrown away **2 :** cast adrift or ashore

[2]castaway *n* **1 :** something that has been thrown away **2 :** a shipwrecked person

caste *n* **1 :** one of the classes into which the people of India were formerly divided **2 :** a division or class of society based on wealth, rank, or occupation **3 :** social rank **:** PRESTIGE

cast·er *n* **1 :** one that casts **2 :** a small container (as for salt or pepper) with holes in the top **3** *or* **cas·tor :** a small wheel that turns freely and is used for supporting furniture

cas·ti·gate *vb* **cas·ti·gat·ed; cas·ti·gat·ing :** to punish or correct with words or blows

cast·ing *n* **1 :** the act or action of one that casts **2 :** something that is cast in a mold **3 :** something (as skin or feathers) that is cast out or off

cast iron *n* **:** a hard and brittle alloy of iron, carbon, and silicon shaped by being poured into a mold while melted

cas·tle *n* **1 :** a large building or group of buildings usually having high walls with towers and a surrounding moat for protection **2 :** a large or impressive house

cast·off *n* **:** a cast-off person or thing

cast–off *adj* **:** thrown away or aside

cas·tor oil *n* **:** a thick yellowish liquid that comes from the seeds (**castor beans**) of a tropical herb and is used as a lubricant and as a strong laxative

cas·trate *vb* **cas·trat·ed; cas·trat·ing :** to remove the sex glands of

ca·su·al *adj* **1 :** happening unexpectedly or by chance **:** not planned or foreseen **2 :** occurring without regularity **:** OCCASIONAL **3 :** showing or feeling little concern **:** NONCHALANT **4 :** meant for informal use — **ca·su·al·ly** *adv*

ca·su·al·ty *n, pl* **ca·su·al·ties 1 :** a serious or fatal accident **:** DISASTER **2 :** a military person lost (as by death) during warfare **3 :** a person or thing injured, lost, or destroyed

cat *n* **1 :** a common furry flesh-eating animal kept as a pet or for catching mice and rats **2 :** any of the group of mammals (as lions, tigers, and wildcats) to which the domestic cat belongs

[1]**cat·a·log** *or* **cat·a·logue** *n* **1 :** a list of names, titles, or articles arranged by some system **2 :** a book or file containing a catalog

[2]**catalog** *or* **catalogue** *vb* **cat·a·loged** *or* **cat·a·logued; cat·a·log·ing** *or* **cat·a·logu·ing 1 :** to make a catalog of **2 :** to enter in a catalog — **cat·a·log·er** *or* **cat·a·logu·er** *n*

ca·tal·pa *n* **:** a tree of America and Asia with broad leaves, bright flowers, and long pods

[1]**cat·a·pult** *n* **1 :** an ancient military machine for hurling stones and arrows **2 :** a device for launching an airplane from the deck of a ship

[2]**catapult** *vb* **1 :** to throw or launch by or as if by a catapult **2 :** to become catapulted

ca·tarrh *n* **:** a red sore state of mucous membrane especially when chronic

ca·tas·tro·phe *n* **1 :** a sudden disaster **2 :** complete failure **:** FIASCO

cat·bird *n* **:** a dark gray songbird that has a call like a cat's mewing

cat·boat *n* **:** a sailboat with a single mast set far forward and a single large sail with a long boom

cat·call *n* **:** a sound like the cry of a cat or a noise expressing disapproval (as at a sports event)

[1]**catch** *vb* **caught; catch·ing 1 :** to capture or seize something in flight or motion **2 :** to discover unexpectedly **3 :** to check suddenly **4 :** to take hold of **5 :** to get tangled **6 :** to hold firmly **:** FASTEN **7 :** to become affected by **8 :** to take or get briefly or quickly **9 :** to be in time for **10 :** to grasp by the senses or the mind **11 :** to play catcher on a baseball team

[2]**catch** *n* **1 :** something caught **:** the amount caught at one time **2 :** the act of catching **3 :** a pastime in which a ball is thrown and caught **4 :** something that checks, fastens, or holds immovable **5 :** a hidden difficulty

catch·er *n* **1 :** one that catches **2 :** a baseball player who plays behind home plate

catch·ing *adj* **1 :** INFECTIOUS 1, CONTAGIOUS **2 :** likely to spread as if infectious

catchy *adj* **catch·i·er; catch·i·est 1 :** likely to attract **2 :** TRICKY 2

cat·e·chism *n* **1 :** a series of questions and answers used in giving instruction and especially religious instruction **2 :** a set of formal questions

cat·e·go·ry *n, pl* **cat·e·go·ries :** a basic division or grouping of things

ca·ter *vb* **1 :** to provide a supply of food **2 :** to supply what is needed or wanted — **ca·ter·er** *n*

cat·er·pil·lar *n* **:** a wormlike often hairy larva of an insect (as a moth or butterfly)

cat·fish *n* **:** any of a group of fishes with large heads and feelers about the mouth

cat·gut *n* **:** a tough cord made from intestines of animals (as sheep) and used for strings of musical instruments and rackets and for sewing in surgery

ca·the·dral *n* **:** the principal church of a district headed by a bishop

cath·o·lic *adj* **1 :** broad in range **2** *cap* **:** of or relating to the Roman Catholic Church

Catholic *n* **1 :** a member of a Christian church tracing its history back to the apostles **2 :** a member of the Roman Catholic Church

cat·kin *n* **:** a flower cluster (as of the willow and birch) in which the flowers grow in close circular rows along a slender stalk

cat·like *adj* **:** like a cat (as in grace or slyness)

cat·nap *n* **:** a very short light nap

cat·nip *n* **:** a plant of the mint family enjoyed by cats

cat–o'–nine–tails *n, pl* **cat–o'–nine–tails :** a whip made of nine knotted cords fastened to a handle

cat·sup *variant of* KETCHUP

cat·tail *n* **:** a tall plant with long flat leaves and tall furry stalks that grows in marshy areas

cat·tle *n, pl* **cattle :** domestic animals with four feet and especially cows, bulls, and calves

cat·walk *n* **:** a narrow walk or way (as along a bridge)

caught *past of* CATCH

caul·dron *or* **cal·dron** *n* **:** a large kettle or boiler

cau·li·flow·er *n* **:** a vegetable closely related to the cabbage that is grown for its white head of undeveloped flowers

[1]**caulk** *vb* **:** to fill up a crack, seam, or joint so as to make it watertight

2caulk *also* **caulk·ing** *n* **:** material used to caulk

1cause *n* **1 :** a person or thing that brings about a result **2 :** a good or good enough reason for something **3 :** something (as a question) to be decided **4 :** something supported or deserving support

2cause *vb* **caused; caus·ing :** to be the cause of

cause·way *n* **:** a raised road or way across wet ground or water

caus·tic *adj* **1 :** capable of eating away by chemical action **:** CORROSIVE **2 :** 1SHARP 8, BITING

1cau·tion *n* **1 :** ADMONITION **2 :** carefulness in regard to danger **:** PRECAUTION

2caution *vb* **:** to advise caution to **:** WARN

cau·tious *adj* **:** showing or using caution — **cau·tious·ly** *adv*

cav·al·cade *n* **1 :** a procession especially of riders or carriages **2 :** a dramatic series (as of related events)

1cav·a·lier *n* **1 :** a mounted soldier **2 :** a brave and courteous gentleman

2cavalier *adj* **1 :** easy and lighthearted in manner **2 :** tending to disregard the rights or feelings of others **:** ARROGANT

cav·al·ry *n, pl* **cav·al·ries :** troops mounted on horseback or moving in motor vehicles

cav·al·ry·man *n, pl* **cav·al·ry·men :** a cavalry soldier

1cave *n* **:** a hollow underground place with an opening on the surface

2cave *vb* **caved; cav·ing :** to fall or cause to fall in or down **:** COLLAPSE

cave·man *n, pl* **cave·men :** a person living in a cave especially during the Stone Age

cav·ern *n* **:** a cave often of large or unknown size

cav·ern·ous *adj* **1 :** having caverns or hollow places **2 :** like a cavern because large and hollow

cav·i·ty *n, pl* **cav·i·ties :** a hollow place

ca·vort *vb* **:** to move or hop about in a lively way

1caw *vb* **:** to make a caw

2caw *n* **:** the cry of a crow or a raven

cay·enne pepper *n* **:** dried ripe hot peppers ground and used to add flavor to food

CD *n* **:** COMPACT DISC

cease *vb* **ceased; ceas·ing :** to come or bring to an end **:** STOP

cease·less *adj* **:** CONSTANT 3

ce·cro·pia moth *n* **:** a silkworm moth that is the largest moth of the eastern United States

ce·dar *n* **:** any of a number of trees having cones and a strong wood with a pleasant smell

cede *vb* **ced·ed; ced·ing :** to give up especially by treaty

ceil·ing *n* **1 :** the overhead inside surface of a room **2 :** the greatest height at which an airplane can fly properly **3 :** the height above the ground of the bottom of the lowest layer of clouds **4 :** an upper limit

cel·e·brate *vb* **cel·e·brat·ed; cel·e·brat·ing 1 :** to perform publicly and according to certain rules **2 :** to observe in some special way (as by merrymaking or by staying away from business) **3 :** 1PRAISE 1

cel·e·brat·ed *adj* **:** widely known and talked about

cel·e·bra·tion *n* **1 :** the act of celebrating **2 :** the activities or ceremonies for celebrating a special occasion

ce·leb·ri·ty *n, pl* **ce·leb·ri·ties 1 :** FAME **2 :** a celebrated person

cel·ery *n* **:** a plant related to the carrots whose crisp leafstalks are used for food

ce·les·ta *n* **:** a keyboard instrument with hammers that strike steel plates to make ringing sounds

ce·les·tial *adj* **1 :** of, relating to, or suggesting heaven **2 :** of or relating to the sky

cell *n* **1 :** a very small room (as in a prison or a monastery) **2 :** a small enclosed part or division (as in a honeycomb) **3 :** a small mass of living matter that is made of protoplasm, includes a nucleus, is enclosed in a membrane, and is the basic unit of which all plants and animals are made up **4 :** a container with substances which can produce an electric current by chemical action — **celled** *adj*

cel·lar *n* **:** a room or set of rooms below the surface of the ground **:** BASEMENT

cel·lo *n, pl* **cel·los :** a large stringed instrument of the violin family that plays the bass part

cel·lo·phane *n* **:** a thin clear material made from cellulose and used as a wrapping

cel·lu·lar *adj* **1 :** of, relating to, or made up of cells **2 :** of, relating to, or being a telephone that connects to others by radio and is part of a system in which a geographical area is divided into small sections each served by a transmitter of limited range

cel·lu·lose *n* **:** a substance that is the chief part of the cell walls of plants and is used in making various products (as paper and rayon)

cell wall *n* **:** the firm outer nonliving boundary of a plant cell

Cel·si·us *adj* **:** relating to or having a thermometer scale on which the interval between the freezing point and the boiling point of water is divided into 100 degrees with 0 representing the freezing point and 100 the boiling point

[1]**ce·ment** *n* **1 :** a powder that is made mainly from compounds of aluminum, calcium, silicon, and iron heated together and then ground, that combines with water and hardens into a mass, and that is used in mortar and concrete **2 :** [2]CONCRETE, MORTAR **3 :** a substance that by hardening sticks things together firmly

[2]**cement** *vb* **1 :** to join together with or as if with cement **2 :** to cover with concrete

ce·men·tum *n* **:** a thin bony layer covering the part of a tooth inside the gum

cem·e·tery *n, pl* **cem·e·ter·ies :** a place where dead people are buried **:** GRAVEYARD

Ce·no·zo·ic *n* **:** an era of geological history lasting from seventy million years ago to the present time in which there has been a rapid evolution of mammals and birds and of flowering plants

[1]**cen·sor** *n* **:** an official who checks writings or movies to take out things thought to be objectionable

[2]**censor** *vb* **:** to examine (as a book) to take out things thought to be objectionable

[1]**cen·sure** *n* **1 :** the act of finding fault with or blaming **2 :** an official criticism

[2]**censure** *vb* **cen·sured; cen·sur·ing :** to find fault with especially publicly

cen·sus *n* **:** a count of the number of people in a country, city, or town

cent *n* **1 :** a hundredth part of the unit of the money system in a number of different countries **2 :** a coin, token, or note representing one cent

cen·taur *n* **:** a creature in Greek mythology that is part man and part horse

cen·te·nar·i·an *n* **:** a person 100 or more years old

[1]**cen·ten·ni·al** *n* **:** a 100th anniversary or a celebration of this event

[2]**centennial** *adj* **:** relating to a period of 100 years

[1]**cen·ter** *n* **1 :** the middle point of a circle or a sphere equally distant from every point on the circumference or surface **2 :** one (as a person or area) that is very important to some activity or concern **3 :** the middle part of something **4 :** a player occupying a middle position on a team

[2]**center** *vb* **1 :** to place or fix at or around a center or central area **2 :** to collect at or around one point

center of gravity : the point at which the entire weight of a body may be thought of as centered so that if supported at this point the body would balance perfectly

cen·ter·piece *n* **:** a piece put in the center of something and especially a decoration (as flowers) for a table

centi- *prefix* **:** hundredth part — used in terms of the metric system

cen·ti·grade *adj* **:** CELSIUS

cen·ti·gram *n* **:** a unit of weight equal to $^1/_{100}$ gram

cen·ti·li·ter *n* **:** a unit of liquid capacity equal to $^1/_{100}$ liter

cen·ti·me·ter *n* **:** a unit of length equal to $^1/_{100}$ meter

cen·ti·pede *n* **:** a small animal that has a long body and many legs and is related to the insects

cen·tral *adj* **1 :** containing or being the center **2 :** most important **:** CHIEF **3 :** placed at, in, or near the center — **cen·tral·ly** *adv*

[1]**Central American** *adj* **:** of or relating to Central America or the Central Americans

[2]**Central American** *n* **:** a person born or living in Central America

central angle *n* **:** an angle with its vertex at the center of a circle and with sides that are radii of the circle

cen·tral·ize *vb* **cen·tral·ized; cen·tral·iz·ing :** to bring to a central point or under a single control

central processing unit *n* **:** PROCESSOR 3

cen·trif·u·gal force *n* **:** the force that tends to cause a thing or parts of a thing to go outward from a center of rotation

cen·tu·ry *n, pl* **cen·tu·ries :** a period of 100 years

ce·ram·ic *n* **1 ceramics** *pl* **:** the art of making things (as pottery or tiles) of baked clay **2 :** a product made by ceramics

[1]**ce·re·al** *adj* **1 :** relating to grain or the plants that it comes from **2 :** made of grain

[2]**cereal** *n* **1 :** a plant (as a grass) that yields grain for food **2 :** a food prepared from grain

cer·e·bel·lum *n, pl* **cer·e·bel·lums** *or* **cer·e·bel·la :** a part of the brain concerned especially with the coordination of muscles and with keeping the body in proper balance

ce·re·bral *adj* **1 :** of or relating to the brain or mind **2 :** of, relating to, or affecting the cerebrum

ce·re·brum *n, pl* **ce·re·brums** *or* **ce·re·bra :** the enlarged front and upper part of the brain that is the center of thinking

[1]**cer·e·mo·ni·al** *adj* **:** of, relating to, or being a ceremony

[2]**ceremonial** *n* **:** a ceremonial act, action, or system

cer·e·mo·ni·ous *adj* **1 :** [1]CEREMONIAL **2 :** given to ceremony **:** FORMAL — **cer·e·mo·ni·ous·ly** *adv*

cer·e·mo·ny *n, pl* **cer·e·mo·nies 1 :** an act

or series of acts performed in some regular way according to fixed rules **2 :** very polite behavior **:** FORMALITY

[1]cer·tain *adj* **1 :** being fixed or settled **2 :** known but not named **3 :** sure to have an effect **4 :** known to be true **5 :** bound by the way things are **6 :** assured in thought or action

[2]certain *pron* **:** certain ones

cer·tain·ly *adv* **1 :** with certainty **:** without fail **2 :** without doubt

cer·tain·ty *n, pl* **cer·tain·ties 1 :** something that is certain **2 :** the quality or state of being certain

cer·tif·i·cate *n* **1 :** a written or printed statement that is proof of some fact **2 :** a paper showing that a person has met certain requirements (as of a school) **3 :** a paper showing ownership

cer·ti·fy *vb* **cer·ti·fied; cer·ti·fy·ing 1 :** to show to be true or as claimed by a formal or official statement **2 :** to guarantee the quality, fitness, or value of officially **3 :** to show to have met certain requirements

ce·ru·le·an *adj* **:** somewhat like the blue of the sky

ces·sa·tion *n* **:** a coming to a stop

chafe *vb* **chafed; chaf·ing 1 :** IRRITATE 1, VEX **2 :** to be bothered **:** FRET **3 :** to warm by rubbing **4 :** to rub so as to wear away or make sore

[1]chaff *n* **1 :** the husks of grains and grasses separated from the seed in threshing **2 :** something worthless

[2]chaff *vb* **:** to tease in a friendly way

cha·grin *n* **:** a feeling of being annoyed by failure or disappointment

[1]chain *n* **1 :** a series of links or rings usually of metal **2 :** something that restricts or binds **:** BOND **3 :** a series of things joined together as if by links

[2]chain *vb* **:** to fasten, bind, or connect with or as if with a chain

chair *n* **1 :** a seat for one person usually having a back and either four legs or a swivel base **2 :** an official seat or a seat of authority or honor **3 :** an office or position of authority or honor **4 :** an official who conducts a meeting

chair·man *n, pl* **chair·men :** CHAIR 4 — **chair·man·ship** *n*

chair·per·son *n* **:** CHAIR 4

chair·wom·an *n, pl* **chair·wom·en :** a woman who conducts a meeting

chaise longue *n* **:** a long chair somewhat like a couch

chaise lounge *n* **:** CHAISE LONGUE

cha·let *n* **1 :** a herdsman's hut in the Alps away from a town or village **2 :** a Swiss dwelling with a roof that sticks far out past the walls **3 :** a cottage built to look like a chalet

chal·ice *n* **:** a drinking cup **:** GOBLET

[1]chalk *n* **1 :** a soft white, gray, or buff limestone made up mainly of very small seashells **2 :** a material like chalk especially when used in the form of a crayon

[2]chalk *vb* **1 :** to rub, mark, write, or draw with chalk **2 :** to record or add up with or as if with chalk

chalk·board *n* **:** BLACKBOARD

chalky *adj* **chalk·i·er; chalk·i·est 1 :** made of or like chalk **2 :** easily crumbled **3 :** very pale

[1]chal·lenge *vb* **chal·lenged; chal·leng·ing 1 :** to halt and demand a password from **2 :** to object to as bad or incorrect **:** DISPUTE **3 :** to demand proof that something is right or legal **4 :** to invite or dare to take part in a contest — **chal·leng·er** *n*

[2]challenge *n* **1 :** an objection to something as not being true, genuine, correct, or proper or to a person (as a juror) as not being qualified or approved **:** PROTEST **2 :** a sentry's command to halt and prove identity **3 :** a demand that someone take part in a duel **4 :** a call or dare for someone to compete in a contest or sport

challenged *adj* **:** having a disability or deficiency

cham·ber *n* **1 :** a room in a house and especially a bedroom **2 :** an enclosed space, cavity, or compartment (as in a gun) **3 :** a meeting hall of a government body (as an assembly) **4 :** a room where a judge conducts business out of court **5 :** a group of people organized into a lawmaking body **6 :** a board or council of volunteers (as businessmen) — **cham·bered** *adj*

cham·ber·lain *n* **1 :** a chief officer in the household of a ruler or noble **2 :** TREASURER

cham·ber·maid *n* **:** a maid who takes care of bedrooms (as in a hotel)

chamber music *n* **:** instrumental music to be performed in a room or small hall

cha·me·leon *n* **:** a lizard that has the ability to change the color of its skin

cham·ois *n, pl* **cham·ois 1 :** a small antelope living on the highest mountains of Europe and Asia **2 :** a soft yellowish leather made from the skin of the chamois or from sheepskin

[1]champ *vb* **:** to bite and chew noisily

[2]champ *n* **:** [1]CHAMPION 2, 3

[1]cham·pi·on *n* **1 :** a person who fights or speaks for another person or in favor of a cause **2 :** a person accepted as better than all others in a sport or in a game of skill **3 :** the winner of first place in a competition

[2]**champion** *vb* **:** to protect or fight for as a champion

cham·pi·on·ship *n* **1 :** the act of defending as a champion **2 :** the position or title of champion **3 :** a contest held to find a champion

[1]**chance** *n* **1 :** the uncertain course of events **2 :** OPPORTUNITY 1 **3 :** [1]RISK, GAMBLE **4 :** PROBABILITY 1 **5 :** a ticket in a raffle

[2]**chance** *vb* **chanced; chanc·ing 1 :** to take place by chance **2 :** to come unexpectedly **3 :** to leave to chance **:** RISK

[3]**chance** *adj* **:** happening by chance

chan·cel·lor *n* **1 :** a high state official (as in Germany) **2 :** a high officer of some universities **3 :** a chief judge in some courts — **chan·cel·lor·ship** *n*

chan·de·lier *n* **:** a lighting fixture with several branches that usually hangs from the ceiling

[1]**change** *vb* **changed; chang·ing 1 :** to make or become different **:** ALTER **2 :** to give a different position, course, or direction to **3 :** to put one thing in the place of another **:** SWITCH, EXCHANGE **4 :** to give or receive an equal amount of money in usually smaller units of value or in the money of another country **5 :** to put fresh clothes or covering on **6 :** to put on different clothes

[2]**change** *n* **1 :** the act, process, or result of changing **2 :** a fresh set of clothes **3 :** money in small units of value received in exchange for an equal amount in larger units **4 :** money returned when a payment is more than the amount due **5 :** money in coins

change·able *adj* **:** able or likely to change

[1]**chan·nel** *n* **1 :** the bed of a stream **2 :** the deeper part of a waterway (as a river or harbor) **3 :** a strait or a narrow sea **4 :** a closed course (as a tube) through which something flows **5 :** a long groove **6 :** a means by which something is passed or carried **7 :** a range of frequencies used by a single radio or television station in broadcasting

[2]**channel** *vb* **chan·neled** *or* **chan·nelled; chan·nel·ing** *or* **chan·nel·ling 1 :** to form a channel in **2 :** to direct into or through a channel

[1]**chant** *vb* **1 :** to sing especially in the way a chant is sung **2 :** to recite or speak with no change in tone

[2]**chant** *n* **1 :** a melody in which several words or syllables are sung on one tone **2 :** something spoken in the style of a chant

cha·os *n* **:** complete confusion and disorder

cha·ot·ic *adj* **:** being in a state of chaos

[1]**chap** *vb* **chapped; chap·ping :** to open in slits **:** CRACK

[2]**chap** *n* **:** [1]FELLOW 4

chap·el *n* **1 :** a building or a room or place for prayer or special religious services **2 :** a religious service or assembly held in a school or college

[1]**chap·er·on** *or* **chap·er·one** *n* **:** an older person who goes with and is responsible for a young woman or a group of young people (as at a dance)

[2]**chaperon** *or* **chaperone** *vb* **chap·er·oned; chap·er·on·ing :** to act as a chaperon

chap·lain *n* **1 :** a member of the clergy officially attached to a special group (as the army) **2 :** a person chosen to conduct religious services (as for a club)

chaps *n pl* **:** a set of leather coverings for the legs used especially by western ranch workers

chap·ter *n* **1 :** a main division of a book or story **2 :** a local branch of a club or organization

char *vb* **charred; char·ring 1 :** to change to charcoal by burning **2 :** to burn slightly **:** SCORCH

char·ac·ter *n* **1 :** a mark, sign, or symbol (as a letter or figure) used in writing or printing **2 :** [1]CHARACTERISTIC **3 :** the group of qualities that make a person, group, or thing different from others **4 :** a person who is unusual or peculiar **5 :** a person in a story or play **6 :** REPUTATION 1 **7 :** moral excellence

[1]**char·ac·ter·is·tic** *n* **:** a special quality or appearance that makes an individual or a group different from others

[2]**characteristic** *adj* **:** serving to stress some special quality of an individual or a group **:** TYPICAL

char·ac·ter·is·ti·cal·ly *adv* **:** in a characteristic way

char·ac·ter·ize *vb* **char·ac·ter·ized; char·ac·ter·iz·ing 1 :** to point out the character of an individual or a group **:** DESCRIBE **2 :** to be characteristic of

char·coal *n* **:** a black or dark absorbent carbon made by heating animal or vegetable material in the absence of air

[1]**charge** *n* **1 :** the amount (as of ammunition or fuel) needed to load or fill something **2 :** an amount of electricity available **3 :** a task, duty, or order given to a person **:** OBLIGATION **4 :** the work or duty of managing **5 :** a person or thing given to a person to look after **6 :** [2]COMMAND 2 **7 :** the price demanded especially for a service **8 :** an amount listed as a debt on an account **9 :** ACCUSATION **10 :** a rushing attack

[2]**charge** *vb* **charged; charg·ing 1 :** [1]FILL 1

2 : to give an electric charge to **3 :** to restore the active materials in a storage battery by passage of an electric current through it **4 :** to give a task, duty, or responsibility to **5 :** [1]COMMAND 1 **6 :** to accuse formally **7 :** to rush against **:** ASSAULT **8 :** to take payment from or make responsible for payment **9 :** to enter as a debt or responsibility on a record **10 :** to ask or set as a price

charg•er *n* **:** a cavalry horse

char•i•ot *n* **:** a vehicle of ancient times that had two wheels, was pulled by horses, and was used in war and in races and parades

char•i•ta•ble *adj* **1 :** freely giving money or help to needy persons **:** GENEROUS **2 :** given for the needy **:** of service to the needy **3 :** kindly in judging other people

char•i•ty *n, pl* **char•i•ties 1 :** love for others **2 :** kindliness in judging others **3 :** the giving of aid to the poor and suffering **4 :** public aid for the poor **5 :** an institution or fund for helping the needy

char•ley horse *n* **:** pain and stiffness in a muscle (as in a leg)

[1]**charm** *n* **1 :** a word, action, or thing believed to have magic powers **2 :** something worn or carried to keep away evil and bring good luck **3 :** a small decorative object worn on a chain or bracelet **4 :** a quality that attracts and pleases

[2]**charm** *vb* **1 :** to affect or influence by or as if by a magic spell **2 :** FASCINATE 2, DELIGHT **3 :** to protect by or as if by a charm **4 :** to attract by grace or beauty

charm•ing *adj* **:** very pleasing

[1]**chart** *n* **1 :** [1]MAP **2 :** a map showing coasts, reefs, currents, and depths of water **3 :** a sheet giving information in a table or lists or by means of diagrams

[2]**chart** *vb* **1 :** to make a map or chart of **2 :** to lay out a plan for

[1]**char•ter** *n* **1 :** an official document granting, guaranteeing, or showing the limits of the rights and duties of the group to which it is given **2 :** a contract by which the owners of a ship lease it to others

[2]**charter** *vb* **1 :** to grant a charter to **2 :** to hire (as a bus or an aircraft) for temporary use

charter school *n* **:** a school supported by taxes but run independently to achieve set goals under a charter between an official body (as a state government) and an outside group (as educators and businesses)

[1]**chase** *n* **1 :** the act of chasing **:** PURSUIT **2 :** the hunting of wild animals **3 :** something pursued

[2]**chase** *vb* **chased; chas•ing 1 :** to follow in order to catch up with or capture **2 :** [1]HUNT 1 **3 :** to drive away or out

chasm *n* **:** a deep split or gap in the earth

chas•sis *n, pl* **chas•sis :** a structure that supports the body (as of an automobile or airplane) or the parts (as of a television set)

chaste *adj* **chast•er; chast•est 1 :** pure in thought and act **:** MODEST **2 :** simple or plain in design

chas•ten *vb* **:** to correct by punishment or suffering **:** DISCIPLINE

chas•tise *vb* **chas•tised; chas•tis•ing :** to punish severely (as by whipping)

chas•ti•ty *n* **:** the quality or state of being chaste

[1]**chat** *vb* **chat•ted; chat•ting :** to talk in a friendly manner of things that are not serious

[2]**chat** *n* **:** a light friendly conversation

chat room *n* **:** an on-line computer site at which any visitor to the site can send messages that immediately appear on the screen for everyone to read

[1]**chat•ter** *vb* **1 :** to make quick sounds that suggest speech but lack meaning **2 :** to talk without thinking, without stopping, or fast **:** JABBER **3 :** to click again and again and without control — **chat•ter•er** *n*

[2]**chatter** *n* **:** the act or sound of chattering

chat•ter•box *n* **:** a person who talks all the time

chat•ty *adj* **chat•ti•er; chat•ti•est 1 :** TALKATIVE **2 :** having the style and manner of friendly conversation

chauf•feur *n* **:** a person hired to drive people around in a car

[1]**cheap** *adj* **1 :** not costing much **2 :** worth little **:** not very good **3 :** gained without much effort **4 :** lowered in one's own opinion **5 :** charging low prices — **cheap•ly** *adv*

[2]**cheap** *adv* **:** at low cost

cheap•en *vb* **:** to make or become cheap or cheaper

[1]**cheat** *vb* **1 :** to take something away from or keep from having something by dishonest tricks **:** DEFRAUD **2 :** to use unfair or dishonest methods to gain an advantage

[2]**cheat** *n* **1 :** an act of cheating **:** DECEPTION, FRAUD **2 :** a dishonest person

[1]**check** *n* **1 :** a sudden stopping of progress **:** PAUSE **2 :** something that delays, stops, or holds back **:** RESTRAINT **3 :** a standard or guide for testing and studying something **4 :** EXAMINATION 1, INVESTIGATION **5 :** a written order telling a bank to pay out money from a person's account to the one named on the order **6 :** a ticket or token showing a person's ownership, identity, or claim to something **7 :** a slip of paper showing the amount due **:** BILL **8 :** a pattern in squares **9 :** material with a design in

squares **10 :** a mark typically ✓ placed beside a written or printed item to show that something has been specially noted

²check *vb* **1 :** to bring to a sudden stop **2 :** to keep from expressing **3 :** to make sure that something is correct or satisfactory **:** VERIFY **4 :** to mark with a check **5 :** to mark with squares **6 :** to leave or accept for safekeeping or for shipment **7 :** to be the same on every point **:** TALLY

check·er·board *n* **:** a board marked with sixty-four squares in two colors and used for games (as checkers)

check·ers *n* **:** a game played on a checkerboard by two players each having twelve pieces

check·up *n* **1 :** INSPECTION, EXAMINATION **2 :** a physical examination

cheek *n* **1 :** the side of the face below the eye and above and beside the mouth **2 :** IMPUDENCE

¹cheep *vb* **:** ¹PEEP, CHIRP

²cheep *n* **:** ¹CHIRP

¹cheer *n* **1 :** state of mind or heart **:** SPIRIT **2 :** good spirits **3 :** something that gladdens **4 :** a shout of praise or encouragement

²cheer *vb* **1 :** to give hope to **:** make happier **:** COMFORT **2 :** to urge on especially with shouts or cheers **3 :** to shout with joy, approval, or enthusiasm **4 :** to grow or be cheerful — usually used with *up*

cheer·ful *adj* **:** full of good spirits **:** PLEASANT — **cheer·ful·ly** *adv* — **cheer·ful·ness** *n*

cheer·less *adj* **:** offering no cheer **:** GLOOMY

cheery *adj* **cheer·i·er; cheer·i·est :** merry and bright in manner or effect **:** CHEERFUL — **cheer·i·ly** *adv* — **cheer·i·ness** *n*

cheese *n* **:** the curd of milk pressed for use as food

cheese·cloth *n* **:** a thin loosely woven cotton cloth

cheesy *adj* **chees·i·er; chees·i·est :** like or suggesting cheese

chee·tah *n* **:** a long-legged African and formerly Asian animal of the cat family that has a spotted coat and that is the fastest animal on land

chef *n* **1 :** a chief cook **2 :** ¹COOK

¹chem·i·cal *adj* **:** of or relating to chemistry or chemicals — **chem·i·cal·ly** *adv*

²chemical *n* **:** a substance (as an acid) that is formed when two or more other substances act upon one another or that is used to produce a change in another substance (as in making plastics)

chem·ist *n* **:** a person trained or engaged in chemistry

chem·is·try *n* **1 :** a science that deals with the composition and properties of substances and of the changes they undergo **2 :** chemical composition and properties

cher·ish *vb* **1 :** to hold dear **2 :** to keep deeply in mind **:** cling to

Cher·o·kee *n, pl* **Cherokee** *or* **Cherokees :** a member of an Indian people originally from the southern Appalachian Mountains

cher·ry *n, pl* **cherries 1 :** the round red or yellow fruit of a tree (**cherry tree**) that is related to the plum **2 :** a medium red

cher·ub *n* **1 :** a painting or drawing of a beautiful child usually with wings **2 :** a chubby rosy child

chess *n* **:** a game of capture played on a board by two players each using sixteen pieces that have set moves

chest *n* **1 :** a container (as a box or case) for storing, safekeeping, or shipping **2 :** a public fund **3 :** the part of the body enclosed by the ribs and breastbone — **chest·ed** *adj*

chest·nut *n* **1 :** a sweet edible nut that grows in burs on a tree (**chestnut tree**) related to the beech **2 :** a reddish brown

chev·ron *n* **:** a sleeve badge of one or more bars or stripes usually in the shape of an upside down V indicating the wearer's rank (as in the armed forces)

¹chew *vb* **:** to crush or grind with the teeth

²chew *n* **1 :** the act of chewing **2 :** something for chewing

chew·ing gum *n* **:** gum usually of sweetened and flavored chicle prepared for chewing

chewy *adj* **chew·i·er; chew·i·est :** requiring chewing

¹chic *n* **:** fashionable style

²chic *adj* **:** STYLISH, SMART

¹Chi·ca·no *n, pl* **Chicanos :** an American of Mexican ancestry

²Chicano *adj* **:** of or relating to Chicanos

chick *n* **1 :** a young chicken **2 :** CHILD 2

chick·a·dee *n* **:** a small bird with fluffy grayish feathers and usually a black cap

¹chick·en *n* **1 :** the common domestic fowl especially when young **:** a young hen or rooster **2 :** the flesh of a chicken for use as food

²chicken *adj* **:** CHICKENHEARTED

chick·en·heart·ed *adj* **:** COWARDLY, TIMID

chicken pox *n* **:** a contagious disease especially of children in which there is fever and the skin breaks out in watery blisters

chick·weed *n* **:** a weedy plant related to the pinks that has small pointed leaves and whitish flowers

chi·cle *n* **:** a gum obtained from the sap of a tropical American tree and used in making chewing gum

chide *vb* **chid** *or* **chid·ed; chid** *or* **chid·den**

or **chided; chid·ing :** to find fault with : SCOLD

[1]**chief** *n* **:** the head of a group **:** LEADER — **in chief :** in the chief position or place

[2]**chief** *adj* **1 :** highest in rank or authority **2 :** most important **:** MAIN

chief·ly *adv* **1 :** above all **2 :** for the most part

chief master sergeant *n* **:** a noncommissioned officer in the Air Force ranking above a senior master sergeant

chief petty officer *n* **:** a petty officer in the Navy or Coast Guard ranking above a petty officer first class

chief·tain *n* **:** a chief especially of a band, tribe, or clan

chief warrant officer *n* **:** a warrant officer in any of the three top grades

chig·ger *n* **:** the larva of some mites that has six legs, clings to the skin, and causes itching

chil·blain *n* **:** a red swollen itchy condition caused by cold that occurs especially on the hands or feet

child *n, pl* **chil·dren 1 :** an unborn or recently born person **2 :** a young person of either sex between infancy and youth **3 :** one's son or daughter of any age

child·birth *n* **:** the act or process of giving birth to a child

child·hood *n* **:** the period of life between infancy and youth

child·ish *adj* **1 :** of, like, or thought to be suitable to children **2 :** showing the less pleasing qualities (as silliness) often thought to be those of children

child·like *adj* **1 :** of or relating to a child or childhood **2 :** showing the more pleasing qualities (as innocence and trustfulness) often thought to be those of children

chili *or* **chile** *n, pl* **chil·ies** *or* **chil·es 1 :** the small very sharply flavored fruit of a pepper plant **2 :** a spicy stew of ground beef and chilies usually with beans

[1]**chill** *n* **1 :** a feeling of coldness accompanied by shivering **2 :** unpleasant coldness

[2]**chill** *adj* **1 :** unpleasantly cold **:** RAW **2 :** not friendly

[3]**chill** *vb* **1 :** to make or become cold or chilly **2 :** to make cool especially without freezing **3 :** to harden the surface of (as metal) by sudden cooling

chilly *adj* **chill·i·er; chill·i·est :** noticeably cold — **chill·i·ness** *n*

[1]**chime** *vb* **chimed; chim·ing 1 :** to make sounds like a bell **:** ring chimes **2 :** to call or indicate by chiming

[2]**chime** *n* **1 :** a set of bells tuned to play music **2 :** the music from a set of bells — usually used in pl. **3 :** a musical sound suggesting bells

chime in *vb* **:** to break into or join in a discussion

chim·ney *n, pl* **chimneys 1 :** a passage for smoke especially in the form of a vertical structure of brick or stone that reaches above the roof of a building **2 :** a glass tube around a lamp flame

chimney sweep *n* **:** a person who cleans soot from chimneys

chimney swift *n* **:** a small dark gray bird with long narrow wings that often attaches its nest to chimneys

chimp *n* **:** CHIMPANZEE

chim·pan·zee *n* **:** an African ape that lives mostly in trees and is smaller than the related gorilla

[1]**chin** *n* **:** the part of the face below the mouth and including the point of the lower jaw

[2]**chin** *vb* **chinned; chin·ning :** to raise oneself while hanging by the hands until the chin is level with the support

chi·na *n* **1 :** porcelain ware **2 :** pottery (as dishes) for use in one's home

chin·chil·la *n* **:** a South American animal that is somewhat like a squirrel and is hunted or raised for its soft silvery gray fur

[1]**Chi·nese** *adj* **:** of or relating to China, the Chinese people, or Chinese

[2]**Chinese** *n, pl* **Chinese 1 :** a person born or living in China **2 :** a group of related languages used in China

chink *n* **:** a narrow slit or crack (as in a wall)

[1]**chip** *n* **1 :** a small piece (as of wood, stone, or glass) cut or broken off **2 :** POTATO CHIP **3 :** a flaw left after a small piece has been broken off **4 :** INTEGRATED CIRCUIT **5 :** a small slice of silicon containing electronic circuits (as for a computer)

[2]**chip** *vb* **chipped; chip·ping 1 :** to cut or break chips from **2 :** to break off in small pieces

chip·munk *n* **:** a small striped animal related to the squirrels

chip·ping sparrow *n* **:** a small North American sparrow that often nests about houses and has a weak chirp as a call

[1]**chirp** *n* **:** the short sharp sound made by crickets and some small birds

[2]**chirp** *vb* **:** to make a chirp

[1]**chis·el** *n* **:** a metal tool with a sharp edge at the end of a usually flat piece used to chip away stone, wood, or metal

[2]**chisel** *vb* **chis·eled** *or* **chis·elled; chis·el·ing** *or* **chis·el·ling :** to cut or shape with a chisel

chiv·al·rous *adj* **1 :** of or relating to chivalry **2 :** having or showing honor, generosity, and courtesy **3 :** showing special courtesy and regard to women

chiv•al•ry *n* **1 :** a body of knights **2 :** the system, spirit, ways, or customs of knighthood **3 :** chivalrous conduct

chlo•rine *n* **:** a chemical element that is a greenish yellow irritating gas of strong odor used as a bleach and as a disinfectant to purify water

[1]**chlo•ro•form** *n* **:** a colorless heavy liquid used especially to dissolve fatty substances and in the past in medicine to deaden the pain of operations but now mostly replaced by less poisonous substances

[2]**chloroform** *vb* **:** to make unconscious or kill with chloroform

chlo•ro•phyll *n* **:** the green coloring matter by means of which green plants produce carbohydrates from carbon dioxide and water

chlo•ro•plast *n* **:** one of the tiny bodies in which chlorophyll is found

chock–full *or* **chuck–full** *adj* **:** full to the limit

choc•o•late *n* **1 :** a food prepared from ground roasted cacao beans **2 :** a beverage of chocolate in water or milk **3 :** a candy made or coated with chocolate

[1]**choice** *n* **1 :** the act of choosing **:** SELECTION **2 :** the power of choosing **:** OPTION **3 :** a person or thing chosen **4 :** the best part **5 :** a large enough number and variety to choose among

[2]**choice** *adj* **choic•er; choic•est :** of very good quality

choir *n* **1 :** an organized group of singers especially in a church **2 :** the part of a church set aside for the singers

[1]**choke** *vb* **choked; chok•ing 1 :** to keep from breathing in a normal way by cutting off the supply of air **2 :** to have the windpipe blocked entirely or partly **3 :** to slow or prevent the growth or action of **4 :** to block by clogging

[2]**choke** *n* **1 :** the act or sound of choking **2 :** something that chokes

choke•cher•ry *n, pl* **choke•cher•ries :** a wild cherry tree with long clusters of reddish black fruits that pucker the mouth

chol•era *n* **:** a dangerous infectious disease of Asian origin in which violent vomiting and dysentery are present

choose *vb* **chose; cho•sen; choos•ing 1 :** to select freely and after careful thought **2 :** DECIDE 3 **3 :** to see fit

choosy *adj* **choos•i•er; choos•i•est :** careful in making choices

[1]**chop** *vb* **chopped; chop•ping 1 :** to cut by striking especially over and over with something sharp **2 :** to cut into small pieces **:** MINCE **3 :** to strike quickly or again and again

[2]**chop** *n* **1 :** a sharp downward blow or stroke (as with an ax) **2 :** a small cut of meat often including a part of a rib **3 :** a short quick motion (as of a wave)

chop•per *n* **1 :** someone or something that chops **2 :** HELICOPTER

[1]**chop•py** *adj* **chop•pi•er; chop•pi•est :** frequently changing direction

[2]**choppy** *adj* **chop•pi•er; chop•pi•est 1 :** rough with small waves **2 :** JERKY

chops *n pl* **:** the fleshy covering of the jaws

chop•stick *n* **:** one of two thin sticks used chiefly in Asian countries to lift food to the mouth

cho•ral *adj* **:** of, relating to, or sung or recited by a chorus or choir or in chorus

cho•rale *n* **1 :** a hymn sung by the choir or congregation at a church service **2 :** CHORUS 1

[1]**chord** *n* **:** a group of tones sounded together to form harmony

[2]**chord** *n* **:** a straight line joining two points on a curve

chore *n* **1 chores** *pl* **:** the regular light work about a home or farm **2 :** an ordinary task **3 :** a dull, unpleasant, or difficult task

cho•re•og•ra•phy *n* **:** the art of dancing or of arranging dances and especially ballets — **cho•re•og•ra•pher** *n*

cho•ris•ter *n* **:** a singer in a choir

chor•tle *vb* **chor•tled; chor•tling :** to chuckle especially in satisfaction

[1]**cho•rus** *n* **1 :** a group of singers **:** CHOIR **2 :** a group of dancers and singers (as in a musical comedy) **3 :** a part of a song or hymn that is repeated every so often **:** REFRAIN **4 :** a song meant to be sung by a group **:** group singing **5 :** sounds uttered by a group of persons or animals together

[2]**chorus** *vb* **:** to speak, sing, or sound at the same time or together

chose *past of* CHOOSE

cho•sen *adj* **1 :** picked to be given favor or special privilege **2 :** picked by God for special protection

chow *n* **:** a muscular dog with a blue-black tongue, a short tail curled close to the back, straight legs, and a thick coat

chow•der *n* **:** a soup or stew made of fish, clams, or a vegetable usually simmered in milk

Christ *n* **:** JESUS

chris•ten *vb* **1 :** BAPTIZE 1 **2 :** to give a name to at baptism **3 :** to name or dedicate (as a ship) in a ceremony like that of baptism

Chris•ten•dom *n* **1 :** the entire body of Christians **2 :** the part of the world in which Christianity is most common

chris•ten•ing *n* : BAPTISM

1**Chris•tian** *n* **1** : a person who believes in Jesus and follows his teachings **2** : a member of a Christian church

2**Christian** *adj* **1** : of or relating to Jesus or the religion based on his teachings **2** : of or relating to Christians **3** : being what a Christian should be or do

Chris•tian•i•ty *n* **1** : CHRISTENDOM 1 **2** : the religion of Christians

Christian name *n* : the personal name given to a person at birth or christening

Christ•mas *n* : December 25 celebrated in honor of the birth of Christ

Christ•mas•tide *n* : the season of Christmas

Christmas tree *n* : a usually evergreen tree decorated at Christmas

chro•mat•ic scale *n* : a musical scale that has all half steps

chrome *n* **1** : CHROMIUM **2** : something plated with an alloy of chromium

chro•mi•um *n* : a bluish white metallic chemical element used especially in alloys

chro•mo•some *n* : one of the rodlike bodies of a cell nucleus that contain genes and divide when the cell divides

chron•ic *adj* **1** : continuing for a long time or returning often **2** : HABITUAL 2 — **chron•i•cal•ly** *adv*

1**chron•i•cle** *n* : an account of events in the order of their happening : HISTORY

2**chronicle** *vb* **chron•i•cled; chron•i•cling** : to record in or as if in a chronicle

chron•o•log•i•cal *adj* : arranged in or according to the order of time — **chron•o•log•i•cal•ly** *adv*

chrys•a•lis *n* : a moth or butterfly pupa that is enclosed in a firm protective case

chry•san•the•mum *n* : a plant related to the daisies that has deeply notched leaves and brightly colored often double flower heads

chub•by *adj* **chub•bi•er; chub•bi•est** : 4PLUMP

1**chuck** *vb* **1** : to give a pat or tap to **2** : 1TOSS 2

2**chuck** *n* **1** : a pat or nudge under the chin **2** : 2TOSS

chuck–full *variant of* CHOCK-FULL

1**chuck•le** *vb* **chuck•led; chuck•ling** : to laugh in a quiet way

2**chuckle** *n* : a low quiet laugh

chuck wagon *n* : a wagon carrying a stove and food for cooking

1**chug** *n* : a dull explosive sound

2**chug** *vb* **chugged; chug•ging** : to move with chugs

1**chum** *n* : a close friend : PAL

2**chum** *vb* **chummed; chum•ming** : to be chums

chum•my *adj* **chum•mi•er; chum•mi•est** : being on close friendly terms : SOCIABLE

chunk *n* : a short thick piece (as of ice)

chunky *adj* **chunk•i•er; chunk•i•est** : STOCKY

church *n* **1** : a building for public worship and especially Christian worship **2** : an organized body of religious believers **3** : public worship

church•yard *n* : a yard that belongs to a church and is often used as a burial ground

1**churn** *n* : a container in which milk or cream is stirred or shaken in making butter

2**churn** *vb* **1** : to stir or shake in a churn (as in making butter) **2** : to stir or shake violently

chute *n* **1** : a sloping plane, trough, or passage down or through which things are slid or dropped **2** : 1PARACHUTE

ci•ca•da *n* : an insect that has transparent wings and a stout body and is related to the true bugs

-cide *n suffix* **1** : killer **2** : killing

ci•der *n* : the juice pressed out of fruit (as apples) and used especially as a drink and in making vinegar

ci•gar *n* : a small roll of tobacco leaf for smoking

cig•a•rette *n* : a small roll of cut tobacco wrapped in paper for smoking

cil•i•um *n, pl* **cil•ia** : any of the structures on the surface of some cells that look like tiny flexible eyelashes

1**cinch** *n* **1** : GIRTH 1 **2** : a sure or an easy thing

2**cinch** *vb* **1** : to fasten or tighten a girth on **2** : to fasten with or as if with a girth

cin•cho•na *n* : a South American tree whose bark yields quinine

cin•der *n* **1** : SLAG **2** : a piece of partly burned coal or wood that is not burning **3** : EMBER **4 cinders** *pl* : 2ASH 1

cin•e•ma *n* **1** : a movie theater **2** : the movie industry

cin•na•mon *n* : a spice made from the fragrant bark of tropical trees related to the Old World laurel

1**ci•pher** *n* **1** : ZERO 1 **2** : an unimportant or worthless person : NONENTITY **3** : a method of secret writing or the alphabet or letters and symbols used in such writing **4** : a message in code

2**cipher** *vb* : to use figures in doing a problem in arithmetic : CALCULATE

1**cir•cle** *n* **1** : a closed curve every point of which is equally distant from a central point within it : the space inside such a closed curve **2** : something in the form of a circle or part of a circle **3** : 1CYCLE 2, ROUND **4**

: a group of people sharing a common interest

²**circle** *vb* **cir•cled; cir•cling** **1 :** to enclose in or as if in a circle **2 :** to move or revolve around **3 :** to move in or as if in a circle

cir•cuit *n* **1 :** a boundary line around an area **2 :** an enclosed space **3 :** a moving around (as in a circle) **4 :** a traveling from place to place in an area (as by a judge) so as to stop in each place at a certain time **:** a course so traveled **5 :** the complete path of an electric current **6 :** a group of electronic parts **7 :** a chain of theaters at which stage shows are shown in turn

cir•cu•i•tous *adj* **1 :** having a circular or winding course **2 :** not saying what one means in simple and sincere language

¹**cir•cu•lar** *adj* **1 :** having the form of a circle **:** ROUND **2 :** passing or going around in a circle **3 :** CIRCUITOUS 2 **4 :** sent around to a number of persons

²**circular** *n* **:** a printed notice or advertisement given or sent to many people

cir•cu•late *vb* **cir•cu•lat•ed; cir•cu•lat•ing** **1 :** to move around in a course **2 :** to pass or be passed from place to place or from person to person

cir•cu•la•tion *n* **1 :** motion around in a course **2 :** passage from place to place or person to person **3 :** the average number of copies (as of a newspaper) sold in a given period

cir•cu•la•to•ry *adj* **:** of or relating to circulation (as of the blood)

circum- *prefix* **:** around **:** about

cir•cum•fer•ence *n* **1 :** the line that goes around a circle **2 :** a boundary line or circuit enclosing an area **3 :** the distance around something

cir•cum•nav•i•gate *vb* **cir•cum•nav•i•gat•ed; cir•cum•nav•i•gat•ing** **:** to go completely around (as the earth) especially by water

cir•cum•po•lar *adj* **1 :** continually visible above the horizon **2 :** surrounding or found near the north pole or south pole

cir•cum•stance *n* **1 :** a fact or event that must be considered along with another fact or event **2 circumstances** *pl* **:** conditions at a certain time or place **3 circumstances** *pl* **:** situation with regard to wealth **4 :** ¹CHANCE 1, FATE

cir•cum•vent *vb* **1 :** to go around **:** BYPASS **2 :** to get the better of or avoid the force or effect of especially by trickery

cir•cus *n* **1 :** a show that usually travels from place to place and that has a variety of exhibitions including riding, acrobatic feats, wild animal displays, and the performances of jugglers and clowns **2 :** a circus performance **3 :** the performers and equipment of a circus

cir•rus *n, pl* **cir•ri** **:** a thin white cloud of tiny ice crystals that forms at a very high altitude

cis•tern *n* **:** an artificial reservoir or tank for storing water usually underground

cit•a•del *n* **1 :** a fortress that sits high above a city **2 :** a strong fortress

ci•ta•tion *n* **1 :** an act or instance of quoting **2 :** QUOTATION 1 **3 :** a formal statement of what a person did to be chosen to receive an award

cite *vb* **cit•ed; cit•ing** **1 :** to quote as an example, authority, or proof **2 :** to refer to especially in praise

cit•i•zen *n* **1 :** a person who lives in a city or town **2 :** a person who owes loyalty to a government and is protected by it

cit•i•zen•ry *n* **:** the whole body of citizens

cit•i•zen•ship *n* **:** the state of being a citizen

cit•ron *n* **1 :** a citrus fruit like the smaller lemon and having a thick rind that is preserved for use in cakes and puddings **2 :** a small hard watermelon used especially in pickles and preserves

cit•rus *adj* **:** of or relating to a group of often thorny trees and shrubs of warm regions whose fruits include the lemon, lime, orange, and grapefruit

city *n, pl* **cit•ies** **1 :** a place in which people live that is larger or more important than a town **2 :** the people of a city

civ•ic *adj* **:** of or relating to a citizen, a city, or citizenship

civ•ics *n* **:** a study of the rights and duties of citizens

civ•il *adj* **1 :** of or relating to citizens **2 :** of or relating to the state **3 :** of or relating to ordinary or government affairs rather than to those of the military or the church **4 :** polite without being friendly **5 :** relating to court action between individuals having to do with private rights rather than criminal action

¹**ci•vil•ian** *n* **:** a person not on active duty in a military, police, or fire-fighting force

²**civilian** *adj* **:** of or relating to a civilian

ci•vil•i•ty *n, pl* **ci•vil•i•ties** **1 :** civil behavior **2 :** COURTESY 1

civ•i•li•za•tion *n* **1 :** an advanced stage (as in art, science, and government) of social development **2 :** the way of life of a people

civ•i•lize *vb* **civ•i•lized; civ•i•liz•ing** **:** to cause to develop out of a primitive state

civil service *n* **:** the branch of a government that takes care of the business of running a state but that does not include the lawmaking branch, the military, or the court system

civil war *n* **:** a war between opposing groups of citizens of the same country

¹clack *vb* **1 :** PRATTLE **2 :** to make or cause to make a clatter

²clack *n* **1 :** rapid continuous talk **:** CHATTER **2 :** a sound of clacking

clad *adj* **:** being covered **:** wearing clothes

¹claim *vb* **1 :** to ask for as rightfully belonging to oneself **2 :** to call for **:** REQUIRE **3 :** to state as a fact **:** MAINTAIN **4 :** to make a claim

²claim *n* **1 :** a demand for something due or believed to be due **2 :** a right to something **3 :** a statement that may be doubted **4 :** something (as an area of land) claimed as one's own

¹clam *n* **:** a shellfish with a soft body and a hinged double shell

²clam *vb* **clammed; clam•ming :** to dig or gather clams

clam•bake *n* **:** an outing where food is cooked usually on heated rocks covered by seaweed

clam•ber *vb* **:** to climb in an awkward way (as by scrambling)

clam•my *adj* **clam•mi•er; clam•mi•est :** unpleasantly damp, soft, sticky, and usually cool — **clam•mi•ly** *adv* — **clam•mi•ness** *n*

¹clam•or *n* **1 :** a noisy shouting **2 :** a loud continous noise **3 :** strong and active protest or demand

²clamor *vb* **:** to make a clamor

clam•or•ous *adj* **:** full of clamor **:** very noisy

¹clamp *n* **:** a device that holds or presses parts together firmly

²clamp *vb* **:** to fasten or to hold together with or as if with a clamp

clan *n* **1 :** a group (as in the Scottish Highlands) made up of households whose heads claim to have a common ancestor **2 :** a group of persons united by some common interest

¹clang *vb* **:** to make or cause to make a loud ringing sound

²clang *n* **:** a loud ringing sound like that made by pieces of metal striking together

¹clank *vb* **1 :** to make or cause to make a clank or series of clanks **2 :** to move with a clank

²clank *n* **:** a sharp short ringing sound

¹clap *vb* **clapped; clap•ping 1 :** to strike noisily **:** SLAM, BANG **2 :** to strike (one's hands) together again and again in applause **3 :** to strike with the open hand **4 :** to put or place quickly or with force

²clap *n* **1 :** a loud noisy crash made by or as if by the striking together of two hard surfaces **2 :** a hard or a friendly slap

clap•board *n* **:** a narrow board thicker at one edge than at the other used as siding for a building

clap•per *n* **:** one (as the tongue of a bell) that makes a clapping sound

clar•i•fy *vb* **clar•i•fied; clar•i•fy•ing 1 :** to make or to become pure or clear **2 :** to make or become more easily understood

clar•i•net *n* **:** a woodwind instrument in the form of a tube with finger holes and keys

clar•i•on *adj* **:** being loud and clear

clar•i•ty *n* **:** clear quality or state

¹clash *vb* **1 :** to make or cause to make a clash **2 :** to come into conflict **3 :** to not match well

²clash *n* **1 :** a loud sharp sound usually of metal striking metal **2 :** a struggle or strong disagreement

¹clasp *n* **1 :** a device for holding together objects or parts of something **2 :** ²GRASP 1, GRIP **3 :** ²EMBRACE

²clasp *vb* **1 :** to fasten with or as if with a clasp **2 :** ¹EMBRACE 1 **3 :** ¹GRASP 1

¹class *n* **1 :** a group of pupils meeting at set times for study or instruction **2 :** the period during which a study group meets **3 :** a course of instruction **4 :** a body of students who are to graduate at the same time **5 :** a group or rank of society **6 :** a group of plants or animals that ranks above the order and below the phylum or division in scientific classification **7 :** a grouping or standing (as of goods or services) based on quality

²class *vb* **:** CLASSIFY

¹clas•sic *adj* **1 :** serving as a standard of excellence **2 :** fashionable year after year **3 :** of or relating to the ancient Greeks and Romans or their culture **4 :** being very good or typical of its kind

²classic *n* **1 :** a written work or author of ancient Greece or Rome **2 :** a great work of art **3 :** something regarded as outstanding of its kind

clas•si•cal *adj* **1 :** of or relating to the classics of literature or art and especially to the ancient Greek and Roman classics **2 :** of or relating to serious music in the European tradition **3 :** concerned with a general study of the arts and sciences

clas•si•fi•ca•tion *n* **1 :** the act of classifying or arranging in classes **2 :** an arrangement in classes

clas•si•fy *vb* **clas•si•fied; clas•si•fy•ing :** to group in classes

class•mate *n* **:** a member of the same class in a school or college

class•room *n* **:** a room in a school or college in which classes meet

¹clat•ter *vb* **1 :** to make or cause to make a rattling sound **2 :** to move or go with a clatter

²clatter *n* **1 :** a rattling sound (as of hard objects striking together) **2 :** COMMOTION

clause *n* **1 :** a separate part of a document (as a will) **2 :** a group of words having its own subject and predicate but forming only part of a complete sentence
clav•i•cle *n* **:** COLLARBONE
[1]**claw** *n* **1 :** a sharp usually thin and curved nail on the finger or toe of an animal (as a cat or bird) **2 :** the end of a limb of a lower animal (as an insect, scorpion, or lobster) that is pointed or like pincers **3 :** something like a claw in shape or use
[2]**claw** *vb* **:** to scratch, seize, or dig with claws
clay *n* **1 :** an earthy material that is sticky and easily molded when wet and hard when baked **2 :** a plastic substance used like clay for modeling
[1]**clean** *adj* **1 :** free of dirt or evil **2 :** free of objectionable behavior or language **3 :** THOROUGH 1, COMPLETE **4 :** having a simple graceful form **:** TRIM **5 :** [1]SMOOTH 1
[2]**clean** *adv* **1 :** so as to clean **2 :** in a clean way **3 :** all the way
[3]**clean** *vb* **:** to make or become clean — **clean•er** *n*
clean•li•ness *n* **:** the condition of being clean **:** the habit of keeping clean
[1]**clean•ly** *adv* **:** in a clean way
[2]**clean•ly** *adj* **clean•li•er; clean•li•est** **1 :** careful to keep clean **2 :** kept clean
cleanse *vb* **cleansed; cleans•ing :** to make clean
cleans•er *n* **:** a substance (as a scouring powder) used for cleaning
[1]**clear** *adj* **1 :** BRIGHT 1, LUMINOUS **2 :** free of clouds, haze, or mist **3 :** UNTROUBLED **4 :** free of blemishes **5 :** easily seen through **6 :** easily heard, seen, or understood **7 :** free from doubt **:** SURE **8 :** INNOCENT **9 :** not blocked or limited — **clear•ly** *adv* — **clear•ness** *n*
[2]**clear** *adv* **1 :** in a clear manner **2 :** all the way
[3]**clear** *vb* **1 :** to make or become clear **2 :** to go away **:** DISPERSE **3 :** to free from blame **4 :** to approve or be approved by **5 :** EXPLAIN 1 **6 :** to free of things blocking **7 :** to get rid of **:** REMOVE **8 :** [4]NET **9 :** to go over or by without touching
[4]**clear** *n* **:** a clear space or part — **in the clear :** free from guilt or suspicion
clear•ance *n* **1 :** the act or process of clearing **2 :** the distance by which one object avoids hitting or touching another
clear•ing *n* **:** an area of land from which trees and bushes have all been removed
cleat *n* **1 :** a wooden or metal device used to fasten a line or a rope **2 :** a strip or projection fastened on or across something to give strength or a place to hold or to prevent slipping
cleav•age *n* **1 :** the tendency of a rock or mineral to split readily in one or more directions **2 :** the action of cleaving **3 :** the state of being cleft
[1]**cleave** *vb* **cleaved** *or* **clove; cleav•ing :** to cling to a person or thing closely
[2]**cleave** *vb* **cleaved** *or* **cleft** *or* **clove; cleaved** *or* **cleft** *or* **clo•ven; cleav•ing :** to divide by or as if by a cutting blow **:** SPLIT
cleav•er *n* **:** a heavy knife used for cutting up meat
clef *n* **:** a sign placed on the staff in writing music to show what pitch is represented by each line and space
[1]**cleft** *n* **1 :** a space or opening made by splitting or cracking **:** CREVICE **2 :** [1]NOTCH 1
[2]**cleft** *adj* **:** partly split or divided
clem•en•cy *n, pl* **clemencies** **1 :** MERCY 1 **2 :** an act of mercy
clench *vb* **1 :** to hold tightly **:** CLUTCH **2 :** to set or close tightly
cler•gy *n, pl* **clergies :** the group of religious officials (as priests, ministers, and rabbis) specially prepared and authorized to lead religious services
cler•gy•man *n, pl* **cler•gy•men :** a member of the clergy
cler•i•cal *adj* **1 :** of or relating to the clergy **2 :** of or relating to a clerk or office worker
[1]**clerk** *n* **1 :** a person whose job is to keep records or accounts **2 :** a salesperson in a store
[2]**clerk** *vb* **:** to act or work as a clerk
clev•er *adj* **1 :** showing skill especially in using one's hands **2 :** having a quick inventive mind **3 :** showing wit or imagination — **clev•er•ly** *adv* — **clev•er•ness** *n*
[1]**click** *vb* **1 :** to make or cause to make a click **2 :** to fit in or work together smoothly **3 :** to select or make a selection especially on a computer by pressing a button on a control device (as a mouse)
[2]**click** *n* **:** a slight sharp noise
click•er *n* **:** REMOTE CONTROL 2
cli•ent *n* **:** a person who uses the professional advice or services of another
cli•en•tele *n* **:** a group of clients
cliff *n* **:** a high steep surface of rock
cli•mate *n* **:** the average weather conditions of a place over a period of years
cli•max *n* **:** the time or part of something that is of greatest interest, excitement, or importance
[1]**climb** *vb* **1 :** to rise little by little to a higher point **2 :** to go up or down often with the help of the hands in holding or pulling **3 :** to go upward in growing (as by winding around something) — **climb•er** *n*
[2]**climb** *n* **1 :** a place where climbing is necessary **2 :** the act of climbing

clime *n* : CLIMATE

[1]clinch *vb* **1 :** to turn over or flatten the end of (as a nail sticking out of a board) **2 :** to fasten by clinching **3 :** to show to be certain or true

[2]clinch *n* **:** a fastening with a clinched nail, bolt, or rivet **:** the clinched part of a nail, bolt, or rivet

cling *vb* **clung; cling·ing 1 :** to hold fast or stick closely to a surface **2 :** to hold fast by grasping or winding around **3 :** to remain close

clin·ic *n* **1 :** a group meeting for teaching a certain skill and working on individual problems **2 :** a place where people can receive medical examinations and usually treatment for minor ailments

[1]clink *vb* **:** to make or cause to make a slight short sound like that of metal being struck

[2]clink *n* **:** a clinking sound

[1]clip *vb* **clipped; clip·ping :** to fasten with a clip

[2]clip *n* **:** a device that holds or hooks

[3]clip *vb* **clipped; clip·ping 1 :** to shorten or remove by cutting (as with shears or scissors) **2 :** to cut off or trim the hair or wool of

[4]clip *n* **1 :** an instrument with two blades for cutting the nails **2 :** a sharp blow **3 :** a rapid pace

clip art *n* **:** ready-made illustrations sold in books or as software from which they may be taken for use in a printed work

clip·board *n* **:** a small board with a clip at the top for holding papers

clip·per *n* **1 :** a person who clips **2 clip·pers** *pl* **:** a device used for clipping especially hair or nails **3 :** a fast sailing ship with usually three tall masts and large square sails

clip·ping *n* **:** something cut out or off

clique *n* **:** a small group of people that keep out outsiders

[1]cloak *n* **1 :** a long loose outer garment **2 :** something that hides or covers

[2]cloak *vb* **:** to cover or hide with a cloak

cloak·room *n* **:** a room (as in a school) in which coats and hats may be kept

[1]clock *n* **:** a device for measuring or telling the time and especially one not meant to be worn or carried by a person

[2]clock *vb* **1 :** to time (as a person or a piece of work) by a timing device **2 :** to show (as time or speed) on a recording device

clock·wise *adv or adj* **:** in the direction in which the hands of a clock turn

clock·work *n* **:** machinery (as in mechanical toys) like that which makes clocks go

clod *n* **1 :** a lump or mass especially of earth or clay **2 :** a clumsy or stupid person

[1]clog *n* **1 :** something that hinders or holds back **2 :** a shoe having a thick usually wooden sole

[2]clog *vb* **clogged; clog·ging :** to make passage through difficult or impossible **:** PLUG

[1]clois·ter *n* **1 :** MONASTERY, CONVENT **2 :** a covered usually arched passage along or around the walls of a court

[2]cloister *vb* **1 :** to shut away from the world **2 :** to surround with a cloister

clop *n* **:** a sound like that of a hoof against pavement

[1]close *vb* **closed; clos·ing 1 :** to stop up **:** prevent passage through **2 :** to fill or cause to fill an opening **3 :** to bring or come to an end **4 :** to end the operation of **5 :** to bring the parts or edges of together **6 :** [1]APPROACH 1

[2]close *n* **:** the point at which something ends

[3]close *adj* **clos·er; clos·est 1 :** having little space in which to move **2 :** SECRETIVE **3 :** lacking fresh or moving air **4 :** not generous **5 :** not far apart in space, time, degree, or effect **6 :** [1]SHORT 1 **7 :** very like **8 :** having a strong liking each one for the other **9 :** strict and careful in attention to details **10 :** decided by a narrow margin — **close·ly** *adv* — **close·ness** *n*

[4]close *adv* **:** [1]NEAR 1

close call *n* **:** a barely successful escape from a difficult or dangerous situation

closed *adj* **1 :** not open **2 :** having mathematical elements that when subjected to an operation produce only elements of the same set

[1]clos·et *n* **1 :** a small room for privacy **2 :** a small room for clothing or for supplies for the house

[2]closet *vb* **1 :** to shut up in or as if in a closet **2 :** to take into a private room for an interview

close–up *n* **:** a photograph taken at close range

clo·sure *n* **1 :** an act of closing **2 :** the condition of being closed

[1]clot *n* **:** a lump made by some substance getting thicker and sticking together

[2]clot *vb* **clot·ted; clot·ting :** to thicken into a clot

cloth *n, pl* **cloths 1 :** a woven or knitted material (as of cotton or nylon) **2 :** a piece of cloth for a certain use **3 :** TABLECLOTH

clothe *vb* **clothed** *or* **clad; cloth·ing 1 :** to cover with or as if with clothing **:** DRESS **2 :** to provide with clothes **3 :** to express in a certain way

clothes *n pl* **:** CLOTHING 1

clothes moth *n* **:** a small yellowish moth whose larvae feed on wool, fur, and feathers

clothes·pin *n* **:** a peg (as of wood) with the

lower part slit or a clamp for holding clothes in place on a line

cloth·ing *n* **1 :** covering for the human body **2 :** COVERING

1cloud *n* **1 :** a visible mass of tiny bits of water or ice hanging in the air usually high above the earth **2 :** a visible mass of small particles in the air **3 :** something thought to be like a cloud — **cloud·less** *adj*

2cloud *vb* **1 :** to make or become cloudy **2 :** to darken or hide as if by a cloud

cloud·burst *n* **:** a sudden heavy rainfall

cloudy *adj* **cloud·i·er; cloud·i·est 1 :** overspread with clouds **2 :** showing confusion **3 :** not clear — **cloud·i·ness** *n*

1clout *n* **:** a blow especially with the hand

2clout *vb* **:** to hit hard

1clove *n* **:** the dried flower bud of a tropical tree used as a spice

2clove *past of* CLEAVE

clo·ven *past participle of* 2CLEAVE

cloven hoof *n* **:** a hoof (as of a cow) with the front part divided into two sections

clo·ver *n* **:** any of various plants grown for hay and pasture that have leaves with three leaflets and usually roundish red, white, yellow, or purple flower heads

1clown *n* **1 :** a rude and often stupid person **2 :** a performer (as in a play or circus) who entertains by playing tricks and who usually wears comical clothes and makeup

2clown *vb* **:** to act like a clown **:** SHOW OFF

1club *n* **1 :** a heavy usually wooden stick used as a weapon **2 :** a stick or bat used to hit a ball in various games **3 :** a group of people associated because of a shared interest **4 :** the meeting place of a club

2club *vb* **clubbed; club·bing :** to beat or strike with or as if with a club

club·house *n* **1 :** a house used by a club **2 :** locker rooms used by an athletic team

club moss *n* **:** a low often trailing evergreen plant that forms spores instead of seeds

1cluck *vb* **:** to make or call with a cluck

2cluck *n* **:** the call of a hen especially to her chicks

clue *n* **:** something that helps a person to find something or to solve a mystery

1clump *n* **1 :** a group of things clustered together **2 :** a cluster or lump of something **3 :** a heavy tramping sound

2clump *vb* **1 :** to walk clumsily and noisily **2 :** to form or cause to form clumps

clum·sy *adj* **clum·si·er; clum·si·est 1 :** lacking skill or grace in movement **2 :** not knowing how to get along with others **3 :** badly or awkwardly made or done — **clum·si·ly** *adv* — **clum·si·ness** *n*

clung *past of* CLING

1clus·ter *n* **:** a number of similar things growing, collected, or grouped closely together **:** BUNCH

2cluster *vb* **:** to grow, collect, or assemble in a cluster

1clutch *vb* **1 :** to grasp or hold tightly with or as if with the hands or claws **2 :** to make a grab

2clutch *n* **1 :** the state of being clutched **2 :** a device for gripping an object **3 :** a coupling for connecting and disconnecting a driving and a driven part in machinery **4 :** a lever or pedal operating a clutch

1clut·ter *vb* **:** to throw into disorder **:** fill or cover with scattered things

2clutter *n* **:** a crowded or confused collection **:** DISORDER

co- *prefix* **1 :** with **:** together **:** joint **:** jointly **2 :** in or to the same degree **3 :** fellow **:** partner

1coach *n* **1 :** a large carriage that has four wheels and a raised seat outside in front for the driver and is drawn by horses **2 :** a railroad passenger car without berths **3 :** a class of passenger transportation in an airplane at a lower fare than first class **4 :** a person who teaches students individually **5 :** a person who instructs or trains a performer or team

2coach *vb* **:** to act as coach

coach·man *n, pl* **coach·men :** a person whose business is driving a coach or carriage

co·ag·u·late *vb* **co·ag·u·lat·ed; co·ag·u·lat·ing :** to gather into a thick compact mass **:** CLOT

coal *n* **1 :** a piece of glowing or charred wood **:** EMBER **2 :** a black solid mineral substance that is formed by the partial decay of vegetable matter under the influence of moisture and often increased pressure and temperature within the earth and is mined for use as a fuel

coarse *adj* **1 :** of poor or ordinary quality **2 :** made up of large particles **3 :** being harsh or rough **4 :** crude in taste, manners, or language — **coarse·ly** *adv* — **coarse·ness** *n*

coars·en *vb* **:** to make or become coarse

1coast *n* **:** the land near a shore

2coast *vb* **1 :** to slide downhill by the force of gravity over snow or ice **2 :** to move along (as on a bicycle when not pedaling) without applying power

coast·al *adj* **:** of, relating to, or located on, near, or along a coast

coast·er *n* **1 :** someone or something that coasts **2 :** a sled or small wagon used in coasting

coast guard *n* **:** a military force that guards a coast

[1]coat *n* **1 :** an outer garment that differs in length and style according to fashion or use **2 :** the outer covering (as fur or feathers) of an animal **3 :** a layer of material covering a surface — **coat•ed** *adj*

[2]coat *vb* **:** to cover with a coat or covering

coat•ing *n* **:** [1]COAT 3, COVERING

coat of arms : the heraldic arms belonging to a person, family, or group or a representation of these (as on a shield)

coat of mail : a garment of metal scales or rings worn long ago as armor

co•au•thor *n* **:** an author who works with another author

coax *vb* **1 :** to influence by gentle urging, special attention, or flattering **2 :** to get or win by means of gentle urging or flattery

cob *n* **:** CORNCOB

co•balt *n* **:** a tough shiny silvery white metallic chemical element found with iron and nickel

cob•bled *adj* **:** paved or covered with cobblestones

cob•bler *n* **1 :** a person who mends or makes shoes **2 :** a fruit pie with a thick upper crust and no bottom crust that is baked in a deep dish

cob•ble•stone *n* **:** a naturally rounded stone larger than a pebble and smaller than a boulder once used in paving streets

co•bra *n* **:** a very poisonous snake of Asia and Africa that puffs out the skin around its neck into a hood when excited

cob•web *n* **1 :** the network spread by a spider **:** SPIDERWEB **2 :** tangles of threads of a cobweb

co•caine *n* **:** a habit-forming drug obtained from the leaves of a South American shrub and sometimes used as a medicine to deaden pain

coc•cus *n, pl* **coc•ci :** a bacterium shaped like a ball

[1]cock *n* **1 :** a male bird **:** ROOSTER **2 :** a faucet or valve for controlling the flow of a liquid or a gas **3 :** a cocked position of the hammer of a gun

[2]cock *vb* **1 :** to draw back the hammer of (a gun) in readiness for firing **2 :** to set or draw back in readiness for some action **3 :** to turn or tip upward or to one side

[3]cock *n* **:** the act of tipping at an angle **:** TILT

cock•a•too *n, pl* **cock•a•toos :** any of several large, noisy, and usually brightly colored crested parrots mostly of Australia

cock•eyed *adj* **1 :** tilted to one side **2 :** FOOLISH

cock•le *n* **:** an edible shellfish with a shell that has two parts and is shaped like a heart

cock•le•bur *n* **:** a plant with prickly fruit that is related to the thistles

cock•le•shell *n* **:** a shell of a cockle

cock•pit *n* **1 :** an open space in the deck from which a small boat (as a yacht) is steered **2 :** a space in an airplane for the pilot or pilot and passengers or pilot and crew

cock•roach *n* **:** a troublesome insect found in houses and ships and active chiefly at night

cocky *adj* **cock•i•er; cock•i•est :** very sure of oneself **:** boldly self-confident

co•coa *n* **1 :** chocolate ground to a powder after some of its fat is removed **2 :** a drink made from cocoa powder

co•co•nut *n* **:** a large nutlike fruit that has a thick husk and grows on a tall tropical palm (**coconut palm**)

co•coon *n* **:** the silky covering which caterpillars make around themselves and in which they are protected while changing into butterflies or moths

cod *n, pl* **cod :** a large food fish found in the deep colder parts of the northern Atlantic Ocean

cod•dle *vb* **cod•dled; cod•dling 1 :** to cook slowly in water below the boiling point **2 :** to treat with very much and usually too much care **:** PAMPER

[1]code *n* **1 :** a collection of laws arranged in some orderly way **2 :** a system of rules or principles **3 :** a system of signals or letters and symbols with special meanings used for sending messages **4 :** GENETIC CODE

[2]code *vb* **cod•ed; cod•ing :** to put in the form of a code

cod•fish *n, pl* **codfish** *or* **cod•fish•es :** COD

cod•ger *n* **:** an odd or cranky man

co•erce *vb* **co•erced; co•erc•ing :** [2]FORCE 1, COMPEL

cof•fee *n* **1 :** a drink made from the roasted and ground seeds of a tropical plant **2 :** the seeds of the coffee plant

cof•fee•pot *n* **:** a covered utensil for preparing or serving coffee

coffee table *n* **:** a low table usually placed in front of a sofa

cof•fer *n* **:** a box used especially for holding money and valuables

cof•fin *n* **:** a box or case to hold a dead body

cog *n* **:** a tooth on the rim of a wheel or gear

cog•i•tate *vb* **cog•i•tat•ed; cog•i•tat•ing :** to think over **:** PONDER

cog•i•ta•tion *n* **:** MEDITATION

cog•wheel *n* **:** a wheel with cogs on the rim

co•he•sion *n* **1 :** the action of sticking together **2 :** the force of attraction between the molecules in a mass

[1]coil *vb* **1 :** to wind into rings or a spiral **2 :** to form or lie in a coil

[2]coil *n* **1 :** a circle, a series of circles, or a

spiral made by coiling **2 :** something coiled

[1]**coin** *n* **1 :** a piece of metal put out by government authority as money **2 :** metal money

[2]**coin** *vb* **1 :** to make coins especially by stamping pieces of metal **:** MINT **2 :** to make metal (as gold or silver) into coins **3 :** to make up (a new word or phrase)

coin•age *n* **1 :** the act or process of coining **2 :** something coined

co•in•cide *vb* **co•in•cid•ed; co•in•cid•ing 1 :** to occupy the same space **2 :** to happen at the same time **3 :** to agree exactly

co•in•ci•dence *n* **1 :** a coinciding in space or time **2 :** two things that happen at the same time by accident but seem to have some connection

coke *n* **:** gray lumps of fuel made by heating soft coal in a closed chamber until some of its gases have passed off

col- — see COM-

col•an•der *n* **:** a utensil with small holes for draining foods

[1]**cold** *adj* **1 :** having a low temperature or one much below normal **2 :** lacking warmth of feeling **:** UNFRIENDLY **3 :** suffering from lack of warmth — **cold•ly** *adv* — **cold•ness** *n*

[2]**cold** *n* **1 :** a condition of low temperature **:** cold weather **2 :** the bodily feeling produced by lack of warmth **:** CHILL **3 :** COMMON COLD

cold–blood•ed *adj* **1 :** lacking or showing a lack of normal human feelings **2 :** having a body temperature that varies with the temperature of the environment **3 :** sensitive to cold

co•le•us *n* **:** a plant of the mint family grown for its many-colored leaves

col•ic *n* **:** sharp pain in the bowels — **colicky** *adj*

col•i•se•um *n* **:** a large structure (as a stadium) for athletic contests or public entertainment

col•lab•o•rate *vb* **col•lab•o•rat•ed; col•lab•o•rat•ing 1 :** to work with others (as in writing a book) **2 :** to cooperate with an enemy force that has taken over one's country

col•lage *n* **:** a work of art made by gluing pieces of different materials to a flat surface

[1]**col•lapse** *vb* **col•lapsed; col•laps•ing 1 :** to break down completely **:** fall in **2 :** to shrink together suddenly **3 :** to suffer a physical or mental breakdown **4 :** to fold together

[2]**collapse** *n* **:** the act or an instance of collapsing **:** BREAKDOWN

col•laps•ible *adj* **:** capable of collapsing or possible to collapse

[1]**col•lar** *n* **1 :** a band, strap, or chain worn around the neck or the neckline of a garment **2 :** a part of the harness of draft animals fitted over the shoulders **3 :** something (as a ring to hold a pipe in place) that is like a collar — **col•lar•less** *adj*

[2]**collar** *vb* **1 :** to seize by or as if by the collar **:** CAPTURE, GRAB **2 :** to put a collar on

col•lar•bone *n* **:** a bone of the shoulder joined to the breastbone and the shoulder blade

col•league *n* **:** an associate in a profession **:** a fellow worker

col•lect *vb* **1 :** to bring or come together into one body or place **2 :** to gather from a number of sources **3 :** to gain or regain control of **4 :** to receive payment for

col•lect•ed *adj* **:** [3]CALM 2

col•lec•tion *n* **1 :** the act or process of gathering together **2 :** something collected and especially a group of objects gathered for study or exhibition **3 :** a gathering of money (as for charitable purposes)

col•lec•tive *adj* **1 :** having to do with a number of persons or things thought of as a whole **2 :** done or shared by a number of persons as a group — **col•lec•tive•ly** *adj*

col•lec•tor *n* **1 :** a person or thing that collects **2 :** a person whose business it is to collect money

col•lege *n* **:** a school higher than a high school

col•le•giate *adj* **1 :** having to do with a college **2 :** of, relating to, or characteristic of college students

col•lide *vb* **col•lid•ed; col•lid•ing 1 :** to strike against each other **2 :** [1]CLASH 2

col•lie *n* **:** a large usually long-coated dog of a Scottish breed used to herd sheep

col•li•sion *n* **:** an act or instance of colliding

col•lo•qui•al *adj* **:** used in or suited to familiar and informal conversation

col•lo•qui•al•ism *n* **:** a colloquial word or expression

co•logne *n* **:** a perfumed liquid made up of alcohol and fragrant oils

[1]**co•lon** *n* **:** the main part of the large intestine

[2]**colon** *n* **:** a punctuation mark : used mostly to call attention to what follows (as a list, explanation, or quotation)

col•o•nel *n* **:** a commissioned officer in the Army, Air Force, or Marine Corps ranking above a lieutenant colonel

[1]**co•lo•ni•al** *adj* **1 :** of, relating to, or characteristic of a colony **2** *often cap* **:** of or relating to the original thirteen colonies that formed the United States

[2]**colonial** *n* **:** a member of or a person living in a colony

col·o·nist *n* **1 :** a person living in a colony **2 :** a person who helps to found a colony

col·o·nize *vb* **col·o·nized; col·o·niz·ing 1 :** to establish a colony in or on **2 :** to settle in a colony

col·on·nade *n* **:** a row of columns usually supporting the base of a roof structure

col·o·ny *n, pl* **col·o·nies 1 :** a group of people sent out by a state to a new territory **:** the territory in which these people settle **2 :** a distant territory belonging to or under the control of a nation **3 :** a group of living things of one kind living together **4 :** a group of people with common qualities or interests located in close association

[1]**col·or** *n* **1 :** the appearance of a thing apart from size and shape when light strikes it **2 :** a hue other than black, white, or gray **3 :** outward show **:** APPEARANCE **4 :** the normal rosy tint of skin **5 :** [1]BLUSH **6 colors** *pl* **:** an identifying flag **7 colors** *pl* **:** military service **8 :** [1]INTEREST 6 **9 :** the quality of sound in music

[2]**color** *vb* **1 :** to give color to **2 :** to change the color of **3 :** MISREPRESENT **4 :** to take on or change color **:** BLUSH

col·or·ation *n* **:** use or arrangement of colors or shades **:** COLORING

color–blind *adj* **:** unable to tell some colors apart

col·ored *adj* **:** having color

col·or·ful *adj* **1 :** having bright colors **2 :** full of variety or interest

col·or·ing *n* **1 :** the act of applying colors **2 :** something that produces color **3 :** the effect produced by the use of color **4 :** natural color **:** COMPLEXION

col·or·less *adj* **1 :** having no color **2 :** WAN, PALE **3 :** [1]DULL 8

co·los·sal *adj* **:** very large **:** HUGE

colt *n* **1 :** FOAL **2 :** a young male horse

col·um·bine *n* **:** a plant related to the buttercups that has leaves with three parts and showy flowers usually with five petals ending in spurs

col·umn *n* **1 :** one of two or more vertical sections of a printed page **2 :** a special regular feature in a newspaper or magazine **3 :** a pillar supporting a roof or gallery **4 :** something like a column in shape, position, or use **5 :** a long straight row (as of soldiers)

col·um·nist *n* **:** a writer of a column in a newspaper or magazine

com- *or* **col-** *or* **con-** *prefix* **:** with **:** together **:** jointly — usually *com-* before *b, p,* or *m, col-* before *l* and *con-* before other sounds

co·ma *n* **:** a deep sleeplike state caused by sickness or injury

[1]**comb** *n* **1 :** a toothed implement used to smooth and arrange the hair or worn in the hair to hold it in place **2 :** a toothed instrument used for separating fibers (as of wool or flax) **3 :** a fleshy crest often with points suggesting teeth on the head of a fowl and some related birds **4 :** [1]HONEYCOMB 1

[2]**comb** *vb* **1 :** to smooth, arrange, or untangle with a comb **2 :** to search over or through carefully

[1]**com·bat** *n* **1 :** a fight or contest between individuals or groups **2 :** [1]CONFLICT 2 **3 :** active military fighting

[2]**com·bat** *vb* **com·bat·ed** *or* **com·bat·ted; com·bat·ing** *or* **com·bat·ting :** to fight with **:** fight against **:** OPPOSE

[1]**com·bat·ant** *n* **:** a person who takes part in a combat

[2]**combatant** *adj* **:** engaging in or ready to engage in combat

com·bi·na·tion *n* **1 :** a result or product of combining or being combined **2 :** a union of persons or groups for a purpose **3 :** a series of letters or numbers which when dialed by a disk on a lock will operate or open the lock **4 :** a union of different things

combination lock *n* **:** a lock with one or more dials or rings marked usually with numbers which are used to open the lock by moving them in a certain order to certain positions

[1]**com·bine** *vb* **com·bined; com·bin·ing :** to join together so as to make or to seem one thing **:** UNITE, MIX

[2]**com·bine** *n* **1 :** a union of persons or groups of persons especially for business or political benefits **2 :** a machine that harvests and threshes grain

com·bus·ti·ble *adj* **1 :** possible to burn **2 :** catching fire or burning easily

com·bus·tion *n* **:** the process of burning

come *vb* **came; come; com·ing 1 :** to move toward **:** APPROACH **2 :** to reach the point of being or becoming **3 :** to add up **:** AMOUNT **4 :** to take place **5 :** ORIGINATE 2, ARISE **6 :** to be available **7 :** [1]REACH 3

co·me·di·an *n* **1 :** an actor who plays comic roles **2 :** an amusing person

com·e·dy *n, pl* **com·e·dies 1 :** an amusing play that has a happy ending **2 :** an amusing and often ridiculous event

come·ly *adj* **come·li·er; come·li·est :** pleasing to the sight **:** good-looking

com·et *n* **:** a bright celestial body that develops a cloudy tail as it moves in an orbit around the sun

come to *vb* **:** to become conscious again

[1]**com•fort** *vb* **1 :** to give hope and strength to : CHEER **2 :** to ease the grief or trouble of

[2]**comfort** *n* **1 :** acts or words that comfort **2 :** the feeling of the one that is comforted **3 :** something that makes a person comfortable

com•fort•able *adj* **1 :** giving comfort and especially physical ease **2 :** more than what is needed **3 :** physically at ease — **com•fort•ably** *adj*

com•fort•er *n* **1 :** one that gives comfort **2 :** [1]QUILT

com•ic *adj* **1 :** of, relating to, or characteristic of comedy **2 :** FUNNY 1

com•i•cal *adj* **:** FUNNY 1, RIDICULOUS — **com•i•cal•ly** *adv*

comic book *n* **:** a magazine made up of a series of comic strips

comic strip *n* **:** a series of cartoons that tell a story or part of a story

com•ma *n* **:** a punctuation mark, used chiefly to show separation of words or word groups within a sentence

[1]**com•mand** *vb* **1 :** to order with authority **2 :** to have power or control over **:** be commander of **3 :** to have for one's use **4 :** to demand as right or due **:** EXACT **5 :** to survey from a good position

[2]**command** *n* **1 :** the act of commanding **2 :** an order given **3 :** the ability to control and use **:** MASTERY **4 :** the authority, right, or power to command **:** CONTROL **5 :** the people, area, or unit (as of soldiers and weapons) under a commander **6 :** a position from which military operations are directed

com•man•dant *n* **:** a commanding officer

com•mand•er *n* **:** a commissioned officer in the Navy or Coast Guard ranking above a lieutenant commander

commander in chief : a person who holds supreme command of the armed forces of a nation

com•mand•ment *n* **:** something given as a command and especially one of the Ten Commandments in the Bible

com•man•do *n, pl* **com•man•dos** *or* **com•man•does** **1 :** a band or unit of troops trained for making surprise raids into enemy territory **2 :** a member of a commando unit

command sergeant major *n* **:** a noncommissioned officer in the Army ranking above a first sergeant

com•mem•o•rate *vb* **com•mem•o•rat•ed; com•mem•o•rat•ing** **1 :** to call or recall to mind **2 :** to observe with a ceremony **3 :** to serve as a memorial of

com•mem•o•ra•tion *n* **1 :** the act of commemorating **2 :** something (as a ceremony) that commemorates

com•mence *vb* **com•menced; com•menc•ing :** BEGIN, START

com•mence•ment *n* **1 :** the act or the time of commencing **:** BEGINNING **2 :** graduation exercises

com•mend *vb* **1 :** to give into another's care **:** ENTRUST **2 :** to speak of with approval **:** PRAISE

com•men•da•tion *n* **:** [2]PRAISE 1, APPROVAL

[1]**com•ment** *n* **1 :** an expression of opinion either in speech or writing **2 :** mention of something that deserves notice

[2]**comment** *vb* **:** to make a comment **:** REMARK

com•men•ta•tor *n* **1 :** a person who makes comments **2 :** a person who reports and discusses news events (as over radio)

com•merce *n* **:** the buying and selling of goods especially on a large scale and between different places **:** TRADE

[1]**com•mer•cial** *adj* **1 :** having to do with commerce **2 :** having financial profit as the chief goal — **com•mer•cial•ly** *adv*

[2]**commercial** *n* **:** an advertisement broadcast on radio or television

com•mer•cial•ize *vb* **com•mer•cial•ized; com•mer•cial•iz•ing :** to manage with the idea of making a profit

[1]**com•mis•sion** *n* **1 :** an order or instruction granting the power to perform various acts or duties **:** the right or duty in question **2 :** a certificate that gives military or naval rank and authority **:** the rank and authority given **3 :** authority to act as agent for another **:** a task or piece of business entrusted to an agent **4 :** a group of persons given orders and authority to perform specified duties **5 :** an act of doing something wrong **6 :** a fee paid to an agent for taking care of a piece of business

[2]**commission** *vb* **1 :** to give a commission to **2 :** to put (a ship) into service

commissioned officer *n* **:** an officer in the armed forces who ranks above the enlisted persons or warrant officers and who is appointed by a commission from the president

com•mis•sion•er *n* **1 :** a member of a commission **2 :** an official who is the head of a government department

com•mit *vb* **com•mit•ted; com•mit•ting** **1 :** to make secure or put in safekeeping **:** ENTRUST **2 :** to place in or send to a prison or mental institution **3 :** to bring about **:** PERFORM **4 :** to pledge or assign to a certain course or use — **com•mit•ment** *n*

com•mit•tee *n* **:** a group of persons appointed or elected to consider some subject of interest or to perform some duty

com•mod•i•ty *n, pl* **com•mod•i•ties :** something produced by agriculture, mining, or manufacture

com•mo•dore *n* **1 :** a former wartime commissioned officer rank in the Navy and Coast Guard between the ranks of captain and rear admiral **2 :** the chief officer of a yacht club **3 :** the senior captain of a line of merchant ships

¹com•mon *adj* **1 :** having to do with, belonging to, or used by everybody **:** PUBLIC **2 :** belonging to or shared by two or more individuals or by the members of a family or group **3 :** ¹GENERAL 1 **4 :** occurring or appearing frequently **5 :** not above the average in rank, excellence, or social position **6 :** falling below ordinary standards (as in quality or manners) **:** INFERIOR **7 :** COARSE 4, VULGAR

²common *n* **:** land (as a park) owned and used by a community — **in common :** shared together

common cold *n* **:** a contagious disease which causes the lining of the nose and throat to be sore, swollen, and red and in which there is usually much mucus and coughing and sneezing

common denominator *n* **:** a common multiple of the denominators of a number of fractions

com•mon•er *n* **:** one of the common people

common multiple *n* **:** a multiple of each of two or more numbers

common noun *n* **:** a noun that names a class of persons or things or any individual of a class and that may occur with a limiting modifier (as *a*, *the*, *some*, or *every*)

¹com•mon•place *n* **:** something that is often seen or met with

²commonplace *adj* **:** often seen or met with **:** ORDINARY

common sense *n* **:** ordinary good sense and judgment

com•mon•wealth *n* **1 :** a political unit (as a nation or state) **2 :** a state of the United States and especially Kentucky, Massachusetts, Pennsylvania, or Virginia

com•mo•tion *n* **:** noisy excitement and confusion **:** TURMOIL

¹com•mune *vb* **com•muned; com•mun•ing :** to be in close accord or communication with someone or something

²com•mune *n* **:** a community in which individuals have close personal ties to each other and share property and duties

com•mu•ni•ca•ble *adj* **:** possible to communicate

com•mu•ni•cate *vb* **com•mu•ni•cat•ed; com•mu•ni•cat•ing 1 :** to make known **2 :** to pass (as a disease) from one to another **:** SPREAD **3 :** to get in touch (as by telephone)

com•mu•ni•ca•tion *n* **1 :** the exchange (as by speech or letter) of information between persons **2 :** information communicated **3 communications** *pl* **:** a system of sending messages (as by telephone) **4 communications** *pl* **:** a system of routes for moving troops, supplies, and vehicles

com•mu•nion *n* **1 :** an act or example of sharing **2 :** a religious ceremony commemorating with bread and wine the last supper of Jesus **3 :** the act of receiving the sacrament **4 :** friendly communication **5 :** a body of Christians having a common faith and discipline

com•mu•nism *n* **1 :** a social system in which property and goods are held in common **2 :** a theory that supports communism

com•mu•nist *n* **1 :** a person who believes in communism **2** *cap* **:** a member or follower of a Communist party or plan for change

com•mu•ni•ty *n, pl* **com•mu•ni•ties 1 :** the people living in a certain place (as a village or city) **:** the area itself **2 :** a natural group (as of kinds of plants and animals) living together and depending on one another for various necessities of life **3 :** a group of people with common interests living together **4 :** people in general **:** PUBLIC **5 :** common ownership or participation

com•mu•ta•tive *adj* **:** being a property of a mathematical operation (as addition or multiplication) in which the result of combining elements is independent of the order in which they are taken

com•mute *vb* **com•mut•ed; com•mut•ing 1 :** to change (as a penalty) to something less severe **2 :** to travel back and forth regularly — **com•mut•er** *n*

¹com•pact *adj* **1 :** closely united or packed **2 :** arranged so as to save space **3 :** not wordy **:** BRIEF — **com•pact•ly** *adv* — **com•pact•ness** *n*

²com•pact *n* **1 :** a small case for cosmetics **2 :** a somewhat small automobile

³com•pact *n* **:** AGREEMENT 2

compact disc *n* **:** a small plastic disc on which information (as music or computer data) is recorded

com•pan•ion *n* **1 :** a person or thing that accompanies another **2 :** one of a pair of matching things **3 :** a person employed to live with and serve another

com•pan•ion•ship *n* **:** FELLOWSHIP 1, COMPANY

com•pan•ion•way *n* **:** a ship's stairway from one deck to another

com•pa•ny *n, pl* **com•pa•nies 1 :** FELLOWSHIP 1 **2 :** a person's companions or associates **3 :** guests or visitors especially at one's home **4 :** a group of persons or things **5 :** a body of soldiers and especially an infantry unit normally led by a captain **6 :** a band of musical or dramatic performers **7 :** the officers and crew of a ship **8 :** an association of persons carrying on a business

com·pa·ra·ble *adj* **:** being similar or about the same

[1]**com·par·a·tive** *adj* **1 :** of, relating to, or being the form of an adjective or adverb that shows a degree of comparison that is greater or less than its positive degree **2 :** measured by comparisons **:** RELATIVE — **com·par·a·tive·ly** *adv*

[2]**comparative** *n* **:** the comparative degree or a comparative form in a language

com·pare *vb* **com·pared; com·par·ing 1 :** to point out as similar **:** LIKEN **2 :** to examine for likenesses or differences **3 :** to appear in comparison to others **4 :** to state the positive, comparative, and superlative forms of an adjective or adverb

com·par·i·son *n* **1 :** the act of comparing **:** the condition of being compared **2 :** an examination of two or more objects to find the likenesses and differences between them **3 :** change in the form and meaning of an adjective or an adverb (as by adding *-er* or *-est* to the word or by adding *more* or *most* before the word) to show different levels of quality, quantity, or relation

com·part·ment *n* **1 :** one of the parts into which a closed space is divided **2 :** a separate division or section

com·pass *n* **1 :** BOUNDARY, CIRCUMFERENCE **2 :** a closed-in space **3 :** [1]RANGE 6, SCOPE **4 :** a device having a magnetic needle that indicates direction on the earth's surface by pointing toward the north **5 :** a device that indicates direction by means other than a magnetic needle **6 :** an instrument for drawing circles or marking measurements consisting of two pointed legs joined at the top by a pivot — usually used in pl.

com·pas·sion *n* **:** pity for and a desire to help another

com·pas·sion·ate *adj* **:** having or showing compassion

com·pat·i·ble *adj* **:** capable of existing together in harmony

com·pa·tri·ot *n* **:** a person from one's own country

com·pel *vb* **com·pelled; com·pel·ling :** to make (as a person) do something by the use of physical, moral, or mental pressure **:** FORCE

com·pen·sate *vb* **com·pen·sat·ed; com·pen·sat·ing 1 :** to make up for **2 :** [1]RECOMPENSE, PAY

com·pen·sa·tion *n* **1 :** something that makes up for or is given to make up for something else **2 :** money paid regularly

com·pete *vb* **com·pet·ed; com·pet·ing :** to strive for something (as a prize or a reward) for which another is also striving

com·pe·tence *n* **:** the quality or state of being competent

com·pe·tent *adj* **:** CAPABLE 1, EFFICIENT

com·pe·ti·tion *n* **1 :** the act or process of competing **2 :** a contest in which all who take part compete for the same thing

com·pet·i·tive *adj* **:** relating to, characterized by, or based on competition

com·pet·i·tor *n* **:** someone or something that competes especially in the selling of goods or services **:** RIVAL

com·pile *vb* **com·piled; com·pil·ing 1 :** to collect into a volume or list **2 :** to collect information from books or documents and arrange it in a new form

com·pla·cence *n* **:** calm or satisfied feeling about one's self or one's position

com·pla·cen·cy *n* **:** COMPLACENCE

com·pla·cent *adj* **:** feeling or showing complacence

com·plain *vb* **1 :** to express grief, pain, or discontent **:** find fault **2 :** to accuse someone of wrongdoing — **com·plain·er** *n*

com·plaint *n* **1 :** expression of grief, pain, or discontent **2 :** a cause or reason for complaining **3 :** a sickness or disease of the body **4 :** a charge of wrongdoing against a person

[1]**com·ple·ment** *n* **:** something that completes or fills **:** the number required to complete or make perfect

[2]**com·ple·ment** *vb* **:** to form or serve as a complement to

com·ple·men·ta·ry *adj* **:** serving as a complement

[1]**com·plete** *adj* **1 :** having no part lacking **:** ENTIRE **2 :** brought to an end **3 :** THOROUGH 1 — **com·plete·ness** *n*

[2]**complete** *vb* **com·plet·ed; com·plet·ing 1 :** to bring to an end **:** FINISH **2 :** to make whole or perfect

com·plete·ly *adv* **:** as much as possible **:** in every way or detail

com·ple·tion *n* **:** the act or process of completing **:** the condition of being complete

com·plex *adj* **1 :** made up of two or more parts **2 :** not simple

complex fraction *n* **:** a fraction with a fraction or mixed number in the numerator or denominator or both

com·plex·ion *n* **1 :** the color or appearance

of the skin and especially of the face **2** **:** general appearance or impression

com•plex•i•ty *n, pl* **com•plex•i•ties** **1 :** the quality or condition of being complex **2 :** something complex

com•pli•cate *vb* **com•pli•cat•ed; com•pli•cat•ing :** to make or become complex or difficult

com•pli•ca•tion *n* **1 :** a confused situation **2 :** something that makes a situation more difficult

1com•pli•ment *n* **1 :** an act or expression of praise, approval, respect, or admiration **2** **compliments** *pl* **:** best wishes

2com•pli•ment *vb* **:** to pay a compliment to

com•pli•men•ta•ry *adj* **1 :** expressing or containing a compliment **2 :** given free as a courtesy or favor

com•ply *vb* **com•plied; com•ply•ing :** to act in agreement with another's wishes or in obedience to a rule

com•po•nent *n* **:** one of the parts or units of a combination, mixture, or system

com•pose *vb* **com•posed; com•pos•ing** **1 :** to form by putting together **2 :** to be the parts or materials of **3 :** to put in order **:** SETTLE

com•posed *adj* **:** being calm and in control of oneself

com•pos•er *n* **1 :** a person who composes **2 :** a writer of music

com•pos•ite *adj* **:** made up of different parts or elements

composite number *n* **:** an integer that is a product of two or more whole numbers each greater than 1

com•po•si•tion *n* **1 :** the act of composing (as by writing) **2 :** the manner in which the parts of a thing are put together **3 :** MAKEUP 1, CONSTITUTION **4 :** a literary, musical, or artistic production **5 :** a short piece of writing done as a school exercise

com•post *n* **:** decayed organic material used to improve soil for growing crops

com•po•sure *n* **:** calmness especially of mind, manner, or appearance

1com•pound *vb* **1 :** to mix or unite together into a whole **2 :** to form by combining separate things

2com•pound *adj* **:** made of or by the union of two or more parts

3com•pound *n* **1 :** a word made up of parts that are themselves words **2 :** something (as a chemical) that is formed by combining two or more parts or elements

4com•pound *n* **:** an enclosed area containing a group of buildings

compound fracture *n* **:** a breaking of a bone in which bone fragments stick out through the flesh

com•pre•hend *vb* **1 :** to understand fully **2 :** to take in **:** INCLUDE

com•pre•hen•sion *n* **:** ability to understand

com•pre•hen•sive *adj* **:** including much **:** INCLUSIVE — **com•pre•hen•sive•ness** *n*

1com•press *vb* **1 :** to press or squeeze together **2 :** to reduce the volume of by pressure

2com•press *n* **:** a pad (as of folded cloth) applied firmly to a part of the body (as to check bleeding)

com•pres•sion *n* **:** the process of compressing **:** the state of being compressed

com•pres•sor *n* **1 :** one that compresses **2 :** a machine for compressing something (as air)

com•prise *vb* **com•prised; com•pris•ing** **1 :** to be made up of **:** consist of **2 :** 2FORM 3

1com•pro•mise *n* **1 :** an agreement over a dispute reached by each side changing or giving up some demands **2 :** the thing agreed upon as a result of a compromise

2compromise *vb* **com•pro•mised; com•pro•mis•ing** **1 :** to settle by compromise **2 :** to expose to risk, suspicion, or disgrace

com•pul•sion *n* **1 :** an act of compelling **:** the state of being compelled **2 :** a force that compels **3 :** a very strong urge to do something

com•pul•so•ry *adj* **1 :** required by or as if by law **2 :** having the power of forcing someone to do something

com•pu•ta•tion *n* **1 :** the act or action of computing **2 :** a result obtained by computing

com•pute *vb* **com•put•ed; com•put•ing :** to find out by using mathematics

com•put•er *n* **:** an automatic electronic machine that can store, recall, and process data

com•put•er•ize *vb* **com•put•er•ized; com•put•er•iz•ing** **1 :** to carry out, control, or produce on a computer **2 :** to equip with computers **3 :** to put in a form that a computer can use

com•rade *n* **:** COMPANION 1

1con *adv* **:** on the negative side

2con *n* **:** an opposing argument, person, or position

con- — see COM-

con•cave *adj* **:** hollow or rounded inward like the inside of a bowl

con•ceal *vb* **1 :** to hide from sight **2 :** to keep secret

con•ceal•ment *n* **1 :** the act of hiding **:** the state of being hidden **2 :** a hiding place

con•cede *vb* **con•ced•ed; con•ced•ing** **1 :** to grant as a right or privilege **2 :** to admit to be true

con•ceit *n* **:** too much pride in oneself or one's ability

con·ceit·ed *adj* **:** VAIN 2
con·ceiv·able *adj* **:** possible to conceive, imagine, or understand
con·ceive *vb* **con·ceived; con·ceiv·ing 1 :** to form an idea of **:** IMAGINE **2 :** THINK 2
con·cen·trate *vb* **con·cen·trat·ed; con·cen·trat·ing 1 :** to bring or come to or direct toward a common center **2 :** to make stronger or thicker by removing something (as water) **3 :** to fix one's powers, efforts, or attentions on one thing
con·cen·tra·tion *n* **1 :** the act or process of concentrating **:** the state of being concentrated **2 :** close mental attention to a subject
con·cept *n* **1 :** 2THOUGHT 4 **2 :** a general idea
1con·cern *vb* **1 :** to relate to **:** be about **2 :** to be of interest or importance to **:** AFFECT **3 :** to be a care, trouble, or distress to **4 :** ENGAGE 3, OCCUPY
2concern *n* **1 :** something that relates to or involves a person **:** AFFAIR **2 :** a state of interest and uncertainty **3 :** a business organization
con·cerned *adj* **:** being worried and disturbed
con·cern·ing *prep* **:** relating to **:** ABOUT
con·cert *n* **1 :** AGREEMENT 1 **2 :** a musical performance by several voices or instruments or by both
con·cer·ti·na *n* **:** a small musical instrument like an accordion
con·cer·to *n, pl* **con·cer·tos :** a musical composition usually in three parts for orchestra with one or more principal instruments
con·ces·sion *n* **1 :** the act or an instance of granting something **2 :** something granted **3 :** a special right or privilege given by an authority
conch *n, pl* **conchs** *or* **conch·es :** a very large sea snail with a tall thick spiral shell
con·cil·i·ate *vb* **con·cil·i·at·ed; con·cil·i·at·ing 1 :** to bring into agreement **:** RECONCILE **2 :** to gain or regain the goodwill or favor of
con·cise *adj* **:** expressing much in few words
con·clude *vb* **con·clud·ed; con·clud·ing 1 :** to bring or come to an end **:** FINISH **2 :** to form an opinion **3 :** to bring about as a result
con·clu·sion *n* **1 :** final decision reached by reasoning **2 :** the last part of something **3 :** a final settlement
con·clu·sive *adj* **:** DECISIVE 1 — **con·clu·sive·ly** *adv*
con·coct *vb* **1 :** to prepare (as food) by putting several different things together **2 :** to make up **:** DEVISE
con·cord *n* **:** a state of agreement
con·course *n* **1 :** a flocking, moving, or flowing together (as of persons or streams) **:** GATHERING **2 :** a place where roads or paths meet **3 :** an open space or hall (as in a mall or railroad terminal) where crowds gather
1con·crete *adj* **1 :** 1MATERIAL 1, REAL **2 :** made of or relating to concrete
2con·crete *n* **:** a hardened mixture of cement, sand, and water with gravel or broken stone used in construction (as of pavements and buildings)
con·cur *vb* **con·curred; con·cur·ring 1 :** to act or happen together **2 :** to be in agreement (as in action or opinion) **:** ACCORD
con·cus·sion *n* **1 :** a sharp hard blow or the effect of this **2 :** injury to the brain by jarring (as from a blow)
con·demn *vb* **1 :** to declare to be wrong **2 :** to declare guilty **3 :** 2SENTENCE **4 :** to declare to be unfit for use
con·dem·na·tion *n* **1 :** 1CENSURE 1, BLAME **2 :** the act of judicially condemning **3 :** the state of being condemned
con·den·sa·tion *n* **1 :** the act or process of condensing **2 :** something that has been condensed
con·dense *vb* **con·densed; con·dens·ing :** to make or become more compact, more concise, closer, or denser **:** CONCENTRATE
con·de·scend *vb* **1 :** to stoop to a level considered lower than one's own **2 :** to grant favors with a show of being better than others
1con·di·tion *n* **1 :** something agreed upon or necessary if some other thing is to take place **2 conditions** *pl* **:** state of affairs **3 :** state of being **4 :** situation in life **5 :** state of health or fitness
2condition *vb* **1 :** to put into the proper or desired condition **2 :** to change the habits of usually by training
con·di·tion·al *adj* **:** depending on a condition
con·dor *n* **:** a very large American vulture having a bare head and neck and a frill of white feathers on the neck
1con·duct *n* **1 :** the act or way of carrying something on **2 :** personal behavior
2con·duct *vb* **1 :** 2GUIDE 1 **2 :** to carry on or out from a position of command **:** LEAD **3 :** BEHAVE 1 **4 :** to have the quality of transmitting light, heat, sound, or electricity
con·duc·tion *n* **1 :** the act of transporting something **2 :** transmission through a conductor
con·duc·tor *n* **1 :** a person in charge of a public means of transportation (as a train) **2 :** a person or thing that directs or leads **3 :** a substance or body capable of transmitting light, electricity, heat, or sound

cone *n* **1 :** the scaly fruit of certain trees (as the pine or fir) **2 :** a solid body tapering evenly to a point from a circular base **3 :** something resembling a cone in shape **4 :** an ice-cream holder **5 :** a cell of the retina of the eye that is sensitive to colored light
con·fec·tion *n* **:** a fancy dish or sweet **:** DELICACY, CANDY
con·fec·tion·er *n* **:** a maker of or dealer in confections (as candies)
con·fec·tion·ery *n, pl* **con·fec·tion·er·ies** **1 :** sweet things to eat (as candy) **2 :** a confectioner's business or place of business
con·fed·er·a·cy *n, pl* **con·fed·er·a·cies** **1 :** a league of persons, parties, or states **2** *cap* **:** the eleven southern states that seceded from the United States in 1860 and 1861
¹con·fed·er·ate *adj* **1 :** united in a league **2** *cap* **:** of or relating to the Confederacy
²confederate *n* **1 :** a member of a confederacy **2 :** ACCOMPLICE **3** *cap* **:** a soldier of or a person who sided with the Confederacy
³con·fed·er·ate *vb* **con·fed·er·at·ed; con·fed·er·at·ing :** to unite in an alliance or confederacy
con·fer *vb* **con·ferred; con·fer·ring** **1 :** BESTOW, PRESENT **2 :** to compare views especially in studying a problem
con·fer·ence *n* **:** a meeting for discussion or exchange of opinions
con·fess *vb* **1 :** to tell of or make known (as something private or damaging to oneself) **2 :** to make known one's sins to God or to a priest
con·fes·sion *n* **1 :** an act of confessing **2 :** an admission of guilt **3 :** a formal statement of religious beliefs
con·fide *vb* **con·fid·ed; con·fid·ing** **1 :** to have or show faith **2 :** to show confidence by telling secrets **3 :** to tell in confidence **4 :** ENTRUST 2
con·fi·dence *n* **1 :** a feeling of trust or belief **2 :** SELF-CONFIDENCE **3 :** reliance on another's secrecy or loyalty **4 :** ²SECRET
con·fi·dent *adj* **:** having or showing confidence — **con·fi·dent·ly** *adv*
con·fi·den·tial *adj* **1 :** ¹SECRET 1 **2 :** ²INTIMATE 2 **3 :** trusted with secret matters — **con·fi·den·tial·ly** *adv*
con·fine *vb* **con·fined; con·fin·ing** **1 :** to keep within limits **2 :** to shut up **:** IMPRISON **3 :** to keep indoors — **con·fine·ment** *n*
con·fines *n pl* **:** the boundary or limits of something
con·firm *vb* **1 :** to make firm or firmer (as in a habit, in faith, or in intention) **:** STRENGTHEN **2 :** APPROVE 2, ACCEPT **3 :** to administer the rite of confirmation to **4 :** to make sure of the truth of
con·fir·ma·tion *n* **1 :** an act of confirming **2 :** a religious ceremony admitting a person to full privileges in a church or synagogue **3 :** something that confirms
con·firmed *adj* **1 :** being firmly established **2 :** unlikely to change
con·fis·cate *vb* **con·fis·cat·ed; con·fis·cat·ing :** to seize by or as if by public authority
con·fla·gra·tion *n* **:** a large destructive fire
¹con·flict *n* **1 :** an extended struggle **:** BATTLE **2 :** a clashing disagreement (as between ideas or interests)
²con·flict *vb* **:** to be in opposition
con·form *vb* **1 :** to make or be like **:** AGREE, ACCORD **2 :** COMPLY
con·for·mi·ty *n, pl* **con·for·mi·ties** **1 :** agreement in form, manner, or character **2 :** action in accordance with some standard or authority
con·found *vb* **:** to throw into disorder **:** mix up **:** CONFUSE
con·front *vb* **1 :** to face especially in challenge **:** OPPOSE **2 :** to cause to face or meet
con·fuse *vb* **con·fused; con·fus·ing** **1 :** to make mentally foggy or uncertain **:** PERPLEX **2 :** to make embarrassed **3 :** to fail to tell apart
con·fu·sion *n* **1 :** an act or instance of confusing **2 :** the state of being confused
con·geal *vb* **1 :** to change from a fluid to a solid state by or as if by cold **:** FREEZE **2 :** to make or become hard, stiff, or thick
con·ge·nial *adj* **1 :** alike or sympathetic in nature, disposition, or tastes **2 :** existing together in harmony **3 :** tending to please or satisfy
con·gest *vb* **:** to make too crowded or full **:** CLOG
¹con·glom·er·ate *adj* **:** made up of parts from various sources or of various kinds
²conglomerate *n* **:** a mass (as a rock) formed of fragments from various sources
con·grat·u·late *vb* **con·grat·u·lat·ed; con·grat·u·lat·ing :** to express pleasure on account of success or good fortune
con·grat·u·la·tion *n* **1 :** the act of congratulating **2 :** an expression of joy or pleasure at another's success or good fortune — usually used in pl.
con·gre·gate *vb* **con·gre·gat·ed; con·gre·gat·ing :** to collect or gather into a crowd or group **:** ASSEMBLE
con·gre·ga·tion *n* **1 :** a gathering or collection of persons or things **2 :** an assembly of persons gathered especially for religious worship **3 :** the membership of a church or synagogue
con·gress *n* **1 :** a formal meeting of delegates for discussion and action **:** CONFER-

DICTIONARY

ENCE **2 :** the chief lawmaking body of a nation and especially of a republic that in the United States is made up of separate houses of senators and representatives

con•gress•man *n, pl* **con•gress•men :** a member of a congress and especially of the United States House of Representatives

con•gress•wom•an *n, pl* **con•gress•wom•en :** a woman member of a congress and especially of the United States House of Representatives

con•gru•ent *adj* **:** having the same size and shape

con•ic *adj* **1 :** CONICAL **2 :** of or relating to a cone

con•i•cal *adj* **:** shaped like a cone

co•ni•fer *n* **:** any of a group of mostly evergreen trees and shrubs (as pines) that produce cones — **co•nif•er•ous** *adj*

1**con•jec•ture** *n* **:** 2GUESS

2**conjecture** *vb* **con•jec•tured; con•jec•tur•ing :** 1GUESS 1, SURMISE

con•junc•tion *n* **1 :** a joining together **:** UNION **2 :** a word or expression that joins together sentences, clauses, phrases, or words

con•jure *vb* **con•jured; con•jur•ing 1 :** to beg earnestly or solemnly **:** BESEECH **2 :** to practice magical arts **3 :** IMAGINE 1

con•nect *vb* **1 :** to join or link together **2 :** to attach by close personal relationship **3 :** to bring together in thought — **con•nec•tor** *n*

con•nec•tion *n* **1 :** the act of connecting **2 :** the fact or condition of being connected **:** RELATIONSHIP **3 :** a thing that connects **:** BOND, LINK **4 :** a person connected with others (as by kinship) **5 :** a social, professional, or commercial relationship **6 :** the act or the means of continuing a journey by transferring (as to another train)

con•nois•seur *n* **:** a person qualified to act as a judge in matters involving taste and appreciation

con•quer *vb* **1 :** to get or gain by force **:** win by fighting **2 :** OVERCOME 1

con•quer•or *n* **:** one that conquers **:** VICTOR

con•quest *n* **1 :** the act or process of conquering **:** VICTORY **2 :** something that is conquered

con•quis•ta•dor *n, pl* **con•quis•ta•do•res** *or* **con•quis•ta•dors :** a leader in the Spanish conquest especially of Mexico and Peru in the sixteenth century

con•science *n* **:** knowledge of right and wrong and a feeling that one should do what is right

con•sci•en•tious *adj* **1 :** guided by or agreeing with one's conscience **2 :** using or done with careful attention

con•scious *adj* **1 :** aware of facts or feelings **2 :** known or felt by one's inner self **3 :** mentally awake or active **4 :** INTENTIONAL — **con•scious•ly** *adv*

con•scious•ness *n* **1 :** the condition of being conscious **2 :** the upper level of mental life involving conscious thought and the will

con•se•crate *vb* **con•se•crat•ed; con•se•crat•ing 1 :** to declare to be sacred or holy **:** set apart for the service of God **2 :** to dedicate to a particular purpose

con•sec•u•tive *adj* **:** following one another in order without gaps

1**con•sent** *vb* **:** to express willingness or approval **:** AGREE

2**consent** *n* **:** approval of or agreement with what is done or suggested by another person

con•se•quence *n* **1 :** something produced by a cause or following from a condition **2 :** real importance

con•se•quent *adj* **:** following as a result or effect

con•se•quent•ly *adv* **:** as a result

con•ser•va•tion *n* **1 :** PROTECTION 1, PRESERVATION **2 :** planned management of natural resources (as timber) to prevent waste, destruction, or neglect

1**con•ser•va•tive** *adj* **1 :** favoring a policy of keeping things as they are **:** opposed to change **2 :** favoring established styles and standards — **con•ser•va•tive•ly** *adv*

2**conservative** *n* **:** a person who holds conservative views **:** a cautious person

con•ser•va•to•ry *n, pl* **con•ser•va•to•ries 1 :** GREENHOUSE **2 :** a place of instruction in some special study (as music)

1**con•serve** *vb* **con•served; con•serv•ing :** to keep in a safe condition **:** SAVE

2**con•serve** *n* **1 :** a candied fruit **2 :** a rich fruit preserve

con•sid•er *vb* **1 :** to think over carefully **:** PONDER, REFLECT **2 :** to treat in a kind or thoughtful way **3 :** to think of in a certain way **:** BELIEVE

con•sid•er•able *adj* **:** rather large in extent, amount, or size — **con•sid•er•ably** *adv*

con•sid•er•ate *adj* **:** thoughtful of the rights and feelings of others

con•sid•er•ation *n* **1 :** careful thought **:** DELIBERATION **2 :** thoughtfulness for other people **3 :** something that needs to be considered before deciding or acting **4 :** a payment made in return for something

con•sign *vb* **1 :** ENTRUST 2 **2 :** to give, transfer, or deliver to another **3 :** to send (as goods) to an agent to be sold or cared for — **con•sign•ment** *n*

con•sist *vb* **:** to be made up or composed

con·sis·ten·cy *n, pl* **con·sis·ten·cies** **1** : degree of compactness, firmness, or stickiness **2** : agreement or harmony between parts or elements **3** : a sticking with one way of thinking or acting

con·sis·tent *adj* : showing consistency — **con·sis·tent·ly** *adv*

con·so·la·tion *n* **1** : the act of consoling : the state of being consoled **2** : something that lessens disappointment, misery, or grief

1con·sole *n* **1** : the part of an organ at which the organist sits and which contains the keyboard and controls **2** : a panel or cabinet on which are dials and switches for controlling an electronic or mechanical device **3** : a radio, phonograph, or television cabinet that stands on the floor

2con·sole *vb* **con·soled; con·sol·ing** : to comfort in a time of grief or distress

con·sol·i·date *vb* **con·sol·i·dat·ed; con·sol·i·dat·ing** **1** : to join together into one whole : UNITE **2** : STRENGTHEN

con·so·nant *n* **1** : a speech sound (as \p\, \n\, or \s\) produced by narrowing or closing the breath channel at one or more points **2** : a letter in the English alphabet other than *a, e, i, o,* or *u*

1con·sort *n* : a wife or husband especially of a king or queen

2con·sort *vb* : to go together as companions : ASSOCIATE

con·spic·u·ous *adj* **1** : easily seen **2** : attracting attention : PROMINENT

con·spir·a·cy *n, pl* **con·spir·a·cies** **1** : the act of conspiring or plotting **2** : an agreement among conspirators **3** : a group of conspirators

con·spir·a·tor *n* : a person who conspires

con·spire *vb* **con·spired; con·spir·ing** **1** : to make an agreement especially in secret to do an unlawful act : PLOT **2** : to act together

con·sta·ble *n* : a police officer usually of a village or small town

con·stan·cy *n* : firmness and loyalty in one's beliefs or personal relationships

con·stant *adj* **1** : always faithful and true **2** : remaining steady and unchanged **3** : occurring over and over again — **con·stant·ly** *adv*

con·stel·la·tion *n* : any of eighty-eight groups of stars forming patterns

con·ster·na·tion *n* : amazement, alarm, or disappointment that makes one feel helpless or confused

con·sti·pate *vb* **con·sti·pat·ed; con·sti·pat·ing** : to cause constipation in

con·sti·pa·tion *n* : difficult or infrequent passage of dry hard material from the bowels

1con·stit·u·ent *n* **1** : one of the parts or materials of which something is made : ELEMENT, INGREDIENT **2** : any of the voters who elect a person to represent them

2constituent *adj* **1** : serving to form or make up a unit or whole **2** : having power to elect or appoint or to make or change a constitution

con·sti·tute *vb* **con·sti·tut·ed; con·sti·tut·ing** **1** : to appoint to an office or duty **2** : SET UP 2 **3** : to make up : FORM

con·sti·tu·tion *n* **1** : the bodily makeup of an individual **2** : the basic structure of something **3** : the basic beliefs and laws of a nation, state, or social group by which the powers and duties of the government are established and certain rights are guaranteed to the people

1con·sti·tu·tion·al *adj* **1** : having to do with a person's bodily or mental makeup **2** : of, relating to, or in agreement with a constitution (as of a nation)

2constitutional *n* : an exercise (as a walk) taken for one's health

con·strain *vb* : COMPEL, FORCE

con·straint *n* **1** : COMPULSION 1, 2 **2** : a keeping back of one's natural feelings

con·strict *vb* : to make narrower or smaller by drawing together : SQUEEZE

con·stric·tion *n* : an act or instance of constricting

con·stric·tor *n* : a snake (as a boa) that kills prey by crushing in its coils

con·struct *vb* : to make or form by combining parts

con·struc·tion *n* **1** : the arrangement of words and the relationship between words in a sentence **2** : the process, art, or manner of constructing **3** : something built or put together : STRUCTURE **4** : INTERPRETATION

construction paper *n* : a thick paper available in many colors for school art work

con·struc·tive *adj* : helping to develop or improve something

con·strue *vb* **con·strued; con·stru·ing** : to understand or explain the sense or intention of

con·sul *n* : an official appointed by a government to live in a foreign country in order to look after the commercial interests of citizens of the appointing country

con·sult *vb* **1** : to seek the opinion or advice of **2** : to seek information from **3** : to talk something over

con·sul·ta·tion *n* **1** : a discussion between doctors on a case or its treatment **2** : the act of consulting

con·sume *vb* **con·sumed; con·sum·ing** **1** : to destroy by or as if by fire **2** : to use up

: SPEND **3 :** to eat or drink up **4 :** to take up the interest or attention of

con·sum·er *n* **1 :** one that consumes **2 :** a person who buys and uses up goods

con·sump·tion *n* **1 :** the act or process of consuming and especially of using up something (as food or coal) **2 :** a wasting away of the body especially from tuberculosis of the lungs

1con·tact *n* **1 :** a meeting or touching of persons or things **2 :** a person one knows who has influence especially in the business or political world

2contact *vb* **1 :** to come or bring into contact **2 :** to get in touch or communication with

3contact *adj* **:** involving or activated by contact

contact lens *n* **:** a thin lens used to correct bad eyesight and worn right over the cornea of the eye

con·ta·gion *n* **1 :** the passing of a disease from one individual to another as a result of some contact between them **2 :** a contagious disease

con·ta·gious *adj* **:** spreading by contagion

con·tain *vb* **1 :** to keep within limits **:** RESTRAIN, CHECK **2 :** to have within **:** HOLD **3 :** to consist of or include

con·tain·er *n* **:** something into which other things can be put (as for storage)

con·tam·i·nate *vb* **con·tam·i·nat·ed; con·tam·i·nat·ing 1 :** to soil, stain, or infect by contact or association **2 :** to make unfit for use by adding something harmful or unpleasant

con·tem·plate *vb* **con·tem·plat·ed; con·tem·plat·ing 1 :** to view with careful and thoughtful attention **2 :** to have in mind **:** plan on

con·tem·pla·tion *n* **1 :** the act of thinking about spiritual things **:** MEDITATION **2 :** the act of looking at or thinking about something for some time **3 :** a looking ahead to some future event

1con·tem·po·rary *adj* **1 :** living or occurring at the same period of time **2 :** MODERN 1

2contemporary *n, pl* **con·tem·po·rar·ies :** a person who lives at the same time or is of about the same age as another

con·tempt *n* **1 :** the act of despising **:** the state of mind of one who despises **2 :** the state of being despised

con·tempt·ible *adj* **:** deserving contempt

con·temp·tu·ous *adj* **:** feeling or showing contempt **:** SCORNFUL

con·tend *vb* **1 :** COMPETE **2 :** to try hard to deal with **3 :** to argue or state earnestly

1con·tent *adj* **:** pleased and satisfied with what one has or is

2content *vb* **:** to make content **:** SATISFY

3content *n* **:** freedom from care or discomfort

4con·tent *n* **1 :** something contained — usually used in pl. **2 :** the subject or topic treated (as in a book) — usually used in pl. **3 :** the important part or meaning (as of a book) **4 :** the amount contained or possible to contain

con·tent·ed *adj* **:** satisfied or showing satisfaction with one's possessions or one's situation in life

con·ten·tion *n* **1 :** an act or instance of contending **2 :** an idea or point for which a person argues (as in a debate or argument) **3 :** COMPETITION 2

con·tent·ment *n* **:** freedom from worry or restlessness **:** peaceful satisfaction

1con·test *vb* **:** to make (something) a cause of dispute or fighting

2con·test *n* **:** a struggle for victory **:** COMPETITION

con·tes·tant *n* **:** one who takes part in a contest

con·ti·nent *n* **1 :** one of the great divisions of land on the globe (as Africa, Antarctica, Asia, Australia, Europe, North America, or South America) **2** *cap* **:** the continent of Europe

con·ti·nen·tal *adj* **:** of or relating to a continent

con·tin·gent *adj* **:** depending on something else that may or may not exist or occur

con·tin·u·al *adj* **1 :** going on without stopping **2 :** occurring again and again at short intervals — **con·tin·u·al·ly** *adv*

con·tin·u·ance *n* **1 :** the act of continuing **2 :** the quality of being continual

con·tin·u·a·tion *n* **1 :** the making longer of a state or activity **2 :** a going on after stopping **3 :** a thing or part by which something is continued

con·tin·ue *vb* **con·tin·ued; con·tinu·ing 1 :** to do or cause to do the same thing without changing or stopping **2 :** to begin again after stopping

con·ti·nu·i·ty *n, pl* **con·ti·nu·i·ties :** the quality or state of being continuous

con·tin·u·ous *adj* **:** continuing without a stop — **con·tin·u·ous·ly** *adv*

con·tort *vb* **:** to give an unusual appearance or unnatural shape to by twisting

con·tor·tion *n* **1 :** a twisting or a being twisted out of shape **2 :** a contorted shape or thing

con·tour *n* **1 :** the outline of a figure, body, or surface **2 :** a line or a drawing showing an outline

contra- *prefix* **1 :** against **:** contrary **:** contrasting **2 :** pitched below normal bass

con·tra·band *n* **1 :** goods forbidden by law to be owned or to be brought into or out of a country **2 :** smuggled goods

[1]con·tract *n* **1 :** an agreement that the law can force one to keep **2 :** a writing made to show the terms and conditions of a contract

[2]con·tract *vb* **1 :** to agree by contract **2 :** to become sick with **:** CATCH **3 :** to draw together and make shorter and broader **4 :** to make or become smaller **:** SHRINK **5 :** to make (as a word) shorter by dropping sounds or letters

con·trac·tion *n* **1 :** the act or process of contracting **:** the state of being contracted **2 :** a shortening of a word or word group by leaving out a sound or letter **3 :** a form (as *don't* or *they've*) produced by contraction

con·tra·dict *vb* **1 :** to deny the truth of a statement **:** say the opposite of what someone else has said **2 :** to be opposed to

con·tra·dic·tion *n* **:** something (as a statement) that contradicts something else

con·tra·dic·to·ry *adj* **:** involving, causing, or being a contradiction

con·tral·to *n, pl* **con·tral·tos 1 :** the lowest female singing voice **:** ALTO **2 :** a singer with a contralto voice

con·trap·tion *n* **:** GADGET

[1]con·trary *n, pl* **con·trar·ies :** something opposite or contrary — **on the contrary :** just the opposite **:** NO

[2]con·trary *adj* **1 :** exactly opposite **2 :** being against what is usual or expected **3 :** not favorable **4 :** unwilling to accept control or advice

[1]con·trast *vb* **1 :** to show noticeable differences **2 :** to compare two persons or things so as to show the differences between them

[2]con·trast *n* **1 :** difference or the amount of difference (as in color or brightness) between adjacent parts **2 :** difference or amount of difference between related or similar things

con·trib·ute *vb* **con·trib·ut·ed; con·trib·ut·ing 1 :** to give along with others **2 :** to have a share in something **3 :** to supply (as an article) for publication especially in a magazine — **con·trib·u·tor** *n*

con·tri·bu·tion *n* **1 :** the act of contributing **2 :** the sum or thing contributed

con·trite *adj* **:** feeling or showing sorrow for some wrong that one has done **:** REPENTANT

con·triv·ance *n* **:** something (as a scheme or a mechanical device) produced with skill and cleverness

con·trive *vb* **con·trived; con·triv·ing 1 :** [2]PLAN 1, PLOT **2 :** to form or make in some skillful or clever way **3 :** to manage to bring about or do

[1]con·trol *vb* **con·trolled; con·trol·ling 1 :** to keep within bounds **:** RESTRAIN **2 :** to have power over

[2]control *n* **1 :** the power or authority to control or command **2 :** ability to control **3 :** SELF-RESTRAINT **4 :** REGULATION **5 :** a device used to start, stop, or change the operation of a machine or system **6 :** something used in an experiment or study to provide a check on results

con·tro·ver·sial *adj* **:** relating to or causing controversy

con·tro·ver·sy *n, pl* **con·tro·ver·sies 1 :** an often long or heated discussion of something about which there is great difference of opinion **2 :** [1]QUARREL 2

co·nun·drum *n* **:** [1]RIDDLE

con·va·lesce *vb* **con·va·lesced; con·va·lesc·ing :** to regain health and strength gradually after sickness or injury

con·va·les·cence *n* **:** the period or process of convalescing

[1]con·va·les·cent *adj* **:** passing through convalescence

[2]convalescent *n* **:** a person who is convalescent

con·vec·tion *n* **:** motion in a gas (as air) or a liquid in which the warmer portions rise and the colder portions sink

con·vene *vb* **con·vened; con·ven·ing 1 :** ASSEMBLE 3 **2 :** to cause to assemble

con·ve·nience *n* **1 :** the quality or state of being convenient **2 :** personal comfort **3 :** OPPORTUNITY 1 **4 :** something that gives comfort or advantage

con·ve·nient *adj* **1 :** suited to a person's comfort or ease **2 :** suited to a certain use **3 :** easy to get to — **con·ve·nient·ly** *adv*

con·vent *n* **1 :** a group of nuns living together **2 :** a house or a set of buildings occupied by a community of nuns

con·ven·tion *n* **1 :** AGREEMENT 2 **2 :** a custom or a way of acting and doing things that is widely accepted and followed **3 :** a meeting of persons gathered together for a common purpose

con·ven·tion·al *adj* **1 :** behaving according to convention **2 :** used or accepted through convention

con·ver·sa·tion *n* **:** talking or a talk between two or more people

con·verse *vb* **con·versed; con·vers·ing :** to have a conversation

con·ver·sion *n* **1 :** the act of converting **:** the state of being converted **2 :** a change in the nature or form of a thing **3 :** a change of religion

[1]con·vert *vb* **1 :** to change from one belief,

religion, view, or party to another **2 :** to change from one form to another **3 :** to exchange for an equivalent

[2]**con·vert** *n* **:** a person who has been converted

[1]**con·vert·ible** *adj* **:** possible to change in form or use

[2]**convertible** *n* **1 :** something that is convertible **2 :** an automobile with a top that can be raised, lowcred, or removed

con·vex *adj* **:** rounded like the outside of a ball or circle

con·vey *vb* **con·veyed; con·vey·ing 1 :** to carry from one place to another **:** TRANSPORT **2 :** to serve as a way of carrying **3 :** IMPART 2, COMMUNICATE

con·vey·ance *n* **1 :** the act of conveying **2 :** something used to carry goods or passengers

[1]**con·vict** *vb* **:** to prove or find guilty

[2]**con·vict** *n* **:** a person serving a prison sentence usually for a long time

con·vic·tion *n* **1 :** the act of convicting **:** the state of being convicted **2 :** the state of mind of a person who is sure that what he or she believes or says is true **3 :** a strong belief or opinion

con·vince *vb* **con·vinced; con·vinc·ing :** to argue so as to make a person agree or believe

con·vinc·ing *adj* **:** causing one to believe or agree **:** PERSUASIVE — **con·vinc·ing·ly** *adv*

con·vulse *vb* **con·vulsed; con·vuls·ing :** to shake violently or with jerky motions

con·vul·sion *n* **1 :** an attack of violent involuntary muscular contractions **:** FIT **2 :** a violent disturbance **:** UPHEAVAL

con·vul·sive *adj* **:** being or producing a convulsion — **con·vul·sive·ly** *adv*

[1]**coo** *vb* **cooed; coo·ing 1 :** to make the soft sound made by doves and pigeons or one like it **2 :** to talk fondly or lovingly

[2]**coo** *n, pl* **coos :** the sound made in cooing

[1]**cook** *n* **:** a person who prepares food for eating

[2]**cook** *vb* **1 :** to prepare food for eating by the use of heat **2 :** to go through the process of being cooked

cook·book *n* **:** a book of cooking recipes and directions

cook·ie *or* **cooky** *n, pl* **cook·ies :** a small sweet cake

cook·out *n* **:** an outing at which a meal is cooked and served outdoors

cook up *vb* **:** to think up **:** DEVISE

[1]**cool** *adj* **1 :** somewhat cold **:** not warm **2 :** not letting or keeping in heat **3 :** [3]CALM 2 **4 :** not friendly or interested **:** INDIFFERENT — **cool·ly** *adv*

[2]**cool** *vb* **:** to make or become cool

[3]**cool** *n* **:** a cool time or place

cool·er *n* **:** a container for keeping food or drink cool

coon *n* **:** RACCOON

[1]**coop** *n* **:** a building for housing poultry

[2]**coop** *vb* **:** to restrict to a small space

coo·per *n* **:** a worker who makes or repairs wooden casks, tubs, or barrels

co·op·er·ate *vb* **co·op·er·at·ed; co·op·er·at·ing :** to act or work together so as to get something done

co·op·er·a·tion *n* **:** the act or process of cooperating

[1]**co·op·er·a·tive** *adj* **1 :** willing to cooperate or work with others **2 :** of, relating to, or organized as a cooperative

[2]**cooperative** *n* **:** an association formed to enable its members to buy or sell to better advantage

[1]**co·or·di·nate** *adj* **:** equal in rank or importance

[2]**co·or·di·nate** *vb* **co·or·di·nat·ed; co·or·di·nat·ing :** to work or cause to work together smoothly

co·or·di·na·tion *n* **:** smooth working together (as of parts)

cop *n* **:** POLICE OFFICER

cope *vb* **coped; cop·ing :** to struggle or try to manage especially with some success

copi·er *n* **1 :** a person who copies **2 :** a machine for making copies (as of letters or drawings)

co·pi·lot *n* **:** an assistant airplane pilot

co·pi·ous *adj* **:** very plentiful **:** ABUNDANT — **co·pi·ous·ly** *adv*

cop·per *n* **1 :** a tough reddish metallic chemical element that is one of the best conductors of heat and electricity **2 :** a copper or bronze coin

cop·per·head *n* **:** a mottled reddish brown poisonous snake of the eastern United States

cop·pice *n* **:** a thicket, grove, or growth of small trees

co·pra *n* **:** dried coconut meat

copse *n* **:** COPPICE

[1]**copy** *n, pl* **cop·ies 1 :** something that is made to look exactly like something else **:** DUPLICATE **2 :** one of the total number of books, magazines, or papers printed at one time **3 :** written or printed material to be set in type

[2]**copy** *vb* **cop·ied; copy·ing 1 :** to make a copy of **:** DUPLICATE **2 :** IMITATE 1 3

[1]**copy·right** *n* **:** the legal right to be the only one to reproduce, publish, and sell the contents and form of a literary or artistic work

[2]**copyright** *vb* **:** to get a copyright on

[1]**cor·al** *n* **1 :** a stony or horny material consisting of the skeletons of tiny colonial sea

animals related to the jellyfishes and including one kind that is red and used in jewelry **2 :** one or a colony of the animals that form coral **3 :** a dark pink

[2]**coral** *adj* **1 :** made of coral **2 :** of the color of coral

coral snake *n* **:** a small poisonous American snake brightly ringed with red, black, and yellow or white

cord *n* **1 :** material like a small thin rope that is used mostly for tying things **2 :** something like a cord **3 :** an amount of firewood equal to a pile of wood eight feet long, four feet high, and four feet wide or 128 cubic feet (about 3.6 cubic meters) **4 :** a rib or ridge woven into cloth **5 :** a ribbed fabric **6 :** a small insulated cable used to connect an electrical appliance with an outlet

cord•ed *adj* **:** having or drawn into ridges or cords

cor•dial *adj* **:** being warm and friendly — **cor•dial•ly** *adv*

cor•dial•i•ty *n* **:** sincere affection and kindness

cor•du•roy *n* **1 :** a heavy ribbed usually cotton cloth **2 corduroys** *pl* **:** trousers made of corduroy **3 :** logs laid crosswise side by side to make a road surface

[1]**core** *n* **1 :** the central part of some fruits (as pineapples or pears) **2 :** the central part of a heavenly body (as the earth or sun) **3 :** the basic or central part of something

[2]**core** *vb* **cored; cor•ing :** to remove the core from

[1]**cork** *n* **1 :** the light but tough material that is the outer layer of bark of a tree (**cork oak**) and is used especially for stoppers and insulation **2 :** a usually cork stopper for a bottle or jug

[2]**cork** *vb* **:** to stop with a cork

[1]**cork•screw** *n* **:** a pointed spiral piece of metal with a handle that is screwed into corks to draw them from bottles

[2]**corkscrew** *adj* **:** like a corkscrew

cor•mo•rant *n* **:** a large black seabird with a long neck and a slender hooked beak

[1]**corn** *n* **1 :** the seeds or grain of a cereal plant (as wheat or oats) **2 :** INDIAN CORN **3 :** a plant whose seeds are corn

[2]**corn** *vb* **:** to preserve by packing with salt or by soaking in salty water

[3]**corn** *n* **:** a hardening and thickening of the skin (as on a person's toe)

corn•cob *n* **:** the woody core on which grains of Indian corn grow

cor•nea *n* **:** the transparent outer layer of the front of the eye covering the pupil and iris

[1]**cor•ner** *n* **1 :** the point or place where edges or sides meet **2 :** the place where two streets or roads meet **3 :** a piece used to mark, form, or protect a corner (as of a book) **4 :** a place away from ordinary life or business **5 :** a position from which escape or retreat is difficult or impossible — **cor•nered** *adj*

[2]**corner** *adj* **1 :** located at a corner **2 :** used or usable in or on a corner

[3]**corner** *vb* **1 :** to drive into a corner **2 :** to put in a difficult position

cor•net *n* **:** a brass musical instrument similar to but shorter than a trumpet

corn•flow•er *n* **:** a European plant related to the daisies that is often grown for its bright heads of blue, pink, or white flowers

cor•nice *n* **1 :** an ornamental piece that forms the top edge of the front of a building or pillar **2 :** an ornamental molding placed where the walls meet the ceiling of a room

corn•meal *n* **:** meal ground from corn

corn•stalk *n* **:** a stalk of Indian corn

corn•starch *n* **:** a fine starch made from Indian corn and used as a thickening agent in cooking

corn syrup *n* **:** a syrup made from cornstarch and used chiefly in baked goods and candy

cor•nu•co•pia *n* **:** a container in the shape of a horn overflowing with fruits and flowers used as a symbol of plenty

corny *adj* **corn•i•er; corn•i•est :** so simple, sentimental, or old-fashioned as to be annoying

co•rol•la *n* **:** the part of a flower that is formed by the petals

cor•o•nary *adj* **:** of or relating to the heart or its blood vessels

cor•o•na•tion *n* **:** the act or ceremony of crowning a king or queen

cor•o•net *n* **1 :** a small crown worn by a person of noble but less than royal rank **2 :** an ornamental wreath or band worn around the head

[1]**cor•po•ral** *adj* **:** of or relating to the body **:** BODILY

[2]**corporal** *n* **:** a noncommissioned officer ranking above a private in the Army or above a lance corporal in the Marine Corps

cor•po•ra•tion *n* **:** a group authorized by law to carry on an activity (as a business) with the rights and duties of a single person

cor•po•re•al *adj* **:** having, consisting of, or relating to a physical body

corps *n, pl* **corps 1 :** an organized branch of a country's military forces **2 :** a group of persons acting under one authority

corpse *n* **:** a dead body

cor•pu•lent *adj* **:** very stout and heavy **:** extremely fat

cor•pus•cle *n* **:** one of the very small cells that float freely in the blood

DICTIONARY

[1]**cor·ral** *n* **:** an enclosure for keeping or capturing animals
[2]**corral** *vb* **cor·ralled; cor·ral·ling** **1 :** to confine in or as if in a corral **2 :** to get hold of or control over
[1]**cor·rect** *vb* **1 :** to make or set right **2 :** to change or adjust so as to bring to some standard or to a required condition **3 :** to punish in order to improve **4 :** to show how a thing can be improved or made right
[2]**correct** *adj* **1 :** meeting or agreeing with some standard **:** APPROPRIATE **2 :** free from mistakes **:** ACCURATE — **cor·rect·ly** *adv* — **cor·rect·ness** *n*
cor·rec·tion *n* **1 :** the act of correcting **2 :** a change that makes something right **3 :** PUNISHMENT 1
cor·re·spond *vb* **1 :** to be alike **:** AGREE **2 :** to be equivalent **3 :** to communicate with a person by exchange of letters
cor·re·spon·dence *n* **1 :** agreement between certain things **2 :** communication by means of letters **:** the letters exchanged
cor·re·spon·dent *n* **1 :** a person with whom another person communicates by letter **2 :** a person who sends news stories or comment to a newspaper, magazine, or broadcasting company especially from a distant place
cor·ri·dor *n* **:** a passage into which rooms open
cor·rode *vb* **cor·rod·ed; cor·rod·ing** **:** to wear away little by little (as by rust or acid)
cor·ro·sion *n* **:** the process or effect of corroding
cor·ro·sive *adj* **:** tending or able to corrode
cor·ru·gate *vb* **cor·ru·gat·ed; cor·ru·gat·ing** **:** to make wrinkles in or shape into wavy folds
[1]**cor·rupt** *vb* **1 :** to change (as in morals, manners, or actions) from good to bad **2 :** to influence a public official in an improper way (as by a bribe)
[2]**corrupt** *adj* **1 :** morally bad **:** EVIL **2 :** behaving in a bad or improper way **:** doing wrong — **cor·rupt·ly** *adv* — **cor·rupt·ness** *n*
cor·rup·tion *n* **1 :** physical decay or rotting **2 :** lack of honesty **3 :** the causing of someone else to do something wrong **4 :** a being changed for the worse
cor·sage *n* **:** a bouquet of flowers usually worn on the shoulder
corse·let *or* **cors·let** *n* **:** the body armor worn by a knight especially on the upper part of the body
cor·set *n* **:** a tight undergarment worn to support or give shape to waist and hips
cos·met·ic *n* **:** material (as a cream, lotion, or powder) used to beautify especially the complexion
cos·mic *adj* **:** of or relating to the whole universe
cosmic ray *n* **:** a stream of very penetrating particles that enter the earth's atmosphere from outer space at high speed
cos·mo·naut *n* **:** a Soviet astronaut
cos·mos *n* **1 :** the orderly universe **2 :** a tall garden plant related to the daisies that has showy white, pink, or rose-colored flower heads
[1]**cost** *n* **1 :** the amount paid or charged for something **:** PRICE **2 :** loss or penalty involved in gaining something
[2]**cost** *vb* **cost; cost·ing** **1 :** to have a price of **2 :** to cause one to pay, spend, or lose
cost·ly *adj* **cost·li·er; cost·li·est** **1 :** of great cost or value **:** EXPENSIVE, DEAR **2 :** made at great expense or sacrifice
[1]**cos·tume** *n* **1 :** style of clothing, ornaments, and hair used especially during a certain period, in a certain region, or by a certain class or group **2 :** special or fancy dress (as for wear on the stage or at a masquerade) **3 :** a person's outer garments
[2]**costume** *vb* **cos·tumed; cos·tum·ing** **1 :** to provide with a costume **2 :** to design costumes for
[1]**cot** *n* **:** a small house **:** COTTAGE, HUT
[2]**cot** *n* **:** a narrow bed often made to fold up
cot·tage *n* **1 :** a small usually frame house for one family **2 :** a small house for vacation use
cottage cheese *n* **:** a very soft cheese made from soured skim milk
[1]**cot·ton** *n* **1 :** a soft fluffy material made up of twisted hairs that surrounds the seeds of a tall plant (**cotton plant**) related to the mallows and that is spun into yarn **2 :** thread, yarn, or cloth made from cotton
[2]**cotton** *adj* **:** made of cotton
cotton gin *n* **:** a machine for removing seeds from cotton
cot·ton·mouth *n* **:** MOCCASIN 2
cot·ton·seed *n* **:** the seed of the cotton plant from which comes a meal rich in protein and an oil used especially in cooking
cot·ton·tail *n* **:** a small rabbit with a white tail
cot·ton·wood *n* **:** any of several poplar trees that have seeds with bunches of hairs suggesting cotton and that include some which grow rapidly
couch *n* **:** a piece of furniture (as a bed or sofa) that one can sit or lie on
cou·gar *n* **:** a large yellowish brown North American wild animal related to the domestic cat
[1]**cough** *vb* **1 :** to force air from the lungs

with a sharp short noise or series of noises **2 :** to get rid of by coughing

[2]**cough** *n* **1 :** a condition in which there is severe or frequent coughing **2 :** an act or sound of coughing

could *past of* CAN **1** — used as a helping verb in the past **2** — used as a polite form instead of *can*

couldn't : could not

coun·cil *n* **:** a group of persons appointed or elected to make laws or give advice

coun·cil·or *or* **coun·cil·lor** *n* **:** a member of a council

[1]**coun·sel** *n* **1 :** advice given **2 :** the discussion of reasons for or against a thing **:** an exchange of opinions **3** *pl* **counsel :** a lawyer engaged in the trial and management of a case in court

[2]**counsel** *vb* **coun·seled** *or* **coun·selled; coun·sel·ing** *or* **coun·sel·ling** **1 :** to give counsel **:** ADVISE **2 :** to seek counsel

coun·sel·or *or* **coun·sel·lor** *n* **1 :** a person who gives counsel **2 :** LAWYER **3 :** a supervisor of campers or activities at a summer camp

[1]**count** *vb* **1 :** to add one by one in order to find the total number in a collection **2 :** to name the numerals in order up to a particular point **3 :** to name the numbers one by one or by groups **4 :** to include in counting or thinking about **5 :** to consider or judge to be **6 :** to include or leave out by or as if by counting **7 :** RELY, DEPEND **8 :** [2]PLAN 1 **9 :** to have value, force, or importance

[2]**count** *n* **1 :** the act or process of counting **2 :** a total arrived at by counting **3 :** any one charge in a legal declaration or indictment

[3]**count** *n* **:** a European nobleman whose rank is like that of a British earl

count·down *n* **:** a counting off of the time remaining before an event (as the launching of a rocket)

[1]**coun·te·nance** *n* **:** the human face or its expression

[2]**countenance** *vb* **coun·te·nanced; coun·te·nanc·ing :** to give approval or tolerance to

[1]**count·er** *n* **1 :** a piece (as of plastic or ivory) used in counting or in games **2 :** a level surface usually higher than a table that is used for selling, serving food, displaying things, or working on

[2]**count·er** *n* **1 :** one that counts **2 :** a device for showing a number or amount

[3]**coun·ter** *vb* **1 :** to act in opposition to **:** OPPOSE **2 :** RETALIATE

[4]**coun·ter** *adv* **:** in another or opposite direction

[5]**coun·ter** *n* **:** an answering or opposing force or blow

[6]**coun·ter** *adj* **:** moving or acting in an opposite way **:** CONTRARY

coun·ter- *prefix* **1 :** opposite **2 :** opposing **3 :** like **:** matching **4 :** duplicate **:** substitute

coun·ter·act *vb* **:** to act against so as to prevent something from acting in its own way

coun·ter·clock·wise *adv or adj* **:** in a direction opposite to that in which the hands of a clock move

[1]**coun·ter·feit** *adj* **1 :** made in exact imitation of something genuine and meant to be taken as genuine **2 :** not sincere

[2]**counterfeit** *vb* **1 :** PRETEND 2 **2 :** to imitate or copy especially in order to deceive — **coun·ter·feit·er** *n*

[3]**counterfeit** *n* **:** something made to imitate another thing with the desire to deceive

coun·ter·part *n* **:** a person or thing that is very like or corresponds to another person or thing

coun·ter·point *n* **:** one or more independent melodies added above or below and in harmony with a given melody

coun·ter·sign *n* **:** a secret signal that must be given by a person wishing to pass a guard **:** PASSWORD

count·ess *n* **1 :** the wife or widow of a count or an earl **2 :** a woman who holds the rank of a count or an earl in her own right

counting number *n* **:** NATURAL NUMBER

count·less *adj* **:** too many to be counted

coun·try *n, pl* **coun·tries** **1 :** REGION 1, DISTRICT **2 :** a land lived in by a people with a common government **3 :** the people of a nation **4 :** open rural land away from big towns and cities

country and western *n* **:** music coming from or imitating the folk music of the southern United States or the Western cowboy

coun·try·man *n, pl* **coun·try·men** **1 :** a person born in the same country as another **:** a fellow citizen **2 :** a person living or raised in the country

coun·try·side *n* **:** a rural area or its people

coun·ty *n, pl* **coun·ties :** a division of a state or country for local government

cou·pé *or* **coupe** *n* **1 :** a carriage with four wheels and an enclosed body seating two persons and with an outside seat for the driver in front **2 :** an enclosed two-door automobile for usually two persons

[1]**cou·ple** *n* **1 :** two persons who are paired together or closely associated **2 :** two things of the same kind that are connected or that are thought of together

[2]**couple** *vb* **cou·pled; cou·pling** **1 :** to join or link together **:** CONNECT **2 :** to join in pairs

cou•plet *n* **:** two rhyming lines of verse one after another

cou•pling *n* **1 :** the act of bringing or coming together **2 :** something that joins or connects two parts or things

cou•pon *n* **1 :** a ticket or form that allows the holder to receive some service, payment, or discount **2 :** a part of an advertisement meant to be cut out for use as an order blank

cour•age *n* **:** the strength of mind that makes one able to meet danger and difficulties with firmness

cou•ra•geous *adj* **:** having or showing courage — **cou•ra•geous•ly** *adv*

[1]**course** *n* **1 :** motion from one point to another **:** progress in space or time **2 :** the path over which something moves **3 :** direction of motion **4 :** a natural channel for water **5 :** way of doing something **6 :** a series of acts or proceedings arranged in regular order **7 :** a series of studies leading to a diploma or a degree **8 :** a part of a meal served at one time **9 :** a continuous level range of brick or masonry throughout a wall — **of course :** as might be expected

[2]**course** *vb* **coursed; cours•ing 1 :** to run through or over **2 :** to move rapidly **:** RACE

[1]**court** *n* **1 :** the home of a ruler **2 :** a ruler's assembly of advisers and officers as a governing power **3 :** the family and people who follow a ruler **4 :** an open space completely or partly surrounded by buildings **5 :** a short street **6 :** a space arranged for playing a certain game **7 :** an official meeting led by a judge for settling legal questions or the place where it is held **8 :** respect meant to win favor

[2]**court** *vb* **1 :** to try to gain or get the support of **:** SEEK **2 :** to seem to be asking for **:** TEMPT **3 :** to seek the liking of

cour•te•ous *adj* **:** showing respect and consideration for others **:** POLITE — **cour•te•ous•ly** *adv* — **cour•te•ous•ness** *n*

cour•te•sy *n, pl* **cour•te•sies 1 :** the quality or state of being courteous **2 :** a courteous act or expression **3 :** something that is a favor and not a right

court•house *n* **1 :** a building in which courts of law are held **2 :** a building in which county offices are housed

court•i•er *n* **:** a member of a royal court

court•ly *adj* **court•li•er; court•li•est :** suitable to a royal court **:** ELEGANT, POLITE

court•ship *n* **:** the act or process of courting or seeking the liking of someone

court•yard *n* **:** [1]COURT 4

cous•in *n* **:** a child of one's uncle or aunt

cove *n* **:** a small sheltered inlet or bay

cov•e•nant *n* **:** a formal or solemn agreement

[1]**cov•er** *vb* **1 :** to provide protection to or against **2 :** to maintain a check on especially by patrolling **3 :** to hide from sight or knowledge **4 :** to place or spread something over **5 :** to dot thickly **6 :** to form a cover or covering over **7 :** to take into account **8 :** to have as one's field of activity or interest **9 :** to pass over or through

[2]**cover** *n* **1 :** something that protects, shelters, or hides **2 :** something that is placed over or about another thing **:** LID, TOP **3 :** a binding or a protecting case **4 :** a covering (as a blanket) used on a bed **5 :** an envelope or wrapper for mail

cov•er•age *n* **1 :** insurance against something **2 :** the value or amount of insurance

cov•er•all *n* **:** an outer garment that combines shirt and pants and is worn to protect one's regular clothes — usually used in pl.

covered wagon *n* **:** a large long wagon with a curving canvas top

cov•er•ing *n* **:** something (as a roof or an envelope) that covers or conceals

cov•er•let *n* **:** BEDSPREAD

[1]**co•vert** *adj* **:** made or done secretly — **co•vert•ly** *adv* — **co•vert•ness** *n*

[2]**covert** *n* **1 :** a hiding place (as a thicket that gives shelter to game animals) **2 :** one of the small feathers around the bottom of the quills on the wings and tail of a bird

cov•et *vb* **:** to wish for greatly or with envy

cov•et•ous *adj* **:** having or showing too much desire for wealth or possessions or for something belonging to another person

cov•ey *n, pl* **coveys 1 :** a small flock (as of quail) **2 :** [1]GROUP

[1]**cow** *n* **:** the mature female of cattle or of an animal (as the moose) of which the male is called *bull*

[2]**cow** *vb* **:** to lower the spirits or courage of **:** make afraid

cow•ard *n* **:** a person who shows dishonorable fear

cow•ard•ice *n* **:** dishonorable fear

cow•ard•ly *adj* **:** being or behaving like a coward — **cow•ard•li•ness** *n*

cow•bell *n* **:** a bell hung around the neck of a cow to tell where it is

cow•bird *n* **:** a small American blackbird that lays its eggs in the nests of other birds

cow•boy *n* **:** a man or boy who works on a ranch or performs at a rodeo

cow•catch•er *n* **:** a strong frame on the front of a railroad engine for moving things blocking the track

cow•er *vb* **:** to shrink away or crouch down shivering (as from fear)

cow•girl *n* **:** a girl or woman who works on a ranch or performs at a rodeo

cow·hand *n* **:** a person who works on a cattle ranch

cow·herd *n* **:** a person who tends cows

cow·hide *n* **1 :** the hide of cattle or leather made from it **2 :** a whip of rawhide or braided leather

cowl *n* **:** a hood or long hooded cloak especially of a monk

cow·lick *n* **:** a small bunch of hair that sticks out and will not lie flat

cow·pox *n* **:** a disease of cattle that when given to humans (as by vaccination) protects from smallpox

cow·punch·er *n* **:** COWBOY

cow·slip *n* **1 :** a common Old World primrose with yellow or purple flowers **2 :** MARSH MARIGOLD

cox·swain *n* **:** the person who steers a boat

coy *adj* **:** falsely shy or modest

coy·ote *n* **:** a small wolf chiefly of western North America

[1]**co·zy** *adj* **co·zi·er; co·zi·est :** enjoying or providing warmth and comfort — **co·zi·ly** *adv* — **co·zi·ness** *n*

[2]**cozy** *n, pl* **co·zies :** a padded covering for a container (as a teapot) to keep the contents hot

[1]**crab** *n* **:** a sea animal related to the lobsters but having a flat shell and a small abdomen pressed against the underside of the body

[2]**crab** *vb* **crabbed; crab·bing :** to find fault **:** COMPLAIN

[3]**crab** *n* **:** a person who is usually cross

crab apple *n* **1 :** a small wild sour apple **2 :** a cultivated apple with small usually brightly colored acid fruit

crab·bed *adj* **:** CRABBY

crab·by *adj* **crab·bi·er; crab·bi·est :** being cross and irritable

crab·grass *n* **:** a weedy grass with coarse stems that root at the joints

[1]**crack** *vb* **1 :** to break or cause to break with a sudden sharp sound **2 :** to make or cause to make a sound of cracking as if breaking **3 :** to break often without completely separating into parts **4 :** to tell (a joke) especially in a clever way **5 :** to lose self-control **:** break down **6 :** to change in tone quality **7 :** to strike or receive a sharp blow

[2]**crack** *n* **1 :** a sudden sharp noise **2 :** a sharp clever remark **3 :** a narrow break or opening **4 :** a broken tone of the voice **5 :** the beginning moment **6 :** a sharp blow **7 :** [2]ATTEMPT

[3]**crack** *adj* **:** of high quality or ability

crack·er *n* **:** a dry thin baked food made of flour and water

[1]**crack·le** *vb* **crack·led; crack·ling 1 :** to make many small sharp noises **2 :** to form little cracks in a surface

[2]**crackle** *n* **:** the noise of repeated small cracks (as of burning wood)

crack–up *n* **1 :** BREAKDOWN **2 :** [2]CRASH 3, WRECK

crack up *vb* **:** to cause or have a crack-up

[1]**cra·dle** *n* **1 :** a baby's bed or cot usually on rockers **2 :** place of beginning **3 :** a framework or support resembling a baby's cradle in appearance or use **4 :** a rocking device used in panning gold **5 :** a support for a telephone receiver

[2]**cradle** *vb* **cra·dled; cra·dling 1 :** to hold or support in or as if in a cradle **2 :** to wash (as earth or sand) in a miner's cradle

craft *n* **1 :** skill in making things especially with the hands **2 :** an occupation or trade requiring skill with the hands or as an artist **3 :** skill in deceiving for a bad purpose **:** CUNNING **4 :** the members of a trade or a trade group **5** *pl usually* **craft :** a boat especially when of small size **6** *pl usually* **craft :** AIRCRAFT

crafts·man *n, pl* **crafts·men 1 :** a person who works at a trade or handicraft **2 :** a highly skilled worker in any field

crafty *adj* **craft·i·er; craft·i·est :** skillful at deceiving others **:** CUNNING — **craft·i·ly** *adv* — **craft·i·ness** *n*

crag *n* **:** a steep rock or cliff

crag·gy *adj* **crag·gi·er; crag·gi·est :** having many crags

cram *vb* **crammed; cram·ming 1 :** to stuff or pack tightly **2 :** to fill full **3 :** to study hard just before a test

[1]**cramp** *n* **1 :** a sudden painful involuntary tightening of a muscle **2 :** sharp pain in the abdomen — usually used in pl.

[2]**cramp** *vb* **1 :** to cause cramp in **2 :** to hold back from free action or expression **:** HAMPER

cran·ber·ry *n, pl* **cran·ber·ries :** a sour bright red berry that is eaten in sauces and jelly and is the fruit of an evergreen swamp plant related to the blueberries

[1]**crane** *n* **1 :** a tall wading bird that looks like a heron but is related to the rails **2 :** a machine with a swinging arm for lifting and carrying heavy weights **3 :** a mechanical arm that swings freely from a center and is used to support or carry a weight

[2]**crane** *vb* **craned; cran·ing :** to stretch one's neck to see better

cra·ni·al *adj* **:** of or relating to the cranium

cra·ni·um *n, pl* **cra·ni·ums** *or* **cra·nia 1 :** SKULL **2 :** the part of the skull enclosing the brain

[1]**crank** *n* **1 :** a bent armlike part with a handle that is turned to start or run machinery **2 :** a person with strange ideas **3 :** a cross or irritable person

2crank *vb* **:** to start or run by turning a crank

cranky *adj* **crank•i•er; crank•i•est :** easily angered or irritated — **crank•i•ness** *n*

cran•ny *n, pl* **cran•nies :** a small break or slit (as in a cliff)

crap•pie *n* **:** either of two sunfishes native to the Great Lakes and Mississippi valley of which the larger and darker one (**black crappie**) is an important sport fish and the other (**white crappie**) is used as a table fish

1crash *vb* **1 :** to break or go to pieces with or as if with violence and noise **:** SMASH **2 :** to fall or strike something with noise and damage **3 :** to hit or cause to hit something with force and noise **4 :** to make or cause to make a loud noise **5 :** to move or force a way roughly and noisily

2crash *n* **1 :** a loud sound (as of things smashing) **2 :** a breaking to pieces by or as if by hitting something **:** SMASH, COLLISION **3 :** the crashing of something **4 :** a sudden weakening or failure (as of a business or prices)

1crate *n* **:** a box or frame of wooden slats or boards for holding and protecting something in shipment

2crate *vb* **crat•ed; crat•ing :** to pack in a crate

cra•ter *n* **1 :** a hollow in the shape of a bowl around the opening of a volcano or geyser **2 :** a hole (as in the surface of the earth or moon) formed by an impact (as of a meteorite)

cra•vat *n* **:** NECKTIE

crave *vb* **craved; crav•ing 1 :** to ask for earnestly **2 :** to want greatly **:** long for

cra•ven *adj* **:** COWARDLY

crav•ing *n* **:** a great desire or longing

craw *n* **1 :** 1CROP 2 **2 :** the stomach of an animal

craw•fish *n, pl* **crawfish :** CRAYFISH

1crawl *vb* **1 :** to move slowly with the body close to the ground **:** move on hands and knees **2 :** to go very slowly or carefully **3 :** to be covered with or have the feeling of being covered with creeping things

2crawl *n* **1 :** the act or motion of crawling **2 :** a swimming stroke that looks a little like crawling

cray•fish *n, pl* **crayfish 1 :** a freshwater shellfish that looks like the related lobster but is much smaller **2 :** a spiny saltwater shellfish that looks like the related lobster but lacks very large claws

1cray•on *n* **:** a stick of white or colored chalk or of colored wax used for writing or drawing

2crayon *vb* **:** to draw or color with a crayon

craze *n* **:** something that is very popular for a short while

cra•zy *adj* **cra•zi•er; cra•zi•est 1 :** having a diseased or abnormal mind **:** INSANE **2 :** not sensible or logical **3 :** very excited or pleased — **cra•zi•ly** *adv* — **cra•zi•ness** *n*

1creak *vb* **:** to make a long scraping or squeaking sound

2creak *n* **:** a long squeaking or scraping noise

creaky *adj* **creak•i•er; creak•i•est :** making or likely to make a creaking sound — **creak•i•ly** *adv*

1cream *n* **1 :** the oily yellowish part of milk **2 :** a food prepared with cream **3 :** something having the smoothness and thickness of cream **4 :** the best part **5 :** a pale yellow

2cream *vb* **1 :** to furnish, prepare, or treat with cream **2 :** to rub or beat (as butter) until creamy

cream•ery *n, pl* **cream•er•ies :** DAIRY 1, 3

creamy *adj* **cream•i•er; cream•i•est 1 :** full of or containing cream **2 :** like cream in appearance, color, or taste — **cream•i•ness** *n*

1crease *n* **:** a line or mark usually made by folding or wrinkling

2crease *vb* **creased; creas•ing 1 :** to make a crease in or on **2 :** to become creased

cre•ate *vb* **cre•at•ed; cre•at•ing :** to cause to exist **:** bring into existence **:** PRODUCE

cre•a•tion *n* **1 :** the act of bringing the world into existence out of nothing **2 :** the act of making, inventing, or producing something **3 :** something created by human intelligence or imagination **4 :** the created world

cre•a•tive *adj* **:** able to create especially new and original things — **cre•a•tive•ly** *adv* — **cre•a•tive•ness** *n*

cre•a•tor *n* **1 :** one that creates or produces **2** *cap* **:** GOD 1

crea•ture *n* **1 :** a living being **2 :** a lower animal **3 :** PERSON 1

cred•i•ble *adj* **:** possible to believe **:** deserving belief — **cred•i•bly** *adv*

1cred•it *n* **1 :** the balance in an account in a person's favor **2 :** trust given to a customer for future payment for goods purchased **3 :** time given for payment **4 :** belief or trust in the truth of something **5 :** good reputation especially for honesty **:** high standing **6 :** a source of honor or pride **7 :** recognition or honor received for some quality or work **8 :** a unit of schoolwork

2credit *vb* **1 :** BELIEVE 2 **2 :** to place something in a person's favor on (a business account) **3 :** to give credit or honor to for something

cred•it•able *adj* **:** good enough to deserve praise

cred·i·tor *n* **:** a person to whom a debt is owed

cred·u·lous *adj* **:** quick to believe especially without very good reasons

creed *n* **1 :** a statement of the basic beliefs of a religious faith **2 :** a set of guiding rules or beliefs

creek *n* **:** a stream of water usually larger than a brook and smaller than a river

creel *n* **:** a basket for holding a catch of fish

[1]**creep** *vb* **crept; creep·ing 1 :** to move along with the body close to the ground or floor **:** move slowly on hands and knees **:** CRAWL **2 :** to move or advance slowly, timidly, or quietly **3 :** to grow or spread along the ground or along a surface

[2]**creep** *n* **1 :** a creeping movement **2 :** a feeling as of insects crawling over one's skin **:** a feeling of horror — usually used in pl.

creep·er *n* **1 :** one that creeps **2 :** a small bird that creeps about trees and bushes in search of insects **3 :** a plant (as ivy) that grows by spreading over a surface

creepy *adj* **creep·i·er; creep·i·est 1 :** having or causing a feeling as of insects creeping on the skin **2 :** causing fear **:** SCARY — **creep·i·ness** *n*

cre·mate *vb* **cre·mat·ed; cre·mat·ing :** to burn (as a dead body) to ashes

cre·ma·tion *n* **:** the act or practice of cremating

crepe *n* **:** a thin crinkled fabric (as of silk or wool)

crepe paper *n* **:** paper with a crinkled or puckered look and feel

crept *past of* CREEP

cre·scen·do *n, pl* **cre·scen·dos** *or* **cre·scen·does :** a gradual increase in the loudness of music

[1]**cres·cent** *n* **1 :** the shape of the visible moon during about the first week after new moon or the last week before the next new moon **2 :** something shaped like a crescent moon

[2]**crescent** *adj* **:** shaped like the new moon

cress *n* **:** any of several salad plants of the mustard group

crest *n* **1 :** a showy growth (as of flesh or feathers) on the head of an animal **2 :** an emblem or design on a helmet (as of a knight) or over a coat of arms **3 :** something forming the top of something else — **crest·ed** *adj*

crest·fall·en *adj* **:** feeling disappointment and loss of pride

crev·ice *n* **:** a narrow opening (as in the earth) caused by cracking or splitting **:** FISSURE

crew *n* **1 :** a gathering of people **2 :** a group of people working together **3 :** the group of people who operate a ship, train, or airplane

crib *n* **1 :** a manger for feeding animals **2 :** a small bed frame with high sides for a child **3 :** a building or bin for storing

[1]**crick·et** *n* **:** a small leaping insect noted for the chirping notes of the males

[2]**cricket** *n* **:** a game played on a large field with bats, ball, and wickets by two teams of eleven players each

cri·er *n* **:** one who calls out orders or announcements

crime *n* **1 :** the doing of an act forbidden by law **:** the failure to do an act required by law **2 :** an act that is sinful, foolish, or disgraceful

[1]**crim·i·nal** *adj* **1 :** being or guilty of crime **2 :** relating to crime or its punishment — **crim·i·nal·ly** *adv*

[2]**criminal** *n* **:** a person who has committed a crime

crim·son *n* **:** a deep purplish red

cringe *vb* **cringed; cring·ing 1 :** to shrink in fear **:** COWER **2 :** to behave in a very humble way **:** FAWN

crin·kle *vb* **crin·kled; crin·kling 1 :** to form or cause little waves or wrinkles on the surface **:** WRINKLE **2 :** [1]RUSTLE 1

crin·kly *adj* **crin·kli·er; crin·kli·est :** full of small wrinkles

[1]**crip·ple** *n* **:** a lame or disabled person

[2]**cripple** *vb* **crip·pled; crip·pling 1 :** to cause to become a cripple **2 :** to make useless or imperfect

cri·sis *n, pl* **cri·ses 1 :** a turning point for better or worse in a disease **2 :** an unstable or critical time or state of affairs

[1]**crisp** *adj* **1 :** being thin and hard and easily crumbled **2 :** pleasantly firm and fresh **3 :** having a sharp distinct outline **4 :** being clear and brief **5 :** pleasantly cool and invigorating **:** BRISK

[2]**crisp** *vb* **:** to make or become crisp

criss·cross *vb* **1 :** to mark with or make lines that cross one another **2 :** to go or pass back and forth

crit·ic *n* **1 :** a person who makes or gives a judgment of the value, worth, beauty, or quality of something **2 :** a person given to finding fault or complaining

crit·i·cal *adj* **1 :** inclined to criticize especially in an unfavorable way **2 :** consisting of or involving criticism or the judgment of critics **3 :** using or involving careful judgment **4 :** of, relating to, or being a turning point or crisis — **crit·i·cal·ly** *adv*

crit·i·cism *n* **1 :** the act of criticizing and especially of finding fault **2 :** a critical remark or comment **3 :** a careful judgment or review especially by a critic

crit·i·cize *vb* **crit·i·cized; crit·i·ciz·ing** **1** : to examine and judge as a critic **2** : to find fault with

[1]**croak** *vb* **1** : to make a deep harsh sound **2** : to speak in a hoarse throaty voice

[2]**croak** *n* : a hoarse harsh sound or cry

[1]**cro·chet** *n* : work done or a fabric formed by crocheting

[2]**crochet** *vb* : to make (something) or create a fabric with a hooked needle by forming and interlacing loops in a thread

crock *n* : a thick pot or jar of baked clay

crock·ery *n* : EARTHENWARE

croc·o·dile *n* : a very large animal related to the alligator that crawls on short legs about tropical marshes and rivers

cro·cus *n* : a plant related to the irises that has grasslike leaves and is often planted for its white, yellow, or purple spring flowers

cro·ny *n, pl* **cro·nies** : a close companion : CHUM

[1]**crook** *vb* : [2]BEND 2, CURVE

[2]**crook** *n* **1** : a shepherd's staff with one end curved into a hook **2** : a dishonest person (as a thief or swindler) **3** : a curved or hooked part of a thing : BEND

crook·ed *adj* **1** : having bends and curves **2** : not set or placed straight **3** : DISHONEST — **crook·ed·ly** *adv* — **crook·ed·ness** *n*

croon *vb* : to hum or sing in a low soft voice

[1]**crop** *n* **1** : a short riding whip **2** : an enlargement just above the stomach of a bird or insect in which food is stored for a while **3** : the amount gathered or harvested : HARVEST **4** : BATCH 3, LOT

[2]**crop** *vb* **cropped; crop·ping** **1** : to remove (as by cutting or biting) the upper or outer parts of : TRIM **2** : to grow or yield a crop (as of grain) : cause (land) to bear a crop **3** : to come or appear when not expected

cro·quet *n* : a game in which players drive wooden balls with mallets through a series of wickets set out on a lawn

cro·quette *n* : a roll or ball of hashed meat, fish, or vegetables fried in deep fat

[1]**cross** *n* **1** : a structure consisting of one bar crossing another at right angles **2** *often cap* : the structure on which Jesus was crucified used as a symbol of Christianity and of the Christian religion **3** : sorrow or suffering as test of patience or virtue **4** : an object or mark shaped like a cross **5** : a mixing of breeds, races, or kinds : the product of such a mixing

[2]**cross** *vb* **1** : to lie or be situated across **2** : to divide by passing through or across (a line or area) : INTERSECT **3** : to move, pass, or extend across or past **4** : to make the sign of the cross upon or over (as in prayer) **5** : to cancel by marking crosses on or by drawing a line through **6** : to place one over the other **7** : to act against : OPPOSE **8** : to draw a line across **9** : to cause (an animal or plant) to breed with one of another kind : produce hybrids **10** : to pass going in opposite directions

[3]**cross** *adj* **1** : lying, falling, or passing across **2** : [2]CONTRARY 1 **3** : hard to get along with : IRRITABLE — **cross·ly** *adv* — **cross·ness** *n*

cross·bar *n* : a bar, piece, or stripe placed crosswise or across something

cross·bones *n pl* : two leg or arm bones placed or pictured as lying across each other

cross·bow *n* : a short bow mounted crosswise near the end of a wooden stock that shoots short arrows

cross–ex·am·ine *vb* **cross–ex·am·ined; cross–ex·am·in·ing** : to question (a person) in an effort to show that statements or answers given earlier were false — **cross–ex·am·in·er** *n*

cross–eyed *adj* : having one or both eyes turned toward the nose

cross·ing *n* **1** : a point where two lines, tracks, or streets cross each other **2** : a place provided for going across a street, railroad tracks, or a stream **3** : a voyage across a body of water

cross·piece *n* : something placed so as to cross something else

cross–ref·er·ence *n* : a reference made from one place to another (as in a dictionary)

cross·roads *n sing or pl* : a place where roads cross

cross section *n* **1** : a cutting made across something (as a log or an apple) **2** : a representation of a cross section **3** : a number of persons or things selected from a group to stand for the whole

cross·walk *n* : a specially paved or marked path for people walking across a street or road

cross·wise *adv* : so as to cross something : ACROSS

cross·word puzzle *n* : a puzzle in which words are filled into a pattern of numbered squares in answer to clues so that they read across and down

crotch *n* : an angle formed by the spreading apart of two legs or branches or of a limb from its trunk

[1]**crouch** *vb* : to stoop or bend low with the arms and legs close to the body

[2]**crouch** *n* : the position of crouching

croup *n* : a children's disease in which a hoarse cough and hard breathing are present

[1]**crow** *n* : a glossy black bird that has a harsh cry

²crow *vb* **1 :** to make the loud shrill sound that a rooster makes **2 :** to make sounds of delight **3 :** ²BOAST 1

³crow *n* **1 :** the cry of a rooster **2 :** a cry of triumph

crow•bar *n* **:** a metal bar used as a lever (as for prying things apart)

¹crowd *vb* **1 :** to press or push forward **2 :** to press close **3 :** to collect in numbers **:** THRONG **4 :** to fill or pack by pressing together

²crowd *n* **1 :** a large number of persons collected together **:** THRONG **2 :** the population as a whole **:** ordinary people **3 :** a group of people having a common interest

¹crown *n* **1 :** a wreath or band especially as a mark of victory or honor **2 :** a royal headdress **3 :** the highest part (as of a tree or mountain) **4 :** the top of the head **5 :** the top part of a hat **6 :** the part of a tooth outside of the gum **7 :** something suggesting a crown **8** *cap* **:** royal power or authority or one having such power **9 :** any of various coins (as a British coin worth five shillings) — **crowned** *adj*

²crown *vb* **1 :** to place a crown on **:** make sovereign **2 :** to declare officially to be **3 :** to give something as a mark of honor or reward **4 :** ²TOP 2 **5 :** to bring to a successful conclusion **:** COMPLETE, PERFECT **6 :** to put an artificial crown on a damaged tooth **7 :** to hit on the head

crow's nest *n* **:** a partly enclosed place to stand high on the mast of a ship for use as a lookout

cru•cial *adj* **1 :** being a final or very important test or decision **:** DECISIVE **2 :** very important **:** SIGNIFICANT

cru•ci•ble *n* **:** a pot made of a substance not easily damaged by fire that is used for holding something to be treated under great heat

cru•ci•fix *n* **:** a cross with a figure of Christ crucified on it

cru•ci•fix•ion *n* **1 :** an act of crucifying **2** *cap* **:** the crucifying of Christ on the cross

cru•ci•fy *vb* **cru•ci•fied; cru•ci•fy•ing 1 :** to put to death by nailing or binding the hands and feet to a cross **2 :** to treat cruelly **:** TORTURE, PERSECUTE

crude *adj* **crud•er; crud•est 1 :** in a natural state and not changed by special treatment **:** RAW **2 :** not having or showing good manners **:** VULGAR **3 :** planned or done in a rough or unskilled way — **crude•ly** *adv* — **crude•ness** *n*

cru•el *adj* **cru•el•er** *or* **cru•el•ler; cru•el•est** *or* **cru•el•lest 1 :** ready to hurt others **2 :** causing or helping to cause suffering — **cru•el•ly** *adv*

cru•el•ty *n, pl* **cru•el•ties 1 :** the quality or state of being cruel **2 :** cruel treatment

cru•et *n* **:** a bottle for holding vinegar, oil, or sauce for table use

¹cruise *vb* **cruised; cruis•ing 1 :** to travel by ship often stopping at a series of ports **2 :** to travel for pleasure **3 :** to travel at the best operating speed

²cruise *n* **:** an act or instance of cruising

cruis•er *n* **1 :** a warship that is smaller than a battleship **2 :** a police car used for patrolling streets and equipped with radio for communicating with headquarters **3 :** a motorboat equipped for living aboard

crul•ler *n* **:** a small sweet cake made of egg batter usually cut in strips or twists and fried in deep fat

¹crumb *n* **1 :** a small piece especially of bread **2 :** a little bit

²crumb *vb* **:** to break into crumbs **:** CRUMBLE

crum•ble *vb* **crum•bled; crum•bling 1 :** to break into small pieces **2 :** to fall to pieces **:** fall into ruin

crum•bly *adj* **crum•bli•er; crum•bli•est :** easily crumbled

crum•ple *vb* **crum•pled; crum•pling 1 :** to press or crush out of shape **:** RUMPLE **2 :** to become crumpled **3 :** ¹COLLAPSE 1

¹crunch *vb* **1 :** to chew or grind with a crushing noise **2 :** to make the sound of being crushed or squeezed

²crunch *n* **:** an act or sound of crunching

¹cru•sade *n* **1** *cap* **:** one of the military expeditions made by Christian countries in the eleventh, twelfth, and thirteenth centuries to recover the Holy Land from the Muslims **2 :** a campaign to get things changed for the better

²crusade *vb* **cru•sad•ed; cru•sad•ing :** to take part in a crusade

cru•sad•er *n* **:** a person who takes part in a crusade

¹crush *vb* **1 :** to squeeze together so as to change or destroy the natural shape or condition **2 :** ¹HUG 1 **3 :** to break into fine pieces by pressure **4 :** OVERWHELM 2 **5 :** OPPRESS 1

²crush *n* **1 :** an act of crushing **2 :** a tightly packed crowd **3 :** a foolish or very strong liking **:** INFATUATION

crust *n* **1 :** the hardened outside surface of bread **2 :** a hard dry piece of bread **3 :** the pastry cover of a pie **4 :** a hard outer covering or surface layer **5 :** the outer part of the earth

crus•ta•cean *n* **:** any of a large group of mostly water animals (as crabs, lobsters, and shrimps) with a body made of segments, a firm outer shell, two pairs of antennae, and limbs that are jointed

crusty *adj* **crust·i·er; crust·i·est** **1 :** having or being a crust **2 :** [3]CROSS 3

crutch *n* **1 :** a support usually made with a piece at the top to fit under the armpit that is used by a lame person as an aid in walking **2 :** something (as a prop or support) like a crutch in shape or use

[1]**cry** *vb* **cried; cry·ing** **1 :** to make a loud call or cry **:** SHOUT, EXCLAIM **2 :** to shed tears **:** WEEP **3 :** to utter a special sound or call **4 :** to make known to the public **:** call out

[2]**cry** *n, pl* **cries** **1 :** a loud call or shout (as of pain, fear, or joy) **2 :** [1]APPEAL 2 **3 :** a fit of weeping **4 :** the special sound made by an animal

cry·ba·by *n, pl* **cry·ba·bies :** a person who cries easily or who complains often

[1]**crys·tal** *n* **1 :** quartz that is colorless and transparent or nearly so **2 :** something transparent like crystal **3 :** a body formed by a substance hardening so that it has flat surfaces in an even arrangement **4 :** a clear colorless glass of very good quality **5 :** the transparent cover over a clock or watch dial

[2]**crystal** *adj* **:** made of or being like crystal **:** CLEAR

crys·tal·line *adj* **1 :** made of crystal or composed of crystals **2 :** like crystal **:** TRANSPARENT

crys·tal·lize *vb* **crys·tal·lized; crys·tal·liz·ing** **1 :** to form or cause to form crystals or grains **2 :** to take or cause to take definite form

cub *n* **1 :** the young of various animals (as the bear, fox, or lion) **2 :** CUB SCOUT

cub·by·hole *n* **:** a snug place (as for storing things)

[1]**cube** *n* **1 :** a solid body having six equal square sides **2 :** the product obtained by multiplying the square of a number by the number itself

[2]**cube** *vb* **cubed; cub·ing** **1 :** to take (a number) as a factor three times **2 :** to form into a cube or divide into cubes

cu·bic *adj* **:** being the volume of a cube whose edge is a specified unit

cu·bi·cal *adj* **1 :** having the form of a cube **2 :** relating to volume

cu·bit *n* **:** a unit of length usually equal to about forty-six centimeters

Cub Scout *n* **:** a member of a program of the Boy Scouts for boys in the first through fifth grades in school

cuck·oo *n, pl* **cuckoos** **1 :** any of several related birds (as a grayish brown European bird) that mostly lay their eggs in the nests of other birds for them to hatch **2 :** the call of the European cuckoo

cu·cum·ber *n* **:** a long usually green-skinned vegetable that is used in salads and as pickles and is the fruit of a vine related to the melons and gourds

cud *n* **:** a portion of food brought up from the first stomach of some animals (as the cow and sheep) to be chewed again

cud·dle *vb* **cud·dled; cud·dling** **1 :** to hold close for warmth or comfort or in affection **2 :** to lie close **:** NESTLE, SNUGGLE

[1]**cud·gel** *n* **:** a short heavy club

[2]**cudgel** *vb* **cud·geled** *or* **cud·gelled; cud·gel·ing** *or* **cud·gel·ling :** to beat with or as if with a cudgel

[1]**cue** *n* **1 :** a word, phrase, or action in a play serving as a signal for the next actor to speak or to do something **2 :** something serving as a signal or suggestion **:** HINT

[2]**cue** *n* **:** a straight tapering stick used in playing billiards and pool

[1]**cuff** *n* **1 :** a band or turned-over piece at the end of a sleeve **2 :** the turned-back hem of a trouser leg

[2]**cuff** *vb* **:** to strike especially with or as if with the palm of the hand **:** SLAP

[3]**cuff** *n* **:** [2]SLAP 1

[1]**cull** *vb* **1 :** to select from a group **2 :** to identify and remove the culls from

[2]**cull** *n* **:** something rejected from a group or lot as not as good as the rest

cul·mi·nate *vb* **cul·mi·nat·ed; cul·mi·nat·ing :** to reach the highest point

cul·pa·ble *adj* **:** deserving blame

cul·prit *n* **1 :** one accused of or charged with a crime or fault **2 :** one guilty of a crime or fault

cul·ti·vate *vb* **cul·ti·vat·ed; cul·ti·vat·ing** **1 :** to prepare land for the raising of crops **2 :** to raise or assist the growth of crops by tilling or by labor and care **3 :** to improve or develop by careful attention, training, or study **:** devote time and thought to **4 :** to seek the company and friendship of

cul·ti·vat·ed *adj* **1 :** raised or produced under cultivation **2 :** having or showing good education and proper manners

cul·ti·va·tion *n* **1 :** the act or process of cultivating especially the soil **2 :** REFINEMENT 2

cul·ti·va·tor *n* **1 :** one (as a farmer) that cultivates something **2 :** a tool or machine for loosening the soil between rows of a crop

cul·tur·al *adj* **:** of or relating to culture — **cul·tur·al·ly** *adv*

cul·ture *n* **1 :** CULTIVATION 1 **2 :** the raising or development (as of a crop or product) by careful attention **3 :** the improvement of the mind, tastes, and manners through careful training **4 :** a certain stage, form, or kind of civilization

cul·tured *adj* **1 :** having or showing refinement in taste, speech, or manners **2 :** produced under artificial conditions
cul·vert *n* **:** a drain or waterway crossing under a road or railroad
cum·ber·some *adj* **:** hard to handle or manage because of size or weight
cu·mu·la·tive *adj* **:** increasing (as in force, strength, or amount) by one addition after another
cu·mu·lus *n, pl* **cu·mu·li :** a massive cloud form having a flat base and rounded outlines often piled up like a mountain
[1]**cu·ne·i·form** *adj* **1 :** shaped like a wedge **2 :** made up of or written with marks or letters shaped like wedges
[2]**cuneiform** *n* **:** cuneiform writing
[1]**cun·ning** *adj* **1 :** skillful and clever at using special knowledge or at getting something done **2 :** showing craftiness and trickery **3 :** CUTE, PRETTY
[2]**cunning** *n* **1 :** SKILL 1, DEXTERITY **2 :** cleverness in getting what one wants often by tricks or deceiving
[1]**cup** *n* **1 :** something to drink out of in the shape of a small bowl usually with a handle **2 :** the contents of a cup **:** CUPFUL **3 :** a trophy in the shape of a cup with two handles **4 :** something like a cup in shape or use
[2]**cup** *vb* **cupped; cup·ping :** to curve into the shape of a cup
cup·board *n* **:** a closet usually with shelves for dishes or food
cup·cake *n* **:** a small cake baked in a mold shaped like a cup
cup·ful *n, pl* **cup·fuls** *or* **cups·ful 1 :** the amount held by a cup **2 :** a half pint **:** eight ounces (about 236 milliliters)
cu·pid *n* **:** a picture or statue of Cupid the Roman god of love often as a winged child with a bow and arrow
cu·pid·i·ty *n* **:** excessive desire for wealth **:** GREED
cu·po·la *n* **1 :** a rounded roof or ceiling **:** DOME **2 :** a small structure built on top of a roof
cur *n* **:** a worthless or mongrel dog
cur·able *adj* **:** possible to cure
cu·rate *n* **:** a member of the clergy who assists the rector or vicar of a church
[1]**curb** *n* **1 :** a chain or strap on a horse's bit used to control the horse by pressing against the lower jaw **2 :** [1]CHECK 2 **3 :** an enclosing border (as of stone or concrete) often along the edge of a street
[2]**curb** *vb* **:** to control by or furnish with a curb
curb·ing *n* **1 :** material for making a curb **2 :** [1]CURB 3
curd *n* **:** the thickened or solid part of sour or partly digested milk
cur·dle *vb* **cur·dled; cur·dling :** to change into curd **:** COAGULATE
[1]**cure** *n* **1 :** a method or period of medical treatment **2 :** recovery or relief from a disease **3 :** [1]REMEDY 1
[2]**cure** *vb* **cured; cur·ing 1 :** to make or become healthy or sound again **2 :** to prepare by a chemical or physical process for use or storage **3 :** to undergo a curing process
cur·few *n* **1 :** a rule requiring certain or all people to be off the streets or at home at a stated time **2 :** a signal (as the ringing of a bell) formerly given to announce the beginning of a curfew **3 :** the time when a curfew is sounded
cu·rio *n, pl* **cu·ri·os :** a rare or unusual article **:** CURIOSITY
cu·ri·os·i·ty *n, pl* **cu·ri·os·i·ties 1 :** an eager desire to learn and often to learn what does not concern one **2 :** something strange or unusual **3 :** an object or article valued because it is strange or rare
cu·ri·ous *adj* **1 :** eager to learn **:** INQUISITIVE **2 :** attracting attention by being strange or unusual **:** ODD — **cu·ri·ous·ly** *adv*
[1]**curl** *vb* **1 :** to twist or form into ringlets **2 :** to take or move in a curved form
[2]**curl** *n* **1 :** a lock of hair that coils **:** RINGLET **2 :** something having a spiral or winding form **:** COIL **3 :** the action of curling **:** the state of being curled
curly *adj* **curl·i·er; curl·i·est 1 :** tending to curl **2 :** having curls
cur·rant *n* **1 :** a small seedless raisin used in baking and cooking **2 :** a sour red or white edible berry produced by a low spreading shrub related to the gooseberry
cur·ren·cy *n, pl* **cur·ren·cies 1 :** common use or acceptance **2 :** money in circulation
[1]**cur·rent** *adj* **1 :** now passing **2 :** occurring in or belonging to the present time **3 :** generally and widely accepted, used, or practiced
[2]**current** *n* **1 :** a body of fluid moving in a specified direction **2 :** the swiftest part of a stream **3 :** the general course **:** TREND **4 :** a flow of charges of electricity
cur·ric·u·lum *n, pl* **cur·ric·u·la** *or* **cur·ric·u·lums :** all the courses of study offered by a school
cur·ry *vb* **cur·ried; cur·ry·ing :** to rub and clean the coat of
[1]**curse** *n* **1 :** a calling for harm or injury to come to someone **2 :** a word or an expression used in cursing or swearing **3 :** evil or misfortune that comes as if in answer to a curse **4 :** a cause of great harm or evil
[2]**curse** *vb* **cursed; curs·ing 1 :** to call upon

divine power to send harm or evil upon **2 :** SWEAR 5 **3 :** to bring unhappiness or evil upon **:** AFFLICT

cur•sor *n* **:** a symbol (as an arrow or blinking line) on a computer screen that shows where the user is working

curt *adj* **:** rudely brief in language

cur•tail *vb* **:** to shorten or reduce by cutting off the end or a part of

[1]**cur•tain** *n* **1 :** a piece of material (as cloth) hung up to darken, hide, divide, or decorate **2 :** something that covers, hides, or separates like a curtain

[2]**curtain** *vb* **1 :** to furnish with curtains **2 :** to hide or shut off with a curtain

[1]**curt•sy** *or* **curt•sey** *vb* **curt•sied** *or* **curt•seyed; curt•sy•ing** *or* **curt•sey•ing :** to lower the body slightly by bending the knees as an act of politeness or respect

[2]**curtsy** *or* **curtsey** *n, pl* **curtsies** *or* **curtseys :** an act of politeness or respect made mainly by women and consisting of a slight lowering of the body by bending the knees

cur•va•ture *n* **1 :** a curving or bending **2 :** the state of being curved

[1]**curve** *vb* **curved; curv•ing 1 :** to turn or change from a straight line or course **2 :** to cause to curve

[2]**curve** *n* **1 :** a bending or turning without angles **:** BEND **2 :** something curved **3 :** a ball thrown so that it moves away from a straight course

[1]**cush•ion** *n* **1 :** a soft pillow or pad to rest on or against **2 :** something like a cushion in use, shape, or softness **3 :** something that serves to soften or lessen the effects of something bad or unpleasant

[2]**cushion** *vb* **1 :** to place on or as if on a cushion **2 :** to furnish with a cushion **3 :** to soften or lessen the force or shock of

cusp *n* **:** a point or pointed end (as on the crown of a tooth)

cus•pid *n* **:** [1]CANINE 1

cuss *vb* **:** SWEAR 5

cus•tard *n* **:** a sweetened mixture of milk and eggs baked, boiled, or frozen

cus•to•di•an *n* **:** one that guards and protects or takes care of

cus•to•dy *n* **1 :** direct responsibility for care and control **2 :** the state of being arrested or held by police

[1]**cus•tom** *n* **1 :** the usual way of doing things **:** the usual practice **2 customs** *pl* **:** duties or taxes paid on imports or exports **3 :** support given to a business by its customers

[2]**custom** *adj* **1 :** made or done to personal order **2 :** specializing in custom work

cus•tom•ary *adj* **1 :** based on or existing by custom **2 :** commonly done or observed

cus•tom•er *n* **:** a person who buys from or uses the services of a company especially regularly

[1]**cut** *vb* **cut; cut•ting 1 :** to penetrate or divide with or as if with an edged tool **:** CLEAVE **2 :** to undergo shaping or penetrating with an edged tool **3 :** to experience the growth of through the gum **4 :** to hurt someone's feelings **5 :** to strike sharply or at an angle **6 :** to make less **7 :** [2]CROSS 2, INTERSECT **8 :** to shape by carving or grinding **9 :** [1]SWERVE **10 :** to go by a short or direct path or course **11 :** to divide into two parts **12 :** to stop or cause to stop **13 :** [1]SNUB

[2]**cut** *n* **1 :** something cut or cut off **2 :** [1]SHARE 1 **3 :** something (as a gash or wound) produced by or as if by cutting **4 :** a passage made by digging or cutting **5 :** a pictorial illustration (as in a book) **6 :** something done or said that hurts the feelings **7 :** a straight path or course **8 :** a cutting stroke or blow **9 :** the way in which a thing is cut, formed, or made **10 :** REDUCTION 1

cute *adj* **cut•er; cut•est 1 :** KEEN 4, SHREWD **2 :** attractive especially in looks or actions

cu•ti•cle *n* **1 :** an outer layer (as of skin or a leaf) often produced by the cells beneath **2 :** a dead or horny layer of skin especially around a fingernail

cut•lass *n* **:** a short heavy curved sword

cut•lery *n* **1 :** cutting tools (as knives and scissors) **2 :** utensils used in cutting, serving, and eating food

cut•let *n* **1 :** a small slice of meat cut for broiling or frying **2 :** a piece of food shaped like a cutlet

cut•out *n* **:** something cut out or intended to be cut out from something else

cut out *vb* **:** to form by cutting

cut•ter *n* **1 :** someone or something that cuts **2 :** a boat used by warships for carrying passengers and stores to and from the shore **3 :** a small sailing boat with one mast **4 :** a small armed boat used by the Coast Guard

cut•ting *n* **:** a part (as a shoot) of a plant able to grow into a whole new plant

cut•tle•fish *n* **:** a sea animal with ten arms that is related to the squid and octopus

cut•up *n* **:** a person who clowns or acts in a noisy manner

cut•worm *n* **:** a moth caterpillar that has a smooth body and feeds on the stems of plants at night

-cy *n suffix, pl* **-cies 1 :** action **:** practice **2 :** rank **:** office **3 :** body **:** class **4 :** state **:** quality

DICTIONARY

cy·a·nide *n* **:** any of several compounds containing carbon and nitrogen and including two very poisonous substances
cy·cad *n* **:** a tropical tree like a palm but related to the conifers
¹cy·cle *n* **1 :** a period of time taken up by a series of events or actions that repeat themselves again and again in the same order **2 :** a complete round or series **3 :** a long period of time **:** AGE **4 :** BICYCLE **5 :** TRICYCLE **6 :** MOTORCYCLE
²cycle *vb* **cy·cled; cy·cling :** to ride a cycle
cy·clist *n* **:** a person who rides a cycle and especially a bicycle
cy·clone *n* **1 :** a storm or system of winds that rotates about a center of low atmospheric pressure in a counterclockwise direction north of the equator and a clockwise direction south of the equator and that moves forward at a speed of thirty to fifty kilometers per hour and often brings heavy rain **2 :** TORNADO
cy·clops *n, pl* **cyclops :** WATER FLEA
cyl·in·der *n* **:** a long round body whether hollow or solid
cy·lin·dri·cal *adj* **:** having the shape of a cylinder
cym·bal *n* **:** either of a pair of brass plates that are clashed together to make a sharp ringing sound and that together form a musical percussion instrument
cy·press *n* **:** any of various evergreen trees that are related to the pines, bear cones, and have strong reddish wood which is not easily damaged by moisture
cyst *n* **1 :** an abnormal sac in a living body **2 :** a covering like a cyst or a body (as a spore) with such a covering
cy·to·plasm *n* **:** the protoplasm of a cell except for the nucleus
czar *n* **:** the ruler of Russia until the 1917 revolution
cza·ri·na *n* **1 :** the wife of a czar **2 :** a woman who has the rank of czar

D

d *n, pl* **d's** *or* **ds** *often cap* **1 :** the fourth letter of the English alphabet **2 :** 500 in Roman numerals **3 :** a grade that shows a student's work is poor
¹dab *n* **1 :** a sudden poke **2 :** a small amount **3 :** a light quick touch
²dab *vb* **dabbed; dab·bing 1 :** to strike or touch lightly **2 :** to apply with light or uneven strokes — **dab·ber** *n*
dab·ble *vb* **dab·bled; dab·bling 1 :** to wet by splashing **:** SPATTER **2 :** to paddle in or as if in water **3 :** to work without real interest or effort — **dab·bler** *n*
dace *n, pl* **dace :** any of several small fishes related to the carps
dachs·hund *n* **:** a small hound with a long body, very short legs, and long drooping ears
dad *n* **:** ¹FATHER 1
dad·dy *n, pl* **daddies :** ¹FATHER 1
dad·dy long·legs *n, pl* **daddy longlegs 1 :** an insect like a spider but with a small rounded body and long slender legs **2 :** a slender two-winged fly with long legs
daf·fo·dil *n* **:** a plant that grows from a bulb and has long slender leaves and yellow, white, or pinkish flowers suggesting trumpets and having a scalloped edge and leaflike parts at the base
daft *adj* **:** FOOLISH, CRAZY — **daft·ly** *adv* — **daft·ness** *n*
dag·ger *n* **:** a short knife used for stabbing
dahl·ia *n* **:** a tall plant related to the daisies and widely grown for its bright flowers
¹dai·ly *adj* **1 :** occurring, done, produced, or issued every day or every weekday **2 :** given or paid for one day
²daily *adv* **:** every day
³daily *n, pl* **dai·lies :** a newspaper published every weekday
¹dain·ty *n, pl* **dain·ties :** DELICACY 1
²dainty *adj* **dain·ti·er; dain·ti·est 1 :** tasting good **2 :** pretty in a delicate way **3 :** having or showing delicate taste — **dain·ti·ly** *adv* — **dain·ti·ness** *n*
dairy *n, pl* **dair·ies 1 :** a place where milk is stored or is made into butter and cheese **2 :** a farm that produces milk **3 :** a company or a store that sells milk products
dairy·ing *n* **:** the business of producing milk or milk products
dairy·maid *n* **:** a woman or girl who works in a dairy
dairy·man *n, pl* **dairy·men :** a man who operates a dairy farm or works in a dairy
da·is *n* **:** a raised platform (as in a hall or large room)
dai·sy *n, pl* **daisies :** any of a large group of plants with flower heads consisting of one or more rows of white or colored flowers like petals around a central disk of tiny often yellow flowers closely packed together
dale *n* **:** VALLEY
dal·ly *vb* **dal·lied; dal·ly·ing 1 :** to act playfully **2 :** to waste time **3 :** LINGER, DAWDLE
dal·ma·tian *n, often cap* **:** a large dog having a short white coat with black or brown spots

[1]**dam** *n* : a female parent — used especially of a domestic animal

[2]**dam** *n* : a barrier (as across a stream) to hold back a flow of water

[3]**dam** *vb* **dammed; dam·ming** : to hold back or block with or as if with a dam

[1]**dam·age** *n* **1** : loss or harm due to injury **2 damages** *pl* : money demanded or paid according to law for injury or damage

[2]**damage** *vb* **dam·aged; dam·ag·ing** : to cause damage to

dam·ask *n* : a fancy cloth used especially for household linen

dame *n* : a woman of high rank or social position

[1]**damn** *vb* **1** : to condemn to everlasting punishment especially in hell **2** : to declare to be bad or a failure **3** : to swear at : CURSE

[2]**damn** *n* : the word *damn* used as a curse

dam·na·ble *adj* : very bad : OUTRAGEOUS — **dam·na·bly** *adv*

[1]**damned** *adj* **damned·er; damned·est** **1** : DAMNABLE **2** : REMARKABLE

[2]**damned** *adv* : to a high degree : VERY

[1]**damp** *n* **1** : a harmful gas found especially in coal mines **2** : MOISTURE

[2]**damp** *vb* : DAMPEN

[3]**damp** *adj* : slightly wet : MOIST — **damp·ly** *adv* — **damp·ness** *n*

damp·en *vb* **1** : to make dull or less active **2** : to make or become damp — **damp·en·er** *n*

damp·er *n* **1** : something that checks, discourages, or deadens **2** : a valve or movable plate for controlling a flow of air

dam·sel *n* : GIRL 1, MAIDEN

[1]**dance** *vb* **danced; danc·ing** **1** : to glide, step, or move through a series of movements usually in time to music **2** : to move about or up and down quickly and lightly **3** : to perform or take part in as a dancer — **danc·er** *n*

[2]**dance** *n* **1** : an act of dancing **2** : a social gathering for dancing **3** : a set of movements or steps for dancing usually in time to special music **4** : the art of dancing

dan·de·li·on *n* : a weedy plant related to the daisies that has a ring of long deeply toothed leaves often eaten as cooked greens or in salad and bright yellow flowers with hollow stems

dan·druff *n* : thin dry whitish flakes that form on the scalp and come off freely

[1]**dan·dy** *n, pl* **dandies** **1** : a man who pays a great deal of attention to his clothes **2** : an excellent or unusual example

[2]**dandy** *adj* **dan·di·er; dan·di·est** : very good

Dane *n* : a person born or living in Denmark

dan·ger *n* **1** : the state of not being protected from harm or evil : PERIL **2** : something that may cause injury or harm

dan·ger·ous *adj* **1** : full of danger **2** : able or likely to injure — **dan·ger·ous·ly** *adv*

dan·gle *vb* **dan·gled; dan·gling** **1** : to hang loosely especially with a swinging or jerking motion **2** : to depend on something else **3** : to cause to dangle

[1]**Dan·ish** *adj* : of or relating to Denmark, the Danes, or Danish

[2]**Danish** *n* **1** : the language of the Danes **2** : a piece of Danish pastry

Danish pastry *n* : a pastry made of rich raised dough

dank *adj* : unpleasantly wet or moist — **dank·ly** *adv* — **dank·ness** *n*

dap·per *adj* : neat and trim in dress or appearance

dap·ple *vb* **dap·pled; dap·pling** : to mark or become marked with rounded spots of color

[1]**dare** *vb* **dared; dar·ing** **1** : to have courage enough for some purpose : be bold enough — sometimes used as a helping verb **2** : to challenge to do something especially as a proof of courage

[2]**dare** *n* : a demand that one do something difficult or dangerous as proof of courage

dare·dev·il *n* : a person so bold as to be reckless

[1]**dar·ing** *adj* : ready to take risks : BOLD, VENTURESOME — **dar·ing·ly** *adv*

[2]**daring** *n* : bold fearlessness : readiness to take chances

[1]**dark** *adj* **1** : being without light or without much light **2** : not light in color **3** : not bright and cheerful : GLOOMY **4** : being without knowledge and culture — **dark·ish** *adj* — **dark·ly** *adv* — **dark·ness** *n*

[2]**dark** *n* **1** : absence of light **2** : a place or time of little or no light

dark·en *vb* **1** : to make or grow dark or darker **2** : to make or become gloomy — **dark·en·er** *n*

dark·room *n* : a usually small lightproof room used in developing photographic plates and film

[1]**dar·ling** *n* **1** : a dearly loved person **2** : [1]FAVORITE

[2]**darling** *adj* **1** : dearly loved **2** : very pleasing : CHARMING

[1]**darn** *vb* : to mend by interlacing threads

[2]**darn** *n* : a place that has been darned

[3]**darn** *n* : [2]DAMN

darning needle *n* : DRAGONFLY

[1]**dart** *n* **1** : a small pointed object that is meant to be thrown **2 darts** *pl* : a game in which darts are thrown at a target **3** : a quick sudden movement **4** : a stitched fold in a garment

²dart *vb* **:** to move or shoot out suddenly and quickly

¹dash *vb* **1 :** to knock, hurl, or shove violently **2 :** ²SMASH 1 **3 :** ¹SPLASH 2 **4 :** DESTROY 1 **5 :** to complete or do hastily **6 :** to move with sudden speed

²dash *n* **1 :** a sudden burst or splash **2 :** a punctuation mark — that is used most often to show a break in the thought or structure of a sentence **3 :** a small amount **:** TOUCH **4 :** liveliness in style and action **5 :** a sudden rush or attempt **6 :** a short fast race **7 :** a long click or buzz forming a letter or part of a letter (as in telegraphy) **8 :** DASHBOARD

dash•board *n* **:** a panel across an automobile or aircraft below the windshield usually containing dials and controls

dash•ing *adj* **:** having clothes or manners that are very fancy and stylish

das•tard *n* **:** a mean and sneaky coward

das•tard•ly *adj* **:** of or like a dastard — **das•tard•li•ness** *n*

da•ta *n sing or pl* **1 :** facts about something that can be used in calculating, reasoning, or planning **2 :** DATUM

da•ta•base *n* **:** a collection of data that is organized especially to be used by a computer

¹date *n* **:** the sweet brownish fruit of an Old World palm (**date palm**)

²date *n* **1 :** the day, month, or year of a happening **2 :** a statement of time on something (as a coin, letter, book, or building) **3 :** APPOINTMENT 3 **4 :** a person with whom one has a social engagement

³date *vb* **dat•ed; dat•ing 1 :** to find or show the date of **2 :** to write the date on **3 :** to make or have a date with **4 :** to belong to or have survived from a time **5 :** to show to be old-fashioned or belonging to a past time

da•tum *n, pl* **da•ta** *or* **datums :** a single piece of information **:** FACT

¹daub *vb* **1 :** to cover with something soft and sticky **2 :** to paint or color carelessly or badly — **daub•er** *n*

²daub *n* **:** something daubed on **:** SMEAR

daugh•ter *n* **1 :** a female child or offspring **2 :** a woman or girl associated with or thought of as a child of something (as a country, race, or religion) — **daugh•ter•ly** *adj*

daugh•ter–in–law *n, pl* **daugh•ters–in–law :** the wife of one's son

daunt *vb* **:** DISCOURAGE 1, INTIMIDATE

daunt•less *adj* **:** bravely determined — **daunt•less•ly** *adv* — **daunt•less•ness** *n*

dau•phin *n* **:** the oldest son of a king of France

dav•en•port *n* **:** a large sofa

da•vit *n* **:** one of a pair of posts fitted with ropes and pulleys and used for supporting and lowering a ship's boat

daw•dle *vb* **daw•dled; daw•dling 1 :** to spend time wastefully **:** DALLY **2 :** to move slowly and without purpose — **daw•dler** *n*

¹dawn *vb* **1 :** to begin to grow light as the sun rises **2 :** to start becoming plain or clear

²dawn *n* **1 :** the time when the sun comes up in the morning **2 :** a first appearance **:** BEGINNING

day *n* **1 :** the time between sunrise and sunset **:** DAYLIGHT **2 :** the time the earth takes to make one turn on its axis **3 :** a period of twenty-four hours beginning at midnight **4 :** a specified day or date **5 :** a specified period **:** AGE **6 :** the time set apart by custom or law for work

day•bed *n* **:** a couch with low head and foot pieces

day•break *n* **:** ²DAWN 1

¹day•dream *n* **:** a happy or pleasant imagining about oneself or one's future

²daydream *vb* **:** to have a daydream — **day•dream•er** *n*

day•light *n* **1 :** the light of day **2 :** DAYTIME **3 :** ²DAWN 1 **4** *pl* **:** normal soundness of the mind

daylight saving time *n* **:** time usually one hour ahead of standard time

day•time *n* **:** the period of daylight

¹daze *vb* **dazed; daz•ing :** to stun especially by a blow

²daze *n* **:** a dazed state

daz•zle *vb* **daz•zled; daz•zling 1 :** to confuse or be confused by too much light or by moving lights **2 :** to confuse, surprise, or delight by being or doing something special and unusual — **daz•zler** *n* — **daz•zling•ly** *adv*

DDT *n* **:** a chemical formerly used as an insecticide but found to damage the environment

de- *prefix* **1 :** do the opposite of **2 :** reverse of **3 :** remove or remove from a specified thing **4 :** reduce **5 :** get off of

dea•con *n* **1 :** an official in some Christian churches ranking just below a priest **2 :** a church member who has special duties (as helping a minister)

¹dead *adj* **1 :** no longer living **:** LIFELESS **2 :** having the look of death **3 :** ¹NUMB 1 **4 :** very tired **5 :** never having lived **:** INANIMATE **6 :** lacking motion, activity, energy, or power to function **7 :** no longer in use **:** OBSOLETE **8 :** lacking warmth, vigor, or liveliness **9 :** ACCURATE, PRECISE **10 :** being sudden and complete **11 :** ¹COMPLETE 1, TOTAL

²dead *n, pl* **dead 1** *dead pl* **:** those that are dead **2 :** the time of greatest quiet

[3]**dead** *adv* **1 :** in a whole or complete manner **2 :** suddenly and completely **3 :** [2]STRAIGHT
dead·en *vb* **:** to take away some of the force of **:** make less
dead end *n* **:** an end (as of a street) with no way out
dead heat *n* **:** a contest that ends in a tie
dead letter *n* **:** a letter that cannot be delivered by the post office or returned to the sender
dead·line *n* **:** a date or time by which something must be done
[1]**dead·lock** *n* **:** a stopping of action because both sides in a struggle are equally strong and neither will give in
[2]**deadlock** *vb* **:** to bring or come to a deadlock
[1]**dead·ly** *adj* **dead·li·er; dead·li·est 1 :** causing or capable of causing death **2 :** meaning or hoping to kill or destroy **3 :** very accurate **4 :** causing spiritual death **5 :** suggestive of death **6 :** [1]EXTREME 1 — **dead·li·ness** *n*
[2]**deadly** *adv* **1 :** in a way suggestive of death **2 :** to an extreme degree
deaf *adj* **1 :** wholly or partly unable to hear **2 :** unwilling to hear or listen — **deaf·ness** *n*
deaf·en *vb* **1 :** to make deaf **2 :** to stun with noise
deaf–mute *n* **:** a person who can neither hear nor speak
[1]**deal** *n* **1 :** an indefinite amount **2 :** one's turn to deal the cards in a card game
[2]**deal** *vb* **dealt; deal·ing 1 :** to give out one or a few at a time **2 :** [1]GIVE 5, ADMINISTER **3 :** to have to do **4 :** to take action **5 :** to buy and sell regularly **:** TRADE — **deal·er** *n*
[3]**deal** *n* **1 :** an agreement to do business **2 :** treatment received **3 :** a secret agreement **4 :** [1]BARGAIN 2
deal·ing *n* **1 :** [3]DEAL 1 **2 :** a way of acting or doing business
dean *n* **1 :** a church official in charge of a cathedral **2 :** the head of a section (as a college) of a university **3 :** an official in charge of students or studies in a school or college — **dean·ship** *n*
[1]**dear** *adj* **1 :** greatly loved or cared about **2** — used as form of address especially in letters **3 :** high-priced **4 :** deeply felt **:** EARNEST — **dear·ly** *adv* — **dear·ness** *n*
[2]**dear** *adv* **:** at a high price
[3]**dear** *n* **:** a loved one **:** DARLING
dearth *n* **:** SCARCITY, LACK
death *n* **1 :** the end or ending of life **2 :** the cause of loss of life **3 :** the state of being dead **4 :** DESTRUCTION 2 — **death·less** *adj* — **death·like** *adj*
death·bed *n* **1 :** the bed a person dies in **2 :** the last hours of life
death·blow *n* **:** a fatal or crushing blow or event
[1]**death·ly** *adj* **:** of, relating to, or suggesting death
[2]**deathly** *adv* **:** in a way suggesting death
de·bar *vb* **de·barred; de·bar·ring :** to keep from having or doing something
de·base *vb* **de·based; de·bas·ing :** to make less good or valuable than before — **de·base·ment** *n*
de·bat·able *adj* **:** possible to question or argue about
[1]**de·bate** *n* **1 :** a discussion or argument carried on between two teams **2 :** DISCUSSION
[2]**debate** *vb* **de·bat·ed; de·bat·ing 1 :** to discuss a question by giving arguments on both sides **:** take part in a debate **2 :** to consider reasons for and against — **de·bat·er** *n*
de·bil·i·tate *vb* **de·bil·i·tat·ed; de·bil·i·tat·ing :** to make feeble **:** WEAKEN
de·bil·i·ty *n, pl* **de·bil·i·ties :** a weakened state especially of health
[1]**deb·it** *vb* **:** to record as a debit
[2]**debit** *n* **:** a business record showing money paid out or owed
deb·o·nair *adj* **:** gaily and gracefully charming — **deb·o·nair·ly** *adv* — **deb·o·nair·ness** *n*
de·bris *n, pl* **de·bris :** the junk or pieces left from something broken down or destroyed
debt *n* **1 :** [1]SIN **2 :** something owed to another **3 :** the condition of owing money
debt·or *n* **:** a person who owes a debt
de·but *n* **1 :** a first public appearance **2 :** the formal entrance of a young woman into society
deb·u·tante *n* **:** a young woman making her debut
deca- *or* **dec-** *or* **deka-** *or* **dek-** *prefix* **:** ten
de·cade *n* **:** a period of ten years
deca·gon *n* **:** a closed figure having ten angles and ten sides
de·cal *n* **:** a design made to be transferred (as to glass) from specially prepared paper
deca·logue *n, often cap* **:** the ten commandments of God given to Moses on Mount Sinai
de·camp *vb* **:** to go away suddenly and usually secretly **:** run away
de·cant·er *n* **:** an ornamental glass bottle used especially for serving wine
de·cap·i·tate *vb* **de·cap·i·tat·ed; de·cap·i·tat·ing :** to cut off the head of **:** BEHEAD
[1]**de·cay** *vb* **:** to weaken in health or soundness (as by aging or rotting)
[2]**decay** *n* **1 :** the state of something that is decayed or decaying **:** a spoiled or rotting

condition **2 :** a gradual getting worse or failing **3 :** a natural change of a radioactive element into another form of the same element or into a different element
[1]**de•cease** *n* **:** DEATH 1
[2]**decease** *vb* **de•ceased; de•ceas•ing :** [1]DIE 1
de•ce•dent *n* **:** a dead person
de•ceit *n* **1 :** the act or practice of deceiving **:** DECEPTION **2 :** a statement or act that misleads a person or causes him or her to believe what is false **:** TRICK
de•ceit•ful *adj* **:** full of deceit **:** not honest — **de•ceit•ful•ly** *adv* — **de•ceit•ful•ness** *n*
de•ceive *vb* **de•ceived; de•ceiv•ing 1 :** to cause to believe what is not true **:** MISLEAD **2 :** to be dishonest and misleading — **de•ceiv•er** *n*
de•cel•er•ate *vb* **de•cel•er•at•ed; de•cel•er•at•ing :** to slow down
De•cem•ber *n* **:** the twelfth month of the year
de•cen•cy *n, pl* **de•cen•cies 1 :** a way or habit of conducting oneself that is decent **:** modest or proper behavior **2 :** something that is right and proper
de•cent *adj* **1 :** meeting an accepted standard of good taste (as in speech, dress, or behavior) **2 :** being moral and good **:** not dirty **3 :** fairly good — **de•cent•ly** *adv*
de•cep•tion *n* **1 :** the act of deceiving **2 :** [1]TRICK 1
de•cep•tive *adj* **:** tending or able to deceive — **de•cep•tive•ly** *adv*
deci- *prefix* **:** tenth part
deci•bel *n* **:** a unit for measuring the relative loudness of sounds
de•cide *vb* **de•cid•ed; de•cid•ing 1 :** to make a judgment on **2 :** to bring to an end **3 :** to make or cause to make a choice
de•cid•ed *adj* **1 :** UNMISTAKABLE **2 :** free from doubt — **de•cid•ed•ly** *adv*
de•cid•u•ous *adj* **:** made up of or having a part that falls off at the end of a period of growth and use
[1]**dec•i•mal** *adj* **1 :** based on the number 10 **:** numbered or counting by tens **2 :** expressed in or including a decimal
[2]**decimal** *n* **:** a proper fraction in which the denominator is 10 or 10 multiplied one or more times by itself and is indicated by a point (**decimal point**) placed at the left of the numerator
deci•me•ter *n* **:** a unit of length equal to one tenth meter
de•ci•pher *vb* **1 :** to translate from secret writing **:** DECODE **2 :** to make out the meaning of something not clear
de•ci•sion *n* **1 :** the act or result of deciding **2 :** promptness and firmness in deciding
de•ci•sive *adj* **1 :** deciding or able to decide a question or dispute **2 :** RESOLUTE **3 :** [1]CLEAR 7, UNMISTAKABLE — **de•ci•sive•ly** *adv* — **de•ci•sive•ness** *n*
[1]**deck** *n* **1 :** a floor that goes from one side of a ship to the other **2 :** something like the deck of a ship **3 :** a pack of playing cards
[2]**deck** *vb* **:** to dress or decorate especially in a showy way
dec•la•ra•tion *n* **1 :** an act of declaring **2 :** something declared or a document containing such a declaration
de•clar•a•tive *adj* **:** making a statement
de•clare *vb* **de•clared; de•clar•ing 1 :** to make known in a clear or formal way **2 :** to state as if certain
[1]**de•cline** *vb* **de•clined; de•clin•ing 1 :** to bend or slope downward **2 :** to pass toward a lower, worse, or weaker state **3 :** to refuse to accept, do, or agree
[2]**decline** *n* **1 :** a gradual weakening in body or mind **2 :** a change to a lower state or level **3 :** the time when something is nearing its end
de•code *vb* **de•cod•ed; de•cod•ing :** to change a message in code into ordinary language
de•com•pose *vb* **de•com•posed; de•com•pos•ing 1 :** to separate a thing into its parts or into simpler compounds **2 :** to break down in decaying — **de•com•pos•er** *n*
de•com•po•si•tion *n* **1 :** the process of decomposing **2 :** the state of being decomposed
dec•o•rate *vb* **dec•o•rat•ed; dec•o•rat•ing 1 :** to make more attractive by adding something nice looking **2 :** to award a decoration of honor to
dec•o•ra•tion *n* **1 :** the act of decorating **2 :** [1]ORNAMENT 1 **3 :** a badge of honor
dec•o•ra•tive *adj* **:** serving to decorate **:** ORNAMENTAL
dec•o•ra•tor *n* **:** a person who decorates especially the rooms of houses
de•co•rum *n* **:** proper behavior
[1]**de•coy** *n* **:** a person or thing (as an artificial bird) used to lead or lure into a trap or snare
[2]**decoy** *vb* **:** to lure by or as if by a decoy
[1]**de•crease** *vb* **de•creased; de•creas•ing :** to grow less or cause to grow less
[2]**de•crease** *n* **1 :** the process of decreasing **2 :** REDUCTION 2
[1]**de•cree** *n* **:** an order or decision given by a person or group in authority
[2]**decree** *vb* **de•creed; de•cree•ing :** to order by a decree
de•crep•it *adj* **:** worn out or weakened by age or use
de•cre•scen•do *n* **:** a gradual decrease in the loudness of music
ded•i•cate *vb* **ded•i•cat•ed; ded•i•cat•ing 1**

: to set apart for some purpose and especially for a sacred or serious purpose : DEVOTE **2 :** to address or write something in (as a book) as a compliment to someone

ded·i·ca·tion *n* **1 :** an act of dedicating **2 :** something written in dedicating a book **3 :** devotion to the point of giving up what one needs or loves

de·duct *vb* **:** to take away an amount of something **:** SUBTRACT

de·duc·tion *n* **1 :** SUBTRACTION **2 :** an amount deducted

[1]**deed** *n* **1 :** a usually fine or brave act or action **:** FEAT **2 :** a legal document containing the record of an agreement or especially of a transfer of real estate

[2]**deed** *vb* **:** to transfer by a deed

deem *vb* **:** to hold as an opinion

[1]**deep** *adj* **1 :** reaching down far below the surface **2 :** reaching far back from the front or outer part **3 :** hard to understand **4 :** located well below the surface or well within the boundaries of **5 :** fully developed **:** PROFOUND **6 :** dark and rich in color **7 :** low in tone **8 :** completely busy — **deep·ly** *adv*

[2]**deep** *adv* **:** to a great depth **:** DEEPLY

[3]**deep** *n* **1 :** a very deep place or part **2 :** OCEAN 1

deep·en *vb* **:** to make or become deep or deeper

deep fat *n* **:** hot fat or oil deep enough in a cooking utensil to cover the food to be fried

deep–fry *vb* **:** to cook in deep fat

deer *n, pl* **deer :** any of a group of mammals that chew the cud and have cloven hoofs and in the male antlers which are often branched

deer·skin *n* **:** leather made from the skin of a deer or a garment made of such leather

de·face *vb* **de·faced; de·fac·ing :** to destroy or mar the face or surface of — **de·face·ment** *n* — **de·fac·er** *n*

[1]**de·fault** *n* **:** failure to do something required by law or duty

[2]**default** *vb* **:** to fail to do one's duty — **de·fault·er** *n*

[1]**de·feat** *vb* **1 :** to bring to nothing **2 :** to win victory over

[2]**defeat** *n* **:** loss of a contest or battle

de·fect *n* **:** a lack of something necessary for completeness or perfection

de·fec·tive *adj* **:** lacking something necessary **:** FAULTY

de·fend *vb* **1 :** to protect from danger or attack **2 :** to act or speak in favor of when others are opposed — **de·fend·er** *n*

de·fense *n* **1 :** the act of defending **2 :** something that defends or protects **3 :** a defensive team — **de·fense·less** *adj*

[1]**de·fen·sive** *adj* **1 :** serving or meant to defend or protect **2 :** of or relating to the attempt to keep an opponent from scoring (as in a game) — **de·fen·sive·ly** *adv*

[2]**defensive** *n* **:** a defensive position or attitude

[1]**de·fer** *vb* **de·ferred; de·fer·ring :** to put off to a future time — **de·fer·ment** *n*

[2]**defer** *vb* **de·ferred; de·fer·ring :** to yield to the opinion or wishes of another

def·er·ence *n* **:** respect and consideration for the wishes of another

de·fi·ance *n* **1 :** an act of defying **2 :** a willingness to resist

de·fi·ant *adj* **:** showing defiance — **de·fi·ant·ly** *adv*

de·fi·cien·cy *n, pl* **de·fi·cien·cies :** the state of being without something necessary and especially something required for health

de·fi·cient *adj* **:** lacking something necessary for completeness or health

def·i·cit *n* **:** a shortage especially in money needed

de·file *vb* **de·filed; de·fil·ing 1 :** to make filthy **2 :** [1]CORRUPT 1 **3 :** [2]DISHONOR — **de·file·ment** *n*

de·fine *vb* **de·fined; de·fin·ing 1 :** to set or mark the limits of **2 :** to make distinct in outline **3 :** to find out and explain the meaning of — **de·fin·er** *n*

def·i·nite *adj* **1 :** having certain or distinct limits **2 :** clear in meaning **3 :** UNQUESTIONABLE — **def·i·nite·ly** *adv* — **def·i·nite·ness** *n*

definite article *n* **:** the article *the* used to show that the following noun refers to one or more specific persons or things

def·i·ni·tion *n* **1 :** an act of defining **2 :** a statement of the meaning of a word or a word group **3 :** clearness of outline or detail

de·flate *vb* **de·flat·ed; de·flat·ing 1 :** to let the air or gas out of something that has been blown up **2 :** to reduce in size or importance

de·flect *vb* **:** to turn aside

de·for·est *vb* **:** to clear of forests

de·form *vb* **:** to spoil the form or the natural appearance of

de·for·mi·ty *n, pl* **de·for·mi·ties 1 :** the condition of being deformed **2 :** a flaw or blemish in something and especially in the body of a person or animal

de·fraud *vb* **:** to take or keep something from by deceit **:** CHEAT

de·frost *vb* **1 :** to thaw out **2 :** to remove ice from — **de·frost·er** *n*

deft *adj* **:** quick and neat in action **:** SKILLFUL — **deft·ly** *adv* — **deft·ness** *n*

de·fy *vb* **de·fied; de·fy·ing 1 :** to challenge

to do something thought to be impossible : DARE **2 :** to refuse boldly to obey or yield to **3 :** to resist the effects of or attempts at

deg·ra·da·tion *n* **1 :** an act of degrading **2 :** the state of being degraded

de·grade *vb* **de·grad·ed; de·grad·ing** **1 :** to reduce from a higher to a lower rank or degree **2 :** to bring to a low state : DEBASE, CORRUPT

de·gree *n* **1 :** a step in a series **2 :** amount of something as measured by a series of steps **3 :** one of the three forms an adjective or adverb may have when it is compared **4 :** a title given (as to students) by a college or university **5 :** one of the divisions marked on a measuring instrument (as a thermometer) **6 :** a 360th part of the circumference of a circle **7 :** a line or space of the staff in music or the difference in pitch between two notes

de·hu·mid·i·fy *vb* **de·hu·mid·i·fied; de·hu·mid·i·fy·ing :** to take moisture from (as the air) — **de·hu·mid·i·fi·er** *n*

de·hy·drate *vb* **de·hy·drat·ed; de·hy·drat·ing** **1 :** to take water from (as foods) **2 :** to lose water or body fluids

de·ice *vb* **de·iced; de·ic·ing :** to free or keep free of ice — **de·ic·er** *n*

de·i·fy *vb* **de·i·fied; de·i·fy·ing :** to make a god of

deign *vb* **:** CONDESCEND 1

de·i·ty *n, pl* **de·i·ties** **1** *cap* **:** GOD 1 **2 :** GOD 2, GODDESS

de·ject·ed *adj* **:** low in spirits — **de·ject·ed·ly** *adv*

de·jec·tion *n* **:** a dejected state

deka- *or* **dek-** — see DECA-

¹de·lay *n* **1 :** a putting off of something **2 :** the time during which something is delayed

²delay *vb* **1 :** to put off **2 :** to stop or prevent for a time **3 :** to move or act slowly

¹del·e·gate *n* **:** a person sent with power to act for another or others

²del·e·gate *vb* **del·e·gat·ed; del·e·gat·ing** **1 :** to entrust to another **2 :** to make responsible for getting something done

del·e·ga·tion *n* **1 :** the act of delegating **2 :** one or more persons chosen to represent others

de·lete *vb* **de·let·ed; de·let·ing :** to take out from something written especially by erasing, crossing out, or cutting

de·le·tion *n* **1 :** an act of deleting **2 :** something deleted

¹de·lib·er·ate *vb* **de·lib·er·at·ed; de·lib·er·at·ing :** to think about carefully

²de·lib·er·ate *adj* **1 :** showing careful thought **2 :** done or said on purpose **3 :** slow in action **:** not hurried — **de·lib·er·ate·ly** *adv* — **de·lib·er·ate·ness** *n*

de·lib·er·a·tion *n* **1 :** careful thought **:** CONSIDERATION **2 :** the quality of being deliberate

del·i·ca·cy *n, pl* **del·i·ca·cies** **1 :** something pleasing to eat that is rare or a luxury **2 :** fineness of structure **3 :** weakness of body **:** FRAILTY **4 :** a situation needing careful handling **5 :** consideration for the feelings of others

del·i·cate *adj* **1 :** pleasing because of fineness or mildness **2 :** able to sense very small differences **3 :** calling for skill and careful treatment **4 :** easily damaged **5 :** SICKLY 1 **6 :** requiring tact — **del·i·cate·ly** *adv*

del·i·ca·tes·sen *n* **:** a store where prepared foods (as salads and cooked meats) are sold

de·li·cious *adj* **:** giving great pleasure especially to the taste or smell — **de·li·cious·ly** *adv* — **de·li·cious·ness** *n*

¹de·light *n* **1 :** great pleasure or satisfaction **:** JOY **2 :** something that gives great pleasure

²delight *vb* **1 :** to take great pleasure **2 :** to give joy or satisfaction to

de·light·ed *adj* **:** very pleased

de·light·ful *adj* **:** giving delight **:** very pleasing — **de·light·ful·ly** *adv*

de·lir·i·ous *adj* **1 :** suffering delirium **2 :** wildly excited — **de·lir·i·ous·ly** *adv*

de·lir·i·um *n* **1 :** a condition of mind in which thought and speech are confused and which often goes along with a high fever **2 :** wild excitement

de·liv·er *vb* **1 :** to set free **:** RESCUE **2 :** ¹TRANSFER 2 **3 :** to help in childbirth **4 :** ²UTTER 2 **5 :** to send to an intended target — **de·liv·er·er** *n*

de·liv·er·ance *n* **:** an act of delivering or the state of being delivered **:** a setting free

de·liv·ery *n, pl* **de·liv·er·ies** **1 :** a setting free (as from something that hampers or holds one back) **2 :** the transfer of something from one place or person to another **3 :** the act of giving birth **4 :** speaking or manner of speaking (as of a formal speech) **5 :** the act or way of throwing

dell *n* **:** a small valley usually covered with trees

del·phin·i·um *n* **:** a tall plant related to the buttercups and often grown for its large stalks of showy flowers

del·ta *n* **:** a piece of land in the shape of a triangle or fan made by deposits of mud and sand at the mouth of a river

de·lude *vb* **de·lud·ed; de·lud·ing :** DECEIVE, MISLEAD

¹del·uge *n* **1 :** a flooding of land by water

: FLOOD **2 :** a drenching rain **3 :** a sudden huge stream of something

²deluge *vb* **del·uged; del·ug·ing** **1 :** ²FLOOD 1 **2 :** to overwhelm as if with a deluge

de·lu·sion *n* **1 :** an act of deluding or the state of being deluded **2 :** a false belief that continues in spite of the facts

de·luxe *adj* **:** very fine or luxurious

delve *vb* **delved; delv·ing** **1 :** DIG **2 :** to work hard looking for information in written records — **delv·er** *n*

¹de·mand *n* **1 :** an act of demanding **2 :** an expressed desire to own or use something **3 :** a seeking or being sought after

²demand *vb* **1 :** to claim as one's right **2 :** to ask earnestly or in the manner of a command **3 :** to call for **:** REQUIRE — **de·mand·er** *n*

de·mean *vb* **de·meaned; de·mean·ing :** to behave or conduct (oneself) usually in a proper way

de·mean·or *n* **:** outward manner or behavior

de·ment·ed *adj* **:** INSANE 1, MAD — **de·ment·ed·ly** *adv*

de·mer·it *n* **:** a mark placed against a person's record for doing something wrong

demi- *prefix* **1 :** half **2 :** one that partly belongs to a specified type or class

demi·god *n* **:** one who is partly divine and partly human

de·mo·bi·lize *vb* **de·mo·bi·lized; de·mo·bi·liz·ing :** to let go from military service

de·moc·ra·cy *n, pl* **de·moc·ra·cies** **1 :** government by the people **:** majority rule **2 :** government in which the highest power is held by the people and is usually used through representatives **3 :** a political unit (as a nation) governed by the people **4 :** belief in or practice of the idea that all people are socially equal

dem·o·crat *n* **:** one who believes in or practices democracy

dem·o·crat·ic *adj* **1 :** of, relating to, or favoring political democracy **2 :** believing in or practicing the idea that people are socially equal — **dem·o·crat·i·cal·ly** *adv*

de·mol·ish *vb* **1 :** to destroy by breaking apart **2 :** to ruin completely **:** SHATTER

de·mon *n* **1 :** an evil spirit **:** DEVIL **2 :** a person of great energy or skill

dem·on·strate *vb* **dem·on·strat·ed; dem·on·strat·ing** **1 :** to show clearly **2 :** to prove or make clear by reasoning **3 :** to explain (as in teaching) by use of examples or experiments **4 :** to show to people the good qualities of an article or a product **5 :** to make a public display (as of feelings or military force)

dem·on·stra·tion *n* **1 :** an outward expression (as a show of feelings) **2 :** an act or a means of demonstrating **3 :** a showing or using of an article for sale to display its good points **4 :** a parade or a gathering to show public feeling

de·mon·stra·tive *adj* **1 :** pointing out the one referred to and showing that it differs from others **2 :** showing feeling freely

dem·on·stra·tor *n* **1 :** a person who makes or takes part in a demonstration **2 :** a manufactured article used for demonstration

de·mor·al·ize *vb* **de·mor·al·ized; de·mor·al·iz·ing :** to weaken the discipline or spirit of

de·mote *vb* **de·mot·ed; de·mot·ing :** to reduce to a lower grade or rank

de·mure *adj* **1 :** MODEST 3 **2 :** pretending to be modest **:** COY — **de·mure·ly** *adv* — **de·mure·ness** *n*

den *n* **1 :** the shelter or resting place of a wild animal **2 :** a quiet or private room in a home **3 :** a hiding place (as for thieves)

de·na·ture *vb* **de·na·tured; de·na·tur·ing :** to make alcohol unfit for humans to drink

den·drite *n* **:** any of the usually branched fibers that carry nerve impulses toward a nerve cell body

de·ni·al *n* **1 :** a refusal to give or agree to something asked for **2 :** a refusal to admit the truth of a statement **3 :** a refusal to accept or believe in someone or something **4 :** a cutting down or limiting

den·im *n* **1 :** a firm often coarse cotton cloth **2 denims** *pl* **:** overalls or pants of usually blue denim

de·nom·i·na·tion *n* **1 :** a name especially for a class of things **2 :** a religious body made up of a number of congregations having the same beliefs **3 :** a value in a series of values (as of money)

de·nom·i·na·tor *n* **:** the part of a fraction that is below the line

de·note *vb* **de·not·ed; de·not·ing** **1 :** to serve as a mark or indication of **2 :** to have the meaning of **:** MEAN

de·nounce *vb* **de·nounced; de·nounc·ing** **1 :** to point out as wrong or evil **:** CONDEMN **2 :** to inform against **:** ACCUSE — **de·nounce·ment** *n* — **de·nounc·er** *n*

dense *adj* **dens·er; dens·est** **1 :** having its parts crowded together **:** THICK **2 :** STUPID 1 — **dense·ly** *adv* — **dense·ness** *n*

den·si·ty *n, pl* **den·si·ties** **1 :** the state of being dense **2 :** the amount of something in a specified volume or area

¹dent *vb* **1 :** to make a dent in or on **2 :** to become marked by a dent

²dent *n* **:** a notch or hollow made in a surface by a blow or by pressure

den•tal *adj* **:** of or relating to the teeth or dentistry — **den•tal•ly** *adv*
dental floss *n* **:** flat thread used for cleaning between teeth
den•ti•frice *n* **:** a powder, paste, or liquid used in cleaning the teeth
den•tin *or* **den•tine** *n* **:** a hard bony material that makes up the main part of a tooth
den•tist *n* **:** a person whose profession is the care, treatment, and repair of the teeth
den•tist•ry *n* **:** the profession or practice of a dentist
den•ture *n* **:** a set of false teeth
de•nude *vb* **de•nud•ed; de•nud•ing :** to strip of covering **:** make bare
de•ny *vb* **de•nied; de•ny•ing 1 :** to declare not to be true **2 :** to refuse to grant **3 :** DISOWN, REPUDIATE
de•odor•ant *n* **:** something used to remove or hide unpleasant odors
de•odor•ize *vb* **de•odor•ized; de•odor•iz•ing :** to remove odor and especially a bad smell from
de•part *vb* **1 :** to go away or go away from **:** LEAVE **2 :** [1]DIE 1 **3 :** to turn aside
de•part•ment *n* **:** a special part or division of an organization (as a government or college)
department store *n* **:** a store having individual departments for different kinds of goods
de•par•ture *n* **1 :** a going away **2 :** a setting out (as on a new course) **3 :** a turning away or aside (as from a way of doing things)
de•pend *vb* **1 :** to rely for support **2 :** to be determined by or based on some action or condition **3 :** [2]TRUST 1, RELY
de•pend•able *adj* **:** TRUSTWORTHY, RELIABLE — **de•pend•ably** *adv*
de•pen•dence *n* **1 :** a condition of being influenced and caused by something else **2 :** a state of being dependent on someone or something **3 :** [1]TRUST 1, RELIANCE
[1]de•pen•dent *adj* **1 :** CONTINGENT **2 :** relying on someone else for support **3 :** requiring something (as a drug) to feel or act normally
[2]dependent *n* **:** a person who depends upon another for support
de•pict *vb* **1 :** to represent by a picture **2 :** to describe in words
de•plete *vb* **de•plet•ed; de•plet•ing :** to reduce in amount by using up
de•plor•able *adj* **1 :** deserving to be deplored **:** REGRETTABLE **2 :** very bad **:** WRETCHED — **de•plor•ably** *adv*
de•plore *vb* **de•plored; de•plor•ing 1 :** to regret strongly **2 :** to consider deserving of disapproval
de•port *vb* **1 :** BEHAVE 1, CONDUCT **2 :** to force (a person who is not a citizen) to leave a country
de•port•ment *n* **:** BEHAVIOR 1
de•pose *vb* **de•posed; de•pos•ing :** to remove from a high office
[1]de•pos•it *vb* **1 :** to place for or as if for safekeeping **2 :** to put money in a bank **3 :** to give as a pledge that a purchase will be made or a service used **4 :** to lay down **:** PUT **5 :** to let fall or sink
[2]deposit *n* **1 :** the state of being deposited **2 :** money that is deposited in a bank **3 :** something given as a pledge or as part payment **4 :** something laid or thrown down **5 :** mineral matter built up in nature
de•pos•i•tor *n* **:** a person who makes a deposit especially of money in a bank
de•pot *n* **1 :** a place where military supplies are kept **2 :** STOREHOUSE 1 **3 :** a railroad or bus station
de•pre•ci•ate *vb* **de•pre•ci•at•ed; de•pre•ci•at•ing 1 :** to lower the price or value of **2 :** BELITTLE **3 :** to lose value
de•press *vb* **1 :** to press down **2 :** to lessen the activity or strength of **3 :** to lower the spirits of **:** make sad and dull
de•pres•sant *adj or n* **:** SEDATIVE
de•pres•sion *n* **1 :** an act of depressing **:** a state of being depressed **2 :** a hollow place or part **3 :** low spirits **4 :** a period of low activity in business with much unemployment
de•pri•va•tion *n* **1 :** an act or instance of depriving **2 :** the state of being deprived
de•prive *vb* **de•prived; de•priv•ing :** to take something away from or keep from having or doing something
depth *n* **1 :** a deep place in a body of water (as a sea or a lake) **2 :** measurement from top to bottom or from front to back **3 :** the innermost part of something **:** MIDDLE, MIDST **4 :** ABUNDANCE, COMPLETENESS **5 :** the quality of being deep
depth charge *n* **:** an explosive for use underwater especially against submarines
dep•u•tize *vb* **dep•u•tized; dep•u•tiz•ing :** to appoint as deputy
dep•u•ty *n, pl* **dep•u•ties :** a person appointed to act for or in place of another
de•rail *vb* **:** to cause to leave the rails — **de•rail•ment** *n*
de•range *vb* **de•ranged; de•rang•ing 1 :** to put out of order **:** DISARRANGE **2 :** to make insane — **de•range•ment** *n*
der•by *n, pl* **der•bies 1 :** a horse race for three-year-olds usually held every year **2 :** a stiff felt hat with a narrow brim and a rounded top
de•ride *vb* **de•rid•ed; de•rid•ing :** to laugh at in scorn **:** make fun of **:** RIDICULE

der·i·va·tion *n* **1 :** the formation of a word from an earlier word or root **2 :** ETYMOLOGY **3 :** ORIGIN 3, SOURCE **4 :** an act or process of deriving

[1]**de·riv·a·tive** *n* **1 :** a word formed by derivation **2 :** something derived

[2]**derivative** *adj* **:** derived from something else — **de·riv·a·tive·ly** *adv*

de·rive *vb* **de·rived; de·riv·ing 1 :** to receive or obtain from a source **2 :** to trace the derivation of **3 :** to come from a certain source

der·mal *adj* **:** of or relating to skin

der·mis *n* **:** the inner sensitive layer of the skin

de·rog·a·to·ry *adj* **:** intended to hurt the reputation of a person or thing

der·rick *n* **1 :** a machine for moving or lifting heavy weights by means of a long beam fitted with ropes and pulleys **2 :** a framework or tower over an oil well for supporting machinery

de·scend *vb* **1 :** to come or go down from a higher place or level to a lower one **2 :** to come down in sudden attack **3 :** to come down from an earlier time **4 :** to come down from a source **:** DERIVE **5 :** to be handed down to an heir **6 :** to sink in a social or moral scale **:** STOOP

de·scen·dant *n* **:** one that is descended from a particular ancestor or family

de·scent *n* **1 :** a coming or going down **2 :** one's line of ancestors **3 :** a downward slope **4 :** a sudden attack

de·scribe *vb* **de·scribed; de·scrib·ing 1 :** to write or tell about **:** give an account of **2 :** to draw the outline of — **de·scrib·er** *n*

de·scrip·tion *n* **1 :** an account of something especially of a kind that presents a picture to a person who reads or hears it **2 :** [1]SORT 1, KIND

de·scrip·tive *adj* **:** serving to describe — **de·scrip·tive·ly** *adv*

des·e·crate *vb* **des·e·crat·ed; des·e·crat·ing :** to treat a sacred place or sacred object shamefully or with great disrespect

de·seg·re·gate *vb* **de·seg·re·gat·ed; de·seg·re·gat·ing :** to end segregation in **:** free of any law or practice setting apart members of a certain race

de·seg·re·ga·tion *n* **:** the act or process or an instance of desegregating

[1]**des·ert** *n* **:** a dry barren region where only a few special kinds of plants can grow without an artificial water supply

[2]**desert** *adj* **:** of, relating to, or being a desert

[3]**de·sert** *n* **1 :** worthiness of reward or punishment **2 :** a just reward or punishment

[4]**de·sert** *vb* **1 :** to leave usually without intending to return **2 :** to leave a person or a thing that one should stay with **3 :** to fail in time of need — **de·sert·er** *n*

de·serve *vb* **de·served; de·serv·ing :** to be worthy of **:** MERIT

de·served·ly *adv* **:** as one deserves

de·serv·ing *adj* **:** WORTHY

[1]**de·sign** *vb* **1 :** to think up and plan out in the mind **2 :** to set apart for or have as a special purpose **:** INTEND **3 :** to make a pattern or sketch of — **de·sign·er** *n*

[2]**design** *n* **1 :** [1]PLAN 2, SCHEME **2 :** a planned intention **3 :** a secret purpose **:** PLOT **4 :** a preliminary sketch, model, or plan **5 :** an arrangement of parts in a structure or a work of art **6 :** a decorative pattern

des·ig·nate *vb* **des·ig·nat·ed; des·ig·nat·ing 1 :** to mark or point out **:** INDICATE **2 :** to appoint or choose for a special purpose **:** NAME **3 :** to call by a name or title

des·ig·na·tion *n* **1 :** an act of designating **2 :** a name, sign, or title that identifies something

de·sign·ing *adj* **:** CRAFTY

de·sir·able *adj* **1 :** having pleasing qualities **:** ATTRACTIVE **2 :** worth having or seeking — **de·sir·ably** *adv*

[1]**de·sire** *vb* **de·sired; de·sir·ing 1 :** to long for **:** wish for in earnest **2 :** to express a wish for **:** REQUEST

[2]**desire** *n* **1 :** a strong wish **:** LONGING **2 :** a wish made known **:** REQUEST **3 :** something desired

de·sist *vb* **:** to stop something one is doing

desk *n* **:** a piece of furniture with a flat or sloping surface for use in writing or reading

[1]**des·o·late** *adj* **1 :** ABANDONED **2 :** having no comfort or companionship **:** LONELY **3 :** left neglected or in ruins **4 :** CHEERLESS, GLOOMY

[2]**des·o·late** *vb* **des·o·lat·ed; des·o·lat·ing :** to make or leave desolate

des·o·la·tion *n* **1 :** the state of being desolated **:** RUIN **2 :** sadness resulting from grief or loneliness

[1]**de·spair** *vb* **:** to give up or lose all hope or confidence

[2]**despair** *n* **1 :** loss of hope **:** a feeling of complete hopelessness **2 :** a cause of hopelessness

des·per·ate *adj* **1 :** being beyond or almost beyond hope **:** causing despair **2 :** reckless because of despair **:** RASH — **des·per·ate·ly** *adv* — **des·per·ate·ness** *n*

des·per·a·tion *n* **:** a state of hopeless despair leading to recklessness

de·spi·ca·ble *adj* **:** deserving to be despised — **de·spi·ca·bly** *adv*

de·spise *vb* **de·spised; de·spis·ing :** to

consider as beneath one's notice or respect : feel scorn and dislike for
de·spite *prep* : in spite of
de·spoil *vb* : to rob of possessions or belongings : PLUNDER — **de·spoil·er** *n*
de·spon·den·cy *n* : MELANCHOLY, DEJECTION
de·spon·dent *adj* : feeling quite discouraged or depressed : being in very low spirits — **de·spon·dent·ly** *adv*
des·pot *n* : a ruler having absolute power and authority and especially one who rules cruelly
des·sert *n* : a course of sweet food, fruit, or cheese served at the end of a meal
des·ti·na·tion *n* : a place that one starts out for or that something is sent to
des·tine *vb* **des·tined; des·tin·ing** **1** : to decide in advance on the future condition, use, or action of **2** : to set aside for a special purpose
des·ti·ny *n, pl* **des·ti·nies** **1** : the fate or lot to which a person or thing is destined **2** : the course of events held to be arranged by a superhuman power
des·ti·tute *adj* **1** : lacking something needed or desirable **2** : very poor
de·stroy *vb* **1** : to put an end to : do away with **2** : [1]KILL 1
de·stroy·er *n* **1** : one that destroys **2** : a small fast warship armed with guns, depth charges, torpedoes, and sometimes missiles
de·struc·ti·ble *adj* : possible to destroy
de·struc·tion *n* **1** : the act or process of destroying something **2** : the state or fact of being destroyed : RUIN **3** : something that destroys
de·struc·tive *adj* **1** : causing destruction **2** : not positive or helpful — **de·struc·tive·ly** *adv* — **de·struc·tive·ness** *n*
de·tach *vb* : to separate from something else or from others especially for a certain purpose — **de·tach·able** *adj*
de·tached *adj* **1** : not joined or connected : SEPARATE **2** : not taking sides or being influenced by others — **de·tached·ly** *adv*
de·tach·ment *n* **1** : SEPARATION 1 **2** : a body of troops or ships sent on special duty **3** : a keeping apart : lack of interest in worldly concerns **4** : IMPARTIALITY
[1]**de·tail** *n* **1** : a dealing with something item by item **2** : a small part : ITEM **3** : a soldier or group of soldiers picked for special duty
[2]**detail** *vb* **1** : to report in detail : give the details of **2** : to select for some special duty
de·tailed *adj* : including many details
de·tain *vb* **1** : to hold or keep in or as if in prison **2** : to stop especially from going on : DELAY — **de·tain·ment** *n*
de·tect *vb* : to learn of the existence, presence, or fact of
de·tec·tion *n* : the act of detecting : the state or fact of being detected : DISCOVERY
[1]**de·tec·tive** *adj* **1** : able to detect or used in detecting something **2** : of or relating to detectives or their work
[2]**detective** *n* : a person (as a police officer) whose business is solving crimes and catching criminals or gathering information that is not easy to get
de·ten·tion *n* **1** : the act of detaining : the state of being detained : CONFINEMENT **2** : a forced delay
de·ter *vb* **de·terred; de·ter·ring** : to discourage or prevent from doing something
[1]**de·ter·gent** *adj* : able to clean : used in cleaning
[2]**detergent** *n* : a substance that is like soap in its ability to clean
de·te·ri·o·rate *vb* **de·te·ri·o·rat·ed; de·te·ri·o·rat·ing** : to make or become worse or of less value
de·ter·mi·na·tion *n* **1** : a coming to a decision or the decision reached **2** : a settling or making sure of the position, size, or nature of something **3** : firm or fixed intention
de·ter·mine *vb* **de·ter·mined; de·ter·min·ing** **1** : to fix exactly and with certainty **2** : to come to a decision **3** : to learn or find out exactly **4** : to be the cause of or reason for
de·ter·mined *adj* **1** : free from doubt **2** : not weak or uncertain : FIRM — **de·ter·mined·ly** *adv*
de·ter·min·er *n* : a word belonging to a group of noun modifiers that can occur before descriptive adjectives modifying the same noun
de·test *vb* : to dislike very much
de·test·able *adj* : causing or deserving strong dislike — **de·test·ably** *adv*
de·throne *vb* **de·throned; de·thron·ing** : to drive from a throne : DEPOSE — **de·throne·ment** *n*
[1]**de·tour** *n* : a roundabout way that temporarily replaces part of a regular route
[2]**detour** *vb* : to use or follow a detour
de·tract *vb* : to take away (as from value or importance)
det·ri·ment *n* : injury or damage or its cause : HARM
dev·as·tate *vb* **dev·as·tat·ed; dev·as·tat·ing** : to reduce to ruin : lay waste
dev·as·ta·tion *n* : the action of devastating : the state of being devastated
de·vel·op *vb* **1** : to make or become plain little by little : UNFOLD **2** : to apply chemicals to exposed photographic material (as a film) in order to bring out the picture **3** : to

bring out the possibilities of : IMPROVE **4** : to make more available or usable **5 :** to gain gradually **6 :** to grow toward maturity — **de·vel·op·er** *n*

de·vel·oped *adj* : having many large industries and a complex economic system

de·vel·op·ment *n* **1 :** the act or process of developing : a result of developing **2 :** the state of being developed

de·vi·ate *vb* **de·vi·at·ed; de·vi·at·ing :** to turn aside from a course, principle, standard, or topic

de·vice *n* **1 :** a scheme to deceive : TRICK **2 :** a piece of equipment or mechanism for a special purpose **3 :** [2]DESIRE 2, WILL

[1]**dev·il** *n* **1** *often cap* : the personal supreme spirit of evil **2 :** an evil spirit : DEMON, FIEND **3 :** a wicked or cruel person **4 :** a reckless or dashing person **5 :** a mischievous person **6 :** a person to be pitied

[2]**devil** *vb* **dev·iled** *or* **dev·illed; dev·il·ing** *or* **dev·il·ling** **1 :** to chop fine and season highly **2 :** [1]TEASE, ANNOY

dev·il·ment *n* : reckless mischief

de·vise *vb* **de·vised; de·vis·ing :** to think up : PLAN, INVENT — **de·vis·er** *n*

de·void *adj* : entirely lacking

de·vote *vb* **de·vot·ed; de·vot·ing** **1 :** to set apart for a special purpose **2 :** to give up to entirely or in part

de·vot·ed *adj* **1 :** completely loyal **2 :** AFFECTIONATE, LOVING — **de·vot·ed·ly** *adv*

de·vo·tion *n* **1 :** a religious exercise or practice (as prayers) especially for use in private worship **2 :** an act of devoting : the quality of being devoted **3 :** deep love or affection

de·vour *vb* **1 :** to eat up greedily **2 :** CONSUME 1 **3 :** to take in eagerly by the senses or mind

de·vout *adj* **1 :** devoted to religion **2** : warmly sincere and earnest — **de·vout·ly** *adv* — **de·vout·ness** *n*

dew *n* : moisture condensed on cool surfaces at night

dew·ber·ry *n, pl* **dew·ber·ries :** a sweet edible berry that grows on a prickly vine and is related to the blackberries

dew·lap *n* : a hanging fold of skin under the neck of some animals

dew point *n* : the temperature at which the moisture in the air begins to turn to dew

dewy *adj* **dew·i·er; dew·i·est :** moist with or as if with dew — **dew·i·ly** *adv* — **dew·i·ness** *n*

dex·ter·i·ty *n, pl* **dex·ter·i·ties** **1 :** skill and ease in bodily activity **2 :** mental skill or quickness

dex·ter·ous *or* **dex·trous** *adj* **1 :** skillful with the hands **2 :** mentally skillful and clever **3 :** done with skill — **dex·ter·ous·ly** *adv* — **dex·ter·ous·ness** *n*

di·a·be·tes *n* : a disease in which too little insulin is produced and the body cannot use sugar and starch in the normal way

di·a·bet·ic *n* : a person with diabetes

di·a·crit·i·cal mark *n* : a mark used with a letter or group of letters to show a pronunciation different from that given a letter or group of letters not marked or marked in a different way

di·a·dem *n* : a band for the head worn especially by monarchs

di·ag·nose *vb* **di·ag·nosed; di·ag·nos·ing** : to recognize (as a disease) by signs and symptoms

di·ag·no·sis *n, pl* **di·ag·no·ses :** the art or act of recognizing a disease from its signs and symptoms

[1]**di·ag·o·nal** *adj* **1 :** running from one corner to the opposite corner of a figure with four sides **2 :** running in a slanting direction — **di·ag·o·nal·ly** *adv*

[2]**diagonal** *n* : a diagonal line, direction, or pattern

[1]**di·a·gram** *n* : a drawing, sketch, plan, or chart that makes something clearer or easier to understand

[2]**diagram** *vb* **di·a·gramed** *or* **di·a·grammed; di·a·gram·ing** *or* **di·a·gram·ming :** to put in the form of a diagram

[1]**di·al** *n* **1 :** the face of a watch or clock **2** : SUNDIAL **3 :** a face or series of marks on which some measurement or other number is shown usually by means of a pointer **4** : a disk usually with a knob or holes that may be turned to operate something (as a telephone)

[2]**dial** *vb* **di·aled** *or* **di·alled; di·al·ing** *or* **di·al·ling :** to use a dial to operate or select

di·a·lect *n* **1 :** a form of a language belonging to a certain region **2 :** a form of a language used by the members of a certain occupation or class

di·a·logue *or* **di·a·log** *n* **1 :** a conversation between two or more persons **2 :** conversation given in a written story or a play

di·am·e·ter *n* **1 :** a straight line that joins two points of a figure or body and passes through the center **2 :** the distance through the center of an object from one side to the other : THICKNESS

di·a·mond *n* **1 :** a very hard mineral that is a form of carbon, is usually nearly colorless, and is used especially in jewelry **2 :** a flat figure ♦ like one of the surfaces of certain cut diamonds **3 :** INFIELD 1

di·a·per *n* : a piece of absorbent material drawn up between the legs of a baby and fastened about the waist

di·a·phragm *n* **1 :** a muscular wall separating the chest from the abdomen **2 :** a thin circular plate (as in a microphone) that vibrates when sound strikes it

di·ar·rhea *n* **:** abnormally frequent and watery bowel movements

di·a·ry *n, pl* **di·a·ries** **1 :** a daily record especially of personal experiences and thoughts **2 :** a book for keeping a diary

¹dice *n, pl* **dice :** a small cube marked on each face with one to six spots and used usually in pairs in games

²dice *vb* **diced; dic·ing :** to cut into small cubes

dick·er *vb* **:** ²BARGAIN, HAGGLE

¹dic·tate *vb* **dic·tat·ed; dic·tat·ing** **1 :** to speak or read for someone else to write down or for a machine to record **2 :** to say or state with authority **:** ORDER

²dictate *n* **:** a statement made or direction given with authority **:** COMMAND

dic·ta·tion *n* **1 :** the giving of orders often without thought of whether they are reasonable or fair **2 :** the dictating of words **3 :** something dictated or taken down from dictation

dic·ta·tor *n* **1 :** a person who rules with total authority and often in a cruel or brutal manner **2 :** a person who dictates — **dic·ta·tor·ship** *n*

dic·ta·to·ri·al *adj* **:** of, relating to, or like a dictator or a dictatorship

dic·tion *n* **1 :** choice of words especially with regard to correctness, clearness, and effectiveness **2 :** ENUNCIATION

dic·tio·nary *n, pl* **dic·tio·nar·ies** **1 :** a book giving the meaning and usually the pronunciation of words listed in alphabetical order **2 :** an alphabetical reference book explaining words and phrases of a field of knowledge **3 :** a book listing words of one language in alphabetical order with definitions in another language

did *past of* DO

didn't : did not

¹die *vb* **died; dy·ing** **1 :** to stop living **2 :** to pass out of existence **3 :** to disappear little by little **4 :** to wish eagerly **5 :** ¹STOP 4

²die *n* **1** *pl* **dice :** ¹DICE **2** *pl* **dies :** a device for forming or cutting material by pressure

die·sel *n* **1 :** DIESEL ENGINE **2 :** a vehicle driven by a diesel engine

diesel engine *n* **:** an engine in which the mixture of air and fuel is compressed until enough heat is created to ignite the mixture

¹di·et *n* **1 :** the food and drink that a person or animal usually takes **2 :** the kind and amount of food selected or allowed in certain circumstances (as ill health)

²diet *vb* **:** to eat or cause to eat less or according to certain rules — **di·et·er** *n*

³diet *adj* **:** reduced in calories

di·e·tary *adj* **:** of or relating to a diet or to rules of diet

di·e·ti·tian *or* **di·e·ti·cian** *n* **:** a person trained to apply the principles of nutrition to the planning of food and meals

dif·fer *vb* **1 :** to be not the same **:** be unlike **2 :** DISAGREE 2

dif·fer·ence *n* **1 :** what makes two or more persons or things different **2 :** a disagreement about something **3 :** REMAINDER 2

dif·fer·ent *adj* **1 :** not of the same kind **2 :** not the same — **dif·fer·ent·ly** *adv*

dif·fer·en·ti·ate *vb* **dif·fer·en·ti·at·ed; dif·fer·en·ti·at·ing** **1 :** to make or become different **2 :** to recognize or state the difference between

dif·fer·en·ti·a·tion *n* **:** the process of change by which immature living structures develop to maturity

dif·fi·cult *adj* **1 :** hard to do or make **2 :** hard to deal with **3 :** hard to understand

dif·fi·cul·ty *n, pl* **dif·fi·cul·ties** **1 :** the state of being difficult **2 :** great effort **3 :** OBSTACLE **4 :** a difficult situation **:** TROUBLE

dif·fi·dent *adj* **1 :** lacking confidence **2 :** RESERVED 1 — **dif·fi·dent·ly** *adv*

dif·fuse *vb* **dif·fused; dif·fus·ing :** to undergo diffusion

dif·fu·sion *n* **:** the mixing of particles of liquids or gases so that they move from a region of high concentration to one of lower concentration

¹dig *vb* **dug; dig·ging** **1 :** to turn up, loosen, or remove the soil **2 :** to form by removing earth **3 :** to uncover or search by or as if by turning up earth **4 :** DISCOVER, UNCOVER **5 :** ¹PROD 1, POKE **6 :** to work hard — **dig·ger** *n*

²dig *n* **1 :** ²POKE, THRUST **2 :** a nasty remark

¹di·gest *n* **:** information in shortened form

²di·gest *vb* **1 :** to think over and get straight in the mind **2 :** to change (food) into simpler forms that can be taken in and used by the body **3 :** to become digested

di·gest·ible *adj* **:** possible to digest

di·ges·tion *n* **:** the process or power of digesting something (as food)

di·ges·tive *adj* **:** of, relating to, or functioning in digestion

dig·it *n* **1 :** any of the numerals 1 to 9 and the symbol 0 **2 :** ¹FINGER 1, ¹TOE 1

dig·i·tal *adj* **1 :** of, relating to, or done with a finger or toe **2 :** of, relating to, or using calculation directly with digits rather than through measurable physical quantities **3 :** of or relating to data in the form of numerical digits **4 :** providing displayed or recorded information in numerical digits from an automatic device — **dig·i·tal·ly** *adv*

dig·ni·fied *adj* **:** having or showing dignity

dig·ni·fy *vb* **dig·ni·fied; dig·ni·fy·ing :** to give dignity or importance to

dig·ni·tary *n, pl* **dig·ni·tar·ies :** a person of high position or honor

dig·ni·ty *n, pl* **dig·ni·ties 1 :** the quality or state of being worthy of honor and respect **2 :** high rank or office **3 :** a dignified look or way of behaving

dike *or* **dyke** *n* **:** a bank of earth thrown up from a ditch or heaped up to form a boundary or to control water

di·lap·i·dat·ed *adj* **:** partly fallen apart or ruined from age or from lack of care

di·late *vb* **di·lat·ed; di·lat·ing :** to make or grow larger or wider

di·lem·ma *n* **:** a situation in which a person has to choose between things that are all bad or unsatisfactory

dil·i·gence *n* **:** careful and continued work

dil·i·gent *adj* **:** showing steady and earnest care and effort — **dil·i·gent·ly** *adv*

dill *n* **:** an herb related to the carrot with fragrant leaves and seeds used mostly in flavoring pickles

dil·ly·dal·ly *vb* **dil·ly·dal·lied; dil·ly·dal·ly·ing :** to waste time **:** DAWDLE

di·lute *vb* **di·lut·ed; di·lut·ing :** to make thinner or more liquid

di·lu·tion *n* **1 :** the act of diluting **:** the state of being diluted **2 :** something (as a solution) that is diluted

1dim *adj* **dim·mer; dim·mest 1 :** not bright or distinct **:** FAINT **2 :** not seeing or understanding clearly — **dim·ly** *adv* — **dim·ness** *n*

2dim *vb* **dimmed; dim·ming 1 :** to make or become dim **2 :** to reduce the light from

dime *n* **:** a United States coin worth ten cents

di·men·sion *n* **:** the length, width, or height of something

di·men·sion·al *adj* **:** of or relating to dimensions

di·min·ish *vb* **1 :** to make less or cause to seem less **2 :** BELITTLE **3 :** DWINDLE — **di·min·ish·ment** *n*

di·min·u·en·do *n, pl* **di·min·u·en·dos** *or* **di·min·u·en·does :** DECRESCENDO

di·min·u·tive *adj* **:** very small **:** TINY

dim·mer *n* **:** a device for regulating the brightness of an electric lighting unit (as the lights of a room)

1dim·ple *n* **:** a slight hollow spot especially in the cheek or chin

2dimple *vb* **dim·pled; dim·pling :** to mark with or form dimples

1din *n* **:** loud confused noise

2din *vb* **dinned; din·ning 1 :** to make a din **2 :** to repeat again and again in order to impress on someone's mind

dine *vb* **dined; din·ing 1 :** to eat dinner **2 :** to give a dinner to

din·er *n* **1 :** a person eating dinner **2 :** a railroad dining car or a restaurant in the shape of one

di·nette *n* **:** a separate area or small room used for dining

ding·dong *n* **:** the sound of a bell ringing

din·ghy *n, pl* **dinghies 1 :** a small light rowboat **2 :** a rubber life raft

din·gle *n* **:** a small narrow wooded valley

din·gy *adj* **din·gi·er; din·gi·est :** rather dark and dirty — **din·gi·ness** *n*

din·ner *n* **1 :** the main meal of the day **2 :** BANQUET

di·no·saur *n* **:** any of a group of extinct mostly land-dwelling reptiles that lived millions of years ago

dint *n* **1 :** the force or power of something **2 :** 2DENT

di·o·cese *n* **:** the district over which a bishop has authority

1dip *vb* **dipped; dip·ping 1 :** to sink or push briefly into a liquid **2 :** to take out with or as if with a ladle **3 :** to lower and quickly raise again **:** drop or sink and quickly rise again **4 :** to sink out of sight **5 :** to slope downward

2dip *n* **1 :** a plunge into water for fun or exercise **:** a short swim **2 :** a downward slope **3 :** something obtained by or used in dipping **4 :** a tasty sauce into which solid food may be dipped

diph·the·ria *n* **:** a contagious disease in which the air passages become coated with a membrane that often makes breathing difficult

diph·thong *n* **:** two vowel sounds joined in one syllable to form one speech sound

di·plo·ma *n* **:** a certificate that shows a person has finished a course or graduated from a school

di·plo·ma·cy *n* **1 :** the work of keeping up relations between the governments of different countries **2 :** skill in dealing with others

dip·lo·mat *n* **1 :** a person whose work is diplomacy **2 :** a person who is good at not saying or doing things that hurt or make people angry

dip·lo·mat·ic *adj* **1 :** of or relating to diplomats and their work **2 :** TACTFUL — **dip·lo·mat·i·cal·ly** *adv*

dip·per *n* **1 :** one that dips **2 :** a ladle or scoop for dipping

dire *adj* **1 :** causing horror or terror

: DREADFUL **2 :** very great — **dire·ly** *adv* — **dire·ness** *n*
¹di·rect *vb* **1 :** to put an address on (as a letter) **2 :** ¹AIM 3, TURN **3 :** to show or tell the way **4 :** to guide the production of **5 :** ¹ORDER 2, COMMAND
²direct *adj* **1 :** going from one point to another without turning or stopping **:** STRAIGHT **2 :** going straight to the point **3 :** being in an unbroken family line — **di·rect·ness** *n*
³direct *adv* **:** DIRECTLY 1
direct current *n* **:** an electric current flowing in one direction only
di·rec·tion *n* **1 :** SUPERVISION, MANAGEMENT **2 :** an order or instruction to be followed **3 :** the path along which something moves, lies, or points
di·rect·ly *adv* **1 :** in a direct course or way **2 :** right away **:** IMMEDIATELY
direct object *n* **:** a word that represents the main goal or the result of the action of a verb
di·rec·tor *n* **:** a person who directs something
di·rec·to·ry *n, pl* **di·rec·to·ries :** a book containing an alphabetical list of names and addresses
dirge *n* **:** a song or hymn of grief
di·ri·gi·ble *n* **:** AIRSHIP
dirk *n* **:** a long dagger with a straight blade
dirt *n* **1 :** a filthy or soiling substance (as mud or dust) **2 :** ²SOIL
¹dirty *adj* **dirt·i·er; dirt·i·est 1 :** soiled or polluted by dirt or impurities **2 :** UNFAIR, MEAN **3 :** INDECENT, VULGAR **4 :** not clear in color **5 :** showing dislike or anger — **dirt·i·ness** *n*
²dirty *vb* **dirt·ied; dirty·ing :** to make or become dirty
dis- *prefix* **1 :** do the opposite of **2 :** deprive of **3 :** expel from **4 :** opposite or absence of **5 :** not
dis·abil·i·ty *n, pl* **dis·abil·i·ties 1 :** the state of being disabled **:** lack of power to do something **2 :** something that disables
dis·able *vb* **dis·abled; dis·abling :** to make unable or incapable **:** CRIPPLE — **dis·able·ment** *n*
dis·ad·van·tage *n* **:** something that makes it hard for a person to succeed or do something
dis·ad·van·ta·geous *adj* **:** making it harder for a person to succeed or do something — **dis·ad·van·ta·geous·ly** *adv* — **dis·ad·van·ta·geous·ness** *n*
dis·agree *vb* **dis·agreed; dis·agree·ing 1 :** to be unlike each other **:** be different **2 :** to have unlike ideas or opinions **3 :** QUARREL **4 :** to have an unpleasant effect
dis·agree·able *adj* **1 :** UNPLEASANT **2 :** having a bad disposition **:** PEEVISH — **dis·agree·ably** *adv*
dis·agree·ment *n* **1 :** the act or fact of disagreeing **2 :** the condition of being different **3 :** a difference of opinion
dis·ap·pear *vb* **1 :** to stop being visible **:** pass out of sight **2 :** to stop existing
dis·ap·pear·ance *n* **:** the act or fact of disappearing
dis·ap·point *vb* **:** to fail to satisfy the hope or expectation of
dis·ap·point·ment *n* **1 :** the act of disappointing **2 :** the condition or feeling of being disappointed **3 :** one that disappoints
dis·ap·prov·al *n* **:** the feeling of not liking or agreeing with something or someone
dis·ap·prove *vb* **dis·ap·proved; dis·ap·prov·ing :** to dislike or be against something
dis·arm *vb* **1 :** to take weapons from **2 :** to reduce the size and strength of the armed forces of a country **3 :** to make harmless **4 :** to remove any feelings of doubt, mistrust, or unfriendliness **:** win over — **dis·ar·ma·ment** *n*
dis·ar·range *vb* **dis·ar·ranged; dis·ar·rang·ing :** to make all mussed up or mixed up — **dis·ar·range·ment** *n*
di·sas·ter *n* **:** something (as a flood or a tornado) that happens suddenly and causes much suffering or loss **:** CALAMITY
di·sas·trous *adj* **:** being or resulting in a disaster — **di·sas·trous·ly** *adv*
dis·band *vb* **:** to break up and stop being a group — **dis·band·ment** *n*
dis·bar *vb* **dis·barred; dis·bar·ring :** to deprive (a lawyer) of the rights of membership in the legal profession — **dis·bar·ment** *n*
dis·be·lief *n* **:** refusal or inability to believe
dis·be·lieve *vb* **dis·be·lieved; dis·be·liev·ing :** to think not to be true or real — **dis·be·liev·er** *n*
dis·burse *vb* **dis·bursed; dis·burs·ing :** to pay out — **dis·burse·ment** *n*
disc *variant of* DISK
¹dis·card *vb* **1 :** to throw down an unwanted playing card from one's hand **2 :** to get rid of as useless or unwanted
²dis·card *n* **1 :** the act of discarding **2 :** something discarded
dis·cern *vb* **:** to see, recognize, or understand something
¹dis·charge *vb* **dis·charged; dis·charg·ing 1 :** to relieve of a load or burden **:** UNLOAD **2 :** SHOOT 1, 2, FIRE **3 :** to set free **4 :** to dismiss from service **5 :** to let go or let off **6 :** to give forth the contents (as a fluid) **7 :** to get rid of by paying or doing
²dis·charge *n* **1 :** the act of discharging, unloading, or releasing **2 :** a certificate of

DICTIONARY

release or payment **3 :** a firing off **4 :** a flowing out (as of blood or pus) **5 :** a firing of a person from a job **6 :** complete separation from military service

dis·ci·ple *n* **1 :** a person who accepts and helps to spread the teachings of another **2 :** APOSTLE 1

¹dis·ci·pline *n* **1 :** strict training that corrects or strengthens **2 :** PUNISHMENT 1 **3 :** habits and ways of acting that are gotten through practice **4 :** a system of rules

²discipline *vb* **dis·ci·plined; dis·ci·plin·ing** **1 :** to punish for the sake of discipline **2 :** to train in self-control or obedience **3 :** to bring under control

disc jockey *n* **:** a radio announcer who plays records

dis·claim *vb* **:** to deny being part of or responsible for

dis·close *vb* **dis·closed; dis·clos·ing :** to make known **:** REVEAL

dis·clo·sure *n* **1 :** an act of disclosing **2 :** something disclosed

dis·col·or *vb* **:** to change in color especially for the worse

dis·col·or·a·tion *n* **1 :** change of color **2 :** a discolored spot

dis·com·fort *n* **:** the condition of being uncomfortable

dis·con·cert *vb* **:** to make confused and a little upset

dis·con·nect *vb* **:** to undo the connection of

dis·con·nect·ed *adj* **:** INCOHERENT — **dis·con·nect·ed·ly** *adv*

dis·con·so·late *adj* **:** too sad to be cheered up — **dis·con·so·late·ly** *adv*

¹dis·con·tent *vb* **:** to make dissatisfied

²discontent *n* **:** the condition of being dissatisfied

dis·con·tent·ed *adj* **:** not contented — **dis·con·tent·ed·ly** *adv*

dis·con·tin·ue *vb* **dis·con·tin·ued; dis·con·tinu·ing :** to bring to an end **:** STOP

dis·cord *n* **:** lack of agreement or harmony

dis·cord·ant *adj* **:** being in disagreement **:** not being in harmony

¹dis·count *n* **:** an amount taken off a regular price

²dis·count *vb* **1 :** to lower the amount of a bill, debt, or charge usually in return for cash or quick payment **2 :** to believe only partly

dis·cour·age *vb* **dis·cour·aged; dis·cour·ag·ing** **1 :** to make less determined, hopeful, or sure of oneself **2 :** DETER **3 :** to try to persuade not to do something — **dis·cour·age·ment** *n*

¹dis·course *n* **1 :** CONVERSATION **2 :** a long talk or composition about a subject

²dis·course *vb* **dis·coursed; dis·cours·ing :** to talk especially for a long time

dis·cour·te·ous *adj* **:** not polite **:** RUDE — **dis·cour·te·ous·ly** *adv*

dis·cour·te·sy *n, pl* **dis·cour·te·sies** **1 :** rude behavior **2 :** a rude act

dis·cov·er *vb* **:** to find out, see, or learn of especially for the first time **:** FIND — **dis·cov·er·er** *n*

dis·cov·ery *n, pl* **dis·cov·er·ies** **1 :** an act of discovering **2 :** something discovered

¹dis·cred·it *vb* **1 :** to refuse to accept as true **2 :** to cause to seem dishonest or untrue

²discredit *n* **:** loss of good name or respect

dis·creet *adj* **:** having or showing good judgment especially in conduct or speech — **dis·creet·ly** *adv*

dis·cre·tion *n* **1 :** good sense in making decisions **2 :** the power of deciding for oneself

dis·crim·i·nate *vb* **dis·crim·i·nat·ed; dis·crim·i·nat·ing** **1 :** to be able to tell the difference between things **2 :** to treat some people better than others without any fair or proper reason

dis·crim·i·na·tion *n* **1 :** the act of discriminating **2 :** the ability to see differences **3 :** the treating of some people better than others without any fair or proper reason

dis·crim·i·na·to·ry *adj* **:** showing discrimination **:** being unfair

dis·cus *n, pl* **dis·cus·es :** an object that is shaped like a disk and hurled for distance in a track-and-field event

dis·cuss *vb* **1 :** to argue or consider fully and openly **2 :** to talk about

dis·cus·sion *n* **:** conversation or debate for the purpose of understanding a question or subject

¹dis·dain *n* **:** a feeling of scorn for something considered beneath oneself — **dis·dain·ful** *adj* — **dis·dain·ful·ly** *adv*

²disdain *vb* **1 :** to think oneself far too good for something or someone **2 :** to refuse because of scorn

dis·ease *n* **1 :** a change in a living body (as of a person or plant) that interferes with its normal functioning **:** ILLNESS **2 :** an instance or a kind of disease — **dis·eased** *adj*

dis·em·bark *vb* **:** to go or put ashore from a ship

dis·en·tan·gle *vb* **dis·en·tan·gled; dis·en·tan·gling :** to straighten out **:** UNTANGLE — **dis·en·tan·gle·ment** *n*

dis·fa·vor *n* **1 :** DISAPPROVAL **2 :** the state of being disliked

dis·fig·ure *vb* **dis·fig·ured; dis·fig·ur·ing :** to spoil the looks of — **dis·fig·ure·ment** *n*

dis·fran·chise *vb* **dis·fran·chised; dis-**

fran·chis·ing : to take away the right to vote — **dis·fran·chise·ment** *n*

¹dis·grace *vb* **dis·graced; dis·grac·ing :** to bring shame to — **dis·grac·er** *n*

²disgrace *n* **1 :** the condition of being looked down on **:** loss of respect **2 :** ¹DISHONOR 1 **3 :** a cause of shame

dis·grace·ful *adj* **:** bringing or deserving disgrace — **dis·grace·ful·ly** *adv* — **dis·grace·ful·ness** *n*

dis·grun·tle *vb* **dis·grun·tled; dis·grun·tling :** to make grouchy or cross

¹dis·guise *vb* **dis·guised; dis·guis·ing 1 :** to change the looks of so as to conceal identity **2 :** to keep from revealing

²disguise *n* **1 :** clothing put on to hide one's true identity or to imitate another's **2 :** an outward appearance that hides what something really is

¹dis·gust *n* **:** the strong dislike one feels for something nasty and sickening

²disgust *vb* **:** to cause to feel disgust — **dis·gust·ed·ly** *adv*

dis·gust·ing *adj* **:** causing disgust — **dis·gust·ing·ly** *adv*

¹dish *n* **1 :** a hollowed out vessel for serving food at table **2 :** the contents of a dish

²dish *vb* **:** to put into a dish **:** SERVE

dis·heart·en *vb* **:** DISCOURAGE 1 — **dis·heart·en·ing·ly** *adv*

di·shev·eled *or* **di·shev·elled** *adj* **:** mussed up **:** UNTIDY

dis·hon·est *adj* **:** not honest or trustworthy — **dis·hon·est·ly** *adv*

dis·hon·es·ty *n* **:** lack of honesty **:** the quality of being dishonest

¹dis·hon·or *n* **1 :** loss of honor or good name **2 :** a cause of disgrace

²dishonor *vb* **:** to bring shame on **:** DISGRACE

dis·hon·or·able *adj* **:** not honorable **:** SHAMEFUL — **dis·hon·or·ably** *adv*

dis·il·lu·sion *vb* **:** to free from mistaken beliefs or foolish hopes — **dis·il·lu·sion·ment** *n*

dis·in·fect *vb* **:** to free from germs that might cause disease

¹dis·in·fec·tant *n* **:** something that frees from germs

²disinfectant *adj* **:** serving to disinfect

dis·in·her·it *vb* **:** to deprive (an heir) of the right to inherit

dis·in·te·grate *vb* **dis·in·te·grat·ed; dis·in·te·grat·ing :** to separate or break up into small parts or pieces

dis·in·te·gra·tion *n* **:** the act or process of disintegrating **:** the state of being disintegrated

dis·in·ter·est·ed *adj* **1 :** not interested **2 :** free of selfish interest — **dis·in·ter·est·ed·ly** *adv* — **dis·in·ter·est·ed·ness** *n*

dis·joint·ed *adj* **:** not clear and orderly — **dis·joint·ed·ly** *adv*

disk *or* **disc** *n* **1 :** something that is or appears to be flat and round **2** *usually disc* **:** a phonograph record **3 :** a round flat plate coated with a magnetic substance on which data for a computer is stored — **disk·like** *adj*

disk·ette *n* **:** FLOPPY DISK

¹dis·like *n* **:** a strong feeling of not liking or approving

²dislike *vb* **dis·liked; dis·lik·ing :** to feel dislike for

dis·lo·cate *vb* **dis·lo·cat·ed; dis·lo·cat·ing :** to displace a bone from its normal connections with another bone

dis·lo·ca·tion *n* **:** the state of being dislocated

dis·lodge *vb* **dis·lodged; dis·lodg·ing :** to force out of a resting place or a place of hiding or defense

dis·loy·al *adj* **:** not loyal — **dis·loy·al·ly** *adv*

dis·loy·al·ty *n, pl* **dis·loy·al·ties 1 :** lack of loyalty **2 :** a disloyal act

dis·mal *adj* **:** very gloomy and depressing

dis·man·tle *vb* **dis·man·tled; dis·man·tling 1 :** to strip of furniture or equipment **2 :** to take completely apart (as for storing or repair) — **dis·man·tle·ment** *n*

¹dis·may *vb* **:** to cause to be unable to act because of surprise, fear, or confusion

²dismay *n* **1 :** sudden loss of courage or determination because of fear **2 :** a feeling of fear or disappointment

dis·miss *vb* **1 :** to send away **2 :** to discharge from an office or job **3 :** to decide not to think about

dis·miss·al *n* **:** the act of dismissing **:** the state or fact of being dismissed

dis·mount *vb* **1 :** to get down from something (as a horse or bicycle) **2 :** to cause to fall off or get off **3 :** to take (as a cannon) off a support **4 :** to take apart (as a machine)

dis·obe·di·ence *n* **:** an act or the fact of disobeying

dis·obe·di·ent *adj* **:** not obeying — **dis·obe·di·ent·ly** *adv*

dis·obey *vb* **dis·obeyed; dis·obey·ing :** to refuse, neglect, or fail to obey

¹dis·or·der *vb* **1 :** to disturb the order of **2 :** to disturb the regular or normal functioning of

²disorder *n* **1 :** lack of order or of orderly arrangement **:** CONFUSION **2 :** an abnormal state of body or mind **:** SICKNESS

dis·or·der·ly *adj* **1 :** not behaving quietly or

well : UNRULY **2 :** not neat or orderly — **dis•or•der•li•ness** *n*

dis•or•ga•nize *vb* **dis•or•ga•nized; dis•or•ga•niz•ing :** to break up the regular arrangement or system of

dis•own *vb* **:** to refuse to accept any longer as one's own

dis•par•age *vb* **dis•par•aged; dis•par•ag•ing :** to speak of as unimportant or not much good : BELITTLE — **dis•par•age•ment** *n*

dis•pas•sion•ate *adj* **:** not influenced by strong feeling **:** CALM, IMPARTIAL — **dis•pas•sion•ate•ly** *adv*

1dis•patch *vb* **1 :** to send away quickly to a certain place or for a certain reason **2 :** 1KILL 1 — **dis•patch•er** *n*

2dispatch *n* **1 :** MESSAGE **2 :** a news story sent in to a newspaper **3 :** SPEED 1

dis•pel *vb* **dis•pelled; dis•pel•ling :** to drive away

dis•pense *vb* **dis•pensed; dis•pens•ing 1 :** to give out in shares : DISTRIBUTE **2 :** ADMINISTER 2 **3 :** to put up or prepare medicine in a form ready for use — **dispense with :** to do or get along without

dis•pens•er *n* **:** a container that gives out something one at a time or a little at a time

dis•perse *vb* **dis•persed; dis•pers•ing :** to break up and scatter

dispir•it *vb* **:** to take away the cheerfulness or enthusiasm of

dis•place *vb* **dis•placed; dis•plac•ing 1 :** to remove from the usual or proper place **2 :** to remove from office **:** DISCHARGE **3 :** to take the place of **:** REPLACE — **dis•place•ment** *n*

1dis•play *vb* **1 :** to put (something) in plain sight **2 :** to make clear the existence or presence of : show plainly

2display *n* **:** a showing of something

dis•please *vb* **dis•pleased; dis•pleas•ing :** to be or do something that makes (a person) cross or not pleased or satisfied

dis•plea•sure *n* **:** a feeling of dislike and irritation **:** DISSATISFACTION

dis•pos•able *adj* **:** made to be thrown away after use

dis•pos•al *n* **1 :** ARRANGEMENT 1 **2 :** a getting rid of **3 :** right or power to use **:** CONTROL

dis•pose *vb* **dis•posed; dis•pos•ing 1 :** to put in place **:** ARRANGE **2 :** to make ready and willing — **dis•pos•er** *n* — **dispose of 1 :** to finish with **2 :** to get rid of

dis•po•si•tion *n* **1 :** ARRANGEMENT 1 **2 :** one's usual attitude or mood **3 :** TENDENCY 2, LIKING

dis•pro•por•tion *n* **:** lack of normal or usual proportions

dis•prove *vb* **dis•proved; dis•prov•ing :** to show to be false

dis•put•able *adj* **:** not yet proved **:** DEBATABLE — **dis•put•ably** *adv*

1dis•pute *vb* **dis•put•ed; dis•put•ing 1 :** ARGUE 2 **2 :** to question or deny the truth or rightness of **3 :** to fight over — **dis•put•er** *n*

2dispute *n* **1 :** ARGUMENT 2, DEBATE **2 :** 1QUARREL 2

dis•qual•i•fy *vb* **dis•qual•i•fied; dis•qual•i•fy•ing :** to make or declare unfit or not qualified

1dis•qui•et *vb* **:** to make uneasy or worried **:** DISTURB

2disquiet *n* **:** an uneasy feeling

dis•qui•et•ing *adj* **:** causing worry or uneasiness — **dis•qui•et•ing•ly** *adv*

1dis•re•gard *vb* **:** to pay no attention to

2disregard *n* **:** the act of disregarding **:** the state of being disregarded

dis•re•pair *n* **:** the condition of needing repair

dis•rep•u•ta•ble *adj* **:** not respectable — **dis•rep•u•ta•bly** *adv*

dis•re•spect *n* **:** lack of respect **:** DISCOURTESY — **dis•re•spect•ful** *adj* — **dis•re•spect•ful•ly** *adv*

dis•robe *vb* **dis•robed; dis•rob•ing :** UNDRESS

dis•rupt *vb* **:** to throw into disorder **:** BREAK UP

dis•sat•is•fac•tion *n* **:** a being dissatisfied

dis•sat•is•fy *vb* **dis•sat•is•fied; dis•sat•is•fy•ing :** to fail to satisfy **:** DISPLEASE

dis•sect *vb* **:** to cut or take apart especially for examination

dis•sen•sion *n* **:** disagreement in opinion **:** DISCORD

1dis•sent *vb* **:** DISAGREE 2 — **dis•sent•er** *n*

2dissent *n* **:** difference of opinion

dis•ser•vice *n* **:** a harmful, unfair, or unjust act

dis•sim•i•lar *adj* **:** not similar **:** DIFFERENT

dis•si•pate *vb* **dis•si•pat•ed; dis•si•pat•ing 1 :** to break up and drive off **:** DISPERSE **2 :** to scatter or waste foolishly **:** SQUANDER

dis•si•pat•ed *adj* **:** enjoying bad, foolish, or harmful activities

dis•si•pa•tion *n* **1 :** the act of dissipating or the state of being dissipated **2 :** a dissipated way of life

dis•so•lute *adj* **:** having or showing bad morals or behavior — **dis•so•lute•ly** *adv* — **dis•so•lute•ness** *n*

dis•solve *vb* **dis•solved; dis•solv•ing 1 :** to mix or cause to mix with a liquid so that the result is a liquid that is the same throughout **2 :** to bring to an end **:** TERMI-

NATE **3 :** to fade away as if by melting or breaking up
dis·so·nance *n* **:** an unpleasant combination of musical sounds
dis·suade *vb* **dis·suad·ed; dis·suad·ing :** to persuade or advise not to do something
dis·tance *n* **1 :** how far from each other two points or places are **2 :** the quality or state of not being friendly **:** RESERVE **3 :** a distant point or region
dis·tant *adj* **1 :** separated in space or time **2 :** REMOTE 1 **3 :** not closely related **4 :** [1]COLD 2, UNFRIENDLY — **dis·tant·ly** *adv*
dis·taste *n* **:** [1]DISLIKE
dis·taste·ful *adj* **:** UNPLEASANT
dis·tend *vb* **:** EXPAND 2, SWELL
dis·till *also* **dis·til** *vb* **dis·tilled; dis·till·ing :** to obtain or purify by distillation — **dis·till·er** *n*
dis·til·la·tion *n* **:** the process of heating a liquid or solid until it sends off a gas or vapor and then cooling the gas or vapor until it becomes liquid
dis·tinct *adj* **1 :** real and different from each other **2 :** easy to see, hear, or understand — **dis·tinct·ly** *adv* — **dis·tinct·ness** *n*
dis·tinc·tion *n* **1 :** the seeing or pointing out of a difference **2 :** DIFFERENCE 1 **3 :** great worth **:** EXCELLENCE **4 :** something that makes a person or thing special or different
dis·tinc·tive *adj* **1 :** clearly marking a person or a thing as different from others **2 :** having or giving a special look or way — **dis·tinc·tive·ly** *adv* — **dis·tinc·tive·ness** *n*
dis·tin·guish *vb* **1 :** to recognize by some mark or quality **2 :** to know the difference **3 :** to set apart as different or special
dis·tin·guish·able *adj* **:** possible to recognize or tell apart from others
dis·tin·guished *adj* **:** widely known and admired
dis·tort *vb* **1 :** to tell in a way that is misleading **:** MISREPRESENT **2 :** to twist out of shape — **dis·tort·er** *n*
dis·tor·tion *n* **:** the act of distorting **:** the state or fact of being distorted
dis·tract *vb* **1 :** to draw the mind or attention to something else **2 :** to upset or trouble in mind to the point of confusion
dis·trac·tion *n* **1 :** the act of distracting **:** the state of being distracted **2 :** complete confusion of mind **3 :** something that makes it hard to pay attention
[1]**dis·tress** *n* **1 :** suffering or pain of body or mind **2 :** DANGER 1 — **dis·tress·ful** *adj*
[2]**distress** *vb* **:** to cause distress to — **dis·tress·ing·ly** *adv*
dis·trib·ute *vb* **dis·trib·ut·ed; dis·trib·ut·ing 1 :** to divide among several or many **2 :** to spread out so as to cover something **3 :** to divide or separate especially into classes **:** SORT — **dis·trib·u·tor** *n*
dis·tri·bu·tion *n* **1 :** the act of distributing **2 :** the way things are distributed **3 :** something distributed
dis·trib·u·tive *adj* **1 :** of or relating to distribution **2 :** producing the same answer when operating on the sum of several numbers as when operating on each and collecting the results — **dis·trib·u·tive·ly** *adv*
dis·trict *n* **1 :** an area or section (as of a city or nation) set apart for some purpose **2 :** an area or region with some special feature
[1]**dis·trust** *n* **:** a lack of trust or confidence **:** SUSPICION — **dis·trust·ful** *adj* — **dis·trust·ful·ly** *adv*
[2]**distrust** *vb* **:** to have no trust or confidence in
dis·turb *vb* **1 :** to interfere with **:** INTERRUPT **2 :** to change the arrangements of **:** move from its place **3 :** to trouble the mind of **:** UPSET **4 :** to make confused or disordered
dis·tur·bance *n* **1 :** the act of disturbing **:** the state of being disturbed **2 :** [2]DISORDER 1, COMMOTION
dis·use *n* **:** lack of use
dis·used *adj* **:** not used any more
[1]**ditch** *n* **:** a long narrow channel or trench dug in the earth
[2]**ditch** *vb* **1 :** to dig a ditch in or around (as for drainage) **2 :** to get rid of **:** DISCARD **3 :** to make a forced landing in an airplane on water
dith·er *n* **:** a very nervous or excited state
dit·ty *n, pl* **ditties :** a short simple song
di·van *n* **:** a large couch often with no back or arms
[1]**dive** *vb* **dived** *or* **dove; div·ing 1 :** to plunge into water headfirst **2 :** SUBMERGE 1 **3 :** to fall fast **4 :** to descend in an airplane at a steep angle **5 :** to shove suddenly into or at something — **div·er** *n*
[2]**dive** *n* **1 :** an act of diving **2 :** a quick drop (as of prices)
di·verse *adj* **:** different from each other **:** UNLIKE — **di·verse·ly** *adv* — **di·verse·ness** *n*
di·ver·sion *n* **1 :** an act or instance of diverting or turning aside **2 :** something that relaxes, amuses, or entertains
di·ver·si·ty *n, pl* **di·ver·si·ties :** the condition or fact of being different
di·vert *vb* **1 :** to turn aside **:** turn from one course or use to another **2 :** to turn the attention away **:** DISTRACT **3 :** to give pleasure to **:** AMUSE
[1]**di·vide** *vb* **di·vid·ed; di·vid·ing 1 :** to separate into two or more parts or pieces **2 :** to give out in shares **3 :** to be or make different in opinion or interest **4 :** to subject to

DICTIONARY

mathematical division **5 :** to branch off **:** FORK — **di•vid•er** *n*

²**divide** *n* **:** WATERSHED 1

div•i•dend *n* **1 :** a sum to be divided and given out **2 :** a number to be divided by another number

¹**di•vine** *adj* **1 :** of or relating to God or a god **2 :** being in praise of God **:** RELIGIOUS, HOLY **3 :** GODLIKE — **di•vine•ly** *adv*

²**divine** *n* **:** a member of the clergy

di•vin•i•ty *n, pl* **di•vin•i•ties 1 :** the quality or state of being divine **2 :** DEITY **3 :** the study of religion

di•vis•i•ble *adj* **:** possible to divide or separate

di•vi•sion *n* **1 :** the act or process of dividing **:** the state of being divided **2 :** a part or portion of a whole **3 :** a large military unit **4 :** something that divides, separates, or marks off **5 :** the finding out of how many times one number is contained in another **6 :** a group of plants that ranks above the class in scientific classification and is the highest group of the plant kingdom

di•vi•sor *n* **:** the number by which a dividend is divided

¹**di•vorce** *n* **1 :** a complete legal ending of a marriage **2 :** complete separation

²**divorce** *vb* **di•vorced; di•vorc•ing 1 :** to make or keep separate **2 :** to end one's marriage legally **:** get a divorce

di•vulge *vb* **di•vulged; di•vulg•ing :** to make public **:** REVEAL, DISCLOSE

dix•ie•land *n* **:** lively jazz music in a style developed in New Orleans

diz•zy *adj* **diz•zi•er; diz•zi•est 1 :** having the feeling of whirling **2 :** confused or unsteady in mind **3 :** causing a dizzy feeling — **diz•zi•ly** *adv* — **diz•zi•ness** *n*

DNA *n* **:** a complicated organic acid that carries genetic information in the chromosomes

¹**do** *vb* **did; done; do•ing; does 1 :** to cause (as an act or action) to happen **:** CARRY OUT, PERFORM **2 :** ²ACT 2, BEHAVE **3 :** to meet one's needs **:** SUCCEED **4 :** ¹FINISH 1 — used in the past participle **5 :** to put forth **:** EXERT **6 :** to work on, prepare, or put in order **7 :** to work at as a paying job **8 :** to serve the purpose **:** SUIT **9** — used as a helping verb (1) before the subject in a question, (2) in a negative statement, (3) for emphasis, and (4) as a substitute for a preceding predicate — **do away with 1 :** to get rid of **2 :** ¹KILL 1

²**do** *n* **:** the first note of the musical scale

doc•ile *adj* **:** easily taught, led, or managed — **doc•ile•ly** *adv*

¹**dock** *vb* **1 :** to cut off the end of **2 :** to take away a part of

²**dock** *n* **1 :** an artificial basin for ships that has gates to keep the water in or out **2 :** a waterway usually between two piers to receive ships **3 :** a wharf or platform for loading or unloading materials

³**dock** *vb* **1 :** to haul or guide into a dock **2 :** to come or go into a dock **3 :** to join (as two spacecraft) mechanically while in space

⁴**dock** *n* **:** the place in a court where a prisoner stands or sits during trial

¹**doc•tor** *n* **:** a person (as a physician or veterinarian) skilled and specializing in the art of healing

²**doctor** *vb* **1 :** to use remedies on or for **2 :** to practice medicine

doc•trine *n* **:** something (as a rule or principle) that is taught, believed in, or considered to be true

doc•u•ment *n* **1 :** a written or printed paper that gives information about or proof of something **2 :** a computer file (as a letter, essay, or chart) typed in by a user

¹**dodge** *n* **:** a sudden movement to one side

²**dodge** *vb* **dodged; dodg•ing 1 :** to move suddenly aside or to and fro **2 :** to avoid by moving quickly **3 :** EVADE — **dodg•er** *n*

dodge ball *n* **:** a game in which players stand in a circle and try to hit a player inside the circle by throwing a large inflated ball

do•do *n, pl* **dodoes** *or* **dodos :** a large heavy bird unable to fly that once lived on some of the islands of the Indian ocean

doe *n* **:** the female of an animal (as a deer) the male of which is called *buck*

do•er *n* **:** one that does

does *present third sing of* DO

doesn't : does not

doff *vb* **:** to take off (as one's hat as an act of politeness)

¹**dog** *n* **1 :** a domestic animal that eats meat and is related to the wolves and foxes **2 :** a device (as a metal bar with a hook at the end) for holding, gripping, or fastening something — **dog•like** *adj*

²**dog** *vb* **dogged; dog•ging :** to hunt, track, or follow like a hound

dog•cart *n* **1 :** a cart pulled by dogs **2 :** a light one-horse carriage with two seats back to back

dog•catch•er *n* **:** an official paid to catch and get rid of stray dogs

dog days *n pl* **:** the hot period between early July and early September

dog–eared *adj* **:** having a lot of pages with corners turned over

dog•fish *n* **:** any of several small sharks often seen near shore

dog•ged *adj* **:** stubbornly determined — **dog•ged•ly** *adv* — **dog•ged•ness** *n*

dog·gy *or* **dog·gie** *n, pl* **doggies :** a usually small or young dog

dog·house *n* **:** a shelter for a dog — **in the doghouse :** in trouble over some wrongdoing

dog·ma *n* **1 :** something firmly believed **2 :** a belief or set of beliefs taught by a church

dog·mat·ic *adj* **1 :** of or relating to dogma **2 :** seeming or sounding absolutely certain about something — **dog·mat·i·cal·ly** *adv*

[1]**dog·trot** *n* **:** a slow trot

[2]**dogtrot** *vb* **dog·trot·ted; dog·trot·ting :** to move at a dogtrot

dog·wood *n* **:** any of several shrubs and small trees with clusters of small flowers often surrounded by four showy leaves that look like petals

doi·ly *n, pl* **doilies :** a small often ornamental mat used on a table

do·ings *n pl* **:** things that are done or that go on

dol·drums *n pl* **1 :** a spell of low spirits **2 :** a part of the ocean near the equator known for its calms

[1]**dole** *n* **1 :** a giving out especially of food, clothing, or money to the needy **2 :** something given out as charity

[2]**dole** *vb* **doled; dol·ing 1 :** to give out as charity **2 :** to give in small portions

dole·ful *adj* **:** full of grief **:** SAD — **dole·ful·ly** *adv* — **dole·ful·ness** *n*

doll *n* **:** a small figure of a human being used especially as a child's plaything

dol·lar *n* **:** any of various coins or pieces of paper money (as of the United States or Canada) equal to 100 cents

dolly *n, pl* **dollies 1 :** DOLL **2 :** a platform on a roller or on wheels for moving heavy things

dol·phin *n* **1 :** a small whale with teeth and a long nose **2 :** either of two large food fishes of the sea

dolt *n* **:** a stupid person — **dolt·ish** *adj* — **dolt·ish·ly** *adv* — **dolt·ish·ness** *n*

-dom *n suffix* **1 :** dignity **:** office **2 :** realm **:** jurisdiction **3 :** state or fact of being **4 :** those having a certain office, occupation, interest, or character

do·main *n* **1 :** land under the control of a ruler or a government **2 :** a field of knowledge or activity

dome *n* **:** a bulge or a rounded top or roof that looks like half of a ball — **domed** *adj*

[1]**do·mes·tic** *adj* **1 :** of or relating to a household or a family **2 :** of, relating to, made in, or done in one's own country **3 :** living with or under the care of human beings **:** TAME — **do·mes·ti·cal·ly** *adv*

[2]**domestic** *n* **:** a household servant

do·mes·ti·cate *vb* **do·mes·ti·cat·ed; do·mes·ti·cat·ing :** to bring under the control of and make usable by humans

do·mi·cile *n* **:** a dwelling place

dom·i·nance *n* **:** the state or fact of being dominant

dom·i·nant *adj* **:** controlling or being over all others — **dom·i·nant·ly** *adv*

dom·i·nate *vb* **dom·i·nat·ed; dom·i·nat·ing :** to have a commanding position or controlling power over

dom·i·neer *vb* **:** to rule or behave in a bossy way

do·min·ion *n* **1 :** ruling or controlling power **:** SOVEREIGNTY **2 :** a territory under the control of a ruler **:** DOMAIN

dom·i·no *n, pl* **dom·i·noes** *or* **dom·i·nos :** one of a set of flat oblong dotted pieces used in playing a game (**dominoes**)

don *vb* **donned; don·ning :** to put on

do·nate *vb* **do·nat·ed; do·nat·ing :** to make a gift of **:** CONTRIBUTE — **do·na·tor** *n*

do·na·tion *n* **:** a giving of something without charge **:** the thing given (as to charity)

done *past participle of* DO

don·key *n, pl* **donkeys 1 :** an animal related to but smaller than the horse that has short hair in mane and tail and very large ears **2 :** a silly or stupid person

do·nor *n* **:** one who gives, donates, or presents — **do·nor·ship** *n*

don't : do not

[1]**doo·dle** *vb* **doo·dled; doo·dling :** to make a doodle — **doo·dler** *n*

[2]**doodle** *n* **:** a scribble, design, or sketch done while thinking about something else

doo·dle·bug *n* **:** ANT LION

[1]**doom** *n* **1 :** a decision made by a court **:** SENTENCE **2 :** a usually unhappy end **:** FATE

[2]**doom** *vb* **1 :** to give judgment against **:** CONDEMN **2 :** to make sure that something bad will happen

dooms·day *n* **:** the day of final judgment **:** the end of the world

door *n* **1 :** a usually swinging or sliding frame or barrier by which an entrance (as into a house) is closed and opened **2 :** a part of a piece of furniture like a house's door **3 :** DOORWAY

door·man *n, pl* **door·men :** a person who tends a door of a building

door·step *n* **:** a step or a series of steps before an outer door

door·way *n* **:** the opening or passage that a door closes

door·yard *n* **:** a yard outside the door of a house

dope *n* **1 :** a thick sticky material (as one used to make pipe joints tight) **2 :** a narcotic substance **3 :** a stupid person **4 :** INFORMATION 2

dop•ey *adj* **dop•i•er; dop•i•est 1 :** lacking alertness and activity **:** SLUGGISH **2 :** STUPID 2

dorm *n* **:** DORMITORY

dor•mant *adj* **:** being in an inactive state for the time being

dor•mer *n* **1 :** a window placed upright in a sloping roof **2 :** the structure containing a dormer window

dor•mi•to•ry *n, pl* **dor•mi•to•ries 1 :** a sleeping room especially for several people **2 :** a residence hall having many sleeping rooms

dor•mouse *n, pl* **dor•mice :** a small European animal that is like a squirrel, lives in trees, and feeds on nuts

dor•sal *adj* **:** of, relating to, or being on or near the surface of the body that in humans is the back but in most animals is the upper surface — **dor•sal•ly** *adv*

do•ry *n, pl* **dories :** a boat with a flat bottom, high sides that curve upward and outward, and a sharp bow

[1]**dose** *n* **:** a measured amount (as of a medicine) to be used at one time

[2]**dose** *vb* **dosed; dos•ing :** to give medicine to

[1]**dot** *n* **1 :** a small point, mark, or spot **2 :** a certain point in time **3 :** a short click forming a letter or part of a letter (as in telegraphy)

[2]**dot** *vb* **dot•ted; dot•ting :** to mark with or as if with dots

dote *vb* **dot•ed; dot•ing :** to be foolishly fond — **dot•er** *n* — **dot•ing•ly** *adv*

[1]**dou•ble** *adj* **1 :** having a twofold relation or character **:** DUAL **2 :** made up of two parts or members **3 :** being twice as great or as many **4 :** folded in two **5 :** having more than the usual number of petals

[2]**double** *vb* **dou•bled; dou•bling 1 :** to make or become twice as great or as many **:** multiply by two **2 :** to make of two thicknesses **3 :** CLENCH 2 **4 :** to become bent or folded usually in the middle **5 :** to take the place of another **6 :** to turn sharply and go back over the same course

[3]**double** *adv* **1 :** DOUBLY **2 :** two together

[4]**double** *n* **1 :** something that is twice another **2 :** a hit in baseball that enables the batter to reach second base **3 :** one that is very like another

double bass *n* **:** an instrument of the violin family that is the largest member and has the deepest tone

dou•ble–cross *vb* **:** BETRAY 2

dou•ble•head•er *n* **:** two games played one right after the other on the same day

dou•ble–joint•ed *adj* **:** having a joint that permits unusual freedom of movement of the parts that are joined

double play *n* **:** a play in baseball by which two base runners are put out

dou•blet *n* **:** a close-fitting jacket worn by men in Europe especially in the sixteenth century

dou•ble–talk *n* **:** language that seems to make sense but is actually a mixture of sense and nonsense

dou•bloon *n* **:** an old gold coin of Spain and Spanish America

dou•bly *adv* **:** to twice the amount or degree

[1]**doubt** *vb* **1 :** to be uncertain about **2 :** to lack confidence in **:** DISTRUST **3 :** to consider unlikely — **doubt•er** *n* — **doubt•ing•ly** *adv*

[2]**doubt** *n* **1 :** uncertainty of belief or opinion **2 :** the condition of being undecided **3 :** a lack of confidence **:** DISTRUST

doubt•ful *adj* **1 :** not clear or certain as to fact **2 :** of a questionable kind **3 :** undecided in opinion **4 :** not certain in outcome — **doubt•ful•ly** *adv*

doubt•less *adv* **1 :** without doubt **2 :** in all probability

dough *n* **1 :** a soft mass of moistened flour or meal thick enough to knead or roll **2 :** MONEY 1, 2

dough•nut *n* **:** a small ring of sweet dough fried in fat

dough•ty *adj* **dough•ti•er; dough•ti•est :** very strong and brave — **dough•ti•ly** *adv* — **dough•ti•ness** *n*

dour *adj* **:** looking or being stern or sullen — **dour•ly** *adv* — **dour•ness** *n*

douse *vb* **doused; dous•ing 1 :** to stick into water **2 :** to throw a liquid on **3 :** to put out **:** EXTINGUISH

[1]**dove** *n* **:** any of various mostly small pigeons

[2]**dove** *past of* DIVE

dowdy *adj* **dowd•i•er; dowd•i•est 1 :** not neatly or well dressed or cared for **2 :** not stylish — **dowd•i•ly** *adv* — **dowd•i•ness** *n*

dow•el *n* **:** a pin or peg used for fastening together two pieces of wood

[1]**down** *adv* **1 :** toward or in a lower position **2 :** to a lying or sitting position **3 :** toward or to the ground, floor, or bottom **4 :** in cash **5 :** in a direction opposite to up **6 :** to or in a lower or worse condition **7 :** from a past time **8 :** to or in a state of less activity

[2]**down** *prep* **:** down in **:** down along **:** down on **:** down through

[3]**down** *vb* **:** to go or cause to go or come down

[4]**down** *adj* **1 :** being in a low position **2 :** directed or going downward **3 :** being at a lower level **4 :** low in spirits **:** DOWNCAST

[5]**down** *n* **:** a low or falling period

[6]**down** *n* **:** a rolling grassy upland — usually used in pl.

[7]**down** *n* **1 :** soft fluffy feathers (as of young birds) **2 :** something soft and fluffy like down — **down•like** *adj*

down•beat *n* **:** the first beat of a measure of music

down•cast *adj* **1 :** low in spirit **:** SAD **2 :** directed down

down•fall *n* **:** a sudden fall (as from power, happiness, or a high position) or the cause of such a fall — **down•fall•en** *adj*

[1]**down•grade** *n* **:** a downward slope (as of a road)

[2]**downgrade** *vb* **down•grad•ed; down•grad•ing :** to lower in grade, rank, position, or standing

down•heart•ed *adj* **:** DOWNCAST 1 — **down•heart•ed•ly** *adv* — **down•heart•ed•ness** *n*

[1]**down•hill** *adv* **:** [1]DOWNWARD 1

[2]**down•hill** *adj* **:** sloping downhill

down payment *n* **:** a part of a price paid when something is bought or delivered leaving a balance to be paid later

down•pour *n* **:** a heavy rain

[1]**down•right** *adv* **:** REALLY, VERY

[2]**downright** *adj* **:** [2]OUTRIGHT 1, ABSOLUTE

down•stage *adv or adj* **:** toward or at the front of a theatrical stage

[1]**down•stairs** *adv* **:** down the stairs **:** on or to a lower floor

[2]**down•stairs** *adj* **:** situated on a lower floor or on the main or first floor

[3]**down•stairs** *n sing or pl* **:** the lower floor of a building

down•stream *adv* **:** in the direction a stream is flowing

down•town *adv or adj* **:** to, toward, or in the main business district

[1]**down•ward** *or* **down•wards** *adv* **1 :** from a higher place or condition to a lower one **2 :** from an earlier time

[2]**downward** *adj* **:** going or moving down

down•wind *adv or adj* **:** in the direction the wind is blowing

downy *adj* **down•i•er; down•i•est 1 :** like down **2 :** covered with down

dow•ry *n, pl* **dowries :** the property that a woman brings to her husband in marriage

[1]**doze** *vb* **dozed; doz•ing :** to sleep lightly — **doz•er** *n*

[2]**doze** *n* **:** a light sleep

doz•en *n, pl* **dozens** *or* **dozen :** a group of twelve

[1]**drab** *n* **:** a light olive brown

[2]**drab** *adj* **drab•ber; drab•best 1 :** of the color drab **2 :** lacking change and interest **:** DULL — **drab•ly** *adv* — **drab•ness** *n*

[1]**draft** *n* **1 :** the act of pulling or hauling **:** the thing or amount pulled **2 :** the act or an instance of drinking or inhaling **:** the portion drunk or inhaled at one time **3 :** a medicine prepared for drinking **4 :** something represented in words or lines **:** DESIGN, PLAN **5 :** a quick sketch or outline from which a final work is produced **6 :** the act of drawing out liquid (as from a cask) **:** a portion of liquid drawn out **7 :** the depth of water a ship needs in order to float **8 :** a picking of persons for required military service **9 :** an order made by one party to another to pay money to a third party **10 :** a current of air **11 :** a device to regulate an air supply (as in a stove)

[2]**draft** *adj* **1 :** used for pulling loads **2 :** TENTATIVE **3 :** ready to be drawn from a container

[3]**draft** *vb* **1 :** to pick especially for required military service **2 :** to make a draft of **:** OUTLINE **3 :** COMPOSE 1, PREPARE — **draft•er** *n*

drafts•man *n, pl* **drafts•men :** a person who draws plans (as for machinery) — **drafts•man•ship** *n*

drafty *adj* **draft•i•er; draft•i•est :** exposed to a draft or current of air — **draft•i•ness** *n*

[1]**drag** *n* **1 :** something without wheels (as a sledge for carrying heavy loads) that is dragged, pulled, or drawn along or over a surface **2 :** something used for dragging (as a device used underwater to catch something) **3 :** something that stops or holds back progress **4 :** a dull event, person, or thing

[2]**drag** *vb* **dragged; drag•ging 1 :** to haul slowly or heavily **2 :** to move with distressing slowness or difficulty **3 :** to pass or cause to pass slowly **4 :** to hang or lag behind **5 :** to trail along on the ground **6 :** to search or fish with a drag

drag•gle *vb* **drag•gled; drag•gling 1 :** to make or become wet and dirty by dragging **2 :** to follow slowly **:** STRAGGLE

drag•net *n* **1 :** a net to be drawn along in order to catch something **2 :** a network of planned actions for going after and catching a criminal

drag•on *n* **:** an imaginary animal usually pictured as a huge serpent or lizard with wings and large claws

drag•on•fly *n, pl* **drag•on•flies :** a large insect with a long slender body and four wings

dra•goon *n* **:** a soldier on horseback

drag race *n* **:** a race for two vehicles at a time from a standstill to a point a quarter mile away

[1]**drain** *vb* **1 :** to draw off or flow off gradually or completely **2 :** to make or become

dry or empty a little at a time **3 :** to let out surface or surplus water **4 :** [1]EXHAUST 3

[2]**drain** *n* **1 :** a means of draining (as a pipe, channel, or sewer) **2 :** the act of draining **3 :** a using up a little at a time

drain•age *n* **1 :** an act of draining **2 :** something that is drained off **3 :** a method of draining **:** system of drains

drain•pipe *n* **:** a pipe for drainage

drake *n* **:** a male duck

dra•ma *n* **1 :** a written work that tells a story through action and speech and is meant to be acted out on a stage **2 :** dramatic art, literature, or affairs

dra•mat•ic *adj* **1 :** of or relating to the drama **2 :** like that of the drama **:** VIVID — **dra•mat•i•cal•ly** *adv*

dra•ma•tist *n* **:** PLAYWRIGHT

dra•ma•tize *vb* **dram•a•tized; dram•a•tiz•ing** **1 :** to make into a drama **2 :** to present or represent in a dramatic manner — **dra•ma•ti•za•tion** *n*

drank *past of* DRINK

[1]**drape** *vb* **draped; drap•ing** **1 :** to decorate or cover with or as if with folds of cloth **2 :** to arrange or hang in flowing lines

[2]**drape** *n* **1 drapes** *pl* **:** DRAPERY 2 **2 :** arrangement in or of folds **3 :** the cut or hang of clothing

drap•ery *n, pl* **drap•er•ies** **1 :** a decorative fabric hung in loose folds **2 :** curtains of heavy fabric often used over thinner curtains

dras•tic *adj* **1 :** acting rapidly and strongly **2 :** severe in effect **:** HARSH — **dras•ti•cal•ly** *adv*

draught *chiefly Brit variant of* DRAFT

[1]**draw** *vb* **drew; drawn; draw•ing** **1 :** to cause to move by pulling **:** cause to follow **2 :** to move or go usually steadily or a little at a time **3 :** ATTRACT 1 **4 :** to call forth **:** PROVOKE **5 :** INHALE **6 :** to bring or pull out **7 :** to bring or get from a source **8 :** to need (a certain depth) to float in **9 :** to take or receive at random **10 :** to bend (a bow) by pulling back the string **11 :** to cause to shrink or pucker **:** WRINKLE **12 :** to leave (a contest) undecided **:** TIE **13 :** to produce a likeness of by making lines on a surface **:** SKETCH **14 :** to write out in proper form — often used with *up* **15 :** FORMULATE **16 :** to produce or make use of a current of air

[2]**draw** *n* **1 :** the act or the result of drawing **2 :** a tie game or contest **3 :** something that draws attention **4 :** a gully shallower than a ravine

draw•back *n* **:** [1]HANDICAP 3

draw•bridge *n* **:** a bridge made to be drawn up, down, or aside to permit or prevent passage

draw•er *n* **1 :** one that draws **2 :** a sliding boxlike compartment (as in a desk) **3 drawers** *pl* **:** an undergarment for the lower part of the body

draw•ing *n* **1 :** an act or instance of drawing lots **2 :** the act or art of making a figure, plan, or sketch by means of lines **3 :** a picture made by drawing

drawing room *n* **:** a formal room for entertaining company

[1]**drawl** *vb* **:** to speak slowly with vowel sounds drawn out beyond their usual length

drawl *n* **:** a drawling way of speaking

draw on *vb* **:** to come closer **:** APPROACH

draw out *vb* **:** to cause or encourage to speak freely

draw•string *n* **:** a string, cord, or tape used to close a bag, control fullness in clothes, or open or close curtains

draw up *vb* **1 :** to arrange (as a body of troops) in order **2 :** to straighten (oneself) to an erect posture **3 :** to bring or come to a stop

dray *n* **:** a strong low cart or wagon without sides for hauling heavy loads

[1]**dread** *vb* **1 :** to fear greatly **2 :** to be very unwilling to meet or face

[2]**dread** *n* **:** great fear especially of harm to come

[3]**dread** *adj* **:** causing great fear or anxiety

dread•ful *adj* **1 :** causing a feeling of dread **2 :** very disagreeable, unpleasant, or shocking — **dread•ful•ly** *adv* — **dread•ful•ness** *n*

dread•nought *n* **:** a very large battleship

[1]**dream** *n* **1 :** a series of thoughts, pictures, or feelings occurring during sleep **2 :** a dreamlike creation of the imagination **:** DAYDREAM **3 :** something notable for its pleasing quality **4 :** a goal that is longed for **:** IDEAL — **dream•like** *adj*

[2]**dream** *vb* **dreamed** *or* **dreamt; dream•ing** **1 :** to have a dream or dreams **2 :** to spend time having daydreams **3 :** to think of as happening or possible — **dream•er** *n*

dream•land *n* **:** an unreal delightful country existing only in imagination or in dreams

dream•less *adj* **:** having no dreams — **dream•less•ly** *adv* — **dream•less•ness** *n*

dreamy *adj* **dream•i•er; dream•i•est** **1 :** tending to spend time dreaming **2 :** having the quality of a dream **3 :** being quiet and soothing **4 :** SUPERB — **dream•i•ly** *adv* — **dream•i•ness** *n*

drea•ry *adj* **drea•ri•er; drea•ri•est :** DISMAL, GLOOMY — **drea•ri•ly** *adv* — **drea•ri•ness** *n*

[1]**dredge** *vb* **dredged; dredg•ing :** to dig or gather with or as if with a dredge — **dredg•er** *n*

[2]**dredge** *n* **1 :** a heavy iron frame with a net

attached to be dragged (as for gathering oysters) over the sea bottom **2 :** a machine for scooping up or removing earth usually by buckets on an endless chain or by a suction tube **3 :** a barge used in dredging

dregs *n pl* **1 :** solids that settle out of a liquid **2 :** the worst or most useless part

drench *vb* **:** to wet thoroughly

1dress *vb* **1 :** to make or set straight (as soldiers on parade) **2 :** to put clothes on **:** CLOTHE **3 :** to wear formal or fancy clothes **4 :** to trim or decorate for display **5 :** to treat with remedies and bandage **6 :** to arrange by combing, brushing, or curling **7 :** to prepare (a meat animal) for food **8 :** to apply fertilizer to

2dress *n* **1 :** CLOTHING 1, APPAREL **2 :** an outer garment with a skirt for a woman or child

1dress•er *n* **:** a piece of furniture (as a chest or a bureau) with a mirror

2dresser *n* **:** a person who dresses in a certain way

dress•ing *n* **1 :** the act or process of one who dresses **2 :** a sauce added to a food (as a salad) **3 :** a seasoned mixture used as a stuffing (as for a turkey) **4 :** material used to cover an injury **5 :** something used as a fertilizer

dress•mak•er *n* **:** a person who makes dresses

dress•mak•ing *n* **:** the process or occupation of making dresses

dress up *vb* **1 :** to put on one's best or formal clothes **2 :** to put on strange or fancy clothes

dressy *adj* **dress•i•er; dress•i•est 1 :** showy in dress **2 :** suitable for formal occasions

drew *past of* DRAW

1drib•ble *vb* **drib•bled; drib•bling 1 :** to fall or let fall in small drops **:** TRICKLE **2 :** 1SLOBBER, DROOL **3 :** to move forward by bouncing, tapping, or kicking

2dribble *n* **1 :** a trickling flow **2 :** the act of dribbling a ball

drib•let *n* **1 :** a small amount **2 :** a falling drop

dri•er *or* **dry•er** *n* **1 :** something that removes or absorbs moisture **2 :** a substance that speeds up the drying of oils, paints, and inks **3** *usually dryer* **:** a device for drying

1drift *n* **1 :** the motion or course of something drifting **2 :** a mass of matter (as snow or sand) piled in a heap by the wind **3 :** a course something appears to be taking **4 :** the meaning of something said or implied

2drift *vb* **1 :** to float or to be driven along by winds, waves, or currents **2 :** to move along without effort or purpose **3 :** to pile up in drifts — **drift•er** *n*

drift•wood *n* **:** wood drifted or floated by water

1drill *vb* **1 :** to bore with a drill **2 :** to teach by means of repeated practice — **drill•er** *n*

2drill *n* **1 :** a tool for making holes in hard substances **2 :** the training of soldiers (as in marching) **3 :** regular strict training and instruction in a subject

3drill *n* **:** a farming implement for making holes or furrows and planting seeds in them

4drill *vb* **:** to sow seeds with or as if with a drill

drily *variant of* DRYLY

1drink *vb* **drank; drunk; drink•ing 1 :** to swallow liquid **2 :** to absorb a liquid **3 :** to take in through the senses **4 :** to drink alcoholic liquor — **drink•er** *n*

2drink *n* **1 :** BEVERAGE **2 :** alcoholic liquor

drink•able *adj* **:** suitable or safe for drinking

1drip *vb* **dripped; drip•ping 1 :** to fall or let fall in or as if in drops **2 :** to let fall drops of liquid

2drip *n* **1 :** a falling in drops **2 :** dripping liquid **3 :** the sound made by falling drops

1drive *vb* **drove; driv•en; driv•ing 1 :** to push or force onward **2 :** to direct the movement or course of **3 :** to go or carry in a vehicle under one's own control **4 :** to set or keep in motion or operation **5 :** to carry through **:** CONCLUDE **6 :** to force to work or to act **7 :** to bring into a specified condition — **driv•er** *n*

2drive *n* **1 :** a trip in a carriage or automobile **2 :** a collecting and driving together of animals **3 :** DRIVEWAY **4 :** an often scenic public road **5 :** an organized usually thorough effort to carry out a purpose **6 :** the means for giving motion to a machine or machine part **7 :** a device that transfers information to and from a storage material (as tape or disks)

drive–in *adj* **:** designed and equipped to serve customers while they remain in their automobiles

drive•way *n* **:** a private road leading from the street to a house or garage

1driz•zle *n* **:** a fine misty rain

2drizzle *vb* **driz•zled; driz•zling :** to rain in very small drops

droll *adj* **:** having an odd or amusing quality — **droll•ness** *n* — **drol•ly** *adv*

drom•e•dary *n, pl* **drom•e•dar•ies 1 :** a speedy camel trained for riding **2 :** the camel of western Asia and northern Africa that has only one hump

1drone *n* **1 :** a male bee **2 :** a lazy person **:** one who lives on the labor of others

²drone *vb* **droned; dron·ing :** to make or to speak with a low dull monotonous hum

³drone *n* **:** a droning sound

drool *vb* **:** to let liquid flow from the mouth **:** SLOBBER

¹droop *vb* **1 :** to sink, bend, or hang down **2 :** to become sad or weak

²droop *n* **:** the condition or appearance of drooping

¹drop *n* **1 :** the amount of liquid that falls naturally in one rounded mass **2 drops** *pl* **:** a dose of medicine measured by drops **3 :** something (as a small round candy) that is shaped like a liquid drop **4 :** an instance of dropping **5 :** the distance of a fall

²drop *vb* **dropped; drop·ping 1 :** to fall or let fall in drops **2 :** to let fall **3 :** to lower in pitch and volume **4 :** SEND 1 **5 :** to let go **:** DISMISS **6 :** to knock down **:** cause to fall **7 :** to go lower **8 :** to make a brief visit **9 :** to pass into a less active state **10 :** to withdraw from membership or from taking part **11 :** LOSE 4

drop·let *n* **:** a tiny drop

drop·out *n* **:** one that drops out especially from school or a training program

drop·per *n* **1 :** one that drops **2 :** a short glass tube with a rubber bulb used to measure out liquids by drops

drought *n* **1 :** lack of rain or water **2 :** a long period of dry weather

¹drove *n* **1 :** a group of animals being driven or moving in a body **2 :** a crowd of people moving or acting together

²drove *past of* DRIVE

drov·er *n* **:** a worker who drives cattle or sheep

drown *vb* **1 :** to suffocate in a liquid and especially in water **2 :** to cover with water **:** FLOOD **3 :** to overpower especially with noise

¹drowse *vb* **drowsed; drows·ing :** to be half asleep **:** sleep lightly

²drowse *n* **:** a light sleep **:** DOZE

drowsy *adj* **drows·i·er; drows·i·est 1 :** ready to fall asleep **2 :** making one sleepy — **drows·i·ly** *adv* — **drows·i·ness** *n*

drub *vb* **drubbed; drub·bing 1 :** to beat severely **2 :** to defeat completely

drudge *n* **:** a person who does hard or dull work

drudg·ery *n, pl* **drudg·er·ies :** hard or dull work

¹drug *n* **1 :** a substance used as a medicine or in making medicines **2 :** medicine used to deaden pain or bring sleep **3 :** a substance that may harm or make an addict of a person who uses it

²drug *vb* **drugged; drug·ging 1 :** to poison with or as if with a drug **2 :** to dull a person's senses with drugs

drug·gist *n* **:** a seller of drugs and medicines **:** PHARMACIST

drug·store *n* **:** a retail store where medicines and often other things are sold **:** PHARMACY

¹drum *n* **1 :** a percussion instrument usually consisting of a metal or wooden cylinder with flat ends covered by tightly stretched skin **2 :** a sound of or like a drum **3 :** an object shaped like a drum

²drum *vb* **drummed; drum·ming 1 :** to beat a drum **2 :** to beat or sound like a drum **3 :** to gather together by or as if by beating a drum **4 :** to drive or force by steady or repeated effort **5 :** to beat or tap in a rhythmic way

drum major *n* **:** the marching leader of a band or drum corps

drum ma·jor·ette *n* **:** a girl who is a drum major

drum·mer *n* **1 :** a person who plays a drum **2 :** a traveling salesman

drum·stick *n* **1 :** a stick for beating a drum **2 :** the lower section of the leg of a fowl

¹drunk *past participle of* DRINK

²drunk *adj* **1 :** being so much under the influence of alcohol that normal thinking and acting become difficult or impossible **2 :** controlled by some feeling as if under the influence of alcohol

³drunk *n* **1 :** a period of drinking too much alcoholic liquor **2 :** a drunken person

drunk·ard *n* **:** a person who is often drunk

drunk·en *adj* **1 :** ²DRUNK 1 **2 :** resulting from being drunk — **drunk·en·ly** *adv* — **drunk·en·ness** *n*

¹dry *adj* **dri·er; dri·est 1 :** free or freed from water or liquid **:** not wet or moist **2 :** having little or no rain **3 :** lacking freshness **:** STALE **4 :** not being in or under water **5 :** THIRSTY 1, 2 **6 :** no longer liquid or sticky **7 :** containing no liquid **8 :** not giving milk **9 :** not producing phlegm **10 :** amusing in a sharp or acid way **11 :** UNINTERESTING **12 :** not sweet — **dry·ly** *adv* — **dry·ness** *n*

²dry *vb* **dried; dry·ing :** to make or become dry

dry cell *n* **:** a small cell producing electricity by means of chemicals in a sealed container

dry–clean *vb* **:** to clean (fabrics) with chemical solvents

dry cleaner *n* **:** one whose business is dry cleaning

dry cleaning *n* **1 :** the cleaning of fabrics with a substance other than water **2 :** something that is dry-cleaned

dryer *variant of* DRIER

dry goods *n pl* **:** cloth goods (as fabrics, lace, and ribbon)
dry ice *n* **:** solidified carbon dioxide used chiefly to keep something very cold
du·al *adj* **:** consisting of two parts **:** having two like parts **:** DOUBLE — **du·al·ly** *adv*
[1]**dub** *vb* **dubbed; dub·bing** **1 :** to make a knight of by a light tapping on the shoulder with a sword **2 :** [2]NAME 1, NICKNAME
[2]**dub** *vb* **dubbed; dub·bing** **:** to add (sound effects) to a film or broadcast
du·bi·ous *adj* **1 :** causing doubt **:** UNCERTAIN **2 :** feeling doubt **3 :** QUESTIONABLE 1 — **du·bi·ous·ly** *adv*
duch·ess *n* **1 :** the wife or widow of a duke **2 :** a woman who holds the rank of a duke in her own right
[1]**duck** *n* **:** any of a group of swimming birds that have broad flat bills and are smaller than the related geese and swans
[2]**duck** *vb* **1 :** to push or pull under water for a moment **2 :** to lower the head or body suddenly **3 :** [2]DODGE 1 **4 :** [2]DODGE 2 **5 :** to avoid a duty, question, or responsibility
[3]**duck** *n* **1 :** a coarse usually cotton fabric rather like canvas **2 ducks** *pl* **:** clothes (as trousers) made of duck
duck·bill *n* **:** PLATYPUS
duck·ling *n* **:** a young duck
duck·weed *n* **:** a very small stemless plant that floats in fresh water
duct *n* **:** a pipe, tube, or vessel that carries something (as a bodily secretion, water, or hot air) — **duct·less** *adj*
ductless gland *n* **:** ENDOCRINE GLAND
dud *n* **1 duds** *pl* **:** CLOTHING **2 :** a complete failure **3 :** a missile that fails to explode
dude *n* **:** a man who pays too much attention to his clothes
[1]**due** *adj* **1 :** owed or owing as a debt or a right **2 :** SUITABLE **3 :** being a result — used with *to* **4 :** required or expected to happen
[2]**due** *n* **1 :** something owed **:** DEBT **2 dues** *pl* **:** a regular or legal charge or fee
[3]**due** *adv* **:** DIRECTLY 1
[1]**du·el** *n* **1 :** a combat between two persons fought with deadly weapons by agreement and in the presence of witnesses **2 :** a contest between two opponents
[2]**duel** *vb* **du·eled** *or* **du·elled; du·el·ing** *or* **du·el·ling** **:** to fight in a duel — **du·el·ist** *n*
du·et *n* **1 :** a musical composition for two performers **2 :** two performers playing or singing together
due to *prep* **:** because of
dug *past of* DIG
dug·out *n* **1 :** a boat made by hollowing out a log **2 :** a shelter dug in a hillside or in the ground **3 :** a low shelter facing a baseball diamond and containing the players' bench
duke *n* **:** a member of the highest rank of the British nobility
[1]**dull** *adj* **1 :** mentally slow **:** STUPID **2 :** LISTLESS **3 :** slow in action **:** SLUGGISH **4 :** not sharp in edge or point **:** BLUNT **5 :** lacking brightness or luster **6 :** not clear and ringing **7 :** CLOUDY 1, OVERCAST **8 :** not interesting **:** TEDIOUS **9 :** slightly grayish — **dull·ness** *or* **dul·ness** *n* — **dul·ly** *adv*
[2]**dull** *vb* **:** to make or become dull
du·ly *adv* **:** in a due or suitable manner, time, or degree
dumb *adj* **1 :** lacking the normal power of speech **2 :** normally unable to speak **3 :** not willing to speak **:** SILENT **4 :** STUPID 1, FOOLISH — **dumb·ly** *adv* — **dumb·ness** *n*
dumb·bell *n* **1 :** a short bar with two weighted balls or disks at the ends usually used in pairs for strengthening the arms **2 :** a stupid person
dumb·found *or* **dum·found** *vb* **:** to cause to become speechless with astonishment **:** AMAZE
dumb·wait·er *n* **:** a small elevator for carrying food and dishes or other small items from one floor to another
dum·my *n, pl* **dummies** **1 :** a person who does not have or seems not to have the power of speech **2 :** a stupid person **3 :** an imitation used as a substitute for something
[1]**dump** *vb* **:** to let fall in a heap **:** get rid of
[2]**dump** *n* **1 :** a place for dumping something (as trash) **2 :** a place for storage of military materials or the materials stored **3 :** a messy or shabby place
dump·ling *n* **:** a small mass of dough cooked by boiling or steaming
dumps *n pl* **:** low spirits
dumpy *adj* **dump·i·er; dump·i·est** **:** short and thick in build — **dump·i·ness** *n*
[1]**dun** *n* **:** a slightly brownish dark gray
[2]**dun** *vb* **dunned; dun·ning** **:** to make repeated demands upon for payment
dunce *n* **:** a stupid person
dune *n* **:** a hill or ridge of sand piled up by the wind
dung *n* **:** FECES
dun·ga·ree *n* **1 :** a heavy cotton cloth **2 dungarees** *pl* **:** pants or work clothes made of dungaree
dun·geon *n* **:** a dark usually underground prison
dung·hill *n* **:** a pile of manure
dunk *vb* **:** to dip (as a doughnut) into liquid (as coffee)

duo *n, pl* **du•os** **1 :** a duet especially for two performers at two pianos **2 :** [1]PAIR 1
[1]**dupe** *n* **:** a person who has been or is easily deceived or cheated
[2]**dupe** *vb* **duped; dup•ing :** to make a dupe of **:** TRICK
du•plex *adj* **:** [1]DOUBLE 2
[1]**du•pli•cate** *adj* **1 :** having two parts exactly the same or alike **2 :** being the same as another
[2]**du•pli•cate** *vb* **du•pli•cat•ed; du•pli•cat•ing** **1 :** to make double **2 :** to make an exact copy of
[3]**du•pli•cate** *n* **:** a thing that is exactly like another
du•pli•ca•tion *n* **1 :** the act or process of duplicating **2 :** the state of being duplicated
du•ra•bil•i•ty *n* **:** ability to last or to stand hard or continued use
du•ra•ble *adj* **:** able to last a long time — **du•ra•ble•ness** *n* — **du•ra•bly** *adv*
du•ra•tion *n* **:** the time during which something exists or lasts
dur•ing *prep* **1 :** throughout the course of **2 :** at some point in the course of
dusk *n* **1 :** the darker part of twilight especially at night **2 :** partial darkness
dusky *adj* **dusk•i•er; dusk•i•est** **1 :** somewhat dark in color **2 :** somewhat dark **:** DIM — **dusk•i•ness** *n*
[1]**dust** *n* **1 :** fine dry powdery particles (as of earth) **:** a fine powder **2 :** the powdery remains of bodies once alive **3 :** something worthless **4 :** the surface of the ground — **dust•less** *adj*
[2]**dust** *vb* **1 :** to make free of dust **:** brush or wipe away dust **2 :** to sprinkle with or as if with fine particles — **dust•er** *n*
dust•pan *n* **:** a pan shaped like a shovel and used for sweepings
dust storm *n* **:** a violent wind carrying dust across a dry region
dusty *adj* **dust•i•er; dust•i•est** **1 :** filled or covered with dust **2 :** like dust
[1]**Dutch** *adj* **:** of or relating to the Netherlands, its people, or the Dutch language
[2]**Dutch** *n* **1 Dutch** *pl* **:** the people of the Netherlands **2 :** the language of the Dutch
Dutch door *n* **:** a door divided so that the lower part can be shut while the upper part remains open
Dutch treat *n* **:** a treat for which each person pays his or her own way
du•ti•ful *adj* **:** having or showing a sense of duty — **du•ti•ful•ly** *adv* — **du•ti•ful•ness** *n*
du•ty *n, pl* **duties** **1 :** conduct owed to parents and those in authority **2 :** the action required by one's position or occupation **3 :** something a person feels he or she ought to do **4 :** a tax especially on imports into a country
[1]**dwarf** *n, pl* **dwarfs** *also* **dwarves** **1 :** a person, animal, or plant much below normal size **2 :** a small legendary being usually pictured as a deformed and ugly person
[2]**dwarf** *vb* **1 :** to prevent from growing to natural size **:** STUNT **2 :** to cause to appear smaller
[3]**dwarf** *adj* **:** of less than the usual size
dwell *vb* **dwelt** *or* **dwelled; dwell•ing** **1 :** to stay for a while **2 :** to live in a place **:** RESIDE **3 :** to keep the attention directed — **dwell•er** *n*
dwell•ing *n* **:** RESIDENCE 2, 3
dwin•dle *vb* **dwin•dled; dwin•dling** **:** to make or become less
[1]**dye** *n* **:** a coloring matter
[2]**dye** *vb* **dyed; dye•ing :** to give a new color to
dye•stuff *n* **:** material used for dyeing
dying *present participle of* DIE
dyke *variant of* DIKE
dy•nam•ic *adj* **:** full of energy **:** ACTIVE, FORCEFUL
[1]**dy•na•mite** *n* **:** an explosive used in blasting
[2]**dynamite** *vb* **dy•na•mit•ed; dy•na•mit•ing** **:** to blow up with dynamite — **dy•na•mit•er** *n*
dy•na•mo *n, pl* **dy•na•mos** **:** a machine for producing electric current
dy•nas•ty *n, pl* **dy•nas•ties** **:** a series of rulers of the same family
dys•en•tery *n* **:** a disease in which much watery material mixed with mucus and blood is passed from the bowels

E

e *n, pl* **e's** *or* **es** *often cap* **1 :** the fifth letter of the English alphabet **2 :** a grade that shows a student's work is failing

[1]**each** *adj* **:** being one of two or more individuals

[2]**each** *pron* **:** each one

[3]**each** *adv* **:** to or for each **:** APIECE

each other *pron* **:** each of two or more in a shared action or relationship

ea•ger *adj* **:** desiring very much **:** IMPATIENT — **ea•ger•ly** *adv* — **ea•ger•ness** *n*

ea•gle *n* **:** any of several large birds of prey noted for keen sight and powerful flight

ea•glet *n* **:** a young eagle

-ean — see -AN

[1]**ear** *n* **1 :** the organ of hearing **2 :** the sense of hearing **3 :** willing or sympathetic attention **4 :** something like an ear in shape or position — **eared** *adj*

[2]**ear** *n* **:** the seed-bearing head of a cereal grass

ear•ache *n* **:** an ache or pain in the ear

ear•drum *n* **:** the membrane that separates the outer and middle parts of the ear and vibrates when sound waves strike it

earl *n* **:** a member of the British nobility ranking below a marquess and above a viscount

[1]**ear•ly** *adv* **ear•li•er; ear•li•est 1 :** at or near the beginning of a period of time or a series **2 :** before the usual time

[2]**early** *adj* **ear•li•er; ear•li•est :** occurring near the beginning or before the usual time

ear•muff *n* **:** one of a pair of coverings joined by a flexible band and worn to protect the ears from cold or noise

earn *vb* **1 :** to get for services given **2 :** to deserve especially as a reward or punishment

ear•nest *adj* **:** not light or playful — **ear•nest•ly** *adv* — **ear•nest•ness** *n*

earn•ings *n pl* **:** money received as wages or gained as profit

ear•phone *n* **:** a device that converts electrical energy into sound and is worn over the opening of the ear or inserted into it

ear•ring *n* **:** an ornament worn on the ear lobe

ear•shot *n* **:** the range within which an unaided human voice can be heard

earth *n* **1 :** [2]SOIL 1 **2 :** areas of land as distinguished from the sea and the air **3** *often cap* **:** the planet that we live on

earth•en *adj* **:** made of earth

earth•en•ware *n* **:** things (as dishes) made of baked clay

earth•ly *adj* **1 :** having to do with or belonging to the earth **:** not heavenly **2 :** IMAGINABLE, POSSIBLE

earth•quake *n* **:** a shaking or trembling of a portion of the earth

earth•worm *n* **:** a worm that has a long body made up of similar segments and lives in damp soil

earthy *adj* **earth•i•er; earth•i•est 1 :** consisting of or like earth **2 :** PRACTICAL 4 **3 :** not polite **:** CRUDE

ear•wig *n* **:** an insect with long slender feelers and a large forcepslike organ at the end of its abdomen

[1]**ease** *n* **1 :** freedom from pain or trouble **:** comfort of body or mind **2 :** freedom from any feeling of difficulty or embarrassment

[2]**ease** *vb* **eased; eas•ing 1 :** to free from discomfort or worry **:** RELIEVE **2 :** to make less tight **:** LOOSEN **3 :** to move very carefully

ea•sel *n* **:** a frame for holding a flat surface in an upright position

eas•i•ly *adv* **1 :** in an easy manner **:** without difficulty **2 :** without doubt or question

[1]**east** *adv* **:** to or toward the east

[2]**east** *adj* **:** placed toward, facing, or coming from the east

[3]**east** *n* **1 :** the direction of sunrise **:** the compass point opposite to west **2** *cap* **:** regions or countries east of a certain point

Eas•ter *n* **:** a Christian church festival observed in memory of the Resurrection

Easter lily *n* **:** a white garden lily that blooms in spring

east•er•ly *adj or adv* **1 :** toward the east **2 :** from the east

east•ern *adj* **1** *often cap* **:** of, relating to, or like that of the East **2 :** lying toward or coming from the east

east•ward *adv or adj* **:** toward the east

easy *adj* **eas•i•er; eas•i•est 1 :** not hard to do or get **:** not difficult **2 :** not hard to please **3 :** free from pain, trouble, or worry **4 :** COMFORTABLE **5 :** showing ease **:** NATURAL

eat *vb* **ate; eat•en; eat•ing 1 :** to chew and swallow food **2 :** to take a meal or meals **3 :** to destroy as if by eating **:** CORRODE — **eat•er** *n*

eat•able *adj* **:** fit to be eaten

eaves *n sing or pl* **:** the lower edge of a roof that sticks out past the wall

eaves•drop *vb* **eaves•dropped; eaves•drop•ping :** to listen secretly to private conversation

[1]**ebb** *n* **1 :** the flowing out of the tide **2 :** a

passing from a high to a low point or the time of this

[2]**ebb** *vb* **1 :** to flow out or away **:** RECEDE **2 :** [1]DECLINE 2, WEAKEN

[1]**eb·o·ny** *n, pl* **eb·o·nies :** a hard heavy wood that wears well and comes from tropical trees related to the persimmon

[2]**ebony** *adj* **1 :** made of or like ebony **2 :** [1]BLACK 1

[1]**ec·cen·tric** *adj* **1 :** acting or thinking in a strange way **2 :** not of the usual or normal kind

[2]**eccentric** *n* **:** an eccentric person

ec·cle·si·as·ti·cal *adj* **:** of or relating to the church or its affairs

[1]**echo** *n, pl* **ech·oes :** the repeating of a sound caused by the reflection of sound waves

[2]**echo** *vb* **ech·oed; echo·ing 1 :** to send back or repeat a sound **2 :** to say what someone else has already said

éclair *n* **:** an oblong pastry with whipped cream or custard filling

[1]**eclipse** *n* **1 :** a complete or partial hiding of the sun caused by the moon's passing between the sun and the earth **2 :** a darkening of the moon caused by the moon's entering the shadow of the earth **3 :** the hiding of any celestial body by another **4 :** a falling into disgrace or out of use or public favor

[2]**eclipse** *vb* **eclipsed; eclips·ing 1 :** to cause an eclipse of **2 :** to be or do much better than **:** OUTSHINE

eco·log·i·cal *adj* **:** of or relating to the science of ecology or the ecology of a particular environment and the living things in it

ecol·o·gist *n* **:** a specialist in ecology

ecol·o·gy *n* **1 :** a branch of science dealing with the relation of living things to their environment **2 :** the pattern of relations between living things and their environment

eco·nom·ic *adj* **1 :** of or relating to economics **2 :** of, relating to, or based on the making, selling, and using of goods and services

eco·nom·i·cal *adj* **1 :** using what one has carefully and without waste **:** FRUGAL **2 :** operating with little waste or at a saving — **eco·nom·i·cal·ly** *adv*

eco·nom·ics *n* **:** the science that studies and explains facts about the making, selling, and using of goods and services

econ·o·mize *vb* **econ·o·mized; econ·o·miz·ing 1 :** to practice economy **:** be thrifty **2 :** to reduce expenses **:** SAVE

econ·o·my *n, pl* **econ·o·mies 1 :** the careful use of money and goods **:** THRIFT **2 :** the way an economic system (as of a country or a period in history) is organized

eco·sys·tem *n* **:** the whole group of living and nonliving things that make up an environment and affect each other

ec·sta·sy *n, pl* **ec·sta·sies :** very great happiness **:** extreme delight

ec·stat·ic *adj* **:** of, relating to, or showing ecstasy

ec·ze·ma *n* **:** a disease in which the skin is red, itchy, and marred by scaly or crusted spots

[1]**-ed** *vb suffix or adj suffix* **1** — used to form the past participle of verbs **2 :** having **:** showing **3 :** having the characteristics of

[2]**-ed** *vb suffix* — used to form the past tense of verbs

[1]**ed·dy** *n, pl* **eddies :** a current of air or water running against the main current or in a circle

[2]**eddy** *vb* **ed·died; ed·dy·ing :** to move in an eddy

[1]**edge** *n* **1 :** the cutting side of a blade **2 :** the line where a surface ends **:** MARGIN, BORDER — **edged** *adj* — **on edge :** NERVOUS 3, TENSE

[2]**edge** *vb* **edged; edg·ing 1 :** to give an edge to **2 :** to move slowly and little by little

edge·ways *or* **edge·wise** *adv* **:** with the edge in front **:** SIDEWAYS

ed·i·ble *adj* **:** fit or safe to eat

edict *n* **:** a command or law given or made by an authority (as a ruler)

ed·i·fice *n* **:** a large or impressive building (as a church)

ed·it *vb* **1 :** to correct, revise, and get ready for publication **:** collect and arrange material to be printed **2 :** to be in charge of the publication of something (as an encyclopedia or a newspaper) that is the work of many writers

edi·tion *n* **1 :** the form in which a book is published **2 :** the whole number of copies of a book, magazine, or newspaper published at one time **3 :** one of several issues of a newspaper for a single day

ed·i·tor *n* **1 :** a person who edits **2 :** a person who writes editorials

[1]**ed·i·to·ri·al** *adj* **1 :** of or relating to an editor **2 :** being or like an editorial

[2]**editorial** *n* **:** a newspaper or magazine article that gives the opinions of its editors or publishers

ed·u·cate *vb* **ed·u·cat·ed; ed·u·cat·ing 1 :** to provide schooling for **2 :** to develop the mind and morals of especially by formal instruction **:** TRAIN — **ed·u·ca·tor** *n*

ed·u·ca·tion *n* **1 :** the act or process of educating or of being educated **2 :** knowledge, skill, and development gained from study or training **3 :** the study or science of the methods and problems of teaching

ed·u·ca·tion·al *adj* **1 :** having to do with education **2 :** offering information or something of value in learning — **ed·u·ca·tion·al·ly** *adv*

[1]**-ee** *n suffix* **1 :** person who receives or benefits from a specified thing or action **2 :** person who does a specified thing

[2]**-ee** *n suffix* **1 :** a certain and especially a small kind of **2 :** one like or suggesting

eel *n* **:** a long snakelike fish with a smooth slimy skin

e'en *adv* **:** EVEN

-eer *n suffix* **:** person who is concerned with or conducts or produces as a profession

e'er *adv* **:** EVER

ee·rie *also* **ee·ry** *adj* **ee·ri·er; ee·ri·est :** causing fear and uneasiness **:** STRANGE

ef·face *vb* **ef·faced; ef·fac·ing :** to erase or blot out completely

[1]**ef·fect** *n* **1 :** an event, condition, or state of affairs that is produced by a cause **2 :** EXECUTION 1, OPERATION **3 :** REALITY 1, FACT **4 :** the act of making a certain impression **5 :** [1]INFLUENCE 1 **6 effects** *pl* **:** personal property or possessions

[2]**effect** *vb* **:** BRING ABOUT

ef·fec·tive *adj* **1 :** producing or able to produce a desired effect **2 :** IMPRESSIVE **3 :** being in actual operation — **ef·fec·tive·ly** *adv* — **ef·fec·tive·ness** *n*

ef·fec·tu·al *adj* **:** producing or able to produce a desired effect

ef·fi·ca·cy *n, pl* **ef·fi·ca·cies :** power to produce effects **:** efficient action

ef·fi·cien·cy *n, pl* **ef·fi·cien·cies :** the quality or degree of being efficient

ef·fi·cient *adj* **:** capable of bringing about a desired result with little waste (as of time or energy) — **ef·fi·cient·ly** *adv*

ef·fort *n* **1 :** hard work of mind or body **:** EXERTION **2 :** a serious attempt **:** TRY

ef·fort·less *adj* **:** showing or needing little or no effort — **ef·fort·less·ly** *adv*

[1]**egg** *vb* **:** INCITE, URGE

[2]**egg** *n* **1 :** a shelled oval or rounded body by which some animals (as birds or snakes) reproduce and from which the young hatches out **2 :** an egg cell usually together with its protective coverings

egg cell *n* **:** a cell produced by an ovary that when fertilized by a sperm cell can develop into an embryo and finally a new mature being

egg·nog *n* **:** a drink made of eggs beaten with sugar, milk or cream, and often alcoholic liquor

egg·plant *n* **:** an oval vegetable with a usually glossy purplish skin and white flesh that is the fruit of a plant related to the tomato

egg·shell *n* **:** the shell of an egg

egret *n* **:** any of various herons that have long plumes during the breeding season

[1]**Egyp·tian** *adj* **:** of or relating to Egypt or the Egyptians

[2]**Egyptian** *n* **1 :** a person who is born or lives in Egypt **2 :** the language of the ancient Egyptians

ei·der *n* **:** a large northern sea duck that is mostly white above and black below and has very soft down

ei·der·down *n* **1 :** the down of the eider used for filling quilts and pillows **2 :** a quilt filled with down

[1]**eight** *adj* **:** being one more than seven

[2]**eight** *n* **:** one more than seven **:** two times four **:** 8

[1]**eigh·teen** *adj* **:** being one more than seventeen

[2]**eighteen** *n* **:** one more than seventeen **:** three times six **:** 18

[1]**eigh·teenth** *adj* **:** coming right after seventeenth

[2]**eighteenth** *n* **:** number eighteen in a series

[1]**eighth** *adj* **:** coming right after seventh

[2]**eighth** *n* **1 :** number eight in a series **2 :** one of eight equal parts

[1]**eight·i·eth** *adj* **:** coming right after seventy-ninth

[2]**eightieth** *n* **:** number eighty in a series

[1]**eighty** *adj* **:** being eight times ten

[2]**eighty** *n* **:** eight times ten **:** 80

[1]**ei·ther** *adj* **1 :** [1]EACH **2 :** being one or the other

[2]**either** *pron* **:** the one or the other

[3]**either** *conj* — used before words or phrases the last of which follows "or" to show that they are choices or possibilities

ejac·u·late *vb* **ejac·u·lat·ed; ejac·u·lat·ing :** EXCLAIM

eject *vb* **:** to drive out or throw off or out

eke out *vb* **eked out; ek·ing out 1 :** to add to bit by bit **2 :** to get with great effort

[1]**elab·o·rate** *adj* **:** worked out with great care or with much detail — **elab·o·rate·ly** *adv*

[2]**elab·o·rate** *vb* **elab·o·rat·ed; elab·o·rat·ing :** to work out in detail

elapse *vb* **elapsed; elaps·ing :** to slip past **:** go by

[1]**elas·tic** *adj* **:** capable of returning to original shape or size after being stretched, pressed, or squeezed together

[2]**elastic** *n* **1 :** an elastic fabric made of yarns containing rubber **2 :** a rubber band

elas·tic·i·ty *n* **:** the quality or state of being elastic

elate *vb* **elat·ed; elat·ing :** to fill with joy or pride

ela·tion *n* **:** the quality or state of being elated

¹el·bow *n* **1 :** the joint of the arm or of the same part of an animal's forelimb **2 :** a part (as of a pipe) bent like an elbow

²elbow *vb* **:** to push or force a way through with the elbows

¹el·der *n* **:** a shrub or small tree related to the honeysuckles that has flat clusters of white flowers followed by fruits like berries

²elder *adj* **:** being older than another person

³elder *n* **1 :** one who is older **2 :** a person having authority because of age and experience **3 :** an official in some churches

el·der·ber·ry *n, pl* **el·der·ber·ries :** the juicy black or red fruit of the elder

el·der·ly *adj* **:** somewhat old **:** past middle age

el·dest *adj* **:** being oldest of a group of people (as siblings)

¹elect *adj* **:** chosen for office but not yet holding office

²elect *vb* **1 :** to select by vote **2 :** to make a choice

elec·tion *n* **:** an electing or being elected especially by vote

elec·tive *adj* **:** chosen or filled by election

elec·tor *n* **:** a person qualified or having the right to vote in an election

electr- *or* **electro-** *prefix* **1 :** electricity **2 :** electric **3 :** electric and **4 :** electrically

elec·tric *or* **elec·tri·cal** *adj* **1 :** of or relating to electricity or its use **2 :** heated, moved, made, or run by electricity **3 :** having a thrilling effect **4 :** giving off sounds through an electronic amplifier — **elec·tri·cal·ly** *adv*

electric eel : a large South American eel-shaped fish having organs that are able to give a severe electric shock

elec·tri·cian *n* **:** a person who installs, operates, or repairs electrical equipment

elec·tric·i·ty *n* **1 :** an important form of energy that is found in nature but that can be artificially produced by rubbing together two unlike things (as glass and silk), by the action of chemicals, or by means of a generator **2 :** electric current

elec·tri·fy *vb* **elec·tri·fied; elec·tri·fy·ing 1 :** to charge with electricity **2 :** to equip for use of electric power **3 :** to supply with electric power **4 :** to excite suddenly and sharply **:** THRILL

elec·tro·cute *vb* **elec·tro·cut·ed; elec·tro·cut·ing :** to kill by an electric shock

elec·trode *n* **:** a conductor (as a metal or carbon) used to make electrical contact with a part of an electrical circuit that is not metallic

elec·trol·y·sis *n* **:** the producing of chemical changes by passage of an electric current through a liquid

elec·tro·lyte *n* **:** a substance (as an acid or salt) that when dissolved (as in water) conducts an electric current

elec·tro·lyt·ic *adj* **:** of or relating to electrolysis or an electrolyte

elec·tro·mag·net *n* **:** a piece of iron encircled by a coil of wire through which an electric current is passed to magnetize the iron

elec·tro·mag·net·ic *adj* **:** of or relating to a magnetic field produced by an electric current

electromagnetic wave *n* **:** a wave (as a radio wave or wave of light) that travels at the speed of light and consists of a combined electric and magnetic effect

elec·tron *n* **:** a very small particle that has a negative charge of electricity and travels around the nucleus of an atom

elec·tron·ic *adj* **1 :** of, relating to, or using the principles of electronics **2 :** operating by means of or using an electronic device (as a computer) — **elec·tron·i·cal·ly** *adv*

electronic mail *n* **:** E-MAIL

elec·tron·ics *n* **:** a science that deals with the giving off, action, and effects of electrons in vacuums, gases, and semiconductors and with devices using such electrons

electron tube *n* **:** a device in which conduction of electricity by electrons takes place through a vacuum or a gas within a sealed container and which has various uses (as in radio and television)

elec·tro·scope *n* **:** an instrument for discovering the presence of an electric charge on a body and for finding out whether the charge is positive or negative

el·e·gance *n* **1 :** refined gracefulness **2 :** decoration that is rich but in good taste

el·e·gant *adj* **:** showing good taste (as in dress or manners) **:** having or showing beauty and refinement — **el·e·gant·ly** *adv*

el·e·gy *n, pl* **el·e·gies :** a sad or mournful poem usually expressing sorrow for one who is dead

el·e·ment *n* **1 :** one of the parts of which something is made up **2 :** something that must be learned before one can advance **3 :** a member of a mathematical set **4 :** any of more than 100 substances that cannot by ordinary chemical means be separated into different substances

el·e·men·ta·ry *adj* **:** of or relating to the beginnings or first principles of a subject

el·e·phant *n* **:** a huge thickset mammal with the nose drawn out into a long trunk and two large curved tusks

el·e·vate *vb* **el·e·vat·ed; el·e·vat·ing :** to lift up **:** RAISE

el·e·va·tion *n* **1 :** height especially above

sea level : ALTITUDE **2 :** a raised place (as a hill) **3 :** the act of elevating : the condition of being elevated
el·e·va·tor *n* **1 :** a device (as an endless belt) for raising material **2 :** a floor or little room that can be raised or lowered for carrying persons or goods from one level to another **3 :** a building for storing grain **4 :** a winglike device on an airplane to produce motion up or down
1elev·en *adj* **:** being one more than ten
2eleven *n* **:** one more than ten : 11
1elev·enth *adj* **:** coming right after tenth
2eleventh *n* **:** number eleven in a series
elf *n, pl* **elves :** an often mischievous fairy
elf·in *adj* **1 :** of or relating to elves **2 :** having a strange beauty or charm
el·i·gi·ble *adj* **:** worthy or qualified to be chosen
elim·i·nate *vb* **elim·i·nat·ed; elim·i·nat·ing :** to get rid of : do away with
elim·i·na·tion *n* **:** a getting rid especially of waste from the body
elk *n* **1 :** the moose of Europe and Asia **2 :** a large North American deer with curved antlers having many branches
el·lipse *n* **:** a closed curve that looks like a circle pulled out on opposite sides
el·lip·ti·cal *or* **el·lip·tic** *adj* **:** of or like an ellipse
elm *n* **:** a tall shade tree with a broad rather flat top and spreading branches
el·o·cu·tion *n* **:** the art of reading or speaking well in public
elo·dea *n* **:** a common floating water plant with small green leaves
elon·gate *vb* **elon·gat·ed; elon·gat·ing :** to make or grow longer
elope *vb* **eloped; elop·ing :** to run away to be married — **elope·ment** *n*
el·o·quence *n* **1 :** speaking or writing that is forceful and able to persuade **2 :** the art or power of speaking or writing with force and in a way to persuade
el·o·quent *adj* **1 :** expressing oneself or expressed clearly and with force **2 :** clearly showing some feeling or meaning — **el·o·quent·ly** *adv*
1else *adv* **1 :** in a different way or place or at a different time **2 :** if the facts are or were different : if not
2else *adj* **1 :** being other and different **2 :** being in addition
else·where *adv* **:** in or to another place
elude *vb* **elud·ed; elud·ing :** to avoid or escape by being quick, skillful, or tricky
elu·sive *adj* **1 :** clever in eluding **2 :** hard to understand or define
elves *pl of* ELF
em- — see EN-

E–mail *n* **:** messages sent and received electronically (as between computer terminals linked by telephone lines)
e–mail *vb* **:** to send E-mail — **e–mailer** *n*
eman·ci·pate *vb* **eman·ci·pat·ed; eman·ci·pat·ing :** to set free from control or slavery : LIBERATE
eman·ci·pa·tion *n* **:** a setting free
em·balm *vb* **:** to treat a dead body so as to preserve it from decay — **em·balm·er** *n*
em·bank·ment *n* **:** a raised bank or wall to carry a roadway, prevent floods, or hold back water
em·bar·go *n, pl* **em·bar·goes :** an order of a government prohibiting commercial shipping from leaving its ports
em·bark *vb* **1 :** to go on or put on board a ship or an airplane **2 :** to begin some project or task
em·bar·rass *vb* **1 :** to involve in financial difficulties **2 :** to cause to feel confused and distressed : FLUSTER
em·bas·sy *n, pl* **em·bas·sies 1 :** an ambassador and his assistants **2 :** the residence or office of an ambassador
em·bed *or* **im·bed** *vb* **em·bed·ded** *or* **im·bed·ded; em·bed·ding** *or* **im·bed·ding :** to set solidly in or as if in a bed
em·bel·lish *vb* **:** to add ornamental details to — **em·bel·lish·ment** *n*
em·ber *n* **:** a glowing piece of coal or wood in the ashes from a fire
em·bez·zle *vb* **em·bez·zled; em·bez·zling :** to take (property entrusted to one's care) dishonestly for one's own use
em·bit·ter *vb* **:** to make bitter : stir bitter feeling in
em·blem *n* **:** an object or a likeness of an object used to suggest a thing that cannot be pictured : SYMBOL
em·body *vb* **em·bod·ied; em·body·ing 1 :** to bring together so as to form a body or system **2 :** to make a part of a body or system **3 :** to represent in visible form
em·boss *vb* **:** to ornament with a raised pattern or design
1em·brace *vb* **em·braced; em·brac·ing 1 :** to clasp in the arms **2 :** to enclose on all sides **3 :** to take up readily or gladly **4 :** TAKE IN 5, INCLUDE
2embrace *n* **:** an encircling with the arms : HUG
em·broi·der *vb* **1 :** to make or fill in a design with needlework **2 :** to decorate with needlework **3 :** to add to the interest of (as a story) with details far beyond the truth
em·broi·dery *n, pl* **em·broi·der·ies 1 :** needlework done to decorate cloth **2 :** the act or art of embroidering
em·bryo *n, pl* **em·bry·os 1 :** an animal in

the earliest stages of growth when its basic structures are being formed **2 :** a tiny young plant inside a seed

[1]**em·er·ald** *n* **:** a precious stone of a rich green color

[2]**emerald** *adj* **:** brightly or richly green

emerge *vb* **emerged; emerg·ing 1 :** to come out or into view (as from water or a hole) **2 :** to become known especially as a result of study or questioning

emer·gen·cy *n, pl* **emer·gen·cies :** an unexpected situation calling for prompt action

em·ery *n, pl* **em·er·ies :** a mineral used in the form of powder or grains for polishing and grinding

-emia *or* **-ae·mia** *n suffix* **:** condition of having a specified disorder of the blood

em·i·grant *n* **:** a person who emigrates

em·i·grate *vb* **em·i·grat·ed; em·i·grat·ing :** to leave a country or region to settle somewhere else

em·i·gra·tion *n* **:** a going away from one region or country to live in another

em·i·nence *n* **1 :** the condition of being eminent **2 :** a piece of high ground **:** HILL

em·i·nent *adj* **:** standing above others in rank, merit, or worth

em·is·sary *n, pl* **em·is·sar·ies :** a person sent on a mission to represent another

emit *vb* **emit·ted; emit·ting :** to give out **:** send forth

emo·tion *n* **1 :** strong feeling **2 :** a mental and bodily reaction (as anger or fear) accompanied by strong feeling

emo·tion·al *adj* **1 :** of or relating to the emotions **2 :** likely to show or express emotion **3 :** expressing emotion — **emo·tion·al·ly** *adv*

em·per·or *n* **:** the supreme ruler of an empire

em·pha·sis *n, pl* **em·pha·ses 1 :** a forcefulness of expression that gives special importance to something **2 :** special force given to one or more words or syllables in speaking or reading **3 :** special importance given to something

em·pha·size *vb* **em·pha·sized; em·pha·siz·ing :** to give emphasis to

em·phat·ic *adj* **:** showing or spoken with emphasis

em·phy·se·ma *n* **:** a disease in which the lungs become stretched and inefficient

em·pire *n* **1 :** a group of territories or peoples under one ruler **2 :** a country whose ruler is called an emperor **3 :** the power or rule of an emperor

[1]**em·ploy** *vb* **1 :** to make use of **2 :** to use the services of **:** hire for wages or salary

[2]**employ** *n* **:** the state of being employed

em·ploy·ee *or* **em·ploye** *n* **:** a person who works for pay in the service of an employer

em·ploy·er *n* **:** one that employs others

em·ploy·ment *n* **1 :** OCCUPATION 1, ACTIVITY **2 :** the act of employing **:** the state of being employed

em·pow·er *vb* **:** to give authority or legal power to

em·press *n* **1 :** the wife of an emperor **2 :** a woman who is the ruler of an empire in her own right

[1]**emp·ty** *adj* **emp·ti·er; emp·ti·est 1 :** containing nothing **2 :** not occupied or lived in **:** VACANT — **emp·ti·ness** *n*

[2]**empty** *vb* **emp·tied; emp·ty·ing 1 :** to make empty **:** remove the contents of **2 :** to transfer by emptying a container **3 :** to become empty **4 :** [1]DISCHARGE 6

emp·ty–hand·ed *adj* **1 :** having nothing in the hands **2 :** having gotten or gained nothing

emp·ty–head·ed *adj* **:** having a merry silly nature

emu *n* **:** an Australian bird that is like but smaller than the related ostrich and runs very fast

em·u·late *vb* **em·u·lat·ed; em·u·lat·ing :** to try hard to equal or do better than

em·u·la·tion *n* **:** ambition or effort to equal or do better than others

emul·si·fy *vb* **emul·si·fied; emul·si·fy·ing :** to make an emulsion of

emul·sion *n* **:** a material consisting of a mixture of liquids so that fine drops of one liquid are scattered throughout the other

en- *also* **em-** *prefix* **1 :** put into or on to **:** go into or on to **2 :** cause to be **3 :** provide with — in all senses usually *em-* before *b, m,* or *p*

[1]**-en** *also* **-n** *adj suffix* **:** made of **:** consisting of

[2]**-en** *vb suffix* **1 :** become or cause to be **2 :** cause or come to have

en·able *vb* **en·abled; en·abling :** to give strength, power, or ability to **:** make able

en·act *vb* **1 :** to make into law **2 :** to act the part of (as in a play) — **en·act·ment** *n*

[1]**enam·el** *vb* **enam·eled** *or* **enam·elled; enam·el·ing** *or* **enam·el·ling :** to cover with or as if with enamel

[2]**enamel** *n* **1 :** a glassy substance used for coating the surface of metal, glass, and pottery **2 :** the hard outer surface of the teeth **3 :** a paint that forms a hard glossy coat

en·camp *vb* **:** to set up and occupy a camp

en·camp·ment *n* **1 :** the act of making a camp **2 :** CAMP

en·case *vb* **en·cased; en·cas·ing :** to enclose in or as if in a case

-ence *n suffix* **:** action or process

en·chant *vb* **1 :** to put under a spell by or as

if by charms or magic **2 :** to please greatly — **en·chant·er** *n* — **en·chant·ment** *n*

en·chant·ing *adj* **:** very attractive **:** CHARMING

en·chant·ress *n* **:** a woman who enchants **:** WITCH, SORCERESS

en·cir·cle *vb* **en·cir·cled; en·cir·cling 1 :** to form a circle around **:** SURROUND **2 :** to pass completely around

en·close *or* **in·close** *vb* **en·closed** *or* **in·closed; en·clos·ing** *or* **in·clos·ing 1 :** to close in all around **:** SURROUND **2 :** to put in the same parcel or envelope with something else

en·clo·sure *or* **in·clo·sure** *n* **1 :** the act of enclosing **2 :** an enclosed space **3 :** something (as a fence) that encloses **4 :** something enclosed (as in a letter)

en·com·pass *vb* **1 :** ENCIRCLE 1 **2 :** INCLUDE

[1]**en·core** *n* **1 :** a demand for the repeating of something on a program made by applause from an audience **2 :** a further appearance or performance given in response to applause

[2]**encore** *vb* **en·cored; en·cor·ing :** to call for an encore

[1]**en·coun·ter** *vb* **1 :** to meet as an enemy **:** FIGHT **2 :** to meet face-to-face or unexpectedly

[2]**encounter** *n* **1 :** a meeting with an enemy **:** COMBAT **2 :** a meeting face-to-face and often by chance

en·cour·age *vb* **en·cour·aged; en·cour·ag·ing 1 :** to give courage, spirit, or hope to **:** HEARTEN **2 :** to give help to **:** AID

en·cour·age·ment *n* **1 :** the act of encouraging **:** the state of being encouraged **2 :** something that encourages

en·croach *vb* **1 :** to take over the rights or possessions of another little by little or in secret **2 :** to go beyond the usual or proper limits

en·crust *also* **in·crust** *vb* **:** to cover with or as if with a crust

en·cum·ber *vb* **1 :** to weigh down **:** BURDEN **2 :** HINDER, HAMPER

-en·cy *n suffix, pl* **-en·cies :** quality or state

en·cy·clo·pe·dia *n* **:** a book or a set of books containing information on all branches of learning in articles arranged alphabetically by subject

[1]**end** *n* **1 :** the part near the boundary of an area **2 :** the point (as of time or space) where something ceases to exist **3 :** the first or last part of a thing **4 :** DEATH 1, DESTRUCTION **5 :** [1]PURPOSE, GOAL

[2]**end** *vb* **:** to bring or come to an end **:** STOP

en·dan·ger *vb* **:** [2]RISK 1

en·dear *vb* **:** to make dear or beloved

en·dear·ment *n* **:** a word or an act that shows love or affection

[1]**en·deav·or** *vb* **:** to make an effort **:** TRY

[2]**endeavor** *n* **:** a serious determined effort

end·ing *n* **:** the final part **:** END

en·dive *n* **:** either of two plants related to the daisies and often used in salads

end·less *adj* **1 :** having or seeming to have no end **2 :** joined at the ends — **end·less·ly** *adv* — **end·less·ness** *n*

en·do·crine gland *n* **:** any of several glands (as the thyroid or pituitary) that secrete hormones directly into the blood

en·dorse *or* **in·dorse** *vb* **en·dorsed** *or* **in·dorsed; en·dors·ing** *or* **in·dors·ing 1 :** to sign one's name on the back of (a check) to obtain payment **2 :** to give one's support to openly — **en·dorse·ment** *n*

en·dow *vb* **1 :** to provide with money for support **2 :** to provide with something freely or naturally

en·dow·ment *n* **:** the providing of a permanent fund for support or the fund provided

end·point *n* **:** either of two points that mark the ends of a line segment or a point that marks the end of a ray

en·dur·ance *n* **:** the ability to put up with strain, suffering, or hardship

en·dure *vb* **en·dured; en·dur·ing 1 :** to continue in existence **:** LAST **2 :** to put up with (as pain) patiently or firmly

end·ways *adv or adj* **1 :** on end **2 :** with the end forward **3 :** [1]LENGTHWISE

en·e·ma *n* **:** the injection of liquid into the bowel or the liquid injected

en·e·my *n, pl* **en·e·mies 1 :** one that hates another **:** one that attacks or tries to harm another **2 :** something that harms or threatens **3 :** a nation with which one's own country is at war or a person belonging to such a nation

en·er·get·ic *adj* **:** having or showing energy **:** ACTIVE, VIGOROUS — **en·er·get·i·cal·ly** *adv*

en·er·gy *n, pl* **en·er·gies 1 :** ability to be active **:** strength of body or mind to do things or to work **2 :** usable power or the resources (as oil) for producing such power

en·fold *vb* **1 :** to wrap up **:** cover with or as if with folds **2 :** [1]EMBRACE 1

en·force *vb* **en·forced; en·forc·ing 1 :** to demand and see that one gets **2 :** to put into force — **en·force·ment** *n*

en·gage *vb* **en·gaged; en·gag·ing 1 :** to pledge (as oneself) to do something **:** PROMISE **2 :** to catch and hold fast (as the attention) **3 :** to take part in something **4 :** to enter into contest or battle with **5 :** to arrange for the services or use of **:** HIRE **6 :** to put or become in gear **:** MESH

en·gaged *adj* **1 :** busy with some activity **2 :** pledged to be married

en·gage·ment *n* **1 :** the act of engaging **:** the state of being engaged **2 :** EMPLOYMENT 2 **3 :** an appointment at a certain time and place **4 :** a fight between armed forces

en·gag·ing *adj* **:** ATTRACTIVE

en·gen·der *vb* **:** to cause to be or develop **:** PRODUCE

en·gine *n* **1 :** a mechanical tool or device **2 :** a machine for driving or operating something especially by using the energy of steam, gasoline, or oil **3 :** [1]LOCOMOTIVE

[1]**en·gi·neer** *n* **1 :** a member of a military group devoted to engineering work **2 :** a person who specializes in engineering **3 :** a person who runs or has charge of an engine or of machinery or technical equipment

[2]**engineer** *vb* **1 :** to plan, build, or manage as an engineer **2 :** to plan out **:** CONTRIVE

en·gi·neer·ing *n* **:** a science by which the properties of matter and the sources of energy in nature are made useful to man in structures (as roads and dams), machines (as automobiles and computers), and products (as plastics and radios)

[1]**En·glish** *adj* **:** of or relating to England, its people, or the English language

[2]**English** *n* **1 :** the language of England, the United States, and some other countries now or at one time under British rule **2 English** *pl* **:** the people of England

English horn *n* **:** a woodwind instrument that is similar to an oboe but is longer and has a deeper tone

en·grave *vb* **en·graved; en·grav·ing 1 :** to cut or carve (as letters or designs) on a hard surface **2 :** to cut lines, letters, figures, or designs on or into (a hard surface) often for use in printing **3 :** to print from a cut surface — **en·grav·er** *n*

en·grav·ing *n* **1 :** the art of cutting something especially into the surface of wood, stone, or metal **2 :** a print made from an engraved surface

en·gross *vb* **:** to take up the whole interest of

en·gulf *vb* **:** to flow over and swallow up

en·hance *vb* **en·hanced; en·hanc·ing :** to make greater or better

enig·ma *n* **:** something hard to understand

en·joy *vb* **1 :** to take pleasure or satisfaction in **2 :** to have for one's use or benefit

en·joy·able *adj* **:** being a source of pleasure

en·joy·ment *n* **1 :** the action or condition of enjoying something **2 :** something that gives pleasure

en·large *vb* **en·larged; en·larg·ing :** to make or grow larger **:** EXPAND

en·large·ment *n* **1 :** an act of enlarging **2 :** the state of being enlarged **3 :** a photographic print made larger than the negative

en·light·en *vb* **:** to give knowledge to

en·list *vb* **1 :** to join the armed forces as a volunteer **2 :** to obtain the help of — **en·list·ment** *n*

en·list·ed man *n* **:** a man or woman serving in the armed forces who ranks below a commissioned officer or warrant officer

en·liv·en *vb* **:** to put life or spirit into **:** make active or cheerful

en·mi·ty *n, pl* **en·mi·ties :** hatred especially when shared **:** ILL WILL

enor·mous *adj* **:** unusually large **:** HUGE — **enor·mous·ly** *adv*

[1]**enough** *adj* **:** equal to the needs or demands

[2]**enough** *adv* **:** in sufficient amount or degree

[3]**enough** *pron* **:** a sufficient number or amount

en·rage *vb* **en·raged; en·rag·ing :** to fill with rage **:** ANGER

en·rich *vb* **1 :** to make rich or richer **2 :** to improve the quality of food by adding vitamins and minerals **3 :** to make more fertile

en·roll *or* **en·rol** *vb* **en·rolled; en·roll·ing :** to include (as a name) on a roll or list

en·roll·ment *or* **en·rol·ment** *n* **1 :** the act of enrolling or being enrolled **2 :** the number of persons enrolled

en route *adv* **:** on or along the way

en·sem·ble *n* **:** a group of musicians or dancers performing together

en·shrine *vb* **en·shrined; en·shrin·ing :** to cherish as if sacred

en·sign *n* **1 :** a flag flown as the symbol of nationality **2 :** a commissioned officer of the lowest rank in the Navy or Coast Guard

en·slave *vb* **en·slaved; en·slav·ing :** to make a slave of

en·sue *vb* **en·sued; en·su·ing :** to come after in time or as a result **:** FOLLOW

en·sure *vb* **en·sured; en·sur·ing :** to make sure, certain, or safe **:** GUARANTEE

en·tan·gle *vb* **en·tan·gled; en·tan·gling 1 :** to make tangled or confused **2 :** to catch in a tangle — **en·tan·gle·ment** *n*

en·ter *vb* **1 :** to come or go in or into **2 :** to put into a list **:** write down **3 :** to become a member or a member of **:** JOIN **4 :** to become a party to or take an interest in something **5 :** PENETRATE 1, PIERCE **6 :** to cause to be admitted (as to a school)

en·ter·prise *n* **1 :** an undertaking requiring courage and energy **2 :** willingness to engage in daring or difficult action **3 :** a business organization or activity

en·ter·pris·ing *adj* **:** bold and energetic in trying or experimenting

en·ter·tain *vb* **1 :** to greet in a friendly way and provide for especially in one's home

: have as a guest **2 :** to have in mind **3 :** to provide amusement for

en·ter·tain·er *n* **:** a person who performs for public entertainment

en·ter·tain·ment *n* **1 :** the act of entertaining or amusing **2 :** something (as a show) that is a form of amusement or recreation

en·thrall *or* **en·thral** *vb* **en·thralled; en·thrall·ing :** to hold the attention of completely **:** CHARM

en·throne *vb* **en·throned; en·thron·ing 1 :** to seat on a throne **2 :** to place in a high position

en·thu·si·asm *n* **:** strong feeling in favor of something

en·thu·si·ast *n* **:** a person filled with enthusiasm

en·thu·si·as·tic *adj* **:** full of enthusiasm **:** EAGER

en·thu·si·as·ti·cal·ly *adv* **:** with enthusiasm

en·tice *vb* **en·ticed; en·tic·ing :** to attract by raising hope or desire **:** TEMPT

en·tire *adj* **:** complete in all parts or respects — **en·tire·ly** *adv*

en·tire·ty *n, pl* **en·tire·ties 1 :** a state of completeness **2 :** [2]WHOLE 2

en·ti·tle *vb* **en·ti·tled; en·ti·tling 1 :** to give a title to **2 :** to give a right or claim to

en·trails *n pl* **:** the internal parts of an animal

[1]**en·trance** *n* **1 :** the act of entering **2 :** a door, gate, or way for entering **3 :** permission to enter **:** ADMISSION

[2]**en·trance** *vb* **en·tranced; en·tranc·ing 1 :** to put into a trance **2 :** to fill with delight and wonder

en·trap *vb* **en·trapped; en·trap·ping :** to catch in or as if in a trap

en·treat *vb* **:** to ask in an earnest way

en·treaty *n, pl* **en·treat·ies :** an act of entreating **:** PLEA

en·trust *or* **in·trust** *vb* **1 :** to give care of something to as a trust **2 :** to give to another with confidence

en·try *n, pl* **en·tries 1 :** the act of entering **:** ENTRANCE **2 :** a place (as a hall or door) through which entrance is made **3 :** the act of making (as in a book or a list) a written record of something **4 :** something entered in a list or a record **5 :** a person or thing entered in a contest

en·twine *vb* **en·twined; en·twin·ing :** to twist or twine together or around

enu·mer·ate *vb* **enu·mer·at·ed; enu·mer·at·ing 1 :** [1]COUNT 1 **2 :** to name one after another **:** LIST

enun·ci·ate *vb* **enun·ci·at·ed; enun·ci·at·ing 1 :** ANNOUNCE 1 **2 :** to pronounce words or parts of words

enun·ci·a·tion *n* **:** clearness of pronunciation

en·vel·op *vb* **:** to put a covering completely around **:** wrap up or in

en·ve·lope *n* **:** an enclosing cover or wrapper (as for a letter)

en·vi·ous *adj* **:** feeling or showing envy — **en·vi·ous·ly** *adv* — **en·vi·ous·ness** *n*

en·vi·ron·ment *n* **1 :** SURROUNDINGS **2 :** the surrounding conditions or forces (as soil, climate, and living things) that influence the form and ability to survive of a plant or animal or ecological community **3 :** the social and cultural conditions that influence the life of a person or human community

en·voy *n* **1 :** a representative sent by one government to another **2 :** MESSENGER

[1]**en·vy** *n, pl* **envies 1 :** a feeling of discontent at another's good fortune together with a desire to have the same good fortune oneself **2 :** a person or a thing that is envied

[2]**envy** *vb* **en·vied; en·vy·ing :** to feel envy toward or because of

en·zyme *n* **:** one of the substances produced by body cells that help bodily chemical activities (as digestion) to take place but are not destroyed in so doing

eon *variant of* AEON

[1]**ep·ic** *adj* **:** of, relating to, or characteristic of an epic

[2]**epic** *n* **:** a long poem that tells the story of a hero's deeds

[1]**ep·i·dem·ic** *adj* **:** spreading widely and affecting large numbers of people at the same time

[2]**epidemic** *n* **1 :** a rapidly spreading outbreak of disease **2 :** something that spreads or develops rapidly like an epidemic disease

epi·der·mis *n* **1 :** a thin outer layer of skin covering the dermis **2 :** any of various thin outer layers of plants or animals

ep·i·sode *n* **:** an event or one of a series of events that stands out clearly in one's life, in history, or in a story

epis·tle *n* **:** [1]LETTER 2

ep·i·taph *n* **:** a brief statement on a tombstone in memory of a dead person

ep·och *n* **:** a period marked by unusual or important events

[1]**equal** *adj* **1 :** exactly the same in number, amount, degree, rank, or quality **2 :** evenly balanced **3 :** having enough strength, ability, or means **:** ADEQUATE — **equal·ly** *adv*

[2]**equal** *vb* **equaled** *or* **equalled; equal·ing** *or* **equal·ling :** to be equal to

[3]**equal** *n* **:** one that is equal to another

equal·i·ty *n, pl* **equal·i·ties :** the condition or state of being equal

equal·ize *vb* **equal·ized; equal·iz·ing :** to make equal or even

equa·tion *n* **1 :** a statement of the equality

DICTIONARY

of two mathematical expressions **2 :** an expression representing a chemical reaction by means of chemical symbols

equa·tor *n* **:** an imaginary circle around the earth everywhere equally distant from the north pole and the south pole

equa·to·ri·al *adj* **1 :** of, relating to, or lying near the equator **2 :** of, coming from, or suggesting the region at or near the equator

eques·tri·an *adj* **:** of or relating to horses or to the riding or riders of horses

equi·lat·er·al *adj* **:** having all sides of equal length

equi·lib·ri·um *n* **1 :** a state of balance between opposing weights, forces, or influences **2 :** the normal bodily adjustment of a person or animal in relation to its environment

equi·nox *n* **:** either of the two times each year when the sun's center crosses the equator and day and night (as on March 21 and September 23) are everywhere of equal length

equip *vb* **equipped; equip·ping :** to make ready for a purpose by supplying what is necessary

equip·ment *n* **1 :** an act of equipping **2 :** supplies and tools needed for a special purpose

[1]**equiv·a·lent** *adj* **:** alike or equal in number, value, or meaning

[2]**equivalent** *n* **:** something equivalent

[1]**-er** *adj suffix or adv suffix* — used to form the comparative degree of adjectives and adverbs of one syllable and of some adjectives and adverbs of two or more syllables

[2]**-er** *also* **-ier** *or* **-yer** *n suffix* **1 :** a person whose work or business is connected with **2 :** a person or thing belonging to or associated with **3 :** a native of **:** resident of **4 :** one that has **5 :** one that produces **6 :** one that does or performs a specified action **7 :** one that is a suitable object of a specified action **8 :** one that is

era *n* **1 :** a period of time starting from some special date or event **2 :** an important period of history

erad·i·cate *vb* **erad·i·cat·ed; erad·i·cat·ing :** to remove by or as if by tearing up by the roots **:** destroy completely

erase *vb* **erased; eras·ing :** to cause to disappear by rubbing or scraping

eras·er *n* **:** something (as a piece of rubber or a felt pad) for erasing marks

era·sure *n* **1 :** an act of erasing **2 :** something erased

[1]**ere** *prep* **:** [2]BEFORE 3

[2]**ere** *conj* **:** [3]BEFORE 2

[1]**erect** *adj* **:** being straight up and down — **erect·ly** *adv* — **erect·ness** *n*

[2]**erect** *vb* **1 :** to put up by fitting together materials or parts **2 :** to set straight up — **erec·tor** *n*

er·mine *n* **:** a weasel of northern regions that is valued for its winter coat of white fur with a tail tipped in black

erode *vb* **erod·ed; erod·ing :** to eat into **:** wear away **:** destroy by wearing away

ero·sion *n* **:** the act of eroding **:** the state of being eroded

err *vb* **1 :** to make a mistake **2 :** to do wrong **:** SIN

er·rand *n* **1 :** a short trip made to take care of some business **2 :** the business done on an errand

er·rant *adj* **1 :** wandering in search of adventure **2 :** straying from a proper course

er·rat·ic *adj* **:** not following the usual or expected course

er·ro·ne·ous *adj* **:** INCORRECT 1

er·ror *n* **:** a failure to be correct or accurate **:** MISTAKE

erupt *vb* **1 :** to burst forth or cause to burst forth **2 :** to break through a surface **3 :** to break out (as with a skin rash)

erup·tion *n* **1 :** a bursting forth **2 :** a breaking out (as of a skin rash) or the resulting rash

-ery *n suffix, pl* **-er·ies 1 :** qualities considered as a group **:** character **:** -NESS **2 :** art **:** practice **3 :** place of doing, keeping, producing, or selling **4 :** collection **:** aggregate **5 :** state or condition

[1]**-es** *n pl suffix* **1** — used to form the plural of most nouns that end in *s*, *z*, *sh*, *ch*, or a final *y* that changes to *i* and of some nouns ending in *f* that changes to *v* **2 :** [1]-s 2

[2]**-es** *vb suffix* — used to form the third person singular present of most verbs that end in *s*, *z*, *sh*, *ch*, or a final *y* that changes to *i*

es·ca·la·tor *n* **:** a moving stairway arranged like an endless belt

es·ca·pade *n* **:** a daring or reckless adventure

[1]**es·cape** *vb* **es·caped; es·cap·ing 1 :** to get away **:** get free or clear **2 :** to keep free of **:** AVOID **3 :** to fail to be noticed or remembered by **4 :** to leak out from some enclosed place

[2]**escape** *n* **1 :** the act of escaping **2 :** a way of escaping

[1]**es·cort** *n* **1 :** one (as a person or group) that accompanies another to give protection or show courtesy **2 :** the man who goes on a date with a woman

[2]**es·cort** *vb* **:** to accompany as an escort

[1]**-ese** *adj suffix* **:** of, relating to, or coming from a certain place or country

[2]**-ese** *n suffix, pl* **-ese 1 :** native or resident of a specified place or country **2 :** language

of a particular place, country, or nationality **3 :** speech or literary style of a specified place, person, or group

Es·ki·mo *n, pl* **Es·ki·mos :** a member of a group of peoples of Alaska, northern Canada, Greenland, and northeastern Siberia

Eskimo dog *n* **:** a sled dog of northern North America

esoph·a·gus *n, pl* **esoph·a·gi :** the tube that leads from the mouth through the throat to the stomach

es·pe·cial *adj* **:** SPECIAL — **es·pe·cial·ly** *adv*

es·pi·o·nage *n* **:** the practice of spying **:** the use of spies

es·py *vb* **es·pied; es·py·ing :** to catch sight of

-ess *n suffix* **:** female

[1]**es·say** *vb* **:** [1]TRY 6

[2]**es·say** *n* **1 :** [2]ATTEMPT **2 :** a usually short piece of writing dealing with a subject from a personal point of view

es·say·ist *n* **:** a writer of essays

es·sence *n* **1 :** the basic part of something **2 :** a substance made from a plant or drug and having its special qualities **3 :** [1]PERFUME 2

[1]**es·sen·tial** *adj* **1 :** forming or belonging to the basic part of something **2 :** important in the highest degree — **es·sen·tial·ly** *adv*

[2]**essential** *n* **:** something that is essential

-est *adj suffix or adv suffix* — used to form the superlative degree of adjectives and adverbs of one syllable and of some adjectives and adverbs of two or more syllables

es·tab·lish *vb* **1 :** to bring into being **:** FOUND **2 :** to put beyond doubt **:** PROVE

es·tab·lish·ment *n* **1 :** the act of establishing **2 :** a place for residence or for business

es·tate *n* **1 :** [1]STATE 1 **2 :** the property of all kinds that a person leaves at death **3 :** a fine country house on a large piece of land

[1]**es·teem** *n* **:** high regard

[2]**esteem** *vb* **:** to think well or highly of

esthetic *variant of* AESTHETIC

[1]**es·ti·mate** *vb* **es·ti·mat·ed; es·ti·mat·ing 1 :** to give or form a general idea of (as the value, size, or cost of something) **2 :** to form an opinion

[2]**es·ti·mate** *n* **1 :** an opinion or judgment especially of the value or quality of something **2 :** an approximation of the size or cost of something

es·ti·ma·tion *n* **1 :** the making of an estimate **:** JUDGMENT **2 :** an estimate formed **:** OPINION

et cet·era : and others of the same kind **:** and so forth **:** and so on

etch *vb* **:** to produce designs or figures on metal or glass by lines eaten into the substance by acid

etch·ing *n* **1 :** the art or process of producing drawings or pictures by printing from etched plates **2 :** a picture made from an etched plate

eter·nal *adj* **1 :** lasting forever **:** having no beginning and no end **2 :** continuing without interruption

eter·ni·ty *n, pl* **eter·ni·ties 1 :** time without end **2 :** the state after death **3 :** a period of time that seems to be endless

-eth — see -TH

ether *n* **1 :** the clear upper part of the sky **2 :** a light flammable liquid used to dissolve fats and as an anesthetic

ethe·re·al *adj* **1 :** HEAVENLY 1 **2 :** very delicate **:** AIRY

eth·i·cal *adj* **1 :** of or relating to ethics **2 :** following accepted rules of behavior

eth·ics *n sing or pl* **1 :** a branch of philosophy dealing with moral duty and with questions of what is good and bad **2 :** the rules of moral behavior governing an individual or a group

eth·nic *adj* **:** of or relating to races or large groups of people classed according to common characteristics and customs — **eth·ni·cal·ly** *adv*

et·i·quette *n* **:** the rules governing the proper way to behave or to do something

-ette *n suffix* **1 :** little one **2 :** female **3 :** imitation

et·y·mol·o·gy *n, pl* **et·y·mol·o·gies :** the history of a word shown by tracing it or its parts back to the earliest known forms and meanings both in its own language and any other language from which it may have been taken

eu·ca·lyp·tus *n, pl* **eu·ca·lyp·ti** *or* **eu·ca·lyp·tus·es :** a tree of a kind native mainly to western Australia and widely grown for shade, timber, gum, and oil

Eu·cha·rist *n* **:** COMMUNION 2

eu·gle·na *n* **:** any of numerous tiny single-celled organisms that contain chlorophyll, swim about by means of a flagellum, and are often classified in science as algae

eu·ro *n, pl* **euros :** a coin or bill used by countries of the European Union

[1]**Eu·ro·pe·an** *adj* **:** of or relating to Europe or the Europeans

[2]**European** *n* **:** a native or resident of Europe

evac·u·ate *vb* **evac·u·at·ed; evac·u·at·ing 1 :** to make empty **:** empty out **2 :** to discharge waste matter from the body **3 :** to remove troops or people from a place of danger

evade *vb* **evad·ed; evad·ing :** to get away from or avoid meeting directly

eval·u·ate *vb* **eval·u·at·ed; eval·u·at·ing** : to find or estimate the value of

eval·u·a·tion *n* : the act or result of evaluating

evan·ge·list *n* : a Christian preacher who goes about from place to place trying to change or increase people's religious feelings

evap·o·rate *vb* **evap·o·rat·ed; evap·o·rat·ing** **1** : to change into vapor **2** : to disappear without being seen to go **3** : to remove some of the water from something (as by heating)

evap·o·ra·tion *n* : the process of evaporating

eve *n* **1** : EVENING **2** : the evening or day before a special day **3** : the period just before an important event

[1]**even** *adj* **1** : being without breaks or bumps **2** : staying the same over a period of time **3** : being on the same line or level **4** : equal in size, number, or amount **5** : [1]EQUAL 2, FAIR **6** : possible to divide by two — **even·ly** *adv* — **even·ness** *n*

[2]**even** *adv* **1** : at the very time : JUST **2** : INDEED **3** — used to stress an extreme or highly unlikely condition or instance **4** : to a greater extent or degree : STILL **5** : so much as

[3]**even** *vb* : to make or become even

eve·ning *n* : the final part of the day and early part of the night

evening star *n* : a bright planet (as Venus) seen in the western sky after sunset

event *n* **1** : something usually of importance that happens **2** : a social occasion (as a party) **3** : the fact of happening **4** : a contest in a program of sports

event·ful *adj* **1** : filled with events **2** : very important

even·tide *n* : EVENING

even·tu·al *adj* : coming at some later time — **even·tu·al·ly** *adv*

ev·er *adv* **1** : at all times : ALWAYS **2** : at any time **3** : in any way

ev·er·glade *n* : a swampy grassland

[1]**ev·er·green** *n* **1** : an evergreen plant (as a pine or a laurel) **2** **evergreens** *pl* : branches and leaves of evergreens used for decorations

[2]**evergreen** *adj* : having leaves that stay green through more than one growing season

ev·er·last·ing *adj* **1** : lasting forever : ETERNAL **2** : going on for a long time or for too long a time — **ev·er·last·ing·ly** *adv*

ev·er·more *adj* : FOREVER 1

ev·ery *adj* : being each of a group or series without leaving out any

ev·ery·body *pron* : every person

ev·ery·day *adj* : used or suitable for every day : ORDINARY

ev·ery·one *pron* : every person

ev·ery·thing *pron* : every thing : ALL

ev·ery·where *adv* : in or to every place or part

evict *vb* : to put out from property by legal action

ev·i·dence *n* **1** : an outward sign : INDICATION **2** : material presented to a court to help find the truth in a matter

ev·i·dent *adj* : clear to the sight or to the mind : PLAIN — **ev·i·dent·ly** *adv*

[1]**evil** *adj* **1** : morally bad : WICKED **2** : causing harm : tending to injure

[2]**evil** *n* **1** : something that brings sorrow, trouble, or destruction **2** : the fact of suffering or wrongdoing

evoke *vb* **evoked; evok·ing** : to call forth or up : SUMMON

evo·lu·tion *n* **1** : the process of development of an animal or a plant **2** : the theory that the various kinds of existing animals and plants have come from kinds that existed in the past

evolve *vb* **evolved; evolv·ing** : to grow or develop out of something

ewe *n* : a female sheep

ex- *prefix* **1** : out of : outside **2** : former

[1]**ex·act** *vb* : to demand and get by force or threat

[2]**exact** *adj* : showing close agreement with fact : ACCURATE — **ex·act·ly** *adv* — **ex·act·ness** *n*

ex·act·ing *adj* : making many or difficult demands upon a person : TRYING

ex·ag·ger·ate *vb* **ex·ag·ger·at·ed; ex·ag·ger·at·ing** : to enlarge a fact or statement beyond what is true

ex·ag·ger·a·tion *n* **1** : the act of exaggerating **2** : an exaggerated statement

ex·alt *vb* **1** : to raise in rank or power **2** : to praise highly

ex·am *n* : EXAMINATION

ex·am·i·na·tion *n* **1** : the act of examining or state of being examined **2** : a test given to determine progress, fitness, or knowledge

ex·am·ine *vb* **ex·am·ined; ex·am·in·ing** **1** : to look at or check carefully **2** : to question closely

ex·am·ple *n* **1** : a sample of something taken to show what the whole is like : INSTANCE **2** : something to be imitated : MODEL **3** : something that is a warning to others **4** : a problem to be solved to show how a rule works

ex·as·per·ate *vb* **ex·as·per·at·ed; ex·as·per·at·ing** : to make angry

ex·as·per·a·tion *n* : extreme annoyance : ANGER

ex·ca·vate *vb* **ex·ca·vat·ed; ex·ca·vat·ing** **1** : to hollow out : form a hole in **2** : to make by hollowing out **3 :** to dig out and remove **4 :** to expose to view by digging away a covering (as of earth)

ex•ca•va•tion *n* **1 :** the act of excavating **2 :** a hollow place formed by excavating

ex•ceed *vb* **1 :** to go or be beyond the limit of **2 :** to be greater than

ex•ceed•ing•ly *adv* **:** to a very great degree

ex•cel *vb* **ex•celled; ex•cel•ling :** to do better than others **:** SURPASS

ex•cel•lence *n* **1 :** high quality **2 :** an excellent quality **:** VIRTUE

ex•cel•lent *adj* **:** very good of its kind — **ex•cel•lent•ly** *adv*

¹ex•cept *prep* **1 :** not including **2 :** other than **:** BUT

²except *vb* **:** to leave out from a number or a whole **:** EXCLUDE

³except *conj* **:** if it were not for the fact that **:** ONLY

ex•cep•tion *n* **1 :** the act of leaving out **2 :** a case to which a rule does not apply **3 :** an objection or a reason for objecting

ex•cep•tion•al *adj* **1 :** forming an exception **2 :** better than average **:** SUPERIOR — **ex•cep•tion•al•ly** *adv*

¹ex•cess *n* **1 :** a state of being more than enough **2 :** the amount by which something is more than what is needed or allowed

²excess *adj* **:** more than is usual or acceptable

ex•ces•sive *adj* **:** showing excess — **ex•ces•sive•ly** *adv*

¹ex•change *n* **1 :** a giving or taking of one thing in return for another **:** TRADE **2 :** the act of substituting one thing for another **3 :** the act of giving and receiving between two groups **4 :** a place where goods or services are exchanged

²exchange *vb* **ex•changed; ex•chang•ing :** to give in exchange **:** TRADE, SWAP

ex•cit•able *adj* **:** easily excited

ex•cite *vb* **ex•cit•ed; ex•cit•ing 1 :** to increase the activity of **2 :** to stir up feeling in **:** ROUSE

ex•cite•ment *n* **1 :** the state of being excited **:** AGITATION **2 :** something that excites or stirs up

ex•cit•ing *adj* **:** producing excitement

ex•claim *vb* **:** to cry out or speak out suddenly or with strong feeling

ex•cla•ma•tion *n* **1 :** a sharp or sudden cry of strong feeling **2 :** strong expression of anger or complaint

exclamation point *n* **:** a punctuation mark ! used mostly to show a forceful way of speaking or strong feeling

ex•clam•a•to•ry *adj* **:** containing or using exclamation

ex•clude *vb* **ex•clud•ed; ex•clud•ing :** to shut out **:** keep out

ex•clu•sion *n* **:** the act of excluding **:** the state of being excluded

ex•clu•sive *adj* **1 :** excluding or trying to exclude others **2 :** ⁴SOLE 2 **3 :** ENTIRE, COMPLETE **4 :** not including — **ex•clu•sive•ly** *adv*

ex•crete *vb* **ex•cret•ed; ex•cret•ing :** to separate and give off waste matter from the body usually as urine or sweat

ex•cre•tion *n* **1 :** the process of excreting **2 :** waste material excreted

ex•cre•to•ry *adj* **:** of or relating to excretion **:** used in excreting

ex•cur•sion *n* **1 :** a brief pleasure trip **2 :** a trip at special reduced rates

ex•cus•able *adj* **:** possible to excuse

¹ex•cuse *vb* **ex•cused; ex•cus•ing 1 :** to make apology for **2 :** to overlook or pardon as of little importance **3 :** to let off from doing something **4 :** to be an acceptable reason for

²ex•cuse *n* **1 :** the act of excusing **2 :** something offered as a reason for being excused **3 :** something that excuses or is a reason for excusing

ex•e•cute *vb* **ex•e•cut•ed; ex•e•cut•ing 1 :** to put into effect **:** CARRY OUT, PERFORM **2 :** to put to death according to a legal order **3 :** to make according to a design

ex•e•cu•tion *n* **1 :** a carrying through of something to its finish **2 :** a putting to death as a legal penalty

¹ex•ec•u•tive *adj* **1 :** fitted for or relating to the carrying of things to completion **2 :** concerned with or relating to the carrying out of the law and the conduct of public affairs

²executive *n* **1 :** the executive branch of a government **2 :** a person who manages or directs

ex•em•pli•fy *vb* **ex•em•pli•fied; ex•em•pli•fy•ing :** to show by example

¹ex•empt *adj* **:** free or released from some condition or requirement that other persons must meet or deal with

²exempt *vb* **:** to make exempt

ex•emp•tion *n* **1 :** the act of exempting **:** the state of being exempt **2 :** something that is exempted

¹ex•er•cise *n* **1 :** the act of putting into use, action, or practice **2 :** bodily activity for the sake of health **3 :** a school lesson or other task performed to develop skill **:** practice work **:** DRILL **4 exercises** *pl* **:** a program of songs, speeches, and announcing of awards and honors

²exercise *vb* **ex•er•cised; ex•er•cis•ing 1 :** to put into use **:** EXERT **2 :** to use again

DICTIONARY

and again to train or develop **3 :** to take part in bodily activity for the sake of health or training

ex•ert *vb* **1 :** to put forth (as strength) **:** bring into play **2 :** to put (oneself) into action or to tiring effort

ex•er•tion *n* **1 :** the act of exerting **2 :** use of strength or ability

ex•hale *vb* **ex•haled; ex•hal•ing** **1 :** to breathe out **2 :** to send forth **:** give off

1ex•haust *vb* **1 :** to draw out or let out completely **2 :** to use up completely **3 :** to tire out **:** FATIGUE

2exhaust *n* **1 :** the gas that escapes from an engine **2 :** a system of pipes through which exhaust escapes

ex•haus•tion *n* **1 :** the act of exhausting **2 :** the condition of being exhausted

1ex•hib•it *vb* **1 :** to show by outward signs **:** REVEAL **2 :** to put on display

2exhibit *n* **1 :** an article or collection shown in an exhibition **2 :** an article presented as evidence in a law court

ex•hi•bi•tion *n* **1 :** the act of exhibiting **2 :** a public showing (as of athletic skill or works of art)

ex•hil•a•rate *vb* **ex•hil•a•rat•ed; ex•hil•a•rat•ing :** to make cheerful or lively

ex•hort *vb* **:** to try to influence by words or advice **:** urge strongly

1ex•ile *n* **1 :** the sending or forcing of a person away from his or her own country or the situation of a person who is sent away **2 :** a person who is expelled from his or her own country

2exile *vb* **ex•iled; ex•il•ing :** to force to leave one's own country

ex•ist *vb* **1 :** to have actual being **:** be real **2 :** to continue to live **3 :** to be found **:** OCCUR

ex•is•tence *n* **1 :** the fact or the condition of being or of being real **2 :** the state of being alive **:** LIFE

1ex•it *n* **1 :** the act of going out of or away from a place **:** DEPARTURE **2 :** a way of getting out of a place

2exit *vb* **:** to go out **:** LEAVE, DEPART

ex•o•dus *n* **:** the going out or away of a large number of people

ex•or•bi•tant *adj* **:** going beyond the limits of what is fair, reasonable, or expected

exo•sphere *n* **:** the outer fringe region of the atmosphere

ex•ot•ic *adj* **:** introduced from a foreign country

ex•pand *vb* **1 :** to open wide **:** UNFOLD **2 :** to take up or cause to take up more space **3 :** to work out in greater detail

ex•panse *n* **:** a wide area or stretch

ex•pan•sion *n* **:** the act of expanding or the state of being expanded **:** ENLARGEMENT

ex•pect *vb* **1 :** to look for or look forward to something that ought to or probably will happen **2 :** to consider to be obliged

ex•pec•tant *adj* **:** looking forward to or waiting for something

ex•pec•ta•tion *n* **:** a looking forward to or waiting for something

ex•pe•di•ent *adj* **:** suitable for bringing about a desired result often without regard to what is fair or right — **ex•pe•di•ent•ly** *adv*

ex•pe•di•tion *n* **1 :** a journey for a particular purpose (as for exploring) **2 :** the people making an expedition

ex•pel *vb* **ex•pelled; ex•pel•ling** **1 :** to force out **2 :** to drive away

ex•pend *vb* **1 :** to pay out **:** SPEND **2 :** to use up

ex•pen•di•ture *n* **1 :** the act of spending (as money, time, or energy) **2 :** something that is spent

ex•pense *n* **1 :** something spent or required to be spent **:** COST **2 :** a cause for spending

ex•pen•sive *adj* **:** COSTLY 1 — **ex•pen•sive•ly** *adv*

1ex•pe•ri•ence *n* **1 :** the actual living through an event or events **2 :** the skill or knowledge gained by actually doing a thing **3 :** something that one has actually done or lived through

2experience *vb* **ex•pe•ri•enced; ex•pe•ri•enc•ing :** to have experience of **:** UNDERGO

ex•pe•ri•enced *adj* **:** made skillful or wise through experience

1ex•per•i•ment *n* **:** a trial or test made to find out about something

2ex•per•i•ment *vb* **:** to make experiments

ex•per•i•men•tal *adj* **:** of, relating to, or based on experiment

1ex•pert *adj* **:** showing special skill or knowledge gained from experience or training — **ex•pert•ly** *adv* — **ex•pert•ness** *n*

2ex•pert *n* **:** a person with special skill or knowledge of a subject

ex•pi•ra•tion *n* **:** an act or instance of expiring

ex•pire *vb* **ex•pired; ex•pir•ing** **1 :** 1DIE 1 **2 :** to come to an end **3 :** to breathe out **:** EXHALE

ex•plain *vb* **1 :** to make clear **:** CLARIFY 2 **2 :** to give the reasons for or cause of — **ex•plain•able** *adj*

ex•pla•na•tion *n* **1 :** the act or process of explaining **2 :** a statement that makes something clear

ex•plan•a•to•ry *adj* **:** giving explanation **:** helping to explain

ex·plic·it *adj* **:** so clear in statement that there is no doubt about the meaning

ex·plode *vb* **ex·plod·ed; ex·plod·ing** **1 :** to burst or cause to burst with violence and noise **2 :** to burst forth

1ex·ploit *n* **:** a brave or daring act

2ex·ploit *vb* **1 :** to get the value or use out of **2 :** to make use of unfairly for one's own benefit

ex·plo·ra·tion *n* **:** the act or an instance of exploring

ex·plore *vb* **ex·plored; ex·plor·ing** **1 :** to search through or into **:** examine closely **2 :** to go into or through for purposes of discovery

ex·plor·er *n* **:** a person (as a traveler seeking new geographical or scientific information) who explores something

ex·plo·sion *n* **1 :** the act of exploding **:** a sudden and noisy bursting (as of a bomb) **2 :** a sudden outburst of feeling

1ex·plo·sive *adj* **1 :** able to cause explosion **2 :** likely to explode — **ex·plo·sive·ly** *adv*

2explosive *n* **:** an explosive substance

ex·po·nent *n* **:** a numeral written above and to the right of a number to show how many times the number is to be used as a factor

1ex·port *vb* **:** to send or carry abroad especially for sale in foreign countries

2ex·port *n* **1 :** something that is exported **2 :** the act of exporting

ex·pose *vb* **ex·posed; ex·pos·ing** **1 :** to leave without protection, shelter, or care **2 :** to let light strike the photographic film or plate in taking a picture **3 :** to put on exhibition **:** display for sale **4 :** to make known

ex·po·si·tion *n* **1 :** an explaining of something **2 :** a public exhibition

ex·po·sure *n* **1 :** an act of making something public **2 :** the condition of being exposed **3 :** the act of letting light strike a photographic film or the time during which a film is exposed **4 :** a section of a roll of film for one picture **5 :** position with respect to direction

ex·pound *vb* **1 :** EXPLAIN 1, INTERPRET **2 :** to talk especially for a long time

1ex·press *adj* **1 :** clearly stated **2 :** of a certain sort **3 :** sent or traveling at high speed

2express *n* **1 :** a system for the special transportation of goods **2 :** a vehicle (as a train or elevator) run at special speed with few or no stops

3express *vb* **1 :** to make known especially in words **2 :** to represent by a sign or symbol **3 :** to send by express

ex·pres·sion *n* **1 :** the act or process of expressing especially in words **2 :** a meaningful word or saying **3 :** a way of speaking, singing, or playing that shows mood or feeling **4 :** the look on one's face — **ex·pres·sion·less** *adj*

ex·pres·sive *adj* **:** expressing something **:** full of expression — **ex·pres·sive·ly** *adv* — **ex·pres·sive·ness** *n*

ex·press·way *n* **:** a divided highway for rapid traffic

ex·pul·sion *n* **:** the act of expelling **:** the state of being expelled

ex·qui·site *adj* **1 :** finely made or done **2 :** very pleasing (as through beauty or fitness) **3 :** very severe **:** INTENSE

ex·tend *vb* **1 :** 1STRETCH 2 **2 :** to hold out **3 :** to make longer **4 :** ENLARGE **5 :** to stretch out or across something

ex·ten·sion *n* **1 :** a stretching out **:** an increase in length or time **2 :** a part forming an addition or enlargement

ex·ten·sive *adj* **:** having wide extent **:** BROAD

ex·tent *n* **1 :** the distance or range over which something extends **2 :** the point, degree, or limit to which something extends

1ex·te·ri·or *adj* **:** EXTERNAL

2exterior *n* **:** an exterior part or surface

ex·ter·mi·nate *vb* **ex·ter·mi·nat·ed; ex·ter·mi·nat·ing** **:** to get rid of completely **:** wipe out

1ex·ter·nal *adj* **:** situated on or relating to the outside **:** OUTSIDE

2external *n* **:** something that is external

ex·tinct *adj* **1 :** no longer active **2 :** no longer existing

ex·tinc·tion *n* **1 :** an act of extinguishing or an instance of being extinguished **2 :** the state of being extinct

ex·tin·guish *vb* **1 :** to cause to stop burning **2 :** to cause to die out **:** DESTROY — **ex·tin·guish·er** *n*

ex·tol *vb* **ex·tolled; ex·tol·ling** **:** to praise highly **:** GLORIFY

1ex·tra *adj* **:** being more than what is usual, expected, or due

2extra *n* **1 :** something extra **2 :** an added charge **3 :** a special edition of a newspaper **4 :** a person hired for a group scene (as in a movie)

3extra *adv* **:** beyond the usual size, amount, or degree

extra- *prefix* **:** outside **:** beyond

1ex·tract *vb* **1 :** to remove by pulling **2 :** to get out by pressing, distilling, or by a chemical process **3 :** to choose and take out for separate use

2ex·tract *n* **1 :** a selection from a writing **2 :** a product obtained by extraction

ex·trac·tion *n* **1 :** an act of extracting **2 :** ORIGIN 1, DESCENT
ex·tra·cur·ric·u·lar *adj* **:** of or relating to those activities (as athletics) that are offered by a school but are not part of the course of study
ex·traor·di·nary *adj* **:** so unusual as to be remarkable — **ex·traor·di·nari·ly** *adv*
ex·trav·a·gance *n* **1 :** the wasteful or careless spending of money **2 :** something that is extravagant **3 :** the quality or fact of being extravagant
ex·trav·a·gant *adj* **1 :** going beyond what is reasonable or suitable **2 :** wasteful especially of money — **ex·trav·a·gant·ly** *adv*
1ex·treme *adj* **1 :** existing to a very great degree **2 :** farthest from a center — **ex·treme·ly** *adv*
2extreme *n* **1 :** something as far as possible from a center or from its opposite **2 :** the greatest possible degree **:** MAXIMUM
ex·trem·i·ty *n, pl* **ex·trem·i·ties** **1 :** the farthest limit, point, or part **2 :** an end part of a limb of the body (as a foot) **3 :** an extreme degree (as of emotion or distress)
ex·tri·cate *vb* **ex·tri·cat·ed; ex·tri·cat·ing** **:** to free from entanglement or difficulty
ex·ult *vb* **:** to be in high spirits **:** REJOICE
ex·ul·tant *adj* **:** full of or expressing joy or triumph — **ex·ul·tant·ly** *adv*
-ey — see -Y
1eye *n* **1 :** the organ of seeing **2 :** the ability to see **3 :** the ability to recognize **4 :** GLANCE **5 :** close attention **:** WATCH **6 :** JUDGMENT 1 **7 :** something like or suggesting an eye **8 :** the center of something — **eyed** *adj* — **eye·less** *adj*
2eye *vb* **eyed; eye·ing** *or* **ey·ing** **:** to look at **:** watch closely
eye·ball *n* **:** the whole eye
eye·brow *n* **:** the arch or ridge over the eye **:** the hair on the ridge over the eye
eye·drop·per *n* **:** DROPPER 2
eye·glass *n* **1 :** a glass lens used to help one to see clearly **2 eyeglasses** *pl* **:** a pair of glass lenses set in a frame and used to help one to see clearly
eye·lash *n* **:** a single hair of the fringe on the eyelid
eye·let *n* **1 :** a small hole (as in cloth or leather) for a lace or rope **2 :** GROMMET
eye·lid *n* **:** the thin movable cover of an eye
eye·piece *n* **:** the lens or combination of lenses at the eye end of an optical instrument (as a microscope or telescope)
eye·sight *n* **:** 1SIGHT 4, VISION
eye·sore *n* **:** something displeasing to the sight
eye·strain *n* **:** a tired or irritated state of the eyes (as from too much use)
eye·tooth *n, pl* **eye·teeth** **:** a canine tooth of the upper jaw
ey·rie *n* **:** AERIE

F

f *n, pl* **f's** *or* **fs** *often cap* **1 :** the sixth letter of the English alphabet **2 :** a grade that shows a student's work is failing
fa *n* **:** the fourth note of the musical scale
fa·ble *n* **1 :** a story that is not true **2 :** a story in which animals speak and act like people and which is usually meant to teach a lesson
fab·ric *n* **1 :** the basic structure **2 :** CLOTH 1 **3 :** a structural plan or material
fab·u·lous *adj* **1 :** like a fable especially in being marvelous or beyond belief **2 :** told in or based on fable
fa·cade *n* **:** the face or front of a building
1face *n* **1 :** the front part of the head **2 :** an expression of the face **3 :** outward appearance **4 :** GRIMACE **5 :** DIGNITY 1, PRESTIGE **6 :** a front, upper, or outer surface **7 :** one of the flat surfaces that bound a solid
2face *vb* **faced; fac·ing** **1 :** to cover the front or surface of **2 :** to have the front or face toward **3 :** to oppose firmly
fac·et *n* **:** one of the small flat surfaces on a cut gem
fa·ce·tious *adj* **:** intended or trying to be funny
face–to–face *adv or adj* **:** in person
fa·cial *adj* **:** of or relating to the face — **fa·cial·ly** *adv*
fa·cil·i·tate *vb* **fa·cil·i·tat·ed; fa·cil·i·tat·ing** **:** to make easier
fa·cil·i·ty *n, pl* **fa·cil·i·ties** **1 :** freedom from difficulty **2 :** ease in doing something **:** APTITUDE **3 :** something that makes an action, operation, or activity easier
fac·sim·i·le *n* **1 :** an exact copy **2 :** a system of transmitting and reproducing printed matter or pictures by means of signals sent over telephone lines
fact *n* **1 :** something (as an event or an act) that really exists or has occurred **2 :** physical reality or actual experience
1fac·tor *n* **1 :** something that helps produce a result **2 :** any of the numbers that when multiplied together form a product
2factor *vb* **:** to find the factors of a number
fac·to·ry *n, pl* **fac·to·ries** **:** a place where goods are manufactured

fac·tu·al *adj* **:** of, relating to, or based on facts — **fac·tu·al·ly** *adv*

fac·ul·ty *n, pl* **fac·ul·ties 1 :** ability to do something **:** TALENT **2 :** one of the powers of the mind or body **3 :** the teachers in a school or college

fad *n* **:** a way of doing or an interest widely followed for a time

fade *vb* **fad·ed; fad·ing 1 :** to dry up **:** WITHER **2 :** to lose or cause to lose brightness of color **3 :** to grow dim or faint

Fahr·en·heit *adj* **:** relating to or having a temperature scale on which the boiling point of water is at 212 degrees above the zero of the scale and the freezing point is at 32 degrees above zero

[1]fail *vb* **1 :** to lose strength **:** WEAKEN **2 :** to die away **3 :** to stop functioning **4 :** to fall short **5 :** to be or become absent or not enough **6 :** to be unsuccessful **7 :** to become bankrupt **8 :** DISAPPOINT, DESERT **9 :** [1]NEGLECT 2

[2]fail *n* **:** FAILURE 1

fail·ing *n* **:** a slight moral weakness or flaw

fail·ure *n* **1 :** a failing to do or perform **2 :** a state of being unable to work in a normal way **3 :** a lack of success **4 :** BANKRUPTCY **5 :** a falling short **6 :** a breaking down **7 :** a person or thing that has failed

[1]faint *adj* **1 :** lacking courage **:** COWARDLY **2 :** being weak or dizzy and likely to collapse **3 :** lacking strength **:** FEEBLE **4 :** not clear or plain **:** DIM — **faint·ly** *adv* — **faint·ness** *n*

[2]faint *vb* **:** to lose consciousness

[3]faint *n* **:** an act or condition of fainting

faint·heart·ed *adj* **:** TIMID

[1]fair *adj* **1 :** attractive in appearance **:** BEAUTIFUL **2 :** not stormy or cloudy **3 :** not favoring one over another **4 :** observing the rules **5 :** being within the foul lines **6 :** not dark **:** BLOND **7 :** neither good nor bad — **fair·ness** *n*

[2]fair *adv* **:** in a fair manner

[3]fair *n* **1 :** a gathering of buyers and sellers at a certain time and place for trade **2 :** an exhibition (as of livestock or farm products) usually along with entertainment and amusements **3 :** a sale of articles for a charitable purpose

fair·ground *n* **:** an area set aside for fairs, circuses, or exhibitions

fair·ly *adv* **1 :** in a manner of speaking **:** QUITE **2 :** in a fair manner **:** JUSTLY **3 :** for the most part **:** RATHER

[1]fairy *n, pl* **fair·ies :** an imaginary being who has the form of a very tiny human being and has magic powers

[2]fairy *adj* **:** of, relating to, or like a fairy

fairy·land *n* **1 :** the land of fairies **2 :** a place of delicate beauty or magical charm

fairy tale *n* **1 :** a story about fairies **2 :** a small lie **:** FIB

faith *n* **1 :** loyalty to duty or to a person **2 :** belief in God **3 :** firm belief even in the absence of proof **4 :** a system of religious beliefs **:** RELIGION

faith·ful *adj* **1 :** RELIABLE **2 :** firm in devotion or support **3 :** true to the facts **:** ACCURATE — **faith·ful·ly** *adv* — **faith·ful·ness** *n*

faith·less *adj* **:** not true to allegiance or duty — **faith·less·ly** *adv* — **faith·less·ness** *n*

[1]fake *adj* **:** [1]COUNTERFEIT

[2]fake *n* **:** a person or thing that is not really what is pretended

[3]fake *vb* **faked; fak·ing 1 :** to change or treat in a way that gives a false effect **2 :** [2]COUNTERFEIT 2 **3 :** PRETEND 1

fal·con *n* **1 :** a hawk trained for use in hunting small game **2 :** any of several small hawks with long wings and swift flight

fal·con·ry *n* **:** the art or sport of hunting with a falcon

[1]fall *vb* **fell; fall·en; fall·ing 1 :** to come or go down freely by the force of gravity **2 :** to come as if by falling **3 :** to become lower (as in degree or value) **4 :** to topple from an upright position **5 :** to collapse wounded or dead **6 :** to become captured **7 :** to occur at a certain time **8 :** to pass from one condition of body or mind to another — **fall short :** be lacking in something

[2]fall *n* **1 :** the act or an instance of falling **2 :** AUTUMN **3 :** a thing or quantity that falls **4 :** a loss of greatness **:** DOWNFALL **5 :** WATERFALL — usually used in pl. **6 :** a decrease in size, amount, or value **7 :** the distance something falls

fal·la·cy *n, pl* **fal·la·cies 1 :** a false or mistaken idea **2 :** false reasoning

fall back *vb* **:** [2]RETREAT

fall·out *n* **:** the usually radioactive particles falling through the atmosphere as a result of the explosion of an atomic bomb

fall out *vb* **:** [2]QUARREL 2

[1]fal·low *n* **:** land for crops that lies idle

[2]fallow *vb* **:** to till without planting a crop

[3]fallow *adj* **:** not tilled or planted

fallow deer *n* **:** a small European deer with broad antlers and a pale yellowish coat spotted with white in summer

[1]false *adj* **fals·er; fals·est 1 :** not true, genuine, or honest **2 :** not faithful or loyal **3 :** not based on facts or sound judgment — **false·ly** *adv* — **false·ness** *n*

[2]false *adv* **:** in a false or misleading manner

false·hood *n* **1 :** [3]LIE **2 :** the habit of lying

fal·si·fy *vb* **fal·si·fied; fal·si·fy·ing :** to make false

fal·si·ty *n, pl* **fal·si·ties** **1 :** something false **2 :** the quality or state of being false

fal·ter *vb* **1 :** to move unsteadily **:** WAVER **2 :** to hesitate in speech **3 :** to hesitate in purpose or action

fame *n* **:** the fact or condition of being known to and usually thought well of by the public **:** RENOWN

famed *adj* **:** known widely and well **:** FAMOUS

fa·mil·ial *adj* **:** of, relating to, or typical of a family

fa·mil·iar *adj* **1 :** closely acquainted **:** INTIMATE **2 :** INFORMAL 1 **3 :** too friendly or bold **4 :** often seen or experienced **5 :** having a good knowledge of

fa·mil·iar·i·ty *n, pl* **fa·mil·iar·i·ties** **1 :** close friendship **:** INTIMACY **2 :** good knowledge of something **3 :** INFORMALITY 1

fa·mil·iar·ize *vb* **fa·mil·iar·ized; fa·mil·iar·iz·ing :** to make familiar

fam·i·ly *n, pl* **fam·i·lies** **1 :** a group of persons who come from the same ancestor **2 :** a group of persons living under one roof or one head **3 :** a group of things sharing certain characteristics **4 :** a social group made up of parents and their children **5 :** a group of related plants or animals that ranks above the genus and below the order in scientific classification

fam·ine *n* **1 :** a very great and general lack of food **2 :** a great shortage

fam·ish *vb* **:** to suffer from hunger **:** STARVE

fam·ished *adj* **:** very hungry

fa·mous *adj* **:** very well-known

fa·mous·ly *adv* **:** very well

1fan *n* **1 :** something (as a hand-waved semicircular device or a mechanism with rotating blades) for producing a current of air **2 :** something like a fan — **fan·like** *adj*

2fan *vb* **fanned; fan·ning** **1 :** to move air with a fan **2 :** to direct a current of air upon with a fan

3fan *n* **:** an enthusiastic follower or admirer

1fa·nat·ic *adj* **:** too enthusiastic or devoted

2fanatic *n* **:** a fanatic person

fan·ci·ful *adj* **1 :** showing free use of the imagination **2 :** coming from fancy rather than reason — **fan·ci·ful·ly** *adv* — **fan·ci·ful·ness** *n*

1fan·cy *vb* **fan·cied; fan·cy·ing** **1 :** 1LIKE 1, ENJOY **2 :** IMAGINE 1

2fancy *n, pl* **fancies** **1 :** the power of the mind to think of things that are not present or real **:** IMAGINATION **2 :** LIKING **3 :** IDEA 2, NOTION

3fancy *adj* **fan·ci·er; fan·ci·est** **1 :** not plain or ordinary **2 :** being above the average (as in quality or price) **3 :** done with great skill and grace — **fan·ci·ly** *adv* — **fan·ci·ness** *n*

fang *n* **1 :** a long sharp tooth by which animals seize and hold their prey **2 :** one of the usually two long hollow or grooved teeth by which a poisonous snake injects its poison — **fanged** *adj*

fan·tas·tic *adj* **1 :** produced by or like something produced by the fancy **2 :** barely believable — **fan·tas·ti·cal·ly** *adv*

fan·ta·sy *or* **phan·ta·sy** *n, pl* **fan·ta·sies** *or* **phan·ta·sies** **1 :** IMAGINATION 1 **2 :** something produced by the imagination

1far *adv* **far·ther** *or* **fur·ther; far·thest** *or* **fur·thest** **1 :** at or to a great distance in space or time **2 :** to a great extent **:** MUCH **3 :** to or at a definite distance or point **4 :** to an advanced point

2far *adj* **far·ther** *or* **fur·ther; far·thest** *or* **fur·thest** **1 :** very distant in space or time **2 :** LONG 3 **3 :** the more distant of two

far·away *adj* **1 :** REMOTE 1, DISTANT **2 :** PREOCCUPIED

1fare *vb* **fared; far·ing :** to get along **:** SUCCEED

2fare *n* **1 :** the money a person pays to travel (as on a bus) **2 :** a person paying a fare **3 :** FOOD 1

1fare·well *n* **:** an expression of good wishes at parting — often used as an interjection

2fare·well *adj* **:** of or relating to a time or act of leaving **:** FINAL

far·fetched *adj* **:** not likely to be true

1farm *n* **1 :** a piece of land used for raising crops or animals **2 :** an area of water where fish or shellfish are grown

2farm *vb* **:** to work on or run a farm — **farm·er** *n*

farm·hand *n* **:** a farm laborer

farm·house *n* **:** the dwelling house of a farm

farm·yard *n* **:** the yard around or enclosed by farm buildings

far–off *adj* **:** distant in time or space

far–reach·ing *adj* **:** EXTENSIVE

far·sight·ed *adj* **1 :** able to see distant things more clearly than near ones **2 :** able to judge how something will work out in the future — **far·sight·ed·ness** *n*

1far·ther *adv* **1 :** at or to a greater distance or more advanced point **2 :** 2BESIDES

2farther *adj* **:** more distant

1far·thest *adj* **:** most distant

2farthest *adv* **1 :** to or at the greatest distance in space or time **2 :** to the most advanced point

fas·ci·nate *vb* **fas·ci·nat·ed; fas·ci·nat·ing** **1 :** to seize and hold the attention of **2 :** to attract greatly

fas·ci·na·tion *n* **:** the state of being fascinated

DICTIONARY

fas·cism *n* **:** a political system headed by a dictator in which the government controls business and labor and opposition is not permitted

fas·cist *n, often cap* **:** one who approves of or practices fascism

¹fash·ion *n* **1 :** the make or form of something **2 :** MANNER 2, WAY **3 :** the popular style of a thing at a certain time

²fashion *vb* **:** to give shape or form to **:** MOLD

fash·ion·able *adj* **:** following the fashion or established style — **fash·ion·ably** *adv*

¹fast *adj* **1 :** firmly placed **2 :** totally loyal **3 :** moving, operating, or acting quickly **4 :** taking a short time **5 :** indicating ahead of the correct time **6 :** not likely to fade

²fast *adv* **1 :** in a fast or fixed way **2 :** to the full extent **:** SOUND **3 :** with great speed

³fast *vb* **1 :** to go without eating **2 :** to eat in small amounts or only certain foods

⁴fast *n* **1 :** the act of fasting **2 :** a period of fasting

fas·ten *vb* **1 :** to attach or join by or as if by pinning, tying, or nailing **2 :** to fix firmly **3 :** to become fixed or joined — **fas·ten·er** *n*

fas·ten·ing *n* **:** something that holds another thing shut or in the right position

fast–food *adj* **:** of, relating to, or specializing in food that can be prepared and served quickly — **fast–food** *n*

fas·tid·i·ous *adj* **:** hard to please **:** very particular

¹fat *adj* **fat·ter; fat·test 1 :** having much body fat **2 :** ¹THICK 1 **3 :** richly rewarding or profitable **4 :** swollen up — **fat·ness** *n*

²fat *n* **1 :** animal or plant tissue containing much greasy or oily material **2 :** any of numerous compounds of carbon, hydrogen, and oxygen that make up most of animal or plant fat and that are important to nutrition as sources of energy **3 :** a solid fat as distinguished from an oil **4 :** the best or richest part

fa·tal *adj* **1 :** FATEFUL **2 :** causing death **:** MORTAL — **fa·tal·ly** *adv*

fa·tal·i·ty *n, pl* **fa·tal·i·ties :** a death resulting from a disaster or accident

fate *n* **1 :** a power beyond human control that is held to determine what happens **:** DESTINY **2 :** something that happens as though determined by fate **:** FORTUNE **3 :** final outcome

fate·ful *adj* **:** having serious results — **fate·ful·ly** *adv* — **fate·ful·ness** *n*

¹fa·ther *n* **1 :** a male parent **2** *cap* **:** GOD 1 **3 :** ANCESTOR **4 :** one who cares for another as a father might **5 :** one deserving the respect and love given to a father **6 :** a person who invents or begins something **7 :** PRIEST — used especially as a title — **fa·ther·hood** *n* — **fa·ther·less** *adj*

²father *vb* **1 :** to become the father of **2 :** to care for as a father

fa·ther–in–law *n, pl* **fa·thers–in–law :** the father of one's husband or wife

fa·ther·land *n* **:** one's native land

fa·ther·ly *adj* **1 :** of or like a father **2 :** showing the affection or concern of a father

¹fath·om *n* **:** a unit of length equal to six feet (about 1.8 meters) used chiefly in measuring the depth of water

²fathom *vb* **1 :** to measure the depth of water by means of a special line **2 :** to see into and come to understand

¹fa·tigue *n* **:** a state of being very tired

²fatigue *vb* **fa·tigued; fa·tigu·ing :** to tire by work or exertion

fat·ten *vb* **:** to make or become fat

fat·ty *adj* **fat·ti·er; fat·ti·est :** containing or like fat

fau·cet *n* **:** a fixture for controlling the flow of a liquid (as from a pipe or cask)

fault *n* **1 :** a weakness in character **:** FAILING **2 :** FLAW, IMPERFECTION **3 :** ERROR **4 :** responsibility for something wrong **5 :** a crack in the earth's crust along which movement occurs — **at fault :** BLAMEWORTHY

fault·less *adj* **:** free from fault **:** PERFECT — **fault·less·ly** *adv* — **fault·less·ness** *n*

faulty *adj* **fault·i·er; fault·i·est :** having a fault or blemish **:** IMPERFECT — **fault·i·ly** *adv* — **fault·i·ness** *n*

faun *n* **:** a Roman god of country life represented as part goat and part man

fau·na *n* **:** the animal life typical of a region, period, or special environment

¹fa·vor *n* **1 :** APPROVAL, LIKING **2 :** a preferring of one side over another **:** PARTIALITY **3 :** an act of kindness **4 :** a small gift or decorative item

²favor *vb* **1 :** to regard with favor **2 :** OBLIGE 3 **3 :** to prefer especially unfairly **4 :** to make possible or easier **5 :** to look like

fa·vor·able *adj* **1 :** showing favor **2 :** PROMISING — **fa·vor·able·ness** *n* — **fa·vor·ably** *adv*

¹fa·vor·ite *n* **:** a person or a thing that is favored above others

²favorite *adj* **:** being a favorite

¹fawn *vb* **1 :** to show affection — used especially of a dog **2 :** to try to win favor by behavior that shows lack of self-respect

²fawn *n* **1 :** a young deer **2 :** a light grayish brown

¹fax *n* **1 :** FACSIMILE 2 **2 :** a machine used

to send or receive material by facsimile **3** **:** something sent or received by facsimile
[2]**fax** *vb* **:** to send material by facsimile
faze *vb* **fazed; faz•ing :** DAUNT
[1]**fear** *vb* **:** to be afraid of **:** feel fear
[2]**fear** *n* **:** a strong unpleasant feeling caused by being aware of danger or expecting something bad to happen
fear•ful *adj* **1 :** causing fear **2 :** filled with fear **3 :** showing or caused by fear — **fear•ful•ly** *adv* — **fear•ful•ness** *n*
fear•less *adj* **:** free from fear **:** BRAVE — **fear•less•ly** *adv* — **fear•less•ness** *n*
fear•some *adj* **:** causing fear
fea•si•ble *adj* **:** possible to do or carry out
[1]**feast** *n* **1 :** a fancy meal **2 :** a religious festival
[2]**feast** *vb* **1 :** to eat well **2 :** [2]DELIGHT 1
feat *n* **:** an act showing courage, strength, or skill
[1]**feath•er** *n* **1 :** one of the light horny growths that make up the outer covering of a bird **2 :** VARIETY 3, SORT — **feath•ered** *adj* — **feath•er•less** *adj*
[2]**feather** *vb* **:** to grow or form feathers
feather bed *n* **1 :** a mattress filled with feathers **2 :** a bed with a feather mattress
feath•ery *adj* **1 :** like a feather or tuft of feathers **2 :** covered with feathers
[1]**fea•ture** *n* **1 :** a single part (as the nose or the mouth) of the face **2 :** something especially noticeable **3 :** a main attraction **4 :** a special story in a newspaper or magazine
[2]**feature** *vb* **fea•tured; fea•tur•ing :** to stand out or cause to stand out
Feb•ru•ary *n* **:** the second month of the year
fe•ces *n pl* **:** body waste that passes out from the intestine
fed•er•al *adj* **:** of or relating to a nation formed by the union of several states or nations
fee *n* **1 :** a fixed charge **2 :** a charge for services
fee•ble *adj* **fee•bler; fee•blest 1 :** lacking in strength or endurance **2 :** not loud — **fee•ble•ness** *n* — **fee•bly** *adv*
[1]**feed** *vb* **fed; feed•ing 1 :** to give food to or give as food **2 :** to take food into the body **:** EAT **3 :** to supply with something necessary (as to growth or operation) — **feed•er** *n*
[2]**feed** *n* **:** food especially for livestock
[1]**feel** *vb* **felt; feel•ing 1 :** to be aware of through physical contact **2 :** to examine or test by touching **3 :** to be conscious of **4 :** to seem especially to the touch **5 :** to sense oneself to be
[2]**feel** *n* **1 :** SENSATION 2, FEELING **2 :** the quality of something as learned through or as if through touch
feel•er *n* **1 :** a long flexible structure (as an insect's antenna) that is an organ of touch **2 :** a suggestion or remark made to find out the views of other people
feel•ing *n* **1 :** the sense by which a person knows whether things are hard or soft, hot or cold, heavy or light **2 :** a sensation of temperature or pressure **3 :** a state of mind **4 feelings** *pl* **:** the state of a person's emotions **5 :** the condition of being aware **6 :** IMPRESSION 4
feet *pl of* FOOT
feign *vb* **:** PRETEND 2
[1]**feint** *n* **:** a pretended blow or attack at one point or in one direction to take attention away from the point or direction one really intends to attack
[2]**feint** *vb* **:** to make a feint
[1]**fe•line** *adj* **1 :** of or relating to cats or the cat family **2 :** like or like that of a cat
[2]**feline** *n* **:** a feline animal **:** CAT
[1]**fell** *vb* **:** to cut or knock down
[2]**fell** *past of* FALL
[1]**fel•low** *n* **1 :** COMPANION 1, COMRADE **2 :** an equal in rank, power, or character **3 :** one of a pair **:** MATE **4 :** a male person
[2]**fellow** *adj* **:** being a companion, mate, or equal
fel•low•man *n, pl* **fel•low•men :** a fellow human being
fel•low•ship *n* **1 :** friendly relationship existing among persons **2 :** a group with similar interests
fel•on *n* **:** [2]CRIMINAL
fel•o•ny *n, pl* **fel•o•nies :** a very serious crime
[1]**felt** *n* **:** a heavy material made by rolling and pressing fibers together
[2]**felt** *past of* FEEL
[1]**fe•male** *adj* **1 :** of, relating to, or being the sex that bears young or lays eggs **2 :** having a pistil but no stamens **3 :** of, relating to, or characteristic of females — **fe•male•ness** *n*
[2]**female** *n* **:** a female being
fem•i•nine *adj* **1 :** [1]FEMALE 1 **2 :** [1]FEMALE 3
fem•i•nism *n* **1 :** the theory that women and men should have equal rights and opportunities **2 :** organized activity on behalf of women's rights and interests — **fem•i•nist** *n or adj*
fen *n* **:** low land covered by water
[1]**fence** *n* **:** a barrier (as of wood or wire) to prevent escape or entry or to mark a boundary
[2]**fence** *vb* **fenced; fenc•ing 1 :** to enclose with a fence **2 :** to practice fencing — **fenc•er** *n*
fenc•ing *n* **:** the sport of having a pretended fight with blunted swords
fend *vb* **1 :** REPEL 1 **2 :** to try to get along without help

fend·er *n* **1 :** a frame on the lower front of a locomotive or streetcar to catch or throw off anything that is hit **2 :** a guard over an automobile or cycle wheel
1fer·ment *vb* **:** to undergo or cause to undergo fermentation
2fer·ment *n* **1 :** something (as yeast) that causes fermentation **2 :** a state of excitement
fer·men·ta·tion *n* **:** a chemical breaking down of an organic material that is controlled by an enzyme and usually does not require oxygen
fern *n* **:** a plant that produces spores instead of seeds and no flowers and whose leaves are usually divided into many parts — **fern-like** *adj*
fe·ro·cious *adj* **:** FIERCE 1, SAVAGE — **fe·ro·cious·ly** *adv* — **fe·ro·cious·ness** *n*
fe·roc·i·ty *n, pl* **fe·roc·i·ties :** the quality or state of being ferocious
1fer·ret *n* **:** a domesticated animal with usually white or light brown or gray fur that is descended from the European polecat
2ferret *vb* **1 :** to hunt with a ferret **2 :** to find by eager searching
Fer·ris wheel *n* **:** an amusement device consisting of a large vertical wheel that is driven by a motor and has seats around its rim
1fer·ry *vb* **fer·ried; fer·ry·ing 1 :** to carry by boat over a body of water **2 :** to cross by a ferry **3 :** to deliver an airplane under its own power **4 :** to transport in an airplane
2ferry *n, pl* **fer·ries 1 :** a place where persons or things are ferried **2 :** FERRYBOAT
fer·ry·boat *n* **:** a boat used to ferry passengers, vehicles, or goods
fer·tile *adj* **1 :** producing much vegetation or large crops **2 :** capable of developing and growing
fer·til·i·ty *n* **:** the condition of being fertile
fer·til·iza·tion *n* **1 :** an act or process of making fertile **2 :** the joining of an egg cell and a sperm cell to form the first stage of an embryo
fer·til·ize *vb* **fer·til·ized; fer·til·iz·ing :** to make fertile or more fertile
fer·til·iz·er *n* **:** material added to soil to make it more fertile
fer·vent *adj* **:** very warm in feeling **:** ARDENT — **fer·vent·ly** *adv*
fer·vor *n* **:** strong feeling or expression
fes·ter *vb* **:** to become painfully red and sore and usually full of pus
fes·ti·val *n* **1 :** a time of celebration **2 :** a program of cultural events or entertainment
fes·tive *adj* **1 :** having to do with a feast or festival **2 :** very merry and joyful
fes·tiv·i·ty *n, pl* **fes·tiv·i·ties 1 :** a festive state **2 :** festive activity **:** MERRYMAKING
1fes·toon *n* **:** an ornament (as a chain) hanging between two points
2festoon *vb* **:** to hang or form festoons on
fetch *vb* **1 :** to go after and bring back **2 :** to bring as a price **:** sell for
fetch·ing *adj* **:** very attractive — **fetch·ing·ly** *adv*
1fet·ter *n* **1 :** a shackle for the feet **2 :** something that holds back **:** RESTRAINT
2fetter *vb* **1 :** to put fetters on **2 :** to keep from moving or acting freely
fe·tus *n* **:** an animal not yet born or hatched but more developed than an embryo
1feud *n* **:** a long bitter quarrel carried on especially between families or clans and usually having acts of violence and revenge
2feud *vb* **:** to carry on a feud
feu·dal *adj* **:** of or relating to feudalism
feu·dal·ism *n* **:** a system of social organization existing in medieval Europe in which a vassal served a lord and received protection and land in return
fe·ver *n* **1 :** a rise of body temperature above normal **2 :** a disease in which fever is present
fe·ver·ish *adj* **1 :** having a fever **2 :** of, relating to, or being fever **3 :** showing great emotion or activity **:** HECTIC — **fe·ver·ish·ly** *adv* — **fe·ver·ish·ness** *n*
1few *pron* **:** not many **:** a small number
2few *adj* **:** not many but some
3few *n* **:** a small number of individuals
fez *n, pl* **fez·zes :** a round red felt hat that usually has a tassel but no brim
fi·as·co *n, pl* **fi·as·coes :** a complete failure
1fib *n* **:** an unimportant lie
2fib *vb* **fibbed; fib·bing :** to tell a fib — **fib·ber** *n*
fi·ber *or* **fi·bre** *n* **:** a long slender threadlike structure
fi·ber·glass *also* **fi·bre·glass** *n* **1 :** glass in the form of fibers used in various products (as filters and insulation) **2 :** a material of plastic and fiberglass
fiber op·tics *n pl* **:** thin transparent fibers of glass or plastic that transmit light throughout their length
fi·brous *adj* **:** containing, consisting of, or like fibers
-fi·ca·tion *n suffix* **:** the act or process of or the result of
fick·le *adj* **:** INCONSTANT — **fick·le·ness** *n*
fic·tion *n* **1 :** something told or written that is not fact **2 :** a made-up story
fic·tion·al *adj* **:** of, relating to, or suggesting fiction — **fic·tion·al·ly** *adv*
fic·ti·tious *adj* **:** not real
1fid·dle *n* **:** VIOLIN

2fiddle *vb* **fid·dled; fid·dling** **1 :** to play on a fiddle **2 :** to move the hands or fingers restlessly **3 :** to spend time in aimless activity **4 :** TAMPER — **fid·dler** *n*

fid·dle·sticks *n* **:** NONSENSE 1 — used as an interjection

fi·del·i·ty *n* **1 :** LOYALTY **2 :** ACCURACY

fidg·et *vb* **:** to move in a restless or nervous way

fidg·ets *n pl* **:** uneasy restlessness shown by nervous movements

fidg·ety *adj* **:** tending to fidget

fief *n* **:** an estate given to a vassal by a feudal lord

1field *n* **1 :** a piece of open, cleared, or cultivated land **2 :** a piece of land put to a special use or giving a special product **3 :** an open space **4 :** an area of activity or influence **5 :** a background on which something is drawn, painted, or mounted

2field *adj* **:** of or relating to a field

3field *vb* **:** to catch or stop and throw a ball

field·er *n* **:** a baseball player other than the pitcher or catcher on the team that is not at bat

field glasses *n pl* **:** a hand-held instrument for seeing at a distance that is made up of two telescopes usually without prisms

field goal *n* **:** a score in football made by kicking the ball through the goal during ordinary play

fiend *n* **1 :** DEMON 1, DEVIL **2 :** a very wicked or cruel person — **fiend·ish** *adj*

fierce *adj* **fierc·er; fierc·est** **1 :** likely to attack **2 :** having or showing very great energy or enthusiasm **3 :** wild or threatening in appearance — **fierce·ly** *adv* — **fierce·ness** *n*

fi·ery *adj* **fi·er·i·er; fi·er·i·est** **1 :** being on fire **2 :** hot like a fire **3 :** full of spirit

fi·es·ta *n* **:** FESTIVAL 1, CELEBRATION

fife *n* **:** a small musical instrument like a flute that produces a shrill sound

1fif·teen *adj* **:** being one more than fourteen

2fifteen *n* **:** one more than fourteen **:** three times five **:** 15

1fif·teenth *adj* **:** coming right after fourteenth

2fifteenth *n* **:** number fifteen in a series

1fifth *adj* **:** coming right after fourth

2fifth *n* **1 :** number five in a series **2 :** one of five equal parts

1fif·ti·eth *adj* **:** coming right after forty-ninth

2fiftieth *n* **:** number fifty in a series

1fif·ty *adj* **:** being five times ten

2fifty *n* **:** five times ten **:** 50

fig *n* **:** an edible fruit that is oblong or shaped like a pear and that grows on a tree related to the mulberry

1fight *vb* **fought; fight·ing** **1 :** to take part in a fight **:** COMBAT **2 :** to try hard **3 :** to struggle against — **fight·er** *n*

2fight *n* **1 :** a meeting in battle or in physical combat **2 :** 1QUARREL 2 **3 :** strength or desire for fighting

1fig·ure *n* **1 :** a symbol (as 1, 2, 3) that stands for a number **:** NUMERAL **2 figures** *pl* **:** ARITHMETIC 2 **3 :** value or price expressed in figures **4 :** the shape or outline of something **5 :** the shape of the body especially of a person **6 :** an illustration in a printed text **7 :** 1PATTERN 3 **8 :** a series of movements in a dance **9 :** an outline traced by a series of movements (as by an ice skater) **10 :** a well-known or important person

2figure *vb* **fig·ured; fig·ur·ing** **1 :** to decorate with a pattern **2 :** CALCULATE 1

fig·ure·head *n* **:** a figure, statue, or bust on the bow of a ship

figure of speech : an expression (as a simile or a metaphor) that uses words in other than a plain or literal way

figure out *vb* **:** to work out in the mind

fil·a·ment *n* **1 :** a fine thread **2 :** a fine wire (as in a light bulb) that is made to glow by the passage of an electric current **3 :** the stalk of a plant stamen that bears the anther — **fil·a·men·tous** *adj*

fil·bert *n* **:** the hazel or its nut

filch *vb* **:** PILFER

1file *n* **:** a steel tool with sharp ridges or teeth for smoothing or rubbing down hard substances

2file *vb* **filed; fil·ing :** to rub, smooth, or cut away with a file

3file *vb* **filed; fil·ing** **1 :** to arrange in order **2 :** to enter or record officially

4file *n* **1 :** a device for keeping papers or records **2 :** a collection of papers or records kept in a file **3 :** a collection of data treated as a unit by a computer

5file *n* **:** a row of persons or things arranged one behind the other

6file *vb* **filed; fil·ing :** to move in a file

fil·ial *adj* **1 :** of, relating to, or suitable for a son or daughter **2 :** being or having the relation of offspring

1fill *vb* **1 :** to make or become full **2 :** to occupy fully **3 :** to spread through **4 :** to stop up **:** PLUG **5 :** to write information on or in **:** COMPLETE **6 :** to do the duties of **7 :** to supply according to directions

2fill *n* **1 :** an amount that satisfies **2 :** material for filling something

fill·er *n* **1 :** one that fills **2 :** a material used for filling

fil·let *n* **:** a piece of lean boneless meat or fish

fill·ing *n* **:** a substance used to fill something else

filling station *n* **:** SERVICE STATION

fil·ly *n, pl* **fillies :** a female foal **:** a young female horse

1film *n* **1 :** a thin coating or layer **2 :** a roll of material prepared for taking pictures **3 :** MOVIE

2film *vb* **1 :** to cover or become covered with film **2 :** to photograph on a film **3 :** to make a movie

film·strip *n* **:** a strip of film for projecting still pictures on a screen

filmy *adj* **film·i·er; film·i·est :** of, like, or made of film

1fil·ter *n* **1 :** a device or a mass of material (as sand) with tiny openings through which a gas or liquid is passed to separate out something which it contains **2 :** a transparent material that absorbs light of some colors and is used for changing light (as in photography)

2filter *vb* **1 :** to pass through a filter **2 :** to remove by means of a filter

filth *n* **:** disgusting dirt

filthy *adj* **filth·i·er; filth·i·est :** disgustingly dirty — **filth·i·ness** *n*

fil·tra·tion *n* **:** the process of filtering

fin *n* **1 :** any of the thin parts that stick out from the body of a water animal and especially a fish and are used in moving or guiding the body through the water **2 :** something shaped like a fin

1fi·nal *adj* **1 :** not to be changed **:** CONCLUSIVE **2 :** coming or happening at the end — **fi·nal·ly** *adv*

2final *n* **1 :** the last match or game of a tournament **2 :** a final examination in a course

fi·na·le *n* **:** the close or end of something (as a musical work)

fi·nal·i·ty *n* **:** the condition of being final

1fi·nance *n* **1 finances** *pl* **:** money available to a government, business, or individual **2 :** the system that includes the circulation of money, the providing of banks and credit, and the making of investments

2finance *vb* **fi·nanced; fi·nanc·ing :** to provide money for

fi·nan·cial *adj* **:** having to do with finance or with finances — **fi·nan·cial·ly** *adv*

fin·an·cier *n* **:** a specialist in finance and especially in the financing of businesses

finch *n* **:** a small songbird (as a sparrow, bunting, or canary) that eats seeds

1find *vb* **found; find·ing 1 :** to come upon by chance **2 :** to come upon by searching, study, or effort **3 :** to decide on **4 :** to know by experience **5 :** to gain or regain the use of — **find fault :** to criticize in an unfavorable way

2find *n* **:** something found

find·er *n* **1 :** one that finds **2 :** a device on a camera that shows the view being photographed

find out *vb* **:** to learn by studying or watching **:** DISCOVER

1fine *n* **:** a sum of money to be paid as a punishment

2fine *vb* **fined; fin·ing :** to punish by a fine

3fine *adj* **fin·er; fin·est 1 :** very small or thin **2 :** not coarse **3 :** very good in quality or appearance — **fine·ly** *adv* — **fine·ness** *n*

4fine *adv* **:** very well

fin·ery *n, pl* **fin·er·ies :** stylish or showy clothes and jewelry

1fin·ger *n* **1 :** one of the five divisions of the end of the hand including the thumb **2 :** something that is like or does the work of a finger **3 :** the part of a glove into which a finger goes — **fin·ger·like** *adj*

2finger *vb* **:** to touch with the fingers **:** HANDLE

fin·ger·board *n* **:** a strip on the neck of a stringed instrument (as a guitar) against which the fingers press the strings to change the pitch

finger hole *n* **:** any of a group of holes in a wind instrument that may be covered with a finger to change the pitch

fin·ger·ling *n* **:** a young fish

fin·ger·nail *n* **:** the hard covering at the end of a finger

1fin·ger·print *n* **:** the pattern of marks made by pressing a finger on a surface especially when the pattern is made in ink in order to identify a person

2fingerprint *vb* **:** to take the fingerprints of

fin·icky *adj* **:** very hard to please **:** FUSSY — **fin·ick·i·ness** *n*

1fin·ish *vb* **1 :** to bring or come to an end **:** COMPLETE, TERMINATE **2 :** to put a final coat or surface on

2finish *n* **1 :** 1END 2, CONCLUSION **2 :** the final treatment or coating of a surface or the appearance given by finishing

fi·nite *adj* **:** having certain limits

Finn *n* **:** a person born or living in Finland

finned *adj* **:** having fins

1Finn·ish *adj* **:** of or relating to Finland, its people, or the Finnish language

2Finnish *n* **:** the language of the Finns

fiord *variant of* FJORD

fir *n* **:** a tall evergreen tree related to the pine that yields useful lumber

1fire *n* **1 :** the light and heat and especially the flame produced by burning **2 :** fuel that is burning (as in a fireplace or stove) **3 :** the destructive burning of something (as a building or a forest) **4 :** a being lively **:** ENTHUSIASM **5 :** the shooting of firearms — **on fire :** actively burning — **under fire 1**

: exposed to the firing of enemy guns **2** : under attack

[2]**fire** *vb* **fired; fir·ing** **1** : to set on fire **2** : EXCITE 2, STIR **3** : to dismiss from employment **4** : to set off : EXPLODE **5** : [1]SHOOT 2 **6** : to subject to great heat

fire·arm *n* : a small weapon from which shot or a bullet is driven by the explosion of gunpowder

fire·bug *n* : a person who sets destructive fires on purpose

fire·crack·er *n* : a paper tube containing an explosive to be set off for amusement

fire engine *n* : a truck equipped to fight fires

fire escape *n* : a stairway that provides a way of escape from a building in case of fire

fire extinguisher *n* : something (as a metal container filled with chemicals) that is used to put out a fire

fire·fight·er *n* : a person whose job is to put out fires

fire·fly *n, pl* **fire·flies** : a small beetle producing a soft light

fire·house *n* : FIRE STATION

fire·man *n, pl* **fire·men** **1** : FIREFIGHTER **2** : a person who tends a fire (as in a large furnace)

fire·place *n* : a structure with a hearth on which an open fire can be built for heating or especially outdoors for cooking

fire·plug *n* : HYDRANT

fire·proof *adj* : not easily burned : made safe against fire

fire·side *n* **1** : a place near the hearth **2** : [1]HOME 1

fire station *n* : a building housing fire engines and usually firefighters

fire·wood *n* : wood cut for fuel

fire·work *n* **1** : a device that makes a display of light or noise by the burning of explosive or flammable materials **2 fireworks** *pl* : a display of fireworks

[1]**firm** *adj* **1** : STRONG 1, VIGOROUS **2** : having a solid compact texture **3** : not likely to be changed **4** : not easily moved or shaken : FAITHFUL **5** : showing no weakness — **firm·ly** *adv* — **firm·ness** *n*

[2]**firm** *n* : BUSINESS 2

fir·ma·ment *n* : the arch of the sky

[1]**first** *adj* **1** : being number one **2** : coming before all others

[2]**first** *adv* **1** : before any other **2** : for the first time

[3]**first** *n* **1** : number one in a series **2** : something or someone that is first

first aid *n* : care or treatment given to an ill or injured person before regular medical help can be gotten

first·hand *adj or adv* : coming right from the original source

first lieutenant *n* : a commissioned officer in the Army, Air Force, or Marine Corps ranking above a second lieutenant

first–rate *adj* : EXCELLENT

first sergeant *n* **1** : a noncommissioned officer serving as the chief assistant to a military commander **2** : a noncommissioned officer ranking above a sergeant first class in the Army or above a gunnery sergeant in the Marine Corps

firth *n* : a narrow arm of the sea

[1]**fish** *n, pl* **fish** *or* **fish·es** **1** : an animal that lives in water — usually used in combination **2** : any of a large group of vertebrate animals that live in water, breathe with gills, and usually have fins and scales — **fish·like** *adj*

[2]**fish** *vb* **1** : to attempt to catch fish **2** : to try to find or to find out something by groping

fish·er·man *n, pl* **fish·er·men** : a person who fishes

fish·ery *n, pl* **fish·er·ies** **1** : the business of catching fish **2** : a place for catching fish

fish·hook *n* : a hook used for catching fish

fishy *adj* **fish·i·er; fish·i·est** **1** : of or like fish **2** : QUESTIONABLE

fis·sion *n* **1** : a splitting or breaking into parts **2** : a method of reproduction in which a living cell or body divides into two or more parts each of which grows into a whole new individual **3** : the splitting of an atomic nucleus with the release of large amounts of energy

fis·sure *n* : a narrow opening or crack

fist *n* : the hand with the fingers doubled tight into the palm

[1]**fit** *adj* **fit·ter; fit·test** **1** : good enough **2** : healthy in mind and body — **fit·ness** *n*

[2]**fit** *n* : a sudden attack or outburst

[3]**fit** *vb* **fit·ted; fit·ting** **1** : to be suitable for or to **2** : to be the right shape or size **3** : to bring to the right shape or size **4** : EQUIP

[4]**fit** *n* **1** : the way something fits **2** : a piece of clothing that fits

fit·ful *adj* : IRREGULAR 4

[1]**fit·ting** *adj* : [2]APPROPRIATE, SUITABLE — **fit·ting·ly** *adv*

[2]**fitting** *n* : a small accessory part

[1]**five** *adj* : being one more than four

[2]**five** *n* **1** : one more than four : 5 **2** : the fifth in a set or series

[1]**fix** *vb* **1** : to make firm or secure **2** : to cause to combine chemically **3** : to set definitely : ESTABLISH **4** : to get ready : PREPARE **5** : [1]REPAIR 1, MEND — **fix·er** *n*

[2]**fix** *n* : an unpleasant or difficult position

fixed *adj* **1** : not changing : SET **2** : not moving : INTENT — **fix·ed·ly** *adv*

fixed star *n* **:** a star so distant that its motion can be measured only by very careful observations over long periods
fix·ture *n* **:** something attached as a permanent part
[1]**fizz** *vb* **:** to make a hissing or sputtering sound
[2]**fizz** *n* **1 :** a hissing or sputtering sound **2 :** a bubbling drink
[1]**fiz·zle** *vb* **fiz·zled; fiz·zling :** to fail after a good start
[2]**fizzle** *n* **:** FAILURE 3
fjord *or* **fiord** *n* **:** a narrow inlet of the sea between cliffs or steep slopes
flab·by *adj* **flab·bi·er; flab·bi·est :** not hard and firm **:** SOFT — **flab·bi·ness** *n*
[1]**flag** *n* **:** a piece of cloth with a special design or color that is used as a symbol (as of a nation) or as a signal
[2]**flag** *vb* **flagged; flag·ging :** to signal with or as if with a flag
[3]**flag** *vb* **flagged; flag·ging :** to become weak
fla·gel·lum *n, pl* **fla·gel·la :** a long whiplike structure by which some tiny plants and animals move
flag·man *n, pl* **flag·men :** a person who signals with a flag
flag·on *n* **:** a container for liquids usually having a handle, spout, and lid
flag·pole *n* **:** a pole from which a flag flies
fla·grant *adj* **:** so bad as to be impossible to overlook — **fla·grant·ly** *adv*
flag·ship *n* **:** the ship carrying the commander of a group of ships and flying a flag that tells the commander's rank
flag·staff *n, pl* **flag·staffs :** FLAGPOLE
flag·stone *n* **:** a piece of hard flat rock used for paving
[1]**flail** *n* **:** a tool for threshing grain by hand
[2]**flail** *vb* **:** to hit with or as if with a flail
flair *n* **:** natural ability
[1]**flake** *n* **:** a small thin flat piece
[2]**flake** *vb* **flaked; flak·ing :** to form or separate into flakes
flaky *adj* **flak·i·er; flak·i·est :** tending to flake — **flak·i·ness** *n*
flam·boy·ant *adj* **:** liking or making a dashing show — **flam·boy·ant·ly** *adv*
[1]**flame** *n* **1 :** the glowing gas that makes up part of a fire **2 :** a condition or appearance suggesting a flame
[2]**flame** *vb* **flamed; flam·ing :** to burn with or as if with a flame
flame·throw·er *n* **:** a device that shoots a burning stream of fuel
fla·min·go *n, pl* **fla·min·gos** *or* **fla·min·goes :** a waterbird with very long neck and legs, scarlet wings, and a broad bill bent downward at the end
flam·ma·ble *adj* **:** capable of being easily set on fire and of burning quickly
[1]**flank** *n* **1 :** the fleshy part of the side between the ribs and the hip **2 :** [1]SIDE 3 **3 :** the right or left side of a formation (as of soldiers)
[2]**flank** *vb* **1 :** to pass around the flank of **2 :** to be located at the side of **:** BORDER
flank·er *n* **:** a football player stationed wide of the formation
flan·nel *n* **:** a soft cloth made of wool or cotton
[1]**flap** *n* **1 :** something broad and flat or limber that hangs loose **2 :** the motion made by something broad and limber (as a sail or wing) moving back and forth or the sound produced
[2]**flap** *vb* **flapped; flap·ping 1 :** to give a quick light blow **2 :** to move with a beating or fluttering motion
flap·jack *n* **:** PANCAKE
[1]**flare** *vb* **flared; flar·ing 1 :** to burn with an unsteady flame **2 :** to shine with great or sudden light **3 :** to become angry **4 :** to spread outward
[2]**flare** *n* **1 :** a sudden blaze of light **2 :** a blaze of light used to signal, light up something, or attract attention **3 :** a device or material used to produce a flare **4 :** a sudden outburst (as of sound or anger) **5 :** a spreading outward **:** a part that spreads outward
[1]**flash** *vb* **1 :** to shine in or like a sudden flame **2 :** to send out in or as if in flashes **3 :** to come or pass very suddenly **4 :** to make a sudden display (as of feeling)
[2]**flash** *n* **1 :** a sudden burst of or as if of light **2 :** a very short time
[3]**flash** *adj* **:** beginning suddenly and lasting only a short time
flash·light *n* **:** a small portable electric light that runs on batteries
flashy *adj* **flash·i·er; flash·i·est :** GAUDY
flask *n* **:** a container like a bottle with a flat or rounded body
[1]**flat** *adj* **flat·ter; flat·test 1 :** having a smooth level surface **2 :** spread out on or along a surface **3 :** having a broad smooth surface and little thickness **4 :** [2]OUTRIGHT 1, POSITIVE **5 :** FIXED 1 **6 :** having nothing lacking or left over **:** EXACT **7 :** INSIPID **8 :** having lost air pressure **9 :** lower than the true musical pitch **10 :** lower by a half step in music **11 :** free from gloss — **flat·ly** *adv* — **flat·ness** *n*
[2]**flat** *n* **1 :** a level place **:** PLAIN **2 :** a flat part or surface **3 :** a note or tone that is a half step lower than the note named **4 :** a sign ♭ meaning that the pitch of a musical

note is to be lower by a half step **5 :** a deflated tire

[3]**flat** *adv* **1 :** on or against a flat surface **2 :** below the true musical pitch

[4]**flat** *n* **:** an apartment on one floor

flat·boat *n* **:** a large boat with a flat bottom and square ends

flat·fish *n* **:** a fish (as the flounder) that swims on its side and has both eyes on the upper side

flat·iron *n* **:** [1]IRON

flat·ten *vb* **:** to make or become flat

flat·ter *vb* **1 :** to praise but not sincerely **2 :** to show too favorably — **flat·ter·er** *n* — **flat·ter·ing·ly** *adv*

flat·tery *n, pl* **flat·ter·ies :** praise that is not deserved or meant

flaunt *vb* **1 :** to wave or flutter in a showy way **2 :** to make too much show of **:** PARADE

[1]**fla·vor** *n* **1 :** the quality of something that affects the sense of taste **2 :** a substance added to food to give it a desired taste — **fla·vored** *adj*

[2]**flavor** *vb* **:** to give or add a flavor to

fla·vor·ing *n* **:** [1]FLAVOR 2

flaw *n* **:** a small often hidden fault

flax *n* **:** a plant with blue flowers that is grown for its fiber from which linen is made and for its seed from which oil and livestock feed are obtained

flax·en *adj* **1 :** made of flax **2 :** having a light straw color

flax·seed *n* **:** the seed of flax from which linseed oil comes and which is used in medicine

flay *vb* **1 :** [2]SKIN **2 :** to scold severely

flea *n* **:** a small bloodsucking insect that has no wings and a hard body

[1]**fleck** *vb* **:** to mark with small streaks or spots

[2]**fleck** *n* **1 :** [1]SPOT 2, MARK **2 :** [1]FLAKE, PARTICLE

fledg·ling *n* **:** a young bird that has just grown the feathers needed to fly

flee *vb* **fled; flee·ing :** to run away or away from **:** FLY

[1]**fleece** *n* **:** the woolly coat of an animal and especially a sheep

[2]**fleece** *vb* **fleeced; fleec·ing :** to take money or property from by trickery

fleecy *adj* **fleec·i·er; fleec·i·est :** covered with, made of, or like fleece

[1]**fleet** *n* **1 :** a group of warships under one command **2 :** a country's navy **3 :** a group of ships or vehicles that move together or are under one management

[2]**fleet** *adj* **:** very swift — **fleet·ly** *adv* — **fleet·ness** *n*

Fleet Admiral *n* **:** the highest ranking commissioned officer in the Navy ranking above an admiral

flesh *n* **1 :** the soft and especially the edible muscular parts of an animal's body **2 :** a fleshy edible plant part (as the pulp of a fruit) — **fleshed** *adj*

fleshy *adj* **flesh·i·er; flesh·i·est 1 :** like or consisting of flesh **2 :** rather stout

flew *past of* FLY

flex *vb* **:** to bend often again and again

flex·i·bil·i·ty *n* **:** the quality or state of being flexible

flex·i·ble *adj* **1 :** possible to bend or flex **2 :** able or suitable to meet new situations — **flex·i·bly** *adv*

[1]**flick** *n* **:** a light snapping stroke

[2]**flick** *vb* **:** to strike or move with a quick motion

[1]**flick·er** *vb* **:** to burn unsteadily

[2]**flicker** *n* **1 :** a quick small movement **2 :** a flickering light

[3]**flicker** *n* **:** a large North American woodpecker

fli·er *or* **fly·er** *n* **1 :** one that flies **2 :** AVIATOR

[1]**flight** *n* **1 :** an act or instance of passing through the air by the use of wings **2 :** a passing through the air or space **3 :** the distance covered in a flight **4 :** a scheduled trip by an airplane **5 :** a group of similar things flying through the air together **6 :** a passing above or beyond ordinary limits **7 :** a continuous series of stairs

[2]**flight** *n* **:** the act of running away

flight·less *adj* **:** unable to fly

flighty *adj* **flight·i·er; flight·i·est 1 :** easily excited **:** SKITTISH **2 :** not wise or sober **:** FRIVOLOUS

flim·sy *adj* **flim·si·er; flim·si·est :** not strong or solid — **flim·si·ly** *adv* — **flim·si·ness** *n*

flinch *vb* **:** to draw back from or as if from pain

[1]**fling** *vb* **flung; fling·ing 1 :** to move suddenly **2 :** to throw hard or without care

[2]**fling** *n* **1 :** an act of flinging **2 :** a time of freedom for pleasure

flint *n* **:** a very hard stone that produces a spark when struck by steel

flint·lock *n* **:** an old-fashioned firearm using a flint for striking a spark to fire the charge

[1]**flip** *vb* **flipped; flip·ping :** to move or turn by or as if by tossing

[2]**flip** *n* **:** an act of flipping **:** TOSS

flip·pant *adj* **:** not respectful **:** SAUCY — **flip·pant·ly** *adv*

flip·per *n* **1 :** a broad flat limb (as of a seal) specialized for swimming **2 :** a flat rubber shoe with the front expanded into a paddle used in swimming

[1]**flirt** *vb* **:** to show a liking for someone of the opposite sex just for the fun of it

[2]**flirt** *n* **:** a person who flirts a lot

flit *vb* **flit·ted; flit·ting :** to move by darting about

[1]**float** *n* **1 :** something that floats in or on the surface of a liquid **2 :** a cork or bob that holds up the baited end of a fishing line **3 :** a floating platform anchored near a shore for the use of swimmers or boats **4 :** a hollow ball that controls the flow or level of the liquid it floats on (as in a tank) **5 :** a vehicle with a platform used to carry an exhibit in a parade

[2]**float** *vb* **1 :** to rest on the surface of a liquid **2 :** to drift on or through or as if on or through a fluid **3 :** to cause to float — **float·er** *n*

[1]**flock** *n* **1 :** a group of animals (as geese or sheep) living or kept together **2 :** a group someone (as a minister) watches over

[2]**flock** *vb* **:** to gather or move in a crowd

floe *n* **:** a sheet or mass of floating ice

flog *vb* **flogged; flog·ging :** to beat severely with a rod or whip

[1]**flood** *n* **1 :** a huge flow of water that rises and spreads over the land **2 :** the flowing in of the tide **3 :** a very large number or amount

[2]**flood** *vb* **1 :** to cover or become filled with water **2 :** to fill as if with a flood

flood·light *n* **:** a lamp that gives a bright broad beam of light

flood·plain *n* **:** low flat land along a stream that is flooded when the steam overflows

flood·wa·ter *n* **:** the water of a flood

[1]**floor** *n* **1 :** the part of a room on which one stands **2 :** the lower inside surface of a hollow structure **3 :** a ground surface **4 :** a story of a building

[2]**floor** *vb* **1 :** to cover or provide with a floor **2 :** to knock down

floor·ing *n* **1 :** [1]FLOOR 1 **2 :** material for floors

[1]**flop** *vb* **flopped; flop·ping 1 :** to flap about **2 :** to drop or fall limply **3 :** [1]FAIL 6

[2]**flop** *n* **1 :** the act or sound of flopping **2 :** FAILURE 3

[1]**flop·py** *adj* **flop·pi·er; flop·pi·est :** being soft and flexible

[2]**floppy** *n, pl* **floppies :** FLOPPY DISK

floppy disk *n* **:** a small flexible plastic disk with a magnetic coating on which computer data can be stored

flo·ra *n* **:** the plant life typical of a region, period, or special environment

flo·ral *adj* **:** of or relating to flowers

flo·ret *n* **:** a small flower

flo·rist *n* **:** a person who sells flowers and ornamental plants

[1]**floss** *n* **1 :** soft thread used in embroidery **2 :** fluffy material full of fibers

[2]**floss** *vb* **:** to use dental floss on (one's teeth)

flo·til·la *n* **:** a fleet of usually small ships

[1]**flounce** *vb* **flounced; flounc·ing :** to move with exaggerated jerky motions

[2]**flounce** *n* **:** a strip of fabric attached by its upper edge

[1]**floun·der** *n* **:** a flatfish used for food

[2]**flounder** *vb* **1 :** to struggle to move or get footing **2 :** to behave or do something in a clumsy way

flour *n* **:** the finely ground meal of a cereal grain and especially of wheat

[1]**flour·ish** *vb* **1 :** to grow well **:** THRIVE **2 :** to do well **:** PROSPER **3 :** to make sweeping movements with

[2]**flourish** *n* **1 :** a fancy bit of decoration added to something (as handwriting) **2 :** a sweeping motion

flout *vb* **:** to show lack of respect for **:** DISREGARD

[1]**flow** *vb* **1 :** to move in a stream **2 :** to glide along smoothly **3 :** to hang loose and waving

[2]**flow** *n* **1 :** an act of flowing **2 :** the rise of the tide **3 :** a smooth even movement **:** STREAM

[1]**flow·er** *n* **1 :** a plant part that produces seed **2 :** a plant grown chiefly for its showy flowers **3 :** the state of bearing flowers **4 :** the best part or example — **flow·ered** *adj* — **flow·er·less** *adj*

[2]**flower** *vb* **:** to produce flowers

flower head *n* **:** a tight cluster of small flowers that are arranged so that the whole looks like a single flower

flowering plant *n* **:** a seed plant whose seeds are produced in the ovary of a flower

flow·er·pot *n* **:** a pot in which to grow plants

flow·ery *adj* **1 :** having many flowers **2 :** full of fine words — **flow·er·i·ness** *n*

flown *past participle of* FLY

flu *n* **1 :** INFLUENZA **2 :** any of several virus diseases something like a cold

fluc·tu·ate *vb* **fluc·tu·at·ed; fluc·tu·at·ing :** to change continually and especially up and down

flue *n* **:** an enclosed passage (as in a chimney) for smoke or air

flu·en·cy *n* **:** the ability to speak easily and well

flu·ent *adj* **1 :** able to speak easily and well **2 :** that is smooth and correct **:** GOOD — **flu·ent·ly** *adv*

[1]**fluff** *n* **:** [7]DOWN, NAP

[2]**fluff** *vb* **:** to make or become fluffy

fluffy *adj* **fluff·i·er; fluff·i·est :** having, covered with, or like down

[1]**flu·id** *adj* **1 :** capable of flowing like a

liquid or gas **2 :** being smooth and easy — **flu·id·ly** *adv*

[2]**fluid** *n* **:** something that tends to flow and take the shape of its container

flung *past of* FLING

flunk *vb* **:** [1]FAIL 6

fluo·res·cent *adj* **1 :** giving out visible light when exposed to external radiation **2 :** producing visible light by means of a fluorescent coating **3 :** extremely bright or glowing

fluo·ri·date *vb* **fluo·ri·dat·ed; fluo·ri·dat·ing :** to add a fluoride to (as drinking water) to reduce tooth decay

fluo·ri·da·tion *n* **:** the act of fluoridating

fluo·ride *n* **:** a compound of fluorine

fluo·rine *n* **:** a yellowish flammable irritating gaseous chemical element

[1]**flur·ry** *n, pl* **flurries 1 :** a gust of wind **2 :** a brief light snowfall **3 :** a brief outburst (as of activity)

[2]**flurry** *vb* **flur·ried; flur·ry·ing :** [1]FLUSTER, EXCITE

[1]**flush** *vb* **:** to begin or cause to begin flight suddenly

[2]**flush** *n* **1 :** an act of flushing **2 :** [1]BLUSH 1

[3]**flush** *vb* **1 :** [2]BLUSH **2 :** to pour water over or through

[4]**flush** *adj* **:** having one edge or surface even with the next

[5]**flush** *adv* **:** so as to be flush

[1]**flus·ter** *vb* **:** to make nervous and confused **:** UPSET

[2]**fluster** *n* **:** a state of nervous confusion

[1]**flute** *n* **:** a woodwind instrument in the form of a hollow slender tube open at only one end that is played by blowing across a hole near the closed end

[2]**flute** *vb* **flut·ed; flut·ing :** to make a sound like that of a flute

[1]**flut·ter** *vb* **1 :** to move the wings rapidly without flying or in making short flights **2 :** to move with a quick flapping motion **3 :** to move about busily without getting much done

[2]**flutter** *n* **:** an act of fluttering

[1]**fly** *vb* **flew; flown; fly·ing 1 :** to move in or pass through the air with wings **2 :** to move through the air or before the wind **3 :** to float or cause to float, wave, or soar in the wind **4 :** to run away **:** FLEE **5 :** to move or pass swiftly **6 :** to operate or travel in an aircraft

[2]**fly** *n, pl* **flies 1 :** a flap of material to cover a fastening in a garment **2 :** the outer canvas of a tent that has a double top **3 :** a baseball hit high in the air

[3]**fly** *n, pl* **flies 1 :** a winged insect **2 :** any of a large group of mostly stout-bodied two-winged insects (as the common housefly) **3 :** a fishhook made to look like an insect

fly·catch·er *n* **:** a small bird that eats flying insects

flyer *variant of* FLIER

fly·ing boat *n* **:** a seaplane with a hull designed to support it on the water

flying fish *n* **:** a fish with large fins that let it jump from the water and move for a distance through the air

fly·pa·per *n* **:** sticky paper to catch and kill flies

fly·speck *n* **:** a spot of feces left by a fly on a surface

fly·way *n* **:** a route regularly followed by migratory birds

[1]**foal** *n* **:** a young animal of the horse family especially while less than one year old

[2]**foal** *vb* **:** to give birth to a foal

[1]**foam** *n* **:** a mass of tiny bubbles that forms in or on the surface of liquids or in the mouths or on the skins of animals

[2]**foam** *vb* **:** to produce or form foam

foamy *adj* **foam·i·er; foam·i·est :** covered with or looking like foam — **foam·i·ness** *n*

fo·cal *adj* **:** of, relating to, or having a focus

[1]**fo·cus** *n, pl* **fo·cus·es** *or* **fo·ci 1 :** a point at which rays (as of light, heat, or sound) meet after being reflected or bent **:** the point at which an image is formed **2 :** the distance from a lens or mirror to a focus **3 :** an adjustment (as of a person's eyes or glasses) that gives clear vision **4 :** a center of activity or interest

[2]**focus** *vb* **fo·cused** *or* **fo·cussed; fo·cus·ing** *or* **fo·cus·sing 1 :** to bring or come to a focus **2 :** to adjust the focus of

fod·der *n* **:** coarse dry food (as stalks of corn) for livestock

foe *n* **:** an enemy especially in war

[1]**fog** *n* **1 :** fine particles of water floating in the air at or near the ground **2 :** a confused state of mind

[2]**fog** *vb* **fogged; fog·ging :** to cover or become covered with fog

fog·gy *adj* **fog·gi·er; fog·gi·est 1 :** filled with fog **2 :** confused as if by fog — **fog·gi·ness** *n*

fog·horn *n* **:** a loud horn sounded in a fog to give warning

fo·gy *n, pl* **fogies :** a person with old-fashioned ideas

foi·ble *n* **:** an unimportant weakness or failing

[1]**foil** *vb* **:** to keep from succeeding or from reaching a goal

[2]**foil** *n* **1 :** a very thin sheet of metal **2 :** something that makes another thing more noticeable by being very different from it

³foil *n* **:** a fencing weapon having a light flexible blade with a blunt point
¹fold *n* **:** an enclosure or shelter for sheep
²fold *vb* **:** to pen up (sheep) in a fold
³fold *vb* **1 :** to double something over itself **2 :** to clasp together **3 :** ¹EMBRACE 1
⁴fold *n* **1 :** a part doubled or laid over another part **:** PLEAT **2 :** a bend produced in a rock layer by pressure **3 :** a crease made by folding something (as a newspaper)
-fold *suffix* **1 :** multiplied by a specified number **:** times — in adjectives and adverbs **2 :** having so many parts
fold•er *n* **1 :** one that folds **2 :** a folded printed sheet **3 :** a folded cover or large envelope for loose papers
fo•li•age *n* **:** the leaves of a plant (as a tree) — **fo•li•aged** *adj*
¹folk *or* **folks** *n pl* **1 :** persons of a certain class, kind, or group **2 folks** *pl* **:** people in general **3 folks** *pl* **:** the members of one's family **:** one's relatives
²folk *adj* **:** created by the common people
folk•lore *n* **:** customs, beliefs, stories, and sayings of a people handed down from generation to generation
folk•sing•er *n* **:** a person who sings songs (**folk songs**) created by and long sung among the common people
folk•tale *n* **:** a story made up and handed down by the common people
fol•low *vb* **1 :** to go or come after or behind **2 :** to be led or guided by **:** OBEY **3 :** to proceed along **4 :** to work in or at something as a way of life **5 :** to come after in time or place **6 :** to result from **7 :** to keep one's eyes or attention on — **fol•low•er** *n* — **follow suit 1 :** to play a card that belongs to the same group (as hearts or spades) as the one led **2 :** to do the same thing someone else has just done
¹fol•low•ing *adj* **:** coming just after
²following *n* **:** a group of followers
follow through *vb* **:** to complete an action
follow up *vb* **:** to show continued interest in or take further action regarding
fol•ly *n, pl* **follies 1 :** lack of good sense **2 :** a foolish act or idea
fond *adj* **1 :** having a liking or love **2 :** AFFECTIONATE, LOVING — **fond•ly** *adv* — **fond•ness** *n*
fon•dle *vb* **fon•dled; fon•dling :** to touch or handle in a tender or loving manner
font *n* **:** a basin to hold water for baptism
food *n* **1 :** material containing carbohydrates, fats, proteins, and supplements (as minerals and vitamins) that is taken in by and used in the living body for growth and repair and as a source of energy for activities **2 :** inorganic substances taken in by green plants and used to build organic nutrients **3 :** organic materials formed by plants and used in their growth and activities **4 :** solid food as distinguished from drink
food chain *n* **:** a sequence of organisms in which each depends on the next and usually lower member as a source of food
food•stuff *n* **:** a substance with food value
¹fool *n* **1 :** a person without good sense or judgment **2 :** JESTER 1
²fool *vb* **1 :** to spend time idly **2 :** to meddle or tamper with something **3 :** to speak or act in a playful way or in fun **:** JOKE **4 :** ²TRICK
fool•har•dy *adj* **fool•har•di•er; fool•har•di•est :** foolishly adventurous or bold
fool•ish *adj* **:** showing or resulting from lack of good sense **:** SENSELESS — **fool•ish•ly** *adv* — **fool•ish•ness** *n*
fool•proof *adj* **:** done, made, or planned so well that nothing can go wrong
¹foot *n, pl* **feet 1 :** the end part of the leg of an animal or person **:** the part of an animal on which it stands or moves **2 :** a unit of length equal to twelve inches (about .3 meter) **3 :** something like a foot in position or use — **on foot :** by walking
²foot *vb* **1 :** to go on foot **2 :** ¹PAY 2
foot•ball *n* **1 :** a game played with a blown up oval ball on a large field by two teams of eleven players that move the ball by kicking, passing, or running with it **2 :** the ball used in football
foot•ed *adj* **1 :** having a foot or feet **2 :** having such or so many feet
foot•fall *n* **:** the sound of a footstep
foot•hill *n* **:** a hill at the foot of higher hills
foot•hold *n* **:** a place where the foot may be put (as for climbing)
foot•ing *n* **1 :** a firm position or placing of the feet **2 :** FOOTHOLD **3 :** position in relation to others **4 :** social relationship
foot•lights *n pl* **:** a row of lights set across the front of a stage floor
foot•man *n, pl* **foot•men :** a male servant who lets visitors in and waits on table
foot•note *n* **:** a note at the bottom of a page
foot•path *n* **:** a path for walkers
foot•print *n* **:** a track left by a foot
foot•sore *adj* **:** having sore feet from walking a lot
foot•step *n* **1 :** a step of the foot **2 :** the distance covered by a step **3 :** FOOTPRINT
foot•stool *n* **:** a low stool to support the feet
foot•work *n* **:** the skill with which the feet are moved (as in boxing)
¹for *prep* **1 :** by way of getting ready **2 :** toward the goal of **3 :** in order to reach **4**

: as being **5 :** because of **6** — used to show who or what is to receive something **7 :** in order to help or defend **8 :** directed at **:** AGAINST **9 :** in exchange as equal to **10 :** with regard to **:** CONCERNING **11 :** taking into account **12 :** through the period of

2for *conj* **:** BECAUSE

1for·age *n* **:** food (as pasture) for browsing or grazing animals

2forage *vb* **for·aged; for·ag·ing :** 1SEARCH 1

for·ay *n* **:** 1RAID

for·bear *vb* **for·bore; for·borne; for·bear·ing 1 :** to hold back **2 :** to control oneself when provoked

for·bid *vb* **for·bade** *or* **for·bad; for·bid·den; for·bid·ding :** to order not to do something

for·bid·ding *adj* **:** tending to frighten or discourage

1force *n* **1 :** POWER 4 **2 :** the state of existing and being enforced **:** EFFECT **3 :** a group of persons gathered together and trained for action **4 :** power or violence used on a person or thing **5 :** an influence (as a push or pull) that tends to produce a change in the speed or direction of motion of something

2force *vb* **forced; forc·ing 1 :** to make (as a person) do something **2 :** to get or make by using force **3 :** to break open by force **4 :** to speed up the development of

force·ful *adj* **:** having much force **:** VIGOROUS — **force·ful·ly** *adv* — **force·ful·ness** *n*

for·ceps *n, pl* **forceps :** an instrument for grasping, holding, or pulling on things especially in delicate operations (as by a jeweler or surgeon)

forc·ible *adj* **1 :** got, made, or done by force or violence **2 :** showing a lot of force or energy — **forc·ibly** *adv*

1ford *n* **:** a shallow place in a body of water where one can wade across

2ford *vb* **:** to cross by wading

1fore *adv* **:** in or toward the front

2fore *adj* **:** being or coming before in time, place, or order

3fore *n* **:** 1FRONT 2

4fore *interj* — used by a golfer to warn someone within range of a hit ball

fore- *prefix* **1 :** earlier **:** beforehand **2 :** at the front **:** in front **3 :** front part of something specified

fore–and–aft *adj* **:** being in line with the length of a ship

fore·arm *n* **:** the part of the arm between the elbow and the wrist

fore·bear *n* **:** ANCESTOR

fore·bod·ing *n* **:** a feeling that something bad is going to happen

1fore·cast *vb* **forecast** *or* **fore·cast·ed; fore·cast·ing :** to predict often after thought and study of available evidence — **fore·cast·er** *n*

2forecast *n* **:** a prediction of something in the future

fore·cas·tle *n* **1 :** the forward part of the upper deck of a ship **2 :** quarters for the crew in the forward part of a ship

fore·fa·ther *n* **:** ANCESTOR

fore·fin·ger *n* **:** INDEX FINGER

fore·foot *n, pl* **fore·feet :** one of the front feet of an animal with four feet

fore·front *n* **:** the very front **:** VANGUARD

forego *variant of* FORGO

fore·go·ing *adj* **:** being before in time or place

fore·gone conclusion *n* **:** something felt to be sure to happen

fore·ground *n* **:** the part of a picture or scene that seems to be nearest to and in front of the person looking at it

fore·hand *n* **:** a stroke (as in tennis) made with the palm of the hand turned in the direction in which the hand is moving

fore·head *n* **:** the part of the face above the eyes

for·eign *adj* **1 :** located outside of a place or country and especially outside of one's country **2 :** belonging to a place or country other than the one under consideration **3 :** relating to or having to do with other nations **4 :** not normal or wanted

for·eign·er *n* **:** a person who is from a foreign country

fore·leg *n* **:** a front leg

fore·limb *n* **:** an arm, fin, wing, or leg that is or occupies the position of a foreleg

fore·man *n, pl* **fore·men :** the leader of a group of workers

fore·mast *n* **:** the mast nearest the bow of the ship

1fore·most *adj* **:** first in time, place, or order **:** most important

2foremost *adv* **:** in the first place

fore·noon *n* **:** MORNING

fore·quar·ter *n* **:** the front half of a side of the body or carcass of an animal with four feet

fore·run·ner *n* **:** one that comes before especially as a sign of the coming of another

fore·see *vb* **fore·saw; fore·seen; fore·see·ing :** to see or know about beforehand

fore·sight *n* **1 :** the act or power of foreseeing **2 :** care for the future **:** PRUDENCE

for·est *n* **:** a growth of trees and underbrush covering a large area — **for·est·ed** *adj*

fore·stall *vb* **:** to keep out, interfere with, or prevent by steps taken in advance

forest ranger *n* **:** a person in charge of the management and protection of a part of a public forest

for·est·ry *n* **:** the science and practice of caring for forests — **for·est·er** *n*

fore·tell *vb* **fore·told; fore·tell·ing :** to tell of a thing before it happens

fore·thought *n* **:** a thinking or planning for the future

for·ev·er *adv* **1 :** for a limitless time **2 :** at all times

for·ev·er·more *adv* **:** FOREVER 1

fore·word *n* **:** PREFACE

[1]**for·feit** *n* **:** something forfeited

[2]**forfeit** *vb* **:** to lose or lose the right to something through a fault, error, or crime

[1]**forge** *n* **:** a furnace or a place with a furnace where metal is shaped and worked by heating and hammering

[2]**forge** *vb* **forged; forg·ing 1 :** to shape and work metal by heating and hammering **2 :** to produce something that is not genuine **:** COUNTERFEIT — **forg·er** *n*

[3]**forge** *vb* **forged; forg·ing :** to move forward slowly but steadily

forg·ery *n, pl* **forg·er·ies 1 :** the crime of falsely making or changing a written paper or signing someone else's name **2 :** something that has been forged

for·get *vb* **for·got; for·got·ten** *or* **for·got; for·get·ting 1 :** to be unable to think of or recall **2 :** to fail by accident to do (something) **:** OVERLOOK

for·get·ful *adj* **:** forgetting easily — **for·get·ful·ly** *adv* — **for·get·ful·ness** *n*

for·get–me–not *n* **:** a small low plant with bright blue flowers

for·give *vb* **for·gave; for·giv·en; for·giv·ing :** to stop feeling angry at or hurt by

for·give·ness *n* **:** the act of forgiving or the state of being forgiven

for·go *or* **fore·go** *vb* **for·went** *or* **fore·went; for·gone** *or* **fore·gone; for·go·ing** *or* **fore·go·ing :** to hold oneself back from **:** GIVE UP

[1]**fork** *n* **1 :** an implement having a handle and two or more prongs for taking up (as in eating), pitching, or digging **2 :** something like a fork in shape **3 :** the place where something divides or branches **4 :** one of the parts into which something divides or branches — **forked** *adj*

[2]**fork** *vb* **1 :** to divide into branches **2 :** to pitch or lift with a fork

for·lorn *adj* **:** sad from being left alone — **for·lorn·ly** *adv*

[1]**form** *n* **1 :** the shape and structure of something **2 :** an established way of doing something **3 :** a printed sheet with blank spaces for information **4 :** a mold in which concrete is placed to set **5 :** [1]SORT 1, KIND **6 :** a plan of arrangement or design (as for a work of art) **7 :** one of the different pronunciations, spellings, or inflections a word may have

[2]**form** *vb* **1 :** to give form or shape to **2 :** DEVELOP 5 **3 :** to come or bring together in making **4 :** to take form **:** come into being

[1]**for·mal** *adj* **:** following established form, custom, or rule — **for·mal·ly** *adv*

[2]**formal** *n* **:** something (as a dress) formal in character

for·mal·i·ty *n, pl* **for·mal·i·ties 1 :** the quality or state of being formal **2 :** an established way of doing something

for·ma·tion *n* **1 :** a forming of something **2 :** something that is formed **3 :** an arrangement of something (as persons or ships)

for·mer *adj* **:** coming before in time

for·mer·ly *adv* **:** at an earlier time

for·mi·da·ble *adj* **1 :** exciting fear or awe **2 :** offering serious difficulties

form·less *adj* **:** having no regular form or shape — **form·less·ly** *adv* — **form·less·ness** *n*

for·mu·la *n* **1 :** a direction giving amounts of the substances for the preparation of something (as a medicine) **2 :** a milk mixture or substitute for feeding a baby **3 :** a general fact or rule expressed in symbols **4 :** an expression in symbols giving the makeup of a substance **5 :** an established form or method

for·mu·late *vb* **for·mu·lat·ed; for·mu·lat·ing :** to state definitely and clearly

for·sake *vb* **for·sook; for·sak·en; for·sak·ing :** to give up or leave entirely

for·syth·ia *n* **:** a bush often grown for its bright yellow flowers that appear in early spring

fort *n* **:** a strong or fortified place

forth *adv* **1 :** onward in time, place, or order **2 :** out into view

forth·com·ing *adj* **1 :** being about to appear **2 :** ready or available when needed

forth·right *adj* **:** going straight to the point clearly and firmly — **forth·right·ly** *adv*

forth·with *adv* **:** without delay **:** IMMEDIATELY

[1]**for·ti·eth** *adj* **:** coming right after thirty-ninth

[2]**fortieth** *n* **:** number forty in a series

for·ti·fi·ca·tion *n* **1 :** the act of fortifying **2 :** something that strengthens or protects

for·ti·fy *vb* **for·ti·fied; for·ti·fy·ing 1 :** to make strong (as by building defenses) **2 :** ENRICH 2, 3

for·ti·tude *n* **:** strength of mind that lets a person meet and put up with trouble

fort·night *n* **:** two weeks

for·tress *n* **:** a fortified place

for·tu·nate *adj* **1 :** bringing some unexpected good **2 :** receiving some unexpected good **:** LUCKY — **for·tu·nate·ly** *adv*

for·tune *n* **1 :** favorable results that come partly by chance **2 :** what happens to a person **:** good or bad luck **3 :** what is to happen to one in the future **4 :** WEALTH

for·tune–tell·er *n* **:** a person who claims to foretell future events

¹for·ty *adj* **:** being four times ten

²forty *n* **:** four times ten **:** 40

for·ty–nin·er *n* **:** a person in the California gold rush of 1849

fo·rum *n* **1 :** the marketplace or public place of an ancient Roman city serving as the center for public business **2 :** a program of open discussion

¹for·ward *adj* **1 :** near, at, or belonging to the front part **2 :** lacking proper modesty or reserve **3 :** moving, tending, or leading to a position in front

²forward *adv* **:** to or toward what is in front

³forward *vb* **1 :** to help onward **:** ADVANCE **2 :** to send on or ahead

⁴forward *n* **:** a player at or near the front of his or her team or near the opponent's goal

for·wards *adv* **:** ²FORWARD

fos·sil *n* **:** a trace or print or the remains of a plant or animal of a past age preserved in earth or rock

¹fos·ter *adj* **:** giving, receiving, or sharing parental care even though not related by blood or legal ties

²foster *vb* **1 :** to give parental care to **2 :** to help the growth and development of

fought *past of* FIGHT

¹foul *adj* **1 :** disgusting in looks, taste, or smell **2 :** full of or covered with dirt **3 :** being vulgar or insulting **4 :** being wet and stormy **5 :** very unfair **6 :** breaking a rule in a game or sport **7 :** being outside the foul lines — **foul·ly** *adv* — **foul·ness** *n*

²foul *n* **1 :** a breaking of the rules in a game or sport **2 :** a foul ball in baseball

³foul *vb* **1 :** to make or become foul or filthy **2 :** to make a foul **3 :** to become or cause to become entangled

foul line *n* **:** either of two straight lines running from the rear corner of home plate through first and third base to the boundary of a baseball field

foul play *n* **:** VIOLENCE 1

¹found *past of* FIND

²found *vb* **:** ESTABLISH 1

foun·da·tion *n* **1 :** the act of founding **2 :** the support upon which something rests

¹found·er *n* **:** a person who founds something

²foun·der *vb* **:** ¹SINK 1

found·ling *n* **:** an infant found after being abandoned by unknown parents

found·ry *n, pl* **foundries :** a building or factory where metals are cast

foun·tain *n* **1 :** a spring of water **2 :** SOURCE 1 **3 :** an artificial stream or spray of water (as for drinking or ornament) or the device from which it comes

fountain pen *n* **:** a pen with ink inside that is fed as needed to the writing point

¹four *adj* **:** being one more than three

²four *n* **1 :** one more than three **:** two times two **:** 4 **2 :** the fourth in a set or series

four·fold *adj* **:** being four times as great or as many

four·score *adj* **:** ¹EIGHTY

four·some *adj* **:** a group of four persons or things

¹four·teen *adj* **:** being one more than thirteen

²fourteen *n* **:** one more than thirteen **:** two times seven **:** 14

¹four·teenth *adj* **:** coming right after thirteenth

²fourteenth *n* **:** number fourteen in a series

¹fourth *adj* **:** coming right after third

²fourth *n* **1 :** number four in a series **2 :** one of four equal parts

Fourth of July *n* **:** INDEPENDENCE DAY

fowl *n, pl* **fowl** *or* **fowls 1 :** BIRD **2 :** a common domestic rooster or hen **3 :** the flesh of a mature domestic fowl for use as food

fox *n* **:** a wild animal closely related to the dog that has a sharp snout, pointed ears, and a long bushy tail

foxy *adj* **fox·i·er; fox·i·est :** cunning and careful in planning and action — **fox·i·ly** *adv* — **fox·i·ness** *n*

foy·er *n* **1 :** a lobby especially in a theater **2 :** an entrance hall

fra·cas *n* **:** a noisy quarrel **:** BRAWL

frac·tion *n* **1 :** a part of a whole **:** FRAGMENT **2 :** a number (as $^1/_2$, $^2/_3$, $^{17}/_{100}$) that indicates one or more equal parts of a whole or group and that may be considered as indicating also division of the number above the line by the number below the line

frac·tion·al *adj* **1 :** of, relating to, or being a fraction **2 :** fairly small

¹frac·ture *n* **1 :** a breaking or being broken (as of a bone) **2 :** damage or an injury caused by breaking

²fracture *vb* **frac·tured; frac·tur·ing :** to cause a fracture in **:** BREAK

frag·ile *adj* **:** easily broken **:** DELICATE

frag·ment *n* **:** a part broken off or incomplete

frag·men·tary *adj* **:** made up of fragments **:** INCOMPLETE

fra·grance *n* **:** a sweet or pleasant smell

fra·grant *adj* **:** sweet or pleasant in smell — **fra·grant·ly** *adv*

frail *adj* **:** very delicate or weak in structure or being

frail·ty *n, pl* **frailties** **1 :** the quality or state of being weak **2 :** a weakness of character

[1]**frame** *vb* **framed; fram·ing** **1 :** [2]FORM 1, CONSTRUCT **2 :** to enclose in a frame

[2]**frame** *n* **1 :** the structure of an animal and especially a human body **:** PHYSIQUE **2 :** an arrangement of parts that give form or support to something **3 :** an open case or structure for holding or enclosing something **4 :** a particular state or mood

[3]**frame** *adj* **:** having a wooden frame

frame·work *n* **:** a basic supporting part or structure

franc *n* **1 :** a French coin or bill **2 :** any of various coins or bills used in countries where French is widely spoken

Fran·co- *prefix* **1 :** French and **2 :** French

frank *adj* **:** free in speaking one's feelings and opinions — **frank·ly** *adv* — **frank·ness** *n*

frank·furt·er *n* **:** a cooked sausage (as of beef or beef and pork)

frank·in·cense *n* **:** a fragrant gum that is burned for its sweet smell

fran·tic *adj* **:** wildly excited

fran·ti·cal·ly *adv* **:** in a frantic way

fra·ter·nal *adj* **1 :** having to do with brothers **2 :** made up of members banded together like brothers

fra·ter·ni·ty *n, pl* **fra·ter·ni·ties :** a society of boys or men (as in a college)

fraud *n* **1 :** TRICKERY, DECEIT **2 :** an act of deceiving **:** TRICK **3 :** a person who pretends to be what he or she is not

fraud·u·lent *adj* **:** based on or done by fraud — **fraud·u·lent·ly** *adv*

fraught *adj* **:** full of some quality

[1]**fray** *n* **:** [2]FIGHT 1, BRAWL

[2]**fray** *vb* **:** to wear into shreds

fraz·zle *n* **:** a tired or nervous condition

[1]**freak** *n* **:** a strange, abnormal, or unusual person, thing, or event

[2]**freak** *adj* **:** being or suggesting a freak **:** IMPROBABLE

[1]**freck·le** *n* **:** a small brownish spot on the skin

[2]**freckle** *vb* **freck·led; freck·ling :** to mark or become marked with freckles

[1]**free** *adj* **fre·er; fre·est** **1 :** having liberty **:** not being a slave **2 :** not controlled by others **3 :** released or not suffering from something unpleasant or painful **4 :** given without charge **5 :** not held back by fear or distrust **:** OPEN **6 :** not blocked **:** CLEAR **7 :** not combined — **free·ly** *adv*

[2]**free** *vb* **freed; free·ing :** to make or set free

[3]**free** *adv* **1 :** in a free manner **:** FREELY **2 :** without charge

freed·man *n, pl* **freed·men :** a person freed from slavery

free·dom *n* **1 :** the condition of being free **:** LIBERTY, INDEPENDENCE **2 :** ability to move or act freely **3 :** the quality of being very frank **:** CANDOR **4 :** free and unlimited use

free·hand *adj or adv* **:** done without mechanical aids

free·man *n, pl* **free·men :** a free person **:** one who is not a slave

free·stand·ing *adj* **:** standing alone or on its own foundation free of attachment or support

free·way *n* **:** an expressway that can be used without paying tolls

[1]**freeze** *vb* **froze; fro·zen; freez·ing** **1 :** to harden into or be hardened into a solid (as ice) by loss of heat **2 :** to be or become uncomfortably cold **3 :** to damage by cold **4 :** to clog or become clogged by ice **5 :** to become fixed or motionless

[2]**freeze** *n* **1 :** a period of freezing weather **:** cold weather **2 :** an act or instance of freezing **3 :** the state of being frozen

freez·er *n* **:** a compartment or room used to freeze food or keep it frozen

freezing point *n* **:** the temperature at which a liquid becomes solid

[1]**freight** *n* **1 :** the amount paid (as to a shipping company) for carrying goods **2 :** goods or cargo carried by a ship, train, truck, or airplane **3 :** the carrying (as by truck) of goods from one place to another **4 :** a train that carries freight

[2]**freight** *vb* **:** to send by freight

freight·er *n* **:** a ship or airplane used to carry freight

[1]**French** *adj* **:** of or relating to France, its people, or the French language

[2]**French** *n* **1 French** *pl* **:** the people of France **2 :** the language of the French

french fry *n, often cap 1st F* **:** a strip of potato fried in deep fat

French horn *n* **:** a circular brass musical instrument with a large opening at one end and a mouthpiece shaped like a small funnel

fren·zied *adj* **:** very excited and upset

fren·zy *n, pl* **frenzies :** great and often wild or disorderly activity

fre·quen·cy *n, pl* **fre·quen·cies** **1 :** frequent repetition **2 :** rate of repetition

[1]**fre·quent** *vb* **:** to visit often

[2]**fre·quent** *adj* **:** happening often — **fre·quent·ly** *adv*

fresh *adj* **1 :** not salt **2 :** PURE 1, BRISK **3 :** not frozen, canned, or pickled **4 :** not stale, sour, or spoiled **5 :** not dirty or rumpled **6 :** NEW 6 **7 :** newly made or received **8 :** IMPUDENT — **fresh·ly** *adv* — **fresh·ness** *n*

fresh·en *vb* **:** to make or become fresh

fresh•et *n* : a sudden overflowing of a stream
fresh•man *n, pl* **fresh•men** : a first year student (as in college)
fresh•wa•ter *adj* : of, relating to, or living in fresh water
[1]**fret** *vb* **fret•ted; fret•ting** : to make or become worried
[2]**fret** *n* : an irritated or worried state
[3]**fret** *n* : a design of short lines or bars
[4]**fret** *n* : one of a series of ridges fixed across the fingerboard of a stringed musical instrument — **fret•ted** *adj*
fret•ful *adj* : likely to fret : IRRITABLE — **fret•ful•ly** *adv* — **fret•ful•ness** *n*
fri•ar *n* : a member of a Roman Catholic religious order for men
fric•tion *n* **1** : the rubbing of one thing against another **2** : resistance to motion between bodies in contact **3** : disagreement among persons or groups
Fri•day *n* : the sixth day of the week
friend *n* **1** : a person who has a strong liking for and trust in another person **2** : a person who is not an enemy **3** : a person who aids or favors something — **friend-less** *adj*
friend•ly *adj* **friend•li•er; friend•li•est** **1** : showing friendship **2** : being other than an enemy — **friend•li•ness** *n*
friend•ship *n* : the state of being friends
frieze *n* : a band or stripe (as around a building) used as a decoration
frig•ate *n* **1** : a square-rigged warship **2** : a modern warship that is smaller than a destroyer
fright *n* **1** : sudden terror : great fear **2** : something that frightens or is ugly or shocking
fright•en *vb* : to make afraid : TERRIFY — **fright•en•ing•ly** *adv*
fright•ful *adj* **1** : causing fear or alarm **2** : SHOCKING, OUTRAGEOUS — **fright•ful•ly** *adv* — **fright•ful•ness** *n*
frig•id *adj* **1** : freezing cold **2** : not friendly — **frig•id•ly** *adv* — **frig•id•ness** *n*
frill *n* **1** : [2]RUFFLE **2** : something added mostly for show
frilly *adj* **frill•i•er; frill•i•est** : having frills
[1]**fringe** *n* **1** : a border or trimming made by or made to look like the loose ends of the cloth **2** : something suggesting a fringe
[2]**fringe** *vb* **fringed; fring•ing** **1** : to decorate with a fringe **2** : to serve as a fringe for
frisk *vb* : to move around in a lively or playful way
frisky *adj* **frisk•i•er; frisk•i•est** : tending to frisk : PLAYFUL, LIVELY
[1]**frit•ter** *n* : a small amount of fried batter often containing fruit or meat
[2]**fritter** *vb* : to waste on unimportant things
friv•o•lous *adj* **1** : of little importance : TRIVIAL **2** : lacking in seriousness : PLAYFUL
frizzy *adj* **frizz•i•er; frizz•i•est** : very curly
fro *adv* : in a direction away
frock *n* : a woman's or girl's dress
frog *n* **1** : a tailless animal with smooth skin and webbed feet that spends more of its time in water than the related toad **2** : an ornamental fastening for a garment — **frog in one's throat** : HOARSENESS
frog•man *n, pl* **frog•men** : a swimmer equipped to work underwater for long periods of time
[1]**frol•ic** *vb* **frol•icked; frol•ick•ing** : to play about happily : ROMP
[2]**frolic** *n* : FUN 1, GAIETY
frol•ic•some *adj* : given to frolic : PLAYFUL
from *prep* **1** — used to show a starting point **2** — used to show a point of separation **3** — used to show a material, source, or cause
frond *n* : a large leaf (as of a palm or fern) with many divisions or something like such a leaf
[1]**front** *n* **1** : a region in which active warfare is taking place **2** : the forward part or surface **3** : the boundary between bodies of air at different temperatures
[2]**front** *vb* : [2]FACE 2
[3]**front** *adj* : of, relating to, or situated at the front
fron•tal *adj* : of, relating to, or directed at the front
fron•tier *n* **1** : a border between two countries **2** : the edge of the settled part of a country
fron•tiers•man *n, pl* **fron•tiers•men** : a person living on the frontier
[1]**frost** *n* **1** : temperature cold enough to cause freezing **2** : a covering of tiny ice crystals on a cold surface formed from the water vapor in the air
[2]**frost** *vb* : to cover with frost or with something suggesting frost
frost•bite *n* : slight freezing of a part of the body or the effect of this
frost•ing *n* **1** : ICING **2** : a dull finish on glass
frosty *adj* **frost•i•er; frost•i•est** **1** : cold enough to produce frost **2** : covered with or appearing to be covered with frost — **frost•i•ly** *adv* — **frost•i•ness** *n*
[1]**froth** *n* : bubbles formed in or on liquids
[2]**froth** *vb* : to produce or form froth
frothy *adj* **froth•i•er; froth•i•est** : full of or made up of froth — **froth•i•ness** *n*
[1]**frown** *vb* **1** : to wrinkle the forehead (as in anger or thought) **2** : to look with disapproval
[2]**frown** *n* : a wrinkling of the brow

froze *past of* FREEZE
frozen *past participle of* FREEZE
fru·gal *adj* **:** careful in spending or using resources — **fru·gal·ly** *adv*
[1]**fruit** *n* **1 :** a pulpy or juicy plant part (as rhubarb or a strawberry) that is often eaten as a dessert and is distinguished from a vegetable **2 :** a reproductive body of a seed plant that consists of the ripened ovary of a flower with its included seeds **3 :** [2]RESULT 1, PRODUCT — **fruit·ed** *adj*
[2]**fruit** *vb* **:** to bear or cause to bear fruit
fruit·cake *n* **:** a rich cake containing nuts, dried or candied fruits, and spices
fruit·ful *adj* **1 :** very productive **2 :** bringing results — **fruit·ful·ly** *adv* — **fruit·ful·ness** *n*
fruit·less *adj* **1 :** not bearing fruit **2 :** UNSUCCESSFUL — **fruit·less·ly** *adv* — **fruit·less·ness** *n*
fruity *adj* **fruit·i·er; fruit·i·est :** relating to or suggesting fruit
frus·trate *vb* **frus·trat·ed; frus·trat·ing 1 :** to prevent from carrying out a purpose **2 :** [1]DEFEAT 1 **3 :** DISCOURAGE 1
frus·tra·tion *n* **:** DISAPPOINTMENT 2, DEFEAT
[1]**fry** *vb* **fried; fry·ing :** to cook in fat
[2]**fry** *n, pl* **fry 1 :** recently hatched or very young fishes **2 :** persons of a particular group
fudge *n* **:** a soft creamy candy often containing nuts
[1]**fu·el** *n* **:** a substance (as oil) that can be burned to produce heat or power
[2]**fuel** *vb* **fu·eled** *or* **fu·elled; fu·el·ing** *or* **fu·el·ling :** to supply with or take on fuel
[1]**fu·gi·tive** *adj* **:** running away or trying to escape
[2]**fugitive** *n* **:** a person who is running away
[1]**-ful** *adj suffix* **1 :** full of **2 :** characterized by **3 :** having the qualities of **4 :** -ABLE
[2]**-ful** *n suffix* **:** number or quantity that fills or would fill
ful·crum *n, pl* **fulcrums** *or* **ful·cra :** the support on which a lever turns in lifting something
ful·fill *or* **ful·fil** *vb* **ful·filled; ful·fill·ing 1 :** ACCOMPLISH **2 :** SATISFY 1 — **ful·fill·ment** *n*
[1]**full** *adj* **1 :** containing as much as possible or normal **2 :** [1]COMPLETE 1 **3 :** plump and rounded in outline **4 :** having much material — **full·ness** *n*
[2]**full** *adv* **1 :** [2]VERY 1 **2 :** COMPLETELY
[3]**full** *n* **1 :** the highest state, extent, or degree **2 :** the complete amount
full moon *n* **:** the moon with its whole disk lighted
ful·ly *adv* **1 :** COMPLETELY **2 :** at least
[1]**fum·ble** *vb* **fum·bled; fum·bling :** to feel about for or handle something clumsily
[2]**fumble** *n* **:** an act of fumbling
[1]**fume** *n* **:** a disagreeable smoke, vapor, or gas — usually used in pl.
[2]**fume** *vb* **fumed; fum·ing 1 :** to give off fumes **2 :** to show bad temper **:** be angry
fu·mi·gate *vb* **fu·mi·gat·ed; fu·mi·gat·ing :** to disinfect by exposing to smoke, vapor, or gas
fun *n* **1 :** someone or something that provides amusement or enjoyment **2 :** a good time **:** AMUSEMENT **3 :** words or actions to make someone or something an object of unkind laughter
[1]**func·tion** *n* **1 :** the action for which a person or thing is specially fitted or used **:** PURPOSE **2 :** a large important ceremony or social affair
[2]**function** *vb* **:** to serve a certain purpose **:** WORK
function key *n* **:** any of a set of keys on a computer keyboard that have or can be programmed to have special functions
fund *n* **1 :** [1]STOCK 4, SUPPLY **2 :** a sum of money for a special purpose **3 funds** *pl* **:** available money
[1]**fun·da·men·tal** *adj* **:** being or forming a foundation **:** BASIC, ESSENTIAL — **fun·da·men·tal·ly** *adv*
[2]**fundamental** *n* **:** a basic part
fu·ner·al *n* **:** the ceremonies held for a dead person (as before burial)
fun·gi·cide *n* **:** a substance used to kill fungi — **fun·gi·cid·al** *adj*
fun·gous *or* **fun·gal** *adj* **:** of, relating to, or caused by fungi
fun·gus *n, pl* **fun·gi** *also* **fun·gus·es :** any of a group of plantlike organisms (as mushrooms, molds, and rusts) that have no chlorophyll and must live on other plants or animals or on decaying material
fun·nel *n* **1 :** a utensil usually shaped like a hollow cone with a tube extending from the point and used to catch and direct a downward flow (as of liquid) **2 :** a large pipe for the escape of smoke or for ventilation (as on a ship)
fun·nies *n pl* **:** comic strips or a section containing comic strips (as in a newspaper)
fun·ny *adj* **fun·ni·er; fun·ni·est 1 :** causing laughter **2 :** STRANGE 3
fur *n* **1 :** a piece of the pelt of an animal **2 :** an article of clothing made with fur **3 :** the hairy coat of a mammal especially when fine, soft, and thick — **furred** *adj*
fu·ri·ous *adj* **1 :** very angry **2 :** very active **:** VIOLENT — **fu·ri·ous·ly** *adv*
furl *vb* **:** to wrap or roll close to or around something

fur·long *n* **:** a unit of length equal to 220 yards (about 201 meters)
fur·lough *n* **:** a leave of absence from duty
fur·nace *n* **:** an enclosed structure in which heat is produced (as for heating a house or for melting metals)
fur·nish *vb* **1 :** to provide with what is needed **2 :** to supply to someone or something
fur·nish·ings *n pl* **:** articles of furniture for a room or building
fur·ni·ture *n* **:** movable articles used to furnish a room
fur·ri·er *n* **:** a dealer in furs
¹fur·row *n* **1 :** a trench made by or as if by a plow **2 :** a narrow groove **:** WRINKLE
²furrow *vb* **:** to make furrows in
fur·ry *adj* **fur·ri·er; fur·ri·est 1 :** like fur **2 :** covered with fur
¹fur·ther *adv* **1 :** ¹FARTHER 1 **2 :** ²BESIDES, ALSO **3 :** to a greater degree or extent
²further *vb* **:** to help forward **:** PROMOTE
³further *adj* **1 :** ²FARTHER **2 :** going or extending beyond **:** ADDITIONAL
fur·ther·more *adv* **:** MOREOVER
fur·ther·most *adj* **:** most distant **:** FARTHEST
fur·thest *adv or adj* **:** FARTHEST
fur·tive *adj* **:** done in a sneaky or sly manner — **fur·tive·ly** *adv* — **fur·tive·ness** *n*
fu·ry *n, pl* **furies 1 :** violent anger **:** RAGE **2 :** wild and dangerous force
¹fuse *vb* **fused; fus·ing 1 :** to change into a liquid or to a plastic state by heat **2 :** to unite by or as if by melting together
²fuse *n* **:** a device having a metal wire or strip that melts and interrupts an electrical circuit when the current becomes too strong
³fuse *n* **1 :** a cord that is set afire to ignite an explosive by carrying fire to it **2** *usually* **fuze :** a device for setting off a bomb or torpedo
fu·se·lage *n* **:** the central body part of an airplane that holds the crew, passengers, and cargo
fu·sion *n* **1 :** a fusing or melting together **2 :** union by or as if by melting **3 :** union of atomic nuclei to form heavier nuclei resulting in the release of enormous quantities of energy
¹fuss *n* **1 :** unnecessary activity or excitement often over something unimportant **2 :** ¹PROTEST 2 **3 :** a great show of interest
²fuss *vb* **:** to make a fuss
fussy *adj* **fuss·i·er; fuss·i·est 1 :** inclined to complain or whine **2 :** needing much attention to details **3 :** hard to please
fu·tile *adj* **:** having no result or effect **:** USELESS — **fu·tile·ly** *adv* — **fu·tile·ness** *n*
fu·til·i·ty *n* **:** the quality or state of being futile
¹fu·ture *adj* **:** coming after the present
²future *n* **1 :** future time **2 :** the chance of future success
fuze *variant of* FUSE
fuzz *n* **:** fine light particles or fibers
fuzzy *adj* **fuzz·i·er; fuzz·i·est 1 :** covered with or looking like fuzz **2 :** not clear — **fuzz·i·ly** *adv* — **fuzz·i·ness** *n*
-fy *vb suffix* **-fied; -fy·ing 1 :** make **:** form into **2 :** make similar to

G

g *n, pl* **g's** *or* **gs** *often cap* **1 :** the seventh letter of the English alphabet **2 :** a unit of force equal to the weight of a body on which the force acts
¹gab *vb* **gabbed; gab·bing :** to talk in an idle way
²gab *n* **:** idle talk **:** CHATTER
gab·ar·dine *n* **:** a firm cloth with diagonal ribs and a hard smooth finish
¹gab·ble *vb* **gab·bled; gab·bling :** ¹CHATTER 2
²gabble *n* **:** loud or fast talk that has no meaning
gab·by *adj* **gab·bi·er; gab·bi·est :** given to talking a lot **:** TALKATIVE
ga·ble *n* **:** the triangular part of an outside wall of a building formed by the sides of the roof sloping down from the ridgepole to the eaves
gad *vb* **gad·ded; gad·ding :** to roam about **:** WANDER
gad·about *n* **:** a person who goes from place to place without much reason
gad·fly *n, pl* **gad·flies 1 :** a large biting fly **2 :** a person who is an annoying pest
gad·get *n* **:** an interesting, unfamiliar, or unusual device
gaff *n* **1 :** an iron hook with a handle **2 :** something hard to take
¹gag *vb* **gagged; gag·ging 1 :** to keep from speaking or crying out by or as if by stopping up the mouth **2 :** to cause to feel like vomiting **:** RETCH
²gag *n* **1 :** something that gags **2 :** ¹JOKE 1, 2
gage *variant of* GAUGE
gai·ety *n, pl* **gai·eties 1 :** MERRYMAKING 1 **2 :** bright spirits or manner
gai·ly *adv* **1 :** in a merry or lively way **2 :** in a bright or showy way
¹gain *n* **1 :** advantage gained or increased **:** PROFIT **2 :** an increase in amount, size, or degree

[2]**gain** *vb* **1 :** to get hold of often by effort or with difficulty **:** WIN **2 :** to get to **:** REACH **3 :** to get advantage **:** PROFIT — **gain·er** *n*

gain·ful *adj* **:** producing gain

gait *n* **:** way of walking or running

[1]**ga·la** *n* **:** a large showy entertainment celebrating a special occasion

[2]**gala** *adj* **:** of or being a gala

ga·lac·tic *adj* **:** of or relating to a galaxy

gal·axy *n, pl* **gal·ax·ies 1 :** MILKY WAY GALAXY **2 :** one of billions of collections of stars, gas, and dust that make up the universe

gale *n* **1 :** a strong wind **2 :** a wind of from about fourteen to twenty-four meters per second **3 :** OUTBURST 1

ga·le·na *n* **:** a bluish gray mineral that is the main ore of lead

[1]**gall** *n* **1 :** bile especially when obtained from an animal and used in the arts or medicine **2 :** insolent boldness

[2]**gall** *n* **:** a sore spot (as on a horse's back) caused by rubbing

[3]**gall** *vb* **1 :** to make sore by rubbing **2 :** IRRITATE 1

[4]**gall** *n* **:** a swelling or growth on a twig or leaf

gal·lant *adj* **1 :** showing no fear **:** BRAVE **2 :** CHIVALROUS 2, NOBLE **3 :** very polite to women

gal·lant·ry *n* **1 :** polite attention shown to women **2 :** COURAGE, BRAVERY

gall·blad·der *n* **:** a small sac in which bile from the liver is stored

gal·le·on *n* **:** a large sailing ship of the time of Columbus and later

gal·lery *n, pl* **gal·ler·ies 1 :** a long narrow room or hall usually with windows along one side **2 :** an indoor structure (as in a theater or church) built out from one or more walls **3 :** a room or hall used for a special purpose (as showing pictures)

gal·ley *n, pl* **galleys 1 :** a large low ship of olden times moved by oars and sails **2 :** the kitchen of a ship

galley slave *n* **:** a person forced to row on a galley

gal·li·vant *vb* **:** GAD

gal·lon *n* **:** a unit of liquid capacity equal to four quarts (about 3.8 liters)

[1]**gal·lop** *vb* **:** to go or cause to go at a gallop

[2]**gallop** *n* **1 :** a fast springing way of running of an animal with four feet and especially a horse **2 :** a ride or run at a gallop

gal·lows *n, pl* **gallows** *or* **gal·lows·es :** a structure from which criminals are hanged

ga·losh *n* **:** an overshoe worn in snow or wet weather

gal·va·nize *vb* **gal·va·nized; gal·va·niz·ing 1 :** to excite or stir by or as if by an electric shock **2 :** to coat with zinc for protection

[1]**gam·ble** *vb* **gam·bled; gam·bling 1 :** to play a game in which something (as money) is risked **:** BET **2 :** to take risks on the chance of gain **:** take a chance

[2]**gamble** *n* **:** something that is risky to do

gam·bler *n* **:** a person who gambles

gam·bol *vb* **gam·boled** *or* **gam·bolled; gam·bol·ing** *or* **gam·bol·ling :** to run or skip about playfully **:** FROLIC

[1]**game** *n* **1 :** AMUSEMENT, PLAY **2 :** a contest carried on according to rules with the players in direct opposition to each other **3 :** animals hunted for sport or for food **4 :** the meat from game animals

[2]**game** *adj* **gam·er; gam·est 1 :** full of spirit or eagerness **2 :** of or relating to animals that are hunted

game·cock *n* **:** a rooster trained for fighting

game·keep·er *n* **:** a person in charge of the breeding and protection of game animals or birds on private land

game·ly *adv* **:** with spirit and courage

game·ness *n* **:** the quality or state of being spirited and courageous

game show *n* **:** a television program on which contestants compete for prizes in a game (as a quiz)

game warden *n* **:** a person who sees that fishing and hunting laws are obeyed

gam·ing *n* **:** the practice of gambling

gam·ma rays *n pl* **:** very penetrating rays like X rays but of shorter wavelength

gamy *adj* **gam·i·er; gam·i·est :** having the flavor of wild game especially when slightly spoiled

gan·der *n* **:** a male goose

gang *n* **1 :** a group of persons working or going about together **2 :** a group of persons acting together to do something illegal

gan·gli·on *n, pl* **gan·glia :** a mass of nerve cells especially outside the brain or spinal cord

gang·plank *n* **:** a movable bridge from a ship to the shore

gan·grene *n* **:** death of body tissue when the blood supply is cut off

gang·ster *n* **:** a member of a gang of criminals

gang·way *n* **1 :** a way into, through, or out of an enclosed space **2 :** GANGPLANK

gan·net *n* **:** a large bird that eats fish and spends much time far from land

gan·try *n, pl* **gantries 1 :** a structure over railroad tracks for holding signals **2 :** a movable structure for preparing a rocket for launching

gap *n* **1 :** an opening made by a break or a coming apart **2 :** an opening between mountains **3 :** a hole or space where something is missing

[1]**gape** *vb* **gaped; gap•ing** **1 :** to open the mouth wide **2 :** to stare with open mouth **3 :** to open or part widely
[2]**gape** *n* **:** an act or instance of gaping
[1]**ga•rage** *n* **:** a building where automobiles or trucks are repaired or kept when not in use
[2]**garage** *vb* **ga•raged; ga•rag•ing :** to keep or put in a garage
[1]**garb** *n* **:** style or kind of clothing
[2]**garb** *vb* **:** CLOTHE 1
gar•bage *n* **:** waste food especially from a kitchen
gar•ble *vb* **gar•bled; gar•bling :** to change or twist the meaning or sound of
[1]**gar•den** *n* **1 :** a piece of ground in which fruits, flowers, or vegetables are grown **2 :** an enclosure for the public showing of plants or animals
[2]**garden** *vb* **:** to make or work in a garden
gar•den•er *n* **:** a person who gardens especially for pay
gar•de•nia *n* **:** a large white or yellowish flower with a fragrant smell
[1]**gar•gle** *vb* **gar•gled; gar•gling :** to rinse the throat with a liquid kept in motion by air forced through it from the lungs
[2]**gargle** *n* **1 :** a liquid used in gargling **2 :** a gargling sound
gar•goyle *n* **:** a waterspout in the form of a strange or frightening human or animal figure sticking out at the roof or eaves of a building
gar•ish *adj* **:** too bright or showy **:** GAUDY
[1]**gar•land** *n* **:** a wreath or rope of leaves or flowers
[2]**garland** *vb* **:** to form into or decorate with a garland
gar•lic *n* **:** a plant related to the onion and grown for its bulbs that have a strong smell and taste and are used to flavor foods
gar•ment *n* **:** an article of clothing
gar•ner *vb* **:** to gather in and store
gar•net *n* **:** a deep red mineral used as a gem
[1]**gar•nish** *vb* **:** to add decorations or seasoning (as to food)
[2]**garnish** *n* **:** something used in garnishing
gar•ret *n* **:** a room or unfinished part of a house just under the roof
[1]**gar•ri•son** *n* **:** a place in which troops are regularly stationed
[2]**garrison** *vb* **1 :** to station troops in **2 :** to send (troops) to a garrison
gar•ter *n* **:** a band worn to hold up a stocking or sock
garter snake *n* **:** any of numerous harmless American snakes with stripes along the back
[1]**gas** *n, pl* **gas•es** **1 :** a substance (as oxygen or hydrogen) having no fixed shape and tending to expand without limit **2 :** a gas or a mixture of gases used as a fuel or to make one unconscious (as for an operation) **3 :** a fluid that poisons the air or makes breathing difficult **4 :** GASOLINE
[2]**gas** *vb* **gassed; gas•sing; gas•ses** **1 :** to treat with gas **2 :** to poison with gas **3 :** to supply with gas
gas•eous *adj* **:** of or relating to gas
[1]**gash** *n* **:** a long deep cut
[2]**gash** *vb* **:** to make a long deep cut in
gas mask *n* **:** a mask connected to a chemical air filter and used to protect the face and lungs from poisonous gases
gas•o•line *n* **:** a flammable liquid made especially from gas found in the earth and from petroleum and used mostly as an automobile fuel
[1]**gasp** *vb* **1 :** to breathe with difficulty **:** PANT **2 :** to utter with quick difficult breaths
[2]**gasp** *n* **1 :** the act of gasping **2 :** something gasped
gas station *n* **:** SERVICE STATION
gas•tric juice *n* **:** an acid liquid made by the stomach that helps to digest food
gate *n* **1 :** an opening in a wall or fence often with a movable frame or door for closing it **2 :** a part of a barrier (as a fence) that opens and closes like a door
[1]**gath•er** *vb* **1 :** to bring or come together **2 :** to pick out and collect **3 :** to gain little by little **4 :** to get an idea **:** CONCLUDE **5 :** to draw together in folds
[2]**gather** *n* **:** the result of gathering cloth **:** PUCKER
gath•er•ing *n* **:** a coming together of people **:** MEETING
gau•cho *n, pl* **gauchos :** a South American cowboy
gaudy *adj* **gaud•i•er; gaud•i•est :** too showy
[1]**gauge** *or* **gage** *n* **1 :** measurement according to a standard **2 :** SIZE 2 **3 :** an instrument for measuring, testing, or registering
[2]**gauge** *or* **gage** *vb* **gauged** *or* **gaged; gaug•ing** *or* **gag•ing** **1 :** to measure exactly **2 :** to find out the capacity or contents of **3 :** [1]ESTIMATE 1, JUDGE
gaunt *adj* **:** very thin and bony (as from illness or starvation)
[1]**gaunt•let** *n* **1 :** a glove made of small metal plates and worn with a suit of armor **2 :** a glove with a wide cuff that covers and protects the wrist and part of the arm
[2]**gauntlet** *n* **:** a double file of persons who beat someone forced to run between them
gauze *n* **:** a thin transparent fabric
gauzy *adj* **gauz•i•er; gauz•i•est :** thin and transparent like gauze
gave *past of* GIVE
gav•el *n* **:** a mallet with which the person in

charge raps to call a meeting or court to order
gawk *vb* **:** to stare stupidly
gawky *adj* **gawk·i·er; gawk·i·est :** AWKWARD 1, CLUMSY — **gawk·i·ly** *adv* — **gawk·i·ness** *n*
gay *adj* **gay·er; gay·est 1 :** MERRY **2 :** brightly colored
1gaze *vb* **gazed; gaz·ing :** to fix the eyes in a long steady look
2gaze *n* **:** a long steady look
ga·zelle *n* **:** a swift graceful antelope with large bright eyes
ga·zette *n* **1 :** NEWSPAPER **2 :** a journal giving official information
gaz·et·teer *n* **:** a geographical dictionary
ga·zil·lion *n* **:** a large number — **gazillion** *adj*
1gear *n* **1 :** EQUIPMENT 2 **2 :** a group of parts that has a specific function in a machine **3 :** a toothed wheel **:** COGWHEEL **4 :** the position the gears of a machine are in when they are ready to work **5 :** one of the adjustments in a motor vehicle that determine the direction of travel and the relative speed between the engine and the motion of the vehicle
2gear *vb* **1 :** to make ready for operation **2 :** to make suitable
gear·shift *n* **:** a mechanism by which gears are connected and disconnected
gee *interj* — used to show surprise or enthusiasm
geese *pl of* GOOSE
Gei·ger counter *n* **:** an instrument for detecting the presence of cosmic rays or radioactive substances
gel·a·tin *n* **1 :** a protein obtained by boiling animal tissues and used especially as food **2 :** an edible jelly formed with gelatin
gem *n* **:** a usually valuable stone cut and polished for jewelry
Gem·i·ni *n* **1 :** a constellation between Taurus and Cancer imagined as twins **2 :** the third sign of the zodiac or a person born under this sign
gen·der *n* **:** SEX 1
gene *n* **:** a unit of DNA that controls the development of a single characteristic in an individual
genera *pl of* GENUS
1gen·er·al *adj* **1 :** having to do with the whole **2 :** not specific or detailed **3 :** not specialized
2general *n* **:** a commissioned officer in the Army, Air Force, or Marine Corps ranking above a lieutenant general
gen·er·al·iza·tion *n* **1 :** the act of generalizing **2 :** a general statement
gen·er·al·ize *vb* **gen·er·al·ized; gen·er·al·iz·ing :** to put in the form of a general rule **:** draw or state a general conclusion from a number of different items or instances
gen·er·al·ly *adv* **:** as a rule **:** USUALLY
General of the Air Force : the highest ranking commissioned officer in the Air Force ranking above a general
General of the Army : the highest ranking commissioned officer in the Army ranking above a general
gen·er·ate *vb* **gen·er·at·ed; gen·er·at·ing :** to cause to come into being
gen·er·a·tion *n* **1 :** those having the same parents and being a step in a line from one ancestor **2 :** a group of individuals born about the same time **3 :** the act of generating something
gen·er·a·tor *n* **:** DYNAMO
gen·er·os·i·ty *n, pl* **gen·er·os·i·ties 1 :** willingness to give or to share **2 :** a generous act
gen·er·ous *adj* **1 :** free in giving or sharing **2 :** ABUNDANT — **gen·er·ous·ly** *adv*
gen·e·sis *n, pl* **gen·e·ses :** a coming into being
ge·net·ic *adj* **:** of or relating to genetics
genetic code *n* **:** the arrangement of chemical groups within the genes by which genetic information is passed on
ge·net·i·cist *n* **:** a specialist in genetics
ge·net·ics *n* **:** a branch of biology that deals with the heredity and variation of living things
ge·nial *adj* **:** pleasantly cheerful — **ge·nial·ly** *adv*
ge·nie *n* **:** a magic spirit believed to take human form and serve the person who calls it
gen·i·tal *adj* **:** of or relating to reproduction or sex
ge·nius *n* **1 :** great natural ability **2 :** a very gifted person
gen·tian *n* **:** an herb with smooth opposite leaves and usually blue flowers
1gen·tile *n, often cap* **:** a person who is not Jewish
2gentile *adj, often cap* **:** of or relating to people not Jewish
gen·til·i·ty *n* **1 :** good birth and family **2 :** the qualities of a well-bred person **3 :** good manners
gen·tle *adj* **gen·tler; gen·tlest 1 :** easily handled **:** not wild **2 :** not harsh or stern **:** MILD **3 :** 1MODERATE 1 — **gen·tle·ness** *n*
gen·tle·folk *n pl* **:** GENTRY 1
gen·tle·man *n, pl* **gen·tle·men 1 :** a man of good birth and position **2 :** a man of good education and social position **3 :** a man with very good manners **4 :** MAN — used

in the plural when speaking to a group of men — **gen·tle·man·ly** *adj*

gen·tle·wom·an *n, pl* **gen·tle·wom·en** **1 :** a woman of good birth and position **2 :** a woman with very good manners **:** LADY 2

gen·tly *adv* **:** in a gentle manner

gen·try *n* **1 :** people of good birth, breeding, and education **2 :** people of a certain class

gen·u·flect *vb* **:** to kneel on one knee and rise again as an act of deep respect

gen·u·ine *adj* **1 :** being just what it seems to be **:** REAL **2 :** HONEST 1, SINCERE — **gen·u·ine·ly** *adv* — **gen·u·ine·ness** *n*

ge·nus *n, pl* **gen·era :** a group of related plants or animals that ranks below the family in scientific classification and is made up of one or more species

geo- *prefix* **1 :** earth **2 :** geographical

geo·chem·is·try *n* **:** chemistry that deals with the earth's crust

geo·graph·ic *or* **geo·graph·i·cal** *adj* **:** of or relating to geography

ge·og·ra·phy *n* **1 :** a science that deals with the location of living and nonliving things on earth and the way they affect one another **2 :** the natural features of an area

geo·log·ic *or* **geo·log·i·cal** *adj* **:** of or relating to geology

ge·ol·o·gist *n* **:** a specialist in geology

ge·ol·o·gy *n* **1 :** a science that deals with the history of the earth and its life especially as recorded in rocks **2 :** the geologic features (as mountains or plains) of an area

geo·mag·net·ic *adj* **:** of or relating to the magnetism of the earth

geo·met·ric *adj* **:** of or relating to geometry

ge·om·e·try *n* **:** a branch of mathematics that deals with points, lines, angles, surfaces, and solids

ge·ra·ni·um *n* **:** an herb often grown for its bright flowers

ger·bil *n* **:** a small Old World leaping desert rodent

germ *n* **1 :** a bit of living matter capable of forming a new individual **2 :** a source from which something develops **3 :** a microbe that causes disease

[1]Ger·man *n* **1 :** a person born or living in Germany **2 :** the language spoken mainly in Germany, Austria, and parts of Switzerland

[2]German *adj* **:** of or relating to Germany, the Germans, or the German language

ger·ma·ni·um *n* **:** a white hard brittle element used as a semiconductor

germ cell *n* **:** a reproductive cell (as an egg or sperm cell)

ger·mi·cide *n* **:** a substance that destroys germs

ger·mi·nate *vb* **ger·mi·nat·ed; ger·mi·nat·ing :** [1]SPROUT

ger·mi·na·tion *n* **:** a beginning of development (as of a seed)

ges·tic·u·late *vb* **ges·tic·u·lat·ed; ges·tic·u·lat·ing :** to make gestures especially when speaking

[1]ges·ture *n* **1 :** a motion of the limbs or body that expresses an idea or a feeling **2 :** something said or done that shows one's feelings

[2]gesture *vb* **ges·tured; ges·tur·ing :** to make or direct with a gesture

get *vb* **got; got** *or* **got·ten; get·ting 1 :** to gain possession of (as by receiving, earning, buying, or winning) **2 :** ARRIVE 1 **3 :** GO 1, MOVE **4 :** BECOME 1 **5 :** [1]CATCH 7 **6 :** to cause to be **7 :** UNDERSTAND 1 **8 :** PERSUADE — **get ahead :** to achieve success (as in business) — **get around 1 :** to get the better of **2 :** EVADE — **get at 1 :** to reach with or as if with the hand **2 :** to turn one's attention to **3 :** to try to prove or make clear — **get away with :** to do (as something wrong) without being caught — **get back at :** to get even with — **get even :** to get revenge — **get even with :** to pay back for a real or imagined injury — **get one's goat :** to make one angry or annoyed — **get over :** to recover from — **get together 1 :** to bring or come together **2 :** to reach agreement — **get wind of :** to become aware of **:** hear about

get along *vb* **1 :** to approach old age **2 :** to meet one's needs **3 :** to stay friendly

get by *vb* **1 :** GET ALONG 2 **2 :** to succeed with the least possible effort or accomplishment

get off *vb* **1 :** START **2 :** to escape punishment or harm

get out *vb* **1 :** ESCAPE **2 :** to become known

get–to·geth·er *n* **:** an informal social gathering

get up *vb* **1 :** to arise from bed **2 :** to rise to one's feet **3 :** PREPARE, ORGANIZE **4 :** DRESS

gey·ser *n* **:** a spring that now and then shoots up hot water and steam

ghast·ly *adj* **ghast·li·er; ghast·li·est 1 :** HORRIBLE, SHOCKING **2 :** like a ghost **:** PALE

ghet·to *n, pl* **ghettos** *or* **ghettoes :** a part of a city in which members of a minority group live because of social, legal, or economic pressure

ghost *n* **:** the spirit of a dead person thought of as living in an unseen world or as appearing to living people

ghost·ly *adj* **ghost·li·er; ghost·li·est :** of, relating to, or like a ghost

ghost town *n* **:** a town deserted because some nearby natural resource has been used up

ghoul *n* **1 :** an evil being of legend that robs graves and feeds on corpses **2 :** someone whose activities suggest those of a ghoul

[1]**gi·ant** *n* **1 :** an imaginary person of great size and strength **2 :** a person or thing that is very large or powerful

[2]**giant** *adj* **:** much larger than ordinary **:** HUGE

giant panda *n* **:** a large black-and-white mammal of the bear family found mainly in central China

gib·ber·ish *n* **:** confused meaningless talk

gib·bon *n* **:** a small ape of southeastern Asia that has long arms and legs and lives mostly in trees

[1]**gibe** *or* **jibe** *vb* **gibed; gib·ing :** [1]JEER

[2]**gibe** *or* **jibe** *n* **:** [2]JEER

gib·let *n* **:** an edible inner organ (as the heart or liver) of a fowl

gid·dy *adj* **gid·di·er; gid·di·est 1 :** having a feeling of whirling or spinning about **:** DIZZY **2 :** causing dizziness **3 :** SILLY 3 — **gid·di·ness** *n*

gift *n* **1 :** a special ability **:** TALENT **2 :** something given **:** PRESENT

gift·ed *adj* **:** having great ability

gig *n* **1 :** a long light boat for a ship's captain **2 :** a light carriage having two wheels and pulled by a horse

giga·byte *n* **:** a unit of computer information storage capacity equal to 1,073,741,824 bytes

gi·gan·tic *adj* **:** like a giant (as in size, weight, or strength)

gig·gle *vb* **gig·gled; gig·gling :** to laugh with repeated short high sounds

Gi·la monster *n* **:** a large black and orange poisonous lizard of the southwestern United States

gild *vb* **gild·ed** *or* **gilt; gild·ing :** to cover with a thin coating of gold

[1]**gill** *n* **:** a unit of liquid capacity equal to a quarter of a pint (about 120 milliliters)

[2]**gill** *n* **:** an organ (as of a fish) for taking oxygen from water

[1]**gilt** *n* **:** gold or something like gold applied to a surface

[2]**gilt** *n* **:** a young female hog

gim·let *n* **:** a small tool for boring

[1]**gin** *n* **:** a machine to separate seeds from cotton

[2]**gin** *vb* **ginned; gin·ning :** to separate seeds from cotton in a gin

[3]**gin** *n* **:** a strong alcoholic liquor flavored with juniper berries

gin·ger *n* **:** a hot spice obtained from the root of a tropical plant and used to season foods (as cookies) or in medicine

ginger ale *n* **:** a soft drink flavored with ginger

gin·ger·bread *n* **:** a dark cake flavored with ginger and molasses

gin·ger·ly *adv* **:** with great caution or care

gin·ger·snap *n* **:** a thin brittle cookie flavored with ginger

ging·ham *n* **:** a cotton cloth in plain weave

gipsy *variant of* GYPSY

gi·raffe *n* **:** a spotted mammal of Africa that has a long neck and chews the cud

gird *vb* **gird·ed** *or* **girt; gird·ing :** to encircle or fasten with or as if with a belt or cord

gird·er *n* **:** a horizontal main supporting beam

[1]**gir·dle** *n* **1 :** something (as a belt or sash) that encircles or binds **2 :** a light corset worn below the waist

[2]**girdle** *vb* **gir·dled; gir·dling 1 :** to bind with or as if with a girdle, belt, or sash **:** ENCIRCLE **2 :** to strip a ring of bark from a tree trunk

girl *n* **1 :** a female child or young woman **2 :** a female servant **3 :** GIRLFRIEND

girl·friend *n* **1 :** a female friend **2 :** a regular female companion of a boy or man

girl·hood *n* **:** the state or time of being a girl

girl·ish *adj* **:** of, relating to, or having qualities often felt to be typical of a girl — **girl·ish·ly** *adv* — **girl·ish·ness** *n*

Girl Scout *n* **:** a member of the Girl Scouts of the United States of America

girth *n* **1 :** a band put around the body of an animal to hold something (as a saddle) on its back **2 :** the measure or distance around something

gist *n* **:** the main point of a matter

[1]**give** *vb* **gave; giv·en; giv·ing 1 :** to hand over to be kept **:** PRESENT **2 :** [1]PAY 1 **3 :** [2]UTTER **4 :** FURNISH, PROVIDE **5 :** to cause to have **6 :** to let someone or something have **7 :** to yield slightly **8 :** to yield as a product **:** PRODUCE — **give way 1 :** to yield oneself without control **2 :** to break down **:** COLLAPSE

[2]**give** *n* **:** the quality of being able to bend under pressure

give in *vb* **1 :** [1]OFFER 2 **2 :** [1]SURRENDER 1, YIELD

giv·en *adj* **1 :** being likely to have or do something **2 :** decided on beforehand

given name *n* **:** a first name (as *John* or *Susan*)

give up *vb* **1 :** to let go **:** ABANDON **2 :** to stop trying **:** QUIT

giz·zard *n* **:** a large muscular part of the

digestive tube (as of a bird) in which food is churned and ground small

gla·cial *adj* **1 :** very cold **2 :** of or relating to glaciers

gla·cier *n* **:** a large body of ice moving slowly down a slope or over a wide area of land

glad *adj* **glad·der; glad·dest 1 :** being happy and joyful **2 :** bringing or causing joy **3 :** very willing — **glad·ly** *adv* — **glad·ness** *n*

glad·den *vb* **:** to make glad

glade *n* **:** a grassy open space in a forest

glad·i·a·tor *n* **:** a person taking part in a fight to the death as public entertainment for the ancient Romans

glad·i·o·lus *n, pl* **glad·i·o·li** *or* **gladiolus** *or* **glad·i·o·lus·es :** a plant with long stiff pointed leaves and stalks of brightly colored flowers

glad·some *adj* **:** giving or showing joy

glam·or·ous *adj* **:** full of glamour

glam·our *or* **glam·or** *n* **1 :** appeal or attractiveness especially when it is misleading **2 :** tempting or fascinating personal attraction

[1]glance *vb* **glanced; glanc·ing 1 :** to strike at an angle and fly off to one side **2 :** to give a quick look

[2]glance *n* **:** a quick look

gland *n* **:** an organ in the body that prepares a substance to be used by the body or given off from it

glan·du·lar *adj* **:** of or relating to glands

[1]glare *vb* **glared; glar·ing 1 :** to shine with a harsh bright light **2 :** to look fiercely or angrily

[2]glare *n* **1 :** a harsh bright light **2 :** a fierce or angry look

glar·ing *adj* **1 :** so bright as to be harsh **2 :** ANGRY, FIERCE **3 :** very noticeable **:** OBVIOUS

[1]glass *n* **1 :** a hard brittle usually transparent substance commonly made from sand heated with chemicals **2 :** something made of glass **3 glasses** *pl* **:** EYEGLASS 2 **4 :** the contents of a glass

[2]glass *vb* **:** to fit or protect with glass

glass·blow·ing *n* **:** the art of shaping a mass of melted glass by blowing air into it through a tube

glass·ful *n* **:** the amount a glass will hold

glass·ware *n* **:** articles of glass

glassy *adj* **glass·i·er; glass·i·est 1 :** like glass (as in smoothness) **2 :** not shiny or bright **:** DULL

[1]glaze *vb* **glazed; glaz·ing 1 :** to set glass in **2 :** to cover with a glassy surface **3 :** to become shiny or glassy in appearance

[2]glaze *n* **:** a glassy surface or coating

gla·zier *n* **:** a person who sets glass in window frames

[1]gleam *n* **1 :** a faint, soft, or reflected light **2 :** a small bright light **3 :** a short or slight appearance

[2]gleam *vb* **1 :** to shine with a soft light **2 :** to give out gleams of light

glean *vb* **1 :** to gather from a field what is left by the harvesters **2 :** to gather (as information) little by little with patient effort

glee *n* **:** great joy **:** DELIGHT

glee club *n* **:** a singing group organized especially as a social activity in a school or college

glee·ful *adj* **:** full of glee

glen *n* **:** a narrow hidden valley

glib *adj* **glib·ber; glib·best :** speaking or spoken with careless ease and often with little regard for the truth — **glib·ly** *adv* — **glib·ness** *n*

[1]glide *vb* **glid·ed; glid·ing :** to move with a smooth silent motion

[2]glide *n* **:** the act or action of gliding

glid·er *n* **1 :** an aircraft without an engine that glides on air currents **2 :** a porch seat hung from a frame (as by chains)

[1]glim·mer *vb* **:** to shine faintly and unsteadily

[2]glimmer *n* **:** a faint unsteady light

[1]glimpse *vb* **glimpsed; glimps·ing :** to catch a quick view of

[2]glimpse *n* **:** a short hurried look

[1]glint *vb* **:** to shine with tiny bright flashes

[2]glint *n* **:** a brief flash

glis·ten *vb* **:** to shine with a soft reflected light

glitch *n* **:** a usually minor problem

[1]glit·ter *vb* **1 :** to sparkle brightly **2 :** to sparkle with light that is harsh and cold **3 :** to be very bright and showy

[2]glitter *n* **:** sparkling brightness

gloat *vb* **:** to gaze at or think about something with great satisfaction and often with mean or selfish satisfaction

glob·al *adj* **1 :** shaped like a globe **2 :** having to do with the whole earth

globe *n* **1 :** a round object **:** BALL, SPHERE **2 :** EARTH 3 **3 :** a round model of the earth or heavens

globe–trot·ter *n* **:** a person who travels widely

glob·u·lar *adj* **:** shaped like a globe **:** SPHERICAL

glob·ule *n* **:** a small round mass

glock·en·spiel *n* **:** a portable musical instrument consisting of a series of metal bars played with hammers

gloom *n* **1 :** partial or complete darkness **2 :** a sad mood

gloomy *adj* **gloom·i·er; gloom·i·est 1 :** partly or completely dark **2 :** SAD 1, BLUE

3 : causing lowness of spirits **4 :** not hopeful : PESSIMISTIC
glo·ri·fi·ca·tion *n* **:** the act of glorifying **:** the state of being glorified
glo·ri·fy *vb* **glo·ri·fied; glo·ri·fy·ing 1 :** to honor or praise as divine **:** WORSHIP **2 :** to give honor and praise to **3 :** to show in a way that looks good
glo·ri·ous *adj* **1 :** having or deserving glory **2 :** having great beauty or splendor **3 :** DELIGHTFUL
[1]**glo·ry** *n, pl* **glories 1 :** praise, honor, and admiration given to a person by others **2 :** something that brings honor, praise, or fame **3 :** BRILLIANCE, SPLENDOR **4 :** HEAVEN 2
[2]**glory** *vb* **glo·ried; glo·ry·ing :** to rejoice proudly **:** be proud or boastful
[1]**gloss** *n* **1 :** brightness from a smooth surface **:** LUSTER, SHEEN **2 :** a falsely attractive surface appearance
[2]**gloss** *vb* **1 :** to give a gloss to **2 :** to smooth over **:** explain away
glos·sa·ry *n, pl* **glos·sa·ries :** a list of the hard or unusual words used in a book given with their meanings
glossy *adj* **gloss·i·er; gloss·i·est :** smooth and shining on the surface
glove *n* **:** a covering for the hand having a separate section for each finger
[1]**glow** *vb* **1 :** to shine with or as if with great heat **2 :** to show strong bright color **3 :** to be or to look warm and flushed (as with exercise)
[2]**glow** *n* **1 :** light such as comes from something that is very hot but not flaming **2 :** brightness or warmth of color **3 :** a feeling of physical warmth (as from exercise) **4 :** warmth of feeling
glow·er *vb* **:** to stare angrily **:** SCOWL
glow·worm *n* **:** an insect or insect larva that gives off light
glu·cose *n* **:** a sugar in plant saps and fruits that is the usual form in which carbohydrate is taken in by the animal body
[1]**glue** *n* **:** a substance used to stick things tightly together
[2]**glue** *vb* **glued; glu·ing :** to stick with or as if with glue
glu·ey *adj* **glu·i·er; glu·i·est 1 :** sticky like glue **2 :** covered with glue
glum *adj* **glum·mer; glum·mest 1 :** [1]SULKY **2 :** seeming gloomy and sad — **glum·ly** *adv* — **glum·ness** *n*
[1]**glut** *vb* **glut·ted; glut·ting 1 :** to make quite full **:** fill completely **2 :** to flood with goods so that supply is greater than demand
[2]**glut** *n* **:** too much of something
glu·ti·nous *adj* **:** like glue **:** STICKY — **glu·ti·nous·ly** *adv*
glut·ton *n* **:** a person or animal that overeats — **glut·ton·ous** *adj* — **glut·ton·ous·ly** *adv*
glut·tony *n, pl* **glut·ton·ies :** the act or habit of eating or drinking too much
glyc·er·in *or* **glyc·er·ine** *n* **:** a sweet thick liquid that is found in various oils and fats and is used to moisten or dissolve things
gly·co·gen *n* **:** a white tasteless starchy substance that is the chief stored carbohydrate of animals
G–man *n, pl* **G–men :** a special agent of the Federal Bureau of Investigation
gnarled *adj* **:** being full of knots, twisted, and rugged
gnash *vb* **:** to strike or grind (the teeth) together (as in anger)
gnat *n* **:** a very small two-winged fly
gnaw *vb* **gnawed; gnaw·ing :** to bite so as to wear away little by little **:** bite or chew upon
gnome *n* **:** one of an imaginary race of dwarfs believed to live inside the earth and guard treasure
gnu *n, pl* **gnu** *or* **gnus :** a large African antelope with a head like that of an ox, curving horns, a short mane, and a tail somewhat like that of a horse
go *vb* **went; gone; go·ing; goes 1 :** to pass from one place to or toward another **2 :** to move away **:** LEAVE **3 :** to become lost, used, or spent **4 :** to continue its course or action **:** RUN **5 :** to make its own special sound **6 :** to be suitable **:** MATCH **7 :** to reach some state
[1]**goad** *n* **1 :** a pointed rod used to keep an animal moving **2 :** something that stirs one to action
[2]**goad** *vb* **:** to drive or stir with a goad
goal *n* **1 :** the point at which a race or journey is to end **2 :** an area to be reached safely in certain games **3 :** [1]PURPOSE **4 :** an object into which a ball or puck must be driven in various games in order to score **5 :** a scoring of one or more points by driving a ball or puck into a goal
goal·ie *n* **:** GOALKEEPER
goal·keep·er *n* **:** a player who defends a goal
goal·post *n* **:** one of two usually upright posts often with a crossbar that serve as the goal in various games
goal·tend·er *n* **:** GOALKEEPER
goat *n* **:** a horned animal that chews the cud and is related to but more lively than the sheep — **goat·like** *adj*
goa·tee *n* **:** a small beard trimmed to a point
goat·herd *n* **:** a person who tends goats
goat·skin *n* **:** the skin of a goat or leather made from it
gob *n* **:** [1]LUMP

[1]gob·ble *vb* **gob·bled; gob·bling :** to eat fast or greedily

[2]gobble *vb* **gob·bled; gob·bling :** to make the call of a turkey or a similar sound

[3]gobble *n* **:** the loud harsh call of a turkey

go–be·tween *n* **:** a person who acts as a messenger or peacemaker

gob·let *n* **:** a drinking glass with a foot and stem

gob·lin *n* **:** an ugly imaginary creature with evil or sly ways

god *n* **1** *cap* **:** the Being considered the holy and ruling power who made and sustains all things of the universe **2 :** a being believed to have more than human powers **3 :** a natural or artificial object worshiped as divine **4 :** something believed to be the most important thing in existence

god·child *n, pl* **god·chil·dren :** a person for whom another person is sponsor at baptism

god·dess *n* **:** a female god

god·fa·ther *n* **:** a boy or man who is sponsor for a child at its baptism

god·less *adj* **1 :** not believing in God or a god **2 :** WICKED 1, EVIL — **god·less·ness** *n*

god·like *adj* **:** like or suitable for God or a god

god·ly *adj* **god·li·er; god·li·est :** DEVOUT 1, PIOUS — **god·li·ness** *n*

god·moth·er *n* **:** a girl or woman who is sponsor for a child at its baptism

god·par·ent *n* **:** a sponsor at baptism

god·send *n* **:** some badly needed thing that comes unexpectedly

goes *present 3d sing of* GO

go–get·ter *n* **:** a very active and aggressive person

gog·gle *vb* **gog·gled; gog·gling 1 :** to roll the eyes **2 :** to stare with bulging or rolling eyes

gog·gle–eyed *adj* **:** having bulging or rolling eyes

gog·gles *n pl* **:** eyeglasses worn to protect the eyes (as from dust, sun, or wind)

go·ings–on *n pl* **:** things that happen

goi·ter *n* **:** a swelling on the front of the neck caused by enlargement of the thyroid gland

gold *n* **1 :** a soft yellow metallic chemical element used especially in coins and jewelry **2 :** gold coins **3 :** MONEY 3 **4 :** a deep yellow

gold·en *adj* **1 :** like, made of, or containing gold **2 :** of the color of gold **3 :** very good or desirable **4 :** being prosperous and happy

gold·en·rod *n* **:** a plant with tall stiff stems topped with rows of tiny yellow flower heads on slender branches

golden rule *n* **:** a rule that one should treat others as one would want others to treat oneself

gold·finch *n* **1 :** a European finch with a yellow patch on each wing **2 :** an American finch that looks like the canary

gold·fish *n* **:** a small usually golden yellow or orange carp often kept in aquariums

gold·smith *n* **:** a person who makes or deals in articles of gold

golf *n* **:** a game played by driving a small ball (**golf ball**) with one of a set of clubs (**golf clubs**) around an outdoor course (**golf course**) and into various holes in as few strokes as possible

golf·er *n* **:** a person who plays golf

gol·ly *interj* — used to express surprise or annoyance

gon·do·la *n* **1 :** a long narrow boat used in the canals of Venice, Italy **2 :** a freight car with no top **3 :** an enclosure that hangs from a balloon and carries passengers or instruments

gone *adj* **1 :** ADVANCED 1 **2 :** INFATUATED **3 :** [1]DEAD 1 **4 :** WEAK 1, LIMP

gon·er *n* **:** one whose case is hopeless

gong *n* **:** a metallic disk that produces a harsh ringing tone when struck

[1]good *adj* **bet·ter; best 1 :** suitable for a use **:** SATISFACTORY **2 :** being at least the amount mentioned **3 :** CONSIDERABLE **4 :** DESIRABLE, ATTRACTIVE **5 :** HELPFUL, KIND **6 :** behaving well **7 :** being honest and upright **8 :** showing good sense or judgment **9 :** better than average

[2]good *n* **1 :** something good **2 :** WELFARE 1, BENEFIT **3 goods** *pl* **:** WARE 2 **4 goods** *pl* **:** personal property **5 goods** *pl* **:** a length of cloth

[1]good–bye *or* **good–by** *interj* — used as a farewell remark

[2]good–bye *or* **good–by** *n* **:** a farewell remark

good–heart·ed *adj* **:** having a kindly generous disposition — **good–heart·ed·ly** *adv* — **good–heart·ed·ness** *n*

good–hu·mored *adj* **:** GOOD-NATURED — **good–hu·mored·ly** *adv* — **good–hu·mored·ness** *n*

good·ly *adj* **good·li·er; good·li·est 1 :** of pleasing appearance **2 :** LARGE, CONSIDERABLE

good–na·tured *adj* **:** having or showing a pleasant disposition — **good–na·tured·ly** *adv*

good·ness *n* **1 :** the quality or state of being good **2 :** excellence of morals and behavior

good–tem·pered *adj* **:** not easily angered or upset

good·will *n* **1 :** kindly feelings **2 :** the value of the trade a business has built up

goody *n, pl* **good·ies :** something especially good to eat

1goof *n* **1 :** a stupid or silly person **2 :** 2BLUNDER

2goof *vb* **:** to make a blunder

goofy *adj* **goof·i·er; goof·i·est :** SILLY 1

goose *n, pl* **geese 1 :** a waterbird with webbed feet that is related to the smaller duck and the larger swan **2 :** a female goose **3 :** the flesh of a goose used as food **4 :** a silly person

goose·ber·ry *n, pl* **goose·ber·ries :** the sour berry of a thorny bush related to the currant

goose bumps *n pl* **:** a roughness of the skin caused by cold, fear, or a sudden feeling of excitement

goose·flesh *n* **:** GOOSE BUMPS

goose pimples *n pl* **:** GOOSE BUMPS

go·pher *n* **1 :** a burrowing animal that is about the size of a rat and has strong claws on the forefeet and very large outside cheek pouches **2 :** a striped ground squirrel of the prairies **3 :** a burrowing American land tortoise

1gore *n* **:** shed or clotted blood

2gore *vb* **gored; gor·ing :** to pierce or wound with a horn or tusk

1gorge *n* **:** a narrow steep-walled canyon or part of a canyon

2gorge *vb* **gorged; gorg·ing :** to eat greedily

gor·geous *adj* **:** very beautiful — **gor·geous·ly** *adv* — **gor·geous·ness** *n*

go·ril·la *n* **:** a very large ape of the forests of central Africa that lives mostly on the ground

gory *adj* **gor·i·er; gor·i·est :** covered with gore

gos·ling *n* **:** a young goose

gos·pel *n* **1** *often cap* **:** the teachings of Christ and the apostles **2 :** something told or accepted as being absolutely true

gos·sa·mer *adj* **:** very light and flimsy

1gos·sip *n* **1 :** a person who repeats stories about other people **2 :** talk or rumors having no worth

2gossip *vb* **:** to spread gossip

got *past of* GET

gotten *past participle of* GET

1gouge *n* **1 :** a chisel with a curved blade for scooping or cutting holes **2 :** a hole or groove made with or as if with a gouge

2gouge *vb* **gouged; goug·ing :** to dig out with or as if with a gouge

gou·lash *n* **:** a beef stew made with vegetables and paprika

gourd *n* **:** the fruit of a vine (**gourd vine**) related to the pumpkin and melon

gour·met *n* **:** a person who appreciates fine food and drink

gov·ern *vb* **1 :** 2RULE 2 **2 :** to influence the actions and conduct of **:** CONTROL

gov·ern·able *adj* **:** possible to govern

gov·ern·ess *n* **:** a woman who teaches and trains a child especially in a private home

gov·ern·ment *n* **1 :** control and direction of public business (as of a city or a nation) **2 :** a system of control **:** an established form of political rule **3 :** the persons making up a governing body

gov·ern·men·tal *adj* **:** of or relating to government or the government

gov·er·nor *n* **1 :** a person who governs and especially the elected head of a state of the United States **2 :** a device attached to an engine for controlling its speed

gov·er·nor·ship *n* **1 :** the office or position of governor **2 :** the term of office of a governor

gown *n* **1 :** a woman's dress **2 :** a loose robe

1grab *vb* **grabbed; grab·bing :** 1SNATCH

2grab *n* **:** the act or an instance of grabbing

1grace *n* **1 :** GOODWILL 1, FAVOR **2 :** a short prayer at a meal **3 :** pleasing and attractive behavior or quality **4 :** the condition of being in favor **5 :** a sense of what is proper **6 :** an extra note or notes in music (as a trill) added for ornamentation **7 :** beauty and ease of movement

2grace *vb* **graced; grac·ing 1 :** to do credit to **:** HONOR **2 :** to make more attractive **:** ADORN

grace·ful *adj* **:** showing grace or beauty in form or action — **grace·ful·ly** *adv* — **grace·ful·ness** *n*

grace·less *adj* **:** lacking grace — **grace·less·ly** *adv* — **grace·less·ness** *n*

gra·cious *adj* **1 :** being kind and courteous **2 :** GRACEFUL — **gra·cious·ly** *adv* — **gra·cious·ness** *n*

grack·le *n* **:** a large blackbird with shiny feathers that show changeable green, purple, and bronze colors

1grade *n* **1 :** a position in a scale of rank, quality, or order **2 :** a class of things that are of the same rank, quality, or order **3 :** a division of a school course representing a year's work **4 :** the group of pupils in a school grade **5 grades** *pl* **:** the elementary school system **6 :** a mark or rating especially in school **7 :** the degree of slope (as of a road or railroad track) **:** SLOPE

2grade *vb* **grad·ed; grad·ing 1 :** to arrange in grades **:** SORT **2 :** to make level or evenly sloping **3 :** to give a grade to **4 :** to assign to a grade

grade school *n* **:** a school including the first six or the first eight grades

grad·u·al *adj* **:** moving or happening by steps or degrees — **grad·u·al·ly** *adv*

[1]**grad·u·ate** *n* **:** a person who has completed the required course of study in a college or school

[2]**grad·u·ate** *vb* **grad·u·at·ed; grad·u·at·ing :** to become a graduate **:** finish a course of study

grad·u·a·tion *n* **1 :** the act or process of graduating **2 :** COMMENCEMENT 2

Graeco- — see GRECO-

[1]**graft** *n* **1 :** a grafted plant **2 :** the act of grafting **3 :** something (as skin or a bud) used in grafting **4 :** something (as money or advantage) gotten in a dishonest way and especially by betraying a public trust

[2]**graft** *vb* **1 :** to insert a twig or bud from one plant into another plant so they are joined and grow together **2 :** to join one thing to another as if by grafting **3 :** to gain money or advantage in a dishonest way — **graft·er** *n*

grain *n* **1 :** the edible seed or seedlike fruit of some grasses (as wheat or oats) or a few other plants (as buckwheat) **2 :** plants that produce grain **3 :** a small hard particle **4 :** a tiny amount **:** BIT **5 :** a unit of weight equal to 0.0648 gram **6 :** the arrangement of fibers in wood — **grained** *adj*

gram *or* **gramme** *n* **:** a unit of mass in the metric system equal to $^1/_{1000}$ kilogram

-gram *n suffix* **:** drawing **:** writing **:** record

gram·mar *n* **1 :** the study of the classes of words and their uses and relations in sentences **2 :** the study of what is good and bad to use in speaking and writing **3 :** speech or writing judged according to the rules of grammar

gram·mat·i·cal *adj* **:** of, relating to, or following the rules of grammar — **gram·mat·i·cal·ly** *adv*

gra·na·ry *n, pl* **gra·na·ries :** a storehouse for grain

grand *adj* **1 :** higher in rank than others **:** FOREMOST **2 :** great in size **3 :** COMPREHENSIVE, INCLUSIVE **4 :** showing wealth or high social standing **5 :** IMPRESSIVE **6 :** very good — **grand·ly** *adv* — **grand·ness** *n*

grand·aunt *n* **:** GREAT-AUNT

grand·child *n, pl* **grand·chil·dren :** a child of one's son or daughter

grand·daugh·ter *n* **:** a daughter of one's son or daughter

gran·dee *n* **:** a man of high rank especially in Spain or Portugal

gran·deur *n* **:** impressive greatness (as of power or nature)

grand·fa·ther *n* **1 :** the father of one's father or mother **2 :** ANCESTOR — **grand·fa·ther·ly** *adj*

grandfather clock *n* **:** a tall clock standing directly on the floor

grand·ma *n* **:** GRANDMOTHER 1

grand·moth·er *n* **1 :** the mother of one's father or mother **2 :** a female ancestor — **grand·moth·er·ly** *adj*

grand·neph·ew *n* **:** a grandson of one's brother or sister

grand·niece *n* **:** a granddaughter of one's brother or sister

grand·pa *n* **:** GRANDFATHER 1

grand·par·ent *n* **:** a parent of one's father or mother

grand·son *n* **:** a son of one's son or daughter

grand·stand *n* **:** the main stand (as on an athletic field) for spectators

grand·un·cle *n* **:** GREAT-UNCLE

gran·ite *n* **:** a very hard rock that is used for building and for monuments

gran·ny *n, pl* **gran·nies :** GRANDMOTHER 1

granny knot *n* **:** a knot that is not very firm and is often made accidentally instead of a square knot

[1]**grant** *vb* **1 :** to agree to **2 :** to give as a favor or right **3 :** to admit (something not yet proved) to be true

[2]**grant** *n* **1 :** the act of granting **2 :** GIFT 2

grape *n* **:** a juicy berry that has a smooth green or whitish to deep red, purple, or black skin and grows in clusters on a woody vine (**grapevine**)

grape·fruit *n* **:** a large fruit with a yellow skin that is related to the orange and lemon

graph *n* **:** a diagram that by means of dots and lines shows a system of relationships between things

-graph *n suffix* **1 :** something written **2 :** instrument for making or sending records

[1]**graph·ic** *adj* **1 :** being written, drawn, printed, or engraved **2 :** told or described in a clear vivid way **3 :** of or relating to the pictorial arts or to printing — **graph·i·cal·ly** *adv*

[2]**graphic** *n* **1 :** a picture, map, or graph used for illustration **2 graphics** *pl* **:** a display (as of pictures or graphs) generated by a computer on a screen or printer

graph·ite *n* **:** a soft black carbon used in making lead pencils and as a lubricant

-g·ra·phy *n suffix, pl* **-g·ra·phies :** writing or picturing in a special way, by a special means, or of a special thing

grap·nel *n* **:** a small anchor with several claws that can be used to anchor a boat or to take and keep a hold on an object (as another boat or something under water)

[1]**grap·ple** *n* **1 :** the act of grappling or seizing **2 :** a device for grappling

[2]**grapple** *vb* **grap·pled; grap·pling 1 :** to

seize or hold with an instrument (as a hook) **2 :** to seize and struggle with another

¹grasp *vb* **1 :** to seize and hold with or as if with the hand **:** GRIP **2 :** to make the motion of seizing **:** CLUTCH **3 :** UNDERSTAND 1, COMPREHEND

²grasp *n* **1 :** the act of grasping **:** a grip of the hand **2 :** ²CONTROL 1, HOLD **3 :** the power of seizing and holding **:** REACH **4 :** ¹UNDERSTANDING 1, COMPREHENSION

grasp•ing *adj* **:** GREEDY 2

grass *n* **1 :** plants suitable for or eaten by grazing animals **2 :** any of a large natural group of green plants with jointed stems, long slender leaves, and stalks of clustered flowers **3 :** GRASSLAND — **grass•like** *adj*

grass•hop•per *n* **:** a common leaping insect that feeds on plants

grass•land *n* **:** land covered with herbs (as grass and clover) rather than shrubs and trees

grassy *adj* **grass•i•er; grass•i•est :** of, like, or covered with grass

¹grate *vb* **grat•ed; grat•ing 1 :** to break into small pieces by rubbing against something rough **2 :** to grind or rub against something with a scratching noise **3 :** to have a harsh effect

²grate *n* **1 :** a frame containing parallel or crossed bars (as in a window) **2 :** a frame of iron bars for holding burning fuel

grate•ful *adj* **1 :** feeling or showing thanks **2 :** providing pleasure or comfort — **grate•ful•ly** *adv* — **grate•ful•ness** *n*

grat•er *n* **:** a device with a rough surface for grating

grat•i•fi•ca•tion *n* **1 :** the act of gratifying **:** the state of being gratified **2 :** something that gratifies

grat•i•fy *vb* **grat•i•fied; grat•i•fy•ing :** to give pleasure or satisfaction to

grat•ing *n* **:** ²GRATE 1

grat•i•tude *n* **:** the state of being grateful

¹grave *n* **:** a hole in the ground for burying a dead body

²grave *adj* **grav•er; grav•est 1 :** deserving serious thought **:** IMPORTANT **2 :** having a serious look or way of acting — **grave•ly** *adv* — **grave•ness** *n*

grav•el *n* **:** small pieces of rock and pebbles larger than grains of sand

grav•el•ly *adj* **1 :** containing or made up of gravel **2 :** sounding harsh or scratchy

grave•stone *n* **:** a monument on a grave

grave•yard *n* **:** CEMETERY

grav•i•tate *vb* **grav•i•tat•ed; grav•i•tat•ing :** to move or be drawn toward something

grav•i•ta•tion *n* **1 :** a force of attraction that tends to draw particles or bodies together **2 :** the act or process of gravitating

grav•i•ty *n, pl* **grav•i•ties 1 :** the condition of being grave **2 :** the attraction of bodies by gravitation toward the center of the earth **3 :** GRAVITATION 1

gra•vy *n, pl* **gravies :** a sauce made from the juice of cooked meat

¹gray *or* **grey** *adj* **1 :** of the color gray **2 :** having gray hair **3 :** lacking cheer or brightness — **gray•ness** *n*

²gray *or* **grey** *n* **1 :** something gray in color **2 :** a color that is a blend of black and white

³gray *or* **grey** *vb* **:** to make or become gray

gray•ish *adj* **:** somewhat gray

¹graze *vb* **grazed; graz•ing 1 :** to eat grass **2 :** to supply with grass or pasture

²graze *vb* **grazed; graz•ing 1 :** to rub lightly in passing **:** barely touch **2 :** to scrape by rubbing against something

³graze *n* **:** a scrape or mark caused by grazing

¹grease *n* **1 :** a more or less solid substance obtained from animal fat by melting **2 :** oily material **3 :** a thick lubricant

²grease *vb* **greased; greas•ing 1 :** to smear with grease **2 :** to lubricate with grease

grease•paint *n* **:** actors' makeup

greasy *adj* **greas•i•er; greas•i•est 1 :** smeared with grease **2 :** like or full of grease

great *adj* **1 :** very large in size **:** HUGE **2 :** large in number **:** NUMEROUS **3 :** long continued **4 :** much beyond the average or ordinary **5 :** IMPORTANT 1, DISTINGUISHED **6 :** remarkable in knowledge or skill **7 :** GRAND 6 — **great•ly** *adv*

great–aunt *n* **:** an aunt of one's father or mother

great–grand•child *n, pl* **great–grand•chil•dren :** a grandson (**great–grandson**) or granddaughter (**great–granddaughter**) of one's son or daughter

great–grand•par•ent *n* **:** a grandfather (**great–grandfather**) or grandmother (**great–grandmother**) of one's father or mother

great–un•cle *n* **:** an uncle of one's father or mother

grebe *n* **:** any of a group of swimming and diving birds related to the loons

Gre•cian *adj* **:** ²GREEK

Gre•co- *or* **Grae•co-** *prefix* **1 :** Greece **:** Greeks **2 :** Greek and

greed *n* **:** greedy desire (as for money or food)

greedy *adj* **greed•i•er; greed•i•est 1 :** having a strong appetite for food or drink **:** very hungry **2 :** trying to grab more than one needs or more than one's share — **greed•i•ly** *adv* — **greed•i•ness** *n*

¹Greek *n* **1 :** a person born or living in Greece **2 :** the language of the Greeks
²Greek *adj* **:** of or relating to Greece, its people, or the Greek language
¹green *adj* **1 :** of the color green **2 :** covered with green vegetation **3 :** made of green plants or of the leafy parts of plants **4 :** not ripe **5 :** not fully processed, treated, or seasoned **6 :** lacking training or experience **7 :** supporting the preservation or improvement of the natural environment (as by controlling pollution) **8 :** helping to preserve the environment (as by being recyclable or not polluting) — **green•ly** *adv* — **green•ness** *n*
²green *n* **1 :** a color that ranges between blue and yellow **2 greens** *pl* **:** leafy parts of plants used for decoration or food **3 :** a grassy plain or plot
green•ery *n, pl* **green•er•ies :** green plants or foliage
green•horn *n* **:** a person who is new at something
green•house *n* **:** a building with glass walls and roof for growing plants
greenhouse effect *n* **:** warming of the lower atmosphere of the earth that occurs when radiation from the sun is absorbed by the earth and then given off again and absorbed by carbon dioxide and water vapor in the atmosphere
green•ish *adj* **:** somewhat green
green•ling *n* **:** any of a group of food and sport fishes of the Pacific coast
green manure *n* **:** a leafy crop (as of clover) plowed under to improve the soil
green thumb *n* **:** an unusual ability to make plants grow
green•wood *n* **:** a forest green with leaves
greet *vb* **1 :** to speak to in a friendly polite way upon arrival or meeting **2 :** to receive or react to in a certain way **3 :** to present itself to — **greet•er** *n*
greet•ing *n* **1 :** an expression of pleasure on meeting someone **2 :** SALUTATION 2 **3 :** an expression of good wishes
gre•gar•i•ous *adj* **:** tending to live together with or associate with others of one's own kind — **gre•gar•i•ous•ly** *adv* — **gre•gar•i•ous•ness** *n*
gre•nade *n* **:** a small bomb designed to be thrown by hand or fired (as by a rifle)
gren•a•dier *n* **:** a member of a European regiment formerly armed with grenades
grew *past of* GROW
grey *variant of* GRAY
grey•hound *n* **:** a tall swift dog with a smooth coat and good eyesight
grid *n* **1 :** a group of electrical conductors that form a network **2 :** a network of horizontal and perpendicular lines (as for locating places on a map)
grid•dle *n* **:** a flat surface or pan on which food is cooked
griddle cake *n* **:** PANCAKE
grid•iron *n* **1 :** a grate with parallel bars for broiling food **2 :** a football field
grief *n* **1 :** very deep sorrow **2 :** a cause of sorrow **3 :** MISHAP
griev•ance *n* **1 :** a cause of uneasiness or annoyance **2 :** a formal complaint
grieve *vb* **grieved; griev•ing 1 :** to cause grief to **2 :** to feel or show grief
griev•ous *adj* **1 :** causing suffering **2 :** SERIOUS 5, GRAVE
¹grill *vb* **1 :** to broil on a grill **2 :** to distress with continued questioning
²grill *n* **1 :** a grate on which food is broiled **2 :** a dish of broiled food **3 :** a simple restaurant
grille *or* **grill** *n* **:** an often ornamental arrangement of bars (as of metal) forming a barrier or screen
grim *adj* **grim•mer; grim•mest 1 :** ¹SAVAGE 2, CRUEL **2 :** harsh in appearance **:** STERN **3 :** UNYIELDING 2 **4 :** FRIGHTFUL 1 — **grim•ly** *adv* — **grim•ness** *n*
¹gri•mace *n* **:** a twisting of the face (as in disgust)
²grim•ace *vb* **grim•aced; grim•ac•ing :** to make a grimace
grime *n* **:** dirt rubbed into a surface
grimy *adj* **grim•i•er; grim•i•est :** full of grime **:** DIRTY
¹grin *vb* **grinned; grin•ning :** to draw back the lips and show the teeth
²grin *n* **:** an act of grinning
¹grind *vb* **ground; grind•ing 1 :** to make or be made into meal or powder by rubbing **2 :** to wear down, polish, or sharpen by friction **3 :** to rub together with a scraping noise **4 :** to operate or produce by or as if by turning a crank
²grind *n* **1 :** an act of grinding **2 :** steady hard work
grind•stone *n* **:** a flat round stone that turns on an axle and is used for sharpening tools and for shaping and smoothing
¹grip *vb* **gripped; grip•ping 1 :** to grasp firmly **2 :** to hold the interest of
²grip *n* **1 :** a strong grasp **2 :** strength in holding **:** POWER **3 :** ¹HANDLE **4 :** a small suitcase
grippe *n* **:** a disease like or the same as influenza
gris•ly *adj* **gris•li•er; gris•li•est :** HORRIBLE, GHASTLY
grist *n* **:** grain to be ground or that is already ground

gris•tle *n* : CARTILAGE — **gris•tli•ness** *n* — **gris•tly** *adj*
grist•mill *n* : a mill for grinding grain
1grit *n* **1 :** rough hard bits especially of sand **2 :** strength of mind or spirit
2grit *vb* **grit•ted; grit•ting :** 1GRIND 3, GRATE
grits *n pl* : coarsely ground hulled grain
grit•ty *adj* **grit•ti•er; grit•ti•est 1 :** containing or like grit **2 :** bravely refusing to yield : PLUCKY — **grit•ti•ness** *n*
griz•zled *adj* : streaked or mixed with gray
griz•zly *adj* **griz•zli•er; griz•zli•est :** GRIZZLED, GRAYISH
grizzly bear *n* : a large powerful usually brownish yellow bear of western North America
1groan *vb* **1 :** to make or express with a deep moaning sound **2 :** to creak under a strain
2groan *n* : a low moaning sound
gro•cer *n* : a dealer in food
gro•cery *n, pl* **gro•cer•ies 1** *groceries pl* : the goods sold by a grocer **2 :** a grocer's store
grog•gy *adj* **grog•gi•er; grog•gi•est :** weak and confused and unsteady on one's feet — **grog•gi•ly** *adv* — **grog•gi•ness** *n*
groin *n* : the fold or area where the abdomen joins the thigh
grom•met *n* : an eyelet of firm material to strengthen or protect an opening
1groom *n* **1 :** a servant especially in charge of horses **2 :** BRIDEGROOM
2groom *vb* **1 :** to make neat and attractive (as by cleaning and brushing) **2 :** to make fit or ready
1groove *n* **1 :** a narrow channel made in a surface (as by cutting) **2 :** 1ROUTINE
2groove *vb* **grooved; groov•ing :** to form a groove in
groovy *adj* **groov•i•er; groov•i•est :** very good : EXCELLENT
grope *vb* **groped; grop•ing 1 :** to feel one's way **2 :** to seek by or as if by feeling around
gros•beak *n* : a finch with a strong conical bill
1gross *adj* **1 :** GLARING 3 **2 :** BIG 1 **3 :** 1THICK 3 **4 :** consisting of a whole before anything is deducted **5 :** COARSE 4, VULGAR
2gross *n* : the whole before anything is deducted
3gross *n, pl* **gross :** twelve dozen
gro•tesque *adj* : very strange and unexpected : FANTASTIC
grot•to *n, pl* **grottoes 1 :** 1CAVE, CAVERN **2 :** an artificial structure like a cave
1grouch *n* **1 :** a fit of bad temper **2 :** a person with a bad disposition
2grouch *vb* : 1GRUMBLE 1, COMPLAIN
grouchy *adj* **grouch•i•er; grouch•i•est** : having a bad disposition : CANTANKEROUS — **grouch•i•ly** *adv* — **grouch•i•ness** *n*
1ground *n* **1 :** the bottom of a body of water **2 grounds** *pl* : SEDIMENT 1 **3 :** a reason for a belief, action, or argument **4 :** the surface or material upon which something is made or displayed or against which it appears **5 :** the surface of the earth : SOIL **6 :** an area used for some purpose **7 grounds** *pl* : the land around and belonging to a building **8 :** an area to be won or defended as if in a battle
2ground *vb* **1 :** to instruct in basic knowledge or understanding **2 :** to run or cause to run aground **3 :** to connect electrically with the ground **4 :** to prevent (a plane or pilot) from flying
3ground *past of* GRIND
ground crew *n* : the mechanics and technicians who take care of an airplane
ground•hog *n* : WOODCHUCK
ground•less *adj* : being without foundation or reason
ground swell *n* : a broad deep ocean swell caused by a distant storm or earthquake
ground•work *n* : FOUNDATION 2
1group *n* : a number of persons or things that form one whole
2group *vb* : to arrange in or put into a group
1grouse *n, pl* **grouse :** a game bird that is much like the domestic fowl
2grouse *vb* **groused; grous•ing :** 1GRUMBLE 1, GROUCH
grove *n* : a small wood or a planting of trees
grov•el *vb* **grov•eled** *or* **grov•elled; grov•el•ing** *or* **grov•el•ling 1 :** to creep or lie face down on the ground (as in fear) **2 :** CRINGE — **grov•el•er** *or* **grov•el•ler** *n*
grow *vb* **grew; grown; grow•ing 1 :** to spring up and develop to maturity **2 :** to be able to live and develop **3 :** to be related in some way by reason of growing **4 :** 1INCREASE, EXPAND **5 :** BECOME 1 **6 :** to cause to grow : RAISE — **grow•er** *n*
1growl *vb* **1 :** to make a rumbling noise **2 :** to make a growl **3 :** 1GRUMBLE 1
2growl *n* **1 :** a deep threatening sound (as of a dog) **2 :** a grumbling or muttered complaint
grown *adj* : having reached full growth : MATURE
1grown–up *adj* : 1ADULT
2grown–up *n* : an adult person
growth *n* **1 :** a stage or condition in growing **2 :** a process of growing **3 :** a gradual increase **4 :** something (as a covering of plants) produced by growing
grow up *vb* : to become adult

DICTIONARY

[1]**grub** *vb* **grubbed; grub•bing** **1 :** to root out by digging **:** DIG **2 :** to work hard
[2]**grub** *n* **1 :** a soft thick wormlike larva (as of a beetle) **2 :** FOOD 1
grub•by *adj* **grub•bi•er; grub•bi•est :** [1]DIRTY 1 — **grub•bi•ly** *adv* — **grub•bi•ness** *n*
[1]**grub•stake** *n* **:** supplies or funds given to a prospector in return for a promise of a share in the finds
[2]**grubstake** *vb* **grub•staked; grub•stak•ing :** to provide with a grubstake
[1]**grudge** *vb* **grudged; grudg•ing :** BEGRUDGE
[2]**grudge** *n* **:** a feeling of sullen dislike that lasts a long time
gru•el *n* **:** a thin porridge
gru•el•ing *or* **gru•el•ling** *adj* **:** calling for much effort
grue•some *adj* **:** HORRIBLE, GHASTLY — **grue•some•ly** *adv* — **grue•some•ness** *n*
gruff *adj* **:** rough in speech or manner **:** HARSH — **gruff•ly** *adv* — **gruff•ness** *n*
[1]**grum•ble** *vb* **grum•bled; grum•bling** **1 :** to complain or mutter in discontent **2 :** [1]RUMBLE
[2]**grumble** *n* **1 :** the act of grumbling **2 :** [2]RUMBLE
grumpy *adj* **grump•i•er; grump•i•est :** GROUCHY, CROSS — **grump•i•ly** *adv* — **grump•i•ness** *n*
[1]**grunt** *vb* **:** to make a grunt — **grunt•er** *n*
[2]**grunt** *n* **:** a deep short sound (as of a hog)
[1]**guar•an•tee** *n* **1 :** GUARANTOR **2 :** the act of guaranteeing **3 :** a promise that something will work the way it should **4 :** SECURITY 2
[2]**guarantee** *vb* **guar•an•teed; guar•an•tee•ing** **1 :** to promise to answer for the debt or duty of another person **2 :** to give a guarantee on or about
guar•an•tor *n* **:** a person who gives a guarantee
[1]**guard** *n* **1 :** the act or duty of keeping watch **2 :** a person or a body of persons that guards against injury or danger **3 :** a device giving protection
[2]**guard** *vb* **1 :** to protect from danger **:** DEFEND **2 :** to watch over so as to prevent escape **3 :** to keep careful watch
guard•ed *adj* **:** CAUTIOUS
guard•house *n* **1 :** a building used as a headquarters by soldiers on guard duty **2 :** a military jail
guard•ian *n* **1 :** a person who guards or looks after something **:** CUSTODIAN **2 :** a person who legally has the care of another person or of that person's property — **guard•ian•ship** *n*
guard•room *n* **:** a room used by a military guard while on duty
guards•man *n, pl* **guards•men :** a member of a military guard
gu•ber•na•to•ri•al *adj* **:** of or relating to a governor
gud•geon *n* **:** any of several small fishes
guer•ril•la *or* **gue•ril•la** *n* **:** a member of a band of persons carrying on warfare but not part of a regular army
[1]**guess** *vb* **1 :** to judge without sure knowledge **2 :** to solve correctly **3 :** THINK 2, BELIEVE — **guess•er** *n*
[2]**guess** *n* **:** an opinion formed by guessing
guess•work *n* **:** work done or results gotten by guessing
guest *n* **1 :** a person entertained in one's house or at one's table **2 :** a person using a hotel, motel, inn, or restaurant
[1]**guf•faw** *n* **:** a burst of loud laughter
[2]**guffaw** *vb* **:** to laugh noisily
guid•ance *n* **:** the act or process of guiding or being guided **:** DIRECTION
[1]**guide** *n* **:** someone or something (as a book) that leads, directs, or shows the right way
[2]**guide** *vb* **guid•ed; guid•ing** **1 :** to show the way to **2 :** DIRECT, INSTRUCT
guide•book *n* **:** a book of information for travelers
guide•post *n* **:** a post with signs giving directions for travelers
guide word *n* **:** either of the terms at the head of a page of an alphabetical reference work (as a dictionary) usually showing the first and last entries on the page
guild *n* **:** an association of persons with similar aims or common interests
guile *n* **:** sly trickery — **guile•ful** *adj* — **guile•ful•ly** *adv*
[1]**guil•lo•tine** *n* **:** a machine for cutting off a person's head with a heavy blade that slides down two grooved posts
[2]**guillotine** *vb* **guil•lo•tined; guil•lo•tin•ing :** to cut off a person's head with a guillotine
guilt *n* **1 :** the fact of having done something wrong and especially something punishable by law **2 :** conduct that causes one to feel shame or regret or the feeling experienced — **guilt•less** *adj*
guilty *adj* **guilt•i•er; guilt•i•est** **1 :** having done wrong **2 :** aware of, suffering from, or showing guilt — **guilt•i•ly** *adv* — **guilt•i•ness** *n*
guin•ea *n* **:** an old British gold coin
guinea fowl *n* **:** an African bird related to the pheasants that has a bare head and neck and usually dark gray feathers with white speckles and is sometimes raised for food
guinea pig *n* **:** a stocky rodent with short ears and a very short tail
guise *n* **1 :** a style of dress **2 :** outward appearance

gui·tar *n* **:** a musical instrument with six strings played by plucking or strumming

gulch *n* **:** RAVINE

gulf *n* **1 :** a part of an ocean or sea extending into the land **2 :** CHASM, ABYSS **3 :** a wide separation (as in age)

gull *n* **:** a waterbird with webbed feet that is usually blue-gray or whitish in color and has a thick strong bill

gul·let *n* **:** THROAT 2, ESOPHAGUS

gull·ible *adj* **:** easily tricked or misled

gul·ly *n, pl* **gullies :** a trench worn in the earth by running water

[1]gulp *vb* **1 :** to swallow eagerly or in large amounts at a time **2 :** to keep back as if by swallowing **3 :** to catch the breath as if after a long drink

[2]gulp *n* **1 :** the act of gulping **2 :** a large swallow

[1]gum *n* **:** the flesh along the jaws at the roots of the teeth

[2]gum *n* **1 :** a sticky substance obtained from plants that hardens on drying **2 :** a substance like a plant gum (as in stickiness) **3 :** CHEWING GUM

[3]gum *vb* **gummed; gum·ming :** to smear, stick together, or clog with or as if with gum

gum·bo *n, pl* **gumbos :** a rich soup thickened with okra pods

gum·drop *n* **:** a candy usually made from corn syrup and gelatin

gum·my *adj* **gum·mi·er; gum·mi·est 1 :** consisting of, containing, or covered with gum **2 :** GLUEY, STICKY

gump·tion *n* **:** [1]SPIRIT 5, COURAGE

[1]gun *n* **1 :** CANNON 1 **2 :** a portable firearm (as a rifle, shotgun, or pistol) **3 :** something like a gun in shape or function **4 :** a discharge of a gun (as in a salute)

[2]gun *vb* **gunned; gun·ning 1 :** to hunt with a gun **2 :** to open the throttle of quickly so as to increase speed

gun·boat *n* **:** a small armed ship for use in coastal waters

gun·fire *n* **:** the firing of guns

gun·man *n, pl* **gun·men :** a criminal armed with a gun

gun·ner *n* **:** a person who operates a gun

gun·nery *n* **:** the use of guns

gunnery sergeant *n* **:** a noncommissioned officer in the Marine Corps ranking above a staff sergeant

gun·ny *n, pl* **gun·nies 1 :** coarse jute sacking **2 :** BURLAP

gun·pow·der *n* **:** an explosive powder used in guns and blasting

gun·shot *n* **1 :** a shot from a gun **2 :** the effective range of a gun

gun·wale *n* **:** the upper edge of a ship's side

gup·py *n, pl* **guppies :** a small tropical minnow often kept as an aquarium fish

[1]gur·gle *vb* **gur·gled; gur·gling 1 :** to flow in a broken uneven noisy current **2 :** to sound like a liquid flowing with a gurgle

[2]gurgle *n* **:** a sound of or like gurgling liquid

[1]gush *vb* **1 :** [1]SPOUT 1 3 **2 :** to be too affectionate or enthusiastic

[2]gush *n* **:** a sudden free pouring out

gush·er *n* **:** an oil well with a large natural flow

gust *n* **1 :** a sudden brief rush of wind **2 :** a sudden outburst (as of emotion)

gusty *adj* **gust·i·er; gust·i·est :** WINDY

[1]gut *n* **1 :** ENTRAILS — usually used in pl. **2 :** the digestive tube or a part of this **3 :** CATGUT **4 guts** *pl* **:** COURAGE

[2]gut *vb* **gut·ted; gut·ting 1 :** to remove the entrails from **2 :** to destroy the inside of

[1]gut·ter *n* **1 :** a trough along the eaves of a house to catch and carry off water **2 :** a low area (as at the side of a road) to carry off surface water

[2]gutter *vb* **1 :** to flow in small streams **2 :** to have wax flowing down the sides after melting through the rim

[1]guy *n* **:** a rope, chain, rod, or wire (**guy wire**) attached to something to steady it

[2]guy *n* **:** PERSON 1, FELLOW

gym *n* **:** GYMNASIUM

gym·na·si·um *n* **:** a room or building for sports events or gymnastics

gym·nast *n* **:** a person who is skilled in gymnastics

gym·nas·tic *adj* **:** of or relating to gymnastics

gym·nas·tics *n sing or pl* **:** physical exercises for developing skill, strength, and control in the use of the body or a sport in which such exercises are performed

Gyp·sy *or* **Gip·sy** *n, pl* **Gyp·sies** *or* **Gip·sies :** a member of a group of people coming from India to Europe long ago and living a wandering way of life

gypsy moth *n* **:** a moth whose caterpillar has a spotty grayish look and does great damage to trees by eating the leaves

gy·rate *vb* **gy·rat·ed; gy·rat·ing :** to move in a circle around a center **:** SPIN

gy·ro·scope *n* **:** a wheel mounted to spin rapidly so that its axis is free to turn in various directions

gy·ro·scop·ic *adj* **:** of or relating to a gyroscope

H

h *n, pl* **h's** *or* **hs** *often cap* **:** the eighth letter of the English alphabet
ha *interj* — used to show surprise or joy
hab•it *n* **1 :** clothing worn for a special purpose **2 :** usual way of behaving **3 :** a way of acting or doing that has become fixed by being repeated often **4 :** characteristic way of growing
hab•it•able *adj* **:** suitable or fit to live in
hab•i•tat *n* **:** the place where a plant or animal grows or lives in nature
hab•i•ta•tion *n* **1 :** the act of living in a place **2 :** a place to live
ha•bit•u•al *adj* **1 :** being or done by habit **2 :** doing or acting by force of habit **3 :** [1]REGULAR — **ha•bit•u•al•ly** *adv* — **ha•bit•u•al•ness** *n*
ha•ci•en•da *n* **1 :** a large estate especially in a Spanish-speaking country **2 :** the main house of a hacienda
[1]**hack** *vb* **1 :** to cut with repeated chopping blows **2 :** to cough in a short broken way **3 :** to write computer programs for enjoyment **4 :** to gain access to a computer illegally
[2]**hack** *n* **:** a short broken cough
[3]**hack** *n* **1 :** a horse let out for hire or used for varied work **2 :** a person who works for pay at a routine writing job **3 :** a writer who is not very good
hack•er *n* **1 :** one that hacks **2 :** a person who is unskilled at a particular activity **3 :** an expert at programming and solving problems with a computer **4 :** a person who illegally gains access to a computer system
hack•les *n pl* **:** hairs (as on the neck of a dog) that can be made to stand up
hack•ney *n, pl* **hack•neys :** a horse for ordinary riding or driving
hack•saw *n* **:** a saw used for cutting hard materials (as metal) that consists of a frame and a blade with small teeth
had *past of* HAVE
had•dock *n, pl* **haddock** *or* **haddocks :** a food fish related to but smaller than the cod
hadn't : had not
haf•ni•um *n* **:** a gray metallic chemical element
hag *n* **1 :** WITCH 1 **2 :** an ugly old woman
hag•gard *adj* **:** having a hungry, tired, or worried look
hag•gle *vb* **hag•gled; hag•gling :** to argue especially over a price — **hag•gler** *n*
ha–ha *interj* — used to show amusement or scorn
hai•ku *n, pl* **haiku 1 :** a Japanese verse form without rhyme having three lines with the first and last lines having five syllables and the middle having seven **2 :** a poem written in this form
[1]**hail** *n* **1 :** small lumps of ice and snow that fall from the clouds sometimes during thunderstorms **2 :** [1]VOLLEY 1
[2]**hail** *vb* **1 :** to fall as hail **2 :** to pour down like hail
[3]**hail** *interj* — used to show enthusiastic approval
[4]**hail** *vb* **1 :** GREET 1, WELCOME **2 :** to call out to — **hail from :** to come from
[5]**hail** *n* **:** an exclamation of greeting, approval, or praise
hail•stone *n* **:** a lump of hail
hail•storm *n* **:** a storm that brings hail
hair *n* **1 :** a threadlike growth from the skin of a person or lower animal **2 :** a covering or growth of hairs (as on one's head) **3 :** something (as a growth on a leaf) like an animal hair — **haired** *adj* — **hair•less** *adj* — **hair•like** *adj*
hair•brush *n* **:** a brush for the hair
hair•cut *n* **:** the act, process, or result of cutting the hair
hair•do *n, pl* **hairdos :** a way of arranging a person's hair
hair•dress•er *n* **:** one who dresses or cuts hair — **hair•dress•ing** *n*
hair•pin *n* **:** a pin in the shape of a U for holding the hair in place
hair–rais•ing *adj* **:** causing terror, excitement, or great surprise
hair•style *n* **:** HAIRDO
hairy *adj* **hair•i•er; hair•i•est :** covered with hair — **hair•i•ness** *n*
[1]**hale** *adj* **:** being strong and healthy
[2]**hale** *vb* **haled; hal•ing :** to force to go
[1]**half** *n, pl* **halves 1 :** one of two equal parts into which something can be divided **2 :** a part of something that is about equal to the remainder **3 :** one of a pair
[2]**half** *adj* **1 :** being one of two equal parts **2 :** amounting to about a half **:** PARTIAL
[3]**half** *adv* **1 :** to the extent of half **2 :** not completely
half brother *n* **:** a brother by one parent only
half•heart•ed *adj* **:** lacking spirit or interest — **half•heart•ed•ly** *adv* — **half•heart•ed•ness** *n*
half–knot *n* **:** a knot in which two rope ends are wrapped once around each other and which is used to start other knots
half–life *n, pl* **half–lives :** the time required for half of the atoms of a radioactive substance to change composition
half sister *n* **:** a sister by one parent only

[1]**half·way** *adv* **:** at or to half the distance

[2]**halfway** *adj* **1 :** midway between two points **2 :** PARTIAL 3

half–wit *n* **:** a very stupid person — **half–wit·ted** *adj*

hal·i·but *n, pl* **halibut** *or* **halibuts :** a very large flatfish much used for food

hall *n* **1 :** a large building used for public purposes **2 :** a building (as of a college) set apart for a special purpose **3 :** an entrance room **4 :** CORRIDOR **5 :** AUDITORIUM

hal·le·lu·jah *interj* — used to express praise, joy, or thanks

hal·low *vb* **:** to set apart for holy purposes **:** treat as sacred

Hal·low·een *n* **:** October 31 observed with parties and with the playing of tricks by children during the evening

hal·lu·ci·na·tion *n* **:** the seeing of objects or the experiencing of feelings that are not real but are usually the result of mental disorder or the effect of a drug

hal·lu·ci·no·gen *n* **:** a drug that causes hallucinations — **hal·lu·ci·no·gen·ic** *adj*

hall·way *n* **:** CORRIDOR

ha·lo *n, pl* **halos** *or* **haloes 1 :** a circle of light around the sun or moon caused by tiny ice crystals in the air **2 :** a circle drawn or painted around the head of a person in a picture as a symbol of holiness

[1]**halt** *vb* **:** HESITATE 1

[2]**halt** *n* **:** [1]END 2

[3]**halt** *vb* **1 :** to stop or cause to stop marching or traveling **2 :** [2]END

hal·ter *n* **1 :** a rope or strap for leading or tying an animal **2 :** a headstall to which a halter may be attached **3 :** a brief blouse usually without a back and fastened by straps around the neck

halve *vb* **halved; halv·ing 1 :** to divide into halves **2 :** to reduce to one half

halves *pl of* HALF

hal·yard *n* **:** a rope for raising or lowering a sail

ham *n* **1 :** a buttock with the connected thigh **2 :** a cut of meat consisting of a thigh usually of pork **3 :** an operator of an amateur radio station

ham·burg·er *or* **ham·burg** *n* **1 :** ground beef **2 :** a sandwich made of a patty of ground beef in a split bun

ham·let *n* **:** a small village

[1]**ham·mer** *n* **1 :** a tool consisting of a head fastened to a handle and used for pounding (as in driving nails) **2 :** something like a hammer in shape or action **3 :** a heavy metal ball with a flexible handle thrown for distance in a track-and-field contest (**hammer throw**)

[2]**hammer** *vb* **1 :** to strike with a hammer **2 :** to fasten (as by nailing) with a hammer **3 :** to produce by or as if by means of repeated blows

ham·mock *n* **:** a swinging cot usually made of canvas or netting

[1]**ham·per** *vb* **:** to keep from moving or acting freely

[2]**hamper** *n* **:** a large basket usually with a cover

ham·ster *n* **:** a stocky rodent with a short tail and large cheek pouches

[1]**hand** *n* **1 :** the part of the arm fitted (as in humans) for handling, grasping, and holding **2 :** a bodily structure (as the hind foot of an ape) like the human hand in function or form **3 :** something like a hand **4 :** [2]CONTROL 1 **5 :** one side of a problem **6 :** a pledge especially of marriage **7 :** HANDWRITING **8 :** ABILITY 1 **9 :** a unit of measure equal to about ten centimeters **10 :** [2]HELP 1, ASSISTANCE **11 :** a part or share in doing something **12 :** an outburst of applause **13 :** the cards held by a player in a card game **14 :** a hired worker **:** LABORER — **at hand :** near in time or place — **by hand :** with the hands — **in hand 1 :** in one's possession or control **2 :** in preparation — **off one's hands :** out of one's care — **on hand 1 :** in present possession **2 :** [3]PRESENT 1 — **out of hand :** out of control

[2]**hand** *vb* **:** to give or pass with the hand

hand·bag *n* **:** a bag used for carrying money and small personal articles

hand·ball *n* **:** a game played by hitting a small rubber ball against a wall or board with the hand

hand·bill *n* **:** a printed sheet (as of advertising) distributed by hand

hand·book *n* **:** a book of facts usually about one subject

hand·car *n* **:** a small railroad car that is made to move by hand or by a small motor

hand·cart *n* **:** a cart drawn or pushed by hand

[1]**hand·cuff** *n* **:** a metal fastening that can be locked around a person's wrist

[2]**handcuff** *vb* **:** to put handcuffs on

hand·ed *adj* **:** using a particular hand or number of hands

hand·ful *n, pl* **handfuls** *or* **hands·ful 1 :** as much or as many as the hand will grasp **2 :** a small amount or number

[1]**hand·i·cap** *n* **1 :** a contest in which one more skilled is given a disadvantage and one less skilled is given an advantage **2 :** the disadvantage or advantage given in a contest **3 :** a disadvantage that makes progress or success difficult

[2]**handicap** *vb* **hand·i·capped; hand·i·cap·ping 1 :** to give a handicap to **2 :** to put at a disadvantage

hand·i·craft *n* **1 :** an occupation (as weaving or pottery making) that requires skill with the hands **2 :** articles made by one working at handicraft

hand·i·ly *adv* **:** in a handy manner **:** EASILY

hand·i·work *n* **:** work done by the hands

hand·ker·chief *n, pl* **hand·ker·chiefs :** a small usually square piece of cloth used for wiping the face, nose, or eyes

[1]**han·dle** *n* **:** the part by which something (as a dish or tool) is picked up or held — **han·dled** *adj*

[2]**handle** *vb* **han·dled; han·dling 1 :** to touch, feel, hold, or move with the hand **2 :** to manage with the hands **3 :** to deal with (as in writing or speaking) **4 :** MANAGE 1, DIRECT **5 :** to deal with or act on **6 :** to deal or trade in — **han·dler** *n*

han·dle·bars *n pl* **:** a bar (as on a bicycle) that has a handle at each end and is used for steering

hand·made *adj* **:** made by hand rather than by machine

hand–me–downs *n pl* **:** used clothes

hand organ *n* **:** a small musical instrument cranked by hand

hand·out *n* **:** something (as food) given to a beggar

hand·rail *n* **:** a rail to be grasped by the hand for support

hands down *adv* **:** without question **:** EASILY

hand·shake *n* **:** a clasping of hands by two people (as in greeting)

hand·some *adj* **hand·som·er; hand·som·est 1 :** CONSIDERABLE **2 :** more than enough **3 :** having a pleasing and impressive appearance

hand·spring *n* **:** a feat of tumbling in which the body turns forward or backward in a full circle from a standing position and lands first on the hands and then on the feet

hand·stand *n* **:** a stunt in which a person balances the body in the air upside down supported on the hands

hand–to–hand *adj* **:** involving bodily contact

hand·work *n* **:** work done by hand and not by machine

hand·writ·ing *n* **:** writing done by hand

handy *adj* **hand·i·er; hand·i·est 1 :** within easy reach **2 :** easy to use or manage **3 :** VERSATILE 2 **4 :** DEXTEROUS 1

[1]**hang** *vb* **hung** *also* **hanged; hang·ing 1 :** to fasten or be fastened to something without support from below **:** SUSPEND **2 :** to kill or be killed by suspending (as from a gallows) by a rope tied around the neck **3 :** to fasten so as to allow free motion forward and backward **4 :** to cause to droop — **hang on to :** to hold or keep with determination

[2]**hang** *n* **1 :** the way in which a thing hangs **2 :** MEANING 1 **3 :** KNACK 1

han·gar *n* **:** a shelter for housing and repairing aircraft

hang·er *n* **:** a device on which something hangs

hang·man *n, pl* **hang·men :** one who hangs criminals

hang·nail *n* **:** a bit of skin hanging loose about a fingernail

hang·out *n* **:** a place where a person spends much idle time or goes often

hang·over *n* **1 :** something (as a surviving custom) that remains from what is past **2 :** a sick uncomfortable state that comes from drinking too much liquor

han·ker *vb* **:** to have a great desire

han·som *n* **:** a light covered carriage that has two wheels and a driver's seat elevated at the rear

Ha·nuk·kah *n* **:** a Jewish holiday lasting eight days and celebrating the cleansing and second dedication of the Temple after the Syrians were driven out of Jerusalem in 165 B.C.

hap·haz·ard *adj* **:** marked by lack of plan, order, or direction — **hap·haz·ard·ly** *adv* — **hap·haz·ard·ness** *n*

hap·less *adj* **:** [1]UNFORTUNATE 1

hap·pen *vb* **1 :** to occur or come about by chance **2 :** to take place **3 :** to have opportunity **:** CHANCE **4 :** to come especially by way of injury or harm

hap·pen·ing *n* **:** something that happens

hap·py *adj* **hap·pi·er; hap·pi·est 1 :** FORTUNATE 1, LUCKY **2 :** being suitable for something **3 :** enjoying one's condition **:** CONTENT **4 :** JOYFUL **5 :** feeling or showing pleasure **:** GLAD — **hap·pi·ly** *adv* — **hap·pi·ness** *n*

hap·py–go–lucky *adj* **:** free from care

ha·rangue *n* **:** a scolding speech or writing

ha·rass *vb* **1 :** to worry and hinder by repeated attacks **2 :** to annoy again and again — **ha·rass·ment** *n*

[1]**har·bor** *n* **1 :** a place of safety and comfort **:** REFUGE **2 :** a part of a body of water (as a sea or lake) so protected as to be a place of safety for ships **:** PORT

[2]**harbor** *vb* **1 :** to give shelter to **2 :** to have or hold in the mind

[1]**hard** *adj* **1 :** not easily cut, pierced, or divided **:** not soft **2 :** high in alcoholic content **3 :** containing substances that prevent lathering with soap **4 :** difficult to put up with **:** SEVERE **5 :** UNFEELING 2 **6 :** carried on with steady and earnest effort **7 :** DILIGENT, ENERGETIC **8 :** sounding as in *cold* and *geese* — used of *c* and *g* **9 :** difficult to do or to understand

[2]**hard** *adv* **1 :** with great effort or energy **2 :** in a violent way **3 :** with pain, bitterness, or resentment

hard copy *n* **:** a copy of information (as from computer storage) produced on paper in normal size

hard disk *n* **1 :** a rigid metal disk used to store computer data **2 :** HARD DRIVE

hard drive *n* **:** a computer-data storage device containing one or more hard disks

hard·en *vb* **1 :** to make or become hard or harder **2 :** to make or become hardy or strong **3 :** to make or become stubborn or unfeeling — **hard·en·er** *n*

hard·head·ed *adj* **1 :** STUBBORN 1 **2 :** using or showing good judgment — **hard·head·ed·ly** *adv* — **hard·head·ed·ness** *n*

hard·heart·ed *adj* **:** showing or feeling no pity **:** UNFEELING — **hard·heart·ed·ly** *adv* — **hard·heart·ed·ness** *n*

hard·ly *adv* **:** only just **:** BARELY

hard·ness *n* **:** the quality or state of being hard

hard palate *n* **:** the bony front part of the roof of the mouth

hard·ship *n* **:** something (as a loss or injury) that is hard to put up with

hard·tack *n* **:** a hard biscuit made of flour and water without salt

hard·ware *n* **1 :** things (as tools, cutlery, or parts of machines) made of metal **2 :** items of equipment or their parts used for a particular purpose

[1]**hard·wood** *n* **:** the usually hard wood of a tree belonging to the group bearing broad leaves as distinguished from the wood of a tree (as a pine) with leaves that are needles

[2]**hardwood** *adj* **:** having or made of hardwood

har·dy *adj* **har·di·er; har·di·est 1 :** BOLD 1, BRAVE **2 :** able to stand weariness, hardship, or severe weather — **har·di·ness** *n*

hare *n* **:** a timid animal like the related rabbit but having young that are born with the eyes open and a furry coat

hare·brained *adj* **:** FOOLISH

hark *vb* **:** LISTEN

[1]**harm** *n* **1 :** physical or mental damage **:** INJURY **2 :** MISCHIEF 1

[2]**harm** *vb* **:** to cause harm to **:** HURT

harm·ful *adj* **:** causing harm **:** INJURIOUS — **harm·ful·ly** *adv* — **harm·ful·ness** *n*

harm·less *adj* **:** not harmful — **harm·less·ly** *adv* — **harm·less·ness** *n*

har·mon·ic *adj* **:** of or relating to musical harmony rather than melody or rhythm — **har·mon·i·cal·ly** *adv*

har·mon·i·ca *n* **:** a small musical instrument held in the hand and played by the mouth **:** MOUTH ORGAN

har·mo·ni·ous *adj* **1 :** having a pleasant sound **:** MELODIOUS **2 :** combining so as to produce a pleasing result **3 :** showing harmony in action or feeling — **har·mo·ni·ous·ly** *adv* — **har·mo·ni·ous·ness** *n*

har·mo·nize *vb* **har·mo·nized; har·mo·niz·ing 1 :** to play or sing in harmony **2 :** to be in harmony — **har·mo·niz·er** *n*

har·mo·ny *n, pl* **har·mo·nies 1 :** the playing of musical tones together in chords **2 :** a pleasing arrangement of parts **3 :** AGREEMENT 1, ACCORD

[1]**har·ness** *n* **:** an arrangement of straps and fastenings placed on an animal so as to control it or prepare it to pull a load

[2]**harness** *vb* **1 :** to put a harness on **2 :** to put to work **:** UTILIZE

[1]**harp** *n* **:** a musical instrument consisting of a triangular frame set with strings that are plucked by the fingers

[2]**harp** *vb* **:** to call attention to something over and over again

[1]**har·poon** *n* **:** a barbed spear used especially for hunting whales and large fish

[2]**harpoon** *vb* **:** to strike with a harpoon

harp·si·chord *n* **:** a keyboard instrument similar to a piano with strings that are plucked

[1]**har·row** *n* **:** a heavy frame set with metal teeth or disks used in farming for breaking up and smoothing soil

[2]**harrow** *vb* **1 :** to drag a harrow over (plowed ground) **2 :** [2]DISTRESS

har·ry *vb* **har·ried; har·ry·ing :** HARASS

harsh *adj* **1 :** having a coarse surface **:** rough to the touch **2 :** disagreeable to any of the senses **3 :** causing physical discomfort **4 :** SEVERE 1 — **harsh·ly** *adv* — **harsh·ness** *n*

[1]**har·vest** *n* **1 :** the season when crops are gathered **2 :** the gathering of a crop **3 :** a ripe crop (as of grain)

[2]**harvest** *vb* **:** to gather in a crop

har·vest·er *n* **1 :** one that gathers by or as if by harvesting **2 :** a machine for harvesting field crops

has *present 3d sing of* HAVE

[1]**hash** *vb* **:** to chop into small pieces

[2]**hash** *n* **1 :** cooked meat and vegetables chopped together and browned **2 :** [2]JUMBLE

hash·ish *n* **:** a drug from the hemp plant that is used for its intoxicating effects

hash over *vb* **:** to talk about **:** DISCUSS

hasn't : has not

hasp *n* **:** a fastener (as for a door) consisting of a hinged metal strap that fits over a staple and is held by a pin or padlock

has·sle *n* **1 :** a loud angry argument **2 :** a

brief fight **3 :** something that annoys or bothers

has·sock *n* **:** a firm stuffed cushion used as a seat or leg rest

haste *n* **1 :** quickness of motion or action **:** SPEED **2 :** hasty action

has·ten *vb* **:** to move or act fast **:** HURRY

hasty *adj* **hast·i·er; hast·i·est 1 :** done or made in a hurry **2 :** made, done, or decided without proper care and thought — **hast·i·ly** *adv*

hat *n* **:** a covering for the head having a crown and usually a brim

[1]**hatch** *n* **1 :** an opening in the deck of a ship or in the floor or roof of a building **2 :** a small door or opening (as in an airplane) **3 :** the cover for a hatch

[2]**hatch** *vb* **1 :** to produce from eggs **2 :** to come forth from an egg **3 :** to develop usually in secret

hatch·ery *n, pl* **hatch·er·ies :** a place for hatching eggs

hatch·et *n* **:** a small ax with a short handle

hatch·way *n* **:** a hatch usually having a ladder or stairs

[1]**hate** *n* **:** deep and bitter dislike

[2]**hate** *vb* **hat·ed; hat·ing :** to feel great dislike toward

hate·ful *adj* **1 :** full of hate **2 :** causing or deserving hate — **hate·ful·ly** *adv* — **hate·ful·ness** *n*

ha·tred *n* **:** [1]HATE

hat·ter *n* **:** a person who makes, sells, or cleans and repairs hats

haugh·ty *adj* **haugh·ti·er; haugh·ti·est :** acting as if other people are not as good as oneself — **haugh·ti·ly** *adv* — **haugh·ti·ness** *n*

[1]**haul** *vb* **1 :** to pull or drag with effort **2 :** to transport in a vehicle

[2]**haul** *n* **1 :** the act of hauling **2 :** an amount collected **3 :** the distance or route over which a load is moved

haunch *n* **1 :** HIP **2 :** HINDQUARTER

[1]**haunt** *vb* **1 :** to visit often **2 :** to come to mind frequently **3 :** to visit or live in as a ghost

[2]**haunt** *n* **:** a place often visited

have *vb, past & past participle* **had;** *present participle* **hav·ing;** *present 3d sing* **has 1 :** to hold for one's use or as property **2 :** to consist of **3 :** to be forced or feel obliged **4 :** to stand in some relationship to **5 :** OBTAIN, GAIN, GET **6 :** to possess as a characteristic **7 :** [2]EXERCISE 1 **8 :** to be affected by **9 :** to be in **:** CARRY ON **10 :** to hold in the mind **11 :** to cause to be **12 :** to cause to **13 :** [1]PERMIT 1 **14 :** [2]TRICK **15 :** to give birth to **16 :** to partake of **17** — used as a helping verb with the past participle of another verb

ha·ven *n* **:** a safe place

haven't : have not

hav·er·sack *n* **:** a bag worn over one shoulder for carrying supplies

hav·oc *n* **1 :** wide destruction **2 :** great confusion and lack of order

Ha·wai·ian *n* **1 :** a person born or living in Hawaii **2 :** the language of the Hawaiians

[1]**hawk** *n* **:** a bird of prey that has a strong hooked bill and sharp curved claws and is smaller than most eagles

[2]**hawk** *vb* **:** to make a harsh coughing sound in clearing the throat

[3]**hawk** *vb* **:** to offer for sale by calling out in the street — **hawk·er** *n*

haw·ser *n* **:** a large rope for towing or tying up a ship

haw·thorn *n* **:** any of several thorny shrubs or small trees with shiny leaves, white, pink, or red flowers, and small red fruits

[1]**hay** *n* **:** any of various herbs (as grasses) cut and dried for use as fodder

[2]**hay** *vb* **:** to cut plants for hay

hay fever *n* **:** a sickness like a cold usually affecting people sensitive to plant pollen

hay·loft *n* **:** a loft in a barn or stable for storing hay

hay·mow *n* **:** HAYLOFT

hay·stack *n* **:** a large pile of hay stored outdoors

hay·wire *adj* **1 :** working badly or in an odd way **2 :** CRAZY 1, WILD

[1]**haz·ard** *n* **:** a source of danger

[2]**hazard** *vb* **:** to risk something **:** take a chance

haz·ard·ous *adj* **:** DANGEROUS — **haz·ard·ous·ly** *adv* — **haz·ard·ous·ness** *n*

[1]**haze** *n* **:** fine dust, smoke, or fine particles of water in the air

[2]**haze** *vb* **hazed; haz·ing :** to make or become hazy or cloudy

ha·zel *n* **1 :** a shrub or small tree that bears an edible nut **2 :** a light brown

ha·zel·nut *n* **:** the nut of a hazel

hazy *adj* **haz·i·er; haz·i·est 1 :** partly hidden by haze **2 :** not clear in thought or meaning **:** VAGUE — **haz·i·ly** *adv* — **haz·i·ness** *n*

H–bomb *n* **:** HYDROGEN BOMB

he *pron* **1 :** that male one **2 :** a or the person **:** [3]ONE 2

[1]**head** *n* **1 :** the part of the body containing the brain, eyes, ears, nose, and mouth **2 :** [1]MIND 2 **3 :** control of the mind or feelings **4 :** the side of a coin or medal usually thought of as the front **5 :** each person among a number **6** *pl* **head :** a unit of number **7 :** something like a head in position or

use **8 :** the place a stream begins **9 :** a skin stretched across one or both ends of a drum **10 :** DIRECTOR, LEADER **11 :** a compact mass of plant parts (as leaves or flowers) **12 :** a part of a machine, tool, or weapon that performs the main work **13 :** a place of leadership or honor **14 :** CLIMAX, CRISIS — **out of one's head :** DELIRIOUS 1 — **over one's head :** beyond one's understanding

²head *adj* **1 :** ²CHIEF 1 **2 :** located at the head **3 :** coming from in front

³head *vb* **1 :** to provide with or form a head **2 :** to be or put oneself at the head of **3 :** to be or get in front of **4 :** to go or cause to go in a certain direction

head•ache *n* **1 :** pain in the head **2 :** something that annoys or confuses

head•band *n* **:** a band worn on or around the head

head•board *n* **:** a board forming the head (as of a bed)

head•dress *n* **:** a covering or ornament for the head

head•ed *adj* **:** having such a head or so many heads

head•first *adv* **:** with the head in front

head•gear *n* **:** something worn on the head

head•ing *n* **:** something (as a title or an address) at the top or beginning (as of a letter)

head•land *n* **:** a point of high land sticking out into the sea

head•light *n* **:** a light at the front of a vehicle

¹head•line *n* **:** a title of an article in a newspaper

²headline *vb* **head•lined; head•lin•ing :** to provide with a headline

¹head•long *adv* **1 :** HEADFIRST **2 :** without waiting to think things through

²headlong *adj* **1 :** ¹RASH, IMPULSIVE **2 :** plunging headfirst

head•mas•ter *n* **:** a man who heads the staff of a private school

head•mis•tress *n* **:** a woman who heads the staff of a private school

head–on *adv or adj* **:** with the front hitting or facing an object

head•phone *n* **:** an earphone held over the ear by a band worn on the head

head•quar•ters *n sing or pl* **:** a place where a leader gives out orders

head•stall *n* **:** an arrangement of straps or rope that fits around the head of an animal and forms part of a bridle or halter

head start *n* **:** an advantage given at the beginning (as to a school child or a runner)

head•stone *n* **:** a stone at the head of a grave

head•strong *adj* **:** always wanting one's own way

head•wait•er *n* **:** the head of the staff of a restaurant or of the dining room of a hotel

head•wa•ters *n pl* **:** the beginning and upper part of a stream

head•way *n* **1 :** movement in a forward direction (as of a ship) **2 :** ¹PROGRESS 2

heal *vb* **1 :** ²CURE 1 **2 :** to return to a sound or healthy condition — **heal•er** *n*

health *n* **1 :** the condition of being free from illness or disease **2 :** the overall condition of the body

health•ful *adj* **:** good for the health — **health•ful•ly** *adv* — **health•ful•ness** *n*

healthy *adj* **health•i•er; health•i•est 1 :** being sound and well **:** not sick **2 :** showing good health **3 :** aiding or building up health — **health•i•ly** *adv* — **health•i•ness** *n*

¹heap *n* **1 :** things or material piled together **2 :** a large number or amount

²heap *vb* **1 :** to throw or lay in a heap **:** make into a pile **2 :** to provide in large amounts **3 :** to fill to capacity

hear *vb* **heard; hear•ing 1 :** to take in through the ear **:** have the power of hearing **2 :** to gain knowledge of by hearing **3 :** to listen to with care and attention — **hear•er** *n*

hear•ing *n* **1 :** the act or power of taking in sound through the ear **:** the sense by which a person hears **2 :** EARSHOT **3 :** a chance to be heard or known

hearing aid *n* **:** an electronic device used by a partly deaf person to make sounds louder

hear•ken *vb* **:** LISTEN

hear•say *n* **:** something heard from another **:** RUMOR

hearse *n* **:** a vehicle for carrying the dead to the grave

heart *n* **1 :** a hollow organ of the body that expands and contracts to move blood through the arteries and veins **2 :** something shaped like a heart **3 :** the part nearest the center **4 :** the most essential part **5 :** human feelings **6 :** COURAGE — **by heart :** so as to be able to repeat from memory

heart•ache *n* **:** ¹SORROW 1, 2

heart•beat *n* **:** a single contracting and expanding of the heart

heart•break *n* **:** very great or deep grief

heart•break•ing *adj* **:** causing great sorrow

heart•bro•ken *adj* **:** overcome by sorrow

heart•en *vb* **:** to give new hope or courage to

heart•felt *adj* **:** deeply felt **:** SINCERE

hearth *n* **1 :** an area (as of brick) in front of a fireplace **2 :** the floor of a fireplace **3 :** ¹HOME 1

hearth•stone *n* **:** a stone forming a hearth

heart•i•ly *adv* **1 :** with sincerity or enthusiasm **2 :** COMPLETELY

heart•less *adj* **:** UNFEELING 2, CRUEL — **heart•less•ly** *adv* — **heart•less•ness** *n*

heart·sick *adj* : DESPONDENT

heart·wood *n* : the usually dark wood in the center of a tree

hearty *adj* **heart·i·er; heart·i·est** **1** : friendly and enthusiastic **2** : strong, healthy, and active **3** : having a good appetite **4** : AMPLE — **heart·i·ness** *n*

[1]**heat** *vb* : to make or become warm or hot

[2]**heat** *n* **1** : a condition of being hot : WARMTH **2** : high temperature **3** : a form of energy that causes a body to rise in temperature **4** : strength of feeling or force of action **5** : a single race in a contest that includes two or more races

heat·ed *adj* **1** : HOT 1 **2** : ANGRY — **heat·ed·ly** *adv*

heat·er *n* : a device for heating

heath *n* **1** : any of a group of low, woody, and often evergreen plants that grow on poor, sour, wet soil **2** : a usually open level area of land on which heaths can grow

[1]**hea·then** *adj* **1** : of or relating to the heathen **2** : UNCIVILIZED 1

[2]**heathen** *n, pl* **heathens** *or* **heathen** **1** : a person who does not know about and worship the God of the Bible : PAGAN **2** : an uncivilized person

heath·er *n* : an evergreen heath of northern and mountainous areas with pink flowers and needlelike leaves

[1]**heave** *vb* **heaved** *or* **hove; heav·ing** **1** : to raise with an effort **2** : HURL, THROW **3** : to utter with an effort **4** : to rise and fall again and again **5** : to be thrown or raised up

[2]**heave** *n* **1** : an effort to lift or raise **2** : a forceful throw **3** : an upward motion (as of the chest in breathing)

heav·en *n* **1** : SKY 1 — usually used in pl. **2** *often cap* : the dwelling place of God and of the blessed dead **3** *cap* : GOD 1 **4** : a place or condition of complete happiness

heav·en·ly *adj* **1** : of or relating to heaven or the heavens **2** : of or relating to the Heaven of God and the blessed dead **3** : entirely delightful

heav·i·ly *adv* **1** : with or as if with weight **2** : in a slow and difficult way **3** : very much

heavy *adj* **heavi·er; heavi·est** **1** : having great weight **2** : hard to put up with **3** : burdened by something important or troubling **4** : having little strength or energy **5** : unusually great in amount, force, or effect — **heav·i·ness** *n*

[1]**He·brew** *adj* : of or relating to the Hebrew peoples or Hebrew

[2]**Hebrew** *n* **1** : a member of any of a group of peoples including the ancient Jews **2** : JEW **3** : the language of the Hebrews

hec·tic *adj* : filled with excitement, activity, or confusion

hecto- *prefix* : hundred

hec·to·me·ter *n* : a unit of length in the metric system equal to 100 meters

he'd : he had : he would

[1]**hedge** *n* : a fence or boundary made up of a thick growth of shrubs or low trees

[2]**hedge** *vb* **hedged; hedg·ing** **1** : to surround or protect with a hedge **2** : to avoid giving a direct or exact answer or promise

hedge·hog *n* **1** : a European mammal that eats insects, has sharp spines mixed with the hair on its back, and is able to roll itself up into a ball **2** : PORCUPINE

hedge·row *n* : a hedge of shrubs or trees around a field

[1]**heed** *vb* : to pay attention to : MIND

[2]**heed** *n* : ATTENTION 1 — **heed·ful** *adj* — **heed·ful·ly** *adv*

heed·less *adj* : not taking heed : CARELESS — **heed·less·ly** *adv* — **heed·less·ness** *n*

[1]**heel** *n* **1** : the back part of the human foot behind the arch and below the ankle **2** : the part of an animal's limb corresponding to a person's heel **3** : one of the crusty ends of a loaf of bread **4** : a part (as of a stocking) that covers the human heel **5** : the solid part of a shoe that supports the heel **6** : a rear, low, or bottom part **7** : a mean selfish person — **heel·less** *adj*

[2]**heel** *vb* : to lean to one side

heft *vb* : to test the weight of by lifting

hefty *adj* **heft·i·er; heft·i·est** : HEAVY 1

heif·er *n* : a young cow

height *n* **1** : the highest point or greatest degree **2** : the distance from the bottom to the top of something standing upright **3** : distance upward

height·en *vb* **1** : to make greater : INCREASE **2** : to make or become high or higher

heir *n* **1** : a person who inherits or has the right to inherit property after the death of its owner **2** : a person who has legal claim to a title or a throne when the person holding it dies

heir·ess *n* : a female heir

heir·loom *n* : a piece of personal property handed down in a family from one generation to another

held *past of* HOLD

he·li·cop·ter *n* : an aircraft supported in the air by horizontal propellers

he·li·port *n* : a place for a helicopter to land and take off

he·li·um *n* : a very light gaseous chemical element that is found in various natural gases, will not burn, and is used in balloons

hell *n* **1** : a place where souls are believed to survive after death **2** : a place or state of punishment for the wicked after death **:** the home of evil spirits **3 :** a place or state of misery or wickedness — **hell·ish** *adj*

he'll : he shall **:** he will

hell·ben·der *n* **:** a large American salamander that lives in water

hel·lo *interj* — used as a greeting or to express surprise

helm *n* **1 :** a lever or wheel for steering a ship **2 :** a position of control

hel·met *n* **:** a protective covering for the head

1help *vb* **1 :** to provide with what is useful in achieving an end **:** AID, ASSIST **2 :** to give relief from pain or disease **3 :** PREVENT 1 **4 :** 1SERVE 9

2help *n* **1 :** an act or instance of helping **:** AID **2 :** the state of being helped **3 :** a person or a thing that helps **4 :** a body of hired helpers

help·er *n* **1 :** one that helps **2 :** a less skilled person who helps a skilled worker

help·ful *adj* **:** providing help — **help·ful·ly** *adv* — **help·ful·ness** *n*

help·ing *n* **:** a serving of food

helping verb *n* **:** a verb (as *am, may*, or *will*) that is used with another verb to express person, number, mood, or tense

help·less *adj* **:** not able to help or protect oneself — **help·less·ly** *adv* — **help·less·ness** *n*

hel·ter–skel·ter *adv* **:** in great disorder

1hem *n* **:** a border of a cloth article made by folding back an edge and sewing it down

2hem *vb* **hemmed; hem·ming 1 :** to finish with or make a hem **2 :** SURROUND

hemi- *prefix* **:** half

hemi·sphere *n* **1 :** one of the halves of the earth as divided by the equator into northern and southern parts (**northern hemisphere**, **southern hemisphere**) or by a meridian into two parts so that one half (**eastern hemisphere**) to the east of the Atlantic ocean includes Europe, Asia, and Africa and the half (**western hemisphere**) to the west includes North and South America and surrounding waters **2 :** a half of a sphere **3 :** either the left or the right half of the cerebrum

hemi·spher·ic *or* **hemi·spher·i·cal** *adj* **:** of or relating to a hemisphere

hem·lock *n* **1 :** a poisonous plant of the carrot family **2 :** an evergreen tree of the pine family

he·mo·glo·bin *n* **:** the coloring material of the red blood cells that carry oxygen from the lungs to the tissues

hem·or·rhage *n* **:** great loss of blood by bleeding

hemp *n* **:** a tall plant grown for its tough woody fiber that is used in making rope and for its flowers and leaves that yield drugs (as marijuana)

hen *n* **1 :** a female domestic fowl **2 :** a female bird

hence *adv* **1 :** from this place **2 :** from this time **3 :** as a result **:** THEREFORE

hence·forth *adv* **:** from this time on

hench·man *n, pl* **hench·men :** a trusted follower or supporter

hep·a·ti·tis *n* **:** a disease which is caused by a virus and in which the liver is damaged and there is yellowing of the skin and fever

hepta- *or* **hept-** *prefix* **:** seven

hep·ta·gon *n* **:** a closed figure having seven angles and seven sides

1her *adj* **:** of or relating to her or herself

2her *pron objective case of* SHE

1her·ald *n* **1 :** an official messenger **2 :** a person who brings news or announces something

2herald *vb* **:** to give notice of **:** ANNOUNCE

he·ral·dic *adj* **:** of or relating to heralds or heraldry

her·ald·ry *n* **:** the art or science of tracing a person's ancestors and determining what coat of arms his or her family has the right to

herb *n* **1 :** a plant with soft stems that die down at the end of the growing season **2 :** a plant or plant part used in medicine or in seasoning foods

her·biv·o·rous *adj* **:** eating or living on plants

1herd *n* **:** a number of animals of one kind kept or living together

2herd *vb* **1 :** to gather or join in a herd **2 :** to form into or move as a herd — **herd·er** *n*

herds·man *n, pl* **herds·men :** one who owns or tends a flock or herd

1here *adv* **1 :** in or at this place **2 :** 1NOW 1 **3 :** to or into this place **:** HITHER

2here *n* **:** this place

here·abouts *or* **here·about** *adv* **:** near or around this place

1here·af·ter *adv* **1 :** after this **2 :** in some future time or state

2hereafter *n* **1 :** 2FUTURE 1 **2 :** life after death

here·by *adv* **:** by means of this

he·red·i·tary *adj* **1 :** capable of being passed from parent to offspring **2 :** received or passing from an ancestor to an heir

he·red·i·ty *n, pl* **he·red·i·ties :** the passing on of characteristics (as looks or ability) from parents to offspring

here·in *adv* **:** in this

here·of *adv* **:** of this

here·on *adv* **:** on this

her·e·sy *n, pl* **her·e·sies** **1 :** the holding of religious beliefs opposed to church doctrine **:** such a belief **2 :** an opinion opposed to a generally accepted belief

her·e·tic *n* **:** a person who believes or teaches something opposed to accepted beliefs (as of a church)

he·ret·i·cal *adj* **:** of, relating to, or being heresy

here·to·fore *adv* **:** HITHERTO

here·up·on *adv* **:** right after this

here·with *adv* **:** with this

her·i·tage *n* **:** something that comes to one from one's ancestors

her·mit *n* **:** one who lives apart from others especially for religious reasons

he·ro *n, pl* **heroes** **1 :** a person admired for great deeds or fine qualities **2 :** one who shows great courage **3 :** the chief male character in a story, play, or poem

he·ro·ic *adj* **1 :** of, relating to, or like heroes **2 :** COURAGEOUS, DARING — **he·ro·ical·ly** *adv*

her·o·in *n* **:** a very harmful drug that comes from morphine

her·o·ine *n* **1 :** a woman admired for great deeds or fine qualities **2 :** the chief female character in a story, poem, or play

her·o·ism *n* **1 :** great courage especially for a noble purpose **2 :** the qualities of a hero

her·on *n* **:** a wading bird that has long legs and a long neck and feeds on frogs, lizards, and small fish

her·ring *n* **:** a widely used food fish of the north Atlantic ocean

hers *pron* **:** that which belongs to her

her·self *pron* **:** her own self

he's : he is **:** he has

hes·i·tan·cy *n* **:** the quality or state of being hesitant

hes·i·tant *adj* **:** feeling or showing hesitation — **hes·i·tant·ly** *adv*

hes·i·tate *vb* **hes·i·tat·ed; hes·i·tat·ing** **1 :** to pause because of forgetfulness or uncertainty **2 :** to speak or say in a weak or broken way

hes·i·ta·tion *n* **:** an act or instance of hesitating

hew *vb* **hewed** *or* **hewn; hew·ing** **1 :** to chop down **2 :** to shape by cutting with an ax

hex *n* **:** a harmful spell **:** JINX

hexa- *or* **hex-** *prefix* **:** six

hexa·gon *n* **:** a closed figure having six angles and six sides

hex·ag·o·nal *adj* **:** having six sides — **hex·ag·o·nal·ly** *adv*

hey *interj* — used to call attention or to express surprise or joy

hey·day *n* **:** the time of greatest strength, energy, or success

hi *interj* — used especially as a greeting

hi·ber·nate *vb* **hi·ber·nat·ed; hi·ber·nat·ing** **:** to pass the winter in a resting state — **hi·ber·na·tor** *n*

hi·ber·na·tion *n* **:** the state of one that hibernates

1hic·cup *n* **:** a gulping sound caused by sudden movements of muscles active in breathing

2hiccup *vb* **hic·cuped** *also* **hic·cupped; hic·cup·ing** *also* **hic·cup·ping** **:** to make a hiccup

hick·o·ry *n, pl* **hick·o·ries** **:** a tall tree related to the walnuts that has strong tough elastic wood and bears an edible nut (**hickory nut**) in a hard shell

1hide *vb* **hid; hid·den** *or* **hid; hid·ing** **1 :** to put or stay out of sight **2 :** to keep secret **3 :** to screen from view

2hide *n* **:** the skin of an animal whether fresh or prepared for use

hide–and–go–seek *n* **:** HIDE-AND-SEEK

hide–and–seek *n* **:** a game in which one player covers his or her eyes and after giving the others time to hide goes looking for them

hide·away *n* **:** 1RETREAT 3, HIDEOUT

hid·eous *adj* **:** very ugly or disgusting **:** FRIGHTFUL — **hid·eous·ly** *adv* — **hid·eous·ness** *n*

hide·out *n* **:** a secret place for hiding (as from the police)

hi·ero·glyph·ic *n* **:** any of the symbols in the picture writing of ancient Egypt

hi–fi *n* **1 :** HIGH FIDELITY **2 :** equipment for reproduction of sound with high fidelity

hig·gle·dy–pig·gle·dy *adv or adj* **:** in confusion **:** TOPSY-TURVY

1high *adj* **1 :** extending to a great distance above the ground **2 :** having a specified elevation **:** TALL **3 :** of greater degree, size, amount, or cost than average **4 :** of more than usual importance **5 :** having great force **6 :** pitched or sounding above some other sound

2high *adv* **:** at or to a high place or degree

3high *n* **1 :** the space overhead **:** SKY **2 :** a region of high barometric pressure **3 :** a high point or level **4 :** the arrangement of gears in an automobile giving the highest speed of travel

high·brow *n* **:** a person of great learning or culture

high fidelity *n* **:** the reproduction of sound with a high degree of accuracy

high·land *n* **:** high or hilly country

1high·light *n* **:** a very interesting event or detail

2highlight *vb* **high·light·ed; high·light·ing** **1 :** EMPHASIZE **2 :** to be a highlight of

high·ly *adv* **1 :** to a high degree **:** very much **2 :** with much approval
high·ness *n* **1 :** the quality or state or being high **2** — used as a title for a person of very high rank
high school *n* **:** a school usually including the ninth to twelfth or tenth to twelfth grades
high seas *n pl* **:** the open part of a sea or ocean
high–spir·it·ed *adj* **:** LIVELY 1
high–strung *adj* **:** very sensitive or nervous
high tide *n* **:** the tide when the water is at its greatest height
high·way *n* **:** a main road
high·way·man *n, pl* **high·way·men :** a person who robs travelers on a road
[1]**hike** *vb* **hiked; hik·ing :** to take a long walk — **hik·er** *n*
[2]**hike** *n* **:** a long walk especially for pleasure or exercise
hi·lar·i·ous *adj* **:** enjoying or causing hilarity **:** MERRY — **hi·lar·i·ous·ly** *adv* — **hi·lar·i·ous·ness** *n*
hi·lar·i·ty *n* **:** noisy fun
[1]**hill** *n* **1 :** a usually rounded elevation of land lower than a mountain **2 :** a little heap or mound of earth **3 :** several seeds or plants planted in a group rather than a row
[2]**hill** *vb* **1 :** to form into a heap **2 :** to draw earth around the roots or base of
hill·bil·ly *n, pl* **hill·bil·lies :** a person from a backwoods area
hill·ock *n* **:** a small hill
hill·side *n* **:** the part of a hill between the top and the foot
hill·top *n* **:** the highest part of a hill
hilly *adj* **hill·i·er; hill·i·est :** having many hills
hilt *n* **:** a handle especially of a sword or dagger
him *pron objective case of* HE
him·self *pron* **:** his own self
hind *adj* **:** being at the end or back **:** REAR
hin·der *vb* **:** to make slow or difficult
hind·quar·ter *n* **:** the back half of a complete side of a four-footed animal or carcass
hin·drance *n* **:** something that hinders **:** OBSTACLE
hind·sight *n* **:** understanding of something only after it has happened
[1]**hinge** *n* **:** a jointed piece on which a door, gate, or lid turns or swings
[2]**hinge** *vb* **hinged; hing·ing 1 :** to attach by or provide with hinges **2 :** DEPEND 2
[1]**hint** *n* **1 :** information that helps one guess an answer or do something more easily **2 :** a small amount **:** TRACE
[2]**hint** *vb* **:** to suggest something without plainly asking or saying it
hin·ter·land *n* **:** a region far from cities
hip *n* **:** the part of the body that curves out below the waist on each side
hip·pie *or* **hip·py** *n, pl* **hippies :** a usually young person who typically has long hair, is against the values and practices of society, and often lives together with others
hip·po *n, pl* **hip·pos :** HIPPOPOTAMUS
hip·po·pot·a·mus *n, pl* **hip·po·pot·a·mus·es** *or* **hip·po·pot·a·mi :** a large hoglike animal with thick hairless skin that eats plants and lives in African rivers
hire *vb* **hired; hir·ing 1 :** [1]EMPLOY 2 **2 :** to get the temporary use of in return for pay **3 :** to take a job
[1]**his** *adj* **:** of or relating to him or himself
[2]**his** *pron* **:** that which belongs to him
[1]**His·pan·ic** *adj* **:** of or relating to people of Latin American origin
[2]**Hispanic** *n* **:** a person of Latin American origin
[1]**hiss** *vb* **1 :** to make a hiss **2 :** to show dislike by hissing
[2]**hiss** *n* **:** a sound like a long \s\ sometimes used as a sign of dislike
his·to·ri·an *n* **:** a person who studies or writes about history
his·tor·ic *adj* **:** famous in history
his·tor·i·cal *adj* **1 :** of, relating to, or based on history **2 :** known to be true — **his·tor·i·cal·ly** *adv*
his·to·ry *n, pl* **his·to·ries 1 :** a telling of events **:** STORY **2 :** a written report of past events **3 :** a branch of knowledge that records and explains past events
[1]**hit** *vb* **hit; hit·ting 1 :** to touch or cause to touch with force **2 :** to strike or cause to strike something aimed at **3 :** to affect as if by a blow **4 :** OCCUR 2 **5 :** to happen to get **:** come upon **6 :** to arrive at — **hit·ter** *n*
[2]**hit** *n* **1 :** a blow striking an object aimed at **2 :** COLLISION **3 :** something very successful **4 :** a batted baseball that enables the batter to reach base safely
hit–and–run *adj* **:** being or involving a driver who does not stop after being in an automobile accident
[1]**hitch** *vb* **1 :** to move by jerks **2 :** to fasten by or as if by a hook or knot **3 :** HITCHHIKE
[2]**hitch** *n* **1 :** a jerky movement or pull **2 :** an unexpected stop or obstacle **3 :** a knot used for a temporary fastening
hitch·hike *vb* **hitch·hiked; hitch·hik·ing :** to travel by getting free rides in passing vehicles — **hitch·hik·er** *n*
hith·er *adv* **:** to this place
hith·er·to *adv* **:** up to this time
HIV *n* **:** a virus that causes AIDS by destroying large numbers of cells that help the human body fight infection

DICTIONARY

hive *n* **1 :** a container for housing honeybees **2 :** a colony of bees **3 :** a place swarming with busy people
hives *n pl* **:** an allergic condition in which the skin breaks out in large red itching patches
ho *interj* — used especially to attract attention
[1]**hoard** *n* **:** a supply usually of something of value stored away or hidden
[2]**hoard** *vb* **:** to gather and store away — **hoard·er** *n*
hoar·frost *n* **:** [1]FROST 2
hoarse *adj* **hoars·er; hoars·est** **1 :** harsh in sound **2 :** having a rough voice — **hoarse·ly** *adv* — **hoarse·ness** *n*
hoary *adj* **hoar·i·er; hoar·i·est** **:** gray or white with age
[1]**hoax** *vb* **:** to trick into thinking something is true or real when it isn't
[2]**hoax** *n* **1 :** an act meant to fool or deceive **2 :** something false passed off as real
[1]**hob·ble** *vb* **hob·bled; hob·bling** **1 :** to walk with difficulty **:** LIMP **2 :** to tie the legs of to make movement difficult
[2]**hobble** *n* **1 :** a limping walk **2 :** something used to hobble an animal
hob·by *n, pl* **hobbies :** an interest or activity engaged in for pleasure
hob·by·horse *n* **1 :** a stick with a horse's head on which children pretend to ride **2 :** ROCKING HORSE
hob·gob·lin *n* **1 :** a mischievous elf **2 :** BOGEY 2
hob·nail *n* **:** a short nail with a large head driven into soles of heavy shoes to protect against wear — **hob·nailed** *adj*
ho·bo *n, pl* **hoboes :** [1]VAGRANT
hock·ey *n* **:** a game played on ice or in a field by two teams who try to drive a puck or ball through a goal by hitting it with a stick
hod *n* **1 :** a wooden tray or trough that has a long handle and is used to carry mortar or bricks **2 :** a bucket for holding or carrying coal
hodge·podge *n* **:** a disorderly mixture
[1]**hoe** *n* **:** a tool with a long handle and a thin flat blade used for weeding and cultivating
[2]**hoe** *vb* **hoed; hoe·ing :** to weed or loosen the soil around plants with a hoe
[1]**hog** *n* **1 :** an adult domestic swine **2 :** a greedy or dirty person
[2]**hog** *vb* **hogged; hog·ging :** to take more than one's share
ho·gan *n* **:** a dwelling of some American Indians made of logs or sticks covered with earth
hog·gish *adj* **:** very selfish or greedy — **hog·gish·ly** *adv* — **hog·gish·ness** *n*
hogs·head *n* **1 :** a very large cask **2 :** a unit of liquid measure equal to sixty-three gallons (about 238 liters)
[1]**hoist** *vb* **:** to lift up especially with a pulley
[2]**hoist** *n* **1 :** an act of hoisting **2 :** a device used for lifting heavy loads
[1]**hold** *vb* **held; hold·ing** **1 :** to have or keep in one's possession or under one's control **2 :** to limit the movement or activity of **:** RESTRAIN **3 :** to make accept a legal or moral duty **4 :** to have or keep in one's grasp **5 :** [1]SUPPORT 4 **6 :** to take in and have within **:** CONTAIN **7 :** to have in mind **8 :** CONSIDER 3, REGARD **9 :** to carry on by group action **10 :** to continue in the same way or state **:** LAST **11 :** to remain fast or fastened **12 :** to bear or carry oneself
[2]**hold** *n* **1 :** the act or way of holding **:** GRIP **2 :** [1]INFLUENCE 1 **3 :** a note or rest in music kept up longer than usual
[3]**hold** *n* **1 :** the part of a ship below the decks in which cargo is stored **2 :** the cargo compartment of an airplane
hold·er *n* **:** one that holds
hold out *vb* **:** to refuse to yield or agree
hold·up *n* **1 :** robbery by an armed robber **2 :** [1]DELAY
hold up *vb* **1 :** [2]DELAY 2 **2 :** to rob while threatening with a weapon
hole *n* **1 :** an opening into or through something **2 :** CAVITY **3 :** DEN 1, BURROW
hol·i·day *n* **1 :** a day of freedom from work especially when celebrating some event **2 :** VACATION
ho·li·ness *n* **1 :** the quality or state of being holy **2** — used as a title for persons of high religious position
[1]**hol·ler** *vb* **:** to cry out **:** SHOUT
[2]**holler** *n* **:** [2]SHOUT, CRY
[1]**hol·low** *n* **1 :** a low spot in a surface **2 :** VALLEY **3 :** CAVITY
[2]**hollow** *adj* **1 :** curved inward **:** SUNKEN **2 :** having a space inside **:** not solid **3 :** suggesting a sound made in an empty place **4 :** not sincere — **hol·low·ly** *adv* — **hol·low·ness** *n*
[3]**hollow** *vb* **:** to make or become hollow
hol·ly *n, pl* **hollies :** an evergreen tree or shrub that has shiny leaves with prickly edges and red berries much used for Christmas decorations
hol·ly·hock *n* **:** a plant with large rounded leaves and tall stalks of bright showy flowers
ho·lo·caust *n* **:** a complete destruction especially by fire
ho·lo·gram *n* **:** a three-dimensional picture made by laser light reflected onto a photographic substance without the use of a camera

hol•ster *n* **:** a usually leather case in which a pistol is carried or worn

ho•ly *adj* **ho•li•er; ho•li•est** **1 :** set apart for the service of God or of a divine being **:** SACRED **2 :** having a right to expect complete devotion **3 :** pure in spirit

hom- *or* **homo-** *prefix* **:** one and the same **:** similar **:** alike

hom•age *n* **1 :** a feudal ceremony in which a person pledges loyalty to a lord and becomes a vassal **2 :** [1]RESPECT 2

[1]**home** *n* **1 :** the house in which one or one's family lives **2 :** the place where one was born or grew up **3 :** HABITAT **4 :** a place for the care of persons unable to care for themselves **5 :** the social unit formed by a family living together **6 :** [1]HOUSE 1 **7 :** the goal or point to be reached in some games — **home•less** *adj*

[2]**home** *adv* **1 :** to or at home **2 :** to the final place or limit

home•land *n* **:** native land

home•like *adj* **:** like a home (as in comfort and kindly warmth)

home•ly *adj* **home•li•er; home•li•est** **1 :** suggesting home life **2 :** not handsome

home•made *adj* **:** made in the home

home•mak•er *n* **:** a person who manages a household especially as a wife and mother — **home•mak•ing** *n or adj*

home page *n* **:** the page of a World Wide Web site that is usually seen first and that usually contains links to the other pages of the site or to other sites

home plate *n* **:** the base that a baseball runner must touch to score

hom•er *n* **:** HOME RUN

home•room *n* **:** a schoolroom where pupils of the same class report at the start of each day

home run *n* **:** a hit in baseball that enables the batter to go around all the bases and score

home•school *vb* **:** to teach school subjects to one's children at home

home•school•er *n* **1 :** one that homeschools **2 :** a child who is homeschooled

home•sick *adj* **:** longing for home and family — **home•sick•ness** *n*

[1]**home•spun** *adj* **1 :** spun or made at home **2 :** made of homespun **3 :** not fancy **:** SIMPLE

[2]**homespun** *n* **:** a loosely woven usually woolen or linen fabric originally made from homespun yarn

[1]**home•stead** *n* **1 :** a home and the land around it **2 :** a piece of land gained from United States public lands by living on and farming it

[2]**homestead** *vb* **:** to acquire or settle on public land for use as a homestead — **home•stead•er** *n*

home•ward *or* **home•wards** *adv or adj* **:** toward home

home•work *n* **:** work (as school lessons) to be done at home

hom•ey *adj* **hom•i•er; hom•i•est** **:** HOMELIKE — **hom•ey•ness** *or* **hom•i•ness** *n*

ho•mi•cide *n* **:** a killing of one human being by another

hom•ing pigeon *n* **:** a racing pigeon trained to return home

hom•i•ny *n* **:** hulled corn with the germ removed

homo- — see HOM-

ho•mog•e•nize *vb* **ho•mog•e•nized; ho•mog•e•niz•ing** **:** to reduce the particles in (as milk or paint) to the same size and spread them evenly in the liquid

ho•mo•graph *n* **:** one of two or more words spelled alike but different in meaning or origin or pronunciation

hom•onym *n* **1 :** HOMOPHONE **2 :** HOMOGRAPH **3 :** one of two or more words spelled and pronounced alike but different in meaning

ho•mo•phone *n* **:** one of two or more words pronounced alike but different in meaning or origin or spelling

hone *vb* **honed; hon•ing** **:** to sharpen with or as if with a fine abrasive stone

hon•est *adj* **1 :** free from fraud or trickery **:** STRAIGHTFORWARD **2 :** not given to cheating, stealing, or lying **:** UPRIGHT, TRUSTWORTHY **3 :** being just what is indicated **:** REAL, GENUINE

hon•es•ty *n* **:** the quality or state of being honest

hon•ey *n* **1 :** a sweet sticky fluid made by bees from the liquid drawn from flowers **2 :** an outstanding example

hon•ey•bee *n* **:** a bee whose honey is used by people as food

[1]**hon•ey•comb** *n* **1 :** a mass of wax cells built by honeybees in their nest to contain young bees and stores of honey **2 :** something like a honeycomb in structure or appearance

[2]**honeycomb** *vb* **:** to make or become full of holes like a honeycomb

hon•ey•dew melon *n* **:** a pale muskmelon with greenish sweet flesh and smooth skin

[1]**hon•ey•moon** *n* **1 :** a holiday taken by a recently married couple **2 :** a period of harmony especially just after marriage

[2]**honeymoon** *vb* **:** to have a honeymoon — **hon•ey•moon•er** *n*

hon•ey•suck•le *n* **:** a climbing vine or a bush with fragrant white, yellow, or red flowers

[1]**honk** *vb* **:** to make a honk

[2]honk *n* **1 :** the cry of a goose **2 :** a sound like the cry of a goose

[1]hon·or *n* **1 :** public admiration : REPUTATION **2 :** outward respect : RECOGNITION **3 :** PRIVILEGE **4** — used especially as a title for an official of high rank (as a judge) **5 :** a person whose worth brings respect or fame **6 :** evidence or a symbol of great respect **7 :** high moral standards of behavior

[2]honor *vb* **1 :** [2]RESPECT **2 :** to give an honor to

hon·or·able *adj* **1 :** bringing about or deserving honor **2 :** observing ideas of honor or reputation **3 :** having high moral standards of behavior : ETHICAL, UPRIGHT

hon·or·ary *adj* **:** given or done as an honor

[1]hood *n* **1 :** a covering for the head and neck and sometimes the face **2 :** something like a hood **3 :** the movable covering for an automobile engine — **hood·ed** *adj*

[2]hood *vb* **:** to cover with or as if with a hood

-hood *n suffix* **1 :** state : condition : quality : nature **2 :** instance of a specified state or quality **3 :** individuals sharing a specified state or character

hood·lum *n* **:** a brutal ruffian : THUG

hood·wink *vb* **:** to mislead by trickery

hoof *n, pl* **hooves** *or* **hoofs** **1 :** a covering of horn that protects the ends of the toes of some animals (as horses, oxen, or swine) **2 :** a hoofed foot (as of a horse) — **hoofed** *adj*

[1]hook *n* **1 :** a curved device (as a piece of bent metal) for catching, holding, or pulling something **2 :** something curved or bent like a hook — **by hook or by crook :** in any way : fairly or unfairly

[2]hook *vb* **1 :** to bend in the shape of a hook **2 :** to catch or fasten with a hook

hook·worm *n* **:** a small worm that lives in the intestines and makes people sick by sucking their blood

hoop *n* **1 :** a circular band used for holding together the strips that make up the sides of a barrel or tub **2 :** a circular figure or object **3 :** a circle or series of circles of flexible material (as wire) used for holding a woman's skirt out from the body

hooray *variant of* HURRAH

[1]hoot *vb* **1 :** to utter a loud shout usually to show disapproval **2 :** to make the noise of an owl or a similar cry **3 :** to express by hoots

[2]hoot *n* **1 :** a sound of hooting **2 :** the least bit

[1]hop *vb* **hopped; hop·ping** **1 :** to move by short quick jumps **2 :** to jump on one foot **3 :** to jump over **4 :** to get aboard by or as if by hopping **5 :** to make a quick trip especially by air

[2]hop *n* **1 :** a short quick jump especially on one leg **2 :** [2]DANCE 2 **3 :** a short trip especially by air

[3]hop *n* **1 :** a twining vine whose greenish flowers look like cones **2 hops** *pl* **:** the dried flowers of the hop plant used chiefly in making beer and ale and in medicine

[1]hope *vb* **hoped; hop·ing :** to desire especially with expectation that the wish will be granted

[2]hope *n* **1 :** [1]TRUST 1 **2 :** desire together with the expectation of getting what is wanted **3 :** a cause for hope **4 :** something hoped for

hope·ful *adj* **1 :** full of hope **2 :** giving hope : PROMISING — **hope·ful·ly** *adv* — **hope·ful·ness** *n*

hope·less *adj* **1 :** having no hope **2 :** offering no hope — **hope·less·ly** *adv* — **hope·less·ness** *n*

hop·per *n* **1 :** one that hops **2 :** an insect that moves by leaping **3 :** a container usually shaped like a funnel for delivering material (as grain or coal) into a machine or a bin **4 :** a tank holding liquid and having a device for releasing its contents through a pipe

hop·scotch *n* **:** a game in which a player tosses a stone into sections of a figure drawn on the ground and hops through the figure and back to pick up the stone

horde *n* **:** MULTITUDE, SWARM

ho·ri·zon *n* **1 :** the line where the earth or sea seems to meet the sky **2 :** the limit of a person's outlook or experience

[1]hor·i·zon·tal *adj* **:** level with the horizon — **hor·i·zon·tal·ly** *adv*

[2]horizontal *n* **:** something (as a line or plane) that is horizontal

hor·mone *n* **:** any of various chemical substances secreted by body cells especially into the blood and acting on cells or organs of the body usually at a distance from the place of origin

horn *n* **1 :** one of the hard bony growths on the head of many hoofed animals (as cattle, goats, or sheep) **2 :** the material of which horns are composed or a similar material **3 :** something made from a horn **4 :** something shaped like a horn **5 :** a musical or signaling instrument made from an animal's horn **6 :** a brass musical instrument (as a trumpet or French horn) **7 :** a usually electrical device that makes a noise like that of a horn — **horned** *adj* — **horn·less** *adj* — **horn·like** *adj*

horned toad *n* **:** a small harmless lizard with scales and hard pointed growths on the skin

hor·net *n* **:** a large wasp that can give a severe sting

horn of plenty : CORNUCOPIA

horny *adj* **horn•i•er; horn•i•est :** like or made of horn
hor•ri•ble *adj* **:** causing horror **:** TERRIBLE — **hor•ri•bly** *adv*
hor•rid *adj* **1 :** HORRIBLE **2 :** very unpleasant **:** DISGUSTING — **hor•rid•ly** *adv*
hor•ri•fy *vb* **hor•ri•fied; hor•ri•fy•ing :** to cause to feel horror
hor•ror *n* **1 :** great and painful fear, dread, or shock **2 :** great dislike **3 :** a quality or thing that causes horror
horse *n* **1 :** a large hoofed animal that feeds on grasses and is used as a work animal and for riding **2 :** a frame that supports something (as wood while being cut) **3 :** a piece of gymnasium equipment used for vaulting exercises — **horse•less** *adj* — **from the horse's mouth :** from the original source
[1]**horse•back** *n* **:** the back of a horse
[2]**horseback** *adv* **:** on horseback
horse•car *n* **1 :** a streetcar drawn by horses **2 :** a car for transporting horses
horse chestnut *n* **:** a shiny brown nut that is unfit to eat and is the fruit of a tall tree with leaves divided into fingerlike parts and large flower clusters shaped like cones
horse•fly *n, pl* **horse•flies :** a large swift two-winged fly the females of which suck blood from animals
horse•hair *n* **1 :** the hair of a horse especially from the mane or tail **2 :** cloth made from horsehair
horse latitudes *n pl* **:** either of two regions in the neighborhoods of 30° north and 30° south of the equator marked by calms and light changeable winds
horse•man *n, pl* **horse•men 1 :** a horseback rider **2 :** a person skilled in handling horses — **horse•man•ship** *n*
horse opera *n* **:** a movie or a radio or television play about cowboys
horse•play *n* **:** rough play
horse•pow•er *n* **:** a unit of power that equals the work done in raising 550 pounds one foot in one second
horse•rad•ish *n* **:** a hot relish made from the root of an herb of the mustard family
horse•shoe *n* **1 :** a protective iron plate that is nailed to the rim of a horse's hoof **2 :** something shaped like a horseshoe **3 horseshoes** *pl* **:** a game in which horseshoes are tossed at a stake in the ground
horse•tail *n* **:** any of a group of primitive plants that produce spores and have hollow stems with joints and leaves reduced to sheaths about the joints
horse•whip *vb* **horse•whipped; horse•whip•ping :** to beat severely with a whip made to be used on a horse
horse•wom•an *n, pl* **horse•wom•en :** a woman skilled in riding on horseback or in handling horses
hors•ey *or* **horsy** *adj* **hors•i•er; hors•i•est :** of or relating to horses or horsemen and horsewomen
ho•san•na *interj* — used as a cry of approval, praise, or love
[1]**hose** *n, pl* **hose** *or* **hos•es 1** *pl hose* **:** STOCKING, SOCK **2 :** a flexible tube for carrying fluid
[2]**hose** *vb* **hosed; hos•ing :** to spray, water, or wash with a hose
ho•siery *n* **:** stockings or socks in general
hos•pi•ta•ble *adj* **1 :** friendly and generous in entertaining guests **2 :** willing to deal with something new — **hos•pi•ta•bly** *adv*
hos•pi•tal *n* **:** a place where the sick and injured are cared for
hos•pi•tal•i•ty *n* **:** friendly and generous treatment of guests
hos•pi•tal•ize *vb* **hos•pi•tal•ized; hos•pi•tal•iz•ing :** to place in a hospital for care and treatment — **hos•pi•tal•iza•tion** *n*
[1]**host** *n* **1 :** ARMY 1 **2 :** MULTITUDE
[2]**host** *n* **:** one who receives or entertains guests
[3]**host** *n, often cap* **:** the bread used in Christian Communion
hos•tage *n* **:** a person given or held to make certain that promises will be kept
hos•tel *n* **:** a place providing inexpensive lodging for use by young travelers
host•ess *n* **:** a woman who receives or entertains guests
hos•tile *adj* **1 :** of or relating to an enemy **2 :** UNFRIENDLY
hos•til•i•ty *n, pl* **hos•til•i•ties 1 :** a hostile state, attitude, or action **2** *hostilities pl* **:** acts of warfare
hot *adj* **hot•ter; hot•test 1 :** having a high temperature **2 :** easily excited **3 :** having or causing the sensation of an uncomfortable degree of body heat **4 :** recently made or received **5 :** close to something sought **6 :** PUNGENT **7 :** RADIOACTIVE **8 :** recently stolen — **hot•ly** *adv* — **hot•ness** *n*
hot•bed *n* **:** a bed of heated earth covered by glass for growing tender plants early in the season
hot dog *n* **:** a frankfurter and especially a cooked one served in a long split roll
ho•tel *n* **:** a place that provides lodging and meals for the public **:** INN
hot•head *n* **:** a person who is easily excited or angered — **hot•head•ed** *adj*
hot•house *n* **:** a heated building enclosed by glass for growing plants
hot plate *n* **:** a small portable appliance for heating or cooking

hot rod *n* **:** an automobile rebuilt for high speed and fast acceleration
hot water *n* **:** a difficult or distressing situation **:** TROUBLE
[1]**hound** *n* **:** a dog with drooping ears and deep bark that is used in hunting and follows game by the sense of smell
[2]**hound** *vb* **:** to hunt, chase, or annoy without ceasing
hour *n* **1 :** one of the twenty-four divisions of a day **:** sixty minutes **2 :** the time of day **3 :** a fixed or particular time **4 :** a measure of distance figured by the amount of time it takes to cover it
hour•glass *n* **:** a device for measuring time in which sand runs from the upper into the lower part of a glass in an hour
[1]**hour•ly** *adv* **:** at or during every hour
[2]**hourly** *adj* **1 :** occurring every hour **2 :** figured by the hour
[1]**house** *n, pl* **hous•es 1 :** a place built for people to live in **2 :** something (as a nest or den) used by an animal for shelter **3 :** a building in which something is kept **4 :** [1]HOUSEHOLD **5 :** FAMILY 1 **6 :** a body of persons assembled to make the laws for a country **7 :** a business firm **8 :** the audience in a theater or concert hall — **on the house :** free of charge
[2]**house** *vb* **1 :** to provide with living quarters or shelter **2 :** CONTAIN 3
house•boat *n* **:** a roomy pleasure boat fitted for use as a place to live
house•boy *n* **:** a boy or man hired to do housework
house•fly *n, pl* **house•flies :** a two-winged fly that is common about houses and often carries disease germs
[1]**house•hold** *n* **:** all the persons who live as a family in one house
[2]**household** *adj* **1 :** of or relating to a household **2 :** FAMILIAR
house•hold•er *n* **:** one who lives in a dwelling alone or as the head of a household
house•keep•er *n* **:** a person employed to take care of a house
house•keep•ing *n* **:** the care and management of a house
house•maid *n* **:** a woman or girl hired to do housework
house•moth•er *n* **:** a woman who acts as hostess, supervisor, and often housekeeper in a residence for young people
house•plant *n* **:** a plant grown or kept indoors
house•top *n* **:** [1]ROOF 1
house•warm•ing *n* **:** a party to celebrate moving into a new home
house•wife *n, pl* **house•wives :** a married woman in charge of a household
house•work *n* **:** the actual labor involved in housekeeping
hous•ing *n* **1 :** dwellings provided for a number of people **2 :** something that covers or protects
hove *past of* HEAVE
hov•el *n* **:** a small poorly built usually dirty house
hov•er *vb* **1 :** to hang fluttering in the air or on the wing **2 :** to move to and fro near a place
[1]**how** *adv* **1 :** in what way **:** by what means **2 :** for what reason **3 :** to what degree, number, or amount **4 :** in what state or condition — **how about :** what do you say to or think of — **how come :** [1]WHY — **how do you do :** HELLO
[2]**how** *conj* **:** in what manner or condition
how•ev•er *adv* **1 :** to whatever degree or extent **2 :** in whatever way **3 :** in spite of that
[1]**howl** *vb* **1 :** to make a loud long mournful sound like that of a dog **2 :** to cry out loudly (as with pain)
[2]**howl** *n* **1 :** a loud long mournful sound made by dogs **2 :** a long loud cry (as of distress, disappointment, or rage) **3 :** COMPLAINT 1 **4 :** something that causes laughter
HTML *n* **:** a computer language that is used to create pages on the World Wide Web that can include text, pictures, sound, video, and links to other Web pages
hub *n* **1 :** the center of a wheel, propeller, or fan **2 :** a center of activity
hub•bub *n* **:** UPROAR
huck•le•ber•ry *n, pl* **huck•le•ber•ries :** a dark edible berry with many hard seeds that grows on a bush related to the blueberry
huck•ster *n* **1 :** PEDDLER, HAWKER **2 :** a writer of advertising
[1]**hud•dle** *vb* **hud•dled; hud•dling 1 :** to crowd, push, or pile together **2 :** to get together to talk something over **3 :** to curl up
[2]**huddle** *n* **1 :** a closely packed group **2 :** a private meeting or conference
hue *n* **1 :** [1]COLOR 1 **2 :** a shade of a color
[1]**huff** *vb* **:** to give off puffs (as of air or steam)
[2]**huff** *n* **:** a fit of anger or temper
huffy *adj* **huff•i•er; huff•i•est 1 :** easily offended **:** PETULANT **2 :** [1]SULKY — **huff•i•ly** *adv* — **huff•i•ness** *n*
[1]**hug** *vb* **hugged; hug•ging 1 :** to clasp in the arms **:** EMBRACE **2 :** to keep close to
[2]**hug** *n* **:** [2]EMBRACE
huge *adj* **hug•er; hug•est :** very large **:** VAST
hulk *n* **1 :** a person or thing that is bulky or clumsy **2 :** the remains of an old or wrecked ship

hulk•ing *adj* **:** very large and strong **:** MASSIVE

1hull *n* **1 :** the outside covering of a fruit or seed **2 :** the frame or body of a ship, flying boat, or airship

2hull *vb* **:** to remove the hulls of — **hull•er** *n*

hul•la•ba•loo *n, pl* **hul•la•ba•loos :** a confused noise **:** HUBBUB, COMMOTION

1hum *vb* **hummed; hum•ming 1 :** to utter a sound like a long \m\ **2 :** to make the buzzing noise of a flying insect **3 :** to sing with closed lips **4 :** to give forth a low murmur of sounds **5 :** to be very busy or active

2hum *n* **:** the act or an instance of humming **:** the sound produced by humming

1hu•man *adj* **1 :** of, relating to, being, or characteristic of people as distinct from lower animals **2 :** having human form or characteristics

2human *n* **:** a human being — **hu•man•like** *adj*

hu•mane *adj* **:** having sympathy and consideration for others — **hu•mane•ly** *adv* — **hu•mane•ness** *n*

1hu•man•i•tar•i•an *n* **:** a person devoted to and working for the health and happiness of other people

2humanitarian *adj* **:** of, relating to, or characteristic of humanitarians

hu•man•i•ty *n, pl* **hu•man•i•ties 1 :** KINDNESS 2, SYMPATHY **2 :** the quality or state of being human **3** *humanities pl* **:** studies (as literature, history, and art) concerned primarily with human culture **4 :** the human race

hu•man•ly *adv* **:** within the range of human ability

1hum•ble *adj* **hum•bler; hum•blest 1 :** not bold or proud **:** MODEST **2 :** expressing a spirit of respect for the wishes of another **3 :** low in rank or condition — **hum•bly** *adv*

2humble *vb* **hum•bled; hum•bling 1 :** to make humble **2 :** to destroy the power of

1hum•bug *n* **1 :** FRAUD 3 **2 :** NONSENSE 1

2humbug *vb* **hum•bugged; hum•bug•ging :** DECEIVE 1

hum•ding•er *n* **:** something striking or extraordinary

hum•drum *adj* **:** MONOTONOUS

hu•mid *adj* **:** MOIST

hu•mid•i•fy *vb* **hu•mid•i•fied; hu•mid•i•fy•ing :** to make (as the air of a room) more moist — **hu•mid•i•fi•er** *n*

hu•mid•i•ty *n, pl* **hu•mid•i•ties :** the degree of wetness especially of the atmosphere **:** MOISTURE

hu•mil•i•ate *vb* **hu•mil•i•at•ed; hu•mil•i•at•ing :** to lower the pride or self-respect of

hu•mil•i•a•tion *n* **1 :** the state of being humiliated **2 :** an instance of being humiliated

hu•mil•i•ty *n* **:** the quality of being humble

hum•ming•bird *n* **:** a tiny brightly colored American bird whose wings make a humming sound in flight

hum•mock *n* **1 :** a rounded mound of earth **:** KNOLL **2 :** a ridge or pile of ice

1hu•mor *n* **1 :** state of mind **:** MOOD **2 :** the amusing quality of something **3 :** the ability to see or report the amusing quality of things

2humor *vb* **:** to give in to the wishes of

hu•mor•ist *n* **:** a person who writes or talks in a humorous way

hu•mor•ous *adj* **:** full of humor **:** FUNNY — **hu•mor•ous•ly** *adv*

hump *n* **1 :** a rounded bulge or lump (as on the back of a camel) **2 :** a difficult part (as of a task) — **humped** *adj*

hump•back *n* **1 :** a humped back **2 :** HUNCHBACK 2 — **hump•backed** *adj*

hu•mus *n* **:** the dark rich part of earth formed from decaying material

1hunch *vb* **1 :** to bend one's body into an arch or hump **2 :** to draw up close together or into an arch

2hunch *n* **1 :** HUMP 1 **2 :** a strong feeling about what will happen

hunch•back *n* **1 :** HUMPBACK 1 **2 :** a person with a humped or crooked back

1hun•dred *n* **1 :** ten times ten **:** 100 **2 :** a very large number

2hundred *adj* **:** being 100

1hun•dredth *adj* **:** coming right after ninety-ninth

2hundredth *n* **:** number 100 in a series

hung *past of* HANG

1hun•ger *n* **1 :** a desire or a need for food **2 :** a strong desire

2hunger *vb* **1 :** to feel hunger **2 :** to have a strong desire

hun•gry *adj* **hun•gri•er; hun•gri•est 1 :** feeling or showing hunger **2 :** having a strong desire — **hun•gri•ly** *adv*

hunk *n* **:** a large lump or piece

1hunt *vb* **1 :** to follow after in order to capture or kill **2 :** to try to find

2hunt *n* **:** an instance or the practice of hunting

hunt•er *n* **1 :** a person who hunts game **2 :** a dog or horse used or trained for hunting **3 :** a person who searches for something

hunts•man *n, pl* **hunts•men :** HUNTER 1

1hur•dle *n* **1 :** a barrier to be jumped in a race (**hur•dles**) **2 :** OBSTACLE

2hurdle *vb* **hur•dled; hur•dling 1 :** to leap over while running **2 :** OVERCOME

hur•dy–gur•dy *n, pl* **hur•dy–gur•dies :** HAND ORGAN

DICTIONARY

hurl *vb* **:** to throw with force

hur·rah *or* **hoo·ray** *also* **hur·ray** *interj* — used to express joy, approval, or encouragement

hur·ri·cane *n* **:** a tropical cyclone with winds of thirty-three meters per second or greater usually accompanied by rain, thunder, and lightning

hur·ried *adj* **1 :** going or working with speed **:** FAST **2 :** done in a hurry — **hur·ried·ly** *adv*

1hur·ry *vb* **hur·ried; hur·ry·ing 1 :** to carry or cause to go with haste **2 :** to move or act with haste **3 :** to speed up

2hurry *n* **:** a state of eagerness or urgent need **:** extreme haste

1hurt *vb* **hurt; hurt·ing 1 :** to feel or cause pain **2 :** to do harm to **:** DAMAGE **3 :** 2DISTRESS, OFFEND **4 :** to make poorer or more difficult

2hurt *n* **1 :** an injury or wound to the body **2 :** SUFFERING 1, ANGUISH **3 :** 1WRONG

hurt·ful *adj* **:** causing injury or suffering

hur·tle *vb* **hur·tled; hur·tling 1 :** to rush suddenly or violently **2 :** to drive or throw violently

1hus·band *n* **:** a married man

2husband *vb* **:** to manage with thrift **:** use carefully

hus·band·ry *n* **1 :** the management or wise use of resources **:** THRIFT **2 :** the business and activities of a farmer

1hush *vb* **:** to make or become quiet, calm, or still **:** SOOTHE

2hush *n* **:** 1QUIET

hush–hush *adj* **:** 1SECRET 1, CONFIDENTIAL

1husk *n* **:** the outer covering of a fruit or seed

2husk *vb* **:** to strip the husk from — **husk·er** *n*

1hus·ky *adj* **hus·ki·er; hus·ki·est :** HOARSE — **hus·ki·ly** *adv* — **hus·ki·ness** *n*

2husky *n, pl* **huskies :** a strong dog with a thick coat used to pull sleds in the Arctic

3husky *n, pl* **huskies :** a husky person or thing

4husky *adj* **hus·ki·er; hus·ki·est :** STRONG 1, BURLY — **hus·ki·ness** *n*

1hus·tle *vb* **hus·tled; hus·tling 1 :** to push, crowd, or force forward roughly **2 :** HURRY

2hustle *n* **:** energetic activity

hus·tler *n* **:** an energetic person who works fast

hut *n* **:** a small roughly made and often temporary dwelling

hutch *n* **1 :** a low cupboard usually having open shelves on top **2 :** a pen or coop for an animal

hy·a·cinth *n* **:** a plant of the lily family with stalks of fragrant flowers shaped like bells

1hy·brid *n* **1 :** an animal or plant whose parents differ in some hereditary characteristic or belong to different groups (as breeds, races, or species) **2 :** something that is of mixed origin or composition

2hybrid *adj* **:** of or relating to a hybrid **:** of mixed origin

hydr- *or* **hydro-** *prefix* **1 :** water **2 :** hydrogen

hy·drant *n* **:** a pipe with a spout through which water may be drawn from the main pipes

hy·drau·lic *adj* **1 :** operated, moved, or brought about by means of water **2 :** operated by liquid forced through a small hole or through a tube — **hy·drau·li·cal·ly** *adv*

hy·dro·car·bon *n* **:** a substance containing only carbon and hydrogen

hy·dro·chlo·ric acid *n* **:** a strong acid formed by dissolving in water a gas made up of hydrogen and chlorine

hy·dro·elec·tric *adj* **:** relating to or used in the making of electricity by waterpower

hy·dro·gen *n* **:** a colorless, odorless, and tasteless flammable gas that is the lightest of the chemical elements

hydrogen bomb *n* **:** a bomb whose great power is due to the sudden release of energy when the central portions of hydrogen atoms unite

hydrogen peroxide *n* **:** a liquid chemical containing hydrogen and oxygen and used for bleaching and as an antiseptic

hy·dro·pho·bia *n* **:** RABIES

hy·dro·plane *n* **1 :** a speedboat whose hull is completely or partly raised as it glides over the water **2 :** SEAPLANE

hy·e·na *n* **:** a large mammal of Asia and Africa that lives on flesh

hy·giene *n* **1 :** a science that deals with the bringing about and keeping up of good health in the individual and the group **2 :** conditions or practices necessary for health

hy·gien·ic *adj* **:** of, relating to, or leading toward health or hygiene — **hy·gien·i·cal·ly** *adv*

hy·gien·ist *n* **:** a person skilled in hygiene and especially in a specified branch of hygiene

hy·grom·e·ter *n* **:** an instrument for measuring the humidity of the air

hymn *n* **:** a song of praise especially to God

hym·nal *n* **:** a book of hymns

hyper- *prefix* **:** excessively

hy·per·link *n* **:** an electronic link that allows a computer user to move directly from a marked place in a hypertext document to another in the same or a different document — **hyperlink** *vb*

hy·per·sen·si·tive *adj* **:** very sensitive
hy·per·text *n* **:** an arrangement of the information in a computer database that allows the user to get other information by clicking on text displayed on the screen
hy·pha *n, pl* **hy·phae :** one of the fine threads that make up the body of a fungus
[1]**hy·phen** *n* **:** a mark - used to divide or to compound words or word elements
[2]**hyphen** *vb* **:** HYPHENATE
hy·phen·ate *vb* **hy·phen·at·ed; hy·phen·at·ing :** to connect or mark with a hyphen
hyp·no·sis *n* **:** a state which resembles sleep but is produced by a person who can then make suggestions to which the hypnotized person will respond
hyp·no·tism *n* **:** the study or act of producing a state like sleep in which the person in this state will respond to suggestions made by the hypnotist
hyp·no·tist *n* **:** a person who practices hypnotism
hyp·no·tize *vb* **hyp·no·tized; hyp·no·tiz·ing :** to affect by or as if by hypnotism
hy·poc·ri·sy *n, pl* **hy·poc·ri·sies :** a pretending to be what one is not or to believe or feel what one does not
hyp·o·crite *n* **:** a person who practices hypocrisy
hy·pot·e·nuse *n* **:** the side of a right triangle that is opposite the right angle
hy·poth·e·sis *n, pl* **hy·poth·e·ses :** something not proved but assumed to be true for purposes of argument or further study or investigation
hy·po·thet·i·cal *adj* **1 :** involving or based on a hypothesis **2 :** being merely supposed — **hy·po·thet·i·cal·ly** *adv*
hys·te·ria *n* **1 :** a nervous disorder in which one loses control over the emotions **2 :** a wild uncontrolled outburst of emotion — **hys·ter·i·cal** *adj* — **hys·ter·i·cal·ly** *adv*
hys·ter·ics *n sing or pl* **:** a fit of uncontrollable laughing or crying **:** HYSTERIA

I

i *n, pl* **i's** *or* **is** *often cap* **1 :** the ninth letter of the English alphabet **2 :** one in Roman numerals
I *pron* **:** the person speaking or writing
-ial *adj suffix* **:** [1]-AL
-ian — see -AN
ibex *n, pl* **ibex** *or* **ibex·es :** a wild goat of the Old World with horns that curve backward
-ibility — see -ABILITY
ibis *n, pl* **ibis** *or* **ibis·es :** a bird related to the herons but having a slender bill that curves down
-ible — see -ABLE
-ic *adj suffix* **1 :** of, relating to, or having the form of **:** being **2 :** coming from, consisting of, or containing **3 :** in the manner of **4 :** associated or dealing with **:** using **5 :** characterized by **:** exhibiting **:** affected with
-ical *adj suffix* **:** -IC
[1]**ice** *n* **1 :** frozen water **2 :** a substance like ice **3 :** a frozen dessert usually made with sweetened fruit juice
[2]**ice** *vb* **iced; ic·ing 1 :** to coat or become coated with ice **2 :** to chill with ice **:** supply with ice **3 :** to cover with icing
ice·berg *n* **:** a large floating mass of ice that has broken away from a glacier
ice·boat *n* **:** a boatlike frame driven by sails and gliding over ice on runners
ice·bound *adj* **:** surrounded or blocked by ice
ice·box *n* **:** REFRIGERATOR
ice·break·er *n* **:** a ship equipped to make and keep open a channel through ice
ice cap *n* **:** a large more or less level glacier flowing outward in all directions from its center
ice–cold *adj* **:** very cold
ice cream *n* **:** a frozen food containing sweetened and flavored cream or butterfat
ice–skate *vb* **:** to skate on ice — **ice skat·er** *n*
ici·cle *n* **:** a hanging mass of ice formed from dripping water
ic·ing *n* **:** a sweet coating for baked goods
icon *n* **1 :** a picture that represents something **2 :** a religious image usually painted on a small wooden panel **3 :** a small picture or symbol on a computer screen that suggests a function that the computer can perform
-ics *n sing or pl suffix* **1 :** study **:** knowledge **:** skill **:** practice **2 :** characteristic actions or qualities
icy *adj* **ic·i·er; ic·i·est 1 :** covered with, full of, or being ice **2 :** very cold **3 :** UNFRIENDLY — **ic·i·ly** *adv* — **ic·i·ness** *n*
I'd : I had **:** I should **:** I would
idea *n* **1 :** a plan of action **:** INTENTION **2 :** something imagined or pictured in the mind **:** NOTION **3 :** a central meaning or purpose
[1]**ide·al** *adj* **1 :** existing only in the mind **2 :** having no flaw **:** PERFECT — **ide·al·ly** *adv*
[2]**ideal** *n* **1 :** a standard of perfection, beauty, or excellence **2 :** a perfect type
iden·ti·cal *adj* **1 :** being one and the same **2 :** being exactly alike or equal

iden·ti·fi·ca·tion *n* **1 :** an act of identifying **:** the state of being identified **2 :** something that shows or proves identity

iden·ti·fy *vb* **iden·ti·fied; iden·ti·fy·ing** **1 :** to think of as identical **2 :** [1]ASSOCIATE 2 **3 :** to find out or show the identity of

iden·ti·ty *n, pl* **iden·ti·ties** **1 :** the fact or condition of being exactly alike **:** SAMENESS **2 :** INDIVIDUALITY 1 **3 :** the fact of being the same person or thing as claimed

id·i·o·cy *n, pl* **id·i·o·cies** **1 :** great lack of intelligence **2 :** something very stupid or foolish

id·i·om *n* **:** an expression that cannot be understood from the meanings of its separate words but must be learned as a whole

id·i·ot *n* **1 :** a person of very low intelligence **2 :** a silly or foolish person

id·i·ot·ic *adj* **:** showing idiocy **:** FOOLISH, STUPID — **id·i·ot·i·cal·ly** *adv*

[1]**idle** *adj* **idler; idlest** **1 :** not based on facts **2 :** not working or in use **3 :** LAZY 1 — **idle·ness** *n* — **idly** *adv*

[2]**idle** *vb* **idled; idling** **1 :** to spend time doing nothing **2 :** to run without being connected for doing useful work — **idler** *n*

idol *n* **1 :** an image worshiped as a god **2 :** a much loved person or thing

idol·ize *vb* **idol·ized; idol·iz·ing** **:** to make an idol of **:** love or admire too much

-ie *also* **-y** *n suffix, pl* **-ies** **:** little one

-ier — see [2]-ER

if *conj* **1 :** in the event that **2 :** WHETHER 1

-ify *vb suffix* **-ified; -ify·ing** **:** -FY

ig·loo *n, pl* **igloos** **:** an Eskimo house often made of blocks of snow and shaped like a dome

ig·ne·ous *adj* **:** formed by hardening of melted mineral material

ig·nite *vb* **ig·nit·ed; ig·nit·ing** **1 :** to set on fire **:** LIGHT **2 :** to catch fire

ig·ni·tion *n* **1 :** the act or action of igniting **2 :** the process or means (as an electric spark) of igniting a fuel mixture

ig·no·ble *adj* **:** DISHONORABLE — **ig·no·bly** *adv*

ig·no·rance *n* **:** the state of being ignorant

ig·no·rant *adj* **1 :** having little or no knowledge **:** not educated **2 :** not knowing **:** UNAWARE **3 :** resulting from or showing lack of knowledge — **ig·no·rant·ly** *adv*

ig·nore *vb* **ig·nored; ig·nor·ing** **:** to pay no attention to

igua·na *n* **:** a very large tropical American lizard with a ridge of tall scales along its back

il- — see IN-

[1]**ill** *adj* **worse; worst** **1 :** [1]EVIL 2 **2 :** causing suffering or distress **3 :** not normal or sound **4 :** not in good health **5 :** [1]UNFORTUNATE 1, UNLUCKY **6 :** UNKIND, UNFRIENDLY **7 :** not right or proper

[2]**ill** *adv* **worse; worst** **1 :** with displeasure **2 :** in a harsh way **3 :** SCARCELY 1, HARDLY **4 :** in a faulty way

[3]**ill** *n* **1 :** the opposite of good **2 :** SICKNESS 2 **3 :** [2]TROUBLE 2

I'll **:** I shall **:** I will

il·le·gal *adj* **:** contrary to law **:** UNLAWFUL — **il·le·gal·ly** *adv*

il·leg·i·ble *adj* **:** impossible to read — **il·leg·i·bly** *adv*

il·le·git·i·mate *adj* **:** not legitimate — **il·le·git·i·mate·ly** *adv*

il·lic·it *adj* **:** not permitted **:** UNLAWFUL — **il·lic·it·ly** *adv*

il·lit·er·a·cy *n* **:** the quality or state of being illiterate

[1]**il·lit·er·ate** *adj* **1 :** unable to read or write **2 :** showing lack of education — **il·lit·er·ate·ly** *adv*

[2]**illiterate** *n* **:** an illiterate person

ill–man·nered *adj* **:** not polite

ill–na·tured *adj* **:** having a bad disposition — **ill–na·tured·ly** *adv*

ill·ness *n* **:** SICKNESS 1 2

il·log·i·cal *adj* **:** not using or following good reasoning — **il·log·i·cal·ly** *adv*

ill–tem·pered *adj* **:** ILL-NATURED

ill–treat *vb* **:** to treat in a cruel or improper way — **ill–treat·ment** *n*

il·lu·mi·nate *vb* **il·lu·mi·nat·ed; il·lu·mi·nat·ing** **1 :** to supply with light **:** light up **2 :** to make clear **:** EXPLAIN

il·lu·mi·na·tion *n* **1 :** the action of illuminating **:** the state of being illuminated **2 :** the amount of light

ill–use *vb* **:** ILL-TREAT

il·lu·sion *n* **1 :** a misleading image presented to the eye **2 :** the state or fact of being led to accept as true something unreal or imagined **3 :** a mistaken idea

il·lu·sive *adj* **:** ILLUSORY

il·lu·so·ry *adj* **:** based on or producing illusion **:** DECEPTIVE

il·lus·trate *vb* **il·lus·trat·ed; il·lus·trat·ing** **1 :** to make clear by using examples **2 :** to supply with pictures or diagrams meant to explain or decorate **3 :** to serve as an example

il·lus·tra·tion *n* **1 :** the action of illustrating **:** the condition of being illustrated **2 :** an example or instance used to make something clear **3 :** a picture or diagram that explains or decorates

il·lus·tra·tive *adj* **:** serving or meant to illustrate

il·lus·tra·tor *n* **:** an artist who makes illustrations (as for books)

il·lus·tri·ous *adj* **:** EMINENT

ill will *n* : unfriendly feeling
im- — see IN-
I'm : I am
[1]**im·age** *n* **1** : something (as a statue) made to look like a person or thing **2** : a picture of a person or thing formed by a device (as a mirror or lens) **3** : a person very much like another **4** : a mental picture of something not present : IMPRESSION **5** : a graphic representation
[2]**image** *vb* **im·aged; im·ag·ing** **1** : to describe in words or pictures **2** : REFLECT 2
imag·in·able *adj* : possible to imagine
imag·i·nary *adj* : existing only in the imagination : not real
imag·i·na·tion *n* **1** : the act, process, or power of forming a mental picture of something not present and especially of something one has not known or experienced **2** : creative ability **3** : a creation of the mind
imag·i·na·tive *adj* **1** : of, relating to, or showing imagination **2** : having a lively imagination — **imag·i·na·tive·ly** *adv*
imag·ine *vb* **imag·ined; imag·in·ing** **1** : to form a mental picture of **2** : THINK 2
[1]**im·be·cile** *n* : a person of such low intelligence as to need help in simple personal care
[2]**imbecile** *or* **im·be·cil·ic** *adj* : of very low intelligence : very stupid
im·be·cil·i·ty *n, pl* **im·be·cil·i·ties** **1** : the quality or state of being imbecile **2** : something very foolish
imbed *variant of* EMBED
im·i·tate *vb* **im·i·tat·ed; im·i·tat·ing** **1** : to follow as a pattern, model, or example **2** : to be or appear like : RESEMBLE **3** : to copy exactly : MIMIC
[1]**im·i·ta·tion** *n* **1** : an act of imitating **2** : [1]COPY 1
[2]**imitation** *adj* : like something else and especially something better
im·i·ta·tive *adj* **1** : involving imitation **2** : given to imitating
im·mac·u·late *adj* **1** : having no stain or blemish : PURE **2** : perfectly clean — **im·mac·u·late·ly** *adv*
im·ma·te·ri·al *adj* : not important : INSIGNIFICANT
im·ma·ture *adj* : not yet fully grown or ripe — **im·ma·ture·ly** *adv*
im·mea·sur·able *adj* : impossible to measure — **im·mea·sur·ably** *adv*
im·me·di·ate *adj* **1** : acting or being without anything else between **2** : being next in line or nearest in relationship **3** : closest in importance **4** : acting or being without any delay **5** : not far away in time or space
im·me·di·ate·ly *adv* **1** : with nothing between **2** : right away
im·mense *adj* : very great in size or amount : HUGE — **im·mense·ly** *adv*
im·men·si·ty *n, pl* **im·men·si·ties** : the quality or state of being immense
im·merse *vb* **im·mersed; im·mers·ing** **1** : to plunge into something (as a fluid) that surrounds or covers **2** : to become completely involved with
im·mi·grant *n* : a person who comes to a country to live there
im·mi·grate *vb* **im·mi·grat·ed; im·mi·grat·ing** : to come into a foreign country to live
im·mi·gra·tion *n* : an act or instance of immigrating
im·mi·nent *adj* : being about to happen — **im·mi·nent·ly** *adv*
im·mo·bile *adj* : unable to move or be moved
im·mo·bi·lize *vb* **im·mo·bi·lized; im·mo·bi·liz·ing** : to fix in place : make immovable
im·mod·est *adj* : not modest — **im·mod·est·ly** *adv*
im·mod·es·ty *n* : lack of modesty
im·mor·al *adj* : not moral : BAD 4 — **im·mor·al·ly** *adv*
im·mo·ral·i·ty *n, pl* **im·mo·ral·i·ties** **1** : the quality or state of being immoral **2** : an immoral act or custom
[1]**im·mor·tal** *adj* : living or lasting forever — **im·mor·tal·ly** *adv*
[2]**immortal** *n* **1** : an immortal being **2** : a person of lasting fame
im·mor·tal·i·ty *n* **1** : the quality or state of being immortal : endless life **2** : lasting fame or glory
im·mov·able *adj* : impossible to move : firmly fixed — **im·mov·ably** *adv*
im·mune *adj* **1** : [1]EXEMPT **2** : having a strong or special power to resist
immune system *n* : the system of the body that fights infection and disease and that includes especially the white blood cells and antibodies and the organs that produce them
im·mu·ni·ty *n, pl* **im·mu·ni·ties** **1** : EXEMPTION 1 **2** : power to resist infection whether natural or acquired (as by vaccination)
im·mu·ni·za·tion *n* : treatment (as with a vaccine) to produce immunity to a disease
im·mu·nize *vb* **im·mu·nized; im·mu·niz·ing** : to make immune
imp *n* **1** : a small demon **2** : a mischievous child
im·pact *n* **1** : a striking together of two bodies **2** : a strong effect
im·pair *vb* : to make less (as in quantity, value, or strength) or worse : DAMAGE
im·pale *vb* **im·paled; im·pal·ing** : to pierce with something pointed

im·part *vb* **1 :** to give or grant from a supply **2 :** to make known

im·par·tial *adj* **:** not partial or biased **:** FAIR, JUST — **im·par·tial·ly** *adv*

im·par·tial·i·ty *n* **:** the quality or state of being impartial

im·pass·able *adj* **:** impossible to pass, cross, or travel

im·pas·sioned *adj* **:** showing very strong feeling

im·pas·sive *adj* **:** not feeling or showing emotion — **im·pas·sive·ly** *adv*

im·pa·tience *n* **1 :** lack of patience **2 :** restless or eager desire

im·pa·tient *adj* **1 :** not patient **2 :** showing or coming from impatience **3 :** restless and eager — **im·pa·tient·ly** *adv*

im·peach *vb* **:** to charge a public official formally with misconduct in office

im·pede *vb* **im·ped·ed; im·ped·ing :** to disturb the movement or progress of

im·ped·i·ment *n* **1 :** something that impedes **2 :** a defect in speech

im·pel *vb* **im·pelled; im·pel·ling :** to urge or drive forward or into action **:** FORCE

im·pend *vb* **:** to threaten to occur very soon

im·pen·e·tra·ble *adj* **1 :** impossible to penetrate **2 :** impossible to understand — **im·pen·e·tra·bly** *adv*

im·pen·i·tent *adj* **:** not penitent

im·per·a·tive *adj* **1 :** expressing a command, request, or strong encouragement **2 :** impossible to avoid or ignore **:** URGENT

im·per·cep·ti·ble *adj* **1 :** not perceptible by the senses or by the mind **2 :** very small or gradual — **im·per·cep·ti·bly** *adv*

im·per·fect *adj* **:** not perfect **:** FAULTY — **im·per·fect·ly** *adv*

im·per·fec·tion *n* **1 :** the quality or state of being imperfect **2 :** FLAW, FAULT

im·pe·ri·al *adj* **:** of or relating to an empire or its ruler — **im·pe·ri·al·ly** *adv*

im·per·il *vb* **im·per·iled** *or* **im·per·illed; im·per·il·ing** *or* **im·per·il·ling :** to place in great danger **:** ENDANGER

im·per·ish·able *adj* **:** INDESTRUCTIBLE — **im·per·ish·ably** *adv*

im·per·son·al *adj* **:** not referring or belonging to a specific person — **im·per·son·al·ly** *adv*

im·per·son·ate *vb* **im·per·son·at·ed; im·per·son·at·ing :** to pretend to be another person

im·per·son·a·tion *n* **:** the act of impersonating

im·per·ti·nence *n* **1 :** the quality or state of being impertinent **2 :** a rude act or remark

im·per·ti·nent *adj* **:** INSOLENT, RUDE — **im·per·ti·nent·ly** *adv*

im·per·turb·able *adj* **:** hard to disturb or upset — **im·per·turb·ably** *adv*

im·per·vi·ous *adj* **:** not letting something enter or pass through

im·pet·u·ous *adj* **:** IMPULSIVE, RASH — **im·pet·u·ous·ly** *adv*

im·pi·ous *adj* **:** not pious **:** IRREVERENT — **im·pi·ous·ly** *adv*

imp·ish *adj* **:** MISCHIEVOUS 3 — **imp·ish·ly** *adv*

im·pla·ca·ble *adj* **:** impossible to please, satisfy, or change — **im·pla·ca·bly** *adv*

im·plant *vb* **:** to fix or set securely or deeply

im·ple·ment *n* **:** an article (as a tool) intended for a certain use

im·pli·cate *vb* **im·pli·cat·ed; im·pli·cat·ing :** to show to be connected or involved

im·pli·ca·tion *n* **1 :** the act of implicating **:** the state of being implicated **2 :** the act of implying **3 :** something implied

im·plic·it *adj* **1 :** understood though not put clearly into words **2 :** ABSOLUTE 2 — **im·plic·it·ly** *adv*

im·plore *vb* **im·plored; im·plor·ing :** to call upon with a humble request **:** BESEECH

im·ply *vb* **im·plied; im·ply·ing :** to express indirectly **:** suggest rather than say plainly

im·po·lite *adj* **:** not polite — **im·po·lite·ly** *adv* — **im·po·lite·ness** *n*

¹im·port *vb* **1 :** ²MEAN 3 **2 :** to bring (as goods) into a country usually for selling

²im·port *n* **1 :** MEANING 1 **2 :** IMPORTANCE **3 :** something brought into a country

im·por·tance *n* **:** the quality or state of being important **:** SIGNIFICANCE

im·por·tant *adj* **1 :** SIGNIFICANT **2 :** having power or authority — **im·por·tant·ly** *adv*

im·por·ta·tion *n* **1 :** the act or practice of importing **2 :** something imported

im·por·tu·nate *adj* **:** making a nuisance of oneself with requests and demands — **im·por·tu·nate·ly** *adv*

im·por·tune *vb* **im·por·tuned; im·por·tun·ing :** to beg or urge so much as to be a nuisance

im·pose *vb* **im·posed; im·pos·ing 1 :** to establish or apply as a charge or penalty **2 :** to force someone to accept or put up with **3 :** to take unfair advantage

im·pos·ing *adj* **:** impressive because of size, dignity, or magnificence

im·pos·si·bil·i·ty *n, pl* **im·pos·si·bil·i·ties 1 :** the quality or state of being impossible **2 :** something impossible

im·pos·si·ble *adj* **1 :** incapable of being or of occurring **2 :** HOPELESS 2 **3 :** very bad or unpleasant — **im·pos·si·bly** *adv*

im·pos·tor *n* **:** a person who pretends to be someone else in order to deceive

im•pos•ture *n* **:** the act or conduct of an impostor

im•po•tence *n* **:** the quality or state of being impotent

im•po•tent *adj* **:** lacking in power or strength — **im•po•tent•ly** *adv*

im•pound *vb* **:** to shut up in or as if in an enclosed place

im•pov•er•ish *vb* **1 :** to make poor **2 :** to use up the strength or richness of

im•prac•ti•cal *adj* **:** not practical — **im•prac•ti•cal•ly** *adv*

im•pre•cise *adj* **:** not clear or exact — **im•pre•cise•ly** *adv*

im•preg•nate *vb* **im•preg•nat•ed; im•preg•nat•ing 1 :** to make fertile or fruitful **2 :** to cause (a material) to be filled with something

im•press *vb* **1 :** to fix in or on one's mind **2 :** to move or affect strongly

im•pres•sion *n* **1 :** the act or process of impressing **2 :** something (as a design) made by pressing or stamping **3 :** something that impresses or is impressed on one's mind **4 :** a memory or belief that is vague or uncertain

im•pres•sion•able *adj* **:** easy to impress or influence

im•pres•sive *adj* **:** having the power to impress the mind or feelings — **im•pres•sive•ly** *adv*

[1]**im•print** *vb* **1 :** to mark by pressure **:** STAMP **2 :** to fix firmly

[2]**im•print** *n* **:** something imprinted or printed **:** IMPRESSION

im•pris•on *vb* **:** to put in prison

im•pris•on•ment *n* **:** the act of imprisoning **:** the state of being imprisoned

im•prob•a•bil•i•ty *n* **:** the quality or state of being improbable

im•prob•a•ble *adj* **:** not probable — **im•prob•a•bly** *adv*

im•prop•er *adj* **:** not proper, right, or suitable — **im•prop•er•ly** *adv*

improper fraction *n* **:** a fraction whose numerator is equal to or larger than the denominator

im•prove *vb* **im•proved; im•prov•ing :** to make or become better — **im•prov•er** *n*

im•prove•ment *n* **1 :** the act or process of improving **2 :** increased value or excellence **3 :** something that adds to the value or appearance (as of a house)

im•prov•i•sa•tion *n* **1 :** the act or art of improvising **2 :** something that is improvised

im•pro•vise *vb* **im•pro•vised; im•pro•vis•ing 1 :** to compose, recite, or sing without studying or practicing ahead of time **2 :** to make, invent, or arrange with whatever is at hand

im•pu•dence *n* **:** impudent behavior or speech **:** INSOLENCE, DISRESPECT

im•pu•dent *adj* **:** being bold and disrespectful **:** INSOLENT — **im•pu•dent•ly** *adv*

im•pulse *n* **1 :** a force that starts a body into motion **2 :** the motion produced by a starting force **3 :** a sudden stirring up of the mind and spirit to do something **4 :** the wave of change that passes along a stimulated nerve and carries information to the brain

im•pul•sive *adj* **1 :** acting or tending to act on impulse **2 :** resulting from a sudden impulse — **im•pul•sive•ly** *adv*

im•pure *adj* **1 :** not pure **:** UNCLEAN, DIRTY **2 :** mixed with something else that is usually not as good — **im•pure•ly** *adv*

im•pu•ri•ty *n, pl* **im•pu•ri•ties 1 :** the quality or state of being impure **2 :** something that is or makes impure

[1]**in** *prep* **1 :** enclosed or surrounded by **:** WITHIN **2 :** INTO 1 **3 :** DURING **4 :** WITH 7 **5** — used to show a state or condition **6** — used to show manner or purpose **7 :** INTO 2

[2]**in** *adv* **1 :** to or toward the inside **2 :** to or toward some particular place **3 :** [1]NEAR 1 **4 :** into the midst of something **5 :** to or at its proper place **6 :** on the inner side **:** WITHIN **7 :** at hand or on hand

[3]**in** *adj* **1 :** being inside or within **2 :** headed or bound inward

[1]**in-** *or* **il-** *or* **im-** *or* **ir-** *prefix* **:** not **:** NON-, UN- — usually *il-* before *l* and *im-* before *b, m,* or *p* and *ir-* before *r* and *in-* before other sounds

[2]**in-** *or* **il-** *or* **im-** *or* **ir-** *prefix* **1 :** in **:** within **:** into **:** toward **:** on — usually *il-* before *l, im-* before *b, m,* or *p, ir-* before *r,* and *in-* before other sounds **2 :** EN-

in•abil•i•ty *n* **:** the condition of being unable to do something **:** lack of ability

in•ac•ces•si•bil•i•ty *n* **:** the quality or state of being inaccessible

in•ac•ces•si•ble *adj* **:** hard or impossible to get to or at

in•ac•cu•ra•cy *n, pl* **in•ac•cu•ra•cies 1 :** lack of accuracy **2 :** ERROR, MISTAKE

in•ac•cu•rate *adj* **:** not right or correct **:** not exact — **in•ac•cu•rate•ly** *adv*

in•ac•tive *adj* **:** not active **:** IDLE

in•ac•tiv•i•ty *n* **:** the state of being inactive

in•ad•e•qua•cy *n, pl* **in•ad•e•qua•cies :** the condition of being not enough or not good enough

in•ad•e•quate *adj* **:** not enough or not good enough

in•ad•vis•able *adj* **:** not wise to do **:** UNWISE

in•alien•able *adj* **:** impossible to take away or give up

inane *adj* **:** silly and pointless — **inane•ly** *adv*

in·an·i·mate *adj* : not living : LIFELESS
in·ap·pro·pri·ate *adj* : not appropriate — **in·ap·pro·pri·ate·ly** *adv*
in·as·much as *conj* : considering that : [2]SINCE 2
in·at·ten·tion *n* : failure to pay attention
in·at·ten·tive *adj* : not paying attention — **in·at·ten·tive·ly** *adv*
in·au·di·ble *adj* : impossible to hear — **in·au·di·bly** *adv*
in·au·gu·ral *adj* : of or relating to an inauguration
in·au·gu·rate *vb* **in·au·gu·rat·ed; in·au·gu·rat·ing** **1** : to introduce into office with suitable ceremonies : INSTALL **2** : to celebrate the opening of **3** : to bring into being or action
in·au·gu·ra·tion *n* : an act or ceremony of inaugurating
in·born *adj* : INSTINCTIVE
in·breed *vb* **in·bred; in·breed·ing** : to breed with closely related individuals
in·can·des·cent *adj* : white or glowing with great heat
incandescent lamp *n* : a lamp whose light is produced by the glow of a wire heated by an electric current
in·ca·pa·ble *adj* : not able to do something
[1]**in·cense** *n* **1** : material used to produce a perfume when burned **2** : the perfume given off by burning incense
[2]**in·cense** *vb* **in·censed; in·cens·ing** : to make very angry
in·cen·tive *n* : something that makes a person try or work hard or harder
in·ces·sant *adj* : going on and on : not stopping or letting up — **in·ces·sant·ly** *adv*
[1]**inch** *n* : a unit of length equal to $^1/_{36}$ yard or 2.54 centimeters
[2]**inch** *vb* : to move a little bit at a time
in·ci·dent *n* : an often unimportant happening that may form a part of a larger event
[1]**in·ci·den·tal** *adj* **1** : happening by chance **2** : of minor importance
[2]**incidental** *n* : something incidental
in·ci·den·tal·ly *adv* : as a matter of less interest or importance
in·cin·er·ate *vb* **in·cin·er·at·ed; in·cin·er·at·ing** : to burn to ashes
in·cin·er·a·tor *n* : a furnace or a container for burning waste materials
in·cise *vb* **in·cised; in·cis·ing** : to cut into : CARVE, ENGRAVE
in·ci·sion *n* : a cutting into something or the cut or wound that results
in·ci·sor *n* : a tooth (as any of the four front teeth of the human upper or lower jaw) for cutting
in·cite *vb* **in·cit·ed; in·cit·ing** : to move to action : stir up : ROUSE
in·clem·ent *adj* : STORMY 1
in·cli·na·tion *n* **1** : an act or the action of bending or leaning **2** : a usually favorable feeling toward something **3** : [1]SLANT, TILT
[1]**in·cline** *vb* **in·clined; in·clin·ing** **1** : to cause to bend or lean **2** : to be drawn to an opinion or course of action **3** : [1]SLOPE, LEAN
[2]**in·cline** *n* : [2]SLOPE 2
in·clined *adj* **1** : having an inclination **2** : having a slope
inclose, inclosure *variant of* ENCLOSE, ENCLOSURE
in·clude *vb* **in·clud·ed; in·clud·ing** : to take in or have as part of a whole
in·clu·sion *n* **1** : an act of including : the state of being included **2** : something included
in·clu·sive *adj* **1** : covering everything or all important points **2** : including the stated limits and all in between
in·cog·ni·to *adv or adj* : with one's identity kept secret
in·co·her·ence *n* : the quality or state of being incoherent
in·co·her·ent *adj* : not connected in a clear or logical way — **in·co·her·ent·ly** *adv*
in·come *n* : a gain usually measured in money that comes in from labor, business, or property
income tax *n* : a tax on the income of a person or business
in·com·pa·ra·ble *adj* : MATCHLESS — **in·com·pa·ra·bly** *adv*
in·com·pat·i·ble *adj* : not able to live or work together in harmony — **in·com·pat·i·bly** *adv*
in·com·pe·tence *n* : the state or fact of being incompetent
in·com·pe·tent *adj* : not able to do a good job — **in·com·pe·tent·ly** *adv*
in·com·plete *adj* : not complete : not finished — **in·com·plete·ly** *adv*
in·com·pre·hen·si·ble *adj* : impossible to understand — **in·com·pre·hen·si·bly** *adv*
in·con·ceiv·able *adj* **1** : impossible to imagine or put up with **2** : hard to believe — **in·con·ceiv·ably** *adv*
in·con·gru·ous *adj* : not harmonious, suitable, or proper — **in·con·gru·ous·ly** *adv*
in·con·sid·er·ate *adj* : careless of the rights or feelings of others
in·con·sis·tent *adj* **1** : not being in agreement **2** : not keeping to the same thoughts or practices : CHANGEABLE
in·con·spic·u·ous *adj* : not easily seen or noticed — **in·con·spic·u·ous·ly** *adv*
[1]**in·con·ve·nience** *n* **1** : the quality or state of being inconvenient **2** : something inconvenient

²inconvenience *vb* **in·con·ve·nienced; in·con·ve·nienc·ing :** to cause inconvenience to

in·con·ve·nient *adj* **:** not convenient — **in·con·ve·nient·ly** *adv*

in·cor·po·rate *vb* **in·cor·po·rat·ed; in·cor·po·rat·ing 1 :** to join or unite closely into a single mass or body **2 :** to make a corporation of

in·cor·po·ra·tion *n* **:** an act of incorporating **:** the state of being incorporated

in·cor·rect *adj* **1 :** not correct **:** not accurate or true **:** WRONG **2 :** showing no care for duty or for moral or social standards — **in·cor·rect·ly** *adv* — **in·cor·rect·ness** *n*

¹in·crease *vb* **in·creased; in·creas·ing :** to make or become greater (as in size)

²in·crease *n* **1 :** the act of increasing **2 :** something added (as by growth)

in·creas·ing·ly *adv* **:** more and more

in·cred·i·ble *adj* **:** too strange or unlikely to be believed — **in·cred·i·bly** *adv*

in·cre·du·li·ty *n* **:** the quality or state of being incredulous

in·cred·u·lous *adj* **:** feeling or showing disbelief **:** SKEPTICAL — **in·cred·u·lous·ly** *adv*

in·crim·i·nate *vb* **in·crim·i·nat·ed; in·crim·i·nat·ing :** to charge with or involve in a crime or fault **:** ACCUSE

incrust *variant of* ENCRUST

in·cu·bate *vb* **in·cu·bat·ed; in·cu·bat·ing 1 :** to sit upon eggs to hatch them by warmth **2 :** to keep under conditions good for hatching or development

in·cu·ba·tion *n* **1 :** an act of incubating **:** the state of being incubated **2 :** the time between infection with germs and the appearance of disease symptoms

in·cu·ba·tor *n* **1 :** an apparatus that provides enough heat to hatch eggs artificially **2 :** an apparatus to help the growth of tiny newborn babies

in·cum·bent *n* **:** the holder of an office or position

in·cur *vb* **in·curred; in·cur·ring :** to bring upon oneself

in·cur·able *adj* **:** impossible to cure — **in·cur·ably** *adv*

in·debt·ed *adj* **:** being in debt **:** owing something — **in·debt·ed·ness** *n*

in·de·cen·cy *n, pl* **in·de·cen·cies 1 :** lack of decency **2 :** an indecent act or word

in·de·cent *adj* **:** not decent **:** COARSE, VULGAR

in·de·ci·sion *n* **:** a swaying between two or more courses of action

in·de·ci·sive *adj* **1 :** not decisive or final **2 :** finding it hard to make decisions — **in·de·ci·sive·ly** *adv* — **in·de·ci·sive·ness** *n*

in·deed *adv* **:** in fact **:** TRULY

in·de·fen·si·ble *adj* **:** impossible to defend

in·def·i·nite *adj* **1 :** not clear or fixed in meaning or details **2 :** not limited (as in amount or length) — **in·def·i·nite·ly** *adv*

indefinite article *n* **:** either of the articles *a* or *an* used to show that the following noun refers to any person or thing of the kind named

in·del·i·ble *adj* **1 :** impossible to erase, remove, or blot out **2 :** making marks not easily removed — **in·del·i·bly** *adv*

in·del·i·cate *adj* **:** not polite or proper **:** COARSE — **in·del·i·cate·ly** *adv*

in·dent *vb* **:** to set (as the first line of a paragraph) in from the margin

in·den·ta·tion *n* **1 :** a cut or dent in something **2 :** the action of indenting or the state of being indented

in·de·pen·dence *n* **:** the quality or state of being independent

Independence Day *n* **:** July 4 observed as a legal holiday in honor of the adoption of the Declaration of Independence in 1776

¹in·de·pen·dent *adj* **1 :** not under the control or rule of another **2 :** not connected with something else **:** SEPARATE **3 :** not depending on anyone else for money to live on **4 :** able to make up one's own mind — **in·de·pen·dent·ly** *adv*

²independent *n* **:** an independent person (as a voter who belongs to no political party)

in·de·scrib·able *adj* **:** impossible to describe — **in·de·scrib·ably** *adv*

in·de·struc·ti·ble *adj* **:** impossible to destroy — **in·de·struc·ti·bly** *adv*

¹in·dex *n, pl* **in·dex·es** *or* **in·di·ces 1 :** a list of names or topics (as in a book) given in alphabetical order and showing where each is to be found **2 :** POINTER 1 **3 :** ¹SIGN 5, INDICATION

²index *vb* **1 :** to provide with an index **2 :** to list in an index

index finger *n* **:** the finger next to the thumb

¹In·di·an *n* **1 :** a person born or living in India **2 :** AMERICAN INDIAN

²Indian *adj* **1 :** of or relating to India or its peoples **2 :** of or relating to the American Indians or their languages

Indian club *n* **:** a wooden club swung for exercise

Indian corn *n* **:** a tall American cereal grass widely grown for its large ears of grain which are used as food or for feeding livestock

Indian pipe *n* **:** a waxy white leafless woodland herb with nodding flowers

Indian summer *n* **:** a period of mild weather in late autumn or early winter

in·di·cate *vb* **in·di·cat·ed; in·di·cat·ing 1 :** to point out or point to **2 :** to state or express briefly

in·di·ca·tion *n* **1 :** the act of indicating **2 :** something that indicates
in·dic·a·tive *adj* **1 :** representing an act or state as a fact that can be known or proved **2 :** pointing out
in·di·ca·tor *n* **1 :** one that indicates **2 :** a pointer on a dial or scale **3 :** [1]DIAL 3, GAUGE 3
indices *pl of* INDEX
in·dict *vb* **:** to charge with an offense or crime **:** ACCUSE — **in·dict·ment** *n*
in·dif·fer·ence *n* **1 :** the condition or fact of being indifferent **2 :** lack of interest
in·dif·fer·ent *adj* **1 :** having no choice **:** showing neither interest nor dislike **2 :** neither good nor bad — **in·dif·fer·ent·ly** *adv*
in·di·gest·ible *adj* **:** not digestible **:** not easy to digest
in·di·ges·tion *n* **:** discomfort caused by slow or painful digestion
in·dig·nant *adj* **:** filled with or expressing indignation — **in·dig·nant·ly** *adv*
in·dig·na·tion *n* **:** anger caused by something unjust or unworthy
in·dig·ni·ty *n, pl* **in·dig·ni·ties** **1 :** an act that injures one's dignity or self-respect **2 :** treatment that shows a lack of respect
in·di·go *n, pl* **in·di·gos** *or* **in·di·goes** **1 :** a blue dye made artificially and formerly obtained from plants (**indigo plants**) **2 :** a dark grayish blue
in·di·rect *adj* **1 :** not straight or direct **2 :** not straightforward **3 :** not having a plainly seen connection — **in·di·rect·ly** *adv* — **in·di·rect·ness** *n*
indirect object *n* **:** an object that represents the secondary goal of the action of its verb
in·dis·creet *adj* **:** not discreet — **in·dis·creet·ly** *adv*
in·dis·cre·tion *n* **1 :** lack of discretion **2 :** an indiscreet act or remark
in·dis·crim·i·nate *adj* **:** showing lack of discrimination
in·dis·pens·able *adj* **:** [1]ESSENTIAL 2 — **in·dis·pens·ably** *adv*
in·dis·posed *adj* **1 :** somewhat unwell **2 :** not willing
in·dis·po·si·tion *n* **:** the condition of being indisposed **:** a slight illness
in·dis·put·able *adj* **:** not disputable **:** UNQUESTIONABLE — **in·dis·put·ably** *adv*
in·dis·tinct *adj* **:** not distinct — **in·dis·tinct·ly** *adv* — **in·dis·tinct·ness** *n*
in·dis·tin·guish·able *adj* **:** impossible to distinguish clearly — **in·dis·tin·guish·ably** *adv*
[1]**in·di·vid·u·al** *adj* **1 :** of or relating to an individual **2 :** intended for one person **3 :** [1]PARTICULAR 1, SEPARATE **4 :** having a special quality **:** DISTINCTIVE 1 — **in·di·vid·u·al·ly** *adv*
[2]**individual** *n* **1 :** a single member of a class **2 :** a single human being
in·di·vid·u·al·i·ty *n, pl* **in·di·vid·u·al·i·ties** **1 :** the qualities that set one person or thing off from all others **2 :** the quality or state of being an individual
in·di·vis·i·ble *adj* **:** impossible to divide or separate — **in·di·vis·i·bly** *adv*
in·doc·tri·nate *vb* **in·doc·tri·nat·ed; in·doc·tri·nat·ing** **1 :** INSTRUCT 1, TEACH **2 :** to teach the ideas, opinions, or beliefs of a certain group
in·doc·tri·na·tion *n* **:** the act or process of indoctrinating
in·do·lence *n* **:** LAZINESS
in·do·lent *adj* **:** LAZY, IDLE
in·dom·i·ta·ble *adj* **:** UNCONQUERABLE — **in·dom·i·ta·bly** *adv*
in·door *adj* **1 :** of or relating to the inside of a building **2 :** done, used, or belonging within a building
in·doors *adv* **:** in or into a building
indorse *variant of* ENDORSE
in·du·bi·ta·ble *adj* **:** being beyond question or doubt — **in·du·bi·ta·bly** *adv*
in·duce *vb* **in·duced; in·duc·ing** **1 :** to lead on to do something **2 :** to bring about **:** CAUSE **3 :** to produce (as an electric current) by induction
in·duce·ment *n* **1 :** the act of inducing **2 :** something that induces
in·duct *vb* **1 :** to place in office **:** INSTALL **2 :** to take in as a member of a military service
in·duc·tion *n* **1 :** the act or process of inducting **2 :** the production of an electrical or magnetic effect through the influence of a nearby magnet, electrical current, or electrically charged body
in·dulge *vb* **in·dulged; in·dulg·ing** **1 :** to give in to one's own or another's desires **:** HUMOR **2 :** to allow oneself the pleasure of having or doing something
in·dul·gence *n* **1 :** the act of indulging **:** the state of being indulgent **2 :** an indulgent act **3 :** something indulged in
in·dul·gent *adj* **:** characterized by indulgence **:** LENIENT — **in·dul·gent·ly** *adv*
in·dus·tri·al *adj* **1 :** of, relating to, or engaged in industry **2 :** having highly developed industries — **in·dus·tri·al·ly** *adv*
in·dus·tri·al·ist *n* **:** a person owning or engaged in the management of an industry
in·dus·tri·al·i·za·tion *n* **:** the process of industrializing **:** the state of being industrialized
in·dus·tri·al·ize *vb* **in·dus·tri·al·ized; in·dus·tri·al·iz·ing** **:** to make or become industrial
in·dus·tri·ous *adj* **:** working hard and

steadily : DILIGENT — **in·dus·tri·ous·ly** *adv*

in·dus·try *n, pl* **in·dus·tries** **1 :** the habit of working hard and steadily **2 :** businesses that provide a certain product or service **3 :** manufacturing activity

-ine *adj suffix* **:** of, relating to, or like

in·ed·i·ble *adj* **:** not fit for food

in·ef·fec·tive *adj* **:** not producing the desired effect — **in·ef·fec·tive·ly** *adv*

in·ef·fec·tu·al *adj* **:** not producing the proper or usual effect — **in·ef·fec·tu·al·ly** *adv*

in·ef·fi·cien·cy *n, pl* **in·ef·fi·cien·cies :** the state or an instance of being inefficient

in·ef·fi·cient *adj* **1 :** not effective **:** INEFFECTUAL **2 :** not able or willing to do something well — **in·ef·fi·cient·ly** *adv*

in·elas·tic *adj* **:** not elastic

in·el·i·gi·bil·i·ty *n* **:** the condition or fact of being ineligible

in·el·i·gi·ble *adj* **:** not eligible

in·ept *adj* **1 :** not suited to the occasion **2 :** lacking in skill or ability — **in·ept·ly** *adv* — **in·ept·ness** *n*

in·equal·i·ty *n, pl* **in·equal·i·ties** **1 :** the quality of being unequal or uneven **2 :** an instance of being uneven

in·ert *adj* **:** unable or slow to move or react — **in·ert·ly** *adv* — **in·ert·ness** *n*

in·er·tia *n* **1 :** a property of matter by which it remains at rest or in motion in the same straight line unless acted upon by some external force **2 :** a tendency not to move or change

in·er·tial *adj* **:** of or relating to inertia

in·es·cap·able *adj* **:** INEVITABLE — **in·es·cap·ably** *adv*

in·ev·i·ta·bil·i·ty *n* **:** the quality or state of being inevitable

in·ev·i·ta·ble *adj* **:** sure to happen **:** CERTAIN — **in·ev·i·ta·bly** *adv*

in·ex·act *adj* **:** INACCURATE — **in·ex·act·ly** *adv* — **in·ex·act·ness** *n*

in·ex·cus·able *adj* **:** not to be excused — **in·ex·cus·ably** *adv*

in·ex·haust·ible *adj* **:** plentiful enough not to give out or be used up — **in·ex·haust·ibly** *adv*

in·ex·o·ra·ble *adj* **:** RELENTLESS — **in·ex·o·ra·bly** *adv*

in·ex·pe·di·ent *adj* **:** not suitable or advisable

in·ex·pen·sive *adj* **:** ¹CHEAP 1 — **in·ex·pen·sive·ly** *adv* — **in·ex·pen·sive·ness** *n*

in·ex·pe·ri·ence *n* **:** lack of experience

in·ex·pe·ri·enced *adj* **:** having little or no experience

in·ex·pli·ca·ble *adj* **:** impossible to explain or account for — **in·ex·pli·ca·bly** *adv*

in·ex·press·ible *adj* **:** being beyond one's power to express **:** INDESCRIBABLE — **in·ex·press·ibly** *adv*

in·fal·li·ble *adj* **1 :** not capable of being wrong **2 :** not likely to fail **:** SURE — **in·fal·li·bly** *adv*

in·fa·mous *adj* **1 :** having an evil reputation **2 :** DETESTABLE — **in·fa·mous·ly** *adv*

in·fa·my *n, pl* **in·fa·mies** **1 :** an evil reputation **2 :** an infamous act

in·fan·cy *n, pl* **in·fan·cies** **1 :** early childhood **2 :** a beginning or early period of existence

¹in·fant *n* **1 :** a child in the first period of life **2 :** ²MINOR

²infant *adj* **1 :** of or relating to infancy **2 :** intended for young children

in·fan·tile *adj* **:** CHILDISH

infantile paralysis *n* **:** POLIO

in·fan·try *n, pl* **in·fan·tries :** a branch of an army composed of soldiers trained to fight on foot

in·fat·u·at·ed *adj* **:** having a foolish or very strong love or admiration

in·fat·u·a·tion *n* **:** the state of being infatuated

in·fect *vb* **1 :** to cause disease germs to be present in or on **2 :** to pass on a germ or disease to **3 :** to enter and cause disease in **4 :** to cause to share one's feelings

in·fec·tion *n* **1 :** the act or process of infecting **:** the state of being infected **2 :** any disease caused by germs

in·fec·tious *adj* **1 :** passing from one to another in the form of a germ **2 :** capable of being easily spread

in·fer *vb* **in·ferred; in·fer·ring** **1 :** to arrive at as a conclusion **2 :** ²SURMISE **3 :** to point out **4 :** HINT, SUGGEST

in·fer·ence *n* **1 :** the act or process of inferring **2 :** something inferred

¹in·fe·ri·or *adj* **1 :** situated lower down (as in place or importance) **2 :** of little or less importance, value, or merit

²inferior *n* **:** an inferior person or thing

in·fe·ri·or·i·ty *n* **1 :** the state of being inferior **2 :** a sense of being inferior

in·fer·nal *adj* **1 :** of or relating to hell **2 :** very bad or unpleasant **:** DAMNABLE — **in·fer·nal·ly** *adv*

in·fer·tile *adj* **:** not fertile

in·fest *vb* **:** to spread or swarm in or over in a troublesome manner

in·fi·del *n* **:** a person who does not believe in a certain religion

in·fi·del·i·ty *n, pl* **in·fi·del·i·ties** **1 :** lack of belief in a certain religion **2 :** DISLOYALTY

in·field *n* **1 :** the diamond-shaped part of a baseball field inside the bases and home plate **2 :** the players in the infield

in·field·er *n* **:** a baseball player who plays in the infield

in·fi·nite *adj* **1 :** having no limits of any kind **2 :** seeming to be without limits — **in·fi·nite·ly** *adv*

in·fin·i·tive *n* **:** a verb form serving as a noun or as a modifier and at the same time taking objects and adverbial modifiers

in·fin·i·ty *n, pl* **in·fin·i·ties 1 :** the quality of being infinite **2 :** a space, quantity, or period of time that is without limit

in·firm *adj* **:** weak or frail in body (as from age or disease)

in·fir·ma·ry *n, pl* **in·fir·ma·ries :** a place for the care and housing of infirm or sick people

in·fir·mi·ty *n, pl* **in·fir·mi·ties :** the condition of being infirm

in·flame *vb* **in·flamed; in·flam·ing 1 :** to excite to too much action or feeling **2 :** to cause to redden or grow hot (as from anger) **3 :** to make or become sore, red, and swollen

in·flam·ma·ble *adj* **1 :** FLAMMABLE **2 :** easily inflamed **:** EXCITABLE

in·flam·ma·tion *n* **1 :** the act of inflaming **:** the state of being inflamed **2 :** a bodily response to injury in which heat, redness, and swelling are present

in·flam·ma·to·ry *adj* **1 :** tending to excite anger or disorder **2 :** causing or having inflammation

in·flat·able *adj* **:** possible to inflate

in·flate *vb* **in·flat·ed; in·flat·ing 1 :** to swell or fill with air or gas **2 :** to cause to increase beyond proper limits

in·fla·tion *n* **1 :** an act of inflating **:** the state of being inflated **2 :** a continual rise in the price of goods and services

in·flect *vb* **1 :** to change a word by inflection **2 :** to change the pitch of a person's voice

in·flec·tion *n* **1 :** a change in the pitch of a person's voice **2 :** a change in a word that shows a grammatical difference (as of number, person, or tense)

in·flec·tion·al *adj* **:** of or relating to inflection

in·flex·i·ble *adj* **1 :** not easily bent or twisted **:** RIGID **2 :** not easily influenced or persuaded **:** FIRM

in·flict *vb* **1 :** to give by or as if by striking **2 :** to cause to be put up with

in·flo·res·cence *n* **:** the arrangement of flowers on a stalk

¹in·flu·ence *n* **1 :** the act or power of producing an effect without apparent force or direct authority **2 :** a person or thing that influences

²influence *vb* **in·flu·enced; in·flu·enc·ing :** to have an influence on

in·flu·en·tial *adj* **:** having influence

in·flu·en·za *n* **:** a very contagious virus disease like a severe cold with fever

in·fo·mer·cial *n* **:** a television program that is a long commercial often including a discussion or demonstration

in·form *vb* **1 :** to let a person know something **2 :** to give information so as to accuse or cause suspicion — **in·form·er** *n*

in·for·mal *adj* **1 :** not formal **2 :** suitable for ordinary or everyday use — **in·for·mal·ly** *adv*

in·for·mal·i·ty *n, pl* **in·for·mal·i·ties 1 :** the quality or state of being informal **2 :** an informal act

in·form·ant *n* **:** a person who informs

in·for·ma·tion *n* **1 :** the giving or getting of knowledge **2 :** knowledge obtained from investigation, study, or instruction **3 :** NEWS 3

information superhighway *n* **:** INTERNET

in·for·ma·tive *adj* **:** giving information **:** INSTRUCTIVE

in·frac·tion *n* **:** VIOLATION

in·fra·red *adj* **:** being, relating to, or producing rays like light but lying outside the visible spectrum at its red end

in·fre·quent *adj* **1 :** seldom happening **:** RARE **2 :** not placed, made, or done at frequent intervals — **in·fre·quent·ly** *adv*

in·fringe *vb* **in·fringed; in·fring·ing 1 :** to fail to obey or act in agreement with **:** VIOLATE **2 :** to go further than is right or fair to another **:** ENCROACH — **in·fringe·ment** *n*

in·fu·ri·ate *vb* **in·fu·ri·at·ed; in·fu·ri·at·ing :** to make furious **:** ENRAGE

in·fuse *vb* **in·fused; in·fus·ing 1 :** to put in as if by pouring **2 :** to steep without boiling — **in·fu·sion** *n*

¹-ing *n suffix* **1 :** action or process **2 :** product or result of an action or process **3 :** something used in or connected with making or doing

²-ing *vb suffix or adj suffix* — used to form the present participle and sometimes to form adjectives that do not come from a verb

in·ge·nious *adj* **:** showing ingenuity **:** CLEVER — **in·ge·nious·ly** *adv*

in·ge·nu·ity *n, pl* **in·ge·nu·ities :** skill or cleverness in discovering, inventing, or planning

in·gen·u·ous *adj* **1 :** FRANK, STRAIGHTFORWARD **2 :** NAIVE 1 — **in·gen·u·ous·ly** *adv* — **in·gen·u·ous·ness** *n*

in·got *n* **:** a mass of metal cast into a shape that is easy to handle or store

in·gra·ti·ate *vb* **in·gra·ti·at·ed; in·gra·ti·at·ing :** to gain favor for by effort

in·gra·ti·at·ing *adj* **1 :** PLEASING **2 :** intended to gain someone's favor — **in•gra•ti•at•ing•ly** *adv*

in•grat•i•tude *n* : lack of gratitude

in•gre•di•ent *n* : one of the substances that make up a mixture

in•hab•it *vb* : to live or dwell in

in•hab•i•tant *n* : one who lives in a place permanently

in•ha•la•tion *n* : the act or an instance of inhaling

in•hale *vb* **in•haled; in•hal•ing** **1** : to draw in by breathing **2** : to breathe in

in•hal•er *n* : a device used for inhaling medicine

in•her•ent *adj* : belonging to or being a part of the nature of a person or thing — **in•her•ent•ly** *adv*

in•her•it *vb* **1** : to get by legal right from a person at his or her death **2** : to get by heredity

in•her•i•tance *n* **1** : the act of inheriting **2** : something inherited

in•hib•it *vb* : to prevent or hold back from doing something

in•hos•pi•ta•ble *adj* : not friendly or generous : not showing hospitality — **in•hos•pi•ta•bly** *adv*

in•hu•man *adj* **1** : lacking pity or kindness **2** : unlike what might be expected by a human — **in•hu•man•ly** *adv*

in•hu•mane *adj* : not humane

in•hu•man•i•ty *n, pl* **in•hu•man•i•ties** : a cruel act or attitude

in•iq•ui•tous *adj* : WICKED 1

in•iq•ui•ty *n, pl* **in•iq•ui•ties** : [1]SIN 1

[1]**ini•tial** *adj* **1** : of, relating to, or being a beginning **2** : placed or standing at the beginning : FIRST

[2]**initial** *n* **1** : the first letter of a name **2** : a large letter beginning a text or a paragraph

[3]**initial** *vb* **ini•tialed** *or* **ini•tialled; ini•tial•ing** *or* **ini•tial•ling** : to mark with an initial or with one's initials

ini•ti•ate *vb* **ini•ti•at•ed; ini•ti•at•ing** **1** : to set going **2** : to admit into a club by special ceremonies

ini•ti•a•tion *n* **1** : the act or an instance of initiating : the process of being initiated **2** : the ceremonies with which a person is made a member of a club

ini•tia•tive *n* **1** : a first step or movement **2** : energy shown in initiating action : ENTERPRISE

in•ject *vb* **1** : to throw or drive into something **2** : to force a fluid into (as a part of the body) for medical reasons

in•jec•tion *n* **1** : an act or instance of injecting **2** : something injected

in•junc•tion *n* : a court order commanding or forbidding the doing of some act

in•jure *vb* **in•jured; in•jur•ing** **1** : to do an injustice to : WRONG **2** : to cause pain or harm to

in•ju•ri•ous *adj* : causing injury

in•ju•ry *n, pl* **in•ju•ries** **1** : an act that damages or hurts **2** : hurt, damage, or loss suffered

in•jus•tice *n* **1** : violation of a person's rights **2** : an unjust act

[1]**ink** *n* : a usually liquid material for writing or printing

[2]**ink** *vb* : to put ink on

in•kling *n* : a vague notion : HINT

ink•stand *n* : a small stand for holding ink and pens

ink•well *n* : a container for ink

inky *adj* **ink•i•er; ink•i•est** **1** : consisting of or like ink **2** : soiled with or as if with ink

in•laid *adj* **1** : set into a surface in a decorative design **2** : decorated with a design or material set into a surface

[1]**in•land** *adj* : of or relating to the part of a country away from the coast

[2]**inland** *n* : the part of a country away from the coast or boundaries

[3]**inland** *adv* : into or toward the arca away from a coast

in–law *n* : a relative by marriage

[1]**in•lay** *vb* **in•laid; in•lay•ing** : to set into a surface for decoration or strengthening

[2]**in•lay** *n* : inlaid work : material used in inlaying

in•let *n* **1** : a small or narrow bay **2** : an opening for intake

in•mate *n* **1** : one of a group living in a single residence **2** : a person confined in an institution (as an asylum or prison)

in•most *adj* : INNERMOST

inn *n* : a place that provides a place to sleep and food for travelers

in•ner *adj* **1** : located farther in **2** : of or relating to the mind or spirit

inner ear *n* : the inner hollow part of the ear that contains sense organs which perceive sound and help keep the body properly balanced

in•ner•most *adj* : farthest inward

in•ning *n* : a division of a baseball game that consists of a turn at bat for each team

inn•keep•er *n* : the person who runs an inn

in•no•cence *n* : the quality or state of being innocent

in•no•cent *adj* **1** : free from sin : PURE **2** : free from guilt or blame **3** : free from evil influence or effect : HARMLESS — **in•no•cent•ly** *adv*

in•noc•u•ous *adj* : not harmful

in•no•va•tion *n* **1** : the introduction of something new **2** : a new idea, method, or device : NOVELTY

in·nu·mer·a·ble *adj* **:** too many to be counted

in·oc·u·late *vb* **in·oc·u·lat·ed; in·oc·u·lat·ing :** to inject a serum, vaccine, or weakened germ into to protect against or treat a disease

in·oc·u·la·tion *n* **1 :** the act or an instance of inoculating **2 :** material used in inoculating

in·of·fen·sive *adj* **1 :** not harmful **2 :** PEACEFUL 1 **3 :** not offensive

in·op·por·tune *adj* **:** INCONVENIENT

¹in·put *n* **1 :** something (as power, a signal, or data) that is put into a machine or system **2 :** the point at which an input is made **3 :** the act of or process of putting in

²input *vb* **in·put·ted** *or* **input; in·put·ting :** to enter (as data) into a computer

in·quest *n* **:** an official investigation especially into the cause of a death

in·quire *vb* **in·quired; in·quir·ing 1 :** to ask about **2 :** to make an investigation **3 :** to ask a question — **in·quir·er** *n* — **in·quir·ing·ly** *adv*

in·qui·ry *n, pl* **in·qui·ries 1 :** the act of inquiring **2 :** a request for information **3 :** a thorough examination

in·quis·i·tive *adj* **1 :** given to seeking information **2 :** tending to ask questions — **in·quis·i·tive·ly** *adv* — **in·quis·i·tive·ness** *n*

in·sane *adj* **1 :** not normal or healthy in mind **2 :** used by or for people who are insane — **in·sane·ly** *adv*

in·san·i·ty *n* **:** the condition of being insane **:** mental illness

in·sa·tia·ble *adj* **:** impossible to satisfy

in·scribe *vb* **in·scribed; in·scrib·ing 1 :** to write, engrave, or print as a lasting record **2 :** to write, engrave, or print something on or in

in·scrip·tion *n* **:** something that is inscribed

in·sect *n* **1 :** a small and often winged animal that has six jointed legs and a body formed of three parts **2 :** an animal (as a spider or a centipede) similar to the true insects

in·sec·ti·cide *n* **:** a chemical used to kill insects

in·se·cure *adj* **:** not safe or secure — **in·se·cure·ly** *adv*

in·se·cu·ri·ty *n* **:** the quality or state of being insecure

in·sen·si·ble *adj* **1 :** UNCONSCIOUS 2 **2 :** not able to feel **3 :** not aware of or caring about something

in·sen·si·tive *adj* **:** not sensitive **:** lacking feeling — **in·sen·si·tive·ly** *adv*

in·sen·si·tiv·i·ty *n* **:** lack of sensitivity

in·sep·a·ra·bil·i·ty *n* **:** the quality or state of being inseparable

in·sep·a·ra·ble *adj* **:** impossible to separate — **in·sep·a·ra·bly** *adv*

¹in·sert *vb* **1 :** to put in **2 :** to set in and make fast

²in·sert *n* **:** something that is or is meant to be inserted

in·ser·tion *n* **1 :** the act or process of inserting **2 :** ²INSERT

¹in·set *n* **:** ²INSERT

²inset *vb* **in·set** *or* **in·set·ted; in·set·ting :** ¹INSERT 2

¹in·side *n* **1 :** an inner side, surface, or space **:** INTERIOR **2 :** ENTRAILS — usually used in pl.

²inside *adv* **1 :** on the inner side **2 :** in or into the interior

³inside *adj* **1 :** of, relating to, or being on or near the inside **2 :** relating or known to a certain few people

⁴inside *prep* **1 :** to or on the inside of **2 :** before the end of **:** WITHIN

in·sid·er *n* **:** a person having information not generally available

in·sight *n* **:** the power or act of seeing what's really important about a situation

in·sig·nia *or* **in·sig·ne** *n, pl* **insignia** *or* **in·sig·ni·as :** an emblem of a certain office, authority, or honor

in·sig·nif·i·cance *n* **:** the quality or state of being insignificant

in·sig·nif·i·cant *adj* **:** not significant **:** UNIMPORTANT — **in·sig·nif·i·cant·ly** *adv*

in·sin·cere *adj* **:** not sincere — **in·sin·cere·ly** *adv*

in·sin·cer·i·ty *n* **:** lack of sincerity

in·sin·u·ate *vb* **in·sin·u·at·ed; in·sin·u·at·ing 1 :** to bring or get in little by little or in a secret way **2 :** ²HINT, IMPLY

in·sip·id *adj* **1 :** having little taste or flavor **:** TASTELESS **2 :** not interesting or challenging **:** DULL

in·sist *vb* **1 :** to place special stress or great importance **2 :** to make a demand

in·sis·tence *n* **:** the quality or state of being insistent

in·sis·tent *adj* **:** demanding attention **:** PERSISTENT — **in·sis·tent·ly** *adv*

in·so·lence *n* **:** lack of respect for rank or authority

in·so·lent *adj* **:** showing insolence — **in·so·lent·ly** *adv*

in·sol·u·bil·i·ty *n* **:** the quality or state of being insoluble

in·sol·u·ble *adj* **1 :** having no solution or explanation **2 :** difficult or impossible to dissolve — **in·sol·u·bly** *adv*

in·spect *vb* **1 :** to examine closely **2 :** to view and examine in an official way

in·spec·tion *n* **:** the act of inspecting

in·spec·tor *n* **:** a person who makes inspections

in·spi·ra·tion *n* **1 :** the act of breathing in

2 : the act or power of arousing the mind or the emotions **3 :** the state of being inspired **4 :** something that is or seems inspired **5 :** an inspiring agent or influence

in•spire *vb* **in•spired; in•spir•ing** **1 :** to move or guide by divine influence **2 :** to give inspiration to : ENCOURAGE **3 :** AROUSE 2 **4 :** to bring about : CAUSE **5 :** INHALE

in•sta•bil•i•ty *n* : the quality or state of being unstable

in•stall *vb* **1 :** to put in office with ceremony **2 :** to set up for use or service

in•stal•la•tion *n* **1 :** the act of installing : the state of being installed **2 :** something installed for use

1in•stall•ment *or* **in•stal•ment** *n* : INSTALLATION 1

2installment *n* : one of the parts of a series

in•stance *n* **1 :** EXAMPLE 1 **2 :** a certain point in an action or process

1in•stant *n* : MOMENT 1

2instant *adj* **1 :** happening or done at once **2 :** partially prepared by the manufacturer so that only final mixing is needed **3 :** made to dissolve quickly in a liquid

in•stan•ta•neous *adj* **1 :** happening in an instant **2 :** done without delay — **in•stan•ta•neous•ly** *adv*

in•stant•ly *adv* : IMMEDIATELY 2

in•stead *adv* : as a substitute

in•stead of *prep* : as a substitute for : rather than

in•step *n* : the arched middle part of the human foot in front of the ankle joint

in•sti•gate *vb* **in•sti•gat•ed; in•sti•gat•ing** : PROVOKE 2, INCITE

in•still *vb* : to put into the mind little by little

in•stinct *n* **1 :** a natural ability **2 :** an act or course of action in response to a stimulus that is automatic rather than learned **3 :** behavior based on automatic reactions

in•stinc•tive *adj* : of or relating to instinct : resulting from instinct — **in•stinc•tive•ly** *adv*

1in•sti•tute *vb* **in•sti•tut•ed; in•sti•tut•ing** **1 :** ESTABLISH 1 **2 :** to set going : INAUGURATE

2institute *n* **1 :** an organization for the promotion of a cause **2 :** a place for study usually in a special field

in•sti•tu•tion *n* **1 :** the act of instituting : ESTABLISHMENT **2 :** an established custom, practice, or law **3 :** an established organization

in•sti•tu•tion•al *adj* : of or relating to an institution

in•struct *vb* **1 :** to help to get knowledge to : TEACH **2 :** to give information to **3 :** to give commands to : DIRECT

in•struc•tion *n* **1 :** LESSON 3 **2 instructions** *pl* : DIRECTION 2, ORDER **3 instructions** *pl* : an outline of how something is to be done **4 :** the practice or method used by a teacher

in•struc•tive *adj* : helping to give knowledge — **in•struc•tive•ly** *adv*

in•struc•tor *n* : TEACHER

in•stru•ment *n* **1 :** a way of getting something done **2 :** a device for doing a particular kind of work **3 :** a device used to produce music **4 :** a legal document (as a deed) **5 :** a measuring device

in•stru•men•tal *adj* **1 :** acting to get something done **2 :** of or relating to an instrument **3 :** being music played on an instrument rather than sung — **in•stru•men•tal•ly** *adv*

in•sub•or•di•nate *adj* : unwilling to obey authority : DISOBEDIENT

in•sub•or•di•na•tion *n* : failure to obey authority

in•sub•stan•tial *adj* **1 :** not real : IMAGINARY **2 :** not firm or solid — **in•sub•stan•tial•ly** *adv*

in•suf•fer•able *adj* : impossible to endure : INTOLERABLE — **in•suf•fer•ably** *adv*

in•suf•fi•cien•cy *n, pl* **in•suf•fi•cien•cies** **1 :** the quality or state of being insufficient **2 :** a shortage of something

in•suf•fi•cient *adj* : not sufficient : INADEQUATE — **in•suf•fi•cient•ly** *adv*

in•su•late *vb* **in•su•lat•ed; in•su•lat•ing** **1 :** to separate from others : ISOLATE **2 :** to separate a conductor of electricity, heat, or sound from other conducting bodies by means of something that will not conduct electricity, heat, or sound

in•su•la•tion *n* **1 :** the act of insulating : the state of being insulated **2 :** material used in insulating

in•su•la•tor *n* **1 :** a material (as rubber or glass) that is a poor conductor of electricity or heat **2 :** a device made of an electrical insulating material and used for separating or supporting electrical conductors

in•su•lin *n* : a hormone from the pancreas that prevents or controls diabetes

1in•sult *vb* : to treat with disrespect or scorn

2in•sult *n* : an act or expression showing disrespect or scorn

in•sur•ance *n* **1 :** the act of insuring : the state of being insured **2 :** the business of insuring persons or property **3 :** a contract by which someone guarantees for a fee to pay someone else for the value of property lost or damaged (as through theft or fire) or usually a specified amount for injury or death **4 :** the amount for which something is insured

DICTIONARY

in·sure *vb* **in·sured; in·sur·ing** **1 :** to give or get insurance on or for **2 :** ENSURE — **in·sur·er** *n*

in·sured *n* **:** a person whose life or property is insured

¹in·sur·gent *n* **:** ²REBEL

²insurgent *adj* **:** REBELLIOUS 1

in·sur·rec·tion *n* **:** an act or instance of rebelling against a government

in·tact *adj* **:** not touched especially by anything that harms

in·take *n* **1 :** a place where liquid or air is taken into something (as a pump) **2 :** the act of taking in **3 :** something taken in

¹in·tan·gi·ble *adj* **1 :** not possible to touch **2 :** not possible to think of as matter or substance

²intangible *n* **:** something intangible

in·te·ger *n* **:** a number that is a natural number (as 1, 2, or 3), the negative of a natural number (as –1, –2, –3), or 0

in·te·gral *adj* **:** needed to make something complete

in·te·grate *vb* **in·te·grat·ed; in·te·grat·ing** **1 :** to form into a whole **:** UNITE **2 :** to make a part of a larger unit **3 :** to make open to all races

integrated circuit *n* **:** a tiny group of electronic devices and their connections that is produced in or on a small slice of material (as silicon)

in·te·gra·tion *n* **:** an act, process, or instance of integrating

in·teg·ri·ty *n* **1 :** the condition of being free from damage or defect **2 :** total honesty and sincerity

in·tel·lect *n* **1 :** the power of knowing **2 :** the capacity for thought especially when highly developed **3 :** a person with great powers of thinking and reasoning

¹in·tel·lec·tu·al *adj* **1 :** of or relating to the intellect or understanding **2 :** having or showing greater than usual intellect **3 :** requiring study and thought — **in·tel·lec·tu·al·ly** *adv*

²intellectual *n* **:** an intellectual person

in·tel·li·gence *n* **1 :** the ability to learn and understand **2 :** NEWS 3, INFORMATION **3 :** an agency that obtains information about an enemy or a possible enemy

in·tel·li·gent *adj* **:** having or showing intelligence or intellect — **in·tel·li·gent·ly** *adv*

in·tel·li·gi·ble *adj* **:** possible to understand — **in·tel·li·gi·bly** *adv*

in·tem·per·ance *n* **:** lack of self-control (as in satisfying an appetite)

in·tem·per·ate *adj* **1 :** not moderate or mild **2 :** lacking or showing a lack of self-control (as in the use of alcoholic drinks) — **in·tem·per·ate·ly** *adv*

in·tend *vb* **:** to have in mind as a purpose or aim **:** PLAN

in·tense *adj* **1 :** ¹EXTREME 1 **2 :** done with great energy, enthusiasm, or effort **3 :** having very strong feelings — **in·tense·ly** *adv*

in·ten·si·fi·ca·tion *n* **:** the act or process of intensifying

in·ten·si·fy *vb* **in·ten·si·fied; in·ten·si·fy·ing** **:** to make or become intense or more intensive **:** HEIGHTEN

in·ten·si·ty *n, pl* **in·ten·si·ties** **1 :** extreme strength or force **2 :** the degree or amount of a quality or condition

¹in·ten·sive *adj* **1 :** involving special effort or concentration **:** THOROUGH **2** — used to stress something

²intensive *n* **:** an intensive word

¹in·tent *n* **1 :** ¹PURPOSE, INTENTION **2 :** MEANING 1

²intent *adj* **1 :** showing concentration or great attention **2 :** showing great determination — **in·tent·ly** *adv* — **in·tent·ness** *n*

in·ten·tion *n* **1 :** a determination to act in a particular way **2 :** ¹PURPOSE, AIM **3 :** MEANING 1, INTENT

in·ten·tion·al *adj* **:** done by intention **:** not accidental — **in·ten·tion·al·ly** *adv*

in·ter *vb* **in·terred; in·ter·ring** **:** BURY 1

inter- *prefix* **1 :** between **:** among **:** together **2 :** mutual **:** mutually **:** reciprocal **:** reciprocally **3 :** located, occurring, or carried on between

in·ter·act *vb* **:** to act upon one another

in·ter·ac·tion *n* **:** the action or influence of people, groups, or things on one another

in·ter·ac·tive *adj* **1 :** active between people, groups, or things **2 :** of, relating to, or allowing two-way electronic communications (as between a person and a computer) — **in·ter·ac·tive·ly** *adv*

in·ter·cede *vb* **in·ter·ced·ed; in·ter·ced·ing** **1 :** to try to help settle differences between unfriendly individuals or groups **2 :** to plead for the needs of someone else

in·ter·cept *vb* **:** to take, seize, or stop before reaching an intended destination — **in·ter·cep·tor** *n*

in·ter·ces·sion *n* **:** the act of interceding

in·ter·ces·sor *n* **:** a person who intercedes

¹in·ter·change *vb* **in·ter·changed; in·ter·chang·ing** **:** to put each in the place of the other **:** EXCHANGE

²in·ter·change *n* **1 :** an act or instance of interchanging **2 :** a joining of highways that permits moving from one to the other without crossing traffic lanes

in·ter·change·able *adj* **:** possible to interchange — **in·ter·change·ably** *adv*

in·ter·com *n* **:** a communication system with a microphone and loudspeaker at each end

in·ter·course *n* **:** dealings between persons or groups

in·ter·de·pen·dence *n* **:** the quality or state of being interdependent

in·ter·de·pen·dent *adj* **:** depending on one another — **in·ter·de·pen·dent·ly** *adv*

[1]in·ter·est *n* **1 :** a right, title, or legal share in something **2 :** WELFARE 1, BENEFIT **3 :** the money paid by a borrower for the use of borrowed money **4 interests** *pl* **:** a group financially interested in an industry or business **5 :** a feeling of concern, curiosity, or desire to be involved with something **6 :** the quality of attracting special attention or arousing curiosity **7 :** something in which one is interested

[2]interest *vb* **1 :** to persuade to become involved in **2 :** to arouse and hold the interest of

in·ter·est·ed *adj* **:** having or showing interest

in·ter·est·ing *adj* **:** holding the attention **:** arousing interest — **in·ter·est·ing·ly** *adv*

in·ter·fere *vb* **in·ter·fered; in·ter·fer·ing 1 :** to be in opposition **:** CLASH **2 :** to take a part in the concerns of others

in·ter·fer·ence *n* **1 :** the act or process of interfering **2 :** something that interferes

in·ter·im *n* **:** INTERVAL 1

[1]in·te·ri·or *adj* **1 :** being or occurring within the limits **:** INNER **2 :** far from the border or shore **:** INLAND

[2]interior *n* **:** the inner part of something

in·ter·ject *vb* **:** to put between or among other things

in·ter·jec·tion *n* **1 :** an interjecting of something **2 :** something interjected **3 :** a word or cry (as "ouch") expressing sudden or strong feeling

in·ter·lace *vb* **in·ter·laced; in·ter·lac·ing :** to unite by or as if by lacing together

in·ter·lock *vb* **:** to lock together

in·ter·lop·er *n* **:** INTRUDER

in·ter·lude *n* **1 :** an entertainment between the acts of a play **2 :** a period or event that comes between others **3 :** a musical composition between parts of a longer composition or of a drama

in·ter·mar·riage *n* **:** marriage between members of different groups

in·ter·mar·ry *vb* **in·ter·mar·ried; in·ter·mar·ry·ing :** to become connected by intermarriage

in·ter·me·di·ary *n, pl* **in·ter·me·di·ar·ies :** GO-BETWEEN

[1]in·ter·me·di·ate *adj* **:** being or occurring in the middle or between — **in·ter·me·di·ate·ly** *adv*

[2]intermediate *n* **:** someone or something that is intermediate

in·ter·ment *n* **:** BURIAL

in·ter·mi·na·ble *adj* **:** ENDLESS 1 — **in·ter·mi·na·bly** *adv*

in·ter·min·gle *vb* **in·ter·min·gled; in·ter·min·gling :** to mix together

in·ter·mis·sion *n* **1 :** [1]PAUSE 1, INTERRUPTION **2 :** a temporary halt (as between acts of a play)

in·ter·mit·tent *adj* **:** starting, stopping, and starting again — **in·ter·mit·tent·ly** *adv*

[1]in·tern *vb* **:** to force to stay within certain limits especially during a war — **in·tern·ment** *n*

[2]in·tern *or* **in·terne** *n* **:** a medical school graduate getting practical experience in a hospital — **in·tern·ship** *n*

[3]in·tern *vb* **:** to work as an intern

in·ter·nal *adj* **1 :** being within something **:** INTERIOR, INNER **2 :** having to do with the inside of the body **3 :** of or relating to the domestic affairs of a country — **in·ter·nal·ly** *adv*

in·ter·na·tion·al *adj* **:** of, relating to, or affecting two or more nations — **in·ter·na·tion·al·ly** *adv*

In·ter·net *n* **:** a communications system that connects groups of computers and databases all over the world

in·ter·plan·e·tary *adj* **:** existing, carried on, or operating between planets

in·ter·play *n* **:** INTERACTION

in·ter·pose *vb* **in·ter·posed; in·ter·pos·ing 1 :** to put between **2 :** to introduce between parts of a conversation **3 :** to be or come between

in·ter·po·si·tion *n* **1 :** the act of interposing **:** the state of being interposed **2 :** something that interposes or is interposed

in·ter·pret *vb* **1 :** to tell the meaning of **:** EXPLAIN, TRANSLATE **2 :** to understand according to one's own belief, judgment, or interest **3 :** to bring out the meaning of — **in·ter·pret·er** *n*

in·ter·pre·ta·tion *n* **:** the act or the result of interpreting

in·ter·pre·ta·tive *adj* **:** designed or serving to interpret

in·ter·pre·tive *adj* **:** INTERPRETATIVE

in·ter·ra·cial *adj* **:** of or involving members of different races

in·ter·re·late *vb* **in·ter·re·lat·ed; in·ter·re·lat·ing :** to bring into or have a relationship with each other

in·ter·re·la·tion *n* **:** relation with each other — **in·ter·re·la·tion·ship** *n*

in·ter·ro·gate *vb* **in·ter·ro·gat·ed; in·ter·ro·gat·ing :** to question thoroughly

in·ter·ro·ga·tion *n* **:** the act of interrogating

interrogation point *n* **:** QUESTION MARK

in·ter·rog·a·tive *adj* **:** asking a question

in·ter·rog·a·to·ry *adj* **:** containing or expressing a question

in·ter·rupt *vb* **1 :** to stop or hinder by breaking in **2 :** to put or bring a difference into

in·ter·rup·tion *n* **:** an act of interrupting **:** a state of being interrupted

in·ter·scho·las·tic *adj* **:** existing or carried on between schools

in·ter·sect *vb* **:** to cut or divide by passing through or across **:** CROSS

in·ter·sec·tion *n* **1 :** the act or process of intersecting **2 :** the place or point where two or more things (as streets) intersect **:** CROSSING **3 :** the set of mathematical elements common to two or more sets

in·ter·sperse *vb* **in·ter·spersed; in·ter·spers·ing 1 :** to insert here and there **2 :** to insert something at various places in or among

in·ter·state *adj* **:** existing between or including two or more states

in·ter·stel·lar *adj* **:** existing or taking place among the stars

in·ter·twine *vb* **in·ter·twined; in·ter·twin·ing :** to twine or cause to twine about one another

in·ter·val *n* **1 :** a space of time between events or states **2 :** a space between things **3 :** the difference in pitch between two tones

in·ter·vene *vb* **in·ter·vened; in·ter·ven·ing 1 :** to come between events, places, or points of time **2 :** to interfere with something so as to stop, settle, or change

in·ter·ven·tion *n* **:** the act or fact of intervening

¹in·ter·view *n* **1 :** a meeting face to face to give or get information or advice **2 :** a written report of an interview for publication

²interview *vb* **:** to meet and question in an interview — **in·ter·view·er** *n*

in·ter·weave *vb* **in·ter·wove; in·ter·wo·ven; in·ter·weav·ing 1 :** to weave together **2 :** INTERMINGLE

in·tes·ti·nal *adj* **:** of or relating to the intestine

in·tes·tine *n* **:** the lower narrower part of the digestive canal in which most of the digestion and absorption of food occurs and through which waste material passes to be discharged

in·ti·ma·cy *n, pl* **in·ti·ma·cies :** the state or an instance of being intimate

¹in·ti·mate *vb* **in·ti·mat·ed; in·ti·mat·ing :** to express (as an idea) indirectly **:** HINT

²in·ti·mate *adj* **1 :** most private **:** PERSONAL **2 :** marked by very close association **3 :** suggesting comfortable warmth or privacy **:** COZY — **in·ti·mate·ly** *adv*

³in·ti·mate *n* **:** a very close friend

in·ti·ma·tion *n* **1 :** the act of intimating **2 :** ¹HINT 1

in·tim·i·date *vb* **in·tim·i·dat·ed; in·tim·i·dat·ing :** to frighten especially by threats

in·tim·i·da·tion *n* **:** the act of intimidating **:** the state of being intimidated

in·to *prep* **1 :** to the inside of **2 :** to the state, condition, or form of **3 :** so as to hit **:** AGAINST

in·tol·er·a·ble *adj* **:** UNBEARABLE — **in·tol·er·a·bly** *adv*

in·tol·er·ance *n* **:** the quality or state of being intolerant

in·tol·er·ant *adj* **:** not tolerant — **in·tol·er·ant·ly** *adv*

in·to·na·tion *n* **:** the rise and fall in pitch of the voice in speech

in·tox·i·cate *vb* **in·tox·i·cat·ed; in·tox·i·cat·ing 1 :** to make drunk **2 :** to make wildly excited or enthusiastic

in·tox·i·ca·tion *n* **1 :** an unhealthy state that is or is like a poisoning **2 :** the state of one who has drunk too much liquor **:** DRUNKENNESS

in·tra·mu·ral *adj* **:** being or occurring within the limits usually of a school

in·tran·si·tive *adj* **:** not having or containing a direct object

in·trep·id *adj* **:** feeling no fear **:** BOLD — **in·trep·id·ly** *adv*

in·tri·ca·cy *n, pl* **in·tri·ca·cies 1 :** the quality or state of being intricate **2 :** something intricate

in·tri·cate *adj* **1 :** having many closely combined parts or elements **2 :** very difficult to follow or understand — **in·tri·cate·ly** *adv*

¹in·trigue *vb* **in·trigued; in·trigu·ing 1 :** ²PLOT 2, SCHEME **2 :** to arouse the interest or curiosity of

²in·trigue *n* **:** a secret or sly scheme often for selfish purposes

in·tro·duce *vb* **in·tro·duced; in·tro·duc·ing 1 :** to bring into practice or use **2 :** to lead or bring in especially for the first time **3 :** to cause to be acquainted **:** make known **4 :** to bring forward for discussion **5 :** to put in **:** INSERT — **in·tro·duc·er** *n*

in·tro·duc·tion *n* **1 :** the action of introducing **2 :** something introduced **3 :** the part of a book that leads up to and explains what will be found in the main part **4 :** the act of making persons known to each other

in·tro·duc·to·ry *adj* **:** serving to introduce **:** PRELIMINARY

in·trude *vb* **in·trud·ed; in·trud·ing 1 :** to force in, into, or on especially where not right or proper **2 :** to come or go in without an invitation or right — **in·trud·er** *n*

in·tru·sion *n* **:** the act of intruding

intrust *variant of* ENTRUST

in·tu·i·tion *n* **:** a knowing or something known without mental effort

in·un·date *vb* **in·un·dat·ed; in·un·dat·ing :** to cover with a flood **:** OVERFLOW

in·un·da·tion *n* **:** [1]FLOOD 1

in·vade *vb* **in·vad·ed; in·vad·ing 1 :** to enter by force to conquer or plunder **2 :** to show lack of respect for — **in·vad·er** *n*

[1]**in·val·id** *adj* **:** not valid

[2]**in·va·lid** *adj* **1 :** SICKLY 1 **2 :** of or relating to a sick person

[3]**in·va·lid** *n* **:** a sick or disabled person — **in·va·lid·ism** *n*

in·val·i·date *vb* **in·val·i·dat·ed; in·val·i·dat·ing :** to weaken or destroy the effect of

in·valu·able *adj* **:** having value too great to be estimated **:** PRICELESS

in·var·i·a·bil·i·ty *n* **:** the quality or state of being invariable

in·vari·able *adj* **:** not changing or capable of change — **in·vari·ably** *adv*

in·va·sion *n* **:** an act of invading

in·vei·gle *vb* **in·vei·gled; in·vei·gling :** to win over or obtain by flattery

in·vent *vb* **1 :** to think up **:** make up **2 :** to create or produce for the first time — **in·ven·tor** *n*

in·ven·tion *n* **1 :** an original device or process **2 :** [3]LIE **3 :** the act or process of inventing

in·ven·tive *adj* **:** CREATIVE

[1]**in·ven·to·ry** *n, pl* **in·ven·to·ries 1 :** a list of items (as goods on hand) **2 :** the act or process of making an inventory

[2]**inventory** *vb* **in·ven·to·ried; in·ven·to·ry·ing :** to make an inventory of

[1]**in·verse** *adj* **1 :** opposite in order, nature, or effect **2 :** being a mathematical operation that is opposite in effect to another operation — **in·verse·ly** *adv*

[2]**inverse** *n* **:** something inverse

in·vert *vb* **1 :** to turn inside out or upside down **2 :** to reverse the order or position of

[1]**in·ver·te·brate** *adj* **:** having no backbone

[2]**invertebrate** *n* **:** an invertebrate animal

[1]**in·vest** *vb* **1 :** to give power or authority to **2 :** BESIEGE 1

[2]**invest** *vb* **1 :** to put out money in order to gain a financial return **2 :** to put out (as effort) in support of a usually worthy cause — **in·ves·tor** *n*

in·ves·ti·gate *vb* **in·ves·ti·gat·ed; in·ves·ti·gat·ing :** to study by close and careful observation — **in·ves·ti·ga·tor** *n*

in·ves·ti·ga·tion *n* **:** the act or process of investigating

in·ves·ti·ture *n* **:** the act of placing in office

in·vest·ment *n* **1 :** the investing of money **2 :** a sum of money invested **3 :** a property in which money is invested

in·vig·o·rate *vb* **in·vig·o·rat·ed; in·vig·o·rat·ing :** to give life and energy to

in·vin·ci·bil·i·ty *n* **:** the quality or state of being invincible

in·vin·ci·ble *adj* **:** impossible to defeat — **in·vin·ci·bly** *adv*

in·vi·o·la·ble *adj* **1 :** too sacred to be treated with disrespect **2 :** impossible to harm or destroy by violence

in·vi·o·late *adj* **:** not violated

in·vis·i·bil·i·ty *n* **:** the quality or state of being invisible

in·vis·i·ble *adj* **1 :** impossible to see **2 :** being out of sight **3 :** IMPERCEPTIBLE 1 — **in·vis·i·ble·ness** *n* — **in·vis·i·bly** *adv*

in·vi·ta·tion *n* **1 :** the act of inviting **2 :** the written or spoken expression by which a person is invited

in·vite *vb* **in·vit·ed; in·vit·ing 1 :** to tend to bring on **2 :** to request the presence or company of **3 :** [1]WELCOME 2

in·vit·ing *adj* **:** ATTRACTIVE — **in·vit·ing·ly** *adv*

in·vo·ca·tion *n* **:** a prayer for blessing or guidance at the beginning of a meeting or a service

[1]**in·voice** *n* **:** a list of goods shipped usually showing the price and the terms of sale

[2]**invoice** *vb* **in·voiced; in·voic·ing :** to make an invoice of

in·voke *vb* **in·voked; in·vok·ing 1 :** to call on for aid or protection (as in prayer) **2 :** to call forth by magic **3 :** to appeal to as an authority or for support

in·vol·un·tary *adj* **1 :** not made or done willingly or from choice **2 :** not under the control of the will — **in·vol·un·tari·ly** *adv*

in·volve *vb* **in·volved; in·volv·ing 1 :** to draw into a situation **:** ENGAGE **2 :** INCLUDE **3 :** to be sure to or need to be accompanied by — **in·volve·ment** *n*

in·volved *adj* **:** COMPLEX 2

in·vul·ner·a·bil·i·ty *n* **:** the quality or state of being invulnerable

in·vul·ner·a·ble *adj* **1 :** impossible to injure or damage **2 :** safe from attack — **in·vul·ner·a·bly** *adv*

[1]**in·ward** *adj* **1 :** situated on the inside **:** INNER **2 :** of or relating to the mind or spirit **3 :** directed toward the interior

[2]**inward** *or* **in·wards** *adv* **1 :** toward the inside or center **2 :** toward the mind or spirit

in·ward·ly *adv* **1 :** in the mind or spirit **2 :** beneath the surface **3 :** to oneself **:** PRIVATELY **4 :** toward the inside

io·dine *n* **1 :** a chemical element found in seawater and seaweeds and used especially in medicine and photography **2 :** a solution of iodine in alcohol used to kill germs

io·dize *vb* **io·dized; io·diz·ing :** to add iodine to
ion *n* **:** an atom or group of atoms that carries an electric charge
-ion *n suffix* **1 :** act or process **2 :** result of an act or process **3 :** state or condition
ion·ize *vb* **ion·ized; ion·iz·ing :** to change into ions
ion·o·sphere *n* **:** the part of the earth's atmosphere beginning at an altitude of about 40 kilometers, extending outward 400 kilometers or more, and containing electrically charged particles
io·ta *n* **:** a tiny amount **:** JOT
IOU *n* **:** a written promise to pay a debt
-ious *adj suffix* **:** -OUS
ir- — see IN-
iras·ci·ble *adj* **:** easily angered
irate *adj* **:** ANGRY — **irate·ly** *adv* — **irate·ness** *n*
ire *n* **:** 2ANGER, WRATH
ir·i·des·cence *n* **:** a shifting and constant change of colors producing rainbow effects
ir·i·des·cent *adj* **:** having iridescence — **ir·i·des·cent·ly** *adv*
irid·i·um *n* **:** a hard brittle heavy metallic chemical element
iris *n* **1 :** the colored part around the pupil of an eye **2 :** a plant with long pointed leaves and large usually brightly colored flowers
1Irish *adj* **:** of or relating to Ireland, its people, or the Irish language
2Irish *n* **1 Irish** *pl* **:** the people of Ireland **2 :** a language of Ireland
irk *vb* **:** to make weary, irritated, or bored
irk·some *adj* **:** causing boredom **:** TIRESOME — **irk·some·ness** *n*
1iron *n* **1 :** a heavy silvery white metallic chemical element that rusts easily, is strongly attracted by magnets, occurs in meteorites and combined in minerals, and is necessary in biological processes **2 :** something made of iron **3 irons** *pl* **:** handcuffs or chains used to bind or to hinder movement **4 :** a device that is heated and used for pressing cloth
2iron *adj* **1 :** made of or relating to iron **2 :** like iron
3iron *vb* **:** to press with a heated iron — **iron·er** *n*
iron·ic *or* **iron·i·cal** *adj* **:** relating to, containing, or showing irony — **iron·i·cal·ly** *adv*
iron lung *n* **:** an apparatus in which a person whose breathing is damaged (as by polio) can be placed to help the breathing
iron·work *n* **1 :** work in iron **2 ironworks** *pl* **:** a mill where iron or steel is smelted or heavy iron or steel products are made
iro·ny *n, pl* **iro·nies 1 :** the use of words that mean the opposite of what one really intends **2 :** a result opposite to what was expected
ir·ra·di·ate *vb* **ir·ra·di·at·ed; ir·ra·di·at·ing 1 :** to cast rays of light on **2 :** to affect or treat with radiations (as X rays)
ir·ra·di·a·tion *n* **1 :** the giving off of radiant energy (as heat) **2 :** exposure to irradiation (as of X rays)
ir·ra·tio·nal *adj* **1 :** not able to reason **2 :** not based on reason — **ir·ra·tio·nal·ly** *adv*
ir·rec·on·cil·able *adj* **:** impossible to bring into harmony
ir·re·cov·er·able *adj* **:** impossible to recover or set right
ir·re·deem·able *adj* **:** impossible to redeem
ir·re·duc·ible *adj* **:** not possible to reduce
ir·re·fut·able *adj* **:** impossible to refute **:** INDISPUTABLE
ir·reg·u·lar *adj* **1 :** not following custom or rule **2 :** not following the usual manner of inflection **3 :** not even or having the same shape on both sides **4 :** not continuous or coming at set times — **ir·reg·u·lar·ly** *adv*
ir·reg·u·lar·i·ty *n, pl* **ir·reg·u·lar·i·ties 1 :** the quality or state of being irregular **2 :** something irregular
ir·rel·e·vance *n* **1 :** the quality or state of being irrelevant **2 :** something irrelevant
ir·rel·e·vant *adj* **:** not relevant — **ir·rel·e·vant·ly** *adv*
ir·re·li·gious *adj* **:** not having or acting as if one has religious emotions or beliefs
ir·rep·a·ra·ble *adj* **:** impossible to get back or to make right — **ir·rep·a·ra·bly** *adv*
ir·re·place·able *adj* **:** impossible to replace
ir·re·press·ible *adj* **:** impossible to repress or control
ir·re·proach·able *adj* **:** being beyond reproach
ir·re·sist·ible *adj* **:** impossible to resist — **ir·re·sist·ibly** *adv*
ir·res·o·lute *adj* **:** uncertain how to act or proceed — **ir·res·o·lute·ly** *adv*
ir·re·spec·tive of *prep* **:** without regard to
ir·re·spon·si·bil·i·ty *n* **:** the quality or state of being irresponsible
ir·re·spon·si·ble *adj* **:** having or showing little or no sense of responsibility — **ir·re·spon·si·bly** *adv*
ir·re·triev·able *adj* **:** impossible to get back — **ir·re·triev·ably** *adv*
ir·rev·er·ence *n* **1 :** lack of reverence **2 :** something said or done that is irreverent
ir·rev·er·ent *adj* **:** not reverent **:** DISRESPECTFUL — **ir·rev·er·ent·ly** *adv*
ir·re·vers·i·ble *adj* **:** impossible to reverse
ir·rev·o·ca·ble *adj* **:** impossible to take away or undo — **ir·rev·o·ca·bly** *adv*
ir·ri·gate *vb* **ir·ri·gat·ed; ir·ri·gat·ing 1 :** to

supply (as land) with water by artificial means **2 :** to flush with a liquid

ir·ri·ga·tion *n* **:** an act or process of irrigating

ir·ri·ta·bil·i·ty *n* **:** the quality or state of being irritable

ir·ri·ta·ble *adj* **:** easily irritated — **ir·ri·ta·bly** *adv*

[1]**ir·ri·tant** *adj* **:** tending to cause irritation

[2]**irritant** *n* **:** something that irritates

ir·ri·tate *vb* **ir·ri·tat·ed; ir·ri·tat·ing 1 :** to cause anger or impatience in **:** ANNOY **2 :** to make sensitive or sore

ir·ri·ta·tion *n* **1 :** the act of irritating **:** the state of being irritated **2 :** [2]IRRITANT

is *present 3d sing of* BE

-ish *adj suffix* **1 :** of, relating to, or being **2 :** characteristic of **3 :** somewhat **4 :** about

isin·glass *n* **:** mica in thin sheets

Is·lam *n* **:** a religion based on belief in Allah as the only God, in Muhammad as his prophet, and in the Koran — **Is·lam·ic** *adj*

is·land *n* **1 :** an area of land surrounded by water and smaller than a continent **2 :** something suggesting an island in its isolation

is·land·er *n* **:** a person who lives on an island

isle *n* **:** a usually small island

is·let *n* **:** a small island

-ism *n suffix* **1 :** act **:** practice **:** process **2 :** manner of action or behavior like that of a specified person or thing **3 :** state **:** condition **4 :** teachings **:** theory **:** cult **:** system

isn't : is not

iso·bar *n* **:** a line on a map to indicate areas having the same atmospheric pressure

iso·late *vb* **iso·lat·ed; iso·lat·ing :** to place or keep apart from others

iso·la·tion *n* **:** the act of isolating **:** the condition of being isolated

isos·ce·les triangle *n* **:** a triangle having two sides of equal length

ISP *n* **:** a company that provides access to the Internet for a fee **:** Internet service provider

[1]**Is·rae·li** *adj* **:** of or relating to the Republic of Israel or the Israelis

[2]**Israeli** *n* **:** a person born or living in the Republic of Israel

Is·ra·el·ite *n* **:** a member of the Hebrew people having Jacob as an ancestor

is·su·ance *n* **:** the act of issuing

[1]**is·sue** *n* **1 :** the action of going, coming, or flowing out **2 :** OFFSPRING, PROGENY **3 :** what finally happens **:** RESULT **4 :** something that is disputed **5 :** a giving off (as of blood) from the body **6 :** the act of bringing out, offering, or making available **7 :** the thing or the whole quantity of things given out at one time

[2]**issue** *vb* **is·sued; is·su·ing 1 :** to go, come, or flow out **2 :** [1]RESULT 1 **3 :** to distribute officially **4 :** to send out for sale or circulation

-ist *n suffix* **1 :** performer of a specified action **:** maker **:** producer **2 :** one who plays a specified musical instrument or operates a specified mechanical device **3 :** one who specializes in a specified art or science or skill **4 :** one who follows or favors a specified teaching, practice, system, or code of behavior

isth·mus *n* **:** a neck of land separating two bodies of water and connecting two larger areas of land

[1]**it** *pron* **1 :** the thing, act, or matter about which these words are spoken or written **2 :** the whole situation **3** — used with little meaning of its own in certain kinds of sentences

[2]**it** *n* **:** the player who has to do something special in a children's game

[1]**Ital·ian** *n* **1 :** a person born or living in Italy **2 :** the language of the Italians

[2]**Italian** *adj* **:** of or relating to Italy, its people, or the Italian language

[1]**ital·ic** *adj* **:** of or relating to a type style with letters that slant to the right (as in *"these characters are italic"*)

[2]**italic** *n* **:** an italic letter or italic type

ital·i·cize *vb* **ital·i·cized; ital·i·ciz·ing 1 :** to print in italics **2 :** UNDERLINE 1

[1]**itch** *vb* **:** to have or cause an itch

[2]**itch** *n* **1 :** an uneasy irritating sensation in the skin **2 :** a skin disorder in which an itch is present **3 :** a restless usually constant desire

itchy *adj* **itch·i·er; itch·i·est :** that itches

it'd : it had **:** it would

-ite *n suffix* **1 :** native **:** resident **2 :** descendant **3 :** adherent **:** follower

item *n* **1 :** a single thing in a list, account, or series **2 :** a brief piece of news

item·ize *vb* **item·ized; item·iz·ing :** to set down one by one **:** LIST

[1]**itin·er·ant** *adj* **:** traveling from place to place

[2]**itinerant** *n* **:** a person who travels about

-itis *n suffix* **:** inflammation of

it'll : it shall **:** it will

its *adj* **:** of or relating to it or itself

it's 1 : it is **2 :** it has

it·self *pron* **:** its own self

-ity *n suffix, pl* **-ities :** quality **:** state **:** degree

I've : I have

-ive *adj suffix* **:** that does or tends to do a specified action

ivo·ry *n, pl* **ivo·ries 1 :** the hard creamy-white material of which the tusks of a tusked mammal (as an elephant) are made **2 :** a very pale yellow

ivy *n, pl* **ivies 1 :** a woody vine with evergreen leaves, small yellowish flowers, and black berries often found growing on buildings **2 :** a plant like ivy

-i·za·tion *n suffix* **:** action **:** process **:** state

-ize *vb suffix* **-ized; -iz·ing** **1 :** cause to be or be like **:** form or cause to be formed into **2 :** cause to experience a specified action **3 :** saturate, treat, or combine with **4 :** treat like **5 :** engage in a specified activity

J

j *n, pl* **j's** *or* **js** *often cap* **:** the tenth letter of the English alphabet

¹jab *vb* **jabbed; jab·bing :** to poke quickly or suddenly with or as if with something sharp

²jab *n* **:** a quick or sudden poke

¹jab·ber *vb* **:** to talk too fast or not clearly enough to be understood

²jabber *n* **:** confused talk **:** GIBBERISH

¹jack *n* **1 :** a playing card marked with the figure of a man **2 :** a device for lifting something heavy a short distance **3 :** JACKASS 1 **4 :** a small six-pointed usually metal object used in a children's game (**jacks**) **5 :** a small national flag flown by a ship **6 :** a socket used with a plug to connect one electric circuit with another

²jack *vb* **:** to move or lift by or as if by a jack

jack·al *n* **:** any of several Old World wild dogs like but smaller than wolves

jack·ass *n* **1 :** a male donkey **2 :** DONKEY 1 **3 :** a stupid person

jack·daw *n* **:** a European bird somewhat like a crow

jack·et *n* **1 :** a short coat or coatlike garment **2 :** an outer cover or casing

Jack Frost *n* **:** frost or frosty weather thought of as a person

jack–in–the–box *n, pl* **jack–in–the–box·es** *or* **jacks–in–the–box :** a small box out of which a comical toy figure springs when the lid is raised

jack–in–the–pul·pit *n, pl* **jack–in–the–pulpits** *or* **jacks–in–the–pul·pit :** a plant that grows in moist shady woods and has a stalk of tiny yellowish flowers protected by a leaf bent over like a hood

¹jack·knife *n, pl* **jack·knives :** a knife with folding blade or blades that can be carried in one's pocket

²jackknife *vb* **jack·knifed; jack·knif·ing :** to double up like a jackknife

jack–of–all–trades *n, pl* **jacks–of–all–trades :** a person who can do several kinds of work fairly well

jack–o'–lan·tern *n* **:** a lantern made of a pumpkin cut to look like a human face

jack·pot *n* **:** a large and often unexpected success or reward

jack·rab·bit *n* **:** a large North American hare with very long ears and long hind legs

jade *n* **:** a usually green mineral used for jewelry and carvings

jag·ged *adj* **:** having a sharply uneven edge or surface — **jag·ged·ly** *adv*

jag·uar *n* **:** a large yellowish brown black-spotted animal of the cat family found from Texas to Paraguay

¹jail *n* **:** PRISON

²jail *vb* **:** to shut up in or as if in a prison

jail·bird *n* **:** a person who is or has been locked up in prison

jail·break *n* **:** escape from prison by the use of force

jail·er *or* **jail·or** *n* **:** a keeper of a prison

ja·lopy *n, pl* **ja·lop·ies :** a worn shabby old automobile or airplane

¹jam *vb* **jammed; jam·ming** **1 :** to crowd, squeeze, or wedge into a tight position **2 :** to put into action hard or suddenly **3 :** to hurt by pressure **4 :** to be or cause to be stuck or unable to work because a part is wedged tight **5 :** to cause interference in (radio or television signals)

²jam *n* **1 :** a crowded mass of people or things that blocks something **2 :** a difficult state of affairs

³jam *n* **:** a food made by boiling fruit with sugar until it is thick

jamb *n* **:** a vertical piece forming the side of an opening (as for a doorway)

jam·bo·ree *n* **1 :** a large jolly get-together **2 :** a national or international camping assembly of boy scouts

¹jan·gle *vb* **jan·gled; jan·gling :** to make or cause to make a harsh sound

²jangle *n* **:** a harsh often ringing sound

jan·i·tor *n* **:** a person who takes care of a building (as a school)

Jan·u·ary *n* **:** the first month of the year

¹Jap·a·nese *adj* **:** of or relating to Japan, its people, or the Japanese language

²Japanese *n, pl* **Japanese** **1 :** a person born or living in Japan **2 :** the language of the Japanese

Japanese beetle *n* **:** a small glossy green or brown Asian beetle that has gotten into the United States where it is a harmful pest whose larvae feed on roots and whose adults eat leaves and fruits

¹jar *vb* **jarred; jar·ring** **1 :** to make a harsh unpleasant sound **2 :** to have a disagreeable effect **3 :** to shake or cause to shake hard

²jar *n* **1 :** a harsh sound **2 :** ²JOLT 1 **3 :** ²SHOCK 3

[3]**jar** *n* **:** a usually glass or pottery container with a wide mouth
jar·gon *n* **1 :** the special vocabulary of an activity or group **2 :** language that is not clear and is full of long words
jas·mine *n* **:** any of various mostly climbing plants of warm regions with fragrant flowers
jas·per *n* **:** an opaque usually red, green, brown, or yellow stone used for making ornamental objects (as vases)
[1]**jaunt** *vb* **:** to make a short trip for pleasure
[2]**jaunt** *n* **:** a short pleasure trip
jaun·ty *adj* **jaun·ti·er; jaun·ti·est :** lively in manner or appearance — **jaun·ti·ly** *adv* — **jaun·ti·ness** *n*
Ja·va man *n* **:** a small-brained prehistoric human known from skulls found in Java
jav·e·lin *n* **1 :** a light spear **2 :** a slender rod thrown for distance in a track-and-field contest (**javelin throw**)
jaw *n* **1 :** either of the bony structures that support the soft parts of the mouth and usually bear teeth on their edge **2 :** a part of an invertebrate animal (as an insect) that resembles or does the work of a jaw **3 :** one of a pair of moving parts that open and close for holding or crushing something
jaw·bone *n* **:** JAW 1
jay *n* **:** a noisy bird related to the crow but with brighter colors
jay·walk *vb* **:** to cross a street in a place or in a way that is against traffic regulations — **jay·walk·er** *n*
jazz *n* **:** lively American music that developed from ragtime
jeal·ous *adj* **1 :** demanding complete faithfulness **2 :** feeling a mean resentment toward someone more successful than oneself **3 :** CAREFUL 1, WATCHFUL — **jeal·ous·ly** *adv*
jeal·ou·sy *n, pl* **jeal·ou·sies :** a jealous attitude or feeling
jeans *n pl* **:** pants made of a heavy cotton cloth
[1]**jeer** *vb* **1 :** to speak or cry out in scorn **2 :** to scorn or mock with jeers
[2]**jeer** *n* **:** a scornful remark or sound **:** TAUNT
Je·ho·vah *n* **:** GOD 1
jell *vb* **1 :** to become as firm as jelly **:** SET **2 :** to take shape
[1]**jel·ly** *n, pl* **jellies :** a soft springy food made from fruit juice boiled with sugar, from meat juices, or from gelatin — **jel·ly·like** *adj*
[2]**jelly** *vb* **jel·lied; jel·ly·ing 1 :** JELL 1 **2 :** to make jelly
jelly bean *n* **:** a chewy bean-shaped candy
jel·ly·fish *n* **:** a free-swimming sea animal related to the corals that has a jellylike body shaped like a saucer
jen·net *n* **:** a female donkey
jeop·ar·dize *vb* **jeop·ar·dized; jeop·ar·diz·ing :** to expose to danger
jeop·ar·dy *n* **:** DANGER 1
[1]**jerk** *n* **1 :** a short quick pull or jolt **2 :** a foolish person
[2]**jerk** *vb* **1 :** to give a quick sharp pull or twist to **2 :** to move with jerks
jer·kin *n* **:** a close-fitting sleeveless jacket that extends to or just over the hips
jerky *adj* **jerk·i·er; jerk·i·est :** moving with sudden starts and stops — **jerk·i·ly** *adv* — **jerk·i·ness** *n*
jer·sey *n, pl* **jerseys 1 :** a knitted cloth (as of wool or cotton) used mostly for clothing **2 :** a close-fitting knitted garment (as a shirt)
[1]**jest** *n* **1 :** a comic act or remark **:** JOKE **2 :** a playful mood or manner
[2]**jest** *vb* **:** to make jests **:** JOKE
jest·er *n* **1 :** a person formerly kept in royal courts to amuse people **2 :** a person who often jests
Je·sus *n* **:** the founder of the Christian religion
[1]**jet** *n* **1 :** a black mineral that is often used for jewelry **2 :** a very dark black
[2]**jet** *vb* **jet·ted; jet·ting :** [1]SPURT 1
[3]**jet** *n* **1 :** a rush of liquid, gas, or vapor through a narrow opening or a nozzle **2 :** a nozzle for a jet of gas or liquid **3 :** JET ENGINE **4 :** JET AIRPLANE
jet airplane *n* **:** an airplane powered by a jet engine
jet engine *n* **:** an engine in which fuel burns to produce a jet of heated air and gases that shoot out from the rear and drive the engine forward
jet plane *n* **:** JET AIRPLANE
jet–pro·pelled *adj* **:** driven forward or onward by a jet engine
jet·sam *n* **:** goods thrown overboard to lighten a ship in danger of sinking
jet stream *n* **:** high-speed winds blowing from a westerly direction several kilometers above the earth's surface
jet·ti·son *vb* **:** to throw out especially from a ship or an airplane
jet·ty *n, pl* **jetties 1 :** a pier built to change the path of the current or tide or to protect a harbor **2 :** a landing wharf
Jew *n* **:** a person who is a descendant of the ancient Hebrews or whose religion is Judaism
jew·el *n* **1 :** an ornament of precious metal often set with precious stones and worn on the person **2 :** a person who is greatly admired **3 :** GEM **4 :** a bearing in a watch made of crystal or a precious stone
jew·el·er *or* **jew·el·ler** *n* **:** a person who

makes or deals in jewelry and related articles (as silverware)

jew•el•ry *n* **:** ornamental pieces (as rings or necklaces) worn on the person

Jew•ish *adj* **:** of or relating to Jews or Judaism

Jew's harp *or* **Jews' harp** *n* **:** a small musical instrument that is held in the mouth and struck with the finger to give off a tone

jib *n* **:** a three-cornered sail extending forward from the foremast

1jibe *variant of* GIBE

2jibe *vb* **jibed; jib•ing 1 :** to shift suddenly from side to side **2 :** to change the course of a boat so that the sail jibes

3jibe *vb* **jibed; jib•ing :** to be in agreement

jif•fy *n, pl* **jiffies :** MOMENT 1

1jig *n* **:** a lively dance

2jig *vb* **jigged; jig•ging :** to dance a jig

1jig•gle *vb* **jig•gled; jig•gling :** to move or cause to move with quick little jerks

2jiggle *n* **:** a quick little jerk

jig•saw *n* **:** a machine saw used to cut curved and irregular lines or openwork patterns

jigsaw puzzle *n* **:** a puzzle made by cutting a picture into small pieces that must be fitted together again

jim•son•weed *n* **:** a coarse poisonous weedy plant related to the potato that is sometimes grown for its showy white or purple flowers

1jin•gle *vb* **jin•gled; jin•gling :** to make or cause to make a light clinking sound

2jingle *n* **1 :** a light clinking sound **2 :** a short verse or song that repeats bits in a catchy way — **jin•gly** *adj*

jinx *n* **:** a bringer of bad luck

jit•ters *n pl* **:** extreme nervousness

jit•tery *adj* **:** very nervous

job *n* **1 :** a piece of work usually done on order at an agreed rate **2 :** something produced by or as if by work **3 :** a regular paying employment **4 :** a special duty or function — **job•less** *adj*

jock•ey *n, pl* **jockeys 1 :** a professional rider in a horse race **2 :** OPERATOR 1

1jog *vb* **jogged; jog•ging 1 :** to give a slight shake or push to **:** NUDGE **2 :** to rouse to alertness **3 :** to move or cause to move at a jog **4 :** to run slowly (as for exercise) — **jog•ger** *n*

2jog *n* **1 :** a slight shake or push **2 :** a slow jolting gait (as of a horse) **3 :** a slow run

3jog *n* **:** a short change in direction

jog•gle *vb* **jog•gled; jog•gling :** to shake or cause to shake slightly

john•ny•cake *n* **:** a bread made of cornmeal, water or milk, and leavening with or without flour, shortening, and eggs

join *vb* **1 :** to come, bring, or fasten together **2 :** ADJOIN **3 :** to come or bring into close association **4 :** to come into the company of **5 :** to become a member of **6 :** to take part in a group activity **7 :** to combine the elements of

1joint *n* **1 :** a part of the skeleton where two pieces come together usually in a way that allows motion **2 :** a part of a plant stem where a leaf or branch develops **:** NODE **3 :** a place where two things or parts are joined — **joint•ed** *adj*

2joint *adj* **1 :** joined together **2 :** done by or shared by two or more — **joint•ly** *adv*

joist *n* **:** any of the small timbers or metal beams laid crosswise in a building to support a floor or ceiling

1joke *n* **1 :** something said or done to cause laughter or amusement **2 :** a very short story with a funny ending that is a surprise **3 :** something not worthy of being taken seriously

2joke *vb* **joked; jok•ing 1 :** to say or do something as a joke **2 :** to make jokes

jok•er *n* **1 :** a person who jokes **2 :** an extra card used in some card games

jok•ing•ly *adv* **:** in a joking manner

jol•li•ty *n* **:** the state of being jolly

1jol•ly *adj* **jol•li•er; jol•li•est :** full of fun or high spirits

2jolly *adv* **:** 2VERY 1

1jolt *vb* **1 :** to move or cause to move with a sudden jerky motion **2 :** to cause to be upset

2jolt *n* **1 :** an abrupt jerky blow or movement **2 :** a sudden shock or disappointment

jon•quil *n* **:** a plant related to the daffodil but with fragrant yellow or white flowers with a short central tube

josh *vb* **1 :** 2KID 1 **2 :** 2JOKE

jos•tle *vb* **jos•tled; jos•tling :** to knock against so as to jar **:** push roughly

1jot *n* **:** the least bit

2jot *vb* **jot•ted; jot•ting :** to write briefly or in a hurry **:** make a note of

jounce *vb* **jounced; jounc•ing :** to move, fall, or bounce so as to shake

jour•nal *n* **1 :** a brief record (as in a diary) of daily happenings **2 :** a daily record (as of business dealings) **3 :** a daily newspaper **4 :** a magazine that reports on things of special interest to a particular group

jour•nal•ism *n* **1 :** the business of collecting and editing news (as for newspapers, radio, or television) **2 :** writing of general or popular interest

jour•nal•ist *n* **:** an editor or reporter of the news

1jour•ney *n, pl* **jour•neys :** a traveling from one place to another

2journey *vb* **jour•neyed; jour•ney•ing :** to go on a journey **:** TRAVEL — **jour•ney•er** *n*

jour•ney•man *n, pl* **jour•ney•men :** a worker who has learned a trade and usually works for another person by the day
¹joust *vb* **:** to take part in a joust **:** TILT
²joust *n* **:** a combat on horseback between two knights with lances
jo•vial *adj* **:** ¹JOLLY — **jo•vial•ly** *adv*
¹jowl *n* **:** loose flesh (as a double chin) hanging from the lower jaw and throat
²jowl *n* **1 :** an animal's jaw and especially the lower jaw **2 :** CHEEK 1
joy *n* **1 :** a feeling of pleasure or happiness that comes from success, good fortune, or a sense of well-being **2 :** something that gives pleasure or happiness
joy•ful *adj* **:** feeling, causing, or showing joy — **joy•ful•ly** *adv* — **joy•ful•ness** *n*
joy•ous *adj* **:** JOYFUL — **joy•ous•ly** *adv* — **joy•ous•ness** *n*
joy•stick *n* **:** a control lever (as for a computer display or an airplane) capable of motion in two or more directions
ju•bi•lant *adj* **:** expressing great joy especially with shouting **:** noisily happy
ju•bi•lee *n* **1 :** a fiftieth anniversary **2 :** time of celebration
Ju•da•ism *n* **:** a religion developed among the ancient Hebrews that stresses belief in one God and faithfulness to the moral laws of the Old Testament
¹judge *vb* **judged; judg•ing 1 :** to form an opinion after careful consideration **2 :** to act as a judge (as in a trial) **3 :** THINK 2
²judge *n* **1 :** a public official whose duty is to decide questions brought before a court **2 :** a person appointed to decide in a contest or competition **3 :** a person with the experience to give a meaningful opinion **:** CRITIC
judg•ment *or* **judge•ment** *n* **1 :** a decision or opinion (as of a court) given after judging **2 :** an opinion or estimate formed by examining and comparing **3 :** the ability for judging
ju•di•cial *adj* **:** of or relating to the providing of justice — **ju•di•cial•ly** *adv*
ju•di•cious *adj* **:** having, using, or showing good judgment **:** WISE — **ju•di•cious•ly** *adv* — **ju•di•cious•ness** *n*
ju•do *n* **:** a Japanese form of wrestling in which each person tries to throw or pin the opponent
jug *n* **:** a large deep usually earthenware or glass container with a narrow mouth and a handle
jug•gle *vb* **jug•gled; jug•gling 1 :** to keep several things moving in the air at the same time **2 :** to mix things up in order to deceive **3 :** to hold or balance insecurely — **jug•gler** *n*
juice *n* **1 :** the liquid part that can be squeezed out of vegetables and fruit **2 :** the fluid part of meat
juicy *adj* **juic•i•er; juic•i•est :** having much juice — **juic•i•ness** *n*
Ju•ly *n* **:** the seventh month of the year
¹jum•ble *vb* **jum•bled; jum•bling :** to mix in a confused mass
²jumble *n* **:** a disorderly mass or pile
jum•bo *n, pl* **jumbos :** something very large of its kind
¹jump *vb* **1 :** to spring into the air **:** LEAP **2 :** to make a sudden movement **:** START **3 :** to have or cause a sudden sharp increase **4 :** to make a hasty judgement **5 :** to make a sudden attack **6 :** to pass over or cause to pass over with or as if with a leap — **jump the gun 1 :** to start in a race before the starting signal **2 :** to do something before the proper time
²jump *n* **1 :** an act or instance of jumping **:** LEAP **2 :** a sudden involuntary movement **:** START **3 :** a sharp sudden increase **4 :** an initial advantage
jum•per *n* **1 :** a loose blouse or jacket often worn by workmen **2 :** a sleeveless dress worn usually with a blouse
jumpy *adj* **jump•i•er; jump•i•est :** NERVOUS 3
jun•co *n, pl* **juncos** *or* **juncoes :** a small mostly gray American finch usually having a pink bill
junc•tion *n* **1 :** an act of joining **2 :** a place or point of meeting
June *n* **:** the sixth month of the year
jun•gle *n* **1 :** a thick or tangled growth of plants **2 :** a large area of land usually in a tropical region covered with a thick tangled growth of plants
¹ju•nior *adj* **1 :** being younger — used to distinguish a son from a father with the same name **2 :** lower in rank **3 :** of or relating to juniors
²junior *n* **1 :** a person who is younger or lower in rank than another **2 :** a student in the next-to-last year (as at high school)
ju•ni•per *n* **:** any of various evergreen trees and shrubs related to the pines but having tiny berrylike cones
¹junk *n* **1 :** old iron, glass, paper, or waste **:** RUBBISH **2 :** a poorly made product
²junk *vb* **:** to get rid of as worthless **:** SCRAP
³junk *n* **:** a sailing ship of Chinese waters
junk food *n* **:** food that is high in calories but low in nutritional content
Ju•pi•ter *n* **:** the planet that is fifth in order of distance from the sun and is the largest of the planets with a diameter of about 140,000 kilometers
ju•ror *n* **:** a member of a jury
ju•ry *n, pl* **juries 1 :** a body of persons

sworn to seek for and try to learn the truth about a matter put before them for decision **2 :** a committee that judges and awards prizes (as at an exhibition)

[1]just *adj* **1 :** having a foundation in fact or reason **:** REASONABLE **2 :** agreeing with a standard of correctness **3 :** morally right or good **4 :** legally right — **just·ly** *adv*

[2]just *adv* **1 :** exactly as wanted **2 :** very recently **3 :** by a very small amount **4 :** by a very short distance **5 :** nothing more than **6 :** [2]VERY 2

jus·tice *n* **1 :** just or right action or treatment **2 :** [2]JUDGE 1 **3 :** the carrying out of law **4 :** the quality of being fair or just

jus·ti·fi·able *adj* **:** possible to justify — **jus·ti·fi·ably** *adv*

jus·ti·fi·ca·tion *n* **1 :** the act or an instance of justifying **2 :** something that justifies

jus·ti·fy *vb* **jus·ti·fied; jus·ti·fy·ing :** to prove or show to be just, right, or reasonable

jut *vb* **jut·ted; jut·ting :** to extend or cause to extend above or beyond a surrounding area

jute *n* **:** a strong glossy fiber from a tropical plant used chiefly for making sacks and twine

[1]ju·ve·nile *adj* **1 :** incompletely developed **:** IMMATURE **2 :** of, relating to, or characteristic of children or young people

[2]juvenile *n* **:** a young person **:** YOUTH

K

k *n, pl* **k's** *or* **ks** *often cap* **1 :** the eleventh letter of the English alphabet **2 :** THOUSAND **3 :** KILOBYTE

kale *n* **:** a hardy cabbage with wrinkled leaves that do not form a head

ka·lei·do·scope *n* **1 :** a tube containing bits of colored glass or plastic and two mirrors at one end that shows many different patterns as it is turned **2 :** a changing pattern or scene

kan·ga·roo *n, pl* **kan·ga·roos :** any of numerous leaping mammals of Australia and nearby islands that feed on plants and have long powerful hind legs, a thick tail used as a support in standing or walking, and in the female a pouch on the abdomen in which the young are carried

ka·o·lin *n* **:** a very pure white clay used in making porcelain

kar·a·o·ke *n* **:** a device that plays music to which the user sings along and that records the user's singing with the music

kar·at *n* **:** a unit of fineness for gold

ka·ra·te *n* **:** an Oriental art of self-defense in which an attacker is defeated by kicks and punches

ka·ty·did *n* **:** any of several large green American grasshoppers with males that make shrill noises

kay·ak *n* **1 :** an Eskimo canoe made of a frame covered with skins except for a small opening in the center **2 :** a boat styled like an Eskimo kayak

ka·zoo *n, pl* **ka·zoos :** a toy musical instrument containing a membrane which produces a buzzing tone when one hums into the mouth hole

KB *n* **:** KILOBYTE

[1]keel *n* **:** a timber or plate running lengthwise along the center of the bottom of a ship and usually sticking out from the bottom

[2]keel *vb* **:** to turn over

keel over *vb* **:** to fall suddenly (as in a faint)

keen *adj* **1 :** having a fine edge or point **:** SHARP **2 :** seeming to cut or sting **3 :** full of enthusiasm **:** EAGER **4 :** having or showing mental sharpness **5 :** very sensitive (as in seeing or hearing) — **keen·ly** *adv* — **keen·ness** *n*

[1]keep *vb* **kept; keep·ing 1 :** to be faithful to **:** FULFILL **2 :** to act properly in relation to **3 :** PROTECT **4 :** to take care of **:** TEND **5 :** to continue doing something **6 :** to have in one's service or at one's disposal **7 :** to preserve a record in **8 :** to have on hand regularly for sale **9 :** to continue to have in one's possession or power **10 :** to prevent from leaving **:** DETAIN **11 :** to hold back **12 :** to remain or cause to remain in a given place, situation, or condition **13 :** to continue in an unspoiled condition **14 :** [1]REFRAIN

[2]keep *n* **1 :** the strongest part of a castle in the Middle Ages **2 :** the necessities of life — **for keeps 1 :** with the understanding that one may keep what is won **2 :** for a long time **:** PERMANENTLY

keep·er *n* **:** a person who watches, guards, or takes care of something

keep·ing *n* **1 :** watchful attention **:** CARE **2 :** a proper or fitting relationship **:** HARMONY

keep·sake *n* **:** something kept or given to be kept in memory of a person, place, or happening

keep up *vb* **1 :** MAINTAIN 1 **2 :** to stay well informed about something **3 :** to continue without interruption **4 :** to stay even with others (as in a race)

keg *n* **1 :** a small barrel holding about 114 liters **2 :** the contents of a keg

kelp *n* **:** a large coarse brown seaweed

ken *n* **1 :** range of vision **:** SIGHT **2 :** range of understanding

ken·nel *n* **1 :** a shelter for a dog **2 :** a place where dogs are bred or housed

kept *past of* KEEP

ker·chief *n, pl* **kerchiefs 1 :** a square of cloth worn as a head covering or as a scarf **2 :** HANDKERCHIEF

ker·nel *n* **1 :** the inner softer part of a seed, fruit stone, or nut **2 :** the whole grain or seed of a cereal

ker·o·sene *or* **ker·o·sine** *n* **:** a thin oil obtained from petroleum and used as a fuel and solvent

ketch *n* **:** a fore-and-aft rigged ship with two masts

ketch·up *n* **:** a thick seasoned sauce usually made from tomatoes

ket·tle *n* **1 :** a pot for boiling liquids **2 :** TEAKETTLE

ket·tle·drum *n* **:** a large brass or copper drum that has a rounded bottom and can be varied in pitch

[1]**key** *n* **1 :** an instrument by which the bolt of a lock (as on a door) is turned **2 :** a device having the form or function of a key **3 :** a means of gaining or preventing entrance, possession, or control **4 :** something (as a map legend) that gives an explanation **:** SOLUTION **5 :** one of the levers with a flat surface that is pressed with a finger to activate a mechanism of a machine or instrument **6 :** a system of seven musical tones arranged in relation to a keynote from which the system is named **7 :** a characteristic way (as of thought) **8 :** a small switch for opening or closing an electric circuit

[2]**key** *vb* **keyed; key·ing 1 :** to regulate the musical pitch of **2 :** to bring into harmony

[3]**key** *adj* **:** of great importance **:** most important

[4]**key** *n* **:** a low island or reef

key·board *n* **1 :** a row of keys by which a musical instrument (as a piano) is played **2 :** a portable electronic musical instrument with a keyboard like that of a piano **3 :** the whole arrangement of keys (as on a typewriter)

key·hole *n* **:** a hole for receiving a key

key·note *n* **1 :** the first and harmonically fundamental tone of a scale **2 :** the fundamental fact, idea, or mood

key·stone *n* **1 :** the wedge-shaped piece at the top of an arch that locks the other pieces in place **2 :** something on which other things depend for support

key up *vb* **:** to make nervous or tense

kha·ki *n* **1 :** a light yellowish brown **2 :** a light yellowish brown cloth used especially for military uniforms

khan *n* **1 :** a Mongolian leader **2 :** a local chieftain or man of rank in some countries of central Asia

ki·bitz·er *n* **:** a person who looks on and often offers unwanted advice especially at a card game

[1]**kick** *vb* **1 :** to strike out or hit with the foot **2 :** to object strongly **:** PROTEST **3 :** to spring back when fired

[2]**kick** *n* **1 :** a blow with the foot **2 :** a sudden moving (as of a ball) with the foot **3 :** the sudden move backward of a gun when fired **4 :** a feeling of or cause for objection **5 :** a feeling or source of pleasure

kick·ball *n* **:** a form of baseball played with a large rubber ball that is kicked instead of hit with a bat

kick·off *n* **:** a kick that puts the ball into play (as in football or soccer)

kick off *vb* **1 :** to make a kickoff **2 :** BEGIN 1

[1]**kid** *n* **1 :** the young of a goat or a related animal **2 :** the flesh, fur, or skin of a kid or something (as leather) made from one of these **3 :** CHILD — **kid·dish** *adj*

[2]**kid** *vb* **kid·ded; kid·ding 1 :** to deceive or trick as a joke **2 :** [1]TEASE — **kid·der** *n*

kid·nap *vb* **kid·napped** *or* **kid·naped; kid·nap·ping** *or* **kid·nap·ing :** to carry away a person by force or by fraud and against his or her will — **kid·nap·per** *or* **kid·nap·er** *n*

kid·ney *n, pl* **kid·neys :** either of a pair of organs near the backbone that give off waste from the body in the form of urine

kidney bean *n* **:** a common garden bean and especially one having large dark red seeds

[1]**kill** *vb* **1 :** to end the life of **:** SLAY **2 :** to put an end to **3 :** to use up **4 :** [1]DEFEAT 1

[2]**kill** *n* **1 :** an act of killing **2 :** an animal killed

kill·deer *n* **:** a grayish brown North American plover that has a shrill mournful call

[1]**kill·er** *n* **:** one that kills

[2]**killer** *adj* **1 :** very impressive or effective **2 :** very difficult **3 :** causing death or ruin

kill·joy *n* **:** a person who spoils the pleasure of others

kiln *n* **:** a furnace or oven in which something (as pottery) is hardened, burned, or dried

ki·lo *n, pl* **kilos :** KILOGRAM

kilo- *prefix* **:** thousand

ki·lo·byte *n* **:** a unit of computer information storage equal to 1024 bytes

ki·lo·gram *n* **:** a metric unit of weight equal to 1000 grams

ki·lo·me·ter *n* **:** a metric unit of length equal to 1000 meters

kilo·watt *n* **:** a unit of electrical power equal to 1000 watts

kilt *n* **:** a knee-length pleated skirt usually of tartan worn by men in Scotland
kil•ter *n* **:** proper condition
ki•mo•no *n, pl* **ki•mo•nos 1 :** a loose robe with wide sleeves that is traditionally worn with a broad sash as an outer garment by the Japanese **2 :** a loose dressing gown worn chiefly by women
kin *n* **1 :** a person's relatives **2 :** KINSMAN
-kin *also* **-kins** *n suffix* **:** little
[1]**kind** *n* **:** a group of persons or things that can be recognized as belonging together or having something in common
[2]**kind** *adj* **1 :** wanting or liking to do good and to bring happiness to others **:** CONSIDERATE **2 :** showing or growing out of gentleness or goodness of heart
kin•der•gar•ten *n* **:** a school or a class for very young children
kind•heart•ed *adj* **:** having or showing a kind and sympathetic nature — **kind•heart•ed•ly** *adv* — **kind•heart•ed•ness** *n*
kin•dle *vb* **kin•dled; kin•dling 1 :** to set on fire **:** LIGHT **2 :** to stir up **:** EXCITE
kin•dling *n* **:** material that burns easily and is used for starting a fire
[1]**kind•ly** *adj* **kind•li•er; kind•li•est 1 :** pleasant or wholesome in nature **2 :** sympathetic or generous in nature — **kind•li•ness** *n*
[2]**kindly** *adv* **1 :** in a willing manner **2 :** in a kind manner **3 :** in an appreciative manner **4 :** in an obliging manner
kind•ness *n* **1 :** a kind deed **:** FAVOR **2 :** the quality or state of being kind
kind of *adv* **:** to a moderate degree **:** SOMEWHAT
[1]**kin•dred** *n* **1 :** a group of related individuals **2 :** a person's relatives
[2]**kindred** *adj* **:** alike in nature or character
kin•folk *n* **:** [1]KINDRED 2
king *n* **1 :** a male ruler of a country who usually inherits his position and rules for life **2 :** a chief among competitors **3 :** the chief piece in the game of chess **4 :** a playing card bearing the figure of a king **5 :** a piece in checkers that has reached the opponent's back row — **king•ly** *adj*
king•dom *n* **1 :** a country whose ruler is a king or queen **2 :** one of the three basic divisions (**animal kingdom**, **plant kingdom**, **mineral kingdom**) into which natural objects are commonly grouped **3 :** a major category in scientific biological classification that ranks above the phylum and division and is the highest and broadest group
king•fish•er *n* **:** any of a group of usually crested birds with a short tail, long sharp bill, and bright feathers
king•let *n* **:** a small bird resembling a warbler
king–size *or* **king–sized** *adj* **:** unusually large
[1]**kink** *n* **1 :** a short tight twist or curl (as in a thread or rope) **2 :** [1]CRAMP 1 **3 :** an imperfection that makes something hard to use or work — **kinky** *adj*
[2]**kink** *vb* **:** to form or cause to form a kink in
-kins — see -KIN
kin•ship *n* **:** the quality or state of being kin
kins•man *n, pl* **kins•men :** a relative usually by birth
kins•wom•an *n, pl* **kins•wom•en :** a woman who is a relative usually by birth
[1]**kiss** *vb* **1 :** to touch with the lips as a mark of love or greeting **2 :** to touch gently or lightly
[2]**kiss** *n* **1 :** a loving touch with the lips **2 :** a gentle touch or contact **3 :** a bite-size candy often wrapped in paper or foil
kit *n* **1 :** a set of articles for personal use **2 :** a set of tools or supplies **3 :** a set of parts to be put together **4 :** a container (as a bag or case) for a kit
kitch•en *n* **:** a room in which cooking is done
kitch•en•ette *n* **:** a small kitchen
kitchen garden *n* **:** a piece of land where vegetables are grown for household use
kite *n* **1 :** a hawk with long narrow wings and deeply forked tail that feeds mostly on insects and small reptiles **2 :** a light covered frame for flying in the air at the end of a long string
kith *n* **:** familiar friends and neighbors or relatives
kit•ten *n* **:** a young cat — **kit•ten•ish** *adj*
kit•ty *n, pl* **kitties :** CAT, KITTEN
ki•wi *n* **:** a New Zealand bird that is unable to fly
knack *n* **1 :** a clever or skillful way of doing something **:** TRICK **2 :** a natural ability **:** TALENT
knap•sack *n* **:** a carrying case or pouch slung from the shoulders over the back
knave *n* **1 :** RASCAL 1 **2 :** [1]JACK 1
knead *vb* **1 :** to work and press into a mass with or as if with the hands **2 :** [2]MASSAGE — **knead•er** *n*
knee *n* **1 :** the joint or region in which the thigh and lower leg come together **2 :** something resembling a knee **3 :** the part of a garment covering the knee
knee•cap *n* **:** a thick flat movable bone forming the front part of the knee
kneel *vb* **knelt** *or* **kneeled; kneel•ing :** to bend the knee **:** support oneself on one's knees
[1]**knell** *vb* **1 :** to ring slowly and solemnly **:** TOLL **2 :** to summon, announce, or warn by a knell
[2]**knell** *n* **1 :** a stroke or sound of a bell espe-

cially when rung slowly for a death, funeral, or disaster **2 :** an indication (as a sound) of the end or failure of something

knew *past of* KNOW

knick·ers *n pl* **:** loose-fitting short pants gathered just below the knee

knick·knack *n* **:** a small ornamental object

[1]**knife** *n, pl* **knives** **1 :** a cutting instrument consisting of a sharp blade fastened to a handle **2 :** a cutting blade in a machine

[2]**knife** *vb* **knifed; knif·ing :** to stab, slash, or wound with a knife

[1]**knight** *n* **1 :** a warrior of olden times who fought on horseback, served a king, held a special military rank, and swore to behave in a noble way **2 :** a man honored by a sovereign for merit and in Great Britain ranking below a baronet **3 :** one of the pieces in the game of chess — **knight·ly** *adj*

[2]**knight** *vb* **:** to make a knight of

knight·hood *n* **1 :** the rank, dignity, or profession of a knight **2 :** the qualities that a knight should have **3 :** knights as a class or body

knit *vb* **knit** *or* **knit·ted; knit·ting** **1 :** to form a fabric or garment by interlacing yarn or thread in connected loops with needles (**knitting needles**) **2 :** to draw or come together closely as if knitted **:** unite firmly **3 :** [2]WRINKLE — **knit·ter** *n*

knob *n* **1 :** a rounded lump **2 :** a small rounded handle **3 :** a rounded hill

[1]**knock** *vb* **1 :** to strike with a sharp blow **2 :** to bump against something **3 :** to make a pounding noise **4 :** to find fault with

[2]**knock** *n* **1 :** a sharp blow **2 :** a severe misfortune or hardship **3 :** a pounding noise

knock·er *n* **:** a device made like a hinge and fastened to a door for use in knocking

knock–kneed *adj* **:** having the legs bowed inward

knoll *n* **:** a small round hill

[1]**knot** *n* **1 :** an interlacing (as of string or ribbon) that forms a lump or knob **2 :** PROBLEM 2 **3 :** a bond of union **4 :** the inner end of a branch enclosed in a plant stem or a section of this in sawed lumber **5 :** a cluster of persons or things **6 :** an ornamental bow of ribbon **7 :** one nautical mile per hour (about two kilometers per hour)

[2]**knot** *vb* **knot·ted; knot·ting** **1 :** to tie in or with a knot **2 :** to unite closely

knot·hole *n* **:** a hole in wood where a knot has come out

knot·ty *adj* **knot·ti·er; knot·ti·est** **1 :** full of knots **2 :** DIFFICULT 3

know *vb* **knew; known; know·ing** **1 :** to have understanding of **2 :** to recognize the nature of **3 :** to recognize the identity of **4 :** to be acquainted or familiar with **5 :** to be aware of the truth of **6 :** to have a practical understanding of **7 :** to have information or knowledge **8 :** to be or become aware

know·ing *adj* **1 :** having or showing special knowledge, information, or intelligence **2 :** shrewdly and keenly alert **3 :** INTENTIONAL — **know·ing·ly** *adv*

know–it–all *n* **:** a person who always claims to know everything

knowl·edge *n* **1 :** understanding and skill gained by experience **2 :** the state of being aware of something or of having information **3 :** range of information or awareness **4 :** something learned and kept in the mind **:** LEARNING

knuck·le *n* **:** the rounded lump formed by the ends of two bones (as of a finger) where they come together in a joint

ko·ala *n* **:** a tailless Australian animal with thick fur and big hairy ears, sharp claws for climbing, and a pouch like the kangaroo's for carrying its young

kohl·ra·bi *n* **:** a cabbage that forms no head but has a fleshy edible stem

kook·a·bur·ra *n* **:** an Australian kingfisher that has a call resembling loud laughter

Ko·ran *n* **:** a book of sacred writings accepted by Muslims as revealed to Muhammad by Allah

[1]**Ko·re·an** *n* **1 :** a person born or living in North Korea or South Korea **2 :** the language of the Koreans

[2]**Korean** *adj* **:** of or relating to North Korea or South Korea, the Korean people, or their language

krill *n* **:** tiny floating sea creatures that are a chief food of whales

kud·zu *n* **:** an Asian vine of the pea family that is widely grown for hay and for use in erosion control and is often a serious weed in the southeastern United States

kum·quat *n* **:** a small citrus fruit with sweet rind and sour pulp that is used mostly in preserves

L

l *n, pl* **l's** *or* **ls** *often cap* **1 :** the twelfth letter of the English alphabet **2 :** fifty in Roman numerals

la *n* **:** the sixth note of the musical scale

lab *n* **:** LABORATORY

¹la·bel *n* **1 :** a slip (as of paper or cloth) attached to something to identify or describe it **2 :** a word or phrase that describes or names something

²label *vb* **la·beled** *or* **la·belled; la·bel·ing** *or* **la·bel·ling 1 :** to attach a label to **2 :** to name or describe with or as if with a label

la·bi·al *adj* **:** of or relating to the lips

¹la·bor *n* **1 :** effort that is hard and usually physical **2 :** the effort involved in giving birth **3 :** something that has to be done **:** TASK **4 :** workers as a body or class

²labor *vb* **1 :** to work hard **:** TOIL **2 :** to move slowly or heavily

lab·o·ra·to·ry *n, pl* **lab·o·ra·to·ries :** a room or building in which experiments and tests are done

Labor Day *n* **:** the first Monday in September observed as a legal holiday to honor the worker

la·bored *adj* **:** produced or done with effort or difficulty

la·bor·er *n* **:** a person who works on jobs that require strength rather than skill

la·bo·ri·ous *adj* **:** requiring much effort — **la·bo·ri·ous·ly** *adv*

labor union *n* **:** an organization of workers designed to help them get better pay and working conditions

¹lace *vb* **laced; lac·ing :** to fasten with a lace

²lace *n* **1 :** a cord or string for pulling and holding together opposite edges (as of a shoe) **2 :** an ornamental net of thread or cord usually with a design

lac·er·ate *vb* **lac·er·at·ed; lac·er·at·ing :** to injure by tearing

lac·er·a·tion *n* **:** a lacerated place or wound

¹lack *vb* **1 :** to be missing **2 :** to need or be without something

²lack *n* **1 :** the fact or state of being absent or needed **2 :** something that is absent or needed

¹lac·quer *n* **:** a material like varnish that dries quickly into a shiny layer (as on wood or metal)

²lacquer *vb* **:** to coat with lacquer

la·crosse *n* **:** a ball game played outdoors using a long-handled stick with a shallow net for catching, throwing, and carrying the ball

lacy *adj* **lac·i·er; lac·i·est :** like or made of lace

lad *n* **:** BOY 1, YOUTH

lad·der *n* **:** a device used for climbing usually consisting of two long pieces of wood, rope, or metal joined at short distances by horizontal pieces

lad·die *n* **:** BOY 1, LAD

lad·en *adj* **:** heavily loaded

¹la·dle *n* **:** a spoon with a long handle and a deep bowl that is used for dipping

²ladle *vb* **la·dled; la·dling :** to take up and carry in a ladle

la·dy *n, pl* **la·dies 1 :** a woman of high social position **2 :** a pleasant well-bred woman or girl **3 :** a woman of any kind or class — often used in speaking to a stranger **4 :** WIFE **5 :** a British noblewoman — used as a title

la·dy·bird *n* **:** LADYBUG

la·dy·bug *n* **:** a small rounded beetle that feeds mostly on plant lice

la·dy·like *adj* **:** WELL-BRED

la·dy·ship *n* **:** the rank of a lady — used as a title

lady's slipper *or* **lady slipper** *n* **:** any of several North American wild orchids whose flowers suggest a slipper in shape

¹lag *n* **:** the act or the amount of lagging

²lag *vb* **lagged; lag·ging :** to move or advance slowly

¹lag·gard *adj* **:** lagging behind **:** SLOW

²laggard *n* **:** a person who lags

la·goon *n* **:** a shallow channel or pond near or connected to a larger body of water

laid *past of* LAY

lain *past participle of* LIE

lair *n* **:** the den or resting place of a wild animal

lake *n* **:** a large inland body of still water

¹lamb *n* **:** a young sheep usually less than one year old

²lamb *vb* **:** to give birth to a lamb

lamb·kin *n* **:** a young lamb

¹lame *adj* **lam·er; lam·est 1 :** not able to get around without pain or difficulty **2 :** being stiff and sore **3 :** not very convincing **:** WEAK — **lame·ly** *adv* — **lame·ness** *n*

²lame *vb* **lamed; lam·ing :** to make or become lame

¹la·ment *vb* **1 :** to mourn aloud **:** WAIL **2 :** to show sorrow for

²lament *n* **1 :** a crying out in sorrow **2 :** a sad song or poem

la·men·ta·ble *adj* **:** REGRETTABLE

lam·en·ta·tion *n* **:** the act of lamenting

lam·i·nat·ed *adj* **:** made of layers of material firmly joined together

lamp *n* **:** a device for producing light

lamp·black *n* **:** a fine black soot made by

burning material incompletely and used especially to color things black

lam·prey *n, pl* **lampreys :** a water animal that looks like an eel but has a sucking mouth with no jaws

[1]**lance** *n* **:** a weapon with a long handle and a sharp steel head used in olden times by knights on horseback

[2]**lance** *vb* **:** to cut open with a small sharp instrument

lance corporal *n* **:** an enlisted person in the Marine Corps ranking above a private first class

[1]**land** *n* **1 :** the solid part of the surface of the earth **2 :** a part of the earth's surface (as a country or a farm) marked off by boundaries **3 :** the people of a country — **landless** *adj*

[2]**land** *vb* **1 :** to go ashore or cause to go ashore from a ship **2 :** to cause to reach or come to rest where planned **3 :** to catch and bring in **4 :** to get for oneself by trying **5 :** to come down or bring down and settle on a surface

land breeze *n* **:** a breeze blowing toward the sea

land·hold·er *n* **:** an owner of land

land·ing *n* **1 :** the act of one that lands **2 :** a place for unloading or taking on passengers and cargo **3 :** the level part of a staircase (as between flights of stairs)

landing field *n* **:** a field where aircraft land and take off

landing strip *n* **:** AIRSTRIP

land·la·dy *n, pl* **land·la·dies 1 :** a woman who owns land or houses that she rents **2 :** a woman who runs an inn or rooming house

land·locked *adj* **1 :** shut in or nearly shut in by land **2 :** kept from leaving fresh water by some barrier

land·lord *n* **1 :** a man who owns land or houses that he rents **2 :** a man who runs an inn or rooming house

land·lub·ber *n* **:** a person who lives on land and knows little or nothing about the sea

land·mark *n* **1 :** something (as a building, a large tree, or a statue) that is easy to see and can help a person find the way to a place near it **2 :** a very important event **3 :** a building of historical importance

land mine *n* **:** a mine placed just below the surface of the ground and designed to be exploded by the weight of vehicles or troops passing over it

land·own·er *n* **:** a person who owns land

[1]**land·scape** *n* **1 :** a picture of natural scenery **2 :** the land that can be seen in one glance

[2]**landscape** *vb* **land·scaped; land·scap·ing :** to improve the natural beauty of a piece of land

land·slide *n* **1 :** the slipping down of a mass of rocks or earth on a steep slope **2 :** the material that moves in a landslide **3 :** the winning of an election by a very large number of votes

lane *n* **1 :** a narrow path or road (as between fences or hedges) that is not used as a highway **2 :** a special route (as for ships) **3 :** a strip of road used for a single line of traffic

lan·guage *n* **1 :** the words and expressions used and understood by a large group of people **2 :** the speech of human beings **3 :** a means of expressing ideas or feelings **4 :** a formal system of signs and symbols that is used to carry information **5 :** the way in which words are used **6 :** the special words used by a certain group or in a certain field **7 :** the study of languages

lan·guid *adj* **:** having very little strength or energy — **lan·guid·ly** *adv* — **lan·guid·ness** *n*

lan·guish *vb* **:** to become weak especially from a lack of something needed or wanted — **lan·guish·er** *n* — **lan·guish·ing** *adj* — **lan·guish·ing·ly** *adv*

lan·guor *n* **1 :** weakness or weariness of body or mind **2 :** a state of dreamy idleness — **lan·guor·ous** *adj* — **lan·guor·ous·ly** *adv*

lank *adj* **1 :** not well filled out **:** THIN **2 :** hanging straight and limp without spring or curl — **lank·ly** *adv* — **lank·ness** *n*

lanky *adj* **lank·i·er; lank·i·est :** being very tall and thin — **lank·i·ly** *adv* — **lank·i·ness** *n*

lan·tern *n* **:** a usually portable lamp with a protective covering

lan·yard *n* **1 :** a short rope or cord used as a fastening on ships **2 :** a cord worn around the neck to hold a knife or whistle **3 :** a strong cord with a hook at one end used in firing cannon

[1]**lap** *n* **:** the front part of a person between the waist and the knees when seated

[2]**lap** *vb* **lapped; lap·ping :** OVERLAP

[3]**lap** *n* **1 :** a part of something that overlaps another part **2 :** one time around a racetrack **3 :** a stage in a trip

[4]**lap** *vb* **lapped; lap·ping 1 :** to scoop up food or drink with the tip of the tongue **2 :** to splash gently

[5]**lap** *n* **:** the act or sound of lapping

lap·dog *n* **:** a dog small enough to be held in the lap

la·pel *n* **:** the part of the front of a collar that is turned back

lap·ful *n, pl* **lap·fuls** *or* **laps·ful :** as much as the lap can hold

¹lapse *n* **1 :** a slight error or slip **2 :** a gradual falling away from a higher to a lower condition **3 :** a gradual passing of time

²lapse *vb* **lapsed; laps·ing 1 :** to slip, pass, or fall gradually **2 :** to become little used **3 :** to come to an end — **laps·er** *n*

lap·top *adj* **:** small enough to be used on one's lap — **laptop** *n*

lar·board *n* **:** ³PORT

lar·ce·ny *n, pl* **lar·ce·nies :** the unlawful taking of personal property without the owner's consent **:** THEFT

larch *n* **:** a tree related to the pine that sheds its needles each fall

¹lard *vb* **:** to smear or soil with grease

²lard *n* **:** a white soft fat from fatty tissue of the hog

lar·der *n* **:** a place where food is kept

large *adj* **larg·er; larg·est :** more than most others of a similar kind in amount or size **:** BIG — **large·ness** *n* — **at large 1 :** not locked up **:** FREE **2 :** as a whole **3 :** representing a whole state or district

large-heart·ed *adj* **:** GENEROUS 1

large intestine *n* **:** the wide lower part of the intestine from which water is absorbed and in which feces are made ready for passage

large·ly *adv* **:** MOSTLY, CHIEFLY

lar·i·at *n* **:** a long light rope used to catch livestock or tie up grazing animals

¹lark *n* **:** any of a group of mostly brownish songbirds of Europe and Asia

²lark *n* **:** something done for fun **:** PRANK

lark·spur *n* **:** a tall branching plant related to the buttercups that is often grown for its stalks of showy blue, purple, pink, or white flowers

lar·va *n, pl* **lar·vae 1 :** a wingless form (as a grub or caterpillar) in which many insects hatch from the egg **2 :** an early form of any animal that at birth or hatching is very different from its parents

lar·yn·gi·tis *n* **:** inflammation of the larynx **:** a sore throat

lar·ynx *n, pl* **la·ryn·ges** *or* **lar·ynx·es :** the upper part of the windpipe that contains the vocal cords

la·ser *n* **:** a device that produces a very powerful beam of light

laser printer *n* **:** a printer for computer output that produces high-quality images formed by a laser

¹lash *vb* **1 :** to move violently or suddenly **2 :** to hit with a whip — **lash·er** *n*

²lash *n* **1 :** a blow with a whip or switch **2 :** the flexible part of a whip **3 :** a sudden swinging blow **4 :** EYELASH

³lash *vb* **:** to tie down with a rope or chain

lash·ing *n* **:** something used for tying, wrapping, or fastening

lass *n* **:** GIRL 1

lass·ie *n* **:** GIRL 1, LASS

¹las·so *vb* **:** to catch with a lasso

²lasso *n, pl* **lassos** *or* **lassoes :** a rope or long leather thong with a slipknot for catching animals

¹last *vb* **1 :** to go on **2 :** to stay in good condition — **last·er** *n*

²last *n* **:** a block shaped like a foot on which shoes are made

³last *adv* **1 :** at the end **2 :** most recently

⁴last *adj* **1 :** following all the rest **:** FINAL **2 :** most recent **3 :** lowest in rank or position **4 :** most unlikely

⁵last *n* **:** a person or thing that is last

last·ing *adj* **:** continuing for a long while — **last·ing·ly** *adv* — **last·ing·ness** *n*

last·ly *adv* **:** at or as the end

¹latch *n* **:** a movable piece that holds a door or gate closed

²latch *vb* **:** to fasten with a latch

¹late *adj* **lat·er; lat·est 1 :** coming or remaining after the usual or proper time **2 :** coming toward the end (as of the day or night) **3 :** having died or recently left a certain position **4 :** RECENT 2 — **late·ness** *n*

²late *adv* **lat·er; lat·est 1 :** after the usual or proper time **2 :** LATELY

late·com·er *n* **:** a person who arrives late

late·ly *adv* **:** not long ago **:** RECENTLY

la·tent *adj* **:** present but not visible or active — **la·tent·ly** *adv*

lat·er·al *adj* **:** being on or directed toward the side — **lat·er·al·ly** *adv*

la·tex *n* **1 :** a milky plant juice that is the source of rubber **2 :** a mixture of water and tiny particles of rubber or plastic used especially in paints

lath *n, pl* **laths :** a thin strip of wood used (as in a wall or ceiling) as a base for plaster

lathe *n* **:** a machine in which a piece of material is held and turned while being shaped by a tool

¹lath·er *n* **1 :** the foam made by stirring soap and water together **2 :** foam from sweating

²lather *vb* **1 :** to spread lather over **2 :** to form a lather

¹Lat·in *adj* **1 :** of or relating to the language of the ancient Romans **2 :** of or relating to Latin America or the Latin Americans

²Latin *n* **1 :** the language of the ancient Romans **2 :** a member of a people whose language and customs have descended from the ancient Romans **3 :** a person born or living in Latin America

Lat·in–Amer·i·can *adj* **:** of or relating to Latin America or its people

Latin American *n* **:** a person born or living in Latin America

lat·i·tude *n* **1 :** the distance north or south of the equator measured in degrees **2 :** REGION 3 **3 :** freedom to act or speak as one wishes

lat·ter *adj* **1 :** relating to or coming near the end **2 :** of, relating to, or being the second of two things referred to

lat·tice *n* **1 :** a structure made of thin strips of wood or metal that cross each other to form a network **2 :** a window or gate having a lattice

[1]laud *n* **:** [2]PRAISE 1, ACCLAIM

[2]laud *vb* **:** [1]PRAISE 1, ACCLAIM

[1]laugh *vb* **:** to show amusement, joy, or scorn by smiling and making sounds (as chuckling) in the throat

[2]laugh *n* **:** the act or sound of laughing

laugh·able *adj* **:** causing or likely to cause laughter — **laugh·able·ness** *n* — **laugh·ably** *adv*

laugh·ing·stock *n* **:** a person or thing that is made fun of

laugh·ter *n* **:** the action or sound of laughing

[1]launch *vb* **1 :** [1]THROW 1 2, HURL **2 :** to set afloat **3 :** to send off especially with force **4 :** to give a start to

[2]launch *n* **:** an act of launching

[3]launch *n* **:** MOTORBOAT

launch·pad *n* **:** a nonflammable platform from which a rocket can be launched

laun·der *vb* **:** to wash or wash and iron clothes — **laun·der·er** *n*

laun·dress *n* **:** a woman whose work is washing clothes

laun·dry *n, pl* **laundries 1 :** clothes or linens that have been laundered or are to be laundered **2 :** a place where laundering is done

laun·dry·man *n, pl* **laun·dry·men :** a man who works in or for a laundry

lau·rel *n* **1 :** a small evergreen European tree with shiny pointed leaves used in ancient times to crown victors (as in sports) **2 :** any of various plants (as the American **mountain laurel**) that resemble the European laurel **3 :** a crown of laurel used as a mark of honor

la·va *n* **1 :** melted rock coming from a volcano **2 :** lava that has cooled and hardened

lav·a·to·ry *n, pl* **lav·a·to·ries 1 :** a small sink (as in a bathroom) **2 :** a room for washing that usually has a toilet **3 :** TOILET 3

lav·en·der *n* **1 :** a European mint with narrow somewhat woolly leaves and stalks of small sweet-smelling pale violet flowers **2 :** a pale purple

[1]lav·ish *adj* **1 :** spending or giving more than is necessary **:** EXTRAVAGANT **2 :** spent, produced, or given freely — **lav·ish·ly** *adv* — **lav·ish·ness** *n*

[2]lavish *vb* **:** to spend, use, or give freely

law *n* **1 :** a rule of conduct or action that a nation or a group of people agrees to follow **2 :** a whole collection of established rules **3 :** a rule or principle that always works the same way under the same conditions **4 :** a bill passed by a legislative group **5 :** [2]POLICE **6** *cap* **:** the first part of the Jewish scriptures **7 :** trial in court **8 :** the profession of a lawyer

law–abid·ing *adj* **:** obeying the law

law·break·er *n* **:** a person who breaks the law

law·ful *adj* **1 :** permitted by law **2 :** approved by law — **law·ful·ly** *adv* — **law·ful·ness** *n*

law·less *adj* **1 :** having no laws **:** not based on or controlled by law **2 :** uncontrolled by law **:** UNRULY — **law·less·ly** *adv* — **law·less·ness** *n*

law·mak·er *n* **:** one who takes part in writing and passing laws **:** LEGISLATOR — **law·mak·ing** *adj or n*

lawn *n* **:** ground (as around a house) covered with grass that is kept mowed

lawn mower *n* **:** a machine used to mow the grass on lawns

lawn tennis *n* **:** TENNIS

law·suit *n* **:** a complaint brought before a court of law for decision

law·yer *n* **:** a person whose profession is to handle lawsuits for people or to give advice about legal rights and duties

lax *adj* **1 :** not firm or tight **:** LOOSE **2 :** not stern or strict — **lax·ly** *adv* — **lax·ness** *n*

[1]lax·a·tive *adj* **:** helpful against constipation

[2]laxative *n* **:** a laxative medicine that is nearly always mild

[1]lay *vb* **laid; lay·ing 1 :** to bring down (as with force) **2 :** to put down **3 :** to produce an egg **4 :** to cause to disappear **5 :** to spread over a surface **6 :** PREPARE 1, ARRANGE **7 :** to put to **:** APPLY

[2]lay *n* **:** the way a thing lies in relation to something else

[3]lay *past of* lie

lay·away *n* **:** something held for a customer until the price is paid

lay away *vb* **:** to put aside for later use or delivery

lay·er *n* **1 :** one that lays something **2 :** one thickness of something laid over another

lay in *vb* **:** to store for later use

lay·man *n, pl* **lay·men 1 :** a person who is not a member of the clergy **2 :** a person who is not a member of a certain profession

lay off *vb* **1 :** to stop employing (a person) usually temporarily **2 :** to let alone

lay·out *n* : [1]PLAN 1, ARRANGEMENT
lay out *vb* **1 :** to plan in detail **2 :** ARRANGE 1, DESIGN
lay up *vb* **1 :** to store up **2 :** to be confined by illness or injury
la·zy *adj* **la·zi·er; la·zi·est 1 :** not willing to act or work **2 :** [1]SLOW 3, SLUGGISH — **la·zi·ly** *adv* — **la·zi·ness** *n*
leach *vb* **1 :** to treat (as earth) with a liquid (as water) to remove something soluble **2 :** to remove (as a soluble salt) by leaching
[1]**lead** *vb* **led; lead·ing 1 :** to guide on a way often by going ahead **2 :** to be at the head of **3 :** to go through : LIVE **4 :** to reach or go in a certain direction
[2]**lead** *n* **1 :** position at the front **2 :** the distance that a person or thing is ahead **3 :** the first part of a news story
[3]**lead** *n* **1 :** a heavy soft gray metallic element that is easily bent and shaped **2 :** AMMUNITION 1 **3 :** a long thin piece of graphite used in pencils
lead·en *adj* **1 :** made of lead **2 :** heavy as lead **3 :** dull gray — **lead·en·ly** *adv* — **lead·en·ness** *n*
lead·er *n* : one that leads or is able to lead — **lead·er·ship** *n*
[1]**leaf** *n, pl* **leaves 1 :** one of the usually flat green parts that grow from a plant stem and that together make up the foliage **2 :** FOLIAGE **3 :** a single sheet of a book making two pages **4 :** a movable part of a table top — **leaf·less** *adj* — **leaf·like** *adj*
[2]**leaf** *vb* **1 :** to grow leaves **2 :** to turn the leaves of a book
leaf·let *n* **1 :** a young or small leaf **2 :** a division of a compound leaf **3 :** PAMPHLET
leaf·stalk *n* : PETIOLE
leafy *adj* **leaf·i·er; leaf·i·est :** having, covered with, or like leaves
[1]**league** *n* **1 :** a group of nations working together for a common purpose **2 :** an association of persons or groups with common interests or goals **3 :** [1]CLASS 7
[2]**league** *vb* **leagued; leagu·ing :** to form a league
[1]**leak** *vb* **1 :** to enter or escape or let enter or escape usually by accident **2 :** to make or become known
[2]**leak** *n* **1 :** a crack or hole that accidentally lets fluid in or out **2 :** something that accidentally or secretly causes or permits loss **3 :** the act of leaking : LEAKAGE
leak·age *n* **1 :** the act or process of leaking **2 :** the thing or amount that leaks
leaky *adj* **leak·i·er; leak·i·est :** letting fluid leak in or out — **leak·i·ness** *n*
[1]**lean** *vb* **1 :** to bend or tilt from a straight position **2 :** to bend and rest one's weight on **3 :** DEPEND 1, RELY **4 :** to tend or move toward in opinion, taste, or desire
[2]**lean** *adj* **1 :** having too little flesh : SKINNY **2 :** containing very little fat **3 :** not large or plentiful — **lean·ness** *n*
lean–to *n, pl* **lean–tos 1 :** a building that has a roof with only one slope and is usually joined to another building **2 :** a rough shelter held up by posts, rocks, or trees
[1]**leap** *vb* **leaped** *or* **leapt; leap·ing 1 :** to jump or cause to jump from a surface **2 :** to move, act, or pass quickly — **leap·er** *n*
[2]**leap** *n* **1 :** an act of leaping : JUMP **2 :** a place leaped over **3 :** a distance leaped
leap·frog *n* **:** a game in which one player bends down and another leaps over the first player
leap year *n* : a year of 366 days with February 29 as the extra day
learn *vb* **learned** *also* **learnt; learn·ing 1 :** to get knowledge of or skill in (by studying or practicing) **2 :** MEMORIZE **3 :** to become able through practice **4 :** to find out **5 :** to gain knowledge
learned *adj* : having or showing knowledge or learning
learn·ing *n* **1 :** the act of a person who learns **2 :** knowledge or skill gained from teaching or study
[1]**lease** *n* **1 :** an agreement by which a person exchanges property (as real estate) for a period of time for rent or services **2 :** the period of time for which property is leased **3 :** a piece of property that is leased
[2]**lease** *vb* **leased; leas·ing :** to give or get the use of (property) in return for services or rent
[1]**leash** *n* : a line for leading or holding an animal
[2]**leash** *vb* : to put on a leash
[1]**least** *adj* : smallest in size or degree
[2]**least** *n* **:** the smallest or lowest amount or degree
[3]**least** *adv* **:** in or to the smallest degree
leath·er *n* **1 :** the tanned skin of an animal **2 :** something made of leather
leath·ery *adj* : like leather
[1]**leave** *vb* **left; leav·ing 1 :** to fail to include or take along **2 :** to have remaining **3 :** to give by will **4 :** to let stay without interference **5 :** to go away from **6 :** to give up **7 :** DELIVER 2
[2]**leave** *n* **1 :** PERMISSION **2 :** permitted absence from one's duty or work **3 :** the act of leaving and saying good-bye **4 :** a period of time during which a person is allowed to be absent from duties
leaved *adj* : having leaves
leaves *pl of* LEAF
leav·ings *n pl* : something left over

[1]**lec•ture** *n* **1 :** a talk that teaches something **2 :** a severe scolding

[2]**lecture** *vb* **lec•tured; lec•tur•ing** **1 :** to give a lecture **2 :** [2]SCOLD — **lec•tur•er** *n*

led *past of* LEAD

ledge *n* **1 :** a piece projecting from a top or an edge like a shelf **2 :** SHELF 2

[1]**lee** *n* **1 :** a protecting shelter **2 :** the side (as of a ship) sheltered from the wind

[2]**lee** *adj* **:** of or relating to the lee

leech *n* **1 :** a bloodsucking worm related to the earthworm **2 :** a person who clings like a leech to another person for what can be gained

leek *n* **:** a garden plant grown for its thick stems which taste like a mild onion

[1]**leer** *vb* **:** to look with a leer

[2]**leer** *n* **:** a mean or nasty glance

leery *adj* **:** SUSPICIOUS 2, WARY

[1]**lee•ward** *n* **:** the lee side

[2]**leeward** *adj* **:** located away from the wind

[1]**left** *adj* **1 :** on the same side of the body as the heart **2 :** located nearer to the left side of the body than to the right

[2]**left** *n* **:** the left side or the part on the left side

[3]**left** *past of* LEAVE

left–hand *adj* **1 :** located on the left **2 :** LEFT-HANDED

left–hand•ed *adj* **1 :** using the left hand better or more easily than the right **2 :** done or made with or for the left hand

left•over *n* **:** something left over

lefty *n, pl* **left•ies :** a left-handed person

leg *n* **1 :** one of the limbs of an animal or person that support the body and are used in walking and running **2 :** the part of the leg between the knee and the foot **3 :** something like a leg in shape or use **4 :** the part of a garment that covers the leg **5 :** a stage or part of a journey

leg•a•cy *n, pl* **leg•a•cies :** something left to a person by or as if by a will

le•gal *adj* **1 :** of or relating to law or lawyers **2 :** based on law **3 :** allowed by law or rules — **le•gal•ly** *adv*

le•gal•i•ty *n, pl* **le•gal•i•ties :** the quality or state of being legal

le•gal•ize *vb* **le•gal•ized; le•gal•iz•ing :** to make legal — **le•gal•iza•tion** *n*

leg•end *n* **1 :** an old story that is widely believed but cannot be proved to be true **2 :** writing or a title on an object **3 :** a list of symbols used (as on a map)

leg•end•ary *adj* **:** of, relating to, or like a legend

leg•ged *adj* **:** having legs

leg•ging *n* **:** an outer covering for the leg usually of cloth or leather

leg•i•ble *adj* **:** clear enough to be read — **leg•i•bly** *adv*

le•gion *n* **1 :** a group of from 3000 to 6000 soldiers that made up the chief army unit in ancient Rome **2 :** ARMY 1 **3 :** a very great number

leg•is•late *vb* **leg•is•lat•ed; leg•is•lat•ing :** to make laws — **leg•is•la•tor** *n*

leg•is•la•tion *n* **1 :** the action of making laws **2 :** the laws that are made

leg•is•la•tive *adj* **1 :** having the power or authority to make laws **2 :** of or relating to legislation — **leg•is•la•tive•ly** *adv*

leg•is•la•ture *n* **:** a body of persons having the power to make, change, or cancel laws

le•git•i•ma•cy *n* **:** the quality or state of being legitimate

le•git•i•mate *adj* **1 :** accepted by the law as rightful **:** LAWFUL **2 :** being right or acceptable — **le•git•i•mate•ly** *adv*

leg•less *adj* **:** having no legs

le•gume *n* **:** any of a large group of plants (as peas, beans, and clover) with fruits that are pods and root nodules containing bacteria that fix nitrogen

lei•sure *n* **1 :** freedom from work **2 :** time that is free for use as one wishes

lei•sure•ly *adj* **:** UNHURRIED

lem•on *n* **1 :** an oval yellow fruit with a sour juice that is related to the orange and grows on a small spiny tree **2 :** something unsatisfactory **:** DUD

lem•on•ade *n* **:** a drink made of lemon juice, sugar, and water

lend *vb* **lent; lend•ing** **1 :** [2]LOAN 1 **2 :** to give usually for a time **3 :** to make a loan or loans — **lend•er** *n*

length *n* **1 :** the measured distance from one end to the other of the longer or longest side of an object **2 :** a measured distance **3 :** amount of time something takes **4 :** the sound of a vowel or syllable as it is affected by the time needed to pronounce it **5 :** a piece of something that is long — **at length** **1 :** very fully **2 :** at the end

length•en *vb* **:** to make or become longer

length•ways *adv* **:** LENGTHWISE

length•wise *adv or adj* **:** in the direction of the length

lengthy *adj* **length•i•er; length•i•est :** very long — **length•i•ly** *adv* — **length•i•ness** *n*

le•nient *adj* **:** being kind and patient — **le•nient•ly** *adv*

lens *n* **1 :** a clear curved piece of material (as glass) used to bend the rays of light to form an image **2 :** a part of the eye that focuses rays of light so as to form clear images

lent *past of* LEND

len•til *n* **:** the flattened round edible seed of a plant related to the pea

Leo *n* **1 :** a constellation between Cancer

and Virgo imagined as a lion **2 :** the fifth sign of the zodiac or a person born under this sign
leop•ard *n* **:** a large cat of Asia and Africa that has a brownish buff coat with black spots
leop•ard•ess *n* **:** a female leopard
le•o•tard *n* **:** a tight one-piece garment worn by dancers or acrobats
le•sion *n* **:** an abnormal spot or area of the body caused by sickness or injury
[1]**less** *adj* **1 :** being fewer **2 :** of lower rank, degree, or importance **3 :** not so much **:** a smaller amount of
[2]**less** *adv* **:** not so much or so well
[3]**less** *n* **1 :** a smaller number or amount **2 :** a thing that is poorer than another
[4]**less** *prep* **:** [1]MINUS 1
-less *adj suffix* **1 :** not having **2 :** not able to be acted on or to act in a specified way
less•en *vb* **:** to make or become less
[1]**less•er** *adj* **:** of smaller size or importance
[2]**lesser** *adv* **:** [2]LESS
les•son *n* **1 :** a part of the Scripture read in a church service **2 :** a reading or exercise assigned for study **3 :** something learned or taught
lest *conj* **:** for fear that
let *vb* **let; let•ting 1 :** to cause to **:** MAKE **2 :** to give use of in return for payment **3 :** to allow or permit to **4 :** to allow to go or pass
-let *n suffix* **1 :** small one **2 :** something worn on
let•down *n* **:** DISAPPOINTMENT 2
let down *vb* **1 :** DISAPPOINT **2 :** RELAX 3
let on *vb* **1 :** ADMIT 3 **2 :** PRETEND 1
let's : let us
[1]**let•ter** *n* **1 :** one of the marks that are symbols for speech sounds in writing or print and that make up the alphabet **2 :** a written or printed communication (as one sent through the mail) **3 letters** *pl* **:** LITERATURE 2 **4 :** the strict or outward meaning **5 :** the initial of a school awarded to a student usually for athletic achievement
[2]**letter** *vb* **:** to mark with letters
letter carrier *n* **:** a person who delivers mail
let•ter•head *n* **1 :** stationery having a printed or engraved heading **2 :** the heading of a letterhead
let•ter•ing *n* **:** letters used in an inscription
let•tuce *n* **:** a garden plant related to the daisies that has large crisp leaves eaten in salad
let up *vb* **1 :** to slow down **2 :** [1]STOP 4, CEASE
leu•ke•mia *n* **:** a dangerous disease in which too many white blood cells are formed
le•vee *n* **1 :** a bank built along a river to prevent flooding **2 :** a landing place along a river
[1]**lev•el** *n* **1 :** a device used (as by a carpenter) to find a horizontal line or surface **2 :** a horizontal line or surface usually at a named height **3 :** a step or stage in height, position, or rank
[2]**level** *vb* **lev•eled** *or* **lev•elled; lev•el•ing** *or* **lev•el•ling :** to make or become level, flat, or even — **lev•el•er** *or* **lev•el•ler** *n*
[3]**level** *adj* **1 :** having a flat even surface **2 :** HORIZONTAL **3 :** of the same height or rank **:** EVEN **4 :** steady and cool in judgment — **lev•el•ly** *adv* — **lev•el•ness** *n*
[1]**le•ver** *n* **1 :** a bar used to pry or move something **2 :** a stiff bar for lifting a weight at one point of its length by pressing or pulling at a second point while the bar turns on a support **3 :** a bar or rod used to run or adjust something
[2]**lever** *vb* **:** to raise or move with a lever
[1]**levy** *n, pl* **lev•ies 1 :** a collection (as of taxes) by authority of the law **2 :** the calling of troops into service **3 :** something (as taxes) collected by authority of the law
[2]**levy** *vb* **lev•ied; levy•ing 1 :** to collect legally **2 :** to raise or collect troops for service
li•a•ble *adj* **1 :** forced by law or by what is right to make good **2 :** not sheltered or protected (as from danger or accident) **3 :** LIKELY 1
li•ar *n* **:** a person who tells lies
[1]**li•bel** *n* **:** something spoken or written that hurts a person's good name
[2]**libel** *vb* **li•beled** *or* **li•belled; li•bel•ing** *or* **li•bel•ling :** to hurt by a libel — **li•bel•er** *or* **li•bel•ler** *n*
lib•er•al *adj* **1 :** not stingy **:** GENEROUS **2 :** being more than enough **3 :** not strict **4 :** BROAD 4 — **lib•er•al•ly** *adv*
lib•er•ate *vb* **lib•er•at•ed; lib•er•at•ing :** to set free
lib•er•ty *n, pl* **lib•er•ties 1 :** the state of those who are free and independent **:** FREEDOM **2 :** freedom to do what one pleases **3 :** the state of not being busy **:** LEISURE **4 :** behavior or an act that is too free
Li•bra *n* **1 :** a constellation between Virgo and Scorpio imagined as a pair of scales **2 :** the seventh sign of the zodiac or a person born under this sign
li•brar•i•an *n* **:** a person in charge of a library
li•brary *n, pl* **li•brar•ies 1 :** a place where especially literary or reference materials (as books, manuscripts, recordings, or films) are kept for use but not for sale **2 :** a collection of such materials
lice *pl of* LOUSE
[1]**li•cense** *or* **li•cence** *n* **1 :** permission

granted by qualified authority to do something **2 :** a paper showing legal permission **3 :** liberty of action that is carried too far

[2]**license** *or* **licence** *vb* **li·censed** *or* **li·cenced; li·cens·ing** *or* **li·cenc·ing :** to permit or authorize by license

li·chen *n* **:** a plant made up of an alga and a fungus growing together

[1]**lick** *vb* **1 :** to pass the tongue over **2 :** to touch or pass over like a tongue **3 :** to hit again and again **:** BEAT **4 :** to get the better of — **lick·ing** *n*

[2]**lick** *n* **1 :** the act of licking **2 :** a small amount **3 :** a place (**salt lick**) where salt is found on the top of the ground and animals come to lick it up

lick·e·ty–split *adv* **:** at top speed

lic·o·rice *n* **1 :** the dried root of a European plant related to the peas or a juice from it used in medicine and in candy **2 :** candy flavored with licorice

lid *n* **1 :** a movable cover **2 :** EYELID — **lid·ded** *adj* — **lid·less** *adj*

[1]**lie** *vb* **lay; lain; ly·ing 1 :** to stretch out or be stretched out (as on a bed or on the ground) **2 :** to be spread flat so as to cover **3 :** to be located or placed **4 :** to be or stay

[2]**lie** *vb* **lied; ly·ing :** to make a statement that one knows to be untrue

[3]**lie** *n* **:** something said or done in the hope of deceiving **:** an untrue statement

[1]**liege** *adj* **1 :** having the right to receive service and loyalty **2 :** owing or giving service to a lord

[2]**liege** *n* **1 :** VASSAL 1 **2 :** a feudal lord

lieu·ten·ant *n* **1 :** an official who acts for a higher official **2 :** a first lieutenant or second lieutenant (as in the Army) **3 :** a commissioned officer in the Navy or Coast Guard ranking above a lieutenant junior grade

lieutenant colonel *n* **:** a commissioned officer in the Army, Air Force, or Marine Corps ranking above a major

lieutenant commander *n* **:** a commissioned officer in the Navy or Coast Guard ranking above a lieutenant

lieutenant general *n* **:** a commissioned officer in the Army, Air Force, or Marine Corps ranking above a major general

lieutenant junior grade *n* **:** a commissioned officer in the Navy or Coast Guard ranking above an ensign

life *n, pl* **lives 1 :** the quality that separates plants and animals from such things as water or rock **:** the quality that plants and animals lose when they die **2 :** all the experiences that make up the existence of a person **:** the course of existence **3 :** BIOGRAPHY **4 :** the period during which a person or thing is alive or exists **5 :** a way of living **6 :** a living being **7 :** [1]SPIRIT 5

life belt *n* **:** a life preserver worn like a belt

life·boat *n* **:** a sturdy boat (as one carried by a ship) for use in an emergency and especially in saving lives at sea

life buoy *n* **:** a life preserver in the shape of a ring

life·guard *n* **:** a guard employed at a beach or swimming pool to protect swimmers from drowning

life jacket *n* **:** a life preserver in the form of a vest

life·less *adj* **:** having no life

life·like *adj* **:** very like something that is alive

life·long *adj* **:** continuing through life

life preserver *n* **:** a device (as a life jacket or life buoy) designed to save a person from drowning by keeping the person afloat

life raft *n* **:** a raft usually made of wood or an inflatable material for use by people forced into the water

life·sav·er *n* **:** a person trained in lifesaving

life·sav·ing *n* **:** the methods that can be used to save lives especially of drowning persons

life–size *or* **life–sized** *adj* **:** of natural size **:** having the same size as the original

life·style *n* **:** the usual way of life of a person, group, or society **:** the way we live

life·time *n* **:** LIFE 4

life vest *n* **:** LIFE JACKET

[1]**lift** *vb* **1 :** to raise from a lower to a higher position, rate, or amount **2 :** to rise from the ground **3 :** to move upward and disappear or become scattered — **lift·er** *n*

[2]**lift** *n* **1 :** the amount that may be lifted at one time **:** LOAD **2 :** the action or an instance of lifting **3 :** help especially in the form of a ride **4** *chiefly British* **:** ELEVATOR 2 **5 :** an upward force (as on an airplane wing) that opposes the pull of gravity

lift·off *n* **:** a vertical takeoff (as by a rocket)

lig·a·ment *n* **:** a tough band of tissue or fibers that holds bones together or keeps an organ in place in the body

[1]**light** *n* **1 :** the bright form of energy given off by something (as the sun) that lets one see objects **2 :** a source (as a lamp) of light **3 :** DAYLIGHT 1 **4 :** public knowledge **5 :** something that helps one to know or understand

[2]**light** *adj* **1 :** having light **:** BRIGHT **2 :** not dark or deep in color

[3]**light** *vb* **light·ed** *or* **lit; light·ing 1 :** to make or become bright **2 :** to burn or cause to burn **3 :** to lead with a light

[4]**light** *adj* **1 :** having little weight **:** not heavy **2 :** not strong or violent **3 :** not hard to bear, do, pay, or digest **4 :** active in motion **5 :** not severe **6 :** free from care

: HAPPY **7 :** intended mainly to entertain — **light·ly** *adv* — **light·ness** *n*
5light *adv* **:** with little baggage
6light *vb* **light·ed** *or* **lit; light·ing 1 :** 2PERCH, SETTLE **2 :** to come by chance
light bulb *n* **:** INCANDESCENT LAMP
1light·en *vb* **1 :** to make or become light or lighter **:** BRIGHTEN **2 :** to grow bright with lightning — **light·en·er** *n*
2lighten *vb* **:** to make or become less heavy — **light·en·er** *n*
light·face *n* **:** a type having light thin lines — **light·faced** *adj*
light·heart·ed *adj* **:** free from worry — **light·heart·ed·ly** *adv* — **light·heart·ed·ness** *n*
light·house *n* **:** a tower with a powerful light at the top that is built on the shore to guide sailors at night
light·ing *n* **:** supply of light or of lights
light·ning *n* **:** the flashing of light caused by the passing of electricity from one cloud to another or between a cloud and the earth
lightning bug *n* **:** FIREFLY
light·proof *adj* **:** not letting in light
light·weight *adj* **:** having less than the usual or expected weight
light–year *n* **:** a unit of length in astronomy equal to the distance that light travels in one year or 9,458,000,000,000 kilometers
lik·able *or* **like·able** *adj* **:** easily liked — **lik·able·ness** *n*
1like *vb* **liked; lik·ing 1 :** to have a liking for **:** ENJOY **2 :** to feel toward **:** REGARD **3 :** CHOOSE 3, PREFER
2like *n* **:** LIKING, PREFERENCE
3like *adj* **1 :** SIMILAR, ALIKE **2 :** similar to or to that of — used after the word modified
4like *prep* **1 :** similar or similarly to **2 :** typical of **3 :** likely to **4 :** such as
5like *n* **:** 3EQUAL, COUNTERPART
6like *conj* **1 :** AS IF **2 :** in the same way that **:** 2AS 2
like·li·hood *n* **:** PROBABILITY 1
1like·ly *adj* **1 :** very possibly going to happen **2 :** seeming to be the truth **:** BELIEVABLE **3 :** giving hope of turning out well **:** PROMISING — **like·li·ness** *n*
2likely *adv* **:** without great doubt
lik·en *vb* **:** COMPARE 1
like·ness *n* **1 :** the state of being like **:** RESEMBLANCE **2 :** a picture of a person **:** PORTRAIT
like·wise *adv* **1 :** in like manner **2 :** ALSO
lik·ing *n* **:** a being pleased with someone or something
li·lac *n* **1 :** a bush having clusters of fragrant grayish pink, purple, or white flowers **2 :** a medium purple
lilt *vb* **:** to sing or play in a lively cheerful manner — **lilt·ing·ly** *adv*
lily *n, pl* **lil·ies :** a plant (as the **Easter lily** or the **tiger lily**) that grows from a bulb and has a leafy stem and showy funnel-shaped flowers
lily of the valley : a low plant related to the lilies that has usually two leaves and a stalk of fragrant flowers shaped like bells
li·ma bean *n* **:** a bean with flat pale green or white seeds
limb *n* **1 :** any of the paired parts (as an arm, wing, or leg) of an animal that stick out from the body and are used mostly in moving or grasping **2 :** a large branch of a tree — **limbed** *adj* — **limb·less** *adj*
1lim·ber *adj* **:** bending easily — **lim·ber·ly** *adv* — **lim·ber·ness** *n*
2limber *vb* **:** to make or become limber
1lime *n* **:** a white substance made by heating limestone or shells that is used in making plaster and cement and in farming
2lime *vb* **limed; lim·ing :** to treat or cover with lime
3lime *n* **:** a small greenish yellow fruit that is related to the lemon and orange
lim·er·ick *n* **:** a humorous poem five lines long
lime·stone *n* **:** a rock formed chiefly from animal remains (as shells or coral) that is used in building and gives lime when burned
lime·wa·ter *n* **:** a colorless water solution that contains calcium and turns white when carbon dioxide is blown through it
1lim·it *n* **1 :** a boundary line **2 :** a point beyond which a person or thing cannot go
2limit *vb* **:** to set limits to
lim·i·ta·tion *n* **1 :** an act or instance of limiting **2 :** the quality or state of being limited
lim·it·less *adj* **:** having no limits
1limp *vb* **:** to walk lamely
2limp *n* **:** a limping movement or gait
3limp *adj* **:** not firm or stiff — **limp·ly** *adv* — **limp·ness** *n*
limy *adj* **lim·i·er; lim·i·est :** containing lime or limestone
lin·den *n* **:** a shade tree with heart-shaped toothed leaves, drooping clusters of yellowish white flowers, and hard fruits like peas
1line *n* **1 :** a long thin cord **2 :** a pipe carrying a fluid (as steam, water, or oil) **3 :** an outdoor wire carrying electricity for a telephone or power company **4 :** a row of letters or words across a page or column **5 lines** *pl* **:** the words of a part in a play **6 :** the direction followed by something in motion **7 :** the boundary or limit of a place or lot **8 :** the track of a railway **9 :** AGREE-

MENT 1, HARMONY **10 :** a course of behavior or thought **11 :** FAMILY 1 **12 :** a system of transportation **13 :** a long narrow mark (as one drawn by a pencil) **14 :** the football players whose positions are along the line of scrimmage **15 :** a geometric element produced by moving a point **:** a set of points **16 :** [1]OUTLINE 1, CONTOUR **17 :** a plan for making or doing something

[2]**line** *vb* **lined; lin•ing 1 :** to mark with a line or lines **2 :** to place or be placed in a line along **3 :** to form a line **:** form into lines

[3]**line** *vb* **lined; lin•ing :** to cover the inner surface of

lin•eage *n* **1 :** the ancestors from whom a person is descended **2 :** people descended from the same ancestor

lin•ear *adj* **1 :** of, relating to, or like a line **:** STRAIGHT **2 :** involving a single dimension

lin•en *n* **1 :** smooth strong cloth or yarn made from flax **2 :** household articles (as tablecloths or sheets) or clothing (as shirts or underwear) once often made of linen

line of scrimmage : an imaginary line in football parallel to the goal lines and running through the place where the ball is laid before each play begins

[1]**lin•er** *n* **:** a ship or airplane of a regular transportation line

[2]**liner** *n* **:** one that lines or is used to line something

line segment *n* **:** SEGMENT 3

line•up *n* **1 :** a line of persons arranged especially for police identification **2 :** a list of players taking part in a game (as baseball)

-ling *n suffix* **1 :** one associated with **2 :** young, small, or minor one

lin•ger *vb* **:** to be slow in leaving **:** DELAY

lin•guist *n* **1 :** a person skilled in languages **2 :** a person who specializes in linguistics

lin•guis•tics *n* **:** the study of human speech including the units, nature, structure, and development of language, languages, or a language

lin•i•ment *n* **:** a liquid medicine rubbed on the skin (as to ease pain)

lin•ing *n* **:** material that lines an inner surface

[1]**link** *n* **1 :** a single ring of a chain **2 :** something that connects **3 :** HYPERLINK

[2]**link** *vb* **:** to join with or as if with links

linking verb *n* **:** an intransitive verb that links a subject with a word or words in the predicate

lin•net *n* **:** a common small European finch often kept as a cage bird

li•no•leum *n* **:** a floor covering with a canvas back and a surface of hardened linseed oil and usually cork dust

lin•seed *n* **:** FLAXSEED

linseed oil *n* **:** a yellowish oil obtained from flaxseed

lint *n* **1 :** loose bits of thread **2 :** [1]COTTON 1

lin•tel *n* **:** a horizontal piece or part across the top of an opening (as of a door) to carry the weight of the structure above it

li•on *n* **:** a large flesh-eating animal of the cat family that has a brownish buff coat, a tufted tail, and in the male a shaggy mane and that lives in Africa and southern Asia

li•on•ess *n* **:** a female lion

lip *n* **1 :** either of the two folds of flesh that surround the mouth **2 :** an edge (as of a flower or a wound) like or of flesh **3 :** the edge of a hollow container especially where it is slightly spread out — **lip•less** *adj* — **lip•like** *adj* — **lipped** *adj*

lip•stick *n* **:** a waxy solid colored cosmetic for the lips usually in stick form

liq•ue•fy *vb* **liq•ue•fied; liq•ue•fy•ing :** to make or become liquid

[1]**liq•uid** *adj* **1 :** flowing freely like water **2 :** neither solid nor gaseous **3 :** like liquid in clearness or smoothness **4 :** made up of or easily changed into cash — **liq•uid•ly** *adv* — **liq•uid•ness** *n*

[2]**liquid** *n* **:** a liquid substance

liq•uor *n* **1 :** a liquid substance or solution **2 :** a strong alcoholic beverage (as whiskey)

[1]**lisp** *vb* **:** to pronounce the sounds \s\ and \z\ as \th\ and \th\

[2]**lisp** *n* **:** the act or habit of lisping

[1]**list** *n* **:** a leaning over to one side

[2]**list** *vb* **:** to lean to one side

[3]**list** *n* **:** a record or catalog of names or items

[4]**list** *vb* **:** to put into a list

lis•ten *vb* **1 :** to pay attention in order to hear **2 :** to give heed **:** follow advice — **lis•ten•er** *n*

list•less *adj* **:** too tired or too little interested to want to do things — **list•less•ly** *adv* — **list•less•ness** *n*

lit *past of* LIGHT

li•ter *n* **:** a metric unit of liquid capacity equal to 1.057 quarts

lit•er•al *adj* **1 :** following the ordinary or usual meaning of the words **2 :** true to fact — **lit•er•al•ly** *adv* — **lit•er•al•ness** *n*

lit•er•ary *adj* **:** of or relating to literature

lit•er•ate *adj* **1 :** well educated **:** WELL-BRED **2 :** able to read and write

lit•er•a•ture *n* **1 :** written works having excellence of form or expression and ideas of lasting and widespread interest **2 :** written material (as of a period or on a subject)

lithe *adj* **:** [1]LIMBER, SUPPLE — **lithe•ly** *adv* — **lithe•ness** *n*

lith•o•sphere *n* **:** the outer part of the solid earth

lit·mus paper *n* **:** paper treated with coloring matter that turns red in acid solutions and blue in alkaline solutions

¹lit·ter *n* **1 :** a covered and curtained couch having poles and used for carrying a single passenger **2 :** a stretcher for carrying a sick or wounded person **3 :** material spread out like a bed in places where farm animals (as cows or chickens) are kept to soak up their urine and feces **4 :** the young born to an animal at a single time **5 :** a messy collection of things scattered about **:** RUBBISH

²litter *vb* **1 :** to cover with litter **2 :** to scatter about in disorder

lit·ter·bug *n* **:** one that litters a public area

¹lit·tle *adj* **lit·tler** *or* **less; lit·tlest** *or* **least** **1 :** small in size **2 :** small in quantity **3 :** small in importance **4 :** NARROW-MINDED, MEAN **5 :** short in duration or extent — **lit·tle·ness** *n*

²little *adv* **less; least :** in a very small quantity or degree

³little *n* **:** a small amount or quantity

Little Dipper *n* **:** a group of seven stars in the northern sky arranged in a form like a dipper with the North Star forming the tip of the handle

li·tur·gi·cal *adj* **:** of, relating to, or like liturgy

lit·ur·gy *n, pl* **lit·ur·gies :** a religious rite or body of rites

¹live *vb* **lived; liv·ing** **1 :** to be alive **2 :** to continue in life **3 :** DWELL 2 **4 :** to pass one's life — **live it up :** to live with great enthusiasm and excitement

²live *adj* **1 :** not dead **:** ALIVE **2 :** burning usually without flame **3 :** not exploded **4 :** of present and continuing interest **5 :** charged with an electric current **6 :** broadcast at the time of production

live·li·hood *n* **:** ²LIVING 3

live·long *adj* **:** during all of

live·ly *adj* **live·li·er; live·li·est** **1 :** full of life **:** ACTIVE **2 :** KEEN 4 **3 :** full of spirit or feeling **:** ANIMATED — **live·li·ness** *n*

liv·en *vb* **:** to make or become lively

live oak *n* **:** any of several American oaks that have evergreen leaves

liv·er *n* **:** a large gland of vertebrates (as fishes and humans) that has a rich blood supply, secretes bile, and helps in storing some nutrients and in forming some body wastes

liv·er·ied *adj* **:** wearing a livery

liv·er·wort *n* **:** any of a group of flowerless plants that are somewhat like mosses

liv·ery *n, pl* **liv·er·ies** **1 :** a special uniform worn by the servants of a wealthy household **2 :** the clothing worn to distinguish an association of persons **3 :** the care and stabling of horses for pay **4 :** the keeping of horses and vehicles for hire or a place (**livery stable**) engaged in this

lives *pl of* LIFE

live·stock *n* **:** animals kept or raised especially on a farm and for profit

live wire *n* **:** an alert active forceful person

liv·id *adj* **1 :** discolored by bruising **2 :** pale as ashes — **liv·id·ly** *adv* — **liv·id·ness** *n*

¹liv·ing *adj* **1 :** not dead **:** ALIVE **2 :** ACTIVE 4 **3 :** true to life

²living *n* **1 :** the condition of being alive **2 :** conduct or manner of life **3 :** what one has to have to meet one's needs

living room *n* **:** a room in a house for general family use

liz·ard *n* **:** any of a group of reptiles having movable eyelids, ears that are outside the body, and usually four legs

lla·ma *n* **:** a South American hoofed animal that chews the cud

lo *interj* — used to call attention or to show wonder or surprise

¹load *n* **1 :** something taken up and carried **:** BURDEN **2 :** a mass or weight supported by something **3 :** something that depresses the mind or spirits **4 :** a charge for a firearm **5 :** the quantity of material loaded into a device at one time

²load *vb* **1 :** to put a load in or on **2 :** to supply abundantly **3 :** to put a load into — **load·er** *n*

¹loaf *n, pl* **loaves** **1 :** a usually oblong mass of bread **2 :** a dish (as of meat) baked in the form of a loaf

²loaf *vb* **:** to spend time idly or lazily — **loaf·er** *n*

loam *n* **:** a soil having the right amount of silt, clay, and sand for good plant growth

loamy *adj* **:** made up of or like loam

¹loan *n* **1 :** money loaned at interest **2 :** something loaned for a time to a borrower **3 :** permission to use something for a time

²loan *vb* **1 :** to give to another for temporary use with the understanding that the same or a like thing will be returned **2 :** LEND 3

loath *or* **loth** *adj* **:** not willing

loathe *vb* **loathed; loath·ing :** to dislike greatly

loathing *n* **:** very great dislike

loath·some *adj* **:** very unpleasant **:** OFFENSIVE — **loath·some·ly** *adv* — **loath·some·ness** *n*

loaves *pl of* LOAF

¹lob *vb* **lobbed; lob·bing :** to send (as a ball) in a high arc by hitting or throwing easily

²lob *n* **:** a lobbed throw or shot (as in tennis)

lob·by *n, pl* **lobbies :** a hall or entry especially when large enough to serve as a waiting room

lobe *n* **:** a rounded part — **lobed** *adj*

lob·ster *n* **:** a large edible sea crustacean with five pairs of legs of which the first pair usually has large claws

[1]**lo·cal** *adj* **1 :** of or relating to position in space **2 :** relating to a particular place — **lo·cal·ly** *adv*

[2]**local** *n* **1 :** a public vehicle (as a bus or train) that makes all or most stops on its run **2 :** a local branch (as of a lodge or labor union)

lo·cal·i·ty *n, pl* **lo·cal·i·ties :** a place and its surroundings

lo·cal·ize *vb* **lo·cal·ized; lo·cal·iz·ing :** to make or become local

lo·cate *vb* **lo·cat·ed; lo·cat·ing 1 :** to state and fix exactly the place or limits of **2 :** to settle or establish in a locality **3 :** to look and find the position of

lo·ca·tion *n* **1 :** the act or process of locating **2 :** a place fit for some use (as a building)

[1]**lock** *n* **:** a small bunch of hair or of fiber (as cotton or wool)

[2]**lock** *n* **1 :** a fastening (as for a door) in which a bolt is operated (as by a key) **2 :** the device for exploding the charge or cartridge of a firearm **3 :** an enclosure (as in a canal) with gates at each end used in raising or lowering boats as they pass from level to level

[3]**lock** *vb* **1 :** to fasten with or as if with a lock **2 :** to shut in or out by or as if by means of a lock **3 :** to make fast by the linking of parts together

lock·er *n* **:** a cabinet, compartment, or chest for personal use or for storing frozen food at a low temperature

lock·et *n* **:** a small ornamental case usually worn on a chain

lock·jaw *n* **:** TETANUS

lock·smith *n* **:** a worker who makes or repairs locks

lock·up *n* **:** PRISON

lo·co *adj* **:** not sane **:** CRAZY

lo·co·mo·tion *n* **:** the act or power of moving from place to place

lo·co·mo·tive *n* **:** a vehicle that moves under its own power and is used to haul cars on a railroad

lo·cust *n* **1 :** a grasshopper that moves in huge swarms and eats up the plants in its course **2 :** CICADA **3 :** a hardwood tree with feathery leaves and drooping flower clusters

lode·stone *n* **1 :** a rocky substance having magnetic properties **2 :** something that attracts strongly

[1]**lodge** *vb* **lodged; lodg·ing 1 :** to provide temporary quarters for **2 :** to use a place for living or sleeping **3 :** to come to rest **4 :** [3]FILE 2

[2]**lodge** *n* **1 :** a house set apart for residence in a special season or by an employee on an estate **2 :** the meeting place of a branch of a secret society

lodg·er *n* **:** a person who lives in a rented room in another's house

lodging *n* **1 :** a temporary living or sleeping place **2 lodgings** *pl* **:** a room or rooms in the house of another person rented as a place to live

loft *n* **1 :** an upper room or upper story of a building **2 :** a balcony in a church **3 :** an upper part of a barn

lofty *adj* **loft·i·er; loft·i·est 1 :** PROUD 1 **2 :** of high rank or fine quality **3 :** rising to a great height — **loft·i·ly** *adv* — **loft·i·ness** *n*

[1]**log** *n* **1 :** a large piece of rough timber **:** a long piece of a tree trunk trimmed and ready for sawing **2 :** a device for measuring the speed of a ship **3 :** the daily record of a ship's speed and progress **4 :** the record of a ship's voyage or of an aircraft's flight **5 :** a record of how something (as a piece of equipment) works in actual use

[2]**log** *vb* **logged; log·ging 1 :** to engage in cutting and hauling logs for timber **2 :** to put details of or about in a log

log·ger·head *n* **:** a very large sea turtle found in the warmer parts of the Atlantic ocean

log·ic *n* **1 :** a science that deals with the rules and tests of sound thinking and reasoning **2 :** sound reasoning

log·i·cal *adj* **1 :** having to do with logic **2 :** according to the rules of logic **3 :** according to what is reasonably expected — **log·i·cal·ly** *adv* — **log·i·cal·ness** *n*

log on *vb* **:** to establish a connection to and begin using a computer or network

-logy *n suffix* **:** area of knowledge **:** science

loin *n* **1 :** the part of the body between the hip and the lower ribs **2 :** a piece of meat (as beef) from the loin of an animal

loi·ter *vb* **1 :** to linger on one's way **2 :** to hang around idly — **loi·ter·er** *n*

loll *vb* **1 :** to hang loosely **:** DANGLE **2 :** to lie around lazily

lol·li·pop *or* **lol·ly·pop** *n* **:** a lump of hard candy on the end of a stick

lone *adj* **1 :** having no companion **2 :** being by itself

lone·ly *adj* **lone·li·er; lone·li·est 1 :** LONE 1 **2 :** not often visited **3 :** longing for companions — **lone·li·ness** *n*

lone·some *adj* **1 :** saddened by a lack of companions **2 :** not often visited or traveled over — **lone·some·ly** *adv* — **lone·some·ness** *n*

[1]**long** *adj* **lon•ger; lon•gest** **1 :** of great length from end to end **:** not short **2 :** having a greater length than breadth **3 :** lasting for some time **:** not brief **4 :** having a stated length (as in distance or time) **5 :** of, relating to, or being one of the vowel sounds \ā, ȧ, ē, ī, ō, ü\ and sometimes \ä\ and \ȯ\

[2]**long** *adv* **1 :** for or during a long time **2 :** for the whole length of **3 :** at a distant point of time

[3]**long** *n* **:** a long time

[4]**long** *vb* **:** to wish for something very much — **long•ing•ly** *adv*

long•hand *n* **:** HANDWRITING

long•horn *n* **:** any of the half-wild cattle with very long horns that were once common in the southwestern United States

long–horned *adj* **:** having long horns or antennae

long•ing *n* **:** an eager desire

long•ish *adj* **:** somewhat long

lon•gi•tude *n* **:** distance measured in degrees east or west of a line drawn (as through Greenwich, England) between the north and south poles

lon•gi•tu•di•nal *adj* **:** placed or running lengthwise — **lon•gi•tu•di•nal•ly** *adv*

long–lived *adj* **:** living or lasting for a long time

long–range *adj* **1 :** capable of traveling or shooting great distances **2 :** lasting over or providing for a long period

long•sight•ed *adj* **:** FARSIGHTED — **long•sight•ed•ness** *n*

long–suf•fer•ing *adj* **:** very patient and forgiving

long–wind•ed *adj* **1 :** too long **2 :** given to talking too long

[1]**look** *vb* **1 :** to use the power of vision **:** SEE **2 :** to appear suitable to **3 :** SEEM 1 **4 :** to turn one's attention or eyes **5 :** [2]FACE 2 — **look after :** to take care of — **look down on :** to regard with contempt — **look up to :** RESPECT 1

[2]**look** *n* **1 :** an act of looking **2 :** the way one appears to others **3 :** appearance that suggests what something is or means

looking glass *n* **:** [1]MIRROR 1

look•out *n* **1 :** a careful watch for something expected or feared **2 :** a high place from which a wide view is possible **3 :** a person who keeps watch

[1]**loom** *n* **:** a device for weaving cloth

[2]**loom** *vb* **:** to come into sight suddenly and often with a dim or strange appearance

loon *n* **:** a large diving bird that lives on fish and has webbed feet, a black head, and a black back spotted with white

[1]**loop** *n* **1 :** an almost oval form produced when something flexible and thin (as a wire or a rope) crosses itself **2 :** something (as a figure or bend) suggesting a flexible loop

[2]**loop** *vb* **:** to make a loop or loops in

loop•hole *n* **:** a way of escaping something

[1]**loose** *adj* **loos•er; loos•est** **1 :** not tightly fixed or fastened **2 :** not pulled tight **3 :** not tied up or shut in **4 :** not brought together in a package or binding **5 :** not respectable **6 :** having parts that are not squeezed tightly together **7 :** not exact or careful — **loose•ly** *adv* — **loose•ness** *n*

[2]**loose** *vb* **loosed; loos•ing** **1 :** to make loose **:** UNTIE **2 :** to set free

loose–leaf *adj* **:** arranged so that pages can be put in or taken out

loos•en *vb* **:** to make or become loose

[1]**loot** *n* **:** something stolen or taken by force

[2]**loot** *vb* **:** [1]PLUNDER — **loot•er** *n*

[1]**lope** *n* **:** a gait with long smooth steps

[2]**lope** *vb* **loped; lop•ing :** to go or ride at a lope

lop–eared *adj* **:** having ears that droop

lop•sid•ed *adj* **:** UNBALANCED 1 — **lop•sid•ed•ly** *adv* — **lop•sid•ed•ness** *n*

[1]**lord** *n* **1 :** a person having power and authority over others **2** *cap* **:** GOD 1 **3** *cap* **:** JESUS **4 :** a British nobleman or a bishop of the Church of England entitled to sit in the House of Lords — used as a title

[2]**lord** *vb* **:** to act in a proud or bossy way toward others

lord•ship *n* **:** the rank or dignity of a lord — used as a title

lore *n* **:** common knowledge or belief

lose *vb* **lost; los•ing** **1 :** to be unable to find or have at hand **:** MISLAY **2 :** to be deprived of **3 :** [2]WASTE 2 **4 :** to be defeated in **5 :** to fail to keep — **los•er** *n* — **lose one's way :** to stray from the right path

loss *n* **1 :** the act or fact of losing something **2 :** harm or distress that comes from losing something **3 :** something that is lost **4 :** failure to win

[1]**lost** *past of* LOSE

[2]**lost** *adj* **1 :** not used, won, or claimed **2 :** unable to find the way **3 :** come or brought to a bad end **4 :** no longer possessed or known **5 :** fully occupied

lot *n* **1 :** an object used in deciding something by chance or the use of such an object to decide something **2 :** FATE 2 **3 :** a piece or plot of land **4 :** a large number or amount

loth *variant of* LOATH

lo•tion *n* **:** a liquid preparation used on the skin for healing or as a cosmetic

lot•tery *n, pl* **lot•ter•ies :** a way of raising money in which many tickets are sold and a few of these are drawn to win prizes

lo•tus *n* **:** any of various water lilies

¹loud *adj* **1 :** not low, soft, or quiet in sound **:** NOISY **2 :** not quiet or calm in expression **3 :** too bright or showy to be pleasing — **loud·ly** *adv* — **loud·ness** *n*
²loud *adv* **:** in a loud manner
loud·speak·er *n* **:** an electronic device that makes sound louder
¹lounge *vb* **lounged; loung·ing 1 :** to move or act in a slow, tired, or lazy way **2 :** to stand, sit, or lie in a relaxed manner
²lounge *n* **1 :** a comfortable room where one can relax or lounge **2 :** SOFA
louse *n, pl* **lice 1 :** a small, wingless, and usually flat insect that lives on the bodies of warm-blooded animals **2 :** PLANT LOUSE
lov·able *adj* **:** deserving to be loved or admired — **lov·able·ness** *n* — **lov·ably** *adv*
¹love *n* **1 :** great and warm affection (as of a child for a parent) **2 :** a great liking **3 :** a beloved person
²love *vb* **loved; lov·ing 1 :** to feel warm affection for **2 :** to like very much — **lov·er** *n*
love·ly *adj* **love·li·er; love·li·est 1 :** very beautiful **2 :** very pleasing — **love·li·ness** *n*
lov·ing *adj* **:** feeling or showing love **:** AFFECTIONATE — **lov·ing·ly** *adv*
¹low *vb* **:** to make the calling sound of a cow **:** MOO
²low *n* **:** the mooing of a cow **:** MOO
³low *adj* **1 :** not high **:** not tall **2 :** lying or going below the usual level **3 :** not loud **:** SOFT **4 :** deep in pitch **5 :** ¹PROSTRATE 3 **6 :** SAD 1 **7 :** less than usual (as in quantity or value) **8 :** COARSE 4, VULGAR **9 :** not favorable **:** POOR — **low·ness** *n*
⁴low *n* **1 :** something that is low **2 :** a region of low barometric pressure **3 :** the arrangement of gears in an automobile that gives the lowest speed of travel
⁵low *adv* **:** so as to be low
¹low·er *adj* **1 :** being below the other of two similar persons or things **2 :** less advanced
²lower *vb* **1 :** to move to a lower level **:** SINK **2 :** to let or pull down **3 :** to make or become less (as in value or amount) **4 :** to make or become lower
low·land *n* **:** low flat country
¹low·ly *adv* **:** in a humble way
²lowly *adj* **low·li·er; low·li·est :** of low rank or condition **:** HUMBLE — **low·li·ness** *n*
loy·al *adj* **1 :** faithful to one's country **2 :** faithful to a person or thing one likes or believes in — **loy·al·ly** *adv*
loy·al·ty *n, pl* **loy·al·ties :** the quality or state of being loyal
loz·enge *n* **:** a small candy often containing medicine
LSD *n* **:** a dangerous drug that causes hallucinations
lu·bri·cant *n* **:** something (as oil or grease) that makes a surface smooth or slippery
lu·bri·cate *vb* **lu·bri·cat·ed; lu·bri·cat·ing 1 :** to make smooth or slippery **2 :** to apply oil or grease to
lu·bri·ca·tion *n* **:** the act or process of lubricating or the state of being lubricated
lu·cid *adj* **1 :** showing a normal state of mind **2 :** easily understood — **lu·cid·ly** *adv* — **lu·cid·ness** *n*
luck *n* **1 :** something that happens to a person by or as if by chance **2 :** the accidental way events occur **3 :** good fortune
lucky *adj* **luck·i·er; luck·i·est 1 :** helped by luck **:** FORTUNATE **2 :** happening because of good luck **3 :** thought of as bringing good luck — **luck·i·ly** *adv*
lu·di·crous *adj* **:** funny because of being ridiculous **:** ABSURD — **lu·di·crous·ly** *adv* — **lu·di·crous·ness** *n*
lug *vb* **lugged; lug·ging :** to find hard to carry or haul
lug·gage *n* **:** BAGGAGE
luke·warm *adj* **1 :** neither hot nor cold **2 :** not very interested or eager
¹lull *vb* **:** to make or become quiet or less watchful
²lull *n* **:** a period of calm (as in a storm)
lul·la·by *n, pl* **lul·la·bies :** a song for helping babies to sleep
¹lum·ber *vb* **:** to move in an awkward way
²lumber *n* **:** timber especially when sawed into boards
³lumber *vb* **:** to cut logs **:** saw logs into lumber
lum·ber·jack *n* **:** a person who works at lumbering
lum·ber·man *n, pl* **lum·ber·men :** a boss lumberjack
lum·ber·yard *n* **:** a place where a stock of lumber is kept for sale
lu·mi·nous *adj* **:** shining brightly — **lu·mi·nous·ly** *adv*
¹lump *n* **:** a small uneven mass (as a chunk or a swelling)
²lump *vb* **1 :** to form into a lump **2 :** to group together
lu·nar *adj* **1 :** of or relating to the moon **2 :** measured by the revolutions of the moon
¹lu·na·tic *adj* **1 :** INSANE 1, CRAZY **2 :** INSANE 2
²lunatic *n* **:** an insane person
¹lunch *n* **1 :** a light meal especially when eaten in the middle of the day **2 :** food prepared for lunch
²lunch *vb* **:** to eat lunch
lun·cheon *n* **1 :** ¹LUNCH 1 **2 :** a formal lunch

lung *n* **:** either of two organs in the chest that are like bags and are the main breathing structure in animals that breathe air

¹lunge *n* **:** a sudden movement forward

²lunge *vb* **lunged; lung·ing :** to push or drive with force

lung·fish *n* **:** any of several fishes that breathe with structures like lungs as well as with gills

lu·pine *n* **:** a plant related to the clovers that has tall spikes of showy flowers like those of sweet peas

¹lurch *n* **1 :** a sudden roll of a ship to one side **2 :** a swaying staggering movement or gait

²lurch *vb* **:** to move with a lurch

¹lure *n* **1 :** something that attracts or draws one on **:** TEMPTATION **2 :** an artificial bait for catching fish

²lure *vb* **lured; lur·ing :** to tempt or lead away by offering some pleasure or advantage **:** ENTICE

lu·rid *adj* **1 :** looking like glowing fire seen through smoke **2 :** SENSATIONAL 2 — **lu·rid·ly** *adv* — **lu·rid·ness** *n*

lurk *vb* **:** to hide in or about a place

lus·cious *adj* **1 :** very sweet and pleasing to taste and smell **2 :** delightful to hear, see, or feel — **lus·cious·ly** *adv* — **lus·cious·ness** *n*

lush *adj* **1 :** very juicy and fresh **2 :** covered with a thick growth — **lush·ly** *adv* — **lush·ness** *n*

lus·ter *or* **lus·tre** *n* **:** a glow of reflected light **:** SHEEN

lus·trous *adj* **:** having luster

lute *n* **:** an old stringed instrument with a body shaped like a pear and usually paired strings played with the fingers

lux·u·ri·ant *adj* **:** growing freely and well — **lux·u·ri·ant·ly** *adv*

lux·u·ri·ous *adj* **1 :** loving pleasure and luxury **2 :** very fine and comfortable — **lux·u·ri·ous·ly** *adv* — **lux·u·ri·ous·ness** *n*

lux·u·ry *n, pl* **lux·u·ries 1 :** very rich, pleasant, and comfortable surroundings **2 :** something desirable but expensive or hard to get **3 :** something pleasant but not really needed for one's pleasure or comfort

¹-ly *adj suffix* **1 :** like **:** similar to **2 :** happening in each specified period of time **:** every

²-ly *adv suffix* **1 :** in a specified manner **2 :** from a specified point of view

lye *n* **:** a dangerous compound containing sodium that dissolves in water and is used in cleaning

lying *present participle of* LIE

lymph *n* **:** a clear liquid like blood without the red cells that nourishes the tissues and carries off wastes

lym·phat·ic *adj* **:** of or relating to lymph

lynx *n, pl* **lynx** *or* **lynx·es :** any of several wildcats with rather long legs, a short tail, and often ears with small bunches of long hairs at the tip

lyre *n* **:** a stringed instrument like a harp used by the ancient Greeks

¹lyr·ic *n* **1 :** a lyric poem **2 lyrics** *pl* **:** the words of a popular song

²lyric *adj* **1 :** suitable for singing **:** MUSICAL **2 :** expressing personal emotion

lyr·i·cal *adj* **:** ²LYRIC

M

m *n, pl* **m's** *or* **ms** *often cap* **1 :** the thirteenth letter of the English alphabet **2 :** 1000 in Roman numerals

ma *n, often cap* **:** ¹MOTHER 1

ma'am *n* **:** MADAM

mac·ad·am *n* **:** a road surface made of small closely packed broken stone

ma·caque *n* **:** any of several mostly Asian monkeys with short tails

mac·a·ro·ni *n, pl* **macaronis** *or* **macaronies :** a food that is made of a mixture of flour and water formed into tubes and dried

mac·a·roon *n* **:** a cookie made of the white of eggs, sugar, and ground almonds or coconut

ma·caw *n* **:** a large parrot of Central and South America with a long tail, a harsh voice, and bright feathers

¹mace *n* **:** a spice made from the dried outer covering of the nutmeg

²mace *n* **:** a fancy club carried before certain officials as a sign of authority

ma·chete *n* **:** a large heavy knife used for cutting sugarcane and underbrush and as a weapon

¹ma·chine *n* **1 :** VEHICLE 2 **2 :** a device that combines forces, motion, and energy in a way that does some desired work

²machine *vb* **ma·chined; ma·chin·ing :** to shape or finish by tools run by machines

machine gun *n* **:** an automatic gun for continuous firing

ma·chin·ery *n* **1 :** a group of machines **2 :** the working parts of a machine **3 :** the people and equipment by which something is done

machine shop *n* **:** a workshop in which metal articles are machined and put together

ma·chin·ist *n* **:** a person who makes or works on machines

mack•er•el *n, pl* **mackerel** *or* **mackerels :** a food fish of the North Atlantic that is green with blue bars above and silvery below
mack•i•naw *n* **:** a short heavy woolen coat
ma•cron *n* **:** a mark {macr} placed over a vowel to show that the vowel is long
mad *adj* **mad•der; mad•dest 1 :** INSANE 1 **2 :** done or made without thinking **3 :** ANGRY **4 :** INFATUATED **5 :** having rabies **6 :** marked by intense and often disorganized activity — **mad•ly** *adv* — **mad•ness** *n*
mad•am *n, pl* **mes•dames** — used without a name as a form of polite address to a woman
[1]**mad•cap** *adj* **:** likely to do something mad or reckless **:** done for fun without thinking
[2]**madcap** *n* **:** a madcap person
mad•den *vb* **:** to make mad
made *past of* MAKE
made–up *adj* **:** showing more imagination than concern with fact
mad•house *n* **:** a place or scene of complete confusion
mag•a•zine *n* **1 :** a storehouse or warehouse for military supplies **2 :** a place for keeping explosives in a fort or ship **3 :** a container in a gun for holding cartridges **4 :** a publication issued at regular intervals (as weekly or monthly)
mag•got *n* **:** a legless grub that is the larva of a two-winged fly
[1]**mag•ic** *n* **1 :** the power to control natural forces possessed by certain persons (as wizards and witches) in folk tales and fiction **2 :** a power that seems mysterious **3 :** something that charms **4 :** the art or skill of performing tricks or illusions as if by magic for entertainment
[2]**magic** *adj* **1 :** of or relating to magic **2 :** having effects that seem to be caused by magic **3 :** giving a feeling of enchantment
mag•i•cal *adj* **:** [2]MAGIC
ma•gi•cian *n* **:** a person skilled in magic
magic lantern *n* **:** an early kind of slide projector
mag•is•trate *n* **1 :** a chief officer of government **2 :** a local official with some judicial power
mag•ma *n* **:** molten rock within the earth
mag•na•nim•i•ty *n* **:** the quality of being magnanimous
mag•nan•i•mous *adj* **1 :** having a noble and courageous spirit **2 :** being generous and forgiving — **mag•nan•i•mous•ly** *adv*
mag•ne•sium *n* **:** a silvery white metallic chemical element that is lighter than aluminum and is used in lightweight alloys
mag•net *n* **:** a piece of material (as of iron, steel, or alloy) that is able to attract iron
mag•net•ic *adj* **1 :** acting like a magnet **2 :** of or relating to the earth's magnetism **3 :** having a great power to attract people
magnetic field *n* **:** the portion of space near a magnetic body within which magnetic forces can be detected
magnetic needle *n* **:** a narrow strip of magnetized steel that is free to swing around to show the direction of the earth's magnetism
magnetic pole *n* **1 :** either of the poles of a magnet **2 :** either of two small regions of the earth which are located near the North and South Poles and toward which a compass needle points
magnetic tape *n* **:** a thin ribbon of plastic coated with a magnetic material on which information (as sound) may be stored
mag•ne•tism *n* **1 :** the power to attract that a magnet has **2 :** the power to attract others **:** personal charm
mag•ne•tize *vb* **mag•ne•tized; mag•ne•tiz•ing :** to cause to be magnetic
mag•ne•to *n, pl* **mag•ne•tos :** a small generator used especially to produce the spark in some gasoline engines
mag•nif•i•cent *adj* **:** having impressive beauty **:** very grand — **mag•nif•i•cent•ly** *adv*
mag•ni•fy *vb* **mag•ni•fied; mag•ni•fy•ing 1 :** to enlarge in fact or appearance **2 :** to cause to seem greater or more important **:** EXAGGERATE
magnifying glass *n* **:** a lens that magnifies something seen through it
mag•ni•tude *n* **:** greatness of size
mag•no•lia *n* **:** a tree or tall shrub having showy white, pink, yellow, or purple flowers that appear before or sometimes with the leaves
mag•pie *n* **:** a noisy black-and-white bird related to the jays
ma•hog•a•ny *n, pl* **ma•hog•a•nies :** a strong reddish brown wood that is used especially for furniture and is obtained from several tropical trees
maid *n* **1 :** an unmarried girl or woman **2 :** a female servant
[1]**maid•en** *n* **:** an unmarried girl or woman
[2]**maiden** *adj* **1 :** UNMARRIED **2 :** [1]FIRST 2
maid•en•hair fern *n* **:** a fern with slender stems and delicate feathery leaves
maid•en•hood *n* **:** the state or time of being a maiden
maiden name *n* **:** a woman's family name before she is married
maid of honor : an unmarried woman who stands with the bride at a wedding
[1]**mail** *n* **1 :** letters, parcels, and papers sent from one person to another through the post office **2 :** the whole system used in the public sending and delivering of mail **3 :** something that comes in the mail

²mail *vb* **:** to send by mail
³mail *n* **:** a fabric made of metal rings linked together and used as armor
mail•box *n* **1 :** a public box in which to place outgoing mail **2 :** a private box (as on a house) for the delivery of incoming mail
mail carrier *n* **:** LETTER CARRIER
mail•man *n, pl* **mail•men :** LETTER CARRIER
maim *vb* **:** to injure badly or cripple by violence
¹main *n* **1 :** physical strength **:** FORCE **2 :** HIGH SEAS **3 :** the chief part **:** essential point **4 :** a principal line, tube, or pipe of a utility system
²main *adj* **1 :** first in size, rank, or importance **:** CHIEF **2 :** PURE 3, SHEER — **main•ly** *adv*
main•land *n* **:** a continent or the main part of a continent as distinguished from an offshore island or sometimes from a cape or peninsula
main•mast *n* **:** the principal mast of a sailing ship
main•sail *n* **:** the principal sail on the mainmast
main•spring *n* **:** the principal spring in a mechanical device (as a watch or clock)
main•stay *n* **1 :** the large strong rope from the maintop of a ship usually to the foot of the foremast **2 :** a chief support
main•tain *vb* **1 :** to keep in a particular or desired state **2 :** to defend by argument **3 :** CARRY ON 3, CONTINUE **4 :** to provide for **:** SUPPORT **5 :** to insist to be true
main•te•nance *n* **1 :** the act of maintaining **:** the state of being maintained **2 :** UPKEEP
main•top *n* **:** a platform around the head of a mainmast
maize *n* **:** INDIAN CORN
ma•jes•tic *adj* **:** very impressive and dignified **:** NOBLE — **ma•jes•ti•cal•ly** *adv*
maj•es•ty *n, pl* **maj•es•ties 1 :** royal dignity or authority **2 :** the quality or state of being majestic **3** — used as a title for a king, queen, emperor, or empress
¹ma•jor *adj* **1 :** greater in number, quantity, rank, or importance **2 :** of or relating to a musical scale of eight notes with half steps between the third and fourth and between the seventh and eighth notes and with whole steps between all the others
²major *n* **:** a commissioned officer in the Army, Air Force, or Marine Corps ranking above a captain
major general *n* **:** a commissioned officer in the Army, Air Force, or Marine Corps ranking above a brigadier general
ma•jor•i•ty *n, pl* **ma•jor•i•ties 1 :** the age at which one is allowed to vote **2 :** a number greater than half of a total **3 :** the amount by which a majority is more than a minority **4 :** a group or party that makes up the greater part of a whole body of persons
¹make *vb* **made; mak•ing 1 :** to cause to occur **2 :** to form or put together out of material or parts **3 :** to combine to produce **4 :** to set in order **:** PREPARE **5 :** to cause to be or become **6 :** ¹DO 1, PERFORM **7 :** to produce by action **8 :** COMPEL **9 :** GET 1, GAIN **10 :** to act so as to be — **make believe :** to act as if something known to be imaginary is real or true — **make good 1 :** FULFILL, COMPLETE **2 :** SUCCEED 3
²make *n* **1 :** the way in which a thing is made **:** STRUCTURE **2 :** ¹BRAND 4
¹make–be•lieve *n* **:** a pretending to believe (as in children's play)
²make–believe *adj* **:** not real **:** IMAGINARY
make out *vb* **1 :** to write out **2 :** UNDERSTAND 1 **3 :** IDENTIFY 3 **4 :** ¹FARE
¹make•shift *n* **:** a thing used as a temporary substitute for another
²makeshift *adj* **:** serving as a temporary substitute
make•up *n* **1 :** the way the parts or elements of something are put together or joined **2 :** materials used in changing one's appearance (as for a play or other entertainment) **3 :** any of various cosmetics (as lipstick or powder)
make up *vb* **1 :** to create from the imagination **2 :** ²FORM 3, COMPOSE **3 :** ¹RECOMPENSE, ATONE **4 :** to become friendly again **5 :** to put on makeup — **make up one's mind :** to reach a decision
mal- *prefix* **1 :** bad **:** badly **2 :** abnormal **:** abnormally
mal•ad•just•ed *adj* **:** not properly adjusted
mal•a•dy *n, pl* **mal•a•dies :** a disease or ailment of body or mind
ma•lar•ia *n* **:** a serious disease with chills and fever that is spread by the bite of one kind of mosquito
¹male *n* **:** an individual that produces germ cells (as sperm) that fertilize the eggs of a female
²male *adj* **1 :** of, relating to, or being the sex that fathers young **2 :** bearing stamens but no pistil **3 :** of, relating to, or like that of males — **male•ness** *n*
mal•for•ma•tion *n* **:** something that is badly or wrongly formed
mal•ice *n* **:** ILL WILL
ma•li•cious *adj* **1 :** doing mean things for pleasure **2 :** done just to be mean — **ma•li•cious•ly** *adv*
¹ma•lign *adj* **:** MALIGNANT 1
²malign *vb* **:** to say evil things about **:** SLANDER

ma•lig•nant *adj* **1 :** evil in influence or result : INJURIOUS **2 :** MALICIOUS 1 **3 :** likely to cause death : DEADLY — **ma•lig•nant•ly** *adv*

mall *n* **1 :** a shaded walk : PROMENADE **2 :** a usually paved or grassy strip between two roadways **3 :** a shopping area in a community with a variety of shops around an often covered space for pedestrians

mal•lard *n* **:** a common wild duck of the northern hemisphere that is the ancestor of the domestic ducks

mal•lea•ble *adj* **:** capable of being beaten out, extended, or shaped by hammer blows

mal•let *n* **1 :** a hammer with a short handle and a barrel-shaped head of wood or soft material used for driving a tool (as a chisel) or for striking a surface without denting it **2 :** a club with a short thick rod for a head and a long thin rod for a handle

mal•low *n* **:** a tall plant related to the hollyhock that has usually lobed leaves and white, rose, or purplish flowers with five petals

mal•nu•tri•tion *n* **:** faulty nourishment

malt *n* **1 :** grain and especially barley soaked in water until it has sprouted **2 :** MALTED MILK

malt•ed milk *n* **:** a beverage made by dissolving a powder made from dried milk and cereals in a liquid (as milk)

mal•treat *vb* **:** to treat in a rough or unkind way : ABUSE

ma•ma *or* **mam•ma** *n* **:** [1]MOTHER 1

mam•mal *n* **:** a warm-blooded animal that feeds its young with milk and has a backbone, two pairs of limbs, and a more or less complete covering of hair

[1]**mam•moth** *n* **:** a very large hairy extinct elephant with tusks that curve upward

[2]**mammoth** *adj* **:** very large : HUGE

mam•my *n, pl* **mammies :** [1]MOTHER 1

[1]**man** *n, pl* **men 1 :** a human being : PERSON **2 :** an adult male human being **3 :** the human race : MANKIND **4 :** a member of the natural family to which human beings belong including both modern humans and extinct related forms **5 :** HUSBAND **6 :** an adult male servant or employee **7 :** one of the pieces with which various games (as chess or checkers) are played

[2]**man** *vb* **manned; man•ning 1 :** to station crew members at **2 :** to do the work of operating

man•age *vb* **man•aged; man•ag•ing 1 :** to look after and make decisions about : be the boss of **2 :** to achieve what one wants to do

man•age•ment *n* **1 :** the managing of something **2 :** the people who manage

man•ag•er *n* **:** a person who manages — **man•ag•er•ship** *n*

man•a•tee *n* **:** a mainly tropical water-dwelling mammal that eats plants and has a broad rounded tail

man•da•rin *n* **:** a high public official of the Chinese Empire

man•date *n* **1 :** an order from a higher court to a lower court **2 :** the instruction given by voters to their elected representatives

man•di•ble *n* **1 :** a lower jaw often with its soft parts **2 :** either the upper or lower part of the bill of a bird **3 :** either of the first pair of mouth parts of some invertebrates (as an insect or crustacean) that often form biting organs

man•do•lin *n* **:** a small stringed instrument with four pairs of strings played by plucking

mane *n* **:** long heavy hair growing from the neck or shoulders of an animal (as a horse or lion) — **maned** *adj*

[1]**ma•neu•ver** *n* **1 :** a planned movement of troops or ships **2 :** a training exercise by armed forces **3 :** skillful action or management

[2]**maneuver** *vb* **1 :** to move in a maneuver **2 :** to perform a maneuver **3 :** to guide skillfully — **ma•neu•ver•able** *adj*

ma•neu•ver•abil•i•ty *n* **:** the quality or state of being maneuverable

man•ga•nese *n* **:** a grayish white brittle metallic chemical element that resembles iron

mange *n* **:** a contagious skin disease usually of domestic animals in which there is itching and loss of hair

man•ger *n* **:** an open box in which food for farm animals is placed

man•gle *vb* **man•gled; man•gling 1 :** to cut or bruise with repeated blows **2 :** to spoil while making or performing

man•go *n, pl* **man•goes** *or* **man•gos :** a juicy somewhat acid tropical fruit that is yellow or reddish and is borne by an evergreen tree related to the sumac

mangy *adj* **mang•i•er; mang•i•est 1 :** having mange or resulting from mange **2 :** SHABBY 2 **3 :** SEEDY 2

man•hole *n* **:** a covered hole (as in a street or tank) large enough to let a person pass through

man•hood *n* **1 :** COURAGE **2 :** the state of being an adult human male **3 :** adult human males

ma•nia *n* **1 :** often violent or excited insanity **2 :** unreasonable enthusiasm

ma•ni•ac *n* **:** a violently insane person

[1]**man•i•cure** *n* **1 :** MANICURIST **2 :** a treatment for the care of the hands and nails

²manicure *vb* **man·i·cured; man·i·cur·ing** : to give a manicure to

man·i·cur·ist *n* : a person who gives manicures

¹man·i·fest *adj* : clear to the senses or to the mind : easy to recognize : OBVIOUS

²manifest *vb* : to show plainly

man·i·fes·ta·tion *n* **1 :** the act of manifesting **2 :** something that makes clear : EVIDENCE

man·i·fold *adj* : of many and various kinds

ma·nip·u·late *vb* **ma·nip·u·lat·ed; ma·nip·u·lat·ing 1 :** to work with the hands or by mechanical means and especially with skill **2 :** to manage skillfully and especially with intent to deceive

man·kind *n* **1 :** human beings **2 :** men as distinguished from women

man·ly *adj* **man·li·er; man·li·est :** having qualities (as courage) often felt to be proper for a man — **man·li·ness** *n*

man–made *adj* : made by people rather than nature

man·na *n* : food supplied by a miracle to the Israelites in the wilderness

man·ne·quin *n* : a form representing the human figure used especially for displaying clothes

man·ner *n* **1 :** ¹SORT 1 **2 :** a way of acting **3 manners** *pl* **:** behavior toward or in the presence of other people

man·ner·ism *n* : a habit (as of looking or moving in a certain way) that one notices in a person's behavior

man·ner·ly *adj* : showing good manners : POLITE

man–of–war *n, pl* **men–of–war :** WARSHIP

man·or *n* : a large estate

man·sion *n* : a large fine house

man·slaugh·ter *n* : the unintentional but unlawful killing of a person

man·tel *n* : a shelf above a fireplace

man·tel·piece *n* **1 :** a shelf above a fireplace along with side pieces **2 :** MANTEL

man·tis *n, pl* **man·tis·es** *or* **man·tes :** an insect related to the grasshoppers and roaches that feeds on other insects which are clasped in the raised front legs

man·tle *n* **1 :** a loose sleeveless outer garment **2 :** something that covers or wraps **3 :** a fold of the body wall of a mollusk that produces the shell material **4 :** the part of the earth's interior beneath the crust and above the central core

¹man·u·al *adj* **1 :** of or relating to the hands **2 :** done or operated by the hands — **man·u·al·ly** *adv*

²manual *n* : HANDBOOK

manual training *n* : training in work done with the hands and in useful arts

¹man·u·fac·ture *n* **1 :** the making of products by hand or machinery **2 :** PRODUCTION 2

²manufacture *vb* **man·u·fac·tured; man·u·fac·tur·ing :** to make from raw materials by hand or machinery — **man·u·fac·tur·er** *n*

ma·nure *n* : material (as animal wastes) used to fertilize land

man·u·script *n* **1 :** a composition or document written by hand especially before the development of printing **2 :** a document submitted for publication **3 :** HANDWRITING

¹many *adj* **more; most 1 :** amounting to a large number **2 :** being one of a large but not fixed number

²many *pron* : a large number

³many *n* : a large number

¹map *n* **1 :** a picture or chart showing features of an area (as the surface of the earth or the moon) **2 :** a picture or chart of the sky showing the position of stars and planets

²map *vb* **mapped; map·ping 1 :** to make a map of **2 :** to plan in detail

ma·ple *n* : any of a group of trees having deeply notched leaves, fruits with two wings, and hard pale wood and including some whose sap is evaporated to a sweet syrup (**maple syrup**) and a brownish sugar (**maple sugar**)

mar *vb* **marred; mar·ring :** to make a blemish on : SPOIL

ma·ra·ca *n* : a musical rhythm instrument made of a dried gourd with seeds or pebbles inside that is usually played in pairs by shaking

mar·a·thon *n* **1 :** a long-distance running race **2 :** a long hard contest

¹mar·ble *n* **1 :** limestone that is capable of taking a high polish and is used in architecture and sculpture **2 :** a little ball (as of glass) used in a children's game (**marbles**)

²marble *adj* : made of or like marble

¹march *vb* **1 :** to move or cause to move along steadily usually with long even steps and in step with others **2 :** to make steady progress — **march·er** *n*

²march *n* **1 :** the action of marching **2 :** the distance covered in marching **3 :** a regular step used in marching **4 :** a musical piece in a lively rhythm with a strong beat that is suitable to march to

March *n* : the third month of the year

mar·chio·ness *n* **1 :** the wife or widow of a marquess **2 :** a woman who holds the rank of a marquess in her own right

mare *n* : an adult female of the horse or a related animal (as a zebra or donkey)

mar·ga·rine *n* : a food product made usually

from vegetable oils and skim milk and used as a spread or for cooking

mar·gin *n* **1 :** the part of a page outside the main body of print or writing **2 :** [1]BORDER 1 **3 :** an extra amount (as of time or money) allowed for use if needed

mari·gold *n* **:** any of several plants related to the daisies that are grown for their yellow or brownish red and yellow flower heads

mar·i·jua·na *n* **:** dried leaves and flowers of the hemp plant smoked as a drug

ma·ri·na *n* **:** a dock or basin providing a place to anchor motorboats and yachts

[1]ma·rine *adj* **1 :** of or relating to the sea **2 :** of or relating to the navigation of the sea **:** NAUTICAL **3 :** of or relating to marines

[2]marine *n* **1 :** the ships of a country **2 :** one of a class of soldiers serving on board a ship or in close cooperation with a naval force

mar·i·ner *n* **:** SEAMAN 1, SAILOR

mar·i·o·nette *n* **:** a doll that can be made to move by means of strings **:** PUPPET

mar·i·tal *adj* **:** of or relating to marriage

mar·i·time *adj* **1 :** of or relating to ocean navigation or trade **2 :** bordering on or living near the sea

[1]mark *n* **1 :** something designed or serving to record position **2 :** something aimed at **:** TARGET **3 :** the starting line of a race **4 :** INDICATION 2 **5 :** a blemish (as a scratch or stain) made on a surface **6 :** a written or printed symbol **7 :** a grade or score showing the quality of work or conduct

[2]mark *vb* **1 :** to set apart by a line or boundary **2 :** to make a mark on **3 :** to decide and show the value or quality of by marks **:** GRADE **4 :** to be an important characteristic of **5 :** to take notice of — **mark·er** *n*

[3]mark *n* **:** a German coin or bill

marked *adj* **1 :** having a mark or marks **2 :** NOTICEABLE

[1]mar·ket *n* **1 :** a meeting of people at a fixed time and place to buy and sell things **2 :** a public place where a market is held **3 :** a store where foods are sold to the public **4 :** the region in which something can be sold

[2]market *vb* **:** to buy or sell in a market

mar·ket·place *n* **:** an open square or place in a town where markets or public sales are held

mark·ing *n* **:** a mark made

marks·man *n, pl* **marks·men :** a person who shoots well — **marks·man·ship** *n*

mar·ma·lade *n* **:** a jam containing pieces of fruit and fruit rind

mar·mo·set *n* **:** a small monkey of South and Central America with soft fur and a bushy tail

mar·mot *n* **:** a stocky animal with short legs, coarse fur, and bushy tail that is related to the squirrels

[1]ma·roon *vb* **:** to put ashore and abandon on a lonely island or coast

[2]maroon *n* **:** a dark red

mar·quess *n* **:** a British nobleman ranking below a duke and above an earl

mar·quis *n* **:** MARQUESS

mar·quise *n* **:** MARCHIONESS

mar·riage *n* **1 :** the legal relationship into which a man and a woman enter with the purpose of making a home and raising a family **2 :** the act of getting married

mar·row *n* **:** a soft tissue rich in fat and blood vessels that fills the cavities of most bones

mar·ry *vb* **mar·ried; mar·ry·ing 1 :** to join in marriage as husband and wife **2 :** to give (as one's child) in marriage **3 :** to take for husband or wife **4 :** to enter into a marriage relationship

Mars *n* **:** the planet that is fourth in order of distance from the sun, is known for its redness, and has a diameter of about 6800 kilometers

marsh *n* **:** an area of soft wet land usually overgrown with grasses and related plants

[1]mar·shal *n* **1 :** a person who arranges and directs ceremonies **2 :** an officer of the highest rank in some military forces **3 :** a federal official having duties similar to those of a sheriff **4 :** the head of a division of a city government

[2]marshal *vb* **mar·shaled** *or* **mar·shalled; mar·shal·ing** *or* **mar·shal·ling :** to arrange in order

marsh·mal·low *n* **:** a soft spongy sweet made from corn syrup, sugar, and gelatin

marsh marigold *n* **:** a swamp plant with shiny leaves and bright yellow flowers like buttercups

marshy *adj* **marsh·i·er; marsh·i·est :** like or being a marsh

mar·su·pi·al *n* **:** any of a group of mammals (as kangaroos and opossums) that do not develop a true placenta and that usually have a pouch on the female's abdomen in which the young are carried

mart *n* **:** a trading place **:** MARKET

mar·ten *n* **:** a slender animal larger than the related weasels that eats flesh and is sought for its soft gray or brown fur

mar·tial *adj* **:** having to do with or suitable for war

mar·tin *n* **1 :** a European swallow with a forked tail **2 :** any of several birds (as the American **purple martin**) resembling or related to the true martin

Mar·tin Lu·ther King Day *n* **:** the third Monday in January observed as a legal holiday in some states of the United States

¹mar·tyr *n* **:** a person who suffers greatly or dies rather than give up his or her religion or principles

²martyr *vb* **:** to put to death for refusing to give up a belief

¹mar·vel *n* **:** something that causes wonder or astonishment

²marvel *vb* **mar·veled** *or* **mar·velled; mar·vel·ing** *or* **mar·vel·ling :** to be struck with astonishment or wonder

mar·vel·ous *or* **mar·vel·lous** *adj* **1 :** causing wonder or astonishment **2 :** of the finest kind or quality — **mar·vel·ous·ly** *adv*

mas·cot *n* **:** a person, animal, or object adopted by a group and believed to bring good luck

mas·cu·line *adj* **1 :** of the male sex **2 :** ²MALE 3

¹mash *vb* **:** to make into a soft pulpy mass

²mash *n* **1 :** a mixture of ground feeds used for feeding livestock **2 :** a mass of something made soft and pulpy by beating or crushing

¹mask *n* **1 :** a cover for the face or part of the face used for disguise or protection **2 :** something that disguises or conceals **3 :** a copy of a face molded in wax or plaster

²mask *vb* **:** CONCEAL, DISGUISE

ma·son *n* **:** a person who builds or works with stone, brick, or cement

ma·son·ry *n, pl* **ma·son·ries 1 :** the art, trade, or occupation of a mason **2 :** the work done by a mason **3 :** something built of stone, brick, or concrete

masque *n* **1 :** ¹MASQUERADE 1 **2 :** an old form of dramatic entertainment in which the actors wore masks

¹mas·quer·ade *n* **1 :** a party (as a dance) at which people wear masks and costumes **2 :** a pretending to be something one is not

²masquerade *vb* **mas·quer·ad·ed; mas·quer·ad·ing 1 :** to disguise oneself **2 :** to pass oneself off as something one is not **:** POSE — **mas·quer·ad·er** *n*

¹mass *n* **1 :** an amount of something that holds or clings together **2 :** BULK 1, SIZE **3 :** the principal part **:** main body **4 :** a large quantity or number **5 masses** *pl* **:** the body of ordinary or common people

²mass *vb* **:** to collect into a mass

Mass *n* **:** a religious service in celebration of the Eucharist

¹mas·sa·cre *n* **:** the violent and cruel killing of a large number of persons

²massacre *vb* **mas·sa·cred; mas·sa·cring :** to kill in a massacre **:** SLAUGHTER

¹mas·sage *n* **:** treatment of the body by rubbing, kneading, and tapping

²massage *vb* **mas·saged; mas·sag·ing :** to give massage to

mas·sive *adj* **:** very large, heavy, and solid

mast *n* **1 :** a long pole that rises from the bottom of a ship and supports the sails and rigging **2 :** a vertical or nearly vertical tall pole — **mast·ed** *adj*

¹mas·ter *n* **1 :** a male teacher **2 :** an artist or performer of great skill **3 :** one having authority over another person or thing **4 :** EMPLOYER **5** — used as a title for a young boy too young to be called *mister*

²master *vb* **1 :** to get control of **2 :** to become skillful at

master chief petty officer *n* **:** a petty officer in the Navy or Coast Guard ranking above a senior chief petty officer

mas·ter·ful *adj* **1 :** tending to take control **:** BOSSY **2 :** having or showing great skill

mas·ter·ly *adj* **:** showing the knowledge or skill of a master

mas·ter·piece *n* **:** a work done or made with supreme skill

master sergeant *n* **:** a noncommissioned officer in the Army ranking above a sergeant first class or in the Air Force ranking above a technical sergeant or in the Marine Corps ranking above a gunnery sergeant

mas·tery *n, pl* **mas·ter·ies 1 :** the position or authority of a master **2 :** VICTORY 1 **3 :** skill that makes one master of something

mast·head *n* **:** the top of a mast

mas·ti·cate *vb* **mas·ti·cat·ed; mas·ti·cat·ing :** ¹CHEW

mas·tiff *n* **:** a very large powerful dog with a smooth coat

¹mat *n* **1 :** a piece of coarse woven or braided fabric used as a floor or seat covering **2 :** a piece of material in front of a door to wipe the shoes on **3 :** a piece of material (as cloth or woven straw) used under dishes or vases or as an ornament **4 :** a pad or cushion for gymnastics or wrestling **5 :** something made up of many tangled strands

²mat *vb* **mat·ted; mat·ting :** to form into a tangled mass

mat·a·dor *n* **:** a bullfighter who plays the chief human part in a bullfight

¹match *n* **1 :** a person or thing that is equal to or as good as another **2 :** a thing that is exactly like another thing **3 :** two people or things that go well together **4 :** MARRIAGE 1 **5 :** a contest between two individuals or teams

²match *vb* **1 :** to place in competition **2 :** to choose something that is the same as another or goes with it **3 :** to be the same or suitable to one another

³match *n* **1 :** a wick or cord that is made to burn evenly and is used for lighting a charge of powder **2 :** a short slender piece of material tipped with a mixture that produces fire when scratched

match·book *n* **:** a small folder containing rows of paper matches

match·less *adj* **:** having no equal **:** better than any other of the same kind — **match·less·ly** *adv*

match·lock *n* **:** a musket with a hole at the rear of the barrel into which a slowly burning cord is lowered to ignite the charge

¹mate *n* **1 :** COMPANION 1, COMRADE **2 :** an officer on a ship used to carry passengers or freight who ranks below the captain **3 :** either member of a married couple **4 :** either member of a breeding pair of animals **5 :** either of two matched objects

²mate *vb* **mat·ed; mat·ing :** to join as mates **:** MARRY

¹ma·te·ri·al *adj* **1 :** of, relating to, or made of matter **:** PHYSICAL **2 :** of or relating to a person's bodily needs or wants **3 :** having real importance — **ma·teri·al·ly** *adv*

²material *n* **1 :** the elements, substance, or parts of which something is made or can be made **2 materials** *pl* **:** equipment needed for doing something

ma·te·ri·al·ize *vb* **ma·te·ri·al·ized; ma·te·ri·al·iz·ing 1 :** to cause to take on a physical form **2 :** to become actual fact

ma·ter·nal *adj* **1 :** of or relating to a mother **2 :** related through one's mother — **ma·ter·nal·ly** *adv*

ma·ter·ni·ty *n* **:** the state of being a mother

math *n* **:** MATHEMATICS

math·e·mat·i·cal *adj* **1 :** of or relating to mathematics **2 :** ²EXACT — **math·e·mat·i·cal·ly** *adv*

math·e·ma·ti·cian *n* **:** a specialist in mathematics

math·e·mat·ics *n* **:** the science that studies and explains numbers, quantities, measurements, and the relations between them

mat·i·nee *or* **mat·i·née** *n* **:** a musical or dramatic performance in the afternoon

mat·ri·mo·ni·al *adj* **:** of or relating to marriage

mat·ri·mo·ny *n* **:** MARRIAGE 1

ma·tron *n* **1 :** a married woman **2 :** a woman who is in charge of the household affairs of an institution **3 :** a woman who looks after women prisoners in a police station or prison

¹mat·ter *n* **1 :** something to be dealt with or considered **2 :** PROBLEM 2, DIFFICULTY **3 :** the substance things are made of **:** something that takes up space and has weight **4 :** material substance of a certain kind or function **5 :** PUS **6 :** a more or less definite quantity or amount **7 :** ¹MAIL 1 — **no matter :** it makes no difference

²matter *vb* **:** to be of importance

mat·ter–of–fact *adj* **:** sticking to or concerned with fact

mat·ting *n* **:** material for mats

mat·tress *n* **1 :** a springy pad for use as a resting place usually over springs on a bedstead **2 :** a sack that can be filled with air or water and used as a mattress

¹ma·ture *adj* **1 :** fully grown or developed **:** ADULT, RIPE **2 :** like that of a mature person

²mature *vb* **ma·tured; ma·tur·ing :** to reach maturity

ma·tu·ri·ty *n* **:** the condition of being mature **:** full development

¹maul *n* **:** a heavy hammer used especially for driving wedges or posts

²maul *vb* **1 :** to beat and bruise severely **2 :** to handle roughly

mauve *n* **:** a medium purple, violet, or lilac

maxi- *prefix* **:** very long or large

max·il·la *n, pl* **max·il·lae 1 :** an upper jaw especially of a mammal **2 :** either of the pair of mouth parts next behind the mandibles of an arthropod (as an insect or a crustacean)

max·im *n* **:** a short saying expressing a general truth or rule of conduct

¹max·i·mum *n, pl* **maximums** *or* **max·i·ma :** the highest value **:** greatest amount

²maximum *adj* **:** as great as possible in amount or degree

may *helping verb, past* **might;** *present sing & pl* **may 1 :** have permission to **2 :** be in some degree likely to **3** — used to express a wish **4** — used to express purpose

May *n* **:** the fifth month of the year

may·be *adv* **:** possibly but not certainly

mayn't : may not

may·on·naise *n* **:** a creamy dressing usually made of egg yolk, oil, and vinegar or lemon juice

may·or *n* **:** an official elected to serve as head of a city or borough

maze *n* **:** a confusing arrangement of paths or passages

MB *n* **:** MEGABYTE

me *pron objective case of* I

mead·ow *n* **:** usually moist and low grassland

mead·ow·lark *n* **:** a bird that has brownish upper parts and a yellow breast and is about as large as a robin

mea·ger *or* **mea·gre** *adj* **1 :** having little flesh **:** THIN **2 :** INSUFFICIENT

¹meal *n* **1 :** the food eaten or prepared for eating at one time **2 :** the act or time of eating

²meal *n* **1 :** usually coarsely ground seeds of a cereal grass and especially of Indian corn **2 :** something like meal in texture

mealy *adj* **meal·i·er; meal·i·est :** like meal — **meal·i·ness** *n*

¹mean *vb* **meant; mean·ing** **1 :** to have in mind as a purpose **:** INTEND **2 :** to intend for a particular use **3 :** to have as a meaning **:** SIGNIFY

²mean *adj* **1 :** low in quality, worth, or dignity **2 :** lacking in honor or dignity **3 :** STINGY 1 **4 :** deliberately unkind **5 :** ASHAMED 1 — **mean·ly** *adv* — **mean·ness** *n*

³mean *adj* **:** occurring or being in a middle position **:** AVERAGE

⁴mean *n* **1 :** a middle point or something (as a place, time, number, or rate) that falls at or near a middle point **:** MODERATION **2 :** ARITHMETIC MEAN **3 means** *pl* **:** something that helps a person to get what he or she wants **4 means** *pl* **:** WEALTH 1 — **by all means :** CERTAINLY 1 — **by any means :** in any way — **by means of :** through the use of — **by no means :** certainly not

me·an·der *vb* **1 :** to follow a winding course **2 :** to wander without a goal or purpose

mean·ing *n* **1 :** the idea a person intends to express by something said or done **2 :** the quality of communicating something or of being important

mean·ing·ful *adj* **:** having a meaning or purpose — **mean·ing·ful·ly** *adv*

mean·ing·less *adj* **:** having no meaning or importance

¹mean·time *n* **:** the time between two events

²meantime *adv* **:** in the meantime

¹mean·while *n* **:** ¹MEANTIME

²meanwhile *adv* **1 :** ²MEANTIME **2 :** at the same time

mea·sles *n sing or pl* **1 :** a contagious disease in which there are fever and red spots on the skin **2 :** any of several diseases (as **German measles**) resembling true measles

mea·sly *adj* **mea·sli·er; mea·sli·est :** so small or unimportant as to be rejected with scorn

mea·sur·able *adj* **:** capable of being measured

¹mea·sure *n* **1 :** EXTENT 2, DEGREE, AMOUNT **2 :** the size, capacity, or quantity of something as fixed by measuring **3 :** something (as a yardstick or cup) used in measuring **4 :** a unit used in measuring **5 :** a system of measuring **6 :** the notes and rests between bar lines on a musical staff **7 :** a way of accomplishing something **8 :** a legislative bill or act

²measure *vb* **mea·sured; mea·sur·ing** **1 :** to find out the size, extent, or amount of **2 :** ¹ESTIMATE 1 **3 :** to bring into comparison **4 :** to give a measure of **:** INDICATE **5 :** to have as its measurement

mea·sure·ment *n* **1 :** the act of measuring **2 :** the extent, size, capacity, or amount of something as fixed by measuring **3 :** a system of measures

measure up *vb* **:** to satisfy needs or requirements

meat *n* **1 :** solid food **2 :** the part of something that can be eaten **3 :** animal and especially mammal tissue for use as food **4 :** the most important part **:** SUBSTANCE — **meat·less** *adj*

me·chan·ic *n* **:** a person who makes or repairs machines

me·chan·i·cal *adj* **1 :** of or relating to machinery **2 :** made or operated by a machine **3 :** done or produced as if by a machine **:** lacking freshness and individuality — **me·chan·i·cal·ly** *adv*

me·chan·ics *n sing or pl* **1 :** a science dealing with the action of forces on bodies **2 :** the way something works or things are done

mech·a·nism *n* **1 :** a mechanical device **2 :** the parts by which a machine operates **3 :** the parts or steps that make up a process or activity

mech·a·nize *vb* **mech·a·nized; mech·a·niz·ing** **1 :** to make mechanical or automatic **2 :** to equip with machinery

med·al *n* **:** a piece of metal often in the form of a coin with design and words in honor of a special event, a person, or an achievement

me·dal·lion *n* **1 :** a large medal **2 :** something like a large medal (as in shape)

med·dle *vb* **med·dled; med·dling :** to interest oneself in what is not one's concern

med·dle·some *adj* **:** given to meddling

media *pl of* MEDIUM

med·i·cal *adj* **:** of or relating to the science or practice of medicine or to the treatment of disease — **med·i·cal·ly** *adv*

med·i·cate *vb* **med·i·cat·ed; med·i·cat·ing** **1 :** to use medicine on or for **2 :** to add medicinal material to

med·i·ca·tion *n* **1 :** the act or process of medicating **2 :** medicinal material

me·dic·i·nal *adj* **:** used or likely to relieve or cure disease — **me·dic·i·nal·ly** *adv*

med·i·cine *n* **1 :** something used to cure or relieve a disease **2 :** a science or art dealing with the prevention, cure, or relief of disease

medicine dropper *n* **:** DROPPER 2

medicine man *n* **:** a member of a primitive tribe believed to have magic powers and called on to cure illnesses and keep away evil spirits

me·di·eval *or* **me·di·ae·val** *adj* **:** of or relating to the Middle Ages

me·di·o·cre *adj* **:** neither good nor bad **:** ORDINARY

med·i·tate *vb* **med·i·tat·ed; med·i·tat·ing** **1 :** to consider carefully **:** PLAN **2 :** to spend time in quiet thinking **:** REFLECT

med·i·ta·tion *n* **:** the act or an instance of meditating

Med·i·ter·ra·nean *adj* **:** of or relating to the Mediterranean sea or to the lands or peoples surrounding it

1**me·di·um** *n, pl* **me·di·ums** *or* **me·dia** **1 :** something that is between or in the middle **2 :** the thing by which or through which something is done **3 :** the substance in which something lives or acts **4 :** a person through whom other persons try to communicate with the spirits of the dead

2**medium** *adj* **:** intermediate in amount, quality, position, or degree

med·ley *n, pl* **medleys** **1 :** MIXTURE 2, JUMBLE **2 :** a musical selection made up of a series of different songs or parts of different compositions

me·dul·la ob·lon·ga·ta *n* **:** the last part of the brain that joins the spinal cord and is concerned especially with control of involuntary activities (as breathing and beating of the heart)

meed *n* **:** something deserved or earned **:** REWARD

meek *adj* **1 :** putting up with injury or abuse with patience **2 :** lacking spirit or self-confidence — **meek·ly** *adv* — **meekness** *n*

1**meet** *vb* **met; meet·ing** **1 :** to come upon or across **2 :** to be at a place to greet or keep an appointment **3 :** to approach from the opposite direction **4 :** to come together **:** JOIN, MERGE **5 :** to be sensed by **6 :** to deal with **7 :** to fulfill the requirements of **:** SATISFY **8 :** to become acquainted **9 :** to hold a meeting

2**meet** *n* **:** a meeting for sports competition

meet·ing *n* **1 :** the act of persons or things that meet **2 :** ASSEMBLY 1

meet·ing·house *n* **:** a building used for public assembly and especially for Protestant worship

mega·byte *n* **:** a unit of computer information storage capacity equal to 1,048,576 bytes

mega·phone *n* **:** a device shaped like a cone that is used to direct the voice and increase its loudness

1**mel·an·choly** *n* **:** a sad or gloomy mood

2**melancholy** *adj* **:** SAD 1

1**mel·low** *adj* **1 :** tender and sweet because of ripeness **2 :** made mild by age **3 :** being clear, full, and pure **:** not coarse — **mel·lowness** *n*

2**mellow** *vb* **:** to make or become mellow

me·lo·di·ous *adj* **:** agreeable to the ear because of its melody — **me·lo·di·ous·ly** *adv* — **me·lo·di·ous·ness** *n*

mel·o·dy *n, pl* **mel·o·dies** **1 :** pleasing arrangement of sounds **2 :** a series of musical notes or tones arranged in a definite pattern of pitch and rhythm **3 :** the leading part in a musical composition

mel·on *n* **:** a fruit (as a watermelon) having juicy and usually sweet flesh and growing on a vine related to the gourds

melt *vb* **1 :** to change from a solid to a liquid usually through the action of heat **2 :** to grow less **:** DISAPPEAR **3 :** to make or become gentle **:** SOFTEN **4 :** to lose clear outline

melting point *n* **:** the temperature at which a solid melts

mem·ber *n* **1 :** a part (as an arm, leg, leaf, or branch) of a person, animal, or plant **2 :** one of the individuals (as persons) or units (as species) making up a group **3 :** a part of a structure

mem·ber·ship *n* **1 :** the state or fact of being a member **2 :** the whole number of members

mem·brane *n* **:** a thin soft flexible layer especially of animal or plant tissue

mem·bra·nous *adj* **:** made of or like membrane

me·men·to *n, pl* **me·men·tos** *or* **me·men·toes** **:** something that serves as a reminder

mem·o·ra·ble *adj* **:** worth remembering **:** not easily forgotten — **mem·o·ra·bly** *adv*

mem·o·ran·dum *n, pl* **mem·o·ran·dums** *or* **mem·o·ran·da** **1 :** an informal record or message **2 :** a written reminder

1**me·mo·ri·al** *adj* **:** serving to preserve the memory of a person or event

2**memorial** *n* **:** something by which the memory of a person or an event is kept alive **:** MONUMENT

Memorial Day *n* **1 :** May 30 once observed as a legal holiday in remembrance of war dead **2 :** the last Monday in May observed as a legal holiday in most states of the United States

mem·o·rize *vb* **mem·o·rized; mem·o·riz·ing** **:** to learn by heart

mem·o·ry *n, pl* **mem·o·ries** **1 :** the power or process of remembering **2 :** the store of things learned and kept in the mind **3 :** the act of remembering and honoring **4 :** something remembered **5 :** the time within which past events are remembered **6 :** a device or part in a computer which can receive and store information for use when wanted **7 :** capacity for storing information

men *pl of* MAN

¹men·ace *n* **1 :** DANGER 2 **2 :** an annoying person

²menace *vb* **men·aced; men·ac·ing :** THREATEN 1

me·nag·er·ie *n* **:** a collection of confined wild animals

¹mend *vb* **1 :** IMPROVE, CORRECT **2 :** to restore to a whole condition **3 :** to improve in health — **mend·er** *n*

²mend *n* **1 :** the process of improving **2 :** a mended place

men·folk *or* **men·folks** *n pl* **:** the men of a family or community

men·ha·den *n, pl* **menhaden :** a fish of the Atlantic coast of the United States that is related to the herrings and is a source of oil and fertilizer

¹me·ni·al *n* **:** a household servant

²menial *adj* **:** of, relating to, or suitable for servants **:** not needing skill

men–of–war *pl of* MAN-OF-WAR

men·stru·a·tion *n* **:** a periodic discharge of bloody fluid from the uterus

-ment *n suffix* **1 :** result, goal, or method of a specified action **2 :** action **:** process **3 :** place of a specified action **4 :** state **:** condition

men·tal *adj* **1 :** of or relating to the mind **2 :** done in the mind — **men·tal·ly** *adv*

men·tal·i·ty *n* **:** mental power **:** ability to learn

men·thol *n* **:** a white crystalline soothing substance from oils of mint

¹men·tion *n* **:** a brief reference to something

²mention *vb* **:** to refer to **:** speak about briefly

menu *n* **1 :** a list of dishes served at or available for a meal **2 :** the dishes or kinds of food served at a meal **3 :** a list shown on a computer screen from which a user can select an operation for the computer to perform

¹me·ow *n* **:** the cry of a cat

²meow *vb* **:** to utter a meow

mer·can·tile *adj* **:** of or relating to merchants or trade

¹mer·ce·nary *n, pl* **mer·ce·nar·ies :** a soldier from a foreign country hired to fight in an army

²mercenary *adj* **1 :** doing something only for the pay or reward **2 :** greedy for money

mer·chan·dise *n* **:** goods that are bought and sold in trade

mer·chant *n* **1 :** a person who carries on trade especially on a large scale or with foreign countries **2 :** STOREKEEPER 2

mer·chant·man *n, pl* **mer·chant·men :** a ship used in trading

merchant marine *n* **1 :** the trading ships of a nation **2 :** the persons who work in a merchant marine

mer·ci·ful *adj* **:** having or showing mercy or compassion — **mer·ci·ful·ly** *adv*

mer·ci·less *adj* **:** having no mercy **:** PITILESS — **mer·ci·less·ly** *adv*

mer·cu·ric *adj* **:** of, relating to, or containing mercury

mer·cu·ry *n* **1 :** a heavy silvery white metallic chemical element that is liquid at ordinary temperatures **2 :** the column of mercury in a thermometer or barometer **3** *cap* **:** the planet that is nearest the sun and has a diameter of about 4700 kilometers

mer·cy *n, pl* **mer·cies 1 :** kind and gentle treatment of a wrongdoer, an opponent, or some unfortunate person **2 :** a kind sympathetic disposition **:** willingness to forgive, spare, or help **3 :** a blessing as an act of divine love **4 :** a fortunate happening

mere *adj, superlative* **mer·est :** nothing more than **:** SIMPLE

mere·ly *adv* **:** nothing else than **:** JUST

merge *vb* **merged; merg·ing :** to be or cause to be combined or blended into a single unit

merg·er *n* **:** a combination of two or more businesses into one

me·rid·i·an *n* **1 :** the highest point reached **2 :** any imaginary semicircle on the earth reaching from the north to the south pole **3 :** a representation of a meridian on a map or globe numbered according to degrees of longitude

me·ringue *n* **1 :** a mixture of beaten white of egg and sugar put on pies or cakes and browned **2 :** a shell made of baked meringue and filled with fruit or ice cream

me·ri·no *n, pl* **me·ri·nos 1 :** a sheep of a breed that produces a heavy fleece of white fine wool **2 :** a fine soft fabric like cashmere

¹mer·it *n* **1 :** the condition or fact of deserving well or ill **2 :** ²WORTH 1, VALUE **3 :** a quality worthy of praise **:** VIRTUE

²merit *vb* **:** to be worthy of or have a right to

mer·i·to·ri·ous *adj* **:** deserving reward or honor **:** PRAISEWORTHY — **mer·i·to·ri·ous·ly** *adv*

mer·maid *n* **:** an imaginary sea creature usually shown with a woman's body and a fish's tail

mer·man *n, pl* **mer·men :** an imaginary sea creature usually shown with a man's body and a fish's tail

mer·ri·ment *n* **:** GAIETY, MIRTH

mer·ry *adj* **mer·ri·er; mer·ri·est 1 :** full of good humor and good spirits **:** JOYOUS **2**

: full of gaiety or festivity — **mer·ri·ly** *adv*
mer·ry–go–round *n* **:** a circular revolving platform fitted with seats and figures of animals on which people sit for a ride
mer·ry·mak·er *n* **:** one taking part in merrymaking
mer·ry·mak·ing *n* **1 :** merry activity **2 :** a festive occasion **:** PARTY
me·sa *n* **:** a hill with a flat top and steep sides
mesdames *pl of* MADAM *or of* MRS.
¹mesh *n* **1 :** one of the spaces enclosed by the threads of a net or the wires of a sieve or screen **2 :** NETWORK 1 2 **3 :** the coming or fitting together of the teeth of two sets of gears
²mesh *vb* **:** to fit together **:** INTERLOCK
Mes·o·zo·ic *n* **:** an era of geological history which extends from the Paleozoic to the Cenozoic and in which dinosaurs are present and the first birds and mammals and flowering plants appear
mes·quite *n* **:** a spiny shrub or small tree of the southwestern United States and Mexico that is related to the clovers
¹mess *n* **1 :** a group of people (as military personnel) who regularly eat together **2 :** the meal eaten by a mess **3 :** a state of confusion or disorder
²mess *vb* **1 :** to take meals with a mess **2 :** to make dirty or untidy **3 :** to mix up **:** BUNGLE **4 :** to work without serious goal **:** PUTTER **5 :** ²FOOL 2, INTERFERE
mes·sage *n* **:** a communication in writing, in speech, or by signals
mes·sen·ger *n* **:** a person who carries a message or does an errand
Messrs. *pl of* MR.
messy *adj* **mess·i·er; mess·i·est :** UNTIDY — **mess·i·ly** *adv* — **mess·i·ness** *n*
met *past of* MEET
met·a·bol·ic *adj* **:** of or relating to metabolism — **met·a·bol·i·cal·ly** *adv*
me·tab·o·lism *n* **:** the processes by which a living being uses food to obtain energy and build tissue and disposes of waste material
¹met·al *n* **1 :** a substance (as gold, tin, copper, or bronze) that has a more or less shiny appearance, is a good conductor of electricity and heat, and usually can be made into a wire or hammered into a thin sheet **2 :** METTLE
²metal *adj* **:** made of metal
me·tal·lic *adj* **1 :** of, relating to, or being a metal **2 :** containing or made of metal
met·al·lur·gi·cal *adj* **:** of or relating to metallurgy
met·al·lur·gy *n* **:** the science of obtaining metals from their ores and preparing them for use
meta·mor·phic *adj* **:** formed by the action of pressure, heat, and water that results in a more compact form
meta·mor·pho·sis *n, pl* **meta·mor·pho·ses** **:** a sudden and very great change especially in appearance or structure
met·a·phor *n* **:** a figure of speech comparing two unlike things without using *like* or *as*
mete *vb* **met·ed; met·ing :** ALLOT
me·te·or *n* **:** one of the small pieces of matter in the solar system that enter the earth's atmosphere where friction may cause them to glow and form a streak of light
me·te·or·ic *adj* **1 :** of or relating to a meteor or group of meteors **2 :** like a meteor in speed or in sudden and temporary brilliance
me·te·or·ite *n* **:** a meteor that reaches the surface of the earth
me·te·o·rol·o·gist *n* **:** a specialist in meteorology
me·te·o·rol·o·gy *n* **:** a science that deals with the atmosphere, weather, and weather forecasting
¹me·ter *n* **1 :** a planned rhythm in poetry that is usually repeated **2 :** the repeated pattern of musical beats in a measure
²meter *n* **:** a measure of length on which the metric system is based and which is equal to about 39.37 inches
³meter *n* **:** an instrument for measuring and sometimes recording the amount of something
-meter *n suffix* **:** instrument for measuring
meth·od *n* **1 :** a certain way of doing something **2 :** careful arrangement **:** PLAN
me·thod·i·cal *adj* **1 :** showing or done or arranged by method **2 :** following a method out of habit **:** SYSTEMATIC — **me·thod·i·cal·ly** *adv*
met·ric *adj* **1 :** of or relating to measurement **2 :** of or relating to the metric system
met·ri·cal *adj* **:** of or relating to meter (as in poetry or music)
metric system *n* **:** a system of weights and measures in which the meter is the unit of length and the kilogram is the unit of weight
metric ton *n* **:** a unit of weight equal to 1000 kilograms
met·ro·nome *n* **:** a device for marking exact musical tempo by regularly repeated ticks
me·trop·o·lis *n* **1 :** the chief or capital city of a country, state, or region **2 :** a large or important city
met·ro·pol·i·tan *adj* **:** of, relating to, or like that of a metropolis
met·tle *n* **:** strength of spirit **:** COURAGE — **on one's mettle :** aroused to do one's best
¹mew *vb* **:** to make a meow or a similar sound

²mew *n* : MEOW
¹Mex·i·can *adj* : of or relating to Mexico or the Mexicans
²Mexican *n* : a person born or living in Mexico
mi *n* : the third note of the musical scale
mi·ca *n* : a mineral that easily breaks into very thin transparent sheets
mice *pl of* MOUSE
micr- *or* **micro-** *prefix* **1** : small : tiny **2** : millionth
mi·crobe *n* : a very tiny and often harmful plant or animal : MICROORGANISM
mi·cro·com·put·er *n* : PERSONAL COMPUTER
mi·cro·film *n* : a film on which something (as printing or a drawing) is recorded in very much smaller size
mi·crom·e·ter *n* **1** : an instrument used with a telescope or microscope for measuring very small distances **2** : MICROMETER CALIPER
micrometer caliper *n* : an instrument having a rod moved by fine screw threads and used for making exact measurements
mi·cro·or·gan·ism *n* : an organism (as a bacterium) of microscopic or less than microscopic size
mi·cro·phone *n* : an instrument in which sound is changed into an electrical effect for transmitting or recording (as in radio or television)
mi·cro·pro·ces·sor *n* : a computer processor contained on an integrated-circuit chip
mi·cro·scope *n* : an instrument with one or more lenses used to help a person to see something very small by making it appear larger
mi·cro·scop·ic *adj* **1** : of, relating to, or conducted with the microscope **2** : so small as to be visible only through a microscope : very tiny — **mi·cro·scop·i·cal·ly** *adv*
¹mi·cro·wave *n* **1** : a radio wave between one millimeter and one meter in wavelength **2** : MICROWAVE OVEN
²microwave *vb* : to cook or heat in a microwave oven
microwave oven *n* : an oven in which food is cooked by the heat produced as a result of penetration of the food by microwaves
¹mid *adj* : being the part in the middle
²mid *prep* : AMID
mid·air *n* : a region in the air some distance above the ground
mid·day *n* : NOON
¹mid·dle *adj* **1** : equally distant from the ends : CENTRAL **2** : being at neither extreme
²middle *n* : the middle part, point, or position : CENTER
middle age *n* : the period of life from about forty to about sixty years of age — **middle–aged** *adj*
Middle Ages *n pl* : the period of European history from about A.D. 500 to about 1500
middle class *n* : a social class between that of the wealthy and the poor
middle school *n* : a school usually including grades 5 to 8 or 6 to 8
mid·dy *n, pl* **middies** **1** : MIDSHIPMAN **2** : a loose blouse with a collar cut wide and square in the back
midge *n* : a very small fly or gnat
midg·et *n* : one (as a person) that is much smaller than usual or normal
mid·night *n* : twelve o'clock at night
mid·rib *n* : the central vein of a leaf
mid·riff *n* **1** : the middle part of the surface of the human body **2** : a part of a garment that covers the midriff
mid·ship·man *n, pl* **mid·ship·men** : a student naval officer
¹midst *n* **1** : the inside or central part **2** : a position among the members of a group **3** : the condition of being surrounded
²midst *prep* : in the midst of
mid·stream *n* : the part of a stream away from both sides
mid·sum·mer *n* **1** : the middle of summer **2** : the summer solstice
mid·way *adv or adj* : in the middle of the way or distance : HALFWAY
mid·win·ter *n* **1** : the middle of winter **2** : the winter solstice
mid·year *n* : the middle of a year
mien *n* : a person's appearance or way of acting that shows mood or personality
¹might *past of* MAY — used as a helping verb to show that something is possible but not likely
²might *n* : power that can be used (as by a person or group)
mightn't : might not
¹mighty *adj* **might·i·er**; **might·i·est** **1** : having great power or strength **2** : done by might : showing great power **3** : great in influence, size, or effect — **might·i·ly** *adv*
²mighty *adv* : ²VERY 1
mi·grant *n* : one that migrates
mi·grate *vb* **mi·grat·ed**; **mi·grat·ing** **1** : to move from one country or region to another **2** : to pass from one region to another on a regular schedule
mi·gra·tion *n* **1** : the act or an instance of migrating **2** : a group of individuals that are migrating
mi·gra·to·ry *adj* **1** : having a way of life that includes making migrations **2** : of or relating to migration

mike *n* **:** MICROPHONE
milch *adj* **:** giving milk **:** kept for milking
mild *adj* **1 :** gentle in personality or behavior **2 :** not strong or harsh in action or effect — **mild·ly** *adv* — **mild·ness** *n*
1mil·dew *n* **1 :** a thin whitish growth of fungus on decaying material or on living plants **2 :** a fungus that grows as a mildew
2mildew *vb* **:** to become affected with mildew
mile *n* **1 :** a measure of distance (**statute mile**) equal to 5280 feet (1609 meters) **2 :** a measure of distance (**geographical mile** or **nautical mile**) equal to about 6076 feet (1852 meters)
mile·age *n* **1 :** an amount of money given for traveling expenses at a certain rate per mile **2 :** distance or distance covered in miles **3 :** the number of miles that something (as a car or tire) will travel before wearing out **4 :** the average number of miles a car or truck will travel on a gallon of fuel
mile·stone *n* **1 :** a stone showing the distance in miles to a stated place **2 :** an important point in progress or development
1mil·i·tary *adj* **1 :** of or relating to soldiers, the army, or war **2 :** carried on by soldiers **:** supported by armed force
2military *n, pl* **military :** members of the armed forces
mi·li·tia *n* **:** a body of citizens having some military training but called into service only in emergencies
1milk *n* **1 :** a whitish liquid secreted by the breasts or udder of a female mammal as food for her young **2 :** a liquid (as a plant juice) like milk
2milk *vb* **:** to draw off the milk of (as by pressing or sucking)
milk·maid *n* **:** DAIRYMAID
milk·man *n, pl* **milk·men :** a person who sells or delivers milk
milk of mag·ne·sia : a white liquid containing an oxide of magnesium in water and used as a laxative
milk shake *n* **:** a drink made of milk, a flavoring syrup, and ice cream shaken or mixed thoroughly
milk tooth *n* **:** one of the first and temporary teeth that in humans number twenty
milk·weed *n* **:** any of a group of plants with milky juice and flowers in dense clusters
milky *adj* **milk·i·er; milk·i·est 1 :** like milk in color or thickness **2 :** full of or containing milk — **milk·i·ness** *n*
Milky Way *n* **1 :** a broad band of light that stretches across the sky and is caused by the light of a very great number of faint stars **2 :** MILKY WAY GALAXY
Milky Way galaxy *n* **:** the galaxy of which the sun and the solar system are a part and which contains the stars that make up the Milky Way
1mill *n* **1 :** a building in which grain is ground into flour **2 :** a machine used in processing (as by grinding, crushing, stamping, cutting, or finishing) raw material **3 :** a factory using machines
2mill *vb* **1 :** to grind into flour or powder **2 :** to shape or finish by means of a rotating cutter **3 :** to give a raised rim to (a coin) **4 :** to move about in a circle or in disorder
3mill *n* **:** one tenth of a cent
mil·len·ni·um *n, pl* **mil·len·nia** *or* **millenniums 1 :** a period of 1000 years **2 :** a 1000th anniversary or its celebration — **mil·len·ni·al** *adj*
mill·er *n* **1 :** a person who works in or runs a flour mill **2 :** a moth whose wings seem to be covered with flour or dust
mil·let *n* **:** an annual grass with clusters of small usually white seeds that is grown as a cereal and for animals to graze
milli- *prefix* **:** thousandth
mil·li·gram *n* **:** a unit of weight equal to $^1/_{1000}$ gram
mil·li·li·ter *n* **:** a unit of capacity equal to $^1/_{1000}$ liter
mil·li·me·ter *n* **:** a unit of length equal to $^1/_{1000}$ meter
mil·li·ner *n* **:** a person who makes, trims, or sells women's hats
1mil·lion *n* **1 :** one thousand thousands **:** 1,000,000 **2 :** a very large number
2million *adj* **:** being 1,000,000
mil·lion·aire *n* **:** a person having a million dollars or more
1mil·lionth *adj* **:** being last in a series of a million
2millionth *n* **:** number 1,000,000 in a series
mil·li·pede *n* **:** an animal that is an arthropod with a long body somewhat like that of a centipede but with two pairs of legs on most of its many body sections
mill·stone *n* **:** either of two circular stones used for grinding grain
mill wheel *n* **:** a waterwheel that drives a mill
mim·eo·graph *n* **:** a machine for making copies of typewritten, written, or drawn matter by means of stencils
1mim·ic *n* **:** one that mimics another
2mimic *vb* **mim·icked; mim·ick·ing 1 :** to imitate very closely **2 :** to make fun of by imitating
min·a·ret *n* **:** a tall slender tower of a mosque with a balcony from which the people are called to prayer
mince *vb* **minced; minc·ing 1 :** to cut or chop very fine **2 :** to act or speak in an un-

naturally dainty way **3 :** to keep (what one says) within the bounds of politeness

mince·meat *n* **:** a mixture of finely chopped and cooked raisins, apples, suet, spices, and sometimes meat that is used chiefly as a filling for pie (**mince pie**)

¹mind *n* **1 :** MEMORY 1 **2 :** the part of a person that feels, understands, thinks, wills, and especially reasons **3 :** INTENTION 1 **4 :** OPINION 1

²mind *vb* **1 :** to pay attention to **:** HEED **2 :** to pay careful attention to and obey **3 :** to be bothered about **4 :** to object to **:** DISLIKE **5 :** to take charge of

mind·ed *adj* **1 :** having a specified kind of mind **2 :** greatly interested in one thing

mind·ful *adj* **:** keeping in mind

¹mine *pron* **:** that which belongs to me

²mine *n* **1 :** a pit or tunnel from which minerals (as coal, gold, or diamonds) are taken **2 :** an explosive buried in the ground and set to explode when disturbed (as by an enemy soldier or vehicle) **3 :** an explosive placed in a case and sunk in the water to sink enemy ships **4 :** a rich source of supply

³mine *vb* **mined; min·ing 1 :** to dig a mine **2 :** to obtain from a mine **3 :** to work in a mine **4 :** to dig or form mines under a place **5 :** to lay military mines in or under — **min·er** *n*

¹min·er·al *n* **1 :** a naturally occurring substance (as diamond or quartz) that results from processes other than those of plants and animals **2 :** a naturally occurring substance (as ore, coal, petroleum, natural gas, or water) obtained for humans to use usually from the ground

²mineral *adj* **1 :** of or relating to minerals **2 :** containing gases or mineral salts

mineral kingdom *n* **:** a basic group of natural objects that includes objects consisting of matter that does not come from plants and animals

min·gle *vb* **min·gled; min·gling 1 :** to mix or be mixed so that the original parts can still be recognized **2 :** to move among others within a group

mini- *prefix* **:** very short or small

¹min·i·a·ture *n* **1 :** a copy on a much reduced scale **2 :** a very small portrait especially on ivory or metal

²miniature *adj* **:** very small **:** represented on a small scale

min·i·mize *vb* **min·i·mized; min·i·miz·ing :** to make as small as possible

¹min·i·mum *n, pl* **min·i·ma** *or* **min·i·mums :** the lowest amount

²minimum *adj* **:** being the least possible

min·ing *n* **:** the process or business of working mines

¹min·is·ter *n* **1 :** a Protestant clergyman **2 :** a government official at the head of a section of government activities **3 :** a person who represents his or her government in a foreign country

²minister *vb* **:** to give aid or service

min·is·try *n, pl* **min·is·tries 1 :** the act of ministering **2 :** the office or duties of a minister **3 :** a body of ministers **4 :** a section of a government headed by a minister

mink *n* **1 :** an animal related to the weasel that has partly webbed feet and lives around water **2 :** the soft thick usually brown fur of a mink

min·now *n* **1 :** any of various small freshwater fishes (as a shiner) related to the carps **2 :** a fish that looks like a true minnow

¹mi·nor *adj* **1 :** less in size, importance, or value **2 :** of or relating to a musical scale having the third tone lowered a half step

²minor *n* **:** a person too young to have full civil rights

mi·nor·i·ty *n, pl* **mi·nor·i·ties 1 :** the state of being a minor **2 :** a number less than half of a total **3 :** a part of a population that is in some ways different from others and that is sometimes disliked or given unfair treatment

min·strel *n* **1 :** an entertainer in the Middle Ages who sang verses and played a harp **2 :** one of a group of entertainers with blackened faces who sing, dance, and tell jokes

¹mint *n* **1 :** any of a group of fragrant herbs and shrubs (as catnip or peppermint) with square stems **2 :** a piece of candy flavored with mint

²mint *n* **1 :** a place where metals are made into coins **2 :** a great amount especially of money

³mint *vb* **1 :** ²COIN 1 **2 :** to make into coin

min·u·end *n* **:** a number from which another number is to be subtracted

min·u·et *n* **:** a slow stately dance

¹mi·nus *prep* **1 :** with the subtraction of **:** LESS **2 :** ¹WITHOUT 2

²minus *adj* **:** located in the lower part of a range

minus sign *n* **:** a sign – used especially in mathematics to indicate subtraction (as in 8–6=2) or a quantity less than zero (as in –10°)

¹min·ute *n* **1 :** the sixtieth part of an hour or of a degree **:** sixty seconds **2 :** MOMENT 1 **3 minutes** *pl* **:** a brief record of what happened during a meeting

²mi·nute *adj* **mi·nut·er; mi·nut·est 1 :** very small **:** TINY **2 :** paying attention to small details — **mi·nute·ly** *adv*

min·ute·man *n, pl* **min·ute·men :** a member of a group of armed men ready to fight at a minute's notice immediately before and during the American Revolution

mir•a•cle *n* **1 :** an extraordinary event taken as a sign of the power of God **2 :** something very rare, unusual, or wonderful

mi•rac•u•lous *adj* **:** being or being like a miracle — **mi•rac•u•lous•ly** *adv*

mi•rage *n* **:** an illusion sometimes seen at sea, in the desert, or over hot pavement that looks like a pool of water or a mirror in which distant objects are glimpsed

1mire *n* **:** heavy deep mud

2mire *vb* **mired; mir•ing :** to stick or cause to stick fast in mire

1mir•ror *n* **1 :** a glass coated on the back with a reflecting substance **2 :** something that gives a true likeness or description

2mirror *vb* **:** to reflect in or as if in a mirror

mirth *n* **:** the state of being happy or merry as shown by laughter

mirth•ful *adj* **:** full of or showing mirth — **mirth•ful•ly** *adv*

mis- *prefix* **1 :** in a way that is bad or wrong **2 :** bad **:** wrong **3 :** opposite or lack of

mis•ad•ven•ture *n* **:** an unfortunate or unpleasant event

mis•be•have *vb* **mis•be•haved; mis•be•hav•ing :** to behave badly

mis•car•ry *vb* **mis•car•ried; mis•car•ry•ing :** to go wrong **:** FAIL

mis•cel•la•neous *adj* **:** consisting of many things of different sorts

mis•chance *n* **1 :** bad luck **2 :** a piece of bad luck **:** MISHAP

mis•chief *n* **1 :** injury or damage caused by a person **2 :** conduct that annoys or bothers

mis•chie•vous *adj* **1 :** harming or intended to do harm **2 :** causing or likely to cause minor injury or harm **3 :** showing a spirit of irresponsible fun or playfulness — **mis•chie•vous•ly** *adv* — **mis•chie•vous•ness** *n*

1mis•con•duct *n* **:** wrong conduct **:** bad behavior

2mis•con•duct *vb* **:** to manage badly

mis•count *vb* **:** to count incorrectly

mis•cre•ant *n* **:** VILLAIN, RASCAL

mis•cue *n* **:** 2MISTAKE 2

mis•deal *vb* **mis•dealt; mis•deal•ing :** to deal in an incorrect way

mis•deed *n* **:** a bad action

mis•di•rect *vb* **:** to direct incorrectly

mi•ser *n* **:** a stingy person who lives poorly in order to store away money

mis•er•a•ble *adj* **1 :** very unsatisfactory **2 :** causing great discomfort **3 :** very unhappy or distressed **:** WRETCHED — **mis•er•a•bly** *adv*

mi•ser•ly *adj* **:** of, relating to, or like a miser

mis•ery *n, pl* **mis•er•ies :** suffering or distress due to being poor, in pain, or unhappy

mis•fit *n* **1 :** something that fits badly **2 :** a person who cannot adjust to an environment

mis•for•tune *n* **1 :** bad luck **2 :** an unfortunate situation or event

mis•giv•ing *n* **:** a feeling of distrust or doubt especially about what is going to happen

mis•guid•ed *adj* **:** having mistaken ideas or rules of conduct

mis•hap *n* **:** an unfortunate accident

mis•judge *vb* **mis•judged; mis•judg•ing :** to judge incorrectly or unjustly

mis•lay *vb* **mis•laid; mis•lay•ing :** to put in a place later forgotten **:** LOSE

mis•lead *vb* **mis•led; mis•lead•ing :** to lead in a wrong direction or into error

mis•place *vb* **mis•placed; mis•plac•ing 1 :** to put in a wrong place **2 :** MISLAY

mis•print *n* **:** a mistake in printing

mis•pro•nounce *vb* **mis•pro•nounced; mis•pro•nounc•ing :** to pronounce in a way considered incorrect

mis•pro•nun•ci•a•tion *n* **:** incorrect pronunciation

mis•read *vb* **mis•read; mis•read•ing 1 :** to read incorrectly **2 :** MISUNDERSTAND 2

mis•rep•re•sent *vb* **:** to give a false or misleading idea of

1miss *vb* **1 :** to fail to hit, catch, reach, or get **2 :** 1ESCAPE 2 **3 :** to fail to have or go to **4 :** to be aware of the absence of **:** want to be with

2miss *n* **:** failure to hit or catch

3miss *n* **1** — used as a title before the name of an unmarried woman **2 :** young lady — used without a name as a form of polite address to a girl or young woman

mis•shap•en *adj* **:** badly shaped

mis•sile *n* **:** an object (as a stone, arrow, bullet, or rocket) that is dropped, thrown, shot, or launched usually so as to strike something at a distance

miss•ing *adj* **1 :** 1ABSENT 1 **2 :** 2LOST 4

mis•sion *n* **1 :** a group of missionaries **2 :** a place where the work of missionaries is carried on **3 :** a group of persons sent by a government to represent it in a foreign country **4 :** a task that is assigned or begun

1mis•sion•ary *adj* **:** of or relating to religious missions

2missionary *n, pl* **mis•sion•ar•ies :** a person sent (as to a foreign country) to spread a religious faith

mis•sive *n* **:** 1LETTER 2

mis•spell *vb* **:** to spell in an incorrect way

mis•spend *vb* **mis•spent; mis•spend•ing :** 2WASTE 2

mis•step *n* **1 :** a wrong step **2 :** 2MISTAKE 2, SLIP

1mist *n* **1 :** particles of water floating in the air or falling as fine rain **2 :** something that keeps one from seeing or understanding clearly

2mist *vb* **1 :** to be or become misty **2 :** to become or cause to become dim or blurred **3 :** to cover with mist

1mis·take *vb* **mis·took; mis·tak·en; mis·tak·ing** **1 :** MISUNDERSTAND 2 **2 :** to fail to recognize correctly

2mistake *n* **1 :** a wrong judgment **2 :** a wrong action or statement

mis·tak·en *adj* **1 :** being in error **:** judging wrongly **2 :** 2WRONG 2, INCORRECT — **mis·tak·en·ly** *adv*

mis·ter *n* **1** *cap* — used sometimes in writing instead of the usual *Mr.* **2 :** SIR 2

mis·tle·toe *n* **:** a green plant with waxy white berries that grows on the branches and trunks of trees

mis·treat *vb* **:** to treat badly **:** ABUSE

mis·tress *n* **:** a woman who has control or authority

1mis·trust *n* **:** 1DISTRUST

2mistrust *vb* **1 :** 2DISTRUST, SUSPECT **2 :** to lack confidence in

misty *adj* **mist·i·er; mist·i·est** **1 :** full of mist **2 :** clouded by or as if by mist **3 :** VAGUE 3, INDISTINCT — **mist·i·ly** *adv* — **mist·i·ness** *n*

mis·un·der·stand *vb* **mis·un·der·stood; mis·un·der·stand·ing** **1 :** to fail to understand **2 :** to take in a wrong meaning or way

mis·un·der·stand·ing *n* **1 :** a failure to understand **2 :** DISAGREEMENT 3, QUARREL

1mis·use *vb* **mis·used; mis·us·ing** **1 :** to use in a wrong way **2 :** 2ABUSE 3, MISTREAT

2mis·use *n* **:** incorrect or improper use

mite *n* **1 :** any of various tiny spiderlike animals often living on plants, animals, and stored foods **2 :** a very small coin or amount of money **3 :** a very small object or creature

mi·to·sis *n, pl* **mi·to·ses :** a process of cell division in which two new nuclei are formed each containing the original number of chromosomes

mitt *n* **1 :** MITTEN **2 :** a baseball catcher's or first baseman's glove

mit·ten *n* **:** a covering for the hand and wrist having a separate division for the thumb only

1mix *vb* **1 :** to make into one mass by stirring together **:** BLEND **2 :** to make by combining different things **3 :** to become one mass through blending **4 :** CONFUSE 1 — **mixer** *n*

2mix *n* **:** MIXTURE 2

mixed *adj* **1 :** made up of two or more kinds **2 :** made up of persons of both sexes

mixed number *or* **mixed numeral** *n* **:** a number (as $1\frac{2}{3}$) made up of a whole number and a fraction

mix·ture *n* **1 :** the act of mixing **2 :** something mixed or being mixed **3 :** two or more substances mixed together in such a way that each remains unchanged

mix-up *n* **:** an instance of confusion

miz·zen *n* **1 :** a fore-and-aft sail set on the mizzenmast **2 :** MIZZENMAST

miz·zen·mast *n* **:** the mast behind or next behind the mainmast

1moan *n* **1 :** a long low sound showing pain or grief **2 :** a mournful sound

2moan *vb* **1 :** COMPLAIN 1 **2 :** to utter a moan

moat *n* **:** a deep wide ditch around the walls of a castle or fort that is usually filled with water

1mob *n* **1 :** the common masses of people **2 :** a rowdy excited crowd

2mob *vb* **mobbed; mob·bing :** to crowd about and attack or annoy

1mo·bile *adj* **1 :** easily moved **:** MOVABLE **2 :** changing quickly in expression

2mo·bile *n* **:** an artistic structure whose parts can be moved especially by air currents

mo·bi·lize *vb* **mo·bi·lized; mo·bi·liz·ing :** to assemble (as military forces) and make ready for action

moc·ca·sin *n* **1 :** a soft shoe with no heel and the sole and sides made of one piece **2 :** a poisonous snake of the southern United States

moccasin flower *n* **:** LADY'S SLIPPER

1mock *vb* **1 :** to treat with scorn **:** RIDICULE **2 :** 3MIMIC 2

2mock *adj* **:** not real **:** MAKE-BELIEVE

mock·ery *n, pl* **mock·er·ies** **1 :** the act of mocking **2 :** a bad imitation **:** FAKE

mock·ing·bird *n* **:** a songbird of the southern United States noted for its sweet song and imitations of other birds

mock orange *n* **:** SYRINGA

1mode *n* **1 :** a particular form or variety of something **2 :** a form or manner of expressing or acting **:** WAY

2mode *n* **:** a popular fashion or style

1mod·el *n* **1 :** a small but exact copy of a thing **2 :** a pattern or figure of something to be made **3 :** a person who sets a good example **4 :** a person who poses for an artist or photographer **5 :** a person who wears and displays garments that are for sale **6 :** a special type of a product

2model *vb* **mod·eled** *or* **mod·elled; mod·el·ing** *or* **mod·el·ling** **1 :** to plan or shape after a pattern **2 :** to make a model of **3 :** to act or serve as a model

3model *adj* **1 :** worthy of being imitated **2 :** being a miniature copy

mo·dem *n* **:** a device that changes electrical signals from one form to another and is used especially to send or receive computer data over a telephone line

[1]**mod·er·ate** *adj* **1 :** neither too much nor too little **2 :** neither very good nor very bad **3 :** not expensive **:** REASONABLE — **mod·er·ate·ly** *adv*

[2]**mod·er·ate** *vb* **mod·er·at·ed; mod·er·at·ing :** to make or become less violent or severe

mod·er·a·tion *n* **1 :** the act of moderating **2 :** the condition of being moderate

mod·ern *adj* **1 :** of, relating to, or characteristic of the present time or times not long past **2 :** of the period from about 1500

mod·ern·ize *vb* **mod·ern·ized; mod·ern·iz·ing :** to make or become modern

mod·est *adj* **1 :** having a limited and not too high opinion of oneself and one's abilities **:** not boastful **2 :** limited in size or amount **3 :** clean and proper in thought, conduct, and dress — **mod·est·ly** *adv*

mod·es·ty *n* **:** the quality of being modest

mod·i·fi·ca·tion *n* **1 :** the act of modifying **2 :** the result of modifying **:** a slightly changed form

mod·i·fi·er *n* **:** a word (as an adjective or adverb) used with another word to limit its meaning

mod·i·fy *vb* **mod·i·fied; mod·i·fy·ing 1 :** to make changes in **2 :** to lower or reduce in amount or scale **3 :** to limit in meaning **:** QUALIFY

mod·u·late *vb* **mod·u·lat·ed; mod·u·lat·ing 1 :** to bring into proper proportion **2 :** to tone down **:** SOFTEN

mod·ule *n* **:** an independent unit of a spacecraft

mo·hair *n* **:** a fabric or yarn made from the long silky hair of an Asian goat

Mohammedan, Mohammedanism *variant of* MUHAMMADAN, MUHAMMADANISM

moist *adj* **:** slightly wet **:** DAMP — **moist·ness** *n*

moist·en *vb* **:** to make moist

mois·ture *n* **:** a small amount of liquid that causes moistness

mo·lar *n* **:** a tooth with a broad surface used for grinding **:** a back tooth

mo·las·ses *n* **:** a thick brown syrup that drains from sugar as it is being made

[1]**mold** *or* **mould** *n* **:** light rich crumbly earth that contains decaying material

[2]**mold** *or* **mould** *n* **1 :** a hollow form in which something is shaped **2 :** something shaped in a mold

[3]**mold** *or* **mould** *vb* **1 :** to work and press into shape **2 :** to form in or as if in a mold

[4]**mold** *n* **1 :** an often woolly surface growth of fungus on damp or decaying material **2 :** a fungus that forms mold

[5]**mold** *vb* **:** to become moldy

mold·er *vb* **:** to crumble to bits by slow decay

mold·ing *n* **1 :** the act or work of a person who molds **2 :** a strip of material having a shaped surface and used as a decoration (as on a wall or the edge of a table)

moldy *adj* **mold·i·er; mold·i·est :** covered with or containing mold

[1]**mole** *n* **:** a small usually brown spot on the skin

[2]**mole** *n* **:** a small burrowing animal with very soft fur and very tiny eyes

mo·lec·u·lar *adj* **:** of or relating to a molecule

mol·e·cule *n* **1 :** the smallest portion of a substance having the properties of the substance **2 :** a very small particle

mole·hill *n* **:** a little ridge of earth pushed up by moles as they burrow underground

mo·lest *vb* **:** to disturb or injure by interfering

mol·li·fy *vb* **mol·li·fied; mol·li·fy·ing :** to soothe in temper or disposition

mol·lusk *n* **:** any of a large group of animals (as clams, snails, and octopuses) most of which live in water and have the body protected by a limy shell

molt *or* **moult** *vb* **:** to shed outer material (as hair, shell, or horns) that will be replaced by a new growth

mol·ten *adj* **:** melted especially by very great heat

mo·lyb·de·num *n* **:** a white metallic chemical element used in some steel to give greater strength and hardness

mom *n* **:** [1]MOTHER 1

mo·ment *n* **1 :** a very brief time **2 :** IMPORTANCE

mo·men·tary *adj* **:** lasting only a moment — **mo·men·tar·i·ly** *adv*

mo·men·tous *adj* **:** very important — **mo·men·tous·ness** *n*

mo·men·tum *n* **:** the force that a moving body has because of its weight and motion

mom·my *n, pl* **mom·mies :** [1]MOTHER 1

mon- *or* **mono-** *prefix* **:** one **:** single **:** alone

mon·arch *n* **1 :** a person who reigns over a kingdom or empire **2 :** a large orange and black American butterfly

mon·ar·chy *n, pl* **mon·ar·chies 1 :** a state or country having a monarch **2 :** the system of government by a monarch

mon·as·tery *n, pl* **mon·as·ter·ies :** a place where a community of monks live and work

mo·nas·tic *adj* **:** of or relating to monks or monasteries

Mon·day *n* **:** the second day of the week

mon·e·tary *adj* **:** of or relating to money

mon·ey *n, pl* **moneys** *or* **mon·ies** **1 :** metal (as gold, silver, or copper) coined or stamped and issued for use in buying and selling **2 :** a printed or engraved certificate (**paper money**) legal for use in place of metal money **3 :** wealth figured in terms of money

money order *n* **:** a piece of paper like a check that can be bought (as at a post office) and that tells another office to pay the sum of money printed on it to the one named

1**Mon·go·lian** *adj* **:** of or relating to Mongolia or the Mongolians

2**Mongolian** *n* **:** a person born or living in Mongolia

mon·goose *n, pl* **mon·goos·es :** a long thin furry animal that eats snakes, eggs, and rodents

1**mon·grel** *n* **:** one (as a plant, person, or thing) of mixed or uncertain kind or origin

2**mongrel** *adj* **:** of mixed or uncertain kind or origin

1**mon·i·tor** *n* **1 :** a pupil in a school picked for a special duty (as keeping order) **2 :** a person or thing that watches or checks something **3 :** a video screen used for display (as of television pictures or computer information)

2**monitor** *vb* **:** to watch or check for a special reason

monk *n* **:** a member of a religious group of men who form a community and promise to stay poor, obey all the laws of their community, and not get married

1**mon·key** *n, pl* **monkeys** **1 :** any of a group of mostly tropical furry animals that have a long tail and that along with the apes are most closely related to humans in the animal kingdom **2 :** a mischievous child

2**monkey** *vb* **mon·keyed; mon·key·ing** **1 :** to act in a mischievous way **2 :** 2TRIFLE 3, FOOL

mon·key·shine *n* **:** PRANK

monkey wrench *n* **:** a wrench with one fixed and one adjustable jaw

monks·hood *n* **:** a tall poisonous Old World plant related to the buttercups that is grown for its white or purplish flowers that are shaped like hoods or as a source of drugs

mono- — see MON-

mono·gram *n* **:** a design usually made by combining two or more of a person's initials

mono·plane *n* **:** an airplane with only one set of wings

mo·nop·o·lize *vb* **mo·nop·o·lized; mo·nop·o·liz·ing :** to get or have complete control over

mo·nop·o·ly *n, pl* **mo·nop·o·lies** **1 :** complete control of the entire supply of goods or a service in a certain market **2 :** complete possession **3 :** a person or group having a monopoly

mono·syl·la·ble *n* **:** a word of one syllable

mo·not·o·nous *adj* **:** boring from being always the same — **mo·not·o·nous·ly** *adv*

mo·not·o·ny *n, pl* **mo·not·o·nies :** a boring lack of change

mon·soon *n* **1 :** a wind in the Indian ocean and southern Asia that blows from the southwest from April to October and from the northeast from October to April **2 :** the rainy season that comes with the southwest monsoon

mon·ster *n* **1 :** an animal or plant that is very unlike the usual type **2 :** a strange or horrible creature **3 :** something unusually large **4 :** an extremely wicked or cruel person

mon·strous *adj* **1 :** unusually large **:** ENORMOUS **2 :** very bad or wrong **3 :** very different from the usual form **:** ABNORMAL — **mon·strous·ly** *adv*

month *n* **:** one of the twelve parts into which the year is divided

1**month·ly** *adj* **1 :** happening, done, or published every month **2 :** figured in terms of one month **3 :** lasting a month

2**monthly** *n, pl* **monthlies :** a magazine published every month

mon·u·ment *n* **1 :** a structure (as a building, stone, or statue) made to keep alive the memory of a person or event **2 :** a work, saying, or deed that lasts or is worth keeping or remembering

1**moo** *vb* **mooed; moo·ing :** to make a moo **:** LOW

2**moo** *n, pl* **moos :** the low sound made by a cow

1**mood** *n* **:** a state or frame of mind **:** DISPOSITION

2**mood** *n* **:** a set of forms of a verb that show whether the action or state expressed is to be thought of as a fact, a command, or a wish or possibility

moody *adj* **mood·i·er; mood·i·est :** often feeling gloomy or in a bad mood — **mood·i·ly** *adv* — **mood·i·ness** *n*

1**moon** *n* **1 :** the natural celestial body that shines by reflecting light from the sun and revolves about the earth in about 29 1/2 days **2 :** SATELLITE 1 **3 :** MONTH

2**moon** *vb* **:** to waste time by daydreaming

moon·beam *n* **:** a ray of light from the moon

moon·light *n* **:** the light of the moon

moon·stone *n* **:** a partly transparent shining stone used as a gem

1**moor** *n* **:** an area of open land that is too wet or too poor for farming

[2]**moor** *vb* **:** to fasten in place with cables, lines, or anchors
moor·ing *n* **1 :** a place where or an object to which a boat can be fastened **2 :** a chain or line by which an object is moored
moor·land *n* **:** land consisting of moors
moose *n* **:** a large deerlike animal with broad flattened antlers and humped shoulders that lives in forests of Canada and the northern United States
[1]**mop** *n* **1 :** a tool for cleaning made of a bundle of cloth or yarn or a sponge fastened to a handle **2 :** something that looks like a cloth or yarn mop
[2]**mop** *vb* **mopped; mop·ping :** to wipe or clean with or as if with a mop
[1]**mope** *vb* **moped; mop·ing :** to be in a dull and sad state of mind
[2]**mope** *n* **:** a person without any energy or enthusiasm
mo·raine *n* **:** a pile of earth and stones left by a glacier
[1]**mor·al** *adj* **1 :** concerned with or relating to what is right and wrong in human behavior **2 :** able or fit to teach a lesson **3 :** [1]GOOD 7, VIRTUOUS **4 :** able to tell right from wrong — **mor·al·ly** *adv*
[2]**moral** *n* **1 :** the lesson to be learned from a story or experience **2 morals** *pl* **:** moral conduct **3 morals** *pl* **:** moral teachings or rules of behavior
mo·rale *n* **:** the condition of the mind or feelings (as in relation to enthusiasm, spirit, or hope) of an individual or group
mo·ral·i·ty *n, pl* **mo·ral·i·ties 1 :** moral quality **:** VIRTUE **2 :** moral conduct
mo·rass *n* **:** MARSH, SWAMP
mor·bid *adj* **:** not healthy or normal
[1]**more** *adj* **1 :** greater in amount, number, or size **2 :** [1]EXTRA, ADDITIONAL
[2]**more** *adv* **1 :** in addition **2 :** to a greater extent — often used with an adjective or adverb to form the comparative
[3]**more** *n* **1 :** a greater amount or number **2 :** an additional amount
more·over *adv* **:** in addition to what has been said **:** BESIDES
morn *n* **:** MORNING
morn·ing *n* **:** the early part of the day **:** the time from sunrise to noon
morning glory *n* **:** a vine that climbs by twisting around something and has large bright flowers that close in the sunshine
morning star *n* **:** any of the planets Venus, Jupiter, Mars, Mercury, or Saturn when rising before the sun
mo·ron *n* **:** a person with less than ordinary mental ability but able to do simple routine work
mor·phine *n* **:** a habit-forming drug made from opium and used often to relieve pain
mor·row *n* **:** the next following day
mor·sel *n* **1 :** a small piece of food **:** BITE **2 :** a small amount **:** a little piece
[1]**mor·tal** *adj* **1 :** capable of causing death **:** FATAL **2 :** certain to die **3 :** very unfriendly **4 :** very great or overpowering **5 :** [1]HUMAN 1 — **mor·tal·ly** *adv*
[2]**mortal** *n* **:** a human being
[1]**mor·tar** *n* **1 :** a strong deep bowl in which substances are pounded or crushed with a pestle **2 :** a short light cannon used to shoot shells high into the air
[2]**mortar** *n* **:** a building material made of lime and cement mixed with sand and water that is spread between bricks or stones so as to hold them together when it hardens
mor·ti·fy *vb* **mor·ti·fied; mor·ti·fy·ing :** to embarrass greatly **:** SHAME
mo·sa·ic *n* **:** a decoration on a surface made by setting small pieces of glass or stone of different colors into another material so as to make patterns or pictures
Moslem *variant of* MUSLIM
mosque *n* **:** a Muslim place of worship
mos·qui·to *n, pl* **mos·qui·toes :** a small two-winged fly the female of which punctures the skin of people and animals to suck their blood
moss *n* **1 :** any of a class of plants that have no flowers and grow as small leafy stems in cushion-like patches clinging to rocks, bark, or damp ground **2 :** any of various plants (as lichens) resembling moss
mossy *adj* **moss·i·er; moss·i·est :** like or covered with moss
[1]**most** *adj* **1 :** the majority of **2 :** greatest in amount or extent
[2]**most** *adv* **1 :** to the greatest or highest level or extent — often used with an adjective or adverb to form the superlative **2 :** to a very great extent
[3]**most** *n* **:** the greatest amount, number, or part
most·ly *adv* **:** for the greatest part
mote *n* **:** a small particle **:** SPECK
mo·tel *n* **:** a building or group of buildings which provide lodgings and in which the rooms are usually reached directly from an outdoor parking area
moth *n, pl* **moths 1 :** CLOTHES MOTH **2 :** an insect that usually flies at night and has mostly feathery antennae and stouter body, duller coloring, and smaller wings than the related butterflies
[1]**moth·er** *n* **1 :** a female parent **2 :** a nun in charge of a convent **3 :** [1]CAUSE 1, ORIGIN — **moth·er·hood** *n* — **moth·er·less** *adj*
[2]**mother** *adj* **1 :** of or having to do with a

mother **2 :** being in the relation of a mother to others **3 :** gotten from or as if from one's mother

[3]**mother** *vb* **:** to be or act as a mother to

moth·er·board *n* **:** the main circuit board especially of a small computer

moth·er–in–law *n, pl* **mothers–in–law :** the mother of one's husband or wife

moth·er·ly *adj* **1 :** of, relating to, or characteristic of a mother **2 :** like a mother **:** MATERNAL

moth·er–of–pearl *n* **:** a hard pearly material that lines the shell of some mollusks (as mussels) and is often used for ornamental objects and buttons

[1]**mo·tion** *n* **1 :** a formal plan or suggestion for action offered according to the rules of a meeting **2 :** the act or process of changing place or position **:** MOVEMENT — **mo·tion·less** *adj* — **mo·tion·less·ness** *n*

[2]**motion** *vb* **:** to direct or signal by a movement or sign

motion picture *n* **1 :** a series of pictures projected on a screen rapidly one after another so as to give the appearance of a continuous picture in which the objects move **2 :** MOVIE 1

mo·ti·vate *vb* **mo·ti·vat·ed; mo·ti·vat·ing :** to provide with a reason for doing something

[1]**mo·tive** *n* **:** a reason for doing something

[2]**motive** *adj* **:** causing motion

mot·ley *adj* **1 :** having various colors **2 :** composed of various often unlike kinds or parts

[1]**mo·tor** *n* **1 :** a machine that produces motion or power for doing work **2 :** [2]AUTOMOBILE — **mo·tored** *adj*

[2]**motor** *adj* **1 :** causing or controlling activity (as motion) **2 :** equipped with or driven by a motor **3 :** of or relating to an automobile **4 :** designed for motor vehicles or motorists

[3]**motor** *vb* **:** [1]DRIVE 3

mo·tor·bike *n* **:** a light motorcycle

mo·tor·boat *n* **:** an often small boat driven by a motor

mo·tor·car *n* **:** [2]AUTOMOBILE

mo·tor·cy·cle *n* **:** a vehicle for one or two passengers that has two wheels and is driven by a motor

mo·tor·ist *n* **:** a person who travels by automobile

mo·tor·ize *vb* **mo·tor·ized; mo·tor·iz·ing :** to equip with a motor or with motor-driven vehicles

motor scooter *n* **:** a motorized vehicle having two or three wheels like a child's scooter but having a seat

motor vehicle *n* **:** a motorized vehicle (as an automobile or motorcycle) not operated on rails

mot·tled *adj* **:** having spots or blotches of different colors

mot·to *n, pl* **mottoes 1 :** a phrase or word inscribed on something (as a coin or public building) to suggest its use or nature **2 :** a short expression of a guiding rule of conduct

mould *variant of* MOLD

moult *variant of* MOLT

mound *n* **:** a small hill or heap of dirt (as one made to mark a grave)

[1]**mount** *n* **:** a high hill **:** MOUNTAIN — used especially before a proper name

[2]**mount** *vb* **1 :** ASCEND, CLIMB **2 :** to get up onto something **3 :** to increase rapidly in amount **4 :** to prepare for use or display by fastening in position on a support

[3]**mount** *n* **:** that on which a person or thing is or can be mounted

moun·tain *n* **1 :** an elevation higher than a hill **2 :** a great mass or huge number

moun·tain·eer *n* **1 :** a person who lives in the mountains **2 :** a mountain climber

mountain goat *n* **:** a goatlike animal of the mountains of western North America with thick white coat and slightly curved black horns

mountain lion *n* **:** COUGAR

moun·tain·ous *adj* **1 :** having many mountains **2 :** like a mountain in size **:** HUGE

moun·tain·side *n* **:** the side of a mountain

moun·tain·top *n* **:** the highest part of a mountain

mount·ing *n* **:** something that serves as a mount **:** SUPPORT

mourn *vb* **:** to feel or show grief or sorrow especially over someone's death — **mourn·er** *n*

mourn·ful *adj* **1 :** full of sorrow or sadness **2 :** causing sorrow — **mourn·ful·ly** *adv* — **mourn·ful·ness** *n*

mourn·ing *n* **1 :** the act of sorrowing **2 :** an outward sign (as black clothes or an arm band) of grief for a person's death

mourning dove *n* **:** a wild dove of the United States named from its mournful cry

mouse *n, pl* **mice 1 :** a furry gnawing animal like the larger related rats **2 :** a person without spirit or courage **3 :** a small movable device that is connected to a computer and used to move the cursor and select functions on the screen — **mouse·like** *adj*

mous·er *n* **:** a cat good at catching mice

moustache *variant of* MUSTACHE

[1]**mouth** *n, pl* **mouths 1 :** the opening through which food passes into the body **:** the space containing the tongue and teeth **2 :** an opening that is like a mouth **3 :** the

DICTIONARY

place where a stream enters a larger body of water

[2]**mouth** *vb* **:** to repeat without being sincere or without understanding

mouth·ful *n* **1 :** as much as the mouth will hold **2 :** the amount put into the mouth at one time

mouth organ *n* **:** HARMONICA

mouth·piece *n* **:** the part put to, between, or near the lips

mov·able *or* **move·able** *adj* **1 :** possible to move **2 :** changing from one date to another

[1]**move** *vb* **moved; mov·ing 1 :** to go from one place to another **2 :** to change the place or position of **:** SHIFT **3 :** to set in motion **:** STIR **4 :** to cause to act **:** INFLUENCE **5 :** to stir the feelings of **6 :** to change position **7 :** to suggest according to the rules in a meeting **8 :** to change residence

[2]**move** *n* **1 :** the act of moving a piece in a game **2 :** the turn of a player to move **3 :** an action taken to accomplish something **:** MANEUVER **4 :** the action of moving **:** MOVEMENT

move·ment *n* **1 :** the act or process of moving **:** an instance of moving **2 :** a program or series of acts working toward a desired end **3 :** a mechanical arrangement (as of wheels) for causing a particular motion (as in a clock or watch) **4 :** RHYTHM 2, METER **5 :** a section of a longer piece of music **6 :** an emptying of the bowels **:** the material emptied from the bowels

mov·er *n* **:** a person or company that moves the belongings of others (as from one home to another)

mov·ie *n* **1 :** a story represented in motion pictures **2 :** a showing of a movie

mov·ing *adj* **1 :** changing place or position **2 :** having the power to stir the feelings or sympathies — **mov·ing·ly** *adv*

moving picture *n* **:** MOTION PICTURE 1

[1]**mow** *n* **:** the part of a barn where hay or straw is stored

[2]**mow** *vb* **mowed; mowed** *or* **mown; mow·ing 1 :** to cut down with a scythe or machine **2 :** to cut the standing plant cover from **3 :** to cause to fall in great numbers — **mow·er** *n*

Mr. *n, pl* **Messrs.** — used as a title before a man's name

Mrs. *n, pl* **mes·dames** — used as a title before a married woman's name

Ms. *n* — often used instead of *Miss* or *Mrs.*

[1]**much** *adj* **more; most :** great in amount or extent

[2]**much** *adv* **more; most 1 :** to a great or high level or extent **2 :** just about **:** NEARLY

[3]**much** *n* **:** a great amount or part

mu·ci·lage *n* **:** a water solution of a gum or similar substance used especially to stick things together

muck *n* **1 :** soft wet soil or barnyard manure **2 :** DIRT 1, FILTH

mu·cous *adj* **1 :** of, relating to, or like mucus **2 :** containing or producing mucus

mu·cus *n* **:** a slippery sticky substance produced especially by mucous membranes (as of the nose and throat) which it moistens and protects

mud *n* **:** soft wet earth or dirt

[1]**mud·dle** *vb* **mud·dled; mud·dling 1 :** to be or cause to be confused or bewildered **2 :** to mix up in a confused manner **3 :** to make a mess of **:** BUNGLE

[2]**muddle** *n* **:** a state of confusion

[1]**mud·dy** *adj* **mud·di·er; mud·di·est 1 :** filled or covered with mud **2 :** looking like mud **3 :** not clear or bright **:** DULL **4 :** being mixed up — **mud·di·ly** *adv* — **mud·di·ness** *n*

[2]**muddy** *vb* **mud·died; mud·dy·ing 1 :** to soil or stain with or as if with mud **2 :** to make cloudy or dull

[1]**muff** *n* **:** a soft thick cover into which both hands can be shoved to protect them from cold

[2]**muff** *vb* **:** to handle awkwardly **:** BUNGLE

muf·fin *n* **:** a bread made of batter containing eggs and baked in a small container

muf·fle *vb* **muf·fled; muf·fling 1 :** to wrap up so as to hide or protect **2 :** to deaden the sound of

muf·fler *n* **1 :** a scarf for the neck **2 :** a device to deaden the noise of an engine (as of an automobile)

mug *n* **:** a large drinking cup

mug·gy *adj* **mug·gi·er; mug·gi·est :** being very warm and humid — **mug·gi·ness** *n*

Mu·ham·mad·an *or* **Mo·ham·med·an** *n* **:** MUSLIM

Mu·ham·mad·an·ism *or* **Mo·ham·med·an·ism** *n* **:** ISLAM

mul·ber·ry *n, pl* **mul·ber·ries :** a tree that bears edible usually purple fruit like berries and has leaves on which silkworms can be fed

[1]**mulch** *n* **:** a material (as straw or sawdust) spread over the ground to protect the roots of plants from heat, cold, or drying of the soil or to keep fruit clean

[2]**mulch** *vb* **:** to cover with mulch

mule *n* **1 :** an animal that is an offspring of a donkey and a horse **2 :** a stubborn person

mule skinner *n* **:** a driver of mules

mu·le·teer *n* **:** a driver of mules

mul·ish *adj* **:** stubborn like a mule — **mul·ish·ly** *adv* — **mul·ish·ness** *n*

mul·let *n* **:** any of various freshwater or saltwater food fishes some mostly gray (**gray mullets**) and others red or golden (**red mullets**)

multi- *prefix* **1 :** many **:** much **2 :** more than two **3 :** many times over

mul·ti·cul·tur·al *adj* **:** of, relating to, or made up of several different cultures together

1mul·ti·ple *adj* **:** being more than one

2multiple *n* **:** the number found by multiplying one number by another

mul·ti·pli·cand *n* **:** a number that is to be multiplied by another number

mul·ti·pli·ca·tion *n* **:** a short way of finding out what would be the result of adding a figure the number of times indicated by another figure

mul·ti·pli·er *n* **:** a number by which another number is multiplied

mul·ti·ply *vb* **mul·ti·plied; mul·ti·ply·ing 1 :** to increase in number **:** make or become more numerous **2 :** to find the product of by means of multiplication

mul·ti·tude *n* **:** a great number of persons or things

mum *adj* **:** SILENT 1 4

1mum·ble *vb* **mum·bled; mum·bling :** to speak so that words are not clear

2mumble *n* **:** speech that is not clear enough to be understood

mum·my *n, pl* **mummies :** a dead body preserved in the manner of the ancient Egyptians

mumps *n sing or pl* **:** an infectious disease in which there is fever and soreness and swelling of glands and especially of those around the jaw

munch *vb* **:** to chew with a crunching sound

mu·nic·i·pal *adj* **:** having to do with the government of a town or city

mu·nic·i·pal·i·ty *n, pl* **mu·nic·i·pal·i·ties :** a town or city having its own local government

mu·ni·tions *n* **:** military equipment and supplies for fighting **:** AMMUNITION

1mu·ral *adj* **:** having to do with a wall

2mural *n* **:** a painting on a wall

1mur·der *n* **:** the intentional and unlawful killing of a human being

2murder *vb* **1 :** to commit murder **2 :** to spoil by performing or using badly — **mur·der·er** *n*

mur·der·ous *adj* **1 :** intending or capable of murder **:** DEADLY **2 :** very hard to bear or withstand — **mur·der·ous·ly** *adv*

murk *n* **:** GLOOM 1, DARKNESS

murky *adj* **murk·i·er; murk·i·est 1 :** very dark or gloomy **2 :** FOGGY 1, MISTY — **murk·i·ness** *n*

1mur·mur *n* **:** a low faint sound

2murmur *vb* **1 :** to make a murmur **2 :** to say in a voice too low to be heard clearly

mus·ca·dine *n* **:** a grape of the southern United States

mus·cle *n* **1 :** an animal body tissue consisting of long cells that can contract and produce motion **2 :** a bodily organ that is a mass of muscle tissue attached at either end (as to bones) so that it can make a body part (as an arm) move **3 :** strength or development of the muscles

mus·cle–bound *adj* **:** having large muscles that do not move and stretch easily

mus·cu·lar *adj* **1 :** of, relating to, or being muscle **2 :** done by the muscles **3 :** STRONG 1

muse *vb* **mused; mus·ing :** PONDER

mu·se·um *n* **:** a building in which are displayed objects of interest in one or more of the arts or sciences

1mush *n* **:** cornmeal boiled in water

2mush *vb* **:** to travel across snow with a sled drawn by dogs

1mush·room *n* **1 :** a part of a fungus that bears spores, grows above ground, and suggests an umbrella in shape **2 :** a fungus that produces mushrooms **3 :** something shaped like a mushroom

2mushroom *vb* **:** to come into being suddenly or grow and develop rapidly

mushy *adj* **mush·i·er; mush·i·est :** soft like mush

mu·sic *n* **1 :** the art of producing pleasing or expressive combinations of tones especially with melody, rhythm, and usually harmony **2 :** compositions made according to the rules of music **3 :** pleasing sounds **4 :** a musical composition set down on paper

1mu·si·cal *adj* **1 :** having to do with music or the writing or performing of music **2 :** pleasing like music **3 :** fond of or talented in music **4 :** set to music — **mu·si·cal·ly** *adv*

2musical *n* **:** a movie or play that tells a story with both speaking and singing

music box *n* **:** a box that contains a mechanical device which uses gears like those of a clock to play a tune

mu·si·cian *n* **:** a person who writes, sings, or plays music with skill and especially as a profession

musk *n* **1 :** a strong-smelling material from a gland of an Asian deer (**musk deer**) used in perfumes **2 :** any of several plants with musky odors

mus·ket *n* **:** a firearm that is loaded through the muzzle and that was once used by infantry soldiers

mus·ke·teer *n* **:** a soldier armed with a musket

musk·mel·on *n* **:** a small round to oval melon with sweet usually green or orange flesh
musk–ox *n* **:** a shaggy animal like an ox found in Greenland and northern North America
musk·rat *n* **:** a North American water animal related to the rats that has webbed hind feet and a long scaly tail and is valued for its glossy usually dark brown fur
musky *adj* **musk·i·er; musk·i·est :** suggesting musk in odor — **musk·i·ness** *n*
Mus·lim *or* **Mos·lem** *n* **:** a person whose religion is Islam
mus·lin *n* **:** a cotton fabric of plain weave
[1]**muss** *n* **:** [2]DISORDER 1, CONFUSION
[2]**muss** *vb* **:** to make untidy
mus·sel *n* **1 :** a sea mollusk that has a long dark shell in two parts and is sometimes used as food **2 :** any of various American freshwater clams with shells from which mother-of-pearl is obtained
must *helping verb, present and past all persons* **must 1 :** to be required to **2 :** to be very likely to
mus·tache *or* **mous·tache** *n* **:** the hair growing on the human upper lip
mus·tang *n* **:** a small hardy horse of western North America that is half wild
mus·tard *n* **:** a yellow powder that is prepared from the seeds of a plant related to the turnips, has a sharp taste, and is used in medicine and as a seasoning for foods
[1]**mus·ter** *n* **1 :** a formal military inspection **2 :** an assembled group **:** COLLECTION
[2]**muster** *vb* **1 :** to call together (as troops) for roll call or inspection **2 :** to bring into being or action
mustn't : must not
musty *adj* **must·i·er; must·i·est :** bad in odor or taste from the effects of dampness or mildew — **must·i·ness** *n*
[1]**mu·tant** *adj* **:** of, relating to, or resulting from mutation
[2]**mutant** *n* **:** a mutant individual
mu·tate *vb* **mu·tat·ed; mu·tat·ing 1 :** to undergo great changes **2 :** to undergo mutation
mu·ta·tion *n* **:** a change in a gene or a resulting new trait inherited by an individual
[1]**mute** *adj* **mut·er; mut·est 1 :** unable to speak **2 :** not speaking **:** SILENT
[2]**mute** *n* **1 :** a person who cannot or does not speak **2 :** a device on a musical instrument that deadens, softens, or muffles its tone
[3]**mute** *vb* **mut·ed; mut·ing :** to muffle or reduce the sound of
mu·ti·late *vb* **mu·ti·lat·ed; mu·ti·lat·ing 1 :** to cut off or destroy a necessary part (as a limb) **:** MAIM **2 :** to make imperfect by cutting or changing
mu·ti·neer *n* **:** a person who is guilty of mutiny
mu·ti·nous *adj* **:** being inclined to or in a state of mutiny — **mu·ti·nous·ly** *adv*
[1]**mu·ti·ny** *n, pl* **mu·ti·nies 1 :** refusal to obey authority **2 :** a turning of a group (as of sailors) against an officer in authority
[2]**mutiny** *vb* **mu·ti·nied; mu·ti·ny·ing :** to refuse to obey authority
mutt *n* **:** a mongrel dog
mut·ter *vb* **1 :** to speak in a low voice with lips partly closed **2 :** [1]GRUMBLE 1
mut·ton *n* **:** the flesh of a mature sheep
mu·tu·al *adj* **1 :** given and received in equal amount **2 :** having the same relation to one another **3 :** shared by two or more at the same time — **mu·tu·al·ly** *adv*
[1]**muz·zle** *n* **1 :** the nose and jaws of an animal **2 :** a fastening or covering for the mouth of an animal to prevent it from biting or eating **3 :** the open end of a gun from which the bullet comes out when the gun is fired
[2]**muzzle** *vb* **muz·zled; muz·zling 1 :** to put a muzzle on **2 :** to keep from free expression of ideas or opinions
my *adj* **:** of or relating to me or myself
my·nah *or* **my·na** *n* **:** an Asian starling that can be trained to pronounce words and is sometimes kept as a cage bird
[1]**myr·i·ad** *n* **:** a large but not specified or counted number
[2]**myriad** *adj* **:** extremely numerous
myrrh *n* **:** a brown slightly bitter fragrant material obtained from African and Arabian trees and used especially in perfumes or formerly in incense
myr·tle *n* **1 :** an evergreen shrub of southern Europe **2 :** [1]PERIWINKLE
my·self *pron* **:** my own self
mys·te·ri·ous *adj* **:** containing a mystery **:** hard to understand **:** SECRET — **mys·te·ri·ous·ly** *adv* — **mys·te·ri·ous·ness** *n*
mys·tery *n, pl* **mys·ter·ies 1 :** something that is beyond human power to understand **2 :** something that has not been explained **3 :** a piece of fiction about a mysterious crime
mys·ti·fy *vb* **mys·ti·fied; mys·ti·fy·ing :** CONFUSE 1
myth *n* **1 :** a legend that tells about a being with more than human powers or an event which cannot be explained or that explains a religious belief or practice **2 :** a person or thing existing only in the imagination
myth·i·cal *adj* **1 :** based on or told of in a myth **2 :** IMAGINARY
my·thol·o·gy *n, pl* **my·thol·o·gies :** a collection of myths

N

n *n, pl* **n's** *or* **ns** *often cap* **:** the fourteenth letter of the English alphabet
-n — see -EN
nab *vb* **nabbed; nab·bing :** [1]ARREST 2
[1]**nag** *n* **:** a usually old or worn-out horse
[2]**nag** *vb* **nagged; nag·ging 1 :** to find fault continually **:** COMPLAIN **2 :** to annoy continually or again and again
na·iad *n, pl* **na·iads** *or* **na·ia·des 1 :** a nymph believed in ancient times to be living in lakes, rivers, and springs **2 :** the larva of an insect (as a dragonfly) that lives in water
[1]**nail** *n* **1 :** the horny scale at the end of each finger and toe **2 :** a slender pointed piece of metal driven into or through something for fastening
[2]**nail** *vb* **:** to fasten with or as if with a nail
nail·brush *n* **:** a brush for cleaning the hands and fingernails
na·ive *or* **na·ïve** *adj* **1 :** being simple and sincere **2 :** showing lack of experience or knowledge — **na·ive·ly** *adv*
na·ked *adj* **1 :** having no clothes on **:** NUDE **2 :** lacking a usual or natural covering **3 :** not in its case or covering **4 :** stripped of anything misleading **:** PLAIN **5 :** not aided by an artificial device — **na·ked·ly** *adv* — **na·ked·ness** *n*
[1]**name** *n* **1 :** a word or combination of words by which a person or thing is known **2 :** REPUTATION 2
[2]**name** *vb* **named; nam·ing 1 :** to give a name to **:** CALL **2 :** to refer to by name **3 :** to nominate for a job of authority **:** APPOINT **4 :** to decide on **:** CHOOSE **5 :** [2]MENTION
[3]**name** *adj* **1 :** of, relating to, or having a name **2 :** well known because of wide distribution
name·less *adj* **1 :** having no name **2 :** not marked with a name **3 :** [1]UNKNOWN, ANONYMOUS **4 :** not to be described — **name·less·ness** *n*
name·ly *adv* **:** that is to say
name·sake *n* **:** a person who has the same name as another and especially one named for another
nan·ny *n, pl* **nannies :** a child's nurse
nanny goat *n* **:** a female domestic goat
[1]**nap** *vb* **napped; nap·ping 1 :** to sleep briefly especially during the day **2 :** to be unprepared
[2]**nap** *n* **:** a short sleep especially during the day
[3]**nap** *n* **:** a hairy or fluffy surface (as on cloth)
nape *n* **:** the back of the neck
naph·tha *n* **:** any of various usually flammable liquids prepared from coal or petroleum and used to dissolve substances or to thin paint
nap·kin *n* **:** a small square of cloth or paper used at table to wipe the lips or fingers and protect the clothes
nar·cis·sus *n, pl* **narcissus** *or* **nar·cis·sus·es** *or* **nar·cis·si :** a daffodil with flowers that have short tubes, grow separately on the stalk, and come in white, yellow, or a combination of both
[1]**nar·cot·ic** *n* **:** a drug (as opium) that in small doses dulls the senses, relieves pain, and brings on sleep but in larger doses is a dangerous poison
[2]**narcotic** *adj* **1 :** acting as or being the source of a narcotic **2 :** of or relating to narcotics or their use or control
nar·rate *vb* **nar·rat·ed; nar·rat·ing :** to tell in full detail — **nar·ra·tor** *n*
nar·ra·tion *n* **1 :** the act or process or an instance of narrating **2 :** [1]NARRATIVE 1
[1]**nar·ra·tive** *n* **1 :** something (as a story) that is narrated **2 :** the art or practice of narrating
[2]**narrative** *adj* **:** of or relating to narration **:** having the form of a story
[1]**nar·row** *adj* **1 :** of slender or less than usual width **2 :** limited in size or extent **3 :** not broad or open in mind or views **4 :** barely successful **:** CLOSE — **nar·row·ly** *adv* — **nar·row·ness** *n*
[2]**narrow** *vb* **:** to make or become narrow
[3]**narrow** *n* **:** a narrow passage connecting two bodies of water — usually used in pl.
nar·row–mind·ed *adj* **:** [1]NARROW 3, INTOLERANT — **nar·row–mind·ed·ly** *adv* — **nar·row–mind·ed·ness** *n*
nar·whal *n* **:** an arctic marine animal about twenty feet long that is related to the dolphin and in the male has a long twisted ivory tusk
[1]**na·sal** *n* **:** a nasal sound
[2]**nasal** *adj* **1 :** of or relating to the nose **2 :** uttered with the nose passage open — **na·sal·ly** *adv*
nas·tur·tium *n* **:** an herb with a juicy stem, roundish leaves, red, yellow, or white flowers, and seeds with a sharp taste
nas·ty *adj* **nas·ti·er; nas·ti·est 1 :** very dirty **:** FILTHY **2 :** INDECENT **3 :** [1]MEAN 4 **4 :** HARMFUL, DANGEROUS **5 :** very unpleasant — **nas·ti·ly** *adv* — **nas·ti·ness** *n*
na·tal *adj* **:** of, relating to, or associated with birth
na·tion *n* **1 :** NATIONALITY 3 **2 :** a community of people made up of one or more na-

tionalities usually with its own territory and government **3 :** a usually large independent division of territory **:** COUNTRY

¹na·tion·al *adj* **:** of or relating to a nation — **na·tion·al·ly** *adv*

²national *n* **:** a citizen of a nation

na·tion·al·ism *n* **:** devotion to the interests of a certain country

na·tion·al·ist *n* **:** a person who believes in nationalism

na·tion·al·is·tic *adj* **1 :** of, relating to, or favoring nationalism **2 :** ¹NATIONAL — **na·tion·al·is·ti·cal·ly** *adv*

na·tion·al·i·ty *n, pl* **na·tion·al·i·ties 1 :** the fact or state of belonging to a nation **2 :** the state of being a separate nation **3 :** a group of people having a common history, tradition, culture, or language

na·tion·al·ize *vb* **na·tion·al·ized; na·tion·al·iz·ing :** to place under government control

na·tion·wide *adj* **:** extending throughout a nation

¹na·tive *adj* **1 :** NATURAL 1 **2 :** born in a certain place or country **3 :** belonging to one because of one's place of birth **4 :** grown, produced, or coming from a certain place

²native *n* **:** one that is native

Native American *n* **:** AMERICAN INDIAN

na·tiv·i·ty *n, pl* **na·tiv·i·ties 1 :** BIRTH 1 **2** *cap* **:** the birth of Christ **:** CHRISTMAS

nat·ty *adj* **nat·ti·er; nat·ti·est :** very neat, trim, and stylish — **nat·ti·ly** *adv* — **nat·ti·ness** *n*

nat·u·ral *adj* **1 :** born in or with one **2 :** being such by nature **:** BORN **3 :** found in or produced by nature **4 :** of or relating to nature **5 :** not made by humans **6 :** being simple and sincere **7 :** LIFELIKE **8 :** being neither sharp nor flat **:** having neither sharps nor flats — **nat·u·ral·ly** *adv* — **nat·u·ral·ness** *n*

nat·u·ral·ist *n* **:** a student of nature and especially of plants and animals as they live in nature

nat·u·ral·i·za·tion *n* **:** the act or process of naturalizing **:** the state of being naturalized

nat·u·ral·ize *vb* **nat·u·ral·ized; nat·u·ral·iz·ing 1 :** to become or cause to become established as if native **2 :** to admit to citizenship

natural number *n* **:** the number 1 or any number (as 3, 12, 432) obtained by adding 1 to it one or more times

natural resource *n* **:** something (as a mineral, forest, or kind of animal) that is found in nature and is valuable to humans

na·ture *n* **1 :** the basic character of a person or thing **2 :** ¹SORT 1, VARIETY **3 :** natural feelings **:** DISPOSITION, TEMPERAMENT **4 :** the material universe **5 :** the working of a living body **6 :** natural scenery

¹naught *or* **nought** *pron* **:** ¹NOTHING 1

²naught *or* **nought** *n* **:** ZERO 1, CIPHER

naugh·ty *adj* **naugh·ti·er; naugh·ti·est :** behaving in a bad or improper way — **naugh·ti·ly** *adv* — **naugh·ti·ness** *n*

nau·sea *n* **1 :** a disturbed condition of the stomach in which one feels like vomiting **2 :** deep disgust **:** LOATHING

nau·se·ate *vb* **nau·se·at·ed; nau·se·at·ing :** to affect or become affected with nausea — **nau·se·at·ing** *adj* — **nau·se·at·ing·ly** *adv*

nau·seous *adj* **1 :** suffering from nausea **2 :** causing nausea

nau·ti·cal *adj* **:** of or relating to sailors, navigation, or ships — **nau·ti·cal·ly** *adv*

na·val *adj* **:** of or relating to a navy or warships

nave *n* **:** the long central main part of a church

na·vel *n* **:** a hollow in the middle of the abdomen that marks the place where the umbilical cord was attached

nav·i·ga·bil·i·ty *n* **:** the quality or state of being navigable

nav·i·ga·ble *adj* **1 :** deep enough and wide enough to permit passage of ships **2 :** possible to steer

nav·i·gate *vb* **nav·i·gat·ed; nav·i·gat·ing 1 :** to travel by water **2 :** to sail over, on, or through **3 :** to steer a course in a ship or aircraft **4 :** to steer or direct the course of (as a boat)

nav·i·ga·tion *n* **1 :** the act or practice of navigating **2 :** the science of figuring out the position and course of a ship or aircraft

nav·i·ga·tor *n* **:** an officer on a ship or aircraft responsible for its navigation

na·vy *n, pl* **navies 1 :** a nation's ships of war **2 :** the complete naval equipment and organization of a nation **3 :** a dark blue

¹nay *adv* **:** ¹NO 2

²nay *n* **:** ³NO 2

Na·zi *n* **:** a member of a political party controlling Germany from 1933 to 1945

Ne·an·der·thal man *n* **:** a long gone ancient human who made tools of stone and lived by hunting

¹near *adv* **1 :** at, within, or to a short distance or time **2 :** ALMOST, NEARLY

²near *prep* **:** close to

³near *adj* **1 :** closely related or associated **2 :** not far away **3 :** coming close **:** NARROW **4 :** being the closer of two — **near·ly** *adv* — **near·ness** *n*

⁴near *vb* **:** to come near **:** APPROACH

near·by *adv or adj* **:** close at hand
near·sight·ed *adj* **:** able to see near things more clearly than distant ones — **near·sight·ed·ly** *adv* — **near·sight·ed·ness** *n*
neat *adj* **1 :** being simple and in good taste **2 :** SKILLFUL 2 **3 :** showing care and a concern for order — **neat·ly** *adv* — **neat·ness** *n*
neb·u·la *n, pl* **neb·u·las** *or* **neb·u·lae :** any of many clouds of gas or dust seen in the sky among the stars
neb·u·lous *adj* **:** not clear **:** VAGUE — **neb·u·lous·ly** *adv* — **neb·u·lous·ness** *n*
1nec·es·sary *adj* **:** needing to be had or done **:** ESSENTIAL — **nec·es·sar·i·ly** *adv*
2necessary *n, pl* **nec·es·sar·ies :** something that is needed
ne·ces·si·tate *vb* **ne·ces·si·tat·ed; ne·ces·si·tat·ing :** to make necessary **:** REQUIRE
ne·ces·si·ty *n, pl* **ne·ces·si·ties 1 :** the state of things that forces certain actions **2 :** very great need **3 :** the state of being without or unable to get necessary things **:** POVERTY **4 :** something that is badly needed
neck *n* **1 :** the part connecting the head and the main part of the body **2 :** the part of a garment covering or nearest to the neck **3 :** something like a neck in shape or position — **necked** *adj* — **neck and neck :** so nearly equal (as in a race) that one cannot be said to be ahead of the other
neck·er·chief *n, pl* **neck·er·chiefs :** a square of cloth worn folded around the neck like a scarf
neck·lace *n* **:** an ornament (as a string of beads) worn around the neck
neck·line *n* **:** the outline of the neck opening of a garment
neck·tie *n* **:** a narrow length of material worn around the neck and tied in front
nec·tar *n* **1 :** the drink of the Greek and Roman gods **2 :** a sweet liquid given off by plants and used by bees in making honey
nec·tar·ine *n* **:** a peach with a smooth skin
née *or* **nee** *adj* **:** BORN 1 — used to identify a woman by her maiden name
1need *n* **1 :** something that must be done **:** OBLIGATION **2 :** a lack of something necessary, useful, or desired **3 :** something necessary or desired
2need *vb* **1 :** to suffer from the lack of something important to life or health **2 :** to be necessary **3 :** to be without **:** REQUIRE
need·ful *adj* **:** 1NECESSARY — **need·ful·ly** *adv* — **need·ful·ness** *n*
1nee·dle *n* **1 :** a slender pointed usually steel device used to make a hole and pull thread through in sewing **2 :** a slender pointed piece of metal or plastic (used for knitting) **3 :** a leaf (as of a pine) shaped like a needle **4 :** a pointer on a dial **5 :** a slender hollow instrument by which material is put into or taken from the body through the skin — **nee·dle·like** *adj*
2needle *vb* **nee·dled; nee·dling :** 1TEASE, TAUNT
nee·dle·point *n* **:** embroidery done on canvas usually in simple even stitches across counted threads
need·less *adj* **:** UNNECESSARY — **need·less·ly** *adv* — **need·less·ness** *n*
nee·dle·work *n* **:** work (as sewing or embroidery) done with a needle
needn't : need not
needs *adv* **:** because of necessity
needy *adj* **need·i·er; need·i·est :** very poor — **need·i·ness** *n*
ne'er *adv* **:** NEVER
ne'er–do–well *n* **:** a worthless person who will not work
ne·gate *vb* **ne·gat·ed; ne·gat·ing 1 :** to deny the existence or truth of **2 :** to cause to be ineffective
ne·ga·tion *n* **:** the action of negating **:** DENIAL
1neg·a·tive *adj* **1 :** making a denial **2 :** not positive **3 :** not helpful **4 :** less than zero and shown by a minus sign **5 :** of, being, or relating to electricity of which the electron is the unit and which is produced in a hard rubber rod that has been rubbed with wool **6 :** having more electrons than protons **7 :** being the part toward which the electric current flows from the outside circuit — **neg·a·tive·ly** *adv* — **neg·a·tiv·i·ty** *n*
2negative *n* **1 :** something that is the opposite of something else **2 :** a negative number **3 :** an expression (as the word *no*) that denies or says the opposite **4 :** the side that argues or votes against something **5 :** a photographic image on film from which a final picture is made
1ne·glect *vb* **1 :** to fail to give the right amount of attention to **2 :** to fail to do or look after especially because of carelessness
2neglect *n* **1 :** an act or instance of neglecting something **2 :** the state of being neglected
ne·glect·ful *adj* **:** tending to neglect **:** NEGLIGENT — **ne·glect·ful·ly** *adv* — **ne·glect·ful·ness** *n*
neg·li·gee *n* **:** a woman's loose robe worn especially while dressing or resting
neg·li·gence *n* **1 :** the state of being negligent **2 :** an act or instance of being negligent
neg·li·gent *adj* **:** likely to neglect things **:** CARELESS — **neg·li·gent·ly** *adv*

neg·li·gi·ble *adj* **:** so small or unimportant as to deserve little or no attention — **neg·li·gi·bly** *adv*

ne·go·tia·ble *adj* **:** possible to negotiate — **ne·go·tia·bil·i·ty** *n*

ne·go·ti·ate *vb* **ne·go·ti·at·ed; ne·go·ti·at·ing** **1 :** to have a discussion with another in order to settle something **2 :** to arrange for by discussing **3 :** to give to someone in exchange for cash or something of equal value **4 :** to be successful in getting around, through, or over — **ne·go·ti·a·tor** *n*

ne·go·ti·a·tion *n* **:** the act or process of negotiating or being negotiated

Ne·gro *n, pl* **Ne·groes** **1 :** a member of any of the original peoples of Africa south of the Sahara **2 :** a person with Negro ancestors — **Negro** *adj*

[1]**neigh** *vb* **:** to make a neigh

[2]**neigh** *n* **:** the long loud cry of a horse

[1]**neigh·bor** *n* **1 :** a person living or a thing located near another **2 :** a fellow human being

[2]**neighbor** *vb* **:** to be near or next to — **neigh·bor·ing** *adj*

neigh·bor·hood *n* **1 :** a place or region near **:** VICINITY **2 :** an amount, size, or range that is close to **3 :** the people living near one another **4 :** a section lived in by neighbors

neigh·bor·ly *adj* **:** of, relating to, or like neighbors **:** FRIENDLY — **neigh·bor·li·ness** *n*

[1]**nei·ther** *conj* **1 :** not either **2 :** also not

[2]**neither** *pron* **:** not the one and not the other

[3]**neither** *adj* **:** not either

ne·on *n* **1 :** a colorless gaseous chemical element found in very small amounts in the air and used in electric lamps **2 :** a lamp in which the gas contains a large proportion of neon **3 :** a sign made up of such lamps

neo·phyte *n* **1 :** a new convert **2 :** BEGINNER, NOVICE

neph·ew *n* **:** a son of one's brother or sister

Nep·tune *n* **:** the planet that is eighth in order of distance from the sun and has a diameter of about 45,000 kilometers

nep·tu·ni·um *n* **:** a radioactive chemical element similar to uranium

nerd *n* **1 :** a person who is socially awkward, unattractive, or not fashionable **2 :** a person who is extremely devoted to study and learning — **nerdy** *adj*

[1]**nerve** *n* **1 :** one of the bands of nerve fibers that join centers (as the brain) of the nervous system with other parts of the body and carry nerve impulses **2 :** FORTITUDE, DARING **3 :** IMPUDENCE **4 nerves** *pl* **:** JITTERS **5 :** the sensitive soft inner part of a tooth — **nerve·less** *adj*

[2]**nerve** *vb* **nerved; nerv·ing** **:** to give strength or courage to

nerve cell *n* **:** a cell of the nervous system with fibers that conduct nerve impulses

nerve fiber *n* **:** any of the slender extensions of a nerve cell that carry nerve impulses

nerve impulse *n* **:** a progressive change of a nerve fiber by which information is brought to or orders sent from the central nervous system

ner·vous *adj* **1 :** of or relating to nerve cells **2 :** of, relating to, or made up of nerves or nervous tissue **3 :** easily excited or upset **4 :** TIMID — **ner·vous·ly** *adv* — **ner·vous·ness** *n*

nervy *adj* **nerv·i·er; nerv·i·est** **1 :** showing calm courage **:** BOLD **2 :** [1]FORWARD 2 **3 :** NERVOUS 3 — **nerv·i·ness** *n*

-ness *n suffix* **:** state **:** condition

[1]**nest** *n* **1 :** a shelter made by a bird for its eggs and young **2 :** a place where the eggs of some animals other than birds are laid and hatched **3 :** a cozy home **:** a snug shelter **4 :** those living in a nest

[2]**nest** *vb* **:** to build or live in a nest

nes·tle *vb* **nes·tled; nes·tling** **1 :** to lie close and snug **:** CUDDLE **2 :** to settle as if in a nest

nest·ling *n* **:** a young bird not yet able to leave the nest

[1]**net** *n* **1 :** a fabric made of threads, cords, ropes, or wires that weave in and out with much open space **2 :** something made of net **3 :** something that traps one as if in a net **4 :** NETWORK 2 **5** *often cap* **:** INTERNET

[2]**net** *vb* **net·ted; net·ting** **1 :** to cover with or as if with a net **2 :** to catch in or as if in a net

[3]**net** *adj* **:** remaining after all charges or expenses have been subtracted

[4]**net** *vb* **net·ted; net·ting :** to gain or produce as profit **:** CLEAR

net·ting *n* **:** NETWORK 1 2

net·tle *n* **:** a tall plant with stinging hairs on the leaves

net·work *n* **1 :** a net fabric or structure **2 :** an arrangement of lines or channels crossing as in a net **3 :** a system of computers connected by communications lines **4 :** a group of connected radio or television stations

neu·ron *n* **:** NERVE CELL

neu·ter *adj* **:** lacking sex organs **:** having sex organs that are not fully developed

[1]**neu·tral** *n* **1 :** one that does not favor either side in a quarrel, contest, or war **2 :** a grayish color **3 :** a position of gears (as in the transmission of a motor vehicle) in which they are not in contact

DICTIONARY

[2]**neutral** *adj* **1 :** not favoring either side in a quarrel, contest, or war **2 :** of or relating to a neutral country **3 :** being neither one thing nor the other **4 :** having no color that stands out : GRAYISH **5 :** neither acid nor basic **6 :** not electrically charged

neu•tral•i•ty *n* **:** the quality or state of being neutral

neu•tral•ize *vb* **neu•tral•ized; neu•tral•iz•ing** **1 :** to make chemically neutral **2 :** to make ineffective — **neu•tral•i•za•tion** *n* — **neu•tral•iz•er** *n*

neu•tron *n* **:** a particle that has a mass nearly equal to that of the proton but no electrical charge and that is present in all atomic nuclei except those of hydrogen

nev•er *adv* **1 :** not ever : at no time **2 :** not to any extent or in any way

nev•er•more *adv* **:** never again

nev•er•the•less *adv* **:** even so : HOWEVER

[1]**new** *adj* **1 :** not old : RECENT **2 :** taking the place of one that came before **3 :** recently discovered or learned about **4 :** not known or experienced before **5 :** not accustomed **6 :** beginning as a repeating of a previous act or thing **7 :** being in a position, place, or state the first time — **new•ness** *n*

[2]**new** *adv* **:** NEWLY, RECENTLY

new•born *adj* **1 :** recently born **2 :** made new or strong again

new•com•er *n* **1 :** one recently arrived **2 :** BEGINNER

new•el *n* **:** a post at the bottom or at a turn of a stairway

new•fan•gled *adj* **:** of the newest style **:** NOVEL

new•ly *adv* **:** not long ago : RECENTLY

new moon *n* **1 :** the moon's phase when its dark side is toward the earth **2 :** the thin curved outline of the moon seen shortly after sunset for a few days after the new moon

news *n* **1 :** a report of recent events **2 :** material reported in a newspaper or news magazine or on a newscast **3 :** an event that is interesting enough to be reported

news•boy *n* **:** a person who delivers or sells newspapers

news•cast *n* **:** a radio or television broadcast of news

news•girl *n* **:** a girl who delivers or sells newspapers

news•man *n, pl* **news•men :** a person who gathers or reports news

news•pa•per *n* **:** a paper that is printed and sold usually every day or weekly and that contains news, articles of opinion, features, and advertising

news•pa•per•man *n, pl* **news•pa•per•men :** a man who owns or works on a newspaper

news•pa•per•wom•an *n, pl* **news•pa•per•wom•en :** a woman who owns or works on a newspaper

news•reel *n* **:** a short motion picture about current events

news•stand *n* **:** a place where newspapers and magazines are sold

news•wom•an *n, pl* **news•wom•en :** a woman who gathers or reports news

newsy *adj* **news•i•er; news•i•est :** filled with news

newt *n* **:** a small salamander that lives mostly in water

New Year's Day *n* **:** January 1 observed as a legal holiday in many countries

[1]**next** *adj* **:** coming just before or after

[2]**next** *prep* **:** NEXT TO

[3]**next** *adv* **1 :** in the nearest place, time, or order following **2 :** at the first time after this

next–door *adj* **:** located in the next building, apartment, or room

[1]**next to** *prep* **1 :** BESIDE 1 **2 :** following right after

[2]**next to** *adv* **:** very nearly : ALMOST

nib *n* **1 :** a pointed object (as the bill of a bird) **2 :** the point of a pen

[1]**nib•ble** *vb* **nib•bled; nib•bling :** to bite or chew gently or bit by bit — **nib•bler** *n*

[2]**nibble** *n* **1 :** an act of nibbling **2 :** a very small amount

nice *adj* **nic•er; nic•est** **1 :** very fussy (as about appearance, manners, or food) **2 :** able to recognize small differences between things **3 :** PLEASING, PLEASANT **4 :** well behaved — **nice•ly** *adv* — **nice•ness** *n*

ni•ce•ty *n, pl* **ni•ce•ties** **1 :** something dainty, delicate, or especially nice **2 :** a fine detail

niche *n* **1 :** an open hollow in a wall (as for a statue) **2 :** a place, job, or use for which a person or a thing is best fitted

[1]**nick** *n* **1 :** a small cut or chip in a surface **2 :** the last moment

[2]**nick** *vb* **:** to make a nick in

[1]**nick•el** *n* **1 :** a hard silvery white metallic chemical element that can be highly polished, resists weathering, and is used in alloys **2 :** a United States coin worth five cents

[2]**nickel** *vb* **nick•eled** *or* **nick•elled; nick•el•ing** *or* **nick•el•ling :** to plate with nickel

[1]**nick•er** *vb* **:** [1]NEIGH, WHINNY

[2]**nicker** *n* **:** [2]NEIGH

[1]**nick•name** *n* **1 :** a usually descriptive name given in addition to the one belonging to an individual **2 :** a familiar form of a proper name

[2]**nickname** *vb* **nick•named; nick•nam•ing :** to give a nickname to

nic•o•tine *n* **:** a poisonous substance found in small amounts in tobacco and used especially to kill insects

niece *n* **:** a daughter of one's brother or sister

nig•gling *adj* **:** PETTY 1

¹nigh *adv* **1 :** near in time or place **2 :** ALMOST, NEARLY

²nigh *adj* **:** ³CLOSE 5, NEAR

night *n* **1 :** the time between dusk and dawn when there is no sunlight **2 :** NIGHTFALL **3 :** the darkness of night

night•club *n* **:** a place of entertainment open at night usually serving food and liquor and having music for dancing

night crawl•er *n* **:** EARTHWORM

night•fall *n* **:** the coming of night

night•gown *n* **:** a loose garment worn in bed

night•hawk *n* **1 :** a bird that is related to the whippoorwill, flies mostly at twilight, and eats insects **2 :** a person who stays up late at night

night•in•gale *n* **:** a reddish brown Old World thrush noted for the sweet song of the male

¹night•ly *adj* **1 :** of or relating to the night or every night **2 :** happening or done at night or every night

²nightly *adv* **1 :** every night **2 :** at or by night

night•mare *n* **1 :** a frightening dream **2 :** a horrible experience — **night•mar•ish** *adj*

night•shirt *n* **:** a nightgown like a very long shirt

night•stick *n* **:** a police officer's club

night•time *n* **:** NIGHT 1

nil *n* **:** ZERO 4, NOTHING

nim•ble *adj* **nim•bler; nim•blest 1 :** quick and light in motion **:** AGILE **2 :** quick in understanding and learning **:** CLEVER — **nim•ble•ness** *n* — **nim•bly** *adv*

nim•bus *n, pl* **nim•bi** *or* **nim•bus•es :** a rain cloud that is evenly gray and that covers the whole sky

nin•com•poop *n* **:** ¹FOOL 1

¹nine *adj* **:** being one more than eight

²nine *n* **1 :** one more than eight **:** three times three **:** 9 **2 :** the ninth in a set or series

¹nine•teen *adj* **:** being one more than eighteen

²nineteen *n* **:** one more than eighteen **:** 19

¹nine•teenth *adj* **:** coming right after eighteenth

²nineteenth *n* **:** number nineteen in a series

¹nine•ti•eth *adj* **:** coming right after eighty-ninth

²ninetieth *n* **:** number ninety in a series

¹nine•ty *adj* **:** being nine times ten

²ninety *n* **:** nine times ten **:** 90

nin•ja *n* **:** a person trained in ancient Japanese arts of fighting and defending oneself and employed especially for espionage and assassinations

nin•ny *n, pl* **ninnies :** ¹FOOL 1

¹ninth *adj* **:** coming right after eighth

²ninth *n* **1 :** number nine in a series **2 :** one of nine equal parts

¹nip *vb* **nipped; nip•ping 1 :** to catch hold of (as with teeth) and squeeze sharply though not very hard **2 :** to cut off by or as if by pinching sharply **3 :** to stop the growth or progress of **4 :** to injure or make numb with cold

²nip *n* **1 :** something that nips **2 :** the act of nipping **3 :** a small portion **:** BIT

³nip *n* **:** a small amount of liquor

nip and tuck *adj or adv* **:** so close that the lead shifts rapidly from one contestant to another

nip•ple *n* **1 :** the part of the breast from which a baby or young animal sucks milk **2 :** something (as the mouthpiece of a baby's bottle) like a nipple

nip•py *adj* **nip•pi•er; nip•pi•est :** CHILLY

nit *n* **:** the egg of a louse

ni•trate *n* **:** a substance that is made from or has a composition as if made from nitric acid

ni•tric acid *n* **:** a strong liquid acid that contains hydrogen, nitrogen, and oxygen and is used in making fertilizers, explosives, and dyes

ni•tro•gen *n* **:** a colorless odorless gaseous chemical element that makes up 78 percent of the atmosphere and forms a part of all living tissues

nitrogen cycle *n* **:** a continuous series of natural processes by which nitrogen passes from air to soil to organisms and back into the air

nitrogen fix•a•tion *n* **:** the changing of free nitrogen into combined forms especially by bacteria (**nitrogen-fixing bacteria**)

ni•tro•glyc•er•in *or* **ni•tro•glyc•er•ine** *n* **:** a heavy oily liquid explosive from which dynamite is made

nit•wit *n* **:** a very silly or stupid person

¹no *adv* **1 :** not at all **:** not any **2 :** not so — used to express disagreement or refusal **3** — used to express surprise, doubt, or disbelief

²no *adj* **1 :** not any **2 :** hardly any **:** very little **3 :** not a

³no *n, pl* **noes** *or* **nos 1 :** an act or instance of refusing or denying by the use of the word *no* **:** DENIAL **2 :** a negative vote or decision **3** *noes or nos pl* **:** persons voting in the negative

no•bil•i•ty *n, pl* **no•bil•i•ties 1 :** the quality or state of being noble **2 :** noble rank **3 :** the class or a group of nobles

[1]**no·ble** *adj* **no·bler; no·blest** **1 :** EMINENT, ILLUSTRIOUS **2 :** of very high birth or rank **3 :** having very fine qualities **4 :** grand in appearance — **no·ble·ness** *n* — **no·bly** *adv*

[2]**noble** *n* **:** a person of noble birth or rank

no·ble·man *n, pl* **no·ble·men :** a man of noble rank

no·ble·wom·an *n, pl* **no·ble·wom·en :** a woman of noble rank

[1]**no·body** *pron* **:** no person **:** not anybody

[2]**nobody** *n, pl* **no·bod·ies :** a person of no importance

noc·tur·nal *adj* **1 :** of, relating to, or happening at night **:** NIGHTLY **2 :** active at night — **noc·tur·nal·ly** *adv*

[1]**nod** *vb* **nod·ded; nod·ding** **1 :** to bend the head downward or forward (as in bowing, going to sleep, or indicating "yes") **2 :** to move up and down **3 :** to show by a nod of the head

[2]**nod** *n* **:** the action of bending the head downward and forward

node *n* **:** a thickened spot or part (as of a plant stem where a leaf develops)

nod·ule *n* **:** a small node (as of a clover root)

no·el *n* **1 :** a Christmas carol **2** *cap* **:** the Christmas season

noes *pl of* NO

[1]**noise** *n* **1 :** a loud unpleasant sound **2 :** [3]SOUND 1 — **noise·less** *adj* — **noise·less·ly** *adv* — **noise·less·ness** *n*

[2]**noise** *vb* **noised; nois·ing :** to spread by rumor or report

noise·mak·er *n* **:** a device used to make noise especially at parties

noisy *adj* **nois·i·er; nois·i·est** **1 :** making noise **2 :** full of noise — **nois·i·ly** *adv* — **nois·i·ness** *n*

[1]**no·mad** *n* **1 :** a member of a people having no fixed home but wandering from place to place **2 :** WANDERER

[2]**nomad** *adj* **:** NOMADIC 2

no·mad·ic *adj* **1 :** of or relating to nomads **2 :** roaming about with no special end in mind

nom·i·nal *adj* **1 :** being such in name only **2 :** very small **:** TRIFLING — **nom·i·nal·ly** *adv*

nom·i·nate *vb* **nom·i·nat·ed; nom·i·nat·ing :** to choose as a candidate for election, appointment, or honor — **nom·i·na·tor** *n*

nom·i·na·tion *n* **1 :** the act or an instance of nominating **2 :** the state of being nominated

nom·i·na·tive *adj* **:** being or belonging to the case of a noun or pronoun that is usually the subject of a verb

nom·i·nee *n* **:** a person nominated for an office, duty, or position

non- *prefix* **:** not

non·al·co·hol·ic *adj* **:** containing no alcohol

non·cha·lance *n* **:** the state of being nonchalant

non·cha·lant *adj* **:** having a confident and easy manner — **non·cha·lant·ly** *adv*

non·com·bat·ant *n* **1 :** a member (as a chaplain) of the armed forces whose duties do not include fighting **2 :** [1]CIVILIAN

non·com·mis·sioned officer *n* **:** an officer in the Army, Air Force, or Marine Corps appointed from among the enlisted persons

non·com·mit·tal *adj* **:** not telling or showing what one thinks or has decided — **non·com·mit·tal·ly** *adv*

non·com·mu·ni·ca·ble *adj* **:** not spread from one individual to another

non·con·duc·tor *n* **:** a substance that conducts heat, electricity, or sound at a very low rate

non·con·form·ist *n* **:** a person who does not conform to generally accepted standards or customs

non·de·script *adj* **:** of no certain class or kind **:** not easily described

[1]**none** *pron* **:** not any **:** not one

[2]**none** *adv* **1 :** not at all **2 :** in no way

non·en·ti·ty *n, pl* **non·en·ti·ties :** someone or something of no importance

[1]**non·es·sen·tial** *adj* **:** not essential

[2]**nonessential** *n* **:** something that is not essential

none·the·less *adv* **:** NEVERTHELESS

non·fic·tion *n* **:** writings that are not fiction

non·flam·ma·ble *adj* **:** not flammable

non·green *adj* **:** having no chlorophyll

non·liv·ing *adj* **:** not living

non·par·ti·san *adj* **:** not partisan **:** not committed to one party or side

non·plus *vb* **non·plussed; non·plus·sing :** to cause to be at a loss as to what to say, think, or do **:** PERPLEX

non·poi·son·ous *adj* **:** not poisonous

non·prof·it *adj* **:** not existing or carried on to make a profit

[1]**non·res·i·dent** *adj* **:** not living in a certain place

[2]**nonresident** *n* **:** a nonresident person

non·sched·uled *adj* **:** licensed to carry pasengers or freight by air whenever demand requires

non·sec·tar·i·an *adj* **:** not limited to a particular religious group

non·sense *n* **1 :** foolish or meaningless words or actions **2 :** things of no importance or value

non·sen·si·cal *adj* **:** making no sense **:** ABSURD — **non·sen·si·cal·ly** *adv*

non·smok·er *n* **:** a person who does not smoke tobacco

non·smok·ing *adj* **1 :** not in the habit of

smoking tobacco **2 :** reserved for the use of nonsmokers
non·stan·dard *adj* **:** not standard
non·stop *adv or adj* **:** without a stop
noo·dle *n* **:** a food like macaroni made with egg and shaped into flat strips — usually used in pl.
nook *n* **1 :** an inner corner **2 :** a sheltered or hidden place
noon *n* **:** the middle of the day **:** twelve o'clock in the daytime
noon·day *n* **:** NOON, MIDDAY
no one *pron* **:** 1NOBODY
noon·tide *n* **:** NOON
noon·time *n* **:** NOON
noose *n* **:** a loop that passes through a knot at the end of a line so that it gets smaller when the other end of the line is pulled
nor *conj* **:** and not
norm *n* **:** 1AVERAGE 2
1nor·mal *adj* **1 :** of the regular or usual kind **:** REGULAR **2 :** of average intelligence **3 :** sound in body or mind — **nor·mal·ly** *adv*
2normal *n* **1 :** one that is normal **2 :** 1AVERAGE 2
nor·mal·cy *n* **:** NORMALITY
nor·mal·i·ty *n* **:** the quality or state of being normal
Nor·man *n* **1 :** one of the Scandinavians who conquered Normandy in the tenth century **2 :** one of the people of mixed Norman and French blood who conquered England in 1066
Norse *n pl* **1 :** people of Scandinavia **2 :** people of Norway
1north *adv* **:** to or toward the north
2north *adj* **:** placed toward, facing, or coming from the north
3north *n* **1 :** the direction to the left of one facing east **:** the compass point opposite to south **2** *cap* **:** regions or countries north of a point that is mentioned or understood
1North American *n* **:** a person born or living in North America
2North American *adj* **:** of or relating to North America or the North Americans
north·bound *adj* **:** going north
1north·east *adv* **:** to or toward the direction between north and east
2northeast *adj* **:** placed toward, facing, or coming from the northeast
3northeast *n* **1 :** the direction between north and east **2** *cap* **:** regions or countries northeast of a point that is mentioned or understood
north·east·er·ly *adv or adj* **1 :** from the northeast **2 :** toward the northeast
north·east·ern *adj* **1** *often cap* **:** of, relating to, or like that of the Northeast **2 :** lying toward or coming from the northeast
north·er·ly *adj or adv* **1 :** toward the north **2 :** from the north
north·ern *adj* **1** *often cap* **:** of, relating to, or like that of the North **2 :** lying toward or coming from the north
northern lights *n pl* **:** AURORA BOREALIS
north·land *n, often cap* **:** land in the north **:** the north of a country or region
north pole *n* **1** *often cap N&P* **:** the most northern point of the earth **:** the northern end of the earth's axis **2 :** the end of a magnet that points toward the north when the magnet is free to swing
North Star *n* **:** the star toward which the northern end of the earth's axis very nearly points
north·ward *adv or adj* **:** toward the north
1north·west *adv* **:** to or toward the direction between north and west
2northwest *adj* **:** placed toward, facing, or coming from the northwest
3northwest *n* **1 :** the direction between north and west **2** *cap* **:** regions or countries northwest of a point that is mentioned or understood
north·west·er·ly *adv or adj* **1 :** from the northwest **2 :** toward the northwest
north·west·ern *adj* **1** *often cap* **:** of, relating to, or like that of the Northwest **2 :** lying toward or coming from the northwest
1Nor·we·gian *adj* **:** of or relating to Norway, its people, or the Norwegian language
2Norwegian *n* **1 :** a person who is born or lives in Norway **2 :** the language of the Norwegians
nos *pl of* NO
1nose *n* **1 :** the part of a person's face or an animal's head that contains the nostrils **2 :** the sense or organ of smell **3 :** something (as a point, edge, or the front of an object) that suggests a nose **4 :** an ability to discover — **nosed** *adj*
2nose *vb* **nosed; nos·ing 1 :** to detect by or as if by smell **:** SCENT **2 :** to touch or rub with the nose **:** NUZZLE **3 :** to search in a nosy way **:** PRY **4 :** to move ahead slowly or carefully
nose·bleed *n* **:** a bleeding at the nose
nose cone *n* **:** a protective cone forming the forward end of a rocket or missile
nose–dive *vb* **nose–dived; nose–div·ing :** to plunge suddenly or sharply
nose dive *n* **1 :** a downward plunge (as of an airplane) **2 :** a sudden sharp drop (as in prices)
nos·tal·gia *n* **:** a wishing for something past
nos·tril *n* **:** either of the outer openings of the nose through which one breathes
nos·trum *n* **:** a medicine of secret formula and doubtful worth **:** a questionable remedy

nosy *or* **nos•ey** *adj* **nos•i•er; nos•i•est** : tending to pry into someone else's business

not *adv* **1** — used to make a word or group of words negative **2** — used to stand for the negative of a group of words that comes before

¹no•ta•ble *adj* **1** : deserving special notice : REMARKABLE **2** : DISTINGUISHED, PROMINENT — **no•ta•bly** *adv*

²notable *n* : a famous person

no•ta•rize *vb* **no•ta•rized; no•ta•riz•ing** : to sign as a notary public to show that a document is authentic

no•ta•ry public *n, pl* **notaries public** *or* **notary publics** : a public officer who witnesses the making of a document (as a deed) and signs it to show that it is authentic

no•ta•tion *n* **1** : the act of noting **2** : ²NOTE 5 **3** : a system of signs, marks, or figures used to give specified information

¹notch *n* **1** : a cut in the shape of a V in an edge or surface **2** : a narrow pass between mountains **3** : DEGREE 1, STEP

²notch *vb* : to cut or make notches in

¹note *vb* **not•ed; not•ing** **1** : to notice or observe with care **2** : to record in writing **3** : to call attention to in speech or writing

²note *n* **1** : a musical sound : TONE **2** : a symbol in music that by its shape and position on the staff shows the pitch of a tone and the length of time it is to be held **3** : the musical call or song of a bird **4** : a quality that shows a feeling **5** : something written down often to aid the memory **6** : a printed comment in a book that helps explain part of the text **7** : DISTINCTION 3 **8** : a short written message or letter **9** : careful notice **10** : a promise to pay a debt **11** : a piano key **12** : frame of mind : MOOD

note•book *n* : a book of blank pages for writing in

not•ed *adj* : well-known and highly regarded

note•wor•thy *adj* : worthy of note : REMARKABLE — **note•wor•thi•ness** *n*

¹noth•ing *pron* **1** : not anything : no thing **2** : one of no interest, value, or importance

²nothing *adv* : not at all : in no way

³nothing *n* **1** : something that does not exist **2** : ZERO 1 4 **3** : something of little or no worth or importance — **noth•ing•ness** *n*

¹no•tice *n* **1** : WARNING **2** : an indication that an agreement will end at a specified time **3** : ATTENTION 1, HEED **4** : a written or printed announcement **5** : a brief published criticism (as of a book or play)

²notice *vb* **no•ticed; no•tic•ing** : to take notice of : pay attention to

no•tice•able *adj* : deserving notice : likely to be noticed — **no•tice•ably** *adv*

no•ti•fi•ca•tion *n* **1** : the act or an instance of notifying **2** : something written or printed that gives notice

no•ti•fy *vb* **no•ti•fied; no•ti•fy•ing** : to give notice to : INFORM

no•tion *n* **1** : IDEA 2 **2** : WHIM **3 notions** *pl* : small useful articles (as buttons, needles, and thread)

no•to•ri•e•ty *n* : the state of being notorious

no•to•ri•ous *adj* : widely known for some bad characteristic — **no•to•ri•ous•ly** *adv*

¹not•with•stand•ing *prep* : in spite of

²notwithstanding *adv* : NEVERTHELESS

nou•gat *n* : a candy consisting of a sugar paste with nuts or fruit pieces

nought *variant of* NAUGHT

noun *n* : a word or phrase that is the name of something (as a person, place, or thing) and that is used in a sentence especially as subject or object of a verb or as object of a preposition

nour•ish *vb* : to cause to grow or live in a healthy state especially by providing with enough good food — **nour•ish•ing** *adj*

nour•ish•ment *n* **1** : something (as food) that nourishes **2** : the act of nourishing : the state of being nourished

¹nov•el *adj* **1** : new and different from what is already known **2** : original or striking in design or appearance

²novel *n* : a long made-up story that usually fills a book

nov•el•ist *n* : a writer of novels

nov•el•ty *n, pl* **nov•el•ties** **1** : something new or unusual **2** : the quality or state of being novel **3** : a small article of unusual design intended mainly for decoration or adornment

No•vem•ber *n* : the eleventh month of the year

nov•ice *n* **1** : a new member of a religious community who is preparing to take the vows of religion **2** : a person who has no previous experience with something : BEGINNER

¹now *adv* **1** : at this time **2** : immediately before the present time **3** : in the time immediately to follow **4** — used to express command or introduce an important point **5** : SOMETIMES **6** : in the present state **7** : at the time referred to

²now *conj* : in view of the fact that : ²SINCE 2

³now *n* : the present time

now•a•days *adv* : at the present time

¹no•where *adv* **1** : not in or at any place **2** : to no place

²nowhere *n* : a place that does not exist

nox•ious *adj* : causing harm

noz•zle *n* : a short tube with a taper or constriction often used on a hose or pipe to direct or speed up a flow of fluid

-n't *adv suffix* **:** not

nu·cle·ar *adj* **1 :** of, relating to, or being a nucleus (as of a cell) **2 :** of or relating to the nucleus of the atom **3 :** produced by a nuclear reaction **4 :** of, relating to, or being a weapon whose destructive power comes from an uncontrolled nuclear reaction **5 :** relating to or powered by nuclear energy

nu·cle·us *n, pl* **nu·clei** **1 :** a central point, group, or mass **2 :** a part of cell protoplasm enclosed in a nuclear membrane, containing chromosomes and genes, and concerned especially with the control of vital functions and heredity **3 :** the central part of an atom that comprises nearly all of the atomic mass and that consists of protons and neutrons except in hydrogen in which it consists of one proton only

nude *adj* **nud·er; nud·est :** not wearing clothes **:** NAKED — **nude·ness** *n*

1nudge *vb* **nudged; nudg·ing :** to touch or push gently (as with the elbow) especially in order to attract attention

2nudge *n* **:** a slight push

nu·di·ty *n* **:** the quality or state of being nude

nug·get *n* **:** a solid lump especially of precious metal

nui·sance *n* **:** an annoying person or thing

null *adj* **:** having no legal force **:** not binding **:** VOID

null and void *adj* **:** NULL

1numb *adj* **1 :** lacking in sensation especially from cold **2 :** lacking feelings **:** INDIFFERENT — **numb·ly** *adv* — **numb·ness** *n*

2numb *vb* **:** to make or become numb

1num·ber *n* **1 :** the total of persons, things, or units taken together **:** AMOUNT **2 :** a total that is not specified **3 :** a quality of a word form that shows whether the word is singular or plural **4 :** NUMERAL **5 :** a certain numeral for telling one person or thing from another or from others **6 :** one of a series

2number *vb* **1 :** 1COUNT 1 **2 :** INCLUDE **3 :** to limit to a certain number **4 :** to give a number to **5 :** to add up to or have a total of

num·ber·less *adj* **:** too many to count

number line *n* **:** a line in which points are matched to numbers

nu·mer·al *n* **:** a symbol or group of symbols representing a number

nu·mer·a·tion *n* **:** a system of counting

nu·mer·a·tor *n* **:** the part of a fraction that is above the line

nu·mer·i·cal *adj* **:** of or relating to number **:** stated in numbers — **nu·mer·i·cal·ly** *adv*

nu·mer·ous *adj* **:** consisting of a large number — **nu·mer·ous·ly** *adv*

num·skull *n* **:** a stupid person

nun *n* **:** a woman belonging to a religious community and living by vows

nun·cio *n, pl* **nun·ci·os :** a person who is the pope's representative to a civil government

nup·tial *adj* **:** of or relating to marriage or a wedding

nup·tials *n pl* **:** WEDDING

1nurse *n* **1 :** a woman employed for the care of a young child **2 :** a person skilled or trained in the care of the sick

2nurse *vb* **nursed; nurs·ing** **1 :** to feed at the breast **2 :** to take care of (as a young child or a sick person) **3 :** to treat with special care

nurse·maid *n* **:** 1NURSE 1

nurs·ery *n, pl* **nurs·er·ies** **1 :** a place set aside for small children or for the care of small children **2 :** a place where young trees, vines, and plants are grown and usually sold

nurs·ery·man *n, pl* **nurs·ery·men :** a person whose occupation is the growing of trees, shrubs, and plants

1nur·ture *n* **1 :** UPBRINGING **2 :** something (as food) that nourishes

2nurture *vb* **nur·tured; nur·tur·ing** **1 :** to supply with food **2 :** EDUCATE 2 **3 :** to provide for growth of

1nut *n* **1 :** a dry fruit or seed with a firm inner kernel and a hard shell **2 :** the often edible kernel of a nut **3 :** a piece of metal with a hole in it that is fastened to a bolt by means of a screw thread **4 :** a foolish or crazy person — **nut·like** *adj*

2nut *vb* **nut·ted; nut·ting :** to gather or seek nuts

nut·crack·er *n* **1 :** a device used for cracking the shells of nuts **2 :** a bird related to the crows that lives mostly on the seeds of pine trees

nut·hatch *n* **:** a small bird that creeps on tree trunks and branches and eats insects

nut·let *n* **1 :** a small nut **2 :** a small fruit like a nut

nut·meg *n* **:** a spice that is the ground seeds of a small evergreen tropical tree

nu·tri·ent *n* **:** a substance used in nutrition

nu·tri·ment *n* **:** something that nourishes

nu·tri·tion *n* **:** the act or process of nourishing or being nourished **:** the processes by which a living being takes in and uses nutrients

nu·tri·tion·al *adj* **:** of or relating to nutrition

nu·tri·tious *adj* **:** providing nutrients **:** NOURISHING

nu·tri·tive *adj* **1 :** NUTRITIONAL **2 :** NUTRITIOUS

nut·ty *adj* **nut·ti·er; nut·ti·est** **1 :** not showing good sense **2 :** having a flavor like that of nuts

nuz·zle *vb* **nuz·zled; nuz·zling** **1 :** to push or rub with the nose **2 :** to lie close **:** NESTLE

ny·lon *n* **:** a synthetic material used in the making of textiles and plastics

nymph *n* **1 :** one of many goddesses in old legends represented as beautiful young girls living in the mountains, forests, and waters **2 :** an immature insect that differs from the adult chiefly in the size and proportions of the body

O

o *n, pl* **o's** *or* **os** *often cap* **1 :** the fifteenth letter of the English alphabet **2 :** ZERO 1

O *variant of* OH

oaf *n* **:** a stupid or awkward person — **oaf·ish** *adj*

oak *n* **:** any of various trees and shrubs related to the beech and chestnut whose fruits are acorns and whose tough wood is much used for furniture and flooring

oak·en *adj* **:** made of or like oak

oar *n* **:** a long pole with a broad blade at one end used for rowing or steering a boat

oar·lock *n* **:** a usually U-shaped device for holding an oar in place

oars·man *n, pl* **oars·men** **:** a person who rows a boat

oa·sis *n, pl* **oa·ses** **:** a fertile or green spot in a desert

oat *n* **1 :** a cereal grass grown for its loose clusters of seeds that are used for human food and animal feed **2 oats** *pl* **:** a crop or the grain of the oat

oath *n, pl* **oaths** **1 :** a solemn appeal to God or to some deeply respected person or thing to witness to the truth of one's word or the sacredness of a promise **2 :** a careless or improper use of a sacred name

oat·meal *n* **1 :** oats husked and ground into meal or flattened into flakes **2 :** a hot cereal made from meal or flakes of oats

obe·di·ence *n* **:** the act of obeying **:** willingness to obey

obe·di·ent *adj* **:** willing to obey **:** likely to mind — **obe·di·ent·ly** *adv*

obe·lisk *n* **:** a four-sided pillar that becomes narrower toward the top and ends in a pyramid

obese *adj* **:** very fat

obey *vb* **obeyed; obey·ing** **1 :** to follow the commands or guidance of **2 :** to comply with **:** carry out

obit·u·ary *n, pl* **obit·u·ar·ies** **:** a notice of a person's death (as in a newspaper)

[1]ob·ject *n* **1 :** something that may be seen or felt **2 :** something that arouses feelings in an observer **3 :** [1]PURPOSE, AIM **4 :** a noun or a term behaving like a noun that receives the action of a verb or completes the meaning of a preposition

[2]ob·ject *vb* **1 :** to offer or mention as an objection **2 :** to oppose something firmly and usually with words

ob·jec·tion *n* **1 :** an act of objecting **2 :** a reason for or a feeling of disapproval

ob·jec·tion·able *adj* **:** arousing objection **:** OFFENSIVE

[1]ob·jec·tive *adj* **1 :** being outside of the mind and independent of it **2 :** being or belonging to the case of a noun or pronoun that is an object of a transitive verb or a preposition **3 :** dealing with facts without allowing one's feelings to confuse them — **ob·jec·tive·ly** *adv*

[2]objective *n* **:** [1]PURPOSE, GOAL

ob·jec·tiv·i·ty *n* **:** the quality or state of being objective

ob·li·gate *vb* **ob·li·gat·ed; ob·li·gat·ing** **1 :** to make (someone) do something by law or because it is right **2 :** OBLIGE 2

ob·li·ga·tion *n* **1 :** an act of making oneself responsible for doing something **2 :** something (as the demands of a promise or contract) that requires one to do something **3 :** something one must do **:** DUTY **4 :** a feeling of being indebted for an act of kindness

oblige *vb* **obliged; oblig·ing** **1 :** [2]FORCE 1, COMPEL **2 :** to earn the gratitude of **3 :** to do a favor for or do something as a favor

oblig·ing *adj* **:** willing to do favors — **oblig·ing·ly** *adv*

oblique *adj* **:** neither perpendicular nor parallel — **oblique·ly** *adv*

oblit·er·ate *vb* **oblit·er·at·ed; oblit·er·at·ing** **:** to remove or destroy completely

obliv·i·on *n* **1 :** the state of forgetting or having forgotten or of being unaware or unconscious **2 :** the state of being forgotten

obliv·i·ous *adj* **:** not being conscious or aware — **obliv·i·ous·ly** *adv* — **obliv·i·ous·ness** *n*

[1]ob·long *adj* **:** different from a square, circle, or sphere by being longer in one direction than the other

[2]oblong *n* **:** an oblong figure or object

ob·nox·ious *adj* **:** very disagreeable **:** HATEFUL — **ob·nox·ious·ly** *adv* — **ob·nox·ious·ness** *n*

oboe *n* **:** a woodwind instrument with two reeds that has a penetrating tone and a range of nearly three octaves

ob•scene *adj* **:** very shocking to one's sense of what is moral or decent

ob•scen•i•ty *n, pl* **ob•scen•i•ties** **1 :** the quality or state of being obscene **2 :** something that is obscene

[1]**ob•scure** *adj* **1 :** [1]DARK 1, GLOOMY **2 :** SECLUDED **3 :** not easily understood or clearly expressed **4 :** not outstanding or famous

[2]**obscure** *vb* **ob•scured; ob•scur•ing :** to make obscure

ob•scu•ri•ty *n, pl* **ob•scu•ri•ties** **1 :** the quality or state of being obscure **2 :** something that is obscure

ob•serv•able *adj* **:** NOTICEABLE — **ob•serv•ably** *adv*

ob•ser•vance *n* **1 :** an established practice or ceremony **2 :** an act of following a custom, rule, or law

ob•ser•vant *adj* **:** quick to take notice **:** WATCHFUL, ALERT — **ob•ser•vant•ly** *adv*

ob•ser•va•tion *n* **1 :** an act or the power of seeing or of fixing the mind upon something **2 :** the gathering of information by noting facts or occurrences **3 :** an opinion formed or expressed after observing **4 :** the fact of being observed

ob•ser•va•to•ry *n, pl* **ob•ser•va•to•ries** **:** a place that has instruments for making observations (as of the stars)

ob•serve *vb* **ob•served; ob•serv•ing** **1 :** to act in agreement with **:** OBEY **2 :** CELEBRATE 2 **3 :** [1]WATCH 5 **4 :** [2]REMARK 2, SAY — **ob•serv•er** *n*

ob•sess *vb* **:** to occupy the mind of completely or abnormally

ob•ses•sion *n* **:** a disturbing and often unreasonable idea or feeling that cannot be put out of the mind

ob•sid•i•an *n* **:** a smooth dark rock formed by the cooling of lava

ob•so•lete *adj* **:** no longer in use **:** OUT-OF-DATE

ob•sta•cle *n* **:** something that stands in the way or opposes **:** HINDRANCE

ob•sti•na•cy *n* **:** the quality or state of being obstinate

ob•sti•nate *adj* **1 :** sticking stubbornly to an opinion or purpose **2 :** not easily overcome or removed — **ob•sti•nate•ly** *adv*

ob•struct *vb* **1 :** to stop up by an obstacle **:** BLOCK **2 :** to be or come in the way of **:** HINDER

ob•struc•tion *n* **1 :** an act of obstructing **:** the state of being obstructed **2 :** something that gets in the way **:** OBSTACLE

ob•tain *vb* **:** to gain or get hold of with effort

ob•tain•able *adj* **:** possible to obtain

ob•tuse *adj* **1 :** not pointed or sharp **:** BLUNT **2 :** measuring more than a right angle **3 :** not quick or keen of understanding or feeling

ob•vi•ous *adj* **:** easily found, seen, or understood — **ob•vi•ous•ly** *adv* — **ob•vi•ous•ness** *n*

oc•ca•sion *n* **1 :** a suitable opportunity **:** a good chance **2 :** the time of an event **3 :** a special event

oc•ca•sion•al *adj* **:** happening or met with now and then — **oc•ca•sion•al•ly** *adv*

oc•cu•pan•cy *n, pl* **oc•cu•pan•cies** **:** the act of occupying or taking possession

oc•cu•pant *n* **:** a person who occupies or takes possession

oc•cu•pa•tion *n* **1 :** one's business or profession **2 :** the taking possession and control of an area

oc•cu•pa•tion•al *adj* **:** of or relating to one's occupation — **oc•cu•pa•tion•al•ly** *adv*

oc•cu•py *vb* **oc•cu•pied; oc•cu•py•ing** **1 :** to take up the attention or energies of **2 :** to fill up (an extent of time or space) **3 :** to take or hold possession of **4 :** to live in as an owner or tenant

oc•cur *vb* **oc•curred; oc•cur•ring** **1 :** to be found or met with **:** APPEAR **2 :** to present itself **:** come by or as if by chance **3 :** to come into the mind

oc•cur•rence *n* **1 :** something that occurs **2 :** the action or process of occurring

ocean *n* **1 :** the whole body of salt water that covers nearly three fourths of the earth **2 :** one of the large bodies of water into which the great ocean is divided

oce•an•ic *adj* **:** of or relating to the ocean

ocean•og•ra•phy *n* **:** a science that deals with the ocean

oce•lot *n* **:** a medium-sized American wildcat that is tawny or grayish and blotched with black

o'•clock *adv* **:** according to the clock

octa- *or* **octo-** *also* **oct-** *prefix* **:** eight

oc•ta•gon *n* **:** a flat figure with eight angles and eight sides

oc•tag•o•nal *adj* **:** having eight sides

oc•tave *n* **1 :** a space of eight steps between musical notes **2 :** a tone or note that is eight steps above or below another note or tone

oc•tet *n* **:** a group or set of eight

Oc•to•ber *n* **:** the tenth month of the year

oc•to•pus *n, pl* **oc•to•pus•es** *or* **oc•to•pi** **:** a marine animal with no shell that has a rounded body with eight long flexible arms about its base which have sucking disks able to seize and hold things (as prey)

oc•u•lar *adj* **:** of or relating to the eye or eyesight

odd *adj* **1 :** not one of a pair or a set **2 :** not capable of being divided by two without leaving a remainder **3 :** numbered with an odd number **4 :** some more than the number mentioned **5 :** not usual, expected, or planned **6 :** not usual or traditional — **odd·ly** *adv* — **odd·ness** *n*

odd·ball *n* **:** a person who behaves strangely

odd·i·ty *n, pl* **odd·i·ties 1 :** something odd **2 :** the quality or state of being odd

odds *n pl* **1 :** a difference in favor of one thing over another **2 :** DISAGREEMENT 1

odds and ends *n pl* **:** things left over **:** miscellaneous things

ode *n* **:** a lyric poem that expresses a noble feeling with dignity

odi·ous *adj* **:** causing hatred or strong dislike **:** worthy of hatred

odom·e·ter *n* **:** an instrument for measuring the distance traveled (as by a vehicle)

odor *n* **1 :** a quality of something that one becomes aware of through the sense of smell **2 :** a smell whether pleasant or unpleasant — **odored** *adj* — **odor·less** *adj*

odor·ous *adj* **:** having or giving off an odor

o'er *adv or prep* **:** OVER

of *prep* **1 :** proceeding from **:** belonging to **2 :** CONCERNING **3** — used to show what has been taken away or what one has been freed from **4 :** on account of **5 :** made from **6** — used to join an amount or a part with the whole which includes it **7 :** that is **8 :** that has **:** WITH 8

[1]**off** *adv* **1 :** from a place or position **2 :** from a course **:** ASIDE **3 :** into sleep **4 :** so as not to be supported, covering or enclosing, or attached **5 :** so as to be discontinued or finished **6 :** away from work

[2]**off** *prep* **1 :** away from the surface or top of **2 :** at the expense of **3 :** released or freed from **4 :** below the usual level of **5 :** away from

[3]**off** *adj* **1 :** more removed or distant **2 :** started on the way **3 :** not taking place **4 :** not operating **5 :** not correct **:** WRONG **6 :** not entirely sane **7 :** small in degree **:** SLIGHT **8 :** provided for

of·fend *vb* **1 :** to do wrong **:** SIN **2 :** to hurt the feelings of **:** DISTRESS

of·fend·er *n* **:** a person who offends

of·fense *or* **of·fence** *n* **1 :** an act of attacking **:** ASSAULT **2 :** an offensive team **3 :** the act of offending **:** the state of being offended **4 :** WRONGDOING, SIN

[1]**of·fen·sive** *adj* **1 :** relating to or made for or suited to attack **2 :** of or relating to the attempt to score in a game or contest **3 :** causing displeasure or resentment — **of·fen·sive·ly** *adv* — **of·fen·sive·ness** *n*

[2]**offensive** *n* **1 :** the state or attitude of one who is making an attack **2 :** [2]ATTACK 1

[1]**of·fer** *vb* **1 :** to present as an act of worship **:** SACRIFICE **2 :** to present (something) to be accepted or rejected **3 :** to present for consideration **:** SUGGEST **4 :** to declare one's willingness **5 :** PUT UP 5

[2]**offer** *n* **1 :** an act of offering **2 :** a price suggested by one prepared to buy **:** BID

of·fer·ing *n* **1 :** the act of one who offers **2 :** something offered **3 :** a sacrifice offered as part of worship **4 :** a contribution to the support of a church

off·hand *adv or adj* **:** without previous thought or preparation

of·fice *n* **1 :** a special duty or post and especially one of authority in government **2 :** a place where business is done or a service is supplied

of·fice·hold·er *n* **:** a person who holds public office

of·fi·cer *n* **1 :** a person given the responsibility of enforcing the law **2 :** a person who holds an office **3 :** a person who holds a commission in the armed forces

[1]**of·fi·cial** *n* **:** OFFICER 2

[2]**official** *adj* **1 :** of or relating to an office **2 :** having authority to perform a duty **3 :** coming from or meeting the requirements of an authority **4 :** proper for a person in office — **of·fi·cial·ly** *adv*

of·fi·ci·ate *vb* **of·fi·ci·at·ed; of·fi·ci·at·ing 1 :** to perform a ceremony or duty **2 :** to act as an officer **:** PRESIDE

off·ing *n* **:** the near future or distance

off–line *adj or adv* **:** not connected to or directly controlled by a computer system

[1]**off·set** *n* **:** something that serves to make up for something else

[2]**offset** *vb* **offset; off·set·ting :** to make up for

off·shoot *n* **:** a branch of a main stem of a plant

[1]**off·shore** *adv* **:** from the shore **:** at a distance from the shore

[2]**off·shore** *adj* **1 :** coming or moving away from the shore **2 :** located off the shore

off·spring *n, pl* **offspring** *also* **off·springs :** the young of a person, animal, or plant

off·stage *adv or adj* **:** off or away from the stage

off–the–rec·ord *adj* **:** given or made in confidence and not for publication

oft *adv* **:** OFTEN

of·ten *adv* **:** many times

of·ten·times *adv* **:** OFTEN

ogle *vb* **ogled; ogling :** to look at (as a person) in a flirting way or with unusual attention or desire

ogre *n* **1 :** an ugly giant of fairy tales and

folklore who eats people **2 :** a dreaded person or object

oh *or* **O** *interj* **1** — used to express an emotion (as surprise or pain) **2** — used in direct address

1-oid *n suffix* **:** something resembling a specified object or having a specified quality

2-oid *adj suffix* **:** resembling **:** having the form or appearance of

1oil *n* **1 :** any of numerous greasy usually liquid substances from plant, animal, or mineral sources that do not dissolve in water and are used especially as lubricants, fuels, and food **2 :** PETROLEUM **3 :** artists' paints made of pigments and oil **4 :** a painting in oils

2oil *vb* **:** to put oil on or in

oil•cloth *n* **:** cloth treated with oil or paint so as to be waterproof and used for shelf and table coverings

oily *adj* **oil•i•er; oil•i•est** **1 :** of, relating to, or containing oil **2 :** covered or soaked with oil — **oil•i•ness** *n*

oint•ment *n* **:** a semisolid usually greasy medicine for use on the skin

1OK *or* **okay** *adv or adj* **:** all right

2OK *or* **okay** *n* **:** APPROVAL

3OK *or* **okay** *vb* **OK'd** *or* **okayed; OK'•ing** *or* **okay•ing :** APPROVE 2, AUTHORIZE

oka•pi *n* **:** an animal of the African forests related to the giraffe

okra *n* **:** a plant related to the hollyhocks and grown for its edible green pods which are used in soups and stews

1old *adj* **1 :** dating from the distant past **:** ANCIENT **2 :** having lasted or been such for a long time **3 :** having existed for a specified length of time **4 :** having lived a long time **5 :** FORMER **6 :** showing the effects of time or use

2old *n* **:** old or earlier time

old•en *adj* **:** of or relating to earlier days

Old English *n* **:** the language of the English people from the earliest documents in the seventh century to about 1100

old–fash•ioned *adj* **1 :** of, relating to, or like that of an earlier time **2 :** holding fast to old ways **:** CONSERVATIVE

Old French *n* **:** the French language from the ninth to the thirteenth century

Old Glory *n* **:** the flag of the United States

old maid *n* **1 :** an elderly unmarried woman **2 :** a very neat fussy person **3 :** a card game in which cards are matched in pairs and the player holding the extra queen at the end loses

old•ster *n* **:** an old person

old–time *adj* **:** 1OLD 1

old–tim•er *n* **1 :** 1VETERAN 1 **2 :** OLDSTER

old–world *adj* **:** having old-fashioned charm

oleo•mar•ga•rine *n* **:** MARGARINE

ol•fac•to•ry *adj* **:** of or relating to smelling or the sense of smell

ol•ive *n* **1 :** an oily fruit that is eaten both ripe and unripe, is the source of an edible oil (**olive oil**), and grows on an evergreen tree with hard smooth shining wood (**olive wood**) **2 :** a yellowish green

Olym•pic *adj* **:** of or relating to the Olympic Games

Olympic Games *n pl* **:** a series of international athletic contests held in a different country once every four years

om•e•lette *or* **om•e•let** *n* **:** eggs beaten with milk or water, cooked without stirring until firm, and folded in half often over a filling

omen *n* **:** a happening believed to be a sign or warning of a future event

om•i•nous *adj* **:** being a sign of evil or trouble to come — **om•i•nous•ly** *adv* — **om•i•nous•ness** *n*

omis•sion *n* **1 :** something omitted **2 :** the act of omitting **:** the state of being omitted

omit *vb* **omit•ted; omit•ting** **1 :** to leave out **:** fail to include **2 :** to leave undone **:** NEGLECT

om•ni•bus *n* **:** BUS

om•nip•o•tent *adj* **:** having power or authority without limit **:** ALMIGHTY

1on *prep* **1 :** over and in contact with **2 :** AGAINST 3 **3 :** near or connected with **4 :** 1TO 1 **5 :** sometime during **6 :** in the state or process of **7 :** 2ABOUT 3 **8 :** by means of

2on *adv* **1 :** in or into contact with a surface **2 :** forward in time, space, or action **3 :** from one to another **4 :** into operation or a position allowing operation

3on *adj* **1 :** being in operation **2 :** placed so as to allow operation **3 :** taking place **4 :** having been planned

1once *adv* **1 :** one time only **2 :** at any one time **:** EVER **3 :** at some time in the past **:** FORMERLY

2once *n* **:** one single time — **at once** **1 :** at the same time **2 :** IMMEDIATELY 2

3once *conj* **:** as soon as **:** WHEN

once–over *n* **:** a quick glance or examination

on•com•ing *adj* **:** coming nearer

1one *adj* **1 :** being a single unit or thing **2 :** being a certain unit or thing **3 :** being the same in kind or quality **4 :** not specified

2one *n* **1 :** the number denoting a single unit **:** 1 **2 :** the first in a set or series **3 :** a single person or thing

3one *pron* **1 :** a single member or individual **2 :** any person

one another *pron* **:** EACH OTHER

one•self *pron* **:** one's own self

one–sid•ed *adj* **1 :** having or happening on

DICTIONARY

one side only **2 :** having one side more developed **3 :** favoring one side

one•time *adj* **:** FORMER

one–way *adj* **:** moving or allowing movement in one direction only

on•go•ing *adj* **:** being in progress or movement

on•ion *n* **:** the edible bulb of a plant related to the lilies that has a sharp odor and taste and is used as a vegetable and to season foods

on–line *adj or adv* **:** connected to, directly controlled by, or available through a computer system

on•look•er *n* **:** SPECTATOR

[1]**on•ly** *adj* **1 :** best without doubt **2 :** alone in or of a class or kind **:** SOLE

[2]**only** *adv* **1 :** as a single fact or instance and nothing more or different **2 :** no one or nothing other than **3 :** in the end **4 :** as recently as

[3]**only** *conj* **:** except that

on•o•mato•poe•ia *n* **:** the forming of a word (as "buzz" or "hiss") in imitation of a natural sound

on•rush *n* **:** a rushing forward

on•set *n* **1 :** [2]ATTACK 1 **2 :** BEGINNING

on•slaught *n* **:** a violent attack

on•to *prep* **:** to a position on or against

[1]**on•ward** *adv* **:** toward or at a point lying ahead in space or time **:** FORWARD

[2]**onward** *adj* **:** directed or moving onward

oo•dles *n pl* **:** a great quantity

[1]**ooze** *n* **:** soft mud **:** SLIME

[2]**ooze** *vb* **oozed; ooz•ing :** to flow or leak out slowly

opal *n* **:** a mineral with soft changeable colors that is used as a gem

opaque *adj* **1 :** not letting light through **:** not transparent **2 :** not reflecting light **:** DULL

[1]**open** *adj* **1 :** not shut or blocked **:** not closed **2 :** not enclosed or covered **3 :** not secret **:** PUBLIC **4 :** to be used, entered, or taken part in by all **5 :** easy to enter, get through, or see **6 :** not drawn together **:** spread out **7 :** not decided or settled **8 :** ready to consider appeals or ideas — **open•ly** *adv* — **open•ness** *n*

[2]**open** *vb* **1 :** to change or move from a shut condition **2 :** to clear by or as if by removing something in the way **3 :** to make or become ready for use **4 :** to have an opening **5 :** BEGIN 1, START — **open•er** *n*

[3]**open** *n* **:** open space **:** OUTDOORS

open–air *adj* **:** OUTDOOR

open–and–shut *adj* **:** [1]PLAIN 3, OBVIOUS

open•heart•ed *adj* **1 :** FRANK **2 :** GENEROUS 1

open•ing *n* **1 :** an act of opening **2 :** an open place **:** CLEARING **3 :** BEGINNING **4 :** OCCASION 1 **5 :** a job opportunity

open letter *n* **:** a letter (as one addressed to an official) for the public to see and printed in a newspaper or magazine

open•work *n* **:** something made or work done so as to show openings through the fabric or material

op•era *n* **:** a play in which the entire text is sung with orchestral accompaniment

opera glasses *n* **:** small binoculars of low power for use in a theater

op•er•ate *vb* **op•er•at•ed; op•er•at•ing 1 :** to work or cause to work in a proper way **2 :** to take effect **3 :** MANAGE 1 **4 :** to perform surgery **:** do an operation on (as a person)

operating system *n* **:** a program or series of programs that controls the operation of a computer and directs the processing of the user's programs (as by assigning storage space and controlling input and output functions)

op•er•a•tion *n* **1 :** the act, process, method, or result of operating **2 :** the quality or state of being able to work **3 :** a certain piece or kind of surgery **4 :** a process (as addition or multiplication) of getting one mathematical expression from others according to a rule **5 :** the process of putting military or naval forces into action **6 :** a single step performed by a computer in carrying out a program

op•er•a•tion•al *adj* **1 :** of or relating to operation or an operation **2 :** ready for operation

op•er•a•tor *n* **1 :** a person who operates something (as a business) **2 :** a person in charge of a telephone switchboard

op•er•et•ta *n* **:** a light play set to music with speaking, singing, and dancing scenes

opin•ion *n* **1 :** a belief based on experience and on seeing certain facts but not amounting to sure knowledge **2 :** a judgment about a person or thing **3 :** a statement by an expert after careful study

opin•ion•at•ed *adj* **:** holding to one's opinions too strongly

opi•um *n* **:** a bitter brownish narcotic drug that is the dried juice of one kind of poppy

opos•sum *n* **:** a common American animal related to the kangaroos that lives mostly in trees and is active at night

op•po•nent *n* **:** a person or thing that opposes another

op•por•tu•ni•ty *n, pl* **op•por•tu•ni•ties 1 :** a favorable combination of circumstances, time, and place **2 :** a chance to better oneself

op•pose *vb* **op•posed; op•pos•ing 1 :** to

be or place opposite to something **2 :** to offer resistance to **:** stand against **:** RESIST

1op·po·site *adj* **1 :** being at the other end, side, or corner **2 :** being in a position to oppose or cancel out **3 :** being as different as possible **:** CONTRARY

2opposite *n* **:** either of two persons or things that are as different as possible

3opposite *adv* **:** on the opposite side

4opposite *prep* **:** across from and usually facing or on the same level with

op·po·si·tion *n* **1 :** the state of being opposite **2 :** the action of resisting **3 :** a group of persons that oppose someone or something **4** *often cap* **:** a political party opposed to the party in power

op·press *vb* **1 :** to cause to feel burdened in spirit **2 :** to control or rule in a harsh or cruel way

op·pres·sion *n* **1 :** cruel or unjust use of power or authority **2 :** a feeling of low spirits

op·pres·sive *adj* **1 :** cruel or harsh without just cause **2 :** causing a feeling of oppression — **op·pres·sive·ly** *adv*

op·tic *adj* **:** of or relating to seeing or the eye

op·ti·cal *adj* **1 :** of or relating to the science of optics **2 :** of or relating to seeing **:** VISUAL **3 :** involving the use of devices that are sensitive to light to get information for a computer

optical fiber *n* **:** a single fiber used in fiber optics

optical illusion *n* **:** ILLUSION 1

op·ti·cian *n* **:** a person who prepares eyeglass lenses and sells glasses

op·tics *n* **:** a science that deals with the nature and properties of light and the changes that it undergoes and produces

op·ti·mism *n* **:** a habit of expecting things to turn out for the best

op·ti·mist *n* **:** an optimistic person

op·ti·mis·tic *adj* **:** showing optimism **:** expecting everything to come out all right **:** HOPEFUL

op·ti·mum *adj* **:** most desirable or satisfactory

op·tion *n* **1 :** the power or right to choose **2 :** a right to buy or sell something at a specified price during a specified period

op·tion·al *adj* **:** left to one's choice **:** not required

op·tom·e·trist *n* **:** a person who prescribes glasses or exercise to improve the eyesight

op·u·lent *adj* **:** having or showing much wealth

or *conj* — used between words or phrases that are choices

1-or *n suffix* **:** one that does a specified thing

2-or *n suffix* **:** condition **:** activity

or·a·cle *n* **1 :** a person (as a priestess in ancient Greece) through whom a god is believed to speak **2 :** the place where a god speaks through an oracle **3 :** an answer given by an oracle

orac·u·lar *adj* **:** of, relating to, or serving as an oracle

oral *adj* **1 :** 2SPOKEN 1 **2 :** of, relating to, given by, or near the mouth — **oral·ly** *adv*

or·ange *n* **1 :** a sweet juicy fruit with a reddish yellow rind that grows on an evergreen citrus tree with shining leaves and fragrant white flowers **2 :** a color between red and yellow

or·ange·ade *n* **:** a drink made of orange juice, sugar, and water

orang·utan *or* **orang·ou·tan** *n* **:** a large ape of Borneo and Sumatra that eats plants, lives in trees, and has very long arms and hairless face, feet, and hands

ora·tion *n* **:** an important speech given on a special occasion

or·a·tor *n* **:** a public speaker noted for skill and power in speaking

or·a·tor·i·cal *adj* **:** of, relating to, or like an orator or oratory — **or·a·tor·i·cal·ly** *adv*

or·a·to·ry *n* **1 :** the art of an orator **2 :** the style of language used in an oration

orb *n* **:** something in the shape of a ball (as a planet or the eye)

1or·bit *n* **:** the path taken by one body circling around another body

2orbit *vb* **1 :** to move in an orbit around **:** CIRCLE **2 :** to send up so as to move in an orbit

or·chard *n* **1 :** a place where fruit trees are grown **2 :** the trees in an orchard

or·ches·tra *n* **1 :** a group of musicians who perform instrumental music using mostly stringed instruments **2 :** the front part of the main floor in a theater

or·ches·tral *adj* **:** of, relating to, or written for an orchestra

or·chid *n* **:** any of a large group of plants with usually showy flowers with three petals of which the middle petal is enlarged into a lip and differs from the others in shape and color

or·dain *vb* **1 :** to make a person a Christian minister or priest by a special ceremony **2 :** 2DECREE **3 :** DESTINE 1, FATE

or·deal *n* **:** a severe test or experience

1or·der *vb* **1 :** to put into a particular grouping or sequence **:** ARRANGE **2 :** to give an order to or for

2order *n* **1 :** a group of people united (as by living under the same religious rules or by loyalty to common needs or duties) **2 orders** *pl* **:** the office of a person in the Christian ministry **3 :** a group of related plants or animals that ranks above the family and below the class in scientific classification **4 :** the arrangement of objects or events in space or time **5 :** the way something should be **6 :** the state of things when law or authority is obeyed **7 :** a certain rule or regulation **:** COMMAND **8 :** good working condition **9 :** a written direction to pay a sum of money **10 :** a statement of what one wants to buy **11 :** goods or items bought or sold — **in order to :** for the purpose of

1or·der·ly *adj* **1 :** being in good order **:** NEAT, TIDY **2 :** obeying orders or rules **:** well-behaved — **or·der·li·ness** *n*

2orderly *n, pl* **or·der·lies 1 :** a soldier who works for an officer especially to carry messages **2 :** a person who does cleaning and general work in a hospital

or·di·nal *n* **:** ORDINAL NUMBER

ordinal number *n* **:** a number that is used to show the place (as first, fifth, twenty-second) taken by an element in a series

or·di·nance *n* **:** a law or regulation especially of a city or town

or·di·nar·i·ly *adv* **:** in the usual course of events **:** USUALLY

1or·di·nary *n* **:** the conditions or events that are usual or normal

2ordinary *adj* **1 :** to be expected **:** NORMAL, USUAL **2 :** neither good nor bad **:** AVERAGE **3 :** not very good **:** MEDIOCRE — **or·di·nar·i·ness** *n*

ord·nance *n* **1 :** military supplies (as guns, ammunition, trucks, and tanks) **2 :** ARTILLERY 1

ore *n* **:** a mineral mined to obtain a substance (as gold) that it contains

or·gan *n* **1 :** a musical instrument played by means of one or more keyboards and having pipes sounded by compressed air **2 :** a part of a person, plant, or animal that is specialized to do a particular task **3 :** a way of getting something done

or·gan·ic *adj* **1 :** relating to an organ of the body **2 :** having parts that fit or work together **3 :** relating to or obtained from living things **4 :** relating to carbon compounds **:** containing carbon

or·gan·ism *n* **1 :** something having many related parts and functioning as a whole **2 :** a living being made up of organs and able to carry on the activities of life **:** a living person, animal, or plant

or·gan·ist *n* **:** a person who plays an organ

or·ga·ni·za·tion *n* **1 :** the act or process of organizing **2 :** the state or way of being organized **3 :** a group of persons united for a common purpose

or·ga·nize *vb* **or·ga·nized; or·ga·niz·ing 1 :** to make separate parts into one united whole **2 :** to arrange in a certain order — **or·ga·niz·er** *n*

ori·ent *vb* **1 :** to set or arrange in a position especially so as to be lined up with certain points of the compass **2 :** to acquaint with an existing situation or environment — **ori·en·ta·tion** *n*

Ori·en·tal *adj* **1 :** 1ASIAN **2 :** of or relating to the region that includes the countries of eastern Asia (as China, Japan, Vietnam, and Korea)

Oriental *n* **:** a member of any of the native peoples of the Orient

ori·ga·mi *n* **:** the art of folding paper into three-dimensional figures or designs without cutting the paper or using glue

or·i·gin *n* **1 :** a person's ancestry **2 :** the rise, beginning, or coming from a source **3 :** basic source or cause

1orig·i·nal *n* **:** something from which a copy or translation can be made

2original *adj* **1 :** of or relating to the origin or beginning **:** FIRST **2 :** not copied from anything else **:** not translated **:** NEW **3 :** able to think up new things **:** INVENTIVE — **orig·i·nal·ly** *adv*

orig·i·nal·i·ty *n* **1 :** the quality or state of being original **2 :** the power or ability to think, act, or do something in ways that are new

orig·i·nate *vb* **orig·i·nat·ed; orig·i·nat·ing 1 :** to bring into being **:** cause to be **:** INVENT, INITIATE **2 :** to come into being — **orig·i·na·tor** *n*

ori·ole *n* **1 :** an Old World yellow and black bird related to the crow **2 :** an American songbird related to the blackbird and bobolink that has a bright orange and black male

1or·na·ment *n* **1 :** something that adds beauty **:** DECORATION **2 :** the act of beautifying

2or·na·ment *vb* **:** DECORATE 1

1or·na·men·tal *adj* **:** serving to ornament **:** DECORATIVE

2ornamental *n* **:** a plant grown for its beauty

or·na·men·ta·tion *n* **1 :** the act or process of ornamenting **:** the state of being ornamented **2 :** something that ornaments

or·nate *adj* **:** decorated in a fancy way — **or·nate·ly** *adv* — **or·nate·ness** *n*

or·nery *adj* **or·neri·er; or·neri·est :** having a bad disposition

1or·phan *n* **:** a child whose parents are dead

2orphan *vb* **:** to cause to become an orphan

or·phan·age *n* **:** an institution for the care of orphans

or·tho·don·tist *n* **:** a dentist who adjusts badly placed or irregular teeth

or·tho·dox *adj* **1 :** holding established beliefs especially in religion **2 :** approved as measuring up to some standard **:** CONVENTIONAL

1-ory *n suffix, pl* **-ories :** place of or for

2-ory *adj suffix* **:** of, relating to, or associated with

os·cil·late *vb* **os·cil·lat·ed; os·cil·lat·ing :** to swing back and forth like a pendulum

os·mo·sis *n* **:** a passing of material and especially water through a membrane (as of a living cell) that will not allow all kinds of molecules to pass

os·prey *n, pl* **ospreys :** a large hawk that feeds chiefly on fish

os·ten·si·ble *adj* **:** shown in an outward way **:** APPARENT — **os·ten·si·bly** *adv*

os·ten·ta·tious *adj* **:** having or fond of unnecessary show

os·tra·cize *vb* **os·tra·cized; os·tra·ciz·ing :** to shut out of a group by the agreement of all

os·trich *n* **:** a very large bird of Africa and the Arabian Peninsula that often weighs 300 pounds and runs very swiftly but cannot fly

1oth·er *adj* **1 :** being the one (as of two or more) left **2 :** 1SECOND 1 **3 :** 1EXTRA, ADDITIONAL

2other *n* **:** a remaining or different one

3other *pron* **:** another thing

oth·er·wise *adv* **1 :** in another way **2 :** in different circumstances **3 :** in other ways

ot·ter *n* **:** a web-footed animal related to the minks that feeds on fish

ouch *interj* — used especially to express sudden pain

ought *helping verb* **1** — used to show duty **2** — used to show what it would be wise to do **3** — used to show what is naturally expected **4** — used to show what is correct

oughtn't : ought not

ounce *n* **1 :** a unit of weight equal to $1/16$ pound (about 28 grams) **2 :** a unit of liquid capacity equal to $1/16$ pint (about 30 milliliters)

our *adj* **:** of or relating to us **:** done, given, or felt by us

ours *pron* **:** that which belongs to us

our·selves *pron* **:** our own selves

-ous *adj suffix* **:** full of **:** having **:** resembling

oust *vb* **:** to force or drive out (as from office or from possession of something)

oust·er *n* **:** the act or an instance of ousting or being ousted

1out *adv* **1 :** in a direction away from the inside, center, or surface **2 :** away from home, business, or the usual or proper place **3 :** beyond control or possession **4 :** so as to be used up, completed, or discontinued **5 :** in or into the open **6 :** ALOUD **7 :** so as to put out or be put out in baseball

2out *prep* **1 :** outward through **2 :** outward on or along

3out *adj* **1 :** located outside or at a distance **2 :** no longer in power or use **3 :** not confined **:** not concealed or covered **4 :** 1ABSENT 1 **5 :** being no longer at bat and not successful in reaching base **6 :** no longer in fashion

4out *n* **:** PUTOUT

out- *prefix* **:** in a manner that goes beyond

out–and–out *adj* **:** THOROUGH 1

out·board motor *n* **:** a small gasoline engine with an attached propeller that can be fastened to the back end of a small boat

out·break *n* **:** something (as an epidemic of measles) that breaks out

out·build·ing *n* **:** a building (as a shed or stable) separate from a main building

out·burst *n* **1 :** a sudden violent expression of strong feeling **2 :** a sudden increase of activity or growth

1out·cast *adj* **:** rejected or cast out

2outcast *n* **:** a person who is cast out by society

out·class *vb* **:** EXCEL, SURPASS

out·come *n* **:** 2RESULT 1

out·cry *n, pl* **out·cries 1 :** a loud and excited cry **2 :** a strong protest

out·dat·ed *adj* **:** OBSOLETE, OUTMODED

out·dis·tance *vb* **out·dis·tanced; out·dis·tanc·ing :** to go far ahead of (as in a race)

out·do *vb* **out·did; out·done; out·do·ing; out·does :** to do better than **:** SURPASS

out·door *adj* **1 :** of or relating to the outdoors **2 :** used, being, or done outdoors

1out·doors *adv* **:** outside a building **:** in or into the open air

2outdoors *n* **1 :** the open air **2 :** the world away from human dwellings

out·er *adj* **1 :** located on the outside or farther out **2 :** being beyond the earth's atmosphere or beyond the solar system

out·er·most *adj* **:** farthest out

out·field *n* **:** the part of a baseball field beyond the infield and between the foul lines

out·field·er *n* **:** a baseball player who plays in the outfield

1out·fit *n* **1 :** the equipment or clothing for a special use **2 :** a group of persons working together or associated in the same activity

2outfit *vb* **out·fit·ted; out·fit·ting :** to supply with an outfit **:** EQUIP — **out·fit·ter** *n*

out·go *n, pl* **outgoes :** EXPENDITURE 2

out·go·ing *adj* **1 :** going out **2 :** retiring from a place or position **3 :** FRIENDLY 1

out·grow *vb* **out·grew; out·grown; out·grow·ing 1 :** to grow faster than **2 :** to grow too large for

out·growth *n* **:** something that grows out of or develops from something else

out·ing *n* **:** a brief usually outdoor trip for pleasure

out·land·ish *adj* **:** very strange or unusual **:** BIZARRE

out·last *vb* **:** to last longer than

¹out·law *n* **:** a lawless person or one who is running away from the law

²outlaw *vb* **:** to make illegal

out·lay *n* **:** EXPENDITURE

out·let *n* **1 :** a place or opening for letting something out **2 :** a way of releasing or satisfying a feeling or impulse **3 :** a device (as in a wall) into which the prongs of an electrical plug are inserted for making connection with an electrical circuit

¹out·line *n* **1 :** a line that traces or forms the outer limits of an object or figure and shows its shape **2 :** a drawing or picture giving only the outlines of a thing **:** this method of drawing **3 :** a short treatment of a subject **:** SUMMARY

²outline *vb* **out·lined; out·lin·ing :** to make or prepare an outline of

out·live *vb* **out·lived; out·liv·ing :** to live longer than **:** OUTLAST

out·look *n* **1 :** a view from a certain place **2 :** a way of thinking about or looking at things **3 :** conditions that seem to lie ahead

out·ly·ing *adj* **:** being far from a central point **:** REMOTE

out·mod·ed *adj* **:** no longer in style or in use

out·num·ber *vb* **:** to be more than in number

out of *prep* **1 :** from the inside to the outside of **:** not in **2 :** beyond the limits of **3 :** BECAUSE OF **4 :** in a group of **5 :** ¹WITHOUT 2 **6 :** FROM 3

out–of–bounds *adv or adj* **:** outside the limits of the playing field

out–of–date *adj* **:** OUTMODED

out–of–door *or* **out–of–doors** *adj* **:** OUTDOOR 2

out–of–doors *n* **:** ²OUTDOORS

out·pa·tient *n* **:** a person who visits a hospital for examination or treatment but who does not stay overnight at the hospital

out·post *n* **1 :** a guard placed at a distance from a military force or camp **2 :** the position taken by an outpost **3 :** a settlement on a frontier or in a faraway place

¹out·put *n* **1 :** something produced **2 :** the information produced by a computer

²output *vb* **out·put·ted** *or* **out·put; out·put·ting :** to produce as output

¹out·rage *n* **1 :** an act of violence or cruelty **2 :** an act that hurts someone or shows disrespect for a person's feelings **3 :** angry feelings caused by injury or insult

²outrage *vb* **out·raged; out·rag·ing 1 :** to cause to suffer violent injury or great insult **2 :** to cause to feel anger or strong resentment

out·ra·geous *adj* **:** going far beyond what is right, decent, or just

¹out·right *adv* **1 :** COMPLETELY **2 :** without holding back **3 :** on the spot **:** INSTANTLY

²out·right *adj* **1 :** being exactly what is said **2 :** given without restriction

out·run *vb* **out·ran; out·run; out·run·ning :** to run faster than

out·sell *vb* **out·sold; out·sell·ing :** to sell or be sold more than

out·set *n* **:** BEGINNING 1, START

out·shine *vb* **out·shone; out·shin·ing 1 :** to shine brighter than **2 :** OUTDO, SURPASS

¹out·side *n* **1 :** a place or region beyond an enclosure or boundary **2 :** an outer side or surface **3 :** the greatest amount or limit **:** ³MOST

²outside *adj* **1 :** of, relating to, or being on the outside **2 :** coming from outside **:** not belonging to a place or group

³outside *adv* **:** on or to the outside **:** OUTDOORS

⁴outside *prep* **:** on or to the outside of **:** beyond the limits of

out·sid·er *n* **:** a person who does not belong to a certain party or group

out·size *adj* **:** unusually large or heavy

out·skirts *n pl* **:** the area that lies away from the center of a place

out·smart *vb* **:** OUTWIT

out·spo·ken *adj* **:** direct or open in expression **:** BLUNT — **out·spo·ken·ly** *adv* — **out·spo·ken·ness** *n*

out·spread *adj* **:** spread out

out·stand·ing *adj* **1 :** UNPAID **2 :** standing out especially because of excellence — **out·stand·ing·ly** *adv*

out·stay *vb* **:** to stay beyond or longer than

out·stretched *adj* **:** stretched out

out·strip *vb* **out·stripped; out·strip·ping 1 :** to go faster or farther than **2 :** to do better than **:** EXCEL

¹out·ward *adj* **1 :** moving or turned toward the outside or away from a center **2 :** showing on the outside

²outward *or* **out·wards** *adv* **:** toward the outside **:** away from a center

out·ward·ly *adv* **:** on the outside **:** in outward appearance

out·weigh *vb* **:** to be greater than in weight or importance

out·wit *vb* **out·wit·ted; out·wit·ting :** to get ahead of by cleverness **:** BEST

out·worn *adj* : no longer useful or accepted
[1]**oval** *n* : a figure or object having the shape of an egg or ellipse
[2]**oval** *adj* : having the shape of an oval : ELLIPTICAL
ova·ry *n, pl* **ova·ries** **1** : an organ of the body in female animals in which eggs are produced **2** : the larger lower part of the pistil of a flower in which the seeds are formed
ova·tion *n* : a making of a loud noise by many people (as by cheering or clapping) to show great liking or respect
ov·en *n* : a heated chamber (as in a stove) for baking, heating, or drying
[1]**over** *adv* **1** : across a barrier or space **2** : in a direction down or forward and down **3** : across the brim **4** : so as to bring the underside up **5** : beyond a limit **6** : more than needed **7** : once more : AGAIN
[2]**over** *prep* **1** : above in place : higher than **2** : above in power or value **3** : on or along the surface of **4** : on or to the other side of : ACROSS **5** : down from the top or edge of
[3]**over** *adj* **1** : being more than needed : SURPLUS **2** : brought or come to an end
[1]**over·all** *adv* : as a whole : in most ways
[2]**overall** *adj* : including everything
over·alls *n pl* : loose pants usually with shoulder straps and a piece in front to cover the chest
over·anx·ious *adj* : much too anxious
over·bear·ing *adj* : acting in a proud or bossy way toward other people
over·board *adv* **1** : over the side of a ship into the water **2** : to extremes of enthusiasm
over·bur·den *vb* : to burden too heavily
over·cast *adj* : clouded over
over·charge *vb* **over·charged; over·charg·ing** : to charge too much
over·coat *n* : a heavy coat worn over indoor clothing
over·come *vb* **over·came; overcome; over·com·ing** **1** : to win a victory over : CONQUER **2** : to make helpless
over·con·fi·dent *adj* : too sure of oneself
over·cooked *adj* : cooked too long
over·crowd *vb* : to cause to be too crowded
over·do *vb* **over·did; over·done; over·do·ing** **1** : to do too much **2** : EXAGGERATE **3** : to cook too long
over·dose *n* : too large a dose (as of a drug)
over·dress *vb* : to dress too well for the occasion
over·due *adj* **1** : not paid when due **2** : delayed beyond an expected time
over·eat *vb* **over·ate; over·eat·en; over·eat·ing** : to eat too much
over·es·ti·mate *vb* **over·es·ti·mat·ed; over·es·ti·mat·ing** : to estimate too highly
over·flight *n* : a passage over an area in an airplane
[1]**over·flow** *vb* **1** : to cover with or as if with water **2** : to flow over the top of **3** : to flow over bounds
[2]**over·flow** *n* **1** : a flowing over : FLOOD **2** : something that flows over : SURPLUS
over·grown *adj* : grown too big
[1]**over·hand** *adj* : made with a downward movement of the hand or arm
[2]**overhand** *adv* : with an overhand movement
overhand knot *n* : a simple knot often used to prevent the end of a cord from pulling apart
[1]**over·hang** *vb* **over·hung; over·hang·ing** : to stick out or hang over
[2]**overhang** *n* : a part that overhangs
[1]**over·haul** *vb* **1** : to make a thorough examination of and make necessary repairs and adjustments on **2** : to catch up with : OVERTAKE
[2]**over·haul** *n* : an instance of overhauling
[1]**over·head** *adv* **1** : above one's head **2** : in the sky
[2]**over·head** *adj* : placed or passing overhead
[3]**over·head** *n* : the general expenses (as for rent or heat) of a business
over·hear *vb* **over·heard; over·hear·ing** : to hear something said to someone else and not meant for one's own ears
over·heat *vb* : to heat too much : become too hot
over·joy *vb* : to make very joyful
[1]**over·land** *adv* : by land rather than by water
[2]**over·land** *adj* : going overland
over·lap *vb* **over·lapped; over·lap·ping** : to place or be placed so that a part of one covers a part of another
[1]**over·lay** *vb* **over·laid; over·lay·ing** : to lay or spread over or across
[2]**over·lay** *n* : something (as a veneer on wood) that is overlaid
over·load *vb* : to put too great a load on
over·look *vb* **1** : to look over : INSPECT **2** : to look down upon from a higher position **3** : to fail to see : MISS **4** : to pass over without notice or blame : EXCUSE
over·lord *n* : a lord over other lords
over·ly *adv* : by too much
[1]**over·night** *adv* **1** : during or through the night **2** : [2]FAST 3, QUICKLY
[2]**overnight** *adj* **1** : done or lasting through the night **2** : staying for the night **3** : for use on short trips
over·pass *n* : a crossing (as of two highways or a highway and a railroad) at different levels usually by means of a bridge

over·pow·er *vb* **1 :** to overcome by greater force **:** DEFEAT **2 :** to affect by being too strong

over·rate *vb* **over·rat·ed; over·rat·ing :** to value or praise too highly

over·ride *vb* **over·rode; over·rid·den; over·rid·ing :** to push aside as less important

over·ripe *adj* **:** passed beyond ripeness toward decay

over·rule *vb* **over·ruled; over·rul·ing 1 :** to decide against **2 :** to set aside a decision or ruling made by someone having less authority

over·run *vb* **over·ran; overrun; over·run·ning 1 :** to take over and occupy by force **2 :** to run past **3 :** to spread over so as to cover

1over·seas *adv* **:** beyond or across the sea

2overseas *adj* **:** of, relating to, or intended for lands across the sea

over·see *vb* **over·saw; over·seen; over·see·ing 1 :** INSPECT 1, EXAMINE **2 :** SUPERINTEND

over·seer *n* **:** a person whose business it is to oversee something

over·shad·ow *vb* **1 :** to cast a shadow over **:** DARKEN **2 :** to be more important than

over·shoe *n* **:** a shoe (as of rubber) worn over another for protection

over·shoot *vb* **over·shot; over·shoot·ing :** to miss by going beyond

over·sight *n* **1 :** the act or duty of overseeing **:** watchful care **2 :** an error or a leaving something out through carelessness or haste

over·sim·pli·fy *vb* **over·sim·pli·fied; over·sim·pli·fy·ing :** to make incorrect or misleading by simplifying too much

over·size *or* **over·sized** *adj* **:** larger than the usual or normal size

over·sleep *vb* **over·slept; over·sleep·ing :** to sleep beyond the usual time or beyond the time set for getting up

over·spread *vb* **overspread; over·spread·ing :** to spread over or above

over·state *vb* **over·stat·ed; over·stat·ing :** to put in too strong terms **:** EXAGGERATE

over·step *vb* **over·stepped; over·step·ping :** to step over or beyond **:** EXCEED

over·stuffed *adj* **:** covered completely and deeply with upholstery

over·sup·ply *n, pl* **over·sup·plies :** a supply that is too large

over·take *vb* **over·took; over·tak·en; over·tak·ing 1 :** to catch up with and often pass **2 :** to come upon suddenly or without warning

1over·throw *vb* **over·threw; over·thrown; over·throw·ing 1 :** OVERTURN 1 **2 :** to cause the fall or end of **:** DEFEAT, DESTROY

2over·throw *n* **:** an act of overthrowing **:** the state of being overthrown **:** DEFEAT, RUIN

over·time *n* **:** time spent working that is more than one usually works in a day or a week

over·ture *n* **1 :** something first offered or suggested with the hope of reaching an agreement **2 :** a musical composition played by the orchestra at the beginning of an opera or musical play

over·turn *vb* **1 :** to turn over **:** UPSET **2 :** 1OVERTHROW 2

1over·weight *n* **1 :** weight that is more than is required or allowed **2 :** bodily weight that is greater than what is considered normal or healthy

2over·weight *adj* **:** weighing more than is right, necessary, or allowed

over·whelm *vb* **1 :** to cover over completely **:** SUBMERGE **2 :** to overcome completely

1over·work *vb* **1 :** to work or cause to work too much or too hard **2 :** to make too much use of

2overwork *n* **:** too much work

ovip·a·rous *adj* **:** reproducing by eggs that hatch outside the parent's body

ovule *n* **:** any of the tiny egglike structures in a plant ovary that can develop into seeds

ovum *n, pl* **ova :** EGG CELL

owe *vb* **owed; ow·ing 1 :** to be obligated to pay, give, or return **2 :** to be in debt to **3 :** to have as a result

owing *adj* **:** due to be paid

owing to *prep* **:** BECAUSE OF

owl *n* **:** a bird with large head and eyes, hooked bill, and strong claws that is active at night and lives on rats and mice, insects, and small birds — **owl·ish** *adj*

owl·et *n* **:** a young or small owl

1own *adj* **:** belonging to oneself or itself

2own *vb* **1 :** to have or hold as property **:** POSSESS **2 :** ADMIT 3, CONFESS 1

own·er *n* **:** a person who owns something

own·er·ship *n* **:** the state or fact of being an owner

ox *n, pl* **ox·en** *also* **ox 1 :** one of our common domestic cattle or a closely related animal **2 :** an adult castrated male of domestic cattle used especially for meat or for hauling loads **:** STEER

ox·bow *n* **:** a bend in a river in the shape of a U

ox·cart *n* **:** a cart pulled by oxen

ox·ford *n* **:** a low shoe laced and tied over the instep

ox·i·da·tion *n* **:** the process of oxidizing

ox·ide *n* **:** a compound of oxygen with another element or with a group of elements

ox·i·dize *vb* **ox·i·dized; ox·i·diz·ing :** to combine with oxygen **:** add oxygen to

ox·y·gen *n* **:** a chemical element found in the air as a colorless odorless tasteless gas that is necessary for life

oys·ter *n* **:** a soft gray shellfish that lives on stony bottoms (**oyster beds**) in shallow seawater, has a shell made up of two hinged parts, and is used as food

ozone *n* **1 :** a faintly blue form of oxygen that is present in the air in small quantities **2 :** pure and refreshing air

ozone layer *n* **:** a layer of the upper atmosphere that is characterized by high ozone content which blocks most of the sun's radiation from entering the lower atmosphere

P

p *n, pl* **p's** *or* **ps** *often cap* **:** the sixteenth letter of the English alphabet

pa *n* **:** [1]FATHER 1

[1]**pace** *n* **1 :** rate of moving forward or ahead **2 :** a manner of walking **3 :** a horse's gait in which the legs on the same side move at the same time **4 :** a single step or its length

[2]**pace** *vb* **paced; pac·ing 1 :** to walk with slow steps **2 :** to move at a pace **3 :** to measure by steps **4 :** to walk back and forth across **5 :** to set or regulate the pace of

pa·cif·ic *adj* **1 :** making peace **:** PEACEABLE **2 :** [3]CALM, PEACEFUL **3** *cap* **:** relating to the Pacific ocean

pac·i·fy *vb* **pac·i·fied; pac·i·fy·ing :** to make peaceful or quiet **:** CALM, SOOTHE

[1]**pack** *n* **1 :** a bundle arranged for carrying especially on the back of a person or animal **2 :** a group of like persons or things **:** BAND, SET

[2]**pack** *vb* **1 :** to put into a container or bundle **2 :** to put things into **3 :** to crowd into so as to fill full **:** CRAM **4 :** to send away — **pack·er** *n*

pack·age *n* **1 :** a bundle made up for shipping **2 :** a box or case in which goods are shipped or delivered

pack·et *n* **:** a small package

pack·ing·house *n* **:** a building for preparing and packing food and especially meat

pact *n* **:** AGREEMENT 2, TREATY

[1]**pad** *vb* **pad·ded; pad·ding :** to walk or run with quiet steps

[2]**pad** *n* **1 :** something soft used for protection or comfort **:** CUSHION **2 :** a piece of material that holds ink used in inking rubber stamps **3 :** one of the cushioned parts of the underside of the foot of some animals (as a dog) **4 :** a floating leaf of a water plant **5 :** a tablet of writing or drawing paper

[3]**pad** *vb* **pad·ded; pad·ding 1 :** to stuff or cover with soft material **2 :** to make longer by adding words

pad·ding *n* **:** material used to pad something

[1]**pad·dle** *vb* **pad·dled; pad·dling :** to move or splash about in the water with the hands or feet **:** WADE

[2]**paddle** *n* **1 :** an instrument like an oar used in moving and steering a small boat (as a canoe) **2 :** one of the broad boards at the outer edge of a waterwheel or a paddle wheel **3 :** an instrument for beating, mixing, or hitting

[3]**paddle** *vb* **pad·dled; pad·dling 1 :** to move or drive forward with or as if with a paddle **2 :** to stir or mix with a paddle **3 :** to beat with or as if with a paddle

paddle wheel *n* **:** a wheel with paddles near its outer edge used to drive a boat

pad·dock *n* **1 :** an enclosed area where animals are put to eat grass or to exercise **2 :** an enclosed area where racehorses are saddled and paraded

pad·dy *n, pl* **paddies :** wet land in which rice is grown

[1]**pad·lock** *n* **:** a removable lock that has a curved piece that snaps into a catch

[2]**padlock** *vb* **:** to fasten with a padlock

[1]**pa·gan** *n* **:** [2]HEATHEN 1

[2]**pagan** *adj* **:** of or relating to pagans or their worship **:** HEATHEN

[1]**page** *n* **1 :** a boy being trained to be a knight in the Middle Ages **2 :** a person employed (as by a hotel or the United States congress) to carry messages or run errands

[2]**page** *vb* **paged; pag·ing :** to call out the name of (a person) in a public place

[3]**page** *n* **1 :** one side of a printed or written sheet of paper **2 :** a large section of computer memory **3 :** the block of information found at a single World Wide Web address

pag·eant *n* **1 :** a grand and fancy public ceremony and display **2 :** an entertainment made up of scenes based on history or legend

pa·go·da *n* **:** a tower of several stories built as a temple or memorial in the Far East

paid *past of* PAY

pail *n* **1 :** a usually round container with a handle **:** BUCKET **2 :** PAILFUL

pail·ful *n, pl* **pail·fuls** *or* **pails·ful :** the amount a pail holds

[1]**pain** *n* **1 :** suffering that accompanies a

bodily disorder (as a disease or an injury) **2 :** a feeling (as a prick or an ache) that is caused by something harmful and usually makes one try to escape its source **3 :** suffering of the mind or emotions **:** GRIEF **4 pains** *pl* **:** great care or effort — **pain•ful** *adj* — **pain•ful•ly** *adv* — **pain•less** *adj*

²pain *vb* **1 :** to cause pain in or to **2 :** to give or feel pain

pains•tak•ing *adj* **:** taking pains **:** showing care — **pains•tak•ing•ly** *adv*

¹paint *vb* **1 :** to cover a surface with or as if with paint **2 :** to make a picture or design by using paints **3 :** to describe clearly — **paint•er** *n*

²paint *n* **:** a mixture of coloring matter with a liquid that forms a dry coating when spread on a surface

paint•brush *n* **:** a brush for applying paint

paint•ing *n* **1 :** a painted work of art **2 :** the art or occupation of painting

¹pair *n, pl* **pairs** *also* **pair 1 :** two things that match or are meant to be used together **2 :** a thing having two similar parts that are connected **3 :** a mated couple

²pair *vb* **1 :** to arrange or join in pairs **2 :** to form a pair **:** MATCH

pa•ja•mas *n pl* **:** loose clothes usually consisting of pants and top that match and that are worn for relaxing or sleeping

¹Pak•i•stani *n* **:** a person born or living in Pakistan

²Pakistani *adj* **:** of or relating to Pakistan or the Pakistanis

pal *n* **:** a close friend

pal•ace *n* **1 :** the home of a ruler **2 :** a large or splendid house

pal•at•able *adj* **:** pleasant to the taste

pal•ate *n* **1 :** the roof of the mouth made up of a bony front part (**hard palate**) and a soft flexible back part (**soft palate**) **2 :** the sense of taste

¹pale *adj* **pal•er; pal•est 1 :** not having the warm color of a healthy person **2 :** not bright or brilliant **3 :** light in color or shade — **pale•ness** *n*

²pale *vb* **paled; pal•ing :** to make or become pale

Pa•leo•zo•ic *n* **:** an era of geological history ending about 230,000,000 years ago which came before the Mesozoic and in which vertebrates and land plants first appeared

pal•ette *n* **1 :** a thin board or tablet on which a painter puts and mixes colors **2 :** the set of colors that a painter puts on a palette

pal•i•sade *n* **1 :** a fence made of poles to protect against attack **2 :** a line of steep cliffs

¹pall *vb* **:** to become dull or uninteresting **:** lose the ability to give pleasure

²pall *n* **1 :** a heavy cloth covering for a coffin, hearse, or tomb **2 :** something that makes things dark and gloomy

pall•bear•er *n* **:** a person who helps to carry or follows a coffin at a funeral

pal•let *n* **1 :** a mattress of straw **2 :** a temporary bed on the floor

pal•lid *adj* **:** ¹PALE 1

pal•lor *n* **:** paleness of face

¹palm *n* **:** any of a group of mostly tropical trees, shrubs, and vines with a simple but often tall stem topped with leaves that are shaped like feathers or fans

²palm *n* **1 :** the under part of the hand between the fingers and the wrist **2 :** a measure of length of about seven to ten centimeters

³palm *vb* **:** to hide in the hand

pal•met•to *n, pl* **pal•met•tos** *or* **pal•met•toes :** a low palm with leaves shaped like fans

palm off *vb* **:** to get rid of or pass on in a dishonest way

pal•o•mi•no *n, pl* **pal•o•mi•nos :** a small strong horse that is light tan or cream in color with a lighter mane and tail

pal•pi•tate *vb* **pal•pi•tat•ed; pal•pi•tat•ing :** ¹THROB 1

pal•sy *n* **1 :** PARALYSIS **2 :** an uncontrollable trembling of the body or a part of the body

pal•try *adj* **pal•tri•er; pal•tri•est :** of little importance **:** PETTY

pam•pas *n pl* **:** wide treeless plains of South America

pam•per *vb* **:** to give someone or someone's desires too much care and attention **:** INDULGE

pam•phlet *n* **:** a short publication without a binding **:** BOOKLET

¹pan *n* **1 :** a shallow open container used for cooking **2 :** a container somewhat like a cooking pan

²pan *vb* **panned; pan•ning :** to wash earthy material so as to collect bits of metal (as gold)

pan•cake *n* **:** a flat cake made of thin batter and cooked on both sides on a griddle

pan•cre•as *n* **:** a large gland in the abdomen that produces insulin and a fluid (**pancreatic juice**) that aids digestion

pan•cre•at•ic *adj* **:** of or relating to the pancreas

pan•da *n* **1 :** a long-tailed mainly plant-eating mammal that is related to and resembles the American raccoon, has long reddish fur, and is found from the Himalayas to China **2 :** GIANT PANDA

pan•de•mo•ni•um *n* **:** wild uproar

pane *n* **:** a sheet of glass (as in a window)

¹pan·el *n* **1 :** a group of persons appointed for some service **2 :** a group of persons taking part in a discussion or quiz program **3 :** a part of something (as a door or a wall) often sunk below the level of the frame **4 :** a piece of material (as plywood) made to form part of a surface (as of a wall) **5 :** a board into which instruments or controls are set

²panel *vb* **pan·eled** *or* **pan·elled; pan·el·ing** *or* **pan·el·ling :** to supply or decorate with panels

pan·el·ing *n* **:** panels joined in a continuous surface

pang *n* **:** a sudden sharp attack or feeling (as of hunger or regret)

¹pan·ic *n* **:** a sudden overpowering fear especially without reasonable cause

²panic *vb* **pan·icked; pan·ick·ing :** to affect or be affected by panic

pan·icky *adj* **1 :** like or caused by panic **2 :** feeling or likely to feel panic

pan·o·rama *n* **:** a clear complete view in every direction

pan out *vb* **:** to give a good result **:** SUCCEED

pan·sy *n, pl* **pansies :** a garden plant related to the violets that has large velvety flowers with five petals usually in shades of yellow, purple, or brownish red

¹pant *vb* **:** to breathe hard or quickly

²pant *n* **:** a panting breath

pan·ta·loons *n pl* **:** PANTS

pan·ther *n* **1 :** LEOPARD **2 :** COUGAR **3 :** JAGUAR

pant·ie *or* **panty** *n, pl* **pant·ies :** a woman's or child's undergarment with short legs or no legs

¹pan·to·mime *n* **1 :** a show in which a story is told by using expressions on the face and movements of the body instead of words **2 :** a showing or explaining of something through movements of the body and face alone

²pantomime *vb* **pan·to·mimed; pan·to·mim·ing :** to tell through pantomime

pan·try *n, pl* **pan·tries :** a small room where food and dishes are kept

pants *n pl* **:** an outer garment reaching from the waist to the ankle or only to the knee and covering each leg separately

pa·pa *n* **:** ¹FATHER 1

pa·pal *adj* **:** of or relating to the pope

pa·paw *n* **1 :** PAPAYA **2 :** the greenish or yellow edible fruit of a North American tree with shiny leaves and purple flowers

pa·pa·ya *n* **:** a yellow edible fruit that looks like a melon and grows on a tropical American tree

¹pa·per *n* **1 :** a material made in thin sheets from fibers (as of wood or cloth) **2 :** a sheet or piece of paper **3 :** a piece of paper having something written or printed on it **:** DOCUMENT **4 :** NEWSPAPER **5 :** WALLPAPER **6 :** a piece of written schoolwork

²paper *vb* **:** to cover or line with paper (as wallpaper)

³paper *adj* **1 :** made of paper **2 :** like paper in thinness or weakness

pa·per·back *n* **:** a book with a flexible paper binding

paper clip *n* **:** a clip of bent wire used to hold sheets of paper together

pa·pery *adj* **:** like paper

pa·poose *n* **:** a baby of North American Indian parents

pa·pri·ka *n* **:** a mild red spice made from the fruit of some sweet peppers

pa·py·rus *n, pl* **pa·py·rus·es** *or* **pa·py·ri 1 :** a tall African plant related to the grasses that grows especially in Egypt **2 :** a material like paper made from papyrus by ancient people and used by them to write on

par *n* **1 :** a fixed or stated value (as of money or a security) **2 :** an equal level **3 :** the score set for each hole of a golf course

par·a·ble *n* **:** a simple story that teaches a moral truth

¹para·chute *n* **:** a folding device of light material shaped like an umbrella and used for making a safe jump from an airplane

²parachute *vb* **para·chut·ed; para·chut·ing :** to transport or come down by parachute

¹pa·rade *n* **1 :** great show or display **2 :** the formation of troops before an officer for inspection **3 :** a public procession **4 :** a crowd of people walking at an easy pace

²parade *vb* **pa·rad·ed; pa·rad·ing 1 :** to march in an orderly group **2 :** SHOW OFF

par·a·dise *n* **1 :** the garden of Eden **2 :** HEAVEN 2 **3 :** a place or state of great happiness

par·a·dox *n* **:** a statement that seems to be the opposite of the truth or of common sense and yet is perhaps true

par·af·fin *n* **:** a white odorless tasteless substance obtained from wood, coal, or petroleum and used in coating and sealing and in candles

¹para·graph *n* **:** a part of a piece of writing that is made up of one or more sentences and has to do with one topic or gives the words of one speaker

²paragraph *vb* **:** to divide into paragraphs

par·a·keet *or* **par·ra·keet** *n* **:** a small parrot with a long tail

¹par·al·lel *adj* **:** lying or moving in the same direction but always the same distance apart

²parallel *n* **1 :** a parallel line or surface **2 :** one of the imaginary circles on the earth's surface parallel to the equator that mark latitude **3 :** agreement in many or most details **4 :** COUNTERPART, EQUAL

³**parallel** *vb* **1 :** to be like or equal to **2 :** to move, run, or extend in a direction parallel with

par·al·lel·o·gram *n* **:** a plane figure with four sides whose opposite sides are parallel and equal

pa·ral·y·sis *n, pl* **pa·ral·y·ses :** partial or complete loss of one's ability to move or feel

par·a·lyze *vb* **par·a·lyzed; par·a·lyz·ing 1 :** to affect with paralysis **2 :** to destroy or decrease something's energy or ability to act

par·a·me·cium *n, pl* **par·a·me·cia** *also* **par·a·me·ciums :** a tiny water animal that is a single cell shaped like a slipper

par·a·mount *adj* **:** highest in importance or greatness

par·a·pet *n* **1 :** a wall of earth or stone to protect soldiers **2 :** a low wall or fence at the edge of a platform, roof, or bridge

¹**para·phrase** *n* **:** a way of stating something again by giving the meaning in different words

²**paraphrase** *vb* **para·phrased; para·phras·ing :** to give the meaning of in different words

par·a·site *n* **1 :** a person who lives at the expense of another **2 :** a plant or animal that lives in or on some other living thing and gets food and sometimes shelter from it

par·a·sit·ic *adj* **:** of or relating to parasites or their way of life **:** being a parasite — **par·a·sit·i·cal·ly** *adv*

par·a·sol *n* **:** a light umbrella used as a protection against the sun

par·a·troop·er *n* **:** a soldier trained and equipped to parachute from an airplane

¹**par·cel** *n* **1 :** a plot of land **2 :** PACKAGE 1

²**parcel** *vb* **par·celed** *or* **par·celled; par·cel·ing** *or* **par·cel·ling 1 :** to divide and give out by parts **2 :** to wrap up into a package

parcel post *n* **:** a mail service that handles packages

parch *vb* **:** to dry up from heat and lack of moisture

parch·ment *n* **1 :** the skin of a sheep or goat prepared so that it can be written on **2 :** a paper similar to parchment

¹**par·don** *n* **1 :** forgiveness for wrong or rude behavior **2 :** a setting free from legal punishment

²**pardon** *vb* **1 :** to free from penalty for a fault or crime **2 :** to allow (a wrong act) to pass without punishment **:** FORGIVE

pare *vb* **pared; par·ing 1 :** to cut or shave off the outside or the ends of **2 :** to reduce as if by cutting

par·ent *n* **1 :** a father or mother of a child **2 :** an animal or plant that produces offspring or seed

par·ent·age *n* **:** a line of ancestors **:** ANCESTRY

pa·ren·tal *adj* **:** of or relating to parents

pa·ren·the·sis *n, pl* **pa·ren·the·ses 1 :** a word, phrase, or sentence inserted in a passage to explain or comment on it **2 :** one of a pair of marks ( ) used to enclose a word or group of words or to group mathematical terms to be dealt with as a unit — **par·en·thet·ic** *or* **par·en·thet·i·cal** *adj*

par·fait *n* **:** a dessert made usually of layers of fruit, syrup, ice cream, and whipped cream

par·ish *n* **1 :** a section of a church district under the care of a priest or minister **2 :** the persons who live in a parish and attend the parish church **3 :** the members of a church **4 :** a division in the state of Louisiana that is similar to a county in other states

parish house *n* **:** a building for the educational and social activities of a church

pa·rish·io·ner *n* **:** a member or resident of a parish

¹**park** *n* **1 :** an area of land set aside for recreation or for its beauty **2 :** an enclosed field for ball games

²**park** *vb* **:** to stop (as an auto or truck) and leave it for a while

par·ka *n* **:** a warm windproof jacket with a hood

park·way *n* **:** a broad landscaped highway

¹**par·ley** *n, pl* **parleys :** a discussion with an enemy

²**parley** *vb* **par·leyed; par·ley·ing :** to hold a discussion of terms with an enemy

par·lia·ment *n* **:** an assembly that is the highest legislative body of a country (as the United Kingdom)

par·lor *n* **1 :** a room for receiving guests and for conversation **2 :** a usually small place of business

pa·ro·chi·al *adj* **:** of, relating to, or supported by a religious body (as a church)

pa·role *n* **:** an early release of a prisoner

parrakeet *variant of* PARAKEET

par·rot *n* **:** a brightly colored tropical bird that has a strong hooked bill and is sometimes trained to imitate human speech

¹**par·ry** *vb* **par·ried; par·ry·ing 1 :** to turn aside an opponent's weapon or blow **2 :** to avoid by a skillful answer

²**parry** *n, pl* **par·ries :** an act or instance of parrying

pars·ley *n, pl* **pars·leys :** a garden plant related to the carrot that has finely divided leaves and is used to season or decorate various foods

pars•nip *n* **:** a vegetable that is the long white root of a plant related to the carrot
par•son *n* **:** [1]MINISTER 1
par•son•age *n* **:** a house provided by a church for its pastor to live in
[1]**part** *n* **1 :** one of the sections into which something is divided **:** something less than a whole **2 :** a voice or instrument **3 :** the music for a voice or instrument **4 :** a piece of a plant or animal body **5 :** a piece of a machine **6 :** a person's share or duty **7 :** one of the sides in a disagreement **8 :** the role of a character in a play **9 :** a line along which the hair is divided
[2]**part** *vb* **1 :** to leave someone **:** go away **2 :** to divide into parts **3 :** to hold apart **4 :** to come apart
par•take *vb* **par•took; par•tak•en; par•tak•ing :** to take a share or part
part•ed *adj* **:** divided into parts
par•tial *adj* **1 :** favoring one side of a question over another **2 :** fond or too fond of someone or something **3 :** of one part only **4 :** not complete — **par•tial•ly** *adv*
par•ti•al•i•ty *n, pl* **par•ti•al•i•ties :** the quality or state of being partial
par•tic•i•pant *n* **:** a person who takes part in something
par•tic•i•pate *vb* **par•tic•i•pat•ed; par•tic•i•pat•ing :** to join with others in doing something
par•tic•i•pa•tion *n* **:** the act of participating
par•ti•ci•ple *n* **:** a word formed from a verb but often used like an adjective while keeping some verb characteristics (as tense and the ability to take an object)
par•ti•cle *n* **:** a very small bit of something
[1]**par•tic•u•lar** *adj* **1 :** relating to one person or thing **2 :** not usual **:** SPECIAL **3 :** being one of several **4 :** concerned about details — **par•tic•u•lar•ly** *adv*
[2]**particular** *n* **:** a single fact or detail
part•ing *n* **:** a place or point where a division or separation occurs
par•ti•san *n* **1 :** a person who aids or approves something (as a party or a point of view) or someone **2 :** a soldier who lives and fights behind enemy lines — **par•ti•san•ship** *n*
[1]**par•ti•tion** *n* **1 :** an act of dividing into parts **2 :** something that divides
[2]**partition** *vb* **1 :** to divide into shares **2 :** to divide into separate parts or areas
part•ly *adv* **:** somewhat but not completely
part•ner *n* **1 :** a person who does or shares something with another **2 :** either one of a married pair **3 :** one who plays with another person on the same side in a game **4 :** one of two or more persons who run a business together
part•ner•ship *n* **1 :** the state of being a partner **2 :** a group of people in business together
part of speech : a class of words (as adjectives, adverbs, conjunctions, interjections, nouns, prepositions, pronouns, or verbs) identified according to the kinds of ideas they express and the work they do in a sentence
partook *past of* PARTAKE
par•tridge *n, pl* **partridge** *or* **par•tridg•es :** any of several plump game birds related to the chicken
part-time *adj* **:** involving fewer than the usual hours
par•ty *n, pl* **par•ties 1 :** a group of persons who take one side of a question or share a set of beliefs **2 :** a social gathering or the entertainment provided for it **3 :** a person or group concerned in some action
[1]**pass** *vb* **1 :** [1]MOVE 1, PROCEED **2 :** to go away **3 :** [1]DIE 1 **4 :** to go by or move past **5 :** to go or allow to go across, over, or through **6 :** to move from one place or condition to another **7 :** HAPPEN 2 **8 :** to be or cause to be approved **9 :** to go successfully through an examination or inspection **10 :** to be or cause to be identified or recognized **11 :** to transfer or throw to another person — **pass•er** *n*
[2]**pass** *n* **1 :** an opening or way for passing along or through **2 :** a gap in a mountain range
[3]**pass** *n* **1 :** SITUATION 4 **2 :** a written permit to go or come **3 :** the act or an instance of passing (as a ball) in a game
pass•able *adj* **1 :** fit to be traveled on **2 :** barely good enough — **pass•ably** *adv*
pas•sage *n* **1 :** the act or process of passing from one place or condition to another **2 :** a means (as a hall) of passing or reaching **3 :** the passing of a law **4 :** a right or permission to go as a passenger **5 :** a brief part of a speech or written work
pas•sage•way *n* **:** a road or way by which a person or thing may pass
pas•sen•ger *n* **:** someone riding on or in a vehicle
passenger pigeon *n* **:** a North American wild pigeon once common but now extinct
pass•er•by *n, pl* **pass•ers•by :** someone who passes by
[1]**pass•ing** *n* **1 :** the act of passing **2 :** DEATH 1
[2]**passing** *adj* **1 :** going by or past **2 :** lasting only for a short time **3 :** showing haste or lack of attention **4 :** used for passing **5 :** showing satisfactory work in a test or course of study
pas•sion *n* **1** *cap* **:** the suffering of Christ

between the night of the Last Supper and his death **2 :** a strong feeling or emotion **3 :** strong liking or desire **:** LOVE **4 :** an object of one's love, liking, or desire

pas•sion•ate *adj* **1 :** easily angered **2 :** showing or affected by strong feeling — **pas•sion•ate•ly** *adv*

pas•sive *adj* **1 :** not acting but acted upon **2 :** showing that the person or thing represented by the subject is acted on by the verb **3 :** offering no resistance — **pas•sive•ly** *adv*

pass out *vb* **:** to become unconscious **:** FAINT

Pass•over *n* **:** a Jewish holiday celebrated in March or April in honor of the freeing of the Hebrews from slavery in Egypt

pass•port *n* **:** a government document that allows a citizen to leave his or her country

pass up *vb* **:** to let go by **:** REFUSE

pass•word *n* **:** a secret word or phrase that must be spoken by a person before being allowed to pass a guard

1past *adj* **1 :** of or relating to a time that has gone by **2 :** expressing a time gone by **3 :** no longer serving

2past *prep* **1 :** 2BEYOND **2 :** going close to and then beyond

3past *n* **1 :** a former time **2 :** past life or history

4past *adv* **:** so as to pass by or beyond

1paste *n* **1 :** dough for pies or tarts **2 :** a soft smooth mixture **3 :** a mixture of flour or starch and water used for sticking things together

2paste *vb* **past•ed; past•ing :** to stick on or together with paste

paste•board *n* **:** a stiff material made of sheets of paper pasted together or of pulp pressed and dried

1pas•tel *n* **1 :** a crayon made by mixing ground coloring matter with a watery solution of a gum **2 :** a drawing made with pastel crayons **3 :** a soft pale color

2pastel *adj* **1 :** made with pastels **2 :** light and pale in color

pas•teur•i•za•tion *n* **:** the process or an instance of pasteurizing

pas•teur•ize *vb* **pas•teur•ized; pas•teur•iz•ing :** to keep a liquid (as milk) for a time at a temperature high enough to kill many harmful germs and then cool it rapidly — **pas•teur•iz•er** *n*

pas•time *n* **:** something (as a hobby) that helps to make time pass pleasantly

pas•tor *n* **:** a minister or priest in charge of a church

pas•to•ral *adj* **1 :** of or relating to shepherds or peaceful rural scenes **2 :** of or relating to the pastor of a church

past•ry *n, pl* **past•ries 1 :** sweet baked goods (as pies) made mainly of flour and fat **2 :** a piece of pastry

1pas•ture *n* **1 :** plants (as grass) for feeding grazing animals **2 :** land on which animals graze

2pasture *vb* **pas•tured; pas•tur•ing 1 :** 1GRAZE 1 **2 :** to supply (as cattle) with pasture

1pat *n* **1 :** a light tap with the open hand or a flat instrument **2 :** the sound of a pat or tap **3 :** a small flat piece (as of butter)

2pat *adj* **pat•ter; pat•test 1 :** exactly suitable **2 :** learned perfectly **3 :** not changing

3pat *vb* **pat•ted; pat•ting :** to tap or stroke gently with the open hand

1patch *n* **1 :** a piece of cloth used to mend or cover a torn or worn place **2 :** a small piece or area different from what is around it

2patch *vb* **:** to mend or cover with a patch

patch up *vb* **:** ADJUST 1

patch•work *n* **:** pieces of cloth of different colors and shapes sewed together

1pat•ent *adj* **1 :** protected by a patent **2 :** OBVIOUS, EVIDENT

2pat•ent *n* **:** a document that gives the inventor of something the only right to make, use, and sell the invention for a certain number of years

3pat•ent *vb* **:** to get a patent for

pa•ter•nal *adj* **1 :** of or relating to a father **:** FATHERLY **2 :** received or inherited from a father **3 :** related through the father

path *n, pl* **paths 1 :** a track made by traveling on foot **2 :** the way or track in which something moves **3 :** a way of life or thought — **path•less** *adj*

pa•thet•ic *adj* **:** making one feel pity, tenderness, or sorrow

path•way *n* **:** PATH 1

pa•tience *n* **:** the ability to be patient or the fact of being patient

1pa•tient *adj* **1 :** putting up with pain or troubles without complaint **2 :** showing or involving calm self-control — **pa•tient•ly** *adv*

2patient *n* **:** a person under medical care and treatment

pa•tio *n, pl* **pa•ti•os 1 :** an inner part of a house that is open to the sky **2 :** an open area next to a house that is usually paved

pa•tri•arch *n* **1 :** the father and ruler of a family or tribe **2 :** a respected old man

pa•tri•ot *n* **:** a person who loves his or her country and enthusiastically supports it

pa•tri•ot•ic *adj* **:** having or showing patriotism

pa•tri•ot•ism *n* **:** love of one's country

1pa•trol *n* **1 :** the action of going around an area for observation or guard **2 :** a person or group doing the act of patrolling **3 :** a part of a troop of Boy Scouts that consists of two or more boys **4 :** a part of a troop of Girl Scouts that usually consists of six or eight girls

[2]**patrol** *vb* **pa·trolled; pa·trol·ling :** to go around an area for the purpose of watching or protecting

pa·trol·man *n, pl* **pa·trol·men :** a police officer who has a regular beat

pa·tron *n* **1 :** a person who gives generous support or approval **2 :** CUSTOMER **3 :** a saint to whom a church or society is dedicated

pa·tron·age *n* **1 :** the help or encouragement given by a patron **2 :** a group of patrons (as of a shop or theater) **3 :** the control by officials of giving out jobs, contracts, and favors

pa·tron·ize *vb* **pa·tron·ized; pa·tron·iz·ing 1 :** to act as a patron to or of **:** SUPPORT **2 :** to be a customer of **3 :** to treat (a person) as if one were better or more important

[1]**pat·ter** *vb* **1 :** to strike again and again with light blows **2 :** to run with quick light steps

[2]**patter** *n* **:** a series of quick light sounds

[1]**pat·tern** *n* **1 :** something worth copying **2 :** a model or guide for making something **3 :** a form or figure used in decoration **:** DESIGN — **pat·terned** *adj*

[2]**pattern** *vb* **:** to make or design by following a pattern

pat·ty *n, pl* **pat·ties :** a small flat cake of chopped food

pau·per *n* **:** a very poor person

[1]**pause** *n* **1 :** a temporary stop **2 :** a sign 𝄐 above a musical note or rest to show that the note or rest is to be held longer

[2]**pause** *vb* **paused; paus·ing :** to stop for a time **:** make a pause

pave *vb* **paved; pav·ing :** to make a hard surface on (as with concrete or asphalt)

pave·ment *n* **1 :** a paved surface (as of a street) **2 :** material used in paving

pa·vil·ion *n* **1 :** a very large tent **2 :** a building usually with open sides that is used as a place for entertainment or shelter in a park or garden

pav·ing *n* **:** PAVEMENT

[1]**paw** *n* **:** the foot of a four-footed animal (as the lion, dog, or cat) that has claws

[2]**paw** *vb* **1 :** to touch in a clumsy or rude way **2 :** to touch or scrape with a paw **3 :** to beat or scrape with a hoof

[1]**pawn** *n* **:** the piece of least value in the game of chess

[2]**pawn** *n* **1 :** something of value given as a guarantee (as of payment of a debt) **2 :** the condition of being given as a guarantee

[3]**pawn** *vb* **:** to leave as a guarantee for a loan **:** PLEDGE

pawn·bro·ker *n* **:** a person who makes a business of lending money and keeping personal property as a guarantee

pawn·shop *n* **:** a pawnbroker's shop

[1]**pay** *vb* **paid; pay·ing 1 :** to give (as money) in return for services received or for something bought **2 :** to give what is owed **3 :** to get revenge on **4 :** to give or offer freely **5 :** to get a suitable return for cost or trouble **:** be worth the effort or pains required — **pay·er** *n*

[2]**pay** *n* **1 :** the act of paying **:** PAYMENT **2 :** the state of being paid or employed for money **3 :** SALARY

pay·able *adj* **:** that may, can, or must be paid

pay·check *n* **:** a check or money received as wages or salary

pay·ment *n* **1 :** the act of paying **2 :** money given to pay a debt

pay off *vb* **1 :** to pay in full **2 :** to have a good result

pay·roll *n* **1 :** a list of persons who receive pay **2 :** the amount of money necessary to pay the employees of a business

pay up *vb* **:** to pay in full especially debts that are overdue

PC *n, pl* **PCs** *or* **PC's :** PERSONAL COMPUTER

pea *n, pl* **peas** *also* **pease 1 :** a vegetable that is the round seed found in the pods of a garden plant (**pea vine**) related to the clovers **2 :** a plant (as the sweet pea) resembling or related to the garden pea

peace *n* **1 :** freedom from public disturbance or war **2 :** freedom from upsetting thoughts or feelings **3 :** agreement and harmony among persons **4 :** an agreement to end a war

peace·able *adj* **:** PEACEFUL 1 3

peace·ful *adj* **1 :** liking peace **:** not easily moved to argue or fight **2 :** full of or enjoying peace, quiet, or calm **3 :** not involving fighting — **peace·ful·ly** *adv* — **peace·ful·ness** *n*

peace·mak·er *n* **:** a person who settles an argument or stops a fight

peace pipe *n* **:** a decorated pipe of the American Indians used for certain ceremonies

peach *n* **1 :** a fruit that is related to the plum and has a sweet juicy pulp, hairy skin, and a large rough stone **2 :** a pale yellowish pink color

pea·cock *n* **:** the male of a very large Asian pheasant with a very long brightly colored tail that can be spread or raised at will, a small crest, and in most forms brilliant blue or green feathers on the neck and shoulders

peak *n* **1 :** the part of a cap that sticks out in

DICTIONARY

front **2 :** the pointed top of a hill or mountain **3 :** a mountain all by itself **4 :** the highest point of development

[1]**peal** *n* **1 :** the sound of bells **2 :** a loud sound **:** a series of loud sounds

[2]**peal** *vb* **:** to give out peals

pea•nut *n* **:** a plant related to the peas that has yellow flowers and is grown for its underground pods of oily nutlike edible seeds which yield a valuable oil (**peanut oil**) or are crushed to form a spread (**peanut butter**)

pear *n* **:** the fleshy fruit that grows on a tree related to the apple and is commonly larger at the end opposite the stem

pearl *n* **1 :** a smooth body with a rich luster that is formed within the shell of some mollusks (as the **pearl oyster** of tropical seas) usually around something irritating (as a grain of sand) which has gotten into the shell **2 :** MOTHER-OF-PEARL **3 :** something like a pearl in shape, color, or value **4 :** a pale bluish gray color

pearly *adj* **pearl•i•er; pearl•i•est :** like a pearl especially in having a shining surface

peas•ant *n* **:** a farmer owning a small amount of land or a farm worker in European countries

pease *pl of* PEA

peat *n* **:** a blackish or dark brown material that is the remains of plants partly decayed in water and is dug and dried for use as fuel

peat moss *n* **:** a spongy brownish moss of wet areas that is often the chief plant making up peat

peb•ble *n* **:** a small rounded stone

pe•can *n* **:** an oval edible nut that usually has a thin shell and is the fruit of a tall tree of the central and southern United States related to the walnuts

pec•ca•ry *n, pl* **pec•ca•ries :** either of two mostly tropical American animals that gather in herds, are active at night, and look like but are much smaller than the related pigs

[1]**peck** *n* **1 :** a unit of capacity equal to one quarter of a bushel **2 :** a great deal **:** a large quantity

[2]**peck** *vb* **1 :** to strike or pick up with the bill **2 :** to strike with a sharp instrument (as a pick)

[3]**peck** *n* **1 :** the act of pecking **2 :** a mark made by pecking

pe•cu•liar *adj* **1 :** one's own **:** of or limited to some one person, thing, or place **2 :** different from the usual **:** ODD

pe•cu•li•ar•i•ty *n, pl* **pe•cu•li•ar•i•ties 1 :** the quality or state of being peculiar **2 :** something peculiar or individual

[1]**ped•al** *n* **:** a lever worked by the foot or feet

[2]**pedal** *vb* **ped•aled** *or* **ped•alled; ped•al•ing** *or* **ped•al•ling :** to use or work the pedals of something

ped•dle *vb* **ped•dled; ped•dling :** to go about especially from house to house with goods for sale

ped•dler *or* **ped•lar** *n* **:** someone who peddles

ped•es•tal *n* **1 :** a support or foot of an upright structure (as a column, statue, or lamp) **2 :** a position of high regard

pe•des•tri•an *n* **:** a person who is walking

pe•di•a•tri•cian *n* **:** a doctor who specializes in the care of babies and children

ped•i•gree *n* **1 :** a table or list showing the line of ancestors of a person or animal **2 :** a line of ancestors

pe•dom•e•ter *n* **:** an instrument that measures the distance one covers in walking

[1]**peek** *vb* **1 :** to look slyly or cautiously **2 :** to take a quick glance — **peek•er** *n*

[2]**peek** *n* **:** a short or sly look

[1]**peel** *vb* **1 :** to strip off the skin or bark of **2 :** to strip or tear off **3 :** to come off smoothly or in bits

[2]**peel** *n* **:** an outer covering and especially the skin of a fruit

[1]**peep** *vb* **:** to make a weak shrill sound such as a young bird makes — **peep•er** *n*

[2]**peep** *n* **:** a weak shrill sound

[3]**peep** *vb* **1 :** to look through or as if through a small hole or a crack **:** PEEK **2 :** to show slightly

[4]**peep** *n* **1 :** a brief or sly look **2 :** the first appearance

[1]**peer** *n* **1 :** a person of the same rank or kind **:** EQUAL **2 :** a member of one of the five ranks (duke, marquis, earl, viscount, and baron) of the British nobility

[2]**peer** *vb* **1 :** to look curiously or carefully **2 :** to come slightly into view **:** peep out

peer•less *adj* **:** having no equal

pee•vish *adj* **:** complaining a lot **:** IRRITABLE — **pee•vish•ly** *adv* — **pee•vish•ness** *n*

pee•wee *n* **:** one that is small

[1]**peg** *n* **1 :** a slender piece (as of wood or metal) used especially to fasten things together or to hang things on **2 :** a piece driven into the ground to mark a boundary or to hold something **3 :** a step or grade in approval or esteem

[2]**peg** *vb* **pegged; peg•ging 1 :** to mark or fasten with pegs **2 :** to work hard

pel•i•can *n* **:** a bird with a large bill, webbed feet, and a great pouch on the lower jaw that is used to scoop in fish for food

pel•la•gra *n* **:** a disease caused by a diet containing too little protein and too little of a necessary vitamin

pel•let *n* **1 :** a little ball (as of food or medicine) **2 :** a piece of small shot

pell–mell *adv* **1 :** in crowded confusion **2 :** in a big hurry

[1]**pelt** *n* **:** a skin of an animal especially with its fur or wool

[2]**pelt** *vb* **1 :** to strike with repeated blows **2 :** HURL, THROW **3 :** to beat or pound against something again and again

pel•vis *n* **:** the bowl-shaped part of the skeleton that supports the lower part of the abdomen and includes the hip bones and the lower bones of the backbone

[1]**pen** *vb* **penned; pen•ning :** to shut in a small enclosure

[2]**pen** *n* **:** a small enclosure especially for animals

[3]**pen** *n* **:** an instrument for writing with ink

[4]**pen** *vb* **penned; pen•ning :** to write with a pen

pe•nal *adj* **:** of or relating to punishment

pe•nal•ize *vb* **pe•nal•ized; pe•nal•iz•ing :** to give a penalty to

pen•al•ty *n, pl* **pen•al•ties 1 :** punishment for doing something wrong **2 :** a loss or handicap given for breaking a rule in a sport or game

pence *pl of* PENNY

[1]**pen•cil** *n* **:** a device for writing or drawing consisting of a stick of black or colored material enclosed in wood, plastic, or metal

[2]**pencil** *vb* **pen•ciled** *or* **pen•cilled; pen•cil•ing** *or* **pen•cil•ling :** to write, mark, or draw with a pencil

pen•dant *n* **:** an ornament (as on a necklace) allowed to hang free

[1]**pend•ing** *prep* **1 :** DURING 1 **2 :** while waiting for

[2]**pending** *adj* **:** not yet decided

pen•du•lum *n* **:** an object hung from a fixed point so as to swing freely back and forth under the action of gravity

pen•e•trate *vb* **pen•e•trat•ed; pen•e•trat•ing 1 :** to pass into or through **:** PIERCE **2 :** to see into or understand

pen•e•tra•tion *n* **1 :** the act or process of penetrating **2 :** keen understanding

pen•guin *n* **:** a seabird that cannot fly, has very short legs, and is found in the cold regions of the southern hemisphere

pen•i•cil•lin *n* **:** an antibiotic that is produced by a mold and is used especially against disease-causing round bacteria

pen•in•su•la *n* **:** a piece of land extending out into a body of water

pe•nis *n, pl* **pe•nes** *or* **pe•nis•es :** a male organ in mammals used for sexual intercourse and for urinating

pen•i•tence *n* **:** sorrow for one's sins or faults

[1]**pen•i•tent** *adj* **:** feeling or showing penitence

[2]**penitent** *n* **:** a penitent person

pen•i•ten•tia•ry *n, pl* **pen•i•ten•tia•ries :** a prison for criminals

pen•knife *n, pl* **pen•knives :** a small jackknife

pen•man *n, pl* **pen•men :** a person who uses a pen **:** WRITER

pen•man•ship *n* **:** writing with a pen **:** style or quality of handwriting

pen name *n* **:** a false name that an author uses on his or her work

pen•nant *n* **1 :** a narrow pointed flag used for identification, signaling, or decoration **2 :** a flag that serves as the emblem of a championship

pen•ni•less *adj* **:** very poor **:** having no money

pen•ny *n, pl* **pennies 1** *or pl* **pence :** a coin of the United Kingdom equal to $^1/_{100}$ pound **2 :** CENT

[1]**pen•sion** *n* **:** a sum paid regularly to a person who has retired from work

[2]**pension** *vb* **:** to grant or give a pension to

pen•sive *adj* **:** lost in sober or sad thought — **pen•sive•ly** *adv* — **pen•sive•ness** *n*

pent *adj* **:** penned up **:** shut up

penta- *or* **pent-** *prefix* **:** five

pen•ta•gon *n* **:** a flat figure having five angles and five sides

pen•tag•o•nal *adj* **:** having five sides

pen•tath•lon *n* **:** an athletic contest made up of five different events in which each person participates

pent•house *n* **:** an apartment built on the roof of a building

pe•on *n* **:** a member of the landless laboring class in Spanish America

pe•o•ny *n, pl* **pe•o•nies :** a plant related to the buttercup that lives for years and is widely grown for its very large usually double white, pink, or red flowers

[1]**peo•ple** *n, pl* **people** *or* **peoples 1 :** a body of persons making up a race, tribe, or nation **2 :** human beings — often used in compounds instead of *persons* **3 :** the persons of a certain group or place

[2]**people** *vb* **peo•pled; peo•pling 1 :** to supply or fill with people **2 :** to dwell on or in

[1]**pep** *n* **:** brisk energy or liveliness

[2]**pep** *vb* **pepped; pep•ping :** to put pep into

[1]**pep•per** *n* **1 :** a product from the fruit of an East Indian climbing shrub that is sharp in flavor, is used as a seasoning or in medicine, and consists of the whole ground dried berry (**black pepper**) or of the ground seeds alone (**white pepper**) **2 :** a plant related to the tomato that is grown for its fruits which may be very sharp in flavor (**hot peppers**) or mild and sweet (**sweet peppers** or **bell peppers**)

[2]**pepper** *vb* **1 :** to season with or as if with pepper **2 :** to hit with a shower of blows or objects

pep·per·mint *n* **:** a mint with stalks of small usually purple flowers that yields an oil (**peppermint oil**) which is sharp in flavor and is used especially to flavor candies

pep·py *adj* **pep·pi·er; pep·pi·est :** full of pep

pep·sin *n* **:** an enzyme that starts the digestion of proteins in the stomach

per *prep* **1 :** to or for each **2 :** ACCORDING TO 1

per an·num *adv* **:** by the year **:** in or for each year **:** ANNUALLY

per cap·i·ta *adv or adj* **:** by or for each person

per·ceive *vb* **per·ceived; per·ceiv·ing 1 :** to become aware of through the senses and especially through sight **2 :** UNDERSTAND 1

[1]**per·cent** *adv or adj* **:** out of every hundred **:** measured by the number of units as compared with one hundred

[2]**percent** *n, pl* **percent :** a part or fraction of a whole expressed in hundredths

per·cent·age *n* **1 :** a part of a whole expressed in hundredths **2 :** a share of profits

per·cep·ti·ble *adj* **:** possible to detect

per·cep·tion *n* **1 :** an act or the result of grasping with one's mind **2 :** the ability to grasp (as meanings and ideas) with one's mind **3 :** a judgment formed from information grasped

[1]**perch** *n* **1 :** a place where birds roost **2 :** a raised seat or position

[2]**perch** *vb* **:** to sit or rest on or as if on a perch

[3]**perch** *n, pl* **perch** *or* **perch·es 1 :** a European freshwater food fish that is mostly olive green and yellow **2 :** any of numerous fishes related to or resembling the European perch

per·chance *adv* **:** PERHAPS

per·co·late *vb* **per·co·lat·ed; per·co·lat·ing 1 :** to trickle or cause to trickle through something porous **:** OOZE **2 :** to prepare (coffee) by passing hot water through ground coffee beans again and again — **per·co·la·tor** *n*

per·co·la·tion *n* **:** the act or process of percolating

per·cus·sion *n* **1 :** a sharp tapping **2 :** the striking of an explosive cap to set off the charge in a gun **3 :** the musical instruments of a band or orchestra that are played by striking or shaking

percussion instrument *n* **:** a musical instrument (as a drum, cymbal, or maraca) sounded by striking or shaking

[1]**pe·ren·ni·al** *adj* **1 :** present all through the year **2 :** never ending **:** CONTINUOUS **3 :** living from year to year

[2]**perennial** *n* **:** a perennial plant

[1]**per·fect** *adj* **1 :** lacking nothing **:** COMPLETE **2 :** thoroughly skilled or trained **:** meeting the highest standards **3 :** having no mistake, error, or flaw — **per·fect·ly** *adv*

[2]**per·fect** *vb* **:** to make perfect

per·fec·tion *n* **1 :** completeness in all parts or details **2 :** the highest excellence or skill **3 :** a quality or thing that cannot be improved

per·fo·rate *vb* **per·fo·rat·ed; per·fo·rat·ing 1 :** to make a hole through **:** PIERCE **2 :** to make many small holes in

per·form *vb* **1 :** to carry out **:** ACCOMPLISH, DO **2 :** to do something needing special skill — **per·form·er** *n*

per·for·mance *n* **1 :** the carrying out of an action **2 :** a public entertainment

[1]**per·fume** *n* **1 :** a pleasant smell **:** FRAGRANCE **2 :** a liquid used to make things smell nice

[2]**per·fume** *vb* **per·fumed; per·fum·ing :** to make smell nice **:** add a pleasant scent to

per·haps *adv* **:** possibly but not certainly **:** MAYBE

per·il *n* **1 :** the state of being in great danger **2 :** a cause or source of danger

per·il·ous *adj* **:** DANGEROUS 1 — **per·il·ous·ly** *adv*

pe·rim·e·ter *n* **1 :** the whole outer boundary of a figure or area **2 :** the length of the boundary of a figure

pe·ri·od *n* **1 :** a punctuation mark . used chiefly to mark the end of a declarative sentence or an abbreviation **2 :** a portion of time set apart by some quality **3 :** a portion of time that forms a stage in the history of something **4 :** one of the divisions of a school day

pe·ri·od·ic *adj* **:** occurring at regular intervals

[1]**pe·ri·od·i·cal** *adj* **1 :** PERIODIC **2 :** published at regular intervals — **pe·ri·od·i·cal·ly** *adv*

[2]**periodical** *n* **:** a periodical publication (as a magazine)

peri·scope *n* **:** an instrument containing lenses and mirrors by which a person (as on a submarine) can get a view that would otherwise be blocked

per·ish *vb* **:** to become destroyed **:** DIE

per·ish·able *adj* **:** likely to spoil or decay

[1]**per·i·win·kle** *n* **:** an evergreen plant that spreads along the ground and has shining leaves and blue or white flowers

[2]**periwinkle** *n* **:** a small snail that lives along rocky seashores

perk *vb* **1 :** to lift in a quick, alert, or bold way **2 :** to make fresher in appearance **3 :** to become more lively or cheerful

perky *adj* **perk·i·er; perk·i·est :** being lively and cheerful

per·ma·nence *n* **:** the quality or state of being permanent

per·ma·nent *adj* **:** lasting or meant to last for a long time **:** not temporary — **per·ma·nent·ly** *adv*

per·me·able *adj* **:** having pores or openings that let liquids or gases pass through

per·me·ate *vb* **per·me·at·ed; per·me·at·ing 1 :** to pass through something that has pores or small openings or is in a loose form **2 :** to spread throughout

per·mis·sion *n* **:** the consent of a person in authority

[1]**per·mit** *vb* **per·mit·ted; per·mit·ting 1 :** to give permission **:** ALLOW **2 :** to make possible **:** give an opportunity

[2]**per·mit** *n* **:** a statement of permission (as a license or pass)

per·ni·cious *adj* **:** causing great damage or harm

per·ox·ide *n* **:** an oxide containing much oxygen (as one of hydrogen used as an antiseptic)

[1]**per·pen·dic·u·lar** *adj* **1 :** exactly vertical **2 :** being at right angles to a line or surface — **per·pen·dic·u·lar·ly** *adv*

[2]**perpendicular** *n* **:** a perpendicular line, surface, or position

per·pe·trate *vb* **per·pe·trat·ed; per·pe·trat·ing :** to bring about or carry out **:** COMMIT — **per·pe·tra·tor** *n*

per·pet·u·al *adj* **1 :** lasting forever **:** ETERNAL **2 :** occurring continually **:** CONSTANT — **per·pet·u·al·ly** *adv*

per·pet·u·ate *vb* **per·pet·u·at·ed; per·pet·u·at·ing :** to cause to last a long time

per·plex *vb* **:** to confuse the mind of **:** BEWILDER

per·plex·i·ty *n, pl* **per·plex·i·ties 1 :** a puzzled or anxious state of mind **2 :** something that perplexes

per·se·cute *vb* **per·se·cut·ed; per·se·cut·ing :** to treat continually in a way meant to be cruel and harmful

per·se·cu·tion *n* **1 :** the act of persecuting **2 :** the state of being persecuted

per·se·ver·ance *n* **:** the act or power of persevering

per·se·vere *vb* **per·se·vered; per·se·ver·ing :** to keep trying to do something in spite of difficulties

per·sim·mon *n* **:** a fruit of orange color that looks like a plum and grows on a tree related to the ebonies

per·sist *vb* **1 :** to keep on doing or saying something **:** continue stubbornly **2 :** to last on and on **:** continue to exist or occur

per·sist·ence *n* **1 :** the act or fact of persisting **2 :** the quality of being persistent **:** PERSEVERANCE

per·sist·ent *adj* **:** continuing to act or exist longer than usual — **per·sist·ent·ly** *adv*

per·son *n* **1 :** a human being — used in compounds especially by those who prefer to avoid *man* in words that apply to both sexes **2 :** the body of a human being **3 :** bodily presence **4 :** reference to the speaker, to the one spoken to, or to one spoken of as shown especially by means of certain pronouns

per·son·age *n* **:** an important or famous person

per·son·al *adj* **1 :** of, relating to, or belonging to a person **:** not public **:** not general **2 :** made or done in person **3 :** of the person or body **4 :** relating to a particular person or his or her qualities **5 :** intended for one particular person **6 :** relating to oneself — **per·son·al·ly** *adv*

personal computer *n* **:** a computer designed for an individual user

per·son·al·i·ty *n, pl* **per·son·al·i·ties 1 :** the qualities (as moods or habits) that make one person different from others **2 :** a person's pleasing qualities **3 :** a person of importance or fame

personal pronoun *n* **:** a pronoun (as *I, you, it,* or *they*) used as a substitute for a noun that names a definite person or thing

per·son·i·fy *vb* **per·son·i·fied; per·son·i·fy·ing :** to think of or represent as a person

per·son·nel *n* **:** a group of people employed in a business or an organization

per·spec·tive *n* **1 :** the art of painting or drawing a scene so that objects in it seem to have their right shape and to be the right distance apart **2 :** the power to understand things in their true relationship to each other **3 :** the true relationship of objects or events to one another

per·spi·ra·tion *n* **1 :** the act or process of perspiring **2 :** salty liquid given off from skin glands

per·spire *vb* **per·spired; per·spir·ing :** to give off salty liquid through the skin

per·suade *vb* **per·suad·ed; per·suad·ing :** to win over to a belief or way of acting by argument or earnest request **:** CONVINCE

per·sua·sion *n* **1 :** the act of persuading **2 :** the power to persuade **3 :** a way of believing **:** BELIEF

per·sua·sive *adj* **:** able or likely to persuade — **per·sua·sive·ly** *adv* — **per·sua·sive·ness** *n*

pert *adj* **1 :** SAUCY 1 **2 :** PERKY

per·tain *vb* **1 :** to belong to as a part, quality, or function **2 :** to relate to a person or thing

per•ti•nent *adj* **:** relating to the subject that is being thought about or discussed **:** RELEVANT

per•turb *vb* **:** to disturb in mind **:** trouble greatly

pe•ruse *vb* **pe•rused; pe•rus•ing 1 :** READ 1 **2 :** to read through carefully

per•vade *vb* **per•vad•ed; per•vad•ing :** to spread through all parts of **:** PERMEATE

per•verse *adj* **:** stubborn in being against what is right or sensible

pe•se•ta *n* **:** a Spanish coin or bill

pe•so *n, pl* **pesos 1 :** an old silver coin of Spain and Spanish America **2 :** a coin of the Philippines or of any of various Latin American countries

pes•si•mist *n* **:** a pessimistic person

pes•si•mis•tic *adj* **1 :** having no hope that one's troubles will end or that success or happiness will come **:** GLOOMY **2 :** having the belief that evil is more common or powerful than good

pest *n* **1 :** PESTILENCE **2 :** a plant or animal that damages humans or their goods **3 :** NUISANCE

pes•ter *vb* **:** to bother again and again

pes•ti•cide *n* **:** a substance used to destroy pests

pes•ti•lence *n* **:** a contagious often fatal disease that spreads quickly

pes•tle *n* **:** a tool shaped like a small club for crushing substances in a mortar

[1]pet *n* **1 :** a tame animal kept for pleasure rather than for use **2 :** a person who is treated with special kindness or consideration

[2]pet *adj* **1 :** kept or treated as a pet **2 :** showing fondness **3 :** [2]FAVORITE

[3]pet *vb* **pet•ted; pet•ting 1 :** to stroke or pat gently or lovingly **2 :** to kiss and caress

pet•al *n* **:** one of the often brightly colored modified leaves that make up the corolla of a flower — **pet•aled** *or* **pet•alled** *adj* — **pet•al•less** *adj*

pet•i•ole *n* **:** the stalk of a leaf

pe•tite *adj* **:** having a small trim figure

[1]pe•ti•tion *n* **1 :** an earnest appeal **2 :** a document asking for something

[2]petition *vb* **:** to make a petition to or for — **pe•ti•tion•er** *n*

pe•trel *n* **:** a small seabird with long wings that flies far from land

pet•ri•fy *vb* **pet•ri•fied; pet•ri•fy•ing 1 :** to change plant or animal matter into stone or something like stone **2 :** to frighten very much

pe•tro•leum *n* **:** a raw oil that is obtained from wells drilled in the ground and that is the source of gasoline, kerosene, and fuel oils

pet•ti•coat *n* **:** a skirt worn under a dress or outer skirt

petting zoo *n* **:** a collection of farm animals or gentle exotic animals for children to pet and feed

pet•ty *adj* **pet•ti•er; pet•ti•est 1 :** small and of no importance **2 :** showing or having a mean narrow-minded attitude — **pet•ti•ly** *adv* — **pet•ti•ness** *n*

petty officer *n* **:** an officer in the Navy or Coast Guard appointed from among the enlisted people

petty officer first class *n* **:** a petty officer in the Navy or Coast Guard ranking above a petty officer second class

petty officer second class *n* **:** a petty officer in the Navy or Coast Guard ranking above a petty officer third class

petty officer third class *n* **:** a petty officer in the Navy or Coast Guard ranking above a seaman

pet•u•lant *adj* **:** easily put in a bad humor **:** CROSS

pe•tu•nia *n* **:** a plant related to the potato grown for its velvety brightly colored flowers that are shaped like funnels

pew *n* **:** one of the benches with backs and sometimes doors set in rows in a church

pe•wee *n* **:** a small grayish or greenish brown bird (as a phoebe) that eats flying insects

pew•ter *n* **1 :** a metallic substance made mostly of tin sometimes mixed with copper or antimony that is used in making utensils (as pitchers and bowls) **2 :** utensils made of pewter

phantasy *variant of* FANTASY

phan•tom *n* **:** an image or figure that can be sensed (as with the eyes or ears) but that is not real

pha•raoh *n* **:** a ruler of ancient Egypt

phar•ma•cist *n* **:** a person skilled or engaged in pharmacy

phar•ma•cy *n, pl* **phar•ma•cies 1 :** the art, practice, or profession of mixing and preparing medicines usually according to a doctor's prescription **2 :** the place of business of a pharmacist **:** DRUGSTORE

phar•ynx *n, pl* **pha•ryn•ges** *also* **phar•ynx•es :** the space behind the mouth into which the nostrils, gullet, and windpipe open — **pha•ryn•geal** *adj*

phase *n* **1 :** the way that the moon or a planet looks to the eye at any time in its series of changes with respect to how it shines **2 :** a step or part in a series of events or actions **:** STAGE **3 :** a particular part or feature **:** ASPECT

pheas•ant *n* **:** a large brightly colored game bird with a long tail that is related to the chicken

phe·nom·e·nal *adj* **:** very remarkable **:** EXTRAORDINARY

phe·nom·e·non *n, pl* **phe·nom·e·na** *or* **phe·nom·e·nons** **1** *pl phenomena* **:** an observable fact or event **2 :** a rare or important fact or event **3** *pl phenomenons* **:** an extraordinary or exceptional person or thing

[1]**-phil** *or* **-phile** *n suffix* **:** lover **:** one having a strong attraction to

[2]**-phil** *or* **-phile** *adj suffix* **:** having a fondness for or strong attraction to

phil·an·throp·ic *adj* **:** of, relating to, or devoted to philanthropy **:** CHARITABLE — **phil·an·throp·i·cal·ly** *adv*

phi·lan·thro·pist *n* **:** a person who gives generously to help other people

phi·lan·thro·py *n, pl* **phi·lan·thro·pies** **1 :** active effort to help other people **2 :** a philanthropic gift **3 :** an organization giving or supported by charitable gifts

phil·o·den·dron *n* **:** any of several plants that can stand shade and are often grown for their showy leaves

phi·los·o·pher *n* **1 :** a student of philosophy **2 :** a person who takes misfortunes with calmness and courage

phil·o·soph·i·cal *or* **phil·o·soph·ic** *adj* **1 :** of or relating to philosophy **2 :** showing the wisdom and calm of a philosopher — **phil·o·soph·i·cal·ly** *adv*

phi·los·o·phy *n, pl* **phi·los·o·phies** **1 :** the study of the basic ideas about knowledge, right and wrong, reasoning, and the value of things **2 :** the philosophical teachings or principles of a person or a group **3 :** calmness of temper and judgment

phlox *n, pl* **phlox** *or* **phlox·es** **:** any of a group of plants grown for their showy clusters of usually white, pink, or purplish flowers

pho·bia *n* **:** an unreasonable, abnormal, and lasting fear of something

phoe·be *n* **:** a common American bird that is grayish brown above and yellowish white below and that eats flying insects

phon- *or* **phono-** *prefix* **:** sound **:** voice **:** speech

[1]**phone** *n* **:** [1]TELEPHONE

[2]**phone** *vb* **phoned; phon·ing :** [2]TELEPHONE

pho·neme *n* **:** one of the smallest units of speech that distinguish one utterance from another

pho·net·ic *adj* **:** of or relating to spoken language or speech sounds

pho·nics *n* **:** a method of teaching beginners to read and pronounce words by learning the sound value of letters, letter groups, and syllables

pho·no·graph *n* **:** an instrument that reproduces sounds recorded on a grooved disk (**phonograph record**)

phos·pho·rus *n* **:** a white or yellowish waxlike chemical element that gives a faint glow in moist air and is necessary in some form to plant and animal life

[1]**pho·to** *n, pl* **photos :** [1]PHOTOGRAPH

[2]**photo** *vb* **:** [2]PHOTOGRAPH

[1]**pho·to·copy** *n* **:** a copy of usually printed material made using a process in which an image is formed by the action of light on an electrically charged surface

[2]**photocopy** *vb* **:** to make a photocopy of — **pho·to·copi·er** *n*

[1]**pho·to·graph** *n* **:** a picture made by photography

[2]**photograph** *vb* **:** to take a picture of with a camera — **pho·tog·ra·pher** *n*

pho·to·graph·ic *adj* **:** obtained by or used in photography

pho·tog·ra·phy *n* **:** the making of pictures by means of a camera that directs the image of an object onto a film made sensitive to light

pho·to·syn·the·sis *n* **:** the process by which green plants form carbohydrates from carbon dioxide and water in the presence of light — **pho·to·syn·thet·ic** *adj*

[1]**phrase** *n* **1 :** a brief expression **2 :** a group of two or more words that express a single idea but do not form a complete sentence

[2]**phrase** *vb* **phrased; phras·ing :** to express in words

phy·lum *n, pl* **phy·la** **:** a group of animals that ranks above the class in scientific classification and is the highest group of the plant kingdom

phys·i·cal *adj* **1 :** of or relating to nature or the world as we see it **:** material and not mental, spiritual, or imaginary **2 :** of the body **:** BODILY **3 :** of or relating to physics — **phys·i·cal·ly** *adv*

phy·si·cian *n* **:** a specialist in healing human disease **:** a doctor of medicine

phys·i·cist *n* **:** a specialist in physics

phys·ics *n* **:** a science that deals with the facts about matter and motion and includes the subjects of mechanics, heat, light, electricity, sound, and the atomic nucleus

phys·i·o·log·i·cal *or* **phys·i·o·log·ic** *adj* **:** of or relating to physiology

phys·i·ol·o·gist *n* **:** a specialist in physiology

phys·i·ol·o·gy *n* **1 :** a branch of biology that deals with the working of the living body and its parts (as organs and cells) **2 :** the processes and activities by which a living being or any of its parts functions

phy·sique *n* **:** the build of a person's body

pi *n, pl* **pis :** the symbol π representing the ratio of the circumference of a circle to its diameter or about 3.1416

pi•a•nist *n* **:** a person who plays the piano

pi•a•no *n, pl* **pianos :** a keyboard instrument having steel wire strings that sound when struck by hammers covered with felt

pi•az•za *n* **1 :** a large open square in an Italian town **2 :** PORCH, VERANDA

pic•co•lo *n, pl* **pic•co•los :** a small flute whose tones are an octave higher than those of the ordinary flute

¹pick *vb* **1 :** to strike or work on with a pointed tool **2 :** to remove bit by bit **3 :** to gather one by one **4 :** CHOOSE 1, SELECT **5 :** to eat sparingly or daintily **6 :** to steal from **7 :** to start (a fight) with someone else deliberately **8 :** to unlock without a key **9 :** to pluck with the fingers or with a pick — **pick•er** *n* — **pick on :** ¹TEASE

²pick *n* **1 :** PICKAX **2 :** a slender pointed instrument **3 :** a thin piece of metal or plastic used to pluck the strings of a musical instrument **4 :** the act or opportunity of choosing **5 :** the best ones

pick•ax *n* **:** a heavy tool with a wooden handle and a blade pointed at one or both ends for loosening or breaking up soil or rock

pick•er•el *n* **:** any of several fairly small fishes that look like the pike

¹pick•et *n* **1 :** a pointed stake or slender post (as for making a fence) **2 :** a soldier or a group of soldiers assigned to stand guard **3 :** a person stationed before a place of work where there is a strike

²picket *vb* **1 :** ²TETHER **2 :** to walk or stand in front of as a picket

¹pick•le *n* **1 :** a mixture of salt and water or vinegar for keeping foods **:** BRINE **2 :** a difficult or very unpleasant condition **3 :** something (as a cucumber) that has been kept in a pickle of salty water or vinegar

²pickle *vb* **pick•led; pick•ling :** to soak or keep in a pickle

pick•pock•et *n* **:** a thief who steals from pockets and purses

pick•up *n* **:** a light truck with an open body and low sides

pick up *vb* **1 :** to take hold of and lift **2 :** to stop for and take along **3 :** to gain by study or experience **:** LEARN **4 :** to get by buying **:** BUY **5 :** to come to and follow **6 :** to bring within range of hearing **7 :** to get back speed or strength

¹pic•nic *n* **1 :** an outdoor party with food taken along and eaten in the open **2 :** a nice experience

²picnic *vb* **pic•nicked; pic•nick•ing :** to go on a picnic

pic•to•graph *n* **:** a diagram showing information by means of pictures

pic•to•ri•al *adj* **1 :** of or relating to pictures **2 :** using pictures

¹pic•ture *n* **1 :** an image of something formed on a surface (as by drawing, painting, printing, or photography) **2 :** a very clear description **3 :** an exact likeness **4 :** MOVIE **5 :** an image on the screen of a television set

²picture *vb* **pic•tured; pic•tur•ing 1 :** to draw or paint a picture of **2 :** to describe very clearly in words **3 :** to form a mental image of **:** IMAGINE

picture graph *n* **:** PICTOGRAPH

pic•tur•esque *adj* **:** like a picture **:** suggesting a painted scene

pie *n* **:** a food consisting of a crust and a filling (as of fruit or meat)

pie•bald *adj* **:** spotted or blotched with two colors and especially black and white

¹piece *n* **1 :** a part cut, torn, or broken from a thing **2 :** one of a group, set, or mass of things **3 :** a portion marked off **4 :** a single item or example **5 :** a definite amount or size in which articles are made for sale or use **6 :** something made or written **7 :** ¹COIN 1

²piece *vb* **pieced; piec•ing 1 :** to repair or complete by adding a piece or pieces **2 :** to make out of pieces

piece•meal *adv* **:** one piece at a time **:** little by little

pied *adj* **:** having blotches of two or more colors

pier *n* **1 :** a support for a bridge **2 :** a structure built out into the water for use as a place to land or walk or to protect or form a harbor

pierce *vb* **pierced; pierc•ing 1 :** to run into or through **:** STAB **2 :** to make a hole in or through **3 :** to force into or through **4 :** to penetrate with the eye or mind **:** see through — **pierc•ing•ly** *adv*

pi•e•ty *n, pl* **pieties :** the state or fact of being pious **:** devotion to one's God

pig *n* **1 :** a swine especially when not yet mature **2 :** a person who lives or acts like a pig **3 :** a metal cast (as of iron) poured directly from the smelting furnace into a mold

pi•geon *n* **:** a bird with a stout body, short legs, and smooth feathers

pi•geon-toed *adj* **:** having the toes turned in

pig•gish *adj* **:** like a pig especially in greed or dirtiness

pig•gy•back *adv or adj* **:** on the back or shoulders

piggy bank *n* **:** a bank for coins often in the shape of a pig

pig•head•ed *adj* **:** STUBBORN 1 2

pig•ment *n* **1 :** a substance that gives color to other substances **2 :** coloring matter in persons, animals, and plants
pigmy *variant of* PYGMY
pig•pen *n* **1 :** a place where pigs are kept **2 :** a dirty place
pig•sty *n* **:** PIGPEN
pig•tail *n* **:** a tight braid of hair
[1]**pike** *n, pl* **pike** *or* **pikes :** a long slender freshwater fish with a large mouth
[2]**pike** *n* **:** a long wooden pole with a steel point used long ago as a weapon by soldiers
[3]**pike** *n* **:** TURNPIKE, ROAD
[1]**pile** *n* **:** a large stake or pointed post driven into the ground to support a foundation
[2]**pile** *n* **1 :** a mass of things heaped together **:** HEAP **2 :** REACTOR 2
[3]**pile** *vb* **piled; pil•ing 1 :** to lay or place in a pile **:** STACK **2 :** to heap in large amounts **3 :** to move or push forward in a crowd or group
[4]**pile** *n* **:** a velvety surface of fine short raised fibers
pil•fer *vb* **:** to steal small amounts or articles of small value
pil•grim *n* **1 :** a person who travels to a holy place as an act of religious devotion **2** *cap* **:** one of the English colonists who founded the first permanent settlement in New England at Plymouth in 1620
pil•grim•age *n* **:** a journey made by a pilgrim
pil•ing *n* **:** a structure made of piles
pill *n* **:** medicine or a food supplement in the form of a small rounded mass to be swallowed whole
[1]**pil•lage** *n* **:** the act of robbing by force especially in war
[2]**pillage** *vb* **pil•laged; pil•lag•ing :** to take goods and possessions by force
pil•lar *n* **1 :** a large post that supports something (as a roof) **2 :** a column standing alone (as for a monument) **3 :** something like a pillar **:** a main support
pil•lo•ry *n, pl* **pil•lo•ries :** a device once used for punishing someone in public consisting of a wooden frame with holes in which the head and hands can be locked
[1]**pil•low** *n* **:** a bag filled with soft or springy material used as a cushion usually for the head of a person lying down
[2]**pillow** *vb* **1 :** to lay on or as if on a pillow **2 :** to serve as a pillow for
pil•low•case *n* **:** a removable covering for a pillow
[1]**pi•lot** *n* **1 :** a person who steers a ship **2 :** a person especially qualified to guide ships into and out of a port or in dangerous waters **3 :** a person who flies or is qualified to fly an aircraft
[2]**pilot** *vb* **:** to act as pilot of
pi•mien•to *also* **pi•men•to** *n, pl* **pi•mien•tos** *also* **pi•men•tos :** a sweet pepper with a mild thick flesh
pim•ple *n* **:** a small swelling of the skin often containing pus — **pim•pled** *adj* — **pim•ply** *adj*
[1]**pin** *n* **1 :** a slender pointed piece (as of wood or metal) usually having the shape of a cylinder used to fasten articles together or in place **2 :** a small pointed piece of wire with a head used for fastening cloth or paper **3 :** something (as an ornament or badge) fastened to the clothing by a pin **4 :** one of ten pieces set up as the target in bowling
[2]**pin** *vb* **pinned; pin•ning 1 :** to fasten or join with a pin **2 :** to hold as if with a pin
pin•a•fore *n* **:** a sleeveless garment with a low neck worn as an apron or a dress
pin•cer *n* **1 pincers** *pl* **:** an instrument with two handles and two jaws for gripping something **2 :** a claw (as of a lobster) like pincers
[1]**pinch** *vb* **1 :** to squeeze between the finger and thumb or between the jaws of an instrument **2 :** to squeeze painfully **3 :** to cause to look thin or shrunken **4 :** to be thrifty or stingy
[2]**pinch** *n* **1 :** a time of emergency **2 :** a painful pressure or stress **3 :** an act of pinching **:** SQUEEZE **4 :** as much as may be picked up between the finger and the thumb
pinch hitter *n* **1 :** a baseball player who is sent in to bat for another **2 :** a person who does another's work in an emergency
pin•cush•ion *n* **:** a small cushion in which pins may be stuck when not in use
[1]**pine** *n* **:** an evergreen tree that has narrow needles for leaves, cones, and a wood that ranges from very soft to hard
[2]**pine** *vb* **pined; pin•ing 1 :** to lose energy, health, or weight through sorrow or worry **2 :** to long for very much
pine•ap•ple *n* **:** a large juicy yellow fruit of a tropical plant that has long stiff leaves with spiny margins
pin•ey *also* **piny** *adj* **:** of, relating to, or like that of pine
pin•feath•er *n* **:** a new feather just breaking through the skin of a bird
pin•ion *n* **1 :** the wing or the end part of the wing of a bird **2 :** [1]FEATHER 1
[1]**pink** *n* **1 :** any of a group of plants with thick stem joints and narrow leaves that are grown for their showy often fragrant flowers **2 :** the highest degree
[2]**pink** *n* **:** a pale red
[3]**pink** *adj* **:** of the color pink

⁴pink *vb* **:** to cut cloth, leather, or paper in an ornamental pattern or with an edge with notches
pink·eye *n* **:** a very contagious disease of the eyes in which the inner part of the eyelids becomes sore and red
pink·ish *adj* **:** somewhat pink
pin·na·cle *n* **1 :** a slender tower generally coming to a narrow point at the top **2 :** a high pointed peak **3 :** the highest point of development or achievement
pin·point *vb* **:** to locate or find out exactly
pint *n* **:** a unit of capacity equal to one half quart or sixteen ounces (about .47 liter)
pin·to *n, pl* **pintos :** a spotted horse or pony
pin·wheel *n* **:** a toy with fanlike blades at the end of a stick that spin in the wind
piny *variant of* PINEY
¹pi·o·neer *n* **1 :** a person who goes before and prepares the way for others to follow **2 :** an early settler
²pioneer *vb* **1 :** to explore or open up ways or regions for others to follow **2 :** to start up something new or take part in the early development of something
pi·ous *adj* **1 :** showing respect and honor toward God **2 :** making a show of being very good
pip *n* **:** a small fruit seed
¹pipe *n* **1 :** a musical instrument or part of a musical instrument consisting of a tube (as of wood) played by blowing **2 :** one of the tubes in a pipe organ that makes sound when air passes through it **3 :** BAGPIPE — usually used in pl. **4 :** a long tube or hollow body for transporting a substance (as water, steam, or gas) **5 :** a tube with a small bowl at one end for smoking tobacco or for blowing bubbles
²pipe *vb* **piped; pip·ing 1 :** to play on a pipe **2 :** to have or utter in a shrill tone **3 :** to equip with pipes **4 :** to move by means of pipes — **pip·er** *n*
pipe·line *n* **:** a line of pipe with pumps and control devices (as for carrying liquids or gases)
¹pip·ing *n* **1 :** the music or sound of a person or thing that pipes **2 :** a quantity or system of pipes **3 :** a narrow fold of material used to decorate edges or seams
²piping *adj* **:** having a high shrill sound
pip·it *n* **:** a small bird like a lark
pi·ra·cy *n, pl* **pi·ra·cies 1 :** robbery on the high seas **2 :** the using of another's work or invention without permission
pi·rate *n* **:** a robber on the high seas **:** a person who commits piracy
pis *pl of* PI
Pi·sces *n* **1 :** a constellation between Aquarius and Aries imagined as two fish **2 :** the twelfth sign of the zodiac or a person born under this sign
pis·ta·chio *n, pl* **pis·ta·chios :** the green edible seed of a small tree related to the sumacs
pis·til *n* **:** the central organ in a flower that contains the ovary and produces the seed
pis·tol *n* **:** a short gun made to be aimed and fired with one hand
pis·ton *n* **:** a disk or short cylinder that slides back and forth inside a larger cylinder and is moved by steam in steam engines and by the explosion of fuel in automobiles
¹pit *n* **1 :** a cavity or hole in the ground **2 :** an area set off from and often sunken below neighboring areas **3 :** a hollow area usually of the surface of the body **4 :** an indented scar (as from a boil) — **pit·ted** *adj*
²pit *vb* **pit·ted; pit·ting 1 :** to make pits in or scar with pits **2 :** to set against another in a fight or contest
³pit *n* **:** a hard seed or stone (as of a cherry)
⁴pit *vb* **pit·ted; pit·ting :** to remove the pits from
¹pitch *n* **1 :** a dark sticky substance left over from distilling tar and used in making roofing paper, in waterproofing seams, and in paving **2 :** resin from pine trees
²pitch *vb* **1 :** to set up and fix firmly in place **2 :** to throw (as hay) usually upward or away from oneself **3 :** to throw a baseball to a batter **4 :** to plunge or fall forward **5 :** ¹SLOPE **6 :** to fix or set at a certain pitch or level **7 :** to move in such a way that one end falls while the other end rises
³pitch *n* **1 :** the action or manner of pitching **2 :** highness or lowness of sound **3 :** amount of slope **4 :** the amount or level of something (as a feeling) — **pitched** *adj*
pitch·blende *n* **:** a dark mineral that is a source of radium and uranium
¹pitch·er *n* **:** a container usually with a handle and a lip used for holding and pouring out liquids
²pitcher *n* **:** a baseball player who pitches
pitch·fork *n* **:** a fork with a long handle used in pitching hay or straw
pit·e·ous *adj* **:** seeking or deserving pity — **pit·e·ous·ly** *adv*
pit·fall *n* **1 :** a covered or camouflaged pit used to capture animals or people **:** TRAP **2 :** a danger or difficulty that is hidden or is not easily recognized
pith *n* **1 :** the loose spongy tissue forming the center of the stem in some plants **2 :** the important part
piti·able *adj* **:** PITIFUL
piti·ful *adj* **1 :** causing a feeling of pity or sympathy **2 :** deserving pitying scorn
piti·less *adj* **:** having no pity **:** MERCILESS

pi·tu·i·tary gland *n* **:** an endocrine organ at the base of the brain producing several hormones of which one affects growth

[1]pity *n* **1 :** a sympathetic feeling for the distress of others **2 :** a reason or cause of pity or regret

[2]pity *vb* **pit·ied; pity·ing :** to feel pity for

[1]piv·ot *n* **1 :** a point or a fixed pin on the end of which something turns **2 :** something on which something else turns or depends **:** a central member, part, or point

[2]pivot *vb* **1 :** to turn on or as if on a pivot **2 :** to provide with, mount on, or attach by a pivot

pix·ie *or* **pixy** *n, pl* **pix·ies :** a mischievous elf or fairy

piz·za *n* **:** an open pie made usually of thinly rolled bread dough spread with a spiced mixture (as of tomatoes, cheese, and ground meat) and baked

plac·ard *n* **:** a large card for announcing or advertising something **:** POSTER

pla·cate *vb* **pla·cat·ed; pla·cat·ing :** to calm the anger of **:** SOOTHE

[1]place *n* **1 :** a short street **2 :** an available space **:** ROOM **3 :** a building or spot set apart for a special purpose **4 :** a certain region or center of population **5 :** a piece of land with a house on it **6 :** position in a scale or series in comparison with another or others **7 :** a space (as a seat in a theater) set aside for one's use **8 :** usual space or use **9 :** the position of a figure in a numeral **10 :** a public square

[2]place *vb* **placed; plac·ing 1 :** to put or arrange in a certain place or position **2 :** to appoint to a job or find a job for **3 :** to identify by connecting with a certain time, place, or happening

place·hold·er *n* **:** a symbol (as *x*, Δ, *) used in mathematics in the place of a numeral

place·kick *n* **:** a kick in football made with the ball held in place on the ground

pla·cen·ta *n* **:** an organ that has a large blood supply and joins the fetus of a mammal to its mother's uterus

pla·gia·rism *n* **:** an act of stealing and passing off as one's own the ideas or words of another

[1]plague *n* **1 :** something that causes much distress **2 :** a cause of irritation **:** NUISANCE **3 :** a destructive epidemic disease

[2]plague *vb* **plagued; plagu·ing 1 :** to strike or afflict with disease or distress **2 :** [1]TEASE, TORMENT

plaid *n* **1 :** TARTAN **2 :** a pattern consisting of rectangles formed by crossed lines of various widths

[1]plain *adj* **1 :** having no pattern or decoration **2 :** open and clear to the sight **3 :** clear to the mind **4 :** FRANK **5 :** of common or average accomplishments or position **:** ORDINARY **6 :** not hard to do **:** not complicated **7 :** not handsome or beautiful

[2]plain *n* **:** a large area of level or rolling treeless land

[3]plain *adv* **:** in a plain manner

plain·tive *adj* **:** showing or suggesting sorrow **:** MOURNFUL, SAD

[1]plait *n* **1 :** a flat fold **:** PLEAT **2 :** a flat braid (as of hair)

[2]plait *vb* **1 :** [1]PLEAT **2 :** [1]BRAID **3 :** to make by braiding

[1]plan *n* **1 :** a drawing or diagram showing the parts or outline of something **2 :** a method or scheme of acting, doing, or arranging

[2]plan *vb* **planned; plan·ning 1 :** to form a plan of or for **:** arrange the parts of ahead of time **2 :** to have in mind **:** INTEND

[1]plane *vb* **planed; plan·ing 1 :** to smooth or level off with a plane **2 :** to remove with or as if with a plane

[2]plane *n* **:** a tool for smoothing wood

[3]plane *adj* **:** HORIZONTAL, FLAT

[4]plane *n* **1 :** a surface any two points of which can be joined by a straight line lying wholly within it **2 :** a level or flat surface **3 :** a level of development **4 :** AIRPLANE

plan·et *n* **:** a celestial body other than a comet or meteor that travels in orbit about the sun

plan·e·tar·i·um *n* **:** a building in which there is a device for projecting the images of celestial bodies on a ceiling shaped like a dome

plan·e·tary *adj* **1 :** of or relating to a planet **2 :** having a motion like that of a planet

plank *n* **:** a heavy thick board

plank·ton *n* **:** the tiny floating plants and animals of a body of water

[1]plant *vb* **1 :** to place in the ground to grow **2 :** to set firmly in or as if in the ground **:** FIX **3 :** to introduce as a habit **4 :** to cause to become established **:** SETTLE **5 :** to stock with something

[2]plant *n* **1 :** any member of the kingdom of living things (as mosses, ferns, grasses, and trees) that usually lack obvious nervous or sense organs and the ability to move about and that have cellulose cell walls **2 :** the buildings and equipment of an industrial business or an institution — **plant·like** *adj*

[1]plan·tain *n* **:** any of several common weeds having little or no stem, leaves with parallel veins, and a long stalk of tiny greenish flowers

[2]plantain *n* **:** a banana plant having greenish

fruit that is larger, less sweet, and more starchy than the ordinary banana

plan·ta·tion *n* **1 :** a group of plants and especially trees planted and cared for **2 :** a planted area (as an estate) cultivated by laborers **3 :** COLONY 1

plant·er *n* **1 :** one (as a farmer or a machine) that plants crops **2 :** a person who owns or runs a plantation **3 :** a container in which ornamental plants are grown

plant kingdom *n* **:** a basic group of natural objects that includes all living and extinct plants

plant louse *n* **:** APHID

plaque *n* **1 :** a flat thin piece (as of metal) used for decoration or having writing cut in it **2 :** a thin film containing bacteria and bits of food that forms on the teeth

plas·ma *n* **:** the watery part of blood, lymph, or milk

1**plas·ter** *n* **:** a paste (as of lime, sand, and water) that hardens when it dries and is used for coating walls and ceilings

2**plaster** *vb* **1 :** to cover or smear with or as if with plaster **2 :** to paste or fasten on especially so as to cover — **plas·ter·er** *n*

plaster of par·is *often cap 2d P* **:** a white powder that mixes with water to form a paste that hardens quickly and is used for casts and molds

1**plas·tic** *adj* **1 :** capable of being molded or modeled **2 :** made of plastic

2**plastic** *n* **:** any of various manufactured materials that can be molded into objects or formed into films or fibers

1**plate** *n* **1 :** a thin flat piece of material **2 :** metal in sheets **3 :** a piece of metal on which something is engraved or molded **4 :** HOME PLATE **5 :** household utensils made of or plated with gold or silver **6 :** a shallow usually round dish **7 :** a main course of a meal **8 :** a sheet of glass coated with a chemical sensitive to light for use in a camera **9 :** an illustration often covering a full page of a book

2**plate** *vb* **plat·ed; plat·ing :** to cover with a thin layer of metal (as gold or silver)

pla·teau *n, pl* **plateaus** *or* **pla·teaux :** a broad flat area of high land

plat·form *n* **1 :** a statement of the beliefs and rules of conduct for which a group stands **2 :** a level usually raised surface (as in a railroad station) **3 :** a raised floor or stage for performers or speakers **4 :** an arrangement of computer components that uses a particular operating system

plat·i·num *n* **:** a heavy grayish white metallic chemical element

pla·toon *n* **:** a part of a military company usually made up of two or more squads

platoon sergeant *n* **:** a noncommissioned officer in the Army ranking above a staff sergeant

plat·ter *n* **:** a large plate especially for serving meat

platy·pus *n* **:** a small water-dwelling mammal of Australia that lays eggs and has webbed feet, dense fur, and a bill that resembles that of a duck

plau·si·ble *adj* **:** seeming to be reasonable — **plau·si·bly** *adv*

1**play** *n* **1 :** exercise or activity for amusement **2 :** the action of or a particular action in a game **3 :** one's turn to take part in a game **4 :** absence of any bad intention **5 :** quick or light movement **6 :** freedom of motion **7 :** a story presented on stage

2**play** *vb* **1 :** to produce music or sound **2 :** to take part in a game of **3 :** to take part in sport or recreation **:** amuse oneself **4 :** to handle something idly **:** TOY **5 :** to act on or as if on the stage **6 :** PRETEND 1 **7 :** to perform (as a trick) for fun **8 :** to play in a game against **9 :** 2ACT 2, BEHAVE **10 :** to move swiftly or lightly **11 :** to put or keep in action — **play hooky :** to stay out of school without permission

play·act·ing *n* **:** an acting out of make-believe roles

play·er *n* **1 :** a person who plays a game **2 :** a person who plays a musical instrument **3 :** a device that reproduces sounds or video images that have been recorded (as on magnetic tape)

player piano *n* **:** a piano containing a mechanical device by which it may be played automatically

play·ful *adj* **1 :** full of play **:** MERRY **2 :** HUMOROUS — **play·ful·ly** *adv* — **play·ful·ness** *n*

play·ground *n* **:** an area used for games and playing

play·house *n* **1 :** THEATER 1 **2 :** a small house for children to play in

playing card *n* **:** any of a set of cards marked to show rank and suit (**spades**, **hearts**, **diamonds**, or **clubs**) and used in playing various games

play·mate *n* **:** a companion in play

play·pen *n* **:** a small enclosure in which a baby is placed to play

play·thing *n* **:** 1TOY 2

play·wright *n* **:** a writer of plays

pla·za *n* **:** a public square in a city or town

plea *n* **1 :** an argument in defense **:** EXCUSE **2 :** an earnest appeal

plead *vb* **plead·ed** *or* **pled; plead·ing 1 :** to argue for or against **:** argue in court **2 :** to answer to a charge **3 :** to offer as a defense, an excuse, or an apology **4 :** to make an earnest appeal **:** BEG

pleas•ant *adj* **1 :** giving pleasure **:** AGREEABLE **2 :** having pleasing manners, behavior, or appearance — **pleas•ant•ly** *adv* — **pleas•ant•ness** *n*

¹please *vb* **pleased; pleas•ing 1 :** to give pleasure or enjoyment to **2 :** to be willing **:** LIKE, CHOOSE

²please *adv* — used to show politeness in asking or accepting

pleas•ing *adj* **:** giving pleasure **:** AGREEABLE — **pleas•ing•ly** *adv*

plea•sur•able *adj* **:** PLEASANT 1

plea•sure *n* **1 :** a particular desire **2 :** a feeling of enjoyment or satisfaction **3 :** something that pleases or delights

¹pleat *vb* **:** to arrange in folds made by doubling material over on itself

²pleat *n* **:** a fold (as in cloth) made by doubling material over on itself

pled *past of* PLEAD

¹pledge *n* **1 :** something handed over to another to ensure that the giver will keep his or her promise or agreement **2 :** something that is a symbol of something else **3 :** a promise or agreement that must be kept

²pledge *vb* **pledged; pledg•ing 1 :** to give as a pledge **2 :** to hold by a pledge **:** PROMISE

plen•te•ous *adj* **:** PLENTIFUL 2

plen•ti•ful *adj* **1 :** giving or containing plenty **:** FRUITFUL **2 :** present in large numbers or amount **:** ABUNDANT — **plen•ti•ful•ly** *adv*

plen•ty *n* **:** a full supply **:** more than enough

pleu•ri•sy *n* **:** a sore swollen state of the membrane that lines the chest often with fever, painful breathing, and coughing

plex•us *n, pl* **plex•us•es** *or* **plex•us :** a network usually of nerves or blood vessels

pli•able *adj* **1 :** possible to bend without breaking **2 :** easily influenced

pli•ant *adj* **:** PLIABLE

pli•ers *n pl* **:** small pincers with long jaws used for bending or cutting wire or handling small things

plight *n* **:** a usually bad condition or state **:** PREDICAMENT

plod *vb* **plod•ded; plod•ding :** to move or travel slowly but steadily

¹plot *n* **1 :** a small area of ground **2 :** the plan or main story of a play or novel **3 :** a secret usually evil scheme

²plot *vb* **plot•ted; plot•ting 1 :** to make a map or plan of **2 :** to plan or scheme secretly — **plot•ter** *n*

plo•ver *n* **:** any one of several shorebirds having shorter and stouter bills than the related sandpipers

¹plow *or* **plough** *n* **1 :** a farm machine used to cut, lift, and turn over soil **2 :** a device (as a snowplow) used to spread or clear away matter on the ground

²plow *or* **plough** *vb* **1 :** to open, break up, or work with a plow **2 :** to move through or cut as a plow does

plow•share *n* **:** the part of a plow that cuts the earth

¹pluck *vb* **1 :** to pull off **:** PICK **2 :** to remove something (as hairs) by or as if by plucking **3 :** to seize and remove quickly **:** SNATCH **4 :** to pull at (a string) and let go

²pluck *n* **1 :** a sharp pull **:** TUG, TWITCH **2 :** COURAGE, SPIRIT

plucky *adj* **pluck•i•er; pluck•i•est :** showing courage **:** BRAVE

¹plug *n* **1 :** a piece (as of wood or metal) used to stop up or fill a hole **2 :** a device usually on a cord used to make an electrical connection by putting it into another part (as a socket)

²plug *vb* **plugged; plug•ging 1 :** to stop or make tight with a plug **2 :** to keep steadily at work or in action **3 :** to connect to an electric circuit

plum *n* **1 :** a roundish smooth-skinned edible fruit that has an oblong stone and grows on a tree related to the peaches and cherries **2 :** a dark reddish purple **3 :** a choice or desirable thing **:** PRIZE

plum•age *n* **:** the feathers of a bird

¹plumb *n* **:** a small weight (as of lead) attached to a line and used to show depth or an exactly straight up-and-down line

²plumb *vb* **:** to measure or test with a plumb

plumb•er *n* **:** a person who puts in or repairs plumbing

plumb•ing *n* **1 :** a plumber's work **2 :** a system of pipes for supplying and carrying off water in a building

plume *n* **1 :** a large or showy feather of a bird **2 :** an ornamental feather or tuft of feathers (as on a hat) — **plumed** *adj*

plum•met *vb* **:** to fall straight down

¹plump *vb* **1 :** to drop or fall heavily or suddenly **2 :** to come out in favor of something

²plump *adv* **1 :** with a sudden or heavy drop **2 :** DIRECTLY 1

³plump *vb* **:** to make or become rounded or filled out

⁴plump *adj* **:** having a pleasingly rounded form **:** well filled out — **plump•ness** *n*

¹plun•der *vb* **:** to rob or steal especially openly and by force (as during war)

²plunder *n* **:** something taken by plundering **:** LOOT

plunge *vb* **plunged; plung•ing 1 :** to thrust or force quickly **2 :** to leap or dive

DICTIONARY

suddenly **3 :** to rush, move, or force with reckless haste **4 :** to dip or move suddenly downward or forward and downward

[2]**plunge** *n* **:** a sudden dive, rush, or leap

[1]**plu•ral** *adj* **:** of, relating to, or being a word form used to show more than one

[2]**plural** *n* **:** a form of a word used to show that more than one person or thing is meant

plu•ral•ize *vb* **plu•ral•ized; plu•ral•iz•ing :** to make plural or express in the plural form

[1]**plus** *adj* **:** falling high in a certain range

[2]**plus** *prep* **:** increased by **:** with the addition of

[1]**plush** *n* **:** a cloth like a very thick soft velvet

[2]**plush** *adj* **:** very rich and fine

plus sign *n* **:** a sign + used in mathematics to show addition (as in 8+6=14) or a quantity greater than zero (as in +10°)

Plu•to *n* **:** the planet that is farthest away from the sun and has a diameter of about 5800 kilometers

plu•to•ni•um *n* **:** a radioactive metallic chemical element formed from neptunium and used for releasing atomic energy

[1]**ply** *vb* **plied; ply•ing 1 :** to use something steadily or forcefully **2 :** to keep supplying **3 :** to work hard and steadily at

[2]**ply** *n, pl* **plies :** one of the folds, layers, or threads of which something (as yarn or plywood) is made up

ply•wood *n* **:** a strong board made by gluing together thin sheets of wood under heat and pressure

pneu•mat•ic *adj* **1 :** of, relating to, or using air, gas, or wind **2 :** moved or worked by the pressure of air **3 :** made to hold or be inflated with compressed air

pneu•mo•nia *n* **:** a serious disease in which the lungs are inflamed

[1]**poach** *vb* **:** to cook slowly in liquid

[2]**poach** *vb* **:** to hunt or fish unlawfully on private property

pock *n* **:** a small swelling like a pimple on the skin (as in smallpox) or the mark it leaves

[1]**pock•et** *n* **1 :** a small bag fastened into a garment for carrying small articles **2 :** a place or thing like a pocket **3 :** a condition of the air (as a down current) that causes an airplane to drop suddenly

[2]**pocket** *vb* **1 :** to put something in a pocket **2 :** to take for oneself especially dishonestly

[3]**pocket** *adj* **:** POCKET-SIZE

pock•et•book *n* **1 :** a case for carrying money or papers in the pocket **2 :** HANDBAG **3 :** amount of income

pock•et•knife *n, pl* **pock•et•knives :** a knife that has one or more blades that fold into the handle and that can be carried in the pocket

pock•et–size *adj* **:** small enough to fit in a pocket

pock•mark *n* **:** the mark left by a pock — **pock•marked** *adj*

pod *n* **:** a fruit (as of the pea or bean) that is dry when ripe and then splits open to free its seeds

po•em *n* **:** a piece of writing often having rhyme or rhythm which tells a story or describes a feeling

po•et *n* **:** a writer of poems

po•et•ic *or* **po•et•i•cal** *adj* **1 :** of, relating to, or like that of poets or poetry **2 :** written in verse

po•et•ry *n* **1 :** writing usually with a rhythm that repeats **:** VERSE **2 :** the writings of a poet

po•go stick *n* **:** a pole with a strong spring at the bottom and two rests for the feet on which a person stands and bounces along

poin•set•tia *n* **:** a tropical plant much used at Christmas with showy usually red leaves that grow like petals around its small greenish flowers

[1]**point** *n* **1 :** a separate or particular detail **:** ITEM **2 :** an individual quality **3 :** the chief idea or meaning (as of a story or a speech) **4 :** [1]PURPOSE, AIM **5 :** a geometric element that has position but no dimensions and is pictured as a small dot **6 :** a particular place or position **7 :** a particular stage or moment **8 :** the sharp end (as of a sword, pin, or pencil) **9 :** a piece of land that sticks out **10 :** a dot in writing or printing **11 :** one of the thirty-two marks indicating direction on a compass **12 :** a unit of scoring in a game — **point•ed** *adj* — **point•less** *adj*

[2]**point** *vb* **1 :** to put a point on **2 :** to show the position or direction of something by the finger or by standing in a fixed position **3 :** to direct someone's attention to **4 :** [1]AIM 1, DIRECT

[1]**point–blank** *adj* **1 :** aimed at a target from a short distance away **2 :** [1]BLUNT 2

[2]**point–blank** *adv* **:** in a point-blank manner

point•er *n* **1 :** something that points or is used for pointing **2 :** a large hunting dog with long ears and short hair that is usually white with colored spots, hunts by scent, and points game **3 :** a helpful hint

point of view : a way of looking at or thinking about something

[1]**poise** *vb* **poised; pois•ing :** to hold or make steady by balancing

[2]**poise** *n* **1 :** the state of being balanced **2 :** a natural self-confident manner **3 :** BEARING 1

[1]**poi•son** *n* **:** a substance that by its chemical action can injure or kill a living thing

[2]**poison** *vb* **1 :** to injure or kill with poison **2 :** to put poison on or in

poison ivy *n* **:** a common woody plant related to the sumacs and having leaves with three leaflets that can cause an itchy rash when touched
poison oak *n* **:** a poison ivy that grows as a bush
poi·son·ous *adj* **:** containing poison **:** having or causing an effect of poison
poison sumac *n* **:** a poisonous American swamp shrub or small tree related to poison ivy
1poke *vb* **poked; pok·ing 1 :** JAB **2 :** to make by stabbing or piercing **3 :** to stick out, or cause to stick out **4 :** to search over or through usually without purpose **:** RUMMAGE **5 :** to move slowly or lazily
2poke *n* **:** a quick thrust **:** JAB
1pok·er *n* **:** a metal rod used for stirring a fire
2po·ker *n* **:** a card game in which each player bets on the value of his or her hand
poky *or* **pok·ey** *adj* **pok·i·er; pok·i·est 1 :** being small and cramped **2 :** so slow as to be annoying
po·lar *adj* **1 :** of or relating to a pole of the earth or the region around it **2 :** coming from or being like a polar region **3 :** of or relating to a pole of a magnet
polar bear *n* **:** a large creamy-white bear of arctic regions
Po·lar·is *n* **:** NORTH STAR
1pole *n* **:** a long slender piece (as of wood or metal)
2pole *vb* **poled; pol·ing :** to push or move with a pole
3pole *n* **1 :** either end of an axis and especially of the earth's axis **2 :** either of the two ends of a magnet **3 :** either of the terminals of an electric battery
Pole *n* **:** a person born or living in Poland
pole·cat *n* **1 :** a brown or black European animal related to the weasel **2 :** SKUNK
pole·star *n* **:** NORTH STAR
pole vault *n* **:** a track-and-field contest in which each athlete uses a pole to jump over a high bar
1po·lice *vb* **po·liced; po·lic·ing :** to keep order in or among
2police *n, pl* **police 1 :** the department of government that keeps order and enforces law, investigates crimes, and makes arrests **2** *police pl* **:** members of a police force
police dog *n* **:** a dog trained to help police
po·lice·man *n, pl* **po·lice·men :** a man who is a police officer
police officer *n* **:** a member of a police force
po·lice·wom·an *n, pl* **po·lice·wom·en :** a woman who is a police officer
1pol·i·cy *n, pl* **pol·i·cies :** a course of action chosen to guide people in making decisions
2policy *n, pl* **pol·i·cies :** a document that contains the agreement made by an insurance company with a person whose life or property is insured
po·lio *n* **:** a once common virus disease often affecting children and sometimes causing paralysis
po·lio·my·eli·tis *n* **:** POLIO
1pol·ish *vb* **1 :** to make smooth and glossy usually by rubbing **2 :** to smooth or improve in manners, condition, or style — **pol·ish·er** *n*
2polish *n* **1 :** a smooth glossy surface **2 :** good manners **:** REFINEMENT **3 :** a substance prepared for use in polishing
1Pol·ish *adj* **:** of or relating to Poland, the Poles, or Polish
2Polish *n* **:** the language of the Poles
po·lite *adj* **po·lit·er; po·lit·est :** showing courtesy or good manners — **po·lite·ly** *adv* — **po·lite·ness** *n*
po·lit·i·cal *adj* **:** of or relating to politics, government, or the way government is carried on — **po·lit·i·cal·ly** *adv*
pol·i·ti·cian *n* **:** a person who is actively taking part in party politics or in conducting government business
pol·i·tics *n sing or pl* **1 :** the science and art of government **:** the management of public affairs **2 :** activity in or management of the business of political parties
pol·ka *n* **:** a lively dance for couples or the music for it
1poll *n* **1 :** the casting or recording of the votes or opinions of a number of persons **2 :** the place where votes are cast — usually used in pl.
2poll *vb* **1 :** to receive and record the votes of **2 :** to receive (votes) in an election **3 :** to cast a vote or ballot at a poll
pol·lack *or* **pol·lock** *n, pl* **pollack** *or* **pollock :** either of two food fishes of the northern Atlantic and the northern Pacific that are related to the cod
pol·len *n* **:** the fine usually yellow dust in the anthers of a flower that fertilizes the seeds
pol·li·nate *vb* **pol·li·nat·ed; pol·li·nat·ing :** to place pollen on the stigma of
pol·li·na·tion *n* **:** the act or process of pollinating
pol·li·wog *or* **pol·ly·wog** *n* **:** TADPOLE
pol·lut·ant *n* **:** something that causes pollution
pol·lute *vb* **pol·lut·ed; pol·lut·ing :** to make impure — **pol·lut·er** *n*
pol·lu·tion *n* **:** the action of polluting or the state of being polluted
po·lo *n* **:** a game played by teams of players on horseback who drive a wooden ball with long-handled mallets
poly- *prefix* **:** many **:** much **:** MULTI-

poly·es·ter *n* **:** a synthetic fiber used especially in clothing

poly·gon *n* **:** a plane figure having three or more straight sides

poly·mer *n* **:** a chemical compound or mixture of compounds that is formed by combination of smaller molecules and consists basically of repeating structural units

pol·yp *n* **:** a small sea animal (as a coral) having a tubelike body closed and attached to something (as a rock) at one end and opening at the other with a mouth surrounded by tentacles

pome·gran·ate *n* **:** a reddish fruit about the size of an orange that has a thick skin and many seeds in a pulp of acid flavor and grows on a tropical Old World tree

1**pom·mel** *n* **:** a rounded knob on the handle of a sword or at the front and top of a saddle

2**pommel** *vb* **pom·meled** *or* **pom·melled; pom·mel·ing** *or* **pom·mel·ling :** PUMMEL

pomp *n* **:** a show of wealth and splendor

pom-pom *or* **pom·pon** *n* **:** a fluffy ball used as trimming on clothing

pomp·ous *adj* **1 :** making an appearance of importance or dignity **2 :** SELF-IMPORTANT — **pomp·ous·ly** *adv* — **pomp·ous·ness** *n*

pon·cho *n, pl* **ponchos 1 :** a Spanish-American cloak like a blanket with a slit in the middle for the head **2 :** a waterproof garment like a poncho worn as a raincoat

pond *n* **:** a body of water usually smaller than a lake

pon·der *vb* **:** to think over carefully

pon·der·ous *adj* **1 :** very heavy **2 :** unpleasantly dull

pond scum *n* **:** a mass of algae in still water or an alga that grows in such masses

pon·iard *n* **:** a slender dagger

pon·toon *n* **1 :** a small boat with a flat bottom **2 :** a light watertight float used as one of the supports for a floating bridge **3 :** a float attached to the bottom of an airplane for landing on water

po·ny *n, pl* **ponies :** a small horse

pony express *n* **:** a rapid postal system that operated across the western United States in 1860–61 by changing horses and riders along the way

poo·dle *n* **:** one of an old breed of active intelligent dogs with heavy coats of solid color

pooh *interj* — used to express contempt or disapproval

1**pool** *n* **1 :** a small deep body of usually fresh water **2 :** something like a pool **3 :** a small body of standing liquid **:** PUDDLE **4 :** SWIMMING POOL

2**pool** *n* **1 :** a game of billiards played on a table with six pockets **2 :** people, money, or things come together or put together for some purpose

3**pool** *vb* **:** to contribute to a common fund or effort

poor *adj* **1 :** not having riches or possessions **2 :** less than enough **3 :** worthy of pity **4 :** low in quality or value — **poor·ly** *adv* — **poor·ness** *n*

1**pop** *vb* **popped; pop·ping 1 :** to burst or cause to burst with a sharp sound **2 :** to move suddenly **3 :** to fire a gun **:** SHOOT **4 :** to stick out

2**pop** *n* **1 :** a short explosive sound **2 :** SODA POP

pop·corn *n* **1 :** corn whose kernels burst open when exposed to high heat to form a white or yellowish mass **2 :** the kernels after popping

pope *n, often cap* **:** the head of the Roman Catholic Church

pop·lar *n* **:** a tree that has rough bark, catkins for flowers, and a white cottonlike substance around its seeds

pop·py *n, pl* **poppies :** a plant with a hairy stem and showy usually red, yellow, or white flowers

pop·u·lace *n* **1 :** the common people **2 :** POPULATION 1

pop·u·lar *adj* **1 :** of, relating to, or coming from the whole body of people **2 :** enjoyed or approved by many people — **pop·u·lar·ly** *adv*

pop·u·lar·i·ty *n* **:** the quality or state of being popular

pop·u·late *vb* **pop·u·lat·ed; pop·u·lat·ing :** to provide with inhabitants

pop·u·la·tion *n* **1 :** the whole number of people in a country, city, or area **2 :** the people or things living in a certain place

pop·u·lous *adj* **:** having a large population

por·ce·lain *n* **:** a hard white ceramic ware used especially for dishes and chemical utensils

porch *n* **:** a covered entrance to a building usually with a separate roof

por·cu·pine *n* **:** a gnawing animal having stiff sharp quills among its hairs

1**pore** *vb* **pored; por·ing :** to read with great attention **:** STUDY

2**pore** *n* **:** a tiny opening (as in the skin or in the soil)

por·gy *n, pl* **porgies :** any of several food fishes of the Mediterranean sea and the Atlantic ocean

pork *n* **:** the fresh or salted flesh of a pig

po·rous *adj* **1 :** full of pores **2 :** capable of absorbing liquids

por·poise *n* **1 :** a sea animal somewhat like a small whale with a blunt rounded snout **2 :** DOLPHIN 1

por·ridge *n* **:** a food made by boiling meal of a grain or a vegetable (as peas) in water or milk until it thickens

[1]port *n* **1 :** a place where ships may ride safe from storms **2 :** a harbor where ships load or unload cargo **3 :** AIRPORT

[2]port *n* **1 :** an opening (as in machinery) for gas, steam, or water to go in or out **2 :** PORTHOLE

[3]port *n* **:** the left side of a ship or airplane looking forward

por·ta·ble *adj* **:** possible to carry or move about

por·tage *n* **:** the carrying of boats or goods overland from one body of water to another

por·tal *n* **:** a grand or fancy door or gate

port·cul·lis *n* **:** a heavy iron gate which can be let down to prevent entrance (as to a castle)

por·tend *vb* **:** to give a sign or warning of beforehand

por·tent *n* **:** a sign or warning that something is going to happen

por·ter *n* **1 :** a person who carries baggage (as at a terminal) **2 :** an attendant on a train

port·fo·lio *n, pl* **port·fo·li·os :** a flat case for carrying papers or drawings

port·hole *n* **:** a small window in the side of a ship or airplane

por·ti·co *n, pl* **por·ti·coes** *or* **por·ti·cos :** a row of columns supporting a roof around or at the entrance of a building

[1]por·tion *n* **:** a part or share of a whole

[2]portion *vb* **:** to divide into portions **:** DISTRIBUTE

por·trait *n* **:** a picture of a person usually showing the face

por·tray *vb* **1 :** to make a portrait of **2 :** to picture in words **:** DESCRIBE **3 :** to play the role of

por·tray·al *n* **:** the act or result of portraying

[1]Por·tu·guese *adj* **:** of or relating to Portugal, its people, or the Portuguese language

[2]Portuguese *n, pl* **Portuguese 1 :** a person born or living in Portugal **2 :** the language of Portugal and Brazil

[1]pose *vb* **posed; pos·ing 1 :** to hold or cause to hold a special position of the body **2 :** to set forth **3 :** to pretend to be what one is not

[2]pose *n* **1 :** a position of the body held for a special purpose **2 :** a pretended attitude

po·si·tion *n* **1 :** the way in which something is placed or arranged **2 :** a way of looking at or considering things **3 :** the place where a person or thing is **4 :** the rank a person has in an organization or in society **5 :** JOB 3

[1]pos·i·tive *adj* **1 :** definitely and clearly stated **2 :** fully confident **:** CERTAIN **3 :** of, relating to, or having the form of an adjective or adverb that shows no degree of comparison **4 :** having a real position or effect **5 :** having the light and shade the same as in the original subject **6 :** being greater than zero and often shown by a plus sign **7 :** of, being, or relating to electricity of a kind that is produced in a glass rod rubbed with silk **8 :** having a deficiency of electrons **9 :** being the part from which the electric current flows to the external circuit **10 :** showing acceptance or approval **11 :** showing the presence of what is looked for or suspected to be present — **pos·i·tive·ly** *adv*

[2]positive *n* **:** the positive degree or a positive form of an adjective or adverb

pos·sess *vb* **1 :** to have and hold as property **:** OWN **2 :** to enter into and control firmly — **pos·ses·sor** *n*

pos·ses·sion *n* **1 :** the act of possessing or holding as one's own **:** OWNERSHIP **2 :** something that is held as one's own property

[1]pos·ses·sive *adj* **1 :** being or belonging to the case of a noun or pronoun that shows possession **2 :** showing the desire to possess or control

[2]possessive *n* **:** a noun or pronoun in the possessive case

pos·si·bil·i·ty *n, pl* **pos·si·bil·i·ties 1 :** the state or fact of being possible **2 :** something that may happen

pos·si·ble *adj* **1 :** being within the limits of one's ability **2 :** being something that may or may not happen **3 :** able or fitted to be or to become

pos·si·bly *adv* **1 :** by any possibility **2 :** PERHAPS

pos·sum *n* **:** OPOSSUM

[1]post *n* **:** a piece of solid substance (as metal or timber) placed firmly in an upright position and used especially as a support

[2]post *vb* **1 :** to fasten on a post, wall, or bulletin board **2 :** to make known publicly as if by posting a notice **3 :** to forbid persons from entering or using by putting up warning notices

[3]post *vb* **1 :** to ride or travel with haste **2 :** to send by mail **:** MAIL **3 :** to make familiar with a subject

[4]post *n* **1 :** the place at which a soldier or guard is stationed **2 :** a place where a body of troops is stationed **3 :** a place or office to which a person is appointed **4 :** a trading settlement

[5]post *vb* **:** to station at a post

post- *prefix* **:** after **:** later **:** following **:** behind

post·age *n* **:** a fee for postal service

post·al *adj* **:** of or relating to the post office or the handling of mail

DICTIONARY

postal card *n* **1 :** a blank card with a postage stamp printed on it **2 :** POSTCARD 1

post·card *n* **1 :** a card on which a message may be sent by mail without an envelope **2 :** POSTAL CARD 1

post·er *n* **:** a usually large sheet with writing or pictures on it that is displayed as a notice, advertisement, or for decoration

pos·ter·i·ty *n* **1 :** the line of individuals descended from one ancestor **2 :** all future generations

post·man *n, pl* **post·men :** LETTER CARRIER

post·mark *n* **:** a mark put on a piece of mail especially for canceling the postage stamp

post·mas·ter *n* **:** a person in charge of a post office

post·mis·tress *n* **:** a woman in charge of a post office

post office *n* **1 :** a government agency in charge of the mail **2 :** a place where mail is received, handled, and sent out

post·paid *adv* **:** with postage paid by the sender

post·pone *vb* **post·poned; post·pon·ing :** to put off till some later time — **post·pone·ment** *n*

post·script *n* **:** a note added at the end of a finished letter or book

[1]**pos·ture** *n* **:** the position of one part of the body with relation to other parts **:** the general way of holding the body

[2]**posture** *vb* **pos·tured; pos·tur·ing :** to take on a particular posture **:** POSE

po·sy *n, pl* **posies 1 :** [1]FLOWER 1, 2 **2 :** BOUQUET

[1]**pot** *n* **1 :** a deep rounded container for household purposes **2 :** the amount a pot will hold

[2]**pot** *vb* **pot·ted; pot·ting 1 :** to put or pack in a pot **2 :** to plant (as a flower) in a pot to grow — often used with *up*

pot·ash *n* **:** potassium or a compound of potassium

po·tas·si·um *n* **:** a silvery soft light metallic chemical element found especially in minerals

po·ta·to *n, pl* **po·ta·toes :** the thick edible underground tuber of a widely grown American plant related to the tomato

potato chip *n* **:** a very thin slice of white potato fried crisp and salted

po·tent *adj* **1 :** having power or authority **2 :** very effective **:** STRONG

po·ten·tial *adj* **:** existing as a possibility — **po·ten·tial·ly** *adv*

pot·hole *n* **:** a deep round hole (as in a stream bed or a road)

po·tion *n* **:** a drink especially of a medicine or of a poison

pot·shot *n* **:** a shot taken in a casual manner or at an easy target

[1]**pot·ter** *n* **:** a person who makes pottery

[2]**potter** *vb* **:** PUTTER

pot·tery *n, pl* **pot·ter·ies 1 :** a place where clay articles (as pots, dishes, and vases) are made **2 :** the art of making clay articles **3 :** articles made from clay that is shaped while moist and hardened by heat

pouch *n* **1 :** a small bag with a drawstring **2 :** a bag often with a lock for carrying goods or valuables **3 :** a bag of folded skin and flesh especially for carrying the young (as on the abdomen of a kangaroo) or for carrying food (as in the cheek of many animals of the rat family)

poul·tice *n* **:** a soft and heated mass usually containing medicine and spread on the body surface to relieve pain, inflammation, or congestion

poul·try *n* **:** birds (as chickens, turkeys, ducks, and geese) grown to furnish meat or eggs for human food

[1]**pounce** *vb* **pounced; pounc·ing 1 :** to swoop on and seize something with or as if with claws **2 :** to leap or attack very quickly

[2]**pounce** *n* **:** an act of pouncing **:** a sudden swooping or springing on something

[1]**pound** *n* **1 :** a measure of weight equal to sixteen ounces (about .45 kilogram) **2 :** a coin or bill used in the United Kingdom and several other countries

[2]**pound** *n* **:** a public enclosure where stray animals are kept

[3]**pound** *vb* **1 :** to crush to a powder or pulp by beating **2 :** to strike heavily again and again **3 :** to move along heavily

pour *vb* **1 :** to flow or cause to flow in a stream **2 :** to let loose something without holding back **3 :** to rain hard

[1]**pout** *vb* **:** to show displeasure by pushing out one's lips

[2]**pout** *n* **:** an act of pouting

pov·er·ty *n* **1 :** the condition of being poor **:** lack of money or possessions **2 :** a lack of something desirable

[1]**pow·der** *vb* **1 :** to sprinkle with or as if with fine particles of something **2 :** to reduce to powder **3 :** to use face powder

[2]**powder** *n* **1 :** the fine particles made (as by pounding or crushing) from a dry substance **2 :** something (as a food, medicine, or cosmetic) made in or changed to the form of a powder **3 :** an explosive used in shooting and in blasting

powder horn *n* **:** a cow or ox horn made into a flask for carrying gunpowder

pow·dery *adj* **1 :** made of or like powder **2 :** easily crumbled **3 :** sprinkled with powder

[1]pow•er *n* **1 :** possession of control, authority, or influence over others **2 :** a nation that has influence among other nations **3 :** the ability to act or to do **4 :** physical might **:** STRENGTH **5 :** the number of times as shown by an exponent a number is used as a factor to obtain a product **6 :** force or energy used to do work **7 :** the rate of speed at which work is done **8 :** the number of times an optical instrument magnifies the apparent size of the object viewed — **pow•er•less** *adj*

[2]power *vb* **:** to supply with power

[3]power *adj* **:** relating to, supplying, or using mechanical or electrical power

pow•er•ful *adj* **:** full of or having power, strength, or influence — **pow•er•ful•ly** *adv*

pow•er•house *n* **1 :** POWER PLANT **2 :** a person or thing having unusual strength or energy

power plant *n* **:** a building in which electric power is generated

pow•wow *n* **1 :** a North American Indian ceremony or conference **2 :** a meeting for discussion

prac•ti•ca•ble *adj* **:** possible to do or put into practice

prac•ti•cal *adj* **1 :** engaged in some work **2 :** of or relating to action and practice rather than ideas or thought **3 :** capable of being made use of **4 :** ready to do things rather than just plan or think about them

practical joke *n* **:** a joke made up of something done rather than said **:** a trick played on someone

prac•ti•cal•ly *adv* **1 :** ACTUALLY **2 :** ALMOST

[1]prac•tice *or* **prac•tise** *vb* **prac•ticed** *or* **prac•tised; prac•tic•ing** *or* **prac•tis•ing** **1 :** to work at often so as to learn well **2 :** to engage in often or usually **3 :** to follow or work at as a profession

[2]practice *also* **practise** *n* **1 :** actual performance **:** USE **2 :** a usual way of doing **3 :** repeated action for gaining skill

prai•rie *n* **:** a large area of level or rolling grassland

prairie chicken *n* **:** a grouse of the Mississippi valley

prairie dog *n* **:** a burrowing animal related to the woodchuck but about the size of a large squirrel that lives in large colonies

prairie schooner *n* **:** a long covered wagon used by pioneers to cross the prairies

[1]praise *vb* **praised; prais•ing** **1 :** to express approval of **2 :** to glorify God or a saint especially in song

[2]praise *n* **1 :** an expression of approval **2 :** [1]WORSHIP 1

praise•wor•thy *adj* **:** worthy of praise

prance *vb* **pranced; pranc•ing** **1 :** to rise onto or move on the hind legs **2 :** to ride on a prancing horse **3 :** [1]STRUT

prank *n* **:** a mischievous act **:** PRACTICAL JOKE

prat•tle *vb* **prat•tled; prat•tling** **:** to talk a great deal without much meaning

prawn *n* **:** an edible shellfish that looks like a shrimp

pray *vb* **1 :** to ask earnestly **:** BEG **2 :** to address God with adoration, pleading, or thanksgiving

prayer *n* **1 :** a request addressed to God **2 :** the act of praying to God **3 :** a set form of words used in praying **4 :** a religious service that is mostly prayers

praying mantis *n* **:** MANTIS

pre- *prefix* **1 :** earlier than **:** before **2 :** beforehand **3 :** in front of **:** front

preach *vb* **1 :** to give a sermon **2 :** to urge publicly **:** ADVOCATE

preach•er *n* **1 :** a person who preaches **2 :** [1]MINISTER 1

pre•am•ble *n* **:** an introduction (as to a law) that often gives the reasons for the parts that follow

pre•car•i•ous *adj* **1 :** depending on chance or unknown conditions **:** UNCERTAIN **2 :** lacking steadiness or security — **pre•car•i•ous•ly** *adv* — **pre•car•i•ous•ness** *n*

pre•cau•tion *n* **1 :** care taken beforehand **2 :** something done beforehand to prevent evil or bring about good results

pre•cede *vb* **pre•ced•ed; pre•ced•ing** **:** to be or go before in importance, position, or time

pre•ce•dent *n* **:** something that can be used as a rule or as a model to be followed in the future

pre•ced•ing *adj* **:** going before **:** PREVIOUS

pre•cious *adj* **1 :** very valuable **2 :** greatly loved **:** DEAR

prec•i•pice *n* **:** a very steep and high face of rock or mountain **:** CLIFF

pre•cip•i•tate *vb* **pre•cip•i•tat•ed; pre•cip•i•tat•ing** **1 :** to cause to happen suddenly or unexpectedly **2 :** to change from a vapor to a liquid or solid and fall as rain or snow **3 :** to separate from a solution

pre•cip•i•ta•tion *n* **1 :** unwise haste **2 :** water or the amount of water that falls to the earth as hail, mist, rain, sleet, or snow

pre•cise *adj* **1 :** exactly stated or explained **2 :** very clear **3 :** very exact **:** ACCURATE — **pre•cise•ly** *adv* — **pre•cise•ness** *n*

pre•ci•sion *n* **:** the quality or state of being precise

pre•co•cious *adj* **:** showing qualities or abilities of an adult at an unusually early age — **pre•co•cious•ly** *adv* — **pre•co•cious•ness** *n*

pre–Co·lum·bi·an *adj* **:** preceding or belonging to the time before the arrival of Columbus in America

pred·a·tor *n* **:** an animal that lives mostly by killing and eating other animals

pred·a·to·ry *adj* **:** living by preying upon other animals

pre·de·ces·sor *n* **:** a person who has held a position or office before another

pre·dic·a·ment *n* **:** a bad or difficult situation **:** FIX

pred·i·cate *n* **:** the part of a sentence or clause that tells what is said about the subject

predicate adjective *n* **:** an adjective that occurs in the predicate after a linking verb and describes the subject

predicate noun *n* **:** a noun that occurs in the predicate after a linking verb and refers to the same person or thing as the subject

pre·dict *vb* **:** to figure out and tell beforehand

pre·dic·tion *n* **1 :** an act of predicting **2 :** something that is predicted

pre·dom·i·nance *n* **:** the quality or state of being predominant

pre·dom·i·nant *adj* **:** greater than others in number, strength, influence, or authority

pre·dom·i·nate *vb* **pre·dom·i·nat·ed; pre·dom·i·nat·ing :** to be predominant

preen *vb* **1 :** to smooth with or as if with the bill **2 :** to make one's appearance neat and tidy

pre·fab·ri·cate *vb* **pre·fab·ri·cat·ed; pre·fab·ri·cat·ing :** to manufacture the parts of something beforehand so that it can be built by putting the parts together

pref·ace *n* **:** a section at the beginning that introduces a book or a speech

pre·fer *vb* **pre·ferred; pre·fer·ring :** to like better

pref·er·a·ble *adj* **:** deserving to be preferred **:** more desirable — **pref·er·a·bly** *adv*

pref·er·ence *n* **1 :** a choosing of or special liking for one person or thing rather than another **2 :** the power or chance to choose **:** CHOICE **3 :** a person or thing that is preferred

¹pre·fix *vb* **:** to put or attach at the beginning of a word **:** add as a prefix

²prefix *n* **:** a letter or group of letters that comes at the beginning of a word and has a meaning of its own

preg·nan·cy *n, pl* **preg·nan·cies :** the state of being pregnant

preg·nant *adj* **1 :** carrying unborn offspring **2 :** full of meaning

pre·hen·sile *adj* **:** adapted for grasping by wrapping around

pre·his·tor·ic *adj* **:** of, relating to, or being in existence in the period before written history began

¹prej·u·dice *n* **1 :** injury or damage to a case at law or to one's rights **2 :** a liking or dislike for one rather than another without good reason

²prejudice *vb* **prej·u·diced; prej·u·dic·ing 1 :** to cause damage to (as a case at law) **2 :** to cause prejudice in

prel·ate *n* **:** a clergyman (as a bishop) of high rank

¹pre·lim·i·nary *n, pl* **pre·lim·i·nar·ies :** something that is preliminary

²preliminary *adj* **:** coming before the main part **:** INTRODUCTORY

prel·ude *n* **1 :** something that comes before and prepares for the main or more important parts **2 :** a short musical introduction (as for an opera) **3 :** a piece (as an organ solo) played at the beginning of a church service

pre·ma·ture *adj* **:** happening, coming, or done before the usual or proper time **:** too early — **pre·ma·ture·ly** *adv*

pre·med·i·tate *vb* **pre·med·i·tat·ed; pre·med·i·tat·ing :** to think about and plan beforehand

¹pre·mier *adj* **:** first in position or importance **:** CHIEF

²premier *n* **:** PRIME MINISTER

¹pre·miere *adj* **:** ²CHIEF 2

²premiere *n* **:** a first showing or performance

prem·ise *n* **1 :** a statement taken to be true and on which an argument or reasoning may be based **2 premises** *pl* **:** a piece of land with the buildings on it

pre·mi·um *n* **1 :** a prize to be gained by some special act **2 :** a sum over and above the stated value **3 :** the amount paid for a contract of insurance

pre·mo·lar *n* **:** any of the teeth that come between the canines and the molars and in humans are normally two in each side of each jaw

pre·mo·ni·tion *n* **:** a feeling that something is going to happen

pre·oc·cu·pied *adj* **:** lost in thought

prepaid *past of* PREPAY

prep·a·ra·tion *n* **1 :** the act of making ready beforehand for some special reason **2 :** something that prepares **3 :** something prepared for a particular purpose

pre·par·a·to·ry *adj* **:** preparing or serving to prepare for something

pre·pare *vb* **pre·pared; pre·par·ing 1 :** to make ready beforehand for some particular reason **2 :** to put together the elements of

pre·pay *vb* **pre·paid; pre·pay·ing :** to pay or pay for beforehand

prep·o·si·tion *n* **:** a word or group of words that combines with a noun or pronoun to form a phrase that usually acts as an adverb, adjective, or noun

prep·o·si·tion·al *adj* : of, relating to, or containing a preposition

pre·pos·ter·ous *adj* : making little or no sense : FOOLISH

pre·req·ui·site *n* : something that is needed beforehand or is necessary to prepare for something else

pre·scribe *vb* **pre·scribed; pre·scrib·ing** **1** : to lay down as a rule of action : ORDER **2** : to order or direct the use of as a remedy

pre·scrip·tion *n* **1** : a written direction or order for the preparing and use of a medicine **2** : a medicine that is prescribed

pres·ence *n* **1** : the fact or condition of being present **2** : position close to a person **3** : a person's appearance

presence of mind : ability to think clearly and act quickly in an emergency

[1]**pres·ent** *n* : something presented or given : GIFT

[2]**pre·sent** *vb* **1** : to introduce one person to another **2** : to take (oneself) into another's presence **3** : to bring before the public **4** : to make a gift to **5** : to give as a gift **6** : to offer to view : SHOW, DISPLAY,

[3]**pres·ent** *adj* **1** : not past or future : now going on **2** : being before or near a person or in sight : being at a certain place and not elsewhere **3** : pointing out or relating to time that is not past or future

[4]**pres·ent** *n* : the present time : right now

pre·sent·able *adj* : having a satisfactory or pleasing appearance

pre·sen·ta·tion *n* **1** : an introduction of one person to another **2** : an act of presenting **3** : something offered or given

pres·ent·ly *adv* **1** : before long : SOON **2** : at the present time : NOW

pres·er·va·tion *n* : a keeping from injury, loss, or decay

[1]**pre·serve** *vb* **pre·served; pre·serv·ing** **1** : to keep or save from injury or ruin : PROTECT **2** : to prepare (as by canning or pickling) fruits or vegetables for keeping **3** : MAINTAIN 1, CONTINUE — **pre·serv·er** *n*

[2]**preserve** *n* **1** : fruit cooked in sugar or made into jam or jelly — often used in pl. **2** : an area where game or fish are protected

pre·side *vb* **pre·sid·ed; pre·sid·ing** **1** : to act as chairperson of a meeting **2** : to be in charge

pres·i·den·cy *n, pl* **pres·i·den·cies** **1** : the office of president **2** : the term during which a president holds office

pres·i·dent *n* **1** : a person who presides over a meeting **2** : the chief officer of a company or society **3** : the head of the government and chief executive officer of a modern republic

pres·i·den·tial *adj* : of or relating to a president or the presidency

[1]**press** *n* **1** : [2]CROWD 1, THRONG **2** : a machine that uses pressure to shape, flatten, squeeze, or stamp **3** : a closet for clothing **4** : the act of pressing : PRESSURE **5** : a printing or publishing business **6** : the newspapers and magazines of a country

[2]**press** *vb* **1** : to bear down upon : push steadily against **2** : to squeeze so as to force out the juice or contents **3** : to flatten out or smooth by bearing down upon especially by ironing **4** : to ask or urge strongly **5** : to force or push one's way

press·ing *adj* : needing one's immediate attention

pres·sure *n* **1** : the action of pressing or bearing down upon **2** : a force or influence that cannot be avoided **3** : the force with which one body presses against another **4** : the need to get things done

pres·tige *n* : importance in the eyes of people : REPUTE

pres·to *adv or adj* : suddenly as if by magic

pre·sume *vb* **pre·sumed; pre·sum·ing** **1** : to undertake without permission or good reason : DARE **2** : to suppose to be true without proof

pre·sump·tion *n* **1** : presumptuous behavior or attitude **2** : a strong reason for believing something to be so **3** : something believed to be so but not proved

pre·sump·tu·ous *adj* : going beyond what is proper — **pre·sump·tu·ous·ly** *adv* — **pre·sump·tu·ous·ness** *n*

pre·tend *vb* **1** : to make believe : SHAM **2** : to put forward as true something that is not true — **pre·tend·er** *n*

pre·tense *or* **pre·tence** *n* **1** : a claim usually not supported by facts **2** : an effort to reach a certain condition or quality

pre·ten·tious *adj* : having or showing pretenses : SHOWY — **pre·ten·tious·ly** *adv* — **pre·ten·tious·ness** *n*

[1]**pret·ty** *adj* **pret·ti·er; pret·ti·est** : pleasing to the eye or ear especially because of being graceful or delicate — **pret·ti·ly** *adv* — **pret·ti·ness** *n*

[2]**pret·ty** *adv* : in some degree : FAIRLY

pret·zel *n* : a brown cracker that is salted and is usually hard and shaped like a loose knot

pre·vail *vb* **1** : to win a victory **2** : to succeed in convincing **3** : to be or become usual, common, or widespread

prev·a·lence *n* : the state of being prevalent

prev·a·lent *adj* : accepted, practiced, or happening often or over a wide area

pre·vent *vb* **1 :** to keep from happening **2 :** to hold or keep back — **pre·vent·able** *adj*

pre·ven·tion *n* **:** the act or practice of preventing something

pre·ven·tive *adj* **:** used for prevention

pre·view *n* **:** a showing of something (as a movie) before regular showings

pre·vi·ous *adj* **:** going before in time or order **:** PRECEDING — **pre·vi·ous·ly** *adv*

¹prey *n* **1 :** an animal hunted or killed by another animal for food **2 :** a person that is helpless and unable to escape attack **:** VICTIM **3 :** the act or habit of seizing or pouncing upon

²prey *vb* **1 :** to seize and eat something as prey **2 :** to have a harmful effect

¹price *n* **1 :** the quantity of one thing given or asked for something else **:** the amount of money paid or to be paid **2 :** ²REWARD **3 :** the cost at which something is gotten or done

²price *vb* **priced; pric·ing 1 :** to set a price on **2 :** to ask the price of

price·less *adj* **:** too valuable to have a price **:** not to be bought at any price

¹prick *n* **1 :** a mark or small wound made by a pointed instrument **2 :** something sharp or pointed **3 :** a sensation of being pricked

²prick *vb* **1 :** to pierce slightly with a sharp point **2 :** to have or to cause a feeling of or as if of being pricked **3 :** to point upward

prick·er *n* **:** ¹PRICKLE 1

¹prick·le *n* **1 :** a small sharp point (as a thorn) **2 :** a slight stinging pain

²prickle *vb* **prick·led; prick·ling :** ²PRICK 2

prick·ly *adj* **prick·li·er; prick·li·est 1 :** having prickles **2 :** being or having a pricking

prickly pear *n* **:** a usually spiny cactus with flat branching joints and a sweet pulpy fruit shaped like a pear

¹pride *n* **1 :** too high an opinion of one's own ability or worth **:** a feeling of being better than others **2 :** a reasonable and justifiable sense of one's own worth **:** SELF-RESPECT **3 :** a sense of pleasure that comes from some act or possession **4 :** something of which one is proud

²pride *vb* **prid·ed; prid·ing :** to think highly of (oneself)

priest *n* **:** a person who has the authority to lead or perform religious ceremonies

priest·ess *n* **:** a woman who is a priest

prim *adj* **prim·mer; prim·mest :** very fussy about one's appearance or behavior — **prim·ly** *adv*

pri·mar·i·ly *adv* **:** in the first place

¹pri·ma·ry *adj* **1 :** first in time or development **2 :** most important **:** PRINCIPAL **3 :** not made or coming from something else **:** BASIC **4 :** of, relating to, or being the heaviest of three levels of stress in pronunciation

²primary *n, pl* **pri·ma·ries :** an election in which members of a political party nominate candidates for office

primary color *n* **:** any of a set of colors from which all other colors may be made with the colors for light being red, green, and blue and for pigments or paint being red, yellow, and blue

pri·mate *n* **:** any of a group of mammals that includes humans together with the apes and monkeys and a few related forms

¹prime *n* **1 :** the first part **:** the earliest stage **2 :** the period in life when a person is best in health, looks, or strength **3 :** the best individual or part

²prime *adj* **1 :** first in time **:** ORIGINAL **2 :** having no factor except itself and one **3 :** first in importance, rank, or quality

³prime *vb* **primed; prim·ing 1 :** to put a first color or coating on (an unpainted surface) **2 :** to put into working order by filling **3 :** to tell what to say beforehand **:** COACH

prime minister *n* **:** the chief officer of the government in some countries

¹prim·er *n* **1 :** a small book for teaching children to read **2 :** a book of first instructions on a subject

²prim·er *n* **1 :** a device (as a cap) for setting off an explosive **2 :** material used to prime a surface

pri·me·val *adj* **:** belonging to the earliest time **:** PRIMITIVE

prim·i·tive *adj* **1 :** of or belonging to very early times **2 :** of or belonging to an early stage of development

primp *vb* **:** to dress or arrange in a careful or fussy manner

prim·rose *n* **:** a low perennial plant with large leaves growing from the base of the stem and showy often yellow or pink flowers

prince *n* **1 :** MONARCH 1 **2 :** the son of a monarch **3 :** a nobleman of very high or the highest rank

prin·cess *n* **:** a daughter or granddaughter of a monarch **:** a female member of a royal family

¹prin·ci·pal *adj* **:** highest in rank or importance **:** CHIEF — **prin·ci·pal·ly** *adv*

²principal *n* **1 :** a leading or most important person or thing **2 :** the head of a school **3 :** a sum of money that is placed to earn interest, is owed as a debt, or is used as a fund

prin·ci·pal·i·ty *n, pl* **prin·ci·pal·i·ties :** a small territory that is ruled by a prince

principal parts *n pl* **:** the infinitive, the past tense, and the past and present participles of an English verb

prin·ci·ple *n* **1 :** a general or basic truth on

which other truths or theories can be based **2 :** a rule of conduct **3 :** a law or fact of nature which makes possible the working of a machine or device

1print *n* **1 :** a mark made by pressure **2 :** something which has been stamped with an impression or formed in a mold **3 :** printed matter **4 :** printed letters **5 :** a picture, copy, or design taken from an engraving or photographic negative **6 :** cloth upon which a design is stamped

2print *vb* **1 :** to put or stamp in or on **2 :** to make a copy of by pressing paper against an inked surface (as type or an engraving) **3 :** to stamp with a design by pressure **4 :** PUBLISH 2 **5 :** PRINT OUT **6 :** to write in separate letters like those made by a typewriter **7 :** to make a picture from a photographic negative

print•er *n* **1 :** a person whose business is printing **2 :** a machine that produces printouts

print•ing *n* **1 :** the process of putting something in printed form **2 :** the art, practice, or business of a printer

printing press *n* **:** a machine that makes printed copies

print•out *n* **:** a printed record produced by a computer

print out *vb* **:** to make a printout of

1pri•or *n* **:** a monk who is head of a priory

2prior *adj* **1 :** being or happening before something else **2 :** being more important than something else

pri•or•ess *n* **:** a nun who is head of a priory

pri•or•i•ty *n, pl* **pri•or•i•ties :** the quality or state of coming before another in time or importance

prior to *prep* **:** in advance of **:** BEFORE

pri•o•ry *n, pl* **pri•o•ries :** a religious house under a prior or prioress

prism *n* **:** a transparent object that usually has three sides and bends light so that it breaks up into rainbow colors

pris•on *n* **:** a place where criminals are locked up

pris•on•er *n* **:** a person who has been captured or locked up

pri•va•cy *n* **1 :** the state of being out of the sight and hearing of other people **2 :** SECRECY 2

1pri•vate *adj* **1 :** having to do with or for the use of a single person or group **:** not public **2 :** not holding any public office **3 :** 1SECRET 1 — **pri•vate•ly** *adv* — **pri•vate•ness** *n*

2private *n* **:** an enlisted person of the lowest rank in the Marine Corps or of either of the two lowest ranks in the Army

pri•va•teer *n* **1 :** an armed private ship permitted by its government to make war on ships of an enemy country **2 :** a sailor on a privateer

private first class *n* **:** an enlisted person in the Army or Marine Corps ranking above a private

priv•et *n* **:** a shrub with white flowers that is related to the lilac and is often used for hedges

priv•i•lege *n* **:** a right or liberty granted as a favor or benefit especially to some and not others

priv•i•leged *adj* **:** having more things and a better chance in life than most people

1prize *n* **1 :** something won or to be won in a contest **2 :** something unusually valuable or eagerly sought

2prize *adj* **1 :** awarded a prize **2 :** awarded as a prize **3 :** outstanding of its kind

3prize *vb* **prized; priz•ing 1 :** to estimate the value of **2 :** to value highly **:** TREASURE

4prize *n* **:** something taken (as in war) by force especially at sea

prize•fight•er *n* **:** a professional boxer

1pro *n, pl* **pros :** an argument or evidence in favor of something

2pro *adv* **:** in favor of something

3pro *n or adj* **:** PROFESSIONAL

pro- *prefix* **:** approving **:** in favor of

prob•a•bil•i•ty *n, pl* **prob•a•bil•i•ties 1 :** the quality or state of being probable **2 :** something probable

prob•a•ble *adj* **:** reasonably sure but not certain of happening or being true **:** LIKELY

prob•a•bly *adv* **:** very likely

pro•ba•tion *n* **:** a period of trial for finding out or testing a person's fitness (as for a job)

1probe *n* **1 :** a slender instrument for examining a cavity (as a deep wound) **2 :** a careful investigation

2probe *vb* **probed; prob•ing 1 :** to examine with or as if with a probe **2 :** to investigate thoroughly

prob•lem *n* **1 :** something to be worked out or solved **2 :** a person or thing that is hard to understand or deal with

pro•bos•cis *n* **:** a long flexible hollow bodily structure (as the trunk of an elephant or the beak of a mosquito)

pro•ce•dure *n* **1 :** the manner or method in which a business or action is carried on **2 :** an action or series of actions

pro•ceed *vb* **1 :** to come from a source **2 :** to go or act by an orderly method **3 :** to go forward or onward **:** ADVANCE

pro•ceed•ing *n* **1 :** PROCEDURE 2 **2 proceedings** *pl* **:** things that happen

pro•ceeds *n pl* **:** the money or profit that comes from a business deal

1pro•cess *n* **1 :** 2ADVANCE 1 **2 :** a series of

actions, motions, or operations leading to some result **3 :** the carrying on of a legal action

²process *vb* **1 :** to change by a special treatment **2 :** to take care of according to a routine **3 :** to take in and organize for use in a variety of ways

pro•ces•sion *n* **1 :** continuous forward movement **:** PROGRESSION **2 :** a group of individuals moving along in an orderly often ceremonial way

pro•ces•sor *n* **1 :** a person or machine that processes **2 :** COMPUTER **3 :** the part of a computer that operates on data

pro•claim *vb* **:** to announce publicly **:** DECLARE

proc•la•ma•tion *n* **1 :** the act of proclaiming **2 :** something proclaimed

pro•cure *vb* **pro•cured; pro•cur•ing 1 :** OBTAIN **2 :** to bring about or cause to be done

¹prod *vb* **prod•ded; prod•ding 1 :** to poke with something **2 :** to stir a person or animal to action

²prod *n* **1 :** something used for prodding **2 :** an act of prodding **3 :** a sharp urging or reminder

¹prod•i•gal *adj* **:** carelessly wasteful

²prodigal *n* **:** somebody who wastes money carelessly

prod•i•gy *n, pl* **prod•i•gies 1 :** an amazing event or action **:** WONDER **2 :** an unusually talented child

¹pro•duce *vb* **pro•duced; pro•duc•ing 1 :** to bring to view **:** EXHIBIT **2 :** to bring forth **:** YIELD **3 :** to prepare (as a play) for public presentation **4 :** MANUFACTURE — **pro•duc•er** *n*

²pro•duce *n* **1 :** something produced **2 :** fresh fruits and vegetables

prod•uct *n* **1 :** the number resulting from the multiplication of two or more numbers **2 :** something produced by manufacture, labor, thought, or growth

pro•duc•tion *n* **1 :** something produced **2 :** the act of producing **3 :** the amount produced

pro•duc•tive *adj* **1 :** having the power to produce plentifully **2 :** producing something

¹pro•fane *vb* **pro•faned; pro•fan•ing :** to treat with great disrespect — **pro•fan•er** *n*

²profane *adj* **:** showing no respect for God or holy things — **pro•fane•ly** *adv* — **pro•fane•ness** *n*

pro•fan•i•ty *n, pl* **pro•fan•i•ties :** profane language

pro•fess *vb* **1 :** to declare openly **2 :** PRETEND 2

pro•fes•sion *n* **1 :** a public declaring or claiming **2 :** an occupation (as medicine, law, or teaching) that is not mechanical or agricultural and that requires special education **3 :** the people working in a profession

¹pro•fes•sion•al *adj* **1 :** of, relating to, or like that of a profession **2 :** taking part in an activity (as a sport) that others do for pleasure in order to make money — **pro•fes•sion•al•ly** *adv*

²professional *n* **:** a person whose work is professional

pro•fes•sor *n* **:** a teacher especially of the highest rank at a college or university

prof•fer *vb* **:** ¹OFFER 2

pro•fi•cient *adj* **:** very good at doing something **:** EXPERT — **pro•fi•cient•ly** *adv*

pro•file *n* **:** something (as a head) seen or drawn from the side

¹prof•it *n* **1 :** the gain or benefit from something **2 :** the gain after all the expenses are subtracted from the total amount received — **prof•it•less** *adj*

²profit *vb* **1 :** to get some good out of something **:** GAIN **2 :** to be of use to (someone)

prof•it•able *adj* **:** producing profit — **prof•it•ably** *adv*

pro•found *adj* **1 :** having or showing great knowledge and understanding **2 :** very deeply felt — **pro•found•ly** *adv* — **pro•found•ness** *n*

pro•fuse *adj* **:** very plentiful — **pro•fuse•ly** *adv* — **pro•fuse•ness** *n*

pro•fu•sion *n* **:** a plentiful supply **:** PLENTY

prog•e•ny *n, pl* **prog•e•nies :** human descendants or animal offspring

¹pro•gram *n* **1 :** a brief statement or written outline (as of a concert or play) **2 :** PERFORMANCE 2 **3 :** a plan of action **4 :** a set of step-by-step instructions that tell a computer to do something with data

²program *vb* **pro•grammed; pro•gram•ming :** to provide with a program

pro•gram•mer *n* **:** a person who creates and tests programs for computers

¹prog•ress *n* **1 :** a moving toward a goal **2 :** gradual improvement

²pro•gress *vb* **1 :** to move forward **:** ADVANCE **2 :** to move toward a higher, better, or more advanced stage

pro•gres•sion *n* **1 :** the act of progressing or moving forward **2 :** a continuous and connected series (as of acts, events, or steps)

pro•gres•sive *adj* **1 :** of, relating to, or showing progress **2 :** taking place gradually or step by step **3 :** favoring or working for gradual political change and social improvement by action of the government — **pro•gres•sive•ly** *adv* — **pro•gres•sive•ness** *n*

pro·hib·it *vb* **1 :** to forbid by authority **2 :** to make impossible
pro·hi·bi·tion *n* **1 :** the act of prohibiting something **2 :** the forbidding by law of the sale or manufacture of alcoholic liquids for use as beverages
¹proj·ect *n* **1 :** a plan or scheme to do something **2 :** a task or problem in school **3 :** a group of houses or apartment buildings built according to a single plan
²pro·ject *vb* **1 :** to stick out **2 :** to cause to fall on a surface
pro·jec·tile *n* **:** something (as a bullet or rocket) that is thrown or driven forward especially from a weapon
pro·jec·tion *n* **1 :** something that sticks out **2 :** the act or process of projecting on a surface (as by means of motion pictures or slides)
pro·jec·tor *n* **:** a machine for projecting images on a screen
pro·lif·ic *adj* **:** producing young or fruit in large numbers
pro·long *vb* **:** to make longer than usual or expected
prom *n* **:** a usually formal dance given by a high school or college class
prom·e·nade *n* **1 :** a walk or ride for pleasure or to be seen **2 :** a place for walking
prom·i·nence *n* **1 :** the quality, condition, or fact of being prominent **:** DISTINCTION **2 :** something (as a mountain) that is prominent
prom·i·nent *adj* **1 :** sticking out beyond the surface **2 :** attracting attention (as by size or position) **:** CONSPICUOUS **3 :** DISTINGUISHED, EMINENT — **prom·i·nent·ly** *adv*
¹prom·ise *n* **1 :** a statement by a person that he or she will do or not do something **2 :** a cause or ground for hope
²promise *vb* **prom·ised; prom·is·ing** **1 :** to give a promise about one's own actions **2 :** to give reason to expect
prom·is·ing *adj* **:** likely to turn out well
prom·on·to·ry *n, pl* **prom·on·to·ries** **:** a high point of land sticking out into the sea
pro·mote *vb* **pro·mot·ed; pro·mot·ing** **1 :** to move up in position or rank **2 :** to help (something) to grow or develop
pro·mo·tion *n* **1 :** a moving up in position or rank **2 :** the promoting of something (as growth of health)
¹prompt *vb* **1 :** to lead to do something **2 :** to remind of something forgotten or poorly learned **3 :** to be the cause of **:** INSPIRE — **prompt·er** *n*
²prompt *adj* **1 :** quick and ready to act **2 :** being on time **:** PUNCTUAL **3 :** done at once **:** given without delay — **prompt·ly** *adv* — **prompt·ness** *n*
prone *adj* **1 :** likely to be or act a certain way **2 :** having the front surface downward — **prone·ness** *n*
prong *n* **1 :** one of the sharp points of a fork **2 :** a slender part that sticks out (as a point of an antler)
prong·horn *n* **:** an animal like an antelope that lives in the treeless parts of the western United States and Mexico
pro·noun *n* **:** a word used as a substitute for a noun
pro·nounce *vb* **pro·nounced; pro·nounc·ing** **1 :** to state in an official or solemn way **2 :** to use the voice to make the sounds of **3 :** to say correctly
pro·nounced *adj* **:** very noticeable
pro·nun·ci·a·tion *n* **:** the act or way of pronouncing a word or words
¹proof *n* **1 :** evidence of truth or correctness **2 :** ¹TEST 1 **3 :** a printing (as from type) prepared for study and correction **4 :** a test print made from a photographic negative
²proof *adj* **:** able to keep out something that could be harmful — usually used in compounds
proof·read *vb* **proof·read; proof·read·ing** **:** to read over and fix mistakes in (written or printed matter) — **proof·read·er** *n*
¹prop *n* **:** something that props or supports
²prop *vb* **propped; prop·ping** **1 :** to keep from falling or slipping by providing a support under or against **2 :** to give help, encouragement, or support to
³prop *n* **:** PROPERTY 3
pro·pa·gan·da *n* **:** an organized spreading of certain ideas or the ideas spread in such a way
prop·a·gate *vb* **prop·a·gat·ed; prop·a·gat·ing** **1 :** to have or cause to have offspring **2 :** to cause (as an idea or belief) to spread out and affect a greater number or wider area
prop·a·ga·tion *n* **:** an act or process of propagating
pro·pel *vb* **pro·pelled; pro·pel·ling** **:** to push or drive usually forward or onward
pro·pel·ler *n* **:** a device having a hub fitted with blades that is made to turn rapidly by an engine and that drives a ship, power boat, or airplane
prop·er *adj* **1 :** referring to one individual only **2 :** belonging naturally to a particular group or individual **:** CHARACTERISTIC **3 :** considered in its true or basic meaning **4 :** having or showing good manners **5 :** APPROPRIATE, SUITABLE
proper fraction *n* **:** a fraction in which the numerator is smaller than the denominator
prop·er·ly *adv* **1 :** in a fit or suitable way **2 :** according to fact

proper noun *n* **:** a noun that names a particular person, place, or thing

prop·er·ty *n, pl* **prop·er·ties** **1 :** a special quality of a thing **2 :** something (as land or money) that is owned **3 :** something other than scenery or costumes that is used in a play or movie

proph·e·cy *n, pl* **proph·e·cies** **1 :** the sayings of a prophet **2 :** something foretold **:** PREDICTION

proph·e·sy *vb* **proph·e·sied; proph·e·sy·ing** **1 :** to speak or write as a prophet **2 :** FORETELL, PREDICT

proph·et *n* **1 :** one who declares publicly a message that one believes has come from God or a god **2 :** a person who predicts the future

pro·phet·ic *adj* **:** of or relating to a prophet or prophecy

1**pro·por·tion** *n* **1 :** the size, number, or amount of one thing or group of things as compared to that of another thing or group of things **2 :** a balanced or pleasing arrangement **3 :** a statement of the equality of two ratios (as $^4/_2 = {}^{10}/_5$) **4 :** a fair or just share **5 :** DIMENSION

2**proportion** *vb* **1 :** to adjust something to fit with something else **2 :** to make the parts of fit well with each other

pro·por·tion·al *adj* **:** being in proportion to something else — **pro·por·tion·al·ly** *adv*

pro·pos·al *n* **1 :** a stating or putting forward of something for consideration **2 :** something proposed **:** PLAN **3 :** an offer of marriage

pro·pose *vb* **pro·posed; pro·pos·ing** **1 :** to make a suggestion to be thought over and talked about **:** SUGGEST **2 :** to make plans **:** INTEND **3 :** to suggest for filling a place or office **4 :** to make an offer of marriage

prop·o·si·tion *n* **1 :** something proposed **2 :** a statement to be proved, explained, or discussed

pro·pri·e·tor *n* **:** a person who owns something **:** OWNER

pro·pri·ety *n, pl* **pro·pri·eties** **1 :** the quality or state of being proper **2 :** correctness in manners or behavior **3** *proprieties pl* **:** the rules and customs of behavior followed by nice people

pro·pul·sion *n* **1 :** the act or process of propelling **2 :** something that propels

pros *pl of* PRO

prose *n* **1 :** the ordinary language that people use in speaking or writing **2 :** writing without the repeating rhythm that is used in verse

pros·e·cute *vb* **pros·e·cut·ed; pros·e·cut·ing** **1 :** to follow up to the end **:** keep at **2 :** to carry on a legal action against an accused person to prove his or her guilt

pros·e·cu·tion *n* **1 :** the act of prosecuting especially a criminal case in court **2 :** the one bringing charges of crime against a person being tried **3 :** the state's lawyers in a criminal case

pros·e·cu·tor *n* **:** a person who prosecutes especially a criminal case as lawyer for the state

1**pros·pect** *n* **1 :** a wide view **2 :** an imagining of something to come **3 :** something that is waited for or expected **:** POSSIBILITY **4 :** a possible buyer or customer **5 :** a likely candidate

2**prospect** *vb* **:** to explore especially for mineral deposits

pro·spec·tive *adj* **1 :** likely to come about **2 :** likely to become — **pro·spec·tive·ly** *adv*

pros·pec·tor *n* **:** a person who explores a region in search of valuable minerals (as metals or oil)

pros·per *vb* **1 :** to succeed or make money in something one is doing **2 :** 1FLOURISH 1, THRIVE

pros·per·i·ty *n* **:** the state of being prosperous or successful

pros·per·ous *adj* **1 :** having or showing success or financial good fortune **2 :** strong and healthy in growth — **pros·per·ous·ly** *adv*

1**pros·trate** *adj* **1 :** stretched out with face on the ground **2 :** spread out parallel to the ground **3 :** lacking strength or energy

2**prostrate** *vb* **pros·trat·ed; pros·trat·ing** **1 :** to throw or put into a prostrate position **2 :** to bring to a weak and powerless condition

pro·tect *vb* **:** to cover or shield from something that would destroy or injure **:** GUARD

pro·tec·tion *n* **1 :** the act of protecting **:** the state of being protected **2 :** a protecting person or thing

pro·tec·tive *adj* **:** giving or meant to give protection — **pro·tec·tive·ly** *adv* — **pro·tec·tive·ness** *n*

pro·tec·tor *n* **:** a person or thing that protects or is intended to protect

pro·tein *n* **:** a nutrient containing nitrogen that is found in all living plant or animal cells, is a necessary part of the diet, and is supplied especially by such foods as meat, milk, and eggs

1**pro·test** *n* **1 :** the act of protesting **2 :** a complaint or objection against an idea, an act, or a way of doing things

2**pro·test** *vb* **1 :** to declare positively **:** ASSERT **2 :** to complain strongly about

1**Prot·es·tant** *n* **:** a member of a Christian

church other than the Eastern Orthodox Church and the Roman Catholic Church

[2]**Protestant** *adj* **:** of or relating to Protestants

pro•ton *n* **:** a very small particle that occurs in the nucleus of every atom and has a positive charge of electricity

pro•to•plasm *n* **:** the usually colorless and jellylike living part of cells

pro•to•zo•an *n* **:** any of a large group of mostly microscopic animals whose body is a single cell

pro•tract *vb* **:** to make longer **:** draw out in time or space

pro•trac•tor *n* **:** an instrument used for drawing and measuring angles

pro•trude *vb* **pro•trud•ed; pro•trud•ing :** to stick out or cause to stick out

proud *adj* **1 :** having or showing a feeling that one is better than others **:** HAUGHTY **2 :** having a feeling of pleasure or satisfaction **:** very pleased **3 :** having proper self-respect — **proud•ly** *adv*

prove *vb* **proved; proved** *or* **prov•en; prov•ing 1 :** to test by experiment or by a standard **2 :** to convince others of the truth of something by showing the facts **3 :** to test the answer to and check the way of solving an arithmetic problem

prov•erb *n* **:** a short well-known saying containing a wise thought **:** MAXIM, ADAGE

pro•ver•bi•al *adj* **:** of, relating to, or being a proverb — **pro•ver•bi•al•ly** *adv*

pro•vide *vb* **pro•vid•ed; pro•vid•ing 1 :** to look out for or take care of beforehand **2 :** to make as a condition **3 :** to give something that is needed

pro•vid•ed *conj* **:** IF 1

pro•vid•er *n* **:** one that provides something

prov•i•dence *n* **1** *often cap* **:** help or care from God or heaven **2** *cap* **:** God as the guide and protector of all human beings **3 :** PRUDENCE, THRIFT

prov•ince *n* **1 :** a part of a country having a government of its own (as one of the divisions of the Dominion of Canada) **2 provinces** *pl* **:** the part or parts of a country far from the capital or chief city **3 :** an area of activity or authority

pro•vin•cial *adj* **1 :** of, relating to, or coming from a province **2 :** lacking the social graces and sophistication of the city

[1]**pro•vi•sion** *n* **1 :** the act of providing **2 :** something done beforehand **3 :** a stock or store of food — usually used in pl. **4 :** [1]CONDITION 1

[2]**provision** *vb* **:** to supply with provisions

prov•o•ca•tion *n* **1 :** the act of provoking **2 :** something that provokes

pro•voc•a•tive *adj* **:** serving or likely to cause a reaction (as interest, curiosity, or anger) — **pro•voc•a•tive•ly** *adv*

pro•voke *vb* **pro•voked; pro•vok•ing 1 :** to cause to become angry **2 :** to bring about

pro•vok•ing *adj* **:** causing mild anger — **pro•vok•ing•ly** *adv*

prow *n* **:** the bow of a ship

prow•ess *n* **1 :** great bravery especially in battle **2 :** very great ability

prowl *vb* **:** to move about quietly and secretly like a wild animal hunting prey — **prowl•er** *n*

proxy *n, pl* **prox•ies 1 :** authority to act for another or a paper giving such authority **2 :** a person with authority to act for another

prude *n* **:** a person who cares too much about proper speech and conduct — **prud•ish** *adj*

pru•dence *n* **:** skill and good sense in taking care of oneself or of one's doings

pru•dent *adj* **1 :** clever and careful in action or judgment **2 :** careful in trying to avoid mistakes — **pru•dent•ly** *adv*

[1]**prune** *n* **:** a dried plum

[2]**prune** *vb* **pruned; prun•ing 1 :** to cut off dead or unwanted parts of a bush or tree **2 :** to cut out useless or unwanted parts (as unnecessary words or phrases in a composition)

[1]**pry** *vb* **pried; pry•ing :** to be nosy about something

[2]**pry** *vb* **pried; pry•ing 1 :** to raise or open or try to do so with a lever **2 :** to get at with great difficulty

pry•ing *adj* **:** rudely nosy

psalm *n* **1 :** a sacred song or poem **2** *cap* **:** one of the hymns that make up the Old Testament Book of Psalms

psy•chi•a•trist *n* **:** a specialist in psychiatry

psy•chi•a•try *n* **:** a branch of medicine dealing with problems of the mind, emotions, or behavior

psy•cho•log•i•cal *adj* **1 :** of or relating to psychology **2 :** directed toward or meant to influence the mind

psy•chol•o•gist *n* **:** a specialist in psychology

psy•chol•o•gy *n* **:** the science that studies facts about the mind and its activities especially in human beings

pu•ber•ty *n* **:** the age at or period during which a person becomes able to reproduce sexually

[1]**pub•lic** *adj* **1 :** of or relating to the people as a whole **2 :** of, relating to, or working for a government or community **3 :** open to all **4 :** known to many people **:** not kept secret **5 :** WELL-KNOWN, PROMINENT — **pub•lic•ly** *adv*

[2]**public** *n* **1 :** the people as a whole **2 :** a group of people having common interests

pub·li·ca·tion *n* **1 :** the act or process of publishing **2 :** a printed work (as a book or magazine) made for sale or distribution

pub·lic·i·ty *n* **1 :** public interest and approval **2 :** something (as favorable news) used to attract public interest and approval

pub·li·cize *vb* **pub·li·cized; pub·li·ciz·ing :** to give publicity to

public school *n* **:** a free school paid for by taxes and run by a local government

pub·lish *vb* **1 :** to make widely known **2 :** to bring printed works (as books) before the public usually for sale — **pub·lish·er** *n*

puck *n* **:** a rubber disk used in hockey

1puck·er *vb* **:** to draw or cause to draw up into folds or wrinkles

2pucker *n* **:** a fold or wrinkle in a normally even surface

pud·ding *n* **:** a soft spongy or creamy dessert

pud·dle *n* **:** a very small pool (as of dirty or muddy water)

pudgy *adj* **pudg·i·er; pudg·i·est :** being short and plump **:** CHUBBY

pueb·lo *n, pl* **pueb·los :** an Indian village of Arizona or New Mexico made up of groups of stone or adobe houses with flat roofs

1Puer·to Ri·can *adj* **:** of or relating to Puerto Rico or the Puerto Ricans

2Puerto Rican *n* **:** a person born or living in Puerto Rico

1puff *vb* **1 :** to blow in short gusts **2 :** to breathe hard **:** PANT **3 :** to send out small whiffs or clouds (as of smoke) **4 :** to swell up or become swollen with or as if with air

2puff *n* **1 :** a quick short sending or letting out of air, smoke, or steam **2 :** a slight swelling **3 :** a soft pad for putting powder on the skin

puf·fin *n* **:** a seabird related to the auks that has a short thick neck and a deep grooved bill marked with several colors

puffy *adj* **puff·i·er; puff·i·est 1 :** blowing in puffs **2 :** BREATHLESS 1 **3 :** somewhat swollen **4 :** like a puff **:** FLUFFY

pug *n* **1 :** a small dog having a thick body, a large round head, a square snout, a curled tail, and usually short hair **2 :** a nose turning up at the tip and usually short and thick

1pull *vb* **1 :** to separate from a firm or a natural attachment **2 :** to use force on so as to cause or tend to cause movement toward the force **3 :** to stretch repeatedly **4 :** 1MOVE 1 **5 :** to draw apart **:** TEAR, REND

2pull *n* **1 :** the act or an instance of pulling **2 :** the effort put forth in moving **3 :** a device for pulling something **4 :** a force that pulls

pul·let *n* **:** a young hen

pul·ley *n, pl* **pulleys :** a wheel that has a grooved rim in which a belt, rope, or chain runs and that is used to change the direction of a pulling force and in combination to increase the force applied for lifting

pull·over *n* **:** a garment (as a sweater) that is put on by being pulled over the head

pull through *vb* **:** to survive a very difficult or dangerous period

pul·mo·nary *adj* **:** of or relating to the lungs

1pulp *n* **1 :** the soft juicy part of a fruit or vegetable **2 :** a mass of vegetable matter from which the moisture has been squeezed **3 :** the soft sensitive tissue inside a tooth **4 :** a material prepared usually from wood or rags and used in making paper

2pulp *vb* **:** to make into a pulp

pul·pit *n* **1 :** a raised place in which a clergyman stands while preaching or conducting a religious service **2 :** preachers in general

pulp·wood *n* **:** wood (as of aspen or spruce) from which wood pulp is made

pulpy *adj* **pulp·i·er; pulp·i·est :** like or made of pulp

pul·sate *vb* **pul·sat·ed; pul·sat·ing :** to have or show a pulse or beats

pul·sa·tion *n* **:** pulsating movement or action

pulse *n* **1 :** a regular beating or throbbing (as of the arteries) **2 :** one complete beat of a pulse or the number of these in a given period (as a minute)

pul·ver·ize *vb* **pul·ver·ized; pul·ver·iz·ing :** to beat or grind into a powder or dust

pu·ma *n* **:** COUGAR

pum·ice *n* **:** a very light porous volcanic glass that is used in powder form for smoothing and polishing

pum·mel *vb* **pum·meled** *or* **pum·melled; pum·mel·ing** *or* **pum·mel·ling :** to strike again and again

1pump *n* **:** a device for raising, moving, or compressing fluids

2pump *vb* **1 :** to raise, move, or compress by using a pump **2 :** to free (as from water or air) by the use of a pump **3 :** to fill by using a pump **4 :** to draw, force, or drive onward in the manner of a pump **5 :** to question again and again to find out something — **pump·er** *n*

pum·per·nick·el *n* **:** a dark rye bread

pump·kin *n* **:** a large round orange or yellow fruit of a vine related to the squash vine that is used as a vegetable or as feed for farm animals

1pun *n* **:** a form of joking in which a person uses a word in two senses

2pun *vb* **punned; pun·ning :** to make a pun

1punch *vb* **1 :** to care for (range cattle) **2 :** to strike with the fist **3 :** to press or strike by or as if by punching **4 :** to pierce or stamp with a punch

²punch *n* **:** a blow with or as if with the fist
³punch *n* **:** a tool for piercing, stamping, or cutting
⁴punch *n* **:** a drink containing several things and often including wine or liquor
punc·tu·al *adj* **:** acting at the right time **:** not late
punc·tu·ate *vb* **punc·tu·at·ed; punc·tu·at·ing :** to mark or divide with punctuation marks
punc·tu·a·tion *n* **1 :** the act of punctuating **2 :** a system of using marks (**punctuation marks**) such as commas and periods to make clear the meaning of written matter
¹punc·ture *n* **1 :** an act of puncturing **2 :** a hole or wound made by puncturing
²puncture *vb* **punc·tured; punc·tur·ing 1 :** to pierce with something pointed **2 :** to make useless or destroy as if by a puncture
pun·gent *adj* **:** giving a sharp or biting sensation — **pun·gent·ly** *adv*
pun·ish *vb* **1 :** to make suffer for a fault or crime **2 :** to make someone suffer for (as a crime)
pun·ish·able *adj* **:** deserving to be punished
pun·ish·ment *n* **1 :** the act of punishing **:** the state or fact of being punished **2 :** the penalty for a fault or crime
¹punk *n* **:** a petty gangster or hoodlum
²punk *adj* **1 :** poor in quality **2 :** UNWELL, SICK
¹punt *vb* **:** to kick a ball dropped from the hands before it hits the ground — **punt·er** *n*
²punt *n* **:** an act or instance of punting a ball
pu·ny *adj* **pu·ni·er; pu·ni·est :** small and weak in size or power
pup *n* **1 :** PUPPY **2 :** one of the young of any of several animals (as a seal)
pu·pa *n, pl* **pu·pae** *or* **pupas :** an insect (as a bee, moth, or beetle) in an intermediate inactive stage of its growth in which it is enclosed in a cocoon or case
pu·pal *adj* **:** of, relating to, or being a pupa
¹pu·pil *n* **:** a child in school or under the care of a teacher
²pupil *n* **:** the opening in the iris through which light enters the eye
pup·pet *n* **1 :** a doll moved by hand or by strings or wires **2 :** one (as a person or government) whose acts are controlled by another
pup·py *n, pl* **puppies :** a young dog
¹pur·chase *vb* **pur·chased; pur·chas·ing :** to get by paying money
²purchase *n* **1 :** an act of purchasing **2 :** something purchased **3 :** a firm hold or grasp or a safe place to stand
pure *adj* **pur·er; pur·est 1 :** not mixed with anything else **:** free from everything that might injure or lower the quality **2 :** free from sin **:** INNOCENT, CHASTE **3 :** nothing other than **:** ABSOLUTE — **pure·ly** *adv* — **pure·ness** *n*
pure·bred *adj* **:** bred from ancestors of a single breed for many generations
¹purge *vb* **purged; purg·ing 1 :** to make clean **2 :** to have or cause frequent bowel movements **3 :** to get rid of
²purge *n* **1 :** an act or instance of purging **2 :** the removal of members thought to be treacherous or disloyal
pu·ri·fi·ca·tion *n* **:** an act or instance of purifying or of being purified
pu·ri·fy *vb* **pu·ri·fied; pu·ri·fy·ing :** to make pure **:** free from impurities
pu·ri·tan *n* **1** *cap* **:** a member of a sixteenth and seventeenth century Protestant group in England and New England opposing formal customs of the Church of England **2 :** a person who practices or preaches or follows a stricter moral code than most people
pu·ri·ty *n* **1 :** freedom from dirt or impurities **2 :** freedom from sin or guilt
pur·ple *n* **:** a color between red and blue
pur·plish *adj* **:** somewhat purple
¹pur·pose *n* **:** something set up as a goal to be achieved **:** INTENTION, AIM — **on purpose :** PURPOSELY
²purpose *vb* **pur·posed; pur·pos·ing :** to have as one's intention **:** INTEND
pur·pose·ful *adj* **:** having a clear purpose or aim — **pur·pose·ful·ly** *adv* — **pur·pose·ful·ness** *n*
pur·pose·ly *adv* **:** with a clear or known purpose
purr *vb* **:** to make the low murmuring sound of a contented cat or a similar sound
¹purse *n* **1 :** a bag or pouch for money **2 :** HANDBAG **3 :** the contents of a purse **:** MONEY 1 **4 :** a sum of money offered as a prize or collected as a present
²purse *vb* **pursed; purs·ing :** to draw into folds
pur·sue *vb* **pur·sued; pur·su·ing 1 :** to follow after in order to catch or destroy **:** CHASE **2 :** to follow with an end in view **3 :** to go on with **:** FOLLOW — **pur·su·er** *n*
pur·suit *n* **1 :** the act of pursuing **2 :** ACTIVITY 2, OCCUPATION
pus *n* **:** thick yellowish matter (as in an abscess or a boil)
¹push *vb* **1 :** to press against with force so as to drive or move away **2 :** to force forward, downward, or outward **3 :** to go or make go ahead
²push *n* **1 :** a sudden thrust **:** SHOVE **2 :** a steady applying of force in a direction away from the body from which it comes
push button *n* **:** a small button or knob that

when pushed operates something usually by closing an electric circuit

push·cart *n* **:** a cart pushed by hand

push·over *n* **1 :** an opponent that is easy to defeat **2 :** something easily done

pushy *adj* **push·i·er; push·i·est :** too aggressive **:** FORWARD

puss *n* **:** CAT 1

pussy *n, pl* **puss·ies :** CAT 1

pussy willow *n* **:** a willow with large silky catkins

put *vb* **put; put·ting 1 :** to place in or move into a particular position **2 :** to bring into a specified state or condition **3 :** to cause to stand for or suffer something **4 :** to give expression to **5 :** to give up to or urge to an activity **6 :** to think something to have **:** ATTRIBUTE **7 :** to begin a voyage — **put forward :** PROPOSE 1

put away *vb* **1 :** to give up **:** DISCARD **2 :** to take in food and drink

put by *vb* **:** to lay aside **:** SAVE

put down *vb* **1 :** to bring to an end by force **2 :** to consider to belong to a particular class or to be due to a particular cause

put in *vb* **1 :** to ask for **2 :** to spend time in a place or activity

put off *vb* **:** DEFER

put on *vb* **1 :** to dress oneself in **2 :** PRETEND 2, SHAM **3 :** 1PRODUCE 4

put down *vb* **1 :** to bring to an end by force **2 :** to consider to belong to a particular class or to be due to a particular cause

put in *vb* **1 :** to ask for **2 :** to spend time in a place or activity

put off *vb* **:** DEFER

put on *vb* **1 :** to dress oneself in **2 :** PRETEND 2, SHAM **3 :** 1PRODUCE 4

put·out *n* **:** the causing of a batter or runner to be out in baseball

put out *vb* **1 :** to make use of **2 :** EXTINGUISH 1 **3 :** 1MAKE 2 **4 :** IRRITATE 1, ANNOY **5 :** to cause to be out (as in baseball)

pu·trid *adj* **1 :** ROTTEN 1 **2 :** coming from or suggesting something rotten

put·ter *vb* **:** to act or work without much purpose

put through *vb* **:** to conclude with success

1put·ty *n, pl* **putties :** a soft cement (as for holding glass in a window frame)

2putty *vb* **put·tied; put·ty·ing :** to cement or seal up with putty

put up *vb* **1 :** to make (as food) ready or safe for later use **2 :** NOMINATE **3 :** to give or get shelter and often food **4 :** 1BUILD 1 **5 :** to make by action or effort — **put up to :** to urge or cause to do something wrong or unexpected — **put up with :** to stand for **:** TOLERATE

1puz·zle *vb* **puz·zled; puz·zling 1 :** CONFUSE 1, PERPLEX **2 :** to solve by thought or by clever guessing

2puzzle *n* **1 :** something that puzzles **:** MYSTERY **2 :** a question, problem, or device intended to test one's skill or cleverness

1pyg·my *also* **pig·my** *n, pl* **pygmies** *also* **pigmies :** a person or thing very small for its kind **:** DWARF

2pygmy *adj* **:** very small

1pyr·a·mid *n* **1 :** a large structure built especially in ancient Egypt that usually has a square base and four triangular sides meeting at a point and that contains tombs **2 :** something that has the shape of a pyramid **3 :** a solid with a polygon for its base and three or more triangles for its sides which meet to form the top

2pyramid *vb* **:** to build up in the form of a pyramid

pyre *n* **:** a heap of wood for burning a dead body

py·thon *n* **:** any of various large snakes of the Old World tropics that are related to the boas

Q

q *n, pl* **q's** *or* **qs** *often cap* **:** the seventeenth letter of the English alphabet

1quack *vb* **:** to make the cry of a duck

2quack *n* **:** a cry made by or as if by quacking

3quack *n* **:** an ignorant person who pretends to have medical knowledge and skill

4quack *adj* **1 :** of, relating to, or like that of a quack **2 :** pretending to cure disease

quadri- *or* **quadr-** *or* **quadru-** *prefix* **1 :** four **2 :** fourth

quad·ri·lat·er·al *n* **:** a figure of four sides and four angles

quad·ru·ped *n* **:** an animal having four feet

qua·dru·plet *n* **1 :** one of four offspring born at one birth **2 :** a combination of four of a kind

1quail *n, pl* **quail** *or* **quails :** any of various mostly small plump game birds (as the bobwhite) that are related to the chicken

2quail *vb* **:** to lose courage **:** shrink in fear

quaint *adj* **1 :** being or looking unusual or different **2 :** pleasingly old-fashioned or unfamiliar — **quaint·ly** *adv* — **quaint·ness** *n*

1quake *vb* **quaked; quak·ing 1 :** to shake usually from shock or lack of stability **2 :** to tremble or shudder usually from cold or fear

[2]quake *n* **:** an instance (as an earthquake) of shaking or trembling

qual·i·fi·ca·tion *n* **1 :** the act or an instance of qualifying **2 :** the state of being qualified **3 :** a special skill, knowledge, or ability that fits a person for a particular work or position **4 :** LIMITATION 1

qual·i·fy *vb* **qual·i·fied; qual·i·fy·ing 1 :** to narrow down or make less general in meaning **:** LIMIT **2 :** to make less harsh or strict **:** SOFTEN **3 :** to fit by training, skill, or ability for a special purpose **4 :** to show the skill or ability needed to be on a team or take part in a contest

qual·i·ty *n, pl* **qual·i·ties 1 :** basic and individual nature **2 :** how good or bad something is **3 :** high social rank **4 :** what sets a person or thing apart **:** CHARACTERISTIC

qualm *n* **1 :** a sudden attack of illness, faintness, or nausea **2 :** a sudden fear **3 :** a feeling of doubt or uncertainty that one's behavior is honest or right — **qualm·ish** *adj*

quan·da·ry *n, pl* **quan·da·ries :** a state of doubt or puzzled confusion

quan·ti·ty *n, pl* **quan·ti·ties 1 :** [2]AMOUNT, NUMBER **2 :** a large number or amount

[1]quar·an·tine *n* **1 :** a halting or forbidding of the moving of people or things out of a certain area to prevent the spread of disease or pests **2 :** a period during which a person with a contagious disease is under quarantine **3 :** a place (as a hospital) where persons are kept in quarantine

[2]quarantine *vb* **quar·an·tined; quar·an·tin·ing :** to put or hold in quarantine

[1]quar·rel *n* **1 :** a cause of disagreement or complaint **2 :** an angry difference of opinion

[2]quarrel *vb* **quar·reled** *or* **quar·relled; quar·rel·ing** *or* **quar·rel·ling 1 :** to find fault **2 :** to argue actively **:** SQUABBLE

quar·rel·some *adj* **:** usually ready to quarrel

[1]quar·ry *n, pl* **quar·ries :** an animal or bird hunted as game or prey

[2]quarry *n, pl* **quar·ries :** an open pit usually for obtaining building stone, slate, or limestone

[3]quarry *vb* **quar·ried; quar·ry·ing 1 :** to dig or take from or as if from a quarry **2 :** to make a quarry in — **quar·ri·er** *n*

quart *n* **:** a measure of capacity that equals two pints (about .95 liter)

[1]quar·ter *n* **1 :** one of four equal parts into which something can be divided **2 :** a United States coin worth twenty-five cents **3 :** someone or something (as a place, direction, or group) not clearly identified **4 :** a particular division or district of a city **5 quarters** *pl* **:** a dwelling place **6 :** MERCY 1

[2]quarter *vb* **1 :** to divide into four usually equal parts **2 :** to provide with lodgings or shelter

[3]quarter *adj* **:** consisting of or equal to a quarter

quar·ter·deck *n* **:** the part of the upper deck that is located toward the rear of a ship

quarter horse *n* **:** a stocky muscular saddle horse capable of high speed over short distances

[1]quar·ter·ly *adv* **:** four times a year

[2]quarterly *adj* **:** coming or happening every three months

[3]quarterly *n, pl* **quar·ter·lies :** a magazine published four times a year

quar·ter·mas·ter *n* **:** an army officer who provides clothing and supplies for troops

quar·tet *also* **quar·tette** *n* **:** a group or set of four

quartz *n* **:** a common mineral often found in the form of colorless transparent crystals but sometimes (as in amethysts, agates, and jaspers) brightly colored

qua·ver *vb* **1 :** [1]TREMBLE 1, SHAKE **2 :** to sound in shaky tones

quay *n* **:** a paved bank or a solid artificial landing for loading and unloading ships

quea·sy *adj* **quea·si·er; quea·si·est 1 :** somewhat nauseated **2 :** full of doubt

queen *n* **1 :** the wife or widow of a king **2 :** a woman who rules a kingdom in her own right **3 :** a woman of high rank, power, or attractiveness **4 :** the most powerful piece in the game of chess **5 :** a playing card bearing the figure of a queen **6 :** a fully developed adult female of social bees, ants, or termites — **queen·ly** *adj*

queer *adj* **:** oddly unlike the usual or normal — **queer·ly** *adv*

quell *vb* **1 :** to put down by force **2 :** [4]QUIET 1, CALM

quench *vb* **1 :** to put out (as a fire) **2 :** to end by satisfying

[1]que·ry *n, pl* **queries 1 :** [1]QUESTION 1 **2 :** a question in the mind **:** DOUBT

[2]query *vb* **que·ried; que·ry·ing 1 :** to put as a question **2 :** to ask questions about especially in order to clear up a doubt **3 :** to ask questions of especially to obtain official or expert information

[1]quest *n* **:** an act or instance of seeking **:** SEARCH

[2]quest *vb* **:** to search for

[1]ques·tion *n* **1 :** something asked **2 :** a topic discussed or argued about **3 :** a suggestion to be voted on **4 :** an act or instance of asking **5 :** OBJECTION 1, DISPUTE

[2]question *vb* **1 :** to ask questions of or about **2 :** to doubt the correctness of

ques·tion·able *adj* **1 :** not certain or exact

: DOUBTFUL **2 :** not believed to be true, sound, or proper

question mark *n* **:** a punctuation mark ? used chiefly at the end of a sentence to indicate a direct question

ques·tion·naire *n* **:** a set of questions to be asked of a number of persons to collect facts about knowledge or opinions

1queue *n* **1 :** PIGTAIL **2 :** a waiting line

2queue *vb* **queued; queu·ing** *or* **queue·ing :** to form or line up in a queue

quib·ble *vb* **quib·bled; quib·bling 1 :** to talk about unimportant things rather than the main point **2 :** to find fault especially over unimportant points — **quib·bler** *n*

1quick *adj* **1 :** very swift **:** SPEEDY **2 :** mentally alert **3 :** easily stirred up — **quick·ly** *adv* — **quick·ness** *n*

2quick *n* **1 :** a very tender area of flesh (as under a fingernail) **2 :** one's innermost feelings

3quick *adv* **:** in a quick manner **:** FAST

quick·en *vb* **1 :** REVIVE 1 **2 :** AROUSE 2 **3 :** to make or become quicker **:** HASTEN **4 :** to begin or show active growth

quick·sand *n* **:** a deep mass of loose sand mixed with water into which heavy objects sink

quick·sil·ver *n* **:** MERCURY 1

quick–tem·pered *adj* **:** easily made angry

quick–wit·ted *adj* **:** mentally alert

1qui·et *n* **:** the quality or state of being quiet

2quiet *adj* **1 :** marked by little or no motion or activity **:** CALM **2 :** GENTLE 2, MILD **3 :** not disturbed **:** PEACEFUL **4 :** free from noise or uproar **:** STILL **5 :** not showy (as in color or style) **6 :** SECLUDED — **qui·et·ly** *adv* — **qui·et·ness** *n*

3quiet *adv* **:** in a quiet manner **:** QUIETLY

4quiet *vb* **1 :** to cause to be quiet **:** CALM **2 :** to become quiet

qui·etude *n* **:** the state of being quiet **:** REST

quill *n* **1 :** a large stiff feather **2 :** the hollow tubelike part of a feather **3 :** a spine of a hedgehog or porcupine **4 :** a pen made from a feather

1quilt *n* **:** a bed cover made of two pieces of cloth with a filling of wool, cotton, or down held together by patterned stitching

2quilt *vb* **:** to stitch or sew together as in making a quilt

quince *n* **:** a hard yellow fruit that grows on a shrubby tree related to the apple and is used especially in preserves

qui·nine *n* **:** a bitter drug obtained from cinchona bark and used to treat malaria

quin·tet *n* **:** a group or set of five

quin·tu·plet *n* **1 :** a combination of five of a kind **2 :** one of five offspring born at one birth

quirk *n* **:** a sudden turn, twist, or curve

quit *vb* **quit; quit·ting :** to finish doing, using, dealing with, working on, or handling **:** LEAVE

quite *adv* **1 :** beyond question or doubt **:** COMPLETELY **2 :** more or less **:** RATHER

quit·ter *n* **:** a person who gives up too easily

1quiv·er *n* **:** a case for carrying arrows

2quiver *vb* **:** to move with a slight trembling motion

3quiver *n* **:** the act or action of quivering

1quiz *n, pl* **quiz·zes :** a short oral or written test

2quiz *vb* **quizzed; quiz·zing :** to ask a lot of questions of

quoit *n* **:** a ring (as of rope) tossed at a peg in a game (**quoits**)

quo·rum *n* **:** the number of members of a group needed at a meeting in order for business to be legally carried on

quo·ta *n* **:** a share assigned to each member of a group

quo·ta·tion *n* **1 :** material (as a passage from a book) that is quoted **2 :** the act or process of quoting

quotation mark *n* **:** one of a pair of punctuation marks " " or ' ' used chiefly to indicate the beginning and end of a direct quotation

quote *vb* **quot·ed; quot·ing :** to repeat (someone else's words) exactly

quo·tient *n* **:** the number obtained by dividing one number by another

R

r *n, pl* **r's** *or* **rs** *often cap* **:** the eighteenth letter of the English alphabet

rab·bi *n, pl* **rab·bis 1 :** 1MASTER 1, TEACHER — used as a term of address for Jewish religious leaders **2 :** a professionally trained leader of a Jewish congregation

rab·bit *n* **:** a gnawing mammal that burrows and is smaller and has shorter ears than the related hare

rab·ble *n* **1 :** a crowd that is noisy and hard to control **:** MOB **2 :** a group of people looked down upon as ignorant and hard to handle

ra·bid *adj* **1 :** very angry **:** FURIOUS **2 :** going to extreme lengths (as in interest or opinion) **3 :** affected with rabies — **ra·bid·ly** *adv* — **ra·bid·ness** *n*

ra·bies *n* **:** a deadly disease of the nervous

system caused by a virus that is usually passed on through the bite of an infected animal

rac·coon *n* **:** a small North American animal that lives in trees, eats flesh, is active mostly at night, and is sometimes hunted for sport, for its edible flesh, or for its coat of long fluffy fur

¹race *n* **1 :** a strong or rapid current of water **2 :** a contest of speed **3 :** a contest involving progress toward a goal

²race *vb* **raced; rac·ing 1 :** to take part in a race **2 :** to go, move, or drive at top speed **3 :** to cause an engine of a motor vehicle in neutral to run fast

³race *n* **1 :** a group of individuals with the same ancestors **2 :** one of the three, four, or five great divisions based on easily seen things (as skin color) into which human beings are usually divided

race·course *n* **:** a place for racing

race·horse *n* **:** a horse bred or kept for racing

rac·er *n* **1 :** one that races or is used for racing **2 :** any of several long slender active snakes (as a common American blacksnake)

race·track *n* **:** a usually oval course on which races are run

ra·cial *adj* **:** of, relating to, or based on race — **ra·cial·ly** *adv*

¹rack *n* **1 :** an instrument of torture for stretching the body **2 :** a frame or stand for storing or displaying things

²rack *vb* **1 :** to cause to suffer torture, pain, or sorrow **2 :** to stretch or strain violently

¹rack·et *n* **:** a light bat consisting of a handle and a frame with a netting stretched tight across it

²racket *n* **1 :** a loud confused noise **2 :** a dishonest scheme for obtaining money (as by cheating or threats)

rack·e·teer *n* **:** a person who gets money or advantages by using force or threats

racy *adj* **rac·i·er; rac·i·est :** full of energy or keen enjoyment

ra·dar *n* **:** a radio device for detecting the position of things in the distance and the direction of moving objects (as distant airplanes or ships)

ra·di·ance *n* **:** the quality or state of being radiant **:** SPLENDOR

ra·di·ant *adj* **1 :** giving out or reflecting rays of light **2 :** glowing with love, confidence, or joy **3 :** transmitted by radiation

radiant energy *n* **:** energy sent out in the form of electromagnetic waves

ra·di·ate *vb* **ra·di·at·ed; ra·di·at·ing 1 :** to send out rays **:** SHINE **2 :** to come forth in the form of rays **3 :** to spread around from or as if from a center

ra·di·a·tion *n* **1 :** the process of radiating and especially of giving off radiant energy in the form of waves or particles **2 :** something that is radiated

ra·di·a·tor *n* **:** a device to heat air (as in a room) or to cool an object (as an automobile engine)

¹rad·i·cal *adj* **1 :** departing sharply from the usual or ordinary **:** EXTREME **2 :** of or relating to radicals in politics — **rad·i·cal·ly** *adv*

²radical *n* **:** a person who favors rapid and sweeping changes especially in laws and methods of government

radii *pl of* RADIUS

¹ra·dio *adj* **1 :** of or relating to radiant energy **2 :** of, relating to, or used in radio

²radio *n, pl* **ra·di·os 1 :** the sending or receiving of signals by means of electromagnetic waves without a connecting wire **2 :** a radio receiving set **3 :** a radio message **4 :** the radio broadcasting industry

³radio *vb* **:** to communicate or send a message to by radio

ra·dio·ac·tive *adj* **:** of, caused by, or exhibiting radioactivity

ra·dio·ac·tiv·i·ty *n* **:** the giving off of rays of energy or particles by the breaking apart of atoms of certain elements (as uranium)

radio wave *n* **:** an electromagnetic wave used in radio, television, or radar communication

rad·ish *n* **:** the fleshy edible root of a plant related to the mustards

ra·di·um *n* **:** a strongly radioactive element found in very small quantities in various minerals (as pitchblende) and used in the treatment of cancer

ra·di·us *n, pl* **ra·dii 1 :** the bone on the thumb side of the human forearm or a corresponding bone in lower forms **2 :** a straight line extending from the center of a circle to the circumference or from the center of a sphere to the surface **3 :** a nearly circular area defined by a radius

raf·fle *n* **:** the sale of chances for a prize whose winner is the one whose ticket is picked at a drawing

¹raft *n* **:** a flat structure (as a group of logs fastened together) for support or transportation on water

²raft *n* **:** a large amount or number

raf·ter *n* **:** one of the usually sloping timbers that support a roof

rag *n* **1 :** a waste or worn piece of cloth **2 rags** *pl* **:** shabby or very worn clothing

rag·a·muf·fin *n* **:** a poorly clothed and often dirty child

¹rage *n* **1 :** very strong and uncontrolled anger **:** FURY **2 :** violent action (as of wind or sea) **3 :** FAD

DICTIONARY

²rage *vb* **raged; rag•ing** **1 :** to be in a rage **2 :** to continue out of control

rag•ged *adj* **1 :** having a rough or uneven edge or outline **2 :** very worn **:** TATTERED **3 :** wearing tattered clothes **4 :** done in an uneven way — **rag•ged•ly** *adv* — **rag•ged•ness** *n*

rag•gedy *adj* **:** RAGGED 2, 3

rag•man *n, pl* **rag•men :** a collector of or dealer in rags

rag•time *n* **:** jazz music that has a lively melody and a steady rhythm like a march

rag•weed *n* **:** a common coarse weed with pollen that irritates the eyes and noses of some persons

¹raid *n* **:** a sudden attack or invasion

²raid *vb* **:** to make a raid on — **raid•er** *n*

¹rail *n* **1 :** a bar extending from one support to another and serving as a guard or barrier **2 :** a bar of steel forming a track for wheeled vehicles **3 :** RAILROAD

²rail *vb* **:** to provide with a railing

³rail *n* **:** any of a family of wading birds related to the cranes and hunted as game birds

⁴rail *vb* **:** to scold or complain in harsh or bitter language

rail•ing *n* **1 :** a barrier (as a fence) made up of rails and their supports **2 :** material for making rails

rail•lery *n, pl* **rail•ler•ies :** an act or instance of making fun of someone in a good-natured way

¹rail•road *n* **1 :** a permanent road that has parallel steel rails that make a track for cars **2 :** a railroad together with the lands, buildings, locomotives, cars, and other equipment that belong to it

²railroad *vb* **:** to work on a railroad

rail•way *n* **:** ¹RAILROAD 1

rai•ment *n* **:** CLOTHING 1

¹rain *n* **1 :** water falling in drops from the clouds **2 :** a fall of rain **3 :** rainy weather **4 :** a heavy fall of objects

²rain *vb* **1 :** to fall as water in drops from the clouds **2 :** to send down rain **3 :** to fall like rain **4 :** to give in large amounts — **rain cats and dogs :** to rain very hard

rain•bow *n* **:** an arc of colors that appears in the sky opposite the sun and is caused by the sun shining through rain, mist, or spray

rain•coat *n* **:** a coat of waterproof or water-resistant material

rain•drop *n* **:** a drop of rain

rain•fall *n* **1 :** ¹RAIN 2 **2 :** amount of precipitation

rain forest *n* **:** a woodland with a high annual rainfall and very tall trees and that is often found in tropical regions

rain•proof *adj* **:** not letting in rain

rain•storm *n* **:** a storm of or with rain

rain•wa•ter *n* **:** water falling or fallen as rain

rainy *adj* **rain•i•er; rain•i•est :** having much rain

¹raise *vb* **raised; rais•ing** **1 :** to cause to rise **:** LIFT **2 :** to give life to **:** AROUSE **3 :** to set upright by lifting or building **4 :** PROMOTE 1, ELEVATE **5 :** ²END **6 :** COLLECT 2 **7 :** to look after the growth and development of **:** GROW **8 :** to bring up a child **:** REAR **9 :** to give rise to **:** PROVOKE **10 :** to bring to notice **11 :** ¹INCREASE **12 :** to make light and airy **13 :** to cause to form on the skin — **rais•er** *n*

²raise *n* **:** an increase in amount (as of pay)

rai•sin *n* **:** a sweet grape dried for food

ra•ja *or* **ra•jah** *n* **:** an Indian prince

¹rake *n* **:** a garden tool with a long handle and a bar with teeth or prongs at the end

²rake *vb* **raked; rak•ing** **1 :** to gather, loosen, or smooth with a rake **2 :** to search through **:** RANSACK **3 :** to sweep the length of with gunfire

³rake *n* **:** a person with bad morals and conduct

¹ral•ly *vb* **ral•lied; ral•ly•ing** **1 :** to bring or come together for a common purpose **2 :** to bring back to order **3 :** to rouse from low spirits or weakness **4 :** ¹REBOUND 2

²rally *n, pl* **rallies** **1 :** the act of rallying **2 :** a big meeting held to arouse enthusiasm

¹ram *n* **1 :** a male sheep **2 :** BATTERING RAM

²ram *vb* **rammed; ram•ming** **1 :** to strike or strike against with violence **2 :** to force in, down, or together by driving or pressing **3 :** ²FORCE 2

RAM *n* **:** RANDOM-ACCESS MEMORY

Ram•a•dan *n* **:** the ninth month of the Islamic calendar observed as sacred with fasting practiced daily from dawn to sunset

¹ram•ble *vb* **ram•bled; ram•bling** **1 :** to go aimlessly from place to place **:** WANDER **2 :** to talk or write without a clear purpose or point **3 :** to grow or extend irregularly

²ramble *n* **:** a long stroll with no particular destination

ram•bler *n* **:** a hardy climbing rose with large clusters of small flowers

ram•bunc•tious *adj* **:** UNRULY — **ram•bunc•tious•ly** *adv* — **ram•bunc•tious•ness** *n*

ram•i•fi•ca•tion *n* **1 :** a branching out **2 :** one thing that comes from another like a branch

ram•i•fy *vb* **ram•i•fied; ram•i•fy•ing :** to spread out or split up into branches or divisions

ramp *n* **:** a sloping passage or roadway connecting different levels

ram•page *n* **:** a course of violent or reckless action or behavior

ram•pant *adj* **:** not checked in growth or spread — **ram•pant•ly** *adv*
ram•part *n* **:** a broad bank or wall raised as a protective barrier
ram•rod *n* **:** a rod for ramming the charge down the barrel in a firearm that is loaded through the muzzle
ram•shack•le *adj* **:** ready to fall down
ran *past of* RUN
¹ranch *n* **1 :** a place for the raising of livestock (as cattle) on range **2 :** a farm devoted to a special crop
²ranch *vb* **:** to live or work on a ranch — **ranch•er** *n*
ran•cid *adj* **:** having the strong disagreeable smell or taste of stale oil or fat — **ran•cid•ness** *n*
ran•cor *n* **:** deep hatred
ran•cor•ous *adj* **:** showing rancor — **ran•cor•ous•ly** *adv*
ran•dom *adj* **:** lacking a clear plan, purpose, or pattern — **ran•dom•ly** *adv* — **ran•dom•ness** *n*
ran•dom–ac•cess *adj* **:** permitting access to stored data in any order the user desires
random–access memory *n* **:** a computer memory that provides the main storage available to the user for programs and data
rang *past of* RING
¹range *n* **1 :** a series of things in a line **2 :** a cooking stove **3 :** open land over which livestock may roam and feed **4 :** the distance a gun will shoot **5 :** a place where shooting is practiced **6 :** the distance or amount included or gone over **:** SCOPE **7 :** a variety of choices within a scale
²range *vb* **ranged; rang•ing 1 :** to set in a row or in proper order **2 :** to set in place among others of the same kind **3 :** to roam over or through **4 :** to come within an upper and a lower limit
rang•er *n* **1 :** FOREST RANGER **2 :** a member of a body of troops who range over a region **3 :** a soldier specially trained in close-range fighting and in raiding tactics
rangy *adj* **rang•i•er; rang•i•est :** tall and slender in body build — **rang•i•ness** *n*
¹rank *adj* **1 :** strong and active in growth **2 :** ¹EXTREME 1 **3 :** having an unpleasant smell — **rank•ly** *adv* — **rank•ness** *n*
²rank *n* **1 :** ³ROW 1, SERIES **2 :** a line of soldiers standing side by side **3 ranks** *pl* **:** the body of enlisted persons in an army **4 :** position within a group **5 :** high social position **6 :** official grade or position
³rank *vb* **1 :** to arrange in lines or in a formation **2 :** to arrange in a classification **3 :** to take or have a certain position in a group
ran•kle *vb* **ran•kled; ran•kling :** to cause anger, irritation, or bitterness
ran•sack *vb* **1 :** to search thoroughly **2 :** to search through in order to rob
¹ran•som *n* **1 :** something paid or demanded for the freedom of a captured person **2 :** the act of ransoming
²ransom *vb* **:** to free from captivity or punishment by paying a price — **ran•som•er** *n*
rant *vb* **:** to talk loudly and wildly — **rant•er** *n*
¹rap *n* **:** a sharp blow or knock
²rap *vb* **rapped; rap•ping :** to give a quick sharp blow **:** ¹KNOCK 1
³rap *vb* **rapped; rap•ping 1 :** to talk freely and informally **2 :** to perform rap music
⁴rap *n* **1 :** an informal talk **:** CHAT **2 :** a rhythmic chanting often in unison of rhymed verses to a musical accompaniment
ra•pa•cious *adj* **1 :** very greedy **2 :** PREDATORY — **ra•pa•cious•ly** *adv* — **ra•pa•cious•ness** *n*
¹rape *n* **:** a plant related to the mustards that is grown for animals to graze on and for its seeds used as birdseed and as a source of oil
²rape *vb* **raped; rap•ing :** to have sexual intercourse with by force
³rape *n* **:** an act of raping
rap•id *adj* **:** very fast — **rap•id•ly** *adv*
ra•pid•i•ty *n* **:** the quality or state of being rapid
rap•ids *n pl* **:** a part of a river where the current flows very fast usually over rocks
ra•pi•er *n* **:** a straight sword with a narrow blade having two sharp edges
rap•port : friendly relationship **:** ACCORD
rapt *adj* **:** showing complete delight or interest
rap•ture *n* **:** a strong feeling of joy, delight, or love
¹rare *adj* **rar•er; rar•est 1 :** not thick or compact **:** THIN **2 :** very fine **:** EXCELLENT **3 :** very uncommon
²rare *adj* **rar•er; rar•est :** cooked so that the inside is still red
rar•e•fy *vb* **rar•e•fied; rar•e•fy•ing :** to make or become less dense or solid
rare•ly *adv* **:** not often **:** SELDOM
rar•i•ty *n, pl* **rar•i•ties 1 :** the quality, state, or fact of being rare **2 :** something that is uncommon
ras•cal *n* **1 :** a mean or dishonest person **2 :** a mischievous person
¹rash *adj* **:** too hasty in decision, action, or speech — **rash•ly** *adv* — **rash•ness** *n*
²rash *n* **:** a breaking out of the skin with red spots (as in measles)
¹rasp *vb* **1 :** to rub with or as if with a rough file **2 :** IRRITATE 1 **3 :** to make a harsh sound
²rasp *n* **1 :** a coarse file with cutting points

instead of lines **2 :** a rasping sound or sensation

rasp·ber·ry *n, pl* **rasp·ber·ries :** a sweet edible red, black, or purple berry

[1]**rat** *n* **1 :** a gnawing animal with brown, black, white, or grayish fur that looks like but is larger than the mouse **2 :** a person who betrays friends

[2]**rat** *vb* **rat·ted; rat·ting 1 :** to betray one's friends **2 :** to hunt or catch rats

[1]**rate** *n* **1 :** a price or charge set according to a scale or standard **2 :** amount of something measured in units of something else — **at any rate :** in any case

[2]**rate** *vb* **rat·ed; rat·ing 1 :** CONSIDER 3, REGARD **2 :** to have a rating **:** RANK **3 :** to have a right to **:** DESERVE

rath·er *adv* **1 :** more willingly **2 :** more correctly or truly **3 :** INSTEAD **4 :** [2]SOMEWHAT

rat·i·fi·ca·tion *n* **:** the act or process of ratifying

rat·i·fy *vb* **rat·i·fied; rat·i·fy·ing :** to give legal approval to (as by a vote)

rat·ing *n* **:** a position within a grading system

ra·tio *n, pl* **ra·tios :** the relationship in number or quantity between two or more things

[1]**ra·tion** *n* **1 :** a food allowance for one day **2 rations** *pl* **:** [1]PROVISION 3 **3 :** the amount one is allowed by authority

[2]**ration** *vb* **1 :** to control the amount one can use **2 :** to use sparingly

ra·tio·nal *adj* **1 :** having the ability to reason **2 :** relating to, based on, or showing reason — **ra·tio·nal·ly** *adv*

ra·tio·nale *n* **:** a basic explanation or reason for something

ra·tio·nal·ize *vb* **ra·tio·nal·ized; ra·tio·nal·iz·ing :** to find believable but untrue reasons for (one's conduct)

rat·ter *n* **:** a dog or cat that catches rats

[1]**rat·tle** *vb* **rat·tled; rat·tling 1 :** to make or cause to make a rapid series of short sharp sounds **2 :** to move with a clatter **3 :** to say or do in a brisk lively way **4 :** to disturb the calmness of **:** UPSET

[2]**rattle** *n* **1 :** a series of short sharp sounds **2 :** a device (as a toy) for making a rattling sound **3 :** a rattling organ at the end of a rattlesnake's tail

rat·tler *n* **:** RATTLESNAKE

rat·tle·snake *n* **:** a poisonous American snake with a rattle at the end of its tail

rat·tle·trap *n* **:** something (as an old car) rickety and full of rattles

rau·cous *adj* **1 :** being harsh and unpleasant **2 :** behaving in a rough and noisy way — **rau·cous·ly** *adv* — **rau·cous·ness** *n*

[1]**rav·age** *n* **:** violently destructive action or effect

[2]**ravage** *vb* **rav·aged; rav·ag·ing :** to attack or act upon with great violence — **rav·ag·er** *n*

rave *vb* **raved; rav·ing 1 :** to talk wildly or as if crazy **2 :** to talk with great enthusiasm

rav·el *vb* **rav·eled** *or* **rav·elled; rav·el·ing** *or* **rav·el·ling :** UNRAVEL 1

[1]**ra·ven** *n* **:** a large shiny black bird like a crow that is found in northern regions

[2]**raven** *adj* **:** shiny and black like a raven's feathers

rav·en·ous *adj* **:** very hungry — **rav·en·ous·ly** *adv*

ra·vine *n* **:** a small narrow valley with steep sides that is larger than a gully and smaller than a canyon

rav·ish *vb* **1 :** to seize and take away by force **2 :** to overcome with a feeling and especially one of joy or delight

raw *adj* **1 :** not cooked **2 :** being in or nearly in the natural state **3 :** lacking a normal or usual finish **4 :** having the skin rubbed off **5 :** not trained or experienced **6 :** unpleasantly damp or cold — **raw·ly** *adv* — **raw·ness** *n*

raw·hide *n* **1 :** a whip of untanned hide **2 :** untanned cattle skin

[1]**ray** *n* **:** a flat broad fish related to the sharks that has its eyes on the top of its head

[2]**ray** *n* **1 :** one of the lines of light that appear to be given off by a bright object **2 :** a thin beam of radiant energy (as light) **3 :** light cast in rays **4 :** any of a group of lines that spread out from the same center **5 :** a straight line extending from a point in one direction only **6 :** a plant or animal structure like a ray **7 :** a tiny bit **:** PARTICLE

ray·on *n* **:** a cloth made from fibers produced chemically from cellulose

raze *vb* **razed; raz·ing :** to destroy completely by knocking down or breaking to pieces **:** DEMOLISH

ra·zor *n* **:** a sharp cutting instrument used to shave off hair

razz *vb* **:** to make fun of **:** TEASE

re *n* **:** the second note of the musical scale

re- *prefix* **1 :** again **2 :** back **:** backward

[1]**reach** *vb* **1 :** to stretch out **:** EXTEND **2 :** to touch or move to touch or take by sticking out a part of the body (as the hand) or something held in the hand **3 :** to extend or stretch to **4 :** to arrive at **:** COME **5 :** to communicate with

[2]**reach** *n* **1 :** an unbroken stretch (as of a river) **2 :** the act of reaching especially to take hold of something **3 :** ability to stretch (as an arm) so as to touch something

re·act *vb* **1 :** to act or behave in response (as to stimulation or an influence) **2 :** to oppose a force or influence — usually used with against **3 :** to go through a chemical reaction

re·ac·tion *n* **1 :** an instance of reacting **2 :** a response (as of body or mind) to a stimulus (as a treatment, situation, or stress) **3 :** a chemical change that is brought about by the action of one substance on another and results in a new substance being formed

re·ac·tion·ary *adj* **:** of, relating to, or favoring old-fashioned political or social ideas

re·ac·tor *n* **1 :** one that reacts **2 :** a device using atomic energy to produce heat

read *vb* **read; read·ing 1 :** to understand language through written symbols for speech sounds **2 :** to speak aloud written or printed words **3 :** to learn from what one has seen in writing or printing **4 :** to discover or figure out the meaning of **5 :** to give meaning to **6 :** to show by letters or numbers — **read between the lines :** to understand more than is directly stated

read·able *adj* **:** able to be read easily

read·er *n* **1 :** one that reads **2 :** a book for learning or practicing reading

read·ing *n* **1 :** something read or for reading **2 :** the form in which something is written **:** VERSION **3 :** the number or fact shown on an instrument

read–only memory *n* **:** a usually small computer memory that contains special-purpose information (as a program) which cannot be changed

read·out *n* **1 :** information from an automatic device (as a computer) that is recorded (as on a disk) or presented in a form that can be seen **2 :** an electronic device that presents information in a form that can be seen

1ready *adj* **read·i·er; read·i·est 1 :** prepared for use or action **2 :** likely to do something **3 :** WILLING 1 **4 :** showing ease and promptness **5 :** available right away **:** HANDY — **read·i·ly** *adv* — **read·i·ness** *n*

2ready *vb* **read·ied; ready·ing :** to make ready **:** PREPARE

ready–made *adj* **:** made beforehand in large numbers

re·al *adj* **1 :** of, relating to, or made up of land and buildings **2 :** not artificial **:** GENUINE **3 :** not imaginary **:** ACTUAL — **re·al·ness** *n*

real estate *n* **:** property consisting of buildings and land

re·al·ism *n* **:** willingness to face facts or to give in to what is necessary

re·al·is·tic *adj* **1 :** true to life or nature **2 :** ready to see things as they really are and to deal with them sensibly — **re·al·is·ti·cal·ly** *adv*

re·al·i·ty *n, pl* **re·al·i·ties 1 :** actual existence **2 :** someone or something real or actual

re·al·iza·tion *n* **:** the action of realizing **:** the state of being realized

re·al·ize *vb* **re·al·ized; re·al·iz·ing 1 :** to bring into being **:** ACCOMPLISH **2 :** to get as a result of effort **:** GAIN **3 :** to be aware of **:** UNDERSTAND

re·al·ly *adv* **1 :** in fact **2 :** without question

realm *n* **1 :** KINGDOM 1 **2 :** field of activity or influence

real time *n* **:** the actual time during which something takes place — **real–time** *adj*

re·al·ty *n* **:** REAL ESTATE

1ream *n* **1 :** a quantity of paper that may equal 480, 500, or 516 sheets **2 reams** *pl* **:** a great amount

2ream *vb* **1 :** to shape or make larger with a reamer **2 :** to clean or clear with a reamer

ream·er *n* **:** a tool with cutting edges for shaping or enlarging a hole

reap *vb* **1 :** to cut (as grain) or clear (as a field) with a sickle, scythe, or machine **2 :** HARVEST

reap·er *n* **1 :** a worker who harvests crops **2 :** a machine for reaping grain

re·ap·pear *vb* **:** to appear again

1rear *vb* **1 :** to put up by building **:** CONSTRUCT **2 :** to raise or set on end **3 :** to take care of the breeding and raising of **4 :** BRING UP **5 :** to rise high **6 :** to rise up on the hind legs

2rear *n* **1 :** the part (as of an army) or area farthest from the enemy **2 :** the space or position at the back

3rear *adj* **:** being at the back

rear admiral *n* **:** a commissioned officer in the Navy or Coast Guard ranking above a captain

re·ar·range *vb* **re·ar·ranged; re·ar·rang·ing :** to arrange again usually in a different way

1rea·son *n* **1 :** a statement given to explain a belief or an act **2 :** a good basis **3 :** 1CAUSE 1 **4 :** the power to think **5 :** a sound mind

2reason *vb* **1 :** to talk with another so as to influence his or her actions or opinions **2 :** to use the power of reason

rea·son·able *adj* **1 :** not beyond what is usual or expected **:** MODERATE **2 :** 1CHEAP 1, INEXPENSIVE **3 :** able to reason — **rea·son·able·ness** *n* — **rea·son·ably** *adv*

re·as·sure *vb* **re·as·sured; re·as·sur·ing 1 :** to assure again **2 :** to give fresh confidence to **:** free from fear

1re·bate *vb* **re·bat·ed; re·bat·ing :** to make a rebate to or give as a rebate

2rebate *n* **:** a returning of part of a payment or of an amount owed

[1]reb·el *adj* **1 :** being or fighting against one's government or ruler **2 :** not obeying
[2]rebel *n* **:** a person who refuses to give in to authority
[3]re·bel *vb* **re·belled; re·bel·ling 1 :** to be or fight against authority and especially the authority of one's government **2 :** to feel or show anger or strong dislike
re·bel·lion *n* **1 :** open opposition to authority **2 :** an open fight against one's government
re·bel·lious *adj* **1 :** taking part in rebellion **2 :** tending to fight against or disobey authority — **re·bel·lious·ly** *adv* — **re·bel·lious·ness** *n*
re·birth *n* **1 :** a new or second birth **2 :** a return to importance
re·born *adj* **:** born again
[1]re·bound *vb* **1 :** to spring back on hitting something **2 :** to get over a disappointment
[2]re·bound *n* **1 :** the action of rebounding **:** RECOIL **2 :** an immediate reaction to a disappointment
[1]re·buff *vb* **:** to refuse or criticize sharply
[2]rebuff *n* **:** a refusal to meet an advance or offer
re·build *vb* **re·built; re·build·ing 1 :** to make many or important repairs to or changes in **2 :** to build again
[1]re·buke *vb* **re·buked; re·buk·ing :** to criticize severely
[2]rebuke *n* **:** an expression of strong disapproval
re·bus *n* **:** a riddle or puzzle made up of letters, pictures, and symbols whose names sound like the syllables and words of a phrase or sentence
re·but *vb* **re·but·ted; re·but·ting :** to prove to be wrong especially by argument or by proof that the opposite is right
[1]re·call *vb* **1 :** to ask or order to come back **2 :** to bring back to mind **3 :** CANCEL 2, REVOKE
[2]re·call *n* **1 :** a command to return **2 :** remembrance of what has been learned or experienced
re·cap·ture *vb* **re·cap·tured; re·cap·tur·ing 1 :** to capture again **2 :** to experience again
re·cede *vb* **re·ced·ed; re·ced·ing 1 :** to move back or away **2 :** to slant backward
[1]re·ceipt *n* **1 :** RECIPE **2 :** the act of receiving **3 receipts** *pl* **:** something received **4 :** a written statement saying that money or goods have been received
[2]receipt *vb* **1 :** to give a receipt for **2 :** to mark as paid
re·ceive *vb* **re·ceived; re·ceiv·ing 1 :** to take or get something that is given, paid, or sent **2 :** to let enter one's household or company **:** WELCOME **3 :** to be at home to visitors **4 :** [2]EXPERIENCE **5 :** to change incoming radio waves into sounds or pictures
re·ceiv·er *n* **1 :** one that receives **2 :** a device for changing electricity or radio waves into light or sound
re·cent *adj* **1 :** of or relating to a time not long past **2 :** having lately appeared to come into being **:** NEW, FRESH — **re·cent·ly** *adv* — **re·cent·ness** *n*
re·cep·ta·cle *n* **:** something used to receive and contain smaller objects
re·cep·tion *n* **1 :** the act or manner of receiving **2 :** a social gathering at which someone is often formally introduced or welcomed **3 :** the receiving of a radio or television broadcast
re·cep·tion·ist *n* **:** an office employee who greets callers
re·cep·tive *adj* **:** able or willing to receive ideas — **re·cep·tive·ly** *adv* — **re·cep·tive·ness** *n*
re·cep·tor *n* **:** a cell or group of cells that receives stimuli **:** SENSE ORGAN
[1]re·cess *n* **1 :** a secret or hidden place **2 :** a hollow cut or built into a surface (as a wall) **3 :** a brief period for relaxation between work periods
[2]recess *vb* **1 :** to put into a recess **2 :** to interrupt for or take a recess
re·ces·sion *n* **:** a period of reduced business activity
re·ces·sive *adj* **:** not dominant
rec·i·pe *n* **:** a set of instructions for making something (as a food dish) by combining various things
re·cip·i·ent *n* **:** one that receives
re·cip·ro·cal *n* **:** one of a pair of numbers (as 9 and $1/9$ or $2/3$ and $3/2$) whose product is one
re·cit·al *n* **1 :** a reciting of something **2 :** a public performance given by one musician **3 :** a public performance by music or dance pupils
rec·i·ta·tion *n* **1 :** a complete telling or listing of something **2 :** the reciting before an audience of something memorized **3 :** a student's oral reply to questions
re·cite *vb* **re·cit·ed; re·cit·ing 1 :** to repeat from memory **2 :** to tell about in detail **3 :** to answer questions about a lesson
reck·less *adj* **:** being or given to wild careless behavior — **reck·less·ly** *adv* — **reck·less·ness** *n*
reck·on *vb* **1 :** [1]COUNT 1, COMPUTE **2 :** to regard or think of as **:** CONSIDER
re·claim *vb* **1 :** to make better in behavior or character **:** REFORM **2 :** to change to a desirable condition or state **3 :** to obtain from a waste product or by-product
rec·la·ma·tion *n* **:** the act or process of reclaiming **:** the state of being reclaimed

re·cline *vb* **re·clined; re·clin·ing** **1 :** to lean backward **2 :** to lie down
rec·og·ni·tion *n* **1 :** the act of recognizing **2 :** special attention or notice
rec·og·nize *vb* **rec·og·nized; rec·og·niz·ing** **1 :** to know and remember upon seeing **2 :** to be willing to acknowledge **3 :** to take approving notice of **4 :** to show one is acquainted with
[1]**re·coil** *vb* **1 :** to draw back **2 :** to spring back to a former position
[2]**recoil** *n* **1 :** the act or action of recoiling **2 :** a springing back (as of a gun just fired) **3 :** the distance through which something (as a spring) recoils
rec·ol·lect *vb* **:** to call to mind **:** REMEMBER
rec·ol·lec·tion *n* **1 :** the act or power of recalling to mind **:** MEMORY **2 :** something remembered
rec·om·mend *vb* **1 :** to present or support as worthy or fit **2 :** to make acceptable **3 :** to make a suggestion **:** ADVISE
rec·om·men·da·tion *n* **1 :** the act of recommending **2 :** a thing or course of action recommended **3 :** something that recommends
[1]**rec·om·pense** *vb* **rec·om·pensed; rec·om·pens·ing :** to pay for or pay back
[2]**recompense** *n* **:** a return for something done, suffered, or given **:** PAYMENT
rec·on·cile *vb* **rec·on·ciled; rec·on·cil·ing** **1 :** to make friendly again **2 :** [1]SETTLE 7, ADJUST **3 :** to make agree **4 :** to cause to give in or accept
re·con·di·tion *vb* **:** to restore to good condition (as by repairing or replacing parts)
re·con·nais·sance *n* **:** a survey (as of enemy territory) to get information
re·con·noi·ter *vb* **:** to make a reconnaissance (as in preparation for military action)
re·con·sid·er *vb* **:** to consider again especially with a view to change
re·con·sid·er·a·tion *n* **:** the act of reconsidering **:** the state of being reconsidered
re·con·struct *vb* **:** to construct again **:** REBUILD, REMODEL
[1]**re·cord** *vb* **1 :** to set down in writing **2 :** to register permanently **3 :** to change sound or visual images into a form (as on magnetic tape) that can be listened to or watched at a later time
[2]**rec·ord** *n* **1 :** the state or fact of being recorded **2 :** something written to preserve an account **3 :** the known or recorded facts about a person or thing **4 :** a recorded top performance **5 :** something on which sound or visual images have been recorded
[3]**rec·ord** *adj* **:** outstanding among other like things
re·cord·er *n* **1 :** a person or device that records **2 :** a musical instrument like a long hollow whistle with eight finger holes
re·cord·ing *n* **:** [2]RECORD 5
[1]**re·count** *vb* **:** to tell all about **:** NARRATE
[2]**re·count** *vb* **:** to count again
[3]**re·count** *n* **:** a counting again (as of election votes)
re·course *n* **1 :** a turning for help or protection **2 :** a source of help or strength
re·cov·er *vb* **1 :** to get back **:** REGAIN **2 :** to regain normal health, self-confidence, or position **3 :** to make up for **4 :** RECLAIM 2
re–cov·er *vb* **:** to cover again
re·cov·ery *n, pl* **re·cov·er·ies :** the act, process, or an instance of recovering
rec·re·a·tion *n* **1 :** a refreshing of mind or body after work or worry **2 :** a means of refreshing mind or body
[1]**re·cruit** *vb* **1 :** to form or strengthen with new members **2 :** to get the services of **3 :** to restore or increase the health or vigor of
[2]**recruit** *n* **:** a newcomer to a field of activity
rect·an·gle *n* **:** a four-sided figure with right angles and with opposite sides parallel
rect·an·gu·lar *adj* **:** shaped like a rectangle
rec·ti·fy *vb* **rec·ti·fied; rec·ti·fy·ing :** to set or make right
rec·tor *n* **:** PASTOR
rec·tum *n, pl* **rec·tums** *or* **rec·ta :** the last part of the large intestine
re·cu·per·ate *vb* **re·cu·per·at·ed; re·cu·per·at·ing :** to regain health or strength
re·cu·per·a·tion *n* **:** a getting back to health or strength
re·cur *vb* **re·curred; re·cur·ring :** to occur or appear again
re·cur·rence *n* **:** the state of occurring again and again
re·cy·cla·ble *adj* **:** that can be recycled
re·cy·cle *vb* **re·cy·cled; re·cy·cling :** to process (as paper, glass, or cans) in order to regain materials for human use
[1]**red** *adj* **red·der; red·dest** **1 :** of the color red **2 :** of or relating to Communism or Communists — **red·ness** *n*
[2]**red** *n* **1 :** the color of fresh blood or of the ruby **2 :** something red in color **3 :** a person who seeks or favors revolution **4 :** COMMUNIST 2
red·bird *n* **:** any of several birds (as a cardinal) with mostly red feathers
red blood cell *n* **:** one of the tiny reddish cells of the blood that have no nuclei and carry oxygen from the lungs to the tissues
red·breast *n* **:** a bird (as a robin) with a reddish breast
red·cap *n* **:** PORTER 1
red cell *n* **:** RED BLOOD CELL
red·coat *n* **:** a British soldier especially during the Revolutionary War

red corpuscle *n* **:** RED BLOOD CELL
red·den *vb* **:** to make or become red
red·dish *adj* **:** somewhat red
re·deem *vb* **1 :** to buy back **2 :** to ransom, free, or rescue through payment or effort **3 :** to free from sin **4 :** to make good **:** FULFILL **5 :** to make up for — **re·deem·er** *n*
re·demp·tion *n* **:** the act or process or an instance of redeeming
red–hand·ed *adv or adj* **:** in the act of doing something wrong
red·head *n* **:** a person having reddish hair
red–hot *adj* **1 :** glowing red with heat **2 :** very active and emotional
re·di·rect *vb* **:** to change the course or direction of
re·dis·cov·er *vb* **:** to discover again
red–let·ter *adj* **:** of special importance **:** MEMORABLE
re·do *vb* **re·did; re·done; re·do·ing :** to do over or again
re·dress *vb* **:** to set right **:** REMEDY
red tape *n* **:** usually official rules and regulations that waste people's time
re·duce *vb* **re·duced; re·duc·ing 1 :** to make smaller or less **2 :** to force to surrender **3 :** to lower in grade or rank **4 :** to change from one form into another **5 :** to lose weight by dieting
re·duc·tion *n* **1 :** the act of reducing **:** the state of being reduced **2 :** something made by reducing **3 :** the amount by which something is reduced
red·wood *n* **:** a tall timber tree of California that bears cones and has a light long-lasting brownish red wood
reed *n* **1 :** a tall slender grass of wet areas that has stems with large joints **2 :** a stem or a growth or mass of reeds **3 :** a thin flexible piece of cane, plastic, or metal fastened to the mouthpiece or over an air opening in a musical instrument (as a clarinet or accordion) and set in vibration by an air current (as the breath)
reef *n* **:** a chain of rocks or ridge of sand at or near the surface of water
[1]**reek** *n* **:** a strong or unpleasant smell
[2]**reek** *vb* **:** to have a strong or unpleasant smell
[1]**reel** *n* **1 :** a device that can be turned round and round and on which something flexible may be wound **2 :** a quantity of something wound on a reel
[2]**reel** *vb* **1 :** to wind on a reel **2 :** to pull by the use of a reel
[3]**reel** *vb* **1 :** to whirl around **2 :** to be in a confused state **3 :** to fall back (as from a blow) **4 :** to walk or move unsteadily **:** STAGGER
[4]**reel** *n* **:** a reeling motion
[5]**reel** *n* **:** a lively folk dance
re·elect *vb* **:** to elect for another term
reel off *vb* **:** to tell or recite rapidly or easily
re·en·ter *vb* **:** to enter again
re·es·tab·lish *vb* **:** to establish again
re·fer *vb* **re·ferred; re·fer·ring 1 :** to send or direct to some person or place for treatment, aid, information, or decision **2 :** to call attention
[1]**ref·er·ee** *n* **1 :** a person to whom something that is to be investigated or decided is referred **2 :** a sports official with final authority for conducting a game or match
[2]**referee** *vb* **ref·er·eed; ref·er·ee·ing :** to act or be in charge of as referee
ref·er·ence *n* **1 :** the act of referring **2 :** a relation to or concern with something **3 :** something that refers a reader to another source of information **4 :** a person of whom questions can be asked about the honesty or ability of another person **5 :** a written statement about someone's honesty or ability **6 :** a work (as a dictionary) that contains useful information
ref·er·en·dum *n, pl* **ref·er·en·da** *or* **ref·er·en·dums :** the idea or practice of letting the voters approve or disapprove laws
[1]**re·fill** *vb* **:** to fill or become filled again
[2]**re·fill** *n* **:** a new or fresh supply of something
re·fine *vb* **re·fined; re·fin·ing 1 :** to bring to a pure state **2 :** to make better **:** IMPROVE
re·fined *adj* **1 :** having or showing good taste or training **2 :** freed from impurities **:** PURE
re·fine·ment *n* **1 :** the act or process of refining **2 :** excellence of manners, feelings, or tastes **3 :** something meant to improve something else
re·fin·ery *n, pl* **re·fin·er·ies :** a building and equipment for refining metals, oil, or sugar
re·fin·ish *vb* **:** to give (as furniture) a new surface
re·fit *vb* **re·fit·ted; re·fit·ting :** to get ready for use again
re·flect *vb* **1 :** to bend or throw back (waves of light, sound, or heat) **2 :** to give back an image or likeness of in the manner of a mirror **3 :** to bring as a result **4 :** to bring disapproval or blame **5 :** to think seriously
re·flec·tion *n* **1 :** the return of light or sound waves from a surface **2 :** an image produced by or as if by a mirror **3 :** something that brings blame or disgrace **4 :** an opinion formed or a remark made after careful thought **5 :** careful thought
re·flec·tor *n* **:** a shiny surface for reflecting light or heat
re·flex *n* **:** an action that occurs automatically when a sense organ is stimulated
reflex act *n* **:** REFLEX

re·for·est *vb* **:** to renew forest growth by planting seeds or young trees

re·for·es·ta·tion *n* **:** the act of reforesting

1re·form *vb* **1 :** to make better or improve by removal of faults **2 :** to correct or improve one's own behavior or habits

2reform *n* **1 :** improvement of what is bad **2 :** a removal or correction of a wrong or an error

ref·or·ma·tion *n* **:** the act of reforming **:** the state of being reformed

re·for·ma·to·ry *n, pl* **re·for·ma·to·ries :** an institution for reforming usually young or first offenders

re·form·er *n* **:** a person who works for reform

re·fract *vb* **:** to cause to go through refraction

re·frac·tion *n* **:** the bending of a ray when it passes at an angle from one medium into another in which its speed is different (as when light passes from air into water)

re·frac·to·ry *adj* **1 :** STUBBORN 3 **2 :** capable of enduring very high temperatures

1re·frain *vb* **:** to hold oneself back

2refrain *n* **:** a phrase or verse repeated regularly in a poem or song

re·fresh *vb* **:** to make fresh or fresher **:** REVIVE — **re·fresh·er** *n*

re·fresh·ment *n* **1 :** the act of refreshing **:** the state of being refreshed **2 :** something (as food or drink) that refreshes — often used in pl.

re·frig·er·ate *vb* **re·frig·er·at·ed; re·frig·er·at·ing :** to make or keep cold or cool

re·frig·er·a·tor *n* **:** a device or room for keeping articles (as food) cool

re·fu·el *vb* **:** to provide with or take on more fuel

ref·uge *n* **1 :** shelter or protection from danger or distress **2 :** a place that provides shelter or protection

ref·u·gee *n* **:** a person who flees for safety usually to a foreign country

1re·fund *vb* **:** to give back **:** REPAY

2re·fund *n* **:** a sum of money refunded

re·fus·al *n* **:** the act of refusing

1re·fuse *vb* **re·fused; re·fus·ing 1 :** to say one will not accept **2 :** to say one will not do, give, or allow something

2ref·use *n* **:** TRASH 1, RUBBISH

re·fute *vb* **re·fut·ed; re·fut·ing :** to prove wrong by argument or evidence — **re·fut·er** *n*

re·gain *vb* **1 :** to gain or get again **:** get back **2 :** to get back to **:** reach again

re·gal *adj* **:** of, relating to, or suitable for a monarch **:** ROYAL — **re·gal·ly** *adv*

re·gale *vb* **re·galed; re·gal·ing 1 :** to entertain richly **2 :** to give pleasure or amusement to

1re·gard *n* **1 :** 2LOOK 1 **2 :** CONSIDERATION 2 **3 :** a feeling of respect **4 regards** *pl* **:** friendly greetings **5 :** a point to be considered

2regard *vb* **1 :** to pay attention to **2 :** to show respect or consideration for **3 :** to have a high opinion of **4 :** to look at **5 :** to think of **:** CONSIDER

re·gard·ing *prep* **:** relating to **:** ABOUT

re·gard·less *adv* **:** come what may

regardless of *prep* **:** in spite of

re·gat·ta *n* **:** a rowing, speedboat, or sailing race or a series of such races

re·gen·er·ate *vb* **re·gen·er·at·ed; re·gen·er·at·ing :** to form (as a lost part) once more

re·gent *n* **1 :** a person who governs a kingdom (as during the childhood of the monarch) **2 :** a member of a governing board (as of a state university)

re·gime *n* **:** a form or system of government or management

reg·i·men *n* **:** a systematic course of treatment

reg·i·ment *n* **:** a military unit made up usually of a number of battalions

re·gion *n* **1 :** an area having no definite boundaries **2 :** VICINITY 2 **3 :** a broad geographical area

re·gion·al *adj* **:** of, relating to, or characteristic of a certain region

1reg·is·ter *n* **1 :** a written record or list containing regular entries of items or details **2 :** a book or system of public records **3 :** a device for regulating ventilation or the flow of heated air from a furnace **4 :** a mechanical device (as a **cash register**) that records items

2register *vb* **1 :** to enter or enroll in a register (as a list of voters, students, or guests) **2 :** to record automatically **3 :** to get special protection for by paying extra postage **4 :** to show by expression and bodily movements

reg·is·tra·tion *n* **1 :** the act of registering **2 :** an entry in a register **3 :** the number of persons registered **4 :** a document showing that something is registered

reg·is·try *n, pl* **reg·is·tries :** a place where registration takes place

1re·gret *vb* **re·gret·ted; re·gret·ting 1 :** to mourn the loss or death of **2 :** to be sorry for

2regret *n* **1 :** sorrow aroused by events beyond one's control **2 :** an expression of sorrow **3 regrets** *pl* **:** a note politely refusing to accept an invitation

re·gret·ful *adj* **:** full of regret — **re·gret·ful·ly** *adv*

re·gret·ta·ble *adj* **:** deserving regret — **re·gret·ta·bly** *adv*

DICTIONARY

re•group *vb* **:** to form into a new grouping

reg•u•lar *adj* **1 :** formed, built, or arranged according to an established rule, law, principle, or type **2 :** even or balanced in form or structure **3 :** steady in practice or occurrence **4 :** following established usages or rules **5 :** [1]NORMAL 1 **6 :** of, relating to, or being a permanent army — **reg•u•lar•ly** *adv*

reg•u•lar•i•ty *n* **:** the quality or state of being regular

reg•u•late *vb* **reg•u•lat•ed; reg•u•lat•ing 1 :** to govern or direct by rule **2 :** to bring under the control of authority **3 :** to bring order or method to **4 :** to fix or adjust the time, amount, degree, or rate of — **reg•u•la•tor** *n*

reg•u•la•tion *n* **1 :** the act of regulating **:** the state of being regulated **2 :** a rule or order telling how something is to be done or having the force of law

re•hears•al *n* **:** a private performance or practice session in preparation for a public appearance

re•hearse *vb* **re•hearsed; re•hears•ing :** to practice in private in preparation for a public performance

[1]reign *n* **1 :** the authority or rule of a monarch **2 :** the time during which a monarch rules

[2]reign *vb* **1 :** to rule as a monarch **2 :** to be usual or widespread

re•im•burse *vb* **re•im•bursed; re•im•burs•ing :** to pay back **:** REPAY — **re•im•burse•ment** *n*

[1]rein *n* **1 :** a line or strap attached at either end of the bit of a bridle to control an animal — usually used in pl. **2 :** an influence that slows, limits, or holds back **3 :** controlling or guiding power

[2]rein *vb* **:** to check, control, or stop by or as if by reins

re•in•car•na•tion *n* **:** rebirth of the soul in a new body

rein•deer *n, pl* **reindeer :** a large deer that has antlers in both the male and the female and is found in northern regions

re•in•force *vb* **re•in•forced; re•in•forc•ing 1 :** to strengthen with extra troops or ships **2 :** to strengthen with new force, assistance, material, or support

re•in•force•ment *n* **1 :** the act of reinforcing **:** the state of being reinforced **2 :** something that reinforces

re•in•state *vb* **re•in•stat•ed; re•in•stat•ing :** to place again in a former position or condition — **re•in•state•ment** *n*

re•it•er•ate *vb* **re•it•er•at•ed; re•it•er•at•ing :** to say or do over again or repeatedly

[1]re•ject *vb* **1 :** to refuse to admit, believe, or receive **2 :** to throw away as useless or unsatisfactory **3 :** to refuse to consider

[2]re•ject *n* **:** a rejected person or thing

re•jec•tion *n* **1 :** the act of rejecting **:** the state of being rejected **2 :** something rejected

re•joice *vb* **re•joiced; re•joic•ing 1 :** to give joy to **:** GLADDEN **2 :** to feel joy

re•join *vb* **1 :** to join again **:** return to **2 :** to reply sharply

re•join•der *n* **:** [2]REPLY

[1]re•lapse *n* **:** a fresh period of an illness after an improvement

[2]re•lapse *vb* **re•lapsed; re•laps•ing :** to slip or fall back into a former condition after a change for the better

re•late *vb* **re•lat•ed; re•lat•ing 1 :** to give an account of **:** NARRATE **2 :** to show or have a relationship to or between **:** CONNECT

re•lat•ed *adj* **:** connected by common ancestry or by marriage

re•la•tion *n* **1 :** the act of telling or describing **2 :** CONNECTION 2 **3 :** a related person **:** RELATIVE **4 :** RELATIONSHIP 2 **5 :** REFERENCE 2, RESPECT **6 relations** *pl* **:** business or public affairs

re•la•tion•ship *n* **1 :** the state of being related or connected **2 :** connection by blood or marriage

[1]rel•a•tive *n* **:** a person connected with another by blood or marriage

[2]relative *adj* **1 :** RELEVANT **2 :** existing in comparison to something else — **rel•a•tive•ly** *adv*

re•lax *vb* **1 :** to make or become loose or less tense **2 :** to make or become less severe or strict **3 :** to rest or enjoy oneself away from one's usual duties

re•lax•a•tion *n* **1 :** the act or fact of relaxing or of being relaxed **2 :** a relaxing activity or pastime

[1]re•lay *n* **1 :** a fresh supply (as of horses or people) arranged to relieve others **2 :** a race between teams in which each team member covers a certain part of the course

[2]re•lay *vb* **re•layed; re•lay•ing :** to pass along by stages

[1]re•lease *vb* **re•leased; re•leas•ing 1 :** to set free (as from prison) **2 :** to relieve from something that holds or burdens **3 :** to give up in favor of another **4 :** to permit to be published, sold, or shown — **re•leas•er** *n*

[2]release *n* **1 :** relief or rescue from sorrow, suffering, or trouble **2 :** a discharge from an obligation **3 :** a giving up of a right or claim **4 :** a setting free **:** the state of being freed **5 :** a device for holding or releasing a mechanism **6 :** the act of permitting publication or performance **7 :** matter released for publication or performance

re•lent *vb* **:** to become less severe, harsh, or strict

re•lent•less *adj* **:** very stern or harsh — **re•lent•less•ly** *adv* — **re•lent•less•ness** *n*

rel•e•vance *n* **:** relation to the matter at hand

rel•e•vant *adj* **:** having something to do with the matter at hand — **rel•e•vant•ly** *adv*

re•li•abil•i•ty *n* **:** the quality or state of being reliable

re•li•able *adj* **:** fit to be trusted **:** DEPENDABLE — **re•li•ably** *adv*

re•li•ance *n* **1 :** the act of relying **2 :** the condition or attitude of one who relies

rel•ic *n* **1 :** an object treated with great respect because of its connection with a saint or martyr **2 :** something left behind after decay or disappearance

re•lief *n* **1 :** removal or lightening of something painful or troubling **2 :** WELFARE 2 **3 :** military assistance in or rescue from a position of difficulty **4 :** release from a post or from performance of a duty **5 :** elevation of figures or designs from the background (as in sculpture) **6 :** elevations of a land surface

re•lieve *vb* **re•lieved; re•liev•ing 1 :** to free partly or wholly from a burden or from distress **2 :** to release from a post or duty **3 :** to break the sameness of — **re•liev•er** *n*

re•li•gion *n* **1 :** the service and worship of God or the supernatural **2 :** a system of religious beliefs and practices

re•li•gious *adj* **1 :** relating to or showing devotion to God or to the powers or forces believed to govern life **2 :** of or relating to religion **3 :** very devoted and faithful — **re•li•gious•ly** *adv* — **re•li•gious•ness** *n*

re•lin•quish *vb* **:** GIVE UP 1 **:** let go of

¹rel•ish *n* **1 :** a pleasing taste **2 :** great enjoyment **3 :** a highly seasoned food eaten with other food to add flavor

²relish *vb* **1 :** to be pleased by **:** ENJOY **2 :** to like the taste of

re•live *vb* **re•lived; re•liv•ing :** to experience again (as in the imagination)

re•luc•tance *n* **:** the quality or state of being reluctant

re•luc•tant *adj* **:** showing doubt or unwillingness — **re•luc•tant•ly** *adv*

re•ly *vb* **re•lied; re•ly•ing :** to place faith or confidence **:** DEPEND

re•main *vb* **1 :** to be left after others have been removed, subtracted, or destroyed **2 :** to be something yet to be done or considered **3 :** to stay after others have gone **4 :** to continue unchanged

re•main•der *n* **1 :** a remaining group or part **2 :** the number left after a subtraction **3 :** the number left over from the dividend after division that is less than the divisor

re•mains *n pl* **1 :** whatever is left over or behind **2 :** a dead body

re•make *vb* **re•made; re•mak•ing :** to make again or in a different form

¹re•mark *n* **1 :** a telling of something in speech or writing **2 :** a brief comment

²remark *vb* **1 :** to take note of **:** OBSERVE **2 :** to make a comment

re•mark•able *adj* **:** worth noticing **:** UNUSUAL — **re•mark•able•ness** *n* — **re•mark•ably** *adv*

re•match *n* **:** a second meeting between the same contestants

re•me•di•al *adj* **:** intended to make something better — **re•me•di•al•ly** *adv*

¹rem•e•dy *n, pl* **rem•e•dies 1 :** a medicine or treatment that cures or relieves **2 :** something that corrects an evil

²remedy *vb* **rem•e•died; rem•e•dy•ing :** to provide or serve as a remedy for

re•mem•ber *vb* **1 :** to bring to mind or think of again **2 :** to keep in mind **3 :** to pass along greetings from

re•mem•brance *n* **1 :** the act of remembering **2 :** something remembered **3 :** something (as a souvenir) that brings to mind a past experience

re•mind *vb* **:** to cause to remember — **re•mind•er** *n*

rem•i•nisce *vb* **rem•i•nisced; rem•i•nisc•ing :** to talk or think about things in the past

rem•i•nis•cence *n* **1 :** a recalling or telling of a past experience **2 reminiscences** *pl* **:** a story of one's memorable experiences

rem•i•nis•cent *adj* **1 :** of, relating to, or engaging in reminiscence **2 :** reminding one of something else

re•miss *adj* **:** careless in the performance of work or duty — **re•miss•ly** *adv* — **re•miss•ness** *n*

re•mit *vb* **re•mit•ted; re•mit•ting 1 :** ²PARDON 2 **2 :** to send money (as in payment) — **re•mit•ter** *n*

re•mit•tance *n* **:** money sent in payment

rem•nant *n* **:** something that remains or is left over

re•mod•el *vb* **re•mod•eled** *or* **re•mod•elled; re•mod•el•ing** *or* **re•mod•el•ling :** to change the structure of

re•mon•strate *vb* **re•mon•strat•ed; re•mon•strat•ing :** ²PROTEST 2

re•morse *n* **:** deep regret for one's sins or for acts that wrong others — **re•morse•ful** *adj* — **re•morse•less** *adj*

¹re•mote *adj* **re•mot•er; re•mot•est 1 :** far off in place or time **2 :** SECLUDED **3 :** not closely connected or related **4 :** small in degree **5 :** distant in manner **:** ALOOF — **re·mote·ly** *adv* — **re·mote·ness** *n*

²remote *n* **:** REMOTE CONTROL

remote control *n* **1 :** control (as by a radio signal) of operation from a point some distance away **2 :** a device for controlling something from a distance

re·mov·able *adj* **:** possible to remove

re·mov·al *n* **:** the act of removing **:** the fact of being removed

re·move *vb* **re·moved; re·mov·ing 1 :** to move by lifting or taking off or away **2 :** to dismiss from office **3 :** to get rid of

re·mov·er *n* **:** something (as a chemical) used in removing a substance

Re·nais·sance *n* **1 :** the period of European history between the fourteenth and seventeenth centuries marked by a fresh interest in ancient art and literature and by the beginnings of modern science **2** *often not cap* **:** a movement or period of great activity in literature, science, and the arts

re·name *vb* **re·named; re·nam·ing :** to give a new name to

rend *vb* **rent; rend·ing :** to tear apart by force

ren·der *vb* **1 :** to obtain by heating **2 :** to furnish or give to another **3 :** to cause to be or become **4 :** PERFORM 2

ren·dez·vous *n, pl* **ren·dez·vous 1 :** a place agreed on for a meeting **2 :** a planned meeting

ren·di·tion *n* **:** an act or a result of rendering

ren·e·gade *n* **:** a person who deserts a faith, cause, or party

re·nege *vb* **re·neged; re·neg·ing :** to go back on a promise or agreement

re·new *vb* **1 :** to make or become new, fresh, or strong again **2 :** to make, do, or begin again **3 :** to put in a fresh supply of **4 :** to continue in force for a new period

re·new·al *n* **1 :** the act of renewing **:** the state of being renewed **2 :** something renewed

re·nounce *vb* **re·nounced; re·nounc·ing 1 :** to give up, abandon, or resign usually by a public declaration **2 :** REPUDIATE 1, DISCLAIM

ren·o·vate *vb* **ren·o·vat·ed; ren·o·vat·ing :** to put in good condition again — **ren·o·va·tor** *n*

re·nown *n* **:** the state of being widely and favorably known

re·nowned *adj* **:** having renown

¹rent *n* **:** money paid for the use of another's property — **for rent :** available for use at a price

²rent *vb* **1 :** to take and hold property under an agreement to pay rent **2 :** to give the possession and use of in return for rent **3 :** to be for rent

³rent *past of* REND

⁴rent *n* **:** an opening (as in cloth) made by tearing

¹rent·al *n* **:** an amount paid or collected as rent

²rental *adj* **:** of, relating to, or available for rent

rent·er *n* **:** a person who pays rent for something (as a place to live)

re·open *vb* **:** to open again

re·or·ga·nize *vb* **re·or·ga·nized; re·or·ga·niz·ing :** to organize again

¹re·pair *vb* **1 :** to put back in good condition **2 :** to make up for

²repair *n* **1 :** the act or process of repairing **2 :** ¹CONDITION 3

rep·a·ra·tion *n* **1 :** the act of making up for a wrong **2 :** something paid by a country losing a war to the winner to make up for damages done in the war

re·past *n* **:** ¹MEAL

re·pay *vb* **re·paid; re·pay·ing 1 :** to pay back **2 :** to make a return payment to

re·pay·ment *n* **:** the act or an instance of paying back

re·peal *vb* **:** to do away with especially by legislative action

¹re·peat *vb* **1 :** to state or tell again **2 :** to say from memory **:** RECITE **3 :** to make or do again — **re·peat·er** *n*

²repeat *n* **1 :** the act of repeating **2 :** something repeated

re·peat·ed *adj* **:** done or happening again and again — **re·peat·ed·ly** *adv*

re·pel *vb* **re·pelled; re·pel·ling 1 :** to drive back **2 :** to turn away **:** REJECT **3 :** to keep out **:** RESIST **4 :** ²DISGUST

re·pel·lent *n* **:** a substance used to keep off pests (as insects)

re·pent *vb* **1 :** to feel sorrow for one's sin and make up one's mind to do what is right **2 :** to feel sorry for something done **:** REGRET

re·pen·tance *n* **:** the action or process of repenting

re·pen·tant *adj* **:** feeling or showing regret for something one has done — **re·pen·tant·ly** *adv*

re·per·cus·sion *n* **1 :** a return action or effect **2 :** a widespread, indirect, or unexpected effect of something said or done

rep·er·toire *n* **:** a list or supply of plays, operas, or pieces that a company or person is prepared to perform

rep·er·to·ry *n, pl* **rep·er·to·ries :** REPERTOIRE

rep·e·ti·tion *n* **1 :** the act or an instance of repeating **2 :** something repeated

re·place *vb* **re·placed; re·plac·ing 1 :** to put back in a former or proper place **2 :** to take the place of **3 :** to put something new in the place of

re·place·ment *n* **1 :** the act of replacing **:** the state of being replaced **2 :** [1]SUBSTITUTE

re·plen·ish *vb* **:** to make full or complete once more — **re·plen·ish·er** *n* — **re·plen·ish·ment** *n*

re·plete *adj* **:** well supplied — **re·plete·ness** *n*

rep·li·ca *n* **:** a very exact copy

[1]**re·ply** *vb* **re·plied; re·ply·ing :** to say or do in answer **:** RESPOND

[2]**reply** *n, pl* **re·plies :** something said, written, or done in answer

[1]**re·port** *n* **1 :** [1]RUMOR **2 :** REPUTATION 1 **3 :** a usually complete description or statement **4 :** an explosive noise

[2]**report** *vb* **1 :** to describe or tell something **2 :** to prepare or present an account of something (as for television or a newspaper) **3 :** to present oneself **4 :** to make known to the proper authorities **5 :** to make a charge of misconduct against — **re·port·er** *n*

report card *n* **:** a report on a student's grades that is regularly sent by a school to the student's parents or guardian

[1]**re·pose** *vb* **re·posed; re·pos·ing 1 :** to lay at rest **2 :** to lie at rest

[2]**repose** *n* **1 :** a state of resting and especially sleep after effort or strain **2 :** freedom from disturbance or excitement **:** CALM

rep·re·sent *vb* **1 :** to present a picture, image, or likeness of **:** PORTRAY **2 :** to be a sign or symbol of **3 :** to act for or in place of

rep·re·sen·ta·tion *n* **1 :** one (as a picture or symbol) that represents something else **2 :** the act of representing **:** the state of being represented (as in a legislative body)

[1]**rep·re·sen·ta·tive** *adj* **1 :** serving to represent **2 :** standing or acting for another **3 :** carried on by elected representatives **4 :** being a typical example of the thing mentioned

[2]**representative** *n* **1 :** a typical example (as of a group or class) **2 :** a person who represents another (as in a legislature)

re·press *vb* **:** to hold in check by or as if by pressure

[1]**re·prieve** *vb* **re·prieved; re·priev·ing :** to delay the punishment of (as a prisoner sentenced to die)

[2]**reprieve** *n* **1 :** a postponing of a prison or death sentence **2 :** a temporary relief

[1]**rep·ri·mand** *n* **:** a severe or formal criticism **:** CENSURE

[2]**reprimand** *vb* **:** to criticize (a person) severely or formally

re·pri·sal *n* **:** an act in return for harm done by another

[1]**re·proach** *n* **1 :** something that calls for blame or disgrace **2 :** an expression of disapproval

[2]**reproach** *vb* **:** to find fault with **:** BLAME

re·pro·duce *vb* **re·pro·duced; re·pro·duc·ing 1 :** to produce again **2 :** to produce another living thing of the same kind — **re·pro·duc·er** *n*

re·pro·duc·tion *n* **1 :** the act or process of reproducing **2 :** [1]COPY 1

re·pro·duc·tive *adj* **:** of, relating to, capable of, or concerned with reproduction

re·proof *n* **:** blame or criticism for a fault

re·prove *vb* **re·proved; re·prov·ing :** to express blame or disapproval of **:** SCOLD

rep·tile *n* **:** any of a group of vertebrates (as snakes, lizards, turtles, and alligators) that are cold-blooded, breathe air, and usually have the skin covered with scales or bony plates

re·pub·lic *n* **1 :** a government having a chief of state who is not a monarch and who is usually a president **2 :** a government in which supreme power lies in the citizens through their right to vote **3 :** a state or country having a republican government

[1]**re·pub·li·can** *n* **:** a person who favors a republican form of government

[2]**republican** *adj* **:** of, relating to, or like a republic

re·pu·di·ate *vb* **re·pu·di·at·ed; re·pu·di·at·ing 1 :** to refuse to have anything to do with **2 :** to refuse to accept, admit, or pay

[1]**re·pulse** *vb* **re·pulsed; re·puls·ing 1 :** to drive or beat back **:** REPEL **2 :** to treat with discourtesy **:** SNUB

[2]**repulse** *n* **1 :** [2]REBUFF, SNUB **2 :** the action of driving back an attacker

re·pul·sive *adj* **:** causing disgust — **re·pul·sive·ly** *adv* — **re·pul·sive·ness** *n*

rep·u·ta·ble *adj* **:** having a good reputation — **rep·u·ta·bly** *adv*

rep·u·ta·tion *n* **1 :** overall quality or character as seen or judged by people in general **2 :** notice by other people of some quality or ability

[1]**re·pute** *vb* **re·put·ed; re·put·ing :** CONSIDER 3

[2]**repute** *n* **1 :** REPUTATION 1 **2 :** good reputation **:** HONOR

[1]**re·quest** *n* **1 :** an asking for something **2 :** something asked for **3 :** the condition of being requested

[2]**request** *vb* **1 :** to make a request to or of **2 :** to ask for

re·qui·em *n* **1 :** a mass for a dead person **2 :** a musical service or hymn in honor of the dead

re·quire *vb* **re·quired; re·quir·ing 1 :** to have a need for **2 :** [1]ORDER 2, COMMAND
re·quire·ment *n* **:** something that is required or necessary
[1]**req·ui·site** *adj* **:** needed for reaching a goal or achieving a purpose
[2]**requisite** *n* **:** REQUIREMENT
re·read *vb* **re·read; re·read·ing :** to read again
[1]**res·cue** *vb* **res·cued; res·cu·ing :** to free from danger or evil **:** SAVE — **res·cu·er** *n*
[2]**rescue** *n* **:** an act of rescuing
re·search *n* **:** careful study and investigation for the purpose of discovering and explaining new knowledge — **re·search·er** *n*
re·sem·blance *n* **:** the quality or state of resembling something else
re·sem·ble *vb* **re·sem·bled; re·sem·bling :** to be like or similar to
re·sent *vb* **:** to feel annoyance or anger at
re·sent·ment *n* **:** a feeling of angry displeasure at a real or imagined wrong, insult, or injury
res·er·va·tion *n* **1 :** an act of reserving **2 :** an arrangement to have something (as a hotel room) held for one's use **3 :** something (as land) reserved for a special use **4 :** something that limits
[1]**re·serve** *vb* **re·served; re·serv·ing 1 :** to keep in store for future or special use **2 :** to hold over to a future time or place **3 :** to arrange to have set aside and held for one's use
[2]**reserve** *n* **1 :** something stored or available for future use **2 reserves** *pl* **:** military forces held back or available for later use **3 :** an area of land set apart **4 :** an act of reserving **5 :** caution in one's words and behavior
re·served *adj* **1 :** cautious in words and actions **2 :** kept or set apart for future or special use
res·er·voir *n* **:** a place where something (as water) is kept in store for future use
re·set *vb* **re·set; re·set·ting :** to set again
re·ship·ment *n* **:** an act of shipping again
re·side *vb* **re·sid·ed; re·sid·ing 1 :** to live permanently and continuously **:** DWELL **2 :** to have its place **:** EXIST
res·i·dence *n* **1 :** the act or fact of residing **2 :** the place where one actually lives **3 :** a building used for a home **4 :** the time during which a person lives in a place
[1]**res·i·dent** *adj* **1 :** living in a place for some length of time **2 :** serving in a full-time position at a certain place
[2]**resident** *n* **:** a person who lives in a place
res·i·den·tial *adj* **1 :** used as a residence or by residents **2 :** suitable for or containing residences
res·i·due *n* **:** whatever remains after a part is taken, set apart, or lost
re·sign *vb* **1 :** to give up by a formal or official act **2 :** to prepare to accept something usually unpleasant
res·ig·na·tion *n* **1 :** an act of resigning **2 :** a letter or written statement that gives notice of resignation **3 :** the feeling of a person who is resigned
re·signed *adj* **:** giving in patiently (as to loss or sorrow) — **re·sign·ed·ly** *adv*
res·in *n* **1 :** a yellowish or brownish substance obtained from the gum or sap of some trees (as the pine) and used in varnishes and medicine **2 :** any of various manufactured products that are similar to natural resins in properties and are used especially as plastics
re·sist *vb* **1 :** to withstand the force or effect of **2 :** to fight against **:** OPPOSE
re·sis·tance *n* **1 :** an act or instance of resisting **2 :** the ability to resist **3 :** an opposing or slowing force **4 :** the opposition offered by a substance to the passage through it of an electric current
re·sis·tant *adj* **:** giving or capable of resistance
res·o·lute *adj* **:** firmly determined — **res·o·lute·ly** *adv* — **res·o·lute·ness** *n*
res·o·lu·tion *n* **1 :** the act of resolving **2 :** the act of solving **:** SOLUTION **3 :** something decided on **4 :** firmness of purpose **5 :** a statement expressing the feelings, wishes, or decisions of a group
[1]**re·solve** *vb* **re·solved; re·solv·ing 1 :** to find an answer to **:** SOLVE **2 :** to reach a firm decision about something **3 :** to declare or decide by a formal resolution and vote
[2]**resolve** *n* **1 :** something resolved **2 :** firmness of purpose
res·o·nance *n* **:** the quality or state of being resonant
res·o·nant *adj* **:** being or making sound with a rich vibrating quality — **res·o·nant·ly** *adv*
[1]**re·sort** *n* **1 :** one that is looked to for help **2 :** HANGOUT **3 :** a place where people go for pleasure, sport, or a change
[2]**resort** *vb* **1 :** to go often or again and again **2 :** to seek aid, relief, or advantage
re·sound *vb* **1 :** to become filled with sound **:** REVERBERATE **2 :** to sound loudly
re·source *n* **1 :** a new or a reserve source of supply or support **2 resources** *pl* **:** a usable stock or supply (as of money or products) **3 :** the ability to meet and deal with situations
re·source·ful *adj* **:** clever in dealing with problems — **re·source·ful·ly** *adv* — **re·source·ful·ness** *n*
[1]**re·spect** *n* **1 :** relation to or concern with

something specified **2 :** high or special regard **:** ESTEEM **3 respects** *pl* **:** an expression of regard or courtesy **4 :** [1]DETAIL 2

[2]**respect** *vb* **1 :** to consider worthy of high regard **:** ESTEEM **2 :** to pay attention to — **re•spect•er** *n*

re•spect•able *adj* **1 :** deserving respect **2 :** decent or correct in conduct **:** PROPER **3 :** fair in size or quantity **4 :** fit to be seen **:** PRESENTABLE — **re•spect•ably** *adv*

re•spect•ful *adj* **:** showing respect — **re•spect•ful•ly** *adv* — **re•spect•ful•ness** *n*

re•spect•ing *prep* **:** CONCERNING

re•spec•tive *adj* **:** not the same or shared **:** SEPARATE — **re•spec•tive•ly** *adv*

re•spell *vb* **:** to spell again or in another way

res•pi•ra•tion *n* **1 :** the act or process of breathing **2 :** the physical and chemical processes (as breathing and oxidation) by which a living being gets the oxygen it needs to live

res•pi•ra•tor *n* **1 :** a device covering the mouth or nose especially to prevent the breathing in of something harmful **2 :** a device used for aiding one to breathe

res•pi•ra•to•ry *adj* **:** of, relating to, or concerned with respiration

re•spire *vb* **re•spired; re•spir•ing :** BREATHE 1

res•pite *n* **1 :** a short delay **2 :** a period of rest or relief

re•splen•dent *adj* **:** shining brightly **:** SPLENDID — **re•splen•dent•ly** *adv*

re•spond *vb* **1 :** to say something in return **:** REPLY **2 :** to act in response **:** REACT

re•sponse *n* **1 :** an act or instance of replying **:** ANSWER **2 :** words said or sung by the people or choir in a religious service **3 :** a reaction of a living being (as to a drug)

re•spon•si•bil•i•ty *n, pl* **re•spon•si•bil•i•ties 1 :** the quality or state of being responsible **2 :** the quality of being dependable **3 :** something for which one is responsible

re•spon•si•ble *adj* **1 :** getting the credit or blame for one's acts or decisions **2 :** RELIABLE **3 :** needing a person to take charge of or be trusted with things of importance — **re•spon•si•bly** *adv*

re•spon•sive *adj* **1 :** giving response **2 :** quick to respond or react in a sympathetic way — **re•spon•sive•ly** *adv* — **re•spon•sive•ness** *n*

[1]**rest** *n* **1 :** [1]SLEEP 1 **2 :** freedom from activity or work **3 :** a state of not moving or not doing anything **4 :** a place for resting or stopping **5 :** a silence in music **6 :** a symbol in music that stands for a certain period of silence in a measure **7 :** something used for support

[2]**rest** *vb* **1 :** to get rest by lying down **:** SLEEP **2 :** to give rest to **3 :** to lie dead **4 :** to not take part in work or activity **5 :** to sit or lie fixed or supported **6 :** DEPEND 2 **7 :** to fix or be fixed in trust or confidence

[3]**rest** *n* **:** something that is left over **:** REMAINDER

re•state•ment *n* **:** a saying again or in another way

res•tau•rant *n* **:** a public eating place

rest•ful *adj* **1 :** giving rest **2 :** giving a feeling of rest **:** QUIET — **rest•ful•ly** *adv* — **rest•ful•ness** *n*

rest•ing *adj* **:** DORMANT

res•tive *adj* **1 :** resisting control **2 :** not being at ease — **res•tive•ly** *adv* — **res•tive•ness** *n*

rest•less *adj* **1 :** having or giving no rest **2 :** not quiet or calm — **rest•less•ly** *adv* — **rest•less•ness** *n*

res•to•ra•tion *n* **1 :** an act of restoring **:** the condition of being restored **2 :** something (as a building) that has been restored

re•store *vb* **re•stored; re•stor•ing 1 :** to give back **:** RETURN **2 :** to put back into use or service **3 :** to put or bring back to an earlier or original state

re•strain *vb* **1 :** to keep from doing something **2 :** to keep back **:** CURB — **re•strain•er** *n*

re•straint *n* **1 :** the act of restraining **:** the state of being restrained **2 :** a restraining force or influence **3 :** control over one's thoughts or feelings

re•strict *vb* **:** to keep within bounds **:** set limits to

re•stric•tion *n* **1 :** something (as a law or rule) that restricts **2 :** an act of restricting **:** the condition of being restricted

re•stric•tive *adj* **:** serving or likely to restrict — **re•stric•tive•ly** *adv* — **re•stric•tive•ness** *n*

[1]**re•sult** *vb* **1 :** to come about as an effect **2 :** to end as an effect

[2]**result** *n* **1 :** something that comes about as an effect or end **2 :** a good effect

re•sume *vb* **re•sumed; re•sum•ing 1 :** to take or occupy again **2 :** to begin again

re•sump•tion *n* **:** the act of resuming

res•ur•rect *vb* **1 :** to raise from the dead **:** bring back to life **2 :** to bring to view or into use again

res•ur•rec•tion *n* **1** *cap* **:** the rising of Christ from the dead **2** *often cap* **:** the rising again to life of all human dead before the final judgment **3 :** a coming back into use or importance

re•sus•ci•tate *vb* **re•sus•ci•tat•ed; re•sus•ci•tat•ing :** to bring back from apparent death or unconsciousness — **re•sus•ci•ta•tor** *n*

DICTIONARY

¹re·tail *vb* **:** to sell in small amounts to people for their own use — **re·tail·er** *n*

²retail *n* **:** the sale of products or goods in small amounts to people for their own use

³retail *adj* **:** of, relating to, or engaged in selling by retail

re·tain *vb* **1 :** to keep in one's possession or control **2 :** to hold safe or unchanged

re·tal·i·ate *vb* **re·tal·i·at·ed; re·tal·i·at·ing :** to get revenge by returning like for like

re·tal·i·a·tion *n* **:** the act or an instance of retaliating

re·tard *vb* **:** to slow up **:** keep back **:** DELAY — **re·tard·er** *n*

re·tard·ed *adj* **:** very slow especially in mind

retch *vb* **:** to vomit or try to vomit

re·ten·tion *n* **1 :** the act of retaining **:** the state of being retained **2 :** the power of retaining

ret·i·na *n, pl* **retinas** *or* **ret·i·nae :** the membrane that lines the back part of the eyeball and is the sensitive part for seeing

re·tire *vb* **re·tired; re·tir·ing 1 :** to get away from action or danger **:** RETREAT **2 :** to go away especially to be alone **3 :** to give up one's job permanently **:** quit working **4 :** to go to bed **5 :** to take out of circulation — **re·tire·ment** *n*

re·tired *adj* **:** not working at active duties or business

re·tir·ing *adj* **:** ¹SHY 2, RESERVED

¹re·tort *vb* **1 :** to answer back **:** reply angrily or sharply **2 :** to reply with an argument against

²retort *n* **:** a quick, clever, or angry reply

re·trace *vb* **re·traced; re·trac·ing :** to go over once more

re·tract *vb* **1 :** to pull back or in **2 :** to take back (as an offer or statement) **:** WITHDRAW

¹re·tread *vb* **re·tread·ed; re·tread·ing :** to put a new tread on the cord fabric of (a tire)

²re·tread *n* **:** a retreaded tire

¹re·treat *n* **1 :** an act of going away from something dangerous, difficult, or disagreeable **2 :** a military signal for turning away from the enemy **3 :** a place of privacy or safety **:** REFUGE **4 :** a period in which a person goes away to pray, think quietly, and study

²retreat *vb* **:** to make a retreat

re·trieve *vb* **re·trieved; re·triev·ing 1 :** to find and bring in killed or wounded game **2 :** to make good a loss or damage **:** RECOVER — **re·triev·er** *n*

ret·ro–rock·et *n* **:** a rocket (as on a space vehicle) used to slow forward motion

ret·ro·spect *n* **:** a looking back on things past

¹re·turn *vb* **1 :** to come or go back **2 :** ²ANSWER 1, REPLY **3 :** to make an official report of **4 :** to bring, carry, send, or put back **:** RESTORE **5 :** ¹YIELD 4, PRODUCE **6 :** REPAY 1

²return *n* **1 :** the act of coming back to or from a place or condition **2 :** RECURRENCE **3 :** a report of the results of voting **4 :** a statement of income to be taxed **5 :** the profit from labor, investment, or business **6 :** the act of returning something (as to an earlier place or condition) **7 :** something given (as in payment)

³return *adj* **1 :** played or given in return **2 :** used for returning

re·union *n* **1 :** the act of reuniting **:** the state of being reunited **2 :** a reuniting of persons after being apart

re·unite *vb* **re·unit·ed; re·unit·ing :** to come or bring together again after being apart

rev *vb* **revved; rev·ving :** to increase the number of revolutions per minute of (a motor)

re·veal *vb* **1 :** to make known **2 :** to show clearly

rev·eil·le *n* **:** a signal sounded at about sunrise on a bugle or drum to call soldiers or sailors to duty

¹rev·el *vb* **rev·eled** *or* **rev·elled; rev·el·ing** *or* **rev·el·ling 1 :** to be social in a wild noisy way **2 :** to take great pleasure

²revel *n* **:** a noisy or merry celebration

rev·e·la·tion *n* **1 :** an act of revealing **2 :** something revealed

rev·el·ry *n, pl* **rev·el·ries :** rough and noisy merrymaking

¹re·venge *vb* **re·venged; re·veng·ing :** to cause harm or injury in return for

²revenge *n* **1 :** an act or instance of revenging **2 :** a desire to repay injury for injury **3 :** a chance for getting satisfaction

re·venge·ful *adj* **:** given to or seeking revenge

rev·e·nue *n* **1 :** the income from an investment **2 :** money collected by a government (as through taxes)

re·ver·ber·ate *vb* **re·ver·ber·at·ed; re·ver·ber·at·ing :** to continue in or as if in a series of echoes

re·vere *vb* **re·vered; re·ver·ing :** to think of with reverence

¹rev·er·ence *n* **:** honor and respect mixed with love and awe

²reverence *vb* **rev·er·enced; rev·er·enc·ing :** to show reverence to or toward

rev·er·end *adj* **1 :** worthy of honor and respect **2** — used as a title for a member of the clergy

rev·er·ent *adj* **:** very respectful — **rev·er·ent·ly** *adv*

rev·er·ie *or* **rev·ery** *n, pl* **rev·er·ies 1**

: [1]DAYDREAM **2 :** the condition of being lost in thought

re·ver·sal *n* **:** an act or the process of reversing

[1]re·verse *adj* **1 :** opposite to a previous or normal condition **2 :** acting or working in a manner opposite to the usual — **re·verse·ly** *adv*

[2]reverse *vb* **re·versed; re·vers·ing 1 :** to turn completely around or upside down or inside out **2 :** ANNUL **3 :** to go or cause to go in the opposite direction

[3]reverse *n* **1 :** something opposite to something else **:** CONTRARY **2 :** an act or instance of reversing **3 :** the back part of something **4 :** a gear that reverses something

re·vert *vb* **:** to come or go back

[1]re·view *n* **1 :** a military parade put on for high officers **2 :** a general survey **3 :** a piece of writing about the quality of a book, performance, or show **4 :** a fresh study of material studied before

[2]review *vb* **1 :** to look at a thing again **:** study or examine again **2 :** to make an inspection of (as troops) **3 :** to write a review about (as a book) **4 :** to look back on — **re·view·er** *n*

re·vile *vb* **re·viled; re·vil·ing :** to speak to or yell at in an insulting way — **re·vil·er** *n*

re·vise *vb* **re·vised; re·vis·ing 1 :** to look over again to correct or improve **2 :** to make a new version of

re·viv·al *n* **1 :** a reviving of interest (as in art) **2 :** a new presentation of a play or movie **3 :** a gaining back of strength or importance **4 :** a meeting or series of meetings led by a preacher to stir up religious feelings or to make converts

re·vive *vb* **re·vived; re·viv·ing 1 :** to bring back or come back to life, consciousness, freshness, or activity **2 :** to bring back into use

re·voke *vb* **re·voked; re·vok·ing :** to take away or cancel

[1]re·volt *vb* **1 :** to rebel against the authority of a ruler or government **2 :** to be or cause to be disgusted or shocked

[2]revolt *n* **:** REBELLION, INSURRECTION

rev·o·lu·tion *n* **1 :** the action by a celestial body of going round in a fixed course **2 :** completion of a course (as of years) **:** CYCLE **3 :** a turning round a center or axis **:** ROTATION **4 :** a single complete turn (as of a wheel) **5 :** a sudden, extreme, or complete change (as in manner of living or working) **6 :** the overthrow of one government and the substitution of another by the governed

rev·o·lu·tion·ary *adj* **1 :** of, relating to, or involving revolution **2 :** [1]RADICAL 2

rev·o·lu·tion·ist *n* **:** a person taking part in or supporting a revolution

rev·o·lu·tion·ize *vb* **rev·o·lu·tion·ized; rev·o·lu·tion·iz·ing :** to change greatly or completely

re·volve *vb* **re·volved; re·volv·ing 1 :** to think over carefully **2 :** to move in an orbit **3 :** ROTATE 1

re·volv·er *n* **:** a pistol having a revolving cylinder holding several bullets all of which may be shot without loading again

re·vue *n* **:** a theatrical entertainment consisting usually of short and often funny sketches and songs

[1]re·ward *vb* **:** to give a reward to or for

[2]reward *n* **:** something (as money) given or offered in return for a service (as the return of something lost)

re·word *vb* **:** to state in different words

re·write *vb* **re·wrote; re·writ·ten; re·writ·ing :** to write over again especially in a different form

rhap·so·dy *n, pl* **rhap·so·dies :** a written or spoken expression of extreme praise or delight

rhea *n* **:** a tall flightless South American bird that has three toes on each foot and is like but smaller than the ostrich

rheu·mat·ic *adj* **:** of, relating to, or suffering from rheumatism — **rheu·mat·i·cal·ly** *adv*

rheu·ma·tism *n* **:** any of several disorders in which muscles or joints are red, hot, and painful

rhi·no *n, pl* **rhino** *or* **rhi·nos :** RHINOCEROS

rhi·noc·er·os *n, pl* **rhi·noc·er·os·es** *or* **rhinoceros :** a large mammal of Africa and Asia with a thick skin, three toes on each foot, and one or two heavy upright horns on the snout

rho·do·den·dron *n* **:** a shrub or tree with long usually shiny and evergreen leaves and showy clusters of white, pink, red, or purple flowers

rhom·bus *n* **:** a parallelogram whose sides are equal

rhu·barb *n* **:** a plant with broad green leaves and thick juicy pink or red stems that are used for food

[1]rhyme *or* **rime** *n* **1 :** close similarity in the final sounds of two or more words or lines of verse **2 :** a verse composition that rhymes

[2]rhyme *or* **rime** *vb* **rhymed** *or* **rimed; rhym·ing** *or* **rim·ing 1 :** to make rhymes **2 :** to end with the same sound **3 :** to cause lines or words to end with a similar sound

rhythm *n* **1 :** a flow of rising and falling sounds produced in poetry by a regular repeating of stressed and unstressed syllables **2 :** a flow of sound in music having regular

DICTIONARY

accented beats **3 :** a movement or activity in which some action repeats regularly

rhyth·mic *or* **rhyth·mi·cal** *adj* **:** having rhythm — **rhyth·mi·cal·ly** *adv*

[1]**rib** *n* **1 :** one of the series of curved bones that are joined in pairs to the backbone of humans and other vertebrates and help to stiffen the body wall **2 :** something (as a piece of wire supporting the fabric of an umbrella) that is like a rib in shape or use **3 :** one of the parallel ridges in a knitted or woven fabric — **ribbed** *adj*

[2]**rib** *vb* **ribbed; rib·bing 1 :** to provide or enclose with ribs **2 :** to form ribs in (a fabric) in knitting or weaving

rib·bon *n* **1 :** a narrow strip of fabric (as silk) used for trimming or for tying or decorating packages **2 :** a long narrow strip like a ribbon **3 :** TATTER 1, SHRED

rice *n* **:** an annual cereal grass widely grown in warm wet regions for its grain that is a chief food in many parts of the world

rich *adj* **1 :** having great wealth **2 :** [1]VALUABLE 1, EXPENSIVE **3 :** containing much sugar, fat, or seasoning **4 :** high in fuel content **5 :** deep and pleasing in color or tone **6 :** ABUNDANT **7 :** FERTILE 1 — **richly** *adv* — **rich·ness** *n*

rich·es *n pl* **:** things that make one rich **:** WEALTH

rick·ets *n* **:** a disease in which the bones are soft and deformed and which usually attacks the young and is caused by lack of the vitamin that controls the use of calcium and phosphorus

rick·ety *adj* **:** SHAKY, UNSOUND

rick·sha *or* **rick·shaw** *n* **:** a small hooded carriage with two wheels that is pulled by one person and was used originally in Japan

[1]**ric·o·chet** *n* **:** a bouncing off at an angle (as of a bullet off a wall)

[2]**ricochet** *vb* **ric·o·cheted; ric·o·chet·ing :** to bounce off at an angle

rid *vb* **rid** *also* **rid·ded; rid·ding :** to free from something **:** RELIEVE

rid·dance *n* **:** the act of ridding **:** the state of being rid of something

[1]**rid·dle** *n* **:** a puzzling question to be solved or answered by guessing

[2]**riddle** *vb* **rid·dled; rid·dling :** to pierce with many holes

[1]**ride** *vb* **rode; rid·den; rid·ing 1 :** to go on an animal's back or in a vehicle (as a car) **2 :** to sit on and control so as to be carried along **3 :** to float or move on water **4 :** to travel over a surface **5 :** CARRY 1 — **rid·er** *n*

[2]**ride** *n* **1 :** a trip on horseback or by vehicle **2 :** a mechanical device (as a merry-go-round) that one rides for fun **3 :** a means of transportation

ridge *n* **1 :** a range of hills or mountains **2 :** a raised strip **3 :** the line made where two sloping surfaces come together — **ridged** *adj*

ridge·pole *n* **:** the highest horizontal timber in a sloping roof to which the upper ends of the rafters are fastened

[1]**rid·i·cule** *n* **:** the act of making fun of someone

[2]**ridicule** *vb* **rid·i·culed; rid·i·cul·ing :** to make fun of **:** DERIDE

ri·dic·u·lous *adj* **:** causing or deserving ridicule **:** ABSURD — **ri·dic·u·lous·ly** *adv* — **ri·dic·u·lous·ness** *n*

riff·raff *n* **:** RABBLE 2

[1]**ri·fle** *vb* **ri·fled; ri·fling 1 :** to search through fast and roughly especially in order to steal **2 :** [1]STEAL 2

[2]**rifle** *n* **:** a gun having a long barrel with spiral grooves on its inside

rift *n* **1 :** an opening made by splitting or separation **:** CLEFT **2 :** a break in friendly relations

[1]**rig** *vb* **rigged; rig·ging 1 :** to fit out (as a ship) with rigging **2 :** CLOTHE 1 2, DRESS **3 :** EQUIP **4 :** to set up usually for temporary use

[2]**rig** *n* **1 :** the shape, number, and arrangement of sails on a ship of one class or type that sets it apart from ships of other classes or types **2 :** apparatus for a certain purpose

rig·ging *n* **:** lines and chains used on a ship especially for moving the sails and supporting the masts and spars

[1]**right** *adj* **1 :** being just or good **:** UPRIGHT **2 :** ACCURATE, CORRECT **3 :** SUITABLE, APPROPRIATE **4 :** STRAIGHT 1 **5 :** of, relating to, located on, or being the side of the body away from the heart **6 :** located nearer to the right hand **7 :** being or meant to be the side on top, in front, or on the outside **8 :** healthy in mind or body — **right·ly** *adv* — **right·ness** *n*

[2]**right** *n* **1 :** the ideal of what is right and good **2 :** something to which one has a just claim **3 :** the cause of truth or justice **4 :** the right side or a part that is on or toward the right side

[3]**right** *adv* **1 :** according to what is right **2 :** in the exact location or position **:** PRECISELY **3 :** in a direct line or course **:** STRAIGHT **4 :** according to truth or fact **5 :** in the right way **:** CORRECTLY **6 :** all the way **7 :** without delay **:** IMMEDIATELY **8 :** on or to the right

[4]**right** *vb* **1 :** to make right (something wrong or unjust) **2 :** to adjust or restore to a proper state or condition **3 :** to bring or bring back to a vertical position **4 :** to become vertical

right angle *n* **:** an angle formed by two lines that are perpendicular to each other — **right–an•gled** *adj*
righ•teous *adj* **:** doing or being what is right — **righ•teous•ly** *adv* — **righ•teous•ness** *n*
right•ful *adj* **:** LAWFUL 2, PROPER — **right•ful•ly** *adv* — **right•ful•ness** *n*
right–hand *adj* **1 :** located on the right **2 :** RIGHT-HANDED **3 :** relied on most of all
right–hand•ed *adj* **1 :** using the right hand more easily than the left **2 :** done or made with or for the right hand **3 :** CLOCKWISE
right–of–way *n, pl* **rights–of–way 1 :** the right to pass over someone else's land **2 :** the right of some traffic to go before other traffic
right triangle *n* **:** a triangle having a right angle
rig•id *adj* **1 :** not flexible **:** STIFF **2 :** STRICT 1, SEVERE — **rig•id•ly** *adv* — **rig•id•ness** *n*
rig•ma•role *n* **:** NONSENSE 1
rig•or *n* **:** a harsh severe condition (as of discipline or weather)
rig•or•ous *adj* **1 :** very strict **2 :** hard to put up with **:** HARSH — **rig•or•ous•ly** *adv* — **rig•or•ous•ness** *n*
rill *n* **:** a very small brook
rim *n* **1 :** an outer edge especially of something curved **2 :** the outer part of a wheel — **rimmed** *adj*
[1]**rime** *n* **:** [1]FROST 2
[2]**rime** *variant of* RHYME
rind *n* **:** a usually hard or tough outer layer
[1]**ring** *n* **1 :** a circular band worn as an ornament or used for holding or fastening **2 :** something circular in shape **3 :** a place for exhibitions (as at a circus) or contests (as in boxing) **4 :** a group of persons who work together for selfish or dishonest purposes — **ringed** *adj* — **ring•like** *adj*
[2]**ring** *vb* **ringed; ring•ing 1 :** to place or form a ring around **:** to throw a ring over (a peg or hook) in a game (as quoits)
[3]**ring** *vb* **rang; rung; ring•ing 1 :** to make or cause to make a rich vibrating sound when struck **2 :** to sound a bell **3 :** to announce by or as if by striking a bell **4 :** to sound loudly **5 :** to be filled with talk or report **6 :** to repeat loudly **7 :** to seem to be a certain way **8 :** to call on the telephone
[4]**ring** *n* **1 :** a clear ringing sound made by vibrating metal **2 :** a tone suggesting that of a bell **3 :** a loud or continuing noise **4 :** something that suggests a certain quality **5 :** a telephone call
ring•lead•er *n* **:** a leader especially of a group of persons who cause trouble
ring•let *n* **:** a long curl
ring•worm *n* **:** a contagious skin disease with discolored rings on the skin
rink *n* **:** a place for skating
[1]**rinse** *vb* **rinsed; rins•ing 1 :** to wash lightly with water **2 :** to cleanse (as of soap) with clear water **3 :** to treat (hair) with a rinse
[2]**rinse** *n* **1 :** an act of rinsing **2 :** a liquid used for rinsing **3 :** a solution that temporarily tints hair
[1]**ri•ot** *n* **1 :** public violence, disturbance, or disorder **2 :** a colorful display
[2]**riot** *vb* **:** to create or take part in a riot
[1]**rip** *vb* **ripped; rip•ping :** to cut or tear open — **rip•per** *n*
[2]**rip** *n* **:** [3]TEAR 2
ripe *adj* **rip•er; rip•est 1 :** fully grown and developed **2 :** having mature knowledge, understanding, or judgment **3 :** [1]READY 1 — **ripe•ness** *n*
rip•en *vb* **:** to make or become ripe
[1]**rip•ple** *vb* **rip•pled; rip•pling 1 :** to become or cause to become covered with small waves **2 :** to make a sound like that of water flowing in small waves
[2]**ripple** *n* **1 :** the disturbing of the surface of water **2 :** a sound like that of rippling water
[1]**rise** *vb* **rose; ris•en; ris•ing 1 :** to get up from lying, kneeling, or sitting **2 :** to get up from sleep or from one's bed **3 :** to return from death **4 :** to take up arms **5 :** to appear above the horizon **6 :** to go up **:** ASCEND **7 :** to swell in size or volume **8 :** to become encouraged **9 :** to gain a higher rank or position **10 :** to increase in amount or number **11 :** ARISE 3 **12 :** to come into being **:** ORIGINATE **13 :** to show oneself equal to a demand or test — **ris•er** *n*
[2]**rise** *n* **1 :** an act of rising **:** a state of being risen **2 :** BEGINNING 1, ORIGIN **3 :** an increase in amount, number, or volume **4 :** an upward slope **5 :** a spot higher than surrounding ground **6 :** an angry reaction
[1]**risk** *n* **:** possibility of loss or injury
[2]**risk** *vb* **1 :** to expose to danger **2 :** to take the risk or danger of
risky *adj* **risk•i•er; risk•i•est :** DANGEROUS 1
rite *n* **1 :** a set form of conducting a ceremony **2 :** a ceremonial act or action
rit•u•al *n* **1 :** an established form for a ceremony **2 :** a system of rites
[1]**ri•val** *n* **:** one of two or more trying to get what only one can have
[2]**rival** *adj* **:** having the same worth
[3]**rival** *vb* **ri•valed** *or* **ri•valled; ri•val•ing** *or* **ri•val•ling 1 :** to be in competition with **2 :** [2]EQUAL
ri•val•ry *n, pl* **ri•val•ries :** the act of rivaling **:** the state of being a rival **:** COMPETITION
riv•er *n* **1 :** a natural stream of water larger than a brook or creek **2 :** a large stream

riv•et *n* **:** a bolt with a head at one end used for uniting two or more pieces by passing the shank through a hole in each piece and then beating or pressing down the plain end so as to make a second head

riv•u•let *n* **:** a small stream

roach *n* **:** COCKROACH

road *n* **1 :** an open way for vehicles, persons, and animals **2 :** PATH 3, ROUTE

road•bed *n* **1 :** the foundation of a road or railroad **2 :** the traveled surface of a road

road•side *n* **:** the strip of land along a road **:** the side of a road

road•way *n* **1 :** the strip of land over which a road passes **2 :** the part of the surface of a road traveled by vehicles

roam *vb* **:** to go from place to place with no fixed purpose or direction — **roam•er** *n*

1roan *adj* **:** of a dark color (as black or brown) sprinkled with white

2roan *n* **:** an animal (as a horse) with a roan coat

1roar *vb* **1 :** to utter a long full loud sound **2 :** to laugh loudly — **roar•er** *n*

2roar *n* **:** a long shout, bellow, or loud confused noise

1roast *vb* **1 :** to cook with dry heat (as in an oven) **2 :** to be or make very hot — **roast•er** *n*

2roast *n* **1 :** a piece of meat roasted or suitable for roasting **2 :** an outing at which food is roasted

3roast *adj* **:** cooked by roasting

rob *vb* **robbed; rob•bing 1 :** to take something away from a person or place in secrecy or by force, threat, or trickery **2 :** to keep from getting something due, expected, or desired — **rob•ber** *n*

rob•bery *n, pl* **rob•ber•ies :** the act or practice of robbing

1robe *n* **1 :** a long loose or flowing garment **2 :** a covering for the lower part of the body

2robe *vb* **robed; rob•ing 1 :** to put on a robe **2 :** 1DRESS 2

rob•in *n* **1 :** a small European thrush with a yellowish red throat and breast **2 :** a large North American thrush with a grayish back and dull reddish breast

ro•bot *n* **1 :** a machine that looks and acts like a human being **2 :** a capable but unfeeling person

ro•bust *adj* **:** strong and vigorously healthy — **ro•bust•ly** *adv* — **ro•bust•ness** *n*

1rock *vb* **1 :** to move back and forth as in a cradle **2 :** to sway or cause to sway back and forth

2rock *n* **1 :** a rocking movement **2 :** popular music played on instruments that are amplified electronically

3rock *n* **1 :** a large mass of stone **2 :** solid mineral deposits **3 :** something like a rock in firmness **:** SUPPORT

rock•er *n* **1 :** a curving piece of wood or metal on which an object (as a cradle) rocks **2 :** a structure or device that rocks on rockers **3 :** a mechanism that works with a rocking motion

1rock•et *n* **1 :** a firework that is driven through the air by the gases produced by a burning substance **2 :** a jet engine that operates like a firework rocket but carries the oxygen needed for burning its fuel **3 :** a bomb, missile, or vehicle that is moved by a rocket

2rocket *vb* **1 :** to rise swiftly **2 :** to travel rapidly in or as if in a rocket

rock•ing chair *n* **:** a chair mounted on rockers

rocking horse *n* **:** a toy horse mounted on rockers

rock 'n' roll *or* **rock and roll** *n* **:** 2ROCK 2

rock salt *n* **:** common salt in large crystals

rocky *adj* **rock•i•er; rock•i•est :** full of or consisting of rocks — **rock•i•ness** *n*

rod *n* **1 :** a straight slender stick or bar **2 :** a stick or bundle of twigs used in whipping a person **3 :** a measure of length equal to $16^1/_2$ feet (about 5 meters) **4 :** any of the sensory bodies shaped like rods in the retina that respond to faint light **5 :** a light flexible pole often with line and a reel attached used in fishing — **rod•like** *adj*

rode *past of* RIDE

ro•dent *n* **:** any of a group of mammals (as squirrels, rats, mice, and beavers) with sharp front teeth used in gnawing

ro•deo *n, pl* **ro•de•os 1 :** a roundup of cattle **2 :** an exhibition that features cowboy skills (as riding and roping)

1roe *n, pl* **roe** *or* **roes 1 :** ROE DEER **2 :** DOE

2roe *n* **:** the eggs of a fish especially while still held together in a membrane

roe•buck *n* **:** a male roe deer

roe deer *n* **:** a small deer of Europe and Asia with erect antlers forked at the tip

rogue *n* **1 :** a dishonest or wicked person **2 :** a pleasantly mischievous person

rogu•ish *adj* **:** being or like a rogue — **rogu•ish•ly** *adv* — **rogu•ish•ness** *n*

role *n* **1 :** a character assigned or taken on **2 :** a part played by an actor or singer **3 :** 1FUNCTION 1

1roll *n* **1 :** a writing that may be rolled up **:** SCROLL **2 :** an official list of names **3 :** something or a quantity of something that is rolled up or rounded as if rolled **4 :** a small piece of baked bread dough

2roll *vb* **1 :** to move by turning over and over on a surface without sliding **2 :** to shape or become shaped in rounded form **3**

: to make smooth, even, or firm with a roller **4 :** to move on rollers or wheels **5 :** to sound with a full echoing tone or with a continuous beating sound **6 :** to go by : PASS **7 :** to flow in a continuous stream **8 :** to move with a side-to-side sway

3**roll** *n* **1 :** a sound produced by rapid strokes on a drum **2 :** a heavy echoing sound **3 :** a rolling movement or action

roll•er *n* **1 :** a turning cylinder over or on which something is moved or which is used to press, shape, or smooth something **2 :** a rod on which something (as a map) is rolled up **3 :** a small wheel **4 :** a long heavy wave on the sea

roller coaster *n* **:** an elevated railway (as in an amusement park) with sharp curves and steep slopes on which cars roll

roller skate *n* **:** a skate that has wheels instead of a runner

rolling pin *n* **:** a cylinder (as of wood) used to roll out dough

ROM *n* **:** READ-ONLY MEMORY

1**Ro•man** *n* **1 :** a person born or living in Rome **2 :** a citizen of an ancient empire centered on Rome **3** *not cap* **:** roman letters or type

2**Roman** *adj* **1 :** of or relating to Rome or the Romans **2** *not cap* **:** of or relating to a type style with upright characters (as in "these definitions")

1**ro•mance** *n* **1 :** an old tale of knights and noble ladies **2 :** an adventure story **3 :** a love story **4 :** a love affair **5 :** an attraction or appeal to one's feelings

2**romance** *vb* **ro•manced; ro•manc•ing :** to have romantic thoughts or ideas

Roman numeral *n* **:** a numeral in a system of figures based on the ancient Roman system

ro•man•tic *adj* **1 :** not founded on fact : IMAGINARY **2 :** IMPRACTICAL **3 :** stressing or appealing to the emotions or imagination **4 :** of, relating to, or associated with love — **ro•man•ti•cal•ly** *adv*

1**romp** *n* **:** rough and noisy play : FROLIC

2**romp** *vb* **:** to play in a rough and noisy way

romp•er *n* **:** a young child's one-piece garment having legs that can be unfastened around the inside — usually used in pl.

1**roof** *n, pl* **roofs 1 :** the upper covering part of a building **2 :** something like a roof in form, position, or purpose — **roofed** *adj*

2**roof** *vb* **:** to cover with a roof

roof•ing *n* **:** material for a roof

roof•tree *n* **:** RIDGEPOLE

1**rook** *n* **:** an Old World bird similar to the related crows

2**rook** *vb* **:** 1CHEAT 1, SWINDLE

3**rook** *n* **:** one of the pieces in the game of chess

rook•ie *n* **:** BEGINNER, RECRUIT

1**room** *n* **1 :** available space **2 :** a divided part of the inside of a building **3 :** the people in a room **4 rooms** *pl* **:** LODGING 2 **5 :** a suitable opportunity

2**room** *vb* **:** to provide with or live in lodgings

room•er *n* **:** LODGER

rooming house *n* **:** a house for renting furnished rooms to lodgers

room•mate *n* **:** one of two or more persons sharing a room or dwelling

roomy *adj* **room•i•er; room•i•est :** SPACIOUS — **room•i•ness** *n*

1**roost** *n* **:** a support on which birds perch

2**roost** *vb* **:** to settle on a roost

roost•er *n* **:** an adult male chicken

1**root** *n* **1 :** a leafless underground part of a plant that stores food and holds the plant in place **2 :** the part of something by which it is attached **3 :** something like a root especially in being a source of support or growth **4 :** SOURCE 1 **5 :** 1CORE 3 **6 :** a word or part of a word from which other words are obtained by adding a prefix or suffix — **root•ed** *adj*

2**root** *vb* **1 :** to form or cause to form roots **2 :** to attach by or as if by roots **3 :** UPROOT 1

3**root** *vb* **:** to turn up or dig with the snout

4**root** *vb* **:** 2CHEER 2 — **root•er** *n*

root beer *n* **:** a sweet drink flavored with extracts of roots and herbs

1**rope** *n* **1 :** a large stout cord of strands (as of fiber or wire) twisted or braided together **2 :** a noose used for hanging **3 :** a row or string (as of beads) made by braiding, twining, or threading

2**rope** *vb* **roped; rop•ing 1 :** to bind, fasten, or tie with a rope **2 :** to set off or divide by a rope **3 :** 1LASSO — **rop•er** *n*

ro•sa•ry *n, pl* **ro•sa•ries :** a string of beads used in counting prayers

1**rose** *past of* RISE

2**rose** *n* **1 :** a showy and often fragrant white, yellow, pink, or red flower that grows on a prickly shrub (**rose•bush**) with compound leaves **2 :** a moderate purplish red

rose•mary *n* **:** a fragrant mint that has branching woody stems and is used in cooking and in perfumes

ro•sette *n* **:** a badge or ornament of ribbon gathered in the shape of a rose

rose•wood *n* **:** a reddish or purplish wood streaked with black and that is valued for making furniture

Rosh Ha•sha•nah *n* **:** the Jewish New Year observed as a religious holiday in September or October

ros•in *n* **:** a hard brittle yellow to dark red substance obtained especially from pine trees and used in varnishes and on violin bows

ros•ter *n* **:** an orderly list usually of people belonging to some group

ros•trum *n, pl* **rostrums** *or* **ros•tra :** a stage or platform for public speaking

rosy *adj* **ros•i•er; ros•i•est 1 :** of the color rose **2 :** PROMISING, HOPEFUL

1rot *vb* **rot•ted; rot•ting 1 :** to undergo decay **:** SPOIL **2 :** to go to ruin

2rot *n* **1 :** the process of rotting **:** the state of being rotten **2 :** a disease of plants or of animals in which tissue decays

ro•ta•ry *adj* **1 :** turning on an axis like a wheel **2 :** having a rotating part

ro•tate *vb* **ro•tat•ed; ro•tat•ing 1 :** to turn about an axis or a center **2 :** to do or cause to do something in turn **3 :** to pass in a series

ro•ta•tion *n* **1 :** the act of rotating especially on an axis **2 :** the growing of different crops in the same field usually in a regular order

rote *n* **:** repeating from memory of forms or phrases with little or no attention to meaning

ro•tor *n* **1 :** the part of an electrical machine that turns **2 :** a system of spinning horizontal blades that support a helicopter in the air

rot•ten *adj* **1 :** having rotted **2 :** morally bad **3 :** very unpleasant or worthless — **rot•ten•ly** *adv* — **rot•ten•ness** *n*

ro•tund *adj* **1 :** somewhat round **2 :** 4PLUMP — **ro•tund•ly** *adv* — **ro•tund•ness** *n*

rouge *n* **:** a cosmetic used to give a red color to cheeks or lips

1rough *adj* **1 :** uneven in surface **2 :** not calm **3 :** being harsh or violent **4 :** coarse or rugged in nature or look **5 :** not complete or exact — **rough•ly** *adv* — **rough•ness** *n*

2rough *n* **1 :** uneven ground covered with high grass, brush, and stones **2 :** something in a crude or unfinished state

3rough *vb* **1 :** ROUGHEN **2 :** to handle roughly **:** BEAT **3 :** to make or shape roughly — **rough it :** to live without ordinary comforts

rough•age *n* **:** coarse food (as bran) whose bulk increases the activity of the bowel

rough•en *vb* **:** to make or become rough

rough•neck *n* **:** a rough person **:** ROWDY

1round *adj* **1 :** having every part of the surface or circumference the same distance from the center **2 :** shaped like a cylinder **3 :** 4PLUMP **4 :** 1COMPLETE 1, FULL **5 :** nearly correct or exact **6 :** LARGE **7 :** moving in or forming a circle **8 :** having curves rather than angles — **round•ish** *adj* — **round•ly** *adv* — **round•ness** *n*

2round *adv* **:** 1AROUND

3round *n* **1 :** something (as a circle or globe) that is round **2 :** a song in which three or four singers sing the same melody and words one after another at intervals **3 :** a round or curved part (as a rung of a ladder) **4 :** an indirect path **5 :** a regularly covered route **6 :** a series or cycle of repeated actions or events **7 :** one shot fired by a soldier or a gun **8 :** ammunition for one shot **9 :** a unit of play in a contest or game **10 :** a cut of beef especially between the rump and the lower leg

4round *vb* **1 :** to make or become round **2 :** to go or pass around **3 :** to bring to completion **4 :** to express as a round number **5 :** to follow a winding course

5round *prep* **:** 2AROUND 123

round•about *adj* **:** not direct

round•house *n, pl* **round•hous•es :** a circular building where locomotives are kept or repaired

round trip *n* **:** a trip to a place and back usually over the same route

round•up *n* **1 :** the gathering together of animals on the range by circling them in vehicles or on horseback and driving them in **2 :** a gathering together of scattered persons or things **3 :** 2SUMMARY

round up *vb* **1 :** to collect (as cattle) by circling in vehicles or on horseback and driving **2 :** to gather in or bring together

round•worm *n* **:** any of a group of worms with long round bodies that are not segmented and that include serious parasites of people and animals

rouse *vb* **roused; rous•ing 1 :** 1AWAKE 1 **2 :** to stir up **:** EXCITE

1rout *n* **1 :** a state of wild confusion or disorderly retreat **2 :** a disastrous defeat

2rout *vb* **1 :** to put to flight **2 :** to defeat completely

1route *n* **:** a regular, chosen, or assigned course of travel

2route *vb* **rout•ed; rout•ing 1 :** to send or transport by a selected route **2 :** to arrange and direct the order of (as a series of factory operations)

1rou•tine *n* **:** a standard or usual way of doing

2routine *adj* **1 :** 2COMMONPLACE, ORDINARY **2 :** done or happening in a standard or usual way — **rou•tine•ly** *adv*

rove *vb* **roved; rov•ing :** to wander without definite plan or direction — **rov•er** *n*

1row *vb* **1 :** to move a boat by means of oars **2 :** to travel or carry in a rowboat

2row *n* **:** an act or instance of rowing

3row *n* **1 :** a series of persons or things in an orderly sequence **2 :** 1WAY 1, STREET

[4]**row** *n* **:** a noisy disturbance or quarrel
row•boat *n* **:** a boat made to be rowed
[1]**row•dy** *adj* **row•di•er; row•di•est :** coarse or rough in behavior — **row•di•ness** *n*
[2]**rowdy** *n, pl* **rowdies :** a rowdy person
roy•al *adj* **1 :** of or relating to a sovereign **:** REGAL **2 :** fit for a king or queen — **roy•al•ly** *adv*
roy•al•ty *n, pl* **roy•al•ties 1 :** royal status or power **2 :** royal character or conduct **3 :** members of a royal family **4 :** a share of a product or profit (as of a mine) claimed by the owner for allowing another to use the property **5 :** payment made to the owner of a patent or copyright for the use of it
[1]**rub** *vb* **rubbed; rub•bing 1 :** to move along the surface of a body with pressure **2 :** to wear away or chafe with friction **3 :** to cause discontent, irritation, or anger **4 :** to scour, polish, erase, or smear by pressure and friction — **rub the wrong way :** to cause to be angry **:** IRRITATE
[2]**rub** *n* **1 :** something that gets in the way **:** DIFFICULTY **2 :** something that is annoying **3 :** the act of rubbing
rub•ber *n* **1 :** something used in rubbing **2 :** an elastic substance obtained from the milky juice of some tropical plants **3 :** a synthetic substance like rubber **4 :** something (as an overshoe) made of rubber
rubber band *n* **:** a continuous band made of rubber for holding things together **:** ELASTIC
rubber stamp *n* **:** a stamp with a printing face of rubber
rub•bish *n* **:** TRASH
rub•ble *n* **:** a confused mass of broken or worthless things
ru•ble *n* **:** a Russian coin or bill
ru•by *n, pl* **rubies 1 :** a precious stone of a deep red color **2 :** a deep purplish red
ruck•us *n* **:** [4]ROW
rud•der *n* **:** a movable flat piece attached at the rear of a ship or aircraft for steering
rud•dy *adj* **rud•di•er; rud•di•est :** having a healthy reddish color — **rud•di•ness** *n*
rude *adj* **rud•er; rud•est 1 :** roughly made **2 :** not refined or cultured **:** UNCOUTH **3 :** IMPOLITE — **rude•ly** *adv* — **rude•ness** *n*
ru•di•ment *n* **:** a basic principle
ru•di•men•ta•ry *adj* **1 :** ELEMENTARY, SIMPLE **2 :** not fully developed
rue *vb* **rued; ru•ing :** to feel sorrow or regret for
rue•ful *adj* **1 :** exciting pity or sympathy **2 :** MOURNFUL 1, REGRETFUL
ruff *n* **1 :** a large round collar of pleated muslin or linen worn by men and women in the sixteenth and seventeenth centuries **2 :** a fringe of long hair or feathers on the neck of an animal or bird
ruf•fi•an *n* **:** a brutal cruel person
[1]**ruf•fle** *vb* **ruf•fled; ruf•fling 1 :** to disturb the smoothness of **2 :** [1]TROUBLE 1, VEX **3 :** to erect (as feathers) in or like a ruff **4 :** to make into or provide with a ruffle
[2]**ruffle** *n* **:** a strip of fabric gathered or pleated on one edge
rug *n* **:** a piece of thick heavy fabric usually with a nap or pile used especially as a floor covering
rug•ged *adj* **1 :** having a rough uneven surface **2 :** involving hardship **3 :** STRONG 9, TOUGH — **rug•ged•ly** *adv* — **rug•ged•ness** *n*
[1]**ru•in** *n* **1 :** complete collapse or destruction **2 ruins** *pl* **:** the remains of something destroyed **3 :** a cause of destruction
[2]**ruin** *vb* **1 :** to reduce to ruins **2 :** to damage beyond repair **3 :** [3]BANKRUPT
ru•in•ous *adj* **:** causing or likely to cause ruin **:** DESTRUCTIVE — **ru•in•ous•ly** *adv*
[1]**rule** *n* **1 :** a guide or principle for conduct or action **2 :** an accepted method, custom, or habit **3 :** the exercise of authority or control **:** GOVERNMENT **4 :** the time of a particular sovereign's reign **5 :** RULER 2
[2]**rule** *vb* **ruled; rul•ing 1 :** [1]CONTROL 2, DIRECT **2 :** to exercise authority over **:** GOVERN **3 :** to be supreme or outstanding in **4 :** to give or state as a considered decision **5 :** to mark with lines drawn along the straight edge of a ruler
rul•er *n* **1 :** [1]SOVEREIGN 1 **2 :** a straight strip (as of wood or metal) with a smooth edge that is marked off in units and used for measuring or as a guide in drawing straight lines
rum *n* **:** an alcoholic liquor made from sugarcane or molasses
[1]**rum•ble** *vb* **rum•bled; rum•bling :** to make or move with a low heavy rolling sound
[2]**rumble** *n* **:** a low heavy rolling sound
[1]**ru•mi•nant** *n* **:** an animal (as a cow) that chews the cud
[2]**ruminant** *adj* **1 :** chewing the cud **2 :** of or relating to the group of hoofed mammals that chew the cud
ru•mi•nate *vb* **ru•mi•nat•ed; ru•mi•nat•ing 1 :** to engage in thought **:** MEDITATE **2 :** to bring up and chew again what has been previously swallowed
[1]**rum•mage** *vb* **rum•maged; rum•mag•ing :** to make an active search especially by moving about, turning over, or looking through the contents of a place or container
[2]**rummage** *n* **:** a confused collection of different articles
rum•my *n* **:** a card game in which each player

DICTIONARY

tries to lay down cards in groups of three or more

1ru•mor *n* **1 :** widely held opinion having no known source **:** HEARSAY **2 :** a statement or story that is in circulation but has not been proven to be true

2rumor *vb* **:** to tell by rumor **:** spread a rumor

rump *n* **1 :** the back part of an animal's body where the hips and thighs join **2 :** a cut of beef between the loin and the round

rum•ple *vb* **rum•pled; rum•pling :** 2WRINKLE, MUSS

rum•pus *n* **:** 4ROW, FRACAS

1run *vb* **ran; run; run•ning 1 :** to go at a pace faster than a walk **2 :** to take to flight **3 :** to move freely about as one wishes **4 :** to go rapidly or hurriedly **5 :** to do something by or as if by running **6 :** to take part in a race **7 :** to move on or as if on wheels **8 :** to go back and forth often according to a fixed schedule **9 :** to migrate or move in schools **10 :** 2FUNCTION, OPERATE **11 :** to continue in force **12 :** to pass into a specified condition **13 :** 1FLOW 1 **14 :** DISSOLVE 1 **15 :** to give off liquid **16 :** to tend to develop a specified feature or quality **17 :** 1STRETCH 2 **18 :** to be in circulation **19 :** 2TRACE 4 **20 :** to pass over, across, or through **21 :** to slip through or past **22 :** to cause to penetrate **23 :** to cause to go **24 :** INCUR — **run into :** to meet by chance

2run *n* **1 :** an act or the action of running **2 :** a continuous series especially of similar things **3 :** sudden heavy demands from depositors, creditors, or customers **4 :** the quantity of work turned out in a continuous operation **5 :** the usual or normal kind **6 :** the distance covered in a period of continuous traveling **7 :** a regular course or trip **8 :** freedom of movement **9 :** a way, track, or path frequented by animals **10 :** an enclosure for animals where they may feed and exercise **11 :** a score made in baseball by a base runner reaching home plate **12 :** 2SLOPE 1 **13 :** a ravel in a knitted fabric

1run•away *n* **1 :** 2FUGITIVE **2 :** a horse that is running out of control

2runaway *adj* **:** running away **:** escaping from control

run–down *adj* **1 :** being in poor condition **2 :** being in poor health

1rung *past participle of* RING

2rung *n* **1 :** a rounded part placed as a crosspiece between the legs of a chair **2 :** one of the crosspieces of a ladder

run–in *n* **:** an angry dispute **:** QUARREL

run•ner *n* **1 :** one that runs **2 :** MESSENGER **3 :** a thin piece or part on or in which something slides **4 :** a slender creeping branch of a plant that roots at the end or at the joints to form new plants **5 :** a plant that forms or spreads by runners **6 :** a long narrow carpet (as for a hall)

run•ner–up *n, pl* **run•ners–up :** the competitor in a contest who finishes next to the winner

run•ny *adj* **:** running or likely to run

run out *vb* **1 :** to come to an end **:** EXPIRE **2 :** to become exhausted or used up — **run out of :** to use up the available supply of

run over *vb* **:** 1OVERFLOW 2

runt *n* **:** an unusually small person or animal

run•way *n* **1 :** a path beaten by animals in going to and from feeding grounds **2 :** a paved strip of ground on a landing field for the landing and takeoff of aircraft

ru•pee *n* **:** any of various coins (as of India or Pakistan)

1rup•ture *n* **1 :** a break in peaceful or friendly relations **2 :** a breaking or tearing apart (as of body tissue) **3 :** a condition in which a body part (as a loop of intestine) bulges through the weakened wall of the cavity that contains it

2rupture *vb* **rup•tured; rup•tur•ing 1 :** to part by violence **:** BREAK **2 :** to produce a rupture in **3 :** to have a rupture

ru•ral *adj* **:** of or relating to the country, country people or life, or agriculture

rural free delivery *n* **:** the free delivery of mail on routes in country districts

ruse *n* **:** 1TRICK 4, ARTIFICE

1rush *n* **:** a grasslike marsh plant with hollow stems used in chair seats and mats

2rush *vb* **1 :** to move forward or act with great haste or eagerness **2 :** to perform in a short time or at high speed **3 :** 1ATTACK 1, CHARGE — **rush•er** *n*

3rush *n* **1 :** a violent forward motion **2 :** a burst of activity or speed **3 :** an eager migration of people usually to a new place in search of wealth

4rush *adj* **:** demanding special speed

1Rus•sian *adj* **:** of or relating to Russia, its people, or the Russian language

2Russian *n* **1 :** a person born or living in Russia **2 :** a language of the Russians

1rust *n* **1 :** a reddish coating formed on metal (as iron) when it is exposed especially to moist air **2 :** a plant disease caused by fungi that makes spots on plants **3 :** a fungus that causes a rust — **rust•like** *adj*

2rust *vb* **:** to make or become rusty

1rus•tic *adj* **1 :** of, relating to, or suitable for the country **2 :** 1PLAIN 5, SIMPLE

2rustic *n* **:** a person living or raised in the country

1rus•tle *vb* **rus•tled; rus•tling 1 :** to make or cause to make a rustle **2 :** to steal (as cattle) from the range — **rus•tler** *n*

²rustle *n* **:** a quick series of small sounds
rusty *adj* **rust·i·er; rust·i·est** **1 :** affected by rust **2 :** less skilled and slow through lack of practice or old age — **rust·i·ness** *n*
¹rut *n* **1 :** a track worn by a wheel or by habitual passage **2 :** ¹ROUTINE
²rut *vb* **rut·ted; rut·ting :** to make a rut in
ru·ta·ba·ga *n* **:** a turnip with a large yellow root
ruth·less *adj* **:** having no pity **:** CRUEL — **ruth·less·ly** *adv* — **ruth·less·ness** *n*
-ry *n suffix, pl* **-ries :** -ERY
rye *n* **:** a hardy cereal grass grown especially for its edible seeds that are used in flour and animal feeds and in making whiskey

S

s *n, pl* **s's** *or* **ss** *often cap* **1 :** the nineteenth letter of the English alphabet **2 :** a grade rating a student's work as satisfactory
¹-s *n pl suffix* — used to form the plural of most nouns that do not end in *s, z, sh, ch,* or *y* following a consonant and with or without an apostrophe to form the plural of abbreviations, numbers, letters, and symbols used as nouns
²-s *adv suffix* — used to form adverbs showing usual or repeated action or state
³-s *vb suffix* — used to form the third person singular present of most verbs that do not end in *s, z, sh, ch,* or *y* following a consonant
-'s *n suffix or pron suffix* — used to form the possessive of singular nouns, of plural nouns not ending in *s,* and of some pronouns
Sab·bath *n* **1 :** the seventh day of the week in the Jewish calendar beginning at sundown on Friday and lasting until sundown on Saturday **2 :** the first day of the week (as Sunday) kept for rest and worship
sa·ber *or* **sa·bre** *n* **:** a cavalry sword with a curved blade
saber–toothed tiger *n* **:** a very large prehistoric cat with long sharp curved eyeteeth
Sa·bin vaccine *n* **:** a material that is taken by mouth to prevent polio
sa·ble *n* **1 :** the color black **2 :** a meat-eating animal of northern Europe and Asia that is related to the marten and prized for its soft rich brown fur
¹sab·o·tage *n* **:** deliberate destruction of or damage to property or machinery (as by enemy agents) to block production or a nation's war effort
²sabotage *vb* **sab·o·taged; sab·o·tag·ing :** to damage or block by sabotage
sac *n* **:** a baglike part of a plant or animal often containing a liquid — **sac·like** *adj*
sa·chem *n* **:** a North American Indian chief
¹sack *n* **1 :** ¹BAG 1 **2 :** a sack and its contents
²sack *vb* **:** to put into a sack
³sack *vb* **:** to loot after capture
⁴sack *n* **:** the looting of a city by its conquerors
sack·ing *n* **:** a strong rough cloth (as burlap) from which sacks are made
sac·ra·ment *n* **:** a religious act or ceremony that is considered especially sacred
sa·cred *adj* **1 :** HOLY 1 **2 :** RELIGIOUS 2 **3 :** deserving to be respected and honored — **sa·cred·ness** *n*
¹sac·ri·fice *n* **1 :** the act or ceremony of making an offering to God or a god especially on an altar **2 :** something offered as a religious act **3 :** an unselfish giving **4 :** a loss of profit
²sacrifice *vb* **sac·ri·ficed; sac·ri·fic·ing** **1 :** to offer or kill as a sacrifice **2 :** to give for the sake of something else **3 :** to sell at a loss
sad *adj* **sad·der; sad·dest** **1 :** filled with sorrow or unhappiness **2 :** causing or showing sorrow or gloom — **sad·ly** *adv* — **sad·ness** *n*
sad·den *vb* **:** to make or become sad
¹sad·dle *n* **1 :** a seat (as for a rider on horseback) that is padded and usually covered with leather **2 :** something like a saddle in shape, position, or use
²saddle *vb* **sad·dled; sad·dling** **1 :** to put a saddle on **2 :** to put a load on **:** BURDEN
saddle horse *n* **:** a horse suited for or trained for riding
sa·fa·ri *n* **:** a hunting trip especially in Africa
¹safe *adj* **saf·er; saf·est** **1 :** free or secure from harm or danger **2 :** successful in reaching base in baseball **3 :** giving protection or security against danger **4 :** HARMLESS **5 :** unlikely to be wrong **:** SOUND **6 :** not likely to take risks **:** CAREFUL — **safe·ly** *adv* — **safe·ness** *n*
²safe *n* **:** a metal chest for keeping something (as money) safe
¹safe·guard *n* **:** something that protects and gives safety
²safeguard *vb* **:** to keep safe
safe·keep·ing *n* **:** the act of keeping safe **:** protection from danger or loss
safe·ty *n* **:** freedom from danger **:** SECURITY
safety belt *n* **:** a belt for holding a person to something (as a car seat)
safety pin *n* **:** a pin that is bent back on itself

DICTIONARY

to form a spring and has a guard that covers the point

saf·fron *n* **1 :** an orange powder used especially to color or flavor foods that consists of the dried stigmas of a crocus with purple flowers **2 :** an orange to orange yellow

1sag *vb* **sagged; sag·ging 1 :** to sink, settle, or hang below the natural or right level **2 :** to become less firm or strong

2sag *n* **:** a sagging part or area

sa·ga *n* **:** a story of heroic deeds

sa·ga·cious *adj* **:** quick and wise in understanding and judging — **sa·ga·cious·ly** *adv* — **sa·ga·cious·ness** *n*

1sage *adj* **:** 2WISE 1 — **sage·ly** *adv*

2sage *n* **:** a very wise person

3sage *n* **1 :** a mint that grows as a low shrub and has grayish green leaves used to flavor foods **2 :** a mint grown for its showy usually scarlet flowers **3 :** SAGEBRUSH

sage·brush *n* **:** a western American plant related to the daisies that grows as a low shrub and has a bitter juice and sharp smell

Sag·it·tar·i·us *n* **1 :** a constellation between Scorpio and Capricorn imagined as a centaur **2 :** the ninth sign of the zodiac or a person born under this sign

sa·gua·ro *n, pl* **sa·gua·ros :** a giant cactus of the southwestern United States

said *past of* SAY

1sail *n* **1 :** a sheet of fabric (as canvas) used to catch enough wind to move boats through the water or over ice **2 :** the sails of a ship considered as a group **3 :** a trip in a sailing vessel

2sail *vb* **1 :** to travel on a boat moved by the wind **2 :** to travel by water **3 :** to move or pass over by ship **4 :** to manage or direct the motion of (a boat or ship moved by the wind) **5 :** to move or glide along

sail·boat *n* **:** a boat equipped with sails

sail·fish *n* **:** a fish related to the swordfish but with a large sail-like fin on its back

sail·or *n* **:** a person who sails

saint *n* **1 :** a good and holy person and especially one who is declared to be worthy of special honor **2 :** a person who is very good especially about helping others

Saint Ber·nard *n* **:** a very large powerful dog bred originally in the Swiss Alps

saint·ly *adj* **:** like a saint or like that of a saint — **saint·li·ness** *n*

sake *n* **1 :** 1PURPOSE **2 :** WELFARE 1, BENEFIT

sal·able *or* **sale·able** *adj* **:** good enough to sell **:** likely to be bought

sal·ad *n* **1 :** a dish of raw usually mixed vegetables served with a dressing **2 :** a cold dish of meat, shellfish, fruit, or vegetables served with a dressing

sal·a·man·der *n* **:** any of a group of animals that are related to the frogs but look like lizards

sa·la·mi *n* **:** a highly seasoned sausage of pork and beef

sal·a·ry *n, pl* **sal·a·ries :** a fixed amount of money paid at regular times for work done

sale *n* **1 :** an exchange of goods or property for money **2 :** the state of being available for purchase **3 :** 1AUCTION **4 :** a selling of goods at lowered prices

sales·clerk *n* **:** a person who sells in a store

sales·man *n, pl* **sales·men :** a person who sells either in a territory or in a store

sales·per·son *n* **:** one who sells especially in a store

sales tax *n* **:** a tax paid by the buyer on goods bought

sales·wom·an *n, pl* **sales·wom·en :** a woman who sells either in a territory or in a store

sa·li·va *n* **:** a watery fluid that contains enzymes which break down starch and is secreted into the mouth from glands in the neck

sal·i·vary *adj* **:** of, relating to, or producing saliva

Salk vaccine *n* **:** a material given by injection to prevent polio

sal·low *adj* **:** of a grayish greenish yellow color

1sal·ly *n, pl* **sallies 1 :** a rushing out to attack especially by besieged soldiers **2 :** a funny remark

2sally *vb* **sal·lied; sal·ly·ing :** to rush out

salm·on *n* **1 :** a large fish (**Atlantic salmon**) of the northern Atlantic Ocean valued for food and sport **2 :** any of several fishes (**Pacific salmon**) of the northern Pacific Ocean valued for food and sport

sa·loon *n* **1 :** a large public hall (as on a passenger ship) **2 :** a place where liquors are sold and drunk **:** BAR

sal·sa *n* **1 :** a spicy sauce of tomatoes, onions, and hot peppers **2 :** popular music of Latin American origin with characteristics of jazz and rock

1salt *n* **1 :** a colorless or white substance that consists of sodium and chlorine and is used in seasoning foods, preserving meats and fish, and in making soap and glass **2 :** a compound formed by replacement of hydrogen in an acid by a metal or group of elements that act like a metal

2salt *vb* **:** to add salt to

3salt *adj* **:** containing salt **:** SALTY

salt·wa·ter *adj* **:** of, relating to, or living in salt water

salty *adj* **salt·i·er; salt·i·est :** of, tasting of, or containing salt

sal·u·ta·tion *n* **1 :** an act or action of greeting **2 :** a word or phrase used as a greeting at the beginning of a letter

[1]**sa·lute** *vb* **sa·lut·ed; sa·lut·ing 1 :** to address with expressions of kind wishes, courtesy, or honor **2 :** to honor by a standard military ceremony **3 :** to give a sign of respect to (as a military officer) especially by a smart movement of the right hand to the forehead

[2]**salute** *n* **1 :** GREETING 1, SALUTATION **2 :** a military show of respect or honor **3 :** the position taken or the movement made to salute a military officer

[1]**sal·vage** *n* **1 :** money paid for saving a wrecked or endangered ship or its cargo or passengers **2 :** the act of saving a ship **3 :** the saving of possessions in danger of being lost **4 :** something that is saved (as from a wreck)

[2]**salvage** *vb* **sal·vaged; sal·vag·ing :** to recover (something usable) especially from wreckage

sal·va·tion *n* **1 :** the saving of a person from the power and the results of sin **2 :** something that saves

[1]**salve** *n* **:** a healing or soothing ointment

[2]**salve** *vb* **salved; salv·ing :** to quiet or soothe with or as if with a salve

[1]**same** *adj* **1 :** not another **:** IDENTICAL **2 :** UNCHANGED **3 :** very much alike

[2]**same** *pron* **:** something identical with or like another

same·ness *n* **1 :** the quality or state of being the same **2 :** MONOTONY

sam·pan *n* **:** a Chinese boat with a flat bottom that is usually moved with oars

[1]**sam·ple** *n* **:** a part or piece that shows the quality of the whole

[2]**sample** *vb* **sam·pled; sam·pling :** to judge the quality of by samples **:** TEST

sam·pler *n* **:** a piece of cloth with letters or verses embroidered on it

san·a·to·ri·um *n* **:** a place for the care and treatment usually of people recovering from illness or having a disease likely to last a long time

sanc·tion *n* **1 :** approval by someone in charge **2 :** an action short of war taken by several nations to make another nation behave

sanc·tu·ary *n, pl* **sanc·tu·ar·ies 1 :** a holy or sacred place **2 :** the most sacred part (as near the altar) of a place of worship **3 :** a building for worship **4 :** a place of safety **5 :** the state of being protected

[1]**sand** *n* **1 :** loose material in grains produced by the natural breaking up of rocks **2 :** a soil made up mostly of sand

[2]**sand** *vb* **1 :** to sprinkle with sand **2 :** to smooth or clean with sand or sandpaper — **sand·er** *n*

san·dal *n* **:** a shoe that is a sole held in place by straps

san·dal·wood *n* **:** the fragrant yellowish heartwood of an Asian tree

sand·bag *n* **:** a bag filled with sand and used as a weight (as on a balloon) or as part of a wall or dam

sand·bar *n* **:** a ridge of sand formed in water by tides or currents

sand dollar *n* **:** a flat round sea urchin

sand·man *n, pl* **sand·men :** a genie said to make children sleepy by sprinkling sand in their eyes

[1]**sand·pa·per** *n* **:** paper that has rough material (as sand) glued on one side and is used for smoothing and polishing

[2]**sandpaper** *vb* **:** to rub with sandpaper

sand·pip·er *n* **:** a small shorebird related to the plovers

sand·stone *n* **:** rock made of sand held together by a natural cement

sand·storm *n* **:** a storm of wind (as in a desert) that drives clouds of sand

[1]**sand·wich** *n* **:** two or more slices of bread or a split roll with a filling (as meat or cheese) between them

[2]**sandwich** *vb* **:** to fit in between things

sandy *adj* **sand·i·er; sand·i·est 1 :** full of or covered with sand **2 :** of a yellowish gray color

sane *adj* **san·er; san·est 1 :** having a healthy and sound mind **2 :** very sensible — **sane·ness** *n*

sang *past of* SING

san·i·tar·i·um *n* **:** SANATORIUM

san·i·tary *adj* **1 :** of or relating to health or hygiene **2 :** free from filth, infection, or other dangers to health

san·i·ta·tion *n* **1 :** the act or process of making sanitary **2 :** the act of keeping things sanitary

san·i·ty *n* **:** the state of being sane

sank *past of* SINK

San·ta Claus *n* **:** the spirit of Christmas as represented by a jolly old man in a red suit

[1]**sap** *n* **:** a watery juice that circulates through a higher plant and carries food and nutrients

[2]**sap** *vb* **sapped; sap·ping :** to weaken or exhaust little by little

sap·ling *n* **:** a young tree

sap·phire *n* **:** a clear bright blue precious stone

sap·wood *n* **:** young wood found just beneath the bark of a tree and usually lighter in color than the heartwood

sar·casm *n* **:** the use of words that normally mean one thing to mean just the opposite usually to hurt someone's feelings or show scorn

sar·cas·tic *adj* **1 :** showing or related to sarcasm **2 :** having the habit of sarcasm — **sar·cas·ti·cal·ly** *adv*

sar·dine *n* **:** a young or very small fish often preserved in oil and used for food

sa·ri *n* **:** a piece of clothing worn mainly by women of India that is a long light cloth wrapped around the body

sar·sa·pa·ril·la *n* **:** the dried root of a tropical American plant used especially as a flavoring

¹sash *n* **:** a broad band of cloth worn around the waist or over the shoulder

²sash *n* **1 :** a frame for a pane of glass in a door or window **2 :** the movable part of a window

¹sass *n* **:** a rude fresh reply

²sass *vb* **:** to reply to in a rude fresh way

sas·sa·fras *n* **:** a tall tree of eastern North America whose dried root bark was formerly used in medicine or as a flavoring

sassy *adj* **sass·i·er; sass·i·est :** given to or made up of sass

sat *past of* SIT

Sa·tan *n* **:** ¹DEVIL 1

satch·el *n* **:** a small bag for carrying clothes or books

sat·el·lite *n* **1 :** a smaller body that revolves around a planet **2 :** a vehicle sent out from the earth to revolve around the earth, moon, sun, or a planet **3 :** a country controlled by another more powerful country

sat·in *n* **:** a cloth (as of silk) with a shiny surface

sat·ire *n* **:** writing or cartoons meant to make fun of and often show the weaknesses of someone or something

sa·tir·i·cal *adj* **:** of, relating to, or showing satire

sat·is·fac·tion *n* **1 :** the act of satisfying **:** the condition of being satisfied **2 :** something that satisfies

sat·is·fac·to·ry *adj* **:** causing satisfaction — **sat·is·fac·to·ri·ly** *adv* — **sat·is·fac·to·ri·ness** *n*

sat·is·fy *vb* **sat·is·fied; sat·is·fy·ing 1 :** to carry out the terms of (as a contract) **2 :** to make contented **3 :** to meet the needs of **4 :** CONVINCE

sat·u·rate *vb* **sat·u·rat·ed; sat·u·rat·ing :** to soak full or fill to the limit

Sat·ur·day *n* **:** the seventh day of the week

Sat·urn *n* **:** the planet that is sixth in distance from the sun and has a diameter of about 115,000 kilometers

sa·tyr *n* **:** a forest god of the ancient Greeks believed to have the ears and the tail of a horse or goat

sauce *n* **1 :** a tasty liquid poured over food **2 :** stewed fruit

sauce·pan *n* **:** a small deep cooking pan with a handle

sau·cer *n* **:** a small shallow dish often with a slightly lower center for holding a cup

saucy *adj* **sauc·i·er; sauc·i·est 1 :** being rude usually in a lively and playful way **2 :** ²TRIM — **sauc·i·ly** *adv* — **sauc·i·ness** *n*

sau·er·kraut *n* **:** finely cut cabbage soaked in a salty mixture

saun·ter *vb* **:** to walk in a slow relaxed way **:** STROLL

sau·ro·pod *n* **:** any of a group of plant-eating dinosaurs (as a brontosaurus)

sau·sage *n* **1 :** spicy ground meat (as pork) usually stuffed in casings **2 :** a roll of sausage in a casing

¹sav·age *adj* **1 :** not tamed **:** WILD **2 :** being cruel and brutal **:** FIERCE — **sav·age·ly** *adv* — **sav·age·ness** *n*

²savage *n* **1 :** a person belonging to a group with a low level of civilization **2 :** a cruel person

sav·age·ry *n, pl* **sav·age·ries 1 :** an uncivilized condition **2 :** savage behavior

¹save *vb* **saved; sav·ing 1 :** to free from danger **2 :** to keep from being ruined **:** PRESERVE **3 :** to put aside for later use **4 :** to keep from being spent, wasted, or lost **5 :** to make unnecessary

²save *prep* **:** ¹EXCEPT

sav·ing *n* **1 :** the act of rescuing **2 :** something saved **3 savings** *pl* **:** money put aside (as in a bank)

sav·ior *or* **sav·iour** *n* **1 :** a person who saves from ruin or danger **2** *cap* **:** JESUS

sa·vo·ry *adj* **:** pleasing to the taste or smell

¹saw *past of* SEE

²saw *n* **1 :** a tool with a tooth-edged blade for cutting hard material **2 :** a machine that operates a toothed blade

³saw *vb* **sawed; sawed** *or* **sawn; saw·ing :** to cut or shape with a saw

⁴saw *n* **:** a common saying **:** PROVERB

saw·dust *n* **:** tiny bits (as of wood) which fall from something being sawed

saw·horse *n* **:** a frame or rack on which wood is rested while being sawed

saw·mill *n* **:** a mill or factory having machinery for sawing logs

saw–toothed *adj* **:** having an edge or outline like the teeth of a saw

sax·o·phone *n* **:** a musical wind instrument with a reed mouthpiece and a bent tubelike metal body with keys

¹say *vb* **said; say·ing 1 :** to express in words **2 :** to give as one's opinion or decision **:** DECLARE **3 :** ¹REPEAT 2, RECITE

2say *n* **1 :** an expression of opinion **2 :** the power to decide or help decide

say·ing *n* **:** PROVERB

scab *n* **1 :** a crust that forms over and protects a sore or wound **2 :** a plant disease in which crusted spots form on stems or leaves

scab·bard *n* **:** a protective case or sheath for the blade of a sword or dagger

scab·by *adj* **scab·bi·er; scab·bi·est 1 :** having scabs **2 :** diseased with scab

sca·bies *n, pl* **scabies :** an itch or mange caused by mites living as parasites in the skin

scaf·fold *n* **1 :** a raised platform built as a support for workers and their tools and materials **2 :** a platform on which a criminal is executed

1scald *vb* **1 :** to burn with or as if with hot liquid or steam **2 :** to pour very hot water over **3 :** to bring to a heat just below the boiling point

2scald *n* **:** an injury caused by scalding

1scale *n* **1 :** either pan of a balance or the balance itself **2 :** an instrument or machine for weighing

2scale *vb* **scaled; scal·ing 1 :** to weigh on scales **2 :** to have a weight of

3scale *n* **1 :** one of the small stiff plates that cover much of the body of some animals (as fish and snakes) **2 :** a thin layer or part (as a special leaf that protects a plant bud) suggesting a fish scale — **scaled** *adj* — **scale·less** *adj* — **scale·like** *adj*

4scale *vb* **scaled; scal·ing 1 :** to remove the scales of **2 :** 2FLAKE

5scale *vb* **scaled; scal·ing 1 :** to climb by or as if by a ladder **2 :** to regulate or set according to a standard — often used with *down* or *up*

6scale *n* **1 :** a series of tones going up or down in pitch in fixed steps **2 :** a series of spaces marked off by lines and used for measuring distances or amounts **3 :** a number of like things arranged in order from the highest to the lowest **4 :** the size of a picture, plan, or model of a thing compared to the size of the thing itself **5 :** a standard for measuring or judging

scale insect *n* **:** any of a group of insects that are related to the plant lice, suck the juices of plants, and have winged males and wingless females which look like scales attached to the plant

1scal·lop *n* **1 :** an edible shellfish that is a mollusk with a ribbed shell in two parts **2 :** any of a series of rounded half-circles that form a border on an edge (as of lace)

2scallop *vb* **1 :** to bake with crumbs, butter, and milk **2 :** to embroider, cut, or edge with scallops

1scalp *n* **:** the part of the skin and flesh of the head usually covered with hair

2scalp *vb* **:** to remove the scalp from

scaly *adj* **scal·i·er; scal·i·est :** covered with or like scales

scamp *n* **:** RASCAL

1scam·per *vb* **:** to run or move lightly

2scamper *n* **:** a playful scampering or scurrying

scan *vb* **scanned; scan·ning 1 :** to read or mark verses so as to show stress and rhythm **2 :** to examine or look over **3 :** to examine with a sensing device (as a scanner) especially to obtain information

scan·dal *n* **1 :** something that causes a general feeling of shame **:** DISGRACE **2 :** talk that injures a person's good name

scan·dal·ous *adj* **1 :** being or containing scandal **2 :** very bad or objectionable

Scan·di·na·vian *n* **:** a person born or living in Scandinavia

scan·ner *n* **:** a device that converts a printed image (as text or a photograph) into a form a computer can use (as for displaying on the screen)

1scant *adj* **1 :** barely enough **2 :** not quite full **3 :** having only a small supply

2scant *vb* **:** to give or use less than needed **:** be stingy with

scanty *adj* **scant·i·er; scant·i·est :** barely enough

1scar *n* **1 :** a mark left after injured tissue has healed **2 :** an ugly mark (as on furniture) **3 :** the lasting effect of some unhappy experience

2scar *vb* **scarred; scar·ring :** to mark or become marked with a scar

scar·ab *n* **:** a large dark beetle used in ancient Egypt as a symbol of eternal life

scarce *adj* **scarc·er; scarc·est 1 :** not plentiful **2 :** hard to find **:** RARE — **scarce·ness** *n*

scarce·ly *adv* **1 :** only just **2 :** certainly not

scar·ci·ty *n, pl* **scar·ci·ties :** the condition of being scarce

1scare *vb* **scared; scar·ing :** to be or become frightened suddenly

2scare *n* **1 :** a sudden fright **2 :** a widespread state of alarm

scare·crow *n* **:** a crude human figure set up to scare away birds and animals from crops

scarf *n, pl* **scarves** *or* **scarfs 1 :** a piece of cloth worn loosely around the neck or on the head **2 :** a long narrow strip of cloth used as a cover (as on a bureau)

scar·la·ti·na *n* **:** a mild scarlet fever

1scar·let *n* **:** a bright red

2scarlet *adj* **:** of the color scarlet

scarlet fever *n* **:** a contagious disease in

which there is a sore throat, a high fever, and a rash

scary *adj* **scar·i·er; scar·i·est :** causing fright

scat *vb* **scat·ted; scat·ting :** to go away quickly

scat·ter *vb* **1 :** to toss, sow, or place here and there **2 :** to separate and go in different ways

scat·ter·brain *n* **:** a flighty thoughtless person — **scat·ter·brained** *adj*

scav·en·ger *n* **1 :** a person who picks over junk or garbage for useful items **2 :** an animal that lives on decayed material

scene *n* **1 :** a division of an act in a play **2 :** a single interesting or important happening in a play or story **3 :** the place and time of the action in a play or story **4 :** the painted screens and slides used as backgrounds on the stage **:** SCENERY **5 :** something that attracts or holds one's gaze **:** VIEW **6 :** a display of anger or misconduct

scen·ery *n* **1 :** the painted scenes used on a stage and the furnishings that go with them **2 :** outdoor scenes or views

sce·nic *adj* **1 :** of or relating to stage scenery **2 :** giving views of natural scenery

¹scent *n* **1 :** an odor left by some animal or person no longer in a place or given off (as by flowers) at a distance **2 :** a usual or particular and often agreeable odor **3 :** power or sense of smell **4 :** a course followed by someone in search or pursuit of something **5 :** ¹PERFUME 2

²scent *vb* **1 :** to become aware of or follow through the sense of smell **2 :** to get a hint of **3 :** to fill with an odor **:** PERFUME

scep·ter *or* **scep·tre** *n* **:** a rod carried by a ruler as a sign of authority

¹sched·ule *n* **1 :** a written or printed list **2 :** a list of the times set for certain events **:** TIMETABLE **3 :** AGENDA, PROGRAM

²schedule *vb* **sched·uled; sched·ul·ing :** to form into or add to a schedule

¹scheme *n* **1 :** a plan or program of something to be done **:** PROJECT **2 :** a secret plan **:** PLOT **3 :** an organized design

²scheme *vb* **schemed; schem·ing :** to form a scheme — **schem·er** *n*

Schick test *n* **:** a test to find out whether a person might easily catch diphtheria

schol·ar *n* **1 :** a student in a school **:** PUPIL **2 :** a person who knows a great deal about one or more subjects

schol·ar·ly *adj* **:** like that of or suitable to learned persons

schol·ar·ship *n* **1 :** the qualities of a scholar **:** LEARNING **2 :** money given a student to help pay for further education

scho·las·tic *adj* **:** of or relating to schools, pupils, or education

¹school *n* **1 :** a place for teaching and learning **2 :** a session of school **3 :** SCHOOLHOUSE **4 :** the teachers and pupils of a school **5 :** a group of persons who share the same opinions and beliefs

²school *vb* **:** TEACH 2, TRAIN

³school *n* **:** a large number of one kind of fish or water animals swimming together

school·bag *n* **:** a bag for carrying schoolbooks

school·book *n* **:** a book used in schools

school·boy *n* **:** a boy who goes to school

school·girl *n* **:** a girl who goes to school

school·house *n, pl* **school·hous·es :** a building used as a place for teaching and learning

school·ing *n* **:** EDUCATION 1

school·mas·ter *n* **:** a man who has charge of a school or teaches in a school

school·mate *n* **:** a fellow pupil

school·mis·tress *n* **:** a woman who has charge of a school or teaches in a school

school·room *n* **:** CLASSROOM

school·teach·er *n* **:** a person who teaches in a school

school·work *n* **:** lessons done at school or assigned to be done at home

school·yard *n* **:** the playground of a school

schoo·ner *n* **:** a ship usually having two masts with the mainmast located toward the center and the shorter mast toward the front

schwa *n* **1 :** an unstressed vowel that is the usual sound of the first and last vowels of the English word *America* **2 :** the symbol ə commonly used for a schwa and sometimes also for a similarly pronounced stressed vowel (as in *cut*)

sci·ence *n* **1 :** a branch of knowledge in which what is known is presented in an orderly way **2 :** a branch of study that is concerned with collecting facts and forming laws to explain them

sci·en·tif·ic *adj* **1 :** of or relating to science or scientists **2 :** using or applying the methods of science — **sci·en·tif·i·cal·ly** *adv*

sci·en·tist *n* **:** a person who knows much about science or does scientific work

scis·sors *n sing or pl* **:** a cutting instrument with two blades fastened together so that the sharp edges slide against each other

scoff *vb* **:** to show great disrespect with mocking laughter or behavior

¹scold *n* **:** a person given to criticizing and blaming others

²scold *vb* **:** to find fault with or criticize in an angry way — **scold·ing** *n*

DICTIONARY

¹scoop *n* **1 :** a large deep shovel for digging, dipping, or shoveling **2 :** a shovellike tool or utensil for digging into a soft substance and lifting out some of it **3 :** a motion made with or as if with a scoop **4 :** the amount held by a scoop
²scoop *vb* **1 :** to take out or up with or as if with a scoop **2 :** to make by scooping
scoot *vb* **:** to go suddenly and fast
scoot·er *n* **1 :** a vehicle consisting of a narrow base mounted between a front and a back wheel and guided by a handle attached to the front wheel **2 :** MOTOR SCOOTER
scope *n* **1 :** space or opportunity for action or thought **2 :** the area or amount covered, reached, or viewed
scorch *vb* **1 :** to burn on the surface **2 :** to burn so as to brown or dry out
¹score *n* **1 :** a group of twenty things **:** TWENTY **2 :** a line (as a scratch) made with or as if with something sharp **3 :** a record of points made or lost (as in a game) **4 :** DEBT 2 **5 :** a duty or an injury kept in mind for later action **6 :** ¹GROUND 3, REASON **7 :** the written or printed form of a musical composition — **score·less** *adj*
²score *vb* **scored; scor·ing 1 :** to set down in an account **:** RECORD **2 :** to keep the score in a game **3 :** to cut or mark with a line, scratch, or notch **4 :** to make or cause to make a point in a game **5 :** ACHIEVE 2, WIN **6 :** ²GRADE 3, MARK
¹scorn *n* **1 :** an emotion involving both anger and disgust **2 :** a person or thing very much disliked
²scorn *vb* **:** to show scorn for
scorn·ful *adj* **:** feeling or showing scorn — **scorn·ful·ly** *adv*
Scor·pio *n* **1 :** a constellation between Libra and Sagittarius imagined as a scorpion **2 :** the eighth sign of the zodiac or a person born under this sign
scor·pi·on *n* **:** an animal related to the spiders that has a long jointed body ending in a slender tail with a poisonous stinger at the end
Scot *n* **:** a person born or living in Scotland
¹Scotch *adj* **:** ¹SCOTTISH
²Scotch *n pl* **:** ²SCOTTISH
scot–free *adj* **:** completely free from duty, harm, or punishment
¹Scot·tish *adj* **:** of or relating to Scotland or the Scottish
²Scottish *n pl* **:** the people of Scotland
scoun·drel *n* **:** a mean or wicked person **:** VILLAIN
¹scour *vb* **1 :** to rub hard with a rough substance in order to clean **2 :** to free or clear from impurities by or as if by rubbing
²scour *n* **:** an action or result of scouring
³scour *vb* **:** to go or move swiftly about, over, or through in search of something
¹scourge *n* **1 :** ²WHIP 1 **2 :** a cause of widespread or great suffering
²scourge *vb* **scourged; scourg·ing 1 :** to whip severely **:** FLOG **2 :** to cause severe suffering to **:** AFFLICT
¹scout *vb* **1 :** to go about in search of information **2 :** to make a search
²scout *n* **1 :** a person, group, boat, or plane that scouts **2 :** the act of scouting **3** *often cap* **:** BOY SCOUT **4** *often cap* **:** GIRL SCOUT
scout·ing *n* **1 :** the act of one that scouts **2** *often cap* **:** the general activities of Boy Scout and Girl Scout groups
scout·mas·ter *n* **:** the leader of a troop of Boy Scouts
scow *n* **:** a large boat with a flat bottom and square ends that is used chiefly for loading and unloading ships and for carrying rubbish
¹scowl *vb* **:** ¹FROWN 1
²scowl *n* **:** an angry look
scram *vb* **scrammed; scram·ming :** to go away at once
¹scram·ble *vb* **scram·bled; scram·bling 1 :** to move or climb quickly on hands and knees **2 :** to work hard to win or escape something **3 :** to mix together in disorder **4 :** to cook the mixed whites and yolks of eggs by stirring them while frying
²scramble *n* **:** the act or result of scrambling
¹scrap *n* **1 scraps** *pl* **:** pieces of leftover food **2 :** a small bit **3 :** waste material (as metal) that can be made fit to use again
²scrap *vb* **scrapped; scrap·ping 1 :** to break up (as a ship) into scrap **2 :** to throw away as worthless
³scrap *n* **:** ¹QUARREL 2, FIGHT
scrap·book *n* **:** a blank book in which clippings or pictures are kept
¹scrape *vb* **scraped; scrap·ing 1 :** to remove by repeated strokes of a sharp or rough tool **2 :** to clean or smooth by rubbing **3 :** to rub or cause to rub so as to make a harsh noise **:** SCUFF **4 :** to hurt or roughen by dragging against a rough surface **5 :** to get with difficulty and a little at a time — **scrap·er** *n*
²scrape *n* **1 :** the act of scraping **2 :** a sound, mark, or injury made by scraping **3 :** a disagreeable or trying situation
¹scratch *vb* **1 :** to scrape or injure with claws, nails, or an instrument **2 :** to make a scraping noise **3 :** to erase by scraping
²scratch *n* **:** a mark or injury made by scratching
scratchy *adj* **scratch·i·er; scratch·i·est :** likely to scratch or make sore or raw

[1]**scrawl** *vb* **:** to write quickly and carelessly **:** SCRIBBLE

[2]**scrawl** *n* **:** something written carelessly or without skill

scraw•ny *adj* **scraw•ni•er; scraw•ni•est :** poorly nourished **:** SKINNY

[1]**scream** *vb* **:** to cry out (as in fright) with a loud and shrill sound

[2]**scream** *n* **:** a long cry that is loud and shrill

[1]**screech** *n* **:** a shrill harsh cry usually expressing terror or pain

[2]**screech** *vb* **:** to cry out usually in terror or pain

[1]**screen** *n* **1 :** a curtain or wall used to hide or to protect **2 :** a network of wire set in a frame for separating finer parts from coarser parts (as of sand) **3 :** a frame that holds a usually wire netting and is used to keep out pests (as insects) **4 :** the flat surface on which movies are projected **5 :** the surface on which the image appears in an electronic display (as on a television set or computer terminal)

[2]**screen** *vb* **1 :** to hide or protect with or as if with a screen **2 :** to separate or sift with a screen

screen saver *n* **:** a computer program that usually displays images on the screen of a computer that is on but not in use so as to prevent damage to the screen

[1]**screw** *n* **1 :** a nail-shaped or rod-shaped piece of metal with a winding ridge around its length used for fastening and holding pieces together **2 :** the act of screwing tight **:** TWIST **3 :** PROPELLER

[2]**screw** *vb* **1 :** to attach or fasten with a screw **2 :** to operate, tighten, or adjust with a screw **3 :** to turn or twist on a thread on or like that on a screw

screw•driv•er *n* **:** a tool for turning screws

[1]**scrib•ble** *vb* **scrib•bled; scrib•bling :** to write quickly or carelessly — **scrib•bler** *n*

[2]**scribble** *n* **:** something scribbled

scribe *n* **1 :** a teacher of Jewish law **2 :** a person who copies writing (as in a book)

scrim•mage *n* **1 :** a confused struggle **2 :** the action between two football teams when one attempts to move the ball down the field

script *n* **1 :** the written form of a play or movie or the lines to be said by a radio or television performer **2 :** a type used in printing that resembles handwriting **3 :** HANDWRITING

scrip•ture *n* **1** *cap* **:** BIBLE 1 **2 :** writings sacred to a religious group

[1]**scroll** *n* **1 :** a roll of paper or parchment on which something is written or engraved **2 :** an ornament resembling a length of paper usually rolled at both ends

[2]**scroll** *vb* **:** to move words or images up or down a display screen as if by unrolling a scroll

[1]**scrub** *n* **1 :** a thick growth of small or stunted shrubs or trees **2 :** one of poor size or quality

[2]**scrub** *vb* **scrubbed; scrub•bing :** to rub hard in washing

[3]**scrub** *n* **:** the act or an instance or a period of scrubbing

scrub•by *adj* **scrub•bi•er; scrub•bi•est 1 :** of poor size or quality **2 :** covered with scrub

scruff *n* **:** the loose skin on the back of the neck

scruffy *adj* **scruff•i•er; scruff•i•est :** dirty or shabby in appearance

scru•ple *n* **1 :** a sense of right and wrong that keeps one from doing as one pleases **2 :** a feeling of guilt when one does wrong **:** QUALM

scru•pu•lous *adj* **:** having or showing very careful and strict regard for what is right and proper **:** CONSCIENTIOUS — **scru•pu•lous•ly** *adv*

scuff *vb* **1 :** to scrape the feet while walking **2 :** to become rough or scratched through wear

[1]**scuf•fle** *vb* **scuf•fled; scuf•fling 1 :** to struggle in a confused way at close quarters **2 :** to shuffle one's feet

[2]**scuffle** *n* **:** a rough confused struggle

scull *n* **1 :** an oar used at the rear of a boat to drive it forward **2 :** one of a pair of short oars **3 :** a boat driven by one or more pairs of sculls

sculp•tor *n* **:** one that sculptures

[1]**sculp•ture** *n* **1 :** the action or art of making statues by carving or chiseling (as in wood or stone), by modeling (as in clay), or by casting (as in melted metal) **2 :** work produced by sculpture

[2]**sculpture** *vb* **sculp•tured; sculp•tur•ing :** to make sculptures

scum *n* **1 :** a film of matter that rises to the top of a boiling or fermenting liquid **2 :** a coating on the surface of still water

scurf *n* **:** thin dry scales or a coating of these (as on a leaf or the skin)

[1]**scur•ry** *vb* **scur•ried; scur•ry•ing :** to move in a brisk way

[2]**scurry** *n, pl* **scur•ries :** the act or an instance of scurrying

[1]**scur•vy** *n* **:** a disease caused by lack of vitamin C in which the teeth loosen, the gums soften, and there is bleeding under the skin

[2]**scurvy** *adj* **scur•vi•er; scur•vi•est :** [1]MEAN 4, CONTEMPTIBLE

[1]**scut•tle** *n* **:** a pail or bucket for carrying coal

[2]**scuttle** *n* **:** a small opening with a lid or cover (as in the deck of a ship)
[3]**scuttle** *vb* **scut·tled; scut·tling :** to sink by cutting holes through the bottom or sides
[4]**scuttle** *vb* **scut·tled; scut·tling :** to run rapidly from view
scythe *n* **:** a tool with a curved blade on a long curved handle that is used to mow grass or grain by hand
sea *n* **1 :** a body of salt water not as large as an ocean and often nearly surrounded by land **2 :** OCEAN 1 **3 :** rough water **4 :** something suggesting a sea's great size or depth
sea anemone *n* **:** a hollow sea animal with a flowerlike cluster of tentacles about its mouth
sea·bird *n* **:** a bird (as a gull) that lives about the open ocean
sea·coast *n* **:** the shore of the sea
sea cucumber *n* **:** a sea animal related to the starfishes and sea urchins that has a long flexible muscular body shaped like a cucumber
sea dog *n* **:** an experienced sailor
sea·far·er *n* **:** a person who travels over the ocean **:** MARINER
[1]**sea·far·ing** *adj* **:** of, given to, or employed in seafaring
[2]**seafaring** *n* **:** a traveling over the sea as work or as recreation
sea·food *n* **:** edible saltwater fish and shellfish
sea·go·ing *adj* **:** suitable or used for sea travel
sea gull *n* **:** a gull that lives near the sea
sea horse *n* **:** a small fish with a head which looks like that of a horse
[1]**seal** *n* **1 :** a sea mammal that swims with flippers, lives mostly in cold regions, mates and bears young on land, eats flesh, and is hunted for fur, hides, or oil **2 :** the soft dense fur of a northern seal
[2]**seal** *n* **1 :** something (as a pledge) that makes safe or secure **2 :** a device with a cut or raised design or figure that can be stamped or pressed into wax or paper **3 :** a piece of wax stamped with a design and used to seal a letter or package **4 :** a stamp that may be used to close a letter or package **5 :** something that closes tightly **6 :** a closing that is tight and perfect
[3]**seal** *vb* **1 :** to mark with a seal **2 :** to close or make fast with or as if with a seal — **seal·er** *n*
sea level *n* **:** the surface of the sea midway between the average high and low tides
sea lion *n* **:** a very large seal of the Pacific Ocean
seal·skin *n* **:** [1]SEAL 2
[1]**seam** *n* **1 :** the fold, line, or groove made by sewing together or joining two edges or two pieces of material **2 :** a layer of a mineral or metal
[2]**seam** *vb* **1 :** to join with a seam **2 :** to mark with a line, scar, or wrinkle
sea·man *n, pl* **sea·men 1 :** a person who helps in the handling of a ship at sea **:** SAILOR **2 :** an enlisted person in the Navy or Coast Guard ranking above a seaman apprentice
seaman apprentice *n* **:** an enlisted person in the Navy or Coast Guard ranking above a seaman recruit
seaman recruit *n* **:** an enlisted person of the lowest rank in the Navy or Coast Guard
seam·stress *n* **:** a woman who earns her living by sewing
sea·plane *n* **:** an airplane that can rise from and land on water
sea·port *n* **:** a port, harbor, or town within reach of seagoing ships
sear *vb* **1 :** to dry by or as if by heat **:** PARCH **2 :** to scorch or make brown on the surface by heat
[1]**search** *vb* **1 :** to go through carefully and thoroughly in an effort to find something **2 :** to look in the pockets or the clothing of for something hidden — **search·ing·ly** *adv*
[2]**search** *n* **:** an act or instance of searching
search engine *n* **:** computer software used to search data (as text or a database) for requested information
search·light *n* **:** a lamp for sending a beam of bright light
sea·shell *n* **:** the shell of a sea creature
sea·shore *n* **:** the shore of a sea
sea·sick *adj* **:** sick at the stomach from the pitching or rolling of a ship — **sea·sick·ness** *n*
sea·side *n* **:** SEACOAST
[1]**sea·son** *n* **1 :** one of the four quarters into which a year is commonly divided **2 :** a period of time associated with something special
[2]**season** *vb* **1 :** to make pleasant to the taste by use of seasoning **2 :** to make suitable for use (as by aging or drying)
sea·son·al *adj* **:** of, relating to, or coming only at a certain season
sea·son·ing *n* **:** something added to food to give it more flavor
[1]**seat** *n* **1 :** something (as a chair) used to sit in or on **2 :** the part of something on which one rests in sitting **3 :** the place on or at which a person sits **4 :** a place that serves as a capital or center — **seat·ed** *adj*
[2]**seat** *vb* **1 :** to place in or on a seat **2 :** to provide seats for

seat belt *n* **:** a strap (as in an automobile or airplane) designed to hold a person in a seat
sea urchin *n* **:** a rounded shellfish related to the starfishes that lives on or burrows in the sea bottom and is covered with spines
sea•wall *n* **:** a bank or a wall to prevent sea waves from cutting away the shore
sea•wa•ter *n* **:** water in or from the sea
sea•weed *n* **:** an alga (as a kelp) that grows in the sea
se•clud•ed *adj* **:** hidden from sight
se•clu•sion *n* **:** the condition of being secluded
¹sec•ond *adj* **1 :** being next after the first **2 :** next lower in rank, value, or importance than the first
²second *adv* **:** in the second place or rank
³second *n* **:** one that is second
⁴second *n* **1 :** a sixtieth part of a minute of time or of a degree **2 :** MOMENT 1, INSTANT
⁵second *vb* **:** to support a motion or nomination so that it may be debated or voted on
sec•ond•ary *adj* **1 :** second in rank, value, or importance **2 :** of, relating to, or being the second of three levels of stress in pronunciation **3 :** derived from or coming after something original or primary
sec•ond•hand *adj* **1 :** not new **:** having had a previous owner **2 :** selling used goods
second lieutenant *n* **:** a commissioned officer of the lowest rank in the Army, Air Force, or Marine Corps
sec•ond•ly *adv* **:** in the second place
sec•ond–rate *adj* **:** of ordinary quality or value
se•cre•cy *n, pl* **se•cre•cies 1 :** the habit of keeping things secret **2 :** the quality or state of being secret or hidden
¹se•cret *adj* **1 :** hidden from the knowledge of others **2 :** done or working in secrecy — **se•cret•ly** *adv*
²secret *n* **:** something kept or planned to be kept from others' knowledge
sec•re•tary *n, pl* **sec•re•tar•ies 1 :** a person who is employed to take care of records and letters for another person **2 :** an officer of a business corporation or society who has charge of the letters and records and who keeps minutes of meetings **3 :** a government official in charge of the affairs of a department **4 :** a writing desk with a top section for books
¹se•crete *vb* **se•cret•ed; se•cret•ing :** to produce and give off as a secretion
²secrete *vb* **se•cret•ed; se•cret•ing :** to put in a hiding place
se•cre•tion *n* **1 :** the act or process of secreting some substance **2 :** a substance formed in and given off by a gland that usually performs a useful function in the body **3 :** a concealing or hiding of something
se•cre•tive *adj* **:** not open or frank
sect *n* **:** a group within a religion which has a special set of teachings or a special way of doing things
¹sec•tion *n* **1 :** a part cut off or separated **2 :** a part of a written work **3 :** the appearance that a thing has or would have if cut straight through **4 :** a part of a country, group of people, or community
²section *vb* **:** to cut into sections
sec•tor *n* **:** a part of an area or of a sphere of activity
sec•u•lar *adj* **1 :** not concerned with religion or the church **2 :** not bound by a monk's vows **:** not belonging to a religious order
¹se•cure *adj* **se•cur•er; se•cur•est 1 :** free from danger or risk **2 :** strong or firm enough to ensure safety **3 :** ¹SURE 5, ASSURED
²secure *vb* **se•cured; se•cur•ing 1 :** to make safe **2 :** to fasten tightly **3 :** to get hold of **:** ACQUIRE
se•cu•ri•ty *n, pl* **se•cu•ri•ties 1 :** the state of being secure **:** SAFETY **2 :** something given as a pledge of payment **3 :** something (as a stock certificate) that is evidence of debt or ownership
se•dan *n* **1 :** SEDAN CHAIR **2 :** a closed automobile seating four or more persons that has two or four doors and a permanent top
sedan chair *n* **:** a portable and often covered chair made to hold one person and to be carried on two poles by two men
se•date *adj* **:** quiet and steady in manner or conduct — **se•date•ly** *adv* — **se•date•ness** *n*
¹sed•a•tive *adj* **:** tending to calm or to relieve tension
²sedative *n* **:** a sedative medicine
sedge *n* **:** a plant that is like grass but has solid stems and grows in tufts in marshes
sed•i•ment *n* **1 :** the material from a liquid that settles to the bottom **2 :** material (as stones and sand) carried onto land or into water by water, wind, or a glacier
sed•i•men•ta•ry *adj* **:** of, relating to, or formed from sediment
se•duce *vb* **se•duced; se•duc•ing :** to persuade to do wrong
¹see *vb* **saw; seen; see•ing 1 :** to have the power of sight **:** view with the eyes **2 :** to have experience of **:** UNDERGO **3 :** to understand the meaning or importance of **4 :** to make sure **5 :** to attend to **6 :** to meet with **7 :** ACCOMPANY 1, ESCORT
²see *n* **1 :** the city in which a bishop's church is located **2 :** DIOCESE

[1]**seed** *n* **1 :** a tiny resting plant closed in a protective coat and able to develop under suitable conditions into a plant like the one that produced it **2 :** a small structure (as a spore or a tiny dry fruit) other than a true seed by which a plant reproduces itself **3 :** the descendants of one individual **4 :** a source of development or growth **:** GERM 2 — **seed·ed** *adj* — **seed·less** *adj*

[2]**seed** *vb* **1 :** [2]SOW 2, PLANT **2 :** to produce or shed seeds **3 :** to take the seeds out of

seed·case *n* **:** a dry hollow fruit (as a pod) that contains seeds

seed·ling *n* **1 :** a young plant grown from seed **2 :** a young tree before it becomes a sapling

seed plant *n* **:** a plant that reproduces by true seeds

seed·pod *n* **:** POD

seedy *adj* **seed·i·er; seed·i·est 1 :** having or full of seeds **2 :** poor in condition or quality

seek *vb* **sought; seek·ing 1 :** to try to find **2 :** to try to win or get **3 :** to make an attempt

seem *vb* **1 :** to give the impression of being **:** APPEAR **2 :** to suggest to one's own mind

seem·ing *adj* **:** APPARENT 3 — **seem·ing·ly** *adv*

seen *past participle of* SEE

seep *vb* **:** to flow slowly through small openings

seer *n* **:** a person who predicts events

[1]**see·saw** *n* **1 :** an up-and-down or backward-and-forward motion or movement **2 :** a children's game of riding on the ends of a plank balanced in the middle with one end going up while the other goes down **3 :** the plank used in seesaw

[2]**seesaw** *vb* **1 :** to ride on a seesaw **2 :** to move like a seesaw

seethe *vb* **seethed; seeth·ing 1 :** to move without order as if boiling **2 :** to be in a state of great excitement

seg·ment *n* **1 :** any of the parts into which a thing is divided or naturally separates **2 :** a part cut off from a figure (as a circle) by means of a line or plane **3 :** a part of a straight line included between two points — **seg·ment·ed** *adj*

seg·re·gate *vb* **seg·re·gat·ed; seg·re·gat·ing :** to set apart from others

seg·re·ga·tion *n* **1 :** an act, process, or instance of segregating **2 :** enforced separation of a race, class, or group from the rest of society

seize *vb* **seized; seiz·ing 1 :** to take possession of by force **2 :** to take hold of suddenly or with force

sei·zure *n* **:** an act of seizing **:** the state of being seized

sel·dom *adv* **:** not often **:** RARELY

[1]**se·lect** *adj* **1 :** chosen to include the best or most suitable individuals **2 :** of special value or excellence

[2]**select** *vb* **:** to pick out from a number or group **:** CHOOSE

se·lec·tion *n* **1 :** the act or process of selecting **2 :** something that is chosen

se·lec·tive *adj* **:** involving or based on selection

se·le·ni·um *n* **:** a gray powdery chemical element used chiefly in electronic devices

self *n, pl* **selves 1 :** a person regarded as an individual apart from everyone else **2 :** a special side of a person's character

self- *prefix* **1 :** oneself or itself **2 :** of or by oneself or itself **3 :** to, with, for, or toward oneself or itself

self–ad·dressed *adj* **:** addressed for return to the sender

self–cen·tered *adj* **:** SELFISH

self–con·fi·dence *n* **:** confidence in oneself and one's abilities

self–con·scious *adj* **:** too much aware of one's feelings or appearance when in the presence of other people — **self–con·scious·ly** *adv* — **self–con·scious·ness** *n*

self–con·trol *n* **:** control over one's own impulses, emotions, or actions

self–de·fense *n* **:** the act of defending oneself or one's property

self–ev·i·dent *adj* **:** having no need of proof

self–gov·ern·ing *adj* **:** having self-government

self–gov·ern·ment *n* **:** government by action of the people making up a community **:** democratic government

self–im·por·tant *adj* **:** believing or acting as if one's importance is greater than it really is

self·ish *adj* **:** taking care of oneself without thought for others — **self·ish·ness** *n*

self·less *adj* **:** not selfish — **self·less·ly** *adv* — **self·less·ness** *n*

self–pro·pelled *adj* **:** containing within itself the means for its own movement

self–re·li·ance *n* **:** trust in one's own efforts and abilities

self–re·spect *n* **1 :** a proper regard for oneself as a human being **2 :** regard for one's standing or position

self–re·straint *n* **:** proper control over one's actions or emotions

self–righ·teous *adj* **:** strongly convinced of the rightness of one's actions or beliefs

self·same *adj* **:** exactly the same

self–serv·ice *n* **:** the serving of oneself with things to be paid for to a cashier usually upon leaving

sell *vb* **sold; sell•ing** **1 :** to betray a person or duty **2 :** to exchange in return for money or something else of value **3 :** to be sold or priced — **sell•er** *n*

selves *pl of* SELF

sem•a•phore *n* **1 :** a device for sending signals that can be seen by the receiver **2 :** a system of sending signals with two flags held one in each hand

sem•blance *n* **:** outward appearance

se•mes•ter *n* **:** either of two terms that make up a school year

semi- *prefix* **1 :** half **2 :** partly **:** not completely **3 :** partial

semi•cir•cle *n* **:** half of a circle

semi•cir•cu•lar *adj* **:** having the form of a semicircle

semi•co•lon *n* **:** a punctuation mark ; that can be used to separate parts of a sentence which need clearer separation than would be shown by a comma, to separate main clauses which have no conjunction between, and to separate phrases and clauses containing commas

semi•con•duc•tor *n* **:** a solid substance whose ability to conduct electricity is between that of a conductor and that of an insulator

1semi•fi•nal *adj* **:** coming before the final round in a tournament

2semi•fi•nal *n* **:** a semifinal match or game

sem•i•nary *n, pl* **sem•i•nar•ies** **1 :** a private school at or above the high school level **2 :** a school for the training of priests, ministers, or rabbis

semi•sol•id *adj* **:** having the qualities of both a solid and a liquid

sen•ate *n* **1 :** the upper and smaller branch of a legislature in a country or state **2 :** a governing body

sen•a•tor *n* **:** a member of a senate

send *vb* **sent; send•ing** **1 :** to cause to go **2 :** to set in motion by physical force **3 :** to cause to happen **4 :** to cause someone to pass a message on or do an errand **5 :** to give an order or request to come or go **6 :** to bring into a certain condition — **send•er** *n*

1se•nior *n* **1 :** a person older or higher in rank than someone else **2 :** a student in the final year of high school or college

2senior *adj* **1 :** being older — used to distinguish a father from a son with the same name **2 :** higher in rank or office **3 :** of or relating to seniors in a high school or college

senior airman *n* **:** an enlisted person in the Air Force who ranks above airman first class but who has not been made sergeant

senior chief petty officer *n* **:** a petty officer in the Navy or Coast Guard ranking above a chief petty officer

senior master sergeant *n* **:** a noncommissioned officer in the Air Force ranking above a master sergeant

sen•sa•tion *n* **1 :** awareness (as of noise or heat) or a mental process (as seeing or smelling) resulting from stimulation of a sense organ **2 :** an indefinite bodily feeling **3 :** a state of excited interest or feeling **4 :** a cause or object of excited interest

sen•sa•tion•al *adj* **:** causing or meant to cause great interest

1sense *n* **1 :** a meaning or one of a set of meanings a word, phrase, or story may have **2 :** a specialized function or mechanism (as sight, taste, or touch) of the body that involves the action and effect of a stimulus on a sense organ **3 :** a particular sensation or kind of sensation **4 :** awareness arrived at through or as if through the senses **5 :** an awareness or understanding of something **6 :** the ability to make wise decisions **7 :** good reason or excuse

2sense *vb* **sensed; sens•ing** **:** to be or become conscious of

sense•less *adj* **1 :** UNCONSCIOUS 2 **2 :** STUPID 2 — **sense•less•ly** *adv* — **sense•less•ness** *n*

sense organ *n* **:** a bodily structure (as the retina of the eye) that reacts to a stimulus (as light) and activates associated nerves so that they carry impulses to the brain

sen•si•bil•i•ty *n, pl* **sen•si•bil•i•ties** **1 :** the ability to receive or feel sensations **2 :** the emotion or feeling of which a person is capable

sen•si•ble *adj* **1 :** possible to take in by the senses or mind **2 :** capable of feeling or perceiving **3 :** showing or containing good sense or reason — **sen•si•ble•ness** *n* — **sen•si•bly** *adv*

sen•si•tive *adj* **1 :** capable of responding to stimulation **2 :** easily or strongly affected, impressed, or hurt **3 :** readily changed or affected by the action of a certain thing — **sen•si•tive•ly** *adv* — **sen•si•tive•ness** *n*

sen•si•tiv•i•ty *n* **:** the quality or state of being sensitive

sen•so•ry *adj* **:** of or relating to sensation or the senses

sen•su•al *adj* **:** relating to the pleasing of the senses

sent *past of* SEND

1sen•tence *n* **1 :** JUDGMENT 1 **2 :** punishment set by a court **3 :** a group of words that makes a statement, asks a question, or expresses a command, wish, or exclamation **4 :** a mathematical statement (as an equation) in words or symbols

[2]**sentence** *vb* **sen·tenced; sen·tenc·ing :** to give a sentence to

sen·ti·ment *n* **1 :** a thought or attitude influenced by feeling **2 :** OPINION 1 **3 :** tender feelings of affection or yearning

sen·ti·men·tal *adj* **1 :** influenced strongly by sentiment **2 :** primarily affecting the emotions

sen·ti·nel *n* **:** SENTRY

sen·try *n, pl* **sentries :** a person (as a soldier) on duty as a guard

se·pal *n* **:** one of the specialized leaves that form the calyx of a flower

[1]**sep·a·rate** *vb* **sep·a·rat·ed; sep·a·rat·ing** **1 :** to set or keep apart **2 :** to make a distinction between **3 :** to cease to be together **:** PART

[2]**sep·a·rate** *adj* **1 :** set or kept apart **2 :** divided from each other **3 :** not shared **:** INDIVIDUAL **4 :** having independent existence

sep·a·rate·ly *adv* **:** apart from others

sep·a·ra·tion *n* **1 :** the act of separating **:** the state of being separated **2 :** a point or line at which something is divided

sep·a·ra·tor *n* **:** a machine for separating cream from milk

Sep·tem·ber *n* **:** the ninth month of the year

sep·tet *n* **:** a group or set of seven

sep·ul·cher *or* **sep·ul·chre** *n* **:** [1]GRAVE, TOMB

se·quel *n* **1 :** an event that follows or comes afterward **:** RESULT **2 :** a book that continues a story begun in another

se·quence *n* **1 :** the condition or fact of following or coming after something else **2 :** [2]RESULT 1, SEQUEL **3 :** the order in which things are or should be connected, related, or dated

se·quin *n* **:** a bit of shiny metal or plastic used as an ornament usually on clothing

se·quoia *n* **1 :** a California tree that grows almost 100 meters tall and has needles as leaves and small egg-shaped cones **2 :** REDWOOD

se·ra·pe *n* **:** a colorful woolen shawl or blanket

ser·e·nade *n* **:** music sung or played at night under the window of a lady

se·rene *adj* **1 :** [1]CLEAR 2 **2 :** being calm and quiet — **se·rene·ly** *adv* — **se·rene·ness** *n*

se·ren·i·ty *n* **:** the quality or state of being serene

serf *n* **:** a servant or laborer of olden times who was treated as part of the land worked on and went along with the land if it was sold

serge *n* **:** a woolen cloth that wears well

ser·geant *n* **1 :** a noncommissioned officer in the Army or Marine Corps ranking above a corporal or in the Air Force ranking above an airman first class **2 :** an officer in a police force

sergeant first class *n* **:** a noncommissioned officer in the Army ranking above a staff sergeant

sergeant major *n* **1 :** the chief noncommissioned officer at a military headquarters **2 :** a noncommissioned officer in the Marine Corps ranking above a first sergeant **3 :** a staff sergeant major or command sergeant major in the Army

[1]**se·ri·al** *adj* **:** arranged in or appearing in parts or numbers that follow a regular order — **se·ri·al·ly** *adv*

[2]**serial** *n* **:** a story appearing (as in a magazine or on television) in parts at regular intervals

se·ries *n, pl* **series :** a number of things or events arranged in order and connected by being alike in some way

se·ri·ous *adj* **1 :** thoughtful or quiet in appearance or manner **2 :** requiring much thought or work **3 :** being in earnest **:** not light or casual **4 :** IMPORTANT 1 **5 :** being such as to cause distress or harm — **se·ri·ous·ly** *adv* — **se·ri·ous·ness** *n*

ser·mon *n* **1 :** a speech usually by a priest, minister, or rabbi for the purpose of giving religious instruction **2 :** a serious talk to a person about his or her conduct

[redacted] *n* **:** a usually large snake

se·rum *n* **:** the liquid part that can be separated from coagulated blood, contains antibodies, and is sometimes used to prevent or cure disease

ser·vant *n* **:** a person hired to perform household or personal services

[1]**serve** *vb* **served; serv·ing** **1 :** to be a servant **2 :** to give the service and respect due **3 :** [2]WORSHIP 1 **4 :** to put in **:** SPEND **5 :** to be of use **:** answer some purpose **6 :** to provide helpful services **7 :** to be enough for **8 :** to hold an office **:** perform a duty **9 :** to help persons to food or set out helpings of food or drink **10 :** to furnish with something needed or desired **11 :** to make a serve (as in tennis)

[2]**serve** *n* **:** an act of putting the ball or shuttlecock in play (as in tennis or badminton)

[1]**ser·vice** *n* **1 :** the occupation or function of serving or working as a servant **2 :** the work or action of one that serves **3 :** [2]HELP 1, USE **4 :** a religious ceremony **5 :** a helpful or useful act **:** good turn **6 :** [2]SERVE **7 :** a set of dishes or silverware **8 :** a branch of public employment or the people working in it **9 :** a nation's armed forces **10 :** an organization for supplying some public

demand or keeping up and repairing something

²**service** *vb* **ser·viced; ser·vic·ing :** to work at taking care of or repairing

ser·vice·able *adj* **1 :** fit for or suited to some use **2 :** lasting or wearing well in use — **ser·vice·able·ness** *n*

ser·vice·man *n, pl* **ser·vice·men :** a male member of the armed forces

service station *n* **:** a place for servicing motor vehicles especially with gasoline and oil

ser·vile *adj* **1 :** of or suitable to a slave **2 :** lacking spirit or independence

serv·ing *n* **:** a helping of food

ser·vi·tude *n* **:** the condition of a slave

ses·sion *n* **1 :** a single meeting (as of a court, lawmaking body, or school) **2 :** a whole series of meetings **3 :** the time during which a court, congress, or school meets

¹**set** *vb* **set; set·ting 1 :** to cause to sit **2 :** to cover and warm eggs to hatch them **3 :** to put or fix in a place or condition **4 :** to arrange in a desired and especially a normal position **5 :** ¹START 5 **6 :** to cause to be, become, or do **7 :** to fix at a certain amount **:** SETTLE **8 :** to furnish as a model **9 :** to put in order for immediate use **10 :** to provide (as words or verses) with music **11 :** to fix firmly **12 :** to become or cause to become firm or solid **13 :** to form and bring to maturity **14 :** to pass below the horizon **:** go down — **set about :** to begin to do — **set forth :** to start out

²**set** *n* **1 :** the act or action of setting **:** the condition of being set **2 :** a number of persons or things of the same kind that belong or are used together **3 :** the form or movement of the body or of its parts **4 :** an artificial setting for a scene of a play or motion picture **5 :** a group of tennis games that make up a match **6 :** a collection of mathematical elements **7 :** an electronic apparatus

³**set** *adj* **1 :** fixed by authority **2 :** not very willing to change **3 :** ¹READY 1

set·back *n* **:** a slowing of progress **:** a temporary defeat

set down *vb* **1 :** to place at rest on a surface **2 :** to land an aircraft

set in *vb* **:** to make its appearance **:** BEGIN

set off *vb* **1 :** to cause to stand out **2 :** to set apart **3 :** to cause to start **4 :** EXPLODE 1 **5 :** to start a journey

set on *vb* **:** to urge to attack or chase

set out *vb* **1 :** UNDERTAKE 1 **2 :** to begin on a course or journey

set·tee *n* **:** a long seat with a back

set·ter *n* **1 :** one that sets **2 :** a large dog that has long hair and is used in hunting birds

set·ting *n* **1 :** the act of one that sets **2 :** that in which something is set or mounted **3 :** the background (as time and place) of the action of a story or play **4 :** a batch of eggs for hatching

¹**set·tle** *vb* **set·tled; set·tling 1 :** to place so as to stay **2 :** to come to rest **3 :** to sink gradually to a lower level **4 :** to sink in a liquid **5 :** to make one's home **6 :** to apply oneself **7 :** to fix by agreement **8 :** to put in order **9 :** to make quiet **:** CALM **10 :** DECIDE 1 **11 :** to complete payment on **12 :** ADJUST 1

²**settle** *n* **:** a long wooden bench with arms and a high solid back

set·tle·ment *n* **1 :** the act of settling **:** the condition of being settled **2 :** final payment (as of a bill) **3 :** the act or fact of establishing colonies **4 :** a place or region newly settled **5 :** a small village **6 :** an institution that gives help to people in a crowded part of a city

set·tler *n* **:** a person who settles in a new region **:** COLONIST

set up *vb* **1 :** to place or secure in position **2 :** to put in operation **:** FOUND, ESTABLISH

¹**sev·en** *adj* **:** being one more than six

²**seven** *n* **:** one more than six **:** 7

¹**sev·en·teen** *adj* **:** being one more than sixteen

²**seventeen** *n* **:** one more than sixteen **:** 17

¹**sev·en·teenth** *adj* **:** coming right after sixteenth

²**seventeenth** *n* **:** number seventeen in a series

¹**sev·enth** *adj* **:** coming right after sixth

²**seventh** *n* **1 :** number seven in a series **2 :** one of seven equal parts

¹**sev·en·ti·eth** *adj* **:** coming right after sixty-ninth

²**seventieth** *n* **:** number seventy in a series

¹**sev·en·ty** *adj* **:** being seven times ten

²**seventy** *n* **:** seven times ten **:** 70

sev·er *vb* **1 :** to put or keep apart **:** DIVIDE **2 :** to come or break apart

¹**sev·er·al** *adj* **1 :** separate or distinct from others **:** DIFFERENT **2 :** consisting of more than two but not very many

²**several** *pron* **:** a small number **:** more than two but not many

se·vere *adj* **se·ver·er; se·ver·est 1 :** very strict **:** HARSH **2 :** serious in feeling or manner **:** GRAVE **3 :** not using unnecessary ornament **:** PLAIN **4 :** hard to bear or deal with — **se·vere·ly** *adv* — **se·vere·ness** *n*

se·ver·i·ty *n* **:** the quality or state of being severe

sew *vb* **sewed; sewn** *or* **sewed; sew·ing 1 :** to join or fasten by stitches **2 :** to work with needle and thread

sew·age *n* **:** waste materials carried off by sewers
¹sew·er *n* **:** one that sews
²sew·er *n* **:** a usually covered drain to carry off water and waste
sew·er·age *n* **1 :** SEWAGE **2 :** the removal and disposal of sewage by sewers **3 :** a system of sewers
sew·ing *n* **1 :** the act, method, or occupation of one that sews **2 :** material being sewed or to be sewed
sex *n* **1 :** either of two divisions of living things and especially humans, one made up of males, the other of females **2 :** the things that make males and females different from each other **3 :** sexual activity
sex·ism *n* **:** distinction and especially unjust distinction based on sex and made against one person or group (as women) in favor of another
sex·ist *adj* **:** based on or showing sexism — **sexist** *n*
sex·tet *n* **:** a group or set of six
sex·ton *n* **:** an official of a church who takes care of church buildings and property
sex·u·al *adj* **1 :** of or relating to sex or the sexes **2 :** of, relating to, or being the form of reproduction in which germ cells from two parents combine in fertilization to form a new individual — **sex·u·al·ly** *adv*
shab·by *adj* **shab·bi·er; shab·bi·est 1 :** dressed in worn clothes **2 :** faded and worn from use or wear **3 :** not fair or generous — **shab·bi·ly** *adv* — **shab·bi·ness** *n*
shack *n* **:** HUT, SHANTY
¹shack·le *n* **1 :** a ring or band that prevents free use of the legs or arms **2 :** something that prevents free action **3 :** a U-shaped metal device for joining or fastening something
²shackle *vb* **shack·led; shack·ling 1 :** to bind or fasten with a shackle **2 :** HINDER
shad *n, pl* **shad :** any of several sea fishes related to the herrings that have deep bodies, swim up rivers to spawn, and are important food fish
¹shade *n* **1 :** partial darkness **2 :** space sheltered from light or heat and especially from the sun **3 shades** *pl* **:** the shadows that gather as darkness falls **4 :** GHOST, SPIRIT **5 :** something that blocks off or cuts down light **6 :** the darkening of some objects in a painting or drawing to suggest that they are in shade **7 :** the darkness or lightness of a color **8 :** a very small difference or amount
²shade *vb* **shad·ed; shad·ing 1 :** to shelter from light or heat **2 :** to mark with shades of light or color **3 :** to show or begin to have slight differences of color, value, or meaning
¹shad·ow *n* **1 :** ¹SHADE 1 **2 :** a reflected image **3 :** shelter from danger or view **4 :** the dark figure cast on a surface by a body that is between the surface and the light **5 :** PHANTOM **6 shadows** *pl* **:** darkness caused by the setting of the sun **7 :** a very little bit **:** TRACE
²shadow *vb* **1 :** to cast a shadow upon **2 :** to cast gloom over **3 :** to follow and watch closely especially in a secret way
shad·owy *adj* **1 :** not realistic **2 :** full of shadow
shady *adj* **shad·i·er; shad·i·est 1 :** sheltered from the sun's rays **2 :** not right or honest — **shad·i·ness** *n*
shaft *n* **1 :** the long handle of a weapon (as a spear) **2 :** one of two poles between which a horse is hitched to pull a wagon or carriage **3 :** an arrow or its narrow stem **4 :** a narrow beam of light **5 :** a long narrow part especially when round **6 :** the handle of a tool or instrument **7 :** a bar to support rotating pieces of machinery or to give them motion **8 :** a tall monument (as a column) **9 :** a mine opening made for finding or mining ore **10 :** an opening or passage straight down through the floors of a building
shag·gy *adj* **shag·gi·er; shag·gi·est 1 :** covered with or made up of a long, coarse, and tangled growth (as of hair or vegetation) **2 :** having a rough or hairy surface — **shag·gi·ly** *adv* — **shag·gi·ness** *n*
¹shake *vb* **shook; shak·en; shak·ing 1 :** to tremble or make tremble **:** QUIVER **2 :** to make less firm **:** WEAKEN **3 :** to move back and forth or to and fro **4 :** to cause to be, become, go, or move by or as if by a shake
²shake *n* **:** the act or motion of shaking
shak·er *n* **:** one that shakes or is used in shaking
shaky *adj* **shak·i·er; shak·i·est :** easily shaken **:** UNSOUND — **shak·i·ly** *adv* — **shak·i·ness** *n*
shale *n* **:** a rock with a fine grain formed from clay, mud, or silt
shall *helping verb, past* **should;** *present sing & pl* **shall 1 :** am or are going to or expecting to **:** WILL **2 :** is or are forced to **:** MUST
¹shal·low *adj* **1 :** not deep **2 :** showing little knowledge, thought, or feeling — **shal·low·ness** *n*
²shallow *n* **:** a shallow place in a body of water — usually used in pl.
¹sham *n* **:** ³COUNTERFEIT, IMITATION
²sham *adj* **:** not real **:** FALSE
³sham *vb* **shammed; sham·ming :** to act in a deceiving way

DICTIONARY

sham•ble *vb* **sham•bled; sham•bling :** to walk in an awkward unsteady way

sham•bles *n sing or pl* **:** a place or scene of disorder or destruction

[1]**shame** *n* **1 :** a painful emotion caused by having done something wrong or improper **2 :** ability to feel shame **3 :** [1]DISHONOR 1, DISGRACE **4 :** something that brings disgrace or causes shame or strong regret

[2]**shame** *vb* **shamed; sham•ing 1 :** to make ashamed **2 :** [2]DISHONOR **3 :** to force by causing to feel shame

shame•faced *adj* **:** seeming ashamed — **shame•faced•ly** *adv* — **shame•faced•ness** *n*

shame•ful *adj* **:** bringing shame **:** DISGRACEFUL — **shame•ful•ly** *adv* — **shame•ful•ness** *n*

shame•less *adj* **:** having no shame — **shame•less•ly** *adv* — **shame•less•ness** *n*

[1]**sham•poo** *vb* **:** to wash the hair and scalp

[2]**shampoo** *n, pl* **sham•poos 1 :** a washing of the hair **2 :** a cleaner made for washing the hair

sham•rock *n* **:** a plant (as some clovers) that has leaves with three leaflets and is used as an emblem by the Irish

shank *n* **1 :** the lower part of the human leg **:** the equivalent part of a lower animal **2 :** the part of a tool that connects the working part with a part by which it is held or moved

shan't : shall not

shan•ty *n, pl* **shanties :** a small roughly built shelter or dwelling

[1]**shape** *vb* **shaped; shap•ing 1 :** to give a certain form or shape to **2 :** DEVISE **3 :** to make fit especially for some purpose **:** ADAPT **4 :** to take on a definite form or quality **:** DEVELOP — **shap•er** *n*

[2]**shape** *n* **1 :** outward appearance **:** FORM **2 :** the outline of a body **:** FIGURE **3 :** definite arrangement and form **4 :** [1]CONDITION 3 — **shaped** *adj*

shape•less *adj* **1 :** having no fixed or regular shape **2 :** not shapely — **shape•less•ly** *adv* — **shape•less•ness** *n*

shape•ly *adj* **shape•li•er; shape•li•est :** having a pleasing shape — **shape•li•ness** *n*

[1]**share** *n* **1 :** a portion belonging to one person **2 :** the part given or belonging to one of a number of persons owning something together **3 :** any of the equal portions into which a property or corporation is divided

[2]**share** *vb* **shared; shar•ing 1 :** to divide and distribute in portions **2 :** to use, experience, or enjoy with others **3 :** to take a part

share•crop *vb* **share•cropped; share•cropping :** to farm another's land for a share of the crop or profit — **share•crop•per** *n*

[1]**shark** *n* **:** any of a group of mostly fierce sea fishes that are typically gray, have a skeleton of cartilage, and include some forms that may attack humans

[2]**shark** *n* **:** a sly greedy person who takes advantage of others

[1]**sharp** *adj* **1 :** having a thin edge or fine point **2 :** brisk and cold **3 :** QUICK-WITTED, SMART **4 :** ATTENTIVE 1 **5 :** having very good ability to see or hear **6 :** ENERGETIC, BRISK **7 :** SEVERE 1, ANGRY **8 :** very trying to the feelings **:** causing distress **9 :** strongly affecting the senses **10 :** ending in a point or edge **11 :** involving an abrupt change **12 :** DISTINCT 2 **13 :** raised in pitch by a half step **14 :** higher than true pitch — **sharp•ly** *adv* — **sharp•ness** *n*

[2]**sharp** *adv* **1 :** in a sharp manner **2 :** at an exact time

[3]**sharp** *n* **1 :** a note or tone that is a half step higher than the note named **2 :** a sign ♯ that tells that a note is to be made higher by a half step

sharp•en *vb* **:** to make or become sharp or sharper — **sharp•en•er** *n*

shat•ter *vb* **1 :** to break or fall to pieces **2 :** to damage badly **:** RUIN, WRECK

[1]**shave** *vb* **shaved; shaved** *or* **shav•en; shav•ing 1 :** to cut or trim off with a sharp blade **2 :** to make bare or smooth by cutting the hair from **3 :** to trim closely

[2]**shave** *n* **1 :** an operation of shaving **2 :** a narrow escape

shav•ing *n* **:** a thin slice or strip sliced off with a cutting tool

shawl *n* **:** a square or oblong piece of cloth used especially by women as a loose covering for the head or shoulders

she *pron* **:** that female one

sheaf *n, pl* **sheaves 1 :** a bundle of stalks and ears of grain **2 :** a group of things fastened together — **sheaf•like** *adj*

shear *vb* **sheared; sheared** *or* **shorn; shear•ing 1 :** to cut the hair or wool from **:** CLIP **2 :** to strip of as if by cutting **3 :** to cut or break sharply — **shear•er** *n*

shears *n pl* **:** a cutting tool like a pair of large scissors

sheath *n, pl* **sheaths 1 :** a case for a blade (as of a knife) **2 :** a covering (as the outer wings of a beetle) suggesting a sheath in form or use

sheathe *vb* **sheathed; sheath•ing 1 :** to put into a sheath **2 :** to cover with something that protects

sheath•ing *n* **:** the first covering of boards or of waterproof material on the outside wall of a frame house or on a timber roof

sheaves *pl of* SHEAF

[1]**shed** *vb* **shed; shed·ding** **1 :** to give off in drops **2 :** to cause (blood) to flow from a cut or wound **3 :** to spread abroad **4 :** REPEL 3 **5 :** to cast (as a natural covering) aside

[2]**shed** *n* **:** a structure built for shelter or storage

she'd : she had **:** she would

sheen *n* **:** a bright or shining condition **:** LUSTER

sheep *n, pl* **sheep** **1 :** an animal related to the goat that is raised for meat or for its wool and skin **2 :** a weak helpless person who is easily led

sheep·fold *n* **:** a pen or shelter for sheep

sheep·herd·er *n* **:** a worker in charge of a flock of sheep

sheep·ish *adj* **1 :** like a sheep **2 :** embarrassed especially over being found out in a fault — **sheep·ish·ly** *adv* — **sheep·ish·ness** *n*

sheep·skin *n* **:** the skin of a sheep or leather prepared from it

[1]**sheer** *adj* **1 :** very thin or transparent **2 :** THOROUGH 1, ABSOLUTE **3 :** very steep — **sheer·ly** *adv* — **sheer·ness** *n*

[2]**sheer** *adv* **1 :** COMPLETELY **2 :** straight up or down

[1]**sheet** *n* **1 :** a broad piece of cloth (as an article of bedding used next to the body) **2 :** a broad piece of paper (as for writing or printing) **3 :** a broad surface **4 :** something that is very thin as compared with its length and width — **sheet·like** *adj*

[2]**sheet** *n* **:** a rope or chain used to adjust the angle at which the sail of a boat is set to catch the wind

sheikh *or* **sheik** *n* **:** an Arab chief

shek·el *n* **1 :** any of various ancient units of weight (as of the Hebrews) **2 :** a coin weighing one shekel

shelf *n, pl* **shelves** **1 :** a flat piece (as of board or metal) set above a floor (as on a wall or in a bookcase) to hold things **2 :** something (as a sandbar or ledge of rock) that suggests a shelf

[1]**shell** *n* **1 :** a stiff hard covering of an animal (as a turtle, oyster, or beetle) **2 :** the tough outer covering of an egg **3 :** the outer covering of a nut, fruit, or seed especially when hard or tough and fibrous **4 :** something like a shell (as in shape, function, or material) **5 :** a narrow light racing boat rowed by one or more persons **6 :** a metal or paper case holding the explosive charge and the shot or object to be fired from a gun or cannon — **shelled** *adj*

[2]**shell** *vb* **1 :** to take out of the shell or husk **2 :** to remove the kernels of grain from (as a cob of Indian corn) **3 :** to shoot shells at or upon

she'll : she shall **:** she will

[1]**shel·lac** *n* **:** a varnish made from a material given off by an Asian insect dissolved usually in alcohol

[2]**shellac** *vb* **shel·lacked; shel·lack·ing** **:** to coat with shellac

shell·fish *n, pl* **shellfish** **:** an invertebrate animal that lives in water and has a shell — used mostly of edible forms (as oysters or crabs)

[1]**shel·ter** *n* **1 :** something that covers or protects **2 :** the condition of being protected

[2]**shelter** *vb* **1 :** to be a shelter for **:** provide with shelter **2 :** to find and use a shelter

shelve *vb* **shelved; shelv·ing** **1 :** to place or store on shelves **2 :** [1]DEFER

shelves *pl of* SHELF

[1]**shep·herd** *n* **:** a person who takes care of sheep

[2]**shepherd** *vb* **:** to care for as or as if a shepherd

shep·herd·ess *n* **:** a woman who takes care of sheep

sher·bet *n* **:** a frozen dessert of fruit juice to which milk, the white of egg, or gelatin is added before freezing

sher·iff *n* **:** the officer of a county who is in charge of enforcing the law

she's : she is **:** she has

Shet·land pony *n* **:** any of a breed of small stocky horses with shaggy coats

[1]**shield** *n* **1 :** a broad piece of armor carried on the arm to protect oneself in battle **2 :** something that serves as a defense or protection

[2]**shield** *vb* **:** to cover or screen with or as if with a shield

[1]**shift** *vb* **1 :** to exchange for another of the same kind **2 :** to change or remove from one person or place to another **3 :** to change the arrangement of gears transmitting power (as in an automobile) **4 :** to get along without help **:** FEND

[2]**shift** *n* **1 :** the act of shifting **:** TRANSFER **2 :** a group of workers who work together during a scheduled period of time **3 :** the period during which one group of workers is working **4 :** GEARSHIFT

shift·less *adj* **:** lacking in ambition and energy **:** LAZY — **shift·less·ly** *adv* — **shift·less·ness** *n*

shifty *adj* **shift·i·er; shift·i·est** **:** not worthy of trust **:** TRICKY — **shift·i·ly** *adv* — **shift·i·ness** *n*

shil·ling *n* **:** an old British coin equal to $^1/_{20}$ pound

shim·mer *vb* **:** to shine with a wavering light **:** GLIMMER

1shin *n* **:** the front part of the leg below the knee

2shin *vb* **shinned; shin·ning :** to climb (as a pole) by grasping with arms and legs and moving oneself upward by repeated jerks

1shine *vb* **shone** *or* **shined; shin·ing** **1 :** to give light **2 :** to be glossy **:** GLEAM **3 :** to be outstanding **4 :** to make bright by polishing

2shine *n* **1 :** brightness from light given off or reflected **2 :** fair weather **:** SUNSHINE **3 :** 2POLISH 1

shin·er *n* **1 :** a small silvery American freshwater fish related to the carp **2 :** an eye discolored by injury **:** a black eye

1shin·gle *n* **1 :** a small thin piece of building material (as wood or an asbestos composition) for laying in overlapping rows as a covering for the roof or sides of a building **2 :** a small sign

2shingle *vb* **shin·gled; shin·gling :** to cover with shingles

shin·ny *vb* **shin·nied; shin·ny·ing :** 2SHIN

shiny *adj* **shin·i·er; shin·i·est :** bright in appearance

1ship *n* **1 :** a large seagoing boat **2 :** a ship's crew **3 :** AIRSHIP, AIRPLANE **4 :** a vehicle for traveling beyond the earth's atmosphere

2ship *vb* **shipped; ship·ping** **1 :** to put or receive on board for transportation by water **2 :** to cause to be transported **3 :** to take into a ship or boat **4 :** to sign on as a crew member on a ship

-ship *n suffix* **1 :** state **:** condition **:** quality **2 :** office **:** rank **:** profession **3 :** skill **4 :** something showing a quality or state of being **5 :** one having a specified rank

ship·board *n* **1 :** a ship's side **2 :** 1SHIP 1

ship·ment *n* **1 :** the act of shipping **2 :** the goods shipped

ship·ping *n* **1 :** the body of ships in one place or belonging to one port or country **2 :** the act or business of a person who ships goods

ship·shape *adj* **:** being neat and orderly **:** TIDY

1ship·wreck *n* **1 :** a wrecked ship **2 :** the loss or destruction of a ship

2shipwreck *vb* **1 :** to cause to experience shipwreck **2 :** to destroy (a ship) by driving ashore or sinking

ship·yard *n* **:** a place where ships are built or repaired

shirk *vb* **1 :** to get out of doing what one ought to do **2 :** AVOID

shirt *n* **1 :** a garment for the upper part of the body usually with a collar, sleeves, a front opening, and a tail long enough to be tucked inside pants or a skirt **2 :** UNDERSHIRT

1shiv·er *vb* **:** to be made to shake (as by cold or fear) **:** QUIVER

2shiver *n* **:** an instance of shivering

1shoal *adj* **:** 1SHALLOW 1

2shoal *n* **1 :** a place where a sea, lake, or river is shallow **2 :** a bank or bar of sand just below the surface of the water

3shoal *n* **:** 3SCHOOL

1shock *n* **:** a bunch of sheaves of grain or stalks of corn set on end in the field

2shock *n* **1 :** the sudden violent collision of bodies in a fight **2 :** a violent shake or jerk **3 :** a sudden and violent disturbance of mind or feelings **4 :** a state of bodily collapse that usually follows severe crushing injuries, burns, or hemorrhage **5 :** the effect of a charge of electricity passing through the body of a person or animal

3shock *vb* **1 :** to strike with surprise, horror, or disgust **2 :** to affect by electrical shock **3 :** to drive into or out of by or as if by a shock

4shock *n* **:** a thick bushy mass (as of hair)

shock·ing *adj* **:** causing horror or disgust — **shock·ing·ly** *adv*

shod·dy *adj* **shod·di·er; shod·di·est :** poorly done or made — **shod·di·ly** *adv* — **shod·di·ness** *n*

1shoe *n* **1 :** an outer covering for the human foot usually having a thick and somewhat stiff sole and heel and a lighter upper part **2 :** something (as a horseshoe) like a shoe in appearance or use

2shoe *vb* **shod** *also* **shoed; shoe·ing :** to put a shoe on **:** furnish with shoes

shoe·horn *n* **:** a curved piece (as of metal) to help in putting on a shoe

shoe·lace *n* **:** a lace or string for fastening a shoe

shoe·mak·er *n* **:** a person who makes or repairs shoes

shoe·string *n* **:** SHOELACE

shone *past of* SHINE

shoo *vb* **:** to wave, scare, or send away by or as if by crying *shoo*

shook *past of* SHAKE

1shoot *vb* **shot; shoot·ing** **1 :** to let fly or cause to be driven forward with force **2 :** to cause a missile to be driven out of **3 :** to cause a weapon to discharge a missile **4 :** to force (a marble) forward by snapping the thumb **5 :** to hit or throw (as a ball or puck) toward a goal **6 :** to score by shooting **7 :** 2PLAY 2 **8 :** to strike with a missile from a bow or gun **9 :** to push or slide into or out of a fastening **10 :** to thrust forward swiftly **11 :** to grow rapidly **12 :** to go, move, or pass rapidly **13 :** to pass swiftly along or through **14 :** to stream out suddenly **:** SPURT — **shoot·er** *n*

[2]**shoot** *n* **1 :** the part of a plant that grows above ground or as much of this as comes from a single bud **2 :** a hunting party or trip

shooting star *n* **:** a meteor appearing as a temporary streak of light in the night sky

[1]**shop** *n* **1 :** a worker's place of business **2 :** a building or room where goods are sold at retail **:** STORE **3 :** a place in which workers are doing a particular kind of work

[2]**shop** *vb* **shopped; shop·ping :** to visit shops for the purpose of looking over and buying goods — **shop·per** *n*

shop·keep·er *n* **:** STOREKEEPER 2

shop·lift·er *n* **:** a person who steals merchandise on display in stores

[1]**shore** *n* **:** the land along the edge of a body of water (as the sea)

[2]**shore** *vb* **shored; shor·ing :** to support with one or more bracing timbers

shore·bird *n* **:** any of various birds (as the plovers) that frequent the seashore

shore·line *n* **:** the line where a body of water touches the shore

shorn *past participle of* SHEAR

[1]**short** *adj* **1 :** not long or tall **2 :** not great in distance **3 :** brief in time **4 :** cut down to a brief length **5 :** not coming up to the regular standard **6 :** less in amount than expected or called for **7 :** less than **:** not equal to **8 :** not having enough **9 :** FLAKY, CRUMBLY **10 :** of, relating to, or being one of the vowel sounds \ə, a, e, i, u̇\ and sometimes \ä\ and \ȯ\ — **short·ness** *n*

[2]**short** *adv* **1 :** with suddenness **2 :** so as not to reach as far as expected

[3]**short** *n* **1 :** something shorter than the usual or regular length **2 shorts** *pl* **:** pants that reach to or almost to the knees **3 shorts** *pl* **:** short underpants **4 :** SHORT CIRCUIT

short·age *n* **:** a lack in the amount needed **:** DEFICIT

short·cake *n* **:** a dessert made usually of rich biscuit dough baked and served with sweetened fruit

short circuit *n* **:** an electric connection made between points in an electric circuit between which current does not normally flow

short·com·ing *n* **:** FAULT 1

short·cut *n* **:** a shorter, quicker, or easier way

short·en *vb* **:** to make or become short or shorter

short·en·ing *n* **:** a fatty substance (as lard) used to make pastry flaky

short·hand *n* **:** a method of rapid writing by using symbols for sounds or words

short·horn *n* **:** any of a breed of beef cattle developed in England and including good producers of milk from which a separate dairy breed (**milking shorthorn**) has come

short–lived *adj* **:** living or lasting only a short time

short·ly *adv* **1 :** in a few words **:** BRIEFLY **2 :** in or within a short time **:** SOON

short–sight·ed *adj* **:** NEARSIGHTED

short·stop *n* **:** a baseball infielder whose position is between second and third base

[1]**shot** *n* **1 :** the act of shooting **2** *pl* **shot :** a bullet, ball, or pellet for a gun or cannon **3 :** something thrown, cast forth, or let fly with force **4 :** [2]ATTEMPT, TRY **5 :** the flight of a missile or the distance it travels **:** RANGE **6 :** a person who shoots **7 :** a heavy metal ball thrown for distance in a track-and-field contest (**shot put**) **8 :** a stroke or throw at a goal **9 :** an injection of something (as medicine) into the body

[2]**shot** *past of* SHOOT

shot·gun *n* **:** a gun with a long barrel used to fire shot at short range

should *past of* SHALL **1 :** ought to **2 :** happen to **3** — used as a politer or less assured form of *shall*

[1]**shoul·der** *n* **1 :** the part of the body of a person or animal where the arm or foreleg joins the body **2 :** the part of a garment at the wearer's shoulder **3 :** a part that resembles a person's shoulder **4 :** the edge of a road

[2]**shoulder** *vb* **1 :** to push with one's shoulder **2 :** to accept as one's burden or duty

shoulder blade *n* **:** the flat triangular bone in a person's or animal's shoulder

shouldn't : should not

[1]**shout** *vb* **:** to make a sudden loud cry (as of joy, pain, or sorrow)

[2]**shout** *n* **:** a sudden loud cry

[1]**shove** *vb* **shoved; shov·ing 1 :** to push with steady force **2 :** to push along or away carelessly or rudely

[2]**shove** *n* **:** the act or an instance of shoving

[1]**shov·el** *n* **1 :** a broad scoop used to lift and throw loose material (as snow) **2 :** as much as a shovel will hold

[2]**shovel** *vb* **shov·eled** *or* **shov·elled; shov·el·ing** *or* **shov·el·ling 1 :** to lift or throw with a shovel **2 :** to dig or clean out with a shovel **3 :** to throw or carry roughly or in a mass as if with a shovel

[1]**show** *vb* **showed; shown** *or* **showed; show·ing 1 :** to place in sight **:** DISPLAY **2 :** REVEAL 2 **3 :** to give from or as if from a position of authority **4 :** TEACH 1, INSTRUCT **5 :** PROVE 2 **6 :** [1]DIRECT 3, USHER **7 :** to be noticeable

[2]**show** *n* **1 :** a display made for effect **2**

: an appearance meant to deceive : PRETENSE **3 :** an appearance or display that is basically true or real **4 :** an entertainment or exhibition especially by performers (as on TV or the stage)

show•boat *n* **:** a river steamboat used as a traveling theater

show•case *n* **:** a protective glass case in which things are displayed

1show•er *n* **1 :** a short fall of rain over a small area **2 :** something like a shower **3 :** a party where gifts are given especially to a bride or a pregnant woman **4 :** a bath in which water is showered on a person or a device for providing such a bath

2shower *vb* **1 :** to wet with fine spray or drops **2 :** to fall in or as if in a shower **3 :** to provide in great quantity **4 :** to bathe in a shower

show•man *n, pl* **show•men 1 :** the producer of a theatrical show **2 :** a person having a special skill for presenting something in a dramatic way

shown *past participle of* SHOW

show off *vb* **:** to make an obvious display of one's abilities or possessions

show up *vb* **1 :** to reveal the true nature of **:** EXPOSE **2 :** APPEAR 2

showy *adj* **show•i•er; show•i•est 1 :** attracting attention **:** STRIKING **2 :** given to or being too much outward display **:** GAUDY — **show•i•ly** *adv* — **show•i•ness** *n*

shrank *past of* SHRINK

shrap•nel *n* **1 :** a shell designed to burst and scatter the metal balls with which it is filled along with jagged fragments of the case **2 :** metal pieces from an exploded bomb, shell, or mine

1shred *n* **1 :** a long narrow piece torn or cut off **:** STRIP **2 :** 2BIT 1, PARTICLE

2shred *vb* **shred•ded; shred•ding :** to cut or tear into shreds

shrew *n* **1 :** a small mouselike animal with a long pointed snout and tiny eyes that lives on insects and worms **2 :** an unpleasant quarrelsome woman

shrewd *adj* **:** showing quick practical cleverness **:** ASTUTE — **shrewd•ly** *adv* — **shrewd•ness** *n*

1shriek *vb* **:** to utter a sharp shrill cry

2shriek *n* **:** a sharp shrill cry

shrike *n* **:** a grayish or brownish bird with a hooked bill that feeds mostly on insects and often sticks them on thorns before eating them

1shrill *vb* **:** to make a high sharp piercing sound **:** SCREAM

2shrill *adj* **:** having a sharp high sound — **shrill•ness** *n* — **shril•ly** *adv*

shrimp *n* **1 :** a small shellfish related to the crabs and lobsters **2 :** a small or unimportant person or thing — **shrimp•like** *adj*

shrine *n* **1 :** a case or box for sacred relics (as the bones of saints) **2 :** the tomb of a holy person (as a saint) **3 :** a place that is considered sacred

shrink *vb* **shrank** *also* **shrunk; shrunk; shrink•ing 1 :** to curl up or withdraw in or as if in fear or pain **2 :** to make or become smaller

shrink•age *n* **:** the amount by which something shrinks or becomes less

shriv•el *vb* **shriv•eled** *or* **shriv•elled; shriv•el•ing** *or* **shriv•el•ling :** to shrink and become dry and wrinkled

1shroud *n* **1 :** the cloth placed over or around a dead body **2 :** something that covers or shelters like a shroud **3 :** one of the ropes that go from the masthead of a boat to the sides to support the mast

2shroud *vb* **:** to cover with or as if with a shroud

shrub *n* **:** a woody plant having several stems and smaller than most trees

shrub•bery *n, pl* **shrub•ber•ies :** a group or planting of shrubs

shrug *vb* **shrugged; shrug•ging :** to draw or hunch up the shoulders usually to express doubt, uncertainty, or lack of interest

shrunk *past & past participle of* SHRINK

shrunk•en *adj* **:** made or grown smaller (as in size or value)

1shuck *n* **:** a covering shell or husk

2shuck *vb* **:** to free (as an ear of corn) from the shuck

1shud•der *vb* **:** to tremble with fear or horror or from cold

2shudder *n* **:** an act of shuddering **:** SHIVER

1shuf•fle *vb* **shuf•fled; shuf•fling 1 :** to push out of sight or mix in a disorderly mass **2 :** to mix cards to change their order in the pack **3 :** to move from place to place **4 :** to move in a clumsy dragging way

2shuffle *n* **1 :** an act of shuffling **2 :** 2JUMBLE **3 :** a clumsy dragging walk

shun *vb* **shunned; shun•ning :** to avoid purposely or by habit

shunt *vb* **1 :** to turn off to one side or out of the way **:** SHIFT **2 :** to switch (as a train) from one track to another

shut *vb* **shut; shut•ting 1 :** to close or become closed **2 :** to close so as to prevent entrance or leaving **:** BAR **3 :** to keep in a place by enclosing or by blocking the way out **:** IMPRISON **4 :** to close by bringing parts together

shut–in *n* **:** a sick person kept indoors

shut•out *n* **:** a game in which one side fails to score

shut•ter *n* **1 :** a movable cover for a window **2 :** a device in a camera that opens to let in light when a picture is taken

1shut•tle *n* **1 :** an instrument used in weaving to carry the thread back and forth from side to side through the threads that run lengthwise **2 :** a vehicle (as a bus or train) that goes back and forth over a short route **3 :** SPACE SHUTTLE

2shuttle *vb* **shut•tled; shut•tling :** to move back and forth rapidly or often

shut•tle•cock *n* **:** a light object (as a piece of cork with feathers stuck in it) used in badminton

1shy *adj* **shi•er** *or* **shy•er; shi•est** *or* **shy•est** **1 :** easily frightened **:** TIMID **2 :** not feeling comfortable around people **:** not wanting or able to call attention to oneself **:** BASHFUL **3 :** having less than a full or an expected amount or number — **shy•ly** *adv* — **shy•ness** *n*

2shy *vb* **shied; shy•ing** **1 :** to draw back in dislike or distaste **2 :** to move quickly to one side in fright

sick *adj* **1 :** affected with disease or ill health **:** not well **2 :** of, relating to, or intended for use in or during illness **3 :** affected with or accompanied by nausea **4 :** badly upset by strong emotion (as shame or fear) **5 :** tired of something from having too much of it **6 :** filled with disgust

sick•bed *n* **:** a bed on which a sick person lies

sick•en *vb* **:** to make or become sick

sick•en•ing *adj* **:** causing sickness or disgust — **sick•en•ing•ly** *adv*

sick•le *n* **:** a tool with a sharp curved metal blade and a short handle used to cut grass

sick•ly *adj* **sick•li•er; sick•li•est** **1 :** somewhat sick **:** often ailing **2 :** caused by or associated with ill health **3 :** not growing well **:** SPINDLY

sick•ness *n* **1 :** ill health **:** ILLNESS **2 :** a specific disease **:** MALADY **3 :** NAUSEA 1

1side *n* **1 :** the right or left part of the trunk of the body **2 :** a place, space, or direction away from or beyond a central point or line **3 :** a surface or line forming a border or face of an object **4 :** an outer part of a thing considered as facing in a certain direction **5 :** a position viewed as opposite to another **6 :** a body of contestants **7 :** a line of ancestors traced back from either parent

2side *adj* **1 :** of, relating to, or being on the side **2 :** aimed toward or from the side **3 :** related to something in a minor or unimportant way **4 :** being in addition to a main portion

3side *vb* **sid•ed; sid•ing :** to take the same side

side•arm *adv* **:** with the arm moving out to the side

side•board *n* **:** a piece of furniture for holding dishes, silverware, and table linen

sid•ed *adj* **:** having sides often of a stated number or kind

side•line *n* **1 :** a line marking the side of a playing field or court **2 :** a business or a job done in addition to one's regular occupation

1side•long *adv* **:** out of the corner of one's eye

2sidelong *adj* **1 :** made to one side or out of the corner of one's eye **2 :** INDIRECT 2

side•show *n* **:** a small show off to the side of a main show or exhibition (as of a circus)

side•step *vb* **side•stepped; side•step•ping** **1 :** to take a step to the side **2 :** to avoid by a step to the side **3 :** to avoid answering or dealing with

side•track *vb* **1 :** to transfer from a main railroad line to a side line **2 :** to turn aside from a main purpose or direction

side•walk *n* **:** a usually paved walk at the side of a street or road

side•ways *adv or adj* **1 :** from one side **2 :** with one side forward **3 :** to one side

side•wise *adv or adj* **:** SIDEWAYS

sid•ing *n* **1 :** a short railroad track connected with the main track **2 :** material (as boards or metal pieces) used to cover the outside walls of frame buildings

si•dle *vb* **si•dled; si•dling :** to go or move with one side forward

siege *n* **1 :** the moving of an army around a fortified place to capture it **2 :** a lasting attack (as of illness)

si•er•ra *n* **:** a range of mountains especially with jagged peaks

si•es•ta *n* **:** a nap or rest especially at midday

sieve *n* **:** a utensil with meshes or holes to separate finer particles from coarser ones or solids from liquids

sift *vb* **1 :** to pass or cause to pass through a sieve **2 :** to separate or separate out by or as if by passing through a sieve **3 :** to test or examine carefully — **sift•er** *n*

1sigh *vb* **1 :** to take or let out a long loud breath often as an expression of sadness or weariness **2 :** to make a sound like sighing **3 :** YEARN

2sigh *n* **:** the act or a sound of sighing

1sight *n* **1 :** something that is seen **:** SPECTACLE **2 :** something that is worth seeing **3 :** something that is peculiar, funny, or messy **4 :** the function, process, or power of seeing **:** the sense by which one becomes aware of the position, form, and color of objects **5 :** the act of seeing **6 :** the presence of an object within the field of vision **7 :** the distance a person can see **8 :** a device (as a small metal bead on a gun barrel) that aids the eye in aiming or in finding the direction of an object

[2]**sight** *vb* **1 :** to get sight of **:** SEE **2 :** to look at through or as if through a sight

sight·less *adj* **:** lacking sight **:** BLIND

sight·seer *n* **:** a person who goes about to see places and things of interest

[1]**sign** *n* **1 :** a motion, action, or movement of the hand that means something **2 :** one of the twelve parts of the zodiac **3 :** a symbol (as + or ÷) indicating a mathematical operation **4 :** a public notice that advertises something or gives information **5 :** something that indicates what is to come **6 :** [1]TRACE 2

[2]**sign** *vb* **1 :** to make or place a sign on **2 :** to represent or show by a sign or signs **3 :** to write one's name on to show that one accepts, agrees with, or will be responsible for **4 :** to communicate by using sign language

[1]**sig·nal** *n* **1 :** a sign, event, or word that serves to start some action **2 :** a sound, a movement of part of the body, or an object that gives warning or a command **3 :** a radio wave that transmits a message or effect (as in radio or television)

[2]**signal** *vb* **sig·naled** *or* **sig·nalled; sig·nal·ing** *or* **sig·nal·ling 1 :** to notify by a signal **2 :** to communicate by signals

[3]**signal** *adj* **1 :** unusually great **2 :** used for signaling

sig·na·ture *n* **1 :** the name of a person written by that person **2 :** a sign or group of signs placed at the beginning of a staff in music to show the key (**key signature**) or the meter (**time signature**)

sign·board *n* **:** a board with a sign or notice on it

sig·nif·i·cance *n* **1 :** MEANING 1 **2 :** IMPORTANCE

sig·nif·i·cant *adj* **1 :** having meaning and especially a special or hidden meaning **2 :** IMPORTANT 1

sig·ni·fy *vb* **sig·ni·fied; sig·ni·fy·ing 1 :** [2]MEAN 3, DENOTE **2 :** to show especially by a sign **:** make known **3 :** to have importance

sign language *n* **:** a system of hand movements used for communication (as by people who are deaf)

sign·post *n* **:** a post with a sign (as for directing travelers)

si·lage *n* **:** fodder fermented (as in a silo) to produce a good juicy feed for livestock

[1]**si·lence** *n* **1 :** the state of keeping or being silent **2 :** the state of there being no sound or noise **:** STILLNESS

[2]**silence** *vb* **si·lenced; si·lenc·ing 1 :** to stop the noise or speech of **:** cause to be silent **2 :** SUPPRESS 1

si·lent *adj* **1 :** not speaking **:** not talkative **2 :** free from noise or sound **:** STILL **3 :** done or felt without being spoken **4 :** making no mention **5 :** not active in running a business **6 :** not pronounced

[1]**sil·hou·ette** *n* **1 :** a drawing or picture of the outline of an object filled in with a solid usually black color **2 :** a profile portrait done in silhouette **3 :** [1]OUTLINE 1

[2]**silhouette** *vb* **sil·hou·ett·ed; sil·hou·ett·ing :** to represent by a silhouette **:** show against a light background

sil·i·con *n* **:** a chemical element that is found combined as the most common element next to oxygen in the earth's crust and is used especially in electronic devices

silk *n* **1 :** a fine fiber that is spun by many insect larvae usually to form their cocoon or by spiders to make their webs and that includes some kinds used for weaving cloth **2 :** thread, yarn, or fabric made from silk **3 :** something suggesting silk

silk·en *adj* **1 :** made of or with silk **2 :** like silk especially in its soft and smooth feel

silk·worm *n* **:** a yellowish hairless caterpillar that is the larva of an Asian moth (**silk moth** or **silkworm moth**), is raised in captivity on mulberry leaves, and produces a strong silk that is the silk most used for thread or cloth

silky *adj* **silk·i·er; silk·i·est :** soft and smooth as silk

sill *n* **1 :** a horizontal supporting piece at the base of a structure **2 :** a heavy horizontal piece (as of wood) that forms the bottom part of a window frame or a doorway

sil·ly *adj* **sil·li·er; sil·li·est 1 :** not very intelligent **2 :** showing a lack of common sense **3 :** not serious or important — **sil·li·ness** *n*

si·lo *n, pl* **silos :** a covered trench, pit, or especially a tall round building in which silage is made and stored

[1]**silt** *n* **1 :** particles of small size left as sediment from water **2 :** a soil made up mostly of silt and containing little clay

[2]**silt** *vb* **:** to choke, fill, cover, or block with silt

[1]**sil·ver** *n* **1 :** a soft white metallic chemical element that takes a high polish and is used for money, jewelry and ornaments, and table utensils **2 :** coin made of silver **3 :** SILVERWARE **4 :** a medium gray

[2]**silver** *adj* **1 :** made of, coated with, or yielding silver **2 :** having the color of silver

[3]**silver** *vb* **:** to coat with or as if with silver

sil·ver·smith *n* **:** a person who makes objects of silver

sil•ver•ware *n* **:** things (as knives, forks, and spoons) made of silver, silver-plated metal, or stainless steel

sil•very *adj* **:** having a shine like silver

sim•i•lar *adj* **:** having qualities in common — **sim•i•lar•ly** *adv*

sim•i•lar•i•ty *n, pl* **sim•i•lar•i•ties :** the quality or state of being similar **:** RESEMBLANCE

sim•i•le *n* **:** a figure of speech comparing two unlike things using *like* or *as*

sim•mer *vb* **1 :** to cook gently at or just below the boiling point **2 :** to be on the point of bursting out with violence or anger

sim•ple *adj* **sim•pler; sim•plest 1 :** INNOCENT 1, MODEST **2 :** not rich or important **3 :** lacking in education, experience, or intelligence **4 :** not fancy **5 :** having few parts **:** not complicated **6 :** ABSOLUTE 2 **7 :** not hard to understand or solve **8 :** EASY 1, STRAIGHTFORWARD

sim•ple•ton *n* **:** a foolish or stupid person

sim•plic•i•ty *n, pl* **sim•plic•i•ties 1 :** the quality or state of being simple or plain and not complicated or difficult **2 :** SINCERITY **3 :** directness or clearness in speaking or writing

sim•pli•fy *vb* **sim•pli•fied; sim•pli•fy•ing :** to make simple or simpler **:** make easier

sim•ply *adv* **1 :** in a clear way **2 :** in a plain way **3 :** DIRECTLY 1, CANDIDLY **4 :** 2ONLY 1, MERELY **5 :** in actual fact **:** REALLY, TRULY

si•mul•ta•neous *adj* **:** existing or taking place at the same time — **si•mul•ta•neous•ly** *adv*

1sin *n* **1 :** an action that breaks a religious law **2 :** an action that is or is felt to be bad

2sin *vb* **sinned; sin•ning :** to be guilty of a sin

1since *adv* **1 :** from a definite past time until now **2 :** before the present time **:** AGO **3 :** after a time in the past

2since *conj* **1 :** in the period after **2 :** BECAUSE

3since *prep* **1 :** in the period after **2 :** continuously from

sin•cere *adj* **1 :** HONEST 2, STRAIGHTFORWARD **2 :** being what it seems to be **:** GENUINE — **sin•cere•ly** *adv*

sin•cer•i•ty *n* **:** freedom from fraud or deception **:** HONESTY

sin•ew *n* **:** TENDON

sin•ewy *adj* **1 :** full of tendons **:** TOUGH, STRINGY **2 :** STRONG 1, POWERFUL

sin•ful *adj* **:** being or full of sin **:** WICKED

sing *vb* **sang** *or* **sung; sung; sing•ing 1 :** to produce musical sounds with the voice **2 :** to express in musical tones **3 :** 1CHANT 2 **4 :** to make musical sounds **5 :** to make a small shrill sound **6 :** to speak with enthusiasm **7 :** to do something with song — **sing•er** *n*

1singe *vb* **singed; singe•ing 1 :** to burn lightly or on the surface **:** SCORCH **2 :** to remove the hair, down, or fuzz from by passing briefly over a flame

2singe *n* **:** a slight burn

1sin•gle *adj* **1 :** not married **2 :** being alone **:** being the only one **3 :** made up of or having only one **4 :** having but one row of petals or rays **5 :** being a separate whole **:** INDIVIDUAL **6 :** of, relating to, or involving only one person

2single *vb* **sin•gled; sin•gling :** to select or distinguish (as one person or thing) from a number or group

3single *n* **1 :** a separate individual person or thing **2 :** a hit in baseball that enables the batter to reach first base

sin•gle–hand•ed *adj* **1 :** done or managed by one person or with one hand **2 :** working alone **:** lacking help

sin•gly *adv* **:** one by one **:** INDIVIDUALLY

1sin•gu•lar *adj* **1 :** of, relating to, or being a word form used to show not more than one **2 :** 1SUPERIOR 2, EXCEPTIONAL **3 :** of unusual quality **:** UNIQUE **4 :** STRANGE 3, ODD

2singular *n* **:** a form of a word used to show that only one person or thing is meant

sin•is•ter *adj* **1 :** 1EVIL 1, CORRUPT **2 :** threatening evil, harm, or danger

1sink *vb* **sank** *or* **sunk; sunk; sink•ing 1 :** to move or cause to move downward so as to be swallowed up **2 :** to fall or drop to a lower level **3 :** to lessen in amount **4 :** to cause to penetrate **5 :** to go into or become absorbed **6 :** to form by digging or boring **7 :** to spend (money) unwisely

2sink *n* **:** a basin usually with water faucets and a drain fixed to a wall or floor

sin•ner *n* **:** a sinful person

si•nus *n* **:** any of several spaces in the skull mostly connected with the nostrils

1sip *vb* **sipped; sip•ping :** to take small drinks of

2sip *n* **1 :** the act of sipping **2 :** a small amount taken by sipping

1si•phon *n* **1 :** a bent pipe or tube through which a liquid can be drawn by air pressure up and over the edge of a container **2 :** a tubelike organ in an animal and especially a mollusk or arthropod used to draw in or squirt out a fluid

2siphon *vb* **:** to draw off by a siphon

sir *n* **1** *cap* — used as a title before the given name of a knight or a baronet **2 —** used without a name as a form of polite address to a man

¹sire *n* **1** *often cap* **:** ¹FATHER 1 **2 :** ANCESTOR **3 :** the male parent of an animal
²sire *vb* **sired; sir·ing :** to become the father of
si·ren *n* **:** a device that makes a loud shrill warning sound and is often operated by electricity
sir·loin *n* **:** a cut of beef taken from the part just in front of the rump
sirup *variant of* SYRUP
si·sal *n* **1 :** a long strong white fiber used to make rope and twine **2 :** a Mexican agave whose leaves yield sisal
sis·ter *n* **1 :** a female person or animal related to another person or animal by having one or both parents in common **2 :** a member of a religious society of women **:** NUN **3 :** a woman related to another by a common tie or interest — **sis·ter·ly** *adj*
sis·ter·hood *n* **1 :** the state of being a sister **2 :** women joined in a group
sis·ter–in–law *n, pl* **sis·ters–in–law 1 :** the sister of one's husband or wife **2 :** the wife of one's brother
sit *vb* **sat; sit·ting 1 :** to rest upon the part of the body where the hips and legs join **2 :** to cause (as oneself) to be seated **3 :** ²PERCH **4 :** to hold a place as a member of an official group **5 :** to hold a session **6 :** to pose for a portrait or photograph **7 :** to be located **8 :** to remain quiet or still
site *n* **1 :** the space of ground a building rests upon **2 :** the place where something (as a town or event) is found or took place **3 :** a place on the Internet at which an individual or organization provides information to others
sit·ting *n* **1 :** an act of one that sits **:** the time taken in such a sitting **2 :** SESSION 1
sitting room *n* **:** LIVING ROOM
sit·u·at·ed *adj* **1 :** having its place **2 :** being in such financial circumstances
sit·u·a·tion *n* **1 :** LOCATION 2, PLACE **2 :** position or place of employment **:** JOB **3 :** position in life **:** STATUS **4 :** the combination of surrounding conditions
¹six *adj* **:** being one more than five
²six *n* **:** one more than five **:** two times three **:** 6
six–gun *n* **:** a revolver having six chambers
six·pence *n* **1 :** the sum of six pence **2 :** an old British coin worth six pence
six–shoot·er *n* **:** SIX-GUN
¹six·teen *adj* **:** being one more than fifteen
²sixteen *n* **:** one more than fifteen **:** four times four **:** 16
¹six·teenth *adj* **:** coming right after fifteenth
²sixteenth *n* **:** number sixteen in a series
¹sixth *adj* **:** coming right after fifth
²sixth *n* **1 :** number six in a series **2 :** one of six equal parts
¹six·ti·eth *adj* **:** coming right after fifty-ninth
²sixtieth *n* **:** number sixty in a series
¹six·ty *adj* **:** being six times ten
²sixty *n* **:** six times ten **:** 60
siz·able *or* **size·able** *adj* **:** fairly large
size *n* **1 :** amount of space occupied **:** BULK **2 :** the measurements of a thing **3 :** one of a series of measures especially of manufactured articles (as clothing) — **sized** *adj*
siz·zle *vb* **siz·zled; siz·zling :** to make a hissing or sputtering noise in or as if in frying or burning
¹skate *n* **:** a very flat fish related to the sharks that has large and nearly triangular fins
²skate *n* **1 :** a metal runner fitting the sole of the shoe or a shoe with a permanently attached metal runner used for gliding on ice **2 :** ROLLER SKATE
³skate *vb* **skat·ed; skat·ing 1 :** to glide along on skates **2 :** to slide or move as if on skates — **skat·er** *n*
skate·board *n* **:** a short board mounted on small wheels that is used for coasting and often for performing athletic stunts — **skate·board·er** *n* — **skate·board·ing** *n*
skein *n* **:** a quantity of yarn or thread arranged in a loose coil
skel·e·tal *adj* **:** of, relating or attached to, forming, or like a skeleton
skel·e·ton *n* **1 :** a firm supporting or protecting structure or framework of a living being **:** the usually bony framework of a vertebrate (as a fish, bird, or human) **2 :** FRAMEWORK
skep·ti·cal *adj* **:** having or showing doubt
¹sketch *n* **1 :** a rough outline or drawing showing the main features of something to be written, painted, or built **2 :** a short written composition (as a story or essay)
²sketch *vb* **1 :** to make a sketch, rough draft, or outline of **2 :** to draw or paint sketches
sketchy *adj* **sketch·i·er; sketch·i·est 1 :** like a sketch **:** roughly outlined **2 :** lacking completeness or clearness
¹ski *n, pl* **skis :** one of a pair of narrow wooden, metal, or plastic strips bound one on each foot and used in gliding over snow or water
²ski *vb* **skied; ski·ing :** to glide on skis — **ski·er** *n*
¹skid *n* **1 :** a support (as a plank) used to raise and hold an object **2 :** one of the logs, planks, or rails along or on which something heavy is rolled or slid **3 :** the act of skidding **:** SLIDE
²skid *vb* **skid·ded; skid·ding 1 :** to roll or

slide on skids **2 :** to slide sideways **3 :** ¹SLIDE 1, SLIP
skiff *n* **1 :** a small light rowboat **2 :** a sailboat light enough to be rowed
ski·ing *n* **:** the art or sport of gliding and jumping on skis
skill *n* **1 :** ability that comes from training or practice **2 :** a developed or acquired ability
skilled *adj* **1 :** having skill **2 :** requiring skill and training
skil·let *n* **:** a frying pan
skill·ful *or* **skil·ful** *adj* **1 :** having or showing skill **:** EXPERT **2 :** done or made with skill — **skill·ful·ly** *adv*
skim *vb* **skimmed; skim·ming 1 :** to clean a liquid of scum or floating substance **:** remove (as cream or film) from the top part of a liquid **2 :** to read or examine quickly and not thoroughly **3 :** to throw so as to skip along the surface of water **4 :** to pass swiftly or lightly over
skim milk *n* **:** milk from which the cream has been taken
skimp *vb* **:** to give too little or just enough attention or effort to or funds for
skimpy *adj* **skimp·i·er; skimp·i·est :** not enough especially because of skimping **:** SCANTY
¹skin *n* **1 :** the hide especially of a small animal or one that has fur **2 :** the outer limiting layer of an animal body that in vertebrate animals (as humans) is made up of two layers of cells forming an inner dermis and an outer epidermis **3 :** an outer or surface layer (as of a fruit) — **skin·less** *adj* — **skinned** *adj*
²skin *vb* **skinned; skin·ning 1 :** to strip, scrape, or rub off the skin of **2 :** to remove an outer layer from (as by peeling)
skin dive *vb* **:** to swim below the surface of water with a face mask and sometimes a portable breathing device — **skin diver** *n*
skin·ny *adj* **skin·ni·er; skin·ni·est :** very thin
¹skip *vb* **skipped; skip·ping 1 :** to move lightly with leaps and bounds **2 :** to bound or cause to bound off one point after another **:** SKIM **3 :** to leap over lightly and nimbly **4 :** to pass over or omit an item, space, or step **5 :** to fail to attend
²skip *n* **1 :** a light bounding step **2 :** a way of moving by hops and steps
skip·per *n* **:** the master of a ship and especially of a fishing, trading, or pleasure boat
¹skir·mish *n* **1 :** a minor fight in war **2 :** a minor dispute or contest
²skirmish *vb* **:** to take part in a skirmish
¹skirt *n* **1 :** a woman's or girl's garment or part of a garment that hangs from the waist down **2 :** either of two flaps on a saddle covering the bars on which the stirrups are hung **3 :** a part or attachment serving as a rim, border, or edging
²skirt *vb* **1 :** ²BORDER 2 **2 :** to go or pass around or about the outer edge of
skit *n* **:** a brief sketch in play form
skit·tish *adj* **:** easily frightened
skulk *vb* **:** to hide or move in a sly or sneaking way
skull *n* **:** the case of bone or cartilage that forms most of the skeleton of the head and face, encloses the brain, and supports the jaws
skunk *n* **1 :** a North American animal related to the weasels and minks that has coarse black and white fur and can squirt out a fluid with a very unpleasant smell **2 :** a mean person who deserves to be scorned
sky *n, pl* **skies 1 :** the upper air **:** the vast arch or dome that seems to spread over the earth **2 :** WEATHER, CLIMATE
sky·lark *n* **:** a European lark noted for its song
sky·light *n* **:** a window or group of windows in a roof or ceiling
sky·line *n* **1 :** the line where earth and sky seem to meet **:** HORIZON **2 :** an outline against the sky
sky·rock·et *n* **:** ¹ROCKET 1
sky·scrap·er *n* **:** a very tall building
sky·writ·ing *n* **:** writing formed in the sky by means of smoke or vapor released from an airplane
slab *n* **:** a flat thick piece or slice (as of stone, wood, or bread)
¹slack *adj* **1 :** CARELESS 2, NEGLIGENT **2 :** not energetic **:** SLOW **3 :** not tight or firm **4 :** not busy or active
²slack *vb* **:** to make or become looser, slower, or less energetic **:** LOOSEN, SLACKEN
³slack *n* **1 :** a stopping of movement or flow **2 :** a part (as of a rope or sail) that hangs loose without strain **3 slacks** *pl* **:** pants especially for informal wear
slack·en *vb* **1 :** to make slower or less energetic **:** slow up **2 :** to make less tight or firm **:** LOOSEN
slag *n* **:** the waste left after the melting of ores and the separation of the metal from them
slain *past participle of* SLAY
slake *vb* **slaked; slak·ing 1 :** QUENCH 2 **2 :** to cause solid lime to heat and crumble by treating it with water
¹slam *n* **1 :** a severe blow **2 :** a noisy violent closing **:** BANG
²slam *vb* **slammed; slam·ming 1 :** to strike or beat hard **2 :** to shut with noisy

force : BANG **3 :** to put or place with force **4 :** to criticize harshly

1slan·der *vb* **:** to make a false and spiteful statement against **:** DEFAME

2slander *n* **:** a false and spiteful statement that damages another person's reputation

slang *n* **:** an informal nonstandard vocabulary composed mostly of invented words, changed words, and exaggerated or humorous figures of speech

1slant *n* **:** a direction, line, or surface that is neither level nor straight up and down **:** SLOPE

2slant *vb* **:** to turn or incline from a straight line or level **:** SLOPE

3slant *adj* **:** not level or straight up and down

slant·wise *adv or adj* **:** so as to slant **:** at a slant **:** in a slanting position

1slap *vb* **slapped; slap·ping 1 :** to strike with or as if with the open hand **2 :** to make a sound like that of slapping **3 :** to put, place, or throw with careless haste or force

2slap *n* **1 :** a quick sharp blow especially with the open hand **2 :** a noise like that of a slap

1slash *vb* **1 :** to cut by sweeping blows **:** GASH **2 :** to whip or strike with or as if with a cane **3 :** to reduce sharply

2slash *n* **1 :** an act of slashing **2 :** a long cut or slit made by slashing

slat *n* **:** a thin narrow strip of wood, plastic, or metal

slate *n* **1 :** a fine-grained usually bluish gray rock that splits into thin layers or plates and is used mostly for roofing and blackboards **2 :** a framed piece of slate used to write on

1slaugh·ter *n* **1 :** the act of killing **2 :** the killing and dressing of animals for food **3 :** destruction of many lives especially in battle

2slaughter *vb* **1 :** 2BUTCHER 1 **2 :** 1MASSACRE

slaugh·ter·house *n, pl* **slaugh·ter·hous·es :** an establishment where animals are killed and dressed for food

Slav *n* **:** a person speaking a Slavic language as a native tongue

1slave *n* **1 :** a person who is owned by another person and can be sold at the owner's will **2 :** one who is like a slave in not being his or her own master **3 :** DRUDGE

2slave *vb* **slaved; slav·ing :** to work like a slave

slave·hold·er *n* **:** an owner of slaves

slav·ery *n* **1 :** hard tiring labor **:** DRUDGERY **2 :** the state of being a slave **:** BONDAGE **3 :** the custom or practice of owning slaves

Slav·ic *adj* **:** of, relating to, or characteristic of the Slavs or their languages

slav·ish *adj* **1 :** of or characteristic of slaves **2 :** following or copying something or someone without questioning

slay *vb* **slew; slain; slay·ing :** 1KILL 1 — **slay·er** *n*

1sled *n* **1 :** a vehicle on runners for carrying loads especially over snow **2 :** a small vehicle with runners used mostly by children for sliding on snow and ice

2sled *vb* **sled·ded; sled·ding :** to ride or carry on a sled

1sledge *n* **:** SLEDGEHAMMER

2sledge *n* **:** a strong heavy sled

sledge·ham·mer *n* **:** a large heavy hammer usually used with both hands

1sleek *vb* **:** 1SLICK

2sleek *adj* **1 :** smooth and glossy as if polished **2 :** having a plump healthy look

1sleep *n* **1 :** a natural periodic loss of consciousness during which the body rests and refreshes itself **2 :** an inactive state (as hibernation or trance) like true sleep **3 :** DEATH — **sleep·less** *adj* — **sleep·less·ness** *n*

2sleep *vb* **slept; sleep·ing :** to take rest in sleep **:** be or lie asleep

sleep·er *n* **1 :** one that sleeps **2 :** a horizontal beam to support something on or near ground level **3 :** a railroad car with berths for sleeping

sleep·walk·er *n* **:** a person who walks about while asleep — **sleep·walk·ing** *n*

sleepy *adj* **sleep·i·er; sleep·i·est 1 :** ready to fall asleep **:** DROWSY **2 :** not active, noisy, or busy — **sleep·i·ness** *n*

1sleet *n* **:** frozen or partly frozen rain

2sleet *vb* **:** to shower sleet

sleeve *n* **1 :** the part of a garment covering the arm **2 :** a part that fits over or around something like a sleeve — **sleeved** *adj* — **sleeve·less** *adj*

1sleigh *n* **:** an open usually horse-drawn vehicle with runners for use on snow or ice

2sleigh *vb* **:** to drive or ride in a sleigh

sleight of hand : skill and quickness in the use of the hands especially in doing magic tricks

slen·der *adj* **1 :** gracefully thin **2 :** narrow for its height **3 :** very little

slept *past of* SLEEP

slew *past of* SLAY

1slice *vb* **sliced; slic·ing 1 :** to cut with or as if with a knife **2 :** to cut into thin flat pieces

2slice *n* **:** a thin flat piece cut from something

1slick *vb* **:** to make sleek or smooth

2slick *adj* **1 :** having a smooth surface **:** SLIPPERY **2 :** CRAFTY, CLEVER

slick·er *n* **:** a long loose raincoat

1slide *vb* **slid; slid·ing 1 :** to move or cause

to move smoothly over a surface : GLIDE **2** : to move or pass smoothly and without much effort

²slide *n* **1 :** the act or motion of sliding **2 :** a loosened mass that slides : AVALANCHE **3 :** a surface down which a person or thing slides **4 :** something that operates or adjusts by sliding **5 :** a transparent picture that can be projected on a screen **6 :** a glass plate for holding an object to be examined under a microscope

¹slight *adj* **1 :** not large or stout **2 :** FLIMSY, FRAIL **3 :** not important : TRIVIAL **4 :** small of its kind or in amount — **slight•ly** *adv*

²slight *vb* **:** to treat without proper care, respect, or courtesy

³slight *n* **1 :** an act or an instance of slighting **2 :** the state or an instance of being slighted

slight•ing *adj* **:** showing a lack of respect or caring

¹slim *adj* **slim•mer; slim•mest 1 :** SLENDER 1 **2 :** very small

²slim *vb* **slimmed; slim•ming :** to make or become slender

slime *n* **1 :** soft slippery mud **2 :** a soft slippery material (as on the skin of a slug or catfish)

slimy *adj* **slim•i•er; slim•i•est 1 :** having the feel or look of slime **2 :** covered with slime

¹sling *vb* **slung; sling•ing 1 :** to throw with a sudden sweeping motion : FLING **2 :** to hurl with a sling

²sling *n* **1 :** a device (as a short strap with a string attached at each end) for hurling stones **2 :** SLINGSHOT **3 :** a device (as a rope or chain) by which something is lifted or carried **4 :** a hanging bandage put around the neck to hold up the arm or hand

³sling *vb* **slung; sling•ing 1 :** to put in or move or support with a sling **2 :** to hang from two points

sling•shot *n* **:** a forked stick with an elastic band attached for shooting small stones

slink *vb* **slunk; slink•ing :** to move or go by or as if by creeping especially so as not to be noticed (as in fear or shame)

¹slip *vb* **slipped; slip•ping 1 :** to move easily and smoothly **2 :** to move quietly : STEAL **3 :** to pass or let pass or escape without being noted, used, or done **4 :** to get away from **5 :** to escape the attention of **6 :** to slide into or out of place or away from a support **7 :** to slide on a slippery surface so as to lose one's balance **8 :** to put on or take off a garment quickly and carelessly

²slip *n* **1 :** a ramp where ships can be landed or repaired **2 :** a place for a ship between two piers **3 :** a secret or quick departure or escape **4 :** a small mistake : BLUNDER **5 :** the act or an instance of slipping down or out of place **6 :** a sudden mishap **7 :** a fall from some level or standard : DECLINE **8 :** an undergarment made in dress length with straps over the shoulders **9 :** PILLOWCASE

³slip *n* **1 :** a piece of a plant cut for planting or grafting **2 :** a long narrow piece of material **3 :** a piece of paper used for some record **4 :** a young and slender person

⁴slip *vb* **slipped; slip•ping :** to take slips from (a plant)

slip•cov•er *n* **:** a cover (as for a sofa or chair) that may be slipped off and on

slip•knot *n* **:** a knot made by tying the end of a line around the line itself to form a loop so that the size of the loop may be changed by slipping the knot

slip•per *n* **:** a light low shoe that is easily slipped on the foot

slip•pery *adj* **slip•per•i•er; slip•per•i•est 1 :** having a surface smooth or wet enough to make something slide or make one lose one's footing or hold **2 :** not to be trusted : TRICKY

slip•shod *adj* **:** very careless : SLOVENLY

slip up *vb* **:** to make a mistake

¹slit *n* **:** a long narrow cut or opening

²slit *vb* **slit; slit•ting :** to make a long narrow cut in : SLASH

slith•er *vb* **:** ¹GLIDE

¹sliv•er *n* **:** a long slender piece cut or torn off : SPLINTER

²sliver *vb* **:** to cut or form into slivers

¹slob•ber *vb* **:** to let saliva or liquid dribble from the mouth

²slobber *n* **:** dripping saliva

slo•gan *n* **:** a word or phrase used by a party, a group, or a business to attract attention (as to its goal, worth, or beliefs)

sloop *n* **:** a sailing boat with one mast and a fore-and-aft mainsail and jib

¹slop *n* **1 :** thin tasteless drink or liquid food **2 :** liquid spilled or splashed **3 :** food waste or gruel fed to animals **4 :** body waste

²slop *vb* **slopped; slop•ping 1 :** to spill or spill something on or over **2 :** to feed slop to

¹slope *vb* **sloped; slop•ing :** to take a slanting direction

²slope *n* **1 :** a piece of slanting ground (as a hillside) **2 :** upward or downward slant

slop•py *adj* **slop•pi•er; slop•pi•est 1 :** wet enough to spatter easily **2 :** careless in work or in appearance

slosh *vb* **1 :** to walk with trouble through water, mud, or slush **2 :** ¹SPLASH 1, 2, 3

[1]**slot** *n* **:** a narrow opening, groove, or passage

[2]**slot** *vb* **slot·ted; slot·ting :** to cut a slot in

sloth *n* **1 :** the state of being lazy **2 :** an animal of Central and South America that hangs back downward and moves slowly along the branches of trees on whose leaves, twigs, and fruits it feeds

[1]**slouch** *n* **1 :** a lazy worthless person **2 :** a lazy drooping way of standing, sitting, or walking

[2]**slouch** *vb* **:** to walk, stand, or sit with a slouch

slough *n* **:** a wet marshy or muddy place

slov·en·ly *adj* **:** personally untidy

[1]**slow** *adj* **1 :** not as smart or as quick to understand as most people **2 :** not easily aroused or excited **3 :** moving, flowing, or going at less than the usual speed **4 :** indicating less than is correct **5 :** not lively or active — **slow·ly** *adv* — **slow·ness** *n*

[2]**slow** *adv* **:** in a slow way

[3]**slow** *vb* **:** to make or go slow or slower

slow·poke *n* **:** a very slow person

sludge *n* **:** a soft muddy mass resulting from sewage treatment

[1]**slug** *n* **:** a long wormlike land mollusk that is related to the snails but has an undeveloped shell or none at all

[2]**slug** *n* **1 :** a small piece of shaped metal **2 :** BULLET **3 :** a metal disk often used in place of a coin

[3]**slug** *n* **:** a hard blow especially with the fist

[4]**slug** *vb* **slugged; slug·ging :** to hit hard with the fist or with a bat

slug·gard *n* **:** a lazy person

slug·ger *n* **:** a boxer or baseball batter who hits hard

slug·gish *adj* **:** slow in movement or reaction — **slug·gish·ly** *adv* — **slug·gish·ness** *n*

[1]**sluice** *n* **1 :** an artificial passage for water with a gate for controlling its flow or changing its direction **2 :** a device for controlling the flow of water **3 :** a sloping trough for washing ore or for floating logs

[2]**sluice** *vb* **sluiced; sluic·ing 1 :** to wash in a stream of water running through a sluice **2 :** [3]FLUSH 2, DRENCH

slum *n* **:** a very poor crowded dirty section especially of a city

[1]**slum·ber** *vb* **:** to be asleep

[2]**slumber** *n* **:** [1]SLEEP

[1]**slump** *vb* **1 :** to drop or slide down suddenly **:** COLLAPSE **2 :** [2]SLOUCH **3 :** to drop sharply

[2]**slump** *n* **:** a big or continued drop especially in prices, business, or performance

slung *past of* SLING

slunk *past of* SLINK

[1]**slur** *n* **1 :** an insulting remark **2 :** STIGMA 1, STAIN

[2]**slur** *vb* **slurred; slur·ring 1 :** to pass over without proper mention or stress **2 :** to run one's speech together so that it is hard to understand

[3]**slur** *n* **:** a slurred way of talking

slush *n* **:** partly melted snow

sly *adj* **sli·er** *or* **sly·er; sli·est** *or* **sly·est 1 :** both clever and tricky **2 :** being sneaky and dishonest **3 :** MISCHIEVOUS 3 — **sly·ly** *adv* — **sly·ness** *n* — **on the sly :** so as not to be seen or caught **:** SECRETLY

[1]**smack** *n* **:** a slight taste, trace, or touch of something

[2]**smack** *vb* **:** to have a flavor, trace, or suggestion

[3]**smack** *vb* **1 :** to close and open the lips noisily especially in eating **2 :** to kiss usually loudly or hard **3 :** to make or give a smack **:** SLAP

[4]**smack** *n* **1 :** a quick sharp noise made by the lips (as in enjoyment of some taste) **2 :** a loud kiss **3 :** a noisy slap or blow

[1]**small** *adj* **1 :** little in size **2 :** few in numbers or members **3 :** little in amount **4 :** not very much **5 :** UNIMPORTANT **6 :** operating on a limited scale **7 :** lacking in strength **8 :** not generous **:** MEAN **9 :** made up of units of little worth **10 :** [1]HUMBLE 3, MODEST **11 :** lowered in pride **12 :** being letters that are not capitals — **small·ness** *n*

[2]**small** *n* **:** a part smaller and usually narrower than the rest

small intestine *n* **:** the long narrow upper part of the intestine in which food is mostly digested and from which digested food is absorbed into the body

small·pox *n* **:** an acute disease in which fever and skin eruptions occur and which is believed to be extinct due to vaccination against the virus causing it

[1]**smart** *adj* **1 :** BRISK, SPIRITED **2 :** quick to learn or do **:** BRIGHT **3 :** SAUCY 1 **4 :** stylish in appearance — **smart·ly** *adv* — **smart·ness** *n*

[2]**smart** *vb* **1 :** to cause or feel a sharp stinging pain **2 :** to feel distress

[3]**smart** *n* **:** a stinging pain usually in one spot

smart al·eck *n* **:** a person who likes to show off

[1]**smash** *n* **1 :** a violent blow or attack **2 :** the action or sound of smashing **3 :** a striking success

[2]**smash** *vb* **1 :** to break in pieces **:** SHATTER **2 :** to drive or move violently **3 :** to destroy completely **:** WRECK **4 :** to go to pieces **:** COLLAPSE

[1]**smear** *n* **:** a spot or streak made by or as if by an oily or sticky substance **:** SMUDGE

[2]**smear** *vb* **1 :** to spread or soil with something oily or sticky **:** DAUB **2 :** to spread over a surface **3 :** to blacken the good name of

[1]**smell** *vb* **smelled** *or* **smelt; smell·ing 1 :** to become aware of the odor of by means of sense organs located in the nose **2 :** to detect by means or use of the sense of smell **3 :** to have or give off an odor

[2]**smell** *n* **1 :** the sense by which a person or animal becomes aware of an odor **2 :** the sensation one gets through the sense of smell **:** ODOR, SCENT

[1]**smelt** *n, pl* **smelts** *or* **smelt :** a small food fish that looks like the related trouts, lives in coastal sea waters, and swims up rivers to spawn

[2]**smelt** *vb* **:** to melt (as ore) in order to separate the metal **:** REFINE

smelt·er *n* **1 :** a person whose work or business is smelting **2 :** a place where ores or metals are smelted

[1]**smile** *vb* **smiled; smil·ing 1 :** to have, produce, or show a smile **2 :** to look with amusement or scorn **3 :** to express by a smile

[2]**smile** *n* **:** an expression on the face in which the lips curve upward especially to show amusement or pleasure

smite *vb* **smote; smit·ten; smit·ing :** to strike hard especially with the hand or a weapon

smith *n* **1 :** a worker in metals **2 :** BLACKSMITH

smithy *n, pl* **smith·ies :** the workshop of a smith and especially of a blacksmith

smock *n* **:** a loose outer garment worn especially for protection of clothing

smog *n* **:** a fog made heavier and thicker by the action of sunlight on air polluted by smoke and automobile fumes

[1]**smoke** *n* **1 :** the gas of burning materials (as coal, wood, or tobacco) made visible by particles of carbon floating in it **2 :** a mass or column of smoke **:** SMUDGE **3 :** the act of smoking tobacco

[2]**smoke** *vb* **smoked; smok·ing 1 :** to give out smoke **2 :** to draw in and breathe out the fumes of burning tobacco **3 :** to drive (as mosquitoes) away by smoke **4 :** to expose (as meat) to smoke to give flavor and keep from spoiling — **smok·er** *n*

smoke de·tec·tor *n* **:** a device that sounds an alarm automatically when it detects smoke

smoke·house *n, pl* **smoke·hous·es :** a building where meat or fish is cured with smoke

smoke·stack *n* **:** a large chimney or a pipe for carrying away smoke (as on a factory or ship)

smoky *adj* **smok·i·er; smok·i·est 1 :** giving off smoke especially in large amounts **2 :** like that of smoke **3 :** filled with or darkened by smoke

[1]**smol·der** *or* **smoul·der** *n* **:** a slow often smoky fire

[2]**smolder** *or* **smoulder** *vb* **1 :** to burn slowly usually with smoke and without flame **2 :** to burn inwardly

[1]**smooth** *adj* **1 :** not rough or uneven in surface **2 :** not hairy **3 :** free from difficulties or things in the way **4 :** moving or progressing without breaks, sudden changes, or shifts **5 :** able to make things seem right or easy or good **:** GLIB — **smooth·ly** *adv* — **smooth·ness** *n*

[2]**smooth** *vb* **1 :** to make smooth **2 :** [1]POLISH 2, REFINE **3 :** to free from trouble or difficulty

smote *past of* SMITE

smoth·er *vb* **1 :** to overcome by depriving of air or exposing to smoke or fumes **:** SUFFOCATE **2 :** to become suffocated **3 :** to cover up **:** SUPPRESS **4 :** to cover thickly

[1]**smudge** *vb* **smudged; smudg·ing :** to soil or blur by rubbing or smearing

[2]**smudge** *n* **1 :** a blurred spot or streak **:** SMEAR **2 :** a smoky fire (as to drive away mosquitoes or protect fruit from frost)

smug *adj* **smug·ger; smug·gest :** very satisfied with oneself — **smug·ly** *adv*

smug·gle *vb* **smug·gled; smug·gling 1 :** to export or import secretly and unlawfully especially to avoid paying taxes **2 :** to take or bring secretly — **smug·gler** *n*

smut *n* **1 :** something (as a particle of soot) that soils or blackens **2 :** a destructive disease of plants (as cereal grasses) in which plant parts (as seeds) are replaced by masses of dark spores of the fungus that causes the disease **3 :** a fungus that causes smut

snack *n* **:** a light meal **:** LUNCH

[1]**snag** *n* **1 :** a stump or stub of a tree branch especially when hidden under water **2 :** a rough or broken part sticking out from something **3 :** an unexpected difficulty

[2]**snag** *vb* **snagged; snag·ging :** to catch or damage on or as if on a snag

snail *n* **1 :** a small slow-moving mollusk with a spiral shell into which it can draw itself for safety **2 :** a person who moves slowly

[1]**snake** *n* **1 :** a limbless crawling reptile that has a long body and lives usually on large insects or small animals and birds **2 :** a horrid or treacherous person

[2]**snake** *vb* **snaked; snak·ing :** to crawl, wind, or move like a snake

snaky *adj* **snak·i·er; snak·i·est** **1 :** of or like a snake **2 :** full of snakes

¹snap *vb* **snapped; snap·ping** **1 :** to grasp or grasp at something suddenly with the mouth or teeth **2 :** to grasp at something eagerly **3 :** to get, take, or buy at once **4 :** to speak or utter sharply or irritably **5 :** to break or break apart suddenly and often with a cracking noise **6 :** to make or cause to make a sharp or crackling sound **7 :** to close or fit in place with a quick movement **8 :** to put into or remove from a position suddenly or with a snapping sound **9 :** to close by means of snaps or fasteners **10 :** to act or be acted on with snap **11 :** to take a snapshot of

²snap *n* **1 :** the act or sound of snapping **2 :** something that is easy and presents no problems **3 :** a small amount **:** BIT **4 :** a sudden spell of harsh weather **5 :** a catch or fastening that closes or locks with a click **6 :** a thin brittle cookie **7 :** SNAPSHOT **8 :** smartness of movement or speech **:** ENERGY

³snap *adj* **1 :** made suddenly or without careful thought **2 :** closing with a click or by means of a device that snaps **3 :** very easy

snap·drag·on *n* **:** a garden plant with stalks of mostly white, pink, crimson, or yellow flowers with two lips

snap·per *n* **1 :** one that snaps **2 :** SNAPPING TURTLE **3 :** an active sea fish important for sport and food

snap·ping tur·tle *n* **:** a large American turtle that catches its prey with a snap of the powerful jaws

snap·py *adj* **snap·pi·er; snap·pi·est** **1 :** full of life **:** LIVELY **2 :** briskly cold **:** CHILLY **3 :** STYLISH, SMART

snap·shot *n* **:** a photograph taken usually with an inexpensive hand-held camera

¹snare *n* **1 :** a trap (as a noose) for catching small animals and birds **2 :** something by which one is entangled, trapped, or deceived

²snare *vb* **snared; snar·ing :** to catch or entangle by or as if by use of a snare

snare drum *n* **:** a small drum with two heads that has strings stretched across its lower head to produce a rattling sound

¹snarl *vb* **:** to get into a tangle

²snarl *n* **1 :** a tangle usually of hairs or thread **:** KNOT **2 :** a tangled situation

³snarl *vb* **1 :** to growl with a showing of teeth **2 :** to speak in an angry way **3 :** to utter with a growl

⁴snarl *n* **:** an angry growl

¹snatch *vb* **:** to take hold of or try to take hold of something quickly or suddenly

²snatch *n* **1 :** an act of snatching **2 :** a brief period **3 :** something brief, hurried, or in small bits

¹sneak *vb* **sneaked** *or* **snuck; sneak·ing :** to move, act, bring, or put in a sly or secret way

²sneak *n* **1 :** a person who acts in a sly or secret way **2 :** the act or an instance of sneaking

sneak·er *n* **:** a canvas shoe with a rubber sole

sneaky *adj* **sneak·i·er; sneak·i·est :** behaving in a sly or secret way or showing that kind of behavior

¹sneer *vb* **1 :** to smile or laugh while making a face that shows scorn **2 :** to speak or write in a scorning way

²sneer *n* **:** a sneering expression or remark

¹sneeze *vb* **sneezed; sneez·ing :** to force out the breath in a sudden loud violent action

²sneeze *n* **:** an act or instance of sneezing

¹snick·er *vb* **:** to give a small and often mean or sly laugh

²snicker *n* **:** an act or sound of snickering

¹sniff *vb* **1 :** to draw air into the nose in short breaths loud enough to be heard **2 :** to show scorn **3 :** to smell by taking short breaths

²sniff *n* **1 :** the act or sound of sniffing **2 :** an odor or amount sniffed

snif·fle *vb* **snif·fled; snif·fling** **1 :** to sniff repeatedly **2 :** to speak with sniffs

snif·fles *n pl* **:** a common cold in which the main symptom is a runny nose

¹snig·ger *vb* **:** ¹SNICKER

²snigger *n* **:** ²SNICKER

¹snip *n* **1 :** a small piece that is snipped off **2 :** an act or sound of snipping

²snip *vb* **snipped; snip·ping :** to cut or cut off with or as if with shears or scissors

¹snipe *n, pl* **snipes** *or* **snipe :** a game bird that lives in marshes and has a long straight bill

²snipe *vb* **sniped; snip·ing :** to shoot from a hiding place (as at individual enemy soldiers) — **snip·er** *n*

snob *n* **:** a person who imitates, admires, or wants to be friends with people of higher position and looks down on or avoids those felt to be less important

snob·bish *adj* **:** of, relating to, or being a snob

¹snoop *vb* **:** to look or search especially in a sneaking or nosy way

²snoop *n* **:** SNOOPER

snoop·er *n* **:** a person who snoops

snoot *n* **:** ¹NOSE 1

¹snooze *vb* **snoozed; snooz·ing :** to take a nap

²snooze *n* **:** a short sleep **:** NAP

¹snore *vb* **snored; snor·ing :** to breathe with a rough hoarse noise while sleeping
²snore *n* **:** an act or sound of snoring
¹snort *vb* **:** to force air through the nose with a rough harsh sound
²snort *n* **:** an act or sound of snorting
snout *n* **1 :** a long projecting nose (as of a pig) **2 :** the front part of a head (as of a weevil) that sticks out like the snout of a pig **3 :** a usually large and ugly human nose
¹snow *n* **1 :** small white crystals of ice formed directly from the water vapor of the air **2 :** a fall of snowflakes **:** a mass of snowflakes fallen to earth
²snow *vb* **1 :** to fall or cause to fall in or as snow **2 :** to cover or shut in with snow
snow·ball *n* **:** a round mass of snow pressed or rolled together
snow·bird *n* **:** a small bird (as a junco) seen mostly in winter
snow–blind *or* **snow–blind·ed** *adj* **:** having the eyes red and swollen and unable to see from the effect of glare reflected from snow — **snow blindness** *n*
snow·bound *adj* **:** shut in by snow
snow·drift *n* **:** a bank of drifted snow
snow·fall *n* **1 :** a fall of snow **2 :** the amount of snow that falls in a single storm or in a certain period
snow·flake *n* **:** a snow crystal **:** a small mass of snow crystals
snow·man *n, pl* **snow·men :** snow shaped to look like a person
snow·mo·bile *n* **:** a motor vehicle designed for travel on snow
snow·plow *n* **:** any of various devices used for clearing away snow
¹snow·shoe *n* **:** a light frame of wood strung with a net (as of rawhide) and worn under one's shoe to prevent sinking into soft snow
²snowshoe *vb* **snow·shoed; snow·shoe·ing :** to go on snowshoes
snow·storm *n* **:** a storm of falling snow
snowy *adj* **snow·i·er; snow·i·est 1 :** having or covered with snow **2 :** white like snow
¹snub *vb* **snubbed; snub·bing :** to ignore or treat rudely on purpose
²snub *n* **:** an act or an instance of snubbing
snub–nosed *adj* **:** having a stubby and usually slightly turned-up nose
snuck *past of* SNEAK
¹snuff *vb* **1 :** to cut or pinch off the burned end of the wick of a candle **2 :** EXTINGUISH 1
²snuff *vb* **:** to draw through or into the nose with force
³snuff *n* **:** powdered tobacco that is chewed, placed against the gums, or drawn in through the nostrils
¹snuf·fle *vb* **snuf·fled; snuf·fling :** to breathe noisily through a nose that is partly blocked
²snuffle *n* **:** the sound made in snuffling
snug *adj* **snug·ger; snug·gest 1 :** fitting closely and comfortably **2 :** COMFORTABLE 1, COZY **3 :** offering protection or a hiding place — **snug·ly** *adv*
snug·gle *vb* **snug·gled; snug·gling 1 :** to curl up comfortably or cozily **:** CUDDLE **2 :** to pull in close to one
¹so *adv* **1 :** in the way indicated **2 :** in the same way **:** ALSO **3 :** ¹THEN 2 **4 :** to an indicated extent or way **5 :** to a great degree **:** VERY, EXTREMELY **6 :** to a definite but not specified amount **7 :** most certainly **:** INDEED **8 :** THEREFORE
²so *conj* **1 :** in order that **2 :** and therefore
³so *pron* **1 :** the same **:** THAT **2 :** approximately that
¹soak *vb* **1 :** to lie covered with liquid **2 :** to place in a liquid to wet or as if to wet thoroughly **3 :** to enter or pass through something by or as if by tiny holes **:** PERMEATE **4 :** to draw out by or as if by soaking in a liquid **5 :** to draw in by or as if by absorption
²soak *n* **:** the act or process of soaking **:** the state of being soaked
¹soap *n* **:** a substance that is usually made by the action of alkali on fat, dissolves in water, and is used for washing
²soap *vb* **:** to rub soap over or into something
soap·stone *n* **:** a soft stone having a soapy or greasy feeling
soap·suds *n pl* **:** SUDS
soapy *adj* **soap·i·er; soap·i·est 1 :** smeared with or full of soap **2 :** containing or combined with soap **3 :** like soap
soar *vb* **:** to fly or sail through the air often at a great height
¹sob *vb* **sobbed; sob·bing 1 :** to cry or express with gasps and catching in the throat **2 :** to make a sobbing sound
²sob *n* **1 :** an act of sobbing **2 :** a sound of or like that of sobbing
¹so·ber *adj* **1 :** not drinking too much **:** TEMPERATE **2 :** not drunk **3 :** having a serious attitude **:** SOLEMN **4 :** having a quiet color **5 :** not fanciful or imagined
²sober *vb* **:** to make or become sober
so–called *adj* **:** usually but often wrongly so named
soc·cer *n* **:** a game played between two teams of eleven players in which a round inflated ball is moved toward a goal usually by kicking
so·cia·ble *adj* **1 :** liking to be around other people **:** FRIENDLY **2 :** involving pleasant social relations

[1]**so·cial** *adj* **1 :** FRIENDLY 1, SOCIABLE **2 :** of or relating to human beings as a group **3 :** living or growing naturally in groups or communities **4 :** of, relating to, or based on rank in a particular society **5 :** of or relating to fashionable society — **so·cial·ly** *adv*

[2]**social** *n* **:** a friendly gathering usually for a special reason

so·cial·ism *n* **:** a theory or system of government based on public ownership and control of the means of production and distribution of goods

so·cial·ist *n* **:** a person who believes in socialism

social studies *n pl* **:** the studies (as civics, history, and geography) that deal with human relationships and the way society works

so·ci·ety *n, pl* **so·ci·et·ies** **1 :** friendly association with others **2 :** human beings viewed as a system within which the individual lives **:** all of the people **3 :** a group of persons with a common interest or purpose **4 :** a part of a community thought of as different in some way **5 :** the group or set of fashionable persons

[1]**sock** *n, pl* **socks** *or* **sox :** a knitted or woven covering for the foot usually reaching past the ankle and sometimes to the knee

[2]**sock** *vb* **:** [1]HIT 1, PUNCH

[3]**sock** *n* **:** [2]PUNCH

sock·et *n* **:** a hollow thing or place that receives or holds something

sock·eye *n* **:** a small Pacific salmon that is the source of most of the salmon with red flesh that we eat

[1]**sod** *n* **:** the layer of the soil filled with roots (as of grass)

[2]**sod** *vb* **sod·ded; sod·ding :** to cover with sod

so·da *n* **1 :** a powdery substance like salt used in washing and in making glass or soap **2 :** SODIUM BICARBONATE **3 :** SODA WATER **4 :** SODA POP **5 :** a sweet drink made of soda water, flavoring, and ice cream

soda fountain *n* **:** a counter where soft drinks and ice cream are served

soda pop *n* **:** a flavored beverage containing carbon dioxide

soda water *n* **:** water with carbon dioxide added

sod·den *adj* **:** SOGGY

so·di·um *n* **:** a soft waxy silver-white chemical element occurring in nature in combined form (as in salt)

sodium bicarbonate *n* **:** a white powder used in cooking and medicine

sodium chlo·ride *n* **:** [1]SALT 1

so·fa *n* **:** a long upholstered seat usually with a back and arms

[1]**soft** *adj* **1 :** having a pleasing or comfortable effect **2 :** not bright or glaring **3 :** quiet in pitch or volume **4 :** smooth or delicate in appearance or feel **5 :** not violent **6 :** EASY 1 **7 :** sounding as in *ace* and *gem* — used of *c* and *g* **8 :** easily affected by emotions **9 :** lacking in strength **10 :** not hard, solid, or firm **11 :** free from substances that prevent lathering of soap **12 :** not containing alcohol — **soft·ness** *n*

[2]**soft** *adv* **:** SOFTLY

soft·ball *n* **1 :** a game like baseball played with a larger ball **2 :** the ball used in softball

soft·en *vb* **:** to make or become soft or softer — **soft·en·er** *n*

soft·ly *adv* **:** in a soft way **:** QUIETLY, GENTLY

soft·ware *n* **:** the programs and related information used by a computer

soft·wood *n* **:** the wood of a cone-bearing tree (as a pine or spruce)

sog·gy *adj* **sog·gi·er; sog·gi·est :** heavy with water or moisture

[1]**soil** *vb* **:** to make or become dirty

[2]**soil** *n* **1 :** the loose finely divided surface material of the earth in which plants have their roots **2 :** COUNTRY 2, LAND — **soil·less** *adj*

[1]**so·journ** *n* **:** a temporary stay

[2]**sojourn** *vb* **:** to stay as a temporary resident

sol *n* **:** the fifth note of the musical scale

so·lar *adj* **1 :** of or relating to the sun **2 :** measured by the earth's course around the sun **3 :** produced or made to work by the action of the sun's light or heat

solar system *n* **:** the sun and the planets, asteroids, comets, and meteors that revolve around it

sold *past of* SELL

[1]**sol·der** *n* **:** a metal or a mixture of metals used when melted to join or mend surfaces of metal

[2]**solder** *vb* **:** to join together or repair with solder

sol·dier *n* **:** a person in military service **:** an enlisted person who is not a commissioned officer

[1]**sole** *n* **:** a flatfish that has a small mouth and small eyes set close together and is a popular food fish

[2]**sole** *n* **1 :** the bottom of the foot **2 :** the bottom of a shoe, slipper, or boot

[3]**sole** *vb* **soled; sol·ing :** to furnish with a sole

[4]**sole** *adj* **1 :** [1]SINGLE 2, ONLY **2 :** limited or belonging only to the one mentioned

sole·ly *adv* **1 :** without another **:** ALONE **2 :** [2]ONLY 2

sol·emn *adj* **1 :** celebrated with religious ceremony **:** SACRED **2 :** [1]FORMAL **3 :** done or made seriously and thoughtfully **4** **:** very serious **5 :** being dark and gloomy **:** SOMBER — **sol·emn·ly** *adv*

so·lem·ni·ty *n, pl* **so·lem·ni·ties** **1 :** a solemn ceremony, event, day, or speech **2** **:** formal dignity

so·lic·it *vb* **1 :** to come to with a request or plea **2 :** to try to get

¹sol·id *adj* **1 :** not hollow **2 :** not loose or spongy **:** COMPACT **3 :** neither liquid nor gaseous **4 :** made firmly and well **5** **:** being without a break, interruption, or change **6 :** UNANIMOUS **7 :** RELIABLE, DEPENDABLE **8 :** of one material, kind, or color — **sol·id·ly** *adv* — **sol·id·ness** *n*

²solid *n* **1 :** something that has length, width, and thickness **2 :** a solid substance **:** a substance that keeps its size and shape

so·lid·i·fy *vb* **so·lid·i·fied; so·lid·i·fy·ing** **:** to make or become solid

so·lid·i·ty *n, pl* **so·lid·i·ties :** the quality or state of being solid

sol·i·taire *n* **:** a card game played by one person alone

sol·i·tary *adj* **1 :** all alone **2 :** seldom visited **:** LONELY **3 :** growing or living alone **:** not one of a group or cluster

sol·i·tude *n* **1 :** the quality or state of being alone or away from others **:** SECLUSION **2** **:** a lonely place

¹so·lo *n, pl* **solos** **1 :** music played or sung by one person either alone or with accompaniment **2 :** an action (as in a dance) in which there is only one performer

²solo *adv or adj* **:** ²ALONE 2

³solo *vb* **:** to fly solo in an airplane

so·lo·ist *n* **:** a person who performs a solo

sol·stice *n* **:** the time of the year when the sun is farthest north (**summer solstice**, about June 22) or south (**winter solstice**, about December 22) of the equator

sol·u·ble *adj* **1 :** capable of being dissolved in liquid **2 :** capable of being solved or explained

so·lu·tion *n* **1 :** the act or process of solving **2 :** the result of solving a problem **3 :** the act or process by which a solid, liquid, or gas is dissolved in a liquid **4 :** a liquid in which something has been dissolved

solve *vb* **solved; solv·ing :** to find the answer to or a solution for

sol·vent *n* **:** a usually liquid substance in which other substances can be dissolved or dispersed

som·ber *or* **som·bre** *adj* **1 :** being dark and gloomy **:** DULL **2 :** showing or causing low spirits

som·bre·ro *n, pl* **som·bre·ros :** a tall hat of felt or straw with a very wide brim worn especially in the Southwest and Mexico

¹some *adj* **1 :** being one unknown or not specified **2 :** being one, a part, or an unspecified number of something **3 :** being of an amount or number that is not mentioned **4 :** being at least one and sometimes all of

²some *pron* **:** a certain number or amount

¹-some *adj suffix* **:** distinguished by a specified thing, quality, state, or action

²-some *n suffix* **:** group of so many members

¹some·body *pron* **:** some person

²somebody *n, pl* **some·bod·ies :** a person of importance

some·day *adv* **:** at some future time

some·how *adv* **:** in one way or another

some·one *pron* **:** some person

¹som·er·sault *n* **:** a moving of the body through one complete turn in which the feet move up and over the head

²somersault *vb* **:** to turn a somersault

some·thing *pron* **1 :** a thing that is not surely known or understood **2 :** a thing or amount that is clearly known but not named **3 :** SOMEWHAT

some·time *adv* **1 :** at a future time **2 :** at a time not known or not specified

some·times *adv* **:** now and then **:** OCCASIONALLY

some·way *adv* **:** SOMEHOW

¹some·what *pron* **:** some amount or extent

²somewhat *adv* **:** to some extent

some·where *adv* **1 :** in, at, or to a place not known or named **2 :** at some time not specified

son *n* **1 :** a male child or offspring **2 :** a man or boy closely associated with or thought of as a child of something (as a country, race, or religion)

so·na·ta *n* **:** a musical composition usually for a single instrument consisting of three or four separate sections in different forms and keys

song *n* **1 :** vocal music **2 :** poetic composition **:** POETRY **3 :** a short musical composition of words and music **4 :** a small amount

song·bird *n* **:** a bird that sings

song·ster *n* **:** a person or a bird that sings

son·ic *adj* **:** using, produced by, or relating to sound waves

sonic boom *n* **:** a sound like an explosion made by an aircraft traveling at supersonic speed

son–in–law *n, pl* **sons–in–law :** the husband of one's daughter

son·ny *n, pl* **son·nies :** a young boy — used mostly to address a stranger

so·no·rous *adj* **1 :** producing sound (as when struck) **2 :** loud, deep, or rich in sound **:** RESONANT

soon *adv* **1 :** without delay **:** before long **2 :** in a prompt way **:** QUICKLY **3 :** [1]EARLY 2 **4 :** by choice **:** WILLINGLY

soot *n* **:** a black powder formed when something is burned **:** the very fine powder that colors smoke

soothe *vb* **soothed; sooth·ing 1 :** to please by praise or attention **2 :** RELIEVE 1 **3 :** to calm down **:** COMFORT

sooth·say·er *n* **:** a person who claims to foretell events

sooty *adj* **soot·i·er; soot·i·est 1 :** soiled with soot **2 :** like soot especially in color

sop *vb* **sopped; sop·ping 1 :** to soak or dip in or as if in liquid **2 :** to mop up (as water)

soph·o·more *n* **:** a student in his or her second year at a high school or college

so·pra·no *n, pl* **so·pra·nos 1 :** the highest part in harmony having four parts **2 :** the highest singing voice of women or boys **3 :** a person having a soprano voice **4 :** an instrument having a soprano range or part

sor·cer·er *n* **:** a person who practices sorcery or witchcraft **:** WIZARD

sor·cer·ess *n* **:** a woman who practices sorcery or witchcraft **:** WITCH

sor·cery *n, pl* **sor·cer·ies :** the use of magic **:** WITCHCRAFT

sor·did *adj* **1 :** very dirty **:** FOUL **2 :** of low moral quality **:** VILE

[1]**sore** *adj* **sor·er; sor·est 1 :** causing distress **2 :** very painful or sensitive **:** TENDER **3 :** hurt or red and swollen so as to be or seem painful **4 :** ANGRY — **sore·ly** *adv* — **sore·ness** *n*

[2]**sore** *n* **:** a sore spot (as an ulcer) on the body usually with the skin broken or bruised and often with infection

sor·ghum *n* **1 :** a tall grass that looks like Indian corn and is used for forage and grain **2 :** syrup from the juice of a sorghum

so·ror·i·ty *n, pl* **so·ror·i·ties :** a club of girls or women especially at a college

[1]**sor·rel** *n* **1 :** an animal (as a horse) of a sorrel color **2 :** a brownish orange to light brown

[2]**sorrel** *n* **:** any of several plants with sour juice

[1]**sor·row** *n* **1 :** sadness or grief caused by loss (as of something loved) **2 :** a cause of grief or sadness **3 :** a feeling of regret

[2]**sorrow** *vb* **:** to feel or express sorrow **:** GRIEVE

sor·row·ful *adj* **1 :** full of or showing sorrow **2 :** causing sorrow

sor·ry *adj* **sor·ri·er; sor·ri·est 1 :** feeling sorrow or regret **2 :** causing sorrow, pity, or scorn **:** WRETCHED

[1]**sort** *n* **1 :** a group of persons or things that have something in common **:** KIND **2 :** PERSON 1, INDIVIDUAL **3 :** general disposition **:** NATURE — **out of sorts 1 :** not feeling well **2 :** easily angered **:** IRRITABLE

[2]**sort** *vb* **:** to separate and arrange according to kind or class **:** CLASSIFY

SOS *n* **1 :** an international radio code distress signal used especially by ships and airplanes calling for help **2 :** a call for help

[1]**so–so** *adv* **:** fairly well

[2]**so–so** *adj* **:** neither very good nor very bad

sought *past of* SEEK

soul *n* **1 :** the spiritual part of a person believed to give life to the body **2 :** the essential part of something **3 :** a person who leads or stirs others to action **:** LEADER **4 :** a person's moral and emotional nature **5 :** human being **:** PERSON

[1]**sound** *adj* **1 :** free from disease or weakness **2 :** free from flaw or decay **3 :** [1]SOLID 4, FIRM **4 :** free from error **5 :** based on the truth **6 :** THOROUGH 1 **7 :** [1]DEEP 5, UNDISTURBED **8 :** showing good sense **:** WISE — **sound·ly** *adv* — **sound·ness** *n*

[2]**sound** *adv* **:** to the full extent

[3]**sound** *n* **1 :** the sensation experienced through the sense of hearing **:** an instance or occurrence of this **2 :** one of the noises that together make up human speech **3 :** the suggestion carried or given by something heard or read **4 :** hearing distance **:** EARSHOT — **sound·less** *adj* — **sound·less·ly** *adv*

[4]**sound** *vb* **1 :** to make or cause to make a sound or noise **2 :** PRONOUNCE 2 **3 :** to make known **:** PROCLAIM **4 :** to order, signal, or indicate by a sound **5 :** to make or give an impression **:** SEEM

[5]**sound** *n* **:** a long stretch of water that is wider than a strait and often connects two larger bodies of water or forms a channel between the mainland and an island

[6]**sound** *vb* **1 :** to measure the depth of (as by a weighted line dropped down from the surface) **2 :** to find or try to find the thoughts or feelings of a person

sound·proof *adj* **:** capable of keeping sound from entering or escaping

sound wave *n* **:** a wave that is produced when a sound is made and is responsible for carrying the sound to the ear

soup *n* **:** a liquid food made from the liquid in which vegetables, meat, or fish have been cooked and often containing pieces of solid food

[1]**sour** *adj* **1 :** having an acid taste **2 :** having become acid through spoiling **3 :** suggesting decay **4 :** not pleasant or friendly **5 :** acid in reaction — **sour·ish** *adj* — **sour·ly** *adv* — **sour·ness** *n*

[2]**sour** *vb* **:** to make or become sour

source *n* **1 :** the cause or starting point of something **2 :** the beginning of a stream of water **3 :** one that supplies information

sou•sa•phone *n* **:** a large circular tuba designed to rest on the player's shoulder and used chiefly in marching bands

1south *adv* **:** to or toward the south

2south *adj* **:** placed toward, facing, or coming from the south

3south *n* **1 :** the direction to the right of one facing east **:** the compass point opposite to north **2** *cap* **:** regions or countries south of a point that is mentioned or understood

1South American *adj* **:** of or relating to South America or the South Americans

2South American *n* **:** a person born or living in South America

south•bound *adj* **:** going south

1south•east *adv* **:** to or toward the southeast

2southeast *n* **1 :** the direction between south and east **2** *cap* **:** regions or countries southeast of a point that is mentioned or understood

3southeast *adj* **:** placed toward, facing, or coming from the southeast

south•east•er•ly *adv or adj* **1 :** from the southeast **2 :** toward the southeast

south•east•ern *adj* **1** *often cap* **:** of, relating to, or like that of the Southeast **2 :** lying toward or coming from the southeast

south•er•ly *adj or adv* **1 :** toward the south **2 :** from the south

south•ern *adj* **1** *often cap* **:** of, relating to, or like that of the South **2 :** lying toward or coming from the south

South•ern•er *n* **:** a person who is born or lives in the South

south•paw *n* **:** a person (as a baseball pitcher) who is left-handed

south pole *n, often cap S&P* **1 :** the most southern point of the earth **:** the southern end of the earth's axis **2 :** the end of a magnet that points toward the south when the magnet is free to swing

south•ward *adv or adj* **:** toward the south

1south•west *adv* **:** to or toward the southwest

2southwest *n* **1 :** the direction between south and west **2** *cap* **:** regions or countries southwest of a point that is mentioned or understood

3southwest *adj* **:** placed toward, facing, or coming from the southwest

south•west•er•ly *adv or adj* **1 :** from the southwest **2 :** toward the southwest

south•west•ern *adj* **1 :** lying toward or coming from the southwest **2** *often cap* **:** of, relating to, or like that of the Southwest

sou•ve•nir *n* **:** something that serves as a reminder

sou'•west•er *n* **:** a waterproof hat with wide slanting brim that is longer in back than in front

1sov•er•eign *n* **1 :** a person (as a king or queen) or body of persons having the highest power and authority in a state **2 :** an old British gold coin

2sovereign *adj* **1 :** highest in power or authority **2 :** having independent authority

sov•er•eign•ty *n, pl* **sov•er•eign•ties 1 :** supreme power especially over a political unit **2 :** freedom from outside control **3 :** one (as a country) that is sovereign

1sow *n* **:** an adult female hog

2sow *vb* **sowed; sown** *or* **sowed; sow•ing 1 :** to plant or scatter (as seed) for growing **2 :** to cover with or as if with scattered seed for growing **3 :** to set in motion **:** cause to exist — **sow•er** *n*

sow bug *n* **:** WOOD LOUSE

sox *pl of* SOCK

soy•bean *n* **:** an annual Asian plant related to the clovers that is widely grown for its edible seeds which yield an oil rich in protein

soybean oil *n* **:** a pale yellow oil that is obtained from soybeans and is used chiefly as a food and in paints and soaps

1space *n* **1 :** a period of time **2 :** a part of a distance, area, or volume that can be measured **3 :** a certain place set apart or available **4 :** the area without limits in which all things exist and move **5 :** the region beyond the earth's atmosphere **6 :** an empty place

2space *vb* **spaced; spac•ing :** to place with space between

space•craft *n, pl* **spacecraft :** a vehicle for travel beyond the earth's atmosphere

space•man *n, pl* **space•men :** a person who travels outside the earth's atmosphere

space•ship *n* **:** SPACECRAFT

space shuttle *n* **:** a spacecraft designed to transport people and cargo between earth and space that can be used repeatedly

space station *n* **:** an artificial satellite designed to stay in orbit permanently and to be occupied by humans for long periods

space suit *n* **:** a suit equipped to keep its wearer alive in space

spa•cious *adj* **:** having ample space

1spade *n* **:** a digging tool made to be pushed into the ground with the foot

2spade *vb* **spad•ed; spad•ing :** to dig with a spade

spa•ghet•ti *n* **:** a food made of a mixture of flour and water and dried in the form of strings that are prepared for eating by boiling

1span *n* **1 :** the distance from the end of the

thumb to the end of the little finger when the hand is stretched wide open **2 :** a limited portion of time **3 :** the spread (as of an arch) from one support to another
²span *vb* **spanned; span•ning 1 :** to measure by or as if by the hand stretched wide open **2 :** to reach or extend across **3 :** to place or construct a span over
³span *n* **:** two animals (as mules) worked or driven as a pair
span•gle *n* **:** SEQUIN
Span•iard *n* **:** a person born or living in Spain
span•iel *n* **:** a small or medium-sized dog with a thick wavy coat, long drooping ears, and usually short legs
¹Span•ish *adj* **:** of or relating to Spain, its people, or the Spanish language
²Spanish *n* **1 :** the language of Spain and the countries colonized by Spaniards **2 Spanish** *pl* **:** the people of Spain
spank *vb* **:** to strike on the buttocks with the open hand
spank•ing *adj* **:** BRISK 1, LIVELY
¹spar *n* **:** a long rounded piece of wood or metal (as a mast, yard, or boom) to which a sail is fastened
²spar *vb* **sparred; spar•ring 1 :** to box or make boxing movements with the fists for practice or in fun **2 :** ²SKIRMISH
¹spare *vb* **spared; spar•ing 1 :** to keep from being punished or harmed **:** show mercy to **2 :** to free of the need to do something **3 :** to keep from using or spending **4 :** to give up especially as not really needed **5 :** to have left over
²spare *adj* **spar•er; spar•est 1 :** held in reserve **2 :** being over what is needed **3 :** somewhat thin **4 :** SCANTY
³spare *n* **1 :** a spare or duplicate piece or part **2 :** the knocking down of all ten bowling pins with the first two balls
spare•ribs *n pl* **:** a cut of pork ribs separated from the bacon strips
spar•ing *adj* **:** careful in the use of money or supplies — **spar•ing•ly** *adv*
¹spark *n* **1 :** a small bit of burning material **2 :** a hot glowing bit struck from a mass (as by steel on flint) **3 :** a short bright flash of electricity between two points **4 :** ²SPARKLE 1 **5 :** ¹TRACE 2
²spark *vb* **1 :** to give off or cause to give off sparks **2 :** to set off
¹spar•kle *vb* **spar•kled; spar•kling 1 :** to throw off sparks **2 :** to give off small flashes of light **3 :** to be lively or active
²sparkle *n* **1 :** a little flash of light **2 :** the quality of sparkling
spar•kler *n* **:** a firework that throws off very bright sparks as it burns
spark plug *n* **:** a device used in an engine to produce a spark that ignites a fuel mixture
spar•row *n* **:** a small brownish bird related to the finches
sparrow hawk *n* **:** a small hawk or falcon
sparse *adj* **spars•er; spars•est :** not thickly grown or settled — **sparse•ly** *adv*
spasm *n* **1 :** a sudden involuntary and usually violent contracting of muscles **2 :** a sudden, violent, and temporary effort, emotion, or outburst
spas•mod•ic *adj* **:** relating to or affected by spasm **:** involving spasms — **spas•mod•i•cal•ly** *adv*
¹spat *past of* SPIT
²spat *n* **:** a cloth or leather covering for the instep and ankle
³spat *n* **:** a brief unimportant quarrel
spa•tial *adj* **:** of or relating to space
¹spat•ter *vb* **1 :** to splash with drops or small bits of something wet **2 :** to scatter by splashing
²spatter *n* **1 :** the act or sound of spattering **2 :** a drop or splash spattered on something **:** a spot or stain due to spattering
spat•u•la *n* **:** a knifelike instrument with a broad flexible blade that is used mostly for spreading or mixing soft substances or for lifting
¹spawn *vb* **:** to produce or deposit eggs or spawn
²spawn *n* **:** the eggs of a water animal (as an oyster or fish) that produces many small eggs
spay *vb* **:** to remove the ovaries of (a female animal)
speak *vb* **spoke; spo•ken; speak•ing 1 :** to utter words **:** TALK **2 :** to utter in words **3 :** to mention in speech or writing **4 :** to use or be able to use in talking
speak•er *n* **1 :** a person who speaks **2 :** a person who conducts a meeting **3 :** LOUDSPEAKER
¹spear *n* **1 :** a weapon with a long straight handle and sharp head or blade used for throwing or jabbing **2 :** an instrument with a sharp point and curved hooks used in spearing fish
²spear *vb* **:** to strike or pierce with or as if with a spear
³spear *n* **:** a usually young blade or sprout (as of grass)
¹spear•head *n* **1 :** the head or point of a spear **2 :** the person, thing, or group that is the leading force (as in a development or an attack)
²spearhead *vb* **:** to serve as leader of
spear•mint *n* **:** a common mint used for flavoring

spe·cial *adj* **1 :** UNUSUAL, EXTRAORDINARY **2 :** liked very well **3 :** UNIQUE 2 **4 :** [1]EXTRA **5 :** meant for a particular purpose or occasion — **spe·cial·ly** *adv*

spe·cial·ist *n* **1 :** a person who studies or works at a special occupation or branch of learning **2 :** a person working in a special skill in the Army in any of the four ranks equal to the ranks of corporal through sergeant first class

spe·cial·ize *vb* **spe·cial·ized; spe·cial·iz·ing 1 :** to limit one's attention or energy to one business, subject, or study **2 :** to change and develop so as to be suited for some particular use or living conditions

spe·cial·ty *n, pl* **spe·cial·ties 1 :** a product of a special kind or of special excellence **2 :** something a person specializes in

spe·cies *n, pl* **species 1 :** a class of things of the same kind and with the same name **:** KIND, SORT **2 :** a category of plants or animals that ranks below a genus in scientific classification and that is made up of individuals able to produce young with one another

spe·cif·ic *adj* **1 :** being an actual example of a certain kind of thing **2 :** clearly and exactly presented or stated **3 :** of, relating to, or being a species

spec·i·fi·ca·tion *n* **1 :** the act or process of specifying **2 :** a single specified item **3 :** a description of work to be done or materials to be used — often used in pl.

spec·i·fy *vb* **spec·i·fied; spec·i·fy·ing 1 :** to mention or name exactly and clearly **2 :** to include in a specification

spec·i·men *n* **:** a part or a single thing that shows what the whole thing or group is like **:** SAMPLE

speck *n* **1 :** a small spot or blemish **2 :** a very small amount **:** BIT

[1]**speck·le** *n* **:** a small mark (as of color)

[2]**speckle** *vb* **speck·led; speck·ling :** to mark with speckles

spec·ta·cle *n* **1 :** an unusual or impressive public display (as a big parade) **2 specta·cles** *pl* **:** a pair of glasses held in place by parts passing over the ears

spec·tac·u·lar *adj* **:** STRIKING, SHOWY

spec·ta·tor *n* **:** a person who looks on (as at a sports event)

spec·ter *or* **spec·tre** *n* **:** GHOST

spec·trum *n, pl* **spec·tra** *or* **spec·trums :** the group of different colors including red, orange, yellow, green, blue, indigo, and violet seen when light passes through a prism and falls on a surface or when sunlight is affected by drops of water (as in a rainbow)

spec·u·late *vb* **spec·u·lat·ed; spec·u·lat·ing 1 :** MEDITATE 2 **2 :** to engage in a business deal in which much profit may be made although at a big risk

spec·u·la·tion *n* **1 :** [2]GUESS **2 :** the taking of a big risk in business in hopes of making a big profit

speech *n* **1 :** the communication or expression of thoughts in spoken words **2 :** something that is spoken **3 :** a public talk **4 :** a form of communication (as a language or dialect) used by a particular group **5 :** the power of expressing or communicating thoughts by speaking

speech·less *adj* **1 :** unable to speak **2 :** not speaking for a time **:** SILENT

[1]**speed** *n* **1 :** quickness in movement or action **2 :** rate of moving or doing

[2]**speed** *vb* **sped** *or* **speed·ed; speed·ing 1 :** to move or cause to move fast **:** HURRY **2 :** to go or drive at too high a speed **3 :** to increase the speed of **:** ACCELERATE

speed·boat *n* **:** a fast motorboat

speed bump *n* **:** a low raised ridge across a roadway (as in a parking lot) to limit vehicle speed

speed·om·e·ter *n* **1 :** an instrument that measures speed **2 :** an instrument that measures speed and records distance traveled

speedy *adj* **speed·i·er; speed·i·est :** moving or taking place fast — **speed·i·ly** *adv*

[1]**spell** *vb* **1 :** to name, write, or print in order the letters of a word **2 :** to make up the letters of **3 :** to amount to **:** MEAN

[2]**spell** *n* **1 :** a spoken word or group of words believed to have magic power **:** CHARM **2 :** a very strong influence

[3]**spell** *n* **1 :** one's turn at work or duty **2 :** a period spent in a job or occupation **3 :** a short period of time **4 :** a stretch of a specified kind of weather **5 :** a period of bodily or mental distress or disorder

[4]**spell** *vb* **:** to take the place of for a time **:** RELIEVE

spell·bound *adj* **:** held by or as if by a spell

spell·er *n* **1 :** a person who spells words **2 :** a book with exercises for teaching spelling

spell·ing *n* **1 :** the forming of words from letters **2 :** the letters composing a word

spelling checker *also* **spell check** *or* **spell checker** *n* **:** a computer program that shows the user any words that might be incorrectly spelled

spend *vb* **spent; spend·ing 1 :** to use up **:** pay out **2 :** to wear out **:** EXHAUST **3 :** to use wastefully **:** SQUANDER **4 :** to cause or allow (as time) to pass

spend·thrift *n* **:** one who spends wastefully

spent *adj* **1 :** used up **2 :** drained of energy

sperm *n* **:** SPERM CELL

sperm cell *n* **:** a male germ cell

sperm whale *n* **:** a large whale of warm seas hunted mostly for its oil (**sperm oil**)

spew *vb* **:** to pour out

sphere *n* **1 :** a body (as the moon) shaped like a ball **2 :** a figure so shaped that every point on its surface is an equal distance from the center of the figure **3 :** a field of influence or activity

spher•i•cal *adj* **:** relating to or having the form of a sphere

sphinx *n* **:** an Egyptian figure having the body of a lion and the head of a man, a ram, or a hawk

¹spice *n* **1 :** a plant product (as pepper or nutmeg) that has a strong pleasant smell and is used to flavor food **2 :** something that adds interest

²spice *vb* **spiced; spic•ing :** to season with or as if with spices

spick–and–span *or* **spic–and–span** *adj* **1 :** quite new and unused **2 :** very clean and neat

spicy *adj* **spic•i•er; spic•i•est 1 :** flavored with or containing spice **2 :** somewhat shocking or indecent

spi•der *n* **1 :** a wingless animal somewhat like an insect but having eight legs instead of six and a body divided into two parts instead of three **2 :** a cast-iron frying pan

spi•der•web *n* **:** the silken web spun by most spiders and used as a resting place and a trap for prey

spig•ot *n* **1 :** a plug used to stop the vent in a barrel **2 :** FAUCET

¹spike *n* **1 :** a very large nail **2 :** one of the metal objects attached to the heel and sole of a shoe (as a baseball shoe) to prevent slipping **3 :** something pointed like a spike

²spike *vb* **spiked; spik•ing 1 :** to fasten with spikes **2 :** to pierce or cut with or on a spike

³spike *n* **1 :** an ear of grain **2 :** a long usually rather narrow flower cluster in which the blossoms grow very close to a central stem

¹spill *vb* **spilled** *also* **spilt; spill•ing 1 :** to cause (blood) to flow by wounding **:** ¹SHED 2 **2 :** to cause or allow to fall, flow, or run out so as to be wasted or scattered **3 :** to flow or run out, over, or off and become wasted or scattered **4 :** to make known

²spill *n* **1 :** an act of spilling **2 :** a fall especially from a horse or vehicle **3 :** something spilled

¹spin *vb* **spun; spin•ning 1 :** to make yarn or thread from (fibers) **2 :** to make (yarn or thread) from fibers **3 :** to form threads or a web or cocoon by giving off a sticky fluid that quickly hardens into silk **4 :** to turn or cause to turn round and round rapidly **:** TWIRL **5 :** to feel as if in a whirl **6 :** to make up and tell using the imagination **7 :** to move swiftly on wheels or in a vehicle **8 :** to make, shape, or produce by or as if by whirling

²spin *n* **1 :** a rapid whirling motion **2 :** a short trip in or on a wheeled vehicle

spin•ach *n* **:** a leafy plant that is grown for use as food

spi•nal *adj* **:** of, relating to, or located near the backbone or the spinal cord — **spi•nal•ly** *adv*

spinal column *n* **:** BACKBONE 1

spinal cord *n* **:** the thick cord of nervous tissue that extends from the brain down the back, fills the cavity of the backbone, and is concerned especially with reflex action

spin•dle *n* **1 :** a slender round rod or stick with narrowed ends by which thread is twisted in spinning and on which it is wound **2 :** something (as an axle or shaft) which is shaped or turned like a spindle or on which something turns

spin•dly *adj* **spin•dli•er; spin•dli•est :** being thin and long or tall and usually feeble or weak

spine *n* **1 :** BACKBONE 1 **2 :** a stiff pointed part growing from the surface of a plant or animal

spine•less *adj* **1 :** lacking spines **2 :** having no backbone **3 :** lacking spirit, courage, or determination

spin•et *n* **1 :** an early harpsichord with one keyboard and only one string for each note **2 :** a small upright piano

spin•ning jen•ny *n, pl* **spin•ning jen•nies :** an early machine for spinning wool or cotton by means of many spindles

spinning wheel *n* **:** a small machine driven by the hand or foot that is used to spin yarn or thread

spin•ster *n* **:** an unmarried woman past the usual age for marrying

spiny *adj* **spin•i•er; spin•i•est :** covered with spines

spi•ra•cle *n* **:** an opening (as in the head of a whale or the abdomen of an insect) for breathing

¹spi•ral *adj* **1 :** winding or circling around a center and gradually getting closer to or farther away from it **2 :** circling around a center like the thread of a screw — **spi•ral•ly** *adv*

²spiral *n* **1 :** a single turn or coil in a spiral object **2 :** something that has a spiral form

³spiral *vb* **spi•raled** *or* **spi•ralled; spi•ral•ing** *or* **spi•ral•ling :** to move in a spiral path

spire *n* **1 :** a pointed roof especially of a tower **2 :** STEEPLE

spi·rea *or* **spi·raea** *n* **:** a shrub related to the roses that bears clusters of small white or pink flowers

[1]**spir·it** *n* **1 :** a force within a human being thought to give the body life, energy, and power **:** SOUL **2** *cap* **:** the active presence of God in human life **:** the third person of the Trinity **3 :** a being (as a ghost) whose existence cannot be explained by the known laws of nature **4 :** [1]MOOD **5 :** a lively or brisk quality **6 :** an attitude governing one's actions **7 :** PERSON 1 **8 :** an alcoholic liquor — usually used in pl. **9 spirits** *pl* **:** a solution in alcohol **10 :** real meaning or intention — **spir·it·less** *adj*

[2]**spirit** *vb* **:** to carry off secretly or mysteriously

spir·it·ed *adj* **:** full of courage or energy

[1]**spir·i·tu·al** *adj* **1 :** of, relating to, or consisting of spirit **:** not bodily or material **2 :** of or relating to sacred or religious matters — **spir·i·tu·al·ly** *adv*

[2]**spiritual** *n* **:** a religious folk song developed especially among Negroes of the southern United States

[1]**spit** *n* **1 :** a thin pointed rod for holding meat over a fire **2 :** a small point of land that runs out into a body of water

[2]**spit** *vb* **spit** *or* **spat; spit·ting 1 :** to cause (as saliva) to spurt from the mouth **2 :** to express by or as if by spitting **3 :** to give off usually briskly **:** EMIT **4 :** to rain lightly or snow in flurries

[3]**spit** *n* **1 :** SALIVA **2 :** the act of spitting **3 :** a foamy material given out by some insects **4 :** perfect likeness

[1]**spite** *n* **:** dislike or hatred for another person with a wish to torment, anger, or defeat — **in spite of :** without being prevented by

[2]**spite** *vb* **spit·ed; spit·ing :** ANNOY, ANGER

spite·ful *adj* **:** filled with or showing spite **:** MALICIOUS — **spite·ful·ly** *adv*

spit·tle *n* **1 :** SALIVA **2 :** [3]SPIT 3

[1]**splash** *vb* **1 :** to hit (something liquid or sloppy) and cause to move and scatter roughly **2 :** to wet or soil by spattering with water or mud **3 :** to move or strike with a splashing sound **4 :** to spread or scatter like a splashed liquid

[2]**splash** *n* **1 :** splashed material **2 :** a spot or smear from or as if from splashed liquid **3 :** the sound or action of splashing

[1]**splat·ter** *vb* **:** [1]SPLASH, SPATTER

[2]**splatter** *n* **:** [2]SPLASH

spleen *n* **:** an organ near the stomach that destroys worn-out red blood cells and produces some of the white blood cells

splen·did *adj* **1 :** having or showing splendor **:** BRILLIANT **2 :** impressive in beauty, excellence, or magnificence **3 :** GRAND 4 — **splen·did·ly** *adv*

splen·dor *n* **1 :** great brightness **2 :** POMP, GLORY

[1]**splice** *vb* **spliced; splic·ing 1 :** to unite (as two ropes) by weaving together **2 :** to unite (as rails or pieces of film) by connecting the ends together

[2]**splice** *n* **:** a joining or joint made by splicing

splint *n* **1 :** a thin flexible strip of wood woven together with others in making a chair seat or basket **2 :** a device for keeping a broken or displaced bone in place

[1]**splin·ter** *n* **:** a thin piece split or torn off lengthwise **:** SLIVER

[2]**splinter** *vb* **:** to break into splinters

[1]**split** *vb* **split; split·ting 1 :** to divide lengthwise or by layers **2 :** to separate the parts of by putting something between **3 :** to burst or break apart or in pieces **4 :** to divide into shares or sections

[2]**split** *n* **1 :** a product or result of splitting **:** CRACK **2 :** the act or process of splitting **:** DIVISION **3 :** the feat of lowering oneself to the floor or leaping into the air with the legs extended in a straight line and in opposite directions

[3]**split** *adj* **:** divided by or as if by splitting

[1]**spoil** *n* **:** stolen goods **:** PLUNDER

[2]**spoil** *vb* **spoiled** *or* **spoilt; spoil·ing 1 :** [1]PLUNDER, ROB **2 :** to damage badly **:** RUIN **3 :** to damage the quality or effect of **4 :** to decay or lose freshness, value, or usefulness by being kept too long **5 :** to damage the disposition of by letting get away with too much

spoil·age *n* **:** the action of spoiling or condition of being spoiled

[1]**spoke** *past of* SPEAK

[2]**spoke** *n* **:** one of the bars or rods extending from the hub of a wheel to the rim

[1]**spoken** *past participle of* SPEAK

[2]**spo·ken** *adj* **1 :** expressed in speech **:** ORAL **2 :** used in speaking **3 :** speaking in a specified manner

spokes·man *n, pl* **spokes·men :** SPOKESPERSON

spokes·per·son *n* **:** a person who speaks for another or for a group

spokes·wom·an *n, pl* **spokes·wom·en :** a woman who is a spokesperson

[1]**sponge** *n* **1 :** a springy mass of horny fibers that forms the skeleton of a group of sea animals, is able to absorb water freely, and is used for cleaning **2 :** any of a group of water animals that have the form of hollow cell colonies made up of two layers and that include those whose skeletons are sponges **3 :** a manufactured product (as of

rubber or plastic) having the springy absorbent quality of natural sponge **4 :** a pad of folded gauze used in surgery and medicine — **sponge·like** *adj*

²sponge *vb* **sponged; spong·ing** **1 :** to clean or wipe with a sponge **2 :** to absorb with or like a sponge **3 :** to get something or live at the expense of another

spongy *adj* **spong·i·er; spong·i·est :** like a sponge in appearance or in ability to absorb **:** soft and full of holes or moisture

¹spon·sor *n* **1 :** a person who takes the responsibility for some other person or thing **2 :** GODPARENT **3 :** a person or an organization that pays for or plans and carries out a project or activity **4 :** a person or an organization that pays the cost of a radio or television program — **spon·sor·ship** *n*

²sponsor *vb* **:** to act as sponsor for

spon·ta·ne·ous *adj* **1 :** done, said, or produced freely and naturally **2 :** acting or taking place without outside force or cause — **spon·ta·ne·ous·ly** *adv*

spontaneous combustion *n* **:** a bursting of material into flame from the heat produced within itself through chemical action

spook *n* **:** GHOST, SPECTER

spooky *adj* **spook·i·er; spook·i·est** **1 :** like a ghost **2 :** suggesting the presence of ghosts

¹spool *n* **:** a small cylinder which has a rim or ridge at each end and a hole from end to end for a pin or spindle and on which material (as thread, wire, or tape) is wound

²spool *vb* **:** to wind on a spool

¹spoon *n* **:** a utensil with a shallow bowl and a handle used especially in cooking and eating

²spoon *vb* **:** to take up in or as if in a spoon

spoon·bill *n* **:** a wading bird related to the ibises and having a bill which widens and flattens at the tip

spoon·ful *n, pl* **spoon·fuls** *or* **spoons·ful** **:** as much as a spoon can hold

spore *n* **:** a reproductive body of various plants and some lower animals that consists of a single cell and is able to produce a new individual — **spored** *adj*

¹sport *vb* **1 :** to amuse oneself **:** FROLIC **2 :** to speak or act in fun **3 :** SHOW OFF

²sport *n* **1 :** PASTIME, RECREATION **2 :** physical activity (as running or an athletic game) engaged in for pleasure **3 :** FUN 3 **4 :** a person thought of with respect to the ideals of sportsmanship

sports·man *n, pl* **sports·men :** a person who engages in or is interested in sports and especially outdoor sports (as hunting and fishing)

sports·man·ship *n* **:** fair play, respect for opponents, and gracious behavior in winning or losing

sports·wom·an *n, pl* **sports·wom·en :** a woman who engages in or is interested in sports and especially outdoor sports

¹spot *n* **1 :** something bad that others know about one **:** FAULT **2 :** a small part that is different (as in color) from the main part **3 :** an area soiled or marked (as by dirt) **4 :** a particular place — **spot·ted** *adj* — **on the spot** **1 :** right away **:** IMMEDIATELY **2 :** at the place of action **3 :** in difficulty or danger

²spot *vb* **spot·ted; spot·ting** **1 :** to mark or be marked with spots **2 :** to single out **:** IDENTIFY

spot·less *adj* **:** free from spot or blemish **:** perfectly clean or pure — **spot·less·ly** *adv* — **spot·less·ness** *n*

¹spot·light *n* **1 :** a spot of light used to show up a particular area, person, or thing (as on a stage) **2 :** public notice **3 :** a light to direct a narrow strong beam of light on a small area

²spotlight *vb* **spot·light·ed** *or* **spot·lit; spot·light·ing** **1 :** to light up with a spotlight **2 :** to bring to public attention

spotted owl *n* **:** a rare brown owl with white spots and dark stripes that is found from British Columbia to southern California and central Mexico

spot·ty *adj* **spot·ti·er; spot·ti·est** **1 :** having spots **2 :** not always the same especially in quality

spouse *n* **:** a married person **:** HUSBAND, WIFE

¹spout *vb* **1 :** to shoot out (liquid) with force **2 :** to speak with a long and quick flow of words so as to sound important **3 :** to flow out with force **:** SPURT

²spout *n* **1 :** a tube, pipe, or hole through which something (as rainwater) spouts **2 :** a sudden strong stream of fluid

¹sprain *n* **1 :** a sudden or severe twisting of a joint with stretching or tearing of ligaments **2 :** a sprained condition

²sprain *vb* **:** to injure by a sudden or severe twist

sprang *past of* SPRING

¹sprawl *vb* **1 :** to lie or sit with arms and legs spread out **2 :** to spread out in an uneven or awkward way

²sprawl *n* **:** the act or posture of sprawling

¹spray *n* **:** a green or flowering branch or a usually flat arrangement of these

²spray *n* **1 :** liquid flying in fine drops like water blown from a wave **2 :** a burst of fine mist (as from an atomizer) **3 :** a device (as an atomizer) for scattering a spray of liquid or mist

³spray *vb* **1 :** to scatter or let fall in a spray

2 : to scatter spray on or into — **spray·er** *n*

spray gun *n* : a device for spraying paints, varnishes, or insect poisons

[1]**spread** *vb* **spread; spread·ing** **1 :** to open over a larger area **2 :** to stretch out : EXTEND **3 :** SCATTER 1, STREW **4 :** to give out over a period of time or among a group **5 :** to put a layer of on a surface **6 :** to cover something with **7 :** to prepare for a meal : SET **8 :** to pass from person to person **9** : to stretch or move apart

[2]**spread** *n* **1 :** the act or process of spreading **2 :** extent of spreading **3 :** a noticeable display in a magazine or newspaper **4** : a food to be spread on bread or crackers **5** : a very fine meal : FEAST **6 :** a cloth cover for a table or bed **7 :** distance between two points

spree *n* : an outburst of activity

sprig *n* : a small shoot or twig

spright·ly *adj* **spright·li·er; spright·li·est** : full of spirit : LIVELY

[1]**spring** *vb* **sprang** *or* **sprung; sprung; spring·ing** **1 :** to appear or grow quickly **2 :** to come from by birth or descent **3 :** to come into being : ARISE **4 :** to move suddenly upward or forward : LEAP **5 :** to have (a leak) appear **6 :** to move quickly by elastic force **7 :** [2]WARP 1 **8 :** to cause to operate suddenly

[2]**spring** *n* **1 :** a source of supply (as of water coming up from the ground) **2 :** the season between winter and summer including in the northern hemisphere usually the months of March, April, and May **3 :** a time or season of growth or development **4 :** an elastic body or device that recovers its original shape when it is released after being squeezed or stretched **5 :** the act or an instance of leaping up or forward **6 :** elastic power or force

spring·board *n* : a flexible board usually fastened at one end and used for jumping high in the air in gymnastics or diving

spring peep·er *n* : a small frog that lives in trees and makes a high peeping sound heard mostly in spring

spring·time *n* : the season of spring

springy *adj* **spring·i·er; spring·i·est** **1** : [1]ELASTIC **2 :** having or showing a lively and energetic movement

[1]**sprin·kle** *vb* **sprin·kled; sprin·kling** **1 :** to scatter in drops **2 :** to scatter over or in or among **3 :** to rain lightly — **sprin·kler** *n*

[2]**sprinkle** *n* **1 :** a light rain **2 :** SPRINKLING

sprin·kling *n* : a very small number or amount

[1]**sprint** *vb* : to run at top speed especially for a short distance — **sprint·er** *n*

[2]**sprint** *n* **1 :** a short run at top speed **2 :** a race over a short distance

sprite *n* : ELF, FAIRY

sprock·et *n* : one of many points that stick up on the rim of a wheel (**sprocket wheel**) shaped so as to fit into the links of a chain

[1]**sprout** *vb* : to produce or cause to produce fresh young growth

[2]**sprout** *n* : a young stem of a plant especially when coming directly from a seed or root

[1]**spruce** *vb* **spruced; spruc·ing** : to make something or oneself neat or stylish in appearance

[2]**spruce** *adj* **spruc·er; spruc·est** : neat or stylish in appearance

[3]**spruce** *n* : an evergreen tree shaped like a cone with a thick growth of short needles, drooping cones, and light soft wood

sprung *past of* SPRING

spry *adj* **spri·er** *or* **spry·er; spri·est** *or* **spry·est** : LIVELY 1, ACTIVE

spun *past of* SPIN

spunk *n* : COURAGE, SPIRIT

[1]**spur** *n* **1 :** a pointed device fastened to the back of a rider's boot and used to urge a horse on **2 :** something that makes one want to do something : INCENTIVE **3 :** a stiff sharp point (as a horny spine on the leg of a rooster) **4 :** a mass of jagged rock coming out from the side of a mountain **5** : a short section of railway track coming away from the main line — **spurred** *adj*

[2]**spur** *vb* **spurred; spur·ring** **1 :** to urge a horse on with spurs **2 :** INCITE

spurn *vb* : to reject with scorn

[1]**spurt** *vb* **1 :** to pour out suddenly : SPOUT **2 :** [1]SQUIRT

[2]**spurt** *n* : a sudden pouring out : JET

[3]**spurt** *n* : a brief burst of increased effort

[4]**spurt** *vb* : to make a spurt

[1]**sput·ter** *vb* **1 :** to spit or squirt bits of food or saliva noisily from the mouth **2 :** to speak in a hasty or explosive way in confusion or excitement **3 :** to make explosive popping sounds

[2]**sputter** *n* : the act or sound of sputtering

[1]**spy** *vb* **spied; spy·ing** **1 :** to watch secretly **2 :** to catch sight of : SEE

[2]**spy** *n, pl* **spies** **1 :** a person who watches the movement or actions of others especially in secret **2 :** a person who tries secretly to get information especially about an unfriendly country or its plans and actions

spy·glass *n* : a small telescope

squab *n* : a young pigeon especially when about four weeks old and ready for use as food

[1]**squab·ble** *n* : a noisy quarrel usually over unimportant things

²squabble *vb* **squab·bled; squab·bling :** to quarrel noisily for little or no reason
squad *n* **1 :** a small group of soldiers **2 :** a small group working or playing together
squad car *n* **:** CRUISER 2
squad·ron *n* **:** a group especially of cavalry riders, military airplanes, or naval ships moving and working together
squal·id *adj* **:** filthy or degraded from a lack of care or money
¹squall *vb* **:** to let out a harsh cry or scream
²squall *n* **:** a sudden strong gust of wind often with rain or snow
squa·lor *n* **:** the quality or state of being squalid
squan·der *vb* **:** to spend foolishly **:** WASTE
¹square *n* **1 :** an instrument having at least one right angle and two or more straight edges used to mark or test right angles **2 :** a flat figure that has four equal sides and four right angles **3 :** something formed like a square **4 :** the product of a number or amount multiplied by itself **5 :** an open place or area where two or more streets meet **6 :** ¹BLOCK 6, 7
²square *adj* **squar·er; squar·est 1 :** having four equal sides and four right angles **2 :** forming a right angle **3 :** multiplied by itself **4 :** having outlines that suggest sharp corners rather than curves **5 :** being a unit of area consisting of a square whose sides have a given length **6 :** having a specified length in each of two equal dimensions **7 :** exactly adjusted **8 :** ¹JUST 3, FAIR **9 :** leaving no balance **:** EVEN **10 :** large enough to satisfy — **square·ly** *adv*
³square *vb* **squared; squar·ing 1 :** to make square **:** form with right angles, straight edges, and flat surfaces **2 :** to make straight **3 :** to multiply a number by itself **4 :** AGREE 4 **5 :** ²BALANCE 1, SETTLE
square knot *n* **:** a knot made of two half-knots tied in opposite directions and typically used to join the ends of two cords
square–rigged *adj* **:** having the principal sails extended on yards fastened in a horizontal position to the masts at their center
square root *n* **:** a factor of a number that when multiplied by itself gives the number
¹squash *vb* **:** to beat or press into a soft or flat mass **:** CRUSH
²squash *n* **:** the fruit of any of several plants related to the gourds that is cooked as a vegetable or used for animal feed
¹squat *vb* **squat·ted; squat·ting 1 :** to crouch by bending the knees fully so as to sit on or close to the heels **2 :** to settle without any right on land that one does not own **3 :** to settle on government land in order to become the owner of the land
²squat *adj* **squat·ter; squat·test 1 :** bent in a deep crouch **2 :** low to the ground **3 :** having a short thick body
³squat *n* **1 :** the act of squatting **2 :** a squatting posture
¹squawk *vb* **1 :** to make a harsh short scream **2 :** to complain or protest loudly or with strong feeling
²squawk *n* **1 :** a harsh short scream **2 :** a noisy complaint
¹squeak *vb* **1 :** to make a short shrill cry **2 :** to get, win, or pass with trouble **:** barely succeed
²squeak *n* **:** a sharp shrill cry or sound
squeaky *adj* **squeak·i·er; squeak·i·est :** likely to squeak
¹squeal *vb* **1 :** to make a sharp long shrill cry or noise **2 :** INFORM 2
²squeal *n* **:** a shrill sharp cry or noise
¹squeeze *vb* **squeezed; squeez·ing 1 :** to press together from the opposite sides or parts of **:** COMPRESS **2 :** to get by squeezing **3 :** to force or crowd in by compressing
²squeeze *n* **:** an act or instance of squeezing
squid *n* **:** a sea mollusk that is related to the octopus but has a long body and ten arms
¹squint *adj* **:** not able to look in the same direction — used of the two eyes
²squint *vb* **1 :** to have squint eyes **2 :** to look or peer with the eyes partly closed
³squint *n* **1 :** the condition of being cross-eyed **2 :** the action or an instance of squinting
¹squire *n* **1 :** a person who carries the shield or armor of a knight **2 :** ¹ESCORT 1 **3 :** an owner of a country estate
²squire *vb* **squired; squir·ing :** to act as a squire or escort for
squirm *vb* **1 :** to twist about like an eel or a worm **2 :** to feel very embarrassed
squir·rel *n* **:** a small gnawing animal (as the common American **red squirrel** and **gray squirrel**) usually with a bushy tail and soft fur and strong hind legs for leaping
¹squirt *vb* **:** to shoot out liquid in a thin stream **:** SPURT
²squirt *n* **1 :** an instrument for squirting liquid **2 :** a small powerful stream of liquid **:** JET **3 :** the action of squirting
¹stab *n* **1 :** a wound produced by or as if by a pointed weapon **2 :** ²THRUST 1 **3 :** ³TRY, EFFORT
²stab *vb* **stabbed; stab·bing 1 :** to wound or pierce with a stab **2 :** ¹DRIVE 2, THRUST
sta·bil·i·ty *n, pl* **sta·bil·i·ties :** the condition of being stable
sta·bi·lize *vb* **sta·bi·lized; sta·bi·liz·ing :** to make or become stable — **sta·bi·liz·er** *n*
¹sta·ble *n* **:** a building in which domestic animals are housed and cared for

2stable *vb* **sta•bled; sta•bling :** to put or keep in a stable

3stable *adj* **sta•bler; sta•blest 1 :** not easily changed or affected **2 :** not likely to change suddenly or greatly **3 :** LASTING **4 :** RELIABLE

stac•ca•to *adj* **1 :** cut short so as not to sound connected **2 :** played or sung with breaks between notes

1stack *n* **1 :** a large pile (as of hay) usually shaped like a cone **2 :** a neat pile of objects usually one on top of the other **3 :** a large number or amount **4 :** CHIMNEY 1, SMOKESTACK **5 :** a structure with shelves for storing books

2stack *vb* **:** to arrange in or form a stack **:** PILE

sta•di•um *n, pl* **sta•di•ums** *or* **sta•dia :** a large outdoor structure with rows of seats for spectators at sports events

staff *n, pl* **staffs** *or* **staves 1 :** a pole, stick, rod, or bar used as a support or as a sign of authority **2 :** something that is a source of strength **3 :** the five parallel lines with their four spaces on which music is written **4** *pl staffs* **:** a group of persons serving as assistants to or employees under a chief **5** *pl staffs* **:** a group of military officers who plan and manage for a commanding officer

staff sergeant *n* **:** a noncommissioned officer in the Army, Air Force, or Marine Corps ranking above a sergeant

staff sergeant major *n* **:** a noncommissioned officer in the Army ranking above a master sergeant

1stag *n* **1 :** an adult male deer especially of the larger kind **2 :** a man who goes to a social gathering without escorting a woman

2stag *adj* **:** intended or thought suitable for men only

1stage *n* **1 :** a raised floor (as for speaking or giving plays) **2 :** a place where something important happens **3 :** the theatrical profession or art **4 :** a step forward in a journey, a task, a process, or a development **:** PHASE **5 :** STAGECOACH

2stage *vb* **staged; stag•ing :** to produce or show to the public on or as if on the stage

stage•coach *n* **:** a coach pulled by horses that runs on a schedule from place to place carrying passengers and mail

1stag•ger *vb* **1 :** to move unsteadily from side to side as if about to fall **:** REEL **2 :** to cause to move unsteadily **3 :** to cause great surprise or shock in **4 :** to place or arrange in a zigzag but balanced way

2stagger *n* **:** a reeling or unsteady walk

stag•nant *adj* **1 :** not flowing **2 :** not active or brisk **:** DULL

stag•nate *vb* **stag•nat•ed; stag•nat•ing :** to be or become stagnant

1stain *vb* **1 :** to soil or discolor especially in spots **2 :** 2COLOR 2, TINGE **3 :** 1CORRUPT 1 **4 :** 1DISGRACE

2stain *n* **1 :** 1SPOT 3, DISCOLORATION **2 :** a mark of guilt or disgrace **:** STIGMA **3 :** something (as a dye) used in staining — **stain•less** *adj*

stainless steel *n* **:** an alloy of steel and chromium that is resistant to stain, rust, and corrosion

stair *n* **1 :** a series of steps or flights of steps for going from one level to another — often used in pl. **2 :** one step of a stairway

stair•case *n* **:** a flight of stairs with their supporting structure and railings

stair•way *n* **:** one or more flights of stairs usually with connecting landings

1stake *n* **1 :** a pointed piece (as of wood) driven or to be driven into the ground as a marker or to support something **2 :** a post to which a person is tied to be put to death by burning **3 :** something that is put up to be won or lost in gambling **4 :** the prize in a contest **5 :** 1SHARE 1, INTEREST — **at stake :** in a position to be lost if something goes wrong

2stake *vb* **staked; stak•ing 1 :** to mark the limits of by stakes **2 :** to fasten or support (as plants) with stakes **3 :** 2BET 1 **4 :** to give money to to help (as with a project)

sta•lac•tite *n* **:** a deposit hanging from the roof or side of a cave in the shape of an icicle formed by the partial evaporating of dripping water containing lime

sta•lag•mite *n* **:** a deposit like an upside down stalactite formed by the dripping of water containing lime onto the floor of a cave

1stale *adj* **stal•er; stal•est 1 :** having lost a good taste or quality through age **2 :** used or heard so often as to be dull **3 :** not so strong, energetic, or effective as before — **stale•ly** *adv* — **stale•ness** *n*

2stale *vb* **staled; stal•ing :** to make or become stale

1stalk *n* **1 :** a plant stem especially when not woody **2 :** a slender supporting structure — **stalked** *adj* — **stalk•less** *adj*

2stalk *vb* **1 :** to hunt slowly and quietly **2 :** to walk in a stiff or proud manner **3 :** to move through or follow as if stalking prey — **stalk•er** *n*

3stalk *n* **1 :** the act of stalking **2 :** a stalking way of walking

1stall *n* **1 :** a compartment for one animal in a stable **2 :** a space set off (as for parking an automobile) **3 :** a seat in a church choir **:** a church pew **4 :** a booth, stand, or counter where business may be carried on or articles may be displayed for sale

²stall *vb* **1 :** to put or keep in a stall **2 :** to stop or cause to stop usually by accident

³stall *n* **:** a trick to deceive or delay

⁴stall *vb* **:** to distract attention or make excuses to gain time

stal·lion *n* **:** a male horse

stal·wart *adj* **:** STURDY, RESOLUTE

sta·men *n* **:** the male organ of a flower that produces pollen and that consists of an anther and a filament

stam·i·na *n* **:** VIGOR 1, ENDURANCE

¹stam·mer *vb* **:** to speak with involuntary stops and much repeating — **stam·mer·er** *n*

²stammer *n* **:** an act or instance of stammering

¹stamp *vb* **1 :** to bring the foot down hard and with noise **2 :** to put an end to by or as if by hitting with the bottom of the foot **3 :** to mark or cut out with a tool or device having a design **4 :** to attach a postage stamp to **5 :** CHARACTERIZE 1

²stamp *n* **1 :** a device or instrument for stamping **2 :** the mark made by stamping **3 :** a sign of a special quality **4 :** the act of stamping **5 :** a small piece of paper or a mark attached to something to show that a tax or fee has been paid

¹stam·pede *n* **1 :** a wild dash or flight of frightened animals **2 :** a sudden foolish action or movement of a crowd of people

²stampede *vb* **stam·ped·ed; stam·ped·ing 1 :** to run or cause (as cattle) to run away in panic **2 :** to act or cause to act together suddenly and without thought

stance *n* **:** way of standing **:** POSTURE

stanch *vb* **:** to stop or check the flow of (as blood)

¹stand *vb* **stood; stand·ing 1 :** to be in or take a vertical position on one's feet **2 :** to take up or stay in a specified position or condition **3 :** to have an opinion **4 :** to rest, remain, or set in a usually vertical position **5 :** to be in a specified place **6 :** to stay in effect **7 :** to put up with **:** ENDURE **8 :** UNDERGO **9 :** to perform the duty of — **stand by :** to be or remain loyal or true to — **stand for 1 :** to be a symbol for **:** REPRESENT **2 :** to put up with **:** PERMIT

²stand *n* **1 :** an act of standing **2 :** a halt for defense or resistance **3 :** a place or post especially where one stands **:** STATION **4 :** a structure containing rows of seats for spectators of a sport or spectacle **5 :** a raised area (as for speakers or performers) **6 :** a stall or booth often outdoors for a small business **7 :** a small structure (as a rack or table) on or in which something may be placed **8 :** POSITION 2

¹stan·dard *n* **1 :** a figure used as a symbol by an organized body of people **2 :** the personal flag of the ruler of a state **3 :** something set up as a rule for measuring or as a model **4 :** an upright support

²standard *adj* **1 :** used as or matching a standard **2 :** regularly and widely used **3 :** widely known and accepted to be of good and permanent value

stan·dard·ize *vb* **stan·dard·ized; stan·dard·iz·ing :** to make standard or alike

standard time *n* **:** the time established by law or by common usage over a region or country

stand by *vb* **1 :** to be present **2 :** to be or get ready to act

¹stand·ing *adj* **1 :** ¹ERECT **2 :** not flowing **:** STAGNANT **3 :** remaining at the same level or amount until canceled **4 :** PERMANENT

²standing *n* **1 :** the action or position of one that stands **2 :** length of existence or service **3 :** POSITION 4, STATUS

stand out *vb* **:** to be easily seen or recognized

stand·point *n* **:** a way in which things are thought about **:** POINT OF VIEW

stand·still *n* **:** the condition of not being active or busy **:** STOP

stand up *vb* **1 :** to stay in good condition **2 :** to fail to keep an appointment with — **stand up for :** DEFEND 2 — **stand up to :** to face boldly

stank *past of* STINK

stan·za *n* **:** a group of lines forming a division of a poem

¹sta·ple *n* **1 :** a piece of metal shaped like a U with sharp points to be driven into a surface to hold something (as a hook, rope, or wire) **2 :** a short thin wire with bent ends that is driven through papers and clinched to hold them together or driven through thin material to fasten it to a surface

²staple *vb* **sta·pled; sta·pling :** to fasten with staples

³staple *n* **1 :** a chief product of business or farming of a place **2 :** something that is used widely and often **3 :** the chief part of something **4 :** fiber (as cotton or wool) suitable for spinning into yarn

⁴staple *adj* **1 :** much used, needed, or enjoyed usually by many people **2 :** ¹PRINCIPAL, CHIEF

sta·pler *n* **:** a device that staples

¹star *n* **1 :** any of those celestial bodies except planets which are visible at night and look like fixed points of light **2 :** a star or especially a planet that is believed in astrology to influence one's life **3 :** a figure or thing (as a medal) with five or more points that represents or suggests a star **4 :** the principal member of a theater or opera company **5 :** a very talented or popular performer

[2]**star** *vb* **starred; star•ring 1 :** to sprinkle or decorate with or as if with stars **2 :** to mark with a star as being special or very good **3 :** to mark with an asterisk **4 :** to present in the role of a star **5 :** to play the most important role **6 :** to perform in an outstanding manner

star•board *n* **:** the right side of a ship or airplane looking forward

[1]**starch** *vb* **:** to stiffen with starch

[2]**starch** *n* **:** a white odorless tasteless substance that is the chief storage form of carbohydrates in plants, is an important food, and has also various household and business uses (as for stiffening clothes)

starchy *adj* **starch•i•er; starch•i•est :** like or containing starch

[1]**stare** *vb* **stared; star•ing :** to look at hard and long often with wide-open eyes

[2]**stare** *n* **:** the act or an instance of staring

star•fish *n* **:** any of a group of sea animals mostly having five arms that spread out from a central disk and feeding mostly on mollusks

[1]**stark** *adj* **1 :** [1]BARREN 2, DESOLATE **2 :** [1]UTTER, ABSOLUTE

[2]**stark** *adv* **:** COMPLETELY

star•light *n* **:** the light given by the stars

star•ling *n* **:** a dark brown or in summer greenish black European bird about the size of a robin that is now common and often a pest in the United States

star•lit *adj* **:** lighted by the stars

star•ry *adj* **star•ri•er; star•ri•est :** full of stars **2 :** of, relating to, or consisting of stars **3 :** shining like stars

Stars and Stripes *n sing or pl* **:** the flag of the United States

[1]**start** *vb* **1 :** to move suddenly and quickly **:** give a sudden twitch or jerk (as in surprise) **2 :** to come or bring into being or action **3 :** to stick out or seem to stick out **4 :** SET OUT 2 **5 :** to set going

[2]**start** *n* **1 :** a sudden movement **2 :** a brief act, movement, or effort **3 :** a beginning of movement, action, or development **4 :** a place of beginning (as of a race)

start•er *n* **:** someone or something that starts something or causes something else to start

star•tle *vb* **star•tled; star•tling 1 :** to cause to move or jump (as in surprise or fear) **2 :** to frighten suddenly but slightly

star•tling *adj* **:** causing a moment of fright or surprise

star•va•tion *n* **:** the act or an instance of starving **:** the condition of being starved

starve *vb* **starved; starv•ing 1 :** to suffer or die or cause to suffer or die from lack of food **2 :** to suffer or cause to suffer from a lack of something other than food

[1]**state** *n* **1 :** manner or condition of being **2 :** a body of people living in a certain territory under one government **:** the government of such a body of people **3 :** one of the divisions of a nation having a federal government

[2]**state** *vb* **stat•ed; stat•ing 1 :** to set by rule, law, or authority **:** FIX **2 :** to express especially in words

state•house *n* **:** the building where the legislature of a state meets

state•ly *adj* **state•li•er; state•li•est 1 :** having great dignity **2 :** impressive especially in size **:** IMPOSING — **state•li•ness** *n*

state•ment *n* **1 :** something that is stated **:** REPORT, ACCOUNT **2 :** a brief record of a business account

state•room *n* **:** a private room on a ship or a train

states•man *n, pl* **states•men :** a person who is active in government and who gives wise leadership in making policies

[1]**stat•ic** *adj* **1 :** showing little change or action **2 :** of or relating to charges of electricity (as one produced by friction) that do not flow

[2]**static** *n* **:** noise produced in a radio or television receiver by atmospheric or electrical disturbances

[1]**sta•tion** *n* **1 :** the place or position where a person or thing stands or is assigned to stand or remain **2 :** a regular stopping place (as on a bus line) **:** DEPOT **3 :** a post or area of duty **4 :** POSITION 4, RANK **5 :** a place for specialized observation or for a public service **6 :** a collection of radio or television equipment for transmitting or receiving **7 :** the place where a radio or television station is

[2]**station** *vb* **:** to assign to or set in a station or position **:** POST

sta•tion•ary *adj* **1 :** having been set in a certain place or post **:** IMMOBILE **2 :** not changing **:** STABLE

sta•tion•ery *n* **:** writing paper and envelopes

station wagon *n* **:** an automobile that is longer on the inside than a sedan and has one or more folding or removable seats but no separate luggage compartment

stat•ue *n* **:** an image or likeness (as of a person or animal) sculptured, modeled, or cast in a solid substance (as marble or bronze)

stat•ure *n* **1 :** natural height (as of a person) **2 :** quality or fame one has gained (as by growth or development)

sta•tus *n* **1 :** position or rank of a person or thing **2 :** state of affairs **:** SITUATION

stat·ute *n* : LAW 4

staunch *adj* **1 :** strongly built : SUBSTANTIAL **2 :** LOYAL 2, STEADFAST — **staunch·ly** *adv*

[1]**stave** *n* **1 :** a wooden stick : STAFF **2 :** one of a number of narrow strips of wood or iron plates placed edge to edge to form the sides, covering, or lining of something (as a barrel or keg)

[2]**stave** *vb* **staved** *or* **stove; stav·ing** **1 :** to break in the staves of **2 :** to smash a hole in : crush or break inward

stave off *vb* : to keep away : ward off

staves *pl of* STAFF

[1]**stay** *n* : a strong rope or wire used to steady or brace something (as a mast)

[2]**stay** *vb* : to fasten (as a smokestack) with stays

[3]**stay** *vb* **1 :** to stop going forward : PAUSE **2 :** [1]REMAIN 3, 4 **3 :** to stand firm **4 :** to live for a while **5 :** [2]CHECK 1, HALT

[4]**stay** *n* **1 :** the action of bringing to a stop : the state of being stopped **2 :** a period of living in a place

[5]**stay** *n* **1 :** [1]PROP, SUPPORT **2 :** a thin firm strip (as of steel or plastic) used to stiffen a garment (as a corset) or part of a garment (as a shirt collar)

[6]**stay** *vb* : to hold up

stead *n* **1 :** [2]AVAIL — used mostly in the phrase *stand one in good stead* **2 :** the place usually taken or duty carried out by the one mentioned

stead·fast *adj* **1 :** not changing : RESOLUTE **2 :** LOYAL 2 — **stead·fast·ly** *adv* — **stead·fast·ness** *n*

[1]**steady** *adj* **steadi·er; steadi·est** **1 :** firmly fixed in position **2 :** direct or sure in action **3 :** showing little change **4 :** not easily upset **5 :** RELIABLE — **stead·i·ly** *adv* — **stead·i·ness** *n*

[2]**steady** *vb* **stead·ied; steady·ing :** to make, keep, or become steady

steak *n* **1 :** a slice of meat and especially beef **2 :** a slice of a large fish (as salmon)

[1]**steal** *vb* **stole; sto·len; steal·ing** **1 :** to come or go quietly or secretly **2 :** to take and carry away (something that belongs to another person) without right and with the intention of keeping **3 :** to get more than one's share of attention during **4 :** to take or get for oneself secretly or without permission

[2]**steal** *n* **1 :** the act or an instance of stealing **2 :** [1]BARGAIN 2

stealth *n* : sly or secret action

stealthy *adj* **stealth·i·er; stealth·i·est** : done in a sly or secret manner — **stealth·i·ly** *adv*

[1]**steam** *n* **1 :** the vapor into which water is changed when heated to the boiling point **2 :** steam when kept under pressure so that it supplies heat and power **3 :** the mist formed when water vapor cools **4 :** driving force : POWER

[2]**steam** *vb* **1 :** to rise or pass off as steam **2 :** to give off steam or vapor **3 :** to move or travel by or as if by the power of steam **4 :** to expose to steam (as for cooking)

steam·boat *n* : a boat driven by steam

steam engine *n* : an engine driven by steam

steam·er *n* **1 :** a container in which something is steamed **2 :** a ship driven by steam **3 :** an engine, machine, or vehicle run by steam

steam·roll·er *n* : a machine formerly driven by steam that has wide heavy rollers for pressing down and smoothing roads

steam·ship *n* : STEAMER 2

steam shovel *n* : a power machine for digging that was formerly operated by steam

steed *n* : a usually lively horse

[1]**steel** *n* **1 :** a hard and tough metal made by treating iron with great heat and mixing carbon with it **2 :** an article (as a sword) made of steel

[2]**steel** *vb* : to fill with courage or determination

[3]**steel** *adj* : made of or like steel

steely *adj* **steel·i·er; steel·i·est** **1 :** made of steel **2 :** like steel (as in hardness or color)

[1]**steep** *adj* **1 :** having a very sharp slope : almost straight up and down **2 :** too great or high — **steep·ly** *adv* — **steep·ness** *n*

[2]**steep** *vb* **1 :** to soak in a liquid **2 :** to fill with or involve deeply

stee·ple *n* **1 :** a tall pointed structure usually built on top of a church tower **2 :** a church tower

stee·ple·chase *n* **1 :** a horse race across country **2 :** a race on a course that has hedges, walls, and ditches to be crossed

[1]**steer** *n* : a castrated bull usually raised for beef

[2]**steer** *vb* **1 :** to control a course or the course of : GUIDE **2 :** to follow a course of action **3 :** to be guided

steering wheel *n* : a wheel for steering something by hand

stego·sau·rus *n* : a large plant-eating dinosaur having bony plates along its back and tail with spikes at the end of the tail

[1]**stem** *n* **1 :** the main stalk of a plant that develops buds and sprouts and usually grows above ground **2 :** a plant part (as a leafstalk or flower stalk) that supports some other part **3 :** the bow of a ship **4 :** a line of ancestors : STOCK **5 :** the basic part of a word to which prefixes or suffixes may be added

6 : something like a stalk or shaft — **stem·less** *adj*

²stem *vb* **stemmed; stem·ming 1 :** to make progress against **2 :** to check or hold back the progress of

³stem *vb* **stemmed; stem·ming 1 :** to come from a certain source **2 :** to remove the stem from

⁴stem *vb* **stemmed; stem·ming :** to stop or check by or as if by damming

stemmed *adj* **:** having a stem

¹sten·cil *n* **1 :** a material (as a sheet of paper, thin wax, or woven fabric) with cut out lettering or a design through which ink, paint, or metallic powder is forced onto a surface to be printed **2 :** a pattern, design, or print produced with a stencil

²stencil *vb* **sten·ciled** *or* **sten·cilled; sten·cil·ing** *or* **sten·cil·ling 1 :** to mark or paint with a stencil **2 :** to produce with a stencil

ste·nog·ra·pher *n* **:** one employed chiefly to take and make a copy of dictation

¹step *n* **1 :** a rest or place for the foot in going up or down **:** STAIR 2 **2 :** a movement made by raising one foot and putting it down in another spot **3 :** a combination of foot and body movements in a repeated pattern **4 :** manner of walking **5 :** FOOTPRINT **6 :** the sound of a footstep **7 :** the space passed over in one step **8 :** a short distance **9 :** the height of one stair **10 steps** *pl* **:** ¹COURSE 3 **11 :** a level, grade, or rank in a scale or series **:** a stage in a process **12 :** ¹MEASURE 7 **13 :** a space in music between two notes of a scale or staff that may be a single degree of the scale (**half step**) or two degrees (**whole step**) — **in step :** with one's foot or feet moving in time with other feet or in time to music

²step *vb* **stepped; step·ping 1 :** to move by taking a step or steps **2 :** ¹DANCE 1 **3 :** to go on foot **:** WALK **4 :** to move at a good speed **5 :** to press down with the foot **6 :** to come as if at a single step **7 :** to measure by steps

step–by–step *adj or adv* **:** moving or happening by steps one after the other

step·fa·ther *n* **:** the husband of one's mother after the death or divorce of one's real father

step·lad·der *n* **:** a light portable set of steps with a hinged frame for steadying

step·moth·er *n* **:** the wife of one's father after the death or divorce of one's real mother

steppe *n* **:** land that is dry, usually rather level, and covered with grass in regions (as much of southeastern Europe and parts of Asia) of wide temperature range

step·ping–stone *n* **1 :** a stone on which to step (as in crossing a stream) **2 :** a means of progress or advancement

step up *vb* **:** to increase especially by a series of steps

-ster *n suffix* **1 :** one that does or handles or operates **2 :** one that makes or uses **3 :** one that is associated with or takes part in **4 :** one that is

ste·reo *n, pl* **ste·re·os 1 :** stereophonic reproduction **2 :** a stereophonic sound system

ste·reo·phon·ic *adj* **:** of or relating to sound reproduction designed to create the effect of listening to the original

ste·reo·scope *n* **:** an optical instrument that blends two pictures of one subject taken from slightly different points of view into one image that seems to be three-dimensional

¹ste·reo·type *vb* **1 :** to make a printing plate by casting melted metal in a mold **2 :** to form a fixed mental picture of

²stereotype *n* **1 :** a printing plate of a complete page made by casting melted metal in a mold **2 :** a fixed idea that many people have about a thing or a group and that may often be untrue or only partly true

ste·reo·typed *adj* **:** following a pattern or stereotype **:** lacking individuality

ste·reo·typ·i·cal *also* **ste·reo·typ·ic** *adj* **:** based on or characteristic of a stereotype — **ste·reo·typ·i·cal·ly** *adv*

ster·ile *adj* **1 :** not able to produce fruit, crops, or offspring **:** not fertile **2 :** free from living germs

ster·il·ize *vb* **ster·il·ized; ster·il·iz·ing :** to make sterile and especially free from harmful germs

¹ster·ling *n* **1 :** British money **2 :** sterling silver **:** articles made from sterling silver

²sterling *adj* **1 :** of or relating to British sterling **2 :** being or made of an alloy of 925 parts of silver with 75 parts of copper **3 :** EXCELLENT

¹stern *adj* **1 :** hard and severe in nature or manner **2 :** firm and not changeable — **stern·ly** *adv* — **stern·ness** *n*

²stern *n* **:** the rear end of a boat

ster·num *n, pl* **ster·nums** *or* **ster·na :** BREASTBONE

stetho·scope *n* **:** an instrument used by doctors for listening to sounds produced in the body and especially in the chest

¹stew *n* **1 :** food (as meat with vegetables) prepared by slow boiling **2 :** a state of excitement, worry, or confusion

²stew *vb* **1 :** to boil slowly **:** SIMMER **2 :** to become excited or worried

stew·ard *n* **1 :** a manager of a very large

home, an estate, or an organization **2 :** a person employed to manage the supply and distribution of food (as on a ship) **3 :** a worker who serves and looks after the needs of passengers (as on an airplane or ship)

stew•ard•ess *n* **:** a woman who looks after passengers (as on an airplane or ship)

1stick *n* **1 :** a cut or broken branch or twig **2 :** a long thin piece of wood **3 :** WALKING STICK 1 **4 :** something like a stick in shape or use

2stick *vb* **stuck; stick•ing 1 :** to stab with something pointed **2 :** to cause to penetrate **3 :** to put in place by or as if by pushing **4 :** to push out, up, into, or under **5 :** to put in a specified place or position **6 :** to remain in a place, situation, or environment **7 :** to halt the movement or action of **8 :** BAFFLE **9 :** to burden with something unpleasant **10 :** to cling or cause to cling **11 :** to become blocked or jammed

stick•er *n* **:** something (as a slip of paper with gum or glue on its back) that can be stuck to a surface

stick•le•back *n* **:** a small scaleless fish with sharp spines on its back

sticky *adj* **stick•i•er; stick•i•est 1 :** ADHESIVE 1 **2 :** coated with a sticky substance **3 :** MUGGY, HUMID **4 :** tending to stick — **stick•i•ness** *n*

stiff *adj* **1 :** not easily bent **2 :** not easily moved **3 :** FIRM 5 **4 :** hard fought **:** STUBBORN **5 :** not easy or graceful in manner **:** FORMAL **6 :** POWERFUL, STRONG **7 :** not flowing easily **:** being thick and heavy **8 :** SEVERE 1 **9 :** DIFFICULT 1 — **stiff•ly** *adv* — **stiff•ness** *n*

stiff•en *vb* **:** to make or become stiff or stiffer — **stiff•en•er** *n*

sti•fle *vb* **sti•fled; sti•fling 1 :** to kill by depriving of or die from lack of oxygen or air **:** SMOTHER **2 :** to keep in check by deliberate effort

stig•ma *n, pl* **stig•ma•ta** *or* **stig•mas 1 :** a mark of disgrace or discredit **2 :** the upper part of the pistil of a flower which receives the pollen grains and on which they complete their development

stile *n* **1 :** a step or set of steps for crossing a fence or wall **2 :** TURNSTILE

sti•let•to *n, pl* **sti•let•tos** *or* **sti•let•toes :** a slender pointed dagger

1still *adj* **1 :** having no motion **2 :** making no sound **3 :** free from noise and confusion **:** QUIET — **still•ness** *n*

2still *vb* **:** to make or become still **:** QUIET

3still *adv* **1 :** without motion **2 :** up to this or that time **3 :** NEVERTHELESS **4 :** 2EVEN 4

4still *n* **:** 1QUIET, SILENCE

5still *n* **1 :** a place where alcoholic liquors are made **2 :** a device used in distillation

still•born *adj* **:** born dead

stilt *n* **1 :** one of a pair of tall poles each with a high step or loop for the support of a foot used to lift the person wearing them above the ground in walking **2 :** a stake or post used to support a structure above ground or water level

stilt•ed *adj* **:** not easy and natural

1stim•u•lant *n* **1 :** something (as a drug) that makes the body or one of its parts more active for a while **2 :** STIMULUS 1

2stimulant *adj* **:** stimulating or tending to stimulate

stim•u•late *vb* **stim•u•lat•ed; stim•u•lat•ing 1 :** to make active or more active **:** ANIMATE, AROUSE **2 :** to act toward as a bodily stimulus or stimulant

stim•u•la•tion *n* **:** an act or result of stimulating

stim•u•lus *n, pl* **stim•u•li 1 :** something that stirs or urges to action **2 :** an influence that acts usually from outside the body to partly change bodily activity (as by exciting a sense organ)

1sting *vb* **stung; sting•ing 1 :** to prick painfully usually with a sharp or poisonous stinger **2 :** to suffer or affect with sharp quick burning pain **3 :** to cause to suffer severely

2sting *n* **1 :** an act of stinging **2 :** a wound or pain caused by or as if by stinging **3 :** STINGER

sting•er *n* **:** a sharp organ by which an animal (as a wasp or scorpion) wounds and often poisons an enemy

sting•ray *n* **:** a very flat fish with a stinging spine on its whiplike tail

stin•gy *adj* **stin•gi•er; stin•gi•est 1 :** not generous **:** giving or spending as little as possible **2 :** very small in amount — **stin•gi•ly** *adv* — **stin•gi•ness** *n*

1stink *vb* **stank** *or* **stunk; stunk; stink•ing 1 :** to give off or cause to have a strong unpleasant smell **2 :** to be of very bad quality

2stink *n* **:** a strong unpleasant smell

stink•bug *n* **:** a bug that gives off a bad smell

stinky *adj* **:** having a strong unpleasant smell

1stint *vb* **:** to be stingy or saving

2stint *n* **:** an amount of work given to be done

1stir *vb* **stirred; stir•ring 1 :** to make or cause to make a usually slight movement or change of position **2 :** to make active (as by pushing, beating, or prodding) **3 :** to mix, dissolve, or make by a continued circular movement **4 :** AROUSE 2

2stir *n* **1 :** a state of upset or activity **2 :** a slight movement **3 :** the act of stirring

stir•ring *adj* **:** LIVELY 3, MOVING

stir•rup *n* **:** either of a pair of small light frames often of metal hung by straps from a saddle and used as a support for the foot of a horseback rider

[1]**stitch** *n* **1 :** a sudden sharp pain especially in the side **2 :** one in-and-out movement of a threaded needle in sewing **:** a portion of thread left in the material after one such movement **3 :** a single loop of thread or yarn around a tool (as a knitting needle or crochet hook) **4 :** a method of stitching

[2]**stitch** *vb* **1 :** to fasten or join with stitches **2 :** to make, mend, or decorate with or as if with stitches **3 :** SEW 2

[1]**stock** *n* **1 stocks** *pl* **:** a wooden frame with holes for the feet or the feet and hands once used to punish a wrongdoer publicly **2 :** the wooden part by which a rifle or shotgun is held during firing **3 :** an original (as a person, race, or language) from which others descend **4 :** the whole supply or amount on hand **5 :** farm animals **:** LIVESTOCK, CATTLE **6 :** the ownership element in a business which is divided into shares that can be traded independently **7 :** liquid in which meat, fish, or vegetables have been simmered — **in stock :** on hand **:** in the store and available for purchase

[2]**stock** *vb* **1 :** to provide with or get stock or a stock **2 :** to get or keep a stock of

[3]**stock** *adj* **1 :** kept regularly in stock **2 :** commonly used **:** STANDARD

stock•ade *n* **1 :** a line of strong posts set in the ground to form a defense **2 :** an enclosure formed by stakes driven into the ground

stock•bro•ker *n* **:** a person who handles orders to buy and sell stocks

stock•hold•er *n* **:** an owner of stock

stock•ing *n* **:** a close-fitting usually knit covering for the foot and leg

stock market *n* **:** a place where shares of stock are bought and sold

stocky *adj* **stock•i•er; stock•i•est :** compact, sturdy, and relatively thick in build **:** THICKSET

stock•yard *n* **:** a yard for stock and especially for keeping livestock about to be slaughtered or shipped

[1]**stole** *past of* STEAL

[2]**stole** *n* **:** a long wide scarf worn about the shoulders

stolen *past participle of* STEAL

[1]**stom•ach** *n* **1 :** the pouch into which food goes after it leaves the mouth and has passed down the throat **2 :** ABDOMEN 1 **3 :** [2]DESIRE 1, LIKING

[2]**stomach** *vb* **:** to bear patiently **:** put up with

stomp *vb* **:** to walk heavily or noisily **:** STAMP

[1]**stone** *n* **1 :** earth or mineral matter hardened in a mass **:** ROCK **2 :** a piece of rock coarser than gravel **3 :** GEM **4 :** a stony mass sometimes present in a diseased organ **5 :** the kernel of a fruit in its hard case **6** *pl usually* **stone :** an English measure of weight equaling fourteen pounds (about 6.5 kilograms)

[2]**stone** *vb* **stoned; ston•ing 1 :** to throw stones at **2 :** to remove the stones of

[3]**stone** *adj* **:** of, relating to, or made of stone

Stone Age *n* **:** the oldest period in which human beings are known to have existed **:** the age during which stone tools were used

stone–blind *adj* **:** completely blind

stone–deaf *adj* **:** completely deaf

stony *adj* **ston•i•er; ston•i•est 1 :** full of stones **2 :** insensitive as stone **:** UNFEELING **3 :** hard as stone

stood *past of* STAND

stool *n* **1 :** a seat without back or arms supported by three or four legs or by a central post **2 :** FOOTSTOOL **3 :** a mass of material discharged from the intestine

[1]**stoop** *vb* **1 :** to bend down or over **2 :** to carry the head and shoulders or the upper part of the body bent forward **3 :** to do something that is beneath one

[2]**stoop** *n* **:** a forward bend of the head and shoulders

[3]**stoop** *n* **:** a porch, platform, or stairway at the entrance of a house or building

[1]**stop** *vb* **stopped; stop•ping 1 :** to close an opening by filling or blocking it **:** PLUG **2 :** to hold back **:** RESTRAIN **3 :** to halt the movement or progress of **4 :** to come to an end **:** CEASE **5 :** to make a visit **:** STAY

[2]**stop** *n* **1 :** [1]END 2, FINISH **2 :** a set of organ pipes of one tone quality **:** a control knob for such a set **3 :** something that delays, blocks, or brings to a halt **4 :** STOPPER, PLUG **5 :** the act of stopping **:** the state of being stopped **6 :** a halt in a journey **:** STAY **7 :** a stopping place

stop•light *n* **1 :** a light on the rear of a motor vehicle that goes on when the driver presses the brake pedal **2 :** a signal light used in controlling traffic

stop•over *n* **:** a stop made during a journey

stop•page *n* **:** the act of stopping **:** the state of being stopped

stop•per *n* **:** something (as a cork or plug) used to stop openings

stop•watch *n* **:** a watch having a hand that can be started and stopped for exact timing (as of a race)

stor•age *n* **1 :** space or a place for storing **2 :** an amount stored **3 :** the act of storing

: the state of being stored **4 :** the price charged for storing something

storage battery *n* **:** a battery that can be renewed by passing an electric current through it

[1]**store** *vb* **stored; stor·ing 1 :** to provide with what is needed **:** SUPPLY **2 :** to place or leave something in a location (as a warehouse, library, or computer memory) to keep for later use or disposal **3 :** to put somewhere for safekeeping

[2]**store** *n* **1 stores** *pl* **:** something collected and kept for future use **2 :** a large quantity, supply, or number **3 :** a place where goods are sold **:** SHOP — **in store :** [1]READY 1

store·house *n, pl* **store·hous·es 1 :** a building for storing goods **2 :** a large supply or source

store·keep·er *n* **1 :** a person in charge of supplies (as in a factory) **2 :** an owner or manager of a store or shop

store·room *n* **:** a room for storing things not in use

stork *n* **:** a large Old World wading bird that looks like the related herons and includes one European form (the **white stork**) that often nests on roofs and chimneys

[1]**storm** *n* **1 :** a heavy fall of rain, snow, or sleet often with strong wind **2 :** a violent outburst **3 :** a violent attack on a defended position

[2]**storm** *vb* **1 :** to blow hard and rain or snow heavily **2 :** to make a mass attack against **3 :** to be very angry **:** RAGE **4 :** to rush about violently

stormy *adj* **storm·i·er; storm·i·est 1 :** relating to or affected by a storm **2 :** displaying anger and excitement — **storm·i·ness** *n*

[1]**sto·ry** *n, pl* **sto·ries 1 :** a report about incidents or events **:** ACCOUNT **2 :** a short often amusing tale **3 :** a tale shorter than a novel **4 :** a widely told rumor **5 :** [3]LIE, FALSEHOOD

[2]**sto·ry** *or* **sto·rey** *n, pl* **sto·ries** *or* **sto·reys :** a set of rooms or an area making up one floor level of a building

stout *adj* **1 :** of strong character **:** BRAVE, FIRM **2 :** of a strong or lasting sort **:** STURDY, TOUGH **3 :** bulky in body **:** FLESHY — **stout·ly** *adv* — **stout·ness** *n*

[1]**stove** *n* **:** a structure usually of iron or steel that burns fuel or uses electricity to provide heat (as for cooking or heating)

[2]**stove** *past of* STAVE

stove·pipe *n* **:** a metal pipe to carry away smoke from a stove

stow *vb* **1 :** to put away **:** STORE **2 :** to arrange in an orderly way **:** PACK **3 :** [2]LOAD 1

stow·away *n* **:** a person who hides (as in a ship or airplane) to travel free

strad·dle *vb* **strad·dled; strad·dling 1 :** to stand, sit, or walk with the legs spread wide apart **2 :** to stand, sit, or ride with a leg on either side of **3 :** to favor or seem to favor two opposite sides of

strag·gle *vb* **strag·gled; strag·gling 1 :** to wander from a straight course or way **:** STRAY **2 :** to trail off from others of its kind — **strag·gler** *n*

[1]**straight** *adj* **1 :** following the same direction throughout its length **:** not having curves, bends, or angles **2 :** not straying from the main point or proper course **3 :** not straying from what is right or honest **4 :** correctly ordered or arranged — **straight·ness** *n*

[2]**straight** *adv* **:** in a straight manner, course, or line

straight·en *vb* **1 :** to make or become straight **2 :** to put in order

straight·for·ward *adj* **:** being plain and honest **:** FRANK — **straight·for·ward·ly** *adv* — **straight·for·ward·ness** *n*

straight·way *adv* **:** IMMEDIATELY 2

[1]**strain** *n* **1 :** a line of ancestors to whom a person is related **2 :** a group of individuals that cannot be told from related kinds by appearance alone **3 :** a quality or disposition that runs through a family or race **4 :** a small amount **:** TRACE **5 :** MELODY 2, AIR

[2]**strain** *vb* **1 :** to stretch or be stretched, pulled, or used to the limit **2 :** to stretch beyond a proper limit **3 :** to try one's hardest **4 :** to injure or be injured by too much or too hard use or effort **5 :** to press or pass through a strainer **:** FILTER

[3]**strain** *n* **1 :** the act of straining **2 :** the state of being strained **3 :** [2]OVERWORK, WORRY **4 :** bodily injury resulting from strain or from a wrench or twist that stretches muscles and ligaments

strained *adj* **1 :** not easy or natural **2 :** brought close to war

strain·er *n* **:** a device (as a screen, sieve, or filter) to hold back solid pieces while a liquid passes through

strait *n* **1 :** a narrow channel connecting two bodies of water **2 :** [1]DISTRESS 1, NEED — often used in pl.

[1]**strand** *n* **:** the land bordering a body of water **:** SHORE, BEACH

[2]**strand** *vb* **1 :** to run, drive, or cause to drift onto a strand **:** run aground **2 :** to leave in a strange or unfavorable place especially without any chance to get away

[3]**strand** *n* **1 :** one of the fibers, threads, strings, or wires twisted or braided to make

a cord, rope, or cable **2 :** something long or twisted like a rope

strange *adj* **strang·er; strang·est** **1 :** of or relating to some other person, place, or thing **2 :** UNFAMILIAR 1 **3 :** exciting curiosity, surprise, or wonder because of not being usual or ordinary **4 :** ill at ease **:** SHY — **strange·ly** *adv* — **strange·ness** *n*

strang·er *n* **1 :** one who is not in the place where one's home is **:** FOREIGNER **2 :** GUEST 1, VISITOR **3 :** a person whom one does not know or has not met

stran·gle *vb* **stran·gled; stran·gling** **1 :** to choke to death by squeezing the throat **2 :** to choke in any way — **stran·gler** *n*

¹**strap** *n* **:** a narrow strip of flexible material (as leather) used especially for fastening, binding, or wrapping

²**strap** *vb* **strapped; strap·ping** **1 :** to fasten with or attach by means of a strap **2 :** BIND 1, 2, CONSTRICT **3 :** to whip with a strap

strap·ping *adj* **:** LARGE, STRONG

strat·a·gem *n* **:** a trick in war to deceive or outwit the enemy

stra·te·gic *adj* **1 :** of, relating to, or showing the use of strategy **2 :** useful or important in strategy

strat·e·gy *n, pl* **strat·e·gies** **1 :** the skill of using military, naval, and air forces to win a war **2 :** a clever plan or method

strato·sphere *n* **:** an upper portion of the atmosphere more than eleven kilometers above the earth where temperature changes little and clouds rarely form

stra·tum *n, pl* **stra·ta** **:** LAYER 2

stra·tus *n, pl* **stra·ti** **:** a cloud extending over a large area at an altitude of from 600 to 2000 meters

straw *n* **1 :** stalks especially of grain after threshing **2 :** a single dry coarse plant stalk **:** a piece of straw **3 :** a slender tube for sucking up a beverage

straw·ber·ry *n, pl* **straw·ber·ries** **:** the juicy edible usually red fruit of a low plant with white flowers and long slender runners

¹**stray** *n* **:** a domestic animal that is wandering at large because it is lost or has been abandoned

²**stray** *vb* **1 :** to wander from a group or from the proper place **:** ROAM **2 :** to go off from a straight or the right course

³**stray** *adj* **1 :** having strayed or been lost **2 :** occurring here and there **:** RANDOM

¹**streak** *n* **1 :** a line or mark of a different color or composition from its background **2 :** a narrow band of light **3 :** a small amount **:** TRACE, STRAIN **4 :** a short series of something — **streaked** *adj*

²**streak** *vb* **1 :** to make streaks in or on **2 :** to move swiftly **:** RUSH

¹**stream** *n* **1 :** a body of water (as a brook or river) flowing on the earth **2 :** a flow of liquid **3 :** a steady series (as of words or events) following one another

²**stream** *vb* **1 :** to flow in or as if in a stream **2 :** to give out a bodily fluid in large amounts **3 :** to become wet with flowing liquid **4 :** to trail out at full length **5 :** to pour in large numbers

stream·er *n* **1 :** a flag that streams in the wind **:** PENNANT **2 :** a long narrow wavy strip (as of ribbon on a hat) suggesting a banner floating in the wind **3 streamers** *pl* **:** AURORA BOREALIS

stream·lined *adj* **1 :** designed or constructed to make motion through water or air easier or as if for this purpose **2 :** made shorter, simpler, or more efficient

street *n* **1 :** a public way especially in a city, town, or village **2 :** the people living along a street

street·car *n* **:** a passenger vehicle that runs on rails and operates mostly on city streets

strength *n* **1 :** the quality of being strong **2 :** power to resist force **3 :** power to resist attack **4 :** intensity of light, color, sound, or odor **5 :** force as measured in numbers

strength·en *vb* **:** to make, grow, or become stronger

stren·u·ous *adj* **1 :** very active **:** ENERGETIC **2 :** showing or requiring much energy — **stren·u·ous·ly** *adv*

strep·to·my·cin *n* **:** a substance produced by a soil bacterium and used especially in treating tuberculosis

¹**stress** *n* **1 :** a force that tends to change the shape of a body **2 :** something that causes bodily or mental tension **:** a state of tension resulting from a stress **3 :** special importance given to something **4 :** relative prominence of sound **:** a syllable carrying this stress **:** ACCENT

²**stress** *vb* **1 :** to expose to stress **:** STRAIN **2 :** ¹ACCENT 1 **3 :** to give special importance to

stress mark *n* **:** a mark used with a written syllable in the respelling of a word to show that this syllable is to be stressed when spoken

¹**stretch** *vb* **1 :** to reach out **:** EXTEND, SPREAD **2 :** to draw out in length or width or both **:** EXPAND, ENLARGE **3 :** to draw up from a cramped, stooping, or relaxed position **4 :** to pull tight **5 :** to cause to reach or continue **6 :** EXAGGERATE **7 :** to become extended without breaking

²**stretch** *n* **1 :** the act of extending or draw-

ing out beyond ordinary or normal limits **2 :** the extent to which something may be stretched **3 :** the act or an instance of stretching the body or one of its parts **4 :** a continuous extent in length, area, or time

stretch·er *n* **1 :** one that stretches **2 :** a light bedlike device for carrying sick or injured persons

strew *vb* **strewed; strewed** *or* **strewn; strew·ing 1 :** to spread by scattering **2 :** to cover by or as if by scattering something

strick·en *adj* **1 :** hit or wounded by or as if by a missile **2 :** troubled with disease, misfortune, or sorrow

strict *adj* **1 :** permitting no avoidance or escape **2 :** kept with great care **:** ABSOLUTE **3 :** carefully observing something (as a rule or principle) **:** EXACT, PRECISE — **strict·ly** *adv* — **strict·ness** *n*

[1]**stride** *vb* **strode; strid·den; strid·ing 1 :** to walk or run with long even steps **2 :** to step over **:** STRADDLE

[2]**stride** *n* **1 :** a long step **:** the distance covered by such a step **2 :** a step forward **:** ADVANCE **3 :** a way of striding

strife *n* **1 :** bitter and sometimes violent disagreement **2 :** [2]STRUGGLE 1, CONTENTION

[1]**strike** *vb* **struck; struck** *or* **strick·en; strik·ing 1 :** GO 1, PROCEED **2 :** to touch or hit with force **3 :** to lower (as a flag or sail) usually in salute or surrender **4 :** to come into contact or collision with **5 :** to make a military attack **:** FIGHT **6 :** to remove or cancel with or as if with the stroke of a pen **7 :** to make known by sounding or cause to sound **8 :** to affect usually suddenly **9 :** to produce by stamping with a die or punch **10 :** to produce by or as if by a blow **11 :** to cause to ignite by scratching **12 :** to agree on the arrangements of **13 :** to make an impression on **14 :** to come upon **:** DISCOVER **15 :** to stop work in order to obtain a change in conditions of work

[2]**strike** *n* **1 :** an act or instance of striking **2 :** a stopping of work by workers to force an employer to agree to demands **3 :** a discovery of a valuable mineral deposit **4 :** a baseball pitch that is swung at or that passes through a certain area over home plate (**strike zone**) and that counts against the batter **5 :** DISADVANTAGE, HANDICAP **6 :** the knocking down of all ten bowling pins with the first ball **7 :** a military attack

strike·out *n* **:** an out in baseball that results from a batter's striking out

strike out *vb* **:** to be out in baseball by getting three strikes as a batter

strik·ing *adj* **:** attracting attention **:** REMARKABLE — **strik·ing·ly** *adv*

[1]**string** *n* **1 :** a small cord used to bind, fasten, or tie **2 :** a thin tough plant structure (as the fiber connecting the halves of a bean pod) **3 :** the gut, wire, or plastic cord of a musical instrument that vibrates to produce a tone **4 strings** *pl* **:** the stringed instruments of an orchestra **5 :** a group, series, or line of objects threaded on a string or arranged as if strung together

[2]**string** *vb* **strung; string·ing 1 :** to provide with strings **2 :** to make tense **3 :** [2]THREAD 4 **4 :** to tie, hang, or fasten with string **5 :** to remove the strings of **6 :** to set or stretch out in a line

string bass *n* **:** DOUBLE BASS

string bean *n* **:** a bean grown primarily for its pods which are eaten before the seeds are full grown

stringed instrument *n* **:** a musical instrument (as a violin, guitar, or banjo) sounded by plucking or striking or by drawing a bow across tight strings

string·er *n* **:** a long strong piece of wood or metal used for support or strengthening in building (as under a floor)

stringy *adj* **string·i·er; string·i·est :** containing, consisting of, or like string

[1]**strip** *vb* **stripped; strip·ping 1 :** to remove clothes **:** UNDRESS **2 :** to remove a covering or surface layer from **3 :** to take away all duties, honors, or special rights **4 :** to remove furniture, equipment, or accessories from **5 :** to tear or damage the thread of a screw or bolt

[2]**strip** *n* **:** a long narrow piece or area

strip–crop·ping *n* **:** the growing of a food crop (as potatoes) in alternate strips with a crop (as grass) that forms sod and helps keep the soil from being worn away

[1]**stripe** *vb* **striped; strip·ing :** to make stripes on

[2]**stripe** *n* **1 :** a line or long narrow division or section of something different in color or appearance from the background **2 :** a piece of material often with a special design worn (as on a sleeve) to show military rank or length of service

striped *adj* **:** having stripes

strive *vb* **strove; striv·en** *or* **strived; striv·ing 1 :** to carry on a conflict or effort **:** CONTEND **2 :** to try hard

strode *past of* STRIDE

[1]**stroke** *vb* **stroked; strok·ing :** to rub gently in one direction

[2]**stroke** *n* **1 :** the act of striking **:** BLOW **2 :** a single unbroken movement especially in one direction **:** one of a series of repeated movements (as in swimming or rowing a boat) **3 :** the hitting of a ball in a game (as golf or tennis) **4 :** a sudden action or

process that results in something being struck **5 :** a sudden or unexpected example **6 :** a sudden weakening or loss of consciousness and powers of voluntary movement that results from the breaking or blocking of an artery in the brain **7 :** effort by which something is done or the results of such effort **8 :** the sound of striking (as of a clock or bell) **9 :** a mark made by a single movement of a brush, pen, or tool

[1]stroll *vb* **:** to walk in a leisurely manner **:** RAMBLE

[2]stroll *n* **:** a leisurely walk **:** RAMBLE

stroll·er *n* **:** a small carriage in which a baby can sit and be pushed around

strong *adj* **stron·ger; stron·gest 1 :** having great power in the muscles **2 :** HEALTHY 1 2, ROBUST **3 :** having great resources **4 :** of a specified number **5 :** PERSUASIVE **6 :** having much of some quality **7 :** moving with speed and force **8 :** ENTHUSIASTIC, ZEALOUS **9 :** not easily injured or overcome **10 :** well established **:** FIRM — **strong·ly** *adv*

strong·hold *n* **:** FORTRESS

strove *past of* STRIVE

struck *past of* STRIKE

struc·tur·al *adj* **1 :** of, relating to, or affecting structure **2 :** used or formed for use in construction

struc·ture *n* **1 :** something built (as a house or dam) **2 :** the manner in which something is built **:** CONSTRUCTION **3 :** the arrangement or relationship of parts or organs

[1]strug·gle *vb* **strug·gled; strug·gling 1 :** to make a great effort to overcome someone or something **:** STRIVE **2 :** to move with difficulty or with great effort

[2]struggle *n* **1 :** a violent effort **2 :** [2]FIGHT 1, CONTEST

strum *vb* **strummed; strum·ming :** to play on a stringed instrument by brushing the strings with the fingers

strung *past of* STRING

[1]strut *vb* **strut·ted; strut·ting :** to walk in a stiff proud way

[2]strut *n* **1 :** a bar or brace used to resist lengthwise pressure **2 :** a strutting step or walk

[1]stub *n* **1 :** a short part remaining after the rest has been removed or used up **2 :** a small part of a check kept as a record of what was on the detached check

[2]stub *vb* **stubbed; stub·bing :** to strike (as the toe) against an object

stub·ble *n* **1 :** the stem ends of herbs and especially cereal grasses left in the ground after harvest **2 :** a rough growth or surface like stubble in a field **:** a short growth of beard

stub·born *adj* **1 :** refusing to change an opinion or course of action in spite of difficulty or urging **2 :** PERSISTENT **3 :** difficult to handle, manage, or treat — **stub·born·ly** *adv* — **stub·born·ness** *n*

stub·by *adj* **stub·bi·er; stub·bi·est :** short and thick like a stub

stuc·co *n, pl* **stuc·cos** *or* **stuc·coes :** a plaster for coating walls

stuck *past of* STICK

stuck–up *adj* **:** VAIN 2, CONCEITED

[1]stud *n* **1 :** one of the smaller vertical braces of the walls of a building to which the wall materials are fastened **2 :** a removable device like a button used to fasten something or as an ornament **3 :** one of the metal cleats used on a snow tire to provide a better grip

[2]stud *vb* **stud·ded; stud·ding 1 :** to supply or cover with or as if with studs **2 :** to set thickly together

stu·dent *n* **:** a person who studies especially in school **:** PUPIL

stu·dio *n, pl* **stu·di·os 1 :** the place where an artist, sculptor, or photographer works **2 :** a place for the study of an art **3 :** a place where movies are made **4 :** a place from which radio or television programs are broadcast

stu·di·ous *adj* **:** devoted to and fond of study

[1]study *n, pl* **stud·ies 1 :** use of the mind to get knowledge **2 :** a careful investigation or examination of something **3 :** a room especially for study, reading, or writing

[2]study *vb* **stud·ied; study·ing 1 :** to use the mind to learn about something by reading, investigating, or memorizing **2 :** to give close attention to

[1]stuff *n* **1 :** materials, supplies, or equipment that people need or use **2 :** writing, speech, or ideas of little value **3 :** something mentioned or understood but not named **4 :** basic part of something **:** SUBSTANCE

[2]stuff *vb* **1 :** to fill by packing or crowding things in **:** CRAM **2 :** OVEREAT, GORGE **3 :** to fill with a stuffing **4 :** to stop up **:** CONGEST **5 :** to force into something **:** THRUST

stuff·ing *n* **1 :** material used in filling up or stuffing something **2 :** a mixture (as of bread crumbs and seasonings) used to stuff meat, vegetables, eggs, or poultry

stuffy *adj* **stuff·i·er; stuff·i·est 1 :** needing fresh air **2 :** stuffed or choked up **3 :** [1]DULL 8

[1]stum·ble *vb* **stum·bled; stum·bling 1 :** to trip in walking or running **2 :** to walk unsteadily **3 :** to speak or act in a clumsy manner **4 :** to come unexpectedly or accidentally

[2]**stumble** *n* **:** an act or instance of stumbling

[1]**stump** *n* **1 :** the part of something (as an arm, a tooth, or a pencil) that remains after the rest has been removed, lost, or worn away **:** STUB **2 :** the part of a tree that remains in the ground after the tree is cut down

[2]**stump** *vb* **1 :** PERPLEX, BAFFLE **2 :** to walk or walk over heavily, stiffly, or clumsily as if with a wooden leg **3 :** [2]STUB

stun *vb* **stunned; stun•ning 1 :** to make dizzy or senseless by or as if by a blow **2 :** to affect with shock or confusion **:** fill with disbelief

stung *past of* STING

stunk *past of* STINK

stun•ning *adj* **1 :** able or likely to make a person senseless or confused **2 :** unusually lovely or attractive **:** STRIKING

[1]**stunt** *vb* **:** to hold back the normal growth of

[2]**stunt** *n* **:** an unusual or difficult performance or act

stu•pe•fy *vb* **stu•pe•fied; stu•pe•fy•ing 1 :** to make stupid, groggy, or numb **2 :** ASTONISH, ASTOUND

stu•pen•dous *adj* **:** amazing especially because of great size or height

stu•pid *adj* **1 :** slow or dull of mind **2 :** showing or resulting from a dull mind or a lack of proper attention **3 :** not interesting or worthwhile — **stu•pid•ly** *adv*

stu•pid•i•ty *n, pl* **stu•pid•i•ties 1 :** the quality or state of being stupid **2 :** a stupid thought, action, or remark

stu•por *n* **:** a condition in which the senses or feelings become dull

stur•dy *adj* **stur•di•er; stur•di•est 1 :** firmly built or made **2 :** strong and healthy in body **:** ROBUST **3 :** RESOLUTE — **stur•di•ly** *adv* — **sturd•i•ness** *n*

stur•geon *n* **:** a large food fish with tough skin and rows of bony plates

[1]**stut•ter** *vb* **:** to speak or say in a jerky way with involuntary repeating or interruption of sounds

[2]**stutter** *n* **:** the act or an instance of stuttering

[1]**sty** *n, pl* **sties :** PIGPEN

[2]**sty** *or* **stye** *n, pl* **sties** *or* **styes :** a painful red swelling on the edge of an eyelid

[1]**style** *n* **1 :** the narrow middle part of the pistil of a flower **2 :** a way of speaking or writing **3 :** an individual way of doing something **4 :** a method or manner that is felt to be very respectable, fashionable, or proper **:** FASHION

[2]**style** *vb* **styled; styl•ing 1 :** to identify by some descriptive term **:** CALL **2 :** to design and make in agreement with an accepted or a new style

styl•ish *adj* **:** having style **:** FASHIONABLE — **styl•ish•ly** *adv* — **styl•ish•ness** *n*

sty•lus *n, pl* **sty•li** *or* **sty•lus•es :** a pointed instrument used in ancient times for writing on wax tablets

[1]**sub** *n* **:** [1]SUBSTITUTE

[2]**sub** *vb* **subbed; sub•bing :** to act as a substitute

[3]**sub** *n* **:** SUBMARINE

sub- *prefix* **1 :** under **:** beneath **:** below **2 :** lower in importance or rank **:** lesser **3 :** division or part of **4 :** so as to form, stress, or deal with lesser parts or relations

sub•di•vide *vb* **sub•di•vid•ed; sub•di•vid•ing 1 :** to divide the parts of into more parts **2 :** to divide into several parts

sub•di•vi•sion *n* **1 :** the act of subdividing **2 :** one of the parts into which something is subdivided

sub•due *vb* **sub•dued; sub•du•ing 1 :** to overcome in battle **2 :** to bring under control **3 :** to reduce the brightness or strength of **:** SOFTEN

sub•head *or* **sub•head•ing** *n* **:** a heading under which one of the divisions of a subject is listed

[1]**sub•ject** *n* **1 :** a person under the authority or control of another **2 :** a person who owes loyalty to a monarch or state **3 :** a course of study **4 :** an individual that is studied or experimented on **5 :** the person or thing discussed **:** TOPIC **6 :** the word or group of words about which the predicate makes a statement

[2]**subject** *adj* **1 :** owing obedience or loyalty to another **2 :** likely to be affected by **3 :** depending on

[3]**sub•ject** *vb* **1 :** to bring under control or rule **2 :** to cause to put up with

sub•lime *adj* **1 :** grand or noble in thought, expression, or manner **2 :** having beauty enough or being impressive enough to arouse a mixed feeling of admiration and wonder

submarine *n* **:** a naval ship designed to operate underwater

sub•merge *vb* **sub•merged; sub•merg•ing 1 :** to put under or plunge into water **2 :** to cover or become covered with or as if with water

sub•mis•sion *n* **1 :** the act of submitting something (as for consideration or comment) **2 :** the condition of being humble or obedient **3 :** the act of submitting to power or authority

sub•mis•sive *adj* **:** willing to submit to others

sub•mit *vb* **sub•mit•ted; sub•mit•ting 1 :** to leave to the judgment or approval of someone else **2 :** to put forward as an opin-

ion, reason, or idea **3 :** to yield to the authority, control, or choice of another
[1]**sub·or·di·nate** *adj* **1 :** being in a lower class or rank **:** INFERIOR **2 :** yielding to or controlled by authority
[2]**subordinate** *n* **:** one that is subordinate
[3]**sub·or·di·nate** *vb* **sub·or·di·nat·ed; sub·or·di·nat·ing :** to make subordinate
sub·scribe *vb* **sub·scribed; sub·scrib·ing 1 :** to make known one's approval by or as if by signing **2 :** to agree to give or contribute by signing one's name with the amount promised **3 :** to place an order (as for a newspaper) with payment or a promise to pay — **sub·scrib·er** *n*
sub·scrip·tion *n* **1 :** an act or instance of subscribing **2 :** a thing or amount subscribed
sub·se·quent *adj* **:** following in time, order, or place — **sub·se·quent·ly** *adv*
sub·set *n* **:** a mathematical set each of whose members is also a member of a larger set
sub·side *vb* **sub·sid·ed; sub·sid·ing 1 :** to become lower **:** SINK **2 :** to become quiet or less
sub·sist *vb* **:** to continue living or being
sub·sis·tence *n* **:** the smallest amount (as of food and clothing) necessary to support life
sub·soil *n* **:** a layer of soil lying just under the topsoil
sub·stance *n* **1 :** ESSENCE 1 **2 :** the most important part **3 :** material of a certain kind **4 :** material belongings **:** WEALTH
sub·stan·dard *adj* **:** being below what is standard
sub·stan·tial *adj* **1 :** made up of or relating to substance **2 :** ABUNDANT **3 :** PROSPEROUS 1 **4 :** firmly constructed **5 :** large in amount
[1]**sub·sti·tute** *n* **:** a person or thing that takes the place of another
[2]**substitute** *vb* **sub·sti·tut·ed; sub·sti·tut·ing 1 :** to put in the place of another **2 :** to serve as a substitute
sub·sti·tu·tion *n* **:** the act or process of substituting
sub·tle *adj* **sub·tler; sub·tlest 1 :** DELICATE 1 **2 :** SHREWD, KEEN **3 :** CLEVER 2, SLY — **sub·tly** *adv*
sub·top·ic *n* **:** a topic (as in a composition) that is a division of a main topic
sub·tract *vb* **:** to take away (as one part or number from another) **:** DEDUCT
sub·trac·tion *n* **:** the subtracting of one number from another
sub·tra·hend *n* **:** a number that is to be subtracted from another number
sub·urb *n* **1 :** a part of a city or town near its outer edge **2 :** a smaller community close to a city **3 suburbs** *pl* **:** the area of homes close to or surrounding a city — **sub·ur·ban** *adj or n*
sub·way *n* **1 :** an underground tunnel **2 :** a usually electric underground railway
suc·ceed *vb* **1 :** to come after **:** FOLLOW **2 :** to take the place of a ruler or leader who has died, resigned, or been removed **3 :** to be successful
suc·cess *n* **1 :** satisfactory completion of something **2 :** the gaining of wealth, respect, or fame **3 :** a person or thing that succeeds
suc·cess·ful *adj* **1 :** resulting or ending well or in success **2 :** gaining or having gained success — **suc·cess·ful·ly** *adv*
suc·ces·sion *n* **1 :** the order, act, or right of succeeding to a throne, title, or property **2 :** a series of persons or things that follow one after another
suc·ces·sive *adj* **:** following in order and without interruption — **suc·ces·sive·ly** *adv*
suc·ces·sor *n* **:** a person who succeeds to a throne, title, property, or office
suc·cor *n* **:** [2]HELP 1, RELIEF
suc·cu·lent *adj* **:** JUICY
suc·cumb *vb* **1 :** to yield to force or pressure **2 :** [1]DIE 1
[1]**such** *adj* **1 :** of a kind just specified or to be specified **2 :** of the same class, type, or sort **:** SIMILAR **3 :** so great **:** so remarkable
[2]**such** *pron* **:** that sort of person, thing, or group
suck *vb* **1 :** to draw in liquid and especially mother's milk with the mouth **2 :** to draw liquid from by action of the mouth **3 :** to allow to dissolve gradually in the mouth **4 :** to put (as a thumb) into the mouth and draw on as if sucking **5 :** ABSORB 1
suck·er *n* **1 :** one that sucks **:** SUCKLING **2 :** a freshwater fish related to the carps that has thick soft lips for sucking in food **3 :** a new stem from the roots or lower part of a plant **4 :** LOLLIPOP **5 :** a person easily fooled or cheated
suck·le *vb* **suck·led; suck·ling :** to feed from the breast or udder
suck·ling *n* **:** a young mammal still sucking milk from its mother
suc·tion *n* **1 :** the act or process of sucking **2 :** the process of drawing something into a space (as in a pump) by removing air from the space **3 :** the force caused by suction
sud·den *adj* **1 :** happening or coming quickly and unexpectedly **2 :** met with unexpectedly **3 :** [1]STEEP 1 **4 :** HASTY 2 — **sud·den·ly** *adv* — **sud·den·ness** *n*
suds *n pl* **1 :** soapy water especially when foamy **2 :** the foam on soapy water

sue *vb* **sued; su•ing :** to seek justice or right by bringing legal action
suede *n* **:** leather tanned and rubbed so that it is soft and has a nap
su•et *n* **:** the hard fat about the kidneys in beef and mutton from which tallow is made
suf•fer *vb* **1 :** to feel pain **2 :** to experience something unpleasant **3 :** to bear loss or damage **4 :** [1]PERMIT — **suf•fer•er** *n*
suf•fer•ing *n* **1 :** the state or experience of one that suffers **2 :** a cause of distress **:** HARDSHIP
suf•fice *vb* **suf•ficed; suf•fic•ing 1 :** to satisfy a need **2 :** to be enough for
suf•fi•cient *adj* **:** enough to achieve a goal or fill a need — **suf•fi•cient•ly** *adv*
suf•fix *n* **:** a letter or group of letters that comes at the end of a word and has a meaning of its own
suf•fo•cate *vb* **suf•fo•cat•ed; suf•fo•cat•ing 1 :** to kill by stopping the breath or depriving of oxygen to breathe **2 :** to be or become choked or smothered **3 :** to have or cause to have a feeling of smothering
suf•fo•ca•tion *n* **:** the act of suffocating or state of being suffocated
suf•frage *n* **:** the right to vote
[1]**sug•ar** *n* **1 :** a sweet substance obtained from sugarcane, sugar beets, or maple syrup **2 :** any of numerous soluble and usually sweet carbohydrates
[2]**sugar** *vb* **1 :** to mix, cover, or sprinkle with sugar **2 :** to make something less hard to take or put up with **3 :** to change to crystals of sugar
sugar beet *n* **:** a large beet with white roots that is grown as a source of sugar
sug•ar•cane *n* **:** a tall strong grass with jointed stems widely raised in tropical regions for the sugar it yields
sugar maple *n* **:** an American maple tree with hard strong wood and a sweet sap that yields maple syrup and maple sugar
sug•gest *vb* **1 :** to put (as a thought or desire) into a person's mind **2 :** to offer as an idea **3 :** to bring into one's mind through close connection or association
sug•ges•tion *n* **1 :** the act or process of suggesting **2 :** a thought or plan that is suggested **3 :** [1]HINT 2
sug•ges•tive *adj* **1 :** giving a suggestion **2 :** full of suggestions **:** PROVOCATIVE **3 :** suggesting something improper or indecent
sui•cide *n* **1 :** the act of killing oneself purposely **2 :** a person who commits suicide
[1]**suit** *n* **1 :** an action in court for enforcing a right or claim **2 :** an earnest request **3 :** COURTSHIP **4 :** a number of things used together **:** SET **5 :** all the playing cards of one kind (as spades) in a pack
[2]**suit** *vb* **1 :** to be suitable or satisfactory **2 :** to make suitable **:** ADAPT **3 :** to be proper for or pleasing with **4 :** to meet the needs or desires of
suit•abil•i•ty *n* **:** the quality or state of being suitable
suit•able *adj* **:** being fit or right for a use or group — **suit•ably** *adv*
suit•case *n* **:** a flat rectangular traveling bag
suite *n* **1 :** a number of connected rooms (as in a hotel) **2 :** a set of matched furniture for a room
suit•or *n* **:** a man who courts a woman
sul•fur *or* **sul•phur** *n* **:** a yellow chemical element that is found widely in nature and is used in making chemicals and paper
sul•fu•rous *or* **sul•phu•rous** *adj* **:** containing or suggesting sulfur
[1]**sulk** *vb* **:** to be sullenly silent or irritable
[2]**sulk** *n* **1 :** the state of one sulking **2 :** a sulky mood or spell
[1]**sulky** *adj* **sulk•i•er; sulk•i•est :** sulking or given to sulking
[2]**sulky** *n, pl* **sulk•ies :** a light vehicle with two wheels, a seat for the driver only, and usually no body
sul•len *adj* **1 :** not sociable **:** SULKY **2 :** GLOOMY 1, DREARY — **sul•len•ly** *adv*
sul•tan *n* **:** a ruler especially of a Muslim state
sul•ta•na *n* **:** the wife, mother, sister, or daughter of a sultan
sul•try *adj* **sul•tri•er; sul•tri•est :** very hot and humid
[1]**sum** *n* **1 :** a quantity of money **2 :** the whole amount **3 :** the result obtained by adding numbers **4 :** a problem in arithmetic
[2]**sum** *vb* **summed; sum•ming :** to find the sum of by adding or counting
su•mac *or* **su•mach** *n* **:** any of a group of trees, shrubs, or woody vines having leaves with many leaflets and loose clusters of red or white berries
sum•ma•rize *vb* **sum•ma•rized; sum•ma•riz•ing :** to tell in or reduce to a summary
[1]**sum•ma•ry** *adj* **1 :** expressing or covering the main points briefly **:** CONCISE **2 :** done without delay
[2]**summary** *n, pl* **sum•ma•ries :** a short statement of the main points (as in a book or report)
[1]**sum•mer** *n* **1 :** the season between spring and autumn which is in the northern hemisphere usually the months of June, July, and August **2 :** YEAR 2
[2]**summer** *vb* **:** to pass the summer
sum•mer•time *n* **:** the summer season

sum•mery *adj* **:** of, relating to, or typical of summer
sum•mit *n* **:** the highest point (as of a mountain) **:** TOP
sum•mon *vb* **1 :** to call or send for **:** CONVENE **2 :** to order to appear before a court of law **3 :** to call into being **:** AROUSE — **sum•mon•er** *n*
sum•mons *n, pl* **sum•mons•es 1 :** the act of summoning **2 :** a call by authority to appear at a place named or to attend to some duty **3 :** a written order to appear in court
sump•tu•ous *adj* **:** very expensive or luxurious
sum up *vb* **:** SUMMARIZE
¹sun *n* **1 :** the celestial body whose light makes our day **:** the member of the solar system round which the planets revolve **2 :** a celestial body like our sun **3 :** SUNSHINE 1
²sun *vb* **sunned; sun•ning 1 :** to expose to or as if to the rays of the sun **2 :** to sun oneself
sun•bathe *vb* **sun•bathed; sun•bath•ing :** ²SUN 2
sun•beam *n* **:** a ray of sunlight
sun•block *n* **:** a strong sunscreen
sun•bon•net *n* **:** a bonnet with a wide curving brim that shades the face and usually a ruffle at the back that protects the neck from the sun
¹sun•burn *vb* **sun•burned** *or* **sun•burnt; sun•burn•ing :** to burn or discolor by the sun
²sunburn *n* **:** a sore red state of the skin caused by too much sunlight
sun•dae *n* **:** a serving of ice cream topped with fruit, syrup, or nuts
Sun•day *n* **:** the first day of the week **:** the Christian Sabbath
Sunday school *n* **:** a school held on Sunday in a church for religious education
sun•di•al *n* **:** a device to show the time of day by the position of the shadow cast onto a marked plate by an object with a straight edge
sun•down *n* **:** SUNSET
sun•dries *n pl* **:** various small articles or items
sun•dry *adj* **:** more than one or two **:** VARIOUS
sun•fish *n, pl* **sunfish** *or* **sun•fish•es :** any of numerous mostly small and brightly colored American freshwater fishes related to the perches
sun•flow•er *n* **:** a tall plant often grown for its large flower heads with brown center and yellow petals or for its edible oily seeds
sung *past of* SING
sun•glass•es *n pl* **:** glasses to protect the eyes from the sun
sunk *past of* SINK
sunk•en *adj* **1 :** lying at the bottom of a body of water **2 :** fallen in **:** HOLLOW **3 :** built or settled below the surrounding or normal level
sun•less *adj* **:** being without sunlight **:** DARK
sun•light *n* **:** SUNSHINE
sun•lit *adj* **:** lighted by the sun
sun•ny *adj* **sun•ni•er; sun•ni•est 1 :** bright with sunshine **2 :** MERRY 1, CHEERFUL
sun•rise *n* **1 :** the apparent rise of the sun above the horizon **:** the light and color that go with this **2 :** the time at which the sun rises
sun•screen *n* **:** a substance used on the skin to help protect it from the sun's ultraviolet radiation
sun•set *n* **1 :** the apparent passing of the sun below the horizon **:** the light and color that go with this **2 :** the time at which the sun sets
sun•shade *n* **:** something (as a parasol) used to protect from the sun's rays
sun•shine *n* **1 :** the sun's light or direct rays **:** the warmth and light given by the sun's rays **2 :** something that spreads warmth or happiness
sun•stroke *n* **:** a disorder marked by high fever and collapse and caused by too much sun
sun•tan *n* **:** a browning of skin exposed to the sun
sun•up *n* **:** SUNRISE
sun•ward *adv or adj* **:** toward or facing the sun
su•per *adj* **1 :** very great **2 :** very good
super- *prefix* **1 :** more than **2 :** extremely **:** very
su•perb *adj* **:** outstandingly excellent, impressive, or beautiful
su•per•com•put•er *n* **:** a large very fast computer used especially for scientific computations
su•per•fi•cial *adj* **1 :** of or relating to the surface or appearance only **2 :** not thorough **:** SHALLOW — **su•per•fi•cial•ly** *adv*
su•per•flu•ous *adj* **:** going beyond what is enough or necessary **:** EXTRA
su•per•he•ro *n* **:** a fictional hero having extraordinary or superhuman powers
su•per•high•way *n* **:** an expressway for high-speed traffic
su•per•hu•man *adj* **:** going beyond normal human power, size, or ability
su•per•in•tend *vb* **:** to have or exercise the charge of
su•per•in•ten•dent *n* **:** a person who looks

after or manages something (as schools or a building)

[1]su·pe·ri·or *adj* **1 :** situated higher up **:** higher in rank, importance, numbers, or quality **2 :** excellent of its kind **:** BETTER **3 :** feeling that one is better or more important than others **:** ARROGANT

[2]superior *n* **1 :** one that is higher than another in rank, importance, or quality **2 :** the head of a religious house or order

su·pe·ri·or·i·ty *n* **:** the state or fact of being superior

[1]su·per·la·tive *adj* **1 :** of, relating to, or being the form of an adjective or adverb that shows the highest or lowest degree of comparison **2 :** better than all others **:** SUPREME

[2]superlative *n* **:** the superlative degree or a superlative form in a language

su·per·mar·ket *n* **:** a self-service market selling foods and household items

su·per·nat·u·ral *adj* **:** of or relating to something beyond or outside of nature or the visible universe

su·per·sede *vb* **su·per·sed·ed; su·per·sed·ing :** to take the place or position of

su·per·son·ic *adj* **1 :** relating to or being vibrations too rapid to be heard **2 :** having a speed from one to five times that of sound

su·per·sti·tion *n* **:** beliefs or practices resulting from ignorance, fear of the unknown, or trust in magic or chance

su·per·sti·tious *adj* **:** of, relating to, showing, or influenced by superstition

su·per·vise *vb* **su·per·vised; su·per·vis·ing :** SUPERINTEND, OVERSEE

su·per·vi·sion *n* **:** the act of supervising **:** MANAGEMENT

su·per·vi·sor *n* **1 :** a person who supervises **2 :** an officer in charge of a unit or an operation of a business, government, or school

sup·per *n* **1 :** the evening meal especially when dinner is eaten at midday **2 :** refreshments served late in the evening especially at a social gathering

sup·plant *vb* **:** to take the place of another usually unfairly

sup·ple *adj* **sup·pler; sup·plest 1 :** ADAPTABLE **2 :** capable of bending or of being bent easily without stiffness, creases, or damage

[1]sup·ple·ment *n* **:** something that supplies what is needed or adds to something else

[2]sup·ple·ment *vb* **:** to add to **:** COMPLETE

sup·ple·men·ta·ry *adj* **:** added as a supplement **:** ADDITIONAL

sup·pli·cate *vb* **sup·pli·cat·ed; sup·pli·cat·ing :** to ask or beg in a humble way **:** BESEECH

sup·pli·ca·tion *n* **:** the act of supplicating

[1]sup·ply *vb* **sup·plied; sup·ply·ing 1 :** to provide for **:** SATISFY **2 :** to make available **:** FURNISH

[2]supply *n, pl* **sup·plies 1 :** the amount of something that is needed or can be gotten **2 :** [2]STORE 1 **3 :** the act or process of supplying something

[1]sup·port *vb* **1 :** to take sides with **:** FAVOR **2 :** to provide evidence for **:** VERIFY **3 :** to pay the costs of **:** MAINTAIN **4 :** to hold up or in position **:** serve as a foundation or prop for **5 :** to keep going **:** SUSTAIN — **sup·port·er** *n*

[2]support *n* **1 :** the act of supporting **:** the condition of being supported **2 :** one that supports

sup·pose *vb* **sup·posed; sup·pos·ing 1 :** to think of as true or as a fact for the sake of argument **2 :** BELIEVE 2, THINK **3 :** [1]GUESS 1

sup·posed *adj* **1 :** believed to be true or real **2 :** forced or required to do something — **sup·pos·ed·ly** *adv*

sup·press *vb* **1 :** to put down (as by authority or force) **:** SUBDUE **2 :** to hold back **:** REPRESS

sup·pres·sion *n* **:** an act or instance of suppressing **:** the state of being suppressed

su·prem·a·cy *n, pl* **su·prem·a·cies :** the highest rank, power, or authority

su·preme *adj* **1 :** highest in rank, power, or authority **2 :** highest in degree or quality **:** UTMOST **3 :** [1]EXTREME 1, FINAL — **su·preme·ly** *adv*

Supreme Being *n* **:** GOD 1

Supreme Court *n* **:** the highest court of the United States consisting of a chief justice and eight associate justices

[1]sure *adj* **sur·er; sur·est 1 :** firmly established **:** STEADFAST **2 :** RELIABLE, TRUSTWORTHY **3 :** having no doubt **:** CONFIDENT **4 :** not to be doubted **:** CERTAIN **5 :** bound to happen **6 :** bound as if by fate

[2]sure *adv* **:** SURELY 2, 3

sure·ly *adv* **1 :** with confidence **:** CONFIDENTLY **2 :** without doubt **3 :** beyond question **:** REALLY

[1]surf *n* **1 :** the waves of the sea that splash on the shore **2 :** the sound, splash, and foam of breaking waves

[2]surf *vb* **1 :** to ride the surf (as on a surfboard) **2 :** to scan a wide range of offerings (as on television or the Internet) for something that is interesting or fills a need

[1]sur·face *n* **1 :** the outside or any one side of an object **2 :** the outside appearance

[2]surface *adj* **1 :** of or relating to a surface **:** acting on a surface **2 :** not deep or real

[3]surface *vb* **sur·faced; sur·fac·ing 1 :** to give a surface to **:** make smooth (as by sanding or paving) **2 :** to come to the surface

surf•board *n* **:** a long narrow board that floats and is ridden in surfing

surf•ing *n* **:** the sport of riding waves in to shore usually while standing on a surfboard

¹surge *vb* **surged; surg•ing** **1 :** to rise and fall with much action **2 :** to move in or as if in waves

²surge *n* **1 :** an onward rush like that of a wave **2 :** a large wave

sur•geon *n* **:** a doctor who specializes in surgery

sur•gery *n, pl* **sur•ger•ies** **1 :** a branch of medicine concerned with the correction of defects, the repair and healing of injuries, and the treatment of diseased conditions by operation **2 :** the work done by a surgeon

sur•gi•cal *adj* **:** of, relating to, or associated with surgery or surgeons

sur•ly *adj* **sur•li•er; sur•li•est** **:** having a mean rude disposition **:** UNFRIENDLY

¹sur•mise *n* **:** a thought or idea based on very little evidence **:** ²GUESS

²surmise *vb* **sur•mised; sur•mis•ing** **:** to form an idea on very little evidence **:** ¹GUESS 1

sur•mount *vb* **1 :** OVERCOME 1 **2 :** to get to the top of **3 :** to be at the top of

sur•name *n* **:** a family name **:** a last name

sur•pass *vb* **1 :** to be greater, better, or stronger than **:** EXCEED **2 :** to go beyond the reach or powers of

¹sur•plus *n* **:** an amount left over **:** EXCESS

²surplus *adj* **:** left over **:** EXTRA

¹sur•prise *n* **1 :** an act or instance of coming upon without warning **2 :** something that surprises **3 :** ASTONISHMENT, AMAZEMENT

²surprise *vb* **sur•prised; sur•pris•ing** **1 :** to attack without warning **:** capture by an unexpected attack **2 :** to come upon without warning **3 :** to cause to feel wonder or amazement because of being unexpected

sur•pris•ing *adj* **:** causing surprise **:** UNEXPECTED — **sur•pris•ing•ly** *adv*

¹sur•ren•der *vb* **1 :** to give oneself or something over to the power, control, or possession of another especially under force **:** YIELD **2 :** RELINQUISH

²surrender *n* **:** the act of giving up or yielding oneself or something into the possession or control of someone else

sur•rey *n, pl* **surreys** **:** a pleasure carriage that has two wide seats and four wheels and is drawn by horses

sur•round *vb* **:** to enclose on all sides **:** ENCIRCLE

sur•round•ings *n pl* **:** the circumstances, conditions, or things around an individual **:** ENVIRONMENT

¹sur•vey *vb* **sur•veyed; sur•vey•ing** **1 :** to look over **:** EXAMINE **2 :** to find out the size, shape, or position of (as an area of land) **3 :** to gather information from **:** make a survey of

²sur•vey *n, pl* **surveys** **1 :** the action or an instance of surveying **2 :** something that is surveyed **3 :** a careful examination to learn facts **4 :** a history or description that covers a large subject briefly

sur•vey•ing *n* **1 :** the act or occupation of a person who makes surveys **2 :** a branch of mathematics that teaches how to measure the earth's surface and record these measurements accurately

sur•vey•or *n* **:** a person who surveys or whose occupation is surveying

sur•viv•al *n* **1 :** a living or continuing longer than another person or thing **2 :** one that survives

sur•vive *vb* **sur•vived; sur•viv•ing** **1 :** to remain alive **:** continue to exist **2 :** to live longer than or past the end of — **sur•vi•vor** *n*

sus•cep•ti•ble *adj* **1 :** of such a nature as to permit **2 :** having little resistance **3 :** easily affected or impressed by

¹sus•pect *adj* **:** thought of with suspicion

²sus•pect *n* **:** a person who is suspected

³sus•pect *vb* **1 :** to have doubts of **:** DISTRUST **2 :** to imagine to be guilty without proof **3 :** to suppose to be true or likely

sus•pend *vb* **1 :** to force to give up some right or office for a time **2 :** to stop or do away with for a time **3 :** to stop operation or action for a time **4 :** to hang especially so as to be free except at one point

sus•pend•er *n* **:** one of a pair of supporting straps that fasten to trousers or a skirt and pass over the shoulders

sus•pense *n* **:** uncertainty or worry about the result of something

sus•pen•sion *n* **1 :** the act or an instance of suspending **2 :** the state of being suspended **3 :** the period during which someone or something is suspended

sus•pi•cion *n* **1 :** an act or instance of suspecting or the state of being suspected **2 :** a feeling that something is wrong **:** DOUBT

sus•pi•cious *adj* **1 :** likely to arouse suspicion **2 :** likely to suspect or distrust **3 :** showing distrust

sus•tain *vb* **1 :** to give support or relief to **:** HELP **2 :** to provide with what is needed **3 :** to keep up **:** PROLONG **4 :** to hold up the weight of **:** PROP **5 :** to keep up the spirits of **6 :** to put up with without giving in **7 :** ²EXPERIENCE **8 :** to allow or uphold as true, legal, or fair **9 :** CONFIRM 1, PROVE

sus•te•nance *n* **1 :** ²LIVING 3, SUBSISTENCE

2 : the act of sustaining **:** the state of being sustained **3 :** ²SUPPORT 2

¹swab *n* **1 :** a yarn mop especially as used on a ship **2 :** a wad of absorbent material usually wound around the end of a small stick and used for applying or removing material (as medicine or makeup)

²swab *vb* **swabbed; swab•bing 1 :** to clean with or as if with a swab **2 :** to apply medication to with a swab

¹swag•ger *vb* **:** to walk with a proud strut

²swagger *n* **:** an act or instance of swaggering

¹swal•low *n* **:** any of a group of small migratory birds with long wings, forked tails, and a graceful flight

²swallow *vb* **1 :** to take into the stomach through the mouth and throat **2 :** to perform the actions used in swallowing something **3 :** to take in as if by swallowing **:** ENGULF **4 :** to accept or believe without question, protest, or anger **5 :** to keep from expressing or showing **:** REPRESS

³swallow *n* **1 :** an act of swallowing **2 :** an amount that can be swallowed at one time

swam *past of* SWIM

¹swamp *n* **:** wet spongy land often partly covered with water

²swamp *vb* **1 :** to fill or cause to fill with water **:** sink after filling with water **2 :** OVERWHELM 2

swampy *adj* **swamp•i•er; swamp•i•est :** of, relating to, or like a swamp

swan *n* **:** a usually white waterbird with a long neck and a heavy body that is related to but larger than the geese

¹swap *vb* **swapped; swap•ping :** to give in exchange **:** make an exchange **:** TRADE

²swap *n* **:** ¹EXCHANGE 1, TRADE

¹swarm *n* **1 :** a large number of bees that leave a hive together to form a new colony elsewhere **2 :** a large moving crowd (as of people or insects)

²swarm *vb* **1 :** to form a swarm and leave the hive **2 :** to move or gather in a swarm or large crowd **3 :** to be filled with a great number **:** TEEM

swar•thy *adj* **swar•thi•er; swar•thi•est :** having a dark complexion

¹swat *vb* **swat•ted; swat•ting :** to hit with a quick hard blow

²swat *n* **:** a hard blow

swath *or* **swathe** *n* **1 :** a sweep of a scythe or machine in mowing or the path cut in one course **2 :** a row of cut grass (as grain)

¹sway *n* **1 :** a slow swinging back and forth or from side to side **2 :** a controlling influence or force **:** RULE

²sway *vb* **1 :** to swing slowly back and forth or from side to side **2 :** to change often between one point, position, or opinion and another **3 :** ²INFLUENCE

swear *vb* **swore; sworn; swear•ing 1 :** to make a statement or promise under oath **:** VOW **2 :** to give an oath to **3 :** to bind by an oath **4 :** to take an oath **5 :** to use bad or vulgar language **:** CURSE

¹sweat *vb* **sweat** *or* **sweat•ed; sweat•ing 1 :** to give off salty moisture through the pores of the skin **:** PERSPIRE **2 :** to collect moisture on the surface **3 :** to work hard enough to perspire

²sweat *n* **1 :** PERSPIRATION 2 **2 :** moisture coming from or collecting in drops on a surface **3 :** the condition of one sweating

sweat•er *n* **:** a knitted or crocheted jacket or pullover

sweat gland *n* **:** any of numerous small skin glands that give off perspiration

Swede *n* **:** a person born or living in Sweden

¹Swed•ish *adj* **:** of or relating to Sweden, the Swedes, or Swedish

²Swedish *n* **:** the language of the Swedes

¹sweep *vb* **swept; sweep•ing 1 :** to remove with a broom or brush **2 :** to clean by removing loose dirt or small trash with a broom or brush **3 :** to move over or across swiftly with force or destruction **4 :** to move or gather as if with a broom or brush **5 :** to touch a surface as if with a brush **6 :** to drive along with steady force **7 :** to move the eyes or an instrument through a wide curve — **sweep•er** *n*

²sweep *n* **1 :** something that sweeps or works with a sweeping motion **2 :** an act or instance of sweeping **3 :** a complete or easy victory **4 :** a curving movement, course, or line **5 :** ¹RANGE 6, SCOPE **6 :** CHIMNEY SWEEP

¹sweep•ing *n* **1 :** the act or action of one that sweeps **2 sweepings** *pl* **:** things collected by sweeping

²sweeping *adj* **1 :** moving or extending in a wide curve or over a wide area **2 :** EXTENSIVE

sweep•stakes *n, sing or pl* **:** a contest in which money or prizes are given to winners picked by chance (as by drawing names from a box)

¹sweet *adj* **1 :** pleasing to the taste **2 :** containing or tasting of sugar **3 :** pleasing to the mind or feelings **:** AGREEABLE **4 :** ¹KINDLY 2, MILD **5 :** FRAGRANT **6 :** pleasing to the ear or eye **7 :** much loved **:** DEAR **8 :** not sour, stale, or spoiled **9 :** FRESH 1 — **sweet•ish** *adj* — **sweet•ly** *adv* — **sweet•ness** *n*

²sweet *n* **1 :** something (as candy) that is sweet to the taste **2 :** ¹DARLING 1, DEAR

sweet corn *n* **:** an Indian corn with kernels

rich in sugar that is cooked as a vegetable while young

sweet·en *vb* **:** to make or become sweet or sweeter

sweet·en·ing *n* **1 :** the act or process of making sweet **2 :** something that sweetens

sweet·heart *n* **:** a person whom one loves

sweet·meat *n* **:** a food (as a piece of candy or candied fruit) rich in sugar

sweet pea *n* **:** a climbing plant related to the peas that is grown for its fragrant flowers of many colors

sweet potato *n* **:** the large sweet edible root of a tropical vine somewhat like a morning glory

sweet wil·liam *n, often cap W* **:** a European pink grown for its thick flat clusters of many-colored flowers

1**swell** *vb* **swelled; swelled** *or* **swol·len; swell·ing 1 :** to enlarge in an abnormal way usually by pressure from within or by growth **2 :** to grow or make bigger (as in size or value) **3 :** to stretch upward or outward **:** BULGE **4 :** to fill or become filled with emotion

2**swell** *n* **1 :** a becoming larger (as in size or value) **2 :** a long rolling wave or series of waves in the open sea **3 :** a very fashionably dressed person

3**swell** *adj* **1 :** STYLISH, FASHIONABLE **2 :** EXCELLENT, FIRST-RATE

swell·ing *n* **:** a swollen lump or part

swel·ter *vb* **:** to suffer, sweat, or be faint from heat

swept *past of* SWEEP

1**swerve** *vb* **swerved; swerv·ing :** to turn aside suddenly from a straight line or course

2**swerve** *n* **:** an act or instance of swerving

1**swift** *adj* **1 :** moving or capable of moving with great speed **2 :** occurring suddenly **3 :** 1READY 3, ALERT — **swift·ly** *adv* — **swift·ness** *n*

2**swift** *adv* **:** SWIFTLY

3**swift** *n* **:** a small usually sooty black bird that is related to the hummingbirds but looks like a swallow

swig *n* **:** the amount drunk at one time **:** GULP

1**swill** *vb* **:** to eat or drink greedily

2**swill** *n* **1 :** 1SLOP 3 **2 :** GARBAGE, REFUSE

1**swim** *vb* **swam; swum; swim·ming 1 :** to move through or in water by moving arms, legs, fins, or tail **2 :** to glide smoothly and quietly **3 :** to float on or in or be covered with or as if with a liquid **4 :** to be dizzy **:** move or seem to move dizzily **5 :** to cross by swimming — **swim·mer** *n*

2**swim** *n* **1 :** an act or period of swimming **2 :** the main current of activity

swimming *adj* **1 :** capable of swimming **2 :** used in or for swimming

swimming pool *n* **:** a tank (as of concrete or plastic) made for swimming

swim·suit *n* **:** a garment for swimming or bathing

1**swin·dle** *vb* **swin·dled; swin·dling :** to get money or property from by dishonest means **:** CHEAT

2**swindle** *n* **:** an act or instance of swindling

swin·dler *n* **:** a person who swindles

swine *n, pl* **swine :** a hoofed domestic animal that comes from the wild boar, has a long snout and bristly skin, and is widely raised for meat

swine·herd *n* **:** a person who tends swine

1**swing** *vb* **swung; swing·ing 1 :** to move rapidly in a sweeping curve **2 :** to throw or toss in a circle or back and forth **3 :** to sway to and fro **4 :** to hang or be hung so as to move freely back and forth or in a curve **5 :** to turn on a hinge or pivot **6 :** to manage or handle successfully **7 :** to march or walk with free swaying movements

2**swing** *n* **1 :** an act of swinging **2 :** a swinging movement, blow, or rhythm **3 :** the distance through which something swings **4 :** a swinging seat usually hung by overhead ropes **5 :** a style of jazz marked by lively rhythm and played mostly for dancing

1**swipe** *n* **:** a strong sweeping blow

2**swipe** *vb* **swiped; swip·ing :** 1STEAL 2

1**swirl** *vb* **:** to move with a whirling or twisting motion

2**swirl** *n* **1 :** a whirling mass or motion **:** EDDY **2 :** whirling confusion **3 :** a twisting shape or mark

1**swish** *vb* **:** to make, move, or strike with a soft rubbing or hissing sound

2**swish** *n* **1 :** a hissing sound (as of a whip cutting the air) or a light sweeping or rubbing sound (as of a silk skirt) **2 :** a swishing movement

1**Swiss** *n, pl* **Swiss :** a person born or living in Switzerland

2**Swiss** *adj* **:** of or relating to Switzerland or the Swiss

1**switch** *n* **1 :** a narrow flexible whip, rod, or twig **2 :** an act of switching **3 :** a blow with a switch or whip **4 :** a change from one thing to another **5 :** a device for adjusting the rails of a track so that a train or streetcar may be turned from one track to another **6 :** SIDING 1 **7 :** a device for making, breaking, or changing the connections in an electrical circuit

2**switch** *vb* **1 :** to strike or whip with or as if with a switch **2 :** to lash from side to side **3 :** to turn, shift, or change by operating a switch **4 :** to make a shift or change

switch•board *n* **:** a panel for controlling the operation of a number of electric circuits used especially to make and break telephone connections

[1]**swiv•el** *n* **:** a device joining two parts so that one or both can turn freely (as on a bolt or pin)

[2]**swivel** *vb* **swiv•eled** *or* **swiv•elled; swiv•el•ing** *or* **swiv•el•ling :** to turn on or as if on a swivel

swollen *past participle of* SWELL

[1]**swoon** *vb* **:** [2]FAINT

[2]**swoon** *n* **:** [3]FAINT

[1]**swoop** *vb* **:** to rush down or pounce suddenly like a hawk attacking its prey

[2]**swoop** *n* **:** an act or instance of swooping

sword *n* **:** a weapon having a long blade usually with a sharp point and edge

sword•fish *n, pl* **swordfish** *or* **sword•fish•es :** a very large ocean food fish having a long swordlike beak formed by the bones of the upper jaw

swords•man *n, pl* **swords•men :** a person who fights with a sword

swore *past of* SWEAR

sworn *past participle of* SWEAR

swum *past participle of* SWIM

swung *past of* SWING

syc•a•more *n* **1 :** the common fig tree of Egypt and Asia Minor **2 :** an American tree with round fruits and bark that forms flakes

syl•lab•ic *adj* **1 :** of, relating to, or being syllables **2 :** not accompanied by a vowel sound in the same syllable

syl•lab•i•cate *vb* **syl•lab•i•cat•ed; syl•lab•i•cat•ing :** SYLLABIFY

syl•lab•i•ca•tion *n* **:** the forming of syllables **:** the dividing of words into syllables

syl•lab•i•fi•ca•tion *n* **:** SYLLABICATION

syl•lab•i•fy *vb* **syl•lab•i•fied; syl•lab•i•fy•ing :** to form or divide into syllables

syl•la•ble *n* **1 :** a unit of spoken language that consists of one or more vowel sounds alone or of a syllabic consonant alone or of either of these preceded or followed by one or more consonant sounds **2 :** one or more letters (as *syl, la,* and *ble*) in a written word (as *syl•la•ble*) usually separated from the rest of the word by a centered dot or a hyphen and used as guides to the division of the word at the end of a line

sym•bol *n* **1 :** something that stands for something else **:** EMBLEM **2 :** a letter, character, or sign used instead of a word to represent a quantity, position, relationship, direction, or something to be done

sym•bol•ic *or* **sym•bol•i•cal** *adj* **:** of, relating to, or using symbols or symbolism

sym•bol•ize *vb* **sym•bol•ized; sym•bol•iz•ing :** to serve as a symbol of

sym•met•ri•cal *or* **sym•met•ric** *adj* **:** having or showing symmetry

sym•me•try *n, pl* **sym•me•tries :** close agreement in size, shape, and position of parts that are on opposite sides of a dividing line or center **:** an arrangement involving regular and balanced proportions

sym•pa•thet•ic *adj* **1 :** fitting one's mood or disposition **2 :** feeling sympathy **3 :** feeling favorable — **sym•pa•thet•i•cal•ly** *adv*

sym•pa•thize *vb* **sym•pa•thized; sym•pa•thiz•ing 1 :** to feel or show sympathy **2 :** to be in favor of something

sym•pa•thy *n, pl* **sym•pa•thies 1 :** a relationship between persons or things in which whatever affects one similarly affects the other **2 :** readiness to think or feel alike **:** similarity of likes, interest, or aims that makes a bond of goodwill **3 :** readiness to favor or support **4 :** the act of or capacity for entering into the feelings or interests of another **5 :** sorrow or pity for another **6 :** a showing of sorrow for another's loss, grief, or misfortune

sym•phon•ic *adj* **:** of or relating to a symphony or symphony orchestra

sym•pho•ny *n, pl* **sym•pho•nies 1 :** harmonious arrangement (as of sound or color) **2 :** a usually long musical composition for a full orchestra **3 :** a large orchestra of wind, string, and percussion instruments

symp•tom *n* **1 :** a noticeable change in the body or its functions typical of a disease **2 :** INDICATION 2, SIGN

syn•a•gogue *or* **syn•a•gog** *n* **:** a Jewish house of worship

syn•apse *n* **:** the point at which a nerve impulse passes from one nerve cell to another

syn•co•pa•tion *n* **:** a temporary accenting of a normally weak beat in music to vary the rhythm

syn•o•nym *n* **:** a word having the same or almost the same meaning as another word in the same language

syn•on•y•mous *adj* **:** alike in meaning

syn•tax *n* **:** the way in which words are put together to form phrases, clauses, or sentences

syn•the•size *vb* **syn•the•sized; syn•the•siz•ing :** to build up from simpler materials

syn•thet•ic *adj* **:** produced artificially especially by chemical means **:** produced by human beings

sy•rin•ga *n* **:** a garden shrub with often fragrant flowers of a white or cream color

sy•ringe *n* **:** a device used to force fluid into or withdraw it from the body or its cavities

syr•up *or* **sir•up** *n* **1 :** a thick sticky solution of sugar and water often containing flavoring or a medicine **2 :** the juice of a fruit or plant with some of the water removed

sys•tem *n* **1 :** a group of parts combined to form a whole that works or moves as a unit **2 :** a body that functions as a whole **3 :** a group of bodily organs that together carry on some vital function **4 :** an orderly plan or method of governing or arranging **5 :** regular method or order **:** ORDERLINESS

sys•tem•at•ic *adj* **1 :** having, using, or acting on a system **2 :** carrying out a plan with thoroughness or regularity — **sys•tem•at•i•cal•ly** *adv*

sys•tem•ic *adj* **:** of or relating to the body as a whole

T

t *n, pl* **t's** *or* **ts** *often cap* **:** the twentieth letter of the English alphabet — **to a T :** just fine **:** EXACTLY

tab *n* **1 :** a short flap or tag attached to something for filing, pulling, or hanging **2 :** a careful watch

tab•by *n, pl* **tabbies** **1 :** a domestic cat with a gray or tawny coat striped and spotted with black **2 :** a female domestic cat

tab•er•na•cle *n* **1** *often cap* **:** a structure of wood hung with curtains used in worship by the Israelites during their wanderings in the wilderness with Moses **2 :** a house of worship

1ta•ble *n* **1 :** a piece of furniture having a smooth flat top on legs **2 :** food to eat **3 :** the people around a table **4 :** short list **5 :** an arrangement in rows or columns for reference

2table *vb* **ta•bled; ta•bling** **1 :** TABULATE **2 :** to put on a table

tab•leau *n, pl* **tableaus** *or* **tab•leaux** **:** a scene or event shown by a group of persons who remain still and silent

ta•ble•cloth *n* **:** a covering spread over a dining table before the places are set

ta•ble•land *n* **:** PLATEAU

ta•ble•spoon *n* **1 :** a large spoon used mostly for dishing up food **2 :** TABLESPOONFUL

ta•ble•spoon•ful *n, pl* **tablespoonfuls** *or* **ta•ble•spoons•ful** **1 :** as much as a tablespoon will hold **2 :** a unit of measure used in cooking equal to three teaspoonfuls (about fifteen milliliters)

tab•let *n* **1 :** a thin flat slab used for writing, painting, or drawing **2 :** a number of sheets of writing paper glued together at one edge **3 :** a flat and usually round mass of material containing medicine

table tennis *n* **:** a game played on a table by two or four players who use paddles to hit a small hollow plastic ball back and forth over a net

ta•ble•ware *n* **:** utensils (as of china, glass, or silver) for use at the table

tab•u•late *vb* **tab•u•lat•ed; tab•u•lat•ing** **:** to put in the form of a table

tac•it *adj* **:** understood or made known without being put into words — **tac•it•ly** *adv*

1tack *n* **1 :** a small nail with a sharp point and usually a broad flat head for fastening a light object or material to a solid surface **2 :** the direction a ship is sailing as shown by the position the sails are set in or the movement of a ship with the sails set in a certain position **3 :** a change of course from one tack to another **4 :** a zigzag movement or course **5 :** a course of action **6 :** a temporary stitch used in sewing

2tack *vb* **1 :** to fasten with tacks **2 :** to attach or join loosely **3 :** to change from one course to another in sailing **4 :** to follow a zigzag course

1tack•le *n* **1 :** a set of special equipment **2 :** an arrangement of ropes and wheels for hoisting or pulling something heavy **3 :** an act of tackling

2tackle *vb* **tack•led; tack•ling** **1 :** to seize and throw (a person) to the ground **2 :** to begin working on

ta•co *n, pl* **tacos** **:** a corn tortilla usually folded and fried and filled with a spicy mixture (as of ground meat and cheese)

tact *n* **:** a keen understanding of how to get along with other people

tact•ful *adj* **:** having or showing tact — **tact•ful•ly** *adv* — **tact•ful•ness** *n*

tac•tic *n* **:** a planned action for some purpose

tac•tics *n sing or pl* **1 :** the science and art of arranging and moving troops or warships for best use **2 :** a system or method for reaching a goal

tac•tile *adj* **:** of or relating to the sense of touch

tact•less *adj* **:** having or showing no tact — **tact•less•ly** *adv* — **tact•less•ness** *n*

tad•pole *n* **:** the larva of a frog or toad that has a long tail, breathes with gills, and lives in water

taf•fy *n, pl* **taffies** **:** a candy made usually of molasses or brown sugar boiled and pulled until soft

1tag *n* **:** a small flap or tab fixed or hanging on something **2 :** an often quoted saying

[2]**tag** *vb* **tagged; tag·ging** **1 :** to put a tag on **2 :** to follow closely and continually

[3]**tag** *n* **:** a game in which one player who is it chases the others and tries to touch one of them to make that person it

[4]**tag** *vb* **tagged; tag·ging** **1 :** to touch in or as if in a game of tag **2 :** to touch a runner in baseball with the ball and cause the runner to be out

[1]**tail** *n* **1 :** the rear part of an animal or a usually slender flexible extension of this part **2 :** something that in shape, appearance, or position is like an animal's tail **3 :** the back, last, or lower part of something **4 :** the side or end opposite the head — **tailed** *adj* — **tail·less** *adj* — **tail·like** *adj*

[2]**tail** *vb* **:** to follow closely to keep watch on

tail·gate *n* **:** a panel at the back end of a vehicle that can be let down for loading and unloading

tail·light *n* **:** a red warning light at the rear of a vehicle

[1]**tai·lor** *n* **:** a person whose business is making or making adjustments in men's or women's clothes

[2]**tailor** *vb* **1 :** to make or make adjustments in (clothes) **2 :** to change to fit a special need

tail·pipe *n* **:** the pipe carrying off the exhaust gases from the muffler of an engine in a car or truck

tail·spin *n* **:** a dive by an airplane turning in a circle

[1]**taint** *vb* **1 :** to affect slightly with something bad **2 :** to rot slightly

[2]**taint** *n* **:** a trace of decay

[1]**take** *vb* **took; tak·en; tak·ing** **1 :** to get control of **:** CAPTURE **2 :** [1]GRASP 1 **3 :** to come upon **4 :** CAPTIVATE **5 :** to receive into the body **6 :** to get possession or use of **7 :** ASSUME 1 **8 :** to be formed or used with **9 :** to adopt as one's own or for oneself **10 :** WIN 3 **11 :** CHOOSE 1, SELECT **12 :** to sit in or on **13 :** to use as a way of going from one place to another **14 :** REQUIRE **15 :** to find out by special methods **16 :** to save in some permanent form **17 :** to put up with **:** ENDURE **18 :** BELIEVE 2 3 **19 :** to be guided by **:** FOLLOW **20 :** to become affected suddenly **21 :** UNDERSTAND 4, INTERPRET **22 :** to react in a certain way **23 :** to carry or go with from one place to another **24 :** REMOVE 3, SUBTRACT **25 :** to do the action of **26 :** to have effect **:** be successful — **tak·er** *n* — **take advantage of 1 :** to make good use of **2 :** to treat (someone) unfairly — **take after :** RESEMBLE — **take care :** to be careful — **take care of :** to do what is needed **:** look after — **take effect 1 :** to go into effect **2 :** to have an intended or expected effect — **take hold :** to become attached or established — **take part :** to do or join in something together with others — **take place :** to come into being and last for a time — used of events or actions

[2]**take** *n* **1 :** the act of taking **2 :** something that is taken **3 :** a bodily reaction that shows a smallpox vaccination to be successful

take back *vb* **:** to try to cancel (as something said)

take in *vb* **1 :** to make smaller **2 :** to receive as a guest **3 :** to allow to join **4 :** to receive (work) to be done in one's home for pay **5 :** to have within its limits **6 :** to go to **7 :** to get the meaning of **8 :** [1]CHEAT 2

take·off *n* **1 :** an imitation especially to mock the original **2 :** an act or instance of taking off from the ground (as by an airplane) **3 :** a spot at which one takes off

take off *vb* **1 :** to take away (a covering) **:** REMOVE **2 :** DEDUCT **3 :** to leave a surface in beginning a flight or leap

take on *vb* **1 :** to begin (a task) or struggle against (an opponent) **2 :** to gain or show as or as if a part of oneself **3 :** [1]EMPLOY 2 **4 :** to make an unusual show of one's grief or anger

take over *vb* **:** to get control of

take up *vb* **1 :** to get together from many sources **2 :** to start something for the first time or after a pause **3 :** to change by making tighter or shorter

tak·ing *adj* **1 :** ATTRACTIVE **2 :** INFECTIOUS 1

talc *n* **:** a soft mineral that has a soapy feel and is used in making talcum powder and for coloring

tal·cum powder *n* **:** a usually perfumed powder for the body made of talc

tale *n* **1 :** something told **2 :** a story about an imaginary event **3 :** [3]LIE **4 :** a piece of harmful gossip

tal·ent *n* **1 :** unusual natural ability **2 :** a special often creative or artistic ability **3 :** persons having special ability — **tal·ent·ed** *adj*

tal·is·man *n, pl* **tal·is·mans :** a ring or stone carved with symbols and believed to have magical powers **:** CHARM

[1]**talk** *vb* **1 :** to express in speech **:** SPEAK **2 :** to speak about **:** DISCUSS **3 :** to cause or influence by talking **4 :** to use a certain language **5 :** to exchange ideas by means of spoken words **:** CONVERSE **6 :** to pass on information other than by speaking **7 :** [2]GOSSIP **8 :** to reveal secret information — **talk·er** *n*

[2]**talk** *n* **1 :** the act of talking **:** SPEECH **2 :** a

way of speaking : LANGUAGE **3 :** CONFERENCE **4 :** [1]RUMOR 2, GOSSIP **5 :** the topic of comment or gossip **6 :** an informal address

talk•a•tive *adj* **:** fond of talking — **talk•a•tive•ness** *n*

talk•ing–to *n* **:** an often wordy scolding

[1]tall *adj* **1 :** having unusually great height **2 :** of a stated height **3 :** made up — **tall•ness** *n*

[2]tall *adv* **:** so as to be or look tall

tal•low *n* **:** a white solid fat obtained by heating fatty tissues of cattle and sheep

[1]tal•ly *n, pl* **tallies 1 :** a device for keeping a count **2 :** a recorded count **3 :** a score or point made (as in a game)

[2]tally *vb* **tal•lied; tal•ly•ing 1 :** to keep a count of **2 :** to make a tally **:** SCORE **3 :** CORRESPOND 1

tal•on *n* **:** the claw of a bird of prey — **tal•oned** *adj*

ta•ma•le *n* **:** seasoned ground meat rolled in cornmeal, wrapped in corn husks, and steamed

tam•bou•rine *n* **:** a small shallow drum with only one head and loose metal disks around the rim that is played by shaking or hitting with the hand

[1]tame *adj* **tam•er; tam•est 1 :** made useful and obedient to humans **:** DOMESTIC 3 **2 :** not afraid of people **3 :** not interesting **:** DULL — **tame•ly** *adv* — **tame•ness** *n*

[2]tame *vb* **tamed; tam•ing 1 :** to make or become gentle or obedient **2 :** [2]HUMBLE — **tam•able** *or* **tame•able** *adj* — **tam•er** *n*

tamp *vb* **:** to drive down or in with several light blows

tam•per *vb* **:** to interfere in a secret or incorrect way

[1]tan *vb* **tanned; tan•ning 1 :** to change hide into leather by soaking in a tannin solution **2 :** to make or become brown or tan in color **3 :** [1]BEAT 1, THRASH

[2]tan *adj* **tan•ner; tan•nest :** of a light yellowish brown color

[3]tan *n* **1 :** a brown color given to the skin by the sun or wind **2 :** a light yellowish brown color

tan•a•ger *n* **:** a very brightly colored bird related to the finches

[1]tan•dem *n* **1 :** a carriage pulled by horses hitched one behind the other **2 :** TANDEM BICYCLE

[2]tandem *adv* **:** one behind another

tandem bicycle *n* **:** a bicycle for two people sitting one behind the other

tang *n* **:** a sharp flavor or smell

tan•ger•ine *n* **:** a Chinese orange with a loose skin and sweet pulp

tan•gi•ble *adj* **1 :** possible to touch or handle **2 :** actually real **:** MATERIAL — **tan•gi•bly** *adv*

[1]tan•gle *vb* **tan•gled; tan•gling :** to twist or become twisted together into a mass hard to straighten out again

[2]tangle *n* **1 :** a tangled twisted mass (as of yarn) **2 :** a complicated or confused state

[1]tank *n* **1 :** an often large container for a liquid **2 :** an enclosed combat vehicle that has heavy armor and guns and a tread which is an endless belt

[2]tank *vb* **:** to put, keep, or treat in a tank

tan•kard *n* **:** a tall cup with one handle and often a lid

tank•er *n* **:** a vehicle or ship with tanks for carrying a liquid

tan•ner *n* **:** a person who tans hides into leather

tan•nery *n, pl* **tan•ner•ies :** a place where hides are tanned

tan•nin *n* **:** a substance often made from oak bark or sumac and used in tanning, dyeing, and making ink

tan•ta•lize *vb* **tan•ta•lized; tan•ta•liz•ing :** to make miserable by or as if by showing something desirable but keeping it out of reach — **tan•ta•liz•er** *n*

tan•trum *n* **:** an outburst of bad temper

[1]tap *n* **:** FAUCET, SPIGOT — **on tap :** on hand **:** AVAILABLE

[2]tap *vb* **tapped; tap•ping 1 :** to let out or cause to flow by making a hole or by pulling out a plug **2 :** to make a hole in to draw off a liquid **3 :** to draw from or upon **4 :** to connect into (a telephone wire) to listen secretly — **tap•per** *n*

[3]tap *vb* **tapped; tap•ping 1 :** to hit lightly **2 :** to make by striking something lightly again and again — **tap•per** *n*

[4]tap *n* **:** a light blow or its sound

[1]tape *n* **1 :** a narrow band of cloth **2 :** a narrow strip or band of material (as paper, steel, or plastic) **3 :** MAGNETIC TAPE **4 :** TAPE RECORDING

[2]tape *vb* **taped; tap•ing 1 :** to fasten, cover, or hold up with tape **2 :** to make a record of on tape

tape deck *n* **:** a device used to play back and often to record on magnetic tapes

tape measure *n* **:** a tape marked off for measuring

[1]ta•per *n* **1 :** a slender candle **2 :** a gradual lessening in thickness or width in a long object

[2]taper *vb* **1 :** to make or become gradually smaller toward one end **2 :** to grow gradually less and less

tape recorder *n* **:** a device for recording on and playing back magnetic tapes

tape recording *n* **:** a recording made on magnetic tape

tap•es•try *n, pl* **tap•es•tries :** a heavy cloth that has designs or pictures woven into it and is used especially as a wall hanging — **tap•es•tried** *adj*

tape•worm *n* **:** a worm with a long flat body that lives in human or animal intestines

tap•i•o•ca *n* **:** small pieces of starch from roots of a tropical plant used especially in puddings

ta•pir *n* **:** a large hoofed mammal of tropical America, Malaya, and Sumatra that has thick legs, a short tail, and a long flexible snout

tap•root *n* **:** a main root of a plant that grows straight down and gives off smaller side roots

taps *n sing or pl* **:** the last bugle call at night blown as a signal to put out the lights

¹tar *n* **:** a thick dark sticky liquid made from wood, coal, or peat

²tar *vb* **tarred; tar•ring :** to cover with or as if with tar

³tar *n* **:** SAILOR

ta•ran•tu•la *n* **1 :** a large European spider whose bite was once believed to cause a wild desire to dance **2 :** any of a group of large hairy spiders of warm regions of North and South America whose bite is sharp but not serious except for some South American species

tar•dy *adj* **tar•di•er; tar•di•est :** not on time **:** LATE — **tar•di•ly** *adv* — **tar•di•ness** *n*

tar•get *n* **1 :** a mark or object to shoot at **2 :** a person or thing that is talked about, criticized, or laughed at **3 :** a goal to be reached

tar•iff *n* **1 :** a list of taxes placed by a government on goods coming into a country **2 :** the tax or the rate of taxation set up in a tariff list

¹tar•nish *vb* **:** to make or become dull, dim, or discolored

²tarnish *n* **:** a surface coating formed during tarnishing

tar•pau•lin *n* **:** a sheet of waterproof canvas

¹tar•ry *vb* **tar•ried; tar•ry•ing 1 :** to be slow in coming or going **2 :** to stay in or at a place

²tar•ry *adj* **:** of, like, or covered with tar

¹tart *adj* **1 :** pleasantly sharp to the taste **2 :** BITING — **tart•ly** *adv* — **tart•ness** *n*

²tart *n* **:** a small pie often with no top crust

tar•tan *n* **:** a woolen cloth with a plaid design first made in Scotland

tar•tar *n* **1 :** a substance found in the juices of grapes that forms a reddish crust on the inside of wine barrels **2 :** a crust that forms on the teeth made up of deposits of saliva, food, and calcium

task *n* **:** a piece of assigned work

tas•sel *n* **1 :** a hanging ornament made of a bunch of cords of the same length fastened at one end **2 :** something like a tassel

¹taste *vb* **tast•ed; tast•ing 1 :** ²EXPERIENCE **2 :** to find out the flavor of something by taking a little into the mouth **3 :** to eat or drink usually in small amounts **4 :** to recognize by the sense of taste **5 :** to have a certain flavor — **tast•er** *n*

²taste *n* **1 :** a small amount tasted **2 :** the one of the special senses that recognizes sweet, sour, bitter, or salty flavors and that acts through sense organs (**taste buds**) in the tongue **3 :** the quality of something recognized by the sense of taste or by this together with smell and touch **:** FLAVOR **4 :** a personal liking **5 :** the ability to choose and enjoy what is good or beautiful

taste•ful *adj* **:** having or showing good taste — **taste•ful•ly** *adv* — **taste•ful•ness** *n*

taste•less *adj* **1 :** having little flavor **2 :** not having or showing good taste — **taste•less•ly** *adv* — **taste•less•ness** *n*

tasty *adj* **tast•i•er; tast•i•est :** pleasing to the taste — **tast•i•ness** *n*

tat•ter *n* **1 :** a part torn and left hanging **:** SHRED **2 tatters** *pl* **:** ragged clothing

tat•tered *adj* **1 :** torn in or worn to shreds **2 :** dressed in ragged clothes

tat•tle *vb* **tat•tled; tat•tling 1 :** PRATTLE **2 :** to give away secrets **:** tell on someone — **tat•tler** *n*

tat•tle•tale *n* **:** a person who lets secrets out

¹tat•too *vb* **tat•tooed; tat•too•ing :** to mark the body with a picture or pattern by using a needle to put color under the skin — **tat•too•er** *n*

²tattoo *n, pl* **tat•toos :** a picture or design made by tattooing

taught *past of* TEACH

¹taunt *n* **:** a mean insulting remark

²taunt *vb* **:** to make fun of or say mean insulting things to

Tau•rus *n* **1 :** a constellation between Aries and Gemini imagined as a bull **2 :** the second sign of the zodiac or a person born under this sign

taut *adj* **1 :** tightly stretched **2 :** HIGH-STRUNG, TENSE **3 :** kept in good order — **taut•ly** *adv* — **taut•ness** *n*

tav•ern *n* **1 :** a place where beer and liquor are sold and drunk **2 :** INN

taw•ny *adj* **taw•ni•er; taw•ni•est :** of a brownish orange color

¹tax *vb* **1 :** to require to pay a tax **2 :** to accuse of something **3 :** to cause a strain on — **tax•er** *n*

²tax *n* **1 :** money collected by the government from people or businesses for public use **2 :** a difficult task

tax•able *adj* **:** subject to tax

tax•a•tion *n* **1 :** the action of taxing **2 :** money gotten from taxes

[1]**taxi** *n, pl* **tax•is :** TAXICAB

[2]**taxi** *vb* **tax•ied; taxi•ing** *or* **taxy•ing 1 :** to go by taxicab **2 :** to run an airplane slowly along the ground under its own power

taxi•cab *n* **:** an automobile that carries passengers for a fare usually determined by the distance traveled

taxi•der•my *n* **:** the art of stuffing and mounting the skins of animals

tax•on•o•my *n* **1 :** the study of classification **2 :** a classification (as of animals) using a system that is usually based on relationship

tax•pay•er *n* **:** a person who pays or is responsible for paying a tax

TB *n* **:** TUBERCULOSIS

tea *n* **1 :** the dried leaves and leaf buds of a shrub widely grown in eastern and southern Asia **2 :** a drink made by soaking tea in boiling water **3 :** a drink or medicine made by soaking plant parts (as dried roots) **4 :** refreshments often including tea served in late afternoon **5 :** a party at which tea is served

teach *vb* **taught; teach•ing 1 :** to show how **2 :** to guide the studies of **3 :** to cause to know the unpleasant results of something **4 :** to give lessons in

teach•er *n* **:** a person who teaches

teaching *n* **1 :** the duties or profession of a teacher **2 :** something taught

tea•cup *n* **:** a cup used with a saucer for hot drinks

teak *n* **:** the hard wood of a tall tree which grows in the East Indies and resists decay

tea•ket•tle *n* **:** a covered kettle that is used for boiling water and has a handle and spout

teal *n* **:** a small wild duck that is very swift in flight

[1]**team** *n* **1 :** two or more animals used to pull the same vehicle or piece of machinery **2 :** a group of persons who work or play together

[2]**team** *vb* **1 :** to haul with or drive a team **2 :** to form a team

team•mate *n* **:** a person who belongs to the same team as someone else

team•ster *n* **:** a worker who drives a team or a truck

team•work *n* **:** the work of a group of persons acting together

tea•pot *n* **:** a pot for making and serving tea

[1]**tear** *n* **:** a drop of the salty liquid that keeps the eyeballs and inside of the eyelids moist

[2]**tear** *vb* **tore; torn; tear•ing 1 :** to pull into two or more pieces by force **2 :** LACERATE **3 :** to remove by force **4 :** to move powerfully or swiftly

[3]**tear** *n* **1 :** the act of tearing **2 :** damage from being torn

tear•drop *n* **:** [1]TEAR

tear•ful *adj* **:** flowing with, accompanied by, or causing tears — **tear•ful•ly** *adv*

[1]**tease** *vb* **teased; teas•ing :** to annoy again and again — **teas•er** *n*

[2]**tease** *n* **1 :** the act of teasing **:** the state of being teased **2 :** a person who teases

tea•spoon *n* **1 :** a small spoon used especially for stirring drinks **2 :** TEASPOONFUL

tea•spoon•ful *n, pl* **teaspoonfuls** *or* **tea•spoons•ful 1 :** as much as a teaspoon can hold **2 :** a unit of measure used especially in cooking and pharmacy equal to about five milliliters

teat *n* **:** NIPPLE 1 — used mostly of domestic animals

tech•ni•cal *adj* **1 :** having special knowledge especially of a mechanical or scientific subject **2 :** of or relating to a single and especially a practical or scientific subject **3 :** according to a strict explanation of the rules — **tech•ni•cal•ly** *adv*

tech•ni•cal•i•ty *n, pl* **tech•ni•cal•i•ties :** something having meaning only to a person with special training

technical sergeant *n* **:** a noncommissioned officer in the Air Force ranking above a staff sergeant

tech•ni•cian *n* **:** a person skilled in the details or techniques of a subject, art, or job

tech•nique *n* **1 :** the manner in which technical details are used in reaching a goal **2 :** technical methods

tech•no•log•i•cal *adj* **:** of or relating to technology

tech•nol•o•gist *n* **:** a specialist in technology

tech•nol•o•gy *n, pl* **tech•nol•o•gies 1 :** the use of science in solving problems (as in industry or engineering) **2 :** a technical method of doing something

ted•dy bear *n* **:** a stuffed toy bear

te•dious *adj* **:** tiring because of length or dullness — **te•dious•ly** *adv* — **te•dious•ness** *n*

tee *n* **:** a peg on which a golf ball is placed to be hit

teem *vb* **:** to be full of something

teen•age *or* **teen•aged** *adj* **:** of, being, or relating to teenagers

teen•ag•er *n* **:** a person in his or her teens

teens *n pl* **:** the years thirteen through nineteen in a person's life

tee•ny *adj* **tee•ni•er; tee•ni•est :** TINY

tee shirt *variant of* T-SHIRT

tee·ter *vb* **1 :** to move unsteadily **2 :** ²SEESAW

tee·ter–tot·ter *n* **:** ¹SEESAW

teeth *pl of* TOOTH

teethe *vb* **teethed; teeth·ing :** to cut one's teeth **:** grow teeth

tele- *or* **tel-** *prefix* **1 :** at a distance **2 :** television

¹**tele·cast** *n* **:** a program broadcast by television

²**telecast** *vb* **telecast** *also* **tele·cast·ed; tele·cast·ing :** to broadcast by television — **tele·cast·er** *n*

tele·gram *n* **:** a message sent by telegraph

¹**tele·graph** *n* **:** an electric device or system for sending messages by a code over connecting wires

²**telegraph** *vb* **1 :** to send by telegraph **2 :** to send a telegram to

te·leg·ra·phy *n* **:** the use of a telegraph

te·lep·a·thy *n* **:** communication which appears to take place from one mind to another without speech or signs

¹**tele·phone** *n* **:** an instrument for transmitting and receiving sounds over long distances by electricity

²**telephone** *vb* **tele·phoned; tele·phon·ing :** to speak to by telephone

¹**tele·scope** *n* **:** an instrument shaped like a long tube that has lenses for viewing objects at a distance and especially for observing objects in outer space

²**telescope** *vb* **tele·scoped; tele·scop·ing :** to slide or force one part into another like the sections of a small telescope

tele·vise *vb* **tele·vised; tele·vis·ing :** to send (a program) by television

tele·vi·sion *n* **1 :** an electronic system of sending images together with sound over a wire or through space by devices that change light and sound into electrical waves and then change these back into light and sound **2 :** a television receiving set **3 :** television as a way of communicating

tell *vb* **told; tell·ing 1 :** ¹COUNT 1 **2 :** to describe item by item **3 :** ¹SAY 1 **4 :** to make known **5 :** to let a person know something **:** to give information to **6 :** ¹ORDER 2 **7 :** to find out by observing **8 :** to act as a tattletale **9 :** to have a noticeable result **10 :** to act as evidence

tell·er *n* **1 :** NARRATOR **2 :** a person who counts votes **3 :** a bank employee who receives and pays out money

¹**tem·per** *vb* **1 :** SOFTEN **2 :** to make a substance as thick, firm, or tough as is wanted **3 :** to heat and cool a substance (as steel) until it is as hard, tough, or flexible as is wanted

²**temper** *n* **1 :** the hardness or toughness of a substance (as metal) **2 :** characteristic state of feeling **3 :** calmness of mind **4 :** an angry mood

tem·per·a·ment *n* **:** a person's attitude as it affects what he or she says or does

tem·per·a·men·tal *adj* **:** having or showing a nervous sensitive temperament — **tem·per·a·men·tal·ly** *adv*

tem·per·ance *n* **1 :** control over one's actions, thoughts, or feelings **2 :** the use of little or no alcoholic drink

tem·per·ate *adj* **1 :** keeping or held within limits **:** MILD **2 :** not drinking much liquor **3 :** showing self-control **4 :** not too hot or too cold

tem·per·a·ture *n* **1 :** degree of hotness or coldness as shown by a thermometer **2 :** level of heat above what is normal for the human body **:** FEVER

tem·pest *n* **1 :** a strong wind often accompanied by rain, hail, or snow **2 :** UPROAR

tem·pes·tu·ous *adj* **:** very stormy — **tem·pes·tu·ous·ly** *adv*

¹**tem·ple** *n* **:** a building for worship

²**temple** *n* **:** the space between the eye and forehead and the upper part of the ear

tem·po *n, pl* **tem·pi** *or* **tempos :** the rate of speed at which a musical composition is played or sung

tem·po·ral *adj* **:** of, relating to, or limited by time

tem·po·rary *adj* **:** not permanent — **tem·po·rar·i·ly** *adv*

tempt *vb* **1 :** to make someone think of doing wrong (as by promise of gain) **2 :** to risk the dangers of — **tempt·er** *n*

temp·ta·tion *n* **1 :** the act of tempting or the state of being tempted **2 :** something that tempts

¹**ten** *adj* **:** being one more than nine

²**ten** *n* **:** one more than nine **:** two times five **:** 10

te·na·cious *adj* **1 :** not easily pulled apart **2 :** PERSISTENT

te·nac·i·ty *n* **:** the quality or state of being tenacious

¹**ten·ant** *n* **1 :** a person who rents property (as a house) from the owner **2 :** OCCUPANT, DWELLER

²**tenant** *vb* **:** to hold or live in as a tenant

¹**tend** *vb* **1 :** to pay attention **2 :** to take care of **3 :** to manage the operation of

²**tend** *vb* **1 :** to move or turn in a certain direction **:** LEAD **2 :** to be likely

ten·den·cy *n, pl* **ten·den·cies 1 :** the direction or course toward something **2 :** a leaning toward a particular kind of thought or action

¹**ten·der** *adj* **1 :** not tough **2 :** DELICATE 4 **3 :** YOUTHFUL 1 **4 :** feeling or showing

love **5 :** very easily hurt — **ten•der•ly** *adv* — **ten•der•ness** *n*

[2]**tender** *vb* **1 :** to offer in payment **2 :** to present for acceptance

[3]**tender** *n* **1 :** [2]OFFER **2 :** something (as money) that may be offered in payment

[4]**tend•er** *n* **1 :** a ship used to attend other ships (as to supply food) **2 :** a boat that carries passengers or freight to a larger ship **3 :** a car attached to a locomotive for carrying fuel or water

ten•der•foot *n, pl* **ten•der•feet** *also* **ten•der•foots :** a person who is not used to a rough outdoor life

ten•der•heart•ed *adj* **:** easily affected with feelings of love, pity, or sorrow

ten•don *n* **:** a strip or band of tough white fiber connecting a muscle to another part (as a bone)

ten•dril *n* **1 :** a slender leafless winding stem by which some climbing plants fasten themselves to a support **2 :** something that winds like a plant's tendril

ten•e•ment *n* **1 :** a house used as a dwelling **2 :** APARTMENT 1 **3 :** a building divided into separate apartments for rent

ten•nis *n* **:** a game played on a level court by two or four players who use rackets to hit a ball back and forth across a low net dividing the court

ten•or *n* **1 :** the next to the lowest part in harmony having four parts **2 :** the highest male singing voice **3 :** a singer or an instrument having a tenor range or part

ten•pins *n* **:** a bowling game played with ten pins

[1]**tense** *n* **:** a form of a verb used to show the time of the action or state

[2]**tense** *adj* **tens•er; tens•est 1 :** stretched tight **2 :** feeling or showing nervous tension **3 :** marked by strain or uncertainty — **tense•ly** *adv* — **tense•ness** *n*

[3]**tense** *vb* **tensed; tens•ing :** to make or become tense

ten•sion *n* **1 :** the act of straining or stretching **:** the condition of being strained or stretched **2 :** a state of mental unrest **3 :** a state of unfriendliness

[1]**tent** *n* **:** a portable shelter (as of canvas) stretched and supported by poles

[2]**tent** *vb* **:** to live in a tent — **ten•ter** *n*

ten•ta•cle *n* **:** one of the long thin flexible structures that stick out about the head or the mouth of an animal (as an insect or fish) and are used especially for feeling or grasping

ten•ta•tive *adj* **:** not final — **ten•ta•tive•ly** *adv*

tent caterpillar *n* **:** any of several caterpillars that spin tent-like webs in which they live in groups

[1]**tenth** *adj* **:** coming right after ninth

[2]**tenth** *n* **1 :** number ten in a series **2 :** one of ten equal parts

te•pee *n* **:** a tent shaped like a cone and used as a home by some American Indians

tep•id *adj* **:** LUKEWARM 1

[1]**term** *n* **1 :** a period of time fixed especially by law or custom **2 terms** *pl* **:** conditions that limit the nature and scope of something (as a treaty or a will) **3 :** a word or expression that has an exact meaning in some uses or is limited to a subject or field **4 :** the numerator or denominator of a fraction **5 :** any one of the numbers in a series **6 terms** *pl* **:** relationship between people

[2]**term** *vb* **:** to apply a term to

[1]**ter•mi•nal** *adj* **:** of, relating to, or forming an end

[2]**terminal** *n* **1 :** a part that forms the end **:** EXTREMITY **2 :** a device at the end of a wire or on a machine for making an electrical connection **3 :** either end of a transportation line or a passenger or freight station located at it **4 :** a device (as in a computer system) used to put in, receive, and display information

ter•mi•nate *vb* **ter•mi•nat•ed; ter•mi•nat•ing :** END, CLOSE

ter•mi•na•tion *n* **1 :** the end of something **2 :** the act of ending something

ter•mi•nus *n, pl* **ter•mi•ni** *or* **ter•mi•nus•es 1 :** final goal **:** END **2 :** either end of a transportation line or travel route

ter•mite *n* **:** a chewing antlike insect of a light color that lives in large colonies and feeds on wood

tern *n* **:** any of numerous small slender sea gulls with black cap, white body, and narrow wings

[1]**ter•race** *n* **1 :** a flat roof or open platform **2 :** a level area next to a building **3 :** a raised piece of land with the top leveled **4 :** a row of houses on raised ground or a slope

[2]**terrace** *vb* **ter•raced; ter•rac•ing :** to form into a terrace or supply with terraces

ter•rain *n* **:** the features of the surface of a piece of land

ter•ra•pin *n* **:** a North American turtle that eats flesh and lives in water

ter•rar•i•um *n, pl* **ter•rar•ia** *or* **ter•rar•i•ums :** a box usually made of glass that is used for keeping and observing small animals or plants

ter•res•tri•al *adj* **1 :** of or relating to the earth or its people **2 :** living or growing on land

ter•ri•ble *adj* **1 :** causing great fear **2 :** very great in degree **:** INTENSE **3 :** very bad — **ter•ri•bly** *adv*

ter•ri•er *n* **:** any of various usually small dogs

originally used by hunters to drive animals from their holes

ter·rif·ic *adj* **1 :** causing terror **:** TERRIBLE **2 :** very unusual **:** EXTRAORDINARY **3 :** very good **:** EXCELLENT — **ter·rif·i·cal·ly** *adv*

ter·ri·fy *vb* **ter·ri·fied; ter·ri·fy·ing :** to frighten greatly

ter·ri·to·ri·al *adj* **:** of or relating to a territory

ter·ri·to·ry *n, pl* **ter·ri·to·ries 1 :** a geographical area belonging to or under the rule of a government **2 :** a part of the United States not included within any state but organized with a separate governing body **3 :** REGION 1, DISTRICT

ter·ror *n* **1 :** a state of great fear **2 :** a cause of great fear

ter·ror·ism *n* **:** the use of threat or violence especially as a means of forcing others to do what one wishes

ter·ror·ize *vb* **ter·ror·ized; ter·ror·iz·ing 1 :** to fill with terror **2 :** to use terrorism against

terse *adj* **ters·er; ters·est :** being brief and to the point **:** CONCISE — **terse·ly** *adv* — **terse·ness** *n*

[1]test *n* **1 :** a means of finding out the nature, quality, or value of something **2 :** a set of questions or problems by which a person's knowledge, intelligence, or skills are measured

[2]test *vb* **:** to put to a test **:** EXAMINE

tes·ta·ment *n* **1 :** either of two main parts (**Old Testament** and **New Testament**) of the Bible **2 :** [2]WILL 3

tes·ti·fy *vb* **tes·ti·fied; tes·ti·fy·ing :** to make a formal statement of what one swears is true

tes·ti·mo·ny *n, pl* **tes·ti·mo·nies :** a statement made by a witness under oath especially in a court

tes·tis *n, pl* **tes·tes :** a male reproductive gland

test tube *n* **:** a plain tube of thin glass closed at one end

tet·a·nus *n* **:** a dangerous disease in which spasms of the muscles occur often with locking of the jaws and which is caused by poison from a germ that enters wounds and grows in damaged tissue

[1]teth·er *n* **:** a line by which an animal is fastened so as to limit where it can go

[2]tether *vb* **:** to fasten by a tether

text *n* **1 :** the actual words of an author's work **2 :** the main body of printed or written matter on a page **3 :** a passage from the Bible chosen as the subject of a sermon **4 :** TEXTBOOK

text·book *n* **:** a book that presents the important information about a subject and is used as a basis of instruction

tex·tile *n* **:** a woven or knit cloth

tex·ture *n* **:** the structure, feel, and appearance of something (as cloth)

-th *or* **-eth** *adj suffix* — used to form numbers that show the place of something in a series

than *conj* **:** when compared to the way in which, the extent to which, or the degree to which

thank *vb* **1 :** to express gratitude to **2 :** to hold responsible

thank·ful *adj* **:** feeling or showing thanks **:** GRATEFUL — **thank·ful·ly** *adv* — **thank·ful·ness** *n*

thank·less *adj* **1 :** UNGRATEFUL **2 :** not appreciated

thanks *n pl* **1 :** GRATITUDE **2 :** an expression of gratitude (as for something received) — **thanks to 1 :** with the help of **2 :** BECAUSE OF

thanks·giv·ing *n* **1 :** the act of giving thanks **2 :** a prayer expressing gratitude **3** *cap* **:** THANKSGIVING DAY

Thanksgiving Day *n* **:** the fourth Thursday in November observed as a legal holiday for public thanksgiving to God

[1]that *pron, pl* **those 1 :** the one seen, mentioned, or understood **2 :** the one farther away **3 :** the one **:** the kind

[2]that *conj* **1 :** the following, namely **2 :** which is, namely **3 :** [2]SO 1 **4 :** as to result in the following, namely **5 :** BECAUSE

[3]that *adj, pl* **those 1 :** being the one mentioned, indicated, or understood **2 :** being the one farther away

[4]that *pron* **1 :** WHO 3, WHOM, [2]WHICH 2 **2 :** in, on, or at which

[5]that *adv* **:** to such an extent or degree

[1]thatch *vb* **:** to cover with thatch

[2]thatch *n* **:** a plant material (as straw) for use as roofing

[1]thaw *vb* **1 :** to melt or cause to melt **2 :** to grow less unfriendly or quiet in manner

[2]thaw *n* **1 :** the action, fact, or process of thawing **2 :** a period of weather warm enough to thaw ice and snow

[1]the *definite article* **1 :** that or those mentioned, seen, or clearly understood **2 :** that or those near in space, time, or thought **3 :** [1]EACH **4 :** that or those considered best, most typical, or most worth singling out **5 :** any one typical of or standing for the entire class named **6 :** all those that are

[2]the *adv* **1 :** than before **2 :** to what extent **3 :** to that extent

the·ater *or* **the·atre** *n* **1 :** a building in which plays or motion pictures are presented **2 :** a place like a theater in form or use **3 :** a place or area where some impor-

tant action is carried on **4 :** plays or the performance of plays
the·at·ri·cal *adj* **:** of or relating to the theater or the presentation of plays
thee *pron, archaic objective case of* THOU
theft *n* **:** the act of stealing
their *adj* **:** of or relating to them or themselves especially as owners or as agents or objects of an action
theirs *pron* **:** that which belongs to them
them *pron objective case of* THEY
theme *n* **1 :** a subject on which one writes or speaks **2 :** a written exercise **3 :** a main melody in a piece of music
them·selves *pron* **:** their own selves
¹then *adv* **1 :** at that time **2 :** soon after that **:** NEXT **3 :** in addition **:** BESIDES **4 :** in that case **5 :** as an expected result
²then *n* **:** that time
³then *adj* **:** existing or acting at that time
thence *adv* **1 :** from that place **2 :** from that fact
thence·forth *adv* **:** from that time on
thence·for·ward *adv* **:** onward from that place or time
the·ol·o·gy *n, pl* **the·ol·o·gies :** the study and explanation of religious faith, practice, and experience
the·o·ry *n, pl* **the·o·ries 1 :** the general rules followed in a science or an art **2 :** a general rule offered to explain experiences or facts **3 :** an idea used for discussion or as a starting point for an investigation
ther·a·peu·tic *adj* **:** MEDICINAL
ther·a·pist *n* **:** a specialist in therapy and especially in methods of treatment other than drugs and surgery
ther·a·py *n, pl* **ther·a·pies :** treatment of an abnormal state in the body or mind
¹there *adv* **1 :** in or at that place **2 :** to or into that place **3 :** in that situation or way
²there *pron* — used to introduce a sentence in which the subject comes after the verb
³there *n* **:** that place
there·abouts *or* **there·about** *adv* **1 :** near that place or time **2 :** near that number, degree, or amount
there·af·ter *adv* **:** after that
there·at *adv* **1 :** at that place **2 :** because of that
there·by *adv* **1 :** by that **2 :** related to that
there·fore *adv* **:** for that reason
there·in *adv* **:** in or into that place, time, or thing
there·of *adv* **1 :** of that or it **2 :** from that cause
there·on *adv* **:** on that
there·to *adv* **:** to that
there·up·on *adv* **1 :** on that thing **2 :** for that reason **3 :** immediately after that **:** at once
there·with *adv* **:** with that
ther·mal *adj* **:** of, relating to, caused by, or saving heat
ther·mom·e·ter *n* **:** an instrument for measuring temperature usually in the form of a glass tube with mercury or alcohol sealed inside and with a scale marked in degrees on the outside
ther·mos *n* **:** a container (as a bottle or jar) that has a vacuum between an inner and an outer wall and is used to keep liquids hot or cold for several hours
ther·mo·stat *n* **:** a device that automatically controls temperature
the·sau·rus *n, pl* **the·sau·ri** *or* **the·sau·rus·es :** a book of words and their synonyms
these *pl of* THIS
the·sis *n, pl* **the·ses 1 :** a statement that a person wants to discuss or prove **2 :** an essay presenting results of original research
they *pron* **:** those individuals **:** those ones
they'd : they had **:** they would
they'll : they shall **:** they will
they're : they are
they've : they have
thi·a·min *n* **:** a member of the vitamin B complex whose lack causes beriberi
¹thick *adj* **1 :** having great size from one surface to its opposite **2 :** heavily built **3 :** closely packed together **4 :** occurring in large numbers **:** NUMEROUS **5 :** not flowing easily **6 :** having haze, fog, or mist **7 :** measuring a certain amount in the smallest of three dimensions **8 :** not clearly spoken **9 :** STUPID 1 — **thick·ly** *adv*
²thick *n* **1 :** the most crowded or active part **2 :** the part of greatest thickness
thick·en *vb* **:** to make or become thick — **thick·en·er** *n*
thick·et *n* **:** a thick usually small patch of bushes or low trees
thick·ness *n* **1 :** the quality or state of being thick **2 :** the smallest of three dimensions
thick·set *adj* **1 :** closely placed or planted **2 :** STOCKY
thief *n, pl* **thieves :** a person who steals **:** ROBBER
thieve *vb* **thieved; thiev·ing :** ¹STEAL 2, ROB
thiev·ery *n, pl* **thiev·er·ies :** THEFT
thiev·ish *adj* **1 :** likely to steal **2 :** of, relating to, or like a thief
thigh *n* **:** the part of a leg between the knee and the main part of the body
thim·ble *n* **:** a cap or cover used in sewing to protect the finger that pushes the needle
¹thin *adj* **thin·ner; thin·nest 1 :** having little size from one surface to its opposite **:** not thick **2 :** having the parts not close to-

DICTIONARY

gether **3 :** having little body fat **4 :** having less than the usual number **5 :** not very convincing **6 :** somewhat weak or shrill — **thin·ly** *adv* — **thin·ness** *n*

2thin *vb* **thinned; thin·ning :** to make or become thin

thine *pron, singular, archaic* **:** YOURS

thing *n* **1 :** AFFAIR 2, MATTER **2 things** *pl* **:** state of affairs **3 :** EVENT 1 **4 :** 1DEED 1, ACHIEVEMENT **5 :** something that exists and can be talked about **6 things** *pl* **:** personal possessions **7 :** a piece of clothing **8 :** 1DETAIL 2 **9 :** what is needed or wanted **10 :** an action or interest that one very much enjoys

think *vb* **thought; think·ing 1 :** to form or have in the mind **2 :** to have as an opinion or belief **3 :** REMEMBER 1 **4 :** to use the power of reason **5 :** to invent something by thinking **6 :** to hold a strong feeling **7 :** to care about — **think·er** *n*

thin·ner *n* **:** a liquid used to thin paint

1third *adj* **:** coming right after second

2third *n* **1 :** number three in a series **2 :** one of three equal parts

1thirst *n* **1 :** a feeling of dryness in the mouth and throat that accompanies a need for liquids **2 :** the bodily condition that produces thirst **3 :** a strong desire

2thirst *vb* **1 :** to feel thirsty **2 :** to have a strong desire

thirsty *adj* **thirst·i·er; thirst·i·est 1 :** feeling thirst **2 :** needing moisture **3 :** having a strong desire **:** EAGER — **thirst·i·ly** *adv*

1thir·teen *adj* **:** being one more than twelve

2thirteen *n* **:** one more than twelve **:** 13

1thir·teenth *adj* **:** coming right after twelfth

2thirteenth *n* **:** number thirteen in a series

1thir·ti·eth *adj* **:** coming right after twenty-ninth

2thirtieth *n* **:** number thirty in a series

1thir·ty *adj* **:** being three times ten

2thirty *n* **:** three times ten **:** 30

1this *pron, pl* **these 1 :** the one close or closest in time or space **2 :** what is in the present or is being seen or talked about

2this *adj, pl* **these 1 :** being the one present, near, or just mentioned **2 :** being the one nearer or last mentioned

3this *adv* **:** to the degree suggested by something in the present situation

this·tle *n* **:** a prickly plant related to the daisies that has usually purplish often showy heads of mostly tubular flowers

thith·er *adv* **:** to that place **:** THERE

thong *n* **:** a strip of leather used especially for fastening something

tho·rax *n, pl* **tho·rax·es** *or* **tho·ra·ces 1 :** the part of the body of a mammal that lies between the neck and the abdomen and contains the heart and lungs **2 :** the middle of the three main divisions of the body of an insect

thorn *n* **1 :** a woody plant (as hawthorn) with sharp briers, prickles, or spines **2 :** a short hard sharp-pointed leafless branch on a woody plant

thorny *adj* **thorn·i·er; thorn·i·est 1 :** full of or covered with thorns **2 :** full of difficulties

thor·ough *adj* **1 :** being such to the fullest degree **:** COMPLETE **2 :** careful about little things — **thor·ough·ly** *adv* — **thor·ough·ness** *n*

1thor·ough·bred *adj* **1 :** bred from the best blood through a long line **2** *cap* **:** of, relating to, or being a member of the Thoroughbred breed of horses

2thoroughbred *n* **1** *cap* **:** any of an English breed of light speedy horses kept mainly for racing **2 :** a purebred or pedigreed animal **3 :** a very fine person

thor·ough·fare *n* **1 :** a street or road open at both ends **2 :** a main road

thor·ough·go·ing *adj* **:** THOROUGH 1

those *pl of* THAT

thou *pron, singular, archaic* **:** YOU

1though *conj* **:** ALTHOUGH

2though *adv* **:** HOWEVER 3, NEVERTHELESS

1thought *past of* THINK

2thought *n* **1 :** the act or process of thinking and especially of trying to decide about something **2 :** power of reasoning and judging **3 :** power of imagining **4 :** something (as an idea or fancy) formed in the mind

thought·ful *adj* **1 :** deep in thought **2 :** showing careful thinking **3 :** considerate of others — **thought·ful·ly** *adv* — **thought·ful·ness** *n*

thought·less *adj* **1 :** not careful and alert **2 :** NEGLIGENT **3 :** not considerate of others — **thought·less·ly** *adv* — **thought·less·ness** *n*

1thou·sand *n* **1 :** ten times one hundred **:** 1000 **2 :** a very large number

2thousand *adj* **:** being 1000

1thou·sandth *adj* **:** coming right after 999th

2thousandth *n* **:** number 1000 in a series

thrash *vb* **1 :** THRESH 1 **2 :** to beat very hard **3 :** to move about violently

1thrash·er *n* **:** one that thrashes

2thrasher *n* **:** an American bird (as the common reddish brown **brown thrasher**) related to the thrushes and noted for its song

1thread *n* **1 :** a thin fine cord formed by spinning and twisting short fibers into a continuous strand **2 :** something suggesting a thread **3 :** the ridge or groove that winds around a screw **4 :** a line of reasoning or train of thought that connects the parts of an argument or story — **thread·like** *adj*

2thread *vb* **1 :** to put a thread in working position (as in a needle) **2 :** to pass through like a thread **3 :** to make one's way through or between **4 :** to put together on a thread **:** STRING

thread·bare *adj* **1 :** worn so much that the thread shows **:** SHABBY **2 :** TRITE

threat *n* **1 :** a showing of an intention to do harm **2 :** something that threatens

threat·en *vb* **1 :** to make threats against **2 :** to give warning of by a threat or sign — **threat·en·ing·ly** *adv*

1three *adj* **:** being one more than two

2three *n* **1 :** one more than two **:** 3 **2 :** the third in a set or series

3–D *adj* **:** THREE-DIMENSIONAL 2

three–dimensional *adj* **1 :** of, relating to, or having the three dimensions of length, width, and height **2 :** giving the appearance of depth or varying distances

three·fold *adj* **:** being three times as great or as many

three·score *adj* **:** SIXTY

thresh *vb* **1 :** to separate (as grain from straw) by beating **2 :** THRASH 3

thresh·er *n* **:** THRESHING MACHINE

threshing machine *n* **:** a machine used in harvesting to separate grain from straw

thresh·old *n* **1 :** the sill of a door **2 :** a point or place of beginning or entering

threw *past of* THROW

thrice *adv* **:** three times

thrift *n* **:** careful management especially of money

thrifty *adj* **thrift·i·er; thrift·i·est** **1 :** tending to save money **2 :** doing well in health and growth

1thrill *vb* **1 :** to have or cause to have a sudden feeling of excitement or pleasure **2 :** 1TREMBLE 2, VIBRATE — **thrill·er** *n*

2thrill *n* **1 :** a feeling of being thrilled **2 :** VIBRATION 3

thrive *vb* **throve** *or* **thrived; thriv·en** *also* **thrived; thriv·ing** **1 :** to grow very well **:** FLOURISH **2 :** to gain in wealth or possessions

throat *n* **1 :** the part of the neck in front of the backbone **2 :** the passage from the mouth to the stomach and lungs **3 :** something like the throat especially in being an entrance or a narrowed part

1throb *vb* **throbbed; throb·bing** **1 :** to beat hard or fast **2 :** to beat or rotate in a normal way

2throb *n* **:** 2BEAT 2, PULSE

throne *n* **1 :** the chair of state especially of a monarch or bishop **2 :** royal power and dignity

1throng *n* **:** a large group of assembled persons **:** CROWD

2throng *vb* **:** 1CROWD 4

1throt·tle *vb* **throt·tled; throt·tling** **1 :** STRANGLE 1, CHOKE **2 :** to reduce the speed of (an engine) by closing the throttle

2throttle *n* **1 :** a valve for regulating the flow of steam or fuel in an engine **2 :** a lever that controls the throttle valve

1through *prep* **1 :** into at one side and out at the other side of **2 :** by way of **3 :** AMONG 1 **4 :** by means of **5 :** over the whole of **6 :** during the whole of

2through *adv* **1 :** from one end or side to the other **2 :** from beginning to end **3 :** to completion **4 :** in or to every part **5 :** into the open

3through *adj* **1 :** allowing free or continuous passage **:** DIRECT **2 :** going from point of origin to destination without changes or transfers **3 :** coming from and going to points outside a local zone **4 :** having reached an end

1through·out *adv* **1 :** EVERYWHERE **2 :** from beginning to end

2throughout *prep* **1 :** in or to every part of **2 :** during the whole period of

throughway *variant of* THRUWAY

throve *past of* THRIVE

1throw *vb* **threw; thrown; throw·ing** **1 :** to send through the air with a quick forward motion of the arm **2 :** to send through the air in any way **3 :** to cause to fall **4 :** to put suddenly in a certain position or condition **5 :** to put on or take off in a hurry **6 :** to move quickly **7 :** to move (as a switch) to an open or closed position **8 :** to give by way of entertainment — **throw·er** *n*

2throw *n* **1 :** an act of throwing **2 :** the distance something is or may be thrown

throw up *vb* **:** 2VOMIT

thrum *vb* **thrummed; thrum·ming :** to play a stringed instrument idly **:** STRUM

thrush *n* **:** any of numerous songbirds that eat insects and are usually of a plain color but sometimes spotted below

1thrust *vb* **thrust; thrust·ing** **1 :** to push or drive with force **:** SHOVE **2 :** PIERCE 1, STAB **3 :** to push forth **:** EXTEND **4 :** to press the acceptance of on someone

2thrust *n* **1 :** a lunge with a pointed weapon **2 :** a military attack **3 :** a forward or upward push

thru·way *or* **through·way** *n* **:** EXPRESSWAY

1thud *n* **:** a dull sound **:** THUMP

2thud *vb* **thud·ded; thud·ding :** to move or strike so as to make a dull sound

thug *n* **:** RUFFIAN

1thumb *n* **1 :** the short thick finger next to

the forefinger **2 :** the part of a glove covering the thumb

²thumb *vb* **1 :** to turn the pages of quickly with the thumb **2 :** to seek or get (a ride) in a passing automobile by signaling with the thumb

thumb·tack *n* **:** a tack with a broad flat head for pressing into a board or wall with the thumb

¹thump *vb* **1 :** to strike or beat with something thick or heavy so as to cause a dull sound **2 :** ³POUND 2, KNOCK

²thump *n* **1 :** a blow with something blunt or heavy **2 :** the sound made by a thump

¹thun·der *n* **1 :** the loud sound that follows a flash of lightning **2 :** a noise like thunder

²thunder *vb* **1 :** to produce thunder **2 :** to make a sound like thunder **3 :** ¹ROAR 1, SHOUT

thun·der·bolt *n* **:** a flash of lightning and the thunder that follows it

thun·der·cloud *n* **:** a dark storm cloud that produces lightning and thunder

thun·der·head *n* **:** a rounded mass of dark cloud with white edges often appearing before a thunderstorm

thun·der·show·er *n* **:** a shower with thunder and lightning

thun·der·storm *n* **:** a storm with thunder and lightning

thun·der·struck *adj* **:** stunned as if struck by a thunderbolt

Thurs·day *n* **:** the fifth day of the week

thus *adv* **1 :** in this or that way **2 :** to this degree or extent **:** SO **3 :** because of this or that **:** THEREFORE

thwart *vb* **:** to oppose successfully

thy *adj, singular, archaic* **:** YOUR

thyme *n* **:** a mint with tiny fragrant leaves used to season foods or formerly in medicine

thy·roid *n* **:** an endocrine gland at the base of the neck that produces a secretion which affects growth, development, and metabolism

thy·self *pron, archaic* **:** YOURSELF

ti *n* **:** the seventh note of the musical scale

¹tick *n* **1 :** an animal with eight legs that is related to the spiders and attaches itself to humans and animals from which it sucks blood **2 :** a wingless fly that sucks blood from sheep

²tick *n* **1 :** a light rhythmic tap or beat (as of a clock) **2 :** a small mark used chiefly to draw attention to something or to check an item on a list

³tick *vb* **1 :** to make a tick or a series of ticks **2 :** to mark, count, or announce by or as if by ticks **3 :** OPERATE 1, RUN **4 :** ²CHECK 4

¹tick·et *n* **1 :** a summons or warning issued to a person who breaks a traffic law **2 :** a document or token showing that a fare or an admission fee has been paid **3 :** a list of candidates for nomination or election **4 :** a slip or card recording a sale or giving information

²ticket *vb* **1 :** to attach a ticket to **:** LABEL **2 :** to give a traffic ticket to

ticket office *n* **:** an office (as of a transportation company or a theater) where tickets are sold and reservations made

¹tick·le *vb* **tick·led; tick·ling 1 :** to have a tingling or prickling sensation **2 :** to excite or stir up agreeably **3 :** AMUSE 2 **4 :** to touch (a body part) lightly so as to excite the surface nerves and cause uneasiness, laughter, or jerky movements

²tickle *n* **:** a tickling sensation

tick·lish *adj* **1 :** sensitive to tickling **2 :** calling for careful handling

tid·al *adj* **:** of or relating to tides **:** flowing and ebbing like tides

tidal wave *n* **1 :** a great wave of the sea that sometimes follows an earthquake **2 :** an unusual rise of water along a shore due to strong winds

tid·bit *n* **1 :** a small tasty piece of food **2 :** a pleasing bit (as of news)

¹tide *n* **1 :** the rising and falling of the surface of the ocean caused twice daily by the attraction of the sun and the moon **2 :** something that rises and falls like the tides of the sea

²tide *vb* **tid·ed; tid·ing :** to help to overcome or put up with a difficulty

tid·ings *n pl* **:** NEWS 3

¹ti·dy *adj* **ti·di·er; ti·di·est 1 :** well ordered and cared for **:** NEAT **2 :** LARGE, SUBSTANTIAL — **ti·di·ness** *n*

²tidy *vb* **ti·died; ti·dy·ing 1 :** to put in order **2 :** to make things tidy

¹tie *n* **1 :** a line, ribbon, or cord used for fastening, joining, or closing **2 :** a part (as a beam or rod) holding two pieces together **3 :** one of the cross supports to which railroad rails are fastened **4 :** a connecting link **:** BOND **5 :** an equality in number (as of votes or scores) **6 :** a contest that ends with an equal score **7 :** NECKTIE

²tie *vb* **tied; ty·ing** *or* **tie·ing 1 :** to fasten, attach, or close by means of a tie **2 :** to form a knot or bow in **3 :** to bring together firmly **:** UNITE **4 :** to hold back from freedom of action **5 :** to make or have an equal score with in a contest

tier *n* **:** a row, rank, or layer usually arranged in a series one above the other

ti·ger *n* **:** a large Asian flesh-eating animal of the cat family that is light brown with black stripes

¹tight *adj* **1 :** so close in structure as not to

allow a liquid or gas to pass through **2** : fixed or held very firmly in place **3** : firmly stretched or drawn : TAUT **4** : fitting too closely **5** : difficult to get through or out of **6** : firm in control **7** : STINGY 1 **8** : very closely packed or compressed **9** : low in supply : SCARCE — **tight·ly** *adv* — **tight·ness** *n*

²tight *adv* **1** : in a firm, secure, or close manner **2** : in a deep and uninterrupted manner : SOUNDLY

tight·en *vb* : to make or become tight

tight·rope *n* : a rope or wire stretched tight on which an acrobat performs

tights *n pl* : a garment closely fitted to the body and covering it usually from the waist down

tight squeeze *n* : a difficult situation that one can barely get through

tight·wad *n* : a stingy person

ti·gress *n* : a female tiger

til·de *n* : a mark ˜ placed especially over the letter *n* (as in Spanish *señor*) to indicate a sound that is approximately \nyə\

¹tile *n* **1** : a thin piece of material (as plastic, stone, concrete, or rubber) used especially for roofs, walls, floors, or drains **2** : a pipe of earthenware used for a drain

²tile *vb* **tiled; til·ing** : to cover with tiles

¹till *prep or conj* : UNTIL

²till *vb* : to work by plowing, sowing, and raising crops on

³till *n* : a drawer for money

till·age *n* : cultivated land

til·ler *n* : a lever used to turn the rudder of a boat from side to side

¹tilt *n* **1** : a contest on horseback in which two opponents charging with lances try to unhorse one another : ²JOUST **2** : ¹SPEED 2 **3** : ¹SLANT

²tilt *vb* **1** : to move or shift so as to slant or tip **2** : to take part in a contest with lances : ¹JOUST

tim·ber *n* **1** : wood suitable for building or for carpentry **2** : a large squared piece of wood ready for use or forming part of a structure

tim·ber·land *n* : wooded land especially as a source of timber

tim·ber·line *n* : the upper limit beyond which trees do not grow (as on mountains)

¹time *n* **1** : a period during which an action, process, or condition exists or continues **2** : part of the day when one is free to do as one pleases **3** : a point or period when something occurs : OCCASION **4** : a set or usual moment or hour for something to occur **5** : an historical period : AGE **6** : conditions of a period — usually used in pl. **7** : rate of speed : TEMPO **8** : RHYTHM 2 **9** : a moment, hour, day, or year as shown by a clock or calendar **10** : a system of determining time **11** : one of a series of repeated instances or actions **12 times** *pl* : multiplied intances **13** : a person's experience during a certain period — **at times** : SOMETIMES — **for the time being** : for the present — **from time to time** : once in a while — **in time 1** : soon enough **2** : as time goes by **3** : at the correct speed in music — **time after time** : over and over again — **time and again** : over and over again

²time *vb* **timed; tim·ing 1** : to arrange or set the time or rate at which something happens **2** : to measure or record the time, length of time, or rate of — **tim·er** *n*

time·keep·er *n* **1** : a clerk who keeps records of the time worked by employees **2** : an official who keeps track of the playing time in a sports contest

time·ly *adj* **time·li·er; time·li·est 1** : coming early or at the right time **2** : especially suitable to the time

time·piece *n* : a device (as a clock or watch) to measure the passing of time

times *prep* : multiplied by

time·ta·ble *n* : a table telling when something (as a bus or train) leaves or arrives

tim·id *adj* : feeling or showing a lack of courage or self-confidence : SHY — **tim·id·ly** *adv* — **tim·id·ness** *n*

tim·o·rous *adj* : easily frightened : FEARFUL — **tim·o·rous·ly** *adv*

tin *n* **1** : a soft bluish white metallic chemical element used chiefly in combination with other metals or as a coating to protect other metals **2** : something (as a can or sheet) made from tinplate

tin·der *n* : material that burns easily and can be used as kindling

tin·foil *n* : a thin metal sheeting usually of aluminum or an alloy of tin and lead

¹tin·gle *vb* **tin·gled; tin·gling** : to feel or cause a prickling or thrilling sensation

²tingle *n* : a tingling sensation or condition

tin·ker *vb* : to repair or adjust something in an unskilled or experimental manner

¹tin·kle *vb* **tin·kled; tin·kling** : to make or cause to make a series of short high ringing or clinking sounds

²tinkle *n* : a sound of tinkling

tin·plate *n* : thin steel sheets covered with tin

tin·sel *n* **1** : a thread, strip, or sheet of metal, paper, or plastic used to produce a glittering effect **2** : something that seems attractive but is of little worth

tin·smith *n* : a worker in tin or sometimes other metals

¹tint *n* **1** : a slight or pale coloring **2** : a shade of a color

[2]**tint** *vb* **:** to give a tint to **:** COLOR
tin·ware *n* **:** objects made of tinplate
ti·ny *adj* **ti·ni·er; ti·ni·est :** very small
[1]**tip** *vb* **tipped; tip·ping 1 :** to turn over **2 :** to bend from a straight position **:** SLANT **3 :** to raise and tilt forward
[2]**tip** *vb* **tipped; tip·ping 1 :** to attach an end or point to **2 :** to cover or decorate the tip of
[3]**tip** *n* **1 :** the usually pointed end of something **2 :** a small piece or part serving as an end, cap, or point
[4]**tip** *n* **:** a piece of useful or secret information
[5]**tip** *vb* **tipped; tip·ping :** to give a small sum of money for a service
[6]**tip** *n* **:** a small sum of money given for a service
[1]**tip·toe** *n* **:** the position of being balanced on the balls of the feet and toes with the heels raised — usually used with *on*
[2]**tiptoe** *adv or adj* **:** on or as if on tiptoe
[3]**tiptoe** *vb* **tip·toed; tip·toe·ing :** to walk tiptoe
[1]**tip·top** *n* **:** the highest point
[2]**tiptop** *adj* **:** EXCELLENT, FIRST-RATE
[1]**tire** *vb* **tired; tir·ing 1 :** to make or become weary **2 :** to wear out the patience or attention of **:** BORE
[2]**tire** *n* **1 :** a metal band that forms the tread of a wheel **2 :** a rubber cushion that usually contains compressed air and fits around a wheel (as of an automobile)
tired *adj* **:** [1]WEARY 1
tire·less *adj* **:** able to work a long time without becoming tired — **tire·less·ly** *adv* — **tire·less·ness** *n*
tire·some *adj* **:** likely to tire one because of length or dullness **:** BORING — **tire·some·ly** *adv*
'tis : it is
tis·sue *n* **1 :** a fine lightweight fabric **2 :** a piece of soft absorbent paper **3 :** a mass or layer of cells usually of one kind that together with their supporting structures form a basic structural material of an animal or plant body
tit *n* **:** NIPPLE 1, TEAT
ti·tan·ic *adj* **:** enormous in size, force, or power **:** GIGANTIC
ti·tle *n* **1 :** a legal right to the ownership of property **2 :** the name given to something (as a book, song, or job) to identify or describe it **3 :** a word or group of words attached to a person's name to show an honor, rank, or office **4 :** CHAMPIONSHIP
tit·mouse *n, pl* **tit·mice :** any of several small birds that have long tails and are related to the nuthatches
TNT *n* **:** an explosive used in artillery shells and bombs and in blasting
[1]**to** *prep* **1 :** in the direction of **2 :** AGAINST 3, ON **3 :** as far as **4 :** so as to become or bring about **5 :** [2]BEFORE 3 **6 :** [1]UNTIL **7 :** fitting or being a part of **8 :** along with **9 :** in relation to or comparison with **10 :** in agreement with **11 :** within the limits of **12 :** contained, occurring, or included in **13 :** TOWARD 3 **14** — used to show the one or ones that an action is directed toward **15 :** for no one except **16 :** into the action of **17** — used to mark an infinitive
[2]**to** *adv* **1 :** in a direction toward **2 :** to a conscious state
toad *n* **:** a tailless leaping amphibian that has rough skin and usually lives on land
toad·stool *n* **:** a mushroom especially when poisonous or unfit for food
[1]**toast** *vb* **1 :** to make (as bread) crisp, hot, and brown by heat **2 :** to warm completely
[2]**toast** *n* **1 :** sliced toasted bread **2 :** a person in whose honor other people drink **3 :** a highly admired person **4 :** an act of drinking in honor of a person
[3]**toast** *vb* **:** to suggest or drink to as a toast
toast·er *n* **:** an electrical appliance for toasting
to·bac·co *n, pl* **to·bac·cos :** a tall plant related to the tomato and potato that has pink or white flowers and broad sticky leaves which are dried and prepared for use in smoking or chewing or as snuff
[1]**to·bog·gan** *n* **:** a long light sled made without runners and curved up at the front
[2]**toboggan** *vb* **:** to slide on a toboggan
[1]**to·day** *adv* **1 :** on or for this day **2 :** at the present time
[2]**today** *n* **:** the present day, time, or age
tod·dler *n* **:** a small child
[1]**toe** *n* **1 :** one of the separate parts of the front end of a foot **2 :** the front end or part of a foot or hoof — **toed** *adj*
[2]**toe** *vb* **toed; toe·ing :** to touch, reach, or kick with the toes
toe·nail *n* **:** the hard covering at the end of a toe
to·ga *n* **:** the loose outer garment worn in public by citizens of ancient Rome
to·geth·er *adv* **1 :** in or into one group, body, or place **2 :** in touch or in partnership with **3 :** at one time **4 :** one after the other **:** in order **5 :** in or by combined effort **6 :** in or into agreement **7 :** considered as a whole
[1]**toil** *n* **:** long hard labor
[2]**toil** *vb* **1 :** to work hard and long **2 :** to go on with effort
toi·let *n* **1 :** the act or process of dressing and making oneself neat **2 :** BATHROOM **3 :** a device for removing body wastes consisting essentially of a bowl that is flushed with water

to·ken *n* **1 :** an outer sign **:** PROOF **2 :** an object used to suggest something that cannot be pictured **3 :** SOUVENIR **4 :** INDICATION 2 **5 :** a piece like a coin that has a special use

told *past of* TELL

tol·er·a·ble *adj* **1 :** capable of being put up with **2 :** fairly good — **tol·er·a·bly** *adv*

tol·er·ance *n* **1 :** ability to put up with something harmful or bad **2 :** sympathy for or acceptance of feelings or habits which are different from one's own

tol·er·ant *adj* **:** showing tolerance — **tol·er·ant·ly** *adv*

tol·er·ate *vb* **tol·er·at·ed; tol·er·at·ing 1 :** to allow something to be or to be done without making a move to stop it **2 :** to stand the action of

1toll *n* **1 :** a tax paid for a privilege (as the use of a highway or bridge) **2 :** a charge paid for a service **3 :** the cost in life or health

2toll *vb* **1 :** to announce or call by the sounding of a bell **2 :** to sound with slow strokes

3toll *n* **:** the sound of a bell ringing slowly

1tom·a·hawk *n* **:** a light ax used as a weapon by North American Indians

2tomahawk *vb* **:** to cut, strike, or kill with a tomahawk

to·ma·to *n, pl* **to·ma·toes :** a red or yellow juicy fruit that is used as a vegetable or in salads and is produced by a hairy plant related to the potato

tomb *n* **1 :** 1GRAVE **2 :** a house or burial chamber for dead people

tom·boy *n* **:** a girl who enjoys things that some people think are more suited to boys

tomb·stone *n* **:** GRAVESTONE

tom·cat *n* **:** a male cat

1to·mor·row *adv* **:** on or for the day after today

2tomorrow *n* **:** the day after today

tom–tom *n* **1 :** a drum (as a traditional Asian, African, or American Indian drum) that is beaten with the hands **2 :** a deep drum with a low hollow tone that is usually played with soft mallets or drumsticks and is often part of a drum set in a band

ton *n* **:** a measure of weight equal either to 2000 pounds (about 907 kilograms) (**short ton**) or 2240 pounds (about 1016 kilograms) (**long ton**) with the short ton being more frequently used in the United States and Canada

1tone *n* **1 :** quality of spoken or musical sound **2 :** a sound on one pitch **3 :** an individual way of speaking or writing **4 :** a shade of color **5 :** a color that changes another **6 :** a healthy state of the body or any of its parts **7 :** common character or quality

2tone *vb* **toned; ton·ing 1 :** to give tone to **:** STRENGTHEN **2 :** to soften or blend in color, appearance, or sound

tongs *n pl* **:** a device for taking hold of something that consists usually of two movable pieces joined at one end

tongue *n* **1 :** an organ of the mouth used in tasting, in taking and swallowing food, and by human beings in speaking **2 :** the power of communication **:** SPEECH **3 :** LANGUAGE 1 **4 :** something like an animal's tongue in being long and fastened at one end

tongue–tied *adj* **:** unable to speak clearly or freely (as from shyness)

1ton·ic *adj* **:** making (as the mind or body) stronger or healthier

2tonic *n* **1 :** a tonic medicine **2 :** the first note of a scale

1to·night *adv* **:** on this present night or the night following this present day

2tonight *n* **:** the present or the coming night

ton·nage *n* **1 :** a tax on ships based on tons carried **2 :** ships in terms of the total number of tons that are or can be carried **3 :** total weight in tons shipped, carried, or mined

ton·sil *n* **:** either of a pair of masses of spongy tissue at the back of the mouth

ton·sil·li·tis *n* **:** a sore reddened state of the tonsils

too *adv* **1 :** in addition **:** ALSO **2 :** to a greater than wanted or needed degree **3 :** 2VERY 1

took *past of* TAKE

1tool *n* **1 :** an instrument (as a saw, file, knife, or wrench) used or worked by hand or machine **2 :** something that helps to gain an end **3 :** a person used by another **:** DUPE

2tool *vb* **1 :** to shape, form, or finish with a tool **2 :** to equip a plant or industry with machines and tools for production

tool·box *n* **:** a box for storing or carrying tools

tool·shed *n* **:** a small building for storing tools

1toot *vb* **1 :** to sound a short blast **2 :** to blow or sound an instrument (as a horn) especially in short blasts

2toot *n* **:** a short blast (as on a horn)

tooth *n, pl* **teeth 1 :** one of the hard bony structures set in sockets on the jaws of most vertebrates and used in taking hold of and chewing food and in fighting **2 :** something like or suggesting an animal's tooth in shape, arrangement, or action **3 :** one of the projections around the rim of a wheel that fit between the projections on another part causing the wheel or the other part to move along — **tooth·less** *adj*

tooth·ache *n* **:** pain in or near a tooth

tooth·brush *n* **:** a brush for cleaning the teeth — **tooth·brush·ing** *n*

toothed *adj* **1 :** having teeth or such or so many teeth **2 :** JAGGED

tooth·paste *n* **:** a paste for cleaning the teeth

tooth·pick *n* **:** a pointed instrument for removing substances caught between the teeth

¹top *n* **1 :** the highest point, level, or part of something **2 :** the upper end, edge, or surface **3 :** the stalk and leaves of a plant and especially of one with roots that are used for food **4 :** an upper piece, lid, or covering **5 :** the highest position

²top *vb* **topped; top·ping 1 :** to remove or cut the top of **2 :** to cover with a top or on the top **3 :** to be better than **4 :** to go over the top of

³top *adj* **:** of, relating to, or at the top

⁴top *n* **:** a child's toy with a tapering point on which it can be made to spin

to·paz *n* **:** a mineral that when occurring as perfect yellow crystals is valued as a gem

top·coat *n* **:** a lightweight overcoat

top·ic *n* **1 :** a heading in an outline of a subject or explanation **2 :** the subject or a section of the subject of a speech or writing

topic sentence *n* **:** a sentence that states the main thought of a paragraph

top·knot *n* **:** a tuft of feathers or hair on the top of the head

top·mast *n* **:** the second mast above a ship's deck

top·most *adj* **:** highest of all

top·ple *vb* **top·pled; top·pling 1 :** to fall from being too heavy at the top **2 :** to push over

top·sail *n* **1 :** the sail next above the lowest sail on a mast in a square-rigged ship **2 :** the sail above the large sail on a mast in a ship with a fore-and-aft rig

top·soil *n* **:** the rich upper layer of soil in which plants have most of their roots

top·sy–tur·vy *adv or adj* **1 :** upside down **2 :** in complete disorder

torch *n* **1 :** a flaming light that is made of something which burns brightly and that is usually carried in the hand **2 :** something that guides or gives light or heat like a torch **3 :** a portable device for producing a hot flame

tore *past of* TEAR

¹tor·ment *n* **1 :** extreme pain or distress of body or mind **2 :** a cause of suffering in mind or body

²tor·ment *vb* **1 :** to cause severe suffering of body or mind to **2 :** VEX 1, HARASS

torn *past participle of* TEAR

tor·na·do *n, pl* **tor·na·does** *or* **tor·na·dos :** a violent whirling wind accompanied by a cloud that is shaped like a funnel and moves overland in a narrow path

¹tor·pe·do *n, pl* **tor·pe·does :** a self-propelled underwater weapon shaped like a cigar that is used for blowing up ships

²torpedo *vb* **tor·pe·doed; tor·pe·do·ing :** to hit with or destroy by a torpedo

tor·pid *adj* **1 :** having lost motion or the power of exertion or feeling **2 :** having too little energy or strength **:** DULL

tor·rent *n* **1 :** a rushing stream of liquid **2 :** ³RUSH 1 2

tor·rid *adj* **:** very hot and usually dry

tor·so *n* **:** the human body except for the head, arms, and legs

tor·ti·lla *n* **:** a round flat bread made of corn or wheat flour and usually rolled with a filling and eaten hot

tor·toise *n* **1 :** any of a family of turtles that live on land **2 :** TURTLE

tor·toise·shell *n* **1 :** the hornlike covering of the shell of a sea tortoise that is mottled brown and yellow and is used for ornamental objects **2 :** any of several brightly colored butterflies

tor·tu·ous *adj* **:** having many twists and turns

¹tor·ture *n* **1 :** the causing of great pain especially to punish or to obtain a confession **2 :** distress of body or mind

²torture *vb* **tor·tured; tor·tur·ing 1 :** to punish or force someone to do or say something by causing great pain **2 :** to cause great suffering to — **tor·tur·er** *n*

¹toss *vb* **1 :** to throw or swing to and fro or up and down **2 :** to throw with a quick light motion **3 :** to lift with a sudden motion **4 :** to be thrown about rapidly **5 :** to move about restlessly **6 :** to stir or mix lightly

²toss *n* **:** an act or instance of tossing

tot *n* **:** a young child

¹to·tal *adj* **1 :** of or relating to the whole of something **2 :** making up the whole **3 :** being such to the fullest degree **4 :** making use of every means to do something — **to·tal·ly** *adv*

²total *n* **1 :** a result of addition **:** SUM **2 :** an entire amount

³total *vb* **to·taled** *or* **to·talled; to·tal·ing** *or* **to·tal·ling 1 :** to add up **2 :** to amount to **:** NUMBER

tote *vb* **tot·ed; tot·ing :** CARRY 1, HAUL

to·tem *n* **1 :** an object (as an animal or plant) serving as the emblem of a family or clan **2 :** a carving or picture representing such an object

totem pole *n* **:** a pole or pillar carved and painted with totems and placed before the

DICTIONARY

houses of Indian tribes of the northwest coast of North America

tot·ter *vb* **1 :** to sway or rock as if about to fall **2 :** to move unsteadily **:** STAGGER

tou·can *n* **:** a brightly colored tropical bird that has a very large beak and feeds on fruit

1touch *vb* **1 :** to feel or handle (as with the fingers) especially so as to be aware of with the sense of touch **2 :** to be or cause to be in contact with something **3 :** to be or come next to **4 :** to hit lightly **5 :** 2HARM **6 :** to make use of **7 :** to refer to in passing **8 :** to affect the interest of **9 :** to move emotionally

2touch *n* **1 :** a light stroke or tap **2 :** the act or fact of touching or being touched **3 :** the special sense by which one is aware of light pressure **4 :** an impression gotten through the sense of touch **5 :** a state of contact or communication **6 :** a small amount **:** TRACE

touch·down *n* **:** a score made in football by carrying or catching the ball over the opponent's goal line

touch·ing *adj* **:** causing a feeling of tenderness or pity

touch pad *n* **:** a flat surface on an electronic device (as a microwave oven) divided into several differently marked areas that are touched to make choices in controlling the device

touch up *vb* **:** to improve by or as if by small changes

touchy *adj* **touch·i·er; touch·i·est 1 :** easily hurt or insulted **2 :** calling for tact or careful handling

1tough *adj* **1 :** strong or firm but flexible and not brittle **2 :** not easily chewed **3 :** able to put up with strain or hardship **4 :** STUBBORN 1 **5 :** very difficult **6 :** LAWLESS 2 — **tough·ness** *n*

2tough *n* **:** 2ROWDY, RUFFIAN

tough·en *vb* **:** to make or become tough

1tour *n* **1 :** a fixed period of duty **2 :** a trip usually ending at the point where it started

2tour *vb* **:** to make a tour of **:** travel as a tourist

tour·ist *n* **:** a person who travels for pleasure

tour·na·ment *n* **1 :** a contest of skill and courage between knights wearing armor and fighting with blunted lances or swords **2 :** a series of contests played for a championship

tour·ni·quet *n* **:** a device (as a bandage twisted tight) for stopping bleeding or blood flow

tou·sle *vb* **tou·sled; tou·sling :** to put into disorder by rough handling

1tow *vb* **:** to draw or pull along behind

2tow *n* **1 :** a rope or chain for towing **2 :** an act or instance of towing **:** the fact or state of being towed **3 :** something (as a barge) that is towed

3tow *n* **:** short broken fiber of flax, hemp, or jute used for yarn, twine, or stuffing

to·ward *or* **to·wards** *prep* **1 :** in the direction of **2 :** along a course leading to **3 :** in regard to **4 :** so as to face **5 :** 2NEAR **6 :** as part of the payment for

tow·el *n* **:** a cloth or piece of absorbent paper for wiping or drying

1tow·er *n* **1 :** a building or structure that is higher than its length or width, is high with respect to its surroundings, and may stand by itself or be attached to a larger structure **2 :** CITADEL 1

2tower *vb* **:** to reach or rise to a great height

tow·er·ing *adj* **1 :** rising high **:** TALL **2 :** reaching a high point of strength or force **3 :** going beyond proper bounds

tow·head *n* **:** a person having soft whitish hair

town *n* **1 :** a compactly settled area that is usually larger than a village but smaller than a city **2 :** CITY 1 **3 :** the people of a town

town·ship *n* **1 :** a unit of local government in some northeastern and north central states **2 :** a division of territory in surveys of United States public lands containing thirty-six square miles (about ninety-three square kilometers)

tow·path *n* **:** a path traveled by people or animals towing boats

tox·ic *adj* **:** of, relating to, or caused by a poison

tox·in *n* **:** a poison produced by an animal, a plant, or germs

1toy *n* **1 :** something of little or no value **2 :** something for a child to play with **3 :** something small of its kind

2toy *vb* **:** to amuse oneself as if with a toy

1trace *n* **1 :** a mark left by something that has passed or is past **2 :** a very small amount

2trace *vb* **traced; trac·ing 1 :** 2SKETCH 1 **2 :** to form (as letters) carefully **3 :** to copy (as a drawing) by following the lines or letters as seen through a transparent sheet placed over the thing copied **4 :** to follow the footprints, track, or trail of **5 :** to study or follow the development and progress of in detail — **trac·er** *n*

3trace *n* **:** either of the two straps, chains, or ropes of a harness that fasten a horse to a vehicle

trace·able *adj* **:** capable of being traced

tra·chea *n, pl* **tra·che·ae 1 :** WINDPIPE **2 :** a breathing tube of an insect

trac·ing *n* **1 :** the act of a person that traces **2 :** something that is traced

1track *n* **1 :** a mark left by something that

has gone by **2 :** PATH 1, TRAIL **3 :** a course laid out for racing **4 :** a way for a vehicle with wheels **5 :** awareness of things or of the order in which things happen or ideas come **6 :** either of two endless metal belts on which a vehicle (as a tank) travels **7 :** track-and-field sports

²track *vb* **1 :** to follow the tracks or traces of **2 :** to make tracks on or with

track–and–field *adj* **:** relating to or being sports events (as racing, throwing, and jumping contests) held on an oval running track and on an enclosed field

¹tract *n* **:** a pamphlet of political or religious ideas and beliefs

²tract *n* **1 :** an indefinite stretch of land **2 :** a defined area of land **3 :** a system of body parts or organs that serve some special purpose

trac•tor *n* **1 :** a vehicle that has large rear wheels or moves on endless belts and is used especially for pulling farm implements **2 :** a short truck for hauling a trailer

¹trade *n* **1 :** the business or work in which a person takes part regularly **:** OCCUPATION **2 :** an occupation requiring manual or mechanical skill **:** CRAFT **3 :** the persons working in a business or industry **4 :** the business of buying and selling items **:** COMMERCE **5 :** an act of trading **:** TRANSACTION **6 :** a firm's customers

²trade *vb* **trad•ed; trad•ing 1 :** to give in exchange for something else **2 :** to take part in the exchange, purchase, or sale of goods **3 :** to deal regularly as a customer

trade•mark *n* **:** a device (as a word) that points clearly to the origin or ownership of merchandise to which it is applied and that is legally reserved for use only by the owner

trad•er *n* **1 :** a person who trades **2 :** a ship engaged in trade

trades•man *n, pl* **trades•men 1 :** a person who runs a retail store **2 :** CRAFTSMAN 1

trades•peo•ple *n pl* **:** people engaged in trade

trade wind *n* **:** a wind blowing steadily toward the equator from an easterly direction

trad•ing post *n* **:** a station or store of a trader or trading company set up in a thinly settled region

tra•di•tion *n* **1 :** the handing down of information, beliefs, or customs from one generation to another **2 :** a belief or custom handed down by tradition

tra•di•tion•al *adj* **1 :** handed down from age to age **2 :** based on custom **:** CONVENTIONAL — **tra•di•tion•al•ly** *adv*

¹traf•fic *n* **1 :** the business of carrying passengers or goods **2 :** the business of buying and selling **:** COMMERCE **3 :** exchange of information **4 :** the persons or goods carried by train, boat, or airplane or passing along a road, river, or air route **5 :** the movement (as of vehicles) along a route

²traffic *vb* **traf•ficked; traf•fick•ing :** ²TRADE 2

trag•e•dy *n, pl* **trag•e•dies 1 :** a serious play that has a sorrowful or disastrous ending **2 :** a disastrous event

trag•ic *adj* **1 :** of or relating to tragedy **2 :** very unfortunate

¹trail *vb* **1 :** to drag or draw along behind **2 :** to lag behind **3 :** to follow in the tracks of **:** PURSUE **4 :** to hang or let hang so as to touch the ground or float out behind **5 :** to become weak, soft, or less

²trail *n* **1 :** something that trails or is trailed **2 :** a trace or mark left by something that has passed or been drawn along **3 :** a beaten path **4 :** a path marked through a forest or mountainous region

trail•er *n* **1 :** a vehicle designed to be hauled (as by a tractor) **2 :** a vehicle designed to serve wherever parked as a dwelling or a place of business

¹train *n* **1 :** a part of a gown that trails behind the wearer **2 :** the followers of an important person **3 :** a moving line of persons, vehicles, or animals **4 :** a connected series **5 :** a connected series of railway cars usually hauled by a locomotive

²train *vb* **1 :** to direct the growth of (a plant) usually by bending, pruning, and tying **2 :** to give or receive instruction, discipline, or drill **3 :** to teach in an art, profession, or trade **4 :** to make ready (as by exercise) for a sport or test of skill **5 :** to aim (as a gun) at a target — **train•er** *n*

train•ing *n* **1 :** the course followed by one who trains or is being trained **2 :** the condition of one who has trained for a test or contest

trait *n* **:** a quality that sets one person or thing off from another

trai•tor *n* **1 :** a person who betrays another's trust or is false to a personal duty **2 :** a person who commits treason

trai•tor•ous *adj* **1 :** guilty or capable of treason **2 :** amounting to treason — **trai•tor•ous•ly** *adv*

¹tramp *vb* **1 :** to walk heavily **2 :** to tread on forcibly and repeatedly **3 :** to travel or wander through on foot

²tramp *n* **1 :** a person who wanders from place to place, has no home or job, and often lives by begging or stealing **2 :** ²HIKE **3 :** the sounds made by the beat of marching feet

tram•ple *vb* **tram•pled; tram•pling 1 :** to tramp or tread heavily so as to bruise, crush, or injure something **2 :** to crush under the feet **3 :** to injure or harm by treating harshly and without mercy

tram·po·line *n* **:** a canvas sheet or web supported by springs in a metal frame used for springing and landing in acrobatic tumbling

trance *n* **1 :** STUPOR **2 :** a condition like sleep (as deep hypnosis) **3 :** a state of being so deeply absorbed in something as not to be aware of one's surroundings

tran·quil *adj* **:** very calm and quiet **:** PEACEFUL

tran·quil·iz·er *n* **:** a drug used to ease worry and nervous tension

tran·quil·li·ty *or* **tran·quil·i·ty** *n* **:** the state of being calm **:** QUIET

trans- *prefix* **1 :** on or to the other side of **:** across **:** beyond **2 :** so as to change or transfer

trans·act *vb* **:** to carry on **:** MANAGE, CONDUCT

trans·ac·tion *n* **1 :** a business deal **2 transactions** *pl* **:** the record of the meeting of a club or organization

trans·at·lan·tic *adj* **:** crossing or being beyond the Atlantic ocean

tran·scend *vb* **1 :** to rise above the limits of **2 :** to do better or more than

trans·con·ti·nen·tal *adj* **:** crossing, extending across, or being on the farther side of a continent

tran·scribe *vb* **tran·scribed; tran·scrib·ing :** to make a copy of

tran·script *n* **1 :** [1]COPY 1 **2 :** an official copy of a student's school record

[1]**trans·fer** *vb* **trans·ferred; trans·fer·ring 1 :** to pass or cause to pass from one person, place, or condition to another **2 :** to give over the possession or ownership of **3 :** to copy (as by printing) from one surface to another by contact **4 :** to move to a different place, region, or job **5 :** to change from one vehicle or transportation line to another

[2]**trans·fer** *n* **1 :** a giving over of right, title, or interest in property by one person to another **2 :** an act or process of transferring **3 :** someone or something that transfers or is transferred **4 :** a ticket allowing a passenger on a bus or train to continue the journey on another route without paying more fare

trans·fix *vb* **:** to pierce through with or as if with a pointed weapon

trans·form *vb* **:** to change completely — **trans·form·er** *n*

trans·for·ma·tion *n* **:** the act or process of transforming **:** a complete change

trans·fu·sion *n* **1 :** a passing of one thing into another **2 :** a transferring (as of blood or salt solution) into a vein of a person or animal

[1]**tran·sient** *adj* **:** not lasting or staying long

[2]**transient** *n* **:** a person who is not staying long in a place

tran·sis·tor *n* **:** a small solid electronic device used especially in radios for controlling the flow of electricity

tran·sit *n* **1 :** a passing through or across **2 :** the act or method of carrying things from one place to another **3 :** local transportation of people in public vehicles **4 :** a surveyor's instrument for measuring angles

tran·si·tion *n* **:** a passing from one state, stage, place, or subject to another **:** CHANGE

tran·si·tive *adj* **:** having or containing a direct object

trans·late *vb* **trans·lat·ed; trans·lat·ing 1 :** to change from one state or form to another **2 :** to turn from one language into another

trans·la·tion *n* **:** the act, process, or result of translating

trans·lu·cent *adj* **:** not transparent but clear enough to allow rays of light to pass through — **trans·lu·cent·ly** *adv*

trans·mis·sion *n* **1 :** an act or process of transmitting **2 :** the gears by which the power is transmitted from the engine to the axle that gives motion to a motor vehicle

trans·mit *vb* **trans·mit·ted; trans·mit·ting 1 :** to transfer from one person or place to another **2 :** to pass on by or as if by inheritance **3 :** to pass or cause to pass through space or through a material **4 :** to send out by means of radio waves

trans·mit·ter *n* **1 :** one that transmits **2 :** the instrument in a telegraph system that sends out messages **3 :** the part of a telephone that includes the mouthpiece and a device that picks up sound waves and sends them over the wire **4 :** the device that sends out radio or television signals

tran·som *n* **1 :** a piece that lies crosswise in a structure (as in the frame of a window or of a door that has a window above it) **2 :** a window above a door or another window

trans·par·en·cy *n* **:** the quality or state of being transparent

trans·par·ent *adj* **1 :** clear enough or thin enough to be seen through **2 :** easily detected — **trans·par·ent·ly** *adv*

trans·pi·ra·tion *n* **:** an act or instance of transpiring

trans·pire *vb* **trans·pired; trans·pir·ing 1 :** to give off or pass off in the form of a vapor usually through pores **2 :** to become known or apparent **3 :** to come to pass **:** HAPPEN

[1]**trans·plant** *vb* **1 :** to dig up and plant again

in another soil or location **2 :** to remove from one place and settle or introduce elsewhere

[2]**trans•plant** *n* **1 :** something transplanted **2 :** the process of transplanting

[1]**trans•port** *vb* **1 :** to carry from one place to another **2 :** to fill with delight

[2]**trans•port** *n* **1 :** the act of transporting **:** TRANSPORTATION **2 :** a state of great joy or pleasure **3 :** a ship for carrying soldiers or military equipment **4 :** a vehicle used to transport persons or goods

trans•por•ta•tion *n* **1 :** an act, instance, or means of transporting or being transported **2 :** public transporting of passengers or goods especially as a business

trans•pose *vb* **trans•posed; trans•pos•ing** **1 :** to change the position or order of **2 :** to write or perform in a different musical key

trans•verse *adj* **:** lying or being across **:** placed crosswise — **trans•verse•ly** *adv*

[1]**trap** *n* **1 :** a device for catching animals **2 :** something by which one is caught or stopped unawares **3 :** a light one-horse carriage with springs **4 :** a device that allows something to pass through but keeps other things out

[2]**trap** *vb* **trapped; trap•ping** **1 :** to catch in a trap **2 :** to provide (a place) with traps **3 :** to set traps for animals especially as a business — **trap•per** *n*

trap•door *n* **:** a lifting or sliding door covering an opening in a floor or roof

tra•peze *n* **:** a short horizontal bar hung from two parallel ropes and used by acrobats

trap•e•zoid *n* **:** a figure with four sides but with only two sides parallel

trap•pings *n pl* **1 :** ornamental covering especially for a horse **2 :** outward decoration or dress

trash *n* **1 :** something of little or no worth **2 :** low worthless persons

[1]**trav•el** *vb* **trav•eled** *or* **trav•elled; trav•el•ing** *or* **trav•el•ling** **1 :** to journey from place to place or to a distant place **2 :** to get around **:** pass from one place to another **3 :** to journey through or over — **trav•el•er** *or* **trav•el•ler** *n*

[2]**travel** *n* **1 :** the act or a means of traveling **2 :** [1]JOURNEY, TRIP — often used in pl. **3 :** the number traveling **:** TRAFFIC

traveling bag *n* **:** a bag carried by hand and designed to hold a traveler's clothing and personal articles

tra•verse *vb* **tra•versed; tra•vers•ing** **:** to pass through, across, or over

[1]**trawl** *vb* **:** to fish or catch with a trawl

[2]**trawl** *n* **:** a large net in the shape of a cone dragged along the sea bottom in fishing

trawl•er *n* **:** a boat used for trawling

tray *n* **:** an open container with a flat bottom and low rim for holding, carrying, or showing articles

treach•er•ous *adj* **1 :** guilty of or likely to commit treachery **2 :** not to be trusted **3 :** not safe because of hidden dangers — **treach•er•ous•ly** *adv*

treach•ery *n, pl* **treach•er•ies** **1 :** a betraying of trust or faith **2 :** an act or instance of betraying trust

[1]**tread** *vb* **trod; trod•den** *or* **trod; tread•ing** **1 :** to step or walk on or over **2 :** to move on foot **:** WALK **3 :** to beat or press with the feet — **tread water :** to keep the body in an up and down position in the water and the head above water by a walking or running motion of the legs helped by moving the hands

[2]**tread** *n* **1 :** a mark made by or as if by treading **2 :** the action, manner, or sound of treading **3 :** the part of something (as a shoe or tire) that touches a surface **4 :** the horizontal part of a step

trea•dle *n* **:** a device worked by the foot to drive a machine

tread•mill *n* **1 :** a device moved by persons treading on steps around the rim of a wheel or by animals walking on an endless belt **2 :** a device having an endless belt on which an individual walks or runs in place for exercise **3 :** a tiresome routine

trea•son *n* **1 :** the betraying of a trust **2 :** the crime of trying or helping to overthrow the government of one's country or cause its defeat in war

[1]**trea•sure** *n* **1 :** wealth (as money or jewels) stored up or held in reserve **2 :** something of great value

[2]**treasure** *vb* **trea•sured; trea•sur•ing** **:** to treat as precious **:** value highly **:** CHERISH

trea•sur•er *n* **:** a person (as an officer of a club) who has charge of the money

trea•sury *n, pl* **trea•sur•ies** **1 :** a place in which stores of wealth are kept **2 :** a place where money collected is kept and paid out **3** *cap* **:** a government department in charge of finances

[1]**treat** *vb* **1 :** to have as a subject especially in writing **2 :** to handle, use, or act toward in a usually stated way **3 :** to pay for the food or entertainment of **4 :** to give medical or surgical care to **:** to use a certain medical care on **5 :** to expose to some action (as of a chemical)

[2]**treat** *n* **1 :** an entertainment given without expense to those invited **2 :** an often unexpected or unusual source of pleasure or amusement

treat•ment *n* **1 :** the act or manner of treating someone or something **2 :** a substance or method used in treating

trea•ty *n, pl* **trea•ties** : an agreement between two or more states or sovereigns

1tre•ble *n* **1** : the highest part in harmony having four parts : SOPRANO 1 **2** : an instrument having the highest range or part **3** : a voice or sound that has a high pitch **4** : the upper half of the musical pitch range

2treble *adj* **1** : being three times the number or amount **2** : relating to or having the range of a musical treble

3treble *vb* **tre•bled; tre•bling** : to make or become three times as much

1tree *n* **1** : a woody plant that lives for years and has a single usually tall main stem with few or no branches on its lower part **2** : a plant of treelike form **3** : something suggesting a tree — **tree•less** *adj* — **tree•like** *adj*

2tree *vb* **treed; tree•ing** : to drive to or up a tree

tree fern *n* : a tropical fern with a tall woody stalk and a crown of often feathery leaves

tre•foil *n* **1** : a clover or related plant having leaves with three leaflets **2** : a fancy design with three leaflike parts

1trek *vb* **trekked; trek•king** : to make one's way with difficulty

2trek *n* : a slow or difficult journey

trel•lis *n* : a frame of lattice used especially as a screen or a support for climbing plants

1trem•ble *vb* **trem•bled; trem•bling** **1** : to shake without control (as from fear or cold) : SHIVER **2** : to move, sound, or happen as if shaken **3** : to have strong fear or doubt

2tremble *n* : the act or a period of trembling

tre•men•dous *adj* **1** : causing fear or terror : DREADFUL **2** : astonishingly large, strong, or great — **tre•men•dous•ly** *adv*

trem•or *n* **1** : a trembling or shaking especially from weakness or disease **2** : a shaking motion of the earth (as during an earthquake)

trem•u•lous *adj* **1** : marked by trembling or shaking **2** : FEARFUL 2, TIMID

trench *n* : a long narrow ditch

1trend *vb* : to have or take a general direction

2trend *n* : general direction taken in movement or change

1tres•pass *n* **1** : 1SIN, OFFENSE **2** : unlawful entry upon someone's land

2trespass *vb* **1** : to do wrong : SIN **2** : to enter upon someone's land unlawfully — **tres•pass•er** *n*

tress *n* : a long lock of hair

tres•tle *n* **1** : a braced frame consisting usually of a horizontal piece with spreading legs at each end that supports something (as the top of a table) **2** : a structure of timbers or steel for supporting a road or railroad over a low place

T. rex *n* : TYRANNOSAUR

tri- *prefix* : three

tri•ad *n* : a chord made up usually of the first, third, and fifth notes of a scale

tri•al *n* **1** : the action or process of trying or testing **2** : the hearing and judgment of something in court **3** : a test of faith or of one's ability to continue or stick with something **4** : an experiment to test quality, value, or usefulness **5** : 2ATTEMPT

tri•an•gle *n* **1** : a figure that has three sides and three angles **2** : an object that has three sides and three angles **3** : a musical instrument made of a steel rod bent in the shape of a triangle with one open angle

tri•an•gu•lar *adj* **1** : of, relating to, or having the form of a triangle **2** : having three angles, sides, or corners **3** : of, relating to, or involving three parts or persons

trib•al *adj* : of, relating to, or like that of a tribe

tribe *n* **1** : a group of people including many families, clans, or generations **2** : a group of people who are of the same kind or have the same occupation or interest **3** : a group of related plants or animals

tribes•man *n, pl* **tribes•men** : a member of a tribe

trib•u•la•tion *n* **1** : distress or suffering resulting from cruel and unjust rule of a leader, persecution, or misfortune **2** : an experience that is hard to bear

tri•bu•nal *n* : a court of justice

1trib•u•tary *adj* : flowing into a larger stream or a lake

2tributary *n, pl* **trib•u•tar•ies** : a stream flowing into a larger stream or a lake

trib•ute *n* **1** : a payment made by one ruler or state to another especially to gain peace **2** : a tax put on the people to raise money for tribute **3** : something given to show respect, gratitude, or affection

tri•cer•a•tops *n, pl* **triceratops** : a large plant-eating dinosaur with three horns, a large bony crest around the neck, and hoofed toes

tri•chi•na *n, pl* **tri•chi•nae** : a small roundworm which enters the body when infected meat is eaten and whose larvae form cysts in the muscles and cause a painful and dangerous disease (**trichinosis**)

1trick *n* **1** : an action intended to deceive or cheat **2** : a mischievous act : PRANK **3** : an unwise or childish action **4** : an action designed to puzzle or amuse **5** : a quick or clever way of doing something **6** : the cards played in one round of a game

2trick *vb* : to deceive with tricks : CHEAT

trick•ery *n, pl* **trick•er•ies** : the use of tricks to deceive or cheat

[1]**trick·le** *vb* **trick·led; trick·ling** **1 :** to run or fall in drops **2 :** to flow in a thin slow stream

[2]**trickle** *n* **:** a thin slow stream

trick or treat *n* **:** a children's Halloween practice of asking for treats from door to door and threatening to play tricks on those who refuse

trick·ster *n* **:** a person who uses tricks

tricky *adj* **trick·i·er; trick·i·est** **1 :** likely to use tricks **2 :** requiring special care and skill

tri·cy·cle *n* **:** a vehicle with three wheels that is moved usually by pedals

tri·dent *n* **:** a spear with three prongs

[1]**tried** *past of* TRY

[2]**tried** *adj* **:** found good or trustworthy through experience or testing

[1]**tri·fle** *n* **1 :** something of little importance **2 :** a small amount (as of money)

[2]**trifle** *vb* **tri·fled; tri·fling** **1 :** to talk in a joking way **2 :** to act in a playful way **3 :** to handle something in an absentminded way **:** TOY

tri·fling *adj* **1 :** not serious **:** FRIVOLOUS **2 :** of little value

trig·ger *n* **:** the part of the lock of a gun that is pressed to release the hammer so that it will fire

[1]**trill** *n* **1 :** a quick movement back and forth between two musical tones one step apart **2 :** [1]WARBLE 1 **3 :** the rapid vibration of one speech organ against another

[2]**trill** *vb* **:** to utter as or with a trill

tril·lion *n* **:** a thousand billions

tril·li·um *n* **:** a plant related to the lilies that has three leaves and a single flower with three petals and that blooms in the spring

[1]**trim** *vb* **trimmed; trim·ming** **1 :** to put ornaments on **:** ADORN **2 :** to make neat especially by cutting or clipping **3 :** to free of unnecessary matter **4 :** to cause (as a ship) to take the right position in the water by balancing the load carried **5 :** to adjust (as an airplane or submarine) for horizontal movement or for motion upward or downward **6 :** to adjust (as a sail) to a desired position — **trim·mer** *n*

[2]**trim** *adj* **trim·mer; trim·mest** **:** neat and compact in line or structure — **trim·ly** *adv*

[3]**trim** *n* **1 :** the state of a ship as being ready for sailing **2 :** good condition **:** FITNESS **3 :** material used for ornament or trimming **4 :** the woodwork in the finish of a building especially around doors and windows

trim·ming *n* **1 :** the action of one that trims **2 :** something that trims, ornaments, or completes **3 trimmings** *pl* **:** parts removed by trimming

trin·ket *n* **:** a small ornament (as a jewel)

trio *n, pl* **tri·os** **1 :** a musical composition for three instruments or voices **2 :** a group or set of three

[1]**trip** *vb* **tripped; trip·ping** **1 :** to move (as in dancing) with light quick steps **2 :** to catch the foot against something so as to stumble **:** cause to stumble **3 :** to make or cause to make a mistake **4 :** to release (as a spring) by moving a catch

[2]**trip** *n* **1 :** a traveling from one place to another **:** VOYAGE **2 :** a brief errand having a certain aim or being more or less regular **3 :** the action of releasing something mechanically **4 :** a device for releasing something by tripping a mechanism

tripe *n* **:** a part of the stomach of a cow used for food

[1]**tri·ple** *vb* **tri·pled; tri·pling** **:** to make or become three times as great or as many

[2]**triple** *n* **1 :** a sum, amount, or number that is three times as great **2 :** a combination, group, or series of three **3 :** a hit in baseball that lets the batter reach third base

[3]**triple** *adj* **1 :** having three units or parts **2 :** being three times as great or as many **3 :** repeated three times

trip·let *n* **1 :** a combination, set, or group of three **2 :** one of three offspring born at one birth

tri·pod *n* **1 :** something (as a container or stool) resting on three legs **2 :** a stand (as for a camera) having three legs

trite *adj* **trit·er; trit·est** **:** so common that the newness and cleverness have worn off **:** STALE — **trite·ness** *n*

[1]**tri·umph** *n* **1 :** the joy of victory or success **2 :** an outstanding victory

[2]**triumph** *vb* **1 :** to celebrate victory or success in high spirits and often with boasting **2 :** to gain victory **:** WIN

tri·um·phal *adj* **:** of or relating to a triumph

tri·um·phant *adj* **1 :** VICTORIOUS, SUCCESSFUL **2 :** rejoicing for or celebrating victory — **tri·um·phant·ly** *adv*

triv·i·al *adj* **:** of little worth or importance

trod *past of* TREAD

trodden *past participle of* TREAD

[1]**troll** *vb* **1 :** to sing the parts of (a song) in succession **2 :** to fish with a hook and line drawn through the water

[2]**troll** *n* **:** a lure or a line with its lure and hook used in trolling

[3]**troll** *n* **:** a dwarf or giant of folklore living in caves or hills

trol·ley *n, pl* **trolleys** **1 :** a device (as a grooved wheel on the end of a pole) that carries current from a wire to an electrically driven vehicle **2 :** a passenger car that runs on tracks and gets its power through a trol-ley **3 :** a wheeled carriage running on an overhead track

trom•bone *n* **:** a brass musical instrument made of a long bent tube that has a wide opening at one end and one section that slides in and out to make different tones

¹troop *n* **1 :** a cavalry unit **2 troops** *pl* **:** armed forces **:** MILITARY **3 :** a group of beings or things **4 :** a unit of boy or girl scouts under a leader

²troop *vb* **:** to move or gather in groups

troop•er *n* **1 :** a soldier in a cavalry unit **2 :** a mounted police officer **3 :** a state police officer

tro•phy *n, pl* **trophies 1 :** something taken in battle or conquest especially as a memorial **2 :** something given to celebrate a victory or as an award for achievement

trop•ic *n* **1 :** either of two parallels of the earth's latitude of which one is about 23$^1/_2$ degrees north of the equator and the other about 23$^1/_2$ degrees south of the equator **2 tropics** *pl, often cap* **:** the region lying between the two tropics

trop•i•cal *adj* **:** of, relating to, or occurring in the tropics

tropical fish *n* **:** any of various small often brightly colored fishes kept in aquariums

¹trot *n* **1 :** a moderately fast gait of an animal with four feet in which a front foot and the opposite hind foot move as a pair **2 :** a human jogging pace between a walk and a run

²trot *vb* **trot•ted; trot•ting 1 :** to ride, drive, or go at a trot **2 :** to cause to go at a trot **3 :** to go along quickly **:** HURRY

¹trou•ble *vb* **trou•bled; trou•bling 1 :** to disturb or become disturbed mentally or spiritually **:** WORRY **2 :** to produce physical disorder in **:** AFFLICT **3 :** to put to inconvenience **4 :** to make an effort

²trouble *n* **1 :** the quality or state of being troubled **:** MISFORTUNE **2 :** an instance of distress or disturbance **3 :** a cause of disturbance or distress **4 :** extra work or effort **5 :** ill health **:** AILMENT **6 :** failure to work normally

trou•ble•some *adj* **1 :** giving trouble or anxiety **2 :** difficult to deal with — **trou•ble•some•ly** *adv* — **trou•ble•some•ness** *n*

trough *n* **1 :** a long shallow open container especially for water or feed for livestock **2 :** a channel for water **:** GUTTER **3 :** a long channel or hollow

trounce *vb* **trounced; trounc•ing 1 :** to beat severely **:** FLOG **2 :** to defeat thoroughly

troupe *n* **:** a group especially of performers on the stage

trou•sers *n pl* **:** PANTS — used chiefly of such a garment for men and boys

trout *n, pl* **trout :** a freshwater fish related to the salmon and valued for food and sport

trow•el *n* **1 :** a small hand tool with a flat blade used for spreading and smoothing mortar or plaster **2 :** a small hand tool with a curved blade used by gardeners

tru•ant *n* **1 :** a person who neglects his or her duty **2 :** a student who stays out of school without permission

truce *n* **1 :** ARMISTICE **2 :** a short rest especially from something unpleasant

¹truck *n* **1 :** ²BARTER **2 :** goods for barter or for small trade **3 :** close association

²truck *n* **:** a vehicle (as a strong heavy wagon or motor vehicle) for carrying heavy articles or hauling a trailer

³truck *vb* **:** to transport on a truck

trudge *vb* **trudged; trudg•ing :** to walk or march steadily and usually with much effort

¹true *adj* **tru•er; tru•est 1 :** completely loyal **:** FAITHFUL **2 :** that can be relied on **:** CERTAIN **3 :** agreeing with the facts **:** ACCURATE **4 :** HONEST 1, SINCERE **5 :** properly so called **:** GENUINE **6 :** placed or formed accurately **:** EXACT **7 :** being or holding by right **:** LEGITIMATE

²true *adv* **1 :** in agreement with fact **:** TRUTHFULLY **2 :** in an accurate manner **:** ACCURATELY **3 :** without variation from type

³true *n* **:** the quality or state of being accurate (as in alignment)

⁴true *vb* **trued; true•ing** *also* **tru•ing :** to bring to exactly correct condition as to place, position, or shape

true–blue *adj* **:** very faithful

truf•fle *n* **:** the edible usually dark and wrinkled fruiting body of a European fungus that grows in the ground

tru•ly *adv* **:** in a true manner

¹trum•pet *n* **1 :** a brass musical instrument that consists of a tube formed into a long loop with a wide opening at one end and that has valves by which different tones are produced **2 :** something that is shaped like a trumpet **3 :** a sound like that of a trumpet

²trumpet *vb* **1 :** to blow a trumpet **2 :** to make a sound like that of a trumpet — **trum•pet•er** *n*

trumpet creeper *n* **:** a North American woody vine having red flowers shaped like trumpets

trumpet vine *n* **:** TRUMPET CREEPER

¹trun•dle *vb* **trun•dled; trun•dling :** to roll along **:** WHEEL

²trundle *n* **1 :** a small wheel or roller **2 :** a cart or truck with low wheels

trundle bed *n* **:** a low bed on small wheels that can be rolled under a higher bed

trunk *n* **1 :** the main stem of a tree apart from branches and roots **2 :** the body of a person or animal apart from the head, arms, and legs **3 :** a box or chest for holding clothes or other articles especially for traveling **4 :** the enclosed space usually in the rear of an automobile for carrying articles **5 :** the long round muscular nose of an elephant **6 trunks** *pl* **:** men's shorts worn chiefly for sports

¹truss *vb* **1 :** to bind or tie firmly **2 :** to support, strengthen, or stiffen by a truss

²truss *n* **1 :** a framework of beams or bars used in building and engineering **2 :** a device worn to hold a ruptured body part in place

¹trust *n* **1 :** firm belief in the character, strength, or truth of someone or something **2 :** a person or thing in which confidence is placed **3 :** confident hope **4 :** financial credit **5 :** a property interest held by one person or organization (as a bank) for the benefit of another **6 :** a combination of firms or corporations formed by a legal agreement and often held to reduce competition **7 :** something (as a public office) held or managed by someone for the benefit of another **8 :** responsibility for safety and well-being

²trust *vb* **1 :** to place confidence **:** DEPEND **2 :** to be confident **:** HOPE **3 :** to place in one's care or keeping **:** ENTRUST **4 :** to rely on or on the truth of **:** BELIEVE **5 :** to give financial credit to

trust•ee *n* **:** a person who has been given legal responsibility for someone else's property

trust•ful *adj* **:** full of trust — **trust•ful•ly** *adv* — **trust•ful•ness** *n*

trust•ing *adj* **:** having trust, faith, or confidence

trust•wor•thy *adj* **:** deserving trust and confidence — **trust•wor•thi•ness** *n*

¹trusty *adj* **trust•i•er; trust•i•est :** TRUSTWORTHY, RELIABLE

²trusty *n, pl* **trust•ies :** a convict considered trustworthy and allowed special privileges

truth *n, pl* **truths 1 :** the quality or state of being true **2 :** the body of real events or facts **3 :** a true or accepted statement **4 :** agreement with fact or reality

truth•ful *adj* **:** telling or being in the habit of telling the truth — **truth•ful•ly** *adv* — **truth•ful•ness** *n*

¹try *vb* **tried; try•ing 1 :** to examine or investigate in a court of law **2 :** to conduct the trial of **3 :** to put to a test **4 :** to test to the limit **5 :** to melt down (as tallow) and obtain in a pure state **6 :** to make an effort to do

²try *n, pl* **tries :** an effort to do something **:** ATTEMPT

try•ing *adj* **:** hard to bear or put up with

try on *vb* **:** to put on (a garment) in order to test the fit

try•out *n* **:** a test of the ability (as of an athlete or an actor) to fill a part or meet standards

T–shirt *also* **tee shirt** *n* **1 :** a cotton undershirt with short sleeves and no collar **2 :** a cotton or wool jersey outer shirt designed like a T-shirt

¹tub *n* **1 :** a wide low container **2 :** an old or slow boat **3 :** BATHTUB **4 :** BATH 1 **5 :** the amount that a tub will hold

²tub *vb* **tubbed; tub•bing :** to wash or bathe in a tub

tu•ba *n* **:** a brass musical instrument of lowest pitch with an oval shape and valves for producing different tones

tube *n* **1 :** a long hollow cylinder used especially to carry fluids **2 :** a slender channel within a plant or animal body **:** DUCT **3 :** a soft container shaped something like a tube whose contents (as toothpaste or glue) can be removed by squeezing **4 :** a hollow cylinder of rubber inside a tire to hold air **5 :** ELECTRONIC TUBE **6 :** TELEVISION — always used with *the* — **tubed** *adj* — **tubeless** *adj* — **tube•like** *adj*

tu•ber *n* **:** a short fleshy usually underground stem (as of a potato plant) bearing tiny leaves like scales each with a bud at its base

tu•ber•cu•lo•sis *n* **:** a disease (as of humans or cattle) which is caused by a bacillus and in which fever, wasting, and formation of cheesy nodules especially in the lungs occur

tu•ber•ous *adj* **:** of, relating to, or like a tuber

tu•bu•lar *adj* **1 :** having the form of or made up of a tube **2 :** made with tubes

¹tuck *vb* **1 :** to pull up into a fold **2 :** to make stitched folds in **3 :** to put or fit into a snug or safe place **4 :** to push in the edges of **5 :** to cover by tucking in bedclothes

²tuck *n* **:** a fold stitched into cloth usually to alter it

Tues•day *n* **:** the third day of the week

¹tuft *n* **1 :** a small bunch of long flexible things (as hairs) growing out **2 :** a bunch of soft fluffy threads used for ornament **3 :** ¹CLUMP 1, CLUSTER

²tuft *vb* **1 :** to provide or decorate with a tuft **2 :** to grow in tufts **3 :** to make (as upholstery) firm by stitching through the stuffing here and there

¹tug *vb* **tugged; tug•ging 1 :** to pull hard **2 :** to move by pulling hard **:** DRAG **3 :** to tow with a tugboat

2tug *n* **1 :** an act of tugging **:** PULL **2 :** a strong pulling force **3 :** a struggle between two people or forces **4 :** TUGBOAT

tug·boat *n* **:** a small powerful boat used for towing ships

tug–of–war *n, pl* **tugs–of–war 1 :** a struggle to win **2 :** a contest in which two teams pull against each other at opposite ends of a rope

tu·ition *n* **:** money paid for instruction (as at a college)

tu·lip *n* **:** a plant related to the lilies that grows from a bulb and has a large cup-shaped flower in early spring

1tum·ble *vb* **tum·bled; tum·bling 1 :** to perform gymnastic feats of rolling and turning **2 :** to fall suddenly and helplessly **3 :** to suffer a sudden downward turn or defeat **4 :** to move or go in a hurried or confused way **5 :** to come to understand **6 :** to toss together into a confused mass

2tumble *n* **1 :** a messy state or collection **2 :** an act or instance of tumbling and especially of falling down

tum·ble·down *adj* **:** DILAPIDATED

tum·bler *n* **1 :** a person (as an acrobat) who tumbles **2 :** a drinking glass **3 :** a movable part of a lock that must be adjusted (as by a key) before the lock will open

tum·ble·weed *n* **:** a plant that breaks away from its roots in autumn and is tumbled about by the wind

tum·my *n, pl* **tummies :** 1STOMACH 1, 2

tu·mor *n* **:** an abnormal growth of body tissue

tu·mult *n* **1 :** UPROAR **2 :** great confusion of mind

tu·mul·tu·ous *adj* **:** being or suggesting tumult

tu·na *n, pl* **tuna** *or* **tunas :** a large sea fish valued for food and sport

tun·dra *n* **:** a treeless plain of arctic regions

1tune *n* **1 :** a series of pleasing musical tones **:** MELODY **2 :** the main melody of a song **3 :** correct musical pitch or key **4 :** AGREEMENT 1, HARMONY **5 :** general attitude — **tune·ful** *adj*

2tune *vb* **tuned; tun·ing 1 :** to adjust in musical pitch **2 :** to come or bring into harmony **3 :** to adjust a radio or television set so that it receives clearly — often used with *in* **4 :** to put (as an engine) in good working order — often used with *up* — **tun·er** *n*

tung·sten *n* **:** a grayish-white hard metallic chemical element used especially for electrical purposes (as for the fine wire in an electric light bulb) and to make alloys (as steel) harder

tu·nic *n* **1 :** a usually knee-length belted garment worn by ancient Greeks and Romans **2 :** a shirt or jacket reaching to or just below the hips

tuning fork *n* **:** a metal instrument that gives a fixed tone when struck and is useful for tuning musical instruments

1tun·nel *n* **:** a passage under the ground

2tunnel *vb* **tun·neled** *or* **tun·nelled; tun·nel·ing** *or* **tun·nel·ling :** to make a tunnel

tun·ny *n, pl* **tun·nies :** TUNA

tur·ban *n* **1 :** a head covering worn especially by Muslims and made of a long cloth wrapped around the head or around a cap **2 :** a woman's small soft hat with no brim

tur·bid *adj* **:** dark or discolored with sediment

tur·bine *n* **:** an engine whose central driving shaft is fitted with a series of winglike parts that are whirled around by the pressure of water, steam, or gas

tur·bot *n, pl* **turbot :** a large brownish flatfish

tur·bu·lent *adj* **:** causing or being in a state of unrest, violence, or disturbance

tu·reen *n* **:** a deep bowl from which food (as soup) is served

turf *n* **:** the upper layer of soil bound into a thick mat by roots of grass and other plants

Turk *n* **:** a person born or living in Turkey

tur·key *n, pl* **turkeys :** a large American bird related to the chicken and widely raised for food

1Turk·ish *adj* **:** of or relating to Turkey, the Turks, or Turkish

2Turkish *n* **:** the language of the Turks

tur·moil *n* **:** a very confused or disturbed state or condition

1turn *vb* **1 :** to move or cause to move around a center **:** ROTATE **2 :** to twist so as to bring about a desired end **3 :** 1WRENCH 2 **4 :** to change in position usually by moving through an arc of a circle **5 :** to think over **:** PONDER **6 :** to become dizzy **:** REEL **7 :** 1UPSET 3 **8 :** to set in another and especially an opposite direction **9 :** to change course or direction **10 :** to go around **11 :** to reach or pass beyond **12 :** to move or direct toward or away from something **13 :** to make an appeal **14 :** to become or make very unfriendly **15 :** to make or become spoiled **16 :** to cause to be or look a certain way **17 :** to pass from one state to another **18 :** 1CHANGE 1, TRANSFORM **19 :** TRANSLATE 2 **20 :** to give a rounded form to (as on a lathe) — **turn a hair :** to be or become upset or frightened — **turn tail :** to turn so as to run away — **turn the trick :** to bring about the desired result — **turn turtle :** OVERTURN 1

2turn *n* **1 :** a turning about a center **2 :** a change or changing of direction, course, or position **3 :** a change or changing of the general state or condition **4 :** a place at which something turns **5 :** a short walk or ride **6 :** an act affecting another **7 :** proper place in a waiting line or time in a schedule **8 :** a period of action or activity **:** SPELL **9 :** a special purpose or need **10 :** special quality **11 :** the shape or form in which something is molded **:** CAST **12 :** a single circle or loop (as of rope passed around an object) **13 :** natural or special skill — **at every turn :** all the time **:** CONSTANTLY, CONTINUOUSLY — **to a turn :** precisely right

turn·about *n* **:** a change from one direction or one way of thinking or acting to the opposite

turn down *vb* **1 :** to fold back or down **2 :** to lower by using a control **3 :** [1]REFUSE 1, REJECT

tur·nip *n* **:** the thick white or yellow edible root of a plant related to the cabbage

turn off *vb* **1 :** to turn aside **2 :** to stop by using a control

turn on *vb* **:** to make work by using a control

turn·out *n* **:** a gathering of people for a special reason

turn out *vb* **1 :** TURN OFF 2 **2 :** to prove to be

turn·pike *n* **1 :** a road that one must pay to use **2 :** a main road

turn·stile *n* **:** a post having arms that turn around set in an entrance or exit so that persons can pass through only on foot one by one

turn·ta·ble *n* **:** a round flat plate that turns a phonograph record

tur·pen·tine *n* **1 :** a mixture of oil and resin obtained mostly from pine trees **2 :** an oil made from turpentine and used as a solvent and as a paint thinner

tur·quoise *n* **:** a blue to greenish gray mineral used in jewelry

tur·ret *n* **1 :** a little tower often at a corner of a building **2 :** a low usually rotating structure (as in a tank, warship, or airplane) in which guns are mounted

tur·tle *n* **:** any of a large group of reptiles living on land, in water, or both and having a toothless horny beak and a shell of bony plates which covers the body and into which the head, legs, and tail can usually be drawn

tur·tle·dove *n* **:** any of several small wild pigeons

tur·tle·neck *n* **:** a high turned-over collar (as of a sweater)

tusk *n* **:** a very long large tooth (as of an elephant) usually growing in pairs and used in digging and fighting — **tusked** *adj*

[1]**tus·sle** *n* **1 :** a physical contest or struggle **2 :** a rough argument or a struggle against difficult odds

[2]**tussle** *vb* **tus·sled; tus·sling :** to struggle roughly **:** SCUFFLE

tus·sock *n* **:** a compact tuft or clump (as of grass)

[1]**tu·tor** *n* **:** a person who has the responsibility of instructing and guiding another

[2]**tutor** *vb* **:** to teach usually individually

TV *n* **:** TELEVISION

twad·dle *n* **:** silly idle talk

twain *n* **:** [2]TWO 1

[1]**twang** *n* **1 :** a harsh quick ringing sound **2 :** nasal speech

[2]**twang** *vb* **1 :** to sound or cause to sound with a twang **2 :** to speak with a nasal twang

'twas : it was

[1]**tweak** *vb* **:** to pinch and pull with a sudden jerk and twist

[2]**tweak** *n* **:** an act of tweaking

tweed *n* **1 :** a rough woolen cloth **2 tweeds** *pl* **:** tweed clothing (as a suit)

[1]**tweet** *n* **:** a chirping sound

[2]**tweet** *vb* **:** [2]CHIRP

tweez·ers *n pl* **:** a small instrument that is used like pincers in grasping or pulling something

[1]**twelfth** *adj* **:** coming right after eleventh

[2]**twelfth** *n* **:** number twelve in a series

[1]**twelve** *adj* **:** being one more than eleven

[2]**twelve** *n* **:** one more than eleven **:** three times four **:** 12

twelve·month *n* **:** YEAR

[1]**twen·ti·eth** *adj* **:** coming right after nineteenth

[2]**twentieth** *n* **:** number twenty in a series

[1]**twen·ty** *adj* **:** being one more than nineteen

[2]**twenty** *n* **:** one more than nineteen **:** four times five **:** 20

twen·ty–first *adj* **:** coming right after twentieth

[1]**twen·ty–one** *adj* **:** being one more than twenty

[2]**twenty–one** *n* **:** one more than twenty **:** 21

twice *adv* **:** two times

twid·dle *vb* **twid·dled; twid·dling :** [1]TWIRL

twig *n* **:** a small shoot or branch

twi·light *n* **:** the period or the light from the sky between full night and sunrise or between sunset and full night

twill *n* **:** a way of weaving cloth that produces a pattern of diagonal lines

[1]**twin** *n* **1 :** either of two offspring produced at one birth **2 :** one of two persons or things closely related to or very like each other

[2]**twin** *adj* **1 :** born with one other or as a pair at one birth **2 :** made up of two similar,

related, or connected members or parts **3 :** being one of a pair

[1]twine *n* **:** a strong string of two or more strands twisted together

[2]twine *vb* **twined; twin•ing 1 :** to twist together **2 :** to coil around a support

[1]twinge *vb* **twinged; twing•ing** *or* **twinge•ing :** to affect with or feel a sudden sharp pain

[2]twinge *n* **:** a sudden sharp stab (as of pain)

[1]twin•kle *vb* **twin•kled; twin•kling 1 :** to shine or cause to shine with a flickering or sparkling light **2 :** to appear bright with amusement **3 :** to move or flutter rapidly

[2]twinkle *n* **1 :** a very short time **2 :** [2]SPARKLE 1, FLICKER

twin•kling *n* **:** [2]TWINKLE 1

[1]twirl *vb* **:** to turn or cause to turn rapidly — **twirl•er** *n*

[2]twirl *n* **:** an act of twirling

[1]twist *vb* **1 :** to unite by winding one thread, strand, or wire around another **2 :** [2]TWINE 2 **3 :** to turn so as to sprain or hurt **4 :** to change the meaning of **5 :** to pull off, rotate, or break by a turning force **6 :** to follow a winding course

[2]twist *n* **1 :** something that is twisted **2 :** an act of twisting **:** the state of being twisted **3 :** a spiral turn or curve **4 :** a strong personal tendency **:** BENT **5 :** a changing of meaning **6 :** something (as a plan of action) that is both surprising and strange **7 :** a lively dance in which the hips are twisted

twist•er *n* **1 :** TORNADO **2 :** WATERSPOUT 2

[1]twitch *vb* **1 :** to move or pull with a sudden motion **:** JERK **2 :** [1]PLUCK 1 **3 :** [2]QUIVER

[2]twitch *n* **1 :** an act of twitching **2 :** a short sharp contracting of muscle fibers

[1]twit•ter *vb* **1 :** to make a series of chirping noises **2 :** to talk in a chattering fashion **3 :** to make or become very nervous and upset

[2]twitter *n* **1 :** a nervous upset state **2 :** the chirping of birds **3 :** a light chattering

[1]two *adj* **:** being one more than one

[2]two *n* **1 :** one more than one **:** 2 **2 :** the second in a set or series

two–dimensional *adj* **:** having the two dimensions of length and width

two•fold *adj* **:** being twice as great or as many

two–way *adj* **1 :** moving or acting or allowing movement or action in either direction **2 :** involving two persons or groups **3 :** made to send and receive messages

two–winged fly *n* **:** an insect belonging to the same group as the housefly

ty•coon *n* **:** a very powerful and wealthy business person

tying *present participle of* TIE

[1]type *n* **1 :** a set of letters or figures that are used for printing or the letters or figures printed by them **2 :** the special things by which members of a group are set apart from other groups **3 :** VARIETY 3

[2]type *vb* **typed; typ•ing 1 :** TYPEWRITE **2 :** to identify as belonging to a type

type•write *vb* **type•wrote; type•writ•ten; type•writ•ing :** to write with a typewriter

type•writ•er *n* **:** a machine that prints letters or figures when a person pushes its keys down

type•writ•ing *n* **1 :** the use of a typewriter **2 :** writing done with a typewriter

[1]ty•phoid *adj* **1 :** of, relating to, or like typhus **2 :** of, relating to, or being typhoid

[2]typhoid *n* **:** a disease in which a person has fever, diarrhea, an inflamed intestine, and great weakness and which is caused by a bacterium (**typhoid bacillus**) that passes from one person to another in dirty food or water

ty•phoon *n* **:** a tropical cyclone in the region of the Philippines or the China Sea

ty•phus *n* **:** a disease carried to people especially by body lice and marked by high fever, stupor and delirium, severe headache, and a dark red rash

typ•i•cal *adj* **:** combining or showing the special characteristics of a group or kind — **typ•i•cal•ly** *adv*

typ•i•fy *vb* **typ•i•fied; typ•i•fy•ing 1 :** REPRESENT 2 **2 :** to have or include the special or main characteristics of

typ•ist *n* **:** a person who uses a typewriter

ty•ran•ni•cal *adj* **:** of, relating to, or like that of tyranny or a tyrant

ty•ran•no•saur *n* **:** a huge North American flesh-eating dinosaur that had small forelegs and walked on its hind legs

ty•ran•no•sau•rus *n* **:** TYRANNOSAUR

tyr•an•ny *n, pl* **tyr•an•nies 1 :** a government in which all power is in the hands of a single ruler **2 :** harsh, cruel, and severe government or conduct **3 :** a tyrannical act

ty•rant *n* **1 :** a ruler who has no legal limits on his or her power **2 :** a ruler who exercises total power harshly and cruelly **3 :** a person who uses authority or power harshly

U

u *n, pl* **u's** *or* **us** *often cap* **1 :** the twenty-first letter of the English alphabet **2 :** a grade rating a student's work as unsatisfactory
ud•der *n* **:** an organ (as of a cow) made up of two or more milk glands enclosed in a common pouch but opening by separate nipples
ugh *interj* — used to indicate the sound of a cough or to express disgust or horror
ug•ly *adj* **ug•li•er; ug•li•est 1 :** unpleasant to look at **:** not attractive **2 :** [1]OFFENSIVE 3 **3 :** not pleasant **:** TROUBLESOME **4 :** showing a mean or quarrelsome disposition — **ug•li•ness** *n*
uku•le•le *n* **:** a musical instrument like a small guitar with four strings
ul•cer *n* **:** an open sore in which tissue is eaten away and which may discharge pus
ul•cer•ate *vb* **ul•cer•at•ed; ul•cer•at•ing :** to cause or have an ulcer
ul•cer•ation *n* **1 :** the process of forming or state of having an ulcer **2 :** ULCER
ul•cer•ous *adj* **:** being or accompanied by ulceration
ul•na *n, pl* **ul•nas** *or* **ul•nae :** the bone on the side of the forearm opposite the thumb
ul•te•ri•or *adj* **:** not seen or made known
ul•ti•mate *adj* **1 :** last in a series **:** FINAL **2 :** [1]EXTREME 1 **3 :** FUNDAMENTAL, ABSOLUTE — **ul•ti•mate•ly** *adv*
ul•ti•ma•tum *n, pl* **ul•ti•ma•tums** *or* **ul•ti•ma•ta :** a final condition or demand that if rejected could end peaceful talks and lead to forceful action
ul•tra *adj* **:** [1]EXTREME 1, EXCESSIVE
ultra- *prefix* **1 :** beyond in space **:** on the other side **2 :** beyond the limits of **:** SUPER- **3 :** beyond what is ordinary or proper **:** too
ul•tra•vi•o•let *adj* **:** relating to or producing ultraviolet light
ultraviolet light *n* **:** waves that are like light but cannot be seen, that lie beyond the violet end of the spectrum, and that are found especially along with light from the sun
um•bil•i•cal cord *n* **:** a cord joining a fetus to its placenta
um•brel•la *n* **:** a fabric covering stretched over folding ribs attached to a rod or pole and used as a protection against rain or sun
umi•ak *n* **:** an open Eskimo boat made of a wooden frame covered with hide
um•pire *n* **:** a sports official who rules on plays
[1]**un-** *prefix* **:** not **:** IN-, NON-
[2]**un-** *prefix* **1 :** do the opposite of **:** DE- 1, DIS- 1 **2 :** deprive of, remove a specified thing from, or free or release from **3 :** completely
un•able *adj* **:** not able
un•ac•count•able *adj* **:** not accountable **:** not to be explained **:** STRANGE — **un•ac•count•ably** *adv*
un•ac•cus•tomed *adj* **:** not accustomed **:** not customary
un•af•fect•ed *adj* **1 :** not influenced or changed **2 :** free from false behavior intended to impress others **:** GENUINE — **un•af•fect•ed•ly** *adv*
un•afraid *adj* **:** not afraid
un•aid•ed *adj* **:** not aided
un•al•loyed *adj* **:** PURE 1 3
unan•i•mous *adj* **1 :** having the same opinion **2 :** showing total agreement
un•armed *adj* **:** having no weapons or armor
un•asked *adj* **:** not asked or asked for
un•as•sum•ing *adj* **:** MODEST 1
un•at•trac•tive *adj* **:** not attractive **:** [1]PLAIN 7
un•avoid•able *adj* **:** INEVITABLE — **un•avoid•ably** *adv*
[1]**un•aware** *adv* **:** UNAWARES
[2]**unaware** *adj* **:** not aware **:** IGNORANT — **un•aware•ness** *n*
un•awares *adv* **1 :** without knowing **:** UNINTENTIONALLY **2 :** without warning **:** by surprise
un•bal•anced *adj* **1 :** not balanced **2 :** not completely sane
un•bear•able *adj* **:** seeming too great or too bad to put up with — **un•bear•ably** *adv*
un•be•com•ing *adj* **:** not becoming **:** not suitable or proper — **un•be•com•ing•ly** *adv*
un•be•lief *n* **:** lack of belief
un•be•liev•able *adj* **:** too unlikely to be believed — **un•be•liev•ably** *adv*
un•be•liev•er *n* **1 :** a person who doubts what is said **2 :** a person who has no religious beliefs
un•bend *vb* **un•bent; un•bend•ing :** RELAX 3
un•bend•ing *adj* **:** not relaxed and easy in manner
un•bi•ased *adj* **:** free from bias
un•bind *vb* **un•bound; un•bind•ing 1 :** to remove a band from **:** UNTIE **2 :** to set free
un•born *adj* **:** not yet born
un•bos•om *vb* **:** to tell someone one's own thoughts or feelings
un•bound•ed *adj* **:** having no limits
un•break•able *adj* **:** not easily broken
un•bro•ken *adj* **1 :** not damaged **:** WHOLE **2 :** not tamed for use **3 :** not interrupted
un•buck•le *vb* **un•buck•led; un•buck•ling :** to unfasten the buckle of (as a belt)

un·bur·den *vb* **1 :** to free from a burden **2 :** to free oneself from (as cares)
un·but·ton *vb* **:** to unfasten the buttons of (as a garment)
un·called–for *adj* **:** not needed or wanted **:** not proper
un·can·ny *adj* **1 :** MYSTERIOUS, EERIE **2 :** suggesting powers or abilities greater than normal for humans — **un·can·ni·ly** *adv*
un·ceas·ing *adj* **:** never stopping **:** CONTINUOUS — **un·ceas·ing·ly** *adv*
un·cer·tain *adj* **1 :** not exactly known or decided on **2 :** not known for sure **3 :** not sure **4 :** likely to change **:** not dependable — **un·cer·tain·ly** *adv*
un·cer·tain·ty *n, pl* **un·cer·tain·ties 1 :** lack of certainty **:** DOUBT **2 :** something uncertain
un·change·able *adj* **:** not changing or capable of being changed
un·changed *adj* **:** not changed
un·chang·ing *adj* **:** not changing or able to change
un·charged *adj* **:** having no electric charge
un·civ·il *adj* **:** IMPOLITE — **un·civ·il·ly** *adv*
un·civ·i·lized *adj* **1 :** not civilized **:** BARBAROUS **2 :** far away from civilization **:** WILD
un·cle *n* **1 :** the brother of one's father or mother **2 :** the husband of one's aunt
un·clean *adj* **1 :** not pure and innocent **:** WICKED **2 :** not allowed for use by religious law **3 :** DIRTY 1, FILTHY — **unclean·ness** *n*
[1]**un·clean·ly** *adj* **:** UNCLEAN 1, 3 — **unclean·li·ness** *n*
[2]**un·clean·ly** *adv* **:** in an unclean manner
un·cleared *adj* **:** not cleared especially of trees or brush
Un·cle Sam *n* **:** the American government, nation, or people pictured or thought of as a person
un·clothed *adj* **:** NAKED 1, 2
un·com·fort·able *adj* **1 :** causing discomfort **2 :** feeling discomfort **:** UNEASY — **un·com·fort·ably** *adv*
un·com·mon *adj* **1 :** not often found or seen **:** UNUSUAL **2 :** not ordinary **:** REMARKABLE — **un·com·mon·ly** *adv* — **un·com·mon·ness** *n*
un·com·pro·mis·ing *adj* **:** not willing to give in even a little — **un·com·pro·mis·ing·ly** *adv*
un·con·cern *n* **:** lack of care or interest **:** INDIFFERENCE
un·con·cerned *adj* **1 :** not involved or interested **2 :** free of worry — **un·con·cern·ed·ly** *adv*
un·con·di·tion·al *adj* **:** without any special exceptions — **un·con·di·tion·al·ly** *adv*
un·con·quer·able *adj* **:** not capable of being beaten or overcome
un·con·scious *adj* **1 :** not aware **2 :** having lost consciousness **3 :** not intentional or planned — **un·con·scious·ly** *adv* — **un·con·scious·ness** *n*
un·con·sti·tu·tion·al *adj* **:** not according to the constitution (as of a government)
un·con·trol·la·ble *adj* **:** hard or impossible to control — **un·con·trol·la·bly** *adv*
un·con·trolled *adj* **:** not being controlled
un·couth *adj* **:** vulgar in conduct or speech **:** CRUDE — **un·couth·ly** *adv*
un·cov·er *vb* **1 :** to make known **2 :** to make visible by removing some covering
un·cul·ti·vat·ed *adj* **:** not cultivated
un·curl *vb* **:** to make or become straightened out from a curled position
un·cut *adj* **1 :** not cut down or cut into **2 :** not shaped by cutting
un·daunt·ed *adj* **:** not discouraged or frightened **:** FEARLESS
un·de·cid·ed *adj* **1 :** not settled **2 :** not having decided
un·de·clared *adj* **:** not announced or openly confessed
un·de·fined *adj* **:** not defined
un·de·ni·able *adj* **:** plainly true — **un·de·ni·ably** *adv*
[1]**un·der** *adv* **1 :** in or into a position below or beneath something **2 :** below some quantity or level **3 :** so as to be covered or hidden
[2]**under** *prep* **1 :** lower than and topped or sheltered by **2 :** below the surface of **3 :** in or into such a position as to be covered or hidden by **4 :** commanded or guided by **5 :** controlled or limited by **6 :** affected or influenced by the action or effect of **7 :** within the division or grouping of **8 :** less or lower than (as in size, amount, or rank)
[3]**under** *adj* **1 :** lying or placed below or beneath **2 :** [1]SUBORDINATE 1
un·der·brush *n* **:** shrubs and small trees growing among large trees
un·der·clothes *n pl* **:** UNDERWEAR
un·der·cloth·ing *n* **:** UNDERWEAR
un·der·dog *n* **:** a person or team thought to have little chance of winning (as an election or a game)
un·der·foot *adv* **1 :** under the feet **2 :** close about one's feet **:** in one's way
un·der·gar·ment *n* **:** a garment to be worn under another
un·der·go *vb* **un·der·went; un·der·gone; un·der·go·ing :** to have (something) done or happen to oneself **:** EXPERIENCE
[1]**un·der·ground** *adv* **1 :** beneath the surface of the earth **2 :** in or into hiding or secret operation

[2]**un·der·ground** *n* **1 :** SUBWAY 2 **2 :** a secret political movement or group
[3]**un·der·ground** *adj* **1 :** being or growing under the surface of the ground **2 :** done or happening secretly
un·der·growth *n* **:** UNDERBRUSH
[1]**un·der·hand** *adv* **:** in a secret or dishonest manner
[2]**underhand** *adj* **1 :** done in secret or so as to deceive **2 :** made with an upward movement of the hand or arm
un·der·hand·ed *adj* **:** [2]UNDERHAND 1 — **un·der·hand·ed·ly** *adv* — **un·der·hand·ed·ness** *n*
un·der·lie *vb* **un·der·lay; un·der·lain; un·der·ly·ing** **1 :** to be under **2 :** to form the foundation of **:** SUPPORT
un·der·line *vb* **un·der·lined; un·der·lin·ing** **1 :** to draw a line under **2 :** EMPHASIZE
un·der·lip *n* **:** the lower lip
un·der·mine *vb* **un·der·mined; un·der·min·ing** **1 :** to dig out or wear away the supporting earth beneath **2 :** to weaken secretly or little by little
[1]**un·der·neath** *prep* **:** directly under
[2]**underneath** *adv* **1 :** below a surface or object **:** BENEATH **2 :** on the lower side
un·der·nour·ished *adj* **:** given too little nourishment — **un·der·nour·ish·ment** *n*
un·der·pants *n pl* **:** pants worn under an outer garment
un·der·part *n* **:** a part lying on the lower side especially of a bird or mammal
un·der·pass *n* **:** a passage underneath something (as for a road passing under a railroad or another road)
un·der·priv·i·leged *adj* **:** having fewer advantages than others especially because of being poor
un·der·rate *vb* **un·der·rat·ed; un·der·rat·ing** **:** to rate too low **:** UNDERVALUE
un·der·score *vb* **un·der·scored; un·der·scor·ing** **:** UNDERLINE
[1]**un·der·sea** *adj* **1 :** being or done under the sea or under the surface of the sea **2 :** used under the surface of the sea
[2]**un·der·sea** *or* **un·der·seas** *adv* **:** under the surface of the sea
un·der·sell *vb* **un·der·sold; un·der·sell·ing** **:** to sell articles cheaper than
un·der·shirt *n* **:** a collarless garment with or without sleeves that is worn next to the body
un·der·side *n* **:** the side or surface lying underneath
un·der·skirt *n* **:** PETTICOAT
un·der·stand *vb* **un·der·stood; un·der·stand·ing** **1 :** to get the meaning of **2 :** to know thoroughly **3 :** to have reason to believe **4 :** to take as meaning something not openly made known **5 :** to have a sympathetic attitude **6 :** to accept as settled
un·der·stand·able *adj* **:** possible or easy to understand — **un·der·stand·ably** *adv*
[1]**un·der·stand·ing** *n* **1 :** ability to get the meaning of and judge **2 :** AGREEMENT 2
[2]**understanding** *adj* **:** having or showing kind or favorable feelings toward others **:** SYMPATHETIC
un·der·study *n, pl* **un·der·stud·ies** **:** an actor who is prepared to take over another actor's part if necessary
un·der·take *vb* **un·der·took; un·der·tak·en; un·der·tak·ing** **1 :** to plan or try to accomplish **2 :** to take on as a duty **:** AGREE
un·der·tak·er *n* **:** a person whose business is to prepare the dead for burial and to take charge of funerals
un·der·tak·ing *n* **1 :** the act of a person who undertakes something **2 :** the business of an undertaker **3 :** something undertaken
un·der·tone *n* **1 :** a low or quiet tone **2 :** a partly hidden feeling
un·der·tow *n* **:** a current beneath the surface of the water that moves away from or along the shore while the surface water above it moves toward the shore
un·der·val·ue *vb* **un·der·val·ued; un·der·valu·ing** **:** to value below the real worth
[1]**un·der·wa·ter** *adj* **:** lying, growing, worn, or operating below the surface of the water
[2]**un·der·wa·ter** *adv* **:** under the surface of the water
un·der·wear *n* **:** clothing worn next to the skin and under other clothing
un·der·weight *adj* **:** weighing less than what is normal, average, or necessary
underwent *past of* UNDERGO
un·der·world *n* **:** the world of organized crime
[1]**un·de·sir·able** *adj* **:** not desirable — **un·de·sir·ably** *adv*
[2]**undesirable** *n* **:** an undesirable person
un·de·vel·oped *adj* **:** not developed
un·di·gest·ed *adj* **:** not digested
un·dig·ni·fied *adj* **:** not dignified
un·dis·cov·ered *adj* **:** not discovered
un·dis·put·ed *adj* **:** not disputed **:** UNQUESTIONABLE
un·dis·turbed *adj* **:** not disturbed
un·do *vb* **un·did; un·done; un·do·ing; un·does** **1 :** UNTIE, UNFASTEN **2 :** UNWRAP, OPEN **3 :** to destroy the effect of **4 :** to cause the ruin of
un·do·ing *n* **1 :** an act or instance of unfastening **2 :** a cause of ruin or destruction
un·done *adj* **:** not done or finished
un·doubt·ed *adj* **:** not doubted
un·doubt·ed·ly *adv* **:** without doubt **:** SURELY

un·dress *vb* **:** to remove the clothes or covering of

un·dy·ing *adj* **:** living or lasting forever **:** IMMORTAL

un·earth *vb* **1 :** to drive or draw from the earth **:** dig up **2 :** to bring to light **:** UNCOVER

un·easy *adj* **un·eas·i·er; un·eas·i·est 1 :** not easy in manner **:** AWKWARD **2 :** disturbed by pain or worry **:** RESTLESS — **un·eas·i·ly** *adv* — **un·eas·i·ness** *n*

un·ed·u·cat·ed *adj* **:** not educated

un·em·ployed *adj* **:** not employed **:** having no job

un·em·ploy·ment *n* **:** the state of being unemployed

un·end·ing *adj* **:** having no ending **:** ENDLESS — **un·end·ing·ly** *adv*

un·equal *adj* **1 :** not alike (as in size or value) **2 :** badly balanced or matched **3 :** not having the needed abilities — **un·equal·ly** *adv*

un·equaled *adj* **:** not equaled

un·even *adj* **1 :** ODD 2 **2 :** not level or smooth **3 :** IRREGULAR 3 **4 :** varying in quality **5 :** UNEQUAL 2 — **un·even·ly** *adv* — **un·even·ness** *n*

un·event·ful *adj* **:** not eventful **:** including no interesting or important happenings — **un·event·ful·ly** *adv*

un·ex·pect·ed *adj* **:** not expected — **un·ex·pect·ed·ly** *adv* — **un·ex·pect·ed·ness** *n*

un·fail·ing *adj* **:** not failing or likely to fail — **un·fail·ing·ly** *adv*

un·fair *adj* **:** not fair, honest, or just — **un·fair·ly** *adv* — **un·fair·ness** *n*

un·faith·ful *adj* **:** not faithful **:** DISLOYAL — **un·faith·ful·ly** *adv* — **un·faith·ful·ness** *n*

un·fa·mil·iar *adj* **1 :** not well known **:** STRANGE **2 :** not well acquainted

un·fa·mil·iar·i·ty *n* **:** the quality or state of being unfamiliar

un·fas·ten *vb* **:** to make or become loose **:** UNDO

un·fa·vor·able *adj* **1 :** not approving **2 :** likely to make difficult or unpleasant — **un·fa·vor·ably** *adv*

un·feel·ing *adj* **1 :** not able to feel **2 :** having no kindness or sympathy **:** CRUEL — **un·feel·ing·ly** *adv*

un·fin·ished *adj* **:** not finished

un·fit *adj* **1 :** not suitable **2 :** not qualified **3 :** UNSOUND 1 2 — **un·fit·ness** *n*

un·fledged *adj* **:** not feathered or ready for flight

un·fold *vb* **1 :** to open the folds of **:** open up **2 :** to lay open to view **:** REVEAL **3 :** to develop gradually

un·fore·seen *adj* **:** not known beforehand

un·for·get·ta·ble *adj* **:** not likely to be forgotten — **un·for·get·ta·bly** *adv*

un·for·giv·able *adj* **:** not to be forgiven or pardoned — **un·for·giv·ably** *adv*

1un·for·tu·nate *adj* **1 :** not fortunate **:** UNLUCKY **2 :** not proper or suitable — **un·for·tu·nate·ly** *adv*

2unfortunate *n* **:** an unfortunate person

un·found·ed *adj* **:** being without a sound basis

un·friend·ly *adj* **un·friend·li·er; un·friend·li·est :** not friendly or favorable **:** HOSTILE — **un·friend·li·ness** *n*

un·fruit·ful *adj* **1 :** not bearing fruit or offspring **2 :** not producing a desired result

un·furl *vb* **:** to open out from a rolled or folded state

un·fur·nished *adj* **:** not supplied with furniture

un·gain·ly *adj* **un·gain·li·er; un·gain·li·est :** CLUMSY 1, AWKWARD — **un·gain·li·ness** *n*

un·god·ly *adj* **un·god·li·er; un·god·li·est 1 :** disobedient to or denying God **:** IMPIOUS **2 :** SINFUL, WICKED **3 :** not normal or bearable

un·gra·cious *adj* **:** not gracious or polite — **un·gra·cious·ly** *adv*

un·grate·ful *adj* **:** not grateful — **un·grate·ful·ly** *adv* — **un·grate·ful·ness** *n*

1un·gu·late *adj* **:** having hooves

2ungulate *n* **:** a hoofed animal

un·hand *vb* **:** to remove the hand from **:** let go

un·hap·py *adj* **un·hap·pi·er; un·hap·pi·est 1 :** not fortunate **:** UNLUCKY **2 :** not cheerful **:** SAD **3 :** not suitable — **un·hap·pi·ly** *adv* — **un·hap·pi·ness** *n*

un·health·ful *adj* **:** not healthful

un·healthy *adj* **un·health·i·er; un·health·i·est 1 :** not good for one's health **2 :** not in good health **:** SICKLY **3 :** HARMFUL, BAD — **un·health·i·ly** *adv*

un·heard *adj* **:** not heard

un·heard–of *adj* **:** not known before

un·hin·dered *adj* **:** not hindered **:** not kept back

un·hitch *vb* **:** to free from being hitched

un·ho·ly *adj* **un·ho·li·er; un·ho·li·est 1 :** not holy **:** WICKED **2 :** UNGODLY 3 — **un·ho·li·ness** *n*

un·hook *vb* **1 :** to remove from a hook **2 :** to unfasten the hooks of

un·horse *vb* **un·horsed; un·hors·ing :** to cause to fall from or as if from a horse

un·hur·ried *adj* **:** not hurried

uni- *prefix* **:** one **:** single

uni·corn *n* **:** an imaginary animal that looks like a horse with one horn in the middle of the forehead

un·iden·ti·fied *adj* **:** not identified

uni·fi·ca·tion *n* **:** the act, process, or result of unifying **:** the state of being unified

[1]uni•form *adj* **1 :** having always the same form, manner, or degree **:** not changing **2 :** of the same form with others — **uni•form•ly** *adv*
[2]uniform *n* **:** special clothing worn by members of a particular group (as an army)
uni•formed *adj* **:** dressed in uniform
uni•for•mi•ty *n, pl* **uni•for•mi•ties :** the quality or state or an instance of being uniform
uniform resource lo•ca•tor *n* **:** URL
uni•fy *vb* **uni•fied; uni•fy•ing :** to make into or become a unit **:** UNITE
un•im•por•tant *adj* **:** not important
un•in•hab•it•ed *adj* **:** not lived in or on
un•in•tel•li•gi•ble *adj* **:** impossible to understand
un•in•ten•tion•al *adj* **:** not intentional — **un•in•ten•tion•al•ly** *adv*
un•in•ter•est•ed *adj* **:** not interested
un•in•ter•est•ing *adj* **:** not attracting interest or attention
un•in•ter•rupt•ed *adj* **:** not interrupted **:** CONTINUOUS
union *n* **1 :** an act or instance of uniting two or more things into one **2 :** something (as a nation) formed by a combining of parts or members **3 :** a device for connecting parts (as of a machine) **4 :** LABOR UNION
Union *adj* **:** of or relating to the side favoring the federal union in the American Civil War
unique *adj* **1 :** being the only one of its kind **2 :** very unusual — **unique•ly** *adv* — **unique•ness** *n*
uni•son *n* **1 :** sameness of musical pitch **2 :** the state of being tuned or sounded at the same pitch or at an octave **3 :** exact agreement
unit *n* **1 :** the least whole number **:** ONE **2 :** a fixed quantity (as of length, time, or value) used as a standard of measurement **3 :** a single thing, person, or group forming part of a whole **4 :** a part of a school course with a central theme
unite *vb* **unit•ed; unit•ing 1 :** to put or come together to form a single unit **2 :** to bind by legal or moral ties **3 :** to join in action
unit•ed *adj* **1 :** made one **2 :** being in agreement
uni•ty *n* **1 :** the quality or state of being one **2 :** the state of those who are in full agreement **:** HARMONY
uni•ver•sal *adj* **1 :** including, covering, or taking in all or everything **2 :** present or happening everywhere — **uni•ver•sal•ly** *adv*
universal resource lo•ca•tor *n* **:** URL
uni•verse *n* **:** all created things including the earth and celestial bodies viewed as making up one system
uni•ver•si•ty *n, pl* **uni•ver•si•ties :** an institution of higher learning that gives degrees in special fields (as law and medicine) as well as in the arts and sciences
un•just *adj* **:** not just **:** UNFAIR — **un•just•ly** *adv*
un•kempt *adj* **1 :** not combed **2 :** not neat and orderly **:** UNTIDY
un•kind *adj* **:** not kind or sympathetic — **un•kind•ly** *adv* — **un•kind•ness** *n*
[1]un•known *adj* **:** not known
[2]unknown *n* **:** one (as a quantity) that is unknown
un•lace *vb* **un•laced; un•lac•ing :** to untie the laces of
un•latch *vb* **:** to open by lifting a latch
un•law•ful *adj* **:** not lawful **:** ILLEGAL — **un•law•ful•ly** *adv*
un•learned *adj* **1 :** not educated **2 :** not based on experience **:** INSTINCTIVE
un•leash *vb* **:** to free from or as if from a leash
un•less *conj* **:** except on the condition that
[1]un•like *adj* **:** DIFFERENT, UNEQUAL — **un•like•ness** *n*
[2]unlike *prep* **1 :** different from **2 :** unusual for **3 :** differently from
un•like•ly *adj* **un•like•li•er; un•like•li•est 1 :** not likely **2 :** not promising — **un•like•li•ness** *n*
un•lim•it•ed *adj* **1 :** having no restrictions or controls **2 :** BOUNDLESS, INFINITE
un•load *vb* **1 :** to take away or off **:** REMOVE **2 :** to take a load from **3 :** to get rid of or be freed from a load or burden
un•lock *vb* **1 :** to unfasten the lock of **2 :** to make known
un•looked–for *adj* **:** not expected
un•loose *vb* **un•loosed; un•loos•ing 1 :** to make looser **:** RELAX **2 :** to set free
un•lucky *adj* **un•luck•i•er; un•luck•i•est 1 :** not fortunate **2 :** likely to bring misfortune **3 :** causing distress or regret — **un•luck•i•ly** *adv* — **un•luck•i•ness** *n*
un•man•age•able *adj* **:** hard or impossible to manage
un•man•ner•ly *adj* **:** not having or showing good manners
un•mar•ried *adj* **:** not married
un•mis•tak•able *adj* **:** impossible to mistake for anything else — **un•mis•tak•ably** *adv*
un•moved *adj* **1 :** not moved by deep feelings or excitement **:** CALM **2 :** staying in the same place or position
un•nat•u•ral *adj* **1 :** not natural or normal **2 :** ARTIFICIAL 3 — **un•nat•u•ral•ly** *adv* — **un•nat•u•ral•ness** *n*
un•nec•es•sary *adj* **:** not necessary — **un•nec•es•sar•i•ly** *adv*
un•nerve *vb* **un•nerved; un•nerv•ing :** to

cause to lose confidence, courage, or self-control
un·no·tice·able *adj* **:** not easily noticed
un·num·bered *adj* **1 :** not numbered **2 :** INNUMERABLE
un·ob·served *adj* **:** not observed
un·oc·cu·pied *adj* **1 :** not busy **2 :** not occupied **:** EMPTY
un·of·fi·cial *adj* **:** not official — **un·of·fi·cial·ly** *adv*
un·pack *vb* **1 :** to separate and remove things that are packed **2 :** to open and remove the contents of
un·paid *adj* **:** not paid
un·paint·ed *adj* **:** not painted
un·par·al·leled *adj* **:** having no parallel or equal
un·pleas·ant *adj* **:** not pleasant — **un·pleas·ant·ly** *adv* — **un·pleas·ant·ness** *n*
un·pop·u·lar *adj* **:** not popular
un·pre·dict·able *adj* **:** impossible to predict
un·prej·u·diced *adj* **:** not prejudiced
un·pre·pared *adj* **:** not prepared
un·prin·ci·pled *adj* **:** not having or showing high moral principles
un·ques·tion·able *adj* **:** being beyond question or doubt — **un·ques·tion·ably** *adv*
un·rav·el *vb* **un·rav·eled** *or* **un·rav·elled; un·rav·el·ing** *or* **un·rav·el·ling 1 :** to separate the threads of **:** UNTANGLE **2 :** SOLVE
un·re·al *adj* **:** not real
un·rea·son·able *adj* **:** not reasonable — **un·rea·son·able·ness** *n* — **un·rea·son·ably** *adv*
un·re·lent·ing *adj* **1 :** not giving in or softening in determination **:** STERN **2 :** not letting up or weakening in energy or pace — **un·re·lent·ing·ly** *adv*
un·re·li·able *adj* **:** not reliable
un·rest *n* **:** a disturbed or uneasy state
un·righ·teous *adj* **:** not righteous — **un·righ·teous·ly** *adv* — **un·righ·teous·ness** *n*
un·ripe *adj* **:** not ripe or mature
un·ri·valed *or* **un·ri·valled** *adj* **:** having no rival
un·roll *vb* **1 :** to unwind a roll of **2 :** to become unrolled
un·ruf·fled *adj* **1 :** not upset or disturbed **2 :** [1]SMOOTH 4
un·ruly *adj* **un·rul·i·er; un·rul·i·est :** not yielding easily to rule or restriction — **un·rul·i·ness** *n*
un·safe *adj* **:** exposed or exposing to danger
un·san·i·tary *adj* **:** not sanitary
un·sat·is·fac·to·ry *adj* **:** not satisfactory — **un·sat·is·fac·to·ri·ly** *adv*
un·sat·is·fied *adj* **:** not satisfied
un·say *vb* **un·said; un·say·ing :** to take back (something said)
un·schooled *adj* **:** not trained or taught
un·sci·en·tif·ic *adj* **:** not scientific — **un·sci·en·tif·i·cal·ly** *adv*
un·scram·ble *vb* **un·scram·bled; un·scram·bling :** to make orderly or clear again
un·screw *vb* **1 :** to remove the screws from **2 :** to loosen or withdraw by turning
un·scru·pu·lous *adj* **:** not scrupulous — **un·scru·pu·lous·ly** *adv*
un·seal *vb* **:** to break or remove the seal of **:** OPEN
un·sea·son·able *adj* **:** happening or coming at the wrong time — **un·sea·son·ably** *adv*
un·sea·soned *adj* **:** not made ready or fit for use (as by the passage of time)
un·seat *vb* **1 :** to throw from one's seat **2 :** to remove from a position of authority
un·seem·ly *adj* **un·seem·li·er; un·seem·li·est :** not polite or proper
un·seen *adj* **:** not seen **:** INVISIBLE
un·self·ish *adj* **:** not selfish — **un·self·ish·ly** *adv* — **un·self·ish·ness** *n*
un·set·tle *vb* **un·set·tled; un·set·tling :** to disturb the quiet or order of **:** UPSET
un·set·tled *adj* **1 :** not staying the same **2 :** not calm **3 :** not able to make up one's mind **:** DOUBTFUL **4 :** not paid **5 :** not taken over and lived in by settlers
un·shaped *adj* **:** imperfect especially in form
un·sheathe *vb* **un·sheathed; un·sheath·ing :** to draw from or as if from a sheath
un·sight·ly *adj* **:** not pleasant to look at **:** UGLY — **un·sight·li·ness** *n*
un·skilled *adj* **1 :** not skilled **2 :** not needing skill
un·skill·ful *adj* **:** not skillful **:** not having skill — **un·skill·ful·ly** *adv*
un·sound *adj* **1 :** not healthy or in good condition **2 :** being or having a mind that is not normal **3 :** not firmly made or placed **4 :** not fitting or true — **un·sound·ly** *adv* — **un·sound·ness** *n*
un·speak·able *adj* **1 :** impossible to express in words **2 :** extremely bad — **un·speak·ably** *adv*
un·spec·i·fied *adj* **:** not specified
un·spoiled *adj* **:** not spoiled
un·sta·ble *adj* **:** not stable
un·steady *adj* **un·stead·i·er; un·stead·i·est :** not steady **:** UNSTABLE — **un·stead·i·ly** *adv*
un·stressed *adj* **:** not stressed
un·suc·cess·ful *adj* **:** not successful — **un·suc·cess·ful·ly** *adv*
un·sup·port·ed *adj* **1 :** not supported or proved **2 :** not held up
un·sur·passed *adj* **:** not surpassed (as in excellence)
un·sus·pect·ing *adj* **:** having no suspicion **:** TRUSTING

un·tan·gle *vb* **un·tan·gled; un·tan·gling** **1** : to remove a tangle from **2** : to straighten out
un·tanned *adj* : not put through a tanning process
un·think·able *adj* : not to be thought of or considered as possible
un·think·ing *adj* : not taking thought : HEEDLESS
un·ti·dy *adj* **un·ti·di·er; un·ti·di·est** : not neat — **un·ti·di·ly** *adv* — **un·ti·di·ness** *n*
un·tie *vb* **un·tied; un·ty·ing** *or* **un·tie·ing** : to free from something that ties, fastens, or holds back
1**un·til** *prep* : up to the time of
2**until** *conj* : up to the time that
1**un·time·ly** *adv* : before a good or proper time
2**untimely** *adj* **1** : happening or done before the expected, natural, or proper time **2** : coming at the wrong time — **un·time·li·ness** *n*
un·tir·ing *adj* : not making or becoming tired : TIRELESS — **un·tir·ing·ly** *adv*
un·to *prep* : 1TO
un·told *adj* **1** : not told or made public **2** : not counted : VAST
un·to·ward *adj* : causing trouble or unhappiness : UNLUCKY
un·trou·bled *adj* : not troubled : free from worry
un·true *adj* **1** : not faithful : DISLOYAL **2** : not correct : FALSE — **un·tru·ly** *adv*
un·truth *n* **1** : the state of being false **2** : 3LIE
un·truth·ful *adj* : not containing or telling the truth : FALSE — **un·truth·ful·ly** *adv* — **un·truth·ful·ness** *n*
un·used *adj* **1** : not accustomed **2** : not having been used before **3** : not being used
un·usu·al *adj* : not usual — **un·usu·al·ly** *adv*
un·ut·ter·able *adj* : being beyond one's powers of description
un·veil *vb* : to show or make known to the public for the first time
un·voiced *adj* : VOICELESS
un·want·ed *adj* : not wanted
un·wary *adj* **un·war·i·er; un·war·i·est** : easily fooled or surprised — **un·war·i·ness** *n*
un·washed *adj* : not having been washed : DIRTY
un·wea·ried *adj* : not tired
un·well *adj* : being in poor health
un·whole·some *adj* : not good for bodily, mental, or moral health
un·wieldy *adj* : hard to handle or control because of size or weight — **un·wield·i·ness** *n*
un·will·ing *adj* : not willing — **un·will·ing·ly** *adv* — **un·will·ing·ness** *n*
un·wind *vb* **un·wound; un·wind·ing** **1** : UNROLL **2** : RELAX 3
un·wise *adj* : not wise : FOOLISH — **un·wise·ly** *adv*
un·wor·thy *adj* **un·wor·thi·er; un·wor·thi·est** : not worthy — **un·wor·thi·ly** *adv* — **un·wor·thi·ness** *n*
un·wrap *vb* **un·wrapped; un·wrap·ping** : to remove the wrapping from
un·writ·ten *adj* : not in writing : followed by custom
un·yield·ing *adj* **1** : not soft or flexible : HARD **2** : showing or having firmness or determination
1**up** *adv* **1** : in or to a higher position : away from the center of the earth **2** : from beneath a surface (as ground or water) **3** : from below the horizon **4** : in or into a vertical position **5** : out of bed **6** : with greater force **7** : in or into a better or more advanced state **8** : so as to make more active **9** : into being or knowledge **10** : for discussion **11** : into the hands of another **12** : COMPLETELY **13** — used to show completeness **14** : into storage **15** : so as to be closed **16** : so as to approach or arrive **17** : in or into pieces **18** : to a stop
2**up** *adj* **1** : risen above the horizon or ground **2** : being out of bed **3** : unusually high **4** : having been raised or built **5** : moving or going upward **6** : being on one's feet and busy **7** : well prepared **8** : going on **9** : at an end **10** : well informed
3**up** *prep* **1** : to, toward, or at a higher point of **2** : to or toward the beginning of **3** : 1ALONG 1
4**up** *n* : a period or state of doing well
5**up** *vb* **upped; up·ping** **1** : to act suddenly or surprisingly **2** : to make or become higher
up·beat *n* : a beat in music that is not accented and especially one just before a downbeat
up·braid *vb* : to criticize or scold severely
up·bring·ing *n* : the process of raising and training
up·com·ing *adj* : coming soon
up·draft *n* : an upward movement of gas (as air)
up·end *vb* : to set, stand, or rise on end
up·grade *vb* **up·grad·ed; up·grad·ing** : to raise to a higher grade or position
up·heav·al *n* : a period of great change or violent disorder
1**up·hill** *adv* **1** : in an upward direction **2** : against difficulties
2**up·hill** *adj* **1** : going up **2** : DIFFICULT 1

up·hold *vb* **up·held; up·hold·ing** **1 :** to give support to **2 :** to lift up
up·hol·ster *vb* **:** to provide with or as if with upholstery — **up·hol·ster·er** *n*
up·hol·stery *n, pl* **up·hol·ster·ies :** materials used to make a soft covering for a seat
up·keep *n* **:** the act or cost of keeping something in good condition
up·land *n* **:** high land usually far from a coast or sea
[1]**up·lift** *vb* **1 :** to lift up **2 :** to improve the moral, mental, or bodily condition of
[2]**up·lift** *n* **:** an act, process, or result of uplifting
up·on *prep* **:** [1]ON 1, 2, 3, 4, 8
[1]**up·per** *adj* **1 :** higher in position or rank **2 :** farther inland
[2]**upper** *n* **:** something (as the parts of a shoe above the sole) that is upper
upper hand *n* **:** ADVANTAGE 1
up·per·most *adj* **1 :** farthest up **2 :** being in the most important position
up·raise *vb* **up·raised; up·rais·ing :** to raise or lift up
[1]**up·right** *adj* **1 :** VERTICAL 2 **2 :** straight in posture **3 :** having or showing high moral standards — **up·right·ly** *adv* — **up·right·ness** *n*
[2]**upright** *n* **1 :** the state of being upright **2 :** something that is upright
up·rise *vb* **up·rose; up·ris·en; up·ris·ing :** [1]RISE 1, 2a, 7
up·ris·ing *n* **:** REBELLION
up·roar *n* **:** a state of commotion, excitement, or violent disturbance
up·root *vb* **1 :** to take out by or as if by pulling up by the roots **2 :** to take, send, or force away from a country or a traditional home
[1]**up·set** *vb* **up·set; up·set·ting** **1 :** to force or be forced out of the usual position **:** OVERTURN **2 :** to worry or make unhappy **3 :** to make somewhat ill **4 :** to cause confusion in **5 :** to defeat unexpectedly
[2]**up·set** *n* **:** an act or result of upsetting **:** a state of being upset
up·shot *n* **:** the final result
up·side *n* **:** the upper side or part
up·side down *adv* **1 :** in such a way that the upper part is underneath and the lower part is on top **2 :** in or into great confusion
upside–down *adj* **1 :** having the upper part underneath and the lower part on top **2 :** showing great confusion
[1]**up·stairs** *adv* **:** up the stairs **:** on or to an upper floor
[2]**up·stairs** *adj* **:** being on or relating to an upper floor
[3]**up·stairs** *n* **:** the part of a building above the ground floor
up·stand·ing *adj* **:** HONEST 2
up·start *n* **:** a person who gains quick or unexpected success and who makes a great show of pride in that success
up·stream *adv* **:** at or toward the beginning of a stream
up·swing *n* **:** a great increase or rise
up to *prep* **1 :** as far as **2 :** in accordance with **3 :** to the limit of
up–to–date *adj* **1 :** lasting up to the present time **2 :** knowing, being, or making use of what is new or recent
up·town *adv* **:** to, toward, or in what is thought of as the upper part of a town or city
[1]**up·turn** *vb* **:** to turn upward or up or over
[2]**up·turn** *n* **:** an upward turning
[1]**up·ward** *or* **up·wards** *adv* **1 :** in a direction from lower to higher **2 :** toward a higher or better state **3 :** toward a greater amount or a higher number or rate
[2]**upward** *adj* **:** turned toward or being in a higher place or level — **up·ward·ly** *adv*
up·wind *adv or adj* **:** in the direction from which the wind is blowing
ura·ni·um *n* **:** a radioactive metallic chemical element used as a source of atomic energy
Ura·nus *n* **:** the planet that is seventh in order of distance from the sun and has a diameter of about 47,000 kilometers
ur·ban *adj* **:** of, relating to, or being a city
ur·chin *n* **1 :** a mischievous or disrespectful youngster **2 :** SEA URCHIN
-ure *suffix* **1 :** act **:** process **2 :** office **:** duty **3 :** body performing an office or duty
urea *n* **:** a compound of nitrogen that is the chief solid substance dissolved in the urine of a mammal and is formed by the breaking down of protein
[1]**urge** *vb* **urged; urg·ing** **1 :** to try to get (something) accepted **:** argue in favor of **2 :** to try to convince **3 :** [2]FORCE 1, DRIVE
[2]**urge** *n* **:** a strong desire
ur·gen·cy *n* **:** the quality or state of being urgent
ur·gent *adj* **1 :** calling for immediate action **2 :** having or showing a sense of urgency — **ur·gent·ly** *adv*
uri·nal *n* **1 :** a container for urine **2 :** a place for urinating
uri·nary *adj* **:** of or relating to urine or the organs producing it
uri·nate *vb* **uri·nat·ed; uri·nat·ing :** to discharge urine
uri·na·tion *n* **:** the act of urinating
urine *n* **:** the yellowish liquid produced by the kidneys and given off from the body as waste
URL *n* **:** the address of a computer or a document on the Internet

urn *n* **1 :** a container usually in the form of a vase resting on a stand **2 :** a closed container with a faucet used for serving a hot beverage

us *pron objective case of* WE

us·able *adj* **:** suitable or fit for use

us·age *n* **1 :** usual way of doing things **2 :** the way in which words and phrases are actually used **3 :** the action of using **:** USE

[1]**use** *n* **1 :** the act of using something **2 :** the fact or state of being used **3 :** way of using **4 :** the ability or power to use something **5 :** the quality or state of being useful **6 :** a reason or need to use **7 :** LIKING

[2]**use** *vb* **used; us·ing 1 :** to put into action or service **:** make use of **2 :** to take into the body **3 :** to do something by means of **4 :** to behave toward **:** TREAT **5** — used with *to* to show a former custom, fact, or state — **us·er** *n*

used *adj* **1 :** SECONDHAND 1 **2 :** having the habit of doing or putting up with something

use·ful *adj* **:** that can be put to use **:** USABLE — **use·ful·ly** *adv* — **use·ful·ness** *n*

use·less *adj* **:** being of or having no use — **use·less·ly** *adv* — **use·less·ness** *n*

us·er–friend·ly *adj* **:** easy to learn, use, understand, or deal with — **user–friendliness** *n*

[1]**ush·er** *n* **:** a person who shows people to seats (as in a theater)

[2]**usher** *vb* **1 :** to show to a place as an usher **2 :** to come before as if to lead in or announce

usu·al *adj* **:** done, found, used or existing most of the time — **usu·al·ly** *adv*

usurp *vb* **:** to take and hold unfairly or by force — **usurp·er** *n*

uten·sil *n* **1 :** a tool or container used in a home and especially a kitchen **2 :** a useful tool

uter·us *n, pl* **uteri :** the organ of a female mammal in which the young develop before birth

util·i·ty *n, pl* **util·i·ties 1 :** the quality or state of being useful **2 :** a business that supplies a public service (as electricity or gas) under special regulation by the government

uti·li·za·tion *n* **:** the action of utilizing **:** the state of being utilized

uti·lize *vb* **uti·lized; uti·liz·ing :** to make use of especially for a certain job

[1]**ut·most** *adj* **:** of the greatest or highest degree or amount

[2]**utmost** *n* **:** the most possible

[1]**ut·ter** *adj* **:** in every way **:** TOTAL — **ut·ter·ly** *adv*

[2]**utter** *vb* **1 :** to send forth as a sound **2 :** to express in usually spoken words

ut·ter·ance *n* **:** something uttered

V

v *n, pl* **v's** *or* **vs** *often cap* **1 :** the twenty-second letter of the English alphabet **2 :** five in Roman numerals

va·can·cy *n, pl* **va·can·cies 1 :** something (as an office or hotel room) that is vacant **2 :** empty space **3 :** the state of being vacant

va·cant *adj* **1 :** not filled, used, or lived in **2 :** free from duties or care **3 :** showing a lack of thought **:** FOOLISH

va·cate *vb* **va·cat·ed; va·cat·ing :** to leave vacant

[1]**va·ca·tion** *n* **1 :** a period during which activity (as of a school) is stopped for a time **2 :** a period spent away from home or business in travel or amusement

[2]**vacation** *vb* **:** to take or spend a vacation — **va·ca·tion·er** *n*

vac·ci·nate *vb* **vac·ci·nat·ed; vac·ci·nat·ing :** to inoculate with weak germs in order to protect against a disease

vac·ci·na·tion *n* **1 :** the act of vaccinating **2 :** the scar left by vaccinating

vac·cine *n* **:** a material (as one containing killed or weakened bacteria or virus) used in vaccinating

vac·il·late *vb* **vac·il·lat·ed; vac·il·lat·ing :** to hesitate between courses or opinions **:** be unable to choose

[1]**vac·u·um** *n, pl* **vac·u·ums** *or* **vac·ua 1 :** a space completely empty of matter **2 :** a space from which most of the air has been removed (as by a pump) **3 :** VACUUM CLEANER

[2]**vacuum** *adj* **:** of, containing, producing, or using a partial vacuum

[3]**vacuum** *vb* **:** to use a vacuum cleaner on

vacuum bottle *n* **:** THERMOS

vacuum cleaner *n* **:** an electrical appliance for cleaning (as floors or rugs) by suction

vacuum tube *n* **:** an electron tube having a high vacuum

[1]**vag·a·bond** *adj* **:** moving from place to place without a fixed home

[2]**vagabond** *n* **:** a person who leads a vagabond life

va·gi·na *n* **:** a canal leading out from the uterus

[1]**va•grant** *n* **:** a person who has no steady job and wanders from place to place

[2]**vagrant** *adj* **1 :** wandering about from place to place **2 :** having no fixed course

vague *adj* **vagu•er; vagu•est 1 :** not clearly expressed **2 :** not clearly understood **3 :** not clearly outlined **:** SHADOWY — **vague•ly** *adv* — **vague•ness** *n*

vain *adj* **1 :** having no success **2 :** proud of one's looks or abilities — **vain•ly** *adv* — **in vain 1 :** without success **2 :** in an unholy way

vain•glo•ri•ous *adj* **:** being vain and boastful — **vain•glo•ri•ous•ly** *adv* — **vain•glo•ri•ous•ness** *n*

vain•glo•ry *n* **:** too much pride especially in what one has done

vale *n* **:** VALLEY

val•e•dic•to•ri•an *n* **:** a student usually of the highest standing in a class who gives the farewell speech at the graduation ceremonies

val•en•tine *n* **1 :** a sweetheart given something as a sign of affection on Saint Valentine's Day **2 :** a greeting card or gift sent or given on Saint Valentine's Day

va•let *n* **:** a male servant or hotel employee who takes care of a man's clothes and does personal services

val•iant *adj* **1 :** boldly brave **2 :** done with courage **:** HEROIC — **val•iant•ly** *adv*

val•id *adj* **1 :** legally binding **2 :** based on truth or fact — **val•id•ly** *adv*

val•i•date *vb* **val•i•dat•ed; val•i•dat•ing :** to make valid

va•lid•i•ty *n* **:** the quality or state of being valid

va•lise *n* **:** TRAVELING BAG

val•ley *n, pl* **valleys :** an area of lowland between ranges of hills or mountains

val•or *n* **:** COURAGE

val•or•ous *adj* **:** having or showing valor **:** BRAVE — **val•or•ous•ly** *adv*

[1]**valu•able** *adj* **1 :** worth a large amount of money **2 :** of great use or service

[2]**valuable** *n* **:** a personal possession (as a jewel) of great value

[1]**val•ue** *n* **1 :** a fair return in goods, services, or money for something exchanged **2 :** worth in money **3 :** worth, usefulness, or importance in comparison with something else **4 :** a principle or quality that is valuable or desirable — **val•ue•less** *adj*

[2]**value** *vb* **val•ued; val•u•ing 1 :** to estimate the worth of **2 :** to think highly of

valve *n* **1 :** a structure in a tube of the body (as a vein) that closes temporarily to prevent passage of material or allows movement of a fluid in one direction only **2 :** a mechanical device by which the flow of liquid, gas, or loose material may be controlled by a movable part **3 :** a device on a brass musical instrument that changes the pitch of the tone **4 :** one of the separate pieces that make up the shell of some animals (as clams) and are often hinged — **valve•less** *adj*

vam•pire *n* **:** the body of a dead person believed to come from the grave at night and suck the blood of sleeping persons

vampire bat *n* **:** a bat of tropical America that feeds on the blood of birds and mammals often including domestic animals

[1]**van** *n* **:** VANGUARD

[2]**van** *n* **:** a usually closed wagon or truck for moving goods or animals

va•na•di•um *n* **:** a metallic chemical element used in making a strong alloy of steel

van•dal *n* **:** a person who destroys or damages property on purpose

van•dal•ism *n* **:** intentional destruction of or damage to property

vane *n* **1 :** WEATHER VANE **2 :** a flat or curved surface that turns around a center when moved by wind or water

van•guard *n* **1 :** the troops moving at the front of an army **2 :** FOREFRONT

va•nil•la *n* **:** a substance extracted from vanilla beans and used as a flavoring for sweet foods and beverages

vanilla bean *n* **:** the long pod of a tropical American climbing orchid from which vanilla is extracted

van•ish *vb* **:** to pass from sight or existence **:** DISAPPEAR

van•i•ty *n, pl* **van•i•ties 1 :** something that is vain **2 :** the quality or fact of being vain **3 :** a small box for cosmetics

van•quish *vb* **:** OVERCOME 1

va•por *n* **1 :** fine bits (as of fog or smoke) floating in the air and clouding it **2 :** a substance in the form of a gas

va•por•ize *vb* **va•por•ized; va•por•iz•ing :** to turn from a liquid or solid into vapor — **va•por•iz•er** *n*

[1]**var•i•able** *adj* **1 :** able to change **:** likely to be changed **:** CHANGEABLE **2 :** having differences **3 :** not true to type — **var•i•able•ness** *n* — **var•i•ably** *adv*

[2]**variable** *n* **1 :** something that is variable **2 :** PLACEHOLDER

var•i•ant *n* **1 :** an individual that shows variation from a type **2 :** one of two or more different spellings or pronunciations of a word

var•i•a•tion *n* **1 :** a change in form, position, or condition **2 :** amount of change or difference **3 :** departure from what is usual to a group

var•ied *adj* **1 :** having many forms or types **2 :** VARIEGATED 2

var·ie·gat·ed *adj* **1 :** having patches, stripes, or marks of different colors **2 :** full of variety

va·ri·ety *n, pl* **va·ri·et·ies** **1 :** the quality or state of having different forms or types **2 :** a collection of different things **:** ASSORTMENT **3 :** something differing from others of the class to which it belongs **4 :** entertainment made up of performances (as dances and songs) that follow one another and are not related

var·i·ous *adj* **1 :** of different kinds **2 :** different one from another **:** UNLIKE **3 :** made up of an indefinite number greater than one

1var·nish *n* **:** a liquid that is spread on a surface and dries into a hard coating

2varnish *vb* **:** to cover with or as if with varnish

var·si·ty *n, pl* **var·si·ties :** the main team that represents a college, school, or club in contests

vary *vb* **var·ied; vary·ing** **1 :** to make a partial change in **2 :** to make or be of different kinds **3 :** DEVIATE **4 :** to differ from the usual members of a group

vas·cu·lar *adj* **:** of, relating to, containing, or being bodily vessels

vase *n* **:** an often round container of greater depth than width used chiefly for ornament or for flowers

vas·sal *n* **:** a person in the Middle Ages who received protection and land from a lord in return for loyalty and service

vast *adj* **:** very great in size or amount — **vast·ly** *adv* — **vast·ness** *n*

vat *n* **:** a large container (as a tub) especially for holding liquids in manufacturing processes

vaude·ville *n* **:** theatrical entertainment made up of songs, dances, and comic acts

1vault *n* **1 :** an arched structure of stone or concrete forming a ceiling or roof **2 :** an arch suggesting a vault **3 :** a room or compartment for storage or safekeeping **4 :** a burial chamber

2vault *vb* **:** to leap with the aid of the hands or a pole

3vault *n* **:** 2LEAP

VCR *n* **:** a device for recording (as television programs) on videocassettes and playing them back

veal *n* **:** a young calf or its flesh for use as meat

vec·tor *n* **:** a creature (as a fly) that carries disease germs

vee·jay *n* **:** an announcer of a program (as on television) that features music videos

veer *vb* **:** to change direction or course

vee·ry *n, pl* **veeries :** a common brownish woodland thrush of the eastern United States

1veg·e·ta·ble *adj* **1 :** of, relating to, or made up of plants **2 :** gotten from plants

2vegetable *n* **1 :** 2PLANT 1 **2 :** a plant or plant part grown for use as human food and usually eaten with the main part of a meal

veg·e·tar·i·an *n* **:** a person who lives on plants and their products

veg·e·ta·tion *n* **:** plant life or cover (as of an area)

veg·e·ta·tive *adj* **1 :** of, relating to, or functioning in nutrition and growth rather than reproduction **2 :** of, relating to, or involving reproduction by other than sexual means

ve·he·mence *n* **:** the quality or state of being vehement

ve·he·ment *adj* **1 :** showing great force or energy **2 :** highly emotional — **ve·he·ment·ly** *adv*

ve·hi·cle *n* **1 :** a means by which something is expressed, achieved, or shown **2 :** something used to transport persons or goods

1veil *n* **1 :** a piece of cloth or net worn usually by women over the head and shoulders and sometimes over the face **2 :** something that covers or hides like a veil

2veil *vb* **:** to cover or provide with a veil

vein *n* **1 :** a long narrow opening in rock filled with mineral matter **2 :** one of the blood vessels that carry the blood back to the heart **3 :** one of the bundles of fine tubes that make up the framework of a leaf and carry food, water, and nutrients in the plant **4 :** one of the thickened parts that support the wing of an insect **5 :** a streak of different color or texture (as in marble) **6 :** a style of expression — **veined** *adj*

veld *or* **veldt** *n* **:** an area of grassy land especially in southern Africa

ve·loc·i·ty *n, pl* **ve·loc·i·ties :** quickness of motion **:** SPEED

1vel·vet *n* **:** a fabric with short soft raised fibers

2velvet *adj* **1 :** made of or covered with velvet **2 :** VELVETY

vel·vety *adj* **:** soft and smooth like velvet

ve·na·tion *n* **:** an arrangement or system of veins

vend *vb* **:** to sell or offer for sale — **vend·er** *or* **ven·dor** *n*

vending machine *n* **:** a machine for selling merchandise operated by putting a coin or coins into a slot

1ve·neer *n* **1 :** a thin layer of wood bonded to other wood usually to provide a finer surface or a stronger structure **2 :** a protective or ornamental facing (as of brick)

2veneer *vb* **:** to cover with a veneer

ven·er·a·ble *adj* **1 :** deserving to be venerated — often used as a religious title **2 :** deserving honor or respect

ven·er·ate *vb* **ven·er·at·ed; ven·er·at·ing :** to show deep respect for

ven·er·a·tion *n* **1 :** the act of venerating **:** the state of being venerated **2 :** a feeling of deep respect

ve·ne·re·al *adj* **:** of or relating to sexual intercourse or to diseases that pass from person to person by it

ve·ne·tian blind *n* **:** a blind having thin horizontal slats that can be adjusted to keep out light or to let light come in between them

ven·geance *n* **:** punishment given in return for an injury or offense

ven·i·son *n* **:** the flesh of a deer used as food

ven·om *n* **:** poisonous matter produced by an animal (as a snake) and passed to a victim usually by a bite or sting

ven·om·ous *adj* **:** having or producing venom **:** POISONOUS

ve·nous *adj* **:** of, relating to, or full of veins

[1]**vent** *vb* **1 :** to provide with an outlet **2 :** to serve as an outlet for **3 :** [3]EXPRESS 1

[2]**vent** *n* **1 :** OUTLET 1, 2 **2 :** an opening for the escape of a gas or liquid

ven·ti·late *vb* **ven·ti·lat·ed; ven·ti·lat·ing 1 :** to discuss freely and openly **2 :** to let in air and especially a current of fresh air **3 :** to provide with ventilation

ven·ti·la·tion *n* **1 :** the act or process of ventilating **2 :** a system or means of providing fresh air

ven·ti·la·tor *n* **:** a device for letting in fresh air or driving out bad or stale air

ven·tral *adj* **:** of, relating to, or being on or near the surface of the body that in man is the front but in most animals is the lower surface

ven·tri·cle *n* **:** the part of the heart from which blood passes into the arteries

ven·tril·o·quist *n* **:** a person skilled in speaking in such a way that the voice seems to come from a source other than the speaker

[1]**ven·ture** *vb* **ven·tured; ven·tur·ing 1 :** to expose to risk **2 :** to face the risks and dangers of **3 :** to offer at the risk of being criticized **4 :** to go ahead in spite of danger

[2]**venture** *n* **:** a task or an act involving chance, risk, or danger

ven·ture·some *adj* **1 :** tending to take risks **2 :** involving risk — **ven·ture·some·ly** *adv* — **ven·ture·some·ness** *n*

ven·tur·ous *adj* **:** VENTURESOME — **ven·tur·ous·ly** *adv* — **ven·tur·ous·ness** *n*

Ve·nus *n* **:** the planet that is second in order of distance from the sun and has a diameter of about 12,200 kilometers

ve·ran·da *or* **ve·ran·dah** *n* **:** a long porch extending along one or more sides of a building

verb *n* **:** a word that expresses an act, occurrence, or state of being

[1]**ver·bal** *adj* **1 :** of, relating to, or consisting of words **2 :** of, relating to, or formed from a verb **3 :** spoken rather than written — **ver·bal·ly** *adv*

[2]**verbal** *n* **:** a word that combines characteristics of a verb with those of a noun or adjective

ver·be·na *n* **:** a garden plant with fragrant leaves and heads of white, pink, red, blue, or purple flowers with five petals

ver·dant *adj* **:** green with growing plants — **ver·dant·ly** *adv*

ver·dict *n* **1 :** the decision reached by a jury **2 :** JUDGMENT 2, OPINION

ver·dure *n* **:** green vegetation

[1]**verge** *n* **1 :** something that borders, limits, or bounds **:** EDGE **2 :** THRESHOLD 2, BRINK

[2]**verge** *vb* **verged; verg·ing :** to come near to being

ver·i·fi·ca·tion *n* **:** the act or process of verifying **:** the state of being verified

ver·i·fy *vb* **ver·i·fied; ver·i·fy·ing 1 :** to prove to be true or correct **:** CONFIRM **2 :** to check or test the accuracy of

ver·mi·cel·li *n* **:** a food similar to but thinner than spaghetti

ver·min *n, pl* **vermin :** small common harmful or objectionable animals (as fleas or mice) that are difficult to get rid of

ver·sa·tile *adj* **1 :** able to do many different kinds of things **2 :** having many uses

ver·sa·til·i·ty *n* **:** the quality or state of being versatile

verse *n* **1 :** a line of writing in which words are arranged in a rhythmic pattern **2 :** writing in which words are arranged in a rhythmic pattern **3 :** STANZA **4 :** one of the short parts of a chapter in the Bible

versed *adj* **:** having knowledge or skill as a result of experience, study, or practice

ver·sion *n* **1 :** a translation especially of the Bible **2 :** an account or description from a certain point of view

ver·sus *prep* **:** AGAINST 1

ver·te·bra *n, pl* **ver·te·brae :** one of the bony sections making up the backbone

[1]**ver·te·brate** *adj* **1 :** having vertebrae or a backbone **2 :** of or relating to the vertebrates

[2]**vertebrate** *n* **:** any of a large group of animals that includes the fishes, amphibians, reptiles, birds, and mammals all of which have a backbone extending down the back of the body

ver·tex *n, pl* **ver·ti·ces** *or* **ver·tex·es 1 :** the point opposite to and farthest from the base of a geometrical figure **2 :** the common endpoint of the sides of an angle

[1]**ver•ti•cal** *adj* **1 :** directly overhead **2 :** rising straight up and down from a level surface — **ver•ti•cal•ly** *adv*

[2]**vertical** *n* **:** something (as a line or plane) that is vertical

ver•ti•go *n, pl* **ver•ti•goes** *or* **ver•ti•gos :** a dizzy state

[1]**very** *adj* **1 :** [2]EXACT, PRECISE **2 :** exactly suitable or necessary **3 :** MERE, BARE **4 :** exactly the same

[2]**very** *adv* **1 :** to a great degree **:** EXTREMELY **2 :** in actual fact **:** TRULY

ves•pers *n pl, often cap* **:** a late afternoon or evening church service

ves•sel *n* **1 :** a hollow utensil (as a cup or bowl) for holding something **2 :** a craft larger than a rowboat for navigation of the water **3 :** a tube (as an artery) in which a body fluid is contained and carried or circulated

[1]**vest** *vb* **1 :** to place or give into the possession or control of some person or authority **2 :** to clothe in vestments

[2]**vest** *n* **:** a sleeveless garment usually worn under a suit coat

ves•ti•bule *n* **:** a hall or room between the outer door and the inside part of a building

ves•tige *n* **:** a tiny amount or visible sign of something lost or vanished **:** TRACE

ves•ti•gial *adj* **:** of, relating to, or being a vestige

vest•ment *n* **:** an outer garment especially for wear during ceremonies or by an official

[1]**vet** *n* **:** VETERINARIAN

[2]**vet** *n* **:** [1]VETERAN 2

[1]**vet•er•an** *n* **1 :** a person who has had long experience **2 :** a former member of the armed forces especially in war

[2]**veteran** *adj* **:** having gained skill through experience

vet•er•i•nar•i•an *n* **:** a doctor who treats diseases and injuries of animals

[1]**vet•er•i•nary** *adj* **:** of, relating to, or being the medical care of animals and especially domestic animals

[2]**veterinary** *n, pl* **vet•er•i•nar•ies :** VETERINARIAN

[1]**ve•to** *n, pl* **vetoes 1 :** a forbidding of something by a person in authority **2 :** the power of a president, governor, or mayor to prevent something from becoming law

[2]**veto** *vb* **1 :** FORBID, PROHIBIT **2 :** to prevent from becoming law by use of a veto

vex *vb* **1 :** to bring trouble, distress, or worry to **2 :** to annoy by small irritations

vex•a•tion *n* **1 :** the quality or state of being vexed **2 :** the act of vexing **3 :** a cause of trouble or worry

via *prep* **:** by way of

vi•a•ble *adj* **1 :** capable of living or growing **2 :** possible to use or apply

via•duct *n* **:** a bridge for carrying a road or railroad over something (as a gorge or highway)

vi•al *n* **:** a small container (as for medicines) that is usually made of glass or plastic

vi•brant *adj* **:** having or giving the sense of life, vigor, or action — **vi•brant•ly** *adv*

vi•brate *vb* **vi•brat•ed; vi•brat•ing :** to swing or cause to swing back and forth

vi•bra•tion *n* **1 :** a rapid motion (as of a stretched cord) back and forth **2 :** the action of vibrating **:** the state of being vibrated **3 :** a trembling motion

vi•bur•num *n* **:** any of a group of shrubs often grown for their broad clusters of usually white flowers

vic•ar *n* **1 :** a minister in charge of a church who serves under the authority of another minister **2 :** a church official who takes the place of or represents a higher official

vi•car•i•ous *adj* **:** experienced or understood as if happening to oneself — **vi•car•i•ous•ly** *adv* — **vi•car•i•ous•ness** *n*

vice *n* **1 :** evil conduct or habits **2 :** a moral fault or weakness

vice- *prefix* **:** one that takes the place of

vice admiral *n* **:** a commissioned officer in the Navy or Coast Guard ranking above a rear admiral

vice pres•i•dent *n* **:** an official (as of a government) whose rank is next below that of the president and who takes the place of the president when necessary

vice•roy *n* **:** the governor of a country who rules as the representative of a king or queen

vice ver•sa *adv* **:** with the order turned around

vi•cin•i•ty *n, pl* **vi•cin•i•ties 1 :** the state of being close **2 :** a surrounding area **:** NEIGHBORHOOD

vi•cious *adj* **1 :** doing evil things **:** WICKED **2 :** very dangerous **3 :** filled with or showing unkind feelings — **vi•cious•ly** *adv* — **vi•cious•ness** *n*

vic•tim *n* **1 :** a living being offered as a religious sacrifice **2 :** an individual injured or killed (as by disease) **3 :** a person who is cheated, fooled, or hurt by another

vic•tim•ize *vb* **vic•tim•ized; vic•tim•iz•ing :** to make a victim of

vic•tor *n* **:** WINNER, CONQUEROR

vic•to•ri•ous *adj* **:** having won a victory — **vic•to•ri•ous•ly** *adv*

vic•to•ry *n, pl* **vic•to•ries 1 :** the defeating

of an enemy or opponent **2 :** success in a struggle against difficulties

vict·ual *n* **1 :** food fit for humans **2 victuals** *pl* **:** supplies of food

vi·cu·ña *or* **vi·cu·na** *n* **:** a wild animal of the Andes that is related to the llama and produces a fine wool

1vid·eo *n* **1 :** TELEVISION **2 :** the visual part of television **3 :** 1VIDEOTAPE 1 **4 :** a videotaped performance of a song

2video *adj* **1 :** relating to or used in the sending or receiving of television images **2 :** being, relating to, or involving images on a television screen or computer display

vid·eo·cas·sette *n* **1 :** a case containing videotape for use with a VCR **2 :** a recording (as of a movie) on a videocassette

videocassette recorder *n* **:** VCR

video game *n* **:** a game played with images on a video screen

1vid·eo·tape *n* **1 :** a recording of visual images and sound (as of a television production) made on magnetic tape **2 :** the magnetic tape used for such a recording

2videotape *vb* **:** to make a videotape of

vie *vb* **vied; vy·ing :** COMPETE

1view *n* **1 :** the act of seeing or examining **2 :** an opinion or judgment influenced by personal feeling **3 :** all that can be seen from a certain place **:** SCENE **4 :** range of vision **5 :** 1PURPOSE **6 :** a picture that represents something that can be seen

2view *vb* **1 :** to look at carefully **2 :** 1SEE 1 — **view·er** *n*

view·point *n* **:** the angle from which something is considered

vig·il *n* **1 :** the day before a religious feast **2 :** a staying awake to keep watch when one normally would be sleeping

vig·i·lance *n* **:** a staying alert especially to possible danger

vig·i·lant *adj* **:** alert especially to avoid danger — **vig·i·lant·ly** *adv*

vig·i·lan·te *n* **:** a member of a group of volunteers organized to stop crime and punish criminals especially when the proper officials are not doing so

vig·or *n* **1 :** strength or energy of body or mind **2 :** active strength or force

vig·or·ous *adj* **1 :** having vigor **2 :** done with vigor — **vig·or·ous·ly** *adv*

Vi·king *n* **:** a member of the Scandinavian invaders of the coasts of Europe in the eighth to tenth centuries

vile *adj* **vil·er; vil·est 1 :** of little worth **2 :** WICKED 1 **3 :** very objectionable — **vile·ly** *adv* — **vile·ness** *n*

vil·i·fy *vb* **vil·i·fied; vil·i·fy·ing :** to speak of as worthless or wicked

vil·la *n* **1 :** an estate in the country **2 :** a large expensive home especially in the country or suburbs

vil·lage *n* **:** a place where people live that is usually smaller than a town

vil·lag·er *n* **:** a person who lives in a village

vil·lain *n* **:** a wicked person

vil·lain·ous *adj* **:** WICKED

vil·lainy *n, pl* **vil·lain·ies :** conduct or actions of or like those of a villain

vil·lus *n, pl* **vil·li :** one of the tiny extensions that are shaped like fingers, line the small intestine, and are active in absorbing nutrients

vim *n* **:** ENERGY 1, VIGOR

vin·di·cate *vb* **vin·di·cat·ed; vin·di·cat·ing 1 :** to free from blame or guilt **2 :** to show to be true or correct **:** JUSTIFY

vin·dic·tive *adj* **:** likely to seek revenge **:** meant to be harmful

vine *n* **:** a plant whose stem requires support and which climbs by tendrils or twining or creeps along the ground — **vine·like** *adj*

vin·e·gar *n* **:** a sour liquid made from cider, wine, or malt and used to flavor or preserve foods

vin·e·gary *adj* **:** like vinegar

vine·yard *n* **:** a field of grapevines

vin·tage *n* **1 :** the grapes grown or wine made during one season **2 :** a usually excellent wine of a certain type, region, and year **3 :** the time when something started or was made

1vi·o·la *n* **:** a hybrid garden flower that looks like but is smaller than a pansy

2vi·o·la *n* **:** an instrument of the violin family slightly larger and having a lower pitch than a violin

vi·o·late *vb* **vi·o·lat·ed; vi·o·lat·ing 1 :** to fail to keep **:** BREAK **2 :** to do harm or damage to **3 :** to treat in a very disrespectful way **4 :** DISTURB 1 — **vi·o·la·tor** *n*

vi·o·la·tion *n* **:** an act or instance of violating **:** the state of being violated

vi·o·lence *n* **1 :** the use of force to harm a person or damage property **2 :** great force or strength

vi·o·lent *adj* **1 :** showing very strong force **2 :** 1EXTREME 1, INTENSE **3 :** caused by force — **vi·o·lent·ly** *adv*

vi·o·let *n* **1 :** a wild or garden plant related to the pansies that has small often fragrant white, blue, purple, or yellow flowers **2 :** a reddish blue

vi·o·lin *n* **:** a stringed musical instrument with four strings that is usually held against the shoulder under the chin and played with a bow

vi·o·lon·cel·lo *n, pl* **vi·o·lon·cel·los :** CELLO

vi·per *n* **:** a snake that is or is believed to be poisonous

vir·eo *n, pl* **vir·e·os :** a small songbird that

DICTIONARY

eats insects and is olive-green or grayish in color

[1]**vir·gin** *n* **1 :** an unmarried woman devoted to religion **2 :** a girl or woman who has not had sexual intercourse

[2]**virgin** *adj* **1 :** not soiled **2 :** being a virgin **3 :** not changed by human actions

Vir·go *n* **1 :** a constellation between Leo and Libra imagined as a woman **2 :** the sixth sign of the zodiac or a person born under this sign

vir·ile *adj* **1 :** having qualities generally associated with a man **2 :** ENERGETIC, VIGOROUS

vir·tu·al *adj* **:** being almost but not quite complete — **vir·tu·al·ly** *adv*

virtual reality *n* **:** an artificial environment which is experienced through sights and sounds provided by a computer and in which one's actions partly decide what happens in the environment

vir·tue *n* **1 :** moral excellence **:** knowing what is right and acting in a right way **2 :** a desirable quality

vir·tu·o·so *n, pl* **vir·tu·o·sos** *or* **vir·tu·o·si :** a person who is an outstanding performer especially in music

vir·tu·ous *adj* **:** having or showing virtue — **vir·tu·ous·ly** *adv*

vir·u·lent *adj* **:** very infectious or poisonous **:** DEADLY

vi·rus *n* **1 :** an agent too tiny to be seen by the ordinary microscope that causes disease and that may be a living organism or may be a very special kind of protein molecule **2 :** a disease caused by a virus **3 :** a usually hidden computer program that causes harm by making copies of itself and inserting them into other programs

vis·count *n* **:** a British nobleman ranking below an earl and above a baron

vis·count·ess *n* **1 :** the wife or widow of a viscount **2 :** a woman who holds the rank of a viscount in her own right

vise *n* **:** a device with two jaws that works by a screw or lever for holding or clamping work

vis·i·bil·i·ty *n* **1 :** the quality or state of being visible **2 :** the degree of clearness of the atmosphere

vis·i·ble *adj* **1 :** capable of being seen **2 :** easily seen or understood **:** OBVIOUS — **vis·i·bly** *adv*

vi·sion *n* **1 :** something seen in the mind (as in a dream) **2 :** a vivid picture created by the imagination **3 :** the act or power of imagination **4 :** unusual ability to think or plan ahead **5 :** the act or power of seeing **:** SIGHT **6 :** the special sense by which the qualities of an object (as color) that make up its appearance are perceived

vi·sion·ary *n, pl* **vi·sion·ar·ies :** a person whose ideas or plans are impractical

[1]**vis·it** *vb* **1 :** to go to see in order to comfort or help **2 :** to call on as an act of friendship or courtesy or as or for a professional service **3 :** to stay with for a time as a guest **4 :** to go to for pleasure **5 :** to come to or upon

[2]**visit** *n* **1 :** a brief stay **:** CALL **2 :** a stay as a guest **3 :** a professional call

vis·i·tor *n* **:** a person who visits

vi·sor *n* **1 :** the movable front upper piece of a helmet **2 :** a part that sticks out to protect or shade the eyes

vis·ta *n* **:** a distant view through an opening or along an avenue

vi·su·al *adj* **1 :** of, relating to, or used in vision **2 :** obtained by the use of sight **3 :** appealing to the sense of sight — **vi·su·al·ly** *adv*

vi·su·al·ize *vb* **vi·su·al·ized; vi·su·al·iz·ing :** to see or form a mental image

vi·tal *adj* **1 :** of or relating to life **2 :** concerned with or necessary to the continuation of life **3 :** full of life and energy **4 :** very important — **vi·tal·ly** *adv*

vi·tal·i·ty *n, pl* **vi·tal·i·ties 1 :** capacity to live and develop **2 :** ENERGY 1

vi·tals *n pl* **:** the vital organs (as heart, lungs, and liver) of the body

vi·ta·min *n* **:** any of a group of organic substances that are found in natural foods, are necessary in small quantities to health, and include one (**vitamin A**) found mostly in animal products and needed for good vision, several (**vitamin B complex**) found in many foods and needed especially for growth, one (**vitamin C**) found in fruits and leafy vegetables and used as an enzyme and to prevent scurvy, and another (**vitamin D**) found in fish-liver oils, eggs, and milk and needed for healthy bone development

vi·va·cious *adj* **:** full of life **:** LIVELY — **vi·va·cious·ly** *adv*

vi·vac·i·ty *n* **:** the quality or state of being vivacious

vi·var·i·um *n, pl* **vi·var·ia** *or* **vi·var·i·ums :** an enclosure for keeping or studying plants or animals indoors

viv·id *adj* **1 :** seeming full of life and freshness **2 :** very strong or bright **3 :** producing strong mental images **4 :** acting clearly and powerfully — **viv·id·ly** *adv* — **viv·id·ness** *n*

vi·vip·a·rous *adj* **:** giving birth to living young rather than laying eggs

viv·i·sec·tion *n* **:** the operating or experimenting on a living animal usually for scientific study

vix·en *n* **:** a female fox

vo·cab·u·lary *n, pl* **vo·cab·u·lar·ies 1 :** a

list or collection of words defined or explained **2 :** a stock of words used in a language, by a group or individual, or in relation to a subject

vo·cal *adj* **1 :** uttered by the voice **:** ORAL **2 :** composed or arranged for or sung by the human voice **3 :** of, relating to, or having the power of producing voice — **vo·cal·ly** *adv*

vocal cords *n pl* **:** membranes at the top of the windpipe that produce vocal sounds when drawn tight and vibrated by the outgoing breath

vo·cal·ist *n* **:** SINGER

vo·ca·tion *n* **1 :** a strong desire for a certain career or course of action **2 :** the work in which a person is regularly employed **:** OCCUPATION

vo·ca·tion·al *adj* **1 :** of, relating to, or concerned with a vocation **2 :** concerned with choice of or training in a vocation — **vo·ca·tion·al·ly** *adv*

vod·ka *n* **:** a colorless alcoholic liquor

vogue *n* **1 :** the quality or state of being popular at a certain time **2 :** a period in which something is in fashion **3 :** something that is in fashion at a certain time

1voice *n* **1 :** sound produced through the mouth by vertebrates and especially by human beings in speaking or shouting **2 :** musical sound produced by the vocal cords **3 :** SPEECH 5 **4 :** a sound similar to vocal sound **5 :** a means of expression **6 :** the right to express a wish, choice, or opinion

2voice *vb* **voiced; voic·ing :** to express in words

voice box *n* **:** LARYNX

voiced *adj* **:** spoken with vibration of the vocal cords

voice·less *adj* **:** spoken without vibration of the vocal cords

voice mail *n* **:** an electronic communication system in which spoken messages are recorded to be played back later

1void *adj* **:** containing nothing **:** EMPTY

2void *n* **:** empty space

vol·a·tile *adj* **1 :** easily becoming a vapor at a fairly low temperature **2 :** likely to change suddenly

vol·ca·nic *adj* **1 :** of or relating to a volcano **2 :** likely to explode

vol·ca·no *n, pl* **vol·ca·noes** *or* **vol·ca·nos** **1 :** an opening in the earth's crust from which hot or melted rock and steam come **2 :** a hill or mountain composed of material thrown out in a volcanic eruption

vole *n* **:** any of various small rodents that look like fat mice or rats with short tails and are sometimes harmful to crops

vo·li·tion *n* **:** the act or power of making one's own choices or decisions **:** WILL

1vol·ley *n, pl* **volleys** **1 :** a group of missiles (as arrows or bullets) passing through the air **2 :** a firing of a number of weapons (as rifles) at the same time **3 :** a bursting forth of many things at once **4 :** the act of volleying

2volley *vb* **vol·leyed; vol·ley·ing** **1 :** to shoot in a volley **2 :** to hit an object (as a ball) while it is in the air before it touches the ground

vol·ley·ball *n* **:** a game played by volleying a large ball filled with air across a net

volt *n* **:** a unit for measuring the force that moves an electric current

volt·age *n* **:** electric force measured in volts

vol·u·ble *adj* **:** having a smooth and fast flow of words in speaking — **vol·u·bly** *adv*

vol·ume *n* **1 :** 1BOOK 1 **2 :** any one of a series of books that together form a complete work or collection **3 :** space included within limits as measured in cubic units **4 :** 2AMOUNT **5 :** the degree of loudness of a sound

vo·lu·mi·nous *adj* **1 :** of great volume or bulk **2 :** filling or capable of filling a large volume or several volumes

vol·un·tary *adj* **1 :** done, given, or made of one's own free will or choice **2 :** not accidental **:** INTENTIONAL **3 :** of, relating to, or controlled by the will — **vol·un·tar·i·ly** *adv*

1vol·un·teer *n* **1 :** a person who volunteers for a service **2 :** a plant growing without direct human care especially from seeds lost from a previous crop

2volunteer *adj* **:** of, relating to, or done by volunteers

3volunteer *vb* **1 :** to offer or give without being asked **2 :** to offer oneself for a service of one's own free will

1vom·it *n* **:** material from the stomach gotten rid of through the mouth

2vomit *vb* **:** to rid oneself of the contents of the stomach through the mouth

vo·ra·cious *adj* **1 :** greedy in eating **2 :** very eager — **vo·ra·cious·ly** *adv*

1vote *n* **1 :** a formal expression of opinion or will (as by ballot) **2 :** the decision reached by voting **3 :** the right to vote **4 :** the act or process of voting **5 :** a group of voters with some common interest or quality

2vote *vb* **vot·ed; vot·ing** **1 :** to express one's wish or choice by or as if by a vote **2 :** to elect, decide, pass, defeat, grant, or make legal by a vote **3 :** to declare by general agreement

vot·er *n* **:** a person who votes or who has the legal right to vote

vouch *vb* **:** to give a guarantee

vouch·safe *vb* **vouch·safed; vouch·saf·ing** **:** to grant as a special favor

[1]**vow** *n* **:** a solemn promise or statement
[2]**vow** *vb* **:** to make a vow **:** SWEAR
vow·el *n* **1 :** a speech sound (as \ə\, \ā\, or \ȯ\) produced without obstruction or audible friction in the mouth **2 :** a letter (as *a, e, i, o, u*) representing a vowel
[1]**voy·age** *n* **:** a journey especially by water from one place or country to another
[2]**voyage** *vb* **voy·aged; voy·ag·ing :** to take a trip — **voy·ag·er** *n*
vul·ca·nize *vb* **vul·ca·nized; vul·ca·niz·ing :** to treat rubber with chemicals in order to give it useful properties (as strength)
vul·gar *adj* **1 :** of or relating to the common people **2 :** having poor taste or manners **:** COARSE **3 :** offensive in language
vul·gar·i·ty *n, pl* **vul·gar·i·ties 1 :** the quality or state of being vulgar **2 :** a vulgar expression or action
vul·ner·a·ble *adj* **1 :** possible to wound or hurt **2 :** open to attack or damage — **vul·ner·a·bly** *adv*
vul·ture *n* **:** a large bird related to the hawks and eagles that has a naked head and feeds mostly on animals found dead
vying *present participle of* VIE

W

w *n, pl* **w's** *or* **ws** *often cap* **:** the twenty-third letter of the English alphabet
wacky *or* **whacky** *adj* **wack·i·er** *or* **whack·i·er; wack·i·est** *or* **whack·i·est :** CRAZY 2, INSANE
[1]**wad** *n* **1 :** a small mass or lump **2 :** a soft plug or stopper to hold a charge of powder (as in cartridges) **3 :** a soft mass of cotton, cloth, or fibers used as a plug or pad
[2]**wad** *vb* **wad·ded; wad·ding :** to form into a wad
[1]**wad·dle** *vb* **wad·dled; wad·dling :** to walk with short steps swaying like a duck
[2]**waddle** *n* **:** a waddling walk
wade *vb* **wad·ed; wad·ing 1 :** to walk through something (as water or snow) that makes it hard to move **2 :** to proceed with difficulty **3 :** to pass or cross by stepping through water
wading bird *n* **:** a shorebird or waterbird with long legs that wades in water in search of food
wa·fer *n* **:** a thin crisp cake or cracker
waf·fle *n* **:** a crisp cake of batter baked in a waffle iron
waffle iron *n* **:** a cooking utensil with two hinged metal parts that come together for making waffles
waft *vb* **:** to move or be moved lightly by or as if by the action of waves or wind
[1]**wag** *vb* **wagged; wag·ging :** to swing to and fro or from side to side
[2]**wag** *n* **1 :** a wagging movement **2 :** a person full of jokes and humor
[1]**wage** *n* **1 :** payment for work done especially when figured by the hour or day **2 wages** *sing or pl* **:** something given or received in return **:** REWARD
[2]**wage** *vb* **waged; wag·ing :** to engage in **:** CARRY ON
[1]**wa·ger** *n* **1 :** [1]BET 1 **2 :** the act of betting
[2]**wager** *vb* **:** to bet on the result of a contest or question — **wa·ger·er** *n*
wag·gish *adj* **:** showing or done in a spirit of harmless mischief
wag·gle *vb* **wag·gled; wag·gling :** to move backward and forward or from side to side
wag·on *n* **:** a vehicle having four wheels and used for carrying goods
waif *n* **:** a stray person or animal
[1]**wail** *vb* **:** to utter a mournful cry
[2]**wail** *n* **:** a long cry of grief or pain
wain·scot *n* **:** the bottom part of an inside wall especially when made of material different from the rest
wain·scot·ing *or* **wain·scot·ting** *n* **:** WAINSCOT
waist *n* **1 :** the part of the body between the chest and the hips **2 :** the central part of a thing when it is narrower or thinner than the rest **3 :** a garment or part of a garment covering the body from the neck to the waist
[1]**wait** *vb* **1 :** to stay in a place looking forward to something that is expected to happen **2 :** to serve food as a waiter or waitress **3 :** [2]DELAY 1
[2]**wait** *n* **1 :** [2]AMBUSH — used chiefly in the expression *lie in wait* **2 :** an act or period of waiting
wait·er *n* **:** a man who serves food to people at tables (as in a restaurant)
waiting room *n* **:** a room for the use of persons waiting (as for a train)
wait·ress *n* **:** a girl or woman who serves food to people at tables
waive *vb* **waived; waiv·ing :** to give up claim to
[1]**wake** *vb* **waked** *or* **woke; waked** *or* **wo·ken; wak·ing 1 :** to be or stay awake **2 :** to stay awake on watch especially over a corpse **3 :** [1]AWAKE 1
[2]**wake** *n* **:** a watch held over the body of a dead person before burial
[3]**wake** *n* **:** a track or mark left by something moving especially in the water

wake•ful *adj* **1 :** VIGILANT **2 :** not sleeping or able to sleep — **wake•ful•ness** *n*

wak•en *vb* **:** [1]AWAKE 1

[1]**walk** *vb* **1 :** to move or cause to move along on foot at a natural slow pace **2 :** to cover or pass over at a walk **3 :** to go or cause to go to first base after four balls in baseball — **walk•er** *n*

[2]**walk** *n* **1 :** a going on foot **2 :** a place or path for walking **3 :** distance to be walked often measured in time required by a walker to cover **4 :** position in life or the community **5 :** way of walking **6 :** an opportunity to go to first base after four balls in baseball

walking stick *n* **1 :** a stick used in walking **2 :** a sticklike insect with a long round body and long thin legs

walk•out *n* **1 :** a labor strike **2 :** the leaving of a meeting or organization as a way of showing disapproval

walk•over *n* **:** an easy victory

[1]**wall** *n* **1 :** a solid structure (as of stone) built to enclose or shut off a space **2 :** something like a wall that separates one thing from another **3 :** a layer of material enclosing space — **walled** *adj*

[2]**wall** *vb* **:** to build a wall in or around

wall•board *n* **:** a building material (as of wood pulp) made in large stiff sheets and used especially for inside walls and ceilings

wal•let *n* **:** a small flat case for carrying paper money and personal papers

wall•eye *n* **:** a large strong American freshwater sport and food fish that is related to the perches but looks like a pike

[1]**wal•lop** *vb* **:** to hit hard

[2]**wallop** *n* **:** a hard blow

[1]**wal•low** *vb* **1 :** to roll about in or as if in deep mud **2 :** to be too much interested or concerned with

[2]**wallow** *n* **:** a muddy or dust-filled hollow where animals wallow

wall•pa•per *n* **:** decorative paper for covering the walls of a room

wal•nut *n* **:** the edible nut (as the American **black walnut** with a rough shell or the Old World **English walnut** with a smoother shell) that comes from trees related to the hickories and including some valued also for their wood

wal•rus *n* **:** a large animal of northern seas related to the seals and hunted for its hide, for the ivory tusks of the males, and for oil

[1]**waltz** *n* **:** a dance in which couples glide to music having three beats to a measure

[2]**waltz** *vb* **:** to dance a waltz — **waltz•er** *n*

wam•pum *n* **:** beads made of shells and once used for money or ornament by North American Indians

wan *adj* **wan•ner; wan•nest :** having a pale or sickly color — **wan•ly** *adv* — **wan•ness** *n*

wand *n* **:** a slender rod (as one carried by a fairy or one used by a magician in doing tricks)

wan•der *vb* **1 :** to move about without a goal or purpose **:** RAMBLE **2 :** to follow a winding course **3 :** to get off the right path **:** STRAY — **wan•der•er** *n*

wan•der•lust *n* **:** a strong wish or urge to travel

wane *vb* **waned; wan•ing 1 :** to grow smaller or less **2 :** to lose power or importance **:** DECLINE

[1]**want** *vb* **1 :** to be without **:** LACK **2 :** to feel or suffer the need of something **3 :** to desire, wish, or long for something

[2]**want** *n* **1 :** [2]LACK 2, SHORTAGE **2 :** the state of being very poor **3 :** a wish for something **:** DESIRE

want•ing *adj* **:** falling below a standard, hope, or need

wan•ton *adj* **1 :** PLAYFUL 1 **2 :** not modest or proper **:** INDECENT **3 :** showing no thought or care for the rights, feelings, or safety of others — **wan•ton•ly** *adv* — **wan•ton•ness** *n*

[1]**war** *n* **1 :** a state or period of fighting between states or nations **2 :** the art or science of warfare **3 :** a struggle between opposing forces

[2]**war** *vb* **warred; war•ring :** to make war **:** FIGHT

[1]**war•ble** *n* **1 :** low pleasing sounds that form a melody (as of a bird) **2 :** the action of warbling

[2]**warble** *vb* **war•bled; war•bling :** to sing with a warble

war•bler *n* **1 :** any of a group of Old World birds related to the thrushes and noted for their musical song **2 :** any of a group of brightly colored American migratory songbirds that eat insects and have a weak call

[1]**ward** *n* **1 :** a part of a hospital **2 :** one of the parts into which a town or city is divided for management **3 :** a person under the protection of a guardian

[2]**ward** *vb* **1 :** to keep watch over **:** GUARD **2 :** to turn aside

[1]**-ward** *also* **-wards** *adj suffix* **1 :** that moves, faces, or is pointed toward **2 :** that is found in the direction of

[2]**-ward** *or* **-wards** *adv suffix* **1 :** in a specified direction **2 :** toward a specified place

war•den *n* **1 :** a person who sees that certain laws are followed **2 :** the chief official of a prison

ward•robe *n* **1 :** a room or closet where clothes are kept **2 :** the clothes a person owns

ware *n* **1 :** manufactured articles or products of art or craft **2 :** items (as dishes) of baked clay **:** POTTERY

ware·house *n, pl* **ware·hous·es :** a building for storing goods and merchandise

war·fare *n* **1 :** military fighting between enemies **2 :** strong continued effort **:** STRUGGLE

war·like *adj* **1 :** fond of war **2 :** of or relating to war **3 :** threatening war

[1]**warm** *adj* **1 :** somewhat hot **2 :** giving off heat **3 :** making a person feel heat or experience no loss of bodily heat **4 :** having a feeling of warmth **5 :** showing strong feeling **6 :** newly made **:** FRESH **7 :** near the object sought **8 :** of a color in the range yellow through orange to red — **warm·ly** *adv*

[2]**warm** *vb* **1 :** to make or become warm **2 :** to give a feeling of warmth **3 :** to become more interested than at first

warm–blood·ed *adj* **1 :** able to keep up a body temperature that is independent of that of the surroundings **2 :** warm in feeling — **warm–blood·ed·ness** *n*

warmth *n* **1 :** gentle heat **2 :** strong feeling

warm–up *n* **:** the act or an instance of warming up

warm up *vb* **1 :** to exercise or practice lightly in preparation for more strenuous activity or a performance **2 :** to run (as a motor) at slow speed before using

warn *vb* **1 :** to put on guard **:** CAUTION **2 :** to notify especially in advance

warn·ing *n* **:** something that warns

[1]**warp** *n* **1 :** the threads that go lengthwise in a loom and are crossed by the woof **2 :** a twist or curve that has developed in something once flat or straight

[2]**warp** *vb* **1 :** to curve or twist out of shape **2 :** to cause to judge, choose, or act wrongly

war·path *n* **:** the route taken by a group of American Indians going off to fight — **on the warpath :** ready to fight or argue

war·plane *n* **:** a military or naval airplane

[1]**war·rant** *n* **1 :** a reason or cause for an opinion or action **2 :** a document giving legal power

[2]**warrant** *vb* **1 :** to be sure of or that **2 :** [2]GUARANTEE 2 **3 :** to call for **:** JUSTIFY

warrant officer *n* **1 :** an officer in the armed forces in one of the grades between commissioned officers and enlisted persons **2 :** a warrant officer of the lowest rank

war·ren *n* **:** a place for keeping or raising small game (as rabbits)

war·rior *n* **:** a person who is or has been in warfare

war·ship *n* **:** a ship armed for combat

wart *n* **:** a small hard lump of thickened skin

warty *adj* **wart·i·er; wart·i·est 1 :** covered with or as if with warts **2 :** like a wart

wary *adj* **war·i·er; war·i·est :** very cautious — **war·i·ly** *adv* — **war·i·ness** *n*

was *past 1st & 3d sing of* BE

[1]**wash** *vb* **1 :** to cleanse with water and usually a cleaning agent (as soap) **2 :** to wet completely with liquid **3 :** to flow along or overflow against **4 :** to remove by the action of water **5 :** to stand washing without injury

[2]**wash** *n* **1 :** articles (as of clothing) in the laundry **2 :** the flow, sound, or action of water **3 :** a backward flow of water (as made by the motion of a boat) **4 :** material carried or set down by water

wash·able *adj* **:** capable of being washed without damage

wash·board *n* **:** a grooved board to scrub clothes on

wash·bowl *n* **:** a large bowl for water to wash one's hands and face

wash·er *n* **1 :** WASHING MACHINE **2 :** a ring (as of metal) used to make something fit tightly or to prevent rubbing

wash·ing *n* **:** [2]WASH 1

washing machine *n* **:** a machine used especially for washing clothes and household linen

wash·out *n* **1 :** the washing away of earth (as from a road) **2 :** a place where earth is washed away **3 :** a complete failure

wash·tub *n* **:** a tub for washing clothes or for soaking them before washing

wasn't : was not

wasp *n* **:** a winged insect related to the bees and ants that has a slender body with the abdomen attached by a narrow stalk and that in females and workers is capable of giving a very painful sting

wasp·ish *adj* **:** [3]CROSS 3, IRRITABLE — **wasp·ish·ly** *adv* — **wasp·ish·ness** *n*

[1]**waste** *n* **1 :** [1]DESERT, WILDERNESS **2 :** WASTELAND **3 :** the action of wasting **:** the state of being wasted **4 :** material left over or thrown away **5 :** material produced in and of no further use to the living body

[2]**waste** *vb* **wast·ed; wast·ing 1 :** to bring to ruin **2 :** to spend or use carelessly or uselessly **3 :** to lose or cause to lose weight, strength, or energy

[3]**waste** *adj* **1 :** being wild and not lived in or planted to crops **:** BARREN **2 :** of no further use

waste·bas·ket *n* **:** an open container for odds and ends to be thrown away

waste·ful *adj* **1 :** wasting or causing waste **2 :** spending or using in a careless or foolish way — **waste·ful·ly** *adv* — **waste·ful·ness** *n*

waste•land *n* **:** land that is barren or not fit for crops
[1]**watch** *vb* **1 :** to stay awake **2 :** to be on one's guard **3 :** to take care of **:** TEND **4 :** to be on the lookout **5 :** to keep one's eyes on — **watch•er** *n*
[2]**watch** *n* **1 :** an act of keeping awake to guard or protect **2 :** close observation **3 :** [1]GUARD 2 **4 :** the time during which one is on duty to watch **5 :** a small timepiece to be worn or carried
watch•dog *n* **:** a dog kept to watch and guard property
watch•ful *adj* **:** ATTENTIVE 1, VIGILANT — **watch•ful•ly** *adv* — **watch•ful•ness** *n*
watch•man *n, pl* **watch•men :** a person whose job is to watch and guard property at night or when the owners are away
watch•tow•er *n* **:** a tower on which a guard or watchman is placed
watch•word *n* **:** PASSWORD
[1]**wa•ter** *n* **1 :** the liquid that comes from the clouds as rain and forms streams, lakes, and seas **2 :** a liquid that contains or is like water **3 :** a body of water or a part of a body of water
[2]**water** *vb* **1 :** to wet or supply with water **2 :** to add water to **3 :** to fill with liquid (as tears)
wa•ter•bird *n* **:** a swimming or wading bird
water buffalo *n* **:** a common oxlike work animal of Asia
water clock *n* **:** a device or machine for measuring time by the fall or flow of water
wa•ter•col•or *n* **1 :** a paint whose liquid part is water **2 :** a picture painted with watercolor **3 :** the art of painting with watercolor
wa•ter•course *n* **1 :** a channel in which water flows **2 :** a stream of water (as a river or brook)
wa•ter•cress *n* **:** a plant related to the mustards that grows in cold flowing waters and is used especially in salads
wa•ter•fall *n* **:** a fall of water from a height
water flea *n* **:** a small active often brightly colored freshwater animal related to the crabs and lobsters
wa•ter•fowl *n* **1 :** a bird that is found in or near water **2 waterfowl** *pl* **:** swimming birds (as wild ducks and geese) hunted as game
wa•ter•front *n* **:** land or a section of a town that borders on a body of water
water hyacinth *n* **:** a floating water plant that often blocks streams in the southern United States
water lily *n* **:** any of a group of water plants with rounded floating leaves and showy often fragrant flowers with many petals
wa•ter•line *n* **:** any of several lines marked on the outside of a ship that match the surface of the water when the ship floats evenly
wa•ter•logged *adj* **:** so filled or soaked with water as to be heavy or hard to manage
wa•ter•mark *n* **1 :** a mark that shows a level to which water has risen **2 :** a mark made in paper during manufacture and visible when the paper is held up to the light
wa•ter•mel•on *n* **:** a large edible fruit with a hard outer layer and a sweet red juicy pulp
water moccasin *n* **:** MOCCASIN 2
water polo *n* **:** a ball game played in water by teams of swimmers
wa•ter•pow•er *n* **:** the power of moving water used to run machinery
[1]**wa•ter•proof** *adj* **:** not letting water through
[2]**waterproof** *vb* **:** to make waterproof
wa•ter•shed *n* **1 :** a dividing ridge (as a mountain range) separating one drainage area from others **2 :** the whole area that drains into a lake or river
wa•ter•spout *n* **1 :** a pipe for carrying off water from a roof **2 :** a slender cloud that is shaped like a funnel and extends down to a cloud of spray torn up from the surface of a body of water by a whirlwind
water strid•er *n* **:** a bug with long legs that skims over the surface of water
wa•ter•tight *adj* **:** so tight as to be waterproof
wa•ter•way *n* **:** a channel or a body of water by which ships can travel
wa•ter•wheel *n* **:** a wheel turned by a flow of water against it
wa•ter•works *n pl* **:** a system of dams, reservoirs, pumps, and pipes for supplying water (as to a city)
wa•tery *adj* **1 :** of or relating to water **2 :** full of or giving out liquid **3 :** being like water **4 :** being soft and soggy
watt *n* **:** a unit for measuring electric power
wat•tle *n* **:** a fleshy flap of skin that hangs from the throat (as of a bird)
[1]**wave** *vb* **waved; wav•ing 1 :** to move like a wave **2 :** to move (as one's hand) to and fro as a signal or in greeting **3 :** to curve like a wave or series of waves
[2]**wave** *n* **1 :** a moving ridge on the surface of water **2 :** a shape like a wave or series of waves **3 :** something that swells and dies away **4 :** a waving motion **5 :** a rolling movement passing along a surface or through the air **6 :** a motion that is somewhat like a wave in water and transfers energy from point to point
wave•length *n* **:** the distance in the line of advance of a wave from any one point to the next similar point
wave•let *n* **:** a little wave
wa•ver *vb* **1 :** to sway one way and the other

2 : to be uncertain in opinion **3 :** to move unsteadily

wavy *adj* **wav·i·er; wav·i·est :** like, having, or moving in waves — **wav·i·ness** *n*

1wax *n* **1 :** a dull yellow sticky substance made by bees and used in building honeycomb **:** BEESWAX **2 :** a substance like beeswax

2wax *vb* **:** to treat with wax

3wax *vb* **1 :** to grow larger or stronger **2 :** BECOME 1, GROW

wax bean *n* **:** a string bean with yellow waxy pods

wax·en *adj* **:** of or like wax

wax myrtle *n* **:** the bayberry shrub

wax·wing *n* **:** a crested mostly brown bird having smooth feathers (as the American **cedar waxwing** with yellowish belly)

waxy *adj* **wax·i·er; wax·i·est 1 :** being like wax **2 :** made of or covered with wax

1way *n* **1 :** a track for travel **:** PATH, STREET **2 :** the course traveled from one place to another **:** ROUTE **3 :** a course of action **4 :** personal choice as to situation or behavior **:** WISH **5 :** the manner in which something is done or happens **6 :** a noticeable point **7 :** 1STATE 1 **8 :** 1DISTANCE 1 **9 :** progress along a course **10 :** a special or personal manner of behaving **11 :** NEIGHBORHOOD 1, DISTRICT **12 :** room to advance or pass **13 :** CATEGORY, KIND

2way *adv* **:** 1FAR 1

way·far·er *n* **:** a traveler especially on foot

way·lay *vb* **way·laid; way·lay·ing :** to attack from hiding

-ways *adv suffix* **:** in such a way, direction, or manner

way·side *n* **:** the edge of a road

way·ward *adj* **1 :** DISOBEDIENT **2 :** opposite to what is wished or hoped for

we *pron* **:** I and at least one other

weak *adj* **1 :** lacking strength of body, mind, or spirit **2 :** not able to stand much strain or force **3 :** easily overcome **4 :** not able to function well **5 :** not rich in some usual or important element **6 :** lacking experience or skill **7 :** of, relating to, or being the lightest of three levels of stress in pronunciation

weak·en *vb* **:** to make or become weak or weaker

weak·fish *n* **:** any of several sea fishes related to the perches (as a common sport and market fish of the eastern coast of the United States)

weak·ling *n* **:** a person or animal that is weak

1weak·ly *adv* **:** in a weak manner

2weakly *adj* **weak·li·er; weak·li·est :** not strong or healthy

weak·ness *n* **1 :** lack of strength **2 :** a weak point **:** FLAW

wealth *n* **1 :** a large amount of money or possessions **2 :** a great amount or number

wealthy *adj* **wealth·i·er; wealth·i·est :** having wealth **:** RICH

wean *vb* **1 :** to get a child or young animal used to food other than its mother's milk **2 :** to turn one away from desiring a thing one has been fond of

weap·on *n* **:** something (as a gun, knife, or club) to fight with

1wear *vb* **wore; worn; wear·ing 1 :** to use as an article of clothing or decoration **2 :** to carry on the body **3 :** 1SHOW 1 **4 :** to damage, waste, or make less by use or by scraping or rubbing **5 :** to make tired **6 :** to cause or make by rubbing **7 :** to last through long use — **wear·er** *n*

2wear *n* **1 :** the act of wearing **:** the state of being worn **2 :** things worn or meant to be worn **3 :** the result of wearing or use

wea·ri·some *adj* **:** TEDIOUS, DULL

wear out *vb* **1 :** to make useless by long or hard use **2 :** 1TIRE 1

1wea·ry *adj* **wea·ri·er; wea·ri·est 1 :** made tired usually from work **2 :** having one's patience, pleasure, or interest worn out **3 :** causing a loss of strength or interest — **wea·ri·ly** *adv* — **wea·ri·ness** *n*

2weary *vb* **wea·ried; wea·ry·ing :** to make or become weary

wea·sel *n* **:** a small slender active animal related to the minks that feeds on small birds and animals (as mice)

1weath·er *n* **:** the state of the air and atmosphere in regard to how warm or cold, wet or dry, or clear or stormy it is

2weather *vb* **1 :** to expose to the weather **2 :** to change (as in color or structure) by the action of the weather **3 :** to be able to last or come safely through

3weather *adj* **:** 1WINDWARD

weath·er·cock *n* **:** a weather vane shaped like a rooster

weath·er·man *n, pl* **weath·er·men :** a person who reports and forecasts the weather

weather vane *n* **:** a movable device attached to something high (as a roof or spire) to show which way the wind is blowing

1weave *vb* **wove; wo·ven; weav·ing 1 :** to form (as cloth) by lacing together strands of material **2 :** 1SPIN 3 **3 :** to make by or as if by lacing parts together **4 :** to move back and forth, up and down, or in and out — **weav·er** *n*

2weave *n* **:** a method or pattern of weaving

1web *n* **1 :** a woven fabric on a loom or coming from a loom **2 :** COBWEB 1 **3 :** something like a cobweb **4 :** a membrane especially when joining toes (as of a duck) **5** *cap* **:** WORLD WIDE WEB

2web *vb* **webbed; web•bing :** to join or surround with a web

web•foot *n, pl* **web•feet :** a foot (as of a duck) having the toes joined by webs — **web–foot•ed** *adj*

wed *vb* **wed•ded** *also* **wed; wed•ding 1 :** MARRY **2 :** to attach firmly

we'd : we had : we should : we would

wed•ding *n* **:** a marriage ceremony

1wedge *n* **1 :** a piece of wood or metal that tapers to a thin edge and is used for splitting (as logs) or for raising something heavy **2 :** something (as a piece of cake or a formation of wild geese flying) with a triangular shape

2wedge *vb* **wedged; wedg•ing 1 :** to fasten or tighten with a wedge **2 :** to crowd or squeeze in tight

wed•lock *n* **:** MARRIAGE 1

Wednes•day *n* **:** the fourth day of the week

wee *adj* **:** very small : TINY

1weed *n* **:** a plant that tends to grow thickly where not wanted and to choke out more desirable plants

2weed *vb* **1 :** to remove weeds from **2 :** to get rid of what is not wanted

weedy *adj* **weed•i•er; weed•i•est 1 :** full of or consisting of weeds **2 :** like a weed especially in coarse strong rapid growth **3 :** very skinny

week *n* **1 :** seven days in a row especially beginning with Sunday and ending with Saturday **2 :** the working or school days that come between Sunday and Saturday

week•day *n* **:** a day of the week except Sunday or sometimes except Saturday and Sunday

week•end *n* **:** the period between the close of one work or school week and the beginning of the next

1week•ly *adj* **1 :** happening, done, produced, or published every week **2 :** figured by the week

2weekly *n, pl* **weeklies :** a newspaper or magazine published every week

weep *vb* **wept; weep•ing :** to shed tears : CRY

weep•ing *adj* **:** having slender drooping branches

weep•ing willow *n* **:** a willow originally from Asia that has slender drooping branches

wee•vil *n* **:** any of various small beetles with a hard shell and a long snout many of which are harmful to fruits, nuts, grain, or trees

weigh *vb* **1 :** to find the weight of **2 :** to think about as if weighing **3 :** to measure out on or as if on scales **4 :** to lift an anchor before sailing **5 :** to have weight or a specified weight

weigh down *vb* **:** to cause to bend down

1weight *n* **1 :** the amount that something weighs **2 :** the force with which a body is pulled toward the earth **3 :** a unit (as a kilogram) for measuring weight **4 :** an object (as a piece of metal) of known weight for balancing a scale in weighing other objects **5 :** a heavy object used to hold or press down something **6 :** 1BURDEN 2 **7 :** strong influence : IMPORTANCE

2weight *vb* **1 :** to load or make heavy with a weight **2 :** to trouble with a burden

weighty *adj* **weight•i•er; weight•i•est 1 :** having much weight : HEAVY **2 :** very important

weird *adj* **1 :** of or relating to witchcraft or magic **2 :** very unusual : STRANGE, FANTASTIC

weirdo *n, pl* **weird•os :** a very strange person

1wel•come *vb* **wel•comed; wel•com•ing 1 :** to greet with friendship or courtesy **2 :** to receive or accept with pleasure

2welcome *adj* **1 :** greeted or received gladly **2 :** giving pleasure : PLEASING **3 :** willingly permitted to do, have, or enjoy something **4** — used in the phrase "You're welcome" as a reply to an expression of thanks

3welcome *n* **:** a friendly greeting

1weld *vb* **1 :** to join two pieces of metal or plastic by heating and allowing the edges to flow together **2 :** to join closely **3 :** to become or be capable of being welded — **weld•er** *n*

2weld *n* **:** a welded joint

wel•fare *n* **1 :** the state of being or doing well **2 :** aid in the form of money or necessities for people who are poor, aged, or disabled

1well *n* **1 :** a source of supply **2 :** a hole made in the earth to reach a natural deposit (as of water, oil, or gas) **3 :** something suggesting a well

2well *vb* **:** to rise to the surface and flow out

3well *adv* **bet•ter; best 1 :** so as to be right : in a satisfactory way **2 :** in a good-hearted or generous way **3 :** in a skillful or expert manner **4 :** by as much as possible : COMPLETELY **5 :** with reason or courtesy **6 :** in such a way as to be pleasing : as one would wish **7 :** without trouble **8 :** in a thorough manner **9 :** in a familiar manner **10 :** by quite a lot

4well *interj* **1** — used to express surprise or doubt **2** — used to begin a conversation or to continue one that was interrupted

5well *adj* **1 :** being in a satisfactory or good state **2 :** free or recovered from ill health : HEALTHY **3 :** FORTUNATE 1

we'll : we shall : we will

well–be•ing *n* **:** WELFARE 1

well–bred *adj* **:** having or showing good manners **:** POLITE
well–known *adj* **:** known by many people
well–nigh *adv* **:** ALMOST
well–to–do *adj* **:** having plenty of money and possessions
¹**Welsh** *adj* **:** of or relating to Wales or the people of Wales
²**Welsh** *n* **:** the people of Wales
welt *n* **:** a ridge raised on the skin by a blow
¹**wel·ter** *vb* **1 :** to twist or roll one's body about **2 :** to rise and fall or toss about in or with waves
²**welter** *n* **:** a confused jumble
wend *vb* **:** to go one's way **:** PROCEED
went *past of* GO
wept *past of* WEEP
were *past 2d sing, past pl, or past subjunctive of* BE
we're : we are
weren't : were not
were·wolf *n, pl* **were·wolves :** a person in folklore who is changed or is able to change into a wolf
¹**west** *adv* **:** to or toward the west
²**west** *adj* **:** placed toward, facing, or coming from the west
³**west** *n* **1 :** the direction of sunset **:** the compass point opposite to east **2** *cap* **:** regions or countries west of a point that is mentioned or understood
west·bound *adj* **:** going west
west·er·ly *adj or adv* **1 :** toward the west **2 :** from the west
¹**west·ern** *adj* **1** *often cap* **:** of, relating to, or like that of the West **2 :** lying toward or coming from the west
²**western** *n, often cap* **:** a story, film, or radio or television show about life in the western United States especially in the last part of the nineteenth century
west·ward *adv or adj* **:** toward the west
¹**wet** *adj* **wet·ter; wet·test 1 :** containing, covered with, or soaked with liquid (as water) **2 :** RAINY **3 :** not yet dry — **wet·ness** *n*
²**wet** *n* **1 :** ¹WATER **2 :** MOISTURE **3 :** rainy weather **:** RAIN
³**wet** *vb* **wet** *or* **wet·ted; wet·ting :** to make wet
we've : we have
¹**whack** *vb* **:** to hit with a hard noisy blow
²**whack** *n* **1 :** a hard noisy blow **2 :** the sound of a whack
whacky *variant of* WACKY
¹**whale** *n* **:** a warm-blooded sea animal that looks like a huge fish but breathes air and feeds its young with its milk
²**whale** *vb* **whaled; whal·ing :** to hunt whales
whale·boat *n* **:** a long rowboat once used by whalers
whale·bone *n* **:** a substance like horn from the upper jaw of some whales
whal·er *n* **:** a person or ship that hunts whales
wharf *n, pl* **wharves** *or* **wharfs :** a structure built on the shore for loading and unloading ships
¹**what** *pron* **1 :** which thing or things **2 :** which sort of thing or person **3 :** that which — **what for :** ¹WHY — **what if 1 :** what would happen if **2 :** what does it matter if
²**what** *adv* **1 :** in what way **:** HOW **2** — used before one or more phrases that tell a cause
³**what** *adj* **1** — used to ask about the identity of a person, object, or matter **2 :** how remarkable or surprising **3 :** ²WHATEVER 1
¹**what·ev·er** *pron* **1 :** anything that **2 :** no matter what **3 :** what in the world
²**whatever** *adj* **1 :** any and all **:** any . . . that **2 :** of any kind at all
wheat *n* **:** a cereal grain that grows in tight clusters on the tall stalks of a widely cultivated grass, yields a fine white flour, is the chief source of bread in temperate regions, and is also important in animal feeds
wheat·en *adj* **:** containing or made from wheat
whee·dle *vb* **whee·dled; whee·dling 1 :** to get (someone) to think or act a certain way by flattering **:** COAX **2 :** to gain or get by coaxing or flattering
¹**wheel** *n* **1 :** a disk or circular frame that can turn on a central point **2 :** something like a wheel (as in being round or in turning) **3 :** something having a wheel as its main part **4 wheels** *pl* **:** moving power **:** necessary parts — **wheeled** *adj*
²**wheel** *vb* **1 :** to carry or move on wheels or in a vehicle with wheels **2 :** ROTATE 1 **3 :** to change direction as if turning on a central point
wheel·bar·row *n* **:** a small vehicle with two handles and usually one wheel for carrying small loads
wheel·chair *n* **:** a chair with wheels in which a disabled or sick person can get about
wheel·house *n, pl* **wheel·hous·es :** a small house containing a ship's steering wheel that is built on or above the top deck
¹**wheeze** *vb* **wheezed; wheez·ing 1 :** to breathe with difficulty and usually with a whistling sound **2 :** to make a sound like wheezing
²**wheeze** *n* **:** a wheezing sound
whelk *n* **:** a large sea snail that has a spiral shell and is used in Europe for food

¹whelp *n* **:** one of the young of an animal that eats flesh and especially of a dog
²whelp *vb* **:** to give birth to whelps
¹when *adv* **1 :** at what time **2 :** the time at which **3 :** at, in, or during which
²when *conj* **1 :** at, during, or just after the time that **2 :** in the event that **:** IF **3 :** ALTHOUGH
³when *pron* **:** what or which time
whence *adv* **1 :** from what place, source, or cause **2 :** from or out of which
when•ev•er *conj or adv* **:** at whatever time
¹where *adv* **1 :** at, in, or to what place **2 :** at or in what way or direction
²where *conj* **1 :** at, in, or to the place indicated **2 :** every place that
³where *n* **:** what place, source, or cause
¹where•abouts *adv* **:** near what place
²whereabouts *n sing or pl* **:** the place where someone or something is
where•as *conj* **1 :** since it is true that **2 :** while just the opposite
where•by *adv* **:** by or through which
where•fore *adv* **:** ¹WHY
where•in *adv* **1 :** in what way **2 :** in which
where•of *conj* **:** of what **:** that of which
where•on *adv* **:** on which
where•up•on *conj* **:** and then **:** at which time
¹wher•ev•er *adv* **:** where in the world
²wherever *conj* **1 :** at, in, or to whatever place **2 :** in any situation in which **:** at any time that
whet *vb* **whet•ted; whet•ting 1 :** to sharpen the edge of by rubbing on or with a stone **2 :** to make (as the appetite) stronger
wheth•er *conj* **1 :** if it is or was true that **2 :** if it is or was better **3** — used to introduce two or more situations of which only one can occur
whet•stone *n* **:** a stone on which blades are sharpened
whew *n* **:** a sound almost like a whistle made as an exclamation chiefly to show amazement, discomfort, or relief
whey *n* **:** the watery part of milk that separates after the milk sours and thickens
¹which *adj* **:** what certain one or ones
²which *pron* **1 :** which one or ones **2** — used in place of the name of something other than people at the beginning of a clause
¹which•ev•er *adj* **:** being whatever one or ones **:** no matter which
²whichever *pron* **:** whatever one or ones
¹whiff *n* **1 :** a small gust **2 :** a small amount (as of a scent or a gas) that is breathed in **3 :** a very small amount **:** HINT
²whiff *vb* **:** to puff, blow out, or blow away in very small amounts
¹while *n* **1 :** a period of time **2 :** time and effort used in doing something
²while *conj* **1 :** during the time that **2 :** ALTHOUGH
³while *vb* **whiled; whil•ing :** to cause to pass especially in a pleasant way
whim *n* **:** a sudden wish or desire **:** a sudden change of mind
¹whim•per *vb* **:** to cry in low broken sounds **:** WHINE
²whimper *n* **:** a whining cry
whim•si•cal *adj* **1 :** full of whims **2 :** DROLL
¹whine *vb* **whined; whin•ing 1 :** to make a shrill troubled cry or a similar sound **2 :** to complain by or as if by whining
²whine *n* **:** a whining cry or sound
¹whin•ny *vb* **whin•nied; whin•ny•ing :** to neigh usually in a low gentle way
²whinny *n, pl* **whinnies :** a low gentle neigh
¹whip *vb* **whipped; whip•ping 1 :** to move, snatch, or jerk quickly or with force **2 :** to hit with something slender and flexible **:** LASH **3 :** to punish with blows **4 :** to beat into foam **5 :** to move back and forth in a lively way
²whip *n* **1 :** something used in whipping **2 :** a light dessert made with whipped cream or whipped whites of eggs
whip•pet *n* **:** a small swift dog that is like a greyhound and is often used for racing
whip•poor•will *n* **:** a bird of eastern North America that flies at night and eats insects and is named from its peculiar call
¹whir *vb* **whirred; whir•ring :** to fly, move, or turn rapidly with a buzzing sound
²whir *n* **:** a whirring sound
¹whirl *vb* **1 :** to turn or move in circles rapidly **2 :** to feel dizzy **3 :** to move or carry around or about very rapidly
²whirl *n* **1 :** a whirling movement **2 :** something that is or seems to be whirling **3 :** a state of busy movement **:** BUSTLE
whirl•pool *n* **:** a rapid swirl of water with a low place in the center into which floating objects are drawn
whirl•wind *n* **:** a small windstorm in which the air turns rapidly in circles
¹whisk *n* **1 :** a quick sweeping or brushing motion **2 :** a kitchen utensil of wire used for whipping eggs or cream
²whisk *vb* **1 :** to move suddenly and quickly **2 :** to beat into foam **3 :** to brush with or as if with a whisk broom
whisk broom *n* **:** a small broom with a short handle used especially as a clothes brush
whis•ker *n* **1 whiskers** *pl* **:** the part of the beard that grows on the sides of the face and on the chin **2 :** one hair of the beard **3 :** a long bristle or hair growing near the mouth of an animal
whis•key *or* **whis•ky** *n, pl* **whis•keys** *or*

whis•kies : a strong drink containing alcohol and usually made from grain

1**whis•per** *vb* **1 :** to speak very low **2 :** to tell by whispering **3 :** to make a low rustling sound

2**whisper** *n* **1 :** a low soft way of speaking that can be heard only by persons who are near **2 :** the act of whispering **3 :** something said in a whisper **4 :** 1HINT 1

1**whis•tle** *n* **1 :** a device by which a shrill sound is produced **2 :** a shrill sound of or like whistling

2**whistle** *vb* **whis•tled; whis•tling 1 :** to make a shrill sound by forcing the breath through the teeth or lips **2 :** to move, pass, or go with a shrill sound **3 :** to sound a whistle **4 :** to express by whistling

whit *n* **:** a very small amount

1**white** *adj* **whit•er; whit•est 1 :** of the color white **2 :** light or pale in color **3 :** pale gray **:** SILVERY **4 :** having a light skin **5 :** 1BLANK 2 **6 :** not intended to cause harm **7 :** SNOWY 1 — **white•ness** *n*

2**white** *n* **1 :** the color of fresh snow **:** the opposite of black **2 :** the white part of something (as an egg) **3 :** white clothing **4 :** a person belonging to a white race

white blood cell *n* **:** one of the tiny whitish cells of the blood that help fight infection

white•cap *n* **:** the top of a wave breaking into foam

white cell *n* **:** WHITE BLOOD CELL

white•fish *n* **:** a freshwater fish related to the trouts that is greenish above and silvery below and is used for food

white flag *n* **:** a flag of plain white raised in asking for a truce or as a sign of surrender

whit•en *vb* **:** to make or become white **:** BLEACH

white oak *n* **:** a large oak tree known for its hard strong wood that lasts well and is not easily rotted by water

white–tailed deer *n* **:** the common deer of eastern North America with the underside of the tail white

1**white•wash** *vb* **1 :** to cover with whitewash **2 :** to try to hide the wrongdoing of

2**whitewash** *n* **:** a mixture (as of lime and water) for making a surface (as a wall) white

whith•er *adv* **1 :** to what place **2 :** to which place

whit•ish *adj* **:** somewhat white

whit•tle *vb* **whit•tled; whit•tling 1 :** to cut or shave off chips from wood **:** shape by such cutting or shaving **2 :** to reduce little by little

1**whiz** *or* **whizz** *vb* **whizzed; whiz•zing :** to move, pass, or fly rapidly with a buzzing sound

2**whiz** *n* **:** a buzzing sound

who *pron* **1 :** what person or people **2 :** the person or people that **3** — used to stand for a person or people at the beginning of a clause

whoa *vb* — used as a command to an animal pulling a load to stop

who•ev•er *pron* **:** whatever person

1**whole** *adj* **1 :** completely healthy or sound in condition **2 :** not cut up or ground **3 :** keeping all its necessary elements in being made ready for the market **4 :** made up of all its parts **:** TOTAL **5 :** not scattered or divided **6 :** each one of the — **whole•ness** *n*

2**whole** *n* **1 :** something that is whole **2 :** a sum of all the parts and elements — **on the whole 1 :** all things considered **2 :** in most cases

whole•heart•ed *adj* **:** not holding back

whole number *n* **:** a number that is zero or any of the natural numbers

1**whole•sale** *n* **:** the sale of goods in large quantities to dealers

2**wholesale** *adj* **1 :** of, relating to, or working at wholesaling **2 :** done on a large scale

3**wholesale** *vb* **whole•saled; whole•sal•ing :** to sell to dealers usually in large lots — **whole•sal•er** *n*

whole•some *adj* **1 :** helping to improve or keep the body, mind, or spirit in good condition **2 :** sound in body, mind, or morals — **whole•some•ness** *n*

whol•ly *adv* **:** to the limit **:** COMPLETELY

whom *pron objective case of* WHO

whom•ev•er *pron objective case of* WHOEVER

1**whoop** *vb* **1 :** to shout or cheer loudly and strongly **2 :** to make the shrill gasping sound that follows a coughing attack in whooping cough

2**whoop** *n* **:** a whooping sound

whooping cough *n* **:** a bacterial disease especially of children in which severe attacks of coughing are often followed by a shrill gasping intake of breath

whooping crane *n* **:** a large white nearly extinct North American crane that has a loud whooping call

whop•per 1 : something huge of its kind **2 :** a monstrous lie

whorl *n* **1 :** a row of parts (as leaves or petals) encircling a stem **2 :** something that whirls or winds

1**whose** *adj* **:** of or relating to whom or which

2**whose** *pron* **:** whose one **:** whose ones

1**why** *adv* **:** for what cause or reason

2**why** *conj* **1 :** the cause or reason for which **2 :** for which

3**why** *n, pl* **whys :** the cause of or reason for something

4**why** *interj* — used to express surprise, uncertainty, approval, disapproval, or impatience

wick *n* **:** a cord, strip, or ring of loosely woven material through which a liquid (as oil) is drawn to the top in a candle, lamp, or oil stove for burning

wick•ed *adj* **1 :** bad in behavior, moral state, or effect **:** EVIL **2 :** DANGEROUS 2 — **wick•ed•ly** *adv* — **wick•ed•ness** *n*

1**wick•er** *n* **1 :** a flexible twig (as of willow) used in basketry **2 :** WICKERWORK

2**wicker** *adj* **:** made of wicker

wick•er•work *n* **:** basketry made of wicker

wick•et *n* **1 :** a small gate or door in or near a larger gate or door **2 :** a small window (as in a bank or ticket office) through which business is conducted **3 :** either of the two sets of three rods topped by two crosspieces at which the ball is bowled in cricket **4 :** an arch (as of wire) through which the ball is hit in the game of croquet

1**wide** *adj* **wid•er; wid•est 1 :** covering a very large area **2 :** measured across or at right angles to length **3 :** having a large measure across **:** BROAD **4 :** opened as far as possible **5 :** not limited **6 :** far from the goal or truth — **wide•ly** *adv* — **wide•ness** *n*

2**wide** *adv* **wid•er; wid•est 1 :** over a wide area **2 :** to the limit **:** COMPLETELY

wide–awake *adj* **:** not sleepy, dull, or without energy **:** ALERT

wid•en *vb* **:** to make or become wide or wider

wide•spread *adj* **1 :** widely stretched out **2 :** widely scattered

1**wid•ow** *n* **:** a woman who has lost her husband by death

2**widow** *vb* **:** to make a widow or widower of

wid•ow•er *n* **:** a man who has lost his wife by death

width *n* **1 :** the shortest or shorter side of an object **2 :** BREADTH 1

wield *vb* **1 :** to use (as a tool) in an effective way **2 :** 2EXERCISE 1

wie•ner *n* **:** FRANKFURTER

wife *n, pl* **wives :** a married woman — **wife•ly** *adj*

wig *n* **:** a manufactured covering of natural or artificial hair for the head

1**wig•gle** *vb* **wig•gled; wig•gling 1 :** to move to and fro in a jerky way **2 :** to proceed with twisting and turning movements

2**wiggle** *n* **:** a wiggling motion

wig•gler *n* **:** WRIGGLER

wig•gly *adj* **wig•gli•er; wig•gli•est 1 :** given to wiggling **2 :** WAVY

wig•wag *vb* **wig•wagged; wig•wag•ging :** to signal by movement of a flag or light

wig•wam *n* **:** an Indian hut made of poles spread over with bark, rush mats, or hides

1**wild** *adj* **1 :** living in a state of nature and not under human control and care **:** not tame **2 :** growing or produced in nature **:** not cultivated by people **3 :** not civilized **:** SAVAGE **4 :** not kept under control **5 :** wide of the intended goal or course — **wild•ly** *adv* — **wild•ness** *n*

2**wild** *n* **:** WILDERNESS

wild boar *n* **:** an Old World wild hog from which most domestic swine derive

wild•cat *n* **:** any of various cats (as an ocelot or bobcat) of small or medium size

wil•der•ness *n* **:** a wild region which is not used for farming and in which few people live

wild•fire *n* **:** a fire that destroys a wide area

wild•flower *n* **:** the flower of a wild plant or the plant bearing it

wild•fowl *n, pl* **wildfowl :** a bird and especially a waterfowl hunted as game

wild•life *n* **:** creatures that are neither human nor domesticated **:** the wild animals of field and forest

1**wile** *n* **:** a trick meant to trap or deceive

2**wile** *vb* **wiled; wil•ing :** 2LURE

1**will** *helping verb, past* **would;** *present sing & pl* **will 1 :** wish to **2 :** am, is, or are willing to **3 :** am, is, or are determined to **4 :** am, is, or are going to **5 :** is or are commanded to

2**will** *n* **1 :** a firm wish or desire **2 :** the power to decide or control what one will do or how one will act **3 :** a legal paper in which a person states to whom the things which he or she owns are to be given after death

3**will** *vb* **1 :** 1ORDER 2, DECREE **2 :** to bring to a certain condition by the power of the will **3 :** to leave by will

will•ful *or* **wil•ful** *adj* **1 :** STUBBORN 1 **2 :** INTENTIONAL — **will•ful•ly** *adv* — **will•ful•ness** *n*

will•ing *adj* **1 :** feeling no objection **2 :** not slow or lazy **3 :** made, done, or given of one's own choice **:** VOLUNTARY — **will•ing•ly** *adv* — **will•ing•ness** *n*

wil•low *n* **1 :** a tree or bush with narrow leaves, catkins for flowers, and tough flexible stems used in making baskets **2 :** the wood of the willow tree

1**wilt** *vb* **1 :** to lose freshness and become limp **2 :** to lose strength

2**wilt** *n* **:** a plant disease (as of tomatoes) in which wilting and browning of leaves leads to death of the plant

wily *adj* **wil•i•er; wil•i•est :** full of tricks **:** CRAFTY

win *vb* **won; win•ning 1 :** to achieve the victory in a contest **2 :** to get by effort or skill **:** GAIN **3 :** to obtain by victory **4 :** to be the victor in **5 :** to ask and get the favor of

wince *vb* **winced; winc•ing :** to draw back (as from pain)

winch *n* **:** a machine that has a roller on which rope is wound for pulling or lifting

1wind *n* **1 :** a movement of the air **:** BREEZE **2 :** power to breathe **3 :** air carrying a scent (as of game) **4 :** limited knowledge especially about something secret **:** HINT **5 winds** *pl* **:** wind instruments of a band or orchestra

2wind *vb* **1 :** to get a scent of **2 :** to cause to be out of breath

3wind *vb* **wound; wind•ing :** to sound by blowing

4wind *vb* **wound; wind•ing 1 :** to twist around **2 :** to cover with something twisted around **:** WRAP **3 :** to make the spring of tight **4 :** to move in a series of twists and turns

5wind *n* **:** 2BEND

wind•break *n* **:** something (as a growth of trees and shrubs) that breaks the force of the wind

wind•fall *n* **1 :** something (as fruit from a tree) blown down by the wind **2 :** an unexpected gift or gain

wind instrument *n* **:** a musical instrument (as a clarinet, harmonica, or trumpet) sounded by the vibration of a stream of air and especially by the player's breath

wind•lass *n* **:** a winch used especially on ships for pulling and lifting

wind•mill *n* **:** a mill or a machine (as for pumping water) worked by the wind turning sails or vanes at the top of a tower

win•dow *n* **1 :** an opening in a wall to admit light and air **2 :** the glass and frame that fill a window opening **3 :** any of the areas into which a computer display may be divided and on which different types of information may be shown

window box *n* **:** a box for growing plants in or by a window

win•dow•pane *n* **:** a pane in a window

wind•pipe *n* **:** a tube with a firm wall that connects the pharynx with the lungs and is used in breathing

wind•proof *adj* **:** protecting from the wind

wind•shield *n* **:** a clear screen (as of glass) attached to the body of a vehicle (as a car) in front of the riders to protect them from the wind

wind•storm *n* **:** a storm with strong wind and little or no rain

wind•up *n* **1 :** the last part of something **:** FINISH **2 :** a swing of a baseball pitcher's arm before the pitch is thrown

wind up *vb* **1 :** to bring to an end **:** CONCLUDE **2 :** to swing the arm before pitching a baseball

1wind•ward *adj* **:** moving or placed toward the direction from which the wind is blowing

2windward *n* **:** the side or direction from which the wind is blowing

windy *adj* **wind•i•er; wind•i•est :** having much wind

wine *n* **1 :** fermented grape juice containing various amounts of alcohol **2 :** the usually fermented juice of a plant product (as a fruit) used as a drink

win•ery *n, pl* **win•er•ies :** a place where wine is made

1wing *n* **1 :** one of the paired limbs or limblike parts with which a bird, bat, or insect flies **2 :** something like a wing in appearance, use, or motion **3 :** a part (as of a building) that sticks out from the main part **4 :** a division of an organization **5 wings** *pl* **:** an area just off the stage of a theater — **wing•like** *adj* — **on the wing :** in flight

2wing *vb* **:** to go with wings **:** FLY

winged *adj* **:** having wings or winglike parts

wing•less *adj* **:** having no wings

wing•spread *n* **:** the distance between the tips of the spread wings

1wink *vb* **1 :** to close and open the eyelids quickly **2 :** to close and open one eye quickly as a signal or hint

2wink *n* **1 :** a brief period of sleep **2 :** a hint or sign given by winking **3 :** an act of winking **4 :** a very short time

win•ner *n* **:** one that wins

1win•ning *n* **1 :** the act of one that wins **2 :** something won especially in gambling — often used in pl.

2winning *adj* **1 :** being one that wins **2 :** tending to please or delight

win•now *vb* **:** to remove (as waste from grain) by a current of air

win•some *adj* **:** 2WINNING 2

1win•ter *n* **1 :** the season between autumn and spring (as the months of December, January, and February in the northern half of the earth) **2 :** YEAR 2

2winter *vb* **1 :** to pass the winter **2 :** to keep, feed, or manage during the winter

win•ter•green *n* **:** a low evergreen plant with white flowers that look like little bells and are followed by red berries which produce an oil (**oil of wintergreen**) used in medicine and flavoring

win•ter•time *n* **:** the winter season

win•try *adj* **win•tri•er; win•tri•est 1 :** of, relating to, or characteristic of winter **2 :** not friendly **:** COLD

1wipe *vb* **wiped; wip•ing 1 :** to clean or dry

by rubbing **2 :** to remove by or as if by rubbing — **wip·er** *n*

[2]**wipe** *n* **:** an act of wiping **:** RUB

wipe out *vb* **:** to destroy completely

[1]**wire** *n* **1 :** metal in the form of a thread or slender rod **2 :** a telephone or telegraph wire or system **3 :** TELEGRAM, CABLEGRAM

[2]**wire** *vb* **wired; wir·ing 1 :** to provide or equip with wire **2 :** to bind, string, or mount with wire **3 :** to send or send word to by telegraph

[1]**wire·less** *adj* **1 :** having no wire **2 :** relating to communication by electric waves but without connecting wires **:** RADIO 2

[2]**wireless** *n* **1 :** wireless telegraphy **2 :** [2]RADIO

wiry *adj* **wir·i·er; wir·i·est 1 :** of or like wire **2 :** being slender yet strong and active

wis·dom *n* **:** knowledge and the ability to use it to help oneself or others

wisdom tooth *n* **:** the last tooth of the full set on each half of each jaw of an adult

[1]**wise** *n* **:** MANNER 2, WAY — used in such phrases as *in any wise, in no wise, in this wise*

[2]**wise** *adj* **wis·er; wis·est 1 :** having or showing good sense or good judgment **:** SENSIBLE **2 :** having knowledge or information — **wise·ly** *adv*

-wise *adv suffix* **1 :** in the manner of **2 :** in the position or direction of **3 :** with regard to

wise·crack *n* **:** a clever and often insulting statement usually made in joking

[1]**wish** *vb* **1 :** to have a desire for **:** WANT **2 :** to form or express a desire concerning

[2]**wish** *n* **1 :** an act or instance of wishing **2 :** something wished **3 :** a desire for happiness or good fortune

wish·bone *n* **:** a bone in front of a bird's breastbone that is shaped like a V

wish·ful *adj* **:** having, showing, or based on a wish

wishy–washy *adj* **:** lacking spirit, courage, or determination **:** WEAK

wisp *n* **1 :** a small bunch of hay or straw **2 :** a thin piece or strand **3 :** a thin streak

wispy *adj* **wisp·i·er; wisp·i·est :** being thin and flimsy

wis·tar·ia *n* **:** WISTERIA

wis·te·ria *n* **:** a woody vine related to the beans that is grown for its long clusters of violet, white, or pink flowers

wist·ful *adj* **:** feeling or showing a timid longing — **wist·ful·ly** *adv* — **wist·ful·ness** *n*

wit *n* **1 :** power to think, reason, or decide **2 :** normal mental state — usually used in pl. **3 :** cleverness in making sharp and usually amusing comments **4 :** witty comments, expressions, or talk **5 :** a witty person

witch *n* **1 :** a woman believed to have magic powers **2 :** an ugly or mean old woman

witch·craft *n* **:** the power or doings of a witch

witch doctor *n* **:** a person who uses magic to cure illness and fight off evil spirits

witch·ery *n, pl* **witch·er·ies 1 :** WITCHCRAFT **2 :** power to charm or fascinate

witch ha·zel *n* **1 :** a shrub with small yellow flowers in late fall or very early spring **2 :** a soothing alcoholic lotion made from witch hazel bark

with *prep* **1 :** AGAINST 2 **2 :** in shared relation to **3 :** having in or as part of it **4 :** in regard to **5 :** compared to **6 :** in the opinion or judgment of **7 :** by the use of **8 :** so as to show **9 :** in the company of **10 :** in possession of **11 :** as well as **12 :** FROM 2 **13 :** BECAUSE OF **14 :** DESPITE **15 :** if given **16 :** at the time of or shortly after **17 :** in support of **18 :** in the direction of

with·draw *vb* **with·drew; with·drawn; with·draw·ing 1 :** to draw back **:** take away **2 :** to take back (as something said or suggested) **3 :** to go away especially for privacy or safety

with·draw·al *n* **:** an act or instance of withdrawing

with·er *vb* **:** to shrink up from or as if from loss of natural body moisture **:** WILT

with·ers *n pl* **:** the ridge between the shoulder bones of a horse

with·hold *vb* **with·held; with·hold·ing :** to refuse to give, grant, or allow

[1]**with·in** *adv* **:** [2]INSIDE

[2]**within** *prep* **1 :** [4]INSIDE 1 **2 :** not beyond the limits of

[1]**with·out** *prep* **1 :** [4]OUTSIDE **2 :** completely lacking **3 :** not accompanied by or showing

[2]**without** *adv* **:** [3]OUTSIDE

with·stand *vb* **with·stood; with·stand·ing 1 :** to hold out against **2 :** to oppose (as an attack) successfully

wit·less *adj* **:** lacking in wit or intelligence **:** FOOLISH

[1]**wit·ness** *n* **1 :** TESTIMONY **2 :** a person who sees or otherwise has personal knowledge of something **3 :** a person who gives testimony in court **4 :** a person who is present at an action (as the signing of a will) so as to be able to say who did it

[2]**witness** *vb* **1 :** to be a witness to **2 :** to give testimony to **:** testify as a witness **3 :** to be or give proof of

wit·ted *adj* **:** having wit or understanding — used in combination

wit·ty *adj* **wit·ti·er; wit·ti·est :** having or showing wit

wives *pl of* WIFE

wiz·ard *n* **1 :** SORCERER, MAGICIAN **2 :** a very clever or skillful person

[1]**wob·ble** *vb* **wob·bled; wob·bling :** to move from side to side in a shaky manner — **wob·bly** *adj*

[2]**wobble** *n* **:** a rocking motion from side to side

woe *n* **:** great sorrow, grief, or misfortune **:** TROUBLE

woe·ful *adj* **1 :** full of grief or misery **2 :** bringing woe or misery

woke *past of* WAKE

woken *past participle of* WAKE

[1]**wolf** *n, pl* **wolves 1 :** a large intelligent doglike wild animal that eats flesh and has ears which stand up and a bushy tail **2 :** a person felt to resemble a wolf (as in craftiness or fierceness) — **wolf·ish** *adj*

[2]**wolf** *vb* **:** to eat greedily

wolf dog *n* **1 :** WOLFHOUND **2 :** the hybrid offspring of a wolf and a domestic dog **3 :** a dog that looks like a wolf

wolf·hound *n* **:** any of several large dogs used in hunting large animals

wol·fram *n* **:** TUNGSTEN

wol·ver·ine *n* **:** a blackish wild animal with shaggy fur that is related to the martens and sables, eats flesh, and is found chiefly in the northern parts of North America

wolves *pl of* WOLF

wom·an *n, pl* **wom·en 1 :** an adult female person **2 :** women considered as a group

wom·an·hood *n* **1 :** the state of being a woman **2 :** womanly characteristics **3 :** WOMAN 2

wom·an·kind *n* **:** WOMAN 2

wom·an·ly *adj* **:** having the characteristics of a woman

womb *n* **:** UTERUS

wom·en·folk *or* **wom·en·folks** *n pl* **:** women especially of one family or group

won *past of* WIN

[1]**won·der** *n* **1 :** something extraordinary **:** MARVEL **2 :** a feeling (as of astonishment) caused by something extraordinary

[2]**wonder** *vb* **1 :** to feel surprise or amazement **2 :** to be curious or have doubt

won·der·ful *adj* **1 :** causing wonder **:** MARVELOUS **2 :** very good or fine — **won·der·ful·ly** *adv*

won·der·ing·ly *adv* **:** in or as if in wonder

won·der·land *n* **:** a place of wonders or surprises

won·der·ment *n* **:** AMAZEMENT

won·drous *adj* **:** WONDERFUL 1

[1]**wont** *adj* **:** being in the habit of doing

[2]**wont** *n* **:** usual custom **:** HABIT

won't : will not

woo *vb* **wooed; woo·ing 1 :** to try to gain the love of **2 :** to try to gain

[1]**wood** *n* **1 :** a thick growth of trees **:** a small forest — often used in pl. **2 :** a hard fibrous material that makes up most of the substance of a tree or shrub within the bark and is often used as a building material or fuel

[2]**wood** *adj* **1 :** WOODEN 1 **2 :** used for or on wood **3** *or* **woods :** living or growing in woodland

wood·bine *n* **:** any of several climbing vines of Europe and America (as honeysuckle)

wood·carv·er *n* **:** a person who carves useful or ornamental things from wood

wood·chuck *n* **:** a reddish brown rodent that hibernates **:** GROUNDHOG

wood·cock *n* **:** a brown game bird that has a long bill and is related to the snipe

wood·craft *n* **:** knowledge about the woods and how to take care of oneself in them

wood·cut·ter *n* **:** a person who cuts wood especially as an occupation

wood·ed *adj* **:** covered with trees

wood·en *adj* **1 :** made of wood **2 :** stiff like wood **:** AWKWARD **3 :** lacking spirit, ease, or charm

wood·land *n* **:** land covered with trees and shrubs **:** FOREST

wood·lot *n* **:** a small wooded section (as of a farm) kept to meet fuel and timber needs

wood louse *n* **:** a small flat gray crustacean that lives usually under stones or bark

wood·peck·er *n* **:** a bird that climbs trees and drills holes in them with its bill in search of insects

wood·pile *n* **:** a pile of wood especially for use as fuel

wood·shed *n* **:** a shed for storing wood and especially firewood

woods·man *n, pl* **woods·men 1 :** a person who cuts down trees as an occupation **2 :** a person skilled in woodcraft

woodsy *adj* **:** of, relating to, or suggestive of woodland

wood thrush *n* **:** a large thrush of eastern North America noted for its loud clear song

wood·wind *n* **:** one of the group of wind instruments consisting of the flutes, oboes, clarinets, bassoons, and sometimes saxophones

wood·work *n* **:** work (as the edge around doorways) made of wood

wood·work·ing *n* **:** the art or process of shaping or working with wood

woody *adj* **wood·i·er; wood·i·est 1 :** being mostly woods **2 :** of or containing wood or wood fibers **3 :** very much like wood

woof *n* **1 :** the threads that cross the warp in weaving a fabric **2 :** a woven fabric or its texture

wool *n* **1 :** soft heavy wavy or curly hair especially of the sheep **2 :** a substance that looks like a mass of wool **3 :** a material (as yarn) made from wool

wool•en *or* **wool•len** *adj* **1 :** made of wool **2 :** of or relating to wool or cloth made of wool

wool•ly *adj* **wool•li•er; wool•li•est :** made of or like wool

1word *n* **1 :** a sound or combination of sounds that has meaning and is spoken by a human being **2 :** a written or printed letter or letters standing for a spoken word **3 :** a brief remark or conversation **4 :** 2COMMAND 2, ORDER **5 :** NEWS **6 :** 1PROMISE 1 **7 words** *pl* **:** remarks said in anger or in a quarrel

2word *vb* **:** to express in words **:** PHRASE

word•ing *n* **:** the way something is put into words

word processing *n* **:** the production of typewritten documents (as business letters) with automated and usually computerized equipment

word processor *n* **1 :** a terminal operated by a keyboard for use in word processing usually having a video display and a magnetic storage device **2 :** software (as for a computer) to perform word processing

wordy *adj* **word•i•er; word•i•est :** using or containing many words or more words than are needed — **word•i•ness** *n*

wore *past of* WEAR

1work *n* **1 :** the use of a person's strength or ability in order to get something done or get some desired result **:** LABOR **2 :** OCCUPATION 1, EMPLOYMENT **3 :** something that needs to be done **:** TASK, JOB **4 :** DEED 1, ACHIEVEMENT **5 :** something produced by effort or hard work **6 works** *pl* **:** a place where industrial labor is done **:** PLANT, FACTORY **7 works** *pl* **:** the working or moving parts of a mechanical device **8 :** the way one works **:** WORKMANSHIP

2work *vb* **worked** *or* **wrought; work•ing 1 :** to do work especially for money or because of a need instead of for pleasure **:** labor or cause to labor **2 :** to perform or act or to cause to act as planned **:** OPERATE **3 :** to move or cause to move slowly or with effort **4 :** to cause to happen **5 :** 1MAKE 2, SHAPE **6 :** to carry on one's occupation in, through, or along **7 :** EXCITE 2, PROVOKE

work•able *adj* **:** capable of being worked or done

work•bench *n* **:** a bench on which work is done (as by mechanics)

work•book *n* **:** a book made up of a series of problems or practice examples for a student to use as part of a course of study

work•er *n* **1 :** a person who works **2 :** one of the members of a colony of bees, ants, wasps, or termites that are only partially developed sexually and that do most of the labor and protective work of the colony

work•ing *adj* **1 :** doing work especially for a living **2 :** relating to work **3 :** good enough to allow work or further work to be done

work•ing•man *n, pl* **work•ing•men :** a person who works for wages usually at common labor or in industry **:** a member of the working class

work•man *n, pl* **work•men 1 :** WORKINGMAN **2 :** a skilled worker (as an electrician or carpenter)

work•man•ship *n* **1 :** the art or skill of a workman **2 :** the quality of a piece of work

work•out *n* **:** an exercise or practice to test or increase ability or performance

work out *vb* **:** to invent or solve by effort

work•shop *n* **:** a shop where work and especially skilled work is carried on

work•sta•tion *n* **1 :** an area with equipment for the performance of a particular task usually by one person **2 :** a computer usually connected to a computer network

world *n* **1 :** EARTH 3 **2 :** people in general **:** HUMANITY **3 :** a state of existence **4 :** a great number or amount **5 :** a part or section of the earth and the people living there

world•ly *adj* **world•li•er; world•li•est :** of or relating to this world

World Wide Web *n* **:** a part of the Internet designed to allow easier navigation of the network through the use of text and graphics that link to other documents

1worm *n* **1 :** any of various long creeping or crawling animals that usually have soft bodies **2 :** a person hated or pitied **3 worms** *pl* **:** the presence of or disease caused by worms living in the body

2worm *vb* **1 :** to move slowly by creeping or wriggling **2 :** to get hold of or escape from by trickery **3 :** to free from worms

wormy *adj* **worm•i•er; worm•i•est :** containing worms

worn *past participle of* WEAR

worn–out *adj* **1 :** useless from long or hard wear **2 :** very weary

wor•ri•some *adj* **1 :** given to worrying **2 :** causing worry

1wor•ry *vb* **wor•ried; wor•ry•ing 1 :** to shake and tear or mangle with the teeth **2 :** to make anxious or upset **:** DISTURB **3 :** to feel or express great concern

2worry *n, pl* **worries 1 :** ANXIETY **2 :** a cause of great concern

1worse *adj comparative of* BAD *or of* ILL **1 :** more bad or evil **:** poorer in quality or worth **2 :** being in poorer health

2worse *n* **:** something worse

[3]**worse** *adv comparative of* BADLY *or of* ILL **:** not as well **:** in a worse way
wors·en *vb* **:** to get worse
[1]**wor·ship** *n* **1 :** deep respect toward God, a god, or a sacred object **2 :** too much respect or admiration
[2]**worship** *vb* **wor·shiped** *or* **wor·shipped; wor·ship·ing** *or* **wor·ship·ping** **1 :** to honor or respect as a divine being **2 :** to regard with respect, honor, or devotion **3 :** to take part in worship or an act of worship — **wor·ship·er** *or* **wor·ship·per** *n*
[1]**worst** *adj superlative of* BAD *or of* ILL **:** most bad, ill or evil
[2]**worst** *adv superlative of* ILL *or of* BADLY **:** in the worst way possible
[3]**worst** *n* **:** a person or thing that is worst
[4]**worst** *vb* **:** to get the better of **:** DEFEAT
wor·sted *n* **1 :** a smooth yarn spun from pure wool **2 :** a fabric woven from a worsted yarn
[1]**worth** *n* **1 :** the quality or qualities of a thing making it valuable or useful **2 :** value as expressed in money **3 :** EXCELLENCE 1
[2]**worth** *prep* **1 :** equal in value to **2 :** having possessions or income equal to **3 :** deserving of **4 :** capable of
worth·less *adj* **1 :** lacking worth **2 :** USELESS
worth·while *adj* **:** being worth the time spent or effort used
wor·thy *adj* **wor·thi·er; wor·thi·est** **1 :** having worth or excellence **2 :** having enough value or excellence — **wor·thi·ness** *n*
would *past of* WILL **1 :** strongly desire **:** WISH **2** — used as a helping verb to show that something might be likely or meant to happen under certain conditions **3 :** prefers or prefer to **4 :** was or were going to **5 :** is or are able to **:** COULD **6** — used as a politer form of *will*
wouldn't : would not
[1]**wound** *n* **1 :** an injury that involves cutting or breaking of bodily tissue (as by violence, accident, or surgery) **2 :** an injury or hurt to a person's feelings or reputation
[2]**wound** *vb* **1 :** to hurt by cutting or breaking tissue **2 :** to hurt the feelings or pride of
[3]**wound** *past of* WIND
wove *past of* WEAVE
woven *past participle of* WEAVE
[1]**wran·gle** *vb* **wran·gled; wran·gling** **1 :** to have an angry quarrel **:** BICKER **2 :** ARGUE 2, DEBATE
[2]**wrangle** *n* **:** [1]QUARREL 2
wran·gler *n* **1 :** a person who wrangles **2 :** a worker on a ranch who tends the saddle horses
[1]**wrap** *vb* **wrapped; wrap·ping** **1 :** to cover by winding or folding **2 :** to enclose in a package **3 :** to wind or roll together **:** FOLD **4 :** to involve completely
[2]**wrap** *n* **:** a warm loose outer garment (as a shawl, cape, or coat)
wrap·per *n* **1 :** what something is wrapped in **2 :** a person who wraps merchandise **3 :** a garment that is worn wrapped about the body
wrap·ping *n* **:** something used to wrap something else **:** WRAPPER
wrap up *vb* **1 :** to bring to an end **2 :** to put on warm clothing
wrath *n* **:** violent anger **:** RAGE
wrath·ful *adj* **1 :** full of wrath **2 :** showing wrath
wreak *vb* **:** to bring down as or as if punishment
wreath *n, pl* **wreaths :** something twisted or woven into a circular shape
wreathe *vb* **wreathed; wreath·ing** **1 :** to form into wreaths **2 :** to crown, decorate, or cover with or as if with a wreath
[1]**wreck** *n* **1 :** the remains (as of a ship or vehicle) after heavy damage usually by storm, collision, or fire **2 :** a person or animal in poor health or without strength **3 :** the action of breaking up or destroying something
[2]**wreck** *vb* **1 :** [2]SHIPWRECK 2 **2 :** to damage or destroy by breaking up **3 :** to bring to ruin or an end
wreck·age *n* **1 :** a wrecking or being wrecked **2 :** the remains of a wreck
wreck·er *n* **1 :** a person who wrecks something or deals in wreckage **2 :** a ship used in salvaging wrecks **3 :** a truck for removing wrecked or broken-down cars
wren *n* **:** any of a group of small brown songbirds (as the **house wren**) with short rounded wings and short erect tail
[1]**wrench** *vb* **1 :** to pull or twist with sudden sharp force **2 :** to injure or cripple by a sudden sharp twisting or straining
[2]**wrench** *n* **1 :** a violent twist to one side or out of shape **2 :** an injury caused by twisting or straining **:** SPRAIN **3 :** a tool used in turning nuts or bolts
wrest *vb* **1 :** to pull away by twisting or wringing **2 :** to obtain only by great and steady effort
[1]**wres·tle** *vb* **wres·tled; wres·tling** **1 :** to grasp and attempt to turn, trip, or throw down an opponent or to prevent the opponent from being able to move **2 :** to struggle to deal with
[2]**wrestle** *n* **:** [2]STRUGGLE 1
wres·tling *n* **:** a sport in which two opponents wrestle each other
wretch *n* **1 :** a miserable unhappy person **2 :** a very bad person **:** WRONGDOER

wretch·ed *adj* **1 :** very unhappy or unfortunate **:** suffering greatly **2 :** causing misery or distress **3 :** of very poor quality **:** INFERIOR

wrig·gle *vb* **wrig·gled; wrig·gling 1 :** to twist or move like a worm **:** SQUIRM, WIGGLE **2 :** to advance by twisting and turning

wrig·gler *n* **1 :** one that wriggles **2 :** a mosquito larva or pupa

wring *vb* **wrung; wring·ing 1 :** to twist or press so as to squeeze out moisture **2 :** to get by or as if by twisting or pressing **3 :** to twist so as to strangle **4 :** to affect as if by wringing

wring·er *n* **:** a machine or device for squeezing liquid out of something (as laundry)

1wrin·kle *n* **1 :** a crease or small fold (as in the skin or in cloth) **2 :** a clever notion or trick

2wrinkle *vb* **wrin·kled; wrin·kling :** to mark or become marked with wrinkles

wrist *n* **:** the joint or the region of the joint between the hand and arm

wrist·band *n* **1 :** the part of a sleeve that goes around the wrist **2 :** a band that goes around the wrist (as for support or warmth)

wrist·watch *n* **:** a watch attached to a bracelet or strap and worn on the wrist

writ *n* **:** an order in writing signed by an officer of a court ordering someone to do or not to do something

write *vb* **wrote; writ·ten; writ·ing 1 :** to form letters or words with pen or pencil **2 :** to form the letters or the words of (as on paper) **3 :** to put down on paper **4 :** to make up and set down for others to read **5 :** to write a letter to

writ·er *n* **:** a person who writes especially as a business or occupation

writhe *vb* **writhed; writh·ing 1 :** to twist and turn this way and that **2 :** to suffer from shame or confusion **:** SQUIRM

writ·ing *n* **1 :** the act of a person who writes **2 :** HANDWRITING **3 :** something (as a letter or book) that is written

1wrong *n* **:** something (as an idea, rule, or action) that is wrong

2wrong *adj* **1 :** not right **:** SINFUL, EVIL **2 :** not correct or true **:** FALSE **3 :** not the one wanted or intended **4 :** not suitable **5 :** made so as to be placed down or under and not to be seen **6 :** not proper — **wrong·ly** *adv* — **wrong·ness** *n*

3wrong *adv* **:** in the wrong direction, manner, or way

4wrong *vb* **:** to do wrong to

wrong·do·er *n* **:** a person who does wrong and especially a moral wrong

wrong·do·ing *n* **:** bad behavior or action

wrong·ful *adj* **1 :** 2WRONG 1, UNJUST **2 :** UNLAWFUL

wrote *past of* WRITE

1wrought *past of* WORK

2wrought *adj* **1 :** beaten into shape by tools **2 :** much too excited

wrung *past of* WRING

wry *adj* **wry·er; wry·est 1 :** turned abnormally to one side **2 :** made by twisting the features

X

x *n, pl* **x's** *or* **xs** *often cap* **1 :** the twenty-fourth letter of the English alphabet **2 :** ten in Roman numerals **3 :** an unknown quantity

Xmas *n* **:** CHRISTMAS

x–ray *vb, often cap X* **:** to examine, treat, or photograph with X rays

X ray *n* **1 :** a powerful invisible ray made up of very short waves that is somewhat similar to light and that is able to pass through various thicknesses of solids and act on photographic film like light **2 :** a photograph taken by the use of X rays

xy·lo·phone *n* **:** a musical instrument consisting of a series of wooden bars of different lengths made to sound the musical scale and played with two wooden hammers

Y

y *n, pl* **y's** *or* **ys** *often cap* **:** the twenty-fifth letter of the English alphabet

1-y *also* **-ey** *adj suffix* **-i·er; -i·est 1 :** showing, full of, or made of **2 :** like **3 :** devoted to **:** enthusiastic about **4 :** tending to **5 :** somewhat **:** rather

2-y *n suffix, pl* **-ies 1 :** state **:** condition **:** quality **2 :** occupation, place of business, or goods dealt with **3 :** whole body or group

3-y *n suffix, pl* **-ies :** occasion or example of a specified action

4-y — see -IE

1yacht *n* **:** a small ship used for pleasure cruising or racing

2yacht *vb* **:** to race or cruise in a yacht

yacht•ing *n* **:** the action, fact, or recreation of racing or cruising in a yacht

yachts•man *n, pl* **yachts•men :** a person who owns or sails a yacht

yak *n* **:** a wild or domestic ox of the uplands of Asia that has very long hair

yam *n* **1 :** the starchy root of a plant related to the lilies that is an important food in much of the tropics **2 :** a sweet potato with a moist and usually orange flesh

[1]**yank** *n* **:** a strong sudden pull **:** JERK

[2]**yank** *vb* **:** [2]JERK 1

Yan•kee *n* **1 :** a person born or living in New England **2 :** a person born or living in the northern United States **3 :** a person born or living in the United States

[1]**yap** *vb* **yapped; yap•ping 1 :** to bark in yaps **2 :** [2]SCOLD, CHATTER

[2]**yap** *n* **:** a quick shrill bark

[1]**yard** *n* **1 :** a small and often fenced area open to the sky and next to a building **2 :** the grounds of a building **3 :** a fenced area for livestock **4 :** an area set aside for a business or activity **5 :** a system of railroad tracks especially for keeping and repairing cars

[2]**yard** *n* **1 :** a measure of length equal to three feet or thirty-six inches (about .91 meter) **2 :** a long pole pointed toward the ends that holds up and spreads the top of a sail

yard•age *n* **1 :** a total number of yards **2 :** the length or size of something measured in yards

yard•arm *n* **:** either end of the yard of a square-rigged ship

yard•mas•ter *n* **:** the person in charge of operations in a railroad yard

yard•stick *n* **1 :** a measuring stick a yard long **2 :** a rule or standard by which something is measured or judged

[1]**yarn** *n* **1 :** natural or manufactured fiber (as cotton, wool, or rayon) formed as a continuous thread for use in knitting or weaving **2 :** an interesting or exciting story

[2]**yarn** *vb* **:** to tell a yarn

yawl *n* **:** a sailboat having two masts with the shorter one behind the point where the stern enters the water

[1]**yawn** *vb* **1 :** to open wide **2 :** to open the mouth wide usually as a reaction to being tired or bored

[2]**yawn** *n* **:** a deep drawing in of breath through the wide-open mouth

ye *pron, archaic* **:** YOU 1

[1]**yea** *adv* **:** [1]YES 1 — used in spoken voting

[2]**yea** *n* **1 :** a vote in favor of something **2 :** a person casting a yea vote

year *n* **1 :** the period of about $365^1/_4$ days required for the earth to make one complete trip around the sun **2 :** a period of 365 days or in leap year 366 days beginning January 1 **3 :** a fixed period of time

year•book *n* **1 :** a book published yearly especially as a report **2 :** a school publication recording the history and activities of a graduating class

year•ling *n* **:** a person or animal that is or is treated as if a year old

year•ly *adj* **:** [1]ANNUAL 1

yearn *vb* **:** to feel an eager desire

yearn•ing *n* **:** an eager desire

year–round *adj* **:** being in operation for the full year

yeast *n* **1 :** material that may be found on the surface or at the bottom of sweet liquids, is made up mostly of the cells of a tiny fungus, and causes a reaction in which alcohol is produced **2 :** a commercial product containing living yeast plants and used especially to make bread dough rise **3 :** any of the group of tiny fungi that form alcohol or raise bread dough

[1]**yell** *vb* **:** to cry or scream loudly

[2]**yell** *n* **1 :** [2]SCREAM, SHOUT **2 :** a cheer used especially in schools or colleges to encourage athletic teams

[1]**yel•low** *adj* **1 :** of the color yellow **2 :** COWARDLY

[2]**yellow** *n* **1 :** the color in the rainbow between green and orange **2 :** something yellow in color

[3]**yellow** *vb* **:** to turn yellow

yellow fever *n* **:** a disease carried by mosquitoes in hot countries

yel•low•ish *adj* **:** somewhat yellow

yellow jacket *n* **:** a small wasp with yellow markings that usually nests in colonies in the ground

[1]**yelp** *n* **:** a quick shrill bark or cry

[2]**yelp** *vb* **:** to make a quick shrill bark or cry

yen *n* **:** a strong desire **:** LONGING

yeo•man *n, pl* **yeo•men 1 :** a naval petty officer who works as a clerk **2 :** a small farmer who cultivates his or her own land

-yer — see [2]-ER

[1]**yes** *adv* **1** — used to express agreement **2** — used to introduce a phrase with greater emphasis or clearness **3** — used to show interest or attention

[2]**yes** *n* **:** a positive reply

[1]**yes•ter•day** *adv* **:** on the day next before today

[2]**yesterday** *n* **1 :** the day next before this day **2 :** time not long past

yes•ter•year *n* **:** the recent past

[1]**yet** *adv* **1 :** [2]BESIDES **2 :** [2]EVEN 4 **3 :** up to now **:** so far **4 :** at this or that time **5 :** up to the present **6 :** at some later time **7 :** NEVERTHELESS

²yet *conj* **:** but nevertheless

yew *n* **:** a tree or shrub with stiff poisonous evergreen leaves, a fleshy fruit, and tough wood used especially for bows and small articles

Yid·dish *n* **:** a language that comes from German and is used by some Jews

¹yield *vb* **1 :** to give up possession of on claim or demand **2 :** to give (oneself) up to a liking, temptation, or habit **3 :** to bear as a natural product **4 :** to return as income or profit **5 :** to be productive **:** bring good results **6 :** to stop opposing or objecting to something **7 :** to give way under physical force so as to bend, stretch, or break **8 :** to admit that someone else is better

²yield *n* **:** the amount produced or returned

¹yip *vb* **yipped; yip·ping :** ²YELP — used chiefly of a dog

²yip *n* **:** a noise made by or as if by yelping

¹yo·del *vb* **yo·deled** *or* **yo·delled; yo·del·ing** *or* **yo·del·ling 1 :** to sing with frequent sudden changes from the natural voice range to a higher range and back **2 :** to call or shout in the manner of yodeling — **yo·del·er** *n*

²yodel *n* **:** a yodeled shout

¹yoke *n* **1 :** a wooden bar or frame by which two work animals (as oxen) are harnessed at the heads or necks for drawing a plow or load **2 :** a frame fitted to a person's shoulders to carry a load in two equal parts **3 :** a clamp that joins two parts to hold or connect them in position **4** *pl usually* **yoke :** two animals yoked together **5 :** something that brings to a state of hardship, humiliation, or slavery **6 :** SLAVERY 2 **7 :** ¹TIE 4, BOND **8 :** a fitted or shaped piece at the shoulder of a garment or at the top of a skirt

²yoke *vb* **yoked; yok·ing 1 :** to put a yoke on **2 :** to attach a work animal to

yo·kel *n* **:** a country person with little education or experience

yolk *n* **:** the yellow inner part of the egg of a bird or reptile containing stored food material for the developing young — **yolked** *adj*

Yom Kip·pur *n* **:** a Jewish holiday observed in September or October with fasting and prayer

¹yon *adj* **:** ²YONDER 2

²yon *adv* **1 :** ¹YONDER **2 :** THITHER

¹yon·der *adv* **:** at or in that place

²yonder *adj* **1 :** more distant **2 :** being at a distance within view

yore *n* **:** time long past

you *pron* **1 :** the one or ones these words are spoken or written to **2 :** ³ONE 2

you'd : you had **:** you would

you'll : you shall **:** you will

¹young *adj* **youn·ger; youn·gest 1 :** being in the first or an early stage of life or growth **2 :** INEXPERIENCED **3 :** recently come into being **:** NEW **4 :** YOUTHFUL 1

²young *n, pl* **young 1** *young pl* **:** young persons **2** *young pl* **:** immature offspring **3 :** a single recently born or hatched animal

youn·gest *n, pl* **youngest :** one that is the least old especially of a family

young·ster *n* **1 :** a young person **:** YOUTH **2 :** CHILD

your *adj* **1 :** of or belonging to you **2 :** by or from you **3 :** affecting you **4 :** of or relating to one **5** — used before a title of honor in addressing a person

you're : you are

yours *pron* **:** that which belongs to you

your·self *pron, pl* **your·selves :** your own self

youth *n, pl* **youths 1 :** the period of life between being a child and an adult **2 :** a young man **3 :** young people **4 :** the quality or state of being young

youth·ful *adj* **1 :** of or relating to youth **2 :** being young and not yet fully grown **3 :** having the freshness of youth — **youth·ful·ly** *adv* — **youth·ful·ness** *n*

you've : you have

¹yowl *vb* **:** ¹WAIL

²yowl *n* **:** a loud long moaning cry (as of a cat)

yo–yo *n, pl* **yo–yos** *also* **yo–yoes :** a thick divided disk that is made to fall and rise to the hand by unwinding and winding again on a string

yuc·ca *n* **:** a plant related to the lilies that grows in dry regions and has stiff pointed leaves at the base of a tall stiff stalk of usually whitish flowers

yule *n, often cap* **:** CHRISTMAS

yule log *n, often cap Y* **:** a large log once put in the fireplace on Christmas Eve as the foundation of the fire

yule·tide *n, often cap* **:** the Christmas season

Z

z *n, pl* **z's** *or* **zs** *often cap* **:** the twenty-sixth letter of the English alphabet

[1]**za·ny** *n, pl* **zanies** **1 :** [1]CLOWN 2 **2 :** a silly or foolish person

[2]**zany** *adj* **za·ni·er; za·ni·est** **1 :** being or like a zany **2 :** FOOLISH, SILLY

zeal *n* **:** eager desire to get something done or see something succeed

zeal·ous *adj* **:** filled with or showing zeal — **zeal·ous·ly** *adv* — **zeal·ous·ness** *n*

ze·bra *n* **:** an African wild animal related to the horses that has a hide striped in black and white or black and buff

ze·bu *n* **:** an Asian domestic ox that differs from the related European cattle in having a large hump over the shoulders and a loose skin with hanging folds

ze·nith *n* **1 :** the point in the heavens directly overhead **2 :** the highest point

zeph·yr *n* **1 :** a breeze from the west **2 :** a gentle breeze

zep·pe·lin *n* **:** a huge long balloon that has a metal frame and is driven through the air by engines carried on its underside

ze·ro *n, pl* **zeros** *or* **zeroes** **1 :** the numerical symbol 0 meaning the absence of all size or quantity **2 :** the point on a scale (as on a thermometer) from which measurements are made **3 :** the temperature shown by the zero mark on a thermometer **4 :** a total lack of anything **:** NOTHING **5 :** the lowest point

zest *n* **1 :** an enjoyable or exciting quality **2 :** keen enjoyment — **zest·ful** *adj* — **zest·ful·ly** *adv* — **zest·ful·ness** *n*

[1]**zig·zag** *n* **1 :** one of a series of short sharp turns or angles in a course **2 :** a line, path, or pattern that bends sharply this way and that

[2]**zigzag** *adv* **:** in or by a zigzag path or course

[3]**zigzag** *adj* **:** having short sharp turns or angles

[4]**zigzag** *vb* **zig·zagged; zig·zag·ging** **:** to form into or move along a zigzag

zinc *n* **:** a bluish white metal that tarnishes only slightly in moist air and is used mostly to make alloys and to give iron a protective coating

zing *n* **1 :** a shrill humming sound **2 :** a lively or energetic quality

zin·nia *n* **:** a tropical American herb related to the daisies that is widely grown for its bright flower heads that last a long time

[1]**zip** *vb* **zipped; zip·ping** **1 :** to move or act with speed and force **2 :** to move or pass with a shrill hissing or humming sound

[2]**zip** *n* **1 :** a sudden shrill hissing sound **2 :** ENERGY 1

[3]**zip** *vb* **zipped; zip·ping** **:** to close or open with a zipper

zip code *or* **ZIP Code** *n* **:** a number consisting of five digits that identifies each postal area in the United States

zip·per *n* **:** a fastener (as for a jacket) consisting of two rows of metal or plastic teeth on strips of tape and a sliding piece that closes an opening by drawing the teeth together — **zip·pered** *adj*

zip·py *adj* **zip·pi·er; zip·pi·est** **:** full of energy **:** LIVELY

zith·er *n* **:** a stringed instrument with usually thirty to forty strings that are plucked with the fingers or with a pick

zo·di·ac *n* **:** an imaginary belt in the heavens that includes the paths of most of the planets and is divided into twelve constellations or signs

zom·bie *or* **zom·bi** *n* **:** a person who is believed to have died and been brought back to life

[1]**zone** *n* **1 :** any of the five great parts that the earth's surface is divided into according to latitude and temperature **2 :** a band or belt that surrounds **3 :** a section set off or marked as different in some way

[2]**zone** *vb* **zoned; zon·ing** **:** to divide into zones for different uses

zoo *n, pl* **zoos** **:** a collection of living animals for display

zoo·log·i·cal *adj* **:** of or relating to zoology

zoological garden *n* **:** a garden or park where wild animals are kept for exhibition

zo·ol·o·gist *n* **:** a specialist in zoology

zo·ol·o·gy *n* **1 :** a branch of biology dealing with animals and animal life **2 :** animal life (as of a region)

[1]**zoom** *vb* **1 :** to speed along with a loud hum or buzz **2 :** to move upward quickly at a sharp angle

[2]**zoom** *n* **1 :** an act or process of zooming **2 :** a zooming sound

zwie·back *n* **:** a usually sweetened bread made with eggs that is baked and then sliced and toasted until dry and crisp

zy·gote *n* **:** the new cell produced when a sperm cell joins with an egg

Abbreviations

Most of these abbreviations are shown in one form only. Variation in use of periods, in kind of type, and in capitalization is frequent and widespread (as *mph, MPH, m.p.h., Mph*)

abbr abbreviation
AD in the year of our Lord
adj adjective
adv adverb
AK Alaska
AL, Ala Alabama
alt alternate, altitude
a.m., A.M. before noon
Am, Amer America, American
amt amount
anon anonymous
ans answer
Apr April
AR Arkansas
Ariz Arizona
Ark Arkansas
assn association
asst assistant
atty attorney
Aug August
ave avenue
AZ Arizona

BC before Christ
bet between
bldg building
blvd boulevard
Br, Brit Britain, British
bro brother
bros brothers
bu bushel

c carat, cent, centimeter, century, chapter, cup
C Celsius, centigrade
CA, Cal, Calif California
Can, Canad Canada, Canadian
cap capital, capitalize, capitalized
Capt captain
ch chapter, church
cm centimeter
co company, county
CO Colorado
COD cash on delivery, collect on delivery
col column
Col colonel, Colorado
Colo Colorado
conj conjunction
Conn Connecticut
cpu central processing unit
ct cent, court
CT Connecticut
cu cubic
CZ Canal Zone

d penny
DC District of Columbia
DDS doctor of dental surgery
DE Delaware
Dec December
Del Delaware
dept department
DMD doctor of dental medicine
doz dozen
Dr doctor
DST daylight saving time

E east, eastern, excellent
ea each
e.g. for example
Eng England, English
esp especially
etc et cetera

f false, female, forte
F Fahrenheit
FBI Federal Bureau of Investigation
Feb February
fem feminine
FL, Fla Florida
fr father, from
Fri Friday
ft feet, foot, fort

g gram
G good
Ga, GA Georgia
gal gallon
GB gigabyte
gen general
geog geographic, geographical, geography
gm gram
gov governor
govt government
gt great
GU Guam

HI Hawaii
hr hour
HS high school
ht height

Ia, IA Iowa
ID Idaho
i.e. that is
IL, Ill Illinois
in inch
IN Indiana
inc incorporated
Ind Indian, Indiana
interj interjection
intrans intransitive

Jan January
jr, jun junior

Kan, Kans Kansas
KB kilobyte
kg kilogram
km kilometer
KS Kansas
Ky, KY Kentucky

l left, liter
La, LA Louisiana
lb pound
Lt lieutenant
ltd limited

m male, meter, mile
MA Massachusetts

Maj major
Mar March
masc masculine
Mass Massachusetts
MB megabyte
Md Maryland
MD doctor of medicine, Maryland
Me, ME Maine
Mex Mexican, Mexico
mg milligram
MI, Mich Michigan
min minute
Minn Minnesota
Miss Mississippi
ml milliliter
mm millimeter
MN Minnesota
mo month
Mo, MO Missouri
Mon Monday
Mont Montana

mpg miles per gallon
mph miles per hour
MS Mississippi
mt mount, mountain
MT Montana

n noun
N north, northern
NC North Carolina
ND, N Dak North Dakota
NE Nebraska, northeast
Neb, Nebr Nebraska
Nev Nevada
NH New Hampshire
NJ New Jersey
NM, N Mex New Mexico
no north, number
Nov November
NV Nevada
NW northwest
NY New York

O Ohio
obj object, objective
Oct October
off office
OH Ohio
OK, Okla Oklahoma
OR, Ore, Oreg Oregon
oz ounce, ounces

p page
Pa, PA Pennsylvania
part participle
pat patent
Penn, Penna Pennsylvania
pg page
pk park, peck
pkg package
pl plural
p.m., P.M. afternoon
PO post office
poss possessive
pp pages
pr pair
PR Puerto Rico
prep preposition
pres present, president
prof professor
pron pronoun
PS postscript, public school
pt pint, point
PTA Parent-Teacher Association
PTO Parent-Teacher Organization

qt quart

r right
rd road, rod
recd received
reg region, regular
res residence
Rev reverend
RFD rural free delivery
RI Rhode Island
rpm revolutions per minute
RR railroad
RSVP please reply
rt right
rte route

S south, southern
Sat Saturday
SC South Carolina
sci science
Scot Scotland, Scottish
SD, S Dak South Dakota
SE southeast
sec second
Sept September
SI International System of Units
sing singular
so south
sq square
sr senior
Sr sister
SS steamship
st state, street
St saint
Sun Sunday
SW southwest

t true
tbs, tbsp tablespoon
TD touchdown
Tenn Tennessee
Tex Texas
Thurs, Thu Thursday
TN Tennessee
trans transitive
tsp teaspoon
Tues, Tue Tuesday
TX Texas

UN United Nations
US United States
USA United States of America
USSR Union of Soviet Socialist Republics
usu usual, usually
UT Utah

v verb
Va, VA Virginia
var variant
vb verb
VG very good
vi verb intransitive
VI Virgin Islands
vol volume
VP vice president
vs versus
vt verb transitive
Vt, VT Vermont

W west, western
WA, Wash Washington
Wed Wednesday
WI, Wis, Wisc Wisconsin
wk week
wt weight
WV, W Va West Virginia
WWW World Wide Web
WY, Wyo Wyoming

yd yard
yr year

Confused, Misused, or Misspelled Words

a/an 'A' is used before a word beginning with a consonant or consonant sound ("a door", "a one-time deal"). 'An' is usually used before a word beginning with a vowel or vowel sound ("an operation"). 'A' is used before 'h' when the 'h' is pronounced ("a headache"); 'an' is used if the 'h' is not pronounced ("an honor").

accept/except The verb 'accept' means "to agree to, receive" ("accept a gift"). 'Except' most often means "not including" ("will visit all national parks except the Grand Canyon").

adapt/adopt The verb 'adapt' means "to change or modify" ("adapt to the warmer climate"); the verb 'adopt' means "to take as one's own" ("adopt a child").

affect/effect The verb 'affect' means to "cause a change in something" ("rain affects plant growth"); the noun 'effect' means "the result" ("the effect of rain on plant growth").

ain't 'Ain't' is used by some people in informal speech to mean "are not," "is not," or "am not," among other things. Because "ain't" is considered very informal, it is not generally used in schoolwork, or in formal speech and writing.

aisle/isle 'Aisle' means "a walkway between seats"; 'isle' is a poetic word meaning "island".

a lot, allot 'A lot', meaning "a great number", is spelled as two words; it is sometimes written incorrectly as 'alot'. 'Allot' is a verb meaning "to give out in portions" ("alloted one hour for homework").

an See 'a/an'.

apt See 'liable/likely/apt'.

as . . . as Is it more correct to say "she is as smart as I" or "she is as smart as me"? Actually, both ways are correct. In comparisons with "as . . . as", it's okay to use either subject pronouns (like "I", "you", "he", "she", "it", "we", and "they") or object pronouns (like "me", "you", "him", "her", "it", "us", and "them") after the second 'as'. However, subject pronouns sound more formal. So you may want to use subject pronouns in your comparisons when you are doing schoolwork, or anytime you are writing or speaking formally.

as/like Sometimes 'as' is used with the same meaning as 'like' ("do as I do"), ("do like I do"). At other times, 'as' means "in the role of" ("acted as a substitute teacher").

as well as When 'as well as' is used in a comparison, the pronoun following the second 'as' is usually in the subject form ("she can spell as well as I [can]", not "she can spell as well as me"). (For a list of subject pronouns, see 'as . . . as'.)

aural/oral 'Aural' and 'oral' are sometimes pronounced the same, but they have different meanings. 'Aural' means "of or relating to the ear or sense of hearing." It comes from the Latin word for "ear"; 'Oral' means "of, relating to, given by, or near the mouth," and comes from a Latin word for "mouth". (See also 'verbal/oral'.)

bare/bear 'Bare' means "without clothes or a covering" ("bare feet"); 'bear' means "to carry".

bazaar/bizarre 'Bazaar' is a fair; 'bizarre' means 'weird'.

beside/besides 'Beside' generally means "next to or at the side of" something; 'besides' means "in addition to".

born/borne 'Born' is having come into life; 'borne' means "carried".

bring/take 'Bring' usually means "to carry to a closer place"; 'take', "to carry to a farther place".

can/may 'Can' usually means "to be able to or know how to" ("they can read and write"); 'may' means "to have permission to" ("may I go?"). In casual conversation, 'can' also means "to have permission to" ("can I go?"), but 'may' is used instead in more formal speech or in writing.

canvas/canvass 'Canvas' is a cloth; 'canvass' means to ask people's opinions.

capital/capitol 'Capital' is the place or city of government; 'capitol' is the building of government.

cereal/serial 'Cereal' is a breakfast food; 'serial' is a story presented in parts.

colonel/kernal 'Colonel' is a military rank; 'kernel' is a part of a seed.

compliment/complement A 'compliment' is a nice thing to say; a 'complement' is something that completes.

council/counsel A 'council' is a group of people meeting; 'counsel' is advice.

country/county 'Country' is a nation; 'county' is a small, local government area.

data This was originally a plural form, but today it is used as both a singular and a plural noun.

desert/dessert 'Desert' (with one 's') is a dry, barren place; 'dessert' (with two 's's) is a sweet eaten after a meal.

die/dye To 'die' is to cease to live; to 'dye' is to change the color of something.

dived/dove Both spellings are common as a past tense of the verb 'dive' ("she dived into the pool", "she dove into the pool").

effect See 'affect/effect'.

except See 'accept/except'.

farther/further 'Farther' usually refers to distance ("he ran farther than I did"). 'Further' refers to degree or extent ("she further explained the situation")

flammable/inflammable Both words mean "capable of catching fire", but 'inflammable' is also sometimes used to mean "excitable",

forth/fourth 'Forth' means "forward"; 'fourth' means "number four in a sequence".

further See 'farther/further'.

good/well 'To feel good' generally means "to be in good health and good spirits." 'To feel well' usually means "to be healthy".

half/half a/a half a The 'l' in 'half' is silent; it is used in writing, but it is not pronounced. 'Half' is often used with the word 'a', which can either come before 'half' or after it ("ate a half sandwich", "ate half a sandwich"). In casual speech, 'a half a' is sometimes used ("ate a half a sandwich"), but it is avoided in more formal speech and in writing.

hanged/hung Both 'hanged' and 'hung' are used as the past tense of the verb 'to hang'. 'Hanged' is used when referring to execution by hanging; 'hung' is used in all other senses.

hardy/hearty 'Hardy' (suggestive of 'hard') means "strong"; 'hearty' (suggestive of 'heart') means "friendly, enthusiastic".

isle See 'aisle/isle'.

its/it's 'Its' means "of or relating to it or itself" ("the dog wagged its tail"). 'It's' is a contraction of 'it is' ("it's polite to say 'thank you' ").

kernel See 'colonel/kernel'.

later/latter 'Later' is the comparative form of 'late'; it means "after a given time" ("they started later than they had intended"). 'Latter' is an adjective that refers to the second of two things mentioned, or the last one of a sequence ("of the two choices, the latter is preferred").

lay/lie 'Lay' means "to put (something) down"; 'lie' means "to put one's body in a flat position",

lead/led These two words are pronounced the same, but have different meanings. 'Lead' is a metal; 'led' is the past tense of the verb 'to lead'.

less/fewer 'Less' is usually used with things that cannot be counted ("there is less sunshine today") and 'fewer' with things that can be counted ("there are fewer people today").

liable/likely/apt All three words mean the same thing, but 'likely' and 'apt' are more often used in situations that could have a positive or neutral outcome ("she's apt to burst out laughing", "they'll likely visit today"). 'Liable' is usually used where there is a possibility of a negative outcome ("you're liable to get hurt").

lie See 'lay/lie'.

like See 'as/like'.

liter/litter A 'liter' is a unit of measurement; 'litter' is a messy collection of things.

loose/lose 'Loose' means "not tight"; 'lose' means "to misplace or fail to win".

marital/martial 'Marital' has to do with marriage; 'martial' has to do with the military.

may See 'can/may'.

moral/morale 'Moral' has to do with high ideals; 'morale' is the state of feelings of a person or group ("after the victory, morale was high").

naval/navel 'Naval' has to do with the Navy; a 'navel' is a belly button.

no way 'No way' is an expression meaning "no" or "not at all." It is used in everyday speech, but is usually considered too casual for formal speech and writing.

oral See 'verbal/oral' and 'aural/oral'.

peace See 'piece/peace'.

pedal/peddle 'Pedal' means "to use or work the pedals of something" ("pedal a bicycle"). 'Peddle' means "to sell from house to house".

piece/peace A 'piece' is a portion of something ("a piece of cake"); 'peace' is the freedom from war or fighting.

precede/proceed 'Precede' means "to go ahead of or come before"; 'proceed' means "to start or move forward".

principal/principle A 'principal' is the head of a school; a 'principle' is a rule or guiding truth. It may help you to remember that 'principal' ends with the word 'pal', and that 'principle' and 'rule' end with the same two letters.

serial See 'cereal/serial'.

set/sit The verb 'set' means "to place (something) down or to arrange or make settled" ("set the date"); 'sit' means "to rest on the part of the body where the hips and legs join".

stationary/stationery Something that is stationary stands still; 'stationery' is paper that is used for writing letters. It's easy to tell these two words apart if you remember that 'stationery' and 'letter' both contain 'er'.

take See 'bring/take'.

than/then 'Than' is a conjunction used to indicate a comparison ("better than that"); 'then' means "at that time" ("then we went home").

there/their 'There' points to a place ("there it is"); 'their' refers to "what belongs to them" ("that is their house").

to/too/two 'To' implies a direction ("went to the store"). 'Too' means "also", "very", or "excessively" ("brought a pen and pencil too", "not too difficult", "too much"). 'Two' is the number 2.

used to/use to The phrases 'used to' and 'use to' are often confused since they have the same pronunciation. 'Used to' is correct in most instances ("we used to go to the lake every summer", "I used to know that"). But when it follows 'did' or 'didn't', the correct spelling is 'use to' ("that didn't use to be a problem").

verbal/oral Both 'verbal' and 'oral' are sometimes used to mean "spoken rather than written" ("a verbal agreement", "an oral agreement"). 'Verbal' can also mean "of, relating to, or formed by a verb," or "of, relating to, or consisting of words." (For more about 'oral,' see 'aural/oral'.)

want See 'won't/want'.

were/we're 'Were' is a past tense verb form of 'be' ("they were very young"); 'we're' is a contraction of 'we are' ("we're glad to see you").

who's/whose The word 'who's' is a contraction of 'who is' ("who's there?"); 'whose' is an adjective indicating ownership or quality ("whose book is this?")

who/whom 'Who' is used as the subject of a clause (where one would use 'he', 'she', or 'they'). 'Whom' is used as the object of a clause (where one would use 'him', 'her', or 'them'), and often follows prepositions like 'to', 'for', 'from', or 'with'. Subject: "Who is coming to the party?" "He is coming to the party." Object: "John is coming with whom?" "John is coming with them."

won't/want 'Won't is a contraction of 'will not' ("I won't go"); 'want' is a verb meaning "to need or desire" ("do you want some milk?").

Xmas 'Xmas' is a shortened form of the word 'Christmas'; the 'X' comes a Greek letter which is the first letter of the Greek word for 'Christ'. 'Xmas' is used in very casual writing, but is inappropriate for formal writing or schoolwork.

your/you're 'Your' is an adjective meaning "that which belongs to you" ("is that your sister?"). 'You're' is a contraction of 'you are' ("you're going, aren't you?").

Ten General Spelling Rules

1) In general, 'i' comes before 'e' except after 'c' or in words like 'neighbor' and 'weigh'.
2) Words that end in a /seed/ sound: 'supersede' is the only word ending in 'sede'; 'exceed', 'proceed' and 'succeed' are the only three words ending in 'ceed'; all others end in 'cede'.
3) Words ending in a hard 'c' sound usually change to 'ck' before adding 'e', 'i', or 'y': picnic → picnicked, picnicking but picnics.
4) Words ending in a stressed single vowel + single consonant usually double the consonant before a suffix: abet → abetted, abetting; begin → beginner.
5) Words ending in silent 'e' usually drop the 'e' before a suffix that begins with a vowel but not before a suffix beginning with a consonant: bone → boned, boning but boneless.
6) Words ending in stressed 'ie' usually change to 'y' before a suffixal 'i': die → dying.
7) Words ending in a double vowel usually remain unchanged before a suffix: agree → agreeable; blue → blueness; coo → cooing. In forming plurals, words ending in 'ss' usually add 'es'
8) Words ending in a consonant plus 'y' usually change the 'y' to 'i' before a suffix: beauty → beautiful; happy → happiness.
9) Words ending in a vowel plus 'y' usually do not change before a suffix: boy → boys; enjoy → enjoying.
10) Words ending in 'll' usually drop one 'l' when adding another word to form a compound: all + ready → already; full + fill → fulfill; hate + full → hateful.

Ten Rules for Forming Plurals

1) Most nouns form the plural by adding 's'. bag → bags.
2) Words that end in silent 'e' usually just add 's': college → colleges.
3) Nouns ending in 's', 'x', 'z', 'ch', and 'sh' usually add 'es': hush → hushes; church → churches; buzz → buzzes.
4) Words ending in a consonant + 'y' usually change the 'y' to 'i' and add 'es': army → armies; sky → skies.
5) Words ending in a vowel + 'y' usually add 's' with no change: bay → bays; boy → boys; key → keys.
6) Words ending in a vowel + 'o' usually add 's' with no change: duo → duos; studio → studios.
7) Words ending in a consonant + 'o': some add 's' and some add 'es': ego → egos; piano → pianos; echo → echoes; tomato → tomatoes.
8) Words ending in 'f' usually change the 'f' to 'v' and add 'es': leaf → leaves; self → selves; thief → thieves.
9) Words ending in 'fe' usually change the 'fe' to 'v' and add 'es': knife → knives; life → lives.
10) Words that are the names of fishes, birds, and mammals usually have an unchanging form for the plural or have the unchanging form and an 's' plural, depending on meaning.

Frequently Misspelled Words

about
accept
accidental
accidentally
accommodate
ache
acquire
across
adapt
address
adopt
affect
afternoon
again
aisle
all right
along
already
always
among
answer
antarctic
anything
anyway
apparent
appear
appearance
April
apt
arctic
attendance
aunt
awhile
balloon
bare
bargain
bazaar
bear
because
before
beginning
believable
believe
beside
besides
between
bicycle
birthday
bizarre
born
borne
bought
boys
bring
brother
brought
build
built
bureau
business
busy
buy
calendar
can
cannot
can't
canvas
canvass
capital
capitol
ceiling
cellar
cemetery
cereal
changeable
chief
children
choose
chose
close
cocoa
colonel
column
coming
commit
commitment
committee
complement
compliment
concede
conceive
conscience
conscious
cough
could
couldn't
council
counsel
country
county
cousin
cylinder
data
debt
definite
dependent
describe
description
desert
dessert
develop
diction
dictionary
didn't
die
different
dived
divine
doctor
does
done
don't
dove
down
dye
early
easily
easy
effect
eight
eighth
eligible
embarrass
encyclopedia
enough
envelop (verb)
envelope (noun)
environment
every
everybody
everything
exceed
except
existence
familiar
farther
father
February
fewer
fine
first
flammable
foreign
forth
forty
fourth
freight
Friday
friend
fulfill
further
getting
goes
going
good-by
good-bye
government
grammar
guess
half
handkerchiefs
hanged
hardy
haven't
having
hear
heard
hearty
height
hello
hoarse
hospital
hour
house
how's
hung
hygiene
illegal
imagine
independence
inflammable
instead
isle
isn't
its
January
judgment
kernel
knew
know
knowledge
laboratory
laid
later
latter
laugh
lay
lead
league
led
leisure
less
letter
liable
library
license
lie
like
likely
liter

litter
little
loose
lose
lovely
loving
lying
maintenance
management
manual
marital
marshal
martial
mathematics
may
maybe
meant
minute
mischief
misspell
moral
morale
morning
mosquito
mosquitoes
mother
movable
naval
navel
neighbor
nice
nickel
niece
ninety
ninth
none
noticeable
nowadays
occur
occurrence
o'clock
offense
often
once
oral
ought
parallel
parliament
peace
pedal
peddle
people
piece
please
pneumonia
prairie
precede
principal
principle
probably
proceed
quiet
quit
quite
raise
raspberry
ready
receipt
receive
recommend
remember
rhyme
rhythm
right
said
sandwich
satellite
Saturday
says
schedule
school
scissors
secretary
separate
serial
set
sheriff
sincerely
sit
somebody
something
sometime
speech
squirrel
stationary
stationery
straight
strength
studying
succeed
sugar
superintendent
supersede
suppose
sure
surely
surprise
synagogue
take
tear
than
their
them
then
there
though
thought
thoughtful
through
Thursday
to
together
tomorrow
tonight
too
trouble
truly
Tuesday
two
tying
unique
until
usable
used to
use to
usual
usually
vacation
vacuum
vegetable
verbal
villain
visible
volume
want
weak
wear
weather
Wednesday
week
weird
were
when
whether
which
who
whole
wholly
whom
who's
whose
witch
women
won't
would
wouldn't
write
writing
wrote
Xmas
X-ray
yacht
yeast
yield
your
you're
youthful
zenith
zodiac

Country Name	Capital	Area	Population (2001)
Afghanistan (W. Asia)	Kabul	251,825 sq. mi.	26,813,000
Albania (Europe)	Tiranë	11,082 sq. mi.	3,091,000
Algeria (N. Africa)	Algiers	919,595 sq. mi.	30,821,000
Andorra (Europe)	Andorra la Vella	181 sq. mi.	66,900
Angola (S. Africa)	Luanda	481,354 sq. mi.	10,366,000
Antigua and Barbuda (Caribbean)	St. John's	170 sq. mi.	71,500
Argentina (South America)	Buenos Aires	1,073,400 sq. mi.	37,487,000
Armenia (W. Asia)	Yerevan	11,484 sq. mi.	3,807,000
Australia (Pacific)	Canberra	2,969,910 sq. mi.	19,358,000
Austria (Europe)	Vienna	32,378 sq. mi.	8,069,000
Azerbaijan (W. Asia)	Baku	33,400 sq. mi.	8,105,000
Bahamas, The (Caribbean)	Nassau	5,382 sq. mi.	298,000
Bahrain (Asia-Persian Gulf)	Manama	268 sq. mi.	701,000
Bangladesh (Asia)	Dhaka	56,977 sq. mi.	131,270,000
Barbados (Caribbean)	Bridgetown	166 sq. mi.	269,000
Belarus (E. Europe)	Minsk	80,153 sq. mi.	9,986,000
Belgium (Europe)	Brussels	11,787 sq. mi.	10,268,000
Belize (Central America)	Belmopan	8,867 sq. mi.	247,000
Benin (W. Africa)	Porto-Novo, Cotonou	44,300 sq. mi.	6,591,000
Bhutan (Asia)	Thimphu	18,150 sq. mi.	692,000
Bolivia (South America)	La Paz, Sucre	424,164 sq. mi.	8,516,000
Bosnia and Herzegovina (Europe)	Sarajevo	19,741 sq. mi.	3,922,000
Botswana (S. Africa)	Gaborone	224,607 sq. mi.	1,586,000
Brazil (South America)	Brasília	3,300,171 sq. mi.	172,118,000
Brunei (S.E. Asia)	Bandar Seri Begawan	2,226 sq. mi.	344,000
Bulgaria (E. Europe)	Sofia	110,971 sq. mi.	7,953,000
Burkina Faso (W. Africa)	Ouagadougou	105,946 sq. mi.	12,272,000
Burundi (Africa)	Bujumbura	10,740 sq. mi.	6,224,000
Cambodia (S.E. Asia)	Phnom Penh	69,898 sq. mi.	12,720,000
Cameroon (W. Africa)	Yaoundé	183,569 sq. mi.	15,803,000
Canada (North America)	Ottawa	3,849,674 sq. mi.	31,081,900
Cape Verde (Atlantic Ocean-off Africa)	Praia	1,557 sq. mi.	446,000
Central African Republic (Africa)	Bangui	240,324 sq. mi.	3,577,000
Chad (Africa)	N'Djamena	495,755 sq. mi.	8,707,000
Chile (South America)	Santiago	292,135 sq. mi.	15,402,000

Country Name	Capital	Area	Population (2001)
China (Asia)	Beijing	3,696,100 sq. mi.	1,274,915,000
Colombia (South America)	Bogotá	440,762 sq. mi.	43,071,000
Comoros (Indian Ocean-off Africa)	Moroni	719 sq. mi.	566,000
Congo, Democratic Republic of the (Africa)	Kinshasa	905,354 sq. mi.	53,625,000
Congo, Republic of the (Africa)	Brazzaville	132,047 sq. mi.	2,894,000
Costa Rica (Central America)	San José	19,730 sq. mi.	3,936,000
Croatia (Europe)	Zagreb	21,359 sq. mi.	4,393,000
Cuba (Caribbean)	Havana	42,804 sq. mi.	11,190,000
Cyprus (Mediterranean)	Nicosia	2,276 sq. mi.	675,000
Czech Republic (Europe)	Prague	30,453 sq. mi.	10,269,000
Denmark (Europe)	Copenhagen	16,639 sq. mi.	5,358,000
Djibouti (E. Africa)	Djibouti	8,950 sq. mi.	461,000
Dominica (Caribbean)	Roseau	285 sq. mi.	71,700
Dominican Republic (Caribbean)	Santo Domingo	48,671 sq. mi.	8,693,000
East Timor (Pacific)	Dili	5,641 sq. mi.	897,000
Ecuador (South America)	Quito	105,037 sq. mi.	12,879,000
Egypt (N. Africa)	Cairo	385,210 sq. mi.	65,239,000
El Salvador (Central America)	San Salvador	8,124 sq. mi.	6,238,000
Equatorial Guinea (W. Africa)	Malabo	10,831 sq. mi.	486,000
Eritrea (E. Africa)	Asmara	46,770 sq. mi.	4,298,000
Estonia (E. Europe)	Tallinn	16,769 sq. mi.	1,363,000
Ethiopia (E. Africa)	Addis Ababa	437,794 sq. mi.	65,892,000
Fiji (Pacific)	Suva	7,055 sq. mi.	827,000
Finland (N. Europe)	Helsinki	130,559 sq. mi.	5,185,000
France (Europe)	Paris	210,026 sq. mi.	59,090,000
Gabon (W. Africa)	Libreville	103,347 sq. mi.	1,221,000
Gambia (W. Africa)	Banjul	4,127 sq. mi.	1,411,000
Georgia (W. Asia)	Tbilisi	26,911 sq. mi.	4,989,000
Germany (Europe)	Berlin	137,846 sq. mi.	82,386,000
Ghana (W. Africa)	Accra	92,098 sq. mi.	19,894,000
Greece (Europe)	Athens	50,949 sq. mi.	10,975,000
Grenada (Caribbean)	St. George's	133 sq. mi.	102,000
Guatemala (Central America)	Guatemala City	42,042 sq. mi.	11,687,000
Guinea (W. Africa)	Conakry	94,926 sq. mi.	7,614,000

Country Name	Capital	Area	Population (2001)
Guinea-Bissau (W. Africa)	Bissau	13,948 sq. mi.	1,316,000
Guyana (South America)	Georgetown	83,044 sq. mi.	776,000
Haiti (Caribbean)	Port-au-Prince	10,695 sq. mi.	6,965,000
Honduras (Central America)	Tegucigalpa	43,433 sq. mi.	6,626,000
Hungary (Europe)	Budapest	35,919 sq. mi.	10,190,000
Iceland (N. Europe)	Reykjavík	39,699 sq. mi.	284,000
India (Asia)	New Delhi	1,222,559 sq. mi.	1,029,991,000
Indonesia (S.E. Asia)	Jakarta	741,052 sq. mi.	212,195,000
Iran (W. Asia)	Tehran	629,315 sq. mi.	63,442,000
Iraq (W. Asia)	Baghdad	167,975 sq. mi.	23,332,000
Ireland (Europe)	Dublin	27,133 sq. mi.	3,823,000
Israel (W. Asia)	Jerusalem	7,886 sq. mi.	6,258,000
Italy (Europe)	Rome	116,324 sq. mi.	57,892,000
Ivory Coast (W. Africa)	Yamoussoukro	124,504 sq. mi.	16,393,000
Jamaica (Caribbean)	Kingston	4,244 sq. mi.	2,624,000
Japan (Pacific-E. Asia)	Tokyo	145,884 sq. mi.	127,100,000
Jordan (W. Asia)	Amman	34,495 sq. mi.	5,182,000
Kazakhstan (W. Asia)	Astana	1,052,100 sq. mi.	14,868,000
Kenya (E. Africa)	Nairobi	224,961 sq. mi.	30,766,000
Kiribati (Pacific)	Bairiki	313 sq. mi.	94,000
Kuwait (W. Asia)	Kuwait City	6,880 sq. mi.	2,275,000
Kyrgyzstan (W. Asia)	Bishkek	77,200 sq. mi.	4,934,000
Laos (S.E. Asia)	Vientiane	91,429 sq. mi.	5,636,000
Latvia (E. Europe)	Riga	24,938 sq. mi.	2,358,000
Lebanon (W. Asia)	Beirut	4,016 sq. mi.	3,628,000
Lesotho (S. Africa)	Maseru	11,720 sq. mi.	2,177,000
Liberia (W. Africa)	Monrovia	37,743 sq. mi.	3,226,000
Libya (N. Africa)	Tripoli	678,400 sq. mi.	5,241,000
Liechtenstein (Europe)	Vaduz	62 sq. mi.	33,000
Lithuania (E. Europe)	Vilnius	25,212 sq. mi.	3,691,000
Luxembourg (Europe)	Luxembourg	999 sq. mi.	444,000
Macedonia (Europe)	Skopje	9,928 sq. mi.	2,046,000
Madagascar (Indian Ocean-off Africa)	Antananarivo	226,658 sq. mi.	15,983,000
Malawi (S. Africa)	Lilongwe	45,747 sq. mi.	10,491,000
Malaysia (S.E. Asia)	Kuala Lumpur	127,354 sq. mi.	22,602,000
Maldives (Indian Ocean-off India)	Male	115 sq. mi.	275,000
Mali (W. Africa)	Bamako	482,077 sq. mi.	11,009,000
Malta (Mediterranean)	Valletta	122 sq. mi.	381,000
Marshall Islands (Pacific)	Majuro	70 sq. mi.	52,300
Mauritania (W. Africa)	Nouakchott	398,000 sq. mi.	2,591,000
Mauritius (Indian Ocean)	Port Louis	720 sq. mi.	1,210,200

Country Name	Capital	Area	Population (2001)
Mexico (North America)	Mexico City	758,449 sq. mi.	99,969,000
Micronesia (Pacific)	Palikir	271 sq. mi.	118,000
Moldova (E. Europe)	Chisinau	13,000 sq. mi.	4,431,000
Monaco (S. Europe)	Monaco	480 acres	30,500
Mongolia (Asia)	Ulaanbaatar	603,930 sq. mi.	2,435,000
Morocco (N. Africa)	Rabat	274,461 sq. mi.	29,237,000
Mozambique (S. Africa)	Maputo	313,661 sq. mi.	19,371,000
Myanmar (S.E. Asia)	Yangon	261,228 sq. mi.	41,995,000
Namibia (S. Africa)	Windhoek	318,580 sq. mi.	1,798,000
Nauru (Pacific)	-----	8 sq. mi.	10,000
Nepal (Asia)	Kathmandu	56,827 sq. mi.	25,284,000
Netherlands, The (Europe)	Amsterdam, The Hague	16,033 sq. mi.	15,968,000
New Zealand (Pacific)	Wellington	104,454 sq. mi.	3,861,000
Nicaragua (Central America)	Managua	50,337 sq. mi.	4,918,000
Niger (W. Africa)	Niamey	458,075 sq. mi.	10,355,000
Nigeria (W. Africa)	Abuja	356,669 sq. mi.	126,636,000
North Korea (E. Asia)	P'yongyang	47,399 sq. mi.	21,968,000
Norway (N. Europe)	Oslo	125,004 sq. mi.	4,516,000
Oman (W. Asia-Arabian Peninsula)	Masqat	119,500 sq. mi.	2,497,000
Pakistan (W. Asia)	Islamabad	307,374 sq. mi.	144,617,000
Palau (Pacific)	Koror	188 sq. mi.	19,700
Panama (Central America)	Panama City	28,950 sq. mi.	2,903,000
Papua New Guinea (Pacific)	Port Moresby	178,704 sq. mi.	5,287,000
Paraguay (South America)	Asunción	157,048 sq. mi.	5,636,000
Peru (South America)	Lima	496,225 sq. mi.	26,090,000
Philippines (Pacific)	Manila	115,860 sq. mi.	78,609,000
Poland (Europe)	Warsaw	120,728 sq. mi.	38,647,000
Portugal (Europe)	Lisbon	35,662 sq. mi.	10,328,000
Qatar (W. Asia)	Doha	4,412 sq. mi.	596,000
Romania (E. Europe)	Bucharest	91,699 sq. mi.	22,413,000
Russia (Europe & Asia)	Moscow	6,592,800 sq. mi.	144,417,000
Rwanda (Africa)	Kigali	10,169 sq. mi.	7,313,000
Saint Kitts-Nevis (Caribbean)	Basseterre	104 sq. mi.	38,800
Saint Lucia (Caribbean)	Castries	238 sq. mi.	158,000
Saint Vincent and the Grenadines (Caribbean)	Kingstown	150 sq. mi.	113,000
Samoa (Pacific)	Apia	1,093 sq. mi.	179,000
San Marino (Europe-in-Italy)	San Marino	24 sq. mi.	27,200

Country Name	Capital	Area	Population (2001)
São Tomé and Príncipe (Atlantic-off Africa)	São Tomé	386 sq. mi.	147,000
Saudi Arabia (W. Asia-Arabian Peninsula)	Riyadh	868,000 sq. mi.	22,757,000
Senegal (W. Africa)	Dakar	75,951 sq. mi.	10,285,000
Serbia and Montenegro (Europe)	Belgrade	39,449 sq. mi.	10,677,000
Seychelles (Indian Ocean-off Africa)	Victoria	176 sq. mi.	80,600
Sierra Leone (W. Africa)	Freetown	27,699 sq. mi.	5,427,000
Singapore (S.E. Asia-off Malaysia)	Singapore	264 sq. mi.	3,322,000
Slovakia (Europe)	Bratislava	18,933 sq. mi.	5,410,000
Slovenia (Europe)	Ljubljana	7,827 sq. mi.	1,991,000
Solomon Islands (Pacific)	Honiara	10,954 sq. mi.	480,000
Somalia (E. Africa)	Mogadishu	246,000 sq. mi.	7,489,000
South Africa (S. Africa)	Pretoria, Cape Town, Bloemfontein	470,693 sq. mi.	43,586,000
South Korea (E. Asia)	Seoul	38,402 sq. mi.	47,676,000
Spain (Europe)	Madrid	195,364 sq. mi.	40,144,000
Sri Lanka (Indian Ocean-off India)	Colombo	25,332 sq. mi.	19,399,000
Sudan (Africa)	Khartoum	966,757 sq. mi.	36,080,000
Surinam (South America)	Paramaribo	63,251 sq. mi.	434,000
Swaziland (S. Africa)	Mbabane	6,704 sq. mi.	1,104,000
Sweden (N. Europe)	Stockholm	173,732 sq. mi.	8,888,000
Switzerland (Europe)	Bern	15,940 sq. mi.	7,222,000
Syria (W. Asia)	Damascus	71,498 sq. mi.	16,729,000
Taiwan (Pacific-Asia)	Taipei	13,969 sq. mi.	22,340,000
Tajikistan (W. Asia)	Dushanbe	55,300 sq. mi.	6,252,000
Tanzania (E. Africa)	Dar es Salaam, Dodoma	364,017 sq. mi.	36,232,000
Thailand (S.E. Asia)	Bangkok	198,115 sq. mi.	61,251,000
Togo (W. Africa)	Lome	21,925 sq. mi.	5,153,000
Tonga (Pacific)	Nuku'alofa	289 sq. mi.	101,000
Trinidad and Tobago (Caribbean)	Port of Spain	1,980 sq. mi.	1,298,000
Tunisia (N. Africa)	Tunis	63,378 sq. mi.	9,828,000
Turkey (Europe-Asia)	Ankara	300,948 sq. mi.	66,229,000
Turkmenistan (W. Asia)	Ashgabat	188,500 sq. mi.	5,462,000
Tuvalu (Pacific)	Fongafale	10 sq. mi.	11,000
Uganda (Africa)	Kampala	93,065 sq. mi.	23,986,000
Ukraine (E. Europe)	Kiev	233,100 sq. mi.	48,767,000
United Arab Emirates (W. Asia-Arabian Peninsula)	Abu Dhabi	32,283 sq. mi.	3,108,000

Country Name	Capital	Area	Population (2001)
United Kingdom of Great Britain and Northern Ireland (Europe)	London	94,248 sq. mi.	59,953,000
United States of America (North America)	Washington, D.C.	3,675,031 sq. mi.	286,067,000
Uruguay (South America)	Montevideo	68,037 sq. mi.	3,303,000
Uzbekistan (W. Asia)	Tashkent	172,700 sq. mi.	25,155,000
Vanuatu (Pacific)	Port-Vila	4,707 sq. mi.	195,000
Venezuela (South America)	Caracas	353,841 sq. mi.	24,632,000
Vietnam (S.E. Asia)	Hanoi	127,816 sq. mi.	79,939,000
Yemen (W. Asia-Arabian Peninsula)	Sanaa	182,278 sq. mi.	18,078,000
Zambia (S. Africa)	Lusaka	290,586 sq. mi.	9,770,000
Zimbabwe (S. Africa)	Harare	150,872 sq. mi.	11,365,000

State Name and Abbreviation	Capital	Area	Population (2000)
Alabama AL	Montgomery	51,705 sq. mi.	4,447,100
Alaska AK	Juneau	591,004 sq. mi.	626,932
Arizona AZ	Phoenix	114,000 sq. mi.	5,130,632
Arkansas AR	Little Rock	53,187 sq. mi.	2,673,400
California CA	Sacramento	158,706 sq. mi.	33,871,648
Colorado CO	Denver	104,247 sq. mi.	4,301,261
Connecticut CT	Hartford	5018 sq. mi.	3,405,565
Delaware DE	Dover	2057 sq. mi.	783,600
Florida FL	Tallahassee	58,664 sq. mi.	15,982,378
Georgia GA	Atlanta	58,910 sq. mi.	8,186,453
Hawaii HI	Honolulu	6471 sq. mi.	1,211,537
Idaho ID	Boise	83,557 sq. mi.	1,293,953
Illinois IL	Springfield	56,400 sq. mi.	12,419,293
Indiana IN	Indianapolis	36,291 sq. mi.	6,080,485
Iowa IA	Des Moines	56,275 sq. mi.	2,926,324
Kansas KS	Topeka	82,277 sq. mi.	2,688,418
Kentucky KY	Frankfort	40,395 sq. mi.	4,041,769
Louisiana LA	Baton Rouge	48,523 sq. mi.	4,468,976
Maine ME	Augusta	33,265 sq. mi.	1,274,923
Maryland MD	Annapolis	10,460 sq. mi.	5,296,486
Massachusetts MA	Boston	8284 sq. mi.	6,349,097
Michigan MI	Lansing	58,527 sq. mi.	9,938,444
Minnesota MN	St. Paul	84,068 sq. mi.	4,919,479
Mississippi MS	Jackson	47,689 sq. mi.	2,844,658
Missouri MO	Jefferson City	69,697 sq. mi.	5,595,211
Montana MT	Helena	147,046 sq. mi.	902,195
Nebraska NE	Lincoln	77,355 sq. mi.	1,711,263
Nevada NV	Carson City	110,561 sq. mi.	1,998,257
New Hampshire NH	Concord	9279 sq. mi.	1,235,786
New Jersey NJ	Trenton	7787 sq. mi.	8,414,350
New Mexico NM	Santa Fe	121,593 sq. mi.	1,819,046
New York NY	Albany	49,576 sq. mi.	18,976,457
North Carolina NC	Raleigh	52,669 sq. mi.	8,049,313
North Dakota ND	Bismarck	70,665 sq. mi.	642,200
Ohio OH	Columbus	41,222 sq. mi.	11,353,140
Oklahoma OK	Oklahoma City	69,956 sq. mi.	3,450,654
Oregon OR	Salem	97,073 sq. mi.	3,421,399
Pennsylvania PA	Harrisburg	45,333 sq. mi.	12,281,054
Rhode Island RI	Providence	1212 sq. mi.	1,048,319
South Carolina SC	Columbia	31,113 sq. mi.	4,012,012
South Dakota SD	Pierre	77,116 sq. mi.	754,844
Tennessee TN	Nashville	42,144 sq. mi.	5,689,283
Texas TX	Austin	266,807 sq. mi.	20,851,820
Utah UT	Salt Lake City	84,899 sq. mi.	2,233,169
Vermont VT	Montpelier	9609 sq. mi.	608,827
Virginia VA	Richmond	40,767 sq. mi.	7,078,515
Washington WA	Olympia	68,192 sq. mi.	5,894,121
West Virginia WV	Charleston	24,181 sq. mi.	1,808,344
Wisconsin WI	Madison	56,154 sq. mi.	5,363,675
Wyoming WY	Cheyenne	97,914 sq. mi.	493,782

The Declaration of Independence

Action of Second Continental Congress, July 4, 1776
The unanimous Declaration of the thirteen United States of America

WHEN *in the Course of human Events, it becomes necessary for one People to dissolve the Political Bands which have connected them with another, and to assume among the Powers of the Earth, the separate and equal Station to which the Laws of Nature and of Nature's God entitle them, a decent Respect to the Opinions of Mankind requires that they should declare the causes which impel them to the Separation.*

WE *hold these Truths to be self-evident, that all Men are created equal, that they are endowed by their Creator with certain unalienable Rights, that among these are Life, Liberty and the Pursuit of Happiness — That to secure these Rights, Governments are instituted among Men, deriving their just Powers from the Consent of the Governed, that whenever any Form of Government becomes destructive of these Ends, it is the Right of the People to alter or to abolish it, and to institute new Government, laying its Foundation on such Principles, and organizing its Powers in such Form, as to them shall seem most likely to effect their Safety and Happiness. Prudence, indeed, will dictate that Governments long established should not be changed for light and transient Causes; and accordingly all Experience hath shewn, that Mankind are more disposed to suffer, while Evils are sufferable, than to right themselves by abolishing the Forms to which they are accustomed. But when a long Train of Abuses and Usurpations, pursuing invariably the same Object, evinces a Design to reduce them under absolute Despotism, it is their Right, it is their Duty, to throw off such Government, and to provide new Guards for their future Security. Such has been the patient Sufferance of these Colonies; and such is now the Necessity which constrains them to alter their former Systems of Government. The History of the present King of Great-Britain is a History of repeated Injuries and Usurpations, all having in direct Object the Establishment of an absolute Tyranny over these States. To prove this, let Facts be submitted to a candid World.*

HE *has refused his Assent to Laws, the most wholesome and necessary for the public Good.*

HE *has forbidden his Governors to pass Laws of immediate and pressing Importance, unless suspended in their Operation till his Assent should be obtained; and when so suspended, he has utterly neglected to attend to them.*

HE *has refused to pass other Laws for the Accommodation of large Districts of People, unless those People would relinquish the Right of Representation in the Legislature, a Right inestimable to them, and formidable to Tyrants only.*

HE *has called together Legislative Bodies at Places unusual, uncomfortable, and distant from the Depository of their public Records, for the sole Purpose of fatiguing them into Compliance with his Measures.*

HE *has dissolved Representative Houses repeatedly, for opposing with manly Firmness his Invasions on the Rights of the People.*

HE *has refused for a long Time, after such Dissolutions, to cause others to be elected; whereby the Legislative Powers, incapable of the Annihilation, have returned to the People at large for their exercise; the State remaining in the mean time exposed to all the Dangers of Invasion from without, and the Convulsions within.*

HE *has endeavoured to prevent the Population of these States; for that Purpose obstructing the Laws for Naturalization of Foreigners; refusing to pass others to encourage their Migrations hither, and raising the Conditions of new Appropriations of Lands.*

HE *has obstructed the Administration of Justice, by refusing his Assent to Laws for establishing Judiciary Powers.*

HE *has made Judges dependent on his Will alone, for the Tenure of their Offices, and the Amount and Payment of their Salaries.*

***HE** has erected a Multitude of new Offices, and sent hither Swarms of Officers to harrass our People, and eat out their Substance.*

***HE** has kept among us, in Times of Peace, Standing Armies, without the consent of our Legislatures.*

***HE** has affected to render the Military independent of and superior to the Civil Power.*

***HE** has combined with others to subject us to a Jurisdiction foreign to our Constitution, and unacknowledged by our Laws; giving his Assent to their Acts of pretended Legislation:*

***FOR** quartering large Bodies of Armed Troops among us;*

***FOR** protecting them, by a mock Trial, from Punishment for any Murders which they should commit on the Inhabitants of these States:*

***FOR** cutting off our Trade with all Parts of the World:*

***FOR** imposing Taxes on us without our Consent:*

***FOR** depriving us, in many Cases, of the Benefits of Trial by Jury:*

***FOR** transporting us beyond Seas to be tried for pretended Offences:*

***FOR** abolishing the free System of English Laws in a neighbouring Province, establishing therein an arbitrary Government, and enlarging its Boundaries, so as to render it at once an Example and fit Instrument for introducing the same absolute Rules into these Colonies:*

***FOR** taking away our Charters, abolishing our most valuable Laws, and altering fundamentally the Forms of our Governments:*

***FOR** suspending our own Legislatures, and declaring themselves invested with Power to legislate for us in all Cases whatsoever.*

***HE** has abdicated Government here, by declaring us out of his Protection and waging War against us.*

***HE** has plundered our Seas, ravaged our Coasts, burnt our Towns, and destroyed the Lives of our People.*

***HE** is, at this Time, transporting large Armies of foreign Mercenaries to compleat the Works of Death, Desolation, and Tyranny, already begun with circumstances of Cruelty and Perfidy, scarcely paralleled in the most barbarous Ages, and totally unworthy the Head of a civilized Nation.*

***HE** has constrained our fellow Citizens taken Captive on the high Seas to bear Arms against their Country, to become the Executioners of their Friends and Brethren, or to fall themselves by their Hands.*

***HE** has excited domestic Insurrections amongst us, and has endeavoured to bring on the Inhabitants of our Frontiers, the merciless Indian Savages, whose known Rule of Warfare, is an undistinguished Destruction, of all Ages, Sexes and Conditions.*

***IN** every stage of these Oppressions we have Petitioned for Redress in the most humble Terms: Our repeated Petitions have been answered only by repeated Injury. A Prince, whose Character is thus marked by every act which may define a Tyrant, is unfit to be the Ruler of a free People.*

***NOR** have we been wanting in Attentions to our British Brethren. We have warned them from Time to Time of Attempts by their Legislature to extend an unwarrantable Jurisdiction over us. We have reminded them of the Circumstances of our Emigration and Settlement here. We have appealed to their native Justice and Magnanimity, and we have conjured them by the Ties of our common Kindred to disavow these Usurpations, which, would inevitably interrupt our Connections and Correspondence. They too have been deaf to the Voice of Justice and of Consanguinity. We must, therefore, acquiesce in the Necessity, which denounces our Separation, and hold them, as we hold the rest of Mankind, Enemies in War, in Peace, Friends.*

***WE**, therefore, the Representatives of the UNITED STATES OF AMERICA, in GENERAL CONGRESS, Assembled, appealing to the Supreme Judge of the World for the Rectitude of our Intentions, do, in the Name, and by Authority of the good People of these Colonies, solemnly Publish and Declare, That these United Colonies are, and of Right ought to be, FREE AND INDEPENDENT STATES; that they are absolved from all Allegiance to the*

British Crown, and that all political Connection between them and the State of Great-Britain, is and ought to be totally dissolved; and that as FREE AND INDEPENDENT STATES, they have full Power to levy War, conclude Peace, contract Alliances, establish Commerce, and to do all other Acts and Things which INDEPENDENT STATES may of right do. And for the support of this Declaration, with a firm Reliance on the Protection of divine Providence, we mutually pledge to each other our Lives, our Fortunes, and our sacred Honor.

John Hancock

GEORGIA, *Button Gwinnett, Lyman Hall, Geo. Walton.*
NORTH-CAROLINA, *Wm. Hooper, Joseph Hewes, John Penn.*
SOUTH-CAROLINA, *Edward Rutledge, Thos Heyward, junr., Thomas Lynch, junr., Arthur Middleton.*
MARYLAND, *Samuel Chase, Wm. Paca, Thos. Stone, Charles Carroll, of Carrollton.*
VIRGINIA, *George Wythe, Richard Henry Lee, Ths. Jefferson, Benja. Harrison, Thos. Nelson, jr., Francis Lightfoot Lee, Carter Braxton.*
PENNSYLVANIA, *Robt. Morris, Benjamin Rush, Benja. Franklin, John Morton, Geo. Clymer, Jas. Smith, Geo. Taylor, James Wilson, Geo. Ross.*
DELAWARE, *Caesar Rodney, Geo. Read.*
NEW-YORK, *Wm. Floyd, Phil. Livingston, Frank Lewis, Lewis Morris.*
NEW-JERSEY, *Richd. Stockton, Jno. Witherspoon, Fras. Hopkinson, John Hart, Abra. Clark.*
NEW-HAMPSHIRE, *Josiah Bartlett, Wm. Whipple, Matthew Thornton.*
MASSACHUSETTS-BAY, *Saml. Adams, John Adams, Robt. Treat Paine, Elbridge Gerry.*
RHODE-ISLAND AND PROVIDENCE, &c., *Step. Hopkins, William Ellery.*
CONNECTICUT, *Roger Sherman, Saml. Huntington, Wm. Williams, Oliver Wolcott.*

Branches of the Government

LEGISLATIVE

Congress, made up of the **Senate** and the **House of Representatives**, has the power to make laws, levy taxes, borrow money, declare war, and regulate commerce between states. Bills must be approved by both houses and signed by the President to become law.

Senate, consists of 100 members (two members elected at large from each state) with each elected for a term of six years; presided over by the Vice President; special responsibility for approving or rejecting Cabinet and Supreme Court appointees and treaties made by the President and has sole power to try all impeachments.

House of Representatives, consists of 435 members (the number of representatives for each state based on population) with each elected for a term of two years; presided over by the Speaker of the House chosen by the majority vote in the House; special responsibility for initiating all bills for raising revenue.

EXECUTIVE

President, elected (by vote of the Electoral College after a popular vote) for a four-year term; serves as chief executive, head of state, and commander-in-chief of the armed forces; responsible for administering the laws, proposing new legislation to Congress, and for meeting with foreign heads of state and making treaties.

Vice President, elected with the President; serves as a stand-in for the President; presides over the Senate but does not vote as a member except when a tie-breaking vote is needed.

Cabinet, appointed by the President with approval of the Senate; acts as advisors to the President; includes the secretaries of the departments of State, the Treasury, Defense, Interior, Agriculture, Commerce, Labor, Health and Human Services, Housing and Urban Development, Transportation, Energy, Education, Veterans Affairs, Homeland Security, and Justice (headed by the Attorney General). The Cabinet may also have other members appointed at the discretion of the President.

JUDICIAL

Supreme Court, consists of a Chief Justice and eight Associate Justices, each appointed for life terms after nomination by the President and approval by the Senate; has original jurisdiction for all cases affecting ambassadors to the United States and public ministers (including the President), and all matters between individual states; has responsibility for hearing appeals of cases from the federal and state court system.

Other courts within the federal Judicial Branch include the **U.S. Tax Court**, the **U.S. Court of International Trade**, the 13 circuit **Courts of Appeals** (including 11 for the districts throughout the states, one in the District of Columbia, and one Federal Circuit), and courts in 94 **Federal Judicial Districts** in the 50 states, D.C., and Puerto Rico.

Laws and How They Are Made

We have had laws ever since people started living together in societies. Laws are rules for people to live by so as to maintain order and peace, and they either require citizens to do something or prohibit them from doing something.

Since the early American colonies were made up mostly of people from England, it is natural that laws in the United States are based on English law. And English law has two distinct forms. In the early days of England, different communities had their own laws, and whenever disputes arose the King would send out judges to the various communities to interprete the local laws. Gradually, these interpretations in one community came to be like those in similar cases in other communities, and eventually the interpretations became the same throughout the country. These interpretations were based on earlier court decisions, those that preceded--were based on "precedent"–and on common practices, and the body of these decisions came to be called "common law."

Common law did not cover all situations, and the king and Parliament passed other laws that applied to the whole country. This group of laws, passed by the legislature, came to be known as "statute law." In the United States, much of English common law and statute law was adopted by the federal government and by the states, and many current court interpretatons are based on precedent as well as on specific laws passed by the Congress.

How Congress Makes Laws

Any member of either the House or Representatives or the Senate may submit a document (a "bill") for consideration to be a law. A member may even "sponsor" a bill proposed by the President.

The procedures are essentially the same in the House of Representatives and the Senate, so a look at what might happen in the House can be used as an example.

When a member wishes to propose a bill, the bill is dropped into a container (called a "hopper") near the desk of the presiding officer, and the clerk assigns a number to the bill. The bill will then generally be referred to hereafter by this number. Then the bill is assigned to an appropriate committee for consideration. There are many committees in each house of the Congress that have responsibility for various areas of government, and the bill will be assigned to the committee that has jurisdiction over the area that is affected by the bill. For example, if the bill deals with agriculture, it will be assigned to the Agriculture Committee; if it involves relations with foreign governments, it will be assigned to the Committee on Foreign Relations.

The bill may be considered by the committee as a whole or assigned to a subcommittee. A bill may also be sent for consideration by several committees. When considering a bill, a committee will listen to arguments for and against the proposal and may make changes or additions to the bill. When finished, the committee will report the bill back to the full house for debate. Each house has its own rules governing debate.

If the House passes the bill, it sends it to the Senate for consideration and the process continues there. In the Senate the bill may be voted on as is, or changed or rejected. If the Senate changes the bill, then it must be sent to a conference committee made up of members of both houses who seek a compromise version, which then must be voted on by both houses.

When a majority of members of both houses have approved the same verson of the bill, the bill is sent to the President for signing into law. The President then has several options. The bill may be signed; it may be rejected (by a "veto") and sent back to Congress; it may be allowed to become law without a signature; or, if Congress adjourns before the President has had the bill for 10 days, it may be allowed to die without a signature (known as a "pocket veto"). A bill that has been vetoed may still become law if each house of Congress approves it with a two-thirds majority vote.

Presidents of the U.S.

Number & Name	Life Dates	Birthplace	in Office	Vice President
1 George Washington	1732—1799	Virginia	1789—1797	John Adams
2 John Adams	1735—1826	Massachusetts	1797—1801	Thomas Jefferson
3 Thomas Jefferson	1743—1826	Virginia	1801—1809	Aaron Burr
				George Clinton
4 James Madison	1751—1836	Virginia	1809—1817	George Clinton
				Elbridge Gerry
5 James Monroe	1758—1831	Virginia	1817—1825	Daniel Tompkins
6 John Quincy Adams	1767—1848	Massachusetts	1825—1829	John C. Calhoun
7 Andrew Jackson	1767—1845	South Carolina	1829—1837	John C. Calhoun
				Martin Van Buren
8 Martin Van Buren	1782—1862	New York	1837—1841	Richard Johnson
9 William Henry Harrison	1773—1841	Virginia	1841	John Tyler[1]
10 John Tyler	1790—1862	Virginia	1841—1845	
11 James Knox Polk	1795—1849	North Carolina	1845—1849	George M. Dallas
12 Zachary Taylor	1784—1850	Virginia	1849—1850	Millard Fillmore[2]
13 Millard Fillmore	1800—1874	New York	1850—1853	
14 Franklin Pierce	1804—1869	New Hampshire	1853—1857	William R. King[3]
15 James Buchanan	1791—1868	Pennsylvania	1857—1861	John Breckinridge
16 Abraham Lincoln	1809—1865*	Kentucky	1861—1865	Hannibal Hamlin
				Andrew Johnson[4]
17 Andrew Johnson	1808—1875	North Carolina	1865—1869	
18 Ulysses Simpson Grant	1822—1885	Ohio	1869—1877	Schuyler Colfax
				Henry Wilson[5]
19 Rutherford Birchard Hayes	1822—1893	Ohio	1877—1881	William Wheeler
20 James Abram Garfield	1831—1881*	Ohio	1881	Chester A. Arthur[6]
21 Chester Alan Arthur	1830—1886	Vermont	1881—1885	
22 Grover Cleveland	1837—1908	New Jersey	1885—1889	Thomas Hendricks[7]
23 Benjamin Harrison	1833—1901	Ohio	1889—1893	Levi P. Morton
24 Grover Cleveland	1837—1908	New Jersey	1893—1897	Adlai Stephenson
25 William McKinley	1843—1901*	Ohio	1897—1901	Garret Hobart
				Theodore Roosevelt[8]
26 Theodore Roosevelt	1858—1919	New York	1901—1909	Charles Fairbanks
27 William Howard Taft	1857—1930	Ohio	1909—1913	James Sherman[9]
28 Woodrow Wilson	1856—1924	Virginia	1913—1921	Thomas Marshall
29 William Gamaliel Harding	1865—1923	Ohio	1921—1923	Calvin Coolidge[10]
30 Calvin Coolidge	1872—1933	Vermont	1923—1929	Charles Dawes
31 Herbert Clark Hoover	1874—1964	Iowa	1929—1933	Charles Curtis
32 Franklin Delano Roosevelt	1882—1945	New York	1933—1945	John Garner
				Henry Wallace
				Harry S. Truman[11]
33 Harry S. Truman	1884—1972	Missouri	1945—1953	Alben Barkley
34 Dwight David Eisenhower	1890—1969	Texas	1953—1961	Richard M. Nixon
35 John Fitzgerald Kennedy	1917—1963*	Massachusetts	1961—1963	Lyndon B. Johnson[12]
36 Lyndon Baines Johnson	1908—1973	Texas	1963—1969	Hubert Humphrey
37 Richard Milhous Nixon[13]	1913—1994	California	1969—1974	Spiro Agnew[13]
				Gerald R. Ford[14]
38 Gerald Rudolph Ford	1913—	Nebraska	1974—1977	Nelson Rockerfeller
39 James Earl Carter, Jr.	1924—	Georgia	1977—1981	Walter Mondale
40 Ronald Wilson Reagan	1911—	Illinois	1981—1989	George H. W. Bush
41 George Herbert Walker Bush	1924—	Massachusetts	1989—1993	J. Danforth Quayle
42 William Jefferson Clinton	1946—	Arkansas	1993—2001	Albert Gore, Jr.
43 George Walker Bush	1946—	Connecticut	2001—	Richard Cheney

* Assassinated in office
[1] assumed presidency in 1841 on death of Harrison
[2] assumed presidency in 1850 on death of Taylor
[3] died in 1853 before taking office
[4] assumed presidency in 1865 on death of Lincoln
[5] died in office in 1875
[6] assumed presidency in 1881 on death of Garfield
[7] died in office in 1885
[8] assumed presidency in 1901 on death of McKinley
[9] died in office in 1912
[10] assumed presidency in 1923 on death of Harding
[11] assumed presidency in 1945 on death of Roosevelt
[12] assumed presidency in 1963 on death of Kennedy
[13] forced to resign from office
[14] assumed presidency in 1974 on resignation of Nixon

Important Events in American History

1565 · First permanent European settlement in what is now the United States established by the Spanish at St. Augustine (Fla.).

1598 · Spanish begin settlements in what is now New Mexico.

1607 · First permanent English settlement established at Jamestown (Va.).

1620 · Pilgrims land Mayflower and establish a colony at Plymouth (Mass.).

1626 · Dutch establish settlement on what is now Manhattan Island (N.Y.).

1629–36 · Colonies established in Massachusetts, Maryland, Connecticut, and Rhode Island.

1643 · New England Confederation, a union of colonies, is governed by the first written constitution in America.

1660 · Parliament introduces Navigation Acts that restrict the shipment of goods to and from the colonies.

1663 · Carolina colony established.

1664 · Duke of York acquires land between the Connecticut and Delaware rivers, naming it New York; later separates a portion for New Jersey colony.

1679–81 · New Hampshire and Pennsylvania colonies established.

1682 · French from Canada explore Mississippi River, claiming entire valley for France and naming the area Louisiana.

1692–93 · Salem witchcraft trials held in Massachusetts.

1704 · Delaware becomes a colony.

1729 · North and South Carolina become colonies.

1732 · Charter granted for Georgia colony.

1749 · Ohio Company organized for colonizing Ohio River Valley, west of the Appalachian Mountains, challenging French dominance in the area.

1754 · Georgia becomes a royal colony.

1763 · After a seven-year war in Europe, France gives to Great Britain all of Canada and Louisiana east of the Mississippi River.

1764 · Parliament passes Sugar Act to raise money in the colonies to pay off war debt; limits much of colonies' independent trade.

1765 · Parliament passes Stamp Act, which is first direct tax on the colonies.

1767 · Townshend Acts: duties imposed on imports to colonies from Britain; colonies resist by boycotting British goods.

1769 · Spanish begin settlements in California.

1770 · Boston Massacre: several colonists shot in clash with British troops at the Customs House.

1773 · Tea Act gives British East India Company a virtual monopoly on tea sales to colonies; Bostonians rebel with Boston Tea Party.

1774 · First Continental Congress meets in Philadelphia to outline grievances with Britain.

1775 · Parliament declares Massachusetts in rebellion; troops sent to restore order. · Minutemen repel British troops at Concord (Mass.); the clash begins the American Revolution. · Second Continental Congress meets in Philadelphia, and serves as the first federal government. · George Washington assumes command of Continental Army. · Kentucky settlements established.

1776 · Continental Congress adopts Declaration of Independence (on July 4th).

1777 · Continental Congress adopts Articles of Confederation; ratified by the states by 1781. · Continental Congress adopts "Stars and Stripes" as national flag.

1781 · Continental Army, with help from French fleet, defeats British at Yorktown (Va.).

1783 · Revolutionary War ends with Treaty of Paris; America given unlimited independence.

1784 · Russians establish settlements in Alaska.

1787 · Constitutional Convention in Philadelphia drafts a federal Constitution. · Delaware becomes first of the original 13 states to ratify new Constitution.

1789 · George Washington unanimously elected first President.

1789 · Congress submits to the states 12 Amendments to the Constitution for ratification; 10 of the 12 are ratified and become the "Bill of Rights" in 1791.

1790 · First United States census taken.

1791 · Vermont becomes 14th state.

1792 · Kentucky becomes 15th state.

1796 · Tennessee becomes 16th state.

1798 · Mississippi organized as a Territory.

1800 · Washington (D.C.) becomes the seat of government.

1803 · Ohio becomes 17th state. · Louisiana Purchase: President Thomas Jefferson purchases from France all of Louisiana Territory (most of the land between the Mississippi River and Rocky Mountains) for $11,250,000 plus the payment of debts of U.S. citizens to France; U.S. claims western part of Florida as part of purchase.

1804–1806 · Lewis and Clark expedition explores Louisiana Territory.

1805 · Michigan organized as a Territory.

1808 · Congress outlaws African slave trade.
1809 · Illinois organized as a Territory.
1812 · Louisiana becomes 18th state.
1814 · "Star Spangled Banner" written by Francis Scott Key during "War of 1812".
1816 · Indiana becomes 19th state.
1817 · Alabama organized as a Territory. · Mississippi becomes 20th state. · Work begins on Erie Canal, 363 mile waterway from Hudson River (in N.Y.) to Lake Erie.
1818 · Illinois becomes 21st state.
1819 · U.S. purchases eastern part of Florida from Spain for $5,000,000. · Arkansas organized as a Territory. · Alabama becomes 22nd state.
1820 · Missouri Compromise: Congressional compromise between the forces for and against slavery to balance the number of free and slave states admitted to the Union. · Maine (a free state) and Missouri (a slave state) become 23rd and 24th states.
1821–80 · Santa Fe Trail, from Missouri to New Mexico, becomes a major route to the Southwest.
1822 · U.S. colony established in Texas (part of Mexico).
1823 · Monroe Doctrine advanced by President James Monroe; sets out policy of discouraging more European colonization of New World.
1830s · Underground Railroad begins and operates for some 30 years as a clandestine route by which fugitive slaves escape from the South.
1836 · Texas declares independence from Mexico after battles, including siege of the Alamo; recognized by U. S. as an independent nation. · Wisconsin organized as a Territory. · Arkansas becomes 25th state.
1837 · Michigan becomes 26th state.
1838 · Trail of Tears: government removes Indians from homelands in Georgia, Tennessee, Arkansas, and Missouri and forces them to march overland to reservations in Oklahoma and Kansas. · Iowa organized as a Territory.
1842–60 · Oregon Trail, a 2000-mile trail from Missouri to Oregon, becomes a major settlement route to the West.
1845 · Florida becomes 27th state. · Texas annexed by U.S. and becomes 28th state.
1846 · Iowa becomes 29th state. · Treaty establishes the northwestern border between U.S. and Canada.
1846–8 · War with Mexico, over annexation of Texas; Treaty of Guadalupe Hidalgo in 1848 gives U.S. rights to New Mexico Territory and California; Mexico gives up all claim to Texas in exchange for $15 million.
1847 · Mormons migrate from Iowa to Utah, arriving at the Great Salt Lake Valley.
1848 · Wisconsin becomes 30th state. · Oregon organized as a Territory. · Gold discovered in California. · Women's Rights Convention in Seneca Falls (N.Y.).
1849 · California gold rush. · Minnesota organized as a Territory.
1850 · Compromise of 1850 between forces for and against slavery, admits California as a free state (31st state), establishes Texas boundaries, establishes New Mexico and Utah as Territories, and abolishes slave trade in District of Columbia.
1853 · Gadsden Purchase: U.S. pays Mexico $10 million for 300,000 square miles, now part of Arizona and New Mexico. · Washington organized as a Territory.
1854 · Kansas and Nebraska organized as Territories. · Chinese immigrants begin arriving in large numbers on the West Coast.
1858 · Minnesota becomes 32nd state.
1859 · Oregon becomes 33rd state. · Abolitionist John Brown attacks government arsenal at Harper's Ferry (Va.); becomes symbol for antislavery cause.
1860 · South Carolina secedes from Union after Abraham Lincoln is elected President. · Pony Express begins overland mail service from Missouri to California.
1861 · Transcontinental telegraph line completed. · Mississippi, Florida, Alabama, Georgia, Louisiana, and Texas secede from Union and with South Carolina form Confederate States of America. · Kansas becomes 34th state. · Civil War begins. Virginia, Arkansas, Tennessee, and North Carolina secede and join Confederacy. · Western counties of Virginia separate from Virginia and form West Virginia, loyal to the Union. · Dakota, Colorado, and Nevada organized as Territories.
1863 · Emancipation Proclamation grants freedom to all slaves in the states joining the Confederacy. · Arizona organized as a Territory. · Battle of Gettysburg; casualties for both sides number more than 40,000 in three days; Abraham Lincoln's Gettysburg Address given later at the dedication of a cemetery at the battlefield.
1864 · Montana organized as a Territory. · Nevada becomes 36th state.
1865 · Confederate General Lee surrenders to General Grant, ending Civil War. · President Abraham Lincoln is assassinated. · Thirteenth Amendment ratified, abolishing slavery.
1867 · Reconstruction of the former Confederate states begins. · Nebraska becomes 37th state. · Alaska purchased from Russia for $7.2 million.

1868 · Wyoming organized as a Territory and grants women the right to vote. · President Andrew Johnson is impeached and later acquitted in a Senate trial.

1869 · Union Pacific and Central Pacific Railroad lines join at Promontory (Utah), establishing first transcontinental railroad.

1872 · Yellowstone established as first national park.

1876 · Colorado becomes 38th state. · Alexander Graham Bell demonstrates the telephone.

1878 · Congress establishes local government for the District of Columbia.

1879 · Thomas Edison introduces the modern electric lightbulb.

1881 · President James Garfield is assassinated.

1883 · Four standard time zones adopted by U.S. and Canadian railroads.

1886 · Statue of Liberty dedicated.

1889 · North Dakota, South Dakota, Montana, and Washington become 39th, 40th, 41st, and 42nd states. · Johnstown (Pa.) and 4 other towns destroyed by flood after dam breaks. · Oklahoma Land rush.

1890 · Oklahoma organized as a Territory. · Idaho and Wyoming become 43rd and 44th states. · Wounded Knee (S. Dak.): Some 200 Sioux Indians massacred by U.S. Cavalry forces; this site later becomes a focal point of Native American protests against the government.

1893 · Colorado gives women the right to vote.

1893 · Hawaii Republic established when Queen Liliuokalani is overthrown with American intervention.

1896 · Utah becomes 45th state.

1897 · First subway in North America opens in Boston (Mass.).

1898 · Annexation of Hawaii by U.S. · Spanish-American War: U.S. invades Cuba to ensure Cuban independence from Spain; U.S. declares war on Spain, conquers Puerto Rico, Guam, Philippines; by Treaty of Paris, Spain abandons Cuba, gives Puerto Rico and Guam to U.S.; U.S. gives Spain $20 million for Philippines.

1900 · Orville and Wilbur Wright fly glider at Kitty Hawk (N.C.).

1901 · Oil found in Texas · President William McKinley is assassinated.

1903 · Panama revolts, seeking independence from Colombia; U.S. supports Panama and in treaty gives Panama $10 million plus $250,000 annually for a 10-mile-wide strip for a canal zone. · Orville Wright flies powered airplane.

1904 · Work begins on Panama Canal.

1906 · Earthquake destroys most of San Francisco.

1907 · Oklahoma becomes 46th state.

1908 · Henry Ford introduces the Model T automobile.

1909 · NAACP formed.

1912 · New Mexico and Arizona become 47th and 48th states. · Alaska organized as a Territory.

1913 · Sixteenth Amendment ratified, establishing a federal income tax.

1914 · In treaty, U.S. agrees to give Colombia $25 million compensation for taking Panama; treaty not ratified until 1921. · Panama Canal opens.

1917 · U.S. declares war on Germany and enters World War I. · Puerto Rico established as a U.S. Territory. · U.S. buys Virgin Islands (Danish West Indies) from Denmark for $25 million.

1918 · Daylight saving time goes into effect. · Armistice signed, ending WWI.

1920 · Nineteenth Amendment ratified, giving women the right to vote. · Eighteenth Amendment, prohibition, goes into effect.

1925 · Nellie Tayloe Ross becomes governor of Wyoming–first woman governor. · "Monkey trial": John Scopes convicted of teaching the theory of evolution in Tennessee in defiance of state law. · Demonstration of television.

1926 · Robert Goddard successfully tests a liquid-fuel rocket.

1929 · Stock market crash leads to an economic depression.

1931 · "Star-Spangled Banner" officially made the national anthem.

1933 · Prohibition ends with ratification of the Twenty-first Amendment.

1934 · U.S. grants independence to Cuba.

1935 · Social Security is established. · Philippines begins United States Commonwealth status.

1941 · U.S. enters World War II after Japan attacks Pearl Harbor Naval Base in Hawaii.

1942–45 · Federal government moves more than 100,000 Japanese immigrants and American citizens of Japanese ancestry from the West Coast into inland relocation camps for the duration of the war. · First American jet airplane test flown.

1945 · Germany surrenders. · First use of atomic bombs: Bombs dropped by U.S. on Japanese cities of Hiroshima and Nagasaki. · Japan surrenders.

1946 · Philippines granted independence. · First general-purpose electronic digital computer introduced.

1947 · Marshall Plan: Secretary of State George Marshall proposes a plan by which the U.S. contributes to the economic recovery of European countries after World

War II. · Electronic transistor is invented.

1948–49 · U.S. and Britain airlift supplies into West Berlin (inside East Germany) after the Soviet Union blockades surface transport.

1949 · North Atlantic Treaty Organization (NATO) established.

1950–53 · Korean War: U.S. troops are sent to support South Korea after North Korea invades; fighting ends with an armistice. · Guam becomes a U.S. Territory.

1954 · McCarthy hearings: Senate Permanent Subcommittee on Investigations, chaired by Senator Joseph McCarthy, holds televised hearings after McCarthy makes unsubstantiated charges of Communist activity in the U.S. Army and accuses the Democratic party of treason. · Brown v. Board of Education of Topeka (Kan.): Supreme Court holds that racial segregation violates the Constitution.

1954–59 · St. Lawrence Seaway is constructed.

1956 · Interstate highway system begins.

1958 · U.S. launches first space satellites; begins "space race" with Soviet Union.

1959 · Alaska and Hawaii become 49th and 50th states.

1961 · Astronaut Alan Shepard becomes first American in space.

1962 · Astronaut John Glenn is first American to orbit the earth. · Cuban Missile Crisis: Confrontation between U.S. and Soviet Union over the presence of Soviet nuclear missiles in Cuba.

1963 · President John Kennedy is assassinated.

1965–73 · Vietnam War: U.S. troops become directly involved in fighting between North and South Vietnam.

1967 · Thurgood Marshall becomes first African-American Supreme Court justice.

1968 · Civil Rights leader Rev. Martin Luther King, Jr. and presidential candidate Robert Kennedy (brother of John) are assassinated.

1969 · U.S. mission lands on the Moon; American astronaut Neil Armstrong becomes first person to walk on the Moon.

1970 · Members of Ohio National Guard fire into a crowd of students protesting the Vietnam War at Kent State University, killing four.

1971 · Twenty-sixth Amendment ratified, giving 18 year olds the right to vote in national elections.

1974 · President Richard Nixon resigns from office after Watergate scandal.

1977 · Treaty (approved by Senate in 1978) gives complete control of Panama Canal to Panama by the year 2000.

1979 · Iranian militants seize the U.S. embassy in Tehran and hold 90 hostages (63 Americans) for more than a year. · Nuclear reactor at Three Mile Island (Pa.) undergoes a partial meltdown.

1981 · Sandra Day O'Connor becomes first woman Supreme Court justice. · Space shuttle *Columbia* completes maiden voyage becoming the first reusable spacecraft.

1986 · Space shuttle *Challenger* explodes after liftoff killing all 7 astronauts aboard, including Christa McAuliffe, a schoolteacher, to be the first private citizen in space.

1991 · Persian Gulf War: U.S. Armed Forces, supported by a coalition of nations, help liberate Kuwait after an earlier invasion by Iraq.

1992 · L.A. Riots: Riots break out in Los Angeles (Calif.) after four white police officers are acquitted of charges of beating a black man.

1993 · Author Toni Morrison becomes the first African-American to win a Nobel Prize.

1995 · A truck bomb explodes outside a federal office building in Oklahoma City (Okla.), killing 168 persons.

1996 · Shannon Lucid sets an American space endurance record by spending 188 days aboard the Mir space station.

1998 · President William Jefferson Clinton becomes the second sitting president to be impeached. He is acquitted in a Senate trial.

1999 · Two high school students go on a shooting rampage at Columbine High School in Colorado, killing 15 people before killing themselves.

2001 · Four U.S. airliners are hijacked by Islamic militants. Two are flown into the twin towers of the World Trade Center in New York City, one into the Pentagon outside Washington, and one crashes in rural Pa. after passengers try to retake the plane.

2002–2003 · In an effort to root out terrorists and governments believed to pose a threat to the world, the U.S., supported by a few allied countries, destroys militant Islamic training camps and the Taliban government in Afghanistan and then sends troops to Iraq to oust that country's leader Saddam Hussein.

2003 · Space shuttle *Columbia* breaks apart and disintegrates in a fiery re-entry, killing the 7 astronauts aboard.

2005 · Hurricane Katrina, considered the most costly natural disaster in American history, hits the Gulf Coast with devastating force, breaching levees and flooding much of New Orleans and destroying entire towns in Mississippi and Louisiana. It is believed responsible for more than 1,300 deaths.

WEIGHTS AND MEASURES

U.S. system

Length

UNIT (abbreviation)	SAME SYSTEM EQUIVALENT	METRIC EQUIVALENT
mile (mi)	5280 feet, 1760 yards	1.609 kilometers
rod (rd)	$5^1/_2$ yards, $16^1/_2$ feet	5.029 meters
yard (yd)	3 feet, 36 inches	0.914 meter
foot (ft or ′)	12 inches, $^1/_3$ yard	30.48 centimeters
inch (in or ″)		2.54 centimeters

Area

UNIT (abbreviation)	SAME SYSTEM EQUIVALENT	METRIC EQUIVALENT
square mile (sq mi or mi^2)	640 acres	2.59 sq. kilometers
acre	4840 sq. yards, 43,560 square feet	4047 square meters
square rod (sq rd or rd^2)	30.25 square yards	25.293 square meters
square yard (sq yd or yd^2)	9 square feet, 1296 square inches	0.836 square meter
square foot (sq ft or ft^2)	144 square inches	0.093 square meter
square inch (sq in or in^2)		6.452 square centimeters

Volume

UNIT (abbreviation)	SAME SYSTEM EQUIVALENT	METRIC EQUIVALENT
cubic yard (cu yd or yd^3)	27 cubic feet, 46,656 cubic inches	0.765 cubic meter
cubic foot (cu ft or ft^3)	1728 cubic inches, 0.037 cubic yard	0.028 cubic meter
cubic inch (cu in or in^3)		16.387 cubic centimeters

Weight

Avoirdupois

UNIT (abbreviation)	SAME SYSTEM EQUIVALENT	METRIC EQUIVALENT
short ton	2000 pounds	0.907 metric ton
long ton	2240 pounds	1.016 metric tons
hundredweight (cwt)		
short hundredweight	100 pounds	45.359 kilograms
long hundredweight	112 pounds	50.802 kilograms
pound (lb also #)	16 ounces, 7000 grains	0.454 kilogram
ounce (oz or oz av)	16 drams, 437.5 grains	28.350 grams
dram (dr or dr av)	27.343 grains	1.772 grams
grain (gr)		0.0648 gram

Troy

UNIT (abbreviation)	SAME SYSTEM EQUIVALENT	METRIC EQUIVALENT
pound (lb t)	12 ounces, 5760 grains	0.373 kilogram
ounce (oz t)	20 pennyweight, 480 grains	31.103 grams
pennyweight (dwt also pwt)	24 grains, $^{1}/_{20}$ ounce	1.555 grams
grain (gr)		0.0648 gram

Apothecaries'

UNIT (abbreviation)	SAME SYSTEM EQUIVALENT	METRIC EQUIVALENT
pound (lb ap)	12 ounces, 5760 grains	0.373 kilogram
ounce (oz ap)	8 drams, 480 grains	31.103 grams
dram (dr ap)	3 scruples, 60 grains	3.888 grams
scruple (s ap)	20 grains, $^{1}/_{3}$ dram	1.296 grams
grain (gr)		0.0648 gram

Capacity

UNIT (abbreviation)	SAME SYSTEM EQUIVALENT	METRIC EQUIVALENT
	U.S. liquid measure	
gallon (gal)	4 quarts	3.785 liters
quart (qt)	2 pints	0.946 liter
pint (pt)	4 gills	0.473 liter
gill (gi)	4 fluid ounces	0.118 liter
fluid ounce (fl oz)	8 fluid drams	29.573 milliliters
fluid dram (fl dr)	60 minims	3.697 milliliters
minim (min)	$^{1}/_{60}$ fluid dram	0.0616 milliliter
	U.S. dry measure	
bushel (bu)	4 pecks	35.239 liters
peck (pk)	8 quarts	8.810 liters
quart (qt)	2 pints	1.101 liters
pint (pt)	$^{1}/_{2}$ quart	0.551 liter

Metric system

Length

UNIT (abbreviation)	SAME SYSTEM EQUIVALENT	U.S. SYSTEM EQUIVALENT
kilometer (km)	1,000 meters	0.621 mile
hectometer (hm)	100 meters	109.361 yards
dekameter (dam)	10 meters	32.81 feet
meter (m)	1 meter	39.370 inches
decimeter (dm)	0.1 meter	3.937 inches
centimeter (cm)	0.01 meter	0.394 inch
millimeter (mm)	0.001 meter	0.039 inch

Area

UNIT (abbreviation)	SAME SYSTEM EQUIVALENT	U.S. SYSTEM EQUIVALENT
square kilometer (sq km or km^2)	1,000,000 square meters	0.39 square mile
hectare (ha)	10,000 square meters	2.47 acres
are (a)	100 square meters	119.60 square yards
square centimeter (sq cm or cm^2)	0.0001 square meter	0.16 square inch

Capacity

UNIT (abbreviation)	SAME SYSTEM EQUIVALENT	U.S. SYSTEM EQUIVALENT
kiloliter (kl)	1,000 liters	28.38 bushels
hectoliter (hl)	100 liters	2.838 bushels
dekaliter (dal)	10 liters	1.14 pecks (Dry) 2.64 gallons (Liquid)
liter (l)	1 liter	0.91 quart (Dry) 1.06 quarts (Liquid)
deciliter (dl)	0.10 liter	0.18 pint (Dry) 0.21 pint (Liquid)
centiliter (cl)	0.01 liter	0.34 fluid ounce
milliliter (ml)	0.001 liter	0.27 fluid dram

Mass and Weight

UNIT (abbreviation)	SAME SYSTEM EQUIVALENT	U.S. SYSTEM EQUIVALENT
metric ton (t)	1,000,000 grams	1.10 tons
kilogram (kg)	1,000 grams	2.20 pounds
hectogram (hg)	100 grams	3.53 ounces
dekagram (dag)	10 grams	0.35 ounce
gram (g or gm)	1 gram	0.035 ounce
decigram (dg)	0.10 gram	1.54 grains
centigram (cg)	0.01 gram	0.15 grain
milligram (mg)	0.001 gram	0.015 grain

Conversion formulas

to convert from (A)	to (B)	multiply (A) number by
cubic yards	cubic meters	.765
cubic feet	cubic meters	.028
cubic inches	cubic centimeters	16.387
square miles	square kilometers	2.59
square yards	square meters	.836
square inches	square centimeters	6.452
miles	kilometers	1.609
inches	centimeters	2.54
pounds	kilograms	.454
ounces	grams	28.35
liquid quarts	liters	.946
fluid ounces	mililiters	29.57

Math Refresher

FRACTIONS

Simple or common fractions are those having a **numerator,** or top number, that is smaller than the **denominator,** or bottom number. The fraction $\frac{3}{4}$ is a simple fraction. An **improper fraction** is one in which the numerator is larger than the denominator. The fraction $\frac{14}{12}$ is an improper fraction.

Fractions can often be **reduced** to a smaller fraction with the same value but with a smaller numerator and denominator. The fraction $\frac{2}{4}$ can be reduced to $\frac{1}{2}$, which has the same value, and $\frac{6}{8}$ can be reduced to $\frac{3}{4}$. Any improper fraction can be reduced to a **mixed number,** that is, one that is the sum of a whole number and a simple fraction (such as $\frac{3}{2}$, which can be reduced to $1\frac{1}{2}$).

To reduce a simple fraction, it is necessary to discover a common **factor** of the numerator and denominator. (Factors are two numbers that can be multiplied together to produce a given number. The number 6, for example, has 2 and 3 as factors.) When the numerator and denominator have a common factor, they can both be divided by that common factor. (This is the same as canceling out these common factors.)

$$\frac{12}{16} = \frac{4\times 3}{4\times 4} = \frac{3}{4}$$

$$\frac{10}{15} = \frac{2\times 5}{3\times 5} = \frac{2}{3}$$

To reduce an improper fraction to a mixed number, divide the numerator by the denominator. This gives a whole number and possibly a remainder. Any remainder can be expressed in the numerator of a simple fraction over the original denominator. This simple fraction may be further reduced, if necessary.

$$\frac{14}{12} = 14 \div 12 = 1\frac{2}{12} = 1\frac{1}{6}$$

$$\frac{13}{5} = 13 \div 5 = 2\frac{3}{5}$$

Changing a mixed number to an improper fraction involves addition of fractions, and this will be covered after the discussion of adding and subtracting fractions.

MULTIPLYING AND DIVIDING FRACTIONS

In multiplying two fractions, the numerators are multiplied and the denominators are multiplied, regardless of whether or not they are the same.

$$\frac{2}{5} \times \frac{7}{6} = \frac{2\times 7}{5\times 6} = \frac{14}{30} = \frac{7}{15}$$

Dividing fractions is a matter of multiplying one fraction, the **dividend,** by the **reciprocal** of the other, the divisor. (The reciprocal of a fraction is the result of reversing the positions of the numerator and denominator—turning the fraction upside down.)

$$\frac{7}{9} \div \frac{1}{5} = \frac{7}{9} \times \frac{5}{1} = \frac{7\times 5}{9\times 1} = \frac{35}{9} = 3\frac{8}{9}$$

ADDING AND SUBTRACTING FRACTIONS

In order to add or subtract two fractions, they need to have the same denominator. If they already have the same denominator, simply add or subtract the numerators and put the result over the common denominator. If the denominators are not the same, one or more of the fractions has to be converted so that both have a common denominator.

Find the lowest number for the denominator that is common to both (the **lowest common denominator** or LCD), that is, the lowest number that has both denominators as factors. One way is to multiply each denominator successively by 1, 2, 3, etc., until you find a multiple that the denominators have in common. This lowest common multiple is the lowest common denominator.

To find the LCD of the fractions $\frac{3}{4}$ and $\frac{1}{6}$, list the multiples of each denominator:

multiples of 4: 4, 8, 12, 16, 20 ...
multiples of 6: 6, 12, 18, 24 ...

The lowest common multiple is 12, which is the lowest common denominator.

Once the LCD is found, the fractions have to be converted to equivalent fractions with the common denominators. To do this, find the factors of the LCD that include the first denominator and the factors of the LCD that include the second denominator. In the example above, the factors of 12 that include the denominator 4 are 3 and 4; the factors of 12 that include the denominator 6 are 2 and 6.

To keep the same value in the new fraction, it is necessary to multiply both the numerator and the denominator by the same number—which is the same as multiplying the fraction by another fraction equal to 1—and this same number is the factor that will result in the LCD—12 in this example. For the fraction $\frac{3}{4}$ that would be $\frac{3}{3}$; for $\frac{1}{6}$ it would be $\frac{2}{2}$.

$$\frac{3}{4}+\frac{1}{6}=\frac{3\times3}{4\times3}+\frac{1\times2}{6\times2}=\frac{9}{12}+\frac{2}{12}=\frac{11}{12}$$

To find the LCD of the fractions $\frac{2}{3}$ and $\frac{4}{5}$, write out the multiples or multiply the denominators together: 3 x 5 = 15

$$\frac{2}{3}+\frac{4}{5}=\frac{2\times5}{3\times5}+\frac{4\times3}{5\times3}=\frac{10}{15}+\frac{12}{15}=\frac{22}{15}=1\frac{7}{15}$$

To subtract, create fractions with the LCD and then perform subtraction:

$$\frac{9}{14}-\frac{1}{7}=\frac{9}{14}-\frac{1\times2}{7\times2}=\frac{9}{14}-\frac{2}{14}=\frac{7}{14}=\frac{1}{2}$$

To change a mixed number to an improper fraction, convert the whole number to a fraction having the same denominator as the fractional part and then add the two fractions together. A whole number is the same as a fraction with that number over "1," and any fraction equal to "1" will have the same number in the numerator and the denominator. Thus, the conversion involves putting the whole number over "1" and multiplying it by a fraction consisting of the value of the original denominator over itself.

$$2\frac{2}{3}=\left(\frac{2\times3}{1\times3}\right)+\frac{2}{3}=\frac{6}{3}+\frac{2}{3}=\frac{8}{3}$$

DECIMAL NUMBERS

Numbers that include a decimal point are considered fractions in which the numerator is the part to the right of the decimal and the denominator is always 10 or a multiple of 10, depending on the number of decimal places. The number 5.3 is a **decimal number** that is the equivalent of a mixed number with 5 as the whole number and $\frac{3}{10}$ as the fraction, and the number 16.348 is equivalent to a mixed number with 16 as the whole number and $\frac{348}{1000}$ as the fraction.

Each position to the right of any given decimal position is one-tenth the value of the position before. Thus, the first position to the right of the decimal point represents tenths, the next position to the right, hundredths, the third position, thousandths, and so on.

To convert a decimal number into a fraction, the whole number is unchanged and the decimal portion is placed over the appropriate power of 10 (depending on the number of digits).

$$1.3 = 1\frac{3}{10}$$

$$3.25 = 3\frac{25}{100}$$

$$2.325 = 2\frac{325}{1000}$$

To convert a fraction into a decimal number, divide the numerator by the denominator.

$$\frac{1}{2} = 1 \div 2 = .5$$

$$\frac{3}{16} = 3 \div 16 = .1875$$

PERCENT

The word **percent** represents "per hundred" or "in a hundred" or "of one hundred parts." In other words, the number expressed as a percent is the number of parts out of 100 possible parts. Percents are often written with a percent sign (%). Thus, 10 percent, or 10%, means "10 parts in 100." A U.S. dollar can be divided into 100 cents, so a quarter (25 cents) can be said to have a value that is 25% of a dollar (a quarter-dollar).

To convert a decimal to a percent, multiply the decimal number by 100 (or move the decimal point two places to the right) and add the percent sign.

$$.35 = \frac{35}{100} \times \frac{100}{1} = 35\%$$

$$3.14 = 314\%$$

To convert percent to a decimal number, remove the percent sign and divide by 100 (or move the decimal point two places to the left).

$$1.6\% = \frac{1.6}{100} = .016$$

$$30.25\% = .3025$$

EXPONENTS AND POWERS

When a number is multiplied by itself, the result is the **square** of the number. When 2 is multiplied by 2 (2 x 2) the result is 4; thus, 4 is the square of 2. When 5 is multiplied by 5, the result is 25; thus, 25 is the square of 5.

This operation can also be expressed by the use of a small, raised number to the right of the factor, called an **exponent,** as 2^2 or 5^2. The exponent tells the number of times the number is taken as a factor in multiplication. Thus, 2^2 and 5^2 can be read as "two squared" and "five squared." The exponent also indicates the **power** of the number. Power indicates the number of times a number is used as a factor (2^2 is read "two to the second power" and 5^2, "five to the second power").

$$3^3 = 3 \times 3 \times 3$$

$$5^4 = 5 \times 5 \times 5 \times 5$$

Exponents can also be negative as well as positive. Where positive exponents indicate the number of times the number itself is used as a factor in multiplication, negative exponents indicate the number of times the reciprocal of the number is used in multiplication. The reciprocal of a whole number is a fraction consisting of "1" over the number.

$$2^{-2} = \frac{1}{2} \times \frac{1}{2} = \frac{1}{4}$$

$$5^{-4} = \frac{1}{5} \times \frac{1}{5} \times \frac{1}{5} \times \frac{1}{5} = \frac{1}{625}$$

SCIENTIFIC NOTATION

Just as exponents are a form of shorthand for indicating operations, **scientific notation** is a form of shorthand for representing large numbers. In scientific notation, a large number is shown as a whole number having a value between 1 and 9 and having a decimal part. This is multiplied by a specified power of 10 (indicated by the exponent).

$$225 = 2.25 \times 10^2$$

The scientific notation has little value in such a small number as 225, but for large numbers, it is quite useful. Take the distance light travels in one year, called a "light-year." This is estimated to be about 9,460,000,000,000 kilometers—that's a "trillion" kilometers. To write it out takes 10 zeros, but in scientific notation, it can be represented in a much more compact form.

$$9.46 \times 10^{12} \textit{ kilometers}$$

On electronic calculators that do not indicate the exponent as a small, raised number, scientific notation is normally indicated by a capital "E," which stands in place of the "x10" in the previous example and indicates that what follows is the exponent of the "10."

The positive exponent shows the number of times 10 is multiplied by itself. It has the effect of moving the decimal point the indicated number of places to the right (to make the number larger). A negative exponent indicates the number of times the reciprocal of ten ("1" over "10") is multiplied by itself. It has the effect of moving the decimal point the indicated number of places to the left (to make the number smaller). Thus, while something like 1.23 x 108 is a very large number (123,000,000)—the multiplication moves the decimal point 8 places to the right—the number 1.23 x 10^{-8} is a very small number: (.0000000123)—the multiplication moves the decimal point 8 places to the left.

AREA MEASUREMENTS

(The examples given here are arbitrary; they can be in any linear measurement—feet, centimeters, inches, meters, etc. Regardless of the measurement used or the type of plane figure, the area is expressed in "square" measurement, that is, square feet, square centimeters, etc.)

A flat, closed figure—that is, one in which all sides come together—is named according to the number of sides it has. A three-sided figure is a **triangle,** a four-sided figure is a **quadrilateral,** a five-sided figure is a **pentagon,** and so forth.

The most common quadrilateral figures are the **square,** which is a four-sided figure with all sides the same length and all angles right angles, and the **rectangle,** a four-sided figure with all angles right angles but only opposite sides the same size. Whether one is talking about a square or a rectangle, one side is considered the length, and an adjacent side is considered the width. To find the area of a square or rectangle, simply multiply the length by the width.

$A = l \times w$

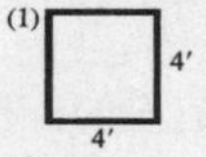

$A(1) = 4 \times 4 = 16$ *square feet*

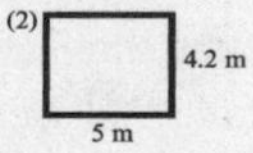

$A(2) = 5 \times 4.2 = 21$ *square meters*

To find the area of a figure that can be viewed as a combination of rectangles, simply find the areas of each component rectangle and add the areas together:

(1) 12 meters by 3 meters

(2) 5 meters by 4 meters

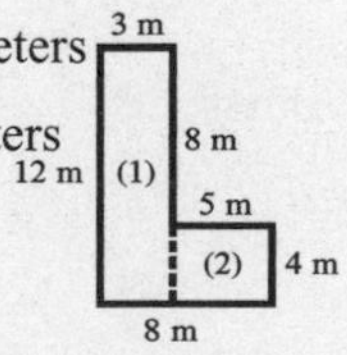

$A = A(1) + A(2)$

$A(1) = 12 \times 3 = 36$

$A(2) = 5 \times 4 = 20$

$A = 36 + 20 = 56$ *square meters*

There are other kinds of four-sided figures: A **parallelogram** is like a rectangle in that opposite sides are parallel, but all four angles are not the same.

$A = b \times h$

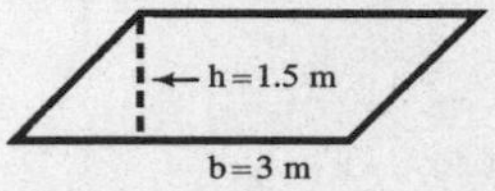

where b is the base length, the length of one of the longest sides, and h is the height, the distance between the two longest sides. The height is a perpendicular constructed from one of the parallel sides to the other.

$A = 3 \times 1.5 = 4.5$ *square meters*

A **trapezoid** is another four-sided figure that is not a rectangle. It is a figure with one set of opposite sides parallel to each other but with the other set not parallel to each other.

$A = \frac{1}{2}(a + b) \times h$

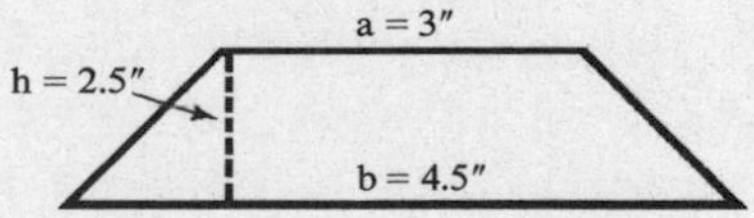

where *a* is the length of one parallel side and *b* is the length of the other parallel side and *h* is the height, or distance between them. The height is a perpendicular constructed from one of the parallel sides to the other.

$A = \frac{1}{2}(3 + 4.5) \times 2.5 = 9.375$ *square inches*

A triangle, which has three sides, has many forms. The **right triangle** is one in which one side is perpendicular to another. An **isosceles triangle** has two sides of equal length. An **equilateral triangle** is one in which all three sides are equal in length.

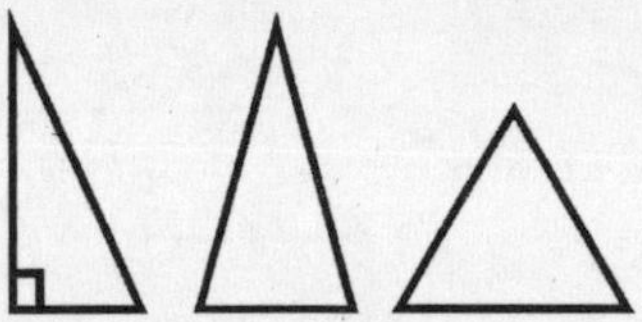

To find the area of a triangle, it is necessary to determine the base and the height. Any side can serve as the base, but in a right triangle the base is usually one of the sides adjacent to the right angle. The height is the perpendicular distance from the base to the opposite angle. For a right triangle, the height is the side that is perpendicular to the base.

$A = \frac{1}{2}\, b \times h$

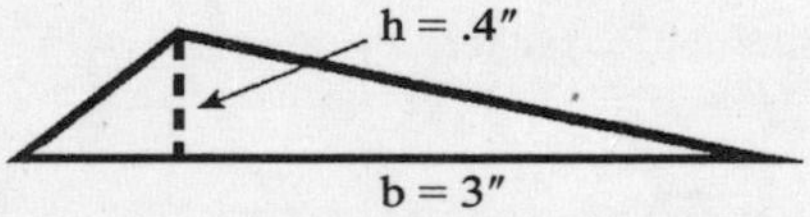

$A = \frac{1}{2}(3) \times .4 = 1.5 \times .4 = .6$ *square inches*

The area of any other plane **polygon,** that is, any other plane figure with three or more sides, would be a combination of all of the enclosed, non-overlapping quadrilateral and triangle areas.

$A = Aa + Ab + Ac$

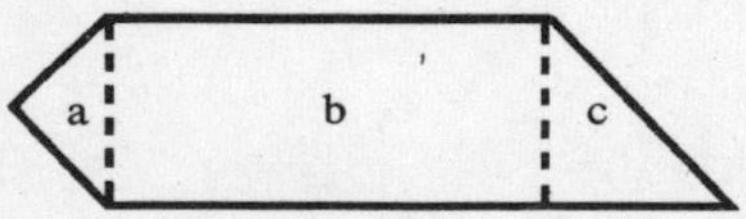

A **circle** is a closed plane figure with no angles. The formula for finding the area of a circle is:

$A = \pi r^2$

The character π represents the ratio of the circumference to the diameter and has the rounded-off value of 3.1416; *r* is the radius or one-half the diameter.

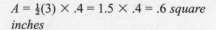

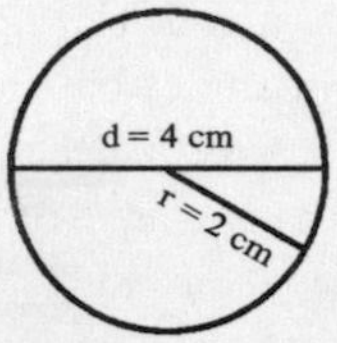

$A = 3.1416 \times 2^2 = 3.1416 \times (2 \times 2)$
$= 12.5664$ *square centimeters*

CONVERSION FROM FAHRENHEIT TO CELSIUS AND CELSIUS TO FAHRENHEIT

To convert from Fahrenheit to Celsius, subtract 32 from the starting temperature and multiply by 5/9. To convert a temperature of 72° Fahrenheit to Celsius:

$$(72 - 32) \times \frac{5}{9} = 40 \times \frac{9}{5} = 22.2°\text{C}$$

To convert from Celsius to Fahrenheit, multiply the starting temperature by 9/5 and add 32. To convert 40° Celsius to Fahrenheit:

$$\left(40 \times \frac{9}{5}\right) + 32 = 72 + 32 = 104°\text{F}$$

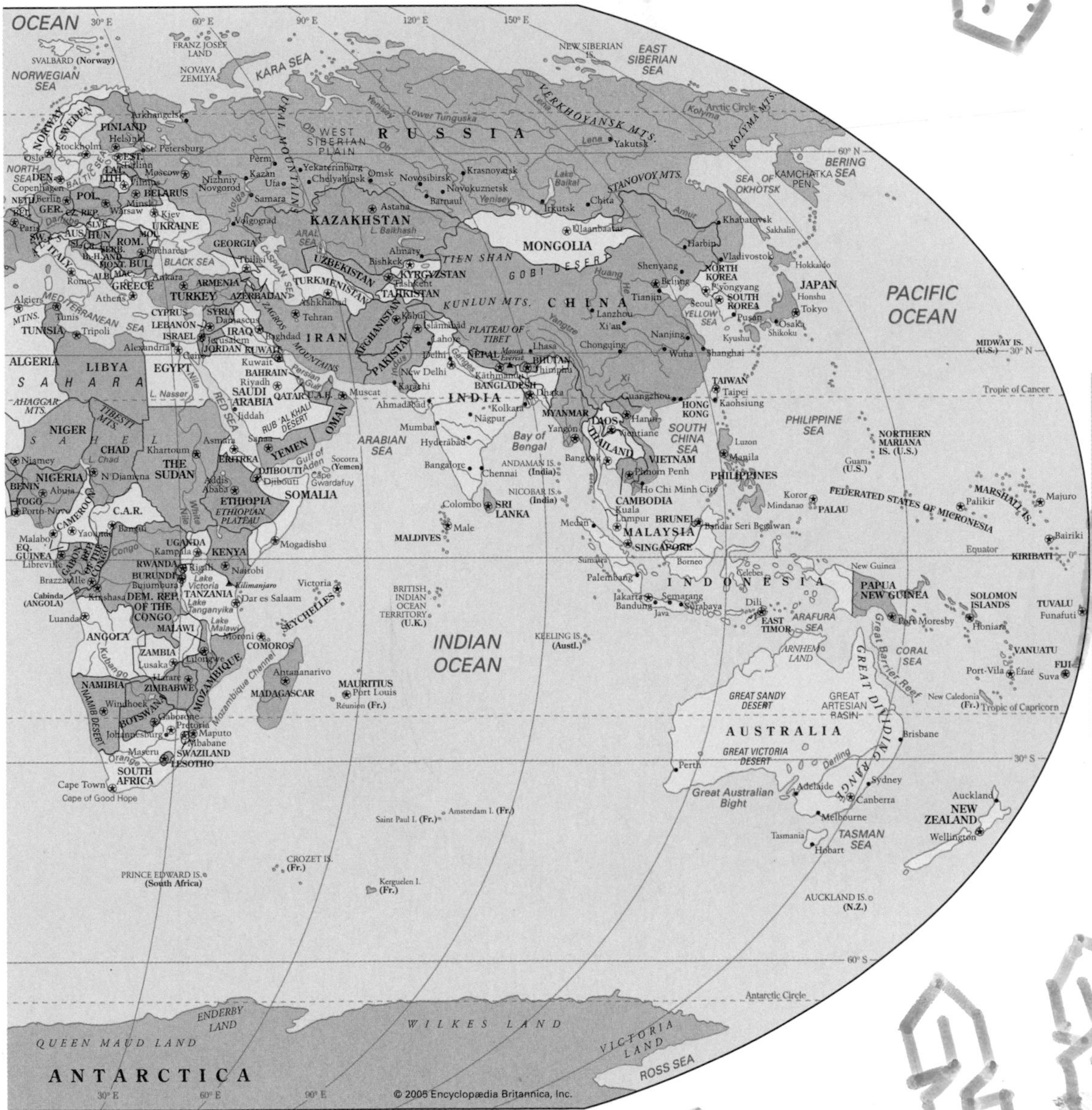
OCEAN
30° E
60° E
90° E
120° E
150° E
FRANZ JOSEF LAND
SVALBARD (Norway)
NORWEGIAN SEA
NOVAYA ZEMLYA
KARA SEA
NEW SIBERIAN IS.
EAST SIBERIAN SEA
Arkhangelsk
FINLAND
Helsinki
St. Petersburg
NORWAY
SWEDEN
Stockholm
Oslo
NORTH SEA
DEN.
Copenhagen
Moscow
Nizhniy Novgorod
Kazan
Perm
Ufa
Yekaterinburg
Chelyabinsk
Omsk
Novosibirsk
Novokuznetsk
Barnaul
Krasnoyarsk
Irkutsk
Chita
Yakutsk
WEST SIBERIAN PLAIN
URAL MOUNTAINS
R U S S I A
VERKHOYANSK MTS.
KOLYMA MTS.
Arctic Circle
STANOVOY MTS.
SEA OF OKHOTSK
KAMCHATKA PEN.
BERING SEA
60° N
Lower Tunguska
Lake Baikal
BELARUS
Minsk
Warsaw
POL.
Berlin
GER.
Paris
Kiev
UKRAINE
Samara
Volgograd
Astana
KAZAKHSTAN
L. Balkhash
ARAL SEA
CASPIAN SEA
Ulaanbaatar
MONGOLIA
Khabarovsk
Sakhalin
Harbin
Vladivostok
Hokkaido
GEORGIA
Tbilisi
Bucharest
ROM.
BLACK SEA
Rome
ITALY
GREECE
Athens
Ankara
TURKEY
ARMENIA
AZERBAIJAN
UZBEKISTAN
TURKMENISTAN
Tashkent
Bishkek
Almaty
KYRGYZSTAN
TAJIKISTAN
TIEN SHAN
GOBI DESERT
Shenyang
Beijing
Tianjin
NORTH KOREA
Pyongyang
SOUTH KOREA
Seoul
Pusan
YELLOW SEA
JAPAN
Honshu
Tokyo
Osaka
Shikoku
Kyushu
PACIFIC OCEAN
Algiers
MEDITERRANEAN SEA
Tunis
TUNISIA
Tripoli
CYPRUS
LEBANON
ISRAEL
SYRIA
Damascus
Jerusalem
JORDAN
IRAQ
Baghdad
Tehran
IRAN
Ashkhabad
AFGHANISTAN
Kabul
Islamabad
Lahore
KUNLUN MTS.
C H I N A
PLATEAU OF TIBET
Lanzhou
Xi'an
Nanjing
Shanghai
Wuhan
Chongqing
MIDWAY IS. (U.S.)
30° N
ALGERIA
LIBYA
S A H A R A
EGYPT
Alexandria
Cairo
Kuwait
KUWAIT
BAHRAIN
Riyadh
SAUDI ARABIA
QATAR
U.A.E.
Muscat
OMAN
L. Nasser
RED SEA
Jiddah
RUB AL KHALI DESERT
PAKISTAN
Karachi
New Delhi
Delhi
NEPAL
Kathmandu
Lhasa
BHUTAN
Thimphu
Mount Everest
BANGLADESH
Dhaka
Kolkata
INDIA
Ahmadabad
Nagpur
Mumbai
Hyderabad
Bangalore
Chennai
ARABIAN SEA
Bay of Bengal
TAIWAN
Taipei
Kaohsiung
Guangzhou
HONG KONG
Tropic of Cancer
AHAGGAR MTS.
NIGER
TIBESTI MTS.
CHAD
L. Chad
Niamey
N'Djamena
Khartoum
THE SUDAN
Asmara
ERITREA
Sanaa
YEMEN
Gulf of Aden
Socotra (Yemen)
DJIBOUTI
Djibouti
Cape Gwardafuy
Addis Ababa
ETHIOPIA
ETHIOPIAN PLATEAU
SOMALIA
MYANMAR
Yangon
LAOS
Hanoi
Vientiane
THAILAND
Bangkok
VIETNAM
Phnom Penh
CAMBODIA
Ho Chi Minh City
SOUTH CHINA SEA
PHILIPPINE SEA
Luzon
Manila
PHILIPPINES
NORTHERN MARIANA IS. (U.S.)
Guam (U.S.)
NIGERIA
Abuja
BENIN
TOGO
Porto-Novo
CAMEROON
C.A.R.
Bangui
Yaoundé
Malabo
EQ. GUINEA
Libreville
GABON
CONGO
Brazzaville
Kinshasa
Cabinda (ANGOLA)
UGANDA
Kampala
KENYA
Nairobi
Mogadishu
RWANDA
Kigali
BURUNDI
Bujumbura
Lake Victoria
Kilimanjaro
TANZANIA
Dar es Salaam
DEM. REP. OF THE CONGO
Lake Tanganyika
ANDAMAN IS. (India)
NICOBAR IS. (India)
Colombo
SRI LANKA
Male
MALDIVES
Medan
Kuala Lumpur
MALAYSIA
SINGAPORE
BRUNEI
Bandar Seri Begawan
Sumatra
Borneo
Celebes
Palembang
Koror
Mindanao
PALAU
FEDERATED STATES OF MICRONESIA
Palikir
MARSHALL IS.
Majuro
Bairiki
Equator
KIRIBATI
0°
Victoria
SEYCHELLES
BRITISH INDIAN OCEAN TERRITORY (U.K.)
I N D O N E S I A
Jakarta
Bandung
Semarang
Surabaya
Java
Dili
EAST TIMOR
New Guinea
PAPUA NEW GUINEA
Port Moresby
SOLOMON ISLANDS
Honiara
TUVALU
Funafuti
Luanda
ANGOLA
MALAWI
Lake Malawi
Moroni
COMOROS
ZAMBIA
Lusaka
Lilongwe
Harare
ZIMBABWE
MOZAMBIQUE
Mozambique Channel
INDIAN OCEAN
KEELING IS. (Austl.)
ARAFURA SEA
ARNHEM LAND
Great Barrier Reef
CORAL SEA
VANUATU
Port-Vila
Éfaté
FIJI
Suva
NAMIBIA
Windhoek
NAMIB DESERT
BOTSWANA
Gaborone
Pretoria
Johannesburg
Maputo
Mbabane
SWAZILAND
Maseru
LESOTHO
Orange
SOUTH AFRICA
Cape Town
Cape of Good Hope
Antananarivo
MADAGASCAR
MAURITIUS
Port Louis
Réunion (Fr.)
GREAT SANDY DESERT
GREAT ARTESIAN BASIN
AUSTRALIA
GREAT DIVIDING RANGE
Brisbane
GREAT VICTORIA DESERT
Darling
Perth
Sydney
Adelaide
Canberra
Great Australian Bight
Melbourne
Tasmania
Hobart
TASMAN SEA
New Caledonia (Fr.)
Tropic of Capricorn
30° S
Auckland
NEW ZEALAND
Wellington
Amsterdam I. (Fr.)
Saint Paul I. (Fr.)
CROZET IS. (Fr.)
PRINCE EDWARD IS. (South Africa)
Kerguelen I. (Fr.)
AUCKLAND IS. (N.Z.)
60° S
Antarctic Circle
ENDERBY LAND
QUEEN MAUD LAND
W I L K E S L A N D
VICTORIA LAND
ROSS SEA
A N T A R C T I C A
© 2005 Encyclopædia Britannica, Inc.

ATLAS

NORTH AMERICA

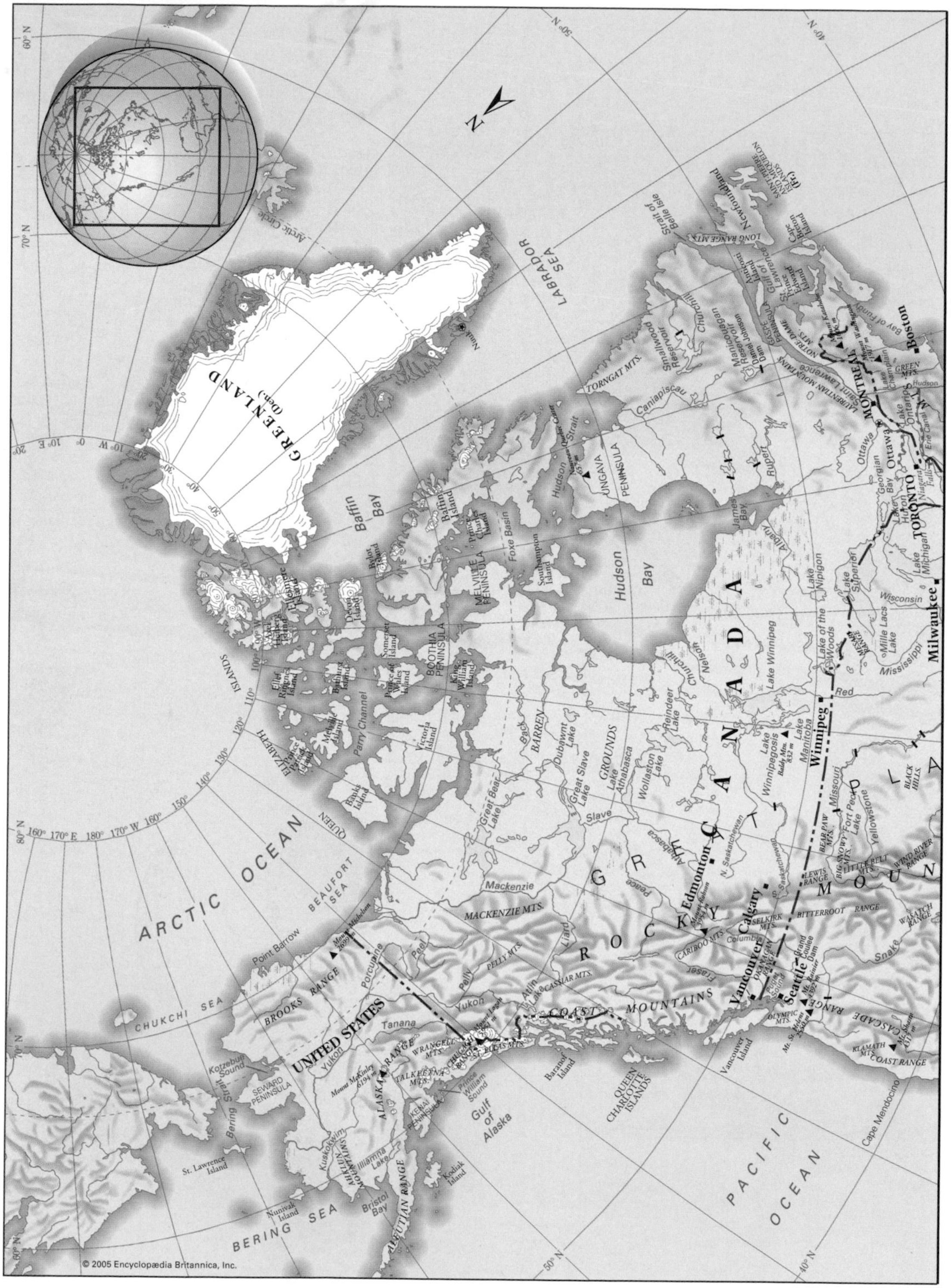

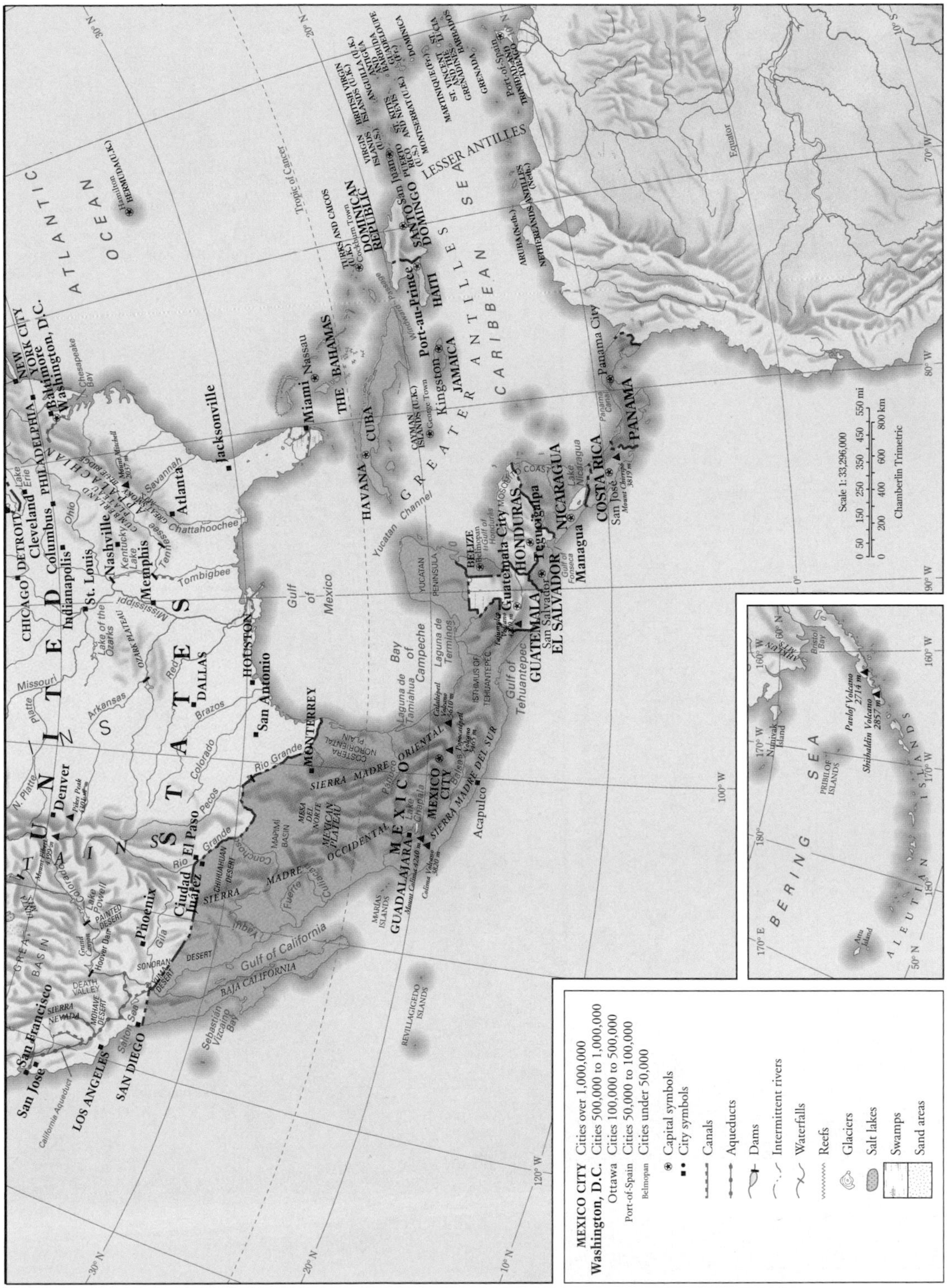
ATLANTIC OCEAN
UNITED STATES
MEXICO
Gulf of Mexico
CARIBBEAN SEA
Gulf of California
BAJA CALIFORNIA
BERMUDA (U.K.)
Hamilton
NEW YORK CITY
Baltimore
Washington, D.C.
PHILADELPHIA
CHICAGO
DETROIT
Cleveland
Columbus
Indianapolis
St. Louis
Nashville
Memphis
Atlanta
Jacksonville
Miami
DALLAS
HOUSTON
San Antonio
Denver
Phoenix
El Paso
Ciudad Juárez
SAN DIEGO
LOS ANGELES
San Francisco
San Jose
MONTERREY
GUADALAJARA
MEXICO CITY
Acapulco
SIERRA MADRE ORIENTAL
SIERRA MADRE OCCIDENTAL
SIERRA MADRE DEL SUR
YUCATAN PENINSULA
BELIZE
Belmopan
GUATEMALA
Guatemala City
EL SALVADOR
San Salvador
HONDURAS
Tegucigalpa
NICARAGUA
Managua
COSTA RICA
San José
PANAMA
Panama City
CUBA
HAVANA
THE BAHAMAS
Nassau
JAMAICA
Kingston
HAITI
Port-au-Prince
DOMINICAN REPUBLIC
SANTO DOMINGO
San Juan
PUERTO RICO
GREATER ANTILLES
LESSER ANTILLES
TRINIDAD AND TOBAGO
Port-of-Spain
Tropic of Cancer
Equator
BERING SEA
ALEUTIAN ISLANDS
PRIBILOF ISLANDS
Scale 1:33,296,000
Chamberlin Trimetric
MEXICO CITY Cities over 1,000,000
Washington, D.C. Cities 500,000 to 1,000,000
Ottawa Cities 100,000 to 500,000
Port-of-Spain Cities 50,000 to 100,000
Belmopan Cities under 50,000
Capital symbols
City symbols
Canals
Aqueducts
Dams
Intermittent rivers
Waterfalls
Reefs
Glaciers
Salt lakes
Swamps
Sand areas

ATLAS

CANADA

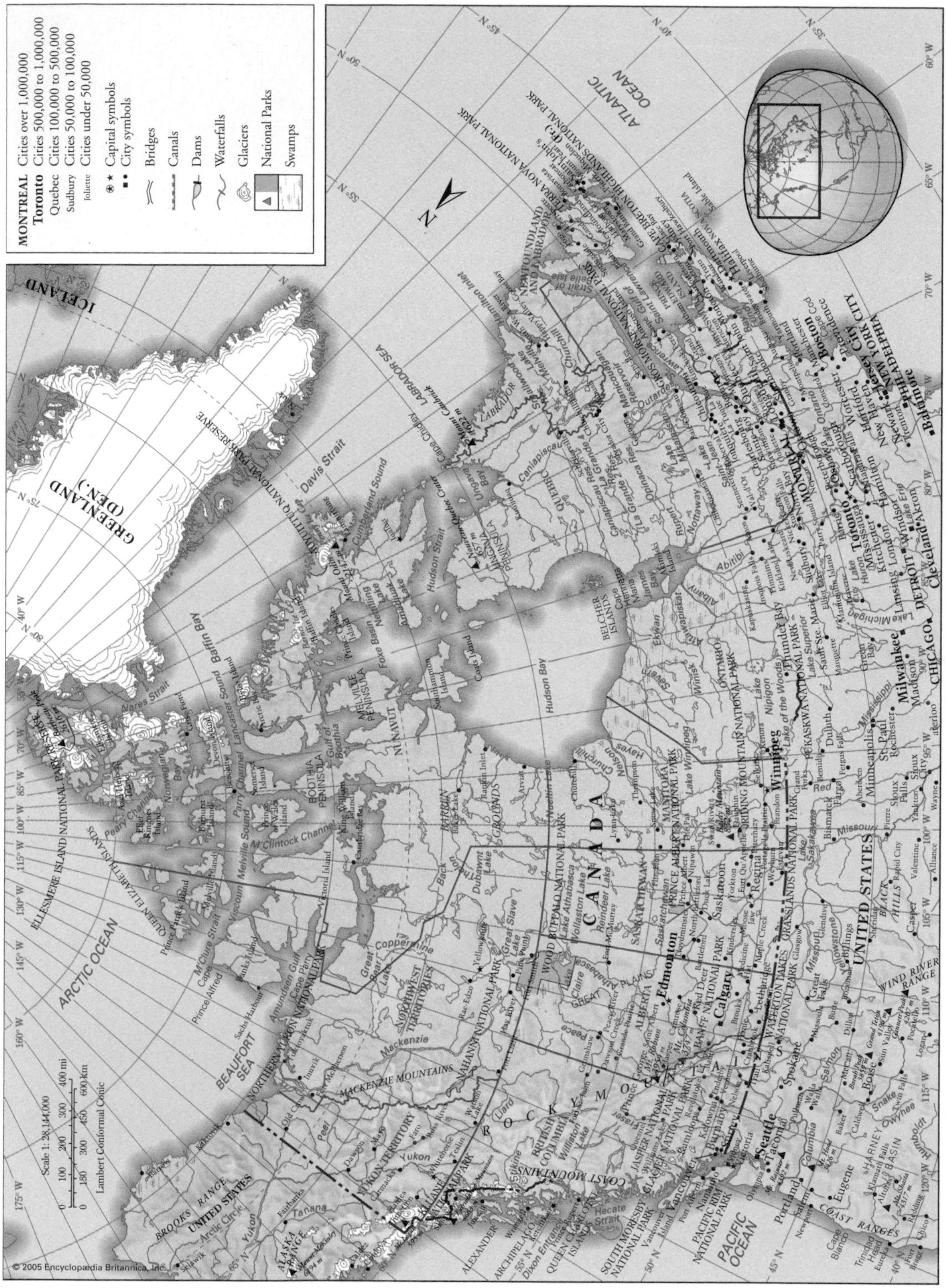
MONTREAL Cities over 1,000,000
Toronto Cities 500,000 to 1,000,000
Quebec Cities 100,000 to 500,000
Sudbury Cities 50,000 to 100,000
Joliette Cities under 50,000
Capital symbols
City symbols
Bridges
Canals
Dams
Waterfalls
Glaciers
National Parks
Swamps
Scale 1: 28,144,000
Lambert Conformal Conic
0 100 200 300 400 mi
0 150 300 450 600 km
ARCTIC OCEAN
ATLANTIC OCEAN
PACIFIC OCEAN
BEAUFORT SEA
LABRADOR SEA
GREENLAND (DEN.)
ICELAND
CANADA
UNITED STATES
Hudson Bay
Baffin Bay
Davis Strait
Hudson Strait
ROCKY MOUNTAINS
MACKENZIE MOUNTAINS
COAST MOUNTAINS
QUEEN ELIZABETH ISLANDS
NUNAVUT
NORTHWEST TERRITORIES
YUKON TERRITORY
BRITISH COLUMBIA
ALBERTA
SASKATCHEWAN
MANITOBA
ONTARIO
QUEBEC
NEWFOUNDLAND AND LABRADOR
NOVA SCOTIA
MONTREAL
Toronto
Ottawa
Quebec
Winnipeg
Edmonton
Calgary
Vancouver
Regina
Saskatoon
Halifax
Seattle
CHICAGO
DETROIT
NEW YORK CITY
PHILADELPHIA
Boston
© 2005 Encyclopædia Britannica, Inc.

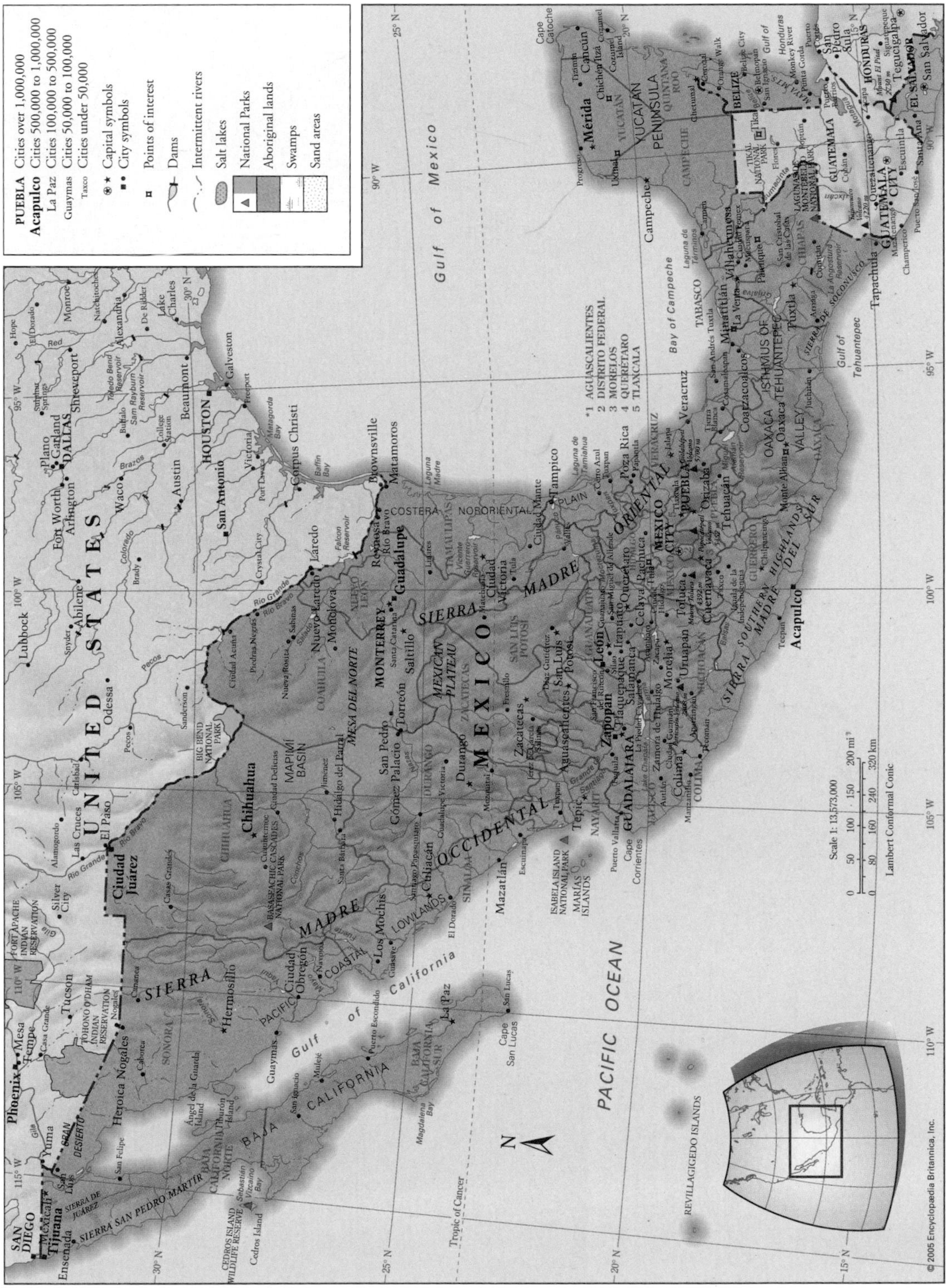
PUBLA Cities over 1,000,000
Acapulco Cities 500,000 to 1,000,000
La Paz Cities 100,000 to 500,000
Guaymas Cities 50,000 to 100,000
Taxco Cities under 50,000
Capital symbols
City symbols
Points of interest
Dams
Intermittent rivers
Salt lakes
National Parks
Aboriginal lands
Swamps
Sand areas
UNITED STATES
MEXICO
Gulf of Mexico
PACIFIC OCEAN
Gulf of California
Bay of Campeche
Gulf of Tehuantepec
SIERRA MADRE OCCIDENTAL
SIERRA MADRE ORIENTAL
SIERRA MADRE DEL SUR
MEXICAN PLATEAU
MESA DEL NORTE
BAJA CALIFORNIA
YUCATAN PENINSULA
ISTHMUS OF TEHUANTEPEC
GUATEMALA
BELIZE
HONDURAS
EL SALVADOR
MEXICO CITY
GUADALAJARA
MONTERREY
*1 AGUASCALIENTES
2 DISTRITO FEDERAL
3 MORELOS
4 QUERETARO
5 TLAXCALA
Tropic of Cancer
REVILLAGIGEDO ISLANDS
Scale 1: 13,573,000
Lambert Conformal Conic
© 2005 Encyclopædia Britannica, Inc.

ATLAS

THE CARIBBEAN

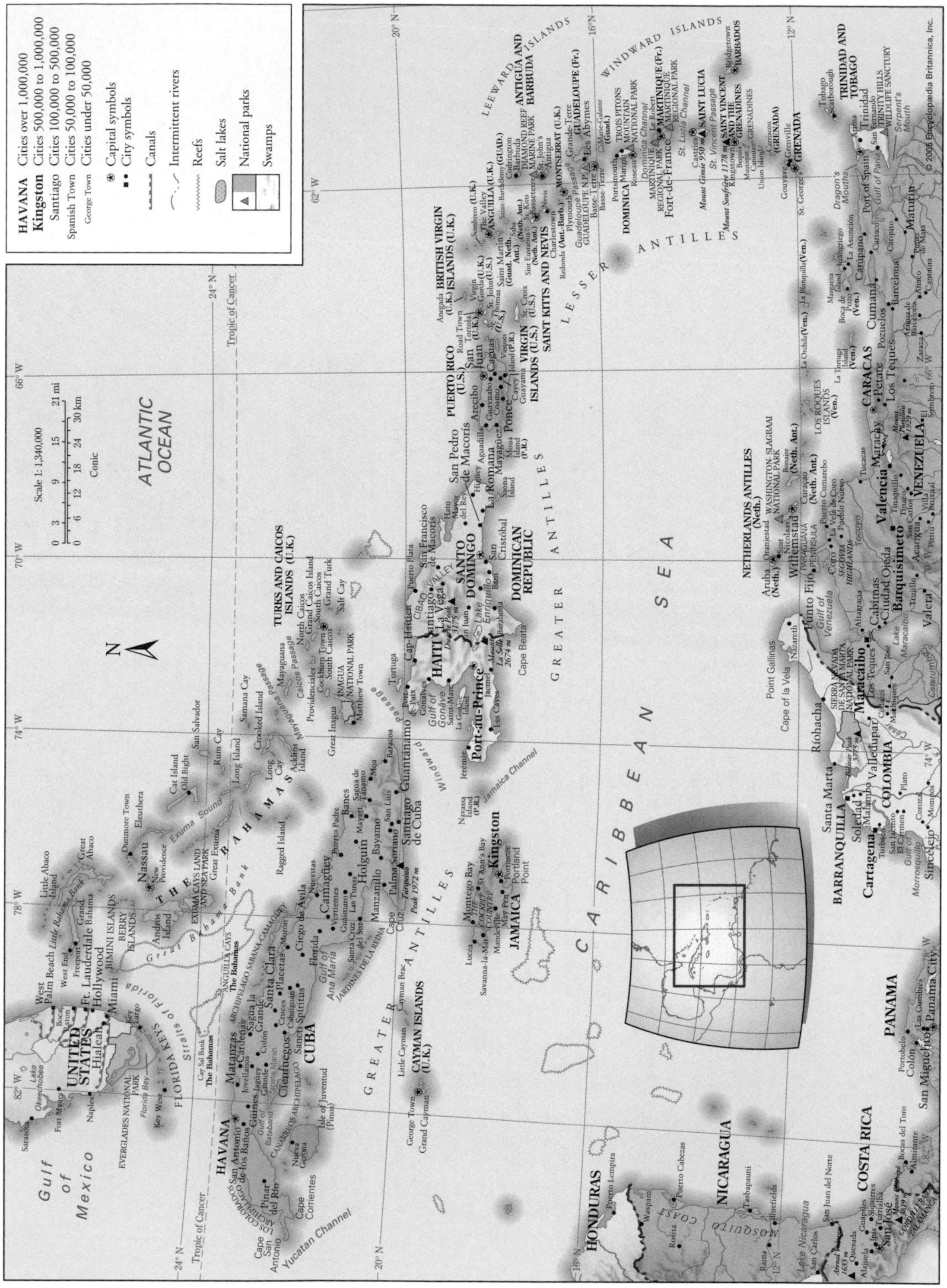

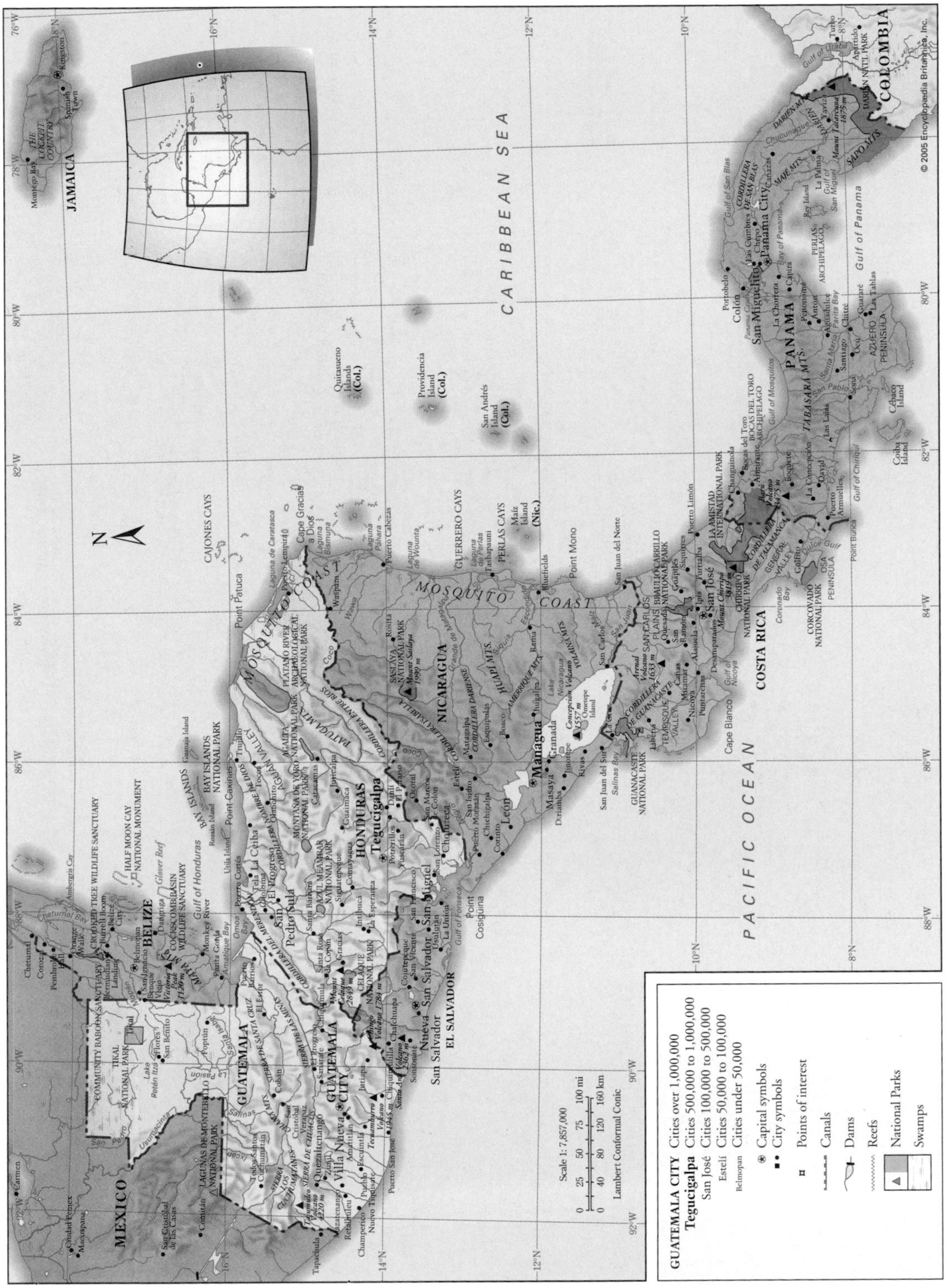
MEXICO
GUATEMALA
BELIZE
HONDURAS
EL SALVADOR
NICARAGUA
COSTA RICA
PANAMA
COLOMBIA
JAMAICA
CARIBBEAN SEA
PACIFIC OCEAN
GUATEMALA CITY
Tegucigalpa
Managua
San José
San Salvador
Panama City
Belmopan
Kingston
MOSQUITO COAST
Gulf of Honduras
Gulf of Fonseca
Gulf of Panama
Scale 1: 7,857,000
Lambert Conformal Conic
GUATEMALA CITY Cities over 1,000,000
Tegucigalpa Cities 500,000 to 1,000,000
San José Cities 100,000 to 500,000
Estelí Cities 50,000 to 100,000
Belmopan Cities under 50,000
Capital symbols
City symbols
Points of interest
Canals
Dams
Reefs
National Parks
Swamps
© 2005 Encyclopædia Britannica, Inc.

SOUTH AMERICA

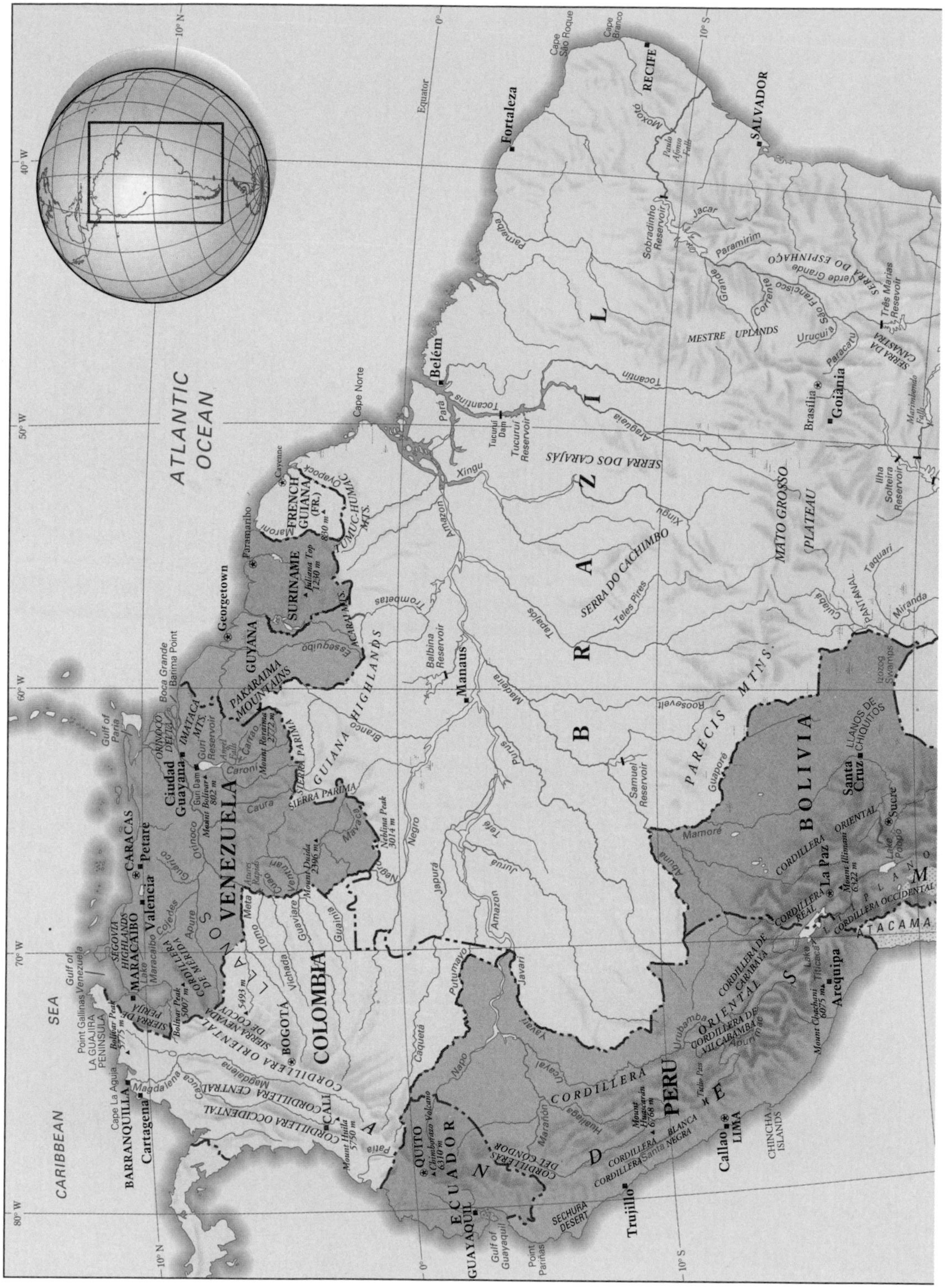

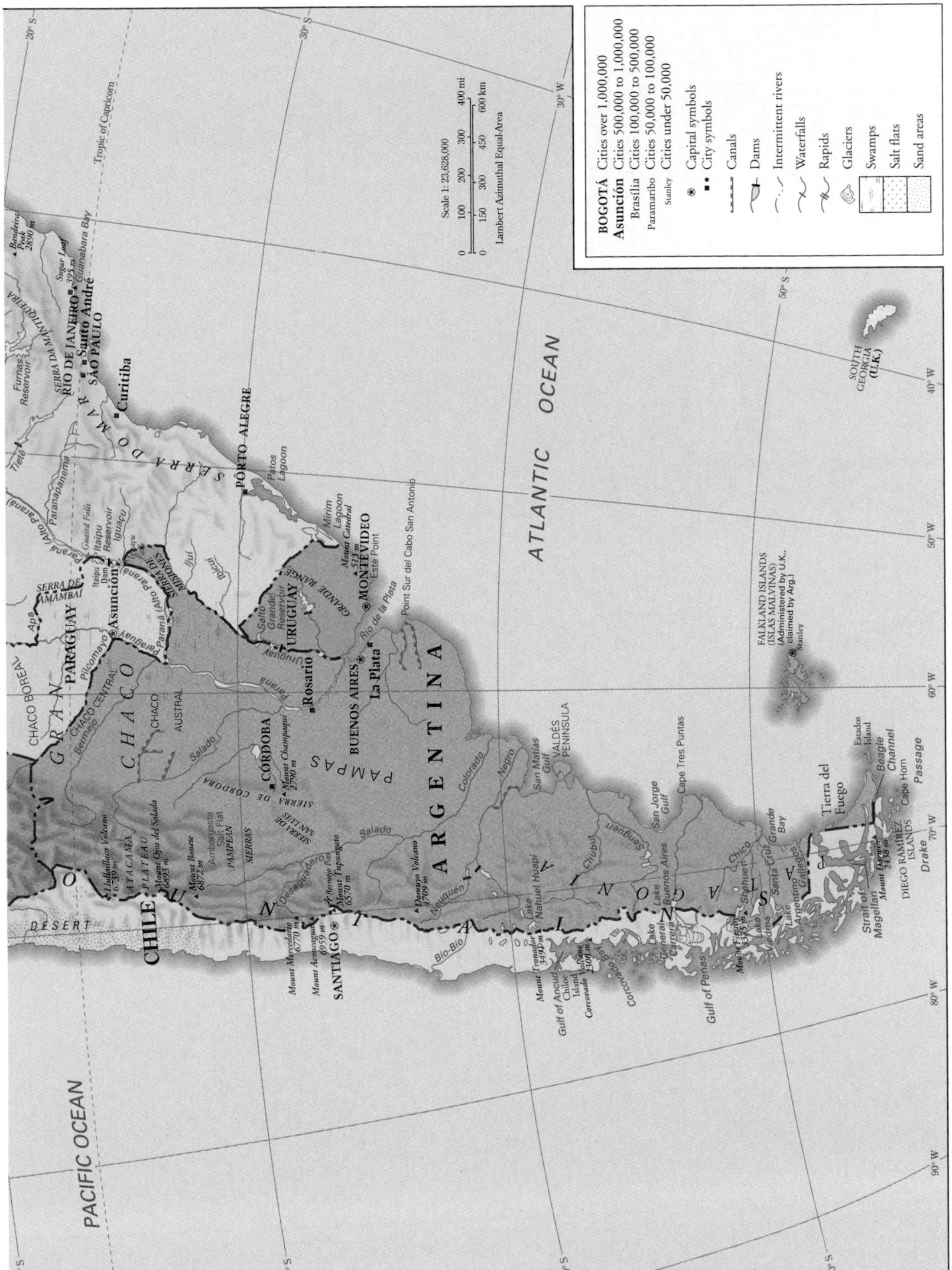
PACIFIC OCEAN
ATLANTIC OCEAN
ARGENTINA
CHILE
URUGUAY
PARAGUAY
GRAN CHACO
PAMPAS
PATAGONIA
BUENOS AIRES
MONTEVIDEO
SANTIAGO
Asunción
Rosario
CÓRDOBA
La Plata
PÔRTO ALEGRE
Curitiba
SÃO PAULO
Santo André
RIO DE JANEIRO
FALKLAND ISLANDS (ISLAS MALVINAS) (Administered by U.K., claimed by Arg.)
Stanley
SOUTH GEORGIA (U.K.)
Tierra del Fuego
Strait of Magellan
Drake Passage
Beagle Channel
Cape Horn
Tropic of Capricorn
BOGOTÁ Cities over 1,000,000
Asunción Cities 500,000 to 1,000,000
Brasília Cities 100,000 to 500,000
Paramaribo Cities 50,000 to 100,000
Stanley Cities under 50,000
Capital symbols
City symbols
Canals
Dams
Intermittent rivers
Waterfalls
Rapids
Glaciers
Swamps
Salt flats
Sand areas
Scale 1: 23,628,000
Lambert Azimuthal Equal-Area
© 2005 Encyclopædia Britannica, Inc.

BRAZIL, BOLIVIA, AND PARAGUAY

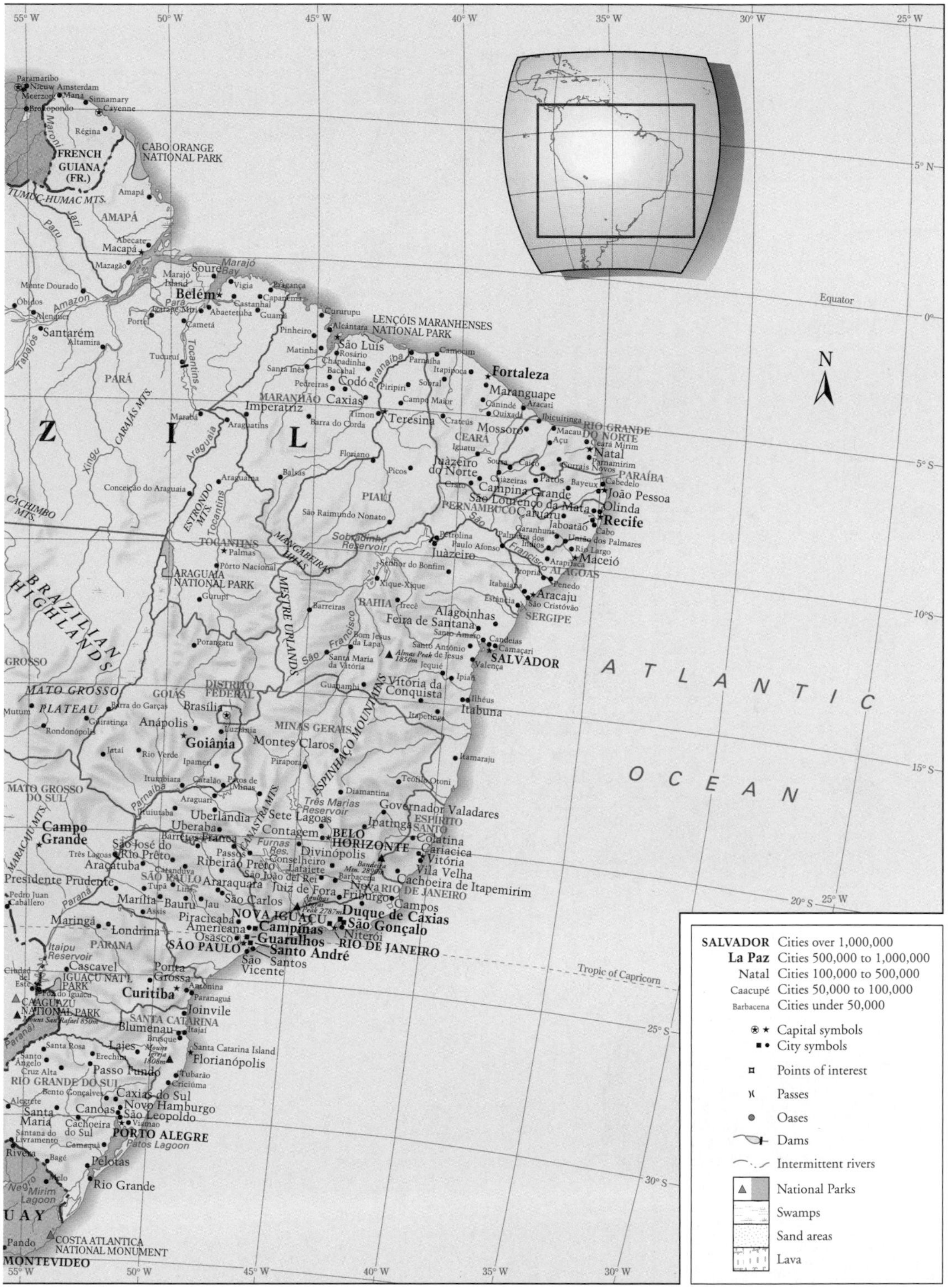

55° W
50° W
45° W
40° W
35° W
30° W
25° W
5° N
0°
5° S
10°S
15° S
20° S
25° S
30° S
Equator
Tropic of Capricorn
N
Paramaribo
Nieuw Amsterdam
Mana
Sinnamary
Cayenne
Régina
FRENCH GUIANA (FR.)
CABO ORANGE NATIONAL PARK
TUMUC-HUMAC MTS.
AMAPÁ
Amapá
Macapá
Mazagão
Marajó Island
Marajó Bay
Soure
Belém
Vigia
Bragança
Capanema
Castanhal
Abaetetuba
Cametá
Monte Dourado
Óbidos
Amazon
Santarém
Altamira
Tucuruí
Tocantins
PARÁ
CARAJÁS MTS.
Xingu
Tapajós
Cururupu
Alcântara
LENÇÓIS MARANHENSES NATIONAL PARK
São Luís
Pinheiro
Matinha
Rosário
Chapadinha
Santa Inês
Bacabal
Pedreiras
Codó
Caxias
MARANHÃO
Imperatriz
Barra do Corda
Timon
Teresina
Parnaíba
Piripiri
Sobral
Camocim
Itapipoca
Fortaleza
Maranguape
Canindé
Aracati
Quixadá
Crateús
Mossoró
CEARÁ
Iguatu
Marabá
Araguatins
Araguaia
Z
I
L
Floriano
Picos
Juàzeiro do Norte
Crato
Sousa
Caicó
Patos
Cajazeiras
Macau
Açu
RIO GRANDE DO NORTE
Ceará Mirim
Natal
Parnamirim
Currais Novos
PARAÍBA
Cabedelo
João Pessoa
Bayeux
Campina Grande
São Lourenço da Mata
Olinda
Recife
Caruaru
Jaboatão
Cabo
Garanhuns
Palmares
Maceió
ALAGOAS
PERNAMBUCO
PIAUÍ
São Raimundo Nonato
Balsas
Conceição do Araguaia
ESTRONDO MTS.
CACHIMBO MTS.
TOCANTINS
Palmas
Pôrto Nacional
Gurupi
ARAGUAIA NATIONAL PARK
MANGABEIRAS HILLS
Sobradinho Reservoir
Petrolina
Paulo Afonso
Juàzeiro
São Francisco
Senhor do Bonfim
Xique-Xique
BRAZILIAN HIGHLANDS
MESTRE URLANDS
Barreiras
BAHIA
Irecê
Alagoinhas
Feira de Santana
Itabaiana
Estância
Aracaju
São Cristóvão
SERGIPE
Penedo
Propriá
Arapiraca
Candeias
Camaçari
SALVADOR
Santo Amaro
Santo Antônio de Jesus
Valença
Jequié
Almas Peak 1850m
Bom Jesus da Lapa
Santa Maria da Vitória
Porangatu
Guanambi
Vitória da Conquista
Ilhéus
Itabuna
Itapetinga
ESPINHAÇO MOUNTAINS
GROSSO
MATO GROSSO PLATEAU
GOIÁS
DISTRITO FEDERAL
Brasília
Barra do Garças
Mutum
Guiratinga
Rondonópolis
Anápolis
Goiânia
Luziânia
Jataí
Rio Verde
Ipameri
MINAS GERAIS
Montes Claros
Pirapora
Itamaraju
Teófilo Otoni
Diamantina
Itumbiara
Catalão
Patos de Minas
MATO GROSSO DO SUL
Três Marias Reservoir
Governador Valadares
Araguari
Ituiutaba
Uberlândia
Sete Lagoas
Ipatinga
ESPÍRITO SANTO
Uberaba
Contagem
BELO HORIZONTE
Colatina
Campo Grande
MARACAJU MTS.
Franca
Furnas Res.
Divinópolis
Cariacica
Vitória
São José do Rio Prêto
Três Lagoas
Araçatuba
Passos
Ribeirão Prêto
Conselheiro Lafaiete
Vila Velha
Cachoeira de Itapemirim
Presidente Prudente
SÃO PAULO
Araraquara
São João del Rei
Barbacena
Juiz de Fora
Nova Friburgo
RIO DE JANEIRO
Campos
Pedro Juan Caballero
Tupã
Lins
Marília
Bauru
Jaú
São Carlos
Assis
Piracicaba
NOVA IGUAÇU
Duque de Caxias
São Gonçalo
Niterói
Maringá
Londrina
Americana
Campinas
Osasco
Guarulhos
SÃO PAULO
RIO DE JANEIRO
Santo André
Santos
São Vicente
Itaipu Reservoir
PARANÁ
Paraná
Cascavel
Ponta Grossa
IGUAÇU NAT'L PARK
Foz do Iguaçu
Curitiba
Antonina
Paranaguá
CAAGUAZÚ NATIONAL PARK
Joinvile
SANTA CATARINA
Blumenau
Itajaí
Brusque
Lajes
Santa Catarina Island
Florianópolis
Santa Rosa
Santo Ângelo
Erechim
Cruz Alta
Passo Fundo
Tubarão
Criciúma
RIO GRANDE DO SUL
Bento Gonçalves
Caxias do Sul
Alegrete
Santa Maria
Canoas
Novo Hamburgo
São Leopoldo
Cachoeira do Sul
Viamão
PORTO ALEGRE
Camaquã
Patos Lagoon
Rivera
Bagé
Pelotas
Rio Grande
Mirim Lagoon
Negro
UAY
COSTA ATLANTICA NATIONAL MONUMENT
Pando
MONTEVIDEO
ATLANTIC
OCEAN
SALVADOR Cities over 1,000,000
La Paz Cities 500,000 to 1,000,000
Natal Cities 100,000 to 500,000
Caacupé Cities 50,000 to 100,000
Barbacena Cities under 50,000
Capital symbols
City symbols
Points of interest
Passes
Oases
Dams
Intermittent rivers
National Parks
Swamps
Sand areas
Lava

ARGENTINA, CHILE, AND URUGUAY

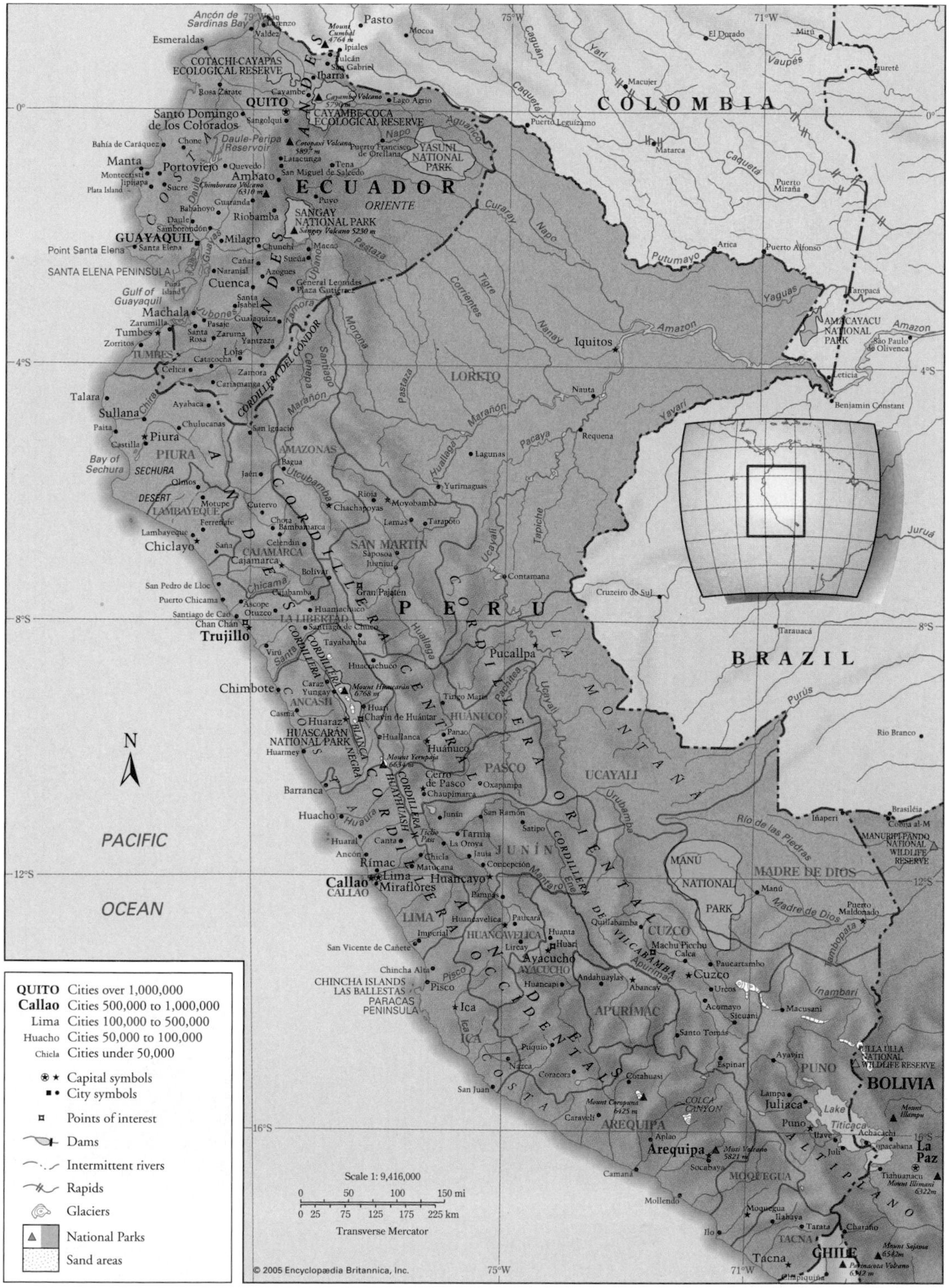

COLOMBIA
ECUADOR
PERU
BRAZIL
BOLIVIA
CHILE
PACIFIC
OCEAN
QUITO
GUAYAQUIL
Callao
Lima
Trujillo
Chiclayo
Piura
Iquitos
Arequipa
Cuzco
Huancayo
Pucallpa
Chimbote
Ayacucho
Tacna
Juliaca
Puno
Cuenca
Machala
Manta
Portoviejo
Ambato
Riobamba
Santo Domingo de los Colorados
Esmeraldas
Ibarra
Huacho
Ica
Pisco
Sullana
Talara
Huánuco
Cerro de Pasco
Huaraz
Cajamarca
La Paz
Pasto
Amazon
Lake Titicaca
YASUNI NATIONAL PARK
SANGAY NATIONAL PARK
HUASCARÁN NATIONAL PARK
MANÚ NATIONAL PARK
AMACAYACU NATIONAL PARK
CORDILLERA DEL CÓNDOR
CORDILLERA CENTRAL
CORDILLERA OCCIDENTAL
CORDILLERA ORIENTAL
LA MONTAÑA
ALTIPLANO
QUITO Cities over 1,000,000
Callao Cities 500,000 to 1,000,000
Lima Cities 100,000 to 500,000
Huacho Cities 50,000 to 100,000
Chicla Cities under 50,000
Capital symbols
City symbols
Points of interest
Dams
Intermittent rivers
Rapids
Glaciers
National Parks
Sand areas
Scale 1: 9,416,000
0 50 100 150 mi
0 25 75 125 175 225 km
Transverse Mercator
© 2005 Encyclopædia Britannica, Inc.

ATLAS

COLOMBIA AND VENEZUELA

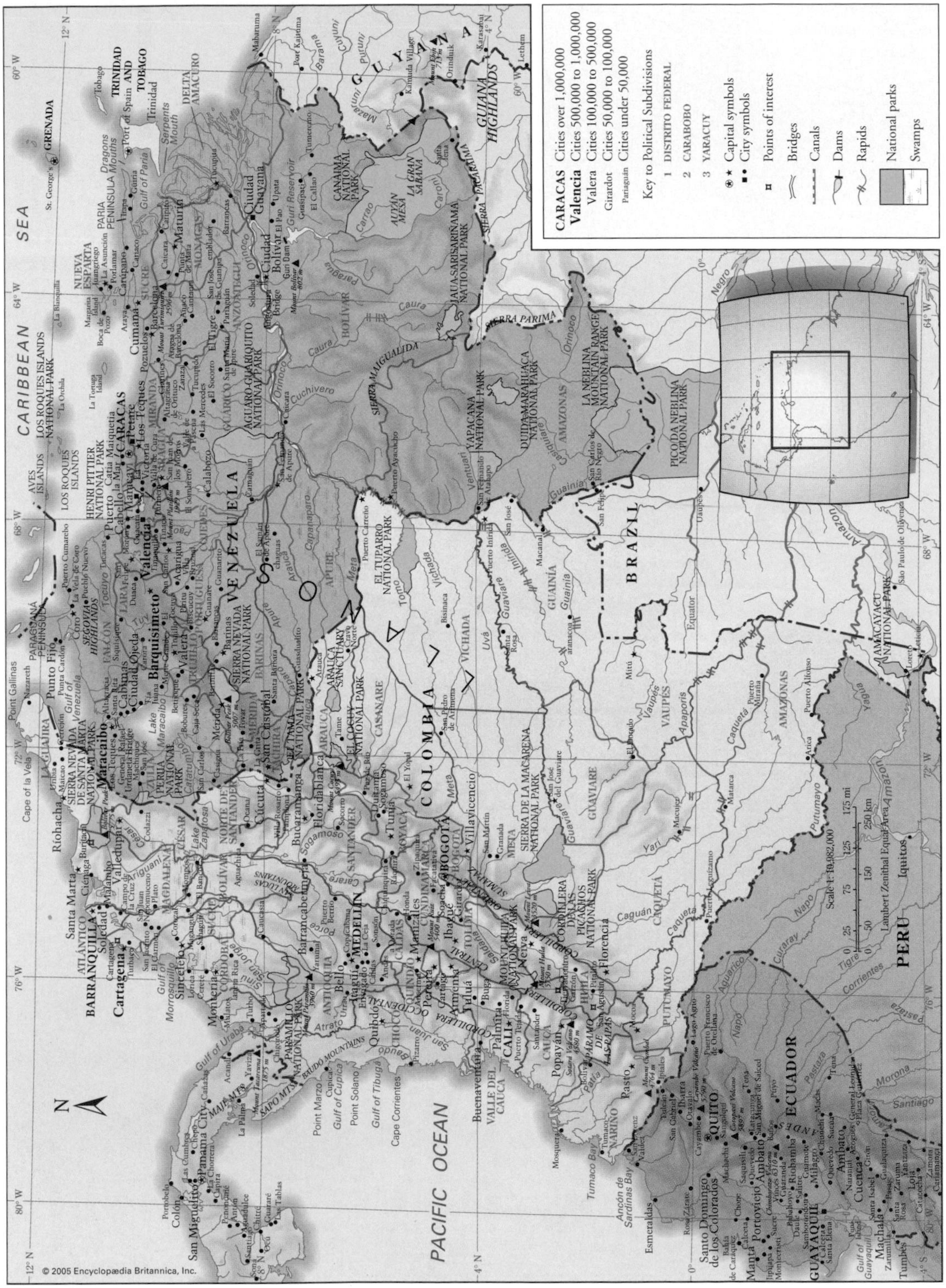

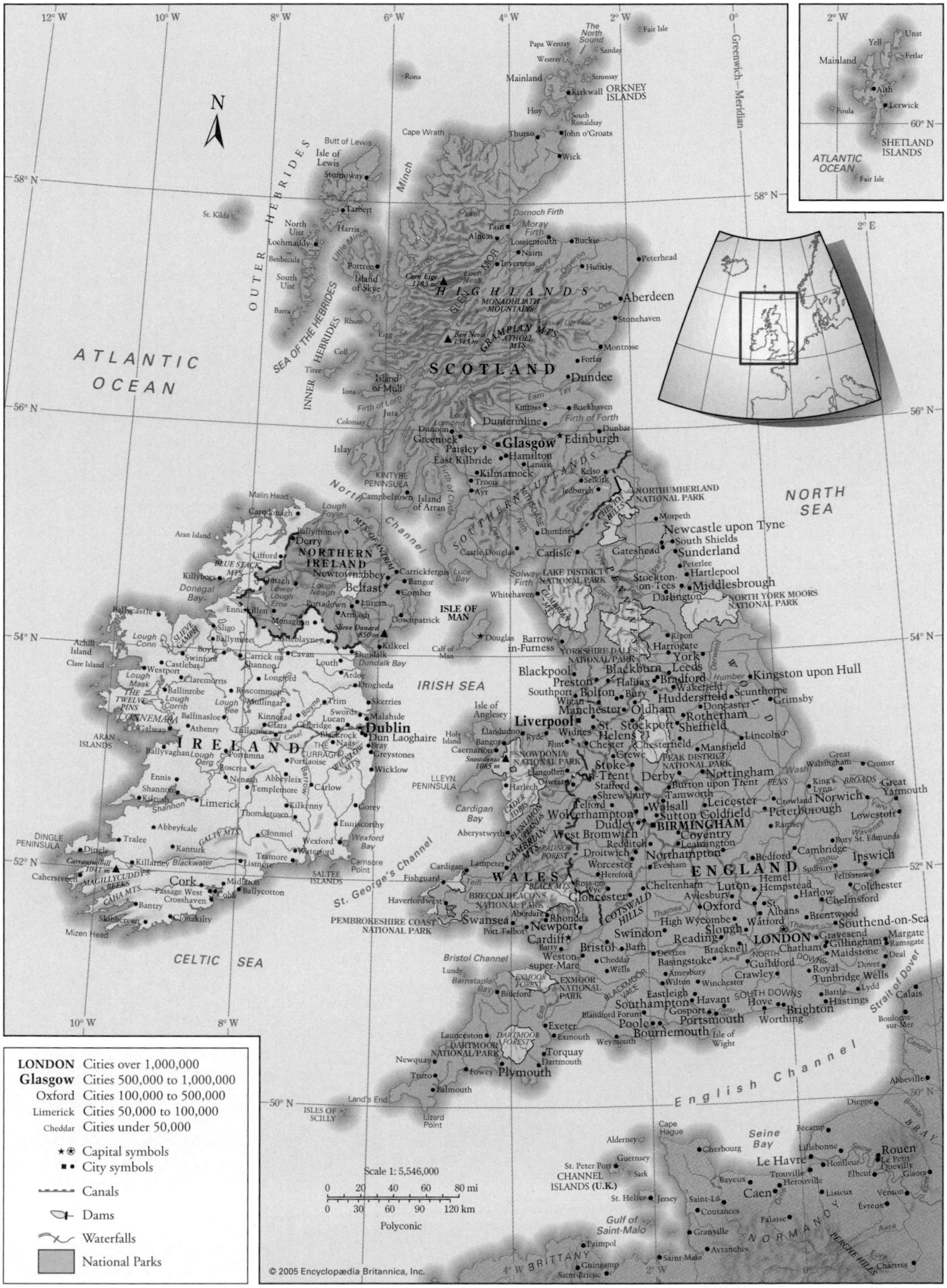
ATLANTIC OCEAN
NORTH SEA
IRISH SEA
CELTIC SEA
English Channel
North Channel
St. George's Channel
Bristol Channel
Strait of Dover
SCOTLAND
NORTHERN IRELAND
IRELAND
WALES
ENGLAND
ISLE OF MAN
ORKNEY ISLANDS
SHETLAND ISLANDS
OUTER HEBRIDES
INNER HEBRIDES
CHANNEL ISLANDS (U.K.)
HIGHLANDS
GRAMPIAN MTS.
SOUTHERN UPLANDS
LONDON
BIRMINGHAM
Glasgow
Edinburgh
Aberdeen
Dundee
Belfast
Dublin
Cork
Limerick
Liverpool
Manchester
Leeds
Sheffield
Bradford
Newcastle upon Tyne
Sunderland
Middlesbrough
Kingston upon Hull
Nottingham
Leicester
Coventry
Norwich
Cambridge
Oxford
Bristol
Cardiff
Swansea
Newport
Southampton
Portsmouth
Brighton
Plymouth
Bournemouth
Greenwich—Meridian
12° W
10° W
8° W
6° W
4° W
2° W
0°
2° E
58° N
56° N
54° N
52° N
50° N
60° N
LONDON Cities over 1,000,000
Glasgow Cities 500,000 to 1,000,000
Oxford Cities 100,000 to 500,000
Limerick Cities 50,000 to 100,000
Cheddar Cities under 50,000
Capital symbols
City symbols
Canals
Dams
Waterfalls
National Parks
Scale 1: 5,546,000
0 20 40 60 80 mi
0 30 60 90 120 km
Polyconic
© 2005 Encyclopædia Britannica, Inc.

EUROPE

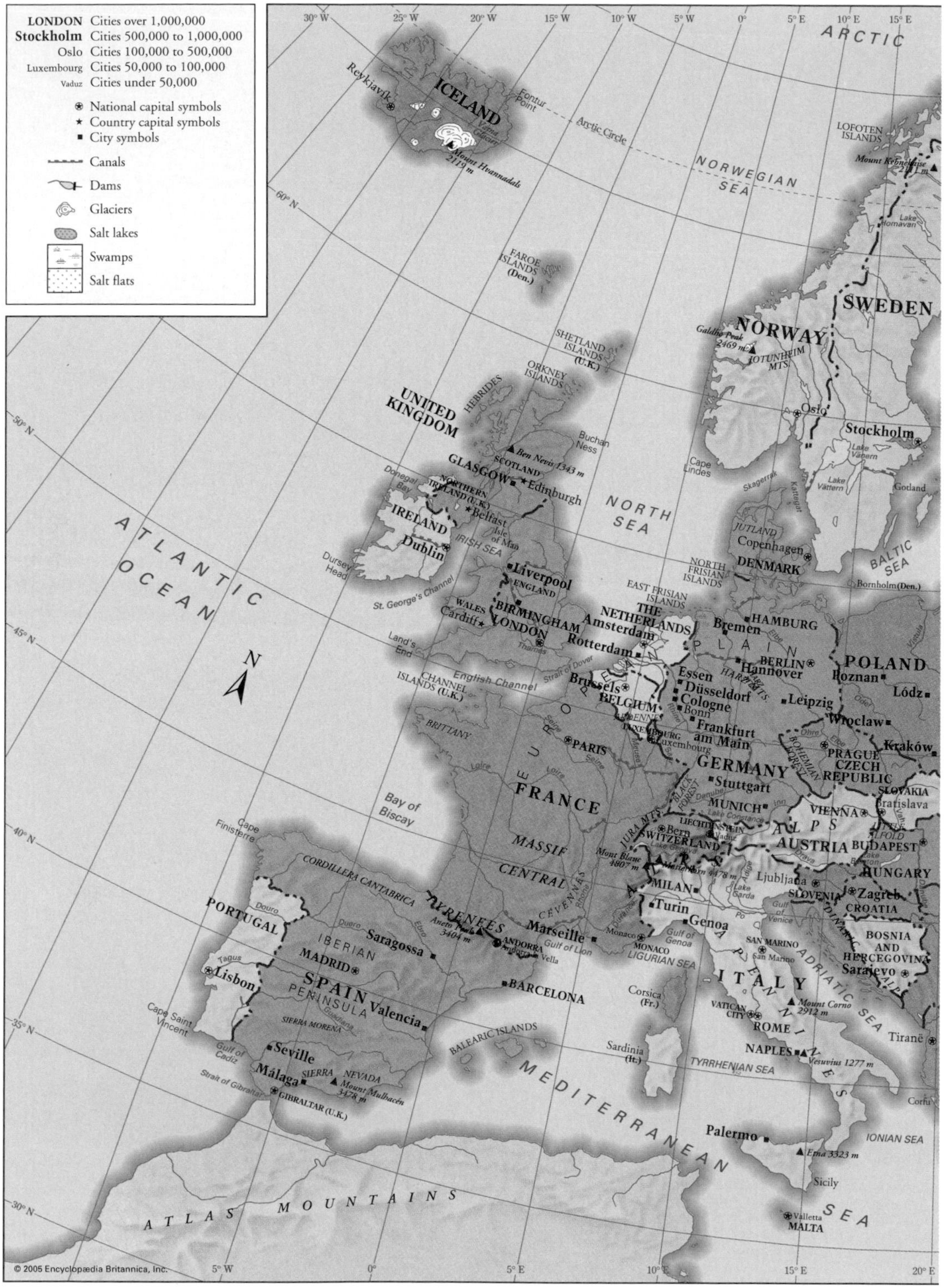

LONDON Cities over 1,000,000
Stockholm Cities 500,000 to 1,000,000
Oslo Cities 100,000 to 500,000
Luxembourg Cities 50,000 to 100,000
Vaduz Cities under 50,000
National capital symbols
Country capital symbols
City symbols
Canals
Dams
Glaciers
Salt lakes
Swamps
Salt flats
ARCTIC
ICELAND
Reykjavík
Arctic Circle
NORWEGIAN SEA
LOFOTEN ISLANDS
FAROE ISLANDS (Den.)
SHETLAND ISLANDS (U.K.)
ORKNEY ISLANDS
HEBRIDES
UNITED KINGDOM
NORWAY
SWEDEN
Oslo
Stockholm
Gotland
NORTH SEA
ATLANTIC OCEAN
SCOTLAND
Edinburgh
GLASGOW
NORTHERN IRELAND (U.K.)
Belfast
IRELAND
Dublin
IRISH SEA
Liverpool
ENGLAND
BIRMINGHAM
WALES
Cardiff
LONDON
St. George's Channel
Land's End
English Channel
CHANNEL ISLANDS (U.K.)
DENMARK
Copenhagen
BALTIC SEA
THE NETHERLANDS
Amsterdam
Rotterdam
Brussels
BELGIUM
HAMBURG
Bremen
BERLIN
Hannover
Essen
Düsseldorf
Cologne
Bonn
Leipzig
Frankfurt am Main
GERMANY
Stuttgart
MUNICH
POLAND
Poznan
Lódz
Wroclaw
Kraków
PRAGUE
CZECH REPUBLIC
SLOVAKIA
Bratislava
VIENNA
AUSTRIA
BUDAPEST
HUNGARY
BRITTANY
PARIS
FRANCE
MASSIF CENTRAL
Bay of Biscay
Cape Finisterre
SWITZERLAND
Bern
Mont Blanc 4807 m
MILAN
Turin
Genoa
Ljubljana
SLOVENIA
Zagreb
CROATIA
BOSNIA AND HERCEGOVINA
Sarajevo
PORTUGAL
Lisbon
SPAIN
IBERIAN PENINSULA
MADRID
Saragossa
BARCELONA
Valencia
Seville
Málaga
GIBRALTAR (U.K.)
PYRENEES
ANDORRA
Marseille
Monaco
LIGURIAN SEA
Corsica (Fr.)
Sardinia (It.)
ITALY
SAN MARINO
VATICAN CITY
ROME
NAPLES
ADRIATIC SEA
TYRRHENIAN SEA
BALEARIC ISLANDS
MEDITERRANEAN SEA
Palermo
Sicily
Etna 3323 m
IONIAN SEA
Valletta
MALTA
ATLAS MOUNTAINS
© 2005 Encyclopædia Britannica, Inc.

OCEAN
BARENTS SEA
Kolguyev Island
KANIN PENINSULA
KOLA PENINSULA
WHITE SEA
Mount Narodnaya 1895 m
TIMAN RIDGE
URAL MOUNTAINS
Lake Inari
Gulf of Bothnia
FINLAND
Lake Saimaa
Lake Onega
Lake Ladoga
Lake Päijänne
Helsinki
Gulf of Finland
ALAND ISLANDS
Tallinn
ESTONIA
Saaremaa
Lake Peipus
ST. PETERSBURG
Riga
LATVIA
LITHUANIA
Kaunas
Vilnius
RUSSIA
MINSK
BELARUS
Gomel
Pripet Marshes
WARSAW
Bug
Vistula
EUROPEAN PLAIN
VALDAI HILLS
Rybinsk Reservoir
Yaroslavl
Gorky Reservoir
MOSCOW
Ryazan
Tula
CENTRAL RUSSIAN UPLAND
Severnaya Dvina
Sukhona
Volga
Oka
Don
Dnieper
RUSSIA
NIZHNY NOVGOROD
KAZAN
Kuybyshev Reservoir
Simbirsk
Tolyattigrad
SAMARA
VOLGA HILLS
Penza
Saratov
Volgograd Reservoir
Kama Reservoir
PERM
Izhevsk
Naberezhnye Chelny
UFA
YEKATERINBURG
CHELYABINSK
Orenburg
Ural
Ob
KAZAKHSTAN
Zhayyk
Emba
MUGODZHAR HILLS
ARAL SEA
CASPIAN DEPRESSION
Astrakhan
CASPIAN SEA
Kara-Bogaz-Gol
KIEV
KHARKIV
VOLGOGRAD
Tsimlyansk Reservoir
UKRAINE
Lviv
Mount Gerlach 2655 m
Kremenchug Reservoir
Luhansk
DNIPROPETROVSK
DONETSK
ROSTOV-NA-DONU
Zaporizhzhya
Kryvyy Rih
Mariupol
KUMA-MANYCH DEPRESSION
MOLDOVA
Mykolayiv
Kakhovka Reservoir
Chisinau
ODESSA
SEA OF AZOV
Krasnodar
CARPATHIAN MTS.
Tisza
GREAT ALFOLD
Dniester
Prut
Siret
ROMANIA
TRANSYLVANIAN ALPS
CRIMEAN PENINSULA
CAUCASUS
BELGRADE
BUCHAREST
Danube
Olt
SERBIA AND MONTENEGRO
BALKAN MTS.
BLACK SEA
GEORGIA
AZERBAIJAN
ARMENIA
SOFIA
BULGARIA
BALKAN
Skopje
MACEDONIA
RHODOPE MTS.
ISTANBUL
ALBANIA
PENINSULA
Lake Van
Lake Urmia
GREECE
AEGEAN SEA
TURKEY
Lake Tuz
Athens
PELOPONNESE
Rhodes
Crete
TURKISH REP. OF NORTHERN CYPRUS (Recognized by Turkey only)
UN Buffer Zone
Nicosia
REPUBLIC OF CYPRUS
Tigris
Euphrates
Scale 1: 18,862,000
0 100 200 300 mi
0 50 150 250 350 450 km
Bonne
20° E
25° E
30° E
35° E
40° E
45° E
50° E
55° E
60° E
65° E
70° E
75° E
80° E
55° N
50° N
45° N
40° N
35° N
30° N

SPAIN AND PORTUGAL

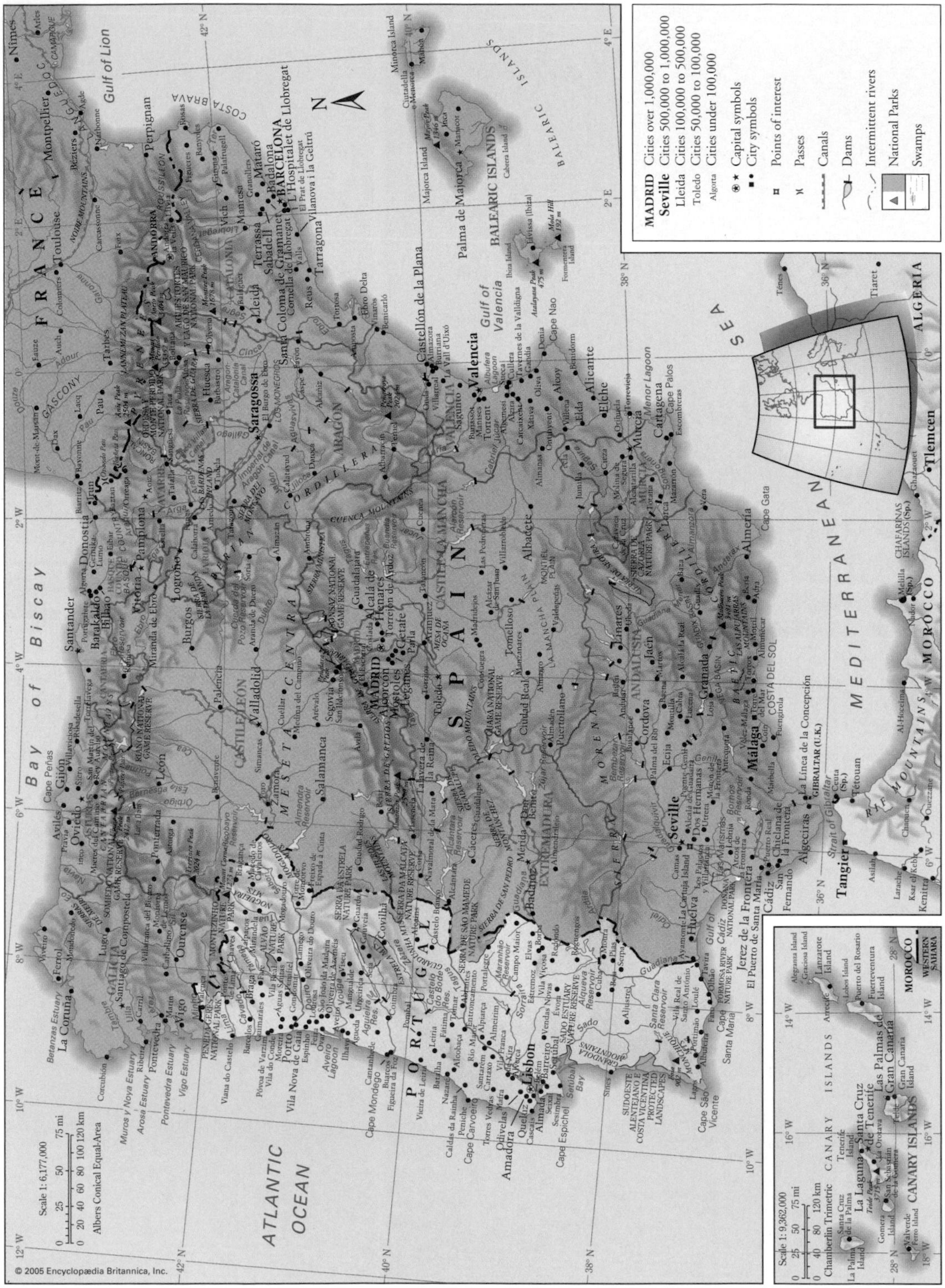

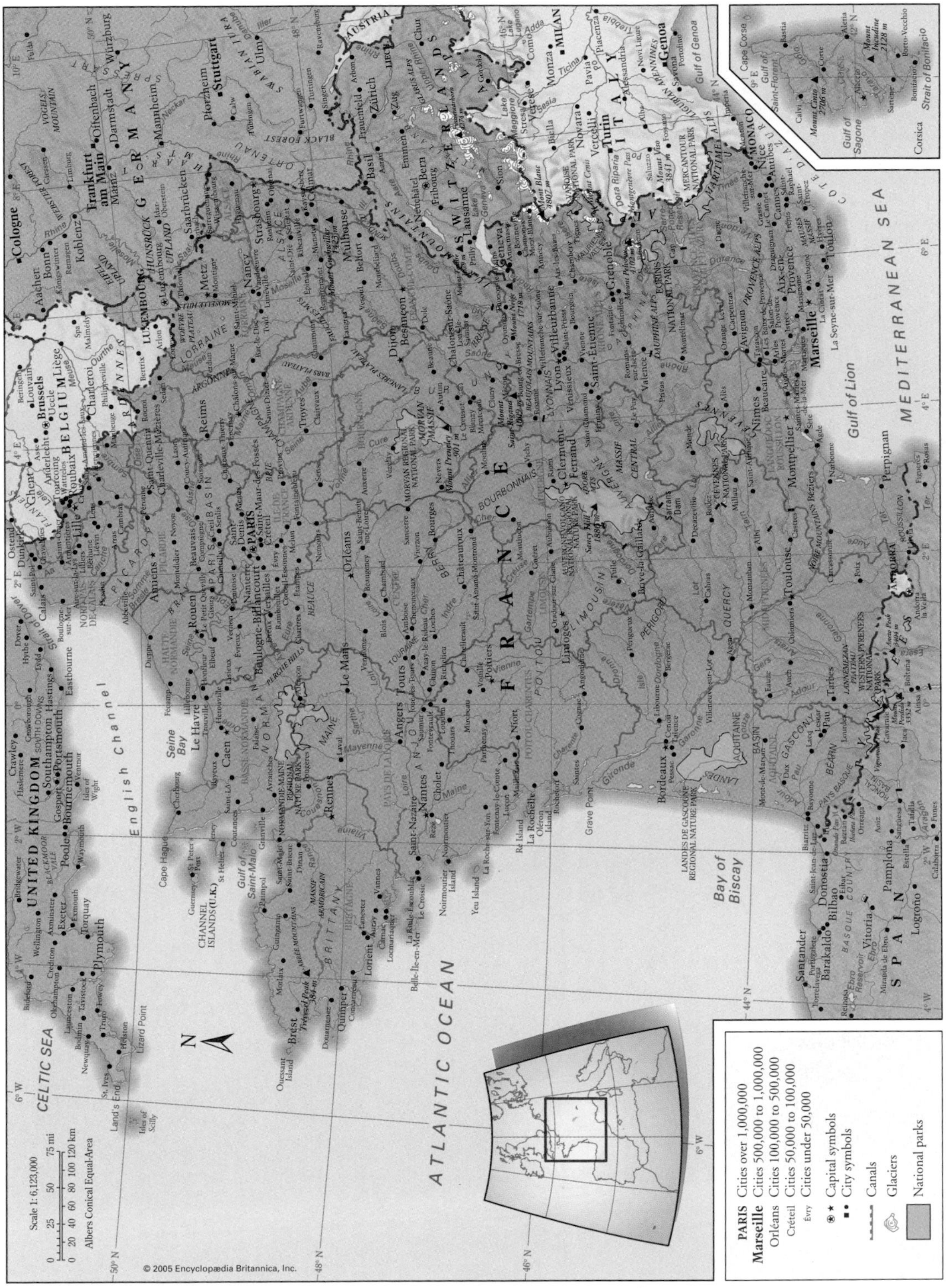

PARIS Cities over 1,000,000
Marseille Cities 500,000 to 1,000,000
Orléans Cities 100,000 to 500,000
Créteil Cities 50,000 to 100,000
Évry Cities under 50,000
Capital symbols
City symbols
Canals
Glaciers
National parks
Scale 1: 6,123,000
0 25 50 75 mi
0 20 40 60 80 100 120 km
Albers Conical Equal-Area
© 2005 Encyclopædia Britannica, Inc.
CELTIC SEA
English Channel
ATLANTIC OCEAN
Bay of Biscay
Gulf of Lion
MEDITERRANEAN SEA
UNITED KINGDOM
BELGIUM
LUXEMBOURG
GERMANY
SWITZERLAND
ITALY
SPAIN
ANDORRA
MONACO
FRANCE
PARIS
Marseille
Lyon
Toulouse
Nice
Nantes
Strasbourg
Montpellier
Bordeaux
Lille
Rennes
Reims
Le Havre
Saint-Étienne
Toulon
Grenoble
Dijon
Angers
Nîmes
Villeurbanne
Clermont-Ferrand
Le Mans
Aix-en-Provence
Brest
Tours
Limoges
Amiens
Perpignan
Metz
Besançon
Orléans
Rouen
Mulhouse
Caen
Nancy
Corsica
Strait of Bonifacio
Gulf of Genoa

ATLAS

ITALY, SLOVENIA, AND CROATIA

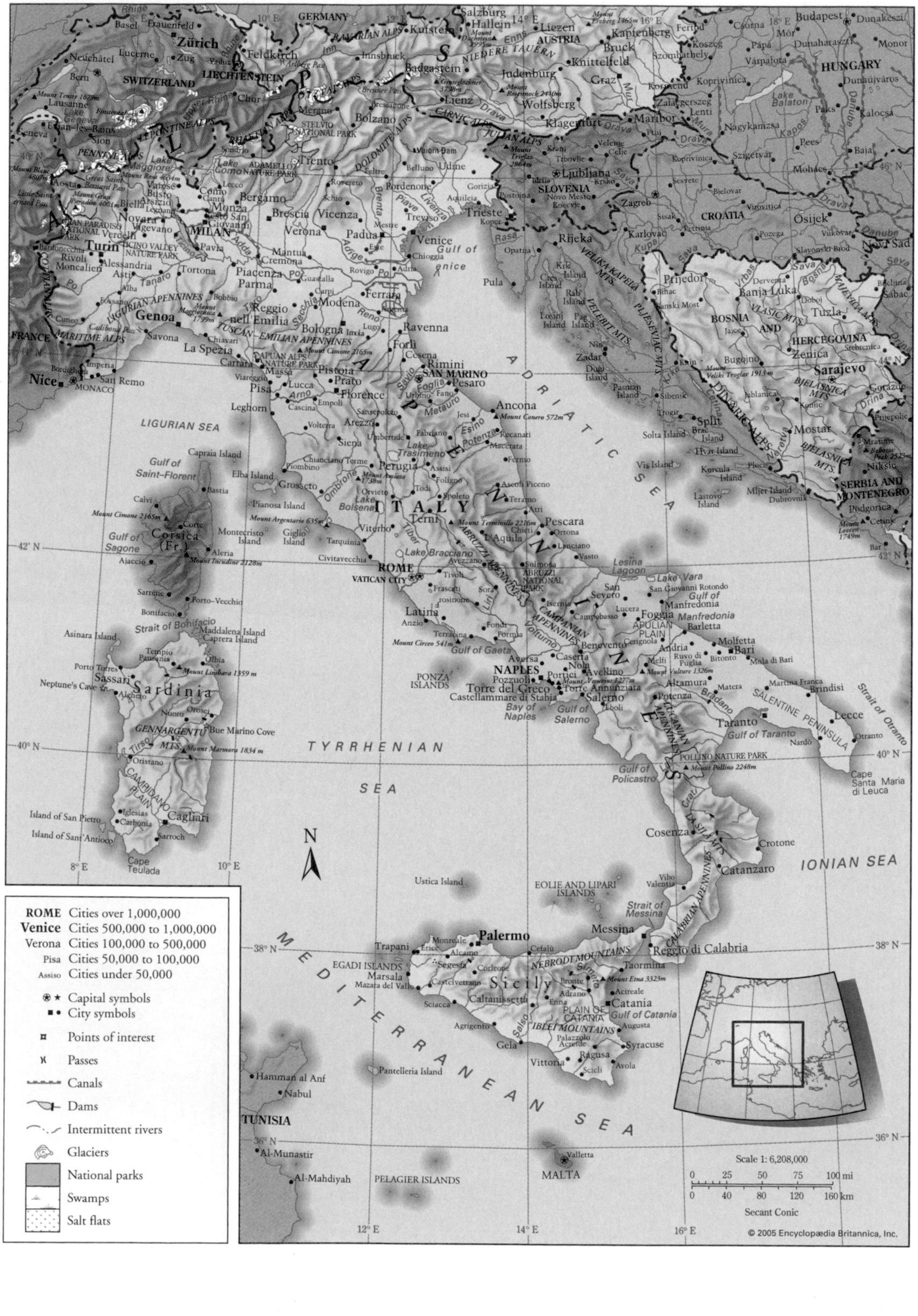

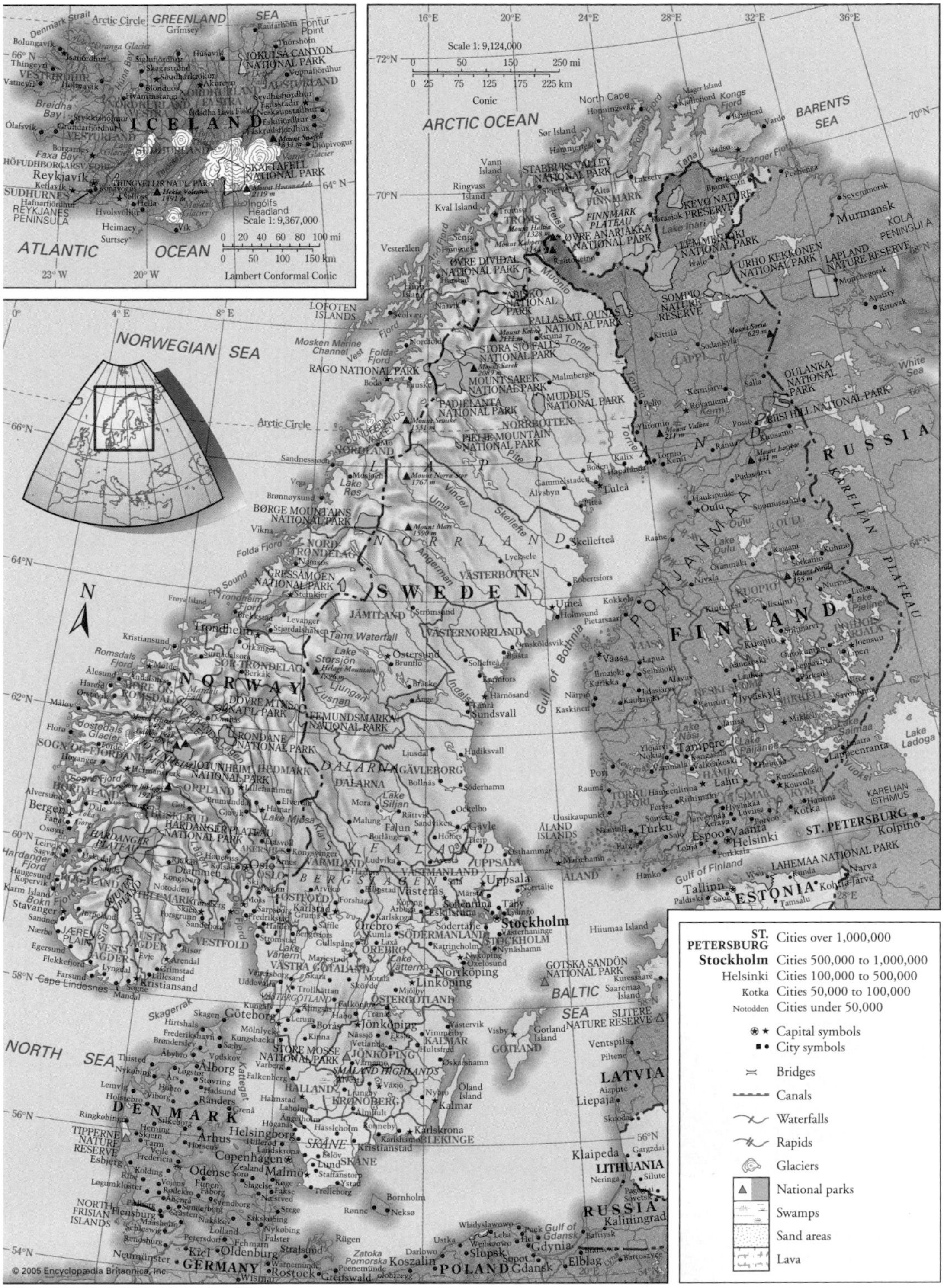
ICELAND
GREENLAND SEA
Arctic Circle
Denmark Strait
Reykjavík
Breidha Bay
Faxa Bay
VATNAJÖKULL
SKAFTAFELL NATIONAL PARK
JÖKULSÁ CANYON NATIONAL PARK
THINGVELLIR NAT'L PARK
Hekla Volcano 1491 m
REYKJANES PENINSULA
Ingólfs Headland
Scale 1: 9,367,000
0 20 40 60 80 100 mi
0 50 100 150 km
Lambert Conformal Conic
ATLANTIC OCEAN
23° W
20° W
Scale 1: 9,124,000
0 50 150 250 mi
0 25 75 125 175 225 km
Conic
ARCTIC OCEAN
BARENTS SEA
NORWEGIAN SEA
NORTH SEA
BALTIC SEA
Gulf of Bothnia
Gulf of Finland
White Sea
Lake Ladoga
North Cape
LOFOTEN ISLANDS
Arctic Circle
NORWAY
SWEDEN
FINLAND
RUSSIA
DENMARK
GERMANY
POLAND
LITHUANIA
LATVIA
ESTONIA
KOLA PENINSULA
KARELIAN PLATEAU
KARELIAN ISTHMUS
Murmansk
ST. PETERSBURG
Oslo
Stockholm
Helsinki
Copenhagen
Tallinn
Bergen
Trondheim
Göteborg
Malmö
Turku
Tampere
Oulu
Luleå
Umeå
Uppsala
Tromsø
Kiruna
Gotland
ÅLAND ISLANDS
Bornholm
Kaliningrad
Gdańsk
Klaipeda
Liepaja
© 2005 Encyclopædia Britannica, Inc.
ST. PETERSBURG Cities over 1,000,000
Stockholm Cities 500,000 to 1,000,000
Helsinki Cities 100,000 to 500,000
Kotka Cities 50,000 to 100,000
Notodden Cities under 50,000
Capital symbols
City symbols
Bridges
Canals
Waterfalls
Rapids
Glaciers
National parks
Swamps
Sand areas
Lava

WESTERN AND CENTRAL EUROPE

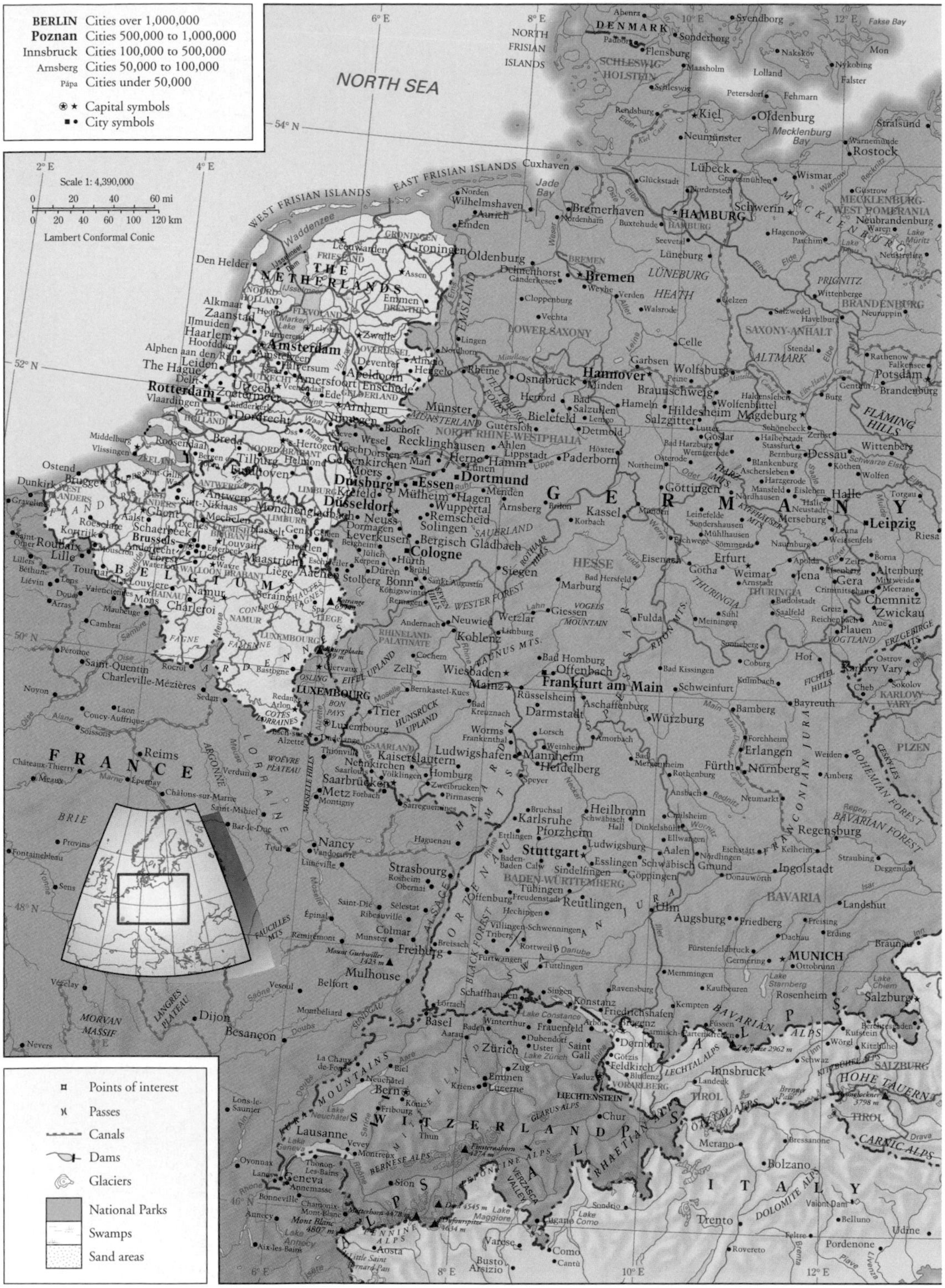

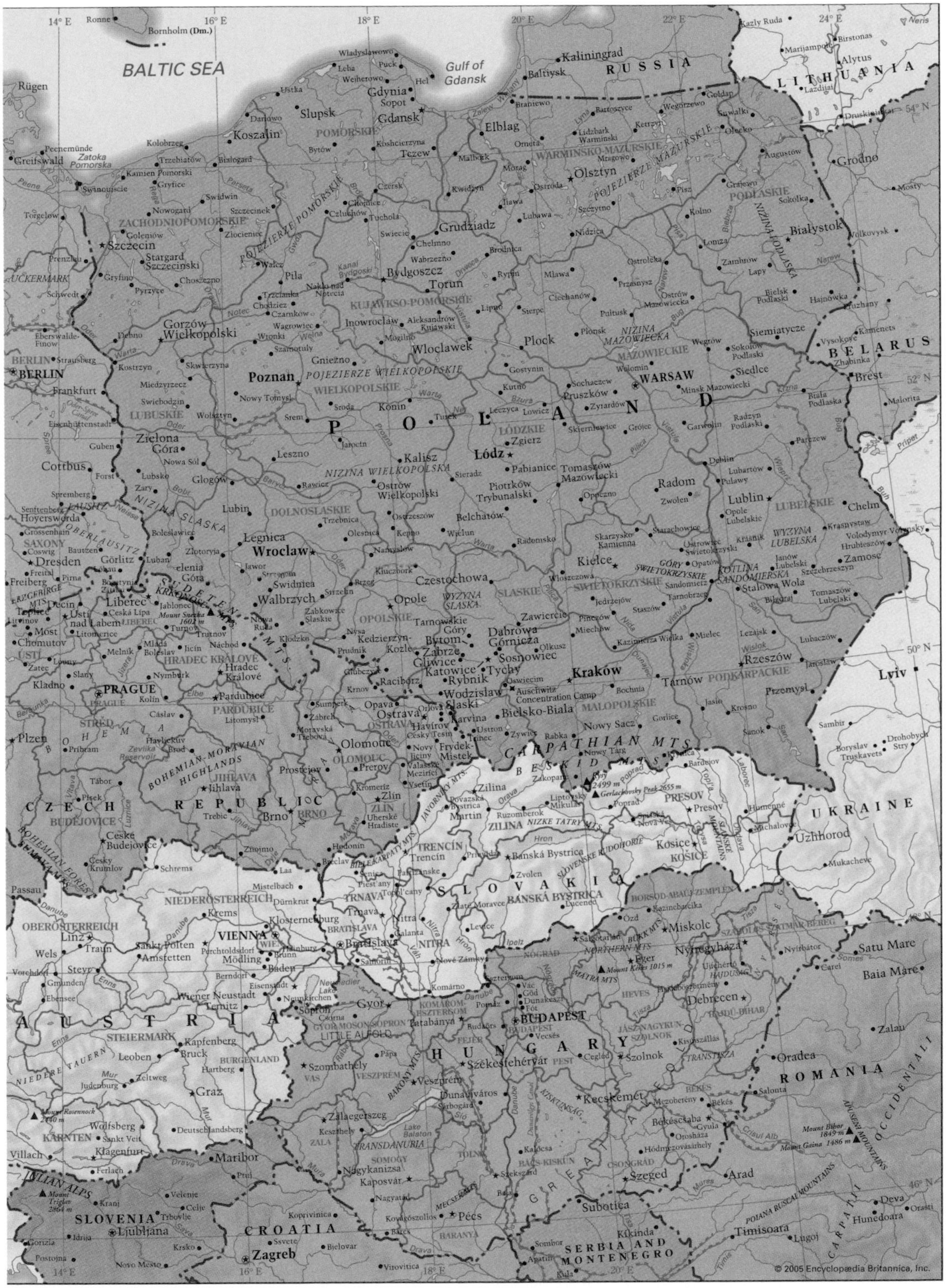
BALTIC SEA
Gulf of Gdansk
RUSSIA
Kaliningrad
LITHUANIA
BELARUS
POLAND
WARSAW
Gdansk
Gdynia
Sopot
Slupsk
Koszalin
Elblag
Olsztyn
Grudziadz
Bydgoszcz
Torun
Bialystok
Grodno
Szczecin
Gorzów Wielkopolski
Poznan
Wloclawek
Plock
Siedlce
Brest
Lódz
Kalisz
Radom
Lublin
Chelm
Kielce
Czestochowa
Wroclaw
Legnica
Opole
Katowice
Kraków
Tarnów
Rzeszów
Przemysl
Lviv
BERLIN
Frankfurt
Cottbus
Dresden
Görlitz
Zielona Góra
Liberec
PRAGUE
Plzen
Hradec Králové
Pardubice
Ostrava
Olomouc
Brno
Jihlava
CZECH REPUBLIC
SLOVAKIA
Zilina
Banská Bystrica
Presov
Kosice
Trencín
Nitra
Bratislava
Uzhhorod
UKRAINE
VIENNA
Linz
AUSTRIA
Graz
Klagenfurt
Innsbruck
HUNGARY
BUDAPEST
Miskolc
Debrecen
Nyíregyháza
Szolnok
Kecskemét
Szeged
Székesfehérvár
Gyor
Pécs
ROMANIA
Oradea
Arad
Timisoara
Satu Mare
Baia Mare
SLOVENIA
Ljubljana
Maribor
CROATIA
Zagreb
SERBIA AND MONTENEGRO
Subotica
CARPATHIAN MTS
SUDETEN MTS
BOHEMIAN FOREST
Danube
Vistula
Oder
© 2005 Encyclopædia Britannica, Inc.

SOUTHEASTERN EUROPE

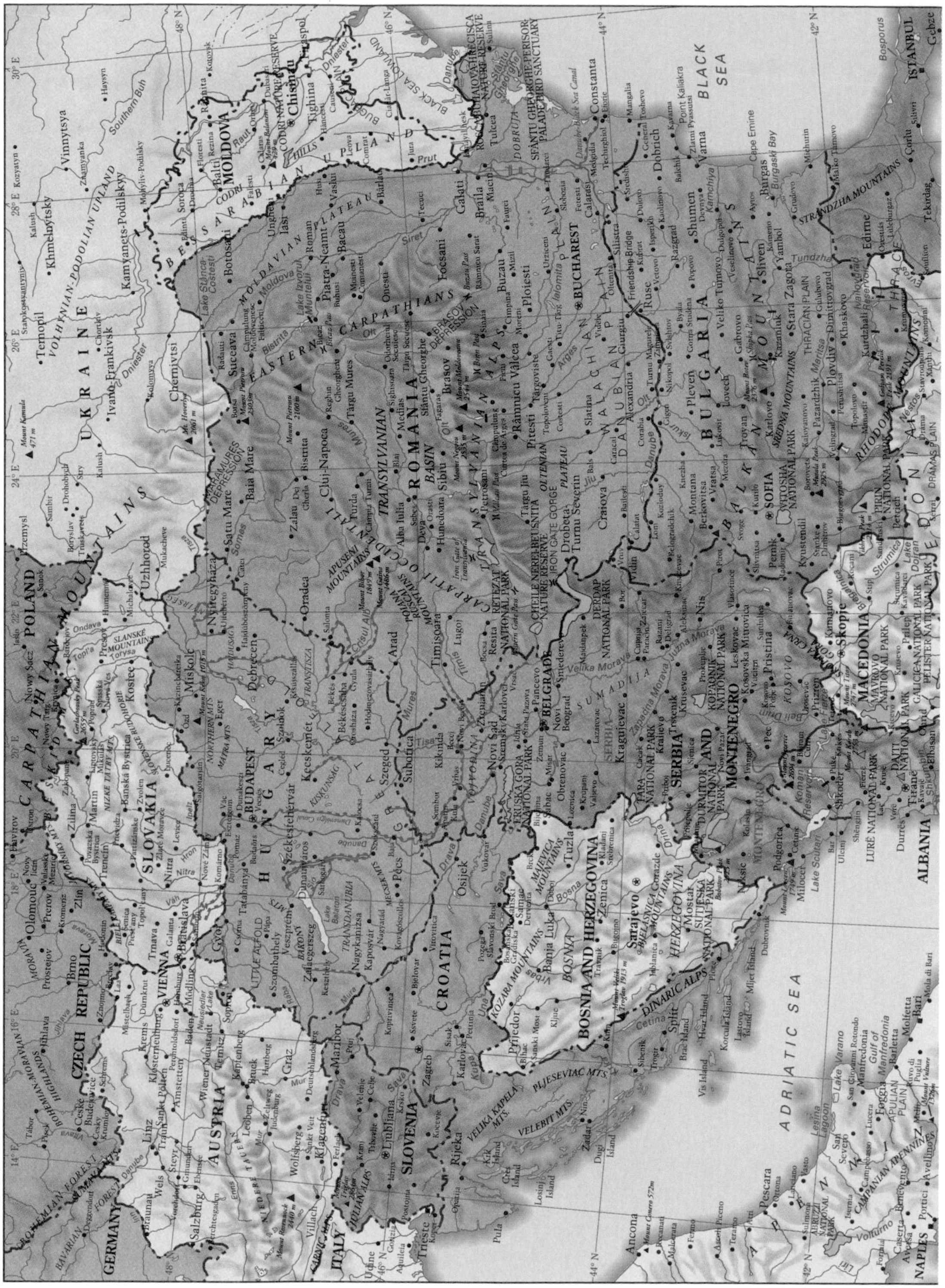

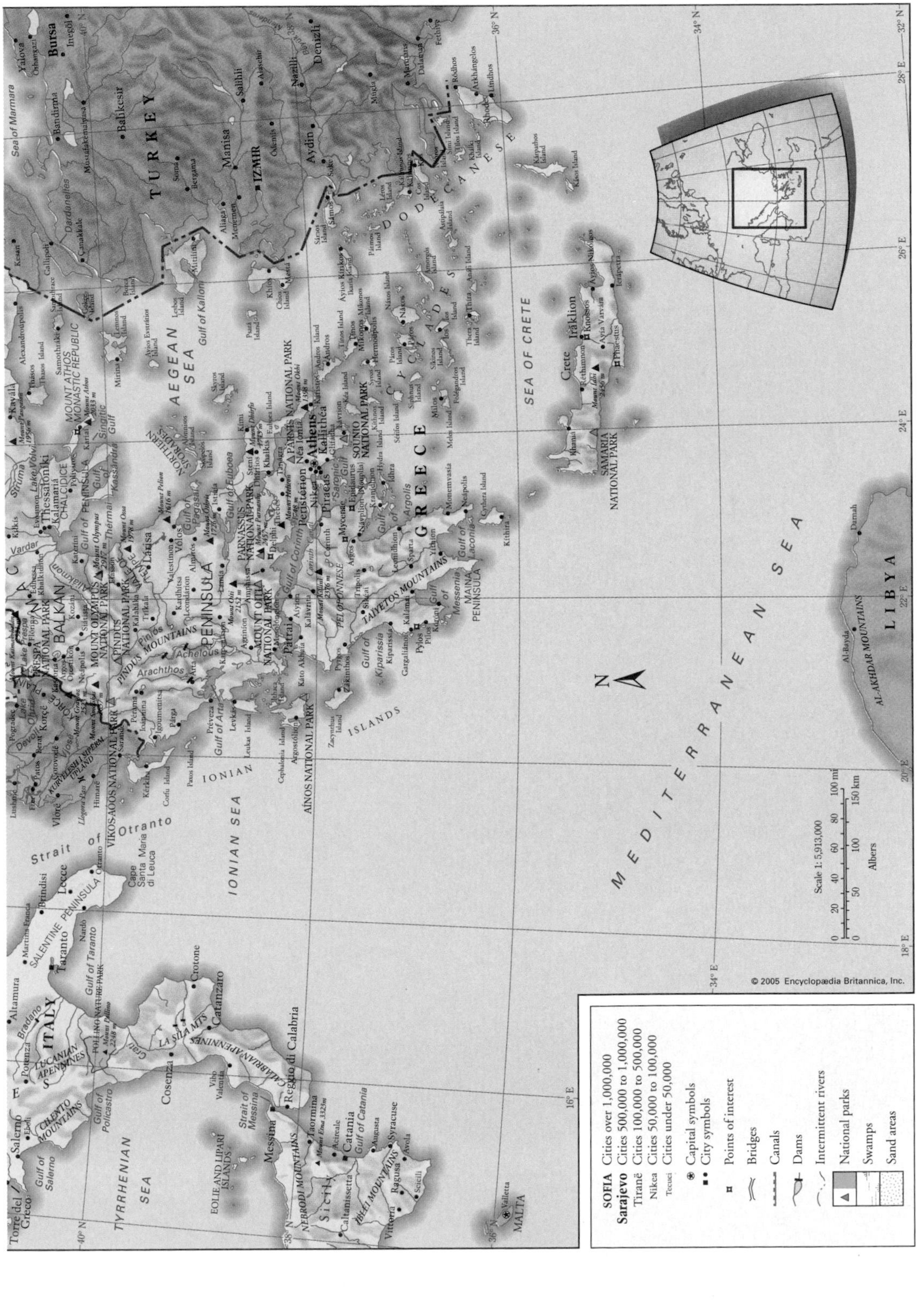
TURKEY
GREECE
ITALY
LIBYA
AEGEAN SEA
IONIAN SEA
TYRRHENIAN SEA
SEA OF CRETE
MEDITERRANEAN SEA
Sea of Marmara
Strait of Otranto
Gulf of Taranto
Gulf of Corinth
DODECANESE
CYCLADES
BALKAN PENINSULA
PELOPONNESE
Athens
Thessaloníki
Piraeus
Pátrai
Lárisa
Iráklion
Crete
Rhodes
IZMIR
Bursa
Balıkesir
Manisa
Aydın
Denizli
Taranto
Brindisi
Lecce
Catanzaro
Crotone
Cosenza
Reggio di Calabria
Messina
Catania
Syracuse
Ragusa
Valletta
MALTA
Scale 1: 5,913,000
Albers
© 2005 Encyclopædia Britannica, Inc.
SOFIA Cities over 1,000,000
Sarajevo Cities 500,000 to 1,000,000
Tiranë Cities 100,000 to 500,000
Nikea Cities 50,000 to 100,000
Tecuci Cities under 50,000
Capital symbols
City symbols
Points of interest
Bridges
Canals
Dams
Intermittent rivers
National parks
Swamps
Sand areas

ATLAS

RUSSIA AND KAZAKSTAN

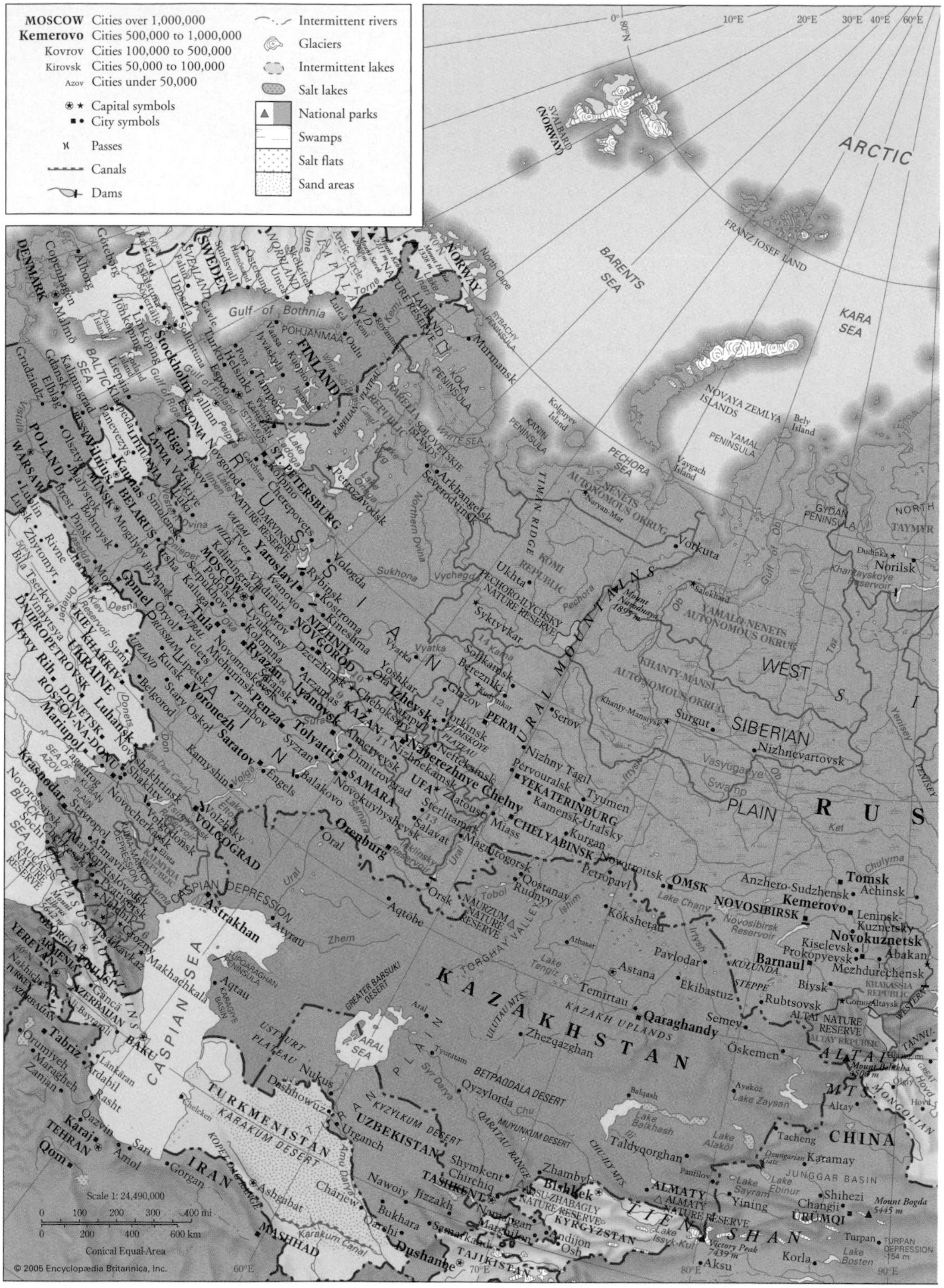

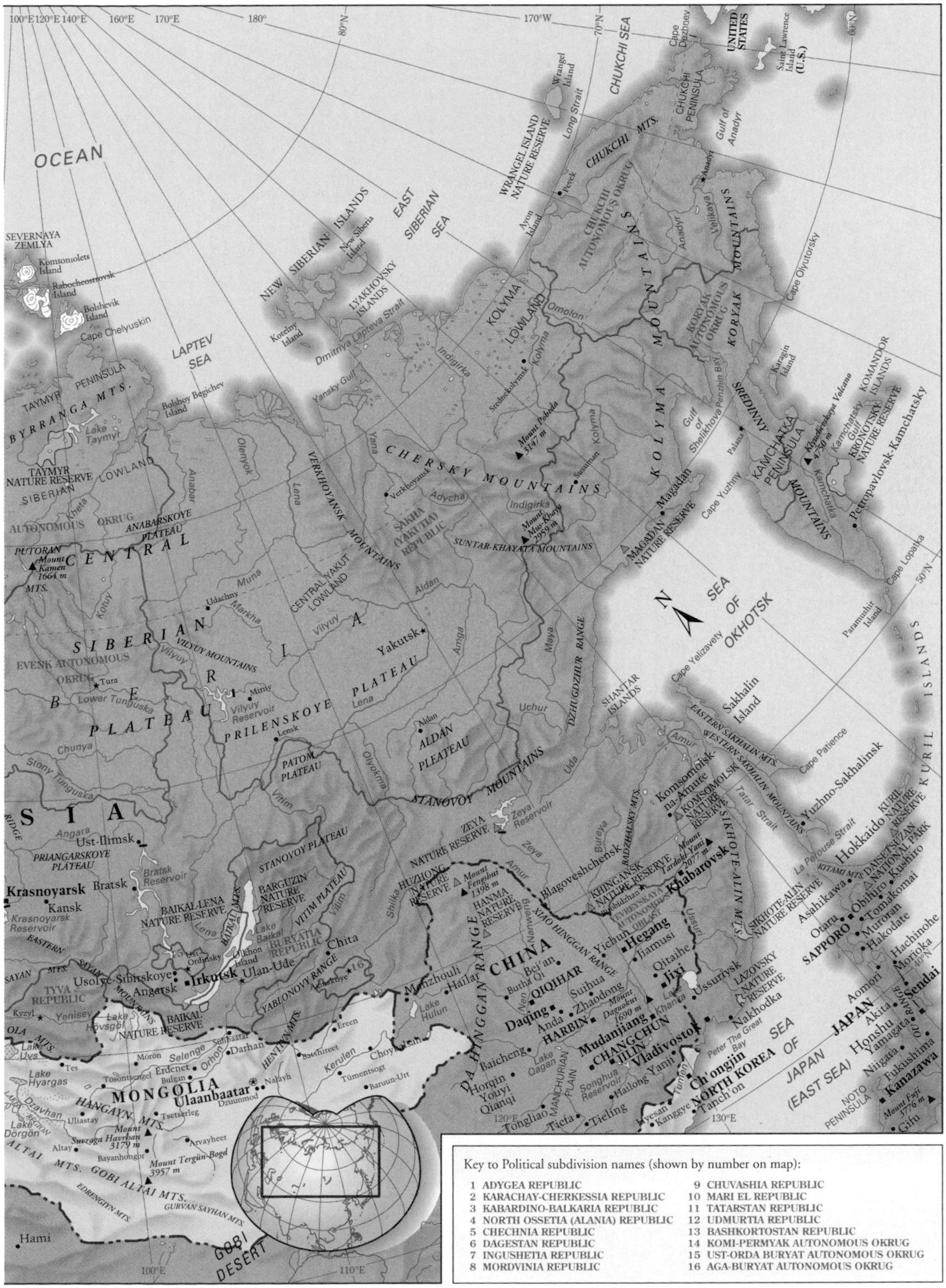
OCEAN
SEVERNAYA ZEMLYA
Komsomolets Island
Rabocheostrovsk Island
Bolshevik Island
Cape Chelyuskin
LAPTEV SEA
NEW SIBERIAN ISLANDS
New Siberia Island
Kotelny Island
LYAKHOVSKY ISLANDS
Dmitriya Lapteva Strait
EAST SIBERIAN SEA
Wrangel Island
WRANGEL ISLAND NATURE RESERVE
Long Strait
CHUKCHI SEA
Cape Dezhnev
UNITED STATES
Saint Lawrence Island (U.S.)
CHUKCHI PENINSULA
Gulf of Anadyr
Anadyr
CHUKCHI MTS.
CHUKCHI AUTONOMOUS OKRUG
Ayon Island
Pevek
KOLYMA LOWLAND
Omolon
KORYAK AUTONOMOUS OKRUG
KORYAK MOUNTAINS
Cape Olyutorsky
Karagin Island
KOMANDOR ISLANDS
KRONOTSKY NATURE RESERVE
Kamchatsky Gulf
Petropavlovsk-Kamchatsky
SREDINNY
KAMCHATKA PENINSULA
Klyuchevskaya Volcano 4750 m
Kamchatka
Penzhin Bay
Gulf of Shelikhova
Palana
KOLYMA MOUNTAINS
Kolyma
Srednekolymsk
Indigirka
Mount Pobeda 3147 m
CHERSKY MOUNTAINS
Susuman
Magadan
MAGADAN NATURE RESERVE
Cape Yuzhny
SEA OF OKHOTSK
Cape Lopatka
Paramushir Island
KURIL ISLANDS
Cape Yelizavety
Sakhalin Island
EASTERN SAKHALIN MTS.
WESTERN SAKHALIN MOUNTAINS
Cape Patience
Yuzhno-Sakhalinsk
Tatar Strait
La Perouse Strait
Hokkaido
KURIL NATURE RESERVE
SHANTAR ISLANDS
TAYMYR PENINSULA
BYRRANGA MTS.
Lake Taymyr
Bolshoy Begichev Island
TAYMYR NATURE RESERVE
SIBERIAN LOWLAND
AUTONOMOUS OKRUG
ANABARSKOYE PLATEAU
PUTORAN MTS.
Mount Kamen 1664 m
CENTRAL SIBERIAN PLATEAU
Anabar
Olenyok
Lena
Yana
Yansky Gulf
VERKHOYANSK MOUNTAINS
Verkhoyansk
Adycha
SAKHA (YAKUTIA) REPUBLIC
Mount Mus-Khaya 2959 m
SUNTAR-KHAYATA MOUNTAINS
CENTRAL YAKUT LOWLAND
Muna
Markha
Udachny
Vilyuy
VILYUY MOUNTAINS
Vilyuy Reservoir
Mirny
Yakutsk
Aldan
Amga
Maya
DZHUGDZHUR RANGE
Uchur
ALDAN PLEATEAU
PRILENSKOYE PLATEAU
Lensk
EVENK AUTONOMOUS OKRUG
Tura
Lower Tunguska
Chunya
Stony Tunguska
PATOM PLATEAU
Olyokma
Vitim
STANOVOY MOUNTAINS
Uda
Amur
Zeya Reservoir
ZEYA NATURE RESERVE
Zeya
Bureya
Komsomolsk-na-Amure
KOMSOMOLSK NATURE RESERVE
SIKHOTE-ALIN MTS.
Mount Yardoki-Yani 2077 m
Khabarovsk
Blagoveshchensk
Ust-Ilimsk
Angara
PRIANGARSKOYE PLATEAU
Bratsk
Bratsk Reservoir
Krasnoyarsk
Kansk
Krasnoyarsk Reservoir
EASTERN SAYAN MTS.
BAIKAL-LENA NATURE RESERVE
BARGUZIN NATURE RESERVE
STANOVOY PLATEAU
VITIM PLATEAU
Lake Baikal
BURYATIA REPUBLIC
Olkhon Island
Chita
Ulan-Ude
Irkutsk
Angarsk
Usolye-Sibirskoye
YABLONOVY RANGE
TYVA REPUBLIC
Kyzyl
Yenisey
Lake Hovsgol
BAIKAL NATURE RESERVE
Mount Fengshui 1398 m
HANMA NATURE RESERVE
DA HINGGAN RANGE
XIAO HINGGAN RANGE
CHINA
Manzhouli
Hailar
Lake Hulun
Bei'an
QIQIHAR
Yichun
Hegang
Jiamusi
Qitaihe
Jixi
Suihua
Daqing
Zhaodong
Anda
HARBIN
Mudanjiang
CHANGCHUN
JILIN
Baicheng
MANCHURIAN PLAIN
Tongliao
Tiefa
Tieling
Vladivostok
Ussuriysk
Nakhodka
LAZOVSKY NATURE RESERVE
Peter The Great Bay
Ch'ongjin
NORTH KOREA
Tanch'on
SEA OF JAPAN (EAST SEA)
JAPAN
Honshu
Aomori
Hachinohe
Morioka
Sendai
Akita
Yamagata
Niigata
Fukushima
Kanazawa
Mount Fuji 3776 m
Gifu
NOTO PENINSULA
SAPPORO
Otaru
Asahikawa
Obihiro
Kushiro
Tomakomai
Muroran
Hakodate
DAISETSUZAN NATIONAL PARK
SIKHOTE-ALIN NATURE RESERVE
MONGOLIA
Ulaanbaatar
Darhan
Erdenet
Selenge
Moron
Bulgan
Choybalsan
Kerulen
Tumentsogt
Baruun-Urt
Ereen
HENTIYN MTS.
HANGAYN MTS.
Tsetserleg
Uliastay
Lake Hyargas
Lake Uvs
Lake Dorgon
Altay
Bayanhongor
Arvayheer
Mount Suvraga Havrhan 3179 m
Mount Tergiin-Bogd 3957 m
GOBI ALTAI MTS.
GURVAN SAYHAN MTS.
GOBI DESERT
Hami
100°E
110°E
120°E
130°E
140°E
160°E
170°E
180°
170°W
80°N
70°N
60°N
50°N
40°N
Key to Political subdivision names (shown by number on map):
1 ADYGEA REPUBLIC
2 KARACHAY-CHERKESSIA REPUBLIC
3 KABARDINO-BALKARIA REPUBLIC
4 NORTH OSSETIA (ALANIA) REPUBLIC
5 CHECHNIA REPUBLIC
6 DAGESTAN REPUBLIC
7 INGUSHETIA REPUBLIC
8 MORDVINIA REPUBLIC
9 CHUVASHIA REPUBLIC
10 MARI EL REPUBLIC
11 TATARSTAN REPUBLIC
12 UDMURTIA REPUBLIC
13 BASHKORTOSTAN REPUBLIC
14 KOMI-PERMYAK AUTONOMOUS OKRUG
15 UST-ORDA BURYAT AUTONOMOUS OKRUG
16 AGA-BURYAT AUTONOMOUS OKRUG

EASTERN EUROPE

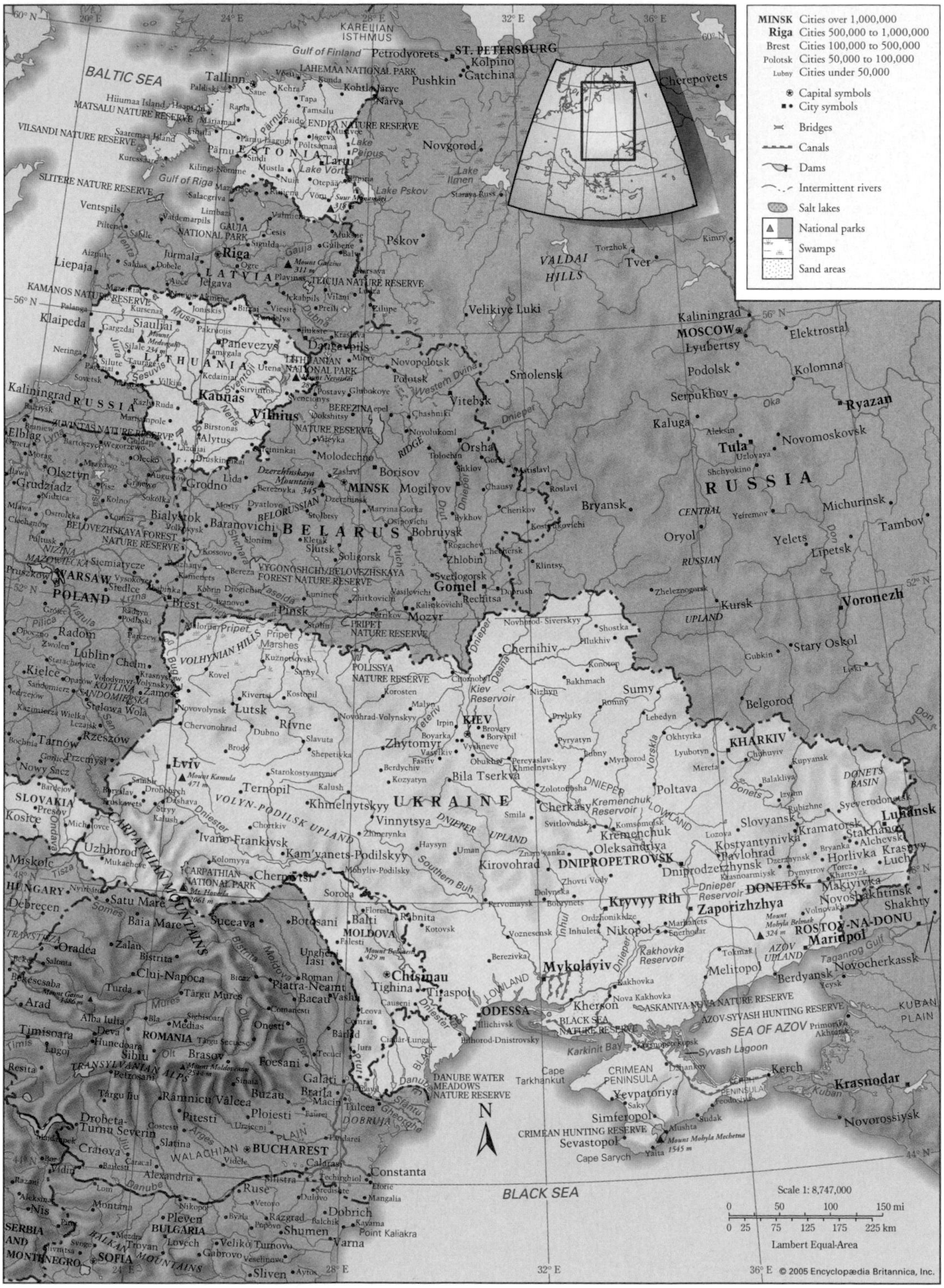

TASHKENT Cities over 1,000,000
Hyderabad Cities 500,000 to 1,000,000
Herat Cities 100,000 to 500,000
Mahabad Cities 50,000 to 100,000
Kasan Cities under 50,000
Capital symbols
City symbols
Points of interest
Canals
Dams
Intermittent rivers
Glaciers
Intermittent lakes
Salt lakes
National parks
Swamps
Salt flats
Sand areas
Scale 1:14,882,000
Lambert Equal-Area
KAZAKHSTAN
UZBEKISTAN
TURKMENISTAN
KYRGYZSTAN
TAJIKISTAN
AFGHANISTAN
PAKISTAN
INDIA
CHINA
IRAN
IRAQ
KUWAIT
OMAN
UNITED ARAB EMIRATES
CASPIAN SEA
ARAL SEA
ARABIAN SEA
Gulf of Oman
Persian Gulf
© 2005 Encyclopædia Britannica, Inc.

ASIA

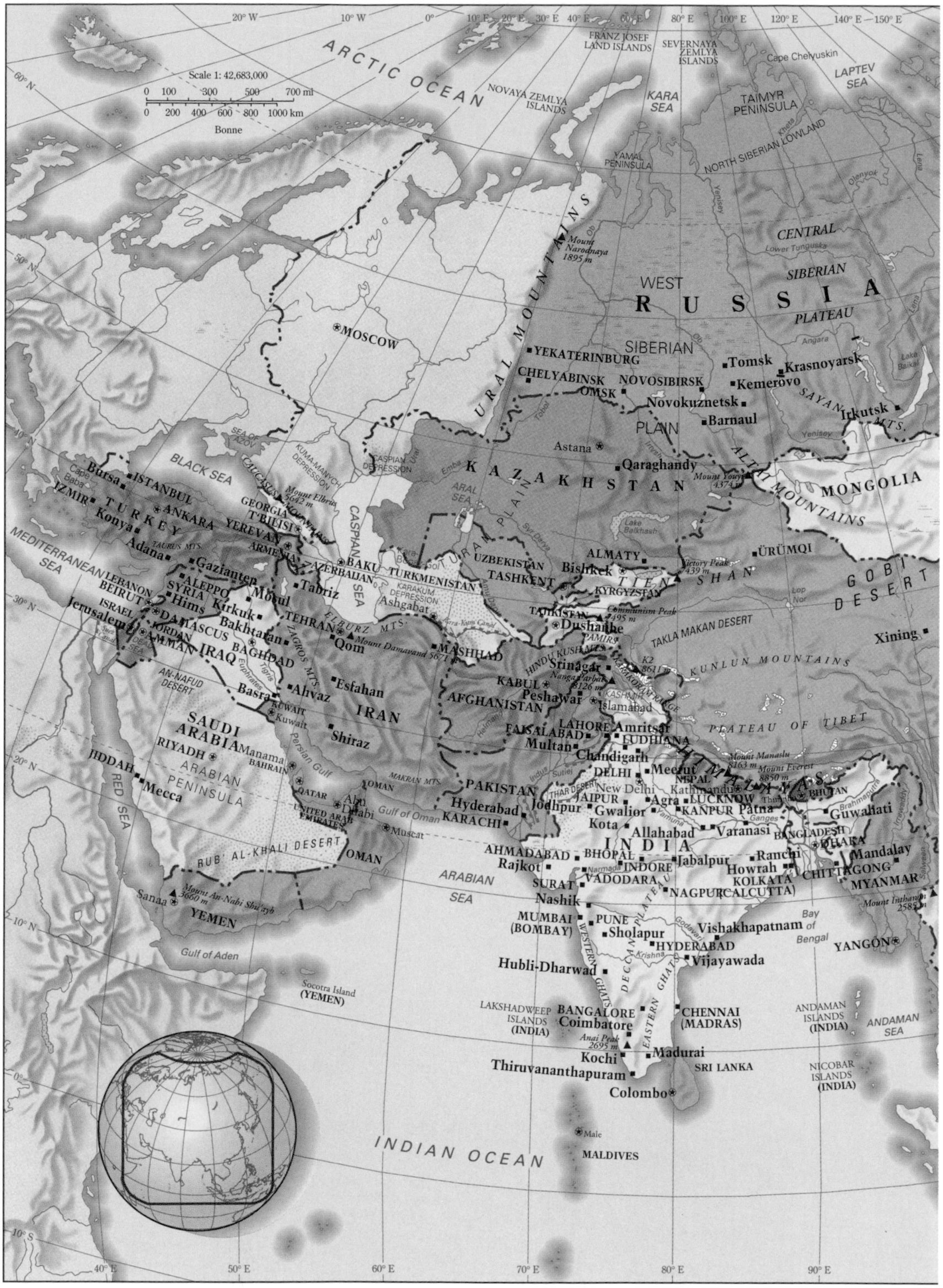

ARCTIC OCEAN
Scale 1: 42,683,000
0 100 300 500 700 mi
0 200 400 600 800 1000 km
Bonne
FRANZ JOSEF LAND ISLANDS
SEVERNAYA ZEMLYA ISLANDS
Cape Chelyuskin
LAPTEV SEA
NOVAYA ZEMLYA ISLANDS
KARA SEA
TAIMYR PENINSULA
YAMAL PENINSULA
NORTH SIBERIAN LOWLAND
CENTRAL SIBERIAN PLATEAU
Lower Tunguska
Mount Narodnaya 1895 m
URAL MOUNTAINS
WEST SIBERIAN PLAIN
RUSSIA
MOSCOW
YEKATERINBURG
CHELYABINSK
NOVOSIBIRSK
OMSK
Tomsk
Krasnoyarsk
Kemerovo
Novokuznetsk
Barnaul
Irkutsk
SAYAN MTS.
Angara
Lake Baikal
Yenisey
Ob
Lena
Olenyok
Tobol
Irtysh
Astana
Qaraghandy
KAZAKHSTAN
ALTAI MOUNTAINS
Mount Youyi 4374 m
MONGOLIA
SEA OF AZOV
BLACK SEA
KUMA-MANYCH DEPRESSION
CASPIAN DEPRESSION
CAUCASUS
Mount Elbrus 5642 m
ARAL SEA
Lake Balkhash
Emba
Syr Darya
Amu Darya
TURAN PLAIN
Bursa
ISTANBUL
Cape Baba
IZMIR
ANKARA
TURKEY
Konya
Adana
TAURUS MTS.
GEORGIA
T'BILISI
YEREVAN
ARMENIA
AZERBAIJAN
BAKU
CASPIAN SEA
MEDITERRANEAN SEA
LEBANON
SYRIA
BEIRUT
ALEPPO
Gaziantep
Hims
DAMASCUS
ISRAEL
JORDAN
Jerusalem
AMMAN
Mosul
Kirkuk
Tabriz
Bakhtaran
BAGHDAD
IRAQ
TEHRAN
Qom
ELBURZ MTS.
Mount Damavand 5671 m
ZAGROS MTS.
Euphrates
Tigris
AN-NAFUD DESERT
Basra
Ahvaz
Esfahan
IRAN
KUWAIT
Kuwait
Shiraz
Persian Gulf
SAUDI ARABIA
RIYADH
Manama
BAHRAIN
ARABIAN PENINSULA
JIDDAH
Mecca
RED SEA
QATAR
Abu Dhabi
UNITED ARAB EMIRATES
Muscat
OMAN
Gulf of Oman
MAKRAN MTS.
RUB' AL-KHALI DESERT
Mount An-Nabi Shu'ayb 3660 m
Sanaa
YEMEN
Gulf of Aden
Socotra Island (YEMEN)
TURKMENISTAN
KARAKUM DEPRESSION
Ashgabat
MASHHAD
UZBEKISTAN
TASHKENT
ALMATY
Bishkek
KYRGYZSTAN
TIEN SHAN
Victory Peak 7439 m
ÜRÜMQI
GOBI DESERT
TAJIKISTAN
Dushanbe
Communism Peak 7495 m
PAMIRS
TAKLA MAKAN DESERT
Lop Nor
Xining
KUNLUN MOUNTAINS
HINDU KUSH
Srinagar
Nanga Parbat 8126 m
K2 8611 m
KARAKORAM RANGE
KASHMIR
KABUL
AFGHANISTAN
Peshawar
Islamabad
PLATEAU OF TIBET
LAHORE
Amritsar
FAISALABAD
Multan
LUDHIANA
Chandigarh
HIMALAYAS
Mount Manaslu 8163 m
Mount Everest 8850 m
DELHI
Meerut
New Delhi
NEPAL
Kathmandu
BHUTAN
Thimphu
PAKISTAN
THAR DESERT
Indus
Sutlej
Hyderabad
KARACHI
JAIPUR
Jodhpur
Agra
Gwalior
LUCKNOW
KANPUR
Patna
Ganges
Yamuna
Brahmaputra
Guwahati
Kota
Allahabad
Varanasi
BANGLADESH
DHAKA
INDIA
AHMADABAD
BHOPAL
Narmada
INDORE
Jabalpur
Ranchi
Howrah
KOLKATA (CALCUTTA)
Mandalay
CHITTAGONG
MYANMAR
Rajkot
SURAT
VADODARA
NAGPUR
Nashik
ARABIAN SEA
MUMBAI (BOMBAY)
PUNE
Sholapur
Godavari
Vishakhapatnam
Bay of Bengal
HYDERABAD
Krishna
Vijayawada
YANGON
Mount Inthanon 2585 m
Irrawaddy
Salween
Hubli-Dharwad
DECCAN PLATEAU
WESTERN GHATS
EASTERN GHATS
LAKSHADWEEP ISLANDS (INDIA)
BANGALORE
Coimbatore
CHENNAI (MADRAS)
ANDAMAN ISLANDS (INDIA)
ANDAMAN SEA
Anai Peak 2695 m
Kochi
Madurai
SRI LANKA
NICOBAR ISLANDS (INDIA)
Thiruvananthapuram
Colombo
Male
MALDIVES
INDIAN OCEAN
20° W
10° W
0°
10° E
20° E
30° E
40° E
60° E
80° E
100° E
120° E
140° E
150° E
60° N
50° N
40° N
30° N
20° N
10° N
0°
10° S
40° E
50° E
60° E
70° E
80° E
90° E

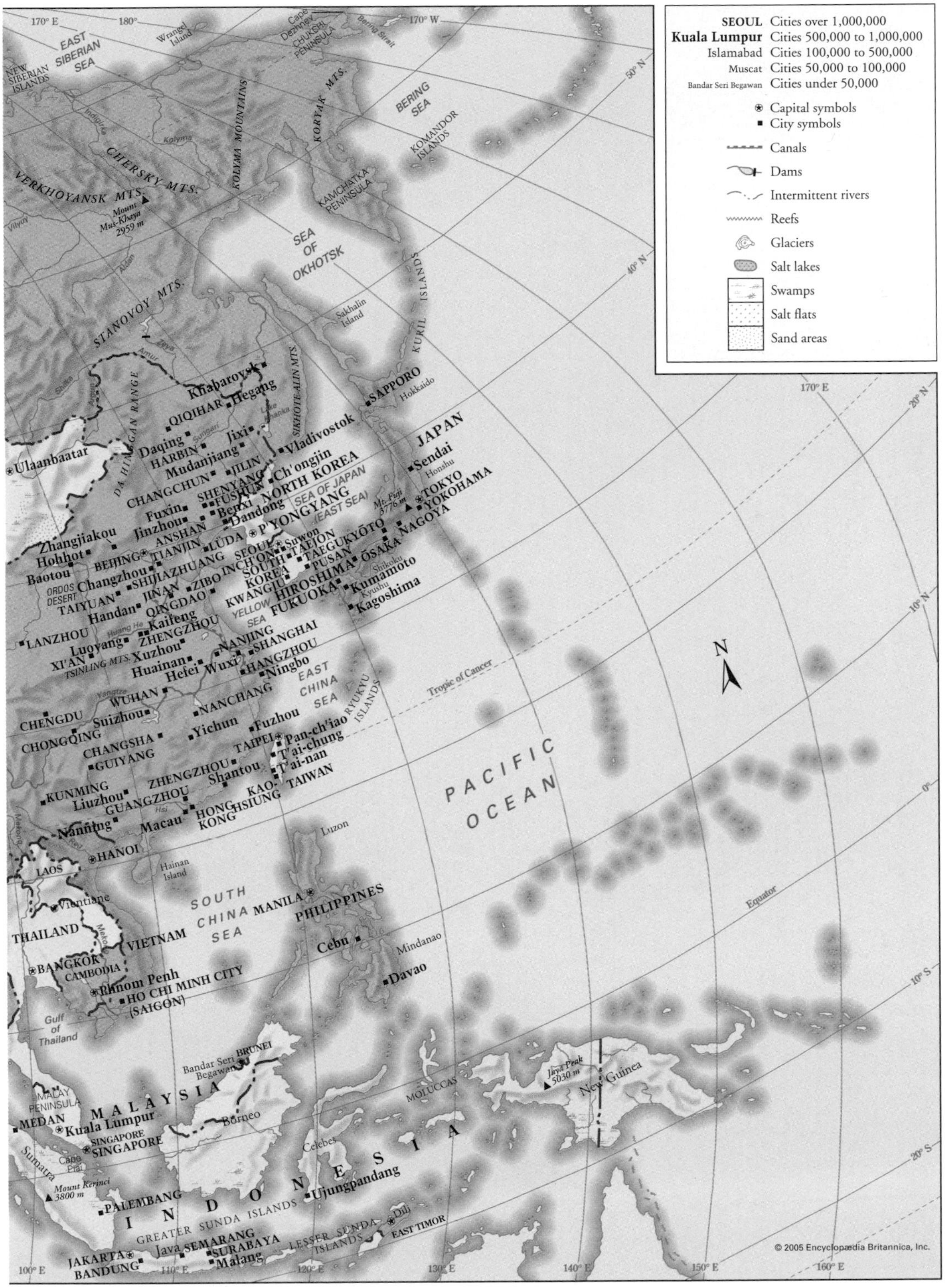
SEOUL Cities over 1,000,000
Kuala Lumpur Cities 500,000 to 1,000,000
Islamabad Cities 100,000 to 500,000
Muscat Cities 50,000 to 100,000
Bandar Seri Begawan Cities under 50,000
Capital symbols
City symbols
Canals
Dams
Intermittent rivers
Reefs
Glaciers
Salt lakes
Swamps
Salt flats
Sand areas
EAST SIBERIAN SEA
NEW SIBERIAN ISLANDS
Wrangel Island
Cape Dezhnev
CHUKCHI PENINSULA
Bering Strait
BERING SEA
KOMANDOR ISLANDS
KORYAK MTS.
KOLYMA MOUNTAINS
CHERSKY MTS.
VERKHOYANSK MTS.
Mount Mus-Khaya 2959 m
KAMCHATKA PENINSULA
SEA OF OKHOTSK
Sakhalin Island
KURIL ISLANDS
STANOVOY MTS.
DA HINGGAN RANGE
SIKHOTE-ALIN MTS.
Khabarovsk
Hegang
QIQIHAR
Daqing
HARBIN
Jixi
Mudanjiang
JILIN
Vladivostok
Ulaanbaatar
CHANGCHUN
SHENYANG
FUSHUN
Ch'ongjin
NORTH KOREA
SEA OF JAPAN (EAST SEA)
SAPPORO
Hokkaido
JAPAN
Sendai
Honshu
TOKYO
YOKOHAMA
Mt. Fuji 3776 m
NAGOYA
ŌSAKA
KYŌTO
Fuxin
Benxi
Dandong
Jinzhou
ANSHAN
P'YONGYANG
Zhangjiakou
Hohhot
BEIJING
TIANJIN
LÜDA
SEOUL
Suwon
TAEJON
TAEGU
INCH'ON
SOUTH KOREA
PUSAN
KWANGJU
HIROSHIMA
Shikoku
Kyushu
FUKUOKA
Kumamoto
Kagoshima
Baotou
ORDOS DESERT
Changzhou
SHIJIAZHUANG
ZIBO
TAIYUAN
JINAN
QINGDAO
Handan
Kaifeng
YELLOW SEA
LANZHOU
Huang He
ZHENGZHOU
Luoyang
XI'AN
TSINLING MTS.
Xuzhou
NANJING
SHANGHAI
Huainan
Hefei
Wuxi
HANGZHOU
Ningbo
EAST CHINA SEA
RYUKYU ISLANDS
Tropic of Cancer
WUHAN
Yangtze
CHENGDU
Suizhou
NANCHANG
CHONGQING
Yichun
Fuzhou
CHANGSHA
GUIYANG
TAIPEI
Pan-ch'iao
T'ai-chung
T'ai-nan
KAO-HSIUNG
TAIWAN
ZHENGZHOU
Shantou
KUNMING
Liuzhou
GUANGZHOU
HONG KONG
Macau
Nanning
HANOI
LAOS
Hainan Island
Luzon
PACIFIC OCEAN
SOUTH CHINA SEA
MANILA
PHILIPPINES
Vientiane
THAILAND
VIETNAM
Cebu
Mindanao
BANGKOK
CAMBODIA
Phnom Penh
HO CHI MINH CITY (SAIGON)
Davao
Gulf of Thailand
Equator
BRUNEI
Bandar Seri Begawan
Jaya Peak 5030 m
New Guinea
MOLUCCAS
MALAY PENINSULA
MALAYSIA
MEDAN
Kuala Lumpur
SINGAPORE
Borneo
Celebes
Sumatra
Cape Prai
Mount Kerinci 3800 m
PALEMBANG
INDONESIA
Ujungpandang
GREATER SUNDA ISLANDS
LESSER SUNDA ISLANDS
Dili
EAST TIMOR
JAKARTA
BANDUNG
Java
SEMARANG
SURABAYA
Malang
170° E
180°
170° W
50° N
40° N
20° N
10° N
0°
10° S
20° S
100° E
110° E
120° E
130° E
140° E
150° E
160° E
N
© 2005 Encyclopædia Britannica, Inc.

CHINA, MONGOLIA, KOREA, AND JAPAN

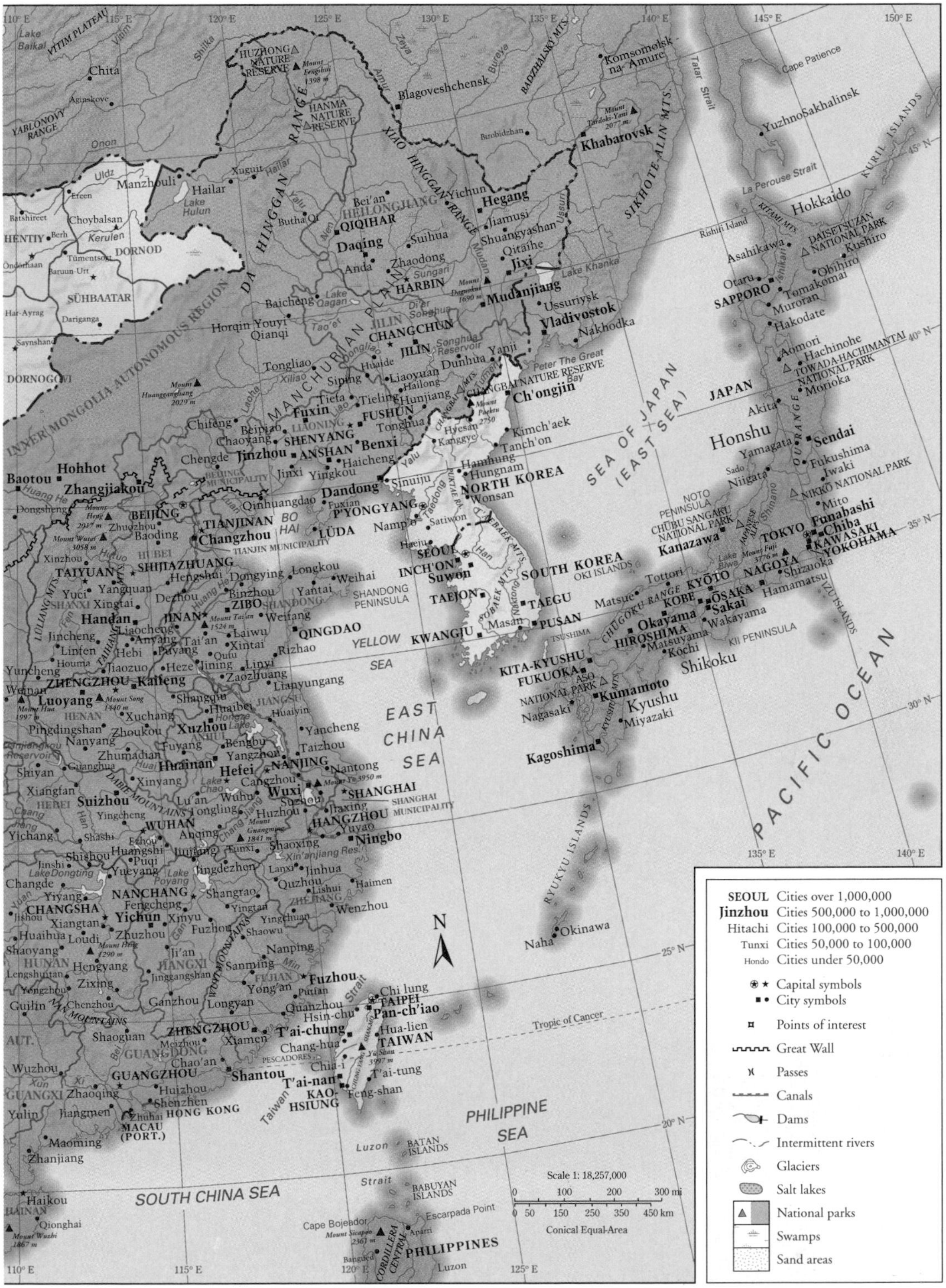
SEOUL Cities over 1,000,000
Jinzhou Cities 500,000 to 1,000,000
Hitachi Cities 100,000 to 500,000
Tunxi Cities 50,000 to 100,000
Hondo Cities under 50,000
Capital symbols
City symbols
Points of interest
Great Wall
Passes
Canals
Dams
Intermittent rivers
Glaciers
Salt lakes
National parks
Swamps
Sand areas
Scale 1: 18,257,000
0 100 200 300 mi
0 50 150 250 350 450 km
Conical Equal-Area
N
SEA OF JAPAN (EAST SEA)
YELLOW SEA
EAST CHINA SEA
PHILIPPINE SEA
SOUTH CHINA SEA
PACIFIC OCEAN
JAPAN
NORTH KOREA
SOUTH KOREA
TAIWAN
PHILIPPINES
HONG KONG
MACAU (PORT.)
INNER MONGOLIA AUTONOMOUS REGION
MANCHURIAN PLAIN
DA HINGGAN RANGE
XIAO HINGGAN RANGE
SIKHOTE-ALIN MTS.
Hokkaido
Honshu
Shikoku
Kyushu
Okinawa
RYUKYU ISLANDS
KURIL ISLANDS
Tropic of Cancer
BEIJING
TIANJINAN
SHANGHAI
NANJING
WUHAN
HARBIN
CHANGCHUN
SHENYANG
P'YONGYANG
SEOUL
PUSAN
TAEGU
TOKYO
YOKOHAMA
NAGOYA
KYOTO
OSAKA
KOBE
SAPPORO
TAIPEI
GUANGZHOU
Vladivostok
Khabarovsk
Blagoveshchensk
Chita
Hohhot
110° E
115° E
120° E
125° E
130° E
135° E
140° E
145° E
150° E
45° N
40° N
35° N
30° N
25° N
20° N

SOUTHEASTERN ASIA

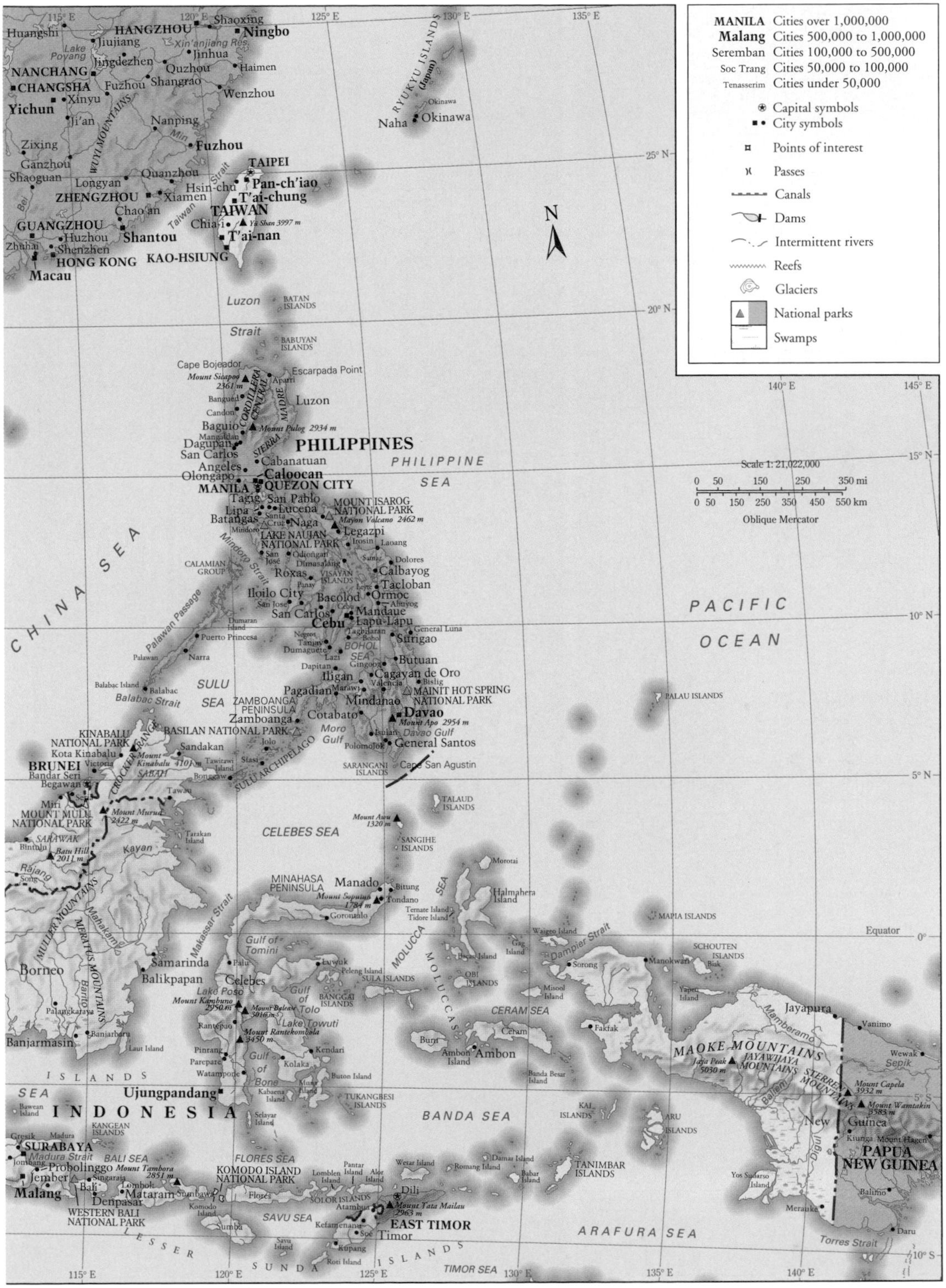
MANILA Cities over 1,000,000
Malang Cities 500,000 to 1,000,000
Seremban Cities 100,000 to 500,000
Soc Trang Cities 50,000 to 100,000
Tenasserim Cities under 50,000
Capital symbols
City symbols
Points of interest
Passes
Canals
Dams
Intermittent rivers
Reefs
Glaciers
National parks
Swamps
Scale 1: 21,022,000
0 50 150 250 350 mi
0 50 150 250 350 450 550 km
Oblique Mercator
N
115° E
120° E
125° E
130° E
135° E
140° E
145° E
25° N
20° N
15° N
10° N
5° N
0°
5° S
10° S
Equator
Huangshi
HANGZHOU
Shaoxing
Ningbo
Jiujiang
Lake Poyang
Xin'anjiang Res.
Jinhua
NANCHANG
Jingdezhen
Quzhou
Haimen
CHANGSHA
Fuzhou
Shangrao
Wenzhou
Xinyu
Yichun
WUYI MOUNTAINS
Ji'an
Nanping
Min
Zixing
Fuzhou
Ganzhou
TAIPEI
Shaoguan
Longyan
Quanzhou
Hsin-chu
Pan-ch'iao
ZHENGZHOU
Xiamen
T'ai-chung
Chao'an
Taiwan Strait
TAIWAN
GUANGZHOU
Chia-i
Yü Shan 3997 m
Huizhou
Shantou
T'ai-nan
Zhuhai
Shenzhen
HONG KONG
KAO-HSIUNG
Macau
RYUKYU ISLANDS (Japan)
Okinawa
Naha
Okinawa
Luzon Strait
BATAN ISLANDS
BABUYAN ISLANDS
Cape Bojeador
Escarpada Point
Mount Sicapoo 2361 m
Aparri
Bangued
CORDILLERA CENTRAL
SIERRA MADRE
Luzon
Candon
Baguio
Mount Pulog 2934 m
Mangaldan
Dagupan
PHILIPPINES
San Carlos
Cabanatuan
Angeles
PHILIPPINE SEA
Olongapo
Caloocan
MANILA
QUEZON CITY
Tagig
San Pablo
MOUNT ISAROG NATIONAL PARK
Lipa
Lucena
Batangas
Santa Cruz
Naga
Mayon Volcano 2462 m
Mindoro
LAKE NAUJAN NATIONAL PARK
Legazpi
Irosin
Laoang
San Jose
Odiongan
Dolores
CALAMIAN GROUP
Dimasalang
Samar
Mindoro Strait
Roxas
VISAYAN ISLANDS
Calbayog
Tacloban
SOUTH CHINA SEA
Panay
Leyte
Iloilo City
Bacolod
Ormoc
Palawan Passage
San Jose
Albuyog
San Carlos
Cebu
Mandaue
PACIFIC OCEAN
Dumaran Island
Cebu
Lapu-Lapu
General Luna
Puerto Princesa
Negros
Tagbilaran
Surigao
Tanjay
Bohol
Palawan
Narra
Dumaguete
BOHOL SEA
Butuan
Lazi
Dapitan
Gingoog
Iligan
Cagayan de Oro
Balabac Island
Balabac
SULU SEA
Bislig
Balabac Strait
Pagadian
Marawi
Valencia
MAINIT HOT SPRING NATIONAL PARK
ZAMBOANGA PENINSULA
Mindanao
PALAU ISLANDS
Zamboanga
Cotabato
Davao
Mount Apo 2954 m
KINABALU NATIONAL PARK
BASILAN NATIONAL PARK
Moro Gulf
Davao Gulf
Kota Kinabalu
Sandakan
Jolo
Isulan
General Santos
BRUNEI
CROCKER RANGE
Mount Kinabalu 4101 m
Tawitawi Island
Siasi
Polomolok
Bandar Seri Begawan
Victoria
SABAH
SULU ARCHIPELAGO
SARANGANI ISLANDS
Cape San Agustin
Bongao
Tawau
Miri
TALAUD ISLANDS
MOUNT MULU NATIONAL PARK
Mount Murud 2422 m
Mount Awu 1320 m
SARAWAK
Tarakan Island
CELEBES SEA
SANGIHE ISLANDS
Bintulu
Batu Hill 2011 m
Kayan
Rajang
Morotai
Song
MINAHASA PENINSULA
Manado
Bitung
Mount Sopután 1784 m
Tondano
Halmahera Island
MOLUCCA SEA
Ternate Island
Tidore Island
Gorontalo
MAPIA ISLANDS
Makassar Strait
MULLER MOUNTAINS
Mahakam
Gulf of Tomini
Waigeo Island
Gag Island
Dampier Strait
SCHOUTEN ISLANDS
MERATUS MOUNTAINS
Samarinda
Palu
Luwuk
Bacan Island
Sorong
Manokwari
Biak
Borneo
Balikpapan
Celebes
Peleng Island
SULA ISLANDS
OBI ISLANDS
MOLUCCAS
Misool Island
Yapen Island
Barito
Lake Poso
Gulf of Tolo
BANGGAI ISLANDS
CERAM SEA
Mount Kambuno 2950 m
Mount Balease 3016 m
Jayapura
Palangkaraya
Lake Towuti
Ceram
Mamberamo
Vanimo
Rantepao
Mount Rantekombola 3450 m
Fakfak
Banjarmasin
Banjarbaru
Laut Island
Pinrang
Kendari
Buru
Ambon
MAOKE MOUNTAINS
Wewak
Parepare
Gulf of Bone
Kolaka
Ambon Island
Jaya Peak 5030 m
JAYAWIJAYA MOUNTAINS
Sepik
ISLANDS
Watampone
Buton Island
Banda Besar Island
STERREN MOUNTAINS
JAVA SEA
Ujungpandang
Kabaena Island
Muna
TUKANGBESI ISLANDS
Mount Capela 3932 m
Bawean Island
INDONESIA
Mount Wamtakin 3583 m
KEI ISLANDS
ARU ISLANDS
Selayar Island
BANDA SEA
New Guinea
Gresik
Madura
KANGEAN ISLANDS
Baliem
Kiunga
Mount Hagen
SURABAYA
BALI SEA
Madura Strait
FLORES SEA
Damar Island
Digul
PAPUA NEW GUINEA
Jombang
Probolinggo
Mount Tambora 2851 m
KOMODO ISLAND NATIONAL PARK
Pantar Island
Wetar Island
Romang Island
Jember
Bali
Lomblen Island
Alor Island
TANIMBAR ISLANDS
Babar Island
Yos Sudarso Island
Malang
Singaraja
Lombok
Dili
Balimo
Denpasar
Mataram
Sumbawa
Flores
SOLOR ISLANDS
Mount Tata Mailau 2963 m
WESTERN BALI NATIONAL PARK
Komodo Island
Atambua
Merauke
SAVU SEA
EAST TIMOR
ARAFURA SEA
Sumba
Kefamenanu
Soe
Timor
Daru
LESSER SUNDA ISLANDS
Savu Island
Kupang
Torres Strait
Roti Island
TIMOR SEA

INDIA

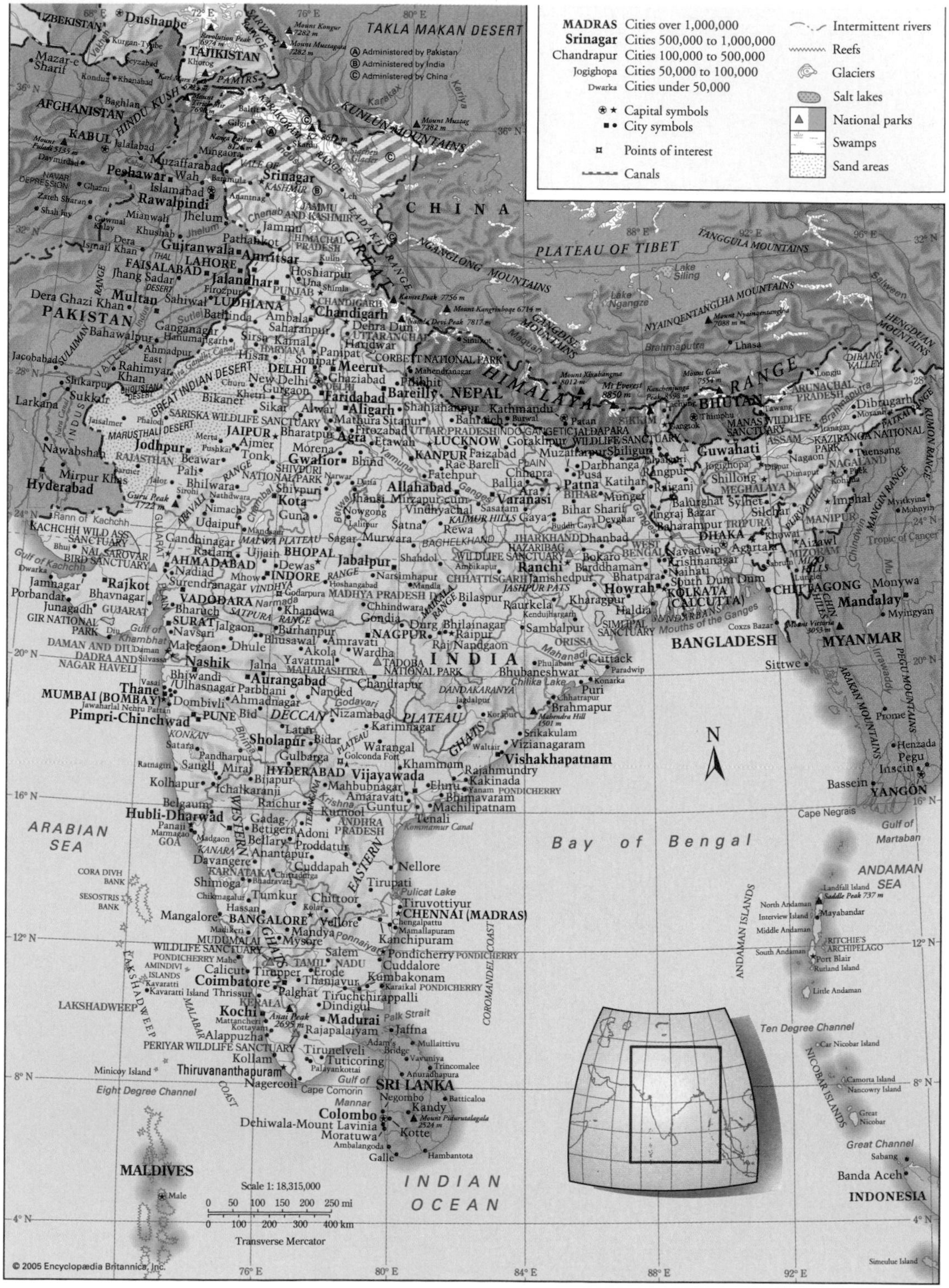
MADRAS Cities over 1,000,000
Srinagar Cities 500,000 to 1,000,000
Chandrapur Cities 100,000 to 500,000
Jogighopa Cities 50,000 to 100,000
Dwarka Cities under 50,000
Capital symbols
City symbols
Points of interest
Canals
Intermittent rivers
Reefs
Glaciers
Salt lakes
National parks
Swamps
Sand areas
Ⓐ Administered by Pakistan
Ⓑ Administered by India
Ⓒ Administered by China
TAKLA MAKAN DESERT
CHINA
PLATEAU OF TIBET
AFGHANISTAN
TAJIKISTAN
PAKISTAN
NEPAL
BHUTAN
BANGLADESH
MYANMAR
INDIA
SRI LANKA
MALDIVES
INDONESIA
HIMALAYA RANGE
GREAT INDIAN DESERT
DECCAN PLATEAU
ARABIAN SEA
Bay of Bengal
INDIAN OCEAN
ANDAMAN SEA
ANDAMAN ISLANDS
NICOBAR ISLANDS
KABUL
Islamabad
DELHI
New Delhi
MUMBAI (BOMBAY)
KOLKATA (CALCUTTA)
CHENNAI (MADRAS)
BANGALORE
HYDERABAD
Kathmandu
Thimphu
DHAKA
Colombo
Male
Scale 1: 18,315,000
0 50 100 150 200 250 mi
0 100 200 300 400 km
Transverse Mercator
© 2005 Encyclopædia Britannica, Inc.

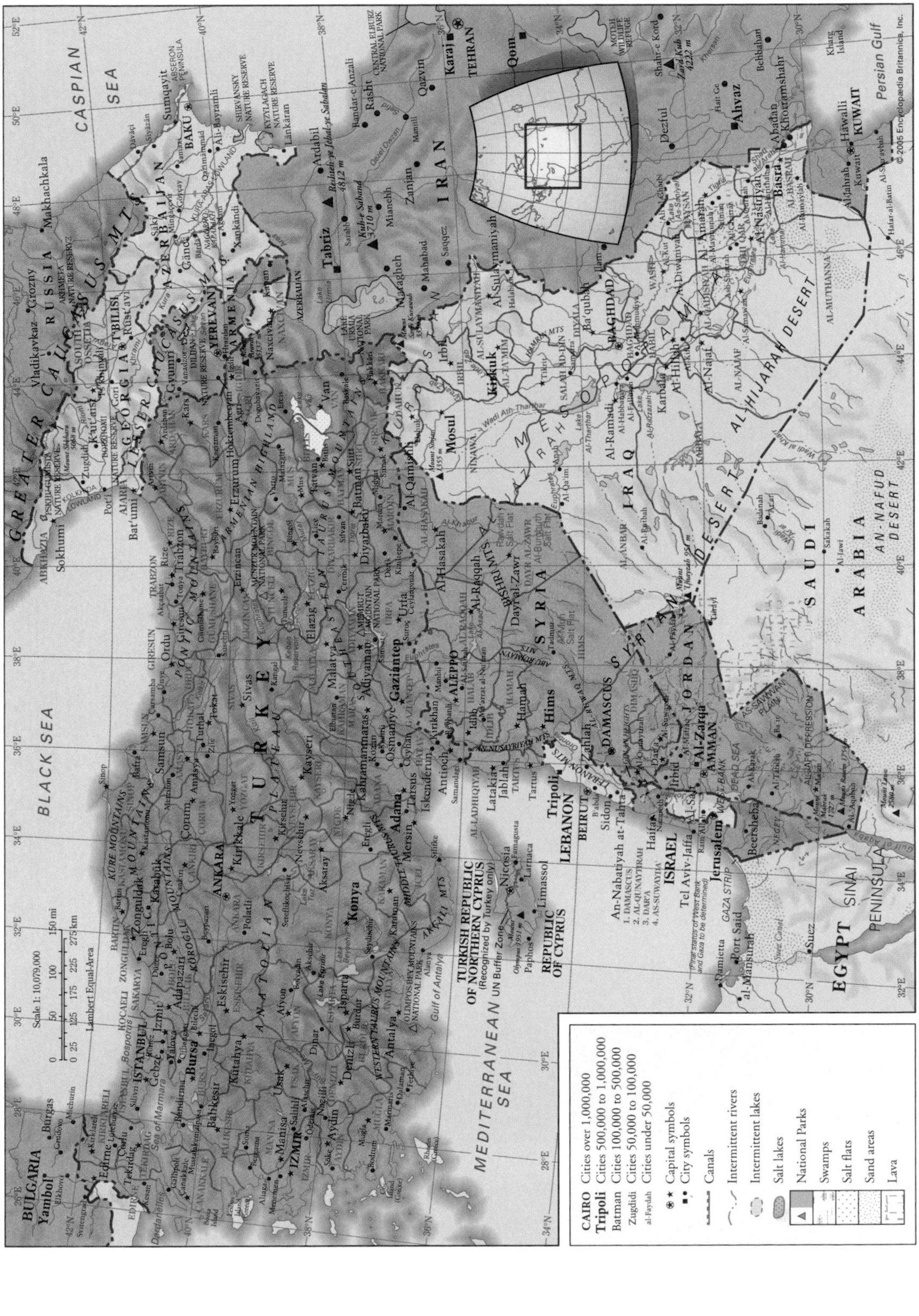
BLACK SEA
CASPIAN SEA
MEDITERRANEAN SEA
Persian Gulf
TURKEY
IRAN
IRAQ
SYRIA
JORDAN
LEBANON
ISRAEL
SAUDI ARABIA
EGYPT
KUWAIT
RUSSIA
GEORGIA
ARMENIA
AZERBAIJAN
BULGARIA
TURKISH REPUBLIC OF NORTHERN CYPRUS (Recognized by Turkey only)
REPUBLIC OF CYPRUS
ANKARA
BAGHDAD
DAMASCUS
BEIRUT
AMMAN
TEHRAN
Jerusalem
Scale 1:10,079,000
Lambert Equal-Area
CAIRO Cities over 1,000,000
Tripoli Cities 500,000 to 1,000,000
Batman Cities 100,000 to 500,000
Zugdidi Cities 50,000 to 100,000
al-Faydah Cities under 50,000
Capital symbols
City symbols
Canals
Intermittent rivers
Intermittent lakes
Salt lakes
National Parks
Swamps
Salt flats
Sand areas
Lava
© 2005 Encyclopædia Britannica, Inc.

AFRICA

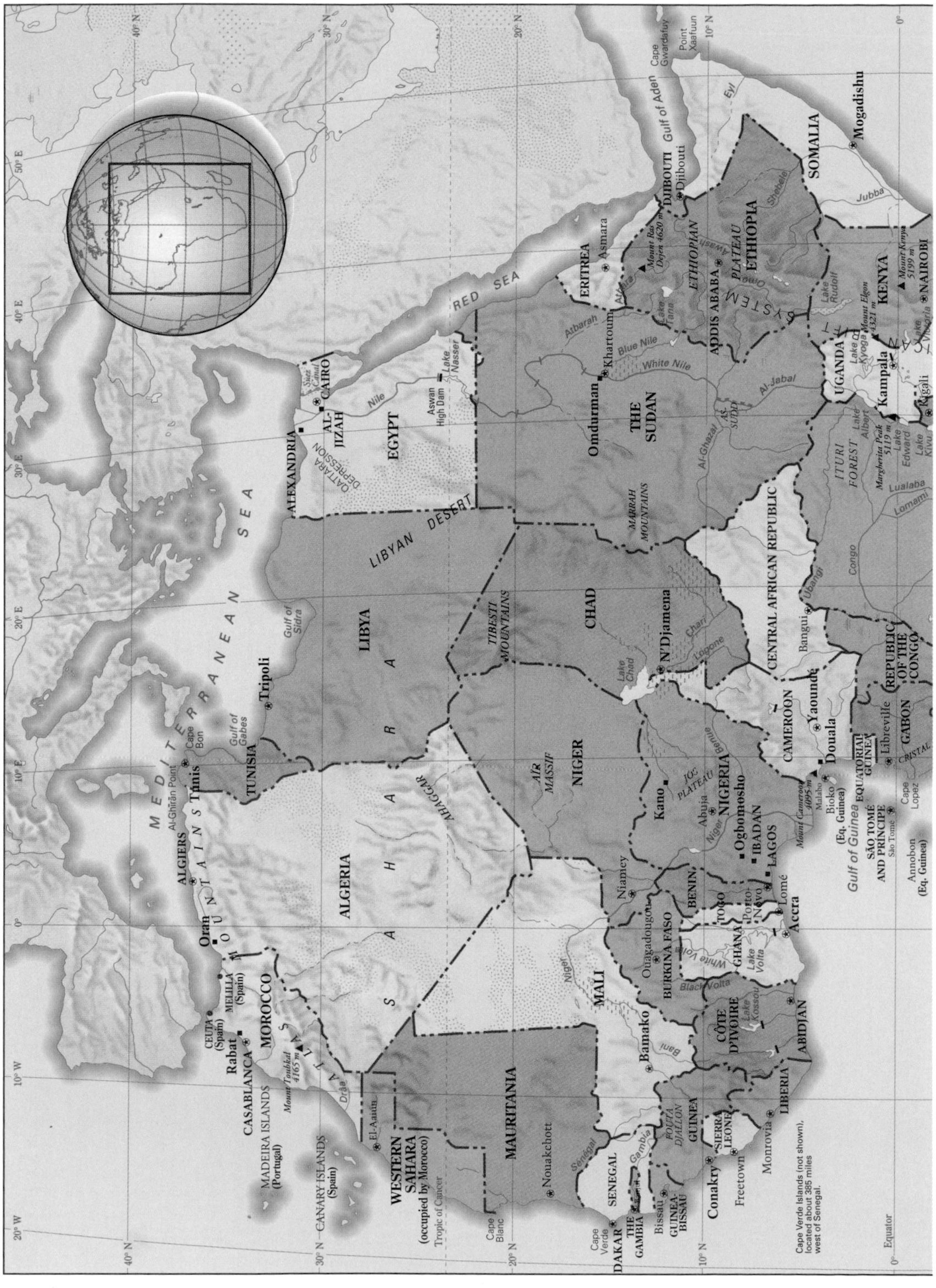

MEDITERRANEAN SEA
RED SEA
Gulf of Aden
Gulf of Guinea
Gulf of Sidra
Gulf of Gabes
SAHARA
LIBYAN DESERT
ATLAS MOUNTAINS
MOROCCO
Rabat
CASABLANCA
CEUTA (Spain)
MELILLA (Spain)
MADEIRA ISLANDS (Portugal)
CANARY ISLANDS (Spain)
WESTERN SAHARA (occupied by Morocco)
El-Aaiún
ALGERIA
ALGIERS
Oran
TUNISIA
Tunis
Cape Bon
LIBYA
Tripoli
EGYPT
CAIRO
AL-JIZAH
ALEXANDRIA
QATTARA DEPRESSION
Aswan High Dam
Lake Nasser
Suez Canal
Nile
MAURITANIA
Nouakchott
MALI
Bamako
NIGER
Niamey
AÏR MASSIF
CHAD
N'Djamena
Lake Chad
TIBESTI MOUNTAINS
THE SUDAN
Khartoum
Omdurman
MARRAH MOUNTAINS
Blue Nile
White Nile
ERITREA
Asmara
DJIBOUTI
Djibouti
ETHIOPIA
ADDIS ABABA
ETHIOPIAN PLATEAU
SOMALIA
Mogadishu
Cape Gwardafuy
Point Xaafuun
KENYA
NAIROBI
Mount Kenya 5199 m
UGANDA
Kampala
Kigali
SENEGAL
DAKAR
Cape Verde
THE GAMBIA
GUINEA-BISSAU
Bissau
GUINEA
Conakry
SIERRA LEONE
Freetown
LIBERIA
Monrovia
CÔTE D'IVOIRE
ABIDJAN
BURKINA FASO
Ouagadougou
GHANA
Accra
Lake Volta
TOGO
Lomé
BENIN
Porto-Novo
NIGERIA
Abuja
Kano
IBADAN
LAGOS
Ogbomosho
JOS PLATEAU
CAMEROON
Yaoundé
Douala
Mount Cameroon 4095 m
EQUATORIAL GUINEA
Malabo
Bioko (Eq. Guinea)
SÃO TOMÉ AND PRINCIPE
Annobon (Eq. Guinea)
GABON
Libreville
Cape Lopez
REPUBLIC OF THE CONGO
CENTRAL AFRICAN REPUBLIC
Bangui
ITURI FOREST
Tropic of Cancer
Equator
Cape Blanc
Cape Verde Islands (not shown), located about 385 miles west of Senegal.

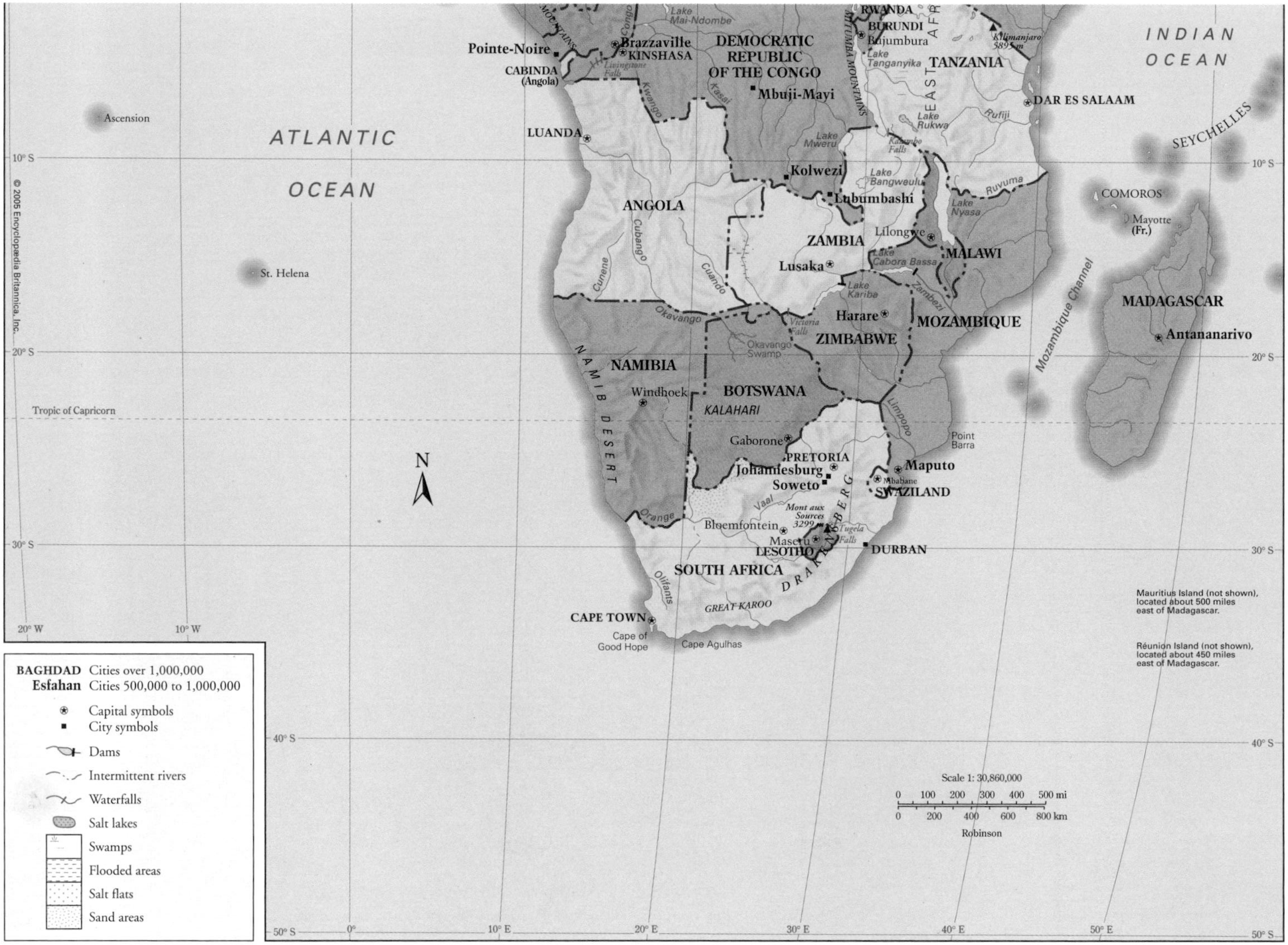

ATLANTIC
OCEAN
INDIAN
OCEAN
Ascension
St. Helena
Tropic of Capricorn
DEMOCRATIC
REPUBLIC
OF THE CONGO
ANGOLA
NAMIBIA
BOTSWANA
ZAMBIA
ZIMBABWE
MOZAMBIQUE
MALAWI
TANZANIA
RWANDA
BURUNDI
SOUTH AFRICA
LESOTHO
SWAZILAND
MADAGASCAR
COMOROS
SEYCHELLES
Mayotte (Fr.)
Pointe-Noire
CABINDA (Angola)
LUANDA
Brazzaville
KINSHASA
Mbuji-Mayi
Kolwezi
Lubumbashi
Lusaka
Harare
Lilongwe
Bujumbura
DAR ES SALAAM
Windhoek
Gaborone
PRETORIA
Johannesburg
Soweto
Bloemfontein
Maseru
Mbabane
Maputo
DURBAN
CAPE TOWN
Antananarivo
Cape of Good Hope
Cape Agulhas
Point Barra
NAMIB DESERT
KALAHARI
GREAT KAROO
MITUMBA MOUNTAINS
DRAKENSBERG
EAST AFRICA
Mozambique Channel
Lake Mai-Ndombe
Lake Tanganyika
Lake Mweru
Lake Bangweulu
Lake Rukwa
Lake Nyasa
Lake Kariba
Lake Cabora Bassa
Okavango Swamp
Victoria Falls
Kalambo Falls
Livingstone Falls
Tugela Falls
Mont aux Sources 3299 m
Kilimanjaro 5895 m
Congo
Kasai
Kwango
Cubango
Cuando
Cunene
Okavango
Zambezi
Limpopo
Orange
Vaal
Olifants
Rufiji
Ruvuma
Mauritius Island (not shown), located about 500 miles east of Madagascar.
Réunion Island (not shown), located about 450 miles east of Madagascar.
Scale 1: 30,860,000
0 100 200 300 400 500 mi
0 200 400 600 800 km
Robinson
N
10° S
20° S
30° S
40° S
50° S
20° W
10° W
0°
10° E
20° E
30° E
40° E
50° E
BAGHDAD Cities over 1,000,000
Esfahan Cities 500,000 to 1,000,000
Capital symbols
City symbols
Dams
Intermittent rivers
Waterfalls
Salt lakes
Swamps
Flooded areas
Salt flats
Sand areas

ATLAS

NORTHERN AFRICA

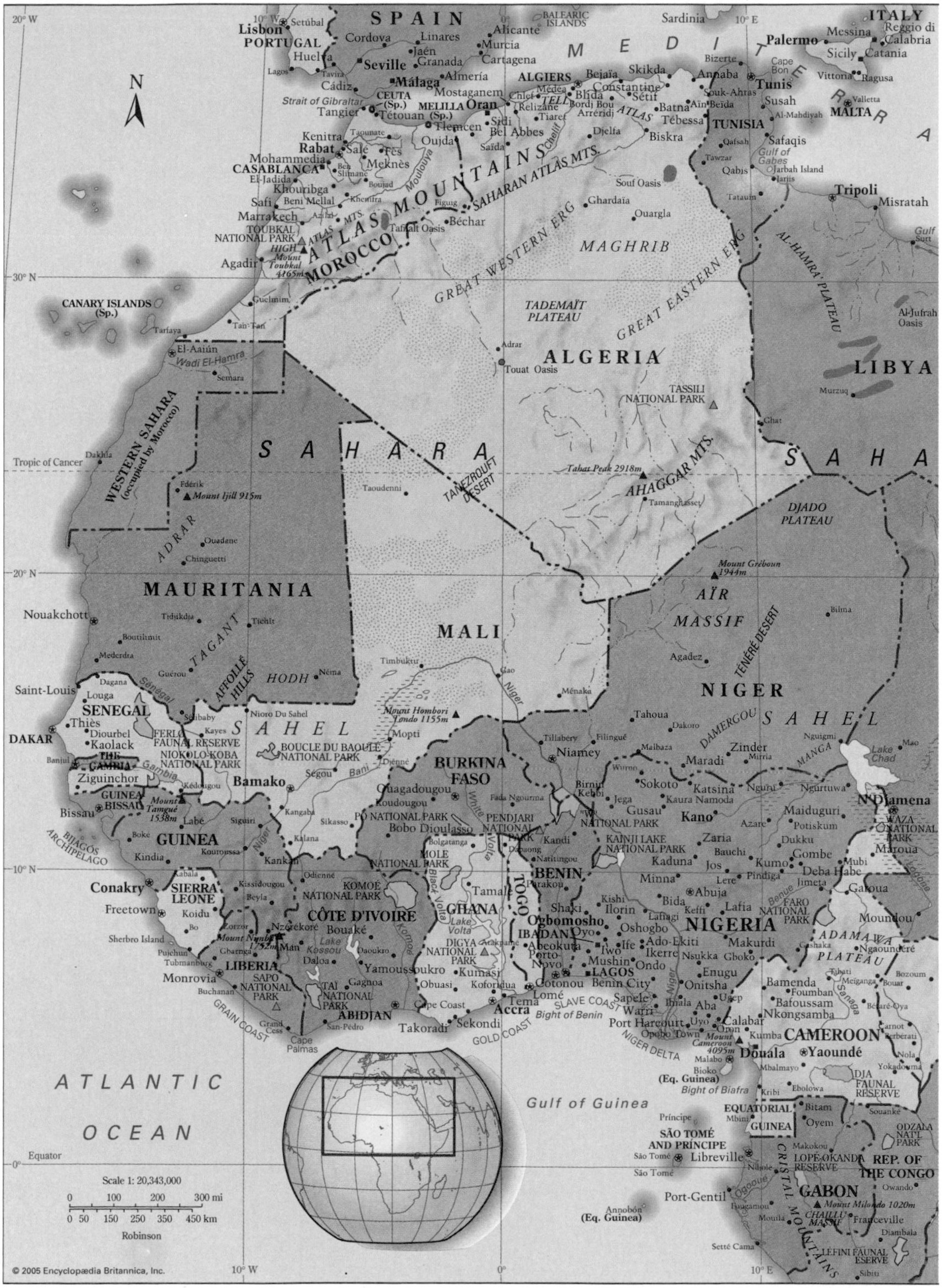

NORTHERN AFRICA

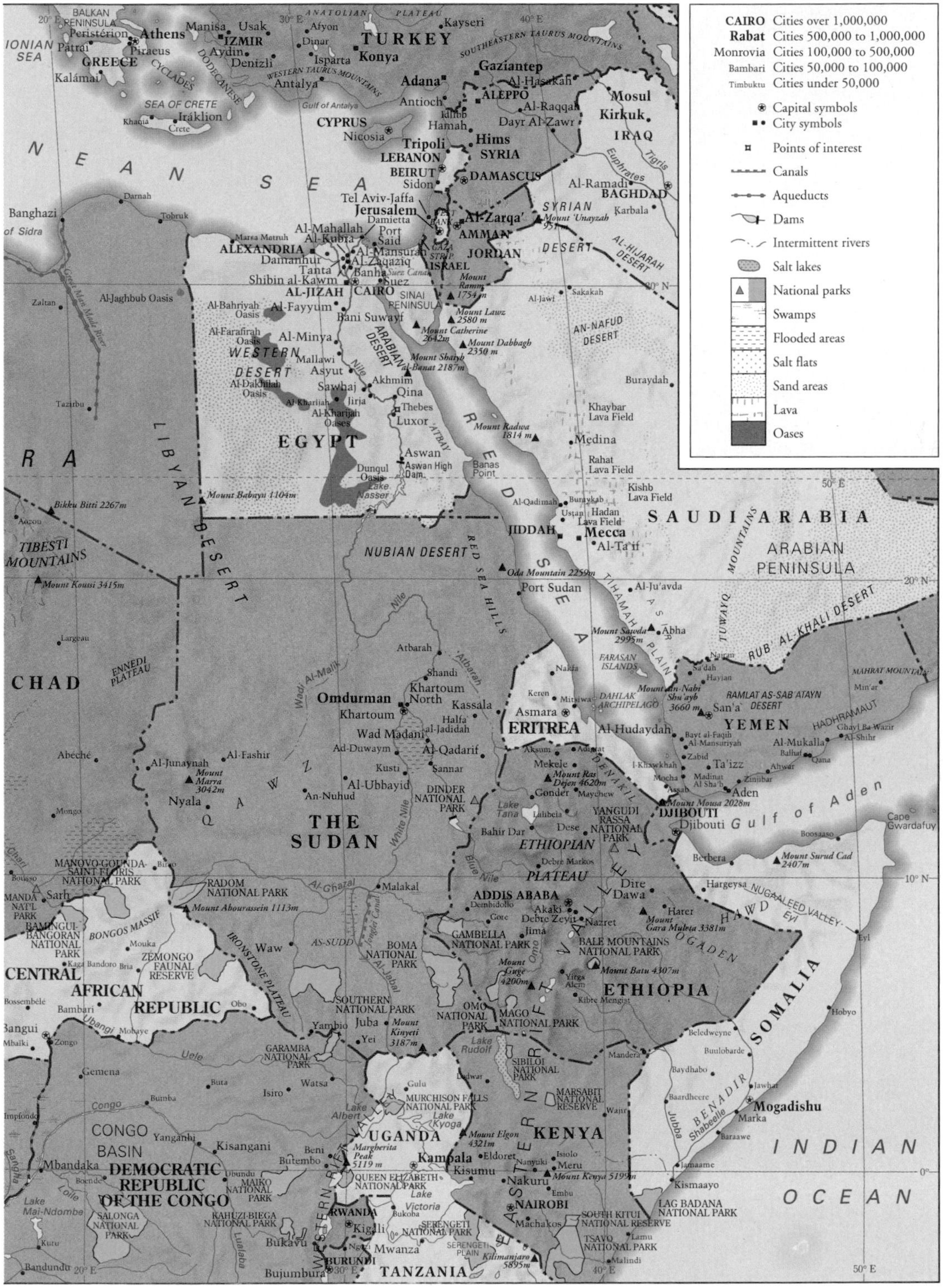

SOUTHERN AFRICA

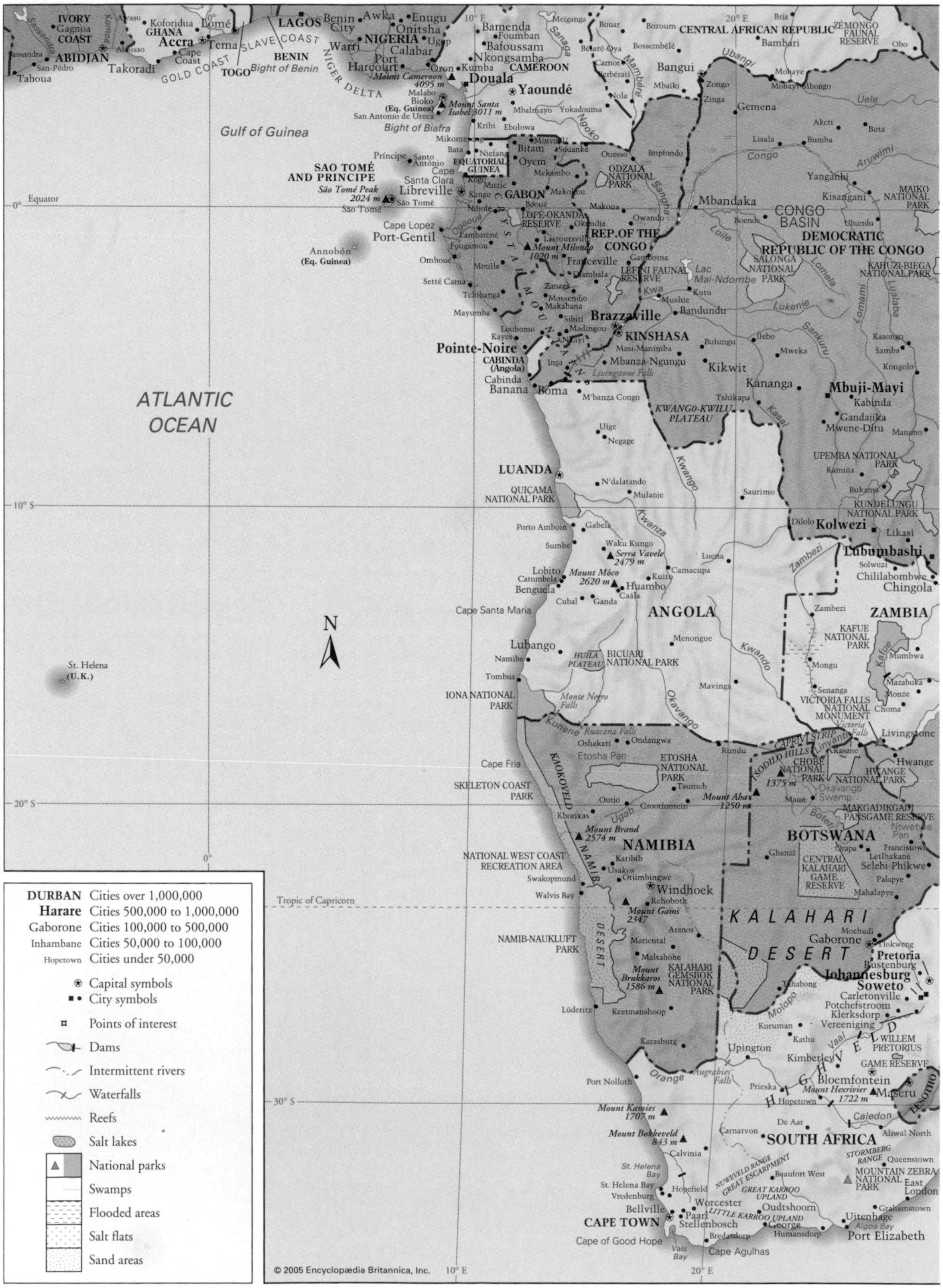

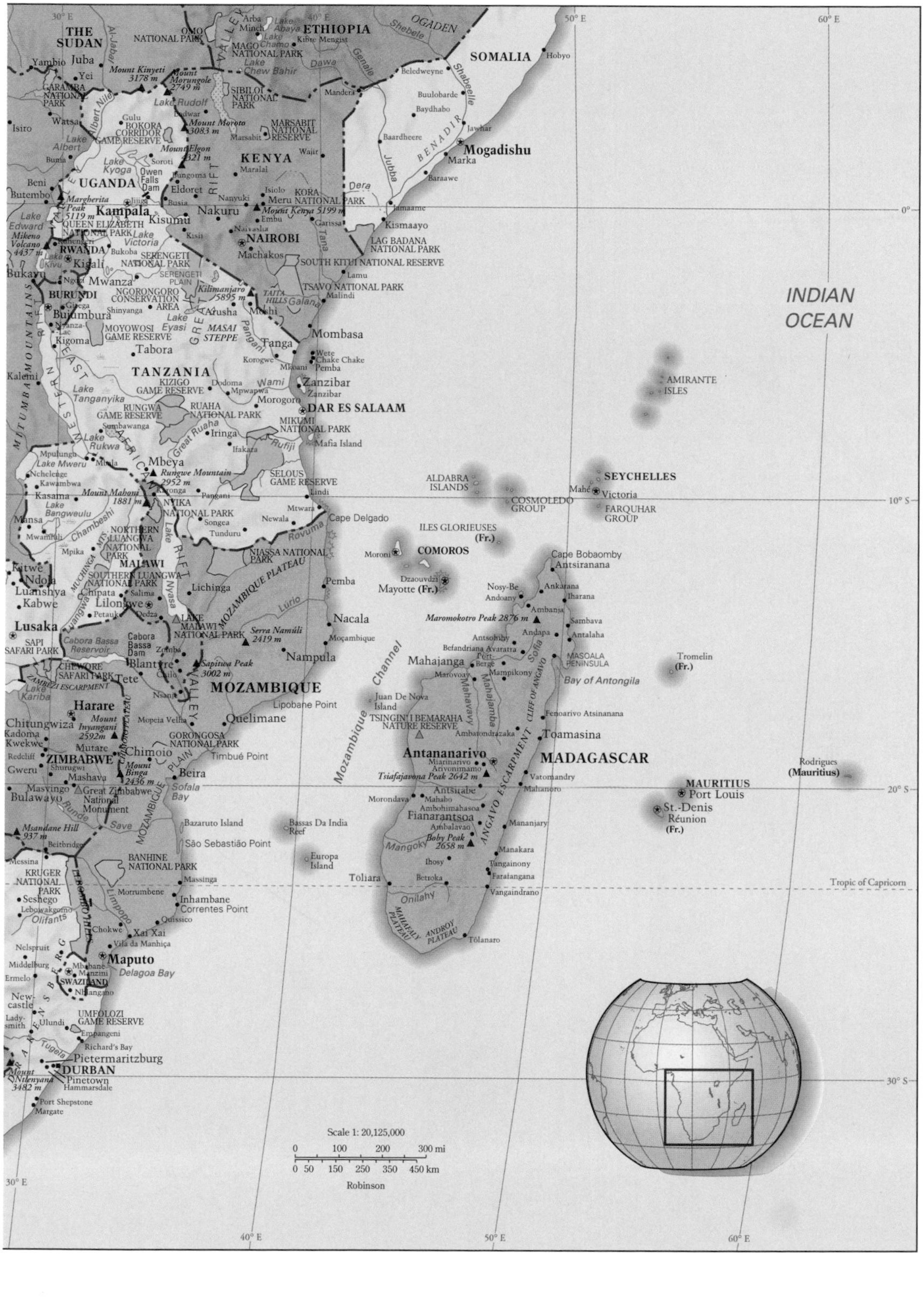
ETHIOPIA
SOMALIA
THE SUDAN
UGANDA
KENYA
RWANDA
BURUNDI
TANZANIA
MALAWI
MOZAMBIQUE
ZIMBABWE
SWAZILAND
MADAGASCAR
COMOROS
SEYCHELLES
MAURITIUS
INDIAN OCEAN
Mozambique Channel
Juba
Mogadishu
Kampala
Nairobi
Kigali
Bujumbura
Mombasa
Zanzibar
DAR ES SALAAM
Lusaka
Lilongwe
Harare
Maputo
DURBAN
Pietermaritzburg
Antananarivo
Toamasina
Fianarantsoa
Toliara
Mahajanga
Antsiranana
Moroni
Victoria
Port Louis
St.-Denis
Réunion
(Fr.)
Mayotte (Fr.)
Tromelin
Rodrigues
(Mauritius)
AMIRANTE ISLES
ALDABRA ISLANDS
COSMOLEDO GROUP
FARQUHAR GROUP
ILES GLORIEUSES
Bay of Antongila
Tropic of Capricorn
Lake Victoria
Lake Tanganyika
Lake Rukwa
Lake Mweru
Lake Kariba
Delagoa Bay
Sofala Bay
Mount Kilimanjaro 5895 m
Mount Kenya 5199 m
Margherita Peak 5119 m
Maromokotro Peak 2876 m
Scale 1: 20,125,000
0 100 200 300 mi
0 50 150 250 350 450 km
Robinson
30° E
40° E
50° E
60° E
0°
10° S
20° S
30° S

ATLAS

ARABIAN PENINSULA

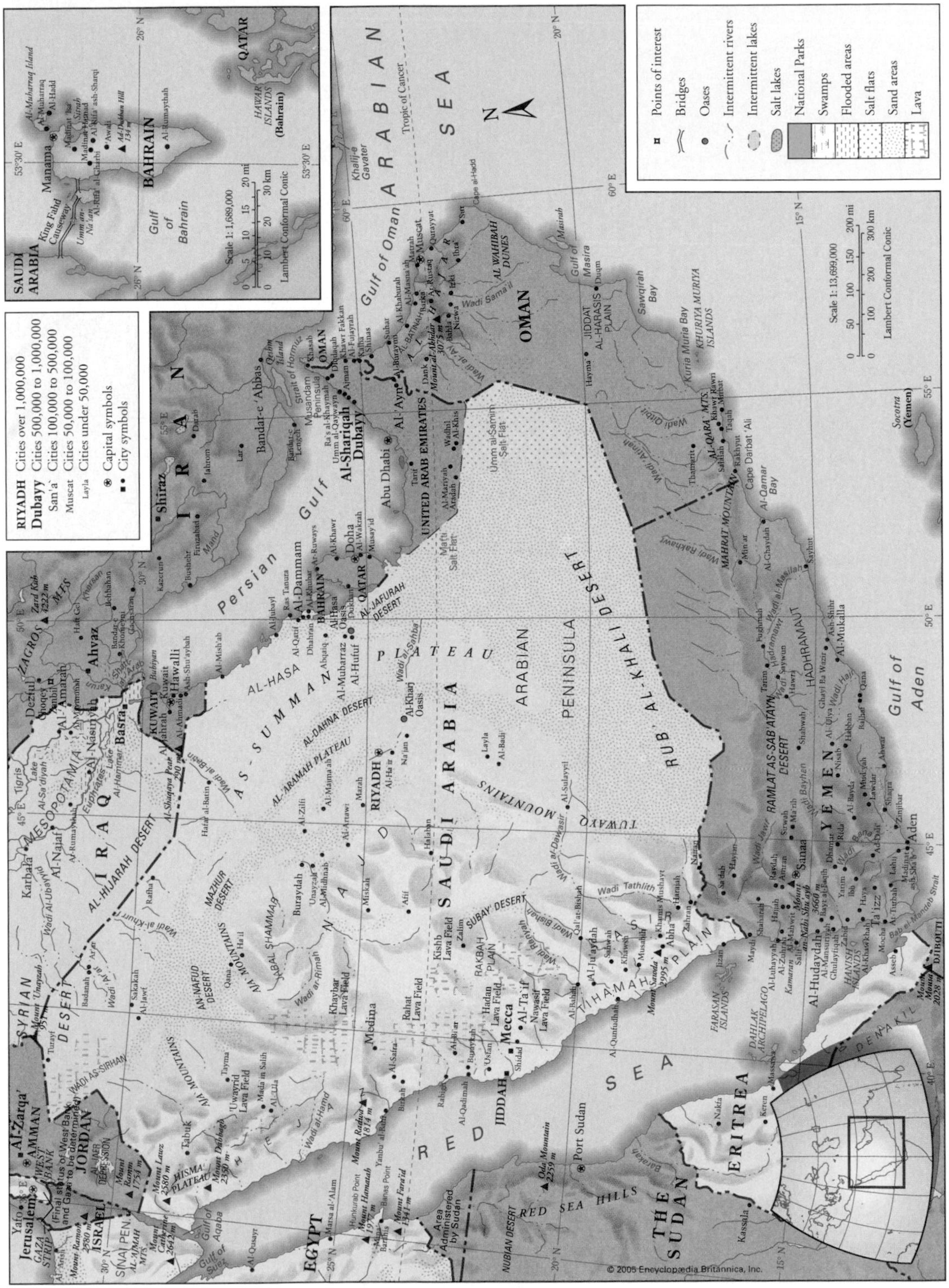

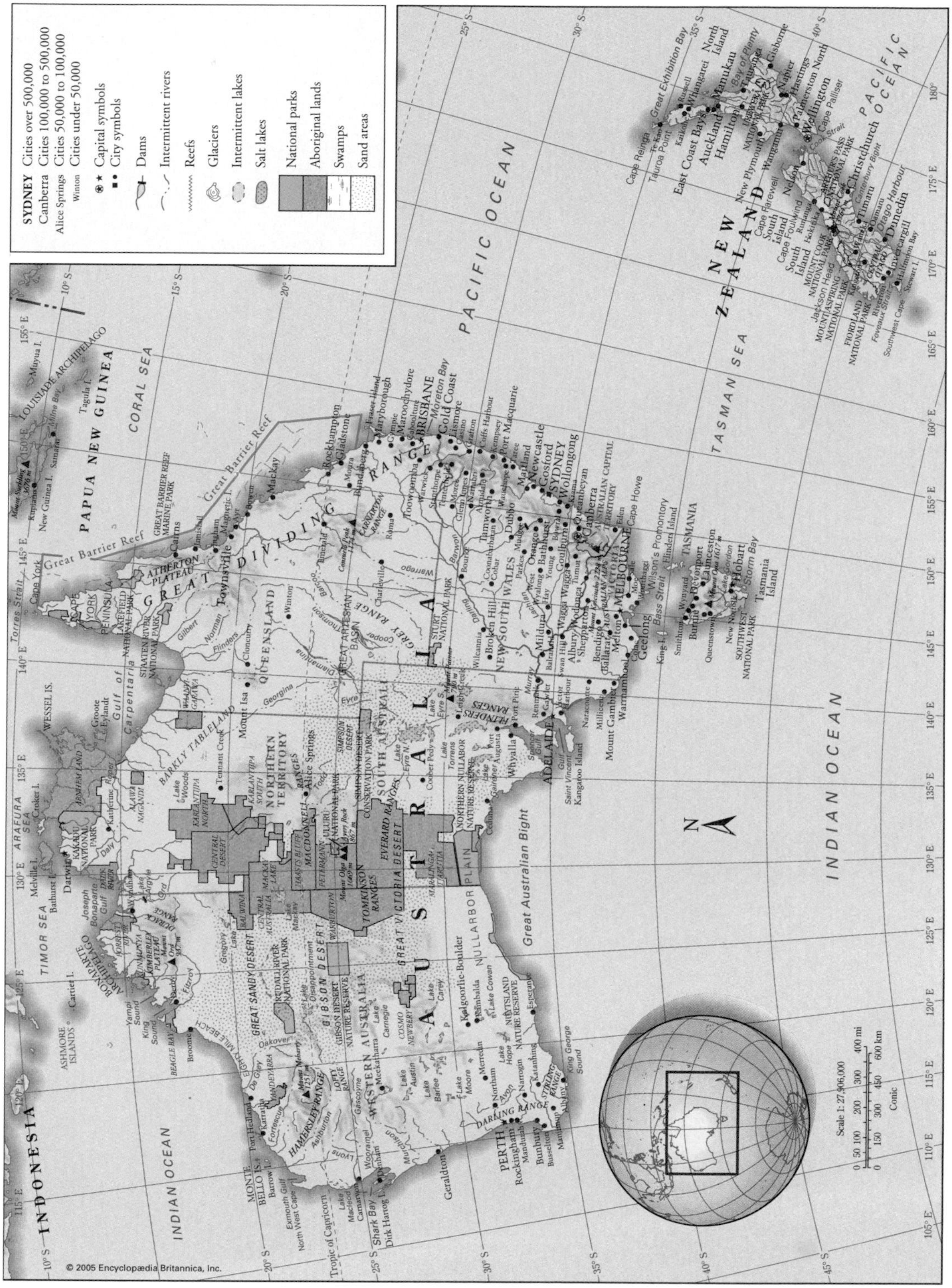
SYDNEY Cities over 500,000
Canberra Cities 100,000 to 500,000
Alice Springs Cities 50,000 to 100,000
Winton Cities under 50,000
Capital symbols
City symbols
Dams
Intermittent rivers
Reefs
Glaciers
Intermittent lakes
Salt lakes
National parks
Aboriginal lands
Swamps
Sand areas
AUSTRALIA
NEW ZEALAND
PAPUA NEW GUINEA
INDONESIA
PACIFIC OCEAN
INDIAN OCEAN
TASMAN SEA
CORAL SEA
TIMOR SEA
ARAFURA SEA
Gulf of Carpentaria
Great Australian Bight
Great Barrier Reef
GREAT DIVIDING RANGE
WESTERN AUSTRALIA
NORTHERN TERRITORY
QUEENSLAND
SOUTH AUSTRALIA
NEW SOUTH WALES
VICTORIA
TASMANIA
AUSTRALIAN CAPITAL TERRITORY
GREAT SANDY DESERT
GIBSON DESERT
GREAT VICTORIA DESERT
SIMPSON DESERT
NULLARBOR PLAIN
BARKLY TABLELAND
PERTH
ADELAIDE
MELBOURNE
SYDNEY
BRISBANE
Canberra
Darwin
Alice Springs
Hobart
Newcastle
Gold Coast
Townsville
Cairns
Geelong
Wollongong
North Island
South Island
Auckland
Wellington
Christchurch
Hamilton
Dunedin
Manukau
Scale 1:27,906,000
Conic
© 2005 Encyclopædia Britannica, Inc.

ATLAS

OCEANIA

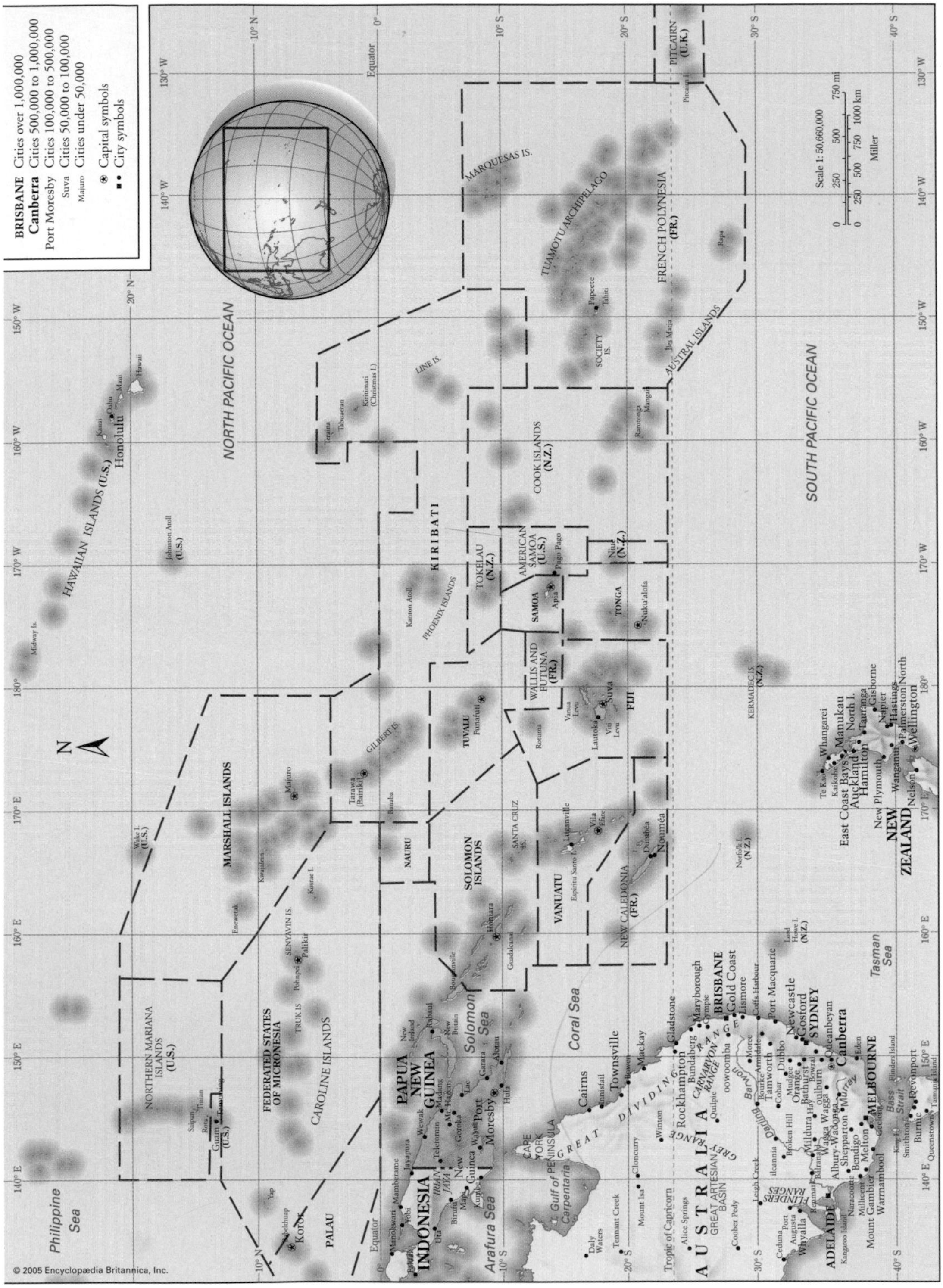
BRISBANE Cities over 1,000,000
Canberra Cities 500,000 to 1,000,000
Port Moresby Cities 100,000 to 500,000
Suva Cities 50,000 to 100,000
Majuro Cities under 50,000
Capital symbols
City symbols
Scale 1: 50,660,000
Miller
NORTH PACIFIC OCEAN
SOUTH PACIFIC OCEAN
Philippine Sea
Coral Sea
Solomon Sea
Arafura Sea
Tasman Sea
Gulf of Carpentaria
Equator
Tropic of Capricorn
HAWAIIAN ISLANDS (U.S.)
Honolulu
Hawaii
Maui
Oahu
Kauai
Midway Is.
Johnston Atoll (U.S.)
Wake I. (U.S.)
NORTHERN MARIANA ISLANDS (U.S.)
Saipan
Tinian
Rota
Guam (U.S.)
MARSHALL ISLANDS
Majuro
Enewetak
Kwajalein
FEDERATED STATES OF MICRONESIA
CAROLINE ISLANDS
SENYAVIN IS.
Palikir
Pohnpei
TRUK IS.
Kosrae I.
Yap
PALAU
Koror
KIRIBATI
GILBERT IS.
Tarawa (Bairiki)
Banaba
PHOENIX ISLANDS
Kanton Atoll
LINE IS.
Kiritimati (Christmas I.)
Tabuaeran
Teraina
NAURU
TUVALU
Funafuti
SOLOMON ISLANDS
Honiara
Guadalcanal
Bougainville
SANTA CRUZ IS.
VANUATU
Vila
Espiritu Santo I.
NEW CALEDONIA (FR.)
Nouméa
Norfolk I. (N.Z.)
Lord Howe I. (N.Z.)
FIJI
Suva
Vanua Levu
Viti Levu
Lautoka
Rotuma
WALLIS AND FUTUNA (FR.)
SAMOA
Apia
AMERICAN SAMOA (U.S.)
Pago Pago
TOKELAU (N.Z.)
TONGA
Nuku'alofa
Niue (N.Z.)
COOK ISLANDS (N.Z.)
Rarotonga
Mangaia
KERMADEC IS. (N.Z.)
FRENCH POLYNESIA (FR.)
MARQUESAS IS.
TUAMOTU ARCHIPELAGO
SOCIETY IS.
Papeete
Tahiti
AUSTRAL ISLANDS
Rapa
PITCAIRN (U.K.)
Pitcairn I.
PAPUA NEW GUINEA
Port Moresby
New Guinea
New Britain
New Ireland
Rabaul
Lae
Madang
Wewak
Mt. Hagen
Goroka
Alotau
INDONESIA
IRIAN JAYA
Jayapura
Manokwari
Sorong
Biak
AUSTRALIA
CAPE YORK PENINSULA
GREAT DIVIDING RANGE
GREAT ARTESIAN BASIN
GREY RANGE
FLINDERS RANGES
CARNARVON RANGE
Cairns
Townsville
Mackay
Rockhampton
Gladstone
Bundaberg
Maryborough
Gympie
BRISBANE
Gold Coast
Lismore
Toowoomba
Coffs Harbour
Port Macquarie
Tamworth
Armidale
Dubbo
Orange
Bathurst
Newcastle
Gosford
SYDNEY
Wollongong
Queanbeyan
Canberra
Wagga Wagga
Albury-Wodonga
Shepparton
Bendigo
Ballarat
MELBOURNE
Geelong
Warrnambool
Mount Gambier
Mildura
Broken Hill
Bourke
Cobar
ADELAIDE
Whyalla
Port Augusta
Ceduna
Kangaroo Island
Coober Pedy
Alice Springs
Tennant Creek
Mount Isa
Cloncurry
Winton
Daly Waters
Bass Strait
Flinders Island
Devonport
Burnie
Queenstown
Tasmania (island)
NEW ZEALAND
North I.
Whangarei
Auckland
Manukau
East Coast Bays
Hamilton
Tauranga
Gisborne
Napier
Hastings
New Plymouth
Wanganui
Palmerston North
Wellington
Nelson
© 2005 Encyclopædia Britannica, Inc.

THESAURUS

Preface to the Thesaurus

This work is more than just a list of synonyms. It is a concise guide to the understanding and use of synonyms. While other books called thesauruses often give just a list of words that are similar in meaning, this work is intended for people who want to learn about the slight differences among English words with similar meanings and to choose the right word for the right situation.

This book consists of a collection of articles that discuss the distinctions in use or meaning among synonyms. In some cases the differences are in range of meaning. In some cases the differences may be in connotations, ideas that come from associations with the word which color the meaning. In some cases the differences may be in restrictions established by current usage.

Each main entry begins with a list of words that are synonymous and a brief statement of the meaning the synonyms have in common:

> **abdicate, renounce, resign** mean to give up formally and definitely.

After this initial sentence, there is a series of statements describing the differences that distinguish the synonyms from one another. The information is clarified by typical examples of use, set inside angle brackets. When the word being discriminated has one or more antonyms, these are indicated by a bold italic word ***antonym***.

> ***Abdicate*** implies a giving up of sovereign power ⟨the king was forced to *abdicate*⟩ or sometimes an evading of responsibility ⟨by walking out he *abdicated* his rights as a father⟩. ***antonym:*** assume, usurp

In addition, the book also contains thousands of cross-reference entries. By means of these entries, every word discussed in each article is entered at its own alphabetical place, followed by a cross-reference to the main entry where it is discussed:

> **desert** See ABANDON.

When a word is discussed at more than one entry and is treated as the same part of speech at each entry, numbered cross-references list all of the entries at which that word is treated:

> **casual 1.** See ACCIDENTAL. **2.** See RANDOM.
> **abandon** *vb* **1. Abandon, desert, forsake** mean to leave without intending to return. . . .
> **2.** See RELINQUISH.

When a word is discussed at more than one entry *and* as a different part of speech, separate cross-reference entries appear:

> **humor** *vb* See INDULGE.
> **humor** *n* **1.** See WIT. **2.** See INDULGE.
> **need** *n* **Need, necessity, exigency** mean a pressing lack of something essential. . . .
> **need** *vb* See LACK.

In the entries listed above, the entry word is followed by an italic part-of-speech label. Such a part-of-speech label appears whenever the same entry word is listed more than once, and it is intended to help the reader identify the appropriate entry and reference. The meanings of the abbreviations used in part-of-speech labels in this book are as follows:

adj adjective   *n* noun   *adv* adverb   *vb* verb

Some cross-references are followed by a number or a part-of-speech label. References like this direct the reader to the desired article when the same word serves as a main-entry word for more than one article:

adventitious See ACCIDENTAL 2.
alternative See CHOICE *n*.
correlate See PARALLEL *n* 2.

English and the Thesaurus

A Brief Look at the English Language

The English language is peculiarly rich in synonyms, which is not surprising considering its history. Over its history of more than a thousand years the language of England has woven together strands of the Celtic language, of earlier Roman words and later church Latin, and then of the Germanic tongues of the early invaders from the European continent.

Because English has so many words derived from Latin and from Greek by way of Latin, the casual observer might guess that English would be—like French, Spanish, and Italian—a Romance language derived from the Latin spoken by the ancient Romans. But although the Romans made a few visits to Britain in the first century A.D., long before the English were there (before there even was an England), English is not a Romance language. English is actually a member of the Germanic group, and thus a sister of such modern languages as Swedish, Dutch, and German.

We often speak of English as having its beginnings with the conquest and settlement of a large part of the island of Britain by Germanic tribes from the European continent in the fifth century, although the earliest written documents of the language belong to the seventh century. Of course these Germanic peoples did not suddenly begin to speak a new language the moment they arrived in England. They spoke the closely related Germanic languages of their continental homelands. And it was from these languages that the English language developed. In fact, the words *English* and *England* are derived from the name of one of these early Germanic peoples, the Angles.

From its beginnings English has been gradually changing and evolving, as language tends to do. To get a sense of how far evolution has taken us from the early tongue, we need only glance at a sample of Old English. Here is the beginning of the Lord's Prayer:

> **Fæder ūre, þu þe eart on heofonum: si þin nama gehālgod. Tōbecume þin rīce. Geweorþe þin willa on eorþan swāswā on heofonum.**

There is a certain continuity between the vocabularies of Old English and Modern English. Of the thousand most common Modern English words, four-fifths are of Old English origin. Of the foreign languages affecting the Old English vocabulary, the most influential was Latin. Church terms especially, like *priest, vicar,* and *mass,* were borrowed from Latin, the language of the church. But words belonging to aspects of life other than the strictly religious, like *cap, inch, kiln, school,* and *noon,* also entered Old English from Latin. The Scandinavians, too, influenced the language of England during the Old English period. From the eighth century on, Vikings from Scandinavia raided and eventually settled in England, especially in the north and the east. In a few instances the influence of a Scandinavian word gave an English word a new meaning. Thus our *dream,* which meant "joy" in Old English, probably took on the now familiar sense "a series of thoughts, images, or emotions occurring during sleep" because its Scandinavian relative *draumr* had that meaning. A considerable number of common words, like *cross, fellow, ball,* and *raise,* also became naturalized as a result of the Viking incursions over the years. The initial consonants *sk-* often reveal the Scandinavian ancestry of words like *sky, skin,* and *skirt,* the last of which has persisted side by side with its native English relative *shirt.*

Additional foreign influence on English came about principally as a result of the Norman Conquest of 1066, which brought England under the rule of French speakers. The English language, though it did not die, was for a long time of only secondary importance in political, social, and cultural matters. French became the language of the upper classes in England. The lower classes continued to speak English, but many French words were borrowed into English. To this circumstance we owe, for example, a number of distinctions between the words used for animals in the pasture and the words for those animals prepared to be eaten. Living animals were under the care of English-speaking peasants; cooked, the animals were served to the French-speaking nobility. *Swine* in the sty became *pork* at the table, *cow* and *calf* became *beef* and *veal.* This Anglo-French also had an influence on the words used in the courts, such as *indict, jury,* and *verdict.*

English eventually reestablished itself as the major language of England, but the language did not lose its habit of borrowing. English still derives much of its learned vocabulary from Latin and Greek. We have also borrowed words from nearly all of the languages in Europe. From Modern French we have such words as *bikini, cliché,* and *discotheque;* from Dutch, *easel, gin,* and *yacht;* from German, *delicatessen, pretzel,* and *swindler;* from Swedish, *ombudsman* and *smorgasbord.* From Italian we have taken *carnival, fiasco,* and *pizza,* as well as many terms from music (including *piano*).

From the period of the Renaissance voyages of discovery through the days when the sun never set upon the British Empire and up to the present, a steady stream of new words has flowed into the language to match the new objects and experiences English speakers have encountered all over the globe. English has drawn words from India (*bandanna*), China (*gung ho*), and Japan (*tycoon*). Arabic has been a prolific source of words over the centuries, giving us *hazard, lute, magazine,* and a host of words beginning with the letter *a,* from *algebra* to *azimuth.*

How Meaning Has Developed

Whether borrowed or created, a word generally begins its life in English with one meaning. Yet no living language is static, and in time words develop new meanings and lose old ones. A word used in a specific sense may be extended, or generalized, to cover a host of similar senses. Our word *virtue* is derived from the Latin *virtus,* which originally meant "manliness." But we apply the term to any excellent quality possessed by man, woman, or beast; even inanimate objects have their *virtues.* In Latin, *decimare* meant "to select and kill a tenth part of" and described the Roman way of dealing with mutinous troops. Its English descendant, *decimate,* now simply means "to destroy a large part of."

The development of meaning can easily be followed in this example. Today when we think of the word *fast* we probably think of the sense involving great speed. But the word's oldest meaning is quite different: "firmly placed" or "immovable," as in "tent pegs set fast in the ground" and "a fast and impassable barrier." It is easy to see how this sense developed expanded uses, such as "a door that is stuck fast and won't open." We see something of this sense in the expression "fast asleep."

In time, users added senses, some of which are common today, from being "unable to leave something, as one's bed" to being "stable and unchangeable," which we find in such uses as "hard and fast rules" or "clothes that are colorfast". Then came the sense of being "steadfast" or "firmly or totally loyal," as in "they were fast friends."

The sense that is most common today, "quick, speedy," came later. It probably developed from an obsolete sense of the adverb meaning "near at hand," which may have led to another meaning "soon." From this obsolete sense of "soon" it is just a short step, in terms of language development, to the sense meaning "quick."

In addition to what could be thought of as a horizontal dimension of change—the extension or contraction of meaning—words also may rise and fall along a vertical scale of value. Perfectly unobjectionable words are sometimes used disparagingly or sarcastically. If we say, "You're a fine one to talk," we are using *fine* in a sense quite different from its usual meaning. If a word is used often enough in negative contexts, the negative coloring may eventually become an integral part of the meaning of the word. A *villain* was once a peasant. His social standing was not high, perhaps, but he was certainly not necessarily a scoundrel. *Scavenger* originally designated the collector of a particular kind of tax in late medieval England. *Puny* meant no more than "younger" when it first passed from French into English and its spelling was transformed. Only later did it acquire the derogatory meaning more familiar to us now.

The opposite process seems to take place somewhat less frequently, but change of meaning to a more positive sense does occasionally occur. In the fourteenth century *nice,* for example, meant "foolish." Its present meaning, of course, is quite different, and the attitude it conveys seems to have undergone a complete reversal from contempt to approval.

What Qualifies as a Synonym?

It is not surprising that with so much to work with, users of English have long been interested in synonyms as an element both in accuracy and in elegance in their expression. Synonyms relieve monotony and enhance expressiveness.

Earlier writers were clear on the meaning of *synonym.* They viewed synonyms as words meaning the same thing. Unfortunately, during the last century or so this simple, clearcut meaning has become blurred. To many publishers of thesauruses the term has come to mean little more than words that are somewhat similar in meaning. But this loose definition is unsuitable for many people, since it deprives them of the guidance needed for finding the precise word in a particular context.

This thesaurus takes a different approach to describing the nature of a synonym. Groups of synonyms are organized around a segment of meaning that two or more words have in common. In order to create these groups, one has to analyze each word carefully, ignoring nonessential aspects such as connotations and implications and try to isolate the basic meaning, which we call an *elementary meaning*.

When we look at the synonymous relationship of words in terms of elementary meanings, the process of choosing synonyms is simpler and more exact. For example, it is easy to see that no term more restricted in definition than another word can be its synonym. For example, *station wagon* and *minivan* cannot be synonyms of *automobile*, nor can *biceps* be a synonym of *muscle*; even though a very definite relationship exists between the members, *station wagon* and *minivan* are types of automobile and *biceps* is a type of muscle. So these words are narrower in their range of application. On the other hand, a word more broadly defined than another word in the dictionary may be considered a synonym of the other word so long as the two words share one or more elementary meanings.

In order to pin down the area of shared meaning for you, each main entry in this work contains after its synonym list a *meaning core* which states the elementary meaning shared by all the words in that particular synonym group. Beyond that, each word in the synonym list is given a discussion to show the subtle differences between this word and all the other words in the list. This discussion is what makes this thesaurus special, and far more helpful than a book that merely lists words with similar meanings.

What is an Antonym?

Like the word *synonym, antonym* has been used by some writers with a great deal of vagueness and often applied loosely to words which show no real oppositeness when compared one to another. As in the case of synonyms, the relation needs to be seen as one between segments of meaning that can be isolated, rather than between words or dictionary senses of words. As is the case with synonyms, antonyms need to have one or more elementary meanings precisely opposite to or negating the same area of meaning of another word. This definition excludes from consideration as antonyms several classes of words that are sometimes treated as antonyms but that actually contain words which neither directly oppose or directly negate the words with which they are said to be antonymous.

For example, some terms have such a relationship to each other that one can scarcely be used without suggesting the other (as *husband* and *wife, father* and *son, buyer* and *seller*), yet there is no real opposition or real negation between such pairs. These are merely *relative terms*—their relation is reciprocal or correlative rather than antonymous.

Complementary terms in a similar way are usually paired and have a reciprocal relationship to the point that one seems incomplete without the other (as in such pairs as *question* and *answer, seek* and *find*). This relation which involves no negation is better seen as sequential than antonymous.

And *contrastive terms* differ sharply from their "opposites" only in some parts of their meaning. They neither oppose nor negate fully, since they are significantly different in range of meaning and applicability, in emphasis, and in the suggestions they convey. An example is *destitute* (a strong word carrying suggestions of misery and distress) which is contrastive rather than antonymous with respect to *rich* (a rather neutral and matter-of-fact term), while *poor* (another neutral and matter-of-fact term) is the appropriate antonym of *rich*. Basically, contrastive words are only opposed incidentally; they do not meet head on.

What then is considered an antonym? True antonyms can be classified in three ways:

Opposites without intermediates: What is *perfect* can be in no way *imperfect;* you cannot at the same time *accept* and *reject* or *agree* and *disagree*.

Opposites with intermediates: Such words make up the extremes in a range of difference and are so completely opposed that the language allows no wider difference. Thus, a scale of excellence might include *superiority, adequacy, mediocrity*, and *inferiority*, but only *superiority* and *inferiority* are so totally opposed that each exactly negates what its opposite affirms.

Reverse opposites: These are words that are opposed in such a way that each means the undoing or nullification of what the other affirms. Such reverse opposites exactly oppose and fully negate the special features of their opposites. Thus, *disprove* so perfectly opposes and so clearly negates the implications of *prove* that it fits the concept of antonym, as does *unkind* with respect to *kind*.

In this book, antonyms, when they fit one of these criteria, are listed after the synonym to which they apply.

A

abandon *vb* **1. Abandon**, **desert**, **forsake** mean to give up completely.

Abandon can suggest complete disinterest in the future of what is given up ⟨they *abandoned* their cat at the end of the summer⟩. ***antonym:*** reclaim

Desert implies a relationship (as of occupancy or guardianship); it can suggest desolation ⟨*deserted* farms growing up to brush⟩ or culpability ⟨soldiers who *desert* their posts⟩. ***antonym:*** cleave to, stick to

Forsake implies a breaking of a close association by repudiation or renunciation ⟨she *forsook* her husband for a career⟩. ***antonym:*** return to, revert to

2. See RELINQUISH.

abandon *n* See UNCONSTRAINT.

abase, **demean**, **debase**, **degrade**, **humble**, **humiliate** mean to lessen in dignity or status.

Abase suggests losing or voluntarily yielding up dignity or prestige ⟨a fine stage actor who *abased* himself by turning to television⟩. ***antonym:*** exalt, extol

Demean suggests unsuitable behavior or association as the cause of loss of status ⟨commercial endorsements *demean* the Olympics⟩.

Debase emphasizes loss of worth or quality ⟨*debase* a currency⟩ and especially deterioration of moral standards ⟨drunkenness has *debased* the Mardi Gras⟩.

Degrade suggests a downward step, sometimes in rank, more often in ethical stature, and typically implies a shameful or corrupt end ⟨the public altercation *degraded* both candidates⟩. ***antonym:*** uplift

Humble frequently replaces ***degrade*** when the disgrace of a reduction in status is to be emphasized ⟨they were delighted to see the bully *humbled* by a boy half his size⟩.

Humiliate implies the severe wounding of one's pride and the causing of deep shame ⟨*humiliated* by his suggestive remarks⟩.

abash See EMBARRASS.

abate 1. See DECREASE. **2. Abate**, **subside**, **wane**, **ebb** mean to die down in force or intensity.

Abate stresses a progressive diminishing ⟨waited until the storm *abated*⟩. ***antonym:*** rise, revive

Subside suggests a falling to a low level and an easing of turbulence ⟨the protests *subsided* after a few days⟩.

Wane adds to ***abate*** an implication of fading or weakening ⟨a *waning* moon⟩ and is often used of something impressive or intense ⟨the public's *waning* interest in spaceflight⟩. ***antonym:*** wax

Ebb suggests a gradual waning, especially of something that commonly comes and goes ⟨vitality often *ebbs* with illness⟩. ***antonym:*** flow (as the tide)

abbey See CLOISTER.

abbreviate See SHORTEN.

abdicate, **renounce**, **resign** mean to give up formally or definitely.

Abdicate implies a giving up of sovereign power ⟨the king was forced to *abdicate*⟩ or sometimes an evading of responsibility such as that of a parent ⟨by walking out he *abdicated* his rights as a father⟩. ***antonym:*** assume, usurp

Renounce may be chosen when the sacrifice, especially to some higher or moral end, is stressed ⟨the king *renounced* his throne to obtain peace⟩. ***antonym:*** arrogate, covet

Resign applies especially to the giving up of an unexpired office or trust ⟨forced to *resign* from office⟩.

aberrant See ABNORMAL.

abet See INCITE.

abeyant See LATENT.

abhor See HATE.

abhorrent 1. See HATEFUL. **2.** See REPUGNANT.

abide **1.** See BEAR. **2.** See CONTINUE. **3.** See STAY 1.

abject See MEAN.

abjure, **renounce**, **forswear**, **recant**, **retract** mean to withdraw one's word or professed belief.

Abjure implies a firm and final rejecting or abandoning under oath ⟨candidates for citizenship must *abjure* allegiance to any foreign power⟩. ***antonym:*** pledge (*as allegiance*), elect (*as a way of life*)

Renounce often equals ***abjure*** but may carry the meaning of ***disclaim*** or ***disown*** ⟨willing to *renounce* his lifelong friends⟩.

Forswear may add to ***abjure*** an implication of perjury or betrayal ⟨cannot *forswear* my principles to win votes⟩.

Recant stresses the withdrawing or denying of something professed or taught ⟨the suspect *recanted* his confession and professed his innocence⟩.

Retract applies to the withdrawing of a promise, an offer, or an accusation ⟨under threat of lawsuit the paper *retracted* the statement⟩.

able, **capable**, **competent**, **qualified** mean having power or fitness for work.

Able suggests ability above the average as revealed in actual performance ⟨proved that she is an *able* Shakespearean actress⟩. ***antonym:*** inept, unable

Capable stresses the having of qualities fitting one for work but does not imply outstanding ability ⟨*capable* of doing simple tasks under supervision⟩. ***antonym:*** incapable

Competent and ***qualified*** imply having the experience or training for adequate performance ⟨a leap that any *competent* ballet dancer can execute⟩ ⟨seek help from a *qualified* medical professional⟩. ***antonym:*** incompetent, unqualified

abnegation See RENUNCIATION.

abnormal, **atypical**, **aberrant** mean deviating markedly from the rule or standard of its kind.

Abnormal frequently suggests strangeness and sometimes deformity or monstrosity ⟨a classic study of *abnormal* personalities⟩. ***antonym:*** normal

Atypical stresses divergence upward or downward from some established norm ⟨a markedly *atypical* reaction to a drug⟩. ***antonym:*** typical, representative

Aberrant implies a departure from the usual or natural type ⟨that joyriding incident must be regarded as an *aberrant* episode in his life⟩. ***antonym:*** true (*to a type*)

abolish, **annihilate**, **extinguish** mean to make nonexistent.

Abolish implies a putting to an end chiefly of things that are the outgrowth of law, customs, and conditions of existence ⟨*abolish* a poll tax⟩. ***antonym:*** establish, institute

Annihilate suggests a complete wiping out of existence of something material or immaterial ⟨homes and cities *annihilated* by enemy attack⟩.

Extinguish is likely to suggest a complete but gradual ending (as by stifling, choking, or smothering) ⟨a religion that was thoroughly *extinguished* by governmental oppression⟩.

abominable See HATEFUL.

abominate See HATE.

abomination, **anathema**, **bugbear**, **bête noire** mean a person or thing that arouses intense dislike.

Abomination suggests the arousal of loathing, disgust, and extreme displeasure ⟨in her opinion all of modern art is an *abomination*⟩.

Anathema suggests that something is so odious that it is dismissed or rejected out of hand ⟨anything that was Yankee was *anathema* to my Southern aunt⟩.

Bugbear suggests something so dreaded that one seeks continually to avoid it ⟨the deficit became an annual congressional *bugbear*⟩.

Bête noire suggests a pet aversion that one habitually or especially avoids ⟨his mooching brother-in-law was the *bête noire* of his life〉.

aboriginal See NATIVE.

abortive See FUTILE.

abound See TEEM.

aboveboard See STRAIGHTFORWARD.

abridge See SHORTEN.

abridgment, **abstract**, **synopsis**, **conspectus**, **epitome** mean a condensed treatment.

Abridgment implies reduction in compass with retention of relative completeness 〈an *abridgment* of a dictionary〉. ***antonym:*** expansion

Abstract applies to a summary of points (as of a treatise, document, or proposed treatment) 〈a published *abstract* of a medical paper〉. ***antonym:*** amplification

Synopsis implies a skeletal presentation of an article or narrative suitable for rapid examination 〈read a *synopsis* of the screenplay〉.

Conspectus suggests a quick overall view of a large detailed subject 〈the book is a *conspectus* of modern American history〉.

Epitome suggests the briefest possible presentation of a complex whole as an ideal example 〈"know thyself" was the *epitome* of Greek philosophy〉.

abrogate See NULLIFY.

abrupt **1.** See PRECIPITATE. **2.** See STEEP.

absolute, **autocratic**, **arbitrary**, **despotic**, **tyrannical** mean exercising power or authority without restraint.

Absolute implies that one is not bound by legal constraints or the control of another 〈King Louis XIV was an *absolute* monarch〉.

Autocratic suggests the egotistical, self-conscious use of power or the haughty imposition of one's own will 〈the flamboyant, *autocratic* director of the ballet company〉.

Arbitrary implies the exercise and usually the abuse of power according to one's momentary inclination 〈his high-handed, *arbitrary* way of running his department〉. ***antonym:*** legitimate

Despotic implies the arbitrary and imperious exercise of absolute power or control 〈the most decadent and *despotic* of the Roman emperors〉.

Tyrannical implies the abuse of absolute power and harsh or oppressive rule 〈a new regime as *tyrannical* as the one it had deposed〉.

absolution See PARDON.

absolve See EXCULPATE.

absorb **1. Absorb**, **imbibe**, **assimilate** mean to take something in so as to become imbued with it.

Absorb is likely to suggest a loss of identity in what is taken in or an enrichment of what takes in 〈a lotion *absorbed* quickly by the skin〉. ***antonym:*** dissipate (*as time, energies*)

Imbibe implies a drinking in and may imply an unconscious taking in whose effect may be significant or profound 〈children *imbibe* the values of their parents〉. ***antonym:*** ooze, exude

Assimilate stresses an incorporation into the substance of the body or mind 〈asked to *assimiliate* a mass of material in a brief time〉.

2. See MONOPOLIZE.

abstain See REFRAIN.

abstemiousness See TEMPERANCE.

abstinence See TEMPERANCE.

abstract See ABRIDGMENT.

abundant See PLENTIFUL.

abuse, **vituperation**, **invective**, **obloquy**, **scurrility**, **billingsgate** mean vehemently expressed condemnation or disapproval.

Abuse implies the anger of the speaker and stresses the harshness of the language 〈charged her husband with verbal *abuse*〉. ***antonym:*** adulation

Vituperation implies fluent and sustained abuse 〈subjected his aide to a torrent of *vituperation*〉. ***antonym:*** acclaim, praise

Invective implies a comparable vehemence but suggests greater verbal and rhetorical skill and may apply to a public denunciation ⟨a politician known for his blistering *invective*⟩.

Obloquy suggests defamation and consequent shame and disgrace ⟨silently endured the *obloquy* of his former friend⟩.

Scurrility implies viciousness of attack and coarseness or foulness of language ⟨a debate that was not an exchange of ideas but an exercise in *scurrility*⟩.

Billingsgate implies practiced fluency and variety of profane or obscene abuse ⟨a *billingsgate* that would make a drunken sailor blush⟩.

abutting See ADJACENT.

abysmal See DEEP 2.

academic **1.** See PEDANTIC. **2.** See THEORETICAL.

accede See ASSENT.

accept See RECEIVE.

acceptation See MEANING.

access See FIT *n*.

accession See FIT *n*.

accident See CHANCE *n*.

accidental **1. Accidental**, **fortuitous**, **casual**, **contingent** mean happening by chance.

Accidental stresses chance or unexpected occurrence ⟨any resemblance to actual persons is entirely *accidental*⟩. ***antonym:*** planned

Fortuitous so strongly suggests chance that it often connotes entire absence of cause ⟨believes that life is more than a series of *fortuitous* events⟩. ***antonym:*** deliberate

Casual stresses lack of real or apparent premeditation or intent ⟨a *casual* encounter between two acquaintances⟩.

Contingent suggests possibility of happening but stresses uncertainty and dependence on other future events ⟨the *contingent* effects of a proposed amendment to the constitution⟩.

2. Accidental, **incidental**, **adventitious** mean not being part of the real or essential nature of something.

Accidental retains its basic notion of chance occurrence but may also imply nonessential character ⟨the essential and *accidental* values of an education⟩. ***antonym:*** essential

Incidental suggests a real, sometimes a designed, relationship but one which is secondary and nonessential ⟨expenses *incidental* to the performance of her job⟩. ***antonym:*** essential

Adventitious implies a lack of essential relationships and may suggest casual addition or irrelevance ⟨avoided elaborate designs with superfluous or *adventitious* elements⟩. ***antonym:*** inherent

accommodate **1.** See ADAPT. **2.** See OBLIGE. **3.** See CONTAIN.

accompany, **attend**, **escort** mean to go along with.

Accompany when referring to persons, usually implies equality of status ⟨*accompanied* his wife to the theater⟩.

Attend implies a waiting upon in order to serve usually as a subordinate ⟨will *attend* the President at the summit meeting⟩.

Escort adds to ***accompany*** implications of protection, ceremony, or courtesy ⟨a motorcade *escorted* the visiting queen⟩.

accomplish See PERFORM.

accomplishment See ACQUIREMENT.

accord *vb* **1.** See AGREE 3. **2.** See GRANT.

accord *n* See HARMONY.

accordingly See THEREFORE.

accountable See RESPONSIBLE.

accoutre See FURNISH.

accredit See APPROVE.

accumulative See CUMULATIVE.

accurate See CORRECT *adj*.

accuse, **charge**, **indict**, **impeach** mean to declare a person guilty of a fault or offense.

Accuse implies a direct, personal declaration ⟨*accused* him of trying to steal his wallet⟩. ***antonym:*** exculpate

Charge usually implies a formal declaration of a serious offense ⟨an athlete *charged* with taking illegal drugs before the race⟩. ***antonym:*** absolve

Indict is usually used in a legal context and implies a formal consideration of evidence prior to a trial ⟨*indicted* by a grand jury for first-degree murder⟩.

Impeach technically refers to a formal charge of malfeasance in office on the part of a public official ⟨the House of Representatives *impeached* President Andrew Johnson for high crimes and misdemeanors⟩.

accustomed See USUAL.

acerbity See ACRIMONY

achieve 1. See PERFORM. **2.** See REACH *vb.*

achievement See FEAT.

acknowledge, **admit**, **own**, **avow**, **confess** mean to disclose against one's will or inclination.

acknowledge implies the disclosing of something that has been or might be concealed ⟨*acknowledged* a lie⟩. ***antonym:*** deny

admit stresses reluctance to disclose, grant, or concede and refers usually to facts rather than their implications ⟨*admitted* that the project was over budget⟩. ***antonym:*** gainsay, disclaim

own implies acknowledging something in close relation to oneself ⟨must *own* that I know little about computers⟩. ***antonym:*** disown, repudiate

avow implies boldly declaring what one might be expected to be silent about ⟨*avowed* hostility toward his parents⟩. ***antonym:*** disavow

confess may apply to an admission of a weakness, failure, omission, or guilt ⟨*confessed* that she had a weakness for sweets⟩. ***antonym:*** renounce (*one's beliefs, principles*)

acme See SUMMIT.

acquaint See INFORM.

acquiesce See ASSENT.

acquire See GET.

acquirement, **acquisition**, **attainment**, **accomplishment** mean a power or skill won through exertion or effort.

Acquirement suggests the result of continued endeavor to cultivate oneself ⟨an appreciation of good music was not one of his *acquirements*⟩.

Acquisition stresses the effort involved and the inherent value of what is gained ⟨the ability to concentrate is a valuable *acquisition*⟩.

Attainment implies a distinguished achievement (in the arts or sciences) and suggests fully developed talents ⟨honored as woman of the year for her many *attainments*⟩.

Accomplishment implies a socially useful skill ⟨mastery of a foreign language is an admirable *accomplishment*⟩.

acquisition See ACQUIREMENT.

acquisitive See COVETOUS.

acquit 1. See BEHAVE. **2.** See EXCULPATE.

acrid See CAUSTIC.

acrimony, **acerbity**, **asperity** mean temper or language marked by irritation, anger, or resentment.

Acrimony implies feelings of bitterness and a stinging verbal attack ⟨a campaign marked by verbal exchanges of intense *acrimony*⟩. ***antonym:*** suavity

Acerbity suggests sourness as well as bitterness and applies especially to mood or temperament ⟨an inbred *acerbity* that pervades even his personal letters⟩. ***antonym:*** mellowness

Asperity suggests quickness of temper and sharpness of resentment, usually without bitterness ⟨told him with some *asperity* to mind his own business⟩. ***antonym:*** amenity

action See BATTLE.

activate See VITALIZE.

actual See REAL.

actuate See MOVE.

acumen See DISCERNMENT.

acute 1. See SHARP. **2. Acute**, **critical**, **crucial** mean full of uncertainty as to outcome.

Acute stresses intensification of conditions leading to a culmination or breaking point ⟨the housing shortage is becoming *acute*⟩.

Critical adds to **acute** implications of imminent change, of attendant suspense, and of decisiveness in the outcome ⟨the war has entered a *critical* phase⟩.

Crucial suggests a dividing of the ways and often implies a test or trial involving the determination of a future course or direction ⟨for the campaign, the coming weeks will be *crucial*⟩.

adamant See INFLEXIBLE.

adapt, **adjust**, **accommodate**, **conform**, **reconcile** mean to bring one thing into correspondence with another.

Adapt implies a ready modification to changing circumstances ⟨they *adapted* themselves to the warmer climate⟩.

Adjust suggests bringing into a close and exact correspondence or harmony as exists between the parts of a mechanism, often by the use of tact or ingenuity ⟨*adjusted* the budget to allow for inflation⟩.

Accommodate may suggest yielding or compromising in order to achieve a correspondence ⟨*accommodated* his political beliefs to those of the majority⟩. ***antonym:*** constrain

Conform applies to bringing into harmony or accordance with a pattern, example, or principle ⟨refused to *conform* to society's idea of woman's proper role⟩.

Reconcile implies the demonstration of the underlying consistency or congruity of things that seem to be incompatible ⟨tried to *reconcile* what they said with what I knew⟩.

adaptable See PLASTIC.

additive See CUMULATIVE.

address See TACT.

adduce See CITE.

adept See PROFICIENT.

adequate See SUFFICIENT.

adhere See STICK.

adherence, **adhesion** mean a sticking to or together.

Adherence suggests a mental or moral attachment ⟨*adherence* to the principles of reform⟩. ***antonym:*** nonadherence

Adhesion implies a physical attachment ⟨the *adhesion* of paint to a surface⟩.

adherent See FOLLOWER.

adhesion See ADHERENCE.

adjacent, **adjoining**, **contiguous**, **abutting**, **tangent**, **conterminous**, **juxtaposed** mean being in close proximity.

Adjacent may or may not imply contact but always implies absence of anything of the same kind in between ⟨the price of the house and the *adjacent* garage⟩. ***antonym:*** nonadjacent

Adjoining definitely implies meeting and touching at some point or line ⟨assigned *adjoining* rooms at the hotel⟩. ***antonym:*** detached, disjoined

Contiguous implies having contact on all or most of one side ⟨offices in all 48 *contiguous* states⟩.

Abutting stresses the termination of one thing along a line of contact with another ⟨land *abutting* on the road⟩.

Tangent implies contact at a single point ⟨a line *tangent* to a curve⟩.

Conterminous applies to objects bordering on each other ⟨crossing the *conterminous* border of France and Germany⟩ or having the same bounds, limits, or ends ⟨the several *conterminous* civil and ecclesiastical parishes of England⟩.

Juxtaposed means placed side by side especially so as to permit comparison and contrast ⟨an ultramodern office building *juxtaposed* to a Gothic church⟩.

adjoining See ADJACENT.

adjourn, **prorogue**, **dissolve** mean to terminate the activities of (as a legislature or meeting).

Adjourn implies suspension until an appointed time or indefinitely ⟨*adjourn* a meeting⟩. ***antonym:*** convene, convoke

Prorogue applies especially to action of the British crown or its representative by which a parliament is adjourned ⟨the king's hasty decision to *prorogue* the parliamentary session⟩.

Dissolve implies permanency and suggests that the body ceases to exist as presently constituted so that an election must be held in order to reconstitute it ⟨the president's decision *dissolved* the committee⟩.

adjure See BEG.

adjust See ADAPT.

administer See EXECUTE.

admire See REGARD.

admission See ADMITTANCE.

admit **1.** See ACKNOWLEDGE. **2.** See RECEIVE.

admittance, **admission** mean permitted entrance.

Admittance is usually applied to mere physical entrance to a locality or a building ⟨members must show their cards upon *admittance* to the club⟩.

Admission applies to entrance or formal acceptance (as into a club) that carries with it rights, privileges, standing, or membership ⟨candidates for *admission* must submit recommendations from two club members⟩.

admixture See MIXTURE.

admonish See REPROVE.

ado See STIR.

adopt, **embrace**, **espouse** mean to take an opinion, policy, or practice as one's own.

Adopt implies accepting something created by another or foreign to one's nature ⟨forced to *adopt* the procedures of the new parent company⟩. ***antonym:*** repudiate, discard

Embrace implies a ready or happy acceptance ⟨eagerly *embraced* the ways and customs of their new homeland⟩. ***antonym:*** spurn

Espouse adds an implication of close attachment to a cause and a sharing of its fortunes ⟨spent her lifetime *espousing* equal rights for women⟩.

adore See REVERE.

adorn, **decorate**, **ornament**, **embellish**, **beautify**, **deck**, **bedeck**, **garnish** mean to enhance the appearance of something by adding something unessential.

Adorn implies an enhancing by something beautiful in itself ⟨a diamond necklace *adorned* her neck⟩. ***antonym:*** disfigure

Decorate suggests the addition of color or interest to what is dull or monotonous ⟨*decorate* a birthday cake with colored frosting⟩.

Ornament implies the adding of something extraneous to heighten or set off the original ⟨a white house *ornamented* with green shutters⟩.

Embellish often stresses the adding of a superfluous or adventitious element ⟨*embellish* a page with floral borders⟩.

Beautify suggests a counteracting of a plainness or ugliness ⟨will *beautify* the park with flower beds⟩. ***antonym:*** uglify

Deck and ***bedeck*** imply the addition of something that contributes to gaiety, splendor, or showiness ⟨a house all *decked* out for the holidays⟩ ⟨*bedecked* with garlands⟩.

Garnish suggests decorating with a small final touch and is used especially in referring to the serving of food ⟨airline food invariably *garnished* with parsley⟩.

adroit **1.** See CLEVER. **2.** See DEXTEROUS.

adult See MATURE.

adultery, **fornication**, **incest** mean illicit sexual intercourse.

Adultery implies unfaithfulness to one's spouse and therefore can be applied only to sexual intercourse between a married person and a partner other than his or her wife or husband ⟨listed *adultery* as grounds for divorce⟩.

Fornication designates sexual intercourse on the part of an unmarried person ⟨religious laws strictly forbidding *fornication*⟩.

Incest refers to sexual intercourse between persons proscribed from marrying on the basis of kinship ties ⟨*incest* involving father and daughter is the most common⟩.

advance 1. Advance, promote, forward, further mean to help (someone or something) to move ahead.

Advance stresses effective assistance in hastening a process or bringing about a desired end ⟨a gesture intended to *advance* the cause of peace⟩. ***antonym:*** retard, check

Promote suggests an open encouraging or fostering ⟨a company trying to *promote* better health among employees⟩ and may denote an increase in status or rank ⟨a student *promoted* to third grade⟩. ***antonym:*** demote

Forward implies an impetus or moral force moving something ahead ⟨a wage increase would *forward* productivity⟩. ***antonym:*** hinder, balk

Further suggests a removing of obstacles in the way of a desired advance ⟨used the marriage to *further* his career⟩. ***antonym:*** hinder, retard

2. See CITE.

advanced See LIBERAL 2.

advantageous See BENEFICIAL.

advent See ARRIVAL.

adventitious See ACCIDENTAL 2.

adventurous, venturesome, daring, daredevil, rash, reckless, foolhardy mean exposing oneself to danger more than dictated by good sense.

Adventurous implies a willingness to accept risks but not necessarily imprudence ⟨*adventurous* pioneers opened the West⟩. ***antonym:*** unadventurous, cautious

Venturesome Implies a jaunty eagerness for perilous undertakings ⟨*venturesome* pilots became popular heroes⟩.

Daring heightens the implication of fearlessness or boldness in courting danger ⟨mountain climbing attracts the *daring* types⟩.

Daredevil stresses ostentation in daring ⟨*daredevil* motorcyclists performing stunts⟩.

Rash suggests imprudence, haste, and lack of forethought ⟨a *rash* decision that you will regret later⟩. ***antonym:*** calculating

Reckless implies heedlessness of probable consequences ⟨a *reckless* driver who endangers others⟩. ***antonym:*** calculating

Foolhardy suggests a recklessness that is inconsistent with good sense ⟨only a *foolhardy* sailor would venture into this storm⟩. ***antonym:*** wary

adversary See OPPONENT.

adverse, antagonistic, counter, counteractive mean so opposed as to cause often harmful interference.

Adverse applies to what is unfavorable, harmful, or detrimental ⟨very sensitive to *adverse* criticism⟩. ***antonym:*** propitious

Antagonistic usually implies mutual opposition and either hostility or incompatibility ⟨neighboring countries were *antagonistic* to the new nation⟩. ***antonym:*** favoring, favorable

Counter applies to forces coming from opposite directions with resulting conflict or tension ⟨the *counter* demands of family and career⟩.

Counteractive implies an opposition between two things that nullifies the effect of one or both ⟨poor eating habits will have a *counteractive* effect on any gains from exercise⟩.

adversity See MISFORTUNE.

advert See REFER 3.

advertise See DECLARE.

advice, counsel mean a recommendation as to a decision or a course of conduct.

Advice implies real or pretended knowledge or experience, often professional or technical, on the part of the one who advises ⟨a book of *advice* for would-be entrepreneurs⟩.

Counsel often stresses the fruit of wisdom or deliberation and may presuppose a weightier occasion, or more authority, or more personal concern on the part of the one giving counsel ⟨the benefit of a father's *counsel*⟩.

advisable See EXPEDIENT.

advise See CONFER.

advocate *vb* See SUPPORT.

advocate *n* See LAWYER.

affable See GRACIOUS.

affair **1. Affair**, **business**, **concern**, **matter**, **thing** mean in general terms something done or dealt with.

Affair suggests action or performance and may imply a process, an operation, a proceeding, an undertaking, or a transaction ⟨the resounding success of the whole *affair*⟩.

Business stresses duty or office and implies an imposed task ⟨concern for quality is everybody's *business*⟩.

Concern suggests personal or direct relationship to something that has bearing on one's welfare, success, or interests ⟨viewed the issue as of no *concern* to them⟩.

Matter generally refers to something being considered or being dealt with ⟨the one remaining *matter* in dispute⟩.

Thing is often used when there is a desire to be vague or inexplicit ⟨a promise to see the *thing* through⟩.

2. See AMOUR.

affect **1. Affect**, **influence**, **touch**, **impress**, **strike**, **sway** mean to produce or have an effect upon.

Affect implies the action of a stimulus that can produce a response or reaction ⟨the sight *affected* him deeply⟩.

Influence implies a force that brings about a change (as in nature or behavior) ⟨our beliefs are *influenced* by our upbringing⟩ ⟨a drug that *influences* growth rates⟩.

Touch may carry a vivid suggestion of close contact and may connote stirring, arousing, or harming ⟨plants *touched* by frost⟩ ⟨his emotions were *touched* by her distress⟩.

Impress stresses the depth and persistence of the effect ⟨only one of the plans *impressed* him⟩.

Strike may convey the notion of sudden sharp perception or appreciation ⟨*struck* by the solemnity of the occasion⟩.

Sway implies the acting of influences that are not resisted or are irresistible, with resulting change in character or course of action ⟨politicians who are *swayed* by popular opinion⟩.

2. See ASSUME.

affectation See POSE.

affecting See MOVING.

affection See FEELING.

affiliated See RELATED.

affinity **1.** See ATTRACTION. **2.** See LIKENESS.

affirm See ASSERT.

affix See FASTEN.

afflict, **try**, **torment**, **torture**, **rack** mean to inflict on a person something that is hard to bear.

Afflict applies to the causing of any pain or suffering or of acute annoyance, embarrassment, or any distress ⟨many aged persons who are *afflicted* with blindness⟩. ***antonym:*** comfort

Try suggests an imposing of something that strains the powers of endurance or self-control ⟨young children often *try* their parent's patience⟩.

Torment suggests persecution or the repeated inflicting of suffering or annoyance ⟨the horses are *tormented* by flies⟩.

Torture implies the unbearable pain or suffering ⟨*tortured* his captive by withholding food⟩.

Rack stresses straining or wrenching ⟨a mind *racked* by guilt⟩.

affluent See RICH.

afford See GIVE.

affront See OFFEND.

afraid See FEARFUL.

age *n* See PERIOD.

age *vb* See MATURE *vb*.

agent See MEAN *n* 2.

aggravate **1.** See INTENSIFY. **2.** See IRRITATE.

aggregate See SUM.

aggression See ATTACK *n* 2.

aggressive, **militant**, **assertive**, **self-assertive**, **pushing**, **pushy** mean obtrusively energetic especially in pursuing particular goals.

Aggressive implies a disposition to dominate often in disregard of others' rights or in determined and energetic pursuit of one's ends ⟨*aggressive* and successful in the business world⟩.

Militant suggests not self-seeking but devotion to a cause, movement, or principle ⟨*militant* environmentalists staged a protest⟩.

Assertive suggests bold self-confidence in expression of opinion ⟨*assertive* speakers dominated the open forum⟩. ***antonym:*** retiring, acquiescent

Self-assertive connotes forwardness or brash self-confidence ⟨a *self-assertive* young executive climbing the corporate ladder⟩.

Pushing and ***pushy*** may apply to ambition or enterprise or to snobbish and crude intrusiveness or officiousness ⟨*pushing* salespeople using high-pressure tactics⟩ ⟨*pushy* people breaking into the line for tickets⟩.

aggrieve See WRONG.

agile, **nimble**, **brisk**, **spry** mean acting or moving with easy quickness.

Agile implies dexterity and ease in physical or mental actions ⟨*agile* at answering questions on a variety of issues⟩. ***antonym:*** torpid

Nimble stresses lightness and swiftness of action or thought ⟨a *nimble* tennis player⟩.

Brisk suggests liveliness, animation, or vigor of movement sometimes with a suggestion of hurry ⟨a *brisk* cleaning-up before the relatives arrived⟩. ***antonym:*** sluggish

Spry stresses an ability for quick action that is unexpected because of age or known infirmity ⟨*spry* older players beating younger opponents⟩. ***antonym:*** doddering

agitate **1.** See DISCOMPOSE. **2.** See SHAKE.

agony See DISTRESS.

agree **1. Agree**, **concur**, **coincide** mean to come into or be in harmony regarding a matter of opinion.

Agree implies complete accord usually attained by discussion and adjustment of differences ⟨on some points we all can *agree*⟩. ***antonym:*** differ, disagree

Concur tends to suggest cooperative thinking or acting toward an end but sometimes implies no more than approval (as of a decision reached by others) ⟨members of the committee *concurred* with his decision⟩. ***antonym:*** contend, altercate

Coincide used more often of opinions, judgments, wishes, or interests than of people, implies an agreement amounting to identity ⟨their wishes *coincide* exactly with my desire⟩.

2. See ASSENT. **3. Agree**, **tally**, **square**, **conform**, **accord**, **comport**, **harmonize**, **correspond**, **jibe** mean to go or exist together without conflict or incongruity.

Agree applies to any precise going, existing, or fitting together ⟨the conclusion *agrees* with the evidence⟩. ***antonym:*** differ (*from*)

Tally implies an agreement between two correct accounts that match not only in overall conclusions but detail by detail ⟨your story *tallies* with earlier accounts⟩.

Square suggests a precise or mathematically exact agreement ⟨force facts to *square* with theory⟩.

Conform implies a fundamental likeness in form, nature, or essential quality ⟨*conform* to local customs⟩. ***antonym:*** diverge

Accord implies perfect fitness in a relation or association (as in character, spirit, quality, or tone) ⟨the speaker's remarks did not *accord* with the sentiments of his listeners⟩. ***antonym:*** conflict

Comport, like ***accord***, stresses the fitness or suitability of a relationship ⟨acts that *comport* with ideals⟩.

Harmonize stresses the blending of dissimilar things to form a congruous or pleasing whole ⟨*harmonize* the conflicting colors through the use of blue⟩. ***antonym:*** clash, conflict

Correspond stresses the way in which dissimilar elements match, complement, or answer to each other ⟨fulfillment seldom *corresponds* to anticipation⟩.

Jibe may sometimes be closely equivalent to ***agree***, sometimes to ***harmonize***, and sometimes to ***accord*** ⟨his actions do not *jibe* with his words⟩.

agreeable See PLEASANT.

aid *vb* See HELP.

aid *n* See ASSISTANT.

aide See ASSISTANT.

aide-de-camp See ASSISTANT.

ail See TROUBLE.

aim See INTENTION.

air *vb* See EXPRESS.

air *n* **1. Air, atmosphere, ether, ozone** mean the invisible mixture of gases which surrounds the earth.

Air refers to the impalpable breathable substance essential to life ⟨the *air* we breathe⟩ or that substance mixed with others ⟨smoggy *air*⟩.

Atmosphere suggests the gaseous layers surrounding the earth or another celestial body ⟨the poisonous *atmosphere* of Venus⟩ or the air which fills a particular place or is in a particular state ⟨the room's stagnant *atmosphere*⟩.

Ether implies a more rarefied or more delicate or subtle medium which was formerly said to fill the upper regions or interstellar space ⟨gods who dwelled in the *ether*⟩ and is used technically to denote a hypothetical medium in space suitable for the transmission of transverse waves ⟨broadcast into the *ether* in hopes someone would hear⟩.

Ozone denotes generally air that is notably pure and refreshing ⟨the vivifying *ozone* of a thunderstorm⟩.

2. See POSE. **3.** See MELODY.

airs See POSE.

akin See SIMILAR.

alacrity See CELERITY.

alarm See FEAR.

albeit See THOUGH.

alert 1. See INTELLIGENT. **2.** See WATCHFUL.

alibi See APOLOGY.

alien See EXTRINSIC.

alienate See ESTRANGE.

align See LINE.

alike See SIMILAR.

alive 1. See AWARE. **2.** See LIVING.

all See WHOLE.

all-around See VERSATILE.

allay See RELIEVE.

allege See CITE.

allegiance See FIDELITY.

alleviate See RELIEVE.

alliance, league, coalition, confederation, federation mean an association to further the common interests of its members.

Alliance applies to an association formed for the mutual benefit of its members ⟨an *alliance* between feminist and religious groups against pornography⟩.

League suggests a more formal compact often with a definite goal ⟨the *League* of Nations⟩ and may be used to suggest association for a bad end ⟨in *league* with the devil⟩.

Coalition applies to a temporary association of parties often of opposing interests ⟨formed a *coalition* government with two other parties⟩.

Confederation applies to a union of independent states under a central government to which powers dealing with common external relations are delegated ⟨the *confederation* formed by the American colonies⟩.

Federation implies any union under the terms of a league or covenant, and specifically a sovereign power formed by a union of states and having a central government and several state and local governments ⟨the United States of America constitutes a *federation*⟩.

allied See RELATED.

allocate See ALLOT.

allot, **assign**, **apportion**, **allocate** mean to give as a share, portion, role, or lot.

Allot implies haphazard or arbitrary distribution with no suggestion of fairness or equality ⟨each child was *alloted* a portion of pie⟩.

Assign stresses an authoritative and fixed allotment but carries no clear implication of an even division ⟨each employee is *assigned* a parking space⟩.

Apportion implies a dividing according to some principle of equal or proportionate distribution ⟨profits were *apportioned* according to a predetermined ratio⟩.

Allocate suggests a fixed appropriation of money, property, territory, or powers to a person or group for a particular use ⟨*allocated* $50,000 for park improvements⟩.

allow See LET.

allowance See RATION.

allude See REFER.

allure See ATTRACT 2.

ally See PARTNER.

almost See NEARLY.

alone, **solitary**, **lonely**, **lonesome**, **lone**, **forlorn**, **desolate** mean isolated from others.

Alone suggests the objective fact of being by oneself with a slight notion of emotional involvement ⟨happier when left *alone* occasionally⟩. ***antonym:*** accompanied

Solitary may indicate isolation as a chosen course ⟨glorying in the calm of her *solitary* life⟩ but more often it suggests sadness and a sense of loss ⟨left *solitary* by the death of his wife⟩.

Lonely adds a suggestion of longing for companionship ⟨felt *lonely* and forsaken⟩.

Lonesome heightens the suggestion of the sadness and poignancy of separation ⟨an only child sometimes leads a *lonesome* life⟩.

Lone may replace ***lonely*** or ***lonesome*** but typically is as objective as ***alone*** ⟨a *lone* robin pecking at the lawn⟩.

Forlorn stresses dejection, woe, and listlessness at separation from someone or something dear ⟨a child lost and *forlorn*⟩.

Desolate implies inconsolable grief at isolation caused by loss or bereavement ⟨her brother's death now left her completely *desolate*⟩.

aloof See INDIFFERENT.

alter See CHANGE.

altercation See QUARREL.

alternate *adj* See INTERMITTENT.

alternate *vb* See ROTATE.

alternative See CHOICE *n*.

although See THOUGH.

altitude See HEIGHT.

amalgam See MIXTURE.

amalgamate See MIX.

amateur, **dilettante**, **dabbler**, **tyro** mean a person who follows a pursuit without attaining proficiency or professional status.

Amateur often applies to one practicing an art without mastery of its essentials ⟨a painting obviously done by an *amateur*⟩, and in sports it may also suggest not so much lack of skill but avoidance of direct remuneration ⟨must remain an *amateur* in order to qualify for the Olympics⟩. ***antonym:*** expert, professional

Dilettante may apply to the lover of an art rather than its skilled practitioner but usually implies elegant trifling in the arts and an absence of serious commitment ⟨a serious art teacher with no patience for *dilettantes*⟩.

Dabbler suggests a lack of serious purpose, desultory habits of work, and lack of persistence ⟨a *dabbler* who never finished a single novel⟩.

Tyro implies inexperience and the attendant incompetence often combined with audacity resulting in crudeness or blundering ⟨a *tyro* who has yet to master the basics of playwriting⟩.

amaze See SURPRISE 2.

ambiguity, **equivocation**, **tergiversation**, **double entendre** mean an expression capable of more than one interpretation.

Ambiguity usually refers to the use of a word or phrase in such a way that it may be taken in either of two senses ⟨the *ambiguity* in the directive's wording caused much confusion⟩. ***antonym:*** lucidity, explicitness

Equivocation suggests that the ambiguity is intentional and the intent is to mislead ⟨a report on the nuclear accident filled with *equivocations*⟩. ***antonym:*** explicitness

Tergiversation stresses the shifting of senses during the course of one's argument and usually suggests evasion or looseness of thought and intentional subterfuge ⟨a thesis that relies on several *tergiversations* of the word "society"⟩.

Double entendre refers to a word or expression allowing two interpretations, one of them being a cover for a subtle, indelicate, or risqué implication ⟨the *double entendres* rife in any bedroom farce⟩.

ambiguous See OBSCURE.

ambition, **aspiration**, **pretension** mean strong desire for advancement or success.

Ambition applies to the desire for personal advancement or preferment and may suggest equally a praiseworthy or an inordinate desire ⟨driven by the *ambition* to be very rich⟩.

Aspiration implies a striving after something higher than oneself and usually implies that the striver is thereby ennobled or uplifted ⟨an *aspiration* to become President someday⟩.

Pretension suggests ardent desire for recognition of accomplishment without actual possession of the necessary ability or qualifications and therefore implies presumption or folly ⟨people with literary *pretensions* frequenting her salon⟩.

amble See SAUNTER.

ambush See SURPRISE 1.

ameliorate See IMPROVE.

amenable **1.** See OBEDIENT. **2.** See RESPONSIBLE.

amend See CORRECT.

amerce See PENALIZE.

amiable, **good-natured**, **obliging**, **complaisant** mean having the desire or disposition to please.

Amiable implies having qualities that make one liked and easy to deal with ⟨a travel club that attracts *amiable* types⟩. ***antonym:*** unamiable

Good-natured implies a cheerful willingness to please or to be helpful and sometimes to permit imposition ⟨a *good-natured* boy always willing to pitch in⟩. ***antonym:*** contrary

Obliging stresses a friendly readiness to be helpful or to accommodate to the wishes of others ⟨our *obliging* innkeeper granted our request⟩. ***antonym:*** disobliging, inconsiderate

Complaisant often implies passivity or a weakly amiable willingness to yield to others through a desire to please or to be agreeable ⟨*complaisant* people who only say what others want to hear⟩. ***antonym:*** contrary, perverse

amicable, **neighborly**, **friendly** mean exhibiting goodwill and an absence of antagonism.

Amicable implies a state of peace and a desire on the part of the parties not to quarrel ⟨maintained *amicable* relations even after the divorce⟩. ***antonym:*** antagonistic

Neighborly implies a disposition to live on good terms with others in necessary proximity and to be helpful and kindly on principle ⟨prompted by *neighborly*

concern to inquire about her health⟩. ***antonym:*** unneighborly, ill-disposed

Friendly stresses cordiality and often warmth or intimacy of personal relations ⟨sought his *friendly* advice on this important matter⟩. ***antonym:*** unfriendly, belligerent

amnesty See PARDON.

amoral See IMMORAL.

amount See SUM.

amour, **liaison**, **intrigue**, **affair** mean an instance of illicit sexual relationship.

Amour stresses passion as the motivating force and often connotes transcience ⟨went from one *amour* to another⟩.

Liaison implies duration but not necessarily permanence of the attachment ⟨known for her *liaison* with a powerful senator⟩.

Intrigue emphasizes the clandestine element in the relationship ⟨frequently drawn to complicated *intrigues*⟩.

Affair is the least specific term and suggests something equivocal rather than definitely illicit about the relationship ⟨had a series of *affairs* after his divorce⟩.

ample 1. See PLENTIFUL. **2.** See SPACIOUS.

amplify See EXPAND.

amulet See FETISH.

amuse, **divert**, **entertain** mean to pass or cause to pass the time pleasantly.

Amuse suggests that the attention is engaged lightly or frivolously ⟨*amuse* yourselves while I prepare dinner⟩. ***antonym:*** bore

Divert implies the distracting of the attention from worry or duty especially by something different, often something light ⟨tired businessmen looking for a comedy to *divert* them⟩.

Entertain suggests supplying amusement or diversion by specially prepared or contrived methods ⟨comedians and pretty girls to *entertain* the troops⟩.

analgesic See ANODYNE 1.

analogous See SIMILAR.

analogue See PARALLEL.

analogy See LIKENESS.

analytic *or* **analytical** See LOGICAL.

analyze, **resolve**, **dissect**, **break down** mean to divide a complex whole into its parts or elements.

Analyze suggests separating or distinguishing the component parts of something (as a substance, a process, or a situation) so as to discover its true nature or inner relationships ⟨*analyzed* the current problem of trade imbalances to discover its basis⟩. ***antonym:*** compose, compound, construct

Resolve often suggests only the separation or division into elements or parts ⟨matter *resolved* by the microscope into distinct cells⟩ or its change of form or metamorphosis ⟨hatred *resolved* by suffering into tenderness⟩. ***antonym:*** blend

Dissect suggests a searching analysis by laying bare parts or pieces for individual scrutiny ⟨commentators *dissected* every word of the President's statement⟩.

Break down implies a methodical reducing of a complex whole to simpler parts or divisions ⟨*break down* the budget to see where the money is going⟩.

anathema See ABOMINATION.

anathematize See EXECRATE.

anatomy See STRUCTURE.

ancient See OLD.

anesthetic See ANODYNE 1.

anecdote See STORY.

anemic See PALE 2.

anger, **ire**, **rage**, **fury**, **indignation**, **wrath** mean emotional excitement induced by intense displeasure.

Anger, the most general term, names the emotional reaction but in itself conveys nothing about intensity or justification or manifesta tion of the state ⟨tried to hide his *anger* at their behavior⟩. ***antonym:*** pleasure, gratification, forbearance

Ire, more frequent in literary contexts, may suggest greater intensity than anger, often with a display of feeling ⟨cheeks flushed dark with *ire*⟩.

Rage suggests loss of self-control from

violence of emotion often with an outward display ⟨screaming with *rage*⟩.

Fury implies overmastering destructive rage verging on madness ⟨in her *fury* she hurled abuse in all directions⟩.

Indignation stresses righteous anger at what one considers unfair, mean, outrageous, or shameful ⟨high-handed behavior that caused general *indignation*⟩.

Wrath is likely to suggest rage or indignation accompanied by a desire or intent to avenge or punish ⟨rose in his *wrath* and struck his tormentor to the floor⟩.

angle See PHASE.

anguish See SORROW.

animadvert See REMARK.

animal See CARNAL.

animate *adj* See LIVING.

animate *vb* See QUICKEN.

animated **1.** See LIVELY. **2.** See LIVING.

animosity See ENMITY.

animus See ENMITY.

annals See HISTORY.

annihilate See ABOLISH.

announce See DECLARE.

annoy **1. Annoy, vex, irk, bother** mean to upset a person's composure.

Annoy implies a wearing on the nerves by persistent and often petty unpleasantness ⟨his constant complaining *annoys* us⟩. ***antonym:*** soothe

Vex implies greater provocation and stronger disturbance and usually connotes anger but sometimes perplexity or anxiety ⟨a problem that *vexes* cancer researchers⟩. ***antonym:*** please, regale

Irk stresses difficulty in enduring and the resulting weariness or impatience ⟨his chronic tardiness *irks* his colleagues⟩.

Bother suggests bewildering or upsetting interference with comfort or peace of mind ⟨that discrepancy *bothers* me⟩. ***antonym:*** comfort

2. See WORRY.

annul See NULLIFY.

anodyne **1. Anodyne, analgesic, anesthetic** mean something used to relieve or prevent pain.

Anodyne may be applied to any agent used primarily to relieve pain whether by dulling the perception of pain or by altering the situation and has a literary rather than a medical connotation ⟨took a long, hard walk as an *anodyne* for disappointment⟩.

Analgesic applies especially to a medicinal preparation used locally or systematically to dull the sensation of pain ⟨used liniment as an *analgesic* for stiff joints⟩. ***antonym:*** irritant

Anesthetic implies a medicinal agent that causes insensibility to pain and other sensations either locally or generally ⟨given an *anesthetic* by the dentist before her tooth was pulled⟩. ***antonym:*** stimulant

2. Anodyne, opiate, narcotic, nepenthe mean something used to dull or deaden the senses or sensibilities.

Anodyne usually suggests something that soothes or calms often by inducing forgetfulness or oblivion ⟨the *anodyne* of religious fervor⟩. ***antonym:*** stimulant, irritant

Opiate implies a substance that causes a dream state and a delusion of happiness and suggests an indifference and false sense of security or well-being ⟨price supports that were an *opiate* for distressed industries⟩.

Narcotic applies to something that literally or figuratively produces sleep, stupor, or lulling drowsiness ⟨beautiful music used as a *narcotic* to escape from the pressures of work⟩.

Nepenthe connotes something sweet and pleasurable that is substituted for something painful ⟨the *nepenthe* of rest after a hard day's work⟩.

anomalous See IRREGULAR.

answer **1. Answer, respond, reply, rejoin, retort** mean to say, write, or do something in return.

Answer implies the satisfying of a question, demand, call, or need ⟨*answered* all the questions on the form⟩.

Respond may suggest a willing or spontaneous and often quick reaction ⟨chose not to *respond* to that comment⟩.

Reply implies making a return commensurate with the original question or demand ⟨an invitation that requires you to *reply* at once⟩.

Rejoin often implies sharpness or pointedness in answering ⟨she *rejoined* quickly to his criticism⟩.

Retort suggests responding to an explicit charge or criticism by way of retaliation ⟨he *retorted* to her every charge with biting sarcasm⟩.

2. See SATISFY 3.

answerable See RESPONSIBLE.

antagonism See ENMITY.

antagonist See OPPONENT.

antagonistic See ADVERSE.

antagonize See OPPOSE.

antecedent *n* See CAUSE.

antecedent *adj* See PRECEDING.

antediluvian See OLD.

anterior See PRECEDING.

anticipate **1.** See FORESEE. **2.** See PREVENT.

anticipation See PROSPECT.

antipathy See ENMITY.

antiquated See OLD.

antique See OLD.

antisocial See UNSOCIAL.

antithetical See OPPOSITE.

anxiety See CARE .

anxious See EAGER.

apathetic See IMPASSIVE.

ape See COPY.

aperture, **interstice**, **orifice** mean an opening that allows passage through or in and out.

Aperture applies to an opening in an otherwise closed or solid surface or structure ⟨light entered through an *aperture* in the castle wall⟩.

Interstice implies an unfilled space or break in a continuous substance or fabric, especially in something loosely woven, coarse-grained, piled, or layered ⟨moss growing in the *interstices* of an old stone wall⟩.

Orifice suggests an opening that functions as a mouth or vent ⟨the *orifice* of the bladder⟩.

apex See SUMMIT.

aplomb See CONFIDENCE.

apocryphal See FICTITIOUS.

apologia See APOLOGY.

apology, **apologia**, **excuse**, **plea**, **pretext**, **alibi** mean matter offered in explanation or defense.

Apology usually applies to an expression of regret for a mistake or wrong with implied admission of guilt or fault and with or without reference to extenuating circumstances ⟨said by way of *apology* that he would have met them if he could⟩.

Apologia, and sometimes ***apology***, implies not admission of guilt or regret but a desire to make clear the grounds for some course, belief, or position ⟨the speech was an effective *apologia* for his foreign policy⟩.

Excuse implies an intent to avoid or remove blame or censure ⟨used his illness as an *excuse* for missing the meeting⟩.

Plea stresses argument or appeal for understanding or sympathy or mercy ⟨her usual *plea* that she was nearsighted⟩.

Pretext suggests subterfuge and the offering of false reasons or motives in excuse or explanation ⟨used any *pretext* to get out of work⟩.

Alibi implies a desire to shift blame or evade punishment and imputes plausibility rather than truth to the explanation offered ⟨his *alibi* failed to withstand scrutiny⟩.

appall See DISMAY.

appalling See FEARFUL 2.

apparent **1. Apparent**, **illusory**, **seeming**, **ostensible** mean not actually being what appearance indicates.

Apparent suggests appearance to unaided senses that is not or may not be proven by more rigorous examination or greater knowledge ⟨the *apparent* cause of the train wreck⟩. ***antonym:*** real

Illusory implies a false impression based on deceptive resemblance or faulty observation, or influenced by emotions that prevent a clear view ⟨the *illusory* happiness of a new infatuation⟩. ***antonym:*** factual, matter-of-fact

Seeming implies a character in the thing observed that gives it the appearance, sometimes through intent, of something else ⟨the *seeming* simplicity of the story⟩.

Ostensible suggests a discrepancy between an openly declared or logically implied aim or reason and the true one ⟨business was the *ostensible* reason for their visit⟩.

2. See EVIDENT.

appear See SEEM.

appease See PACIFY.

apperception See RECOGNITION.

appetizing See PALATABLE.

appliance See IMPLEMENT.

applicable See RELEVANT.

apply **1.** See USE *vb.* **2.** See RESORT.

appoint See FURNISH.

apportion See ALLOT.

apposite See RELEVANT.

appraise See ESTIMATE.

appreciable See PERCEPTIBLE.

appreciate **1. Appreciate, value, prize, treasure, cherish** mean to hold in high estimation.

Appreciate often connotes understanding sufficient to allow enjoyment or admiration of a thing's excellence ⟨*appreciates* fine wine⟩. ***antonym:*** despise

Value implies rating a thing highly for its intrinsic worth ⟨*values* our friendship⟩.

Prize implies taking a deep pride in or setting great store by something one possesses ⟨all people *prize* their freedom⟩.

Treasure emphasizes jealously safeguarding something considered precious ⟨*treasured* mementos of her youth⟩.

Cherish implies a special love and care for an object of attachment ⟨*cherishes* her children above all⟩. ***antonym:*** neglect

2. See UNDERSTAND.

apprehend See FORESEE.

apprehension, foreboding, misgiving, presentiment mean a feeling that something undesirable will or is about to happen.

Apprehension implies a mind preoccupied with fear and anxiety ⟨approached the dangerous undertaking with great *apprehension*⟩. ***antonym:*** confidence

Foreboding suggests fear that is oppressive, unreasoning, or indefinable ⟨the deserted streets filled me with strange *forebodings*⟩.

Misgiving suggests uneasiness and mistrust ⟨had my *misgivings* about her from the start⟩.

Presentiment implies a vague or uncanny sense that something, often unpleasant, is bound to happen ⟨a *presentiment* that some of our group would not survive⟩.

apprehensive See FEARFUL 1.

apprentice See NOVICE.

apprise See INFORM.

approach See MATCH.

appropriate *vb* **Appropriate, preempt, arrogate, usurp, confiscate** mean to seize high-handedly.

Appropriate suggests making something one's own or converting to one's own use without authority or with questionable right ⟨just *appropriated* the tools meant to be shared by all⟩.

Preempt implies beforehandedness in taking something desired or needed by others ⟨news of the crisis *preempted* much of the regular programming⟩.

Arrogate implies insolence, presumption, and exclusion of others in seizing rights, powers, or functions ⟨White House staffers *arrogated* powers belonging to cabinet members⟩. ***antonym:*** renounce, yield

Usurp implies unlawful or unwarranted

intrusion into the place of another and seizure of what is his by custom, right, or law ⟨her new stepmother had *usurped* her place in the household⟩. ***antonym:*** abdicate

Confiscate always implies seizure through exercise of authority ⟨customs officers *confiscate* all contraband⟩.

appropriate *adj* See FIT *adj*.

approve, **endorse**, **sanction**, **accredit**, **certify** mean to have or express a favorable opinion of or about someone or something.

Approve implies commendation or agreement and may suggest a judicious attitude ⟨the parents *approve* of the marriage⟩. ***antonym:*** disapprove

Endorse suggests an explicit statement of support ⟨publicly *endorsed* her for Senator⟩.

Sanction implies both approval and authorization and may suggest the providing of a standard ⟨the President *sanctioned* covert operations⟩. ***antonym:*** interdict

Accredit and ***certify*** usually imply official endorsement attesting conformity to set standards ⟨the board voted to *accredit* the college⟩ ⟨must be *certified* to teach⟩.

approximately See NEARLY.

apropos See RELEVANT.

apt **1.** See FIT *adj*. **2.** See QUICK.

aptitude See GIFT.

arbitrary See ABSOLUTE.

archaic See OLD.

arcane See MYSTERIOUS.

arch See SAUCY.

ardent See IMPASSIONED.

ardor See PASSION.

arduous See HARD.

argot See DIALECT.

argue See DISCUSS.

arid See DRY.

arise **1.** See SPRING. **2.** See RISE 2.

aristocracy **1.** See OLIGARCHY. **2. Aristocracy**, **nobility**, **gentry**, **elite**, **society** mean a body of people constituting a socially superior caste.

Aristocracy usually refers to those persons of superior birth, breeding, and social station ⟨plantation families constituted the *aristocracy* of the antebellum South⟩ or to an ideally superior caste without reference to a definite group ⟨the *aristocracy* of intellectuals⟩. ***antonym:*** people, proletariat

Nobility refers to persons of a privileged and titled class that ranks just below royalty ⟨the duke ranks highest in British *nobility*⟩.

Gentry refers to a class of leisured, well-bred persons who are considered gentlefolk but are without hereditary titles ⟨a private school favored by generations of the *gentry*⟩.

Elite refers to the members of any group or class who are judged highest by social or cultural standards ⟨acknowl edged to be among the *elite* few of the artistic set⟩. ***antonym:*** rabble

Society refers to that class of people who are celebrated for their active social life, conspicuous leisure, and fashionable sports and clothes ⟨the famed lavish balls of Newport *society*⟩

arm See FURNISH.

aroma See SMELL.

aromatic See ODOROUS.

arouse See STIR.

arrange **1.** See NEGOTIATE. **2.** See ORDER.

arrant See OUTRIGHT.

array See LINE.

arrival, **advent** mean the reaching of a destination.

Arrival emphasizes the preceding travel or movement ⟨an *arrival* delayed by fog and ice⟩. ***antonym:*** departure

Advent applies to a momentous or conspicuous arrival or an appearance upon a scene especially for the first time ⟨the *advent* of a new age in space travel⟩. ***antonym:*** exit

arrogant See PROUD.

arrogate See APPROPRIATE *vb*.

art, **skill**, **cunning**, **artifice**, **craft** mean the faculty of executing expertly what one has planned or devised.

Art distinctively implies a personal, unanalyzable creative power ⟨an *art* for saying the right thing⟩.

Skill stresses technical knowledge and proficiency ⟨the *skills* required of a surgeon⟩.

Cunning suggests ingenuity and subtlety in devising, inventing, or executing ⟨a mystery thriller written with great *cunning*⟩.

Artifice suggests mechanical skill especially in imitating things in nature but implies a lack of real creative power and a degree of artificiality ⟨a painter with much of the *artifice* of Rubens and none of the art⟩.

Craft may imply ingenuity and skill but tends to suggest expertness in workmanship and facility in the use of tools ⟨a saltcellar wrought with *craft* worthy of Cellini⟩.

artful See SLY.

article See THING.

articulate See VOCAL 1, 2.

articulation See JOINT.

artifice **1.** See ART. **2.** See TRICK.

artificial, **factitious**, **synthetic**, **ersatz** mean brought into being not by nature but by human art or effort.

Artificial is applicable to anything that is not the result of natural processes or conditions ⟨the state is an *artificial* society⟩ but especially to something that has a counterpart in nature or imitates something natural ⟨*artificial* teeth⟩. ***antonym:*** natural

Factitious applies chiefly to emotions or states of mind not naturally caused or spontaneously aroused but artfully produced to serve some end ⟨created a *factitious* demand for the product⟩. ***antonym:*** bonafide, veritable

Synthetic applies especially to a manufactured substance or to a natural substance so treated that it acquires the appearance or qualities of another and may substitute for it ⟨*synthetic* furs⟩.

Ersatz often implies the use of an inferior substitute for a natural product ⟨served *ersatz* cream with the coffee⟩. ***antonym:*** genuine

artless See NATURAL.

ascend **1. Ascend, mount, climb, scale** mean to move upward or toward a summit.

Ascend implies progressive upward movement ⟨the car *ascended* the steep grade⟩. ***antonym:*** descend

Mount suggests a getting up upon something raised ⟨*mount* a horse⟩. ***antonym:*** dismount

Climb connotes the effort involved in upward movement and is used when difficulty is implicit in the situation ⟨*climb* a tree to rescue a cat⟩. ***antonym:*** descend

Scale suggests skill and adroitness in upward movement ⟨*scale* a high wall to freedom⟩.

2. See RISE.

ascendancy See SUPREMACY.

ascertain See DISCOVER.

ascetic See SEVERE.

ascribe, **attribute**, **assign**, **impute**, **credit**, **charge** mean to lay something to the account of a person or thing.

Ascribe suggests an inferring or conjecturing of a cause, quality, or authorship not outwardly apparent ⟨none of the frivolity commonly *ascribed* to teenagers⟩.

Attribute may suggest the plausibility and appropriateness of the indicated relation ⟨*attribute* the project's failure to poor planning⟩.

Assign implies ascribing with certainty or after deliberation ⟨an investigatory panel *assigned* blame to top officials⟩.

Impute suggests ascribing something that brings discredit by way of accusation or blame ⟨tried to *impute* sinister motives to my actions⟩.

Credit implies ascribing a thing or especially an action to a person or other thing as its agent, source, or explanation ⟨*credited* his insecurities to an unhappy childhood⟩.

Charge implies a fixing upon a person or thing of the responsibility for a fault, crime, or evil ⟨*charged* with the crime of murder⟩.

ashen See PALE 1.

ashy See PALE 1.

asinine See SIMPLE.

ask **1. Ask, question, interrogate, query, inquire** mean to address a person in order to acquire information.

Ask implies no more than the putting of a question ⟨*ask* for directions⟩.

Question usually suggests the asking of a series of questions ⟨*questioned* them about every detail of the trip⟩. ***antonym:*** answer

Interrogate suggests formal or official systematic questioning ⟨the prosecutor *interrogated* the witness all day⟩.

Query implies a desire for authoritative information or confirmation ⟨*queried* the reference librarian about the book⟩.

Inquire implies a searching for facts or for truth often specifically by asking questions ⟨began to *inquire* into the charges of espionage⟩.

2. Ask, request, solicit mean to seek to obtain by making one's wants known.

Ask implies no more than the statement of the desire ⟨*ask* a favor of a friend⟩.

Request implies greater formality and courtesy ⟨*requests* the pleasure of your company at the ball⟩.

Solicit suggests a calling attention to one's wants or desires, often publicly, in the hope of having them satisfied ⟨a classified ad that *solicits* a situation as a babysitter⟩.

asocial See UNSOCIAL.

aspect See PHASE.

asperity See ACRIMONY.

asperse See MALIGN *vb.*

asphyxiate See SUFFOCATE.

aspiration See AMBITION.

assail See ATTACK *vb.*

assassinate See KILL.

assault *n* See ATTACK *n* 1.

assault *vb* See ATTACK *vb.*

assemble See GATHER 1.

assent, consent, accede, acquiesce, agree, subscribe mean to concur with what has been proposed.

Assent implies an act involving the understanding or judgment and applies to propositions or opinions ⟨potential members must *assent* to the organization's credo⟩. ***antonym:*** dissent

Consent involves the will or feelings and indicates compliance with what is requested or desired ⟨*consented* to their daughter's wish to go on the trip⟩. ***antonym:*** dissent

Accede implies a yielding, often under pressure, of assent or concession ⟨officials *acceded* to every demand of the prisoners⟩. ***antonym:*** demur

Acquiesce implies tacit acceptance or forbearance of opposition ⟨usually *acquiesces* to his wife's wishes⟩. ***antonym:*** object

Agree sometimes implies previous difference of opinion or attempts at persuasion, negotiation, or discussion ⟨finally *agreed* to give him a raise⟩. ***antonym:*** protest (*against*), differ (*with*)

Subscribe implies not only consent or assent but hearty approval and willingness to go on record ⟨totally *subscribed* to the free enterprise system⟩. ***antonym:*** boggle

assert **1. Assert, declare, affirm, protest, avow** mean to state positively usually in anticipation or in the face of denial or objection.

Assert implies stating confidently or even brashly without need for proof or regard for evidence ⟨*asserted* that modern music is just noise⟩. ***antonym:*** deny, controvert

Declare stresses the making of an open or public statement ⟨the jury *declared* the defendant guilty⟩.

Affirm implies conviction and willingness to stand by one's statement because of evidence, experience, or faith ⟨*affirmed* the existence of an afterlife⟩. ***antonym:*** deny

Protest stresses affirmation, especially in the face of denial or doubt ⟨*protested* that he had never had a more splendid meal⟩.

Avow stresses frank declaration and acknowledgment of personal responsibility for what is declared ⟨*avowed* that all investors would be repaid in full⟩.

2. See MAINTAIN.

assertive See AGGRESSIVE.

assess See ESTIMATE.

assiduous See BUSY.

assign **1.** See ALLOT. **2.** See ASCRIBE. **3.** See PRESCRIBE.

assignment See TASK.

assimilate See ABSORB.

assimilation See RECOGNITION.

assist See HELP.

assistant, **helper**, **coadjutor**, **aid**, **aide**, **aide-de-camp** mean a person who takes over part of the duties of another, especially in a subordinate capacity.

Assistant applies to such a person, regardless of the status of the work ⟨a carpenter's *assistant*⟩.

Helper often implies apprenticeship in a trade or status as an unskilled laborer ⟨a mother's *helper* who performs the duties of a nursemaid⟩.

Coadjutor implies equality except in authority and may be used of a coworker or a volunteer ⟨viewed the librarian as *coadjutor* of her researches⟩.

Aid and ***aide*** are often interchangeable ⟨a nurse's *aid*⟩ ⟨a teacher's *aide*⟩, but ***aide*** frequently and ***aid*** rarely denotes a special, highly qualified assistant who acts as an advisor ⟨the President and his chief *aides* formulating domestic policy⟩.

Aide and ***aide-de-camp*** designate specifically a military officer who personally attends a general, a sovereign, a president, or a governor, often as an escort but sometimes with definite duties ⟨instructed his *aide-de-camp* to keep the press away⟩.

associate See JOIN.

assorted See MISCELLANEOUS.

assuage See RELIEVE.

assume **1. Assume**, **affect**, **pretend**, **simulate**, **feign**, **counterfeit**, **sham** mean to put on a false or deceptive appearance.

Assume often implies a justifiable motive rather than an intent to deceive ⟨*assumed* an air of cheerfulness for the sake of the patient⟩.

Affect implies making a false show of possessing, using, or feeling something, usually for effect ⟨willing to *affect* an interest in art in order to impress her⟩.

Pretend implies an overt and sustained false profession of what is ⟨*pretended* not to know about her husband's affair⟩.

Simulate suggests an assumption of the characteristics of something else by a close imitation ⟨the training chamber *simulates* a weightless atmosphere⟩.

Feign implies more artful invention than ***pretend***, less specific imitation than ***simulate*** ⟨*feigned* sickness in order to stay home from school⟩.

Counterfeit implies imitation that achieves an extremely high degree of verisimilitude ⟨*counterfeited* drunkenness so perfectly that many forgot he was acting⟩.

Sham stresses an obvious intent to deceive with falseness that fools only the gullible ⟨*shammed* a most unconvincing limp⟩.

2. See PRESUPPOSE.

assurance **1.** See CERTAINTY. **2.** See CONFIDENCE.

assure See ENSURE.

astonish See SURPRISE 2.

astound See SURPRISE 2.

astute See SHREWD.

asylum See SHELTER.

athirst See EAGER.

athletics, **sports**, **games** mean physical activities engaged in for exercise or play.

Athletics is a collective term applied to exercises for which one acquires and maintains agility, skill, and stamina usually in order to compete as an individual or a member of a team ⟨played amateur and professional *athletics*⟩.

Sports implies forms of physical activity that give pleasure or diversion, and sometimes lacks the connotation of vigorous skill, training, and competition ⟨finds more opportunity for *sports* in the summer⟩.

Games suggests athletic or sports contests that require extensive rules ⟨the intricate rules of *games* that use a ball or puck⟩ or denotes a meet held for competition chiefly in track-and-field events ⟨winners from the Pan-American and Pan-African *games*⟩.

atmosphere **1.** See AIR. **2. Atmosphere**, **feeling**, **aura** mean an intangible quality that gives something an individual and distinctly recognizable character.

Atmosphere implies a quality that accrues to something or that pervades it as a whole and that determines the impression given by that thing ⟨a country inn with a warm and friendly *atmosphere*⟩.

Feeling implies that something has distinctive qualities that create a definite if unanalyzable impression ⟨a garden with a definite country *feeling*⟩.

Aura suggests an ethereal or mysterious quality that seems to emanate from a person or thing ⟨a movie queen with an unmistakable *aura* of glamour⟩.

atom See PARTICLE.

atrocious See OUTRAGEOUS.

attach See FASTEN.

attack *n* **1. Attack**, **assault**, **onslaught**, **onset** mean an attempt to injure, destroy, or defame.

Attack, whether on person or character, suggests animosity or enmity as its cause but may imply such motives as cruelty, partisanship, or criticism ⟨a speech *attacking* governmental policies⟩.

Assault implies more violence and malice or viciousness and often the infliction of greater damage than ***attack***, sometimes with specific legal or military connotations ⟨a victim of a brutal *assault*⟩.

Onslaught suggests a vigorous, destructive attempt to overwhelm by force of momentum or numbers or intensity ⟨succumbed to the *onslaught* of the disease⟩.

Onset applies both to the initial attack and to any successive renewal of vigor in the attack ⟨troops preparing for a fresh *onset* from the enemy⟩.

2. Attack, **aggression**, **offense**, **offensive** mean action in a struggle for supremacy, either military or athletic, which must be defended against.

Attack implies the initiation of action, often sudden and violent ⟨sustained running *attack* resulting in an early touchdown⟩.

Aggression stresses a lack of provocation and a desire for conquest or domination, chiefly by military invasion of another's territory ⟨pledged never to fight a war of *aggression*⟩. ***antonym:*** resistance

Offense characterizes the position or methods of the attackers with specific reference to their desire for supremacy ⟨went on the *offense* to gain as much ground as possible⟩.

Offensive implies vigorously aggressive action, especially in war, or it denotes a particular episode marked by such action ⟨launched an economic *offensive* to stave off a recession⟩.

3. See FIT *n*.

attack *vb* **Attack**, **assault**, **assail**, **bombard**, **storm** mean to make a more or less violent onset upon.

Attack implies aggressively taking the initiative in a struggle ⟨seek new ways to *attack* the problem of poverty⟩.

Assail implies attempting to conquer or break down resistance by repeated blows or shots ⟨*assailed* the enemy with artillery fire⟩.

Assault suggests a direct attempt to overpower by suddenness and violence of onslaught in a direct confrontation ⟨commando troops *assaulted* the building from all sides⟩.

Bombard applies to attacking continuously and devastatingly with bombs or shells ⟨*bombarded* the city nightly⟩.

Storm implies an attempt to sweep from its path every obstacle to victory ⟨a fortress that has never been *stormed*⟩.

attain See REACH.

attainment See ACQUIREMENT.

attempt, **try**, **endeavor**, **essay**, **strive** mean to make an effort to accomplish an end.

Attempt stresses the initiation or beginning of an effort and often suggests the strong possibility of failure ⟨will *attempt* to photograph the rare bird⟩.

Try stresses effort or experiment made to test or prove something ⟨*tried* several times to find a solution⟩.

Endeavor heightens the implications of exertion and difficulty and connotes a striving to fulfill a duty ⟨*endeavored* to find survivors of the crash⟩.

Essay implies difficulty but also suggests tentative trying or experimenting ⟨had *essayed* dramatic roles on two earlier occasions⟩.

Strive implies exertion against great difficulty and specifically suggests persistent effort ⟨continues to *strive* for a lasting peaceful solution⟩.

attend **1.** See ACCOMPANY. **2.** See TEND.

attentive See THOUGHTFUL 2.

attest See CERTIFY.

attitude See POSITION 1.

attorney See LAWYER.

attract, **allure**, **charm**, **captivate**, **fascinate**, **bewitch**, **enchant** mean to draw another by exerting an irresistible or powerful influence.

Attract applies to any degree or kind of ability to exert influence to draw ⟨a university that *attracts* students from around the world⟩. ***antonym:*** repel

Allure implies an enticing by what is fair, pleasing, or seductive ⟨the excitement of the city *allures* young people⟩. ***antonym:*** repel

Charm may suggest magic and implies a power to evoke or attract admiration ⟨*charmed* by the beauty of that serene isle⟩. ***antonym:*** disgust

Captivate implies an often transitory capturing of the fancy or feelings ⟨her grace and beauty *captivated* us all⟩. ***antonym:*** repulse

Fascinate suggests a magical influence and tends to stress the ineffectiveness of attempts to resist or escape ⟨a story that continues to *fascinate* children⟩.

Bewitch implies exertion of an overwhelming power of attraction ⟨*bewitched* by the promise of great wealth⟩.

Enchant stresses the power to evoke delight or joy or ecstatic admiration in the one affected ⟨hopelessly *enchanted* by his dashing looks and deep voice⟩. ***antonym:*** disenchant

attraction, **affinity**, **sympathy** mean the relationship existing between things or persons that are naturally or involuntarily drawn together.

Attraction implies the possession by one thing of a quality that tends to draw another to it ⟨a curious *attraction* between people of opposite temperaments⟩.

Affinity implies a susceptibility or predisposition on the part of the one attracted ⟨a student with an *affinity* for mathematics⟩.

Sympathy implies a reciprocal relation between two things that are both susceptible to the same influence ⟨shared a glance of mutual *sympathy*⟩. ***antonym:*** antipathy

attribute *vb* See ASCRIBE.

attribute *n* **1.** See QUALITY. **2.** See SYMBOL.

atypical See ABNORMAL.

audacity See TEMERITY.

augment See INCREASE.
aura See ATMOSPHERE.
auspicious See FAVORABLE.
austere See SEVERE.
authentic, genuine, veritable, bona fide mean being actually and exactly what is claimed.

Authentic implies being fully trustworthy as according with fact or actuality ⟨the *authentic* story⟩. ***antonym:*** spurious

Genuine implies accordance with an original or a type without counterfeiting, admixture, or adulteration ⟨*genuine* maple syrup⟩, or it may stress sincerity ⟨*genuine* piety⟩. ***antonym:*** counterfeit, fraudulent

Veritable implies a correspondence with truth and typically conveys a suggestion of affirmation ⟨in the grip of anxiety that drove him into a *veritable* trance⟩ or asserts the suitability of a metaphor ⟨*veritable* hail of questions⟩. ***antonym:*** factitious

Bona fide can apply when sincerity of intention is in question ⟨*bona fide* sale of securities⟩. ***antonym:*** counterfeit, bogus

authenticate See CONFIRM.
author See MAKER.
authority 1. See INFLUENCE. **2.** See POWER 3.
autocratic See ABSOLUTE.
automatic See SPONTANEOUS.
autonomous See FREE *adj*.
avaricious See COVETOUS.
avenge, revenge mean to punish a person who has wronged oneself or another.

Avenge suggests that the ends of justice are being served or another is being vindicated or a merited punishment is being administered ⟨*avenged* the insult to his honor⟩.

Revenge implies a desire to retaliate or get even and therefore connotes states of malice, spite, or unwillingness to forgive ⟨angry determination to *revenge* herself for the slight⟩.

average, mean, median, norm mean something that represents a middle point between extremes.

Average is exactly or approximately the quotient obtained by dividing the sum total of a set of figures by the number of figures ⟨scored an *average* of 85 in a series of five tests⟩. ***antonym:*** maximum, minimum

Mean may be an average, or it may represent value midway between two extremes ⟨annual temperature *mean* of 50°⟩ ⟨the tranquil *mean* between misery and ecstasy⟩.

Median applies to the value that represents the point at which there are as many instances above as there are below ⟨the *average* of a group of persons earning 3, 4, 5, 8, and 10 dollars a day is 6 dollars, whereas the *median* is 5 dollars⟩.

Norm denotes the computed or estimated average of performance of a significantly large group, class, or grade and implies a standard of reference ⟨scores about the *norm* for 5th grade arithmetic⟩.

averse See DISINCLINED.
avert See PREVENT 2.
avid See EAGER.
avoid See ESCAPE.
avow 1. See ACKNOWLEDGE. **2.** See ASSERT.
await See EXPECT.
awake See AWARE.
awaken See STIR *vb*.
award See GRANT.
aware, cognizant, conscious, sensible, alive, awake mean having knowledge of something.

Aware implies vigilance in observing or alertness in drawing inferences from what is observed ⟨*aware* of a greater number of police officers out and about⟩. ***antonym:*** unaware

Cognizant implies possession of special or certain knowledge as from firsthand sources ⟨as yet, not fully *cognizant* of all the facts⟩. ***antonym:*** ignorant

Conscious implies that one is focusing

one's attention on something already perceptible to the mind or senses ⟨*conscious* that my heart was pounding away⟩. ***antonym:*** unconscious

Sensible implies direct or intuitive perception especially of intangibles or of emotional states or qualities ⟨a doctor who was *sensible* of the woman's deep depression⟩. ***antonym:*** insensible (*of* or *to*)

Alive suggests vivid awareness of or acute sensitivity to something ⟨we were fully *alive* to the momentousness of the occasion⟩. ***antonym:*** blind (*to*)

Awake implies that one has become alive to something and is on the alert ⟨ a country not *awake* to the dangers of persistent inflation⟩.

awe See REVERENCE.

awful See FEARFUL 2.

awkward, **clumsy**, **maladroit**, **inept**, **gauche** mean not marked by ease and smoothness (as of performance or movement).

Awkward is widely applicable and may suggest unhandiness, inconvenience, lack of control, embarrassment, or lack of tact ⟨a dinner party marked by periods of *awkward* silence⟩. ***antonym:*** handy, deft, graceful

Clumsy implies stiffness and heaviness and so may connote inflexibility, unwieldiness, ponderousness, or lack of ordinary skill ⟨a writer with a persistently *clumsy* style⟩. ***antonym:*** dexterous, adroit, facile

Maladroit suggests a deficiency of tact and a tendency to create awkward situations ⟨a *maladroit* handling of a delicate situation⟩. ***antonym:*** adroit

Inept often implies inappropriateness, futility, and absurdity ⟨blamed the conviction on his *inept* defense attorney⟩. ***antonym:*** apt, adept, able

Gauche implies the effects of shyness, inexperience, or ill breeding ⟨always felt *gauche* and unsophisticated at formal parties⟩.

B

babel See DIN.

baby See INDULGE.

back **1.** See RECEDE. **2.** See SUPPORT.

backbone See FORTITUDE.

background, **setting**, **environment**, **milieu**, **mise-en-scène** mean the place, time, and circumstances in which something occurs.

Background refers to those aspects of a stage or picture most remote from the viewer and against or in front of which the actions or figures are set ⟨city streets visible in the *background*⟩ and by extension often refers to the circumstances or events that precede a phenomenon or development ⟨a *background* that prepared her well for the task⟩.

Setting describes the time, place, and conditions in which the characters act in a piece of literature, art, or drama ⟨chose a 19th-century *setting* for her novel⟩ and suggests that one is looking at a real-life situation as though it were a dramatic or literary representation ⟨a social reformer who was born into the most unlikely social *setting*⟩.

Environment applies to all the external factors that have a formative influence on one's physical, mental, or moral development ⟨the kind of *environment* that produces juvenile delinquents⟩.

Milieu applies especially to the physical and social surroundings of a person or group of persons ⟨an intellectual *milieu* conducive to bold experimentation in the arts⟩.

Mise-en-scène strongly suggests the use of properties to achieve a particular atmosphere or theatrical effect ⟨a tale of the occult with a carefully crafted *mise-en-scène*⟩.

backslide See LAPSE *vb*.

bad, **evil**, **ill**, **wicked**, **naughty** mean not morally good or ethically acceptable.

Bad may apply to any degree or kind of reprehensibility ⟨the *bad* guys in a Western⟩. ***antonym:*** good

Evil is a stronger term than ***bad*** and usually carries a baleful or sinister connotation ⟨*evil* men who would even commit murder⟩. ***antonym:*** exemplary, salutary

Ill may imply malevolence or vice ⟨paid dearly for his *ill* deeds⟩. ***antonym:*** good

Wicked usually connotes malice and malevolence ⟨a *wicked* person who delighted in the suffering of others⟩.

Naughty applies either to trivial misdeeds or to matters impolite or amusingly risqué ⟨looked up all the *naughty* words in the dictionary⟩.

badger See BAIT.

baffle See FRUSTRATE.

bag See CATCH.

bait, **badger**, **heckle**, **hector**, **chivy**, **hound** mean to harass persistently or annoyingly by efforts to break down.

Bait implies wanton cruelty or delight in persecuting a helpless victim ⟨siblings *baited* each other constantly⟩.

Badger implies pestering so as to drive a person to confusion or frenzy ⟨*badgered* her father for a raise in her allowance⟩.

Heckle implies persistent interruptive questioning of a speaker in order to confuse or discomfit ⟨drunks *heckled* the stand-up comic⟩.

Hector carries an implication of bullying, scolding, and domineering that breaks the spirit ⟨as a child he had been *hectored* by his father⟩.

Chivy suggests persecution by teasing or nagging ⟨*chivied* her husband to the breaking point⟩.

Hound implies unrelenting pursuit and persecution ⟨*hounded* on all sides by creditors⟩.

balance *vb* See COMPENSATE.

balance *n* See SYMMETRY.

bald See BARE.

baleful See SINISTER.

balk See FRUSTRATE.

balky See CONTRARY.
balmy **1.** See SOFT. **2.** See ODOROUS.
ban See FORBID.
banal See INSIPID.
bane See POISON.
baneful See PERNICIOUS.
banish, **exile**, **deport**, **transport** mean to remove by authority or force from a state or country.

Banish implies compulsory removal from a country not necessarily one's own ⟨a country that once *banished* the Jesuits⟩.

Exile may imply compulsory removal or an enforced or voluntary absence from one's own country ⟨a writer who *exiled* himself from South Africa⟩.

Deport implies a sending out of a country, often back to his or her country of origin, an alien who has illegally entered or whose presence is judged inimical to the public welfare ⟨*deported* many foreign criminals⟩.

Transport implies a sending of a convicted criminal to a particular place, often an overseas penal colony ⟨a convict who was *transported* to Australia⟩.

bank See RELY.
bankrupt See DEPLETE.
barbarian, **barbaric**, **barbarous**, **savage** mean characteristic of uncivilized people.

Barbarian often implies a state midway between tribal savagery and full civilization ⟨traded with *barbarian* peoples to the north⟩. ***antonym:*** civilized

Barbaric tends to imply a wild profusion and lack of restraint that is indicative of crudity of taste and lack of self-restraint ⟨punished the animal with *barbaric* cruelty⟩. ***antonym:*** restrained, refined, subdued

Barbarous is more likely to imply uncivilized cruelty or ruthlessness or sometimes complete lack of cultivated taste and refinement ⟨outlawed the *barbarous* practices of war⟩. ***antonym:*** civilized, humane

Savage in its basic use implies less advance toward civilization than ***barbarian*** ⟨a *savage* tribe with a gathering economy⟩ and in its extended use is ordinarily very close to ***barbarous*** ⟨a *savage* attack⟩. ***antonym:*** civilized

barbaric See BARBARIAN.
barbarous **1.** See BARBARIAN. **2.** See FIERCE.
bare, **naked**, **nude**, **bald**, **barren** mean deprived of naturally or conventionally appropriate covering.

Bare implies the absence of what is additional, superfluous, ornamental, or dispensable ⟨a bleak apartment with *bare* walls⟩. ***antonym:*** covered

Naked suggests complete absence of protective or ornamental covering but may imply a state of nature, of destitution, of defenselessness, or of simple beauty ⟨poor, half-*naked* children shivering in the cold⟩.

Nude applies especially to the unclothed human figure ⟨a *nude* model posing for art students⟩. ***antonym:*** clothed

Bald implies actual or seeming absence of natural covering and may suggest a severe plainness or lack of adornment ⟨a *bald* mountain peak⟩.

Barren often suggests aridity or impoverishment or sterility through absence of natural or appropriate covering ⟨*barren* plains with few shrubs and no trees⟩.

barefaced See SHAMELESS.
barren **1.** See BARE. **2.** See STERILE.
barrister See LAWYER.
base *n* **Base**, **basis**, **foundation**, **ground**, **groundwork** mean something on which another thing is built up and by which it is supported.

Base implies an underlying element that supports or seems to support something material or immaterial ⟨the *base* of a column⟩. ***antonym:*** top

Basis, similar in meaning, is rarely used of material things and usually carries a more definite implication of support

⟨used those facts as the *basis* of her argument⟩.

Foundation tends to imply solidity in what underlies and supports and fixity or stability in what is supported ⟨the beliefs rested on a *foundation* of firm conviction⟩. ***antonym:*** superstructure

Ground suggests solidity and is likely to imply a substratum comparable to the earth in its capacity to support and sometimes to justify ⟨behavior that was *ground* for dismissal⟩.

Groundwork can apply to a substructure but is used chiefly in a figurative sense ⟨laid the *groundwork* for future negotiations⟩. ***antonym:*** superstructure

base *adj* **Base**, **low**, **vile** mean deserving of contempt because beneath what is expected of the average person.

Base stresses the ignoble and may suggest cruelty, treachery, greed, or grossness ⟨real estate developers with *base* motives⟩. ***antonym:*** noble

Low may connote crafty cunning, vulgarity, or immorality and regularly implies an outraging of one's sense of decency or propriety ⟨refused to listen to such *low* talk⟩.

Vile, the strongest of these words, tends to suggest disgusting depravity or foulness ⟨a *vile* remark⟩ ⟨the *vilest* of crimes⟩.

bashful See SHY.

basis See BASE.

bathos See PATHOS.

batter See MAIM.

battle, **engagement**, **action** mean a meeting, often military, between opposing forces.

Battle describes general and prolonged combat or can imply a major extended struggle or controversy ⟨fighting a losing *battle* for basic civility⟩.

Engagement stresses actual combat between forces and may apply to a major battle or a minor skirmish; in extended uses it tends to replace the suggestion of hostility with one of interaction ⟨sought to create an *engagement* between students and teachers⟩.

Action stresses the active give-and-take of offensive and defensive efforts or of attaining an end or resisting a pressure ⟨sounded the call to *action* on behalf of environmentalists⟩.

bear 1. See CARRY. **2. Bear**, **suffer**, **endure**, **abide**, **tolerate**, **brook**, **stand** mean to put up with something trying or painful.

Bear usually implies the power to sustain what is distressing or hurtful without flinching or breaking ⟨forced to *bear* one personal tragedy after another⟩.

Suffer often suggests acceptance or passivity rather than courage or patience in bearing ⟨never *suffered* a single insult to go unchallenged⟩.

Endure implies meeting trials and difficulties with continued firm resolution ⟨*endured* years of rejection and neglect⟩.

Abide suggests acceptance without resistance or protest ⟨I cannot *abide* her chronic rudeness⟩.

Tolerate suggests overcoming or successfully controlling an impulse to resist, avoid, or resent something injurious or distasteful ⟨*tolerated* his affairs for the sake of the children⟩.

Brook implies self-assertion and defiance ⟨will not *brook* restraint⟩.

Stand emphasizes even more strongly the ability to bear without discomposure or flinching ⟨she cannot *stand* teasing⟩.

bearing, **deportment**, **demeanor**, **mien**, **manner**, **carriage** mean the outward manifestation of personality or attitude.

Bearing is the most general of these words but now usually implies characteristic posture ⟨a woman of regal *bearing*⟩.

Deportment suggests actions or behavior as formed by breeding or training in regard to the amenities of life ⟨a child with atrocious *deportment*⟩.

Demeanor suggests one's attitude as expressed by behavior among others ⟨the haughty *demeanor* of a head waiter⟩.

Mien refers both to bearing and demeanor often as indicative of mood ⟨a *mien* of supreme self-satisfaction⟩.

Manner implies characteristic or customary way of moving and gesturing in a social context ⟨the imperious *manner* of a man used to giving orders⟩.

Carriage applies chiefly to habitual posture in standing or walking ⟨the kind of *carriage* learned at elite private schools⟩.

beat See CONQUER.

beautiful, **lovely**, **handsome**, **pretty**, **comely**, **fair** mean sensuously or aesthetically pleasing.

Beautiful applies to whatever excites the keenest of pleasure to the senses and stirs intellectual or spiritual emotion ⟨*beautiful* mountain scenery⟩. ***antonym:*** ugly

Lovely applies to a narrower range of emotional excitation rather than to intellectual or spiritual pleasure ⟨a *lovely* melody⟩. ***antonym:*** unlovely, plain

Handsome suggests aesthetic pleasure resulting from proportion, symmetry, or elegance ⟨a *handsome* Georgian mansion⟩.

Pretty applies to superficial or insubstantial attractiveness that pleases by its delicacy, grace, or charm ⟨a painter of conventionally *pretty* scenes⟩.

Comely is like ***handsome*** in suggesting cool approval rather than emotional response ⟨the *comely* grace of a dancer⟩. ***antonym:*** homely

Fair suggests beauty based on purity, flawlessness, or freshness ⟨looking for fashion models with *fair* faces⟩. ***antonym:*** foul, ill-favored

beautify See ADORN.

bedeck See ADORN.

beg, **entreat**, **beseech**, **implore**, **supplicate**, **adjure**, **importune** mean to ask or request urgently.

Beg suggests earnestness or insistence especially in asking for a favor ⟨children *begging* to stay up later⟩.

Entreat implies an effort to persuade or to overcome resistance in another ⟨*entreated* him to change his mind⟩.

Beseech implies eagerness, anxiety, or solicitude ⟨I *beseech* you to have mercy⟩.

Implore adds a suggestion of greater urgency or anguished appeal ⟨*implored* her not to leave him⟩.

Supplicate suggests a posture of humility ⟨with bowed heads they *supplicated* their lord⟩.

Adjure implies advising as well as pleading and suggests the involving of something sacred ⟨in God's name I *adjure* you to cease⟩.

Importune suggests an annoying persistence in trying to break down resistance to a request ⟨*importuned* his mother nearly every day to buy him a new bike⟩.

begin, **commence**, **start**, **initiate**, **inaugurate** mean to take the first step in a course, process, or operation.

Begin is the most general and applies especially to less formal contexts ⟨school *begins* at eight⟩ ⟨*began* to wash the dishes⟩. ***antonym:*** end

Commence suggests greater formality ⟨let the games *commence*⟩. ***antonym:*** conclude

Start suggests a getting or setting into motion ⟨the procession *started* out slowly⟩. ***antonym:*** stop

Initiate suggests the taking of a first step of a process or series ⟨*initiated* the custom of annual gift giving⟩. ***antonym:*** consummate

Inaugurate implies a ceremonial beginning ⟨the discovery of penicillin *inaugurated* a new medical age⟩.

beguile See DECEIVE.

behave, **conduct**, **deport**, **comport**, **acquit** mean to act or to cause or allow oneself to do something in a certain way.

Behave may apply to the meeting of a standard of what is proper or decorous

⟨*behaved* very badly throughout the affair⟩. ***antonym:*** misbehave

Conduct implies action or behavior that shows one's capacity to control or direct oneself ⟨*conducted* herself with unfailing good humor⟩. ***antonym:*** misconduct

Deport implies behaving in conformity with conventional rules of discipline or propriety ⟨an ingenue who *deports* herself in the best tradition⟩.

Comport suggests conduct measured by what is expected or required of one in a certain class or position ⟨*comported* themselves as the gentlemen they were⟩.

Acquit applies to action under stress that deserves praise or meets expectations ⟨*acquitted* himself well in his first battle⟩.

behindhand See TARDY.

behold See SEE 1.

beholder See SPECTATOR.

belie See MISREPRESENT.

belief **1. Belief**, **faith**, **credence**, **credit** mean an assent to the truth of something offered for acceptance.

Belief suggests mental acceptance but may or may not imply certitude in the believer ⟨my *belief* that I had caught all the errors⟩. ***antonym:*** unbelief, disbelief

Faith always suggests certitude even where there is no evidence or proof ⟨an unshakable *faith* in God⟩. ***antonym:*** doubt

Credence suggests intellectual assent without implying anything about the validity of the grounds for assent ⟨a theory given little *credence* by scientists⟩.

Credit implies assent on grounds other than direct proof ⟨give no *credit* to idle rumors⟩.

2. See OPINION.

believable See PLAUSIBLE.

believe See KNOW.

belittle See DECRY.

bellicose See BELLIGERENT.

belligerent, **bellicose**, **pugnacious**, **combative**, **quarrelsome**, **contentious** mean having an aggressive or truculent attitude.

Belligerent implies being actively at war or engaged in hostilities ⟨*belligerent* nations respected the country's neutrality⟩. ***antonym:*** friendly

Bellicose suggests a disposition to fight ⟨an intoxicated person in a *bellicose* mood⟩. ***antonym:*** pacific, amicable

Pugnacious suggests a disposition that takes pleasure in personal combat ⟨a *pugnacious* student always getting into scraps⟩. ***antonym:*** pacific

Combative, like **pugnacious**, connotes readiness to fight on the basis of a genuine cause ⟨assumed a *combative* stance under questioning⟩. ***antonym:*** pacifistic

Quarrelsome stresses an ill-natured readiness to fight without good cause ⟨the stifling heat made us all *quarrelsome*⟩.

Contentious implies perverse and irritating fondness for arguing and quarreling ⟨wearied by her *contentious* disposition⟩. ***antonym:*** peaceable

bemoan See DEPLORE.

bend See CURVE.

beneficial, **advantageous**, **profitable** mean bringing good or gain.

Beneficial implies especially promoting health or well-being ⟨legislation that would be *beneficial* to the elderly⟩. ***antonym:*** harmful, detrimental

Advantageous stresses a choice or preference that brings superiority or greater success in attaining an end ⟨took up a more *advantageous* position⟩. ***antonym:*** disadvantageous

Profitable implies the yielding of useful or lucrative returns ⟨seeking *profitable* ways to use their time⟩. ***antonym:*** unprofitable

benign See KIND.

benignant See KIND.

bent See GIFT.

berate See SCOLD.

beseech See BEG.

bestow See GIVE.

bête noire See ABOMINATION.
betray See REVEAL.
better See IMPROVE.
bewail See DEPLORE.
bewilder See PUZZLE.
bewitch See ATTRACT.
bias *n* See PREDILECTION.
bias *vb* See INCLINE.
bid **1.** See COMMAND. **2.** See INVITE.
big See LARGE.
billingsgate See ABUSE.
bind See TIE.
birthright See HERITAGE.
biting See INCISIVE.
bit See PARTICLE.
bizarre See FANTASTIC.
blamable See BLAMEWORTHY.
blame See CRITICIZE.
blameworthy, **blamable**, **guilty**, **culpable** mean deserving reproach or punishment.

Blameworthy and ***blamable*** acknowledge the censurable quality of the act or the agent but imply nothing about the degree of reprehensibility ⟨conduct adjudged *blameworthy* by a military court⟩ ⟨an accident for which no one is *blamable*⟩. ***antonym:*** blameless

Guilty implies responsibility for or consciousness of crime, sin, or, at least, grave error or misdoing ⟨the defendant was found *guilty*⟩. ***antonym:*** innocent

Culpable is weaker than ***guilty*** and is likely to connote malfeasance or errors of ignorance, omission, or negligence ⟨a clear case of *culpable* neglect on the part of the landlord⟩.

blanch See WHITEN.
bland **1.** See SOFT. **2.** See SUAVE.
blandish See COAX.
blank See EMPTY.
blasé See SOPHISTICATED.
blatant See VOCIFEROUS.
blaze, **flame**, **flare**, **glare**, **glow** mean a brightly burning light or fire or something suggesting this.

Blaze implies rapidity in kindling of material and the radiation of intense heat and light ⟨the crackle and *blaze* of dry oak logs⟩ ⟨the angry *blaze* of her eyes⟩.

Flame suggests a darting tongue or tongues of fire ⟨the *flames* rose above the burning building⟩.

Flare stresses a sudden rapid burst of fire or flame against a dark background (as of a dying fire) ⟨the sudden *flare* of a match⟩ and implies both suddenness and intensity ⟨a *flare* of temper⟩.

Glare is likely to connote unendurable brilliance ⟨the *glare* of a searchlight⟩.

Glow is more likely to suggest a temperate burning that yields light without flame or glare, or gentle warmth and radiance ⟨the comforting *glow* of coals on the hearth⟩.

bleach See WHITEN.
bleak See DISMAL.
blemish, **defect**, **flaw** mean an imperfection that mars or damages.

Blemish suggests something that affects only the surface or appearance ⟨fair skin completely devoid of *blemishes*⟩. ***antonym:*** immaculateness

Defect implies a lack, often hidden, of something that is essential to completeness or perfect functioning ⟨the smoke detector failed because of a mechanical *defect*⟩.

Flaw suggests a small defect in continuity or cohesion that is likely to cause failure under stress ⟨a *flaw* in a pane of glass⟩.

blench See RECOIL.
blend See MIXTURE.
blithe See MERRY.
block See HINDER.
bloodless See PALE 2.
bloody, **sanguinary**, **sanguine**, **gory** mean affected by or involving the shedding of blood.

Bloody is applied especially to things that are actually covered with blood or are made up of blood ⟨*bloody* hands⟩.

Sanguinary applies especially to something attended by, or someone bent on, bloodshed ⟨the Civil War was America's most *sanguinary* conflict⟩.

Sanguine is applied specifically to bleeding, bloodthirstiness, or the color of blood ⟨one of the most *sanguine* of the Jacobean revenge tragedies⟩. ***antonym:*** bloodless

Gory suggests a profusion of blood and slaughter ⟨exceptionally *gory,* even for a teenage horror movie⟩.

blot See STIGMA.

blot out See ERASE.

blowsy See SLATTERNLY.

bluff, **blunt**, **brusque**, **curt**, **crusty**, **gruff** mean abrupt and unceremonious in speech or manner.

Bluff connotes a good-natured outspokenness and unconventionality ⟨a bartender with a *bluff* manner⟩. ***antonym:*** smooth, suave

Blunt suggests directness of expression in disregard of others' feelings ⟨a *blunt* appraisal of the performance⟩. ***antonym:*** tactful, subtle

Brusque applies to an abrupt sharpness or ungraciousness ⟨a *brusque* response to a civil question⟩. ***antonym:*** unctuous, bland

Curt implies disconcerting shortness or rude conciseness ⟨a *curt* comment about the cause of the foul-up⟩. ***antonym:*** voluble

Crusty suggests a harsh or surly manner that may conceal an inner kindliness ⟨a *crusty* exterior that conceals a heart of gold⟩.

Gruff suggests a hoarse or husky speech which may imply bad temper but more often implies embarrassment or shyness ⟨puts on a *gruff* pose in front of strangers⟩.

blunder See ERROR.

blunt **1.** See BLUFF. **2.** See DULL.

board See HARBOR.

boast, **brag**, **vaunt**, **crow** mean to express in speech pride in oneself or one's accomplishments.

Boast often suggests ostentation and exaggeration ⟨ready to *boast* of every trivial success⟩, but it may imply proper and justifiable pride ⟨the town *boasts* one of the best hospitals in the area⟩. ***antonym:*** depreciate

Brag suggests conceit, crudity, and artlessness in glorifying oneself ⟨boys *bragging* to each other⟩. ***antonym:*** apologize

Vaunt usually connotes more pomp and bombast than **boast** and less crudity or naïveté than **brag** ⟨used the occasion to *vaunt* the country's military might⟩.

Crow usually implies exultant boasting or blatant bragging ⟨loved to *crow* about his triumphs⟩.

boat, **vessel**, **ship**, **craft** mean a floating structure designed to carry persons or goods over water.

Boat is sometimes applied generally to all such structures, but more specifically denotes a small, typically open structure operated by oars, paddles, poles, sails, or a motor ⟨took the *boat* out without any paddles⟩.

Vessel suggests chiefly a large seagoing boat used to contain or transport persons or commodities or to serve as a base of operations ⟨a fleet of fishing *vessels*⟩.

Ship stresses the navigational aspect of a large seagoing vessel and has connotations of individuality and romance ⟨the beauty of the great sailing *ships*⟩.

Craft applies to any boat or ship that plies the water and is often a vague or general term ⟨small *craft* darting in all directions⟩.

bodily, **physical**, **corporeal**, **corporal**, **somatic** mean of or relating to the human body.

Bodily suggests contrast with *mental* or *spiritual* ⟨an intellectual who had *bodily* needs⟩.

Physical suggests less explicitly an organic structure ⟨their ordeal left them at the point of *physical* exhaustion⟩.

Corporeal suggests the substance of which the body is composed ⟨a divinity who assumed *corporeal* existence⟩.

Corporal applies chiefly to things that affect or involve the body ⟨a teacher who still used *corporal* punishment⟩.

Somatic implies contrast with *psychical* and is free of theological and poetic connotations ⟨*somatic* reactions to the drug⟩.

boisterous See VOCIFEROUS.

bombard See ATTACK *vb*.

bombast, **rhapsody**, **rant**, **fustian** mean speech or writing characterized by high-flown pomposity or pretentiousness.

Bombast implies verbose grandiosity or inflation of style disproportionate to the thought ⟨pedestrian ideas dressed up with *bombast*⟩.

Rhapsody applies to an ecstatic or effusive utterance governed more by the feelings than by logical thought and may specifically describe an excess of more or less incoherent praise ⟨she went into *rhapsodies* over their new house⟩ .

Rant stresses extravagance or violence in expressing something ⟨the *rants* and ravings of political fanatics⟩.

Fustian stresses the banality of what is expressed ⟨dimestore novels bursting with romantic *fustian*⟩.

bona fide See AUTHENTIC.

bondage See SERVITUDE.

bon vivant See EPICURE.

bookish See PEDANTIC.

boorish, **churlish**, **loutish**, **clownish** mean uncouth in manner or appearance.

Boorish implies rudeness of manner due to lack of culture, insensitiveness to others' feelings, or unwillingness to be agreeable ⟨your *boorish* behavior at the wedding reception⟩. ***antonym:*** gentlemanly

Churlish suggests surliness, unresponsiveness, and ungraciousness ⟨*churlish* remarks made during a television interview⟩. ***antonym:*** courtly

Loutish implies bodily awkwardness together with crude stupidity ⟨her *loutish* boyfriend spoiled the cocktail party⟩.

Clownish suggests ill-bred awkwardness, ignorance or stupidity, ungainliness, and often a propensity for absurd antics ⟨*clownish* conduct that was out of keeping with the solemn occasion⟩. ***antonym:*** urbane

boost See LIFT.

bootleg See SMUGGLED.

bootless See FUTILE.

booty See SPOIL.

border, **margin**, **verge**, **edge**, **rim**, **brim**, **brink** mean a line or outer part that marks the limit of something.

Border refers to the part of a surface just within a boundary ⟨the magazine cover's red *border*⟩ or to the boundary itself ⟨across international *borders*⟩.

Margin denotes a border or definite width or distinguishing character ⟨a *margin* of one inch on the page's left side⟩.

Verge applies to the line marking an extreme limit or termination of something ⟨an empire that extended to the *verge* of the known world⟩.

Edge denotes the line of termination made by two converging surfaces as of a blade or a box ⟨the *edge* of a table⟩.

Rim applies to an edge of something circular or curving ⟨the *rim* of a wagon wheel⟩.

Brim applies to the upper inner rim of something hollow ⟨fill the cup to the *brim*⟩.

Brink denotes the edge of something that falls away steeply ⟨walked to the *brink* of the cliff⟩ and may imply abrupt transition ⟨nations on the *brink* of peace⟩.

boredom See TEDIUM.

bother See ANNOY.

bough See SHOOT.

bountiful See LIBERAL 1.

bouquet See FRAGRANCE.

box See STRIKE 2.

brag See BOAST.

branch See SHOOT.

brand See STIGMA.

brandish See SWING 1.

brash See SHAMELESS.

brave, **courageous**, **unafraid**, **fearless**, **intrepid**, **valiant**, **valorous**, **dauntless** mean having or showing no fear when faced with something dangerous, difficult, or unknown.

Brave indicates lack of fear in a larming or difficult circumstances ⟨a *brave* kitten hissing at the much bigger dog⟩. ***antonym:*** craven

Courageous implies temperamental stoutheartedness and readiness to meet danger or difficulties ⟨*courageous* stance before the unruly crowd⟩. ***antonym:*** pusillanimous

Unafraid indicates simple lack of fright or fear ⟨faced the future *unafraid*⟩. ***antonym:*** afraid

Fearless may indicate lack of fear or, more positively, undismayed resolution ⟨took a *fearless* stance against powerful opponents⟩. ***antonym:*** fearful

Intrepid suggests daring in meeting danger or fortitude in enduring it ⟨*intrepid* pioneers struggling westward⟩.

Valiant implies resolute courage and fortitude whether in facing danger or attaining some end ⟨her *valiant* efforts to perfect her technique⟩. ***antonym:*** timid, dastardly

Valorous suggests illustrious accomplishments ⟨the *valorous* deeds of King Arthur's knights⟩.

Dauntless emphasizes determination, resolution, and fearlessness ⟨held their *dauntless* position to the end⟩. ***antonym:*** poltroon

brazen See SHAMELESS.

breach, **infraction**, **violation**, **transgression**, **trespass**, **infringement** mean the breaking of a law, duty, or obligation.

Breach implies failure to keep a promise ⟨sued for *breach* of contract⟩. ***antonym:*** observance

Infraction usually implies the breaking of a law or obligation ⟨an *infraction* of the school rules⟩. ***antonym:*** observance

Violation implies the flagrant disregard of the law or the rights of others and often suggests the exercise of force or violence ⟨the police interference was a *violation* of the right to free assembly⟩.

Transgression, often with a moral connotation, applies to any act that goes beyond the limits prescribed by law, rule, or order ⟨censured for repeated financial *transgressions*⟩.

Trespass implies an encroachment upon the rights, the comfort, or the property of others ⟨a would-be burglar who was arrested for *trespass*⟩.

Infringement implies an encroachment upon a legally protected right or privilege ⟨any unauthorized reproduction constitutes an *infringement* of the book's copyright⟩.

break down See ANALYZE.

bridle **1.** See RESTRAIN. **2.** See STRUT.

brief, **short** mean lacking length.

Brief applies primarily to duration and may imply condensation, conciseness, or occasionally intensity ⟨a *brief* speech⟩. ***antonym:*** prolonged, protracted

Short may imply sudden stoppage or incompleteness ⟨the interview was rather *short*⟩. ***antonym:*** long

bright **1. Bright**, **brilliant**, **radiant**, **luminous**, **lustrous** mean shining or glowing with light.

Bright implies emitting or reflecting a high degree of light ⟨one of the *brightest* stars in the sky⟩. ***antonym:*** dull, dim

Brilliant implies intense often sparkling brightness ⟨*brilliant* diamonds⟩. ***antonym:*** subdued

Radiant stresses the emission or seeming emission of rays of light ⟨an imposing figure in *radiant* armor⟩.

Luminous implies emission of steady, suffused, glowing light by reflection or in surrounding darkness ⟨*luminous* white houses dot the shore⟩.

Lustrous stresses an even, rich light from a surface that reflects brightly without sparkling or glittering ⟨the *lustrous* sheen of fine satin⟩.

2. See INTELLIGENT.

brilliant **1.** See BRIGHT. **2.** See INTELLIGENT.

brim See BORDER.

brink See BORDER.

brisk See AGILE.

bristle See STRUT.
brittle See FRAGILE.
broach See EXPRESS.
broad, **wide**, **deep** mean having horizontal extent.
Broad is preferred when full horizontal extent is considered ⟨*broad* shoulders⟩. ***antonym:*** narrow
Wide is more common when units of measurement are mentioned ⟨rugs eight feet *wide*⟩ or applied to unfilled space between limits ⟨a *wide* doorway⟩. ***antonym:*** strait
Deep may indicate horizontal extent away from the observer or from a front or peripheral point ⟨a *deep* cupboard⟩ ⟨*deep* woods⟩. ***antonym:*** shallow
brook See BEAR.
browbeat See INTIMIDATE.
brusque See BLUFF.
bucolic See RURAL.
bugbear See ABOMINATION.
build See PHYSIQUE.
bulge See PROJECTION.
bulk, **mass**, **volume** mean the aggregate that forms a body or unit.
Bulk implies an aggregate that is impressively large, heavy, or numerous ⟨the darkened *bulks* of skyscrapers towered over him⟩.
Mass suggests an aggregate made by piling together things of the same kind ⟨the cave held a *mass* of pottery⟩.
Volume applies to an aggregate without shape or outline and capable of flowing or fluctuating ⟨a tremendous *volume* of water⟩.
bulldoze See INTIMIDATE.
bully See INTIMIDATE.
bunch See GROUP.
burdensome See ONEROUS.
burglary See THEFT.
burlesque See CARICATURE.
bury See HIDE.
business **1. Business**, **commerce**, **trade**, **industry**, **traffic** mean activity concerned with the supplying and distribution of commodities.
Business may be an inclusive term but specifically designates the activities of those engaged in the purchase or sale of commodities or in related financial transactions ⟨the *business* section of the newspaper⟩.
Commerce and ***trade*** imply the exchange and transportation of commodities especially on a large scale ⟨full power to regulate interstate *commerce*⟩ ⟨seek ways to increase foreign *trade*⟩.
Industry applies to the producing of commodities, especially by manufacturing or processing ⟨*industry* has overtaken agriculture in the South⟩.
Traffic applies to the operation and functioning of public carriers of goods and persons ⟨*traffic* managers have rediscovered the railroads⟩ or to the activities of those engaged in the exchange of commodities ⟨*traffic* in contraband goods⟩. **2.** See WORK 2. **3.** See AFFAIR 1.
bustle See STIR *n.*
busy, **industrious**, **diligent**, **assiduous**, **sedulous** mean actively engaged or occupied.
Busy chiefly stresses activity as opposed to idleness or leisure ⟨too *busy* to spend time with the children⟩. ***antonym:*** idle, unoccupied
Industrious implies characteristic or habitual devotion to work ⟨they are by nature an *industrious* people⟩. ***antonym:*** slothful, indolent
Diligent suggests earnest application to some specific object or pursuit ⟨very *diligent* in her pursuit of a degree⟩. ***antonym:*** dilatory
Assiduous stresses careful and unremitting application ⟨mastered the piano only after *assiduous* practice⟩. ***antonym:*** desultory
Sedulous implies painstaking and persevering application ⟨a *sedulous* reconstruction of the events of that night⟩.
butchery See MASSACRE.
butt in See INTRUDE.
bystander See SPECTATOR.

C

cabal See PLOT.
cadence See RHYTHM.
cajole See COAX.
calamity See DISASTER.
calculate, **compute**, **estimate**, **reckon** mean to determine something mathematically.

Calculate is usually preferred in reference to highly intricate and precise processes that produce a result not readily proven by physical confirmation ⟨*calculated* when the comet would next appear⟩.

Compute is the term for reaching an exact result by simpler though often lengthy arithmetic processes ⟨*computed* the interest at a quarterly rate⟩.

Estimate applies chiefly to the forecasting of costs or trends and suggests a seeking of usable but tentative and approximate results ⟨the mechanic *estimated* the cost of repairs⟩.

Reckon usually suggests the simpler arithmetical processes or the use of methods such as can be carried in one's head ⟨*reckoned* the number of yards of fabric needed⟩.

caliber See QUALITY 2.
call *vb* See SUMMON.
call *n* See VISIT.
calling See WORK 2.
callow See RUDE.
calm, **tranquil**, **serene**, **placid**, **peaceful** mean quiet and free from disturbance or harm.

Calm often implies a contrast with a foregoing or nearby state of agitation or violence ⟨the protests ended, and the streets were *calm* again⟩. ***antonym:*** stormy, agitated

Tranquil suggests a deep quietude or composure ⟨the *tranquil* beauty of a formal garden⟩. ***antonym:*** troubled

Serene stresses an unclouded and lofty tranquility ⟨a woman of *serene* beauty⟩.

Placid suggests lack of excitement or agitation and an equable temper and may imply a degree of complacency ⟨led a very *placid* existence⟩. ***antonym:*** choleric

Peaceful implies a state of repose often in contrast with or following strife or turmoil ⟨a former firebrand grown *peaceful* in his old age⟩. ***antonym:*** turbulent

calumniate See MALIGN.
cancel See ERASE.
cancer See TUMOR.
candid See FRANK.
canon See LAW.
cant See DIALECT.
canting See HYPOCRITICAL.
capable See ABLE.
capacious See SPACIOUS.
capitulate See YIELD.
capitulation See SURRENDER.
caprice, **freak**, **whim**, **vagary**, **crotchet** mean an irrational, fanciful, or impractical idea or desire.

Caprice stresses lack of apparent motivation and suggests willfulness ⟨by sheer *caprice* she quit her job⟩.

Freak implies an impulsive change of mind made apparently without cause ⟨struck by a *freak* notion⟩.

Whim implies a fantastic, humorous turn of mind or inclination ⟨an odd antique that was bought on a *whim*⟩.

Vagary stresses the erratic, irresponsible, or extravagant character of the notion or desire ⟨recently he had been prone to strange *vagaries* of taste⟩.

Crochet implies perversely eccentric opinion or preference especially on trivial matters ⟨a serious scientist equally known for his bizarre *crotchets*⟩.

capricious See INCONSTANT.
captious See CRITICAL.
captivate See ATTRACT.
capture See CATCH.
cardinal See ESSENTIAL.

care, concern, solicitude, anxiety, worry mean a troubled or engrossed state of mind or the thing that causes this.

Care implies oppression of the mind by responsibility or apprehension ⟨a face worn by a host of *cares*⟩.

Concern implies a troubled state of mind and the interest, relation, affection, or responsibility that produces it ⟨your happiness is my only *concern*⟩. ***antonym:*** unconcern

Solicitude implies great concern or apprehension and connotes either thoughtful or hovering attentiveness ⟨behaved with typical maternal *solicitude*⟩. ***antonym:*** neglectfulness, unmindfulness

Anxiety stresses anguished uncertainty or fear of misfortune or failure ⟨plagued by *anxiety* and self-doubt⟩. ***antonym:*** security

Worry suggests prolonged fretting over matters that may or may not be real cause for anxiety ⟨a businessman's endless list of *worries*⟩.

careful, meticulous, scrupulous, punctilious mean showing close attention to detail.

Careful implies great concern for persons or matters in one's charge and attentiveness and cautiousness in avoiding mistakes ⟨a *careful* worker⟩. ***antonym:*** careless

Meticulous may imply either extreme carefulness or a finicky caution over small points ⟨*meticulous* scholarship⟩.

Scrupulous applies to what is proper, fitting, or ethical ⟨*scrupulous* honesty⟩. ***antonym:*** remiss

Punctilious implies minute, even excessive attention to fine points ⟨*punctilious* observance of ritual⟩.

caress, fondle, pet, cuddle mean to show affection by touching or handling.

Caress implies expression of affection by gentle stroking or patting ⟨the *caress* of a soft breeze⟩ .

Fondle implies doting fondness and sometimes lack of dignity; it may suggest more intimacy and less gentleness than ***caress*** ⟨*fondle* a baby⟩.

Pet applies to caressing or fondling children or animals ⟨*pet* a cat⟩ but may also apply to excessive indulgence ⟨a spoiled *petted* child⟩ or to amorous fondling in which it may suggest undue familiarity ⟨decided not to *pet* with her boyfriend⟩.

Cuddle applies to a close but gentle embracing designed to soothe and comfort ⟨*cuddle* a frightened puppy⟩.

caricature, burlesque, parody, travesty mean a comic or grotesque imitation.

Caricature implies ludicrous exaggeration of the characteristic or peculiar features of a subject ⟨the movie is a *caricature* of the novel⟩.

Burlesque implies mockery either through treating a trivial subject in a mock-heroic style or through giving a serious or lofty subject a frivolous treatment ⟨a *burlesque* that treats a petty quarrel as a great battle⟩.

Parody applies especially to treatment of a subject in the style of a well-known author or work through subtle and sustained exaggeration or distortion ⟨a witty *parody* of a popular soap opera⟩.

Travesty implies use of an extravagant or absurd style that at once demeans the user and the topic ⟨this production is a *travesty* of a classic opera⟩.

carnage See MASSACRE.

carnal, fleshly, sensual, animal mean having a physical orientation or origin.

Carnal may mean only this but more often carries a derogatory connotation of an action or manifestation of a person's lower nature ⟨a woman who was victimized by her own *carnal* appetites⟩. ***antonym:*** spiritual, intellectual

Fleshly, similar in meaning, is somewhat less derogatory than ***carnal*** ⟨a saint who wrote at length on his *fleshly* temptations⟩.

Sensual may apply to any gratification of a bodily desire or pleasure but commonly implies sexual appetite or bodily satisfaction ⟨a place infamous for providing *sensual* delight⟩.

Animal stresses a relation to physical as distinguished from rational nature ⟨led a mindless, *animal* existence⟩. ***antonym:*** rational

carping See CRITICAL.

carriage See BEARING.

carry, **bear**, **convey**, **transport** mean to move something from one place to another.

Carry tends to emphasize the means by which something is moved or the fact of supporting off the ground while moving ⟨*carried* the basket on her head⟩.

Bear stresses the effort of sustaining or the importance of what is carried ⟨*bear* the banner aloft⟩.

Convey suggests the continuous movement of something in mass ⟨the pipeline *conveys* oil for more than a thousand miles⟩.

Transport implies the orderly moving of something often over great distances to its destination ⟨trucks *transporting* farm produce to market⟩.

cartel See MONOPOLY.

case See INSTANCE.

cast **1.** See DISCARD. **2.** See THROW.

castigate See PUNISH.

casual **1.** See ACCIDENTAL. **2.** See RANDOM.

cataclysm See DISASTER.

catastrophe See DISASTER.

catch **1. Catch**, **capture**, **trap**, **snare**, **entrap**, **ensnare**, **bag** mean to come to possess or control by or as if by seizing.

Catch implies the seizing of something that has been in motion or in flight or in hiding ⟨*caught* the dog as it ran by⟩. ***antonym:*** miss

Capture suggests taking by overcoming resistance or difficulty ⟨*capture* an enemy stronghold⟩.

Trap, ***snare***, ***entrap***, ***ensnare*** imply seizing by some device that holds the one caught at the mercy of one's captor. ***Trap*** and ***snare*** apply more commonly to physical seizing ⟨*trap* animals⟩ ⟨*snared* butterflies with a net⟩. ***Entrap*** and ***ensnare*** more often are figurative ⟨*entrapped* the witness with a trick question⟩ ⟨a sting operation that *ensnared* burglars⟩.

Bag implies success in seizing a difficult quarry by skill, stealth, or artifice, often with the suggestion of a hunter's craft ⟨*bagged* a brace of pheasants⟩.

2. See INCUR.

cause, **determinant**, **antecedent**, **reason**, **occasion** mean something that produces an effect or result.

Cause applies to any event, circumstance, or condition that brings about or helps bring about a result ⟨an icy road was the *cause* of the accident⟩.

Determinant applies to a cause that fixes the nature of what results ⟨heredity may be a *determinant* of heart disease⟩.

Antecedent applies to that which has preceded and may therefore be in some degree responsible for what follows ⟨the *antecedents* of the famine⟩. ***antonym:*** consequence

Reason applies to a traceable or explainable cause of a known effect ⟨the *reason* I was late was that my car would not start⟩.

Occasion applies to a particular time or situation at which underlying causes become effective ⟨the assassination was the *occasion* of the war⟩.

caustic, **mordant**, **acrid**, **scathing** mean stingingly incisive.

Caustic suggests a biting wit ⟨*caustic* comments about her singing ability⟩. ***antonym:*** genial

Mordant suggests a wit that is used with deadly effectiveness ⟨*mordant* reviews put the play out of its misery⟩.

Acrid implies bitterness and often malevolence ⟨a speech marked by *acrid* invective⟩. ***antonym:*** benign, kindly

Scathing implies indignant attacks delivered with fierce or withering severity ⟨a *scathing* satire of corporate life⟩.

caution See WARN.

cautious, **circumspect**, **wary**, **chary** mean prudently watchful and discreet in the face of danger or risk.

Cautious implies the exercise of forethought or prudence usually prompted by fear of danger ⟨a *cautious* driver⟩. ***antonym:*** adventurous, temerarious

Circumspect stresses prudence, discretion, vigilance, and the surveying of all possible consequences before acting or deciding ⟨the panel must be *circumspect* in assigning blame⟩. ***antonym:*** audacious

Wary emphasizes suspiciousness and alertness in watching for danger and cunning in escaping it ⟨be *wary* of those claiming to have all the answers⟩. ***antonym:*** foolhardy, brash

Chary implies a cautious reluctance to give, act, or speak freely ⟨I am *chary* of signing papers I have not read⟩.

cease See STOP.

celebrate See KEEP.

celebrated See FAMOUS.

celerity, **alacrity** mean quickness in movement or action.

Celerity implies speed in working ⟨got dinner ready with remarkable *celerity*⟩. ***antonym:*** leisureliness

Alacrity stresses eager promptness in response to suggestion or command ⟨the students volunteered with surprising *alacrity*⟩. ***antonym:*** languor

censorious See CRITICAL.

censure See CRITICIZE.

ceremonial, **ceremonious**, **formal**, **conventional** mean marked by attention to or adhering strictly to prescribedforms.

Ceremonial and ***ceremonious*** both imply strict attention to what is prescribed by custom or by ritual, but *ceremonial* applies to things that are associated with ceremonies ⟨a *ceremonial* offering⟩, *ceremonious* to persons given to ceremony or to acts attended by ceremony ⟨a *ceremonious* old man⟩. ***antonym:*** unceremonious, informal

Formal applies both to things prescribed by and to persons obedient to custom and may suggest stiff, restrained, or old-fashioned behavior ⟨a *formal* report on the summit meeting⟩ ⟨a *formal* manner⟩. ***antonym:*** informal

Conventional implies accord with general custom and usage and may suggest a lack of originality or independence ⟨*conventional* courtesy⟩ ⟨*conventional* standards of beauty⟩. ***antonym:*** unconventional

ceremonious See CEREMONIAL.

certain See SURE.

certainty, **certitude**, **assurance**, **conviction** mean a state of being free from doubt.

Certainty may stress the existence of objective proof ⟨claims that cannot be confirmed with any scientific *certainty*⟩. ***antonym:*** uncertainty

Certitude may emphasize a faith strong enough to resist all attack ⟨believed in his innocence with a fair degree of *certitude*⟩. ***antonym:*** doubt

Assurance implies confidence rather than certainty and implies reliance on one's own powers or methods, or trust in another ⟨as much *assurance* as is ever possible where hurricanes are concerned⟩. ***antonym:*** mistrust, dubiousness

Conviction usually implies previous doubt or uncertainty and stresses a subjective, rational reaction to evidence ⟨holds firm *convictions* about everything⟩.

certify **1. Certify, attest, witness, vouch** mean to testify to the truth or genuineness of something.

Certify usually applies to a written statement, especially one carrying a signature or seal ⟨*certified* that the candidate had met all requirements⟩.

Attest applies to oral or written testimony usually from experts or witnesses and often under oath or by word of honor ⟨*attested* the authenticity of the document⟩.

Witness applies to the subscribing of one's own name as evidence of the genuineness of a document ⟨two persons who *witnessed* the signing of the will⟩.

Vouch suggests that the one who testifies is a competent authority or a reliable person who will stand behind an affirmation ⟨willing to *vouch* for the woman's integrity⟩.

2. See APPROVE.

certitude See CERTAINTY.

champion See SUPPORT.

chance *n* **Chance**, **accident**, **fortune**, **luck**, **hap**, **hazard** mean something that happens without an apparent cause or as a result of unpredictable forces.

Chance is the most general term and may imply determination by irrational, uncontrollable forces ⟨left things to *chance*⟩ or degree of probability ⟨a *chance* of one in ten⟩. ***antonym:*** law

Accident emphasizes lack of intention ⟨met by happy *accident*⟩. ***antonym:*** design, intent

Fortune often refers to the hypothetical cause of what happens fortuitously ⟨favored by *fortune*⟩ or the outcome of a problematical undertaking ⟨the *fortunes* of war⟩.

Luck, less dignified than ***fortune***, has connotations of gambling ⟨her good *luck* held⟩ and can imply success or a happy outcome ⟨I wish you *luck*⟩.

Hap usually denotes what falls or has already fallen to one's lot ⟨a position won by *hap*⟩.

Hazard is used when the influence of existing conditions or accompanying circumstances is present but not predictable ⟨partners chosen by *hazard*⟩.

chance *vb* See HAPPEN.

chance *adj* See RANDOM.

change, **alter**, **vary**, **modify** mean to make or become different.

Change implies making either an essential difference often amounting to a loss of original identity or a substitution of one thing for another ⟨*changed* the shirt for a larger size⟩.

Alter implies the making of a difference in some particular respect without suggesting loss of identity ⟨slightly *altered* the original design⟩. ***antonym:*** fix

Vary stresses a breaking away from sameness, duplication, or exact repetition ⟨you can *vary* the speed of the conveyor belt⟩.

Modify suggests a difference that limits, restricts, or adapts to a new purpose ⟨*modified* the building for use by the handicapped⟩.

character **1.** See DISPOSITION. **2.** See QUALITY. **3.** See TYPE.

characteristic, **individual**, **peculiar**, **distinctive** mean revealing a special quality or identity.

Characteristic applies to something that distinguishes or identifies a person, thing, or class ⟨responded with his *characteristic* wit⟩.

Individual stresses qualities that distinguish one from other members of the same group or class ⟨a highly *individual* writing style⟩. ***antonym:*** common

Peculiar stresses the rarity or uniqueness of qualities possessed by a particular individual or class or kind ⟨an eccentricity that is *peculiar* to the British⟩.

Distinctive indicates qualities distinguishing and uncommon and often worthy of recognition or praise ⟨her *distinctive* aura of grace and elegance⟩. ***antonym:*** typical

charge *vb* **1.** See ACCUSE. **2.** See COMMAND. **3.** See ASCRIBE.

charge *n* See PRICE.

charity See MERCY.

charm *vb* See ATTRACT.

charm *n* See FETISH.

charter See HIRE.

chary See CAUTIOUS.

chase See FOLLOW 2.

chaste, **pure**, **modest**, **decent** mean free from all taint of what is lewd or salacious.

Chaste primarily implies a refraining from acts or even thoughts or desires that are not virginal or not sanctioned by marriage vows ⟨maintained *chaste* relations until marriage⟩. ***antonym:*** lewd, wanton, immoral

Pure implies innocence and absence of temptation rather than control of one's impulses and actions ⟨the *pure* of heart⟩. ***antonym:*** impure, immoral

Modest stresses absence of characteristics of dress or behavior unbefitting one who is pure and chaste ⟨her dress was always modest⟩. ***antonym:*** immodest

Decent stresses regard for what is considered seemly or proper ⟨*decent* people didn't go to such movies⟩. ***antonym:*** indecent, obscene

chasten See PUNISH.

chastise See PUNISH.

cheap See CONTEMPTIBLE.

cheat, **cozen**, **defraud**, **swindle** mean to get something by dishonesty or deception.

Cheat suggests using deceit or trickery that is intended to escape observation ⟨*cheated* on the written examination⟩.

Cozen implies artful persuading or flattering to attain a thing or a purpose ⟨always able to *cozen* her doting grandfather out of a few dollars⟩.

Defraud stresses depriving someone of what is rightfully his or her own and usually connotes deliberate perversion of the truth ⟨her own lawyer *defrauded* her of her inheritance⟩.

Swindle implies large-scale cheating by means of misrepresentation or abuse of confidence chiefly in order to obtain money ⟨widows *swindled* of their savings by con artists⟩.

check See RESTRAIN.

cheek See TEMERITY.

cheerful See GLAD.

cheerless See DISMAL.

cherish See APPRECIATE.

chide See REPROVE.

chimerical See IMAGINARY.

chivalrous See CIVIL.

chivy See BAIT.

choice *n* **Choice**, **option**, **alternative**, **preference**, **selection**, **election** mean the act or opportunity of choosing or the thing chosen.

Choice suggests the opportunity or privilege to choose freely from a number of alternatives ⟨total freedom of *choice* in the matter⟩.

Option implies a specifically given power to choose among mutually exclusive items ⟨the *option* of paying now or later⟩.

Alternative implies a necessity to choose one and reject another possibility ⟨the *alternatives* were peace with dishonor or war⟩.

Preference suggests personal bias and predilection as a basis of choice ⟨stated a *preference* for red-haired women⟩.

Selection implies a wide range of choice and often the need of thought or discrimination in choosing ⟨a store offering a wide *selection* of furniture⟩.

Election implies a formal choosing, typically for an explicit role, duty, or function ⟨the careful *election* of college courses⟩.

choice *adj* **Choice**, **exquisite**, **elegant**, **rare**, **dainty**, **delicate** mean having qualities that appeal to a cultivated taste.

Choice stresses preeminence in quality or kind ⟨a *choice* bit of gossip⟩. ***antonym:*** indifferent

Exquisite implies a perfection in workmanship or design that appeals only to very sensitive taste ⟨an *exquisite* gold bracelet⟩.

Elegant applies to what is rich and luxurious but restrained by good taste ⟨an *elegant* dining room with genuine French antiques⟩.

Rare suggests a uncommon excellence ⟨refuses to drink any but the *rarest* of wines⟩.

Delicate implies exquisiteness, subtlety,

or fragility ⟨the play's *delicate* charm was lost on screen⟩. ***antonym:*** gross

Dainty suggests smallness coupled with exquisiteness ⟨precious, *dainty* food that leaves you hungry⟩. ***antonym:*** gross

choke See SUFFOCATE.

choleric See IRASCIBLE.

chore See TASK.

chronic See INVETERATE.

chronicle See HISTORY.

chunky See STOCKY.

churlish See BOORISH.

chutzpah See TEMERITY.

circadian See DAILY.

circle See SET *n.*

circuit See PERIMETER.

circumference See PERIMETER.

circumscribe See LIMIT.

circumspect See CAUTIOUS.

circumstance See OCCURRENCE.

circumstantial, **minute**, **particular**, **detailed** mean dealing with a matter fully and usually point by point.

Circumstantial implies a description, narrative, or report that fixes something in time and space with precise details and happenings ⟨a *circumstantial* account of our visit⟩. ***antonym:*** abridged, summary

Minute implies thorough and meticulous attention to the smallest details ⟨a *minute* examination of a fossil⟩.

Particular implies zealous attention to every detail ⟨a *particular* description of the scene of the crime⟩.

Detailed stresses abundance rather than completeness of detail ⟨a *detailed* description of the event⟩.

circumvent See FRUSTRATE.

citation See ENCOMIUM.

cite **1.** See SUMMON. **2.** See QUOTE. **3. Cite**, **advance**, **allege**, **adduce** mean to bring forward as in explanation, proof, or illustration.

Cite implies a bringing forward of something as relevant or specific to an inquiry or discussion ⟨asked to *cite* a single piece of legislation enacted to relieve the situation⟩.

Advance stresses the notion of bringing forward for consideration or study ⟨the idea has been *advanced* as a theoretical possibility⟩.

Allege often carries a strong suggestion of doubt about the validity of what is brought forward ⟨tried the *alleged* perpetrator⟩ and sometimes amounts to a disclaimer of responsibility for the assertion ⟨the existence, real or *alleged*, of ghosts⟩.

Adduce more specifically applies to a bringing forth of evidence, facts, instances, or arguments in support of a position or contention ⟨reasons *adduced* by those who doubt the reality of UFOs⟩.

citizen, **subject**, **national** mean a person owing allegiance to and entitled to the protection of a sovereign state.

Citizen is preferred for one who owes allegiance to a state in which sovereign power is retained by the people and who shares in the political rights of those people ⟨the inalienable rights of a free *citizen*⟩. ***antonym:*** alien

Subject implies allegiance to a personal sovereign such as a monarch ⟨the king enjoys the loyalty of his *subjects*⟩. ***antonym:*** sovereign

National designates one who may claim the protection of a state and applies especially to one living or traveling outside that state ⟨American *nationals* currently in Europe⟩.

civil, **polite**, **courteous**, **gallant**, **chivalrous** mean observant of the forms required by good breeding.

Civil often suggests little more than the avoidance of overt rudeness ⟨a *civil* reply that showed a lack of real enthusiasm⟩. ***antonym:*** uncivil, rude

Polite commonly implies polish of speech and manners with sometimes an absence of cordiality ⟨a conversation as *polite* as it was condescending⟩. ***antonym:*** impolite

Courteous implies more actively considerate or dignified politeness ⟨clerks who were unfailingly *courteous* to customers⟩. ***antonym:*** discourteous

Gallant suggests spirited and dashing behavior and ornate expressions of courtesy ⟨a *gallant* suitor of the old school⟩. ***antonym:*** ungallant

Chivalrous suggests high-minded and self-sacrificing attentions ⟨a *chilvarous* display of duty⟩. ***antonym:*** churlish

claim See DEMAND.

clamor See DIN.

clamorous See VOCIFEROUS.

clandestine See SECRET.

clear 1. Clear, **transparent**, **translucent**, **limpid** mean capable of being seen through.

Clear implies absence of cloudiness, haziness, or muddiness ⟨*clear* water⟩. ***antonym:*** turbid

Transparent applies to whatever can be seen through clearly and sharply ⟨a *transparent* sheet of film⟩. ***antonym:*** opaque

Translucent applies to what permits the passage of light but not a clear view of what lies beyond ⟨*translucent* frosted glass⟩.

Limpid suggests the soft clearness of pure water ⟨*limpid* blue eyes⟩. ***antonym:*** turbid

2. Clear, **perspicuous**, **lucid** mean quickly and easily understood.

Clear implies freedom from obscurity, ambiguity, or undue complexity ⟨the instructions were perfectly *clear*⟩. ***antonym:*** unintelligible, obscure

Perspicuous applies to a style that is simple and elegant as well as clear ⟨the *perspicuous* beauty of Shakespeare's sonnets⟩.

Lucid suggests a clear logical coherence and evident order of arrangement ⟨an amazingly *lucid* description of nuclear physics⟩. ***antonym:*** obscure, vague, dark

3. See EVIDENT.

clear-cut See INCISIVE.

cleave 1. See STICK. **2.** See TEAR.

clemency See MERCY.

clever 1. See INTELLIGENT. **2. Clever**, **adroit**, **cunning**, **ingenious** mean having or showing practical wit or skill in contriving.

Clever stresses physical or mental quickness, deftness, or aptitude ⟨a person *clever* with horses⟩.

Adroit often implies a shrewd or skillful use of expedients to achieve one's purpose ⟨an *adroit* negotiator of business deals⟩. ***antonym:*** maladroit

Cunning implies great skill in constructing or creating ⟨a writer who is *cunning* in his manipulation of the reader⟩.

Ingenious suggests brilliance or cleverness in inventing or discovering ⟨an *ingenious* computer engineer⟩.

climax See SUMMIT.

climb See ASCEND.

cling See STICK.

clique See SET *n.*

cloak See DISGUISE.

clog See HAMPER.

cloister, **convent**, **monastery**, **nunnery**, **abbey**, **priory** mean a place of retirement from the world for members of a religious community.

Cloister stresses the idea of seclusion from the world for either sex ⟨kept a strict silence within the *cloister* walls⟩.

Convent may refer to a retreat for either sex or may refer to a retreat for nuns and stresses the idea of community of living ⟨the shared labor of life within the *convent*⟩.

Monastery refers to a cloister for monks and may indicate a community that combines the cloistered life with teaching, preaching, or other work ⟨left his job on Wall Street and entered a *monastery*⟩.

Nunnery, often interchangeable with ***convent***, refers to a cloister for nuns ⟨found life in a *nunnery* too restrictive⟩.

Abbey denotes a monastery or a nunnery governed by an abbot or an abbess ⟨took the message to the abbot at the *abbey*⟩.

Priory indicates a community governed by a prior or prioress ⟨summoned the inhabitants of the *priory* for matins⟩.

close *vb* **Close**, **end**, **conclude**, **finish**, **complete**, **terminate** mean to bring or come to a stopping point or limit.

Close usually implies that something has been in some way open as well as unfinished ⟨*close* a debate⟩.

End conveys a strong sense of finality and implies a development which has been carried through ⟨*ended* his life⟩. ***antonym:*** begin

Conclude may imply a formal closing (as of a meeting) ⟨the service *concluded* with a blessing⟩. ***antonym:*** open

Finish may stress completion of a final step in a process ⟨after it is painted, the house will be *finished*⟩.

Complete implies the removal of all deficiencies or a successful finishing of what has been undertaken ⟨the resolving of this last issue *completes* the agreement⟩.

Terminate implies the setting of a limit in time or space ⟨your employment *terminates* after three months⟩. ***antonym:*** initiate

close *adj* **1. Close**, **dense**, **compact**, **thick** mean massed tightly together.

Close applies to something made up of separate items that are or seem pressed together ⟨paintings hung *close* together⟩. ***antonym:*** open

Dense implies compression of parts or elements so close as to be almost impenetrable ⟨the *dense* growth in a tropical rain forest⟩. ***antonym:*** sparse

Compact suggests a firm, neat union or effective consolidation of parts within a small compass ⟨a *compact,* muscular body⟩.

Thick implies a concentrated condensed abundance of parts or units ⟨a *thick* head of hair⟩.

2. See STINGY.

clownish See BOORISH.

cloy See SATIATE.

clumsy See AWKWARD.

cluster See GROUP.

clutch *vb* See TAKE.

clutch *n* See HOLD.

coadjutor See ASSISTANT.

coalesce See MIX.

coalition See ALLIANCE.

coarse, **vulgar**, **gross**, **obscene**, **ribald** mean offensive to good taste or moral principles.

Coarse implies roughness, rudeness, crudeness, or insensitivity of spirit, behavior, or language ⟨found the *coarse* humor of her coworkers offensive⟩. ***antonym:*** fine, refined

Vulgar often implies boorishness or ill-breeding ⟨a loud, *vulgar* laugh⟩.

Gross stresses crude animal inclinations and lack of refinement ⟨*gross* eating habits make others lose their appetites⟩. ***antonym:*** delicate, dainty, ethereal

Obscene stresses impropriety, indecency, or nasty obnoxiousness ⟨*obscene* language that violated the broadcasters' code⟩. ***antonym:*** decent

Ribald applies to what is amusingly or picturesquely vulgar or indecent or crudely earthy ⟨entertained the campers with *ribald* songs⟩.

coax, **cajole**, **wheedle**, **blandish** mean to influence or gently urge by caressing or flattering.

Coax suggests an artful, gentle pleading in an attempt to gain one's ends ⟨*coaxed* their friends into staying for dinner⟩. ***antonym:*** bully

Cajole suggests enticing or alluring through beguilement ⟨*cajoled* by his friend into trying the exotic dish⟩.

Wheedle stresses the use of soft words, artful flattery, or seductive appeal ⟨*wheedled* the old man out of his money⟩.

Blandish suggests open flattery and the obvious use of charm in an effort to win over ⟨a salesclerk not above shamelessly *blandishing* customers⟩.

cocksure See SURE.

coerce See FORCE.
coeval See CONTEMPORARY.
cogent See VALID.
cogitate See THINK 2.
cognate See RELATED.
cognizant See AWARE.
cohere See STICK.
coincide See AGREE 1.
coincident See CONTEMPORARY.
collate See COMPARE.
colleague See PARTNER.
collect See GATHER.
collected See COOL.

color, **hue**, **shade**, **tint**, **tinge** mean a property of a visible thing that is recognizable in the light and is distinguished from other properties, such as shape, size, and texture.

Color is the ordinary and generic term for this property and specifically applies to the property of things seen as red, yellow, blue, and so on as distinguished from gray, black, or white ⟨gave the white room touches of *color*⟩.

Hue may be a close synonym of ***color*** ⟨flowers of many *hues*⟩ but suggests gradation or modification of colors ⟨the many green *hues* of spring⟩.

Shade more usually indicates a gradation of a color or hue according to lightness or brightness ⟨use a paler *shade* of blue for the curtains⟩.

Tint usually applies to color that is pale or faint or diluted (as with white) ⟨the rose *tints* of the evening sky⟩.

Tinge distinctively applies to color that modifies other color by mingling with or overlaying ⟨embarrassment brought a *tinge* of red to her pale cheeks⟩.

colorable See PLAUSIBLE.
colossal See ENORMOUS.
combat See OPPOSE.
combative See BELLIGERENT.
combine See JOIN.
comely See BEAUTIFUL.

comfort, **console**, **solace** mean to give or offer help in relieving suffering or sorrow.

Comfort implies imparting cheer, strength, or encouragement as well as lessening pain ⟨a message intended to *comfort* the grieving family⟩. ***antonym:*** afflict, bother

Console emphasizes the alleviating of grief or the mitigating of the sense of loss ⟨*consoled* herself by remembering the good times⟩.

Solace suggests a lifting of spirits often from loneliness or boredom as well as from pain or grief ⟨*solaced* himself by reading books and writing poetry⟩.

comfortable, **cozy**, **snug**, **easy**, **restful** mean enjoying or providing circumstances of contentment and security.

Comfortable applies to anything that encourages serenity, well-being, or complacency as well as physical ease ⟨began to feel *comfortable* in her new surroundings⟩. ***antonym:*** uncomfortable, miserable

Cozy suggests comfortableness derived from warmth, shelter, ease, and friendliness ⟨a *cozy* neighborhood coffee shop⟩.

Snug suggests having just enough of something for comfort and safety but no more ⟨a *snug* little cottage⟩.

Easy implies relief from or absence of anything likely to cause physical or mental discomfort or constraint ⟨our host had a warm, *easy* manner⟩. ***antonym:*** disquieting, disquieted

Restful applies to whatever induces or contributes to rest or relaxation ⟨a quiet *restful* inn where indolence is encouraged⟩.

comic See LAUGHABLE.
comical See LAUGHABLE.

command *vb* **Command**, **order**, **bid**, **enjoin**, **direct**, **instruct**, **charge** mean to issue orders.

Command implies authority and some degree of formality and impersonality in the official exercise of authority ⟨when his superior *commands,* a soldier obeys⟩. ***antonym:*** comply, obey

Order may add the notion of the peremptory or arbitrary exercise of power ⟨*ordered* his men about like slaves⟩.

Bid suggests giving orders directly and orally ⟨*bade* her fix a drink for him⟩. ***antonym:*** forbid

Enjoin implies the giving of an order or direction authoritatively and urgently and often with admonition or solicitude ⟨our guide *enjoined* us to be quiet in the cathedral⟩.

Direct connotes expectation of obedience and usually concerns specific points of procedure or method ⟨*directed* her assistant to hold all calls⟩.

Instruct sometimes implies greater explicitness or formality ⟨the judge *instructed* the jury to ignore the remark⟩.

Charge adds to ***enjoin*** an implication of imposing as a duty or responsibility ⟨*charged* by the President with a covert mission⟩.

command *n* See POWER 3.

commemorate See KEEP.

commence See BEGIN.

commensurable See PROPORTIONAL.

commensurate See PROPORTIONAL.

comment See REMARK.

commentate See REMARK.

commerce See BUSINESS.

commingle See MIX.

commit, **entrust**, **confide**, **consign**, **relegate** mean to assign to a person or place especially for safekeeping.

Commit may express the general idea of delivering into another's charge ⟨*commit* his child to the sitter⟩ or the special sense of transferring to a superior power or to a place of custody ⟨*committed* the person to prison⟩.

Entrust implies committing with trust and confidence ⟨the president is *entrusted* with broad powers⟩.

Confide implies entrusting with assurance or reliance ⟨*confided* all power over my financial affairs to my attorney⟩.

Consign suggests a transferring that removes something from one's immediate control ⟨*consigned* my paintings to a gallery for sale⟩.

Relegate implies a consigning to a particular class, position, or sphere, often with a suggestion of getting rid of ⟨*relegated* to an obscure position in the company⟩.

commodious See SPACIOUS.

common, **ordinary**, **plain**, **familiar**, **popular**, **vulgar** mean generally met with and not in any way special, strange, or unusual.

Common implies usual everyday quality or frequency of occurrence ⟨a *common* error⟩ ⟨lacked *common* honesty⟩ and may additionally suggest inferiority or coarseness ⟨his *common* manners shocked her family⟩. ***antonym:*** uncommon, exceptional

Ordinary stresses accordance in quality or kind with the regular order of things ⟨an *ordinary* pleasant summer day⟩ ⟨a very *ordinary* sort of man⟩. ***antonym:*** extraordinary

Plain suggests ordinariness and homely simplicity ⟨she comes from *plain,* hardworking stock⟩. ***antonym:*** fancy, ornamental

Familiar stresses the fact of being generally known and easily recognized ⟨a *familiar* melody⟩. ***antonym:*** unfamiliar, strange

Popular applies to what is accepted by or prevalent among people in general sometimes in contrast to upper classes or special groups ⟨a hero typically found in *popular* fiction⟩. ***antonym:*** unpopular, esoteric

Vulgar, otherwise similar to ***popular***, is likely to carry derogatory connotations of inferiority or coarseness ⟨goods designed to appeal to the *vulgar* taste⟩.

2. See RECIPROCAL.

common sense See SENSE.

commotion, **tumult**, **turmoil**, **upheaval** mean great physical, mental, or emotional excitement.

Commotion suggests disturbing, sometimes violent, bustle or hubbub ⟨the unexpected dinner guests caused quite a *commotion*⟩.

Tumult suggests a shaking up or stirring up that is accompanied by uproar, din, or great disorder ⟨the town was in a *tumult* over the war news⟩.

Turmoil suggests a state devoid of calm and seething with excitement ⟨a well-ordered life that was suddenly thrown into great *turmoil*⟩.

Upheaval suggests a violent and forceful thrusting that results in a heaving up or an overthrowing ⟨a nation in need of peace after years of *upheaval*⟩.

compact See CLOSE *adj*.

compare, **contrast**, **collate** mean to set side by side in order to show likenesses and differences.

Compare implies an aim of showing relative values or excellences by bringing out characteristic qualities whether similar or divergent ⟨wanted to *compare* the convention facilities of the two cities⟩.

Contrast implies an aim of emphasizing differences ⟨*contrasted* the computerized system with the old filing cards⟩.

Collate implies minute and critical comparison in order to note points of agreement or divergence ⟨data from police districts across the country will be *collated*⟩.

compass *vb* See REACH.

compass *n* **1.** See PERIMETER. **2.** See RANGE.

compassion See SYMPATHY.

compatible See CONSONANT.

compel See FORCE.

compendious See CONCISE.

compendium, **syllabus**, **digest**, **survey**, **sketch**, **précis** mean a brief treatment of a subject or topic.

A ***compendium*** gathers together and presents in concise or outline form all the essential facts and details of a subject ⟨a *compendium* of computer technology⟩.

A ***syllabus*** gives the material necessary for a comprehensive view of a whole subject often in the form of a series of heads or propositions ⟨a *syllabus* for a college history course⟩.

A ***digest*** presents material gathered from many sources and arranged for ready and convenient accessibility ⟨a *digest* of world opinion on the Central America question⟩.

A ***survey*** is a brief but comprehensive treatment presented often as a preliminary to further study or discussion ⟨a *survey* of current trends in higher education⟩.

A ***sketch*** is a slight and tentative treatment subject to later change and amplification ⟨a *sketch* of the proposal⟩.

A ***précis*** is a concise statement of essential facts or points, often in the style or tone of the original ⟨a *précis* of the lengthy article⟩.

compensate **1. Compensate**, **countervail**, **balance**, **offset** mean to make up for what is excessive or deficient, helpful or harmful in another.

Compensate implies making up a lack or making amends for loss or injury ⟨*compensated* for an injury on the job⟩.

Countervail suggests counteracting a bad or harmful influence or overcoming the damage suffered through it ⟨a compassionate heart *countervailed* his short temper⟩.

Balance implies the equalizing or adjusting of two or more things that are contrary or opposed so that no one outweighs the other in effect ⟨in sentencing prisoners, the judge *balanced* justice and mercy⟩.

Offset implies neutralizing one thing's good or evil effect by the contrary effect of another ⟨overeating will *offset* the benefits of exercise⟩.

2. See PAY.

compete **1. Compete**, **contend**, **contest** mean to strive to gain the mastery or upper hand.

Compete implies a struggle to overcome or get the better of in an activity involv-

THESAURUS

ing rivalry between or among two or more participants and may sometimes connote an incentive or inducement ⟨teams *competed* for the championship⟩.

Contend stresses the need for fighting or struggling against opposition that has equal or better chances of succeeding ⟨hope *contended* with despair⟩.

Contest implies a competing or a contending in a debate, dispute, or controversy, an athletic competition, or a physical struggle in an effort to prove one's mastery or superiority ⟨a hotly *contested* election⟩.

2. See RIVAL.

competent **1.** See ABLE. **2.** See SUFFICIENT.

complaisant See AMIABLE.

complete *vb* See CLOSE *vb*.

complete *adj* See FULL.

complex, **complicated**, **intricate**, **involved**, **knotty** mean having confusingly interrelated parts.

Complex suggests the unavoidable result of bringing together various parts, notions, or details and does not imply a fault or failure ⟨a *complex* problem that calls for a *complex* solution⟩. ***antonym:*** simple

Complicated applies to what offers difficulty in understanding, solving, or dealing with ⟨baffled by the *complicated* budgetary procedures⟩. ***antonym:*** simple

Intricate suggests difficulty of understanding or appreciating quickly because of perplexing interweaving or interacting of parts ⟨the *intricate* balance of power among nations⟩.

Involved implies extreme complication and often disorder ⟨an *involved* explanation that clarifies nothing⟩.

Knotty suggests complication and entanglement that make solution or understanding improbable ⟨*knotty* questions concerning free expression and censorship⟩.

complexion See DISPOSITION.

complicated See COMPLEX.

comply See OBEY.

component See ELEMENT.

comport **1.** See AGREE 3. **2.** See BEHAVE.

composed See COOL.

composite See MIXTURE.

composure See EQUANIMITY.

compound See MIXTURE.

comprehend **1.** See INCLUDE. **2.** See UNDERSTAND.

compress See CONTRACT.

compunction **1.** See PENITENCE. **2.** See QUALM.

compute See CALCULATE.

conceal See HIDE.

concede See GRANT.

conceive See THINK 1.

concept See IDEA.

conception See IDEA.

concern **1.** See AFFAIR 1. **2.** See CARE.

conciliate See PACIFY.

concise, **terse**, **succinct**, **laconic**, **summary**, **pithy**, **compendious** mean very brief in statement or expression.

Concise suggests the removal of whatever is superfluous or elaborative ⟨a *concise* study of the situation⟩. ***antonym:*** redundant

Terse implies pointed, elegant conciseness ⟨a *terse* reply that ended the conversation⟩.

Succinct implies precise expression without waste of words ⟨a *succinct* letter of resignation⟩. ***antonym:*** discursive

Laconic implies brevity to the point of seeming rude, indifferent, or mysterious ⟨a *laconic* people who are cold to strangers⟩. ***antonym:*** verbose

Summary suggests the statement of main points with no elaboration or explanation ⟨a *summary* listing of the year's main events⟩. ***antonym:*** circumstantial

Pithy adds to ***succinct*** or ***terse*** the implication of richness of meaning or substance ⟨the play's dialogue is studded with *pithy* one-liners⟩.

Compendious applies to a treatment at

once full in scope and brief and concise in treatment ⟨a *compendious* report giving all that is known about the disease⟩.

conclude 1. See CLOSE *vb.* **2.** See INFER.

conclusive, **decisive**, **determinative**, **definitive** mean bringing to an end.

Conclusive applies to reasoning or logical proof that puts an end to debate or questioning ⟨*conclusive* evidence of criminal guilt⟩. ***antonym:*** inconclusive

Decisive may apply to something that ends a controversy, a contest, or any uncertainty ⟨the *decisive* battle of the war⟩. ***antonym:*** indecisive

Determinative adds an implication of giving a fixed character, course, or direction ⟨the *determinative* influence in her life⟩.

Definitive applies to what is put forth as final and permanent ⟨the *definitive* biography of Jefferson⟩. ***antonym:*** tentative, provisional

concoct See CONTRIVE.

concord See HARMONY.

concourse See JUNCTURE.

concur See AGREE 1.

condemn See CRITICIZE.

condense See CONTRACT.

condescend See STOOP.

condition *n* See STATE.

condition *vb* See PREPARE.

condone See EXCUSE.

conduce, **contribute**, **redound** mean to lead to an end.

Conduce implies having a predictable tendency to further an end ⟨a country setting that *conduces* to relexation⟩. ***antonym:*** ward off

Contribute applies to one factor out of a group of influential factors that furthers an end or produces a result ⟨their studies *contributed* much to our knowledge of the past⟩.

Redound implies a leading to an unplanned end or state by a flow of consequences ⟨such good results can only *redound* to our credit⟩.

conduct 1. Conduct, **manage**, **control**, **direct** mean to use one's powers to lead, guide, or dominate.

Conduct implies a leader's taking responsibility for or supervising the acts and achievements of a group ⟨in charge of *conducting* the negotiations⟩.

Manage implies direct handling and manipulating or maneuvering toward a desired result ⟨ *manages* the financial affairs of the company⟩.

Control implies a regulating or restraining in order to keep within bounds or on a course ⟨try to *control* the number of people using the park⟩.

Direct implies constant guiding and regulating so as to achieve smooth operation ⟨*directs* the day-to-day running of the store⟩.

2. See BEHAVE.

confederate See PARTNER.

confederation See ALLIANCE.

confer 1. Confer, **consult**, **advise**, **parley**, **treat**, **negotiate** mean to engage in discussion in order to reach a decision or settlement.

Confer implies comparison of views or opinions and usually an equality between participants ⟨the executives *confer* weekly about current business problems⟩.

Consult adds to ***confer*** the implication of seeking or taking counsel ⟨before acting, the president *consulted* with his aides⟩.

Advise applies especially to the seeking and giving of opinions regarding personal matters ⟨before deciding to run, he *advised* with friends⟩.

Parley implies a conference for the sake of settling differences ⟨the government refusing to *parley* with the rebels⟩.

Treat implies the existence of a common will to adjust differences or a need for diplomacy ⟨warring nations ready to *treat* for peace⟩.

Negotiate suggests compromise or bargaining ⟨unwilling to *negotiate* with terrorists⟩.

2. See GIVE.

confess See ACKNOWLEDGE.

confide See COMMIT.

confidence, **assurance**, **self-possession**, **aplomb** mean a state of mind or a manner marked by easy coolness and freedom from uncertainty, diffidence, or embarrassment.

Confidence stresses faith in oneself and one's powers without any suggestion of conceit or arrogance <had the *confidence* that comes only from long experience>. ***antonym:*** diffidence

Assurance carries a stronger implication of certainty and may suggest arrogance or lack of objectivity in assessing one's own powers <moved among the guests with great *assurance*>. ***antonym:*** diffidence, alarm

Self-possession implies an ease or coolness under stress that reflects perfect self-control and command of one's powers <she answered the insolent question with complete *self-possession*>.

Aplomb implies a manifest self-possession in trying or challenging situations <handled the horde of reporters with great *aplomb*>. ***antonym:*** shyness

configuration See FORM.

confine See LIMIT.

confirm, **corroborate**, **substantiate**, **verify**, **authenticate**, **validate** mean to attest to the truth or validity of something.

Confirm implies the removing of doubts by an authoritative statement or indisputable fact <*confirmed* reports of troop movements>. ***antonym:*** deny

Corroborate suggests the strengthening of evidence that is already partly established or accepted <witnesses *corroborated* his story>. ***antonym:*** contradict

Substantiate implies the offering of evidence that demonstrates or proves a contention <claims that have yet to be *substantiated*>.

Verify implies the establishment of correspondence of actual facts or details with those proposed or guessed at <all statements of fact in the article have been *verified*>.

Authenticate implies establishing genuineness by adducing legal or official documents or expert opinion <handwriting experts *authenticated* the diaries>. ***antonym:*** impugn

Validate implies establishing validity by authoritative affirmation or certification or by factual proof <*validate* a passport>. ***antonym:*** invalidate

confirmed See INVETERATE.

confiscate See APPROPRIATE *vb*.

conflict See DISCORD.

confluence See JUNCTURE.

conform **1.** See ADAPT. **2.** See AGREE 3.

conformation See FORM.

confound **1.** See PUZZLE. **2.** See MISTAKE.

confuse See MISTAKE.

confute See DISPROVE.

congenial See CONSONANT.

congenital See INNATE.

congratulate, **felicitate** mean to express pleasure in the joy, success, or prospects of another.

Congratulate, the more common and more intimate term, implies that the one to whom pleasure is expressed is the recipient of good fortune <*congratulate* the groom at his wedding>.

Felicitate, more formal in tone, implies that the recipient of the expression is regarded as happy or is wished happiness <*felicitated* the parents of the new child>.

congregate See GATHER.

congruous See CONSONANT.

conjecture, **surmise**, **guess** mean to draw an inference from slight evidence.

Conjecture implies forming an opinion or judgment upon evidence insufficient for definite knowledge <scientists could only *conjecture* about the animal's breeding cycle>.

Surmise implies even slighter evidence and suggests the influence of imagination or suspicion ⟨*surmised* the real reason for the generous gift⟩.

Guess stresses a hitting upon a conclusion either wholly at random or from very uncertain evidence ⟨you would never *guess* that they were wealthy⟩.

conjugal See MATRIMONIAL.

connect See JOIN.

connubial See MATRIMONIAL.

conquer, **defeat**, **vanquish**, **overcome**, **surmount**, **subdue**, **subjugate**, **reduce**, **overthrow**, **rout**, **beat**, **lick** mean to get the better of by force or strategy.

Conquer implies a major action, all-inclusive effort, and a more or less permanent result ⟨working to *conquer* this pernicious disease⟩.

Defeat implies merely the fact of getting the better of an adversary at a particular time often with no more than a temporary checking or frustrating ⟨*defeated* her opponent in the tennis match⟩.

Vanquish suggests a significant action of a certain dignity usually in the defeat of a person rather than a thing ⟨*vanquished* her opponent in the championship match⟩.

Overcome implies an opposing, often fixed, obstacle that can be dealt with only with difficulty or after a hard struggle ⟨*overcome* a legal obstacle⟩.

Surmount implies surpassing or exceeding rather than overcoming in a face-to-face confrontation ⟨severe technical problems to be *surmounted*⟩.

Subdue implies bringing under control by or as if by overpowering ⟨the police *subdued* the unruly man⟩. ***antonym:*** awaken, waken

Subjugate stresses bringing into and keeping in subjection and often implies a humbled or servile state in what is subjugated ⟨*subjugated* the minority populations⟩.

Reduce implies surrender and submission usually as the result of overwhelming by or as if by military action ⟨a city *reduced* by a month-long seige⟩.

Overthrow stresses the bringing down or destruction of enemy power ⟨a futile attempt to *overthrow* the leader⟩.

Rout suggests such complete defeat as to cause flight or complete dispersion and disorganization of the adversary ⟨the guerrillas *routed* the attacking force⟩.

Beat, close to but less formal than ***defeat***, is somewhat neutral though it may imply the finality associated with *vanquish* ⟨*beat* an opponent at cards⟩.

Lick is likely to imply a complete humbling or reduction to ineffectiveness of the one defeated ⟨*lick* a problem⟩.

conquest See VICTORY.

conscientious See UPRIGHT.

conscious See AWARE.

consecrate See DEVOTE.

consecutive, **successive** mean following one after the other.

Consecutive stresses immediacy in following, regularity or fixedness of order, and the close connection of the units ⟨named the numbers from one to ten in *consecutive* order⟩. ***antonym:*** inconsecutive

Successive is applicable to things that follow regardless of differences in duration, extent, or size or of the length of the interval between the units ⟨weakened progressively by *successive* illnesses⟩.

consent See ASSENT.

consequence **1.** See EFFECT. **2.** See IMPORTANCE.

consequently See THEREFORE.

conserve See SAVE 2.

consider, **study**, **contemplate**, **weigh** mean to think about in order to increase one's knowledge or to arrive at a judgment or decision.

Consider may suggest giving thought to in order to reach a suitable conclusion, opinion, or decision ⟨refused even to *consider* my proposal⟩.

Study implies sustained purposeful concentration and attention that will reveal details and minutiae ⟨*study* the budget before making sweeping cuts⟩.

Contemplate stresses the focusing of one's thoughts on something, often without indication of purpose or result ⟨*contemplate* the consequences of such a decision⟩.

Weigh implies the making of an attempt to reach the truth or arrive at a decision by balancing conflicting claims or evidence ⟨*weigh* the pros and cons of the case⟩.

considerate See THOUGHTFUL 2.

consign See COMMIT.

consistent See CONSONANT.

console See COMFORT.

consonance See HARMONY.

consonant, **consistent**, **compatible**, **congruous**, **congenial**, **sympathetic** mean being in agreement with or agreeable to another.

Consonant implies the absence of elements making for discord or difficulty ⟨a motto *consonant* with the company's philosophy⟩. ***antonym:*** inconsonant

Consistent may stress absence of contradiction between things or between details of the same thing ⟨behavior that is not *consistent* with her general character⟩. ***antonym:*** inconsistent

Compatible suggests a capacity for existing or functioning together without disagreement, discord, or interference ⟨looking for a *compatible* roommate⟩. ***antonym:*** incompatible

Congruous suggests a pleasing effect resulting from fitness or appropriateness of elements ⟨modern furniture is not *congruous* with a colonial house⟩. ***antonym:*** incongruous

Congenial implies a generally satisfying harmony between personalities or a fitness to one's personal taste ⟨did not find the atmosphere of the bar *congenial*⟩. ***antonym:*** uncongenial, antipathetic (*of persons*), abhorrent (*of tasks or duties*)

Sympathetic suggests a more subtle or quieter kind of harmony ⟨a music critic not very *sympathetic* to rock⟩.

conspectus See ABRIDGMENT.

conspicuous See NOTICEABLE.

conspiracy See PLOT.

constant **1.** See CONTINUAL. **2.** See FAITHFUL.

constituent See ELEMENT.

constitution See PHYSIQUE.

constrain See FORCE.

constrict See CONTRACT.

consult See CONFER.

consume **1.** See WASTE. **2.** See MONOPOLIZE.

contain, **hold**, **accommodate** mean to have or be capable of having within.

Contain implies the actual presence of a specified substance or quantity within something ⟨the can *contains* about a quart of oil⟩.

Hold implies the capacity of containing or keeping ⟨the container will *hold* a gallon of liquid⟩.

Accommodate implies holding without crowding or inconvenience ⟨the banquet hall can *accommodate* 500 diners⟩.

contaminate, **taint**, **pollute**, **defile** mean to make impure or unclean.

Contaminate implies intrusion of or contact with dirt or foulness from an outside source ⟨water *contaminated* by industrial wastes⟩. ***antonym:*** purify

Taint stresses the loss of purity or cleanliness that follows contamination ⟨the scandal *tainted* the rest of his political career⟩.

Pollute, sometimes interchangeable with ***contaminate***, may imply that the process which begins with contamination is complete and that what was pure or clean has been made foul, poisoned, or filthy ⟨*polluted* the waters of the lake, so that it became in parts no better than an open cesspool⟩.

Defile implies befouling of what could or should have been kept clean and pure or held sacred and suggests violation or desecration ⟨*defile* a hero's memory with slanderous innuendo⟩. ***antonym:*** cleanse, purify

contemn See DESPISE.

contemplate **1.** See CONSIDER. **2.** See SEE 1.
contemplative See THOUGHTFUL 1.
contemporaneous See CONTEMPORARY.
contemporary, **contemporaneous**, **coeval**, **synchronous**, **simultaneous**, **coincident** mean existing or occurring at the same time.

Contemporary is likely to apply to people and what relates to them ⟨Abraham Lincoln was *contemporary* with Charles Darwin⟩.

Contemporaneous applies to events ⟨Victoria's reign was *contemporaneous* with British hegemony⟩.

Coeval implies contemporaneousness at some remote time or for a long period and refers usually to periods, ages, eras, or eons ⟨the rise of the leisure class was *coeval* with the flowering of the arts⟩.

Synchronous implies exact correspondence between or during usually brief periods of time, and especially in periodic intervals ⟨the *synchronous* action of a bird's wings in flight⟩.

Simultaneous implies exact coincidence at a point of time ⟨a *simultaneous* ringing of church bells miles apart⟩.

Coincident is applied to events that happen at the same time and may be used in order to avoid implication of causal relationship ⟨the end of World War II was *coincident* with a great vintage year⟩.

contemptible, **despicable**, **pitiable**, **sorry**, **scurvy**, **cheap** mean arousing or deserving scorn.

Contemptible may imply any quality provoking scorn or a low standing in any scale of values ⟨a *contemptible* bigot and liar⟩. ***antonym:*** admirable, estimable, formidable

Despicable may imply utter worthlessness and usually suggests arousing an attitude of moral indignation ⟨the *despicable* crime of child abuse⟩. ***antonym:*** praiseworthy, laudable

Pitiable applies to what inspires mixed contempt and pity and often attributes weakness to the agent ⟨the play is his *pitiable* attempt at tragedy⟩.

Sorry may stress pitiable or ridiculous inadequacy, wretchedness, or sordidness ⟨the orphanage was a very *sorry* place⟩.

Scurvy adds to ***despicable*** an implication of arousing disgust ⟨the offer of help turned out to be a *scurvy* trick⟩.

Cheap may imply contemptibility resulting from undue familiarity or accessibility ⟨treatment that made her feel *cheap*⟩ but more often implies contemptible pettiness or meanness ⟨critics who condemned the book with *cheap* remarks⟩. ***antonym:*** noble

contend See COMPETE.
content See SATISFY 1.
contention See DISCORD.
contentious See BELLIGERENT.
conterminous See ADJACENT.
contest See COMPETE.
contiguous See ADJACENT.
continence See TEMPERANCE.
continent See SOBER.
contingency See JUNCTURE.
contingent See ACCIDENTAL.
continual, **continuous**, **constant**, **incessant**, **perpetual**, **perennial** mean characterized by continued occurrence or recurrence.

Continual implies a close or unceasing succession or recurrence ⟨*continual* showers the whole weekend⟩. ***antonym:*** intermittent

Continuous usually implies an uninterrupted flow or spatial or temporal extension ⟨the *continuous* roar of the falls⟩. ***antonym:*** interrupted

Constant implies uniform or persistent occurrence or recurrence ⟨lived in *constant* pain⟩. ***antonym:*** fitful

Incessant implies ceaseless or uninterrupted activity that is viewed as undesirable or distasteful ⟨the *incessant* quarreling frayed her nerves⟩. ***antonym:*** intermittent

Perpetual suggests unfailing repetition or lasting duration ⟨the fear of *perpetual*

torment after death⟩. ***antonym:*** transitory, transient

Perennial implies enduring existence often through constant renewal ⟨a *perennial* source of controversy⟩.

continue, **last**, **endure**, **abide**, **persist** mean to exist over a period of time or indefinitely.

Continue applies to a process going on without ending ⟨the stock market will *continue* to rise⟩.

Last, especially when unqualified, may stress existing beyond what is normal or expected ⟨buy shoes that will *last*⟩.

Endure adds an implication of resistance to destructive forces or agents ⟨in spite of everything, her faith *endured*⟩. ***antonym:*** perish

Abide implies a stable and constant existing, especially as opposed to mutability ⟨through 40 years of marriage, their love *abided*⟩. ***antonym:*** pass

Persist suggests outlasting the normal or appointed time and often connotes obstinacy or doggedness ⟨the sense of guilt *persisted*⟩. ***antonym:*** desist

continuous See CONTINUAL.

contort See DEFORM.

contour See OUTLINE.

contraband See SMUGGLED.

contract **1.** See INCUR. **2. Contract**, **shrink**, **condense**, **compress**, **constrict**, **deflate** mean to decrease in bulk or volume.

Contract applies to a drawing together of surfaces or particles or a reduction of area, volume, or length ⟨caused his muscles to *contract*⟩. ***antonym:*** expand

Shrink implies a contracting or a loss of material and stresses a falling short of original dimensions ⟨the sweater will *shrink* if washed improperly⟩. ***antonym:*** swell

Condense implies a reducing of something homogeneous to greater compactness without significant loss of content ⟨*condense* an essay into a single paragraph⟩. ***antonym:*** amplify

Compress implies a pressing into a small compass and definite shape, usually against resistance ⟨*compressed* the comforter to fit the box⟩. ***antonym:*** stretch, spread

Constrict implies a narrowing by contraction or squeezing ⟨the throat is *constricted* by too tight a collar⟩.

Deflate implies a contracting by reducing the internal pressure of a contained substance and stresses the limp or empty state that results ⟨*deflated* his tires to get better traction⟩. ***antonym:*** inflate

contradict See DENY.

contradictory See OPPOSITE.

contrary **1.** See OPPOSITE. **2. Contrary**, **perverse**, **restive**, **balky**, **wayward** mean inclined to resist authority, control, or circumstances.

Contrary implies a temperamental unwillingness to accept orders or advice ⟨the most *contrary* child in my class⟩. ***antonym:*** complaisant

Perverse may imply wrongheaded, determined, unwholesome, or cranky opposition to what is reasonable or generally accepted ⟨offered the most *perverse* argument for declaring war⟩.

Restive suggests unwillingness or obstinate refusal to submit to discipline or follow orders and often suggests restlessness or impatience with control ⟨a *restive* horse who refused to stand still⟩.

Balky suggests a refusal to proceed or acquiesce in a desired direction or course of action ⟨workers became *balky* when asked to accept pay cuts⟩.

Wayward suggests strong-willed capriciousness and irregularity in behavior ⟨*wayward* inmates isolated from the others⟩.

contrast See COMPARE.

contravene See DENY.

contribute See CONDUCE.

contrition See PENITENCE.

contrive, **devise**, **invent**, **frame**, **concoct** mean to find a way of making or doing something or of achieving an end by the exercise of one's mind.

Contrive implies ingenuity or cleverness in planning, designing, or scheming ⟨*contrive* a way of helping them without their knowing it⟩.

Devise stresses mental effort rather than ingenuity and often implies the reflection and experimentation that precede the bringing of something into being ⟨*devise* new dishes to tempt the palate⟩.

Invent contains some notion of finding and suggests originating, especially after reflection, as the result of happy accident ⟨the telescope was *invented* by Galileo⟩.

Frame implies the exact fitting of one thing to another, as of words to thought or of the means to the end ⟨*frame* a proper reply to the letter⟩.

Concoct suggests a bringing together of ingredients in new or unexpected ways that enhance their effectiveness ⟨*concoct* a plausible excuse for his lateness⟩.

control *vb* See CONDUCT.

control *n* See POWER 3.

controvert See DISPROVE.

conundrum See MYSTERY.

convene See SUMMON.

convent See CLOISTER.

conventional See CEREMONIAL.

converse See SPEAK.

convert See TRANSFORM.

convey See CARRY.

conviction **1.** See CERTAINTY. **2.** See OPINION.

convincing See VALID.

convoke See SUMMON.

convulse See SHAKE.

convulsion See FIT.

convulsive See FITFUL.

cool, **composed**, **collected**, **unruffled**, **imperturbable**, **nonchalant** mean actually or apparently free from agitation or excitement.

Cool may imply calmness, deliberateness, or dispassionateness ⟨kept a *cool* head during the emergency⟩. ***antonym:*** ardent, agitated

Composed implies freedom from agitation as a result of self-discipline or a sedate disposition ⟨the *composed* pianist gave a flawless concert⟩. ***antonym:*** discomposed, anxious

Collected implies a concentration of the mind or spirit that eliminates or overcomes distractions ⟨even in heated debate she remains very *collected*⟩. ***antonym:*** distracted, distraught

Unruffled suggests apparent serenity and poise in the face of setbacks or in the midst of excitement ⟨his mother remained *unruffled* during the wedding⟩. ***antonym:*** ruffled, excited

Imperturbable implies a temperament that is cool or assured even under severe provocation ⟨a guest speaker who maintained an air of *imperturbable* civility⟩. ***antonym:*** choleric, touchy

Nonchalant stresses an easy coolness of manner or casualness that suggests indifference or unconcern ⟨*nonchalant* as ever, she ignored the crying baby⟩.

copartner See PARTNER.

copious See PLENTIFUL.

copy *vb* **Copy**, **imitate**, **mimic**, **ape**, **mock** mean to make something so that it resembles an existing thing.

Copy suggests the duplicating of an original as closely as possible ⟨*copied* the painting and sold the fake as an original⟩. ***antonym:*** originate

Imitate suggests the following of a model or a pattern but may allow for some variation and may imply inferiority in the product ⟨*imitate* a poet's style⟩.

Mimic implies a close copying (as of voice or mannerism) often for fun, ridicule, or lifelike simulation ⟨pupils *mimic* their teacher⟩.

Ape may suggest the presumptuous, slavish, or inept imitating of a superior original ⟨American fashion designers *aped* their European colleagues⟩.

Mock usually implies imitation, particularly of sounds or movements, with derisive intent ⟨*mocking* a vain man's manner⟩.

copy *n* See REPRODUCTION.

coquet See TRIFLE.

cordial See GRACIOUS.

corner See MONOPOLY.

corporal See BODILY.

corporeal **1.** See BODILY. **2.** See MATERIAL.

correct *vb* **1. Correct**, **rectify**, **emend**, **remedy**, **redress**, **amend**, **reform**, **revise** mean to make right what is wrong.

Correct implies taking action to remove errors, faults, deviations, or defects ⟨*corrected* all her spelling errors⟩.

Rectify implies a more effective action to make something conform to a rule or standard of what is right, just, or properly controlled or directed ⟨a major error in judgment that should be *rectified* at once⟩.

Emend specifically implies correction of a text or manuscript ⟨*emend* the text to match the first edition⟩. ***antonym:*** corrupt (*a text, passage*)

Remedy implies the removing or making harmless of a cause of trouble, harm, or evil ⟨set out to *remedy* the evils of the world⟩.

Redress implies making compensation or reparation for an unfairness, injustice, or imbalance ⟨we must *redress* past social injustices⟩.

Amend implies making corrective changes that are usually slight ⟨a law that needs to be *amended*⟩. ***antonym:*** debase, impair

Reform implies corrective changes that are more drastic ⟨plans to *reform* the entire court system⟩.

Revise suggests a careful examination of something and the making of necessary changes ⟨forced to *revise* the production schedule⟩.

2. See PUNISH.

correct *adj* **Correct**, **accurate**, **exact**, **precise**, **nice**, **right** mean conforming to fact, standard, or truth.

Correct usually implies freedom from fault or error ⟨socially *correct* dress⟩. ***antonym:*** incorrect

Accurate implies fidelity to fact or truth attained by exercising care ⟨an *accurate* description of the whole situation⟩. ***antonym:*** inaccurate

Exact stresses a very strict agreement with fact, standard, or truth ⟨a suit tailored to *exact* measurements⟩.

Precise adds to ***exact*** an emphasis on sharpness of definition or delimitation ⟨the *precise* terms of the contract⟩. ***antonym:*** loose

Nice stresses great, sometimes excessive, precision and delicacy of action, adjustment, or discrimination ⟨makes *nice* distinctions between freedom and license⟩.

Right is close to ***correct*** but has a stronger positive emphasis on conformity to fact or truth rather than mere absence of error or fault ⟨the *right* thing to do⟩. ***antonym:*** wrong

correlate See PARALLEL *n* 2.

correspond See AGREE 3.

corroborate See CONFIRM.

corrupt *vb* See DEBASE.

corrupt *adj* See VICIOUS.

cost See PRICE.

costly, **expensive**, **dear**, **valuable**, **precious**, **invaluable**, **priceless** mean having a high value or valuation, especially in terms of money.

Costly implies high price and may suggest sumptuousness, luxury, or rarity ⟨the *costliest* of delicacies grace her table⟩. ***antonym:*** cheap

Expensive may further imply a price beyond the thing's value or the buyer's means ⟨the resort's shops seemed rather *expensive*⟩. ***antonym:*** inexpensive

Dear implies a relatively high or exorbitant price or excessive cost usually due to factors other than the thing's intrinsic value ⟨coffee was *dear* during the war⟩. ***antonym:*** cheap

Valuable may suggest worth measured in usefulness or enjoyableness as well as in market value ⟨iron ore was a *valu-*

able commodity⟩. ***antonym:*** valueless, worthless

Precious applies to what is of great or even incalculable value because scarce or irreplaceable ⟨our *precious* natural resources⟩. ***antonym:*** cheap, worthless

Invaluable implies such great worth as to make valuation all but impossible ⟨a good education is *invaluable*⟩. ***antonym:*** worthless

Priceless, used like ***invaluable*** in a hyperbolical sense, adds a note of even greater intensiveness ⟨a bon mot that was *priceless*⟩.

coterie See SET *n*.

counsel 1. See ADVICE. **2.** See LAWYER.

counselor See LAWYER.

count See RELY.

countenance See FACE.

counter See ADVERSE.

counteractive See ADVERSE.

counterfeit *vb* See ASSUME.

counterfeit *n* See IMPOSTURE.

counterpart See PARALLEL *n* 2.

countervail See COMPENSATE.

courage, **mettle**, **spirit**, **resolution**, **tenacity** mean mental or moral strength to resist opposition, danger, or hardship.

Courage implies firmness of mind and will in the face of danger or extreme difficulty ⟨the *courage* to support unpopular causes⟩. ***antonym:*** cowardice

Mettle suggests an ingrained capacity for meeting strain or difficulty with fortitude and resilience ⟨a challenge that will test your *mettle*⟩.

Spirit also suggests a quality of temperament enabling one to hold one's own or keep up one's morale when opposed or threatened ⟨too many failures had broken the *spirit* of the man⟩.

Resolution stresses firm determination to achieve one's ends ⟨the strong *resolution* of the pioneer women⟩.

Tenacity adds to ***resolution*** implications of stubborn persistence and unwillingness to admit defeat ⟨won the argument through sheer *tenacity*⟩.

courageous See BRAVE.

court See INVITE.

courteous See CIVIL.

cover See SHELTER *n*.

covert See SECRET.

covet See DESIRE.

covetous, **greedy**, **acquisitive**, **grasping**, **avaricious** mean having or showing a strong desire for possessions and especially material possessions.

Covetous implies inordinate desire, often for what is rightfully another's ⟨*covetous* of his brother's success⟩.

Greedy stresses lack of restraint and often of discrimination in desire ⟨soldiers *greedy* for glory⟩.

Acquisitive implies both eagerness to possess and ability to acquire and keep ⟨mansions that were the pride of the *acquisitive* class⟩. ***antonym:*** sacrificing, abnegating

Grasping adds an implication of eagerness and selfishness and often suggests use of unfair or ruthless means ⟨*grasping* developers defrauded the homesteaders⟩.

Avaricious implies obsessive acquisitiveness especially of hoardable wealth and strongly suggests stinginess ⟨*avaricious* thrift that left them morally bankrupt⟩. ***antonym:*** generous

cow See INTIMIDATE.

cowardly, **pusillanimous**, **gutless**, **craven**, **dastardly** mean having or showing a lack of courage.

Cowardly implies a weak or ignoble lack of courage ⟨the *cowardly* retreat of the army⟩. ***antonym:*** brave

Pusillanimous suggests a contemptible timidity or lack of courage ⟨*pusillanimous* politicians feared crossing him⟩.

Craven suggests extreme faintheartedness and lack of resistance ⟨secretly despised the *craven* toadies around her⟩.

Dastardly implies behavior that is both cowardly and despicably treacherous or outrageous ⟨a *dastardly* attack on unarmed civilians⟩.

cower See FAWN.

coy See SHY.

cozen See CHEAT.
cozy See COMFORTABLE.
crabbed See SULLEN.
crack See JEST 1.
craft **1.** See ART. **2.** See BOAT.
crafty See SLY.
cranky See IRASCIBLE.
crass See STUPID.
crave See DESIRE.
craven See COWARDLY.
crawl See CREEP.
craze See FASHION.
crazed See INSANE.
crazy See INSANE.
create See INVENT.
creator See MAKER.
credence See BELIEF.
credible See PLAUSIBLE.
credit *vb* See ASCRIBE.
credit *n* **1.** See BELIEF. **2.** See INFLUENCE.

creep, **crawl** mean to move along a surface in a prone or crouching posture.

Creep is more often used of quadrupeds or of human beings who move on all fours and proceed slowly, stealthily, or silently ⟨the cat *crept* up on the mouse⟩.

Crawl is applied to animals with no legs or many small legs that seem to move by drawing the body along a surface or to human beings who imitate such movement ⟨the injured man tried to *crawl* to the door⟩.

crime See OFFENSE 2.
cringe See FAWN.
cripple **1.** See MAIM. **2.** See WEAKEN.
crisis See JUNCTURE.
crisp **1.** See FRAGILE. **2.** See INCISIVE.
criterion See STANDARD.

critical **1. Critical**, **hypercritical**, **faultfinding**, **captious**, **carping**, **censorious** mean inclined to look for and point out faults and defects.

Critical may imply an effort to see a thing clearly and truly in order to judge or value it fairly ⟨a *critical* essay on modern drama⟩. ***antonym:*** uncritical

Hypercritical suggests a tendency to lose objectivity and to judge by unreasonably strict standards ⟨petty, *hypercritical* disparagement of other people's success⟩.

Faultfinding implies persistent, picayune, often ill-informed criticism and a querulous or exacting temperament ⟨a *faultfinding* theater reviewer⟩.

Captious suggests a readiness to detect trivial faults or raise objections on trivial grounds ⟨no point is too minute for this *captious* critic to overlook⟩. ***antonym:*** appreciative

Carping implies an ill-natured or perverse finding of fault ⟨the *carping* editorial writer soon wearied readers⟩. ***antonym:*** fulsome

Censorious implies a disposition to be severely critical and condemnatory ⟨the *censorious* tone of the papal encyclical⟩. ***antonym:*** eulogistic

2. See ACUTE.

criticize, **reprehend**, **blame**, **censure**, **reprobate**, **condemn**, **denounce** mean to find fault with openly.

Criticize implies finding fault especially with methods or intentions ⟨*criticized* the police for using violence⟩. ***antonym:*** praise

Reprehend implies both criticism and severe rebuke ⟨*reprehends* the self-centeredness of today's students⟩.

Blame may imply simply the opposite of praise but more often suggests the placing of responsibility or guilt for wrongdoing ⟨*blames* herself for the accident⟩.

Censure carries a stronger suggestion of authority and of more or less formal reprimand than ***blame*** ⟨a Senator formally *censured* by his peers⟩. ***antonym:*** commend

Reprobate implies strong disapproval or firm refusal to sanction ⟨*reprobated* his son's adulterous adventures⟩.

Condemn suggests an unqualified and final judgment that is unfavorable and merciless ⟨*condemn* the government's racial policies⟩.

Denounce adds to ***condemn*** the implication of a public declaration ⟨stood and *denounced* the war⟩. ***antonym:*** eulogize

crooked, **devious**, **oblique** mean not straight or straightforward.

Crooked may imply the presence of material curves, bends, or twists ⟨a *crooked* road⟩, or it may imply departure from a right and proper course and then usually suggests cheating or fraudulence ⟨set up a *crooked* deal to force his partner out of the business⟩. ***antonym:*** straight

Devious implies a departure from a direct or usual course ⟨returned home by a *devious* route to avoid the waiting bully⟩; in application to persons or their acts or practices it is likely to imply unreliability, shiftiness or trickiness, or sometimes obscurity ⟨gained an inheritance by *devious* means⟩. ***antonym:*** straightforward

Oblique implies departure from a horizontal or vertical direction ⟨an *oblique* line dividing a rectangle into two equal triangles⟩ and can suggest indirection or lack of straightforwardness ⟨made an *oblique* but damning attack on his character⟩.

cross See IRASCIBLE.

crotchet See CAPRICE.

crow See BOAST.

crowd, **throng**, **crush**, **mob**, **horde** mean an assembled multitude of people.

Crowd implies a massing together and often a loss of individuality ⟨a small *crowd* greeted the returning athletes⟩.

Throng strongly suggests movement and shoving or pushing ⟨a *throng* of reporters followed the President⟩.

Crush emphasizes the compact concentration of the group, the difficulty of individual movement, and the attendant discomfort ⟨a *crush* of fans waited outside the theater⟩.

Mob implies a disorderly crowd with the potential or the intent for violence ⟨heard an angry *mob* outside the jail⟩.

Horde suggests a rushing or tumultuous crowd, often of inferior, rude, or savage character, often linked by common interests or problems ⟨a *horde* of shoppers looking for bargains⟩.

crucial See ACUTE.

crude See RUDE.

cruel See FIERCE.

crush *vb* **Crush**, **quell**, **extinguish**, **suppress**, **quash** mean to bring to an end by destroying or defeating.

Crush implies a force that destroys all opposition or brings an operation to a halt ⟨a rebellion that was brutally *crushed*⟩.

Quell means to overwhelm completely and to reduce to submission, inactivity, or passivity ⟨statements intended to *quell* the fears of the people⟩. ***antonym:*** foment

Extinguish suggests ending something as abruptly and completely as putting out a flame ⟨hopes for a promising life *extinguished* by a single bullet⟩. ***antonym:*** inflame

Suppress implies a conscious determination to subdue ⟨the government *suppressed* all opposition newspapers⟩.

Quash implies a sudden and summary extinction ⟨the army *quashed* the rebellion⟩.

crush *n* See CROWD.

crusty See BLUFF.

cryptic See OBSCURE.

cuddle See CARESS.

cuff See STRIKE.

culmination See SUMMIT.

culpable See BLAMEWORTHY.

cumbersome See HEAVY.

cumbrous See HEAVY.

cumulative, **accumulative**, **additive**, **summative** mean increasing or produced by the addition of new material of the same or similar kind.

Cumulative implies a constant increase (as in amount or power) by successive additions, accretions, or repetitions ⟨the *cumulative* effect of taking a drug for many months⟩.

Accumulative may distinctively imply that something has reached its maximum or greatest magnitude through many additions ⟨the *accumulative* impact of a well-ordered sales presentation⟩.

Additive implies that something is capable of assimilation to or incorporation in something else or of growth by additions ⟨as new art forms arise, we develop an *additive* notion of what art is⟩.

Summative implies that something is capable of association or combination with others so as to create a total effect ⟨the *summative* effect of the show's music, dancing, and staging⟩.

cunning *n* See ART.

cunning *adj* **1.** See CLEVER. **2.** See SLY.

curb See RESTRAIN.

cure, **heal**, **remedy** mean to rectify an unhealthy or undesirable condition.

Cure implies the restoration to health after disease ⟨searched for new medications to *cure* the dread disease⟩.

Heal may also apply to this but commonly suggests a restoring to soundness of an affected part after a wound or sore ⟨his wounds were slow to *heal*⟩.

Remedy suggests the correction or relief of a morbid or evil condition through the use of a substance or measure ⟨vainly searched for something to *remedy* her arthritis⟩.

curious, **inquisitive**, **prying** mean interested in what is not one's personal or proper concern.

Curious, a neutral term, connotes an active desire to learn or to know ⟨children are *curious* about everything⟩. ***antonym:*** incurious, uninterested

Inquisitive suggests impertinent and habitual curiosity and persistent quizzing and peering after information ⟨dreaded the visits of their *inquisitive* relatives⟩. ***antonym:*** incurious

Prying implies busy meddling and officiousness ⟨*prying* neighbors who refuse to mind their own business⟩.

current *adj* See PREVAILING.

current *n* See TENDENCY.

curse See EXECRATE.

cursory See SUPERFICIAL.

curt See BLUFF.

curtail See SHORTEN.

curve, **bend**, **turn**, **twist** mean to swerve or cause to swerve from a straight line or course.

Curve implies following or producing a line suggesting the arc of a circle or ellipse ⟨the road *curves* sharply to the left⟩.

Bend suggests a yielding to force and implies a distortion from the anticipated, normal, or desirable straightness ⟨metal rods *bend* under the immense weight⟩. ***antonym:*** straighten

Turn implies change of direction essentially by rotation and not usually as a result of force or pressure ⟨the comet will *turn* toward the earth⟩.

Twist implies the influence of a force having a spiral effect throughout the object or course involved ⟨the *twisted* wreckage of the spacecraft⟩.

custom See HABIT.

customary See USUAL.

cutting See INCISIVE.

cynical, **misanthropic**, **pessimistic**, **misogynistic** mean deeply distrustful.

Cynical implies having a sneering disbelief in sincerity or integrity or sometimes a vicious disregard of the rights or concerns of others ⟨always *cynical* about other people's motives⟩.

Misanthropic suggests a rooted distrust and dislike of human beings and their society ⟨a zoologist who had grown *misanthropic* in recent years⟩. ***antonym:*** philanthropic

Pessimistic implies having a gloomy, distrustful view of life and things in general ⟨a philosopher *pessimistic* about the future of the human race⟩. ***antonym:*** optimistic

Misogynistic applies to a man having a deep-seated distrust of and aversion to women ⟨a *misogynistic* scientist more at home in his laboratory⟩.

D

dabbler See AMATEUR.

daily, **diurnal**, **quotidian**, **circadian** mean of each or every day.

Daily is used with reference to the ordinary concerns of the day or daytime and may refer to weekdays as contrasted with holidays and weekends and may also imply an opposition to ***nightly*** ⟨the *daily* grind⟩.

Diurnal is used in contrast to ***nocturnal*** and occurs chiefly in poetic or technical contexts ⟨*diurnal* mammals that are active by day⟩.

Quotidian emphasizes the quality of daily recurrence and may imply a commonplace, routine, or everyday quality to what it describes ⟨found solace in *quotidian* concerns⟩.

Circadian, a chiefly technical term, differs from ***daily*** or ***quotidian*** in implying only approximate equation with the twenty-four hour day ⟨*circadian* rhythms in insect behavior⟩.

dainty **1.** See CHOICE *adj.* **2.** See NICE.

dally **1.** See DELAY 2. **2.** See TRIFLE.

damage See INJURE.

damn See EXECRATE.

damp See WET.

dangerous, **hazardous**, **precarious**, **perilous**, **risky** mean bringing or involving the chance of loss or injury.

Dangerous applies to whatever may cause harm or loss unless dealt with carefully ⟨soldiers on a *dangerous* mission⟩. ***antonym:*** safe, secure

Hazardous implies great and continuous risk of harm or failure and small chance of successfully avoiding disaster ⟨claims that smoking is *hazardous* to your health⟩.

Precarious suggests insecurity and uncertainty resulting from danger or hazard ⟨has only a *precarious* hold on reality⟩.

Perilous strongly implies the immediacy of danger ⟨the situation at the foreign embassy has grown *perilous*⟩.

Risky often applies to a known and voluntarily accepted danger ⟨shy away from *risky* investments⟩.

dank See WET.

daredevil See ADVENTUROUS.

daring See ADVENTUROUS.

dark **1. Dark**, **dim**, **dusky**, **murky**, **gloomy** mean more or less deficient in light.

Dark, the general term, implies utter or virtual lack of illumination ⟨a *dark* cave⟩. ***antonym:*** light

Dim suggests too weak a light for things to be clearly visible ⟨a clandestine meeting in a *dim* bar⟩. ***antonym:*** bright, distinct

Dusky suggests deep twilight and a close approach to darkness ⟨trudging through *dusky* woods at day's end⟩.

Murky implies a heavy obscuring darkness such as that caused by smoke, fog, or dust in air or mud in water ⟨fish cannot live in the river's *murky* waters⟩.

Gloomy implies serious interference with the normal radiation of light and con notes cheerlessness and pessimism ⟨a *gloomy* room in the basement of the house⟩. ***antonym:*** brilliant

2. See OBSCURE.

dastardly See COWARDLY.

daunt See DISMAY.

dauntless See BRAVE.

dawdle See DELAY 2.

dead, **defunct**, **deceased**, **departed**, **late** mean devoid of life.

Dead is applied literally to what is deprived of vital force but is used figuratively of anything that has lost any attribute of life, such as energy, activity, or radiance ⟨a *dead* engine⟩. ***antonym:*** alive

Defunct stresses cessation of active existence or operation ⟨a *defunct* television series⟩. ***antonym:*** alive, live

Deceased, ***departed***, and ***late*** apply to persons who have died recently.

Deceased occurs especially in legal use ⟨the rights of the *deceased* must be acknowledged⟩; ***departed*** usually occurs as a euphemism ⟨pray for our *departed* mother⟩; and ***late*** applies especially to a person in a specific relation of status ⟨the *late* president of the company⟩.

deadly, **mortal**, **fatal**, **lethal** mean causing or capable of causing death.

Deadly applies to whatever is certain or very likely to cause death ⟨a *deadly* disease⟩.

Mortal appplies to what has caused or is about to cause death ⟨a *mortal* wound⟩. ***antonym:*** venial (*especially of a sin*)

Fatal stresses the inevitability of eventual death or destruction ⟨*fatal* consequences⟩.

Lethal applies to something that is bound to cause death or exists for the destruction of life ⟨*lethal* gas⟩.

deal **1.** See DISTRIBUTE. **2.** See TREAT.

dear See COSTLY.

debar See EXCLUDE.

debase **1.** **Debase**, **vitiate**, **deprave**, **corrupt**, **debauch**, **pervert** mean to cause deterioration or lowering in quality or character.

Debase implies a loss of position, worth, value, or dignity ⟨issued a *debased* coinage⟩. ***antonym:*** elevate, amend

Vitiate implies the impairment or destruction of purity, validity, or effectiveness by introduction of a fault or defect ⟨partisanship and factionalism *vitiated* our foreign policy⟩.

Deprave implies moral deterioration by evil thoughts or influences ⟨hoping to banish *depraved* thoughts⟩.

Corrupt implies loss of soundness, purity, or integrity through the action of debasing or destroying influences ⟨believes that jargon *corrupts* the language⟩.

Debauch implies a demoralizing or debasing through sensual indulgence ⟨led a *debauched* life after the divorce⟩.

Pervert implies a twisting or distorting from what is natural or normal so as to debase it completely ⟨*perverted* the original goals of the institute⟩.

2. See ABASE.

debate See DISCUSS.

debauch See DEBASE.

debilitate See WEAKEN.

decadence See DETERIORATION.

decay, **decompose**, **rot**, **putrefy**, **spoil** mean to undergo destructive dissolution.

Decay implies a slow and not necessarily complete change from a state of soundness or perfection ⟨a *decaying* Southern mansion⟩.

Decompose stresses a breaking down by chemical change and often implies a corruption ⟨the body was badly *decomposed*⟩.

Rot implies decay and decomposition, usually of matter, and often connotes foulness ⟨grain left to *rot* in warehouses⟩.

Putrefy stresses the offensive quality of what decays or rots ⟨corpses *putrefying* on the battlefield⟩.

Spoil applies chiefly to the decomposition of foods ⟨be on guard against *spoiled* mayonnaise⟩.

deceased See DEAD.

deceitful See DISHONEST.

deceive, **mislead**, **delude**, **beguile** mean to lead astray or to frustrate by underhandedness.

Deceive implies imposing a false idea or belief that causes confusion, bewilderment, or helplessness ⟨the salesman tried to *deceive* me about the car⟩. ***antonym:*** undeceive, enlighten

Mislead implies a leading astray from the truth that may or may not be intentional ⟨I was *misled* by the confusing sign⟩.

Delude implies deceiving so thoroughly as to make one a fool or to make one unable to distinguish the false from the true ⟨we were *deluded* into thinking we were safe⟩. ***antonym:*** enlighten

Beguile stresses the use of charm and persuasion to deceive ⟨his ingratiating ways *beguiled* us all⟩.

decency See DECORUM.

decent See CHASTE.

deception, **fraud**, **double-dealing**, **subterfuge**, **trickery** mean the acts or practices of or the means used by one who deliberately deceives.

Deception may or may not imply blameworthiness, since it may be used of cheating or swindling as well as of arts or games designed merely to mystify ⟨magicians are masters of *deception*⟩.

Fraud always implies guilt and often criminality in act or practice ⟨indicted for *fraud*⟩.

Double-dealing suggests duplicity or treachery or action contrary to one's professed attitude ⟨the guerillas accused the go-between of *double-dealing*⟩.

Subterfuge suggests deception by the adoption of a stratagem or the telling of a lie in order to escape responsibility or duty or to gain an end ⟨obtained the papers by *subterfuge*⟩.

Trickery implies ingenious or dishonest acts intended to dupe or cheat ⟨will resort to any *trickery* to gain her ends⟩.

decide, **determine**, **settle**, **rule**, **resolve** mean to come or cause to come to a conclusion.

Decide implies previous consideration and a cutting off of doubt, wavering, debate, or controversy ⟨will *decide* tonight where to build the school⟩.

Determine implies a fixing of the identity, character, scope, bounds, or direction of something ⟨*determined* the cause of the problem⟩.

Settle implies the arrival at a conclusion that brings to an end all doubt, wavering, or dispute ⟨the court's decision *settles* the matter⟩.

Rule implies a determination by judicial or administrative authority ⟨the judge *ruled* that the evidence was inadmissible⟩.

Resolve implies an expressed or clear decision or determination to do or refrain from doing something ⟨both nations *resolved* to stop terrorism⟩.

declare **1. Declare**, **announce**, **publish**, **proclaim**, **promulgate**, **advertise** mean to make known publicly.

Declare implies explicitness and usually formality in making known ⟨the referee *declared* the contest a draw⟩.

Announce implies a declaration, especially for the first time, of something that is of interest or is intended to satisfy curiosity ⟨*announced* their engagement at a party⟩.

Publish implies making public, especially through print ⟨*published* the list of winners in the paper⟩.

Proclaim implies a clear, forceful, authoritative oral declaring ⟨the president *proclaimed* a national day of mourning⟩.

Promulgate implies the proclaiming of a dogma, doctrine, or law ⟨*promulgated* an edict of religious toleration⟩.

Advertise applies to calling public attention to something by widely circulated statements, often marked by extravagance or lack of restraint ⟨*advertised* a new model of vacuum cleaner⟩.

2. See ASSERT.

decisive See CONCLUSIVE.

deck See ADORN.

decline *vb* **Decline**, **refuse**, **reject**, **repudiate**, **spurn** mean to turn away by not accepting, receiving, or considering.

Decline implies courteous refusal especially of offers or invitations ⟨*declined* the invitation to dinner⟩. ***antonym:*** accept

Refuse suggests more decisiveness or ungraciousness and often implies the denial of something expected or asked for ⟨*refused* them the loan they needed⟩.

Reject implies a peremptory refusal by or as if by sending away or discarding ⟨*rejected* the plan as unworkable⟩. ***antonym:*** accept, choose, select

Repudiate implies a casting off or disowning as untrue, unauthorized, or unworthy of acceptance ⟨*repudiated* the values of their parents⟩. ***antonym:*** adopt

Spurn stresses contempt or disdain in rejecting or repudiating ⟨*spurned* his amorous advances⟩. ***antonym:*** crave, embrace

decline *n* See DETERIORATION.

decolorize See WHITEN.

decompose See DECAY.

decorate See ADORN.

decorum, **decency**, **propriety**, **dignity**, **etiquette** mean observance of the rules governing proper conduct.

Decorum suggests conduct that is in accordance with good taste or with a code of rules governing behavior under certain conditions ⟨had failed to exhibit the *decorum* expected of an army officer⟩. ***antonym:*** indecorum, license

Decency implies behavior consistent with normal self-respect or humane feeling for others, or with what is fitting to a particular profession or condition in life ⟨maintained a strict *decency* in dress⟩. ***antonym:*** indecency

Propriety suggests an artificial standard of what is correct in conduct or speech ⟨regarded the *propriety* expected of a society matron as stifling⟩. ***antonym:*** impropriety

Dignity implies reserve or restraint in conduct prompted less by obedience to a code than by a sense of personal integrity or status ⟨conveyed a quiet *dignity* and sincerity that won him respect⟩.

Etiquette is the usual term for the detailed rules governing manners and conduct and for the observance of these rules ⟨the *etiquette* peculiar to the U.S. Senate⟩.

decoy See LURE.

decrease, **lessen**, **diminish**, **reduce**, **abate**, **dwindle** mean to grow or make less.

Decrease suggests a progressive decline in size, amount, numbers, or intensity ⟨slowly *decreased* the amount of pressure⟩. ***antonym:*** increase

Lessen suggests a decline in amount rather than in number ⟨has been unable to *lessen* her debt at all⟩.

Diminish emphasizes a perceptible loss and implies its subtraction from a total ⟨his muscular strength has *diminished* with age⟩.

Reduce implies a bringing down or lowering ⟨*reduce* your caloric intake⟩.

Abate implies a reducing of something excessive or oppressive in force or amount ⟨voted to *abate* the tax⟩. ***antonym:*** augment, intensify (*hopes, fears, a fever*)

Dwindle implies a progressive lessening and is applied to things capable of growing visibly smaller or disappearing ⟨their provisions *dwindled* slowly but surely⟩.

decree See DICTATE.

decrepit See WEAK.

decry, **depreciate**, **disparage**, **belittle**, **minimize** mean to express a low opinion of something.

Decry implies open condemnation with intent to discredit ⟨*decried* their do-nothing attitude⟩. ***antonym:*** extol

Depreciate implies a representing of something as being of less value than commonly believed ⟨critics *depreciate* his plays for being unabashedly sentimental⟩. ***antonym:*** appreciate

Disparage implies depreciation by indirect means such as slighting or invidious comparison ⟨*disparaged* golf as recreation for the middle-aged⟩. ***antonym:*** applaud

Belittle suggests a contemptuous attitude and an effort to make something seem small ⟨inclined to *belittle* the achievements of others⟩. ***antonym:*** aggrandize, magnify

Minimize connotes an effort to make something seem as small as possible ⟨do not try to *minimize* the danger involved⟩. ***antonym:*** magnify

dedicate See DEVOTE.
deduce See INFER.
deep **1.** See BROAD. **2. Deep, profound, abysmal** mean having great extension downward or inward.

Deep is the more general term, stressing the fact rather than the degree of extension downward from a surface or sometimes backward or inward from a front or outer part ⟨a *deep* river⟩; when applied to persons or mental processes, it implies the presence of or need for great intellectual activity or emotional conviction ⟨felt *deep* concern for his brother's safety⟩. ***antonym:*** shallow

Profound connotes exceedingly great depth ⟨the *profound* depths of the sea⟩ and may imply the need or presence of thoroughness ⟨a *profound* thinker⟩. ***antonym:*** shallow

Abysmal carries the idea of ***abyss*** and implies fathomless distance downward, backward, or inward ⟨on the brink of the *abysmal* precipice⟩ or often of measureless degree, especially with words denoting a lack of something ⟨*abysmal* ignorance⟩.

deep-rooted See INVETERATE.
deep-seated See INVETERATE.
deface, disfigure mean to mar the appearance of.

Deface, usually applied to inanimate things, implies superficial injuries that impair the surface appearance ⟨*deface* a building with graffiti⟩.

Disfigure implies deeper or more permanent injury to the surface and permanent impairment of the attractiveness or beauty of a person or thing ⟨a face *disfigured* by scars⟩. ***antonym:*** adorn

defame See MALIGN.
defeat See CONQUER.
defect See BLEMISH.
defend **1. Defend, protect, shield, guard, safeguard** mean to keep secure from danger or against attack.

Defend denotes warding off or repelling actual or threatened attack ⟨a large army needed to *defend* the country⟩. ***antonym:*** combat, attack

Protect implies the use of something as a bar to the admission or impact of what may attack, injure, or destroy ⟨*protect* one's eyes from the sun with dark glasses⟩.

Shield suggests the intervention of a cover or barrier against imminent danger or actual attack ⟨tried to *shield* her child from the real world⟩.

Guard implies protecting with vigilance and force against expected danger ⟨all White House entrances are well *guarded*⟩.

Safeguard implies the taking of precautionary protective measures against merely potential danger ⟨individual rights must be *safeguarded* whatever the cost⟩.

2. See MAINTAIN.

defer **1. Defer, postpone, suspend, stay** mean to delay an action or proceeding.

Defer implies a deliberate putting off to a later date or time ⟨*deferred* payment of the loan⟩. ***antonym:*** advance

Postpone implies an intentional deferring usually to a definite time ⟨the game was *postponed* until Saturday⟩.

Suspend implies a temporary stopping with an added suggestion of waiting until some expressed or implied condition is satisfied ⟨all business has been *suspended* while repairs are being made⟩.

Stay suggests the stopping or checking by an intervening obstacle, agency, or authority ⟨measures intended to *stay* the rapid rate of inflation⟩.

2. See YIELD.

deference See HONOR.
defile See CONTAMINATE.
define See PRESCRIBE.
definite See EXPLICIT.
definitive See CONCLUSIVE.
deflate See CONTRACT.
deform, distort, contort, warp mean to mar or spoil by or as if by twisting.

Deform may imply a changing of shape,

appearance, character, or nature through stress, injury, or some accident of growth ⟨relentless winds *deformed* the pines into bizarre shapes⟩.

Distort implies a wrenching from the natural, normal, or true shape, form, or direction ⟨the odd camera angle *distorts* his face in the photograph⟩.

Contort suggests an extreme distortion that is grotesque or painful ⟨a degenerative bone disease had painfully *contorted* the child's body⟩.

Warp indicates an uneven shrinking that bends or twists parts out of a flat plane ⟨*warped* floorboards⟩.

defraud See CHEAT.

deft See DEXTEROUS.

defunct See DEAD.

degenerate See VICIOUS.

degeneration See DETERIORATION.

degrade See ABASE.

deign See STOOP.

dejected See DOWNCAST.

dejection See SADNESS.

delay 1. Delay, **retard**, **slow**, **slacken**, **detain** mean to cause to be late or behind in movement or progress.

Delay implies a holding back, usually by interference, from completion or arrival ⟨bad weather *delayed* our return⟩. ***antonym:*** expedite, hasten

Retard applies chiefly to motion and suggests a slowing, often by interference ⟨language barriers *retarded* their rate of learning⟩. ***antonym:*** accelerate, advance, further

Slow, often used with *up* or *down*, also implies a reduction of speed, often with deliberate intention ⟨the engineer *slowed* the train⟩. ***antonym:*** speed *up*

Slacken suggests an easing up or relaxing of power or effort ⟨he needs to *slacken* his pace if he intends to finish the race⟩. ***antonym:*** quicken

Detain implies a holding back beyond a reasonable or appointed time, often with resulting delay ⟨unexpected business had *detained* her⟩.

2. Delay, **procrastinate**, **lag**, **loiter**, **dawdle**, **dally** mean to move or act slowly so as to fall behind.

Delay usually implies a putting off (as a beginning or departure) ⟨a tight schedule means we cannot *delay* any longer⟩. ***antonym:*** hasten, hurry

Procrastinate implies blameworthy delay especially through laziness, hesitation, or apathy ⟨*procrastinates* about making every decision⟩. ***antonym:*** hasten, hurry

Lag implies failure to maintain a speed or rate set by others ⟨we *lag* behind other countries in shoe production⟩.

Loiter implies delay while in progress, especially in walking ⟨*loitered* at several store windows before going to church⟩.

Dawdle more clearly suggests idleness, aimlessness, or a wandering mind ⟨children *dawdling* on their way home from school⟩.

Dally suggests delay through trifling or vacillation when promptness is necessary ⟨stop *dallying* and get to work⟩. ***antonym:*** hasten

delectation See PLEASURE.

delete See ERASE.

deleterious See PERNICIOUS.

deliberate *vb* See THINK 2.

deliberate *adj* See VOLUNTARY.

delicate See CHOICE *adj*.

delight See PLEASURE.

delirium See MANIA.

deliver See RESCUE.

delude See DECEIVE.

delusion, **illusion**, **hallucination**, **mirage** mean something believed to be or accepted as true or real that is actually false or unreal.

Delusion implies self-deception or deception by others concerning facts or situations and typically suggests a disordered state of mind ⟨suffered from a *delusion* that his family hated him⟩.

Illusion implies ascribing truth or reality to something that seems to be true or real but in fact is not ⟨clung to the *illusion* of happiness⟩.

Hallucination implies the perception of visual or other sensory impressions that have no reality but are the product of disordered function ⟨suffered from terrifying *hallucinations*⟩.

Mirage is comparable with the foregoing words in an extended sense in which it applies to a vision, dream, hope, or aim that is illusory ⟨the dream of peace was but a *mirage*⟩.

demand, **claim**, **require**, **exact** mean to ask or call for something as due or as necessary or as strongly desired.

Demand implies peremptoriness and insistence and often the claiming of a right to make requests that are to be regarded as commands ⟨the physician *demanded* payment of her bill⟩.

Claim implies a demand for the delivery or concession of something due as one's own or one's right ⟨*claimed* to be the first to describe the disease⟩. ***antonym:*** disclaim, renounce

Require suggests the imperative quality that arises from inner necessity, compulsion of law or regulation, or the exigencies of the situation ⟨the patient *requires* constant attention⟩.

Exact implies not only demanding but getting what one demands ⟨*exact* a promise from a friend⟩.

demean See ABASE.

demeanor See BEARING.

demented See INSANE.

demonstrate See SHOW 1.

demur See QUALM.

denounce See CRITICIZE.

dense **1.** See CLOSE *adj* 1. **2.** See STUPID.

deny, **gainsay**, **contradict**, **traverse**, **impugn**, **contravene** mean to refuse to accept as true or valid.

Deny implies a firm refusal to accept as true, to grant or concede, or to acknowledge the existence or claims of ⟨tried to *deny* the charges⟩. ***antonym:*** confirm, concede

Gainsay implies an opposing, usually by disputing, of the truth of what another has said ⟨no one dares *gainsay* the truth of what I've said⟩. ***antonym:*** admit

Contradict implies an open or flat denial of the truth of an assertion and usually suggests that the reverse is true ⟨her report *contradicts* every point of his statement to the press⟩. ***antonym:*** corroborate

Traverse, chiefly a legal term, implies a formal denial (as of an allegation or the justice of an indictment) ⟨*traversed* the accusation of fraud in his opening remarks⟩. ***antonym:*** allege

Impugn suggests a forceful, direct attacking, disputing, or contradicting of something or someone, often by prolonged argument ⟨dared to *impugn* his motives⟩. ***antonym:*** authenticate, advocate

Contravene implies not so much an intentional opposition as some inherent incompatibility ⟨laws against whaling that *contravene* Eskimo tradition⟩. ***antonym:*** uphold (*law, principle*), allege (*right, claim, privilege*)

depart **1.** See GO. **2.** See SWERVE.

departed See DEAD.

depend See RELY.

deplete, **drain**, **exhaust**, **impoverish**, **bankrupt** mean to deprive of something essential to existence or potency.

Deplete implies a reduction in number or quantity and the actual or potential harm done by such a reduction ⟨we cannot afford to *deplete* our natural resources⟩. ***antonym:*** renew, replace

Drain implies a gradual withdrawal and ultimate deprivation of what is necessary to a thing's existence and functioning ⟨a series of personal tragedies *drained* him of hope⟩.

Exhaust stresses a complete emptying or using up ⟨a theme that can never be *exhausted*⟩.

Impoverish suggests a deprivation of something essential to vigorous well-being ⟨without the arts we would lead an *impoverished* existence⟩. ***antonym:*** enrich

Bankrupt suggests impoverishment to the point of imminent collapse ⟨war had *bankrupted* the nation of manpower and resources⟩.

deplore, **lament**, **bewail**, **bemoan** mean to express grief or sorrow for something.

Deplore implies strong objection or sorrowful condemnation regarding the loss or impairment of something of value ⟨*deplores* the bad manners of today's young people⟩.

Lament implies a strong and demonstrative expression of sorrow ⟨never stopped *lamenting* the loss of their only son⟩. ***antonym:*** exult, rejoice

Bewail implies sorrow, disappointment, or protest finding outlet in loud words or cries ⟨fans *bewailed* the defeat of their team⟩. ***antonym:*** rejoice

Bemoan suggests great lugubriousness in such utterances ⟨purists continually *bemoan* the corruption of the language⟩. ***antonym:*** exult

deport **1.** See BANISH. **2.** See BEHAVE.

deportment See BEARING.

deprave See DEBASE.

depreciate See DECRY.

depreciatory See DEROGATORY.

depressed See DOWNCAST.

depression See SADNESS.

deranged See INSANE.

deride See RIDICULE.

derive See SPRING.

derogatory, **depreciatory**, **disparaging**, **slighting**, **pejorative** mean designed or tending to belittle.

Derogatory often applies to expressions or modes of expression that are intended to detract or belittle by suggesting something that is discreditable ⟨does not consider the word "politician" a *derogatory* term⟩. ***antonym:*** complimentary

Depreciatory is often applied to writing or speech that tends to lower a thing in value or status ⟨her habit of referring to the human body in the most *depreciatory* of ways⟩. ***antonym:*** appreciative

Disparaging implies an intent to depreciate by the use of oblique or indirect methods ⟨a *disparaging* look at some popular heroes⟩.

Slighting may imply mild disparagement, indifference, or even scorn ⟨made brief but *slighting* references to the other candidates in the race⟩.

Pejorative is applied especially to words whose basic meaning has been given a derogatory twist ⟨"egghead" is a *pejorative* term for an intellectual⟩.

description See TYPE.

descry See SEE 1.

desecration See PROFANATION.

desert See ABANDON.

design **1.** See INTENTION. **2.** See PLAN.

desire, **wish**, **want**, **crave**, **covet** mean to have a longing for something.

Desire stresses the strength of feeling and often implies strong intention or fixed aim ⟨*desires* to start a new life in another state⟩.

Wish often implies a general or transient longing for the unattainable ⟨she *wished* that there were some way she could help⟩.

Want specifically suggests a longing for something that would fill a felt need ⟨*want* to have a family⟩.

Crave stresses the force of physical appetite or emotional need ⟨*crave* sweets constantly⟩. ***antonym:*** spurn

Covet implies strong envious desire, typically for what belongs to another ⟨one of the most *coveted* honors in the sports world⟩. ***antonym:*** renounce (*something desirable*)

desist See STOP.

desolate **1.** See ALONE. **2.** See DISMAL.

despairing See DESPONDENT.

desperate See DESPONDENT.

despicable See CONTEMPTIBLE.

despise, **contemn**, **scorn**, **disdain**, **scout** mean to regard as unworthy of one's notice or consideration.

Despise may suggest an emotional response ranging from strong dislike to loathing ⟨*despises* those who show any sign of weakness⟩. ***antonym:*** appreciate

Contemn, more intellectual, implies a vehement condemnation of a person or thing as low, vile, feeble, or ignominious ⟨*contemns* the image of women promoted by advertisers⟩.

Scorn implies a ready or indignant and profound contempt ⟨*scorns* the very thought of retirement⟩. ***antonym:*** respect

Disdain implies an arrogant aversion to what is regarded as base or unworthy ⟨*disdained* all manner of popular music⟩. ***antonym:*** favor, admit

Scout suggests derision or abrupt rejection or dismissal ⟨*scouted* any suggestion that their son was other than angelic⟩.

despoil See RAVAGE.

despondent, **despairing**, **desperate**, **hopeless** mean having lost all or nearly all hope.

Despondent implies a deep dejection arising from a conviction of the uselessness of further effort ⟨*despondent* over the death of her father⟩. ***antonym:*** lighthearted

Despairing suggests the slipping away of all hope and often an accompanying despondency ⟨*despairing* appeals for the return of the kidnapped boy⟩. ***antonym:*** hopeful

Desperate implies such despair as prompts reckless action or violence in the face of anticipated defeat or frustration ⟨one last *desperate* attempt to turn the tide of the war⟩.

Hopeless suggests despair and the cessation of effort or resistance and often implies acceptance or resignation ⟨the situation of the trapped miners is *hopeless*⟩. ***antonym:*** hopeful

despotic See ABSOLUTE.

destiny See FATE.

destitution See POVERTY.

destruction See RUIN *n.*

desultory See RANDOM.

detached See INDIFFERENT.

detail See ITEM.

detailed See CIRCUMSTANTIAL.

detain 1. See DELAY 1. **2.** See KEEP 2.

deterioration, **degeneration**, **decadence**, **decline** mean a falling from a higher to a lower level in quality, character, or vitality.

Deterioration implies impairment of such valuable qualities as vigor, resilience, or usefulness ⟨the *deterioration* of her memory in recent years⟩. ***antonym:*** improvement, amelioration

Degeneration stresses physical, intellectual, or moral retrogression ⟨the *degeneration* of his youthful idealism⟩. ***antonym:*** regeneration

Decadence presupposes a previous attainment of maturity or excellence and implies a turn downward with a consequent loss in vitality or energy ⟨cited rock music as a sign of cultural *decadence*⟩. ***antonym:*** rise, flourishing

Decline suggests a more markedly downward direction and greater momentum as well as more obvious evidence of deterioration ⟨the meteoric rise and *decline* of his career⟩.

determinant See CAUSE.

determinative See CONCLUSIVE.

determine 1. See DECIDE. **2.** See DISCOVER.

detest See HATE.

detestable See HATEFUL.

detrimental See PERNICIOUS.

devastate See RAVAGE.

devastation See RUIN *n.*

develop See MATURE.

deviate See SWERVE.

devious See CROOKED.

devise See CONTRIVE.

devote, **dedicate**, **consecrate**, **hallow** mean to set apart for a particular and often higher end.

Devote is likely to imply a giving up or setting apart because of compelling motives ⟨*devoted* his evenings to study⟩.

Dedicate implies solemn and exclusive devotion to a sacred or serious use or purpose ⟨*dedicated* her life to medical research⟩.

Consecrate stresses investment with a solemn or sacred quality ⟨*consecrate* a church to the worship of God⟩.

Hallow, often differing little from ***dedicate*** or ***consecrate***, may distinctively imply an attribution on intrinsic sanctity ⟨battleground *hallowed* by the blood of patriots⟩.

devotion See FIDELITY.

devout, **pious**, **religious**, **pietistic**, **sanctimonious** mean showing fervor in the practice of religion.

Devout stresses genuine feeling and a mental attitude that leads to solemn reverence and fitting observance of rites and practices ⟨a pilgrimage that is the goal of *devout* believers⟩.

Pious applies to the faithful and dutiful performance of religious duties and maintenance of outwardly religious attitudes ⟨a *pious* family that faithfully observes the Sabbath⟩. ***antonym:*** impious

Religious may imply devoutness and piety but it emphasizes faith in a deity and adherence to a way of life in keeping with that faith ⟨a basically *religious* man, although not a regular churchgoer⟩. ***antonym:*** irreligious

Pietistic stresses the emotion al as opposed to the intellectual aspects of religion ⟨regarded religious articles as *pietistic* excess⟩.

Sanctimonious implies pretentions to holiness or smug appearance of piety ⟨a *sanctimonious* preacher without mercy or human kindness⟩.

dexterity See READINESS.

dexterous, **adroit**, **deft** mean ready and skilled in physical movement or sometimes mental activity.

Dexterous implies expertness with consequent facility and ability in manipulation ⟨a *dexterous* handling of a volatile situation⟩. ***antonym:*** clumsy

Adroit implies dexterity but may also stress resourcefulness or artfulness or inventiveness in coping with situations as they arise ⟨the *adroit* host of a radio call-in show⟩. ***antonym:*** maladroit

Deft emphasizes lightness, neatness, and sureness of touch or handling ⟨a *deft* interweaving of the novel's several subplots⟩. ***antonym:*** awkward

dialect, **vernacular**, **lingo**, **patois**, **jargon**, **cant**, **argot**, **slang** mean a form of language that is not recognized as standard.

Dialect applies commonly to a form of language found regionally or among the uneducated ⟨the *dialect* of the Cajuns in Louisiana⟩.

Vernacular applies to the everyday speech of the people in contrast to that of the learned ⟨the doctor used the *vernacular* in describing the disease⟩.

Lingo is a mildly contemptuous term for any language or form of language not readily understood ⟨foreign tourists speaking some strange *lingo*⟩.

Patois designates the speech used in a bilingual section or country, especially the mixed English and French spoken in some parts of Canada ⟨children chattering happily in the local *patois*⟩.

Jargon applies to a technical or esoteric language used by a profession, trade, or cult ⟨educationese is the *jargon* of educational theorists⟩.

Cant is applied derogatorily to language that is both peculiar to a group or class and marked by hackneyed or unclear expressions ⟨the *cant* of TV sportscasters⟩.

Argot is applied to a peculiar, often almost secret, language of a clique or other closely knit group ⟨the *argot* of narcotics smugglers⟩.

Slang designates a class of mostly recently coined and frequently short-lived terms or usages informally preferred to standard language as being forceful, novel, or voguish ⟨the ever-changing *slang* of college students⟩.

dictate, **prescribe**, **ordain**, **decree**, **impose** mean to issue something to be followed, observed, obeyed, or accepted.

Dictate implies an authoritative directive given orally or as if orally ⟨in matters of love, do as the heart *dictates*⟩.

Prescribe implies an authoritative pronouncement that is clear, definite, and incontrovertible ⟨the *prescribed* procedure for requesting new supplies⟩.

Ordain implies institution, establishment, or enactment by a supreme or unquestioned authority ⟨nature has *ordained* that we humans either swelter or shiver⟩.

Decree implies a formal pronouncement by one of great or absolute authority ⟨the Pope *decreed* that next year will be a Holy Year⟩.

Impose implies a subjecting to what must be borne, endured, or submitted to ⟨morality cannot be *imposed* by law⟩.

dictatorial, **magisterial**, **dogmatic**, **doctrinaire**, **oracular** mean imposing one's will or opinions on others.

Dictatorial stresses autocratic, high-handed methods and a domineering manner ⟨a *dictatorial* manner that alienates her colleagues⟩.

Magisterial stresses assumption or use of prerogatives appropriate to a magistrate or schoolmaster in forcing acceptance of one's opinions ⟨the *magisterial* tone of his arguments implies that only a fool would disagree⟩.

Dogmatic implies being unduly and arrogantly positive in laying down principles and expressing opinions ⟨very *dogmatic* about deciding what is art and what is not⟩.

Doctrinaire implies a disposition to follow abstract or personal theories and doctrines in teaching, framing laws, or deciding policies affecting people ⟨a *doctrinaire* conservative unable to deal with complex realities⟩.

Oracular implies the real or implied possession of hidden knowledge and the manner of one who delivers opinions in cryptic phrases or with pompous dogmatism ⟨for three decades she was the *oracular* voice of fashion⟩.

difference See DISCORD.

different, **diverse**, **divergent**, **disparate**, **various** mean unlike in kind or character.

Different may imply little more than separateness but it may also imply contrast or contrariness ⟨*different* foods from *different* lands⟩. ***antonym:*** identical, alike, same

Diverse implies both distinctness and marked contrast ⟨such *diverse* interests as dancing and football⟩. ***antonym:*** identical, selfsame

Divergent implies movement away from each other and unlikelihood of ultimate meeting or reconciliation ⟨went on to pursue very *divergent* careers⟩. ***antonym:*** convergent

Disparate emphasizes essential incongruity or incompatibility ⟨*disparate* notions of freedom⟩. ***antonym:*** comparable, analogous

Various stresses the number of sorts or kinds ⟨*various* methods have been tried⟩. ***antonym:*** uniform, cognate

difficult See HARD.

difficulty, **hardship**, **rigor**, **vicissitude** mean something obstructing one's course and demanding effort and endurance if one's end is to be attained.

Difficulty can apply to any condition, situation, experience, or task which presents a problem hard to solve or seemingly beyond one's ability to suffer or surmount ⟨they were determined to succeed; they met and solved each *difficulty* as it arose⟩.

Hardship stresses extreme suffering, toil, or privation but does not necessarily imply either effort to overcome or patience in enduring ⟨faced many *hardships* that long, hard winter⟩.

Rigor suggests a hardship necessarily imposed upon one by, for example, an austere religion, a trying climate, or an exacting undertaking ⟨endured the *rigors* of a rite of initiation⟩. ***antonym:*** amenity

Vicissitude applies to an inevitable difficulty or hardship that occurs in connection with life or a way of life, a career, or a course of action ⟨the *vicissitudes* of life left them tired, bitter, and alone⟩.

diffident See SHY.

diffuse See WORDY.

digest See COMPENDIUM.

dignity See DECORUM.

digress See SWERVE.

dilapidate See RUIN *vb*.

dilate See EXPAND.

dilemma See PREDICAMENT.

dilettante See AMATEUR.

diligent See BUSY.

dim See DARK.

diminish See DECREASE.

diminutive See SMALL.

din, **uproar**, **pandemonium**, **hullabaloo**, **babel**, **hubbub**, **clamor**, **racket** mean a disturbing or confusing welter of sounds or a situation marked by such a welter.

Din suggests prolonged and deafening clangor or insistent ear-splitting metallic sounds ⟨the *din* of a machine shop⟩. ***antonym:*** quiet

Uproar suggests tumult or wild disorder or often the sound of a multitude noisily or riotously protesting, arguing, or defying ⟨remarks that threw the crowd into an *uproar*⟩.

Pandemonium suggests the tumultuous din produced when a crowd or group becomes uncontrollably boisterous ⟨*pandemonium* erupted as soon as the teacher left the room⟩.

Hullabaloo suggests great excitement, stormy protest, and an interruption of peace and quiet rather than vociferous turmoil ⟨resubmitted his proposal after the *hullabaloo* died down⟩.

Babel stresses the confusing and seemingly meaningless mass of sound that results from a mingling of languages and vocal qualities ⟨the incomprehensible *babel* of everyone talking at once⟩.

Hubbub denotes the confusing mixture of sounds characteristic of the incessant movement of activities and business ⟨the *hubbub* of city streets⟩.

Clamor and ***racket*** stress the psychological effect of a combination of sounds or any excessively noisy scene and imply annoyance and disturbance ⟨the *clamor* of pigs demanding food⟩ ⟨impossible to hear oneself think amid the *racket*⟩.

diplomatic See SUAVE.

direct *vb* **1.** See COMMAND. **2.** See CONDUCT.

direct *adj* **Direct**, **immediate** mean uninterrupted.

Direct suggests unbroken connection between one thing and another, for example, between cause and effect, source and issue, or beginning and end ⟨had a *direct* bearing on the case⟩.

Immediate stresses the absence of any intervening medium or influence ⟨had *immediate* knowledge about the situation⟩.

directly See PRESENTLY.

dirty, **filthy**, **foul**, **nasty**, **squalid** mean either physically or morally unclean or impure.

Dirty emphasizes the presence of dirt more than an emotional reaction to it ⟨children *dirty* from play⟩ or stresses meanness or despicableness ⟨a *dirty* little secret⟩. ***antonym:*** clean

Filthy carries a strong suggestion of offensiveness and of gradually accumulated dirt that begrimes and besmears ⟨a stained greasy floor, utterly *filthy*⟩ or extreme obscenity ⟨*filthy* language⟩. ***antonym:*** neat, spic and span

Foul implies extreme offensiveness and an accumulation of what is rotten or stinking ⟨a *foul*-smelling open sewer⟩ or disgusting obscenity or loathesome behavior ⟨a record of *foul* deeds⟩. ***antonym:*** fair, undefiled

Nasty applies to what is actually foul or is repugnant to one used to or expecting freshness, cleanliness, or sweetness ⟨it's a *nasty* job to clean up after a sick cat⟩, although in practice it is often no more than a synonym of *unpleasant* or *disagreeable* ⟨his answer gave her a *nasty* shock⟩.

Squalid adds to the idea of dirtiness and filth that of slovenly neglect ⟨living in *squalid* poverty⟩ or sordid baseness and dirtiness ⟨had a series of *squalid* affairs⟩.

disable See WEAKEN.

disaffect See ESTRANGE.

disallow See DISCLAIM.

disaster, **catastrophe**, **calamity**, **cataclysm** mean an event or situation that is or is regarded as a terrible misfortune.

Disaster implies an unforeseen, ruinous, and often sudden misfortune that happens either through lack of foresight or through some hostile external agency ⟨the war proved to be a *disaster* for the country⟩.

Catastrophe implies a disastrous conclusion and emphasizes finality ⟨speculation about the *catastrophe* that befell Atlantis⟩.

Calamity stresses a grievous misfortune involving a great personal or public loss ⟨the father's sudden death was a *calamity* for the family⟩. ***antonym:*** boon

Cataclysm, originally a deluge or geological convulsion, applies to any event or situation that produces an upheaval or complete reversal of an existing order ⟨the French Revolution ranks as one of the *cataclysms* of the modern era⟩.

disavow See DISCLAIM.

disbelief See UNBELIEF.

disburse See SPEND.

discard, **cast**, **shed**, **slough**, **scrap**, **junk** mean to get rid of as of no further use, value, or service.

Discard implies the letting go or throwing away of something that has become useless or superfluous though often not intrinsically valueless ⟨*discard* any clothes you are unlikely to wear again⟩.

Cast, especially when used with *off*, *away*, and *out*, implies a forceful rejection or repudiation ⟨*cast* off her friends when they grew tiresome⟩.

Shed refers to the seasonal or periodic casting of natural parts, such as antlers, hair, skin, or leaves, and to the discarding of whatever has become burdensome or uncomfortable ⟨*shed* her tight shoes at the first opportunity⟩.

Slough implies the shedding of tissue, as from a scar or wound, or the discarding of what has become objectionable or useless ⟨finally *sloughed* off her air of jaded worldliness⟩.

Scrap suggests a throwing away or breaking up as worthless but implies the possibility of salvage or further utility ⟨all the old ideas of warfare had to be *scrapped*⟩.

Junk is close to ***scrap*** but tends to stress finality in disposal ⟨those who would *junk* our entire educational system⟩.

discern See SEE 1.

discernment, **discrimination**, **perception**, **penetration**, **insight**, **acumen** mean a power to see what is not evident to the average mind.

Discernment stresses accuracy, as for example, in reading character or motives or appreciating art ⟨had not the *discernment* to know who her friends really were⟩.

Discrimination stresses the power to distinguish and select what is true or appropriate or excellent ⟨acquire *discrimination* by looking at a lot of art⟩.

Perception implies quick and often sympathetic discernment and delicacy of feeling ⟨a novelist of keen *perception*⟩.

Penetration implies a searching mind that goes beyond what is obvious or superficial ⟨has not the *penetration* to see beneath their deceptive facade⟩.

Insight suggests depth of discernment coupled with sympathetic understanding

⟨a documentary providing *insight* into the plight of the homeless⟩. ***antonym:*** obtuseness

Acumen implies consistent penetration combined with keen practical judgment ⟨a theater director of reliable critical *acumen*⟩. ***antonym:*** obtuseness

discharge See PERFORM.

disciple See FOLLOWER.

discipline **1.** See PUNISH. **2.** See TEACH.

disclaim, **disavow**, **repudiate**, **disown**, **disallow** mean to refuse to admit, accept, or approve.

Disclaim implies a refusal to accept either a rightful claim or an imputation made by another ⟨*disclaimed* in equal measure the virtues and vices attributed to her⟩. ***antonym:*** claim

Disavow implies a vigorous denial of personal responsibility, acceptance, or approval ⟨the radical group *disavowed* any responsibility for the bombing⟩. ***antonym:*** avow

Repudiate implies a rejection or denial of something that had been previously acknowledged, recognized, or accepted ⟨*repudiated* the socialist views of his college days⟩. ***antonym:*** own

Disown implies a vigorous rejection or renunciation of something with which one formerly had a close relationship ⟨*disowned* his allegiance to the country of his birth⟩. ***antonym:*** own

Disallow implies the withholding of sanction or approval and sometimes suggests complete rejection or condemnation ⟨IRS auditors *disallowed* that deduction⟩. ***antonym:*** allow

disclose See REVEAL.

discomfit See EMBARRASS.

discompose, **disquiet**, **disturb**, **perturb**, **agitate**, **upset**, **fluster** mean to destroy capacity for collected thought or decisive action.

Discompose implies a minor degree of loss of self-control or self-confidence especially through emotional stress ⟨*discomposed* by the heckler's shouts⟩. ***antonym:*** compose

Disquiet suggests loss of sense of security or peace of mind and often the resulting uncertainty or fear ⟨the *disquieting* news of a tragic accident⟩. ***antonym:*** quiet, tranquilize, soothe

Disturb implies interference with one's mental processes or emotional balance by worry, perplexity, or fear ⟨the puzzling discrepancy *disturbed* me⟩.

Perturb implies deep disturbance of mind and emotions ⟨*perturbed* by her husband's strange behavior⟩. ***antonym:*** compose

Agitate suggests obvious external signs of nervous or emotional excitement ⟨in his *agitated* state he was unfit to go to work⟩. ***antonym:*** calm, tranquilize

Upset implies the disturbance of normal or habitual functioning by disappointment, distress, or grief ⟨constant bickering that greatly *upsets* their son⟩.

Fluster suggests a bewildered agitation caused by unexpected or sudden demands ⟨his amorous advances completely *flustered* her⟩.

disconcert See EMBARRASS.

disconsolate See DOWNCAST.

discontinue See STOP.

discord, **strife**, **conflict**, **contention**, **dissension**, **difference**, **variance** mean a state or condition marked by a lack of agreement or harmony.

Discord implies an intrinsic or essential lack of harmony that produces quarreling, factiousness, or antagonism between persons or things ⟨years of *discord* had left their mark on the political party⟩. ***antonym:*** concord, harmony

Strife emphasizes a struggle for superiority rather than a fundamental disharmony or incompatibility ⟨during his reign the empire was free of *strife*⟩. ***antonym:*** peace, accord

Conflict usually stresses the action of forces in opposition but it may also imply an incompatibility or irreconcilability, such as of duties or desires ⟨a *conflict* of professional interests⟩. ***antonym:*** harmony

Contention applies to strife or competition that shows itself in quarreling, disputing, or controversy ⟨several points of *contention* between the two sides⟩.

Dissension implies strife or discord and stresses a division into factions ⟨religious *dissensions* threatened to split the colony⟩. ***antonym:*** accord, comity

Difference, often in the plural, suggests actual incompatibility or impossibility of reconciliation because of dissimilarity in opinion, character, or nature ⟨decided to negotiate a reconciliation of their *differences*⟩.

Variance implies discord or strife between persons or things arising from a difference in nature, opinion, or interest ⟨cultural *variances* delayed the process of national unification⟩.

discover 1. Discover, **ascertain**, **determine**, **unearth**, **learn** mean to find out something not previously known to one.

Discover may apply to something requiring exploration or investigation or to a chance encounter and always implies the prior existence of what becomes known ⟨*discovered* the source of the river⟩.

Ascertain implies an awareness of ignorance or uncertainty and a conscious effort to find the facts or the truth ⟨will try to *ascertain* the population of the region⟩.

Determine, largely scientific or legal in usage, emphasizes the intent to establish the facts or to decide a dispute or controversy ⟨unable to *determine* the exact cause of the disease⟩.

Unearth implies a bringing to light of something forgotten or hidden ⟨*unearth* old records⟩.

Learn implies acquiring knowledge either with little effort or conscious intention ⟨*learned* the truth by chance⟩ or by study and practice ⟨spent years *learning* Greek⟩.

2. See INVENT. **3.** See REVEAL.

discrete See DISTINCT.

discrimination See DISCERNMENT.

discuss, **argue**, **debate**, **dispute** mean to discourse about something in order to reach conclusions or to convince others of the validity of one's position.

Discuss implies a sifting of possibilities by presenting considerations pro and con ⟨*discussed* the need for widening the expressway⟩.

Argue implies the often heated offering of reasons or evidence in support of convictions already held ⟨*argued* that the project would be too costly⟩.

Debate suggests formal or public argument between opposing parties ⟨*debated* the merits of the proposed constitutional amendment⟩; it may also apply to deliberation with oneself ⟨I'm *debating* whether I should go⟩.

Dispute implies contentious or heated argument ⟨scientists *dispute* the reasons for the extinction of the dinosaurs⟩. ***antonym:*** concede

disdain See DESPISE.

disdainful See PROUD.

disembarrass See EXTRICATE.

disencumber See EXTRICATE.

disentangle See EXTRICATE.

disfigure See DEFACE.

disgrace, **dishonor**, **disrepute**, **shame**, **infamy**, **ignominy**, **opprobrium** mean the loss of esteem and good repute and the enduring of reproach and contempt.

Disgrace often implies loss of favor or complete humiliation and sometimes ostracism ⟨his conviction for bribery brought *disgrace* upon his family⟩. ***antonym:*** respect, esteem

Dishonor emphasizes the loss of honor that one has previously enjoyed or the loss of self-esteem ⟨prefer death to life with *dishonor*⟩. ***antonym:*** honor

Disrepute stresses loss of one's good name or the acquiring of a bad reputation ⟨a once-proud name now fallen into *disrepute*⟩. ***antonym:*** repute

Shame implies particularly humiliating disgrace or disrepute and is likely to stress the strong emotional reaction of the one affected 〈could hardly live with the *shame*〉. ***antonym:*** glory, pride

Infamy implies notoriety as well as exceeding shame 〈a gangster whose name retains an enduring *infamy*〉.

Ignominy stresses the almost unendurable contemptibility or despicableness of the disgrace 〈suffered the *ignominy* of being brought back in irons〉.

Opprobrium adds to ***disgrace*** the notion of being severely reproached or condemned 〈bring *opprobrium* on oneself by expulsion from school〉.

disguise, **cloak**, **mask**, **dissemble** mean to alter the dress or appearance so as to conceal the identity, intention, or true feeling.

Disguise implies a deceptive changing of appearance or behavior that serves to conceal an identity, a motive, or an attitude 〈*disguised* himself as a peasant to escape detection〉.

Cloak suggests the assumption of something that covers and conceals identity or intention completely 〈*cloaks* her greed and self-interest in the rhetoric of philosophy〉. ***antonym:*** uncloak

Mask suggests the prevention of recognition of a thing's true character usually by some obvious means and does not always imply deception or pretense 〈a smiling front that *masks* a will of iron〉.

Dissemble stresses simulation for the purpose of deceiving and disguising especially feelings and opinions 〈*dissembled* madness to survive the intrigues at court〉. ***antonym:*** betray

dishonest, **deceitful**, **mendacious**, **lying**, **untruthful** mean unworthy of trust or belief.

Dishonest implies a willful perversion of truth in order to deceive, cheat, or defraud 〈a swindle usually involves *dishonest* people〉. ***antonym:*** honest

Deceitful usually implies an intent to mislead and commonly suggests a false appearance or duplicitous behavior 〈learned of the secret of his *deceitful* partner〉. ***antonym:*** trustworthy

Mendacious, less forthright than ***lying***, may suggest bland or even harmless mischievous deceit and often suggests a habit of telling untruths 〈his sea stories became increasingly *mendacious*〉. ***antonym:*** veracious

Lying implies a specific act or instance rather than a habit or tendency and suggests guilt 〈a conviction based upon testimony of a *lying* witness〉. ***antonym:*** truthtelling

Untruthful is a less harsh term than ***lying*** and stresses a discrepancy between what is said or represented and the facts or reality of the situation rather than an intent to deceive 〈the version given in her memoirs is *untruthful* in several respects〉. ***antonym:*** truthful

dishonor See DISGRACE.

disillusioned See SOPHISTICATED.

disinclined, **hesitant**, **reluctant**, **loath**, **averse** mean lacking the will or desire to do something indicated.

Disinclined implies lack of taste for or inclination toward something and may imply disapproval 〈*disinclined* to go out in bad weather〉. ***antonym:*** inclined

Hesitant implies a holding back through fear, uncertainty, or disinclination 〈*hesitant* about asking her for a date〉.

Reluctant implies a holding back through resistance or unwillingness 〈I'm *reluctant* to blame anyone just now〉.

Loath implies lack of harmony between what one anticipates doing and one's opinions, predilections, or liking 〈*loath* to believe that he could do anything right〉. ***antonym:*** anxious

Averse implies a turning away from what is distasteful or unwelcome 〈seems *averse* to anything requiring work〉. ***antonym:*** avid (*of* or *for*), athirst (*for*)

disinterested See INDIFFERENT.
disloyal See FAITHLESS.
dismal, **dreary**, **cheerless**, **dispiriting**, **bleak**, **desolate** mean devoid of all that is cheerful and comfortable.
Dismal may imply extreme gloominess or somberness that is utterly depressing ⟨a *dismal* day of unrelenting rain⟩.
Dreary implies a sustained gloom, dullness, or tiresomeness that discourages or enervates ⟨spent her days alone in a *dreary* apartment⟩.
Cheerless stresses a pervasive, disheartening joylessness or hopelessness ⟨faced a *cheerless* life as a drudge⟩. ***antonym:*** cheerful
Dispiriting implies a disheartening or lessening of morale or determination ⟨problems that made for a *dispiriting* start for their new venture⟩. ***antonym:*** inspiriting
Bleak implies a chilly, dull barrenness that disheartens and lacks any notions of cheer, shelter, or comfort ⟨a *bleak,* windswept landscape offering no refuge for the wayward traveler⟩.
Desolate implies that something disheartens by being utterly barren, lifeless, uninhabitable, or abandoned ⟨the long trek into the country's *desolate* interior⟩.
dismay, **appall**, **horrify**, **daunt** mean to unnerve or deter by arousing fear, apprehension, or aversion.
Dismay implies a loss of power to proceed because of a sudden fear or anxiety or because one does not know how to deal with a situation ⟨*dismayed* to find herself the center of attention⟩. ***antonym:*** cheer
Appall implies that one is faced with that which perturbs, confounds, or shocks ⟨*appalled* by your utter lack of concern⟩. ***antonym:*** nerve, embolden
Horrify stresses a reaction of horror or revulsion from what is ghastly or hideously offensive ⟨the scope of the famine is quite *horrifying*⟩.
Daunt suggests a cowing, subduing, disheartening, or frightening in a venture requiring courage ⟨problems that would *daunt* even the most intrepid of reformers⟩. ***antonym:*** enhearten
dismiss See EJECT.
disown See DISCLAIM.
disparage See DECRY.
disparaging See DEROGATORY.
disparate See DIFFERENT.
dispassionate See FAIR.
dispatch *n* See HASTE.
dispatch *vb* See KILL.
dispel See SCATTER.
dispense See DISTRIBUTE.
disperse See SCATTER.
dispirited See DOWNCAST.
dispiriting See DISMAL.
displace See REPLACE.
display See SHOW 2.
dispose See INCLINE.
disposition, **temperament**, **temper**, **complexion**, **character**, **personality** mean the dominant quality or qualities distinguishing a person or group.
Disposition implies customary moods and attitudes toward the life around one ⟨a boy of cheerful *disposition*⟩.
Temperament implies a pattern of innate characteristics that result from one's specific physical, emotional, and mental makeup ⟨an artistic *temperament* inherited from his mother⟩.
Temper implies the qualities acquired through experience that determines how a person or group meets difficulties or handles situations ⟨the national *temper* has always been one of optimism⟩.
Complexion implies some distinctive quality of mood, attitude, and way of thinking that determines the impression produced on others ⟨a leader of severe and authoritarian *complexion*⟩.
Character applies to the aggregate of moral qualities by which a person is judged apart from his intelligence, competence, or special talents ⟨a woman of resolute *character*⟩.

Personality applies to an aggregate of qualities that distinguish one as an individual ⟨a somber *personality* not to everyone's liking⟩.

disprove, **refute**, **confute**, **rebut**, **controvert** mean to show or try to show by presenting evidence that something is not true.

Disprove implies the successful demonstration by any method of the falsity or invalidity of a claim or argument ⟨the view that one can neither prove nor *disprove* the existence of God⟩. ***antonym:*** prove, demonstrate

Refute stresses a logical method of disproving and suggests adducing of evidence, bringing forward of witnesses or authorities, and close reasoning ⟨*refuted* every piece of his argument⟩.

Confute implies reducing an opponent to silence by an overwhelming refutation or by such methods as raillery, denunciation, or sarcasm ⟨a triumphal flight that *confuted* all of the doubters⟩.

Rebut suggests formality of method but not assurance of success in answering an opponent's argument, evidence, or testimony ⟨give the opposing side time to *rebut*⟩.

Controvert stresses both the denial of and the attempt to disprove what is put forward without necessarily implying success in refutation ⟨a thesis that withstood every attempt to *controvert* it⟩. ***antonym:*** assert

dispute See DISCUSS.

disquiet See DISCOMPOSE.

disregard See NEGLECT.

disrepute See DISGRACE.

dissect See ANALYZE.

dissemble See DISGUISE.

dissension See DISCORD.

dissipate **1.** See SCATTER. **2.** See WASTE.

dissolve See ADJOURN.

distant, **far**, **far-off**, **faraway**, **remote**, **removed** mean not close in space, time, or relationship.

Distant stresses separation and implies an obvious interval whether long or short ⟨went to live in a *distant* city⟩.

Far in most of its uses applies to what is a long way off ⟨retreat to the *far* reaches of the wilderness⟩. ***antonym:*** near, nigh

Far-off stresses distance and is often preferred when distance in time is specifically implied ⟨some *far-off* day⟩. ***antonym:*** near-at-hand

Faraway differs little from ***far-off*** but may sometimes connote a hazy remoteness or even obscurity ⟨began to have a *far-away* look in her eyes⟩. ***antonym:*** near, nigh

Remote suggests a far removal from one's point of view, time, or location and is likely to connote a consequent lessening of importance to oneself ⟨spent her life on a *remote* island⟩. ***antonym:*** close, adjacent

Removed carries a stronger implication of separateness and may suggest a contrast not only in time and space but in character or quality ⟨ sought a quiet retreat, *removed* from the everyday world and its tensions⟩. ***antonym:*** adjoining

distasteful See REPUGNANT.

distend See EXPAND.

distinct **1. Distinct**, **separate**, **several**, **discrete** mean not being each and every one the same.

Distinct indicates that something is distinguished by the mind or eye as being apart or different from others ⟨each and every bowl is hand-decorated and *distinct*⟩. ***antonym:*** indistinguishable

Separate often stresses lack of connection in space or time or a difference in identity between the things in question ⟨the two schools are *separate* and unequal⟩.

Several indicates distinctness, difference, or separation from similar items ⟨a survey of the *several* opinions of the new building⟩.

Discrete strongly emphasizes individuality and lack of material connection despite apparent similarity or continuity

⟨two *discrete* issues are being confused here⟩.
2. See EVIDENT.
distinctive See CHARACTERISTIC.
distinguished See FAMOUS.
distort See DEFORM.
distract See PUZZLE.
distress *n* **Distress**, **suffering**, **misery**, **agony** mean the state of being in great trouble or in pain of body or mind.
Distress implies an external cause of great physical or mental strain and stress and is likely to connote the possibility of or the need for relief ⟨news of the hurricane put everyone in great *distress*⟩.
Suffering implies conscious endurance of pain or distress and often a stoical acceptance ⟨the *suffering* of earthquake victims⟩.
Misery stresses the unhappiness attending distress or suffering and often connotes sordidness, abjectness, or dull passivity ⟨the poor live with *misery* every day⟩. ***antonym:*** felicity, blessedness
Agony suggests pain too intense to be borne by body or mind ⟨in *agony* over their daughter's suicide⟩.
distress *vb* See TROUBLE.
distribute, **dispense**, **divide**, **deal**, **dole** mean to give out, usually in shares, to each member of a group.
Distribute implies an apportioning by separation of something into parts, units, or amounts and a spreading out of those parts equally, systematically, or at random ⟨*distributed* the work to all employees⟩. ***antonym:*** collect, amass
Dispense suggests the giving of a carefully weighed or measured portion to each of a group according to need or as a right or as due ⟨*dispensed* medicine during the epidemic⟩.
Divide stresses the separation of a whole into parts before giving out or delivering and implies that the parts are equal ⟨three charitable groups *divided* the proceeds⟩.
Deal emphasizes the allotment of something piece by piece in turn to each of the members of a group ⟨*deal* out equipment and supplies to each soldier⟩.
Dole implies a scantiness or niggardliness in the amount dispensed ⟨*doled* out the little food there was⟩.
disturb See DISCOMPOSE.
dither See SHAKE 1.
diurnal See DAILY.
dive See PLUNGE.
diverge See SWERVE.
divergent See DIFFERENT.
diverse See DIFFERENT.
divert See AMUSE.
divide **1.** See DISTRIBUTE. **2.** See SEPARATE.
divine See FORESEE.
division See PART.
divorce See SEPARATE.
divulge See REVEAL.
docile See OBEDIENT.
doctrinaire See DICTATORIAL.
doctrine, **dogma**, **tenet** mean a principle accepted as valid and authoritative.
Doctrine may imply authoritative teaching backed by acceptance by a body of believers or adherents ⟨a catechism of religious *doctrines*⟩ but *doctrine* can be used more broadly to denote a formulated theory that is supported by evidence, backed by authority, and proposed for acceptance ⟨the *doctrine* of organic evolution⟩.
Dogma implies a doctrine that is laid down as true and beyond dispute ⟨in 1870 Pope Pius IX defined the *dogma* of papal infallibility⟩ and may connote arbitrary or even arrogant insistence on authority or imposition by authority ⟨the *dogma* that the king can do no wrong⟩.
Tenet stresses acceptance and belief rather than teaching and applies to a principle held or adhered to and implies a body of adherents ⟨the *tenets* of socialism⟩.
dogged See OBSTINATE.
dogma See DOCTRINE.
dogmatic See DICTATORIAL.

doldrums See TEDIUM.
dole *n* See RATION.
dole *vb* See DISTRIBUTE.

dominant, **predominant**, **paramount**, **preponderant**, **sovereign** mean superior to all others in power, influence, or importance.

Dominant applies to something that is uppermost because it rules or controls ⟨a *dominant* wolf⟩. ***antonym:*** subordinate

Predominant applies to something that exerts, often temporarily, the most marked influence on a person or a situation ⟨at the time fear was my *predominant* emotion⟩. ***antonym:*** subordinate

Paramount implies supremacy in importance, rank, or jurisdiction ⟨inflation was the *paramount* issue in the campaign⟩.

Preponderant applies to an element or factor that outweighs all others with which it may come into comparison in influence, power, number, or effect ⟨*preponderant* evidence in his favor⟩.

Sovereign indicates quality or rank to which everything else is clearly subordinate or inferior ⟨the *sovereign* power resides in the people⟩.

domineering See MASTERFUL.
dominion See POWER 3.
donate See GIVE.
doom See FATE.
dormant See LATENT.
double-dealing See DECEPTION.
double entendre See AMBIGUITY.
doubt See UNCERTAINTY.

doubtful, **dubious**, **problematic**, **questionable** mean not affording assurance of the worth, soundness, or certainty of something or someone.

Doubtful is likely to impute worthlessness, unsoundness, failure, or uncertainty ⟨still *doubtful* about the cause of the explosion⟩. ***antonym:*** positive

Dubious stresses suspicion, mistrust, or hesitation ⟨*dubious* about the practicality of the scheme⟩. ***antonym:*** cocksure, reliable, trustworthy

Problematic applies especially to things or situations whose existence, meaning, or realization is highly uncertain ⟨whether the project will ever be finished is *problematic*⟩. ***antonym:*** unproblematic

Questionable may imply no more than the existence of doubt but usually suggests doubt about propriety or well-grounded suspicions ⟨a real estate agent of *questionable* honesty⟩. ***antonym:*** authoritative, unquestioned

dour See SULLEN.
dowdy See SLATTERNLY.

downcast, **dispirited**, **dejected**, **depressed**, **disconsolate**, **woebegone** mean affected by or showing very low spirits.

Downcast implies being overcome by shame, mortification, or loss of hope or confidence and an utter lack of cheerfulness ⟨negative reviews left the actors feeling *downcast*⟩. ***antonym:*** elated

Dispirited implies extreme low-spiritedness and discouragement resulting from failure to accomplish what one wants or to achieve one's goal ⟨*dispirited,* the doomed explorers resigned themselves to failure⟩. ***antonym:*** high-spirited, inspirited

Dejected implies a sudden but often temporary severe loss of hope, courage, or vigor ⟨a crushing defeat that left the team in a *dejected* mood⟩. ***antonym:*** animated

Depressed may imply either a temporary or a chronic low-spiritedness and may indicate a serious inability to be normally happy and active ⟨*depressed* by his failures to the point of suicide⟩. ***antonym:*** exhilarated, animated

Disconsolate implies being inconsolable or very uncomfortable ⟨*disconsolate* motorists leaning against their disabled car⟩. ***antonym:*** cheerful

Woebegone suggests a defeated, spiritless condition and emphasizes the impression of dejection and discouragement produced by facial expression, posture, and surroundings ⟨a rundown, *woebegone* motel on an empty back road⟩.

drag See PULL.

drain See DEPLETE.

dramatic, **theatrical**, **melodramatic**, **histrionic** mean having a character or effects typical of acted plays.

Dramatic applies to a speech, action, gesture, or situation capable of stirring the imagination and emotions deeply ⟨a *dramatic* meeting of world leaders⟩.

Theatrical implies a crude appeal to the emotions through artificiality or exaggeration in gesture, action, or vocal expression ⟨a *theatrical* oration⟩.

Melodramatic suggests an exaggerated emotionalism or an inappropriate theatricalism ⟨making a *melodramatic* scene in public⟩.

Histrionic applies to tones, gestures, and motions and suggests a deliberate affectation or staginess ⟨a *histrionic* show of grief⟩.

draw See PULL.

dread See FEAR.

dreadful See FEARFUL 2.

dreary See DISMAL.

drench See SOAK.

drift See TENDENCY.

drill See PRACTICE.

drive See MOVE.

droll See LAUGHABLE.

drowsy See SLEEPY.

drudgery See WORK 1.

drunk, **drunken**, **intoxicated**, **inebriated**, **tipsy**, **tight**, **plastered** mean considerably and conspicuously affected by alcohol.

Drunk and ***drunken*** are the plainspoken, direct, and inclusive terms ⟨arrived at the party already *drunk*⟩ ⟨a *drunken* man stumbled out of the bar⟩ but *drunken* may imply habitual excess in drinking and also applies to whatever proceeds from intoxication ⟨a *drunken* brawl⟩. ***antonym:*** sober

Intoxicated is a more formal, less derogatory term and likely to be used in legal or medical contexts ⟨arrested for driving while *intoxicated*⟩. ***antonym:*** sober

Inebriated implies such a state of intoxication that exhilaration, noise, or undue excitement results ⟨the *inebriated* revelers bellowed out songs⟩.

Tipsy may imply only slight drunkenness and the consequent lessening of muscular and mental control ⟨a *tipsy* patron began making unwelcome amorous advances⟩.

Tight usually suggests obvious drunkenness ⟨at midnight he returned, *tight* as a drum⟩.

Plastered refers to one who has become wholly incompetent through intoxication ⟨so *plastered* they could not stand up⟩.

drunken See DRUNK.

dry, **arid** mean lacking or deficient in moisture.

Dry may suggest freedom from noticeable moisture either as a characteristic or a desirable state ⟨a *dry* climate⟩ or it may suggest deficiency of moisture or the lack or loss of normal or needed moisture ⟨the spring has gone *dry*⟩ or lack of those qualities in anything that compel interest or attention or in a person indicate vitality, warmth, or responsiveness ⟨possessed a *dry* manner and a droning voice⟩. ***antonym:*** wet

Arid implies destitution or deprivation of moisture and extreme dryness; in its typical applications to regions or territory it suggests waste or desert lands ⟨a bare *arid* stretch of country⟩; it may also suggest absence of those qualities that mark a thing as worthwhile, fruitful, or significant ⟨presented an *arid* paper devoid of intellectual content⟩. ***antonym:*** moist, verdant

dubiety See UNCERTAINTY.

dubious See DOUBTFUL.

ductile See PLASTIC.

dudgeon See OFFENSE 1.

dulcet See SWEET.

dull 1. Dull, **blunt**, **obtuse** mean not sharp, keen, or acute.

Dull suggests a lack or loss of keenness, zest, or pungency ⟨a *dull* pain⟩. ***antonym:*** sharp, poignant, lively

Blunt suggests an inherent lack of sharpness or quickness of feeling or perception ⟨even a person of his *blunt* sensibility was moved⟩. ***antonym:*** keen, sharp

Obtuse implies such bluntness as makes one insensitive in perception, speech, or imagination ⟨too *obtuse* to realize that she had deeply hurt us⟩. ***antonym:*** acute

2. See STUPID.

dumb See STUPID.

dumbfound See PUZZLE.

dumpy See STOCKY.

dupe, **gull**, **trick**, **hoax** mean to deceive by underhanded means for one's own ends.

Dupe suggests unwariness in the person deluded ⟨*duped* us into buying a lemon of a car⟩.

Gull stresses credulousness or readiness to be imposed on or made a fool of ⟨you are so easily *gulled* by these contest promoters⟩.

Trick implies an intent, not always vicious, to delude by means of a ruse or fraud ⟨special effects can *trick* moviegoers into believing anything⟩.

Hoax implies the contriving of an elaborate or adroit imposture in order to deceive ⟨*hoaxed* the public by broadcasting news of a Martian invasion⟩.

duplicate See REPRODUCTION.

durable See LASTING.

dusky See DARK.

duty 1. See FUNCTION. **2.** See TASK.

dwell See RESIDE.

dwindle See DECREASE.

E

eager, **avid**, **keen**, **anxious**, **athirst** mean moved by a strong and urgent desire or interest.

Eager implies ardor and enthusiasm and sometimes impatience at delay or restraint ⟨*eager* to get started on the trip⟩. ***antonym:*** listless

Avid adds to ***eager*** the implication of insatiability or greed ⟨young pleasure-seekers *avid* for the next thrill⟩. ***antonym:*** indifferent, averse

Keen suggests intensity of interest and quick responsiveness in action ⟨very *keen* on the latest styles and fashions⟩.

Anxious suggests earnest desire but emphasizes fear of frustration, failure, or disappointment ⟨*anxious* to know that they got home safely⟩. ***antonym:*** loath

Athirst stresses yearning or longing but not necessarily readiness for action ⟨*athirst* for adventure on her first trip to India⟩.

earn See GET.

earnest See SERIOUS.

earsplitting See LOUD.

earthly, **mundane**, **worldly** mean belonging to or characteristic of the earth.

Earthly often implies a contrast with what is heavenly or spiritual ⟨abandoned *earthly* concerns and entered a convent⟩.

Mundane implies a relation to the immediate concerns and activities of human beings and stresses what is transitory and impermanent or practical and ordinary ⟨a *mundane* discussion of finances⟩. ***antonym:*** eternal

Worldly implies indifference to spiritual matters and preoccupation with the mundane and the satisfaction of the appetites ⟨nightclub habitués with a *worldly* air⟩. ***antonym:*** otherworldly

ease See READINESS.

easy **1. Easy**, **facile**, **simple**, **light**, **effortless**, **smooth** mean not demanding undue effort or involving difficulty.

Easy is applicable either to persons or things imposing tasks or making demands or to activities required by such tasks or demands ⟨an *easy* college course requiring little work⟩. ***antonym:*** hard

Facile chiefly applies to something that is achieved or gains its ends apparently without effort and implies lack of restraint, undue haste, or shallowness ⟨offers only *facile* solutions to complex problems⟩. ***antonym:*** arduous (*referring to the thing accomplished*), constrained, clumsy (*referring to the agent or the method*)

Simple stresses ease in understanding or apprehending because free from complication, intricacy, or elaboration ⟨a *simple* problem in arithmetic⟩. ***antonym:*** complicated, difficult

Light stresses freedom from what is burdensome or difficult and exacting, and often suggests quickness of movement ⟨her novels are pretty *light* stuff⟩. ***antonym:*** heavy, arduous, burdensome

Effortless stresses the appearance of ease and implies the prior attainment of artistry or expertness ⟨a champion figure skater moving with *effortless* grace⟩. ***antonym:*** painstaking

Smooth stresses the absence or removal of all difficulties, hardships, or obstacles from a course or career ⟨made *smooth,* swift progress up the corporate ladder⟩. ***antonym:*** labored

2. See COMFORTABLE.

ebb See ABATE.

eccentric See STRANGE.

eccentricity, **idiosyncrasy** mean singularity in behavior or an instance of this.

Eccentricity retains its basic notion of being off center and in this use stresses divergence from the usual or customary ⟨led a life of charming *eccentricities*⟩.

Idiosyncrasy stresses a strongly individual and independent quality and is likely to imply a following of one's peculiar bent or temperament ⟨a style marked by *idiosyncrasy*⟩.

economical See SPARING.

ecstasy, **rapture**, **transport** mean intense exaltation of mind and feelings.

Ecstasy may apply to any strong emotion (such as joy, fear, rage, or adoration) that can entrance ⟨the sculptor was in *ecstasy* when his work was unveiled⟩. ***antonym:*** depression

Rapture implies intense bliss or utter delight ⟨in speechless *rapture* during the entire wedding⟩.

Transport applies to any powerful emotion that lifts one out of oneself and provokes vehement expression or frenzied action ⟨in a *transport* of rage after reading the article⟩.

edge See BORDER.

educate See TEACH.

educe, **evoke**, **elicit**, **extract**, **extort** mean to draw out something hidden, latent, or reserved.

Educe implies the development and bringing out of something potential or latent ⟨*educe* from common sense the best solution to the problem⟩.

Evoke implies a strong stimulus that arouses an emotion or an interest or recalls an image or memory from the past ⟨a song that *evokes* many memories⟩.

Elicit implies some effort or skill in drawing forth a response and often implies resistance in the object of effort ⟨unable to *elicit* a straight answer from the candidate⟩.

Extract implies the use of force or pressure in obtaining answers or information ⟨*extract* testimony from a hostile witness⟩.

Extort suggests a wringing or wresting of something from one who resists strongly ⟨*extorted* the money from his father-in-law⟩.

eerie See WEIRD.

efface See ERASE.

effect *n* **Effect**, **consequence**, **result**, **issue**, **outcome** mean a condition or occurrence traceable to a cause.

Effect designates something that necessarily and directly follows upon or occurs by reason of a cause ⟨the *effects* of radiation on the body⟩. ***antonym:*** cause

Consequence implies a direct but looser or remoter connection with a cause and usually implies that the cause is no longer operating ⟨a single act that had far-reaching *consequences*⟩. ***antonym:*** antecedent

Result applies often to the last in a series of effects ⟨the end *result* was a growth in business⟩.

Issue applies to a result that ends or solves a problem, a difficulty, or a conflict ⟨a successful *issue* that rendered all the controversy moot⟩.

Outcome suggests the final result of complex or conflicting causes or forces ⟨the *outcome* of generations of controlled breeding⟩.

effect *vb* See PERFORM.

effective, **effectual**, **efficient**, **efficacious** mean producing or capable of producing a result.

Effective stresses the actual production of or the power to produce an effect ⟨an *effective* rebuttal⟩. ***antonym:*** ineffective, futile

Effectual suggests the accomplishment of a desired result or the fulfillment of a purpose especially as viewed after the fact ⟨the measures to halt crime proved *effectual*⟩. ***antonym:*** ineffectual, fruitless

Efficient suggests an acting or a potential for action or use in such a way as to avoid loss or waste of energy in effecting, producing, or functioning ⟨an *efficient* small car⟩. ***antonym:*** inefficient

Efficacious suggests possession of a special quality or virtue that gives effective power ⟨a detergent that is *efficacious* in removing grease⟩. ***antonym:*** inefficacious, powerless

effectual See EFFECTIVE.

effeminate See FEMALE.
efficacious See EFFECTIVE.
efficient See EFFECTIVE.
effort, **exertion**, **pains**, **trouble** mean the active use of energy in producing a result.

Effort often suggests a single action or attempt or persistent activity and implies the calling up or directing of energy by the conscious will ⟨made the supreme *effort* and crossed the finish line first⟩. ***antonym:*** ease

Exertion may describe the bringing into effect of any power of mind or body or it may suggest laborious and exhausting effort ⟨a job not requiring much physical *exertion*⟩.

Pains implies toilsome or solicitous effort by a conscientious agent ⟨take *pains* to do the job well⟩.

Trouble implies effort that inconveniences or wastes time and patience ⟨went to a lot of *trouble* to get the right equipment⟩.

effortless See EASY.
effrontery See TEMERITY.
egregious See FLAGRANT.
eject, **expel**, **oust**, **evict**, **dismiss** mean to drive or force out.

Eject carries an especially strong implication of throwing or thrusting out from within ⟨*ejected* the obnoxious patron from the bar⟩. ***antonym:*** admit

Expel stresses a voluntary, often permanent thrusting out or driving away ⟨a student *expelled* from college⟩. ***antonym:*** admit

Oust implies removal or dispossession by power of the law, by force, or by compulsion of necessity ⟨issued a general order *ousting* all foreigners⟩.

Evict chiefly applies to a turning out of house and home by a legal or comparable process ⟨*evicted* for nonpayment of rent⟩.

Dismiss implies a getting rid of something unpleasant or troublesome by refusing to consider it further ⟨simply *dismissed* the quarrel from her mind⟩.

elastic, **resilient**, **springy**, **flexible**, **supple** mean able to endure strain without being permanently altered or injured.

Elastic implies the property of resisting deformation by stretching ⟨slacks that come with an *elastic* waistband⟩. ***antonym:*** rigid

Resilient implies the ability to recover shape quickly when the deforming force or pressure is removed ⟨a good running shoe has a *resilient* innersole⟩.

Springy stresses both the ease with which something yields to pressure and the quickness of its return to original shape ⟨the cake is done when the top is *springy*⟩. ***antonym:*** rigid, springless

Flexible applies to something which may or may not be resilient or elastic but which can be bent or folded without breaking ⟨*flexible* plastic tubing⟩. ***antonym:*** inflexible

Supple applies to something that can be readily bent, twisted, or folded without any sign of injury ⟨shoes made of luxurious, *supple* leather⟩. ***antonym:*** stiff

elect See SELECT.
election See CHOICE *n.*
electrify See THRILL.
elegant See CHOICE *adj.*
element, **component**, **constituent**, **ingredient**, **factor** mean one of the parts, substances, or principles of a compound or complex whole.

Element applies to any such part and often connotes irreducible simplicity ⟨the basic *elements* of the gothic novel⟩. ***antonym:*** compound, composite

Component stresses the separate identity or distinguishable character of the elements ⟨able to identify every *component* of his firearm⟩. ***antonym:*** composite, complex

Constituent stresses the essential and formative relationship of the elements, substances, or qualities to the whole ⟨analyzed the *constituents* of the compound⟩. ***antonym:*** aggregate, whole

Ingredient applies to any of the substances which can be combined to form a mixture that has qualities that may be different from those of the constituents ⟨the *ingredients* of a cocktail⟩.

Factor applies to any constituent or element whose presence actively helps to perform a certain kind of work or produce a particular result ⟨price was a *factor* in her decision to buy⟩.

elevate See LIFT.
elevation See HEIGHT.
elicit See EDUCE.
eliminate See EXCLUDE.
elite See ARISTOCRACY.
elongate See EXTEND.
eloquent See VOCAL 2.
elucidate See EXPLAIN.
elude See ESCAPE.
emanate See SPRING.
emancipate See FREE *vb*.
emasculate See UNNERVE.

embarrass, **discomfit**, **abash**, **disconcert**, **rattle**, **faze** mean to distress by confusing or confounding.

Embarrass implies some influence that impedes thought, speech, or action ⟨*embarrassed* to admit that she liked the movie⟩.

Discomfit implies a hampering or frustrating accompanied by confusion ⟨persistent heckling *discomfited* the speaker⟩.

Abash presupposes some initial self-confidence that receives a sudden check by something that produces shyness, shame, or a conviction of inferiority ⟨completely *abashed* by her swift and cutting retort⟩. ***antonym:*** embolden, reassure

Disconcert implies an upsetting of equanimity or assurance producing uncertainty or hesitancy ⟨*disconcerted* by the sight of the large audience⟩.

Rattle implies a disorganizing agitation that impairs thought and judgment and undermines normal poise and composure ⟨a tennis player not at all *rattled* by television cameras⟩.

Faze, found chiefly in negative phrases, suggests a loss of assurance or equanimity, often sudden and thorough ⟨a veteran teacher *fazed* by nothing⟩.

embellish See ADORN.
emblem See SYMBOL.
embolden See ENCOURAGE.
embrace **1.** See ADOPT. **2.** See INCLUDE.
emend See CORRECT *vb*.
emergency See JUNCTURE.
eminent See FAMOUS.
emotion See FEELING.
empathy See SYMPATHY.
employ See USE *vb*.
employment See WORK 2.
empower See ENABLE.

empty **1. Empty**, **vacant**, **blank**, **void**, **vacuous** mean lacking contents which could or should be present.

Empty suggests a complete absence of contents ⟨an *empty* bucket⟩. ***antonym:*** full

Vacant suggests an absence of appropriate contents or occupants ⟨a *vacant* apartment⟩. ***antonym:*** occupied

Blank stresses the absence of any significant, relieving, or intelligible features on a surface ⟨a *blank* wall⟩.

Void suggests absolute emptiness as far as the mind or senses can determine ⟨a statement *void* of meaning⟩.

Vacuous suggests the emptiness of a vacuum and especially the lack of intelligence or significance ⟨a *vacuous* facial expression⟩.

2. See VAIN.

emulate See RIVAL 1.

enable, **empower** mean to make one able to do something.

Enable implies provision of the means or opportunity to do something ⟨a job that *enables* them to live with dignity⟩.

Empower refers to the provision of the power or the delegation of the authority to do something ⟨a law which *empowers* the courts to try such cases⟩.

enchant See ATTRACT.

encomium, **eulogy**, **panegyric**, **tribute**, **citation** mean a formal expression of praise.

Encomium implies warm enthusiasm in praise of a person or a thing ‹the subject of several spirited *encomiums* at the banquet›.

Eulogy applies to a prepared speech, especially a funeral oration or an essay extolling the virtues and services of a person ‹delivered the *eulogy* at the funeral›. ***antonym:*** calumny, tirade

Panegyric suggests an elaborate often rhetorical or poetic compliment ‹coronations once inspired *panegyrics*›.

Tribute implies deeply felt praise conveyed either through words or through a significant act ‹a book of *tributes* marking his fifty years of service›.

Citation applies to the formal praise accompanying the mention of a person in a military dispatch or in awarding an honor ‹a *citation* noting her lasting contribution to biology›.

encourage, **inspirit**, **hearten**, **embolden** mean to fill with courage or strength of purpose.

Encourage suggests the raising of one's confidence especially by an external agency ‹the teacher's praise *encouraged* the student to try even harder›. ***antonym:*** discourage

Inspirit implies the instilling of life, energy, courage, or vigor into something ‹pioneers *inspirited* by the stirring accounts of the explorers›. ***antonym:*** dispirit

Hearten implies the lifting of a dispiritedness or despondency by an infusion of fresh courage or zeal ‹a hospital patient *heartened* by the display of moral support›. ***antonym:*** dishearten

Embolden implies the giving of courage sufficient to overcome timidity or reluctance ‹a successful climb *emboldened* her to try more difficult ones›. ***antonym:*** abash

encroach See TRESPASS.

end *n* **1. End**, **termination**, **ending**, **terminus** mean the point or line beyond which something does not or cannot go.

End is the inclusive term, implying the final limit in time or space, in extent of influence, or in range of possibility ‹the report put an *end* to all speculation›. ***antonym:*** beginning

Termination applies to the end of something having predetermined limits or being complete or finished ‹the *termination* of a lease›. ***antonym:*** inception, source

Ending often includes the portion leading to the actual final point ‹a film marred by a contrived *ending*›. ***antonym:*** beginning

Terminus applies commonly to a point toward which one moves or progresses ‹Chicago is the *terminus* for many air routes›. ***antonym:*** starting point

2. See INTENTION.

end *vb* See CLOSE *vb*.

endeavor See ATTEMPT.

endemic See NATIVE.

ending See END.

endorse See APPROVE.

endure 1. See BEAR. **2.** See CONTINUE.

enemy, **foe** mean an individual or a group who shows hostility or ill will to another.

Enemy stresses antagonism that may range from a deep hatred or a will to harm and destroy to no more than active or evident dislike or a habit of preying upon ‹a man with many friends and no *enemies*›.

Foe, preferred in rhetorical or poetic use, stresses active fighting or struggle rather than emotional reaction ‹a *foe* of all injustice›. ***antonym:*** friend

energetic See VIGOROUS.

energize See VITALIZE.

energy See POWER 1.

enervate See UNNERVE.

enfeeble See WEAKEN.

engagement See BATTLE.

engaging See SWEET.

engineer See GUIDE.

engross See MONOPOLIZE.

enhance See INTENSIFY.

enigma See MYSTERY.

enigmatic See OBSCURE.
enjoin See COMMAND.
enjoy See HAVE.
enjoyment See PLEASURE.
enlarge See INCREASE.
enliven See QUICKEN.

enmity, **hostility**, **antipathy**, **antagonism**, **animosity**, **rancor**, **animus** mean deep-seated dislike or ill will or a manifestation of such a feeling.

Enmity suggests positive hatred which may be open or concealed ⟨an unspoken *enmity* seethed between the two⟩. ***antonym:*** amity

Hostility suggests a strong, open enmity showing itself in attacks or aggression ⟨a history of *hostility* between the two nations⟩.

Antipathy implies a natural or logical basis for one's hatred or dislike, suggesting repugnance or a desire to avoid or reject ⟨a natural *antipathy* for self-important upstarts⟩. ***antonym:*** taste (*for*), affection (*for*)

Antagonism suggests a clash of temperaments leading readily to hostility ⟨a long-standing *antagonism* between the banker and his prodigal son⟩. ***antonym:*** accord, comity

Animosity suggests anger, intense ill will, and vindictiveness that threaten to hurt or destroy ⟨*animosity* that eventually led to revenge⟩. ***antonym:*** good will

Rancor stresses bitter brooding or the nursing of a grudge or grievance ⟨*rancor* filled every line of his letters⟩.

Animus implies strong prejudice and often malevolent or spiteful ill will ⟨my objections are devoid of any personal *animus*⟩. ***antonym:*** favor

ennui See TEDIUM.

enormous, **immense**, **huge**, **vast**, **gigantic**, **colossal**, **mammoth** mean exceedingly or excessively large.

Enormous suggests an exceeding of all ordinary bounds in size or amount or degree and often adds an implication of abnormality or monstrousness ⟨the *enormous* expense of the program⟩. ***antonym:*** tiny

Immense implies size far in excess of ordinary measurements or accustomed concepts ⟨the *immense* size of the new shopping mall⟩.

Huge commonly suggests an immensity of size, bulk, or capacity ⟨quickly incurred a *huge* debt⟩.

Vast suggests extreme largeness or broadness and immensity of extent ⟨the *vast* Russian steppes⟩.

Gigantic stresses the contrast with the size of others of the same kind ⟨a *gigantic* sports stadium⟩.

Colossal applies especially to something of stupendous or incredible dimensions ⟨a *colossal* statue of Lincoln⟩.

Mammoth suggests both hugeness and ponderousness of bulk ⟨a *mammoth* boulder⟩.

enough See SUFFICIENT.
enrapture See TRANSPORT 2.
ensnare See CATCH.
ensue See FOLLOW.

ensure, **insure**, **assure**, **secure** mean to make a thing or person sure.

Ensure implies a virtual guarantee ⟨the government has *ensured* the safety of the foreign minister⟩.

Insure sometimes stresses the taking of necessary measures beforehand to make a result certain or to provide for any probable contingency ⟨careful planning should *insure* the success of the party⟩.

Assure distinctively implies the removal of doubt, worry, or uncertainty from the mind ⟨I *assure* you that no one will be harmed⟩. ***antonym:*** alarm

Secure implies the taking of action to ensure safety, protection, or certainty against adverse contingencies ⟨*secure* their cooperation by payment of a large fee⟩.

enter, **penetrate**, **pierce**, **probe** mean to make way into something.

Enter, the most general of these, may imply either going in or forcing a way in

⟨*entered* the city in triumph⟩. ***antonym:*** issue (*from*)

Penetrate carries a strong implication of an impelling force or compelling power that achieves entrance ⟨no bullet has ever *penetrated* a vest of that material⟩.

Pierce adds to ***penetrate*** a clear implication of an entering point or wedge ⟨a fracture in which the bone *pierces* the skin⟩.

Probe implies a penetration to investigate or explore something hidden from easy observation or knowledge ⟨*probed* the depths of the sea⟩.

entertain **1.** See AMUSE. **2.** See HARBOR.

enthuse See THRILL.

enthusiasm See PASSION.

entice See LURE.

entire **1.** See PERFECT . **2.** See WHOLE.

entrance See TRANSPORT 2.

entrap See CATCH.

entreat See BEG.

entrench See TRESPASS.

entrust See COMMIT.

envious, **jealous** mean begrudging another possession of something desirable.

Envious stresses a coveting of something such as riches or attainments which belongs to another or of something such as success or good luck which has come to another and may imply an urgent, even malicious desire to see the other person dispossessed of what gives gratification, or it may imply no more than a mild coveting without desire to injure ⟨we are all *envious* of your new dress⟩.

Jealous is likely to stress intolerance of a rival for the possession of what one regards as peculiarly one's own possession or due, but sometimes it implies no more than intensely zealous efforts to keep or maintain what one possesses; it often carries a strong implication of distrust, suspicion, enviousness, or sometimes anger ⟨stabbed by a *jealous* lover⟩.

environment See BACKGROUND.

envisage See THINK 1.

envision See THINK 1.

ephemeral See TRANSIENT.

epicure, **gourmet**, **gastronome**, **gourmand**, **bon vivant** mean one who takes pleasure in eating and drinking.

Epicure implies fastidiousness and voluptuousness of taste ⟨a delicacy that only an *epicure* would appreciate⟩.

Gourmet applies to a connoisseur in food and drink and suggests discriminating enjoyment ⟨*gourmets* rate the restaurant highly⟩.

Gastronome stresses the possession of expert knowledge and appreciation of fine food and wine and of the rituals of preparation and serving them ⟨an annual banquet that attracts *gastronomes* from all over⟩.

Gourmand implies a less fastidious or discerning appreciation of food and wine, but a hearty interest in an enjoyment of them ⟨a robust dinner fit for an eager *gourmand*⟩.

Bon vivant stresses liveliness and spirit in the enjoyment of fine food and drink in company ⟨*bon vivants* rang in the New Year in style⟩.

epicurean See SENSUOUS.

episode See OCCURRENCE.

epitome See ABRIDGMENT.

epoch See PERIOD.

equable See STEADY.

equal *adj* See SAME.

equal *vb* See MATCH.

equanimity, **composure**, **sangfroid**, **phlegm** mean the quality of one who is self-possessed and not easily disturbed or perturbed.

Equanimity suggests a habit of mind that is disturbed rarely or only under great strain ⟨accepted fortune's slings and arrows with great *equanimity*⟩.

Composure implies great controlling of emotional or mental agitation by an effort of will or as a matter of habit ⟨maintained his *composure* even under hostile questioning⟩. ***antonym:*** discomposure, perturbation

Sangfroid implies great coolness and steadiness under strain perhaps stemming from a constitutional coldness ⟨an Olympian diver of remarkable *sangfroid*⟩.

Phlegm implies insensitiveness and suggests apathy or sluggishness rather than self-control ⟨possessed of a temperamental *phlegm* unaffected by good news and bad news alike⟩.

equip See FURNISH.

equitable See FAIR.

equity See JUSTICE.

equivalent See SAME.

equivocal See OBSCURE.

equivocate See LIE.

equivocation See AMBIGUITY.

era See PERIOD.

eradicate See EXTERMINATE.

erase, **expunge**, **cancel**, **efface**, **obliterate**, **blot out**, **delete** mean to strike out or remove something so that it no longer has any effect or existence.

Erase implies the act of rubbing or wiping out, as of letters or impressions, often in preparation for correction or replacement by new matter ⟨*erase* what you wrote and start over⟩.

Expunge stresses a removal or destruction that leaves no trace ⟨*expunged* all references to the deposed leader⟩.

Cancel implies an action, as marking, revoking, or neutralizing, that nullifies or invalidates a thing ⟨a crime that *cancelled* all her good deeds⟩.

Efface implies the removal of an impression, imprint, or image by damage to or elimination of the surface on which it appears or removal of every visible sign of its existence ⟨coins with dates *effaced* by wear⟩.

Obliterate implies a covering up or smearing over or utter destruction that removes all traces of a thing's existence ⟨an outdoor mural almost *obliterated* by graffiti⟩.

Blot out, like ***obliterate***, suggests a rendering of something indecipherable or nonexistent by smearing over or hiding completely ⟨*blotted out* the offensive passage with black ink⟩.

Delete implies a deliberate exclusion, or a marking to direct exclusion, of written matter ⟨his editor *deleted* all unflattering references to others⟩.

erratic See STRANGE.

error, **mistake**, **blunder**, **slip**, **lapse**, **faux pas** mean a departure from what is true, right, or proper.

Error suggests the existence of a standard or guide and implies a straying from the right course through failure to make effective use of this ⟨one *error* in planning lost the battle⟩.

Mistake implies misconception or inadvertence and usually expresses less criticism than ***error*** ⟨dialed the wrong number by *mistake*⟩.

Blunder regularly imputes stupidity or ignorance as a cause and connotes some degree of blame ⟨a political campaign noted mostly for its series of *blunders*⟩.

Slip stresses inadvertence or accident and applies especially to trivial but embarrassing mistakes ⟨during the speech I made several *slips*⟩.

Lapse stresses forgetfulness, weakness, or inattention as a cause ⟨apart from a few grammatical *lapses,* the paper is good⟩.

Faux pas is applied to a mistake in etiquette ⟨committed a grievous *faux pas* by drinking from the finger bowl⟩.

ersatz See ARTIFICIAL.

erudite See LEARNED.

erudition See KNOWLEDGE.

escape, **avoid**, **evade**, **elude**, **shun**, **eschew** mean to get away or keep away from something.

Escape stresses the fact of getting away or being passed by not necessarily through effort or by conscious intent ⟨nothing *escapes* her sharp eyes⟩.

Avoid stresses forethought and caution in keeping clear of danger or difficulty ⟨with careful planning we can *avoid* the fate of previous expeditions⟩. ***antonym:*** face, meet

Evade implies adroitness, ingenuity, or lack of scruple in escaping or avoiding ⟨*evaded* the question by changing the subject⟩.

Elude implies a slippery or baffling quality in the person or thing that gets away ⟨what she sees in him *eludes* me⟩.

Shun often implies an avoiding as a matter of habitual practice or policy and may imply repugnance or abhorrence ⟨you have *shunned* their company⟩.

Eschew implies an avoiding or abstaining from as unwise or distasteful or immoral ⟨a playwright who *eschews* melodrama and claptrap⟩. ***antonym:*** choose

eschew See ESCAPE.

escort See ACCOMPANY.

especial See SPECIAL.

espy See SEE 1.

espouse See ADOPT.

essay See ATTEMPT.

essential, **fundamental**, **vital**, **cardinal** mean so important as to be indispensable.

Essential implies belonging to the very nature of a thing and therefore being incapable of removal without destroying the thing itself or altering its character ⟨conflict is an *essential* element in drama⟩.

Fundamental applies to something that forms a foundation without which an entire system or complex whole would collapse ⟨the *fundamental* principles of democracy⟩.

Vital suggests something that is necessary to a thing's continued existence or operation ⟨air bases that are *vital* to our national security⟩.

Cardinal suggests something on which an outcome turns or actively depends ⟨one of the *cardinal* events of the Civil War⟩. ***antonym:*** negligible

establish See SET *vb.*

esteem See REGARD.

estimate **1. Estimate**, **appraise**, **evaluate**, **value**, **rate**, **assess** mean to judge something with respect to its worth or significance.

Estimate implies a judgment, considered or casual, that precedes or takes the place of actual measuring or counting or testing out ⟨*estimated* that there were a hundred people there⟩.

Appraise commonly implies the fixing by an expert of the monetary worth of a thing, but it may be used of any intent to give a critical judgment ⟨a real estate agent *appraised* the house⟩.

Evaluate suggests an attempt to determine either the relative or intrinsic worth of something in terms other than monetary ⟨instructors will *evaluate* all students' work⟩.

Value comes close to ***appraise*** but does not imply expertness of judgment ⟨a watercolor *valued* by the donor at $500⟩.

Rate adds to ***estimate*** the notion of placing a thing in a scale of value ⟨an actress who is *rated* highly by her peers⟩.

Assess implies a rendering of a critical appraisal for the purpose of assigning a taxable value or for understanding or interpreting or as a guide to action ⟨officials are still trying to *assess* the damage⟩.

2. See CALCULATE.

estrange, **alienate**, **disaffect**, **wean** mean to cause one to break a bond of affection or loyalty.

Estrange implies the development of indifference or hostility with consequent loss of sympathy or divorcement ⟨had become *estranged* from their family after years of neglect⟩. ***antonym:*** reconcile

Alienate may or may not suggest separation but always implies loss of affection or interest ⟨managed to *alienate* all her coworkers with her arrogance⟩. ***antonym:*** unite, reunite

Disaffect refers to those from whom loyalty is expected or demanded and stresses the effects, such as rebellion or discontent, of alienation without actual separation ⟨a coup led by *disaffected* party members⟩. ***antonym:*** win (*over*)

Wean implies a commendable separation from something on which one is weakly or immaturely dependent ⟨*wean* yourself from a bad habit⟩. ***antonym:*** addict

ether See AIR.

ethical See MORAL.

etiolate See WHITEN.

etiquette See DECORUM.

eulogy See ENCOMIUM.

evade See ESCAPE.

evaluate See ESTIMATE.

evanescent See TRANSIENT.

even 1. See LEVEL. **2.** See STEADY.

event See OCCURRENCE.

eventual See LAST.

evict See EJECT.

evidence See SHOW 1.

evident, **manifest**, **patent**, **distinct**, **obvious**, **apparent**, **plain**, **clear** mean readily perceived or apprehended.

Evident implies the presence of visible signs which point to a definite conclusion ⟨an *evident* fondness for the company of friends⟩. ***antonym:*** inevident

Manifest implies an external display so evident that little or no inference is required ⟨her *manifest* joy upon receiving the award⟩. ***antonym:*** latent

Patent applies to a cause, effect, or significant feature that is clear and unmistakable once attention has been drawn to it ⟨*patent* defects in the item when sold⟩. ***antonym:*** latent

Distinct implies such sharpness of outline or definition that no unusual effort to see or hear or comprehend is required ⟨my offer met with a *distinct* refusal⟩. ***antonym:*** indistinct, nebulous

Obvious implies such ease in discovering or accounting for that it often suggests conspicuousness in the thing or little need for perspicacity in the observer ⟨the motives are *obvious* to all but the most obtuse⟩. ***antonym:*** obscure, abstruse

Apparent may imply conscious exercise of elaborate reasoning as well as inference from evidence ⟨the absurdity of the charge is *apparent* to all who know him⟩. ***antonym:*** unintelligible

Clear implies an absence of anything that confuses the mind or obscures the issues ⟨it's *clear* now what's been going on⟩. ***antonym:*** obscure

evil See BAD.

evince See SHOW 1.

evoke See EDUCE.

exact *adj* See CORRECT *adj.*

exact *vb* See DEMAND.

exacting See ONEROUS.

exaggeration, **overstatement**, **hyperbole** mean an overstepping of the bounds of truth, especially in describing the extent, size, kind, or amount of something.

Exaggeration implies an unwillingness to be held down by the facts, or a bias so great that one cannot clearly see or accurately estimate the exact situation ⟨unable to tell the story without *exaggeration*⟩. ***antonym:*** understatement

Overstatement suggests a simple exceeding of the truth ⟨a style that avoids *overstatement*⟩. ***antonym:*** understatement

Hyperbole suggests a desire, often literary, to create a planned impression or effect through extravagance in statement ⟨sang her praises through poetic *hyperbole*⟩. ***antonym:*** litotes

examine See SCRUTINIZE.

example 1. See INSTANCE. **2.** See MODEL.

exasperate See IRRITATE.

exceed, **surpass**, **transcend**, **excel**, **outdo**, **outstrip** mean to go or be beyond a stated or implied limit, measure, or degree.

Exceed implies going beyond a limit set by authority or established by custom or by prior achievement ⟨*exceed* the speed limit⟩.

Surpass suggests superiority in quality, merit, or skill ⟨the book *surpassed* our expectations⟩.

Transcend implies a rising or extending notably above or beyond ordinary limits ⟨*transcended* the values of their peers⟩.

Excel implies an attaining of preeminence in achievement, accomplishment, or quality and may suggest superiority to all others ⟨*excels* in mathematics⟩.

Outdo applies to a bettering or exceeding of what has been done before ⟨*outdid* herself this time⟩.

Outstrip suggests a succeeding or surpassing in a race or competition ⟨*outstripped* other firms in selling the new plastic⟩.

excel See EXCEED.

excessive, **immoderate**, **inordinate**, **extravagant**, **exorbitant**, **extreme** mean going beyond a normal or acceptable limit.

Excessive implies an amount or degree too great to be reasonable or endurable ⟨punishment that was deemed *excessive*⟩. ***antonym:*** deficient

Immoderate implies lack of desirable or necessary restraint ⟨an *immoderate* amount of time spent on grooming⟩. ***antonym:*** moderate

Inordinate implies an exceeding of limits dictated by reason or good judgment ⟨an *inordinate* portion of their budget goes to entertainment⟩. ***antonym:*** temperate

Extravagant implies a wild, lawless, prodigal, or foolish wandering from proper and accustomed limits ⟨*extravagant* claims for the product⟩. ***antonym:*** restrained

Exorbitant implies a departure from accepted standards regarding amount or degree ⟨a menu with *exorbitant* prices⟩. ***antonym:*** just (*price, charge*)

Extreme may imply an approach to the farthest limit possible or conceivable but commonly means only to a notably high degree ⟨views concerning marriage that are a bit *extreme*⟩.

excite See PROVOKE.

exclude, **debar**, **eliminate**, **suspend** mean to shut or put out.

Exclude implies a keeping out of what is already outside by or as if by closing some barrier ⟨children under 17 are *excluded* from the movie⟩. ***antonym:*** admit, include

Debar stresses the effectiveness of an existent barrier in excluding a person or class from what is open or accessible to others ⟨arbitrary standards that effectively *debar* most female candidates⟩. ***antonym:*** admit

Eliminate implies the getting rid of what is already within, typically as a constituent part or element ⟨a company's plans to *eliminate* a fourth of its work force⟩.

Suspend implies temporary and usually disciplinary removal, as from a membership in an organization, or restraining, as from functioning or expression ⟨a student *suspended* for possession of drugs⟩.

exclusive See SELECT.

exculpate, **absolve**, **exonerate**, **acquit**, **vindicate** mean to free from a charge or burden.

Exculpate implies a clearing from blame or burden ⟨I cannot *exculpate* myself of the charge of overenthusiasm⟩. ***antonym:*** accuse

Absolve implies a release either from an obligation that binds the conscience or from the consequences of its violation ⟨*absolved* the subject from his oath of allegiance⟩. ***antonym:*** hold (*to*), charge (*with*)

Exonerate implies a complete clearance from an accusation or charge and from any attendant suspicion of blame or guilt ⟨a committee *exonerated* the governor from charges of bribery⟩. ***antonym:*** incriminate

Acquit implies a decision in one's favor with respect to a definite charge ⟨*acquitted* of murder by a jury⟩. ***antonym:*** convict

Vindicate may refer to things as well as persons that have been subjected to critical attack or imputation of guilt, weakness, or folly, and implies a clearing through proof of the injustice or unfairness of such criticism or blame ⟨an investigation *vindicated* the senator on all counts⟩. ***antonym:*** calumniate

excuse *vb* **Excuse**, **condone**, **pardon**, **forgive** mean to exact neither punishment nor redress.

Excuse may refer to the overlooking of specific acts especially in social or conventional situations or to the person responsible for these ⟨*excuse* an interruption⟩. ***antonym:*** punish

Condone implies that one passes over without censure or punishment a kind of behavior, such as dishonesty or violence, that involves a serious breach of a moral, ethical, or legal code ⟨a society that *condones* alcohol but not drugs⟩.

Pardon implies that one remits a penalty due for an admitted or established offense or refrains from exacting punishment ⟨*pardon* a criminal⟩. ***antonym:*** punish

Forgive implies that one gives up all claim to requital and all resentment or desire for revenge ⟨*forgave* their previous lapses⟩.

excuse *n* See APOLOGY.

execrate, **curse**, **damn**, **anathematize** mean to denounce violently and indignantly.

Execrate implies intense loathing and usually passionate fury ⟨*execrated* the men who had molested his family⟩. ***antonym:*** eulogize

Curse implies angry denunciation by blasphemous oaths or profane imprecations ⟨*cursed* the fate that had brought them to this pass⟩. ***antonym:*** bless

Damn, like ***curse***, suggests the invoking of divine vengeance with fervor but is more informal ⟨*damns* the city council for not anticipating the problem⟩.

Anathematize implies solemn denunciation of an evil or an injustice ⟨preachers *anathematizing* pornography⟩.

execute, **administer** mean to carry out the declared intent of another.

Execute stresses the enforcing of the specific provisions of a law, will, commission, or command ⟨charged with failing to *execute* the order⟩.

Administer implies the continuing exercise of delegated authority in pursuance of only generally indicated goals rather than specifically prescribed means of attaining them ⟨the agency in charge of *administering* Indian affairs⟩.

2. See KILL. **3.** See PERFORM.

exemplar See MODEL.

exercise See PRACTICE.

exertion See EFFORT.

exhaust **1.** See DEPLETE. **2.** See TIRE.

exhibit See SHOW 2.

exigency **1.** See JUNCTURE. **2.** See NEED.

exiguous See MEAGER.

exile See BANISH.

exonerate See EXCULPATE.

exorbitant See EXCESSIVE.

expand, **amplify**, **swell**, **distend**, **inflate**, **dilate** mean to increase in size or volume.

Expand may apply whether the increase comes from within or without and regardless of manner, whether by growth, unfolding, or addition of parts ⟨our business has *expanded* with every passing year⟩. ***antonym:*** contract, abridge

Amplify implies the extension or enlargement of something that is inadequate ⟨*amplify* the statement with some details⟩. ***antonym:*** abridge, condense

Swell implies gradual expansion beyond a thing's original or normal limits ⟨the bureaucracy *swelled* to unmanageable proportions⟩. ***antonym:*** shrink

Distend implies outward expansion caused by pressure from within ⟨a stomach *distended* by gas⟩. ***antonym:*** constrict

Inflate implies distension by or as if by the introduction of a gas or something insubstantial and suggests a resulting instability and liability to sudden change ⟨an *inflated* ego⟩. ***antonym:*** deflate

Dilate applies especially to the expansion of diameter and suggests a widening of something circular ⟨dim light causes the pupils of the eyes to *dilate*⟩. ***antonym:*** constrict, circumscribe, attenuate

expect, **hope**, **look**, **await** mean to anticipate in the mind some occurrence or outcome.

Expect implies a high degree of certainty and involves the idea of preparing or envisioning ⟨I *expect* to be finished by Tuesday⟩. ***antonym:*** despair (*of*)

Hope implies little certainty but suggests confidence or assurance in the possibility that what one desires or longs for will happen ⟨she *hopes* to find a job soon⟩. ***antonym:*** despair (*of*), despond

Look, followed by *for*, suggests a degree of expectancy and watchfulness rather than confidence or certainty ⟨we *look* for great things in the new year⟩; followed by *to,* it suggests strongly a counting on or a freedom from doubt ⟨*looked* to their children to care for them in old age⟩. ***antonym:*** despair (*of*)

Await often adds to ***look*** for the implication of being ready, mentally or physically ⟨we *await* your decision⟩. ***antonym:*** despair

expedient *adj* **Expedient**, **politic**, **advisable** mean dictated by practical or prudent motives.

Expedient usually implies a choice that is immediately advantageous without regard for ethics or consistent principles ⟨a truce was the *expedient* answer⟩. ***antonym:*** inexpedient

Politic stresses practicality, judiciousness, and tactical value but usually implies material or self-centered motives ⟨converted to Catholicism when it was *politic* to do so⟩.

Advisable applies to what is practical, prudent, or advantageous, without the derogatory connotations of ***expedient*** and ***politic*** ⟨it's *advisable* to say nothing at all⟩. ***antonym:*** inadvisable

expedient *n* See RESOURCE.

expedition See HASTE.

expeditious See FAST.

expel See EJECT.

expend See SPEND.

expense See PRICE.

expensive See COSTLY.

expert See PROFICIENT.

explain, **expound**, **explicate**, **elucidate**, **interpret** mean to make something clear or understandable.

Explain implies making plain or intelligible what is not immediately obvious or clearly known ⟨the doctor *explained* what the operation would entail⟩. ***antonym:*** obfuscate

Expound implies a careful often elaborate or learned explanation ⟨a professor *expounding* the theory of relativity⟩.

Explicate adds to ***expound*** the idea of a developed or detailed analysis of a topic ⟨a passage that critics have been inspired to *explicate* at length⟩.

Elucidate stresses the throwing of light upon as explanation, exposition, or illustration ⟨a newspaper report that *elucidated* the reason for the crime⟩.

Interpret adds to ***explain*** the implication of the need for imagination or sympathy or special knowledge to make something clear ⟨*interprets* the play as an allegory about good and evil⟩.

explicate See EXPLAIN.

explicit, **express**, **specific**, **definite** mean perfectly clear in meaning.

Explicit implies such verbal plainness and distinctness that there is no need for inference and no reason for ambiguity or difficulty in understanding ⟨the dress code is *explicit*⟩. ***antonym:*** ambiguous

Express implies both explicitness and direct and forceful utterance ⟨her *express* wish was to be cremated⟩.

Specific applies to what is precisely and fully referred to or treated in detail or particular ⟨two *specific* criticisms of the proposal⟩. ***antonym:*** vague

Definite stresses precise, clear statement or arrangement that leaves no uncertainty or indecision ⟨the law is *definite* regarding such cases⟩. ***antonym:*** indefinite, equivocal

exploit See FEAT.

expose See SHOW 2.

exposed See LIABLE.

expostulate See OBJECT.

expound See EXPLAIN.

express *vb* **Express**, **vent**, **utter**, **voice**, **broach**, **air** mean to let out or make known what one thinks or feels.

Express suggests an impulse to reveal in words, gestures, or actions, or through what one creates or produces ⟨paintings that *express* the artist's loneliness⟩.

Vent stresses a strong inner compulsion to express something such as a pent-up emotion, especially in a highly emotional manner ⟨her stories *vent* the frustrations of women⟩. ***antonym:*** bridle

Utter implies the use of the voice not necessarily in articulate speech ⟨would occasionally *utter* words of encouragement⟩.

Voice implies expression or formulation in words but not necessarily by vocal utterance ⟨an editorial *voicing* the concerns of many⟩.

Broach suggests the disclosing for the first time of something long thought over or reserved for a suitable occasion ⟨*broached* the subject of a divorce⟩.

Air implies an exposing or parading of one's views often in order to gain relief or sympathy or attention ⟨cabinet members publicly *airing* their differences⟩.

express *adj* See EXPLICIT.

expression See PHRASE.

expunge See ERASE.

exquisite See CHOICE *adj*.

extemporaneous, **improvised**, **impromptu**, **offhand**, **unpremeditated** mean composed, done, or devised at the moment and not beforehand.

Extemporaneous stresses the demands imposed by the occasion or situation and may imply a certain sketchiness or roughness ⟨an *extemporaneous* shelter prompted by the sudden storm⟩.

Improvised implies the constructing or devising of something without advance knowledge, thought, or preparation and often without the necessary or proper equipment ⟨*improvised* a barbecue pit at the campground⟩.

Impromptu stresses the immediacy and the spontaneity of the thing composed or devised ⟨an *impromptu* speech at an awards ceremony⟩.

Offhand strongly implies casualness, carelessness, or indifference ⟨his *offhand* remarks often got him into trouble⟩.

Unpremeditated suggests some strong, often suddenly provoked emotion that impels one to action ⟨*unpremeditated* murder⟩. ***antonym:*** premeditated

extend, **lengthen**, **elongate**, **prolong**, **protract** mean to draw out or add to so as to increase in length.

Extend implies a drawing out of extent in space or time and may also imply increase in width, scope, area, influence or range ⟨*extend* welfare services⟩. ***antonym:*** abridge, shorten

Lengthen suggests an increase of length in either time or space ⟨*lengthen* the school year⟩. ***antonym:*** shorten

Elongate usually implies increase in spatial length and frequently suggests stretching ⟨the dancer's ability to *elongate* her body⟩. ***antonym:*** abbreviate, shorten

Prolong suggests chiefly increase in duration especially beyond usual, normal, or pleasing limits ⟨*prolonged* illness⟩. ***antonym:*** curtail

Protract adds to ***prolong*** implications of needlessness, vexation, or indefiniteness ⟨*protracted* litigation⟩. ***antonym:*** curtail

exterior See OUTER.

exterminate, **extirpate**, **eradicate**, **uproot**, **wipe out** mean to effect the destruction or abolition of something.

Exterminate implies complete and immediate extinction by killing off ⟨failed attempts to *exterminate* the mosquitoes⟩.

Extirpate implies extinction of a race, family, species, kind, or sometimes an idea or doctrine by destruction or by removal of its means of propagation ⟨having *extirpated* the last vestiges of the religion⟩.

Eradicate implies the driving out or elimination of something that has taken root or established itself firmly ⟨polio had virtually been *eradicated*⟩.

Uproot implies a forcible or violent removal and stresses displacement or dislodgment rather than immediate destruction ⟨the war had *uprooted* thousands⟩. ***antonym:*** establish

Wipe out can imply extermination or suggest a canceling or obliterating ⟨*wipe out* the entire population⟩.

external See OUTER.

extinguish **1.** See CRUSH. **2.** See ABOLISH.

extirpate See EXTERMINATE.

extort See EDUCE.

extract See EDUCE.

extraneous See EXTRINSIC.

extravagant See EXCESSIVE.

extreme See EXCESSIVE.

extricate, **disentangle**, **untangle**, **disencumber**, **disembarrass** mean to free from what binds or holds back.

Extricate implies the use of force or ingenuity in freeing from a difficult position or situation ⟨a knack for *extricating* himself from damaging political rows⟩.

Disentangle suggests a painstaking separation of something from what enmeshes or entangles ⟨a biography that *disentangles* the myth from the man⟩. ***antonym:*** entangle

Untangle is sometimes used in place of ***disentangle*** ⟨*untangled* a web of deceit⟩. ***antonym:*** entangle, tangle

Disencumber implies a release from something that clogs or weighs down or imposes a heavy burden ⟨a science article *disencumbered* of scientific jargon⟩. ***antonym:*** encumber

Disembarrass suggests a release from something that embarrasses by impeding or hindering ⟨*disembarrassed* herself of her frivolous companions⟩.

extrinsic, **extraneous**, **foreign**, **alien** mean external to a thing, its essential nature, or its original character.

Extrinsic applies to what is distinctly outside the thing in question or is not contained in or derived from its essential nature ⟨sentimental attachment that is *extrinsic* to the house's market value⟩. ***antonym:*** intrinsic

Extraneous applies to what is on or comes from the outside and may or may not be capable of becoming an essential part ⟨*extraneous* arguments that obscure the real issue⟩. ***antonym:*** relevant

Foreign applies to what is so different as to be rejected or repelled or, if admitted, to be incapable of becoming identified or assimilated by the thing in question ⟨inflammation resulting from a *foreign* body in the eye⟩. ***antonym:*** germane

Alien is stronger than ***foreign*** in suggesting such strangeness as leads to opposition, repugnance, or incompatibility ⟨a practice that is totally *alien* to our democratic principles⟩. ***antonym:*** akin, assimilable

exuberant See PROFUSE.

eyewitness See SPECTATOR.

F

fabricate See MAKE.
fabulous See FICTITIOUS.
face, countenance, visage, physiognomy mean the front part of the head from forehead to chin.
Face is the simple, direct, and also the inclusive term ⟨a strikingly handsome *face*⟩.
Countenance applies to a face as seen and as revealing a mood, character, or attitude ⟨the benign *countenance* of my grandmother⟩.
Visage suggests attention to shape and proportions of the face and sometimes to the impression it gives or the changes in moods it reflects ⟨a penetrating gaze and an aquiline nose gave him a birdlike *visage*⟩.
Physiognomy suggests attention to the contours and characteristic expression as indicative of race, temperament, disease, or qualities of mind or character ⟨a youth with the *physiognomy* of a warrior⟩.
facet See PHASE.
facetious See WITTY.
facile See EASY.
facility See READINESS.
facsimile See REPRODUCTION.
factitious See ARTIFICIAL.
factor See ELEMENT.
faculty 1. See GIFT. **2.** See POWER 2.
fad See FASHION.
fag See TIRE.
failing See FAULT.
fair 1. Fair, just, equitable, impartial, unbiased, dispassionate, objective mean free from favor toward either or any side.
Fair implies an elimination of one's own feelings, prejudices, and interests so as to achieve a proper balance of conflicting interests ⟨a *fair* decision by a judge⟩. ***antonym:*** unfair
Just implies an exact following of a standard of what is right and proper ⟨a *just* settlement of territorial claims⟩. ***antonym:*** unjust
Equitable implies a freer and less rigorous standard than ***just*** and suggests fair and equal treatment of all concerned ⟨provides for the *equitable* distribution of his property⟩. ***antonym:*** inequitable, unfair
Impartial stresses an absence of favor or prejudice in making a judgment ⟨arbitration by an *impartial* third party⟩. ***antonym:*** partial
Unbiased implies even more strongly an absence of all prejudice and implies the firm intent to be fair to all ⟨your *unbiased* opinion of the whole affair⟩. ***antonym:*** biased
Dispassionate suggests freedom from emotional involvement or from the influence of strong feeling and often implies cool or even cold judgment ⟨a *dispassionate* summation of the facts⟩. ***antonym:*** passionate, intemperate
Objective stresses a tendency to view events or persons as apart from oneself and one's own interest or feelings ⟨it's impossible for me to be *objective* about my own child⟩. ***antonym:*** subjective
2. See BEAUTIFUL.
faith See BELIEF.
faithful, loyal, constant, staunch, steadfast, resolute mean firm in adherence to whatever one owes allegiance.
Faithful implies unswerving adherence to a person or thing or to the oath or promise by which a tie was contracted ⟨*faithful* to her marriage vows⟩. ***antonym:*** faithless
Loyal implies firm resistance to any temptation to desert or betray ⟨the army remained *loyal* to the czar⟩. ***antonym:*** disloyal
Constant stresses continuing firmness of emotional attachment without necessarily implying strict obedience to promises or vows ⟨*constant* lovers⟩. ***antonym:*** inconstant, fickle
Staunch suggests fortitude and resolu-

tion in adherence and imperviousness to influences that would weaken it ⟨a *staunch* defender of free speech⟩.

Steadfast implies a steady and unwavering course in love, allegiance, or conviction ⟨*steadfast* in their support of democratic principles⟩. ***antonym:*** capricious

Resolute emphasizes firm determination to adhere to a cause or purpose ⟨*resolute* in his determination to see justice done⟩.

faithless, **false**, **disloyal**, **traitorous**, **treacherous**, **perfidious** mean untrue to someone or something that has a right to expect one's fidelity or allegiance.

Faithless applies to any failure to keep a promise or pledge or to any breach or betrayal of obligation, allegiance, or loyalty ⟨*faithless* allies refused to support the sanctions⟩. ***antonym:*** faithful

False stresses the fact of failing to be true in any manner or degree ranging from fickleness to cold treachery ⟨betrayed by *false* friends⟩. ***antonym:*** true

Disloyal implies a lack of complete faithfulness in thought or words or actions to a friend, cause, leader, or country ⟨accused the hostages of being *disloyal* to their country⟩. ***antonym:*** loyal

Traitorous implies either actual treason or a serious betrayal of trust ⟨*traitorous* acts punishable by death⟩.

Treacherous implies readiness to betray trust or confidence ⟨the victim of *treacherous* allies⟩.

Perfidious adds to ***treacherous*** the implication of an incapacity for fidelity or reliability and of baseness or vileness ⟨repeated and *perfidious* violations of the treaty⟩.

fake See IMPOSTURE.

false See FAITHLESS.

falsify See MISREPRESENT.

falter See HESITATE.

familiar **1. Familiar**, **intimate** mean closely acquainted.

Familiar suggests the ease, informality, and absence of reserve or constraint natural among members of a family or acquaintances of long standing ⟨resent being addressed by strangers in a *familiar* tone⟩. ***antonym:*** aloof

Intimate stresses the closeness and intensity rather than the mere frequency or continuity of personal association and suggests either deep mutual understanding or the sharing of deeply personal thoughts and feelings ⟨their love letters became increasingly *intimate*⟩.

2. See COMMON.

famous, **renowned**, **celebrated**, **noted**, **notorious**, **distinguished**, **eminent**, **illustrious** mean known far and wide.

Famous implies little more than the fact of being, sometimes briefly, widely and popularly known ⟨a *famous* television actress⟩. ***antonym:*** obscure

Renowned implies more glory and acclamation ⟨one of the most *renowned* figures in sports history⟩.

Celebrated implies popular notice and attention especially in print ⟨the most *celebrated* beauty of her day⟩. ***antonym:*** obscure

Noted suggests well-deserved public attention ⟨the *noted* mystery writer⟩. ***antonym:*** unnoted

Notorious frequently adds to ***famous*** pejorative implications of questionableness or evil ⟨a *notorious* gangster⟩.

Distinguished implies acknowledged excellence or superiority ⟨a *distinguished* scientist who recently won the Nobel Prize⟩. ***antonym:*** undistinguished

Eminent implies conspicuousness for outstanding quality or character and is applicable to one rising above others of the same class ⟨a conference of the country's most *eminent* writers⟩.

Illustrious stresses enduring and merited honor and glory attached to a deed or person ⟨the *illustrious* deeds of national heroes⟩. ***antonym:*** infamous

fanciful See IMAGINARY.

fancy See THINK 1.

fantastic **1. Fantastic**, **bizarre**, **grotesque** mean conceived, made, or carried out without evident reference or adherence to truth or reality.

Fantastic may connote unrestrained extravagance in conception or remoteness from reality or merely ingenuity of decorative invention ⟨*fantastic* theories about the origins of life⟩.

Bizarre applies to the sensationally odd or strange and implies violence of contrast or incongruity of combination ⟨a *bizarre* pseudo-medieval castle⟩. ***antonym:*** chaste, subdued

Grotesque may apply to what is conventionally ugly but artistically effective, or it may connote ludicrous awkwardness or incongruity, often with sinister or tragic overtones ⟨*grotesque* statues adorn the cathedral⟩.

2. See IMAGINARY.

far See DISTANT.

faraway See DISTANT.

far-off See DISTANT.

fascinate See ATTRACT.

fashion *n* **1. Fashion**, **style**, **mode**, **vogue**, **fad**, **rage**, **craze** mean the usage, as in dressing, decorating, or living, that is accepted by those who want to be up-to-date.

Fashion is the most general term and applies to any way of dressing, behaving, writing, or performing that is favored at any one time or place or by any group ⟨the current *fashion* for Russian ballet dancers⟩.

Style often implies a distinctive fashion adopted by people of wealth or taste ⟨a media mogul used to traveling in *style*⟩.

Mode suggests the fashion of the moment among those anxious to appear elegant and sophisticated ⟨sleek, tanned bodies are the *mode* at such resorts⟩.

Vogue stresses the prevalence or wide acceptance of a fashion ⟨a novelist who is no longer much in *vogue*⟩.

Fad suggests caprice in taking up or in dropping a fashion ⟨nothing is more dated than last year's *fad*⟩.

Rage stresses intense enthusiasm in adopting a fad ⟨Cajun food was quite the *rage*⟩.

Craze, like ***rage***, emphasizes senseless enthusiasm in pursuing a fad ⟨a sport that is more than a passing *craze*⟩.

2. See METHOD.

fashion *vb* See MAKE.

fast, **rapid**, **swift**, **fleet**, **quick**, **speedy**, **hasty**, **expeditious** mean moving, proceeding, or acting quickly.

Fast applies particularly to a moving object ⟨a *fast* horse⟩. ***antonym:*** slow

Rapid emphasizes the movement itself ⟨a *rapid* current⟩. ***antonym:*** deliberate, leisurely

Swift suggests great rapidity coupled with ease of movement ⟨returned the ball with one *swift* stroke⟩. ***antonym:*** sluggish

Fleet adds the implication of lightness and nimbleness ⟨*fleet* runners⟩.

Quick suggests promptness and the taking of little time ⟨a *quick* wit⟩. ***antonym:*** sluggish

Speedy implies quickness of successful accomplishment and may also suggest unusual velocity ⟨a *speedy* recovery⟩. ***antonym:*** dilatory

Hasty suggests hurry and precipitousness and often connotes carelessness and resultant confusion or inefficiency ⟨a *hasty* inspection⟩.

Expeditious suggests efficiency together with rapidity of accomplishment ⟨an *expeditious* processing of a merchandise order⟩. ***antonym:*** sluggish

fasten, **fix**, **attach**, **affix** mean to make something stay firmly in place.

Fasten implies an action such as tying, buttoning, nailing, locking, or otherwise securing ⟨*fastened* the horse to a post⟩. ***antonym:*** unfasten, loosen, loose

Fix usually implies a driving in, implanting, or embedding in an attempt to secure something ⟨*fix* the stake in the earth⟩.

Attach suggests a connecting or uniting by or as if by a bond, link, or tie in order to keep things together ⟨*attach* the W-2 form here⟩. ***antonym:*** detach

Affix implies an imposing of one thing on another by such means as gluing, impressing, or nailing ⟨*affix* your address label here⟩. ***antonym:*** detach

fastidious See NICE.

fatal See DEADLY.

fate, destiny, lot, portion, doom mean a predetermined state or end.

Fate implies an inevitable and sometimes an adverse outcome ⟨the *fate* of the mariners remains unknown⟩.

Destiny implies something foreordained and often suggests a great or noble course or end ⟨our country's *destiny*⟩.

Lot suggests a distribution by fate or destiny ⟨it was her *lot* to die childless⟩.

Portion implies the apportioning of good and evil ⟨the *portion* that has been meted out to me⟩.

Doom distinctly stresses finality and implies a grim or calamitous fate ⟨if the rebellion fails, our *doom* is certain⟩.

fateful See OMINOUS.

fatigue See TIRE.

fatuous See SIMPLE.

fault, failing, frailty, foible, vice mean an imperfection or weakness of character.

Fault implies a failure, not necessarily culpable, to reach some standard of perfection in disposition, action, or habit ⟨a woman of many virtues and few *faults*⟩. ***antonym:*** merit

Failing suggests a minor shortcoming in character of which one may be unaware ⟨procrastination is one of my *failings*⟩. ***antonym:*** perfection

Frailty implies a general or chronic proneness to yield to temptation ⟨a fondness for chocolate is the most human of *frailties*⟩.

Foible applies to a harmless or endearing weakness or idiosyncrasy ⟨*foibles* that make him all the more lovable⟩.

Vice can be a general term for any imperfection or weakness, but it often suggests violation of a moral code or the giving of offense to the moral sensibilities of others ⟨gambling and drunkenness were the least of his *vices*⟩.

faultfinding See CRITICAL.

faux pas See ERROR.

favor See OBLIGE.

favorable, auspicious, propitious mean pointing toward a happy outcome.

Favorable implies that the persons involved are approving or helpful or that the circumstances are advantageous ⟨*favorable* weather conditions for a rocket launch⟩. ***antonym:*** unfavorable, antagonistic

Auspicious suggests the presence of signs and omens promising success ⟨an *auspicious* beginning for a great partnership⟩. ***antonym:*** inauspicious, ill-omened

Propitious, milder than ***auspicious***, describes events or conditions that constitute favorable indications and implies a continuing favorable condition ⟨the time was not *propitious* for starting a new business⟩. ***antonym:*** unpropitious, adverse

fawn, toady, truckle, cringe, cower mean to act or behave abjectly before a superior.

Fawn implies seeking favor by servile flattery or exaggerated attention and submissiveness ⟨waiters *fawning* over a celebrity⟩. ***antonym:*** domineer

Toady suggests the attempt to ingratiate oneself by an abjectly menial or subservient attitude ⟨never misses an opportunity to *toady* to his boss⟩.

Truckle implies the subordination of oneself and one's desires, opinions, or judgment to those of a superior ⟨the rich are used to seeing others *truckle*⟩.

Cringe suggests a bowing or shrinking in physical or mental distress or in fear or servility ⟨*cringing* before a blow⟩.

Cower suggests a display of abject fear before someone who threatens or domineers ⟨as an adult he still *cowered* before his father⟩.

faze See EMBARRASS.

fealty See FIDELITY.

fear 1. Fear, **dread**, **fright**, **alarm**, **panic**, **terror**, **horror**, **trepidation** mean painful agitation in the presence or anticipation of danger.

Fear, often the most general term, implies anxiety and loss of courage ⟨*fear* of the unknown⟩. ***antonym:*** fearlessness

Dread usually adds the idea of intense reluctance to face or meet a person or situation and suggests aversion as well as anxiety ⟨the *dread* of having to face her mother⟩.

Fright implies the shock of sudden, startling fear ⟨imagine our *fright* at being awakened by screams⟩.

Alarm suggests a sudden and intense apprehension produced by newly perceived awareness of immediate danger ⟨view the situation with *alarm*⟩. ***antonym:*** assurance, composure

Panic implies unreasoning and overmastering fear causing hysterical, disordered, and useless activity ⟨news of the invasion caused great *panic*⟩.

Terror implies the most extreme degree of consternation or fear ⟨immobilized with *terror*⟩.

Horror adds the implication of shuddering abhorrence or aversion before a sight, activity, or demand that causes fear ⟨harbored a secret *horror* of dark, close places⟩. ***antonym:*** fascination

Trepidation adds to ***dread*** the implications of timidity, trembling, and hesitation ⟨raised the subject of marriage with some *trepidation*⟩.

2. See REVERENCE.

fearful 1. Fearful, **apprehensive**, **afraid** mean disturbed by fear.

Fearful implies a timorous or worrying temperament more often than a real cause for fear ⟨the child is *fearful* of loud noises⟩. ***antonym:*** fearless, intrepid

Apprehensive suggests having good reasons for fear and implies a premonition of evil or danger ⟨*apprehensive* that war would break out⟩. ***antonym:*** confident

Afraid often suggests weakness or cowardice and regularly implies inhibition of action or utterance ⟨*afraid* to speak the truth⟩. ***antonym:*** unafraid, sanguine

2. Fearful, **awful**, **dreadful**, **frightful**, **terrible**, **terrific**, **appalling**, **horrible**, **horrific**, **shocking** mean of a kind to cause grave distress of mind. Additionally, all these words have a lighter, chiefly conversational value in which they mean little more than *extreme*.

Fearful applies to what produces fear, agitation, loss of courage, or mere disquiet ⟨a *fearful* predicament⟩. ***antonym:*** reassuring

Awful implies the creating of an awareness of transcendent or overpowering force, might, or significance ⟨waited in the *awful* dark for their rescuers to come⟩.

Dreadful applies to what fills one with shuddering fear or loathing and strikes one as at least disagreeable or extremely unpleasant ⟨cancer is a *dreadful* disease⟩.

Frightful implies such a startling or outrageous quality as produces utter consternation or a paralysis of fear ⟨a *frightful* tornado⟩.

Terrible suggests painfulness too great to be endured or a capacity to produce and prolong extreme and agitating fear ⟨caught in the grip of the *terrible* maelstrom⟩.

Terrific applies to something intended or fitted to inspire terror as by its size, appearance, or potency ⟨a *terrific* outburst of fury⟩.

Appalling describes what strikes one with dismay as well as with terror or horror ⟨had to perform the operation under *appalling* conditions⟩. ***antonym:*** reassuring

Horrible applies to something the sight

of which induces fear or terror combined with loathing or aversion and suggests hatefulness or hideousness ⟨the *horrible* carnage of war⟩.

Horrific suggests qualities or properties intended or suited to produce a horrible effect ⟨a *horrific* account of the tragedy⟩.

Shocking implies characteristics which startle because they are contrary to expectations, standards of good taste, rational thought, or moral sense ⟨fond of *shocking* stories⟩.

fearless See BRAVE.

feasible See POSSIBLE.

feat, **exploit**, **achievement** mean a remarkable deed.

Feat applies to an act involving strength or dexterity or daring ⟨the *feat* of crossing the Atlantic in a balloon⟩.

Exploit suggests an adventurous, brilliant, or heroic act ⟨his celebrated *exploits* as a spy⟩.

Achievement implies hard-won success in the face of difficulty or opposition ⟨honored for her *achievements* as a chemist⟩. ***antonym:*** failure

fecund See FERTILE.

federation See ALLIANCE.

fee See WAGE.

feeble See WEAK.

feel See TOUCH.

feeling **1. Feeling**, **emotion**, **affection**, **sentiment**, **passion** mean a subjective reaction or response to a person, thing, or situation.

Feeling denotes any response marked by such qualities as pleasure, pain, attraction, or repulsion and may imply nothing about the nature or intensity of the response ⟨whatever *feelings* I had for him are gone⟩.

Emotion carries a strong implication of excitement or agitation and, like ***feeling***, encompasses both positive and negative responses ⟨a play in which the *emotions* are real⟩.

Affection applies to feelings that are also inclinations or likings ⟨memoirs filled with *affection* and understanding⟩. ***antonym:*** antipathy

Sentiment implies refined, perhaps romantic, and sometimes artificial or affected emotion with an intellectual component ⟨her feminist *sentiments* are well known⟩.

Passion suggests a powerful or controlling emotion marked by urgency of desire ⟨revenge became his ruling *passion*⟩.

2. See SENSATION. **3.** See ATMOSPHERE.

feign See ASSUME.

feint See TRICK.

felicitate See CONGRATULATE.

felicitous See FIT *adj*.

female, **feminine**, **womanly**, **womanlike**, **womanish**, **effeminate**, **ladylike** mean of, characteristic of, or like a female, especially of the human species.

Female (opposed to *male*) applies to plants and animals as well as persons and stresses the fact of sex ⟨the more numerous *female* births as compared to male⟩. ***antonym:*** male

Feminine applies to qualities or attributes or attitudes characteristic of women and not shared by men ⟨a *feminine* approach to a problem⟩. ***antonym:*** masculine

Womanly suggests the qualities of the mature woman, especially those qualities that make her effective as wife and mother or indicate the absence of mannish qualities ⟨possessed all the *womanly* virtues⟩. ***antonym:*** unwomanly, manly

Womanlike is more likely to suggest characteristically feminine faults and foibles ⟨displayed *womanlike* rage at the slight⟩.

Womanish is often used derogatorily in situations in which manliness might naturally be expected ⟨shed *womanish* tears at his loss⟩. ***antonym:*** mannish

Effeminate emphasizes the softer and more delicate aspects of womanly nature and in its usual application to men implies lack of virility or masculinity ⟨a country grown weak and *effeminate* on its wealth⟩. ***antonym:*** virile

Ladylike suggests decorous propriety ⟨all three were *ladylike* and well brought-up girls⟩.

feminine See FEMALE.

ferocious See FIERCE.

fertile, **fecund**, **fruitful**, **prolific** mean producing or capable of producing offspring or fruit.

Fertile implies the power to reproduce in kind or to assist in reproduction and growth ⟨*fertile* soil⟩, or it may suggest readiness of invention and development ⟨a most *fertile* imagination⟩. ***antonym:*** infertile, sterile

Fecund emphasizes abundance or rapidity in bearing fruits or offspring or projects, inventions, or works of art ⟨came from a remarkably *fecund* family⟩. ***antonym:*** barren

Fruitful adds to ***fertile*** and ***fecund*** the implication of desirable or useful results ⟨undertook *fruitful* research in virology⟩. ***antonym:*** unfruitful, fruitless

Prolific stresses rapidity of spreading or multiplying by or as if by natural reproduction ⟨one of the most *prolific* writers of science fiction⟩. ***antonym:*** barren, unfruitful

fervent See IMPASSIONED.

fervid See IMPASSIONED.

fervor See PASSION.

fetid See MALODOROUS.

fetish, **talisman**, **charm**, **amulet** mean an object believed to have the power to avert evil or attract good.

Fetish is applied to an object that is regarded as sacred or magical or to something that is cherished unreasonably or obsessively ⟨make a *fetish* of the Bill of Rights⟩.

Talisman, primarily applicable to an astrological figure or image held to have magical power, such as to heal or protect, can also denote something that seems to exert a magical, extraordinary, and usually happy influence ⟨wore the ring as a *talisman*⟩.

Charm applies to an object or a formula of words believed to repel evil spirits or malign influences or to attract their opposites ⟨a *charm* against the evil eye⟩; it may also apply to some quality that is appealing or attractive ⟨captivated by the *charm* of the old inn⟩.

Amulet applies especially to something worn or carried on the person as a protection against evil, danger, or disease ⟨protected by an *amulet* of jaguar teeth⟩.

fetter See HAMPER.

fib See LIE.

fickle See INCONSTANT.

fictitious, **fabulous**, **legendary**, **mythical**, **apocryphal** mean having the nature of something imagined or mentally invented.

Fictitious implies fabrication and suggests artificiality or contrivance more than deliberate falsification or deception ⟨all names used in the broadcast are *fictitious*⟩. ***antonym:*** historical

Fabulous stresses the marvelous or incredible character of something without necessarily implying impossibility or actual nonexistence ⟨a land of *fabulous* riches⟩.

Legendary suggests the elaboration of invented details and distortion of historical facts produced by popular tradition ⟨the *legendary* courtship of Miles Standish⟩.

Mythical implies a fanciful, often symbolic explanation of facts or the creation of beings and events ⟨*mythical* creatures such as centaurs⟩. ***antonym:*** historical

Apocryphal implies an unknown or dubious source or origin or may imply that the thing itself is dubious or inaccurate ⟨a book that repeats many *apocryphal* stories⟩.

fidelity, **allegiance**, **fealty**, **loyalty**, **devotion**, **piety** mean faithfulness to something to which one is bound by pledge or duty or by a sense of what is right or appropriate.

Fidelity implies strict and continuing faithfulness to an obligation, trust, or duty ⟨*fidelity* in the performance of one's duties⟩. ***antonym:*** faithlessness, perfidy

Allegiance suggests an adherence like that of a citizen to his country and implies an unswerving fidelity maintained despite conflicting obligations or claims ⟨a politician who owes *allegiance* to no special interest⟩. ***antonym:*** treachery, treason

Fealty implies a fidelity acknowledged by the individual and as compelling as a sworn vow ⟨a critic's only *fealty* is to truth⟩. ***antonym:*** perfidy

Loyalty implies a personal and emotional faithfulness that is steadfast in the face of any temptation to renounce, desert, or betray ⟨valued the *loyalty* of his friends⟩. ***antonym:*** disloyalty

Devotion stresses zeal and service amounting to self-dedication ⟨a painter's *devotion* to her artistic vision⟩.

Piety stresses fidelity to obligations regarded as natural and fundamental and the observance of duties required by such fidelity ⟨filial *piety* demands that I visit my parents⟩. ***antonym:*** impiety

fierce, **ferocious**, **barbarous**, **savage**, **cruel** mean showing fury or malignity in looks or actions.

Fierce applies to humans and animals that inspire terror because of their wild and menacing appearance or fury in attack or to qualities, expressions, or events characteristic of these ⟨a battle marked by *fierce* fighting⟩. ***antonym:*** tame, mild

Ferocious implies extreme fierceness and unrestrained violence and brutality ⟨signs warned of a *ferocious* dog⟩. ***antonym:*** tender

Barbarous implies a ferocity or mercilessness regarded as unworthy of civilized people ⟨the *barbarous* treatment of prisoners⟩. ***antonym:*** clement

Savage implies the absence of inhibitions restraining civilized people filled with rage, lust, hate, fear, or other violent passions ⟨*savage* reviews of the new play⟩.

Cruel implies indifference to suffering or even positive pleasure in witnessing or inflicting it ⟨the *cruel* jokes of young children⟩.

figure See FORM.

filch See STEAL.

filthy See DIRTY.

final See LAST.

financial, **monetary**, **pecuniary**, **fiscal** mean of or relating to money.

Financial implies money matters conducted on a large scale or involving some degree of complexity ⟨a business deal secured through a complex *financial* arrangement⟩.

Monetary refers to money as coined, distributed, or circulating ⟨the country's basic *monetary* unit is the peso⟩.

Pecuniary implies reference to practical money matters as they affect the individual ⟨a struggling single mother constantly in *pecuniary* difficulties⟩.

Fiscal refers to money as providing public revenue or to the financial affairs of an institution or corporation ⟨the *fiscal* year of the United States ends on June 30⟩.

fine See PENALIZE.

finicky See NICE.

finish See CLOSE *vb*.

fire See LIGHT.

firm, **hard**, **solid** mean having a texture or consistency that resists deformation.

Firm implies such compactness and coherence and often elasticity of substance as to resist pulling, distorting, or pressing ⟨a *firm* mattress with good back support⟩. ***antonym:*** loose, flabby

Hard implies impenetrability and nearly complete but inelastic resistance to pressure or tension ⟨a diamond is one of the *hardest* substances known⟩. ***antonym:*** soft

Solid implies a texture of uniform density so as to be not only firm but also resistant to external deforming forces ⟨*solid* furniture that will last⟩.

fiscal See FINANCIAL.

fit *adj* **Fit**, **suitable**, **meet**, **proper**, **appropriate**, **fitting**, **apt**, **happy**, **felicitous** mean right with respect to some end, need, use, or circumstance.

Fit stresses adaptability and sometimes special readiness for use or action ⟨the vessel is now *fit* for service⟩. ***antonym:*** unfit

Suitable implies an answering to requirements or demands ⟨shopped for clothes *suitable* for camping⟩. ***antonym:*** unbecoming, unsuitable

Meet suggests a rightness or just proportioning and suitability ⟨a tip that was *meet* for the services rendered⟩. ***antonym:*** unmeet

Proper suggests a suitability through essential nature or accordance with custom ⟨the *proper* role of the First Lady⟩. ***antonym:*** improper

Appropriate implies eminent or distinctive fitness ⟨a golf bag is an *appropriate* gift for a golfer⟩. ***antonym:*** inappropriate

Fitting implies harmony of mood or tone or purpose ⟨*fitting* subjects for dinner table conversation⟩.

Apt connotes a fitness marked by nicety and discrimination ⟨a speech laced with some *apt* quotations⟩. ***antonym:*** inapt, inept

Happy suggests what is effectively or successfully appropriate ⟨a *happy* choice of words⟩. ***antonym:*** unhappy

Felicitous suggests an aptness that is opportune, telling, or graceful ⟨a *felicitous* note of apology⟩. ***antonym:*** infelicitous

fit *n* **Fit**, **attack**, **access**, **accession**, **paroxysm**, **spasm**, **convulsion** mean a sudden seizure or spell resulting from an abnormal condition of body or mind.

Fit sometimes designates a sudden seizure or period of increased activity characteristic of a disease ⟨fell unconscious in a *fit*⟩ or sometimes refers to a temporary sudden or violent mood or period of activity ⟨works by *fits* and starts⟩.

Attack implies a sudden and often violent onslaught but connotes nothing about length or duration ⟨an *attack* of melancholy⟩.

Access and ***accession*** distinctively imply the initiation of an attack or fit ⟨an *access* of sudden rage⟩ or the intensification of a mood or state of mind to the point where control is lost or nearly lost ⟨driven mad by an *accession* of guilt⟩.

Paroxysm refers to the sudden occurrence or intensification of a symptom or a state and to its recurrence ⟨*paroxysms* of fear⟩.

Spasm connotes sudden involuntary muscular contractions ⟨suffered from *spasms* of his back muscles⟩ or possession by some emotion or state that momentarily grips and paralyzes ⟨seized by *spasms* of fear⟩.

Convulsion suggests repeated spasms that alternately contract and relax the muscles and produce violent contortions and distortions ⟨a face distorted by *convulsions* of unsuppressed anger⟩.

fit *vb* See PREPARE.

fitful, **spasmodic**, **convulsive** mean lacking steadiness or regularity in movement.

Fitful implies intermittence and a succession of starts and stops or risings and fallings ⟨the *fitful* beginnings of a new enterprise⟩. ***antonym:*** constant

Spasmodic adds to ***fitful*** the implication of violent intensity of activity, effort, or zeal alternating with lack of intensity ⟨*spasmodic* trading on the stock exchange⟩.

Convulsive suggests the breaking of regularity or quiet by uncontrolled movement and usually connotes distress of body, mind, or spirit ⟨the *convulsive* shocks of the earthquake⟩.

fitting See FIT *adj.*

fix *n* See PREDICAMENT.

fix *vb* **1.** See FASTEN. **2.** See SET *vb.*

flabbergast See SURPRISE 2.

flabby See LIMP.

flaccid See LIMP.

flagrant, **glaring**, **egregious**, **gross**, **rank** mean conspicuously bad or objectionable.

Flagrant applies usually to offenses or errors so bad that they can neither escape notice nor be condoned ⟨*flagrant* abuse of the office of president⟩.

Glaring implies painful or damaging obtrusiveness of something that is conspicuously wrong, faulty, or improper ⟨*glaring* errors in judgment⟩. ***antonym:*** unnoticeable

Egregious is applicable to something that stands out by reason of its bad quality or because it is in poor taste ⟨made an *egregious* error⟩.

Gross implies the exceeding of reasonable or excusable limits of badness as applied to attitudes, qualities, or faults ⟨*gross* carelessness on your part⟩. ***antonym:*** petty

Rank applies to what is openly and extremely objectionable and utterly condemned ⟨it's *rank* heresy to say that⟩.

flair See LEANING.

flame See BLAZE.

flare See BLAZE.

flash, **gleam**, **glance**, **glint**, **sparkle**, **glitter**, **glisten**, **glimmer**, **shimmer** mean to send forth light.

Flash implies a sudden and transient burst of bright light ⟨lightning *flashed*⟩.

Gleam suggests a steady light seen through an obscuring medium or against a dark background ⟨the lights of the town *gleamed* in the valley below⟩.

Glance suggests a bright darting light reflected from a moving surface ⟨sunlight *glanced* off the hull of the boat⟩.

Glint implies a quickly glancing or gleaming light ⟨steel bars *glinted* in the moonlight⟩.

Sparkle suggests innumerable moving points of bright light ⟨the *sparkling* waters of the gulf⟩.

Glitter connotes a brilliant sparkling or gleaming ⟨*glittering* diamonds⟩.

Glisten applies to the soft, persistent sparkle from or as if from a wet or oily surface ⟨rain-drenched sidewalks *glistened* under the street lamps⟩.

Glimmer suggests a faint, obscured, or wavering gleam ⟨a lone light *glimmered* in the distance⟩.

Shimmer implies a soft tremulous gleaming or a blurred reflection ⟨a *shimmering* satin dress⟩.

flashy See GAUDY.

flat **1.** See INSIPID. **2.** See LEVEL.

flatulent See INFLATED.

flaunt See SHOW 2.

flavor See TASTE 1.

flaw See BLEMISH.

fleer See SCOFF.

fleet See FAST.

fleeting See TRANSIENT.

fleshly See CARNAL.

flexible See ELASTIC.

flightiness See LIGHTNESS.

flimsy See LIMP.

flinch See RECOIL.

fling See THROW.

flippancy See LIGHTNESS.

flirt See TRIFLE.

floppy See LIMP.

flourish **1.** See SUCCEED. **2.** See SWING 1.

flout See SCOFF.

flow See SPRING.

fluctuate See SWING 2.

fluent See VOCAL 2.

fluid See LIQUID.

flurry See STIR *n.*

flush See LEVEL.

fluster See DISCOMPOSE.

foe See ENEMY.

fog See HAZE.

foible See FAULT.

foil See FRUSTRATE.

follow 1. Follow, **succeed**, **ensue**, **supervene** mean to come after something or someone.

Follow may apply to a coming after in time, position, understanding, or logical sequence 〈speeches *followed* the dinner〉. ***antonym:*** precede

Succeed implies a coming after immediately in a sequence determined by some rational cause or rule, such as natural order, inheritance, election, or laws of rank 〈she *succeeded* her father as head of the business〉.

Ensue commonly suggests a logical consequence or naturally expected development 〈after the lecture, a general discussion *ensued*〉.

Supervene suggests the following by something added or conjoined and often unforeseen or unpredictable 〈events *supervened* that brought tragedy into his life〉.

2. Follow, **chase**, **pursue**, **trail** mean to go after or on the track of someone or something.

Follow is the comprehensive term and usually implies the lead or guidance of one going before, but, in itself, gives no clue as to the purpose of the one that follows 〈*follow* a path to town〉. ***antonym:*** precede

Chase implies speed in following, sometimes in order to catch what flees and sometimes to turn or drive away what advances 〈*chasing* the boys out of the orchard〉.

Pursue usually suggests an attempt to overtake, reach, or attain often with eagerness or persistence, sometimes with hostile intent 〈*pursued* the bandits on foot〉.

Trail implies a following in the tracks of one gone before 〈*trail* along behind the leader〉.

follower, **adherent**, **disciple**, **partisan** mean one who attaches himself to another.

Follower denotes a person who attaches himself either to the person or beliefs of another 〈an evangelist and his *followers*〉. ***antonym:*** leader

Adherent suggests a close and persistent attachment 〈*adherents* to the cause〉. ***antonym:*** renegade

Disciple implies a devoted allegiance to the teachings of one chosen or accepted as a master 〈*disciples* of Gandhi〉.

Partisan suggests a zealous often prejudiced attachment 〈*partisans* of the President〉.

foment See INCITE.

fondle See CARESS.

foolhardy See ADVENTUROUS.

foolish See SIMPLE.

forbear See REFRAIN.

forbearing, **tolerant**, **lenient**, **indulgent** mean not inclined by nature, disposition, or circumstances to be severe or rigorous.

Forbearing implies patience under provocation and deliberate abstention from harsh judgment, punishment, or vengeance 〈the most *forbearing* of music teachers〉. ***antonym:*** unrelenting

Tolerant implies a freedom from bias or dogmatism and a reluctance to judge or restrict others harshly who hold opinions or doctrines different from one's own 〈a very *tolerant* attitude towards dissenters〉. ***antonym:*** intolerant

Lenient implies softness of temper and a relaxation of discipline or rigor 〈*lenient* parents pay for it later〉. ***antonym:*** stern, exacting

Indulgent implies compliancy, mercifulness, and a willingness to make concessions out of charity or clemency 〈an aunt *indulgent* of her nephews' and nieces' shortcomings〉. ***antonym:*** strict

forbid, **prohibit**, **interdict**, **inhibit**, **ban** mean to debar one from using or doing something or to order that something not be used or done.

Forbid implies absolute proscription and expected obedience of an order from one in authority 〈smoking is *forbidden* in the building〉. ***antonym:*** permit

Prohibit suggests the issuing of laws, statutes, or regulations ⟨*prohibited* the manufacture and sale of firearms⟩. ***antonym:*** permit

Interdict implies prohibition by civil or ecclesiastical authority for a given time or a declared purpose ⟨*interdicted* trade with belligerent nations⟩. ***antonym:*** sanction

Inhibit implies the imposition of restraints or restrictions that amount to prohibitions, not only by authority but also by the requirements of a situation or by voluntary self-restraint ⟨laws that *inhibit* the growth of free trade⟩. ***antonym:*** allow

Ban suggests prohibition stemming from legal or social pressure and strongly connotes condemnation or disapproval ⟨*banned* the new music video⟩.

force *vb* **Force**, **compel**, **coerce**, **constrain**, **oblige** mean to make someone or something yield.

Force is the general term and implies the overcoming of resistance by the exertion of strength, power, weight, stress, or duress ⟨*forced* the prisoner to sign the confession⟩.

Compel typically requires a personal or personalized object and suggests the working of authority or of an irresistible force ⟨all workers are *compelled* to pay taxes⟩.

Coerce suggests the overcoming of resistance or unwillingness by actual or threatened severe violence or intimidation ⟨*coerced* by gangsters into selling his business⟩.

Constrain suggests a forcing by constricting, confining, or binding action or choice ⟨*constrained* by my conscience to see that justice was done⟩.

Oblige implies the constraint of necessity, law, reason, or duty ⟨I am *obliged* to inform you of your rights⟩.

force *n* See POWER 1.

foreboding See APPREHENSION.

forecast See FORETELL.

foregoing See PRECEDING.

foreign See EXTRINSIC.

foreknow See FORESEE.

forerunner, **precursor**, **harbinger**, **herald** mean one who goes before or announces the coming of another.

Forerunner is applicable to anything that serves as a sign, omen, or warning of something to come ⟨the international incident was a *forerunner* to war⟩.

Precursor applies to a person or thing that paves the way for the success or accomplishment of another ⟨18th century poets who were *precursors* of the Romantics⟩.

Harbinger and ***herald*** both apply, chiefly figuratively, to one that proclaims or announces the coming or arrival of a notable event or person ⟨robins, the *harbingers* of spring⟩ ⟨the *herald* of a new age in medical science⟩.

foresee, **foreknow**, **divine**, **apprehend**, **anticipate** mean to know or prophesy beforehand.

Foresee implies nothing about how the knowledge is derived and may apply to ordinary reasoning and experience ⟨no one could *foresee* the economic crisis⟩.

Foreknow stresses prior knowledge and implies supernatural assistance, as through revelation ⟨if only we could *foreknow* our own destinies⟩.

Divine adds to ***foresee*** the suggestion of exceptional wisdom or discernment ⟨a European traveler who *divined* the course of American destiny⟩.

Apprehend implies foresight mingled with uncertainty, anxiety, or dread ⟨*apprehended* that his odd behavior was a sign of a troubled soul⟩.

Anticipate implies such foreknowledge as leads or allows one to take action about or respond emotionally to something before it happens ⟨the servants *anticipated* our every need⟩.

forestall See PREVENT 1.

foretaste See PROSPECT.

foretell, **predict**, **forecast**, **prophesy**, **prognosticate** mean to tell beforehand.

Foretell applies to the telling of a future event by any procedure or from any source of information ⟨seers *foretold* of calamitous events⟩.

Predict commonly implies inference from facts or from accepted laws of nature ⟨astronomers *predicted* the return of the comet⟩.

Forecast adds the implication of anticipating eventualities and differs from ***predict*** in being usually concerned with probabilities rather than certainties ⟨*forecast* a snowfall of six inches⟩.

Prophesy connotes inspired or mystic knowledge of the future, especially as the fulfilling of divine threats or promises, or implies great assurance in predicting ⟨preachers *prophesying* a day of divine retribution⟩.

Prognosticate suggests prediction based on the learned or skilled interpretation of signs or symptoms ⟨economists are *prognosticating* a slow recovery⟩.

forewarn See WARN.

forge See MAKE.

forget See NEGLECT.

forgetful, **oblivious**, **unmindful** mean losing from one's mind something once known or learned.

Forgetful implies a heedless or negligent habit of or propensity for failing to remember ⟨*forgetful* of my duties as host⟩.

Oblivious suggests a failure to notice or remember as a result of external causes or conditions or of a determination to ignore ⟨lost in thought, *oblivious* to the rushing crowd around her⟩.

Unmindful may suggest inattention and heedlessness or a deliberate disregard ⟨a crusading reformer who was *unmindful* of his family's needs⟩. ***antonym:*** mindful, solicitous

forgive See EXCUSE.

forlorn See ALONE.

form *n* **Form**, **figure**, **shape**, **conformation**, **configuration** mean outward appearance.

Form usually suggests reference to both internal structure and external outline and often the principle that gives unity to the whole ⟨an architect who appreciates the interplay of *forms*⟩.

Figure applies chiefly to the form as determined by bounding or enclosing outlines ⟨cutting doll *figures* out of paper⟩.

Shape, like ***figure***, suggests an outline but carries a stronger implication of the enclosed body or mass ⟨the *shape* of the monument was pyramidal⟩.

Conformation implies a complicated structure composed of harmoniously related parts ⟨a *conformation* that is well-proportioned and symmetrical⟩.

Configuration refers to the pattern formed by the disposition and arrangement of component parts ⟨modular furniture allows for a number of *configurations*⟩.

form *vb* See MAKE.

formal See CEREMONIAL.

former See PRECEDING.

fornication See ADULTERY.

forsake See ABANDON.

forswear **1.** See ABJURE. **2.** See PERJURE.

forth See ONWARD.

forthright See STRAIGHTFORWARD.

fortitude, **grit**, **backbone**, **pluck**, **guts** mean courage and staying power.

Fortitude stresses firmness in enduring physical or mental hardships and suffering ⟨a trip that tested their *fortitude*⟩. ***antonym:*** pusillanimity

Grit stresses unyielding resolution and indomitableness in the face of hardship or danger ⟨*grit* beyond her years⟩. ***antonym:*** faintheartedness

Backbone emphasizes resoluteness of character and implies either ability to stand firm in the face of opposition or such determination and independence as requires no support from without ⟨held their own as long as they kept their *backbone*⟩. ***antonym:*** spinelessness

Pluck implies a willingness to fight or continue against odds ⟨fought on with *pluck* and courage⟩.

Guts, considered by some to be not entirely polite, stresses fortitude and stamina and implies effectiveness and determination in facing and coping with what alarms or repels or discourages ⟨lacked the *guts* to pull it off⟩. ***antonym:*** gutlessness

fortuitous See ACCIDENTAL.

fortunate See LUCKY.

fortune See CHANCE.

forward *adv* See ONWARD.

forward *vb* See ADVANCE.

foul See DIRTY.

foundation See BASE *n*.

foxy See SLY.

fragile 1. Fragile, **frangible**, **brittle**, **crisp**, **friable** mean easily broken.

Fragile implies extreme delicacy of material or construction and need for careful handling ⟨a *fragile* antique chair⟩. ***antonym:*** durable

Frangible implies an inherent susceptibility to being broken without implying weakness or delicacy ⟨*frangible* stone used as paving material⟩.

Brittle implies hardness together with lack of elasticity or flexibility or toughness ⟨elderly patients with *brittle* bones⟩. ***antonym:*** supple

Crisp implies a firmness and brittleness desirable especially in some foods ⟨*crisp* lettuce⟩.

Friable applies to substances that are easily crumbled or pulverized ⟨*friable* soil⟩.

2. See WEAK.

fragment See PART.

fragrance, **perfume**, **bouquet**, **scent**, **incense**, **redolence** mean a sweet or pleasant odor.

Fragrance suggests the pleasant odors of flowers or other growing things ⟨household cleansers with the *fragrance* of pine⟩. ***antonym:*** stench, stink

Perfume may suggest a stronger or heavier odor and applies especially to a prepared or synthetic liquid ⟨the *perfume* of lilacs filled the room⟩.

Bouquet, often used of wine, implies a delicate, complex odor that suggests the distinctive, savory quality of its source ⟨the *bouquet* of ripe apples⟩.

Scent is very close to ***perfume*** but more neutral in connotation ⟨furniture polish with a fresh lemon *scent*⟩.

Incense applies to the smoke from burning spices and gums and suggests a pleasing odor ⟨the exotic *incense* of a Middle Eastern bazaar⟩.

Redolence implies a mixture of fragrant or pungent odors ⟨the *redolence* of a forest after a rain⟩.

fragrant See ODOROUS.

frail See WEAK.

frailty See FAULT.

frame See CONTRIVE.

framework See STRUCTURE.

frangible See FRAGILE.

frank, **candid**, **open**, **plain** mean showing willingness to tell what one feels or thinks.

Frank stresses lack of reticence in expressing oneself and connotes freedom from shyness, secretiveness, or considerations of tact or expedience ⟨*frank* discussions on arms control⟩. ***antonym:*** reticent

Candid suggests expression marked by sincerity and honesty especially in offering unwelcome criticism or opinion ⟨a *candid* appraisal of her singing ability⟩. ***antonym:*** evasive

Open implies frankness and candor but suggests more artlessness than ***frank*** and less earnestness than ***candid*** ⟨young children are *open* and artless in saying what they think⟩. ***antonym:*** close, clandestine

Plain suggests outspokenness and freedom from affectation or subtlety in expression ⟨was very *plain* about telling them to leave⟩.

fraud **1.** See DECEPTION. **2.** See IMPOSTURE.

freak See CAPRICE.

free *adj* **Free**, **independent**, **autonomous**, **sovereign** mean not subject to the rule or control of another.

Free stresses the complete absence of external control and the full right to make all of one's own decisions ⟨you're *free* to do as you like⟩.

Independent implies a standing alone; applied to a state it implies lack of connection with any other having power to interfere with its citizens, laws, or policies ⟨the struggle for Ireland to become *independent*⟩. ***antonym:*** dependent

Autonomous stresses independence combined with freedom; or, applied politically, independence in matters pertaining to self-government ⟨the establishment of *autonomous* school districts⟩.

Sovereign stresses the absence of a superior or dominant power and implies supremacy within one's own domain or sphere ⟨a *sovereign* nation not subject to the laws of another⟩.

free *vb* **Free**, **release**, **liberate**, **emancipate**, **manumit** mean to set loose from restraint or constraint.

Free implies a usually permanent removal from whatever binds, confines, entangles, or oppresses ⟨*freed* the animals from their cages⟩.

Release suggests a setting loose from confinement, restraint, or a state of pressure or tension ⟨*released* his anger by exercising⟩. ***antonym:*** detain

Liberate stresses particularly the resulting state of freedom ⟨*liberated* the novel from Victorian inhibitions⟩.

Emancipate implies the liberation of a person from subjection or domination ⟨labor-saving devices that *emancipated* women from housework⟩. ***antonym:*** enslave

Manumit implies emancipation from slavery ⟨the proclamation *manumitted* the slaves⟩. ***antonym:*** enslave

freedom, **liberty**, **license** mean the power or condition of acting without compulsion.

Freedom has a broad range of application and may imply anything from total absence of restraint to merely a sense of not being unduly hampered or frustrated ⟨*freedom* of the press⟩. ***antonym:*** necessity

Liberty suggests the power to choose or the release from former restraint or compulsion ⟨the prisoners were willing to fight for their *liberty*⟩. ***antonym:*** restraint

License implies unusual freedom granted because of special circumstances ⟨poetic *license*⟩ or may connote an abuse of freedom by willfully following one's own course without regard for propriety or the rights of others ⟨the editorial takes considerable *license* with the facts⟩. ***antonym:*** decorum

frenzy See MANIA 2.

frequently See OFTEN.

fresh See NEW.

friable See FRAGILE.

friendly See AMICABLE.

fright See FEAR.

frightful See FEARFUL 2.

fritter See WASTE.

frivolity See LIGHTNESS.

frown, **scowl**, **glower**, **lower** mean to put on a dark or threatening countenance or appearance.

Frown implies a stern face and contracted brows that express concentration, bewilderment, anger, displeasure, or contempt ⟨the teachers *frowned* on my boyish pranks⟩. ***antonym:*** smile

Scowl suggests a similar facial expression that conveys bad humor, sullenness, or resentful puzzlement ⟨a grumpy old man who *scowled* habitually⟩.

Glower implies a direct defiant brooding stare or glare as in contempt or defiance ⟨the natives merely *glowered* at the invading tourists⟩.

Lower suggests a menacing darkness or

gloomy anger and refers either to persons or to skies that promise bad weather ⟨*lowered* as he went about his work, never uttering a word⟩.

frowzy See SLATTERNLY.

frugal See SPARING.

fruitful See FERTILE.

fruitless See FUTILE.

frustrate, **thwart**, **foil**, **baffle**, **balk**, **circumvent**, **outwit** mean to check or defeat another's desire, plan, or goal.

Frustrate implies making vain or ineffectual all efforts, however vigorous or persistent ⟨*frustrated* all attempts at government reform⟩. ***antonym:*** fulfill

Thwart suggests a frustrating or checking by deliberately crossing or opposing one making headway ⟨the park department is *thwarted* by public indifference to littering⟩.

Foil implies a checking or defeating so as to discourage further effort ⟨her parents *foiled* my efforts to see her⟩.

Baffle implies a frustrating by confusing or puzzling ⟨*baffled* by the maze of rules and regulations⟩.

Balk suggests the interposing of obstacles or hindrances ⟨legal restrictions *balked* police efforts to control crime⟩. ***antonym:*** forward

Circumvent implies a frustrating by means of a particular stratagem ⟨*circumvented* the law by finding loopholes⟩. ***antonym:*** conform (*to laws, orders*), cooperate (*with persons*)

Outwit suggests craft and cunning in frustrating or circumventing ⟨the rebels *outwitted* the army repeatedly⟩.

fugitive See TRANSIENT.

fulfill **1.** See PERFORM. **2.** See SATISFY 3.

full, **complete**, **plenary**, **replete** mean containing all that is wanted or needed or possible.

Full implies the presence or inclusion of everything that is wanted or required by something or that can be held, contained, or attained by it ⟨a *full* schedule of appointments⟩. ***antonym:*** empty

Complete applies when all that is needed or wanted is present ⟨the report does not give a *complete* picture of the situation⟩. ***antonym:*** incomplete

Plenary adds to ***complete*** the implication of fullness without qualification and strongly suggests absoluteness ⟨given *plenary* power as commander in chief⟩. ***antonym:*** limited

Replete stresses abundance of supply and implies being filled to the brim or to satiety ⟨a speech *replete* with innuendos and half-truths⟩.

fulsome, **oily**, **unctuous**, **oleaginous**, **slick** mean too obviously extravagant or ingratiating to be accepted as genuine or sincere.

Fulsome implies that something which is essentially good has been carried to an excessive and offensive degree ⟨the *fulsome* flattery of a celebrity interviewer⟩.

Oily implies an offensively ingratiating quality and sometimes suggests a suavity or benevolence or kindliness that masks a sinister or dubious intent ⟨*oily* land developers trying to persuade older residents to sell⟩.

Unctuous implies the hypocritical adoption of a grave, devout, or spiritual manner ⟨the *unctuous* pleading of the First Amendment by pornographers⟩.

Oleaginous may be used in place of ***oily*** to suggest pomposity or to convey a mocking note ⟨an *oleaginous* host fawning over the female guests⟩.

fun, **jest**, **sport**, **game**, **play** mean action or speech that provides amusement or arouses laughter.

Fun usually implies laughter or gaiety but may imply merely a lack of serious or ulterior purpose ⟨played cards just for *fun*⟩. ***antonym:*** earnestness, seriousness

Jest implies lack of earnestness in what is said or done and may suggest a hoaxing or teasing ⟨took seriously remarks said only in *jest*⟩. ***antonym:*** earnest

Sport applies especially to the arousing

of laughter against someone by raillery or ridicule ⟨teasing begun in *sport* ended in an ugly brawl⟩.

Game is close to ***sport*** and often stresses mischievous or malicious fun but may also apply to any activity carried on in a spirit of fun ⟨habitually made *game* of their poor relations⟩.

Play stresses the opposition to *earnest* or *serious* and connotes the absence of any element of malice or mischief ⟨pretended to strangle his brother in *play*⟩.

antonym: work

function 1. Function, office, duty, province mean the acts or operations expected of a person or thing.

Function, applicable to anything living, natural, or constructed, implies a definite end or purpose that the thing in question serves or a particular kind of work it is intended to perform ⟨the *function* of the stomach is to digest food⟩.

Office is typically applied to the function or service expected of a person by reason of his or her trade, profession, or special relationship to others ⟨exercised the *offices* of both attorney and friend⟩.

Duty applies to a task or responsibility imposed by one's occupation, rank, status, or calling ⟨the lieutenant governor had a few official *duties*⟩.

Province applies to a function, office, or duty that naturally or logically falls within one's range of jurisdiction or competence ⟨it is not the governor's *province* to set foreign policy⟩.

2. See POWER 2.

fundamental See ESSENTIAL.

funny See LAUGHABLE.

furnish, equip, outfit, appoint, accoutre, arm mean to supply one with what is needed.

Furnish implies the provision of any or all essentials for performing a function or serving an end ⟨a sparsely *furnished* apartment⟩.

Equip suggests the provision of something making for efficiency in action or use ⟨a fully *equipped* kitchen with every modern appliance⟩.

Outfit implies provision of a complete list or set of articles as for a journey, an expedition, or a special occupation ⟨*outfitted* the whole family for a ski trip⟩.

Appoint implies provision of complete and usually elegant or elaborate equipment or furnishings ⟨a lavishly *appointed* penthouse apartment⟩.

Accoutre suggests the supplying of personal dress or equipment for a special activity ⟨the fully *accoutred* members of a polar expedition⟩.

Arm implies provision for effective action or operation especially in war ⟨*armed* to the teeth⟩.

2. See PROVIDE.

further See ADVANCE.

furtive See SECRET.

fury See ANGER.

fuse See MIX.

fuss See STIR *n.*

fussy See NICE.

fustian See BOMBAST.

fusty See MALODOROUS.

futile, vain, fruitless, bootless, abortive mean barren of or producing no result.

Futile may connote completeness of the failure or unwisdom of the undertaking ⟨a *futile* search for survivors of the crash⟩. ***antonym:*** effective

Vain usually implies simple failure to achieve a desired result ⟨a *vain* attempt to get the car started⟩.

Fruitless comes close to ***vain*** but often suggests long and arduous effort or severe disappointment ⟨*fruitless* efforts to obtain a lasting peace⟩. ***antonym:*** fruitful

Bootless, chiefly literary, applies to petitions or efforts to obtain relief ⟨a *bootless* request for aid⟩.

Abortive suggests failure before plans are matured or activities begun ⟨an *abortive* attempt to escape⟩. ***antonym:*** consummated

G

gag See JEST.
gain 1. See GET. **2.** See REACH.
gainsay See DENY.
gall See TEMERITY.
gallant See CIVIL.
gallantry See HEROISM.
gambit See TRICK *n.*
game See FUN.
games See ATHLETICS.
gamut See RANGE.
gape See GAZE.
garble See MISREPRESENT.
garish See GAUDY.
garner See REAP.
garnish See ADORN.
garrulous See TALKATIVE.
gastronome See EPICURE.
gather 1. Gather, **collect**, **assemble**, **congregate** mean to come or bring together into a group, mass, or unit.

Gather, the most general term, is usually neutral in connotation or may suggest plucking and culling or harvesting ⟨a crowd *gathers* whenever there is excitement⟩. ***antonym:*** scatter

Collect often implies careful selection or orderly arrangement with a definite end in view ⟨*collected* books on gardening⟩. ***antonym:*** disperse, distribute

Assemble implies an ordered union or organization of persons or things and a conscious or definite end for their coming or being brought together ⟨the country's leading experts on aeronautics *assembled* under one roof⟩. ***antonym:*** disperse

Congregate implies a spontaneous flocking together into a crowd or huddle, usually of similar types ⟨persons were forbidden to *congregate* under martial law⟩. ***antonym:*** disperse

2. See REAP.
3. See INFER.

gauche See AWKWARD.
gaudy, **tawdry**, **garish**, **flashy**, **meretricious** mean vulgarly or cheaply showy.

Gaudy implies a tasteless use of overly bright, often clashing colors or excessive ornamentation ⟨circus performers in *gaudy* costumes⟩. ***antonym:*** quiet

Tawdry applies to what is at once gaudy and cheap and sleazy ⟨*tawdry* saloons along the waterfront⟩.

Garish describes what is distressingly or offensively bright ⟨*garish* signs on the casinos⟩. ***antonym:*** somber

Flashy implies an effect of brilliance quickly and easily revealed to be shallow or vulgar ⟨a *flashy* nightclub act with leggy chorus girls⟩.

Meretricious stresses falsity and may describe a tawdry show that beckons with a false allure or promise ⟨a *meretricious* wasteland of nightclubs and bars⟩.

gauge See STANDARD.
gaunt See LEAN.
gay See LIVELY.
gaze, **gape**, **stare**, **glare**, **peer**, **gloat** mean to look attentively.

Gaze implies fixed and prolonged attention, as in wonder, admiration, or abstractedness ⟨*gazing* at the waves breaking along the shore⟩.

Gape suggests an openmouthed and often stupid wonder ⟨a crowd *gaped* at the man threatening to jump⟩.

Stare implies a direct open-eyed gazing denoting curiosity, disbelief, or insolence ⟨kept *staring* at them as they tried to eat⟩.

Glare suggests a fierce or angry staring ⟨silently *glared* back at her accusers⟩.

Peer suggests a straining to see more closely or fully, often with narrowed eyes and as if through a small opening ⟨*peered* at the bird through his binoculars⟩.

Gloat implies prolonged or frequent gazing, often in secret and with deep or malignant satisfaction ⟨*gloated* over the treasure⟩.

general See UNIVERSAL.

generic See UNIVERSAL.
generous See LIBERAL 1.
genial See GRACIOUS.
genius See GIFT.
gentle See SOFT.
gentry See ARISTOCRACY.
genuine See AUTHENTIC.
germane See RELEVANT.
get **1. Get**, **obtain**, **procure**, **secure**, **acquire**, **gain**, **win**, **earn** mean to come into possession of.

Get is a very general term and may or may not imply effort or initiative ⟨*got* a car for my birthday⟩.

Obtain suggests the attainment of something sought for with some expenditure of time and effort ⟨*obtained* statements from all of the witnesses⟩.

Procure implies effort in obtaining something for oneself or for another ⟨in charge of *procuring* supplies for the office⟩.

Secure implies difficulty in obtaining or keeping safely in one's possession or under one's control ⟨an ad agency that *secured* many top accounts⟩.

Acquire often suggests an adding to what is already possessed ⟨*acquired* a greater appreciation of music⟩. ***antonym:*** forfeit

Gain suggests struggle or competition and usually a material value in the thing obtained ⟨gradually *gained* a reputation as a skilled musician⟩. ***antonym:*** lose

Win suggests that favoring qualities or circumstances played a part in the gaining ⟨*won* the admiration of his fellow actors⟩. ***antonym:*** lose

Earn implies a correspondence between one's effort and what one gets by it ⟨a compelling performance that *earned* her many awards⟩.

2. See INDUCE.

ghastly, **grisly**, **gruesome**, **macabre**, **grim**, **lurid** mean horrifying and repellent in appearance or aspect.

Ghastly suggests the terrifying aspects of bloodshed, death, corpses, and ghosts ⟨a *ghastly* portrait of life after a nuclear war⟩.

Grisly and ***gruesome*** suggest additionally the results of extreme violence or cruelty and an appearance that inspires shuddering or horror ⟨the case of an unusually *grisly* murder⟩ ⟨the *gruesome* history of the Nazi death camps⟩.

Macabre implies a marked or excessive preoccupation with the horrible aspects especially of death ⟨a *macabre* tale of premature burial⟩.

Grim suggests a fierce and forbidding aspect ⟨the *grim* face of the executioner⟩.

Lurid suggests shuddering fascination with violent death and especially with murder ⟨the tabloids wallowed in the crime's *lurid* details⟩.

gibe See SCOFF.

gift, **faculty**, **aptitude**, **bent**, **talent**, **genius**, **knack** mean a special ability or unusual capacity for doing something.

Gift often implies special favor by God, nature, or fortune ⟨the *gift* of a beautiful singing voice⟩.

Faculty applies to an innate or acquired ability for a particular accomplishment or function ⟨a rare *faculty* for remembering people's names⟩.

Aptitude implies an innate capacity as well as a natural liking for some activity ⟨a boy with a definite mechanical *aptitude*⟩.

Bent is nearly equal to ***aptitude*** but it stresses inclination perhaps more than ability ⟨a family that has always had an artistic *bent*⟩.

Talent suggests a marked natural ability that needs to be developed ⟨allowed her dancing *talent* to go to waste⟩.

Genius suggests impressive inborn creative ability and often the inner drive that forces its possessor to achieve ⟨the *genius* of Mozart⟩.

Knack implies a comparatively minor but special ability making for ease and dexterity in performance ⟨has the *knack* for making swift, cutting retorts⟩.

gigantic See ENORMOUS.

give, **present**, **donate**, **bestow**, **confer**, **afford** mean to convey to another.

Give, the general term, is applicable to any passing over of anything by any means ⟨*give* alms⟩ ⟨*give* a boy a ride on a pony⟩ ⟨*give* my love to your mother⟩.

Present carries a note of formality and ceremony ⟨*presented* him with the keys to the city⟩.

Donate is likely to imply a publicized giving such as to charity ⟨*donate* a piano to the orphanage⟩.

Bestow implies the conveying of something as a gift and may suggest condescension on the part of the giver ⟨*bestow* unwanted advice⟩.

Confer implies a gracious giving, such as a favor or honor ⟨the Pope *conferred* the rank of cardinal on three bishops⟩.

Afford implies a giving or bestowing usually as a natural or legitimate consequence of thc character of the giver ⟨the trees *afforded* us a welcome shade⟩.

glad, **happy**, **cheerful**, **lighthearted**, **joyful**, **joyous** mean characterized by or expressing the mood of one who is pleased or delighted.

Glad may convey polite conventional expressions of pleasure ⟨we are so *glad* you could come⟩ or it may convey the idea of an actual lifting of spirits, delight, or even elation ⟨a face that makes me *glad*⟩. ***antonym:*** sad

Happy implies a sense of well-being and complete content ⟨nothing made him so *happy* as to be at home with his family⟩. ***antonym:*** unhappy, disconsolate

Cheerful suggests a strong spontaneous flow of good spirits ⟨broke into a *cheerful* song as he strode along⟩. ***antonym:*** cheerless

Lighthearted stresses freedom from worry, care, and discontent ⟨went off to school, *lighthearted* and gay⟩. ***antonym:*** despondent

Joyful usually suggests an emotional reaction to a situation that calls forth rejoicing of happiness or elation ⟨heard the news with a *joyful* heart⟩. ***antonym:*** joyless

Joyous is more likely to apply to something that is by its nature filled with joy or a source of joy ⟨sang song after *joyous* song⟩. ***antonym:*** lugubrious

glance See FLASH.

glare **1.** See GAZE. **2.** See BLAZE.

glaring See FLAGRANT.

gleam See FLASH.

glean See REAP.

glee See MIRTH.

glib See VOCAL 2.

glimmer See FLASH.

glint See FLASH.

glisten See FLASH.

glitter See FLASH.

gloat See GAZE.

gloom See SADNESS.

gloomy **1.** See DARK. **2.** See SULLEN.

glorious See SPLENDID.

glossy See SLEEK.

glow See BLAZE.

glower See FROWN.

glum See SULLEN.

glut See SATIATE.

gluttonous See VORACIOUS.

go **1. Go**, **leave**, **depart**, **quit**, **withdraw**, **retire** mean to move out of or away from the place where one is.

Go is the general term and is commonly used as the simple opposite of *come* ⟨*go* away for the day⟩. ***antonym:*** come

Leave stresses the fact of separation from someone or something ⟨*leave* one's hometown to take a new job⟩.

Depart carries a stronger implication of separation than ***leave*** and is likely to suggest formality ⟨a plane that *departs* this evening⟩. ***antonym:*** arrive, abide, remain

Quit may add to ***leave*** the notion of freeing, ridding, or disentangling from something that burdens or tries ⟨*quit* a dull job⟩.

Withdraw suggests a deliberate removal for good reason ⟨the visitors *withdrew* when the doctor came into the room⟩.

Retire implies distinctively renunciation, retreat, or recession ⟨*retire* from the world to a monastery⟩. ***antonym:*** advance

2. See RESORT.

goad See MOTIVE.

goal See INTENTION.

good-natured See AMIABLE.

gorge See SATIATE.

gorgeous See SPLENDID.

gory See BLOODY.

gossip See REPORT.

gourmand See EPICURE.

gourmet See EPICURE.

govern, **rule** mean to exercise power or authority in controlling others.

Govern implies a keeping in a straight course or smooth operation for the good of the individual or the whole ⟨the British monarch reigns, but the prime minister *governs*⟩.

Rule may imply no more than a possessing of the power to lay down laws or issue commands that must be obeyed but often suggests the exercising of despotic or arbitrary power ⟨the emperor *ruled* with an iron hand⟩.

grab See TAKE.

grace See MERCY.

gracious, **cordial**, **affable**, **genial**, **sociable** mean markedly pleasant and easy in social intercourse.

Gracious implies courtesy and kindly consideration ⟨her *gracious* acceptance of the award⟩. ***antonym:*** ungracious

Cordial stresses warmth and heartiness ⟨our *cordial* host greeted us at the door⟩.

Affable implies easy approachability and readiness to respond pleasantly to conversation or requests or proposals ⟨the dean of students was surprisingly *affable*⟩. ***antonym:*** reserved

Genial stresses cheerfulness and even joviality ⟨the emcee must be a *genial* extrovert⟩. ***antonym:*** caustic, saturnine

Sociable suggests a genuine liking and need for the companionship of others and a readiness to engage in social intercourse ⟨*sociable* people enjoying an ocean cruise⟩. ***antonym:*** unsociable

grand, **magnificent**, **imposing**, **stately**, **majestic**, **grandiose** mean large and impressive.

Grand adds to greatness of size or conception the implications of handsomeness and dignity ⟨a mansion with a *grand* staircase⟩.

Magnificent implies an impressive largeness proportionate to scale without sacrifice of dignity or good taste ⟨*magnificent* paintings and tapestries⟩. ***antonym:*** modest

Imposing implies great size and dignity but stresses impressiveness ⟨large, *imposing* buildings line the avenue⟩. ***antonym:*** unimposing

Stately may suggest impressive size combined with poised dignity, erect bearing, handsome proportions, and ceremonious deliberation of movement ⟨the *stately* procession proceeded into the cathedral⟩.

Majestic combines the implications of ***imposing*** and ***stately*** and adds a suggestion of solemn grandeur ⟨a *majestic* waterfall⟩.

Grandiose implies a size or scope exceeding ordinary experience but is most commonly applied derogatorily to inflated pretension or absurd exaggeration ⟨*grandiose* schemes of world conquest⟩.

grandiose See GRAND.

grant, **concede**, **vouchsafe**, **accord**, **award** mean to give as a favor or a right.

Grant implies the giving to a claimant or petitioner, often a subordinate, of something that could be withheld ⟨*granted* them another month to finish the work⟩.

Concede implies requested or demanded yielding of something reluctantly in response to a rightful or compelling claim ⟨even her critics *concede* she can be charming⟩. ***antonym:*** deny

Vouchsafe implies the granting of something as a courtesy or an act of gracious condescension ⟨the star refused to *vouchsafe* an interview⟩.

Accord implies the giving to another of what is due or proper or in keeping with the other's character or status ⟨*accorded* all the honors befitting a head of state⟩. ***antonym:*** withhold

Award implies the giving of what is deserved or merited after a careful weighing of pertinent factors ⟨*awarded* the company a huge defense contract⟩.

graphic, **vivid**, **picturesque**, **pictorial** mean giving a clear visual impression especially in words.

Graphic stresses the evoking of a clear lifelike image ⟨a *graphic* account of his combat experiences⟩.

Vivid stresses the intense vital quality of either the description or the response to it ⟨a *vivid* re-creation of an exciting history⟩.

Picturesque suggests the presence of features notable for qualities such as distinctness, unfamiliarity, sharp contrast, and charm ⟨Dickens is famous for his *picturesque* characters⟩.

Pictorial implies representation of a vivid picture with emphasis on colors, shapes, and spatial relations ⟨a *pictorial* style of poetry marked by precise, developed imagery⟩.

grasp **1.** See TAKE. **2.** See HOLD.

grasping See COVETOUS.

grateful **1. Grateful**, **thankful** mean feeling or expressing gratitude.

Grateful is employed to express a proper sense of favors received from another person or persons ⟨*grateful* for the company⟩. ***antonym:*** ungrateful

Thankful is often preferred to express one's acknowledgment of divine favor or of what is vaguely felt to be providential ⟨be *thankful* that you were not badly hurt⟩. ***antonym:*** thankless, unthankful

2. See PLEASANT.

gratifying See PLEASANT.

gratuitous See SUPEREROGATORY.

grave See SERIOUS.

great See LARGE.

greedy See COVETOUS.

green See RUDE.

grief See SORROW.

grievance See INJUSTICE.

grieve, **mourn**, **sorrow** mean to feel or express sorrow or grief.

Grieve implies actual mental suffering, whether it is shown outwardly or not and connotes the concentration of one's mind on one's loss, trouble, or cause of distress ⟨still *grieves* for her dead child⟩. ***antonym:*** rejoice

Mourn stresses the outward expressions of grief, sincere or conventional, and usually suggests a specific cause such as the death of someone loved or respected ⟨a nation *mourns* the loss of its hero⟩.

Sorrow, interchangeable with either ***grieve*** or ***mourn*** when sincere mental distress is implied, stresses the sense of regret or loss and of deep sadness and suggests an inner distress rather than outward expressions of grief ⟨*sorrowed* with great dignity⟩.

grim See GHASTLY.

grind See WORK 1.

grip See HOLD.

grisly See GHASTLY.

grit See FORTITUDE.

gross **1.** See COARSE. **2.** See FLAGRANT.

grotesque See FANTASTIC.

ground See BASE *n.*

groundwork See BASE *n.*

group, **cluster**, **bunch**, **parcel**, **lot** mean a collection or assemblage of separate units.

Group implies some unifying relationship and ordinarily a degree of physical closeness ⟨a *group* of people waiting for a bus⟩.

Cluster basically refers to a group of things growing together ⟨a *cluster* of grapes> but it is often extended to persons or things that form small groups especially within larger masses <cataloging *clusters* of stars>.

Bunch is likely to imply a natural or homogeneous association of similar things or persons <a *bunch* of bananas>.

Parcel is likely to convey an impression of disapproval <the whole story was a *parcel* of lies>.

Lot applies to persons or things that are associated or that have to be dealt with as a whole <the books were sold in *lots*>.

grovel See WALLOW.

grown-up See MATURE *adj*.

grudge See MALICE.

gruesome See GHASTLY.

gruff See BLUFF.

guard See DEFEND 1.

guess See CONJECTURE.

guide, **lead**, **steer**, **pilot**, **engineer** mean to direct in a course or show the way to be followed.

Guide implies intimate knowledge of the way and of all its difficulties and dangers <*guided* the other scouts through the darkened cave>. ***antonym:*** misguide

Lead implies a going ahead to show the way and often to keep those that follow under control and in order <the flagship *led* the fleet>. ***antonym:*** follow

Steer implies an ability to keep to a chosen course and stresses the capacity for maneuvering correctly <*steered* the ship through the narrow channel>.

Pilot suggests special skill or knowledge used in guiding over a dangerous, intricate, or complicated course <successfully *piloted* the bill through the Senate>.

Engineer implies guidance by one who finds ways to avoid or overcome difficulties in achieving an end or carrying out a plan <*engineered* his son's election to the governorship>.

guilty See BLAMEWORTHY.

gull See DUPE.

gumption See SENSE.

gush See POUR.

gusto See TASTE 2.

guts See FORTITUDE.

H

habit **1. Habit**, **habitude**, **practice**, **usage**, **custom**, **use**, **wont** mean a way of acting that has become fixed through repetition.

Habit implies a doing unconsciously or without premeditation and often compulsively ⟨the *habit* of constantly tapping his fingers⟩.

Habitude suggests a fixed attitude or usual state of mind ⟨greeted her friends warmly from *habitude*⟩.

Practice suggests an act or method followed with regularity and usually through choice ⟨our *practice* is to honor all major credit cards⟩.

Usage suggests a customary action so generally followed that it has become a social norm ⟨western-style dress is now common *usage* in international business⟩.

Custom applies to a practice or usage so steadily associated with an individual or group as to have almost the force of unwritten law ⟨the *custom* of mourners wearing black at funerals⟩.

Use stresses the fact of customary usage and its distinctive quality ⟨conform to the *uses* of polite society⟩.

Wont applies to an habitual manner, method, or practice distinguishing an individual or group ⟨as was her *wont,* she slept until noon⟩.

2. See PHYSIQUE.

habitual See USUAL.

habitude See HABIT 1.

hackneyed See TRITE.

hale See HEALTHY.

hallow See DEVOTE.

hallucination See DELUSION.

hamper, **trammel**, **clog**, **fetter**, **shackle**, **manacle** mean to hinder or impede in moving, progressing, or acting.

Hamper implies the encumbering or embarrassing effect of any impeding or restraining influence ⟨*hampered* the investigation by refusing to cooperate⟩. ***antonym:*** assist (*as a person*), expedite (*as work*)

Trammel suggests hindering by or as if by or confining within a net ⟨rules that serve only to *trammel* the artist's creativity⟩.

Clog usually implies a slowing by something extraneous or encumbering ⟨feels that free enterprise is *clogged* by government regulation⟩.

Fetter suggests a restraining so severe that freedom to move or progress is almost lost ⟨a nation that is *fettered* by an antiquated class system⟩.

Shackle and ***manacle*** are stronger than ***fetter*** and suggest total loss of the power to move, to progress, or to act ⟨a mind *shackled* by stubborn pride and prejudice⟩ ⟨hatred can *manacle* the soul⟩.

handle **1. Handle**, **manipulate**, **wield** mean to manage dexterously or efficiently.

Handle implies directing an acquired skill to the accomplishment of immediate ends ⟨*handled* the crisis with cool efficiency⟩.

Manipulate implies adroit handling and often suggests the use of craft or fraud to attain one's ends ⟨brutally *manipulates* other people for his own selfish ends⟩.

Wield implies mastery and vigor in handling a tool or a weapon or in exerting influence, authority, or power ⟨the news media *wield* a tremendous influence on the electorate⟩.

2. See TOUCH. **3.** See TREAT.

handsome See BEAUTIFUL.

hanger-on See PARASITE.

hanker See LONG.

hap See CHANCE.

haphazard See RANDOM.

happen, **chance**, **occur**, **transpire** mean to come about.

Happen is the ordinary and general term applying to whatever comes about with or without obvious causation or intention ⟨remembering an incident that *happened* in his childhood⟩.

Chance regularly implies absence of design or apparent lack of causation ⟨a man he *chanced* to know⟩.

Occur stresses presentation to sight or attention ⟨such events, when they *occur*, fascinate the public⟩.

Transpire implies a leaking out so as to become known or apparent ⟨the meeting *transpired* as planned⟩.

happy **1.** See FIT *adj.* **2.** See GLAD. **3.** See LUCKY.

harass See WORRY.

harbinger See FORERUNNER.

harbor, **shelter**, **entertain**, **lodge**, **house**, **board** mean to provide a place, such as one's home, quarters, or confines, where someone or something may stay or be kept for a time.

Harbor implies provision of a place of refuge especially for an evil, hunted, or harmful person or animal ⟨*harbor* thieves⟩ or suggests the holding in the mind of thoughts, wishes, or designs, especially evil or harmful ones ⟨*harbored* thoughts of suicide⟩.

Shelter suggests the place or thing that affords protection or a retreat, especially from such things as the elements, attackers, or a bombardment ⟨*sheltered* themselves from the posse in the hayloft⟩.

Entertain implies the giving of hospitality, often with special efforts to insure pleasure and comfort, to a guest ⟨*entertained* lavishly most nights⟩ or suggests consideration of ideas, notions, or fears ⟨privately *entertained* a theory about the education of children⟩.

Lodge implies the supplying of a place to stay, often temporary ⟨*lodged* the wanderers for the night⟩ or the reception into the mind or any place in which a thing may be deposited or imbedded ⟨a series of events that are *lodged* in her memory⟩.

House implies shelter like that of a building with a roof and walls that offers protection from the weather ⟨found a nest *housed* in a tree⟩.

Board implies the provision of meals or of room and meals for compensation ⟨*boarded* with the Smiths⟩.

hard **1. Hard**, **difficult**, **arduous** mean demanding great exertion or effort.

Hard implies the opposite of all that is easy ⟨farming is *hard* work⟩. ***antonym:*** easy

Difficult implies the presence of obstacles to be surmounted or complications resolved and suggests the need of skill, patience, endurance, or courage ⟨a *difficult* decision requiring much thought⟩. ***antonym:*** simple

Arduous stresses the need for laborious and persevering exertion ⟨the *arduous* task of rebuilding the town⟩. ***antonym:*** light, facile

2. See FIRM.

hardihood See TEMERITY.

hardship See DIFFICULTY.

harm See INJURE.

harmonize See A GREE 3.

harmony **1. Harmony**, **consonance**, **accord**, **concord** mean the state resulting when different things come together without clashing or disagreement.

Harmony implies a beautiful effect achieved by the agreeable interrelation, blending, or arrangement of parts in a complex whole ⟨a resort in splendid *harmony* with its natural setting⟩. ***antonym:*** conflict

Consonance implies the fact or means by which harmony is achieved through coincidence and concurrence ⟨immediate *consonance* of action and custom⟩. ***antonym:*** dissonance (*in music*), discord

Accord may imply personal agreement or goodwill or the absence of friction or ill will ⟨parents and teachers are in *accord* on this issue⟩. ***antonym:*** dissension, strife, antagonism

Concord adds to ***accord*** implications of peace and amity ⟨a planned utopian community in which all would live in *concord*⟩. ***antonym:*** discord

2. See SYMMETRY.

harry See WORRY.

harsh See ROUGH.

harvest See REAP.

haste, hurry, speed, expedition, dispatch mean quickness in movement or action.

Haste implies urgency, undue hastiness, and often rashness in persons ⟨why this headlong *haste* to get married?⟩. ***antonym:*** deliberation

Hurry often has a strong suggestion of agitated bustle or confusion ⟨in the *hurry* of departure she forgot her toothbrush⟩.

Speed suggests swift efficiency in movement or action ⟨exercises to increase your reading *speed*⟩.

Expedition stresses ease or efficiency of performance ⟨made plans with *expedition*⟩. ***antonym:*** procrastination

Dispatch carries a suggestion of promptness in bringing matters to a conclusion ⟨regularly paid her bills with the greatest possible *dispatch*⟩. ***antonym:*** delay

hasty See FAST.

hate, detest, abhor, abominate, loathe mean to feel strong aversion or intense dislike for.

Hate implies an emotional aversion often coupled with enmity or malice ⟨*hated* his former friend with a passion⟩. ***antonym:*** love

Detest suggests violent antipathy or dislike, but without active hostility or malevolence ⟨I *detest* moral cowards⟩. ***antonym:*** adore

Abhor implies a deep, often shuddering repugnance from or as if from fear or horror ⟨child abuse is a crime *abhorred* by all⟩. ***antonym:*** admire

Abominate suggests strong detestation and often moral condemnation ⟨virtually every society *abominates* incest⟩. ***antonym:*** esteem, enjoy

Loathe implies utter disgust and intolerance ⟨*loathed* self-appointed moral guardians⟩. ***antonym:*** dote on

hateful, odious, abhorrent, detestable, abominable mean deserving of or arousing intense dislike.

Hateful applies to something or someone that arouses active hatred and hostility ⟨the *hateful* prospect of another war⟩.

antonym: lovable, sympathetic

Odious applies to that which is disagreeable or offensive or arouses repugnance ⟨you apparently find the plain truth *odious*⟩.

Abhorrent characterizes that which outrages a sense of what is right, decent, just, or honorable ⟨the *abhorrent* practice of stereotyping minority groups⟩.

antonym: admirable

Detestable suggests something deserving extreme contempt ⟨his *detestable* habit of passing the blame to subordinates⟩. ***antonym:*** adorable

Abominable suggests something fiercely condemned as vile or unnatural ⟨the *abominable* living conditions of the plantation slaves⟩. ***antonym:*** laudable, delightful, enjoyable

haughty See PROUD.

haul See PULL.

have, hold, own, possess, enjoy mean to keep, control, retain, or experience as one's own.

Have is a general term carrying no specific implication of a cause or reason for regarding the thing had as one's own ⟨they *have* plenty of money⟩.

Hold suggests stronger control, grasp, or retention and suggests continuity or actual occupation ⟨*held* absolute power over the whole country⟩.

Own implies a natural or legal right to regard as one's property and under one's full control ⟨*own* property in several states⟩.

Possess is often the preferred term when referring to an intangible such as a characteristic, a power, or a quality ⟨*possesses* a first-rate intellect⟩.

Enjoy implies the having of something as one's own or for one's use ⟨a company that *enjoyed* a fine reputation⟩.

havoc See RUIN *n.*

hazard See CHANCE.

hazardous See DANGEROUS.

haze, mist, fog, smog mean an atmospheric condition that deprives the air of its transparency.

Haze implies a diffusion of smoke or dust or light vapor sufficient to blur vision but not to obstruct it ⟨mountains rendered blue by the *haze*⟩.

Mist implies a suspension of water droplets, floating and slowly falling through the air, that impairs but does not cut off vision ⟨hair damp from the *mist*⟩.

Fog implies a denser suspension than a mist, with power to enshroud and to cut off vision more or less completely ⟨visibility reduced to inches by the *fog*⟩.

Smog applies to a haze, mist, or fog made thicker and darker by the smoke and fumes of an industrial area ⟨cast a pall of *smog* over the city⟩.

headlong See PRECIPITATE.

headstrong See UNRULY.

heal See CURE.

healthful, healthy, wholesome, salubrious, salutary mean conducive or favorable to the health or soundness of mind or body.

Healthful implies a beneficial contribution to a healthy condition ⟨*healthful* diet will provide more energy⟩. ***antonym:*** unhealthful

Healthy, like ***healthful***, applies to what promotes good health and vigor ⟨a *healthy* climate⟩. ***antonym:*** unhealthful

Wholesome applies to what benefits, builds up, or sustains physically, mentally, or spiritually or to what is not detrimental to health or well-being ⟨*wholesome* foods⟩ ⟨the movie is *wholesome* family entertainment⟩. ***antonym:*** noxious, unwholesome

Salubrious applies chiefly to the helpful effects of climate or air that is devoid of harshness or extremes ⟨the *salubrious* climate of the American Southwest⟩. ***antonym:*** insalubrious

Salutary describes something corrective or beneficially effective, even though it may in itself be unpleasant ⟨a *salutary* warning that resulted in increased production⟩. ***antonym:*** deleterious, unsalutary

healthy 1. Healthy, sound, wholesome, robust, hale, well mean enjoying or indicative of good health.

Healthy implies the possession of full strength and vigor or freedom from signs of disease or may apply to what manifests or indicates these conditions ⟨the doctor pronounced the whole family *healthy*⟩. ***antonym:*** unhealthy

Sound emphasizes the absence of disease, weakness, or malfunction ⟨an examination showed his heart to be *sound*⟩.

Wholesome implies appearance and behavior indicating soundness and balance or equilibrium ⟨she looks especially *wholesome* in her tennis togs⟩.

Robust implies the opposite of all that is delicate or sickly and connotes vigor and health shown by muscularity, fresh color, a strong voice, and an ability to work long and hard ⟨a lively, *robust* little boy⟩. ***antonym:*** frail, feeble

Hale applies particularly to robustness in old age ⟨still *hale* at the age of eighty⟩. ***antonym:*** infirm

Well implies merely freedom from disease or illness ⟨she has never been a *well* person⟩. ***antonym:*** ill, unwell

2. See HEALTHFUL.

hearsay See REPORT.

hearten See ENCOURAGE.

heartfelt See SINCERE.

hearty See SINCERE.

heave See LIFT.

heavy, **weighty**, **ponderous**, **cumbrous**, **cumbersome** mean having great weight.

Heavy implies that something has greater density or thickness or sometimes power than the average of its kind or class ⟨a *heavy* child for his age⟩. ***antonym:*** light

Weighty suggests actual as well as relative heaviness ⟨really *weighty* parcels are shipped by freight⟩ or implies a momentous or highly important character ⟨pondered *weighty* matters late into the night⟩. ***antonym:*** weightless

Ponderous implies having great weight because of size and massiveness with resulting great inertia and clumsiness ⟨*ponderous* galleons were outmaneuvered by smaller vessels⟩.

Cumbrous and ***cumbersome*** imply heaviness and massive bulkiness that make a thing difficult to grasp, move, carry, or manipulate ⟨abandoned the *cumbrous* furniture rather than move it⟩ ⟨the old cameras were *cumbersome* and inconvenient⟩.

heckle See BAIT.

hector See BAIT.

height, **altitude**, **elevation** mean vertical distance either between the top and bottom of something or between a base and something above it.

Height refers to any vertical distance whether great or small ⟨a wall two meters in *height*⟩. ***antonym:*** depth

Altitude refers to vertical distance above the surface of the earth or above sea level or to the vertical distance above the horizon in angular measurement ⟨fly at an *altitude* of 10,000 meters⟩.

Elevation is used especially in reference to vertical height above sea level on land ⟨Denver is a city with a high *elevation*⟩.

heighten See INTENSIFY.

heinous See OUTRAGEOUS.

help **1. Help**, **aid**, **assist** mean to supply what is needed to accomplish an end.

Help carries a strong implication of advance toward an objective ⟨*helped* to find a cure for the disease⟩. ***antonym:*** hinder

Aid suggests the need of help or relief and so imputes weakness to the one aided and strength to the one aiding ⟨an army of volunteers *aided* the flood victims⟩.

Assist suggests a secondary role in the assistant or a subordinate character in the assistance ⟨*assisted* the chief surgeon during the operation⟩.

2. See IMPROVE.

helper See ASSISTANT.

hence See THEREFORE.

herald See FORERUNNER.

hereditary See INNATE.

heritage, **inheritance**, **patrimony**, **birthright** mean something which one receives or is entitled to receive by succession, as from a parent or predecessor.

Heritage may apply to anything that is passed on not only to an heir or heirs but to the succeeding generation or generations ⟨want, the *heritage* of waste⟩.

Inheritance refers to what passes from parents to children, such as money, property, or character traits, or to the fact or means of inheriting ⟨brown eyes, her *inheritance* from her father⟩.

Patrimony applies to the money or property inherited from one's father, but also generally to one's ancestral inheritance ⟨the intellectual *patrimony* of the Renaissance⟩.

Birthright generally implies the rights to which one is entitled by nativity, as by being a native-born citizen or a descendant of a particular family ⟨honor that was their *birthright*⟩.

heroism, **valor**, **prowess**, **gallantry** mean conspicuously courageous behavior.

Heroism implies superlative courage especially in fulfilling a high purpose against odds ⟨the boy's outstanding act of *heroism* during the fire⟩. ***antonym:*** pusillanimity

Valor implies illustrious bravery and vigorous audacity in fighting ⟨awarded the army's highest honor for *valor* in battle⟩. ***antonym:*** pusillanimity, pusillanimousness

Prowess stresses skill as well as bravery in both arms and other pursuits ⟨demonstrated her *prowess* with a bow and arrow⟩.

Gallantry implies dash and spirit as well as courage and an indifference to danger or hardship ⟨special forces with a proud tradition of *gallantry*⟩. ***antonym:*** dastardliness

hesitant See DISINCLINED.

hesitate, **waver**, **vacillate**, **falter** mean to show irresolution or uncertainty.

Hesitate implies pausing before deciding or acting or choosing ⟨*hesitated* before answering the question⟩.

Waver implies hesitation after seeming to reach a decision and so connotes weakness or a retreat ⟨*wavered* in his support of the rebels⟩.

Vacillate implies prolonged hesitation from inability to reach a firm decision and suggests the play of opposing factors that results in indecision ⟨*vacillated* until it was too late and events were out of control⟩.

Falter implies a wavering or stumbling and often connotes nervousness, lack of courage, or outright fear ⟨never once *faltered* during her testimony⟩.

heterogeneous See MISCELLANEOUS.

hide, **conceal**, **screen**, **secrete**, **bury** mean to withhold or withdraw from sight or observation.

Hide may or may not suggest intent ⟨a house *hidden* by trees⟩.

Conceal usually implies intent and often specifically implies a refusal to divulge ⟨*concealed* the weapon in a pocket⟩. ***antonym:*** reveal

Screen implies an interposing of something that shelters and hides or merely obscures ⟨*screened* her true identity from her colleagues⟩.

Secrete suggests a depositing, often by stealth, in a place screened from view or unknown to others ⟨*secreted* the cocaine in the hold of the ship⟩.

Bury implies a covering with or submerging in something that hides completely ⟨*buried* the note in a pile of papers⟩.

hideous See UGLY.

high, **tall**, **lofty** mean above the average in height.

High implies marked extension upward and is applied chiefly to things which rise from a base or foundation ⟨a *high* hill⟩ or are placed at a conspicuous height above a lower level ⟨a *high* ceiling⟩. ***antonym:*** low

Tall applies to what grows or rises high by comparison with others of its kind and usually implies relative narrowness ⟨a *tall* thin man⟩.

Lofty suggests great or imposing altitude ⟨*lofty* mountain peaks⟩.

hilarity See MIRTH.

hinder, **impede**, **obstruct**, **block** mean to interfere with the activity or progress of.

Hinder stresses harmful or annoying delay or interference with progress ⟨the rain *hindered* our climbing⟩. ***antonym:*** further

Impede implies making forward progress difficult by clogging, hampering, or fettering ⟨tight clothing *impeded* my movement⟩. ***antonym:*** assist, promote

Obstruct implies interfering with something in motion or in progress by the often intentional placing of obstacles in the way ⟨the view was *obstructed* by billboards⟩.

Block implies the complete obstructing of passage or progress ⟨boulders *blocked* the road⟩.

hint See SUGGEST.

hire, **let**, **lease**, **rent**, **charter** mean to engage or grant for use at a price.

Hire implies the act of engaging or taking for use ⟨we *hired* a car for the summer⟩.

Let suggests the granting of use ⟨decided to *let* the cottage to a young couple⟩.

Lease strictly implies a letting under the terms of a contract but is often applied to the act of hiring on a lease ⟨the diplomat *leased* an apartment for a year⟩.

Rent stresses the payment of money for the full use of property and may imply either hiring or letting ⟨instead of buying a house, they decided to *rent*⟩.

Charter applies to the hiring or letting of a public vessel or vehicle usually for exclusive use ⟨*charter* a bus to go to the game⟩.

history, **chronicle**, **annals** mean a written record of events.

History implies more than a mere recital of occurrences and regularly entails order and purpose in narration and usually a degree of interpretation of the events recorded ⟨studied American *history*⟩.

Chronicle applies strictly to any recital of events in chronological order without interpretation ⟨recited a lengthy *chronicle* of their disastrous trip⟩.

Annals tends to emphasize the progress or succession of events from year to year and need not imply a discursive treatment or a continued narrative ⟨kept meticulous *annals* of the senate's activities⟩.

histrionic See DRAMATIC.

hit See STRIKE.

hoax See DUPE.

hoist See LIFT.

hold *vb* **1.** See CONTAIN. **2.** See HAVE.

hold *n* **Hold**, **grip**, **grasp**, **clutch** mean the power of getting or keeping in possession or control.

Hold is widely applicable and may imply mere possession or control, or possession or control firmly maintained ⟨tried to keep a *hold* on his temper⟩.

Grip regularly suggests a firm or tenacious hold ⟨had a firm *grip* on the reins of power⟩.

Grasp differs from ***grip*** chiefly in suggesting a power to reach out and get possession or control of something ⟨success was almost within his *grasp*⟩.

Clutch implies a seizing and holding with or as if with the avidity or rapacity of a bird of prey ⟨stayed out of the extortioner's *clutches*⟩.

hollow See VAIN.

homage See HONOR.

homely See PLAIN.

homogeneous See SIMILAR.

honest See UPRIGHT.

honesty, **honor**, **integrity**, **probity** mean uprightness of character or action.

Honesty implies refusal to lie, steal, or deceive in any way ⟨a politician of scrupulous *honesty*⟩. ***antonym:*** dishonesty

Honor suggests an active or anxious regard for the standards of one's profession, calling, or position ⟨a keen sense of *honor* in business matters⟩. ***antonym:*** dishonor, dishonorableness

Integrity implies trustworthiness and incorruptibility to a degree that one is incapable of being false to a trust, responsibility, or pledge ⟨her unimpeachable *integrity* as a journalist⟩. ***antonym:*** duplicity

Probity implies tried and proven honesty or integrity ⟨a judge with a reputation for *probity*⟩.

honor **1. Honor**, **homage**, **reverence**, **deference** mean respect and esteem shown to another.

Honor may apply to the recognition of one's right to great respect or to any expression of such recognition ⟨an *honor* just to be nominated⟩. ***antonym:*** dishonor

Homage adds the implication of accompanying praise or tributes or esteem from those who owe allegiance ⟨for centuries dramatists have paid *homage* to Shakespeare⟩.

Reverence implies profound respect mingled with love, devotion, or awe ⟨have the greatest *reverence* for my father⟩.

Deference implies a yielding or submitting to another's judgment or preference out of respect or reverence ⟨refused to show any *deference* to senior staffers⟩. ***antonym:*** disrespect

2. See HONESTY.

honorable See UPRIGHT.

hope See EXPECT.

hopeless See DESPONDENT.

horde See CROWD.

horrible See FEARFUL 2.

horrific See FEARFUL 2.

horrify See DISMAY.

horror See FEAR.

hostility See ENMITY.

hound See BAIT.

house See HARBOR.

hubbub See DIN.

hue See COLOR.

huff See OFFENSE 1.

huge See ENORMOUS.

hullabaloo See DIN.

humble *adj* **Humble**, **meek**, **modest**, **lowly** mean lacking all signs of pride, aggressiveness, or self-assertiveness.

Humble may suggest a virtuous absence of pride or vanity or it may suggest undue self-depreciation or humiliation ⟨a quiet life as a simple, *humble* parish priest⟩. ***antonym:*** conceited

Meek may suggest mildness or gentleness of temper or it may connote undue submissiveness ⟨the refugees were *meek* and grateful for whatever they got⟩. ***antonym:*** arrogant

Modest implies a lack of boastfulness or conceit, without any implication of abjectness ⟨sincerely *modest* about her singing talents⟩. ***antonym:*** ambitious

Lowly stresses lack of pretentiousness ⟨a volunteer willing to accept the *lowliest* hospital duties⟩. ***antonym:*** pompous

humble *vb* See ABASE.

humbug See IMPOSTURE.

humid See WET.

humiliate See ABASE.

humor *vb* See INDULGE.

humor *n* **1.** See WIT. **2.** See MOOD.

humorous See WITTY.

hunger See LONG.

hurl See THROW.

hurry See HASTE.

hurt See INJURE.

hyperbole See EXAGGERATION.

hypercritical See CRITICAL.

hypocritical, **sanctimonious**, **pharisaical**, **canting** mean affecting more virtue or religious devotion than one actually possesses.

Hypocritical implies an appearance of goodness, sincerity, or piety by one who is deficient in these qualities or who is corrupt, dishonest, or irreligious ⟨had no use for such *hypocritical* gestures⟩. ***antonym:*** sincere

Sanctimonious implies an affectation or merely outward show of holiness or piety ⟨made a *sanctimonious* appearance in church every week⟩. ***antonym:*** unsanctimonious

Pharisaical stresses close adherence to outward forms and a censorious attitude toward others' defects in these respects, coupled with little real concern for spiritual matters ⟨always under the gaze of *pharisaical* neighbors⟩.

Canting implies the use of religious or pietistic language without evidence of underlying religious feeling ⟨a *canting* moralist⟩.

hypothesis, **theory**, **law** mean a formulation of a general or abstract principle that is derived from observed data and that explains that data.

Hypothesis implies insufficiency of evidence to provide more than a tentative explanation ⟨an *hypothesis* regarding the extinction of the dinosaurs⟩.

Theory implies a greater range of evidence and greater likelihood of truth than ***hypothesis*** ⟨the *theory* of evolution⟩.

Law emphasizes certainty and truth and implies a statement about order and relationships that has been found to be invariable under a particular set of conditions ⟨the *law* of gravitation⟩.

hysteria See MANIA.

I

idea, **concept**, **conception**, **thought**, **notion**, **impression** mean what exists in the mind as a representation or as a formulation.

Idea may apply to a mental image or formulation of something seen or known or imagined, to a pure abstraction, or to something assumed or vaguely sensed ⟨a mind filled with innovative *ideas*⟩.

Concept may apply to the idea formed after consideration of instances of a category or, more broadly, to any widely accepted idea of what a thing ought to be ⟨a society with no *concept* of private property⟩.

Conception, often interchangeable with ***concept***, stresses the process of imagining or formulating and often applies to a peculiar or individual idea rather than to a widely held one ⟨the writer's *conception* of such a situation⟩.

Thought is likely to suggest the result of reflecting, reasoning, or meditating rather than of imagining ⟨commit your *thoughts* to paper⟩.

Notion suggests an idea not much resolved by analysis or reflection and may suggest the tentative, capricious, or accidental ⟨the oddest *notions* fly in and out of her head⟩.

Impression applies to an idea or notion resulting immediately from some external stimulation ⟨the first *impression* is of soaring height⟩.

ideal See MODEL.

identical See SAME.

identification See RECOGNITION.

idiom See PHRASE.

idiosyncrasy See ECCENTRICITY.

idle 1. See INACTIVE. **2.** See VAIN.

ignite See LIGHT.

ignoble See MEAN.

ignominy See DISGRACE.

ignorant, **illiterate**, **unlettered**, **untutored**, **unlearned** mean not having knowledge.

Ignorant may imply a general condition ⟨an *ignorant* fool⟩ or it may apply to lack of knowledge or awareness of a particular thing ⟨he's *ignorant* of nuclear physics⟩. ***antonym:*** cognizant, conversant, informed

Illiterate applies to either an absolute or a relative inability to read and write ⟨much of that country's population is still *illiterate*⟩. ***antonym:*** literate

Unlettered implies ignorance of the knowledge gained by being educated or by reading ⟨a literary reference that is meaningless to the *unlettered*⟩. ***antonym:*** educated, lettered

Untutored may imply lack of schooling in the arts and ways of civilization ⟨strange megalithic monuments left by an *untutored* people⟩.

Unlearned suggests ignorance of advanced or scholarly subjects ⟨a poet who speaks to the *unlearned*⟩. ***antonym:*** erudite, learned

ignore See NEGLECT.

ilk See TYPE.

ill See BAD.

illegal See UNLAWFUL.

illegitimate See UNLAWFUL.

ill-favored See UGLY.

illicit See UNLAWFUL.

illiterate See IGNORANT.

illusion See DELUSION.

illusory See APPARENT.

illustration See INSTANCE.

illustrious See FAMOUS.

ill will See MALICE.

imaginary, **fanciful**, **visionary**, **fantastic**, **chimerical**, **quixotic** mean unreal or unbelievable.

Imaginary applies to something which is fictitious and purely the product of one's imagination ⟨a chronic sufferer of several *imaginary* illnesses⟩. ***antonym:*** actual, real

Fanciful suggests something affected or created by the free play of the imagination ‹the *fanciful* characters created by Lewis Carroll›. ***antonym:*** realistic

Visionary applies to something that seems real and practical to its conceiver but is impractical or incapable of realization ‹*visionary* schemes for creating a rural utopia›.

Fantastic implies fanciful incredibility or strangeness beyond belief ‹a *fantastic* world inhabited by prehistoric monsters›.

Chimerical applies to what is wildly or fantastically visionary or improbable ‹*chimerical* plans for restoring the British Empire›. ***antonym:*** feasible

Quixotic implies a devotion to romantic or chivalrous ideals unrestrained by ordinary prudence and common sense ‹the *quixotic* notion that absolute equality is attainable›.

imagine See THINK 1.

imbibe See ABSORB.

imbue See INFUSE.

imitate See COPY.

immediate See DIRECT *adj*.

immense See ENORMOUS.

immoderate See EXCESSIVE.

immoral, **unmoral**, **nonmoral**, **amoral** mean not moral.

Immoral implies a positive and active opposition to what is moral and may designate whatever is counter to accepted ethical principles or the dictates of conscience ‹*immoral* ideas and conduct›. ***antonym:*** moral

Unmoral implies a lack of ethical perception and moral awareness or a disregard of moral principles ‹possessed the *unmoral* conscience of a newborn baby›.

Nonmoral implies that the thing described is patently outside the sphere where moral judgments are applicable ‹whether your car runs or not is a *nonmoral* issue›.

Amoral is often applied to something that is not customarily exempted from moral judgment ‹a review that called the film *amoral*›.

impair See INJURE.

impartial See FAIR.

impassioned, **passionate**, **ardent**, **fervent**, **fervid**, **perfervid** mean showing intense feeling.

Impassioned implies warmth and intensity without violence and suggests fluent verbal or artistic expression ‹an *impassioned* plea for international understanding›. ***antonym:*** unimpassioned

Passionate implies great vehemence and often violence and wasteful diffusion of emotion ‹*passionate* denunciations of American arrogance›. ***antonym:*** dispassionate

Ardent implies an intense degree of zeal, devotion, or enthusiasm ‹an *ardent* admirer of the novels of Jane Austen›. ***antonym:*** cool

Fervent stresses sincerity and steadiness of emotional warmth or zeal ‹*fervent* Christians on a pilgrimage›.

Fervid suggests warmly spontaneous and often feverishly urgent emotion ‹*fervid* love letters that suggested mental unbalance›.

Perfervid implies the expression of exaggerated, insincere, or overwrought feelings ‹wary of such *perfervid* expresssions of selfless patriotism›.

impassive, **stoic**, **phlegmatic**, **apathetic**, **stolid** mean unresponsive to something that might normally excite interest or emotion.

Impassive stresses the absence of any external sign of emotion in action or facial expression ‹just sat there with an *impassive* look›. ***antonym:*** responsive

Stoic implies an apparent indifference to pleasure or especially to pain, often as a matter of principle or self-discipline ‹remained resolutely *stoic* even in the face of adversity›.

Phlegmatic implies a temperament or constitution hard to arouse ‹a *phlegmatic* person immune to amorous advances›.

Apathetic may imply a puzzling or deplorable indifference or inertness ⟨charitable appeals met an *apathetic* response⟩. ***antonym:*** alert

Stolid implies an habitual absence of interest, responsiveness, or curiosity about anything beyond an accustomed routine ⟨a *stolid* woman, wedded to routine⟩.

impeach See ACCUSE.

impede See HINDER.

impel See MOVE.

imperative See MASTERFUL.

imperious See MASTERFUL.

impertinent, **officious**, **meddlesome**, **intrusive**, **obtrusive** mean given to thrusting oneself into the affairs of another.

Impertinent implies exceeding the bounds of propriety in showing interest or curiosity or in offering advice ⟨a little brat asking *impertinent* questions⟩.

Officious implies the offering of services or attentions that are unwelcome or annoying ⟨an *officious* salesman followed me outside⟩.

Meddlesome stresses an annoying and usually prying interference in others' affairs ⟨*meddlesome* old gossips with nothing to do⟩.

Intrusive implies a tactless or otherwise objectionable curiosity about or a thrusting of oneself into the company or affairs of others ⟨an *intrusive* interruption in our conversation⟩. ***antonym:*** retiring, unintrusive

Obtrusive stresses improper or offensive conspicuousness of interfering actions ⟨*obtrusive* relatives monopolizing the wedding photographs⟩. ***antonym:*** unobtrusive, shy

imperturbable See COOL.

impetuous See PRECIPITATE.

implant, **inculcate**, **instill**, **inseminate**, **infix** mean to introduce into the mind.

Implant implies teaching that makes for permanence of what is taught ⟨*implanted* an enthusiasm for reading in her students⟩.

Inculcate implies persistent or repeated efforts to impress on the mind ⟨*inculcated* in him high moral standards⟩.

Instill stresses gradual, gentle imparting of knowledge over a long period of time ⟨*instill* traditional values in your children⟩.

Inseminate applies to a sowing of ideas in many minds so that they spread through a class or nation ⟨*inseminated* an unquestioning faith in technology⟩.

Infix stresses firmly inculcating a habit of thought ⟨*infixed* a chronic cynicism⟩.

implement, **tool**, **instrument**, **appliance**, **utensil** mean a relatively simple device for performing work.

Implement may apply to anything necessary to perform a task ⟨lawn and gardening *implements*⟩.

Tool suggests an implement adapted to facilitate a definite kind of stage of work and suggests the need of skill ⟨a carpenter's *tools*⟩.

Instrument suggests a tool or device capable of performing delicate or precise work or one precisely adapted to the end it serves ⟨the surgeon's *instruments*⟩.

Appliance refers to a tool or instrument utilizing a power source and often adapted to a special purpose ⟨modern *appliances* that take the drudgery out of housework⟩.

Utensil applies to a device, tool, or vessel, usually with a particular function, used in domestic work or some routine unskilled activity ⟨knives, graters, and other kitchen *utensils*⟩.

implore See BEG.

imply **1.** See SUGGEST. **2.** See INCLUDE.

import **1.** See MEANING. **2.** See IMPORTANCE.

importance, **consequence**, **moment**, **weight**, **significance**, **import** mean a quality or aspect that is felt to be of great worth, value, or influence.

Importance implies a judgment by which superior worth or influence is ascribed to something or someone ⟨there are no cities of *importance* in this area⟩. ***antonym:*** unimportance

Consequence may imply importance in social rank but more generally implies importance because of probable or possible effects ⟨whatever style you choose is of little *consequence*⟩.

Moment implies conspicuous or self-evident consequence ⟨a decision of very great *moment*⟩.

Weight implies a judgment of the immediate relevant importance of something that must be taken into account or that may seriously affect an outcome ⟨idle chitchat of no particular *weight*⟩.

Significance implies a quality or character that should mark a thing as important or of consequence but that may or may not be self-evident or recognized ⟨time would reveal the *significance* of that casual act⟩. ***antonym:*** insignificance

Import is essentially interchangeable with **significance** ⟨a speech of enormous *import*⟩.

importune See BEG.

impose See DICTATE.

imposing See GRAND.

imposture, **fraud**, **sham**, **fake**, **humbug**, **counterfeit** mean a thing which pretends to be one thing in nature, character, or quality but is really another.

Imposture applies to any situation in which a spurious object or performance is passed off as genuine ⟨the movie's claim of social concern is an *imposture*⟩.

Fraud usually implies a deliberate perversion of truth but, applied to a person, may imply no more than pretense and hypocrisy ⟨a diary that was exposed as a *fraud*⟩.

Sham applies to a fraudulent but close imitation of a real thing or action ⟨condemned the election as a *sham* and a travesty of democracy⟩.

Fake implies an imitation of or substitution for the genuine but does not necessarily imply dishonesty as a motive ⟨these are *fakes*, the real jewels being in the vault⟩.

Humbug suggests elaborate pretense that may be deliberate or may result from self-deceit ⟨the diet business is populated with *humbugs*⟩.

Counterfeit applies especially to the close imitation of something valuable ⟨20-dollar bills that were *counterfeits*⟩.

impotent **1.** See POWERLESS. **2.** See STERILE.

impoverish See DEPLETE.

impregnate See SOAK.

impress See AFFECT.

impression See IDEA.

impressive See MOVING.

impromptu See EXTEMPORANEOUS.

improper See INDECOROUS.

improve, **better**, **help**, **ameliorate** mean to make more acceptable or bring nearer some standard.

Improve, the general term, applies to what is capable of being made better whether it is good or bad ⟨measures to *improve* the quality of medical care⟩. ***antonym:*** impair, worsen

Better, more vigorous and homely than ***improve***, differs little from it in meaning ⟨immigrants hoping to *better* their lot in life⟩. ***antonym:*** worsen

Help implies a bettering that still leaves room for improvement ⟨a coat of paint would *help* that house⟩.

Ameliorate implies making more tolerable or acceptable conditions that are hard to endure ⟨a cancerous condition that cannot be *ameliorated* by chemotherapy⟩. ***antonym:*** worsen, deteriorate

improvised See EXTEMPORANEOUS.

impudent See SHAMELESS.

impugn See DENY.

impulse See MOTIVE.

impulsive See SPONTANEOUS.

impute See ASCRIBE.

inactive, **idle**, **inert**, **passive**, **supine** mean not engaged in work or activity.

Inactive applies to anyone or anything not in action or in use or at work ⟨a playwright who's been *inactive* for several years⟩. ***antonym:*** active, live

Idle applies to persons, their powers, or their implements that are not busy or occupied ⟨tractors were *idle* in the fields⟩. ***antonym:*** busy

Inert as applied to things implies powerlessness to move or to affect other things ⟨*inert* ingredients in drugs⟩; as applied to persons it suggests an inherent or habitual indisposition to activity ⟨an *inert* citizenry uninterested in social change⟩. ***antonym:*** dynamic, animated

Passive implies immobility or lack of normally expected response to an external force or influence and often suggests deliberate submissiveness or self-control ⟨a *passive* individual incapable of strong emotion⟩. ***antonym:*** active

Supine applies only to persons and commonly implies abject or cowardly inertia or passivity as a result of apathy or indolence ⟨remained *supine* in the face of verbal abuse⟩. ***antonym:*** alert

inane See INSIPID.

inaugurate See BEGIN.

inborn See INNATE.

inbred See INNATE.

incense See FRAGRANCE.

incentive See MOTIVE.

inception See ORIGIN.

incessant See CONTINUAL.

incest See ADULTERY.

incident See OCCURRENCE.

incidental See ACCIDENTAL 2.

incisive, **trenchant**, **clear-cut**, **cutting**, **biting**, **crisp** mean having or showing or suggesting a keen alertness of mind.

Incisive implies a power to impress the mind by directness and decisiveness ⟨an *incisive* command that left no room for doubt⟩.

Trenchant implies an energetic cutting or probing that defines differences sharply and clearly or reveals what is hidden ⟨a *trenchant* critic of political pretensions⟩.

Clear-cut suggests the absence of any blurring, ambiguity, or uncertainty of statement or analysis ⟨made a *clear-cut* distinction between the two military actions⟩.

Cutting implies a ruthless accuracy or directness that is wounding to the feelings and may suggest sarcasm, harshness, or asperity ⟨makes the most *cutting* remarks with that quiet voice⟩.

Biting adds a greater implication of harsh vehemence or ironic force and suggests a power to impress deeply the mind or memory ⟨a *biting* commentary on the election⟩.

Crisp suggests both incisiveness and vigorous terseness ⟨jurors were impressed by the witness's *crisp* answers⟩.

incite, **instigate**, **abet**, **foment** mean to spur to action or to exite into activity.

Incite stresses a stirring up and urging on and may or may not imply active prompting ⟨charged with *inciting* a riot⟩. ***antonym:*** restrain

Instigate definitely implies responsibility for the initiating of another's action and often connotes underhandedness or evil intention ⟨*instigated* a conspiracy against the commander⟩.

Abet implies both the assisting and encouraging of some action already begun ⟨accused of aiding and *abetting* the enemy⟩. ***antonym:*** deter

Foment implies a persistence in goading in regard to something already in seething activity ⟨years of *fomenting* kept the flame of rebellion burning⟩. ***antonym:*** quell

incline 1. See SLANT. **2. Incline, bias, dispose, predispose** mean to influence one to have or take an attitude toward something.

Incline implies a tendency to favor one of two or more actions or conclusions ⟨*inclined* to do nothing for the moment⟩. ***antonym:*** disincline, indispose

Bias suggests a settled and predictable leaning in one direction and connotes unfair prejudice ⟨*biased* against young urban professionals⟩.

Dispose suggests an affecting of one's mood or temper so as to incline one toward something or someone ⟨the sunny day *disposed* her to think more positively⟩. ***antonym:*** indispose

Predispose implies the operation of a disposing influence well in advance of the opportunity to manifest itself ⟨fictional violence *predisposes* them to accept violence in real life⟩.

include, **comprehend**, **embrace**, **involve**, **imply** mean to contain within as a part or portion of the whole.

Include suggests that the thing contained forms a constituent, component, or subordinate part of a larger whole ⟨the price of dinner *includes* dessert⟩. ***antonym:*** exclude

Comprehend implies that something comes within the scope or range of a statement, definition, or concept ⟨his notion of manners *comprehends* more than just table etiquette⟩.

Embrace implies a reaching out and gathering of separate items into or within a whole ⟨her faith *embraces* both Christian and non-Christian beliefs⟩.

Involve suggests an entangling of a thing with a whole, often as a natural or inevitable cause or consequence ⟨a procedural change that will *involve* more work for everyone⟩.

Imply, otherwise close to ***involve***, suggests that something's presence can be inferred with more or less certainty from a hint ⟨smoke often *implies* fire⟩.

inconstant, **fickle**, **capricious**, **mercurial**, **unstable** mean lacking firmness or steadiness in such things as purpose or devotion.

Inconstant implies an incapacity for steadiness and an inherent tendency to change ⟨the supply of materials was too *inconstant* to depend on⟩. ***antonym:*** constant

Fickle suggests unreliability because of perverse changeability and incapacity for steadfastness ⟨performers discover how *fickle* the public can be⟩. ***antonym:*** constant, true

Capricious suggests motivation by sudden whim or fancy and stresses unpredictability ⟨an utterly *capricious* manner of selecting candidates⟩. ***antonym:*** steadfast

Mercurial implies a rapid changeability in mood, especially between depression and elation ⟨so *mercurial* in temperament that no one knew what to expect⟩. ***antonym:*** saturnine

Unstable implies an incapacity for remaining in a fixed position or on a steady course and, when applied to persons, suggests a lack of emotional balance ⟨in love she was impulsive and *unstable*⟩. ***antonym:*** stable

increase, **enlarge**, **augment**, **multiply** mean to make or become greater or more numerous.

Increase used intransitively implies progressive growth in size, amount, or intensity ⟨his waistline *increased* with age⟩; used transitively it may imply simple not necessarily progressive addition ⟨*increased* her land holdings⟩. ***antonym:*** decrease

Enlarge implies an expanding or extending that makes something greater in size or capacity ⟨*enlarged* the restaurant to its present capacity⟩.

Augment implies an addition in size, extent, number, or intensity to what is already well grown or well developed ⟨an inheritance that only *augmented* his fortune⟩. ***antonym:*** abate

Multiply implies increase in number by natural generation, by splitting, or by indefinite repetition of a process ⟨with each tampering the problems *multiplied*⟩.

incredulity See UNBELIEF.

inculcate See IMPLANT.

incur, **contract**, **catch** mean to bring something, usually unwanted, upon oneself.

Incur usually implies responsibility for the acts that bring about what is incurred ⟨a couple who adopts a child *incurs* a great responsibility⟩.

Contract more strongly implies effective acquisition but often no definite responsibility for the act of acquiring; it also suggests a meeting between two things that permits transmission of something from one to the other ⟨*contract* a disease⟩.

Catch implies the acqui ring of infection and in its broader use implies an acquiring through personal contact or association ⟨*caught* their interest⟩.

incurious See INDIFFERENT.

indecent See INDECOROUS.

indecorous, **improper**, **unseemly**, **indecent**, **unbecoming**, **indelicate** mean not conforming to what is accepted as right, fitting, or in good taste.

Indecorous suggests a violation of accepted standards of good manners ⟨your *indecorous* manners marred the wedding reception⟩. ***antonym:*** decorous

Improper applies to a broader range of transgressions of rules not only of social behavior but of ethical practice or logical procedure or prescribed method ⟨the *improper* use of campaign contributions⟩. ***antonym:*** proper

Unseemly adds a suggestion of special inappropriateness to a situation or an offensiveness to good taste ⟨married again with *unseemly* haste⟩. ***antonym:*** seemly

Indecent implies great unseemliness or gross offensiveness especially in referring to sexual matters ⟨a scene judged *indecent* by the censors⟩. ***antonym:*** decent

Unbecoming suggests behavior or language that is felt to be beneath or unsuited to one's character or status ⟨conduct *unbecoming* an officer⟩. ***antonym:*** becoming, seemly

Indelicate implies a lack of modesty or of tact or of refined perception of feeling ⟨*indelicate* expressions for bodily functions⟩. ***antonym:*** delicate, refined

indefatigable, **tireless**, **untiring**, **unwearied**, **unflagging** mean capable of prolonged and strenuous effort.

Indefatigable implies persistent and unremitting activity or effort ⟨an *indefatigable* champion of women's rights⟩. ***antonym:*** fatigable

Tireless implies a remarkable energy or stamina ⟨honored as a teacher of *tireless* industry and limitless patience⟩.

Untiring implies the extraordinary ability to go on continuously and without interruption ⟨*untiring* researchers who fight against the disease⟩.

Unwearied stresses the apparent absence of any sign of fatigue in the person or thing concerned ⟨detectives remain *unwearied* in their search for the killer⟩.

Unflagging stresses the absence of any diminution or relaxation in one's efforts or powers ⟨an *unflagging* attention to detail⟩. ***antonym:*** flagging

indelicate See INDECOROUS.

indemnify See PAY.

independent See FREE.

indict See ACCUSE.

indifferent **1. Indifferent**, **unconcerned**, **incurious**, **aloof**, **detached**, **disinterested** mean not showing or feeling interest.

Indifferent implies neutrality of attitude from lack of inclination, preference, or prejudice ⟨*indifferent* to the dictates of fashion⟩. ***antonym:*** avid

Unconcerned suggests such indifference as arises from unconsciousness or from a lack of sensitivity or regard for others' needs or troubles ⟨*unconcerned* about the problems of the homeless⟩. ***antonym:*** concerned

Incurious implies an inability to take a normal interest due to dullness of mind or to self-centeredness ⟨*incurious* about the world beyond their village⟩. ***antonym:*** curious, inquisitive

Aloof suggests a cool reserve arising from a sense of superiority or disdain for inferiors or from shyness or suspicion

⟨remained *aloof* from the other club members⟩. ***antonym:*** familiar, outgoing

Detached implies an objective aloofness achieved through absence of prejudice or selfishness ⟨observed family gatherings with *detached* amusement⟩. ***antonym:*** interested, selfish

Disinterested implies a circumstantial freedom from concern for personal or especially financial advantage that enables one to judge or advise without bias ⟨a panel of *disinterested* observers to act as judges⟩. ***antonym:*** interested, prejudiced, biased

2. See NEUTRAL.

indigence See POVERTY.

indigenous See NATIVE.

indignation See ANGER.

indiscriminate, **wholesale**, **sweeping** mean including all or nearly all within the range of choice, operation, or effectiveness.

Indiscriminate implies lack of consideration of individual merit or worth in giving, treating, selecting, or including ⟨*indiscriminate* praise⟩. ***antonym:*** selective, discriminating

Wholesale stresses extensiveness and action upon all within range of choice, operation, or effectiveness ⟨*wholesale* vaccination of a population⟩.

Sweeping suggests a reaching out to draw everyone or everything into one mass and usually carries a strong implication of indiscriminateness ⟨*sweeping* generalizations⟩.

individual **1.** See CHARACTERISTIC. **2.** See SPECIAL.

indolent See LAZY.

induce, **persuade**, **prevail**, **get** mean to move one to act or decide in a certain way.

Induce implies an influencing of the reason or judgment often by pointing out the advantages or gains that depend upon the desired decision ⟨*induced* them to vote for his proposal⟩.

Persuade implies appealing as much to the emotions as to reason by such things as pleas, entreaty, or expostulation in attempting to win over ⟨*persuaded* them to obey the ceasefire⟩. ***antonym:*** dissuade (*from*)

Prevail, usually used with *on* or *upon*, carries a strong implication of overcoming opposition or reluctance with sustained argument or pressure or cogent appeals ⟨*prevailed* upon them to stay for the night⟩.

Get, the most neutral of these terms, can replace any of them, especially when the method by which a decision is brought about is irrelevant or is deliberately not stressed ⟨finally *got* the boy to do his homework⟩.

inducement See MOTIVE.

indulge, **pamper**, **humor**, **spoil**, **baby**, **mollycoddle** mean to show undue favor or attention to a person's desires and feelings.

Indulge implies excessive compliance and weakness in gratifying another's or one's own wishes or desires ⟨*indulged* herself with food at the slightest excuse⟩. ***antonym:*** discipline

Pamper implies inordinate gratification of an appetite or desire for luxury and comfort ⟨*pampered* by the conveniences of modern living⟩. ***antonym:*** chasten

Humor stresses a yielding to a person's moods or whims ⟨*humored* him by letting him tell the story⟩.

Spoil stresses the injurious effects of indulging or pampering on character ⟨fond but foolish parents *spoil* their children⟩.

Baby suggests excessive and often inappropriate care, attention, or solicitude ⟨*babying* students by not holding them accountable⟩.

Mollycoddle suggests an excessive degree of care and attention to another's health or welfare ⟨refused to *mollycoddle* her teenaged patients⟩.

indulgent See FORBEARING.

industrious See BUSY.

industry See BUSINESS.

inebriated See DRUNK.
inept See AWKWARD.
inerrable See INFALLIBLE.
inerrant See INFALLIBLE.
inert See INACTIVE.
inexorable See INFLEXIBLE.
infallible, inerrable, inerrant, unerring mean having or showing the inability to make errors.

Infallible may imply that one's freedom from error is divinely bestowed ⟨fundamentalists believe in an *infallible* Bible⟩. ***antonym:*** fallible

Inerrable may be preferable when one wishes to avoid any association with religious or papal infallibility ⟨no reference source should be considered *inerrable*⟩. ***antonym:*** errable

Inerrant stresses the fact that no mistakes were made ⟨an *inerrant* interpretation of the most demanding role in drama⟩. ***antonym:*** errant

Unerring stresses reliability, sureness, exactness, or accuracy ⟨a photographer with an *unnerring* eye for beauty⟩.

infamous See VICIOUS.
infamy See DISGRACE.
infer, deduce, conclude, judge, gather mean to arrive at a mental conclusion.

Infer implies the formulating of an opinion, a principle, a decision, or a conclusion by reasoning from evidence ⟨from that remark, I *inferred* that they knew each other⟩.

Deduce adds to ***infer*** the special implication of drawing a particular inference from a generalization ⟨from that we can *deduce* that man is a mammal⟩.

Conclude implies an arriving at a logically necessary inference at the end of a chain of reasoning ⟨*concluded* that only he could have committed the crime⟩.

Judge stresses a critical testing of the premises or examination of the evidence on which a conclusion is based ⟨*judge* people by their actions, not words⟩.

Gather suggests a direct or intuitive forming of a conclusion from hints or implications ⟨*gathered* that the couple wanted to be alone⟩.

infertile See STERILE.
infirm See WEAK.
infix See IMPLANT.
inflate See EXPAND.
inflated, flatulent, tumescent, tumid, turgid mean swollen by or as if by fluid beyond normal size.

Inflated implies expansion by or as if by introduction of gas ⟨an *inflated* balloon⟩ or a stretching or extending often by artificial or questionable means ⟨*inflated* currency with little real buying power⟩. ***antonym:*** pithy

Flatulent applies basically to distension of the belly by internally generated gases or suggests something seemingly full but actually without substance ⟨read a series of bombastic, *flatulent* poems⟩.

Tumescent suggests the process of becoming swollen or bloated or the result of this process ⟨politicians enraptured with their own *tumescent* rhetoric⟩.

Tumid implies swelling or bloating usually beyond what is normal or wholesome or desirable ⟨took a sharp blow to his *tumid* pride⟩.

Turgid is likely to be preferred when normal swelling rather than bloating is described ⟨a *turgid* plant stem⟩; it can also suggest an unrestrained, undisciplined manner accompanied by such faults as overemotionalism or bombast ⟨an author known for her *turgid* prose⟩.

inflexible 1. Inflexible, inexorable, obdurate, adamant mean unwilling to alter a predetermined course or purpose.

Inflexible implies rigid adherence or even slavish conformity to established principle ⟨*inflexible* in her demands⟩. ***antonym:*** flexible

Inexorable implies relentlessness of purpose or ruthlessness or finality or, especially when applied to things, inevitableness ⟨the *inexorable* path of progress⟩. ***antonym:*** exorable

Obdurate stresses hardness of heart and

insensitivity to appeals for mercy or the influence of divine grace ⟨an *obdurate* governor who refused to grant clemency⟩.

Adamant suggests extraordinary strength of will and implies utter immovability in the face of all temptation or entreaty ⟨was *adamant* that the project be completed on time⟩. ***antonym:*** yielding

2. See STIFF.

influence *n* **Influence**, **authority**, **prestige**, **weight**, **credit** mean power exerted over the minds or behavior of others.

Influence may apply to a force or power exercised consciously or unconsciously to guide or determine a course of action or an effect ⟨used all of her *influence* to get the bill passed⟩.

Authority implies power from a source such as personal merit or learning to compel devotion or allegiance or acceptance ⟨a policy that has the *authority* of the school board behind it⟩.

Prestige implies the ascendancy given by conspicuous excellence or recognized superiority ⟨the *prestige* of the newspaper⟩.

Weight implies measurable or decisive influence in determining acts or choices ⟨the wishes of the President obviously had much *weight*⟩.

Credit suggests influence that arises from proven merit or reputation for inspiring confidence and admiration ⟨the *credit* that he had built up in the town⟩. ***antonym:*** discredit

influence *vb* See AFFECT.

inform, **acquaint**, **apprise**, **notify** mean to make one aware of something.

Inform implies the imparting of knowledge especially of facts or occurrences necessary for an understanding of a matter or as a basis for action ⟨*informed* us of the crisis⟩.

Acquaint lays stress on introducing to or familiarizing with ⟨*acquainted* myself with the basics of the game⟩.

Apprise implies the communicating of something of special interest or importance to the recipient ⟨*apprise* me of any rallies in the stock market⟩.

Notify implies the formal communication of something requiring attention or demanding action ⟨*notified* them that their mortgage payment was due⟩.

infraction See BREACH.

infrequent, **uncommon**, **scarce**, **rare**, **sporadic** mean not common or abundant.

Infrequent implies occurrence at wide intervals in space or time ⟨family visits that were *infrequent* and brief⟩. ***antonym:*** frequent

Uncommon suggests something that occurs or is found so infrequently as to be exceptional or extraordinary ⟨smallpox is now *uncommon* in many countries⟩. ***antonym:*** common

Scarce implies a falling short of a standard or required abundance ⟨jobs were *scarce* during the Depression⟩. ***antonym:*** abundant

Rare suggests extreme scarcity or infrequency and often implies consequent high value ⟨*rare* first editions of classics fetch high prices⟩.

Sporadic implies occurrence in scattered instances or isolated outbursts ⟨*sporadic* cases of the genetic disorder⟩. ***antonym:*** frequent

infringe See TRESPASS.

infringement See BREACH.

infuse, **suffuse**, **imbue**, **ingrain**, **inoculate**, **leaven** mean to introduce one thing into another so as to affect it throughout.

Infuse implies a pouring in and permeating of something that gives new life or vigor or significance ⟨new members *infused* the club with new enthusiasm⟩.

Suffuse implies a spreading through or over of something that gives a distinctive color or quality ⟨a room *suffused* with light and cheerfulness⟩.

Imbue implies a permeating so deep and so complete that the very substance and nature of the thing affected are altered

⟨*imbued* her students with intellectual curiosity⟩.

Ingrain suggests the indelible stamping or deep implanting of a quality, idea, or trait ⟨clung to *ingrained* habits and beliefs⟩.

Inoculate implies an imbuing or implanting with a germinal idea and often suggests surreptitiousness or subtlety ⟨tried to *inoculate* the child with a taste for opera⟩.

Leaven implies introducing something that enlivens, tempers, or alters the total quality ⟨a serious play *leavened* with comic moments⟩.

ingenious See CLEVER.

ingenuous See NATURAL.

ingrain See INFUSE.

ingredient See ELEMENT.

inheritance See HERITAGE.

inhibit See FORBID.

iniquitous See VICIOUS.

initiate See BEGIN.

injure, harm, hurt, damage, impair, mar mean to affect someone or something so as to rob it of soundness or strength or to reduce its value, usefulness, or effectiveness.

Injure implies the inflicting of anything detrimental to one's looks, comfort, health, or success ⟨an accident that *injured* him physically and emotionally⟩. ***antonym:*** aid

Harm often stresses the inflicting of pain, suffering, or loss ⟨careful not to *harm* the animals⟩. ***antonym:*** benefit

Hurt implies the inflicting of a wound to the body or to the feelings ⟨*hurt* by her callous remarks⟩. ***antonym:*** benefit

Damage suggests the inflicting of an injury that lowers value or impairs usefulness ⟨a table that was *damaged* in shipping⟩. ***antonym:*** repair

Impair suggests a making less complete or efficient by deterioration or diminution ⟨years of smoking had *impaired* his health⟩. ***antonym:*** improve, repair

Mar applies to disfigurement or maiming that spoils perfection or well-being ⟨the text is *marred* by numerous typos⟩.

injury See INJUSTICE.

injustice, injury, wrong, grievance mean an act that inflicts undeserved damage, loss, or hardship on a person.

Injustice applies to any act that involves unfairness to another or violation of rights ⟨the *injustices* inflicted by society⟩.

Injury applies specifically to an injustice for which there is a legal remedy ⟨a libeled reputation is legally considered an *injury*⟩.

Wrong applies in law to any act punishable according to the criminal code and connotes a flagrant injustice ⟨a crusading reporter determined to right society's *wrongs*⟩.

Grievance applies to any circumstance or condition that, in the opinion of the one affected, constitutes an injustice or gives just grounds for complaint ⟨a committee for investigating employee *grievances*⟩.

innate, inborn, inbred, congenital, hereditary mean not acquired after birth.

Innate applies to qualities or characteristics that are part of one's inner essential nature ⟨a person with an *innate* sense of his own superiority⟩. ***antonym:*** acquired

Inborn suggests a quality or tendency either actually present at birth or so marked and deep-seated as to seem so ⟨her *inborn* love of the rugged, outdoorsy life⟩. ***antonym:*** acquired

Inbred suggests something acquired from parents, either by heredity or nurture, or deeply rooted and ingrained ⟨a person with *inbred* extremist political views⟩.

Congenital applies to things acquired before or at birth during fetal development ⟨a *congenital* heart murmur⟩.

Hereditary applies to things acquired before or at birth and transmitted from one's ancestors ⟨eye color is *hereditary*⟩.

inoculate See INFUSE.
inordinate See EXCESSIVE.
inquire See ASK 1.
inquisitive See CURIOUS.
insane, **mad**, **crazy**, **crazed**, **demented**, **deranged**, **lunatic**, **maniac** mean having or showing an unsound mind or being unable to control one's rational processes.

Insane implies that one is unable to function safely and competently in everyday life and is not responsible for one's actions ⟨adjudged *insane* after a period of observation⟩. ***antonym:*** sane

Mad strongly suggests wildness, rabidness, raving, or complete loss of self-control ⟨drove her husband *mad* with jealousy⟩.

Crazy may suggest such mental breakdown as comes from old age or may suggest a distraught or wild state of mind induced by intense emotion ⟨*crazy* with grief⟩; when applied to a scheme, project, or notion, it usually suggests the product of a disordered mind ⟨got those *crazy* ideas into her head⟩. ***antonym:*** sane

Crazed, often used instead of ***crazy***, implies the existence of a temporary disorder, usually with a specific cause ⟨stampeding cattle *crazed* with fear⟩.

Demented suggests mental unsoundness that manifests itself by apathy or incoherence in thought, speech, or action ⟨years of solitary confinement had left him *demented*⟩.

Deranged stresses a clear loss of mental balance or order resulting in a functional disorder ⟨assassinated by a *deranged* anarchist⟩.

Lunatic may be the equivalent of ***insane*** or may imply no more than extreme folly ⟨invested in one *lunatic* scheme after another⟩.

Maniac is close to ***mad*** and often suggests violence, fury, or raving ⟨once behind the wheel, she turns into a *maniac* driver⟩.

inscrutable See MYSTERIOUS.
inseminate See IMPLANT.
insert See INTRODUCE.
insight See DISCERNMENT.
insinuate **1.** See INTRODUCE. **2.** See SUGGEST.
insipid, **vapid**, **flat**, **jejune**, **banal**, **wishy-washy**, **inane** mean devoid of qualities that make for spirit and character.

Insipid implies a lack of sufficient taste or savor to please or interest ⟨*insipid* art and dull prose⟩. ***antonym:*** sapid, zestful

Vapid suggests a lack of liveliness, freshness, sparkle, force, or spirit ⟨a potentially exciting story given a *vapid* treatment⟩.

Flat applies to things that have lost their sparkle or zest and become dull and lifeless ⟨although well-regarded in its day, this novel now seems *flat*⟩.

Jejune suggests a lack of rewarding or satisfying substance and connotes barrenness, aridity, or meagerness ⟨on close reading the poem comes across as *jejune*⟩.

Banal stresses the presence of trite and commonplace elements and the complete absence of freshness, novelty, or immediacy ⟨a *banal* tale of unrequited love⟩. ***antonym:*** original

Wishy-washy implies that essential or striking qualities are so weak or diluted as to seem utterly insipid or vapid ⟨a set of *wishy-washy* opinions on national issues⟩.

Inane implies a lack of any significant or convincing quality or of any sense or point ⟨an *inane* interpretation of the play⟩. ***antonym:*** deep, profound

insolent See PROUD.
inspect See SCRUTINIZE.
inspirit See ENCOURAGE.
instance *n* **Instance**, **case**, **illustration**, **example**, **sample**, **specimen** mean something that exhibits the distinguishing characteristics of the category to which it belongs.

Instance applies to any individual person, act, or thing that may be offered to illustrate or explain, or prove or disprove a general statement ⟨an *instance* of history repeating itself⟩.

Case applies to an instance that directs attention to a real or assumed occurrence or situation that is to be considered, studied, or dealt with ⟨a *case* of mistaken identity⟩.

Illustration applies to an instance offered as a means of clarifying or illuminating a general statement ⟨an *illustration* of Murphy's law⟩.

Example applies to a typical, representative, or illustrative instance or case ⟨a typical *example* of bureaucratic waste⟩.

Sample implies a random part or unit taken as representative of the larger whole to which it belongs ⟨show us a *sample* of your work⟩.

Specimen applies to any example or sample of a whole or to an example or sample carefully selected to illustrate important or typical qualities ⟨one of the finest *specimens* of the jeweler's art⟩.

instance *vb* See MENTION.

instigate See INCITE.

instill See IMPLANT.

instinctive **1. Instinctive**, **intuitive** mean not based on ordinary processes of reasoning.

Instinctive implies a relation to instinct and stresses the automatic quality of the reaction or the fact that it occurs below the level of conscious thought and volition ⟨an *instinctive* response to an emergency⟩. ***antonym:*** reasoned

Intuitive implies a relation to intuition and suggests activity above and beyond the level of conscious reasoning ⟨an *intuitive* understanding of the complexities of the situation⟩. ***antonym:*** ratiocinative

2. See SPONTANEOUS.

instruct **1.** See COMMAND. **2.** See TEACH.

instrument **1.** See IMPLEMENT. **2.** See MEAN *n* 2.

insult See OFFEND.

insure See ENSURE.

insurrection See REBELLION.

intact See PERFECT.

integrity **1.** See HONESTY. **2.** See UNITY.

intelligent, **clever**, **alert**, **quick-witted**, **bright**, **smart**, **knowing**, **brilliant** mean mentally keen or quick.

Intelligent stresses superiority of mind and success in coping with new situations or in solving problems ⟨an *intelligent* person could assemble it in 10 minutes⟩. ***antonym:*** unintelligent

Clever implies native ability or aptness and sometimes suggests a lack of more substantial qualities ⟨a hack writer who was somewhat *clever* with words⟩. ***antonym:*** dull

Alert stresses quickness in perceiving and understanding ⟨*alert* to new developments in technology⟩.

Quick-witted implies promptness in finding answers or in devising expedients in moments of danger or challenge ⟨no match for her *quick-witted* opponent⟩.

Bright suggests cleverness, especially in liveliness of mind or talk or manner ⟨a press secretary who was very young but very *bright*⟩. ***antonym:*** dense, dull

Smart implies cleverness combined with an alertness or quick-wittedness that allows one to get ahead ⟨a *smart* girl with her eye out for the right opportunity⟩. ***antonym:*** stupid

Knowing suggests the possession of information or knowledge that is necessary or useful and can also suggest sophistication or secretiveness ⟨difficult to deceive a *knowing* consumer⟩.

Brilliant implies such unusual, and outstanding keenness of intellect as to excite admiration ⟨a *brilliant* scientist⟩. ***antonym:*** dense, dull

intensify, **aggravate**, **heighten**, **enhance** mean to increase markedly in measure or degree.

Intensify implies a deepening or strengthening of a thing or of its characteristic quality ⟨police *intensified* their investigation⟩. ***antonym:*** temper, mitigate, allay, abate

Aggravate implies an increasing in gravity or seriousness of something already bad or undesirable ⟨the problem has been *aggravated* by neglect⟩. ***antonym:*** alleviate

Heighten suggests a lifting above the ordinary or accustomed ⟨special effects *heightened* the sense of terror⟩.

Enhance implies a raising or strengthening above the normal of such qualities as desirability, value, or attractiveness ⟨shrubbery *enhanced* the grounds of the estate⟩.

intent See INTENTION.

intention, **intent**, **purpose**, **design**, **aim**, **end**, **object**, **objective**, **goal** mean what one intends to accomplish or attain.

Intention implies little more than what one has in mind to do or bring about ⟨announced his *intention* to marry⟩.

Intent suggests clearer formulation or greater deliberateness ⟨the clear *intent* of the law⟩. ***antonym:*** accident

Purpose suggests a more settled determination or more resolution ⟨she stopped for a *purpose*, not for an idle chat⟩.

Design implies a more carefully calculated plan and carefully ordered details and sometimes scheming ⟨the order of events was by *design,* not by accident⟩.

Aim adds implications of effort clearly directed toward attaining or accomplishing ⟨pursued her *aims* with great courage⟩.

End stresses the intended effect of action often in distinction or contrast to the action or means as such ⟨will use any means to achieve his *end*⟩.

Object may equal ***end*** but more often applies to a more individually determined wish or need ⟨the *object* of the research study⟩.

Objective implies something tangible and immediately attainable ⟨their *objective* is to seize the oil fields⟩.

Goal suggests something attained only by prolonged effort and hardship ⟨worked years to achieve her *goal*⟩.

intentional See VOLUNTARY.

intercalate See INTRODUCE.

intercede See INTERPOSE.

interdict See FORBID.

interfere **1.** See INTERPOSE. **2.** See MEDDLE.

interject See INTRODUCE.

interlope See INTRUDE.

intermeddle See MEDDLE.

intermission See PAUSE.

intermittent, **recurrent**, **periodic**, **alternate** mean occurring or appearing in interrupted sequence.

Intermittent stresses breaks in continuity ⟨an *intermittent* correspondence with a distant relative⟩. ***antonym:*** incessant, continual

Recurrent stresses repetition and reappearance ⟨the boy suffered from *recurrent* illness⟩.

Periodic implies recurrence at essentially regular intervals ⟨*periodic* appearances of a comet⟩.

Alternate may apply to two contrasting things appearing repeatedly one after the other or to every second member of a series ⟨club meetings on *alternate* Tuesdays⟩.

interpolate See INTRODUCE.

interpose **1. Interpose**, **interfere**, **intervene**, **mediate**, **intercede** mean to come or go between.

Interpose implies no more than this ⟨a road *interposed* between the house and the beach⟩.

Interfere implies a getting in the way or otherwise hindering ⟨noise *interfered* with my concentration⟩.

Intervene may imply a coming between two things in space or time or a stepping in to halt or settle a quarrel or conflict ⟨family duties *intervened,* and the work came to a halt⟩.

Mediate implies an intervening between hostile factions or conflicting ideas or principles ⟨chosen to *mediate* between union and management⟩.

Intercede implies an acting in behalf of another, often an offender, to seek mercy or forgiveness ⟨asked to *intercede* on the daughter's behalf⟩.

2. See INTRODUCE.

interpret See EXPLAIN.

interrogate See ASK 1.

interstice See APERTURE.

intervene See INTERPOSE.

intimate *adj* See FAMILIAR.

intimate *vb* See SUGGEST.

intimidate, **cow**, **bulldoze**, **bully**, **browbeat** mean to frighten into submission.

Intimidate implies an inducing of fear or a sense of inferiority in another ⟨*intimidated* by all the other bright young freshmen⟩.

Cow implies a reduction to a state where the spirit is broken or all courage is lost ⟨not at all *cowed* by the odds against making it in show business⟩.

Bulldoze implies an intimidating or an overcoming of resistance usually by urgings, demands, or threats ⟨*bulldozed* the city council into approving the plan⟩.

Bully implies an intimidation through swaggering threats or insults ⟨tourists being *bullied* by taxi drivers⟩. ***antonym:*** coax

Browbeat implies a cowing through arrogant, scornful, contemptuous, or insolent treatment ⟨inmates were routinely *browbeaten* by the staff⟩.

intoxicated See DRUNK.

intractable See UNRULY.

intrepid See BRAVE.

intricate See COMPLEX.

intrigue 1. See PLOT. **2.** See AMOUR.

introduce, **insert**, **insinuate**, **interpolate**, **intercalate**, **interpose**, **interject** mean to put between or among others.

Introduce is a general term for bringing or placing a thing or person into a group or body already in existence ⟨*introduced* a new topic into the conversation⟩. ***antonym:*** withdraw, abstract

Insert implies a putting into a fixed or open space between or among other things ⟨*insert* a clause in the contract⟩. ***antonym:*** abstract, extract

Insinuate implies a slow, careful, sometimes artful introduction ⟨slyly *insinuated* himself into their confidence⟩.

Interpolate applies to the inserting of something extraneous or spurious ⟨*interpolated* her own comments into the report⟩.

Intercalate suggests an intrusive inserting of something into an existing series or sequence ⟨a book in which new material is *intercalated* with old⟩.

Interpose suggests the inserting of an obstruction or cause of delay ⟨rules that *interpose* barriers between children and creativity⟩.

Interject implies an abrupt or forced introduction of something that breaks in or interrupts ⟨quickly *interjected* a question⟩.

introductory See PRELIMINARY.

intrude, **obtrude**, **interlope**, **butt in** mean to thrust oneself or something in without invitation or authorization.

Intrude suggests rudeness or officiousness in invading another's property, time, or privacy ⟨didn't mean to *intrude* upon the family's private gathering⟩.

Obtrude may imply the mere fact of pushing something into view, or it may stress the impropriety or offensiveness of the intrusion ⟨hesitant about *obtruding* her opinions when they were not welcome⟩.

Interlope implies placing oneself in a position that has injurious or adverse consequences ⟨*interloping* nouveaux riches who didn't belong in the club⟩.

Butt in implies an abrupt or offensive intrusion lacking in ceremony, propriety, or decent restraint ⟨in-laws who *butt in* and tell newlyweds what to do⟩.

intrusive See IMPERTINENT.

intuition See REASON.

invade See TRESPASS.

invalidate See NULLIFY.
invaluable See COSTLY.
invective See ABUSE.
inveigle See LURE.
invent **1. Invent**, **create**, **discover** mean to bring something new into existence.

Invent implies fabricating something useful usually as a result of the use of the imagination or ingenious thinking or experiment ⟨*invented* numerous energy-saving devices⟩.

Create implies an evoking or causing of life out of or as if out of nothing ⟨*created* few lasting works of art⟩.

Discover presupposes preexistence of something and implies a finding of what is hidden or an exploring of the unknown rather than a making ⟨attempts to *discover* the source of the Nile⟩.

2. See CONTRIVE.

invert **1.** See TRANSPOSE. **2.** See REVERSE.
inveterate, **confirmed**, **chronic**, **deep-seated**, **deep-rooted** mean firmly established.

Inveterate applies to something, such as a habit, attitude, or feeling, of such long existence as to be almost ineradicable or unalterable ⟨an *inveterate* smoker⟩.

Confirmed implies a growing stronger and firmer with the passage of time so as to resist change or reform ⟨a *confirmed* bachelor⟩.

Chronic suggests the long duration of something usually undesirable that resists attempts to alleviate or cure ⟨sick and tired of his *chronic* complaining⟩.

Deep-seated applies to qualities or attitudes so firmly established as to become part of the very structure ⟨a *deep-seated* fear of heights⟩. ***antonym:*** skin-deep

Deep-rooted applies to something deeply established and of lasting endurance ⟨the causes of the problem are *deep-rooted* and cannot be eliminated overnight⟩.

invidious See REPUGNANT.
inviolable See SACRED.
inviolate See SACRED.
invite, **bid**, **solicit**, **court** mean to request or encourage someone or something to respond or to act.

Invite commonly implies a formal or courteous requesting of one's presence or participation but may also apply to a tacit or unintended attracting or tempting ⟨a movie remake that *invites* comparison with the original⟩.

Bid implies the making of an effort or appeal to win or attract or the offering of a tempting opening for something ⟨*bidding* for their sympathy⟩.

Solicit suggests urgency rather than courtesy in encouraging or asking ⟨continually *solicited* our advice⟩.

Court suggests an endeavoring to win something, such as favor, or to gain something, such as love, by suitable acts or words ⟨a candidate *courting* the votes of young urban professionals⟩.

involve See INCLUDE.
involved See COMPLEX.
iota See PARTICLE.
irascible, **choleric**, **splenetic**, **testy**, **touchy**, **cranky**, **cross** mean easily angered or enraged.

Irascible implies a tendency to be angered on slight provocation ⟨teenagers got a rise out of the *irascible* old man⟩.

Choleric may suggest impatient excitability and unreasonableness in addition to an irritable frame of mind ⟨a *choleric* invalid who tried the nurses' patience⟩. ***antonym:*** placid, imperturbable

Splenetic suggests moroseness, and a bad rather than a hot temper ⟨the *splenetic* type that habored a grudge⟩.

Testy suggests irascibility over small annoyances ⟨everyone grew *testy* under the emotional strain⟩.

Touchy implies readiness to take offense and undue irritability or sensitiveness ⟨*touchy* about references to her weight⟩. ***antonym:*** imperturbable

Cranky suggests an habitual fretful irritability with those who fail to conform to one's set notions, fixed ideas, or unvarying standards ⟨*cranky* neighbors much given to complaining⟩.

Cross suggests a temporary irascibility or grumpy irritability as from disappointment or discomfort ⟨a squabble that left her feeling *cross* all day⟩.

ire See ANGER.

irenic See PACIFIC.

irk See ANNOY.

ironic See SARCASTIC.

irony See WIT.

irrational, **unreasonable** mean not governed or guided by reason or not having the power to reason.

Irrational can imply mental derangement but it more often suggests lack of control by or open conflict with reason ⟨our world which often seems *irrational*⟩. ***antonym:*** rational

Unreasonable is likely to suggest guidance by some force other than reason such as ambition, greed, or stubbornness that makes or shows one deficient in good sense ⟨make *unreasonable* demands on a friend⟩. ***antonym:*** reasonable

irregular, **anomalous**, **unnatural** mean not conforming to, in accordance with, or explainable by rule, law, or custom.

Irregular implies a lack of accord with a law or regulation imposed for the sake of uniformity in methods, practice, or conduct ⟨concerned about her *irregular* behavior⟩. ***antonym:*** regular

Anomalous implies not conforming to what might be expected because of the class or type to which the thing in question belongs or the laws that govern its existence ⟨an *anomalous* example of 18th century domestic architecture⟩.

Unnatural suggests what is contrary to nature or to principles or standards felt to be essential to the well-being of civilized society and often suggests reprehensible abnormality ⟨treated their prisoners of war with *unnatural* cruelty⟩. ***antonym:*** natural

irritate, **exasperate**, **nettle**, **provoke**, **aggravate**, **rile**, **peeve** mean to excite a feeling of angry annoyance.

Irritate implies an often gradual arousing of angry feelings that may range from impatience to rage ⟨her constant nagging *irritated* him to no end⟩.

Exasperate suggests galling annoyance or vexation and the arousing of extreme impatience ⟨his *exasperating* habit of putting off every decision⟩. ***antonym:*** appease, mollify

Nettle suggests a light and sharp but transitory stinging or piquing ⟨your high-handed attitude *nettled* several people⟩.

Provoke implies an arousing of strong annoyance or vexation that may excite to action ⟨remarks that were made solely to *provoke* him⟩. ***antonym:*** gratify

Aggravate implies persistent, often petty, goading that leads to displeasure, impatience, or anger ⟨the *aggravating* drone of self-important politicians⟩. ***antonym:*** appease

Rile implies the inducing of an angry or resentful agitation ⟨the new rules *riled* the employees⟩.

Peeve suggests the arousing of fretful, often petty, or querulous irritation ⟨she is easily *peeved* after a sleepless night⟩.

isolation See SOLITUDE.

issue *n* See EFFECT.

issue *vb* See SPRING.

item, **detail**, **particular** mean one of the distinct parts of a whole.

Item applies to each thing that is specified separately in a list or in a group of things that might be separately listed or enumerated ⟨ordered every *item* on the list⟩.

Detail applies to one of the small component parts of a larger whole, and may specifically denote one of the minutiae that lends finish or character to the whole ⟨leave the petty *details* to others⟩.

Particular stresses the smallness, singleness, and especially the concreteness of a detail or item ⟨a verbal attack that included few *particulars*⟩.

iterate See REPEAT.

J

jade See TIRE.
jam See PREDICAMENT.
jargon See DIALECT.
jealous See ENVIOUS
jeer See SCOFF.
jejune See INSIPID.
jerk, **snap**, **twitch**, **yank** mean to make a sudden sharp quick movement.
Jerk stresses suddenness and abruptness and is likely to imply a movement both graceless and forceful ⟨gave the dog's leash a quick *jerk*⟩.
Snap implies a sharp quick action abruptly terminated, as in biting, seizing, locking, or breaking suddenly ⟨the crocodile *snapped* at the child but missed⟩.
Twitch applies to a light, sudden, and sometimes spasmodic movement that usually combines tugging and jerking ⟨the sleeping cat, its body *twitching* as it dreamt⟩.
Yank implies a quick and heavy tugging and pulling ⟨*yank* the bedclothes over one's head⟩.
jest 1. Jest, **joke**, **quip**, **witticism**, **wisecrack**, **crack**, **gag** mean something said or done for the purpose of evoking laughter.
Jest applies to any utterance not seriously intended, whether sarcastic, ironic, witty, or merely playful ⟨wry *jests* that were lost on her unsophisticated friends⟩.
Joke may apply to an act intended to fool or deceive someone, or to a story or remark designed to promote good humor ⟨he's very good at taking a *joke*⟩.
Quip suggests a quick, neatly turned, witty remark ⟨whatever the topic, she's ready with a quick *quip*⟩.
Witticism implies a clever and often biting or ironic remark ⟨many felt the sting of that critic's *witticisms*⟩.
Wisecrack suggests a sophisticated or knowing witticism and may suggest flippancy or unfeelingness ⟨a comic known for abrasive *wisecracks*⟩.
Crack implies a sharp, witty, often sarcastic remark or retort ⟨responded to the challenge with a series of biting *cracks*⟩.
Gag applies especially to a brief, laughter-provoking, foolish remark or act ⟨a frivolous person, given to *gags*⟩.
2. See FUN.
jibe See AGREE 3.
job 1. See TASK. **2.** See POSITION 2.
jocose See WITTY.
jocular See WITTY.
jocund See MERRY.
join, **combine**, **unite**, **connect**, **link**, **associate**, **relate** mean to bring or come together into some manner of union.
Join implies a bringing into some degree of contact or conjunction of clearly discrete things ⟨*joined* forces in an effort to win⟩. ***antonym:*** disjoin, part
Combine implies a merging or mingling that obscures the identity of each unit ⟨*combine* the ingredients for a cake⟩. ***antonym:*** separate
Unite stresses the bond by which two or more individual entities are joined and implies somewhat greater loss of separate identity ⟨the colonies *united* to form a republic⟩. ***antonym:*** alienate, disunite, divide
Connect suggests a loose or external attachment with little or no loss of identity ⟨a bridge *connects* the island to the mainland⟩. ***antonym:*** disconnect
Link may imply strong attachment or inseparability of elements ⟨a name forever *linked* with liberty⟩. ***antonym:*** sunder
Associate stresses the mere fact of occurrence or existence together in space or in logical sequence ⟨opera is popularly *associated* with high society⟩.
Relate suggests the existence of a real or presumed natural or logical connection ⟨the two events were not *related*⟩.
joint, **articulation**, **suture** mean the place where or the mechanism by which two things are united.

Joint is the most inclusive term and is freely applicable to either a natural or a man-made structure ⟨the complicated flexible *joint* of the elbow⟩.

Articulation, chiefly an anatomical term in this sense, can apply to any joint, with particular emphasis on the fitting together of the parts involved, and is likely to be used when the mechanism of a joint or the elements entering into its construction are under consideration ⟨the ball-and-socket structure of highly movable *articulations*⟩ or when the process or method of joining is involved ⟨the finely-crafted *articulation* of the parts⟩.

Suture is used of a joint that suggests a seam in linear form or lack of mobility or that has been formed by sewing ⟨the joints between the two parts of a bean or pea pod called *sutures*⟩.

joke See JEST.

jollity See MIRTH.

jolly See MERRY.

jot See PARTICLE.

jovial See MERRY.

joy See PLEASURE.

joyful See GLAD.

joyous See GLAD.

judge See INFER.

judgment See SENSE.

judicious See WISE.

junction, **confluence**, **concourse** mean an act, state, or place of meeting or uniting.

Junction is likely to apply to the meeting or uniting of material things such as roads, rivers, or railroads ⟨a town grew up at the *junction* of the two rivers⟩.

Confluence suggests a flowing movement by which things or persons seem to merge and mingle ⟨the turbulent *confluence* of two cultures⟩.

Concourse places emphasis on a rushing or hurrying together of persons or things to form a great crowd ⟨a fortuitous *concourse* of atoms⟩ and it may apply to a place where people throng to and fro ⟨hurried across the *concourse* to the gate where the train was waiting⟩.

juncture, **pass**, **exigency**, **emergency**, **contingency**, **pinch**, **straits**, **crisis** mean a critical or crucial time or state of affairs.

Juncture stresses the significant concurrence or convergence of events that is likely to lead to a turning point ⟨at an important *juncture* in our country's history⟩.

Pass implies a bad or distressing state or situation brought about by a combination of causes ⟨things have come to a sorry *pass* when it's not safe to be on the streets⟩.

Exigency stresses the pressure of necessity or the urgency of demands created by a juncture or pass ⟨made no effort to provide for *exigencies*⟩.

Emergency applies to a sudden or unforeseen situation requiring prompt action to avoid disaster ⟨the presence of mind needed to deal with *emergencies*⟩.

Contingency implies an emergency or exigency that is regarded as possible or even probable but uncertain of occurrence ⟨*contingency* plans prepared by the Pentagon⟩.

Pinch implies a juncture, especially in personal affairs, that exerts pressure and demands vigorous counteractive action, but to a less intense degree than ***exigency*** or ***emergency*** ⟨this will do in a *pinch*⟩.

Straits applies to a troublesome or dangerous situation from which escape is difficult ⟨in dire *straits* since the death of their father⟩.

Crisis applies to a juncture whose outcome will make a decisive difference ⟨the fever broke and the *crisis* passed⟩.

junk See DISCARD.

jurisdiction See POWER.

just **1.** See FAIR. **2.** See UPRIGHT.

justice, **equity** mean the art, practice, or obligation of rendering to another what is his, her, or its due.

Justice may apply to an ideal abstraction, to a quality of mind reflecting this, to a quality of inherent truth and fairness, or to the treatment due one who has transgressed a law or who seeks relief when wronged or threatened ⟨refused to allow such travesties of *justice* while she was judge⟩. ***antonym:*** injustice

Equity stresses the notions of fairness and impartiality and implies a justice that transcends the strict letter of the law and is in keeping with what is reasonable rather than with what is merely legal ⟨divided the pie with absolute *equity* among the greedy children⟩. ***antonym:*** inequity

justify **1.** See MAINTAIN. **2. Justify**, **warrant** mean to be what constitutes sufficient grounds for doing, using, saying, or preferring something.

Justify may be preferred when the stress is on providing grounds that satisfy conscience as well as reason ⟨an end that surely did not *justify* such harsh means⟩.

Warrant is especially appropriate when the emphasis is on something that requires an explanation or reason rather than an excuse and is likely to suggest support by the authority of precedent, experience, or logic ⟨the deposits have shown enough ore to *warrant* further testing⟩.

juxtaposed See ADJACENT.

K

keen **1.** See EAGER. **2.** See SHARP.

keep **1. Keep**, **observe**, **celebrate**, **commemorate** mean to notice or honor a day, occasion, or deed.

Keep suggests a customary or wonted noticing without anything untoward or inappropriate ⟨*keep* the Sabbath⟩. ***antonym:*** break

Observe suggests marking the occasion by ceremonious performance of required acts or rituals ⟨not all holidays are *observed* nationally⟩. ***antonym:*** break, violate

Celebrate suggests the acknowledging of an occasion by festivity or indulgence ⟨traditionally *celebrates* Thanksgiving with a huge dinner⟩.

Commemorate suggests the marking of an occasion by observances that remind one of origin and significance ⟨*commemorate* Memorial Day with the laying of wreaths⟩.

2. Keep, **retain**, **detain**, **withhold**, **reserve** mean to hold in one's possession or under one's control.

Keep may suggest a holding securely of something tangible or intangible in one's possession, custody, or control ⟨*keep* this while I'm gone⟩. ***antonym:*** relinquish

Retain implies continued keeping, especially against threatened seizure or forced loss ⟨managed to *retain* their dignity even in poverty⟩.

Detain suggests a keeping through a delay in letting go ⟨*detained* them for questioning⟩.

Withhold implies a restraint in letting go or a refusal to let go, often for good reason ⟨*withheld* information from the authorities⟩. ***antonym:*** accord

Reserve suggests a keeping in store for other or future use ⟨*reserve* some of your energy for the last mile⟩.

kibitzer See SPECTATOR.

kick See OBJECT.

kill, **slay**, **murder**, **assassinate**, **dispatch**, **execute** mean to deprive of life.

Kill merely states the fact of death by an agency of some sort in some manner ⟨frost *killed* the plants⟩.

Slay is a chiefly literary term implying a killing marked by deliberateness and violence ⟨*slew* thousands of the enemy⟩.

Murder specifically implies a killing with stealth and motive and premeditation and therefore full moral responsibility ⟨convicted of *murdering* his parents⟩.

Assassinate applies to a deliberate killing openly or secretly often for impersonal or political motives ⟨terrorists *assassinated* the Senator⟩.

Dispatch stresses quickness and directness in putting to death ⟨*dispatched* the sentry with a single stab⟩.

Execute stresses a putting to death as a legal penalty ⟨to be *executed* by firing squad at dawn⟩.

kind *adj* **Kind**, **kindly**, **benign**, **benignant** mean showing or having a gentle, considerate nature.

Kind stresses a disposition to be sympathetic and helpful ⟨a *kind* heart beneath a gruff exterior⟩. ***antonym:*** unkind

Kindly stresses more the expression of a sympathetic nature, mood, or impulse ⟨take a *kindly* interest in the poor of the community⟩. ***antonym:*** unkindly, acrid

Benign implies mildness and mercifulness and applies more often to gracious or gentle acts or utterances of a superior rather than an equal ⟨the belief that a *benign* supreme being controls destiny⟩. ***antonym:*** malign

Benignant implies serene mildness and kindliness that produce a favorable or beneficial effect ⟨cultural exchange programs have a *benignant* influence in world affairs⟩. ***antonym:*** malignant

kind *n* See TYPE.

kindle See LIGHT.

kindly See KIND *adj.*
kindred See RELATED.
knack See GIFT.
knock See TAP.
knotty See COMPLEX.
know, **believe**, **think** mean to hold something in one's mind as true or as being what it purports to be.

Know stresses assurance and implies sound logical or factual information as its basis ⟨what we don't *know,* we can find out⟩.

Believe, too, stresses assurance but implies trust and faith rather than evidence as its basis ⟨no longer *believed* in the Tooth Fairy⟩.

Think suggests probability rather than firm assurance and implies mental appraisal of pertinent circumstances as its basis ⟨*thinks* she will do well on the test⟩.

knowing See INTELLIGENT.
knowledge, **learning**, **erudition**, **scholarship** mean what is or can be known by an individual or by mankind.

Knowledge applies to facts or ideas acquired by study, investigation, observation, or experience ⟨rich in the *knowledge* gained from life⟩. ***antonym:*** ignorance

Learning applies to knowledge acquired especially through formal, often advanced, schooling and close application ⟨a book that is evidence of the author's vast *learning*⟩.

Erudition strongly implies the acquiring or possession of profound, recondite, or bookish learning ⟨an *erudition* unusual even for a classicist⟩. ***antonym:*** illiteracy

Scholarship implies the possession of learning characteristic of the advanced scholar in a specialized field of study or investigation ⟨a work of first-rate literary *scholarship*⟩.

L

labor See WORK 1.

lack, want, need, require mean to be without something essential or greatly desired.

Lack may imply either an absence or a shortage in supply ⟨a club that *lacked* a room to meet in⟩.

Want adds to ***lack*** the implication of needing or desiring urgently ⟨you may have whatever you *want*⟩.

Need stresses urgent necessity more than absence or shortage ⟨everyone *needs* a friend⟩.

Require is often interchangeable with ***need*** but it may heighten the implication of urgent necessity ⟨a situation that *required* drastic measures⟩.

laconic See CONCISE.

ladylike See FEMALE.

lag See DELAY.

lament See DEPLORE.

languor See LETHARGY.

lank See LEAN.

lanky See LEAN.

lapse *n* See ERROR.

lapse *vb* **Lapse, relapse, backslide** mean to fall back from a higher or better state or condition into a lower or poorer one.

Lapse usually presupposes attainment of a high level of something such as of morals, manners, or habits and implies an abrupt departure from this level or standard; it may reflect culpability or grave weakness or, sometimes, mere absentmindedness ⟨suffered a momentary *lapse* of manners⟩.

Relapse presupposes definite improvement or an advance, toward, for example, health or a higher state, and implies a severe, often dangerous reversal of direction ⟨a young person *relapsing* into childishness⟩.

Backslide, similar in presuppositions and implications to ***relapse***, is restricted almost entirely to moral and religious lapses, and tends more than the other words to suggest unfaithfulness to duty or to allegiance or to principles once professed ⟨kept a constant vigil lest he *backslide*⟩.

larceny See THEFT.

large, big, great mean above average in magnitude, especially physical magnitude.

Large may be preferred when dimensions or extent or capacity or quantity or amount are being considered ⟨a *large* meal⟩, or when breadth, comprehensiveness, or generosity are stressed ⟨tried to respond to some *large* issues⟩. ***antonym:*** small

Big emphasizes bulk or mass or weight or volume ⟨a *big* book⟩ or impressiveness or importance ⟨yearned mainly to be a *big* man on campus⟩. ***antonym:*** little

Great may sometimes imply physical magnitude, usually with connotations of wonder, surprise, or awe ⟨the *great* canyon cut by the Colorado River⟩, but it more often implies eminence, distinction, or supremacy ⟨possessed a very *great* talent⟩. ***antonym:*** little

lassitude See LETHARGY.

last *adj* **Last, final, terminal, eventual, ultimate** mean following all others in time, order, or importance.

Last applies to something that comes at the end of a series but does not always imply that the series is completed or has stopped ⟨the *last* news we had of him⟩. ***antonym:*** first

Final applies to that which definitely closes a series, process, or progress ⟨the *final* day of school⟩. ***antonym:*** initial

Terminal may indicate a limit of extension, growth, or development ⟨the *terminal* phase of a disease⟩. ***antonym:*** initial

Eventual applies to something that is bound to follow sooner or later as the final effect of causes already in operation and implies a definite ending of a sequence of preliminary events ⟨the *eventual* defeat of the enemy⟩.

Ultimate implies the last degree or stage of a long process or a stage beyond which further progress or change is impossible ⟨the *ultimate* collapse of civilization⟩.

last *vb* See CONTINUE.

lasting, **permanent**, **durable**, **stable** mean enduring for so long as to seem fixed or established.

Lasting implies a capacity to continue indefinitely ⟨a book that left a *lasting* impression on me⟩. ***antonym:*** fleeting

Permanent adds the implication of being designed or planned or expected to stand or continue indefinitely ⟨a *permanent* living arrangement⟩. ***antonym:*** temporary, ad interim (*of persons*)

Durable implies power of resistance to destructive agencies that exceeds that of others of the same kind or sort ⟨*durable* fabrics⟩.

Stable implies lastingness or durability because deep-rooted or balanced or established and therefore resistant to being overturned or displaced ⟨a *stable* government⟩. ***antonym:*** unstable, changeable

late **1.** See TARDY. **2.** See DEAD. **3.** See MODERN.

latent, **dormant**, **quiescent**, **potential**, **abeyant** mean not now manifest or showing signs of activity or existence.

Latent applies to a concealed power or quality that is not yet in sight or action but may emerge and develop in the future ⟨a *latent* sadism that emerged during the war⟩. ***antonym:*** patent

Dormant suggests the inactivity of something, such as a feeling or power, as though it were sleeping and capable of renewed activity ⟨a *dormant* passion existed between them⟩. ***antonym:*** active, live

Quiescent suggests a usually temporary cessation of activity ⟨political tensions were *quiescent* for the moment⟩.

Potential applies to what does not yet have existence, nature, or effect but has the capacity for having it and is likely soon to do so ⟨a toxic waste dump that is a *potential* disaster⟩. ***antonym:*** active, actual

Abeyant applies to what is for the time being held off or suppressed ⟨an *abeyant* distrust of the neighbors⟩. ***antonym:*** active, operative

laughable, **ludicrous**, **ridiculous**, **comic**, **comical**, **risible**, **droll**, **funny** mean provoking laughter or mirth.

Laughable applies to anything that occasions laughter whether intentionally or unintentionally ⟨her attempts at roller-skating were *laughable*⟩.

Ludicrous suggests absurdity or preposterousness that excites both laughter and scorn and sometimes pity ⟨a spy thriller with a *ludicrous* plot⟩.

Ridiculous suggests extreme absurdity, foolishness, or contemptibility ⟨a *ridiculous* portrayal of wartime combat⟩.

Comic applies especially to that which arouses thoughtful or wry amusement ⟨Falstaff is one of Shakespeare's great *comic* characters⟩. ***antonym:*** tragic

Comical applies to that which arouses unrestrained spontaneous hilarity ⟨his *comical* appearance would have tested a saint⟩. ***antonym:*** pathetic

Risible connotes that which causes laughter or is funny ⟨a *risible* account of their mishap⟩.

Droll suggests laughable qualities arising from oddness, quaintness, or deliberate waggishness ⟨amused us with *droll* stories of questionable veracity⟩.

Funny, interchangeable with any of the other terms, may suggest curiousness or strangeness as the basis of a laughable quality ⟨had a *funny* feeling about the whole encounter⟩. ***antonym:*** unfunny

lavish See PROFUSE.

law **1. Law**, **rule**, **regulation**, **precept**, **statute**, **ordinance**, **canon** mean a principle governing action or procedure.

Law implies imposition by a sovereign authority and the obligation of obedience on the part of all who are subject to that authority ⟨obey the *law*⟩. ***antonym:*** chance

Rule suggests closer relation to individual conduct and may imply restriction, usually in regard to a specific situation, for the sake of an immediate end ⟨the *rules* of a game⟩.

Regulation implies prescription by authority in order to control an organization, situation, or system ⟨*regulations* affecting nuclear power plants⟩.

Precept commonly suggests something advisory and authoritative but not obligatory that is communicated typically through teaching ⟨the *precepts* of effective writing⟩. ***antonym:*** practice, counsel

Statute implies a law enacted by a legislative body ⟨a *statute* requiring the use of seat belts⟩.

Ordinance applies to an order governing some detail of procedure or conduct enforced by a limited authority such as a municipality ⟨a city *ordinance*⟩.

Canon in religious use applies to a law of a church; in nonreligious use it suggests a principle or rule of behavior or procedure commonly accepted as a valid guide ⟨a house that violates all the *canons* of good taste⟩.

2. See HYPOTHESIS.

lawful, **legal**, **legitimate**, **licit** mean being in accordance with law.

Lawful may apply to conformity with law of any sort, such as natural, divine, common, or canon ⟨the *lawful* sovereign⟩. ***antonym:*** unlawful

Legal applies to what is sanctioned by law or in conformity with the law, especially as it is written or administered by the courts ⟨*legal* residents of the state⟩. ***antonym:*** illegal

Legitimate may apply to a legal right or status but also, in extended use, to a right or status supported by tradition, custom, or accepted standards ⟨a perfectly *legitimate* question about finances⟩. ***antonym:*** illegitimate, arbitrary (*powers, means*)

Licit applies to a strict conformity to the provisions of the law and applies especially to what is regulated by law ⟨the *licit* use of the drug by hospitals⟩. ***antonym:*** illicit

lawyer, **counselor**, **barrister**, **counsel**, **advocate**, **attorney**, **solicitor** mean one authorized to practice law.

Lawyer applies to anyone versed in the principles of law and authorized to practice law in the courts or to act as legal agent or advisor ⟨the best defense *lawyer* in town⟩.

Counselor applies to one who accepts court cases and gives advice on legal problems ⟨met with their legal *counselor*⟩.

Barrister, the British equivalent of ***counselor***, emphasizes court pleading which in English practice is permitted in higher courts only to barristers ⟨*barristers* before the bench in wigs and robes⟩.

Counsel can be equivalent to ***counselor*** but is typically used collectively to designate a group of lawyers acting for a legal cause in court ⟨*counsel* for the prosecution⟩.

Advocate is similar in implication to ***counselor*** and ***barrister***, but it is used chiefly in countries such as Scotland where the legal system is based on Roman law ⟨acted as *advocate* in the trial⟩.

Attorney is often used interchangeably with ***lawyer***, but in precise use it denotes a lawyer who acts as a legal agent for a client in such matters as conveying property, settling wills, or defending or prosecuting a civil law case ⟨*attorney* for the deceased⟩.

Solicitor is the British term corresponding to ***attorney*** with, however, emphasis on the transaction of legal business for a client as distinct from actual court pleading ⟨sent his *solicitor* to negotiate on his behalf⟩.

lax **1.** See LOOSE. **2.** See NEGLIGENT.

lazy, **indolent**, **slothful** mean not easily aroused to action or activity.

Lazy suggests a disinclination to work or to take trouble and is likely to imply idleness or dawdling even when at work ⟨his habitually *lazy* son⟩. ***antonym:*** industrious

Indolent suggests a love of ease and a settled dislike of movement or activity ⟨the summer's heat made us all *indolent*⟩. ***antonym:*** industrious

Slothful implies a temperamental inability to act promptly or speedily when promptness or speed is called for ⟨the agency is usually *slothful* about fulfilling requests⟩. ***antonym:*** industrious

lead See GUIDE.

league See ALLIANCE.

lean *n* **Lean**, **spare**, **lank**, **lanky**, **gaunt**, **rawboned**, **scrawny**, **skinny** mean thin because of an absence of excess flesh.

Lean stresses lack of fat and of curving contours ⟨a *lean* racehorse⟩. ***antonym:*** fleshy

Spare suggests leanness from abstemious living or constant exercise ⟨the *spare* form of a long-distance runner⟩. ***antonym:*** corpulent

Lank implies tallness as well as leanness ⟨the pale, *lank* limbs of a prisoner of war⟩.

Lanky suggests awkwardness and loose-jointedness as well as thinness ⟨a *lanky* youth, all arms and legs⟩. ***antonym:*** burly

Gaunt implies marked thinness or emaciation as from overwork, undernourishment, or suffering ⟨her *gaunt* face showed the strain of poverty⟩.

Rawboned suggests a large ungainly build without implying undernourishment ⟨*rawboned* lumberjacks squeezed into the booth⟩.

Scrawny suggests extreme thinness and slightness or shrunkenness ⟨*scrawny* kitten⟩. ***antonym:*** brawny, fleshy, obese

Skinny implies leanness that suggests deficient strength and vitality ⟨*skinny* fashion models⟩. ***antonym:*** fleshy

lean *vb* See SLANT.

leaning, **propensity**, **proclivity**, **penchant**, **flair** mean a strong instinct or liking for something.

Leaning suggests a liking or attraction not strong enough to be decisive or uncontrollable ⟨accused of having socialist *leanings*⟩. ***antonym:*** distaste

Propensity implies a deeply ingrained or innate and usually irresistible longing ⟨the natural *propensity* of in-laws to offer advice⟩. ***antonym:*** antipathy

Proclivity suggests a strong natural or habitual proneness usually to something objectionable or evil ⟨movies that reinforce viewers' *proclivities* for violence⟩.

Penchant implies a strongly marked taste for something or an irresistible attraction by something ⟨has a *penchant* for overdramatizing his troubles⟩.

Flair implies an instinctive attraction that leads someone to something ⟨a woman with a real *flair* for business⟩.

learn See DISCOVER.

learned, **scholarly**, **erudite** mean possessing or manifesting unusually wide and deep knowledge.

Learned implies academic knowledge gained by long study and research and is applicable to persons, their associations, or their writings and professional publications ⟨members of a *learned* society⟩.

Scholarly implies learning and applies particularly to persons who have attained mastery of a field of knowledge or to their utterances, ideas, or writings ⟨a *scholarly* study of the causes of war⟩.

Erudite, sometimes interchangeable with ***learned*** and ***scholarly***, can imply a love of learning for its own sake, a taste for out-of-the-way knowledge, or even mere pedanticism ⟨a mind filled with *erudite* and arcane lore⟩.

learning See KNOWLEDGE.
lease See HIRE.
leave *vb* **1.** See GO. **2.** See LET.
leave *n* See PERMISSION.
leaven See INFUSE.
leech See PARASITE.
legal See LAWFUL.
legend See MYTH.
legendary See FICTITIOUS.
legitimate See LAWFUL.
lengthen See EXTEND.
lenient **1.** See FORBEARING. **2.** See SOFT.
lenity See MERCY.
lessen See DECREASE.
let **1. Let**, **allow**, **permit**, **suffer**, **leave** mean not to forbid or prevent.

Let may imply a positive giving of permission but more often implies failure to prevent either through inadvertence and negligence or through lack of power or effective authority ⟨the goalie *let* the ball get by her⟩.

Allow implies little more than a forbearing to prohibit or to exert this power ⟨a teacher who *allows* her pupils to do as they like⟩. ***antonym:*** inhibit

Permit implies express willingness or acquiescence ⟨the park *permits* powerboats on the lake⟩. ***antonym:*** prohibit, forbid

Suffer can be close to ***allow*** or may distinctively imply indifference or reluctance ⟨*suffered* themselves to be photographed⟩.

Leave stresses the implication of noninterference in letting or allowing or permitting and can suggest the departure of the person who might interfere ⟨*left* them to resolve the matter among themselves⟩.

2. See HIRE.

lethal See DEADLY.
lethargy, **languor**, **lassitude**, **stupor**, **torpor** mean physical or mental inertness.

Lethargy implies a drowsiness or aversion to activity such as is induced by disease, injury, or drugs ⟨months of *lethargy* followed my skiing accident⟩. ***antonym:*** vigor

Languor suggests inertia induced by an enervating climate or illness or soft living or love ⟨*languor* induced by a tropical vacation⟩. ***antonym:*** alacrity

Lassitude stresses listlessness or indifference resulting from fatigue or poor health ⟨a deepening depression marked by *lassitude*⟩. ***antonym:*** vigor

Stupor implies a deadening of the mind and senses by or as if by shock, narcotics, or intoxicants ⟨lapsed into a *stupor* following a night of drinking⟩.

Torpor implies a state of suspended animation as of hibernating animals but may suggest merely extreme sluggishness ⟨a once-alert mind now in a state of *torpor*⟩. ***antonym:*** animation

level, **flat**, **plane**, **even**, **smooth**, **flush** mean having a surface without bends, curves, or irregularities, and with no part higher than any other.

Level applies to a horizontal surface that lies on a line parallel with the horizon ⟨the vast prairies are nearly *level*⟩.

Flat applies to any surface devoid of noticeable curvatures, prominences, or depressions ⟨the work surface must be totally *flat*⟩.

Plane applies to any real or imaginary flat surface in which a straight line between any two points on it lies wholly and continuously within that surface ⟨the *plane* sides of a crystal⟩.

Even applies to a surface that is noticeably flat or level or to a line that is observably straight ⟨trim the hedge so that it is *even*⟩. ***antonym:*** uneven

Smooth applies to a flat or even surface especially free of irregularities ⟨a *smooth* dance floor⟩. ***antonym:*** rough

Flush applies to a surface or line that forms a continuous surface or line with another surface or line ⟨the river's surface is now *flush* with the top of the banks⟩.

levity See LIGHTNESS.

liable 1. Liable, **open**, **exposed**, **subject**, **prone**, **susceptible**, **sensitive** mean being by nature or through circumstances likely to experience something adverse.

Liable implies a possibility or probability of incurring something because of position, nature, or the action of forces beyond one's control ⟨unless you're careful, you're *liable* to fall⟩. ***antonym:*** exempt, immune

Open stresses ease of access and a lack of protective barriers ⟨a claim that is *open* to question⟩. ***antonym:*** closed

Exposed suggests lack of protection or powers of resistance against something actually present or threatening ⟨the town's *exposed* position makes it impossible to defend⟩.

Subject implies an openness for any reason to something that must be suffered or undergone ⟨all reports are *subject* to editorial revision⟩. ***antonym:*** exempt

Prone stresses natural tendency or propensity to incur something ⟨a person who is *prone* to accidents⟩.

Susceptible implies conditions existing in one's nature or individual constitution that make one unusually open to something, especially something deleterious ⟨young children are *susceptible* to colds⟩. ***antonym:*** immune

Sensitive implies a readiness to respond to or be influenced by forces or stimuli ⟨her eyes are *sensitive* to light⟩. ***antonym:*** insensitive

2. See RESPONSIBLE.

liaison See AMOUR.

libel See MALIGN *vb*.

liberal 1. Liberal, **generous**, **bountiful**, **munificent** mean giving freely and unstintingly.

Liberal suggests openhandedness in the giver and largeness in the thing or amount given ⟨a teacher *liberal* in bestowing praise⟩. ***antonym:*** close

Generous stresses warmhearted readiness to give more than the size or importance of the gift ⟨a friend's *generous* offer of assistance⟩. ***antonym:*** stingy

Bountiful suggests lavish, unremitting generosity in giving or providing ⟨*bountiful* grandparents spoiling the children⟩.

Munificent suggests splendid or princely lavishness in giving ⟨the Queen was especially *munificent* to her favorite⟩.

2. Liberal, **progressive**, **advanced**, **radical** mean freed from or opposed to what is orthodox, established, or conservative.

Liberal implies a greater or less degree of emancipation from convention, tradition, or dogma and may suggest either pragmatism and tolerance or unorthodoxy, extremism, and laxness ⟨a politician's *liberal* tendencies⟩. ***antonym:*** authoritarian

Progressive is likely to imply a comparison with what is backward or reactionary and a readiness to forsake old methods and beliefs for new ones that hold more promise ⟨went to the most *progressive* school her parents could find⟩. ***antonym:*** reactionary

Advanced applies to what is or seems to be ahead of its proper time and can connote liberalism and mental daring or extreme foolhardiness and experimental impracticality ⟨a man with *advanced* ideas⟩. ***antonym:*** conservative

Radical is likely to imply willingness to destroy the institutions which conserve the ideas or policies condemned and comes close to *revolutionary* in meaning ⟨an idea conceived by a group of *radical* reformers⟩. ***antonym:*** conservative

liberate See FREE *vb*.

liberty See FREEDOM.

license See FREEDOM.

licit See LAWFUL.

lick See CONQUER.

lie, **prevaricate**, **equivocate**, **palter**, **fib** mean to tell an untruth.

Lie is the blunt term, imputing dishonesty to the speaker ⟨to *lie* under oath is a serious crime⟩.

Prevaricate softens the bluntness of ***lie*** by implying a quibbling or an evading or confusing of the issue ⟨during the hearings the witness did his best to *prevaricate*⟩.

Equivocate implies the using of ambiguous words in an attempt to mislead or deceive ⟨*equivocated,* dodged questions, and generally misled her inquisitors⟩.

Palter implies the making of unreliable statements of fact or intention or insincere promises ⟨a cad *paltering* with a naive, young girl⟩.

Fib applies to the telling of a trivial untruth ⟨*fibbed* about the price of the suit⟩.

lift, **raise**, **rear**, **elevate**, **hoist**, **heave**, **boost** mean to move from a lower to a higher place or position.

Lift usually implies exerting effort to overcome the resistance of weight ⟨*lift* the chair while I vacuum⟩. ***antonym:*** lower

Raise carries an implication of bringing up to the vertical or to a high position ⟨soldiers *raising* a flagpole⟩.

Rear can be used in place of ***raise*** but can also be used meaning to raise itself ⟨a steeple *rearing* into the sky⟩.

Elevate may replace ***lift*** or ***raise*** especially when exalting or enhancing is implied ⟨*elevated* the musical tastes of the public⟩. ***antonym:*** lower

Hoist implies the lifting of something heavy, especially by mechanical means ⟨*hoisted* the cargo on board⟩.

Heave implies lifting with a great effort or strain ⟨struggled to *heave* the heavy crate⟩.

Boost suggests assisting to climb or advance by a push ⟨*boosted* his brother over the fence⟩.

light *adj* See EASY.

light *vb* **Light**, **kindle**, **ignite**, **fire** mean to start something to burn.

Light is likely to imply an action for a specific end, such as illuminating, heating, or smoking ⟨*light* a fire in the stove⟩. ***antonym:*** extinguish

Kindle may connote difficulty in setting combustible materials alight and is appropriate when special preparations are needed ⟨we *kindled* the bonfire just after dark⟩ or may connote an exciting, arousing, or stimulating ⟨a look that *kindled* a responsive spark⟩. ***antonym:*** smother

Ignite, like ***kindle***, stresses successful lighting but is more likely to apply to highly flammable materials ⟨*ignite* a firecracker⟩, or it may imply a stirring into activity ⟨a love of learning *ignited* by her first-grade teacher⟩.

Fire suggests blazing and rapid combustion and is usually used with respect to something that ignites readily and burns fiercely ⟨*fire* a haystack⟩ or may imply an inspiring, as with passion, zeal, or desire, to energetic activity ⟨an imagination *fired* with a thousand new ideas⟩.

lighten See RELIEVE.

lighthearted See GLAD.

lightness, **levity**, **frivolity**, **flippancy**, **volatility**, **flightiness** mean gaiety or indifference when seriousness is called for.

Lightness implies a lack of weight and seriousness and sometimes an instability or careless heedlessness in character, mood, or conduct ⟨the only bit of *lightness* in a dreary, ponderous drama⟩. ***antonym:*** seriousness

Levity suggests trifling or unseasonable gaiety ⟨injected a moment of *levity* in the solemn proceedings⟩. ***antonym:*** gravity

Frivolity suggests irresponsible indulgence in gaieties or in idle speech or conduct ⟨a playgirl living a life of uninterrupted *frivolity*⟩. ***antonym:*** seriousness, staidness

Flippancy implies an unbecoming levity especially in speaking of grave or sacred matters ⟨spoke of the bombing with annoying *flippancy*⟩. ***antonym:*** seriousness

Volatility implies such lightness or fickleness of disposition as prevents long attention to any one thing ⟨the *volatility* of the public interest in foreign aid⟩.

Flightiness implies extreme volatility that may approach loss of mental balance ⟨the *flightiness* of my grandmother in her old age⟩. ***antonym:*** steadiness, steadfastness

like See SIMILAR.

likely See PROBABLE.

likeness, **similarity**, **resemblance**, **similitude**, **analogy**, **affinity** mean agreement or correspondence in details.

Likeness implies a close correspondence ⟨a remarkable *likeness* to his late father⟩. ***antonym:*** unlikeness

Similarity often implies that things are merely somewhat alike ⟨some *similarity* between the two cases⟩. ***antonym:*** dissimilarity

Resemblance implies similarity chiefly in appearance or in external or superficial qualities ⟨statements that bear no *resemblance* to the truth⟩. ***antonym:*** difference, distinction

Similitude applies chiefly when the abstract idea of likeness is under consideration ⟨the *similitude* of environments was rigidly maintained⟩. ***antonym:*** dissimilitude, dissimilarity

Analogy implies comparison of things that are basically unlike and is more apt to draw attention to likeness or parallelism in relations rather than in appearance or qualities ⟨pointed out the *analogies* to past situations⟩.

Affinity suggests a cause such as kinship or sympathetic experience or historical influence in common that is responsible for the similarity ⟨a writer with a striking *affinity* for American Indian culture⟩.

limb See SHOOT.

limber See SUPPLE.

limit, **restrict**, **circumscribe**, **confine** mean to set bounds for.

Limit implies the setting of a point or line, as in time, space, speed, or degree, beyond which something cannot or is not permitted to go ⟨visits are *limited* to 30 minutes⟩. ***antonym:*** widen

Restrict suggests a narrowing or tightening or restraining within or as if within an encircling boundary ⟨laws intended to *restrict* the freedom of the press⟩.

Circumscribe stresses a restriction in every direction and by clearly defined boundaries ⟨the work of the investigating committee was carefully *circumscribed*⟩. ***antonym:*** dilate, expand

Confine suggests severe restraint within bounds that cannot or must not be passed and a resulting cramping, fettering, or hampering ⟨our freedom of choice was *confined* by finances⟩.

limp, **floppy**, **flaccid**, **flabby**, **flimsy**, **sleazy** mean deficient in firmness of texture, substance, or structure.

Limp implies a lack or loss of stiffness or body and a resulting tendency to droop ⟨a faded flower on a *limp* stem⟩.

Floppy applies to something that sags or hangs limply and is likely to suggest flexibility and a natural or intended lack of stiffness ⟨wore a large *floppy* garden hat that shaded her eyes⟩.

Flaccid applies primarily to living tissues and implies a loss of normal and especially youthful firmness or a lack of force or energy or substance ⟨a *flaccid* resolve that easily gave way⟩. ***antonym:*** resilient

Flabby in its application to material things is very close to ***flaccid***, but it also suggests spinelessness, spiritlessness, or lethargy ⟨a *flabby* substitute for a hero⟩. ***antonym:*** firm

Flimsy applies to something of such looseness of structure or insubstantiality of texture as to be unable to stand up under strain; it may also stress a lack of real worth or of capacity for endurance ⟨a *flimsy* excuse⟩.

Sleazy implies a flimsiness due to cheap or careless workmanship and may stress a lack or inferiority of standards ⟨a *sleazy* tale of second-rate intrigue⟩.

limpid See CLEAR 1.

line, **align**, **range**, **array** mean to arrange in a line or lines.

Line implies a setting in single file or parallel rows 〈*line* up prisoners for identification〉.

Align stresses the bringing of points or parts that should be in a straight line into correct adjustment or into correspondence 〈*align* the front and rear wheels of an automobile〉.

Range stresses orderly disposition, sometimes by aligning but often by separating into classes according to some plan 〈students *ranged* in groups by age and gender〉.

Array applies especially to a setting in battle order and therefore suggests readiness for action or use as well as ordered arrangement 〈a splendid collection of legal talent *arrayed* against the prosecution〉. ***antonym:*** disarray

linger See STAY.

lingo See DIALECT.

link See JOIN.

liquid, **fluid** mean composed of particles that move easily and flowingly and change their relative position without perceptible break in continuity.

Liquid applies to substances that, like water, are only slightly compressible and are capable of conversion, under suitable conditions of pressure and temperature, into gases 〈watched as a *liquid* tear rolled down the child's cheek〉, or it implies a softness or transparency 〈heard with joy the *liquid* song of the hermit thrush〉. ***antonym:*** solid, vaporous

Fluid is applicable to both liquids and gases or it can be opposed to *rigid*, fixed, unchangeable and apply to whatever is essentially unstable or to what tends to flow easily or freely 〈the *fluid* nature of international relations〉. ***antonym:*** solid

lissome See SUPPLE.

lithe See SUPPLE.

lithesome See SUPPLE.

little See SMALL.

live See RESIDE.

lively, **animated**, **vivacious**, **sprightly**, **gay** mean keenly alive and spirited.

Lively suggests briskness, alertness, or energy 〈a *lively* hour of news and information〉. ***antonym:*** dull

Animated applies to what is spirited, active, and sparkling 〈an *animated* discussion of current events〉. ***antonym:*** depressed, dejected

Vivacious suggests an activeness of gesture and wit, often playful or alluring 〈a *vivacious* party hostess〉. ***antonym:*** languid

Sprightly suggests lightness and spirited vigor of manner or of wit 〈a tuneful, *sprightly* musical revue〉.

Gay stresses complete freedom from care and exuberantly overflowing spirits 〈the *gay* spirit of Paris in the 1920s〉. ***antonym:*** grave, sober

livid See PALE 1.

living, **alive**, **animate**, **animated**, **vital** mean having or showing life.

Living applies to organic bodies having life as opposed to those from which life has gone 〈*living* artists〉. ***antonym:*** lifeless

Alive, opposed to *dead*, is like ***living***, but follows the word it modifies 〈toss the lobster into the pot while it's still *alive*〉. ***antonym:*** dead, defunct

Animate is used chiefly in direct opposition to *inanimate* to denote things alive or capable of life 〈a child seemingly afraid of every *animate* object〉. ***antonym:*** inanimate

Animated is applied to that which becomes alive and active or is given motion simulating life 〈an *animated* cartoon〉. ***antonym:*** inert

Vital implies the energy and especially the power to grow and reproduce that are characteristic of life 〈all of his *vital* functions seemed normal〉.

loath See DISINCLINED.

loathe See HATE.

location See PLACE.

locution See PHRASE.

lodge **1.** See HARBOR. **2.** See RESIDE.

lofty See HIGH.

logical, **analytic**, **analytical**, **subtle** mean having or showing skill in thinking or reasoning.

Logical may imply a capacity for orderly thinking or, more especially, the power to impress others that clearness of thought and freedom from bias underlie the products of one's thinking ⟨an infuriatingly *logical* mind, utterly devoid of emotion⟩. ***antonym:*** illogical

Analytic, often as the variant ***analytical***, stresses the power to simplify what is complicated or complex or what is chaotic or confused by separating and recombining elements in a logical manner ⟨proceeded by precise *analytic* processes to find the hidden cause⟩.

Subtle basically implies a capacity to penetrate below the surface and perceive fine distinctions and minute relations, and it usually connotes exceptional skill in reasoning and analysis ⟨saw the heart of the crisis through *subtle* logic⟩. ***antonym:*** dense (*in mind*), blunt (*in speech*)

logistics See STRATEGY.

loiter See DELAY 2.

lone See ALONE.

lonely See ALONE.

lonesome See ALONE.

long, **yearn**, **hanker**, **pine**, **hunger**, **thirst** mean to have a strong desire for something.

Long implies a wishing with one's whole heart for something remote or not easily attainable ⟨*longed* for some peace and quiet⟩.

Yearn suggests an eager, restless, or painful longing ⟨*yearned* for a career on the stage⟩. ***antonym:*** dread

Hanker suggests the uneasy promptings of unsatisfied appetite or desire ⟨always *hankering* for more money⟩.

Pine implies a languishing or a fruitless longing for what is impossible of attainment ⟨*pined* for a long-lost love⟩.

Hunger implies an insistent or impatient craving or a compelling need like that for food ⟨*hungered* for a business of his own⟩.

Thirst suggests a compelling need like that for liquid ⟨*thirsted* for absolute power⟩.

look **1.** See EXPECT. **2.** See SEE 2. **3.** See SEEM.

looker-on See SPECTATOR.

loose, **relaxed**, **slack**, **lax** mean not tightly bound, held, restrained, or stretched.

Loose is widely referable to persons or things free from a usual or former restraint ⟨a book with a *loose* page⟩ or to something not firmly or tightly held or connected between points of contact ⟨drive with *loose* reins⟩ or to a substance or fabric with particles or filaments in open arrangement ⟨a *loose*-woven woolen⟩. ***antonym:*** strict, tight

Relaxed implies a loss of some tightness, tension, strictness, or rigidity; it may also imply an easing of rather than a freeing from what restrains ⟨the *relaxed* discipline of the last few days of school⟩. ***antonym:*** stiff

Slack, otherwise close to ***relaxed***, may stress lack of firmness and steadiness ⟨an overweight body, pudgy and *slack*⟩. ***antonym:*** taut, tight

Lax stresses lack of steadiness, firmness, and tone or, in respect to immaterial things, may stress lack of needed or proper steadiness and firmness ⟨a *lax* administration⟩. ***antonym:*** rigid

loot See SPOIL.

loquacious See TALKATIVE.

lordly See PROUD.

lot **1.** See FATE. **2.** See GROUP.

loud, **stentorian**, **earsplitting**, **raucous**, **strident** mean marked by intensity or volume of sound.

Loud applies to any volume above normal and may suggest undue vehemence or obtrusiveness ⟨a *loud* obnoxious person⟩. ***antonym:*** low, soft

Stentorian, chiefly used of voices, implies great power and range ⟨an actor with a *stentorian* voice⟩.
Earsplitting implies loudness that is physically oppressive and shrilly discomforting ⟨the *earsplitting* sound of a siren⟩.
Raucous implies a loud harsh grating tone, especially of voice, and may suggest rowdiness ⟨a barroom filled with the *raucous* shouts of drunken revelers⟩.
Strident implies a rasping discordant but insistent quality, especially of voice ⟨the *strident* voices of hecklers⟩.

loutish See BOORISH.
lovely See BEAUTIFUL.
low See BASE *adj*.
lower See FROWN.
lowly See HUMBLE.
loyal See FAITHFUL.
loyalty See FIDELITY.
lucid See CLEAR 2.
luck See CHANCE.

lucky, **fortunate**, **happy**, **providential** mean meeting with or producing unforeseen success.
Lucky stresses the agency of chance in bringing about a favorable result ⟨the *lucky* day I met my future wife⟩. ***antonym:*** luckless, unlucky
Fortunate suggests being rewarded beyond one's deserts or expectations ⟨have been *fortunate* in my business investments⟩. ***antonym:*** unfortunate
Happy combines the implications of ***lucky*** and ***fortunate*** with its more common meaning of being blessed ⟨a life that has been a series of *happy* accidents⟩. ***antonym:*** unhappy
Providential more definitely implies the help or intervention of a higher power in the coming of good or the averting of evil fortune ⟨it was *providential* that rescuers arrived in the nick of time⟩.

ludicrous See LAUGHABLE.
lull See PAUSE.
luminous See BRIGHT.
lunatic See INSANE.

lure, **entice**, **inveigle**, **decoy**, **tempt**, **seduce** mean to draw one from a usual, desirable, or proper course or situation into one considered unusual, undesirable, or wrong.
Lure implies a drawing into danger, evil, or difficulty through attracting and deceiving ⟨*lured* naive investors with get-rich-quick schemes⟩. ***antonym:*** revolt, repel
Entice suggests a drawing by artful or adroit means ⟨advertising designed to *entice* new customers⟩. ***antonym:*** scare (*off*)
Inveigle implies an enticing by cajoling or flattering ⟨*inveigled* her suitor into proposing marriage⟩.
Decoy implies a luring away or into entrapment by artifice and false appearances ⟨the female bird attempted to *decoy* us away from her nest⟩.
Tempt implies the exerting of an attraction so strong that it overcomes the restraints of conscience or better judgment ⟨*tempted* him to abandon his diet⟩.
Seduce implies a leading astray by persuasion or false promises ⟨*seduced* young runaways into the criminal life⟩.

lurid See GHASTLY.

lurk, **skulk**, **slink**, **sneak** mean to behave furtively so as to escape attention.
Lurk implies a lying in wait in a place of concealment and often suggests an evil intent ⟨suspicious men *lurking* in alleyways⟩.
Skulk suggests furtive movement and cowardice or fear or sinister intent ⟨spied something *skulking* in the shadows⟩.
Slink implies a stealthiness in moving to escape attention and may connote sly caution ⟨during the festivities, I *slunk* away⟩.
Sneak may add an implication of entering or leaving a place or evading a difficulty by furtive, indirect, or underhanded methods ⟨he *sneaked* out after the others had fallen asleep⟩.

lush See PROFUSE.
lustrous See BRIGHT.
lusty See VIGOROUS.
luxuriant See PROFUSE.
luxurious **1. Luxurious**, **sumptuous**, **opulent** mean ostentatiously rich or magnificent.

Luxurious applies to what is choice and costly and suggests gratification of the senses and desire for comfort 〈a millionaire's *luxurious* penthouse apartment〉. ***Sumptuous*** applies to what is overwhelmingly or extravagantly rich, splendid, or luxurious 〈an old-fashioned grand hotel with a *sumptuous* lobby〉. ***Opulent*** suggests a flaunting of luxuriousness, luxuriance, or costliness 〈an *opulent* wedding intended to impress the guests〉.

2. See SENSUOUS.
lying See DISHONEST.

M

macabre See GHASTLY.
machination See PLOT.
mad See INSANE.
magisterial See DICTATORIAL.
magnificent See GRAND.

maim, **cripple**, **mutilate**, **batter**, **mangle** mean to injure so severely as to cause lasting damage.

Maim implies the loss or injury of a limb or member usually through violence ⟨a swimmer *maimed* by a shark⟩.

Cripple implies the loss or serious impairment of an arm or leg ⟨the fall *crippled* her for life⟩.

Mutilate implies the cutting off or removal of an essential part of a person or thing thereby impairing its completeness, beauty, or function ⟨a poignant drama *mutilated* by inept acting⟩.

Batter implies a pounding with series of blows that bruises deeply, deforms, or mutilates ⟨a ship *battered* by fierce storms at sea⟩.

Mangle implies a tearing or crushing that leaves deep extensive wounds or lacerations ⟨thousands are *mangled* every year by auto accidents⟩.

maintain, **assert**, **defend**, **vindicate**, **justify** mean to uphold as true, right, just, or reasonable.

Maintain stresses firmness of conviction, and is likely to suggest persistent or insistent upholding of a cause and may suggest aggressiveness or obtrusiveness ⟨steadfastly *maintained* his client's innocence⟩.

Assert suggests a determination to make others accept one's claim of one's position ⟨fiercely *asserted* that credit for the discovery belonged to her⟩.

Defend implies maintaining one's claim in the face of attack or criticism ⟨I need not *defend* my wartime record⟩.

Vindicate implies a successful defending ⟨his success *vindicated* our faith in him⟩.

Justify implies a showing to be true, right, acceptable, or valid by appeal to a standard or to precedent ⟨threats to public safety *justified* such drastic steps⟩.

majestic See GRAND.

majority, **plurality** mean a number or quantity or part larger than some other expressed or implied, particularly in reference to an election.

Majority implies that the winning candidate or opinion has received more votes than the other candidates or opinions combined; that is, the winning vote is in excess of half the votes cast ⟨elected to the senate by a very slim *majority*⟩.

Plurality merely implies that the winner has more votes than any other candidate or opinion, whether a majority of the total or not ⟨a *plurality* of the voters defeated the referendum⟩.

make, **form**. **shape**, **fashion**, **fabricate**, **manufacture**, **forge** mean to cause to come into being.

Make applies to any action of producing or creating whether by an intelligent agency or blind forces and whether the product has material or immaterial existence ⟨the factory *makes* furniture⟩.

Form implies the generating of a definite outline, structure, or design in the thing produced ⟨*form* a plan⟩.

Shape suggests the impressing of a form upon some material by some external agent ⟨*shaped* shrubbery into animal figures⟩.

Fashion suggests the use of inventive power or ingenuity ⟨*fashioned* a bicycle out of spare parts⟩.

Fabricate suggests a uniting of many parts into a whole and often implies an ingenious inventing of something false ⟨*fabricated* an exotic background for her biography⟩.

Manufacture implies a making repeatedly by a fixed process and usually by machinery ⟨*manufacture* shoes⟩.

Forge implies a making or devising or concocting by great physical or mental effort ⟨*forged* an agreement after months of negotiating⟩.

make-believe See PRETENSE.

maker, **creator**, **author** mean one who brings something new into being or existence. (When written with an initial capital letter all three terms are used to designate God or the Supreme Being.)

Maker is likely to imply a close and immediate relationship between the one who makes and the thing that is made and an ensuing responsibility for what is turned out ⟨thought of herself as a *maker* of tales⟩.

Creator stresses a bringing into existence of what the mind conceives and is likely to suggest originality and delving into the unknown ⟨a robot, ultimately destructive of his *creator*⟩.

Author applies to one who originates something and who is the source of its being and as such wholly responsible for its existence ⟨the *author* of several books⟩.

makeshift See RESOURCE.

maladroit See AWKWARD.

male See MASCULINE.

malevolence See MALICE.

malice, **malevolence**, **ill will**, **spite**, **malignity**, **malignancy**, **spleen**, **grudge** mean the desire or wish to see another experience pain, injury, or distress.

Malice implies a deep-seated often unexplainable desire to see another suffer ⟨felt no *malice* for their former enemies⟩, or it may suggest a causeless passing mischievous impulse ⟨a rascal full of *malice*⟩. ***antonym:*** charity

Malevolence suggests a bitter persistent hatred and may suggest inherent evil that is likely to be expressed in malicious conduct ⟨deep *malevolence* governed his every act⟩. ***antonym:*** benevolence

Ill will implies a feeling of antipathy that is of limited duration and usually lacks any element of mental turmoil ⟨a directive that provoked *ill will* among the employees⟩. ***antonym:*** goodwill, charity

Spite implies a petty feeling of envy and resentment that is often expressed in small harassments and meanness ⟨petty insults inspired only by *spite*⟩.

Malignity implies deep passion and relentless driving force ⟨never viewed her daughter-in-law with anything but *malignity*⟩. ***antonym:*** benignity

Malignancy suggests aggressive maliciousness that comes from a basically evil or injurious nature ⟨proceeded to treat the employees with insupportable *malignancy*⟩. ***antonym:*** benignity

Spleen suggests the wrathful release of latent spite or persistent malice ⟨quick to vent his *spleen* at incompetent subordinates⟩.

Grudge implies a harbored or cherished feeling of resentment or ill will that seeks satisfaction ⟨never one to harbor a *grudge*⟩.

malign *adj* See SINISTER.

malign *vb* **Malign**, **traduce**, **asperse**, **vilify**, **calumniate**, **defame**, **slander**, **libel** mean to injure by speaking ill of.

Malign suggests a specific and often subtle misrepresentation but may not always imply deliberate lying ⟨the most *maligned* monarch in British history⟩. ***antonym:*** defend

Traduce stresses the resulting ignominy and distress to the victim ⟨so *traduced* the governor that he was driven from office⟩.

Asperse implies a continued attack on a reputation often by indirect or insinuated detraction ⟨each candidate *aspersed* the other's motives⟩.

Vilify implies an attempting to destroy a reputation by open and direct abuse ⟨no President was more *vilified* by the press⟩. ***antonym:*** eulogize

Calumniate imputes malice to the speaker and falsity to his or her assertion ⟨threatened with a lawsuit for publicly *calumniating* the company⟩. ***antonym:*** eulogize, vindicate

Defame stresses the actual loss of or injury to one's good name ⟨forced to pay a substantial sum for *defaming* her reputation⟩. ***antonym:*** laud, puff

Slander stresses the suffering of the victim from oral or written calumniation ⟨town gossips carelessly *slandered* their good name⟩.

Libel implies the printing or writing and publication or circulation of something that defames a person or his or her reputation ⟨sued the magazine for *libel*⟩.

malignancy 1. See MALICE. **2.** See TUMOR.

malignity See MALICE.

malleable See PLASTIC.

malodorous, **stinking**, **fetid**, **noisome**, **putrid**, **rancid**, **rank**, **fusty**, **musty** mean having a bad or unpleasant smell.

Malodorous may range from the unpleasant to the strongly offensive ⟨*malodorous* unidentifiable substances in the refrigerator⟩.

Stinking suggests the foul or disgusting ⟨prisoners were held in *stinking* cells⟩.

Fetid implies an odor which is peculiarly offensive ⟨skunk cabbage is a *fetid* weed⟩. ***antonym:*** fragrant

Noisome adds a suggestion of being harmful or unwholesome as well as offensive ⟨a *noisome* toxic waste dump⟩. ***antonym:*** balmy

Putrid implies particularly the sickening odor of decaying organic matter ⟨the typically *putrid* smell of a fish pier⟩.

Rancid suggests foulness of both taste and smell, usually of fatty substances that have spoiled ⟨the unmistakable stink of *rancid* butter⟩.

Rank suggests a strong, unpleasant, but not necessarily foul smell ⟨rooms filled with the *rank* smoke of cigars⟩. ***antonym:*** balmy

Fusty suggets lack of fresh air and sunlight and implies prolonged uncleanliness ⟨the *fusty* rooms of a bus station⟩.

Musty implies staleness marked by dampness, darkness, and moldiness ⟨the *musty* odor of a damp cellar⟩.

mammoth See ENORMOUS.

manacle See HAMPER.

manage See CONDUCT.

maneuver See TRICK.

manful See MASCULINE.

mangle See MAIM.

mania, **delirium**, **frenzy**, **hysteria** mean a state marked by exaggerated reactions and a loss of emotional, mental, or nervous control.

Mania usually implies excessive or unreasonable enthusiasm ⟨a society with a *mania* for football⟩.

Delirium adds the notion of extreme emotional excitement ⟨in a *delirium* of ecstasy at the thought of seeing her again⟩. ***antonym:*** apathy

Frenzy suggests loss of self-control and violent agitation often manifested in action ⟨shoppers driven to a *frenzy* during the annual sale⟩.

Hysteria implies emotional instability that is often marked by swift transitions of mood ⟨the *hysteria* of the fans⟩.

maniac See INSANE.

manifest *adj* See EVIDENT.

manifest *vb* See SHOW 1.

manipulate See HANDLE.

manlike See MASCULINE.

manly See MASCULINE.

manner 1. See BEARING. **2.** See METHOD.

mannerism See POSE.

mannish See MASCULINE.

manufacture See MAKE.

manumit See FREE *vb*.

many-sided See VERSATILE.

mar See INJURE.

margin See BORDER.

marital See MATRIMONIAL.

mark See SIGN.

marshal See ORDER.

martial, **warlike**, **military** mean of or characteristic of war.

Martial suggests especially the pomp and circumstance of war ⟨standing in *martial* array⟩.

Warlike is more likely to imply the spirit or temper or acts that lead to or accompany war ⟨spouting *warlike* rhetoric⟩. ***antonym:*** unwarlike

Military may imply reference to war, to arms, or to armed forces ⟨a *military* expedition⟩ and may be specifically opposed to *civil* or *civilian* ⟨*military* law⟩ or restricted to land, or land and air, forces as opposed to *naval* ⟨*military* and naval attachés⟩. ***antonym:*** unmilitary

masculine, **male**, **manly**, **manlike**, **mannish**, **manful**, **virile** mean of, characteristic of, or like a male, especially of the human species.

Masculine applies to qualities or attributes or attitudes characteristic of men and not shared by women ⟨a *masculine* physique⟩. ***antonym:*** feminine

Male is broadly applicable to plants, animals, and persons and stresses the fact of sex ⟨a *male* tiger⟩. ***antonym:*** female

Manly suggests the qualities of the mature man, especially the finer qualities of a man or the powers and skills that come with maturity ⟨wounded his *manly* pride⟩. ***antonym:*** unmanly, womanly

Manlike is more likely to suggest characteristically masculine faults and foibles ⟨exhibited a thoroughly *manlike* disregard for details⟩, but sometimes its reference is to human beings in general and then it suggests resemblance to the human kind ⟨an early hominid, vaguely *manlike* in appearance⟩.

Mannish is often used derogatorily in situations in which womanliness might naturally be expected or wanted ⟨adopted an aggressively *mannish* stance⟩ but in more neutral use, especially as applied to styles and dress, it carries little more than a suggestion of actual masculinity ⟨dressed nattily in a *mannish* suit of tweed⟩. ***antonym:*** womanish

Manful stresses sturdiness and resolution ⟨a *manful* effort to achieve success⟩.

Virile suggests the qualities of fully developed manhood but is at once stronger in emphasis and more specific in many of its applications than ***manly*** or ***masculine*** ⟨a man of eighty yet still strong and *virile*⟩ and in more general applications is likely to imply manful vigor ⟨walked with a *virile* stride⟩. ***antonym:*** effeminate, impotent

mask See DISGUISE.

mass See BULK.

massacre, **slaughter**, **butchery**, **carnage**, **pogrom** mean a great and usually wanton killing of human beings.

Massacre implies promiscuous and wholesale slaying, especially of those not in a position to defend themselves ⟨arrived in time to view the aftermath of the *massacre*⟩.

Slaughter implies extensive and ruthless killing as in a battle or a massacre ⟨went meekly, like lambs to the *slaughter*⟩.

Butchery adds to ***slaughter*** the implication of exceeding cruelty and complete disregard of the sufferings of the victims ⟨barbarians engaged in savage *butchery* of the conquered people⟩.

Carnage stresses bloodshed and great loss of life ⟨saw scenes of the crash and attendant *carnage*⟩.

Pogrom describes an organized massacre and looting of defenseless people, carried on usually with official connivance ⟨a governmentally sanctioned *pogrom* against other ethnic groups⟩.

masterful, **domineering**, **imperious**, **peremptory**, **imperative** mean tending to impose one's will on others.

Masterful implies a strong personality and ability to act authoritatively ⟨her *masterful* personality soon dominated the movement⟩.

Domineering suggests an overbearing or tyrannical manner and an obstinate determination to enforce one's will ⟨*domineering* older siblings, ordering the younger ones about⟩. ***antonym:*** subservient

Imperious implies a commanding nature or manner and often suggests arrogant assurance ⟨an *imperious* executive used to getting his own way⟩. ***antonym:*** abject

Peremptory implies an abrupt dictatorial manner coupled with an unwillingness to tolerate disobedience or dissent ⟨a *peremptory* style that does not allow for compromise⟩.

Imperative implies peremptoriness arising more from the urgency of the situation than from an inherent will to dominate ⟨an *imperative* appeal for assistance⟩.

match, **rival**, **equal**, **approach**, **touch** mean to come up to or nearly up to the standard of something else.

Match implies that one thing is the mate rather than the duplicate of another, as in power, strength, beauty, or interest ⟨feels that no language can *match* French for clarity and exactness⟩.

Rival suggests a close competition, as for superiority or in excellence ⟨a voice which none could *rival*⟩.

Equal implies such close equivalence, as in quantity, worth, or degree, that no question concerning a difference or deficiency can arise ⟨a love of glory *equaled* only by a fear of shame⟩.

Approach implies such closeness in matching or equaling that the difference, though detectable, scarcely matters ⟨a beauty *approaching* perfection⟩.

Touch suggests close equivalence, as in quality or value, and is typically used in negative constructions ⟨as for durability, no current product can *touch* the new product⟩.

material **1. Material**, **physical**, **corporeal**, **phenomenal**, **sensible**, **objective** mean of or belonging to the world of actuality or to things apparent to the senses.

Material implies formation out of tangible matter, but may imply a contrast to *spiritual*, *ideal*, or *intangible* ⟨*material* possessions⟩. ***antonym:*** immaterial

Physical applies to what is perceived directly by the senses or can be measured or calculated and may contrast with *mental*, *spiritual*, or *imaginary* ⟨the benefits of *physical* exercise⟩. ***antonym:*** spiritual

Corporeal implies having the tangible qualities of a body, such as shape, size, or resistance to force ⟨artists have portrayed angels as *corporeal* beings⟩. ***antonym:*** incorporeal

Phenomenal applies to what is known or perceived through the senses and experience rather than by intuition or rational deduction ⟨scientists concerned only with the *phenomenal* world⟩. ***antonym:*** noumenal

Sensible stresses the capability of being readily or forcibly known through the senses ⟨the earth's rotation is not *sensible* to us⟩. ***antonym:*** insensible

Objective may stress material existence apart from a subject perceiving it ⟨tears are the *objective* manifestation of grief⟩. ***antonym:*** subjective

2. See RELEVANT.

matrimonial, **marital**, **conjugal**, **connubial**, **nuptial** mean of, relating to, or characteristic of marriage.

Matrimonial and ***marital*** apply to whatever has to do with marriage and the married state ⟨enjoyed 40 years of *matrimonial* bliss⟩ ⟨a *marital* relationship built upon mutual trust and understanding⟩.

Conjugal specifically applies to married persons and their relations ⟨inmates of the prison now have *conjugal* rights⟩.

Connubial refers to the married state ⟨a *connubial* contract of no legal standing⟩.

Nuptial usually refers to marriage or to the marriage ceremony ⟨busy all week with the *nuptial* preparations⟩.

matter See AFFAIR.

matter-of-fact See PROSAIC.

mature *adj* **Mature**, **ripe**, **adult**, **grown-up** mean fully developed.

Mature stresses completion of development; when applied to persons it implies attainment of the prime of life and powers ⟨a writer with a deft, *mature* style⟩, whereas in application to things it is more likely to imply completion of a course, process, or period ⟨reinvested the *matured* bonds⟩. ***antonym:*** immature

Ripe stresses readiness, as for use, enjoyment, or action ⟨a people *ripe* for democracy⟩. ***antonym:*** unripe, green

Adult is very close to ***mature***, especially when applied to living things; in extended use it is likely to imply successful surmounting of the weaknesses of immaturity ⟨an *adult* approach to a problem⟩. ***antonym:*** juvenile, puerile

Grown-up may be preferred to ***adult*** when an antithesis to *childish* is desired ⟨adults incapable of *grown-up* behavior⟩. ***antonym:*** childish, callow

mature *vb* **Mature**, **develop**, **ripen**, **age** mean to come or cause to come to be fit for use or enjoyment.

Mature, in its basic application to living things, stresses fullness of growth and attainment of adult characteristics ⟨*matured* nicely during her college years⟩.

Develop stresses the unfolding of what is latent and the attainment of what is possible to the species and potential to the individual ⟨a child who had not yet *developed* a cynical outlook⟩.

Ripen emphasizes the approach to or attainment of the peak of perfection ⟨bided his time, waiting for his hatred to *ripen*⟩.

Age may equal ***mature*** when applied to the young but more often it implies approach to the period of decline or decay ⟨wine and cheese improve as they *age*⟩.

meager, **scanty**, **scant**, **skimpy**, **exiguous**, **spare**, **sparse** mean falling short of what is normal, necessary, or desirable.

Meager implies the absence of elements, qualities, or numbers necessary to a thing's richness, substance, or potency ⟨a *meager* portion of meat⟩. ***antonym:*** ample, copious

Scanty stresses insufficiency in amount, quantity, or extent ⟨supplies too *scanty* to last the winter⟩. ***antonym:*** ample, plentiful, profuse

Scant suggests a falling short of what is desired or desirable rather than of what is essential ⟨accorded the guests *scant* welcome⟩. ***antonym:*** plentiful, profuse

Skimpy usually suggests niggardliness or penury as the cause of the deficiency ⟨tacky housing developments on *skimpy* lots⟩.

Exiguous implies a marked deficiency in number or measure that makes the thing described compare unfavorably with others of its kind ⟨trying to function and thrive despite *exiguous* resources⟩. ***antonym:*** capacious, ample

Spare may suggest a slight falling short of adequacy or merely an absence of superfluity ⟨a *spare,* concise style of writing⟩. ***antonym:*** profuse

Sparse implies a thin scattering of units ⟨a *sparse* population⟩. ***antonym:*** dense

mean *adj* **Mean**, **ignoble**, **abject**, **sordid** mean below the normal standards of human decency and dignity.

Mean suggests having repellent characteristics, such as small-mindedness, ill temper, or cupidity, or it may stress inferiority and suggest poverty or penury ⟨a *mean,* rundown neighborhood⟩.

Ignoble suggests a loss or lack of some essential high quality of mind or spirit ⟨*ignoble* collectors who view artworks merely as investments⟩. ***antonym:*** noble, magnanimous

Abject may imply degradation, debasement, or servility ⟨the *abject* poverty of her youth⟩. ***antonym:*** exalted (*as in rank*), imperious (*as in manner*)

Sordid is stronger than all of these in stressing dirtiness and physical or spiritual degradation and abjectness ⟨a *sordid* story of murder and revenge⟩.

mean *n* **1.** See AVERAGE. **2. Mean, instrument, agent, medium** mean something or someone necessary or useful in effecting an end.

Mean, now usually in the plural ***means***, is very general and may apply to anything or anyone that serves an end ⟨had no *means* of traveling but his own two feet⟩.

Instrument, as applied to persons, implies a secondary role, sometimes as a tool, sometimes as a dupe ⟨used him as the *instrument* of her ambitions⟩ and, as applied to things, is likely to suggest a degree of fitness or adaptation for use as a tool ⟨politics, a powerful *instrument* for change⟩.

Agent applies to a person who acts to achieve an end conceived by another ⟨dealt with a real estate *agent*⟩ or to a thing that produces an immediate effect or definite result ⟨salt, an *agent* in the melting of ice⟩.

Medium applies to a usually intangible means of conveying, transmitting, or communicating ⟨resorted to sign language as a *medium* of communication⟩.

meander See WANDER.

meaning, sense, acceptation, signification, significance, import mean an idea which is conveyed to the mind.

Meaning is the general term used of anything, such as a word, sign, poem, or action, requiring or allowing of interpretation ⟨the poem's *meaning* has been fiercely debated⟩.

Sense denotes the meaning or a particular meaning of a word or phrase ⟨used "nighthawk" in its figurative *sense*⟩.

Acceptation is used of a sense of a word or phrase as regularly understood by most people ⟨the writer isn't using "sane" in its common *acceptation*⟩.

Signification denotes the established meaning of a term, symbol, or character ⟨any Christian would immediately know the *signification* of "INRI"⟩.

Significance applies to a covert as distinguished from the ostensible meaning of an utterance, act, or work of art ⟨an agreement that seemed to have little *significance* at the time⟩.

Import suggests momentousness and denotes the meaning or impression a speaker conveyed through language ⟨failed at first to appreciate the *import* of the news⟩.

mechanical See SPONTANEOUS.

meddle, interfere, intermeddle, tamper mean to concern oneself with someone or something officiously, impertinently, or indiscreetly.

Meddle suggests officiousness and an acting without right or permission of those properly concerned ⟨they will tolerate no *meddling* in their affairs⟩.

Interfere implies a meddling in such a way as to hinder, interrupt, frustrate, disorder, or defeat, although not necessarily with conscious intent ⟨the rain *interfered* with their game⟩.

Intermeddle suggests a meddling impertinently and officiously and in such a way as to interfere ⟨government agencies *intermeddling* in their business⟩.

Tamper implies a seeking to make unwarranted alterations, to perform meddlesome experiments, or to exert an improper influence, and may but need not suggest corruption or clandestine operation ⟨obvious signs that the lock had been *tampered* with⟩.

meddlesome See IMPERTINENT.

median See AVERAGE.

mediate See INTERPOSE.

meditate See PONDER.

meditative See THOUGHTFUL 1.

medium See MEAN *n*.

meek See HUMBLE.

meet *adj* See FIT *adj*.

meet *vb* See SATISFY 3.

melancholia See SADNESS.

melancholy See SADNESS.

melodramatic See DRAMATIC.

melody, air, tune mean a clearly distinguishable succession of rhythmically ordered tones.

Melody stresses the sweetness and beauty of the sound produced and often suggests the expressiveness or moving power of a carefully wrought pattern ⟨a poignant *melody*⟩.

Air is likely to apply to an easily remembered succession of tones which identifies a simple musical composition, such as a ballad or waltz, but in technical use it applies to the dominating melody, usually carried by the upper voices, of a piece of vocal music ⟨hummed a lovely Celtic *air*⟩.

Tune can denote a usually simple musical composition or the air that gives it its character ⟨can you remember the *tune* of "America"?⟩.

member See PART.

memorable See NOTEWORTHY.

memory, remembrance, recollection, reminiscence mean the capacity for or the act of remembering, or the thing remembered.

Memory applies both to the capacity to bring back what one has once experienced or known and to what is remembered ⟨no *memory* of that incident⟩. ***antonym:*** oblivion

Remembrance applies to the act of remembering or the fact of being remembered ⟨any *remembrance* of his deceased wife was painful⟩. ***antonym:*** forgetfulness

Recollection suggests the act of consciously bringing back to mind often with some effort or the thing brought back ⟨after a moment's *recollection* he produced the name⟩.

Reminiscence suggests the act of recalling incidents, experiences, or feelings from a remote past or things so recalled ⟨recorded my grandmother's *reminiscenses* of her Iowa girlhood⟩.

menace See THREATEN.

mend, repair, patch, rebuild mean to put into good order something that is injured, damaged, or defective.

Mend implies the making whole or sound of something that is broken, torn, or injured ⟨the wound *mended* slowly⟩.

Repair applies to the mending of more extensive damage or dilapidation requiring professional skill or special equipment ⟨the car needs to be *repaired* by a mechanic⟩.

Patch implies an often temporary or hasty mending of a rent or breach with new material ⟨*patch* potholes with asphalt⟩.

Rebuild suggests the making like new of something without completely replacing it ⟨a *rebuilt* television is cheaper than a brand-new one⟩.

mendacious See DISHONEST.

menial See SUBSERVIENT.

mention, name, instance, specify mean to make clear or specific by referring to something explicitly.

Mention indicates a calling attention to, either by name or by clear but incidental reference ⟨failed to *mention* the incident⟩.

Name implies the clear mentioning of a name and therefore may suggest greater explicitness ⟨*named* three people as participants in the crime⟩.

Instance may indicate a clear specific reference or citation as a typical example or special case ⟨failed in her attempt to *instance* a clear example⟩.

Specify implies the making of a statement so precise, explicit, and detailed that misunderstanding is impossible ⟨use only ingredients and amounts *specified*⟩.

mercurial See INCONSTANT.

mercy, charity, clemency, grace, lenity mean a showing of or a disposition to show kindness or compassion.

Mercy implies compassion that forbears punishing even when justice demands it or that extends help even to the lowliest or most undeserving ⟨admitted his guilt and then begged for *mercy*⟩.

Charity stresses benevolence and goodwill as shown in generosity and in broad understanding and tolerance of others ⟨show a little *charity* for the weak-willed⟩. ***antonym:*** ill will, malice

Clemency implies a mild and merciful disposition in one having the power or duty of judging and punishing ⟨a judge little inclined to show *clemency*⟩. ***antonym:*** harshness

Grace implies a benign attitude and a willingness to grant favors or make concessions ⟨the victor's *grace* in treating the vanquished⟩.

Lenity implies extreme, even undue, lack of severity in punishing and may suggest a weak softness ⟨criticized the courts for excessive *lenity*⟩. ***antonym:*** severity

meretricious See GAUDY.

merge See MIX.

merry, **blithe**, **jocund**, **jovial**, **jolly** mean showing high spirits or lightheartedness.

Merry suggests cheerful, joyous, uninhibited enjoyment of frolic or festivity ⟨a *merry* group of holiday revelers⟩.

Blithe suggests carefree, innocent, or even heedless gaiety ⟨arrived late in her usual *blithe* way⟩. ***antonym:*** atrabilious, morose

Jocund stresses gladness marked by liveliness, elation and exhilaration of spirits ⟨good news had left him in a *jocund* mood⟩.

Jovial suggests the stimulation of conviviality and good fellowship or the capacity for these ⟨grew increasingly *jovial* with every drink⟩.

Jolly suggests high spirits expressed in laughing, bantering, and jesting and a determination to keep one's companions easy and laughing ⟨our *jolly* host enlivened the party⟩. ***antonym:*** somber

metamorphose See TRANSFORM.

meter See RHYTHM.

method, **mode**, **manner**, **way**, **fashion**, **system** mean the means or procedure followed in achieving an end.

Method implies an orderly, logical, and effective arrangement usually in steps ⟨effective *methods* of birth control⟩.

Mode implies an order or course followed by custom, tradition, or personal preference ⟨the preferred *mode* of transportation⟩.

Manner is close to ***mode*** but may imply a procedure or method that is individual or distinctive ⟨a highly distinctive *manner* of conducting⟩.

Way is very general and may be used in place of any of the preceding words ⟨her usual slapdash *way* of doing things⟩.

Fashion may suggest a peculiar or characteristic but perhaps superficial or ephemeral way of doing something ⟨rushing about, in typical New Yorker *fashion*⟩.

System suggests a fully developed or carefully formulated method often emphasizing the idea of rational orderliness ⟨follows no *system* in playing the horses⟩.

methodize See ORDER.

meticulous See CAREFUL.

métier See WORK 2.

mettle See COURAGE.

microscopic See SMALL.

mien See BEARING.

might See POWER 1.

mild See SOFT.

milieu See BACKGROUND.

militant See AGGRESSIVE.

military See MARTIAL.

mimic See COPY.

mind **1.** See OBEY. **2.** See TEND.

mingle See MIX.

miniature See SMALL.

minimize See DECRY.

minute **1.** See CIRCUMSTANTIAL. **2.** See SMALL.

mirage See DELUSION.

mirth, **glee**, **jollity**, **hilarity** mean a mood or temper of joy and high spirits that is expressed in laughter, play, or merrymaking.

Mirth implies lightness of heart, love of gaiety, and ready laughter ⟨family gatherings that were the occasions of much *mirth*⟩. ***antonym:*** melancholy

Glee stresses exultation shown in laughter, cries of joy, or sometimes malicious delight ⟨cackled with *glee* at their misfortune⟩. ***antonym:*** gloom

Jollity suggests exuberance or lack of restraint in mirth or glee ⟨his endless flow of jokes added to the *jollity*⟩. ***antonym:*** somberness

Hilarity suggests loud or irrepressible laughter or high-spirited boisterousness ⟨a dull comedy not likely to inspire much *hilarity*⟩.

misanthropic See CYNICAL.

miscellaneous, **assorted**, **heterogeneous**, **motley**, **promiscuous** mean a group, collection, or mass, or the things that make up a group, collection, or mass, marked by diversity or variety.

Miscellaneous implies a mixture of many kinds showing few signs of selection and often suggesting dependence on chance ⟨a *miscellaneous* assortment of jars and bottles⟩.

Assorted implies a selection that includes various kinds or involves considerations of tastes or needs ⟨a box of *assorted* cookies⟩.

Heterogeneous applies to masses or groups in which diverse or varied individuals or elements are in proximity or relationship by chance ⟨the *heterogeneous* structure of granite⟩. ***antonym:*** homogeneous

Motley adds the suggestion of discordance in the individuals or elements or their striking contrast to each other and carries a depreciative connotation ⟨a *motley* aggregation of curs and mongrels⟩.

Promiscuous usually implies selection that is completely devoid of discrimination or restriction and that results in disorderly confusion ⟨gave all the money away in *promiscuous* acts of charity⟩.

mischance See MISFORTUNE.

mise-en-scène See BACKGROUND.

miserable, **wretched** mean deplorably or contemptibly bad or mean.

Miserable implies that a person is in a state of misery that may arise in extreme distress of body or mind or in pitiable poverty or degradation ⟨looked *miserable,* with eyes red and swollen from crying⟩; in reference to things, it suggests such meanness or inferiority or unpleasantness that it arouses utter dislike or disgust in an observer ⟨what *miserable* weather⟩. ***antonym:*** comfortable

Wretched stresses the unhappiness or despondency of a person exposed to a grave distress, such as want, grief, oppression, affliction, or anxiety ⟨wretched survivors of the terrible flood⟩; applied to things, it stresses extreme or deplorable badness ⟨made a life as best they could in their *wretched* hovel⟩.

miserly See STINGY.

misery See DISTRESS.

misfortune, **mischance**, **mishap**, **adversity** mean adverse fortune or an instance of this.

Misfortune may apply either to the incident or conjunction of events that is the cause of an unhappy change of fortune or to the ensuing state of distress ⟨never lost hope even in the depths of *misfortune*⟩. ***antonym:*** happiness, prosperity

Mischance applies especially to a situation involving no more than slight inconvenience or minor annoyance ⟨took the wrong road by *mischance*⟩.

Mishap applies to a trivial instance of bad luck ⟨the usual *mishaps* that are part of a family vacation⟩.

Adversity applies to a state of grave or persistent misfortune ⟨had never experienced much *adversity* in life⟩. ***antonym:*** prosperity

misgiving See APPREHENSION.

mishap See MISFORTUNE.

mislay See MISPLACE.

mislead See DECEIVE.

misogynistic See CYNICAL.

misplace, **mislay** mean to put in a wrong place so as to be as unavailable as if lost.

Misplace implies a putting of something in other than its customary or usual place, but often it suggests a setting or fixing of something where it should not be ⟨her confidence in him was *misplaced*⟩.

Mislay usually implies a misplacing in the basic sense but stresses a forgetting of the place in which the thing has been put and therefore often means to lose, usually temporarily ⟨I have *mislaid* my glasses⟩.

misrepresent, **falsify**, **belie**, **garble** mean to present or represent in a manner contrary to the truth.

Misrepresent usually implies an intent to deceive and may suggest deliberate lying and often bias, prejudice, or a will to be unfair ⟨*misrepresent* the value of property offered for sale⟩.

Falsify implies a tampering with or distorting of facts or reality that is usually, but not necessarily, deliberate and intended to deceive ⟨*falsify* the records of a business to conceal embezzlement⟩.

Belie implies an impression given that is at variance with fact; it stresses contrast but does not ordinarily suggest intent ⟨an agility that *belies* her age⟩. ***antonym:*** attest

Garble implies mutilation or distortion of such things as reports, testimony, or translations that may or may not be intentional but that regularly creates a wrong impression of the original ⟨the victims of badly *garbled* accounts⟩.

mist See HAZE.

mistake *n* See ERROR.

mistake *vb* **Mistake**, **confuse**, **confound** mean to mix things up or take one thing to be another.

Mistake implies that one fails to recognize a thing or to grasp its real nature and therefore identifies it with something not itself ⟨*mistake* synthetic fur for real⟩. ***antonym:*** recognize

Confuse suggests that one fails to distinguish two things that have similarities or common characteristics ⟨*confuse* moral and political issues⟩. ***antonym:*** differentiate

Confound implies that one mixes things up so hopelessly as to be unable to detect their differences or distinctions and usually connotes mental bewilderment or a muddled mind ⟨hopelessly *confounded* by the wealth of choices available⟩. ***antonym:*** distinguish, discriminate

mistrust See UNCERTAINTY.

mite See PARTICLE.

mitigate See RELIEVE.

mix, **mingle**, **commingle**, **blend**, **merge**, **coalesce**, **amalgamate**, **fuse** mean to combine or to be combined into a more or less uniform whole.

Mix implies a homogeneous product, but may or may not imply loss of each element's identity ⟨*mix* the salad greens⟩.

Mingle usually suggests that the elements are still somewhat distinguishable or separately active ⟨fear *mingled* with anticipation in my mind⟩.

Commingle implies a closer or more thorough unity and harmoniousness ⟨a sense of duty *commingled* with a fierce pride⟩.

Blend implies that the elements as such disappear in the resulting mixture ⟨*blended* several teas to create a balanced brew⟩.

Merge suggests a combining in which one or more elements are lost in the whole ⟨in her mind reality and fantasy *merged*⟩.

Coalesce implies an affinity in the merging elements and usually a resulting organic unity ⟨telling details that *coalesce* into a striking portrait⟩.

Amalgamate suggests the forming of a close union rather than a loss of individual identities ⟨immigrants that were readily *amalgamated* into the population⟩.

Fuse stresses oneness and indissolubility of the resulting product ⟨a building in which modernism and classicism are *fused*⟩.

mixture, **admixture**, **blend**, **compound**, **composite**, **amalgam** mean a product formed by the combination of two or more things.

Mixture, the most general term, often implies miscellaneousness ⟨planted a *mixture* of seeds to get a colorful bed of flowers⟩.

Admixture suggests that one or more elements has an alien character ⟨an *admixture* of coffee and roasted nuts⟩.

Blend implies the thorough mingling of similar elements or ingredients ⟨an expression that was a *blend* of pity and fear⟩.

Compound suggests the union of two or more distinguishable or analyzable parts, elements, or ingredients ⟨a *compound* of elegance and frivolity⟩.

Composite implies that the constituent elements have been artificially or fortuitously combined ⟨a population that is the *composite* of many races⟩.

Amalgam suggests a complex mixture or the final form into which it hardens ⟨a beneficent attitude that was an *amalgam* of generosity and disdain⟩.

mob See CROWD.

mobile See MOVABLE.

mock **1.** See COPY. **2.** See RIDICULE.

mode **1.** See FASHION. **2.** See METHOD.

model, **example**, **pattern**, **exemplar**, **ideal** mean someone or something set or held before one for guidance or imitation.

Model applies to something taken or proposed as worthy of imitation ⟨a performance that is a *model* of charm and intelligence⟩.

Example applies to something, especially a person, to be imitated or, in some contexts, on no account to be imitated but to be regarded as a warning ⟨for better or worse, children follow the *example* of their parents⟩.

Pattern suggests a clear and detailed archetype or prototype ⟨American industry set a *pattern* for others to follow⟩.

Exemplar suggests either a faultless example to be emulated or a perfect typification ⟨cited Hitler as the *exemplar* of power-mad egomania⟩.

Ideal implies the best possible exemplification either in reality or in conception ⟨never found a suitor who matched her *ideal*⟩.

moderate *adj* **Moderate**, **temperate** mean not excessive in degree, amount, or intensity.

Moderate is likely to connote absence or avoidance of excess ⟨proceeded at a *moderate* rate of speed⟩. ***antonym:*** immoderate

Temperate connotes deliberate restraint or restriction and is opposed to *inordinate* and *intemperate* ⟨a person of modest, *temperate* virtues⟩. ***antonym:*** intemperate, inordinate

moderate *vb* **Moderate**, **qualify**, **temper** mean to modify so as to avoid an extreme or to keep within bounds.

Moderate stresses reduction of what is excessive without necessarily reaching an optimum ⟨the sun *moderated* the chill⟩.

Qualify emphasizes a restricting that more precisely defines and limits ⟨*qualified* her praise with some doubts about the project⟩.

Temper strongly implies an accommodating to a special need or requirement and is likely to suggest a counterbalancing or mitigating addition ⟨*temper* justice with mercy⟩. ***antonym:*** intensify

modern **1. Modern**, **recent**, **late** mean having taken place, come into existence, or developed in times close to the present.

Modern may apply to anything that is not ancient or medieval ⟨a *modern* ship set next to an ancient trireme⟩ or anything that bears the marks of a period nearer in time than another ⟨*modern* methods of harvesting replaced the scythe⟩ or to whatever is felt to be new, fresh, or up-to-date ⟨wearing the very latest *modern* hairstyle⟩. ***antonym:*** antique, ancient

Recent usually lacks such implications and applies to a date that approximates the immediate past more or less precisely according to the nature of the thing qualified ⟨a *recent* change of plans⟩.

Late usually implies a series or succession of which the one described is the most recent in time ⟨the *late* war⟩, but it can sometimes be less indefinite and equivalent to "not long ago being" ⟨the firm's new director of research was the *late* professor of chemistry at the state university⟩.

2. See NEW.

modest 1. See CHASTE. **2.** See HUMBLE. **3.** See SHY.

modify See CHANGE.

moist See WET.

mollify See PACIFY.

mollycoddle See INDULGE.

moment See IMPORTANCE.

momentary See TRANSIENT.

monastery See CLOISTER.

monetary See FINANCIAL.

monopolize, **engross**, **absorb**, **consume** mean to take up completely.

Monopolize, the most general term, means to possess or control completely ⟨*monopolized* their attention⟩.

Engross sometimes implies getting a material control of ⟨*engross* a market by buying up available supplies⟩, but more often it implies an unprotested monopolizing of time, attention, or interest ⟨*engrossed* with a new magazine⟩.

Absorb is often interchangeable with ***engross*** but it tends to carry a hint of submission to pressure rather than ready acceptance ⟨grinding tasks that *absorbed* her efforts⟩.

Consume implies a monopolization of one's time, interest, or attention ⟨*consumed* with a desire to climb every mountain in the range⟩.

monopoly, **corner**, **pool**, **syndicate**, **trust**, **cartel** mean a method of or system for controlling prices.

Monopoly implies exclusive control of a public service or exclusive power to buy or sell a commodity in a particular market ⟨our modern electric utilities are controlled and regulated *monopolies*⟩.

Corner applies to a temporary effective monopoly of something sold on an exchange so that buyers are forced to pay the price asked ⟨maintained his *corner* on wheat for three days⟩.

Pool applies to a combining of interests and joint undertaking by apparently competing companies to regulate output and manipulate prices ⟨refused to join the commodities *pool*⟩.

Syndicate, in financial circles, refers to a temporary association of individuals or firms to effect a particular piece of business; in more general terms, it applies to a combination of things, such as newspapers, business firms, or criminals, interested in a common project or enterprise and often carries suggestions of monopoly ⟨own a horse through the *syndicate*⟩.

Trust historically applies to a merger of companies in which control is vested in trustees and stockholders exchange their stock for trust certificates in the new company, but it is often extended to any large or complex combination of business interests especially when felt to represent a threat to healthy competition ⟨prosecuted for violation of *trust* laws⟩.

Cartel commonly implies an international combination for controlling production and sale of one or more products ⟨carried on delicate negotiations with the oil *cartel*⟩.

monstrous 1. Monstrous, **prodigious**, **tremendous**, **stupendous** mean extremely impressive.

Monstrous implies a departure from the normal in such qualities as size, form, or character and often carries suggestions of deformity, ugliness, or fabulousness ⟨the *monstrous* waste of the project⟩.

Prodigious suggests a marvelousness exceeding belief, usually in something felt as going far beyond a previous maximum of goodness, greatness, intensity, or size ⟨made a *prodigious* effort and rolled the stone aside⟩.

Tremendous may imply a power to terrify or inspire awe ⟨the *tremendous* roar of the cataract⟩, but in more general use it means little more than very large or great or intense ⟨success gave him *tremendous* satisfaction⟩.

Stupendous implies a power to stun or astound, usually because of size, numbers, complexity, or greatness beyond one's power to describe ⟨a *stupendous* volcanic eruption that destroyed the city⟩. **2.** See OUTRAGEOUS.

mood, **humor**, **temper**, **vein** mean a state of mind in which an emotion or set of emotions gains ascendancy.

Mood, the most general term, imputes pervasiveness and compelling quality to the principal emotion and may apply not only to the frame of mind but to its expression ⟨the melancholy *mood* of the poem⟩.

Humor implies a mood that is imposed on one by one's special temperament or one's physical or mental condition at the moment ⟨in ill *humor* and out of sorts through fatigue⟩.

Temper applies to a mood dominated by a single strong emotion, often that of anger ⟨gave vent to his bad *temper* in a series of angry yowls⟩.

Vein suggests a transitory mood or humor usually without any profound temperamental or physical basis ⟨spoke in the same humorous *vein*⟩.

moral, **ethical**, **virtuous**, **righteous**, **noble** mean conforming to a standard of what is right and good.

Moral implies conformity to established codes or accepted notions of right and wrong ⟨the basic *moral* values of a community⟩.

Ethical may suggest the involvement of more difficult or subtle questions of rightness, fairness, or equity and usually implies the existence of or conformance to an elevated code of standards ⟨his strict *ethical* code would not tolerate it⟩. ***antonym:*** unethical

Virtuous implies the possession or manifestation of moral excellence in character ⟨a person not conventionally religious, but *virtuous* in all other respects⟩. ***antonym:*** vicious

Righteous stresses guiltlessness or blamelessness and often suggests sanctimoniousness ⟨responded to the charge with *righteous* indignation⟩. ***antonym:*** iniquitous

Noble implies moral eminence and freedom from anything petty, mean, or dubious in conduct and character ⟨had only the *noblest* of reasons for pursuing the case⟩. ***antonym:*** base (*of actions*), atrocious (*of acts, deeds*)

morally See VIRTUALLY.

mordant See CAUSTIC.

morose See SULLEN.

mortal See DEADLY.

motive *adj* See MOVABLE.

motive *n* **Motive**, **impulse**, **incentive**, **inducement**, **spur**, **goad** mean a stimulus to action.

Motive implies an emotion or desire operating on the will and causing it to act ⟨a crime without apparent *motive*⟩.

Impulse suggests a driving power arising from personal temperament or constitution ⟨my first *impulse* was to hit him⟩.

Incentive applies to an external influence, such as an expected reward or a hope, that incites to action ⟨a bonus was offered as an *incentive* for meeting the deadline⟩.

Inducement suggests a motive prompted

by the deliberate enticements or allurements of another ⟨offered a watch as an *inducement* to subscribe⟩.

Spur applies to a motive that stimulates the faculties or increases energy or ardor ⟨fear was the *spur* that kept me going⟩.

Goad suggests a motive that keeps one going against one's will or desire ⟨the need to earn a living is the daily *goad*⟩.

antonym: curb

motley See MISCELLANEOUS.

mount 1. See ASCEND. **2.** See RISE.

mourn See GRIEVE.

movable, **mobile**, **motive** mean capable of moving or of being moved.

Movable applies to what can be moved or to what is not fixed in position or date ⟨an engine with just a few *movable* parts⟩. ***antonym:*** immovable, stationary

Mobile stresses facility and ease in moving or, occasionally, in being moved ⟨a *mobile* radio-transmitting unit⟩. ***antonym:*** immobile

Motive applies to an agent capable of causing movement or impelling to action ⟨diesel engines supply the *motive* power for the ship⟩.

move, **actuate**, **drive**, **impel** mean to set or keep in motion.

Move is very general and implies no more than the fact of changing position ⟨the force that *moves* the moon around the earth⟩.

Actuate stresses transmission of power so as to work or set in motion ⟨turbines are *actuated* by the force of a current of water⟩.

Drive implies imparting forward and continuous motion and often stresses the effect rather than the impetus ⟨a ship *driven* aground by hurricane winds⟩.

Impel suggests a greater impetus producing more headlong action ⟨burning ambition *impelled* her to the seat of power⟩.

moving, **impressive**, **poignant**, **affecting**, **touching**, **pathetic** mean having the power to produce deep and usually somber emotion.

Moving may apply to any stirring that produces a strong emotional effect including thrilling, agitating, saddening, or evoking pity or sympathy ⟨a *moving* appeal for charitable contributions⟩.

Impressive implies such forcefulness as compels attention, admiration, wonder, or conviction ⟨an *impressive* list of achievements⟩. ***antonym:*** unimpressive

Poignant applies to what keenly or sharply affects one's sensibilities ⟨a *poignant* documentary on the plight of the homeless⟩.

Affecting is close to ***moving*** but often suggests pathos ⟨an *affecting* reunion of a mother and her child⟩.

Touching implies a capacity to arouse tenderness or compassion ⟨the *touching* innocence in a child's eyes⟩.

Pathetic implies a capacity to move to pity or sometimes contempt ⟨*pathetic* attempts to justify gross negligence⟩.

mulct See PENALIZE.

mulish See OBSTINATE.

multiply See INCREASE.

mundane See EARTHLY.

munificent See LIBERAL 1.

murder See KILL.

murky See DARK.

muse See PONDER.

muster See SUMMON.

musty See MALODOROUS.

mutilate See MAIM.

mutiny See REBELLION.

mutual See RECIPROCAL.

mysterious, **inscrutable**, **arcane** mean beyond one's powers to discover, understand, or explain.

Mysterious suggests a quality that excites wonder, curiosity, or surmise yet baffles attempts to explain it ⟨couldn't account for the *mysterious* noise upstairs⟩.

Inscrutable applies to something that defies one's efforts to examine or investigate it or to interpret its significance or meaning ⟨sat calmly with an *inscrutable* look on her face⟩.

Arcane implies a quality that is beyond comprehension because known or knowable only to the possessor of a restricted body of knowledge ⟨a book filled with spells and *arcane* lore⟩.

mystery, **problem**, **enigma**, **riddle**, **puzzle**, **conundrum** mean something which baffles or perplexes.

Mystery applies to what cannot be fully understood by human reason or less strictly to whatever resists or defies explanation ⟨the *mystery* of the stone monoliths on Easter Island⟩.

Problem applies to any question or difficulty calling for a solution or causing concern ⟨the *problems* created by high technology⟩. ***antonym:*** solution

Enigma applies to an utterance or behavior that is difficult to interpret ⟨his suicide was an *enigma* his family never understood⟩.

Riddle suggests an enigma or problem involving paradox or apparent contradiction ⟨the *riddle* of the reclusive billionaire⟩.

Puzzle applies to an enigma or problem involving paradox or apparent contradiction that challenges ingenuity for its solution ⟨the mechanisms of heredity were long a *puzzle* for scientists⟩.

Conundrum applies to a riddle or puzzle whose answer involves a pun or less often to a problem whose solution can only be speculative ⟨posed *conundrums* to which there are no practical solutions⟩.

myth, **legend**, **saga** mean a traditional story of ostensibly historical content whose origin has been lost or forgotten.

Myth is varied in application and connotation and can apply to a fanciful explanation as of a natural phenomenon, social practice, or belief ⟨*myths* of ancient Greece⟩ or a story, belief, or notion commonly held to be true but utterly without fact ⟨the *myth* that money buys happiness⟩.

Legend typically applies to a story, incident, or notion attached to a particular person or place that purports to be historical though in fact unverifiable or incredible ⟨the *legend* of Paul Bunyan⟩.

Saga may refer to a long, continued, heroic story that deals with a person or a group and is historical or legendary or a mixture of both ⟨the building of the railroad was part of the great *saga* of the West⟩.

mythical See FICTITIOUS.

N

naive See NATURAL.
naked See BARE.
name See MENTION.
narcotic See ANODYNE 2.
narrative See STORY.
nasty See DIRTY.
national See CITIZEN.

native, indigenous, endemic, aboriginal mean belonging to a locality.

Native implies birth or origin in a place or region and may suggest compatibility with it ⟨a *native* New Yorker⟩. ***antonym:*** alien, foreign

Indigenous applies to species or races and adds to ***native*** the implication of not having been introduced from elsewhere ⟨maize is *indigenous* to America⟩. ***antonym:*** naturalized, exotic

Endemic implies being ***indigenous*** and peculiar to or restricted to a region ⟨edelweiss is *endemic* in the Alps⟩. ***antonym:*** exotic, pandemic

Aboriginal implies having no known race preceding in occupancy of the region ⟨the *aboriginal* peoples of Australia⟩.

natural 1. Natural, ingenuous, naive, unsophisticated, artless mean free from pretension or calculation.

Natural implies lacking artificiality and self-consciousness and having a spontaneousness suggesting the natural rather than the man-made ⟨her unaffected, *natural* quality comes across on film⟩.

Ingenuous implies inability to disguise or conceal one's feelings or intentions and usually implies candid frankness and lack of reserve ⟨the *ingenuous,* spontaneous utterances of children⟩. ***antonym:*** disingenuous, cunning

Naive suggests lack of worldly wisdom often connoting credulousness and unchecked innocence ⟨in money matters she was distressingly *naive*⟩.

Unsophisticated implies a lack of experience and training necessary for social ease and adroitness ⟨the store intimidates *unsophisticated* customers⟩. ***antonym:*** sophisticated

Artless suggests a naturalness resulting from unawareness of the effect one is producing on others ⟨gave an *artless* impromptu speech at the dinner⟩. ***antonym:*** artful, affected

2. See REGULAR.

nature See TYPE.
naughty See BAD.

nearest, next mean closest in time, place, or degree.

Nearest indicates the highest degree of propinquity, as in space, time, or kinship ⟨named the baby after their *nearest* relative⟩.

Next usually implies immediate succession or precedence in an order, a series, or a sequence ⟨the *next* day⟩ but in legal usage defines the closest degree of kinship ⟨notified the victim's *next* of kin⟩.

nearly, almost, approximately, well-nigh mean within a little of being, becoming, reaching, or sufficing.

Nearly implies mere proximity ⟨we were *nearly* home when the accident happened⟩.

Almost stresses a falling short or deficiency ⟨*almost* out of her mind with grief⟩.

Approximately suggests that the difference is of no practical importance and that there is a reasonable approach to accuracy ⟨weather forecasts cannot be more than *approximately* accurate⟩.

Well-nigh implies the closest approach short of identity ⟨they found him *well-nigh* dead from cold⟩.

neat, tidy, trim mean manifesting care and orderliness.

Neat implies clearness, be it manifested in freedom from dirt and soil ⟨her house is as *neat* as a pin⟩ or in freedom from clutter, complication, or confusion ⟨*neat* workmanship⟩ or in freedom from any admixture ⟨took whiskey *neat*⟩. ***antonym:*** filthy

Tidy suggests pleasing neatness and order diligently maintained ⟨a *tidy* desk with everything in its proper place⟩. ***antonym:*** untidy

Trim implies both neatness and tidiness, but it stresses the smartness and spruceness of appearance that is given by clean lines and excellent proportions ⟨a *trim* yacht⟩. ***antonym:*** frowsy

necessity See NEED.

need *n* **Need**, **necessity**, **exigency** mean a pressing lack of something essential.

Need implies pressure and urgency ⟨children have a *need* for affection⟩ and may suggest distress or indispensability ⟨the *need* for a new water supply⟩.

Necessity is likely to stress imperative demand or compelling cause ⟨call me only in case of *necessity*⟩.

Exigency adds the implication of unusual difficulty or restriction imposed by special circumstances ⟨coped as best they could with the *exigencies* of the famine⟩.

need *vb* See LACK.

nefarious See VICIOUS.

negate See NULLIFY.

negative See NEUTRAL.

neglect, **omit**, **disregard**, **ignore**, **overlook**, **slight**, **forget** mean to pass over without giving due attention.

Neglect implies giving insufficient attention to something that has a claim to one's care or attention ⟨habitually *neglected* his studies⟩. ***antonym:*** cherish

Omit implies a leaving out of a part of a whole ⟨*omit* a verse of a song⟩ or a neglecting entirely ⟨*omitted* to remove the telltale fingerprints⟩.

Disregard suggests voluntary inattention ⟨*disregarded* the wishes of the other members⟩. ***antonym:*** regard

Ignore implies a failure, sometimes deliberate, to regard something obvious ⟨*ignored* the snide remarks of passersby⟩. ***antonym:*** heed, acknowledge

Overlook suggests a disregarding or ignoring through haste or lack of care ⟨in my rush I *overlooked* some relevant examples⟩.

Slight implies a contemptuous or disdainful disregarding or omitting ⟨*slighted* several worthy authors in her survey⟩.

Forget may suggest either a willful ignoring or a failure to impress something on one's mind ⟨*forget* what others say and listen to your conscience⟩. ***antonym:*** remember

neglectful See NEGLIGENT.

negligent, **neglectful**, **lax**, **slack**, **remiss** mean culpably careless or indicative of such carelessness.

Negligent implies culpable inattention to one's duty or business ⟨I had been *negligent* in my letter-writing⟩. ***antonym:*** attentive

Neglectful adds an implication of laziness or deliberate inattention ⟨a society callously *neglectful* of the poor⟩. ***antonym:*** attentive

Lax implies a blameworthy lack of needed strictness, severity, or precision ⟨a reporter who is *lax* about getting the facts straight⟩. ***antonym:*** strict, stringent

Slack implies want of due or necessary diligence or care through indolence, sluggishness, or indifference ⟨the *slack* workmanship and slipshod construction⟩.

Remiss implies blameworthy carelessness shown in slackness, forgetfulness, or negligence ⟨had been *remiss* in her domestic duties⟩. ***antonym:*** scrupulous

negotiate **1.** See CONFER. **2. Negotiate**, **arrange** mean to bring about through an exchange of views and wishes and agreement reached by bargaining and compromise.

Negotiate suggests that the dealings are carried on by diplomatic, business, or legal agencies ⟨*negotiate* a new contract⟩.

Arrange implies dealings intended for

the restoration or establishment of order or those carried out between private persons or their representatives ⟨*arrange* a marriage, as they did long ago⟩.

neighborly See AMICABLE.

neophyte See NOVICE.

neoplasm See TUMOR.

nepenthe See ANODYNE 2.

nerve See TEMERITY.

nervous See VIGOROUS.

nettle See IRRITATE.

neutral, **negative**, **indifferent** mean lacking decisiveness or distinctness.

Neutral implies a quality, an appearance, or a reaction that belongs to neither of two opposites or extremes and often connotes vagueness, indefiniteness, indecisiveness, or ineffectualness ⟨maintained a *neutral* position in the argument⟩.

Negative carries a stronger implication of absence of positive or affirmative qualities and commonly implies lack of effect, activity, or definite and concrete form ⟨won't accomplish anything with such a *negative* attitude⟩. ***antonym:*** affirmative

Indifferent implies a quality, a character, or an appearance that is not readily categorized, especially as good or bad, right or wrong, and that, therefore, is unlikely to stir up strong feeling or elicit firm opinions ⟨she was a hard worker but an *indifferent* student⟩.

new, **novel**, **modern**, **original**, **fresh** mean having recently come into existence or use or into a particular state or condition.

New may apply to what is freshly made and unused ⟨*new* brick⟩ or has not been known or experienced before ⟨starts his *new* job⟩. ***antonym:*** old

Novel applies to what is not only new but strange or unprecedented ⟨a *novel* approach to the problem⟩.

Modern applies to what belongs to or is characteristic of the present time or the present era ⟨the life-style of the *modern* woman⟩. ***antonym:*** ancient, antique

Original applies to what is or produces the first of its kind to exist ⟨a man without one *original* idea⟩. ***antonym:*** dependent, banal, trite

Fresh applies to what is or seems new or has not lost its qualities of newness, such as liveliness, energy, or brightness ⟨a *fresh* start⟩. ***antonym:*** stale

next See NEAREST.

nice **1. Nice**, **dainty**, **fastidious**, **finicky**, **particular**, **fussy**, **squeamish** mean having or showing exacting standards.

Nice implies fine discrimination in perception and evaluation ⟨makes a *nice* distinction between an artist and a craftsman⟩.

Dainty suggests a tendency to reject what does not conform to one's delicate taste or sensibility ⟨when camping, one cannot afford to be *dainty* about food⟩.

Fastidious implies having very high and often capricious ethical, artistic, or social standards ⟨a woman too *fastidious* to tolerate messy little boys⟩.

Finicky implies an affected, often exasperating, fastidiousness ⟨small children are usually *finicky* eaters⟩.

Particular implies an insistence that one's exacting standards be met ⟨a customer who is very *particular* about his fried eggs⟩.

Fussy adds a connotation of querulousness to ***finicky*** and ***particular*** ⟨very *fussy* about the starch in his shirts⟩.

Squeamish suggests an oversensitive or prudish readiness to be nauseated, disgusted, or offended ⟨*squeamish* about erotic art⟩.

2. See CORRECT *adj*.

niggardly See STINGY.

night See NIGHTLY.

nightly, **nocturnal**, **night** mean of, relating to, or associated with the night.

Nightly may mean no more than this, but more often it carries a strong implication of recurrence and is appropriate when the reference is to something that happens night after night ⟨awaited her *nightly* dreams⟩. ***antonym:*** daily

Nocturnal distinctively implies what is active at night ⟨small creatures of *nocturnal* habit⟩. ***antonym:*** diurnal

Night, often interchangeable with ***nocturnal***, may be preferred when a more casual term is desired ⟨waiting for the *night* train⟩ but distinctively describes a person who works at night ⟨*night* nurses⟩ and things that occur or are intended for use at night ⟨*night* baseball⟩.

nimble See AGILE.

nobility See ARISTOCRACY.

noble See MORAL.

nocturnal See NIGHTLY.

noise See SOUND.

noiseless See STILL.

noisome See MALODOROUS.

nonchalant See COOL.

nonmoral See IMMORAL.

nonplus See PUZZLE.

nonsocial See UNSOCIAL.

norm See AVERAGE.

normal See REGULAR.

notable See NOTEWORTHY.

note *n* See SIGN 1.

note *vb* See SEE 1.

noted See FAMOUS.

noteworthy, **notable**, **memorable** mean having a quality that attracts attention.

Noteworthy implies a quality, especially of excellence, that merits or attracts attention ⟨a *noteworthy* collection of stories⟩.

Notable is likely to connote a special feature, such as an excellence, a virtue, a value, or a significance, that makes the thing or person worthy of notice ⟨a *notable* performance of Hamlet⟩.

Memorable stresses worthiness of remembrance, sometimes as an intrinsic quality, sometimes as a matter personal to the rememberer ⟨a *memorable* occasion⟩.

notice See SEE 1.

noticeable, **remarkable**, **prominent**, **outstanding**, **conspicuous**, **salient**, **signal**, **striking** mean attracting notice or attention.

Noticeable applies to something unlikely to escape observation ⟨a piano recital with no *noticeable* errors⟩. ***antonym:*** unnoticeable

Remarkable applies to something so extraordinary or exceptional as to demand attention or comment ⟨a film of *remarkable* intelligence and wit⟩.

Prominent applies to something that commands notice by standing out against its surroundings or background ⟨a doctor who occupies a *prominent* position in the town⟩. ***antonym:*** inconspicuous

Outstanding applies to something that rises above and excels others of the same kind ⟨honored for her *outstanding* contributions to science⟩. ***antonym:*** commonplace

Conspicuous applies to something that is obvious and unavoidable to the sight or mind ⟨the *conspicuous* waste of the corrupt regime⟩. ***antonym:*** inconspicuous

Salient applies to something of significance that thrusts itself into attention ⟨list the *salient* points of the speech⟩.

Signal applies to what deserves attention as being unusually significant ⟨a *signal* contribution to sculpture⟩.

Striking applies to something that impresses itself powerfully and deeply upon the mind or vision ⟨the backwardness of the area is *striking* even to casual observers⟩.

notify See INFORM.

notion See IDEA.

notorious See FAMOUS.

novel See NEW.

novice, **apprentice**, **probationer**, **postulant**, **neophyte** mean one who is a beginner in something, such as a trade, a profession, a career, or a skill.

Novice stresses inexperience ⟨a ski slope designed for *novices*⟩. ***antonym:*** doyen, old hand, old-timer, veteran

Apprentice applies to a beginner serving under a master or teacher and stresses subordination more than inexperience ⟨bricklayer's *apprentice*⟩.

Probationer applies to a beginner on trial for a period of time in which he or she must demonstrate aptitude ⟨among the graduate students who were *probationers* in the field⟩.

Postulant designates a candidate on probation, especially for admission to a religious order ⟨gives advice to young *postulants* in the community⟩.

Neophyte usually suggests initiation and is applicable to one who is new to and learning the ways of something, such as an association, a science, or an art, and often connotes youthful eagerness and unsophistication ⟨could easily tell the eager *neophytes* from the jaded professionals⟩.

noxious See PERNICIOUS.

nude See BARE.

nugatory See VAIN.

nullify, negate, annul, abrogate, invalidate mean to deprive of effective or continued existence.

Nullify implies counteracting completely the force, effectiveness, or value of something ⟨his critical insights are *nullified* by tiresome puns⟩.

Negate implies the destruction or canceling out of one of two mutually exclusive things by the other ⟨a relationship *negated* by petty jealousies⟩.

Annul suggests a neutralizing or a making ineffective or nonexistent often by legal or official action ⟨the treaty *annuls* all previous agreements⟩.

Abrogate is like ***annul*** but more definitely implies a legal or official purposeful act ⟨a law that would *abrogate* certain diplomatic privileges⟩. ***antonym:*** establish, fix

Invalidate implies a making of something powerless or unacceptable by a declaration of its logical or moral or legal unsoundness ⟨the absence of witnesses *invalidates* the will⟩. ***antonym:*** validate

number See SUM.

nunnery See CLOISTER.

nuptial See MATRIMONIAL.

O

obdurate See INFLEXIBLE.

obedient, **docile**, **tractable**, **amenable** mean submissive to the will or control of another.

Obedient implies compliance with the demands or requests of one in authority ⟨cadets must be *obedient* to their commanding officer⟩. ***antonym:*** disobedient, contumacious

Docile implies a predisposition to submit readily to control or guidance ⟨a *docile* child who never caused trouble⟩. ***antonym:*** indocile, ungovernable, unruly

Tractable suggests having a character that permits easy handling or managing ⟨Indian elephants are more *tractable* than their African cousins⟩. ***antonym:*** intractable, unruly

Amenable suggests a willingness to yield to or cooperate with advice, demands, or contrary suggestions ⟨he's usually *amenable* to suggestions and new ideas⟩. ***antonym:*** recalcitrant, refractory

obey, **comply**, **mind** mean to follow the direction of another.

Obey is the general term and implies ready or submissive yielding to authority ⟨*obeyed* her parents⟩. ***antonym:*** disobey, command, order

Comply, often used with *with*, is likely to imply complaisance, dependence, or lack of a strong opinion ⟨willing to *comply* with the opinion of the majority⟩. ***antonym:*** command, enjoin

Mind is likely to be used in connection with children or juniors and in admonition or warning ⟨children must *mind* their parents⟩ or in a weaker sense can carry the implication of heeding or at tending in order to conform or comply ⟨*mind* you, he never spoke to me about it⟩.

object *vb* **Object**, **protest**, **remonstrate**, **expostulate**, **kick** mean to oppose by arguing against.

Object stresses dislike or aversion ⟨*objected* to his sweeping generalizations⟩. ***antonym:*** acquiesce

Protest suggests an orderly presentation of objections in speech or writing ⟨an open letter *protesting* the government's foreign policy⟩. ***antonym:*** agree

Remonstrate implies an attempt to persuade or convince by warning or reproving ⟨*remonstrated* on his son's free-spending ways at college⟩.

Expostulate suggests an earnest explanation of one's objection and firm insistence on the merits of one's stand ⟨*expostulated* at length on the reasons for her decision⟩.

Kick suggests more informally a strenuous protesting or complaining ⟨everybody *kicks* when taxes are raised⟩.

object *n* **1.** See INTENTION. **2.** See THING.

objective *adj* **1.** See FAIR. **2.** See MATERIAL.

objective *n* See INTENTION.

oblige **1.** See FORCE. **2. Oblige**, **accommodate**, **favor** mean to do a service or courtesy.

Oblige implies the putting of someone into one's debt by doing something that is pleasing ⟨ingenuous and eager to *oblige* everyone⟩ and is commonly used in conventional acknowledgment of small courtesies ⟨much *obliged* for their warm hospitality⟩. ***antonym:*** disoblige

Accommodate, when used of services, can replace **oblige** or can imply gracious compliance and consideration ⟨a most *accommodating* host⟩ or connote the intent to be of assistance ⟨willing to *accommodate* their unusual requests⟩. ***antonym:*** discommode

Favor implies the rendering of a service out of goodwill and without imposing an obligation on or expecting a return from the one favored ⟨luck *favored* him in all his enterprises⟩; it can sometimes carry a suggestion of gratuitousness or of patronizing ⟨*favor* a friend with unsought advice⟩.

obliging See AMIABLE.

oblique See CROOKED.

obliterate See ERASE.

oblivious See FORGETFUL.

obloquy See ABUSE.

obnoxious See REPUGNANT.

obscene See COARSE.

obscure, **dark**, **vague**, **enigmatic**, **cryptic**, **ambiguous**, **equivocal** mean not clearly understandable.

Obscure implies a hiding or veiling of meaning through some inadequacy of expression or withholding of full knowledge ⟨the poem is *obscure* to those unlearned in the classics⟩. ***antonym:*** distinct, obvious

Dark implies an imperfect or clouded revelation often with ominous, mysterious, or sinister overtones ⟨muttered *dark* hints of revenge⟩. ***antonym:*** lucid

Vague implies a lack of clear definition or formulation because of inadequate conception or consideration ⟨*vague* promises of reimbursement were made⟩. ***antonym:*** definite, specific, lucid

Enigmatic stresses a puzzling, mystifying quality ⟨left behind *enigmatic* works on alchemy⟩. ***antonym:*** explicit

Cryptic implies a purposely concealed meaning and often an intent to perplex or challenge ⟨a *cryptic* message only a spy could decode⟩.

Ambiguous applies to a difficulty of understanding arising from the use, usually inadvertent, of a word or words of multiple meanings ⟨an *ambiguous* directive that could be taken either way⟩. ***antonym:*** explicit

Equivocal applies to the deliberate use of language open to differing interpretations with the intention of deceiving or evading ⟨the prisoner would give only *equivocal* answers⟩. ***antonym:*** unequivocal

obsequious See SUBSERVIENT.

observe **1.** See KEEP 1. **2.** See SEE 1.

observer See SPECTATOR.

obsolete See OLD.

obstinate, **dogged**, **stubborn**, **pertinacious**, **mulish** mean fixed and unyielding in course or purpose.

Obstinate implies usually a perverse or unreasonable persistence ⟨a President who was resolute but never *obstinate*⟩. ***antonym:*** pliant, pliable

Dogged suggests a tenacious, and sometimes sullen and unwavering, persistence ⟨pursued the story with *dogged* perseverance⟩. ***antonym:*** faltering

Stubborn implies innate sturdiness or immovability in resisting attempts to change or abandon a course or opinion ⟨swallow your *stubborn* pride and admit that you are wrong⟩. ***antonym:*** docile

Pertinacious suggests an annoying or irksome persistence ⟨a *pertinacious* salesman who wouldn't take no for an answer⟩.

Mulish implies a settled and thoroughly unreasonable obstinacy ⟨a *mulish* determination to stick with a lost cause⟩.

obstreperous See VOCIFEROUS.

obstruct See HINDER.

obtain See GET.

obtrude See INTRUDE.

obtrusive See IMPERTINENT.

obtuse See DULL.

obviate See PREVENT 2.

obvious See EVIDENT.

occasion See CAUSE.

occupation See WORK 2.

occur See HAPPEN.

occurrence, **event**, **incident**, **episode**, **circumstance** mean something that happens or takes place.

Occurrence implies any happening without intent, volition, or plan ⟨a meeting that was a chance *occurrence*⟩.

Event usually implies an occurrence of some importance and frequently one having evident antecedent causes ⟨the sequence of *events* following the assassination⟩.

Incident suggests an occurrence of brief

duration or relatively slight importance ⟨one of the minor *incidents* of the war⟩.

Episode stresses the distinctiveness or apartness of an incident ⟨recounted some amusing *episodes* from his youth⟩.

Circumstance implies a specific detail attending an action or event ⟨couldn't remember the exact *circumstances*⟩.

odd See STRANGE.

odious See HATEFUL.

odor See SMELL.

odorous, **fragrant**, **redolent**, **aromatic**, **balmy** mean emitting and diffusing scent.

Odorous applies to whatever has a strong distinctive smell whether pleasant or unpleasant ⟨*odorous* cheeses should be tightly wrapped⟩. ***antonym:*** malodorous, odorless, scentless

Fragrant applies to things such as flowers or spices with sweet or agreeable odors that give sensuous delight ⟨roses that were especially *fragrant*⟩. ***antonym:*** fetid

Redolent applies usually to a place or thing that diffuses or is impregnated with odors ⟨the kitchen was often *redolent* of garlic and tomatoes⟩.

Aromatic applies to things emitting pungent, often fresh odors ⟨an *aromatic* blend of rare teas⟩. ***antonym:*** acrid

Balmy applies to things which have a delicate and soothing aromatic odor ⟨the soft, *balmy* air of a summer evening⟩.

offend, **outrage**, **affront**, **insult** mean to cause hurt feelings or deep resentment.

Offend may indicate a violation, often inadvertent, of the victim's sense of what is proper or fitting ⟨hoped that my remarks had not *offended* her⟩.

Outrage implies offending beyond endurance and calling forth extreme feelings ⟨corruption that *outrages* every citizen⟩.

Affront implies treating with deliberate rudeness or contemptuous indifference to courtesy ⟨a movie that *affronts* your intelligence⟩. ***antonym:*** gratify

Insult suggests a wanton and deliberate causing of humiliation, hurt pride, or shame ⟨managed to *insult* every guest at the party⟩. ***antonym:*** honor

offense **1. Offense**, **resentment**, **umbrage**, **pique**, **dudgeon**, **huff** mean an emotional response to a slight or indignity.

Offense implies a marked state of hurt displeasure ⟨takes deep *offense* at racial slurs⟩.

Resentment suggests a longer lasting indignation or smoldering ill will ⟨harbored a life-long *resentment* of his brother⟩.

Umbrage implies a feeling of being snubbed or ignored ⟨took *umbrage* at a lecturer who debunked American legends⟩.

Pique applies to a transient feeling of wounded vanity ⟨in a *pique* she foolishly declined the invitation⟩.

Dudgeon suggests an angry fit of indignation ⟨walked out of the meeting in high *dudgeon*⟩.

Huff implies a peevish short-lived spell of anger, usually at a petty cause ⟨in a *huff* she threw the ring in his face⟩.

2. Offense, **sin**, **vice**, **crime**, **scandal** mean a transgression of law or custom.

Offense applies to the infraction of any law, rule, or code ⟨at that school no *offense* went unpunished⟩.

Sin implies an offense against moral or religious law or an offense of any sort that is felt to be highly reprehensible ⟨the *sin* of blasphemy⟩.

Vice applies to a habit or practice that degrades or corrupts ⟨gambling was traditionally the gentleman's *vice*⟩.

Crime implies a serious offense punishable by the law of the state ⟨the *crime* of murder⟩.

Scandal applies to an offense that outrages the public conscience or damages the integrity of an organization or group ⟨the affair was a public *scandal*⟩.

3. See ATTACK *n* 2.

offensive See ATTACK *n* 2.

offer, **proffer**, **tender**, **present**, **prefer** mean to lay, set, or put something before another for acceptance.

Offer implies a putting before one of something which may be accepted or rejected ⟨*offer* a suggestion⟩.

Proffer suggests that one is at liberty to accept or reject what is offered, and stresses the voluntariness, spontaneity, and courtesy of the agent ⟨*proffered* assistance to the elderly man⟩.

Tender implies modesty, humility, or gentleness on the part of the one who makes the offer ⟨*tender* our thanks⟩ and serves as an idiomatic or polite term in certain phrases ⟨*tender* a resignation⟩.

Present suggests ceremonious exhibition ⟨*presented* to the queen⟩ or the offering of something for use or pleasure ⟨a letter *presented* on a silver tray⟩.

Prefer retains a sense close to ***offer*** in legal usage ⟨*prefer* an indictment⟩.

offhand See EXTEMPORANEOUS.

office 1. See FUNCTION. **2.** See POSITION 2.

officious See IMPERTINENT.

offset See COMPENSATE.

oft See OFTEN.

often, **frequently**, **oft**, **oftentimes** mean again and again in more or less close succession.

Often tends to stress the number of times a thing occurs without regard to the interval of recurrence ⟨they *often* come to dinner⟩. ***antonym:*** seldom

Frequently usually emphasizes repetition, especially at short intervals ⟨saw her as *frequently* as he could⟩. ***antonym:*** rarely, seldom

Oft, close to ***often*** in meaning, is used chiefly in compound adjectives ⟨an *oft*-told tale⟩ or occasionally in formal discourse ⟨a man *oft* seen but seldom understood⟩.

Oftentimes may be preferred for intonational reasons or as a more florid word ⟨a demeanor *oftentimes* vague and distracted⟩.

oftentimes See OFTEN.

oily See FULSOME.

old, **ancient**, **venerable**, **antique**, **antiquated**, **antediluvian**, **archaic**, **obsolete** mean having come into existence or use in the more or less distant past.

Old may apply to either actual or relative length of existence ⟨an *old* sweater of mine⟩. ***antonym:*** new

Ancient applies to occurrence, existence, or use in or survival from the distant past ⟨*ancient* accounts of dragons⟩. ***antonym:*** modern

Venerable stresses the hoariness and dignity of great age ⟨the family's *venerable* patriarch⟩.

Antique applies to what has come down from a former or ancient time ⟨collected *antique* Chippendale furniture⟩. ***antonym:*** modern, current

Antiquated implies that something is discredited or outmoded or otherwise inappropriate to the present time ⟨*antiquated* teaching methods⟩. ***antonym:*** modernistic, modish

Antediluvian suggests that something is so antiquated and outmoded that it might have come from the time before the flood and Noah's ark ⟨an *antediluvian* mode of travel⟩.

Archaic implies that something has the character or characteristics of a much earlier time ⟨the play used *archaic* language to convey a sense of period⟩. ***antonym:*** up-to-date

Obsolete implies qualities that have gone out of currency or habitual practice ⟨this nuclear missile will make all others *obsolete*⟩. ***antonym:*** current

oleaginous See FULSOME.

oligarchy, **aristocracy**, **plutocracy** mean government by, or a state governed by, the few.

Oligarchy is applicable to any government or state in which power is openly or virtually in the hands of a favored few ⟨the many *oligarchies* of ancient Greece⟩.

Aristocracy basically and historically implies the rule of the best citizens, but in its more usual use it implies power vested in a privileged class, often regarded as superior in birth and breeding ⟨a revolution that toppled the *aristocracy*⟩.

Plutocracy implies concentration of power in the hands of the wealthy and is regularly derogatory ⟨successful attempts to prevent the state from becoming a *plutocracy*⟩.

ominous, **portentous**, **fateful** mean having a menacing or threatening aspect.

Ominous implies a menacing, alarming character foreshadowing evil or disaster ⟨*ominous* rumbling from a dormant volcano⟩.

Portentous suggests being frighteningly big or impressive but not threatening ⟨the *portentous* voice of the host of a televised mystery series⟩.

Fateful stresses momentousness or decisive importance ⟨the *fateful* conference that led to war⟩.

omit See NEGLECT.

omnipresent, **ubiquitous** mean present or existent everywhere.

Omnipresent in its strict sense is a divine attribute equivalent to *immanent*, but more commonly it implies presence or prevalence ⟨the residents of that neighborhood have an *omnipresent* sense of fear⟩.

Ubiquitous implies a quality being so active or so numerous as to seem to be everywhere ⟨*ubiquitous* tourists toting their *omnipresent* cameras⟩.

onerous, **burdensome**, **oppressive**, **exacting** mean imposing hardship.

Onerous stresses laboriousness and heaviness and is likely to imply irksomeness and distastefulness ⟨the *onerous* task of informing the family of his death⟩.

Burdensome suggests a quality that causes physical and especially mental strain ⟨*burdensome* government regulations⟩. ***antonym:*** light

Oppressive implies extreme and often intolerable harshness or severity in what is imposed ⟨found the pressure to conform socially *oppressive*⟩. ***antonym:*** unoppressive

Exacting implies rigor or sternness or extreme fastidiousness in the one demanding and extreme care and precision in the one who or thing that meets these demands ⟨an *exacting* employer⟩. ***antonym:*** unexacting

onlooker See SPECTATOR.

onset See ATTACK *n* 1.

onslaught See ATTACK *n* 1.

onward, **forward**, **forth** mean in the act of advancing or going ahead, as in a movement, progression, series, or sequence.

Onward can stress progress or advance toward a definite goal, end, or place ⟨struggled ever *onward* and upward⟩.

Forward more definitely implies movement or advance with reference to what lies before rather than behind ⟨an event to which we all look *forward*⟩ or in a succession as of incidents or steps ⟨episodes that moved the plot slowly *forward*⟩. ***antonym:*** backward

Forth, often interchangeable with ***forward***, may imply a bringing forward (as into knowledge, availability, or view) of something previously obscured ⟨set *forth* the charges against them⟩.

open **1.** See FRANK. **2.** See LIABLE.

opiate See ANODYNE 2.

opinion, **view**, **belief**, **conviction**, **persuasion**, **sentiment** mean a judgment one holds to be true.

Opinion implies a conclusion thought out yet open to dispute ⟨each expert seemed to be of a different *opinion*⟩.

View suggests an opinion more or less colored by the feeling, sentiment, or bias of the holder ⟨very assertive in stating his *views*⟩.

Belief implies deliberate acceptance and intellectual assent ⟨a firm *belief* in a supreme being⟩.

Conviction applies to a firmly and seriously held belief ⟨a *conviction* that she was right⟩.

Persuasion suggests a belief grounded

on assurance often arising from feelings or wishes rather than from evidence or arguments of its truth ⟨was of the *persuasion* that Republicans were better for business⟩.

Sentiment suggests a settled opinion reflective of one's feelings ⟨her feminist *sentiments* were well-known⟩.

opponent, **antagonist**, **adversary** mean one who expresses or manifests an opposite position.

Opponent implies little more than position on the other side, as in a debate, election, contest, or conflict ⟨*opponents* of the project cite cost as a factor⟩. ***antonym:*** exponent, proponent

Antagonist implies sharper, often more personal, opposition in a struggle for supremacy ⟨a formidable *antagonist* in the struggle for corporate control⟩. ***antonym:*** supporter

Adversary may carry an additional implication of active hostility ⟨two peoples that have been bitter *adversaries* for centuries⟩. ***antonym:*** ally

opportune See SEASONABLE.

oppose, **combat**, **resist**, **withstand**, **antagonize** mean to set oneself against someone or something.

Oppose can apply to a range, from mere objection to bitter hostility or active warfare ⟨*opposed* the plan to build a nuclear power plant⟩.

Combat stresses the forceful or urgent nature of actively countering something ⟨*combat* the disease by educating the public⟩. ***antonym:*** champion, defend

Resist implies an overt recognition of a hostile or threatening force and a positive effort to counteract, ward off, or repel it ⟨struggled valiantly to *resist* the temptation⟩. ***antonym:*** submit, abide

Withstand suggests a more passive, yet often successful, resistance ⟨unable to *withstand* peer pressure⟩.

Antagonize implies an arousing of resistance or hostility in another ⟨statements that *antagonized* even his own supporters⟩. ***antonym:*** conciliate

opposite, **contradictory**, **contrary**, **antithetical** mean being so far apart as to be or seem irreconcilable.

Opposite applies to things that stand in sharp contrast or in conflict ⟨they held *opposite* views on foreign aid⟩. ***antonym:*** same

Contradictory applies to two things that completely negate each other so that if one is true or valid the other must be untrue or invalid ⟨made *contradictory* predictions about the stock market⟩. ***antonym:*** corroboratory, confirmatory

Contrary implies extreme divergence or diametrical opposition of such things as opinions, motives, intentions, or ideas ⟨*contrary* accounts of the late president's character⟩.

Antithetical stresses clear and unequivocally diametrical opposition ⟨a law that is *antithetical* to the basic idea of democracy⟩.

oppress See WRONG.

oppressive See ONEROUS.

opprobrium See DISGRACE.

option See CHOICE *n.*

opulent **1.** See LUXURIOUS. **2.** See RICH.

oracular See DICTATORIAL.

oral **1.** See VOCAL. **2. Oral**, **verbal** mean involving the use of words.

Oral, the narrower term, implies utterance and speech and is distinctively applicable to whatever is delivered, communicated, transacted, or carried on directly from one to another by word of mouth ⟨an *oral* examination⟩.

Verbal stresses the use of words and may apply to what is either spoken or written ⟨situations in which signals replace *verbal* communication⟩.

orbit See RANGE.

ordain See DICTATE.

order **1. Order**, **arrange**, **marshal**, **organize**, **systematize**, **methodize** mean to put persons or things into their proper places in relation to each other.

Order suggests a straightening out so as to eliminate confusion ⟨*ordered* her business affairs before going on extended leave⟩. ***antonym:*** disorder

Arrange implies a setting in a fit, suitable, or right sequence, relationship, or adjustment ⟨a bouquet of elaborately *arranged* flowers⟩. ***antonym:*** derange, disarrange

Marshal suggests a gathering and arranging in preparation for a particular operation or for effective management or use ⟨an argument won by carefully *marshalled* facts⟩.

Organize implies an arranging so that the whole aggregate works as a unit in which each element has a proper place and function ⟨*organized* the volunteers into teams⟩. ***antonym:*** disorganize

Systematize implies an arranging according to a definite and predetermined scheme ⟨billing procedures that have yet to be *systematized*⟩.

Methodize suggests the imposing of an orderly procedure rather than a fixed scheme ⟨*methodizes* every aspect of her daily living⟩.

2. See COMMAND.

ordinance See LAW.

ordinary See COMMON.

organize See ORDER.

orifice See APERTURE.

origin, **source**, **inception**, **root**, **provenance** mean the point at which something begins its course or existence.

Origin applies to the things or persons from which something is ultimately derived and often to the causes operating before the thing itself comes into being ⟨an investigation into the *origins* of baseball⟩.

Source applies more often to the point where something springs into being ⟨the *source* of the Nile⟩. ***antonym:*** termination, outcome

Inception stresses the beginning of the existence of something without implying anything about causes ⟨the business has been a success since its *inception*⟩. ***antonym:*** termination

Root suggests a first, ultimate, or fundamental source often not readily discerned ⟨a need to find the real *root* of violence⟩.

original See NEW.

originate See SPRING.

ornament See ADORN.

oscillate See SWING.

ostensible See APPARENT.

ostentatious See SHOWY.

otiose See VAIN.

oust See EJECT.

out-and-out See OUTRIGHT.

outcome See EFFECT.

outdo See EXCEED.

outer, **outward**, **outside**, **external**, **exterior** mean being or placed without something.

Outer tends to retain its comparative force and apply to what is farther out from something described as *inner* ⟨the *outer* layer of skin is called the epidermis⟩ or is farther than another thing from a center ⟨shed one's *outer* garments⟩. ***antonym:*** inner

Outward commonly implies motion or direction away from, or the reverse of, what is inward ⟨given to *outward* display⟩ or implies what is apparent, as opposed to what is within or is spiritual or mental ⟨an *outward* show of courage belied his inward terror⟩. ***antonym:*** inward

Outside usually implies a position on or a reference to the outer parts or surface of a thing ⟨a shutter covered the *outside* of the window⟩; it also tends to apply to what is beyond some implied limit ⟨looked for causes in *outside* influences⟩. ***antonym:*** inside

External, close to ***outside*** in meaning, may be preferred when location beyond or away from the thing under consideration is implied ⟨directed their attention to *external* events⟩. ***antonym:*** internal

Exterior, also close to ***outside***, may be preferred when location on the surface or outer limits of the thing is implied ⟨gave the *exterior* of the building a fresh coat of paint⟩. ***antonym:*** interior

outfit See FURNISH.

outlandish See STRANGE.

outline, contour, profile, silhouette mean the line that bounds and gives form to something.

Outline applies to a continuous line marking the outer limits or edges of a body or mass ⟨chalk *outlines* of the bodies on the sidewalk⟩.

Contour stresses the quality (such as smooth, curved, rough, or irregular) of an outline or a bounding surface ⟨a car with smoothly flowing *contours*⟩.

Profile suggests a representation of something in side view in simple outline ⟨drew a *profile* of his daughter⟩ or a varied and sharply defined outline against a lighter background ⟨a ship in *profile* against the sky⟩ or sometimes a nonmaterial outline, such as one built up of data ⟨furnished a *profile* of the operation⟩.

Silhouette suggests a shape, especially of a head or figure, with all detail blacked out in shadow and only the outline clearly defined ⟨a photograph of two figures in *silhouette* on a mountain ridge⟩.

outlook See PROSPECT.

outrage See OFFEND.

outrageous, monstrous, heinous, atrocious mean enormously bad or horrible.

Outrageous implies exceeding the limits of what is right or decent or bearable or tolerable ⟨*outrageous* terrorist acts against civilians⟩.

Monstrous applies to what is inconceivably, abnormally, or fantastically wrong, absurd, or horrible ⟨a *monstrous* waste of the taxpayers' money⟩.

Heinous implies such flagrant evil or such conspicuous enormity as inevitably excites hatred or horror ⟨*heinous* crimes that exceeded normal wartime actions⟩. ***antonym:*** venial

Atrocious implies such merciless cruelty, savagery, or contempt of ordinary values as excites condemnation ⟨decent people cannot condone such *atrocious* treatment of prisoners⟩. ***antonym:*** humane, noble

outright, out-and-out, unmitigated, arrant mean without limit or qualification.

Outright implies that what is described has gone to the extreme and can be made neither better nor worse or is past recall ⟨he is an *outright* fool⟩.

Out-and-out applies to what is completely as described at all times or in every part or from every point of view ⟨this is an *out-and-out* fraud⟩.

Unmitigated applies to what is or seems to be so utterly what it is as to be beyond the possibility of being lessened, softened, or relieved ⟨an *unmitigated* evil⟩.

Arrant applies to something that is all that is implied by the term, usually a term of abuse, that follows ⟨an *arrant* coward⟩.

outside See OUTER.

outstanding See NOTICEABLE.

outstrip See EXCEED.

outward See OUTER.

outwit See FRUSTRATE.

overbearing See PROUD.

overcome See CONQUER.

overdue See TARDY.

overflow See TEEM.

overlook See NEGLECT.

oversight, supervision, surveillance mean a careful watching.

Oversight attributes the power or right to act to the watcher and implies the intent to assure the good condition or effective functioning of what is watched ⟨a manager with *oversight* of all phases of the operation⟩.

Supervision carries a much stronger implication of authoritative powers and responsibilities ⟨responsible for the *supervision* of the entire district⟩.

Surveillance implies a close, detailed, even prying watch kept on something and especially on a person felt likely to require unexpected or immediate attention ⟨police *surveillance* of known criminals⟩.

overstatement See EXAGGERATION.

overthrow See CONQUER.

own 1. See ACKNOWLEDGE. **2.** See HAVE.

ozone See AIR.

P

pacific, **peaceable**, **peaceful**, **irenic**, **pacifist**, **pacifistic** mean affording or promoting peace.

Pacific applies chiefly to persons or to utterances, acts, influences, or ideas that tend to maintain peace or conciliate strife ⟨adopted a *pacific* attitude at the conference⟩. ***antonym:*** bellicose

Peaceable stresses enjoyment of peace as a way of life and may imply absence of any intent to behave aggressively ⟨a *peaceable* gathering⟩. ***antonym:*** contentious, acrimonious

Peaceful suggests absence of strife or contention as well as of all disturbing influences ⟨*peaceful* solitude⟩.

Irenic, often used with relation to religious controversy, may describe attitudes and measures likely to allay dispute ⟨issued an *irenic* interpretation of the canon⟩. ***antonym:*** acrimonious

Pacifist stresses opposition, and especially active opposition, to war or violence, typically on moral or conscientious grounds ⟨a *pacifist* group on the campus⟩. ***antonym:*** combative

Pacifistic is close to ***pacifist***, but ordinarily applies only to things ⟨a determinedly *pacifistic* outlook⟩.

pacifist See PACIFIC.

pacifistic See PACIFIC.

pacify, **appease**, **placate**, **mollify**, **propitiate**, **conciliate** mean to ease or quiet the anger or disturbance of someone or something.

Pacify suggests a smoothing or calming or the quelling of insurrection ⟨a sincere apology seemed to *pacify* his rage⟩. ***antonym:*** anger

Appease implies the quieting of agitation or insistent demands by making concessions ⟨nothing seemed to *appease* their appetite for territorial expansion⟩. ***antonym:*** exasperate

Placate suggests a changing of resentment or bitterness to goodwill ⟨bought flowers to *placate* his irate wife⟩. ***antonym:*** enrage

Mollify implies the softening of anger or the soothing of hurt feelings by positive action ⟨a promise of a hearing *mollified* the demonstrators⟩. ***antonym:*** exasperate

Propitiate implies the averting of anger or malevolence or the winning of favor especially of a powerful person ⟨*propitiated* his mother-in-law by getting the clean-cut look⟩.

Conciliate suggests the ending of an estrangement by persuasion, concession, or settling of differences ⟨America's efforts to *conciliate* the nations of the Middle East⟩. ***antonym:*** antagonize

pains See EFFORT.

palatable, **appetizing**, **savory**, **tasty**, **toothsome** mean agreeable or pleasant to the taste.

Palatable often applies to something that is unexpectedly found to be agreeable ⟨surprised to find Indian food quite *palatable*⟩. ***antonym:*** unpalatable, distasteful

Appetizing suggests a whetting of the appetite and applies to aroma and appearance as well as taste ⟨select from a cart filled with *appetizing* desserts⟩. ***antonym:*** disgusting, nauseating

Savory applies to both taste and aroma and suggests piquancy and often spiciness ⟨egg rolls filled with various *savory* fillings⟩. ***antonym:*** bland

Tasty implies a pronounced and appetizing taste ⟨stale shrimp that were far from *tasty*⟩. ***antonym:*** bland

Toothsome stresses the notion of agreeableness and sometimes implies tenderness or lusciousness ⟨a dazzling array of *toothsome* hors d'oeuvres⟩.

palate See TASTE 2.

pale **1. Pale**, **pallid**, **ashen**, **ashy**, **wan**, **livid** mean deficient in natural or healthy color or in vividness or intensity of hue.

Pale implies relative nearness to white and deficiency of depth and brilliance of color ⟨her dress was a very *pale* rose⟩.
Pallid is likely to suggest deprivation of natural color and connote abnormality ⟨his *pallid* face reveals the strain he has been under⟩.
Ashen and ***ashy*** imply a pale grayish color suggestive of ashes and stress an unwholesome or portentous pallor ⟨the *ashen* sky of a winter's afternoon⟩ ⟨hoping for color to return to his *ashy* cheeks⟩.
Wan suggests the blanched appearance associated with waning vitality and is likely to denote a sickly paleness ⟨the *wan* paleness of the fading moon⟩.
Livid basically means leaden-hued and is used of things that have lost their normal coloring and assumed a dull grayish tinge ⟨the *livid* red of the sun seen through fog⟩.
2. Pale, **anemic**, **bloodless** mean weak and thin in substance or vital qualities, as though drained of blood.
Pale stresses lack of color, character, vigor, force, or energy; it may also imply a failure to measure up to the requirements of a type or standard ⟨a *pale* imitation of the original⟩. ***antonym:*** brilliant
Anemic implies deficiency in the elements that contribute especially to intellectual or spiritual vigor or richness ⟨the *anemic* support of the arts in this country⟩. ***antonym:*** full-blooded, florid
Bloodless suggests the absence of such qualities as vitality, warmth, color, and human emotion that are necessary to life or lifelikeness ⟨presented a *bloodless* portrait of the great national hero⟩. ***antonym:*** sanguine, plethoric

pall See SATIATE.
pallid See PALE 1.
palpable See PERCEPTIBLE.
palpate See TOUCH.
palter See LIE.
pamper See INDULGE.
pandemonium See DIN.
panegyric See ENCOMIUM.
panic See FEAR.
parade See SHOW 2.
parallel *adj* See SIMILAR.
parallel *n* **1.** See COMPARISON. **2. Parallel**, **counterpart**, **analogue**, **correlate** mean one that corresponds to or closely resembles another.
Parallel implies that the two things being compared are so like that their lack of divergence suggests parallel lines ⟨drew a *parallel* between their experiences⟩.
Counterpart suggests a complementary and sometimes an obverse relationship ⟨gave the balls to her *counterpart* on the other team⟩.
Analogue usually implies a more remote likeness and may involve a comparison made to clarify, enlighten, or demonstrate ⟨saw faith in technology as an *analogue* to earlier beliefs in supernatural forces⟩.
Correlate applies to what corresponds to something else from another point of view or in another order of viewing ⟨debated whether higher interest rates are a *correlate* of economic prosperity⟩.

paramount See DOMINANT.
parasite, **sycophant**, **toady**, **hanger-on**, **leech**, **sponge** mean an obsequious flatterer or self-seeker.
Parasite applies to one who clings to a person of wealth, power, or influence or is useless to society ⟨a jet-setter with the usual entourage of *parasites*⟩.
Sycophant adds to this a strong suggestion of fawning, flattery, or adulation ⟨a military dictator who would only listen to *sycophants*⟩.
Toady emphasizes the servility and snobbery of the self-seeker ⟨the president's own *toady* made others grovel⟩.
Hanger-on, usually contemptuous, refers to someone who habitually keeps company with or depends unduly on others for favors ⟨kept tripping on her *hangers-on*⟩.

Leech stresses persistence in clinging to or bleeding another for one's own advantage ⟨*leeches* who abandoned her when the money ran out⟩.

Sponge stresses the parasitic laziness, dependence, opportunism, and pettiness of the cadger ⟨her brother, a shiftless *sponge,* often came by for a free meal⟩.

parcel See GROUP.

pardon *vb* See EXCUSE.

pardon *n* **Pardon**, **amnesty**, **absolution** mean a lifting of penalty or punishment.

Pardon, often ambiguous, denotes a release not from guilt but from a penalty imposed by an authority ⟨received a *pardon* from the governor at the last moment⟩. ***antonym:*** punishment

Amnesty implies a pardon that is extended to a whole class or to a community ⟨declared an *amnesty* for all tax evaders⟩.

Absolution in ecclesiastical and especially Roman Catholic use refers to a pardon extended for sins confessed and atoned for and implies that the eternal punishment for sin has been removed ⟨asked for and was granted *absolution*⟩. ***antonym:*** condemnation

pardonable See VENIAL.

parley See CONFER.

parody See CARICATURE.

paroxysm See FIT *n*.

parsimonious See STINGY.

part *n* **Part**, **portion**, **piece**, **member**, **division**, **section**, **segment**, **fragment** mean something less than the whole to which it belongs.

Part is a general term appropriate when indefiniteness is required ⟨they ran only *part* of the way⟩. ***antonym:*** whole

Portion implies an assigned or allotted part ⟨cut the pie into six *portions*⟩.

Piece stresses separateness and applies to a separate or detached part of a whole ⟨a puzzle with 500 *pieces*⟩.

Member suggests one of the functional units composing a body ⟨an arm is a bodily *member*⟩.

Division applies to a large or diversified part made as if by cutting ⟨the manufacturing *division* of the company⟩.

Section is like ***division*** but applies to a relatively small or uniform part ⟨the entertainment *section* of the newspaper⟩.

Segment applies to a part separated or marked out by or as if by natural lines of cleavage ⟨the retired *segment* of the population⟩.

Fragment applies to a part produced by or as if by breaking off or shattering or left after the rest has been used, eaten, worn away, or lost ⟨only a *fragment* of the play still exists⟩.

part *vb* See SEPARATE.

partake See SHARE.

participate See SHARE.

particle, **bit**, **mite**, **smidgen**, **whit**, **atom**, **iota**, **jot**, **tittle** mean a very small or insignificant piece or part.

Particle implies an amount of a substance or quality that is within the range of visual or mental perception ⟨a rumor without a *particle* of truth⟩.

Bit suggests the least feasible amount, extent, or degree ⟨a movie that was a *bit* too violent⟩.

Mite may stress either smallness in size or minuteness in amount ⟨doesn't have a *mite* of suspicion⟩.

Smidgen may go even further in stressing minuteness or scarcity ⟨left them without even a *smidgen* of hope⟩.

Whit, used chiefly in negative phrases, implies the least conceivable amount ⟨cared not a *whit* about their opinion⟩.

Atom suggests the very smallest size or amount possible ⟨not an *atom* of dust escaped his attention⟩.

Iota and ***jot*** are used interchangeably to mean the smallest or most minute detail or amount ⟨tried to remove the last *iota* of doubt⟩ ⟨added not a *jot* to their knowledge⟩.

Tittle has the same meaning as ***iota*** and ***jot*** but is usually used in the phrase *jot or* *tittle* ⟨didn't care a *jot or tittle* about the opinions of others⟩.

particular *adj* **1.** See CIRCUMSTANTIAL. **2.** See NICE. **3.** See SINGLE. **4.** See SPECIAL.

particular *n* See ITEM.

partisan See FOLLOWER.

partner, **copartner, colleague**, **ally**, **confederate** mean an associate.

Partner implies an associate in business or one of two associates, as in some games, a dance, or marriage ⟨now, all change *partners*⟩. ***antonym:*** rival

Copartner may add little to ***partner***, or it may distinctively imply a fellow partner ⟨the actions of one partner may commit his or her *copartners*⟩.

Colleague applies usually to an associate in office or in professional or academic relations ⟨presented a lecture to her *colleagues*⟩.

Ally suggests an often temporary association in a common cause ⟨agreed to act as *allies* for the duration of the conflict⟩. ***antonym:*** adversary

Confederate often suggests a closer or more permanent union for strength and solidarity ⟨joined his *confederates* in a toast to the new undertaking⟩. ***antonym:*** adversary

pass See JUNCTURE.

passion **1.** See FEELING. **2. Passion**, **fervor**, **ardor**, **enthusiasm**, **zeal** mean intense emotion compelling action.

Passion applies to an emotion that is deeply stirring or ungovernable ⟨developed a *passion* for reading⟩.

Fervor implies a warm and steady emotion ⟨read the poem aloud with great *fervor*⟩.

Ardor suggests warm and excited feeling likely to be fitful or short-lived ⟨the *ardor* of their honeymoon soon faded⟩. ***antonym:*** coolness, indifference

Enthusiasm applies to lively or eager interest in or admiration for a proposal or cause or activity ⟨never showed much *enthusiasm* for sports⟩. ***antonym:*** apathy

Zeal implies energetic and unflagging pursuit of an aim or devotion to a cause ⟨preaches with the *zeal* of the converted⟩. ***antonym:*** apathy

passionate See IMPASSIONED.

passive See INACTIVE.

pastoral See RURAL.

pat See SEASONABLE.

patch See MEND.

patent See EVIDENT.

pathetic See MOVING.

pathos, **poignancy**, **bathos** mean a quality that moves one to pity or sorrow.

Pathos, common in critical and literary use, typically suggests the arousal of aesthetic rather than acute and personal emotional response ⟨a drama more noted for its *pathos* than its plot⟩.

Poignancy may be preferred when the genuineness of the thing's emotional quality and of the emotions it arouses need to be stressed ⟨felt the full *poignancy* of their last days together⟩.

Bathos is often applied to a false or pretentious pathos and typically implies a maudlin sentimentality more likely to arouse disgusted contempt than the emotion it seeks to elicit ⟨could not tell the story of his last failed romance without descending into *bathos*⟩.

patois See DIALECT.

patrimony See HERITAGE.

pattern See MODEL.

pause, **recess**, **respite**, **lull**, **intermission** mean a temporary cessation.

Pause stresses the fact of stopping and ordinarily implies an expectation of resumption, as of movement or activity ⟨spoke during a *pause* in the music⟩.

Recess implies a temporary suspension of work or activity ⟨children playing during the morning school *recess*⟩.

Respite implies a period of relief, as from labor, suffering, or war, or of delay, as before being sentenced or before having to pay money due ⟨enjoyed the brief *respite* between attacks⟩.

Lull implies a temporary cessation or,

more often, marked decline, as in the violence of a storm or in business activity ⟨the storm strengthened again after a *lull*⟩.

Intermission implies a break in continuity and is especially applicable to an interval available for some new or special activity ⟨no one should work day after day without *intermission*⟩.

paw See TOUCH.

pay *vb* **Pay**, **compensate**, **remunerate**, **satisfy**, **reimburse**, **indemnify**, **repay**, **recompense** mean to give money or its equivalent in return for something.

Pay implies the discharge of an obligation incurred ⟨we *pay* taxes in exchange for government services⟩.

Compensate implies a counterbalancing of services rendered or help given ⟨an attorney well *compensated* for her services⟩.

Remunerate more clearly suggests a paying for services rendered and may extend to payment that is generous or not contracted for ⟨promised to *remunerate* the searchers handsomely⟩.

Satisfy implies the paying of what is demanded or required by law ⟨all creditors will be *satisfied* in full⟩.

Reimburse implies a return of money that has been expended for another's benefit ⟨the company will *reimburse* employees for expenses incurred⟩.

Indemnify implies the promised or actual making good of a loss, injury, or damage suffered through accident, disaster, or warfare ⟨the government can not *indemnify* the families of military casualties⟩.

Repay stresses the paying back of an equivalent in kind or amount ⟨*repay* a loan⟩.

Recompense suggests due return in amends, friendly repayment, or reward ⟨the hotel *recompensed* us with a free bottle of champagne⟩.

pay *n* See WAGE.

peaceable See PACIFIC.

peaceful **1.** See CALM. **2.** See PACIFIC.

peak See SUMMIT.

peculiar **1.** See CHARACTERISTIC. **2.** See STRANGE.

pecuniary See FINANCIAL.

pedantic, **academic**, **scholastic**, **bookish** mean too narrowly concerned with learned matters.

Pedantic implies ostentation in learning and stodginess in expression and may connote absorption in scholarly matters to the exclusion of truly significant issues ⟨gave an infuriatingly *pedantic* discourse on the matter⟩.

Academic is likely to stress abstractness and a lack of practical experience and interests that deprive one of the ability to deal with realities ⟨the economist's concerns seemed more *academic* than practical⟩.

Scholastic is likely to imply aridity, formalism, adherence to the letter, and sometimes subtlety ⟨presented a hopelessly *scholastic* argument⟩.

Bookish may suggest learning derived from books rather than actualities ⟨had about him an effete, *bookish* air⟩.

peer See GAZE.

peeve See IRRITATE.

pejorative See DEROGATORY.

penalize, **fine**, **amerce**, **mulct** mean to punish by depriving of something.

Penalize usually presupposes a violation of an order, rule, or law intended to maintain discipline or ensure propriety; it also implies a penalty such as forfeiture of money, advantage, or privilege or imposition of a handicap ⟨*penalize* late taxpayers by adding interest to their bills⟩.

Fine implies a monetary penalty fixed within certain limits by law ⟨the library *fines* careless borrowers a few cents a day to encourage prompt return of books⟩.

Amerce implies a penalty left to the discretion of the judge and may refer to a nonpecuniary penalty ⟨the judge *amerced* the offender in the sum of fifty dollars〉.

Mulct implies subjection to a superior power that can legally or illegally enforce penalties and especially monetary penalties for failure to conform to its discipline or edicts and is likely to stress the helplessness of the victim and the arbitrariness of the penalizing power 〈a rash of arson designed to *mulct* the terrorized shopkeepers〉.

penchant See LEANING.

penetrate See ENTER.

penetration See DISCERNMENT.

penitence, repentance, contrition, compunction, remorse mean regret for sin or wrongdoing.

Penitence implies sad and humble realization of and regret for one's misdeeds 〈willing to forgive when faced with the outward signs of *penitence*〉.

Repentance adds the implication of an awareness of one's shortcomings and a resolve to change 〈a complete change of character accompanied his *repentance*〉.

Contrition stresses the sorrowful regret that accompanies true penitence 〈the beatings were usually followed by tearful expressions of *contrition*〉.

Compunction implies a painful sting of conscience for past or especially for contemplated wrongdoing 〈have no *compunctions* about taking back what is mine〉.

Remorse suggests prolonged and insistent self-reproach and mental anguish for past wrongs and especially for those whose consequences cannot be remedied 〈swindlers are not usually plagued by feelings of *remorse*〉.

pensive See THOUGHTFUL 1.

penurious See STINGY.

penury See POVERTY.

perceive See SEE 1.

perceptible, sensible, palpable, tangible, appreciable, ponderable mean apprehensible as real or existent.

Perceptible applies to what can be discerned, often to a minimal extent, by the senses 〈a *perceptible* difference in sound〉. ***antonym:*** imperceptible

Sensible applies to whatever is clearly apprehended through the senses or impresses itself strongly on the mind 〈a *sensible* change in weather〉. ***antonym:*** insensible

Palpable applies either to what has physical substance or to what is obvious and unmistakable 〈the tension in the air was almost *palpable*〉. ***antonym:*** insensible, impalpable

Tangible suggests what is capable of being handled or grasped either physically or mentally 〈submitted the gun as *tangible* evidence〉. ***antonym:*** intangible

Appreciable applies to what is distinctly discernible by the senses or definitely measurable 〈an *appreciable* increase in temperature〉. ***antonym:*** inappreciable

Ponderable suggests having definitely measurable weight or importance especially as distinguished from what is so intangible as to elude such determination 〈exerted a *ponderable* influence on world events〉.

perception See DISCERNMENT.

peremptory See MASTERFUL.

perennial See CONTINUAL.

perfect, whole, entire, intact mean not lacking or faulty in any respect.

Perfect implies the soundness and the excellence of every part, element, or quality of a thing, frequently as an unattainable or theoretical state 〈a *perfect* set of teeth〉. ***antonym:*** imperfect

Whole suggests a completeness or perfection that can be sought and attained or lost and regained 〈an experience that made him feel a *whole* man again〉.

Entire implies perfection deriving from integrity, soundness, or completeness 〈recorded the *entire* Beethoven corpus〉. ***antonym:*** impaired

Intact implies retention of an original or natural perfection that might easily have been lost 〈somehow the building survived the storm *intact*⟩. ***antonym:*** defective

perfervid See IMPASSIONED.

perfidious See FAITHLESS.

perform, **execute**, **discharge**, **accomplish**, **achieve**, **effect**, **fulfill** mean to carry out or into effect.

Perform implies action that follows established patterns or procedures or fulfills agreed-upon requirements and often connotes special skill or experience ⟨*performed* gymnastics on the parallel bars⟩.

Execute stresses the carrying out of what exists in design or in intent ⟨*executed* the heist exactly as planned⟩.

Discharge implies execution and completion of appointed duties or tasks ⟨*discharged* his duties promptly and effectively⟩.

Accomplish stresses the successful completion of a process rather than the means of carrying it out ⟨*accomplished* in a year what had taken others a lifetime⟩. ***antonym:*** undo

Achieve adds to ***accomplish*** the implication of conquered difficulties ⟨a nation struggling to *achieve* greatness⟩. ***antonym:*** fail

Effect adds to ***achieve*** an emphasis on the inherent force in the agent capable of surmounting obstacles ⟨a dynamic personality who *effected* sweeping reforms⟩.

Fulfill implies a complete realization of implied responsibilities or plans or ends or possibilities ⟨the rare epic that *fulfills* its ambitions⟩. ***antonym:*** frustrate, fail in

perfume See FRAGRANCE.

perilous See DANGEROUS.

perimeter, **periphery**, **circuit**, **compass**, **circumference** mean a continuous line enclosing an area.

Perimeter applies to the line bounding any area or the surface bounding a solid ⟨walked the *perimeter* of the property every evening⟩.

Periphery, though sometimes interchangeable with ***perimeter***, is likely to apply to the actual edge, border, or boundary of something concrete ⟨explore the *periphery* of the island⟩ or to limits which cannot be exceeded ⟨the *periphery* of consciousness⟩.

Circuit applies to a route, or often a journey, around a periphery or sometimes to any path that comes back to its point of beginning ⟨the hands of the clock made a *circuit* of the face⟩.

Compass is likely to refer to the area or space enclosed within a perimeter or to the ground that figuratively might be passed over by the leg of a compass in describing a circle ⟨taxed all the land within the *compass* of the town⟩.

Circumference applies to the line that describes a circle or an ellipse or the length of such a line, or to something felt to have a center ⟨built fires within the *circumference* of the camp⟩.

period, **epoch**, **era**, **age** mean a portion or division of time.

Period may designate an extent of time of any length ⟨*periods* of economic prosperity⟩.

Epoch applies to a period begun or set off by some significant or striking quality, change, or series of events ⟨the steam engine marked a new *epoch* in industry⟩.

Era suggests a period of history marked by a new or distinct order of things ⟨the *era* of global communications⟩.

Age is used frequently of a fairly well-defined period dominated by a prominent figure or feature ⟨the *age* of Samuel Johnson⟩.

periodic See INTERMITTENT.

periphery See PERIMETER.

perjure, **forswear** mean to violate one's oath or make a false swearer of oneself.

Perjure, in general as distinct from technical legal use, implies making a liar of oneself whether under oath or not ⟨refused to *perjure* himself on anyone's behalf〉.

Forswear implies a violation of an oath, promise, or vow or sometimes of something, such as one's principles or beliefs, that is as sacred as an oath 〈*forswore* the laws of her country in order to save the life of her child〉.

permanent See LASTING.

permission, **leave**, **sufferance** mean sanction granted by one in authority to act or to do something.

Permission implies the power or authority to grant or refuse what is asked 〈refused strangers *permission* to hunt on his land〉. ***antonym:*** prohibition

Leave may be preferred to ***permission*** in conventionally courteous phrases 〈by your *leave,* we'll be going now〉 or in official reference to permission to leave one's duties 〈he was given *leave* to take care of emergency business〉.

Sufferance implies a neglect or refusal to forbid or interfere and therefore suggests a tacit permission that may be withdrawn 〈you are here on *sufferance,* and must watch quietly if you are to stay〉.

permit See LET.

pernicious, **baneful**, **noxious**, **deleterious**, **detrimental** mean exceedingly harmful.

Pernicious implies irreparable harm done through evil or insidious corrupting or undermining 〈the claim that pornography has a *pernicious* effect on society〉. ***antonym:*** innocuous

Baneful implies injury through poisoning or destroying influence 〈the *baneful* notion that discipline destroys creativity〉. ***antonym:*** beneficial

Noxious applies to what is both offensive and injurious to the health of body or mind 〈*noxious* fumes emanating from a chemical plant〉. ***antonym:*** wholesome, sanitary

Deleterious applies to what has an often unsuspected or unanticipated harmful effect, especially on the living body 〈megadoses of vitamins can have *deleterious* effects〉. ***antonym:*** salutary

Detrimental implies something obviously, but not necessarily extremely, harmful to the thing it affects 〈the *detrimental* effects of prolonged fasting〉. ***antonym:*** beneficial

perpendicular See VERTICAL.

perpetual See CONTINUAL.

perplex See PUZZLE.

persecute See WRONG.

persevere, **persist** mean to continue in a course in the face of difficulty or opposition.

Persevere implies an admirable determination and suggests both refusal to be discouraged, as by failure, doubts, or difficulties, and a steadfast pursuit of an end or undertaking 〈*persevered* doggedly in his efforts to get good grades〉.

Persist often suggests a disagreeable or annoying quality, for it stresses pertinacity more than courage or patience and is likely to imply self-willed opposition to advice, remonstrance, disapproval, or conscience 〈the infuriating teasing that *persisted* despite all her attempts to stop it〉. ***antonym:*** desist

persist **1.** See PERSEVERE. **2.** See CONTINUE.

personality See DISPOSITION.

perspicacious See SHREWD.

perspicuous See CLEAR 2.

persuade See INDUCE.

persuasion See OPINION.

pert See SAUCY.

pertinacious See OBSTINATE.

pertinent See RELEVANT.

perturb See DISCOMPOSE.

perverse See CONTRARY.

pervert See DEBASE.

pessimistic See CYNICAL.

pester See WORRY.

pet See CARESS.

petite See SMALL.

pharisaical See HYPOCRITICAL.

phase, **aspect**, **side**, **facet**, **angle** mean

one of the possible ways of viewing or being presented to view.

Phase implies a change in appearance often without clear reference to an observer ⟨the second *phase* of the investigation⟩.

Aspect may stress the point of view of an observer and its limitation of what is seen or considered ⟨an article that considers the financial *aspect* of divorce⟩.

Side stresses one of several aspects from which something may be viewed ⟨a broadcast that told only one *side* of the story⟩.

Facet implies one of a multiplicity of sides that are similar to one another in some respect ⟨explores the many *facets* of life in New York City⟩.

Angle suggests an aspect seen from a very restricted or specific point of view ⟨find a fresh *angle* for covering the political convention⟩.

phenomenal See MATERIAL.

phlegm See EQUANIMITY.

phlegmatic See IMPASSIVE.

phrase, **idiom**, **expression**, **locution** mean a group of words which together express a notion and which may be used as part of a sentence.

Phrase is applicable to any group of words that recurs frequently but is likely to suggest some distinctive quality, such as triteness, pithiness, or pointedness ⟨a poem made up of several trite *phrases* strung together⟩.

Idiom applies to a combination of word elements which is peculiar to the language in which it occurs either in its grammatical relationships or in its nonliteral meaning ⟨"to keep house," "to catch cold," and "to strike a bargain" are *idioms*⟩.

Expression may be preferred when reference to a way of expressing oneself is accompanied by a qualifying adjective, phrase, or clause ⟨that's an odd *expression*⟩.

Locution, a somewhat bookish word, may be chosen when reference is to phrases that are idiomatically peculiar to a language, a group, or a person ⟨a pet *locution* of the author⟩.

physical **1.** See BODILY. **2.** See MATERIAL.

physiognomy See FACE.

physique, **build**, **habit**, **constitution** mean bodily makeup or type.

Physique applies to the structure, appearance, or strength of the body as characteristic of an individual or a race ⟨a people of sturdy *physique*⟩.

Build, freely interchangeable with ***physique***, may stress the body's conformation, calling attention to such qualities as size, structure, and weight ⟨a horse of chunky *build*⟩.

Habit implies reference to the body as the outward evidence of characteristics that determine one's physical and mental capabilities and condition ⟨a woman of tranquil mien and languorous *habit*⟩.

Constitution applies to the makeup of the body as affected by the complex of physical and mental conditions which collectively determine its state ⟨a robust, healthy *constitution*⟩.

picked See SELECT.

pickle See PREDICAMENT.

pictorial See GRAPHIC.

picturesque See GRAPHIC.

piece See PART.

pierce See ENTER.

pietistic See DEVOUT.

piety See FIDELITY.

pilfer See STEAL.

pillage *vb* See RAVAGE.

pillage *n* See SPOIL.

pilot See GUIDE.

pinch See JUNCTURE.

pine See LONG.

pinnacle See SUMMIT.

pious See DEVOUT.

piquant See PUNGENT.

pique *n* See OFFENSE 1.

pique *vb* **1.** See PROVOKE. **2.** See PRIDE.

pitch **1.** See THROW. **2.** See PLUNGE.

piteous See PITIFUL.

pithy See CONCISE.

pitiable **1.** See PITIFUL. **2.** See CONTEMPTIBLE.

pitiful, piteous, pitiable mean arousing or deserving pity or compassion.

Pitiful applies especially to what excites pity or sometimes commiseration because it is felt to be deeply pathetic ⟨a long line of *pitiful* refugees⟩, but it can also apply to what excites pitying contempt ⟨a *pitiful* excuse⟩. ***antonym:*** cruel

Piteous implies not so much the effect on the observer as the quality in the thing that may excite the pity ⟨heard from afar their *piteous* cries for help⟩.

Pitiable, otherwise very close to ***pitiful***, almost always implies a contemptuous commiseration, though contempt may be weakly or strongly connoted ⟨faced a weak, *pitiable* resistance from the opposition party⟩.

pittance See RATION.

pity See SYMPATHY.

placate See PACIFY.

place **1. Place, position, location, situation, site, spot, station** mean the point or portion of space occupied by or chosen for a thing.

Place, the most general of these terms, carries the implication of having dimensions in space, although the dimensions may be large or small and the limits may not be clearly defined ⟨the *place* where I was born⟩.

Position can be used in relation to abstract as well as concrete things and usually implies place in relation to something in particular ⟨an instrument used to indicate the *position* of the aircraft⟩.

Location is used in relation to concrete things and implies a fixed but not necessarily a clearly definite place ⟨knows the *location* of every historical building in town⟩.

Situation adds to ***location*** a more specific note about the character of the surroundings ⟨liked the *situation* of the house halfway up the hill⟩.

Site, close to ***situation***, carries a clearer reference to the land on which something, such as a building, a group of buildings, or a town, is built ⟨built the new factory on the *site* of the old one⟩.

Spot implies a restricted, particular place, clearly defined in extent ⟨called back that she had found the perfect *spot* for the picnic⟩.

Station suggests the place where a person or thing stands or is set to stand and connotes the accompanying responsibility, as in performance of duty or participation ⟨waiters standing expectantly at their *stations*⟩.

2. See POSITION 2.

placid See CALM.

plague See WORRY.

plain **1.** See COMMON. **2.** See EVIDENT. **3. Plain, homely, simple, unpretentious** mean free from all ostentation or superficial embellishment.

Plain stresses lack of anything such as ornamentation or affectation likely to catch the attention ⟨a *plain* house on a quiet street⟩, or it may suggest elegance ⟨the furnishings were *plain* with very simple classic lines⟩ or frugality ⟨she set a *plain* but abundant table⟩ or, with reference to personal appearance, lack of positive beauty that does not go to the extreme of ugliness ⟨drawn to that *plain* and kindly face⟩. ***antonym:*** lovely

Homely may suggest easy familiarity or comfortable informality without ostentation ⟨a comfortable, *homely* room⟩; in application to personal appearance, it implies something between *plain* and *ugly* ⟨a *homely* mutt⟩. ***antonym:*** comely, bonny

Simple, very close to ***plain*** in its references to situations and things, may stress personal choice as the source of the quality described ⟨lived the *simple* life⟩ and regularly connotes lack of complication or ostentation ⟨gave a *simple,* straightforward answer to the question⟩. ***antonym:*** elaborate

Unpretentious stresses lack of vanity or affectation and may praise a person ⟨soft-spoken and *unpretentious*⟩ but in reference to a thing may convey either praise or depreciation ⟨an *unpretentious* and battered old car⟩. ***antonym:*** pretentious

4. See FRANK.

plan, **design**, **plot**, **scheme**, **project** mean a method devised for making or doing something or achieving an end.

Plan implies mental formulation and sometimes graphic representation of a method or course of action ⟨studied the *plans* for the proposed industrial park⟩.

Design often suggests a definite pattern and some degree of achieved order or harmony ⟨*designs* for three new gowns⟩.

Plot implies a laying out in clearly distinguished sections with attention to their relations and proportions ⟨outlined the *plot* of the new play⟩.

Scheme stresses calculation of the end in view and may apply to a plan motivated by craftiness and self-interest ⟨a *scheme* to swindle senior citizens of their savings⟩.

Project often stresses enterprise, imaginative scope, or vision but sometimes connotes ponderous or needless extension ⟨a *project* to develop the waterfront⟩.

plane See LEVEL.

plastered See DRUNK.

plastic, **pliable**, **pliant**, **ductile**, **malleable**, **adaptable** mean susceptible of being modified in form or nature.

Plastic applies to substances soft enough to be molded yet capable of hardening into a final fixed form ⟨*plastic* materials allow the sculptor greater freedom⟩.

Pliable suggests something easily bent, folded, twisted, or manipulated ⟨headphones that are *pliable* and can be bent to fit⟩. ***antonym:*** unpliable

Pliant may stress flexibility and sometimes connote springiness or, in persons, submissiveness ⟨select an athletic shoe with a *pliant* sole⟩. ***antonym:*** impliant

Ductile applies to what can be drawn out or extended with ease ⟨copper is one of the most *ductile* of metals⟩.

Malleable applies to what may be pressed or beaten into shape ⟨the *malleable* properties of gold enhance its value⟩. ***antonym:*** refractory

Adaptable implies the capability of being easily modified to suit other conditions, needs, or uses ⟨computer hardware that is *adaptable*⟩. ***antonym:*** inadaptable, unadaptable

plausible, **credible**, **believable**, **colorable**, **specious** mean outwardly acceptable as true or genuine.

Plausible implies genuineness or reasonableness at first sight or hearing usually with some hint of a possibility of being deceived ⟨a *plausible* excuse⟩. ***antonym:*** implausible

Credible implies apparent worthiness of belief especially because of support by known facts or sound reasoning ⟨his story is perfectly *credible* to one who knows his background⟩. ***antonym:*** incredible

Believable can apply to what seems true because within the range of possibility or probability or known facts ⟨presented a play with *believable* characters⟩. ***antonym:*** unbelievable

Colorable refers to something which on its face seems true or that is capable to some extent of being sustained or justified ⟨a theory supported by *colorable* evidence⟩.

Specious stresses plausibility usually with a clear implication of dissimulation or fraud ⟨*specious* piety⟩. ***antonym:*** valid

play See FUN.

plea See APOLOGY.

pleasant, **pleasing**, **agreeable**, **grateful**, **gratifying**, **welcome** mean highly acceptable to or delighting the mind or senses.

Pleasant stresses a quality inherent in an object ⟨a *pleasant* evening⟩. ***antonym:*** unpleasant, distasteful

Pleasing, close to ***pleasant***, stresses the effect that something has on one ⟨a *pleasing* arrangement of colors⟩. ***antonym:*** displeasing, repellent

Agreeable applies to what is in accord with one's tastes or liking ⟨an *agreeable* companion⟩. ***antonym:*** disagreeable

Grateful implies satisfaction, relief, or comfort yielded by what is pleasing or agreeable ⟨the fire threw a *grateful* warmth into the room⟩. ***antonym:*** obnoxious

Gratifying implies mental pleasure arising usually from a satisfying of one's hopes, desires, conscience, or vanity ⟨a *gratifying* sense of accomplishment⟩.

Welcome is stronger than ***pleasing*** and ***grateful*** in stressing the pleasure given by satisfying a prior need or longing ⟨as *welcome* as rain after a long drought⟩. ***antonym:*** unwelcome

pleasing See PLEASANT.

pleasure, **delight**, **joy**, **delectation**, **enjoyment** mean the agreeable emotion accompanying the possession or expectation of what is good or greatly desired.

Pleasure stresses a feeling of satisfaction or gratification rather than visible happiness ⟨take *pleasure* in one's possessions⟩. ***antonym:*** displeasure

Delight usually reverses this emphasis and stresses lively expression of obvious satisfaction ⟨the *delight* of grandparents in a new grandchild⟩. ***antonym:*** disappointment, discontent

Joy may imply a more deep-rooted rapturous emotion than either ***pleasure*** or ***delight*** ⟨felt a profound *joy* at the sight⟩. ***antonym:*** sorrow, misery, abomination

Delectation suggests amusement, diversion, or entertainment in reaction to pleasurable experience ⟨presented a variety of skits for their *delectation*⟩.

Enjoyment stresses a gratification or happiness resulting from a pleasurable experience ⟨derived great *enjoyment* from her books and her music⟩. ***antonym:*** abhorrence

plenary See FULL.

plentiful, **ample**, **abundant**, **copious** mean more than sufficient without being excessive.

Plentiful implies a great or rich supply, often of something that is not regularly or universally available ⟨peaches are *plentiful* this summer⟩. ***antonym:*** scanty, scant

Ample implies a generous sufficiency to satisfy a particular requirement ⟨an *ample* amount of food to last the winter⟩. ***antonym:*** scant, meager

Abundant suggests an even greater or richer supply than does ***plentiful*** ⟨has surprisingly *abundant* energy for a woman her age⟩. ***antonym:*** scarce

Copious stresses largeness of supply rather than fullness or richness ⟨*copious* examples of bureaucratic waste⟩. ***antonym:*** meager

pliable See PLASTIC.

pliant See PLASTIC.

plight See PREDICAMENT.

plot 1. See PLAN. **2. Plot**, **intrigue**, **machination**, **conspiracy**, **cabal** mean a plan secretly devised to accomplish an evil or treacherous end.

Plot implies careful foresight in planning a complex scheme ⟨foiled an assassination *plot*⟩.

Intrigue suggests secret underhanded maneuvering in an atmosphere of duplicity ⟨finagled the nomination by means of back-room *intrigues*⟩.

Machination implies a contriving of annoyances, injuries, or evils and imputes hostility or treachery to the contrivers ⟨through *machinations* she pieced together a publishing empire⟩.

Conspiracy implies a secret agreement

among several people, often, but not always, involving treason or great treachery ⟨a *conspiracy* of oil companies to set prices⟩.

Cabal typically applies to intrigue, often involving persons of some eminence, to accomplish some end favorable to its members but injurious to those affected ⟨the infamous *cabal* against General Washington⟩.

ploy See TRICK.

pluck See FORTITUDE.

plumb See VERTICAL.

plume See PRIDE.

plunder See SPOIL.

plunge, **dive**, **pitch** mean to throw oneself or to throw or thrust something forward and downward into or as if into deep water.

Plunge stresses the force of the movement and may imply entry into any penetrable substance or into a state or condition in which one is overwhelmed or immersed ⟨he *plunged* eagerly into the new course of studies⟩.

Dive suggests intent and may imply more deliberateness and more skill than ***plunge*** ⟨pilots trained to *dive,* climb, and bank in unison⟩.

Pitch is likely to stress lack of all intent or design ⟨she caught her heel in a crack and *pitched* to the ground⟩ or may imply the alternate forward and backward plunging of a ship or a spaceship ⟨struggled to control the capsule as it *pitched* and yawed⟩.

plurality See MAJORITY.

plutocracy See OLIGARCHY.

pogrom See MASSACRE.

poignancy See PATHOS.

poignant **1.** See MOVING. **2.** See PUNGENT.

poise See TACT.

poison, **venom**, **virus**, **toxin**, **bane** mean material that when present in or introduced into a living organism produces a deadly or injurious effect.

Poison is applicable to any deadly or noxious substance (such as strychnine, arsenic, or carbon monoxide) or to anything felt as having a comparable effect ⟨a relationship destroyed by the *poison* of jealousy⟩.

Venom applies to a poison-containing fluid secreted by an animal such as a snake, bee, or spider and injected into another animal in defensive or predatory action; it may also imply a malignant hostility ⟨a review full of *venom*⟩.

Virus applies to what is felt to have a corrupting quality poisonous to mind and spirit ⟨the *virus* of apathy⟩ or to a submicroscopic agent of infection working with insidious deadliness or destructiveness ⟨the *virus* that causes AIDS⟩.

Toxin denotes a complex organic poison produced by a living organism, especially a bacterium or virus ⟨the *toxins* causing the plague⟩; it may also imply an insidious undermining effect like that of a bacterial toxin ⟨a nation undermined by the *toxin* of ethnic divisiveness⟩.

Bane may apply to any cause of ruin, destruction, or tribulation ⟨the *bane* of his existence⟩.

polite See CIVIL.

politic **1.** See EXPEDIENT. **2.** See SUAVE.

pollute See CONTAMINATE.

ponder, **meditate**, **muse**, **ruminate** mean to consider or examine attentively or deliberately.

Ponder implies a careful weighing of a problem or prolonged inconclusive thinking about a matter ⟨*pondered* at length the various recourses open to him⟩.

Meditate implies a definite focusing of one's thoughts on something so as to understand it deeply ⟨the sight of ruins prompted her to *meditate* upon human vanity⟩.

Muse suggests a more or less focused and persistent but languid and inconclusive turning over in the mind as if in a dream, a fancy, or a remembrance

⟨*mused* upon the adventures of the heroines of gothic novels⟩.

Ruminate implies going over the same matter in one's thoughts again and again but suggests little of either purposive thinking or rapt absorption ⟨the product of fifty years of *ruminating* on the meaning of life⟩.

ponderable See PERCEPTIBLE.

ponderous See HEAVY.

pool See MONOPOLY.

popular See COMMON.

portentous See OMINOUS.

portion 1. See FATE. **2.** See PART.

pose *n* **Pose, air, airs, affectation, mannerism** mean an adopted way of speaking or behaving.

Pose implies an attitude deliberately assumed in order to impress others or to call attention to oneself ⟨her shyness was just a *pose*⟩.

Air may suggest natural acquirement through environment or way of life ⟨years of living in Europe had given him a sophisticated *air*⟩.

Airs always implies artificiality and pretentiousness ⟨a snobby couple much given to putting on *airs*⟩.

Affectation applies to a trick of speech or behavior that strikes the observer as insincere ⟨his foreign accent is an *affectation*⟩.

Mannerism applies to an acquired peculiarity of behavior or speech that has become a habit ⟨gesturing with a cigarette was her most noticeable *mannerism*⟩.

pose *vb* See PROPOSE.

posit See PRESUPPOSE.

position 1. Position, stand, attitude mean a point of view or way of regarding something.

Position implies reference to a question at issue or a matter about which there is a difference of opinion ⟨the candidate discussed his *position* on the war⟩.

Stand is similar to ***position*** but connotes a strongly held or expressed opinion ⟨took a *stand* against continuing any government subsidies⟩.

Attitude is likely to apply to a point of view colored by personal or party feeling and as much the product of temperament or emotion as of thought or conviction ⟨he took a humorous *attitude* toward life⟩.

2. Position, place, situation, office, post, job mean employment for wages or salary.

Position may be preferred where the employment suggests higher status or more dignity in the work involved ⟨my brother has a *position* as research director in the new company⟩.

Place often implies little more than employment for remuneration ⟨she has lost her *place* as a cook⟩.

Situation adds an emphasis on a place needing to be filled ⟨obtained a *situation* as clerk to the city council⟩.

Office applies to a position of trust or authority especially in public service ⟨has held the *office* of county treasurer for many years⟩.

Post suggests a position involving some degree of responsibility ⟨took a *post* as governess in an aristocratic household⟩ or sometimes onerous duties ⟨a new *post* in the foreign service⟩.

Job, a very general term, stresses the work involved ⟨his first *job* was in public-school teaching⟩ and is especially appropriate when physical labor is in question ⟨seasonal *jobs*⟩.

3. See PLACE.

positive See SURE.

possess See HAVE.

possible 1. Possible, practicable, feasible mean capable of being realized.

Possible implies that a thing may certainly exist or occur given the proper conditions ⟨contends that life on other planets is *possible*⟩. ***antonym:*** impossible

Practicable applies to something that may be easily or readily effected by available means or under current conditions ⟨when television became *practicable*⟩ . ***antonym:*** impracticable

Feasible applies to what is likely to work or be useful in attaining the end desired ⟨commercially *feasible* for mass production⟩. ***antonym:*** unfeasible, infeasible, chimerical

2. See PROBABLE.

post See POSITION 2.

postpone See DEFER.

postulant See NOVICE.

postulate See PRESUPPOSE.

potential See LATENT.

pother See STIR *n.*

pour, stream, gush, sluice mean to send forth or come forth copiously.

Pour suggests abundant emission ⟨it never rains but it *pours*⟩ and may sometimes imply a coming in a course or stream from or as if from a spout ⟨workers *poured* from the subway exits⟩.

Stream suggests a flowing through a channel or from an opening or the abundance or continuousness of that flow ⟨tears *streamed* from her eyes⟩.

Gush implies a sudden and copious outpouring of or as if of something released from confinement ⟨blood *gushed* from the wound⟩.

Sluice implies the operation of something like a sluice or flume for the control of the flow of water and regularly suggests a sudden abundant streaming ⟨rainwater *sluicing* through the gutters⟩.

poverty, indigence, penury, want, destitution mean the state of one who is poor or with insufficient resources.

Poverty may cover a range from extreme want of necessities to a falling short of having comfortable means ⟨the extreme *poverty* of many Americans⟩. ***antonym:*** riches

Indigence implies seriously straitened circumstances and the accompanying hardships ⟨the *indigence* of her years as a graduate student⟩. ***antonym:*** affluence, opulence

Penury suggests a cramping or oppressive lack of resources, especially money ⟨given the *penury* of their lifestyle, few suspected their wealth⟩. ***antonym:*** luxury

Want implies extreme poverty that deprives one of the basic necessities of life ⟨lived in a constant state of *want*⟩.

Destitution suggests such utter lack of resources as threatens life through starvation or exposure ⟨the widespread *destitution* in countries beset by famine⟩. ***antonym:*** opulence

power 1. Power, force, energy, strength, might mean the ability to exert effort.

Power may imply latent or exerted physical, mental, or spiritual ability to act or be acted upon ⟨the incredible *power* of flowing water⟩. ***antonym:*** impotence

Force implies the actual effective exercise of power ⟨used enough *force* to push the door open⟩.

Energy applies to power expended or capable of being transformed into work ⟨a social reformer of untiring *energy*⟩.

Strength applies to the quality or property of a person or thing that makes possible the exertion of force or the withstanding of strain, pressure, or attack ⟨use weight training to build your *strength*⟩. ***antonym:*** weakness

Might implies great or overwhelming power or force ⟨all of his *might* was needed to budge the boulder⟩.

2. Power, faculty, function mean the ability of a living being to perform in a given way.

Power may apply to any such ability, whether acting primarily on a physical or a mental level ⟨*power* to think clearly⟩.

Faculty applies to those powers which are the possession of every normal human being and especially to those that are associated with the mind ⟨sensory *faculties*⟩.

Function applies to any special ability or capacity of a body part or system or to any special ability of the mind that contributes to the life of a living organism

⟨the primary *function* of the eye is vision⟩.

3. Power, authority, jurisdiction, control, command, sway, dominion mean the right to govern or rule or determine.

Power implies possession of ability to wield coercive force, permissive authority, or substantial influence ⟨the *power* of the President to mold public opinion⟩.

Authority implies the granting of power for a specific purpose within specified limits ⟨gave her attorney the *authority* to manage her estate⟩.

Jurisdiction applies to official power exercised within prescribed limits ⟨the bureau that has *jurisdiction* over Indian affairs⟩.

Control stresses the power to direct and restrain ⟨you are responsible for students under your *control*⟩.

Command implies the power to make arbitrary decisions and compel obedience ⟨the respect of the men under his *command*⟩.

Sway suggests the extent or scope of exercised power or influence ⟨an empire that extended its *sway* over the known world⟩.

Dominion stresses sovereign power or supreme authority ⟨a world government that would have *dominion* over all nations⟩.

powerless, impotent mean unable to effect one's purpose, intention, or end.

Powerless denotes merely lack of power or efficacy which is often temporary or relative to a specific purpose or situation ⟨claimed he was *powerless* to make the change⟩. ***antonym:*** powerful, efficacious

Impotent implies powerlessness coupled with persistent weakness or complete ineffectiveness ⟨stormed about in *impotent* rage⟩. ***antonym:*** potent

practicable 1. Practicable, practical mean capable of being put to use or turned to account.

Practicable applies to what has been proposed and seems feasible but has not been actually tested in use ⟨the question of whether colonies in space are *practicable*⟩.

Practical applies to things and to persons and implies proven success in meeting the demands of actual living or use ⟨the copier is the most *practical* machine in the office⟩. ***antonym:*** impractical, unpractical

2. See POSSIBLE.

practical See PRACTICABLE.

practically See VIRTUALLY.

practice *n* See HABIT.

practice *vb* **Practice, exercise, drill** mean to perform or make perform repeatedly.

Practice may imply a doing habitually or regularly ⟨*practice* one's profession⟩ or a doing over and over for the sake of acquiring proficiency or skill ⟨*practice* on the piano each day⟩.

Exercise implies a keeping at work and often suggests the resulting strengthening or developing ⟨*exercise* muscles by active play⟩.

Drill connotes an intent to fix as a habit and stresses repetition as a means of training and discipline ⟨*drill* schoolchildren in pronunciation⟩.

precarious See DANGEROUS.

precedence See PRIORITY.

preceding, antecedent, foregoing, previous, prior, former, anterior mean being before.

Preceding usually implies being immediately before in time or in place ⟨the last sentence of the *preceding* paragraph⟩. ***antonym:*** following

Antecedent applies to order in time and may suggest a causal or logical relation ⟨study the revolution and its *antecedent* economic conditions⟩. ***antonym:*** subsequent, consequent

Foregoing applies to what has preceded, chiefly in discourse ⟨a restatement of the *foregoing* paragraph⟩. ***antonym:*** following

Previous implies existing or occurring earlier ⟨a *previous* marriage⟩. ***antonym:*** subsequent, consequent

Prior often adds to ***previous*** an implication of greater importance ⟨the prices in this catalogue supersede all *prior* prices⟩.

Former implies always a definite comparison or contrast with something that is latter ⟨the *former* name of the company⟩. ***antonym:*** latter

Anterior applies to position before or ahead of, usually in space, sometimes in time or order ⟨the *anterior* lobe of the brain⟩. ***antonym:*** posterior

precept See LAW.

precious See COSTLY.

precipitate, headlong, abrupt, impetuous, sudden mean showing undue haste or unexpectedness.

Precipitate stresses lack of due deliberation and implies prematureness of action ⟨the army's *precipitate* withdrawal⟩. ***antonym:*** deliberate

Headlong stresses rashness and lack of forethought of persons or acts ⟨a *headlong* flight from arrest⟩.

Abrupt stresses curtness and a lack of warning or ceremony ⟨an *abrupt* refusal⟩. ***antonym:*** deliberate, leisurely

Impetuous stresses extreme impatience or impulsiveness ⟨it's a bit *impetuous* to propose marriage on the third date⟩.

Sudden stresses unexpectedness and sharpness or impetuousness of action ⟨flew into a *sudden* rage⟩.

precipitous See STEEP.

précis See COMPENDIUM.

precise See CORRECT *adj.*

preciseness See PRECISION.

precision, preciseness mean the quality or state of being precise.

Precision regularly suggests a desirable or sought-for quality and connotes such contributing factors as exactitude, care, devoted workmanship, or thoughtful choice ⟨chose her words with great care and *precision*⟩.

Preciseness more often suggests a less than desirable quality and is likely to connote such contributing factors as rigidity, severity and strictness, or overnicety in observance of rules or proprieties ⟨spoke each sentence with an annoying and intimidating *preciseness*⟩.

preclude See PREVENT 2.

precursor See FORERUNNER.

predicament, dilemma, quandary, plight, fix, jam, pickle mean a situation from which escape is difficult.

Predicament suggests a difficult situation usually offering no satisfactory or easy solution ⟨the *predicament* posed by increasing automation⟩.

Dilemma implies a predicament presenting a choice between equally unpleasant or unacceptable alternatives ⟨faced with the *dilemma* of putting him in a nursing home or caring for him ourselves⟩.

Quandary stresses the puzzlement and perplexity of one faced by a dilemma ⟨in a *quandary* about how to repair it⟩.

Plight suggests an unfortunate or trying situation ⟨a study of the *plight* of the homeless⟩.

Fix and ***jam*** are informal equivalents of ***plight*** but are more likely to suggest involvement through some error, fault, or wrongdoing ⟨constantly getting their son out of some *fix*⟩ ⟨in a real financial *jam* now that she's lost her job⟩.

Pickle implies a particularly distressing or sorry plight ⟨conflicting obligations that put me in a real *pickle*⟩.

predict See FORETELL.

predilection, prepossession, prejudice, bias mean an attitude of mind that predisposes one to favor something or take a stand without full consideration or knowledge.

Predilection implies a strong liking deriving from one's temperament or experience ⟨teenagers with a *predilection* for gory horror movies⟩.

Prepossession suggests a fixed conception likely to preclude objective judgment of anything counter to it ⟨a slave to his *prepossessions*⟩.

Prejudice usually implies an unfavorable prepossession and connotes a feeling rooted in suspicion, fear, or intolerance ⟨strong *prejudices* that are based upon neither reason nor experience⟩.

Bias implies an unreasoned and unfair distortion of judgment in favor of or against a person or thing ⟨society shows a *bias* against overweight people⟩.

predispose See INCLINE.

predominant See DOMINANT.

preempt See APPROPRIATE *vb*.

preen See PRIDE.

prefatory See PRELIMINARY.

prefer See OFFER.

preference See CHOICE *n*.

prejudice See PREDILECTION.

preliminary, **introductory**, **preparatory**, **prefatory** mean serving to make ready the way for something else.

Preliminary refers to what must be done or prepared or acquired before some other state or activity becomes possible ⟨held a *preliminary* discussion to set up the agenda for the meeting⟩.

Introductory refers to the first steps in a process and usually applies to what sets something (such as an action, a work, or a process) going ⟨the speaker's *introductory* remarks established his point of view⟩. ***antonym:*** closing, concluding

Preparatory comes close to ***preliminary*** in meaning but emphasizes preparedness for or against what is expected to ensue ⟨take *preparatory* protective measures against a predicted hurricane⟩.

Prefatory usually implies a desire on the part of someone to prepare others for such activities as hearing, action, or understanding ⟨made some *prefatory* remarks before introducing the speaker⟩.

premise See PRESUPPOSE.

preparatory See PRELIMINARY.

prepare, **fit**, **qualify**, **condition**, **ready** mean to make someone or something ready.

Prepare implies an often complicated process of making or getting ready ⟨*prepare* the ground for a crop⟩.

Fit implies a making suitable to a particular end or objective ⟨schools that don't *fit* students for further education⟩.

Qualify stresses the idea that fitness for a particular situation, such as an office, duty, or function, requires the fulfillment of necessary conditions, such as the taking of a course of study, an examination, or an oath ⟨*qualified* for third grade by passing all subjects in second grade⟩.

Condition implies getting into or bringing to a state that is proper or necessary to satisfy a particular purpose or use ⟨a program that *conditioned* him for the event⟩ or sometimes merely a state that is the inevitable result of past events and impacts ⟨*conditioned* to violence as a way of life⟩.

Ready emphasizes a putting or getting into order especially for use or action ⟨*ready* a room for a committee meeting⟩.

preponderant See DOMINANT.

prepossession See PREDILECTION.

prerequisite See REQUIREMENT.

prescribe 1. See DICTATE. **2. Prescribe**, **assign**, **define** mean to fix arbitrarily or authoritatively.

Prescribe implies an intent to provide explicit direction or clear guidance to those who accept or are bound by one's authority ⟨the Constitution *prescribes* the conditions under which it may be amended⟩.

Assign implies an arbitrary but not despotic determination, allotment, or designation for the sake of an end such as harmonious functioning, smooth routine, or proper or efficient operation ⟨*assign* a worker to the late shift⟩.

Define stresses an intent to mark boundaries so as to prevent confusion, conflict, or overlap ⟨*defined* clearly the limits of their freedom⟩.

prescription See RECEIPT.

present 1. See GIVE. **2.** See OFFER.

presentiment See APPREHENSION.

presently, shortly, soon, directly mean after a little while.

Presently is a term of rather vague implications as to the extent of time indicated ⟨the doctor will be here *presently*⟩.

Shortly typically implies a following quickly or without avoidable delay ⟨you will receive the report *shortly* after the tests are completed⟩.

Soon may imply that the thing narrated or predicted happened or will happen without much loss of time ⟨your sister should be home very *soon*⟩.

Directly implies something happening with little or a minimum of delay ⟨*directly* after graduation he joined the family business⟩.

preserve See SAVE.

pressure See STRESS.

prestige See INFLUENCE.

presume See PRESUPPOSE.

presuppose, presume, assume, postulate, premise, posit mean to take something for granted as the basis for action or reasoning.

Presuppose may imply a hazy or imperfectly realized belief or an uncritical acceptance ⟨a work which *presupposes* a knowledgeable readership⟩, or it may imply the necessity of accepting something that must logically be true ⟨an effect *presupposes* a cause⟩.

Presume suggests that whatever is taken for granted is entitled to belief until it is disproved ⟨*presumed* innocent until proven guilty⟩.

Assume indicates arbitrary or deliberate acceptance of something not proven or demonstrated ⟨had *assumed* that the family would welcome his return⟩.

Postulate suggests advancing an assumption that cannot be proven but that is accepted as true because it serves as the basis for some thought or action ⟨ordinary humans must *postulate* the reality of time and space⟩.

Premise indicates laying down a position from which an inference can be drawn or stating facts and principles fundamental to an argument ⟨an argument *premised* on a belief in the value of a formal education⟩.

Posit suggests the selecting of a proposition on subjective or arbitrary grounds ⟨a company that *posits* an eager consumer for each of its new products⟩.

pretend See ASSUME.

pretense, pretension, make-believe mean the offering of something false or deceptive as real or true.

Pretense may denote false show or the evidence of it ⟨a person utterly devoid of *pretense*⟩, or it may apply to something such as an act, an appearance, or a statement intended to convince others of the reality of something that in fact lacks reality ⟨gained their confidence under false *pretenses*⟩.

Pretension is often used in the sense of false show and implies an unwarranted belief in one's desirable qualities that results from conceit or self-deception ⟨harbored *pretensions* to wealth and good breeding⟩.

Make-believe applies chiefly to pretenses that arise out of a strong or vivid imagination, as of a child or poet ⟨delighted in her world of *make-believe*⟩.

pretension 1. See AMBITION. **2.** See PRETENSE.

pretentious See SHOWY.

pretext See APOLOGY.

pretty See BEAUTIFUL.

prevail See INDUCE.

prevailing, prevalent, rife, current mean generally circulated, accepted, or used in a certain time or place.

Prevailing stresses predominance ⟨the *prevailing* medical opinion regarding smoking⟩.

Prevalent implies only frequency ⟨dairy farms were once *prevalent* in the area⟩.

Rife implies a growing prevalence or

rapid spread ⟨during the epidemic rumors were *rife*⟩.

Current applies to what is subject to change and stresses prevalence at a particular time or present moment ⟨the *current* migration towards the Sunbelt⟩. ***antonym:*** antique, antiquated, obsolete

prevalent See PREVAILING.

prevaricate See LIE.

prevent 1. Prevent, anticipate, forestall mean to deal with beforehand.

Prevent implies the taking of advance measures against something possible or probable ⟨measures taken to *prevent* an epidemic⟩.

Anticipate may imply a getting ahead of another by being a precursor or forerunner or the checking of another's intention by acting first ⟨*anticipated* the firing so she decided to quit first⟩. ***antonym:*** consummate

Forestall implies a getting ahead so as to stop or interrupt something in its course or to render something ineffective or harmless ⟨a government order that effectively *forestalled* a free election⟩.

2. Prevent, preclude, obviate, avert, ward off mean to stop something from coming or occurring.

Prevent implies the existence of or the placing of an insurmountable obstacle ⟨the blizzard *prevented* us from going⟩. ***antonym:*** permit

Preclude implies the existence of some factor that shuts out every possibility of a thing's happening or taking effect ⟨an accident that *precluded* a career in football⟩.

Obviate suggests the use of forethought to avoid the necessity for unwelcome or disagreeable actions or measures ⟨his resignation *obviated* the task of firing him⟩.

Avert implies the taking of immediate and effective measures to avoid, repel, or counteract threatening evil ⟨deftly *averted* a hostile corporate takeover⟩.

Ward off suggests a close encounter and the use of defensive measures ⟨a hot drink to *ward off* a chill⟩. ***antonym:*** conduce to

previous See PRECEDING.

prey See VICTIM.

price, charge, cost, expense mean what is given or asked in exchange for something.

Price designates what is asked, especially for goods and commodities ⟨the *price* of vegetables has risen sharply⟩.

Charge is close to ***price*** but applies especially to services ⟨what is the *charge* for hauling away a load of brush⟩ and can apply additionally to what is imposed on one as a financial burden ⟨*charged* them $3.00 each⟩.

Cost applies to what is given or surrendered for something, often specifically the payment of price asked ⟨the *cost* of a new car⟩.

Expense often designates the aggregate amount actually disbursed for something ⟨our *expenses* were higher last month⟩.

priceless See COSTLY.

pride *n* **Pride, vanity, vainglory** mean the quality or feeling of a person who is firmly convinced of his or her own excellence or superiority.

Pride may imply either justified or unjustified self-esteem, and it may refer to real or imagined merit or superiority or to feelings of proper respect for oneself and one's standards or to blatant and arrogant conceit ⟨took *pride* in her marks⟩. ***antonym:*** humility, shame

Vanity implies an excessive desire to win notice, approval, or praise and connotes self-centeredness and may suggest concentration on trivia ⟨a woman of enormous *vanity*⟩.

Vainglory suggests excessive boastful pride often manifested in an arrogant display of one's vaunted qualities ⟨resorted to bragging and *vainglory* to get his own way⟩.

pride *vb* **Pride, plume, pique, preen** mean to congratulate oneself because of something one is, has, or has done or achieved.

Pride usually implies a taking of credit for something that brings honor or gives just cause for pride ⟨he *prides* himself on his ancestry⟩.

Plume adds the implication of obvious, often vain display of one's satisfaction and commonly suggests less justification ⟨*plumed* herself on the obedience of her staff⟩.

Pique differs from ***plume*** chiefly in carrying a hint of stirred-up pride, usually in some special accomplishment ⟨*piques* himself on his ability to speak French well⟩.

Preen occasionally replaces ***plume***, sometimes with a slight suggestion of adorning oneself with one's virtues or accomplishments ⟨*preened* herself on her awards⟩.

prior See PRECEDING.

priority, **precedence** mean the act, the fact, or the right of being in front or going ahead of another.

Priority is the usual term in law and the sciences and in questions involving simple time relations of events ⟨the right to inherit a title depends mainly on *priority* of birth⟩, but in questions involving things such as debts or cases or needs to be met which cannot be taken care of at one time, *priority* suggests a rule of arrangement that determines the order of procedure, often by relative importance ⟨assigned teaching top *priority*⟩.

Precedence is often close to ***priority*** ⟨it is our intent to give them *precedence* over you⟩, but it most typically implies an established order which gives preference to those of superior rank, dignity, or position ⟨a formal procession that observed the proper order of *precedence*⟩.

priory See CLOISTER.

prize *n* See SPOIL.

prize *vb* See APPRECIATE.

probable, **possible**, **likely** mean not currently certain but such as may be or become true or actual.

Probable applies to what is supported by evidence that is strong but not conclusive ⟨a *probable* cause of the accident⟩. ***antonym:*** certain, improbable

Possible applies to what lies within the known limits of performance, attainment, nature, or mode of existence of a thing or person regardless of the chances for or against its actuality ⟨it is *possible* that she went home without telling us⟩.

Likely differs from ***probable*** in implying more superficial or more general grounds for judgment or belief and from ***possible*** in imputing much greater chance of being true or occurring ⟨the *likely* result of their quarrel is continued bickering⟩. ***antonym:*** unlikely

probationer See NOVICE.

probe See ENTER.

probity See HONESTY.

problem See MYSTERY.

problematic See DOUBTFUL.

procedure See PROCESS.

proceed See SPRING.

proceeding See PROCESS.

process, **procedure**, **proceeding** mean the series of such things as actions, operations, or motions involved in the accomplishment of an end.

Process is particularly appropriate when progress from a definite beginning to a definite end is implied and the sequence of events can be divided into a sequence of steps or stages ⟨the *process* of digestion⟩.

Procedure stresses the method followed or the routine to be followed ⟨achieved success despite disdain for normal *procedure*⟩.

Proceeding applies not only to the sequence of events, actions, or operations but also to any one of these events, actions, or operations and stresses the items involved rather than their relation or the end in view ⟨had little patience with bureaucratic *proceedings*⟩.

proclaim See DECLARE.
proclivity See LEANING.
procrastinate See DELAY.
procure See GET.
prodigal *adj* See PROFUSE.
prodigal *n* See SPENDTHRIFT.
prodigious See MONSTROUS.
proffer See OFFER.
proficient, **adept**, **skilled**, **skillful**, **expert** mean having or manifesting the great knowledge and experience necessary for success in a skill, trade, or profession.
Proficient implies a thorough competence derived from training and practice ⟨a translator thoroughly *proficient* in Russian⟩. ***antonym:*** incompetent
Adept implies special aptitude as well as proficiency ⟨*adept* at handling large numbers in his head⟩. ***antonym:*** bungling, inapt, inept
Skilled stresses mastery of technique ⟨a delicate operation requiring a *skilled* surgeon⟩. ***antonym:*** unskilled
Skillful implies individual dexterity in execution or performance ⟨a shrewd and *skillful* manipulation of public opinion⟩. ***antonym:*** unskillful
Expert implies extraordinary proficiency and often connotes knowledge as well as technical skill ⟨*expert* in the identification and evaluation of wines⟩. ***antonym:*** amateur
profile See OUTLINE.
profitable See BENEFICIAL.
profligate See SPENDTHRIFT.
profound See DEEP 2.
profuse, **lavish**, **prodigal**, **luxuriant**, **lush**, **exuberant** mean giving or given out in great abundance.
Profuse implies pouring forth without restraint or in a stream ⟨uttered *profuse* apologies⟩. ***antonym:*** spare, scanty, scant
Lavish suggests an unstinted or unmeasured or extravagant profusion ⟨a *lavish* wedding reception of obvious expense⟩. ***antonym:*** sparing
Prodigal implies reckless or wasteful lavishness threatening to lead to exhaustion of resources ⟨*prodigal* spending exhausted the fortune⟩. ***antonym:*** parsimonious, frugal
Luxuriant suggests a rich and splendid abundance ⟨the *luxuriant* vegetation of a tropical rain forest⟩.
Lush suggests rich, soft luxuriance at, or slightly past, the peak of perfection ⟨nude portraits that have a *lush,* sensual quality⟩.
Exuberant implies marked vitality, vigor, or creative power in what produces abundantly or luxuriantly ⟨a fantasy writer with an *exuberant* imagination⟩. ***antonym:*** austere, sterile
prognosticate See FORETELL.
progressive See LIBERAL 2.
prohibit See FORBID.
project See PLAN.
projection, **protrusion**, **protuberance**, **bulge** mean an extension beyond the normal line or surface.
Projection implies a jutting out especially at a sharp angle ⟨those *projections* along the wall are safety hazards⟩.
Protrusion suggests a thrusting out so that the extension seems an excrescence or a deformity ⟨the bizarre *protrusions* of a coral reef⟩.
Protuberance implies a growing or swelling out from a surface in rounded form ⟨a skin disease marked by warty *protuberances*⟩.
Bulge suggests an expansion or swelling of a surface caused by pressure within or below ⟨*bulges* soon appeared in the tile floor⟩.
prolific See FERTILE.
prolix See WORDY.
prolong See EXTEND.
prominent See NOTICEABLE.
promiscuous See MISCELLANEOUS.
promote See ADVANCE.
prompt See QUICK.
promulgate See DECLARE.
prone **1.** See LIABLE. **2. Prone**, **supine**, **prostrate**, **recumbent** mean lying down.

Prone implies a position with the front of the body turned toward the supporting surface ⟨push-ups require the body to be in a *prone* position⟩. ***antonym:*** erect

Supine implies lying on one's back and suggests inertness or abjectness ⟨lying *supine* upon a couch⟩.

Prostrate implies lying full-length as in submission, defeat, or physical collapse ⟨a runner fell *prostrate* at the finish line⟩.

Recumbent implies the posture of one lying at ease or in comfortable repose ⟨he was *recumbent* in his hospital bed⟩. ***antonym:*** upright, erect

propel See PUSH.

propensity See LEANING.

proper See FIT *adj.*

property See QUALITY 1.

prophesy See FORETELL.

propitiate See PACIFY.

propitious See FAVORABLE.

proportion See SYMMETRY.

proportional, **proportionate**, **commensurate**, **commensurable** mean in due ratio to something else.

Proportional may apply to several closely related things that change without altering their relations ⟨medical fees are *proportional* to one's income⟩.

Proportionate applies to one thing that bears a reciprocal relationship to another ⟨a punishment not at all *proportionate* to the offense⟩. ***antonym:*** disproportionate

Commensurate stresses an equality between things different from but in some way dependent on each other ⟨the salary will be *commensurate* with experience⟩. ***antonym:*** incommensurate

Commensurable more strongly implies a common scale by which two quite different things can be shown to be significantly equal or proportionate ⟨equal pay for jobs that are *commensurable* in worth⟩. ***antonym:*** incommensurable

proportionate See PROPORTIONAL.

propose, **propound**, **pose** mean to set before the mind for consideration.

Propose fundamentally implies an invitation to consider, discuss, settle, or agree upon some clearly stated question or proposition ⟨*proposed* marriage⟩ ⟨*propose* a solution⟩ or an offering of someone as a candidate ⟨*proposed* his colleague for attorney general⟩.

Propound implies the stating of a question or proposition for discussion usually without personal bias or without any attempt to prove or disprove on the part of the propounder ⟨*propounded* the thesis that all great music is inspired⟩.

Pose, very close to ***propound***, is likely to imply that no attempt will be or can be made to seek an immediate answer ⟨*pose* a question for your consideration⟩.

propound See PROPOSE.

propriety See DECORUM.

prorogue See ADJOURN.

prosaic, **prosy**, **matter-of-fact** mean having a plain, practical, unimaginative quality or character.

Prosaic implies an opposition to *poetic* and usually suggests a commonplace unexciting quality and the absence of everything that would stimulate feeling or awaken great interest ⟨a downtown with a certain mundane, *prosaic* air⟩.

Prosy stresses dullness or tediousness and when applied to persons usually implies a tendency to talk or write at length in a boring and uninviting manner ⟨wrote them a dull, *prosy* letter⟩.

Matter-of-fact implies a disinterest in the imaginative, speculative, visionary, romantic, or ideal; it may connote down-to-earth practicality and accuracy in detail ⟨a *matter-of-fact* account of their adventure⟩ but often it suggests preoccupation with the obvious and a neglect of more subtle values ⟨took a very *matter-of-fact* attitude toward her illness⟩.

prospect, **outlook**, **anticipation**, **foretaste** mean an advance realization of something to come.

Prospect implies expectation of a particular event, condition, or development of definite interest or concern ⟨the appealing *prospect* of a quiet weekend⟩.

Outlook suggests a usually general forecasting of the future ⟨a favorable *outlook* for the state's economy⟩.

Anticipation implies a prospect or outlook that involves advance suffering or enjoyment of what is foreseen ⟨reviewing his notes in *anticipation* of the next meeting⟩. ***antonym:*** retrospect

Foretaste implies an actual though brief or partial experiencing of something that will come later in full force ⟨the frost was a *foretaste* of winter⟩.

prosper See SUCCEED.

prostrate See PRONE.

prosy See PROSAIC.

protect See DEFEND 1.

protest 1. See ASSERT. **2.** See OBJECT.

protract See EXTEND.

protrusion See PROJECTION.

protuberance See PROJECTION.

proud, **arrogant**, **haughty**, **lordly**, **insolent**, **overbearing**, **supercilious**, **disdainful** mean showing superiority toward others or scorn for inferiors.

Proud may suggest a feeling or attitude of pleased satisfaction in oneself or one's accomplishments that may or may not be justified and may or may not be demonstrated offensively ⟨a *proud* man, unwilling to admit failure⟩. ***antonym:*** humble, ashamed

Arrogant implies a claiming for oneself of more consideration or importance than is warranted and often suggests an aggressive, domineering manner ⟨an *arrogant* business executive used to being kowtowed to⟩. ***antonym:*** meek, unassuming

Haughty suggests a blatantly displayed consciousness of superior birth or position ⟨a *haughty* manner that barely concealed his scorn⟩. ***antonym:*** lowly

Lordly implies pomposity or an arrogant display of power ⟨a *lordly* indifference to the consequences of their carelessness⟩.

Insolent implies insultingly contemptuous haughtiness ⟨suffered the stares of *insolent* waiters⟩. ***antonym:*** deferential

Overbearing suggests a tyrannical manner or an intolerable insolence ⟨wearied by demands from her *overbearing* in-laws⟩. ***antonym:*** subservient

Supercilious implies a cool, patronizing haughtiness ⟨*supercilious* parvenus with their disdainful sneers⟩.

Disdainful suggests a more active and openly scornful superciliousness ⟨*disdainful* of their pathetic attempts⟩. ***antonym:*** admiring, respectful

provide, **supply**, **furnish** mean to give or get what is desired by or needed for something.

Provide suggests foresight and stresses the idea of making adequate preparation by stocking or equipping ⟨*provide* suitable accommodations⟩.

Supply may stress the idea of replacing, of making up what is needed, or of satisfying a deficiency ⟨foods that *supply* needed protein and vitamins to the diet⟩.

Furnish may emphasize the idea of fitting with whatever is needed or, sometimes, normal or desirable ⟨the porcupine, *furnished* by nature with a built-in defense⟩.

providential See LUCKY.

province See FUNCTION.

provisional, **tentative** mean not final or definitive.

Provisional applies to something that is adopted only for the time being and will be discarded when the final or definitive form is established or when the need for it otherwise comes to an end ⟨a *provisional* government⟩. ***antonym:*** definitive

Tentative applies to something that is of the nature of a trial or experiment or serves as a test of practicability or feasibility ⟨our plans are still *tentative*—subject to change without notice⟩. ***antonym:*** definitive

provoke 1. Provoke, **excite**, **stimulate**, **pique**, **quicken** mean to rouse someone or something into being, doing, or feeling.

Provoke directs attention to the response called forth and often applies to an angry or vexed or extreme reaction ⟨my stories usually *provoke* laughter⟩.

Excite implies a stirring up or moving profoundly ⟨news that *excited* anger and frustration⟩. ***antonym:*** soothe, quiet (*persons*), allay (*fears, anxiety*)

Stimulate suggests a rousing out of lethargy, quiescence, or indifference ⟨the challenge *stimulated* them to work faster⟩. ***antonym:*** unnerve, deaden

Pique suggests stimulating by mild irritation or challenge ⟨that remark *piqued* my interest⟩.

Quicken implies beneficially stimulating and making active or lively ⟨the high salary *quickened* her desire to have the job⟩. ***antonym:*** arrest

2. See IRRITATE.

prowess See HEROISM.

prudent See WISE.

prying See CURIOUS.

publish See DECLARE.

pugnacious See BELLIGERENT.

pull, **draw**, **drag**, **haul**, **tug** mean to cause to move in the direction determined by an applied force.

Pull is the general term but may emphasize the force exerted rather than the resulting motion ⟨to open the drawer, *pull* hard⟩.

Draw implies a smoother, steadier motion and generally a lighter force than ***pull*** ⟨a child *drawing* his sled across the snow⟩.

Drag suggests great effort overcoming resistance or friction ⟨*dragged* the dead body across the room⟩.

Haul implies sustained pulling or dragging, especially of heavy or bulky objects ⟨a team of horses *hauling* supplies⟩.

Tug applies to strenuous often spasmodic efforts to move something ⟨the little girl *tugged* at her mother's hand⟩.

punch See STRIKE 2.

punctilious See CAREFUL.

pungent, **piquant**, **poignant**, **racy** mean sharp and stimulating to the mind or the senses.

Pungent implies a sharp, stinging, or biting quality, especially of odors ⟨a cheese with a *pungent* odor⟩. ***antonym:*** bland

Piquant suggests a power to whet the appetite or interest through a mildly pungent or provocative quality ⟨grapefruit juice gave the punch its *piquant* taste⟩. ***antonym:*** bland

Poignant suggests something that is sharply or piercingly effective in stirring one's consciousness or emotions ⟨upon her departure he felt a *poignant* sense of loss⟩. ***antonym:*** dull

Racy implies possession of a strongly characteristic natural quality that is fresh and unimpaired ⟨the spontaneous, *racy* prose of the untutored writer⟩.

punish, **chastise**, **castigate**, **chasten**, **discipline**, **correct** mean to inflict a penalty on in requital for wrongdoing.

Punish implies the imposing of a penalty for violation of law, disobedience, or wrongdoing ⟨*punished* for stealing⟩. ***antonym:*** excuse, pardon

Chastise may apply to either the infliction of corporal punishment or to verbal censure or denunciation ⟨*chastised* his son for neglecting his studies⟩.

Castigate implies a severe, typically public lashing with words ⟨an editorial *castigating* the entire city council⟩.

Chasten suggests any affliction or trial that leaves one humbled or subdued but improved and strengthened ⟨a stunning election defeat that left him *chastened*⟩. ***antonym:*** pamper, mollycoddle

Discipline implies a punishing or chastising in order to bring or keep under control ⟨the duty of parents to *discipline* their children⟩.

Correct implies a punishing aimed at reforming an offender ⟨the function of prison is to *correct* the wrongdoer⟩.

pure See CHASTE.
purloin See STEAL.
purpose See INTENTION.
pursue See FOLLOW 2.
pursuit See WORK 2.
push, shove, thrust, propel mean to cause to move ahead or aside by the application of force.
Push implies the application of force by a body already in contact with the body to be moved ⟨*push* the door open⟩.
Shove implies a strong and often fast, sudden, or rough pushing that forces something along or aside ⟨*shoved* the man out of my way⟩.
Thrust suggests less steadiness and greater violence than ***push*** and implies the application of a single abrupt movement or action ⟨*thrust* the money into my hand and ran away⟩.
Propel suggests a driving rapidly forward or onward by a force or power that imparts motion ⟨ships *propelled* by steam⟩.
pushing See AGGRESSIVE.
pushy See AGGRESSIVE.
pusillanimous See COWARDLY.
putrefy See DECAY.
putrid See MALODOROUS.
put up See RESIDE.
puzzle *vb* **Puzzle, perplex, bewilder, distract, nonplus, confound, dumbfound** mean to baffle and disturb mentally.
Puzzle implies the presenting of a problem difficult to solve ⟨a persistent fever which *puzzled* the doctor⟩.
Perplex adds a suggestion of worry and uncertainty especially about making a necessary decision ⟨an odd change of personality that *perplexed* her friends⟩.
Bewilder stresses a confusion of mind that hampers clear and decisive thinking ⟨the number of videotapes available *bewilders* consumers⟩.
Distract implies agitation or uncertainty induced by conflicting preoccupations or interests ⟨a political scandal that *distracted* the country for two years⟩. ***antonym:*** collect (*one's thoughts, powers*)
Nonplus implies a bafflement that causes complete blankness of mind ⟨she was utterly *nonplussed* by the abrupt change in plans⟩.
Confound implies temporary mental paralysis caused by astonishment or profound abasement ⟨tragic news that *confounded* us all⟩.
Dumbfound suggests an intense but momentary confounding or astounding ⟨*dumbfounded* by her rejection of his marriage proposal⟩.
puzzle *n* See MYSTERY.

Q

quail See RECOIL.
quaint See STRANGE.
quake See SHAKE 1.
qualified See ABLE.
qualify 1. See PREPARE. **2.** See MODERATE *vb.*
quality 1. Quality, property, character, attribute mean an intelligible feature by which a thing may be identified or understood.

Quality is a general term applicable to any trait or characteristic whether material or immaterial, individual or generic ⟨a star whose acting had a persistently amateurish *quality*⟩.

Property implies a characteristic that belongs to a thing's essential nature and may be used to describe a type or species ⟨asked them to name the basic *properties* of mammals⟩.

Character applies to a peculiar and distinctive quality of an individual or a class ⟨each of the island's villages has a distinctive *character*⟩.

Attribute implies a quality ascribed to a thing or a being ⟨a man with none of the traditional *attributes* of a popular hero⟩.

2. Quality, stature, caliber mean distinctive merit or superiority.

Quality, used in the singular, implies a complex of properties that together produce a high order of excellence, virtue, or worth ⟨of a *quality* not often found anymore⟩.

Stature is likely to suggest height reached or development attained and to connote considerations of prestige and eminence ⟨chose a new leader of great *stature*⟩.

Caliber suggests unusual but measurable extent or range of quality or powers, such as ability or intellect, or sometimes of deviation from a norm or standard ⟨a man of very low moral *caliber*⟩.

qualm, scruple, compunction, demur mean a misgiving about what one is doing or going to do.

Qualm implies an uneasy fear that one is not following one's conscience or better judgment ⟨no *qualms* about traveling in the Middle East⟩.

Scruple implies a doubt of the rightness of an act on grounds of principle ⟨a lawyer totally devoid of *scruples*⟩.

Compunction implies a spontaneous feeling of responsibility and compassion for a potential victim ⟨not likely to have *compunctions* about knocking out his opponent⟩.

Demur implies hesitation caused by objection or resistance to an outside suggestion or influence ⟨accepted her resignation without *demur*⟩.

quandary See PREDICAMENT.
quantity See SUM.
quarrel, wrangle, altercation, squabble, spat, tiff mean an angry dispute.

Quarrel implies a heated verbal clash followed by strained or severed relations ⟨a bitter *quarrel* that ended their friendship⟩.

Wrangle suggests a noisy, insistent, often futile dispute ⟨an ongoing *wrangle* over the town's finances⟩.

Altercation suggests noisy, heated verbal quarreling often with blows ⟨a violent *altercation* between pro- and anti-abortion groups⟩.

Squabble implies childish and unseemly wrangling over a petty matter ⟨the children constantly *squabble* over toys⟩.

Spat implies a lively but brief dispute over a trifle ⟨the couple averages a *spat* a week⟩.

Tiff suggests a trivial dispute marked by ill humor or hurt feelings but without serious consequence ⟨a *tiff* that was forgotten by dinnertime⟩.

quarrelsome See BELLIGERENT.
quarry See VICTIM.

quash See CRUSH.
quaver See SHAKE 1.
queer See STRANGE.
quell See CRUSH.
query See ASK 1.
question See ASK 1.
questionable See DOUBTFUL.
quick **1.** See FAST. **2. Quick, prompt, ready, apt** mean able to respond without delay or hesitation or indicative of such ability.

Quick stresses instancy of response and is likely to connote native rather than acquired power ⟨a *quick* mind⟩. ***antonym:*** sluggish

Prompt is more likely to connote training and discipline that fits one for instant response ⟨the *prompt* response of emergency medical technicians⟩.

Ready suggests facility or fluency in response ⟨backed by a pair of *ready* assistants⟩.

Apt stresses the possession of qualities, such as high intelligence, a particular talent, or a strong bent, that make quick effective response possible ⟨an *apt* student⟩.

quicken **1. Quicken, animate, enliven, vivify** mean to make alive or lively.

Quicken stresses a sudden arousal or renewal of physical, spiritual, or intellectual life or activity especially in something inert ⟨the arrival of spring *quickens* the earth⟩. ***antonym:*** deaden

Animate emphasizes the imparting of motion or vitality to what was previously deficient in or lacking such a quality ⟨telling details that *animate* the familiar story⟩.

Enliven suggests a stimulating influence that arouses from dullness or torpidity ⟨*enlivened* his lecture with humorous anecdotes⟩. ***antonym:*** deaden, subdue

Vivify implies a freshening or energizing through the imparting or renewal of vitality ⟨her appearance *vivifies* a dreary drawing-room drama⟩.

2. See PROVOKE.

quick-witted See INTELLIGENT.
quiescent See LATENT.
quiet See STILL.
quip See JEST.
quit **1.** See STOP. **2.** See GO.
quiver See SHAKE 1.
quixotic See IMAGINARY.
quote, cite, repeat mean to speak or write again something already said or written by another.

Quote usually implies precise repetition of the words of another for a particular purpose ⟨illustrate the use of a word by *quoting* classical and modern authors⟩, but sometimes *quote* is applied to a more general referral to someone as author or source of information ⟨don't *quote* me as your authority⟩.

Cite is likely to stress the idea of mentioning for a particular reason, such as proof of a thesis or substantiation of a position taken, with or without the idea of quoting another's exact words ⟨his analysis of the causes of student unrest has been *cited* in several recent judicial opinions⟩.

Repeat stresses the mere fact of saying or writing again the words or presenting the ideas of another often with no reference to the source and little concern for precision ⟨*repeat* a scandalous story told one in confidence⟩.

quotidian See DAILY.

R

rack See AFFLICT.
racket See DIN.
racy See PUNGENT.
radiant See BRIGHT.
radical See LIBERAL 2.
rage **1.** See ANGER. **2.** See FASHION.
rail See SCOLD.
raise See LIFT.
rally See STIR *vb.*
ramble See WANDER.
rampant See RANK.
rancid See MALODOROUS.
rancor See ENMITY.
random, **haphazard**, **chance**, **casual**, **desultory**, **hit-or-miss** mean determined by accident rather than design.

Random stresses chance and lack of definite aim, fixed goal, or regular procedure ⟨a *random* sampling of public opinion⟩. ***antonym:*** purposive

Haphazard applies to what is done without regard for regularity or fitness or ultimate consequence ⟨his selection of college courses was entirely *haphazard*⟩.

Chance applies to what comes or happens to one or is done or made without prearrangement, foreknowledge, or preparation ⟨a *chance* encounter⟩ ⟨a *chance* acquaintance⟩.

Casual suggests a leaving things to chance and a working or acting without deliberation, intention, or purpose ⟨a *casual* tour of the sights⟩. ***antonym:*** deliberate

Desultory implies a jumping or skipping from one thing to another without method or system and a consequently inconsistent performance and lack of continuity ⟨a *desultory* discussion of current events⟩. ***antonym:*** assiduous

Hit-or-miss applies to what is so haphazard as to lack all apparent plan, aim, system, or care ⟨a real *hit-or-miss* operation⟩.

range *n* **Range**, **gamut**, **compass**, **sweep**, **scope**, **reach**, **orbit** mean the extent that lies within the powers of something to cover or control.

Range is a general term indicating the extent of one's perception or the extent of powers, capabilities, or possibilities ⟨the entire *range* of human experience⟩.

Gamut suggests a graduated series running from one possible extreme to another ⟨a performance that ran the *gamut* of emotions⟩.

Compass implies a sometimes limited or bounded extent of perception, knowledge, or activity ⟨your concerns lie beyond the narrow *compass* of this study⟩.

Sweep suggests extent, often circular or arc-shaped, of motion or activity ⟨the book covers the entire *sweep* of criminal activity⟩.

Scope is applicable to a predetermined and limited area of activity that is somewhat flexible within those limits ⟨as time went on, the *scope* of the investigation widened⟩.

Reach suggests an extent of perception, knowledge, ability, or activity attained to or experienced by stretching out ⟨a goal well within *reach*⟩.

Orbit suggests an often circumscribed range of activity or influence within which forces work toward accommodation ⟨within that restricted *orbit* they tried to effect social change⟩.

range *vb* **1.** See LINE. **2.** See WANDER.
rank **1. Rank**, **rampant** mean growing or increasing at an immoderate rate.

Rank implies vigorous, luxuriant, and often unchecked or excessive growth ⟨the *rank* plant life of the tropics⟩.

Rampant implies rapid and often wild or unrestrained spreading and can be applied both to what literally grows and to what increases as if by physical growth ⟨diseases that are *rampant* in the region⟩.

2. See FLAGRANT. **3.** See MALODOROUS.
ransom See RESCUE.

rant See BOMBAST.
rap See TAP.
rapacious See VORACIOUS.
rapid See FAST.
rapture See ECSTASY.
rare 1. See CHOICE. **2.** See INFREQUENT.
rash See ADVENTUROUS.
rate See ESTIMATE.
ration, **allowance**, **pittance** mean the amount of food, supplies, or money allotted to an individual.

Ration implies apportionment and, often, equal sharing; basically, it applies to the daily supply of food provided for one individual, such as a prisoner or a milk cow, but it is freely extended to things in short supply that are made available either equally or equitably in accord with need ⟨gasoline *rations* in wartime vary with the special needs of different individuals⟩.

Allowance stresses granting rather than sharing what is in restricted supply ⟨each child was given an *allowance* as soon as he or she became old enough to handle money⟩.

Pittance stresses meagerness or miserliness and may apply indifferently to a ration, an allowance, an alms, a dole, or a wage ⟨managed to survive on a mere *pittance*⟩.

rational, **reasonable** mean having or manifesting the power to reason or being in accordance with the dictates of reason.

Rational usually implies the power to make logical inferences and to draw conclusions that enable one to understand things ⟨a *rational* being⟩; in applications to things conceived or formulated, it stresses satisfactoriness in terms of reason ⟨engaged in *rational* discourse⟩. ***antonym:*** irrational, demented, absurd

Reasonable emphasizes the possession or use of practical sense, justice, and fairness and the avoidance of needless error ⟨willing to grant any *reasonable* request⟩. ***antonym:*** unreasonable

rattle See EMBARRASS.
raucous See LOUD.
ravage, **devastate**, **waste**, **sack**, **pillage**, **despoil** mean to lay waste by plundering or destroying.

Ravage implies a violent, severe, and often cumulative depredation and destruction ⟨a hurricane that *ravaged* the Gulf coast⟩.

Devastate implies the complete ruin and desolation of a wide area ⟨the atomic bomb that *devastated* Hiroshima⟩.

Waste may imply a less complete destruction or one produced by a slower or less violent process ⟨years of drought had *wasted* the area⟩. ***antonym:*** conserve, save

Sack implies the looting and destroying of a place ⟨barbarians *sacked* ancient Rome⟩.

Pillage implies ruthless plundering at will but without the completeness suggested by ***sack*** ⟨settlements *pillaged* by Vikings⟩.

Despoil applies to the looting or robbing of a place or person without suggesting accompanying destruction ⟨the Nazis *despoiled* the art museums of Europe⟩.

ravenous See VORACIOUS.
ravish See TRANSPORT.
raw See RUDE.
rawboned See LEAN.
reach *n* See RANGE.
reach *vb* **Reach**, **gain**, **compass**, **achieve**, **attain** mean to arrive at a point or end by effort or work.

Reach may be used with reference to anything arrived at by any degree of effort ⟨after a long climb we *reached* the top of the hill⟩.

Gain is likely to imply a struggle to reach a contemplated or desired goal or end ⟨*gained* a measure of self-confidence from the experience⟩. ***antonym:*** forfeit, lose

Compass implies the exerting of efforts to get around difficulties and transcend limitation, and often connotes skill or craft in management ⟨an actress taking on the most difficult role that her skills could *compass*⟩.

Achieve can stress the skill or endurance as well as the effort involved in reaching an end ⟨*achieved* the success that was her due⟩. ***antonym:*** miss

Attain stresses the spur of aspiration or ambition and suggests a reaching for the extreme, the unusual, or the difficult ⟨vowed not to relax his efforts until peace was *attained*⟩.

readiness, **ease**, **facility**, **dexterity** mean the power of doing something without evidence of effort.

Readiness emphasizes the quickness or promptitude with which something is done ⟨indicated her *readiness* for the task⟩.

Ease implies absence of strain or care or hesitation with resulting smooth efficiency in performance ⟨answer a series of questions with *ease*⟩. ***antonym:*** effort

Facility is often very close to ***ease*** but sometimes suggests a slick superficiality rather than true ease ⟨a *facility* with words that was almost too glib⟩.

Dexterity implies proficient skill such as results from training and practice ⟨handled the class with the *dexterity* of a master⟩. ***antonym:*** clumsiness

ready *adj* See QUICK.

ready *vb* See PREPARE.

real, **actual**, **true** mean corresponding to known facts.

Real is likely to stress genuineness and especially correspondence between appearance and essence ⟨a *real* diamond⟩. ***antonym:*** unreal, apparent, imaginary

Actual stresses the fact of existence or fidelity to the existent as opposed to the nonexistent, abstract, or hypothetical ⟨the *actual* tests of this missile have not yet been made⟩. ***antonym:*** ideal, imaginary

True can stress conformity to the real especially as a model or standard ⟨the ladybug is not a *true* bug but a beetle⟩ or conformity to the pertinent facts that are known or knowable ⟨the *true* version of events⟩. ***antonym:*** false

realize See THINK 1.

reap, **glean**, **gather**, **garner**, **harvest** mean to do the work or a particular part of the work of collecting ripened crops.

Reap basically applies to the cutting down and usually collecting of ripened grain, and often suggests a return or requital ⟨hoped to *reap* the rewards of hard work⟩.

Glean implies a stripping of a field or plant that has already been gone over once and applies to any gathering up of useful bits from here and there and especially of such as have been overlooked by others ⟨*gleaned* new evidence from the site of the crime⟩.

Gather applies to any collecting or bringing together of material, such as the produce of a farm or garden, and stresses amassing or accumulating ⟨*gathered* information⟩.

Garner implies the storing of produce reaped or gathered and can apply to any laying away of a store ⟨a collection of maxims *garnered* from her neighbors⟩.

Harvest may imply any or all of these agricultural practices or may apply to any gathering in or husbanding ⟨*harvested* a bumper crop⟩.

rear See LIFT.

reason *n* **1.** See CAUSE. **2. Reason**, **understanding**, **intuition** mean the power of the intellect by which human beings attain truth or knowledge.

Reason refers to the faculty for order, sense, and rationality in thought, inference, and conclusion about perceptions ⟨tried to approach each problem with calm and *reason*⟩.

Understanding may widen the scope of ***reason*** to include most thought processes leading to comprehension and also the resultant state of knowledge ⟨research that led to a new *understanding* of the disease⟩.

Intuition stresses quick knowledge or comprehension without evident orderly reason, thought, or cogitation ⟨responded on the basis of *intuition*⟩.

reason *vb* See THINK 2.

reasonable See RATIONAL.

rebellion, **revolution**, **uprising**, **revolt**, **insurrection**, **mutiny** mean an armed outbreak against powers in authority.

Rebellion implies an open, organized armed resistance that is often unsuccessful ⟨the *rebellion* failed for lack of popular support⟩.

Revolution applies to a successful rebellion resulting in a major change in constituted authority ⟨the American *Revolution*⟩.

Uprising implies a brief, limited, and often immediately ineffective rebellion ⟨quickly put down the *uprising*⟩.

Revolt implies an armed uprising that quickly fails or succeeds ⟨a *revolt* by the young Turks that surprised party leaders⟩.

Insurrection differs from ***revolt*** in suggesting more intransigence and less organized purpose ⟨Nat Turner's unsuccessful slave *insurrection*⟩.

Mutiny applies to insubordination or insurrection especially against military or naval authority ⟨the famous *mutiny* aboard the Bounty⟩.

rebuild See MEND.

rebuke See REPROVE.

rebut See DISPROVE.

recalcitrant See UNRULY.

recall 1. See REMEMBER. **2.** See REVOKE.

recant See ABJURE.

recede, **retreat**, **retrograde**, **retract**, **back** mean to move backward.

Recede implies a gradual withdrawing from a forward or high fixed point in time, space, or attitude ⟨the flood waters gradually *receded*⟩. ***antonym:*** proceed, advance

Retreat implies a withdrawal from a point or position reached, typically in response to some pressure ⟨under cross-examination he *retreated* from that statement⟩. ***antonym:*** advance

Retrograde implies a movement contrary to what is expected, normal, or natural, and is the reverse of progress ⟨infant mortality rates *retrograding* to earlier levels⟩.

Retract implies a drawing back or in from an extended or outward position ⟨a cat *retracting* its claws⟩. ***antonym:*** protract

Back is used with *up*, *down, out*, or *off* to refer to any retrograde or reversed motion ⟨*backed* off when her claim was challenged⟩.

receipt, **recipe**, **prescription** mean a formula or set of directions for the compounding of ingredients especially in cookery and medicine.

Receipt often denotes a formula for a homemade or folk medical remedy ⟨a family *receipt* for a cough syrup⟩.

Recipe is broadly applicable and can denote not only a formula or set of instructions for doing or making something but also a method or procedure for attaining some end ⟨revealed their *recipe* for success⟩; in cookery it is the standard term for a set of directions for preparing a made dish ⟨tried a new *recipe* for scalloped oysters⟩.

Prescription refers to a physician's instruction to a pharmacist for the compounding or dispensing of a medicine or to a medicine compounded or dispensed ⟨wanted to get a *prescription* for a sleep aid⟩; it is sometimes extended to other formulas or formulations with a suggestion of the precision expected in medical directions ⟨a candidate with a clear *prescription* for economic recovery⟩.

receive, **accept**, **admit**, **take** mean to permit to come into one's possession, presence, group, mind, or substance.

Receive can imply a welcoming recognition ⟨*receive* guests with open arms⟩, but more often it implies that something comes or is allowed to come into one's possession or presence while one is passive ⟨*received* the news without comment⟩.

Accept adds to ***receive*** an implication of some degree of positive acquiescence or consent even if tacit ⟨refused to *accept* a valuable gift from a comparative stranger⟩. ***antonym:*** reject

Admit carries strong implications of permission, allowance, or sufferance ⟨*admit* new members to a club⟩. ***antonym:*** eject, expel

Take carries the notion of accepting or at least of making no positive protest against receiving, and often of almost welcoming on principle, what is offered, conferred, or inflicted ⟨a man who *took* whatever fortune sent him⟩.

recent See MODERN.

recess See PAUSE.

recipe See RECEIPT.

reciprocal, mutual, common mean shared or experienced by each of those concerned.

Reciprocal implies an equal return or counteraction by each of two sides toward or against or in relation to the other ⟨allies with a *reciprocal* defense agreement⟩.

Mutual applies to feelings or actions shared or experienced by two and may suggest an accompanying reciprocity, equality, or interaction ⟨two people with a *mutual* physical attraction⟩.

Common does not suggest reciprocity but merely a sharing with others ⟨a couple with many *common* interests⟩. ***antonym:*** individual

reciprocate, retaliate, requite, return mean to give back usually in kind or in quantity.

Reciprocate implies a more or less equivalent exchange or a paying back of what one has received ⟨*reciprocated* their hospitality by inviting them for a visit⟩.

Retaliate usually implies a paying back of injury in exact kind by way of vengeance ⟨the enemy *retaliated* by executing their prisoners⟩.

Requite implies a paying back according to one's preference and often not equivalently ⟨*requited* her love with cold indifference⟩.

Return implies a paying back of something usually in kind but sometimes by way of contrast ⟨*returned* their kindness with ingratitude⟩.

reckless See ADVENTUROUS.

reckon **1.** See CALCULATE. **2.** See RELY.

reclaim See RESCUE.

recognition, identification, assimilation, apperception mean a form of cognition that relates a perception of something new to knowledge already acquired.

Recognition implies that the thing now perceived has been previously perceived and that the mind is aware of the fact that the two things are the same thing or identical ⟨encouraged by the patient's *recognition* of his mother⟩.

Identification adds to ***recognition*** the implication of such prior knowledge as permits one to recognize the thing as an individual member of a class ⟨bird calls aid in the *identification* of species⟩.

Assimilation implies that the mind responds to new ideas, facts, and experiences by interpreting them in the light of what is already known, thereby making them an integral part of one's body of knowledge ⟨proceeded rapidly with the *assimilation* of new material⟩.

Apperception implies that the mind responds to new facts, ideas, or situations when and only when it can relate them to what is already known ⟨limited by my *apperceptions* of reality⟩.

recoil, shrink, flinch, wince, blench, quail mean to draw back in fear or distaste.

Recoil implies a start of a movement away prompted by shock, fear, or disgust ⟨*recoils* at the sight of blood⟩. ***antonym:*** confront, defy

Shrink suggests an instinctive recoiling

through sensitiveness, scrupulousness, or cowardice ⟨refused to *shrink* from responsibilities⟩.

Flinch implies a failure to endure pain or to face something dangerous or frightening with resolution ⟨faced her accusers without *flinching*⟩.

Wince suggests a slight involuntary physical recoiling from what pains, frightens, or disgusts ⟨*winced* when the new secretary called him by his first name⟩.

Blench implies fainthearted, fearful flinching ⟨never *blenched* even as his head was lowered on the guillotine⟩.

Quail suggests a shrinking and cowering in fear ⟨*quailed* at the fury of the storm⟩.

recollect See REMEMBER.

recollection See MEMORY.

recompense See PAY.

reconcile See ADAPT.

recrudesce See RETURN.

rectify See CORRECT *vb.*

recumbent See PRONE.

recur See RETURN.

recurrent See INTERMITTENT.

redeem See RESCUE.

redolence See FRAGRANCE.

redolent See ODOROUS.

redound See CONDUCE.

redress See CORRECT *vb.*

reduce 1. See CONQUER. **2.** See DECREASE.

redundant See WORDY.

reel, **whirl**, **stagger**, **totter** mean to move or seem to move uncertainly and irregularly or with such loss of control as occurs in extreme weakness or in intoxication.

Reel usually suggests a turning round and round or a sensation of so turning or being turned, but it may also imply a being thrown off balance ⟨a boxer *reeling* from the blow⟩.

Whirl is often used like ***reel*** ⟨their heads *whirling* with confusion⟩, but it more frequently implies swiftness or impetuousness of movement ⟨dancers *whirling* about the stage⟩.

Stagger stresses loss of control and uncertainty of movement, typically of a person walking while weak, intoxicated, or heavily burdened but sometimes simply of someone meeting with difficulty or adverse conditions ⟨*staggered* by the sheer enormity of the task⟩.

Totter not only implies weakness or unsteadiness that causes uncertain movement but often also hints at the approach of complete collapse ⟨watched closely as the oligarchy *tottered*⟩.

refer 1. See RESORT. **2. Refer**, **allude**, **advert** mean to call or direct attention to something.

Refer usually implies the intentional introduction and distinct and specific mention and sometimes judging ⟨*referred* to her claims as fantasy⟩.

Allude suggests an indirect mention by a hint, roundabout expression, or figure of speech ⟨*alluded* to incidents previously unknown⟩.

Advert usually implies a slight or glancing reference in a text or utterance ⟨a theory *adverted* to here but discussed later⟩.

reflect See THINK 2.

reflective See THOUGHTFUL 1.

reform See CORRECT *vb.*

refractory See UNRULY.

refrain, **abstain**, **forbear** mean to keep oneself voluntarily from doing or indulging in something.

Refrain is likely to suggest the checking of a passing impulse ⟨*refrain* from laughter in church⟩.

Abstain usually implies deliberate renunciation or self-denial on principle and often permanency of intent ⟨a vegetarian who *abstains* from all meat⟩. ***antonym:*** indulge

Forbear usually implies self-restraint rather than self-denial, be it from patience, charity, or clemency or from discretion or stoicism ⟨taught himself to *forbear* such expressions of anger⟩.

refresh See RENEW.

refuge See SHELTER *n.*
refuse See DECLINE.
refute See DISPROVE.
regard, **respect**, **esteem**, **admire** mean to recognize the worth of a person or thing.

Regard is a general term that is usually qualified ⟨he is not highly *regarded* in the profession⟩. ***antonym:*** despise

Respect implies a considered evaluation or estimation as the basis of recognition or worth ⟨after many years they came to *respect* her views⟩. ***antonym:*** abuse, misuse, scorn

Esteem implies a high valuation and a consequent warmth of feeling or attachment ⟨no citizen of the town was more highly *esteemed*⟩. ***antonym:*** abominate

Admire suggests a usually enthusiastic but uncritical appreciation and often deep affection ⟨*admired* the natural beauty of the scene⟩. ***antonym:*** abhor

regret See SORROW.
regular, **normal, typical**, **natural** mean being of the sort or kind that is expected as usual, ordinary, or average.

Regular stresses conformity to a rule, standard, or pattern ⟨the *regular* monthly meeting of the organization⟩. ***antonym:*** irregular

Normal implies lack of deviation from what has been discovered or established as the most usual or expected ⟨*normal* behavior for a two-year-old boy⟩. ***antonym:*** abnormal

Typical implies showing all important traits of a type, class, or group and may suggest lack of marked individuality ⟨a *typical* small town in America⟩. ***antonym:*** atypical, distinctive

Natural applies to what conforms to a thing's essential nature, function, or mode of being ⟨the *natural* love of a mother for her child⟩. ***antonym:*** unnatural, artificial, adventitious

regulation See LAW.
reimburse See PAY.
reiterate See REPEAT.
reject See DECLINE.
rejoin See ANSWER.
rejuvenate See RENEW.
relapse See LAPSE.
relate See JOIN.
related, **cognate**, **kindred**, **allied**, **affiliated** mean connected by or as if by close family ties.

Related can imply connection by blood or marriage or a correspondingly close connection ⟨in separate but *related* incidents⟩. ***antonym:*** unrelated

Cognate applies to things that are generically alike, have a common ancestor or source, or derive from the same root or stock ⟨*cognate* words in various languages, such as *pater, Vater,* and *father*⟩.

Kindred stresses family relations ⟨an isolated community most of whose members were *kindred*⟩ but in more common applications is likely to stress shared interests or tastes or congeniality ⟨felt it to be the meeting of *kindred* souls⟩. ***antonym:*** alien

Allied may imply connection by marriage or voluntary association rather than by origin or blood ⟨*allied* through his wife with several prominent English families⟩ or remote biological relationship, but it is more likely to stress relationship based on common characters, qualities, aims, or effects ⟨DDT and *allied* insecticides⟩. ***antonym:*** unallied

Affiliated, often close to ***allied***, distinctively tends to stress a dependent relation like that of a child to a parent ⟨all blood banks *affiliated* with the Red Cross⟩ and may connote a loose union in which the associated elements are more or less independent ⟨the network and its *affiliated* stations⟩. ***antonym:*** unaffiliated

relaxed See LOOSE.
release See FREE *vb.*
relegate See COMMIT.
relent See YIELD.
relevant, **germane**, **material**, **pertinent**, **apposite**, **applicable**, **apropos** mean relating to or bearing upon the matter at hand.

Relevant implies a traceable, significant, logical connection ⟨use any *relevant* evidence to support your argument⟩. ***antonym:*** extraneous

Germane may additionally imply a fitness for or appropriateness to the situation or occasion ⟨a topic not *germane* to our discussion⟩. ***antonym:*** foreign

Material implies so close a relationship that it cannot be altered without obvious deleterious effect ⟨the scene is *material* to the rest of the play⟩. ***antonym:*** immaterial

Pertinent stresses a clear and decisive relevance ⟨a *pertinent* observation that cut to the heart of the matter⟩. ***antonym:*** impertinent, foreign

Apposite suggests a marked and felicitous relevance ⟨the anecdotes in his sermons are always *apposite*⟩. ***antonym:*** inapposite, inapt

Applicable applies to something such as a general rule or principle that may be brought to bear upon or used fittingly in reference to a particular case, instance, or problem ⟨a precedent that is not *applicable* in this case⟩. ***antonym:*** inapplicable

Apropos suggests what is both relevant and opportune ⟨for your term paper use only *apropos* quotations⟩. ***antonym:*** unapropos

relieve, **alleviate**, **lighten**, **assuage**, **mitigate**, **allay** mean to make something less grievous or more tolerable.

Relieve implies a lifting of enough of a burden to make it endurable or even temporarily forgotten ⟨took drugs to *relieve* the pain⟩. ***antonym:*** intensify

Alleviate implies a temporary or partial lessening of pain or distress ⟨new buildings that will help to *alleviate* the housing shortage⟩. ***antonym:*** aggravate

Lighten implies a reducing of a burdensome or depressing weight and often connotes a cheering influence ⟨good news that *lightened* his worries⟩.

Assuage implies the softening or sweetening of what is harsh or disagreeable ⟨hoped that a vacation would *assuage* the pain of the divorce⟩. ***antonym:*** exacerbate, intensify

Mitigate suggests a moderating or countering of the effects of something inflicting or likely to inflict pain or distress ⟨ocean breezes *mitigated* the intense heat⟩. ***antonym:*** intensify

Allay implies an effective calming or soothing especially of fears or alarms ⟨the encouraging report *allayed* their fears⟩. ***antonym:*** intensify

religious See DEVOUT.

relinquish, **yield**, **resign**, **surrender**, **abandon**, **waive** mean to give up completely.

Relinquish may suggest some regret, reluctance, or weakness in the giving up ⟨*relinquished* her crown with bittersweet feelings⟩. ***antonym:*** keep

Yield implies a concession of compliance or submission to force ⟨I *yield* to your greater expertise in this matter⟩.

Resign emphasizes a voluntary relinquishment or sacrifice without struggle ⟨*resigned* rather than work under the new terms⟩.

Surrender implies a giving up to an external compulsion or demand after a struggle to retain or resist ⟨forced to sign a document *surrendering* all claims to the land⟩.

Abandon stresses finality and completeness in giving up ⟨*abandon* all hope⟩. ***antonym:*** cherish (*as hopes*), restrain (*oneself*)

Waive implies a conceding or forgoing with little or no compulsion ⟨*waived* the right to a trial by jury⟩.

relish See TASTE 2.

reluctant See DISINCLINED.

rely, **trust**, **depend**, **count**, **reckon**, **bank** mean to have or place full confidence.

Rely, used with *on* and *upon*, implies a judgment based on experience or association that someone or something will never fail in giving or doing what one expects ⟨a man one can *rely* on in an emergency⟩.

Trust, used with *in* or *to*, implies assurance based on faith that another will not fail one ⟨*trusted* in her own strength⟩.

Depend, used with *on* or *upon*, implies a resting on someone or something for support or assistance and often connotes weakness or lack of self-sufficiency ⟨lost the compass on which their lives *depended*⟩.

Count and ***reckon***, both used with ***on***, imply a taking into one's calculations as certain or assured ⟨*counted* on his sister for help⟩ ⟨a speaker who *reckons* on the intelligence of her audience⟩, or they may mean little more than *expect* ⟨they *counted* on staying with friends⟩ ⟨*reckoned* they could always go home⟩.

Bank, used with *on*, expresses near or absolute certainty ⟨you can *bank* on his honesty⟩.

remain See STAY 1.

remark 1. See SEE 1. **2. Remark, comment, commentate, animadvert** mean to make observations or pass judgment.

Remark implies little more than a desire to notice and call attention to something ⟨*remark* on a friend's taste in dress⟩.

Comment stresses often critical interpretation ⟨refused to *comment* about the situation⟩.

Commentate is sometimes substituted for ***comment*** to suggest a purely expository or interpretive intent ⟨*commentating* knowledgeably on current events⟩.

Animadvert implies a remarking or commentating usually of scholarly caliber or based on careful judgment ⟨willing to *animadvert* at length on topics in her field⟩ but often emphasizes the passing of an adverse judgment ⟨elders *animadverting* on the content of rock music⟩.

remarkable See NOTICEABLE.

remedy 1. See CORRECT *vb.* **2.** See CURE.

remember, recollect, recall, remind, reminisce mean to bring an image or idea from the past into the mind.

Remember implies a keeping in memory that may be effortless or unwilled ⟨*remembers* that day as though it were yesterday⟩. ***antonym:*** forget

Recollect implies bringing back to mind what is lost or scattered ⟨as near as I can *recollect*⟩.

Recall suggests a summoning back to mind and often a telling of what is brought back ⟨can't *recall* the words of the song⟩.

Remind suggests a jogging of one's memory by an association or similarity ⟨that *reminds* me of a story⟩.

Reminisce implies a casual often nostalgic recalling of experiences long past and gone ⟨old college friends like to *reminisce*⟩.

remembrance See MEMORY.

remind See REMEMBER.

reminisce See REMEMBER.

reminiscence See MEMORY.

remiss See NEGLIGENT.

remonstrate See OBJECT.

remorse See PENITENCE.

remote See DISTANT.

removed See DISTANT.

remunerate See PAY.

rend See TEAR.

renew, restore, refresh, renovate, rejuvenate mean to make like new.

Renew implies so extensive a remaking or replacing that what had become faded or disintegrated now seems like new ⟨efforts to *renew* a failing marriage⟩. ***antonym:*** wear out

Restore implies a return to an original or perfect state after damage, depletion, or loss ⟨*restored* a fine piece of furniture⟩.

Refresh implies the supplying of something necessary to restore lost strength, animation, or power ⟨lunch *refreshed* my energy⟩. ***antonym:*** jade, addle

Renovate suggests a renewing by cleansing, repairing, or rebuilding ⟨the apartment has been entirely *renovated*⟩.

Rejuvenate suggests the restoration of

youthful vigor, powers, and appearance ⟨the change in jobs *rejuvenated* her spirits⟩.

renounce **1.** See ABDICATE. **2.** See ABJURE.

renovate See RENEW.

renowned See FAMOUS.

rent See HIRE.

renunciation, **abnegation**, **self-abnegation**, **self-denial** mean voluntary surrender or forgoing of something desired or desirable.

Renunciation commonly connotes personal sacrifice for a higher end ⟨widely admired for his voluntary *renunciation* of power⟩.

Abnegation and ***self-abnegation*** both imply a high degree of unselfishness or a capacity for putting aside personal interest or desires ⟨undertook all her duties with an air of *abnegation*⟩ ⟨modesty verging on *self-abnegation*⟩. ***antonym:*** indulgence, self-indulgence

Self-denial usually applies to an act or a practice and implies a forbearance from gratifying one's desires, whatever the motive ⟨the *self-denial* involved in following a rigid diet⟩. ***antonym:*** self-indulgence

repair See MEND.

repartee See WIT.

repay See PAY.

repeal See REVOKE.

repeat **1. Repeat**, **reiterate**, **iterate** mean to say or do again.

Repeat stresses the fact of uttering, presenting, or doing again one or more times ⟨*repeated* the joke over and over⟩.

Reiterate usually implies one repetition after another especially of something that is said ⟨*reiterated* her views on the matter at every opportunity⟩.

Iterate means the same as ***reiterate*** but is rarer and has a bookish feel ⟨an ancient theme *iterated* by many noted authors⟩.

2. See QUOTE.

repellent See REPUGNANT.

repentance See PENITENCE.

replace, **displace**, **supplant**, **supersede** mean to put someone or something out of a usual or proper place or into the place of another.

Replace implies a filling of a place once occupied by something lost, destroyed, or no longer usable or adequate ⟨the broken window will have to be *replaced*⟩.

Displace implies an ousting or dislodging or crowding out, often preceding a replacement ⟨thousands had been *displaced* by the floods⟩.

Supplant implies either a dispossessing or usurping of another's place, possessions, or privileges or an uprooting of something and its replacement with something else ⟨discovered that he had been *supplanted* in her affections by another⟩.

Supersede implies the replacing of a person or thing that has become superannuated, obsolete, or otherwise inferior ⟨the new edition *supersedes* all previous ones⟩.

replete See FULL.

replica See REPRODUCTION.

reply See ANSWER.

report, **rumor**, **gossip**, **hearsay** mean common talk or an instance of it that spreads rapidly.

Report is likely to suggest some ground for belief unless specifically qualified as being false, untrue, or wild ⟨it was common *report* that they were living together⟩.

Rumor applies to a report that flies about, often gains in detail as it spreads, but lacks both an evident source and clear-cut evidence of its truth ⟨unsubstantiated *rumors* that spread like wildfire⟩.

Gossip applies primarily to the idle, often personal, chatter that is the chief source and means of propagating rumors or reports ⟨wrote a *gossip* column for the local paper⟩.

Hearsay stresses the source of a rumor or report as what is heard rather than what is seen or known directly ⟨rumored by *hearsay* to have a personal stake in the deal⟩ and in its application to evidence retains this implication of indirect and imperfect knowledge of the facts ⟨based his prosecution on *hearsay* evidence⟩.

reprehend See CRITICIZE.

repress See SUPPRESS.

reprimand See REPROVE.

reproach See REPROVE.

reprobate See CRITICIZE.

reproduction, **duplicate**, **copy**, **facsimile**, **replica** mean something that closely resembles a thing previously made, produced, or written.

Reproduction implies an exact or close imitation of an existing thing ⟨*reproductions* from the museum's furniture collection⟩. ***antonym:*** original

Duplicate implies a double or counterpart exactly corresponding to an original in all significant respects ⟨make a *duplicate* of the key⟩.

Copy applies especially to one of a number of things reproduced mechanically ⟨*copies* of the report were issued to all⟩. ***antonym:*** original

Facsimile suggests a close reproduction in the same materials that may differ in scale ⟨a *facsimile* of an illuminated medieval manuscript⟩.

Replica emphasizes the closeness of likeness and is specifically used of a reproduction made exactly like the original ⟨*replicas* of the ships used by Columbus⟩.

reprove, **rebuke**, **reprimand**, **admonish**, **reproach**, **chide** mean to criticize adversely.

Reprove implies an often kindly censuring or blaming intended to correct a fault ⟨gently *reproved* her table manners⟩.

Rebuke suggests a sharp or stern reproof ⟨the papal letter *rebuked* dissenting church officials⟩.

Reprimand implies a severe, formal, and often public or official rebuke ⟨a general officially *reprimanded* for speaking out of turn⟩.

Admonish suggests an earnest or friendly warning and counseling ⟨*admonished* by my parents to control expenses⟩. ***antonym:*** commend

Reproach connotes the conveying of dissatisfaction or displeasure through criticism or faultfinding ⟨were severely *reproached* for their late return⟩.

Chide suggests the expression of disappointment or displeasure through mild reproof or scolding ⟨*chided* by their mother for not keeping their room clean⟩. ***antonym:*** commend

repudiate **1.** See DECLINE. **2.** See DISCLAIM.

repugnant, **repellent**, **abhorrent**, **distasteful**, **obnoxious**, **invidious** mean so unlikable as to arouse antagonism or aversion.

Repugnant applies to something that is so alien to one's ideas, principles, or tastes as to arouse resistance or loathing ⟨regards boxing as a *repugnant* sport⟩. ***antonym:*** congenial

Repellent suggests a generally forbidding or unpleasant quality that causes one to back away ⟨the public display of grief was *repellent* to her⟩. ***antonym:*** attractive, pleasing

Abhorrent implies a repugnance that causes active antagonism ⟨practices that are *abhorrent* to the American political system⟩. ***antonym:*** congenial

Distasteful implies a contrariness to one's tastes or inclinations ⟨a family to whom displays of affection are *distasteful*⟩. ***antonym:*** agreeable, palatable

Obnoxious suggests an objectionableness, often on personal grounds, too great to tolerate ⟨the colonists found the tea tax especially *obnoxious*⟩. ***antonym:*** grateful

Invidious applies to what cannot be used or performed without creating ill will, odium, or envy <the *invidious* task of deciding custody of the child>.

request See ASK 2.

require **1.** See DEMAND. **2.** See LACK.

requirement, **requisite**, **prerequisite** mean something regarded as necessary for success or perfection.

Requirement may imply something more or less arbitrarily demanded, especially by those with a right to lay down conditions <college entrance *requirements*>.

Requisite implies something indispensable for the end in view or otherwise essential and not arbitrarily demanded <education is a prime *requisite* of a free society>.

Prerequisite applies to a requisite that must be available in advance or acquired as a preliminary <a chemistry course that was a *prerequisite* to further study in biology>.

requisite See REQUIREMENT.

requite See RECIPROCATE.

rescind See REVOKE.

rescue, **deliver**, **redeem**, **ransom**, **reclaim**, **save** mean to set free from confinement, risk or danger.

Rescue implies a freeing from imminent danger by prompt or vigorous action <*rescue* the crew of a sinking ship>.

Deliver implies the releasing usually of a person from confinement, temptation, slavery, suffering, or something that distresses <*delivered* his people from bondage>.

Redeem implies a releasing from bondage or penalties by giving what is demanded or necessary as an equivalent <*redeemed* her from a life of boredom>.

Ransom specifically applies to a buying out of captivity <subjects forced to *ransom* their king>.

Reclaim suggests a bringing back to a former state or condition of someone or something abandoned or debased <*reclaimed* long-abandoned farms>. ***antonym:*** abandon

Save may replace any of the foregoing terms, or it may further imply a preserving or maintaining for usefulness or continued existence <a social worker who *saved* youths from life as criminals>. ***antonym:*** lose, waste, damn

resemblance See LIKENESS.

resentment See OFFENSE.

reserve See KEEP 2.

reserved See SILENT.

reside, **live**, **dwell**, **sojourn**, **lodge**, **stay**, **put up** mean to have as one's habitation or domicile.

Reside expresses the idea that a person keeps or returns to a particular place as his or her fixed, settled, or legal abode <*reside* happily in New Hampshire>.

Live may stress the idea of actually spending one's time and carrying out the activities of one's family life <*lived* for years in the house next door>.

Dwell, a close synonym of these words, is likely to appear in elevated language <longed to *dwell* amongst trees and hills>.

Sojourn distinctively implies a temporary habitation or abode or a more or less uncertain place or way of living <*sojourned* for a while in the south of France>.

Lodge also suggests a habitation for a time and may connote restricted accommodations such as in a hotel or rooming house <chose to *lodge* there for the night>.

Stay is the term commonly used in place of ***sojourn*** or ***lodge*** <*stayed* at that hotel for the entire week>.

Put up is the equivalent of ***lodge*** and usually suggests the status of a guest <decided to *put up* at her sister's house for the weekend>.

resign **1.** See ABDICATE. **2.** See RELINQUISH.

resilient See ELASTIC.

resist See OPPOSE.

resolute See FAITHFUL.

resolution See COURAGE.

resolve **1.** See DECIDE. **2.** See ANALYZE.

resort *vb* **Resort**, **refer**, **apply**, **go**, **turn** mean to have recourse to something when in need of help or relief.

Resort may imply that one has encountered difficulties impossible to surmount without help ⟨found he could get no relief unless he *resorted* to the courts⟩.

Refer suggests a need for authentic information or authoritative action and recourse to a source of this ⟨whenever you come to an unfamiliar word, *refer* to your dictionary⟩.

Apply suggests having direct recourse, as by a letter or in person, to one able to supply what is needed ⟨*apply* to a bank for a loan⟩.

Go and ***turn*** are more general but often more picturesque or more dramatic terms that suggest action or movement in seeking aid or relief ⟨the president *went* directly to the people with his plan⟩ ⟨*turned* to his mother for comfort⟩.

resort *n* See RESOURCE.

resource, **resort**, **expedient**, **shift**, **makeshift**, **stopgap** mean something one turns to in the absence of the usual means or source of supply.

Resource applies to anything one falls back upon ⟨haven't exhausted all of my *resources* yet⟩.

Resort is like ***resource*** but is used mostly with *last* or in the phrase "to have *resort* to" ⟨favor a sales tax only as a last *resort*⟩.

Expedient may apply to any device or contrivance used when the usual one is not at hand or not possible ⟨the flimsiest of *expedients* ends the tale⟩.

Shift implies a tentative or temporary imperfect expedient and often connotes dubiousness or trickery ⟨her desperate *shifts* and dodges fooled no one⟩.

Makeshift implies an inferior expedient adopted because of urgent need or countenanced through indifference ⟨the space heater was supposed to be only a *makeshift*⟩.

Stopgap applies to something used temporarily as an emergency measure ⟨the farm aid bill is no more than a *stopgap*⟩.

respect See REGARD.

respite See PAUSE.

resplendent See SPLENDID.

respond See ANSWER.

responsible, **answerable**, **accountable**, **amenable**, **liable** mean subject to an authority that may hold one to account.

Responsible implies the holding of a specific or formal office, duty, or trust ⟨the bureau *responsible* for revenue collection⟩.

Answerable suggests a relationship between one having a moral or legal obligation and an authority charged with oversight of its observance ⟨a fact-finding committee *answerable* only to the President⟩.

Accountable suggests the imminence of retribution for unfulfilled trust or violated obligation ⟨in a democracy the politicians are *accountable* to the voters⟩. ***antonym:*** unaccountable

Amenable stresses the fact of subjection to review, censure, or control by a designated authority and a limitation of power ⟨laws are *amenable* to judicial review⟩. ***antonym:*** independent (*of*), autonomous

Liable implies an obligation under the law to answer in case of default ⟨will not be *liable* for his ex-wife's debts⟩ or may suggest merely a contingent obligation ⟨all citizens *liable* for jury duty⟩.

restful See COMFORTABLE.

restive See CONTRARY.

restore **1.** See RENEW. **2. Restore**, **revive**, **revivify**, **resuscitate** mean to regain or cause to regain signs of life and vigor.

Restore implies a return to consciousness, health, or vigor often by the use of remedies or treatments ⟨hearing can sometimes be *restored* by surgery⟩.

Revive may imply recovery from a deathlike state, such as a stupor or faint ⟨*revive* him from a faint with cold water⟩ but is widely applicable to restoration to a flourishing state ⟨the showers *revived* the withering crops⟩.

Revivify tends to suggest adding of new life and carries a weaker suggestion than ***revive*** of prior depletion ⟨a good night's sleep *revivifies* the strongest person⟩.

Resuscitate commonly implies a restoration to consciousness by arduous efforts to overcome a serious impairment ⟨*resuscitate* a nearly drowned person with artificial respiration⟩ and can suggest a restoring to vitality of someone or something in which life seems nearly or wholly extinct ⟨labored to *resuscitate* her old interest in sports⟩.

restrain, **check**, **curb**, **bridle** mean to hold back from or control in doing something.

Restrain suggests a holding back by force or persuasion from acting or from going to extremes ⟨*restrained* themselves from trading insults⟩. ***antonym:*** impel, incite, activate, abandon (*oneself*)

Check implies the restraining or impeding of a progress, activity, or impetus ⟨deep mud *checked* our progress⟩. ***antonym:*** accelerate, advance, release

Curb suggests an abrupt or drastic checking or a restricting or restraining that tends to moderate ⟨learn to *curb* your appetite⟩. ***antonym:*** spur

Bridle implies a keeping under control by subduing or holding in ⟨they could no longer *bridle* their interest⟩. ***antonym:*** vent

restrict See LIMIT.
result See EFFECT.
resuscitate See RESTORE.
retain See KEEP 2.
retaliate See RECIPROCATE.
retard See DELAY.
reticent See SILENT.
retire See GO.
retort See ANSWER.
retract **1.** See ABJURE. **2.** See RECEDE.
retreat *vb* See RECEDE.
retreat *n* See SHELTER.
retrench See SHORTEN.
retrograde See RECEDE.

return **1. Return**, **revert**, **recur**, **recrudesce** mean to go or come back.

Return may imply a going back to a starting place or source or to a former or proper place or condition ⟨*returned* home to an enthusiastic welcome⟩.

Revert is likely to imply a going back to a former, often a lower, condition ⟨*reverted* to an earlier, less civilized state⟩, but it can also apply to a returning after interruption ⟨after careful consideration he *reverted* to his first decision⟩.

Recur implies a return, often repeated returns, of something that has happened or been experienced before ⟨suffered from *recurring* headaches⟩.

Recrudesce implies a returning to life or activity especially of something that has been suppressed or kept under control ⟨after an initial subsidence the epidemic *recrudesced* with renewed vigor⟩.

2. See RECIPROCATE.

reveal, **discover**, **disclose**, **divulge**, **tell**, **betray** mean to make known what has been or should be concealed.

Reveal suggests an unveiling of what is not clear to human vision and may apply to a supernatural or inspired revelation ⟨the belief that divine will is *revealed* in the Bible⟩ or a simple disclosure ⟨an act that *revealed* his true nature⟩. ***antonym:*** conceal

Discover implies an uncovering of matters kept secret and not previously known ⟨a step-by-step comparison that *discovered* a clear case of plagiarism⟩.

Disclose may also imply a discovering but more often suggests an imparting of information previously kept secret ⟨candidates must *disclose* their financial assets⟩.

Divulge implies a disclosure involving some impropriety or breach of confidence ⟨refused to *divulge* confidential information⟩.

Tell implies an imparting of necessary or

useful information ⟨never *told* her that he was married⟩.

Betray implies a divulging that represents a breach of faith or an involuntary or unconscious disclosure ⟨a blush that *betrayed* her embarrassment⟩.

revenge See AVENGE.

revengeful See VINDICTIVE.

revere, **reverence**, **venerate**, **worship**, **adore** mean to regard with profound respect and honor.

Revere stresses deference and tenderness of feeling ⟨a tradition *revered* by generations of scholars⟩. ***antonym:*** flout

Reverence presupposes an intrinsic merit and inviolability in the one honored and a corresponding depth of feeling in the one honoring ⟨the general *reverenced* the army's code of honor⟩.

Venerate implies a holding as holy or sacrosanct because of character, association, or age ⟨national heroes who are still *venerated*⟩.

Worship implies homage usually expressed in words or ceremony to a divine being or to a person to whom exalted character or outstanding merit is imputed ⟨*worships* the memory of her husband⟩.

Adore, close to ***worship***, implies love and stresses the notion of an individual and personal attachment ⟨a doctor who is practically *adored* by her patients⟩. ***antonym:*** blaspheme

reverence *n* **1.** See HONOR. **2. Reverence**, **awe**, **fear** mean the emotion inspired by something that arouses one's deep respect or veneration.

Reverence stresses a recognition of the sacredness or inviolability of the person or thing which stimulates the emotion ⟨demonstrated a lack of *reverence* for the truth⟩.

Awe fundamentally implies a sense of being overwhelmed or overcome by great superiority or impressiveness and may suggest such varied reactions as standing mute, adoration, profound reverence, terror, or submissiveness ⟨stood in *awe* of his talent⟩.

Fear in the sense here considered occurs chiefly in religious use and implies awed recognition of divine power and majesty ⟨lived in *fear* of the Lord⟩. ***antonym:*** contempt

reverence *vb* See REVERE.

reverse **1. Reverse**, **transpose**, **invert** mean to change to the opposite position.

Reverse may imply change in order, side, direction, or meaning ⟨*reversed* his position on the arms agreement⟩.

Transpose implies a change in order or relative position of units often through exchange of position ⟨anagrams are formed by *transposing* the letters of a word or phrase⟩.

Invert applies to a change from one side to another by a turning upside down or inside out ⟨a typo consisting of a whole line of *inverted* type⟩.

2. See REVOKE.

revert See RETURN 1.

revile See SCOLD.

revise See CORRECT *vb*.

revive See RESTORE.

revivify See RESTORE.

revoke, **reverse**, **repeal**, **rescind**, **recall** mean to undo something previously done.

Revoke implies a calling back that annuls or abrogates what was previously done ⟨had his license *revoked* for ninety days⟩.

Reverse usually applies specifically to a high court's action in overthrowing a disputed law, decree, or court decision ⟨the court of appeals *reversed* the opinion of the circuit court⟩; when applied to actions or judgments of a non-judicial nature, it implies an upsetting of what was previously done ⟨convinced the umpire to *reverse* his decision⟩.

Repeal usually implies revocation of a law or ordinance by the legislative body that made it ⟨*repealed* the parking ban⟩.

Rescind implies the exercise of proper authority in abolishing or making void ⟨*rescinded* their earlier decision in a new vote⟩.

Recall, a less technical term, can replace

any of the others ⟨*recall* a bid in bridge⟩.

revolt See REBELLION.

revolution See REBELLION.

rhapsody See BOMBAST.

rhythm, meter, cadence mean the more or less regular rise and fall in intensity of sounds that is associated especially with poetry and music.

Rhythm implies movement and flow as well as an agreeable succession of rising and falling sounds and the recurrence at fairly regular intervals of a stress, such as a prolonged syllable or an accented note ⟨moved gracefully to the *rhythm*⟩.

Meter implies the reduction of rhythm to system and measure and the establishment of a definite rhythmical pattern ⟨an epic in hendecasyllabic *meter*⟩.

Cadence may be equivalent to ***rhythm*** or to ***meter*** or may stress variety in ordered sequence, often with falling or rising effects ⟨the gentle *cadence* of the local dialect⟩.

ribald See COARSE.

rich, wealthy, affluent, opulent mean having goods, property, and money in abundance.

Rich implies having more than enough to gratify normal needs or desires ⟨one of the *richest* nations in the world⟩. ***antonym:*** poor

Wealthy stresses the abundant possession of property and intrinsically valuable things ⟨retired from politics a *wealthy* man⟩. ***antonym:*** indigent

Affluent suggests prosperity and increasing wealth ⟨an *affluent* society⟩. ***antonym:*** impecunious, straitened

Opulent suggests lavish expenditure and ostentatious display of great wealth ⟨*opulent* mansions⟩. ***antonym:*** destitute, indigent

riddle See MYSTERY.

ridicule, deride, mock, taunt, twit mean to make an object of laughter of.

Ridicule implies a deliberate often malicious belittling ⟨consistently *ridiculed* everything she said⟩.

Deride suggests a contemptuous and often bitter ridiculing ⟨*derided* their efforts to start their own business⟩.

Mock implies a scornful deriding often ironically expressed by mimicry or sham deference ⟨youngsters began to *mock* the helpless old man⟩.

Taunt suggests a jeeringly reproachful insult or derisive challenging ⟨terrorists *taunted* the hostages⟩.

Twit usually suggests mild or good-humored teasing ⟨students *twitted* their teacher about his tardiness⟩.

ridiculous See LAUGHABLE.

rife See PREVAILING.

right See CORRECT *adj.*

righteous See MORAL.

rigid 1. See STIFF. **2. Rigid, rigorous, strict, stringent** mean extremely severe or stern.

Rigid implies uncompromising inflexibility ⟨the school's admission standards are *rigid*⟩. ***antonym:*** lax

Rigorous implies the imposition of hardship and difficulty ⟨the *rigorous* training of recruits⟩. ***antonym:*** mild

Strict emphasizes undeviating conformity to rules, standards, or requirements ⟨their doctor put them on a *strict* diet⟩. ***antonym:*** lenient

Stringent suggests restrictions or limitations that curb or coerce ⟨the judge's ruling is a *stringent* interpretation of the law⟩.

rigor See DIFFICULTY.

rigorous See RIGID.

rile See IRRITATE.

rim See BORDER.

rip See TEAR.

ripe See MATURE *adj.*

ripen See MATURE *vb.*

rise 1. See SPRING. **2. Rise, arise, ascend, mount, soar** mean to move or come up from a lower to a higher level.

Rise is used in reference to persons or animals that get up from a lying or sitting position ⟨*rise* every morning at five⟩ or to things that seem to come up into view or to lift themselves up ⟨hills *rising* from the plain⟩ or to fluid that is sent upward by some natural force ⟨watched the river *rising*⟩. ***antonym:*** decline, set (*as the sun*)

Arise comes close to ***rise*** but is somewhat more rhetorical or poetic ⟨*arose* slowly, brushing the dust of the street from his clothes⟩. ***antonym:*** recline, slump

Ascend suggests a continuous or progressive upward movement or climbing ⟨the sun *ascends* the sky until noon⟩. ***antonym:*** descend

Mount, close to ***ascend***, implies a gradual upward movement toward an even higher level or degree ⟨felt her hopes *mount* as the race went on⟩. ***antonym:*** drop

Soar usually connotes a continuous, often swift, ascent into high altitudes especially intellectually, spiritually, or aesthetically ⟨the brilliant product of a *soaring* imagination⟩.

risible See LAUGHABLE.

risky See DANGEROUS.

rival **1.** See MATCH. **2. Rival**, **compete**, **vie**, **emulate** mean to strive to equal or surpass.

Rival usually suggests an attempt to outdo each other ⟨success that *rivaled* hers⟩.

Compete stresses a struggle for an objective that may be conscious but is typically a quite impersonal striving ⟨athletes *competing* in college sports⟩.

Vie suggests a less intense effort but a more conscious awareness of an opponent than ***compete*** ⟨*vied* with one another for her attention⟩.

Emulate implies a conscious effort to equal or surpass one that serves as a model ⟨strove to *emulate* his teachers⟩.

rive See TEAR.

roam See WANDER.

robbery See THEFT.

robust See HEALTHY.

rock See SHAKE 2.

root See ORIGIN.

rot See DECAY.

rotate, **alternate** mean to succeed or cause to succeed each other in turn.

Rotate, which may be used of two or more, implies an indefinite repetition of the order of succession ⟨farmers who learned to *rotate* crops⟩.

Alternate, which is referable only to two, implies repetition but does not carry as strong a suggestion of continuity as ***rotate*** ⟨*alternate* heat and cold in treating a sprain⟩.

rough **1. Rough**, **harsh**, **uneven**, **rugged**, **scabrous** mean not smooth or even.

Rough implies the presence of detectable inequalities on the surface, such as points, bristles, ridges, or projections ⟨a *rough* wooden board⟩. ***antonym:*** smooth

Harsh implies a surface or texture distinctly unpleasant to the touch ⟨the *harsh* fabric chafed his skin⟩. ***antonym:*** pleasant, mild

Uneven implies a lack of regularity in height, breadth, or quality ⟨an old house with *uneven* floors⟩. ***antonym:*** even

Rugged implies irregularity or roughness of land surface and connotes difficulty of travel ⟨follow the *rugged* road up the mountain⟩.

Scabrous implies scaliness or prickliness of surface and may connote an unwholesome, decayed, or diseased appearance ⟨an allergic condition that results in *scabrous* hands⟩. ***antonym:*** glabrous, smooth

2. See RUDE.

rouse See STIR *vb*.

rout See CONQUER.

rove See WANDER.

rude, **rough**, **crude**, **raw**, **callow**, **green**, **uncouth** mean lacking in the qualities that make for finish or perfection in development or use.

Rude implies ignorance of or indifference to good form or materials ⟨fashioned a *rude* structure⟩ or may suggest intentional discourtesy ⟨consistently *rude* behavior toward her in-laws⟩.

Rough is likely to stress lack of polish and gentleness ⟨the *rough* manners of a man used to living in the outback⟩. ***antonym:*** gentle

Crude may apply to thought or behavior that is gross, obvious, or primitive or ignorant of what is highly developed or fully civilized ⟨the *crude* antics of college students on spring break⟩. ***antonym:*** consummate, finished

Raw suggests being unprocessed, untested, inexperienced, or unfinished ⟨charged with turning *raw* youths into young men⟩.

Callow applies to the immature and suggests such youthful qualities as naïveté, simplicity, and lack of sophistication ⟨the insensitivity of *callow* youth⟩. ***antonym:*** full-fledged, grownup

Green implies inexperience and lack of assurance, especially in a new or complex situation and often simplicity or gullibility ⟨tested the mettle of the *green* recruits⟩. ***antonym:*** experienced, seasoned

Uncouth implies strangeness in comparison to what is felt to be normal, finished, or excellent, whether because crude and clumsy or because lacking in polish and grace ⟨behavior that was unbearably *uncouth*⟩.

rugged See ROUGH.

ruin *n* **Ruin, havoc, devastation, destruction** mean the bringing about of or the results of disaster.

Ruin suggests collapse and is applicable to whatever has given way or fallen apart through decay, corruption, neglect, or loss ⟨the old house had fallen to *ruin*⟩.

Havoc suggests an agent that pillages, destroys, or ravages and the resulting confusion and disorder ⟨the *havoc* left by the earthquake⟩.

Devastation implies a widespread laying waste, as by war or a natural catastrophe, but it is also applicable to something that overwhelms an individual with comparable decisiveness ⟨tried to overcome the *devastation* of losing a spouse⟩.

Destruction suggests an utter undoing by or as if by demolition or annihilation ⟨saw the rapid *destruction* of his entire life's work⟩.

ruin *vb* **Ruin, wreck, dilapidate** mean to subject to forces that are destructive of soundness, worth, or usefulness.

Ruin usually suggests the action of destructive agencies and the ending of the value, beauty, or well-being of something or someone or the loss of something vital ⟨a reputation *ruined* by ugly rumors⟩.

Wreck implies a ruining by or as if by crashing or being shattered and is likely to suggest damage that is beyond repair ⟨health *wrecked* by dissipation⟩.

Dilapidate historically implies ruin resulting from neglect or abuse but in more general use implies a shabby, run-down, or tumbledown condition without direct suggestion of culpability ⟨drove a *dilapidated* car⟩.

rule *n* See LAW.

rule *vb* **1.** See DECIDE. **2.** See GOVERN.

ruminate See PONDER.

rumor See REPORT.

rural, rustic, pastoral, bucolic mean relating to or characteristic of the country.

Rural suggests open country and farming ⟨a diminishing portion of the island remains *rural*⟩. ***antonym:*** urban, citified

Rustic suggests a contrast with city life and connotes rudeness and lack of polish ⟨a hunting lodge filled with *rustic* furniture and decoration⟩.

Pastoral implies an idealized simplicity and peacefulness and apartness from the world ⟨the *pastoral* setting of an exclusive health resort⟩.

Bucolic may refer to either the charming and desirable or the undesirable aspects of country life ⟨fed-up city dwellers imagining a *bucolic* bliss⟩ ⟨trapped in a *bucolic* nightmare⟩.

ruse See TRICK.

rustic See RURAL.

ruth See SYMPATHY.

S

sack See RAVAGE.

sacred, **sacrosanct**, **inviolate**, **inviolable** mean protected by law, custom, or respect against abuse.

Sacred implies either a setting apart for a special use ⟨the battered chair by the fireside that was *sacred* to father⟩ or a special quality that leads to an almost religious reverence ⟨a *sacred* memory⟩.

Sacrosanct in general use may retain its religious implication of the utmost of sacredness, or it may take on an ironic quality and suggest a supposed rather than a real sacredness ⟨failed to accept that such public figures were *sacrosanct*⟩.

Inviolate applies to such things as laws, agreements, institutions, or persons which for one reason or another are secure from abuse or injury, and it stresses the fact of not having been violated ⟨the *inviolate* beauty of the wilderness⟩. ***antonym:*** violated

Inviolable, while close to ***inviolate***, implies a character that is secure from violation ⟨the *inviolable* sanctity of the law⟩.

sacrosanct See SACRED.

sadness, **depression**, **melancholy**, **melancholia**, **dejection**, **gloom** mean the state of mind of one who is unhappy or low-spirited.

Sadness is a general term that carries no suggestion of the cause, extent, or exact nature of low spirits ⟨a feeling of *sadness* marked the farewell dinner⟩. ***antonym:*** gladness

Depression suggests a condition in which one feels let down, disheartened, despondent, or enervated ⟨under a doctor's care for severe *depression*⟩. ***antonym:*** bouyancy

Melancholy suggests a mood of sad and serious but not wholly unpleasant pensiveness ⟨old love letters that gave her cause for *melancholy*⟩. ***antonym:*** exhilaration

Melancholia applies to a disordered mental state characterized by settled deep depression ⟨fell into a state of *melancholia* after her husband's death⟩.

Dejection implies a usually passing mood of one who is downcast or dispirited from a natural or logical cause ⟨a struggling actor used to periods of *dejection*⟩. ***antonym:*** exhilaration

Gloom applies to either the extreme sadness of the person afflicted by any of these moods or conditions or the atmosphere or the effect on others created by one so afflicted ⟨a universal *gloom* engulfed the devastated town⟩. ***antonym:*** glee

safe, **secure** mean free from danger or risk.

Safe can imply that a risk has been run without incurring harm or damage ⟨arrived home *safe* and sound⟩ or can stress freedom from risk ⟨kept her *safe* from harm⟩ or can suggest a character that eliminates or minimizes risk ⟨*safe* investments⟩. ***antonym:*** dangerous, unsafe

Secure usually stresses a freedom from anxiety or apprehension of danger or risk based on grounds that appear sound and sufficient ⟨reached a *secure* harbor before the storm broke⟩. ***antonym:*** insecure, precarious, dangerous

safeguard See DEFEND.

saga See MYTH.

sagacious See SHREWD.

sage See WISE.

salary See WAGE.

salient See NOTICEABLE.

salubrious See HEALTHFUL.

salutary See HEALTHFUL.

same, **selfsame**, **very**, **identical**, **equivalent**, **equal** mean not different or not differing from one another or others.

Same may imply that the things under consideration are one thing or, although distinct, have no appreciable difference

⟨we took the *same* route on the *same* day⟩. ***antonym:*** different

Selfsame always implies that the things under consideration are one thing and not two or more things ⟨it was the *selfsame* ring I had lost years ago⟩. ***antonym:*** diverse

Very, like ***selfsame***, implies identity ⟨you're the *very* person I've been looking for⟩.

Identical may imply self-sameness or suggest absolute agreement in all details ⟨their test answers were *identical*⟩. ***antonym:*** nonidentical, diverse

Equivalent implies amounting to the same thing in worth or significance ⟨two houses of *equivalent* market value⟩. ***antonym:*** different

Equal implies correspondence in value, magnitude, or some specified quality and therefore equivalence ⟨divided it into *equal* shares⟩. ***antonym:*** unequal

sample See INSTANCE.

sanctimonious **1.** See DEVOUT. **2.** See HYPOCRITICAL.

sanction See APPROVE.

sanctuary See SHELTER.

sane See WISE.

sangfroid See EQUANIMITY.

sanguinary See BLOODY.

sanguine See BLOODY.

sap See WEAKEN.

sapient See WISE.

sarcasm See WIT.

sarcastic, **satiric**, **ironic**, **sardonic** mean marked by bitterness and a power or intent to cut or sting.

Sarcastic applies to what intentionally inflicts pain by deriding, taunting, or ridiculing ⟨a critic famous for his *sarcastic* remarks⟩.

Satiric implies an intent to censure by ridicule and reprobation ⟨a *satiric* look at contemporary sexual mores⟩.

Ironic implies an attempt to be amusing or provocative by saying something startlingly or surprisingly different from, and often the opposite of, what is meant ⟨made the *ironic* observation that the goverment could always be trusted⟩.

Sardonic implies a scornful, mocking, or derisive disbelief or doubt that is manifested by either verbal or facial expression ⟨surveyed the scene with a *sardonic* smile⟩.

sardonic See SARCASTIC.

sate See SATIATE.

satiate, **sate**, **surfeit**, **cloy**, **pall**, **glut**, **gorge** mean to fill completely or to excess.

Satiate and ***sate*** may sometimes imply only complete satisfaction but more often suggest fullness that has destroyed interest or desire ⟨movies that purported to *satiate* their appetite for violence⟩ ⟨audiences were *sated* with dizzying visual effects⟩.

Surfeit implies a fullness to the point of nausea or disgust ⟨*surfeited* themselves with junk food⟩. ***antonym:*** whet

Cloy stresses the disgust or boredom resulting from such surfeiting ⟨sentimental pictures that *cloy* after a while⟩. ***antonym:*** whet

Pall emphasizes the loss of ability to stimulate interest or appetite ⟨even a tropical paradise begins to *pall* after ten trips⟩.

Glut implies an excess in feeding or supplying that chokes or impedes ⟨bookstores *glutted* with diet books⟩. ***antonym:*** stint

Gorge suggests a glutting to the point of bursting or choking ⟨*gorged* themselves with chocolate⟩.

satiny See SLEEK.

satire See WIT.

satiric See SARCASTIC.

satisfy **1. Satisfy**, **content** mean to appease one's desires or longings.

Satisfy implies the full appeasement not only of desires or longings but of needs or requirements ⟨*satisfied* her fondest desire⟩. ***antonym:*** tantalize

Content implies an appeasement to the point where one is not disquieted or disturbed even though every wish is not fully gratified ⟨refused to *content* herself with the answer⟩.

2. See PAY. **3. Satisfy, fulfill, meet, answer** mean to measure up to a set of criteria or requirements.

Satisfy implies adequacy to an end or need in view and often suggests a standard of comparison ⟨*satisfied* all the requirements for her degree⟩.

Fulfill, often interchangeable with ***satisfy***, may imply more abundance or richness in measuring up to a need that is less calculable, more immeasurable ⟨a son who *fulfilled* his father's fondest hopes⟩.

Meet implies an exactness of agreement between a requirement and what is submitted to fill it ⟨designed to *meet* the demands of today's students⟩.

Answer usually implies the simple satisfaction of a demand, need, or purpose often in a temporary or expedient manner ⟨a solution that *answered* their immediate need⟩.

saturate See SOAK.

saturnine See SULLEN.

saucy, pert, arch mean flippant and bold in manner or attitude.

Saucy is likely to stress levity with a hint of smartness or amusing effrontery ⟨made a *saucy* retort⟩. ***antonym:*** deferential

Pert implies a saucy freedom that may verge on presumption or affectation ⟨amused by the boy's *pert* answers⟩ and sometimes also suggests sprightliness or cleverness ⟨held her head at a *pert* angle⟩. ***antonym:*** coy

Arch usually implies a coquettish or roguish audacity or mischievous mockery ⟨known for sly wit and *arch* posturing⟩.

saunter, stroll, amble mean to walk slowly and more or less aimlessly.

Saunter suggests a leisurely pace and an idle and carefree mind ⟨*sauntered* down the road⟩.

Stroll implies the pursuit of an objective, such as sight-seeing or exercise, without haste and often without predetermined path ⟨*strolled* past shops and through the market⟩.

Amble can replace either ***saunter*** or ***stroll*** but distinctively suggests an easy effortless gait ⟨*ambled* through the crowd, greeting each guest⟩.

savage 1. See FIERCE. **2.** See BARBARIAN.

save 1. See RESCUE. **2. Save, preserve, conserve** mean to keep secure from injury, decay, or loss.

Save in this connection can imply the taking of measures to protect against danger of loss, injury, or destruction ⟨*saved* his papers in a vault⟩. ***antonym:*** spend, consume

Preserve stresses a resistance to destructive agencies and implies the use of methods and efforts to keep something intact or in existence ⟨*preserve* food for winter use⟩.

Conserve suggests a keeping sound and unimpaired and implies the avoidance of undue use or of waste or loss or damage ⟨took every possible measure to *conserve* fuel⟩. ***antonym:*** waste, squander

savoir faire See TACT.

savor See TASTE 1.

savory See PALATABLE.

say, utter, tell, state mean to put into words.

Say basically means to articulate words ⟨*say* each word carefully and clearly⟩, but it may be used in reporting something voiced ⟨he *said* he would be home soon⟩ or in implying the fact of putting in speech or writing ⟨be careful what you *say* to that man⟩.

Utter stresses the use of the voice and the act of putting into spoken words ⟨*uttered* a faint response⟩ and is appropriate for reference to vocal sounds other than words ⟨*utter* a hoarse laugh⟩.

Tell stresses the imparting of an idea or information and may refer to either spoken or written communication or other method to present an idea ⟨an attempt to *tell* the story of her life⟩.

State may replace ***say*** when the added implication of clearness and definiteness is needed ⟨*state* one's objections to a proposal⟩.

scabrous See ROUGH.

scale See ASCEND.

scan See SCRUTINIZE.

scandal See OFFENSE 2.

scant See MEAGER.

scanty See MEAGER.

scarce See INFREQUENT.

scathing See CAUSTIC.

scatter, **disperse**, **dissipate**, **dispel** mean to cause to separate or break up.

Scatter implies the action of a force that drives parts of units irregularly in many directions ⟨the bowling ball *scattered* the pins⟩. ***antonym:*** gather

Disperse implies a wider separation of units and a complete breaking up of the mass or group ⟨police *dispersed* the crowd⟩. ***antonym:*** assemble, congregate, collect

Dissipate stresses a complete disintegration or dissolution and final disappearance ⟨the fog was *dissipated* by the morning sun⟩. ***antonym:*** accumulate, concentrate (*efforts, thoughts*)

Dispel stresses a driving away or getting rid of by or as if by scattering ⟨an authoritative statement that *dispelled* all doubt⟩.

scent **1.** See FRAGRANCE. **2.** See SMELL.

scheme See PLAN.

scholarly See LEARNED.

scholarship See KNOWLEDGE.

scholastic See PEDANTIC.

school See TEACH.

scoff, **jeer**, **gibe**, **fleer**, **sneer**, **flout** mean to show one's contempt through derision or mockery.

Scoff stresses a deriding motivated by insolence, disrespect, or incredulity ⟨*scoffed* at the religious faith of others⟩.

Jeer suggests a coarser more undiscriminating derision ⟨the crowd *jeered* the visiting team⟩.

Gibe implies a taunting either good-naturedly or in sarcastic derision ⟨*gibed* at him for repeatedly missing the ball⟩.

Fleer suggests a grinning or grimacing derisively ⟨some freshmen were greeted by *fleering* seniors⟩.

Sneer stresses an insulting by contemptuous facial expression, phrasing, or tone of voice ⟨*sneered* at anything even remotely romantic⟩.

Flout stresses a showing of contempt by refusal to heed or by denial of a thing's truth or power ⟨*flouted* the conventions of polite society⟩. ***antonym:*** revere

scold, **upbraid**, **berate**, **rail**, **revile**, **vituperate** mean to reproach angrily and abusively.

Scold implies a rebuking in irritation or ill temper justly or unjustly ⟨relieved her frustrations by *scolding* the children⟩.

Upbraid implies a censuring on definite and usually justifiable grounds ⟨the governor *upbraided* his aides for poor research⟩.

Berate suggests a prolonged and often abusive scolding ⟨*berated* continually by a violent, abusive father⟩.

Rail, used with *at* or *against*, stresses an unrestrained berating ⟨*railed* loudly at the whims of fate⟩.

Revile implies a scurrilous, abusive attacking prompted by anger or hatred ⟨a President vehemently *reviled* in the press⟩. ***antonym:*** laud

Vituperate suggests a violent, abusive reviling ⟨a preacher more given to *vituperating* than to inspiring⟩. ***antonym:*** acclaim

scope See RANGE.

scorn See DESPISE.

scout See DESPISE.

scowl See FROWN.

scrap See DISCARD.

scrawny See LEAN.

screen See HIDE.

scruple See QUALM.

scrupulous **1.** See CAREFUL. **2.** See UPRIGHT.

scrutinize, scan, inspect, examine mean to look at or over carefully and usually critically.

Scrutinize stresses the application of close observation and attention to minute detail ⟨closely *scrutinized* the bill from the hospital⟩.

Scan implies a surveying from point to point that often suggests a cursory overall observation ⟨quickly *scanned* the wine list⟩.

Inspect implies a searching scrutinizing for errors or defects ⟨*inspected* the restaurant for health-code violations⟩.

Examine suggests a scrutinizing or investigating in order to determine the nature, condition, or quality of a thing ⟨*examined* the gems to see whether they were genuine⟩.

scurrility See ABUSE.

scurvy See CONTEMPTIBLE.

seasonable, timely, well-timed, opportune, pat mean peculiarly appropriate to the time or situation.

Seasonable implies appropriateness to the season or being perfectly fitted to the occasion or situation ⟨*seasonable* weather⟩. ***antonym:*** unseasonable

Timely applies to what occurs or appears at the time or moment when it is most useful or valuable ⟨a *timely* warning⟩. ***antonym:*** untimely

Well-timed applies to what is so timely as to suggest care, forethought, or design ⟨a *well-timed* remark that stifled objections⟩. ***antonym:*** ill-timed

Opportune describes something that comes, often by chance, at the best possible moment and works to the advantage of those concerned ⟨an idea that arose from an *opportune* remark⟩. ***antonym:*** inopportune

Pat may apply to what is notably apt, ready, or well-suited to the occasion ⟨a *pat* remark⟩ or to what is so very apt as to be suspect ⟨offered an alibi that seemed too *pat*⟩.

seclusion See SOLITUDE.

secret, covert, stealthy, furtive, clandestine, surreptitious, underhanded mean existing or done without attracting observation or attention.

Secret implies concealment on any grounds for any motive ⟨a *secret* meeting⟩.

Covert stresses the fact of not being open or declared ⟨*covert* operations against guerrilla forces⟩. ***antonym:*** overt

Stealthy suggests taking pains to avoid being seen or heard especially in some misdoing ⟨the *stealthy* movements of a cat burglar⟩.

Furtive implies a sly or cautious stealthiness ⟨exchanged *furtive* smiles across the room⟩. ***antonym:*** forthright, barefaced, brazen

Clandestine implies secrecy usually for an evil or illicit purpose ⟨a *clandestine* drug deal in a back alley⟩. ***antonym:*** open

Surreptitious applies to action or behavior done secretly often with skillful avoidance of detection and in violation of custom, law, or authority ⟨compromised his diet with *surreptitious* snacking⟩. ***antonym:*** brazen

Underhanded stresses fraudulent or deceptive intent ⟨a car dealership guilty of *underhanded* practices⟩. ***antonym:*** aboveboard

secrete See HIDE.

secretive See SILENT.

section See PART.

secure *adj* See SAFE.

secure *vb* **1.** See ENSURE. **2.** See GET.

sedate See SERIOUS.

seduce See LURE.

sedulous See BUSY.

see **1. See, behold, descry, espy, view, survey, contemplate, observe, notice, remark, note, perceive, discern** mean to take cognizance of something by physical or sometimes mental vision.

See may be used to imply little more than the use of the organs of vision ⟨he cannot *see* the crowd for he is blind⟩ but more commonly implies a recognition or appreciation of what is before one's eyes ⟨went to *see* a ballgame⟩ or the exercise of other powers including a vivid imagination ⟨I can *see* her plainly now, as she looked forty years ago⟩ or mental sight ⟨he was the only one who *saw* the truth⟩ or powers of inference ⟨though he appeared calm, I could *see* he was inwardly agitated⟩.

Behold carries a stronger implication of ocular impression and of distinct recognition and also suggests looking at what is seen ⟨never *beheld* such beauty⟩.

Descry often suggests an effort to discover or a looking out for someone or something despite difficulties such as distance, darkness, or concealment ⟨could barely *descry* his form in the gathering darkness⟩.

Espy usually implies skill in detection of what is small, or is not clearly within the range of vision, or is trying to escape detection ⟨at last *espied* the narrow path along the cliff⟩.

View usually implies the mental or physical seeing of what is spread before one or what can be examined in detail and often implies a particular way of looking at a thing or a particular purpose in considering it ⟨*view* a painting from various angles⟩.

Survey more often implies a detailed scrutiny or inspection by the eyes or the mind so that one has a picture or idea of something as a whole ⟨carefully *surveyed* the scene before entering the room⟩.

Contemplate implies a fixing of the eyes upon something in abstraction, in enjoyment, or in reference to some end in view ⟨a relaxed moment *contemplating* the sunset⟩.

Observe implies a heeding and not passing over and may carry an implication of directed attention ⟨closely *observed* their reaction⟩.

Notice often implies some definite reaction to what is seen or sometimes heard, felt, or sensed, such as making a mental note of it or a remark about it ⟨*noticed* with alarm that the door was unlocked⟩.

Remark is likely to suggest a registering mentally of one's impression and a judging or criticizing of what is noticed ⟨disdainfully *remarked* the apparent camaraderie between them⟩.

Note often suggests a recording of one's impressions sometimes by a mental note, but sometimes in writing or in speech ⟨he carried a map and *noted* every stream and every hill that we passed⟩.

Perceive carries a stong implication of the use of the mind in observation and implies an apprehension or obtaining of knowledge of a thing, not only though the sense of sight but through any of the senses ⟨*perceived* the rock to be made of granite⟩ and often connotes keen mental vision or special insight and penetration ⟨was able to *perceive* the danger of their situation⟩.

Discern, like **descry**, often implies little more than a making out of something by means of the eyes ⟨*discerned* an eagle high overhead⟩ but more distinctively implies the powers of deeply perceiving and of distinguishing or discriminating what the senses perceive ⟨tried hard to *discern* her meaning⟩.

2. See, look, watch mean to perceive something by use of the eyes.

See stresses the fact of receiving visual impressions ⟨she *sees* well with her new glasses⟩.

Look stresses the directing of the eyes to or the fixing of the eyes on something ⟨*looked* long and hard at his receding form⟩.

Watch implies a following of something with one's eyes so as to keep it under constant observation ⟨*watching* the clock as closely as a cat *watches* a mouse⟩.

seem, **look**, **appear** mean to give the impression of being as stated without necessarily being so in fact.

Seem is likely to suggest an opinion based on subjective impressions and personal reaction ⟨*seemed* to be strong and healthy⟩.

Look implies an opinion based on general visual impression ⟨*looked* exactly like his picture⟩.

Appear may convey the same implications as ***look*** but often it suggests an obviously distorted impression ⟨an explanation that *appeared* to be true⟩.

seeming See APPARENT.

segment See PART.

seize See TAKE.

select, **elect**, **picked**, **exclusive** mean set apart by some superior character or quality.

Select refers to one chosen with discrimination in preference to others of the same class ⟨the hotel caters to a *select* clientele⟩ or may be used in the sense of *superior* or *exceptional* with little or no suggestion of choice ⟨aimed at a *select* audience⟩. ***antonym:*** indiscriminate

Elect stresses the notion of being chosen and carries a strong implication of admission to a restricted or inner circle and often one of special privilege ⟨considered herself among the *elect*⟩.

Picked commonly applies to what is conspicuously superior and may suggest the best available ⟨the candidates were all *picked* citizens⟩.

Exclusive basically implies a character that sets apart or rules out whatever is not compatible or congruous ⟨presented as a set of contradictory and mutually *exclusive* demands⟩ but in respect to persons, groups, or institutions is likely to suggest a feeling of superiority as the basis for ruling out what is felt as beneath imposed standards or fastidious and critical requirements ⟨membership in an *exclusive* club⟩. ***antonym:*** inclusive

selection See CHOICE *n*.

self-abnegation See RENUNCIATION.

self-assertive See AGGRESSIVE.

self-denial See RENUNCIATION.

self-possession See CONFIDENCE.

selfsame See SAME.

sensation, **sense**, **feeling**, **sensibility** mean the power to respond or the act of responding to stimuli.

Sensation may center attention on the fact of perception through or as if through the sense organs, with or without comprehension ⟨felt a tingling *sensation*⟩ but often suggests not only recognition but also intellectual and emotional reactions ⟨bothered by the *sensation* that he was being ignored⟩.

Sense may differ little from ***sensation*** ⟨as the fire burned lower a *sense* of chill crept over them⟩ or it may be applied specifically to any one of the basic perceptive powers ⟨the *sense* of smell⟩, but in its typical application to the power or act of responding to stimuli it tends to stress intellectual awareness and full consciousness ⟨a *sense* of frustration⟩.

Feeling may apply to sensations such as touch, heat, cold, or pressure that are perceived through the skin ⟨so cold she had no *feeling* in her fingers⟩ or to a complex response to stimulation involving sensation, emotion, and a degree of thought ⟨had a vague *feeling* of unease⟩ or to the power to respond ⟨a sentient, *feeling* being⟩.

Sensibility often replaces ***feeling*** in this last use, especially when a keenly impressionable nature is to be implied ⟨a creature of gentle nature and great *sensibility*⟩ or excessive or affected responsiveness suggested ⟨made a great show of effete *sensibilities*⟩. ***antonym:*** insensibility

sense **1.** See SENSATION. **2. Sense**, **common sense**, **gumption**, **judgment**,

wisdom mean ability to reach intelligent conclusions.

Sense implies a reliable ability to judge and decide with soundness, prudence, and intelligence ⟨hasn't the *sense* to come in out of the rain⟩.

Common sense suggests an average degree of such ability often with native shrewdness but without sophistication or special knowledge ⟨*common sense* tells me it's wrong⟩.

Gumption suggests a readiness to use or apply common sense and stresses initiative or drive ⟨a shrewd businessman known for his *gumption*⟩.

Judgment implies sense tempered and refined by experience, training, and maturity ⟨*judgment* is required of a camp counselor⟩.

Wisdom implies sense and judgment far above average ⟨the *wisdom* that comes from years of experience⟩. ***antonym:*** folly, injudiciousness

3. See MEANING.

sensibility See SENSATION.

sensible **1.** See AWARE. **2.** See MATERIAL. **3.** See PERCEPTIBLE. **4.** See WISE.

sensitive See LIABLE.

sensual **1.** See CARNAL. **2.** See SENSUOUS.

sensuous, **sensual**, **luxurious**, **voluptuous**, **sybaritic**, **epicurean** mean relating to or providing pleasure through gratification of the senses.

Sensuous implies gratification for the sake of aesthetic pleasure ⟨the *sensuous* delights of a Reubens painting⟩.

Sensual tends to imply the gratification of the senses or the indulgence of the physical appetites as ends in themselves ⟨a man who indulged his *sensual* appetites⟩.

Luxurious suggests the providing of or indulgence in sensuous pleasure inducing bodily ease and languor and a grateful peace of mind ⟨a vacation devoted to *luxurious* self-indulgence⟩. ***antonym:*** ascetic

Voluptuous implies more strongly an abandonment to sensual or sensuous pleasure for its own sake ⟨promised a variety of *voluptuous* pleasures⟩. ***antonym:*** ascetic

Sybaritic suggests voluptuousness of an overrefined sort, especially with regard to food, drink, and surroundings ⟨indulged in a *sybaritic* feast⟩.

Epicurean implies a catering to or indulging in the satisfaction of refined and fastidious physical pleasures ⟨enjoyed a gently *epicurean* way of life⟩.

sentiment **1.** See FEELING. **2.** See OPINION.

separate *vb* **Separate**, **part**, **divide**, **sever**, **sunder**, **divorce** mean to become or cause to become disunited or disjointed.

Separate may imply any of several causes such as dispersion, removal of one from others, or presence of an intervening thing ⟨*separated* her personal life from her career⟩. ***antonym:*** combine

Part implies the separating of things or persons from close union or association ⟨an argument that *parted* the friends permanently⟩. ***antonym:*** unite

Divide implies a separating into pieces, groups, or sections by cutting, breaking, or branching ⟨civil war *divided* the nation⟩. ***antonym:*** unite

Sever implies violence especially in the removal of a part or member ⟨his arm had been *severed* by a chain saw⟩.

Sunder suggests a violent rending or wrenching apart ⟨a friendship *sundered* only by death⟩.

Divorce implies a separating of two things that commonly interact and belong together ⟨would *divorce* scientific research from moral responsibility⟩.

separate *adj* **1.** See DISTINCT. **2.** See SINGLE.

serene See CALM.

serious, **grave**, **solemn**, **sedate**, **staid**, **sober**, **earnest** mean not light or frivolous.

Serious implies a concern for what really matters ⟨prefers gothic romances to *serious* fiction⟩. ***antonym:*** light, flippant

Grave implies both seriousness and dignity in expression or attitude ⟨read the pronouncement in a *grave* voice⟩. ***antonym:*** gay

Solemn suggests an impressive gravity utterly free from levity ⟨the *solemn* occasion of a coronation⟩.

Sedate implies a composed and decorous seriousness ⟨amidst the frenzy of activity the bride remained *sedate*⟩. ***antonym:*** flighty

Staid suggests a settled, accustomed sedateness and prim self-restraint ⟨her dinner parties were *staid* affairs⟩. ***antonym:*** unstaid

Sober stresses a seriousness of purpose and absence of levity or frivolity ⟨an objective and *sober* look at the situation⟩. ***antonym:*** gay

Earnest suggests a sincerity or often zealousness of purpose ⟨an *earnest* attempt at dramatizing the Bible⟩. ***antonym:*** frivolous

servile See SUBSERVIENT.

servitude, **slavery**, **bondage** mean the state of being subject to a master.

Servitude, often vague or rhetorical in application, implies in general lack of liberty to do as one pleases ⟨lived in *servitude* to the daily grind⟩ or, more specifically, lack of freedom to determine one's course of action or way of life ⟨a man sentenced to penal *servitude*⟩.

Slavery implies subjection to a master who owns one's person and may treat one as property ⟨captured and sold into *slavery*⟩ or sometimes a comparable subservience to something that dominates like a master ⟨in *slavery* to his own ambition⟩.

Bondage implies a being bound by law or by other, usually physical, constraint in a state of complete subjection ⟨the *bondage* of the Hebrews in Egypt⟩.

set *n* **Set**, **circle**, **coterie**, **clique** mean a more or less closed and exclusive group of persons.

Set applies to a comparatively large, typically social, group of persons bound together by common interests or tastes ⟨the hunting *set*⟩.

Circle implies a common center of the group, such as a person, an activity, or a cause ⟨a peaceful family *circle*⟩.

Coterie applies to a small, select, or exclusive circle ⟨political aspirants, each with a *coterie* of advisors⟩.

Clique is likely to suggest a selfish or arrogant exclusiveness and is especially applicable to a small inner or dissident group within a larger set or circle ⟨a high school made up of combative *cliques*⟩.

set *vb* **Set**, **settle**, **fix**, **establish** mean to put securely in position.

Set stresses the fact of placing in a definite, often final position or situation or relation ⟨*set* food on the table⟩.

Settle carries a stronger suggestion of putting in a place or condition of stability, ease, or security ⟨*settled* themselves gradually in their new home⟩ and may imply a decisiveness or finality in ordering or adjusting something previously disturbed or unsettled ⟨*settle* doubts with a clear explanation⟩. ***antonym:*** unsettle

Fix stresses permanence and stability ⟨*fixed* the pole firmly in the ground⟩. ***antonym:*** alter, abrogate (*a custom, rule, or law*)

Establish is likely to give less stress to the fact of putting something in place than to subsequent fostering and care that helps it become stable and fixed ⟨do not transplant a tree once it is *established*⟩. ***antonym:*** uproot, abrogate (*a right, privilege, or quality*)

setting See BACKGROUND.

settle **1.** See DECIDE. **2.** See SET *vb*.

sever See SEPARATE.

several See DISTINCT.

severe, **stern**, **austere**, **ascetic** mean

given to or marked by strict discipline and firm restraint.

Severe implies standards enforced without indulgence or laxity and may suggest harshness ⟨the *severe* dress of the Puritans⟩. ***antonym:*** tolerant, tender

Stern stresses inflexibility and inexorability of temper or character ⟨a *stern* judge who seemed immune to pleas for mercy⟩. ***antonym:*** soft, lenient

Austere stresses absence of warmth, color, or feeling and may imply rigorous restraint, simplicity, or self-denial ⟨the view that modern architecture is *austere,* brutal, and inhuman⟩. ***antonym:*** luscious (*of fruits*), warm, ardent (*of persons, feelings*), exuberant (*of style, quality*)

Ascetic implies abstention from pleasure and comfort or self-indulgence as a measure of self- or spiritual discipline ⟨the *ascetic* life of the monastic orders⟩. ***antonym:*** luxurious, voluptuous

shackle See HAMPER.

shade See COLOR.

shake 1. Shake, **tremble**, **quake**, **totter**, **quiver**, **shiver**, **shudder**, **quaver**, **wobble**, **teeter**, **shimmy**, **dither** mean to exhibit vibrating, wavering, or oscillating movement often as an evidence of instability.

Shake can apply to any such movement, often with a suggestion of roughness and irregularity ⟨he *shook* with fear⟩.

Tremble applies specifically to a slight, rapid shaking ⟨her body *trembling* with fear⟩.

Quake may be used in place of ***tremble*** but it commonly carries a stronger implication of violent shaking or of extreme agitation either from an internal convulsion, such as an earthquake, or from an external event that rocks a person or thing to its foundations ⟨a stern lecture that made them *quake*⟩.

Totter usually suggests great physical weakness such as that associated with infancy, extreme old age, or disease and often connotes a shaking that makes movement extremely difficult and uncertain or that forebodes a fall or collapse ⟨the mast *tottered* before it fell⟩.

Quiver may suggest a slight, very rapid shaking ⟨aspen leaves *quiver* in the slightest breeze⟩, or it may suggest fear or passion and an implication of emotional tension ⟨the little boy's lips *quivered* as he tried not to cry⟩.

Shiver typically suggests the effect of cold that produces a momentary quivering ⟨came into the house snow-covered and *shivering*⟩, but it may apply to a quivering that results from an anticipation, a premonition, a foreboding, or a vague fear ⟨*shivered* at the sight of the ancient gravestone⟩.

Shudder usually suggests a brief or temporary shaking that affects the entire body or mass and is the effect of something horrible or revolting ⟨*shuddered* uncontrollably at the eerie shrieks⟩.

Quaver sometimes implies irregular vibration and fluctuation, especially as an effect of something that disturbs ⟨the *quavering* flame of the candle⟩ but often stresses tremulousness especially in reference to voices affected by weakness or emotion ⟨made her plea in a voice *quavering* with fear⟩.

Wobble implies an unsteadiness that shows itself in tottering, or in a quivering characteristic of a mass of soft flesh or soft jelly, or in a shakiness characteristic of rickety furniture ⟨his table *wobbles*⟩.

Teeter implies an unsteadiness that reveals itself in seesawing motions ⟨an inebriated man *teetering* as he stands⟩.

Shimmy suggests the fairly violent shaking of the body from the shoulders down which is characteristic of the dance of that name and, therefore, may suggest vibrating motions of an abnormal nature ⟨the *shimmying* of unbalanced front wheels of an automobile⟩.

Dither implies a shaking or a hesitant vacillating movement often as a result of nervousness, confusion, or lack of purpose ⟨*dithered* incoherently⟩.

2. Shake, **agitate**, **rock**, **convulse** mean to move up and down or to and fro with some violence.

Shake often carries a further implication of purpose ⟨*shake* well before using⟩.

Agitate suggests a violent and prolonged tossing or stirring ⟨strong winds *agitated* the leaves on the trees⟩. ***antonym:*** quiet, lull, still

Rock suggests a swinging or swaying motion that is likely to result from violent impact or upheaval ⟨the entire city was *rocked* by the explosion⟩.

Convulse suggests a violent pulling or wrenching as of a body in a paroxysm ⟨we were *convulsed* with laughter⟩.

shallow See SUPERFICIAL.

sham *n* See IMPOSTURE.

sham *vb* See ASSUME.

shame See DISGRACE.

shameless, **brazen**, **barefaced**, **brash**, **impudent** mean characterized by boldness and a lack of a sense of shame.

Shameless implies a lack of effective restraints, such as modesty, an active conscience, or a sense of decency ⟨told a *shameless* lie⟩.

Brazen adds to ***shameless*** an implication of defiant insolence ⟨stood up to him with *brazen* arrogance⟩. ***antonym:*** bashful

Barefaced implies absence of all efforts to disguise or mask one's transgression and connotes extreme effrontery ⟨a *barefaced* lie⟩. ***antonym:*** furtive

Brash stresses impetuousness and may imply heedlessness and temerity ⟨won them over with his *brash* but charming manner⟩. ***antonym:*** wary

Impudent adds to ***shameless*** implications of bold or pert defiance of considerations of modesty or decency ⟨a rude and *impudent* reply to a polite question⟩. ***antonym:*** respectful

shape *n* See FORM.

shape *vb* See MAKE.

share, **participate**, **partake** mean to have, get, or use in common with another or others.

Share may imply that one as the original holder grants to another the partial use, enjoyment, or possession of a thing, or may merely imply a mutual use or possession ⟨*shared* my tools with the others⟩.

Participate implies a having or taking part in an undertaking, activity, or discussion ⟨students are encouraged to *participate* in outside activities⟩.

Partake implies accepting or acquiring a share especially of food or drink ⟨invited everyone to *partake* freely of the refreshments⟩.

sharp, **keen**, **acute** mean having or showing alert competence and clear understanding.

Sharp implies quick perception, clever resourcefulness, or sometimes devious cunning ⟨*sharp* enough to know a con job when he saw one⟩. ***antonym:*** dull, blunt

Keen suggests quickness, enthusiasm, and a clear-sighted, penetrating mind ⟨a *keen* observer of the political scene⟩. ***antonym:*** blunt

Acute implies a power to penetrate and may suggest subtlety and depth and sharpness of insight ⟨an *acute* sense of what is linguistically effective⟩. ***antonym:*** obtuse

shed See DISCARD.

sheer See STEEP.

shelter *n* **Shelter**, **cover**, **retreat**, **refuge**, **asylum**, **sanctuary** mean the state or a place in which one is safe or secure from what threatens or disturbs.

Shelter implies temporary protection of a shield or roof from something that would harm or annoy ⟨seek *shelter* from the storm in a cave⟩.

Cover stresses concealment and often applies to a natural shelter or something similarly protective ⟨advanced under *cover* of darkness⟩. ***antonym:*** exposure

Retreat stresses usually voluntary retirement from danger or annoyance and escape to a safe, secure, or peaceful place ⟨built themselves a country *retreat*⟩.

Refuge implies an attempt to flee from whatever threatens or harasses ⟨sought *refuge* in the deserted house⟩.

Asylum adds to ***refuge*** the implication of the finding of safety and of exemption from seizure ⟨asked for and was granted political *asylum*⟩.

Sanctuary stresses the claim of a refuge to reverence or inviolability ⟨established a wildlife *sanctuary*⟩.

shelter *vb* See HARBOR.

shield See DEFEND.

shift See RESOURCE.

shimmer See FLASH.

shimmy See SHAKE 1.

ship See BOAT.

shiver See SHAKE 1.

shocking See FEARFUL 2.

shoot, **branch**, **bough**, **limb** mean one of the members of a plant that are outgrowths from a crown or from a main base or one of its divisions.

Shoot stresses actual growing and is applicable chiefly to new growth from a bud ⟨allowed only the strongest *shoots* to grow⟩.

Branch suggests a spreading out by dividing and subdividing and applies typically to a matured member arising from a primary stem or trunk or from a division or subdivision of one of these ⟨*branches* silhouetted against the sky⟩.

Bough may replace ***branch***, in reference to a tree or shrub, especially when the notion of foliage or blossom or fruit is prominent ⟨pine *boughs* for Christmas decoration⟩.

Limb is likely to apply to a main branch arising directly from a trunk ⟨the great *limbs* of the old oak⟩.

shopworn See TRITE.

short See BRIEF.

shorten, **curtail**, **abbreviate**, **abridge**, **retrench** mean to reduce in extent.

Shorten implies a reduction in length or duration ⟨*shorten* the speech to fit the allotted time⟩. ***antonym:*** lengthen, elongate, extend

Curtail adds an implication of cutting that in some way deprives of completeness or adequacy ⟨ceremonies *curtailed* because of the rain⟩. ***antonym:*** prolong, protract

Abbreviate implies a making shorter usually by omitting or cutting off some part ⟨hostile questioning that *abbreviated* the interview⟩. ***antonym:*** lengthen, extend

Abridge implies a reduction in compass or scope with retention of essential elements and relative completeness of the result ⟨the *abridged* version of the novel⟩. ***antonym:*** expand, extend

Retrench suggests a reduction in extent of something felt to be excessive ⟨falling prices forced the company to *retrench*⟩.

short-lived See TRANSIENT.

shortly See PRESENTLY.

shove See PUSH.

show **1. Show**, **manifest**, **evidence**, **evince**, **demonstrate** mean to reveal outwardly or make apparent.

Show implies that what is revealed must be inferred from acts, looks, or words ⟨careful not to *show* what he feels⟩.

Manifest implies a plainer, more direct, and more immediate revelation ⟨*manifested* musical ability at an early age⟩. ***antonym:*** suggest

Evidence suggests a serving as proof of the actuality or existence of something ⟨her deep enmity is *evidenced* by her silent glare⟩.

Evince implies a showing by outward marks or signs ⟨he *evinced* no interest in the project⟩.

Demonstrate implies a showing by action or by display of feelings or evidence ⟨*demonstrated* her appreciation in her own way⟩.

2. Show, **exhibit**, **display**, **expose**, **parade**, **flaunt** mean to present in such a way as to invite notice or attention.

Show implies a presenting to view so that others may see or look at ⟨*showed* her snapshots to the whole group⟩. ***antonym:*** disguise

Exhibit stresses a putting forward prominently or openly ⟨*exhibit* paintings at a gallery⟩.

Display emphasizes putting in a position so as to be seen to advantage or with great clearness ⟨*display* sale items⟩.

Expose suggests a bringing forth from concealment and a displaying, often with a suggestion of unmasking ⟨sought to *expose* the hypocrisy of the town fathers⟩.

Parade implies an ostentatious or arrogant displaying ⟨*parading* their piety for all to see⟩.

Flaunt suggests a shameless, boastful, often offensive parading ⟨nouveaux riches *flaunting* their wealth⟩.

showy, **pretentious**, **ostentatious** mean given to or making excessive outward display.

Showy implies an imposing or striking appearance but usually suggests cheapness or poor taste ⟨the *showy* costumes of the circus performers⟩.

Pretentious implies an appearance of importance not justified by the thing's value or the person's standing ⟨for a family-style restaurant, the menu was far too *pretentious*⟩. ***antonym:*** unpretentious

Ostentatious stresses conspicuous or vainglorious display or parade that may or may not be showy or pretentious ⟨very *ostentatious,* even for a debutante party⟩. ***antonym:*** unostentatious

shrewd, **sagacious**, **perspicacious**, **astute** mean acute in perception and sound in judgment.

Shrewd stresses the possession or effect of practical, hardheaded cleverness and wise, although sometimes selfish, judgment ⟨a *shrewd* judge of character⟩.

Sagacious suggests wisdom, penetration, farsightedness, and mature keenness of judgment ⟨a series of *sagacious* investments tripled her wealth⟩.

Perspicacious implies unusual power to see into and understand what is puzzling or hidden ⟨the *perspicacious* counselor saw through his facade⟩. ***antonym:*** dull

Astute suggests shrewdness, perspicacity, and artfulness and, often, an incapacity for being fooled ⟨an *astute* player of party politics⟩. ***antonym:*** gullible

shrink **1.** See CONTRACT. **2.** See RECOIL.

shrivel See WITHER.

shudder See SHAKE 1.

shun See ESCAPE.

shy, **bashful**, **diffident**, **modest**, **coy** mean not inclined to be forward or obtrude oneself.

Shy implies a timid reserve and a shrinking from familiarity or contact with others ⟨*shy* in front of total strangers⟩. ***antonym:*** bold, obtrusive

Bashful implies a frightened or hesitant shyness characteristic of immaturity ⟨the *bashful* boy rarely told us how he felt about anything⟩. ***antonym:*** brash, forward

Diffident stresses a distrust of one's own ability, opinion, or powers that causes hesitation in acting or speaking ⟨felt *diffident* about raising an objection⟩. ***antonym:*** confident

Modest suggests absence of undue confidence or conceit or of boldness or self-assertion ⟨very *modest* about reciting his achievements⟩.

Coy implies an assumed or affected shyness ⟨don't be misled by her *coy* demeanor⟩.

side See PHASE.

sign **1. Sign**, **mark**, **token**, **note**, **symptom** mean a discernible indication of what is not itself directly perceptible.

Sign applies to any indication to be perceived by the senses or the reason ⟨interpreted her smile as a good *sign*⟩.

Mark suggests something impressed on or inherently characteristic of a thing often in contrast to something outwardly evident ⟨the bitter experience left its *mark* on him⟩.

Token applies to something that serves as a proof or offers evidence of something intangible ⟨this gift is a *token* of our esteem⟩.

Note suggests a distinguishing mark or characteristic ⟨a *note* of despair pervades her poetry⟩.

Symptom suggests detectable outward indication of an internal change or abnormal condition ⟨rampant violence is a *symptom* of that country's decline⟩.

2. Sign, **signal** mean something, such as a gesture or action, by which a command or wish is expressed or a thought made known.

Sign is applicable to any means by which one conveys information without verbal communication ⟨made a *sign* to the others to wait while he reconnoitered⟩.

Signal usually applies to a conventional and readily recognizable sign that conveys a command, a direction, or a warning ⟨saw the coach's *signal*⟩ or it may apply to a mechanical device that performs a comparable function ⟨waiting for a traffic *signal* to change to green⟩.

signal *adj* See NOTICEABLE.

signal *n* See SIGN 2.

significance **1.** See IMPORTANCE. **2.** See MEANING.

signification See MEANING.

silent **1. Silent**, **taciturn**, **reticent**, **reserved**, **secretive** mean showing restraint in speaking.

Silent implies a habit of saying no more than is needed ⟨her husband was the *silent* type, not given to idle chatter⟩. ***antonym:*** talkative

Taciturn implies a temperamental disinclination to speech and usually connotes unsociability ⟨the locals are *taciturn* and not receptive to outsiders⟩. ***antonym:*** garrulous

Reticent implies a reluctance to speak out or at length, especially about one's own affairs ⟨strangely *reticent* about his plans⟩. ***antonym:*** frank, unreticent

Reserved implies reticence and suggests the restraining influence of caution or formality in checking easy informal exchange ⟨a *reserved* and distant demeanor⟩. ***antonym:*** effusive

Secretive, too, implies reticence but usually carries a disparaging suggestion of lack of frankness or of an often ostentatious will to conceal something that might reasonably be made known ⟨a *secretive* public official usually stingy with news stories⟩.

2. See STILL.

silhouette See OUTLINE.

silken See SLEEK.

silky See SLEEK.

silly See SIMPLE.

similar, **analogous**, **like**, **alike**, **akin**, **parallel**, **homogeneous**, **uniform**, **identical** mean closely resembling each other.

Similar implies such likeness as allows the possibility of being mistaken for another ⟨ all the houses in the development are *similar*⟩. ***antonym:*** dissimilar

Analogous applies to things having many similarities but belonging to essentially different categories ⟨*analogous* political systems⟩.

Like implies resemblance or similarity ranging from virtual identity to slight similarity ⟨found people of *like* mind⟩. ***antonym:*** unlike

Alike implies having close resemblance even though obviously distinct ⟨siblings who looked *alike*⟩. ***antonym:*** unlike, different

Akin suggests essential rather than apparent likeness ⟨diseases *akin* to one another in their effects⟩. ***antonym:*** alien

Parallel suggests a marked likeness in the course of development of two things ⟨the *parallel* careers of two movie stars⟩.

Homogeneous implies likeness of a number of things in kind, sort, or class

⟨a *homogeneous* population⟩. ***antonym:*** heterogeneous

Uniform implies consistent likeness and lack of variation in existence, appearance, or operation ⟨*uniform* application of the law⟩.

Identical indicates either essential sameness or exact correspondence without detectable or significant difference ⟨shared *identical* concerns⟩. ***antonym:*** different

similarity See LIKENESS.

similitude See LIKENESS.

simple 1. See EASY. **2.** See PLAIN. **3. Simple, foolish, silly, fatuous, asinine** mean actually or apparently deficient in intelligence.

Simple implies a degree of intelligence inadequate to cope with anything complex or involving mental effort or implies a failure to use one's intelligence ⟨*simple* peasants afraid of revolutionary ideas⟩. ***antonym:*** wise

Foolish implies the character of being or seeming unable to use judgment, discretion, or good sense ⟨*foolish* people believed the ghost story⟩. ***antonym:*** smart

Silly suggests failure to act as a rational being by showing lack of common sense or by ridiculous behavior ⟨the *silly* stunts of vacationing college students⟩. ***antonym:*** sensible

Fatuous implies contemptuous foolishness, inanity, and disregard of reality ⟨the *fatuous* responses of over-ambitious politicians⟩. ***antonym:*** sensible

Asinine suggests utter and contemptible failure to use normal rationality or perception ⟨a soap opera with an especially *asinine* plot⟩. ***antonym:*** judicious, sensible

simulate See ASSUME.

simultaneous See CONTEMPORARY.

sin See OFFENSE 2.

sincere, wholehearted, heartfelt, hearty, unfeigned mean genuine in feeling or expression.

Sincere stresses absence of hypocrisy, feigning, or any falsifying embellishment or exaggeration ⟨offered a *sincere* apology⟩. ***antonym:*** insincere

Wholehearted suggests sincerity and earnest devotion without reservation or misgiving ⟨promised our *wholehearted* support to the cause⟩.

Heartfelt suggests depth of genuine feeling outwardly expressed ⟨a gift that expresses our *heartfelt* gratitude⟩.

Hearty suggests honesty, warmth, and exuberance in the display of feeling ⟨received a *hearty* welcome at the door⟩. ***antonym:*** hollow

Unfeigned stresses spontaneity and absence of pretense or simulation ⟨her *unfeigned* delight at receiving the award⟩.

single, sole, unique, separate, solitary, particular mean one as distinguished from two or more or all others.

Single implies being unaccompanied or unsupported by or not combined or united with any other ⟨a *single* example will suffice⟩. ***antonym:*** multiple

Sole applies to the only one that exists, acts, has power or relevance, or should be considered ⟨my *sole* reason for moving there⟩.

Unique applies to the only one of its kind or character in existence ⟨the medal is *unique,* for no duplicates were made⟩.

Separate stresses discreteness and disconnectedness or unconnectedness from every other one ⟨a country with a *separate* set of problems⟩.

Solitary implies being both single and isolated ⟨television was her *solitary* link to the outside world⟩.

Particular implies singular or numerical distinctness from other instances, examples, or members of a class ⟨a *particular* kind of wine⟩. ***antonym:*** general

singular See STRANGE.

sinister, baleful, malign mean seriously threatening evil or disaster.

Sinister applies to what threatens by appearance or reputation, and suggests a general or vague feeling of fear or apprehension on the part of the observer ⟨a *sinister* aura surrounded the place⟩.

Baleful imputes perniciousness or destructiveness that works either openly or covertly ⟨the *baleful* influence of superstition and fanaticism⟩. ***antonym:*** beneficent

Malign applies to something inherently evil or harmful ⟨the *malign* effects of smoking on one's health⟩. ***antonym:*** benign

situation **1.** See PLACE. **2.** See POSITION 2. **3.** See STATE.

site See PLACE.

skeleton See STRUCTURE.

skepticism See UNCERTAINTY.

sketch See COMPENDIUM.

skill See ART.

skilled See PROFICIENT.

skillful See PROFICIENT.

skimpy See MEAGER.

skinny See LEAN.

skulk See LURK.

slack **1.** See LOOSE. **2.** See NEGLIGENT.

slacken See DELAY 1.

slander See MALIGN.

slang See DIALECT.

slant, **slope**, **incline**, **lean** mean to diverge or to cause to diverge from the vertical or horizontal.

Slant implies a noticeable physical divergence but implies nothing about the degree of divergence ⟨handwriting that was characterized by *slanting* letters⟩.

Slope, often interchangeable with ***slant***, may be preferred when reference is made to a gradual divergence of a side or surface ⟨the land *slopes* to the east⟩.

Incline is likely to suggest the intervention of an external force, such as bending or tipping ⟨graciously *inclined* her head in response to the cheers⟩.

Lean may stress a definite directing of an inclination ⟨*leaned* the ladder against the wall⟩ or a literal or figurative resting or intent to rest against a support ⟨*lean* back in an easy chair⟩.

slap See STRIKE.

slatternly, **dowdy**, **frowzy**, **blowsy** mean deficient in neatness, freshness, and smartness, especially in dress or appearance.

Slatternly stresses notions of slovenliness, unkemptness, and sordidness ⟨a run-down *slatternly* apartment⟩.

Dowdy is likely to suggest a complete lack of taste resulting from a combination of the untidy, drab, and tasteless ⟨an old hotel with an imposing but *dowdy* appearance⟩. ***antonym:*** smart

Frowzy may describe a lazy lack of neatness, order, and cleanliness ⟨a *frowzy* old office⟩ or it may apply to a natural and not unwholesome disorder ⟨a thicket *frowzy* with underbrush⟩ or it may suggest drab misery and squalor ⟨tried her best to overcome the *frowzy* circumstances under which she grew up⟩. ***antonym:*** trim, smart

Blowsy implies dishevelment or disorder ⟨looked *blowsy* and dissolute⟩ to which is often added a notion of crudity or coarseness or grossness ⟨songs carelessly belted out by a *blowsy* singer⟩. ***antonym:*** smart, spruce, dainty

slaughter See MASSACRE.

slavery See SERVITUDE.

slavish See SUBSERVIENT.

slay See KILL.

sleazy See LIMP.

sleek, **slick**, **glossy**, **silken**, **silky**, **satiny** mean having a smooth bright surface or appearance.

Sleek suggests a smoothness or brightness resulting from attentive grooming or excellent physical condition ⟨a *sleek* racehorse⟩.

Slick suggests extreme smoothness that results in an unsafe or slippery surface ⟨slipped and fell on the *slick* floor⟩.

Glossy suggests a surface that is smooth and highly polished ⟨photographs having a *glossy* finish⟩.

Silken and ***silky*** imply the smoothness and luster as well as the softness of silk

⟨*silken* hair⟩ ⟨expensive dresses made of *silky* fabrics⟩.

Satiny applies to what is soft and smooth and shining ⟨a flower's *satiny* petals⟩.

sleepy, **drowsy**, **somnolent**, **slumberous** mean affected by or inducing a desire to sleep.

Sleepy applies to whatever seems about to fall asleep or to whatever leads to such a state ⟨a *sleepy* little town⟩.

Drowsy carries a stronger implication of the heaviness or languor associated with sleepiness than of an actual need for sleep ⟨grew *drowsy* in the stuffy room⟩.

Somnolent is likely to suggest the sluggishness or inertness accompanying sleepiness more than the actual impulse to sleep ⟨the *somnolent* air of a tropical noon⟩.

Slumberous may replace any of the other terms; distinctively it may connote quiescence or the repose of latent powers ⟨felt the sea's *slumberous* power⟩.

slender See THIN.

slick See SLEEK.

slight *adj* See THIN.

slight *vb* See NEGLECT.

slighting See DEROGATORY.

slim See THIN.

sling See THROW.

slink See LURK.

slip See ERROR.

slope See SLANT.

slothful See LAZY.

slough See DISCARD.

slow See DELAY 1.

sluice See POUR.

slumberous See SLEEPY.

sly, **cunning**, **crafty**, **tricky**, **foxy**, **artful** mean attaining or seeking to attain one's ends by devious means.

Sly implies furtiveness, lack of candor, and skill in concealing one's aims and methods ⟨a *sly* corporate-takeover scheme⟩.

Cunning suggests the inventive use of sometimes limited intelligence in overreaching or circumventing ⟨relentlessly *cunning* in her pursuit of the governorship⟩. ***antonym:*** ingenuous

Crafty implies cleverness and subtlety of method ⟨a *crafty* trial lawyer⟩.

Tricky suggests unscrupulous shiftiness and unreliability ⟨a *tricky* interviewer who usually got what she wanted from her subject⟩.

Foxy implies a shrewd and wary craftiness usually based on experience in devious dealing ⟨a *foxy* thief got away with her jewels⟩.

Artful implies insinuating or alluring indirectness in dealing and often connotes sophistication or coquetry or cleverness ⟨*artful* matchmaker⟩. ***antonym:*** artless

small, **little**, **diminutive**, **petite**, **minute**, **tiny**, **microscopic**, **miniature** mean noticeably below average in size.

Small is often interchangeable with ***little***, but it applies more to relative size determined by capacity, value, or number ⟨a *small* amount⟩. ***antonym:*** large

Little is more absolute in implication and often connotes less magnitude that is usual, expected, or desired ⟨your pathetic *little* smile⟩. ***antonym:*** big, great

Diminutive implies exceptional or abnormal smallness ⟨the *diminutive* gymnast outshone her larger competitors⟩.

Petite applies chiefly to girls and women and implies marked smallness and trimness ⟨specializing in clothing for *petite* women⟩.

Minute implies extreme smallness ⟨a beverage with only a *minute* amount of caffeine⟩.

Tiny is an informal equivalent to ***minute*** ⟨*tiny* cracks have formed in the painting⟩. ***antonym:*** huge

Microscopic applies to what is so minute it can only be seen under a microscope ⟨found a *microscopic* defect⟩.

Miniature applies to an exactly proportioned reproduction on a very small scale ⟨a doll house complete with *miniature* furnishings⟩.

smart See INTELLIGENT.

smell, **scent**, **odor**, **aroma** mean the quality that makes a thing perceptible to the olfactory sense.

Smell implies solely the sensation without suggestion of quality or character or source ⟨an odd *smell* permeated the room⟩.

Scent applies to the characteristic smell given off by a substance, an animal, or a plant and stresses the source of the sensation ⟨dogs trained to detect the *scent* of narcotics⟩.

Odor may imply a stronger or more readily distinguished scent or it may be equivalent to ***smell*** ⟨a type of cheese with a very pronounced *odor*⟩.

Aroma suggests a somewhat penetrating, pervasive, or sometimes pungent, but usually pleasant odor ⟨the *aroma* of freshly ground coffee⟩. ***antonym:*** stink, stench

smidgen See PARTICLE.

smite See STRIKE.

smog See HAZE.

smooth **1.** See EASY. **2.** See LEVEL. **3.** See SUAVE.

smother See SUFFOCATE.

smuggled, **bootleg**, **contraband** mean transported in defiance of the law.

Smuggled applies to what is brought in or taken out of an area, especially to avoid payment of taxes or contravene the law ⟨*smuggled* diamonds⟩.

Bootleg refers to a material substance offered for sale or distribution in defiance of prohibition or legal restrictions on its use ⟨*bootleg* whiskey⟩.

Contraband, often interchangeable with ***smuggled***, specifically applies to something whose exportation to belligerents is prohibited and which is therefore liable to seizure ⟨seized a shipment of *contraband* merchandise at the border⟩.

snap See JERK.

snare See CATCH.

snatch See TAKE.

sneak See LURK.

sneer See SCOFF.

snug See COMFORTABLE.

soak, **saturate**, **drench**, **steep**, **impregnate** mean to permeate or be permeated with a liquid.

Soak implies a usually prolonged immersion that results in a thorough wetting, softening, or dissolving ⟨*soak* the clothes to remove the stains⟩.

Saturate implies an absorption until no more liquid can be held ⟨gym clothes *saturated* with sweat⟩.

Drench implies a thorough wetting by something that may pour down or may be poured ⟨the cloudburst *drenched* us to the skin⟩.

Steep suggests an immersion and soaking that results in the extraction of an essence by the liquid ⟨*steep* tea in boiling water⟩.

Impregnate implies a thorough interpenetration of one thing by another ⟨a cake strongly *impregnated* with brandy⟩.

soar See RISE.

sober **1. Sober**, **temperate**, **continent**, **unimpassioned** mean having or manifesting mastery of oneself and one's appetites.

Sober implies moderation in the use of food and especially drink and may suggest composure under stress and freedom from emotional excess ⟨a calm *sober* disposition well-fitted to function in an emergency⟩. ***antonym:*** excited, drunk

Temperate stresses moderation and implies such control that one never exceeds the bounds of what is right or proper ⟨maintained her equanimity and her *temperate* outlook⟩. ***antonym:*** intemperate

Continent stresses deliberate self-restraint especially in regard to expressing feelings or satisfying sexual desires ⟨a nation known for its frugal and *continent* leaders⟩. ***antonym:*** incontinent

Unimpassioned may imply a subduing of feeling or passion by rationality ⟨presented a reserved, *unimpassioned* appearance⟩ but often it connotes a resulting coldness or hardness of heart ⟨prosecuted the case with *unimpassioned* loathing⟩. ***antonym:*** impassioned

2. See SERIOUS.

sobriety See TEMPERANCE.

sociable See GRACIOUS.

society See ARISTOCRACY.

soft, **bland**, **mild**, **gentle**, **lenient**, **balmy** mean devoid of harshness, roughness, or intensity.

Soft implies a subduing of all that is vivid, intense, or forceful until it is agreeably soothing ⟨took a walk in the *soft* evening air⟩. ***antonym:*** hard, stern

Bland implies the absence of anything that might disturb, stimulate, or irritate and may suggest insipidness ⟨spent a week on a *bland* diet⟩. ***antonym:*** pungent, piquant, savory, tasty

Mild stresses moderation or restraint of force or intensity ⟨*mild* weather⟩ and is often applied to what induces a feeling of quiet beauty or serenity ⟨spoke to the patient in a *mild* tone⟩. ***antonym:*** fierce, harsh

Gentle applies to things that are pleasant and agreeable rather than harsh, rough, fierce, strong, or irritating, and that produce a sense of placidity or tranquility or restrained power ⟨a *gentle* rain⟩. ***antonym:*** rough, harsh

Lenient stresses a relaxing, softening, or calming influence ⟨the *lenient* effect of lanolin⟩. ***antonym:*** caustic

Balmy suggests refreshment and sometimes exhilaration, frequently coupled with a suggestion of fragrance ⟨an unusually *balmy* day in early spring⟩.

sojourn See RESIDE.

solace See COMFORT.

sole See SINGLE.

solemn See SERIOUS.

solicit **1.** See ASK 2. **2.** See INVITE.

solicitor See LAWYER.

solicitude See CARE.

solid See FIRM.

solidarity See UNITY.

solitary **1.** See ALONE. **2.** See SINGLE.

solitude, **isolation**, **seclusion** mean the state of one who is alone.

Solitude stresses aloneness and a lack of contact and may imply being cut off by wish or compulsion from one's usual associates ⟨the *solitude* enjoyed by the long-distance trucker⟩.

Isolation stresses often involuntary detachment or separation from others ⟨the oppressive *isolation* of the village during winter⟩.

Seclusion suggests a shutting away or keeping apart from others and often connotes a deliberate withdrawal from the world or retirement to a quiet life ⟨lived in bucolic *seclusion* surrounded by his art collection⟩.

somatic See BODILY.

somnolent See SLEEPY.

soon See PRESENTLY.

sophisticated, **worldly-wise**, **worldly**, **blasé**, **disillusioned** mean experienced in the ways of the world.

Sophisticated implies either refinement, urbanity, cleverness, and cultivation ⟨guests at her salon were rich and *sophisticated*⟩ or artificiality of manner, overrefinement, and absence of enthusiasm ⟨too *sophisticated* to enjoy the carnival rides⟩. ***antonym:*** unsophisticated

Worldly-wise suggests a close knowledge of the affairs and manners of society and a concentration on material ends and aims ⟨a *worldly-wise* woman with a philosophy of personal independence⟩.

Worldly, close to ***worldly-wise***, stresses alienation from spiritual interests and dedication to happiness in this world ⟨chose to focus on *worldly* concerns⟩. ***antonym:*** unworldly

Blasé implies a lack of responsiveness to common joys as a result of a real or affected surfeit of experience and cultivation ⟨*blasé* travelers who claimed to have been everywhere⟩.

Disillusioned applies to someone who

has lost all illusions and hope as a result of experience and who lacks enthusiasm or ideals ‹saw the world around him through scornful, *disillusioned* eyes›.

sordid See MEAN.

sorrow *n* **Sorrow, grief, anguish, woe, regret** mean distress of mind.

Sorrow implies a sense of loss or a sense of guilt and remorse ‹a nation united in *sorrow* upon the death of the President›. ***antonym:*** joy

Grief implies a poignant sorrow for an immediate cause ‹gave his father much *grief*›. ***antonym:*** joy

Anguish suggests a torturing often persistent grief or dread ‹the *anguish* felt by the hostages›. ***antonym:*** relief

Woe implies a deep or inconsolable distress or misery ‹cries of *woe* echoed throughout the bombed city›.

Regret implies a pain caused by deep disappointment, fruitless longing, or unavailing remorse ‹never felt a moment of *regret* following the divorce›.

sorrow *vb* See GRIEVE.

sorry See CONTEMPTIBLE.

sort See TYPE.

soul, spirit mean an immaterial entity distinguishable from the body.

Soul may be preferred when emphasis is on the entity as having functions, responsibilities, aspects, or destiny ‹praying for the *souls* of the dead› or when the emphasis is on relation or connection to a material entity to which it gives life or power ‹set out to save the *soul* of the nation›. ***antonym:*** body

Spirit may be chosen when the stress is upon the quality, the constitution, or the activity of the entity ‹a man fervent in *spirit*› or it may suggest an antithesis to something material ‹enforced the *spirit* rather than the letter of the law›.

sound *adj* **1.** See HEALTHY. **2.** See VALID.

sound *n* **Sound, noise** mean a sensation or effect resulting from stimulati on of the auditory receptors.

Sound is applicable to anything that is heard and in itself is completely neutral in implication ‹loud *sounds* of laughter›. ***antonym:*** silence

Noise applies to a sound that is disagreeably loud or harsh or constantly or irritatingly perceptible ‹the constant *noise* and bustle of the city› or inappropriate to the situation and therefore disturbing ‹wakened by a *noise* at the door late at night›.

source See ORIGIN.

sovereign **1.** See DOMINANT. **2.** See FREE *adj*.

spacious, commodious, capacious, ample mean larger in extent or capacity than the average.

Spacious implies great length and breadth and sometimes height ‹a mansion with a *spacious* front lawn›. ***antonym:*** strait

Commodious stresses roominess and comfortable freedom from hampering constriction ‹a *commodious* and airy penthouse apartment›. ***antonym:*** incommodious

Capacious stresses the ability to hold, contain, or retain in exceptional quantity or to an exceptional degree ‹a *capacious* suitcase›. ***antonym:*** exiguous

Ample implies having a greater size, expanse, or amount than that deemed adequate and may suggest fullness or bulk or freedom from cramping restrictions ‹we have *ample* means to buy the house›. ***antonym:*** meager, circumscribed

spare **1.** See LEAN. **2.** See MEAGER.

sparing, frugal, thrifty, economical mean careful in the use of one's money or resources.

Sparing stresses abstention and restraint ‹mother was *sparing* in the use of butter›. ***antonym:*** lavish

Frugal implies simplicity and temperance and suggests absence of luxury and display ‹carried on in the *frugal* tradition of the Yankees›. ***antonym:*** wasteful

Thrifty stresses good management and industry as well as frugality ⟨the store prospered under his *thrifty* management⟩. ***antonym:*** wasteful

Economical stresses prudent management, lack of wastefulness, and efficient use of resources ⟨trucking remains an *economical* means of transport⟩. ***antonym:*** extravagant

sparkle See FLASH.

sparse See MEAGER.

spasm See FIT *n*.

spasmodic See FITFUL.

spat See QUARREL.

speak, **talk**, **converse** mean to articulate words so as to express one's thoughts.

Speak may refer to any utterance, however coherent or disconnected, and with or without reference to hearers ⟨too hoarse to *speak* clearly⟩.

Talk usually implies one or more listeners and related conversation or discourse ⟨*talk* over a problem with an adviser⟩.

Converse implies an interchange in talk of thoughts and opinions ⟨a multitude of subjects on which they happily *conversed*⟩.

special, **especial**, **specific**, **particular**, **individual** mean of or relating to one thing or class.

Special stresses having a distinctive quality, character, identity, or use ⟨airline passengers who require *special* meals⟩.

Especial may add implications of preeminence or preference ⟨a matter of *especial* importance⟩.

Specific implies a unique and peculiar relationship to a kind or category or individual ⟨children with *specific* nutritional needs⟩. ***antonym:*** nonspecific, unspecific, generic

Particular stresses the distinctness of something as an individual ⟨an Alpine scene of *particular* beauty⟩. ***antonym:*** general, universal

Individual implies unequivocal reference to one of a class or group ⟨valued each *individual* opinion⟩. ***antonym:*** general

specific 1. See EXPLICIT. **2.** See SPECIAL.

specify See MENTION.

specimen See INSTANCE.

specious See PLAUSIBLE.

spectator, **observer**, **beholder**, **looker-on**, **onlooker**, **witness**, **eyewitness**, **bystander**, **kibitzer** mean one who sees or looks upon something.

Spectator can be used for one that attends an exhibition, performance, or entertainment which does not involve an appeal to the sense of hearing ⟨*spectators* at a football game⟩; more broadly it denotes one who is felt to be wholly apart from whatever is presented to the attention ⟨considered herself a *spectator* in the game of life⟩.

Observer may or may not imply an intent to see, but usually suggests that one attends closely to details and often keeps a record of them ⟨earned a reputation as a keen *observer* of current mores⟩.

Beholder sometimes carries a strong implication of watching or regarding intently and is often applicable to one who has looked intently upon a person or thing and obtained a clear and accurate impression ⟨a judgment left to the eye of the *beholder*⟩.

Looker-on and ***onlooker*** suggest casualness or detachment and lack of participation ⟨there was a great crowd of *lookers-on* at the fire⟩ ⟨the surgeon refused to operate in the presence of *onlookers*⟩.

Witness specifically denotes one who has firsthand knowledge and therefore is competent to give testimony ⟨presented a set of *witnesses* who had lived through the tragedy⟩.

Eyewitness more explicitly implies actual sight as the source of knowledge ⟨there were no *eyewitnesses* of the collision⟩.

Bystander primarily denotes one who stands by when something is happening ⟨the policeman took the names of all the *bystanders*⟩ or as merely being present at a place ⟨a *bystander* was injured by the explosion⟩.

Kibitzer specifically applies to one who watches a card game by looking over the shoulders of the players and who may annoy them by offering advice; it may also apply to an onlooker who meddles or makes unwelcome suggestions ⟨a group composed equally of players and *kibitzers*⟩.

speculate See THINK 2.

speculative **1.** See THEORETICAL. **2.** See THOUGHTFUL 1.

speed See HASTE.

speedy See FAST.

spend, **expend**, **disburse** mean to pay out for something received or expected.

Spend suggests the mere fact of paying out ⟨*spend* a nickel for candy⟩ or implies a draining or depleting or exhausting of what is used ⟨*spent* months trying to find a satisfactory house⟩. ***antonym:*** save

Expend is likely to be chosen with reference to public or business rather than private spending and to imply an outlaying of large amounts ⟨vowed to *expend* money on education if elected⟩.

Disburse implies a paying out of money from a fund, but it may also imply distribution, such as to pensioners or heirs, and often stresses an acting under authority ⟨needed a court decree to *disburse* the funds⟩.

spendthrift, **prodigal**, **profligate**, **waster**, **wastrel** mean a person who dissipates resources foolishly and wastefully.

Spendthrift stresses lack of prudence in spending and usually implies imbalance between income and outgo ⟨known in college as a real *spendthrift*⟩.

Prodigal suggests such lavish expenditure as can deplete the most abundant resources ⟨a *prodigal* who squandered his parents' hard-earned money⟩.

Profligate may imply the habits of a spendthrift but stresses dissipation of resources and powers and suggests debauchery and dissoluteness more than waste ⟨an aging rock star forced to abandon his life as a *profligate*⟩.

Waster may come close to ***spendthrift*** but carries a stronger implication of worthlessness and often suggests an idle ne'er-do-well ⟨scorned by all as an idle *waster*⟩.

Wastrel stresses disreputable worthlessness and typically applies to one who has profligate and dissolute habits ⟨worked hard to earn a reputation as a bounder and a *wastrel*⟩.

spirit **1.** See COURAGE. **2.** See SOUL.

spite See MALICE.

spleen See MALICE.

splendid, **resplendent**, **gorgeous**, **glorious**, **sublime**, **superb** mean extraordinarily or transcendently impressive.

Splendid implies an outshining of the usual or customary ⟨the royal wedding was a *splendid* occasion⟩. ***antonym:*** unimpressive

Resplendent suggests a glowing or blazing splendor ⟨the church was *resplendent* in its Easter decorations⟩.

Gorgeous implies a rich or showy or elaborate splendor especially in display of color ⟨a *gorgeous* red dress⟩.

Glorious suggests a radiance that heightens beauty or a state of being that is eminently worthy of admiration, renown, or distinction ⟨a *glorious* sunset over the ocean⟩. ***antonym:*** inglorious

Sublime implies an exaltation or elevation almost beyond human comprehension ⟨the *sublime* grandeur of the thunderous falls⟩.

Superb suggests a magnificence, brilliance, grandeur, splendor, or excellence of the highest conceivable degree ⟨a three-star restaurant offering *superb* cuisine⟩.

splenetic See IRASCIBLE.

split See TEAR.

spoil *n* **Spoil**, **pillage**, **plunder**, **booty**, **prize**, **loot** mean something taken from another by force or craft.

Spoil, more commonly ***spoils***, applies to what belongs by right or custom to the victor in war or political contest ⟨a governor who relished doling out the *spoils* of office⟩.

Pillage applies to things taken with more open violence or lawlessness ⟨filled his capital city with the *pillage* of Europe⟩.

Plunder applies to what is taken not only in war but in robbery, banditry, grafting, or swindling ⟨a fortune that was the *plunder* of years of political corruption⟩.

Booty implies plunder that is to be shared among confederates ⟨the thieves planned to divide their *booty* later⟩.

Prize applies to spoils captured on the high seas or in the territorial waters of the enemy ⟨a pirate ship ruthlessly seizing *prizes*⟩.

Loot applies especially to what is taken from victims of a catastrophe ⟨prowlers searched the storm-damaged cottages for *loot*⟩.

spoil *vb* **1.** See DECAY. **2.** See INDULGE.

sponge See PARASITE.

spontaneity See UNCONSTRAINT.

spontaneous, **impulsive**, **instinctive**, **automatic**, **mechanical** mean acting or activated without deliberation.

Spontaneous implies lack of prompting and connotes naturalness ⟨a *spontaneous* burst of applause⟩. ***antonym:*** studied

Impulsive implies acting under stress of emotion or the spirit of the moment, seemingly without thought or volition ⟨*impulsive* acts of violence⟩. ***antonym:*** deliberate

Instinctive stresses spontaneous action involving neither judgment nor will ⟨blinking is an *instinctive* reaction⟩. ***antonym:*** intentional

Automatic implies prompt action engaging neither the mind nor the emotions and connotes a predictable and unvarying response ⟨his denial was *automatic*⟩.

Mechanical stresses the lifeless, often perfunctory character of the response ⟨over the years her style of teaching became *mechanical*⟩.

sporadic See INFREQUENT.

sport See FUN.

sports See ATHLETICS.

spot See PLACE.

sprain See STRAIN.

sprightly See LIVELY.

spring, **arise**, **rise**, **originate**, **derive**, **flow**, **issue**, **emanate**, **proceed**, **stem** mean to come up or out of something into existence.

Spring implies a rapid or sudden emergence ⟨a brilliant idea that had *sprung* out of nowhere⟩.

Arise may convey the fact of coming into existence or notice often with no suggestion of prior state ⟨a vicious rumor *arose*⟩ or may imply causation ⟨mistakes often *arise* from haste⟩.

Rise, sometimes interchangeable with ***arise***, distinctively stresses gradual growth or ascent ⟨as time passed legends about the house *rose*⟩. ***antonym:*** abate

Originate implies a definite source or starting point ⟨the theory did not *originate* with Darwin⟩.

Derive implies a prior existence in another form ⟨their system of justice *derives* from British colonial law⟩.

Flow adds to ***spring*** a suggestion of abundance or ease of inception ⟨the belief that all good *flows* from God⟩.

Issue suggests an emerging from confinement or from a receptacle ⟨shouts of joy *issued* from the team's locker room⟩.

Emanate applies to the passage of something immaterial such as a principle or thought but carries little suggestion of a causal force ⟨serenity *emanated* from her⟩.

Proceed stresses place of origin, derivation, parentage, or logical cause ⟨bitterness that *proceeded* from an unhappy marriage⟩.

Stem implies an originating by dividing or branching off from something as an outgrowth or subordinate development

⟨a whole new industry *stemmed* from the discovery⟩.

springy See ELASTIC.

spry See AGILE.

spur See MOTIVE.

spurn See DECLINE.

squabble See QUARREL.

squalid See DIRTY.

squander See WASTE.

square See AGREE 3.

squat See STOCKY.

squeamish See NICE.

stable See LASTING.

stagger See REEL.

staid See SERIOUS.

stain See STIGMA.

stalwart See STRONG.

stammer, **stutter** mean to speak stumblingly.

Stammer implies a temporary inhibition from fear, embarrassment, or shock ⟨*stammered* his thanks, overcome with embarrassment⟩.

Stutter is likely to suggest a habitual defect characterized by repetition of sounds, but it may apply to a similar manifestation due to a temporary cause ⟨*stutters* when excited⟩ or even, as may *stammer*, to something suggesting the pattern of a stutterer ⟨the engine *stuttered* then came to life⟩.

stand *n* See POSITION 1.

stand *vb* See BEAR.

standard, **criterion**, **gauge**, **yardstick**, **touchstone** mean a means of determining what a thing should be.

Standard applies to any authoritative rule, principle, or measure by which the qualities, worth, or nature of something can be measured ⟨the book is a classic by any *standard*⟩.

Criterion may apply to anything used as a test of quality whether formulated as a rule or principle or not ⟨in art there are no hard-and-fast *criteria*⟩.

Gauge applies to a means of testing a particular dimension such as thickness, depth, or diameter, or a particular quality or aspect ⟨congressional mail is not always an accurate *gauge* of public opinion⟩.

Yardstick is an informal substitute for ***standard*** or ***criterion*** that suggests quantity more often than quality ⟨the movie was a flop by most *yardsticks*⟩.

Touchstone suggests a simple test of the authenticity or value of something intangible ⟨fine service is one *touchstone* of a first-class restaurant⟩.

stare See GAZE.

start See BEGIN.

state *n* **State**, **condition**, **situation**, **status** mean the way in which one manifests existence or the circumstances under which one exists or by which one is given a definite character.

State most often implies the sum of the qualities involved in an existence at a particular time and place ⟨the present *state* of the economy⟩.

Condition more distinctly implies the effect of immediate or temporary influences ⟨was left in a feeble *condition* after his illness⟩.

Situation implies an arrangement of circumstances that makes for a particular resulting condition, such as of embarrassment, advantage, or difficulty ⟨struggled to keep abreast of the changing political *situation*⟩.

Status applies to one's state or condition as determined with some definiteness, especially for legal administrative purposes or by social or economic considerations ⟨improved her *status* within the company⟩.

state *vb* See SAY.

stately See GRAND.

station See PLACE.

stature See QUALITY 2.

status See STATE.

statute See LAW.

staunch See FAITHFUL.

stay **1. Stay**, **remain**, **wait**, **abide**, **tarry**, **linger** mean to continue to be in one place for a noticeable time.

Stay stresses continuance in a place or sometimes a situation and may connote the status of a visitor ⟨*stayed* in the same job for over forty years⟩.

Remain is often used interchangeably with ***stay*** but distinctively means to stay behind or to be left after others have gone ⟨only one *remained* in the building after the alarm was given⟩. ***antonym:*** depart

Wait implies a staying in expectation or in readiness ⟨*wait* for an answer to a letter⟩.

Abide implies a prolonged staying or remaining behind and suggests either settled residence or patient waiting for some outcome ⟨a culture whose influence will long *abide*⟩. ***antonym:*** depart

Tarry suggests a staying or a failing to proceed when it is time to do so ⟨*tarried* too long and missed the train⟩.

Linger, close to ***tarry***, may add an implication of deliberate delaying or unwillingness to depart ⟨*lingered* over a second cup of coffee⟩.

2. See DEFER. **3.** See RESIDE.

steadfast See FAITHFUL.

steady, **even**, **equable** mean not varying throughout a course or extent.

Steady implies regularity and lack of fluctuation or interruption of movement ⟨ran the race at a *steady* pace⟩ or fixity in position ⟨*steady* as a rock⟩. ***antonym:*** unsteady, nervous, jumpy

Even suggests a levelness or lack of variation in quality or character ⟨read the statement in an *even* voice⟩.

Equable implies a lack of extremes or of sudden sharp changes ⟨an *equable* climate⟩. ***antonym:*** variable, changeable

steal, **pilfer**, **filch**, **purloin** mean to take from another without that person's knowledge or permission.

Steal may apply to any surreptitious taking of something either tangible or intangible ⟨*steal* jewels⟩ ⟨*stole* a look at her⟩.

Pilfer implies a repeated stealing by stealth in small amounts ⟨dismissed for *pilfering* from the company⟩.

Filch adds to ***pilfer*** a suggestion of quickness ⟨*filched* an apple when the man looked away⟩.

Purloin stresses a removing or carrying off for one's own use or purposes ⟨had *purloined* a typewriter and other office equipment⟩.

stealthy See SECRET.

steep *adj* **Steep**, **abrupt**, **precipitous**, **sheer** mean having an incline approaching the perpendicular.

Steep implies such sharpness of pitch that ascent or descent is very difficult ⟨a *steep* staircase leading to the attic⟩.

Abrupt implies a sharper pitch and a sudden break in the level ⟨a beach with an *abrupt* drop-off⟩. ***antonym:*** sloping

Precipitous applies to steepness approaching the vertical ⟨the airplane went into a *precipitous* nosedive⟩.

Sheer suggests an unbroken perpendicular expanse ⟨climbers able to ascend *sheer* cliffs⟩.

steep *vb* See SOAK.

steer See GUIDE.

stem See SPRING.

stentorian See LOUD.

stereotyped See TRITE.

sterile, **barren**, **impotent**, **unfruitful**, **infertile** mean lacking the power to produce offspring or bear fruit.

Sterile implies inability to reproduce or to bear literal or figurative fruit through or as if through an organic defect ⟨a *sterile* imagination⟩. ***antonym:*** fertile

Barren, basically applicable to a female or a marriage that does not produce offspring, may imply a lack of normal or expected return or profit ⟨a *barren* victory⟩. ***antonym:*** fecund

Impotent applies to the male and implies inability to copulate or reproduce ⟨an operation that made him temporarily *impotent*⟩.

Unfruitful may replace ***barren*** in any of its applications with the emphasis on not bearing fruit ⟨an *unfruitful* enterprise⟩. ***antonym:*** fruitful, prolific

Infertile is often interchanged with ***sterile*** ⟨an *infertile* egg⟩ but it may imply deficiency rather than absence of fertility ⟨an *infertile* strain of beef cattle⟩. ***antonym:*** fertile

stern See SEVERE.

stick, adhere, cohere, cling, cleave mean to become closely attached.

Stick implies an attachment by affixing or by or as if by being glued together ⟨the gummed label will *stick* when pressed⟩.

Adhere is often interchangeable with ***stick*** but sometimes implies a growing together of parts normally distinct ⟨muscle fibers will *adhere* following surgery⟩.

Cohere suggests a sticking together of parts so that they form a unified mass ⟨eggs will make the mixture *cohere*⟩.

Cling implies an attachment by or as if by hanging on with arms or tendrils ⟨always *cling* to a capsized boat⟩.

Cleave stresses closeness and strength of attachment ⟨barnacles *cleaving* to the hull of a boat⟩. ***antonym:*** part

stiff, rigid, inflexible, tense, wooden mean difficult to bend or enliven.

Stiff may apply to any degree of this condition ⟨muscles will become *stiff* if they are not stretched⟩. ***antonym:*** supple, relaxed

Rigid applies to something so stiff that it cannot be bent without breaking ⟨a *rigid* surfboard⟩. ***antonym:*** elastic

Inflexible stresses lack of suppleness or pliability ⟨for adequate support, rock-climbers wear shoes with *inflexible* soles⟩. ***antonym:*** flexible

Tense suggests a stretching or straining to the point where elasticity or flexibility is lost ⟨*tense* nerves⟩. ***antonym:*** expansive

Wooden suggests the hard inflexibility and dry rigidity of wood and connotes stiffness and lack of life and often clumsy or heavy deadness ⟨moved in a stark *wooden* manner⟩.

stifle See SUFFOCATE.

stigma, brand, blot, stain mean a mark of shame or discredit.

Stigma may imply dishonor or public shame ⟨tried to avoid the *stigma* of bankruptcy⟩ but more often it applies to a negative attitude or judgment attached to something in order to bring discredit or disapproval ⟨the increasing *stigma* attached to smoking in the workplace⟩.

Brand carries stronger implications of disgrace and infamy and may suggest the impossibility of removal or concealment or the resulting social ostracism and public condemnation ⟨bore the *brand* of corruption and deceit⟩.

Blot and ***stain*** imply a blemish that diminishes but does not extinguish the honor of a name or reputation ⟨a *blot* on the family name⟩ ⟨wanted there to be no *stain* on her record⟩.

still, quiet, silent, noiseless mean making no stir or noise.

Still applies to what is motionless and adds the implication of hush or absence of sound ⟨the *still,* dark night⟩. ***antonym:*** stirring, noisy

Quiet, like ***still***, may imply absence of perceptible motion or sound or of both but it is likely to stress absence of excitement or turbulence and connote tranquillity, serenity, or repose ⟨a *quiet* town⟩. ***antonym:*** unquiet

Silent may apply to motion or stir unaccompanied by sound and carries a strong impression of silence ⟨a submarine equipped for *silent* running⟩. ***antonym:*** noisy

Noiseless, also applicable to soundless motion, usually connotes absence of commotion or of sounds of activity or movement ⟨a cat slowly advancing on *noiseless* feet⟩. ***antonym:*** noisy

stimulate See PROVOKE.

stingy, close, niggardly, parsimonious, penurious, miserly mean being unwilling or showing unwillingness to share with others.

Stingy implies a marked lack of generosity ⟨a *stingy* child, not given to sharing⟩. ***antonym:*** generous

Close suggests keeping a tight grip on one's money and possessions ⟨folks who are very *close* when charity calls⟩. ***antonym:*** liberal

Niggardly implies giving or spending the very smallest amount possible ⟨gave his wife a *niggardly* household allowance⟩. ***antonym:*** bountiful

Parsimonious suggests a frugality so extreme as to lead to stinginess ⟨a *parsimonious* attitude with no room for luxuries⟩. ***antonym:*** prodigal

Penurious implies niggardliness that gives an appearance of actual poverty ⟨the *penurious* old woman left behind a fortune⟩.

Miserly suggests penuriousness motivated by obsessive avariciousness and a morbid pleasure in hoarding ⟨a *miserly* man indifferent to the cries of the needy⟩.

stinking See MALODOROUS.

stint See TASK.

stipend See WAGE.

stir *n* **Stir**, **bustle**, **flurry**, **pother**, **fuss**, **ado** mean signs of excitement or hurry accompanying an act, action, or event.

Stir suggests brisk or restless movement or reaction, usually of a crowd ⟨caused a great *stir*⟩. ***antonym:*** tranquillity

Bustle implies a noisy, obtrusive, often self-important activity ⟨the hustle and *bustle* of city life⟩.

Flurry stresses nervous agitation and undue haste ⟨a *flurry* of activity⟩.

Pother implies flurry and fidgety activity and may additionally stress commotion or confusion ⟨the *pother* made by unexpected guests⟩.

Fuss is close to ***pother*** but adds the notion of needless worry or effort ⟨wondered what all the *fuss* was about⟩.

Ado may suggest fussiness or waste of energy ⟨go to work without more *ado*⟩ or it may imply trouble or difficulty to be overcome ⟨there was much *ado* before their affairs were sorted out⟩.

stir *vb* **Stir**, **rouse**, **arouse**, **awaken**, **waken**, **rally** mean to shift from acquiescence or torpor into activity or action.

Stir usually implies an exciting to action or expression of what is latent or dormant by something that agitates or disturbs ⟨news events that *stirred* the public⟩; it may also imply the evocation of deep and agitating but usually pleasant emotion ⟨a sight that *stirred* pity⟩.

Rouse suggests an incitement to vigorous activity and ensuing commotion from a state of rest by startling or frightening ⟨*roused* from sleep by cries of panic⟩.

Arouse often means little more than to start into action with no hint of consequent action ⟨made no effort to *arouse* their fears⟩. ***antonym:*** quiet, calm

Awaken and ***waken*** frequently imply an ending of sleep or connote the stimulating of spiritual or mental powers into activity ⟨*awakened* the conscience of the nation⟩ ⟨gradually *wakening* to love's delights⟩. ***antonym:*** subdue

Rally implies a gathering together of diffused forces that stirs up or rouses from lethargy or inaction to action ⟨*rallied* her strength to overcome the blow⟩.

stocky, **thickset**, **thick**, **chunky**, **stubby**, **squat**, **dumpy** mean being or having a body that is relatively compact in form.

Stocky suggests broad compact sturdiness ⟨a *stocky*, powerful man⟩.

Thickset implies a thick, solid, burly body ⟨a wrestler's *thickset* physique⟩.

Thick is more often used for body parts than of body, build ⟨*thick* legs⟩. ***antonym:*** thin

Chunky applies to a body type that is ample but robust and solid ⟨a *chunky* fullback⟩.

Stubby stresses lack of height or length and real or apparent breadth ⟨*stubby* fingers that seemed incapable of delicate precision⟩.

Squat is likely to suggest an unshapely lack of height ⟨a *squat* little man in rumpled clothes⟩. ***antonym:*** lanky

Dumpy is likely to suggest short, lumpish gracelessness of body ⟨an ill-fitting dress that made her look *dumpy*⟩.

stoic See IMPASSIVE.

stolid See IMPASSIVE.

stoop, **condescend**, **deign** mean to descend from one's level of rank or dignity to do something.

Stoop may imply a descent in dignity or from a higher moral plane to a lower one ⟨how can you *stoop* to such childish name-calling⟩.

Condescend usually implies an assumed superiority and a patronizing stooping by one of high rank or position to interact with social inferiors ⟨a plant manager *condescending* to mingle with the employees⟩. ***antonym:*** presume

Deign suggests a reluctant condescension of someone haughty, arrogant, or contemptuous ⟨scarcely *deigned* to speak with her poor relations⟩.

stop, **cease**, **quit**, **discontinue**, **desist** mean to suspend or cause to suspend activity.

Stop applies to action or progress or to what is operating or progressing and may imply suddenness or definiteness ⟨*stopped* the conversation⟩. ***antonym:*** start

Cease applies to states, conditions, or existence and may imply gradualness and a degree of finality ⟨by nightfall the fighting had *ceased*⟩.

Quit may stress either finality or abruptness in stopping or ceasing ⟨the engine faltered, sputtered, then *quit* altogether⟩.

Discontinue applies to the stopping of an accustomed activity or practice ⟨we have *discontinued* the manufacture of that item⟩. ***antonym:*** continue

Desist implies forbearance or restraint as a motive for stopping or ceasing ⟨*desisted* from further efforts to persuade them⟩. ***antonym:*** persist

stopgap See RESOURCE.

storm See ATTACK *vb*.

story, **narrative**, **tale**, **anecdote**, **yarn** mean a recital of happenings that is less elaborate than a novel.

Story is the most general term, applicable to legendary lore ⟨the *story* of Arthur⟩ or to an oral or written, factual or fictitious, prose or verse account, typically designed to inform or entertain and characteristically dealing with a series of related incidents or events ⟨repeat the *story* of the opera⟩.

Narrative is more likely to imply factual than imaginative content ⟨his journal is the only surviving *narrative* of the expedition⟩.

Tale may suggest a leisurely and loosely organized recital often of legendary or imaginative happenings ⟨*tales* of the Greek heroes⟩.

Anecdote applies to a brief story featuring a small, discrete, and often humorous incident that may illustrate some truth or principle or illuminate some matter ⟨a biography replete with charming *anecdotes*⟩.

Yarn is likely to suggest a rambling and rather dubious tale of exciting adventure, often marvelous or fanciful and without clear-cut outcome ⟨*yarns* spun around the campfire⟩.

stout See STRONG.

straightforward, **forthright**, **aboveboard** mean free from all that is dishonest or secretive.

Straightforward applies to what is consistently direct and free from deviations or evasiveness ⟨a *straightforward* answer⟩. ***antonym:*** devious, indirect

Forthright applies to something that goes straight to the point without swerving or hesitating ⟨a *forthright* approach to the problems on campus⟩. ***antonym:*** furtive

Aboveboard describes an action or

method that is free of all traces of deception or duplicity ⟨a chief executive who managed to be honest and *aboveboard* in all her dealings⟩. ***antonym:*** underhand, underhanded

strain **1.** See STRESS. **2. Strain**, **sprain** mean an injury to a part of the body through overstretching.

Strain, the more general and less technical term, usually suggests overuse, overexercise, overexertion, or overeffort as a cause and implies injury that may vary from slight soreness or stiffness to a disabling damage ⟨slipped and got a bad *strain* in his back⟩.

Sprain regularly implies injury to a joint, usually from a wrenching that stretches and tears its ligaments or enclosing membrane, resulting in swelling, pain, and disablement of the joint ⟨twisted her ankle and suffered a bad *sprain*⟩.

straits See JUNCTURE.

strange, **singular**, **unique**, **peculiar**, **eccentric**, **erratic**, **odd**, **queer**, **quaint**, **outlandish** mean departing or varying from what is ordinary, usual, or to be expected.

Strange stresses unfamiliarity and may apply to the foreign, the unnatural, the unaccountable, or the new ⟨immigrants adjusting to *strange* new customs⟩. ***antonym:*** familiar

Singular suggests individuality or puzzling strangeness ⟨a *singular* feeling of impending disaster⟩.

Unique implies an absence of peers and the fact of being without a known parallel ⟨a career that is *unique* in the annals of science⟩.

Peculiar implies a marked distinctiveness ⟨problems *peculiar* to inner-city areas⟩.

Eccentric suggests a divergence from the usual or normal especially in behavior ⟨the *eccentric* eating habits of young children⟩.

Erratic stresses a capricious and unpredictable wandering or deviating from the normal or expected ⟨disturbed by his friend's *erratic* behavior⟩.

Odd applies to a possibly fantastic departure from the regular or expected ⟨an *odd* sense of humor⟩.

Queer suggests a dubious sometimes sinister oddness ⟨puzzled by the *queer* happenings since her arrival⟩.

Quaint suggests an old-fashioned but pleasant oddness ⟨a *quaint* and remote village in the mountains⟩.

Outlandish applies to what is uncouth, bizarre, or barbaric ⟨islanders having *outlandish* customs and superstitions⟩.

strangle See SUFFOCATE.

stratagem See TRICK.

strategy, **tactics**, **logistics** mean an aspect of military science.

Strategy applies to the art or science of fundamental military planning for the overall effective use of forces in war ⟨sought a *strategy* that would maximize the use of air power⟩.

Tactics applies to the handling of forces in the field or in action and suggests the actual presence of an enemy force ⟨known for their daring *tactics* in battle⟩.

Logistics is the art or science of military supply and transportation, both planning and implementation in all their aspects ⟨wrestled with the *logistics* of the campaign⟩.

stray See WANDER.

stream See POUR.

strength See POWER.

strenuous See VIGOROUS.

stress, **strain**, **pressure**, **tension** mean the action or effect of force exerted upon or within a thing.

Stress and ***strain*** are the most comprehensive terms and apply to a force tending to deform a body ⟨the weight of the snow put *stress* on the roof⟩ ⟨bolts snapping under the tremendous *strain* of the impact⟩.

Pressure commonly applies to a stress characterized by a weighing down upon or a pushing against a surface ⟨normal atmospheric *pressure*⟩.

Tension applies to either of two balancing forces causing or tending to cause elongation of an elastic body or to the stress resulting in the body ⟨tested the *tension* on the tightrope⟩.

strict See RIGID.

strident **1.** See LOUD. **2.** See VOCIFEROUS.

strife See DISCORD.

strike **1. Strike**, **hit**, **smite**, **slap**, **swat**, **punch** mean to come or bring into contact with a sharp blow.

Strike basically may imply the aiming and dealing of a blow with the hand or with a weapon or tool and usually with moderate or heavy force ⟨*strike* a nail with a hammer⟩.

Hit is likely to stress the impact of the blow or the reacting of the target aimed at ⟨*hit* a snake with a stick⟩.

Smite, somewhat rhetorical or bookish, is likely to stress the injuriousness or destructiveness of the contact and to suggest such motivations as hot anger or a desire for vengeance ⟨fell as if *smitten* by a heavy blow⟩.

Slap primarily applies to a striking with the open hand and implies a sharp or stinging blow with or as if with the palm of the hand ⟨waves *slapped* against the boat⟩.

Swat suggests a forceful slapping blow with an instrument such as a flyswatter or a bat ⟨*swat* a baseball out of the ballpark⟩.

Punch implies a quick sharp blow with or as if with the fist ⟨*punch* a man in the nose⟩.

2. See AFFECT.

striking See NOTICEABLE.

stringent See RIGID.

strive See ATTEMPT.

stroll See SAUNTER.

strong, **stout**, **sturdy**, **stalwart**, **tough**, **tenacious** mean showing power to resist or to endure.

Strong may imply power derived from muscular vigor, large size, structural soundness, or intellectual or spiritual resources ⟨a *strong* desire to succeed⟩. ***antonym:*** weak

Stout suggests an ability to endure stress, pain, or hard use without giving way ⟨wear *stout* boots when hiking⟩.

Sturdy implies strength derived from vigorous growth, determination of spirit, or solidity of construction ⟨people of *sturdy* independence⟩. ***antonym:*** decrepit

Stalwart suggests an unshakable dependability and connotes great physical, mental, or spiritual strength ⟨*stalwart* supporters of the environmental movement⟩.

Tough implies great firmness and resiliency ⟨a *tough* political opponent⟩. ***antonym:*** fragile

Tenacious suggests strength in seizing, retaining, clinging to, or holding together ⟨*tenacious* of their right to privacy⟩.

structure, **anatomy**, **framework**, **skeleton** mean the parts of or the arrangement of parts in a whole.

Structure, the most general term, refers to any whole, natural or artificial, material or immaterial, and may be used specifically of the parts or arrangements that give a whole its characteristic form or nature ⟨studied the *structure* of the atom⟩.

Anatomy applies principally to the structure of an organism or any of its parts ⟨the *anatomy* of the heart⟩ but is likely to stress examination of parts and study of their relation to a whole ⟨described the *anatomy* of a political campaign⟩.

Framework is used chiefly with reference to an artificial supporting construction that serves as a prop or guide but is not visible in the finished whole ⟨the *framework* of a sofa⟩.

Skeleton applies to the bony framework

of the animal body ⟨found only the *skeleton* of a mouse⟩ or may imply either a carefully developed and articulated design or a sketchy conception of the whole that serves as a starting point ⟨roughed out the *skeleton* of the novel⟩.

strut, **swagger**, **bristle**, **bridle** mean to assume an air of dignity or importance.

Strut suggests a pompous affectation of dignity, especially in gait or bearing ⟨*strutted* like a peacock⟩.

Swagger implies an ostentatious conviction of one's own superiority, often manifested in insolent gait and overbearing manner ⟨*swaggered* onto the field⟩.

Bristle implies an aggressive manifestation sometimes of anger or of zeal but often of an emotion that causes one to show one's sense of dignity or importance ⟨an accusation that made her *bristle*⟩.

Bridle usually suggests an awareness of a threat to one's dignity or state and a reaction of hostility or resentment ⟨local government leaders who *bridled* against interference⟩.

stubborn See OBSTINATE.

stubby See STOCKY.

study See CONSIDER.

stupendous See MONSTROUS.

stupid, **dull**, **dense**, **crass**, **dumb** mean lacking in or seeming to lack power to absorb ideas or impressions.

Stupid implies a slow-witted or dazed state of mind that may be either congenital or temporary ⟨you're too *stupid* to know what's good for you⟩. ***antonym:*** intelligent

Dull suggests a slow or sluggish mind such as results from disease, depression, or shock ⟨monotonous work that left his mind *dull*⟩. ***antonym:*** clever, bright, sharp

Dense implies a thickheaded imperviousness to ideas or impressions ⟨was too *dense* to take a hint⟩. ***antonym:*** subtle, bright

Crass suggests a grossness of mind precluding discrimination or delicacy ⟨a *crass,* materialistic people⟩. ***antonym:*** brilliant

Dumb applies to an exasperating obtuseness or lack of comprehension ⟨too *dumb* to figure out what's going on⟩.

stupor See LETHARGY.

sturdy See STRONG.

stutter See STAMMER.

style See FASHION.

suave, **urbane**, **diplomatic**, **bland**, **smooth**, **politic** mean pleasantly tactful and well-mannered.

Suave suggests a specific ability to deal with others easily and without friction ⟨a luxury restaurant with an army of *suave* waiters⟩. ***antonym:*** bluff

Urbane implies high cultivation and poise coming from wide social experience ⟨the *urbane* host of a television series⟩. ***antonym:*** rude, clownish, bucolic

Diplomatic stresses an ability to deal with ticklish situations tactfully and effectively ⟨be *diplomatic* in asking them to leave⟩. ***antonym:*** undiplomatic

Bland emphasizes mildness of manner and absence of irritating qualities ⟨a *bland* manner suitable for early morning radio⟩. ***antonym:*** brusque

Smooth suggests often an excessive, deliberately assumed suavity ⟨the *smooth* sales pitch of a car dealer⟩. ***antonym:*** bluff

Politic implies a shrewd as well as tactful and suave handling of people and situations ⟨an ambassador's wife must be *politic* and discreet⟩.

subdue See CONQUER.

subdued See TAME.

subject *n* See CITIZEN.

subject *adj* See LIABLE.

subjugate See CONQUER.

sublime See SPLENDID.

submission See SURRENDER.

submissive See TAME.

submit See YIELD.

subscribe See ASSENT.

subservient, **servile**, **slavish**, **menial**,

obsequious mean showing or characterized by extreme compliance or abject obedience.

Subservient implies the compliant or cringing manner of one conscious of a subordinate position ⟨domestic help was expected to be properly *subservient*⟩. ***antonym:*** domineering, overbearing

Servile suggests lowly status and mean or fawning submissiveness ⟨a political boss and his entourage of *servile* hangers-on⟩. ***antonym:*** authoritative

Slavish suggests abject or debased servility ⟨the *slavish* condition of migrant farm workers⟩. ***antonym:*** independent

Menial stresses humbleness and degradation associated with one who works at an economically or socially inferior occupation ⟨wanted to escape from a life of *menial* jobs⟩.

Obsequious implies fawning or sycophantic compliance and exaggerated deference of manner ⟨waiters who are *obsequious* in the presence of celebrities⟩. ***antonym:*** contumelious

subside See ABATE.

substantiate See CONFIRM.

subterfuge See DECEPTION.

subtle See LOGICAL.

succeed 1. See FOLLOW 1. **2. Succeed, prosper, thrive, flourish** mean to attain or be attaining a desired end.

Succeed implies an antithesis to *fail* and is widely applicable to persons and things ⟨*succeeded* in her third try for public office⟩. ***antonym:*** fail

Prosper carries an implication of continued or long-continuing and usually increasing success ⟨*prosper* in business⟩.

Thrive adds the implication of vigorous growth often because of or in spite of specified conditions ⟨plants that *thrive* in acid soil⟩. ***antonym:*** languish

Flourish implies a state of vigorous growth and expansion without signs of decadence or decay but also without any suggestion of how long this state will be maintained ⟨attitudes that *flourished* in the Middle Ages⟩. ***antonym:*** languish

successive See CONSECUTIVE.

succinct See CONCISE.

succumb See YIELD.

sudden See PRECIPITATE.

suffer 1. See BEAR. **2.** See LET.

sufferance See PERMISSION.

suffering See DISTRESS.

sufficient, enough, adequate, competent mean being what is necessary or desirable.

Sufficient suggests a quantity or scope that closely meets a need ⟨had supplies *sufficient* to last a month⟩. ***antonym:*** insufficient

Enough is less exact and more approximate than **sufficient** ⟨do you have *enough* food?⟩.

Adequate may imply barely meeting a requirement ⟨the room was *adequate,* no more⟩. ***antonym:*** inadequate, unadequate

Competent suggests measuring up to all requirements without question or being adequately adapted to an end ⟨a *competent* income for their way of life⟩.

suffocate, asphyxiate, stifle, smother, choke, strangle mean to interrupt the normal course of breathing.

Suffocate is likely to imply the impossibility of breathing because of the absence of oxygen, the presence of noxious gases, or interference with the passage of air to and from the lungs ⟨*suffocating* under the sand which had fallen upon him⟩.

Asphyxiate is likely to refer to situations involving death through lack of oxygen or presence of toxic gas ⟨several people were *asphyxiated* by chlorine escaping from the wrecked train⟩.

Stifle is appropriately used to refer to situations where breathing is difficult or impossible because of inadequate fresh air ⟨the room's *stifling* atmosphere⟩.

Smother is usable in situations in which the supply of oxygen is or seems inadequate for life and often suggests a deadening pall of smoke, dust, or impurities in the air ⟨*smothered* by a blanket of volcanic ash⟩.

Choke suggests positive interference with breathing, for example by compression, obstruction, or severe inflammation of the throat ⟨*choke* on a bit of apple⟩.

Strangle, similar to ***choke***, more consistently implies a serious or fatal interference ⟨*strangled* to death by the assailant⟩.

suffuse See INFUSE.

suggest, **imply**, **hint**, **intimate**, **insinuate** mean to convey an idea indirectly.

Suggest may stress a putting into the mind by an association of ideas, an awakening of a desire, or an initiating of a train of thought ⟨an actress who can *suggest* a whole character with one gesture⟩. ***antonym:*** express

Imply is close to ***suggest*** but may indicate a more definite or logical relation of the unexpressed idea to the expressed ⟨pronouncements that *imply* he has lost touch with reality⟩. ***antonym:*** express

Hint implies the use of slight or remote suggestion with a minimum of overt statement ⟨*hinted* that she might have a job lined up⟩.

Intimate stresses delicacy of suggestion without connoting any lack of candor ⟨*intimated* that he was ready to pop the question⟩.

Insinuate applies to the conveying of a usually unpleasant idea in a sly underhanded manner ⟨*insinuated* that the neighbors were not what they appeared to be⟩.

suitable See FIT *adj*.

sulky See SULLEN.

sullen, **glum**, **morose**, **surly**, **sulky**, **crabbed**, **saturnine**, **dour**, **gloomy** mean showing a forbidding or disagreeable mood.

Sullen implies a silent ill humor and a refusal to be sociable or cooperative ⟨remained *sullen* throughout the party⟩.

Glum suggests a silent dispiritedness ⟨the whole team was *glum* following the defeat⟩. ***antonym:*** cheerful

Morose adds to ***glum*** an element of bitterness ⟨became *morose* after the death of his wife⟩. ***antonym:*** blithe

Surly implies sullenness, gruffness, and churlishness of speech or manner ⟨a *surly* young man⟩. ***antonym:*** amiable

Sulky suggests childish resentment expressed in peevish sullenness ⟨a period of *sulky* behavior followed every argument⟩.

Crabbed applies to a forbidding, ill-natured harshness of manner ⟨his *crabbed* exterior was only a pose⟩.

Saturnine describes a heavy, forbidding, taciturn gloom or suggests a bitter, sardonic manner ⟨a *saturnine* wit⟩. ***antonym:*** genial, mercurial

Dour suggests a superficially severe, obstinate, and grim bitterness ⟨a disposition to match the landscape, *dour* and unfriendly⟩.

Gloomy implies a depression in mood making for seeming sullenness, dourness, or glumness ⟨bad news that put everyone in a *gloomy* mood⟩. ***antonym:*** cheerful

sum, **amount**, **number**, **aggregate**, **total**, **whole**, **quantity** mean all that is present in a group or mass.

Sum applies to the result of addition of numbers or particulars ⟨thought of his car as more than the *sum* of its parts⟩.

Amount implies the result of combining sums or weights or measures into a whole ⟨the *amount* of cotton raised last year⟩.

Number suggests a countable aggregate of persons or things ⟨a large *number* of apples⟩.

Aggregate implies a counting or considering together of all the distinct individuals or particulars of a group or collection ⟨errors that are individually insignificant but that in their *aggregate* destroy confidence⟩.

Total suggests the completeness or inclusiveness of the result and may stress magnitude in the result ⟨counted a *total* of 328 paying customers⟩.

Whole, close to ***total***, emphasizes unity in what is summed up ⟨wanted the individual elements to create a cohesive *whole*⟩.

Quantity applies to things measured in bulk, even though they can be counted ⟨a *quantity* of carrots⟩ or to anything that is measurable in extent, duration, volume, magnitude, intensity, or value ⟨the *quantity* of work performed⟩.

summary See CONCISE.

summative See CUMULATIVE.

summit, **peak**, **pinnacle**, **climax**, **apex**, **acme**, **culmination** mean the highest point attained or attainable.

Summit implies the topmost level attainable ⟨a singer at the *summit* of his career⟩.

Peak suggests the highest point reached in a course or during a specific length of time ⟨an artist working at the *peak* of her powers⟩.

Pinnacle suggests a dizzying and often insecure height ⟨the *pinnacle* of success⟩.

Climax implies the highest point in an ascending series ⟨the moon landing marked the *climax* of the program⟩.

Apex implies the point where all ascending lines or processes converge and in which everything is concentrated ⟨Dutch culture reached its *apex* in the 17th century⟩. ***antonym:*** nadir

Acme implies a level of quality representing the perfection of a thing ⟨a statue that was once deemed the *acme* of beauty⟩.

Culmination suggests an apex that is the outcome of a growth or development ⟨the bill marked the *culmination* of the civil rights movement⟩.

summon, **call**, **cite**, **convoke**, **convene**, **muster** mean to demand the presence of.

Summon implies the exercise of authority and may imply a mandate, an imperative order, or urgency ⟨*summoned* by the court to appear as a witness⟩.

Call may be used less formally and less emphatically for ***summon*** ⟨the President *called* Congress for a special session⟩.

Cite implies a summoning to court usually to answer a charge ⟨*cited* to answer the charge of drunken driving⟩.

Convoke implies a summons to assemble, especially for deliberative or legislative purposes ⟨*convoked* an assembly of the world's leading scientists⟩.

Convene is somewhat less formal or emphatic than ***convoke*** ⟨*convened* the students in the school auditorium⟩.

Muster suggests a calling up of a number of things that form a group in order that they may be exhibited, displayed, or utilized as a whole for some purpose ⟨*muster* the troops for an inspection⟩.

sumptuous See LUXURIOUS.

sunder See SEPARATE.

superb See SPLENDID.

supercilious See PROUD.

supererogatory, **gratuitous**, **uncalled-for**, **wanton** mean done without need, compulsion, warrant, or provocation.

Supererogatory implies a giving above or beyond what is required by rule and may suggest the adding of something not needed or not wanted ⟨an abrupt man who regarded the usual pleasantries as *supererogatory*⟩.

Gratuitous may apply to a voluntary giving without expectation of return ⟨provided *gratuitous* services⟩ but usually applies to something offensive or unpleasant given or done without provocation ⟨a *gratuitous* insult⟩.

Uncalled-for implies a gratuitous impertinence or logical absurdity ⟨resented her *uncalled-for* advice⟩. ***antonym:*** required

Wanton implies not only a lack of provocation but a malicious, arbitrary, or sportive motive ⟨the *wanton* destruction of property by vandals⟩.

superficial, **shallow**, **cursory**, **uncritical** mean lacking in depth, comprehensiveness, or solidity.

Superficial implies a concern only with obvious or surface aspects or an avoidance of fundamental matters ⟨a *superficial* examination of the wound⟩. ***antonym:*** exhaustive, radical

Shallow is more generally derogatory in implying lack of depth in knowledge, reasoning, emotions, or character ⟨a *shallow* interpretation of the character Hamlet⟩. ***antonym:*** deep

Cursory suggests haste and casualness that lead to a lack of thoroughness or a neglect of details ⟨even a *cursory* reading of the work will reveal that⟩. ***antonym:*** painstaking

Uncritical implies a superficiality or shallowness unbefitting to a critic or sound judge ⟨her *uncritical* acceptance of his excuses⟩. ***antonym:*** critical

supersede See REPLACE.

supervene See FOLLOW 1.

supervision See OVERSIGHT.

supine **1.** See INACTIVE. **2.** See PRONE.

supplant See REPLACE.

supple **1.** See ELASTIC. **2. Supple**, **limber**, **lithe**, **lithesome**, **lissome** mean showing freedom and ease in bodily movements.

Supple stresses flexibility of muscles and joints and perfect coordination, ease, and rapidity in movement ⟨the light *supple* spring of a cat⟩. ***antonym:*** stiff

Limber implies flexibility and ease and quickness in moving but does not stress excellence of coordination or grace ⟨her long *limber* fingers moved over the keyboard⟩.

Lithe suggests a slender supple body and nimble graceful movements ⟨the *lithe* form of a tiger⟩.

Lithesome may suggest a strength and vigor that makes for sure graceful movement ⟨drew back the bow with a single *lithesome* effort⟩.

Lissome may imply a light easy supple grace in bearing or movement ⟨*lissome* as a bird in flight⟩.

supplicate See BEG.

supply See PROVIDE.

support, **uphold**, **advocate**, **back**, **champion** mean to favor actively someone or something that meets opposition.

Support is least explicit about the nature of the assistance given ⟨people who *support* the development of the area⟩. ***antonym:*** buck

Uphold implies extended support given to something attacked ⟨*upheld* the legitimacy of the military action⟩. ***antonym:*** contravene, subvert

Advocate stresses a verbal urging or pleading ⟨*advocated* a return to basics in public school education⟩. ***antonym:*** impugn

Back suggests a supporting by lending assistance to one failing or falling ⟨allies refused to *back* the call for sanctions⟩.

Champion suggests the public defending of those who are unjustly attacked or too weak to advocate their own cause ⟨*championed* the rights of minorities⟩.

suppress **1.** See CRUSH. **2. Suppress**, **repress** mean to hold back more or less forcefully one that seeks an outlet.

Suppress implies a putting down or keeping back completely, typically by the exercise of great or oppressive power or violence ⟨*suppressed* the revolt⟩ ⟨*suppress* an impulse⟩.

Repress implies little more than a checking or restraining and often suggests that the thing restrained may break out anew or in a different way ⟨had difficulty in *repressing* his curiosity⟩.

supremacy, **ascendancy** mean the position of being first, as in rank, power, or influence.

Supremacy implies superiority over all others that is usually perfectly apparent or generally accepted ⟨the *supremacy* of Shakespeare among English dramatists⟩.

Ascendancy sometimes implies supremacy, but its chief idea is either that of emerging domination or of autocratic use of power ⟨struggled to maintain their *ascendancy* over the other teams in the league⟩.

sure, **certain**, **positive**, **cocksure** mean having no doubt or uncertainty.

Sure usually stresses a subjective or intuitive feeling of assurance ⟨felt *sure* that he had forgotten something⟩. ***antonym:*** unsure

Certain may apply to a basing of a conclusion or conviction on definite grounds or indubitable evidence ⟨scientists are now *certain* what caused the explosion⟩. ***antonym:*** uncertain

Positive intensifies sureness or certainty and may imply opinionated conviction or the forceful expression of it ⟨she is *positive* that he is the killer⟩. ***antonym:*** doubtful

Cocksure implies presumptuous or careless positiveness ⟨you're always so *cocksure* about everything⟩. ***antonym:*** dubious, doubtful

surfeit See SATIATE.

surly See SULLEN.

surmise See CONJECTURE.

surmount See CONQUER.

surpass See EXCEED.

surprise 1. Surprise, **waylay**, **ambush** mean to attack unawares.

Surprise in technical military use may imply strategic planning and secrecy in operations intended to catch an enemy unawares ⟨*surprised* an enemy camp⟩, but general use is more likely to suggest a chance catching unawares ⟨police *surprised* a burglar leaving the house⟩.

Waylay commonly implies a lying in wait along a public way, often in concealment ⟨highwaymen who *waylaid* all travelers⟩, but sometimes it merely implies an intercepting and detaining ⟨a teacher *waylaid* by questioning students⟩.

Ambush tends to evoke the image of would-be attackers concealed in a thicket and is often used with reference to guerrilla warfare ⟨he had been *ambushed* by rebel forces⟩ but is equally applicable to other situations where the primary image is pertinent ⟨*ambushed* by joy⟩.

2. Surprise, **astonish**, **astound**, **amaze**, **flabbergast** mean to impress forcibly through unexpectedness.

Surprise stresses the causing of surprise, amazement, or wonder through being unexpected or unanticipated at a particular time or place ⟨*surprised* to find his mother in a bar⟩.

Astonish implies a surprising so great as to seem incredible ⟨the young player *astonished* the chess masters⟩.

Astound stresses a stunning or overwhelming emotional effect resulting from unprecedented or unbelievable but true occurrences ⟨news of the atomic bomb *astounded* everyone⟩.

Amaze suggests an effect of bewilderment, perplexity, or wonder ⟨*amazed* by the immense size of the place⟩.

Flabbergast may suggest a dumbfounding astonishment and bewilderment or dismay ⟨*flabbergasted* by his daughter's precocious comments⟩.

surrender *n* **Surrender**, **submission**, **capitulation** mean the yielding up of one's person, forces, or possessions to another person or power.

Surrender in both military and general use is likely to imply a complete yielding and a dependence on the mercy or humanity of a stronger power ⟨called for the unconditional *surrender* of all enemy forces⟩.

Submission stresses the acknowledgment of the power or authority of another and often suggests loss of independence ⟨hung his head in a gesture of *submission*⟩. ***antonym:*** resistance

Capitulation may stress conditions elaborated between parties to a surrender but is likely to stress completeness or finality of yielding ⟨forced their *capitulation* to her demands⟩.

surrender *vb* See RELINQUISH.

surreptitious See SECRET.

surveillance See OVERSIGHT.

survey *n* See COMPENDIUM.

survey *vb* See SEE 1.

susceptible See LIABLE.

suspend **1.** See DEFER 1. **2.** See EXCLUDE.

suspicion See UNCERTAINTY.

suture See JOINT.

swagger See STRUT.

swarm See TEEM.

swat See STRIKE.

sway *vb* **1.** See AFFECT. **2.** See SWING 2.

sway *n* See POWER 3.

sweep See RANGE.

sweeping See INDISCRIMINATE.

sweet, **engaging**, **winning**, **winsome**, **dulcet** mean distinctly pleasing or charming and free of all that is irritating or distasteful.

Sweet is likely to be a term of mild general approval for what pleases or attracts without stirring deeply ⟨what a *sweet* little cottage⟩ but can sometimes suggest a cloying excess of what is pleasing in moderation ⟨a *sweet,* overpowering aroma⟩. ***antonym:*** sour, bitter

Engaging is likely to stress the power of attracting and often of holding favorable attention ⟨an *engaging* smile⟩. ***antonym:*** loathesome

Winning, otherwise close to ***engaging***, is likely to stress the power of a person to please or delight ⟨a girl with a ready smile and very *winning* ways⟩.

Winsome implies a generally pleasing and engaging quality and often a childlike charm and innocence ⟨had an indefinably *winsome* quality⟩.

Dulcet suggests an appealing and gratifying or soothing quality ⟨the *dulcet* tones of a harp⟩. ***antonym:*** grating

swell See EXPAND.

swerve, **veer**, **deviate**, **depart**, **digress**, **diverge** mean to turn aside from a straight course.

Swerve suggests a usually somewhat abrupt physical, mental, or moral turning ⟨suddenly *swerved* to avoid hitting an animal⟩.

Veer implies a major change in direction often under an outside influence ⟨at that point the road *veers* to the right⟩.

Deviate implies a turning from a customary or prescribed course and often implies irregularity ⟨the witness never *deviated* from her story⟩.

Depart suggests a deviation from a traditional or conventional course or type ⟨a book that *departs* from the usual memoirs of a film star⟩.

Digress applies to a departing from the subject at hand ⟨frequently *digressed* during his lecture⟩.

Diverge may equal ***depart*** but usually suggests a branching of a single path into two or more leading in different directions ⟨after medical school their paths *diverged*⟩. ***antonym:*** converge

swift See FAST.

swindle See CHEAT.

swing **1. Swing**, **wave**, **flourish**, **brandish**, **thrash** mean to wield or cause to move to and fro or up and down.

Swing implies a regular or uniform movement usually to and fro ⟨*swing* the rope back and forth⟩.

Wave usually implies a smooth or continuous motion ⟨a flag *waving* in the breeze⟩.

Flourish suggests a vigorous, ostentatious, or graceful movement of something held in the hand ⟨*flourishing* her racket, she challenged me to a match⟩.

Brandish implies a threatening or menacing motion ⟨*brandishing* his fist, he vowed vengeance⟩.

Thrash suggests a vigorous, abrupt, violent movement ⟨a child *thrashing* about in a tantrum⟩.

2. Swing, **sway**, **oscillate**, **vibrate**, **fluctuate**, **waver**, **undulate** mean to move to and fro, up and down, or back and forth.

Swing implies a movement through an

arc of something attached at one end or one side ⟨the door suddenly *swung* open⟩.

Sway implies a slow swinging or teetering movement ⟨the bridge *swayed* a little and then fell⟩.

Oscillate stresses a usually rapid alternation between extremes of direction ⟨a fan that *oscillates* will cool more effectively⟩.

Vibrate suggests the rapid oscillation of an elastic body under stress or impact ⟨the *vibrating* strings of a piano⟩.

Fluctuate suggests a constant irregular changing of level, intensity, or value ⟨monetary exchange rates *fluctuate* constantly⟩.

Waver stresses an irregular motion suggestive of reeling or tottering ⟨his whole body *wavered* as he crossed the finish line⟩.

Undulate suggests a gentle wavelike motion ⟨an *undulating* sea of grass⟩.

sybaritic See SENSUOUS.

sycophant See PARASITE.

syllabus See COMPENDIUM.

symbol, **emblem**, **attribute** mean a perceptible thing that stands for something unseen or intangible.

Symbol is applicable to an outward sign of something spiritual or immaterial ⟨a king's crown is the *symbol* of his sovereignty and his scepter the *symbol* of his authority⟩.

Emblem may apply to a pictorial device or representation chosen as the symbol of a person, a nation, a royal line, or other institution that has adopted it ⟨the fleur-de-lis is the *emblem* of French royalty⟩.

Attribute, with ***emblem***, may apply to an object that is conventionally represented in art as an accompanying symbol of a character or of a personified abstraction ⟨the blindness that is the *attribute* of Justice⟩.

symmetry, **proportion**, **balance**, **harmony** mean a quality in design that gives aesthetic pleasure and which depends on the proper relating of parts to each other and to the effect of the whole.

Symmetry implies a median line or axis on either side of which the details correspond in size, form, and placement ⟨the *symmetry* of a Greek temple⟩.

Proportion implies a grace or beauty that stems from the measured fitness of every detail and the consequent perfection of the whole ⟨a statue of perfect *proportion*⟩. ***antonym:*** disproportion

Balance is sometimes equivalent to ***symmetry*** but distinctively suggests equality of values and a massing of different things such as light and shade or contrasting colors that offset each other ⟨a painting in which light and dark were in perfect *balance*⟩. ***antonym:*** imbalance

Harmony suggests the pleasing aesthetic impression produced by something that manifests symmetry, proportion, or balance, singly or in combination ⟨achieved *harmony* through the imaginative use of color⟩.

sympathetic See CONSONANT.

sympathy **1.** See ATTRACTION. **2. Sympathy**, **pity**, **compassion**, **ruth**, **empathy** mean a feeling for or a capacity for sharing in the interests or distress of another.

Sympathy is the most general term, ranging in meaning from friendly interest or agreement in taste to emotional identification ⟨felt *sympathy* for his political beliefs⟩.

Pity implies tender or sometimes slightly contemptuous sympathy or sorrow for one in distress ⟨he felt a tender *pity* for her⟩.

Compassion implies tenderness and understanding and a desire to aid or spare ⟨treated the sick with great *compassion*⟩ but can be quite impersonal in its reference ⟨justice tempered with *compassion*⟩.

Ruth is likely to suggest pity or compassion resulting from the softening of a stern or indifferent spirit ⟨an old man ignorant of the healing effects of *ruth*⟩. ***Empathy*** implies a capacity for vicarious feeling, but the feeling need not be one of sorrow nor involve agreement ⟨lacked capacity for *empathy* for the plight of others⟩.

symptom See SIGN 1.
synchronous See CONTEMPORARY.
syndicate See MONOPOLY.
synopsis See ABRIDGMENT.
synthetic See ARTIFICIAL.
system See METHOD.
systematize See ORDER.

T

taciturn See SILENT.

tact, address, poise, savoir faire mean skill and grace in dealing with others.

Tact implies delicate and considerate perception of what is fit or appropriate under given circumstances ⟨use *tact* when inquiring about the divorce⟩. ***antonym:*** awkwardness

Address stresses dexterity and grace in dealing with new and trying situations and may imply success in attaining one's ends ⟨brought off her first dinner party with remarkable *address*⟩. ***antonym:*** maladroitness, gaucherie

Poise may imply both tact and address but stresses self-possession and ease in meeting difficult situations ⟨the *poise* of one who has been officiating all his life⟩.

Savoir faire is likely to stress worldly experience and a sure awareness of what is proper or expedient in various situations ⟨has little of the *savoir faire* expected of a Washington hostess⟩.

tactics See STRATEGY.

taint See CONTAMINATE.

take **1. Take, seize, grasp, clutch, snatch, grab** mean to get hold of by or as if by catching up with the hand.

Take is a general term applicable to any manner of getting something into one's possession or control ⟨*take* some salad from the bowl⟩.

Seize implies a sudden and forcible effort in getting hold of something tangible or in apprehending something fleeting or elusive when intangible ⟨*seized* the crook as he tried to escape⟩.

Grasp stresses a laying hold of so as to have firmly in possession ⟨firmly *grasp* the handle and pull⟩.

Clutch suggests avidity or anxiety in seizing or grasping and may imply failure in taking or holding ⟨frantically *clutching* the bush at the edge of the cliff⟩.

Snatch suggests a more sudden or quick action ⟨*snatched* a doughnut before running out the door⟩ and may carry a connotation of stealth ⟨*snatch* a purse⟩.

Grab implies roughness or rudeness and often implies arrogant or vulgar disregard for the rights of others ⟨roughly *grabbed* her by the arm⟩.

2. See RECEIVE.

tale See STORY.

talent See GIFT.

talisman See FETISH.

talk See SPEAK.

talkative, loquacious, garrulous, voluble mean given to talk or talking.

Talkative may imply a readiness to engage in talk or a disposition to enjoy conversation ⟨not the *talkative* type who would enjoy a party⟩. ***antonym:*** silent

Loquacious suggests fluency and ease in speaking or an undue talkativeness ⟨the corporation needs a spokesperson who is *loquacious* and telegenic⟩.

Garrulous implies prosy, rambling, or tedious loquacity ⟨forced to endure a *garrulous* companion the whole trip⟩. ***antonym:*** taciturn

Voluble suggests a free, easy, and unending loquacity ⟨the Italians are a *voluble* people⟩. ***antonym:*** curt

tall See HIGH.

tally See AGREE 3.

tame, subdued, submissive mean docilely tractable or incapable of asserting one's will.

Tame implies a lack of independence and spirit that permits or results from domination by others ⟨a friendship that rendered her uncharacteristically *tame*⟩. ***antonym:*** fierce, untamed, wild

Subdued generally implies a loss of vehemence, intensity, or force and may suggest the quietness or meekness of one dependent, chastised, or timorous ⟨a meek, *subdued* attitude⟩. ***antonym:*** unsubdued

Submissive implies the state of mind of

one who has yielded his or her will to control by another and who unquestioningly obeys or accepts ⟨*submissive* to authority⟩. ***antonym:*** rebellious

tamper See MEDDLE.

tang See TASTE 1.

tangent See ADJACENT.

tangible See PERCEPTIBLE.

tantalize See WORRY.

tap, **knock**, **rap**, **thump**, **thud** mean to strike or hit audibly.

Tap implies making a light blow usually repeated ⟨*tap* on the window to attract a friend's attention⟩.

Knock implies a firmer blow, sometimes amounting to a pounding or hammering, and a correspondingly louder sound ⟨the messenger *knocked* loudly to awaken us⟩.

Rap suggests a smart vigorous striking on a hard surface that produces a sharp quick sound or series of sounds ⟨the chairman *rapped* for order⟩.

Thump implies a solid pounding or beating that produces a dull booming sound ⟨heard the *thumping* and banging of carpenters working on the floor below⟩.

Thud places more emphasis on the sound and often implies the result of something falling or striking rather than of something being struck ⟨heard the severed tree limbs *thud* as they fell⟩.

tardy, **late**, **behindhand**, **overdue** mean not arriving or doing or occurring at the set, due, or expected time.

Tardy implies a lack of promptness or punctuality or a lateness that results from slowness in progress or, more often, from delay in starting ⟨made excuses for his *tardy* arrival⟩. ***antonym:*** prompt

Late usually stresses a failure to come or take place at the time due because of procrastination, slowness, or interference ⟨he was *late* for work most mornings⟩. ***antonym:*** early, punctual, prompt

Behindhand applies to the situation of persons who have fallen into arrears or whose development, progress, or action is slower than normal ⟨*behindhand* in their mortgage payments⟩.

Overdue may apply to what has become due but not been dealt with ⟨an *overdue* library book⟩ or what has been expected or scheduled but has not arrived ⟨our guests are long *overdue*⟩ or what might logically have occurred or appeared long before ⟨produced *overdue* tax reform⟩. ***antonym:*** early

tarry See STAY.

task, **duty**, **job**, **chore**, **stint**, **assignment** mean a piece of work to be done.

Task implies usually a specific piece of work imposed by a person in authority or by circumstance ⟨performed a variety of *tasks* for the company⟩.

Duty implies an obligation to perform or a responsibility for performance ⟨the *duties* of a lifeguard⟩.

Job applies to a piece of work voluntarily performed or to an assigned bit of menial work and may sometimes suggest difficulty or importance ⟨took on the *job* of turning the company around⟩.

Chore implies a minor routine activity necessary for maintaining a household or farm and may stress the drabness of such activity ⟨every child had a list of *chores* to do⟩.

Stint implies a carefully allotted or measured quantity of assigned work or service ⟨during his *stint* as governor⟩.

Assignment implies a definite limited task assigned by one in authority ⟨your *assignment* did not include interfering with others⟩.

taste **1. Taste**, **flavor**, **savor**, **tang** mean that property of a substance which makes it perceptible to the gustatory sense.

Taste merely indicates the property ⟨the fundamental *tastes* are acid, sweet, bitter, and salt⟩.

Flavor suggests the interaction of the senses of taste and smell ⟨a head cold seems to spoil the *flavor* of most foods⟩.

Savor suggests delicate or pervasive flavor appealing to a sensitive palate ⟨sipping slowly to get the full *savor* of the wine⟩.

Tang implies a sharp penetrating flavor or savor ⟨there was a *tang* of vinegar in the dressing⟩.

2. Taste, **palate**, **relish**, **gusto**, **zest** mean a liking for or enjoyment of something because of the pleasure it gives.

Taste implies a specific liking or interest, whether natural or acquired ⟨had a *taste* for music⟩ or a discerning appreciation based on informed aesthetic judgment ⟨excellent *taste* in wines⟩. ***antonym:*** antipathy

Palate implies a liking based on pleasurable sensation ⟨the discriminating *palate* of a tea taster⟩.

Relish suggests a capacity for keen gratification ⟨seemed to utter the denunciation with great *relish*⟩.

Gusto implies a hearty relish that goes with high spirits and vitality ⟨sang all the old songs with *gusto*⟩.

Zest implies eagerness and avidity in doing, making, encountering, or experiencing ⟨possessed a *zest* for life⟩.

tasty See PALATABLE.

taunt See RIDICULE.

taut See TIGHT.

tawdry See GAUDY.

teach, **instruct**, **educate**, **train**, **discipline**, **school** mean to cause to acquire knowledge or skill.

Teach applies to any manner of imparting information or skill so that others may learn ⟨*taught* them how to ski⟩.

Instruct suggests a methodical or formal teaching ⟨*instruct* the recruits in calisthenics at boot camp⟩.

Educate implies an attempting to bring out and develop latent capabilities ⟨*educate* students so that they are prepared for the future⟩.

Train stresses an instructing and drilling with a specific end in view ⟨*trained* foreign pilots to operate the new aircraft⟩.

Discipline implies a subordinating to a master or a subjection to control ⟨*disciplined* herself to exercise daily⟩.

School implies a training or disciplining especially in what is hard to master or to bear ⟨*schooled* myself not to flinch at the sight of blood⟩.

tear, **rip**, **rend**, **split**, **cleave**, **rive** mean to separate forcibly.

Tear implies a pulling apart by force that leaves jagged edges ⟨*tear* up lettuce for a salad⟩.

Rip implies a pulling apart in one rapid uninterrupted motion often along a seam or joint ⟨*ripped* the jacket along the seams⟩.

Rend, often rhetorical in tone, implies violent or ruthless severing or sundering ⟨an angry mob *rent* his clothes⟩.

Split implies a cutting or breaking apart in a continuous, straight, and usually lengthwise direction or in the direction of grain or layers ⟨*split* logs for firewood⟩.

Cleave implies a forceful splitting or cutting with a blow of an edged weapon or tool ⟨a bolt of lightning *cleaved* the giant oak⟩.

Rive suggests action rougher and more violent than ***split*** or ***cleave*** ⟨a friendship *riven* by jealousy⟩.

tease See WORRY.

tedium, **boredom**, **ennui**, **doldrums** mean a state of dissatisfaction and weariness.

Tedium is likely to suggest dullness and lowness of spirits resulting from irksome inactivity or sameness or monotony of occupation ⟨could scarcely bear the *tedium* of listening to one long lecture after another⟩.

Boredom adds suggestions of listlessness, dreariness, and unrest that accompany an environment or situation or company that fails to stimulate or challenge ⟨seeks distraction from the *boredom* of housework⟩.

Ennui stresses profound dissatisfaction or weariness of spirit and often suggests physical depression as well as boredom

⟨a life of self-indulgence that later left him subject to feelings of *ennui*⟩.

Doldrums applies to a period of depression marked by listlessness, lagging spirits, and despondency ⟨failed to rouse her from the *doldrums*⟩ or implies a dull inactive state ⟨the stock market has been in the *doldrums* lately⟩.

teem, **abound**, **swarm**, **overflow** mean to be plentifully supplied with or rich in.

Teem implies productiveness or fecundity ⟨the rivers *teemed* with fish and the woods with game⟩.

Abound implies plenitude in numbers or amount and usually stresses profusion ⟨the sturdy maples with which the local forests *abound*⟩. ***antonym:*** fail, fall short

Swarm usually stresses motion and thronging, but it may suggest infestation ⟨tenements that *swarmed* with rats and other vermin⟩.

Overflow adds to ***abound*** the notion of glutting or of exceeding something's or someone's capacity to contain or use ⟨*overflowing* with human kindness⟩.

teeter See SHAKE 1.

tell 1. See REVEAL. **2.** See SAY.

telling See VALID.

temerity, **audacity**, **hardihood**, **effrontery**, **nerve**, **cheek**, **gall**, **chutzpah** mean conspicuous or flagrant boldness.

Temerity suggests presumptuous boldness arising from rashness and contempt of danger ⟨had the *temerity* to ask for a favor after that insult⟩. ***antonym:*** caution

Audacity implies a disregard of restraints commonly imposed by convention or prudence ⟨an entrepreneur with *audacity* and vision⟩. ***antonym:*** circumspection

Hardihood suggests firmness of purpose in daring and defiance ⟨no serious scientist has the *hardihood* to claim that⟩. ***antonym:*** cowardice, timidity

Effrontery implies shameless and arrogant disregard of propriety or courtesy ⟨had the *effrontery* to tell me how to do my job⟩.

Nerve, an informal equivalent for ***effrontery***, stresses hardihood ⟨the *nerve* of that guy⟩.

Cheek, also a substitute for ***effrontery***, implies impudent self-assurance ⟨has the *cheek* to bill herself as a singer⟩.

Gall is like ***nerve*** and ***cheek*** but emphasizes insolence ⟨had the *gall* to demand some evidence⟩.

Chutzpah adds to ***nerve*** and ***gall*** the notion of supreme self-confidence ⟨her *chutzpah* got her into the exclusive party⟩.

temper *n* **1.** See DISPOSITION. **2.** See MOOD.

temper *vb* See MODERATE *vb*.

temperament See DISPOSITION.

temperance, **sobriety**, **abstinence**, **abstemiousness**, **continence** mean self-restraint in the gratification of appetites and desires.

Temperance implies habitual moderation and the exercise of discretion in any activity; in reference to the use of intoxicating beverages it implies not moderation but abstention ⟨exercise *temperance* in all activities⟩. ***antonym:*** excess

Sobriety suggests avoidance of excess, often specifically of the excess of drinking that leads to intoxication; it may also connote seriousness and the avoidance of ostentation ⟨a sect noted for its *sobriety* of dress⟩. ***antonym:*** insobriety, drunkenness, excitement

Abstinence implies voluntary deprivation ⟨practiced *abstinence* when it came to dessert⟩. ***antonym:*** self-indulgence

Abstemiousness implies habitual self-restraint, moderation, and frugality, especially in eating or drinking ⟨lived a life of frugality and *abstemiousness*⟩. ***antonym:*** gluttonous

Continence emphasizes self-restraint in regard to impulses and desires ⟨a style of writing marked by *continence* and craft⟩; it finds its typical application in regard to sexual indulgence where it may imply either complete chastity or avoidance of excess ⟨a society that encouraged sexual *continence* in all its members⟩. ***antonym:*** incontinence

temperate **1.** See SOBER. **2.** See MODERATE *adj*.

tempt See LURE.

tenacious See STRONG.

tenacity See COURAGE.

tend, **attend**, **mind**, **watch** mean to take charge of or look after someone or something.

Tend suggests the need for constant or recurring attention ⟨a shepherd *tending* his flock⟩.

Attend is more likely to stress a taking charge and is, therefore, appropriate when a professional service or skilled activity is involved ⟨the doctor who *attended* his mother⟩.

Mind, otherwise close to ***tend***, distinctively suggests a guarding or protecting from injury or harm or failure ⟨a neighbor who *minds* their children after school⟩.

Watch, often close to ***mind***, may imply a more constant or more professional relationship or suggest an actual need to forestall danger ⟨a guard hired to *watch* the store at night⟩.

tendency, **trend**, **drift**, **tenor**, **current** mean movement in a particular direction or with a particular character.

Tendency implies an inclination sometimes amounting to an impelling force ⟨the *tendency* to expand the limits of what is art⟩.

Trend applies to the general direction maintained by a winding or irregular course ⟨the long-term *trend* of the stock market is upward⟩.

Drift may apply to a tendency whose direction or course may be determined by external forces ⟨the *drift* of the population away from large cities⟩, or it may apply to an underlying or obscure trend of meaning or discourse ⟨a racist *drift* runs through all of his works⟩.

Tenor stresses a clearly perceptible direction and a continuous, undeviating course ⟨a suburb seeking to maintain its *tenor* of tranquility⟩.

Current implies a clearly defined but not necessarily unalterable course or direction ⟨an encounter that altered forever the *current* of my life⟩.

tender See OFFER.

tenet See DOCTRINE.

tenor See TENDENCY.

tense **1.** See STIFF. **2.** See TIGHT.

tension See STRESS.

tentative See PROVISIONAL.

tenuous See THIN.

tergiversation See AMBIGUITY.

terminal See LAST.

terminate See CLOSE *vb*.

termination See END.

terminus See END.

terrible See FEARFUL 2.

terrific See FEARFUL 1.

terror See FEAR.

terse See CONCISE.

testy See IRASCIBLE.

thankful See GRATEFUL.

theatrical See DRAMATIC.

theft, **larceny**, **robbery**, **burglary** mean the act or crime of stealing.

Theft implies the taking and removing of another's property without the person's consent and usually by stealth ⟨the *theft* of an idea may hurt far more than the *theft* of money⟩.

Larceny, chiefly in legal use, applies to simple direct theft in which the property of one person is taken into the possession of another ⟨*larceny* is "grand" or "petty" according to the value of the goods taken⟩.

Robbery in strict use implies violence or the threat of violence employed in the taking of another's property ⟨the messenger was attacked and seriously injured in the course of a *robbery*⟩.

Burglary implies a forced and unlawful entering of enclosed premises for the purpose of committing a felony, usually that of larceny or robbery ⟨lived in constant fear of *burglary*⟩.

then See THEREFORE.

theoretical, **speculative**, **academic** mean concerned principally with abstractions and theories.

Theoretical may apply to branches of learning which deal with the inferences drawn from observed facts and the laws and theories which explain these ⟨the discoveries of *theoretical* physics that form the bases for applied physics⟩, but it may often imply a divorce from reality or actuality that gives a distorted view of things or a lack of testing and experience in actual use ⟨considered both the *theoretical* and the practical aspects of the problem⟩. ***antonym:*** applied

Speculative may go beyond ***theoretical*** in stressing a concern with theorizing and often implies a daring use of the imagination in the manipulation of ideas ⟨proposed a startling new theory that was fascinating but highly *speculative*⟩.

Academic in this use is likely to be derogatory and regularly stresses a tendency to concentrate, often overconcentrate, on the abstract to the neglect of reality or practical concerns ⟨a knowledge of human nature that was purely *academic*⟩.

theory See HYPOTHESIS.

therefore, **hence**, **consequently**, **then**, **accordingly** mean as a result or concomitant.

Therefore stresses the logically deduced conclusion that it introduces ⟨it was raining hard and *therefore* we stayed inside⟩.

Hence, though often interchangeable with ***therefore***, is more likely to stress the importance of what precedes ⟨a meal badly overcooked and *hence* inedible⟩.

Consequently tends to suggest good and reasonable grounds or a strong logical possibility ⟨he said he would come; *consequently* we will wait for him⟩.

Then, when used to indicate logical sequence, is employed chiefly in the consequent clause or conclusion in a conditional sentence ⟨if A and B are mutually exclusive possibilities and A is true, *then* B is false⟩.

Accordingly usually indicates logical or causal sequence but connotes naturalness or usualness in the consequence rather than necessity or inevitability ⟨knew where the edges of the driveway were and plowed the snow *accordingly*⟩.

thick **1.** See CLOSE *adj.* **2.** See STOCKY.

thickset See STOCKY.

thin, **slender**, **slim**, **slight**, **tenuous** mean not thick, broad, abundant, or dense.

Thin implies comparatively little extension between surfaces or in diameter ⟨*thin* wire⟩, or it may suggest lack of substance, richness, or abundance ⟨soup that was *thin* and tasteless⟩. ***antonym:*** thick

Slender implies leanness or spareness often with grace and good proportion ⟨the *slender* legs of a Sheraton chair⟩.

Slim applies to a slenderness that suggests fragility or scantiness ⟨a *slim* chance of success⟩. ***antonym:*** chubby

Slight implies smallness as well as thinness ⟨the *slight* build of a professional jockey⟩.

Tenuous implies extreme thinness, sheerness, or lack of substance and firmness ⟨the sword hung by a few *tenuous* threads⟩. ***antonym:*** dense

thing **1.** See AFFAIR. **2. Thing**, **object**, **article** mean something considered as having actual, distinct, and demonstrable existence.

Thing may apply not only to whatever can be known directly through the senses but also to something whose existence may be inferred from its signs and effects; in more restricted use it may refer to an entity existing in space and time as opposed to one existing only in thought ⟨virtue is not a *thing* but an attribute of a *thing*⟩ or to an inanimate entity as opposed to living beings and especially persons ⟨she treasures each *thing* she buys⟩.

Object stresses existence separate from the observer and typically applies to something that is or can be set before one to be viewed, considered, or contemplated ⟨concentrated on the atom as an *object* of study⟩ or that has body and usually substance and shape ⟨stumbled over some unseen *object* in the dark room⟩.

Article is used chiefly of objects that are thought of as members of a group or class ⟨picked up several *articles* of clothing that the boy had dropped⟩.

think **1. Think**, **conceive**, **imagine**, **fancy**, **realize**, **envisage**, **envision** mean to form an idea of something.

Think implies the entrance of an idea into one's mind with or without deliberate consideration or reflection ⟨I just *thought* of a good story⟩.

Conceive suggests the forming and bringing forth and usually developing of an idea, plan, or design ⟨*conceive* of a plan to rescue the hostages⟩.

Imagine stresses a visualization ⟨*imagine* a permanently operating space station⟩.

Fancy suggests an imagining often unrestrained by factual reality but spurred by desires ⟨*fancied* himself a super athlete⟩.

Realize stresses a grasping of the significance of what is vividly conceived or imagined ⟨*realized* the enormity of the task ahead⟩.

Envisage and ***envision*** imply a conceiving or imagining that is especially clear or detailed ⟨*envisaged* a totally computerized operation⟩ ⟨*envisioned* a world free from hunger and want⟩.

2. Think, **cogitate**, **reflect**, **reason**, **speculate**, **deliberate** mean to use one's powers of conception, judgment, or inference.

Think is general and may apply to any mental activity, but used alone it often suggests the attainment of clear ideas or conclusions ⟨a course that really teaches you to *think*⟩.

Cogitate implies a deep or intent thinking ⟨quietly sitting and *cogitating*⟩.

Reflect suggests the unhurried consideration of something called or recalled to the mind ⟨*reflected* on fifty years of married life⟩.

Reason stresses a consecutive logical thinking ⟨*reasoned* that the murderer and victim knew each other⟩.

Speculate implies a reasoning about things that are theoretical or problematic ⟨historians have *speculated* about the fate of the Lost Colony⟩.

Deliberate suggests a slow or careful reasoning and consideration before forming an opinion or idea or reaching a conclusion or decision ⟨the jury *deliberated* for five hours⟩.

3. See KNOW.

thirst See LONG.

though, **although**, **albeit** mean in spite of the fact.

Though can be used to introduce an established fact ⟨*though* we have put men on the moon, we have not stopped wars⟩ or a hypothesis or admission of possibility or probability ⟨they decided to go on, *though* rain seemed likely⟩ and is the usual term to introduce a contrary-to-fact or imaginary condition ⟨*though* they may come, we will never give in⟩.

Although, in most uses interchangeable with ***though***, may introduce an assertion of fact ⟨*although* she ran faster than ever before, she did not win⟩.

Albeit is especially appropriate when the idea of admitting something that seems or suggests a contradiction is to be stressed ⟨a thorough, *albeit* slow, examination⟩.

thought See IDEA.

thoughtful **1. Thoughtful**, **reflective**, **speculative**, **contemplative**, **meditative**, **pensive** mean characterized by or showing the power to engage in thought, especially concentrated thinking.

Thoughtful may imply either the act of thinking in a concentrated manner or the disposition to apply oneself to careful and serious thought about specific problems or questions ⟨demonstrated his *thoughtful* mind⟩. ***antonym:*** thoughtless

Reflective suggests the use of analysis or logical reasoning with a definite aim ⟨a philosopher of *reflective* bent⟩.

Speculative suggests a tendency to think about things so abstract or unknowable that any conclusions are bound to be uncertain; the term often implies theorizing with little consideration of the evidence ⟨theories about the origins of the universe that are as yet *speculative*⟩.

Contemplative implies an attention fixed on the object of thought or a habit of mind ⟨hoped for a calmer, more *contemplative* life in retirement⟩.

Meditative suggests a tendency to ponder or muse over something but without necessarily any purpose other than pleasure ⟨allowed himself the luxury of a few *meditative* minutes every day⟩.

Pensive, not always distinguishable from ***meditative***, may carry suggestions of dreaminess, wistfulness, or melancholy ⟨a rainy day conducive to *pensive* reflection⟩.

2. Thoughtful, **considerate**, **attentive** mean mindful of others.

Thoughtful usually implies unselfish concern for others and a capacity for anticipating another's needs or wants ⟨the thank-you note was a *thoughtful* gesture⟩. ***antonym:*** thoughtless, unthoughtful

Considerate stresses concern for the feelings or distresses of others ⟨a manner both courtly and *considerate*⟩. ***antonym:*** inconsiderate

Attentive emphasizes continuous thoughtfulness often shown by repeated acts of kindness ⟨a wonderfully *attentive* host⟩. ***antonym:*** inattentive, neglectful

thrash See SWING 1.

threadbare See TRITE.

threaten, **menace** mean to announce or forecast impending danger or evil.

Threaten may imply an attempt to dissuade or influence by promising punishment for failure to obey ⟨*threaten* a child with a spanking if he teases the baby⟩, or it may apply to an impersonal warning of something dire, disastrous, or disturbing ⟨heavy clouds that *threaten* rain⟩.

Menace stresses a definitely hostile or alarming quality in what portends ⟨conditions that *menace* the stability of society⟩.

thrifty See SPARING.

thrill, **electrify**, **enthuse** mean to fill with emotions that stir or excite.

Thrill suggests being pervaded by usually agreeably stimulating emotion that sets one atingle with pleasure, horror, or excitement ⟨a *thrilling* detective story⟩.

Electrify suggests a sudden, violent, startling stimulation comparable to that produced by an electric current ⟨the news *electrified* the community⟩.

Enthuse implies an arousing or experiencing of enthusiasm ⟨was *enthused* about the new vacuum cleaner⟩.

thrive See SUCCEED.

throng See CROWD.

throw, **cast**, **toss**, **fling**, **hurl**, **pitch**, **sling** mean to cause to move swiftly through space by a propulsive movement or a propelling force.

Throw is general and interchangeable with the other terms but may specifically imply a distinctive propelling motion with the arm ⟨*throws* the ball with great accuracy⟩.

Cast usually implies lightness in the thing thrown and sometimes a scattering ⟨*cast* bread crumbs to the birds⟩.

Toss suggests a light or careless or aimless throwing and may imply an upward motion ⟨*tossed* her racket on the bed⟩.

Fling stresses a vigorous throwing with

slight aim or control ⟨*flung* the ring back in his face⟩.

Hurl implies a powerful and forceful driving as in throwing a massive weight ⟨*hurled* the intruder out the window⟩.

Pitch suggests a throwing carefully at a target ⟨*pitch* horseshoes⟩ or lightness and casualness ⟨*pitch* trash in the basket⟩.

Sling suggests propelling with a sweeping or swinging motion, usually with force and suddenness ⟨*slung* the bag over his shoulder⟩.

thrust See PUSH.

thud See TAP.

thump See TAP.

thwart See FRUSTRATE.

tidy See NEAT.

tie, **bind** mean to make fast or secure.

Tie implies the use of a line, such as a rope or chain or strap, to attach one thing that may move to another that is stable ⟨*tie* the boat securely to the dock⟩. ***antonym:*** untie

Bind implies the use of a band or bond to attach two or more things firmly together ⟨used wire to *bind* the gate to the fence post⟩. ***antonym:*** loose, unloose, unbind

tiff See QUARREL.

tight **1. Tight**, **taut**, **tense** mean drawn or stretched to the limit or to the point where there is no looseness or slackness.

Tight implies a drawing together or around something in such a way that there is little or no slack or a binding or constricting results ⟨a *tight* belt⟩ or stresses the idea of squeezing or restraining unmercifully ⟨found themselves in unbearably *tight* quarters⟩. ***antonym:*** loose

Taut suggests the pulling of a rope or fabric to the limit or until there is no give or slack ⟨walked across the *taut* rope to safety⟩ or is likely to stress especially nervous strain ⟨nerves that were *taut* and on edge⟩. ***antonym:*** slack

Tense may be preferred when the tightness or tautness results in or manifests itself in severe physical or mental tension or strain ⟨the crouching cat, *tense* and ready to spring⟩. ***antonym:*** relaxed

2. See DRUNK.

timely See SEASONABLE.

timid, **timorous** mean so fearful and apprehensive as to hesitate or hold back.

Timid stresses lack of courage and daring and implies extreme cautiousness and a fear of venturing into the unfamiliar or the uncertain ⟨a *timid* investor impairing his capital in a vain search for complete security⟩. ***antonym:*** bold

Timorous stresses a usually habitual domination by fears and apprehensions of often imaginary risks that leads one to shrink terrified from any exhibition of independence or self-assertion ⟨a *timorous* personality unsuited to door-to-door selling⟩. ***antonym:*** assured

timorous See TIMID.

tinge See COLOR.

tint See COLOR.

tiny See SMALL.

tipsy See DRUNK.

tire, **weary**, **fatigue**, **exhaust**, **jade**, **fag** mean to make or become unable or unwilling to continue.

Tire implies a draining of one's strength or patience ⟨the long ride *tired* us out⟩.

Weary stresses a tiring until one is unable to endure more ⟨*wearied* of the constant arguing⟩.

Fatigue suggests the causing of great lassitude through excessive strain or undue effort ⟨*fatigued* by the long, hard climb⟩. ***antonym:*** rest

Exhaust implies the complete draining of physical or mental strength by hard exertion ⟨shoveling snow *exhausted* him⟩.

Jade suggests a weariness or fatiguing that deprives one of all freshness and eagerness ⟨*jaded* with the endless round of society parties⟩. ***antonym:*** refresh

Fag implies a drooping with fatigue ⟨arrived home, all *fagged* out by a day's shopping⟩.

tireless See INDEFATIGABLE.
tittle See PARTICLE.
toady *n* See PARASITE.
toady *vb* See FAWN.
toil See WORK 1.
token See SIGN 1.
tolerant See FORBEARING.
tolerate See BEAR.
tool See IMPLEMENT.
toothsome See PALATABLE.
torment See AFFLICT.
torpor See LETHARGY.
torture See AFFLICT.
toss See THROW.
total *adj* See WHOLE.
total *n* See SUM.
totter **1.** See REEL. **2.** See SHAKE 1.
touch **1. Touch**, **feel**, **palpate**, **handle**, **paw** mean to get or produce or affect with a sensation by or as if by bodily contact.

Touch stresses the act and may imply bodily contact or the use of an implement ⟨*touch* paint with a finger to see if it is dry⟩, or it may imply immaterial contact ⟨we were *touched* by his concern⟩.

Feel stresses the sensation induced or experienced ⟨*felt* to see that no bones were broken⟩.

Palpate stresses the feeling of the surface of a body as a means of examining its internal condition ⟨the doctor *palpated* the abdomen and detected a swollen mass⟩.

Handle implies examination or exploration with hands or fingers to determine qualities such as texture, weight, or condition ⟨heavier fabrics can be appreciated better by actually *handling* them, feeling the substance and texture⟩.

Paw is likely to imply clumsy or offensive handling ⟨*pawed* eagerly through the box of prizes⟩.

2. See AFFECT. **3.** See MATCH.
touching See MOVING.
touchstone See STANDARD.
touchy See IRASCIBLE.
tough See STRONG.
toxin See POISON.
toy See TRIFLE.
trace, **vestige**, **track** mean a perceptible sign made by something that has passed.

Trace may suggest any line, mark, or discernible effect left behind ⟨an animal species believed to have vanished without a *trace*⟩.

Vestige applies to a tangible reminder such as a fragment or remnant of what is past and gone ⟨boulders that are *vestiges* of the last ice age⟩.

Track implies a continuous line of marks or footprints or scent that can be followed ⟨the fossilized *tracks* of dinosaurs⟩.

track See TRACE.
tractable See OBEDIENT.
trade See BUSINESS.
traduce See MALIGN.
traffic See BUSINESS.
trail See FOLLOW 2.
train See TEACH.
traipse See WANDER.
traitorous See FAITHLESS.
trammel See HAMPER.
tranquil See CALM.
transcend See EXCEED.
transfigure See TRANSFORM.
transform, **metamorphose**, **transmute**, **convert**, **transmogrify**, **transfigure** mean to change a thing into a different thing or form.

Transform implies a major change in form, nature, or function ⟨*transformed* a small company into a corporate giant⟩.

Metamorphose suggests an abrupt or startling change induced by or as if by magic or a supernatural power or the proceeding of a process of natural development ⟨*metamorphosed* awkward girls into graceful ballerinas⟩.

Transmute implies a fundamental transforming into a higher element or thing ⟨*transmuted* a shopworn tale into a psychological masterpiece⟩.

Convert implies a change fitting something for a new or different use or function ⟨*converted* the boys' room into a guest bedroom⟩.

Transmogrify suggests an extreme, often grotesque or preposterous metamorphosis ⟨the prince was *transmogrified* into a frog⟩.

Transfigure implies a change that exalts or glorifies ⟨ecstasy *transfigured* her face⟩.

transgression See BREACH.

transient, **transitory**, **ephemeral**, **momentary**, **fugitive**, **fleeting**, **evanescent**, **short-lived** mean lasting or staying only a short time.

Transient applies to what is actually short in its duration or stay ⟨a hotel catering primarily to *transient* guests⟩. ***antonym:*** perpetual

Transitory applies to what is by its nature or essence bound to change, pass, or come to an end ⟨fame in the movies is *transitory*⟩. ***antonym:*** everlasting, perpetual

Ephemeral implies brevity of life or duration ⟨much slang is *ephemeral*⟩. ***antonym:*** perpetual

Momentary suggests coming and going quickly, often merely as a brief interruption of a more enduring state or course ⟨my feelings of guilt were only *momentary*⟩. ***antonym:*** agelong

Fugitive implies passing so quickly as to make apprehending difficult ⟨in winter the days are short and sunshine is *fugitive*⟩.

Fleeting is close to ***fugitive*** but stresses the difficulty or impossibility of holding back from flight ⟨a life with only *fleeting* moments of joy⟩. ***antonym:*** lasting

Evanescent suggests momentary existence, a quick vanishing, and an airy or fragile quality ⟨the story has an *evanescent* touch of whimsy that is lost on stage⟩.

Short-lived implies extreme brevity of life or existence, often of what might be expected to last or live longer ⟨*short-lived* satisfaction⟩. ***antonym:*** agelong, long-lived

transitory See TRANSIENT.

translucent See CLEAR 1.

transmogrify See TRANSFORM.

transmute See TRANSFORM.

transparent See CLEAR 1.

transpire See HAPPEN.

transport *n* See ECSTASY.

transport *vb* **1.** See CARRY. **2. Transport**, **ravish**, **enrapture**, **entrance** mean to carry away by strong and usually pleasurable emotion.

Transport implies the fact of being intensely moved by an emotion, as delight or rage, that exceeds ordinary limits and agitates or excites ⟨children *transported* with delight at the thought of Christmas⟩.

Ravish can imply a seizure by emotion and especially by joy or delight ⟨*ravished* by the sight of the tropical sunset⟩.

Enrapture implies a putting into a state of rapture and usually suggests an intense, even ecstatic, delight, often in one of the arts ⟨young girls *enraptured* with the ballet before them⟩, but sometimes it stresses the bemusing aspects of rapture and then suggests a bedazzling or suppressing of the powers of clear thinking ⟨a campaign that failed to *enrapture* the voters⟩.

Entrance usually suggests being held as spellbound as if in a trance by something that awakens an overmastering emotion ⟨a naive ingenuousness that *entranced* them⟩.

3. See BANISH.

transpose See REVERSE.

trap See CATCH.

travail See WORK 1.

traverse See DENY.

travesty See CARICATURE.

treacherous See FAITHLESS.

treasure See APPRECIATE.

treat **1.** See CONFER 1. **2. Treat**, **deal**, **handle** mean to have to do with in a specified manner.

Treat in the sense of doing about, serving, or coping with is usually accompanied by context indicating attitude, temperament, or point of view that determines behavior or manner ⟨*treat* the subject realistically in an essay⟩.

Deal, used with *with*, may suggest a managing, controlling, or authoritative disposing ⟨*dealt* with each problem as it arose⟩.

Handle usually suggests manipulation and a placing, using, directing, or disposing with or as if with the hand ⟨*handle* an ax skillfully⟩.

tremble See SHAKE 1.

tremendous See MONSTROUS.

trenchant See INCISIVE.

trend See TENDENCY.

trepidation See FEAR.

trespass *n* See BREACH.

trespass *vb* **Trespass**, **encroach**, **entrench**, **infringe**, **invade** mean to make inroads upon the property, territory, or rights of another.

Trespass implies an unwarranted, unlawful, or offensive intrusion ⟨warned people about *trespassing* on their land⟩.

Encroach suggests gradual or stealthy intrusion upon another's territory or usurpation of rights or possessions ⟨on guard against laws that *encroach* upon our civil rights⟩.

Entrench suggests establishing and maintaining oneself in a position of advantage or profit at the expense of others ⟨opposed to regulations that *entrench* upon free enterprise⟩.

Infringe implies an encroachment clearly violating a right or prerogative of another ⟨a product that *infringes* upon another's patent⟩.

Invade implies a definite, hostile, and injurious entry into the territory or sphere of another ⟨practices that *invade* our right to privacy⟩.

tribute See ENCOMIUM.

trick *n* **Trick**, **ruse**, **stratagem**, **maneuver**, **gambit**, **ploy**, **artifice**, **wile**, **feint** mean an indirect means to gain an end.

Trick may imply deception, roguishness, illusion, and either an evil or harmless intent ⟨used every *trick* in the book to get the teacher's attention⟩.

Ruse stresses an attempt to mislead by giving a false impression ⟨secured a papal audience through a clever *ruse*⟩.

Stratagem implies a ruse used to entrap, outwit, circumvent, or surprise an opponent or enemy ⟨a series of *stratagems* that convinced both sides he was their agent⟩.

Maneuver suggests adroit and skillful manipulation of persons or things to solve a problem or avoid difficulty ⟨a bold *maneuver* that won him the nomination⟩.

Gambit applies to a trick or tactic used to gain an advantage, often by harassing or embarrassing an opponent ⟨tried a new *gambit* in the peace negotiations⟩.

Ploy may add to ***gambit*** a suggestion of finesse or roguishness ⟨tried a new *ploy* in order to gain entrance⟩.

Artifice implies ingenious contrivance or invention ⟨his fawning smile was just an *artifice*⟩.

Wile suggests an attempt to entrap or deceive with false allurements ⟨used all his *wiles* to win his uncle's favor⟩.

Feint implies a diversion or distraction of attention away from one's real intent ⟨ballcarriers use *feints* to draw defensemen out of position⟩.

trick *vb* See DUPE.

trickery See DECEPTION.

tricky See SLY.

trifle, **toy**, **dally**, **flirt**, **coquet** mean to deal with or act toward someone or something without serious purpose.

Trifle may imply such varied attitudes as playfulness, unconcern, indulgent contempt, or light amorousness ⟨*trifled* with her boyfriend's feelings⟩.

Toy implies an acting without full attention or serious exertion of one's powers ⟨*toying* with the idea of taking a cruise⟩.

Dally suggests an indulging in thoughts

or plans or activity merely as an amusement or pastime ⟨likes to *dally* with the idea of writing a book someday⟩.

Flirt implies a superficiality of interest or attention that soon passes to another object ⟨*flirted* with one college major after another⟩.

Coquet implies an attracting of interest or admiration or a trifling in love without serious intention ⟨brazenly *coquetted* with the husbands of her friends⟩.

trim See NEAT.

trite, **hackneyed**, **stereotyped**, **threadbare**, **shopworn** mean lacking the freshness that evokes attention or interest.

Trite applies to a once effective phrase or idea spoiled by too long familiarity ⟨"you win some, you lose some" is a *trite* expression⟩. ***antonym:*** original, fresh

Hackneyed applies to what has been worn out by overuse as to become dull and meaningless ⟨all of the metaphors and images in the poem are *hackneyed*⟩. ***antonym:*** unhackneyed

Stereotyped implies falling invariably into the same imitative pattern or form ⟨views of American Indians that are *stereotyped* and out-of-date⟩. ***antonym:*** changeful

Threadbare applies to what has been used or exploited until its possibilities of interest have been totally exhausted ⟨a mystery novel with a *threadbare* plot⟩.

Shopworn suggests a loss from constant use of qualities that appeal or arouse interest ⟨used phrases too *shopworn* to generate any interest or convey any praise⟩.

triumph See VICTORY.

trouble *n* See EFFORT.

trouble *vb* **Trouble**, **distress**, **ail** mean to cause to be uneasy or upset.

Trouble suggests a loss of tranquillity and implies a disturbing element that interferes with efficiency, convenience, comfort, health, or peace of mind ⟨*troubled* by sleeplessness⟩.

Distress implies subjection to strain or pressure and resulting tension, pain, worry, or grief ⟨*distressed* by the sight of suffering⟩.

Ail implies that something unspecified has gone wrong and often suggests a will to find the cause with an eye to aid or correction ⟨what *ails* that naughty child?⟩.

truckle See FAWN.

true See REAL.

trust *n* See MONOPOLY.

trust *vb* See RELY.

truth, **veracity**, **verity**, **verisimilitude** mean the quality of keeping close to fact or reality and avoiding distortion or misrepresentation.

Truth may apply to an ideal abstraction that conforms to a universal or generalized reality or quality of statements, acts, or feelings that adhere to reality and avoid error or falsehood ⟨swore to the *truth* of the statement he had made⟩. ***antonym:*** untruth, lie, falsehood

Veracity implies rigid and unfailing adherence to, observance of, or respect for truth ⟨a politician not known for his *veracity*⟩. ***antonym:*** unveracity

Verity designates the quality of a state or thing that is exactly what is purports to be or accords completely with the facts ⟨test the *verity* of his remarks⟩ or refers to things felt to be of lasting, ultimate, or transcendent truth ⟨a teacher still believing in the old *verities* of school pride and loyalty⟩.

Verisimilitude implies the quality of an artistic or literary representation that causes one to accept it as true to life or to human experience ⟨a novel about contemporary marriage that was praised for its *verisimilitude*⟩.

try 1. See AFFLICT. **2.** See ATTEMPT.

tug See PULL.

tumescent See INFLATED.

tumid See INFLATED.

tumor, **neoplasm**, **malignancy**, **cancer** mean an abnormal growth or mass of tissue.

Tumor is applicable to any such growth on or in the body of a person, animal, or plant and to various other enlargements ⟨removed a benign *tumor* from his skull⟩.

Neoplasm is likely to replace ***tumor***, especially in technical use, when reference is to a more or less unrestrained growth of cells without evident function or to a mass formed by such growth ⟨identified the growth as a *neoplasm*⟩.

Malignancy applies to a neoplasm that because of unrestrained proliferation and tendency to invade tissues constitutes a menace to life ⟨X rays revealed a *malignancy* in the lung⟩.

Cancer is the usual popular and technical term for a malignant neoplasm ⟨kept her worries about the *cancer* to herself⟩.

tumult See COMMOTION.

tune See MELODY.

turgid See INFLATED.

turmoil See COMMOTION.

turn **1.** See CURVE. **2.** See RESORT.

twist See CURVE.

twit See RIDICULE.

twitch See JERK.

type, kind, sort, nature, ilk, description, character mean a number of individuals thought of as a group because of a common quality or qualities.

Type may suggest strong and clearly marked similarity throughout the items included so that the distinctiveness of the group is obvious ⟨one of three basic body *types*⟩.

Kind may be indefinite and involve any criterion of classification whatever ⟨that *kind* of ice cream⟩ or may suggest natural or intrinsic criteria ⟨a zoo with animals of every *kind*⟩.

Sort, often close to ***kind***, may suggest a note of disparagement ⟨the *sort* of newspaper dealing in sensational stories⟩.

Nature may imply inherent, essential resemblance rather than obvious or superficial likenesses ⟨two problems of a similar *nature*⟩.

Ilk may suggest grouping on the basis of status, attitude, or temperament ⟨cynics of that *ilk*⟩.

Description implies a group marked by agreement in all details of a type as described or defined ⟨not all individuals of that *description* are truly psychotic⟩.

Character stresses the distinguishing or individualizing criteria that mark the group ⟨a society with little of the *character* of an advanced culture⟩.

typical See REGULAR.

tyrannical See ABSOLUTE.

tyro See AMATEUR.

U

ubiquitous See OMNIPRESENT.

ugly, **hideous**, **ill-favored**, **unsightly** mean neither pleasing nor beautiful, especially to the eye.

Ugly may apply not only to what is not pleasing to the eye but to what offends another sense or gives rise to repulsion, dread, or moral distaste in the mind ⟨a street of small drab *ugly* houses⟩. ***antonym:*** beautiful

Hideous stresses personal reaction and the horror of loathing induced by something felt as outwardly or inwardly extremely ugly ⟨a hurricane that caused *hideous* destruction⟩. ***antonym:*** lovely

Ill-favored applies especially to personal appearance and implies ugliness to the sense of sight without in itself suggesting a resulting distaste or dread ⟨self-conscious about his *ill-favored* features⟩. ***antonym:*** well-favored, fair

Unsightly is likely to refer to a material thing on which the eye dwells with no pleasure and connotes a suggestion of distaste ⟨a dump that sat as an *unsightly* blot on the landscape⟩. ***antonym:*** sightly

ultimate See LAST.

umbrage See OFFENSE.

unafraid See BRAVE.

unbecoming See INDECOROUS.

unbelief, **disbelief**, **incredulity** mean the attitude or state of mind of one who does not believe.

Unbelief stresses absence of belief especially in respect to something above or beyond one's experience or capacity ⟨received news of the disaster with an attitude of *unbelief*⟩. ***antonym:*** belief

Disbelief implies a positive rejection of something stated or advanced ⟨regarded his explanation with *disbelief*⟩. ***antonym:*** belief

Incredulity suggests a disposition to refuse belief or acceptance ⟨greeted her announcement with *incredulity*⟩. ***antonym:*** credulity

unbiased See FAIR.

uncalled-for See SUPEREROGATORY.

uncanny See WEIRD.

uncertainty, **doubt**, **dubiety**, **skepticism**, **suspicion**, **mistrust** mean lack of sureness about someone or something.

Uncertainty stresses lack of certitude that may range from a mere falling short of certainty to an almost complete lack of definite knowledge especially about an outcome or result ⟨general *uncertainty* about the program's future⟩. ***antonym:*** certainty

Doubt suggests both uncertainty and inability to make a decision ⟨plagued by *doubts* about his upcoming marriage⟩. ***antonym:*** certitude, confidence

Dubiety stresses a lack of sureness that leads to a wavering between conclusions ⟨in times of crisis a leader must be free of all *dubiety*⟩. ***antonym:*** decision

Skepticism implies a habitual state of mind or customary reaction characterized by unwillingness to believe without conclusive evidence ⟨an economic forecast that was met with *skepticism*⟩. ***antonym:*** gullibility

Suspicion stresses lack of faith in the truth, reality, fairness, or reliability of something or someone ⟨viewed the new neighbors with *suspicion*⟩.

Mistrust implies a genuine doubt based upon suspicion ⟨had a great *mistrust* of all doctors⟩. ***antonym:*** assurance, trust

uncommon See INFREQUENT.

unconcerned See INDIFFERENT.

unconstraint, **abandon**, **spontaneity** mean a free and uninhibited expression of thoughts or feelings or a mood or style marked by this.

Unconstraint expresses the fact of freely yielding to impulse and can replace either of the other terms though it is less positive in implication ⟨lived a life of complete *unconstraint*⟩. ***antonym:*** constraint

Abandon may add an implication of loss of self-control ⟨weep with *abandon*⟩ or of the absence or impotence of any check on full, free, or natural expression of feeling ⟨ate with *abandon* the whole time we were on vacation⟩. ***antonym:*** self-restraint

Spontaneity suggests an unstudied naturalness and may connote freshness, lack of deliberation, or obedience to the impulse of the moment ⟨a welcome full of warm *spontaneity*⟩.

uncouth See RUDE.
uncritical See SUPERFICIAL.
unctuous See FULSOME.
underhanded See SECRET.
undermine See WEAKEN.
understand, **comprehend**, **appreciate** mean to have a clear or complete idea of.

Understand may stress the fact of having attained a mental grasp of something ⟨*understood* the instructions⟩.

Comprehend stresses the mental process of arriving at a result ⟨failed to *comprehend* the entire process⟩.

Appreciate implies a just estimation of a thing's value and is often used in reference to what is likely to be misjudged ⟨failed to *appreciate* the risks involved⟩.

understanding See REASON.
undulate See SWING.
unearth See DISCOVER.
unerring See INFALLIBLE.
uneven See ROUGH.
unfeigned See SINCERE.
unflagging See INDEFATIGABLE.
unfruitful See STERILE.
ungovernable See UNRULY.
uniform See SIMILAR.
unimpassioned See SOBER.
union See UNITY.
unique **1.** See SINGLE. **2.** See STRANGE.
unite See JOIN.
unity, **solidarity**, **integrity**, **union** mean a combining of parts or elements or individuals into an effective whole or the quality of a whole made up of closely associated parts.

Unity implies oneness especially of what is varied and diverse in its elements or parts ⟨a multiplicity of styles effectively combined into a *unity* of architectural design⟩.

Solidarity implies a unity in a group or class that enables it to manifest its strength and exert its influence as one ⟨an ethnic minority with a strong sense of *solidarity*⟩.

Integrity implies unity that indicates exactitude of association and interdependence of the parts and completeness and perfection of the whole ⟨a farcical scene that destroys the play's *integrity*⟩.

Union implies a thorough integration and harmonious cooperation of the parts or the body or organization that results from such a uniting ⟨the *union* of thirteen diverse colonies to form one nation⟩.

universal, **general**, **generic** mean characteristic of, relating to, comprehending, or affecting all or the whole.

Universal implies reference to every one without exception in the class, category, or genus considered ⟨declared *universal* amnesty⟩. ***antonym:*** particular

General implies reference to all or nearly all ⟨the theory has met *general* acceptance⟩ or, in reference to such things as words, language, ideas, or notions, suggests lack of precision ⟨got the *general* idea⟩.

Generic implies reference to every member of a genus and is applicable especially to items such as qualities, characteristics, or likenesses that serve as identifying guides ⟨*generic* likenesses among all dogs⟩. ***antonym:*** specific

unlawful, **illegal**, **illegitimate**, **illicit** mean not being in accordance with law.

Unlawful implies lack of conformity with law of any sort ⟨*unlawful* conduct⟩. ***antonym:*** lawful

Illegal often stresses lack of conformity to what is sanctioned by the law as defined by statute and administered by courts ⟨an *illegal* U-turn⟩. ***antonym:*** legal

Illegitimate tends to be narrow in reference and usually applies to children born out of wedlock or to a relation leading to such a result ⟨their union was *illegitimate*⟩, but it may refer to something that is not proper according to rules of logic or to authorities or to precedent ⟨an *illegitimate* inference⟩. ***antonym:*** legitimate

Illicit may imply lack of conformance with a regulatory law ⟨*illicit* distilling⟩, but it is also applied to something obtained, done, or maintained unlawfully, illegally, or illegitimately ⟨an *illicit* affair⟩. ***antonym:*** licit

unlearned See IGNORANT.

unlettered See IGNORANT.

unman See UNNERVE.

unmindful See FORGETFUL.

unmitigated See OUTRIGHT.

unmoral See IMMORAL.

unnatural See IRREGULAR.

unnerve, **enervate**, **unman**, **emasculate** mean to deprive of strength or vigor and the capacity for effective action.

Unnerve implies a marked often temporary loss of courage, self-control, or power to act ⟨*unnerved* by the near midair collision⟩.

Enervate suggests a gradual physical or moral weakening through such debilitating influences as climate, disease, luxury, or indolence until one is too feeble to make an effort ⟨totally *enervated* after a week's vacation⟩. ***antonym:*** harden, inure

Unman implies a loss of manly vigor, fortitude, or spirit ⟨the sight of blood usually *unmanned* him⟩.

Emasculate stresses a depriving of characteristic force by removing something essential ⟨an amendment that *emasculates* existing gun-control laws⟩.

unpremeditated See EXTEMPORANEOUS.

unpretentious See PLAIN.

unreasonable See IRRATIONAL.

unruffled See COOL.

unruly, **ungovernable**, **intractable**, **refractory**, **recalcitrant**, **willful**, **headstrong** mean not submissive to government or control.

Unruly implies unwillingness to submit to discipline or incapacity for discipline and often connotes waywardness or turbulence of disposition ⟨*unruly* children⟩. ***antonym:*** tractable, docile

Ungovernable implies either incapacity for or escape from control or guidance by oneself or others or a state of being unsubdued ⟨*ungovernable* rage⟩. ***antonym:*** governable, docile

Intractable suggests stubborn resistance to guidance or control ⟨the farmers were *intractable* in their opposition to the hazardous-waste dump⟩. ***antonym:*** tractable

Refractory stresses resistance to attempts to manage or to mold ⟨special schools for *refractory* children⟩. ***antonym:*** malleable, amenable

Recalcitrant suggests determined resistance to or rebellious and deliberate defiance of the will or authority of another ⟨acts of sabotage by a *recalcitrant* populace⟩. ***antonym:*** amenable

Willful implies an obstinate and often capricious determination to have one's own way ⟨a *willful* disregard for the rights of others⟩. ***antonym:*** biddable

Headstrong suggests self-will that is impatient of restraint, advice, or suggestion ⟨a *headstrong* young army officer bent on engaging the enemy⟩.

unseemly See INDECOROUS.

unsightly See UGLY.

unsocial, **asocial**, **antisocial**, **nonsocial** mean not social and therefore opposed to what is social.

Unsocial implies a distaste for the society of others or an aversion to close association and interaction with others ⟨a very *unsocial* temperament⟩. ***antonym:*** social

Asocial applies more often to behavior,

thoughts, or acts viewed objectively and implies a lack of all the qualities conveyed by the word *social*, and rather stresses a self-centered, individualistic, egocentric orientation ⟨dreaming is an *asocial* act⟩. ***antonym:*** social

Antisocial applies to things such as acts, ideas, or movements that are felt as harmful to or destructive of society or the social order or institutions ⟨tried to discourage *antisocial* behavior among her students⟩. ***antonym:*** social

Nonsocial applies to what cannot be described as *social* in any relevant sense ⟨*nonsocial* bees⟩.

unsophisticated See NATURAL.

unstable See INCONSTANT.

untangle See EXTRICATE.

untiring See INDEFATIGABLE.

untruthful See DISHONEST.

untutored See IGNORANT.

unwearied See INDEFATIGABLE.

upbraid See SCOLD.

upheaval See COMMOTION.

uphold See SUPPORT.

upright, **honest**, **just**, **conscientious**, **scrupulous**, **honorable** mean having or showing a strict regard for what is morally right.

Upright implies a strict adherence to moral principles ⟨ministers of the church must be *upright* and unimpeachable⟩.

Honest stresses recognition of and adherence to such virtues as truthfulness, candor, and fairness ⟨doctors must be *honest* with the terminally ill⟩. ***antonym:*** dishonest

Just stresses a conscious choice and regular practice of what is right or equitable ⟨a reputation for being entirely *just* in business dealings⟩.

Conscientious implies an active moral sense governing all one's actions and stresses painstaking efforts to follow one's conscience ⟨*conscientious* in doing all of her chores⟩. ***antonym:*** unconscientious, conscienceless

Scrupulous, like ***conscientious***, connotes the action of a moral sense in all one's doings, but distinctively it stresses meticulous attention to details of morality or conduct ⟨*scrupulous* in carrying out the terms of the will⟩. ***antonym:*** unscrupulous

Honorable suggests a firm holding to codes of right behavior and the guidance of a high sense of honor and duty ⟨the *honorable* thing would be to resign my position⟩. ***antonym:*** dishonorable

uprising See REBELLION.

uproar See DIN.

uproot See EXTERMINATE.

upset See DISCOMPOSE.

urbane See SUAVE.

usage See HABIT.

use *n* **1. Use**, **usefulness**, **utility** mean a capacity for serving an end or purpose.

Use implies little more than suitability for employment for some purpose specified or implied ⟨she hated to throw away anything that might have some *use*⟩.

Usefulness is employed chiefly with reference to definite concrete things that serve or are capable of serving a practical purpose ⟨demonstrated the *usefulness* of the gadget⟩. ***antonym:*** uselessness

Utility may differ from ***usefulness***, especially in technical use, by implying a measurable property or one that can be viewed as an abstraction ⟨a college major of no immediate *utility*⟩.

2. See HABIT.

use *vb* **Use**, **employ**, **utilize**, **apply** mean to put into service especially to attain an end or to give a practical value.

Use implies availing oneself of something as a means or instrument to an end ⟨willing to *use* any means to achieve her goals⟩.

Employ suggests the using of a person or thing that is available but idle, inactive, or disengaged by putting him, her, or it to some work or profitable activity ⟨your time might have been better *employed* by reading⟩.

Utilize may suggest the discovery of a new, profitable, or practical use for something that might be overlooked or wasted ⟨meat processors *utilize* every part of the animal⟩.

Apply stresses the bringing of one thing into contact or relation with something else in such a way that it proves useful or acquires practical value ⟨*applied* specific rules to the situation⟩.

usefulness See USE.

usual, **customary**, **habitual**, **wonted**, **accustomed** mean familiar through frequent or regular repetition.

Usual stresses the absence of strangeness or unexpectedness and is applicable to whatever is normal ⟨my *usual* order for lunch⟩. ***antonym:*** unusual

Customary applies to what accords with the practices, conventions, or usages of an individual or community ⟨a *customary* waiting period before remarrying⟩. ***antonym:*** occasional

Habitual suggests a practice settled or established by much repetition ⟨an *habitual* exercise regime that served her well⟩. ***antonym:*** occasional

Wonted stresses habituation but usually applies to what is favored, sought, or purposefully cultivated ⟨his *wonted* pleasures had lost their appeal⟩. ***antonym:*** unwonted

Accustomed is less emphatic than ***wonted*** or ***habitual*** in suggesting fixed habit or invariable custom ⟨accepted the compliment with her *accustomed* modesty⟩. ***antonym:*** unaccustomed

usurp See APPROPRIATE.

utensil See IMPLEMENT.

utility See USE *n.*

utilize See USE *vb.*

utter **1.** See EXPRESS. **2.** See SAY.

V

vacant See EMPTY.
vacillate See HESITATE.
vacuous See EMPTY.
vagary See CAPRICE.
vague See OBSCURE.
vain **1. Vain, nugatory, otiose, idle, empty, hollow** mean being without worth or significance.

Vain implies either absolute or relative absence of value or worth ⟨it is *vain* to think that we can alter destiny⟩.

Nugatory suggests triviality or insignificance ⟨a monarch with *nugatory* powers⟩.

Otiose suggests that something serves no purpose and is either an encumbrance or a superfluity ⟨not a single scene in the film is *otiose*⟩.

Idle suggests a lack of capacity for worthwhile use or effect ⟨it is *idle* to speculate on what might have been⟩.

Empty and ***hollow*** suggest a deceiving lack of real substance, soundness, genuineness, or value ⟨an *empty* attempt at reconciliation⟩ ⟨a *hollow* victory that benefited no one⟩.

2. See FUTILE.

vainglory See PRIDE *n.*
valiant See BRAVE.
valid, sound, cogent, convincing, telling mean having such force as to compel serious attention and usually acceptance.

Valid implies being supported by objective truth or generally accepted authority ⟨absences will be excused for *valid* reasons⟩. ***antonym:*** invalid, fallacious, sophistic

Sound implies a basis of flawless reasoning or solid grounds ⟨a *sound* proposal for combating terrorism⟩. ***antonym:*** unsound, fallacious

Cogent may stress either weight of sound argument and evidence or lucidity of presentation ⟨the prosecutor's *cogent* summation won over the jury⟩.

Convincing suggests a power to overcome doubt, opposition, or reluctance to accept ⟨a documentary that makes a *convincing* case for court reform⟩.

Telling stresses an immediate and crucial effect striking at the heart of a matter and may or may not imply soundness and validity ⟨a *telling* example of the bureaucratic mentality⟩.

validate See CONFIRM.
valor See HEROISM.
valorous See BRAVE.
valuable See COSTLY.
value **1.** See APPRECIATE. **2.** See ESTIMATE.
vanity See PRIDE *n.*
vanquish See CONQUER.
vapid See INSIPID.
variance See DISCORD.
various See DIFFERENT.
vary See CHANGE.
vast See ENORMOUS.
vaunt See BOAST.
veer See SWERVE.
vein See MOOD.
venerable See OLD.
venerate See REVERE.
vengeful See VINDICTIVE.
venial, pardonable mean not warranting punishment or the imposition of a penalty.

Venial usually implies an opposition to *grave*, *serious*, or *grievous* ⟨*venial* acts as opposed to truly criminal ones⟩ or, in theological use, to *mortal*, and consequently it applies to what is trivial, harmless, or unwitting ⟨mistakes that were *venial* and easily overlooked⟩. ***antonym:*** heinous, mortal

Pardonable implies that there is excuse of justification that makes the fault or error unworthy of consideration ⟨spoke with *pardonable* pride of his daughter's success⟩. ***antonym:*** unpardonable

venom See POISON.

vent See EXPRESS.
venturesome See ADVENTUROUS.
veracity See TRUTH.
verbal See ORAL.
verbose See WORDY.
verge See BORDER.
verify See CONFIRM.
verisimilitude See TRUTH.
veritable See AUTHENTIC.
verity See TRUTH.
vernacular See DIALECT.
versatile, **many-sided**, **all-around** mean marked by or showing skill or ability or capacity or usefulness of many kinds.

Versatile, applied to persons, stresses variety of aptitude and facility that allows one to turn from one activity to another without loss of effectiveness or skill ⟨a skilled and *versatile* performer⟩; applied to things, it stresses their multiple and diverse qualities, uses, or possibilities ⟨needed a vehicle that was *versatile* and reliable⟩.

Many-sided, applied to persons, stresses breadth or diversity of interests or accomplishments ⟨a *many-sided* scholar, critically aware of yesterday, today, and tomorrow⟩; applied to things, it stresses diversity of aspects, attributes, or uses ⟨a *many-sided* public-policy debate⟩.

All-around implies completeness or symmetry of development and connotes general competence more often than special or outstanding ability ⟨an *all-around* athlete and sportsman⟩.

vertical, **perpendicular**, **plumb** mean being at right angles to a baseline.

Vertical suggests a line or direction rising straight upward toward a zenith ⟨the side of the cliff is almost *vertical*⟩. ***antonym:*** horizontal

Perpendicular may stress the straightness of a line making a right angle with any other line, not necessarily a horizontal one ⟨the parallel bars are *perpendicular* to the support posts⟩.

Plumb stresses an exact verticality determined by the earth's gravity (as with a plumb line) ⟨make sure that the wall is *plumb*⟩.

very See SAME.
vessel See BOAT.
vestige See TRACE.
vex See ANNOY.
vibrate See SWING 2.
vice **1.** See FAULT. **2.** See OFFENSE 2.
vicious, **villainous**, **iniquitous**, **nefarious**, **infamous**, **corrupt**, **degenerate** mean highly reprehensible or offensive in character, nature, or conduct.

Vicious may directly oppose *virtuous* in implying moral depravity, or it may connote malignancy, cruelty, or destructive violence ⟨a *vicious* gangster wanted for murder⟩. ***antonym:*** virtuous

Villainous applies to any evil, depraved, or vile conduct or characteristic ⟨*villainous* behavior that must be punished⟩.

Iniquitous implies absence of all signs of justice or fairness ⟨an *iniquitous* tyrant, ruling by fear and intimidation⟩. ***antonym:*** righteous

Nefarious suggests flagrant breaching of time-honored laws and traditions of conduct ⟨pornography, prostitution, and organized crime's other *nefarious* activities⟩. ***antonym:*** exemplary

Infamous suggests shameful and scandalous wickedness ⟨*infamous* for their crimes⟩. ***antonym:*** illustrious

Corrupt stresses a loss of moral integrity or probity causing betrayal of principle or sworn obligations ⟨city hall was filled with *corrupt* politicians⟩.

Degenerate suggests having sunk from a higher to an especially vicious or enervated condition ⟨a *degenerate* regime propped up by foreign support⟩. ***antonym:*** regenerate

vicissitude See DIFFICULTY.
victim, **prey**, **quarry** mean one killed or injured for the ends of the one who kills or injures.

Victim basically applies to a living being killed as a sacrifice to a divinity, but in more general use it applies to one killed, injured, ruined, or badly treated either by a ruthless person or by an impersonal power that admits of no effective resistance ⟨*victims* of wars and disasters⟩.

Prey basically applies to animals hunted and killed for food by other animals and is often extended to a victim of something suggestive of a rapacious predator ⟨consumers who are easy *prey* for advertisers⟩.

Quarry basically applies to a victim of the chase and in more general use may apply to one pursued intensely as well as to one actually taken by the hunter or pursuer ⟨the private investigator stalked her *quarry* relentlessly⟩.

victory, **conquest**, **triumph** mean a successful outcome in a contest or struggle.

Victory stresses the fact of winning against an opponent or against odds ⟨won an upset *victory* in the election⟩. ***antonym:*** defeat

Conquest stresses the subjugation or mastery of a defeated opponent, be it a personal antagonist or a difficult undertaking ⟨the *conquest* of space⟩.

Triumph suggests a brilliant or decisive victory or an overwhelming conquest and usually connotes the acclaim and personal satisfaction accruing to the winner ⟨crossed the finish line, her arms aloft in *triumph*⟩. ***antonym:*** defeat

vie See RIVAL.

view *n* See OPINION.

view *vb* See SEE 1.

vigilant See WATCHFUL.

vigorous, **energetic**, **strenuous**, **lusty**, **nervous** mean having great vitality and force.

Vigorous further implies showing undepleted or undiminished capacity for activity or freshness or robustness ⟨still *vigorous* and sharp in her seventieth year⟩. ***antonym:*** languorous, lethargic

Energetic suggests a capacity for intense, sometimes bustling or forced, activity ⟨an *energetic* wife, mother, and career woman⟩. ***antonym:*** lethargic

Strenuous suggests what is arduous or challenging and evokes a consistently vigorous response ⟨moved to Alaska in search of the *strenuous* life⟩.

Lusty implies exuberant energy and capacity for enjoyment ⟨a huge meal to satisfy their *lusty* appetites⟩. ***antonym:*** effete

Nervous suggests especially the forcibleness and sustained effectiveness resulting from mental vigor ⟨a *nervous* energy informs his sculptures⟩.

vile See BASE *adj*.

vilify See MALIGN.

villainous See VICIOUS.

vindicate 1. See EXCULPATE. **2.** See MAINTAIN.

vindictive, **revengeful**, **vengeful** mean showing or motivated by a desire for vengeance.

Vindictive tends to stress the reaction as inherent in the nature of the individual and is appropriate when no specific motivating grievance exists ⟨not a *vindictive* bone in his body⟩, but sometimes it implies a persistent emotion, based on real or fancied wrongs, that may manifest itself in implacable malevolence or in mere spiteful malice ⟨a *vindictive* person plotting revenge⟩.

Revengeful and ***vengeful*** are more likely to suggest the state of one specifically provoked to action and truculently ready to seek or take revenge; both terms may also apply to an agent or weapon by which vengeance can be attained ⟨an insult that provoked a *revengeful* spirit in its target⟩ ⟨trained his children to be his *vengeful* agents⟩.

violation See BREACH.

virile See MASCULINE.

virtually, **practically**, **morally** mean not absolutely or actually, yet so nearly so that the difference is negligible.

Virtually may imply a merely apparent difference between outward seeming and inner reality ⟨the prime minister is *virtually* the ruler of his country⟩.

Practically implies a difference between what meets ordinary or practical demands and what qualifies in some formal or absolute way ⟨the road is *practically* finished; cars can use it all the way⟩.

Morally implies a difference between what satisfies one's judgment and what constitutes legal or logical proof ⟨the jurors were *morally* certain of the defendant's guilt but the lack of conclusive evidence demanded a verdict of "not guilty"⟩.

virtuous See MORAL.

virus See POISON.

visage See FACE.

visionary See IMAGINARY.

visit, **visitation**, **call** mean a coming to stay with another temporarily and usually briefly.

Visit applies to any such coming, be it long or short, and whatever its nature or cause or purpose ⟨spent the summer on a *visit* to her English cousins⟩.

Visitation applies chiefly to a formal or official visit made by one in authority often for a special purpose such as inspection or counseling ⟨parochial *visitations* of a bishop⟩.

Call applies to a brief, usually formal visit for social or professional purposes ⟨the salesmen were expected to make at least ten *calls* each day⟩.

visitation See VISIT.

vital **1.** See ESSENTIAL. **2.** See LIVING.

vitalize, **energize**, **activate** mean to arouse to activity, animation, or life.

Vitalize may stress the arousal of something more or less inert or lifeless, often by communicating an impetus or force ⟨took steps to *vitalize* the local economy⟩ or an imparting of significance or interest to something ⟨a set of images that *vitalize* the story⟩. ***antonym:*** atrophy

Energize implies an arousing to activity or a readying for activity by an imparting of strength or a providing with a source of energy ⟨a speech that *energized* the sales force for what lay ahead⟩.

Activate implies a passing from an inactive to an active state and stresses the influence of an external agent in arousing to activity ⟨a switch in the office *activates* all the outdoor lights⟩. ***antonym:*** arrest

vitiate See DEBASE.

vituperate See SCOLD.

vituperation See ABUSE.

vivacious See LIVELY.

vivid See GRAPHIC.

vivify See QUICKEN.

vocal **1. Vocal**, **articulate**, **oral** mean uttered by the voice or having to do with such utterance.

Vocal implies the use of the voice, but not necessarily of speech or language ⟨preferred *vocal* to instrumental music⟩.

Articulate implies the use of distinct intelligible language ⟨so enraged that he was scarcely capable of *articulate* speech⟩. ***antonym:*** inarticulate

Oral implies the use of the voice rather than the hand (as in writing or signaling in communication) ⟨legend is the *oral* transmission of tradition⟩. ***antonym:*** written

2. Vocal, **articulate**, **fluent**, **eloquent**, **voluble**, **glib** mean being able to express oneself clearly or easily.

Vocal usually implies ready responsiveness to an occasion for expression or free and usually forceful, insistent, or emphatic voicing of one's ideas or feelings ⟨one of the president's most *vocal* critics⟩.

Articulate implies the use of language which exactly and distinctly reveals or conveys what it seeks to express ⟨questioned the validity of literary criticism coming from those who are themselves hardly *articulate*⟩. ***antonym:*** inarticulate

Fluent stresses facility in speaking or writing and copiousness in the flow of words ⟨seemed to be *fluent* on any subject⟩; it can also apply to facility and ease in the use of a foreign language ⟨had a *fluent* command of idiomatic French⟩.

Eloquent usually implies fluency but it suggests also the stimulus of powerful emotion and its expression in fervent and moving language ⟨moved by the *eloquent* words of the Gettysburg Address⟩.

Voluble is usually somewhat derogatory and suggests a flow of language that is not easily stemmed ⟨indulge in *voluble* explanations⟩. ***antonym:*** stuttering, stammering

Glib is also usually derogatory and implies superficiality or emptiness in what is said or slipperiness or untrustworthiness in the speaker ⟨a *glib* reply⟩ ⟨known for his *glib* tongue⟩.

vociferous, **clamorous**, **blatant**, **strident**, **boisterous**, **obstreperous** mean so loud or insistent as to compel attention.

Vociferous implies a vehement deafening shouting or calling out ⟨*vociferous* cries of protest and outrage⟩ or an insistent, urgent presentation of requests, excuses, or demands ⟨made *vociferous* demands⟩.

Clamorous may imply insistency as well as vociferousness in demanding or protesting ⟨*clamorous* demands for prison reforms⟩. ***antonym:*** taciturn

Blatant implies an offensive bellowing or insensitive, conspicuous, or vulgar loudness ⟨a *blatant* and abusive drunkard⟩. ***antonym:*** decorous, reserved

Strident suggests a harsh and discordant noise ⟨heard the *strident* cry of the crow⟩.

Boisterous suggests a noisiness and turbulence due to high spirits and release from restraint ⟨a *boisterous* crowd of partygoers⟩.

Obstreperous suggests unruly and aggressive noisiness and resistance to restraint or authority ⟨the *obstreperous* demonstrators were removed from the hall⟩.

vogue See FASHION.

voice See EXPRESS.

void See EMPTY.

volatility See LIGHTNESS.

voluble **1.** See TALKATIVE. **2.** See VOCAL 2.

volume See BULK.

voluntary, **intentional**, **deliberate**, **willful**, **willing** mean done or brought about of one's own will.

Voluntary implies freedom and spontaneity of choice or action without external compulsion ⟨*voluntary* enlistment in the armed services⟩. ***antonym:*** involuntary, instinctive

Intentional stresses an awareness of an end to be achieved ⟨the *intentional* concealment of vital information⟩. ***antonym:*** unintentional, instinctive

Deliberate implies full consciousness of the nature of one's act and its consequences ⟨the *deliberate* sabotaging of a nuclear power plant⟩. ***antonym:*** impulsive

Willful adds to ***deliberate*** the implication of an obstinate determination to follow one's own will or choice ⟨*willful* ignorance⟩.

Willing implies a readiness and eagerness to accede to or anticipate the wishes of another ⟨a *willing* accomplice in a bank robbery⟩. ***antonym:*** unwilling

voluptuous See SENSUOUS.

voracious, **gluttonous**, **ravenous**, **rapacious** mean excessively greedy.

Voracious applies especially to habitual gorging with what satisfies an appetite ⟨teenagers are often *voracious* eaters⟩.

Gluttonous applies to delight in eating or acquiring things especially beyond the point of necessity or satiety ⟨an admiral who had a *gluttonous* appetite for glory⟩. ***antonym:*** abstemious

Ravenous implies excessive hunger and suggests violent or grasping methods of dealing with whatever satisfies an appetite ⟨football practice usually gives them *ravenous* appetites⟩.

Rapacious often suggests excessive and utterly selfish acquisitiveness or avarice ⟨*rapacious* land developers indifferent to the ruination of the environment⟩.

vouch See CERTIFY.

vouchsafe See GRANT.

vulgar **1.** See COARSE. **2.** See COMMON.

W

wage, **salary**, **stipend**, **pay**, **fee** mean the price paid for services or labor.

Wage, often used in the plural ***wages***, applies to an amount paid usually on an hourly basis and chiefly at weekly intervals especially for physical labor ⟨dirty and difficult jobs should command a higher *wage*⟩.

Salary applies to compensation at a fixed, often annual, rate that is paid in installments at regular intervals and suggests that the services performed require training or special ability ⟨negotiated for a higher *salary*⟩.

Stipend adds to ***salary*** the notion of a regular income such as a pension or scholarship paid without concurrently performed service ⟨received a fellowship that included a small *stipend*⟩.

Pay can replace any of the foregoing and is the one of these terms freely used in combination or as a modifier ⟨waiting for *pay* day⟩ ⟨lost his *pay* envelope⟩.

Fee applies to the price asked, usually in the form of a fixed charge, for a specific professional service ⟨a pianist's *fee* for a concert⟩.

wait See STAY.

waive See RELINQUISH.

waken See STIR *vb*.

wallow, **welter**, **grovel** mean to move heavily or clumsily because or as if impeded or out of control.

Wallow basically implies a lurching or rolling to and fro, as of a hog in the mire or a ship in a troubled sea, and may imply complete self-abandonment ⟨*wallowing* in self-pity⟩ or absorption ⟨*wallowed* in the romantic music⟩.

Welter is likely to carry a stronger implication of being helplessly at the mercy of outside forces ⟨a tide of refugees, many of whom *weltered,* adrift on the sea, for days⟩.

Grovel implies a crawling or wriggling close to the ground in abject fear, self-abasement, or utter degradation ⟨*groveled* for forgiveness⟩.

wan See PALE 1.

wander, **stray**, **roam**, **ramble**, **rove**, **range**, **traipse**, **meander** mean to move about more or less aimlessly from place to place.

Wander implies an absence of or an indifference to a fixed course ⟨found her *wandering* about the square⟩.

Stray carries a stronger suggestion of a deviation from a fixed or proper course and may connote a being lost ⟨*strayed* into the underbrush⟩.

Roam suggests a wandering about freely and often far afield and often connotes enjoyment ⟨liked to *roam* through the woods⟩.

Ramble stresses carelessness and indifference to one's course or objective and suggests a straying beyond bounds or an inattention to guiding details ⟨the speaker *rambled* on without ever coming to the point⟩.

Rove suggests vigorous and sometimes purposeful roaming ⟨armed brigands *roved* through the countryside⟩.

Range adds to ***rove*** an emphasis on the extent of territory covered and is often used when literal wandering is not implied ⟨a lecture that *ranged* over much of both Eastern and Western philosophy⟩.

Traipse implies an erratic if purposeful and vigorous course ⟨*traipsed* all over town looking for the right dress⟩.

Meander implies a winding or intricate course suggestive of aimless or listless wandering ⟨the river *meanders* for miles through rich farmland⟩.

wane See ABATE.

want *n* See POVERTY.

want *vb* **1.** See DESIRE. **2.** See LACK.

wanton See SUPEREROGATORY.

warlike See MARTIAL.

ward off See PREVENT 2.

warn, **forewarn**, **caution** mean to let one

know of approaching or possible danger or risk.

Warn may range in meaning from simple notification of something to be watched for or guarded against to admonition or threats of violence or reprisal ⟨the weather bureau *warned* coastal areas to prepare for a hurricane⟩.

Forewarn stresses timeliness and regularly implies warning in advance of a foreseen risk or danger ⟨they had been *forewarned* of the danger, and were prepared when it arose⟩.

Caution stresses giving advice that puts one on guard or suggests precautions against either a prospective or a present risk or peril ⟨the doctor *cautioned* him against overeating⟩.

warp See DEFORM.

warrant See JUSTIFY.

wary See CAUTIOUS.

waste 1. See RAVAGE. **2. Waste**, **squander**, **dissipate**, **fritter**, **consume** mean to spend or expend futilely or without gaining a proper or reasonable or normal return.

Waste usually implies careless or prodigal expenditure ⟨*wasted* her money on frivolous items⟩, but it may also imply fruitless or useless expenditure ⟨why *waste* time trying to help people who want no help?⟩. ***antonym:*** save, conserve

Squander stresses reckless and lavish expenditure that tends to exhaust resources ⟨*squandered* all their time and energy playing tennis⟩.

Dissipate implies loss by extravagance and commonly stresses exhaustion of the store or stock ⟨eventually realized they had *dissipated* all their resources⟩.

Fritter, usually used with *away*, implies expenditure on trifles, bit by bit, or without commensurate return ⟨*frittered* away the entire afternoon on aimless pursuits⟩.

Consume can imply a wasting or squandering as entirely as if by devouring ⟨built a fire that *consumed* the entire stock of wood⟩.

waster See SPENDTHRIFT.

wastrel See SPENDTHRIFT.

watch 1. See SEE 2. **2.** See TEND.

watchful, **vigilant**, **wide-awake**, **alert** mean being on the lookout especially for danger or opportunity.

Watchful is the least explicit term ⟨played under the *watchful* eyes of their mothers⟩. ***antonym:*** unwatchful

Vigilant suggests intense, unremitting, wary watchfulness ⟨*vigilant* taxpayers forestalled all attempts to raise taxes⟩.

Wide-awake stresses keen awareness of and watchfulness for opportunities and developments more often than for dangers ⟨*wide-awake* observers will recall other summit meetings⟩.

Alert stresses readiness or promptness in meeting a problem or a danger or in seizing an opportunity ⟨*alert* traders anticipated the stock market's slide⟩.

wave See SWING 1.

waver 1. See HESITATE. **2.** See SWING 2.

way See METHOD.

waylay See SURPRISE 1.

wayward See CONTRARY.

weak, **feeble**, **frail**, **fragile**, **infirm**, **decrepit** mean not strong enough to endure strain, pressure, or strenuous effort.

Weak applies to deficiency or inferiority in strength or power of any sort ⟨a *weak* government likely to topple soon⟩. ***antonym:*** strong

Feeble suggests extreme weakness inviting pity or disdain ⟨a *feeble* attempt to resist the enemy attack⟩. ***antonym:*** robust

Frail implies delicacy and slightness of constitution or structure and liability to failure or destruction ⟨a once-robust man now *frail* with disease⟩. ***antonym:*** robust

Fragile suggests frailty, inability to resist rough usage, and liability to destruction ⟨a *fragile* beauty that the camera cannot convey⟩. ***antonym:*** durable

Infirm suggests instability, unsoundness, and insecurity due to loss of strength from old age, crippling illness, or temperamental vacillation ⟨an *infirm* old woman confined to her home⟩. ***antonym:*** hale

Decrepit implies being worn-out or broken down from long use or old age ⟨the *decrepit* butler had been with the family for years⟩. ***antonym:*** sturdy

weaken, **enfeeble**, **debilitate**, **undermine**, **sap**, **cripple**, **disable** mean to lose or cause to lose strength, energy, or vigor.

Weaken may imply the loss of physical strength, health, soundness, or stability or of quality, intensity, or effective power ⟨a disease that *weakens* the body's defenses against infection⟩. ***antonym:*** strengthen

Enfeeble implies an obvious and pitiable weakening to the point of helplessness ⟨so *enfeebled* by arthritis that he requires constant care⟩. ***antonym:*** fortify

Debilitate suggests a less marked or more temporary impairment of strength or vitality ⟨the operation has a temporary *debilitating* effect⟩. ***antonym:*** invigorate

Undermine suggests a weakening by something working surreptitiously and insidiously and implies a caving in or breaking down ⟨a poor diet *undermines* your health⟩. ***antonym:*** reinforce

Sap is close to ***undermine*** but adds a suggestion of a draining of strength ⟨drugs had *sapped* his ability to think⟩.

Cripple implies the causing of a serious loss of functioning power through damaging or removing an essential part or element ⟨inflation had *crippled* the economy⟩.

Disable suggests a usually sudden crippling or enfeebling of strength or competence ⟨*disabled* soldiers received an immediate discharge⟩. ***antonym:*** rehabilitate

wealthy See RICH.

wean See ESTRANGE.

weary See TIRE.

weigh See CONSIDER.

weight 1. See IMPORTANCE. **2.** See INFLUENCE.

weighty See HEAVY.

weird, **eerie**, **uncanny** mean mysteriously strange or fantastic.

Weird may imply an unearthly or supernatural strangeness or it may stress queerness or oddness ⟨*weird* creatures from another world⟩.

Eerie suggests an uneasy or fearful consciousness that mysterious and malign powers are at work ⟨an *eerie* calm preceded the bombing raid⟩.

Uncanny implies an unpleasant or disquieting strangeness or mysteriousness ⟨bore an *uncanny* resemblance to his dead wife⟩.

welcome See PLEASANT.

well See HEALTHY.

well-nigh See NEARLY.

well-timed See SEASONABLE.

welter See WALLOW.

wet, **damp**, **dank**, **moist**, **humid** mean more or less covered or soaked with liquid.

Wet usually implies saturation but may suggest a covering of a surface with water or something such as paint not yet dry ⟨slipped on the *wet* pavement⟩. ***antonym:*** dry

Damp implies a slight or moderate absorption and often connotes an unpleasant degree of moisture ⟨clothes will mildew if stored in a *damp* place⟩.

Dank implies a more distinctly disagreeable or unwholesome dampness and often connotes a lack of fresh air and sunshine ⟨a prisoner in a cold, *dank* cell⟩.

Moist applies to what is slightly damp or not entirely dry ⟨treat the injury with *moist* heat⟩.

Humid applies to the presence of an oppressive amount of water vapor in warm air ⟨the hot, *humid* conditions brought on heatstroke⟩.

wheedle See COAX.

whim See CAPRICE.

whirl See REEL.

whit See PARTICLE.

whiten, blanch, bleach, decolorize, etiolate mean to change from an original or natural color to white or nearly white.

Whiten implies a making white or whiter, often by a surface application ⟨the snow fell softly, *whitening* the roofs and streets⟩. ***antonym:*** blacken

Blanch implies a whitening either by the removal of color ⟨*blanched* when she saw the accident⟩ or by preventing it from developing ⟨*blanch* celery by covering the stalks with earth⟩.

Bleach implies the action of light or chemicals in removing or reducing color ⟨*bleach* hair with peroxide⟩.

Decolorize implies the deprivation of color by a process such as bleaching or blanching ⟨a process to *decolorize* raw sugar⟩. ***antonym:*** color

Etiolate is a scientific term chiefly in reference to plants from which sunlight has been excluded and the natural coloring of chlorophyll has not been formed ⟨*etiolated* plants look sickly⟩.

whole *adj* **1. Whole, entire, total, all** mean including everything or everyone without exception.

Whole implies that nothing has been omitted, ignored, abated, or taken away ⟨read the *whole* book⟩. ***antonym:*** partial

Entire may suggest a state of completeness or perfection from which nothing has been taken or to which nothing can be added ⟨the *entire* population was wiped out⟩. ***antonym:*** partial

Total implies that everything has been counted, weighed, measured, or considered ⟨the *total* number of people present⟩ or may suggest the absence of all reservation ⟨a *total* eclipse⟩. ***antonym:*** partial

All may equal ***whole, entire***, or ***total*** ⟨*all* their money went to pay the rent⟩. ***antonym:*** part (*of*)

2. See PERFECT.

whole *n* See SUM.

wholehearted See SINCERE.

wholesale See INDISCRIMINATE.

wholesome 1. See HEALTHFUL. **2.** See HEALTHY.

wicked See BAD.

wide See BROAD.

wide-awake See WATCHFUL.

wield See HANDLE.

wile See TRICK.

willful 1. See UNRULY. **2.** See VOLUNTARY.

willing See VOLUNTARY.

win See GET.

wince See RECOIL.

winning See SWEET.

winsome See SWEET.

wipe out See EXTERMINATE.

wisdom See SENSE.

wise, sage, sapient, judicious, prudent, sensible, sane mean having or showing sound judgment.

Wise suggests great understanding of people and of situations and unusual discernment and judgment in dealing with them and may imply a wide range of experience, knowledge, or learning ⟨*wise* enough to know what really mattered in life⟩. ***antonym:*** simple

Sage suggests wide experience, great learning, and wisdom ⟨sought the *sage* advice of her father in times of crisis⟩.

Sapient suggests great sagacity and discernment ⟨the *sapient* observations of a veteran foreign correspondent⟩.

Judicious stresses a capacity for weighing and judging and for reaching wise decisions or just conclusions ⟨*judicious* parents using kindness and discipline in equal measure⟩. ***antonym:*** injudicious, asinine

Prudent applies to someone who is rich in practical wisdom and hence able to exercise self-restraint and sound judgment ⟨a *prudent* decision to wait out the storm⟩. ***antonym:*** imprudent

Sensible applies to action guided and restrained by good sense and rationality ⟨a *sensible* woman who was not fooled by flattery⟩. ***antonym:*** absurd, foolish

Sane stresses mental soundness, prudent rationality, and levelheadedness ⟨remained *sane* even as the war raged around him⟩. ***antonym:*** insane

wisecrack See JEST.

wish See DESIRE.

wishy-washy See INSIPID.

wit, **humor**, **irony**, **sarcasm**, **satire**, **repartee** mean a mode of expression intended to arouse amused interest or evoke laughter.

Wit suggests the power to evoke laughter by remarks showing verbal felicity or ingenuity and swift perception especially of the incongruous ⟨appreciate the *wit* of Wilde and Shaw⟩.

Humor implies an ability to perceive the ludicrous, the comical, and the absurd in human life and to express these usually with keen insight and sympathetic understanding and without bitterness ⟨a person with a finely honed sense of *humor*⟩.

Irony applies to a manner of expression in which the intended meaning is the opposite of the expressed meaning ⟨with wry *irony,* he said, "Thank God I'm an atheist!"⟩.

Sarcasm applies to savagely humorous expression frequently in the form of irony that is intended to cut or wound ⟨a cynic much given to heartless *sarcasm*⟩.

Satire applies to writing that exposes or ridicules conduct, doctrines, or institutions either by direct criticism or more often through irony, parody, or caricature ⟨the play is a *satire* on contemporary living arrangements⟩.

Repartee implies the power or art of answering quickly, pointedly, or wittily or to an interchange of such responses ⟨a partygoer well known for razor-sharp *repartee*⟩.

withdraw See GO.

wither, **shrivel**, **wizen** mean to lose or cause to lose freshness and smoothness of appearance.

Wither implies a loss of vital moisture, such as sap or tissue fluids, with consequent fading or drying up ⟨*withered* leaves⟩ or suggests a comparable loss of vigor, vitality, or animation ⟨interest that *withered* as the hard work increased⟩. ***antonym:*** flourish

Shrivel carries a stronger impression of a becoming wrinkled or crinkled or shrunken ⟨leaves *shrivel* in the hot sun⟩.

Wizen may be preferred when the notions of shrinking in size and accompanying wrinkling of the surface are stressed, especially if the shrinking is caused by aging, deprivation, or failing vitality ⟨the *wizened* old man⟩ ⟨the *wizened* face of the starving child⟩.

withhold See KEEP 2.

withstand See OPPOSE.

witness *n* See SPECTATOR.

witness *vb* See CERTIFY.

witticism See JEST.

witty, **humorous**, **facetious**, **jocular**, **jocose** mean provoking or intended to provoke amusement or laughter.

Witty suggests cleverness and quickness of mind and often a caustic tongue ⟨a film critic remembered for his *witty* reviews⟩.

Humorous applies broadly to anything that evokes usually genial laughter and may contrast with ***witty*** in suggesting whimsicality or eccentricity ⟨laced her lectures with *humorous* anecdotes⟩.

Facetious stresses a desire to produce laughter and may be derogatory in implying clumsy, dubious, or ill-timed attempts at wit or humor ⟨*facetious* comments that were not appreciated at the funeral⟩. ***antonym:*** lugubrious

Jocular implies a usually habitual, often temperamental fondness for jesting and joking ⟨a *jocular* fellow whose humor often brightened spirits⟩.

Jocose suggests habitual waggishness or playfulness that is often clumsy or inappropriate ⟨the dim-witted took his *jocose* proposals seriously⟩. ***antonym:*** lugubrious

wizen See WITHER.

wobble See SHAKE 1.

woe See SORROW.

woebegone See DOWNCAST.

womanish See FEMALE.

womanlike See FEMALE.

womanly See FEMALE.

wont See HABIT.

wonted See USUAL.

wooden See STIFF.

wordy, **verbose**, **prolix**, **diffuse**, **redundant** mean using more words than necessary to express thought.

Wordy may also imply loquaciousness or garrulousness ⟨a *wordy* speech that said nothing⟩. ***antonym:*** laconic

Verbose suggests a resulting dullness, obscurity, or lack of incisiveness or precision ⟨*verbose* position papers that no one reads⟩. ***antonym:*** concise, laconic

Prolix suggests unreasonable and tedious dwelling on details ⟨habitually transformed brief anecdotes into *prolix* sagas⟩.

Diffuse stresses lack of the organization and compactness that make for pointedness of expression and strength of style ⟨*diffuse* memoirs that are so many shaggy-dog stories⟩. ***antonym:*** succinct

Redundant implies superfluity resulting from needless repetition or overelaboration ⟨emended the text by removing whatever was *redundant*⟩. ***antonym:*** concise

work **1. Work**, **labor**, **travail**, **toil**, **drudgery**, **grind** mean activity involving effort or exertion.

Work may imply activity of body, of mind, of a machine, or of a natural force, or it may apply to effort expended or to the product of such effort ⟨too tired to do any *work*⟩. ***antonym:*** play

Labor applies to physical or intellectual work involving great and often strenuous, onerous, or fatiguing exertion ⟨believes that farmers are poorly paid for their *labor*⟩.

Travail is a somewhat bookish term for labor involving pain or suffering ⟨years of *travail* were lost when the building burned⟩.

Toil implies prolonged and fatiguing labor ⟨his lot would be years of backbreaking *toil*⟩.

Drudgery suggests dull and irksome labor ⟨a job with a good deal of *drudgery*⟩.

Grind implies dreary, monotonous labor exhausting to mind or body ⟨the *grind* of performing the play eight times a week⟩.

2. Work, **employment**, **occupation**, **calling**, **pursuit**, **métier**, **business** mean a specific sustained activity engaged in especially in earning one's living.

Work may apply to any purposeful activity whether remunerative or not ⟨her *work* as a hospital volunteer⟩.

Employment implies work for which one has been engaged and for which one is being paid ⟨*employment* will be terminated in cases of chronic tardiness⟩.

Occupation implies work in which one engages regularly or by preference, especially as a result of training or experience ⟨his *occupation* as a trained auto mechanic⟩.

Calling applies to an occupation viewed as a vocation or profession to which one has been drawn by one's nature, tastes, or aptitudes ⟨I feel the ministry is my true *calling*⟩.

Pursuit suggests a trade, profession, or avocation followed with zeal or steady interest ⟨her family considered medicine the only proper *pursuit*⟩.

Métier implies a calling or pursuit for which one believes oneself to be especially fitted ⟨from childhood I considered acting my *métier*⟩.

Business may be used in the sense of ***work*** or ***occupation*** but often suggests activity in commerce or the management of money and affairs <the *business* of managing a hotel>.

worldly **1.** See EARTHLY. **2.** See SOPHISTICATED.

worldly-wise See SOPHISTICATED.

worry *vb* **Worry**, **annoy**, **harass**, **harry**, **plague**, **pester**, **tease**, **tantalize** mean to torment to the point of destroying one's peace of mind or to disturb or irritate acutely by persistent acts.

Worry implies an incessant goading or attacking that drives one to desperation or defeat <pursued a policy of *worrying* the enemy>.

Annoy implies a disturbing of one's composure or peace of mind by intrusion, interference, or petty attacks <you're doing that just to *annoy* me>.

Harass implies petty persecutions or burdensome demands that wear down, distract, or weaken <*harassed* on all sides by creditors>.

Harry may imply a heavy, driving oppression or maltreatment <*harried* mothers trying to cope with small children>.

Plague implies a painful, persistent, and distressing affliction <*plagued* all her life by poverty>.

Pester implies a continuous harassment with petty, persistent attacks <the bureau was constantly *pestered* with trivial complaints>.

Tease suggests an attempt to break down one's resistance or rouse to wrath by persistent raillery or petty tormenting <malicious children *teased* the dog>.

Tantalize stresses the repeated awakening of expectation and then its frustration <*tantalizing* clues as to the origins of the universe>. ***antonym:*** satisfy

worry *n* See CARE.

worship See REVERE.

wrangle See QUARREL.

wrath See ANGER.

wreck See RUIN *vb*.

wretched See MISERABLE.

wrong *n* See INJUSTICE.

wrong *vb* **Wrong**, **oppress**, **persecute**, **aggrieve** mean to injure unjustly or outrageously.

Wrong implies inflicting injury either unmerited or out of proportion to what one deserves <a penal system that had *wronged* him>.

Oppress suggests inhumane imposing of burdens one cannot endure or exacting more than one can perform <a people *oppressed* by a warmongering tyrant>.

Persecute implies a relentless and unremitting subjection to annoyance or suffering <the boy was *persecuted* by his playmates>.

Aggrieve implies suffering caused by an infringement or denial of rights <a legal aid society representing *aggrieved* minority groups>.

YZ

yank See JERK.
yardstick See STANDARD.
yarn See STORY.
yearn See LONG.
yield **1.** See RELINQUISH. **2. Yield, submit, capitulate, succumb, relent, defer** mean to give way to someone or something that one can no longer resist.

Yield in reference to a person implies being overcome by force or entreaty ⟨*yielded* to their pleas for popcorn⟩ but in reference to a thing implies such qualities as elasticity or weakness that facilitate a giving way ⟨a mattress that *yielded* to pressure⟩. ***antonym:*** withstand

Submit suggests a full surrendering after resistance or conflict to the will or control of another ⟨voluntarily *submitted* to an inspection of the premises⟩. ***antonym:*** resist, withstand

Capitulate stresses the fact of ending all resistance and may imply either a coming to terms, as with an adversary, or submission to an irresistible opposing force ⟨the college president *capitulated* to the protesters' demands⟩.

Succumb implies weakness and helplessness in the one that gives way or an overwhelming power in the one that overcomes ⟨a stage actor *succumbing* to the lure of Hollywood⟩.

Relent implies a yielding through pity or mercy by one who holds the upper hand ⟨finally *relented* and let the children stay up late⟩.

Defer implies a voluntary yielding or submitting out of respect or reverence for or deference and affection toward another ⟨I *defer* to your superior expertise in these matters⟩. ***antonym:*** withstand

zeal See PASSION.
zest See TASTE